2nd Fully Revised & Enlarged Edition

Essence of Horticulture

NIPA GENX ELECTRONIC RESOURCES & SOLUTIONS P. LTD.
New Delhi-110 034

2nd Fully Revised & Enlarged Edition

Essence of Horticulture

A Comprehensive Guide for ARS/NET/SRF/JRF and M.Sc./Ph.D. Entrance Tests in Horticulture

M. S. Patil
Assistant Professor of Horticulture
NARP, ZARS, Solapur - 413002
Mahatma Phule Krishi Vidyapeeth
Rahuri, Maharashtra

A. R. Karale
Ex. Associate Dean
College of Horticulture, Pune - 411005
Mahatma Phule Krishi Vidyapeeth
Rahuri. Maharashtra

C. D. Badgujar
Associate Professor of Horticulture
BRS, Jalgaon - 425002
Mahatma Phule Krishi Vidyapeeth
Rahuri, Maharashtra

J. D. Adiga
Principal Scientist
ICAR- Directorate of Cashew Research
Puttur - 574 202, Karnataka

NIPA GENX ELECTRONIC RESOURCES & SOLUTIONS P. LTD.
New Delhi-110 034

NIPA GENX ELECTRONIC RESOURCES & SOLUTIONS P. LTD.

101,103, Vikas Surya Plaza, CU Block
L.S.C.Market, Pitam Pura, New Delhi-110 034
Ph : +91 11 27341616, 27341717, 27341718
E-mail:newindiapublishingagency@gmail.com
www: www.nipabooks.com

For customer assistance, please contact
Phone: + 91-11-27 34 17 17 Fax: + 91-11- 27 34 16 16
E-Mail: feedbacks@nipabooks.com

ISBN: 978-93-90591-46-6

Composed and Designed by NIPA.

Preface to the First Edition

A secret of life is not just enjoyment but getting education through experience

— Swami Vivekananda

Most of the Agricultural Universities, Institutes, Organizations and Government selection agencies have made competitive examinations as the basis for choosing candidates. The questions asked in these examinations are of objective type, large in number and of varied nature. It requires quick answering within a specified period of time to secure high merit and assured success.

The aspirants have to search a lot of printed and e-material to cover each topic of syllabus thoroughly. This is so because there is hardly any high quality book available on horticulture that covers the entire syllabus of this subject for competitive examinations. Keeping this in mind, a sincere effort has been made to write this book named '**Essence of Horticulture**' covering various branches of horticulture. This book contains quite an adequate material for seven Divisions of Horticulture, namely, Fruit science, Vegetable science, Floriculture and Landscape Gardening, Plantation crops, Spices and Condiments, Medicinal and Aromatic Plants and Post Harvest Technology.

The book has been written keeping in view the pattern of different horticulture/ agriculture competitive entrance examinations viz. JRF, SRF, ARS, ASRB, NET & Ph.D. (Horticulture). We hope that this book will be useful for U.G, P.G. and Ph.D. horticulture students, teachers and horticulture people across the country.

Special appreciation is expressed to the many contributors who have helped and contributed in providing the questions from different divisions and for their helpful suggestions during the preparation of the manuscript. We are thankful to Dr. V.K. Garande, Mr. C.Y. Dhumal, Dr. Manoj Nazir, Dr. P. Pavan Kumar from various disciplines of Horticulture for their help and valuable suggestion. We also thank to New India Publishing Agency to bring the excellent format of this book.

We have attempted to bring this information as much as possible but all the information available on the subject cannot be presented in a text of this size. This presentation is our compromise.

We will feel more satisfied if this book can serve the purpose of students to succeed in various competitive examinations.

All suggestions for future improvement for this book will be greatly solicited.

Pune

M.S.Patil
A.R. Karale
C.D. Badgujar
J.D. Adiga

Preface to the Second Edition

Preface to the Second Edition

The 2nd edition of the book: Essence of Horticulture brought out after 07 years of its 1st edition, which was very widely taken by students, and this revised edition is prepared after taking necessary feedbacks from faculty and students, has been divided into 08 sections spread over 1620 pages

01. General Horticulture
02. Fruit Science
03. Vegetable Science
04. Floriculture and Landscape Architecture
05. Plantation Crops
06. Spices and Condiments
07. Medicinal and Aromatic Plants
08. Postharvest Technology

Most of the Agricultural Universities, Institutes, Organizations and Government selection agencies have made competitive examinations as the basis for choosing candidates. The questions asked in these examinations are of objective type, large in number and of varied nature. It requires quick answering within a specified period of time to secure high merit and assured success.

The aspirants have to search a lot of printed and e-material to cover each topic of syllabus thoroughly. The book has been written keeping in view the latest pattern of different horticulture/ agriculture competitive entrance examinations viz. JRF, SRF, ARS, ASRB, NET & Ph.D. (Horticulture). We hope that this book will be useful for U.G, P.G. and Ph.D. horticulture students, teachers and horticulture people across the country.

Special appreciation is expressed to the many contributors who have helped and contributed in providing the questions from different divisions and for their helpful suggestions during the preparation of the manuscript.

We are thankful to Dr. V.K. Garande, Mr. C.Y. Dhumal, Dr. Manoj Nazir, Dr. P. Pavan Kumar from various disciplines of Horticulture for their help and valuable suggestion. We also thank to NIPA to bring the excellent format of this book.

All suggestions for future improvement for this book will be greatly solicited.

M.S.Patil
A.R. Karale
C.D. Badgujar
J.D. Adiga

Contents

Preface to the First Edition .... *v*

Preface to the Second Edition .... *vii*

GENERAL HORTICULTURE **1**

1. BASICS OF HORTICULTURE 1
2. HORTICULTURAL INSTITUTES 11
3. PLANT PROTECTION CHEMICALS 17
4. PLANT GROWTH REGULATORS: 20
   - 4.1 Growth promoters: 20
     - 4.1.1. Auxin 20
     - 4.1.2. Gibberellin 22
     - 4.1.3. Cytokinin 22
     - 4.1.4. Ethylene 23
   - 4.2 Growth retardants 24
   - 4.3 Growth inhibitors: 24
     - 4.3.1 Abscissic acid (ABA) 24
   - 4.4 Morphactins 25
   - 4.5 Use of growth regulators in fruit crops 27
   - 4.6 Use of growth regulators in flower crops 29
5. NUTRITIVE VALUE OF HORTICULTURAL CROPS 29
6. MINERAL NUTRITION 33
   - 6.1 Role and deficiency symptoms of minerals 37
   - 6.2 Characterization levels of nutrients in soil and plants 40
   - 6.3 Leaf nutrient analysis 40
   - 6.4 Precision farming in horticulture 54
   - 6.5 Organic farming 55
7. NURSERY MANAGEMENT 58
   - 7.1 Types of nurseries 58
   - 7.2 Greenhouse structures 59

8. SOIL-LESS CULTIVATION OF HORTICULTURAL CROPS 68
8.1 Media 70
9. AGRI-EXPORT ZONES (AEZs) OF HORTICULTURAL CROPS 70
10. INTELLECTUAL PROPERTY RIGHTS 71
11. BIO-DIVERSITY OF HORTICULTURAL CROPS 74
12. INFORMATICS IN HORTICULTURE 81
13. BIO-TECHNOLOGY OF HORTICULTURAL CROPS 81
13.1 Tissue culture media and their applications 84
13.2 Somaclonal variation and variants released as varieties for commercial cultivation 86
13.3 Somatic hybridization/ Protoplast fusion/ Para-sexual hybridization 86
13.4 Embryo rescue 87
13.5 Molecular markers 87
13.6 Transgenics in horticultural crops 94
13.7 Artificial seeds/ synthetic seeds 113
14. HORTI-SILVI- PASTORAL SYSTEM 114
15. NANOTECHNOLOGY 115
16. VERTICAL/ URBAN FARMING 117
17. HORTICULTURE JOURNALS and MAGAZINES 117

2. FRUIT SCIENCE 119

1. GENERAL POMOLOGY 119
2. LAYOUT OF ORCHARD 120
2.1 SYSTEMS OF PLANTING 121
2.1.1 High density planting (HDP) 122
3. TRAINING AND PRUNING 123
3.1 Canopy architecture management 124
3.1.1 Objectives of canopy architecture management 124
3.1.1.1 Considerations of canopy management 124
3.2 Training 124
3.2.1 Methods of training 125
3.3 Pruning 127
4. PROPAGATION OF FRUIT CROPS 128
4.1 Seed/ Sexual propagation/ Amphimixis 128
4.1.1 Seed dormancy 129

4.1.2 Methods to break dormancy 129

4.1.3 Seed storage 130

4.2 Asexual/ Vegetative/ Clonal propagation: 130

4.2.1 Cutting 130

4.2.2 Budding 131

4.2.3 Grafting 132

4.2.4 Layering 133

4.2.5 Parthenogenesis: arthenogenesis 134

4.2.6 Polyembryony 134

4.2.7 Apomixis 135

4.2.8 Chimera/ Bud sports/ Bud mutations and induced mutation 136

4.2.9 Special vegetative structures 136

4.2.10 Use of rootstocks in fruit crops 137

5. SEEDLESSNESS IN HORTICULTURAL CROPS 138

6. CLASSIFICATION OF FRUIT CROPS 139

6.1 Based on botany 139

6.2 Based on longevity of fruit crops 144

6.3 Based on stem morphology 144

6.4 Based on fruit morphology 144

6.5 Based on fruit size 145

6.6 Based on respiratory behaviour: 145

6.7 Based on rate of ethylene production 145

6.8 Based on photoperiodic response 145

6.9 Based on specificity to soil texture 146

6.10 Based on soil topography 146

6.11 Based on salt tolerance (E.C.) limit 146

6.12 Based on relative soil pH tolerance 146

6.13 Based on bearing habit 146

6.14 Based on flowering habit i.e. photo-thermal requirement (Kozlowski, 1971) 147

6.15 Based on type of inflorescence 147

6.16 Based on pollination agents 147

6.17 Based on type of pollination: 148

6.18 Based on self incompatibility 148

6.19 Based on type of placentation 149

6.20 Based on ploidy level 149
6.21 Based on growth curve: 149
6.22 Based on shade tolerance: 150
6.23 Based on drought tolerance 150
6.24 Based on storage life 150
6.25 Based on chill sensitive fruits and safe temperature 150
6.26 Based on derivation of fruits from various plant tissues (Coombe, 1976) 150
6.27 Based on edible portion 151
6.28 Based on colour compounds 151
6.29 Based on aromatic and volatile compounds 151
6.30 Based on bitterness due to flavonoids and terpenoids 152
6.31 Based on acid present in fruit crops 152
6.32 Based on pectin and acid content 153
6.33 Predominating biochemical constituents of some stone fruits 153
7. ACTINIDIACEAE 153
7.1 Kiwi fruit 153
8. ANACARDIACEAE (POISON IVY FAMILY) 157
8.1 Mango 157
8.2 Cashewnut 179
8.3 Charoli 190
8.4 Pistachio nut 191
8.5 Marking nut 193
9. ANNONACEAE 194
9.1 Custard apple 194
10. APOCYNACEAE 198
10.1 Karonda 198
11. ARACACEAE (PALMAE) 201
11.1 Datepalm 201
12. BORAGINACEAE (EHRETIACEAE) 207
12.1 Lasoda 207
13. BROMELIACEAE 209
13.1 Pineapple 209
14. CACTACEAE 220
14.1 Dragon fruit 220
14.2 Prickly pear or Opuntia 222

15. CARICACEAE 223
15.1 Papaya 223
16. CLUSIACEAE (GUTTIFERAE) 233
16.1 Kokum 233
16.2 Mangosteen 235
17. CORYLACEAE (BETULACEAE) 238
17.1 Hazelnut 238
18. EBENACEAE 239
18.1 Persimmon 239
19. ELAEGNACEAE 244
19.1 Seabuckthorn 244
20. ERICACEAE 244
20.1 Cranberry 244
20.2 Blueberry 245
21. FABACEAE 247
21.1 Tamarind 247
21.2 Khejri 252
22. FAGACEAE 252
22.1 Chestnut 252
23. JUGLANDACEAE 254
23.1 Persian walnut 254
23.2 Pecan nut 258
24. LAURACEAE 263
24.1 Avocado 263
25. MALPIGHIACEAE 270
25.1 West Indian Cherry 270
26. MALVACEAE (BOMBACACEAE) 270
26.1 Durian 270
27. MORACEAE 274
27.1 Fig 274
27.2 Jackfruit 279
27.3 Bread fruit 284
27.4 Mulberry 284
28. MUSACEAE 285
28.1 Banana 285

29. MYRICACEAE 310
29.1 Kaphal 310
30. MYRTACEAE 310
30.1 Guava 310
30.2 J amun 320
31. OLEACEAE (ELAEOCARPACEAE) 324
31.1 Olive 324
32. OXALIDACEAE 329
32.1 Carambola 329
33. PASSIFLORACEAE 331
33.1 Passion fruit 331
34. PHYLLANTHACEAE (EUPHORBIACEAE) 335
34.1 Aonla 335
35. PROTEACEAE 339
35.1 Macadamia nut 339
36. PUNICACEAE (LYTHRACEAE) LOOSESTRIFE FAMILY 342
36.1 Pomegranate 342
37. RHAMNACEAE (BUCK THORN FAMILY) 350
37.1 Ber 350
38. ROSACEAE 354
38.1 Apple 354
38.2 Pear 368
38.3 Peach 373
38.4 Plum 381
38.5 Cherry 386
38.6 Apricot 391
38.7 Almond 393
38.8 Strawberry 397
38.9 Loquat 407
38.10 Quince 409
38.11 Raspberry 410
39. RUBIACEAE 412
39.1 Noni 412

40. RUTACEAE (ORANGE FAMILY) 413
40.1 Mandarin orange 421
40.2 Sweet orange 428
40.3 Lime and Lemons 430
40.4 Pummelo 435
40.5 Grape fruit 436
40.6 Bael 442
40.7 Woodapple 447
41. SAPINDACEAE 448
41.1 Litchi (syn. Lychee) 448
41.2 Rambutan/ Ramtum 456
41.3 Longan 458
42. SAPOTACEAE 460
42.1 Sapota 460
42.2 Khirni 463
42.3 Mahua 464
42.4 Egg fruit 466
43. SOLANACEAE 468
43.1 Cape gooseberry 468
44. TILIACEAE (BASSWOOD FAMILY) 469
44.1 Phalsa 469
44.2 Jamaica cherry 471
45. VITACEAE 471
45.1 Grape 471
46. PROTECTED CULTIVATION OF FRUIT CROPS 494
46.1 OTHER UNDERUTILIZED FRUIT CROPS 494

3. VEGETABLE SCIENCE 497

1. GENERAL OLERICULTURE 497
2. VEGETABLE GARDENING 501
2.1 Vertical farming/ Urban farming 501
2.2 Micro-green vegetables 502
3. PROTECTED CULTIVATION OF VEGETABLE CROPS 503
4. VEGETABLE GRAFTING 506
5. CLASSIFICATION OF VEGETABLE CROPS 511

5.1 Based on botany 511

5.2 Based on life cycle 516

5.3 Based on transplanting age 516

5.4 Based on photoperiod in relation to flowering, bulbing and tuberization 516

5.5 Formation of underground strage organs in response to photoperiod 516

5.6 Based on flowering response of vegetables to vernalization 516

5.7 Based on temperature requirement and hardiness 517

5.8 Based on inflorescence type 517

5.9 Based on soil acidity/soil reaction (pH) tolerance 517

5.10 Based on soil salinity/ salt tolerance 517

5.11 Based on frost hardiness 517

5.12 Based on water requirement 518

5.13 Based on average feeder root depth (Fulton, 1986) 518

5.14 Based on rooting depth and amount of irrigation water needed 518

5.15 Based on respiratory activity 518

5.16 Based on climacteric peak 518

5.17 Based on storage life 519

5.18 Based on seed storability under cold conditions 519

5.19 Based on useful compounds 519

5.20 Based on anti-nutritional factor (toxic substance) present 519

5.21 Based on edible colour rich varieties in India 520

5.22 Based on optimum soil moisture range 520

5.23 Aroma containing compounds 520

5.24 Based on photosynthesis pathway 521

5.25 Based on acid present 521

5.26 Based on pollination mechanism 521

5.26.1 Autogamy 521

5.26.2 Allogamy 522

5.27 Floral biology of vegetable crops 522

5.28 Based on inbreeding (production of offspring by closely related parents) depression 524

5.29 Based on male sterility (MS) systems 524

5.30 Morphological markers for functional type male sterility identification and production of hybrid seed 525

5.31 Estimation of combining ability: 526
5.32 Based on genetic mechanism for hybrid seed development in cucurbits: 526
5.33 Based on tendril types in cucurbits: 526
5.34 Based on derivation of vegetable from plant tissue 526
5.35 Based on edible part 527
5.36 Effect of ethylene 527
5.37 Critical moisture period and impact of water deficit on vegetable crops (Fulton, 1986) 528
5.38 Sufficient and critical level of nutrients in leaf tissue 529
5.39 Removal of primary nutrients from the soil 529
5.40 Biochemical basis of disease/ pest resistance 530
5.41 Provision of primary type of nutrients 530
5.42 Centers conserving crop germplasm in medium and long term storage units 531

6. BREEDING METHODS FOLLOWED IN VEGETABLE CROPS: 533
6.1 General information 533
6.2 Quantitative genetics 534
6.3 Self incompatibility (SI) 535
6.4 Male sterility 537
6.5 Selection 539
6.6 Heterosis 540
6.7 Intergeneric hybridization 541
6.8 Interspecific hybridization 541
6.9 Special breeding techniques 542
6.10 Mutation breeding 543
6.11 Polyploidy breeding 545
6.12 Bio-technological applications 547

7. AMARANTHACEAE5 548
7.1 Amaranths 548

8. ALLIACEAE 553
8.1 Onion 553
8.2 Garlic 571
8.3 Leek 577
8.4 Chive 579
8.5 Shallot (syn. Aggregatum onion, Multiplier onion) 581

8.6 Welsh onion 583

8.7. Tree onion 583

8.8 Rakkyo 584

9. APIACEAE/ (UMBELLIFERAE) 584

9.1 Carrot 584

9.2 Parsley 599

9.3 Celery 602

10. ARACEAE 607

10.1 Elephant foot yam 607

10.2 Taro 611

10.3 Tannia 619

11. ASTERACEAE 620

11.1 Lettuce 620

11.2 Globe artichoke/ French artichoke/ Green artichoke 629

11.3 Jerusalem artichoke/ Girasole/ Sunchoke 631

11.4 Chichory/ Endive 632

12. BASELLACEAE 633

12.1 Basella 633

13. CHENOPODIACEAE (GOOSEFOOT FAMILY) 635

13.1 Garden beet/ Beet root 635

13.2 Palak 640

13.3 Spinach 643

13.4 French spinach 648

13.5 Bathua 648

13.6 Ceylon spinach 649

13.7 Swiss chard 650

13.8 Some spinach-like vegetables 650

14. CONVOLVULACEAE/ (MORNING GLORY FAMILY) 651

14.1 Sweet potato 651

14.2 Water spinach 662

15. CRUCIFERAE 663

15.1 Cabbage 666

15.2 Cauliflower (syn. Heading broccoli) 676

15.3 Sprouting broccoli/ Broccoli 685

15.4 Radish 689
15.5 Knol khol/ Kohlrabi 697
15.6. Turnip 698
15.7 Brussels sprout 701
15.8 Kale 703
15.9 Collard 704
15.10 Chinese cabbage 705
15.11 Horseradish 708
15.12 Rutabaga 710
16. CUCURBITACEAE (GOURD FAMILY) 711
16.1 Cucumber 712
16.2 Gherkin 728
16.3 Water melon 730
16.3 Musk melon 740
16.4 Round melon (syn. *Praecitrullus fistulosus*, *C. fistulosus*) 748
16.5 Long melon/ *Kakri* 748
16.6 Snap melon/ *Phoot*/ *Kakadia* 750
16.7 Other minor melons 750
16.8 Bottle gourd (syn. *L. vulgaris*, *L. leucantha*) 750
16.9 Bitter gourd 756
16.10 Sweet gourd/ *Kakrol* 762
16.11 Spine gourd/ *Kartoli* 764
16.12 Snake gourd (syn. *T. anguina*) 764
16.13 Pointed gourd 766
16.14 Ash gourd 769
16.15 Ridge gourd 771
16.16 Sponge gourd (syn. *L. aegyptiaca*) 775
16.17 Pumpkin 777
16.18 Summer squash/ Zucchini 784
16.19 Winter Squash (syn. *C. angyrosperma, C. maxima*) 788
16.20 Chow chow 789
16.21 Ivy gourd (syn. *C. cordifolia*, *C. grandis*, *Ciphlandra indica*) 791
16.22 *Meetha karela* 793
17. DIOSCOREACEAE 793
17.1 Yam 793

18. EUPHORBIACEAE/ SPURGE FAMILY 801
18.1 Cassava 802
18.2 Chekkurmanis (*Madura keera*) 811
19. FABACEAE 812
19.1 Fenugreek 812
19.2 Agathi/ *Hadga* 817
20. LABIATAE 817
20.1 Coleus (Chinese potato/ *koorka*) 817
21. LEGUMINOSAE 819
21.1 Garden pea/ vegetable pea 820
21.2 French bean/ Snap bean 834
21.3 Cowpea 845
21.4 Cluster bean 859
21.5 Dolichos bean 865
21.6 Lima bean 872
21.7 Broad bean 875
21.8 Winged bean 877
21.9 Yam bean 882
21.10 Soybean 886
21.11 Velvet bean 893
21.12 Sword bean 893
21.13 Jack bean 894
21.14 Other minor beans/ legume vegetables 896
22. LILIACEAE 896
22.1 Asparagus 896
23. MALVACEAE 904
23.1 Okra 904
24. MARANTACEAE 914
24.1 Queensland arrow root 914
24.2 West Indian arrow root 915
25. MORINGACEAE 915
25.1 Drumstick 915
26. ONOCLEACEAE 919
26.1 Fiddlehead fern 919

27. POACEAE (GRAMINEAE) ... 919
27.1 Sweet corn ... 919
28. POLYGONACEAE (BUCKWHEAT FAMILY) ... 927
28.1 Rhubarb ... 927
28.2 Sorrel ... 929
29. PORTULACACEAE ... 930
29.1 Portulaca ... 930
30. SOLANACEAE ... 931
30.1 Tomato ... 931
30.2 Brinjal ... 960
30.3 Chilli ... 976
30.4 Paprika ... 996
30.5 Capsicum or pepper ... 998
30.6 Potato ... 1002
30.7 Tomatillo ... 1023
31. TETRAGONIACEAE (AIZOACEAE) ... 1023
31.1 New Zealand Spinach ... 1023
32. TRAPACEAE (CYPERACEAE) ... 1024
32.1 Chinese water chestnut ... 1024
33. USE OF PLANT GROWTH REGULATORS IN VEGETABLE CROPS ... 1025
34. SEED PRODUCTION OF VEGETABLE CROPS ... 1026
34.1 Seed Labeling, Testing, and Certification ... 1030
34.2 Seed storability in different vegetables ... 1032
35. MUSHROOMS ... 1033

4. FLORICULTURE AND LANDSCAPE ARCHITECTURE ... 1045

1. GENERAL FLORICULTURE ... 1045
2. IMPROVEMENT OF FLOWERS THROUGH OUTCROSSING ... 1051
2.1 Breeding methods followed in flower crops ... 1051
2.2 Species involved in cross breeding ... 1052
2.3 Flower breeders in India ... 1053
3. CLASSIFICATION OF FLOWER CROPS ... 1054
3.1 Based on botany ... 1054
3.2 Based on pollination mechanism ... 1056

3.2.1 Autogamy ... 1056
3.2.2 Allogamy ... 1056
3.3 Based on photosynthetic pathway ... 1058
3.4 Based on day length requirement ... 1058
3.5 Based on seed storage behaviour ... 1058
3.6 Based on endopsperm content ... 1059
3.7 Based on type of inflorescence ... 1059
3.8 Based on fruit type ... 1059
3.9 Based on type of carotenoids ... 1059
3.10 Morphological markers for identification ... 1059
4. PROPAGATION OF ORNAMENTAL CROPS ... 1060
4.1 Sexual propagation ... 1060
4.1.1 Methods of breaking seed dormancy ... 1060
4.2 Asexual propagation ... 1060
4.3 Vegetative propagation ... 1061
5. PRINCIPLES OF GARDENING ... 1062
6. HISTORY OF GARDENS ... 1064
6.1 FORMAL TYPE ... 1066
6.1.1. Mughal gardens ... 1066
6.1.2. Roman/ Italian gardens ... 1067
6.1.3. French gardens ... 1067
6.2 INFORMAL TYPE ... 1068
6.2.1. Japanese gardens ... 1068
6.2.2. English gardens ... 1068
6.3 FREE TYPE ... 1069
7. WATER GARDEN ... 1071
8. ROCK GARDEN ... 1071
9. MARSH/ BOG GARDEN ... 1072
10. SUNKEN GARDEN ... 1072
11. TERRACE GARDEN ... 1072
12. VERTICAL GARDEN ... 1072
13. TERRARIUM ... 1073
14. FLOWER ARRANGEMENT ... 1073
14.1 Dry flower technology ... 1074

15. ANNUALS 1077
15.1 Classification 1078
15.1.1 Based on height 1078
15.1.2 Based on hardiness 1078
15.1.3 Based on colour 1078
15.1.4 Based on commercial value 1079
15.1.5 Based on purpose 1079
15.1.6 Based on soil requirement 1080
15.2 Exotic and Indian bred varieties in different annual flowers 1081
15.3 Seed production of annual flowers 1082
16. SHRUBS 1083
16.1 Classification 1083
16.2 Propagation method 1083
17. CLIMBERS 1085
17.1 Classification based on purpose 1085
17.2 Modified organs 1085
18. TREES 1086
18.1 Classification based on purpose 1088
18.2 Important trees 1089
19. PALMS 1091
20. HEDGE 1094
21. EDGE 1095
22. BULBOUS PLANTS 1095
23. HOUSE PLANTS/ INDOOR PLANTS 1096
24. TOPIARY 1098
25. LAWN 1098
26. CACTI AND SUCCULENTS 1101
27. BONSAI/ MINIATURE PLANT/ PLANT SCULPTURE 1104
28. FERNS 1105
29. BIO-AESTHETIC PLANNING 1106
30. ESSENTIAL OIL EXTRACTION 1106
31. ACANTHACEAE 1108
31.1 Crossandra 1108
32. AGAVACEAE 1110

32.1 Tuberose 1110

33. ALSTROEMERIACEAE 1113

33.1 Alstroemeria 1113

34. AMARANTHACEAE 1114

34.1 Gomphrena 1114

35. AMARYLLIDACEAE 1115

35.1 Amaryllis (syn. Hippeastrum) 1115

35.2 Daffodil 1119

35.3 Day lily 1119

36. APOCYNACEAE 1119

36.1 Periwinkle (syn. Vinca) 1119

36.2 Adenium 1123

37. ARACEAE 1123

37.1 Anthurium 1123

37.2 Calla lily 1129

38. ASTERACEAE (COMPOSITAE) 1131

38.1 Chrysanthemum 1131

38.2 Marigold 1148

38.3 China aster 1154

38.4 Dahlia 1157

38.5 Gerbera 1163

38.6 Gaillardia 1166

38.7 Zinnia 1168

38.8 Calendula (Pot marigold) 1171

38.9 Garden cosmos 1172

39. BALSAMINACEAE 1175

39.1 Balsam 1175

40. CARYOPHYLLACEAE (PINK FAMILY) 1179

40.1 Carnation 1179

40.2 Gypsophila 1185

41. CRUCIFERAE 1186

41.1 Stock 1186

42. GERANIACEAE 1189

42.1 Geranium 1189

43. HELICONIACEAE 1195

43.1 Heliconia ... 1195

44. IRIDACEAE ... 1196

44.1 Gladiolus ... 1196

44.2 Iris ... 1208

45. LABIATAE ... 1208

45.1 Salvia ... 1208

46. LILIACEAE ... 1212

46.1 Lilium ... 1212

46.2 Tulip ... 1217

47. MALVACEAE/ (MALLOW FAMILY) ... 1222

47.1 Hibiscus ... 1222

47.2 Hollyhock ... 1227

48. NELUMBONACEAE ... 1229

48.1 Lotus ... 1229

49. NYCTAGINACEAE ... 1232

49.1 Bougainvillea ... 1232

50. NYMPHAEACEAE ... 1240

50.1 Water lily ... 1240

51. OLEACEAE (OLIVE FAMILY) ... 1244

51.1 Jasmine ... 1244

52. ORCHIDACEAE ... 1252

52.1 Orchids ... 1252

53. PLANTAGINACEAE (SCROPHULARIACEAE) ... 1262

53.1 Snapdragon ... 1262

54. PLUMBAGINACEAE ... 1264

54.1 Statice ... 1264

55. POLEMONEACEAE ... 1267

55.1 Phlox ... 1267

56. ROSACEAE ... 1269

56.1 Rose ... 1269

57. SOLANACEAE ... 1289

57.1 Petunia ... 1289

58. STRELITZIACEAE ... 1292

58.1 Bird of paradise ... 1292

59. VERBENACEAE ... 1294

59.1 Verbena 1294

60. VIOLACEAE 1296

60.1 Pansy 1296

61. PROTECTED CULTIVATION OF FLOWER CROPS 1300

62. PHYSIOLOGICAL DISORDERS OF FLOWER CROPS 1302

63. HORTICULTURE ASSOCIATIONS AND SOCIETIES 1303

64. INTERNET AND INFO-TECH SERVICES IN FLORICULTURE INDUSTRY 1303

65. BOOKS ON FLORICULTURE AND LANDSCAPE GARDENING 1304

5. PLANTATION CROPS 1305

1. GENERAL INFORMATION 1305

2. ARACACEAE/ PALMAE 1307

2.1 Coconut 1307

2.2 Arecanut 1322

2.3 Palmyrah palm/ *Tadgul* 1329

2.4 Oil palm/ *Tel tad* / Red oil palm 1332

3. EUPHORBIACEAE (MORACEAE) 1342

3.1 Rubber 1342

4. RUBIACEAE (MADDER FAMILY) 1352

4.1 Coffee 1352

5. STERCULIACEAE (MALVACEAE) 1367

5.1 Cocoa 1367

6. THEACEAE (CAMELLIACEAE) 1376

6.1 Tea 1376

6. SPICES AND CONDIMENTS 1389

1. GENERAL INFORMATION 1389

2. CLASSIFICATION OF SPICES AND CONDIMENTS 1395

2.1 Based on botany 1395

2.2 Based on growth habit 1395

2.3 Based on plant part used 1396

2.4 Based on important flavor, taste compounds 1396

2.5 Based on colour compounds 1397

2.6 Based on isolation distance for seed spices 1397

2.7 Based on salinity/ alkalinity tolerance limit in seed spices 1397
2.8 Seed standards for seed spices 1397
2.9 Critical stages of irrigating seed spices 1398
3. APIACEAE (UMBELLIFERAE) 1399
3.1 Coriander/ *Dhania* 1399
3.2 Fennel/*Saunf* 1403
3.3 Anise/*Vilayati saunf* 1405
3.4 Cumin/*Jeera* 1406
3.5 Asafoetida/ *Heeng* 1407
3.6 Dill/ *Sowa* 1408
3.7 Ajowain 1408
3.8 Nigella/ *Kala jeera* 1409
3.9 Caraway 1410
4. IRIDACEAE 1410
4.1 Saffron 1410
5. MYRISTICACEAE 1412
5.1 Nutmeg 1412
6. MYRTACEAE (LAURACEAE) 1417
6.1 Clove 1417
6.2 a. Cinnamon 1420
6.2 b. Cassia 1425
6.3 All spice 1425
7. ORCHIDACEAE 1427
7.1 Vanilla 1427
8. PARMELIACEAE 1432
8.1 Black stone flower 1432
9. PIPERACEAE 1432
9.1 Black pepper 1432
9.2 Betel vine/ *Tambuli*/ *Pan* 1442
10. RUTACEAE 1447
10.1 Curry leaf 1447
11. ZINGIBERACEAE 1448
11.1 Small cardamom 1448
11.2 Large cardamom 1458

11.3 Turmeric 1462

11.4 Ginger 1469

12. Other minor spice 1473

7. MEDICINAL AND AROMATIC PLANTS 1475

1. GENERAL INFORMATION 1475

2. CLASSIFICATION OF MEDICINAL AND AROMATIC PLANTS 1477

3. MEDICINAL PLANTS 1478

3.1. ACANTHACEAE 1478

3.1.1 Adathoda 1478

3.1.2 Kalmegh 1478

3.2. APIACEAE 1479

3.2.1 Dill 1479

3.2.2. Indian pennywort 1479

3.3. APOCYNACEAE 1479

3.3.1 Sarpagandha 1479

3.4. ARACEAE 1480

3.4.1 Sweet flag 1480

3.5. ASCLEPIDACEAE 1480

3.5.1 Madhunashini 1480

3.6. ASTERACEAE 1480

3.6.1 Bhrangraj 1480

3.6.2 Stevia 1480

3.6.3 Sweet worm wood 1480

3.6.4 Chrysanthemum 1481

3.7. BURSERACEAE 1481

3.7.1 Guggul 1481

3.8. COMBRETACEAE 1481

3.8.1 Behada 1481

3.9. CONVOLVULACEAE 1481

3.9.1 Shankhapushpi 1481

3.10. COSTACEAE 1482

3.10.1 Costus 1482

3.11. DIOSCOREACEAE 1482

3.11.1 Medicinal yam 1482
3.12. EUPHORBIACEAE 1482
3.12.1 Jamal gota 1483
3.13. FABACEAE 1483
3.13.1 Babchi 1483
3.13.2 Cow hedge 1483
3.13.3 Indian liquorice 1484
3.14. GINKGOACEAE 1484
3.14.1 Siberian ginseng 1484
3.15. LAMIACEAE 1484
3.15.1 Medicinal coleus 1484
3.16. LEGUMINOSAE 1485
3.16.1 Senna 1485
3.17. LILIACEAE 1486
3.17.1 Safed musli 1486
3.17.2 Aloe 1487
3.17.3 Asparagus 1488
3.18. LYTHRACEAE 1488
3.18.1 Henna/ Mehendi 1488
3.19. MENISPERMACEAE 1488
3.19.1 *Giloe/ Gulvel* 1488
3.20. PAPAVERACEAE 1488
3.20.1 Opium poppy 1488
3.21. PLANTAGINACEAE 1489
3.21.1 Isabgol/ *Psyllium* 1489
3.21.2 *Brahmi* 1491
3.22. PIPERACEAE 1491
3.22.1 Long pepper/ *Pipali* 1491
3.23. PLUMBAGINACEAE 1491
3.23.1 Chitrak 1491
3.24. RUBIACEAE 1491
3.24.1 Cinchona 1491
3.24.2 Ipecac 1492
3.25. SCROPHULARIACEAE 1492

3.25.1 Foxglove/ *Tilpushpi* 1492

3.26. SOLANACEAE 1492

3.26.1 Ashwagandha 1492

3.26.2 Belladonna 1493

3.26.3 Datura 1494

3.26.4 Henbane 1494

3.26.5 Medicinal solanum 1494

4. AROMATIC PLANTS 1495

4.1. ASTERACEAE 1495

4.1.1 Davana 1495

4.1.2 Chamomile 1495

4.2. APIACEAE 1495

4.2.1 Celery 1495

4.3. CANNABINACEAE 1495

4.3.1 Hops 1495

4.4. LAMIACEAE 1496

4.4.1 Patchouli 1496

4.4.2 Basil/ *Tulsi* 1496

4.4.3 Rosemary 1497

4.4.4 Melissa 1498

4.4.5 Thyme 1498

4.4.6 Lavender 1501

4.4.7 Japanese mint 1501

4.4.8 Common mint 1502

4.4.9 Bergamot mint 1503

4.4.10 Pepper mint 1503

4.5. MALVACEAE 1504

4.5.1 Ambrette 1504

4.6. MYRTACEAE 1504

4.6.1 Eucalyptus 1504

4.7. PANDANACEAE 1504

4.7.1 Screwpine 1504

4.8. POACEAE (GRAMINAE) 1505

4.8.1 Lemon grass 1505

4.8.2 Java citronella 1506

4.8.3 Palmarosha grass 1507
4.9. SANTALACEAE 1507
4.9.1 Sandalwood 1507
4.10. VITEVERACEAE 1508
4.10.1 Vetiver grass 1508

8. POST HARVEST TECHNOLOGY 1511

1. GENERAL INFORMATION 1511
2. INVENTIONS AND DISCOVERIES 1518
3. FOOD LAWS 1519
4. CONTAINERS AND PACKING 1520
5. POST HARVEST MANAGEMENT OF HORTICULTURAL CROPS 1521
5.1. Post-harvest losses 1522
5.1.1. Pre-harvest factors to reduce losses 1523
5.1.2. Post-harvest factors 1523
5.1.2.1. Degreening 1523
5.1.2.2. Pre-cooling 1523
5.1.2.3. Curing 1524
5.1.2.4. Disinfection 1524
5.1.2.5. Waxing 1524
5.1.2.6. Ripening 1526
5.1.2.7. Packaging 1526
5.1.2.8. Ethylene absorbents 1527
5.1.2.9. Anti-transpirants 1527
5.1.2.10. Transportation 1527
5.1.2.11. Storage 1527
5.1.2.11.1 Low cost cold storage technology 1528
5.1.2.11.2 High cost cold storage technology 1529
5.1.2.11.3 Controlled atmosphere (CA) storage 1531
5.1.2.11.4 Modified atmosphere (MA) storage 1532
5.1.2.11.5 Hypobaric (HB) storage 1532
5.1.2.11.6 Use of ultra-high pressure 1533
5.1.2.11.7 Super critical extraction technology 1533
5.2 Post harvest management of flower crops 1534
5.2.1. Harvesting stages of flowers 1534

5.2.2. Grading, packing and transport 1536
5.2.3. Storage techniques of flowers 1536
6. HORTICULTURAL CROP RESIDUE AND PROCESSING WASTE FOR VALUE ADDED PRODUCTS 1539
7. PROCESSING TECHNOLOGY OF HORTICULTURAL CROPS 1542
7.1 Preservation by high temperature 1545
7.2 Preservation by low temperature i.e. freezing 1547
7.2.1 Isocoric freezing technology 1549
7.3 Preservation by chemical preservatives 1549
7.4 Preservation by carbonation/carbonated beverages 1551
7.5 Preservation by irradiation 1552
7.6 Preservation by anti-biotics 1554
7.7 CANNING 1555
7.7.1 Peeling 1557
7.7.2 Blanching 1557
7.7.3 Sulphuring 1558
7.7.4 Syruping 1558
7.7.5 Brining 1558
7.7.6 Classification of fruits and vegetables based on pH content 1559
7.7.7 Spoilage of canned foods 1550
7.8 Preservation by dehydration 1561
7.9 Jam 1563
7.10 Jelly 1564
7.11 Marmalade 1565
7.12 Other products 1566
7.13 Vinegar 1567
7.14 Pickles/ Chutney 1568
7.15 Fruit based beverages 1570
7.15.1 Unfermented/ Non-alcoholic fruit beverages 1573
7.15.2 Fermented fruit beverages 1574
7.16 Stepping preservation of vegetables 1577
7.17 Bio-preservation of vegetables 1578
7.18 Sauces/ ketchups 1578
7.19 Tomato processing 1579

7.20 Major products 1580
7.21 Papain 1580
7.22 Jaggery preparation 1581
7.23 Food colour 1581
7.24 Food additives 1582
7.25 Food spoilage 1582
7.25.1 Useful bacteria 1582
7.25.2 Type of spoilage 1584
7.25.3 Post-harvest diseases of fruit crops 1584
7.25.4 Chemicals used to extend shelf life of fruits 1585

1

GENERAL HORTICULTURE

1. BASICS OF HORTICULTURE

- Definition of farmer (National Policy for Farmers, 2001): A person actively engaged in the economic and/or livelihood activity of growing crops and producing other primary agricultural commodities and w'll include all agriculture operational holders, cultivators, agriculture labourers, share croppers, tenants, poultry and livestock rearers, fishers, beekeepers, gardeners, pastoralists, non-corporate planters and planting labours, as well as persons engaged in various farming related occupations such as sericulture, vermiculture, and agroforestry. It also includes tribal families/ persons engaged in shifting cultivation and in the collection, use and sale of minor and non-timber forest produce.
- C. Linnaeus's system of classification is published in book 'Species Plantarum' in 1753.
- Best and highly recognized natural system of classification: G. Bentham and J.D. Hooker in their book 'Genera Plantarum'.
- Majority of present day botanical institutions and publications follow Engler and Prantl's scheme of classification.
- Horticulture word derived from Latin word: *Hortus* meaning 'Garden' and *cultura* means 'cultivation'.
- Father of horticulture: Thomas Andrew Knight, John Lindley, Liberty Hyde Bailey.
- World renowned horticulturists: Mr. S. Percy Lancaster, Dr. Jules Janick, Dr. G.S. Cheema.
- Farmers in space: Drs. Scott Kelly and Kjell Lindgren.
- Future crops to be sent in space: Red romaine lettuce and Chinese cabbage.
- In 1989, Dr. Stephen de Felis proposed idea of Nutrient + Pharmaceutical= Nutriceutical agriculture.
- Father of vegetables: L. H. Bailey.
- Global Horticulture was initiated in 2006 after 26th International Horticultural Congress in Toronto in 2002.
- The sub-tropical region on India lies between latitude 15^0 and 30^0 N of equator.
- The temperate fruits, nuts and berry crops require chilling (above freezing temperature) for resumption of growth and fruiting.

- 1st book in horticulture: Fruit growing in India: W.B. Hayes (1945) & related to litchi.
- India ranks 1st with 179.8 million ha of net crop area (9.6% of the global net crop area).
- India has 2nd highest irrigated area (70.4 million ha) next to China (71.74 million ha).
- India ranks 1st among the rainfed countries in the world having 78 million ha and thus constituting 64 % of the country's net sown area being rainfed.
- Net sown area of the country is 43% of total geographical area along with cropping intensity of 142 %.
- Of the total horticulture production, only 67% is used for domestic consumption, 30% is sunjected to post harvest loss, 2% for export and 0.8% for processing,
- India has just 1% share of world trade in fresh fruits and vegetables.
- India is blessed with 6 ecosystems, 15 major agro-climatic regions/zones and 46 different soil types out of total 60 types of soil in the world.
- In India, more than 20 cropping systems are practiced, of which rice-wheat and rice-rice are most important. The rice-wheat cropping system (RWCS) of the Indo-Gangetic plains in the country has revolutionized agriculture during the green revolution.
- In India, 67% of total holdings are by marginal farmers with average holding of just 0.39 ha, and 17.9% small farmers with average farm size of 1.42 ha.
- Altogether, marginal and small farmers possess 85% of total holdings and cultivate 44.6% area with average farm size of just 0.6 ha.
- Out of total 138.11 million operational holdings, only 39.41% used certified seeds while 26.96% used seeds of notified varieties.
- Block-chain/ Back-bone technology: Trace back to the farmer and give him his due, while maintaining supply chain network by filling the gaps in system.
- Horticulture sector has emerged as a growth engine for India's agriculture sector.
- Horticultural Society of India (HSI) was established in 1942.
- 1st president of HSI: Dr. G.S. Cheema.
- 1st Indian Horticulture Congress was held in 2004.
- Brown revolution: Related with leather and cocoa production.
- Golden revolution: Related with overall horticulture, honey, fruit production (Apple).
- Grey revolution: Promotion of manures and fertilizers.
- Pink revolution: Related with onion production.
- Rainbow revolution: Over all horticulture production.
- Blue revolution: Related with fishery. India ranks 2nd in the world in total fisheries production (6.3% share).
- Father of Golden revolution: Dr. K.L. Chadha.
- Dr. Harbhajan Singh is called as 'Indian Vavilov'.

- Dual factor stimulus of flowering i.e. dual factor hypothesis was given by Chakraborty.
- 'KIRAN'- Knowledge Innovation Repository of Agriculture in the North-East.
- Mission for Integrated Development of Horticulture (MIDH) was launched in 2014-15 to propel Indian horticulture to realize its potential.
- NHM, NHB, CDB and CIH play major role in horticultural mission.
- Horticulture Mission for North-East and Himalayas (HMNEH).
- National Horticulture Board (NHB) was established in 1984.
- National Initiative on Climate Resilient Agriculture (NICRA): Network project of ICAR launched in 2011.
- The Stern Committee is associated with economic impact of climate change.
- Council for Energy, Environment and Water is related with climate change.
- United Nations Climate Change Conference (COP24) held at Katowice, Poland from 3-14 December, 2018 (recent climate change conference).
- Concept of 'Climate Smart Agriculture' put forth by FAO.
- India's 1st Agromet Forecast Centre inaugurated at UAS, Dharwad, Karnataka. (Main objective is to accurate reports on weather which would enable the farmers to protect the crops and get a good yield).
- UNO established Inter-governmental Panel on Climate Change (IPCC).
- Nobel prize winners for the year 2021: Dr. Clouse Hasalman (Germany), Dr. Gorgeo Parisi (Rome) and Dr. Skewkukoro Manabe (Japan) for Foundation of scientific theories and development of 1st computer model on climate change and its effects on earth.
- Initiative by Govt. of India: Green India Mission.
- National target for 5 years (2015-16 to 2020-21): Tree plantation program on 1,67,153 ha area. Among this, only 1,17,507 ha area only.
- Deficit in tree plantation: 30% in Green India Mission.
- Leading states fulfilled 100% target: Mizoram, Odisha, Punjab, Karnataka, Sikkim.
- As per the report of Global Bio-Geo-Chemical Cycles, published in the International Journal of Science (Abigale and Morledge, 2021)-
    1. Atmosphere is fully saturated with CO_2 and has attained 410 ppm concentration as against normal 300 ppm.
    2. Increased CO_2 content caused drastic decline in evaporation and photosynthesis activities.
    3. Increased CO_2 causes increase in leaf thickness, a micro parameter to measure changes in climatic conditions.
- UNO has declared 5 R's should be taken care of to reduce ill effects of climate change 1) Reduce, 2) Refuse 3) Re-use 4) Recycle 5) Recover.

- United Nations Conference on Environment and Development (UNCED), also known as the "Rio de Janeiro Earth Summit" held on June, 1992.
- United Nations Framework Convention on Climate Change (UNFCCC), 1992.
- National Action Plan on Climate Change (NAPCC).
- State Action Plans on Climate Change (SAPCC).
- United Nations Environment Programme (UNEP).
- Nobel Peace prize for the year 2020 was awarded to World Food Program.
- As per WHO, per capita consumption of fruits &vegetables: 440 g/ person.
- As per RDA (Recommended Dietary Allowance), per capita consumption of fruits (ICMR recommendation): 184 g/person/ day.
- As per RDA, per capita consumption of vegetables (ICMR recommendation): 300 g/person/ day(50 g green leafy vegetables + 50 g roots and tubers + 200 g other vegetables).
- Per capita gross availability of fruits (2018-19): 201.5 grams per day.
- Per capita gross availability of vegetables (2018-19): 388.72 grams per day.
- ICAR recognized 8 agro-ecological zones for effective land use planning.
- Planning commission recognized 15 agro-climatic zones for effective land use planning.
- NBSS & LUP, Nagpur recognized 21 agro-ecological regions.
- Growing period of arid zone (90 days); semi-arid zone (90-150 days); sub-arid zone (150-210 days); humid zone (210-270 days); pre humid zone (270 days).
- Defoliation cause maleness while defloration cause femaleness.
- Broad leaved fruit trees suffer, if temperature < 5^0C.
- Optimum temperature for most fruits and vegetables development: 22-27^0C.
- Maximum temperature for most fruits and vegetables development: 40-52^0C.
- High humidity leads to 1. Brown rot of peaches 2. Apple scab 3. Black rot and downy mildew of grapes 4. Reduces photosynthetic activity.
- Spores of Lycopodium are commercially known as: Vegetable sulphur as they used to cure stomach disorder.
- In orchard, area under roads and buildings should not exceed 10% of total area.
- Trees which shed their leaves in winter are called: Deciduous.
- Trees which shed their leaves in summer are called: Caudocous.
- Fruits having anti-oxidant value: Blueberry, Blackberry, Strawberry, Plums, Raspberry, Banana, Sweet orange, Red grapes, Cherries, Kiwi fruit.
- Vegetables having highest anti-oxidant values: Black bean, Kidney bean.
- Plant Quarantine Act (DIP Act) became operational in year 1914.

- Best combination of diversified horticulture: Floriculture + Apiculture.
- Kraft: German name used to mention paper strength are made from *Pinus rom*.
- 'Drupe' type of fruit develop from superior ovary.
- Carotene that contains -OH group is xanthophyll.
- Equilibrium Relative Humidity (ERH) of pure water: 100%.
- Water activity can be calculated by- ERH/100 (For water it is-1.0).
- NAFED is related to agricultural marketing.
- Term 'neutraceutical' was coined in 1989 by F. De Felice.
- Sikkim Chief Minister Shri. Pawan Kumar Chamling: Greenest chief minister of India.
- To test the residue monitoring plan for export purposes, APEDA has developed systems for export viz. GrapeNet for grape; AnarNet for pomegranate; CitrusNet for citrus, MangoNet for mango, BananaNet for banana, BetelNet for betelnut leaves, and VegNet for vegetable crops.
- Pollinators such as bees, birds and bats affect 35% of world's crop production.
- 'Agrowon': A daily newspaper solely dedicated to agriculture has received place in Limca book of records in 2013.
- First website for 7528 fungi: www.fungifromindia.com another link www.mycobank.org
- India ranks 7th in micro-irrigation system.
- National Mission on Micro-irrigation (NMMI), launched in 2008 to enhance water use efficiency.
- Yield increase through micro-irrigation system: 52% in banana, 23% in grapes, 50% in sweet lime and 45% in pomegranate.
- Water-use efficiency: Ratio of water used in plant metabolism to water lost by plant through transpiration.
- Amino acid synthesized during drought tolerance: Proline.
- Plant Quarentine Act came into force in 1914.
- National Agriculture Marketing (NAM), an online trading portal for farm produce launched on 14th April, 2016.
- Agrivoltaic (production of solar photovoltaic power as well as crops on same piece of land).
- Model Contract farming Act passed on-May, 2018 and it will provide adequate confidence to farmers and incentives to sponsors to enter into contract.
- Govt. of India Constituted Agri-export policy for farmers on- 9 Dec, 2018 (aim: to double agri. exports to 60 billion $ by 2022).
- Year 2020: International Year of Plant Health. Importance of Nutri farming for health awareness.

- Year 2021: International Year of Fruits & Vegetables. Consumption of 440 g of fruits and vegetables/ head/ day is recommended.
- Rainbow diet: Concept for colourful & complete diet for well fitness, more energetic diet to control body weight loss & to increase resistance power.
- Country's biggest horti-fair was held at IIHR, Bengaluru during 5-8th February, 2020.
- GMP: Good Management Practices.
- GHP: Good Healthy Practices.
- New concept of Govt. of India: Agro-waste utilization for generation of ethanol.
- Butterfly of Maharashtra state: Blue Mormon.
- September month is recognized as butterfly month.
- Maharashtra is 1st state in India gave recognition/ identity to butterfly.
- Non-dairy milk is obtained from soybean, almond, coconut.
- Earth is also known as 'Blue Planet' because of vastness of water preserved.
- On earth, only 1-2% water is suitable for human use.
- Israel desalinates 90% of sea water used in households and then recycles 90% of its sewage water for agriculture.
- National Agricultrue Innovation Fund (NAIF) is raized by ICAR to help start up projects related to agriculture.
- 1st Indian scientist who used electronics in agriculture: Dr. Omprakash Kulkarni. He has credited with 19 patents. Recently, he has developed an instrument to detect rots in storage of agriculture produce.
- 1st state in the country to flag off India's 1st fruit train: Andhra Pradesh.

  Note: A fruit train was flagged from Tadipatri railway station in A.P. carrying a load of 980 mt of locally grown bananas to Jawaharlal Nehru Port in Mumbai from where the consignment will be exported to Iran (Bananas exported under brand name 'Happy Bananas').
- Top five global innovations in horticulture:
  1. Urban agriculture, Smart design, and Vertical farms
  2. The Drones and the Robot Bees-Pollinator.
  3. Artificial Intelligence, Internet of Things (IoT) and Automation- Driverless Tractor.
  4. Block Chain Technology and
  5. CRISPR and Genetic Editing.

Area, Production and productivity of horticultural commodities:

- For the 1st time horticulture contribution exceeded the combined production of food grains and oilseeds in 2013-14.

- Percentage of gross cultivated area utilized by horticulture: 16%.
- Horticulture production has increased by 30% in the last five years.
- Horticultural crops contribute 13.08% of total cropped area.
- Contribution of horticulture to agriculture GDP (2017-18): 38% and 52% of export earnings in agriculture.
- Contribution of horticulture to agriculture GDP (2020-21): 29.5%.
- During 2020-21, horticulture sector contributes over 326.58 million MT (188.91 million MT of vegetables & 102.03 million MT of fruits) of production in the country growing at an impressive decadal rate of 4.8%.
- Total area under horticulture (2018-19): 25.87 million ha.
- Total horticulture production (2019-20): 313.35 million tonnes (0.84% higher than the previous year) than 310.74 million tonnes (2018-19).
- Total productivity of horticulture crops (2018-19): 12.3 million tonnes/ha.
- Total fruit production (2019-20): 95.74 million tonnes as against 97.77 million tonnes (2018-19).
- Total vegetable production (2019-20): 188.01 million tonnes as against 183.17 million tonnes (2018-19).
- Total flower production (2019-20): 2.8 million tonnes as against 2.9 million tonnes (2018-19).
- Total spices production (2018-19): 8.61 million tonnes.
- India ranks 1st in productivity of grapes, banana, cassava, peas, ginger, and papaya.
- India ranks 1st in cauliflower production, 2nd on onion, tomato, brinjal, peas and 3rd in cabbage.
- India's rank in fruit production: 2nd (1st China).
- India's rank in vegetable production: 2nd (1st China).
- India's share in world production of fruits: 13%.
- India's share in world production of vegetables: 10.7%.
- Export growth of fresh fruits and vegetables is 14% in terms of value and processed fruits and vegetables is 16.27%.
- Export of fresh fruits from India was <1% of total quantity of fruits produced (2018-19).
- At world's level, export of fruits and vegetables has been increased by 115% in 2000 to 2018.
- India is largest producer of Coconut, Cashew nut, Tea, Mango, Sapota, Banana, Mangosteen, Guava, Acid limes, Aonla and Spices.
- During 2016-17, India exported fruits and vegetables worth Rs. 7474.14 crores which comprised of fruits worth Rs. 2771.32 crores and vegetables worth Rs. 4702.78 crores.

- Mangoes, Walnuts, Grapes, Bananas, Pomegranates account for larger portion of fruits exported from the country while Onions, Okra, Bitter gourd, Green chilli, Mushrooms and Potatoes contribute largely to the vegetable export basket.
- Over the last decade, the area under horticulture grew by about 2.7% per annum and annual production increased by 7.0%.
- During 2017-18, highest annual growth of 9.5% is seen in fruit production.
- During 2017-18, the annual growth in citrus fruits is quite high (10.48%).
- During 2018-19, total fruit production was highest in Andhra Pradesh followed by Uttar Pradesh and Maharashtra.
- During 2018-19, total vegetable production, was highest in West Bengal (23,045 thousand tones) followed by Uttar Pradesh (18,545 thousand tones) and Madhya Pradesh.
- During 2017-18, highest production of flowers (loose) was recorded in Tamil Nadu (343.65 thousand tones) followed by Karnataka (211.50 thousand tones).
- During 2020-21, India's horticultural production is estimated to be 326.6 million metric tones.
- Production share of fruits: Banana (33.4%), Mango (20.7%), Papaya (6.3%), Guava (4.1%), Grapes (2.9%), Apple (2.8%), Sapota (2.8%), Pineapple (2%), Pomegranate (5%), Litchi (0.7%) and others (11.1%).
- Production share of vegetables: Potato (25.5%), Onion (11.9%), Tomato (11.5%).
- Production share of plantation crops: Coconut (91.47%), Cashew nut (4.62%), Areca nut (3.82%).
- Production share of major spices: Chilli (25.26%), Garlic (21.19%), Turmeric (20.14%), Ginger (11.09%).

India's share in export trends and rank (2018-19)

- Cucumber and gherkins- 24%, 1st.
- Onion- 12.3%, 3rd.
- Walnut-2.3 %, 7th.
- Fresh mangoes-2%, 2nd.
- Other fresh fruits-7.1%, 6th.
- Mango pulp-5.4 %, 5th.
- Mango- 3.88%, 7th
- Grape- 3.09%, 10th.
- Dried processed vegetables- 4.71%, 4th.
- Fruit and vegetable seeds- 2.19%, 13th.
- Other fresh vegetables- 0.80%, 19th.
- Floriculture- 0.42%, 24th.

- States leading in fruit production: Andhra Pradesh (13%), Maharashtra (11%), Uttar Pradesh (11%), Gujarat (9%), Karnataka (8%).
- States leading in vegetable production: Uttar Pradesh (15%), West Bengal (15%), Madhya Pradesh (10%), Bihar (8%).
- States leading in flower production: West Bengal (27%), Karnataka (13%), Odisha (11%).
- States leading in loose flower production: Tamil Nadu (19%), Karnataka (13%), Madhya Pradesh (10%).
- States leading in spices production: Andhra Pradesh (14.84%), Rajasthan (13.25%). Gujarat (12.27%), Madhya Pradesh (9.76%), Telangana (8.82%).
- States leading in plantation crops production: Kerala (31.71%), Tamil Nadu (24.76%), Karnataka (24.56%), Andhra Pradesh (7.05%), Maharashtra (2.67%).

	Area (million ha)	Production (million MT)	Productivity (MT/ha)
Fruits	6.48	92.85	14.33
Vegetables	10.29	175.01	17.01
Flowers & aromatics	0.94	3.28	3.48
Plantation crops	3.68	16.87	4.59
Spices	3.54	7.08	2.0
Total horticultural crops	**24.93**	**295.16**	**11.84**

Role of honey in Indian economy

- Honey is called as 'natural immunity booster'.
- Pure honey is a golden gift of nature to humanity to improve intelligence, healthy lean body & unmatched stamina.
- Honey contains 76% fructose, 3.2-4.2 pH and specific gravity 1.35-1.44. It is the only product which cannot be spoiled.
- Natural honey has high commercial value i.e. for edible & medicinal purposes.
- In honey production, China ranks 1st in the world & produces 4.50 lakh tonnes/annum.
- At present, India's honey production is hardly 1.25 lakh tonnes/ annum.
- Major producers of honey: Maharashtra, Gujarat, Rajasthan, Karnataka, Uttar Pradesh, Bihar, Himachal Pradesh.
- In terms of honey production, 3.5 times increase has been achieved.
- India ranks 5th in total world's production of honey.
- India is on the door steps of 'Honey revolution'.
- Sweet revolution: Term related with honey production.
- Seminar on Baswant honey bee festival and Honey revolution, 2021 was organized at Pimpalgaon Baswant, Nashik, Maharashtra.
- In last 5 years, honey production has been increased by 57.58%.
- Honey production (2019-20): 76150 ton production; 28378.42 ton export with 116.13% increase in export.

- Export during 2018-19: 61,333 tones worth rs. 732.18 crores.
- Honey was exported to USA, UAE, Saudi Arabia, Morocco, and Qatar.
- At present, there are 1.30 crores colonies of honey bees in India & stands 1st in world scenario.
- Value added products: Herbal honey, honey milk, honey wine, honey cubes.
- Unifloral honey-nector is collected from single flora blossoms.
- Multifloral honey- collected from multiple source flora.
- Genuine honey is delicious, sweet, has specific aroma, colour, taste and sweetness disappears within 15 seconds from tongue while sweetness of adulterated honey remains up to 15 minutes.
- Cross pollination by honey bee is most effective and cheapest method of enhancing crop yield.
- The increase in yields of various horticultural & agronomical crops due to pollination by honey bees ranges from 5-25%.
- As per report of National Commission on Agriculture, tremendous increase in fruit/ seed setting in self pollinated crops, due to bee pollination viz. Litchi (10246%), Onion (9878%), Apple (6950%), Grapes (6700%), Pears (6014%), Plums (2739%), and Cabbage (300%).
- Pollination power of honey bees for enhancing crop productivity remains to be tapped in India.
- Required 3-9 bee colonies/ha for adequate pollination.
- Indigenous bee spp. commonly found are- *Apis florea*, *A. dorsata*, and *A. cerena* (most abundant).
  - *A. dorsata*: Yield 30-35 kg honey and 2-3 kg wax/ colony/ year. Effective pollinator.
  - *A. florea*: Yield 300-500 g honey/ colony/ year. Due to small size, bees enter inside the flowers & make pollination easily.
  - *A. cerena indica*: Yield 5-7 kg honey and 1-2 kg wax/ colony/ year. Can be reared in boxes and transported at many places.
  - *A. mellifera*: European honey bees introduced to India during later part of 19th century. Responsible for honey revolution in India. Yield 40-50 kg honey and 4-5 kg wax/ colony/ year. It is much more productive than indigenous *Acerana indica*.
  - *Trigona iridipennis*: Honey collected by these bees is considered to be medicinal purpose & highly efficient for pollination of polyhouse grown crops.
- Average yield of honey from domestic bees is quite low (6-10 kg/ colony/year).
- Bees are highly useful for production of royal jelly.
- 100 gram honey yields 304 calories energy and glucose & fructose sugar's are available from honey.

- Other products:
  - Venum (used in orthrotise & Api-therapy).
  - Pollens- major food for honey bees & also used in medicine & protein production.
  - Royal jelly- widely used for fertility problems in human beings.
  - Wax: widely used in cosmetic industry, tanning industry for bating hides & candle production.
  - Propolis: has medicinal value in filling of injuries.
  - Honey: major product has medicinal values.

2. HORTICULTURAL INSTITUTES

- 1st Regional Fruit Research Station in Uttar Pradesh was established at Saharanpur.
- Trust for Advancement of Agricultural Sciences (TAAS), New Delhi
- North East Institute of Science and Technology (NEIST), Jorhat, Assam.
- National Herbarium of Cultivated Plants (NHCP), New Delhi.
- Horticulture Produce Co-operative Marketing Society (HOPCOMS), Karnataka.
- Indian Institute of Standardization has been renamed as Bureau of Indian Standards (BIS).
- 'Mousam Bhavan' is located at New Delhi.
- NARP was launched by Govt. of India in 1979.
- National Academy of Agricultural Sciences (NAAS), New Delhi registered on 5th June, 1990.
- Maharashtra Association of Cultivated Sciences for Agriculture Research on agronomic crops (MACS), Baramati, Pune.
- 1st Agri-Food Bio-technology Institute: NABI, Chandigarh.

National

Fruit science

Name of institute	Location
Central Arid Zone Research Institute (CAZRI)	Jodhpur, Rajasthan
Central Citrus Research Institute (earlier NRCC, 1986)	Nagpur, Maharashtra
Central Institute for Sub-tropical Horticulture (CISH) earlier Central Mango Research Station	Lucknow, Uttar Pradesh
Central Institute for Temperate Horticulture (CITH)	Srinagar, Jammu & Kashmir
Central Institute for Arid Horticulture (CIAH)	Bikaner, Rajasthan
Central Institute of Horticulture (CIH)	Mediziphema, Nagaland
Central Island Agricultural Research Institute (CARI)	Port Blair, Andaman and Nicobar Islands
National Research Centre for Banana (NRCB, 1993)	Tiruchirapalli, Tamil Nadu
National Research Centre for Chikoo (NRCC)	Thane, Maharashtra
National Research Centre for Grapes (NRCG, 1997)	Pune, Maharashtra
National Research Centre for Litchi (NRCL)	Muzzaffarpur, Bihar
National Research Centre of Noni (NRCN)	Salavakkam, Chennai
National Research Centre on Pomegranate (NRCP)	Solapur, Maharashtra
National Referral Laboratory for Pesticide Residue Monitoring in Grapes	Pune, Maharashtra

Vegetable science:

Name of institute	Location
Central Potato Research Institute (CPRI)	Shimla, Himachal Pradesh
Central Tuber Crops Research Institute (CTCRI, 1963)	Thiruvananthapuram, Kerala
Directorate of Mushroom Research (DMR)	Solan, Himachal Pradesh
National Centre for Mushroom Research & Training	Solan, Himachal Pradesh
Indian Onion and Garlic Research Institute-IOGRI (earlier- Directorate of Onion and Garlic Research (DOGR, 1994)	Rajgurunagar (Pune), Maharashtra
Indian Institute of Vegetable Research (IIVR)	Varanasi, Uttar Pradesh
Indian Institute Soybean Research (IISR)	Indore, Madhya Pradesh
National Horticultural Research and Development Foundation (NHRDF) (earlier AARDF)	Nashik, Maharashtra

Floriculture:

Name of institute	Location
Directorate of Floricultural Research (DFR)	Pune, Maharashtra
Institute of Himalayan Bioresource Technology (IHBT, 1983) (under CSIR)	Palampur, Himachal Pradesh
Institute of Bioresources and Sustainable Development (IBSD)	Imphal, Meghalaya
Orchid Research and Development Centre (ORDC)	Bhalokpong, Arunachal Pradesh
National Research Centre for Orchids (NRCO, 1996)	Gangtok, Sikkim
National Botanical Research Institute (NBRI, 1953)	Lucknow, Uttar Pradesh
National Research Centre for Makhana (NRCM)	Darbhanga, Bihar
Regional Plant Resource Centre (RPRC, 1985)	Bhubaneshwar, Odisha

Medicinal and aromatic plants:

Name of institute	Location
Central Council for Research on Ayurveda and Siddha (CCRAS)	New Delhi
Central Council for Research on Indian Medicine and Homeopathy (CCRIMH)	New Delhi
Central Institute for Medicinal and Aromatic Plants (CIMAP) (under CSIR)	Lucknow, Uttar Pradesh
Central Drug Research Institute (CDRI) (under CSIR)	Lucknow, Uttar Pradesh
Directorate of Cinchona and other Medicinal Plants	Darjeeling, Kolkata
Directorate of Medicinal and Aromatic Plants Research (DMAPR)	Anand, Gujarat
Indian Institute of Integrative Medicines (IIIM) earlier RRL (under CSIR)	Jammu Tawi, Jammu
Institute of Ayurveda and Integrative Medicine	Bengaluru, Karnataka
Medicinal and Aromatic Plants Research Station	Odakkali, Kerala
National Bureau of Plant Genetic Resources (NBPGR, 1976)	New Delhi
National Medicinal Plants Board (NMPB)	New Delhi
National Institute of Nutrition (NIN)	Hyderabad
Regional Research Laboratory (under CSIR)	Jorhat, Assam
Regional Research Laboratory (under CSIR)	Bhubaneshwar, Odisha
Regional Research Laboratory (under CSIR)	Thiruvananthapuram, Kerala

Plantation crops:

Name of institute	Location
Cashew Export Promotion Council of India (CEPC, 1955)	Ernakulum, Kerala
Central Arecanut Research Station (CARS, 1956)	Vittal, Karnataka
Central Arecanut and Cocoa Marketing and Processing Co-operative Limited (CAMPCO)	Mangalore, Karnataka
Central Coffee Research Institute (CCRI, 1946)	Chikmagalur, Karnataka
Central Institute of Coir Technology	Bangaluru, Karnataka
Central Coir Research Institute	Alappuzha, Kerala
Central Plantation Crops Research Institute (CPCRI, 1970)	Kozhikode, Kerala
Coconut Development Board (CDB, 1981)	Kochi, Kerala
Coffee Board	Bengaluru, Karnataka
Directorate of Cashew Research (DCR) (earlier NRCC, 1986)	Puttur, Karnataka
Coir Board	Kochi, Kerala
Directorate of Cashew nut and Cocoa Development (DCCD)	Kochi, Kerala
Directorate of Arecanut and Spices Development (DASD)	Kozhikode, Kerala
Indian Institute of Oil Palm Research (earlier DOPR)	West Godavari, AP
Oil Palm India Limited (OPIL)	Kerala
Oil Palm Research Centre (OPRC)	Thodupuzha, Kerala
Palmyra Research Station	Srivilliputhur, Tamil Nadu
Quality Upgradation Laboratory and Technical Consultancy Centre	Kollam, Kerala.
Rubber Research Institute of India (RRII, 1995)	Kottayam, Kerala
Rubber Board	Kottayam, Kerala
Tea Board	Kolkata
United Planters' Association of Southern India (UPASI, 1893)	Coonoor, Tamil Nadu
UPASI Tea Research Foundation (UPASI TRF)	Coimbatore, Tamil Nadu
Central Coir Research Institute	Alappuzha, Kerala

Spices:

Name of institute	Location
Cardamom Board (1986)	
Indian Institute of Spices Research (IISR, 1986)	Kozhikode, Kerala
Indian Cardamom Research Institute (ICRI, 1978)	Myladumpara, Kerala
National Research Centre for Seed Spices (NRCSS, 2000)	Ajmer, Rajasthan
Pepper Research Station	Panniyur, Kerala
Spice Board	Kochi, Kerala
Cardamom Research Centre	Appangala, Karnataka

Post harvest technology:

Name of institute	Location
Agricultural and Processed Food Products Export Development Authority (APEDA)	New Delhi
Central Food Laboratory (CFL)	Kolkata, WB
Central Food Technological Research Institute (CFTRI, 1950)	Mysore, Karnataka

Central Research Institute for Post-Harvest Engineering and Technology (CIPHET)	Ludhiana, Punjab
Defense Food Research Laboratory (DFRL)	Mysore, Karnataka
Food Preservation and Canning Institute (FPCI)	Lucknow, UP
Food Research and Standardization Technology (FRSL)	Ghaziabad, UP
Indian Institute of Crop Processing Technology (IICPT)	Thanjavur, Tamil Nadu
National Centre for HACCP Certification	Thiruvananthapuram, Kerala
National Institute of Food Technology Entrepreneurship and Management (NIFTEM)	Kundli, Haryana
National Institute of Post-Harvest Technology (NIPHT)	Pune, Maharashtra
National Agricultural Cooperative Marketing Federation of India Ltd. (NAFED)	New Delhi
Public Health Laboratory (PHL)	Pune, Maharashtra

Other institutes:

Name of institute	Location
Agricultural Research Institute	Barhi, Jharkhand
Bhabha Atomic Research Centre (BARC)	Mumbai, Maharashtra
Centre for Cellular Molecular Biology (CCMB)	Hyderabad, Telangana
Central Plant Protection Training Institute (CPPTI)	Hyderabad, Telangana
Centre for Protected Cultivation Technology (CPCT)	IARI, New Delhi
Central Fertilizer Quality Control Institute & Training Institute	Faridabad, Haryana
Centre for High Altitude Biology (CHAB)	Ribling, Lahaul & Spiti, HP
Central Agricultural Research Institute (CARI)	Port Blair, Andeman & Nicobar Islands
Central Coastal Agricultural Research Institute (CCARI)	Goa
Directorate of Plant Protection, Quarantine and Storage (DPPQS)	Faridabad, Uttar Pradesh
Directorate of Knowledge Management in Agriculture (DKMA)	New Delhi
Defense Institute of Bio-Energy Research (DIBER) rechristened from Defence Agricultural Laboratory (DARL, 1990)	Pithoragarh, Uttarakhand
Fragrance and Flavour Development Centre (FFDC)	Kannauj, Uttar Pradesh
ICAR Research Complex for Eastern Region (RCER)	Patna, Bihar
ICAR Research Complex for North Eastern Hilly Region (RCNEHR)	Meghalaya
indian council of Agricultural Skills (ICAS)	New Delhi
Indian Institute of Bio-diversity (IIB)	Itanagar, Arunachal Pradesh
Indian Institute of Science Education & Research (IISER)	Bhopal, Madhya Pradesh
Indian Institute of Toxicology (IIT)	Pune, Maharashtra
Indian Institute of Natural Resins and Gums (IINRG)	Ranchi, Jharkhand
Indian Agricultural Research Institute (IARI)	New Delhi
Indian Institute of Agricultural Biotechnology (IIAB)	Ranchi, Jharkhand
Indian Institute of Horticulture Research (IIHR)	Bengaluru, Karnataka
India Meteorological Department (IMD)	Pune, Maharashtra
Institute of Bio-resource Management and Sustainable Use	Manipur
National Bio-diversity Authority of India (NBAI)	Chennai, Tamil Nadu
Institute of Forest Genetics and Tree Breeding (IFGTB)	Coimbatore, Tamil Nadu
Institute of Genomics and Integrative Biology (IGIB) (under CSIR)	New Delhi

Institute of Horticulture Technology (IHT, 2009)	New Delhi
National Agricultural Co-operative Marketing Federation of India Limited (NAFED)	New Delhi
National Research Centre for Integrated Pest Management (NRCIPM)	New Delhi
National Institute of Hydrology (NIH)	Roorkee, Uttarakhand
National Institute of Plant Health Management (NIPHM)	Hyderabad, Telangana
National Institute of Plant Genome Research (NIPGR)	New Delhi
National Agri-Food Biotechnology Institute (*NABI*)	Mohali, Chandigarh
National Bureau of Agriculturally Important Insects (NBAII)	Bengaluru, Karnataka
National Bureau of Agriculturally Important Micro-organisms (NBAIM)	Kushmaur, Uttar Pradesh
National Centre for Integrated Pest Management (NCIPM)	New Delhi
National Centre for Cell Science (NCCS)	Pune, Maharashtra
National Research Centre on DNA Fingerprinting (NRCDF)	NBPGR, New Delhi
National Herbarium of Cultivated Plants (NHCP)	NBPGR, New Delhi
National Horticulture Board (NHB)	Gurgaon, Haryana
National Institute of Biotic Stress Management (NIBSM)	Raipur, Chhattisgarh
National Institute of Abiotic Stress Management (NIASM)	Malegaon (Baramati) Maharashtra
National Centre for Integrated Farming Research (NCIFR)	Motihari, Bihar
National Centre for Cold-chain Development (NCCD)	New Delhi
National Centre for Medium Range Weather Forecasting (NCMRWF)	New Delhi
National Organic Farming Research Institute (NOFRI)	Tadong, Sikkim
National Research Centre for Weed Science (NRCWS)	Jabalpur, Madhya Pradesh
National Remote Sensing Agency (NRSA)	Hyderabad, Telangana
National Institute of Agriculture Marketing (NIAM)	Jaipur, Rajasthan

International:

Name of the institute	Location
Asian Pacific Coconut Community (APCC)	Jakarta, Indonesia
Asia and Pacific Seed Association	Bangkok, Thailand
Association of Natural Rubber Producing Countries (ANRPC)	Kuala Lumpur, Malaysia
Association of Cut Flower Growers	Haslett, USA
Association of Specialty Cut Flower Growers	West College Oberlin, USA
Association for the Development of the International Exchange of food and Agricultural Products and Technology (ADEPTA)	France
Bio-diversity International (earlier IBPGR, 1974)	Rome, Italy
Bio-diversity International Banana and Plantain (earlier INIBAP)	Montpellier, France
Central Institute for Tropical Agriculture (CIAT)	Cali, Columbia
Chartered Institute of Horticulture (earlier IIH)	Brazil
Coffee Rust Research Centre (CRRC)	Oeiras, Portugal
Corporation Research Centre for Oil Palm (CENIPPALMA)	Columbia
French National Institute for Agricultural Research (INRA)	France
Global Horticulture Initiative (GHI)	Rome, Italy
Horticulture Research International (HRI)	Wellesbourne, UK
Honduran Agricultural Research Foundation (FHIA)	Honduras
Institute of Enology and Viticulture	Japan

Institute of Grapevine Breeding	Germany
Institute of Introduction and Plant Resources (IIPR)	Sadovo, Bulgaria
Institute of Agricultural and Fishery Research (IAFR)	Belgium
International Atomic Energy Agency (IAEA)	Vienna, Austria
International Center for Underutilized Crops (ICUC)	Sri Lanka
International Horticulture Innovation and Training Centre (IHITC)	Jaipur, Rajasthan
International Centre for Genetic Engineering and Biotechnology (ICGBE)	Trieste, Italy
International Federation of Organic Agriculture Movements (IFOAM, 1972)	Bonn, Germany
International Network for Bamboo and Rattan (INIBAR)	Beijing, China
International Horticulture Innovation and Training Centre (IHITC)	Jaipur, Rajasthan
International Food Policy Research Institute (IFPRI)	Washington, USA
International Fruit Genetics (IFG)	California, USA
International American Spice Trade Associations	Washington D.C., USA
International Bulb Research Centre (IBRC)	Vennestraat, the Netherlands
International Flower Market (IFM)	Alsmeer, the Netherland
International Flower Bulb Centre (IFBC)	The Netherlands
International Fragrance Association (IFRA)	Geneva, Switzerland
International Society for Horticultural Science (ISHS)	Leuven, Belgium
International Society for Silicon in Agriculture (ISSA)	Sweden
International Crop Research Institute for Semi-arid Tropics (ICRISAT)	Hyderabad, Andhra Pradesh
International Olive Oil Council (IOOC)	Madrid, Spain
International Coconut Genetics Network (ICGN)	Rome
International Coconut Gene Bank (ICGB)	Indonesia, Brazil, Papua New Guinea and Cote d Ivoire
International Coconut Gene Bank- South Asia (ICG)	Kidu, Karnataka
International Cocoa Gene Bank (ICG)	Trinidad & CEPLAC, Brazil
International Council for Research in Agroforestry (World Agroforestry Centre)	Nairobi, Kenya
International Pepper Community (IPC)	Jakarta, Indonesia
International Potato Centre (CIP, 1971)	Lima, Peru
International Protea Association	South Africa
International Rubber Research and Development Board (IRRDB)	Kuala Lumpur, Malaysia
International Rubber Association	London
International Seed Testing Association (ISTA)	Zurich, Switzerland
International Institute of Tropical Agriculture (IITA)	Ibadan, Nigeria
International Institute of Ayurveda (IIA)	Coimbatore, Tamil Nadu
International Organisation for Standardisation (ISO)	Budapest, Hungary
International Tropical Fruits Network (ITFN)	Malaysia
John Innes Horticultural Institute (JIHI)	England
Leibniz Institute of Vegetable and Ornamental Crops (IGZ)	Erfurt, Germany
Malaysian Agricultural Research and Development Institute (MARDI)	Malaysia
National Institute of Agriculture Science and Technology (NIASI)	Suwan, Republic of Korea
National Institute of Horticulture and Herbal Science (NIHHS)	South Korea
National Wine & Grape Research Centre	Australia
National Vegetable Research Station (NVRS)	Wellesbourne, UK
National Root Crops Research Institute (NRCRI)	Nigeria
Nigeria Institute for Oil Palm Research (NIFOR)	Nigeria
Palm Oil Research Institute of Malaysia (PORIM)	Malaysia

Regional Agricultural Research and Development Centre (RARDC)	Sri Lanka
Research Institute for Ornamental Horticulture	Czech Republic
Research Institute of Horticulture (earlier Research Institute of Pomology and Floriculture)	Poland
Taiwan Banana Research Institute (TBRI)	Taiwan
United Nations Environment Programme (UNEP)	Nairobi
World Vegetable Centre (previously Asian Vegetable Research and Development Centre, AVRDC)	Taiwan
World Coconut Germplasm Centre (WCGC)	Andaman and Nicobar Islands, Port Blair, India
World Cocoa Foundation	USA
World Intellectual Property Organization (WIPO, 1967)	Geneva
World Trade Organization (WTO, 1995)	Rome, Italy

3. PLANT PROTECTION CHEMICALS:

- Term 'weed' was 1st used by Jethrotull.
- Word 'fungicide' has been derived from Latin *caedere* i.e. to kill.
- Weeds cause huge losses in yield to an extent of 37%.
- In world, use of herbicides is maximum i.e. 43.6% followed by insecticides 29.7%, fungicides 20.6% and other chemicals 6.1%.
- In India, use of herbicide is only 12% & more than 75% use of insecticides.
- In India, herbicides are mainly used in tea, coffee estates and to control weeds in spices and soybean crop.
- Marth and Mitchell were the 1st to introduced 2,4-D as a herbicide in USA in 1944.
- Systemic/Selective herbicides: Atrazine, Butachlor, Propanil, MCPA, 2,4-D, etc.
- Contact/Non-selective herbicides : Paraquat, Diquat. Simazine, Glyphosate.
- Pre-emergence herbicides: Alachlor, Butachlor, Triflurodine, Fluchloraline, Oxyfluraline, Oxydiozone, Pendimethalin, Simazine.
- Post-emergence herbicides: Paraquat, Gramoxone, Glyphosate, Diuron, Diquat, Atrazine, Bromacil, Chloroxeuron, 2, 4-D.
- Glyphosate: Kills the weeds by inhibiting biosynthesis of glutamine.
- 2,4-D: Selective translocated herbicide for dicots.
- Diuron: Pre-emergent, persistent & non-selective herbicide.
- Herbicides having low residual toxicity: Diquat, Paraquat.
- Herbicides having high residual toxicity: Diuron, Atrazine.
- In integrated weed management use of herbicides as per need and label claim is most important.
- After Bhopal gas tragedy pesticide that was banned is Aldicarb.
- 'Agent Orange' is the code name for the herbicide and defoliant- contaminated with TCDD.
- Bordeaux mixture, a fungicide (copper + lime @ 1%) was discovered in France by P.M. Millardet in 1872 working on downy mildew of grape.

- In India, products based on only four plants namely pyrethrum, neem, nicotine and citronella are registered under the Insecticides Act 1968.

Different classes of herbicides:

Class	Examples
Acetamides and analides	Alachlor, Acetochlor, Metolochlor, Propachlor, Propanil
Carbamates and thiocarbamates	Asulam, Terbucarb, Thiobencarb
Chlorophenoxy herbicides	2,4-D, 2,4-DP, 2,4,5-T, MCPA, MCPB, MCPP, Dicamba
Dipyridyls	Paraquat, Diquat
Heavy metals	Lead arsenate, Arsenicals
Nitrophenolic and dinitrocresolic herbicides	Dinitrophenol, Dinitrocresol, Dinoseb, Dinosulfon,
Pentachlorophenol	Pentachlorophenol
Phosphonates	Glyphosate, Glyfusinate, Fosamine ammonium
Triazines	Atrazine, Simazine, Cyanazine, Propazine
Urea derivatives	Diuron, Flumeturon, Linuron, Rimsulfuron, Tebuthiuron

Mechanism of insect resistance:

- o Anti-biosis- mechanism of interfering/ destructing life cycle of insect.
- o Non-preference/ anti-xenosis- avoidance of plants by insects in search of food/ ovipositional site/shelter.
- o Tolerance- ability to withstand insect infestation.

- Largest per hectare pesticide consuming country: Taiwan.
- Organophosphate group insecticides have highest consumption in India.
- Imported pesticides: Carbaryl followed by Chlorpyrifos.
- Indigenous pesticides: BHC followed by Monocrotophos, Endosulfan.
- Insecticide Act: 1968.
- Total registered pesticides in India (2018): 287.
- Total number of pesticides banned in India: 29.
- Central Insecticides Board and Registration Committee (CIB & RC): To facilitate the registration of safe, efficacious and quality pesticides for domestic use and export.
- Andhra Pradesh, Maharashtra and Punjab are top three states contributing to 45% of pesticide consumption in India (cibrc.nic.in).
- Pesticide banned in India for use in agriculture: Heptachlor and Maleic hydrazide/ IBA and IAA/ Chlormequat chloride and 6-BA/ Chlorpyrifos and triadimefon.
- Recently banned: Phospamidon
- Term 'IPM' was coined by Bartlett (1956).
- Chitin inhibitors: Diflubenzuron
- Antiseptic: Zinc oxide
- Fumigant: Methyl bromide.

- Pyrethrum: Organic origin
- Principal producer of pyrethrum is Kenya.
- Synthetic pyrethroids are called 4th generation insecticides.
- Pyrethroids disrupt functioning of Central nervous system (knock down action on insects).
- Allethrin / Divinyl pyrethrin: 1st synthetic pyrethroid.
- Most toxic and maximum residual effect insecticide group: Organochlorine.
- Quickly decomposed leaving no toxic residues: Organophosphorus e.g. DDVP, Nuvon, Phorate, Malathion.
- Ovicidal insecticide: Methomyl.
- Degradation of pesticide is maximum in clayey soil.
- 1st truly anticoagulant rodenticide: Warfarin.
- 1st systemic fungicide: Bavistin. First used in Kashmir valley to save apple orchards from scab.
- 1st indigenously developed fungicide: 'Contaf' by Rallis.
- 1st bio-insecticide on commercial scale in 1938: Sporeine.
- 1st report of insecticidal resistance in world: San Jose Scale.
- Govt. of India made mandatory to put QR code on insecticide bottle to check spurious pesticides.
- Father of nematology: N.A. Cobb.
- *Bacillus thuringiensis* (*Bt*) produces toxin which act as natural insecticide.
- *Bt* was reported by E. Berliner from flour moth (*Ephestia cautella*).
- *Bt* strain effective against lepidopteron pests: Kurstaki and Aizawai.
- *Myrothecium roridum LG7* fungus delignifies parthenium weed is isolated from decayed wood.
- *Arthrobacter cepacia*: Used to degrade chlorinated and nitroaromatic pesticide residues.

Name of disease/ pest/weed	Botanical name	Managed by
Soft rot	*Erwinia carotovora*	*Pseudomonas fluorescence*
Diseases of black pepper, cardamom, ginger, turmeric	-	*Trichoderma harzianum*
Seed fly	*Agromyza lantanae*	*Thecla echion*
Aphid, thrips & mites	-	*Chrysoperla carnea*
Bud borer, codling moth	*Helicoverpa* & *Cydia pomonella*	Baculo viruses
Root knot nematodes	*Meloidogyne incognita*	*Pochonia chlamydosporia*
Cardamom thrips	*Sciothrips cardamomi*	*Lecanicillium psalliotae*
Lantana weed	*Lantana camera*	Larvae of totricid moth (*Crocidosema lantana*)

Congress grass	*Parthenium hysterophorus*	*Zygogramma bicolorata, Diacrisia oblique*
Dodder	*Cuscuta spp.*	Insect- *Melanagromyza cuscutae, Smicronyx cuscutae*
Nut grass or Motha	*Cyperus rotundus*	Insect- *Bactra vermosana*
Anode- weed of Malvaceae	*Anoda cristata*	Fungi- *Alternaria macrospora, Puccinia heterospora*
Water hyacinth	*Eichhornia crassipes*	Fungus- *Cercospora roclmanii*

- Director General of Health Services: Chairman of Central Insecticide Board of India.
- In India, Destructive Insects and Pests Act (DIPA) was promulgated during 1914.
- Safest method to dispose of left over insecticide: Burying below the soil.
- 1st attempt in use of natural enemy in world: Red ant (*Oecophylla smaragidna*) to control leaf chewing insects on mandarins.
- Earliest attempt at introduction of natural enemy in India: *Rodolia cardinalis*.

Main crop	Trap crop	Insect controlled
Potato	Potato	Colorado beetle
Cauliflower	Marigold	Blossom beetle
Tomato	Cucumber	Cotton white fly
	Maize	Maize earworm
	Marigold	American bollworm
Cucurbits	Maize	Fruit fly

4. PLANT GROWTH REGULATORS:

- K.V. Thimann (1948) designated plant hormones by the term phyto-hormones to distinguish from animal hormones.
- As per him, these are organic compound produced naturally in higher plants, controlling growth or other physiological functions at a site remote from its place of production and active in minute amounts.
- Presence of growth regulating hormones in plants was 1st suggested by J. Sachs (1980).
- In 1785, Duhamel Du Monceau was 1st to conclude that formation of roots was caused by descending sap.
- Discovery of photoperiodism: Garner and Allard.
- Bio-stimulant: Group of substances from natural origin that contribute to boosting of plant yield and nutrient uptake, while reducing the dependency on chemical fertilizers e.g. bio-fertilizers, bio-pesticides, etc.

4.1 Growth promoters:

4.1.1. Auxin:

- The term 'Auxin' was used by Frits W. Went (Holland) in 1905.

- Auxin was 1st isolated in 1926.
- Auxin name was given by Kogl and Haagen Smit (1933).
- Auxin-'a' was isolated from human urine and auxin-'b' from corn germ oil.
- Word auxin: Greek word *auxein* meaning to grow or increase.
- Bio-assay of auxin: *Avena* curvature test and oat coleoptile test.
- 'Acid growth hypothesis' explains mechanism of action.
- Precursor: Tryptophan
- Element involved in auxin biosynthesis: Zn.
- Nature of auxin: Acidic.
- Natural auxin (Went's auxin): Indole-3- Acetic acid (IAA).
- Synthetic auxin: IBA, NAA, 2,4-D, IPA (Indole Propionic Acid), 2,4,5-T, MCPA, TIBA (2,3,5-Triiodobenzoic acid), 2-NOA (2-napthoxyacetic acid).
- IAA is degraded (photo-oxidation) by light at 375 nm and 445 nm.
- IAA is commonly known as 'heteroauxin'.
- Rhizocaline: Growth hormone synthesized in the shoot, which controls development of both lateral and adventitious roots.
- In 1936-37, Merck prepared 1st synthetic auxin 'Hormodin' (for rooting of cuttings) under a patent of Boyce Thompson Institute of upstate New York.
- In 1944, P. Zimmerman discovered 2,4-D.
- Involved in tropistic growth movements which include downward growth of roots, upward growth of shoots and leaves towards light.
- Inhibits lateral shoot development.
- Synthesized in shoot and root tip, young expanding leaves.
- Glucobrassicin is a free auxin.
- Glucobrassicin is present in savoy cabbage.
- 1st anti-auxin: g-phenyl butyric acid.
- Anti-auxin substances: TIBA, NTA, DCA.

Role:

a) Polar translocation (apex to downward movement).
b) Promote/restore apical dominance
c) Promote or inhibit delay abscission of leaves, flower, fruits or fruit thinning.
d) Stimulate cell/ shoot elongation.
e) Promotes adventitious roots.
f) Induce callus formation.
g) Promote epinastic responses.
h) Produce parthenocarpic fruits in tomato, brinjal and oranges.
i) NAA @ 25-50 ppm induces greater fruit set and used as spray solution on tree.

4.1.2. Gibberellin:

- Yabuta and Hayashi, 1st isolated highly active crystalline substance in 1929 and designated as 'Gibberellin A'.
- In 1925, E. Kurosawa, investigated problem of unusual symptom of hyper elongation which characterizes the foolish disease of rice. This is due to fungus *Gibberella fujikuroi*.
- In 1938, Yabuta and Sumiki isolated gibberellins A and B from fungal culture. Subsequently, gibberellin-C was isolated by acid treatment of gibberellin-A.
- In 1954, Brian *et al*. made discovery of different fermentation product which they named as 'gibberellic acid'.
- Precursor: Kaurene
- Synthesized in young leaves.
- Rich in autonomic parthenocarpic fruit.
- Anti-gibberellin action: Paclobutrazol (Cultar/ PP 333), Flurprimidol, Ancymidol (control tree size), AMO-1618 (control tree size), Phosphon-D, Cycocel.

Role:

a) Stimulate cell elongation, cell division (internode elongation).
b) Promotes seed germination i.e. more ratio of GA to ABA.
c) Induction of flowering in long day plant.
d) Prevention of genetic and physiological dwarfism.
e) Breaking dormancy (seed, tuber ad shoot)
f) Stimulates bolting in rosette plants.
g) Replace/ overcome chilling requirement in temperate fruits and light requirement of plants.
h) Increase sugar level of fruits due to increased amylase activity.
i) Gibberellic acid is enhanced by exposing plants to red light.
j) Possess pollenicide effect.
k) Induces maleness in fruits.
l) Induce parthenocarpy in loquat and guava.
m) Acts antagonistically with ABA.

4.1.3. Cytokinin:

- Called as 'juvenile hormone'.
- Richmond Lang effect (delay of senescence) is characteristic feature.
- Skoog and Miller coined auxin-cytokinin hypothesis.
- Skoog *et al*. discovered 'Kinetin'.

- 1st cytokinin hormone in plants was identified by Lethan *et al*. from corn seeds and named as 'Zeatin'.
- Precursor: 5'-AMP (Isopentenyl group)
- Natural occurring cytokinins: Zeatin, Adenine, dihydrozeatin, dimethylallyl adenine (DMAA and Methylthio Zeatin).
- Synthetic cytokinins: Kinetin, Benzyl adenine, Tetrahydropyranyl benzyl adenine (PBA), Ethoxyethyl adenine, CPPU [1-(2-chloro-4-pyridyl)-3-phenyl urea].
- Synthesized in shoot and root apices, developing seeds, growing buds, cambium and embryonic axis.
- Natural occurrence: Coconut milk, maize endosperm, apple fruitlets, plant exudates, etc.

Role:

a) Initiation of cell division

b) Delaying/ retard senescence (Richmond lang effect)

c) Differentiation of cells (interact with auxin)

d) Induces flowering in short day plants.

e) Breaking dormancy.

f) Sex reversal in grapes.

g) Induce parthenocarpy and increase fruit size.

4.1.4. Ethylene:

- Gaseous hormone
- Precursor: Methionine (amino acid).
- History began with observations of Neljubow (1901) that ethylene gas alter tropistic responses of roots.
- Gane (1934) discovered ethylene.
- Crocker (1935) proposed that ethylene was plant hormone.
- Conversion of methionine to ethylene was demonstrated by Bour *et al*. (1971).
- Ethylene liberating compounds: Ethrel (2-chloroethyl phosponic acid).
- 1-Methylcyclopropene (1-MCP): For delayed ripening i.e. competitive inhibitor of ethylene action in plant tissues.
- Inhibitor of ethylene biosynthesis: AVG.
- Absorbant: Potassium permanganate ($KMnO_4$)

Role:

a) Stimulates shoot, root growth and differentiation.

b) Enhance latex flow in rubber

c) Stimulates leaf, flower and fruit abscission and senescence (phyto-gerontological hormone)
d) Induction of flowering in pineapple.
e) Initiation of ripening in citrus, banana, tomato, mango, bael.
f) Apical dominance arrested.
g) Stimulate lateral growth.
h) Chlorophyll decomposition induced.
i) Promote seed germination.
j) Mechanical harvesting of apple, cherries, pears, etc.

4.2 Growth retardants:

- Also called as 'Anti-gibberellins' e.g. 2,4 DNC, AMO 1618, Phosphon-D, Phosphon-S, CCC, B-995 or Alar (B-9) or SADH.

Role:

- Retardation of stem elongation.
- Preventing cell division.
- Accelerate flower initiation.
- Inhibit root development.
- Inhibit staminate flower production.
- Block synthesis of gibberellins.
- Increase IAA oxidase activity.

4.3 Growth inhibitors:

a) Phenolic inhibitors: Benzoic acid, Salicylic acid, Cinnamic acid, Caffeic acid, p-Coumaric acid, Ferulic acid, Coumarin, Juglone, Scopoletin, Naringenin, Chlorogenic acid.
b) Synthetic inhibitors and abscissic acid: MH and TIBA. They interfere with auxin metabolism-lower auxin concentration.

4.3.1 Abscissic acid (ABA):

- Natural plant hormone/ Terpenoid phytohormone.
- Eagles and Wareing extracted from birth leaves (*Betulus* sp.).
- Okhuma *et al.* isolated this substance in young cotton fruit.
- Stress hormone.
- Excess shade causes production of ABA.
- Strongest senescence stimulator.
- Precursor: Sesquiterpenoid pathway (Mevalonic acid)

- Synthesized in terminal bud (1st synthesized in plastid and final synthesis occur in cytosol in plant cell).

Role:

a) Bud dormancy and seed maturation processes.
b) Stimulates closure of stomata and reduces transpirational water loss.
c) Induction and maintenance of dormancy
d) Induction of desiccation/ drought tolerance (concentration increases up to 30 fold).
e). Disease resistance
f) Protecting cells from dehydration.
g) Accelerates loss of chlorophyll.
h) Inhibit germination.
i) Increase yield of tubers.
j) Delay sprouting of tubers.
k) Induce male sterility.
l) Aids for mechanical harvesting.
m) Waterlogging increases ABA content in roots and aerial parts off plant.

4.4 Morphactins:

- In 1964, Schneider reported first time new type of growth regulators.
- Synthetic derivatives fluorine-a carboxylic acid.

Role:

- Inhibition of apical buds and favour emergence of lateral buds, resulting dwarfism.
- Prolong bud dormancy or delay bud break.
- Inhibit shoot elongation.
- Inhibition of flowering.

Chemical	Active ingredient	Common name	Commercial use
-	6-Benzyl amino purine	6- Benzyl adenine	Senescence delayer, tillering agent
Ethephon/ Ethrel/ Cepha	2-chloroethyl phosphonic acid	Ethylene	Fruit ripening, sugarcane ripener, colour enhancer, gameticide, breaking seed dormancy, sex changer, enhance latex flow in rubber, abscission agent, degreening in citrus
Plantgard	2,4-dichlorophenoxyacetic acid (low concentration)	2,4-D	Control fruit drop, root inducer, enhance fruit set, induce parthenocarpy
MH-30, Sproutstop	1,2 dihydro-3,6 pyridazinedion	Maleic hydrazide (MH)	Growth retardant, control sprout, suckers, & axillary buds, induces femaleness in fruits
GA_3, Gibrosol	Gibberellic acid	Gibberellin	Enhance germination & post harvest life in apple. Increase fruit size in grape, apple
SARODEX, Rapid root, Quick root	3-indole butyric acid	IBA	Rooting hormone
Chamatkar, Whitegold, Marvel	Mepiquat chloride	MC	Enhance tuber and bulb growth, pod set, fruit set
Combine, BR-120	22, 23 tetrahydroxy 24-methyl, 6,7- lactone	Brassinolide along with GA	Growth stimulant, grape berry growth enhancer.
Regine-8	2,3,5- tri iodo benzoic acid	TIBA	Growth enhancer, stimulant
VIPUL, Mixatol, Miraculan	1-hydroxy triacontane	Tricontanol	Growth stimulant
Fruitone, Planofix	1-Napthalene acetic acid	NAA	Root inducer, enhance fruit set, prevent post harvest fruit drop
Hydrogen cyanamide	-	-	Advances onset of flowering & shoot extension; shortens length of flowering period; best results obtained at 3% a.i.
Paclobutrazol	-	(Cultar) Triazine group compound	Height retardant; reduce internode elongation
Cycocel, Lihocin	2-chloroethyl trimethyl ammonium chloride (CCC)	Chloromequat	Lodging reducer, pigment former, delay senescence, enhance fruit set, reduce plant size, tillering & branching
Alar (B-9)	Succinic acid-2,2-dimethyl hydrazine (SADH)	Daminozide	Growth retardant, germination inhibitor, induce flowering, delay senescence, sex changer, widely used in floriculture industry as foliar spray

4.5 Use of growth regulators in fruit crops:

Crop	Growth regulator	Effects	Stage of application
Mango (Alphonso, Dashehari, Banginpalli)	NAA @ 200 ppm	Reduction of fruit drop	Pea stage
	NAA @ 200 ppm	Reduce floral malformation	Time of fruit bud differentiation (Sept-Oct)
	2,4-D	To control pre-harvest fruit drop	-
	P_{333} (Paclobutrazol/ Cultar) 1.25 to 10 g a.i./tree	Control of vegetative flush & manipulation of flowering; reduce tree height in cv. Alphonso	Applied in Aug-Sept.
	GA_3	Recurrent flowering	-
Citrus (Mandarins & its hybrids)	2,4-D @ 20 ppm	To control pre-harvest fruit drop	-
	NAA @ 100-500 ppm	Fruit thinning	-
	GA_3	Delay fruit senescence	-
Avocado	2,4-D @ 20-25 ppm	Reduction of fruit drop	-
Grape	GA_3 @ 10-40 ppm	Enlargement of panicle growth	-
	GA_3 @ 10 ppm	Rachis elongation	One month after forward pruning
	GA_3 @ 30-40 ppm + CPPU @ 2 ppm	Berry elongation	Bajra grain size berry stage
	CCC @ 250-500 ppm	Suppression of vine growth (reduce internode length) & increase fruitfulness of buds	After back pruning (5 leaf stage)
	GA_3 @ 50 ppm	Berry thinning	50% bloom stage
	GA_3 @ 30-40 ppm + cytokinins	Bunch elongation	Bunch dipping at 6-7 mm berry size
	4-CPA @ 10 ppm	Increase the pedicel thickness	-
	NAA @ 20-50 ppm	Post harvest berry drop	-
	Cytokinin	Increase berry size	After pruning
	HCN	To hasten bud break in winter pruning	-
Banana	2,4-D @ 20 ppm	Removal of seediness	Poovan variety
	Ethrel @ 500 ppm	Accelerate ripening	-

Guava	IBA @ 3000 ppm	Promote roots in air layering	-
	NAA @ 80-100 ppm	To reduce rainy season yield	-
	NAA 800 ppm + deblossoming	Maximum yield in winter season	-
	NAD @ 50 ppm	Enhance high blossom drop	-
Sapota	NAA @ 120 ppm	Increase fruit set	-
Pineapple	Ethephon @ 100 ppm	Uniform flowering	All months
	Ethephon combined with (urea 2% + Ca/Na carbonate @ 0.04%)	Uniform flowering	March-May
	NAA @ 10-20 ppm	Flower induction	Less effective
	NAA @ 200-300 ppm	Increase fruit size	After fruit size
Date palm	Ethephon @ 500-1000 ppm	Enhance early flowering	To avoid rainy season
	Ethephon @ 100-400 ppm	Flower or fruit thinning agent	-
Apple	NAA @ 2-10 ppm	Effective thinning agent	-
	NAA + Sevin	Heavy thinning	-
	NAA @ 10 ppm	Prevent pre-harvest fruit drop	-
	NAA	Reduce rootstock suckers	
Peach	Ethephon @ 100-300 ppm	Fruit thinning	Before pit hardening stage
Plum	NAA @ 25-75 ppm	Fruit thinning	Japanese plum
Longan	CPPU @ 40 ppm twice	Improves shoot growth, leaf area, photosynthesis rate, yield & improved fruit quality	5 & 20 days after full bloom
	MH @ 50-400 ppm	Increased fruit yield with improved eating quality	45-50 days after flowering

4.6 *Use of growth regulators in flower crops*:

- Auxin synergist: TIBA, Coumarin.
- Anti-auxin: Trans-cinnamic acid.
- Epinastic: Acetylene, Ethylene, Carbon monoxide.
- GA_3 induces flowering in long day plants.
- Daminozide/ Alar/ B-9: Very expensive and widely used for flower induction.

Control of plant height:

- SADH: Chrysanthemum.
- Cycocel, Alar: Chrysanthemum, Poinsettia.
- Phosphon-D: Lily.
- B-Nine: Dahlia.
- Maleic hydrazide: Bougainvillea.
- Paclobutrazol (spray): Geranium, Hibiscus, Poinsettia.
- Paclobutrazol (drench): Pot chrysanthemum and bulb crops.
- Uniconazole: Easter lily, Geranium, Azalea, Poinsettia.

5. NUTRITIVE VALUE OF HORTICULTURAL CROPS:

- Term 'Nutrification' is coined by Lachance.
- Daily requirement of vitamin A for healthy vision: 750 μg/day (2300-3000 IU).
- Daily requirement of vitamin D is 200 IU/day (1 IU=0.3 μg).
- Most fruits & vegetables are not rich source of Vit. B.
- Cobalt is a component of Vit. B_{12}.
- Vitamin that is not found in fruits or vegetables: Vit B_{12}.
- Vitamin C (ascorbic acid): Thermo-sensitive & anti-oxidant vitamin. It is destroyed by sulphur treatment.
- Vitamin C: Isolated by C.G. King and Waugh in lemon juice.
- Selenium: Strong anti-oxidant capacity.
- Vitamin K_1: Inhibit banana ripening.
- Folic acid 1st found in spinach leaves.
- Green leafy vegetables: Rich source of folic acid.
- Major mineral present in fruits and vegetables: Potassium.
- Catabolism process results in release of energy.
- Vegetables are deficient in fat content (<0.1% in most of the vegetables).
- Maximum fibre content: Asparagus.
- Soil sampling from different layers up to 1.5 m provide better assessment of soil fertility status for fruit crops.

- Phytochemicals in fruits and vegetables and their contribution as a group- Vit. C- 91%, Vit. A- 48%, Folacin- 30%, Vit. B_6- 75%, Vit. B_1- 17%, Niacin- 15% in diet.
- Calcium present in dark green leaves: 70-400 mg/100 g.

Mineral	Deficiency induced diseases	Fruit		Vegetable	
		Name	Quantity	Name	Quantity
Carbohydrate	-	Raisin	77.3%	Tapioca	38.1%
		Dry apricot	72.8 %	Sweet potato	28.2%
		Dry karonda	67.1%	Potato	22.6%
		Date	67.8%	-	-
Protein	-	Cashew	21.2%	Lima bean	7.9 g/ 100g
		Almond	20.88 %	Pea	7.2 g/ 100g
		-	-	Cowpea	4.3 g/ 100g
Fat	-	Walnut	64.5 %	Potato	118 g/100g
		Almond	58.9 %	-	-
Fibre	Diabetes & heart diseases	Guava	6.9 %	Potato	752 g/ 100g
		Almond	0.23%	Chilli	6.8 g/ 100g
Calcium	Osteoporosis (reduce bone density), muscular cramps & skeletal pain, teeth pain & blood pressure	Litchi	0.21%	Agathi	1130 mg/ 100g
		Dry karonda	0.16%	Curry leaves	83 mg/ 100g
Phosphorus	-	Almond	0.49%	Amaranths	800 mg/ 100 g
		Cashew nut	0.45%	Garlic	310 mg/ 100 g
		Walnut	0.38%		
Iron	Anemia, weakness & fatigue, affects immune system	Dry karonda	39.1 mg/100 g	Broccoli & Brussels' sprout	38.5 mg/100g
		Date	10.6 %	Amaranths	25.5mg/100g
Iodine	Goiter, retarded growth	-	-	Okra	33.31 ig/kg

Potassium	Hypokalemia, muscular cramps, irregular heart-beat, kidney & lung failure	Banana	422 mg/100 g	Spinach	605 mg/ 100g
		Apricot	259 mg/ 100 g	Potato	568 mg/ 100g
Sodium	Weight loss & nervous breakdown	-	-	Celery, Green onion	-
Calorific value (Kcal)	-	Walnut	687 /100 g	Tapioca	338 /100g
		Almond	655 /100 g	Garlic	142/100g
		Cashew nut	596 /100 g	Lima bean	105/100g
		Date	283 /100 g	-	-
Vitamin A (Retinol/ Axerophthol)	Alzamire, Night blindness (Nyctalopia), Xerophthalmia cause Kertaomalacia, Xerosis	Aman palm	51667 IU/ 100g	Kale	20000 IU/ 100g
		Mango	4800 IU/ 100 g	Curry leaf	12600 IU/ 100g
		Papaya	2020 IU/ 100 g	Bathua leaves	11300 IU/ 100g
				Colocasia leaves	10278 IU/ 100g
				Beet leaves	9770 IU/ 100g
				Sprouting broccoli	9000 IU/ 100g
				Turnip	5000 IU/ 100 g
Vitamin B_1 (Thiamine)	Beriberi, paralysis, loss of sensitivity of skin, heart enlargement	Cashew nut	630 mg/ 100 g	Chilli	0.55 mg/ 100 g
		Walnut	450 mg/ 100 g	Palak	0.26mg/ 100g
				Pea	0.25 mg/100g
Vitamin B_2 / Vitamin G (Riboflavin)	Ariboflavinosis (Angular stomatitis, Sore tongue cracking in mouth angles, redness & burning of eyes, Scaliness of skin), sore throat, anorexia cataract, loss of appetite	Bael	1191 mg/ 100 g	Palak	0.56 mg/100g
		Papaya	250 mg/ 100 g	Chilli	0.39 mg/100g
				Radish leaves	0.38 mg/ 100g
		Litchi	122.5 mg/ 100 g	Fenugreek	0.31 mg/ 100g
Vitamin B_3 (Niacin or Nicotinic acid)	Pellagra (black tongue), Dermatitis, Glossitis	Nuts	-	Palak	3.3 mg/ 100g
				Amaranths	1 mg/ 100g
				Sweet potato	
Vitamin B_5 (Pantothenic acid)	Paresthesia	Avocado	-	Mushroom	3.6 mg/ 100g

Vitamin B_6 (Pyridoxine or Adermin)	Convulsions in infants, Oral ulcer, kidney disease, Anaemia	-	-	All vegetables	-
Vitamin B_7 (Biotin or Vitamin H)	Dermatitis, Enteritis	Walnut	-	Broccoli	-
Vitamin B_9 (Folate, Folacin or Pteroy/ glutamic acid)	Macrocytic anemia (Megaloblastic anaemia)	Sweet orange	-	Cabbage, Kale, Broccoli	-
Vitamin B_{12} (Cyanocobalamin)	Pemiocin anaemia (reduction in RBCs)	Coconut water	-	-	-
Vitamin C (Ascorbic acid)	Scurvy, swelling of gums	Barbados cherry	1000-4000 mg/ 100 g	Drumstick leaves	220 mg/ 100g
		Aonla	600 mg/ 100 g	Kale	187 mg/ 100g
		Guava	299 mg/100 g	Brussels sprout	185 mg/ 100g
		-	-	Coriander leaves	135 mg/ 100g
		-	-	Chilli	111 mg/ 100g
				Broccoli	109 mg/ 100g
Vitamin D (Calciferol) D_2- Ergocalciferol D_3- Cholecalciferol	Rickets, Osteomalacia	-	-	-	-
Vitamin E (Tocopherol)	Sterility (less fertility), liver necrosis, degeneration of kidney	Avocado	2.07 mg/ 100 g	Spinach	2.03 mg/ 100g
Vitamin K (Phylloquinone or coagulating vitamin or Anti-hemorrhagic vitamin)	Bleeding disorders, non-clotting of blood	-	-	Kale, Spinach	
		-			
Overall nutritive index	-	Pomegranate	13	-	-
		Fig	11	-	-
Roughages	-	-	-	Amaranths	-
Vegetable milk	-	-	-	Pea pods	-
				Cabbage leaves	-

6. MINERAL NUTRITION:

- Nutrients absorbed by the plants from soil are called mineral nutrients.
- Process of absorption, translocation and assimilation of nutrients by plants is known as mineral nutrition.
- Weathering of minerals and mineralization of organic matter make the nutrients availability to plants.
- English word "Fertilizer" was derived from Latin word "*Fertil*".
- Carbon sink: It is a natural reservoir (forest, ocean) that stores carbon-containing chemical compounds accumulated over an indefinite period of time. The process by which carbon sinks remove carbon dioxide from the atmosphere is known as carbon sequestration.
- Carbon sequestration: A natural or artificial process by which carbon dioxide is removed from the atmosphere and held in solid or liquid form to mitigate global warming and to avoid climate change.
- Carbon dating or Radio-carbon dating: Determination of the age or date of organic matter from the relative proportions of the carbon isotopes carbon-12 and carbon-14 that it contains. The ratio between them changes as radioactive carbon-14 decays and is not replaced by exchange with the atmosphere.
- Carbon or Emission trading: (Article 17 of Kyoto protocol). It is a market-based approach to controlCO_2pollution by providing economic incentives for achieving emission reductions.
- Carbon foot printing: The amount of greenhouse gases released into the atmosphere as a result of the activities of a particular individual, organization, or community. It is expressed in equivalent tons of CO_2 e.g. If a car consumes 7.5 liter diesel per 100 km, then a drive of 300 km distance consumes 3 x 7.5 = 22.5 liter diesel, which adds 22.5 x 2.7 kg = 60.75 kg CO_2 to your personal carbon footprint.

Fuel type	**Unit**	**CO_2 emitted per unit**
Petrol	1 liter	2.3 kg
Gasoline	1 liter	2.3 kg
Diesel	1 liter	2.7 kg
Oil (heating)	1 liter	3 kg

- Carbon sequestration crops: Coconut (7.54 $MtC.y^{-1}$), cashew (3.06 $MtC.y^{-1}$), rubber (2.36 $MtC.y^{-1}$), arecanut (1.45 $MtC.y^{-1}$), tea (1.23 $MtC.y^{-1}$), coffee (1.03 $MtC.y^{-1}$), cocoa (0.38 $MtC.y^{-1}$) and oil palm (0.07 $MtC.y^{-1}$).
- Plantation crops have potential to sequester about 17 Mt of carbon every year.
- Bamboo absorbs about 400 kg of CO_2 a year and emits 35% more O_2/ ha.
- IARI has developed 'Pusa Soil Testing and Fertilizer Recommendation Meter' for facilitating the reach of soil testing at the farmers' doorstep.

- India ranks 3rd in fertilizer production and 2nd in consumption (China is first in fertilizer consumption).
- During 2017-18, total fertilizer consumption in India: 26.79 million metric tons (MMT).
- During 2016-17, per hectare consumption of fertilizers in India: 135 kg/ha.
- Per hectare consumption: 1st Punjab- 266 kg/ ha, 2nd Andhra Pradesh- 244 kg/ ha, 3rd Tamil Nadu- 227 kg/ ha.
- Lowest fertilizer consumption states: Nagaland, Arunachal Pradesh, Sikkim.
- During 2017-18, total import of fertilizers: 15.44 mmt (Urea- 5.98 mt, DAP- 4.22 mt, NP/ NPK- 0.5 mt & MoP-4.74 mt).
- All potash fertilizers viz., KCl and K_2SO_4 used in India is imported from Jordan and Tunisia.
- During 2017-18, total production of N and P fertilizers in India: 18.14 mmt (N fert. 13.42, P fert. 4.72 mmt).
- Optimum use of NPK ratio: 4: 2:1.
- During 2017-18, NPK use ratio in India: 6.2: 2.5: 1.
- Overall rate of nutrient application in fruits is 145.5 kg/ha and nutrient ratio: 1.6:1:1.
- Overall rate of nutrient application in fruits is 170 kg/ha and nutrient ratio: 2.2:1.3:1.
- Nutrient removal pattern is highest for potash.
- Fertilizer Control Order (FCO) was passed in 1985.
- Fertilizer Movement Order (FMO) on 31st December, 1960.
- Essential nutrients: 17.
- Basic elements of plant: C, H, O constitute 96% of total dry matter of plant. Among them C and O constitute 45% each.
- Macro nutrients: N, P, K, Ca, Mg, S (>100 μg/g dry matter).
  - Primary nutrients- required in large quantity: N, P, K.
  - Secondary nutrients- Ca, Mg, S.
- Micro nutrients: Cl, Fe, B, Mn, Zn, Cu, Mo, Ni (<100 μg/g dry matter) required in traces.
- Micro nutrient is also known as – trace element/ Oligo-element/ Spurned elements.
- Energy exchange elements are H & O.
- Metal nutrients: K, Fe, Ca, Mg, Mn, Zn, Cu.
- 1st micronutrient discovered: Fe.
- Criteria of essentiality of nutrients: Arnon and Stout (1939).
- Nicholas (1961) proposed the term 'Functional or Metabolism nutrients'.
- Nutrient mobility concept: Bray.
- 1st Agricultural chemist of ICAR: J.W. Leather.

- The concept of leaf sampling for nutrient sampling is given by Lutherd and Smith.
- The vertical section of the soil showing the various layers from the surface to the unaffected parent material is known as 'soil profile'.
- Top most mineral horizon is 'A' horizon.
- Soil structure: Arrangement of soil particles and their aggregate into certain defined order.
- Law of minimum was given by V. N. Liebig (1840).
- 1st soil classification system: Developed by Russian scientist Dokuchaev (1880)
- The U.S classification system the soil orders: 10.
- Particle density of soil is also known as true density.
- Generally the particle density of normal soil: 2.65 gram/cm^3.
- Bulk density of normal soil: 1.33 g/cm^3.
- Formula of porosity of soil = 100- (bulk density ÷ Particle density)
- Cation exchange capacity (CEC) of montmorillonite clay: 60-100 me/ 100 g.
- Formula of bulk density = wt. of soil ÷ volume of solids and pores.
- The term pH was introduced by Sorensen (1909).
- K & Na content in soil is estimated by Flame Photometer.
- Crop logging technique: Demonstrated by H. F. Clements.
- In soil, heat is transferred through conduction.
- Soil Health Card Scheme: Launched by Govt. of India in July, 2015.
- Studies by National Productivity Council (NPC), recommendations of Soil Health Card has led to a decrement of 8-10% in use of chemical fertilizers and increased productivity by 5-6%.
- Estimated extent of salt affected soils in India: 17.42 million ha.
- Net arable land: 120 million ha.
- Lateritic soils are less erodible than black soils.
- Histosols are called as organic soils.
- Loamy soil: Maximum microbial activity.
- Soil suitable for most of the crops: Sandy loam.
- Soils favorable for nematode growth: Sandy loam.
- Red colour in the red soils: Presence of various oxides of irons.
- Element found in meristematic tissue: K.
- Fertile soils are saturated with Ca and Mg ions.
- In 1923, it was reported that 'B' is essential for cell structure of plants.
- Soil sterilant: Copper sulphate.

- Silicon is important for soybeans. It increases phosphorous availability by 40-60%. Use of silicon increases root length (21.8%), root volume (19.31%), root tips (32.81%) and plant volume (34.81%).
- Spray of salicilic acid @ 2 ml/ litre of water at 21, 36 and 51 days after sowing increases soybean yield by 31%.
- Silicon increased yields of proteins (3 q/ha), oil (2.2 q/ha) and reduction in incidence of pests and diseases is observed.
- Fertigation: Application of fertilizers through irrigation. Maximum (30-40%) fertilizer use efficiency.
- C: N ratio concept was given by Klebs (1913).
- Term C: N ratio was coined by Karaus and Kraybill in 1919.
- Low C: N ratio, promotes vegetative growth while high C: N ratio, promotes flowering.
- C: N ratios: Humus (10:1); organic matter (12: 1); saw dust (400: 1); legume crops (20-30: 1); crop residue i.e. FYM (100: 1).
- Desirable C: N ratio: Humus (9-12: 1); organic manures (12-20: 1); FYM (20 : 1); dried leaves of tree (25: 1); glyricidia leaves & young branches (13: 1); subabool leaves (7: 1); maize garbage & leaves (60: 1).
- Higher the ratio, more is the time required for decomposition of residual material in soil.
- Lower C: N ratio makes availability of N, P, S and other minor minerals in chemical form for easy abortion for the plants.
- C: N ratio > 20 : 1 leads to soil fixation of minerals and their non-availability to plants.
- Nutrient Based Subsidy (NBS) scheme started during 2010-11: Fixed rate of subsidy is announced on nutrients.
- The NBS covers three macro nutrients (N, P and K) and two micro nutrients (Zn and B).
- New Urea policy-2015: The government allowed the urea producers to produce up to 100% of production as neem coated urea.
- *Azotobacter plaque* test: Used to determine deficiency of lime, P and K.
- *Aspergillus niger* test: Used to determine deficiency of Ca, Cu, Mg, Mo, etc. in soil.
- *Cunninghamella plaque* test: Used to determine phosphate content in soil.

Nutrient use efficiency of applied nutrients:

- N varies from 20-40% of soil application.
- P_2O_5 varies from 5-20% of soil application.
- Ca varies from 30-40% of foliar sprays.
- Ca varies from 30-40% of foliar sprays.

- Mg varies from 10-20% of soil application / 40-50% of foliar sprays.
- S varies from 20-40% of foliar sprays.
- Fe varies from 5% of soil application/ 30-50% of foliar sprays.
- Mn varies from 5-10% of soil application/ 30-50% of foliar sprays.
- Zn varies from 5% of soil application/ 25-50% of foliar sprays.
- B varies from 10-20% of soil application/ 50-60% of foliar sprays.
- Mo varies from 50-60% of foliar sprays.
- Efficiency of Ca and Mg is higher in acidic soils and relatively low in alkaline soils.
- SSP and SOP and micronutrients supply sulphur.
- Sulphur can be applied as amendment.

Organic matter-

- Soils rich in organic carbon are show resistance to thrips.
- Hilly areas- >1%.
- Mangroves- 10-30%

Classification	Nature of nutrient	Examples
Mobility in soil	1. Mobile	NO_3^-, SO_4^-, B, Cl, Mn
	2. Less mobile	NH_4^{++++}, Ca^{++}, Mg^{++}, K^+, Cu^{++}
	3. Immobile	H_2PO_4 —, HPO_4^-, Zn^{++}, Pb
Mobility in plants	1. Highly mobile	N, P, K, Mg, Mo
	2. Moderately mobile	Zn, Fe, Cu, Mn, S
	3. Immobile	Ca, B
Functions in plants	1. Useful in energy storage, bonding (structural elements, more active & vital for living tissue)	N, S, P
	2. As regulators and carriers	K, Ca, Mg
	3. As catalyst and activators	Fe, Mn, Zn, Cu, B, Mo, Cl

6.1 Role and deficiency symptoms of minerals

- Compared to nitrogen, foliar uptake of potassium is relatively slow and phosphorous is absorbed most slowly.
- Foliar spray of Urea, KCl, P/ K_2SO_4@ 2% concentration is recommended.
- Excess application of Zn leads to imbalance of Fe + Cu.
- Efficiency of minerals in fruit crops: N (20-30%), P (5-15%) and K (70-80%).
- Potassium fertilizers are less mobile than nitrogenous one and more mobile than phosphatic fertilizers and leached heavily.
- Starter solution: Application of solution of N, P_2O_5 and K_2O in the ratio 1:2:1 and 1:1:2 to young plants at the time of transplanting.
- In high soil pH: Fe, Mn, Zn, Cu, B nutrients become deficient.

- Cobalt is essential for development of rhizobium bacteria.
- Seed treatment of Cobalt nitrate @ 1 g for 10 kg French beans increases production by 2 times.
- Rhizobium bacteria produces vit. B_{12} which causes rapid cell division in plants.
- Presence of pink coloured root nodules helps more in nitrogen fixation process in legume crops.
- Gris (1843) discovered iron.
- Role of manganese in plant was 1st observed by Mchaijne in 1922.
- Role of zinc in plant growth was demonstrated by Sommer and Lipman in 1986.
- Functions of copper was discovered by Lipman and Mchaijne in 1932.
- Warington in 1923, 1st identified essentiality of boron.
- Arnon and Stout in 1939 described importance of molybdenum.
- Hoffer (1986) developed 3 types of testing tissues for assessing nutritional deficiencies.
- Bhargava (2002) suggested use of youngest mature leaf or petiole for analysis.

Nutrient	Role	Deficiency symptoms
N	• Structural constituent of cell • Vegetative growth • Delay maturity	Chlorosis observed in older leaves; stunted growth; late flower production
P	• Growth &development of roots, flowers, seeds & maturing fruits; • Structural component of membrane system; • Essential constituent of DNA, RNA, NADP, ATP & ADP; • Enhance nodule formation in legume crops	Anthocyanin production in older leaves
K	• Opening & closing of stomata i.e. Osmotic regulation, • Maintains cytoplasm pH • Reduction of lodging of plants • Improves colour, flavor & size of fruits, • Formation and accumulation of starch& sugar • Sugar translocation • Carotenoid biosynthesis	• Older leaves to new leaves • Necrotic spots in leaves
Ca	• Maintain membrane integrity as calcium pectate • Maintain chromosome structure • Regulation of enzyme activity	1st appear on shoot tip
Mg	• Constituent of chlorophyll, protoplasm & chromosome • Activate enzyme systems • Synthesis of RNA primealigo adenylase	1st appear on older leaves, (yellowing of leaf margin)
S	• Constituent ofcysteine, methionine, • Stabilization of protein structure	Chlorosis 1st observed on young leaves

Fe	• Key element of respiration, N_2 fixation, electron transfer • Synthesis of chlorophyll & nucleic acid • Reduction of nitrate & sulphates	Interveinal chlorosis 1st observed on younger leaves
Mn	• Key element in respiration, • Electron transfer in photolysis of water	Chlorosis on older leaves
Cu	• Oxidation-reduction reaction, activity of ethylene in fruit ripening • Utilization of protein as well as nodule formation • Influences water permeability of xylem vessels	Chlorosis on terminal leaves
Zn	• Synthesis of tryptophan, RNA • Essential for CO_2 evolution and utilization • Important for anaerobic respiration • Sugar regulation & transformation of –CHO. • Essential component of enzymes • Promotes seed maturation • Formation of auxins and growth promoting substances	Short internodes, little leaf symptoms noticed on old & new leaves
B	• Salt absorption & translocation of sugars, starch, nitrogen & phosphates, • Pollen graingermination &growth • Regulation of stomata opening • Lignifications, xylem differentiation & carbohydrate metabolism • Movements of hormones & sugars • Seed set and fruit development • Cell division & development	• Corky area in cortex • Browning in core region • Suppressed fruit formation • Blossom blast • Suppressed development of terminal /apical bud
Mo	• Role in N_2 metabolism, constituent of enzyme- nitrogenous and nitrate reductase. • Helps in fixation of atmospheric N_2 in legume crops (nodule formation). • Availability increases as soil pH increases	Yellow spots in leaves
Cl	• Involved in O_2 evolution in photosynthesis, • Maintain turgor pressure in guard cells	• Blotchy leaf chlorosis & necrosis; • Bronzing and wilting of leaves

6.2 Characterization levels of nutrients in soil and plants:

Nutrient	Critical level	
	Soil	Plants
Sulphur	8.30 ppm	<0.15-0.2 ppm
Calcium	< 25% of CEC	<0.2%
Magnesium	< 4% of CEC	< 0.1-2%
Zinc	0.6 ppm	< 15-20 ppm
Manganese	2 ppm	< 20 ppm
Copper	0.2 ppm	< 4 ppm
Iron	2.5-4.5 ppm	< 50 ppm
Boron	0.5 ppm	< 20 ppm
Molybdenum	0.2 ppm	< 0.1 ppm

6.3 Leaf nutrient analysis:

Fruit crops:

- Diagnostic leaf to be used for analysis has been standardized for different fruit crops.

Crop	Index tissue	Growth stage/ time	Particulars	Sample size
Acid lime	Leaf	September-October	3-5 months old leaf from new flush- 1st leaf of shoot	30
Almond	Leaf	3rd leaf from top	Beginning of bloom	15
Apple	Leaf	Mid July to August	Mid shoot leaves from current season & terminal shoots on tree periphery. 2 leaves/ terminal shoot	100
Apricot	Leaf	Early June to mid-July	Fully expanded leaves from mid-shoot current growth	50
Avocado	Leaf	-	5-7 months old non-fruiting terminal shoots	50
Banana	Petiole	Bud differentiation 16th leaf stage	Petiole of 3rd open leaf from apex or leaf lamina 20 cm^2 in central part of leaf	15
Ber	Leaf	2 months after pruning	16th leaf from apex from secondary or tertiary shoot	40
Cashew nut	Leaf	At beginning of flowering	4th leaf from tip of mature branches	15
Cherry	Leaf	July-August	Fully expanded leaves, mid-shoot current growth	50
Coconut	Leaf	5 years old tree & leaflets from either side of middle portion of 14th leaf	Youngest open leaf 14th (adult) & 4th (young)	20% of palms in garden & bulked together

Cocoa	Leaf	Bloom initiation	3rd leaf from apex	15
Custard apple	Leaf	2 months after new growth	5th leaf from apex	30
Fig	Leaf	April or August crop	Fully expanded leaves, mid shoot current growth	20
Ginger	Leaf	105-195 days after planting	-	-
Grape (double pruning)	Petioles opposite to bunch	Bud differentiation, 45 days after pruning	5th petiole from base for yield forecast	200
Guava	Leaf	August (rainy season crop) or December (winter season crop) & 50-60 days old leaves	3rd& 4th leaf pair from apex	30
Litchi	Leaf	6 months from autumn flush	2nd pair of leaflets from tip	30
Macadamia nut	Leaf	Summer	6-7 months old leaves	50
Mandarin	Leaf	June	3-5 month old leaf from spring flush, 2nd leaf from base August-October month from *ambia bahar*	50
Mango	Leaf	Recently matured leaf	Vegetative shoot, 5 month old, middle leaf in shoot	30
Papaya	Petiole	6 months after planting	6th petiole from apex	20
Passion fruit	Leaf	Leaf against first open flower	6th leaf from apex	50
Pear	Leaf	From middle of terminal shoot growth	2-4 weeks after terminal bud formation	50
Peach	Leaf	Mid shoot leaves	Fruiting or non-fruiting spurs in mid-summer	25
Phalsa	Leaf	1 month after pruning	4th leaf from apex	40
Pineapple	Leaf	4-6 months	Middle 1/3rd portion of white basal portion of 4th leaf from apex	10
Plum	Leaf	Jan-February	Leaves from middle of current season's growth	25
Pomegranate	Leaf	Bud differentiation in April for February crop	8th leaf from apex	50
Sapota	Leaf	September	10th leaf from apex	30
Strawberry	Leaf	September	10th leaf from apex	30
Rambutan	Leaf	May	3rd pair of mature leaves from non fruiting or flowering terminal of bearing trees	50
Rubber	Leaf	September	4 basal leaves of terminal position	30

Vegetable crops (Donahue *et al.*, 1990; Lorenz and Bartz, 1967)

Crop	Plant part to sample	Stage of growth	Sample size
Crop	Plant part to sample	Stage of growth	Sample size
Potato	4th to 6th leaf from growing tip	Early growth (35-40 days after planting)	-
Tomato	4th to 6th leaf from growing tip	Early bloom	-
Chilli & sweet pepper	Young mature leaves	Early fruit set	-
Cauliflower	Young mature outside leaves	Button stage of curd	-
Cabbage	1st mature leaf from central whorl	Prior to heading	-
Broccoli	Young mature leaves	1st bud formation stage	-
Brussels sprout	Young mature leaves	Mid growth	-
Muskmelon, cucumber, etc.	Leaf + petiole	Mature 5thleaf from tip when flower start forming small fruit	12
Watermelon	Leaf + petiole	Mature 5thleaf from tip when flower start forming small fruit	12
Beans	2-3 fully developed leaves at top of plant	Initial flowering	-
Pea	Leaves from 3rd node down from top of plant	Initial flowering	-
Root crops	Young mature leaves from central rings	Prior to root enlargement	-
Bulb crops	Young mature leaves from centre	Prior to bulbing	-
Celery	Petiole of youngest fully elongated leaf (30-38 cm)	Mid growth (30-35 cm tall)	-
Lettuce (head type)	Midrib of wrapper leaf	Heading	-
Lettuce (leaf type)	Youngest mature leaf	Mid growth	-
Leafy greens (palak, spinach, etc.)	Youngest mature leaf	Mid growth	-
Sweet potato	4th to 6th leaf from growing tip	Prior to root enlargement	-
Asparagus	Top 10 cm of new fern branch	Mid growth of fern	15
Sweet corn	Entire leaf at the ear node	Tasseling	-

Flower crops:

Crop	Plant part to sample	Stage of growth	Sample size
Azalea	Most recent fully developed leaf	-	50
Begonia	Most recent fully developed leaf	-	20
Bougainvillea	Most recent fully developed leaf	-	25
Cactus	Most recent fully developed leaf	-	15
Carnation	5th & 6th leaf pair of non-flowering shoots	-	50
Jasmine	Most recent fully developed leaf	-	50
Chrysanthemum	4th leaf from tip (omit-unfurled)	Bud burst	25
Croton	Most recent fully developed leaf	-	12
Fern	Most recent fully developed leaf	-	15
Ficus	Most recent fully developed leaf	-	50
Geranium	Most recent fully developed leaf	-	15
Gerbera	Most recent fully developed leaf	-	15
Gladiolus	Most recent fully developed leaf	-	12
Hibiscus	Most recent fully developed whole leaf	-	15
Ixora	Most recent fully developed leaf	-	25
Lilly	Most recent fully developed leaf	-	15
Orchid	Most recent fully developed leaf	-	12
Rose	Most recent fully developed compound, 5th leaflet leaf	Flower bud pea size	10

Fertilizers:

- Best time of application of fertilizers: June and July.
- Denitrification occurs in waterlogged soils.
- Preservatives used to decrease nitrogen losses in FYM and cattle urine: Gypsum and super phosphate.
- The word compost is derived from the Latin word "COMPONERE" to mean put together.
- A typical compost earthworm is *Eisenia fetida*, *Eudrilus eugeniae*, *Perionyx excavatus*.
- The process of composting was first initiated in England during First World War (1914 -1918).
- The Agricultural Development Company (ADCO) process of composting was patented at Rothamsted Experimental Station, England.
- Activated compost process was developed by Fowler and Ridge in 1922 at Indian Institute of Science, Bengaluru.
- Indore process is developed in India by Howard and Wardat Indian Institute of Plant Industry, Indore.
- Vermi-composting is done under thatched roof to protect worms against rain & sun.

- Complex fertilizers: 2 or more essential nutrients.
- Fertilizer mixture: Mixture of 2 or more fertilizers.
- Fertilizer grade: Expression that indicates percentage of plant nutrients e.g. 15:15:15.
- Fertilizer ratio: Relative proportion of three major plant nutrients e.g. 1:1:1.
- Conditioner: Organic substance which help to keep mixtures non-caking and free flowing e.g. paddy husk, groundnut husk, neem husk.
- Neutralizer: Substance used to neutralize the residual effect e.g. limestone.
- Filler: Material used for making up the weight e.g. fine sand, ash, paddy husk.
- Fertilization utilization rate under favourable conditions for N is 50-70%, P- 10-25% and K- 50-60%.
- Customized fertilizers (CFs): Unique, ready-to-use granulated fertilizers designed to optimize utilization of nutrients to obtain quality crops, high farm productivity and profitability.
- Government of India designated CFs as a separate category under the Fertilizer Control Order, effective from 2008.
- NFCL: 1st company in India to receive official approval for CFs from the Department of Agriculture and Cooperation, the Ministry of Agriculture, GoI, for manufacture and marketing.
- 4R is the centre stage of right fertilization programme: Right source, Right rate, Right time, and Right place to apply fertilizers. It is a nutrient stewardship concept was introduced by Bruulsema *et al.* (2009).
- DRIS (Diagnosis and Recommendation Integrated System):
  - It represents holistic approach to mineral nutrition of crops.
  - It has impact on integrated set of norms representing-
    - a) Calibration of plant tissues.
    - b) Soil composition.
    - c) Environmental parameters and
    - d) Farming practices as functions of yield of crops (Beaufils, 1973).
  - Advantages of DRIS approach:
    - a) Its ability to make diagnosis at any stage of crop development.
    - b) To list the nutrients in order of importance, which are responsible for limiting the yields.
    - c) To fulfill the diagnosis and productive use of leaf analysis.
    - d) To increase chances of obtaining higher yields and quality.
- For calculation of DRIS index, formulae for petiole/ leaf nutrients (N, P,K, Ca, Mg, S, Fe, Mn, Zn, Cu) and yields for grapes, mango and acid lime have been worked out by Bhargava (1999).

- Approaches used for nutrient diagnosis-
    - a) Uni-variate: CVA (critical value approach).
    - b) Bi-variate: DRIS.
    - c) Multi-variate: CND (compositional nutrient diagnosis) and PCA (principal component analysis).
- CND nutrient norms for Anab-e-Shahi grapes indicate that greater requirement of nutrients during BDS (bud initiation and differentiation stage) than to FS (flowering stage).

a) *Inorganic*

- The 1st ammonia plant was established in 1913 by Fritz Haber and Carp Bosch at Oppau, Germany for Badische, Anilin and Soda-Fabric A.G (BASF). The process is called Haber–Bosch process.
- Ammonium sulphate: Oldest synthetic fertilizer. Applied for alkaline & water logged soils.
- Calcium ammonium nitrate (CAN): Hygroscopic, neutral and explosive fertilizer. Applied for acidic soil.
- F. Wholer (German chemist), 1st prepared urea in 1828 (Commercial production started in 1922).
- Nitrogen form in urea: Amide.
- Urea $[CO(NH_2)_2]$ is an organic fertilizer.
- Toxic substance present in urea: Biuret.
- Biuret % in urea: 1.5%.
- Neem coated Urea (45 Kg bag) was incorporated as regular fertilizer in 2010.
- Indigenous manufacturing of neem coated Urea started in 2014.
- Neem coated urea is sold at 5% above the MRP to recover the cost of coating. It save loss of urea by 20-30%.
- 100 % neem coated production of urea made mandatory in 2015.
- Nano urea in liquid form has been developed by Indian Farmer's Fertilizer Co-operative (IFFCO) Ltd.
- Liquid form of nano urea has been developed 1st time in the world.
- IFFCO-Bio-Nano-technology research centre has been established in Gujarat.
- Liquid form of urea is substitute for crystal/ granular form.
- Half litre of nano urea contain 40,000 ppm nitrogen and equals to 50 kg granular urea.
- GOI has included IFFCO nano urea in fertilizer control order of 1985.
- Online sale counter is available on www.iffcobazar.in

- Phosphatic fertilizers fixes immediately in soil after application.
- Most important source of cadmium (Cd) pollution: Phosphate fertilizers.
- India imports 'K' fertilizer (KCl i.e. Muriate of Potash) mainly from Germany and France.
- Nitrogen is available both in anionic and cationic form.
- Higher concentration of 'K' in plants and 'Ca' in soils, induces boron deficiency.
- 1st fertilizer used: Calcium nitrate.
- Sodium nitrate: 1st nitrogenous fertilizer; useful in acidic soils.
- Phosphorus fertilizer for acidic soil: Rock phosphate.
- Ammonium chloride: Not suitable for solanaceous crops.
- Olivin: Good source of Magnesium.
- 'Ca' ion forms the most stable metal-EDTA chelate.
- Micronutrients most widely deficient in Indian soils: Zn and Fe.
- Zn and Fe are compatible with each other.
- Boron is absorbed by roots as undissociated boric acid [$B(OH)_3$ or H_3BO_3].
- Excessive use of 'NO_3' results in 'Fe' deficiency.
- Dry matter yield is increased with an application of nitrogenous fertilizers.
- The range of deficiency and toxicity is narrow in 'Mo' micronutrient.
- Single Super Phosphate: Oldest artificially produced fertilizer and its manufacture dates back to 1842, when J.B. Lawes prepared for the 1st time in England by treating rock phosphate with H_2SO_4.
- High performance of rock phosphate to supply P to crop plants is expected in acidic soil.
- The Latin/ German word for the element with symbol K is "Kalium". It is derived from the Arab word 'el-kali' means ash.
- Potassium content of earth crust is 2.40% whereas the content of phosphorus is only 0.11%.
- Recently, Geological Survey of India has reported the occurrence of K-deposits in Leh (J & K) and Bikaner (Rajasthan).
- Potassium schoenite a double salt of K_2SO_4 and $MgSO_4$ (Epsom salt) is recently being produced on a pilot scale at Bhavanagar (Gujarat).
- Dolomite, Lime stone, Sand Coal, Ash: Filler material in fertilizer mixture.
- Herbigation: Application of herbicides through irrigation.
- Dry herbicides: Mixture of herbicides + fertilizers.
- Calcium content is maximum in burnt lime (70%) followed by hydrated lime (50%).
- Magnesium content is maximum in magnesium oxide (45%) followed by Kiserite (18.2%), Epsom salt (10%).

- **Largest source of sulphur: Volcanic eruptions.**
- In high soil pH: Fe, Mn, Zn, Cu, B nutrients become deficient.

Fertilizer	**N (%)**	**P_2O_5 (%)**	**K_2O (%)**	**S (%)**	**Ca (%)**	**Mg (%)**
Urea	46	-	-	-	-	-
Neem/ sulphur coated urea	36-38	-		-	-	-
Anhydrous ammonia	82.2	-	-	-	-	-
Ammonium sulphate	20.6	-	-	23.7	-	-
Ammonium nitrate	33.5	-	-	-	-	-
Ammonium sulphate nitrate	26	-	-	-	-	-
Ammonium chloride (NH_4Cl)	25	-	-	-	-	-
Sodium nitrate	16	-	-	-	-	-
Single super phosphate (SSP)	-	16	-	12.5	19.5	0.3
Triple super phosphate (TSP)	-	42.5	-	-	-	-
Dicalcium phosphate	-	26	-	-	-	-
Mono ammonium phosphate (MAP)	11	55	-	-	-	-
Diammonium phosphate (DAP)	18	46				
Rock phosphate	-	20-30	-	-	-	-
Basic sludge	-	14-18	-	-	33.9	3.4
Calcium nitrate [$Ca(NO_3)_2$]	15	-	-	-	-	-
Calcium ammonium nitrate (CAN)	25	-	-	-	8	4.5
Calcium cyanamide	22	-	-	-	39	-
Calcium sulphate [$(CaSO_4).2H_2O$]	-	-	-	18.5	23.3	-
Muriate of potash (KCl)	-	-	58	-	-	-
Sulphate of potash (K_2SO_4)(0:0:50)	-	-	50	17	-	-
Mono potassium phosphate (0:52:34)	-	52	34	-	-	-
Mono ammonium phosphate (12:61:0)	12	61	0	-	-	-
Potassium nitrate (KNO_3) (13:0:45)	13	0	45	-	-	-

Element	**Fertilizers and nutrient content (%)**
Copper (Cu)	Copper sulphate (25)
Zinc (Zn)	Zinc sulphate (22-35)
Boron (B)	Borax (11)
Manganese (Mn)	Manganese sulphate (24.30)
Molybdenum (Mo)	Sodium molybdate (37-39); Ammonium molybdate (54)
Ferrous (Fe)	Ferrous sulphate (20); Fe EDTA (12); Fe EDDHA (6)

Fertilizers compatibility:

	Urea	Ammonium nitrate	Ammonium sulphate	Calcium nitrate	Potassium nitrate	Potassium chloride	Potassium sulphate	Ammonium phosphate	Fe, Zn, Cu, Mn, sulphate	Fe, Zn, Cu, Mn, chelate	Magnesium sulphate	Phosphonic acid	Sulphuric acid	Nitric acid
Urea	C													
Ammonium nitrate	C	C												
Ammonium sulphate	C	C	C											
Calcium nitrate	C	C	X	C										
Potassium nitrate	C	C	C	C	C									
Potassium chloride	C	C	C	C	C	C								
Potassium sulphate	C	C	R	X	C	R	C							
Ammonium phosphate	C	C	C	X	C	C	C	C						
Fe, Zn, Cu, Mn, sulphate	C	C	C	X	C	C	R	X	C					
Fe, Zn, Cu, Mn, chelate	C	C	C	R	C	C	C	R	C	C				
Magnesium sulphate	C	C	C	X	C	C	R	X	C	C	C			
Phosphonic acid	C	C	C	X	C	C	C	C	C	R	C	C		
Sulphuric acid	C	C	C	X	C	C	R	C	C	C	C	C	C	
Nitric acid	C	C	C	C	C	C	C	C	C	X	C	C	C	C

C- compatible, X- incompatible, R-Reduced solubility

b) *Organic*

- Biogas contains 50-60% methane, 40% CO_2 and H_2.
- Concentrated: Bone meal, horn meal, blood meal, meat meal, fish meal, Guano, Oil cakes.
  - Edible oil cake: Ground nut, Gingelly cake, etc.
  - Non-edible cake: Castor cake, Neem cake, etc.
- Best concentrated manure: Bone meal.
- Neem tree is regarded as a "village dispensary".
- Neem seed contains 0.2 to 0.3 % azadirechtin.
- Queen of compost: Vermicompost.

Manures & cakes	N (%)	P_2O_5 (%)	K_2O (%)
F.Y.M	0.75	0.20	0.50
Vermicompost	3.0	1.0	1.5
Groundnut cake	7.3	1.5	1.3
Safflower cake	7.8-7.0	2.2-2.3	1.9-2.0
Sesamum cake	6.2-6.3	2.0-2.1	1.2-1.3
Linseed cake	5.5-5.6	1.4-1.5	1.2-1.3
Castor cake	5.5-5.8	1.8-1.9	1.0-1.1
Cotton seed cake	3.9-4.0	1.8-1.9	1.0-1.1
Neem cake	5.2-5.9	1.0-1.1	1.4-1.5
Press mud cake	1.0-1.5	4.5	2.0
Night soil	1.2-1.3	0.8-1.0	0.4-0.5
Sheep dung & urine mixture	0.95	0.35	1.0
Sludge activated	5-6	3-3.5	0.5-0.7
Blood meal	10-12	1.0-1.5	0.6-0.9
Fish meal	4-10	3-3.9	0.3-1.5
Bone meal	3-4	20-25	Nil
Wood ash	0.5-1.9	1.6-4.2	2.3-12

$$\text{Quantity of fertilizer required (Q)} = \frac{\text{Total quantity of mixture (M) x Parts of nutrients in grade (T)}}{\text{Percentage of nutrients in fertilizer (F)}}$$

Actual amount of fertilizers required by crop:

- Conversion factor from N_2 into protein: 6.25.

Required quantity of nutrients	Multiplication factor	Quantity of fertilizers needed
Nitrogen	4.854	Ammonium sulphate
	2.222	Urea
	3.846	Ammonium sulphate nitrate
	4.000	Ammonium chloride
Phosphoric acid	6.250	Single super phósphate
	3.125	Double super phosphate
	2.083	Triple super phosphate
Potash	1.66	Muriate of potash
	2.00	Sulphate of potash

Lime requirement of different soil types (Kg/ha)

pH of soil	Sandy loam	Loam	Clay loam
5.0	1125	1687	2675
5.5	975	1462	2275
6.0	375	562	875
6.2	225	337	525

Sulphur requirement of different soil types (Kg/ha)

pH of soil	Sandy	Clay
7.5	400-600	800-1000
8.0	1000-1500	1500-2000
8.5	1500-2000	1500-2000
9.0	2000-3000	2000-3000

c) *Bio-fertilizers* and *green manures*:

- Saprophytes- *Aspergillus*, *Penicillium*, *Trichoderma*.
- Approx. 20 gram of rhizobium culture is required to treat one kg seed.
- One packet of rhizobium culture contains 20 gram of rhizobium culture.
- Activity of bio-fertilizers is highly related to soil pH.
- Genes responsible for N fixation: *Nif* genes.
- Micronutrient responsible for N fixation: Molybdenum.
- Micronutrient constituent of N & K: Molybdenum.
- Plants absorb 'N' in nitrate form.
- Conversion of ammonia to nitrate occurs in presence of nitrosomonas.
- Conversion of nitrite to nitrate occurs in presence of nitrobacter.
- Molybdenum seed treatment could also enhance N fixation.
- Incorporate green manure crops into soil at flowering stage e.g. sunhemp (7-8 weeks), dhaincha (5-6 weeks).

Bio-fertilizer capsules:

- Based on nanotechnology.
- Developed by Indian Institute of Spices Research, Kozhikode.
- Granted patent for microbial encapsulation technology (patent no. 361021 on March, 2021) from Govt. of India.
- Bio-encapsulation technique (comprising colony forming units up to 10^{12}) is the 1st in the world.
- Use of one bio-capsule/ acre is recommended. It is suitable for monocots and dicots.

- Bio-capsule can be used for spices (ginger, turmeric), vegetables (onion) and fruit crops.
- Bio-capsule types & related crops:
  - Rhizo capsule- N supply to leguminous crops.
  - Aceto capsule- N supply to sweet potato and sugarcane crop.
  - Azospirilium capsule- N supply to all crops.
  - Azo capsules- N supply to non-leguminous crops.
  - PSB capsules- P supply to all crops.
  - Potash Grow capsule- Supplies K to all crops.
  - NPK capsule- for all crops.
  - Zinc Grow capsule- for all oil seed crops.
- Mode of utilization:
  a) One capsule is soaked in 5 lit of semi-hot cold water for a night. Seed is treated with 1 lit solution before sowing/ planting.
  b) Remaining 200 lit solution can be used in form of soil application at root zone or through foliar sprays or through drip & sprinkler system.
- 1st successful trial on ginger crop in Mysuru. Yield increment by 8 tons/ acre, reduction in disease incidence by 10%.
- Cost: Rs. 360/ capsule.

Green manure crops:

- Sunhemp (*Crotolaria juncea*):
- Pillipesera (*Phaseolus trilobus*):
- Dhaincha/ Koliniji (*Sesbania bispinosa* or *S. aculeata*): Flood tolerant, alkaline and water logged soils.
- *Sesbania rostrata*: Stem nodule formation and fastest nitrogen fixing crop:
- Guar (*Cyamopsis tetragonoloba*)
- Indigo (*Indigofera tinctoria*)
- Wild indigo (*Tephrosia purpurea*): Drought tolerant legume.
- Glyricidia (*Glyricidia sepium*):
- Cowpea (*Vigna unguiculata* or *V. sinensis*):
- Green gram/Mung : *Phaseolus aureus* or *Vigna radiata*):
- Black gram/Urd (*Phaseolus mungo* or *Vigna mungo*):
- Horse gram (*Macrotyloma uniflorum*):
- Cluster bean/ Guar (*Cyamopsis tetragonaloba*):
- Berseem (*Trifolium alexandrium*):

- Karanj (*Miletttia pinnata* syn. *Pongamia pinnata*):
- Genus *Myrica*: Non-leguminous angiosperm nodulated by *Frankia* spp.
- Subabul (*Leucaena leucocephala*):
- Agase (*Sesbania grandiflora*):
- Eupatorium (*Chromolaena odorata*):
- Neem (*Melia azadiracta*):
- Cassia (*Cassia siamea*):
- Ipomea (*Ipomoea carnea*):
- Yekka (*Calotropis gigantia*):

Seed rate and biomass production of green manure crops:

Green manure crop	Seed rate (kg/ha)	Biomass yield (t/ha)
Sunhemp	25-40	21
Dhaincha	20-25	26
Cow pea	25-30	15
Indigo	25-30	12
Wild Indigo	25-40	16
Green gram	15	10
Black gram	15	10
Cluster bean	12-15	10

Nutrient content of green manures:

Name	N (%)	P_2O_5 (%)	K_2O (%)
Sunhemp	0.89	0.12	0.51
Cowpea	0.71	0.15	0.58
Dhaincha	0.68	0.13	0.40
Green gram	0.82	0.18	0.52
Black gram	0.82	0.18	0.52
Horse gram	0.91	0.18	0.65
Glyricidia	0.68	0.16	0.30
Pongamia	0.16	0.14	0.49

Method and area of application:

- Seed inoculants: *Rhizobium*- legume crops.
- *Rhizobium* species for legume crops: Garden pea (*R. leguminosporum*), Soy bean (*R. japonicum*), Cow pea (*Rhizobium* spp.), Alfa-alfa (*R. meliloti*).
- Soil inoculants: Blue green algae, *Azotobacter*- vegetables, fruits, spices, ornamental flowers.
- Seed and soil inoculants: VAM fungi-variety of plants.
- Carrier based BGA- banana.

- Association with plants- Azospirillum- vegetables, fruits, flowers.
- Azo-compost: Preparation of compost using nitrogen fixing bacteria. It is cheapest source of nitrogen among all organic manures.
- Symbiotic nitrogen fixing legume bacterial inoculants- *Rhizobium, Actinomycets alni*.
- Free living organism-*Azotobactor, Clostridium* (actinomycetes) e.g. Vegetable crops.
- Term 'Mycorrhiza' was coined by A.B. Frank in 1883.
- Vesicular Arbuscular Mycorrhiza (VAM) increases availability of phosphorus.
- PSB and VAM absorb and release phosphorous for better utilization of growing plants.
- VAM fungi have extremely broad range of hosts.
- Useful VAM: *Glomus fasciculatum*, *G. mosseae*, *G. etunicatum*, *G. tenue*.

Advantages of VAM:

- o Increase growth of seedlings in nursery.
- o Reduces phosphorus requirement.
- o Increase survival rate and development of micropropagated plantlets.
- o Increase resistance to biotic and abiotic stresses.
- o Make uniformity in crops.
- o Improve rooting of cuttings.
- o Improve uptake of minor elements and water.
- o Produce plant hormone, increase activity of nitrogen fixing organisms in root zone.

- Hartig net is formed by ectomycorrhiza.
- Blue Green Algae (BGA): A prokaryote also known as cyanobacteria e.g. Anabaena, Nostoc (Heterocyst).
- Free water fern- *Azolla*.
- Phosphate solubilizers- *Pseudomonas*, *Aspergillus*, *Bacillus*, *Penicillium*.
- Ectotrophic mycorrhizae- Basidiomycetes.
- Endotrophic mycorrhizae- *Glomus*, *Gigaspore*, *Acaulospore*, *Entrophospora*, *Sclerocystis*.
- *Economic benefits of biofertilizers-*

1. 1 kg *Rhizobium* = 100 kg N = 214.5 kg urea.
2. 1 kg *Azotobacter*/ *Azospirillum* = 40 kg N = 85.8 kg urea.
3. 1 kg BGA = 2 kg N = 4.2 kg urea.

6.4 Precision farming in horticulture

- High tech horticulture and precision famring assume greater significance.
- In India, concept of precision farming was promoted in the year 2001.
- Plasticulture Development Centres were redisigned into PFDC i.e. Precision Farming Development Centre.
- Assigned to work on precision farming models on different crops.
- High tech horticulture and precision farming were launced during 10th five year plan.
- PFDC working on-
    - o Drip irrigation, sprinkler irrigation and fertigation.
    - o *In situ* moisture conservation.
    - o Anti-hail nets and anit-bird nets.
    - o Shade nets.
    - o Protected cultivation of fruits, vegetables and floriculture crops.
    - o LDPE lined water storage tanks.
    - o Microirrigation.
    - o Precision farming includes computers, geographical information systems, global positioning systems, sensors and application control.
- Scope for precision farming:
    - o Application of technologies and principles in horticulture production for improving crop performance and environmental quality.
    - o Efficient management of resources for hi-tech interventions such as microirrigation, fertigation, protected/ green house cultivation, soil and leaf nutrient based fertilizer management, mulching for in situ moisture conservation, micropropagation, bio-technology for germplasm, genetically modified crops, use of bio-fertilizers, HDP, hi-tech mechanization, green foods, soil-less culture and biological control, etc.
- Precision farming in horticulture:
    - o Climatic variations tend to have adverse effects on yield and production of crops.
    - o Technology of protected cultivation is well adopted in Europe and USA.
    - o Japan and China are leading in controlled sphere production of horticultural crops.
    - o In India, protected cultivation is making break through in banana, grape, pomegranate, cashew nut, capsicum, peppers, chilli, cucumber, potato, tomato, musk melons, sweet corn, baby corn, and selected flowers.
- About 17 PFDCs have been established in different agro-climatic regions under NHM.

6.5 Organic farming:

- The term 'organic' was first used in relation to farming by Northbourne (1940) in his book *Look to the Land*: 'the farm itself should have a biological completeness; it must be a living entity, it must be a unit which has within itself a balanced organic life'.
- Masanobu Fukuoka is a pioneer of 'natural farming' from Japan.
- He wrote a book 'The One Straw Revolution' in 1975 in Japanese language and later translated in English in 1978.
- Permaculture: Design system which integrates raising crops and animals with careful water management.
- Pioneer of Zero budget farming: Mr. Subhash Palekar.
- FAO provides support to organic farming in developing countries.
- Organic farming movements have spread to Asia and Africa too.
- Survery of International Trade Centre during year 2000 indicate that demand for organic products is growing rapidly in many world markets, but supply is not attuned.
- International trade in organic foods shows annual growth rate of 20-22%.
- Demand for organic products is growing fast @ 20% per annum in USA, European Union and Japan.
- Worldwide 1.8 million farm house hold in 162 countries practice organic farming in 37 m ha land.
- Global market for organic food reached 89.7 billion US dollars in 2016.
- The regions with the largest areas of organically managed agricultural land are Oceania (12.1 million hectares), Europe (8.2 million hectares) and Latin America (8.1 million hectares).
- Major developed countries have been able to convert 2-10% of their cultivated area into organic farming.
- The countries with most agriculture land of organic: Australia (27 Mha), Argentina (3.8 Mha), USA (1.9 Mha) and China (1.6 Mha).
- Leading country in adoption of organic farming in European Union: Germany.
- The countries with the highest numbers of producers: India (340'000 producers), Uganda (180'000) and Mexico (130'000). More than one third of organic producers are in Africa.
- India ranks 1st in the number of organic farmers and 9th in terms of area under organic farming.
- India is slow in adoption of organic farming.
- Leading country in world: Australia (27.15 Mha).
- Total area under organic certification in India: 1.5 million ha.

- Total number of organic producers in India: 8.35 lakhs.
- Total organic production in India: 1.35 Million tones.
- Total area under organic farming in India: 27.7 lakh hectares.
- Organic farming is practiced in 12 states in about 4.72 million hectares.
- Number of organic farming models developed by ICAR: 45.
- Organic states: Sikkim (1st declared on 18th January, 2016), Uttarakhand (2nd), Tripura, and Tamil Nadu.
- State with largest area under organic certification: Madhya Pradesh > Himachal Pradesh > Rajasthan.
- India produced around 1.35 million MT (2015-16) of certified organic products which includes all varieties of food products.
- India exported organic products 515 million USD in 2017-18.
- More than 30% of world's organic producers are in India.
- Organic food market is growing at 25-30%.
- Domestic organic food market would touch USD 1.36 billion by 2020.
- Organic pulses and food grains took lion's share of the market.
- 1st organic farming institute to be set up in Vadodara, Gujarat.
- Major horticultural products produced in India: Organic tea and niche market for spices, fruits and vegetables.
- Largest exported organic product in India- Oilseeds (50%) > Processed food products >Cereals & millets > Tea >Pulses >Spices.
- India has good potential to export organically grown coffee, vegetables, herbs, nuts, cosmetics, etc.
- Organic certification of Agricultural products will be done by Govt. of Maharashtra and head quarter at Akola.
- MOPFFA: Maha Organic Residue Free Farmers Association.
- Portal launched by central government for e-marketing of organic products: Jaivik kheti.
- A company owned by ICAR-DARE, under Ministry of Agriculture and farmers Welfare: Agri-innovate India.
- ICAR award for organic farming: Haldhar award.
- Residue free and Organic Mission India issues 'Sir Albert Howard Organic Farming Sustainability' award.
- Institute of organic farming is located at UAS, Dharwad.
- On an average, in organic field there is 39% increase in organic carbon and 22.3% increase in soil carbon stock.
- Carbon sequestration is 301 kg/ ha/year under organic farming while it is only 43 kg/ ha/year under conventional farming in cabbage.

- In organically produced vegetables, 17-25% higher vit. C, 30% proteins and 39% higher lycopene content is recorded.
- Benefits from adoption of organic farming:
  - High price premiums for the organic products.
  - Conservation of natural resources in terms of improved soil fertility and water quality.
  - Prevention of soil erosion.
  - Prevention of natural and agro-bio-diversity.
  - Economical and social benefits
  - Protection of ecosystem, flora, fauna and increased bio-diversity.
  - Food security
  - Protection of environment.

Methods of farming:

- Conversion period: Time between start of organic management and certification of crops.
- Bio-dynamic farming: Aims to treat the farm as a living system. It was initiated in Germany in 1924.
- Concept of biodynamic agriculture: Rudolf Steiner.
- Rishi Krishi: Practiced in Madhya Pradesh.
- Natueco farming: Based on the principle of ecosystem networking of nature.

Regulatory mechanisms:

- India has adopted NPOP (National Programme for Organic Production working under Ministry of Commerce) with national standards.
- NPOP launched in May, 2000under FTDR act and subsequent accreditation and certification program in October, 2001.
- Logo India Organic was released in July, 2002 to support NPOP.
- Implementation of NPOP is ensured by formation of NAPP (National Accreditation Policy and Programme).
- The NPOP is administered, monitored and implemented for benefit of farmers, processorers, traders and consumers.
- Implementing agency for NPOP: APEDA.
- NSOP: National Standards of Organic Production.
- To promote organic farming, agriculture ministry is implementing various schemes viz. National Project on Organic Farming; National Horticulture Mission; Technology Mission for North-East and Rastriya Krishi Vikas Yojana.

- The organic Agricultural Produce Grading and Marketing Rules, 2009 provide for grading and certification of all kinds of fruits and vegetables grown organically as per the standards prescribed in National Program for Organic Residues.
- Foreign Trade Development and Regulation Act (FTDR) is responsible for export requirement.
- APEDA: Regulation of organic production and export under the brand name 'India Organic'. Regulates certification of organic products.
- APEDA: Implementing agency for NPOP.
- APEDA: Nodal Agency for Promoting export-oriented production and development of the Scheduled products
- APEDA's website gives training and information of organic operators through net system.
- Apex body of organic certification: National Accreditation Body (NAB).
- Indian Organic Certification (IOC) process granted at world level during 2004.
- National Centre of Organic Farming (NCOF): Ghaziabad, Uttar Pradesh working under Ministry of Agriculture and Farmers Welfare (GOI).
- International Federation of Organic Agriculture Movements (IFOAM), conceptual support for a globally unified certification database. It helps in production and certification of organic produce.
- Agencies accrediated are APEDA, Coffee Board, Tea Board, Spices Board.
- Regulations cover exports, imports and domestic trade or organic products.

Greenhouse gases:

- Contribution of greenhouse gases to global warming: CO_2 (60%), Nitrous oxide (5%), Chloro-fluro Carbon (CFC-5%), CH_4 (15%), etc.
- About 50% of the total methane emissions are from agriculture sector.
- Fertilizers add 0.6-1.2% of the world's greenhouse gases.
- Concentration of CO_2 has increased from a pre-industrial value of 280 to 393 ppm in 2010.
- Green house effect: The process whereby green house gases released into atmosphere cause heat to be trapped into rather than escaping into space.

7. NURSERY MANAGEMENT

7.1 Types of nurseries-

- It is a place where young plants are raised under intensive care for later transplanting to field.
- Seeds Act and the Nursery Registration Act have been in operation since December 1966.

- Nursery Registration Act is presently in force in respect of horticulture nurseries only in the States of Punjab, Maharashtra, Himachal Pradesh, Uttar Pradesh, Uttarakhand, Jammu and Kashmir, Orissa and Tamil Nadu.
- Only 30-40% demand of planting material is being met by existing infrastructure.
- Temporary nursery- Flying nursery.
- Post entry quarantine (PEQ) is required for cuttings and saplings.

7.2 Greenhouse structures:

- Greenhouse technology was 1st used in England.
- Presently, China is the world leader in cultivating horticultural crops under protected condition.
- Climate controlled greenhouses were 1st established in India by Indo-American Hybrid Seed Company (IAHS) in 1965.
- Polyhouses gives 5-6 times higher production compared to open field.
- Glasshouses are very popular in the Netherlands.
- 'Sea of Plastics', a 50,000 acre world's largest complex of a series of greenhouse is located at Almeria in Spain.
- Greenhouse structures should be designed to resist a 130 km/hr wind velocity.
- Galvanized iron (GI) pipes have coating of aluminum and zinc.
- Aluminum and hot dipped galvanized iron pipes are comparatively maintenance free.
- Chromated copper arsenate and ammonical copper arsenate are water based preservatives those are applied to the wood that come into contact with the soil.
- Red wood or cypress (natural decay resistant woods) can be used in desert or tropical regions, but they are expensive.
- World's Largest Solar Park is situated at Bhadla, Jodhpur, Rajasthan which spread across 14,000 acres, generating 2245 MW energy.
- NCPAH: National Committee on Plasticulture Applications in Horticulture, New Delhi, 1981.
- CPCT: Centre for Protected Cultivation, IARI, New Delhi.
- PDC: Plasticulture Development Centre.
- Open roof greenhouse was developed by Art Van Wingerden in 1990.
- Open greenhouses protect from rain and hail.
- Most suitable greenhouses in Indian condition: Quonset type or Arch roofed type.
- Most suitable greenhouses for hilly region: Gable type poly-tunnel.
- Portable mini-tunnels are suitable for nursery plants.

- Walk in tunnel or naturally ventilated or low tunnel polyhouse: Low cost, unheated, semi-permanent structures wisely used for off season vegetable production of cucurbits.
- Low plastic tunnels: Off season vegetable production.
- Ideal central height of greenhouse for mango and papaya: 5.5 to 6.5 m.
- Unit heater system: Most common and least expensive heating system.
- Rain shelters: Protect vegetables against the impact of heavy rainfall.
- The standard size of hot frame is 0.9 x 1.8 m.
- Multi-span/gutter connected greenhouse: Most popular & oriented in N-S direction.
- Propagation benches for rooting of cuttings, grafting are maintained 6^0C warmer than temperature for growing of crop.
- Hot beds: Used for growing small tender seedlings, rooting of cuttings.
- Lath house: Provides shade to young tender seedlings or rooted cuttings.
- Cold frames: Used for hardening of rooted cuttings.
- Net house: Suitable for cacti, succulents and orchids.
- Phytotron: Most expensive type of protected structure.
- National Phytotron Facility is located at IARI, New Delhi in 1997.
- Coloured plastic mulch: Reduce insect damage e.g. yellow mulch: Repel whitefly.
- Black mulch: For soil moisture conservation, weed control and increase in soil heat.
- Mulching paper has thickness about 100μ (0.012 to 0.031 mm).
- Transparent mulch (30-40 μ thick): Increase soil temperature (soil solarization).
- Forage crops for animal feeding: Maize, Cowpea, pulse crops, etc.

***Characters of cladding material*:**

- Glass has highest light transmission (95%) and long life.
- Polyethylene film having thickness 150-200μ (800-1000 gauge or 200-250 gsm) is generally used as cladding material for polyhouses.
- Acrylic sheet is highly weather resistant and does not fade and become yellow with age.
- The most recent addition of green house film plastic covering is Tefzel T2 film (ethylene tetrafluoroethylene). Anticipated life expectancy is 20 years with light transmission capacity of 95% and is greater than that of any other green house covering material.

Type	Durability	Transmission		Maintenance
		Light	Heat	
Polyethylene	One year	90%	70%	Very high
Polyethylene UV resistant	Three years	90%	70%	High
Fiber Glass	Seven years	90%	5%	Low
Tedlar coated Fiber Glass	Fifteen years	90%	5%	Low
Double strength Glass	Fifty years	90%	5%	Low
Poly carbonate	Fifty years	90%	5%	Very low

***Light management in greenhouse*:**

- Shade nets are manufactured using HDPE (High density polyethylene) having 25-75% shade.
- Foliage plants are burned at light intensities >2000-3000 foot candles.
- Silver coloured shade nets are used to control aphids.
- Insect proof net houses (40-50 mesh size) are used for virus free crop production: Tomato, brinjal & sweet pepper.
- Red and grey coloured shade nets: Suitable for growing *Codiaeum.*
- Grey net: Suitable for growing *Hosta, Livistonia, Monstera.*
- Poinsettia and kalanchoe are more sensitive to light than chrysanthemum.
- In chrysanthemum, red wavelength causes plants to flower 4 weeks earlier.
- In photo-sensitive plants, flower bud induction without disturbing dark period is possible using mixture of 80% red and 20% blue LED i.e. light emitting diode.
- Plastic sheets with special reflectance spectra are used as reflective mulch on floor or benches where pot plants are grown in commercial green houses.
  a) White plastic mulch absorbs UV & increases light intensity at the plants.
  b) Red plastic mulch is used to improve flavor in soft fruits.
  c) Silver plastic mulch reflect near UV, visible or near IR light and improves grape quality and increased productivity.
- Photosynthesis does not increase at light intensities > 32.2 klux.
- Shade nets are designed to protect plants from UV rays.
  - Photosynthetically active radiation (PAR) or visible light spectrum: 400-700 nm.
  - In Ultra violet or blue light range (430-450 nm i.e. shorter wavelength). Growth is retarded. Plant become hard and dark in colour.
  - UV-A (315-400 nm)- influence stem and leaf development.
  - UV-B (300-315 nm)- influence flower colour formation.
  - Far red light range: 650-670 nm (longer wavelength). Growth is soft and internodes are long. Cause greenhouse effect.
  - Near infra-red radiation (NIR, 700-3000 nm) - for heating the green house and suitable for temperate countries.

- Red and blue spectrum are most essential for photosynthesis.
- Ideal balance for photosynthesis is 92% red LED and 8% blue LED.
- Red light absorption spectrum i.e. 660 nm contributes maximum to plant.
- Red light combined with blue light encourages flowering, seeding and fruiting.
- Blue lightis responsible for vegetative growth and it is indispensable to morphologically healthy growth of plants.
- UV radiation to 740 nm spectrum is known to control various aspects of plant growth and flowering.
- Visible light spectrum can affect compactness of shape, time of flowering and final yields.
- In food or medicinal plants this spectrum can change plant's chemical content, which affects flavor, colour and nutritional and/ or pharmaceutical values.

***Humidity management in greenhouse*:**

- Desirable level of relative humidity in greenhouse: 50-60%.
- Mist chamber: Used for rooting of leaf cutting and droplet size is 10-500 μ.
- Reduction of greenhouse temperature is done by using evaporative cooling method.
- Temperature differential between indoors and outdoors is greatest at roof.
- Most common summer cooling system in greenhouses: Fan and Pad.
- Fan and pad system works on the principle of evaporative cooling system.
- For effective cooling, distance between fan and pad: 30-60 m.
- The pad was composed of excelsior (wood shreds), but today it is commonly made of a cross-fluted-cellulose material.

***CO_2 enrichment in greenhouse*:**

- In general, the percentage of carbon dioxide in the atmosphere is 0.035% (345 ppm).
- Optimum CO_2 required for crop growth: 1000-2000 ppm.
- CO_2 enrichment increases the vegetative growth on an average 13% and reproductive output by an average of 31% of plants.
- CO_2 should be injected only in day time.
- CO_2 enrichment is beneficial only in C_3 plants.
- CO_2 compensation point in C_3 plants is at 50-150 ppm whereas in C_4 plants it is at 10-20 ppm.
- CO_2 accepter in C_3 plant is RuBP (Ribulose-1, 5-bisphosphate) and in C_4 plant is Phosphoenol pyruvate (PEP).
- 1st stable product in C_3 plant is Phospho glyceric acid (PGA) and in C_4 plant is Oxaloacetic acid (OAA).
- Kreb's cycle is also called Tricarboxylic acid (TCA) cycle.

Irrigation management in greenhouse:

- Sprinkler irrigation can save up to 35-50% water and also useful for saving vegetables from frost.
- Drip irrigation was developed by Simca Blass in 1959 in Isreal.
- Pitcher irrigation: Indigenous method of micro-irrigation.
- Total area under micro-irrigation system in India: 11.58 Mha (Drip -5.75 Mha).
- States having maximum area under micro-irrigation system in India: Rajasthan (1.68 mha), Andhra Pradesh, Maharashtra (94,000 ha).
- States with highest area under drip: Maharashtra (8,81,550 ha), Andhra Pradesh (8,23,833 ha), Gujarat (4,23,771 ha).
- States with highest area under sprinkler: Rajasthan (15,02,329 ha), Haryana (5,38,608 ha), Karnataka (4,23,406 ha).
- Most agriculture sprinklers are slow rotation types.
- Application efficiency is 90 to 95%, compared with sprinkler at 70% and furrow irrigation at 60 to 80%,
- Devised drip and sprinkler irrigation system saves water (30-50%), labour (50%), fertilizer (30-40%) and increase yield (12-76%).
- Low pressure drip irrigation system is found to be more suitable and economical for small greenhouses.
- Drip irrigation is used in only 1% of the total irrigated area.
- Drip system: Operating pressure is 1.0-1.5 kg/cm^2.
- Foggers: Operating pressure is 2.0-2.5 kg/cm^2 and droplet size is < 10 μ.
- Sprinklers: Operating pressure 2.5-3.5 kg/cm^2 and droplet size is 0.5-4 mm.
- Micro-sprinkler: Operating pressure >1.5 kg/cm^2.
- Most soil types use 2.0 lph emitters and are more economical. For sandy soil use 4.0 lph emitters.
- Drip emitters: Most susceptible to clogging.
- About 10% pressure drop is permitted between two ends of laterals.
- Lateral pipes are made up of LDPE and dia. varies from 12-20 mm.
- In-line drippers are most commonly used for vegetable and flower cultivation.
- On-line drippers are used for landscaping and orchard crops.
- Useful life of micro-irrigation system: 7-10 years.
- Sprinklers spray water through atmosphere and designed to wet specific volume of soil around individual tree. It is most suitable for below canopy irrigation.
- Drip is paint source of water and wets specific volume of soil by direct application around root zone.
- Hygroscopic water: Water held tightly to the surface of soil particles by adsorption forces.

- Capillary water: Water held by force of surface as continuous film around soil particles and in capillary space.
- Capillary water is held between tension of 31 and 1/3rd atmosphere.
- Available water: Water between field capacity & permanent wilting point.
- Infiltration: Movement of water from the surface into the soil.
- Percolation: Vertical movement of water in soil.
- Water moves freely in response to gravitational force and drain out of the soil: Gravitational water.
- One ha cm of irrigation is equal to 1,00,000 liters.

Conversion of data:

Area-

- 1 R (i.e. 1 guntha) = 33 feet x 33 feet = 1089 sq. ft =101 m^2.
- 1 ha= 2.47 acres= 10,000 sq. m.
- 1 acre= 40 R= 4047 sq. m. = 43,560 sq. ft.= 0.404 ha= 4.8 Bighas.
- 1 square inch = 6.451 square centimetres.

Mass-

- 1 kg = 2.20462 pounds.
- 1 gram (g) = 1000 milligrams (mg).
- 1 mg = 1000 micrograms (µg).
- 1 µg = 1000 nanograms (ng).
- 1 ounce (oz) = 28.4 g.
- 1 pound (lb) = 16 oz= 453.6 g.
- 1 g = 15.4 grains.
- 1 grain = 65 mg.
- 1 ton = 907 Kg.
- 1 Mg = 1.1 ton.

Volume-

- 1 litre (l) = 1000 millilitres (ml).
- 1 ml = 1000 microlitres (µl).
- 1 gallon = 3.78 litres.
- 1 Pint = 0.473 litre.
- 1 litre = 2.11 pints.
- 1 bushel = 35.24 litres
- 1 litre = 0.0284 bushel.
- 1 cubic foot = 28.3 litres.

Length-

- 1 meter (m) = 1000 millimetres (mm).
- 1 mm = 1000 micros (μ).
- 1 μ = 1000 millimicrons (mμ).
- 1 inch = 2.54 centimetres (cm).
- 1 cm = 0.39 inch.
- 1 foot = 0.305 metre (m).
- 1 mile = 1.609344 km = 8 furlong = 1760 yards.
- 1 furlong = 660 ft = 220 yards.
- 1 yard = 91.44 cm.

Weight-volume relationship-

- 1000 ml (1 litre) = 1,000 ppm = 0.1%.
- 10000 ml (10 litres) = 100 ppm = 0.01%.
- 1 ppm= Percent x 10,000= 1 mg/1 lit.

Temperature-

- Unit of heat measurement: British thermal unit (Btu).
- 1 Calorie= 4.1868 J = 0.003968321 Btu.
- 1 Btu= 251.9958 Calorie = 1055.056 Joule.
- 1 Joule= 0.239 calorie.
- Specific heat of water: 1 Cal/ gram.
- 1 Kg of LPG yields 4200 Kcal energy.
- 1 Kg wood yield only 1700-2200 Kcal energy.
- Rad: Unit of energy that has been absorbed from radiation.
- 1 rad=0.01 gray (Gy).

Thermometer scale	Freezing point (degree)	Boiling point (degree)
Celsius (^{0}C)	0	100
Fahrenheit (^{0}F)	32	212
Reumer (^{0}R)	0	80
Kelvin (^{0}K)	273	373

Pressure-

- 1 gauge= 0.254 microns.
- 1 kg/cm^2 = 14.22 psi.
- 1 HP = 746 watts = 632 Kcal.
- 1 atmospheric pressure =14.7 psi =760 mm Hg.
- 1 bar= 10^5 Pascal = 10^5 N/m^2.

Water measurement-

- 1 acre foot = 0.123 hectare meter.
- 1 hectare meter = 8.1 acre feet.
- 1 acre inch = 1.028 hectare centimeter.
- 1 hectare centimeter = 0.973 acre inch

Yield and rate-

- 1 pound/ acre = 1.12 kg/ ha.
- 1 kg/ha = 0.893 pound/ acre.
- 1 ton/ acre = 2.24 Mg/ ha.
- 1 Mg/ ha = 0.446 ton/ acre.
- 1 gallon/ acre = 9.35 l/ha.
- 1 l/ha = 0.107 gallon / acre.

Conversion formula:

- ppm to per cent = ppm/ 10,000.
- Percent to ppm = % x 10,000.
- ^{0}F to ^{0}C = 5/9 x (^{0}F – 32).
- ^{0}C to ^{0}F = (^{0}C – 9/5) + 32.
- Vitamin A (μg/100g)= Vitamin A (IU/100g) x 0.6
- Vitamin A (IU/100g)= Vitamin A (μg/100g) / 0.6
- 1 g carbohydrate= 4 Kcal.
- 1 g protein = 4 Kcal.
- 1 g fat = 9 Kcal.
- 0.6 μg β-carotene = 1 IU. vitamin A.
- 1 foot candle= 10.7639 Lux.
- 1 Lux= 0.0929 foot candle. It is unit for measurement of light.
- 1 ha cm of water = 10,000 liters.

***Growth and development*:**

- Certain amount of heat energy is required for plants to grow, produce flowers and fruits. This energy is directly related to time and temperature.
- Effect of temperature on flowering and fruit development suggest the use of degree days/ heat summation can more accurately predicts the harvest date.
- Zero point is the temperature below which the particular plant ceases growth.
- Heat unit: Mathematical expression of plant and temperature relationships expressed as degree days/ growing degree days.
- A heat unit means a degree above a daily mean of 18^{0}C between flowering, fruit development and ripening period.

- Heat unit is called differently as degree days, remainder index system, growing degree days, total thermal units, and warmth index (for forest species).
- Heat units = Daily temperature (max.) + Daily temperature (min.) ÷ 2, minus base temperature.
- Almond: Requires maximum number of heat units for crop maturity.
- Reaumer, a French scientist in 1735 was 1st to develop concept of heat units.
- Arnold (1958) developed various methods to determine base temperature. One of the method is 'X intercept method'
- Gilmore and Regers (1958) used 5^0C base temperature.
- Zero point: It is the temperature below which particular plant ceases growth e.g. For citrus (12.22 ^0C), cherry (-1.11^0C), date palm (-12.22^0C), ber (7.22^0C), litchi (15^0C), mango (10^0C).
- Constant factor for estimating heat units is 10^0C.

Crop	Variety and heat units required to reach maturity	Base temperature (^0C)
Litchi	Shahi (813), Calcuttia (1014)	15
Date palm	Kuchh area of Gujarat (1800-2000); arid zone (4200-5000); Halaway (1951-3101); Medjool (2648-3650); Zahidi (2322-3479); Khalas (2357-3281); Sewi (2244-3281); Khadraway (2213-3342); Sharman (2411-3567); Hayani (2460-3168); Zagloul (2227-3631); Barhee (2323 & never attains full dang stage)	10
Grape	Early maturing (1600-2000); late maturing (>3000); Pearl of Casaba (1570-1600); Black Muscat (2080-2160); Thompson Seedless (1600-2000); Gulabi (3508), Anab-e-Shahi (3526), Bangalore Blue (3562), Kandhari (3207), Bhokari (3284), Concord (*V. labrusca* 2747)	10
Strawberry	Regina (174), Talisman (215), Shasta (201),	06
Mango	* Very early maturing (<1800) e.g. Himsagar, Bombay Green, Alphonso, Krishna Bhog, Gulabkhas, Safeda, Banginpalli (1426-1445). * Early maturing (1800-2000) e.g. Langra, Dashehari, Himsagar. * Medium maturing (2000-2200) e.g. Vanraj, Hybrid 7/4. * Late maturing (2200-2400) e.g. Mallika, Amrapali, Chausa, Totapuri, Neelum * Very late maturing (>2400) e.g. Hur, Baneshan, Alampur, Neelgoa.	10
Ber	Gola (1980-2236); Kaithali (2236-2566); Umran (2516-2920)	7.2
Banana	1930 degree days	9.8
Apple	Different cvs. (2457-2756); Red Delicious (1659-1705)	7.2
Apricot	6 weeks post bloom period	7.2
Pear	42 days post bloom period; Bartlett (2240-2296)	4.44
Peach	25 days post bloom period	21.11
Yellow passion fruit	Flower opening in January (861.7), Fruit set in April (867.6)	10
Pecan nut	5000 (warm temperate climate) and 1200-1700 (Nilgiri hills)	10
Arecanut	7244-8866	10

***Heat units for vegetable crops*:**

- The concept of heat units is used to make predictions crop maturity.
- This was introduced in 1940s to facilitate harvest scheduling.
- It is based on the principle that quantity of heat and not day's from planting, determine when a crop will mature.
- Base temperature is defined on physiological basis as lowest temperature at which plant development will proceed.
- The standard base temperatures for onion (1.66^{0}C), egg plant (15.5^{0}C), tomato (15-20^{0}C) due to hot set and cold set varieties, cucumber (12.7 & 15.5^{0}C), garden pea (4.4^{0}C), sweet corn (4.4^{0}C).
- Harvest dates is ascertained by accounting of cumulative heat units.

Crop	Variety and heat units required to reach maturity	Base temperature (^{0}C)
Pea	Alaska (644-672); Early Sweet (734), Champ (790); Dawn (610); Nugget (823); Resistant Early Perfection No. 326 (846); Alderman (918); Bolero (840); Dark Skin Perfection (848); Freezer No. 626 (818); Lotus (756); Spring (834); Trumpet (672)	4.4

8. SOIL-LESS CULTIVATION OF HORTICULTURAL CROPS:

- System of growing plants in soilless crop cultivatipon i.e. in nutrient medium.
- Hydroponics derived from two Greek words: Hydro- water and ponos- labour.
- Hydroponics is traditionally known as 'Solution culture'.
- Father of hydroponics: Dr. William F. Gericke.
- It was commercialized in 1960-70s.
- This technology is better exploited under polyhouse.
- In India, 1st introduced at Kalimpong, Darjeeling, West Bengal.
- It has 4 methods: Water culture, Drip culture and Gravel culture, Coco peat culture.
- Drip culture/ Slop culture is also known as 'sand culture'.
- Soilless culture: Growing plants in medium other than soil.
- Soilless culture techniques : Nutrient Film Technique (NFT), Tube culture, Aeroponics and Aquaponics.
- NFT: True hydroponic system developed by Dr. Allan Corper.
- Benefits of NFT: More production per unit area; efficient use of water and fertilizers; crop growth period can be drastically reduced; crop intensity can be increased; root growth is excellent due to supply of oxygen.

- Nutrient solution with high phosphate level is usually not recommended for water culture.
- Major benefit: Residue free production.
- Proper aeration is major key to success in hydroponics.
- Country having maximum area under hydroponics: Israel
- First crop raised in hydroponics in 1973: Tomato cv. Pipo.
- Vegetables suited for cultivation: Palak, Coriander, Fenugreek, Lettuce and medicinal plants.
- Plant roots are exposed to nutrient solution e.g. Tomato, Cucumber.
- Aeroponics: Plants grown in trough or container; roots are suspended and sprayed with nutrient mist. It is suitable for short statured plant.
- Aquaponics: Combined structure of growing fish and plants.
- Nutrient solution replaced once in 4-6 days interval.
- International Working Group of Soilless Culture (IWGSC) was established at Washington.
- Tensiometer is not suitable for soilless media based greenhouse cultivation.
- Time domain reflectometry TDR based soil moisture gadgets are suitable for soilless medium.
- Crop water productivity: Crop production per unit of water consumption. It is latest concept for evaluation of irrigation method. It is very high for greenhouse based crops.
- BCKV, Kalyani has standardized hydroponic cultivation of tomato, brinjal and PAU, Ludhiana standardized aeroponic cultivation of potato.
- DARL, Pithoragarh has standardized techniques of commercial cultivation of tomato, cucumber, capsicum using hydroponics in polyhouse.
- Tomato (cv. Marglobe) and cucumber (cv. Long Green) yield 1466 and 980 q/ha, respectively compared with 470 and 105 q/ha in open field at Almora.

***Criteria for cultivation of vegetable crops in hydroponics*:**

- Continuous supply of oxygen in fertigation media is highly essential.
- Use of thermocol/ floating sheet with net cup holes at specified distances.
- Roots of crop should be always dipped in solution media.
- Solution media should have-

a) pH between 5.5-6.0.

b) Total total salts range between 550-800 mg/litre.

c) Salinity range between 0.8-1.2 dS/m.

- Avoid direct contact of sunlight with solution media.

Crop	pH	Salinity (dS/m)	Total soluble salts (mg/lit)	Light intensity (Lux)
Palak/ Indian spinach	5.5-6.5	1.8-2.3	1260-1610	1000-1200
Lettuce	5.5-6.0	1.1-1.2	550-800	900-1000
Celery	6.5	1.8-2.4	1260-1680	1200-1400

8.1 Media:

- Rockwool was discovered in 1969 by Bovre and Knoblauch.
- Perlite and sphagnum moss holds 3-4 times its weight in water.
- Sphagnum moss is dehydrated remains of acid bog plants of genus *Sphagnum*.
- Coco peat/ Coco dust: Good drainage and porosity (25-30%).
- Ratio of coco peat, vermiculite and perlite for rooting medium: 3:1:1.
- In Europe and Africa, coco peat is very popular media.
- Perlite: Neutral (volcanic origin) & fastest uptake rate of nutrients. Useful material for routine and shipping cuttings when there are specific plant quarantine regulations.
- Peat: Widely used & acidic in nature. It has good air and water holding capacity.
- Vermiculite: Micaceous mineral; chemically hydrated magnesium-aluminium-iron silicate. Rich in Ca and Mg. Very light in weight.
- Rockwool: Aeration to roots.
- Pumice: Made up of aluminium silicate and small quantities of potassium and sodium.
- Leaf mold: Maple, Oak, Sycamore and Elm are suitable for leaf mold.
- Saw dust and wood shavings: Processed wood material.
- pH of sphagnum moss: 3.5-4.0.
- pH of vermiculite: 6.0-6.5.
- pH of perlite: 6.0-7.5.

9. AGRI-EXPORT ZONES (AEZs) OF HORTICULTURAL CROPS:

- Concept of AEZ has been introduced by Govt. of India in 2001 under 16th chapter of EXIM policy.
- Total number of AEZs in India: 60.
- Nodal agency to coordinate the efforts on AEZs: APEDA.

Product (s)	State (s)
Pineappie	Tripura & West Bengal
Gherkins, Rose onion, Flowers, Vanilla	Karnataka (Shimoga, Uttara Kannada, Dakshina Kannada, Udupi & Chikmagalur districts)
Litchi	Uttaranchal& West Bengal
Cut flowers, Mangoes, Cashew nut	Tamil Nadu

Flowers	Uttarakhand, Maharashtra, Karnataka, Sikkim
Mango (Alphonso & Kesar), Grape & grape wine, Pomegranate, Banana, Oranges, Onion, Floriculture park	Maharashtra & Gujarat
Mangoes, Mango pulp, Grapes, Chilli, fresh vegetables & Gherkins	Andhra Pradesh
Apples, Walnut	Jammu and Kashmir & Himachal Pradesh
Potatoes, Onion,Garlic, Sweet orange	Madhya Pradesh
Cabbage, Broccoli, Okra, Peas, Carrot, Baby corn, Green chilli, Green beans, Tomato, Potatoes	Punjab
Potatoes, Mangoes, Vegetables	Uttar Pradesh
Litchi & vegetables	Bihar
Mangoes, Vegetables,Dehydrated Onion & Garlic	Gujarat
Potatoes, Mangoes, Vegetables, Darjeeling tea	West Bengal
Orchids, Ginger & Cherry Pepper	Sikkim
Ginger, Turmeric	Odisha
Vegetables	Jharkhand
Horticultural products, Medicinal plants	Kerala
Fresh & processed ginger	Assam
Medicinal & aromatic plants	Uttarakhand, Kerala
Coriander, Cumin	Rajasthan

10. INTELLECTUAL PROPERTY RIGHTS:

- A right conferred for plant variety protection system is PBR (Plant Breeders Right).
- Indian IPR protection of varieties: *Sui generis* means 'a system of its own'.
- New plant varieties registered under PPV & FR Act.
- Protection of Plant Varieties of Farmer's Right Act (PPVFRA), came into force in 2001 with its headquarter at New Delhi.
- Present chairman of PPVFRA: Dr. K.V. Prabhu. (1st chairman- Dr. R.R. Hanchinal).
- It is a kind of hybrid rights.
- Protection of new varieties: Novelty, Distinctness, Uniqueness, Stability (N-DUS).
- Royal Horticulture Society (RHS) colour chart is used in DUS testing.
- UPOV (The International Union for the Protection of New Varieties of Plant): It is an International Convention for the Protection of New Varieties of Plants. It was signed in Paris in 1961 and enforced in 1968.
- Head quarter of UPOV, Geneva, Switzerland, 1968.
- The current Secretary-General of UPOV is Francis Gurry.
- UPOV, 2001: Granting to provide and promote an effective system of plant variety protection.
- Bio-prospecting: In search for commercially valuable biochemical and genetic resources in plants, animals and microorganisms.
- Bio-piracy: Is the theft or unsurpation of genetic materials especially plants and other biological materials by the patent process.
- Trade Related aspects of Intellectual Property Rights i.e. TRIPS (it covers IPR related aspects).

- Patent Cooperation Treaty (PCT).
- Traditional Knowledge and Digital Library (TKDL).
- Copy Right Office, New Delhi
- Patent office in India: Kolkata.
- Indian Patent Act, 2005.
- Patent provides protection for 20 years.
- Under UPOV, protection for all trees and vines is granted for 25 years.
- Under PPVFRA, protection for all trees and vines is granted for 18 years; other crops 15 years; extant notified varieties 15 year from the date of notification of variety.
- Geographical indication (GI) is a sign or mark attributed to goods of any category.
- In Europe, there are 1300 GI quality tags have been allocated to different commodities through WIPO, Lisbon norms.
- 1st quarantine law was passed in France.
- The GI tags are given as per the Geographical Indications of Goods (Registration and Protection) Act,1999 and came into force in 15th September, 2003.
- GI tags are issued by the Geographical Indication Registry under the Department of Industry Promotion and Internal Trade, Ministry of Commerce and Industry.
- Headquarter of GI office, Chennai, Tamil Nadu.
- In India, total 290 GI tags allowed in all commodities.
- In agriculture commodities, out of 129 GI tags, maximum GI tags bagged by Maharashtra (26), followed by Karnataka (15), Kerala (13) and Tamil Nadu (6).
- 1st product to get a GI tag in India: Darjeeling Tea in 2004.
- 1st Indian alcoholic drink registered for GI tag from Goa in 2009: Feni.
- Nagpur Santra has received global Good Agricultural Practices (GAP) certificate.
- Malabar pepper originated as chance seedling and has hot and biting taste
- Recently, Govt. of India has curtailed registration fee to Rs. 10 only.
- Alphonso mango grown in Junnar & Ambegaon tahsils of Pune district of Maharashtra known as *'Junneri Hapus'*- brand submitted proposal for GI tag.
- Validity of GI tag: 10 years.
- Farmers submitted highest number of applications for seeking PVP certificates in cereals (75%) (maximum in rice i.e. 5596), pulses (80%), oilseeds (62%), plantation crops (78%), fruits (95%), ornamentals (43%), condiments and spices (93%) and aromatic and medicinal plants (96%).
- In cash crops, potato occupied top rank in proposals submitted by farmers for 39 varieties.
- Shri. N. M. Kaspate, a farmer was given breeder's right for his custard apple variety NMK-1 (syn. Golden) under PPVFRA.
- www.upov.int, www.plantauthority.gov.in

- Essentially Derived Varieties (EDV).
- Genetic Use Restriction Technology (GURT) e.g. Terminator gene.
- Organization for Economic Cooperation and Development (OECD), France.
- Transgenic Biosafety Protocol: Cartagena Protocol, 2003.

DUS testing centers:

Crop	Main centers and sub-centers
Mango	CISH, Lucknow, IIHR, Bengaluru & RFRS, Vengurla
Grape	NRCG, Pune
Tamarind	CHES, Godhra
Jamun	CISH, Lucknow
Papaya	IIHR, Bengaluru & TNAU, Coimbatore
Walnut	CITH, Srinagar
Tomato, Brinjal, Okra, Garden pea	IIVR, Varanasi &IIHR, Bengaluru
Cauliflower, Cabbage	IIVR, Varanasi & IARI Regional station, Katrain
Potato	CPRI, Shimla, CPRS, Modipuram, CPRS, Jalandhar
Onion, Garlic	DOG, Pune & IARI, New Delhi
Chrysanthemum &Rose	IARI, New Delhi, IIHR, Bengaluru& NBRI, Lucknow
Jasmine	IIHR, Bengaluru & TNAU, Coimbatore
Damask rose, Periwinkle	CIMAP, Lucknow
Bougainvillea	IARI, New Delhi & NBRI, Lucknow
Orchids (*Cymbidium*, *Dendrobium*,*Vanda*)	NRCO, Sikkim; SFRI, Itanagar & KAU, Thrissur
Marigold	IARI, New Delhi
Tuberose, Gladiolus	DFR, Pune & IIHR, Bengaluru
China aster	MPKV, Rahuri & IIHR, Bengaluru
Turmeric, Ginger	IISR, Calicut &ICAR-NEH region, Barapani
Black pepper	IISR, Calicut
Small cardamom	IISR, Calicut &ICRI, Mylamdumpara
Coriander	NRCSS, Ajmer &DMAPR, Anand
Coconut	CPCRI, Kasargod
Isabgol	DMAPR, Anand
Field mint, Ashwagandha, Brahmi	CIMAP, Lucknow

Geographical indications/ Quality tag/ Branding	States/ country
Darjeeling-Green Tea and White Tea; Laxman Bhog Mango' Khirsapati (Himsagar) Mango (2008); Fazli mango grown in the district of Malda; Kohitur-Mango	West Bengal
Mysore-Agarbatti, Sandalwood oil & soap, Betel leaf (2005) & Mallige (2007, jasmine); Udupi-Mallige (jasmine); Hadagali & Shankarapura Mallige (jasmine); Nanjanagud-Banana; Coorg- Arabica coffee; Coorg-Green cardamom (syn. Coorg Clipped Cardamom, 2007) & Oranges (2005); Devanahalli-Pummelo; Appemidi-Mango; Kamalapur-Red banana; Byadagi-Chilli, Udupi-Mattu Gulla brinjal; Bengaluru-Bangalore Blue (grapes); Bangaluru-Pink (Rose) onion (2015); Chikmagalur-Arabica coffee; Bababudangiri-Arabica coffee,Monsooned-Malabar Robusta coffee (2007); Monsooned Malabar Arabica Coffee (2007); Sirsi-Supari (arecanut);	Karnataka

Kangra-Tea	Himachal Pradesh
Malabar-Pepper (2007), Alleppey-Green cardamom (2007); Vazhakkulam-Pineapple; Wayanad-Robusta coffee; Chengalikodan-Nendran Banana; Central Travancore-Jaggery; Tirur-Betel leaf	Kerala
Allahabad Surkha-Guava;Malihabadi-Dusseheri mango (2008)	Uttar Pradesh
Uttarakhand-Tejpatta or Tamalpatra (2016)	Uttarakhand
Eathomozhy-Tall coconut (2008); Nilgiri (Orthodox) logo; Virupakshi-Hill banana (2008); Sirumalai- Hill banana (2008); Madurai-Mallige (jasmine); Erode-Turmeric; Kodaikanal-Malai Poondu (i.e. Hill Garlic);	Tamil Nadu
Naga-Chilli; Naga-Tree Tomato;	Nagaland
Arunachal-Orange	Arunachal Pradesh
Sikkim-Large cardamom;	Sikkim
Mizo-Chilli (cv. Bird's Eye, 2004);	Mizoram
Tripura-Queen pineapple	Tripura
Assam-Orthodox Logo;Karbi Anglong-Ginger (2015); Tejpur-Litchi (2015); Kaji Nemu (2022)	Assam
Kachai-Lemon	Manipur
Memong Narang (mandarin orange); Khasi Mandarin;	Meghalaya
Shahi-Litchi; Jardalu-Mango;Magahi Paan (Betel leaf)	Bihar
Feni-Wine; Khola-Chilli; Moira-Banana; Harmal-Chilli	Goa
Guntur-Sannam Chilli; Krishna-Banginpalli (Mango); Araku valley-Arabica coffee; Mahabaleshwar-Strawberry; Alibagh-White onion (2021); Nashik-Grapes;	Andhra Pradesh
Nagpur-Orange; Jalna-Sweet orange; Jalgaon-Brinjal (for *bharta* making) & Basrai-Banana (2016), Marathwada Kesar Mango; Solapur-Pomegranate; Sangli-Turmeric & Raisins; Devgad- *Hapus* (i.e. Alphonso mango);Ratnagiri-Alphonso mango; Lasalgaon-Onion;Purandar-Fig; Beed-Custard apple; Vengurla-Cashew nut; Dahano-Gholvad Chikoo (Sapota); Bhivapuri (Nagpur)-Chilli; Vidharbha-Waygao turmeric; Satara- *Waghya ghevada* (i.e. French bean, 2016); Sindhudurg & Ratnagiri Kokum;	Maharashtra
Gir- Kesar Mango; Kandhamal-Haldi	Gujarat
Ganjam-Kewda flower &Kewda rooh; Kandhamal-Haladi (2020);	Odisha
Kashmir-Saffron (2020); Gucchi-Mushroom (2021)	Jammu & Kashmir
Cherimoya Kumbe-Custard apple; White Maize (2006)	Peru, South America
Wall-the-known-Apple	Italy,
Banano-the-Costa Rica-Banana (2010)	Costa Rica
Chacha wine	Georgia

11. BIO-DIVERSITY OF HORTICULTURAL CROPS:

- Genetic resources: Backbone of crop improvement in horticulture.
- Term 'genetic resources' was coined by O. Frankel.
- Concept of gene pool was given by 'Harlan and de Wet'.
- Most recent theory of 'Centre of Origin' is given by Harlan and de Wet.

- N.I. Vavilov proposed 8 main Centres of Diversity.
- Concept of 'Mega gene centres': Zeven and Zhukovsky.
- In 2006, IPGRI and INIBAP changed their operating names to Bio-diversity International.
- Global research development organization investigates conservation and use of agricultural and forest bio-diversity for improved nutrition, livelihood sustainability and productive and resilient ecosystems.
- Essential for sustainable nutritional security.
- 1st plant genetic resources centre of the world: Leningrad, Russia.
- Year 2010: International Year of Bio-diversity.
- Global diversity in fruit and vegetable crops is estimated to be about 3,400 species.
- India is one of 17 mega bio-diversity hot spot regions of the world.
- India comprises 12% of total global plant wealth.
- India is rich in medicinal plants bio-diversity having 2.4% world's area and 8% global diversity.
- India has rich fauna of beneficial insects.
- India is endowed with large germplasm pool (72,000 germplasm accessions of cultivated, wild and related taxa in arid zone fruit crops, vegetables, spices, condiments, plantation and tuber crops) is scientifically conserved in various institutes.
- The natural enemy bio-diversity has been quantified for each of horticultural and plantation crop pests.
- Several measures have been recommended to conserve and enhance natural bio-diversity.
- About 33% of plants that occur in India are endemic.
- Endemicity of Indian orchids is very high and nearly 29% of recorded taxa are endemic.
- India being the cradle of bio-diversity for banana.
- *Araucaria cookii*: Endangered species declared in 2013.
- Oil palm is endemic to tropical lowlands of West and Central Africa.
- Field gene bank of oil palms is maintained at DOPR, Regional station, Palode, Thiruvananthapuram.
- Shirui lily is endangered species in Manipur.
- Prishnparni (*Uraria picta*): Critically endangered dashmool drug.
- *Exacum bicolor* (Family- Gentianaceae) an endemic garden plant in peninsular India (Kerala) is *ex-situ* conserved through seeds.
- Mauna Kea silversword (*Argyroxiphiun sandwicense*): Highly endangered flowering plant. It only flower once in their lifetime.

- Safed chippi (*Sonneratia alba*): Marshy land tree, locally known as *Kandavalan vruksha* has been declared as State tree of Maharashtra. Maharashtra is 1st state in India which gave highest status to this tree.
- The Flora of British India by Sir J.D. Hooker (1872-1897) is considered to be the National Flora of India.
- Flora of the upper Gangetic plain, and of the adjacent Siwalik and sub-Himalayan tracts was described by Duthie (1905).
- Forest Flora of the Chakrata, Dehra Dun and Saharanpur Forest Divisions were compiled by Kanjilal and Gupta in (1928).
- Japanese botanist Akirra Miyawaki has evolved a new method to create forest on scientific way. Use of local plant species is stressed. Such forests have been created in Sangli district of Maharashtra, India.
- McCann in 1959 described about 100 Beautiful Trees of India.
- A book on flowering trees and shrubs in India was compiled by Cowen.
- Bio-diversity of given region is assessed in terms of species richness.
- Tropics alone account 5 million species of total richness.
- International Treaty on Plant Genetic Resources for Food and Agriculture (ITPGRFA).
- Nagoya protocol (2014): Access to genetic resources and equal sharing of benefits arising from their utilization
- Cartagena protocol (2003): An important international environmental protocol and biosafety as a supplement to the Convention on Biological Diversity which aims to ensure safe handling, transport and use of living modified organisms resulting from modern bio-technology that may have adverse effects on biological diversity.
- Convention on Biological Diversity (CBD): 1st international agreement to study bio-diversity in India.
- CBD provides the facility of prior informed consent or material transfer agreement. It was signed during Earth Summit at Rio de Janeiro, 1992.
- Diversity Act of India, 2002.
- Largest and oldest Center of Diversity: China
- Crop origin center having highest diversity: Hindustan
- Idea of biosphere reserve was initiated by UNESCO in 1973-74.
- Environment Protection Act, Govt. of India was enacted in 1986.
- 1st planned ecotourism in India: Thenmala Ecotourism, Dist. Kollam, Kerala.
- ISO 14000: Monitoring of environmental quality.
- HGR: Horticultural Genetic Resources.
- IIHR, Bengaluru has developed the technologies for conservation of nuclear genetic diversity for many horticultural crops.

- Salient Valley National Park, Kerala.
- No. of biosphere reserve in India: 19.
- 1st biosphere reserve in India: Nilgiri biosphere reserve.
- State having 2 bio-diversity reserves: Assam.
- New biosphere reservc, declared in 2012 is Achanakmar in Amarkantak.
- National Bio-diversity Board, New Delhi (enacted in 2003).
- National Gene Bank was established at New Delhi in 1983.
- NBPGR: Nodal agency for implementation of plant germplasm registration.
- NBPGR ranks 3rd in collection of valuable heritage in the world after the USA and China.
- At NBPGR, nearly 4.52 lakhs seed species including 2.7 lakhs Indian seed species have been conserved in the gene bank.
- Bio-diversity 'Hot Spots' was given by Meyer.
- Total bio-diversity hot spots in the world: 36.
- Total land space covered by hot spots on earth: 2.3%.
- India and adjoining countries to it comprises 4 bio-diversity hot spots.
- Total agro-bio-diversity hot spots in India: 25.
- About 90% tree coverage from these four hot spots has been destroyed and bio-diversity is in danger zone.
- About 25 species of flora and fauna have been destroyed.
- Similar to Flora (plants) and Fauna (animals & creatures), Funga (Fungus spp.) category is accepted by scientists all over the world.
- IUCN and SSP (Species for Survival Commission) have given special status/ classification to fungus spp. as Funga.
- To indicate multipurpose and special roles of fungi, a new category of Funga is accepted by Royal Botanical Garden.
- Till date, fungus spp. were classified under botanical category of Flora.
- In biological sciences, varieties of fungus spp. are widely used in bio-degradation, carbon sequence analysis, anti-biotic medicines and fermented foods (bread, cake) juices/ wine (beer) products.
- Centre for Science and Environment conducts status review of world environment and publishes reports every year.
- Western Ghats, North-East India and Eastern Himalaya: Three hot spots of species diversity of turmeric and ginger due to immense variation in climatic and geographical conditions.
- 'Valley of flowers' in Himachal Pradesh is a part of Nanda Devi Biosphere Reserve. It conserves 300 rare species of wild flowers.

- Rich diversity in fruits and their wild relatives (400 fruit plants) is in North-Eastern region followed by western peninsular and western Himalaya.
- Rich diversity in North-Eastern region is citrus, mango and banana.
- Rich diversity in North-Western and Eastern Himalayan regions is for *Pyrus, Rubus, Ribes* and *Prunus*.
- Bio-diversity of pepper is great in evergreen forest of Western Ghats. Out of 17 species, 11 are endemic.
- Fruit crop having narrow genetic diversity in India: Phalsa.
- Fruit crop having greater bio-diversity in India: Apricot.
- '*Kaas* plateau' (*pathar*), Dist. Satara in Maharashtra: Also known as 'Valley of flowers' declared as World Heritage site by UNESCO in July, 2012 for coloured flower species. It has >850 botanical species including regional and extinct species.
- efloraofindia (eFI) website: A database of Indian plants have been developed by the members of efloraofindia Google Group during 2010.
- CITES (the Convention on International Trade in Endangered Species of Wild Fauna and Flora).
- After China, Indian Himalayas are the world's 2nd largest seabuckthorn resources.
- India has 7% of the world's orchid genetic diversity contributing 1,330 species in 186 genera.
- Indian orchid wealth serve as a foundation of world's orchid industry.
- Orchids and rhododendron sanctuary is situated at Sikkim.
- Ganeshkhind fruit research station, Pune and Landorkhori, Jalgaon of Maharashtra, Bramhagiri hills of Nashik regionreceived status of heritage site by Govt. of Maharashtra.
- Indian National Plant Genetic Resources Management System is National Active Germplasm Site (NAGs), ICAR.
- National Active Germplasm Site (NAGs) for mango is located at CISH, Lucknow.
- NAGs for amaranth, French bean, temperate fruits are instead of is located at NBPGR Regional station, Shimla.
- National Agriculture Science Museum (NASM), New Delhi.
- Threatened species is a broad term that is used for species that fall into categories like vulnerable, endangered, rare and extinct.
- International Union for Conservation of Nature and Natural Resources (IUCN) predicted that 60,000 species of flowering plants could become extinct by 2050.
- The Botanical Survey of India has brought out 'Red book' of threatened plants.
- 'Red Data Book' related to categories of threatened, endangered and extinct species of any region.
- On the global level, the IUCN published Red Data Book.

- About 12% Indian fauna has been enlisted in Red Data Book during 2020-21.
- Its opposite is the Green Book, which lists rare plants growing in protected areas like botanical gardens.
- A mimeographed Green Book for India has already been published. It deals with about a hundred rare plant species growing in protected life sanctuary and garden of Botanical Survey of India.
- The UNEP has complied endangered species of the world under the name Blue Book.
- Passport data: Permanent record giving brief description and other details of the varieties.

Methods of conservation of genetic resources (germplasm)/ bio-diversity (flora and fauna):

- National Gene Fund: Established by Govt. of India on 26th March 2007 for supporting conservation and sustainable use of genetic resources including *in situ* and *ex situ* conditions.
- Germplasm conservation of rare/ endangered plant seeds and tissues: Meristem, embryo or recalcitrant seeds stored in liquid nitrogen.
- In India, maximum fruit germplasm is maintained through *in situ* conservation.
- Germplasm conservation is attempted in 3 forms: Storage of recalcitrant seeds, vegetative propagules and clonal propagules.
- Most common method of germplasm conservation: Seed collection.
- Words '*in vitro*' and '*in vivo*' have Latin origin.
- *Ex situ* conservation: Conservation of material outside its natural habitat e.g. cryo-bank, seed gene banks, field gene banks, botanical gardens, arboretum, *in vitro* repositories, DNA bank, herbal seed/ garden, long term storage of seeds, perennial fruit crops.
- *In situ* / On farm conservation: Conservation of diversity in its natural habitat by NBPGR and NAGS e.g. Wild species, land races, bio-sphere reserve, gene sanctuaries, sacred groves, National parks and traditional farmers' varieties/ genotypes.
- Word 'cryo-preservation' was derived from Greek words 'cryo' meaning 'cold' and 'preserve' to 'maintain'.
- *In vitro* conservation: High-tech techniques for germplasm conservation-
  - Comprises storage at low temperature i.e. cryopreservation (-154 to -196^{0}C) which arrest all metabolic activity resulting in storage of material indefinitely. Particularly recommended for rare or endangered and recalcitrant seed species. It is most successful for cell cultures e.g. Germplasm of apple, *Prunus* spp., blue berry, gooseberry and currents.

   - Pollen cryopreservation is used for hybridization purpose of plants which do not flower at the same time e.g. mango, papaya, gladiolus, carnation, gerbera, coconut and other fruit crops was attempted at IIHR.
   - DNA storage: DNA libraries store total genomic information of germplasm.
   - New techniques based on vetrification is more effective than conventional methods.
- Citrus Gene Sanctuary (NOKREK Biosphere Reserve), Meghalaya is the 1st gene sanctuary for conservation of endangered *Citrus* species.

Celebration of days:

- 21st March: World Forest Day.
- 22nd March: World Water Day to tackle water crisis.
- 22nd April: World Earth Day.
- 20th May: World Honey bee Day. Theme of the year 2021 is 'Bee Engaged'
- 21st May: International Tea Day.
- 22nd May: World Bio-diversity Day.
- 31st May: World Anti-Tobacco Day.Theme of the year 2021 is 'Say No to Tobacco'.
- 5th June: World Environment Day. Established in 1972 by United Nations on the first day of the Stockholm Conference on the Human Environment.
- 7th June: World Food Safety Day.
- 28th July: World Nature Conservation Day. Theme of the year 2021 is 'Conserve the Nature, Conserve the Future'.
- 20th August: World Honey Day.
- 2nd September: World Coconut Day.
- 16th September: World Ozone Day. Theme of the year 2021 is 'Ozone, a roof to life'. The celebration of ozone day was started in 1995.
- 18th September: World Bamboo Day since 2009.
- 22nd September: World Rose Day.
- 29th September: International Coffee Day.
- 1st October: World Coffee Day.
- 13th October: World Fertilizer Day.
- 16th October: World Food Day. This day is celebrated in the memory of establishment of FAO by UN. Food is the medicine. Good food is the foundation of genuine happiness as stated by Auguste Escoffier.
- 3rd December: National Agri-Education Day on the birth anniversary of Dr. Rajendra Prasad.
- 23rd December: Farmer's Day (Kisan Diwas).

12. INFORMATICS IN HORTICULTURE:

- Silent revolution: Geo-informatics in agriculture.
- IT plan for Agriculture Sector (AGRISNET) was submitted to Ministry of Agriculture in 1997 to establish "Indian Agriculture on-line" and revised in 2000.
- AGMARKNET: Agricultural Marketing Information Network. It is joint venture of DMI and Ministry of Agriculture.
- NADAMS: National Agricultural Drought Advisory and Management System.
- AGRIS: Agricultural Resources Information System.
- ARISNET: Agricultural Research and Information System include word Network
- ACINET: Agricultural Credit Informatics Network.
- VERCON: Visual Extension, Research and Communication Network, developed by FAO in 2001.
- ICT: Information and Communication Technology.
- ARIS: Agricultural Research Information System, established by ICAR in 1995.
- Var TRAC: Computer software/ bioinformatics tool for speedy identification of variety on morphological and DNA fingerprint data.

13. BIO-TECHNOLOGY OF HORTICULTURAL CROPS:

- Bio-technology is powerful tool to compliment traditional breeding.
- Term 'bio-technology' was coined by Karl Ereky.
- Greek word '*Bios*' means life and Latin word '*fortificare*' means make strong.
- The process by which nutritional quality of food crops (essential micronutrients) is improved through agronomic practices, conventional plant breeding and modern bio-technology.
- Bio-fortified varieties are rich in iron, zinc, proteins, glucosinolates, kunitz, trypsin inhibitors.
- Bio-fortified crops are released in 27 countries.
- E.g. of bio-fortified crops: Iron rich banana, beta-carotene rich banana (super banana), zinc rich pomegranate, ascorbic acid rich guava, carotene and iodine rich tomato (Golden tomato), iron and zinc rich potato, anthocyanin rich brinjal, carotene rich cauliflower, anthocyanin rich red cabbage, iron and calcium rich okra, selenium rich onion, iodine rich lettuce, anthocyanin rich sweet potato, carotene rich cassava, iron and zinc rich cowpea, iron and zinc rich common bean, lysine and tryptophan rich maize.
- Sunbean: Fusion of sunflower and French beans via fusion of plant cells.
- Chemotaxonomy: Pollen morphology is widely used to identify cultivars from diverse locations.
- Traps have been designed for invasive pests like Pin worm (*Tuta absoluta*) in tomato.

- Diagnostic kits like dip sticks (lateral flow immune strips) for BBrMV & CMV in banana.
- Lateral flow technology for potato viruses.
- NASH detection for banana bunchy top virus/ banana streak virus.
- Real time LAMP assays for viruses in spices have been developed.

***Micropropagation*:**

- Concept of tissue culture dates back to 1878 when a German botanist Hermann Vochting said that from a small piece, a whole plant can be regenerated.
- Totipotency in plants: Vasil and Hildebrancdt (1964)
- Father of tissue culture: Gottlieb Haberlandt
- G. Haberlandt (1902): Cultivation of artificial embryos on nutritional media.
- Commercial tissue culture began in USA in 1970 with the sale of orchids.
- In India, commercial tissue culture started in 1987 with establisement of commercial unit for large-scale production of cardamom by M/s. A.V. Thomas & Co. in Kerala. The protocol ofr cardamom was developed by Dr. R.S. Nadgauda and Dr. A. F. Mascarenhas at NCL, Pune. This was followed by another tissue culture facility at Indo-American Hybrid Seed Company at Bengaluru in 1988.
- During Vth Five Year Plan (2005), Govt. of India listed micropropagation of plants as an industrial activity and declared it as 'Hi-Tech Industry'.
- Kott (1922): Made successful attempt in culturing cut root tips of pea and maize in Liebig's meat extract.
- Micropropagation promotes monoculture.
- *In vitro* multiplication of plants from small tissue.
- Micropropagation is 1st standardized for strawberry.
- Meristem culture: Morel and Martin (1952) to produce virus free plants.
- *In vitro* pollination and fertilization is used to overcome pre-fertilization barriers.
- Embryo/ Ovary/ Ovule culture: To study physiology of fruit development, overcome post-fertilization barriers, shortening breeding cycle and break seed dormancy e.g. Seedless grape, Peach, Sweet cherry.
- Tukey (1933) who 1stcultured Sweet Cherry embryo on artificial medium.
- At present, about 45% area in banana is under tissue culture plants followed by sugarcane (31%), ornamentals (14%), spices (6%) and medicinal plants at 4%.
- Variegated cv. of *Ficus benjamina* 'Golden Princess' is obtained by gamma irradiation of tissue cultured plants.
- Cultivars of *F. benjamina* like 'Reginald' is originated as spontaneous mutant during micropropagation.

- Protoplast fusion has been employed in crops like potato, tomato, carrot, citrus, brassica, atropa, datura, etc.
- Stephen *et al*. (1990) utilized protoplast fusion to transfer polima type CMS from *B. napus* cv. Polima Karat to broccoli Green Comet.
- Cryopreservation methods have been reported in chrysanthemum, carnation, rose, camellia, etc.
- Natural surfactant: *Reetha* (*Sapindus mukorossi*).
- Agar agar is a Malaysian word. It is produced from red algae/ sea weed *Gelidium* and *Gracilaria*.
- Disinfectant used in checking of viral diseases through implements: Trisodium phosphate.
- Word 'Clone' is derived from Greek.
- Double haploids (DH): Production of 100 % homozygous plants.
- Haploid induction 1st developed by Guha and Maheswari (1966) in *Datura innoxia*.
- Haploid plants develop from male gametophyte (anther culture) i.e. Androgenesis
- Androgenesis has been used for Brinjal, Pepper, Cabbage, Cauliflower, Potato, Asparagus, Carrot.
- Gynogenesis: Haploids develop from female gametophyte e.g. Sugar beet, Onion, Gerbera.
- Somaclones: Plants derived from any type of somatic cell culture.
- Diverse cytoplasm can be fixed together by protoplast culture.
- Cybrids or cytoplasmic hybrid: A somatic hybrid containing nuclear genome of one of the two parents and cytoplasmic genomes of both parents is known as cybrid.
- Application of cybrid: Direct transfer of CMS from donor to recipient lines e.g. Citrus, petunia.
- Protocols for micropropagation of banana, papaya, strawberry, orchids and anthurium have been commercially adopted.
- Coated or pelleted seeds are now becoming common in small seeded vegetables.
- Cell suspension culture is used for secondary metabolites production.
- Hormone used to promote somatic embryogenesis: ABA.
- Most effective surface sterilizing agents: Alcohol 70% & $HgCl_2$.
- Polysaccharides from jackfruit and tamarind seeds have been used as encapsulating agent.
- BARC, Trombay has mandate on floriculture in micropropagation.
- National Facility for Virus Diagnosis and Quality Control of Tissue Culture plants: NBPGR, New Delhi with five satellite centres.
- National Centre for Quality Control of Tissue Culture Raised Plant Material: CPRI, Shimla.

- National Certification System for Tissue Culture Raised Plants (NCS-TCP) works under Dept. of Bio-technology, Ministry of Science and Technology as the certification agency.
- Micropropagation of plants is identified as industrial activity by GOI under 1 (D&R) Act of 1951 and effective since 1991.
- Most preferred carbon source in tissue culture: Sucrose.
- Department of Bio-technology (DBT) has set up tissue culture pilot plants for mass propagation of forest tree species in 1989. In 1997, this was upgraded to micro-propagation technology park.
- Poly Hydroxy Butyrate (PHB): Used as substrate for production of bio-degradable plastic.
- Blue bio-technology: Application of bio-technology to marine or aquatic biology.
- Industrial bio-technology: Application of bio-technology to agriculture process.
- Vitrification: Development of succulent and translucent shoots. It is a physiological disorder during *in vitro* multiplication. It can be minimized by using high agar content, low incubation temperature of culture vessels with better aeration, short culture duration and low levels of cytokinins.

13.1 Tissue culture media and their applications:

- pH of nutrient medium: 5.6-5.8.
- Incubation temperature of culture room: 25 ± 2^0C.
- Autoclaving is done at 121^0C at 25 psi for 15-20 min.

Name of medium	Uses
White	Root culture
Nitsch	Culture of excised floral parts
Murashige and Skoog	Callus culture
B_5 (Gamborg's medium)	Cell & protoplast culture
Anderson	Shoot proliferation in rhododendron
Schenk and Hildebrandt	Monocot culture
Woody Plant medium	Woody plant culture
Knob's solution	Embryo culture
Modified Vacin and Went medium, Knudson C, Burgeff N_3f	Orchid culture

Micropropagation followed in fruit crops:

Methods followed	Crops
Shoot tip & Meristem culture	Banana, Cashew nut, Citrus, Grape, Mangosteen, Papaya, Pineapple, Strawberry
Embryo culture/ embryo rescue	Banana, Custard apple, Grape, Guava, Persimmon, Sapota,
Anther culture	Papaya, Litchi, Grape,
Somatic embryogenesis	Avocado, Banana, Ber, Date palm, Grape, Guava, Mango, Papaya, Pomegranate, Sapota
Protoplast fusion/ culture	Avocado, Banana, Papaya, Guava,
Somaclonal variation	Banana

Micropropagation followed in vegetable crops:

Methods followed	Crops
Shoot tip culture	Parsley, Taro
Anther culture	Potato, Brinjal, Chilli, Capsicum
Embryo and ovule culture	Watermelon, Okra, Brinjal, Cucurbits, Chilli
Gynogenesis	Onion
Androgenesis	Asparagus, Brinjal, Carrot, Cabbage, Cauliflower, Pepper, Potato
Somaclonal variation	Potato, Tomato, Lettuce, Garlic, Celery, Carrot
Somatic hybridization	Brinjal, Carrot, *Brassica* genus
Protoplast culture	Carrot

Micropropagation followed in ornamental crops:

Methods followed	Crops
Meristem culture	Carnation, Gladiolus, Lilium, Orchids,
Embryo rescue/ Ovary culture	Amaryllis, Balsam, Calla lily, Carnation, Cosmos, Hibiscus, LA, LO hybrids of lilium, Orchids, Pelargonium, Rose, Statice, Tulip
Ovule culture	Alstroemeria, Chrysanthemum, Lilium, Pelargonium, Tulip,
Anther/ Double haploid culture	African violet, Anthurium, Calla lily, Carnation, Chrysanthemum, Easter lily, Geranium, Gerbera, Orchids, Pelargonium, Petunia, Phlox, Rose, Tuberose, Tulip
Somatic embryogenesis	Alstroemeria, Anthurium, Carnation, Chrysanthemum, Cyclamen, Day lily, Geranium, Gladiolus, Gerbera, Lilium, Marigold, Orchids, Pansy, Periwinkle, Poinsettia, Rose, Tulip
Somatic hybridization	Geranium, Hibiscus, Lilium, Petunia,
Protoplast culture	Anthurium, Carnation, Chrysanthemum, Day lily, Gypsophila, Lilium, Lotus, Orchids, Pelargonium, Petunia, Snapdragon, Stock, Rose
Callus culture	Dieffenbachia, Rose, Gladiolus, Gerbera, *Ficus benjamina*, *Begonia rex*, *Pepromia obtusifolia*, *Philodendron,* Spathiphyllum, Syngonium

Micropropagation followed in spice crops:

Methods followed	Crops
Shoot tip culture	Black pepper, Large cardamom, Small cardamom, Cinnamon, Chinese cassia, Ginger, Turmeric, Vanilla, Saffron, Kalazira, Fennel, Anise, Celery
Ovule culture	Vanilla
Anther/ Double haploid culture	Ginger
Somatic embryogenesis	Saffron
Protoplast culture	Black pepper, Cardamom, Ginger, Vanilla
In vitro hybridization	Ginger, Turmeric, Vanilla

Micropropagation followed in medicinal plants:

Methods followed	Crops
Meristem culture	Aloe, Dioscorea, Geranium, Neem, Patchouli, Stevia
Callus mediated organo genesis	Medicinal yam, Ipecac, Asparagus, Henbane, Mint,
Somatic embryo genesis	Ashwagandha, Periwinkle, Gloriosa, Senna, Nightshade

***Micropropagation followed in plantation and forest crops*:**

Methods followed	Crops
Shoot tip culture	Tea, Bamboo, Teak, White teak, Eucalyptus, *Populus*,
Somatic embryo genesis	Coconut
Embryo & ovule culture	Coconut
Anther culture	Coconut

13.2 Somaclonal variation and variants released as varieties for commercial cultivation:

- Variation arised in the somatic tissue generated by the use of tissue culture (Larkin and Scowcroft, 1981).
- Causes of variation:
  a) Chromosomal changes
  b) Enhanced amplification of certain genes
  c) Mitotic crossing over
  d) Cytoplasmic-genetic changes and
  e) Methylation of genes.
- The technique has been exploited-
  a) In peach cvs. Sunhigh and Red haven for bacterial (leaf spot & canker) diseases.
  b) Apple cv. Green Sleeves for bacterial (fire blight) disease.
  c) Strawberry cv. Morioka for fungal (black spot) disease.
  d) In apple rootstock, M-26 & MM-106 for fungal (phytophthora) disease.
  e) In Giant Cavendish banana for fusarium wilt race-4 disease.
  f) Williams banana for yellow & black sigatoka disease.

Crop	Somaclonal variant	Parent variety	Features
Brassica juncea	Pusa Jaikisan	Varuna	17.4% higher yield over parent
Java citronella	Bio-13	-	More oil & citronellol
Geranium	Velvet	Rober's Lemon Rose	Polyploid somaclone
Khesari (*Lathyrus sativus*)	Ratan	-	Low in nutro-toxins
Sweet potato	Scarlet	-	Darker & more stable colour & disease resistant. Derived from shoot tip culture of a clone

13.3 Somatic hybridization/ Protoplast fusion/ Para-sexual hybridization:

- It is a technique of protoplast fusion from two diverse parents to combine nuclear and cytoplasmic genomes of the organisms (Liu *et al.*, 2005).
- Fusion of two somatic cells of different species, genera and family to overcome sexual incompatibility.

- In citrus, somatic hybrids have been developed and studied well.
- A somatic hybrid is written as: A+B.
- Applications:

a) Crop genetic improvement by overcoming sexual incompatibility or reproductive barriers.

b) By creating novel combinations of nuclear and cytoplasmic genomes.

c) For somatic hybridization, citrus has served as model crop for

1. Direct use as scion or rootstock
2. Cybrid production to induce seedlessness in commercial cvs.
3. Somatic hybrids are used as pollen parents to induce seedlessness through triploidy
4. Partially combining the genomes from donar parents into receipient through irradiation/ asymmetric fusion.

13.4 Embryo rescue:

- Aseptically culturing the developing embryo after excising from the ovule and/ or culturing ovule/ ovary to save embryo.
- 1st use of embryo culture by E. Hanning (1904) in crucifers.
- In fruit crops, Tukey (1933) 1st cultured cherry embryo on artificial medium.
- Applications:

a) Grape- Cross between Muscat Hamburg (*V. vinifera*) x *V. amurensis*- release of Beichun variety with high resistance to PM & anthracnose.

b) Grape- Cross between Thompson Seedless x Concord- release of blue black seedless grape variety Thomcord in 2003.

c) Grape- Cross between complex seedless hybrid (C-33-30 x C-103-41): release of cv. Sweet Scarlet in USA in 2004.

d) Peach- Release of cv. May Fire nectarine and Gold Creast (Ramming and Tanner, 1987).

13.5 Molecular markers:

- Previous century belonged to 'Green' revolution and present century belongs to 'Gene' revolution.
- Concept of association of marker with quantitative traits was 1st proposed by Sax in 1923.
- DNA combing: Stretching a piece of DNA.
- 1st concept of genetic map was presented by Alfred H. Sturtevant, 1913.
- 1st genetic map of chromosome was published in 1911 by T.H.Morgan working on *Drosophila melanogaster*.
- Widely used for cultivar identification, genetic diversity studies & cluster analysis.

- 1st molecular marker: RFLP, 1980
- To minimize linkage drag, need to identification of flanking marker: <5 cM.
- Primers are named using KeyGene nomenclature.
- Term 'Marker Assisted Selection' (MAS) was 1st used by Beckmann and Soller (1986).
- Southern hybridization: DNA-DNA hybridization. Developed by S.M. Southern (1925)
- Northern hybridization: DNA-RNA hybridization.
- Western hybridization: Protein hybridization.
- Common method of RNA extraction: Trizol method.
- Common method of DNA extraction: CTAB (cytyl trimethyl ammonium bromide) method.
- PCR: Polymerase Chain Reaction. It was developed by Dr. Karry Mullis in 1985.
- In PCR, multiplication of DNA takes place by geometric progression.
- Serological and PCR based diagnostics were developed for banana, citrus, grapes, black pepper.
- Sequence of PCR: Denaturation-Anneealing-Extension.
- PCR proceeds in 3 distinct steps governed by temperature as denaturing, annealing and synthesis.
- Thermostable enzyme in PCR: *Taq* (*Thermus aquaticus*) DNA polymerase. It is soil bacterium extracted from hot springs of sulphur.
- Morphological markers: Seed colour, leaf shape, leaf surface, seed size, cotyledon colour, etc.
- DNA marker: PCR based markers e.g. RAPD, AFLP, SSR
- SDS-PAGE: Poly Acrylamide Gel Electrophoresis. It separates proteins based on their charge and molecular weight ratio.
- Dominant markers: RAPD, AFLP, ISSR,
- Co-dominant markers: RFLP, SSR, SCAR, SRAP, STS, SNP.
- 1st generation marker: RFLP
- 2nd generation markers: RAPD, AFLP, STS, SSR
- 3rd generation marker: SNP
- 4th generation markers: CAPS, DART, GBS.
- DAF (DNA Amplification Fingerprinting): Single short oligonucleotide used and produce a range of up to 100 short amplified fragments of varying lengths.
- AP-PCR (Arbitrarily Primed PCR): Almost similar to RAPD, but longer primers used.
- SCAR (Sequence Characterized Amplified Regions): The desired fragment is eluted from the gel, cloned, sequenced and primers designed complementary to its end sequences.
- Term 'genomics' was coined by T. Roderick.

- Genome scanning for expressed genes: EST, SRAP, TRAP
- Highly informative marker i.e. very high polymorphism: SSR (microsatellite)
- Marker system used for identification of clones: CAPS and SNP.
- Markers using array technology: Microarray, DART (whole genome scanning).
- Expressed Sequence Tags (ESTs) are used to make DNA marker in gene discovery research.
- Directed Amplification of Minisatellite DNA (DAMD) marker technique can be used for identifying hybrids resulted from a cross between cultivars.
- NIL: Near Isogenic Lines are developed through repeated random backcrossing.
- NIL: Commonly used for mapping QTLs.
- RIL: Recombinant Inbred Lines are homozygous selfed or sib mated progeny of individuals of an F_2 population up to F_7-F_8.
- Haploid plants in tomato using anther culture: Greshop and Doy (1972).
- True breeding lines or permanent/ immortal populations: RIL and DH.
- Shortest method to detect QTLs is BSA (Bulked segregants analysis).
- Marker Assisted backcrossing (MABC) marker used to assess the presence of introgressed gene or QTL.
- MABC term coined by Tankley (1983).
- NGS: Next Generation Sequencing
- BOLD system: Barcode of Life Data Systems Database.
- CBOL: Consortium for Barcode of Life.
- IBOL: International Barcode of Life.
- GWAS: Genome Wide Association Study.
- Gene chip: Microarray chip.
- Background selection: Markers used to accelerate the return to recipient parent genotype at other loci. The strategy was proposed by Hillel (1990).
- Physical map is measured by base pairs (bp).
- National Genomic Resources Repository Conserves- Cloned genes.
- *Agrobacterium rhizogenes* was 1st identified as a pathogen in apples and named as *Phytomonas rhizogenes* (Riker *et al.*, 1930). Renamed as *A. rhizogenes* (Conn, 1942).
- In 2001, reclassified and named as *Rhizobium rhizogenes* because of phylogenetic similarity between *Agrobacterium* and *Rhizobium* based on 16S rDNA analysis (Young *et al.*, 2001).
- Bio-printing: Use of 3D printing technology with materials that incorporate viable living cells e.g. to produce tissue for reconstructive surgery.
- Hairy root culture for secondary metabolite production are induced by transforming plant cells with *Agrobacterium rhizogenes*.
- Mg^{2+} ions are required for type II restriction enzymes.

- Association mapping (linkage disequilibrium) is used in black pepper, cardamom & coconut.
- Cisgenesis: Genetic modification of a recipient plant with introducing a natural gene from a crossable-sexually compatible plant.

Linkage map:

- Gene mapping is localization of a marker on chromosome.
- Genetic map is representation of genes on chromosome arranged in linear order with distances between loci expressed as parent recombination (map unit).
- Distancebetween loci is measured in centi-morgans (cM).
- One linkage map unit is 1% recombination.
- One map unit = one centi morgan = 1% recombination between loci.
- Comparative mapping used for analysis of genes and QTLs.
- Orthologous gene: Genes in different species that originated by vertical descent from a single gene of last common ancestor.
- 1st map in apple was constructed by European consortium derived from cross cvs. Prima x Fiesta.
- Another linkage map with F_2 progeny from cross of Fiesta x Discovery.
- Comparison between apple and *prunus* maps suggests a high degree of synteny (i.e. two or more genes residing on same chromosome) between two genera.

QTL mapping:

- Term quantitative trait loci (QTL) first coined by Gelderman (1975).
- Concept of quantitative genetics: Fisher, Wright, Haldane
- Most common method of QTL mapping is interval mapping.
- Ideal cM distance for QTL cloning is 2 cM or less.
- Fine mapping of high resolution QTL: 25-100 Kb
- First tagged QTL in plants: *fw2.2* (fruit weight in Tomato).
- Gene pyramiding in solanaceous vegetables (brinjal, tomato) is in progress.

Genomics:

- Sum total of all an individual organism's genes.
- Study of DNA (genotype), mRNA (transcriptome), protein (proteome) level.
- Term genomics was coined by Dr. Tom Roderick
- Complete decoding of the genome of free living organism *Haemophilus influenzae* heralded beginning of genomics era in 1995.
- Variation in genome size: 125 Mbp (*A. thaliana*) to 110,000 Mbp (*Fritillaria assyriaca*).
- Variation in genome sizes may be understood through C-value paradox which shows no correlation between genome size and biological and complexity.

- Structural genomics: Describe 3D structure of every protein encoded by given genome.
- Functional genomics: Understanding the function of genes and other parts of genome.
- Proteomics: A complete set of protein present in a single cell.
- Transcriptomics: A complete set of mRNA present in single cell.
- Metabolomics: A complete set of metabolites present in single cell.
- Tranplastomic: Transfer of chloroplast.
- Introgressiomics: Use of wild relatives in breeding for adaptation to climate change.
- Nutrigenomics: Emerging science which enables nutri-innovations 64x cels-innovations by studying diet-gene interactions.
- Comparative genomics: Study of similarities and differences in structure and function of hereditary information across taxa.

Sequencing technologies:

- Genome sequencing has unveiled the mystery about various genes, the phyllogenetic relationships and evolutionary history of the sequenced fruit crops, vegetable crops and medicinal plants.
- Methods of sequencing: SGS-GRR (Second generation sequence- Glycine rich repeats), CBC, WGS (whole genome shotgun).
- 1st bacterial genome sequenced: *Haemophilus influenzae.*
- 1st multicellular organism sequenced: *Caenorhabditis elegans.*
- 1st plant genome sequenced in 2000: *Arabidopsis thaliana* (125 Mb).
- 1st crop plant sequenced: Rice.
- 1st non-grassy plant sequenced: Banana.
- 1st fruit crop sequenced and 5th plant genome completed: Papaya.
- 1st plant genome sequenced using short read sequencing technology: *Cucumis sativus* var. *sativus*.
- 2nd generation sequencing: Illumina system and Pyro-sequencing e.g. Roche GS20, Roche GS FLX-454, SOLiD system, Helicose system and Sanger sequencing.
- 3rd generation sequencing: True single-molecule sequencing (t-SMS).

Completed genome sequence:

- Recently database of Rosaceae (apple, pear, peach, plum, apricot, cherry) has been developed. It comprises 246 markers (235 RFLP & 11 isozymes) from almond (cv. Texas) x peach (cv. Early Gold) cross. The map had 8 linkage groups with distance of 491 cM.
- 1st oil palm microsatellite data base (OpSatDB) was developed.
- Diagnostic markers have been developed to distinguish Pisifera, Dura and Tenera hybrids at seedling stage.

Crop	Genome size	Mapping population	Completed year
Mango	450 Mbp	-	-
Grape	504.6 Mbp	Pinot Noir (putative genes 33,514)	Velasco *et al*. (2007)
Papaya (1st transgenic fruit)	372.3 Mbp	Sun Up (putative genes 28,027)	Ming *et al*. (2008)
Apple	742.3 Mbp	Golden Delicious (putative genes 57,386 + 31,678 transposable related ORFs)	Velasco *et al*. (2010)
Strawberry	250 Mbp	*Fragaria vesca*	2011
Banana	523 Mbp	Double haploid-Pahang (*Musaa cuminata* spp. *malaccensis*) (putative genes 36,542)	2012
Date palm	658 Mbp	Khalas (*Phoenix dactylifera*)	2011
Pear	527 Mbp	*Pyrus* x *bretschneideri*	2013
Peach	265 Mbp	Lovell	2013
	300 Mbp	*Prunus persica*	2009
Sweet orange	367 Mbp	Ridge pineapple	2013
Kiwi fruit	758 Mbp	Hangyang	2013
Pineapple	445 Mbp	-	-
Pomegranate	357Mbp	Bhagwa	-
Guava	496 Mbp	-	-
Blueberry	600 Mbp		
Potato (1st sequenced tuber veg.)	844 Mbp	*S. tuberosum* group Tuberosum RH89-039-16 & *S. tuberosum* group Phureja DM-1-3-516R44	2011
Chinese cabbage	283.8 Mbp	Chiifu-401-42	2011
Brassica oleracea	600 Mbp	-	2005
Brassica rapa var. *pekinensis*	500 Mbp	-	2010
Brassica napus	1200 Mbp	-	2009
Tomato	950 Mbp	Heinz 1706	2012

Current tomato	739 Mbp	*S. pimpinellifolium* LA1589	2012
Cucumber	367 Mbp	Chinese Long '9930' (putative genes 26,682)	Huang *et al.* (2009)
Melon	450 Mbp	Double haploid line- DHL92 (putative genes 27,427)	2012
Watermelon (1st sequenced veg.)	375 Mbp	-	Garcia-Mas *et al.* (2012)
Soybean	1100 Mbp	*Glycine max* (putative genes 46,430)	2008
Cassava	770 Mbp	*Manihot esculentum*	2010
Coconut	450 Mbp	Chowghat Green Dwarf	-
Black pepper	530 Mbp	Thottumuriyan (putative genes 12,725)	2018
Turmeric	1.02 Mbp	17 varieties (putative genes 19,474)	2021
Lotus	929 Mbp	-	2013
Birdsfoot trefoil	472 Mbp	*Lotus japonicus*	2008
Snapdragon	430 Mbp	*Antirrhinum majus*	1995
Rose	600 Mbp	-	-
Gulvel (1st sequenced medicinal plant)	1.01 Mbp	*Tinospora cordifolia* (putative genes 19,474)	Sharma *et al.* (2021)
Periwinkle	1500 Mbp	Wild type of *C. roseus*	2012
Barrel medic	500 Mbp	*Medicago truncatula*	2009
Maize	2865 Mbp	*Zea mays* (putative genes 32,540)	2008
Poplar tree (syn. Black cotton wood)	485 Mbp	*Populus trichocarpa* (putative genes 45,654)	2006

Mbp: Megabase pair

13.6 Transgenics in horticultural crops:

- Study of knowledge obtained from genetics to alter the reproduction and hereditary process of organism.
- It deals in cloning, *in vitro* fertilization, species hybridization or direct manipulation of the genetic material itself by recombinant DNA technology.
- Transgenics/ Genetically modified/ Genetically engineered/ Recombinant DNA/ Chimeric DNA/ Gene transplantation/ Gene splicing.
- Cohen and Boyer (1973): 1st to use plasmid as vector in *E. coli*. They developed recombinant DNA technology.
- Vector: It is self replicating DNA molecule.
- 1st self-replicating, synthetic bacterial cell was constructed by Craig Venter.
- Father of genetic engineering: Paul Berg (1979).
- Father of DNA bar coding: Paul Harbour.
- Dermatoglyphics: Science of fingerprinting.
- Gene pyramiding: Combining 2 or more major genes.
- Gene silencing: Used for virus resistance via protein inhibition.
- Gene editing: A type of genetic engineering in which DNA is inserted, deleted, modified or replaced in the genome OR an ability to make highly specific changes in DNA sequence of living organism.
- CRISPR (Clustered Regularly Interspaced Short Palindromic Repeats): A powerful gene editing technology (genetic scissors) that scientist uses to change DNA of plants, animals, microorganisms and even humans with extremely high precision.
- The Royal Swedish Academy of Sciences awarded the Nobel Prize in Chemistry 2020 to Dr. Emmanuelle Charpentier and Dr. Jennifer Doudna received Nobel prize for the development of a method 'CRISPR/ Cas9' for genome editing.
- Up to 1980, production of transgenic plants was restricted to tobacco, tomato and petunia of the family Solanaceae. Now more than 40 dicot species transgenic plants have been produced.
- Natural genetic engineer: *Agrobacterium tumefaciens*.
- *Agrobacterium* is a bacterium that introduces DNA into plants.
- *Bacillus thuringiensis* (*Bt*) was discovered by S. Ishiwata in Germany.
- In India, *Bt* kit was developed by Central Institute of Cotton Research, Nagpur.
- Genentech: 1st transgenic company established in 1976.
- New technology of genetic engineering was ushered in 1979.
- Second generation GM crops/ Stacked trait GM crops = GM varieties with modified quality traits.
- Year 1982: 1st genetic transformation of a plant cell from petunia.

- Year 1983: 1st genetic transformation of plant cells by Ti plasmid: Petunia plants resistant to anti-biotics.
- Year 1985: 1st proof that modified plants pass their new traits to offsprings in petunia.
- Year 2001: 1st salt resistant transgenic tomato plants were produced.
- Year 2003: Decaffeinated transgenic coffee.
- Year 2008: Transgenic *Bt*- brinjal approved in India for large scale multiplication of seed.
- Year 2020: Indefinite moratorium imposed by MoFE (India) on transgenic *Bt* brinjal.
- 1st transgenic plant: Tobacco (anti-biotic resistance) developed by Belgium Biotech Company in 1983.
- Total area under GM crops in world: 189.8 million hectares in 26 countries.
- About 44 countries (mainly European) import GM crops for food, animal feed, & processing purpose.
- Leading countries in transgenic use: USA> Brazil > Argentina>India> Canada
- Crops having highest area under cultivation in world: Soybean >Maize > Cotton> Canola.
- 1st country to commercialize transgenic crop: China (1993) with introduction of virus resistant tobacco.
- In Spain and Portugal insect resistant GM maize is grown.
- India ranks 5th in terms of cultivation of GM crops/ biotech crops.
- India has the 4th largest area (11.07 mha) planted under GM crops, according to the International Service for the Acquisition of Agri-Biotech Applications (ISAA).
- In India, 1st conventional release of transgenic plant was done in 1995.
- *Bt*-cotton is the only GM crop cultivated in India.
- Country's 1st genetically-modified cotton variety was developed by PAU, Ludhiana: PAU *Bt*-1 and F-1861.
- GM crops those approved for field trial by Government of India: Rice, Cotton, Maize (corn), Mustard, Brinjal and Chickpea.
- GM fruit crops: Apple, Banana, Papaya, Grape rootstock, Grapefruit, Plum, Guava, Cranberry, Sweet orange, Kagzi lime, Trifoliate orange, Kiwi fruit.
- 1st country to grow *Bt* brinjal (or give approval for cultivation): Bangladesh. They got 30% increase in yield and 71-90% savings on insecticides. This was followed by Philippines.
- 1st woody plant to be transformed and express foreign gene: Walnut.
- 1st successful practical example of transgenic fruit crop: Papaya e.g. Sun Up.
- For importing transgenic seed material in India for research purpose permission from Department of Bio-technology, GOI, is mandatory.

- Genetic Engineering Approval Committee (GEAC) works under Ministry of Environment, Forest and Climate Change, under the Environment Protection Act, 1986, GOI.
- GEAC approves testing or field trials and release of transgenic varieties.
- Brinjal is the 1st food crop and 1st vegetable crop which has been approved by GEAC for commercial cultivation in October, 2009.
- Model plants used for genetic studies: *Arabidopsis thaliana*, *Antirrhinum majus*, Petunia, *Mirabilis jalapa* and carrot.
- In India, network project on development of transgenic crops involves Banana, Brinjal, Cassava, Papaya, Potato and Tomato.
- Field experiments using transgenic began in 1995 and 1st trial on transgenic rape seed containing *Barnase/ Barstar* gene for male sterility.
- Area that gaining popularity in use of plants as a source of edible vaccine for diseases like cholera and rabies.
- Ideal hosts for expression of Hepatitis B surface antigen (*HbsAg*) are Banana, Cherry tomato, Potato.
- 1st transgenic potato: 'Amp Flora' (EH92-527-1) developed by German company, BASF Plant Science for paper pulp production and animal feed purpose. It contains 80% amylopectin and 20% amylase.
- 1st microbial enzyme used in food production: Chymosin.
- 1st pesticide producing crop: Potato (1995) using *Bacillus thuringiensis*.
- 1st food to increase its nutrient value: Golden rice (2000).
- 1st animal to be approved for food use: AquAdvantage salmon (2015).
- 1st white button mushroom modified using the CRISPR technique.
- 1st genetically modified (browning free) apple via RNAi mediated gene silencing: Arctic apple (2015).
- 1st fruit crop in which genome editing was attempted in India: Banana. Work on genome editing was started at NABI, Mohali.
- 1st report of transgenic snapdragon was reported by Klemm *et al*. (1991).
- 1st report of transgenic carnation was reported by Woodson and Goldsbrough (1989).
- Ethylene Forming Enzyme (EFE) is presently known as ACC oxidase.
- *Etrl-1*-gene: Ethylene insensitive gene.
- *AP1* gene: Induce precocity in fruits over its expression.
- Genes used for shortening juvenility period in fruit crops: *LEAFY*, *APETALA*, *MdTFL*.
- Genetic engineering of flower structure modification can be brought out by tinkering MADS-box genes.
- Nourishing gene '*Meg1*' regulates transfer of nutrients from plant to seed.

- Stability of transgene expression is tested by exposing tissues to propionic acid or butyric acid.
- Potato is highly amenable to *Agrobacterium* mediated gene transfer.
- In potato, resistance to virus can also be achieved by transferring a gene that produces defective movement protein (MP).
- In potato, transgenic plants expressing a mutant MP of one virus can also confer resistance to several other viruses e.g. MP of PLRV also restricts movement of PVX, PVY and PLRV.
- *Cry1Ab* gene is tolerant to potato tuber moth and cultivars Desiree, Stunta, Sangerna, Cruza-148 and CIP advanced breeding line 'LT-8' are resistant to potato tuber moth.
- Amylase free transgenic potato cultivars have been commercially released in Netherlands in 1996-97.
- Potato cvs. Russet Burbank and Atlantics have been produced, that express *BN* to *S*-gene of Brazil nut (*Bertholletia excelsa*) which produces methionine rich proteins that contains 19% methionine and 8% cystenine.
- Synthetic gene named 'HEAAE' (High Essential Amino Acid Encoding) which produces 80% essential amino acid is transferred to potato clones K-2, K-7. Protein analysis of transformed plant showed that HEAAE protein comprises 0.2 to 0.35% of total plant protein with 1.1% increase in essential amino acid.
- Commonly used natural anti-bacterial genes for bacterial resistance: Attacin, Chick pea isozyme, T4 phage isozymes, P22 phage genes and lactoferin.
- Genes for herbicide tolerance: *bar* (from *Streptomyces hygroscopicus*), *als*, *aroA*.
- Genes for nematode resistance: *Collagenase*, *Bt-exotoxin*, *cpTi* (cowpea trypsin inhibitor).
- The Cartagena protocol on bio-safety (CPB) originated from Convention on biological diversity (CBD) in 2000 and came into force in 2003.
- The *Ti* plasmid of *Agrobacterium tumifaciens* contains an important gene that codes for the *isopentenyl AMP synthase* enzyme that is involved in the rapid cell division.
- Real Time (RT) PCR is very specific, sensitive and reproducible and widely used to detect RNA viruses in ornamental plants.
- NCS-TCP developed by Dept. of Biotechnology.

Methods of gene transfer:

a) Biological mutagens: Transposon and retrotransposon.

b) Phototrophs can be differentiated from auxotrophs very efficiently by using replica plating.

c) Vector gene transfer: *Agrobacterium* mediated, Agroinfection.

d) Direct gene transfer: Microinjection, particle bombardment (use of gold or tungsten particles).

Transfer method	Crops
Agrobacterium tumefaciens mediated	Passion fruit, Papaya, Peach, Kiwi fruit, Pecan nut, Walnut, Strawberry, Citrange, Apple, Sweet potato, Anthurium, Snapdragon, Cyclamen, Chrysanthemum, Carnation, Lisianthus, Gerbera, Gladiolus, Gypsophila, Kalanchoe, *Lilium longiflorum*, *Pelargoniumdomesticum*, *Pelargoniumhortorum*, Petunia, *Rosahybrida*
Agrobacterium rhizogenes mediated	Snapdragon, Petunia, *Rosahybrida*
Microprojectile bombardment	Cranberry, Papaya, Banana, Sweet potato, *Dendrobium* orchid, Lisianthus, *Liliumlongiflorum*, Tulip
Protoplast mediated	Strawberry, Banana, Lemon
Electroporation	Mandarin, Sweet potato
Laser cell perforation	*Brassica napus*, *Impatiens*
Biolistic mediated	*Dendrobium* orchid, Lisianthus, *Tulipa gesneriana*
Polyethylene glycol mediated	Rough lemon

Transgenic activities:

Crop(s)	Useful gene(s)/ QTLs	Function(s)/ Trait
	Biotic stress	
1. Fungi		
Tomato	*Defensin* gene from chilli	Resistance to fungal pathogens
	Samdc (S-adenosyl methionine carboxylase) gene	Biotic resistance
	chi194, a wheat endochitinase gene	Resistance to tomato wilt
	Wasabi defensin (*WD*) gene from *Wasabia japonica*	Fungal resistance
	Chitinase, glucanase & thaumatin	Fungal resistance
	1-1, 1-3 gene from *S. habrochaites*	Early blight resistance
	Ol-1, Ol-2, Ol-3 gene from *S. habrochaites, L. parviflorum*	Powdery mildew resistance
	Ph-1, Ph-2, Ph-3 from *S. pimpinellifolium*	Late blight resistance
	l, l-1, l-2, l-2C, l-3 from *S. pimpinellifolium, S. pennellii*	Fusarium wilt resistance
Brinjal	*Glucanase* gene from alfalfa	Resistance to verticillium wilt & fusarium wilt
Potato	*RB* gene & tobacco *osmotin* gene; Soybean *glucanase* gene; Glucose oxidase gene from *Aspergillus niger*; Osmotin gene; Osmotin homologue from *S. commersonii*	Late blight resistance
	Synthetic analogue of *cercopin B* gene	Bacterial resistance
	Isozyme gene cloned from bacteriophage T4	Soft rot resistance
	Cucumber *class III Chi C* gene	black scurf resistance

	Chitinase C gene from *Streptomyces griseus & bar* gene	Early blight resistance
Vegetable Brassicas	*Permantis* gene	Damping off resistance
	*Chitinase*gene	Downy mildew (DM), soft rot & black rot resistance
	*Glucanase*gene	Wire stem resistance
	*Thionin*gene	Leaf spot resistance
	*RIP*gene	Cabbage yellow resistance
	*Osmotin*gene	White rust resistance
	Trypsin inhibitor, CaMv capsid. Antisense CaMv gene VI & *BcP-1*gene	Other useful genes
Carrot	Tobacco *class I Chi C gene*	Gray mold resistance
	AtNPR1 gene from *Arabidopsis thaliana*	Bacterial & fungal pathogen resistance
Pepper	Pepper *esterase* gene (*PepEST*)	Anthracnose resistance
Banana cv. Rasthali	*Ace-AMP-1* gene	Fusarium wilt resistance
Banana	*HrAp* gene from capsicum	Fusarium wilt resistance
Pomegranate	Plant ferredoxin protein gene	Bacterial blight resistance
	Xa-21 from rice	Nodal blight resistance
Peach	*Vr-2*	Powdery mildew (PM) resistance
Sweet orange	*nptII, PR-5*	Fungal resistance
	AtNPR-1 gene from Arabidopsis thaliana	Huanglongbing disease resistance
Grape	Endogenous grapevine antifungal gene; Rice *chitinase* gene (*RCC-2*); *VvNPR-1,1* gene from *V. vinifera*; *stilbene synthase* gene, *VqSTS-6* from wild grape *V. quinquangularis*; *RNAi* mediated silencing of *MLO-7* gene	PM resistance
	Agrobacterium oncogene-silencing gene	Resistance to crown gall
	rpfF gene from *Xylella fastidiosa*	Resistance to Pierce's disease
Apple	*Malus pumila NPR-1* (*MpNPR-1*) gene	Fungal & bacterial resistance
	HcrVf2 gene from wild apple	Scab resistance
	Mh-NPR1 gene from *Malus hupehensis*	Resistance to PM
	DIPM-1, DIPM-2, DIPM-4 gene	Fire blight resistance
	Attacin E gene in cv. Royal Gala, M_7 rootstock	Bacterial soft rot resistance
Litchi	Bacterial *chitinase* (*ChiB*) gene	Resistance to Phomopsis light
	Chitinase gene (rice derived)	Fungal resistance
Mango	*Defensin JI* gene from bell pepper	Resistance against anthracnose
Strawberry	Rice *chitinase* gene	PM resistance
	Osmotin	Resistance against gray mold & wilt
	Thaumatin II gene from *Thaumatococcus danielli*	Resistance to gray mold
	Chitinase & glucanse gene	Resistance to gray mold
	B-1-3- glucanase	Resistance to anthracnose crown rot
	B-1-3- glucanase from *Trichoderma harzianum*	Resistance to crown gall
Kiwi fruit	Soybean *β-1-3-glucanase* gene	Resistance to gray mold
Guava	*Trichoderma endochitinase* gene	Resistance to wilt

Pomegranate	*NPT II*, *GFP* gene	Fungal resistance
Soybean	*Rpp-1*, *Rpp-2*, *Rpp-3*, *Rpp-4*	Rust resistance
Coffee	*SH*[3] gene from *C. liberica*	Rust resistance
Maize	Caffeoyl-CoA O- methyl- transferase	Leaf blight, leaf spot & gray mold
Black pepper	*CaRGA-2* gene	Resistance to Phytophthora
Chrysanthemum	*OgPAE-1* gene	White rust resistance
	Rice chitinase gene (*RCC-2*)	Gray mold resistance
Pelargonium	Anti-microbial protein *Ace-AMP1* from onion	Gray mold resistance
Carnation	Osmotin glucanse & chitinase gene	Fusarium wilt resistance
Gerbera	*Pmr* gene	Powdery mildew resistance
Rose	Chitinase transgene	Black spot resistance
	Rdr-1 gene	Black spot resistance
	Anti-microbial protein (*Ace-AMP1*) gene	Powdery mildew resistance
	β-1-3 glucanase (from rice), & anti-bacterial T4-lysozyme (from barley)	Powdery mildew & black spot resistance
	Celery gene mannitol dehydrogenase	Gray mold resistance
Petunia	cDNA clone '*ech-42*'	Botrytis blight resistance
2. Virus		
Banana	BBTV, BBrMV coat protein (*cp*) gene	Virus resistance
	ihp-RNA-Rep and *ihp-RNA-ProRep*	Resistance to BBTV
Strawberry	Coat protein (*cp*) gene from strawberry mild yellow edge pote X virus	Resistance to strawberry mild yellow edge potex virus
Citrus	CTV coat protein (*cp*) gene	Virus resistance
Papaya	PRSV coat protein (*cp*) gene	Virus resistance
Plum, Apricot	PPV coat protein	Plum pox virus (PPV) resistance
Kagzi lime	*npt II*, *sgfp*, *p-23*	Virus resistance
Grapefruit	Coat protein (*cp*) gene, *GUS*, *npt II*	*Citrus tristeza* virus resistance
	Agglutin Coat protein (*cp*) gene, GUS	*Aphid resistance*
Grape	Coat protein (*cp*) gene, heat shock 90 homologous gene, *npt II*	Grapevine Fan Leaf Neo virus & Grapevine Chrome Mosaic Virus resistance
Watermelon	WMV cp gene	Virus resistance
	Chimeric gene construct containing truncated *ZYMV-cp* & *PRSV Wcp* genes	Resistance to ZYMV & PRSV W
Potato	Coat protein (*cp*) gene of Indian isolate of PVY	Potato virus Y (PVY) resistance
	ds RNA of coat protein gene of PVY	Resistance to PVY
	Anti-sense RNA technology	PVX, PVS & PLRV resistance
	Coat protein (*cp*) gene	PVX, PVY and PVX + PVY & PLRV resistance
Tomato	T- Replicase genes (*Ty-1*, *Ty-2*, *Ty-3*, *Ty-4*, *ty-5*, *Ty-6*) from *Solanum habrochaites*, *S. chilense*	Tomato leaf curl virus (TOLCV) resistance
	Tm-1, *Tm-2*, *Tm-2a* from *S. habrochaites*, *S. peruvianum*	Tobacco mosaic virus resistance
	N gene	TOSPO virus resistance

	Coat protein (*cp*) gene	Tomato yellow leaf curl virus resistance
	Sw-5 from *S. peruvianum*	Tomato spotted wilt virus resistance
	Cmr from *S. chilense*	Cucumber mosaic virus resistance
French bean	MYMV gene	Rust & virus resistance
Cowpea	*PR*-1 (pathogenesis related proteins-1)	Disease resistance
	Beta-1-3-glucanase	Colletotrichum resistance
Sweet potato	Coat protein (*cp*) gene & phospho transferase (*hpt*) gene	Sweet potato feathery mottle virus (SPFMV) resistance
Cucumber	Satellite RNA, *cp* gene	CMV resistance
Peas	Coat protein (*cp*) gene from AMV	Alfalfa Mosaic virus resistance
	Replicase (*Nib*) from Pea Seed Born mosaic virus	Pea Seed Born mosaic virus resistance
Poinsettia	*RNAi*	Resistance to poinsettia mosaic virus
Lilium	Defective *cucumber mosaic virus replicase gene*	Resistance to CMV
Chrysanthemum	Nucleocapsid gene	TOSPO virus resistance
	RNA specific ribonuclease *pac-1* from *Schizosaccharomyces pombe* as vector	Virus & viroid resistance
	Pac-1; *ORF-5* encoding the CVB coat protein	Virus & viroid resistance
Gladiolus	Coat protein (*cp*) gene in either sense or anti-sense orientation	Bean yellow mosaic virus resistance
Carnation	Coat protein (*cp*) gene	Resistance to virus
3. Bacteria		
Apple	*Attacin E* gene	Bacterial blight resistance
Potato	*Enteric-b-defensin* (EBD) gene from cow through *Agrobacterium*	Bacterial resistance
	Lysozyme, Tachyplesin, Pectate lyase, Glucose oxidase	Soft rot resistance
Cauliflower	*Brassica napus-2*, *Chitinase* gene	Black rot & soft rot resistance
Tomato	*Rx-1, Rx-2, Rx-3* gene from *S. lycopersicum, S. pennellii*	Bacterial spot resistance
	Pto gene from *S. pimpinellifolium*	Bacterial speck resistance
	Rrs 3.0-12.0 gene from *S. pimpinellifolium, S. peruvianum*	Bacterial wilt resistance
	At NPR1 gene from *Arabidopsis thaliana*	Resistance to bacterial pathogen
Bean	*Phaseolotoxin*	Halo blight resistance
Carnation	*Oat thionin* gene (*ASTHI-1*)	Bacterial wilt resistance
Anthurium	Anti-microbial peptide (AMP)	Bacterial blight tolerance
4. Insects		
Banana	Maize *cystatin* gene (*CC-II*)	Reniform nematode resistance
	Cystatin gene (*OC-1ÄD86*)	Burrowing nematode resistance
Strawberry	*CpTi* (cowpea protease trypsin inhibitor) gene	Vine weevil resistance
Kiwi fruit	Synthetic chimeric gene *sbt Cry1Ac*	Fruit piercing moth resistance
Walnut	*Cry1Ac* gene from *Bt*, *GUS* & *NPTII*	Navel orange worm resistance
Cranberry	*Bt, ICP, GUS* gene	Navel orange worm resistance
Apple	*Cry1A* & *IPC*	Navel orange worm resistance

	Er-3 gene from cv. Aotea-1	Woolly apple aphid resistance
Tomato	*Cry 1Ac, Cry 1Ab, Cry 1H, Cry 9c, Cry 3A, CpTi*	Fruit borer resistance
	Mi, Mi-1, Mi-2, Mi-3, Mi-9 from *S. peruvianum*	Root knot nematode resistance
Brinjal	Synthetic*Cry1Ab, Cry 1Ac, Cry1Aa3*	Shoot & fruit borer resistance
	Cry1Fa1	Insect resistance
	Modified rice *cystatin* gene (OC-1ΔD86)	Root knot nematode resistance
	Cry 3Bb	Colorado potato beetle resistance (coleopteran toxic)
Cauliflower	*Cry 1Ab*	Diamond back moth resistance
	Cry 1Ac	Cabbage butterfly, Diamond back moth, stem borer, hairy caterpillar, cut worm resistance
	Cry1Ba, Cry1ca, Bar	Insect resistance
	Cry2A	Thrips resistance
	Snowdrop lectin gene	Aphid resistance
	Trypsin inhibitor gene	Diamond back moth & hairy caterpillar resistance
Cabbage	*Cry 1Hc/ Cry 9C, Cry1B, Cry1Ab*	Lepidopteron insect resistance
	Cry 2A	Thrips resistance
	Snow drop lectin gene	Aphid resistance
Potato	*Cry 1Ab*	Potato tuber moth & leaf eating caterpillar resistance
	Cystatin gene (*OC-IΔD86*)	Root knot nematode resistance
	Cry 3Aa	Colorado potato beetle resistance
	Snow drop lectin gene (Galanthes nivalis agglutinin i.e. GNA)	Potato aphid tolerance
	Expression of double gene construct i.e. (GNA + WAI i.e. Wheat α-amylase inhibitor) or GNA + BCH i.e. protein bean chitinase	Peach potato aphid resistance
Peas	*Alpha amylase inhibitor* (*α-Ai-1*) gene	Pea weevil resistance
Squash	Coat protein (*cp*) gene	Virus resistance
Cowpea	*Alpha AI-Pv* seed protein gene (*Alpha amylase inhibitor*); *chitinase* gene	Bruchid insect resistance
	Bt- gene	Maruca pod borer & pod bug resistance
	Copwea trypsin inhibitor (*CpTi*) gene	Insect resistance
Garden pea	Coat protein (*cp*) from *Alfalfa mosaic virus* (AMV)	Pea weevil resistance
Peach	*Rm1*	Green peach aphid resistance
Grapefruit	*Agglutinin*	Aphid resistance
Sweet potato	*Cry IIIA* delta-endotoxin gene from *Bt* var. *tenebrionis*	Resistance to sweet potato weevil cv. Jewel
Lettuce	*BPT-1*	Resistance to lepidopteran pest
Okra	*Cry1Ac* gene to develop variety 'Event OE-17A'	Fruit & shoot borer resistance

Lilium	*Rice cystatin* gene, *OC-IΔD86*	Root lesion nematode resistance
Chrysanthemum	*CmWRKY48* transcription factor & Protease inhibitor sea anemone equistatin (*SAE*) gene	Aphid resistance
	Cry1Ab gene	Insect toxicity
	nptII, *GUS*, *cry1Ab*	Insect resistance
	Potato multicystatin	Western flower thrips resistance
	aphidicidal gene, *Gcs* (Gamma-Cadinene Synthase)	Resistance against aphids in *C. morifolium*
Maize	*Cry1Ab* gene	Corn borer resistance
	Abiotic stress	
Potato	Tobacco Osmotin gene	Water stress tolerance
	One gene (Invertase inhibitor) from potato itself	Reduced conversion of sucrose to glucose & fructose leading to reduced acrylamide
	E. coli bet *A* gene encoding choline dehydrogenase	Enhanced salt stress resistance (glycine betaine level)
	Cod A gene from *Arthrobacter globiformis*	Drought tolerance
	Stns LTP1 gene	Heat, drought & salinity tolerance
	Cu/Zn SOD from *Manihot esculenta*	Heat tolerance
	Bar gene	Bialaphos tolerance
	Cu-Zn-SOD (enzyme superoxide dismutase) gene of tomato	Herbicide tolerance
Sugar beet	Phosphinothricin acetyl transferase gene from *Streptomyces viridochromogenes* & Enolpyruvylshikimate-3-phosphate synthase gene from *Agrobacterium* strain CP-4 and truncated glyphosate oxidoreductase gene from *Ochrobactrum anthropi*	Herbicide tolerance
Tomato	GST (gluthaione-S-transferase)	Herbicide detoxification
	AtDREB1A	Water deficit stress tolerance
	Sly-miR169c	Drought tolerance
	Osmyb-4 (rice gene)	Drought tolerance
	Yeast *SAMDC* gene	Heat tolerance
	cAPX gene	UV-B & heat stress tolerance; chilling & salinity tolerance
	Na^+/H^+ antiporter gene (*TaNHX2*) from wheat	Salinity tolerance
	Unedited *NAD9*	Increased lycopene content
Cherry tomato	*GalUR* gene (*D-galacturonic acid reductase gene*) derived from strawberry	Salinity tolerance
Sweet potato	*SoBADH* (*Spinacia oleracea* derived from *betaine aldehyde dehydrogenase* gene)	Salinity, oxidative stress & chilling tolerance
Chilli pepper	*Osmotin* gene	Salinity tolerance
Bottle gourd	*AVP1* gene	Salinity tolerance
Cowpea	*GST* (glucutathione-S-transferase)	Drought tolerance
Soybean	*fs-1*, *fs-2* gene	Abnormal flower structure
Guava	*CBF-1*, *CBF-2* and *CBF-3*	Cold hardiness
Cranberry	*bar, aphII*	Herbicide resistance

Trifoliate orange	*nptII, AhBADH*	Enhanced salt resistance
Citrus	*Yeast HAL-2 gene*	Salinity tolerance
Apple	*Osmyb4*	Drought & cold tolerance
	MdC1PK61	Salt, drought & chilling tolerance
	MdNHX1 gene	Salinity tolerance
	Bar gene in Tamarillo, Royal Gala	Herbicide tolerance
	Als gene	Herbicide resistance
Banana	*MusaWRKY71 & MusaSAP1*	Multiple abiotic stress tolerance
	MusaDHN-1 gene	Drought & salinity tolerance
Citrus	*P5CS gene; P5CSF129A gene*	Drought tolerance
Kiwi fruit	*AtNHX1 gene*	Salinity tolerance
Mulberry	*Osmotin gene*	Salinity & drought tolerance
	Hval gene	Salinity, drought & cold tolerance
Pineapple	*Bar gene*	Bialaphos tolerance
Papaya	*Bar chimeric gene*	Herbicide (Phosphinothrinocin) resistance
Pear	*SAMDC2 gene &SPDS gene*	Salinity tolerance
Strawberry	*Osmotin*	Salinity tolerance
Anthurium	*CBF-1* gene	Low temperature tolerance
Chrysanthemum	*CmWRKY-1 transcription factor derived from C. morifolium*	Drought tolerance
	CmWRKY-17 transcription factor from *C. morifolium*	Salinity tolerance
	CgDREBa	Drought & salinity tolerance
	CgHSP70 gene from C. morifolium; At DREB1A gene	Heat tolerance
	ICE-1 gene from *C. dichrum*	Cold tolerance
	Phosphomannose-isomerase (*Pmi*) &*Vgb* (from bacterium *Vitreoscilla stercoraria*)	Water logging tolerance & antibiotic resistance
	Dehydration responsive element binding factor gene	Freezing, delayed flowering & drought tolerance
Gerbera	*GUS* gene	Kenamycin resistance e.g. Terra Regina
Lotus	*Nn CIPK* (calcineurin B-like protein kinase) gene	Salinity tolerance
Petunia	*CBF-3* gene from *Arabidopsis*	Cold tolerance
Phalaenopsis	*LTP* (liquid transfer protein) gene from rice	Enhanced cold tolerance
Rhododendron	*Fro-2* gene from *Arabidopsis thaliana*	Enhanced resistance to iron deficiency
Rose	*RcXET & MtDREBIC gene*	Freezing & drought tolerance
	AtDREB2A-CA gene; RrNHX1	Salinity tolerance
	Post harvest life & quality	
Banana, Pineapple	*ACC* synthase	Delayed ripening
Pineapple	-	Increased production of lycopene
Mango, Apple	*ACC* synthase & *ACC* oxidase (i.e. shelf life gene)	Delayed ripening
Mango	Ripening inhibitor (*rin*) gene	Delay ripening

Red banana	*Hepatitis B* surface antigen	Edible vaccine; pharmaceutical production
Strawberry	Pectate lyase	Improved fruit quality
Grape	*VviAGL1-1*	Seedless nature
Guava	*CBF-1, CBF-2 &CBF-3*	Cold hardiness
Papaya	*EST-116, ESTS, FSH-11, FSH-19*	Female to male (or) hermaphrodite
Apple	PPO suppression transgene, *npt II*	Reduced polyphenol oxidase
	Polyphenol oxidase antisense, *PGAS-1, PGAS-2*	
	Arctic™& Golden Delicious via RNA imediated gene silencing	Non-browning phenotypei.e. browning free apple
	rolA gene	Dwarf stature i.e. shortened internodes
	rolB, *rolC* gene	Improved rooting ability & root architecture
	Co gene; *ipt* gene	Columnar shape; modification of tree structure
	RiT DNA in M_{26} rootstock	Higher rooting & well developed root system
Raspberry	*S-adenosyl methionine hydrolase*	Fruit ripening
Peach	*Di-2*	Double flower
	Pl	Weeping growth habit
Plum	Early continuous flowering (ECF) gene	Early flowering
Kiwi fruit	*npt-II, rol*A, *rolB*, *rolC* gene	Improved rooting
Tomato	*ACC* synthase in anti-sense orientation	Controlled fruit ripening
	LeETR-4 gene	Early ripening
	Rin, nor, alc, Nr genes	Delay ripening
	Polygalacturonasse (PG) gene in anti-sense orientation	Delay fruit softening
	Deoxyhypusine synthase (DHS)	Delayed post harvest softening
	A-galactosidase-4 (TBG-4) gene	Improved fruit quality
	Phytoene synthase gene, *NAD-9*	Increased carotenoid content
	Geraniol synthase gene	Modified flavor & aroma
	sp gene	Indeterminate habit
	Ctx-B & *Tcp* antigen of *Vibrio cholera*	Edible vaccine development
	Glycoprotein (G-protein)	Edible vaccine against rabies
	Hepatitis E virus	Edible oral vaccine
	Rol B gene	Induction of parthenocarpy
	Thaumatin gene from katemfe (*Thaumatococcus daniellii*)	Increase taste
	Arabidopsis thaliana H^+/ cation exchanger (*CAX*) gene	Prolonged shelf life
	Yeast spermidine synthase (*ySpdSyn*) gene	Increased shelf life
	RNAi based silencing of mitochondrial *APX* gene	Increased vitamin content
	LeEXP1 gene	Enhanced fruit softening in cv. Pusa Uphar

	RNAi mediated suppression of *DET-1* gene	Improved carotenoid & flavonoid content
	RNAi mediated *Lyc* gene	Increased concentration of lycopene
	RNAi gene construct of *ACO1* gene	Increased shelf life in cv. MI-1
	SlIAA-9 gene	Induced parthenocarpy in cv. Micro-Tom & Alisa Craig
	Sucr gene from *L. chmielewskii*	Increased fruit sucrose accumulation
	Yeast (TPS-1) *Trihalose 6-phosphate* synthase	Tolerance to drought, salt & oxidative stress
	Osmy b-4 gene from rice	Tolerance to drought, stress, virus development
	Sweet pepper *ferredoxin-l-protene*	Disease resistance to bacteria
Brinjal	*Iaah* gene, *DefH 9-iaa M* gene	Parthenocarpic fruit development
Melons	*ACC* oxidase, SAM hydrolase	Reduced ethylene production
Watermelon	*ClPDS* gene	To develop *ClPDS* gene knockouts for albino phenotype
	Lycopene beta-cyclase (LCYB) gene & CAPS marker	Canary yellow & red flesh colour
Muskmelon	Rabies glycoprotein genes	Edible vaccine development
Cantaloupe	*S-adenosylmethionine hydrolase* gene	Modified fruit ripening
Onion cv. Sunion	Gene silencing of lachrymatory factor synthase enzyme	Production of 'tearless' onion
Potato	*Am-1* gene from *Amaranths hypochondriacus*	Protein rich potato (41% increase)
	Genes for modification of starch	Alteration of starch biosynthesis
	Starch production gene	Chips with less fat
	Invertase inhibitor (*inhh*) gene from tobacco	Reduced sugar accumulation during storage
	PHYA gene	Reduced plant height
	Starch branching enzyme gene (*glg B*) of *E. coli*	Increased degree of branching in amylopectin by 25%
	RNAi-based silencing of beta-carotene hydroxylase gene (*bch*); anthocyanins and ascorbic acid by over expression of strawberry *GalUR* gene	Increased β-carotene in tubers
	Supression of Granule bound starch synthase (*gbss*) gene by anti-sense orientation	Yield amylose free or waxy starch (1st successful genetic modification of starch done in 1991)
Cassava	Granule bound starch synthase (*gbss*)gene	Produce & store amylase free starch
	glg c from *E. coli*	Increased shoot & root biomass
	ASP-1	Elevated levels of proline & serine amino acids
	AmA-1	Increase in protein content
Cauliflower	*Bar*, *Barnase*, *Barstar* genes from *Bacillusamyloliquefaciens*	Superior hybrids; stable male sterile lines & herbicide resistance
	Or gene	Enhanced β-carotene (provitamin A) content
	BoCAL gene	Altered inflorescence
Broccoli	*BoCAL* gene	Altered inflorescence

Radish	Suppression of photoperiodic gene *GIGANTEA*	Late flowering (delay in bolting)
Radicchio rosso	*Barnase* gene from *Bacillus amyloliquefaciens*	Male sterile plants
Garden pea	*st* & *af* gene	Leafless (reduced stipule size)
Carrot	*Thaumatin II* from *Thaumatococcusdaniellii*	Flavour improvement
Sweet potato	*GUS* A, *npt* II, *hpt*, cowpea trypsin inhibitor, SPFMV-S coat protein (*cp*) gene	Transgenic plants
	Starch granule bound starch synthase (GBSSI)	Starch synthesis
	RNAi mediated *SBE-II* gene	Increased level of amylase for digestive health
Maize	*ZmCIPK-15*	Decides root direction & controls growth angle of developing roots up to 10^0 & this gene also helps in absorbance of nitrogen from deeper zone of soil strata; mutant of this gene helps in formation of straight roots
Strawberry, Cucumber, Navel orange, Clementine, Watermelon, Brinjal	*DefH9-iaaM*	Parthenocarpy fruits
Coffee	*RNAi* mediated *CaMXMT*-1 gene	Reduced alkaloid content (Decaffeinated coffee)
Ornamental crops	Mutated *etr-1* gene from *Arabidopsis* & flower specific promoter, *fbp-1*	Flower longevity
Antirrhinum	*MIXTA*	Pigment intensity of petal
	MAX	More axillary branching
	Leafy	Floral meristems
	floricaula (*flo*) & squamosa (*squa*)	Change in phyllotaxy from spiral to whorled
	Agropine type *Ri* T-DNA plasmid	Dwarf phenotype with small flowers
	Brassinostenoid gene (*BRI1*)	Dwarf plants
	Agamous gene	Floral architecture
	Del gene	Pattern of red anthocyanin pigmentation
	cos gene	Formation of flavonoids in flowers
	Divaricata gene	Asymmetrical corolla shape in ventral region
	Rosea-1, Rosea-2, & *Venosa*	Control intensity & pattern of magenta anthocyanin pigmentation
	pallida, *Niv* gene	Variegation in flower colour
	Clavata-1, Clavata-2 & *Clavata-3*	Regulate of shoot meristem maintenance
	Wuschel	Regulate shoot meristem initiation
Carnation	*rolC* gene	Better rooting ability

	ACC oxidase, *ACC* synthase, Anti-sense *aco* gene, *sACS* transgene	Increased shelf life
	Flavonol synthesis	White to mauve
	F3'H gene	Violet orange to cream
	etr1-1 from petunia	Decreased ethylene level
Chrysanthemum	Flavonol synthesis	Pink to white
	F3'H gene &*F3'5'H* gene	Flower colour modification
	chalcone synthase (*chs*) cDNA gene	Fully white or very pale pink flowers in cv. Money Maker
	Narningenin chalcone synthase *chs* gene & pansy *F3'5'H* gene	Violet & white colours in cv. Money Maker
	Carotenoid cleavage dioxygenase 4-RNAi (*CmCCD4a*)	Control of carotenoid formation in ray petals
	RNAi suppression of *Cm F3'H* gene & over-expression of *Seneciocruentus F3'5'* gene	Bright red flower
	Ls gene	Less branching
	Ipt gene	Increased branching & reduced internodal length
	Ap-1 gene	Speed up time to flowering
	ERS-1 gene	Slows down yellowing of leaves
	GA insensitive (*gai*)gene	Dwarf plants
	Rice *phyA*, Tobacco *phytochrome B-1* (*PHYB-1*) gene	Shorter plant, large branch angle
Cyclamen	Anti-sense orientation of *F-3'H* gene	Orange and brick-red coloured flower
Gerbera	Chalcone synthase (*CHS*) & *dfr* gene	Red to pink & cream coloured flower
	GA insensitive (*gai*) gene	Stem elongation & plant height
	gglo-1, *gdef*-1, *RCD*-1 in anti-sense orientation	Modified floral & plant morphology
	Trichomeless (glossy leaf) gene (*Trl*)	Shiny scalloped-leaves
Gentian	*CHS* gene	Production of white flowers
Orchids/ Lily	MADS-box	Ectopic expression changes the second round of petals into calyx
Pelargonium	Senescence specific gene promoter *pSAG12::ipt* &-*tmr* gene	Delayed leaf senescence & produced long lived plants
	barnase chimaeric gene (from pea anther)	No pollen grains in modified anther structure
	rolC encodes for cytokinin β glucosidase from *E. coli* & *npt* II	Reduction in plant height; dwarf & super dwarf phenotypes
	CP_4EPSPS	Increased resistance to herbicide
	Agropine strain A_4 & LBA9402	Increase in essential oil content of leaves
Petunia	*Lc* regulatory gene from maize	Flower colour modification from white to red
	Anti-sense *GA20 oxidase* gene	Reduced rate of stem elongation
	Isopentenyl transferase (*ipt*) gene	Increased cytokinin production
	DFR gene from gerbera	Production of brick red /orange flowers

	Chalcone synthase (*CHS*) gene	Production of abnormal anthers & purple to white flowers
	Flavonoid biosynthesis	White to pale yellow flowers
	Flavonol synthesis &*DFR* gene	White to pink flowers
	F3'5' gene	Red to deep purple flowers
	Anti-sense *BoACO1* from broccoli	Reduced ethylene biosynthesis i.e. delay in flower senescence
	EPSPS (5-enol-pyruvylshikimate-3-phosphate synthase) gene	Herbicide tolerance
	acc &*aco* genes in anti-sense orientation	Delayed leaf senescence
	gai gene from *Arabidopsis thaliana*	Dwarf plants
Rose	Anthocyanin biosynthesis	Red to Pink/ light red/ magenta red flowers
	npt II &*rolA,B,C*	Improved adventitious rooting of cuttings
	AGAMOUS gene	Double flower form
	CHS gene	Petal colour modification
	Viola *F3'5'H* gene (delphinidin biosynthesis) & *Iris* x *hollandica* DFR gene	Novel bluish flower colour
	RhAN-1, RhAN-2, RhAN-11	More anthocyanin accumulation in leaves
	TCP3SRDX	Increased number of leaflets
	YAB1SRDX	Gypsophila like shape & novel flowers
	Anti-bacterial protein Nos*NptII CecB*	Prolonged vase life
Limonium	*rol A, rol B, rol C*	More dwarfness, increased number of flowers & early flowering
Torenia fournieri	Anthocyanin biosynthesis	Blue to white flowers
	Cytochrome P450 gene	Blue to red flowers
Verbena	*F3'5'H* gene i.e. butterfly pea gene from *Clitoria ternatea*	Altered flower colour in cv. Temari Sakura
Water lily	Chimaeric *NPT-II* gene & nopaline *synthase* gene	Removal of natural barriers in gene exchange

***Transgenic varieties*:**

Crop	Trait	Product name	Year of release	Organization
Fruit crops				
Papaya	Resistance to PRSV	SunUp	1998	Cornell University
	Resistance to PRSV	UH Rainbow	2008	University of Hawaii
	Resistance to PRSV	Laie Gold	1992	University of Hawaii
	Resistance to PRSV	Khaknuan, Thapra-2,	-	From Thailand
Banana	Rich in pro-vitamin A i.e. Phytoene synthase (*PSY2a*) gene isolated from Asupina banana found in Papua New Guinea	Super Banana i.e. β-carotene rich banana	2014	Queensland University of Technology
Plum	Resistance to Plum Pox Virus (PPV)	Honey Sweet	2009	USDA, ARS
Apple	Glufosinate tolerance, Glyphosate tolerance, Coleopterian insect resistance, Lepidopterian insect tolerance, mannose metabolism	Agri Sure™, Viptera™	-	-
Vegetable crops				
Tomato	Increase in shelf life	Endless Summer	1995	DNA Plant Tech.
	Increase in carotenoids phytoene, lycopene, β-carotene & lutein	Ailsa Craig	-	-
	Enhanced vase life	Flavr Savr	1994	Calgene Company
Brinjal	Resistance to fruit and shoot borer using *Cry1 Ac* gene	*Bt* brinjal	-	Mahyco seeds
Lettuce	Increased tocopherol	Chung-Chima	-	-
Soybean	Water stress tolerance gene from sunflower & incorporated in cv. HT-Bt	HB-4	-	Bio-Saras Crop Solution, Argentina
Summer Squash	Resistance to watermelon mosaic virus-2 & zucchini yellow mosaic virus	Freedom-II	1992	Asgrow Seed Co.
Radish	Transgenic by 'floral dip method'	Jin Ju Dae Pyong	2001	-
Potato	Resistance to Colorado beetle	New Leaf™	1995	Monsanto Co.
	Resistance to Colorado beetle	Elizabeth	2010	Monsanto Co.

	Resistance to Potato Leaf Roll virus (PLRV)	New Leaf Plus	1998	Monsanto Co.
	Resistance to late blight (from *S. bulbocastanum*)	Fortuna	2011	BASFPlant Science
	Reduced acrylamide production, modified starch quality & black spot bruise tolerance	Innate™	-	-
Soybean	Glyphosate tolerance & modified oil quality	Vistive Gold™	-	-
	Glyphosate tolerance	Round Up Ready	1995	Monsanto Co.
	Resistance to glufosinate ammonium herbicide	Liberty Link™	1996	Agro-Euo
	Tolerance Sulphonyl urea herbicide	STS™		
Maize	Resistance to corn borer	Maximizer	1996	Ciba Geigy
	Resistance to corn borer	Guard	1996	Monsanto Co.
Flower crops				
Antirrhinum	Dwarf, decrease in apical dominance & increased number of flowers	Floral Carpet	1992	-
Anthurium	Resistance to bacterial blight	Marian Seefurth, Abe Pink, Kanzako No.2, Kalapana, Centennial, Paradise Pink, UH1060, Rudolph (pink heart shaped spathe), Tropic Ice, Tropic Flame 1-9 (red tulip type cupped spathe)	-	University of Hawaii
Carnation	Modified flower colour (violet)	Moon Dust, Moon Shadow, Moon Vista, Moon Shade, Moon Lite, Moon Aqua	2003	Florigene company
	Improved rooting ability	White Sim	-	-
Chrysanthemum	Change of colour	Money Maker, Iridon, Pictor, White Hurricane, White Snowdon, Yamate Shiro	-	-
Gerbera	Altered flower colour	Terra Regina	-	-
Lilium	Resistance to CMV	Four transgenic lines	2011	-
Orchids	Cymbidium mosaic virus resistance in *Dendrobium*	*D.* x Joquelyn Thomas Uniwai	2003	University of Hawaii
	Cymbidium mosaic virus resistance *Dendrobium*	*D.* x Joquelyn Hawaii Uniwai Pearl	2003	University of Hawaii
	Hygromycin resistance in *Phalaenopsis*	68 transgenic lines	2006	-
Pansy	Dwarf plants	Development of 5 lines	2010	-
Pelargonium	No pollen grains	*Pelargonium zonale*	1998	-
	Improved oil quality	LZ-3, 14 TG, *P. graveolens* cv. Hemanti	2007	-

	Reduced growth of plants, delayed flowering	*P.* x *domesticum*	2012	-
	Resistance to gray mold	Scented geranium cv. Frensham	1999	-
	Kanamycin resistance in shoots and roots	Regal pelargonium cvs. Alaska, Dubonnet, Hazel Cherry, Her Majesty, NC Faiss, Mrs. James Rodgers, White Chiffon	2002	-
	Kanamycin resistance in shoots and roots	Zonal pelargonium cvs. Orange Appeal, White Elite, White Multibloom, White Orbit	2004	-
Petunia	Altered plant morphology	Dainty Lady	2010	-
Rose	Increased oil content	GM hybrid rose	-	AgroBioInstitute, Bulgeria
	Improved rooting of cuttings	*R. hybrida* cv. Money Way	1997	-
	Blue coloured rose	Applause, Blue Moon, Blue Perfume, Blue Nile	2009	Australian firm Florigene Ltd. along with Japanese firm Suntroy Ltd.
	Petal colour modification	*R. hybrida* cv. Royalty	1994	-
	More anthocyanin accumulation in leaves	*R. hybrida* cv. Lavande	2012	-
	Enhanced transformation efficiency	*R. hybrida* cv. Tineke	2004	-
	Partial resistance to PM & black spot	*R. hybrida* cv. Heckenzauber, Pariser Charme	2001	-
	Enhanced resistance to PM	*R. hybrida* cv. Carefree Beauty	2003	-
	Resistance to black spot	*R. hybrida* cv. Glad Tidings	1998	-
	Resistance to black spot	*R. multiflora*	2010	-
	Salinity stress tolerance	*R. chinensis*	2009	-
	Salinity stress tolerance	*R. chinensis*	2009	-
	Freezing & drought tolerance	*R. chinensis*	2016	-
	Salinity stress tolerance	*R. rugosa*	2015	-
	Water stress tolerance	Front 'N Center	1994	-
Statice	Pot culture	Super-Compact type hybrid 'L-116'	2003	-
Tulip	-	*T. eichleri, T. fosteriana, T. biflora, T. turkestanica&T. gesnerianacvs.* Apeldoorn, Christmas Marvel, Lustige Witwe, Prominence, Monte Carlo	-	-

13.7 Artificial seeds/ synthetic seeds:

- Term 'artificial seed' was coined by Murashige in 1977.
- Somatic embryos/ shoot apex/ nodal micro-cuttings are encapsulated in bio-degradable synthetic polymer based gel matrix (e.g. Sodium alginate) along with mycorrhiza.
- Synthetic seed in banana was developed by BARC, Mumbai.
- Protocols for production of 'synseed' have been developed in mulberry, banana and mango.
- Commonly used hydrogels: Sodium alginate, Calcium alginate, Carrageenan, Guar gum, Sodium pectate, Tannic acid, Copper sulphate, etc.
- In India, technique of synthetic seeds has been standardized and practiced for sandle wood and mulberry at BARC, Mumbai.

Advantages and limitations:

a) Can be stored for years without loss of viability.
b) Easy to handle
c) Useful as unit of delivery.
d) Don't need hardening in green houses.
e) Can be directly sown in soil.
f) High cost of production.

Plant species	Propagule/ explant used	Size
Guava (*Psidium guajava*)	Somatic embryos	8-14 weeks old
Black pepper (*Piper nigrum*)	Shoot buds	0.3-0.5 mm long
Ginger (*Zinziber officinalis*)	Somatic embryos	0.3-0.5 cm long
Cardamom (*Elettaria cardamomum*)	Callus	0.2-0.4 cm long
Turmeric (*Curcuma longa*)	Adventitious buds	0.3-0.5 mm long
Vanilla (*Vanilla planifolia*)	Shoot buds	0.3-0.5 cm long
Cinnamon (*Cinnamomum verum*)	Shoot buds	0.2-0.4 cm long
Anise (*Pimpinella anisum*)	Callus	1.5-2.5 mm dia
Celery (*Apium graveolens*)	Somatic embryos	< 1.0 mm dia.
Carrot (*Daucus carota*)	Somatic embryos	< 1.0 mm dia.
Lettuce (*Lactuca sativa*)	Somatic embryos	1.5-2.5 mm dia.
Loblolly pine (*Pinus taeda*)	Somatic embryos	< 1.0 mm dia.
Mulberry (*Morus indica*)	Axillary buds	0.5 cm dia.
Sandelwood (*Santalum album*)	Somatic embryos	< 1.0 mm dia.
Periwinkle (*Catharanthus roseus*)	Somatic embryos	< 1.0 mm dia.
Indian valerian (*Valeriana wallichii*)	Axillary buds	0.3-0.5 mm long
Medicinal yam (*Dioscorea floribunda*)	Axillary shoot buds	0.3-0.5 cm long
Indian henbane (*Hyoscyamus muticus*)	Adventitious shoot buds	0.2-0.4 cm long
Picrorhiza (*Picrorrhiza kurroa*)	Axillary shoot buds	0.3-0.5 cm long
Rhubarb (*Rheum emodi*)	Adventitious shoot buds	0.2-0.5 cm long
Patchouli (*Pogostemon patchouli*)	Axillary buds	0.3-0.5 cm long

14. HORTI-SILVI- PASTORAL SYSTEM:

- Total forest area in India (2020-21): 7,12,249 km^2 i.e. 80.73 million ha (24.56% of geographical area).
- States having maximum forest area: Madhya Pradesh, Arunachal Pradesh, Chhattisgarh, Odisha, Maharashtra.
- India has entered in 2nd stage of green mission.
- Padmashri awardee tribal woman named 'Tulasi Gowda' nicknamed as 'Encyclopedia of Forest' due to her vast knowledge of diverse species of plants and herbs- despite not having any formal education.
- Padmashri awardee farmer named 'Sundaram Verma' grew 50,000 trees with water saving technique 'dryland agroforestry' in Shekawati village of Rajasthan.
- Padmashri awardee tribal woman named 'Smt. Rahibai Popere' nicknamed as 'seed mother' conserved and established seed bank preserving hundreds of varieties of crops.
- Bamboo is fastest growing woody plant in the world. It can grow up to 35 inches in a single day.
- For atomic energy production, bamboo is only alternative to coal.
- Bamboo is known as 'Green gold or Kalpa grass or Poor man's timber'.
- Bamboo is considered as 'carbon credit crop'.
- Bamboo absorbs more CO_2. It has highest growth rate compared to other agro-forestry crops.
- As per reports of NTPC (National Thermal Power Corporation) bamboo can act as green corridor for more energy production.
- Bio-mass energy production from bamboo & coal is equal in proportion i.e. energy released by burning of 1 kg bamboo equals to energy released by 1 kg coal.
- Western Ghat region of Maharashtra accounts for 10 bamboo species growing stock.
- Botanically, *Studoxytenanthera stocksii* comprises 'Mess' and 'Managa' varieties.
- 'Mess' variety is newly nominated as 'Madhavi'. It grows up to 30-55 feet. Sturdy nature & widely used in building construction & furniture preparation. Widely cultivated in Bhor, Velha & Mulshi tehsils of Pune district.
- Plant Bamboo Movement has been initiated by World Bamboo Organization to increase the awareness about bamboo globally.
- National Bamboo Mission and Atal Bamboo Plantation schemes are implemented by central government.
- Under these two schemes, about 6 thousand ha land has been brought under bamboo cultivation in Maharashtra during 2019-20 and 2020-21.
- Bamboo species for agarbatti industry: *Bambusa tulda*, *B. cacherensis*, *B. pallida*.
- Bamboo species for timber purpose: *B. giganteus*, *B. brandisii*.

- Beema bamboo (*Bambusa balcova*): Sterile and thornless Indian variety.
- Heavenly bamboo (*Nandina domestica*).
- Japanese bamboo (*Apluda hindsii*).
- Golden bamboo or fish pole bamboo (*Phyllostachys aurea*).
- Tortise shell bamboo (*Phyllostachys heterocycla*).
- Sweet bamboo (*Dendrocalamus asper*): Best for gastrointestinal uses.
- Co-operative movement on bamboo cultivation in India has been initiated by Pasha Patel Ex. President, State Agril. Prices Commission Board.
- World Bamboo Foundation has been established at USA.
- 1st World Bamboo conference held in Thailand in 2009 under chairmanship of Mr. Kamesh Salam.
- Natural habitats of bamboo: India and China.
- India has 130 bamboo species.
- India's rank in bamboo cultivation: 14th.
- North-Eastern region accounts for 2/3rd of India's bamboo growing stock.
- It can address 4 global challenges: Shelter security, livelihood security, ecological security, and food security.
- Institute completely devoted to all aspects of bamboo: CSIR.
- Very soft toilet tissue paper has been prepared.
- Nation Mission on Bamboo: 1st run by China.
- Bamboo Society of India works for overall development of crop cultivation & industrial application.
- Calorific value: 4600-5400 cal/ kg.
- Viscose staple fiber (VSF) from bamboo cellulose: An excellent raw material for premium clothing.
- World's 1st refinery project on ethanol production from bamboo will be initiated in Assam from August, 2022.

15. NANOTECHNOLOGY:

- It is the design, characterization, production and application of structures, devices and systems by controlling shape and size at nanometric scale.
- It has provided new solutions to problems in plants, food and nutrition science and offers new approaches to rational selection of raw materials or processing of such materials to enhance quality of plant products.
- It act as tool for molecular treatment of diseases, rapid disease detection, enhancing the ability of plants to absorb nutrients, increasing efficiency of pesticides, herbicides, etc.

- Term 'nanotechnology' was coined by N. Taniguichi in 1974 at Univ. of Tokyo, Japan in a paper entitled "On the Basic Concept of Nano-Technology".
- It is understanding and control of matter at dimension of 1-100 nm.
- Carbon nanotubes (CNTs) can be used for site specific delivery of materials. CNTs effectively penetrate seed coat, thereby influence seed germination and plant growth via better water permeation and breaking of seed dormancy.
- Anti-microbial capability of silver nanoparticles are employed in household products such as textiles, food storage containers, home appliances and in medical devices.
- Example of Nano based Small Delivery System: Halloysite i.e. aluminosilicate clay mineral.
- Nano pesticide: Nano particles of ZnO, SiO_2 and TiO_2 used for bacteria and green algae.
- Nano particles used for reclamation of heavy particles: Amphiphylic Polyurethane, Zeravalent Iron and Zeolite.
- 'Nano-encapsulation' can be used to improve the insecticidal value.
- Nano silver is a new material having anti-microbial activity.
- Nano-fertilizers: Urea, DAP.
- Chile: Leading country in use of nanotechnology in post harvest management of fruits.
- IIT, Mumbai: Leading organization in the field of nanotechnology.
- Potato minitubers can benefit from anti-microbial effect of nano silver before transplantation in field by staying healthier for longer time in soil.
- In *in vitro* studies olive plants, addition of nano silver @ 4 mg/l into medium was effective in controlling internal microbial contaminations of explants with no harmful effects.
- Nano silicon improves germination rate, root length, dry weight of shoot under salinity level of 25 mM NaCl in tomato seeds.
- Application of 100 ppm silver nanoparticles showed maximum inhibition of fungal hyphae in cucumbers and pumpkins.
- In saffron, using nano silver, number of roots, root length, root fresh and dry weight, leaves fresh weight were reduced by flooding stress.
- Asparagus spears coated by silver nanoparticles could be kept in good quality for 25 days at 2^0C and for 20 days at 10^0C.
- Rose flowers treated with 8-HQS (200 ppm) + nano silver (2 ppm) had highest flower diameter, fresh weight o dry weight ratio and vase life.
- Silver nanoparticles controls contamination in vase solution of gerbera.
- Biologically synthesized silver nanoparticles using medicinal plants such as *Boswellia ovalifolioata*, *Shorea tumbeggaia*, *Svensonia hyderobadensis*, *Thespesia*

populnea and *Vinca rosea* possess anti-bacterial and anti-fungal action against *Escherichia coli, Proteus vulgaris, Curvularia lanata, Aspergillus* spp., *Rhizopus arrhizus* and *Pseudomonas aeruginosa*.

- Green synthesis of silver nanoparticles from leaf extracts of *Euphorbiahirta*, *Nerium indicum* are highly effective against *Streptococcus pyrogens*, *Bacillus subtilis*, *Salmonella typhi* and *Citrobacter* spp.
- Bionatrol, a specified emulsion nano particle from soybean oil, as a non toxic natural bio-insecticide and minimum risk pesticide was proved better against two-spotted spider mites, aphids, white flies in cucumber.

16. VERTICAL/ URBAN FARMING:

- Revolution has been done in San Francisco in vertical farming of medicinal plants and vegetables.
- Possible to save 90% water & 99% area in comparison to traditional farming.
- Use of robots and drone technology has tremendous potential.
- Possible to maintain extreme quality fruits, vegetables, medicinal plants.
- Possible throughout year at any place in the world.
- In future, hardly 2 acres vertical farming will be equal to 720 acres traditional farming.
- Compared to plane lands, it may yield 400 times more production/ acre.
- Non-GM crops can be cultivated without herbicides and insecticides.
- 100% energy requirement can be fulfilled from non-traditional sources.
- Concept was 1st put forward by Dickson Despommier, professor emeritus at Columbia University.
- Crops grown: Spinach, Amaranth, Mint, Lettuce, Kale, Basil, Coriander, Fenugreek, Tomato, Brinjal, Strawberry.

17. HORTICULTURE JOURNALS and MAGAZINES:

- Horticultural Review: Edited by Jules Janick and published by Wiley-Blackwell.

Name of journal	**Periodicity**	**Name of magazine**	**Periodicity**
Name of journal	Periodicity	Name of magazine	Periodicity
Indian Journal of Horticulture	Quarterly	Floriculture Today	Monthly (Media Today)
Journal of Asian Horticulture	Quarterly	Spice India	Monthly (Spices Board)
The Orissa Journal of Horticulture	Half-yearly	Indian Coffee	Monthly (Indian Coffee Board)
South Indian Horticulture	Yearly	Indian Farming	Monthly (ICAR)
Potato Journal	Quarterly	Indian Horticulture	Bi-monthly (ICAR)
Indian Journal of Arecanut, Spices and Medicinal Plants	Quarterly	Plant Horti-Tech	Yearly (Institute for Plantation and *Horti* Culture Management)

Journal of Horticulture Science	Half-yearly	*Phal-Phool* (hindi)	Bi-monthly (ICAR)
* HortScience	Bi-monthly	*Kheti* (hindi)	Monthly (ICAR)
* Hort Technology	Quarterly	Plant Variety Journal of India	Monthly (PPVFRA)
* Journal of the American Society for Horticulture Science	Quarterly		
Scientia Horticulturae	Monthly		
Acta Horticulturae	Monthly		
Journal of Horticultural Science and Biotechnology	Monthly		
Journal of Plantation crops	Monthly		
Journal of Spices and Aromatic crops	Monthly		
Indian Coconut Journal	Monthly		
Corm- The Journal of Floriculture	Half-yearly		
Coconut Research & Development Journal (CORD)	Semi-annual		

* Foreign Journal published by The American Society for Horticulture Science

2

FRUIT SCIENCE

1. GENERAL POMOLOGY

- Word pomology: Derived from Greek word '*pome*' means 'development of fruit from inferior ovary' and '*logos*' means 'to study'.
- Father of systematic pomology: De Candolle.
- T. A. Knight attempted 1st artificial hybridization in fruit crops.
- Luther Burbank: 1st to consider fruit breeding as a commercial endeavour.
- Fruits produced in sub-tropics account for about 40% of India's total fruit basket.
- Degreening temperature for most horticulture crops: 27°C.
- Winter flowering in sub-tropical fruits creates frost damage.
- Out of total 210 varieties/ hybrids released in fruit crops; 70% are clonal selections and 30% are hybrids.
- In case of hybridization of fruit crops, selection must be made in F_1 generation.
- Fruit research in India was 1st started in 1905.
- All India Coordinated Research Network on Underutilized Crops is at NBPGR, New Delhi.
- Above centre has released 1st variety Mansha Marudhana (RMT-59) of tumba (*Citrulus colocynthis*).
- Maharashtra state is known as 'Fruit bowl of India'.
- Term 'vernalization' was coined by Lysenko.
- Appropriate temperature for vernalization: 1-7°C.
- Transgraft has transgenic rootstock.
- Concept of Effective Pollination Period (EPP): Williams.
- Syllepsis: Continuous development of lateral from terminal meristem to establish a shoot without an evident intervening period of rest of lateral meristem and branches so formed are referred as 'syllaptic branches' e.g. Dry land fruit crops viz. mango, ber, pomegranate, etc.
- Total growing period (available period for crop growth) in arid zone: 90 days.
- Cisgenesis: Genetic modification of a recipient plant with introducing a natural gene from a crossable-sexually compatible plant.

- Fruit crops flowers thrice a year: Mandarins, Sweet oranges, Guava, Pomegranate, Lime.
- Ratio of 'chlorophyll a' to 'chlorophyll b'in plants is 3:1 and is highest in C_4 plants.
- Superfood: International food and beverage industry introduced the term 'superfood' during the mid-2000s to encourage consumers to eat more fresh and processed fruit and vegetables. The first use of this term appeared in an article in the August number of the journal 'Nature Nutrition' by Aaron Ross.
- Super fruits: A nutrient-rich fruit considered to be especially beneficial for health and well-being. They are packed with extremely high levels of anti-oxidants, fibers, vitamins, minerals, polyphenols and other nutrients that improve health. These are rich in anti-oxidants, phytochemicals e.g. Acai berries, Avocado, Baobabs, Blackberry, Blueberry, Cashew apple, Cranberry, Chokeberry, Dragon fruit, Gojiberry, Longan, Lycheeberry, Mango, Mangosteen, Maquiberry, Noni, Pomegranate, Raspberry, Seabuckthorn, Strawberry, Surinam cherry, Yumberry and certain banana varieties.

National fruits of different countries

Country	Name of fruit	Country	Name of fruit
Afghanistan	Pomegranate	Iran	Pomegranate
Armenia	Apricot	Jamaica	Ackee (*Blighia sapida*)
Austria	Apple	Japan	Japanese persimmon
Azerbaijan	Pomegranate	Malaysia	Rambutan
Bangladesh	Jack fruit	Mexico	Avocado
Brazil	Cupuacu (*Theobroma grandiflorum*)	New Zealand	Kiwi fruit
Cambodia	Banana (*M. aromatica*)	Pakistan	Mango
Central African Republic	Banana	Phillipines	Filipino mango
China	Fuzzy kiwi fruit, Jujube (*Ziziphus jujuba*)	Serbia	Plum
Colombia	Borojo (*Alibertia patinoi*), Curuba (*Passiflora mollissima*)	Sri Lanka	Jackfruit
Cuba	Mamey (*Pouteria sapota*)	Spain	Grape
Germany	Apple	South Korea	Asian pear
India	Mango		

2. LAYOUT OF ORCHARD

- Planting of trees should be such that intercept maximum solar energy.
- Every 3rd tree in every 3rd row should be pollinizer in self incompatible varieties.
- Evergreen tree should be planted in the front and deciduous behind.
- Total orchard area under roads, buildings, paths, tube-wells is 10%.

- Filler plants must be quick growing and early fruiting.
- Suitable plants for bio-fencing: Agave, *Pithecolobium dulci*, *Thevetia peruviana*, *Carissa carandas*.
- Suitable hedge plants: Duranta, *Lantana camera, Tecoma stans*, *Prosopis julifera*, *Opuntia* spp., *Clerodendron inerme, Inga dulcis*.
- Windbreaks have its effectiveness for a distance about 4 times its height.
- Windbreaks are planted in north-west side of orchard.
- Trees suitable as wind breaks: *Polyalthia longifolia, Azadirachta indica, Pterospermum acerifolium, Syzygium* spp., *Carissa carandas*, *Grevillea robusta*.
- South-West direction is most sensitive to sun burn effects in plants.

2.1 SYSTEMS OF PLANTING

1. Square system: Simplest and ubiquitous system of planting. More commonly followed.
2. Rectangular system: Used in high density planting (HDP) e.g. Grape, Phalsa and Peach.
3. Cluster system: Accommodates nearly twice the population of square system.
4. Triangular: Accommodates 11% lesser number of plants than square system. Mostly used in high density planting (HDP). Intercultural operations difficult.
5. Hexagonal/ Septuple/ Equilateral triangle: Accommodates 15% more plants than square system. Very difficult to layout.
6. Quincunx/ Diagonal: Most suitable in highly fertile soils and near urban/ periurban areas. Accommodates 1.5-2 times more plants than square system. Adopted when tree spacing exceeds 10 m or slow growing fruit tree. Filler plants are generally used e.g. Banana, Guava, Kinnow, Phalsa, Papaya, Peach, Pomegranate and Plum. In this system, pollinating trees are placed at the corner positions, to facilitate removal of central tree, thus changing over to square system without affecting cross pollination.
7. Contour system: Followed in hills & undulated land (slope >10%) to minimize land erosion and to conserve soil moisture.
8. Terrace system: Extension of contour system. Planting in flat strip of land formed across a sloping side of a hill, lying level along the contours. Double hedge contour system accommodates 22% higher than single hedge system. Hedge row planting system is commercially followed in mechanized fruit cultivation e.g. Apple, Pineapple.
9. Single hedge row planting system: Guava.
10. Double/ Hedge row system: Very intensive form of rectangular system. Distance between trees in a row is half to one third the distance between rows e.g. pineapple.
11. Full-field system: Most efficient system for maximum light interception.
12. HYTEC (Hybrid Tree Cone) system: New system for apples, designed for unique climate of Washington. Suitable rootstocks are M-9, M-26 and Mark.
13. Multi row and bed system: Apple.

2.1.1 High density planting (HDP)

- Accommodation of the maximum possible number of the plants per unit area to get the maximum possible profit per unit of tree volume without impairing the soil fertility status.
- Modern tool of plant architecture management.
- Multistoried cropping system was adopted for coconut, arecanut, ber & aonla.
- High density planting is 1st established in apple in Europe (England) in 1962 with the development of Malling and Merton series of rootstock. Subsequently this system was adopted in peach, plum, sweet cherry and pear.
- HDP has been possible by development of dwarfing rootstock like 'M-9' and 'M-26' in apple, 'Quince-A' for pear, peach with almond hybrids (GF-677, GF-557) for peach and 'Cold' in cherry.
- Use of growth regulators such as B-9, which dwarfs the trees and encourages early bud production.
- Super HDP/ Meadow orcharding isdeveloped to utilize vertical and horizontal spaces.
- Meadow orchard/ Ultra High Density planting (UHDP)
  - Modern method of fruit cultivation using small or dwarf tree with modified canopy.
  - Dense population of 20,000-70,000 trees/ ha.
  - Objective: Mechanization of all orchard activities.
  - Originated in Israel.
  - 1st developed by J.P. Hudson (1971) in apple (spur type) in Israel.
- Amenable fruit crops for meadow orchard e.g. Peach (5m x 1m = 2000 plants/ha); Mango-Alphonso, Emam Pasand, Dashehari, Amrapali (3m x 2m = 1666 plants/ha) and guava (2m x 1m = 5000 plants/ha).
- In India, meadow orchard is commercially adapted in guava developed by CISH, Lucknow. It is based on principle of regular topping and hedging of plants.
- Training method followed in HDP orchard: Central leader system.
- Key to success of HDP: Control of tree canopy size by using genetically dwarf varieties. dwarfing rootstock, pruning technique and plant growth redulating chemicals.
- Canopy volume: $(\text{E-W spread} + \text{N-S spread} \div 2)^2 \times \text{canopy height} \times 0.5236$.

Fruit crops	Varieties	Spacing (m)	No. of plants/ha	System of planting
Mango	Amrapali	2.5 x 2.5	1600	Triangular system
	Arka Aruna	-	-	-
	Kesar	3 x 1 or 2 x 4	3333	Triangular system
	Alphonso	5 x 5	400	Square system
Banana	Robusta	1.5 x 1.5	4400	Square system
	Dwarf Cavendish	1.5 x 1.5	4400	Square system
	Grand Naine, Basrai	1 x 1.2 x 2	5200	Paired row system
Papaya	Pusa Nanha	1.2 x 1.2	6944	Square system
Pomegranate	Bhagwa	5 x 2	1000	Square system
Pineapple	Kew & Giant Kew	25 x 35 x 90 cm	64,000	Double row system
		25 x 35 x 75 cm	72,727	Double row system
Guava	Allahabad Safeda, Lalit	1 x 2	5000	Double hedge row
Aonla	Neelum	5 x 5	400	Hedge row
Sapota	PKM-3	5 x 5	-	Square system
Peach	Red Heaven	-	-	-
Cherry	Meteor	-	-	-
Strawberry	Chandler	30 x 20 cm	55,000-60,000	-
Litchi	-	4.5 x 4.5 x 9	329	Double hedge row
Coconut	-	5 x 5	280	Double hedge row
Lemon	Pant Lemon, Assam Lemon	4 x3	833	Square system
Sweet orange	Katol	6 x 3	562	Rectangular system
Cashew nut	H-130, BPP-11	5 x 4	500	Square system
Mandarin orange	Kinnow	1.8 x 1.8	3,000	Square system

3. TRAINING AND PRUNING

- Trunk: Main stem of plant.
- Head: Point on the trunk from which first branch arise.
- Scaffold branches: Main branches arising from the head are known as scaffold branches.
- Crotch: The angle made by scaffold limb to the trunk or the secondary branch to scaffold limb is called crotch. The crotch should be broad and not narrow.
- Leader: The main growing branch from ground level upto the tip dominating all other branches.
- Spur: Numerous shoot growth which are abundant over the fruit trees and upon which most of the fruit is borne.
- Water shoots: These are extraordinary vigorous vegetative shoots which grow from the high points on the main branches in upright direction at the expense of main branches.

- Water suckers: Arise from adventitious buds on the roots or underground parts of the stem of the tree or growth appearing on rootstock portion.
- Alternate bearing index in fruit crops should be 0-1.

3.1 Canopy architecture management

- Canopy architecture management is-
  a) Essential tree management operation.
  b) Starts from 1st year of plant establishement.
  c) Enables the plant to produce high quality and quantity by providing proper framework, more fruiting area and utilization of available resources.

3.1.1 Objectives of canopy architecture management

1. To restore root/shoot ratio.
2. To obtain specific form of the plant.
3. To develop specific geometry within plants and its overall topography.
4. To maintain optimum balance between vegetative and reproductive parts.
5. Pruning for dwarfing.
6. Promotion of maximum shoots/ fruiting points.
7. Vegetative growth and fruiting or yield have antagonistic effects.
8. Apical dominance is a natural phenomenon.

3.1.1.1 *Considerations of canopy management*:

1. Conservation of stored food
2. Maintain root : shoot : fruit ratio by pinching rather pruning.
3. Pruning time and severity.
4. Provision of more light and air inside the canopy for stereo fruiting and better colour development.
5. Boosting up of canopy formation.
6. Development of single canopy with multiple root system concept.
7. Exploring the possibility of mechanization in pruning.

3.2 Training

- Pruning for form is termed as 'training'.
- Training is done to maintain proper shape, canopy of tree and develop good frame work.
- Training controls distribution of fruiting wood and has little effect on fruit bearing.
- Multi storyed cropping is practiced in Karnataka and Kerala.

- Free Air Temperature Increment (FATI) technology: Increase in canopy temperature in fields.
- 'Crotch angle' is related to training practice.
- For better canopy, crotch angle should be 45^0.

3.2.1 Methods of training

1. Central leader system or Closed centered one: It develops pyramidal canopy shape.Main trunk extends from the soil surface to total height of tree. Several side branches grow at different heights in various directions.
   - Advantages: Such trees are structurally best suited to bear crop load and to resist the damage from strong winds.
   - Disadvantages: Trees under this system grow too tall and are less spreading. Tree management (spraying, pruning, thinning and harvesting) is difficult. Shading effect on interior canopy (the lower branches of such trees may be so much in shade that the fruit may not be able to develop proper colour).
2. Open centre system or Vase shaped system: Oldest system of training. Main trunk is allowedto grow upto 1.0 m by cutting within a year of planting. 3-5 lateral branches are allowed to develop from short main stem. Widely used for peaches and is good for mechanical harvesting. Adapted where sunlight is limiting factor. Frost injury is major problem. Exclusively used for Peach, Plum and Nectarines.
   - Advantages: The trees so trained allow maximum sunshine to reach their branches. Better clouration of fruits on the interior side of the tree. Trees are more fruitful and low spreading tree greatly facilitate operations like spraying, pruning, thinning and harvesting.
   - Disadvantages: Such trees are structurally weak, and their limbs are more likely to break with crop load and strong winds. This system does not only need severe pruning to start with but also constant effort to maintain its form through drastic pruning treatment.
3. Modified leader: Most widely adopted/ accepted for commercial fruit cultivation. A leader develops on the young tree until it reaches the height of 2-3 m and then the growth is restricted.
   - Advantages: The branches are well distributed, allowing plenty of sunshine to reach the interior of the tree. The tree is structurally strong and not prone to limb breakage. Spraying, pruning and harvesting may be done easily
4. Other systems of training:
   - Bower system or pendal or arbor or pergola system. Least expensive and have C: B ratio of 1 : 2.09.
   - Telephone system or cverhead trellis system. This was introduced by Prof. N. Gopalkrishnan during 1960 in Pune. Vine is grown up to 160 cm. This system is suitable for high temperature regions.

- Cordons are single stemmed tree system developed in Germany. It is used in gardens as a catalogue of varieties.
- Head system: Shrubs trained to a single stem. Vines become bushy and occupy less space.
- Kniffin system was developed by William Kniffin in 1850 in New York as 'four cane system'. It is similar to Espalier system of training.
- 'Tatura trellis' (V- shaped) system of training: 1st developed in Australia by Chalmer and Vandan Eude. It develops flat canopy. One of the highest yielding systems.
- Lincoln method of training was 1st developed in New Zealand.
- Spindle bush method of training was 1st developed in Germany by Schnitz Hubsh and Heinrichs.
- Slender spindle bush system is modification of dwarf pyramid.
- Dwarf pyramid: Trees spaced like 'Christmas tree'.
- Solen: Low domed form of training adopted to tip bearing cultivars of temperate fruits.
- Multi-row and bed system was developed by Palmer and Jackson.
- Hedge row plantation: Distance within the rows-close and between the rows-wide. Trees planted fairly close 4 feet in rows, 12 feet apart and grown as small bushy trees that develop into a continuous or hedge row habit. Trees are kept 10 feet in height.
- Palmette: Refers to shape of a palm leaf, an open fan or an open hand with spread fingers.
- Meadow or Bed orchard: It offers complete mechanization of both pruning and harvesting coupled with chemical control of weeds.
- Solaxe system: Tree is trained to a central leader, but limb positioning is done towards horizontal to overcome apical dominance e.g. Apple.
- Centrifugal system: Artificial extension is carried out more specifically on underside as well as proximal part of the fruiting branch and around the vertical trunk, where shaded laterals have poor fruit set, size, colour and soluble solids e.g. apple.

Training systems	Examples
Central leader, Hedge row	Walnut, Pecan nut, apple
Open center	Peach, Japanese plum, Nectarines
Modified central leader, Vertical axis system, Spindle	European plum, Pear
Central leader, Modified centre, Palmette, V-shape, Y-trellis,	Sweet cherry
Bower system, Extended 'Y' system	Grape
Espalier system (training on walls, trellies & fences), Spindle bush system, HYTEC (Hybrid tree cone)	Apple

Espalier system	Guava
Cordons, Tatura trellis (syn. Bird's eye view training)	Peach
Single stem system	Citrus, Fig, Annona
Multiple stem system	Pomegranate
Two arm kniffin system	Passion fruit
Lincoln canopy system	Raspberry
T-bar & pergola system	Kiwi fruit
Hedge row	Apricot
Matted row	Strawberry
Palmette system (modification of central leader)	Jamun

3.3 Pruning

Definition: Removal of portion of a tree especially shoots, roots, limbs, buds or nipping away of the terminal parts to correct or maintain tree structure.

- Most suitable time: November-December.
- Improves size and colour of fruits.

Objectives

- Regulation of shape, growth of tree.
- Enhance production and quality of fruits.
- Divert sap flow towards fruiting areas.

Methods of pruning

1. Heading back: Removal of terminal portion of shoot, branches or limbs ($1/4^{th}$ or $2/3^{rd}$ of shoot) leaving its basal portion to encourage development of secondary branches.
   - Reduce tree size by topping and heading back.
   - Skirting: Removal of low hanging branches leaving 7-10 cm e.g. Mango.
   - Tip pruning: Removal of young vegetative flushes prior to flowering e.g. Mango.
   - Containment pruning: Used in HDP of temperate fruit crops.
2. Thinning out: Entire branch is cut right from base. It allows more or sunlight to enter interior of tree because of its opening effect e.g. Mango, Loquat, Quince, Olive.

Pruning intensity

- Light pruning: Guava, Kinnow, Litchi
- Slightly severe pruning: Apple
- Heavy/ severe pruning: Phalsa, Ber, Mulberry.
- Summer pruning forms an essential part in bower system of training.

Special pruning techniques

- Fruits having self thinning capacity: Mango and Apple.
- Pollarding: Severe pruning of plant after attaining maximum desirable height (8-12 feet). Tree top is cut drastically during dormant period.
- Coppicing: Tree cut back to leave a short stump. New growth emerges from stump.
- Pleaching: Used in row tree. Pruning can develop into hedge.
- Topiary: Plants are trained into formal shape.
- Rejuvenation: Done in old senile unproductive orchards during dormancy at a height of 2.5-4 m depending upon tree structure.

Special techniques	Purpose	Examples
Root pruning: Removal of roots 40 cm away from plants	To make dwarf, induce flowering, fruitfulness & determining flowering time	Mandarin orange
Ringing/ cinturing: Removal of complete ring of bark from branch or trunk	To increase fruit bud formation	Mango, Grape, Persimmon, Litchi
Dehorning: Removal of overcrowded & intermingled branches; removal of all wood leaving 7-10 cm thick stub all over tree	To induce flowering	Mango
Notching: Partial ringing of branches above a dormant lateral bud	To induce fruiting branches & increase bearing area	Fig
Nicking: Partial ringing of branches below a dormant bud	To increase flowering shoots & induce spurs from buds	Apple, Fig
Bending: Bending of branches or shoots	To increase lateral branches & fruit production	Guava (Allahabad region)
Thinning: Removal of part flower bud or small fruits from heavy crop	To increase fruit size & reduce alternate bearing tendency	Grapes, Peach, Plum, Quince
Girdling: Removal of 2-3 mm strip of barks around stem	To increase berry size	Grapes, Litchi
Leaf pruning: Removal of old & senescent leaves	-	Date palm
Fruit stripping: Removing all or infested fruits from trees &also to remove insect pests e.g. codling moth larvae, feeding inside the fruit	Reducing pest population	Apple

4. PROPAGATION OF FRUIT CROPS

4.1 Seed/ Sexual propagation/ Amphimixis

- Seed quality is best, if pure seed is >98%, moisture content 6-8% and 60-70% germination e.g. Papaya, Acid lime, Phalsa, Jamun, Mangosteen.
  - Endospermic/ albuminous seeds e.g. Cranberry, Blueberry, Olive.
  - Non-endospermic seeds e.g. Mango, Tamarind, Jack fruit, Ber.
- Epigeal germination: Mango, Jack fruit, Tamarind, Cashewnut.

4.1.1 Seed dormancy

- Inability of viable seed to germinate in favorable conditions.

A. Exogenous dormancy

i) Physical/ Seed coat dormancy: Apricot, Ber, Cherry, Guava, Olive, Peach, Pecannut, Plum, Walnut.

ii) Chemical dormancy: Citrus, Pear, Grapes, Stone fruits.

B. Endogenous dormancy

i) Morphological dormancy (Rudimentary and linear embryo):

ii) Physiological dormancy (ABA): e.g. Apple, Apricot, Cherry, Grape, Pear, Peach, Plum, Strawberry.

C. Double dormancy: e.g. Legume trees.

4.1.2 Methods to break dormancy

A. Scarification: Softening the seed coat to make permeable to water and gases.

i) Mechanical: Cracking of seed with hammer, rubbing with sand paper e.g. Ber, Walnut, Peach, Avocado.

ii) Hot water (77-100^{0}C): Guava, Strawberry

iii) Acid (H_2SO_4 or HCl): Guava (3 min), Ber, Chironji (5-76 h) & HNO_3: Strawberry (0.25%)

B. Stratification (moist chilling)

- Seeds subjected to low temperature. Seeds are placed in sand box @ 0.5-5^{0}C for 1-5 months e.g. Apple, Pear, Peach, Apricot, Cherry, Avocado.
- Seeds place in running water for leaching of inhibitors e.g. Grapes, Strawberry.

C. Use of chemicals

- KNO_3 (0.2%) e.g. Guava, Ber
- Thiourea (5000 ppm or 0.5-3%) e.g. Peach, Plum.

D. Use of hormones:

- GA_3 (100-500 ppm) e.g. Apple, Cherry, Peach, Strawberry, Hazelnut.
- Ethrel (500-1000 ppm) e.g. Guava, Strawberry.
- BA (10-20 ppm) e.g. Apple, Peach.

E. Cryopreservation (liquid nitrogen @ -196^{0}C & liquid carbon dioxide @ -43^{0}C).

F. Cryoprotectants: Glycerol, Dimethyl sulphoxide (DMSO).

G. Seed priming: Procedures followed to overcome dormancy in freshly harvested fruits.

i) Osmo-conditioning: 20-30 % polyethylene glycol (PEG).

ii) Infusion: Hormones, fungicides or insecticides and antidotes are infused into dormant seeds through organic solutions like acetone and dichloromethane.

iii) Fluid drilling: Seeds are suspended in sodium alginate, guar gum and synthetic clay.

iv) Soaking seeds in salt solution is method of halo priming.

4.1.3 Seed storage

Based on longevity *vis-a-vis* seed moisture content and response to drying (Roberts, 1973). Seeds are classified into 2 groups-

- Orthodox (desiccation tolerant) seeds: Seeds can tolerate loss of moisture and their longevity can be increased by preserving them at low temperature e.g. most temperate fruits.
- Recalcitrant (desiccation sensitive) seeds: Seeds do not remain viable for long time at low temperature, not capable to withstand dehydration and sown immediately after extraction. Viability is affected on drying and unable to preserve at sub-zero temperature e.g. most tropical fruits.
- Cryoprservation: Material is stored in liquid nitrogen maintained at a -196^{0}C using cryoprotectants. The most commonly used chemicals are glycerol and DMSO (Dimethyl sulphoxide) e.g. Embryos of coconut and jackfruit.

Orthodox seeds	Recalcitrant seeds
Apple, Banana, Ber, Cashew, Custard apple, Date palm, Fig, Grape, Guava, Lime, Lemons, Mandarin orange, Mulberry, Papaya, Passion fruit, Peach, Phalsa, Plum, Pineapple, Pomegranate, Sweet orange	Avocado, Barbados cherry, Bread fruit, Carambola, Cocoa, Coconut, Coffee, Citrus, Durian, Jack fruit, Litchi, Loquat, Mango, Mangosteen, Oil palm, Rambutan, Rubber & seeds of many forest trees

4.2 Asexual/ Vegetative/ Clonal propagation:

- Multiplication of any plant from any vegetative parts of plant.
- Basic process of normal vegetative growth: Mitosis.
- Genetically uniform materials derived from single individual: Clone.
- Day temperature (21-27^{0}C) and night temperature (15^{0}C) are satisfactory for rooting.
- Most common rooting hormone: IBA.
- Thickness of polythene strip used in propagation: 100µ.
- In quick dip method, the basal portion is dipped for 5 seconds to 2 minutes.

4.2.1 Cutting

- Bottom heat technique: A novel technique for rooting semi-hardwood cuttings developed by Reddy and Majumder (1975) at IARI, New Delhi. Cuttings are treated with 5000 ppm IBA. These cuttings are inserted in rooting medium in a chamber maintained at 30±2^{0}C e.g. Aonla, Guava, Mango, Macadamia nut.

Methods of cutting

a) Hardwood cutting: Length of cutting 10-45 cm containing atleast two buds e.g. Grape, Fig, Pomegranate, Kiwifruit, Hazelnut, Chestnut, Quince, Mulberry, Pear, Plum, Phalsa, Olive, Gooseberry.

b) Semi-hardwood cutting: Mostly used in evergreen fruit and few flower crops e.g. Aonla, Guava, Jack fruit, Lemon, Mango. Treat cuttings with IBA @ 5000 ppm for rooting.

c) Root cutting: Roots 1 cm thick and 10-15 cm tall are used e.g. Apple, Blackberry, Breadfruit, Fig, Kiwifruit, Mulberry, Pecan nut, Peach, Raspberry, Wild pear.

d) Leaf bud cutting: A leaf-bud cutting consists of a leaf blade, petiole and a short piece of stem with attached axillary bud of actively growing leaf.g. Black raspberry, Blackberry, Boysenberry, Lemon, Camellia, Maple.

4.2.2 Budding

- Normally done in when there is good sap flow in plants.
- Healing of bud union- formation of cambium tissue i.e. paranchymatous cells.
- Dedifferentiation of secondary xylem and phloem takes place after 36-48 days of budding.
- Under favorable conditions bud union is completed within 6-7 weeks.

Methods of budding

a) 'T'/Shield budding (thin bark): e.g. Aonla, Peach, Plum, Rose, Sweet orange.

b) Inverted 'T' budding: Widely used in high rainfall areas e.g. Chestnut.

c) Patch budding: e.g. Annona, Aonla, Ber, Citrus, Jackfruit, Jamun, Mango.

d) Ring/ Annular budding: Aonla, Peach, Pecan nut Pecannut.

e) Chip budding: Grape (for nematode and phylloxera tolerant rootstock), Apple and Pear.

f) Forkert budding (modification of patch budding): e.g. Aonla, Custard apple, Jamun.

g) Spring budding: e.g. Citrus.

h) June budding: e.g. Apricot, Aonla, Ber, Cherry, Peach, Plum.

i) Fall budding: e.g. Mango, Guava, Ber, Bael, Jackfruit, Walnut, Chestnut.

j) Microbudding: 45-60 day old micro-buds are used e.g. Citrus, Cocoa, Tamarind, Aonla, Wood apple.

   - First developed by Skaria and Zhang in 2000 in Texas.
   - Can be performed on 5-6 months old rootstock (Rough lemon/ Rangpur lime).
   - Marketable buddlings can be produced 6-8 months earlier compared to conventional buddings.
   - Fast and year round multiplication of planting material is possible.

- Success of microbudding is at par with conventional budding (70-80%).
- Rootstocks are given wedge shaped cut and tender scion bud is inserted inside the wedge cut.
- It is covered with microtip for proper union.
- Microtip caps are removed after sprouting of scion.
- Days taken for sprouting (13-15 days) compared to 26-37 in conventional method.

4.2.3 Grafting

- Grafting cannot be attempted in monocots because of absence of cambium tissue.
- Wood: Combination of secondary xylem and pith.
- Bridge formation is due to callus formation.
- Successful graft: Cambium tissue.
- Optimum temperature for callus formation for grafting: 27-30^{0}C.
- Callus formation starts 1-7 days after grafting.
- Interstock use: Overcome incompatibility.
- Intravarietal grafting: Elberta peach on Elberta peach, Mango.
- Interspecific grafting: Japanese plum grafted on peach.
- Intergeneric grafting: *Citrus* spp. On Trifoliate orange; Sathgudi on Wood apple; Sapota on Pala.
- Shoot tip grafting is used to produce virus free citrus plants, physiological and histological studies of grafting and incompatibility.
- Green finger: Practice of speedy grafting of fruit citrus trees.

Methods of grafting

a) Inarching/ Embracing/Approach grafting:
   - Scion and stock should of same thickness.
   - Not normally followed except e.g. Mango, Sapota.
   - Inarching, if employed to rejuvenate old damaged tree is known as adjuvant grafting.

b) Tongue grafting: e.g. Apple, Pear, Walnut.

c) Softwood/ *in situ* grafting (March-September):
   - Effective in dry, hot weather or low precipitation are as e.g. Avocado, Cashew nut, Mango, Tamarind.

d) Epicotyl/ Stone grafting:
   - Rapid, economic and efficient multiplication of mango (2 weeks old seedling), Jack fruit and Cashew nut (8-10 days old seedlings) in Konkan region of Maharashtra.

e) Veneer grafting
   - Most ideal for establishing *in situ* orchard and top working of old unproductive orchard.
   - 1st developed by Lynch (1941).
   - Mango is commercially propagated by this method in north India.

f) Bridge/ Repair grafting:
   - Useful for the purpose of repairs.
   - To repair plants damaged by frost, rodents or insects during early spring.
   - Used to save severe damaged tree trunk.

g) Cleft or Wedge grafting:
   - Used for top working and rejuvenating old orchards e.g. Fig, Grapes, Hazelnut, Mango, Mangosteen, Pear, Pecannut, Sapota, Walnut.

h) Saddle grafting: e.g. Grape, Rhododendron

i) Whip/ Splice grafting: Apple, Pear

j) Double working:
   - Bartlett pear on quince dwarfing rootstock by using interstock as 'Old Home'.
   - Interstock is used in double working for overcoming graft incompatibility.

k) Top working/ Top grafting: Changing the established plants, trees with desired cultivars e.g. Apple, Mango, Cashew nut, Kokum, Nutmeg.

l) Tube and stick method: Developed by AVRDC, Taiwan for tomato and modified method of that followed in Passion fruit, Bael, Wood apple, Sweet orange with 60-90% success.

m) Shoot tip grafting/ Micrografting:
   - Technique involves grafting of small shoot tip scion (0.1 to 0.3 mm) on to young (2 week old) decapitated seedlings as rootstock growing *in vitro*.
   - Pre-treatment of dipping both scion and excised portion of young rootstock for 10 min in 6-BAP (0.5 ppm) gives higher survival.
   - Success of micrografting is higher with 75 g/ litre of sucrose.
   - To avoid transplantation shock, hardening process in essential.

4.2.4 Layering

- Ideal time (February-March and June-July).
- Removal of cambium is essential practice.
- Basis of rooting: Etiolation.
- Etiolation means growing particular plant part in darkness (branch is covered in soil).
- Commonly used medium: Sphagnum moss.

Methods of layering

a) Simple/ Tongue layering: Guava.

b) Tip layering: The tips of these shoots are buried 5-10 cm deep in soil. Rooting takes place near the tip of current season's shoot which is bent to the ground e.g. Blackberry, Raspberry, Dewberry.

c) Serpentine/ Compound layering: Modification of simple layering in which one-year-old branch is alternatively covered and exposed. The exposed part of stem should have at least one bud to develop a new shoot e.g. American grapes, Muscadine grape, *Jasminum* spp.

d) Trench/ Continuous layering: It consists of growing a plant or branch of a plant in a horizontal position in the base of trench and filling in soil around the new shoots e.g. Apple, Cherry, Pear, Plum, Walnut.

e) Mound/ Stooling: Simplest method for multiplication of scion varieties. Plant is headed back to 15 cm above the ground level during dormant season e.g. Apple and Pear roostocks, Guava, Plum, Cherry, Hazelnut, Pecannut, Mango, Jackfruit, Litchi.

f) Air/ Goottee/ Marcottage/ Pot layering/ Circumportion: Introduced from China. The moist rooting medium (moss grass) is wrapped with the help of small polythene strip 200-300 gauge. Rooting in air layers generally commences within 25-30 days and layers are ready for transplanting within 3 months e.g. Litchi, Guava, Mango, Longan, Persian lime, Ficus, Elephant apple, Rose apple, Watery apple, Star aonla.

4.2.5 Parthenogenesis: arthenogenesis

Development of embryo directly from egg cell with or without pollination but without fertilization. Fruit develop parthenocarpically still they produce viable seeds e.g. Maize, Mangosteen, Strawberry.

4.2.6 Polyembryony

Formation of more than one embryo.

- Term coined by Brau (1859).
- It is controlled by heterozygous dominant gene and absence of dominant allele leads It is an example of facultative apomixis.
- In polyembronic species, extra embryos are formed by nuceller cells (2n), integuments (2n), synergids (n) and antipodal cells (n), etc.
- Polyembrony in mango is apomictic process in which many maternally derived embryos arise from nucellus surrounding the developing zygotic embryo e.g. Olour, Kurukkan, Chandrakaran, Vellaicollumban.
- They are free from virus and source of haploids.
- Polyembryonic stock induces more scion-vigour than monoembryonic.
- Also noticed in Citrus, Jamun, Mahua, Almond, Kiwi, Mangosteen, Peach and Strawberry.

- Nucellar/ Adventitious polyembryony: Embryos arise from diploid sporophytic cells outside the embryo sac i.e. cells of the nucellus, integuments e.g. Citrus, Mango. Identified by uniformity in colour of emerging leaves. It breeds true to type.
- Cleavage polyembryony: Coconut.

4.2.7 Apomixis

- Derived from Greek word '*Apo*' (away from) and '*mixis*' (act of mixing or mingling).
- Formation of embryo with asexual means is apomixes (seeds are formed without union of gametes).
- Development of embryo without usual process of meiosis and fertilization.
- Seeds formed in this way are of vegetative in origin.
- 1st discovered by Leeuwenhock (1719) in *Citrus aurantium*.
- Asexual reproduction through seeds.
- Term coined by Hacke (1893).
- Apomictic seedlings are true to type and free from virus.
- Apomictic apple species are commercially propagated by seed viz., *Malus sikkimensis, M. hupehensis, M. sargenti, M. toringoides*, *Ribes*.
- Seed borne viruses: Psorosis in citrus, mosaic in peach, cherry and almond.
- Apomixis is most common in Poaceae, Asteraceae, Rosaceae & Rutaceae.
  a) Obligate apomixes: When apomixes is the only method of reproduction in plant species.
  b) Facultative apomixes: If gametic and apomictic reproduction occurs in the same plant.

Maheshwari (1950) classified apomixis into 3 groups

1. Recurrent apomixis/ Diploid parthenogenesis/ Somatic apospory/ Gametophytic apomixis: The embryo develops from the diploid egg cell (diploid parthenogenesis) or from some other diploid cells of the embryo sac, with out fertilization (diploid apogamy). As a result, the egg has the normal diploid number of chromosomes, as in the mother plant e.g. Apple, Onion, Raspberry.
   - Diplospory: Embryo sac develops from megaspore mother cell.
   - Apospory: Embryo sac develops from any vegetative cell of ovule.
2. Non-recurrent apomixis/ Nucellar apomixis/ Adventitious embryony/ Androgamy: The embryo develops directly, either from the haploid egg cell (haploid parthenogenesis) or some other haploid cells (synergids or antipodal cells) of the embryo sac (haploid apogamy or pseudogamy). Plants produced by this method contain only one set of chromosomes, these are sterile and the process is not continued for more than one generation. Such type of apomixis are of rare occurrence and is primarily of genetic interest e.g. Maize, *Solanum nigrum, Lilium* spp.

3. Adventitious apomixis/ Adventitious embryony/ Nucellar embryony: Embryo develops from any diploid sporophytic cell e.g. cells of the nucellus (usually), integument, etc. e.g. Citrus, Rose. In addition to such embryo, regular embryo within the embryo sac may also develop simultaneously and gives polyembryony condition as in Citrus and Opuntia.
4. Vegetative apomixis (Bulbils): In this case the flowers in an inflorescence are replaced by bulbils or vegetative buds, which often sprout into new plants while they are still on the mother plant. This type of apomixis is found in some species of *Allium, Agave, Dioscorea, Pao*, etc.

Advantages

- Faster multiplication of genetically uniform individuals.
- Hybrid vigour can permanently be fixed.
- Efficient exploitation of maternal effect is possible from generation to generation.

Disadvantage

- Nuisance when breeder desires to obtain sexual progeny.

4.2.8 Chimera/ Bud sports/ Bud mutations and induced mutation

- Plant part composed of genetically different layer e.g. 'Ruby Red' grapefruit.
- It is a single cell event.
- Term 'chimera' coined by Hans Winkler (1907).
- Variation in leaves.
- Commonly used mutagen in fruit crops: EMS.
- Sectorial chimera: Unstable.
- Periclinal chimera: Most stable e.g. Red coloured apples (Starking Delicious, Richa Red) and Pear, Thornless blackberry.

4.2.9 Special vegetative structures

- Sucker: It is a shoot which arises on a plant below the ground e.g. Banana, Pineapple.
- Offset: It is a lateral shoot or branch which is developed from base of the main stem e.g. Date palm, Pineapple.
- Runner/ stolon: Specialized stem which is produced from the leaf axil at the crown of plant and prostrate horizontally. After root formation in the new plant, the contact with the mother plant is automatically detached and new plant can be separated and planted e.g. Strawberry, *Oxalis corniculata*, Bugle (*Ajuga*).
- Root suckers: e.g. Bread fruit, Charoli, Bael.
- Rhizome/ underground stem: Modified stem structure in which the main axis of the plant grows horizontally just below or on the surface of the ground e.g. Banana.

- Slip and crown: Plant part at the surface of ground from which new shoots are produced e.g. Pineapple (best planting material), Strawberry.

4.2.10 Use of rootstocks in fruit crops

- Father of clonal rootstocks: Gardener.
- Lopping of rootstock: Removal of upper part of rootstock after setting of buds.

Stock-scion relationship

A. Effect of stock on scions

1. Tree height and nature of growth: Apple rootstocks viz. M-27 (extremely dwarf), M-9 (very dwarf), M-7 (semi-dwarf), M-2 (invigorating).
2. Fruiting: Marked reduction in tree height, decrease in yield per tree.
3. Size and quality of fruits: In Washington Naval orange, fruit size is large on sour orange and smaller on Palestine sweet lime. Use of sour orange results in smooth, thin skinned, juicy fruit in sweet orange, tangerine and grape fruit.
4. Winter hardiness and disease resistance: In apple, M-XI and M-XVI impart winter hardiness while MM-104, MM-109 resistant to woolly aphids.

B. Effect of scion on rootstocks

- Scion cv. has strong bearing on root growth pattern of stock plant.
- Budding of 'Red Astrachan' on apple seedlings results in fibrous roots with few tap roots while budding on 'Oldenburg' or 'Faneuse' causes development of 2-3 strong tap roots and no fibrous roots.

Graft incompatibility in fruit crops

- Incompatibility of scion and rootstock.

Types

1. Partial incompatibility e.g. Kinnow grafted on trifoliate orange and mosambi on Troyer, Carrizo and Citrumelo.
2. Localised incompatibility.
   - It can be overcome by interstock.
   - Results from actual contact between stock and scion and can be overcome by inserting mutual compatible interstock in between them.
   - Symptoms- bark cell necrosis, wood discontinuity e.g. Pear and quince graft (need interstock); Apricot and plum graft.
3. Translocalised incompatibility.
   - Can be checked by inserting mutual compatible interstock.

- Symptoms
  - Phloem degeneration due to accumulation of assimilates in scion and disturb water conductivity resulting to starvation of root system and death of scion e.g. Peach scion grafted in plum rootstock.
  - Production of substances by one of graft components (e.g. prunacin- a cyanogenic glucoside in pear-quince combination) toxic to other may impair formation of successful union.

4. Delayed incompatibility.
   - Black line fornation in tree e.g. Walnut grafted on *J. hindsii* or paradox and sapota on *Bassia latifolia*.
   - Paga (*Prunus cerasoides*): Common rootstock of cherry shows delayed incompatibility.
   - Khasi mandarin, Valencia Late, Blood Red and Washington Navel grafted on Pani jamir (*C. limon*) showed delayed incompatibility.

5. SEEDLESSNESS IN HORTICULTURAL CROPS

- Parthenocarpy: Development of fruit without fertilization or pollination and without seeds.
- Term parthenocarpy is coined by Null (1902).
- Stenospermocarpy term coined by Stout (1936).
- Origin of grape stenospermocarpy e.g. Sultanine and Black Manuka.
- Seedlessness in grapes is extensively studied by Dr. H.P. Olmo (1934).
- Stebbins (1958) stated that apomictic condition is recessive to sexuality although polyploidy apomictic show tendency towards dominance.

Types of parthenocarpy

a) Natural/ Obligatory/ Automatic parthenocarpy: Development of seedless fruit due to genetic sterility e.g. Banana, Japanese persimmon, Pineapple.

b) Facultative parthenocarpy: Production of seeded or seedless fruit due to environmental stimulation e.g. Mandarin orange (Clemenules, Satsuma); Sweet orange (Washington Navel Orange); Lime (Tahiti lime - due to triploidy); Pummelo hybrid (Oroblanco); Grape.

c) Vegetativeparthenocarpy: Natural parthenocarpy arises without any stimulation e.g. Apple, Banana, Bread fruit, Pineapple, Fig, Pear, Persimmon.

d) Spontaneous mutant of seedless fruits: Apple, Citrus.

e) Stimulative/ ationemic parthenocarpy i.e. Development of parthenocarpic fruit require an external stimulus e.g. Watermelon, Pear, Himalayan blackberry, Bread fruit, Cacao, Mango (Sindhu), Grape (Black Corianth), Litchi.

f) Stenospermocarpy: Fruits develop from normal pollination and fertilization but abortion of embryo leads seedlessness e.g. Grape (Thompson Seedless, Pusa Seedless, Beauty Seedless), Seedless Jamun.

6. CLASSIFICATION OF FRUIT CROPS

- Biggest family: Rutaceae
- Smallest family: Passifloraceae, Proteaceae and Punicaceae.
- Temperate fruits: Fruit crops growing where winter is distinctly cold, deciduous and undergoes dormancy during winter season.
- Tropical fruits: Plants growing in region between tropic of cancer (23^0 27 N) and tropic of capricon (23^0 27 S latitude).
- Sub-tropical fruits: Fruits crops grown between temperate and tropical climatic conditions.

6.1 Based on botany

A. Simple fruit

Derived from single ovary of one flower.

- *Drupe*: Fleshy, one or more chambered and one or more seeded fruit developing from monocarpellary or syncarpous pistil e.g. Mango, Cashew nut, Charoli, Plum, Peach.
- *Berry*: Fruit derived from superior (sometimes inferior) ovary in which entire ovary wall develops into a fleshy, often juicy and edible pericarp e.g. Banana, Papaya, Grape.
- *Capsule*: Arises out of pistil with either superior or inferior ovary.
- *Achene*: Single seeded, small, dry fruit with seed attached to wall of the ovary at one point.
- *Pome* e.g. Apple, Pear, Quince.
- *Hesperidium* e.g. Citrus.
- *Amphisarca* e.g. Wood apple.
- *Balusta* e.g. Pomegranate.

B. Aggregate fruit

Develop from numerous ovaries of same flower.

- *Etaerio of berries* e.g. Custard apple,
- *Etaerio of druplets* e.g. Blackberry, Longan.

C. Multiple fruit

Produced from ripened ovaries of crowded on same inflorescence.

- *Syconium* e.g. Fig.

- *Sorosis* e.g. Jack fruit, Pineapple, Mulberry, Bread fruit.

Family	Common Name	Botanical name	2n=	Origin	Botanical form of fruit
Monocots					
Aracaceae (Palmae)	Date palm	*Phoenix dactylifera*	36	West Asia	Drupe
	Doum palm	*Hyphaene thebaica*	26	-	
	Peach palm	*Bactris gasipaes*	28	-	
Bromeliaceae	Pineapple	*Ananas comosus*	50 (2x), 75 (3x), 100 (4x)	Brazil	Aggregate berry/ Sorosis
Musaceae	Banana	*Musa paradisica*	22 (2x), 33 (3x), 44 (4x)	Indo-Malaya	Multiseeded berry
	Plantain	*M. acuminata*		Indo-Burma	
Dicots					
Actinidiaceae	Kiwi fruit	*Actinidia deliciosa*	58 (2x) , 174 (6x)	China	Berry
Anacardiaceae	Mango	*Mangifera indica*	40	S-E Asia	Drupe (modified berry)
	Hog plum	*Spondias dulcis*	24	T. America	
	Indian hog plum	*S. pinnata*	24	T. America	
	Cashew nut	*Anacardium occidentale*	42	Brazil	Cotyledon
	Pistachio nut	*Pistachia vera*	30	Iran	Drupe
	Charoli	*Buchanania lanzan*	22	India	Nut
	Marking nut	*Semecarpus anacardium*	-	Tropical Asia	Nut
Annonaceae	Custard apple	*Annona squamosa*	14	West Indies	Etaerio of berry
	Bullock's heart	*A. reticulata*	14	West Indies	
	Sour sop	*A. muricata*	14	S. America	
	Cherimoya	*A. cherimoya*	14	Bolivia	
	Atemoya	*A. atemoya*	14	Man made hybrid	
Apocynaceae	Karonda	*Carissa carandas*	12	India	Berry
	Natal plum	*C. grandiflora*	22	S. Africa	
Boraginaceae (Ehretiaceae)	Lasoda	*Cordia myxa* (syn. *C. dichotoma*)	48	India	Berry
Cactaceae	Dragon fruit	*Hylocereus undatus*	22	Mexico	Berry
	Prickly pear	*Opuntia ficus indica*	88	S. Mexico	Berry

Caricaceae	Papaya	*Carica papaya*	18	Tropical America	Berry
Clusiaceae (Guttiferae)	Kokum	*Garcinia indica* (syn. *G. purpurea*)	48 (2x), 54 (2x)	India	Berry
	Mangosteen	*G. mangostana*	24	S.E. Asia	Berry
Corylaceae (Betulaceae)	Hazelnut	*Corylus avellana*	22	Turkey	Nut
Ebenaceae	Japanese persimmon	*Diospyras kaki*	90 (6x), 60 (4x)	China	Berry
	Mabola persimmon	*D. discolor,D. mabola*			
	Gaub	*D. peregrine*			
	Tendu	*D. tomentosa*			
	American persimmon	*D. virginiana*			
Elaegnaceae	Sea buckthorn	*Hippophae rhamnoides*	24	Europe	Single seeded drupe
Ericaceae	Cranberry	*Vaccinium oxycoccus*	24 (2x)	N. America	Berry
	Blueberry	*Vaccinium corymbosum*	24 (2x), 36 (3x), 48 (4x), 72 (6x)	N. America	Berry
Fabaceae (Leguminosae)	Tamarind	*Tamarindus indica*	24	India	Pod (lomentum)
	Khejri	*Prosopis cineraria*	54	India	-
Fagaceae	Chestnut	*Castanea mollissima*	24	China	Nut
Juglandaceae	Walnut	*Juglans regia*	32	C. Asia	Nut (modified berry)
	Pecan nut	*Carya illinoensis*	32	N. America	Nut
Lauraceae	Avocado	*Persea americana*	24	C. America	Berry
Malpighiaceae	West Indian cherry	*Malpighia punicifolia*	40	Trinidad	Drupe
Malvaceae (Bombacaceae)	Durian	*Durio zibethinus*	56 (2x)	Malaysia	Aril
Moraceae	Jack fruit	*Artocarpus heterophyllus* (syn. *A. integrifolia*)	56 (4x)	Western ghats of India	Sorosis (multiple fruit)
	Aini	*A. hirsuta*	56 (4x)		
	Monkey jack	*A. lakoocha*	56 (4x)		
	Bread fruit	*A. altilis*	56 (2n)	Malaya	Syncarp
	Mulberry	*Morus alba*	28 (2x), 308 (44x)	China	Syncarp

	Edible fig	*Ficus carica*	26	West Asia	Syconium
Myricaceae	Kaphal	*Myrica esculenta*	-	-	-
Myrtaceae	Guava	*Psidium guajava*	22	T. America	Many seeded berry
	Pineapple guava	*Feijoa sellowiana*	22	S. Brazil	
	Malay rose apple	*Syzygium malaccense*	44	Malaya Archipelago	Drupe
	Water rose apple	*S. aqueum*	22	-	Berry
	Rose apple	*S. jambos*	28	Malaya Archipelago & Burma	Drupe
	Jamun	*S. cumini*	40	India	
Oleaceae	Indian olive	*Olea cuspidata*	46	Mediterranean	Drupe
	Olive	*O. europaea*			
Oxalidaceae	Carambola	*Averrhoa carambola*	24	Indonesia	Fleshy berry
Passifloraceae	Passion fruit	*Passiflora edulis*	18	Brazil	Fleshy berry
Phyllanthaceae (Euphorbiaceae)	Aonla	*Emblica officinalis* (syn. *Phyllanthus emblica*)	28	S-E Asia	Capsule (modified berry)
Proteaceae	Macadamia nut	*Macadamia integrifolia*	48	Australia	Nut
Punicaceae (Lythraceae)	Pomegranate	*Punica granatum*	16	Iran.	Balusta (Modified berry)
Rhamnaceae	Ber	*Zizyphus mauritiana*	48 (4x)	Indo-China	Drupe
Rosaceae	Apple	*Malus domestica*	34 (2x)	S-W Asia	Pome without grit cells
	Pear	*Pyrus communis*	34	Western China	Pome with grit cells
	Quince	*Cydonia oblonga* (syn. *C. vulgaris*)	34	Iran & Turkey	Pome
	Loquat	*Eriobotrya japonica*	34	East China	Pome
	Almond	*Prunus communis*	16 (2x)	Central Asia	Drupe (1 seeded stone)
	Apricot	*Prunus armeniaca*	16	China & C. Asia	Drupe
	Peach	*Prunus persia*	16	China	Drupe (1 seeded stone)
	Plum	*Prunus domestica*	16 (2x, Japan);48 (6x, Europe)	China	Drupe (1 seeded stone)

	Raspberry	*Rubus occidentalis*	14	N. America	Etaerio of berries
	Strawberry	*Fragaria x ananassa*	14 (2x), 28 (4x), 56(8x)	France	Etaerio of achenes
	Sweet cherry	*Prunus avium*	16	Asia Minor	Drupe
	Sour cherry	*P. cerasus*	18	West Asia	
Rubiaceae	Noni	*Morinda citrifolia*	44 (2x)	S.E. Asia	Berry
Rutaceae	Bael	*Aegle marmelos*	18 (2x)	India	Amphisarca (multiseeded berry)
	Wood apple	*Feronia limonia*	18	India	
	Mandarin	*Citrus reticulata*	18	N-E India	Hesperidium (modified berry: single enlarged ovary surrounded by lathery peel)
	Sweet orange	*C. sinensis*	18	N-E India	
	Kagzi lime	*C. aurantifolia*	18	Iran	
	Grape fruit	*C. paradisi*	18	South China	
	Lemon	*C. limon*	18	S-E Asia	
	Pummelo	*C. grandis*	18	Malaysia	
	Sweet lime	*C. limettoides*	18	India	
Sapindaceae	Litchi	*Litchi chinensis*	30	South China	Nut
	Rambutan	*Nephelium lappaceum*	22	Malayan Archipelago	Berry
	Longan	*Dimocarpous longan*	20	S. Asia	Berry
	Ackee/ Vegetable brain	*Blighia sapida*	32	Africa	Berry
Sapotaceae	Sapota	*Manilkara acharas*	26 (2x)	South Mexico	Berry
	Khirni	*Manilkara hexandra*	26	S. Asia	
	Mahua	*Madhuca latifolia*	24	Asia	
	Egg fruit	*Pouteria campechiana*	28	T. America	
Solanaceae	Cape gooseberry	*Physalis peruviana*	48 (4x)	Peru	Berry
Tiliaceae	Phalsa	*Grewia subinaequalis* (syn. *G. asiatica*)	36	India	Berry
	Jamaica cherry	*Muntingia calabura*	26	S. America	
Vitaceae	Grape	*Vitis vinifera*	38 (2x)	Western Asia	Berry

6.2 Based on longevity of fruit crops

Life span	Fruit crops
Seasonal	Cape gooseberry, Tree tomato
1-2 years	Pineapple, Banana
4-5 years	Strawberry, Papaya, Cranberry
15-30 years	Raspberry, Passion fruit, Annona, Phalsa
20-40 years	Aonla, Ber, Guava, Orange, Peach, Plum, Pomegranate, Star apple, Rose apple
35-70 years	Apricot, Apple, Coconut, Fig, Palmyra palm
50-100 years	Avocado, Jack fruit, Jamun, Litchi, Mango, Pear, Persimmon, Rambutan
100-300 years	Pecan nut, Walnut
1000 years	Sweet chestnut

6.3 Based on stem morphology

Highly developed stem	Mango, Jackfruit, Walnut, Tamarind
Moderately developed stem	Apple, Litchi, Sapota, Guava
Shrub-like trees	Peach, Pomegranate, Fig, Pummelo, Rose apple
Shrub	Lime, Lemon, Barbadose cherry, Karonda
Semi-shrubs or brambles	Indian hog plum, Blackberry
Vine	Grapes, Passion fruit
Herbaceous perennials	Strawberry, Pineapple, Banana, Papaya
Herbaceous annuals	Cape gooseberry
Ramblers	Cranberry

6.4 Based on fruit morphology

Depending on number of ovaries involved in fruit formation, fruits are usually divided into three groups: simple, aggregate and multiple fruits.

I. Simple fruits: Derived from single or syncarpus pistil of a single flower with or without accessory organ. These are further classified as dehiscent, indehiscent and fleshy type.

   a) Dehiscent: No fruit crops only legumes.

   b) Indehiscent: Hazelnut, Pecannut, Chestnut, Cashewnut, etc.

   c) Schizocarpic: Tamarind (lomentum type).

   d) Fleshy fruits:

II. Aggegate fruits: Derived from numerous ovaries of a single flower (etaerio).

III. Multiple fruits: Derived from fusion of many ripened ovaries and receptacles of many flowers.

6.5 Based on fruit size

Size class on weight basis (g)	Fruit crops
Very light (50)	Cashew nut, Date, Ber, Grape, Karambola, Litchi, Strawberry, Lime, Jamun, Rose apple, Star apple, Cherry, Peach, Plum
Light (50-100)	Lemon, Rambutan, Sapota, Orange, Persimmon
Medium light (100-250)	Apple, Banana, Guava, Bullock heart, Mango (certain varieties), Pear
Medium (250-500)	Mango, Pummelo, Grape fruit
Medium to heavy (500-1000)	Avocado, Coconut, Palmyra palm
Heavy (1000-5000)	Papaya, Pineapple, Soursop, Durian
Very heavy (5000)	Jack fruit

6.6 Based on respiratory behaviour:

- Term 'climacteric rise' was 1st used by Kidd and West (1927).
- Most ethylene sensitive fruits: Strawberry and raspberry.
- In guava some cv. are climacteric e.g. Pedro Sato and others are non-climacteric e.g. Allahabad Safeda.

Climacteric (Sharp rise in respiration harvesting)	Non-climacteric (Steady respiration at the time of after harvesting)
Annona, Apricot, Apple, Avocado, Banana, Bael, Blueberry, Cranberry, Fig, Guava, Jack fruit, Kiwi fruit, Mango, Papaya, Passion fruit, Persimmon, Sapota, Peach, Nectarine, Pear, Plum, Raspberry, Strawberry	Aonla, Ber, Cashew nut, Carambola, Cherry, Citrus (orange, grape fruit), Fig, Grape, Jamun, Kafal, Kinnow, Lemon, Litchi, Loquat, Pineapple, Pomegranate, Phalsa, Prickly pear, Rambutan

6.7 Based on rate of ethylene production

- Threshold level of ethylene in fruits and vegetables is 0.1 ppm (0.1 µl).
- Highest ethylene production: i) Apple - (25-2500 µl/l), ii) Passion fruit- 446-530 µl/l.

Level of ethylene	Rate (µl/Kg/hr)	Examples
Very low	< 0.1	Grape, Citrus(0.1-2.0), Pomegranate
Low	0.1-1.0	Pineapple (0.2-0.4)
Medium	1-10	Mango, Banana (3), Guava, Fig (1-10), Litchi (1-5)
High	10-100	Apple, Papaya, Avocado, Plum, Ber (100), Pear (75-100)
Very high	>100	Passion fruit, Sapota, Apple, Cherimoya (219)

6.8 Based on photoperiodic response

Long day plant	Short day plant	Day neutral plant
Passion fruit, Apple	Strawberry, Pineapple cv. Smooth Cayenne	Papaya, Guava, Banana, Sapota, Olive

6.9 Based on specificity to soil texture

Sandy soil	Loamy soil	Clayey soil
Date palm, Palmyra palm, Coconut, Cashew, Ber, Khirni, Wood apple	Apple, Plum, Citrus, Grapes, Mango, Banana, Papaya, Sapota	Chestnut, Palmyra palm, some species of Jamun & Fig

6.10 Based on soil topography

Semi-arid tropical region	Arid sub-tropical region	Semi-arid temperate region	Arid temperate region
Custard apple, Jackfruit, Tamarind	Fig, Plum, Wood apple, Ber, Aonla	Pecan nut, Chestnut	Walnut, gharis, Oleaster, Chilgoza, Pistachio nut

6.11 Based on salt tolerance (E.C.) limit

Sensitive (0-4 dSm^{-1})	Moderately tolerant (4-6 dSm^{-1})	Tolerant (6-8 dSm^{-1})	Highly tolerant (8-16 dSm^{-1})
Grape fruit, Orange, Lemon, Lime, Avocado, Pear, Apple, Cherry, Plum, Strawberry, Almond	Peach, Papaya, Banana, Grape, Mango, Custard apple, Phalsa	Sapota, Pomegranate, Fig, Olive, Guava, Aonla, Cashewnut	Ber, Jamun, Date palm, Coconut, Khirni

6.12 Based on relative soil pH tolerance

- Oxylophytes: Any plant that tolerates or thrives in acidic soil.

Sensitive (pH 5.5-6.0)	Slightly tolerant (pH 6.0-6.8)	Moderately tolerant (pH 6.8-7.2)	Highly tolerant to alkaline soil (pH 7.2-8.0)
Bael, Fig, Plum, Raspberry, Strawberry, Wood apple, Gooseberry	Apple, Almond, Mango, Citrus, Banana, Guava, apple, Date palm, Papaya, Peach, Kiwi, Cashewnut, Carambola,	Avocado, Jackfruit, Orange, Pineapple, Litchi, Loquat, Longan, Passion fruit, Chestnut, Cranberry,	Aonla, Ber, Custard Guava, Jamun, Olive, Phalsa

6.13 Based on bearing habit

Bearing habit	Fruit crops
Fruit buds borne terminally and giving rise to inflorescene without leaves	Mango, cherry
Fruit buds borne terminally and unfolding to produce leafy shoots which terminate in flower clusters	Apple
Fruit buds borne terminally and unfolding to produce leafy shoots with flower or flower clusters	Guava
Fruit buds borne laterally containing flower parts only and giving rise to inflorescence without leaves	Citrus
Fruit buds borne laterally and unfolding to produce leafy shoots, terminally in flower clusters	Grape, Cashew nut
Fruit buds borne laterally and unfolding to produce leafy shoots with flower clusters in leafy axils	Fig

Terminal		Axillary/ lateral		Mixed
Old season	Current	Old season	Current	Citrus, Carambola,
Mango, Banana, Pineapple, Litchi	Jackfruit, Loquat, Pecan nut, Chestnut	Apple, Avocado, Fig, Pear, Peach, Jamun, Pistachionut, Walnut, Persimmon (1 year)	Custard apple, Grape, Guava, Papaya, Phalsa, Orange, Passion fruit, Plum, Coconut, Kiwi fruit	Pomegranate, Walnut, Cocoa

6.14 Based on flowering habit i.e. photo-thermal requirement (Kozlowski, 1971)

Flowering habit	Fruits
Ever flowering habit	Fig, Papaya
Non-seasonal flowering fruits	Mango, Coconut
Gregarious flowering fruits	Quince
Seasonal flowering fruits	Apple, Guava, Litchi, Pear, Peach, Plum

6.15 Based on type of inflorescence

Type	Fruit crops
A. Racemose	
i) Solitary	• Almond, Apricot, Guava, Peach, Quince, Trifoliate Orange
ii) Raceme	• Blackberry, Gooseberry, Raspberry, Blueberry, Wild cherry, Avocado
iii) Catkin	• Chestnut, Mulberry, Pecan nut, Walnut
iv) Corymbose	• Pear
B. Cymose	
i) Panicle	• Grape, Litchi, Loquat, Mango, Pistachio nut, Cashew nut, Carambola, Rubber
ii) Solitary	• Citrus, Papaya, Persimmon, Phalsa, Sapota, Strawberry
iii) Fasicle	• Ber, Cherry, Plum, Sweet orange
C. Spadix	• Banana, Date palm, Coconut, Arecanut, Oil palm, Palmyra palm
D. Hypanthodium	• Fig

6.16 Based on pollination agents

- Anemophily (wind): Aonla, Coconut, Cashew nut, Chestnut, Date palm, Jack fruit, Papaya, Pomegranate, Sapota, Walnut, Pecan nut, Custard apple.
- Entomophily (insect): Almond, *Annona* spp., Apple, Ber, Cherry, Citrus, Fig, Guava, Litchi, Mango, Pear, Peach, Plum, Strawberry, Tamarind, Oil palm.
- Ornithophily (bird): Banana, Pineapple (Humming bird).
- Myrmecophily (ants): Passion fruit,
- Chiropterophily (bats): Durian and Dragon fruit.
- Hymenopterophily (bees):

- Melittophily (small bees):
- Cantharophily (beetles):
- Malacophily (snails and slugs):
- Phalaenophily (moths):
- Psychophily (butterflies):
- Sphingophily (hawk moth & nocturnal Lepidoptera):

6.17 Based on type of pollination:

Self pollination (Autogamy)	Cross pollination (Allogamy)
Hermaphrodite/ perfect / bisporangiate flowers:	Unisexuality/ dicliny:
i) Cleistogamy: Grape, Sapota, Papaya cv. Sunrise	i) Monoecious: Banana, Pecan nut, Muscadine grape, Walnut, Aonla, Hazelnut, Jack fruit, Tall coconut
ii) Homogamy: Apricot, Citrus, Peach, Phalsa, Dwarf coconut	ii) Dioecious: Papaya, Date palm, *V. rotundifolia*, Kokum, Kiwi fruit, Pistachio nut, Lasoda, Mangosteen, Kaphal, Seabuckthorn, Persimmon
	iii) Gynodioecious: Fig, Papaya.
	iv) Andromonoecious: Mango, Cashew nut

6.18 Based on self incompatibility

A. Homomorphic

i) Sporophytic: Aonla, Mango.

ii) Gametophytic: Apple, Apricot, Almond, Ber, Cherry, Citrus, Loquat, Pineapple, Pear, Plum, Coffee, Cocoa.

B. Type of dichogamy

i) Protandry: *A. muricata*, Passion fruit, Sapota, Walnut, Coconut, Macadamia nut.

ii) Protogyny: Avocado, Banana, Fig, Pomegranate, Plum, All *Annona* spp., Tamarind, Strawberry.

iii) Heterodichogamy: Pistachionut, Pecan nut, Sapota.

iv) Protogynous diurnally synchronous dichogamy (PDSD): Avocado.

v) Duodichogamy: Chestnut, Avocado.

vi) Heterostyly or distyly:

a) Pin type-Litchi, Pomegranate, Sapota.

b) Thrum type- Almond, Carambola, Litchi.

6.19 Based on type of placentation

Type of placentation	Crops
Axile	Banana, Citrus
Marginal	Litchi
Parietal	Papaya
Basal	Ber

6.20 Based on ploidy level

I. Euploidy
   - Exact multiple of haploid (X) chromosome.
   - Chromosome number not exact multiple of basic chromosome mosome (X).

II. Aneuploidy: Not exact multiple of haploid (X) chromosome e.g Guava cv. Aneuploid-82.

Allo-polyploid	Auto-polyploid
1. Allo-tetraploid/Amphidiploid: Mango	1. Autotriploid: Cultivated banana, Tahiti lime, Seedless guava.
2. Allo-hexaploid: European plum	2. Auto-tetraploid: Aonla, Bael, Litchi, Jackfruit, Phalsa, Ber (cv. Umran), Rambutan.
3. Allo-octaploid: Mango cv.	3. Auto-hexaploid: Persimmon, Kiwi fruit.
Vellaicollumban (8x=80), Strawberry.	4. Auto-octaploid: Ber cvs. Gola & Illaichi

6.21 Based on growth curve:

- Growth is maximum during exponential phase.
- Standard growth curve of plants is sigmoidal.
- Fleshy dry drupes represent double sigmoid while dry drupes represent single sigmoid growth curve.

Growth curve	Examples
Single sigmoid	Apple, Avocado, Banana (seeded), Bael, Ber (cvs. Gola, Umran, Kaithali), Carambola, Jack fruit, Jamun, Kagzi lime, Satsuma mandarin, Lemon, Mango, Papaya, Passion fruit, Pear, Pineapple, Pomegranate, Rambutan, Strawberry, Sweet orange, Durian, Jamun, Nutmeg
Double sigmoid	Almond, Aonla, *Annona* spp., Banana (seedless), Ber (cvs. Baramasi, Kadaka, Pewandi, Jogia, Thornless, Sandhura Narnaul), Blueberry, Date palm, Fig, Grape, Guava, Mango (cv. Sindhu), Olive, Persimmon, Raspberry, Sapota, Stone fruits (Apricot, Peach, Plum, Nectarine Cherry), Sweet cherry, Tamarind, Strawberry cv. Reiko
Triple sigmoid	Kiwi fruit

6.22 Based on shade tolerance:

Level	Examples
Highly shade tolerant	Carambola, Bilimbi (cucumber tree), Annonas
Moderately shade tolerant	Banana, Mangosteen, , Rose apple, Cocoa, Tea, Coffee
Highly shade sensitive	Citrus, Guava, Mango, Tamarind
Under polyethylene/ Shade net cultivation	Grape, Strawberry, Sweet orange

6.23 Based on drought tolerance:

Highly tolerant	Karonda, Custard apple, Ber, Wood apple, Aonla, Date palm, Fig, Persimmon, Bael, Flacourtia
Moderately tolerant	Tamarind, Grape fruit, Mango, Lemon, Jackfruit, Sapota
Sensitive	Orange, Papaya, Apple, Banana, Mangosteen

6.24 Based on storage life:

Very perishable (0-4 weeks)	Perishable (4-8 weeks)	Semi-perishable (6-12 weeks)	Low perishable (12-16 weeks)	Very low perishable (>16 weeks)
Apricot, Banana, Berry fruits, Cherry, Fig, Loquat, Mango, Strawberry	Avocado, Grape, Mandarin, Nectarine, Passion fruit, Peach, Pineapple, Plum	Coconut, Oranges	Apple, Grape fruit, Lemon, Pear, Pomegranate	Dry fruits & dry vegetables

6.25 Based on chill sensitive fruits and safe temperature

Temperature (^{0}C)	Products
3	Jujube
4	Avocado (few cvs.), Litchi, Tamarillo
5	Cactus pear, Durian, Guava, Longan, Mandarin, Orange, *Feijoa*
7	Avocado (few cvs.), Olive, Pineapple, Pomegranate
10	Carambola, Lime, Mango, Papaya, Grapefruit, Passion fruit, Rambutan, Water melon, some melons
13	Banana, Breadfruit, Cherimoya, Mangosteen, Jackfruit

6.26 Based on derivation of fruits from various plant tissues (Coombe, 1976):

i) Peduncle: Fig, Pineapple, Cashew apple

ii) Accessory tissue: Apple, Pineapple

iii) Receptacle: Strawberry

iv) Pericarp: Grape, Jackfruit (bulb & fleshy perianth)

v) Mesocarp: Peach, Jujube, Tamarind, Nectarines.

vi) Endoderm interlocular tissue: Orange

vii) Outer layer of testa: Pomegranate

viii) Aril: Mangosteen

6.27 Based on edible portion:

Fruit crops	Edible part (s)
Custard apple, Avocado, Ber, Date palm	Pericarp
Grape	Pericarp & placenta
Mango, Papaya, Sapota, Passion fruit, Mulberry, Tamarind, Charoli	Mesocarp
Banana, Aonla, Apricot	Mesocarp & endocarp
Olive, Peach, Plum, Persimmon, Phalsa, Cherry, Jamun, Karonda	Mesocarp & epicarp
Cashew apple	Fleshy peduncle
Litchi, Rambutan, Durian	Juicy/ fleshy aril
Fig	Fleshy receptacle
Apple, Pear, Quince, Strawberry, Loquat	Fleshy thalamus
Guava	Thalamus & pericarp
Bael, Wood apple	Succulent placenta
Pineapple	Thalamus
Jack fruit	Bracts, perianth & seeds
Citrus	Juicy placenta hairs
Pomegranate, Rambutan	Juicy seed coat (aril)
Pecan nut, Pistachio nut, Cashew nut, Almond, Walnut	Cotyledons
Macadamia nut	White cream coloured kernel or embryo

6.28 Based on colour compounds:

Flesh colour	Pigment	Fruit crops
Orange	β-carotene	Pineapple, Mango cv. Amrapali
Orange	Caricaxanthin	Papaya
Orange-yellow	Flavonoids	Peach, Papaya, Orange, Tangerine
Red	Lycopene	Papaya, Guava cv. Arka Kiran
Red-purple	Anthocyanin	Grape, Pomegranate, Blackberry, Raspberry, Blueberry, Phalsa, Jamun, Strawberry
Pink-red	Lycopene	Grapefruit
Green	Chlorophyll	Guava
Yellow	Xanthophyll	Guava
Yellow	Quercetin & quercitron	White and red grapes
Yellow-green	Lutein & zeaxanthin	Avocado
Yellow with white to cream	Flavonoids	Dragon fruit
Deep purple + red violet	β-cyanin	

6.29 Based on aromatic and volatile compounds:

- Aroma of most of fruits is due to esters.

Fruit	Aromatic compound	Volatile compound (aroma/ flavour)
Almond	-	Benzaldehyde
Apple	Hexanal (green)	Ethyl-2-methyl butyrate (ripe); Pentyl valerate
Banana	Hexanal (green); Eugenol (ripe); Isopentanol (over ripe)	Isopentyl acetate (ripe)
Cherry	-	Methyl anthrinilate
Durian	-	Hydrogen sulphide
Grape	Muscat flavour	Methyl anthranilate (foxiness)
Jackfruit	Isopentyl isovalerate & butyl isovalerate	-
Lemon	Citral	-
Sweet orange	Valencene	Citral
Mango	Peach like flavour (lactone)	Terpenes, Flavanones
Oranges	-	Octyl acetate
Papaya	-	Linalool
Peach	-	Lactones
Pineapple	-	Methyl propionate esters
Raspberry	1-(p-Hydroxyphenyl)-3-butanone	-
Strawberry	-	Ethyl butyrate
Mangosteen	-	Hexyl acetate
Tamarind	-	2-acetyl-furan & 5-methyl-furfural

6.30 Based on bitterness due to flavonoids and terpenoids:

- Almond, peach and cherry kernels- amygdalin (a glycoside gives bitter taste).
- Raw olive fruits- presence of glycoside (oleuropein).

Fruits	Flavonoids	Terpenoids
Orange & lemon	Hesperidin (tasteless glycoside)	Neral and geranial
Grapefruit	Naringenin & Limonin (bitter taste)	Nootakatone

6.31 Based on acid present in fruit crops:

a) Citric acid: All types of berries, Apricot, Mango, Citrus, Guava, Pear, Persimmon, Pineapple, Strawberry.

b) Malic acid: Apple, Banana, Cashew apple, Cherry, Grape, Litchi, Kokum, Mango, Melon, Plum, Peach, Pear.

c) Tartaric acid: Grape, Tamarind.

d) Chlorogenic acid: Mulberry (leaves), Apricot, Cherry, Peach, Plum.

e) Oleic acid: Olive.

f) Isocitric acid: Blackberry.

6.32 Based on pectin and acid content:

Rich in pectin and acid	Wood apple, Jamun, Grape, Sour guava, Lemon, Sour orange, Sour plum, Sour Crab apple, Loquat
Rich in pectin and low acid	Unripe banana, Fig, Sour cherry, Ripe guava, Pear, Peel of orange & Grape fruit
Low in pectin and rich acid	Pineapple, Sweet cherry, Sour peach, Sour apricot
Low in pectin and acid	Pomegranate, Raspberry, Ripe apricot, Ripe peach

6.33 Predominating biochemical constituents of some stone fruits:

Biochemical constituent	Apricot	Cherry	Peach	Plum
Sugars	Sucrose	Glucose & fructose	Sucrose	Glucose & fructose
Organic acid	Citric acid	Malic acid	Malic acid	Malic acid
Pigments	Carotenoids	Ddi-glucoside of cynidinkeracyanin chloride	Anthocyanin (cyanidin-3-monoglucoside)	Anthocyanin (cyanidin-3-rutinoside)
Flavouring compound	Mycene, Limonene, etc.	Methyl anthranilate & methyl salicylate	Lactones	Benzaldehyde
Vitamin	Vit. C	Vit. C	Vit. C	Vit. C
Phenol	Chlorogenic acid & P-coumaric acid	Chlorogenic acid	Chlorogenic acid, catechin, cynidin	Neo-chlorogenic acid
Minerals	Potassium	Potassium	Potassium	Potassium

7. ACTINIDIACEAE

7.1 Kiwi fruit

- Eulogized as 'Chinese gooseberry or China's miracle fruit or Horticultural wonder of New Zealand or Yang-tao'.
- National symbol of New Zealand.
- Commercially grown in New Zealand, Italy, USA, China, Japan, Australia, France, Chile & Spain.
- 1st introduced and planted as an ornamental plant in Lal Bagh botanical garden, Bengaluru.
- Leading producer: Italy.
- Extensively cultivated in H.P., U.P., J & K, Sikkim, Meghalaya, Arunachal Pradesh, Nilgiri hills.
- State having largest producer of Kiwi fruit in India: Manipur.
- An agricultural engineer from Arunachal Pradesh Mrs. Tage Rita is India's 1st kiwi wine brewer.

- Successfully cultivated at 800-1500 m MSL and rainfall of 150 cm/ annum.
- Female flowers have infertile pollen.
- Deciduous and functionally dioecious vine having large heart shaped leaves.
- Flowers: Small, off-white & fragrant.
- Fruits: Brown, flattened, ovoid (upto 5 cm), furry (hairy) fruits are thin skinned and firm with luscious green pulp containing many tiny black seeds around the centre.
- Food value: Very rich in vit. C.
- Skin is good source of flavonoids.
- Flower colour: Creamy white to yellowish.
- Pollination agent: Honey bee.
- Kiwi requires 700-800 chilling hours (< 7^0C) to break rest period.
- High temperature (> 35^0C) causes leaf scorching.
- Cultivation needs atleast 240 frost free days.
- Days required for bud break to flowering: 50 days (at high temperature) to 80 days (at lower temperature).
- Plant can withstand -12^0C temperature when fully dormant.
- Propagation method: Seeds and hard wood, semi-hard wood and soft wood cuttings (commercial propagation).
- Seeds require 10 weeks stratification at 4.4^0C
- Seed germination: Seed soaking in 2500-5000 ppm GA_3 for 24 h.
- Hard wood cutting in January-February with IBA @ 500 ppm.
- Semi-hard wood cuttings in July with IBA @ 4000-5000 ppm.
- Soft wood cuttings root easier & earlier in mist chamber than hard wood cuttings. IBA + NAA @ 2500 ppm each is used and 70-75% success is achieved.
- Ideal methods of grafting: Whip and tongue grafting in January-February on kiwi seedlings.
- In 'T' and chip budding: Highest bud take (95%) during mid-February.
- Chip budding performed in 1st fortnight of July and September gives highest bud take.
- Scion sticks can be stored at 4^0C in refrigerator.
- Pollination agent: Honey bees.
- Major factor affecting fruit development: Inadequate pollination.
- Hand pollination in early morning results in more number of seeds per ovary, longer and heavier fruits compared with bee pollination.
- Flowers that open earlier have longer ovary and set larger seeds leading to larger fruits.

- Fruit softening is retarded by use of ethylene absorbents during storage for 6 months without refrigeration.
- Type of supporting structure for training: Kniffin or T-bar or Telephone or Pergola.
- Planting distance varies according to variety and system of training.
- Planting distance: T-bar: 4m x 5-6 m & for pergola 6 m x 6m.
- Growth and fruiting habit: Only basal 3-6 buds of current season's growth are productive.
- Male and female vines are trained and pruned in same manner.
- After bloom, male vines are pruned more severely than female vines.
- Heading back of laterals is done during dormant season retaining 8-10 buds.
- Pruning cycle comprises:
  a) Summer pruning means shortening back of fruiting arms to develop side shoots and thinning out of criss-cross branches. Fruits are borne on side shoots.
  b) Dormant or hard pruning means cutting back of fruiting laterals of 2 vegetative buds and completed by mid-February each year.
- With summer pruning, pinching the terminal portion bearing shoot at petal fall improves fruit size.
- Winter pruning is restricted to maintain fruiting arms, lateral growth of old fruiting arms or spurs to three different lengths.
- Hand thinning intensity retains 2-6 flowers/ fruitlets per fruiting lateral.
- Chemical thinning agent: NAA @ 50-100 ppm.
- Planting ratio for commercial orchard: 1 male: 6-8 female.
- Interplanting of Chinese gooseberry as male plants can be used for fruit production.
- Group of 3-4 colonies of honey bees at the end of each block of 0.5-0.7 ha area is advisable.
- Total phenotypic gender expression: 6 types.
- Gender change is due to bud mutation in a mature male vine.
- Kiwi requires high Cl because its deficiency adversely affects growth of shoots and roots.
- Fruit maturity is earlier at lower altitude and later at higher altitude due to temperature variation.
- Harvesting season: October-December.
- Fruits having 6.2^0 brix are ideal for harvesting.
- Larger fruit berries are harvested first.
- Use overhead sprinklers for frost protection.
- No. of plants/ ha: 550.
- Yield: 20 T/ha.
- Major problems in cultivation: Sunscald and heat stress.

- At ambient temperature, fruit firmness decreases after 4 hours while in CA storage after 6 months.
- Highly susceptible to residual herbicides viz. Bromocil, Terbacil, Chlorthiamid & Dichlobeint.
- Fruits can be stored in good condition without refrigeration up to 8 weeks.
- Cold storage conditions: At -0.6 to 0^0C for 4-6 months.
- CPPU @ 500 ppm as dip treatment two weeks after petal fall enhances fruit wt, size, yield and proportion of 'A' grade fruit.
- Value added products: Fruits make a soothing lip balm. Juices, jams and jellies also prepared.

Species:

Botanical name	Features
Actinidia chinensis var. *deliciosa*	Hexaploid; available in India
Actinidia chinensis var. *deliciosa*	Hexaploid (2n=6x=174); available in India
A. chinensis var. *chinensis*	Diploid (2n=2x=58); available in India
A. chinensis var. *hispida*	Hexaploid (2n=6x=174)
A. chinensis var. *setosa*	-
A. arguta	1. Know as'... 'Siberian kiwi or baby kiwi or Tara vine or hardy kiwi: Self fertile; deeply toothed leaves, fragrant; white flowers with purple anthers; fruits green, sweet & insipid in taste; copious sap is drinkable; cold tolerant. 2. Issai: Self fertile veriety has hairless fruits.
A. kolomikta	Less vigorous; large oblong leaves; tolerates shade; single white flowers are sweetly perfumed; bear long, yellowish sweet berries & tolerant to cold
A. polygama	Native of Japan; large heart shaped leaves; white fragrant flowers; yellow coloured edible fruits & tolerant to cold

Varieties

- Jenny: Self fertile, very high yielding (90 kg/ vine), susceptible to cold.

Name	Breeding method	Features
Staminate (pollinizer) cultivars		
Tomari	-	Flowers in cluster of 5; late flowering; good pollinizer for cv. Hayward & Monty.
Motus	-	-
Matua	-	Short hairs on peduncle; early flowering; susceptible to cold
Pistillate cultivars		
Allison	-	Prolific cultivar; bear only female flower; fruits tapering; low in ascorbic acid; sweet taste; most suitable for Himachal Pradesh
Monty	-	Prolific cultivar; late maturing; oblong fruits; require thinning; high in acidity; medium in sugar content; most suitable for Himachal Pradesh

Abbott	-	Early flowering & maturing, very sweet in taste; oblong fruits covered with dense fruits; low in ascorbic acid content; low chilling requirement
Hayward	Chance seedling developed by 'Hayward Wright'	Shy bearing & borne single; tendency of biennial bearing, late maturing and more suitable to higher altitude (needs winter rest of 800 h for 0-7^{0}C); most popular in world; susceptible to cold hardiness
Bruno	-	Very heavy bearer; rich in vit. C; best stigma disposition (i.e. all stigmas close to stamen) for bee pollination; longest among all cultivars; suitable for lower altitude; tapering stem end; low chilling requirement
Wilkin Spur	Bud sport of Hayward	-

Grading system

- Grade A: >70g.
- Grade B: 40-70g.

Diseases, pests and disorders:

- Crown gall (*Agrobacterium tumefaciens*): Major disease.
- Armillaria root rot (*Armillaria novae-zelandia*): Spray 1% Bordeaux mixture.
- Leaf spot (*Alternaria* spp.):
- Sclerotinia rot (*Sclerotinia sclerotiorum*): Damp weather is congenial for its growth.
- Storage rot (*Botrytis cinerea*): Major storage disease.
- Ripe rot (*Botryosphaeria dothidea*):
- Bacterial leaf blight (*Pseudomonas viridiflava*): Infects leaves and flowers.
- Brown headed leaf roller (*Ctenopseustis obliquana*):
- Greedy scale (*Hemiberlesia rapax*):
- Passion vine hopper (*Scolypopa australtis*): Cause significant loss.
- Two spotted mite (*Tetranychus urticae*):
- Root knot nematode: Cause severe damage.
- Flats: Improper pollination.
- Sunscald and heat stress: Major problems in cultivation.
- Fruit piercing moth (*Oraesia fullonia*): Major pest.
- Highly susceptible to residual herbicides viz. Bromocil, Terbacil, Dichlobenit and Chlorthiamid.

8. ANACARDIACEAE (POISON IVY FAMILY)

8.1 Mango

- Eulogized as 'King of tropical fruits or National fruit of India or Pride fruit of India or Ambasidor of Indian fruits or Choicest fruit of India or King of fruits in India or Pride of garden or Health promoting fruit or Bathroom fruit or Symbol of love'.
- Area under mango cultivation in world: 4.72 million ha.

- Hiuen Tsang: 1st foreigner to bring mango to the notice of outside world.
- Photographs of cv. Kesar have appeared on special cover and postage stamp by Indian Post's & Telegraph, Govt. of India released during 2021.
- 1st introduced in Brazil.
- Head quarter of International Mango Registration Society: IARI, New Delhi.
- In India, there are 7 Centers of diversity comprising native land races, local selections and elite cultivars (Yadav and Rajan, 1993).
- Golden period of mango cultivation: Mughal period.
- Akbar the Great (1555-1605) planted 1.0 lakh mango trees (Lakhi Bagh) in Darbhanga (District. Bihar).
- Central Mango Research Station (CMRS) was established in 1972 at Lucknow, later renamed as Central Institute of Horticulture for Northern Plains (CIHNP) in 1984 and Central Institute of Sub-tropical Horticulture (CISH) in 1995.
- Flowers yield tannins (15%), otto (*mango attar*) & have curative properties to treat diarrhoea and chronic dysentery.
- Bark yields mangiferine & tannins (16-20%) useful against diphtheria & rheumatism.
- Stem and trunk exude gum & wood has variety of uses.
- Characteristic feature of Anacardiaceae: Resinous canals.
- Adapted to tropical and sub-tropical climate.
- Cannot be grown on commercial scale in areas above 600 m.
- Major exporter in the world: Mexico.
- Major importer from India: UAE, UK, USA, Kuwait.
- Major exporters: Mexico (14.1%), Peru (12.1%), Brazil (11.4%), Thailand (11.4%), India (5%), Spain (3.5%), Pakistan (2.6%).
- India's share in total world's production: 50%.
- Share of U.P. in countries total mango production: 23.47%.
- Average productivity of mango in U.P. (1-1.25 t/ha).
- In USA, mangoes are acidic and used for juice purpose.
- Productivity is highest in Brazil (15.6 t/ha), Indonesia, Mexico, Pakistan (10.5 tha), India (7 t/ha).
- Largest mango producing states: Andhra Pradesh, Uttar Pradesh, Bihar.
- Average productivity of cv. Alphonso in Konkan region is 2.5 T/ha.
- Mango occupies 37% of area.
- Temperature, rainfall, wind velocity and altitude influence growth and fruiting.
- Cannot stand severe frost.
- High temperature accompanied by low humidity and high winds affect trees adversely.
- Dry period before blossoming is conducive to profuse flowering.

- Rains during flowering interferes with pollination and cause damage to ripening fruits.
- Strong winds/ cyclones during fruiting season blows away the crop completely.
- Mango belt: Lucknow region.
- Availability of mango in India: March to mid-August.
- Mango flowers and matures first in South India (at Kanyakumari, Tamil Nadu in January) followed by Central and North-West India (at Uttar Pradesh in July).
- Two crops are taken in Kanyakumari.
- Cultivation should be avoided in black soil.
- Neelum mango is available for 10 months i.e. April-August in Theni district of Tamil Nadu.
- Longevity of mango seeds: Normal 30 days (4-5 weeks) & maximum up to 80 days.
- Viability of stone can be increased by storing in polyethylene bags with charcoal, vermiculite and saw dust.
- Composition of unripe fruits: 90% moisture, 0.7% proteins, 8.8%-CHO, 0.1% fats and minerals (Ca, Fe, P, carotenes, riboflavins & ascorbic acid) 3 mg/100 g.
- Ripe mango is rich in Mg, K followed by Na and P. It gives 74 Kcal/ 100 g energy.
- Mango stone i.e. kernel contain 9.5% protein and 8-10% fat.

Varietal composition and variations

- Tannins in flesh (0.16%) & skin (0.105%) is responsible for astringency.
- Moisture (70.2-83%), TSS (12.9-20.8%), crude proteins (0.38-0.62%), ash content (0.49-0.58%), total sugars (10-17.3%) on fresh weight basis.
- Essential amino acids (alanine, aspartic acid, lysine, leucine, cysteine, arginine & methionine) accounts for 10-40 mg/ 100 g of edible pulp.
- Fruit weight ranges from 100-670 g and pulp percentage between 53-86.
- Carotenoid pigments, beta carotene increase with ripening and vit. C registers sharp fall.
- Green mangoes contains folic acid, thiamin, & riboflavin.
- Optimum temperature for growth: 23.8-26.6^{0}C.
- Temperature <12 and > 34^{0}C is dangerous for crop growth.
- Good varieties have 20% TSS but cvs. Saheb Pasand (27.8^0 Brix) followed by Xavier (24.8^0 Brix) have highest TSS.
- Chloride containing fertilizers are toxic.
- Most popular method of planting: Square method.
- Training is done in 2-3 year old plants.
- Heading back is done in November-December.
- Mango stone if stored at 5-8^{0}C loose complete viability after 20 days.

- 1st attempt to introduce the mango into the USA came in 1833.
- 1st consignment of mango cvs. exported to Japan: Langra and Chausa.
- Parameters suggested to predict rootstock vigour: Stomatal count, chlorophyll fractions, leaf area, dry matter, moisture content and phenolic content.
- Phenolic contents and bark percentage have significant negative correlation with vigour while chlorphyll fractions have significant positive correlation with vigour.
- Stomata count/ unit area: Good indication of tree size e.g. Kalapadi (8.93), Taimuria (9.44), Dashehari (17.68).
- Epicotyl grafting, Softwood grafting, stool layering are easy techniques to multiply selected varieties.
- The Portuguese introduced grafting technique.
- Inarch grafting: Most popular in south India. It was was suggested by S.K. Mukherjee.
- Veneer grafting: Most popular in north India.
- Softwood grafts are raised in 10 x 14 inch size 200 gauge black polybags.
- Cashew seedlings reported to be graft compatible with mango scions and mango fruit on cashew rootstock were almost double in size of normal fruit with smaller seeds and free from fibre.
- *In vitro* propagation for somatic embryogenesis: Nucellus is best explants having 83% success.
- Most ideal method for top working: Side grafting.
- Bottom heat root technique: Developed by Reddy and Majumder (1975) at IARI, New Delhi.
- Ratio of edible to non-edible part: 3 : 4.
- South Indian varieties: Polyembryonic, true to type seedlings.
- North Indian varieties: Monoembryonic, vegetative propagation is needed.
- In polyembryonic varieties, the seedlings emerge from nuceller embryo.
- Polyembryonic rootstocks impart better vigour to scion compared to monoembronic.
- Monoembryonic varieties may revert to polyembryony under different sets of soil and climatic conditions.
- Single tap root is indication of monoembryony.
- More than one tap root with equal number of shoots means variety is polyembryonic.
- Uniformity in colour of emerging leaves of seedlings is an indication of nucellar origin.
- Nucellar seedlings can be distinguished from the zygotic seedling on the basis of their greater vigour one month after germination.
- Regular bearing habit: Shoot growth on the fruiting twig in the same season of fruiting and emergence of new growth flushes, simultaneously with fruiting or immediately after harvest.

- Maximum number seedlings originate from single polyembryonic seed: 30 (normally 3-8).
- Red blush colour of mango: Anthocyanin.
- 60-90 leaves are sufficient for development of one fruit.
- The florigenic promoter, synthesized in leaves, determines flowering in mango.
- Floral differentiation and inflorescence expansion takes place simultaneously.
- Vegetative bud is narrower and more sharply pointed at apical end than fruit bud.
- Pollen production is higher in late flush than in early flush and mean fruit set is negligible in early flush.
- High temperature during panicle development leads to more number of perfect flowers.
- Low temperature during panicle development leads to less number of perfect flowers i.e. more number of male flowers.
- Mango panicle contains both male and hermaphrodite flowers.
- Average percentage of hermaphrodite flowers: 20.
- No. of flowers/ panicle: 1000-6000.
- Sex ratio (male: perfect flowers): Arka Puneet (13:1), Kesar (11:1), Alphonso, Sindhu, Ratna (4:1), Amrapali, Mallika (3.5:1),
- Bisexual/ perfect flowers: Highest in Langra (69.8%) and lowest in Rumani (0.47%), Dashehari (30.6%), Chausa (42.9%), Bangalora (6.6-21%), Mulgoa (5.07-8.44%), Baneshan (3.67%), Bombay Green (9.2%), Himsagar (8.4%), Neelum (16-56%), Alphonso (10%), Fazli (15%), Pairi (32.5%).
- Fruit set in shy bearing cvs.: 0.1%.
- Pollination agents: House fly (*Musca domestica*), *Melipona* sp. (small Dipterous fly) and *Syrphidae* sp. (kind of hover fly), Stingless bees (*Trigona biroi*), honey bees (*Apis cerena*, *A. mellifera, A. florea, A. dorsata*), *Eristalinus arvorum* and *Chrysomya megacephala*.
- Caging technique was standardized by Sharma *et al*. (1972) at IARI, New Delhi.
- Growing points of panicles serves as active sink, monopolizing the supply of metabolites and leads to its tip bearing habit.
- 'Pinching off' of terminal bud is practiced in Amrapali.
- Translocation of phosphorus is involved in alternate bearing.
- Differentiation and development of flower buds starts from December and overs by mid March.
- Period between floral initiation and anthesis: 4 weeks.
- In north India, flower bud differentiation takes place in August while in tropical and sub-tropical India during early October and reaches peak at November.

- Fruit bud differentiation (FBD) in India: During autumn & early winter i.e. October-December.
- FBD in cv. Baramasi: Twice in a year (May-June and September-October). It is a hereditary character and in cvs. Langra, Dashehari, Rumani, Totapuri Red Small and Brindabani (October-January).
- Fruit bud differentiation is not influenced by photoperiodic condition.
- It takes a fortnight for tiny bud to open into flower.
- Cv. Safeda Malihabad contains 13 amino acids.
- Free amino acids i.e. glycine, alanine, serine and threonine are higher before FBD.
- Argenine and phenyl alanine level increase in differentiated buds as they develop.
- Trifactor hypothesis by Kulkarni (2004) explains flowering beaviour based on hormonal regulation.
- The most noticeable impact of climate change: Erratic flowering.
- Severe pruning in old mango trees is advised to improve copper and zinc status in floral and non-floral parts.
- Smudging i.e. smoking the tree, is a special cultural operation to induce offseason or early flowering in Philippines.
- Causes of floral malformation: North Indian conditions, fluctuation in temperature during flowering.
- Temperature has strong environmental stimulus in flowering.
- Intermittent rains disturb flush in mango.
- Flowering is suppressed by gibberellins.
- Vivipary occurs in autumn mango cv. Kesar.
- 'Desapping' is practiced in India.
- Optimum temperature during pollination and fertilization: 20^0C.
- Stigma receptivity is upto 72 h- 5 days after anthesis.
- Anthesis time: 9-10 AM and completed by afternoon.
- Maximum pollen grain germination: Pollination performed between 10 AM to 12 noon on day of anthesis.
- Pollen viability is upto 10-20 days at ambient temperature. It is highest in Chausa (94.3%), Krishnabhog (91.4%), Langra (90.8%).
- Time required for pollen germination: 1 ½ h.
- Like fruit, the mango seed also show sigmoid growth.
- Branching pattern: Sylleptic.
- Specific gravity is the pivotal maturity index for mango.
- Maturity indices:
  - Slight colour development of the shoulder or fullness of the shoulders;

- º Change in colour of pedicel from green to brown;
- º Growth of fibers on the stone/ corrugations;
- º Flow of latex from stalk i.e. fast drying latex;
- º Computation of heat units or cumulative degree days or summation of days taken from flowering to maturity (12-16 weeks after fruit set i.e. 110-125days);
- º Tapka stage;
- º Specific gravity: Alphonso, Pairi (1.01 to 1.02); Dashehari (<1.0);
- º Appearance of bloom (i.e. opening of lenticels) on fruit surface.
- º Pressure test reading of 2 kg/cm^2.
- º Starch: acid ratio: 4 or more.

- Foliar application of 4% Urea during March-April for higher yield.
- Spray of Elsystin 0.1% and Folic acid @ 0.20% increases fruit set.
- Methyl bromide and Methyl formate: Inhibit ripening of mango.
- Prevention of pre-harvest fruit drop: Alar @ 100 ppm or 2,4-D @ 20 ppm, NAA @ 200 ppm.
- Existance of self sterility in cv. Dashehari 1st time reported in 1962 by Singh *et al*.
- Cold storage conditions: 10-12^{0}C for 85-90% R.H. for mature fruit 6-7^{0}C & for ripened fruit 20^{0}C.
- CA storage conditions: 10-15^{0}C at 3-7% O_2, 5-8% CO_2.
- Chilling injury in mango: <8^{0}C.
- Temperature for hydrocooling: 12-15^{0}C.
- Mango leather is called '*Am Paper*'.
- Mango pulp has minimum 12% TSS.
- Artificial ripening of mango is induced by ethrel.
- Amount of ethylene gas generated during ripening of Alphonso fruits: 0.02 to 0.18 ppm.
- Cultar inhibits gibberellin biosynthesis, restricts the vegetative phase and increases reproductive phase.
- 'Cultar' @ 4-5 g/tree is recommended for regular bearing.
- Pallet packaging is done in mango.
- Use of paper bags (25 cm x 20 cm), 1 month after fruit set is recommended.
- DIVA and Flora map have been generated for mapping biodiversity in mango.
- In somatic hybridization, nucellus tissue is used along with GA_3 + 6-BAP.
- Young and unripe fruits have acidic taste and are utilized for culinary purposes as well as for preparing pickles, chutneys & *amchur*.

- Ripe fruits are utilized in preparing squash, nectar, jam, mango leather, toffee, cereal flakes, powder & baby food.
- Mango slices and canned pulp cater the needs of consumers during off season.
- Amchur/ Acidulant spice: Dehydrated product from unripe mango flesh in the form of peeled slices or powder used for acidification of curries.
- Value added products: Cereal flakes, custard powder, juice, juice powder, nectar, leather, jam, wine.
- Starch obtained from kernels is used in textile, jute, paper industry.
- Neelum, Mulgoa and Pairi could be stored for 9-12 months using frozen technique.
- Best temperature for ripening of cold stored fruits: 15.5-21.0^{0}C and takes 6 days to ripen.
- EMS (1.5%) and NMU (0.05%): Effective dose for Dashehari and Neelum.
- Irradiation beyond 5 Kr is lethal.
- LD_{50} of ã-rays for Neelum (3.9 Krad), Dashehari (2.9 Krad) and Mallika (2.4 Krad).
- Pre-selection criteria for dwarfness:
  - Higher phloem: xylem ratio (> 1.0= least vigorous, 0.6-1.0 medium and <0.6 = most vigourous).
  - Higher phenolics in apical bud.
  - Lower stomatal density.
- Requirements for getting phytosanitory certificate: Farm registration under MangoNet, global GAP certificate, packhouse recommended by APEDA, certificate of free from insecticide residues, free from fruit fly, stone weevil, mealy bugs, treatment with vapour heat treatment (VHT), etc.
- In 2007, USA accepted import of irradiated Indian mangoes.

Species

- Name arbor *Mangifera* (tree producing mango) was 1st used by Bontius in 1658 and *M. indica* in 1753 by Linnaeus.
- Seven centres of diversity are recognized in India with maximum diversity located in humid tropical regions.
- Edible fruits of relatively inferior fruit quality: *M. sylvatica*, *M. foetida*, *M. odorata*, *M. caesia*, *M. altissima*, *M. grifith*, *M. cochinchinensis*, *M. langinifera*, *M. pajang*, *M. longipes*, *M. macrocarpa*, *M. pentandra*, *M. zeylanica*.
- Occurrence of wild forms of *M. indica* and allied species originate through amphidiploidy.
- Morphological features used for classification: Flower disc, fertile stamen, labyrinthine seed or not.

- Most recent classification of genus *Mangifera*: Kostermand and Bompard (1993). As per them, mango contains 69 species. Most of species included in 2 sub-genera *Mangifera* (47 species) and *Limus* (11 species) with another 11 species occupying an uncertain position.
- Four sections of genus *Mangifera*: *Marchandara* (01 species), *Euantherae* (3 species), *Rawa* (9 species) and *Mangifera* (34 species).
- Mango species having Indian origin: *M. indica*, *M. andamanica*, *M. camptosperma*, *M. sylvatica*, *M. khasiana*.
- Endangered mango species: *M. flava*, *M. cochinchinensis*, *M. reba*.
- Wild mangoes and *M. sylvatica*: Reported in North-Eastern parts of India.
- Natural hybridization occurred between *M. indica* and *M. sylvatica*.
- *M. andamanica*: Reported in Andaman group Islands.
- *M. zeylanica* (Etamba): Reported in Sri Lanka.

Features	**Species**
Distinctive taste (white pulp, sweet, fragrant)	*M. caesia* var. *wani*
Fruits peeled like banana, endemic & ornamental tree (largest fruit (20 cm dia. & rose-red blossoms)	*M. pajang*
Good parent for breeding free-stone mangoes	*M. similis*
Completely free from fibre (i.e. fibreless)	*M. magnifica*
Off season bearing habit	*M. rufocostata*, *M. swintonioides*
Twice a year fruiting & hence good parent for crossing	*M. indica* var. *mekongensis*
Rootstock for water-logged condition	*M. decandra*, *M. inocarpoides*
Labyrinthine type seed; rootstock for undulated soils & water-logged condition	*M. gedebe*
Rootstock for water-logged condition	*M. grifith*
Rootstock for salinity tolerance	*M. zeylanica*
Rootstock for undulated soils & resistant to anthracnose	Indo-Chinese originated species *M. laurina*
Bear tetramerous flowers & resistant to leaf hopper	*M. altissima*
Resistant to fruit fly	*M. camptosperma*, *M. andamanica*
Highest TSS (21.7^0 Brix)	*M. odorata*
Small fruits, purple or black coloured fruits, distinctive taste & prolific bearer; found in Kalimantan, Indonesia	*M. casturi*
Restricted to mountain region of 1000-1700 m MSL	*M. dongnaiensis* from Vietnam
Polyembryonic, good fruit quality	*M. sylvatica*
Small & narrow leaves	*M. khasiana*
Good quality fruits	*M. foetida*, *M. caesia*, *M. torgenda*
Plum mango	*Bouea oppositifolia*
Five stamens, good pollinizer & endangered	*M. pentandra*
Rare species & endemic to Phillipines	*M. merrillii*
Endangered & flowering occurs once in every 5-10 years	*M. lagenifera*
Highly astringent fruits	*M. foetida*

Rootstocks

Polyembryonic (indigenous): Olour, Goa Kasargod, Salem, Pahutan, Kurukkan, Nileshwar Dwarf, Ambalavi, Moovandan, Mylepalium, Nekkare, K-2

Polyembryonic (exotic): Cambodiana, Carabao, Cecile, Corazon, Higgins, Kitchner, Paho, Pahutan, Peach, Apricot, Turpentine, Pico, Starch, Sabre, Saigon, Samini, Simmonds, Strawberry (Philippines), Kensington (Australia)

Monoembryonic: Rumani, Dashehari, Florigon

1. Bahaduran, Kurrukan, Moovandan, Nekkere, Olour:Salt tolerant;
2. Muvandan, Chausa, Olour: Very vigorous;
3 Vellaicollumban: Allooctaploid/ allopolyploid (2n=8x=80):Dwarfing for Alphonso & Dashehari;
4. Bappakai: Best for Neelum, Dashehari;
5. Kalapadi, Ambalavi, Belkhas, Parikhas: Dwarf;
6 Totapuri Red Small & Olour: Dwarf;
7. K-2: Dwarf
8. '13/1'from Isreal: Tolerant to calcareous soils & salinity & alkanity;
9. Naomi from Israel:Smooth skin & red pigmented;
10. Gomera-1, 2, 3 from Spain: Salt tolerant;
11. M-13-3: Dwarf

Tolerate high salinity & dwarfing effect on Dashehari

Varieties

- Mango was grown in England under green house conditions as early as 1690 and cv. Kew was fruiting during 1818.
- Maximum diversity of mango is seen in Uttar Pradesh.
- Hartless (1913): 1st to emphasize importance of floral characters in mango classification.
- Wester (1920): Gave descriptive list of mango varieties in India.
- Popenoe (1932): 1st to classify varieties on the basis of fruit characters, panicle axis colour, pubescence on panicle and number of embryos in seed.
- Mukherjee (1948) classified varieties based on fruit shape.
- Sturrock (1951) used artificial key for identification of varieties in Florida using characters of fruits alone.
- Polyembryonic phenomenon in mango was 1st reported by Belling (1908).
- Hayes (1970) reported that polyembryonic stock induce more scion vigour than monoembryonic one.
- Mango ideotype (Singh, 1960):
    - Dwarf and suitable for HDP.
    - Fruits medium in size (200 g wt.) with golden apricot colour on ripening.
    - Red blush on cheeks.
    - Fruits must have high pulp: stone ratio.
    - Flesh should be firm, fibreless with excellent sugar: acid blend and pleasing aroma.
    - Regular bearer.

- Gighly tolerant to diseases and malformation.
- Stable &pleasant flavour on processing as in Alphonso.
- Good keeping quality.
- High ratio of edible to non-edible matter (3.31 to 4.0).

- Mulgoa: Mother of all Floridan coloured cultivars was introduced by USDA at Florida during 1889. It give rise a seedling in 1910 which named as 'Haden'. Most of Floridan cvs. Were selected as 2nd and 3rd generation seedling from OP seedling of 'Mulgoa'.
- 1st generation mangoes: Haden, Keitt (seedling of Mulgoa.)
- 2nd generation mangoes: Eldon, Glen, Tommy Atkins, Lippens, Zill, Sensation (seedling of Haden).
- 3rd generation mangoes: Irwin (seedling of Lippens).
- 'Turpentine': Other parent of Floridan mango varieties.
- Majority of Floridan cvs. Were descended from only four monoembryonic Indian cvs. viz. Mulgoa, Sandesha, Amini and Bombay together with polyembryonic 'Turpentine' from West Indies.
- Dwarf mango cultivars have more phloem : xylem ratio.
- 1st introduction of mango into Florida occurred in 1861 from Cuba.
- Haji Kalimullah, a mango grower popularly known as 'Mango Man', developed a new variety named 'Doctor Mango'. It belongs to 'Dussheri' type.
- Term 'Commons' in Australian mango germplasm refers to Kensingtin Pride and its clones.
- Apple Mango: Famous mango cv. of Kenya, having hard skin like apple.
- Intervarital hybridization work was 1st initiated by Burns and Prayag in 1921 at Pune.
- 'Alphonso' mangoes named after 'Afonso de Albuquerque' who introduced the fruit to Goa.
- Export oriented varieties: Kesar (51%), Banginpalli (32%), Alphonso (13%), Rataul, Mallika, Himsagar, etc. (4%).
- Variety popular in eastern states of India: Rataul. It is only variety exported from Pakistan.
- Multiple cropping varieties: Royale Specia, Thambuva, Thephala, Baramasi, Bobbilipunasa.
- Erratic/ unusual varieties: Chitla Afaq, Croton (variegated fruits); Baramasi, Dofasli (flower twice or thrice a year); Kacha Mitha (eaten as raw & lack acidity).
- Resistant to Ceratocystis blight (*Ceratocystis fimbriata*): Carabao, Mangua d'Agua, Pico. Used as rootstock.
- Maximum fruit drop and alternate bearer: Langra, Dashehari.

- Anthracnose and stem end rot resistant: Pulihora.
- Source of dwarfing (lacks apical dominance): Creeper.
- Trailing tree characters: Latara.
- World's expensive sweetest mango: Taiyo-no-Tamago which means 'Egg of the Sun' from Japan.
- Resistant to mango malformation: Alib, Ellaichi, Bhaduran.
- Free from powdery mildew: Latif, Hurr, Lal Sundari.
- Off season bearing: Neelum, Niranjan, Rumani, MDCH-2.
- Madhulika (MDCH-1) and STH-1: Most precocious varieties and off season bearing.
- Chausa variety of Pakistan posed competition with Indian Alphonso in US market during 2011.
- Columbian farmer Orlando Barrera and Reina Marroqun recorded world's heaviest mango about 4.25 kg. It was recorded in Guinness World Records.
- Early mango varieties: Malda and Pairi (in north India) and Banginpalli (in south India).
- Malavia Bhog: Polyembryonic dwarf type from Manipur.
- Kalapady: Shoots bear twice in same season.
- Mallika: Introduced by Dr. Pijush K. Majumdar.
- Vanraj: Called as 'sugar-free mango' (TSS 6%); suitable for diabetic patients.
- Sonaro, Glenn, Keitt: Called as 'sugar-free' because they contain 4-6% TSS.
- Best combiner: Neelum.
- Dwarf cultivars: Kalepadi.
- Slicing purpose: Alphonso, Dashehari, Neelum
- Best for pulp and table purpose: Indira Sona and Indira Gaurav.
- Sucking purpose: Indira Mohini & Indira Raswanti
- Pickling purpose: Indira Achar, Indira Maya, Indira Bhushan, Ramkela, Phule Abhiruchi.
- Wine purpose: Bombay Green, Dashehari, Fazli, Chausa, Langra, Mallika.
- Most susceptible to water logged conditions: Malbhog.
- Cv. Mulgoa is monoembryonic in India but polyembryonic in Florida.
- Highest vitamin C: Bombay Green. It is used as pollinizer variety.
- Totapuri Red Small: Dwarfing rootstock, regular bearer, very short juvenile phase & hence used as male parent in hybridization because there is no effect of female parent.
- Cvs. Janardan Pasand, Suvarnarekha: Impart colour to hybrids.
- Recently introduced variety for colour improvement: Sensation.
- Natural parthenocarpy occurs in 'Thambva' variety of Andhra Pradesh.

- Most suitable filler crop in orchard: Papaya.
- Most suitable intercrop in bearing young orchard: Soybean and cowpea.
- In mango hybridization programme, 'Bangalora' is not considered as suitable parent because hybrid possess prominent beak with poor quality fruit.
- Hybrid varieties developed by Reliance Industries: Niranjan, Jumbo Kesar (syn. Bajrang).
- Malavia Bhog: Polyembryonic, dwarf type from Manipur.
- In Philippines, chemical used for flower forcing: KNO_3 (2-8%, 1-2 times) or NH_4NO_3 (1-4%, 1-2 times).
- Improvement of earlier flowering and fruiting: KNO_3 @ 1%.
- Parthenocarpy can be induced with spray of benzyl adenine @ 250 ppm (at anthesis) and later combination of NAA (10 ppm) and GA_3 @ 250 ppm at 15 days interval.
- Embryonic culture of cv. 'Hindi' has been transformed with ripening genes in anti-sense orientation.
- CHM-7: Clonal selection from germplasm. Free from fruit fly. Fruit wt.- 200-250g; TSS- 18-22^0 Brix; Yield- 70-110 kg/ tree.
- Rootstock purpose: Carillo, Sabre, 4/9, Gomera-1, Gomera-3.
- Neophysis: Phenomenon where growth of nucellus embryo suppress growth of zygotic embryo e.g. Carabao, Turpentine, Paho.
- Graft union success is inversely related to phenol content in scion.
- Prevalance of self incompatibility was 1st confirmed in cv. Dashehari.
- Self incompatible cultivars: Dashehari, Langra, Chausa, Bombay Green.
- Dashehari is cross incompatible with Chausa and Safeda Malihabad while cross compatible with Langra, Rataul and Bombay Green.
- Langra is cross incompatible with Alphonso, Bombay Green, Chausa, Fazali, Rataul, Surkh Burma and Safeda Malihabad.
- Chausa is cross incompatible with Bombay Green and Rataul while cross compatible with Langra and Safeda Malihabad.
- Lowest phenol content occurs in Dashehari and Totapuri. Hence, highest percentage of grafting success (90 %); while Alphonso contains highest phenols and hence lowest grafting success (35-55 %).
- R_2F_2: Developed in Australia is seedling selection of 'Kent'.

Varieties	Breeding method	Features
Irwin, Kent, Zilete, Haden, Sensation, Zill & Julie	Introduced from Miami, Florida (USA)	Contribute colour, heavy crop (300 kg/ tree) & resistance to anthracnose
Carabao, Corazon, Paho, Phautan, Senora, Strawberry	Introduced from Philippines	Polyembryonic
Pico	Introduced from Philippines	Neophysis is absent
Amolie	Introduced from Belgium	-
Sweet	Introduced from Thailand	-
Ambalavi	Introduced from Sri Lanka	Produce 5 crops
Tirunelveli Yellow mango	Introduced from Sri Lanka	Year round fruits
Eldon	Introduced from Brazil	Excellent shelf life; table purpose
Shelly, Tango	Introduced from Isreal	Sweet & sour flavour with milky aroma
Miyazaki	Introduced from Japan	Red coloured
Panxi Hongmang	Introduced from China; selection from 'Luzonmang'	Purple red skin
Haden, Keitt	Seedling selection of 'Mulgoa'	6% TSS
Tommy Atkins	Seedling selection of 'Haden'	Tolerant to anthracnose but susceptible to fruit fly
Osteen, Zill	Seedling selection of 'Haden'	-
Tainong 1, Matoumang, Dazhonmang	Chance seedlings	From China
Celebration	Seedling selection of unknown parent	From Australia, glossy skin with red blush
Dyke and Palmer	Unknown origin	
Golden Nuggets & Brooks	Seedling selection of 'Sandersha'	-
Neldica	Seedling selection of 'Palmer'	-
Alphonso (syn. Gundu Badami, Khader, Hapus)	Selection	Retains flavour even after processing; most suitable for canning & export but susceptible to spongy tissue
Rumang	Clonal selection from Xiangmang	From China, oblate-spindle shaped fruits
Red Blush	Clonal selection from Alphonso	-
Cardoz Mankhurad	Clonal selection from Goa Mankhurad	Regular bearer; large fruits; excellent quality
Pairi	Selection	Regular bearer & early maturing
Gulab Khas	Selection	Rosy flavor, late, good keeping quality; regular & heavy bearer
Manipur I & Manipur II	Selection	From N-E India, dwarf, precocious, polyembryonic & regular bearer
Rangkuai	Selection	From Indo-Burma border i.e. Mizoram
Himsagar	Selection	Regular bearer & pleasant flavour; self incompatible; best for desserts & soft drinks
Krishenbhog	Selection	Popular in West Bengal & Turpentine flavour
Totapuri (syn. Bangalora, Kallamai, Kilimookku, Collector)	Selection	Dwarf; fruits 500-600 g wt., regular bearer; very thin stone; suitable for salad, pickles & soft drinks i.e. processing

Rajapuri	Selection	Very large 2-3 kg fruits, distinct beak; regular bearer
Mulgoa	Selection	Late season & shy bearing
Langra (syn. David Ford, Tikari)	Selection	Biennial, mid-season & most popular in north India; highest perfect flowers (69.8%); strong turpentine flavor & higher ascorbic acid content; resistant to fruit fly
Saikheda	Selection from Gangakhed tehsil	Suitable for pickling; regular bearing; harvesting between June-August
Ellaichi	Selection	Fruit wt. 54 g; free from floral malformation
Bombay Green (syn. Sarauli, Malda, Bombai, Nagan)	Selection	Resistant to bacterial canker but highly susceptible to both vegetative & floral malformation; biennial bearing
Chausa	Selection	Late maturing; sweetest (12 % TSS); susceptible to floral malformation
Fazli	-	Popular in Bihar & West Bengal; regular bearer; possess lateral inflorescence
Zardalu	-	Round shape; regular bearing
Sunder Raja	Clonal selection	-
Shelly	Tommy Atkins x Keitt	From Isreal, late ripening
Tango	Naomi x Tommy Atkins	From Isreal
Kensington Red	Kensington off type x Kensington Pride	From Australia, very juicy, aromatic
Alpha	Mallika x Van Dyke	From Brazil
Beta	Amrapali x Winters	From Brazil
Bhadauran	Neelum x Dashehari	Tolerant to mango malformation
Suverna	Alphonso x Neelum	Regular bearer & free from spongy tissue
Prabha Sankar	Bombay x Kalapady	Regular bearer & late season
Rosica	Mutant of Peruvian cv. Rosado de Ica	Precocious & regular bearer, large fruits; monoembryonic
Davis Haden	Mutant of 'Haden'	Large fruits
Hongmang 6	Mutant of of Chinese cv. Zill	Purplish-red skin, dark yellow flesh
IAC 100 Bourbon	Mutant of 'Bourbon'	Resistant to wilt
Vanlaxmi	Mutant of farmer's selection of 'Vanraj'	Regular & heavy bearer
IARI, New Delhi		
Mallika (1971)	Neelum x Dashehari	1st regular & heavy bearer hybrid released; mid-season variety; β carotene 10392 µg/ 100 g.; wide adaptability
Amrapali (1979)	Dashehari x Neelum	Regular & precocious bearer, dessert variety; suitable for nector making; β carotene 16830 µg/100 g
Pusa Pitambar	Amrapali x Lal Sundari	Yellow colour variety
Pusa Arunima (2002)	Amrapali x Sensation	Regular bearer; high quality; attractive colour
Pusa Surya (2002)	Selection from 'Eldon' introduced from USA	Regular bearer; high quality; attractive peel colour

Pusa Lalima (2012)	Dashehari x Sensation	Red colour variety
Pusa Pratibha	Amrapali x Sensation	Regular bearer
Pusa Shreshth	Amrapali x Sensation	Regular bearer; mod. tolerant to hoppers &mealy bugs
Pusa Manohari (H-8-11) 2020	Amrapali x Lal Sundari	Regular bearer; thin skin; fruit wt. 319 g; TSS 22.16%; 67% pulp; tolerant to mango malformation
Pusa Deepshikha (H-11-2) 2020	Amrapali x Sensation	Dwarf; regular bearer; fruit wt. 353 g; 71% pulp; TSS 18.66%
IIHR, Bengaluru (CHES, Bhubaneswar)		
Arka Aruna (IIHR-10) 1992	Banginpalli x Alphonso	Regular bearer; dwarf & suitable for HDP; free from spongy tissue
Arka Puneet (IIHR-13) 1992	Alphonso x Banginpalli	Regular bearer & suitable for canning; red blush; free from spongy tissue & fruit fly
Arka Neelkiran (1992)	Alphonso x Neelum	Regular bearer; deep yellow pulp; free from spongy tissue & suitable for export
Arka Anmol (1996)	Alphonso x Janardhan Pasand	Regular bearer; free from spongy tissue & suitable for export
Arka Udaya	Amrapali x Arka Anmol	Semi-vigorous, cluster bearing; late season; TSS (24 ^{0}Brix); 12-15 days shelf life
Arka Suprabhath (H-14) 2019	Amrapali x Arka Anmol	Double cross hybrid; regular bearer and cluster bearing; yield (35-40 kg/plant); fruit wt. 240-250 g; TSS 22^0 Brix; carotenoids 8.35 mg/100 g; acidity 0.12%; 8-10 days shelf life
Arka Neelachal Kesari	Clonal selection from Gulab Khas	Early; 60-70 kg fruits/plant; high TSS; free from fruit fly infestation
CISH, Lucknow		
Dashehari-51 (syn. Akshay) 1998	Clonal selection from 'Dashehari'	Tolerant to mango hopper, malformation & high temperature; regular bearer
Ambika (syn. CISH-1) 2000	Amrapali x Janardan Pasand	Regular bearer, late ripening, yellow colour with red blush, scanty fiber, firm flesh; suitable for domestic & export markets
Arunika (2008)	Amrapali x Vanraj	High carotene & high TSS
Dashehari	Local selection Malihabad place near Lucknow	Mid season; oval shape, regular bearer; suitable for canning but susceptible to mango malformation; fiberless; high fruit retention
CISH-M-2	Dashehari x Chausa	Late season; dark yellow colour; scanty fibre & firm flesh
BAU, Sabour		
Alfazali (1980)	Alphonso x Fazli	Tall; regular bearer, late maturing, free from spongy tissue, malformation & fruit fly
Sundar Langra (1980)	Langra x Sunder Pasand	Regular bearer & free from malformation
Safari (1989)	Gulabkhas x Bombai	Red blush at base; 74% pulp recovery
Jawahar (1980)	Gulabkhas x Mahmood Bahar	Semi-dwarf; regular & precocious bearer; high pulp (79.5%), fibreless, very sweet

Menaka (1991)	Seedling seedling of Gulabkhas	Mid season, late maturity; red blush on basal side of fruit; mod. storage life
Subhash (1991)	Chance seedling selection from Zardalu	Similar to Langra; 24% TSS; acidity 0.294%
Mahmood Bahar (1951)	Bombai x Kalapadi	Sturdy, regular bearer, good quality
Prabha Sankar (1951)	Bombai x Kalapadi	Regular bearer
Sabri (1989)	Gulabkhas x Bombai	Regular bearer, very sweet, fibreless
Sabour Mango-1 (H-60-1) 2016	Sundar Pasand x Langra	-
MPKV, Rahuri		
Phule Abhiruchi (syn. GK-PM-5) 2014	Selection	Acidity (3.3%); fruit wt. (250 g); yield (45 kg/tree); suitable for pickle purpose
Sai Sugandh	Kesar x Totapuri	Monoembryonic; regular bearer; free from malformation, spongy tissue, stone weevil; suitable for export & pulp; TSS 22%
Dr BSKKV, Dapoli (FRS, Vengurla)		
Konkan Raja (2010)	Bangalora x Himmayuddin	Suitable for table purpose; regular bearer; free from spongy tissue; yield 90-100 fruits tree (65 kg/tree)
Konkan Samrat (2014)	Alphonso x Tommy Atkins	Regular & precocious bearing; pulp 73%; TSS 20^0 Brix; high percent of perfect flowers (27.52%); cluster bearing; heat resistant; free from spongy tissue; yield 17 kg/ tree; tolerant to fruit fly; ideal for table purpose
Neelum	Kasaladdu	Monoembryonic, regular bearer & late season; susceptible to bacterial canker
Ratna (1981)	Neelum x Alphonso	Regular bearer; pulp percent 78.62%; big seedless fruits; yield 250-300 fruits/ tree; free from spongy tissue; suitable as pollinizer
Sindhu (1992)	Ratna x Alphonso (back cross hybrid)	Regular bearer, seedless (papery seed), cluster bearing; yield 200-250 fruits/ tree; free from spongy tissue
Konkan Ruchi (1999)	Neelum 287 x Alphonso 900	Pickle purpose, regular bearer; pulp recovery 78%; yield 250 fruits/ tree
Suverna (2009)	Alphonso x Neelum	Cluster bearing & large fruits (284 g); high TSS (22.5^{0}B); low acidity (0.24%) & suitable for table purpose; 260-280 fruits/ tree; yield 72-75 q/ha
VNMKV, Parbhani		
Parbhani Bhushan/ Parbhani Hapus	Local selection from Pimpri Deshmukh village	Similar to Alphonso; high pulp to stone ratio (4:1); regular bearer; free from spongy tissue
Neeranjan	Local selection	Off season variety; regular bearing in October
GBPUA & T, Pantnagar		
Pant Chandra	Clonal selection	Fruit colour at maturity remains green; mid-season variety; yield (150 kg/

		tree&120 q/ha); fruit wt. 15 g; TSS-18^0 Brix; adopted to hilly or valley areas of Uttarakhand
Pant Sinduri (2004)	-	-
NAU, Navsari (FRS, Paria)		
Kesar	Selection	Suitable for processing; possess saffron fragrance
Sonpari	Alphonso x Baneshan	Regular bearer; heavy yielder; fruit wt. 360-550 g; TSS 19.7^0 Brix; good for table purpose; 10 days shelf life
Neelphonso (1986)	Neelum x Alphonso	Dwarf; late ripening in July; regular bearer; suitable for table & juice making; free from spongy tissue; mod. resistant to fruit fly
Neeleshwari (1986)	Neelum x Dashehari	Dwarf; non-fibrous; firm texture; regular bearer; high TSS; Vit.C
Neeleshan Gujarat	Neelum x Baneshan	Dwarf, regular bearer
TNAU, Coimbatore (FRS, Paiyur & HC & RI, Periyakulum)		
Paiyur-1 (1992)	Clonal selection from 'Neelum'	Dwarf; regular bearer; excellent taste &suitable for HDP
PKM-1 (1980)	Chinnaswarnarekha x Neelum	Regular bearer; high yielding & bear in cluster
PKM-2 (1982)	Neelum x Mulgoa	Regular bearer with excellent fruit quality
ANGRAU, Andhra Pradesh (FRS, Sangareddy)		
Manjira (1985)	Rumani x Neelum	Precocious; regular & heavy bearer; high yielding; suitable for HDP
Banginpalli (syn. Baneshan, Safeda, Chapta)	-	Early; fruits of 400-500 g; regular bearer; maximum shelf life; early variety in south India
Rumani	Selection	Apple shaped variety in Tamil Nadu; regular, heavy bearer; undergoes change in sex ratio in north India
A.U. Rumani (1985)	Rumani x Mulgoa	Fruit large; regular, heavy yielder & fibreless; juicy & sweet
FRS, Kodur (Andhra Pradesh)		
Neeludin	Neelum x Himayuddin	Regular bearer; small fruits (200 g); fibreless & aromatic
Neelgoa	Neelum x Para Mulgoa	Regular bearer
Neeleshan (1986)	Neelum x Baneshan	Dwarf; late maturing; regular bearer & suitable for canning
Swarnajehangir	Chinnasuvarnarekha x Jehangir	Regular bearer, prolific bearer & fiberless
No. 2/2	Neelum x Banganpalli	Regular bearer, good quality fruits
SKUAST, Jammu		
Jammu Mango (2018)	Selection	-
UAS, Bengaluru		
Aishwarya (2004)	Clonal selection from Alphonso	Free from spongy tissue
IGKV, Raipur, Chhattisgarh		
Indira Sona	-	Best for pulp & table purpose

Indira Gaurav	-	Best for pulp & table purpose
Indira Mohini	-	Best for sucking purpose
Raswanti	-	Best for sucking purpose
Indira Achar	-	Suitable for pickle purpose
Indira Maya	-	Suitable for pickle purpose
Indira Bhushan	-	Suitable for pickle purpose

Other popular varieties: Borsha, Dalimbya, Kohitur, Salebhai-ni-Amdi, Shendriya, Kavasji Patel, Fajri Zafrani, Taimuriya, Gopal Bhog, Samar-Behisht Chausa, Amimgola Behuta, Madhurima, Summer Behuta, Nuzvid Chinna Rasalu

APEDA's standards for export

a) Magness Taylor pressure gauge tester- to test the toughness of fruits- 2 kg/cm^2.

b) TSS- 7.8^0 Brix.

c) pH of pulp: 4.0

d) Sea route: TSS 7-9^0 Brix & 20-25 days keeping quality.

e) Air ways: TSS 10-13^0 Brix & 17-20 days keeping quality.

f) Pre-cooling chamber temperature: 12-13^{0}C.

g) Refer can container: Maintain 12^{0}C & 75% R.H.

h) VHT (at 46.5^{0}C) varies with fruit weight as-

   i) Fruit wt. 400 g or less- 65 min. duration of treatment.

   ii) Fruit wt. 400-570 g- 75 min. duration of treatment.

   iii) Japan banned export of mangoes in 1986 followed by America.

   iv) Hot water treatment at 52^{0}C for 2-3 min. is mandatory for export purpose.

Export standards and grading system

- VHT facility is located at Vashi, Navi Mumbai.
- Hot water treatment plant is located at Horegaon, Mumbai and Nachane, Ratnagiri.
- Precooling at 12^{0}C for 6 h after harvest.
- TSS 8-10% and along with fruit stalk.
- Wooden box (45 cm x30 cm x30 cm); packaging capacity 16-18 kg.

Particulars	Variety	Middle East/ Germany	Netherlands*/ U.K./S. Korea*	Japan, New Zealand*	USA	Australia**
Weight	Alphonso	200-250 g	250-300 g	250-300 g	250-300 g	200-300 g
	Kesar	200-250 g	225-250 g	225-250 g	250-300 g	250-300 g
Packing	-	1 dozen (2.5 kg or more)	1 dozen (2.5 kg)	1 dozen (2.5 kg)	1 dozen (3.5 kg)	1 dozen (3.5 kg)
Export	-	Via ship or air	Via air	Via air	Via air	Via air

* VHT compulsory; ** gamma ray treatment mandatory.

Size group	Fruit wt. (g)	Max. variation (g)
A	200-350	75
B	351-550	100
C	551-800	125

Inheritance of characters:

- Negative linkage between regularity of bearing and fruit quality.
- Genetic marker of cv. Totapuri Red Small: Purple coloured new leaves and inflorescence & dominant beak.
- Inverse correlation exist between temperature and incidence of malformation.
- Positive correlation exist between incidence of floral malformation and both the enzyme activity and phenolic content.

Characters	Inheritance pattern
Tree size	* Upright habit dominant over spreading habit. * Spreading habit dominant over dwarfness.
Bearing characters	* Biennial bearing dominant over regular bearing & short juvenile habit * Precocity of bearing- recessive genes.
Bearing in bunches	Bunch bearing dominant over single fruit per panicle
Trifoliate leaves	Dominant gene
Fruit size	Polygenes, additive & transgressive segregation
Skin colour	Red dominant over green & influenced by duplicate genes
Small stone, presence of beak & sinus	Dominant gene
New leaf & panicle colour in cv. Totapuri	Dominant gene
Pulp colour	Light yellow dominant over orange
Long juvenile phase	Incompletely dominant over short phase
Polyembryony, bunch bearing habit & biennial bearing	Single dominant gene
Dwarfism, regular bearing, precocity, resistance to floral malformation & spongy tissue	Recessive gene
Bacterial canker resistance	Under cytoplasmic maternal control

Pests and diseases

- Most serious pest: Mango hopper (*Amritodus atkinsoni, Idioscopus niveosparsus*). Spray oil formulation of *Metarhizium anisopliae* @ 0.5 ml/litre.
- Most serious storage disease: Anthracnose (*Colletotrichum gloeosporioides*).
- Most serious disease during flowering: Powdery mildew (*Oidium mangiferae*). It can transform 'on year' of flowering to 'off year'.
- Bacterial canker (*Xanthomonas campestris* pv. *mangiferae*) Cv. Neelum is susceptible and transmits disease, when used as female parent.
- Sooty mold (*Capnoidum* spp.).
- Phoma blight (*Phoma glomeratum*).

- Mango seed weevil (*Sternochetus mangiferae*): Serious losses to fruits.
- Gall midge (*Erosomya mangiferae*): Form small galls on leaves.
- Fruit flies are attracted to a chemical compound present in mangoes called gamma-octalactone.
- Trap with methyl eugenol and Malathion: Fruit fly.
- No. of fruit fly traps/ ha: 10-15.
- In Vapour heat treatment (VHT) chamber temperature of is raised up to 50^{0}C or more and fruit core temperature is raised up to 47.5^{0}C for 20 min.
- VHT is done for stone weevil before transport to Japanese and Korean marketwhile gamma irradiation of fruits is done for USA market.
- Hot water dip treatment for insect-pest infestation: 48^{0}C for 60 min.
- Hot water brushing technology (56 64^{0}C for 15-20 min) was developed by Fallik *et al.* at Agricultural Research Organization, Isreal.
- Discoloration of pulp near stone is due to stone weevil.
- Grease painting/ sticky band is done to control mealy bugs.
- Loranthus (*Loranthus longiflorus/ Dendrophthoe falcata/ Elytranthe capitellata*): Partial stem parasite & most destructive parasite. Damage up to 60-90%. Cutting of infected branches from host plant is recommended.

Physiological disorders

- Spongy tissue: 1st observed by Cheema and Dani in 1934 in Alphonso.
- Internal fruit necrosis: 1st noticed by Sant Ram (1972).
- Dashehari, Amrapaliare the most while Langra and Chausaare least susceptible to internal fruit necrosis.
- Boron content in leaves (31-96 ppm) and fruits (7-20 ppm) show inverse relation with internal fruit necrosis (16-21 %).
- Black tip: 1st observed by Woodhouse in 1909. It is more prominent in 6-8 weeks old fruits in north India.
- Mango malformation: Fungus was 1st reported in India by Marries in 1891 at Darbhanga, Bihar. Spray of NAA @ 100-200 ppm during October reduces malady. Malformed leaves have more free and less bound amino acids.
- Vegetative malformation or bunchy top (nursery seedling) more common than floral malformation (bearing stage).These shoots show higher concentration of reducing, non-reducing polysaccharides, total carbohydrates and less nitrogen fractions. Chromatography and bioassay studies indicate that higher levels of inhibitors and low levels of auxins in malformed shoots. Remedy-Spray tree with NAA @ 200 ppm in 1st week of October followed by deblossoming once at bud burst stage.
- In floral malformation, panicles are characterized by condensed mass of male flowers. Incidence is much higher in early flush of panicles than late emerged panicles.

- Mangiferin (i.e. malformin) inhibits growth of *Fusarium moniliforme*, a known biotic agent associated in development of mango malformation.
- Anti-malformin chemicals: Ascorbic acid, glutathione, $AgNO_3$ and $K_2S_2O_3$.
- Skin abrasion, chilling injury and heat injury.
- Mango can withstand deficiency of 'P' but not 'K'.
- Leaf scorching is due to 'K' deficiency or 'Cl' toxicity. Excess application of Muriate of Potash fertilizer. Very common during winter months. Foliar spray of Sulphate of potash @ 5%.
- Fruit pitting: Zn deficiency. More severe in Dashehari, Amrapali and Chausa.
- Jelly seed: Due to mesocarp break down in the vicinity of seed. Tommy Atkins is susceptible.
- Black flesh: Reported in Mexico, in cv. Haden when fruit stored at 13°C for more than 20 days.

Name of disorder	Cause	Remedy
Biennial bearing	High temperature, C: N ratio, hormone imbalance	Soil application of paclobutrazol/ cultar
Chilling injury	Storage < 10°C	-
Spongy tissue/ Internal breakdown (loss 30%)	Convective heat/ temperature arising from soil/ over heating, storage in polythene bags or polyvinyl chloride wraps, post harvest exposure to sunlight & waxing, High dose of N	GA_3 @ 50 ppm; sod culture more effective than mulch; Apply $CaCl_2$ as post harvest dip; pre-cooling at cold water at 10°C; Ethephon @ 500 ppm
Fruit splitting	B & Ca deficiency	-
Internal fruit necrosis/ Taper tip (post-harvest disorder)	B deficiency & high soil pH	Spray borax @ 10 g/litre
Lumpy tissue (called heb in Thailand)	-	-
Riceyness	Serious in cv. Carabao	-
Black tip/ Girdle necrosis/ Chimney disease	Brick kilns fumes containing SO_2, C_2H_4, CO, CO_2	Spray 2 % Na_2CO_3 or 0.6 % borax before flowering & at fruit set
Malformation (most serious)	B deficiency; high temperature, nutrition, auxins	Apply 200 ppm NAA in October; deblossoming
Fruit drop	Nutrition imbalance	Spray NAA or 2,4-D @ 20 ppm
Little leaf	Zn deficiency	Spray 1-2 % $ZnSO_4$
Clustering/ *Jhumka*	Low temperature; improper pollination & fertilization	-
Soft nose/ Tip pulp/ Insidious fruit rot/ Yeasty fruit rot	Ca deficiency & heavy N application	-
Lenticel browning/ discoloration	-	Dip in 150 ppm ascorbic acid for 5-10 min.
Low yield	Zn deficiency	-

8.2 Cashewnut

- Eulogized as 'Gold mine of waste land or Plough crop or Dollar earning crop or King of dry fruits or Wonder nut or Zero cholesterol nut or Forex earning crop or Commodity of commerce'.
- English name cashew is derived from Portugese name *'caju'*.
- Chromosome number: 2n=24, 30, 40 to 42.

Anacardium occidentale	**Commercially cultivated for edible kernels**
A. pumilum	Dwarf root stock
A. gigantium	Originated from Surinam: biggest apple (220 g)
A. nanum	Dwarf
A. rhinocarpus, A. spruceanum	Possess hardwood; used as root stock
A. macropcarpum	Centre of diversity in Amazon region

- Cashew apple is regarded as a remedy for scurvy, cough, cold and purgative.
- Apple is not eaten because of its astringent and acrid principles but contains 4-5 times as much vit. C as citrus.
- Crop is produced in more than 32 countries in the world.
- Prior to 2002, India was leading producer of raw cashews in the world in terms of area utilization in production. Now, the Vietnam has took over the lead from India.
- India provides around 55% supply of cashew kernels in the world and imports raw nuts from African countries to meet the demand of processing industries.
- Introduced to India in Malabar Coast by Portuguese during 16th century for afforestation and soil conservation purpose owing to its hardy and drought resistance characters.
- Cashew kernels gained importance in the beginning of 20th century.
- USA is largest importer of cashew kernels.
- Country leading in cashew nut export: Vietnam.
- Total world production: 34,29,696 tones.
- India: 1st country to exploit international trade in cashew kernels.
- Ranks 3rd in international trade of tree nuts with 20% market after hazel nut (29%) and almond (21%).
- Vietnam and Brazil: Major competitors to India for cashew production and export.
- World's processed cashew production: 14 lakh tones.
- Contribution in world export: Vietnam (21.8%), Ivory Coast (8.1%), India (4.8%), Ghana (3.2%), Netherlands (2.3%).
- Major user's in world: India (3,01,719 T), America (1,43,256 T), Germany (35,930 T).
- India contributes 23% of world's total raw cashew production.

- India's productivity: 750 kg/ha (710-805 kg/ha).
- Highest productivity: Maharashtra (1.5 T/ha) i.e. west-coast areas.
- Leading states in production: Maharashtra (2,70,000 T), Andhra Pradesh (1,17,000 T), Odisha (98,950 T), Karnataka (89,450 T), Kerala (88, 180 T).
- Largest producer: Maharashtra (33%), Andhra Pradesh (17%), Odisha (15%).
- India is 3rd largest consumer of cashew kernels in the world next to USA and EU.
- Cashew processing units are first emerged in Kerala.
- Kerala and Tamil Nadu serve as nucleus centre of cashew trade and together process around 70% of total quantity.
- National Cashew Field Gene Bank (NCFGB) is maintained at DCR, Puttur.
- Cultivation is restricted to 27^{0}N and 28^{0}S latitude with altitude below 700 m MSL where temperature does not fall below 20^{0}C.
- It is sun-loving tree and does not tolerate excessive shade.
- Optimum temperature for growth: 24-28^{0}C.
- Minimum threshold temperature for cultivation: 13^{0}C.
- pH>8.0 is unsuitable for cultivation. It is highly sensitive to water logging.
- Cashew apple contains Vit. C (261.5 mg/100 g), malic acid (0.35%), riboflavin and sugar.
- Cashew apple juice is good remedy for scurvy, cough, cold & purgative. It contains 10-12.5% reducing sugars and 0.35% malic acid.
- Kernel/ cashewnut contains fat (47%), protein (21.2%) and –CHO (22.3%).
- Cashew proteins are complete with all essential amino acids.
- Energy supply: 6000 calories/ Kg.
- Seed is borne outside the fruit.
- Seeds show epigeal germination.
- Parthenocarpy is absent in cashew.
- Kidney shaped nut called achene is true drupe.
- Cashew apple (a pseudo fruit or false fruit): Swollen pedicel develop from peduncle and used for squash, syrup, pickle, toffee, etc.
- Gleaning: Term used for collection of fallen fruits.
- Perfect flowers are larger in size than staminate flowers.
- Fruit maturity: Mature fruits sink while immature fruits float.
- Pollination agents: Insects viz. Halaetid bees (*Lasioglossum* sp.), Indian stingless bees (*Tetragonula iridipennis*), flies, wind.
- Pollen grains from staminate flowers give higher germination.
- Fruit type: Drupaceous nut.

- Main season of panicle emergence: October-January.
- Flowering appears in 3 distinct phases which is highly stable genetic character.
- Flowering sequence:
  - 1st male phase with 90-100% male flowers is of 3 days.
  - Followed by mixed phase (0-60% male & 0-20% hermaphrodite) is of 70 days.
  - 2nd male phase (with 0-6.7% male flowers) is of 13 days.
- Maximum number of hermaphrodite flowers appear in January.
- More number of hermaphrodite flowers found in middle portion of panicle in southern side of tree.
- Rains during flowering cause tea mosquito bug and *Colletotrichum* infection.
- Flowering duration: 85 days.
- Raw cashew is a kidney shaped nut with leathery outer skin & thin hard inner skin.
- Cashewnut takes 45-60 days after flowering to reach maturity.
- Inflorescence type: Indeterminate panicle of polygamomonoecious (i.e. staminate and hermaphrodite flowers).
- Panicle bears 200-1600 flowers of which 10% are hermaphrodite.
- Ratio of perfect flowers to staminate varies from 0.45 to 24.9%.
- Percentage of perfect flowers in hybrids: 12.3-13.3%.
- Perfect flowers 10% of which 85% are fertilized and only 4-6% are carried to final maturity.
- Anthesis time: 11.30 AM to 2 PM.
- Staminate flowers contain 4 staminodes and one well developed stamen.
- In hermaphrodite flower, stamen is shorter than stigma leading to cross pollination.
- Staminate flowers have 8-11 stamens of unequal size.
- Type of ovary: Unilocular.
- Mean fruit set: 3-6%.
- Percent fruit set: OP (3%), Paper roll (17.84%) and hand pollination (55%).
- Pollen fertility: 94%.
- Stigma receptivity: 48 h from anthesis.
- Both cross and self pollination occur.
- Cause of fruit drop: High temperature (39-42°C) during marble stage of fruit development.
- NAA @ 10 ppm or 2,4-D @ 10 ppm or IBA @ 50 ppm controls fruit drop.
- Intensive branch produce panicles.
- After fruit set, nut develops quickly and reaches full size in 3-4 weeks after flowering.

- After that pedicel enlarges to produce cashew apple.
- Nut grows much faster than apple but in later stages, apple increases in size more rapidly and out grows the nut.
- Deblossoming is done in 1st two years and 3rd year onwards allowed to flowering.
- *In situ* conservation of germplasm is done only in the Amazon forests of Brazil.
- Collect seednuts from mother trees having intensive branching and high percentage of flower bearing laterals, large proportion of bisexual flowers and fruit set of >5 nuts/ panicle.
- Best period for collection of seed nuts: March-April.
- Rootstocks are produced by seeds.
- Days taken for seed nut germination: 15-20 days after sowing.
- Propagation methods: Veneer grafting, side grafting, tip grafting, cleft grafting, air layering.
- Forcing of scion shoot for 7-10 days prior to grafting is necessary.
- Epicotyl or softwood grafting: Most successful and commercially viable method (100 % success) on 4-8 days old seedlings in November.
- Problem in mound layering or stooling: Absence of tap roots in seedlings.
- Air layering with 75 ppm IBA in lanolin give 88% rooting.
- Patch/ forkert budding during dry season give 99% success.
- Preferable branching type: Intensive branching.
- Rejuvenation of senile cashew plantation: Top working and softwood grafting.
- Top working: Beheading (20-25 years old trees at 0.5m height) is done during December-February.
- For top working, cleft grafting is commonly used.
- Advantages of top working: Precocity and increased productivity.
- Scion banks can be established by top working.
- Ideal age of rootstocks for softwood grafting: 45-60 days.
- *In vitro* micro-grafting is successful.
- Raising rootstock from irradiated (40-60 Gy) seedlings and grafting on them induces dwarfism in grafts.
- NRC-492: Dwarf rootstock.
- HDP: 4m x 4m accommodates 625 plants/ha.
- System of planting: Square or triangular.
- Soil application of cultar (0.5 g a.i./plant) to grafts twice (1 and 3 months after sprouting) induces dwarfism in nursery stage.
- Harvesting season: March-May.

- Average national yield of nuts: 3 kg/tree/year.
- Average national yield of cashew apple: 8-10 times of nut yield.
- Recommended intercrops: Pineapple, tapioca, green gram, black gram, turmeric, ginger, cucurbits, colocasia, etc.
- Protective irrigation @ 200 liters/ plant once in 15 days during summer and 80 liters/ plant during remaining season.
- *In situ* moisture conservation techniques: Modified crescent bund and coconut husk burial facilitate rain water harvest.
- Florites Sedger: Grown in houses of Uttar Pradesh.
- Cashew apple waste (CAW): Source of energy for livestock and poultry.
- Fruit juices of cashew can be utilized for production of alcohol.
- Feni: Fermented product of cashew apple juice. It is produced using consortium of local microbial strain during fermentation process.
- Cashew wine is a light yellow alcoholic drink, with alcohol content of 6-12%.
- Feni contain 40-42% alcohol.
- Cashew processing is mostly manual in India.
- Processing means recovery of kernels from raw nuts by manual or mechanical means.
- Manual shelling gives higher yield of wholes 90-95% compared to mechanical.
- Steps in processing: Moisture conditioning, roasting, shelling, kernel drying, peeling, grading & packing.
- Conditioning: Sprinkling of water on dried nuts to bring optimum moisture level to 15-25%.
- Roasting: Makes shell brittle. It is done to separate adhering shell from kernels.
- Methods of processing: Drum roasting, steam boiling (most popular) and oil bath roasting (traditional).
- In drum roasting, rate of shelling and out turn of wholes is high but loss of shell liquid.
- In oil bath roasting, shell is heated & cell walls get separated and release oil in bath.
- Oil bath roasting, mode of processing, was introduced in 1970.
- Conditioned nuts are passed through CSNL bath heated to 170-200^{0}C for 1-2 minutes.
- In steam roasting, raw nuts are steam cooked at 120-140 lbs/ sq.inch pressure.
- Best quality kernels are obtained from drum roasting.
- Commonly used drier for drying kernel: Broma dryer.
- Kernel drying temperature: 70-100^{0}C for 6-12 h.
- Moisture content of dried kernel: 2-4%.
- Drying of kernels after shelling, in hot chambers at 70-80^{0}C for 6-8 h facilitates peeling of testa & prevents fungal attack in storage.

- If moisture exceeds 75%, kernel becomes susceptible to microbial attack.
- Commercial cashew processing units are functioning in Kerala.
- Nuts are sun dried to reduce moisture from 25 to < 9%.
- Nuts are shelled to remove kernels.
- Peeling process involves removal of testa from kernels.
- Shelling % in hybrids: 25.3 to 32.2%.
- Output of manual shelling: 15-20 kg in 8 h with 90% whole kernels.
- High shelling cultivars should have a shelling percentage of more than 28.
- Cashew Nut Shell Liquid (CNSL): Naturally occurring phenol, obtained from mesocarp of shell during processing as byproduct.
- CNSL is raw material for paints, varnishes, resins, brake linings, rubber compounding resins, polymer based industries and industrial and decorative laminates, cure craks on sole of feet.
- About 30-35% CNSL is present in shell, which amounts to approximately 67% of nut.
- Cardanol and Anacardic acid of shell possess powerful rubefacient & vesicant properties.
- Main market for CNSL: Japan.
- Expeller extraction is commonly followed for CNSL.
- About 7 kg crude oil can be extracted from 100 kg shell.
- Wt. of 100 nuts: 500-655 grams.
- Number of nuts/ kg: 120-130.
- Nut size is determined on the basis of number of nuts accommodate in one kg.

Grading

- Quality control & Inspection Act 1963 recognizes 26 export grades of kernels.
- The grading standards developed in India refer to: WW (white wholes) & whether kernels are white or scorched, broken, butts, splits and small pieces, etc.
- Grade indicates number of kernels/ lb of weight.
- Whole (no split on the kernel) grade contain 6 grades.
- Largest kernels come in grade W-210 (440-460/ kg) and smallest grade is W-500 (1000-1100/ kg).
- W-180 grade is known as Special Large Wholes.
- Quality export grade: W-180, W-210, W-240, W-320, W-450, W-50.
- Highest grade in cashew: W-180.
- Bold cashew variety/ hybrid: H-1591.

- Defective broken bits of cashew nut are known as 'Splits'.

Grades of cashew (as per Cashew Export Promotion Council of India)

White wholes	Scorched wholes	Dessert wholes	White pieces	Scorched pieces	Dessrt pieces
WW 180	SW 180	SWS (scorched whole seconds)	B (Butts)	SB (Scorched buts)	SPS (Scorched pieces seconds)
WW 210	SW 210	-	S (Splits)	-	-
WW 240	SW 240	-	LWP (Large white pieces)	SS (Scorched splits)	-
WW 320	SW 320	DW (Dessert wholes)	SWP (Small white pieces)	SP (Scorched pieces)	DP (Dessert pieces)
WW 450	SW 450	-	-	-	-
WW 500	SW 500	-	Baby bits (BB)	SSP (Scorched small pieces)	-

- The size grading of kernels is based on number of kernels per pound e.g. Jhargram-1 (280 per pound) and Puttur selection (210 per pound).
- VITA-PACK: Machine used for packaging of kernels.
- Packing is done 10 kg capacity tin boxes filled with CO_2.
- For export purpose, kernels are packed in air-tight cans/ cases/ boxes of 11.35 kg (25 pounds) net wt. and two such cases are put in wooden case.
- For seasoning, cashew nuts are kept under moist condition for 24-30 h.
- Cashew nut, cococnut and casuarina form a popular crop combination in coastal tracts.

Varieties

- Hybrid vigour is reported in crosses involving exotic parents with greater genetic diversity than crosses between local types.
- Varieties are characterized by colour (yellow or red) and shape (round, pear, elongated) of apple.
- Irradiation of cashew bud sticks with gamma rays @ 1-2 Kr led to 100% sprouting & variation in leaf shape, leaf thickness and leaf venation.
- LD_{50} of cashew bud sticks: 3 Kr.

Name	Breeding method	Features
Directorate of Cashew Research, Puttur		
NRCC Selection-1 (1989)	Selection from VTH-107 /31 (3/8 Simhachalam)	Yield 10 kg/tree; nut wt. 7.6 g; 5 fruits/bunch; 28.8% shelling; W-210 grade
NRCC Selection-2 (1989)	Selection from VTH 40/11	Yield 9 kg/tree; nut wt. 9.2 g; 5 fruits/bunch; 28.6% shelling; W-210 grade
Bhaskara (2006)	Selection	Yield 10.7 kg/tree; nut wt. 7.4 g; 8.6 fruits/bunch; 30.6% shelling; W-240 grade; escapes the attack of TMB

Nethra Vaman (H-130) 2020	NRCC Sel-2 x Bhedasi	Dwaf; bold nuts (13 g); long flowering duration; apple colour yellow; 29.5% shelling; kernel grade W-110-150; suitable for HDP
Nethra Jumbo-1 (H-126) 2021	NRCC Sel-2 x Bhedasi	Dwarf; possess jumbo size nut (i.e. W-210, 11-12 g);less fibre content; pruning responsive; fruit wt. 50 g; seed wt. 5.5 g; good for export
Nethra Ganga	NRCC Sel-2 x Bhedasi	Pruning responsive; precocious & suitable for HDP; yield less than cv. Nethra Jumbo-1
ICAR Research Complex for Goa, Panaji		
Goa Cashew-1 (syn. Balli-2) 1999	Selection	Yield 7 kg/tree; nut wt. 7.6 g; 30% shelling; W-210 grade
Goa Cahsew-2 (syn. Tiswadi-3) 2007	Selection	Nut yield 7.5 kg/tree; nut wt. 9.8 g; kernel wt. 2.6 g; shelling 29.6%; kernel grade W-180; apple colour yellow orange;
Goa Cashew-3 (syn. Ganj-2) 2017	Selection	Nut wt. 8.2 g; 29.5% shelling; yield (10-12 kg/tree); kernel wt. 2.26-2.28 g; kernel grade W-210 to W-240; yellow apple; juice content 69.17%; TSS 12.2^0 Brix
Goa Cashew-4 (syn. KN-2/98) 2017	Selection	Nut wt. 8.2g; 29.6% shelling; nut yield (12-15 kg/tree); kernel wt. 2.68g; kernel grade W-210 to W-240; red colour apple; 71.14 % juice & TSS 13.8^0 Brix
UHS, Bagalkot (HRS, Ullal)		
Ullal-1 (1984)	Selection from 8/46 Taliparamba area	1st variety released by any state for commercial cultivation; yield 16 kg/tree; nut wt. 6.7 g; 30.7% shelling; kernel grade W-210; long duration of flowering
Ullal-2 (1984)	Selection from 3/67 Guntur area	Late flowering (Dec-March); yield 9 kg/ tree; nut size medium with 6 g nut wt; shelling percentage 30.5; apple colour-light red; kernel grade W-240
Ullal-3 (1993)	Selection from tree no 5/37	Yield 14.7 kg/tree; nut wt. 7 g; 30% shelling, W-210 grade; very short duration of flowering
Ullal-4 (1994)	Selection from tree no 2/77	Yield 9.5 kg/tree; nut wt. 7.2 g; 31% shelling, W-210 grade
UN-50 (1995)	Selection from tree no 2/27	Yield 10.5 kg/tree; nut wt. 9 g; 32.8% shelling; W-180 grade
UAS, Bengaluru (ARS, Chintamani)		
Chintamani-1 (1993)	Seedling Selection from germplasm accession of 8/46	Yield 7.2 kg/tree; nut wt. 6.9 g; shelling 31%, W-210 grade
Chintamani-2 (2007)	Seedling selection	Yield 12.4 kg/tree; nut wt. 7.9g; 30% shelling; kernel wt. 2.35 g; kernel grade W-210; apple colour red purple; juice content 60%
Dr YSRAPHU, Andhra Pradesh (CRS, Bapatla)		
BPP-1 (1980)	Hybrid of (Tree No.1 x Tree No.273)	Yield (10 kg/tree); 13% perfect flowers; nut wt. 5 g; shelling percentage 27.5; kernel protein 19.8%; apple yellow coloured; juice content 57%; kernel grade W 400; 27.5% shelling; withdrawn from recommendation
BPP-2 (1980)	Hybrid of (Tree No.1 x Tree No.273)	Yield (11 kg/tree); nuts small with nut wt. 4g; 25.7% shelling; protein content 21.3%; juice content 67%; 8-10 fruits/ panicle; kernel grade W-450; withdrawn from recommendation

BPP-3 (1980)	Selection from the germplasm collected from 3/3 Simhachalam	Yield 11 kg/tree; nut wt. 4.8g; 28.1% shelling; protein content 19.0%; juice content 67%; kernel grade W-400; withdrawn from recommendation
BPP-4 (1980)	Selection from germplasm accession of 9/8 Epurupalem	Yield 10.5 kg/tree; nut wt. 6g; 23% shelling; protein content 18.1%; apple yellow coloured & conical; kernel grade W-400
BPP-5 (1980)	Selection from germplasm accession Tree No.1	Yield 11 kg/tree; nut wt.5.2g; 24% shelling; protein content 16.8%; juice content 64%; kernel grade W-400; withdrawn from recommendation
BPP-6 (1980)	Selection from germplasm collection Tree No. 56	Yield 10.5 kg/tree; nut wt.5.2g; 24% shelling; protein content 20.3%; juice content 74%; kernel grade W-400
BPP-8 (1993)	Hybrid of (Tree No.1 x Tree No.39)	Yield 14 kg/tree; nut wt. 8.2g; shelling percentage 29%; kernel grade W 210
BPP-10 (2006)	Clonal selection	Cluster & regular bearer; nut wt. 8.10 g; apple yellow coloured; nut yield 14.9 kg/ tree; 29.3% shelling; kernel grade W-210; yield (22 t/ ha)
BPP-11 (2015)	Clonal selection	Cluster bearing & regular bearer; nut wt. 6.8 g; apple colour yellow; nut yield (14.7 kg/tree); 28% shelling; kernel grade W-240; yield (16-20 t/ ha); suitable for HDP
KAU, Thrissur (CRS, Madakkathara & CRS, Anakkayam)		
Anakkayam-1 (1985)	Selection of tree No. 139 from Baptla	Short flowering duration; yield 35 kg/tree; nut wt. 6 g & shelling percentage 28; apple colour pink; apple wt. 67.5g; kernel grade W 280; suitable for HDP
Sulabha (1996)	Selection from tree no. K-10-2	Intensive branching; bold nuts with 9.8 g nut wt.; yield 21.9 kg; 29.4% shelling; kernel wt. 2.88g; grade W-210; apple colour- light orange
Mridula (1996)	Selection	Dwarf
Dharashree (1996)	Hybrid of (T 30 x Brazil-18)	Yield 15 kg/ tree; nut wt. 7.8 g; 30.5% shelling; kernel wt. 2.4g; grade W-240; apple colour yellowish pink
Priyanka (H-1591) 1995	Hybrid of (BLA-139-1 x K-30-1)	Yield 16.9 kg/tree; nut wt. 10.8 g; 26.5% shelling; W-180 grade; export oriented variety
Anagha (1998)	Hybrid of (T 20 x K -30-1)	Yield 13.7 kg/ tree; nut wt. 10g; 29% shelling; kernel wt. 2.9g; grade W-180; apple colour orange red
BLA-39-4	Tree No. 39 of Baptla	Short flowering duration; 26.8% shelling; nut wt. 6.3 g; yield 20 kg; kernel grade W-210
NDR-2-1	Selection from Naduvellur	Short flowering duration; 26.2% shelling; nut wt. 7.2 g; yield 17.1 kg; kernel grade W-210
Madakkathara-1 (1987)	Selection from tree no. BLA 39-4	Yield 13.8 kg/tree; nut wt. 6.2 g; 26.8% shelling; W-280 grade
Madakkathara-2 (1987)	Selection from tree no. NDR-2-1	Yield 17 kg/tree; nut wt. 7.3 g; 26.2% shelling; W-240 grade
K-22-1 (1987)	Selection from Tree No. K-22 of Kottarakara	Short flowering duration; kernel wt. 1.6 g; kernel grade W-280; yield 13.2 kg/tree; nut wt. 6.2 g; 26.5% shelling
Kanaka (H-1598) 1993	Hybrid of (BLA-139-1 x H-3-13)	Early; yield 19 kg/tree; nut wt. 6.8 g; 31% shelling; W-210 grade
Dhana (H-1608) 1993	Hybrid of (ALGD-1 x K-30-1)	Yield 17.5 kg/tree; nut wt. 9.5 g; 28% shelling; W-210 grade; suitable for HDP

Amrutha (H-1597) 1999	Hybrid of (BLA-139-1 x H-3-13)	Yield 18.4 kg/tree; nut wt. 7.2 g; 31.6% shelling; W-210 grade
Damodara (2002)	Hybrid of (Anakkayam-1 x H-3-13)	Nut yield 13.65 kg/tree; nut wt. 8.2 g; kernel wt. 2 g; 27% shelling; kernel grade W-240; tolerant to TMB
Poornima (2006)	Hybrid of (BLA 139-1 x K-30-1)	Nut yield 14 kg/tree; nut wt. 7.8 g; kernel wt. 2.6 g; 31% shelling; kernel grade W-210; juice TSS 13.3^0 Brix
Raghava (2002)	Hybrid of (ALGD-1 x K- 30-1)	Nut yield 14.65 kg/tree; nut wt. 9.2 g; kernel wt. 2.3 g; 26.6% shelling; kernel grade W-210
Akshaya (1998)	Hybrid of (H-4-7 x K-30-1)	Yield 11 kg/ tree; nut wt. 11g; 28.4% shelling; kernel wt. 3.12g; grade W-180; apple yellow coloured
Sree (2010)	Selection	Tolerant to TMB
Dr BSKKV, Dapoli (RFRS, Vengurla)		
Vengurla-1 (1974)	Seedling selection from 'Ansur-1'	Early flowering; yield 15 kg/tree; nut wt. 6.2 g; 31% shelling; W-240 grade; 1st cashew variety released by a state in India
Vengurla- 2 (1979)	Seedling selection from West Bengal i.e. WBDC -VI- (Vengurla 37/3)	Small nuts; apple colour-pinkish red; W-320 grade; 230 nuts/ kg; yield 15-30 kg/tree; not recommended by university
Vengurla- 3 (1982)	Hybrid of (Vengurla-1 x Vetore 56)	Yellow colour of apple; 25% perfect flowers; 7 fruits/ panicle; 27% shelling;W-210 grade; 110 nuts/ kg; yield 15-20 q/ha; not recommended by university
Vengurla-4 (1982)	Hybrid of (Midnapur Red x Vetore 56)	High sex ratio; 35% perfect flowers; 6 fruits/ panicle; yield 17.2 kg/tree; nut wt. 7.7 g; 31% shelling; cluster bearing; W-210 grade
Vengurla-5 (1984)	Hybrid of (Ansur Early x Mysore Kotekar 1/61)	Highest nut yield (220 nuts/ kg); 50.5% perfect flowers; 3-4 fruits/ panicle; 30% shelling; W-400 grade; not recommended by university
Vengurla- 6 (1992)	Hybrid of (Vetore-56 x Ansur-1)	Yield 13.8 kg/tree; nut wt. 8 g; shelling 28%, W-210 grade
Vengurla-7 (1997)	Hybrid of (Vengurla-3 x M-10/4)	Yield 18.5 kg/tree; nut wt. 10 g; 30.5% shelling; W-180 grade
Vengurla-8 (2002)	Hybrid of (Vengurla-4x VRI-1)	Yield 15-20 kg /tree; bold nuts with 86 nuts/ kg; red apple; juice recovery 85%;
Vengurla-9 (2015)	Hybrid of (Vengurla-4x Vridhachalam-1)	Nut wt. 8.9g; yield 16 kg/tree; 29.5% shelling; apple colour reddish yellow
BCKV, Kalyani (RRS, Jhargram, West Bengal)		
Bidhan Jhargram-1 (1989)	Selection from T.No.16 originally collected from Bapatla	Intensive branching habit; fruit yield 8.5 kg/tree with small nut (5 g nut wt.; shelling percentage 30; kernel grade W- 320
Bidhan Jhargram-2 (2014)	Selection made from seedling plantation of H-2/15	Apple is golden yellow with juice content 68.9%; nut wt. 9.2 g kernel wt. 2.85g; shelling percentage 32%; kernel grade W 180; yield 13.5 kg/tree in 7th harvest
TNAU, Coimbatore (RRS, Vridhachalam)		
VRI- 1 (1981)	Selection from germplasm	'M-10-4' collected from Vazhisodhanipalayam Yield 7.2 kg/tree; nut wt. 5g; 28% shelling; kernel grade W 320; withdrawn from recommendation
VRI- 2 (1985)	Selection from the germplasm 'M-44/3'	Variety is prepotent (capable of giving good seedling progenies irrespective of male parents): yield 7.4 kg/

	(Tree No. 1668) collected from Katthupalli village	tree; nut wt. 5.1 g; 28.3% shelling; kernel grade W 320; apple colour pinkish yellow; failure variety due to chaffy & light wt.; suitable for HDP
VRI- 3 (1991)	Seedling selection from germplasm 'M-26/2'	Yield 10 kg/ tree; nut wt. 7.2 g; 29% shelling; kernel grade W 210; wider acceptance among farmers; suitable for HDP
VRI- 4 (2000)	Selection from Vazhisodanipalayam	Yield (3320 kg/ ha); nut wt. 6.63 g; nut yield 18.10 kg/ tree; 28.5% shelling
VRI- 5 (2001)	Hybrid of (CG 26 x ICGS 44)	Profuse branches with more secondary branches; 75% shelling; red testa; dormancy for 45 days; yield 2133 Kg/ha
VRI-6 (2006)	Hybrid of (ALR 2 x VG 9513)	Tolerant to LLS, rust & PBND; yield 2600 kg/ha; identified for release as all India variety
VRI-7 (2008)	Hybrid of (TMV 1 x JL 24)	Yield 1865 kg/ha; suitable for rainfed condition, 72% shelling & 48% oil.
VRI-8 (2016)	Hybrid of (ALR 3 x AK 303)	Yield 2700 kg/ha; mod. Resistant to LLS, rust; 70% shelling; 49% oil; medium bold kernels
VRI (CW)-H-1 (2009)	Hybrid of (VRI-3 x M 26/10)	Cluster bearing (6-10 fruits/panicle); bold nuts (7.2 g); kernel wt. (2.2 g); high shelling (30.5%); suitable for export (W-210); easy peeling testa; yield (14.5 kg/ tree, 2900 kg/ha)
OUAT, Bhubaneshwar		
Bhubaneshwar-1 (1989)	Selection from seedling progeny of WBDC-V (36/3 Vengurla)	Cluster bearing (12 fruits/ bunch); yield 10 kg/tree; nut wt. 4.6 g; 32% shelling; kernel grade W 320; suitable for sandy & lateritic soils
Jagannath (syn. BH-6)	Selection	Mid season flowering (Jan-Mar); bold nuts with 8.6 g nut wt.; nut yield 2.1 t/ha (10.5 kg/tree); 32.5% shelling
Balabhadra (syn. BH-85)	Selection	Early flowering (Dec-Feb); bold nuts with 7.4 g nut wt.; nut yield 2.0 t/ha (10.0 kg/tree); 30% shelling
IGKV, Raipur		
Indira Kaju-1 (2010)	Clonal selection from germplasm	High nut yield (15.53 kg/plant) & cold tolerant

Pests, disease and disorders

- Major pests: Tea mosquito bug (*Helopeltis antonii*), Cashew stem and root borers.
- Tea mosquito bug (TMB) as vector cause inflorescence blight making 30-40% loss.
- Cashew stem and root borer (*Plocaederus ferrugineus*): Spray Chlorpyrifos 20 EC @ 0.2%.
- Inflorescence blight (*Phomopsis anacardii*):
- Die back or pink disease (*Pellicularia salmonicolour*): Prevalent during rainy season.
- Anthracnose (*Colletotrichum gloeosporioides*): Severe crop loss.
- Damping off: Severe in nursery.
- Little leaf: Zinc deficiency.

- Leaf necrosis: Iron deficiency.
- Yellow leaf spot: Mo deficiency.

Inheritance of characters

- Nut yield is positively correlated with flowering intensity, ratio of bisexual flowers, total number of flowering shoots/ area and number of fruit set.
- Nut weight is positively correlated with height of seedlings.
- Leaf area is directly associated with productivity.

8.3 Charoli

- Eulogized as 'Cudappah almond or Char or Piyal or Chiraulic or Jungle berry or Chironji'.
- Excellent tree of agroforestry & social forestry.
- Assumes significance in waste land development and dry land horticulture.
- Boon for tribal community.
- Kernals are rich in protein (25-30%), oleic acid, oil (33.5%).
- Saponifiable part of oil contains 20% linoleic acid.
- Flowers: small, sessile, white in terminal or axillary panicles.
- Fruit: Single seeded drupe with scanty flesh.
- Nut is valued in Unani and Ayurveda systems of medicine.
- Kernal ointment is used for curing skin diseases.
- Mesocarp (thickest tissue) of ripe fruit is edible in raw/ roasted form.
- Gum is used for dressing textiles.
- Wood has strong timber value, used in furniture, match box factory.
- Good association with sal and teak.
- Seed treatment for germination: 5-7% Sulfuric acid.
- Seed sowing depth: 2-3 cm.
- Days taken for seed germination: 25-35.
- Germination percentage: 63-78%.
- Number of seeds/ kg: 3810.
- Number of fruits/ kg: 1110.
- Yield: 20-25 kg/tree and 2-3 kg kernels (nuts).
- Flowers in spring and fruits available in summer season.
- Ripening time: 3rd week of April to 2nd week of May.
- Ground suckers can be used for planting.
- Leaves as fodder to buffaloes.

- Value added products: Puddings from oily kernels & juice from pulp of fruits, sweet oil from kernels can substitute olive/ almond oil, ointment of kernels is used to cure itching of skin and removes blemishes from face.

Varieties

- C-7, Hazaribagh, Bhimbandh, Adhaura, Dalma.

Genetic diversity and elite accessions

- Earliest flowering genotypes (1st week of February): CPT-1, CPT-5, CPT-10, CPT-15, CPT-17, CPT-19, CPT-22.
- Late flowering (4th week of February): CPT-13.
- Maximum panicle length (35.11 cm) in CPT-1 and least (14.2 cm) in CPT-18.
- Highest percentage of perfect flowers (13.10%) in CPT-12, and least in CPT-18.

Name	Breeding method	Features
Thar Priya (2014)	Selection	Dwarf; precocious & regular bearer; suitable for HDP; TSS 23.9^0 Brix; 1.24% acidity; yield 11.90 kg/plant; fruit wt. 1.15 g; vit. C (48.70 mg/ 100g); 31.36% kernel protein
CHES-C-2	Selection	Spreading; regular bearer; fruit wt. 1.31 g; TSS 21.2%; vit. C. 46.50 mg/ 100g; kernel protein 30.7%; kernel wt. 0.13 g
CHES-C-7	Selection from Kada Dam (Panchamahal dist.)	Peak flowering 1st week of February; peak fruit set 3rd week of February; peak period of fruit ripening 3rd week of February; panicle length 26 cm; fruit wt. 1.26 g; kernel wt. 0.12 g; TSS 22%; total sugars 13%; vit. C 50 mg/ 100 g; protein 30.5%

8.4 Pistachio nut

- Eulogized as 'Smiling nut'.
- Crop of cold arid region, deciduous and grown for edible nuts.
- Nuts are eaten raw, but are most commonly roasted and salted.
- Most expensive variety of nuts to buy.
- Cultivated since ancient times in Italy during late Roman period.
- Introduction from USA to Himachal Pradesh.
- Iran: World's largest producing country.
- Highly biennial bearer and dioecious.
- Drought tolerant (dry temperature zone).
- Grown on poor, dry, hilly soils where other nuts will not thrive.
- Inflorescence: Panicle.
- Flowers: Inconspicuous and protandrous.

- Only male staminate tree is needed for 6 female pistillate trees.
- Masses of small pointed red fruits are produced on pistillate trees.
- Smooth twin-shelled nuts contains small, oval, green kernel.
- Flowering period: 1st week of April- April end.
- Pollination agent: Wind.
- Flowers are devoid of corolla.
- Training method: Modified central leader with 4-5 main scaffold limbs.
- Tree need remedial pruning during mid-summer.
- Heading back is practiced to stimulate lateral growth.
- Reguvenation by top working.
- Chilling hours required to break dormancy: 600-1500 h.
- If chilling is <600 h: Flowering and foliation is delayed, leaves show abnormality, abnormal flowers and reduction in nut production.
- Oil content in kernel: 55%.
- Propagation method: T-budding, Chip budding.
- There is varying success in vegetative propagation by budding, grafting, layering & at different timings of the year.
- Reddish wrinkled fruits borne in cluster.
- Shell splits longitudinally along suture.
- Harvesting:
  a) Green husked nuts hang severally on panicles are cut-off, dried and dehusked.
  b) Kernels are best stored in their shells, which open automatically of roasted.
- Yield: 20-30 kg dry hulled nuts/ tree.

Species:

- *Pistacia integerrima*: Rootstock resistant to verticillium wilt.
- *P. terebinthus*: Cyprus Terpentine tree. Cultivated for resin, which oozes from the whole tree & brown nuts have edible oily kernels. Used as pollinator.
- *P. khinjuk*: Egyptian pistach.
- *P. chinensis*: Chinese pistachio is small, hardy, unproductive shrub and has oriental value.
- *P. lentiscus*: Evergreen mastic tree. Nuts yield edible oil, but this tree is grown mainly for resin obtained from bark incisions. Its oil is used for chewing gum and medicines.

Varieties:

- Seedling pistachios are hybrids of these two (*P. terebinthus* x *P. chinensis*) species and this has prevented improvement of pistachio nuts.

- Continuous cross hybridization with Terebinth (Cyprus Terpentine tree) has prevented crop improvement.
- Momtaz, Owhadi, Kalehghouchi: Popular in Iran.
- Kerman: Popular in USA. Biennial in nature.
- Peters: Male cv. and source of pollen.
- Ibrahim, Safeed Shasti, Wahedi, Bronte, Red Aleppo, Trabonella, Buenzle, Bronte, Minassian, Lost Hills, Randy.

Pests, diseases and disorders:

- Red spider mite:
- Verticillium wilt: Most serious.
- Oak root fungus (*Armillaria mellea*).
- Alternate bearing

8.5 Marking nut

- Eulogized as '*Bibba* or *bhilawa*'.
- Drought tolerant and grown as rainfed crop.
- Requires dry and hot climate during flowering and fruiting.
- Propagation: Seed and softwood grafting in July.
- 2-3 irrigations beneficial in fruit development period (Oct-Nov.).
- Nuts harvested in December-January.
- Maturity index: Hypocarp turns yellow and nut become dark black.
- Bearing starts 4-5th year of planting.
- Yield: 50-80 kg fruits/plant.
- NaOH @ 1% followed by KMS (0.4%) treatment to remove blemishes.
- Bhilawa shell liquid (BSL) i.e oil is separated by heating and collected in earthern pots. It is widely used in paints, varnish industry.

Variety

Name	Breeding method	Features
VNMKV, Parbhani		
Selection-3 (2000)	Selection	Flowering in June;harvesting in November;nut wt. 3.5 g; 25% oil; yield 10-12 kg nuts/ tree

9. ANNONACEAE

9.1 Custard apple

- Eulogized as 'Fruit of poor people or Sherbet fruit or Evening flower scent bearing fruit crop'.
- Largest producer of Cherimoya in world: Spain.
- Atemoya is considered as 'Mandate fruit'.
- Area and productivity in India: 55,000 ha; 8.44 T/ha.
- Share of Maharashtra in India's productivity: 28%.
- Productivity of Maharashtra: 7.36 T/ha.
- Annual fruit export from India: 100 tons.
- Annual pulp production: 2000 tons.
- Sensitive to frost.
- Dried seed kernel contains 30% oil. Used in soap and paint industry.
- Flowering occurs extra axillary, singly or in clusters or on current season growth or old wood.
- Fruit is syncarpia formed by fusion of pistil (carpel) and receptacle into a fleshy mass or aggregate fruit.
- Edible portion: Pericarp.
- Custard apple contains 20% sugar.
- Food value is higher than that of mango, fig and grapes.
- Calorific value: 75 Kcal/100g.
- Nutrition score: 96.
- Bitter taste to leaves: Alkaloid annonaine, liriodenine, noryshinsunine and reticuline.
- Flowering period: Spring to end of rainy season.
- Anthesis time: 5.30-8.30 AM and 2.30-5.30 PM.
- Anther dehiscence: Throughout day but maximum between 12 noon to 2 PM.
- Stigma receptivity: A day before anthesis to 2-3 h after anthesis.
- Pollination agent: Wind.
- Dichogamy: Responsible for poor fruit set.
- Hand pollination is practiced to enhance fruit set.
- Metaxenia is reported.
- Propagation method: Seed, *in situ* cleft grafting (60% success).
- Seed germination: Seed treated with 350-500 ppm GA_3.
- 12-14 months old seedlings are used as rootstock for budding.
- *In situ* cleft grafting: Recommended for drought prone areas with 60% success.

- Cherimoya and *A. squamosa* are graft compatible with atemoya.
- In Spain, 'Pina', 'Cholan' and '604-6' are used as dwarfing rootstock.
- In Brazil, *Rollinia* spp. and *R. emarginata* have root rot tolerance.
- A Spanish cherimoya local selection 'Negrito' is used for heavy and poor soils.
- Planting system: Square or triangular system.
- Harvesting stage for long distance transport: Firm.
- Maturity indices:
  - Days taken from fruit set: 120-140.
  - Colour of fruit changes from dark green to light green.
  - Comparatively the fruit become soft to touch.
  - The inner areolar space widens.
  - The skin between segments turns from creamy yellow.
  - Fruits are harvested in firm condition.
- Centrifugal process is developed by CFTRI, Mysuru for separation of gritty portion from pulp of custard apple.
- Pulp heated at 62^0C and above for 8 months at pH 4.0 develops bitterness.
- Training system: Single stem.
- Compound and sticky nature of pollen grains.
- Fruit set takes place in rainy season.
- Only 0.5 to 5 % flowers set and bear fruits.
- Increase in fruit set: NAA @ 100 ppm.
- Seed viability: 3-4 years.
- Decline in custard apple is associated with water stagnation.
- Fruits storage up to 7 days with 8% wax emulsion + 400 ppm 2,4-D or 2,4,5-T.
- Chemical used for defoliation: Potassium iodide (KI).
- Value added products: Pulp, ice cream industry, powder, jam, fermented liquors, wine.
- Microorganism used in wine preparation: *Saccharomyces cervisiae* var. *elliposoide*.

Species:

- Largest collection of custard apple in India: FRS, Sangareddy.
- Cherimoya is considered to be best fruit among Annonaceae family.
- Among chrimoya types, 'Finger printed' has juicy pulp and very few seeds; 'Smooth cherimoya' is finest; 'Mammillate' has acidic pulp with pineapple flavor adopted in Nilgiri hills and 'Umbonate' has acidic pulp, thick skinand used for making soft drinks and *sherbet*.

- Chemotaxonomy indicates that in *A. glabra*, one genome has been contributed by *A. muricata*.
- All *Annona* spp. Are protogynous except *A. muricata* (protandrous).

Name	Botanical name	Features
Sitaphal/ Sweet sop/ Sugar apple/ Atakatal/ Sharifa/ Custard apple	*A. squamosa* var. green	Common cultivated species; most hardy & escape rom animal damage; susceptible to bacterial root wilt (*Ralstonia solanacearum*)
Sour sop/ Prickly custard apple/ Hanumanphal	*A. muricata*	Heart shaped & fibreless fruit; possess mango like flavor; possess soft spines towards apex; largest annona in world; used as rootstock; graft-compatible with *A. montana* and *A. muricata*
Atemoya/ Prithviphalambu	*A. atemoya* (*A. cherimola* x *A. squamosa*)	Propagated by grafting/ budding on *A. squamosa*; need pollination (for every three rows of atemoya, one row of custard apple)
Lakshmanphal/ Cherimoya	*A. cherimola*	Best fruits among all annona; acidic sweet flavor; less gritty, more buttery; resistant to bacterial root wilt; mostly grown in Assam & Telangana
Bullock's heart/ Ramphal/ West Indian custard apple	*A. reticulata*	More common in south India than north India. Heart shaped yellowish red fruits in April-May (carpels are fused to form rind marked with hexagonal areoles). Late season crop. Less sugar content. Fruit ripen in 8 months; survive long dry periods (drought tolerant), vigorous, grows in pH 5-8; used as rootstock; resistant to *Rhizoctonia*, *Fusarium*, *Phytophthora*, *Cylindrocladium*, *Sclerotium*
Pond apple	*A. glabra*	Tetraploid (2n=4x=28); less vigorous; best rootstock; dwarf; tolerant to flooding & damp soil conditions. It has golden yellow skin with coloured flesh; used as rootstock
Ilama/ White annona	*A. diversifolia*	Fruit pulp like apricot flavor; popular in Mexico; survive long dry periods, vigorous; grows in pH 5-8
Mountain soursop	*A. montana*	Used for fruit quality improvement
Soncoya	*A. purpurea*	Orange flesh, plesant aroma; used as resistant source for fruit cracking because of thick & non-cracking skin
Eoshto	*A. scleroderma*	Used in breeding program for thick hard shell
-	*A. glomerata*	Tolerant to flood condition

Varieties:

- Different cultivars of A. squamosal viz. Green, Red and Yellow types belong to true squamosal & others are hybrids between *A. squamosa* and *A. cherimola*.
- Balanagar, Barbados Seedling, British Guinea, Kakarlapahad, Mehboobnagar, Washinghton, Pink Mammoth, 07005, Wasington 98787, Island Gem.
- Red sitaphal (*A. squamosa* var. red) and yellow sitaphal (*A. squamosa* var. yellow): Used as morphological markers.

- NMK-1 (syn. Golden), NMK-2, NMK-3, Finger Prints, Saraswati-7: Farmer's selections.
- Tropic Sun.

Varieties	Breeding method	Features
IIHR, Bengaluru		
Arka Sahan (1995)	Interspecific F_1hybrid of Island Gem (*A. atemoya*) x Mammoth (*A. squamosa*)	Fruit wt. 450 g; few seeds (10/100g pulp); TSS (31^0 brix); 70% pulp recovery; 6 days shelf life; fused aeroles; creamy white flesh colour; show pseudo-metaxenic property; required assisted pollination for fruit set
Arka Neelachal Vikram	Clonal selection from cv. Balanagar	Fruit wt. 220 g; high yield;TSS 24^0B; low seed content; high keeping quality
MPKV, Rahuri		
Phule Janaki (2017)	*A. atemoya* x *A.squamosa* (Island Gem x 7/17)	Fruit wt. (392 g); TSS (25.54^0Brix); yield (57 fruits/ tree; 21 kg/tree); mod. resistant to mealy bugs, fruit spot & leaf spot
Phule Purander (JWC-1) 2017	Selection from local germplasm from Purander tehsil	Big aromatic fruits (366 g); less seeds (38); TSS (23.56^0Brix); yield (140 fruits/ plant; 51 kg/tree); high pulp (59%); mod. Resistant to mealy bugs & fruit rot.
VNMKV, Parbhani		
Godavari	Seedling selection from survey undertaken in Kandhar tehsil of Nanded dist.	Fruit wt. 750 g; TSS 32^0 Brix; total sugars 25%
Other varieties		
APK (Ca)-1 (2003)	Clonal selection from Courtallam (*A. reticulata*)	Drought tolerant & suitable for arid tracts in Tamil Nadu
Atemoya, Cutemoya	Custard apple x Cherimoya	Shy bearing habit; large sized fruits with few seeds
African Pride, Red Isreal	Cherimoya x Custard apple	-
Dharur-6	Selection	Big fruits (400 g); TSS (24.49^0 Brix); sugar-12; suitable for processing

Inheritance of characters:

- Heart shape of fruit dominant to oblate or cylindrical shape.
- Fruit size, seed count/ fruit and quality parameters: Polygenes.
- Correlation between shoot size and fruit size.

Pests and diseases:

- Fruit rot (*Phytophthora citrophthora*) and *P. nicotiana*: Major disease.
- Mealy bug (*Planococcus pacificus*); Major destructive pest. *Cryptolemus montrozeri* is predator.
- Fruit fly: New pest.

- Alternaria leaf spot: Cause heavy loss. Spray Dithane Z-78 @ 0.25%.
- 'Stone fruit': Fruits turn brown-black and become hard. Major physiological disorder. Malnutrition and lack of moisture increases stony fruit.
- Fruit cracking: Due to differential moisture supply.
- Anthracnose/ Glomerella fruit spot (*Glomerella cingulata*): Serious disease. Spray Dithane M-45 @ 0.2%.
- Woodiness: Presence of seed pockets and gritty lump.
- Tree decline is caused by water stagnation.
- Poor fruit set is due to dichogamy mechanism.

10. APOCYNACEAE

10.1 Karonda

- Eulogized as 'Java plum or Christ thorn or *Kali maina* or Indian cherry'.
- Shrub potential as bio-fence.
- Hardy, evergreen, spiny and drought tolerant and behave as xerophyte.
- Fruits are very useful for curing anaemia and have anti-scorbutic properties.
- Karonda has dichotomous branching habit.
- Fruits sour and astringent in taste.
- Types (A) Green fruited (B) White fruited (C) Dark purple fruited.
- Nutrient composition/ 100 g edible portion:

General composition	Fresh fruits	Dried fruits
Energy value (Cal)	42	364
Proteins (%)	1.1	2.3
Water content (%)	91	18.2
Total carbohydrate (%)	2.9	67.1
Fat (%)	2.9	9.6
Minerals (%)	-	2.8
Calcium (mg)	2.1	160
Phosphorous (mg)	28	60
Iron (mg)	-	39
Vit. C (mg)	200	500

- Very useful to cure anaemia.
- Fruits are richest source of iron and contains good amount of vit. C.
- Fruits are used in medicine industry due to higher contents of alkaloids, flavonoids, saponins, cardiac glucosides, tri-termenoids, phenolic compounds and tannins.
- Ripe fruits are richest source of pectins.

- 90% pulp and 10% seed portion.
- Can tolerate soil pH 5 to 8.
- Planting distance for bio-fencing: 1-1.5 m and require 300-400 plants for planting the boundry of 1 ha land.
- Planting distance as orchard: 3m x 3m and orchard at 4m x 4m.
- Training system: Single or double system.
- Bears white tubular fragrant flowers in terminal clusters of 2-12 and crops twice a year.
- Flowering season: February-March.
- Days taken from tiny bud to anthesis: 18.
- Anthesis time: 3-6 PM.
- Anther dehiscence time: 4-7 PM on same day.
- Stigma receptivity: Up to one day after anthesis.
- Difficult to root species.
- Air layering in July and stem cuttings treated with 5000 ppm IBA give easy rooting in rainy season.
- Difficult to root species.
- Propagation method: Seeds treated with cow urine slurry or GA_3 improves germination.
- Propagation through stem cutting and air layering in beginning of monsoon is easy. Treatment of ringed shoots/ cuttings with 5000 ppm IBA improves rooting.
- Seed viability: 1-3 months.
- Application of cow urine by ring method or through drip irrigation improves flower and fruit formation and increased yield.
- Fruit ripening: July-August.
- Maturity indices:
  - Days from fruit set: 100-120 days and contains high pectin.
  - Fruit colour changes from deep green to deep maroon/purple.
  - Specific gravity- >1.0.
  - Fruits become soft, fruit stalk dries.
- Yield: 3-5 kg fruits/ plant and 3-5 t/acre.
- Fruits are highly perishable and can be stored for 2-3 days.
- Fruits can be stored for 6 months in SO_2 solution (2000 ppm).
- Value added products: Candy, syrup, pickle, nector, RTS, jam, jelly, chutney.

Species:

- Karonda (*Carissa carandas*): Cultivated and grows wild in India in Western peninsula.
- Natal plum (*C. grandiflora*): Introduced from South Africa (EC-37515). Slow growing, papery skin and 12-17 small circular seeds. It is used as rootstock.
- *C. ovata*: Jam preparation. Originated in Australia.
- *C. edulis*: Introduced from USA (EC-35932). Scented flowers. Berry contains 2-7 small seeds. Good source of ascorbic acid (500 mg/100 g).
- *C. spinarum*: Hardiest species. Leaves are used as source of tannin.
- *C. bispinosa* (syn. *C. Arduma*).
- *C. inermis*: Grows wild in India in Western peninsula.
- *C. paucinerva*: Grows wild in India in dry tracts.

Varieties:

- Maroon coloured: Selection from Faizabad.
- White Pink Blush: Promising selection.

Variety	Breeding method	Salient features
IIHR, Bengaluru (CHES, Chettalli)		
CHES-K-II-7	Seedling selection from Konkan region	Bushy (2-3 m tall); almost seedless (0.3 seeds/ fruit); flowers in Feb-March; pulp 88.48%; fruit wt. 12-14 g; TSS 11.5^{0}brix, acidity- 0.76%; yield 3000-3100 fruits/ plant (4 year old)
CHES-K-V-6	Seedling selection from Konkan region	Bushy; 2-3 m tall, flowers in Feb–March; fruit wt. 13-15 g; TSS -14^{0}brix, acidity- 0.44% , vit. C (7.30mg/100 g); yield (4 year old) 1200-1500 fruits/ plant
CIAH, Bikaner (CHES, Godhra)		
Thar Kamal (2015)	Seedling selection	Yield (13 kg/plant); acidity (0.64%); TSS (9.54^0 Brix); vit. C (30.41 mg/100g); suitable for HDP
CHES-K-1	Collection from CHES campus, Vejalpur	Peak flowerin in March & fruits ripen in June; fruit wt. 6 g; pulp wt. 4.64 g; TSS 10.63%; acidity 0.97%; vit |C (26.39 mg/ 100 g)
CISH, Lucknow		
CISH Kr-11	Seedling selection	TSS (6.10^0 Brix), ascorbic acid (16.8 mg/100 g)
CAZRI, Jodhur		
Maru Gaurav	Seedling selection	Very high yield (40 kg/plant); pulp 88.5%; TSS 9.4^0 Brix
CZK-2011	Seedling selection	Pulp 88.48%; TSS 9.4%; vit. C (35.88 mg/ 100 g)
CZK-2022	Seedling selection	Higher pulp; TSS 8.5%; vit. C (37.80 mg/ 100 g)
CZK-2031	Seedling selection	More pulp; TSS 6.1%; vit. C (37.40 mg/ 100 g)
GBPUA & T, Pantnagar		
Pant Manohar (1995)	Seedling selection	Pulp 28.28%; fruit size 2.13 cm x 1.69 cm; TSS 3.93%; acidity 1.82%; yield 27 kg/ plant
Pant Sudarshan (1995)	Seedling selection	Pulp 88.48%; fruit size 2.16 cm x 1.69 cm; TSS 3.45%; acidity 1.89%; yield 29 kg/plant

Pant Suverna (1996)	Seedling selection	Pulp 88.25%; fruit size 2.16 cm x 1.66 cm; TSS 3.90%; acidity 1.85%; yield 22 kg/plant
DrBSKKV, Dapoli		
Konkan Bold (2004)	Seedling selection	Early bearing; bold fruits (12-15 g); cluster bearing; pulp 92%; high vit. C; sweet taste & excellent quality; yield 35 kg/ tree.

Inheritance of characters:

- Positive association between size of berry with number of seeds, weight of seed and weight of skin.
- Negative association between fruit number/ branch and fruit diameter, fruit length, pomace and seed weight/ fruit.

Diseases:

- Anthracnose (*Colletotrichum inamdarri*): Appears on leaves wounded by thorns.
- Bacterial canker (*Xanthomonas campestris* pv. *carissa*): Raised spots on upper leaf surface.

11. ARACACEAE (PALMAE)

11.1 Datepalm

- Eulogized as 'Head in fire and foot in water crop or Prominent tree of the desert oases or *Khajoor'*.
- Oldest fruit known to mankind.
- Earliest fruit grown by man as early as 7000 B.C.
- Unbranched stem.
- Moroccon cultivars have chromosome number 2n=26.
- Modo: About 3-4 palm trees arise from single plant.
- Iraq: largest date growing country.
- Contribution of Egypt in world production: 16.6%.
- Maximum area under cultivation in world: Egypt (36,000 ha).
- Principal date growing countries: Iraq, Saudi Arabia, Iran, Egypt, Lihila, Pakistan, Morocco, Tunisia, Sudan, USA, Spain.
- Contribution of Arabian countries of total world's production: 24.2%.
- Suitable places i.e. 'Gold mine for date' in India: North-Western India i.e. Kachchh region of Gujarat.
- Limiting factor for cultivation in north India: Frost.
- Highly nutritious fruit.
- Edible portion:86%.
- Nutrient composition: / 100 g edible portion: Moisture (20.1%), protein (1.4%), -CHO (86.2%), sucrose (72.2%), glucose and fructose (1.4%), and fibre (2.5%).

- Chemical composition of seed: -CHO (57%), protein (6%), lipid (10%).
- 1 kg fully ripe fresh dates provide approximately 3150 calories.
- Excellent dates contain 75-80% carbohydrates (in form of invert sugars), 2.5% oil and 2% proteins.
- Date fruits contain 50 to 75% digestable sugars on dry weight basis.
- Pulp wt.: Varies from 4.61 to 32.70 g.
- Pulp to stone ratio: 4.83 to 30.72.
- Seed wt.: 0.65 to 1.90 g.
- Date palm tolerates pH upto 9-10.
- Ideal temperature for flowering and fruit ripening: 25-29^{0}C.
- In arid zone, heat unit required to ripen the fruits: 4200-5000 (above base 10^{0}C).
- Early monsoon rains is harmful in cultivation of date palm.
- Inflorescence: Branched spadix.
- Bearing starts from 4-5th year.
- Anthesis season: March-April.
- Propagation method: Axillary offshoots i.e. sucker (ideal 20-35 cm dia., and 15-30 kg wt.).
- Recent propagation technique: Repetative somatic embryogenesis (RSE) using apical buds.
- Tree does not have continuous cambium layer.
- Single palm yield 10-25 offshoots during first 10-15 years of life.
- Offshoots separation time: February-March and August-September.
- Offshoots are cut by means of specially designed chisel.
- Number of offshoots produced in entire life span: 20-30.
- Basal 60-120 cm of offshoot is left bare of leaves and top youngest 10-12 leaves around bud are retained.
- Ideal bunch to leaf ratio for quality fruit production: 1: 6.
- Number of leaves retained for one fruit cluster: 7-9.
- Number of green leaves per palm for good yield: 75-100.
- Number of leaves produced per year: 20 and no leaf removal is done for 5 years.
- Bunches are protected from rain by wax paper/ alkathene covers.
- Best season of planting: June-July.
- Planting distance: 6m x 6m (278 plants/ha) or 8m x 8m (156 plants/ha).
- Planting distance with for offshoot: 3-4 m (Gujarat) and 9m (Arizona, USA).

- Trees start fruiting after 5 years of planting.
- Fruit growth follows double sigmoid pattern having 5 stages of growth as-
    - Haba bouk: (starts after fertilization).
    - Chimri: (depressed growth of 4 weeks stage after set) of 4-9 weeks.
    - Khalal: (slow increase in fruit wt.) of 4-5 weeks.
    - Rutab: (loss in fruit wt.) of 4 weeks period.
    - Tamar: (gain in wt.) of 1 week.
- Pollens are harvested within 24 h to avoid loss of pollen.
- Spines from leaves around bunches are cut during spring to facilitate pollination.
- Pollination agents: Wind, bees and other insects.
- Spathes emerge during February-March in N-W India and flower opening in March-April.
- Pollination must be done during first 2-3 days of spathe opening.
- Oldest and simplest pollination technique: Placing an entire male flower spathe in crown.
- When female spathe crack open, 2-3 strands of male flowers are inserted in it.
- Mechanical or hand pollination is most successful.
- Trailer mounted palm duster is used for pollination.
- 10% male plants should be raised in orchard to provide adequate pollen grains.
- 1 male flower is sufficient for 40-50 female flowers for pollination.
- 2-3 male plants are enough for pollination 100 female plants.
- Dried pollen (with 10% moisture) can be stored with $CaCl_2$ at room temperature for 2-3 weeks or in refrigerator at 4-5^{0}C.
- Exploitation of metaxenia: To induce earliness, in qualityimprovement.
- Pollen grains affects shape, size & time of ripening.
- Selection of good pollinizers is important, since metaxenia effect is common.
- Manifestation of metaxenia has been reported by Dr. Stoler in 1971.
- Fruit set of 50-80% is considered sufficient for full crop.
- Ideal temperature for fruit set: 24-27^{0}C or more.
- Low temperature results in poor fruit set.
- Method to overcome poor fruit set due to low temperature: Placing paper bags over flower clusters at the time of pollination.
- Number of fruits to be left per palm: 1300-1600.
- Bunch removal later than 10 weeks after pollination is avoided.
- Removal of inner strands in each cluster is suggested as outer stands have larger berries.

- Best month for leaf pruning: June than in February.
- Spines from leaves around bunches are also cut during spring to facilitate pollination.
- Ethephon: Effective fruit thinning agent.
- Percentage of thinning: Khadrawy (40-50%), Zahidi (50-60%), Halaway (50-55%), Dayri (30%), Deglet Noor (25-30%).
- For early ripening: Ethephon @ 500-1000 ppm at colour break stage.
- Ethephon @ 2000 ppm, decrease fruit size and hastens ripening.
- GA_3 @ 400 ppm, increase fruit size and delayed ripening.
- Unpollinated bunches treated with GA_3 @ 50 ppm results higher percentage of seedless fruits.
- Duration of Haba bouk (Habamboo) stage: Pollination to 4 weeks.
- Growth/ ripening stages of date from fruit set:

1. Gandora or Chimri: Fully grown, hard, green in colour.
2. Soft dates/ Doka or Khalal: Full grown, hard, yellow to yellowish red and dark red coloured fruits with 35-42% moisture. Fruits are ready for fresh consumption this stage onwards.
3. Dang or Rutab: Translucent and starts softening from tip (convertion of disaccharides into monosaccharides).
4. Pind or Tamar: Fully ripe, mature, soft. Fruits are suitable for dehydration and storage purpose. Pind stage is never attained in India.In middle-east, N. Africa and USA fruits are harvested at this stage when fruits contain 60-84% sugar.

- In India, for fresh consumption, date is harvested at doka stage. They are useful for processing of dry date or dehydrated soft or chhuharas or *kharik* (dehydration in oven at 49^{0}C) contain 25-28% moisture.
- In other countries, for fresh consumption, dates are harvested at dangstage.
- Since 'Doka or Dang' fruits cannot be stored and curing must be done.
- Making of chhuhara: Doka stage fruits are boiled for 5-10 min and dried in solar dryer/ air circulating over at 48-50^{0}C for 70-95 h or sun dried for 80-120 h.
- Making of soft dates (Pind khajoor): Dipping full doka/ dang fruits in boiling water for 20-30 seconds and dehydrated in oven at 42^{0}C.
- Artificial ripening & curing is attempted, if fruits are harvested before ripening.
- Ripening process is related with enzyme activity in fruits.
- Enzymes related with fruit ripening: Cellulose, polygalacturonase & invertase.
- Fruit quality depends on hydrolic enzyme activity.
- Yield: 70-75 kg/ year/ plant.
- Neera: A water-based non-alcoholic health drink containing 12.16% sugar.
- Date syrup prepared from pulp is known as 'Dibis'.

- A liquor named 'Arrack' is popular in Iraq.
- RTS is prepared from Doka fruits by standardizing fruit juice to 14% TSS & 0.3% acidity by additing sugar and citric acid.
- Khadrawy: Developed by somatic embryogenesis.
- Shotgun draft genome is now available.
- Standardization of cloning technique: Dr. Brent Tisserat from USA.
- USDA scientists used liquid nitrogen to freeze date palm tissues.

Species:

- Genetic diversity (i.e. gold mine of genetic resources) exists only in 'Kachchh region', Gujarat.
- *Phoenix dactylifera*: Generic name given by Theophrastus. Word '*dactylos*' means 'fingers' and '*ferre*' means 'to bear'.
- *P. sylvestris* (Indian wine palm or *shindi*): Grows wild. Originated in India. Source for jaggery and drink-toddy/ neera.
- *P. humilis*: Most dwarfing and wild species found in Western and Eastern Ghats hills.
- *P. atlantica*: False date palm.
- *P. canariensis*: Ornamental date palm (i.e.Canaray island palm). Source of fusarium resistance.
- *P. reclinata*: Dwarf palm. Edible fruits.
- *P. farinifera*: Pigmy palm. Edible fruits.
- *P. roebelenii*: Dwarf date palm.

Varieties:

- Breeding work was started in USA in1948.
- Date palm improvement program 1st started in 1955 to 1962 at RFRS, Abhohar (Punjab).
- Suckers were introduced in 1978 under AICFIPs at Bikaner, Abhohar, Hisar, Mundra.
- Intergeneric hybridization with coconut pollen (7-47 %) is successful.
- Most of Egyptian date palm varieties exhibit alternate bearing habit.

Invert sugar date or Soft date	Remain soft till tamar/ pind stage & all cane sugar is converted to invert sugar during ripening e.g. Shamran, Saidy (from Libiya), Halaway, Hayani, etc.
Semi-dry or semi-soft	Have rutab stage e.g. Dayri, Deglet Noor, Zahidi
Dry or Sucrose or Cane sugar date or Bread type date	Do not have rutab stage; retain good amount of sucrose on full ripening e.g. Thoory, Zahidi, Dayri

Name	Features
Deglet Noor	Finest date in the world; highly susceptible to black nose
Khalas	Mid season; suitable for raw eating & processing
Halaway	Early ripening; soft date; suitable for raw eating; TSS 34%; chhuhara recovery 40%; tolerant to rains, early
Khuneizi	Early ripening; red fruits; TSS 32%; suitable for raw eating; yield 40 kg/ tree
Medjool	Late ripening; big & soft date; TSS 28.6%; suitable for making chhuhara; developed by somatic embryogenesis; highest demand in world market
Shamran	Uneven ripening; soft date; suitable for making chhuhara; TSS 35.2%
Zahidi	Soft date; late ripening; TSS 29.6%; suitable for making chhuhara
Khadarawy	Soft date; suitable for making chhuhara; highly astringent; TSS 30.2%; susceptible to V-cut disorder
Zagloul	Red coloured soft date; TSS 28%; suitable for making RTS; yield 150 kg fruits/ tree
Hayani	Soft date; suitable for making RTS (date juice); highly susceptible to black nose
Sewi	TSS 39.6%; suitable for raw eating; yield 50 kg/ tree; highest demand in world market
Barhee	Late ripening; suitable for raw eating; TSS 32%; highest demand in world market
Chip-Chap	Suitable for making chhuhara

Diseases, pests and disorders:

- Termites, thrips (*Adihetrothrip jambudvipae*) and Indian palm weevil (*Rhynchophorus ferrugineus*): Damage bearing trees.
- Birds: Use wire cage.
- Major problem in cultivation of India: Rain damage. Cvs. Zahidi, Barhee, Medjool are resistant.

Name	Causal organism	Remarks & remedy
Graphiloa or false smut or leaf spot	*Graphiola phoenicus*	Common disease; apply Bordeaux paste
Bayoud or Vascular fusariosis	*Fusarium oxysporum* f.sp. *albedinis*	Most devastating disease in Morocco
Black scald	Unknown cause	-
Black nose	High humidity & rainfall; occurs at khalaal stage	Abnormally shriveled & darkened tip of fruits; Bagging of fruits; Avoid excess moisture; Plant intercrops
White nose	Reported in Iraq due to presence of dry wind at early Rutab stage	Hydration may correct the condition
Cross cuts (V-cuts)	Due to anatomical defect in fruit stalks and fronds	
Barhee	Unusual bending of crown and 1st reported in California	Do staking
Fruit rot	Poor ventilation in cluster	Thinning of fruits
Bastard offshoot	Deformed growth of vegetative buds due to bud mite *Makiella phoenicis*	-
Frost damage	-	Keep plantation wet
Cigar hoeing beetle	*Lasioderma testaceum*	Storage pest & attack stored date
Black headed caterpillar	*Nephantis serinopa*	Inject Monocrotophos @ 5-10 ml/litre through roots
Red palm weevil	-	Apply lindane dust & use wire cages

12. BORAGINACEAE (EHRETIACEAE)

12.1 Lasoda

- Eulogized as 'Indian cherry or Gonda or Sebesten or Cherry of desert or Assyrian plum or Pidar or *Bhokar*'.
- Quick growing dioecious, broad leaved, deciduous, less acidic fruit tree having xerophytic characters.
- Fast growing tree used as wind break and thrives under adverse soil and climatic conditions.
- Leathery leaves and sunken stomata makes plant to survive under arid regions.
- Suitable as monoculture as well as component of agroforestry systems in arid and semi-arid systems.
- Grown as storey component crop.
- Wood used for making ornamental furniture/ toys/ agricultural implements, leaves as fodder & making leaf bowls, fibres from bark for caulking boats, rearing of lac insects and ripe fruits for preparing liquors.
- Fruits have medicinal values as anti-helmentic, diuretic, demulcent and expectorant.
- Fruit has mucilaginous pulp (70%).
- Sticky, mucilaginous pulp is eaten to suppress cough, chest complaints and sore throat.
- Tender fruits are used for vegetable purpose and pickles.
- Composition of ripe fruits/ 100 g edible portion: Moisture (83.64%), protein (1.30 g), -CHO (12.50 g), pectin (4.13%) and minerals like Ca (40 mg), K (1.60%), P (65 mg).
- Edible kernels are used to cure ring worms.
- Seed contains 32 g water, 46 g fat per 100 g.
- Pulp: stone ratio: 3.10.
- Principal fatty acids: Palmitic acid, Stearicacid, Arachidic acid, Behenic acid, Oleic acid, and Linoleic acid.
- Propagation method: Seeds sown in April-May and transplanted in July-August and T-budding (96% success) in August.
- Patch budding in July on seedling stock gives 90% success.
- Planting distance: 6m x 6m (rainfed) to 8m x 8m (irrigated).
- Pruning: Removal of water suckers, criss-cross branches and weak/ dried shoots are pruned regularly.
- Flowering season: Mid-February to March.
- Flowering duration: 40-50 days.
- Anthesis time: 6-9 PM.

- Development of flower buds: 21-22 days.
- Only 2% flowers form fruit.
- Time of fruit setting: March.
- Time of fruit ripening: June.
- Bearing behaviour: Cluster of 5-9 fruits.
- Harvesting method: Pluck tender fruits with fruit stalk in April.
- Colour of ripened fruits: Light pink.
- Yield: 100-120 kg/year.
- Fruits are sweet in taste (9.7^0 Brix).
- Pulp recovery: More than 70%.
- GA_3 @ 100 ppm gives highest fruit set.
- Irrigation is withheld in winter to induce defoliation.
- Tender fruits are blanched in 1% NaCl solution while processing for dehydration.

Species:

Botanical name	Features
Cordia alliodora	Good source of timber & biomass production in forest
C. gharaf	Occurs in arid & semi-arid regions
C. rothii	-
C. sebestena	Ornamental tree with orange flowers
C. dichotoma (syn. *C. myxa*)	Cultivated

Varieties:

Name	Breeding method	Features
CIAH, Bikaner		
Thar Bold (CIAH/ LS-3)	Clonal selection	Prolific & early bearer; bold fruits; yield 1.5-2 q/tree/year; fruits suitable for making vegetables, pickles, fresh eating & dehydration purpose
CAZRI, Jodhpur		
Maru Samridhi (2018)	Seedling selection	Regular bearer; starts fruiting after 3rd year; flowering occurs in Feb-March; fruits mature in April-May; fruit wt. 10.5 g; crude protein 11.06%; fibre 13.4%; yield (85 kg /plant)

Pest and disease:

- Leaf gall midge: Minor pest.
- Fruit borer: Minor pest.

13. BROMELIACEAE

13.1 Pineapple

- Eulogized as 'King of fruits or Friendship fruit or Heaven fruit or Golden Queen'.
- Pineapple is a Spanish word '*Pina*' based on appearance of fruit which resembles a pine cone. The name '*Ananas'* which later become generic name, is derived from Tupi-Guarani Indian name 'Nana'.
- Rightly termed as a 'Boon for dry land agriculture'.
- 1st introduced in India at Goa by Portuguese.
- Largest producer in world: Thailand.
- India is the 6th largest country producing 14 thousand tones annually.
- Leading state in production: West Bengal.
- Most bromeliads are epiphytes but pineapple is terrestrial.
- Plant is suited to xerophytic conditions.
- It is CAM, monocarpic (each stem flowers only once & dies after fruiting), herbaceous perennial plant.
- In CAM plants, CO_2 is reduced to organic acids (citric & malic acid) which accumulates in leaves at night and reduced to sugars during day.
- 80% of pineapple production in India is consumed by processing industry.
- Upper leaf surface is green while lower leaf surface (epidermis) is silvery white, due to presence of trichomes (multicellular hairs with short stalk).
- Trichomes absorb water from atmosphere and reduce transpiration.
- Edible portion develops from peduncle i.e. thalamus.
- Hapas: Stem outgrowth produced in transition zone between stem and peduncle.
- Stem part of pineapple is known as 'butts' or 'stumps'.
- In export trade, crown is taken as indication of fruit quality.
- Type of leaf: Radical.
- 'Piping' type leaf: Completely spineless leaf form, completely smooth and margins folded over. Maipure group belongs to this.
- Natural flowering period: December-March.
- Inflorescence: Compact spike (100-200 reddish purple sessile florets, spirally arranged&self sterile).
- Inflorescence emergence stage is known as 'Red bud or Red heart' because of 5-7 reddish peduncle bracts at its base.
- On an average, 5-10 flowers open every day.
- Anthesis time: 6-9 AM in acropetal manner (from base to apex) and takes 10-20 days for completion.

- Number of functional leavesfor flower formation and fruit setting: 35-60.
- Flower has 6 stamens, narrow style with trilobed stigma.
- The inferior ovary has 3 united carpels with 10-15 ovules in each of the 3 loculi.
- Number of seeds after pollination: 2000-3000.
- Pollination agent: Humming bird (reported only in South America).
- Fruit set: By vegetative parthenocarpy.
- If fertilization has not occurred, the ovule will fall after 7 h of anthesis.
- Pineapple produces only one fruit per plant during its life time, by transforming the apical meristem to inflorescence.
- Each fruitlet is a called as 'drupe'.
- North East India produces world best quality due to high TSS and less fibre.
- Most suitable intercrop in banana, coconut and arecanut.
- Early, uniform and increased flowering is noticed under dense shade.
- Pineapple produces seedless fruits because of incompatibility of germ cells, but most of the cultivars are cross fertile.
- Extraction of strong white leaf fibres used for preparing stiff fine fabric called 'pina-cloth' and cordage (rope) preparation.
- Pineapple does not contain starch.
- Bromelin: Proteolatic enzyme which improves protein digestion.
- Optimum temperature for cultivation: 22-32^{0}C.
- Temperature difference of 4^{0}C between day and night is desirable.
- Optimum soil pH for growth: 5-6.
- Commonly used explants for tissue culture: Axillary buds.
- Ideal planting material: Slips (300-450 g) and suckers (450 g).
- Suckers arise from leaf axil just below ground level.
- Slips: Leafy branches attached below the fruit and are developed from axillary buds on peduncle.
- Crowns can be used for multiplication of planting material.
- In Philippines, 60,000-62,000 plants/ ha is commonly followed.
- In India, 15,000-20,000 plants/ ha is followed.

Plant population	**Distance recommended by IIHR, Bengaluru**
43,500	30 cm (p to p in row) x 60 cm (r to r) x 90 cm (trench to trench)
53,000	25 cm x 60 cm x 90 cm
63,500	22.5 cm x 45 cm x 90 cm

- Recommended population density in India: 43,500 (Meghalaya i.e. 30 (plant to plant) x 60 (row to row) x 90 cm (trench to trench) to 56,437 (Konkan region).

- High plant density (HDP) of 64,000 plants/ha (25 x 35 x 90 cm) is ideal for sub-tropical and mild humid condition whereas, 72,727 plants/ha (25 x 35 x 75 cm) is ideal for tropical humid condition. Population of 90,000 plants/ha is followed in Brazil.
- HDP is associated with increased yield, increased production of slips and suckers per unit area, non-lodging of plants and shade to fruits.
- In wider spacing, 20-25% fruits get sun burn.
- Take atleast 2 ratoon crops under HDP.
- In shortage of planting material, take 15 leaf cuttings from crown for planting in nursery.
- Year round availability of fruits is possible by: 1) Planting of suckers, slips and crown at regular intervals from July-December 2) Application of flower inducing chemicals between 335 and 365 days after planting.
- Planting time under rainfed (hills) conditions: June-August.
- Single row system: Mostly used for ratoon crop.
- Trench planting is widely practiced in India.
- Earthing up around the stem should be done after fertilizer application and after harvest of fruit to prevent lodging.
- In commercial production, only 1 or 2 ratoon crops are taken.
- Ratooning is practiced in Assam for more than 25-30 years.
- Partial crown pinching (45 days after fruit set) increases fruit size by 15-20%.
- Common recommended ratooning system is 4-5 years.
- Crop tolerates up to 80% soil moisture depletion in 30 cm soil layer without affecting yield.
- Curing of planting material for 2 weeks period is recommended.
- Ripening is faster by keeping fruit upside down.
- Role of urea: Increase absorption capacity of plant system.
- $CaCO_3$ increase ethylene release by regulating the pH of ethephon.
- Ammonium sulphate: Best source of N fertilizer (dose @ 16 g N/plant/year) as soil application and urea as foliar spray give more yield.
- Nitrogen is applied in 6 split doses, first in 2nd month and last within a year after planting.
- For irrigated/ rainfed ratoon crop, N @ 10 g & 12 g/ plant, respectively be added.
- Apply K@ 12 g/ plant in 2 split doses, during 2nd and 6th month after planting.
- Nutrient analysis leaf: 'D' leaf stage (recently matured with maximum physiological activity, 4th leaf from apex and oriented at 45^0).
- Fruits those mature in winter are acidic.
- Fruit stalk of pineapple if cut into bits is called as 'disc' and can be used for propagation.

- Maturity indices:
  - o Harvesting period: 15-22 weeks (4½ to 5½ months or 115-130 days) after flowering or 11-12 months after planting;
  - o Flattening of eyes.
  - o Tips of the bracts projecting at the eyes start drying;
  - o Emiting a strong flavor;
  - o Specific gravity: 0.98-1.02.
  - o TSS: 12-14^0 Brix and low acidity (0.5-0.6%)
  - o TSS: acid ratio: 21-27.
  - o Term 'three quarterful or full three quarter'.
  - o For canning and distant market: Fully mature fruits.
  - o For table purpose: Golden yellow colour.
- Ripening signs: Rapid loss of shell chlorophyll, flesh pH and respiration rate reach minimum and begins to ripe, volatile esters accumulate rapidly, shell brix increases, flesh pigments increase rapidly while shell pigments decline and titrable acid reaches a peak and begin to decline.
- Suckers produce 1st crop in 15-18 months; slips take 20-22 months and crown requires >24 months.
- Yield:
  a) Plant density- 43,500: 65 T/ha
  b) Plant density- 53,000-63,500: 80-100 t/ha.
  c) Ratoon- 1st and 2nd crop range between 50-60% of plant crop.
- Follow desuckering after harvest of fruits, leaving only one sucker on mother plant & remove all slips.
- In tropical areas, pineapple could be stored well (20 days) when refrigerated at 10-13^{0}C.
- CA storage conditions : 5% O_2 and 10% CO_2.
- PGRs (NAA, Ethephon) are applied to induce flowering, when plants have attained at least 35-40 functional leaves.
- Induction of flowering with auxin was 1st reported in 1939.
- Response to NAA was 1st described by Clark and Kerns (1942).
- Chemicals effective in flower induction: NAA (10 & 15 ppm), ethrel or ethephon (25 ppm), Calcium carbide (0.5-2%) in June and NAA based compounds like Planofix and Celmone. These are added into core of plant.
- Inducing offseason flowering: Ethrel @ 100 ppm.
- Flower enhancement: Ethephon @ 10 ppm + Urea 2% or 2% Urea + 0.04% Sodium carbonate + NAA @ 50 ml/ plant applied at 30-40 leaf stage for induction & regulation of uniform flowering and enhanced fruit weight.

- NAA (in form of Planofix @ 200-300 ppm) at 2-3 months after fruit set increases fruit size by 15-20%.
- Spray of NAA at 6 weeks (45 days) after emergence of inflorescence increases fruit weight, size, acidity and delays fruit maturity.
- Long duration storage: Fruits treated with NAA (500 ppm) and GA_3 (100 ppm).
- GA_3 delays development of yellow colour while NAA enhances it and prevents storage rot.
- Ethrel (5 litre/ha) applied 9 days before actual harvest enhances uniform and rapid colouration.
- Problematic weed: *Cynodon dactylon*.
- Pre-emergent herbicide: Bromacil @ 3 kg a.i/ ha + Diuron @ 2 kg a.i./ha.
- Packing: 12 fruits placed vertically standing on stalk in two layers and packed in wooden box.
- Spray of para-chloro-phenoxyacetic acid 10 days before harvest reduces physiological breakdown during transport and storage.
- Cut end of fruit stalk dipped in 10% benzoic acid to check fungal attack.
- Most common method of preservation: Canning.
- Among the canned fruits, pineapple is important next to peaches.
- Fruit characters essential for canning: Broad flat fruitlets, shallow blossom cup, translucent flesh & small core.
- In pineapple stomata close during day time.
- Number of stomates: 180/ mm^2 in Cayenne and less in triploid (132) and tetraploid hybrids (105).
- Copper fungicides are never used as spray to leaves cause severe scorching.
- Seed extraction: Mature seeds are collected by cutting the fruit into 8-10 longitudinal sections and removing the flesh adjacent to core and then by bending sections.
- Dried seeds are treated with concentrated H_2SO_4 for 30-60 seconds.
- Seeds are kept in fumigant like Carbon disulphide for 48 h.
- Seedlings are cultured in sterilized sand for 30-40 days and then transplanted at 15-18 months age.
- Seedlings take 16-30 months to reach fruiting stage.
- DIANA: Micro computer based expert system which helps in diagnosis of pineapple disorders.
- Del Monte launches GM pineapple with pink flesh and sweet flavour.

Species:

- Smith (1932) established two genera *Ananas* (produce slips but never stolons) and *Pseudoananas*.

- Most pineapple varieties are diploids (2n=2x=50), whereas tetraploids have extra large fruits and lower sugar content.
- Somatic mutation is very common in pineapple cultivars.
- Fruits of *A. ananassoides* and *A. erectifolius* become dry at maturity with little flesh.
- Wild forms are more vigorous, smaller fruits and more palatable.
- *A. comosus* varieties produce seedless fruits because of self incompatibility of germ cells.
- Genetic hybrid between *Cayenne* and *Pseudoananas* produce only 5-10% viable seeds.

Botanical name	Features
Ananas microstachys (wild Brazilian pineapple)	Ancestor of cultivated pineapple
A. macrodontes (earlier *Pseudoananas sagenarius*)	Seedy; self fertile (produce 10% fertile seeds), tetraploid (2n=4x=100); produce elongated stolons & compatible with *A. comosus*; resistant to wilt
A. erectifolius	Seedy; fibre cloth yielding & almost spineless & fibreless leaves; fruits become dry at maturity with little flesh
A. ananassoides	Seedy; fruits become dry at maturity with little flesh; high sugar & acid; distinct flavour; small core; cultivated for fibre; resistant to nematode, wilt, heart rot & root rot
A. bracteatus	Progenitor of pineapple; produce fleshy edible (seedy) fruit; large fruit &smallest core; resistant to wilt, heart rot & root rot; cultivated in Paraguay basin area.
A. sagenarius	Immune to heart rot, root rot & resistant to wilt
A. comosus	Only self incompatible spp.; flesh palatable & fruits are seedless
A. comosus var. *variegates*	Ornamental spp. (red coloured fruit & variegated leaves)
A. fritzmuelleri	Produce fleshy edible (seedy) fruit & cultivated for fiber

Varieties:

- Major obstacles in hybridization: Gametophytic SI, poor seed germination and seedling establishment. Use intermittent mist for higher seed germination.
- Both triploid and tetraploid cvs. Are self incompatible and hence seedless.
- Cultivated seedless pineapple is the result of natural mutation in wild seeded pineapple but most of cultivars are cross fertile.
- Cross compatibility: Most varieties of *A. comosus* are cross fertile, compatible, produce viable F_1 seeds and fertile F_1 plants, when crossed with other species.
- Mass selection is widely used for crop improvement.
- Botanical or horticultural classification of varieties is lacking.
- *Ananas comosus* produces viable F_1 seed and fertile fertile F_1 plant when crossed with *A. ananassoides*.
- 1st breeding work was started by Webber (1905) in Florida.

- Hume and Miller (1904) divided varieties into 3 groups on the basis of general similarity of characters viz. Queen, Cayenne, Red Spanish.
- Johnson (1935) published list of 135 varieties and some of them were synonymous.
- Leal and Soule (1977) classified varieties on the basis of flower colour, fruit shape and spine characteristics.
- The pineapple classification was given by Smith and Downs (1979).
- Py *et al*. (1987) classified all varieties into 5 groups:

Name	Features
I. Varieties of Cayenne group	
Smooth Cayenne or Cayenne group	Triploid (2n=3x=75); spineless leaves; quantitative short day; leaves smooth with few spiny tip; fruits cylindrical; fruitlets or eyes are typically broad & flat; rind dark orange; flesh pale yellow; fruit wt. 2.3 kg; low in fibre & acid content; most ideal for canning; most important & commercially cultivated in Hawaii, Philippines, Australia, South Africa, Kenya, Mexico, Cuba; shy suckering; resistant to gummosis but highly susceptible to pineapple mealy bug wilt.
Kew	Fiberless variety, leading commercial variety of India; shy suckering & highly suitable for canning; eyes broad & shallow; TSS 12-16^0 Brix;
Giant Kew	Similar to Kew except plant size & fruits larger than Kew; late fruiting suckering; suitable for canning
Charlotte Rothschild	Grown in Kerala and Goa; similar to Kew in fruit characteristics & taste
Hilo Cayenne	Produce numerous suckers & no slips; bears small cylindrical fruits
Perolera	Leaves entirely smooth, fruit cylindrical weighing 3-4 Kg
Monte Lirio	Round fruits with white flesh; good aroma & flavour
II. Varieties of Queen group	
Queen group	Commercially grown in Australia, South Africa & N-E India. Earliest, leaves spiny; grown in hills; best dessert variety; fruits conical shaped; fruit wt. 1.1 to 0.5 kg; rind yellow; flesh deep yellow, sweet, low in acid; uniform ripening; suitable for juice making; unsuitable for canning owing to deep small eyes; flesh crisp (less fibrous) less juicy, many slips & sucker formation; (TSS- 15-16^0 Brix); acidity (0.6-0.8%); ripen in June-July; produce more slips & suckers; resistant to pineapple wilt e.g. Jaldhup, Kew, Giant Kew, Queen, Mauritius, Bakhat
Mauritius	Mainly grown in some parts of Meghalaya & Kerala. Mid-season variety of Queen group; red skinned & yellow skinned are observed; exclusively grown for table purpose; suitable for juice production
Ripley Queen	Selection from 'Queen'; fruits conical shaped
Mac Gregor	Selection from 'Queen'; vigorous & bigger fruits
James Queen or Z-Queen	Mutant of 'Natal Queen' & natural tetraploid; large fruit
III. Indigenous types from Assam	
Assam a. Lakhat- sour type	Indigenous types & under Queen group.Indigenous from West
b. Jaldhup- sweet type	Bengal. Acidic blend & have alcoholic flavour
Baruipur Local, Haricharanvita, Silliguri, Darjeeling	Popular in West Bengal districts; 1-2 crowns/fruit; heavy suckering & slips

IV. Varieties of Spanish group

Spanish group	Fruits globose shaped; fruit wt. 0.9 to 1.8 kg; deep eyes; reddish orange skin; pale yellow to white flesh; spicy taste; spiny leaves; resistant to mealy bug &wilt but susceptible to gummosis e.g. Red Spanish, Singapore Spanish, Castilla, Green Selangor
Red Spanish	Hardy, vigorous; fruit wt. 1-1.5 kg; almost square shaped; used as table fruit for fresh consumption; resistant to pineapple wilt, heart rot & root rot
Singapore Spanish (syn. Ruby)	Cylindrical fruits; excellent fruit shape; fruit wt. 1.5-2.3 Kg; deep eyes; canning purpose
Masmerah (1970)	Clonal selection from cultivar population of 'Singapore Spanish'; cylindrical fruits
Cumanesa	Natural sport of 'Red Spanish'
Cabezonia or Bull Head	Natural tetraploid variant of 'Red Spanish'; fruits conical shaped; fruit wt. 1.8 to 2.75 kg; fruits orange yellow coloured; grown in Florida & West Indies.
Valera Amarilla	Strain of 'Red Spanish'; cylindrical fruits; eyes very deep & flesh pale yellow
Puerto Rico	Clonal selection from OP seedlings cross of 'Red Spanish'; excellent flavour, good shape &size; resistant to mealy bug, wilt & gummosis
PR-1-67	Hybrid of 'Red Spanish x Cayenne x' from Puerto Rico; spineless & tolerant to mealy bug
PR-1-56	Hybrid of 'Red Spanish x Cayenne' from Puerto Rico; fruit wt. 2.5 kg; sweet white flesh; spiny, less fibre & resistant to mealy bug
V. Varieties of Pernambuco/ Eleuthera group	
Abacaxi group	Fruits conical shaped; fruit wt. 1.4 kg; rind yellow, flesh pale yellow; spiny leaves; sweetest & best flavoured fruit e.g. Sugar Loaf, Percla
Sugar Loaf	Conical fruits; fruit wt. 0.75 to 1.5 kg; grown in S. America
Papelon, Black Jamaica	Strains of Sugar Loaf
Other varieties	
Maipure group	Fruits cylindrical to ovoid; fruit wt. 0.8 to 2.9 kg; flesh deep yellow; sweeter than Cayenne; aromatic, very juicy; leaves completely smooth with piping e.g. Maipure, Randon, Leg Rija.
Simhachalam	Popular in Andhra Pradesh
Pandora	Not commercially cultivated
KAU, Thrissur (Pineapple Research Station, Vazhakulam)	
Amritha	1st hybrid (Kew x Ripley Queen) released in India; small crown; spiny leaves; fruits cylindrical; fruit wt. 1.5-2 kg; flesh pale yellow & non-fibrous; yield 85 T/ha; high TSS
Exotic hybrids/ selections	
N67-10 (1985)	Vegetative selection from 'Smooth Cayenne' by OPARC, Okinawa; few slips & suckers; oblong shape; yellowish white flesh; suitable for processing
Soft Touch (Okinawa No. 1) 1999	Hybrid of 'Smooth Cayenne x 1-43-880' in Japan; 6 slips; fruit ovate shape; red skin; creamy white flesh; fruit wt. 1 kg; peach like aroma; ripen in mid-July
Bogor	Hybrid of 'Smooth Cayenne x Singapore Spanish' in Japan
Gold Barrel (2009)	Hybrid of 'Cream Pineapple x McGregor- T-1'; fruits oblong; fruit

	wt. 1.4 kg; flesh yellow; good sensitivity to ethephon
Honey Bright (1999)	Hybrid of 'Mitsubishi Smooth Cayenne x 1-43-908'; fruits oblong; flesh light yellow; matures in mid-August
Summer Gold (2004)	Hybrid of 'Cream Pineapple x McGregor- ST-1'; frutis oblong; light yellow flesh; mature in early August
Queensland Cayenne	Dual purpose cv. selected from 'Smooth Cayenne'
Tainung No. 6 (Apple Pineapple)	Hybrid of 'Yellow Maurititius x Smooth Cayenne' at Taiwan; spiny; fruit ball shaped; fruit wt. 1.3 kg; suitable for fresh market
Tainung No. 11 (Perfum)	Hybrid of 'Smooth Cayenne x Queen' at Taiwan; spiny; fruits cylindrical; fruit wt. 1 kg; flesh pale yellow; good resistance to transport; suitable for Japanese fresh market
Tainung No. 13 (Winter Honey)	Taiwan cv.; spiny tip; fruits conical shaped; fruit wt. 1.2 kg; flesh deep yellow; strong fragrance
Tainung No. 16 (Sweet Honey) 1995	Hybrid of 'Smooth Cayenne x Rough' at Taiwan; spiny tip; fruits football shaped; fruit wt. 1.3 kg; flesh pale yellow
Tainung No. 17 (Golden Diamond) 1998	Hybrid of 'Smooth Cayenne x Rough' at Taiwan; spiny tip; fruits cylindrical shaped; fruit wt. 1.4 kg; flesh deep yellow coloured; mod. Susceptible to mealy bug wilt; suitable for export
Tainung No. 18 (Golden Osmanthus) 2000	Hybrid of 'Smooth Cayenne x Queen' at Taiwan; spiny tip; fruits conical shaped; fruit wt. 1 kg; flesh yellow golden
Tainung No. 19 (Honey Treasure) 2001	Hybrid of 'Smooth Cayenne x Rough' at Taiwan; spiny tip; fruits cylindrical shaped; fruit wt. 1-1.6 kg; flesh golden coloured
Tainung No. 20 (Milky Pineappie) 2004	Imported variety 'Monte Lirio' at Taiwan; spineless; fruits round-cylindrical shaped; fruit wt. 0.5-1.3 kg; flesh white; low fibre; popular in Taiwan
Tainung No. 21 (Golden) 2005	2nd generation hybrid of 'Smooth Cayenne x Queen x Singapore Spanish' at Taiwan; fruits cylindrical shaped; fruit wt. 1.3 kg; flesh intense yellow; free from stem-end splitting, pineapple core rupture & cracking peel
Tainung No. 22 (Honey Fragrance) 2012	Hybrid of 'Smooth Cayenne x Queen' at Taiwan; fruits cylindrical; fruit wt. 1.8 kg; flesh yellow
Alexandria	Selection from 'Ripley Queen'
Yeppoon Gold	Clone of 'Smooth Cayenne'
PQM-1	Clonal selection of 'Queen'; vigorous; spiny; few slips; fruits cylindrical; fruit wt. 1.3 kg;

- Key to identification of varieties on the basis of-
  - Presence of thorns on leaf margins
  - Leaf colour
  - Fruit weight
  - Fruit shape
  - Internal and external colour of fruit
  - Locule depth
  - Fruitlet orientation.
- It takes about 36 months from initial cross to emerge a new variety.

- Most breeding programmes start with 'Cayenne'.
- Plants, fruits and shoots of 'Queen' variety are smaller than 'Cayenne'.
- Triploid genotypes (2n=3x=75): Cayenne BR-59, Spanish GU 75-2, Dosindios BR-47.
- Masmerah: Released in 1970 in Malaysia from cv. Singapore Spanish.
- Puerto Rico: Clonal selection from OP cross of 'Red Spanish'. It is resistant to mealy bugs, wilt & gummosis.
- Josapine: 1st hybrid developed at Malaysian Agricultural Research and Development Institute (MARDI), Malaysia.
- Flhoran-41: Red pineapple with golden yellow flesh was developed at The French Agricultural Research Centre for International Development (CIRAD), Montpellier, France.
- Bumanguesa: Sport of 'Perolera'. Produce red fruits.
- Nang Li: Thailand variety has captured world market. It belongs to 'honey pineppale' group, thornless, small, highly scented and sweetest.
- Mutations reported in cv. Cayenne: Paper Leaf, BI, Collar-of-Slip, White Flowers, Flowering Beauty, Nubbin, Seedy.
- Exotic hybrids:
  - Typhone No.1 and Typhone No.3 from Taiwan (dwarf and high yield).
  - Hybrid-7: Valera Morendi x Kew.
  - Hybrid 8: Kew x Queen.
  - SRK SS 3AB: Sarawak x Singapore Spanish. Cylindrical fruits, suitable for canning.
  - MARDI Hybrid-1 (SSSC-1 AB): Smooth Cayenne x Singapore Spanish. Renamed as 'Nanas Johar'. High yield with good canning character.
  - MARDI Hybrid-3 (SRK SS-3): Smooth Cayenne x Singapore Spanish. Good for canning.
  - Valera Amrilla: Perotera x Red Spanish.
  - MD-2 (Golden Ripe or Extra Sweet): Leading cultivar in Hawaii.

Grading system:

Size group/ class	Fruit wt. (Kg)
A/ Extra	1.5 & over
B/ 1st	1.1 to 1.5
C/ 2nd	0.8 to 1.0
D/ 3rd	< 0.8
Baby	About 550 g

Inheritance of characters:

- Collins and Kerns (1946) reported inheritance of 3 leaf types- spiny tips, spiny and pipping (complete spineless leaf).
- Spiny tip and spiny character (entire leaf margin bears spine): Phenotypic expression of single pair of allele.
- Correlation between leaf N & K at 5th month after planting with yield in Kew pineapple is reported.

Character	Inheritance pattern
Spiny tip	Monogenic dominant (*SS*, *Ss*) over entire spiny
Fruit size, quality (sugar & acid)	Polygenic
Green leaf colour	Incompletely dominant over purple
Piping of leaves	Non-linked pair of alleles with dominant gene (piping) *P* epistatic to *S* and *s*

Pests, diseases and disorders:

Name	Causal organism	Remarks & remedy
Mealy bug wilt	Mealy bugs/ lace bugs (*Pseudococcus brevips*)	Serious pest & vector for wilt; bronze/ red coloration of 3rd & 4th leaf whorls; 10-15% yield loss; Cayenne group most susceptible; *Anagrus coccidonus* & *Hambletonia pseudoclonia* are natural parasites; apply Disyston @ 1.5 kg/ ha at plant base
Fruit sucking beetle	*Carpophilus dimidiatus*	Attack ripen fruits & cause fruit rot
Termites	*Odototernes spp.*	Soil drenching with 0.1% Chlorpyrifos
Stem borer	*Metamasius ritchiei*	-
Scale	*Diaspis bromeliae*	-
Base rot/ Butt rot/ Leaf rot/ Fruit rot	*Ceratostomella paradoxa*	Spray Dithane-Z-78 @ 0.3%
Heart rot/ Stem rot/ Stump rot/ Root rot	*Phytophthora cinnamon* & *P. parasitica*	Emits foul smell; predominant in alkaline soil and severe in dry and wet regions. Spray Dithane-Z-78 @ 0.3% or Foltaf @ 0.4%.
Black rot/ soft rot	-	Spray Benomyl @ 3000 ppm
Yellow spot	TOSPO wilt virus (vector- thrips)	Spray systemic insecticides
Internal brown spot/Black heart	Fruits exposed to low temperature (<7.2ºC for 10 h)	-
Sunscald	Exposure of fruits to sun rays	Cover the fruits with butter paper
Fruit & crown fasciation (deformed fruits)	Prolonged ratooning	Related to high vigour of plant; high soil fertility & warm weather favours this malady; take long time to flower than normal
Multiple crowns	Genetic, climatic & edaphic factors	Presence of more than one/ innumerable (even up to 25) crowns & top of fruit become flat, incipid in taste, more corky & unfit for canning; observed in Cayenne (Kew) group

Injection	Due to excessive chilling	-
Dry fruit & bottle neck fruit	-	Lower fruitlets develop normally and upper ones do not develop
Long Tom	-	Fruit abnormality distinguished by excess length & smaller diameter
Crooked neck	Zn & Cu deficiency	Deformation of plant (curling/ twisting/ bending of inner & heart leaves horizontally & downward in bunches); spray 1% $ZnSO_4$ & $CuSO_4$ @ 25-40 kg is basal dressing be applied
Marble	Seasonal & varietal variation	
Yellow spots on leaf lamina	Zn deficiency	Curling & twisting of heart leaves
Irregular flowering	-	Apply 50 ml NAA solution into heart of plant at 35-40 functional leaves.
Excess slips	High N fertilization, rainfall & low temperature	Collar of slip is typified by presence of large number of slips from stem close to fruit base; fruit remain small, tampered with nobs at base;

14. CACTACEAE

14.1 Dragon fruit

- Eulogized as 'Noble Woman or Queen of the Night or Belle of the Night or Night blooming cactus or Strawberry pear or Cinderella plant or Jesus in the cradle'.
- Commonly known as 'pitahaya or pitaya or *Kamalam*' in Asian countries.
- Highly branched, terrestrial or epiphytic vine type succulent cactus plant having sprawling or creeping habit with fleshy stem.
- Wonder crop for rockery, barren lands and water scarcity areas.
- Cultivated around the world in tropical region.
- Leading countries: Veitnam and Thailand.
- Major cultivated in Gujarat and Maharashtra.
- Fruit is assuming importance owing to its high economic returns & export potential.
- Demand is growing in domestic markets and hardly 7% demand is fulfilled.
- India is exporting fresh red coloured fruits to UK, Dubai & Kingdom of Baharin through APEDA.
- Maharashtra Dragon fruit grower's association has been formed on similar lines of Maha Mango, Maha Grapes/ Maha Anar, etc.
- Vietnam has received Global GAP certificate.
- Fruits control constipation, type II diabetes, heart diseases, blood pressure, cholesterol level, joint pains, asthama and colon cancer.
- 100 g edible fruits contain 85.30 g water, Sodium (39 mg), protein (3.57 g), vit. C (6.4 mg), -CHO (82.14 g), fibres (1.8 g), sugars (82.14 g), calcium (107 mg), fat (0%) and 67.70 Kcal energy.

- Flesh and skin contains high calcium pectate and used as jelling agent in fruit processing industry.
- Contain Omega-3 and 6-polyunsaturated fatty acids.
- Three types:

Botanical name	Skin colour
Hylocereus undatus	Red skin (anthocyanin & betacyanin) with white pulp with black seeds
H. megalanthus	Yellow skin (flavonoids) with white pulp with black seeds
H. costaricensis, H. polyrhizus	Red skin with reddish purple (betacyanin) pulp with black seeds
H. purpusii	Red skin (anthocyanin & betacyanin) with red pulp

- Edible colour is prepared from rind.
- 5 flushes in a year.
- Flowering time: May-September.
- Flowers are big sized, white coloured & bloom during night hours.
- Highly cross pollinated crop.
- Pollination agents: Bats, honey bees and moths.
- Self incompatibility reported (Crane and Balerdi (2005).
- Fruit type: Berry.
- Pulp content: 70-80%.
- Optimum temperature for cultivation: 20-30^{0}C & can tolerate up to 40^{0}C for few days.
- High temperature and bright sun light cause sunburn of fruits and maintenance of 20-30% shade is highly beneficial.
- Optimum soil pH: 5.5-6.5.
- Can not tolerate water logged soils and cause stem & root rotting as well as severe flower and fruit drop.
- Drip irrigation is highly preferred.
- Water stress in April-May causes more flower formation in rainy season.
- Life span: 15-20 years.
- Propagation method: Seeds and 20 cm long cutting.
- Plants raised from seeds have mixed inheritance & show highly variable performance.
- Dark green coloured, 20-25 cm long & 0.5-0.7 cm thick cuttings are taken from 1-2 year old shoots.
- Rooted cuttings are ready for transplantation within 3-4 weeks.
- Vine is allowed to grow on single stem with the help of stakes.
- Head system of training is followed.
- Trellising: Main stem allowed to climb concrete or wooden pillars, fence, walls/ trees.

- Planting distance: 2 m x 2 m (2,500 plants/ha) or 3 m x 3 m (1,110 plants/ ha), 4 m x 3 m (834 plants/ ha).
- Fruit weight: 300-600 g.
- Fertilization: In light soils, 500 g N + 500 g P + 300 g K applied in 4 split doses during 1st and 2nd year of planting. After 3rd year onwards, 800 g N + 900 g P + 550 g K in 6 split doses after fruit harvesting, before flowering, after full blooming, during fruit setting & at full development stages gave beneficial results.
- Mixed planting of varieties is recommended for better fruit set.
- Flowering and fruit bearing starts 18-24 months after planting.
- Days required from anthesis to fruit maturity: 30-45 days.
- Harvesting period: September-December.
- Yield: 10-30t/ ha/year.
- Storage: At 10^{0}C for 30-45 days.
- Value added products: Jam, jelly, candy, syrup & wine.

Diseases and disorders:

- Fruit rot/ splitting: Due to over watering and high rainfall.
- Stem rot of stem (*Xanthomonas campestris*):
- Anthracnose: Spray copper fungicide.
- Brown spots on fruits (*Dithiorella*):
- Sunburn
- Unopened flower and fruitlet drop: Nutritional and hormonal imbalance. Less pollination.
- Jelly formation: Deficiency of Ca, B and K. High ethylene production.

14.2 Prickly pear or Opuntia

- Used as fruit, vegetable and fodder.
- Highest water use efficiency among drought resistant plants.
- Propagation: 1 year old cladodes of 500-1000 g weight.
- Planting distance: 3m x 3m.
- Flowers appear on terminal cladodes of 1 year old age in summer after 3 years of planting.
- Pollination agent: Bees.
- Young cladodes are called as 'Nopalitos'.
- Cactus pear show alternate bearing tendency.
- Fruit ripening takes after 80-90 days.
- Formative pruning is required.

- Spring: Best time for pruning.
- Harvesting: 2 years after planting.
- Yield: 10-15 T/ha.
- Widely used to blend guava, RTS beverage to improve nutritive value, colour, and overall acceptability.

Pests and diseases:

- Phycitid moth (*Cactoblastis cactorum*):
- Cochineal (*Dactylopius opuntiale*):
- Bacterial soft rot (*Erwinia* spp.):
- Foot rot (*Phytophthora cactorum*):
- Wilt (*Fusarium oxysporum*):

15. CARICACEAE

15.1 Papaya

- Eulogized as 'Wonder fruit of tropics or Tree melon or Melon tree or Backyard fruit or Breakfast fruit or Papaw'.
- Introduced in India during 16th century by Portuguese.
- Ranks 2nd to mango as source of precursor of vitamin A.
- India is 2nd largest producer (5.64 MT) of papaya in world.
- Mostly cultivated under protected cultivation.
- Monoaxial fruit plant.
- Highest remunerative crop than any other fruits.
- Provides more income/ha next to banana.
- India is largest producer of papaya in the world.
- Edible portion: 75%.
- Sensitive to frost, strong winds and highly susceptible to water logging.
- Papaya is thermosensitive crop.
- Vivipary (seed germination in over-ripe fruits) is observed.
- Female trees exhibit parthenocarpy.
- Though propagated by seed do not have much variability.
- Continuous flowering and fruiting crop.
- Unripe fruits and young leaves are used as vegetable for cooking.
- Papain: Dried milky latex oozing from immature fruits when lanced with sharp blade.
- Latex obtained from ½ to ¾th mature fruits (70-90 days from fruit set).
- Latex when dried yields a powder.

- Coagulated latex produces 25% of dried powder containing 6-10% moisture.
- About 1/6th of dried powder is papain.
- Papain contains 72.2% protein.
- 90-100 days old, fully matured but not ripe fruits are selected for tapping of latex.
- Yield of papain highest in long fruited type and in the month of October.
- Annual yield of papain: 200-300 g/tree with maximum 450 gram.
- Yield of papain/ ha/ year: 250-350 kg.
- Each fruit produce 5-8 g papain depending upon variety.
- Papain yield is greatly influenced by-

  A. Season:

  1. Flow of latex is low if temperature is <10°C.
  2. Papain yield fluctuate from May to October and lowest yield in September.

  B. Fruit size:

  1. Positive correlation between girth (breadth) / length (oblong or long fruited) / weight of fruits and papain yield.
  2. Fruits measuring 1255 to 1544 sq. cm size give highest papain yield.

  C. Fruit maturity: Unripe and fully grown (3 months old) fruits are used for tapping.

  D. Varieties:

  1. Improved strain called 'Botanist's Selection' from Sri Lanka.
  2. Red Panama yields 21 kg of dry papain/ ha.
  3. Red fleshed and Philippine Selection yield as high as 6 g papain/ fruit.
  4. In India, CO.2 evolved from Selection-7 yield 100-120 kg papain/ acre.

- Papain test unit: FCC i.e. Food Chemical Codex or USP i.e. United States Pharmacopeia.
- One FCC papain unit is defined as that quantity of enzyme that liberates the equivalent of 1 μg of tyrosine per hour under the conditions of the assay (pH 6.0 and 40°C).
- Papain strength is measured by tyrosine unit.
- Latex collected everytime from immature fruits is dried at 50-55°C.
- Potassium meta-bisulphite @ 0.05% or 350 ppm is added to liquid latex to extend storage life of papain.
- Papain uses: Meat tendering in manufacture of leather and clarifying beer, treatment of ulcer, textile and garment cleaning, pre-shrinking of wool, manufacturing chewing gum, degumming natural silk, rayon, dentral and face cream, extracting oil from liver of 'Tuna fish', preparing digestive medicines, pharmaceutical industry, paper and adhesive manufacture, sewage disposal,
- Enzyme present in dried milky latex of papaya (papain) is pepsin. This protease, proteinage or proteolytic enzyme helps in both digestion of protein rich foods and milk clotting.

- Quality and grade of papain is determined by colour and enzyme activity (tyrosine unit) in 3 groups-
  - Crude papain- white brown to brown.
  - Crude papain in flake/ powder as semi-refined.
  - Spray dried crude papain of higher activity in powder form as refined papain.
- Refined papain having activity of 800-1000 units or higher is preferred in world trade.
- Papain can be stored for 6 months in air-tight glass/ tin container.
- Carpine alkaloid from milk latex: Diuretic and heart stimulant.
- Pigments found: Cryptoxanthin, Carotenoid, Caricaxanthin (yellow).
- Lycopene content: 2.0 to 5.3 mg/ 100 g.
- 1 g seed contain 20 seeds.
- Planting 3 seedlings per pit in dioecious variety is recommended.
- No male plants in cvs. Coorg Honey Dew, Solo, Sun Rise Solo, CO.3, Pusa Delicious and Pusa Majesty. Hence, only single seedling per pit.
- Seed rate: 400-500 g/ha (dioecious varieties) and 250-300 g/ha (gynodioecious varieties).
- Mature fruit contains 500-1000 seeds.
- Average wt. of 1000 seeds: 27-33 gram.
- Dioecious varieties produce more seeds (300-350 kg/ha) compared to gynodioecious varieties (100-150 kg/ha).
- Fruit thinning promotes formation of large fruits of regular shape.
- Moisture content of seed in storage: 7-9%.
- Seed viability: 45 days at ambient temperature but for 4 years at 10^0C.
- Ferulic acid (10^{-3} M) also retains seed viability in cv. CO.1
- Optimum temperature for seed germination: 30^0C.
- Days required for seed germination: 15-20.
- Thiourea (100-200 ppm) or GA_3 (200 ppm) improves seed germination.
- Cuttings: With intermittent mist and bottom heat technique gives 80-90% rooting.
- Explant used for *in vitro* propagation: Shoot tips.
- Irrigation by ring method.
- Highly cross pollinated: Wind.
- Cleistogamy occurs in cv. Sunrise.
- Gelatinous cover preventing seed germination: Sarcotesta.
- Optimum temperature for cultivation: 30-35^0C.
- High temperature leads to female sterility: 35^0C.

- Optimum soil pH for cultivation: 6.5 to 7.
- Sib-mating (brother-sister mating) is practiced in papaya. It means crossing of female (sister) and male (brother) progenies of same parent. It is done to obtain nucleus or breeder's seed.
- Patch nudding during September gives 90% success on 2 months old rootstock with Pusa Dwarf scion.
- Metaxenia is reported in papaya.
- Female plants are more productive than hermaphrodite ones.
- Amino acid 'proline' is present and cystein is absent in female plants.
- Level of tryptophan is twice in female plants compared to other forms.
- High uptake of nutrients during flowering and harvesting stages.
- Maleness is due to defoliation, high phenolic compounds and high soil pH.
- Femaleness can be induced with GA_3 @ 50 ppm or TIBA @ 100 ppm.
- GA_3 @ 10 and 100 ppm on young seedlings increased growth and fresh weight.
- MH and SADH hastens flowering, fruiting at lower nodes & increased fruit set.
- CCC increase pulp thickness & pectin content (82%) and advances flowering.
- Normal spacing: 1.8 m x 1.8 m while spacing for papain 1.6 m x 1.6 m.
- HDP: 1.2 m x 1.2 m (6944 plants/ha) e.g. Pusa Nanha.
- Potassium is required for TSS content of latex and enzyme activity.
- 'P' fertilizer on yield is more pronounced than that of N and K.
- Papaya is not economical after 2.5-3 years.
- Annual yield: 250-375 kg/ha/year.
- Days required to flowering to reach maturity: 125-140.
- Maturity indices:
  - Light green with tinge of yellow epical end of fully developed fruit;
  - Firm green with moisture of 86% and TSS 10.67^0 brix.
  - Ripe 33% for long distance and 85.5% colour development for localmarket;
  - Fruits show streaks of yellow to purple colour.
  - When latex seizes to be milky and becomes watery.
- Osmotic dehydration (tooty fruity) is done for concentration of fruit pieces.
- Protected cultivation of fruit crops helps in overcoming the problem of PRSV.
- Callus culture: ½ MS + 0.5 mg kinetin/ litre.
- Loop-mediated Isothermal Amplification (LAMP) technique: Does not require prior DNA purification and used for sex determination.
- Cold storage temperature: 7-13^{0}C for 21 days.
- CA storage: (2% O_2, 5% CO_2, 16^{0}C temperature) extend shelf life by two weeks.
- Waxing also enhances shelf life.

Species:

- Badilio (1993) divided genus *Carica* into two sections: *Carica* and *Vasconcella*.
- Babaco (*C. pentagona*): Parthenocarpic species for greenhouse and vegetatively propagated.
- Genus *Vasconcella*: Largest genus.
- *V. parviflora*, *V. quercifolia*, *V. candicans*: Bridging species for *V. pubescens* and *V. cundinamarcensis*.

Common name/ Botanical name	Features
Common papaya (*C. papaya*)	Polygamous; closely related to *V. peltata* and they have arisen by hybridization; only species producing edible fruits; susceptible to virus
Mountain papaya (*C. cundinamarcensis*), *C. cauliflora*	Fruits 7.5-10 cm long, stands lower temperature; ripens from May to August; dioecious & mosaic virus resistant
C. goudottiana, *C. parviflora*	Dioecious & susceptible to virus; resistant to phytophthora
C. pennata	Dioecious & resistant to frost
C. pubescens, *C. stipulata*, *C. candicans*	Dioecious, resistant to distortion ring spot virus
C. horivitziana	Dioecious & susceptible to virus
C. pentagona	Dioecious & resistant to frost
C. quercifolia	Hardiest; resistant to virus
C. monoica	Monoecious & susceptible to virus; grown in Amazon basin
C. microcarpa	Dioecious & susceptible to virus
V. quercifolia	Ornamental
C. pubescence, *V. stipulata*, *V. cauliflora*	Ring spot virus resistant
C. gracilis	Ornamental species
C. erythrocarpa	Fruit has thin red flesh; resistant to virus
C. heilbornii (*C. pubescens* x *C. stipulata*)	Resistant to distortion ring spot virus
C. peltata	Closely related species from south Mexico

Sex forms:

- Polygamous: predominantly 3 sex forms- male (staminate), female (pistillate) and hermaphrodite flowers.
- Sexual variants are due to sex expression in hermaphrodite flowers. It is influenced by temperature and soil moisture condition.
- Long days and high temperature favours femaleness in CO.1 papaya.
- Classification based on sex forms and flowers was proposed by Storey (1958): 8 sex forms-
  - Staminate flowers are produced by male plants.
  - Teratological staminate flowers by sex reverting male plants.
  - Reduced elongata.
  - Elongata.
  - Carpelloid elongata.
  - Pentandria
  - Carpelloid pentandrial flowers by hermaphrodite plants.

- º Pistillate flowers by pistillate plants.
- Hofmeyr (1938) and Storey (1941) studied about sex determining genes.
- Maleness (staminate) genotype (M_1rrm). Male flowers are produced on long stalk.
- Female (pistillate) genotype (mm): Most stable sex form.
- Bisexual (hermaphrodite) genotype: M_2m.
- Sex reversing male: M_1RR_m (homozygous male) or M_1Rr_m (heterozygous male).
- Red skin colour is present only in gynodioecious varieties.
- Carpelloidy formation: <20 ^{0}C, low elevation or cool winter.
- Staminal carpelloidy: Abnormal development of stamens into fleshy carpel like structure i.e. stamen become part of fruit resulting cat face appearance.
- In dioecious variety, reproductive organ is unisexual.
- Sterility: Normally reproductive hermaphrodite trees change into maleness i.e. only male flowers are produced.
- 10% male plants are planted where dioecious varieties are cultivated.
- Three seedlings/ pit in dioecious varieties and no male plants in gynodioecious varieties. Hence, only one seedling per pit.
- Removal of male plants is necessary in dioecious varieties to maintain sex ratio maintained as 1 male: 20 females.
- Hermaphrodite: female ratio in gynodioecious variety: 3:1 and hermaphrodite serves as pollen source.
- Production of gynodioecious lines: Hermaphrodite x hermaphrodite (M_2m x M_2m).
- Gynodioecious varieties breed true-to-type and 2 sex forms i.e. pistillate and hermaphrodite are found.
- Pure male and pistillate sex forms are stable.
- Lethal combination of gene: M_1M_1.
- Prediction of sex of nursery seedlings by colorimetric test for leaf extracts was true upto 88% in female and 67% in males.

Crossability behaviour-

Group I	*C. monoica, C. microcarpa, C. cauliflora, C. candamarcensis*	Easily crossable with each other & produce viable seeds
Group II	*C. papaya*	Cross between group I & II do not form mature seeds & immature embryo is cultivated through embryo culture
Group III	*C. goudottiana*	Cross between group II and III not successful
	C. minoica x *C. goudottiana*; *C. parviflora* x *C. goudottiana*; *C. goudottiana* x *C. monoica*; *C. cauliflora* x *C. pennata*	Produce viable seeds
	C. parviflora x *C. goudottiana*; *C. cauliflora* x *C. monoica*	Heterosis is observed

Varieties:

- Dai (1960): 1st reported heterosis in Philippine x Solo.
- In India, papaya breeding was started in 1950.
- The earliest breeding was started in Tamil Nadu Agricultural University, Coimbatore, in 1954.
- A papaya improvement programme was started at the Regional Fruit Research Station, Pusa, Bihar, in early 1966.
- Food and Drug administration of USA declared transgenic papaya are safe for human consumption in 1997.
- Hortus Gold: Developed by Dr. J.D. Hofmeyer.
- Honey Gold: Developed from 'Hortus Gold' by Allan in 1981.
- Sun Up: Transgenic of cv. Sun Set. Developed by Dr. Dennis Gonsalves in 1998 from Cornell University. Red fleshed and PRSV resistant.
- Exotic varieties popular in India: Red Lady (syn. Taiwan 786; gynodioecious; blood red coloured flesh; elongated fruits).
- Hybrid 'Sinta' (orange yellow flesh & very sweet).
- Transgenic varieties (Laie Gold, Rainbow) is developed from coat protein gene in Hawaii during 1992 using microprojectile bombardment.
- *C. papaya* x *V. quercifolia* and *C. papaya* x *V. cauliflora*: Hybrids exhibit resistance to PRSV.
- Yellow Lady: Developed by Mahabeej, Maharashtra.
- Barwani: Popular variety.
- RTCP-3, Iceberry, Greenberry.

Varieties	Breeding method	Features
Hortus Gold, Honey Gold, Kaapmuiden	Introduced from South Africa	Golden yellow fruits with high sugar content
Santa Cruz Giant, Cedros, Singapore	Introduced from Trinidad	-
Semangka, Thailand, Bangkok	Introduced from Indonesia	-
Improved Peterson, Guinea Gold, Airline 57	Introduced from Australia	-
Honey Dew (syn. Madhu Bindu)	Introduction from Hawaii	Gynodioecious; extra fine pulp
Khaknuan, Thapra 2	Introduction from Thailand	Transgenic PRSV resistant varieties
Cavity Special, Sinta	-	Popular in Philippines
Kapoho Solo	-	Solo cvs. Popular in Hawaii; yellow flesh

Tainung-2	-	Main cv. of Taiwan occupying 90% area
Tainung- 10-Orange Baby	-	Popular in Taiwan
Dai Loan Tim, Sieu Lun Cao San	-	Popular in Vietnam; purple coloured
Khaek Dam, Khaek Nuan, Dampit	-	Popular in Indonesia
IARI Regional Station, Pusa, Bihar		
Ranchi	Local selection	Popular; all 3 sex forms observed & highly variable
Pusa Delicious (Pusa 1-15) 1982	Sib-mating & selection from cv. Ranchi	Gynodioecious; papain extraction; deep orange coloured flesh
Pusa Majesty (Pusa 22-3) 1982	Sib-mating & selection from cv. Ranchi	Gynodioecious, tolerant to virus & nematode; orange coloured flesh
Pusa Giant (Pusa 1-45V) 1982	Sib-mating & selection from cv. Ranchi	Dioecious; suitable for vegetable, tooty fruity & canning; tolerant to strong winds
Pusa Dwarf (Pusa 1-45D) 1982	Sib-mating & selection from cv. Ranchi	Dioecious; suitable for HDP & nutritional/ kitchen garden
Pusa Nanha (1982)	Gamma ray mutant (15 kR) of local type in M_3 generation	Extremely dwarf; dioecious; suitable for HDP, kitchen gardening, pot & roof cultivation; tolerant to water logging
IIHR, Bengaluru		
Coorg Honey Dew (1959)	Chance seedling of 'Honey Dew'	1st variety developed in India; gynodioecious, dwarf & heavy bearing; papain extraction; orange flesh
Pink Red Fleshed (1992)	Selection	Gynodioecious & good dessert variety
Arka Surya (1996)	Heterosis breeding of (Sun Rise Solo x Pink Flesh Sweet)	Gynodioecious, red pulp, fruit wt. 800 g; low cavity index (17%); 14^0B TSS; yield 60-80 kg/ plant
Arka Prabhat	(Arka Surya x Tainung-1) x Local Dwarf	Gynodioecious & deep red pulp; low cavity index; TSS 14^0B
TNAU, Coimbatore		
CO.1 (1972)	Sib-mating selection from Ranchi type	Dwarf, dioecious; fruit round-oval; orange yellow flesh
CO.2 (1973)	Pure line selection from local Ranchi type (Selection-7)	Red flesh; suitable for papain extraction; 4-6 g papain/ fruit
CO.3 (1983)	Hybrid derivative of (CO.2 x Sun Rise Solo)	Gynodioecious; suitable for home gardening; red flesh
CO.4 (1983)	CO.1 x Washington	Dioecious; dwarf; high papain content (800-900 kg/ha); yellow flesh; TSS 13^0Brix
CO.5 (1985)	Inbred selection of 'Washington'	Dwarf; highest papain extraction (1500-1600 kg dried papain/ ha)

CO.6 (1986)	Inbred selection of 'Pusa Majesty'	Dioecious; dual purpose (both table & latex); latex (7-8 g/ fruit)
CO.7 (1997)	Hybrid derivative of (Coorg Honey Dew x CP-75)	Gynodioecious, red flesh; TSS 16.5^0 Brix with low stamen carpellody
CO.8 (2014)	7th generation selection from sibmating population of 'CO.2 x Red anthered teratological male'	Dioecious, red flesh; 75-80 fruits/tree; fruit wt. 2.2 kg; highly suitable for processing & papain extraction
P-7-2, P-7-9, P-7-15, Goa-1, Goa-2	-	Cold tolerant & gynodioecious lines
MPKV, Rahuri		
Pune Selection 1 & 3	Selection	Dioecious; tolerant to PRSV
Phule Vijaya (2018)	Selection	Dioecious; resistant to PRSV, yellow flesh; 78% pulp; avg.wt. 1.33 kg
GBPAU & T, Pantnagar		
Pant Papaya-1 (1984)	Seedling selection	Dioecious; dwarf; heavy yielder; resistant to anthracnose
Pant Papaya-2 (1984)	Seedling selection	Dioecious; tolerant to frost & wet condition; fruits medium-large
Pant Papaya-3 (1984)	Seedling selection	Dioecious; tolerant to frost & water logging
PAU, Ludhiana		
Punjab Sweet	Selection	Dioecious, frost tolerant
Other varieties		
UH Rainbow	Transgenic (Sun Up x Kapoho Solo)	Vigorous; full fruit columns; yield: 20 t/ha; PRSV resistant
Laie Gold	Transgenic (Rainbow F_2 x Red Kamiya)	Vigorous; full fruit columns; PRSV resistant
Solo	Transgenic developed by J.E. Higgins	Gynodioecious; grown in Hawaii; fruits small, deeply ribbed, pyriform shaped; flesh yellowish orange coloured; TSS 14^0 Brix; revolutionized papaya cultivation
Maradol	Transgenic	Self incompatible; resistant to anthracnose
Sun Rise, Sun Set	Transgenic	Solo cvs. Popular in Hawaii
Sun Rise Solo	Inbred selection from Line 9 (Pink Solo) x Kariya Solo (farmer's selection)	Gynodioecious; Hawaiian cv.; high carotene content; pyriform fruit shape
Washington	-	Oldest cv.; round-ovate fruits, sweet flavour; stem have purple ring at node & petiole dark purple
PL-13/96	Seedling selection from Pune Selection-3	Pink coloured flesh
HPSC-3	Tripura Local x Honey Dew	Resistant to papaya mosaic pote x virus; high yield (198 t/ ha); papain yield (5 g/fruit)
Waimanalo (1972), Wilder	-	Gynodioecious; orange yellow flesh; popular in Hawaii

Farm selection 1, Chakalua, Haldwani, Nainital	-	Farmer developed varieties
CPL	Selection from cv. Homestead	Plant parts purple coloured & serve as marker gene
Eksotica	Malaysian variety developed by back crossing (Local Subang x Sun Rise Solo)	Gynodioecious; high yield; TSS 13-15^0 Brix; female plants produce round fruits & hermaphrodite plants produce pyriform fruits
Thailand	-	Gynodioecious; very sweet; deep red flesh
Malay Yellow	Yellow mutant from Malaysia	-
Saipan Red	-	Red flesh line from Micronesia
Higgins	-	Gynodioecious; export purpose variety of Hawaii; suitable for dry areas
CP-60	CO.1 x Washington	Yellow flesh & purple tinge on stem, petile & flowers
CP-81	CO.2 x Sun Rise Solo	Hermaphrodite; red flesh
CP-75	Pusa Delicious x CO.2	-

Inheritance of characters:

- 1st time heterosis in intervarietal hybrids is upto 111% over parents for yield was reported by Dai (1960).
- PMSM1 and PMSM2: Male specific markers (sex determination).
- Papaya sex form is controlled by 3 alleles of a single gene with pleiotropic effects: M_1, M_2 and m.
- Maleness is controlled by satellite chromosome.

Characters	Inheritance pattern
Sex reversal	Single dominant gene (*RR*)
Flower colour	Yellow dominant over white
Stem colour	Purple dominant to red
Leaf structure	Ruegose recessive to smooth leaf
Leaf surface	Waxy recessive to flat bladed
Albino plant colour	*a*- Albino plant recessive to normal green
Plant height	*d*-Dwarf recessive to tall
Diminutive plant (short slender trunk, small leaves)	*dp*- Diminutive plant recessive to large plant
Crimpled leaf	*cp*- Crimpled leaf recessive to normal leaf
Red flesh (pulp)	*r*- Red flesh recessive to yellow flesh
Seed coat colour	*B*- Grey dominant to black colour
Red skin colour	Dominant gene
Succulent pulp	Dominant gene

Pests, diseases and disorders:

- The term "papaya ring spot" was first coined by Jensen.
- Papaya is highly sensititve to diamethoate, chlorpyriphos and omite pesticides.
- Cross protection technique is used.

Name	Causal organism	Remarks & remedy
Papaya fruit fly	*Bactrocera papayae* (*Toxotrypana curvicauda*)	Serious pest; introduced into Florida in 1905, mostly from the West Indies
Mealy bug	*Paracoccus marginatus*	Outbreak occurs in Tamil Nadu during 2009. Biocontrol agent: *Acerophagus papaya* (parasitoid)
Red spider mite	-	Most destructive
White fly	*Bemisia tabaci*	Spray Acetamiprid 20 SP @ 1%.
Collar rot/ Stem rot	*Pythium aphanidermatum*	Soil borne & more severe
Fruit rot & root rot	*Phytophthora palmivora*	Most damaging disease during rains; use copper based fungicides
Anthracnose	*Colletotrichum gloeo sporioides*	Major storage disease
Damping off	*Rhizoctonia, Pythium, Phytophthora*	Most serious & common disease in nursery
Papaya leaf curl	White fly (*Bemisea tabaci*)	Major problem in north India
Papaya Ring Spot Virus (PRSV)	Aphids	Major problem in India. It was 1st recorded in western India in 1958
Papaya sticky disease (syn. Meleira)	-	Viral disease
Phoma spot	*Stagonosporopsis caricae*	-
Deformed papaya fruits with bumpy skin surface	B deficiency	-
Burning of leaf tips and margins	Excess B application in soil	
Skin freckling	Ca deficiency	Wrap young fruits with white paper bags

16. CLUSIACEAE (GUTTIFERAE)

16.1 Kokum

- Eulogized as 'Mangosteen oil tree or *ratamba* or Kokum butter tree or Zero attention crop or Manik of Konkan or Pearl of Konkan'.
- Genus *Garcinia* is a large one (>200 species) of evergreen polygamous trees, shrubs and herbs.
- Sex forms: 3 (female, male and hermaphrodite).
- Sex of seedling plant is known after 7 to 8 years of planting.
- Seeding progeny give 50% of each sex.
- Male plants serve as only pollinizers.
- Plants are known for their oil glands or secretary canals of cavities, which contain yellow or brightly coloured resins.

- Kokum rind contains natural red pigment (2-3%) anthocyanin and seed kernel contains 32-35% fat i.e. kokum butter.
- Fruit contains substantial amount of malic acid and very small quantity of tartaric and citric acid.
- Fruit rind also contains fat soluble yellow pigment garcinol.
- Kokum butter is used in confectionary, cosmetics, soap, candles and ointments.
- For better sunlight availability pruning is attempted once in a year.
- Branching patter: Dimorphic.
- Two types of branches: Orthotropic (main shoot) and plagiotropic (branches).
- Plagiotropic shoots bear fruits and flowers.
- Two sprays of KNO_3@ 3% twice a year (January-February) is essential for more fruit set, good quality and early maturity.
- Saponification value: 189.
- Inarch grafting on 10-18 months old seedlings gives 90% success.
- Softwood grafting on 22 weeks old seedling in October is highly successful.
- Planting distance: 6m x 6 m.
- Flowering season: October to February.
- Fruit harvesting: March to June.
- Maturity index: Fruit colour changes from greenish to reddish.
- Yield: 60-80 kg/fruits/ tree.
- Avoid water stress.
- Herbicide: Gramoxone @ 4 ml/lit + 2% urea.
- For juice extraction, fruits are crushed at 60°C with >1.6% juice recovery having TSS 14.8% and total anthocyanins (73 mg/100 ml).
- Value added products: Kokam syrup (amrit kokum), Kokam agal (brined kokam juice), brined ripe kokum rind (amsul) and natural food colour.

Species:

- Kokum (*G. indica*syn. *G. purpurea*): Evergreen and dioecious.
- Gambage (*G. cambogia*, *G. xanthochymus*): Androdioecious.
- White kokum (*G. morella*): Evergreen,
- Malabar tamarind/ Kadam pulli (*G. gummigutta*):
- *G. cowa* (syn. *G. kydia*): Spice and condiment with medicinal properties.
- Male plants serves only as pollinizers.
- Fruit rind contains 'citrin' i.e. Hydroxy Citric acid (1,2-dihydroxy propane-1,2,3-tricarboxylic acid). Widely used against obesity and weight management.
- Possess anti-oxidant property.

- Processsed rind is an excellent substitute for tamarind in cooking.
- Ovary is two to eight celled ovules with axile placentation.
- Rinds are preserved by rubbing with salt and coconut oil.

Varieties:

- KK-87, KK-155, IC 136687-3, KK-76, KK-149, KK-153, Vengurla-43, MLDK-5 (thick rind of >50 mm).

Name	Breeding method	Features
Dr BSKKV, Dapoli		
Konkan Amruta (1997)	Selection from Shirgaon local	Early; apple shaped fruits; fruit wt. (30 g); yield (140 kg/ tree); long shelf life
Konkan Hatis (2005)	Selection	Female type & require planting of 5-6% male trees for pollination; bold fruits; thick rind; fruit wt. 90-95 g; 5-6 seeds/ fruit; fruits apple shaped; TSS 9.2^0 Brix; acidity 5.1%; yield (250 kg fruits/ tree/ year of 7th year);
Vengurla-43	Clonal selection	-
IIHR, Bengaluru (CHES, Chettalli)		
CHES Ko-5/6	Seedling selection	-
CHES GI-V-8	Seedling selection	Fruit wt. 75-85g; fruits dull red colored; 4-5 seeds/ fruit, rind dark red, flesh white; rind recovery 62%; TSS 13.5^0 Brix; vit. C (62 mg/100g); yield (300-500 fruits/tree)
CHES GI-VIII-5	Seedling selection	Fruit wt. 50-60 g; fruit dull red coloured; 6-7 seeds/fruit, rind dark red, flesh white; rind recovery 59.5%; TSS 14.1^{0}Brix; vit. C (64 mg/ 100 g); yield (1000-1200 fruits/ tree)
CHES GI-V-4	Seedling selection	Fruit wt. 45-50 g; fruits dull red coloured, rind dark red, flesh white; rind recovery 48%; TSS 14.5^0 Brix; vit. C. 36 mg/100g pulp; yield (1000-1250 fruits/ tree)
CHES GG-V-1	Seedling selection	Malabar tamarind type; fruit wt. 75-85g; fruits dull yellow colored, 6-7 seeds/fruit; flesh white, 8 segments, juicy and acid; seeds not attached to flesh; rind recovery 62%; TSS 13.5^{0}brix; vit. C 62 mg/100g; yield 400-700 fruits/ tree

16.2 Mangosteen

- Eulogized as 'Queen of tropical fruits or Finest fruit of the world or Mystery fruit or Fruit of Gods or Energy tablet'.
- National fruit of Thailand.
- Leading country in production: Thailand.
- Widely cultivated in Indonesia, Malaysia, Burma, Philippines, and Sri Lanka.
- Successfully fruited in English green houses in 1855.
- 1st domesticated in Thailand and introduced in India in 1881.
- Natural staple food for man.
- Fruit is rich source of natural 'xanthone' compound having medicinal value.

- Fruit cortex (rind): Used in tannary due to high tannin (13%) content. Ideal for treating cancer, tuberculosis and leukemia.
- Thick rind is rich in tannic acid and dyes.
- Cortex is used in treating chronic diarrhoea, uretural irritation, gynorrhea, etc.
- Anti-neoplasic activity: Gamma-mangostin.
- Ultra tropical fruit crop is due to adaptation to high temperature and humidity.
- Dioecious and shade tolerant tree.
- Longest pre-bearing cycle.
- Highly susceptible to frost and below 5^{0}C, plants are killed.
- *Garcinia mangostana* is an obligate agamo-sperm (2n=88-90) which reproduces by adventitious budding of proembryos from ovular tissues. This hampers cultivar improvement.
- Allotetraploid tree arises from natural hybridization between *G. malaccensis* (2n=42) and *G. hombroniana* (2n=48) which are facultative agamosperms.
- Flowers are sessile and fruit is berry.
- Fruits are round, smooth, purplish/ reddish brown coloured cortex (rind) which is about 0.6 cm thickness, with rosette of dead petals around the stalk and an odd 'flower' shaped button on the other end.
- Inside the fruit 4-6 segments are found but only 1-2 of them contain seeds that have size and shape of shrivelled almond.
- Pearl white, soft and juicy edible pulp has sweet, pleasant flavour is edible.
- Seed development is through diploid parthenogenesis.
- Inner bark of tree contains gummy bitter latex.
- Only fruit in which glucose is readily available form for instant energy.
- Red coloured rind: Cyanidin-3-glucoside.
- Aroma of fleshy aril: Hexyl acetate.
- Number of carpels: 4-8.
- Only female trees are known.
- Lack of genetic variation: Dearth of male trees and lack of pollination
- Type of fruit development: Parthenogenesis (nucellar origin).
- Propagation method: Seeds (apomictic/ azygotic i.e. asexual origin from nucellar tissue)- recalcitrant and polyembryonic (2-4 seedlings).
- Seedlings are slow growing and reach 15 cm height and 2-3 years.
- Slow and poor growth of seedlings is attributed to lack of adequate fibrous lateral roots.
- Seed propagation is considered as major barrier in cultivation.

- Seed viability: Within a month to maximum of 8 weeks.
- Commercial propagation: Cleft grafting.
- Softwood grafting using sweet/ sour rootstock and scion from one year old shoot gives 50% survival.
- Scion sticks collected from plagiotropic branches exhibit lateral spreading growth which is undesirable.
- Scion from terminal portions exhibit orthotropic shoots is desirable for commercial scale.
- Air layering is practiced with less success due to poor rooting.
- Tissue culture using seed explants is highly successful.
- Planting time: May-September.
- Biennial bearing is reported.
- Planting distance: 7m x 7m to 10m x 10m.
- Pruning: Only remedial pruning is necessary. Avoid severe pruning.
- Average time of fruit bearing: 8-10 years after planting.
- Contribution of seed to total fruit weight: 2%.
- Fruit weight: 16-18 g.
- Number of seeds/ fruit: 5-7.
- In south Indian hilly areas, it flowers twice a year (August-October (main crop) and April-May).
- Fruit require about 120-150 days to reach maturity after flowering.
- Harvesting stage: Green brown to dark brown or reddish purple.
- Harvesting is done along with peduncle.
- Yield: 23-25 kg from 20 years old bearing tree or 500-1500 fruits/ tree.
- Storage period: 20-25 days at room temperature.
- Keeping quality is longer compared to other tropical fruits.
- At 4-6^{0}C with 85-90% R.H., fruits can be stored upto 50 days without much loss in aroma and flavour.
- Major problem in cultivation: Slow growth rate of tree and lack of root hairs.
- Value added products: Jelly, paste, syrup, canned fruit segments.
- During processing, fine aroma is lost and hence, fresh fruit are normally consumed.

Species:

- Occurrence of natural variability is limited due to asexual origin of seeds.

Name	Salient features
G. dulcis	Wild spp. bear edible sour fruits; yellow coloured fruits found in Moluccas; grown as fruit tree in Thailand
G. cambogia	Small, yellow pulped, yellow fruit; used as rootstocks on account of well developed root system
G. mangostana	Medicine as anti-inflammatory, anti-diarrhoea & dysentery
G. cowa or Cowa mangosteen	Young leaves as food additive in Thai food; it has bigger, ribbed & apricot coloured fruits which are too acidic & unsuitable for dessert, but makes good preserves
G. schomburgkiana	Fruits are made into preserve
G. hanburyii	Gum resin as purgative % for colouring
G. xanthochymus	Young shoots & mature fruits as vegetable; used as rootstock
G. thorelii	Source of poles. Tree is tall & slender
G. livingstonei	Small fruited, large seed & little sour flesh; used as rootstock
G. morella	Common in South-East Asia & plant also provides orange-red resin, gamboge

Variety:

- Jolo: Famous variety in Phillippines bears large sized fruits and tasty pulp.
- Many local varieties are found in East Indies.

Pest and physiological disorders:

- Leaf eating caterpillar: Major pest.
- Gamboge: Excessive exudation of yellow gum/ latex from branches and fruit pericarp due to high pH.
- Translucent Flesh Disorder (TFD): Major limiting factor in cultivation (Pamplona and Garcia, 2001). Caused by heavy rainfall during pre-harvest i.e. development and growth. Affected fruits show lower titratable acid percentage and soluble solid concentration. Specific gravity of affected fruit is > 1.
- Splitting of fruits: Ca deficiency and heavy irrigation after severe dry spell.
- Little leaf: Mycoplasma and Zn deficiency.
- Irregular fruit shape: Insect damage.
- Fruit cracking, yellow gumming, hardening of pericarp.

17. CORYLACEAE (BETULACEAE)

17.1 Hazelnut

- Eulogized as 'Filbert or Cobnut or Barcelona nut or European hazel'.
- Produced commercially in Turkey, Italy and USA.
- Extensively used in confectionery to make praline and nutella.
- Wild type or Turkish hazelnut (*Corylus colurna*): Grown in Shimla, Himachal Pradesh.
- Cultivated (*C. avellana*).
- Nut yield: 0.85 to 2.9 kg/tree.

- Kernel wt: 1.41 g.
- Nut wt: 3.26 g.
- Blanching treatment is needed to kernels.
- Removal of suckers is a common practice.
- **Varieties**: Tonda Romana, Tonda di Giffoni, Tonda della Langhe.

18. EBENACEAE

18.1 Persimmon

- Eulogized as 'Ebony tree or Japanese persimmon'.
- Introduced from Japan by A.N. Lee in 1921 at Kullu valley of Himachal Pradesh.
- Fruits of tropical origin grown in temperate region does not require chilling.
- Dioecious and deciduous fruit crop.
- It bears only pistillate flowers and exhibit vegetative parthenocarpy.
- Edible portion: Epicarp and mesocarp.
- Rich in vitamin A: 2710 IU/ 100g.
- Pollination agent: Honey bee.
- Planting of pollinizer: 10-15% of total population.
- Artificial pollination is practiced to overcome unfruitfulness.
- Planting time: Winter (January-February) when trees are dormant.
- Planting density: Dwarf cvs. (Jiro) at 5 m x 2.5 m (800 plants/ha); semi-dwarf cv. (Fuyu) at 5 m x 3 m (600 plants/ha); vigorous cv. at 6 m x 4.5 m (370 plants/ha).
- Flowering time: February (after completion of dormancy/ rest period).
- Fruit bud differentiation: Mid-July-August.
- Fruiting time: August.
- Stamen and anthers appear in early April and pistil afterwards.
- Blossom thinning is more effective than fruit thinning done 10 days before anthesis.
- Rootstock seed require stratification for 60-90 days for germination.
- Propagation methods: Whip grafting (adopted for smaller diameter stocks), cleft grafting and vener grafting (adopted for large diameter stocks), tongue grafting (60-65% success), green grafting (followed in summer & commercially adopted in New Zealand), T-budding (80% success in spring & early autumn).
- Commercial propagation: Inarching on its own rootstock: *D. lotus*.
- Extensively used as rootstock in Japan: Saijo seedlings.
- Heading back or thinning out is practiced to produce stronger shoots.
- Highly astringent fruit: Due to presence of tannins ($C_{14}H_{20}O_9$).

- Removal of astringency means polymerization of tannins and not converting tannins to sugars.
- Removal of astringency of from fruits is done by:
  - Spray ethephon @ 500 ppm for 15-24 h;
  - Fruits exposed to fumes of ethanol for 10-15 days (1 kg fruits in 4-5 ml);
  - CO_2 charged atmosphere: Temperature of fruits increased to 25°C then 1.3 to 1.6 kg/m² CO_2 is treated per 300 kg fruits for 20-14 h.
  - 20 kg fruits require 240 g dry ice for 5 days treatment.
- Seed formation plays an important role in removing astringency taste and improves fruit set in PVNA type.
- In cv. Nishimurawase, more than 4 seeds are essential to remove astringency.
- It looses astringency when packed with kieffer pear, tomatoes, mangosteen and passion fruit.
- Flowers appear in spring on new growth.
- Optimum soil pH: 6 to 6.8.
- Days required for stratification: 60-90 days.
- Chilling requirement: 100-200 h below 7.2°C.
- Night temperature at 20 ± 2°C advances anthesis.
- Temperature of 8-11°C for 888 h. is enough to complete dormancy of astringent persimmons.
- During dormancy period, astringent cvs. can tolerate and survive as low as -15°C.
- Temperature for perfect sweet persimmon production: 14.6 to 15.7°C.
- Seedlings difficult to transport due to tap root system and few fibrous roots.
- Cincturing or girdling......... in training and pruning part: Practice of removal of bark strip around the trunk.
- Main sugars in mature fruit: Fructose, glucose, sucrose, sorbitol and inositol.
- Major acids: Malic and Citric acid.
- Increase in fruit diameter follows double sigmoid growth curve each year.
- Maturity indices:
  - Full development of fruit;
  - Colour development;
  - Brix level at time of maturity (14 to 17°);
  - Early harvest results in lack of colour, sweetness and flavour;
  - Fruits harvested by clipping, leaving calyx and short stem attached to fruit.
- MA storage condition: 0°C and 85% R.H. upto 18 weeks.
- CA storage condition: 9% CO_2 + 2% O_2 increases shelf life upto 4 months.
- Value added products: Dried fruits, pickles, vinegar, wine.

Species:

- Saijo seedlings are extensively used as rootstock in Japan.
- *D. virginiana* is cross incompatible with *D. kaki* and *D. lotus*.

Common name	Botanical name	Features & cultivars
Asian Date plum	*Diospyros lotus*	Very vigorous; graft compatible with *D. kaki*; mostly consumed fresh; used as rootstock; susceptible to crown gall
Japanese or Oriental or Sweet persimmon	*D. kaki*	Tetraploid & hexaploid with (2n=60, 90); dioecious
-	*D. glandulosa* (syn. *D. roxburghii*)	Progenitor of *D. kaki*; diploid (2n=30)
-	*D. oleifera*	Used as rootstock
American persimmon	*D. virginiana*	2n=90; rootstock adapted to damp heavy soils & very cold hardy conditions; small fruits, sweeter than *D. kaki*; heavy suckering; highly susceptible to Cephalosporium wilt and scion growth variable & non vigorous. Source of wood for golf club heads e.g. Early Golden, Ruby, Miller
Black sapota	*D. nigra*	-
Mabola persimmon (syn. Velvet apple)	*D. discolor*	Dioecious; edible fruits; ornamental value

Training and pruning:

- Dwarf and semi-dwarf: Modified central leader system.
- Vigorous tree: Palmette or vase-system.
- Trellising systems viz. Tatura, Lincoln and espalier systems.
- Spindle bush: Recommended for HDP.
- Pruned twice a year: At dormant stage and at peak growing period.
- Blossom thinning is important than fruit thinning.
- Cincturing or girdling and GA improves fruit wt. and size.
- Optimum time is 10 days before anthesis and fruit thinning at end of physiological drop.
- Chemical for fruit thinning: NAA @ 10 ppm.
- Control of physiological fruit drop: GA_3 @ 50 ppm.

Varieties:

- Most of cultivars have originated in Japan.
- Countries producing sweet persimmons: Japan, Korea, Brazil, Israel, New Zealand, USA, Italy.
- Cultivars are classified as pollination-constant (PC) if the flesh colour of fruit turns orange-yellow and pollination-variant (PV) if formation of seed causes change in flavour and colour of mesocarp adjacent to seed.

- Non-astringent cvs. require warmer conditions (> 1400 h. sunshine & 16-22^{0}C) for best fruit quality than astringent types (for cooler areas).
- Astringent cvs. are suitable for cooler areas.
- Difference between sweet and astringent types are in quality and size of tannin cells (smaller in 'sweet' than all other types).
- Astringent (A) varieties: Nightingale, Flat Seedless, Triumph, Hyakuma, Hiratanenashi, Shakoku, Giombo, Amankaki, Hachiya, Flat seedless,
- Non-astringent (NA) varieties: Hana Fuyu, Twenteeth Century, Matsumoto, Suruga.
- Oriental persimmons are not astringent when firm.
- Most preferred fruit: PCNA type i.e. perfect sweet persimmons e.g. Gosho, and Matsumotowase (susceptible to anthracnose).
- PVNA type: Imperfect sweet persimmon.
- PCA type: Perfect astringent cultivars e.g. Saijo, Atago.
- PVA type: Imperfect astringent cultivars.
- Varieties of PCNA type are most prone to cracking.
- American cvs.: Early Golden, Ruby, Miller.
- Japanese cvs. Tonewase and Shinsyu respond to artificial pollination after disbudding.

Name	Breeding method	Features
Fuyu (1902)	-	PCNA type; fruit wt. 220 g; high sugar content with no acidity & astringency; 4-5 seeds/ fruits; late variety; rare or weak parthenocarpy; need pollinizer; graft incompatible with *D. lotus*; susceptible to anthracnose
Sujika	-	Formation of white lines on the rind of fruit
Rossiyanka	Interspecific hybridization of (*D. virginiana* x *D. kaki*) followed by embryo culture	Fruits larger than its female parent & contained 1.5 times more sugar than male parent; medium in astringency; resistant to low temperature
Nikitskaya Bordovaya	Chance seedling	-
Nishimurawase	OP seedling of (Fuyu x PVNA type)	PVNA type; fruit has >4 seeds; large fruits; orange red skin; yellow flesh; ripens in late September; susceptible to anthracnose
Fuyuhana (syn. Pomelo)	Fuyu x Hanogosho	Excellent fruit quality
Ito	Fuyu x Oku-Ogosho	PCNA type; small fruits 180 g; 14-16% TSS; early mature; susceptible to anthracnose
Jiro	-	PCNA type; susceptible to cracking; 1-2 seed/ fruit; very sweet in taste; susceptible to anthracnose
Izu	-	Early; orange red fruits; excellent quality
Maekawa Jiro	-	Large fruit size, dark orange colour; mid-season, excellent quality
Daeandangam	Chance seedling	PCNA type; 13% TSS; soft flesh & abundant juice

Kyongsanbansi	Chance seedling	PCA type; 1-2 seeds/ fruit; ripen in October
Sagoksi	-	PCA type; strong parthenocarpic habit; used as interstock for dwarf scion cultivars; suitable for processing
Hiratanenashi	-	PVA type; most leading cv. of Japan; orange yellow skin; strong parthenocarpic habit; susceptible to anthracnose
Hachiya (syn. Fuji)	-	PVA type; large fruit (> 300 g); oblong shape; suiable for processing; commercially grown in India & California
Tonewase	Bud sport of Hiratanenashi	PVA type; grown under protected cultivation; susceptible to anthracnose
Goldener	Chance seedling from native germplasm	Soft flesh & good flavour; fruit detach from calyx when mature;
Owens	-	Oblate shape; fine flavour; seedless fruits; late bearing
Cheongdobansi	-	Strong parthenocarpic habit
Kojongsi	-	PCA types; small, oblong fruits; strong parthenocarpic habit; less post harvest fruit drop; suitable for processing
Goldener	Chance seedling from native American spp.	Soft flesh; fruit detach from calyx; bears late even if grafted
Owens	-	Oblong shaped seedless fruits; largest tree in USA

Inheritance of characters:

- Sex forms and pulp astringency: Polygenes.
- Small fruit size dominant over large fruit.

Disease, pests and disorders:

- Cephalosporium wilt (*Cephalosporium diospyri*).
- Crown gall:
- Cercospora leaf spot:
- Calyx cavity dehiscence (syn. Calyx end cracking): Serious problem in cvs. Izu and Suruga due to high N and moisture deficiency.
- Mealy bugs:
- Fruit fly:
- Skin russeting: Due to high temperature and excess nitrogen application.
- Fruit drop and calyx cavity: Low moisture and high nitrogen.
- Green spot and black spot: Storage disorder.
- Micronutrient (Mg, Mn, Ca) deficiency is more prominent in young trees.
- Green blotch: Excess Mn.
- Sujika: Refers formation of white lines on fruit rind.
- Major problems: Alternate bearing, poor setting.
- Fruit drop: Spray GA_3 @ 50 ppm or Tom a toton @ 15 ppm.

19. ELAEGNACEAE

19.1 Seabuckthorn

- Eulogized as 'Brahmphal or Amil or Tarwar or Amesh or Gold mine of wasteland in cold desert or Store house of vitamins or Holy plant of hilly regions'.
- Typical dry temperature plant, thorny and dioecious shrub having drought resistant capacity.
- Grown at 2000-3000 m above MSL.
- Suitableplant for pharmaceutical, cosmetic and food industry.
- Oil is rich in vit. E and β-carotene and used as folk medicine in China, Tibet and India.
- Seabuckthorn has capacity to fix atmospheric nitrogen through *Frankia* symbiosis.
- Fruits highly acidic with exotic flavour.
- Vitamin C content: 3-4 times higher than aonla and 10-15 times higher than kiwi fruit.
- Controls soil erosion and reclamation of degraded lands.
- Propagation: IBA @ 400 ppm to semi-hardwood cuttings during March.

Species:

- *Hippophae salicifolia*: Most common in Uttarakhand.
- *H. tibetana*: Common in Garhwal and Kumaon region.

20. ERICACEAE

20.1 Cranberry

- Evergreen dwarf shrub having wiry, long & sparsly leafed stems.
- Raw cranberries have been marketed as a 'superfruit'.
- Popular fruit of Sweden.
- Leaves and fruits are used medicinally.
- Cowberry is eaten to cure diarrhea.
- Section: *Oxycocus*.
- Self fertile in nature.
- Inflorescence: Racemose.
- Flowers: Tiny, yellow & pink blooms & appear in early summer.
- Fruits methods: Cluster of round, red coloured berries which are sour in taste.
- Propagation: Seeds and tip layering.
- In tip layering, rooting takes place near the tip of current season's shoot which is bent to the ground. Rooted layers are detached and planted during spring season.

- Most of these berries prefer slightly acidic soils.
- Only terminal pruning is required.
- Fruits are used for making jelly, tarts & pies.
- False bloom: Disorder associated with excess water.

Species:

- American cranberry (*V. macrocarpon*): Similar to cranberry but larger in size & edible berries.
- Cowberry or Foxberry (*V. vitis* var. *idaea*): It is also similar, more densely leafed, with rounded ends & clusters of berries which are more acidic in taste to eat raw but excellent for culinary purposes.
- Mortinia (*V. floribundum*): It is from Ecuador, is evergreen shrub with heavy racemes of rose-pink blooms followed by masses of red berries.
- *V. praestans*: It is from East Asia & Japan, is prostrate, creeping, deciduous shrub with sweet, fragrant, glossy red berries.
- *V. nummularia*: It is evergreen shrub with hairy stems & small black berries and resembles to cowberry.

20.2 Blueberry

- Eulogized as 'Mood fruit'.
- 1st fruit garnered as 'superfruit' title.
- Tree crop having maximum polyphenols.
- Deciduous or evergreen shrub.
- Plants are utilized for ornamental gardening and agroforestry development.
- Flower buds of high bush can tolerate -30^{0}C to -35^{0}C temperature.
- Factors affecting production: Spring frost and fluctuation in winter temperature.
- Chilling hours required: 650-850 h at < 7.2^{0}C.
- Suitable soil pH for growth: 4.2-5.2
- Richest source of anti-oxidants.
- Pollination agent: Honey bees.
- Propagation methods: Hardwood cuttings, grafting, tissue culture.
- Type of Seed germination: Photoblastic.
- Seed stratification: At 3-4^{0}C for 1 month.
- Increased fruit set: Up to 70%.
- Pruning: During dormant season.
- Flowering period: August-November.

- Ethephon @ 200 ppm increases flower initiation.
- Fruit maturity: November-March.
- Harvesting: May-July.
- Harvesting m^thod: Hand picking for dessert fruits and mechanical for processing.
- 3-7 pickings at weekly interval.
- Shelf life: 4-5 days at ambient condition.
- Value added products: Jam, jelly, sauces, juice, table wine.

Species:

Common name	Botanical name	Features
Highbush blueberry	*Vaccinium corymbosum*	Commercially cultivated in N. America and New Zealand
South eastern highbush blueberry	*V. atrococcum & V. australe*	-
Rabbit eye blueberry	*V. ashei*	
Lowbush blueberry	*V. angustifolium*	
Canadian blueberry	*V. myrtilloides*	-
Huckle berry or Dryland blueberry	*V. lirsutium*	-

Varieties:

- Low chilling requirements: Sharp Blue (150 h), Emerald and Jewel (200 h), Windsor and Spring High (225 h), Bright Well, Chaucer and Woodard (400 h), Climax (450 h), Tif Blue and Powder Blue (550 h).

Name	Features
Barkeley	Upright, hardy; mid-late season cv.; resistant to cracking
Blue Crop	Upright, hardy; drought resistant; cold tolerant; excellent export & keeping quality
Blue Ray	Upright, hardy; mid season cv.
Collins	Upright, hardy; early-mid season
Coville	Medium hardy; late season; good dessert quality; resistant to cracking
Early Blue	Upright, hardy; good flavour; resistant to cracking
Herbert	Dwarf; mid season
Jersey	Upright, hardy; lack aroma; tolerant to canker
Rubel	Upright; small fruits; suitable for processing

Pests and diseases:

- Aphid (*Illionoia pepperi*): Vector for virus.
- Sharp nosed leaf hopper (*Scaphytopius magdalensis*): Vector for stunt virus.
- Nematode (*Xiphinema americanum*): Most harmful.
- Maggot (*Rhagoletis pomonella*):
- Birds:

- Mummy berry (*Monilinia vaccinii-corymbosi*)
- Stem canker (*Botryosphaeria corticis*): Severe defoliation.
- Root rot (*Phytophthora cinnamomi*): Most serious.
- Fruit rot (*Colletotrichum gloeosporoides*):
- Shoe string virus: Vector- Aphids.

21. FABACEAE

21.1 Tamarind

- Eulogized as 'Indian date or Kalpavriksha for dry land'.
- Monotypic genus.
- It is very versatile spice.
- Excellent tree for social forestry, agro-forestry, waste lands development & dryland horticulture.
- Tolerates upto 45% exchangeable sodium.
- India faces competition from Thailand in exports.
- It has become hot stuff for patents in USA, Japan, Germany and India.
- Patents issued to CSIR: Production of tartaric acid from pulp.
- Patents issued to Hindustan Gums and Chemicals for use of kernel powder as thickner in textile printing paste.
- Among spices, occupy 6th position in terms of export value.
- India is largest producer & consumer of tamarind pulp in the world.
- India exports tamarind in various forms i.e. fresh, dried, powdered, paste, seed & flour meal to various countries.
- Major importers of Indian tamarind: France, Germany, Netherlands, USA, UK, Japan, Egypt, Syria, Sri Lanka, UAE, Switzerland, Saudi Arabia, Yemen Arab Republic.
- Applications: As an anti-obesity agent, anti-inflammatory, laxative, refrigerant, printing compositions, hair dyeing, cosmetics and pharmaceuticals.
- Manila tamarind/ *Jungle jalebee* (*Pithecellobium dulce*):
- Wood is valued as firewood due to high calorific value.
- In sour type: 4.80 to 38.94% sugar content.
- Fruit pulp provides 230-283 Kcal energy per 100 g.
- Pod: useful part (55% pulp, 34% seed, 11% shell and fibre).
- 100 kg pod weight yield 40 kg pulp + 20 kg seed + 40 kg shell & fibrous material.
- Pulp recovery: 80% (sour type); 60% (sweet type).
- Pulp contains 12.2 to 23.8% tartaric acid.

- Tartaric acid in sweet type: 2 to 3.2% with 39.1 to 47.7% sugar content.
- Pigments present: Chrisanthemin (red pulp); Leucoanthocyanin (brown pulp); Anthoxanthin (leaves); Xanthophyll (yellow flowers); Vitexene i.e. mixture of anthoxanthins (pulp).
- Free sugars in ripe pulp: D-glucose (47.7%), D-mannose (24.5%), D-maltose (20.4%), D-arabinose (2.8%).
- In ripe pulp, tartaric acid (in combined form as potassium bi-tartarate + calcium tartarate) ranges from 12.2-23.8%.
- Major amino acid in pulp: Proline serine & 5-methyl furfural.
- Seed contains 63% starch, 16% protein and 5.5% oil.
- Seed testa contains condensed type of tannins to the extent of 20-24%.
- Seed powder, if added (0.125 to 1%) to soil improves soil structure, water holding capacity & availability of nitrogen.
- Seedling trees exhibit strong biennial/ irregular bearing habit.
- Seed propagation is avoided do not breed true-to-type.
- Quantitative long day plant.
- Optimum temperature for growth: 8-45^{0}C.
- Flowers borne on current season's growth.
- Blossom bud differentiation begins with resumption of vegetative growth just after leaf fall.
- Two types of growth habits: Orthotropic, plagiotropic.
- Pollination agents: Flies, bees and red ants.
- Extreme low level of selfing & apomixis is absent.
- Self incompatible and predominantly protogynous.
- Reasons for low fruit set: Pollen limitations & floral abnormalities.
- Red & yellow dye are prepared from flowers.
- Leaflets folding after darkness: Free tartaric acid.
- Training and pruning is essential.
- Anthesis time: 4.30 am to 8.30 am with peak at 6.30 am.
- Anther dehiscence: 10.30 am to 11.30 am.
- Pollen viability: Up to 12 h at ambient condition and upto 30 days at 4^{0}C.
- Stigma receptivity: Day prior to anthesis upto 2 days after anthesis.
- Number of flowers/ inflorescence: 10-36 (red pulp type), 20-40 (sour & sweet pulp type).
- Days from bud to anthesis: 18-33 days.

- Single inflorescence blooms in 12-19 days.
- Fruit set under natural condition: 3-5%.
- Fruit set by artificial pollination: 56%.
- Congenial period for *in situ* soft wood grafting: Mid- January to mid February.
- Patch budding gives 96 % success (mid April-mid June) for quicker multiplication.
- Modified ring budding (94 % success) on 9 months old seedlings in June is good.
- Micrografting is performed on 3 months old saplings in June-July.
- Micropropagation is also practiced.
- *In vitro* rhizogenesis from micro shoots of axillary buds.
- Light pruning, removal of terminal branches during April results in more flowers.
- VAM fungal inoculated seedlings show better height and biomass production.
- Number of seeds/kg: 1800-2000.
- IBA @ 1000 ppm helps in early rooting in softwood cuttings (of 6-8 inch long from 1-2 year old branches in April) in mist chamber.
- Best rooting in June followed by September-October.
- HDP system: 10 x 5 m (250 trees/ha).
- Fruit maturity period: February-March.
- Maturity indices:
  - Days from flowering: 250-270.
  - Ripening starts on tree itself after diwali season and in December onwards fruit ripen.
  - Pods get suppressed.
  - Drastic reduction in fruit mature content from 80 to 20% causes separation of peel from pulp.
- Yield: 200-300 kg pods/ annum.
- Alcoholic beverage prepared by CFTRI, Mysuru: Tamarind vermouth.
- Important character in trade: Extra white endocarp membrane locally known as '*phool patti*'.
- Pulp contains 12% fibres, 1.27% pectin and preservative @ 600 ppm sodium benzoate.
- Pulp separation: Hydrolic basket press method or Brush type pulper process & can be stored for 1 year at 5^0C.
- Removal of water by vacuum evaporator & contains 65-68% total soluble solids.
- Pulp darkening: Non-enzymatic browning.
- Weight loss in pulp during storage is very low (0.18%) in black polyethylene bags.

- Processing and value addition:
  1. Extraction of pulp: Stickiness of pulp is due to low water content. Water dilution (1 part pulp : 2 part water) method is widely used with 13.2^0 brix & excellent flavor.
  2. Tartarate pectin: Prepared from pulp by integrated method & potassium bi-tartarate is separated & finally alcohol is prepared by fermentation.
  3. Juice concentrate: From 5 kg pulp, 3.46 kg free flowing concentrate can be obtained with 75^0 brix, 18% acidity & 2.2 pH.
  4. Pulp powder: Rich ın Ca, K & Cu. Free flowing nature has 9% moisture, 8.5% acidity & total reducing sugars 18.5 to 25%.
  5. Clarified juice: Transparent juice is obtained by gelatin process.
  6. Beverage: Contains 9-12% pulp & 21.5^0 brix, pasteurized at 85^{0}C & stored ar 29.4^{0}C. It is used for wine and vermouth preparations.
  7. Syrup: Contains 20-24% pulp & 56.7^0 brix is maintained.
  8. Tamarind kernel powder (TKP):
     a) Seeds are dried for 8 h in cabinet drier & milled in machine.
     b) Decorticated grounded seed yields 51% TKP and of the testa (seed husk) 33% on seed weight basis.
     c) Powder is mixed with 0.5% sodium bisulphate to prevent enzymic deterioration.
     d) TKP widely used in textile and paper adhesive industry, for jelly, fortified bread, biscuits and in confectionary industry for manufacturing chocolates.
     e) Testa also contains colouring agents & water soluble tannins (20-40%) and used in leather industry.
     f) Seed extract is used for starching of woolen & jute industry & for joining wooden planks in wood industry.
  9. Tender flowers eaten as vegetables & source of golden yellow coloured honey.
  10. Leaves contain 12-15% proteins & yield reddish yellow dye.
  11. Seed oil: TKP yields amber coloured fatty oil (6-8%) by solvent extraction method & used in paints, varnishes, giving shiny finish to toys, soap making, burning lamps & edible purposes after refining.

Varieties:

- On the basis of fruit size and shape (Bailey, 1947):
  - East Indian type: Long pods with 6-12 seeds.
  - West Indian type: Short pods with 1-4 seeds.

- Sweet type: Less acidic, grown in South-East Asia and used for dessert purpose e.g. Makham Waan, Secthong breed, Manila Sweet, Ajanta, Pratisthan, Selection No. 263).
- Sour type: Highly acidic, pulp is commercically marketed e.g. Urigam, Cumbum.
- Yellow or brown pulp type and reddish pulp type or *rakta chinch*- covers various shades of pink pulped fruits are well known.
- Red type is sweeter than brown type due to low content of free acids. Used for making preserve e.g. Yogeshwari.
- Jagdish (Farmer's selection).

Name	Breeding method	Features
TNAU, Coimbatore (HC & RI, Periyakulum)		
PKM-1 (1992)	Clonal selection from local type 'Endapuli'	Early bearer; fruits in cluster of 3-7; high pulp recovery (39%); sour type; straight pods; TSS 23-24^{0}Brix; seed wt. 6 g; suitable for HDP
Urigam	Selection	Pod shape curved; sweet pulp
Cumbum	Selection	-
CIAH, Bikaner (CHES, Godhra)		
Goma Prateek (2010)	Selection	Long pod (16.70 cm); pod wt. 26.70 g; TSS 21^{0}Brix; acidity 14.06 %; vit. C (17.53 mg/100g); 500-600 kg fruits/ tree;
IIHR, Bengaluru		
Lakshamana (2020)	Farmer's selection from Tumkur district	Pod length 25.4 cm; 24 pods/kg; 8 seeds/ pod; yield 251 kg/ tree
VNMKV, Parbhani		
Selection No. 263 (1987)	Selection from old trees	Regular bearer; straight pods; TSS 24-25^0 Brix; seed wt. 5 g; fruits 15 cm long; pulp brown; pulp 45%; highly acidic (18% acidity); yield 8-10 q fruits/ tree
Ajintha	Selection	Regular bearer; upright growth; seed wt. 6 g; TSS 27^0 Brix; less acidity 7.13%; yield 1-3 q/ tree/ year
Shivai (2018)	Selection from local area	Regular bearer; pod length (20-22 cm), pod wt. (35.33 g), yield (50-150 kg/tree); brown pulp; TSS 41.6^{0}Brix; 31.2% acidity
Pratisthan	Selection from local area	Regular bearer; pod length 7.5 cm; yellowish red coloured pulp; pod shape curved; 61% pulp; 12% seed, 27% shell; 18% acidity; TSS 24-25.2^{0}Brix; seed wt. 5 g; yield 2-3 q fruits/ tree
Yogeshwari	Selection from local area	Regular bearer; red type; sweet type; acidity 11.25%; 60% pulp; yield 7-12 q fruits/ tree
MPKV, Rahuri		
TS-1	Selection	-
TS-2	Selection	-
TR-1	Selection	Red type
Phule Shravani (RHRT-14) 2021	Selection	Sweet & bold fruit size; acidity 8.38%; TSS 24%; fruit wt. 27 g; yield 78.44 kg/tree; ascorbic acid 1.35%

UAS, Dharwad		
DTS-1 (1996)	Clonal selection	Regular bearer; high yielding
DTS-2	Clonal selection	Regular bearer; high yielding
Dr PDKV, Akola		
Akola Smruti (AKT-10) 2007	Selection	Regular bearer; pods slightly curved; fruit wt. 18.53 g; TSS 17.2^0 Brix; acidity 14.43%; TSS: acid ratio 4.56; yield 1.68 q/ tree
Dr YSRHU, Andhra Pradesh (HRS, Anantarajupet)		
Ananth Rudhira	Selection	Blood red color of flesh even at immature stage

Pests, diseases and disorders:

- Scales, mealy bugs and fruit borers: Sporadic pests.
- Seed borer (*Sitophilus linearis*): Active throughout year. Fumigate with methyl bromide.
- Beetle (*Coryoborus gonogra*): Major pest of dried tamarind.
- Rice moth (*Corcyra cepholonica*): Feeds on seeds & silky coccons are conspicuous.
- Fig moth/ Almond moth (*Ephestia cautella*): Affects pulp.
- Rice weevil (*Sitophilus oryzae*):
- Bacterial leaf spot:
- Yellow mold (*Aspergillus flavus*): Infects germinating seeds & seedlings.
- Alternate bearing:

Inheritance of characters:

- Fruit thickness negatively correlated with fibre weight, seed weight and seed number.
- Origin of sweet tamarind: Point mutation and sweetness is rare trait governed by recessive genes.

21.2 Khejri

- Eulogized as 'Life line tree of 'Thar Desert' or *Kalpavriksha* of Indian desert.
- Highly drought tolerant tree and most compatible agroforestry component under arid regions.
- Pod powder is used in preparation of bakery items.
- Fully ripe pods are edible and contain 9-14% protein and 6-16% sugars.
- Propagation: Patch budding (March-April) give 70% success.
- Trees are lopped (pruned) during mid. December to induce new shoots.
- **Variety:** Thar Shobha (4.25 kg tender pods and 6 kg dry fodder/ year).

22. FAGACEAE

22.1 Chestnut

- Monoecious with flowers borne on long spikes (catkins).

- Cultivated for nuts, timber and grace the landscape.
- Commercially grown in Italy, Spain, Portugal, China and Japan.
- Rich in -CHO (85% of dry matter), starch (50% of dry matter), sucrose (25%), pectin (7%) and proteins.
- Thrives best between 30-50^0 latitudes and in temperate Himalayas up to 2700 m MSL.
- Predominant sugars: Raffinose, stachyose and sucrose.
- Albumin: 20% of total protein.
- Japanese chestnut (*Castanea crenata*): 2n=24 and resistant to blight.
- European/ Spanish/ Sweet chestnut (*C. sativa* syn. *C. vesca*): Highest longevity. Cultivated for nuts and timber. Exhibit duodichogamy (sequential maturation of staminate flowers, female flowers of bisexual catkins & then male flowers of bisexual catkins).
- Chinese chestnut (*C. mollissima*): Resistant to blight.
- American chestnut (*C. dentata*): Susceptible to blight.
- Dwarf or bush chestnut (*C. pumila* var. *pumila*): Native to Eastern USA.
- Deciduous and monoecious.
- Limiting factors: High temperature in July-August and Frost (-4 to -6^{0}C) in Sept.-Oct.
- Major cause of graft failure: Fluted or grooved wood of stem.
- Dwarfing rootstock: Chinkapins.
- Seed treatment: Stratification in moist medium at 0-2^{0}C for 2 months before sowing.
- Difficult to root from cutting.
- Propagation method: Inverted 'T' budding on *C. mollissima* in June and cleft grafting in March.
- Ideal time of planting: November-December.
- Training method: Central leader.
- FBD takes place in July-August followed by dormancy up to February followed by active growth period from March-April.
- Anthesis time: Early June.
- Pollination agents: Wind and insects.
- Total growth period from leaf emergence to fruit ripening: 150-190 days.
- Maturity index for mechanical harvesting: Dropping of 4-9% nut.
- Optimum drying time: 100 h (10% moisture content).
- Yield: 45% (from green to dried chestnut).

Varieties:

Name	Breeding method	Features
Abundance	Seedling selection	Excellent flavour & pellicle separates easily
Sleeping Giant	Chinese chestnut x hybrid	Shiny, conical nuts; resistant to blight
Willoka	OP seedling	Large & good quality nuts
Nanking	-	Regular bearer; nuts dark brown in colour
AU-Leader	-	Resistant to blight; high yielder; produce large nuts
AU-Homestead	-	Blight resistant; high yield
Orrin	-	Prolific bearer; cold tolerant; dark nuts; good keeping quality
Shihou		Resistant to gall wasp

Pests and diseases:

- Weevil (*Curculio auriger*, *C. sayi*): Damage nuts.
- Gall wasp (*Dryocosmus kuriphilus*): Use of parasite *Torymus sinensis*.
- Asiatic oak weevil (*Crytepistomus castaneus*): Both grub and adult cause damage.
- Mites (*Oligonychus bicolor*, *Tetranychus urticae*):
- Blight (*Endothia parasitica*): Stem injection with systemic fungicide MBC (methyl-1-2 benzimadazole carbamate).
- Blossom end rot (*Glomerella cingulata*):
- Ink disease/ root rot (*Phytophthora cinnamomi*, *P. cambivora*): Destructive disease of chestnut. Prevalent in poorly drained soil. Soil drenching with Metalaxyl or foliar application of Phosethyl-AL.

23. JUGLANDACEAE

23.1 Persian walnut

- Eulogized as 'King of nuts or *Akhrot*'.
- Generic name 'Juglans' from Roman word 'Jovis Glans' means Gland of Jove.
- Main walnut consumers: Greece, Germany, Spain (0.5 kg per capita).
- USA is leading producer of walnut with 20% world walnut production.
- Largest (98%) walnut producing state in India: Jammu and Kashmir.
- Most valuable exchange earning nut crop.
- 'Butt of gun' is manufactured from walnut wood.
- Resistant to gas pollution (in vicinity of copper smelting plant).
- Walnut contains Omega-3-fatty acid (good fats) which boosts L-Dopa (dopamine) synthesis.
- The nut contains 14-20% protein and richest source (60-70%) of fat (linoleic acid).

- Contain high anti-oxidant (Vit. E) and fibres.
- Immature fruits are rich in ascorbic acid.
- Juglone: Cyanogenic glycoside synthesized in leaves.
- Flowering period: April-May.
- Type of dichogamy: Protandry.
- Male flowers (catkins) are borne terminally while female flowers laterally.
- Pollen grains loose viability with 24 h of anthesis.
- Stigma receptivity: From 3 days to upto a week.
- Apomixis type: Diplosporic.
- Pollination agent: Wind.
- Every 8th row of pollinizers should be planted perpendicular to usual direction of wind.
- Period from flowering to maturity: 135-160 days.
- Pellicle: Thin brown skin surrounding the meat of nut.
- Normal spacing: 9 m x 9 m.
- HDP in hedge row system: 3.5 m x 5 m.
- Training system: Goblet system.
- Ideal training system: Modified central leader.
- Nut shape and weight is variable.
- Rancidity in kernels occurs at very high temperature >43^{0}C.
- Drying temperature for fruits: 44.5^{0}C.
- Propagation method: Cleft tongue or splice technique in mid-January.
- Stool layering is highly successful.
- Micropropagation is 1st attempted in 1980 and improved in 1995.
- Temperature of 29-32^{0}C near harvesting results in well filled kernels.
- Maturity index: Cracking of fruit peel or wall is physiological maturity.
- Harvesting stage: Packing Tissue turn Brown (PTB) stage, achieved at 19-21 weeks after blooming.
- Reduction of walnut hull dehiscence: Ethephon @ 2000 ppm.
- Hulling of walnut: Spray instead of application of ethephon.
- Moisture percentage for storage: 8-12%.
- Nuts can be stored upto 12 months in CA storage at 10^{0}C and 60% R.H.

Species:

Common name	Botanical name	Features
Oil nut	*Juglans cinerea*	Possess 24.6% protein
Peruvian walnut	*J. neotropica*	-
Persian/ English/ Carpathian/ Dioscaryon/ white walnut	*J. regia*	Most widely used seedling rootstock in India; cold hardy & survive up to -40^{0}C; most cvs. belong to this group; nuts light coloured; large & free; reduces tree size both as stock and interstem; when used as rootstock cause black line disease
Japanese walnut	*J. ailantifolia* (syn. *J. sieboldiana*)	Nuts smooth & rugose nearly round with hard shell
-	*J. hindsii*	Nuts adhering to hull; useful as rootstock; tolerant to water logged soils
Black walnut	*J. nigra*	Nuts thick & hard shelled
-	*J. californica*	Nuts small smooth, hard shelled & adhering to hull
Cinerea walnut/ Trachy caryon/ Butternut of USA	*J. cinera*	Fairly cold hardy; nuts elongated, very hard, rough with adhering hull
Texas blacknut	*J. microcarpa*	Nuts small, round, very hard, smooth shell with adhering hull
Arizona black nut	*J. major*	Nearly round, smooth, shell hard with adhering hull

Varieties:

- Indian walnuts are generally seedling origin producing poor quality nuts.
- Roopa, Lake English, Placentia, Wilson.
- Main constraints in breeding: Long selection period, giant tree size.
- Portuguese cv. Rego: Apomictic fruits.

Name	Breeding method	Features
Chandler (1963)	Californian cv.	Lateral bearer; excellent nut & kernel; susceptible to blight; best pollinator 'Cisco & Franquette'
Chico (1956)	Californian cv.	Used in hedge row orchard; precocious bearer, susceptible to blight; best pollinator 'Serr'
Fernor (1990)	French cv.	Lateral bearer; specific pollinator 'Fernette'
Franquette	French cv.	High chilling requirement; pollinator 'Meylannaise & Ronde de Montignac'
Hartley (1909)	Farmer's selection	Very low lateral fruiting buds; less tolerant to abiotic stress; susceptible to blight; pollinator 'Amigo & Franquette'
Serr (1948)	Californian cv.	PFA level is > 75%; not recommended
Vina (1948)	Californian cv.	Willow growth habit; susceptible to blight & sunburn
Tulare (1966)	Californian cv.	Precocious bearer; used in hedge row orchard
Tahama	Waterloo x Payne	80% lateral fruiting; prolific bearer; shell seal is very weak
Eureka	European cv.	Medium nut size; kernel light brown; female sterile
Vitosha	Bulgarian cv.	Soft shelled; resistant to frost; 68% oil content; suitable for higher altitudes

Viktor	Yugoslavian cv.	Homogamous, inclined to apomixis; very small nuts; resistant to cold
Raikov	Bulgarian hybrid	Precocious & regular bearer
Beijing 861	Seedling selection from China	Precocious bearer; 65% kernel; slightly astringent; 21% protein
Grape Walnut	China cv.	Cluster bearing (15);
Govind	Selection	30% lateral flowers; creamish white kernels
AS-1	Chilean cv.	Best pollinizer 'Amigo & Chico'
Payne	Indian cv.	Self fruitful (dichogamy absent); 1st cv. having lateral bearing habit; no need of pollinator; suitable for HDP; susceptible to codling moth & blight
Waterloo	Introduced from USA	-
CITH, Srinagar		
CITH Walnut - 1	Chance seedling	Protogynous; nuts are large, long trapezoid; yield 60 kg/ tree at 40 years age; commence bearing in 4th year; kernel recovery (46.96%); susceptible to moisture stress
CITH Walnut - 2	Chance seedling	Protogynous; nutslarge, long trapezoid; kernel recovery (51.27%); kernel wt. 9.9 g; yield 60 kg/ tree at 35 years age; commence bearing in 4th year; field tolerant to pests
CITH Walnut - 3	Chance seedling	Protogynous; nuts are large, long trapezoid; kernel recovery (54.55%); kernel wt. 9.9 g; yield 60 kg/ tree at 25 years age; commence bearing in 4th year; very good acceptance; field tolerance to pests except white grub & susceptible to moisture stress
CITH Walnut - 4	Chance seedling	Protandrous; nuts are large, kernel bold (11.54 g); kernel recovery (59.39%); yield 60 kg/ tree at 25 years age; commence bearing in 4thyear; very good acceptance; field tolerant to pests except white grub; nut yield 45kg/ tree at 30 years age
CITH Walnut 5	Chance seedling	Protandrous; nuts are large; bold kernel (10.40 g); yield 50 kg/ tree at 30 years age; field tolerant to pests except white grub
CITH-W-426	Chance seedling	Cluster type; promising lines for yield & quality
CITH-W-427	Chance seedling	Cluster type; promising lines for yield & quality
IARI, New Delhi		
Pusa Khor	Seedling selection	Fruiting after 2nd year; oil content 55%, regular & heavy bearer; suitable for ultra-HDP; shelling 48%; self cracking
SKUAST, Srinagar (J&K)		
Hamdan (2001)	Clonal selection	Nut wt. 14 g; smooth texture; shelling ability 54%
Suleiman (2001)	Clonal selection	Precocious bearer; nut wt. 20 g; smooth texture; round shape; shelling ability 50%
Karan (syn. Bulbul Dun)	Clonal selection	Peppery shell; high shelling %; >60% kernel recovery
Chakrata No.14	Clonal selection	Thin shelled; good filling & amber coloured kernel

Use of rootstocks:

- Black More, Tutle 16, 31, German Seedlings.
- Interspecific hybrids: Walnut hybrid (*J. nigra* x *J. regia*), Royal (*J. nigra* x *J. hindsii*), Paradox (*J. hindsii* x *J. nigra*; vigorous, mod. resistant tophytophthora & nematode).

Pests, diseases and disorders:

- Walnut weevil: Feed on kernel.
- Walnut aphid.
- Codling moth (*Cydia pomonella*): As per International marketing rules the damage should be < 1%.
- Navel orange worm (*Amyelois transiella*):
- Bacterial blight (*Xanthomonas arboricola* pv. *juglandis*): 80% damage. Spread through contaminated pollen.
- Anthracnosis (*Gnomonia leptostyla*):
- Downy leaf spot.
- Walnut canker or die back.
- Black line (*Phytophthora* spp.): English walnut grafted on 'Paradox' results indelayed incompatibility and is caused by Cherry leaf roll virus.
- Black nut: Due to hot summer with low humidity.
- Snake heads: B deficiency.
- Pistillate flower abscission (PFA): Major problem.

23.2 Pecan nut

- Eulogized as 'Queen of nuts' in USA.
- Most important nut fruit of the world and ranks 5th in production.
- Introduced in India in 1935 at Palampur, Himachal Pradesh.
- Widely cultivated in H.P., hills of U.P., J & K valley and in Nilgiri hills.
- Largely grown for timber purpose.
- These are very large (up to 30 m height) fast growing trees with pinnate leaves.
- Fruits deficit in cellular endosperm.
- Fruit composition: Kernels have high nutritional & calorific value i.e. 11-12% proteins, 70% fats, vit. B_1, vit. B_2 and phosphoric acid.
- Heterodichogamy: Both protogynynous and protandrous nature is observed. Number of days of overlap of pistil receptivity and actual pollen shedding range from 0-8 days.
- It is highly cross pollinated and rarely self pollinated.
- Male flowers (catkin) and female flowers (spike) borne in mixed flower bud.
- Fruits: Pointed, round, cylindrical (up to 5 cm or 2 inch) nut.
- Fruits have green leathery outer skin that is peeled off to reveal, reddish smooth shelled nut, encloses walnut like kernels.

- Pollination agent: Wind.
- Number of leaves for optimum kernel quality: 8-10.
- Major problem: Irregular and biennial bearing.
- Planting method: Square system at 8-10 m spacing.
- HDP is coupled with dwarf growth habit & light pruning.
- Before planting pecan orchard, placement of pollinizers should be thought off.
- Optimum soil pH: 5.6-6.4.
- Very sensitive to alkaline soils.
- Full grown trees are prone to Zn and Mn deficiency.
- Soils should have proper aeration since restricted soil aeration induces partial stomatal closure, decreases leaf number leaf area, trunk and dry weight of roots.
- Grows well in warm temperate climate.
- Crop requires 3 months coldest (temperature between 7.2^{0}C-12.8^{0}C) period and atleast 400 h chilling (at or below 7.2^{0}C) for better growth and development.
- Requires 240-280 days growing season with mean temperature above 26.7^{0}C is optimum during growth period.
- Heat units (above 10^{0}C) required: 5000 degree days during 7 months to nut growing season.
- Pollens of cvs. Stuart and Desirable can be stored at 5^{0}C for 2 months.
- Pollens maintained at -12^{0}C for 2 years.
- Days for vegetative growth: 211-247 days.
- Loose viability very soon and stored well at low temperature (0^{0}C) after harvesting till stratification.
- Propagation method: Seed and vegetative means.
- Seeds are stratified in moist sand at 3^{0}C for 12-16 weeks or incubated at 35^{0}C for 4 week's period.
- Seeds are also used to raise rootstock seedlings.
- Vegetative propagation: Cutting, stooling, tongue grafting and patch budding.
- Cuttings of 20 cm long and 1.5-3 cm dia. from juvenile root (3 year old) are taken.
- Rooting of hardwood cutting: Improved by girdling the shoots 5 weeks prior to actual cutting.
- Cutting in mid-December from juvenile trees and January-February from mature tree root better.
- Annular (ring) budding in May-June end gives high success.
- Tongue grafting in winter (early March) has been most successful.

- In India, seedling rootstocks of pecan cvs. Nellis and Burkett are used for budding/ grafting purpose.
- Clonal propagation by stooling in combination with girdling and IBA (3000-6000 ppm) gives good success.
- Trees are more prone to Zn and Mn deficiency and foliar sprays @ 0.5% is suggested.
- Herbicide used: Diuron and Simazine (2-5 kg/ha) & Paraquat @ 1 kg/ ha to control broad leaved weeds.
- To check soil erosion, leguminous cover crops can be taken in summer.
- Peach can be planted as filler crop.
- Suitable intercrops: Leguminous cover crops and vegetables.
- Mulching with dry grass is recommended.
- Irrigation method: Flooding/ Basin/ Furrow/ Sprinkler or Drip.
- Irrigation in late season, before shuck opening reduces stick tight & viviparous nuts.
- Irrigation also improves kernel yield, nut weight, diameter, oil content & appearance of nuts.
- Training: Central leader system is adopted.
- It is terminal bearer and require remedial (light to moderate) pruning.
- Heavy pruning results in extremely vigorous growth with no production.
- Fruit drop is severe problem is cultivation.
- Fruit thinning of over crowded trees is beneficial by spraying ethephon @ 25-200 ppm.
- Days taken from anthesis to fruit maturity: 240-280 days.
- Fruit maturity: Late September to last week of October.
- Maturity indices:
  - Opening of husk around nut;
  - Coloured dots and streak markings on shell;
  - Decrease of kernel moisture content;
  - Change in shell colour from white to light brown along suture when Shuck splits open (dehisce) easily from shell.
- Nuts are harvested with the help of bamboo poles.
- Harvesting period: October-January since early harvesting impair nut quality.
- Nuts are separated from shucks and sun dried and stored in dry place.
- Yield: 20-25 kg nuts/tree and (100-120 nuts/ kg).
- Drying: Moisture content reduced from 13-14% to 5% by drying nuts at room temperature for 72 h.

Species:

- All the species belong to *Carya* are together known as 'hickories'.
- Shagbark hickory (*Carya ovata*): Sweet kernel but poor cracking quality.
- Shelbark hickory (*C. laciniosa*): Sweet kernel but poor cracking quality.
- Mockernut hickory (*C. tomentosa*): Sweet kernel but poor cracking quality.
- *C. cordiformis*: Nut having bitter taste.
- *C. glabra*: Pig nut.

Varieties:

- P.J. Conner, USA worked extensively.
- Parameters for selection of cultivars: nut size, shell thickness, cracking.
- Western cultivars are unsuitable for humid areas due to susceptibility to scab.
- Superior cultivar should have more than 55% kernel.
- Transgenic: Elliot 6, Schley 5/3.
- Protandrous cvs. for HDP: Halber, Cherokee.
- Protogynous cvs.: Curtis, Elliot.
- Western: Precocious & very prolific bearer, self pollinated & suitable for HDP. Nuts thin shelled, medium in size, kernel 54-59% of nut, high quality. Highly susceptible to scab & unsuitable for humid areas.
- Wichita· Protogynous, well suited for small tree culture, 20-30 nuts/kg, kernels 60% of nut.
- Desirable: Protandrous, regular and prolific bearer, kernel 52% of nut & best pollinizer for cv. Stuart. Resistant to scab. Good inshell trade product.
- Mohawk: Protogynous, precocious, nuts very large (16-23 nuts/kg), kernel 55-60% of high quality.
- Stuart: Protogynous, very large nuts (23 nuts/ kg), kernels 44-50% of nut. Resistant to scab.
- Chicksaw: Protogynous, very prolific, mature in last week of September, large nut size (25 -32 nuts/ kg), kernels 52-58% of nut. Suitable for HDP.
- Burkett: Protogynous, regular bearer but prone to fruit drop, mature in 2nd week of October, large nut size (24 nuts/ kg), kernels 57% of nut.
- Mahan: Protogynous, early maturing, large nut size (20 nuts/kg) & kernels 57% of nut.
- Western Schley: Protandrous, regular bearer, large nut size (26 nuts/ kg), kernels 58% of nut.
- Cheyenne (Clark x Odom): Protandrous, very precocious & highly prolific bearer, nut size (25-32 nuts/kg), kernels 57% of nut, and suitable for HDP.

- Stuart: Prototgynous, late bearing, large nut size (23 nuts/ kg), kernel 44-50% of nut, resistant to scab.
- Avalon: Prototgynous, resistant to scab.
- Moreland: Resistant to bunchy tumor, shuck disease, liver spot, *G. nerviseda*, *Mycosphaerella dendroides* and brown leaf spot.
- Desirable: Prolific and regular bearer, protandrous.
- Gloria Grande, Sumner: Protogynous, scab resistant.
- Western (Seedling x Taxes): Self pollinated, suitable for HDP, susceptible to scab.
- Melrose: Resistant to *Fusarium effusum* and shuck.
- Pawnee (Mohawk x Starking Hardy Giant): High kernels, resistant to leaf blotch.
- Surprise: Protandrous, large nuts, scab resistance.
- Houma (Desirable x Curtis): Nut size 8.2 g, 55% kernel; protandrous.
- Osage (Major x Evers): 54% kernels; resistant to pecan scab, leaf blotchand *Gnomonia nerviseda*.
- Oconee (Schley x Barton): Protandrous, alternate bearer, nuts large.
- Salopek (Wichita x Onliwon): 59% kernels; protogynous.
- Nellis: Protandrous, regular bearer, mature in 3rd week of October & kernel contant 49.4%, suitable for HDP.
- New cvs.: Kanza, Shawnee, Kiowa, Nacono, Apalachee.

Diseases, pests and disorders:

- Under cool climate of Britain, pecan suffers from coral spot disease, which needs pruning before it spreads.
- American pecans suffer from many pests and diseases.
- Pecan scab (*Cladosporium caryigenum*): Black spots on leaves.
- Leaf blotch (*Mycospharella dendroides*, *M. caryigenai*):
- Brown leaf spot (*Cercospora fusca*): Severe in humid region.
- Liver spot (*Gnomonia caryae*):
- Crown gall (*Agrobacterium tumefaciens*):
- Bunch: Viral disease.
- Hickory shuck worm (*Lasperesia caryana*): Cause premature nut fall.
- Weevil (*Curculio caryae*): Cause damage in orchard and during storage.
- Fall web worm (*Hyphantria cunea*):
- Pecan nut case borer (*Acrobasis caryae*):
- Pecan leaf case borer (*Acrobasis juglandis*):

- Black aphods (*Myzocallis caryaefolia*):
- Leaf miner (*Stigmella juglandifoliella*):
- Mite (*Tetranychus hicoriae*):
- Blossom splitting: B deficiency.
- Rosette: Zn and Mn deficiency cause bronzing/ crinkling of leaves and leads to die back of branches. Spray 0.5% $ZnSO_4$/ $MnSO_4$.
- Mouse ear: Mn deficiency. Container grown trees show small, rounded, cupped and slightly wrinkled leaflets.
- Leaf scorching: Associated with very wet/ dry soils.

Inheritance of characters:

- Correlation: Filling of nuts is negatively correlated with their number on the tree.

24. LAURACEAE

24.1 Avocado

- Eulogized as 'Butter fruit or 21st century fruit or Fruit of New World or Alligator fruit or Alligator Pear or Poor Man's Butter or World's most nutritive fruit or Aristocrat of salad fruit'.
- Archeologists in Peru have found domesticated avocado seeds buried with Incan mummies dating back to 750 BC.
- 1st introduced in India from Ceylon (Sri Lanka) in 1942.
- It is a tasteless fruit and not suitable for canning and cooking.
- Major producers: Mexico, Brazil, USA, Israel, New Zealand, South America, South Africa.
- Mexico: Largest producer and exporter in world and America is major importer.
- Dense and evergreen tree grows up to 80 feet height.
- In India, it is grown as backyard tree.
- Intake of avocado improves cholesterol levels in human body.
- It can keep the eyes, gums, liver and heart healthy. It also helps to ease osteoarthritis, combat metabolic syndrome and prevent food poisoning and liver damage.
- Pulp of avocado makes an ideal natural ingredient for face masks and for skin moisturizers.
- Calorific value: High (twice to that of banana i.e. 245 calories/ 100 g) but sugar content is low. Hence, recommended as high energy food for diabetics.
- Mesocarp is rich in oil content.
- Fruit is rich source of oil ranges from 3-30%- used in cosmetic industry.

- Persin: Fungicidal toxin present in fruit.
- Composition of fruit: Pulp (60-62%), skin (20-22%), seeds (15-20%).
- Nutritional composition/ 100 g edible portion: Fat (24-26.4%), protein (2.1%), low sugar (1%), rich in K, Fe, vit. B complex, rich in vit. E, minerals (1.32%), mono unsaturated fatty acids and no cholesterol.
- Requires more energy to grow a fruit than an apple because of fruit oil content.
- Most resistant to cold temperature.
- At temperature (-0.5 to 3.5^{0}C) only Mexican race survive.
- Optimum temperature for growth (20-28^{0}C) and can withstand 10-15^{0}C.
- High humidity (> 60%) during flowering and fruit setting is necessary to secure good crop.
- Flowers and fruits are rarely produced in cool temperate zones due to low light intensity and reduced day light h.
- It flourish in shelter and in sunshine.
- Optimum pH for cultivation: 5-7.
- Extremely sensitive to poor drainage and cannot withstand waterlogged soils.
- Inflorescence: Compound panicle of raceme.
- Flower is structurally bisexual but functionally unisexual.
- Flowers are functionally pistillate during first opening and staminate during second opening.
- Flower number is drastically reduced at short days.
- West Indian race set no fruits in sub-tropical climate.
- Reasons for low fruit set: Ovule sterility; pollination problem; degeneration of ovule; defective seed development.
- Self pollination is not possible due to differential opening time of both flowers.
- Peak flowering period: December-January.
- Single tree is unfruitful and mixed planting of varieties is desirable.
- Pollination agent: Honey bee and wasps.
- Protogynous dichogamy condition of avocado was 1st noticed by Nirody (1922).
- Protogynous diurnally synchronous dichogamy (PDSD): 1st reported by Bergh (1969).
- Concept of botanical varieties/ types A and B (based on the pattern of opening of flowers): Bergh and Ellstrand (1986).
- Planting ratio of both A and B groups: 1: 1 or 2: 1 and with cv. Hass 4: 1 is desirable.
- Vivipary is observed.
- Fruit type: Single seeded berry.
- Propagation methods: Seeds, cuttings, side grafting (veneer, cleft grafting, approach grafting and chip/ shield budding) are most successful (75% success).

- Seedling may not breed true-to-type.
- Days taken for seed germination: 50-95.
- Seed soaking in water for 8 h or removal of seed coat before sowing or a thin slice at top & bottom may hastens germination.
- Seed viability increased by storing in dry peat / sand at 5^{0}C.
- Seed viability after extraction: 2-3 weeks.
- Fresh seeds are sown soon after extraction from the fruit.
- More number of seedlings are obtained from single seed by lengthwise splitting into 4-6 parts with a piece of embryo in each part.
- Leaf cuttings from young seedlings root more readily than old trees.
- Shield & chip budding on older stocks is highly successful.
- Rootstocks:
  - Duke seedlings are cold hardy & resistant to root rot.
  - Pollock stocks can overcome salilnity problems.
  - Purple/ green variety imparts vigour to scion.
  - Budding/ grafting on 30-40 cm tall, robust, succulent seedlings is generally practiced.
- Both graft and cross incompatibility is reported.
- Bottom heat technique (constant 26^{0}C) + IBA treatment is adopted in rooting through cuttings.
- Seeds are planted in nursery at 30 cm x 60 cm and transplanted to polybags when they putforth 4-5 leaves.
- When seedlings reach 80-90 cm in height, can be transplanted to main field.
- Planting distance: 10m x 7m (140 plants/ha).
- Square system is adopted. Distance varies from 6 to 12 m on the square.
- HDP: 5m x 5m (400 plants/ha).
- Optimum temperature for flower induction: < 25^{0}C.
- Flowers are produced on young branches at the periphery of tree.
- Short days drastically reduces flower number but accelerates flowering.
- Shelterbelts/ wind breaks are essential to protect trees from hot dry winds.
- Trunks of young trees are white washed.
- Planting of several cultivars with over-lapping or simultaneous flowering periods is recommended to produce fruits.
- Pruning: Heading back in tall growing varieties e.g. Pollock.
- Trees can sustain hard pruning.
- Heavy pruning results in excessive vegetative growth.

- Since it is shallow rooted crop, water stress causes wilting and/or shedding of fruits and flowers.
- Cannot withstand waterlogging and saline conditions.
- Irrigation method: basin and sprinkler irrigation.
- TSS of pulp: 6.8-7.1^0 Brix.
- Seed raised trees fruit after 5-7 years and grafted 3-5 years.
- Harvesting time: July-August-September.
- Maturity indices:
  - Reduction in glossy luster of fruit skin & colour fading from green to dark crimson to purple;
  - In Purple variety, fruits show purplish blush.
  - In Green variety, fruits develop yellow tinge and glossy shine diminishes.
  - Fruits are ready for eating if slightly soft when pressed.
  - Picking poles are used for harvesting of fruits.
  - Change in seed coat colour from yellowish white to dark brown;
  - Period from flowering to harvesting: 6 months (tropical); 12-18 months (temperate region);
  - Fruit size;
  - Less oil content in mesocarp.
  - Well matured fruis ripen n 4-5 days after harvesting.
- Ripening takes place at 15-21^{0}C and hampered above 30^{0}C.
- Fruits developed without embryos are cylindrical in shape and smaller.
- Seeded fruits are 8-10 times larger than seedless due to greater cell size and number.
- Seedless fruits are called as 'cukes' and resemble to cucumber.
- Cell division continues till fruit maturity which leads to variable fruit size.
- Fruits remain hard as long as they stay on tree and soften only after harvest.
- Fruits picked from same tree at same time differ in ripening time by 10 days.
- Fruit firmness: Assessed by acoustic measurement.
- Girdling of alternate bearing varieties (Pollock, Fuerte) increase the yield.
- Yield: 100-500 fruits/ tree.
- Inoculation of VAM fungus (*Glomus fasciculatum*) enhances growth of plantlets.
- CA storage: 2% O_2 + 10% CO_2 at 7.2^{0}C for 3-4 weeks.
- Fruits can be kept for a month in cold storage at 7-8^{0}C with 80-90% R.H.
- Fruits exposed to ethylene @ 10 ppm for 36-48 h ripen in 3-4 days.
- Prompt pre-cooling reduces internal discolouration during storage.

- Fruit softnening can be prolonged by wrapping by polyethylene bags and storage at gradually decreasing temperature.
- Pulp preservation: Freezing and used as sandwich filling or spread in ice creams and milk shakes.
- Recommended herbicide: Simazine and Monouron.
- Constraints in cultivation: Bienniel bearing and fruit drop.
- Somatic embryo development through gamma irradiation (10 Gy) has been successful in cv. Fuerte.

Ecological races (sub-species):

- Mexican race scion on rootstock of same race shows most salt sensitiveness.
- All the 3 races are intercrossable and have produced hundreds of cultivars suitable for Mediterranean to tropical climate.
- Sub-genus *Eriodaphne* imparts resistance to root rot.
- *Persea schiedeana*, *P. floccosa*, *P. americana* var. *nubigeana*: Dwarf.
- Most of the races are originated as chance seedlings.

Particulars	**Mexican race (*Persea americana* var. *drymifolia*)**	**Guatemalan race (*P. americana* var. *guatemalensis*)**	**West Indian race (*P. americana* var. *americana*)**
Group	A	B	C
Leaf scent	Anise scented	Lack leaf scent	Lack leaf scent
Climate	Semi-tropical	Sub-tropical	Tropical
Cold (frost) tolerance	High	Medium	Low
Salt tolerance	Low	Medium	High
Oil content	30%	8-15%	3-10%
Fruit size	Small	Large	Large
Fruit wt.	< 250 g	Upto 600 g	Upto 1 kg
Fruit skin	Smooth	Thick, brittle	Smooth, glossy
Seed size	Large, loosely fit in cavity	Small, tightly held in cavity	Large, loosely fit in cavity
Fruit shape	Roundish	Oval	Pear
Months to mature	6-8	9-12	6-9
Varieties	Duke, Topa, Camperon, Cholula, Peuminas, Mexicola, Pernod, Goff Fried	Lula, Hass, Green, Fuerte, Nabal, Benik, Nabal, Itzamna, Taylor Linda	Pollock, Purple, Black Prince, Simmonds, Elgin, Gimball, Huntley, Peterson, Waldin
Rooting ability	Easy & best; easy to root	Intermediate	Most difficult
Rootstock utility	Hardy, impart dwarfness, cold resistant, salt sensitive & widely preferred as rootstock in California	More sensitive to cold, highly susceptible to high pH, chlorosis & verticillium wilt	Preferred in warmer climates & for saline soils; highly susceptible to high pH chlorosis & verticillium wilt

Varieties:

- Named varieties grown in world are chance seedlings e.g. Mexican race selections- Campeon, Cholula, Peuminas.
- Paradenia Purple Hybrid (PPH): Borne in clusters.
- Cvs. belong to Mexican race: Duke, Pernod, Gottfried.
- Cvs. belong to Guatemalan race: Taylor, Linda, Queen, Nabal, Benik & Ilsamma.
- Cvs. belong to West Indian race: Black Prince, Peterson, Simmond, Fuchsia and Waldin.
- Horshim: High yielding variety from Israel.
- Adi (Hass x Horshim): Pale yellow flesh, fruit wt. 230 g; nutty flavour.
- Grown in India: Purple Green, Peradeniya Purple hybrid.
- Rootstocks resistant to root rot/ die back (*Phytophthora cinnamomi*): Barr, Bounty, Borchard, Day, Duke-9, Dusa, Fairchild, G-1033, G-6, Moaz, Martin Grande, Steddon, Thomas, Uzi, Zentmyer.
- Mexicola: Small fruited.
- Toro Canyon: Tolerant to root rot & salinity.
- Mt-4: Dwarf.
- Topa-Topa: Uniform germination & provide thick shoots for tip-grafting but very susceptible to root rot & salinity.
- Elgin, Gimball & Huntley: Local selections from Jamaica.

Name	Breeding method	Features
Fuerte (1911)	Inter-racial hybrid of Mexican x Guatemalan race collected by Carl Schmidt at Mexico	Most leading cultivar in the world; spreading & alternate bearing nature; fruit wt. (225-450 g); grown in India; oil content (18-26%); pyriform fruit shape; alternate bearer & cold resistant; can be left on tree even after maturity; highly susceptible to anthracnose & stem end rot
Hass	Chance seedling of unknown parentage by Mr. Rudolph Hass at California	Predominantly Guatemalan race but with some Mexican genes; self fertile; world famous variety, fruit skin turn purple on ripening; can be left on tree even after maturity
Pollock	Originated in Miami	West Indian race; grown in India & alternate bearer; fruit oblong to pear shaped; very large, up to 5 lbs (2.27 kg); skin smooth; flesh green near skin, oil content (3-5%); large seed; season: early July to Aug. or Oct.; shy-bearing; overcome salinity problem
Duke-7		Mod. resistant to root rot, soft fruit rot, anthracnose & frost
Gwen	Selection of 'Thille' from University of California	Pale green flesh available late winter through late summer
Bacon (1928)	Inter-racial hybrid of Mexican x Guatemalan	Fruit wt. 170- 510 g; skin thin, green & glossy with leathery texture; early maturing with very pale yellow-green flesh; recovery 61%

Zutano (1926)	Inter-racial hybrid of Mexican x Guatemalan & selected by W. L. Ruitt	Pear shaped, large fruit with shiny think, yellow green skin & light textured pale green flesh with light taste; recovery 65 %; susceptible to anthrocnose & mod. susceptible to *Phytophthora* root rot
Pinkerton (1959)	Guatemalan hybrid as 'Rincon' seedling on the property of J. and W. Pinkerton	Semi dwarf; fruit pyriform; fruit wt. 230-425 g; small seed size; cream coloured flesh; recovery 82%; resistant to anthracnose
Lula	-	Fast growing; pyriform shape; fruit wt. 400-680 g; oil content (12-15%); suitable for tropical climate; resistant to root rot
Green	-	Large fruits (450-650 g); oval shape; thick brittle skin
Purple	-	West Indian race; pear shaped fruits; fruit wt. (300-500 g); pulp soft, greenish yellow, firm & nutty flavour; thick brittie skin; popular in south India and Maharashtra
Ettinger	Inter-racial hybrid of Mexican x Guatemalan	Oblong fruits with bright green, shiny skin
TNAU, Coimbatore (HRS, Thadiyankudisai)		
TDK-1 (1997)	Selection from germplasm	Early maturing; suitable for HDP; fruit wt. (600-650 g); yield 26.4 T/ha; TSS 8^0 brix, fat 23.8%, protein 1.35%.
IIHR, Bengaluru regional station (CHES, Chettalli)		
Arka Supreme (2020)	Seedling selection of unknown origin	Regular bearer; flowering behaviour type 'A' category; flowers in March-April & June-July; fruits borne in clusters of 3-5, fruit wt. 367-428 g; TSS 7.8 ^{0}Brix; fat 20%; 0.45% fibre; pulp pale yellow coloured; recovery 60%; yield 175-200 fruits/tree & 370-400 kg/ plant.

Pests and diseases:

- Greedy scale (*Hemiberlesia rapax*): Major pest.
- Fruit spot (*Colletotrichum gloeosporioides*): Important and serious disease results in shedding of young fruits.
- Fruit softening (*Fusarium solani*, *F. sambucinum*):
- Leaf spot (*Cercospora purpurea*):
- Scab (*Sphaceloma perseae*):
- Root rot (*Phytophthora cinnamomi*): Most serious in poorly drained soils or high water table. Drench with Ridomil @ 1 g/10 lit.
- Trunk canker (*P. citricola*):
- Sun blotch: Viral disease transmitted by pollen, grafts or seeds.
- Anthracnose: Furete is susceptible.
- Stem end rot (*Dothiorella dominicana*): Heavy loss from fruit set
- Duke stem pitting: Eradication is only way of management.

Physiological disorders:

- Stamimoidy: Conversion of other flower parts to stamens.

- Pistilloidy: Conversion of other flower parts to pistils.
- 'Dry neck or Ring neck' is most common.
- Internal/ mesocarp discolouration: Due to polyphenol oxidase enzyme and can be reduced by prompt precooling.
- Chilling injury: Fruits stored at 0-4^{0}C for longer than 3-4 weeks.
- Tip burn: Cl toxicity: Most prevalent in spring season. Leaves show necrosis of tips and margins.
- Grey pulp: More prevalent in warm areas i.e low moisture. Fruit unfit for storage and maketing.
- Pulp spot: Black discolouration of vascular bundles at cut end of fruit stalk.
- Fruit drop: Common problem due to very cool weather or dry hot winds at blooming time.
- Irradiation results in excessive flesh browning.
- Fizzles:
- Apoplexy:

25. MALPIGHIACEAE

25.1 West Indian Cherry

- Eulogized as 'Puerto Rican cherry'.
- Tropical evergreen shrub.
- West Indian cherry [syn. Barbados cherry (*Malpighia glabra*)]: Slow growing, prickly shrub and cultivated as hedge plant.
- Fruits of *M. glabra* are used against diarrhea, dysentery and liver disorder.
- Fruits are eaten raw or processed.
- Green fruits are richest source of ascorbic acid (1000-4000 mg/ 100 g) than ripe fruits.
- Tree bark contains tannins (26%) and yield dye of brown colour.
- Ideal fruit for kitchen garden.
- Propagation method: Seed, cutting, ground layering.
- Spacing: 2m x 2m.
- Suitable filler crop for mango, papaya, guava.
- Flowering season: May-November.

26. MALVACEAE (BOMBACACEAE)

26.1 Durian

- Eulogized as 'King of fruits in Indonesia or Pride of tropical South East Asia or Civet fruit or Mother of all fruits'

- Malayan word 'duri' meaning thorn/ spike and species name 'zibethinus' is derived from Italian word 'zibetto' meaning 'strong smelling'.
- Scientific name of durian fruit denotes 'the spiny fruit that has an overpowering smell'.
- An infamous fruit, banned from airlines due to revolting smell.
- Commercially grown in Indonesia, Malaysia and Thailand.
- Thailand: Largest producer in the world.
- Root decoction and leaves are used to cure fever and jaundice, respectively.
- Arils of ripe fruits can be used in fresh and in processed form.
- Seeds can be easily separated from pulp and are edible when fried/ roasted/ boiled.
- Medicinal uses: Pharmacological properties viz. decoction of roots is used to treat fever and that of leaves & roots to check inflammation, infections and to treat jaundice.
- Composition of fruit/ 100 g: Water (65 g), -CHO (27.09 g), fat (5.33 g), protein (1.47 g), dietary fibres (3.8 g), vit. C (19.7 mg), minerals like K (436 mg), and energy (160 kcal).
- Pulp is rich in sugars (12%), -CHO (34%), protein (2.8 g), fat (2.5 g), fibre (1.4 g) and vit. A (10 IU), vit. C: 33 mg, vit. E and minerals like Fe and B.
- Fruits have aphrodisiac property.
- Tall, evergreen, highly shade tolerant, long living tree: 80-150 years.
- Thrives best in humid climate & high rainfall areas (200 cm is minimum requirement).
- Optimum soil pH: 5 to 6.5.
- Trees are highly susceptible to strong winds.
- Growth is severely affected if mean daily temperature drops below 22^{0}C.
- Susceptible to drought and low temperature (< 8^{0}C cause cold injury).
- Flowers: Strongly fragrant, 2-3 inches long and appear in stalked clusters of 1-45 individual flowers/ cluster.
- Flower clusters hang from main & smaller branches or are cauliflorus in nature.
- Period of 3-4 weeks dry weather is essential for stimulation of flowering.
- Appearance of tiny bud to anthesis requires one month duration.
- Flowers are hermaphrodite & fleshy epicalyx comprises 5 united sepals + 5 petals + epicalyx colour matches with colour of edible pulp.
- Trees with yellowish flowers produce yellow fleshed durians, the most common ones.
- White or reddish petaled flowers produce white or reddish fleshed fruits.

- Botanically, fruit is a capsule & edible portion is called as 'aril' i.e. seeds surrounded by edible pulp.
- Tree produces thorny fruits like jackfruit with unique appearance, taste, flavour and aroma.
- Flesh is pale yellow to red & taste-nutty & sweet, which emits strong distinctive odour.
- Compositicıı of durian aroma: Different species have differential aromas due to mixtures of volatile compounds including easters, ketones and organosulphur compounds.
- Fruit flavour: Hydrogen sulphide, ethyl hydrosulphide and dialkyl polysulphide.
- Aril constitutes 33% of total fruit weight.
- Fruits are ovoid to ellipsoid, very large (25 x 20 cm) weighing up to 4-5 kg with thorny (short, sharp spikes) surface, green initially and yellow after ripening with a long stalk.
- The 5 loculed fruit has 2-3 seeds in each locule, surrounded by light coloured, mealy, sweet aril and the white edible pulp.
- Husk colour: Greenish to yellowish tan-brown. Hard outer husk is covered with sharp, prickly thorns.
- Propagation method: Seed.
- Sexual propagation is discouraged since seeds create genetic heterozygosity and have long gestation period.
- Seeds have very short viability and do not store well even at low temperature.
- Seed spread through elephants.
- Seed germinate in 3-4 days & subsequent growth of seedlings is very rapid.
- Saplings ready for planting in 14-18 months.
- Commercial propagation: Cleft grafting in June-September.
- Two months old seedling rootstocks of same species are used for budding/ grafting purpose.
- Modified forkert/ patch budding & inarch or approach grafting is widely practiced for vegetative propagation.
- Air layering and propagation by cuttings are impractical.
- System of planting: Square system.
- Planting distance: 10m x 10m; 6 m x 6m (HDP).
- Planting of more than one variety/ clone with over-lapping or simultaneous flowering period in orchard is recommended for cross pollination and better fruit set.
- Flowering period: January-February.
- Fruits are available 2 times in a year generally during May- September.

- Paclobutrazol @ 750-1500 ppm induce highest flowering intensity, early flowering.
- Seedlings have long juvenile period and take 10 years to bear a crop while grafted trees are precocious in bearing and produce crop in 4-5 years.
- Anthesis: From 3 PM to about mid-night.
- Self pollination rarely occurs.
- Pollination agents: Bats (*Eoncyteris spelea*) and flying fox (*Pteropus hypomelanus*), moths.
- Hand pollination of unopened blossoms gives more fruit set than pollination of fully opened flowers.
- Self incompatibility due to protogynous nature is observed.
- Metaxenia effect influence fruit and seed characters.
- Five locules per fruit having 2-3 seeds in each locule.
- Only remedial pruning is adopted after harvesting to clear off dried and old twigs.
- Young plants are prone to desiccation and hence, regular irrigation is practiced.
- Maturity indices:
  - Fruits take 3 ½ months to reach maturity from fruit set.
  - Fruit spine colour changes from dark green to light green with browning tips;
  - Fruits are ready to eat when its husk begins to crack.
  - Rich aroma develops as fruits mature & reach its peak in 3-4 days after harvesting;
  - Flattening and far apart spines on the rind;
  - Tip of spines become soft and can be pulled off easily by fingers;
  - Fruits are smooth & soft to touch.
  - Immature fruits are used for vegetable purpose.
- Economic yield starts after 10 years of planting.
- Yield: 100-120 fruits/ tree.
- Ripe fruits deteriorate rapidly and can not be transported over longer distance.
- Ripe fruits can last for 4 days under refrigeration and mature fruits can be stored up to 14 days at 10-15^{0}C or can be frozen for 2-3 months.
- Arils can be preserved for 3 months at -24^{0}C.
- Storage: 6-8 weeks at 4-6^{0}C and 85-90% R.H.
- Arils can be processed into durian cake (lempok), durian jelly (tempoyak), paste, candy and roasted seeds.
- Jelly prepared from over ripe fruits is sour in taste.
- Dehydrated powder can be prepared by spray/ drum drying.
- Powder is used as flavouring ingredient for beverages, pastry, ice cream, etc.

Species:

Following each species is variable for fruit size, fruit colour and leaf area.

- *Durio zibethinus*: Fruits ovoid to ellipsoid in shape, large in size, weigh upto 5 kg with thorny surface and olive green in colour. It possesses rotten onion like odour (organosulphur) due to thiol & thioethers compounds.
- *D. testudinarum*: Produce edible fruits.
- *D. graveolens* (red fleshed durian): Produce edible fruits. Emit fragrance of roasted almonds.
- *D. gradiflorous*: Produce edible fruits.
- *D. dulcis* (red durian): Produce edible fruits. It has deep caramel flavour with turpentine odour.
- *D. oxyleyanus*: Produce edible fruits.
- *D. kutejensis*: Produce edible fruits.
- *D. suluk*:
- Tarap: Eulogized as 'Marang' is F_1 hybrid between Durian and jack fruit. This fruit has thorny surface and highly objectionable odour.

Varieties:

- Trees have great inherent tendency towards genetic diversity in every way, from chromosome levels to flavour, aroma, appearance & texture.
- Promising cvs. with small seeds and free from objectionable flavour have market demand viz. Bojol, Chance, Deception, D-24, D-99 (Gob Kecil), D-123 (Chanee), Frog, Gibbon, Golden Pillow, Gombat, Hepe, Kanyao, Ketan, Kob Champa, Lalong, Long Stem, Mong Thong, Otong, Transvestite.

Pests, disease and disorder:

- Hawk moth (*Daphnusa ocellaris*): Serious pest.
- Durian psyllids (*Allocaridara malayensis*). Serious pest.
- Mealy bugs.
- Fruit borer:
- Leaf cutters:
- Phytophthora root rot.
- Flesh burn: Boron deficiency.

27. MORACEAE

27.1 Fig

- Eulogized as 'Forbidden fruit'.
- Fig tree denotes 'peace and prosperity'.

- Large shrub or deciduous tree.
- Most salt and drought tolerant crop.
- Required light intensity for photosynthesis: 40 Klux.
- Optimum leaf temperature for photosynthesis: 25^{0}C.
- Can withstand temperature as low as -12^{0}C to -9.5^{0}C.
- Suitable for clayey soils.
- Fig is gynodioecious species.
- Possess laxative property.
- 1st fruit to be domesticated and 1st processed fruit in human civilization.
- About 90% of the figs produced in the world are dried.
- India imports dried figs valued about Rs. 650 crores from Afghanistan, Turkey and California.
- Calorific value: 269 Kcal.
- Nutrition score: 49.
- Rich in sugar next to dates.
- It is a soft fruit purple or green skin and lot of small seeds inside.
- TSS of fresh fruit: 16% while dried 52%.
- Fresh fig is highly perishable and consists of 84% pulp and 16% skin.
- One of the 1st fruit preserved by drying.
- When dormant, mature tree withstand -12^{0}C to -9.5^{0}C.
- Highest fibre content among fruits.
- Rich in protein and digestive enzyme 'Ficin'.
- Ficin (Rennin) has 30-100 times more milkclotting activity than animal rennin.
- Pruning time: December.
- Training system: Single stem (open vase system).
- Type of inflorescence: Hyphanthodium.
- Pollination type: Cross pollination is known as 'Caprification'.
- Pollination agent: Female wasp (*Blastophaga psenes*).
- Fruit buds borne laterally which unfold to produce leafy shoots with flower cluster in leaf axil.
- Diploid apogamy is induced in *F. carica* and *F. afghanistanica* by application of *Lilium candidum* pollen.
- Adenosine triphosphate stimulated apomicitic seed development in *F. carica.*
- Naphthyl acetamide stimulated apomicitic seed development in *F. afghanistanica*
- Commercial propagation: Hardwood cutting.

- *Ficus glomerata*: Rootstock for root knot nematode resistance.
- Cv. Brown Turkey is also used as rootstock.
- Tissue culture: Recent mode of propagation.
- Tree enters inactive phase during October to January.
- Fiddle leaf fig (*F. lyrata*).
- Afghanistan fig (*F. afghanistanica*): Triploid. Embryo culture is successful.
- Wild Himalayan fig or Bedu (*F. palmata*): Decidious tree. Fruits equivalent to cultivated fig in taste, flavour and nutrition contents.
- 'Breba': Parthenocarpically produced crop on previous season's wood i.e. *khatta bahar*.
- *Khatta bahar*: Fruits formed during March-April & ripened in rainy season.
- *Mitha bahar*: Fruits produced on current season's growth. Fruits ripened during February-March.
- Based on pollination pattern and sex of flower: 4 classes of fig.

Group	**Features**	**Pollination pattern & sex**	**Varieties**
Common fig/ Edible fig/ Adriatic fig/ White fig	Mostly grown in India (Indigenous to India); pale green or pale yellow coloured	Long stylled pistillate flower	Poona Fig, Conadria, Mission, Kadota, Black Ischia, Brown Turkey, Brunswick
Smyrna fig/ Calimyrna fig	Commercially important; superior nutty flavour due to fertile seeds, extensively grown in Europe; most suitable for dehydration	Fruit develop only after pollination; possess long styllled pistillate flower	Calimyrna, Zidi, Taranimt
San Pedro fig	Intermediate between common fig and Smyrna fig	1st crop is breba (complete partheno-carpic); 2nd crop developed if flowers are pollinated	Dauphine, Lampeiria, King, Gentile, San Pedro
Wild fig/ Capri fig/ Male fig/ Goat fig	Most primitive type; monoecious & used as pollinizer, non-edible	Short style pistillate flower & functional staminate (male) flower	Samson, Standford Brawley

- Common fig varieties grown in California are grown parthenocarpically doesn't require caprification.
- Figs grown in India are parthenocarpic & do not need any cross pollination from wild fig.
- Chemical serves as an alternative to caprification: CPA.
- Capri fig produces 3 crops/ year. Spring crop is known as 'profiche' while summer crop is known as 'mommoni'.

- Wild fig has functional staminate flowers.
- Smyrna figs have only female flowers.
- Smyrna and Capri figs often grown together to provide pollen source.
- Black mission figs are extremely sweet (24-26^0 Brix).
- Hard pruning is given in October to get fruits in summer.
- Notching is done in July on atleast 8 months old shoots for production of laterals on vigorous upright branches.
- Only 1-2 buds on each shoot are activated by notching.
- Pre-girdling of canes 30 days before taking cuttings, results in quick and increased rooting.
- Excessing water in soil heavily cause fruit splitting.
- Irrigation at fruit ripening results in production of insipid fruits.
- Irrigated fig plants show greater shoot growth and yield.
- Fruits from irrigated trees are heavier by 13.5-16%.
- Fruit ripening period: In western India (March-May); Northern India (May-July); South India (bears twice in June-July and February-May).
- Best source of nitrogen: Ammonium sulphate.
- Dormex is used to break bud dormancy.
- Maturity indices:
  - Days from fruit set: 120-140.
  - Fruits become soft, slightly wilts at neck and hangs down from their own weight.
  - Change in fruit colour (dark green to reddish purple).
  - Sudden increase in fruit size.
  - Opening of ostiole.
  - Increase in sugar content (20%).
  - No milky latex flows at cut end of stalk.
- Production of parthenocarpic fruits: NAA or IBA @ 25 ppm.
- Before drying, fruits are subjected to sulphur fumigation & dried at 70-72^{0}C.
- At end of process, weight is reduced to 1/3rd of fresh weight.

Varieties:

- Dinakar: Developed from cv. 'Daulatabad Fig'.
- Badka: Bluish black fruits and found in Himachal Pradesh.
- Black Ischia, Brown Turkey: Grown in western India.
- California Mission, California Gold: Highly suitable for dried fig making.
- Marseilles: Grown at an elevation of 1500 m MSL.

- Others: Kabul, Bangalore, Lucknow,
- Cvs. Azendjar, Taranimt, Zidi, Hunt, Celeste: Resistant to nematodes.

Name	Breeding method	Features
YCD-1 (Timla fig) 1993	Introduction	Reddish-purple fruits; fruit dia.7 cm; yield 4000 fruits/ tree; bearing is throughout the year
Deanna (1986)	Introduction from USA	Fruit produced parthenocarpically; pyriform shape; TSS 18^{0}Brix; for drying purpose; grown under Bangalore condition
Conadria (1986)	Introduction from USA	Drying purpose & suitable for HDP; grown under Bangalore condition
Excel (1986)	Introduction from USA	Fruit produced parthenocarpically; pyriform shape; fruit wt. 35-50 g; TSS 20^{0}Brix; for drying purpose; for canning purpose & suitable for HDP
DiRedo	Introduction from USA	Skin light yellow; fruit globose; fruit wt. 50-60 g; good for drying
Flanders	Introduction from USA	Skin light tawny violet strips; fruit pyriform; fruit wt. 45-54 g; good for fresh consumption
Yvonne	Introduction from USA	Skin canary yellow; fruit ovoid; fruit wt. 45-55 g; fruit drop in short time
Saleeb	Introduction from USA	Skin light green; fruit oblate; fruit wt. 48-60 g; matures early
Phule Rajewadi (JWF-6) 2015	Selection	Big fruits; mod. resistant to rust & suitable for processing
Poona fig	*F. carica* x *F. glomerata*	For table purpose

Diseases and pest:

- Rust (*Cerotelium fici*): Serious and common disease in all fig growing countries. Obligate parasite. Spray Chlorothalonil 0.2% + Carbendazim 0.1% or Copper oxy-Chloride @ 0.4%.
- Fig mosaic: Viral disease.
- Leaf spot (*Cylindrocladium scoparium*):
- Anthracnose (*Sphaceloma facicaricae*):
- Rhizopus rot (*Rhizopus stolonifer*):
- Fig moth (*Ehestia cantella*): Dried figs are more susceptible.
- Indian meal moth (*Plodia interpunctella*): Dried figs are more susceptible.

Physiological disorders:

- Sunburn: Due to excess pruning.
- Fruit splitting: Due to sudden change in atmospheric humidity and soil moisture level.
- Fruit drop: Due to excess heat, drought, cold nights, light frost and lack of pollination.

27.2 Jackfruit

- Eulogized as 'Poor man's food or Vegeterian meat'.
- World's largest tree borne edible fruit (30-40 kg).
- Mainly cultivated in Sri Lanka, India, Thailand, Malaysia, Mauritius, Indonesia, Philippines, Nepal, Myanmar and Bangladesh.
- Malaysia, Thailand and Philippines: Exporter of fresh fruits to Singapore and Hong Kong.
- Average productivity: 2-27 T/ha.
- Adapted to tropical and sub-tropical climate.
- Optimum soil pH: 5.5 to 7.5.
- Fruit consist of 4 parts: Bulbs/ flakes (37-40%), perigones i.e. unfertilized or aborted flowers (18-20%), rind (20-22%) and seeds (20-23%).
- High value timber (resistant to white ants).
- Tetraploid species: 2n=56.
- Suitable for homestead farming and high density multispecies cropping systems.
- It contains 20% of carbohydrates, latex from bark contains resin and fruit rind is rich source of pectin.
- Cold and frost susceptible.
- Fruit flesh rich source of β-carotene: 500-580 IU/100g.
- Most expensive fruit in Britain.
- Botanically it is a multiple fruit.
- Major sugars: Fructose, glucose, sucrose in all parts except spiny rind.
- Lectine: Natural protein found in jack fruit- used for cancer treatment.
- Soft fleshed types are suitable for culinary purpose.
- Major protein from seed: 'Jacalin' inhibited the growth of HIV infection in *in vitro*.
- Seed is separated by horny endocarpus enclosed by sub-gelatinous exocarpus.
- Milky white sap (latex) has bateriolytic activity equal to that of of papaya latex.
- Vivipary is observed.
- Bearing habit: Cauliflorous (fruit emergence from main trunk).
- Flowering months: December-March.
- Off seasoning flowering: September-October.
- Two growth flushes: July-September and March-May.
- Anthesis time: 2 to 3 PM.
- Anther dehiscence: 3 to 4 PM.
- Stigma receptivity: For 36 h.

- Special fruiting branchlets are called as 'foot stalks'.
- Inflorescence: Spike covered by two spathes.
- Inflorescence axis, ovary and perianth all grow simultaneously.
- Ratio of male to female inflorescence: Higher proportion of male inflorescence than female.
- Male spike on terminal branches in central and peripheral regions.
- After dehiscence, male spike turns black and drop down.
- Staminate spikes drop about 15 days after their emergence.
- Male inflorescence has sweet scent of honey and burnt sugar.
- Length and diameter of female inflorescence is larger than males.
- Female spike on fruit stalks which appear on trunk and on main branches in central region of tree.
- Only female spike develop into multiple fruit.
- Uniform, regular shape and size is correlated with adequate pollinated flowers of female spikes.
- Pollination agents: Wind and insect.
- Sex distribution: 96% male spikes and 3-40% female spikes.
- Surface of young male spike is smooth while female is granular.
- Male spike reach maturity 3-5 days before female ones.
- Pollination and fertilization of spike completes with 3-6 days of anthesis.
- Fruit size and shape may be small and irregular in less pollinated fruits.
- Partially pollinated female spikes bear small fruits with irregular shape.
- Fruit set under open pollination is 75% and can be improved by hand pollination.
- Lack of pollination leads to dropping of female spikes.
- Common method of propagation: Seed.
- Problems in seed propagation: Seed viability and storage period.
- *In vitro* clonal propagation is practiced.
- Critical moisture content for seed viability: 39 %.
- Seed viability: 1 month (80%).
- Soaking seeds in NAA @ 25 ppm for 24 h improves germination.
- Seed germination period: 3-8 weeks.
- Grafting methods: Veneer, epicotyl (8-10 days old seedlings in April-May) and softwood.
- Etiolated cuttings: 84% success under mist.
- Planting time: June-September.

- Planting system: Square or hexagonal.
- Highly susuceptible to water logging.
- It responds well to irrigation between flowering and fruiting.
- Fruit drop: Natural mechanism of physiological thinning.
- Fruit development period: February-June.
- Light pruning of shoot tips causes lateral bud break and makes tree more compact and dwarf.
- Removal of water sprcuts, old flowering shoots and upright branches with parasitic plants at end of rainy seaspn increases light penetration to inner canopy.
- Maturity indices:
  - o Days from fruit set: 180-270 days.
  - o Tapping i.e. dull, hollow sound is produced when fruit is snapped at maturity;
  - o Last leaf of peduncle turns yellow;
  - o Fruit colour change from green to faint dull green;
  - o Flattening of spines on the rind (spines become well developed and wide spaced);
  - o Rind is soft, flesh is crispy and pale yellow;
  - o Thickening of latex;
  - o Development of aroma.
  - o After dehiscence male spike turns black due to growth of mold.
  - o Tender jackfruit used for culinary purpose is harvested before the hardening of seeds.
- Fruits ripen from March-June, April-September or June-August in various parts of the world.
- Off season fruiting from September to December or round the year fruiting is reported.
- Fruit harvest period: June-July.
- Normally, fruits ripen in 3-10 days at ambient temperature (20-35^{0}C) depending in maturity.
- Storage temperature: 11-12.5^{0}C at 85-90 % R.H.
- Large number of products have been developed from raw, tender and ripe fruits and seeds.
- For culinary purpose, tender fruits are harvested within 2-3 months after fruit setting before seeds hardened.
- Tender fruit is mainly consumed as vegetable and in processed form as pickle, papad, chips and canned.
- Yield: 10 T/ha (150-250 fruits/ tree).

Species:

Botanical name	Features
Artocarpus mariannensis	Contribution to evolution of domesticated spp.
Monkey jack (*A. lakoocha*)	Wet meat is product. Very small edible fruits (5-7 cm in dia.)
Chempedak (*A. champeden, A. polyphema*)	Smallest fruit with unpleasant flavour. Bears strong fruits & strong odour
Elasticus (*A. elasticus*)	Edible pulp & seed
Rudrakshi/ Aini (*A. hirsuta*)	Semi-wild in Western Ghats and bears edible fruits. Used as rootstock. Timber is valuable in making implements and furniture
A. heterophyllus (syn. *A. integrifolia*)	Tetraploid (2n=4x=56) and has separate male and female flowers

Varieties:

- Singapore or Ceylon Jack: Introduced from Ceylon in 1947 at Tamil Nadu- Off season and highly precocious variety.
- Muttam Varikka: Local variety from Kerala weighing 7 kg.
- Gulabi: Local selection and rose scented.
- Hazari: Bear more number of fruits.
- Champa: Flavourlike champak flower.
- Burliar-1: Selection from FRS, Burliar.
- Kappa/ Firm flesh: Large fruit, crisp pulp, small seeds, scanty juice.
- Barka/ Soft flesh: Smaller fruit, juicy pulp, large seeds.
- Rudrakshi: Pummelo size fruit with inferior quality. Retains characters even seed propagated.
- Elite types: Padmaraj, Narayani.
- Baramasi, Dofala: Used as vegetable.
- Rasdar, Khajwa, Sugandh: Uttar Pradesh type.
- Exotic: Golden Nugget, Black Gold, Lemon Gold, Honey Gold.
- Krishnagiri: Farmer's selection from Talegaon Dhandhere, Dist. Pune.
- Prashanti: Farmer's selection from Moodbidri, Karnataka.

Name	Breeding method	Features
IIHR, Bengaluru (CHES, Hirehalli)		
Siddu (2017)	Selection from tree at farmers's field of Chelur village of Tumkur district	Small sized fruits (2-5 Kg); fruit wt. 2.44 kg; yield (450 kg/ tree); irregular fruit shape; 450 fruits/ tree; coppery red flakes;TSS 31^0 Brix; carotenoids (4.43 mg/100 g); lycopene (1.12 mg/100g)
Shankara (2017)	Selection from tree at farmers' field of Chowdlapura village of Tumkur district	Rich in neutraceuticals; Small fruits (2-5 Kg); fruit wt. 2.73 kg; yield (460 kg/tree); irregular fruit shape; 450 fruits/ tree; coppery red flakes; TSS 28^0 Brix; carotenoids (5.83 mg/100 g); lycopene (2.26 mg/100g)
CG-16	Clonal selection	Fruit size 7 kg; red crispy flakes

ICAR Research Complex for Eastern Region, Patna (HARP, Ranchi)		
Swarna Manohar (2004)	Selection from local landraces	Fruit wt. 13.7 kg; TSS-18.0^0 Brix; total sugar 8.33%; yield 550 kg/tree; suitable for table purpose
Swarna Poorti (2004)	Selection from local landraces	Fruit wt. 4.2 kg; TSS-18.0^0 Brix; total sugar 7.46%; yield 120 kg/tree; suitable for vegetable purpose
TNAU, Coimbatore		
PLR-1 (1992)	Clonal selection from Panikkan-kuppam local of Panruti taluk of Tamil Nadu	Fully ripe fruits have flat stigmatic surface instead of spiny surface; off season variety & suitable for HDP; fruit wt. 12 kg containing 115-120 bulbs
PLR (J) 2 (2007)	Clonal selection from Pathirak-kotai local area	High yield (110 fruits/ tree/ year); highly palatable; mosaic resistant
Pechiparai-1 i.e. PPI-1 (1996)	Clonal selection from Mulagu-moodu local area	Yield (107 fruits/ tree/ annum); bears twice a year in April-June & November-December
Hybrid jack	Singapore Jack x Velippala	Precocious bearing; carpels big and sweet than parents
MPKV, Rahuri		
Narali Phanas	Clonal selection	-
Dr BSKKV, Dapoli		
Konkan Prolific (2004)	Seedling selection	1st variety from Konkan region; oblong shape; firm flesh; yield: 420 kg/ tree
GBPUA & T, Pantnagar (HRC, Patharchatta)		
Pant Garima (2004)	Selection	Tall, light brown fruit colour; fruit wt. 5 kg; good for cooking & table purpose
Pant Mahima (2004)	Selection	Tall, light brown fruit colour; fruit wt. 6.5 kg; good for cooking & table purpose
NDUA & T, Faizabad		
NJT-1, 2, 3, 4	Selection	Large fruits; low fibre; suitable for table & culinary purpose
NJC- 1,2, 3, 4	Selection	Small fruits; thin rind; soft flesh; low fibre; suitable for culinary purpose

Pests, diseases and disorder:

- Fruit and shoot borer (*Diaphania casesalis*): Major pest.
- Inflorescence rhizopus rot: Major disease: attack male spikes, premature shedding of tender fruits.
- Fruit rot/ inflorescence rot/ soft rot (*Rhizopus artocarpi*): Serious disease and affected fruits fall early.
- Brown weevil (*Ochyromera artocarpi*):
- Pink disease (*Botryobasidium salmonicolor*):
- Leaf spot (*Phyllosticta artocarpina*):
- Dieback of twigs (*Botryodiplodia theobromae*):

27.3 Bread fruit

- Regarded as 'Tree vegetable or *Vilayati* jackfruit'.
- Monoecious but dicholinous tree (bearing male and female inflorescence on specialized laterals).
- Grown in homestead gardens in Kerala.
- Only seeds are cooked and used for culinary purposes.
- Seedless bread fruit contain high amount of carbohydrate (27.98%).
- Seedless breadfruit is propagated by root cutting, air layering or root suckers while
- seeded bread fruit is propagated by seed.
- Male flowers are produced on long catkins.
- Morphologically both seeded and seedless fruits are similar.
- Seedless types used as vegetable and seeded type as rootstocks.
- *A. rigidus*: Seedling rootstock for budding.
- Fruit size: 10-15 cm in diameter.
- Fruits ready for harvest 60-90 days after emergence.
- Harvesting season: February-May.
- Maturity index: Fruit colour changes from green to yellowish green.
- Female inflorescence emerges from bract in morning (7-11 AM).
- Individual flower takes 72 h for opening in successive stages.
- Female flower receptive after 3 days of emergence.
- Artificial pollination increases fruit set.
- Seedless fruit contains 28% starch and used as staple food in Polynesia.
- Horizontal planting of root suckers is best planting material method (90% success).
- Discoloration or browning of fruit rind is associated with long distance transport and storage.
- **Variety**: Yellow Heart.

Disease and disorder:

- Soft rot (*Rhizopus artocarpi*) is most common fungus leading to rotting and fruit drop.
- Chilling injury: Bread fruit is stored at a temperature < 12^0C.

27.4 Mulberry

- Nutrient composition/ 100 g edible portion: Moisture (85.5%), protein (0.7%), fat (0.4%) fat, -CHO (12.2%), vit. C (1741 mg).
- Individual berry is known as 'pseudocarp'.
- Seed weight is more in polyploids than diploids.
- Seed contain 25-35% drying oil.

- Polyembryony is rarely reported.
- Male catkin is longer than female.
- Male flowers in cluster.
- Female catkin is axillary and shorter than male.
- Pollination agent: Wind.
- Fruits highly perishable and used for table purpose.
- Fruits contain cent percent edible portion and 85.5% moisture.
- Deciduous and pruned regularly in December-January.
- Optimum temperature for growth: 14-28^{0}C.
- Propagation method: Seed, stem cutting, grafting and trench layering.
- Yield: 20-40 kg fruits/ year/ tree.

Species:

- Triploids are grown in Japan.

Name	Botanical name	Features
Black mulberry	*Morus nigra*	Polyploid and valued for fruits; withstand as low as 3^{0}C; parthenocarpy is reported
-	*M. alba*	Indigenous to China; cultivated for fruits & timber
-	*M. alba* var. *atropurpurea*	Grown for rearing silkworms
-	*M. laevigata*	Natural tetraploid grown in eastern Himalayas; wild species cultivated in Assam
-	*M. indica*	Indian varieties belong to this species
-	*M. serrata*	Grown in temperate Himalayas
-	*M. multicaulis*	Indigenous to Russia; resistant to cold

Varieties:

Name	Breeding method	Features
CIAH, Bikaner		
Thar Harit	Selection	Fruit mature in 38-42 days; yield (33 kg/plant); fruit wt. (3.76 g); TSS (31.5^0 Brix); acidity (0.42%); vit. C (23.7 mg); total flavonoids (0.72 mg/g); total anti-oxidant activity (CUPRAC 4.30 μM TE/ g); tolerant to low & high temperature; suitable for table & processing purpose
Thar Lohit	Selection	Low & high temperature tolerant; fruit wt. 10-12 g; TSS (20.8^0 Brix); acidity (1.6%); vit. C (11.2 mg); total flavonoids (0.96 mg/g); total anti-oxidant activity (CUPRAC 6.81 μM TE/ g); neutraceutical rich; yield (12-26 kg/plant); suitable for table & processing purpose

28. MUSACEAE

28.1 Banana

- Eulogized as 'Adam's fig or Antacid fruit or Tree of wisdom or Tree of Paradise or Apple of paradise or *Kalpataru* or Plant of virtues or Antique fruit crop or Vascular plant or Versatile food for the mankind or Wonder berry or Baby fruit or Calcifuge crop or Powerhouse of nutrition or Powerhouse of nutraceuticals'.

- It is symbol of prosperity and fertility.
- 1st plant cultivated, 1st food of man and 1st fruit offered to babies.
- It is cultivated between 8^{0}N to 28^{0}N latitudes and upto altitude of 1500 m in tropics.
- Export oriented countries: UAE followed by Europe, Russiam Japan.
- Major importers of Indian banana: Iran, Iraq, UAE, etc.
- About 23% of world banana are produced in India.
- In India, banana contributes to 31.72% of total fruit production.
- Contribution of banana to agriculture GDP: 2.5%.
- It is 4th important food crop in terms of gross value after paddy, wheat and milk products.
- Among fruits, it occupies maximum area i.e. 2 lakh ha in India.
- Area in Maharashtra: 80,000 ha.
- Total production of banana in India is 29.8 MT from 0.85 million hectares.
- Export of banana from Maharashtra to Arabian countries (2018-19): 1 lakh 95 thousand tones.
- Maximum productivity of banana: 63 t/ha.
- Productivity is highest in Gujarat followed by Maharashtra, Tamil Nadu.
- Capital city of banana in India: Jalgaon, Maharashtra.
- National Banana Day: 21st April.
- Major constraints in cultivation: High/ chilling temperatures, wind and excess/ stress of water.
- It is nutrient loving plant and most delicious fruit of world.
- It is naturally slightly radioactive because of its potassium (P_{40}) content. It is used in nuclear communication to compare radiation levels and exposures.
- Systematic cultivation was 1st started in South East Asia.
- Suitable for vaccine preparation to control Hepatitis B.
- International Network for the Improvement of Banana and Plantain, France (INIBAP) now BIOVERSITY was established in 1985. It maintains largest banana germplasm.
- India is major centre of *Musa* diversity in South East Asia.
- World's largest banana biodiversity is found in New Guinea.
- BAPNET: Network activity between South Asia and South-East Asian countries, HQ. Philippines.
- PROMUSA: Global programme for banana and plantain improvement.
- MGIS: Musa Germplasm Information System.

- FHIA (Fundacion Hondurena de Investigation Agricola), Hondurus.
- Banana 'Makes These Bodies Sing' is a theme of Australian banana industry to attract children.
- The 'Clean and Green' is another promotional idea of Australian banana industry where assured chemical residue status of fruit is guaranteed.
- BARC, Trombay is developing bio-fortified (iron rich) banana for improved nutritional quality.
- Banana genome sequencing initiated in cv. Pahang (*M. acuminata ssp. malaccensis*).
- Its genome is 4 times larger than *Arabidopsis* and 2.5 times larger than strawberry.
- Banana underwent its whole genome duplication thrice during its evolution like wheat, rice, brassica, etc.
- Banana as a group of crops consisting of dessert banana, cooking banana, plantain, pome, silk and others.
- Plantain means cooking banana.
- In ripe banana, starch is converted into sucrose, fructose and glucose.
- Banana is rich source of carotenoids i.e. alpha carotene and beta carotene.
- Double/ dual factor hypothesis of flowering: Chailakhyanin (1961).
- Half of bananas of the world are eaten raw & ripe and about half are eaten as cooked vegetable.
- Globally, plantain contributes to 21% of total production for food consumption.
- Cavendish group has largest area and production and contribution is more than 50% to total production.
- Grown as catch crop in coconut plantation till palm start yielding.
- Grown as nurse crop during initial 3-4 years for provide shade to arecanut seedling.
- Banana is staple food of South Africa due to rich –CHO with calorific value of 67-137 per 100 g fruit.
- It is rich source of potassium (422 mg/100 g) used in nervous impulses.
- Ripe banana peels constitute 22-30% of whole fruit.
- Male bud or 'heart': Used as vegetable in India.
- Most suitable for high blood pressure patients.
- Good source of L-Dopa (Dopamine) to cure Parkinson disease.
- Edible portion: 71%.
- Crop satisty all the basic human needs like food, fodder and roofing.
- It offers edible fruits in all three major ploidy status viz. 2x, 3x and 4x.
- Largest producer of tissue cultured plants (750 million/ annum) in the world: Jain Irrigation Systems Limited, Jalgaon.

- Monoclone culture has resulted in large scale damage in India and world.
- All wild types are diploids while most of cultivated bananas are triploids in nature.
- Growth in volume of seeded banana is sigmoid and that of parthenocarpic fruit is not sigmoid.
- Tzudir (1980) 1st reported double sigmoid growth pattern of fruits.
- Growth curve: Edible clones of *M. acuminata* (concave) and *M. balbisiana* (convex).
- In parts of Thanjavur and Tiruchirappalli districts of Tamil Nadu, banana is cultivated exclusively for leaves.
- Optimum soil pH for cultivation: 6.5-7.5 and can be grown up to 8.5 with organic amendments.
- In India, it is successfully grown from 8^0N to 28^0N latitudes with 15-35^0C temperature and rainfall of 500-2000 mm/ year.
- Low threshold temperature for growth: 11^0C. Basrai, Amritsagar, Rasthali are susceptible to frost damage. Poovan and Hill bananas (Sirumalai, Virupakshi) can withstand low temperature.
- Growth of banana is influenced by temperature. It grows well at temperature of 20-30^0C (26.5^0C).
- Temperature >36-38^0C cause scorching effect with increased transpiration.
- Banana plant produces roughly one leaf per week.
- Leaf longevity: 55-165 days.
- Average time interval between emergences of successive leaves (phylocron) for tropical climate: 7 days.
- Lower leaf numbers are produced in tropics than sub-tropical areas.
- Each leaf is normally larger than its predecessors.
- Leaf is rolled from one margin to other i.e. convolute.
- Prior to bunch emergence, last 2-3 leaves produced are smaller in size.
- Phyllotactic pattern changes gradually from 1/3 to 2/5 to 3/7 to 4/9.
- Minimum number of leaves for optimum crop production: 10-12.
- About 35-40 leaves are formed till flowering.
- Differentiation of bunch (shooting) occurs after production of 45 leaves in Gros Michel; 23 leaves in Dwarf Cavendish and 32 leaves in Robusta.
- Rolling nature of leaf lamina is known as 'vernation'.
- Largest leaf produced by plant is termed as 'climax leaf' while smallest leaf i.e. flag leaf (shot blade) formed just before flowering protects the bunch from rain and sun.
- Average life span of a single leaf: 70-200 days.
- After shooting, bunch weight contributes to 32.17% of total fresh weight at harvest.

- Maximum leaf area of individual leaf at 7th month after planting: 1.37 m^2.
- Inflorescence initiates in the heart of pseudostem 3-6 months prior to shooting.
- Inflorescence: Spadix (female, male and hermaphrodite flowers in the same floral stalk).
- Inflorescence produces series of different types of flowers viz. (female, male & hermaphrodite) in same floral stalk.
  - Normally pistillate flowers are basal portion (develops into fruits) with deciduous staminate flowers e.g. Poovan, Monthan. And male buds continuously produce staminate flowers till fruit ripening.
  - In 2nd group of inflorescence, male bud is absent. The whole inflorescence bears pistillate flowers and hence all flowers develop into fruits e.g. Thatilla Kunnan, Ayirank, Rasthali, Moongli.
  - In 3rd group of inflorescence, basal flowers develop into fruits followed by persistent male flowers which are again followed by deciduous male flowers. Bracts of male flowers are deciduous e.g. Rasthali, Chakkrakeli.
- Flowering cannot be induced by changing day length or by vernalization.
- Age of the plant is dominant factor for flower production.
- Banana produces different types of flowers- female, hermaphrodite and male in same stalk.
- Flowers present in basal side of peduncle: Female.
- Female flowers develop during period of development of last 2-3 leaves.
- Flowers are arranged in 2 series, numbering about 7 to 14 in pairs.
- Floral development occurs before stem elongation.
- Flower differentiates in sequence of sepals, followed by stamens and then carpels.
- Most effective time for pollination: 7 AM to 10.30 AM.
- Dwarf Cavendish and Robusta produce 5,000 pollens of which 4-5% are fertile.
- Cv. Waths produce 10,500 pollens of which 14.9% are fertile.
- Wild cultivars of *M. acuminata* and *M. balbisiana* produce 40,000-50,000 pollens of which 65% are fertile.
- Pollen viability is influenced by genome and ploidy level.
- Pollen viability is highest in *M. balbisiana*.
- 4% pollen viability in Nendran provides scope for developing male parents for genetic improvement of French plantain.
- Edible banana rarely contain pollen.
- Fruit derived from inferior ovary.
- Fruit in seeded banana is derived from developing seeds while in seedless banana fruit develops through endogenous auxin stimulation.

- Edible pulp in parthenocarpic fruits and seeded banana is mostly develops from starchy parenchyma from outer lining of locule.
- Ovary is trilocular with axile placentation.
- Most of the seeds (74.9%) are found in distal 1/3rd of fruit.
- Banana seeds are very hard in nature.
- Banana cv. having seeds: Valery (AAA Cavendish group).
- Cross between 'Bobby Tannap' (AAB) x 'Calcutta 4' (AA) produced 219 seeds/ bunch.
- Cross between 'Gros Michel' (AAA) x 'Pisang Lilin' (AA) produced 60 seeds/ bunch.
- First row of all hands account for 56.5% of total number of fruits.
- Fruits of upper hands have higher pulp: skin weight ratio than those in lower hands.
- Botanically, rhizome is a modified stem.
- Root system lies within 15 cm of soil and requires superficial intercultivation.
- Pure *acuminata* diploids & triploids produce large number of suckers than *balbisiana* derivatives.
- Cv. Monthan is exception in producing large number of suckers.
- Setting of only one sucker for ratooning is important to maintain higher productivity.
- Sword sucker with narrow leaves is preferred to broad leaved water sucker.
- Ideal weight of sword sucker: 450-750 g.
- Fruiting age varies according to size of sucker at planting.
- A part from sword suckers, cut rhizomes (1.5-2.0 kg) called 'bits' and emerging suckers called 'peepers' are used for propagation.
- Sucker production is characteristic of each variety conditioned by level of ploidy.
- Tetraploids are larger in plant stature but poor in sucker production.
- Pseudostem girth is related with more sucker production as in diploid Anaikomban (AA) & triploid Monthan (ABB).
- Banana clones (Robusta, Wather, Monthan) having higher number of functional leaves produce profuse suckers than Poovan (Champa) and tetraploids.
- Increased leaf area in diploids, triploids & tetraploids has relation to increased sucker production.
- Reasons for increased sucker production: Higher photosynthetic area and increased elaboration of metabolites.
- Corm size has no direct influence on sucker production e.g. Tetraploid cv. Klue Teparod has largest corm size but poor in sucker production.
- Number of swollen buds on corm has positive association with number of sucker production.

- Disinfection of planting material: Dipping in Monocrotophos (0.5%) and Bavistin (0.2%).
- Cultivation problems: Female sterility and viruses.
- Karnataka state is pioneer in tissue culture protocol.
- Production level can be increased by use of tissue cultured plants.
- In India, 90% plantation is traditionally through suckers and hardly 10% through tissue culture.
- Most widely used tissue culture method: Shoot tip culture.
- Generally, 3-5% variants are permissibie in micropropagation.
- Popular tissue culture variety: Grand Naine.
- Advisable number of ratoons for tissue cultured plants: 2-3 times.
- Rate of multiplication through shoot tip (5 mm) culture is lowest in ABB genome and maximum in AAA genome.
- Multiple shoot production is possible at the end of 7th culture cycle (11-21 plants with 95% survival). MS medium with NAA @ 1 mg/litre is better in root initiation.
- *In vivo* macropropagation (by *in situ* or *ex situ*) can produce 20-25 shoots/ sucker.
- By tissue culture method (sucker induction by chemical BAP) about 156 plantlets could be produced in a span of 8 months.
- Virus indexing of Cucumber Mosaic virus and Banana Streak virus is done in tissue culture with ELISA, PCR and NASH techniques.
- Embryonic cell suspension of banana cv. Rasthali have been transformed with '*S*' gene of Hepatitis B surface antigen (HbsAg) using *Agrobacterium* mediated transformation at BARC, Mumbai.
- Ripe banana fruit contain over 26% sugar.
- In cv. Monthan, only glucose sugar is found.
- 'Fei' group from Australimusa in Pacific Islands: Richest source of carotenoids. They are referred as 'Karat' bananas.
- Setting up of followers is one of the most crucial operations in cultivation.
- Desuckering, propping and mattocking are important cultural practices followed in banana.
- Desuckering:
  - o Removal of surplus and unwanted suckers.
  - o Two ways of desuckering- pouring kerosene and damaging with crowbar, 2,4-D.
  - o It is done at 3 times in a year but once in 45 days is common practice
- Mattocking: Practice of sequential cutting of pseudostem after bunch harvest. It is originated from Jamaica.

- Propping: Supporting to pseudostem at the time of bunch emergence.
- Denavelling: Removal of male flower bud after appearance of last hand on bunch for nutrient diversion.
- Dual purpose of denavelling: Saving of mobilization of food into unwanted sink of plant and use of male bud as vegetable.
- Production systems:
  a) Homestead/ backyard cultivation in traditional banana growing regions.
  b) Mixed cultivation as commercial shade crop for coffee, coconut and arecanut plantations.
  c) Intercropping with ginger, turmeric, yams, tapioca, vegetable crops and gourds to exploit maximum income/ unit area.
  d) Multistory system in coastal areas with HDP features and semi-tall banana Poovan and Ney Poovan are preferred.
- In Tamil Nadu, banana is specially grown for leaf production.
- Fertilization accounts for 20-30% of total cost of production.
- Correct time of fertilizer application: Planting to bunch emergence.
- In Dwarf Cavendish cvs., application of fertilizers should be completed within 100 days of planting and before initiation of inflorescence.
- In wetlands areas, split application of fertilizers is as- 1st (40-50 days), 2nd (70-80 days), 3rd (110-120 days) after planting.
- Nutrition based on leaf nutrient analysis improves finger filling & bunch weight.
- Suitable fertilizer in fertigation: Potassium nitrate.
- Planting distance for cultivation: 2.1m x 2.1m (Poovan, Rasthali, Nendran and Robusta); 1.8m x 1.8m (Basrai, Kulhan, Rajapuri).
- Planting distance for leaf production: Wider spacing at 2.6 to 3 m and 6 to 9 plants/ clump.
- Planting time followed in Maharashtra: *Mrig baug* (June-July) and *Kande baug* (October-November).
- Planting systems:
  a) Pit planting is practiced in garden land system for biennial plantations.
  b) Trench method is especially followed in wetland system of cultivation (Cauvery delta of Tamil Nadu).
  c) Furrow method and double row system is followed in annual planting systems e.g. in Gujarat and Mahashtra.
  d) HDP for high yield/ unit area in Dwarf Cavendish/ Robusta/ Grand Naine/ Poovan/ Nendran cvs.
- Rainfed crop is taken in west coast and hills of south India.

- AAA, AAB clones are grown under irrigated condition while ABB clones as rainfed crop.
- Normal furrow, basin, trench and flood irrigation is followed.
- Water requirement: 1800-2200 mm and through drip irrigation 10-25 litres/plant.
- Drip irrigation induces earliness & improved yield and saves 40-50% water.
- Multi-storey system is commonly followed in coastal Karnataka and Kerala.
- Crop duration: 6 to 16 months.
- Vegetative phase (1-6 months) is crucial for weed control. Weed causes 60-70% yield loss.
- Wheat straw and banana straw as mulch material (12.5 kg/plant) proves beneficial.
- Recommended herbicide: Diuron @ 3 kg in 1200 lit or Gramaxone (Paraquat) @ 1.5 lit in 1200 lit of water, MSMA (Ansar or Deconate) @ 30 g/ lit/ ha.
- Strong wind is a threat for successful banana production.
- Polyethylene cover 0.1mm thickness can protect bunches from hail damage.
- Bunch covering with perforated white polyethylene bagsin November is essential practice in Dwarf Cavendish and Silk group for attractive colour of fruits.It avoids direct exposure of peduncles to sun, increases yield by 25-30% and avoids secondary infection of *Colletotrichum*.
- Two spray of 0.5% KH_2PO_4 or KNO_3+ 1% Urea at fruit development stage increases the fruit weight and bunch weight.
- Dehanding of last fruitful hands (after emergence of 7th or 8th hand) is done to meet export standard of Basrai banana.
- Maturity indices:
  - Days from flower emergence (100-120) or 12-15 months (dwarf cvs.) and 15-18 months (tall cvs.) after planting or 3-4 months from flowering to harvest;
  - Disappearance of angularity (ridge of surface become angular to round);
  - Brittleness of the floral ends, should fall with slight touch;
  - Bunch usually takes 90-120 days to mature after shooting;
  - Bunches are harvested when the top leaves starts drying;
  - Caliper grade.
  - Pulp to peel ratio varies from 1: 1.44 in Anaikomban clone to 1: 5.04 in Kunnan; in Robusta banana: 1.08 (30 days after flowering) to 2.30 (harvest stage).
  - Fruits are harvested after attainment of 3/4th full stage.
- Under irrigated condition, cv. Dwarf Cavendish take 95-107 days to reach 3¾thof full maturity.
- An unripe firm green banana contains 0.1-2.1% TSS, 19.5-21.5% starch.
- A fully ripe banana contains 75.6% moisture, 20.4% TSS, 1.2% starch.

- Ripened banana contains more sucrose than glucose and fructose.
- Organic acid content increase with increase in ripening.
- For long distance transportation, harvesting is done at ¾ (75-80%) maturity.
- Delatexing is done with detergent or sodium hypochlorite solution.
- Cold storage conditions: 17-21^{0}C (green) and 14-15^{0}C (ripe) @ 90-95% R.H. for 2-3 weeks.
- CA storage conditions: 12-16^{0}C at 2-5% O_2, 2-5% CO_2.
- Ethylene source in banana ripening: Ripened banana.
- Ripening of bunches is done in commercial low cost closed ripening chambers.
- Bananas are commercially ripened using ethylene gas @ 100-300 ppm.
- Cheapest source for inducing artificial ripening of banana: Calcium carbide.
- Use of acetylene gas generated from CaC_2 for banana ripening was started during 1932.
- Ethylene absorbant ($KMNO_4$ at 50 g) is used to delay ripening up to 5 days.
- In Maharashtra and Tamil Nadu, smoke treatment is commonest method to induce ripening.
- Polyethylene bags (100 gauge) with 0.2% holes enhance shelf life under room temperature.
- Skin coating with waxol (12% wax emulsion) prolongs shelf life by 10 days.
- Fungicidal wax coating (400 ppm TBZ) reduces weight loss, spoilage and delay in ripening.
- About 20-25% of banana is completely damaged before it reaches consumer.
- Fruits harvested at 105 days of maturity are suitable for chip making.
- Value added products: Banana fig (sun-dried slices of banana), banana pulp or puree, soft drinks, banana juice, fruit bar (osmotic dehydration), banana chips, banana brandy, banana powder, canning of banana (Cavendish and Lal kela), starch from pseudostem, pulp powder, banana flour, stem candy, thokku (pickle from flower), dehydration of core slice, etc.
- Large quantities of beer are made in Uganda and Tanzania.
- Paper board, tissue paper prepared out of pseudostem.
- Leaf industry is popular in Tamil Nadu.
- Banana leaf forms healthy, hygienic and biological eating plate.
- Two ratoons are meant for leaf production.
- For production of small bunch 4-5 leaves/ plant are kept and rest are cut and marketed.
- Leaf industry has turn over of Rs. 125 millions annually.
- Flower bud differentiation (bunch initiation) occurs within pseudostem within 5 months of planting.

- In Dwarf Cavendish, emergence of 11th last leaf indicates start of fruit bud differentiation.
- Ethylene triggers the vegetative bud to floral one.
- Seedlessness of banana is controlled by spray of 2, 4-D @ 25 ppm.
- Highest pollen output is in the flowers borne on 10th node of the rachis while highest *in vitro* germination is from flowers on 20th node.
- For pollen studies use of flowers on the 10th node has been suggested as standard procedure.
- Among wild species, *M. balbisiana* produced maximum number (47142) of pollen grains/ anther followed by *M. acuminata* (40119) and *M. laterita* (38540).
- Among cultivars, Ney Vannan x *M. balbisiana* has maximum pollen grains (31450) followed by Boddles Altafort (24050) and Pisang Lilin (15710).
- Synthetic seed (Synseed) technology for banana has been developed at BARC, Trombay and CPMB, Hyderabad.
- Synseed technology involves use of shoot apex, nodal microcuttings or somatic embryos encapsulated in an alginate based gel matrix, serving as synthetic seed.
- Advantage of Synseed: Can be stored and used when needed and more easily transportable.
- PCR based technique for indexing micropropagated banana for BBMV has been developed.
- Most banana fruits show negative geotropism.
- Intercropping plantain generates highest income and gives positive effect on rubber trees.
- Horn plantain: Important intercrop with coffee in Columbia and many African countries.
- Kaolin spray @ 8% on leaves in summer months till onset of monsoon is useful.
- Tipping of floral parts 8-12 days after emergence induces earliness in maturity and eliminates use of fungicide in controlling finger tip disease.
- Storage life can be prolonged using sealed polyethylene bags containing $KMnO_4$-.
- It is possible to cultivate banana in green house.
- In West Indies, banana for export are frequently grown in association with coconut.
- Waste utilization: Black and brown coloured organic shoe polish has been developed ffrom banana fruit rind by the students from Savitribai Phule Pune University.
- Requirements for getting phytosanitory certificate: Farm registration, global GAP certificate, packhouse recommended by APEDA, certificate of free from insecticide residues, free from white fly, bacteria, virus, etc.
- Wooden crates having internal dimensions of 42 cm x 32 cm x 29cm has been recommended for long distance transportation.

- Codex quality standards for export:
  - Minimum 14 cm long with 2-7 cm dia.
  - Hands with flown out fingers are not accepted.
  - CFB box- 5 ply 52 x 38 x 24 cm (top) and 51 x 37 x 23 cm (bottom) with more than 6% ventilation.
  - Single layer packing by keeping tips up and crown downside.
  - 6-7 hands/ carton and between each layer of fruits polyurethane foam sheet as cushion.
  - Polyethylene lining of 100 gauge thickness is must inside box.
  - Carton net weight: 12 kg.
  - Stored in pre-ccoling chamber at 13-14^{0}C.

Grading system:

- A net weight of 11 kg should be packed in carton of 55 x 30 x 21 cm.

Size	Bunch wt. (Kg)	Number of fruits in bunch
Extra	40-45	230-240
Large	30-35	160-190
Medium	15-26	150-160
Small	10-12	135-140
Extra small	Less than 7	90-100

Species:

- South-East Asia region: Cradle of *Musa* genus.
- Basic chromosome number varies from 7-11 while basic chromosome number of all edible banana is X=11.
- Markku and De Langhe (2001) described various sub-species of *M. acuminata*.
- Genus *Ensete*: Referred as 'False banana'. Useful as fiber, vegetable and ornamental. Absence of lateral buds on the corm. Only corm and pseudostem are used as food. Originated in Asia. In Ethiopia, it is considered as 'Tree of the poor' or 'Tree against hunger' and National crop of Ethiopia.
- Genus *Ensete* (X=9, 10, 11) has 8 species of which *M. ventricosa* is grown in Ethiopia as food crop. Suckers freely produced.
  - *E. glaucum*, *E. superbum*, *E. livingstoniana*, *E. proboscidea*, *E. gelletti*, *E. edule*, *E. homslei*, *E. perrier*.
- Genus *Musella* has only 1 species i.e. *M. lasiocarpa* (Chinese dwarf banana).
- Genus *Musa* has 5 sections:
  - *Eumusa* (n=11), 2n=22 in wild & 22, 33, 44 in edible varieties.Of the 11 species of section *Eumusa*, 56% of total diversity is found in India. Used as vegetable,

fruit and for fibre e.g. *M. acuminata*, *M. balbisiana*, *M. basjoo*, *M. schizocarpa*, *M. itinerans*, *M. sikkimensis*, *M. cheesmani*, *M. nagensium*, *M. halabanensis*, *M. ochracea*. Inflorescence pendent/ semi-pendent, bracts dull in colour. Parthenocarpy present.

- *Rhodochlamys* (n=11). Parthenocarpy absent and ornamental. *M. ornata*, *M. velutina*, *M. sanguinea*, *M. laterita*, *M. rubra*, *M. aurantiaca*, *M. manii*, *M. rosacea*grown as ornamental plants. Inflorescence erect, flowers few, usually in single series
- *Australimusa* (n=10). Inflorescence pendent/ semi-pendent/ erect. Fruits edible, parthenocarpic & female sterile. Erect fruit bunch, red sap, yellow flesh & orange skin. Fehi banana is ornamental. Used for fibre extraction (Mannila hemp). Fruits eaten after cooking e.g. *M. textillis*, *M. maclayi*, *M. peekelii*, *M. jackeyi*, *M. lolodensis*, *M. bukensis*.
- *Callimusa* (n=10). Small statured ornamental plant, erect inflorescence & purplish bracts. Parthenocarpy absent e.g. *M. beccarii*, *M. borneensis*, *M. coccinea*, *M. flaviflora*, *M. gracilis*, *M. violascens*, *M. salaccensis*.
- *Incertae sedis* (n=7, 9).Largest herb, growing to more than 10 m height e.g. *M. ingens*, *M. boman*, *M. lasiocarpa*.

- Vast majority of cultivated/edible bananas belong to '*Eumusa*' and derived from *M. acuminata* (AA genome) and *M. balbisiana* (BB genome) and their hybrids. They are developed by vegetative parthenocarpy.
- Four sub-species of *M. acuminata* viz. *malaccensis*, *microcarpa*, *burmannica* and *siamaea* show relative homogeneity and 5th *ssp. banksii* is more distant phenotypically.
- *M. acuminata ssp. burmannica* and *malaccensis* contribute good gene source of resistance to black sigatoka disease complex.
- Both seeded and parthenocarpic diploid balbisiana freely hybridizes with acuminata to evolve diverse forms.
- Major banana growing area in India is occupied by clones of AAB.
- ABB genomic group of Klue Teparod was reclassified by Jenny *et al.* (1997).
- Musa landraces are designated as-
  - AAA= Dessert banana e.g. Cavendish. Cooking & beer bananas of East Africa.
  - AAB= Plantain & dessert banana of Brazil and India.
  - ABB= Cooking bananas of Asia. Predominantly constitute hardy culinary types.
- Plantain landraces have been defined into 4 sub-groups based on their inflorescence morphology *viz.*
  - True horn plantain- incomplete inflorescence, hermaphrodite & male flowers absent. Bear only female flowers.
  - False horn plantain- Variegated banana. Incomplete inflorescence, hands with large fingers followed by few hermaphrodite flowers.

- French horn plantain- incomplete inflorescence, hands with large fingers & many hermaphrodite flowers.
- French plantain- Mother of all plantains and basis of banana based food. Complete inflorescence, hands with many fruits with persistent male bud at ripening e.g. Nendran and Tiger banana.

- Simmonds (1962) provided 1st exhaustive account of evolution of this genus.
- Genetic classification of banana (15 character scoring technique): Simmonds and Shepherd (1955).

Sl.No.	Character	*M. acuminata* (Score 1)	*M. balbisiana* (Score 5)
1.	Pseudostem colour	More or less-heavily marked with brown black blotches	Blotches slight or absent
2.	Petiolar canal	Margin erect or spreading with scarious wings below not clasping pseudostem	Margin not winged below clasping pseudostem
3.	Peduncle	Usually downy, hairy and short	Glabrous
4.	Pedicel	Short	Long
5.	Ovules	2 regular rows in each locule	4 irregular rows in each locule
6.	Bract curling	Bracts reflex & roll back after opening	Bracts lift but do not roll back
7.	Bract shape	Lanceolate or narrowly ovate, tapering sharply from the shoulder	Broadly ovate, not tapering sharply
8.	Bract apex	Acute	Obtuse
9.	Bract shoulder	Usually high (ratio less than 0.28)	Usually low (ratio more than 0.3)
10.	Bract colour	Red, dull purple or yellow inside	Distinctive brownish purple outside bright crimson inside
11.	Colour fading	Inside bract colour fades to yellow towards base	Inside bract colour continuous towards base
12.	Bract scars	Prominent	Scarcely prominent
13.	Free tepal of male flower	Variably corrugated below the apex	Rarely corrugated tip
14.	Male flower colour	Creamy white	Variably flushed with pink
15.	Stigma colour	Orange or rich yellow	Cream, pale yellow or pale pink

Other morphological characters used for classification—

- Stooling habit: *M. acuminata* are loosely clumped with erect pseudostem while *M. balbisiana* tightly clumped and having widely divergent pseudostem.
- Pigmentation: Leaf sheaths, petioles and midribs are more pigmented in *M. acuminata* than *M. balbisiana*.

- Scoring technique: Total score from 15 (15x1) for pure *M. acuminata* to 75 (15x5) for pure *M. balbisiana*. Cultivars would have large score if it is derived from *M. balbisiana* and smaller if derived from *M. acuminata*.

Taxonomic classification of edible banana (Simmonds and Shepherd, 1982)

Genome constitution	Ploidy level	Genome score & nomenclature (examples)
Accuminata cvs.		
AA	2x	16-23 'Matti'
AAA	3x	15-21 'Gros Michel', 'Cavendish', 'Robusta'
AAAA (not encounted in nature)	4x	15-20 'Bodles Altafort' (synthetic hybrid of West Indies)
Hybrid cvs.		
AB	2x	46-49 'Ney Poovan'
AAB	3x	26-46 'Champa'
ABB	3x	59-63 'Kancha kela', 'Bluggoe'
BBB	3x	70-75 'Saba'
ABBB	4x	63-69 'Klue Teparod', 'Bhat Manohar'.
AAAB	4x	'Atan'
AABB	4x	'Kalamagol', 'Goldfinger'

Classification according to Silayoi and Chom Chalow (1987) based on Thai banana gene bank scoring basis

Genome constitution	Ploidy level	Score
AA/ AAA	2x/3x	15-25
AAB	3x	26-46
AB	2x	-
ABB	3x	59-63
ABBB	4x	-
BB/BBB	2x/3x	70-75

- Modified score card was developed by NRCB, Tiruchirapalli (Singh and Uma, 1996).

Genome constitution	Score
AA/ AAA	15-25
AAB	26-45
AB	46-49
ABB	59-65
ABBB	66-69
BB/BBB	70-75

- Edibility, seedlessness and vigour are due to triploidy.
- All triploid (AAA) dessert bananas of commerce are highly susceptible to sigatoka leaf spot while all ABB clones are resistant.
- Reduced restitution of gametes are observed in banana.
- Cavendish group never set seeds when pollinated with diploid and not used in breeding programme because of female sterility.
- *M. cavendishii* is cultivated only in sub-tropical areas (thrives outside the tropics) where temperature never goes below 18^{0}C.

- Major culinary types in world: Monthan and Bluggoe (starch specific triploids ABB).
- Leaves of *M. balbisiana* form basis of leaf industry (wrapping material, dining plates, substitute for umbrella, source of roofing) in Manipur.
- Starchiness, hardiness and frost resistance is contributed by 'B' genome.
- International team has sequenced genome of *M. acuminata*, resistant to panama wilt.

Species	Features
M. acuminata ssp. *malaccensis*	Flower used as vegetable & field resistant to nematodes
M. agharkarii	Non-stoloniferous
M. acuminata	Originated in Malayan region; polymorphic; source of today's edible banana; plant slender; short duration; highly female fertile with > 100 seeds/ fruit; slender fruits; pulp mucilagenous & acidic; leaf spot resistance
M. acuminata ssp. *burmanncoides*	Resistant to panama wilt, nematode & sigatoka leaf spot; extensively used in global breeding programmes
M. balbisiana	Called as 'Starchy or Devil's banana; originated in Indo-Burma region; hardy; no parthenocarpy; long duration crop (18-26 months); large fruit size & strong attachment of fruit; clump forming; tolerant to cold, drought; immune to most fungal & bacterial diseases
M. basjoo (Used in Japan); *M. textilis*	Most cold hardy; used as fiber yielding/ textile crop
M. acuminata ssp. banksii	Contribution of parthenocarpic origin
M. ornata, M. flaviflora, M. coccinea, M. gracilis, M. violascens, M. aurantiaca, M. rubra, M. rosacea, M. manii, M. sanguine	Ornamental spp. (coloured flower buds & used in bouquet making)
M. rubra	Dwarf & suitable for growing in pots
M. laterita	Dwarf; ornamental spp.; major donor source to black sigatoka resistant gene, fusarium wilt; most drought tolerant & remain dormant in summer
M. velutina	Self pollinating & self peeling banana; ornamental type; coloured flower buds & used in bouquet making
M. violascens	Used in bouquet making
M. itinerans	Popularly referred as 'walking banana'; found in Vietnam; highly drought tolerant; 4-6 hands; >150 seeds/ fruit; dull green fruit colour
M. chiliocarpa e.g. Kluai Roi Wi of Thailand	>40 hands that almost touch the ground; large number of hands
M. nagensium	Conspicuous black pseudostem; orange flesh, very sweet (32° brix) with 80-100 big, shiny & warty bold seeds; self pollinated &highly female fertile
M. sikkimensis	Maroon pseudostem; small bunch with 4-6 hands
M. swarnaphalya	Maroon pseudostem; 6-8 fruits/ hand
M. sapientum	Triploid (3n) AAB. It has persistent male buds.

Varieties:

- Hybridization and polyploidy played dominant role in evolution of cultivated banana.
- Hindrance in crop improvement: Female sterility and parthenocarpy.
- Cv. Basrai was 1st time introduced at GFE station, Pune in 1924. Have high female sterility.
- Banana breeding work was started at Imperial College of Agriculture, Trinidad in 1922. Tetraploid hybrid IC-I [Gros Michel (AAA) x *M. acuminata* (AA)] was highly resistant to panama wilt. It exhibit poor bunch characters.
- Hybridization work at Central Banana Research Station, Aduthurai, Tamil Nadu was started in 1949.
- Bud mutation in Indian bananas is very common perhaps due to spontaneous rearrangement of chromosomes in somatic meristem and structural reassortment.
- Dwarf Cavendish group forms main stay of Indian bananas. It contributes to 58% of total production.
- FATOM-1: Early flowering mutant derived from *in vitro* gamma irradiated meristem culture of cv. 'Grand Naine' released in Malaysia. It is selection from M_1V_4 generation and flowers within 9 months. Bunch wt. 26 kg.
- GCTCV-219: Philippine selection of 'Giant Cavendish' tissue cultured variant from Taiwan Banana Research Institute. Resistant to strain tropical race-4. Plants take longer time to bear fruits. Bunch smaller but fingers are very sweet in taste.
- SH-3142: Synthetic diploid hybrid having burrowing nematode resistance.
- Pisang Mas: Tetraploid variety developed through colchicine.
- Cavendish: Form main stay of global banana industry.
- Dwarf Cavendish and Robusta: Widely adapted commercial banana.
- Varieties for leaf industry: Poovan, Monthan, Karpuravalli.
- Vegetable type cooking bananas: Monthan, Bonthan, CN-1, Ney Vannan, Nendran, Cardaba, Saba.
- Gandevi: Selection (Hanuman or Padalse) from Basrai.
- 'Mutiara' (from Malaysia) and 'Novaria' (from Austria) varieties were released via *in vitro* mutagenesis using gamma rays from cv. Grand Naine. Flowers earlier (by 10 weeks) than parent. Tolerant to black sigatoka and fusarium wilt disease.
- Cv. Manguthamang, a parthenocarpic diploid (BB) is popular cooking vegetable (fruits) in Arunachal Pradesh.
- Cv. Matti: Acuminata diploid (AA) is commercially grown landrace of Tamil Nadu and Kerala. Known for its medicinal properties and typical finger orientation.Resistant to sigatoka and male sterility.
- Cv. Anikonban: Resistant to nematodes & Panama wilt.
- Cv. Sanna Chen Kadali: Acuminata diploid (AA) has red pigmentation on pseudostem, skin and long slender fruits.

- Cv. Namarai (AA):Popular among tribals for its tolerance to long spells of drought, panama wilt
- Cv. Manoranjitham (AAA) is fragrant banana of India having coral jasmine scent; unique to Indian sub-continent; immune to leaf spot disease; highly female fertile and found only in Tamil Nadu.
- At Coimbatore, cvs. Poovan, Rasthali, Peyan, Thote, Peykunnan, Rajavazhai, Ney Vennan are used as female parents for developing commercial triploids.
- Tetraploid breeding: Triploid female (AAA) x improved diploid male (AA or AB).
- Dessert banana varieties: Dwarf Cavendish, Champa, Rasthali, Lakatan, Latudan.
- Varieties for making banana fig: Giant Governor, Gros Michel, High Gate, Robusta, Harichal, Red Banana, Kannan, Pachakadali.
- Kadali, Surya Kadali, Ambala Kadali: Indigenous diploid has small fruits with sweet taste. Ecotypes used for commercial and religious ceremonies in Kerala.
- Mutika (AAA) and Lujugira (AAA): Used for brewing of beer in Eastern Africa.
- Cultivars belonging to AB group do not produce pollens.
- High Gate and Cocos (AAA) are semi-dwarf mutants of 'Gros Michel'.
- Low Gate: Shortest, dwarf mutant of 'Gros Michel'.
- Motta Poovan (AAB) is bud sport of Poovan. Fruits have round apex.
- Krishna Vazhai: Natural mutant of Virupakshi.
- Bhimkol, Athiakol, Attikol and Manohar are wild *M. balbisiana* diploid (BB) fruits having full of soft seeds with mucilaginous pulp and cultivated for preparation of baby food.
- Empty seeded and soft seeded 'Bhimkol' is consumed as dessert fruit resembling edible feel of pomegranate.
- Elavazhai: Seeded, diploid and wild type. Mainly used as leaves for making dining plates.
- Jahajee (*M. paradisiaca*) from Nagaland: Resistant to virus diseases, short crop duration, suitable for HDP.
- In cv. Nendran alone, more than 6 mutations have been recognized viz. Moongli, Attu Nendran, Nana Nendran, Myndoli, Velathan, Nenu Nendran; cv. Rasthali gave rise to Ayirankai Rasthali (meaning 1000 fruited Rasthali); cv. Red Banana gave rise to Ambala Kadali, Erachi Vazhai, Mishri; cv. Dwarf Cavendish gave rise to Pedda Pacha Arati, Harichal; cv. Kannan gave rise to Thattilla Kannan, Vennettu Kannan, Than Kannan, Adakka Kannan.
- In 'Moongli', there is no male phase and plants bear 1-2 hands with big fruit.
- Barhari Malbhog: Sport of Malbhog.
- Monthan gave rise to bud sports viz. Sambal Monthan, Sambrani Monthan, Nalla Montha Bathees, Pidi Montha, Thellatti Montha.

- Thattilla Kannan: Mutant of Kunnan. Male phase absent.
- Klue Home Thong: Mutant.
- Dichotomous mutant is from 'Benin' variety.
- Ambemohor: Farmer's selection variety. Bunch wt. 26-36 kg, late maturing.
- Blue Java (*M. acuminata* x *M. balbisiana*): ABB genome, hardy, cold-tolerant; peel bright blue with creamy white flesh coloured banana cultivar known for its sweet aromatic fruit in Hawaii. It has ice cream like consistency and flavour reminiscent of vanilla. It is originated from South East Asia. It is also known as 'ice cream banana' They require 4.4^0C for optimum growth. They contain fair amount to fibre, several anti-oxidants, vit. B6, vit. C and plenty of K, Mg, Cu, Mn and proteins.
- Konkan Safed Velchi: Yield (25 t/ha); small fingers, firm flesh, high fragrance.
- Kovvur Bonth Selection: High yielding cooking type, 35 kg/ bunch.
- Bio-fortified varities rich in carotenoids: Apantu (AAB-plantain), Bira (AAB-Pacific plantain), Pelipita (ABB-plantain), To'o (AA-dessert).
- *M. acuminata* 'Calcutta 4': Field resistance to nematodes and black sigatoka.

Common name	Synonym & breeding method	Genome	Specific features
Poovan (syn. Alpan/ Dora Vazhai/ Karpura Chakkarakeli)	Champa	AAB	Choicest table banana; perennial; suitable for multistory cropping; hard lump, highly resistant to panama wilt; susceptible to banana streak virus
	Lal Velchi	-	Severely affected by banana streak virus.
	Palayankodan	AAB	Dessert type; drought tolerant & suitable for ratoon
	Mysore	AAB	Pink pigmentation on ventral side of midrib; susceptible to banana streak virus & leading dessert cultivar of south India. Good for diabetic patients; resistant to biotic &abiotic stress; crop duration 11-14 months
	H-531	AAB	Yield 13-15 kg/bunch; resistant to nematode & fusarium wilt
	Popoulu	AAB	Indigenous to Pacific region; fruits are plump-square ended & noticeably thick india., most fruits are 2-3 times as long as they are wide; best choice for making chips; tastier than cv. Nendran & crispy like potato chips
NeyPoovan (syn. Nhali poovan/ Safed Velchi/ Elakkibale/ Rasa Kadli)	-	ABB	Fetch double price than other cultivars; horizontal bunch orientation; small fruits packed closely having good keeping quality; popular in south India; excellent aroma; suitable for multistory cropping system
Karpuravalli (syn.	-	ABB	Very hardy; field tolerance to sigatoka, drought, salt,

Pisang Awak)			wind; suitable for long distance transport; suitable for making baby food, juice & wine
Monthan	Montha	ABB	Tall & robust growing; resistant to drought & good for culinary & chips purpose; crop duration of 12-16 months
	Kanchkela		-
Dwarf Cavendish	Basrai	AAA	Leading commercial variety; highly resistant to Panama wilt & susceptible to bunchy top; crop duration is 10-16 months
	Kadali	AAB	Leading commercial cultivar
	Pacha Vazhai	-	Green rinded ripe fruits
	Kuzhi Vazhai	-	Less prone to storm damage
	Manoranjitham	AAA	Fragrant skin, immune to leaf spot & highly female fertile
Robusta (syn. Bombay Green/ Pedda Pacha Arati/ Bor Jahaji)	Harichal	AAA	Semi-tall sport of Dwarf Cavendish; highly susceptible to sigatoka leaf spot but immune to Panama wilt
Rasthali (syn. Silk fig/ Amrutapani/ Malbhog/ Rasbale)	Martman	AAB	Choicest table variety; crop duration of 15-16 months; green stem with brownish blotches; reddish margin of petiole & leaf sheath; hard lumps & fruit cracking are major physiological disorders
	Mutheli	-	Hard lump & fruit cracking
Hill banana (syn. Krishna Vazhai) pome group	Virupakshi	ABB	Elite banana of south India; suitable for higher elevation; characteristic apple flavour & keeping quality; immune to leaf spot & well suited for rainfed agriculture
	Vella Vazhai & ecotype Sirumalai	-	Perennial banana system
	Kaali Laden	-	Fruits have unique aroma and flavour (taste). Suitable for jam making
	Rajapuri (syn. Walha)		Resistant to cold
Nendran (French Plantain)	Ethakai	AAB	Good keeping quality (15 days) & dual purpose variety. Remain starchy even on ripening; horizontal bunch orientation; products are exported to Gulf countries
	Rajeli		Most prized cooking variety used in Kerala. Good for making chips
	Plantain		Cooking type
Red Banana	Sevazhai/ Lal kela	AAA	Red skin; long duration of cropping- 16 months, grown only in backyard gardens; shy yielding; susceptible to multidiseases; orange yellow pulp
	Ambala Kadali, Erachi Vazhai	AAA	Mutant of red banana
Kannan	-	AB	Angular bunch orientation; popular dessert variety & used for making baby food; resistant to frost

KAU, Thrissur			
BRS-1 (H-1)	Agniswar (AB) x Pisang Lilin (AA)	AAB	Slightly acidic fruits; bunch wt. 14-16 kg; resistant to Sigatoka leaf spot, fusarium wilt, rhizome weevil & nematodes
BRS-2 (H-2)	Vannan (AAB) x Pisang Lilin (AA)	AAB	Compact bunch; bunch wt. 14 kg with 8 hands & 118 fruits; slightly acidic fruits; tolerant to leaf spot, fusarium wilt & burrowing nematode
TNAU, Coimbatore			
CO.1 (H-135)	Kadali x [Kallar Ladan (AAB) x *M. balbisiana* clone Sawai (BB)]	ABB	Similar to Lalkela; develops acid/ apple flavour when grown at high altitude (1200 m)
H-212	Karpuravalli (ABB) x Pisang Lilin (AA)	AB	Highly tolerant to nematode; bunch wt. 13 kg; very akin to Ney Poovan
NPH-02-01	H-201 x Anikonban	AAB	Akin to Laden; resistant to wilt & leaf spot; tolerant to nematode; adapted to grow on hill slopes of south India; developed by TNAU, Coimbatore
H-9617	Karpuravalli x H-201	ABB	Akin to Karpuravalli; resistant to nematodes; excellent bunch quality; bunch wt. 26 kg
H-531	Poovan x Pisang Lilin	AAB	Akin to Poovan; resistant to nematode & fusarium wilt
FHIA, Honduras			
FHIA-1 (Goldfinger)	Patra Ana x SH 3142	AAAB (pome type)	1st man made hybrid developed in Honduras; global hybrid; pome group & apple like flavour; resistant to black sigatoka, fusarium wilt & burrowing nematode
FHIA-2	Williams x SH 3393	AAAA	Highly resistant to sigatoka & susceptible to fusarium wilt
FHIA-3	SH 3486 x SH 3320	AABB	Hybrid developed in Honduras; drought tolerant, dual purpose & resistant to sigatoka
FHIA-6	Maqueno x SH 3437	AAAB	Plantain resistant to black sigatoka, higher yield
FHIA-17	High Gate x SH 3362	AAAA	Resistant to sigatoka
FHIA-19, FHIA-20, FHIA-22,	-	-	High yield
FHIA-21	AVP-67 x Pisang Jari Buaya	AAAB (plantain type)	Resistant to black sigatoka & fusarium wilt; excellent when fried green & baked ripe; good for cooking & chips
FHIA-25	-	-	Resistant to nematode & fusarium wilt
IITA, Nigeria			
BITA-1	Bluggoe (ABB) x Calcutta-4 (AA)	AABB	Tetraploid; resistant to sigatoka & fusarium wilt
BITA-2	Pisang Awak (ABB) x *M. balbisiana* (BB)	ABBB	Tetraploid; resistant to sigatoka & fusarium wilt

BITA-3	TMB x 5295-1	ABBB	Tetraploid; low partial resistance to black sigatoka
PITA-2	Obino L'Ewai (AAB) x Calcutta-4 (AA)	AAAB (plantain type)	Tetraploid; excellent fruit quality; resistant to black sigatoka & high yield
PITA-5	Bobby Tennap (AARB) x Pisang Lilin (AA)	AAAB	French plantain hybrid; partially resistant to black sigatoka; resistant to pseudostem weevil
PITA-9	Agbagba FR (AAAB) x Calcutta-4 (AA)	AAAB	False Horn plantain hybrid; partially resistant to black sigatoka; sweet & aromatic yellow pulp; resistant to pseudostem weevil
PITA-14	Mbi Egome-1 (AAB) x Calcutta-4 (AA)	AAAB	partially resistant to black sigatoka
NRCB, Tiruchirapalli			
Udhayam	Single plant selection from 'Karpuravalli' Pisang Awak group	ABB	Dwarf; mature in 15-16 months; cylindrical bunch with 13-15 hands; 15-20 fruits/ hand; bunch wt. 30-35 kg; TSS 30-32^0 brix; yield 37 kg/plant; tolerant to sigatoka & nematode; suitable for long distance & processing industry; ideal for wind prone areas
Namwa Khom (syn. Dwarf Karpuravali)	-	ABB	Dwarf; withstand wind damage; no propping require; dessert variety; suited for HDP
NRCB Selection-12	Exotic introduction	ABB	Short duration; short maturing time (50-55 days); yield 15 kg; single fruit wt. 150 g; suitable for making snacks
NRCB Selection-10	Exotic introduction	ABB	Dwarf; lesser in crop duration
Kaveri Haritha (NRCB Sel.08) 2019	-	ABB	Huge bunch; 10-11 hands; bunch wt. 28-30 kg; suitable for all soils except marginal soil; 25 days earlier than cv. Monthan.
Kaveri Kanya (NRCB Sel.03) 2019	-	ABB	10-12 hands; bunch wt. 26-28 kg; dual purpose; suitable for homestead garden; wind tolerant
Kaveri Saba (NRCB Sel.09) 2019	Exotic introduction	ABB	8-9 hands/bunch; bunch wt. 26-29 kg; duration 360-390 days; drought & salinity tolerant; more suitable for marginal cultivation & saline sodic soils with pH ranging from 8.8 to 9.0; used for both culinary & dessert purpose; suitable for flour making & resistant starches which could be used in health and soup mixes, bakeries & extruded products like pasta, noodles, etc.
Kaveri Sugantham (2019)	Selection from somaclonal variant of tissue cultured Manoranjitham	ABB	Crop duration 13-14 months; bunch weight is 18-22 kgs with 12-14 hands and 17-20 fingers per hand; resistant to fusarium wilt; suitable for making ice-cream
Kaveri Kalki (2019)	Exotic introduction	ABB	Dwarf; require no propping; 12 months duration; bunch wt. 17-20 kg; 13-15 hands; 16-18 fruits/ hand; TSS 31^0 brix

Saba	Pisang Kapok x Pisang Nipah x Kluai Hin	BBB	Cooking banana found in Philippines; tolerant to water stress
MPKV, Rahuri			
Phule Pride (BRS- 2013-3)	-	-	Dwarf, heat resistant banana selected from cv. Grand Naine; tolerant to lodging & sigatoka. No need of propping & no bunch chocking.
Other cvs.			
CRBP-39	-	Plantain type	Resistant to black sigatoka & high yield
Boddles Altafort	Gros Michel (AAA) x Pisang Lilin (AA)	AAAA	Synthetic tetraploid/ artificial hybrid
Klue Teparod	-	AABB	Natural tetraploid
Lady Finger (EC160160)	Introduction from Australia	AB	Resistant to bunchy top
Grand Naine	France	AAA	Tall mutant of Dwarf Cavendish; require propping; highest production in India; dessert & processing quality; susceptible to Sigatoka & nematodes; resistant to fusarium wilt race 1 & 2
Pisang Lilin, Tongat, Anaikomban, Hatidat, Matti, Siguzani, Namarai, Kadali, Sanna Chen Kadali	-	AA	Resistant to panama wilt & nematode but susceptible to sigatoka
Karupuravalli, Kannan	-	ABB	Tolerant to drought, salt, wind. Suitable for making baby food, juice & wine
Marau, Pora, Kokopo, Pisang Mas, Pisang Jari Buaya, Pisang Batuau, Saba Gia Hiu, Vudu Papua	-	-	Resistant to *R. similis*

Other varieties: Amrit Sagar, Mannan, Chingan (popular in Kerala); Peyan, Anaikomban (popular in Tamil Nadu); Sugandhi, Bhurkel, Sahastraphali, Ambeli (popular in Maharashtra); Bental (popular in Odisha; culinary tall banana), Kamal Vikas A-One (farmer's selection from Raver tehsil of Jalgaon dist.; 9 hands with 150 fingers & 7-12 inches finger length)

Bunch and fruit characters of banana clones:

Clone	Bunch wt. (kg)	Hands/bunch	Fingers/ bunch	Fruit wt. (g)	Peel/ pulp ratio
Anaikomban	6.65	5.5	68	86.66	1.44
Kunnan	6.86	6.4	64.56	105.20	5.04
Robusta	20.62	7.8	110.56	171.33	2.57
Poovan	12.28	9.9	135.13	82.20	3.50
Monthan	10.83	5.2	55.30	186.46	2.00
Hybrid Sawai	9.50	6.2	80.16	95.23	2.03
Klue Teparod	7.80	6.6	72.80	89.13	4.00

Inheritance of characters:

- Flowering: Controlled by 3 genes viz. *MaFT1*, *MaFT2*, *MaFT5*.
- Number of fingers, petiole length, finger's weight, and volume shows high genetic advance and high heritability.
- Triploids show higher values than diploids for bunch characters.
- Quality characters are more influenced by genomic constitution than ploidy level.
- Uptake of P is positively correlated with ploidy level.

Characters	Inheritance pattern
Parthenocarpy	Single dominant gene (P_1) & 3 complementary genes (Dominant gene P_1, P_2, P_3) with modifier genes. It arises from mutation in A genome species.
Persistance of bracts & flowers on male axis of bunch	Complementary genes which can express only in presence of parthenocarpy
Seed sterility	Cytogenetic factor
Albinism	2 independent recessive alleles with complementary gene action
Apical dominance	Recessive (*ad*) while dominant allele (*Ad*) improves suckering
Resistant to black sigatoka disease	Recessive (*bsi*) with additive effect
Resistant to yellow sigatoka disease	Polygenic & dominant
Suckering	Dominant (*ad*) & conditioned by level of ploidy
Dwarfism	Monogenic recessive (*dw*) or Monogenic dominant (*Dw*)
Bunch orientation	Oligogenic trait regulated by epistatic effect of 3 dominant loci
Fruit size	Epistasis of *bsi* and *Pi* loci.
Host plant response to weevil	*S* gene exhibit partial dominance towards resistance
Panama wilt resistance	Polygenic
Burrowing nematode resistance	Oligogenic & dominant

Pests and diseases:

- Meredith (1970) prepared monograph of diseases.
- Heart leaf & 1st unfurled leaf are major sites of infection of ascospores & conidia.
- Average yield losses due to nematodes: 20%.
- Growing of sunhemp, sesamum, marigold, brinjal, cucurbits is effective in managing nematodes.
- Anthracnose affects fruits in storage. Poovan is susceptible to this.
- Sigatoka leaf spot disease of banana was first observed in Sigatoka valley in Fiji (1913). Fruit development is adversely affected.
- Cabbage top: 1st observed in Fiji (1891). It is introduced from Ceylon/ Sri Lanka in 1940.
- Tetrazolium test is used for banana bunchy top virus detection.
- Panama wilt: Rasthali and Kanthali groups are highly susceptible. Gross Michel is susceptible, Basarai is immune and Poovan is resistant to this disease.

- Cavendish group is completely immune (inherited resistance) to Panama wilt. Rotation of banana with cane has benefited. Slightly alkaline soils show better resistance.
- Banana cultivars are screened for virus by ELISA test.
- Leaf and fruit scarring beetle (*Colaspis hypochlora*):

Name	Causal organism & vector	Remarks & management
Rhizome weevil	*Cosmopolitus sordidus*	Most serious pest in Nendran; *Plaesius javanicus* (biological control)
Pseudostem weevil	*Odiphorous longicollis*	Serious pest
Thrips	*Thrips florum* & *Astrothrips parvilimbus*	Damage young fruits
Spiral nematode	*Helicotylenchus multicinctus*	Most serious in North-Eastern hilly region of India
Root lesion nematode	*Pratylenchus coffeae*	Most serious; cv. Chinia & Pedathi resistant
Burrowing nematode	*Radopholus similis*	Most destructive
Cyst nematode	*Heterodera oryzicola*	Serious problem in Kerala
Moko wilt/ Bacterial wilt	*Pseudomonas solanacerum* vector: insect visiting flowers	Presence of yellow fingers on green stem
Rhizome rot/ Tip over/ bacterial soft rot	*Erwinia carotovora*	100% crop loss; soil drenching with bleaching powder; Spray streptomycin (4 g) + Carbendazim (300 ppm) during rainy season
Leaf spot	*Cercospora musae*	Introduced from Java
Black sigatoka	*Mycosphaerella fijiensis*	-
Yellow sigatoka leaf spot	*Mycosphaerella musicola*	Most serious disease in sub-tropical conditions
Cigar end rot	*Verticillium theobromae* (air borne fungus)	-
Infectious chlorosis	Cucumber Mosaic virus	-
Banana Bunchy top virus (BBTV)/ Cabbage top	Viral disease caused by aphids (*Pentalonia nigronervosa*)	Introduced from Sri Lanka in 1940; Spray Metasystox or Parathion @ 0.5%
Kokkan/ Banana Bract Mosaic Virus (BBMV)	Aphids	1st reported in Kerala
Panama wilt	*Fusarium oxysporium f. sp. cubense* (soil borne)	1st major disease reported; severe in acidic, warm & wet soil
Finger tip	-	Serious in HDP
Banana Streak Virus (BSV)	Mealy bug (*Planococcus citri*)	Dwarf Cavendish, Giant Cavendish, Nendran, Red banana are susceptible
Infectious chlorosis virus (ICV)	Insect vector	Robusta, Grand Naine, Poovan are susceptible
Blood disease	-	Serious in Indonesia
Pseudostem heart rot	*Botryodiplodia*, *Fusarium* spp.	Champa: Highly susceptible
Erwinia rot	-	Serious in Mrig season planting; unknown cause

Physiological disorders:

Name	Cause & features	Remedy
Neer Vazhai	Fruits ooze out watery fluid when cut. Immature unfilled fingers, lanky bunch & delayed shooting-transmitted through infected suckers	Nendran is susceptible
Kotta Vazhai	Enlarged ovules within immature fruits; Poovan susceptible-unknown cause	Spray 2, 4-D @ 120 ppm
Orange chlorosis, improper finger filling, leaf bending, rapid leaf desiccation	K deficiency	Apply potash fertilizers
Blue disease	Mg deficiency	-
Bunchy top crowns, narrow pointed & chlorotic young leaves	Zn deficiency	-
Pulpa crema or yellow pulp	Abnormal and premature development of fruits; Excess K; deficient N & S	-
Curved hands	Excess of Phosphorus	-
Hard lump	Serious in cv. Rasthali	-
November dump	Low temperature	-
Degrain	Droping of ripe fruits due to rotting of pedicel (due to high N: P ratio)	-
Choke throat	Temperature < 10^0C leads to impeded inflorescence or bunch development	-
Gooseflesh	Peel turn brown; common during dry winter	-
White leaf	Unbalanced nitrogen in soil	-
Crown distortion	Wind velocity (> 40-60 km/hr)	-
Male bud fasciation & multiple male buds in bunch	*M. nagensium* is susceptible	-

29. MYRICACEAE

29.1 Kaphal

- Eulogized as 'Bay berry or Box myrtle or Box berry'.
- Evergreen dioecious tree found about 1300-2100 m above MSL.
- Non leguminous angiosperm nodulated by *Frankia* spp.
- Fruit type: Drupe.
- Fruits ripen in May.
- Highly perishable fruit with low shelf life (2-3 days).
- Value added products: Squash and jam.

30. MYRTACEAE

30.1 Guava

- Eulogized as 'Apple of tropics or Poor man's apple or Fruit of masses'.

- Introduced in India by Portuguese in 17th century.
- Brazil stands 3rd in production in world.
- Guava germplasm in Mexican state is known as 'media China' or 'China'.
- Insensitive to photoperiod and catagorized as C_3 plant.
- India is largest producer followed by Brazil and Mexico.
- Maximum productivity in India: Uttar Pradesh.
- Ideal fruit crop for nutritional security (nutraceutical fruit) in India.
- Most useful for avoiding scurvy disease.
- Characteristic aroma of fruits: β-caryophyllene.
- Covers 35% of area among tropical fruit crops.
- Most suitable for multistoried cropping system.
- Edible portion: 100%.
- Nutrient composition/ 100 g edible portion: Proteins (2.55 g), -CHO (14.32 g), dietary fiber (6.9%), sugar (8.92 g) and calories (68 kcal).
- Rich source of vit. C (260-300 mg/100g). It is highest in fruit peel at mature stage.
- Pink fleshed varieties are poor in vit. C content than white fleshed ones.
- Phyto-drug rich in flavonoid-quercetin for treating acute diarrhoea has been developed from leaves.
- Most suitable for jelly making because of high pectin (1.42%) content.
- Pectin content should not exceed 2.4%.
- Yearly water requirement: 206 mm.
- Water requirement for yielding 1 kg guava: 68.02 litres.
- Water logging (high water table) and frost are limiting factors in cultivation.
- Trees are resistant to drought.
- Optimum soil pH for cultivation: 4.5-8.5.
- Favourable pH for spread of guava wilt: 7.5-9.0.
- Optimum temperature for flowering and fruiting: 23-28^{0}C.
- Temperature <7^{0}C in winter ceases growth and leaves become purple.
- Light requirement: >925 mol/m^2/s.
- Type of placentation: Axile.
- Type of inflorescence: Cyme on current season growth in leaf axil.
- Pollination agent: Honey bees (*Apis cerana*, *A. dorsata*, *A. florea*) and other insects.
- Buds take 30-45 days to develop into flower.
- Anthesis time: 5.00-6.30 AM.
- Anther dehiscence: 15-30 minutes after anthesis and up to 2 h.
- Stigma receptivity: Within 2-3 h after flower opening and remains upto 4 days.
- Fruit formation is noticed after 12 days from flowering.

- Fruit quality of winter crops is best when night temperature <10^{0}C and it escapes the attack of fruit flies also.
- Guava is harvested throughout year except May and June.
- Seedless varieties are autotriploids due to ovule sterility and chromosome aberrations.
- Acid used in seed germination: Hydrochloric acid.
- Scarification: Hot water treatment at 60-70^{0}C.
- Easiest and cheapest method of propagation: Stooling.
- Stooling: Maximum rooting (@ 7500 ppm IBA in lanolin paste) during 1st week of August.
- Stooling method was suggested by Pathak and Saroj (1988).
- Inarching method was suggested by Mukherjee and Majumder (1983).
- Softwood cutting under mist gives 44% rooting with IBA after 1 month.
- Air layering (IBA 3000 ppm), inarch grafting and forkert budding are successful.
- Cleft grating: New method of propagation for tolerance to root knot nematode.
- Recently CISH, Lucknow recommends wedge grafting (93-97%) for rapid and mass multiplication utilizing polyethylene cap.
- In Maharashtra, commercially propagated by tongue layering.
- Cutting: Pre-conditioning of stock plant with ethrel (200 ppm) followed by semi-hardwood cutting with 250 ppm IBA.
- Normal spacing: 6 m x 6 m.
- Double hedge row planting system (20 plants in 441 sq. m area).
- Super HDP in Allahabad Safeda @ 3 m x 6 m (555 plants/ ha) and meadow orchard system @ 2 m x 1 m (5,000 plants/ha) coupled with regular topping and heading back.
- Meadow orcharding technique was developed for horizontal utilization of space.
- HDP reduces TSS, sugars and ascorbic acid but increases titrable acidity.
- B: C ratio of UHDP for a period of 5 years is 3.1 as compared to 2.9 in traditional system orcharding.
- Rejuvenation technology involves heading back of tree in May and pruning of shoots to 50% of total length in October for rainy season crop and 2nd shoot pruning in May for winter crop.
- Crop regulation includes restricted irrigation, root pruning, deblossoming, bending, fruit thinning and pruning.
- Guava shows tendency of alternate pattern i.e. less yield after heavy fruit load in previous year.
- Fruit thinning i.e. alternate index, is practiced in Europe from 32-84% similar to pecan trees.
- Bending in guava: Practiced in Maharashtra and western India.

Concept behind branch bending:

- New concept of inducing off season flowering in guava.
- Bending of branches can regulate the bahar or crop regulation.
- Bending of old branches produce new shoots and flowers 30 and 60 days after bending treatment, respectively.
- Autumn bending in cv. Allahabad Safeda is better for yield potential compared to different bahars and summer bending.
- Autumn bending (October) process results in early emergence of shoots, flowering, fruit setting and more number of fruits per branch.
- Summer bending (April-May) process results in profuse flowering, fruiting and high fruit weight and fetches higher market price.
- Bending technique also produces shoots on old branches.
- Fruits produced by this technique are superior in quality and free from hazardous chemicals for crop regulation.
- Lucknow-49 does not require bending.

- Pruning: Above 90 cm, lateral shoots are not allowed to grow.
- To induce multiple cropping, concurrent pruning technique is done during May, September and December.
- In few places, pruning thrice a year viz. March, May and October with 50% reduction in shoot length is practiced.
- Pruning of branchlets to their half length (50%) on entire tree in May-June results in shortening of shoot growth and higher production.
- Maximum 3 crops/ year are taken in Maharashtra and Tamil Nadu.
- Due to severe fruit drop, 34 to 56% fruits reach maturity.
- Rainy season (inferior quality) crop can be removed by spray of 10% urea on Allahabad Safeda and 20% on Lucknow-49 at the time of peak flowering period. This resulted in increase of good quality fruits in winter season by 3-4 times.
- PGRs used in thinning flowers and manipulating cropping season: NAA @ 80-100 ppm at 10% anthesis), 2,4-D or ethephon @ 1800 ppm or KI @ 500 ppm.
- To reduce rainy season crop: Deblossoming with NAA @ 600 ppm + Urea @ 1.5%.
- GA_3 induces parthenocarpic fruits.
- 50% pruning intensity and use of paclobutrazol @ 1500 ppm is recommended for early yield.
- In ripe guava, reduction in astringency is due to enzyme polyphenol oxidase.
- Most preferred *bahar* treatment: *Mrig bahar*.
- Best quality guava is produced from *hasta bahar*.

- Maturity indices:
  - Colour break stage (green firm fruit)
  - Days from flowering to maturity: 140-160.
  - Specific gravity: 1.00
  - Fruit firmness (> 13 kg cm^2) at green mature stage.
- Seed viability: 6 months.
- Chemicals used to retain seed viability: Potassium nitrate 1%, Ferulic acid 10^{-3} M, Para hydroxyl benzoic acid 10^{-3} M.
- In Europe, somatic embryogenesis using mesocarp has been successful and 85% embryos have been developed into plantlets.
- *In vitro* clonal propagation of cv. Pant Prabhat using nodal segments is successful at G.B. Pant Univ. Agri. and Tech., Pantnagar.
- Micropropagation of 'Lucknow-49' was successfully attempted at CIAH, Bikaner.
- Low dose of gamma irradiation kill all stages of fruit fly or hot water treatment (49^0C for 20 min.) is recommended.
- Cold storage temperature: For 4 weeks at 8-10^0C at 80-90% R.H. and at 5^0C upto 1 month in ventilated polybags.
- MAP storage: 0.5 to 2% ventilated polybags of 200-600 gauge thickness.
- CA storage: CO_2> 5% and O_2< 5% enhances shelf life up to 1 month.
- TSS, pH, keeping quality of jelly are affected by pulp wt., core wt., non-reducing sugars, fruit length, fruit wt., pectin content and acidity of fruit.
- Dehydrated slices from firm & ripe fruits: Thick (1.5 cm) slices dipped (4.5 h) in 60^0 Brix sugar syrup + 0.05% KMS + 0.1% citric acid and drying in cabinet at 58^0C.
- HDPE pouches (200 gauge) best to retain leather quality.
- Jelly prepared from cv. Khaja is free from *Penicillium* spp. Upto 16 months.
- Protein rich guava cheese can be prepared from pulp.
- Paclobutrazol mediated somatic embryogenesis has been attempted at CISH, Lucknow.
- Synthetic seed production: 8-14 weeks old somatic embryos were encapsulated in 2% sodium alginate and cultured in 3% sucrose supplemented with full strength MS medium.

Species:

- Genus *Psidium* contains 150 species.
- The common guava, formerly classified as *P. pyriferum* (pear shaped) and *P. pomiferum* (round shaped) based on their shape.
- *P. sartorianum*, *P. longipes*: Introduced from USA.

- *P. molle* and *P. guajava* are cross compatible and resistant to wilt but reciprocal cross is incompatible.
- *P. araucanum*: Large tree with membranous leaves. Fruits globose and pear shaped.
- *P. acutangulum*: Tree, round to pear shaped fruits.
- *P. pomiferum*: Apple shaped fruits.
- At Lucknow condition, higher yield of cv. Allahabad Safeda was obtained when grafted on *P. cattleianum* rootstock but bigger fruits, high ascorbic acid, TSS and total and reducing sugars were maximum on *P. cujavillis* (Singh *et al*., 1976).

Common name	Botanical name	Features
Brazilian/ Guinea/ Castilian guava	*Psidium guineense* (syn. *P. areca, P. schiedeanum*)	Small fruits with poor quality; resistant to wilt; dwarfing rootstock; slow growing; fruits distintly dotted with glands; contains numerous hard seeds
Chinese/ Costa Rican guava	*P. chinensis* (syn. *P. friedrichsthalianum*)	Tall tree; globose small sour fruits with high acid content; compatible & dwarfing rootstock; high vit. C; resistant to nematode & wilt; tolerant to spiraling white fly; good for jelly making; possess suckering habit
Red strawberry guava	*P. cattleianum* var. *cattleianum* (syn. *P. littorale* var. *longipes*)	Malaysian spp; purplish red or light yellow skin with small round fruits & good for quality; very fragrant; dwarfing rootstock; fruits lacks muskiness; resistant to fusarium wilt & nematode
Cattley/ Lemon guava	*P. cattleianum* var. *lucidium* (syn. *P. littorale* var. *littorale*)	Resistant to wilt & yellow type; fruits small, acidic & sulphur yellow in colour
Guisaro guava	*P. molle*	Bushy & resistant to wilt; dwarfing rootstock; leaf apex pointed & lower part of leaf velvety in appearance
Philippine guava	-	Resistant to wilt
Mountain guava	*P. montanum*	Shrub & poor fruit quality; more seedy; poor fruit quality
Pineapple guava/ New Zealand banana	*Feijoa sellowiana*	Introduced from southern Brazil; potential crop in hills of India
-	*P. pumilum*	Highest sugar content spp. & highly dwarfing rootstock; high TSS & total sugars
-	*P. arayan*	Resistant to nematode
-	*P. cujavillis*	Highest vit. C & used as rootstock
-	*P. cumunii*	Resistant to wilt

Varieties:

- Guava improvement work was initiated by G.S. Cheema and Deshmukh in 1907 at FRS, Ganeshkhind, Pune. Lucknow-49 was developed by them in 1927.
- Aneuploid breeding appears to be beneficial where large number of seeds is disadvantage.
- Guava Purple and Lalit: Donors for pink flesh colour.
- Highly seeded or less seeded types are diploids whereas seedlessness is due to autoploidy-triploids (2n=3x=33) and not as a result of parthenocarpy.

- Cvs. L-49, Apple Colour and Behat Coconut are cross incompatible.
- Seedless varieties are shy bearer and produce 2 types of fruits: Partially seeded and completely seedless.
- Red fleshed varieties are rich in starch, crude fibre & tannin content but low in vit. C.
- Baruipur: Commercial variety of West Bengal.
- Rose Supreme, Red Indian and Ruby: Selection from Florida.
- Bangkok Golden Apple (Thai cv. x Indonesian seedless):
- Banarasi Surkha: Pink pulp, outer skin yellow, hard and maximum seeds.
- Navalur: Grown in Dharwad region. Hardy, drought tolerant, resistant to canker.
- Khaja-2, Khaja-4: Recommended for jelly preparation.
- Cuban Red Dwarf: Propagated by rooted cuttings.

Name	Breeding method	Features
Beaumont	Introduced exotic type	Bright pink pulp; acidic type; suitable for cooking. Prone to styler end rot. This character is inherited to hybrids
Patillo, Hong Kong Pink, Indonesian Seedless, Blitch, Suprime Mild Fleshed	Exotic type	Cultivated in Hawaii; suitable for jelly making
Centeno Prolific, Farlong	Exotic type	Cultivated in Trinidad
Rosa, Blanca, Crema	Exotic type	Cultivated in Ecuador
Pei-pa	Exotic type	Local cv. from Taiwan; most resistant to wilt (*Myxosporium psidii*)
Sangam, TG sel. 5/12	Exotic type	Varieties of Taiwan guava
Taiwan guava	Introduction	Leaf, shoot, fruit skin & pulp deep purple in colour
Ben-dov	Selection	Commercial variety of Isreal. Pear shaped fruits, white pulp, sweet flavour, very short life; sensitive to mechanicai damage
Fan Retief, Frank Malharbe	-	Standard cvs. of South Africa; rich in vit.C (1114 mg/ 100 g).
CISH, Lucknow		
Harijha	Selection	Popular in Bihar
Allahàbad Safeda	Selection	Most popular in Uttar Pradesh;free from bronzing; globose fruit shape; high TSS
Allahabad Surkha	Selection from local 'Red flesh type'	Dark pink flesh & large pink fruit
Allahabad Round	Selection	Parthenocarpic variety
Chittidar	Selection	Numerous red dots on fruits; highest TSS
Dhawal	Selection	Heavy bearer; soft seeded, sweet with muskiness
Lalima	Selection	Crimson coloured fruits
CISH-G-1, G-2, G-5, G-6	Seedling selection from local red flesh type	Red pulp & long shelf life
Lalit (CISH-G-3) 2002	Seedling selection from local red flesh type	Red pulp; suitable for table & processing; good for pink coloured beverage

Shweta	OP selection of red coloured type	Fruits snow-white coloured; soft seeds; TSS 13.2^0Brix; vit. C 300 mg/ 100g
CISH-G-4	Selection from 'Shweta'	Apple colour fruits
CISH-G-14	Half-sib selection of 'Allahabad Safeda'	TSS 12.5^0 Brix; soft seeded
IARI, New Delhi		
Pusa Srijan (syn. Aneuploid No. 82)	Aneuploid of hybrid between (Seedless x Allahabad Safeda)	Tetrasomic (2n+2=24); Dwarfing rootstock for Allahabad Safeda, suitable for HDP & tolerant to wilt
MPKV, Rahuri (FRS, Pune)		
Lucknow-49 (syn. Sardar)	Selection from 'Allahabad Safeda'	National variety; highest vit. C; tolerant to guava wilt; more susceptible to bronzing than Allahabad Safeda
Nagpur Seedless	Selection	Few seeds, white flesh, small fruit size
Phule Amrut (2021)	Selection	Fruits greenish-yellow coloured; medium sized; red pulp with good taste & soft seeds
ANGRAU, Andhra Pradesh (FRS, Sangareddy)		
Safed Jam	Allahabad Safeda x Kohir	Few soft seeds; suitable for juice making
Kohir Safeda	Kohir x Allahabad Safeda	White flesh with soft seeds; suitable for juice making
PAU, Ludhiana (RFRS, Bahadurgarh, Patiala)		
Punjab Pink (syn. Punjab Apple Guava)	[(Portugal x L-49) x Apple Colour]	Semi-vigorous; round canopy; dark red creamy flesh; TSS 11.8%
Punjab Bold (H-17-16)	-	-
IIHR, Bengaluru		
Arka Amulya	Allahabad Safeda x Triploid seedless	White flesh with few soft seeds; globose fruit shape; tolerant to spiraling white fly
Arka Mridula (IIHR-selection-8)	OP seedling selection of 'Allahabad Safeda'	Dwarf, smooth white flesh with soft seeds; globose fruit shape; high TSS; pectin 1%; suitable for jelly making
Arka Kiran	Kamsari x Purple Local	Pinkish red flesh, round shaped; soft seeded variety; fruit wt.200-220 g; yield 30-35 t/ha; 6-7 mg/100 g lycopene; suitable for HDP & processing
Arka Rashmi	Kamsari x Purple Local	Bio-fortified var; pinkish red flesh, soft seeded; ascorbic acid (235 mg/ 100 g)
H-21	Red Flesh x Arka Mridula	Deep red pulp, soft seeds
Arka Poorna (2018)	Purple local x Allahabad Safeda	Fruit wt. 180-220g; white pulp; seed softness (9.0-12 kg/ cm^2); TSS ($10-12^0$Brix); suitable for table & osmotic dehydration
Hybrid-58	Allahabad Safeda x Lucknow-49	White flesh with few soft seeds
Hybrid 16-1	Apple Colour x Allahabad Safeda	Semi-vigorous; skin bright red all over; few seeds; high TSS
CCSHAU, Hisar		

Hisar Safeda	Allahabad Safeda x Seedless	White flesh, upright growth, round fruit
Hisar Surkha	Apple Colour x Banarasi Surkha	Pink flesh
DrYSRUH, Andhra Pradesh (FRS, Anantharajupet)		
H-1	Red Fleshed x Saharanpur Seedless	Fruit medium; smooth with thin skin; sweet; moderate seed content
H-2	Smooth Green x Nagpur Seedless	Fruit medium; smooth with thin skin; sweet; less seed content; soft seed
H-3	Allahabad x Red Fleshed	Fruit medium; smooth with thin skin; white flesh; sweet; moderate seed content
H-4	Smooth Green x Saharanpur Seedless	Fruit medium; smooth with thin skin; white flesh; sweet; many seeds & easily crushed
H-5	Red Fleshed x Nagpur Seedless	Fruit medium; smooth with thin skin; white flesh; sweet; moderate seed content
H-6	Banarasi x Allahabad	Fruit medium; smooth with thin skin; cream flesh; sweet; less seeds
MPUA & T, Udaipur		
MPUAT S-1	-	Apple colour, red skinned, soft seed, TSS 18.2%
MPUAT S-2	-	Greenish yellow coloured skin; TSS 16%
Other varieties		
TRY (G)-1 (syn. Acio)	Selection	Developed by Soil salinity reseaech centre, Tiruchirapalli; offseason; harvesting in July-August; & Dec-Feb; fruits pyriform shaped; white pulp & aromatic; resistant to fruit fly, drought hardy & tolerant to sodicity, mites, scales & wilt
Apple Colour (syn. Sebia)	Selection	Red skin (due to lycopene); pulp white; tolerant to anthracnose & fruit canker; donor parent in breeding
Red Flesh (syn. Hafsi)	Selection	Red flesh; seeds less but hard; globose fruit shape
Hafsi 35, Hafsi 46	Selection	Suitable for nectar preparation
Behat Coconut	Selection	Commercially grown; globose fruit shape; seedless (due to triploidy); good yielder; high TSS
Supreme Mild Fleshed	Selection	Suitable for jelly making
Pant Prabhat	Local selection	Soft seeded
Dhareedar	Local selection	Large fruit, soft seed & sweetest pulp
G. Vilas Pasand	-	-

Seedless varieties: Saharanpur Seedless (triploid), Srinageri Seedless

Grading system:

Size code	Weight (g)	Diameter (mm)
A	>350	>95
B	251-350	86-95
C	201-250	76-85
D	151-200	66-75
E	101-150	54-65
F	61-100	43-53

Inheritance of characters:

- Hard seed and pink/ red pulp is linked character.
- Negative correlation between fruit number and average fruit weight.
- Trunk girth is positively associated with fruit yield.

Characters	Inheritance pattern
Pulp colour	Red dominant over white & governed by single dominant gene
Firm pulp texture	Dominant trait
Bold seed	Monogenically dominant over soft seed
Female sterility	Triploidy & genic factors are responsible
Fruit shape	Obovoid shape dominant over round (oblate) & pyriform

Pests, diseases and disorders:

- Mumification is observed in plants affected with guava wilt.
- Parasitic algae: *Cephaleorros mycoideae*.
- Bottle neck: Use of different rootstock and highest with Behat Coconut.

Common name	Causal organism	Remarks & remedy
Fruit fly	*Daucus dorsalis* (syn. *Bactrocera diversus*)	Most serious pest during monsoon; summer ploughing, use of methyl eugenol & yellow sticky traps & release parasitoid like *Opius compensates*, *Spalangia philippinensis*
Fruit borer	*Deudorix isocrates*	Apply biopesticide
Mealy bug	*Plannococcus citri*	Spray 0.1% nicotine sulphate
Scale	*Pulvinaria psidii*	Serious pest in north India
Tea mosquito bug	*Helopeltis antonii*	-
Root knot nematode	*M. incognita*	23.77% yield loss;apply carbofuran @ 60 g/plant; apply *Paecilomyces lilacinus* @ 25 g/plant
Guava wilt or quick wilt	*Fusarium oxysporum f.sp. psidii*	Most prevalent in north India. 1st reported in 1935 from Allahabad. It is most severe in alkaline soils; use of bioagent *Aspergillus niger*, resistant rootstocks, regulating irrigation are only remedies
Anthracnose	*Gloeosporium psidii*	Most common disease. Plants die back from top of branch
Stem canker	*Physalospora psidii*	-
Fruit canker	*Pestalotiopsis psidii*	Spray Cuman L @ 4 ml/ litre
Bronzing	P, K, Zn deficiency	Severe during rainy season; spray DAP @ 0.3 % & SOP @ 0.5 %. More severe in Entisols
Die back	-	Apply 1.8 kg/ha lime or gypsum
Corky fruits	-	Spray 0.3% borax; maintain effective micronutrient status
Fatio	Nutritional deficiency	-
Rusetting	Mg deficiency	-

30.2 Jamun

- Eulogized as 'Indian black berry or Java plum or Black plum'.
- Hardy fruit crop and panacea for many ailments.
- Used as avenue, evergreen tree or wind break or bonsai purpose and highly suitable for agroforestry.
- India exports seeds to West Indies, Europe and Malaysia.
- Hermaphrodite flowers are good source of nector and light yellow in colour.
- Fruits are good source of 'Fe' and effective against diabetics, heart and liver troubles.
- Nutritive value/ 100g: Protein (0.7-0.13 g), fat (0.15-0.3 g), crude fiber (0.3-0.9 g), -CHO (14 g), potassium (55 mg), vit. A (80 IU), ascorbic acid (5.7-18 mg), anti-oxidants (1871 µg/ ml AEAC unit).
- Astringency: Gallic acid and tannins.
- Total tannins: 386.25 to 428.75 mg/ 100g.
- Purple colour: Anthocyanin (1.56%).
- Total anthocyanin: 210.5 to 242.5 mg/ 100g.
- Flavour of fruit: Dihydrocarvyl acetate, geranyl butyrate and terpenyl valerate.
- Distinctive foxy/ grape flavour: Methyl anthranilate.
- Alkaloid present in seed: Jambosin.
- Glycoside present in seed: Jambolin, Antimellin.
- Major sugars: Glucose and fructose.
- Major acid: Malic acid (0.59%), oxalic acid.
- Can be grown on wide range of soils- calcareous, saline sodic soils and marshy areas.
- It does not prefer very heavy and light sandy soils.
- Requires dry weather at flowering and fruit setting.
- Seeds of jamun have no dormancy hence fresh seed need to be sown.
- Seed powder: Reduce quantity of sugar in urine very quickly.
- Pollination agents: Honey bee (*Apis dorsata*), house fly, wind and gravity.
- Anthesis time: 8 AM to 1 PM.
- Anther dehiscence time: 9 AM to 2 PM.
- Flowering period: February-April.
- Fruit develop in 3 phases: 1st (slow; 15-52 days after set), 2nd (rapid; 52-58 days after set), 3rd (slow; 58-60 days after set).
- Fruiting occurs in clusters of 10 to 40 fruits/ inflorescence.
- Seeds show polyembryony up to 30-40%. Hence, nuceller/apomictic seedlings used to produce true-to-type plants.
- Seeds sown at 4-5 cm deep at 25 cm x 15 cm.

- Seed germinate 10-15 days after sowing.
- Propagation method: Seed.
- Softwood grafting and patch budding is the most common method of propagation.
- *In situ* patch budding is done in March-April.
- Wedge grafting on 6-12 months old seedlings is practiced.
- Planting distance: 8m x 8m and for HDP at 5m x 5m (400 plants/ha).
- Do not require pruning except removing diseased, dry and crisscross twigs.
- Seedling tree starts bearing at 9-10 years whereas budded takes 5-6 years.
- Branch girdling is done in October on 3rd order branches for higher yield.
- Tree need number of pickings, since all fruits do not ripen at a time.
- Maturity indices:
  - Days from full bloom: 60-65 days.
  - Fruit colour change from green to deep red or bluish black.
  - TSS to acid ratio: 6.94 to 10.25.
- Yield: 50-70 kg/ plant/ year.
- Ripening period: May-June.
- Top working: Rejuvenation of old and unproductive trees.
- Seed viability: 5-10 days.
- Critical moisture for safe storage of seeds: 45-50% with 80% germination.
- Seed stored at -10^{0}C gives 96% germination after 26 days of storage.
- Major problem: Heavy flower and fruit drop.
- Flower and fruit drop in 3 phases: 65% drop in first 4-5 weeks of flowering; 19-21% drop in 35-50 days of full bloom; 12-15% flower reach maturity from full bloom.
- Fruit set: Spray GA_3 @ 60 ppm 1st at 15 days from full bloom & 2nd at initial fruit set.
- Value added products: Jelly, jam, squash, RTS and vinegar.

Species:

- Genus *Syzygium* contain 1,100 species.
- Cross of water apple x rose apple is successful. Hybrid yielded fragrant, sweet & seeded fruits.

Common name	Botanical name	Features
Rose apple/Safed jamun/ Gulab jamun/ Poma rosa/Malabar plum/ Plum rose/ Jamrosa	*Syzygium jambos*	Tetraploid & polyembryonic; ornamental; yellow coloured fruits; insipid in taste with high pectin
Java plum	*S. cumini*	Cultivated
Watery rose apple/ Water cherry/ Water apple	*S. aqueum*	Edible fruits used for syrup & beverage making; cultivated for wood purpose; much branched; found up to 1350 m MSL

Mountain apple/ Malay apple	*S. malaccense*	Large fruits; medicinal property; used for jam & pickle making
Wild Jamun	*S. fruticosum*	Avenue tree & used as wind break
Wax jamun/ Wax apple/ Wax jumbo	*S. samarangense* (syn. *S. javanicum*)	Fruits edible; flowering in February-March; most popular in Malaysia; flesh white, spongy, juicy, aromatic & sweet-sour in taste; compatible rootstock for watery rose apple; pollen incompatible; used for jam, jelly making
Surinam cherry/ Pitanga cherry	*S. uniflora*	Small tree; deep crimson coloured fruits with spicy taste; used for jam, jelly making
Magenta Lilly Pilly	*S. paniculatum*	Fruits deep magenta colour & contain single seed
Blue Lilly Pilly	*S. oleosum*	Small tree & purplish red fruits
Wild rose apple	*S. densiflorum*	Rootstock against termite attack
Water berry/ Water bloom/ Water pear	*S. guineense*	Fruits ovoid or ellipsoid; juicy
-	*S. claviflorum*	Fruits acidic & edible from Andaman
Clove	*S. aromaticum*	Conical evergreen tree
-	*S. mappaceum*	Ornamental plant
-	*S. bracteatum*	Dwarf & ornamental plant found in Arunachal Pradesh, Assam, Meghalaya
-	*S. amottlanum*	Edible fruit
-	*S. zeylanicum*	Aromatic edible fruits of pea size; found in Western Ghats
-	*S. travancoricum*	Medicinal plant; found in Kerala only
-	*S. bourdillonii*	Endemic to Western Ghats (Kerala) & critically endangered

Varieties:

- Seedless jamun is popularly known as 'Jamun bedana'.
- CHES-M-1 (wax jamun): Yield- 50-70 kg/tree.
- RNC-26, RNC-11: High pulp.
- V-6, V-7, V-8: Seedless, high pulp and minimum seed wt.

Name	Breeding method	Features
CIAH, Bikaner (CHES, Godhra)		
Goma Priyanka (2010)	Selection	Semi-dwarf; suitable for HDP; fruit wt. 19.6 g; TSS 15.10^0 Brix; acidity 0.37 %; vit. C (45.40 mg/100 g); yield (62 kg/ plant)
Thar Kranti (2016)	Selection	Fruit wt. (20.90 g); TSS (18.40^0 Brix); acidity 0.36 %; vit. C (45.20 mg/ 100 g); yield (68 kg/ plant)
Jamwant	Selection	Rich in neutraceuticals; vit.C(49.88 mg/ 100g); TSS 16-17^0 Brix
Ra Jamun	Selection	Most common type in North India; large-sized (length 2.5-3.5cm), oblong, deep purple fruits having purple pink, juicy, sweet pulp, small seed
GJ-2	Selection at CHES	Maximum flowering during March; fruit wt. 20 g; 85% pulp, TSS 18.0^{0}Brix; 0.38% acidity; Total sugar 12.50%; vit. C (45.43

		mg/100g); yield (48-50 kg/ tree at 6th year age)
GJ-8	Selection at CHES	Fruit wt. 17 g; 83% pulp, TSS 16.0°Brix; 0.4% acidity; Total sugar 11.20%; vit. C (47.12 mg/100g); yield (12 kg/ plant)
GJ-19	Selection at CHES	Fruit wt. 20.50 g; 82.86% pulp; TSS (11.10° Brix); 0.36% acidity; vit. C (44 mg/100g)
GJ-23	Selection at CHES	Fruit wt. 20.00 g, 84.45% pulp, TSS 12° Brix; 0.32% acidity, vit. C (44 mg/100 g)
GJ-40	Selection at CHES	Fruit wt. 22 g, TSS-14.10° brix, fruit ripen during mid. May; 0.39% acidity; vit. C (46.10mg /100g)
Katha Jamun	Seleciton	Fruit wt. 8 g; 70.0% pulp, TSS 9° Brix; 0.42% acidity, vit. C (34mg/100g)
CISH, Lucknow		
CISH-J-28	Selection	-
CISH-J-30	Selection	-
CISH-J-33	Selection	-
CISH-J-37 (2008)	Selection	Upright growing; fruits oblong; TSS-16.4° brix, 92% pulp, fruit wt. 24 g; seed wt. >2 g; vit. C (49.88 mg/ 100 g); total anti-oxidant value 38.30 mg AEAC/g; yield 50 kg at 6th years age
CISH-J-40	Selection	Fruit wt. (17.23 g); pulp 91%; TSS 12.4° Brix; 0.76% acidity; vit. C (29.54 mg/100 g)
CISH-J-42 (2008)	Selection	Seedless (stenospermocarpy- facultative parthenocarpy); round shaped fruits; 1.56% anthocyanin; seed wt. >2 g; pulp 98%, TSS 14.7°Brix; vit. C(34.14 mg/100 g); total anti-oxidant value (15.54 mg AEAC/g); yield (60-90 kg at 10th years age); shelf life 5-7 days; good for processing
CISH-Jamwant (2019)	Selection	Pulp (90%); high level of vit. C and anti-oxidants, bio-active compounds; suitable for processing
BHU, Varanasi		
Selection-1	Selection	Fruit wt. (14.55g); seed wt. (1.73g), high pulp (90.05); TSS 21.23%; total sugar (20.24%)
GAU, Junagarh		
Paras	Seedling Selection	Popular in Gujarat; sweet & large sized fruits
BAU, Bihar		
Rajendra Jamun-1	Selection	Early (May-June); high yield (450 kg/ tree); TSS 18.2° Brix; acidity 0.31%; fruit wt. 12.86 g; 88.40% pulp
DrBSKKV, Dapoli		
Konkan Bahadoli (2004)	Selection from Bahadoli village	Regular bearer; big fruits (14-16 g), long keeping quality; regular & cluster bearer; yield (70-80 kg/ tree at 10 years age); fruit wt. 14-16 g; TSS 16° Brix
UHS, Bagalkot		
Gokak-1	Selection	Spreading nature; fruits elliptic; seed wt. 1.7-2 g; TSS <12° Brix
Gokak-2	Selection	Spreading nature; fruits elliptic; seed wt. 1.7-2 g; TSS <12° Brix
Gokak-3	Selection	Semi-spreading nature; fruits elliptic; seed wt. 1.7-2 g; TSS <12° Brix
NDUA & T, Faizabad		
Narendra Jamun-6	Selection	Seedless; oblong fruits; higher fruit wt. & higher pulp: seed ratio
Other		
Krishnagiri	-	-
Panchamrut	Farmers' selection	-
Krian Duat	Selection	Fruits with purple flesh; more astringent than white fleshed types

Disease, pests and disorder:

- Leaf spot and fruit rot (*Glomerella cingulata*): Major disease make fruits shrivel.
- Leaf eating caterpillar (*Corea subtilis*): Cause serious damage.
- Fruit fly: Damage up to 100%.
- Bark eating caterpillar (*Inderbela tetraonis, I. quadrinotata*).
- White fly (*Dialeurodes eugeniae*):
- Squirrels & birds.

31. OLEACEAE (ELAEOCARPACEAE)

31.1 Olive

- Eulogized as 'Green gold'.
- Oldest known cultivated tree of the world.
- Symbol of prosperity and peace.
- Associated with 'Emblem of the United Nations'.
- Green olives are considered to be 'Green Gold' in Greece.
- At present, olive is cultivated in 39 countries and olive oil in 29 countries.
- Commercially grown in France, Spain, California, Australia and China.
- Largest producer of olive oil: Spain followed by Italy, Greece, Turkey, Syria, Algeria, Morocco, Egypt, Tunisia, and adjoining Gulf countries.
- Per capita consumption of oil is highest (17 lit.) in Greece followed by Italy and Spain (10 lit.).
- Oil producing fruit.
- 1st oil production was carried out in 1803 in California.
- Ancient Greeks protected olive trees by legislation as early as 6th century B.C.
- Ripe olive contains proteins (2%), oil (14%), vit. A, B, C and 1% fibre and 650 calories per pound of fresh weight.
- Tablespoon oil contains 120 calories, 1.8% protein, 21% fat, 2.6% -CHO, 1.5% fibre, and no cholesterol.
- Oil is rich source of polyunsaturated fatty acids and is free from cholesterol.
- Oil is rich in minerals, Fe, Ca, P, vit. A, vit. E, oleic acid (70-80%) and linoleic cid (7-12%).
- Oil has many industrial as well as culinary uses. It is edible and possesses therapeutic value.
- About 92% olives are used for oil extraction.
- Oil is used for medicinal purpose and clinically advocated for hypertension, coronary heart disease, muscular pains, textile lubricant, perfumed soap, cometics, pefumery industry and burning of lamps.
- Oil consumption helps to reduce LDL & to raise HDL forms for cholesterol in blood.

- Oil helps in reduction of breast and skin cancer and coronary heart diseases, heals wounds, cures insomnia, ulcer and cholera.
- Wonderful oil is named as 'liquid gold'.

Species:

Botanical name	Features
Olea europaea var. *communis*	Edible olive
O. europaea var. *oleaster* or *O. europaea* var. *sylvestris*	Wild olive; used as rootstock
O. chrysophylla	Wild ancestor
O. glandulifera	Fruits inedible
O. cuspidata (Indian olive)	Flowers bisexual, pulp scanty & not pleasant
O. leucocarpa	Rare species of white olive.

- Olive tree has high (more) alternate bearing.
- Highest quality of oil is obtained at an altitude of 160 m MSL.
- It rarely fruit well outside the Mediterranean climatic regions.
- Olive wood is resistant to decay.
- Tree height: 10 m.
- Evergreen and self fertile in nature.
- Flowers: Inconspicuous, fragrant white flowers.
- Flowering period: April-May.
- Flowering duration: 6-17 days.
- Pollination agent: Wind.
- Flowers borne in axils of opposite leaves of previous season growth.
- Fruits: Initially green coloured fruits ripen to brown or blue-purplish-black or ivory white & contains single large stone.
- Bearing habit: Laterally on previous year's growth.
- Fruit bud differentiation: 2-3 months prior to flowering.
- Natural fruit set: < 5%.
- Leaf removal and shading reduces flower formation by 50%.
- Long juvenile phase accompanied with self incompatibility hampers crop improvement.
- Optimum soil pH for cultivation: 6.5-7.5.
- Tolerant to high soil pH (8.5), salinity, excess boron and drought.
- Soil pH > 6.5 adversely affect growth and productivity.
- Critical factor for cultivation: Temperature.
- Tolerates 0-35^{0}C temperature but optimum is 15-20^{0}C.
- Constant temperature of 12.5^{0}C promotes staminate flower production.
- Chilling requirement: 7-20^{0}C (for 400-2000 h) is essential to break rest period and to promote fruitfulness.

- Occurrence of autumn frost is more harmful & affects fruit maturation and oil accumulation.
- Hail storms at pre-bloom, bloom and post-bloom period causes abscission of flowers and results in low fruit set and heavy fruit drop and induces irregular or alternate bearing in trees.
- Planting distance: 6m x 8m (150-300 plants/ha); planting density of 83 to 125 plants/ acre as per rainfall.
- Rectangular system is adopted at 8 m x 5 m or 6m x 5 m with density of 250-333 plants/ ha.
- NaOH (1.5-2%) removes oleuropein before pickle preparation.
- Flesh to stone ratio: 5:1 or more is suitable for processing.
- Well defined classes of olive fruit utilization: Table and mill type.
- Mill olives contain more oil and less sugar and water than table olives.
- Oleuropein: Bitter glucoside in fruits.
- Glucose is predominant sugar followed by fructose, mannitol.
- Ovuli: Rounded, smooth barked growths at base of trunk.
- Sensitive to flooding and environmental moisture, tolerant to high pH.
- Tree requires 950 mm water during entire growing season.
- It donot tolerate wet soils for prolonged periods.
- Planting system: January-February in irrigated areas.
- Training method followed: Espalier, open cylinder, monocone, polycone, pyramid, shrubby goblet, Y-form and cordon.
- Remedial pruning is required to remove dead and diseased or crossing branches.
- Bearing trees are pruned immediately after harvest to encourage new growth of floral buds.
- Pruning month: November-February.
- Rejuvenative pruning: Increases yield but decreases oil content.
- Hard pruning in 'on' year & lighter in off year decreases degree of alternate bearing.
- Pruning wounds are immediately disinfected with bordeaux paint.
- Crop regulation: Fruit thinning from 6-20 days after full bloom.
- Coppicing after 10 years is an alternative method of orchard management.
- Girdling (removal of 15 mm band of bark) 30 days before full bloom increases individual fruit weight.
- Optimum rate of water in one irrigation: 1 to 1.5 cu.m/tree.
- Three stages of irrigation: Before flowering, at fruit set, maturity period.
- Propagation methods: Seeds, hardwood cutting (3-4 year old), soft wood cuttings (1 year old), hard wood cuttings (3-4 years old), suckers and ovules (masses of callus tissue formed at base of trunk or old trees) and cleft grafting during March-May.

- Seed propagation is not advocated due to heterozygous progeny and long juvenile period.
- Seeds are used to raise rootstock seedlings.
- Seeds require bottom heat technique for successful germination.
- Feather grafting is done in March-May.
- Germination frequency is higher in seeds collected at 4-6 months after full bloom.
- Chilling of seeds at 10^{0}C for 2-4 weeks improves germination percentage.
- For rooting of cuttings, bottom heat technique (18-22^{0}C) with IBA @ 3000-3500 ppm.
- Cutting taken in winter root better taken other times of year.
- Seedling rootstocks of Frantoio, Maraiclo, Leccino, Cipressino, Mignolo, Ogliolo and Canino are used.
- In Indian condition, rootstock of *Olea cuspidata* is vigorous than *O. europaea* var. Argequina.
- Budding on Azeitera rootstock gives better success.
- An old tree often throws suckers and can be used for replacement.
- Control of fruit drop: Spray NAA @ 30 ppm.
- Control of suckers: Glyphosate + MCPA.
- Gramxaone @ 2-3 litre/ ha effectively control perennial weeds.
- Soil treatment with 2,4 or 6 g paclobutrazol in February increase yield by 20%.
- Bearing trees need borax @ 200 g/tree once in alternate years.
- Staking to young plants, removal of undesirable suckers and mulching with white polythene film is essential.
- Fruit maturity: 3-4 months (100-110 days) after flowering.
- Fruits of Indian olive are collected in September-October.
- Harvesting period: November-March.
- Harvesting stage for table purpose:
  - Colour changes from green to yellowish green.
  - White juice exudes from mesocarp.
- Harvesting stage for oil/ preserving purpose:
  - Relationship between refractive index and oil content.
  - Fruits harvested at 29-30 weeks after flowering.
  - Fruits turn violet to black colour and oil content reach up to 20-30%.
  - Cv. Local Gorgan has 43.51% oil content per fruit.
  - Delayed harvest results in acidic oil with poor quality, bitterness and aroma.
- Green unripe fruits are marketed for pickle purpose. Pickle cultivars are harvested at 25 weeks after flowering.

- Milking: Method of harvesting preferred for pickling type cvs.: Mesocarp exudes white juice when squeezed at this stage.
- Greatest deterioration of olives takes place between harvesting & processing.
- Yield: 32-86 kg green ripe fruits/ tree.
- Tree bear 25 kg fruits when about 8 years old.
- Fruit storage: Low temperature (5^0C)
- French green olives can be stored at 5 to 7.5^0C and 90-95% R.H.
- Post harvest management:
  - Raw fruits are bitter due to presence of glucoside oleuropein.
  - Bitternesss is removed by soaking in 1-2% lye solution followed by leaching with water.
  - Exposure to air during this process allows oxidation of phenolic compounds yields black table olives.
  - Extraction of oil is done by cold processing, centrifuging or by percolation method.
  - Canned olives are prepared by adding hot brine solution and pasteurizing at 240^0 F for 1 hr.
- Acidity >3.3% is termed as lampante indicating lamp oil and not used for human consumption.
- Olive fruits are processed within 24 h to obtain quality oil.
- Oil is extracted through mechanization process.
- Saponification value of oil: 188-198.
- Oil that is squeezed out without heat or excess pressure is called 'extra virgin oil'.
- Cheaper grades of oils are produced by heating or adding hot water to the mass.
- Exposure of oil to oxygen results in rancidity.
- Sub-grades of virgin oil based on acidity and flavour:

Extra virgin oil	Oleic acid <0.8% by wt. & excellent flavour
Fine virgin oil	Acidity < 2%
Ordinary olive oil	Acidity upto 3.3%
Refined oil	Acidity < 0.3%
Blended oil	Acidity < 1%
Residual oil/ Olive pomace oil	Extracted by chemical solvents

Varieties:

- Oil purpose: Frontoio (23-25.87% oil), Pendulino, Aglandean (23-24% oil), Coratina (23-25% oil), Leccino (25-30% oil), Cardia (20-21% oil), Canino, Ascolanaterena and Picual.
- Pickle/ Table purpose: Manzanillo, Sevillano, Ascolano (high pulp to stone ratio), Caratina, Queen, Calamta, Cornicabra, Barouni, Chemlali, Mission, Picholine, and Attica.

- Salt tolerant: Frantoio (highly sensitive to frost), Pocama, Hamed, Verdale, Picual.
- Landscaping purpose: Swan Hill, Majestic Beauty, Little Ollie.
- Winter hardy varieties are characterized by few small or large stomata.
- Leaf spot and cold resistant: Ascolana, Ascolana Terena.
- Drought resistant: Canino, Carolea.
- 'Oblonga' rootstock is resistant to verticillium wilt.
- 'ES17' rootstock reduces canopy growth and suitable for HDP.

Disease and pest:

- Phylloxera causes serious damage to olive plantations.
- Fruit fly (*Dacus oleae*) cv. Cilli is used as trap crop.
- Leaf spot/ Peacock eye/ peacock spot (*Cycloconium oleaginum*).
- Olive shield (*Macrophoma dalmatica*).
- Olive canker:
- Olive knot (*Pseudomonas savastana*):
- Black scale (*Saissetia oleae*). Biological control- *Metaphycus zebratus*.
- Olive bark beetle (*Phloeotribus scarabaeoides*).
- Olive psylla (*Euphyllaura pakistanica*).
- Pierce's disease (*Xylella fastidiosa*): Spread through insects.

32. OXALIDACEAE

32.1 Carambola

- Eulogized as 'Star fruit or Sour tasting fruit or *Kamrakh* or *Bilami* or Cucumber tree or Tree sorrel or Five corner fruit'.
- Species: *Averrhoa carambola* (syn. *A. bilimbi*).
- Word 'Carambola' is derived from Sanskrit word.
- Commercially grown in South-East Asia and the Indian sub-continent.
- Fruit cum ornamental tree and pulp is used as substitute for tamarind.
- Root extract used as antidote for poisoning.
- Fruits are used against internal hemorrhoids and rectal bleeding.
- Fruits are often used for making jelly & preserves than as a dessert fruit. Pulp of immature fruits is used for cleaning brasswares.
- Produce gherkin like fruits, used for salad, juice, pickles, candy, preserve and jam.
- Fruits used for pickling and culinary purposes.
- Crushed leaves as used for chicken pox, intestinal parasites, scabies, headache and paste on bite of poisonous creatures.
- Fruit contain 100% edible portion since skin is extremely thin.

- Highly shade tolerant fruit crop.
- Prefers warm moist climate and can be grown up to 1200 m MSL.
- Both alkaline and acidic soils are suitable.
- Fruits rich source of vit. A (570-700 IU/ 100 g), B, C together with minerals and Fe.
- Produce bisexual and heterodistylous flowers and fruits on trunk (cauliflorus).
- Short styled cvs. are self incompatible while long styled are self fertile.
- Individual tree may produce either long styled or short styled flowerd but never both.
- Fruits borne in clusters.
- Anthesis time: 8-10 AM.
- Flower: Panicle of pinkish flowers.
- Fruits: Golden-yellow, cylindrical/oval-elliptical, 3-5 ribbed (prominent angles), & star shaped fruit measures 12-15 cm in length and droop down the branches.
- The acidic nature of pulp is due to oxalic acid.
- Pollination agent: Honey bee (*Apis mellifera*).
- Only 16% fruits reach final maturity.
- Fruit set occurs on 5 shoot types i.e. new, ripening, side, submain, main shoots.
- Largest fruit weight from side shoots (372 g) followed by ripening shoots (365 g) and main shoots (320 g).
- Highest TSS (7.6^0 Brix) from ripening and new shoots.
- Fruit length and fruit thickness is greatest in fruits from ripening shoots.
- Propagation methods: Seeds, budding, layering and wedge grafting.
- Seeds require treatment for germination.
- Seeds have low viability and sown fresh.
- One year old seedlings are used as rootstocks.
- Shield budding and veneer or approach grafting are commonly used.
- Planting distance: 8m x 8m (280 trees/ha).
- Bearing time: July to September to January-February.
- Roostock for calcareous soils in Florida: M-18960.
- Zinc deficiency is common.
- Major problem: Heterostyly condition.
- Sour type (strong taste): Presence of oxalic acid and tannins.
- Sweet type fruits contain oxalic acid (0.96%) and malic acid (0.06%).
- Glucose sugar present in both types.
- Training system: Vase or palmette system.
- Only remedial pruning is needed.
- Plant produces flowers and fruits even on the trunk (cauliflorus bearing).

- Three flushes of flowering in India viz. April-May, July-August and September-October.
- Fruits are borne round the year.
- Days required from flowering to maturity: 100-108.
- Peak harvesting during January-February and September-October.
- Seedling takes 4-5 years to come to bearing and grafted produce crop in 1-2 years.
- Maturity index: 25-75% of fruit surface turns yellow.
- Harvesting stage: Mature fruits drop down.
- Yield: 80 kg/ tree.
- Enzyme responsible for softening process of fruit: Exopolygalacturonase.
- Ethylene and CO_2 production are lower in ripening fruits.
- Life span of fruit: 18 days at room temperature.

Varieties:

- Two types of fruits:
  - Sour (tart) type: Contain 1% acid.
  - Sweet type: Contain 0.4% acid with 5% sugar e.g. Arkin, Dah Pon, New Comb, Thai Knight, Malviya Carambola-1.
- Chinese type: Fuang Tung (very sweet).
- Brazilian type: Rich in vit. C.
- Columbia type: Icambola (sour taste).
- Taiwan type: Tean Ma (sweet taste), Min Tao (very sweet).
- Hawaiian type: Golden Star (sour taste).
- Short styled: B-2, B-8, B-10, Wheeler, Pat Chun, Kembangan, Thai Knight.
- Long styled: B-1, B-6, B-11, B-16, Starking, Maha, Arkin.

Pests and diseases:

- Fruit fly /Melon fly/ Oriental fruit fly/ Caribbean fruit fly (*Anastrepha suspensa*):
- Fruit borer (*Encoenogenes* spp.)
- Fruit sucking moth (*Othreis fullonica*).
- Cercospora leaf spot:
- Anthracnose (*Colletotrichum gloeosporioides*):

33. PASSIFLORACEAE

33.1 Passion fruit

- Produce hen's egg size fruit.
- Perennial woody vine.

- Brazil: Largest producer in the world.
- Taiwan and Kenya accounts for 80-90% of world's production.
- India's productivity: 1.47 T/ha.
- Dried flowers contain an alkaloid 'passiflorin' which is used for relieving pain and inducing sleep.
- Long day plant requiring day length excess of 10.5 h to flowering and fruiting.
- Optimum temperature for growth: 20-30^{0}C and highly sensitive to frost.
- Optimum soil pH for growth: 5.5 to 7.5.
- Good source of pro-vitamin A, ascorbic acid, riboflavin, niacin and high mineral content.
- Fructose and glucose are major sugars in purple and yellow passion fruit.
- Sucrose is highest in tetraploid hybrids (*P. edulis* x *P. incarnata*).
- Citric acid is predominant in yellow colour followed by tetraploid and purple fruits.
- Bisexual flowers borne singly in axils of leaves at terminal region of new growth, 4-5 cm in dia., colourful and fragrant.
- Self incompatibility is reported in yellow types except purple type and hybrids between golden and purple forms.
- RDF of 100 g Ammonium sulphate, 50 g SSP, 100 g MOP/ vine/ year is optimum.
- HDP: Double row planting at 2-4 m x 2.5-5 m accomodates 500-1300 vines/ ha.
- Anthesis time: Yellow (12.30-1.00 pm) and purple (7-7.30 am).
- Anther dehiscence occurs before anthesis in winter in yellow types and no dehiscence in summer.
- Pollination agents: Honey bees, hover fly, carpenter bee.
- Highly precocious in flowering and fruiting.
- Pollination is not effective during rainy season.
- Commercial propagation: Seed which are recalcitrant in nature.
- Micrografting (i.e. *in vitro* shoot tip grafting) is also practiced.
- Ideal training system: Two arm kniffin system.
- Training is done weekly while pruning is restricted to lower parts during winter when vines are dormant.
- Juvenile phase lasts for 80±10 days and flowering phase begins at plant age 195 days.
- Flowers form on above 24th node.
- Harvesting time: 2 main periods: August-December and March-May.
- Fruit bearing starts from 10th month and full bearing reaches by 16-19 months.
- Pollen germination is reduced below 20^{0}C.
- Fruit matures in 30-35 days after flowering and 60-65 days afterfruit set.
- Specific gravity of ripened fruit: 0.976.

- Maximum fruit size is attained at 25-30 days after fruit set.
- Fruits contain many seeds (up to 30) which are covered with juicy endosperm.
- Ripe fruit contains 33% juice which is highly acidic (5%).
- Yield is highest between November-April and lowest in September.
- Slightly purple coloured fruits along with small portion of stem should be picked up.
- New varieties can be improved by somatic cell technique through protoplast culture.
- Yellow passion fruit have stronger transmission ability than related species.
- Yield: 1-1.5 kg fruits/ vine/year; 5-10 T/ha (purple); 30-50 T/ha (yellow); 20-25 T/ha (hybrids).
- Spray of 20 ppm CPPU after 2 weeks of full bloom improves fruit size, increase pulp: pit ratio.
- Storage: Up to 4-5 weeks at 5^0C and 80-90% R.H.

Species:

- Among 400 species, 381 species have ornamental value and 19 species produce edible fruits.
- Key for identification to species-
  - Leaf shape and size;
  - Flower size;
  - Colour of petals;
  - Corona filaments.
- *P. edulis* and *P. incarnata*: Fruit growth (diameter) follow sigmoid growth curve.
- Use of wild spp. *P. setacea*, *P. odontophyla* and *P. nitida* to develop interspecific hybrids resistant to woodiness, virus, root knot nematode and to obtain large fruit size.
- *P. giberti*: Tolerant to Fusarium wilt.
- *P. edulis* grafted on *P. edulis* var. *flavicarpa*, provides virus free plants.

Common name	Botanical name	Features
Purple passion fruit	*Passiflora edulis*	Native of Brazil; more productive, higher elevation
Golden / yellow passion fruit	*P. edulis* var. *flavicarpa*	Native of Hawaii; resistant to fusarium wilt, phytophthora blight, alternaria leaf spot & nematode
Blue passion fruit	*P. coerulea*	Resistant to fusarium wilt, phytophthora stem rot, bacterial spot, tolerant to viruses; tolerant to nematodes, waterlogging & chilling injury/ cold tolerance; used as rootstock for *P. edulis* in South Africa
Banana passion fruit	*P. mollissima*	
Water lemon/ Golden apple/ Bell apple/ Yellow Granadilla	*P. laurifolia*	Native of T. America; white yellow juicy pulp

Sweet Granadilla	*P. ligularis*	-
Maypops	*P. incarnata*	Cold hardy
Giant granadilla	*P. quadrangularis*	Very large fruit; oblong shape; heavy cropping
Sweet calabash	*P. maliformis*	Self incompatible
Banana passion fruit	*P. mollissima*	Suited to 2000-3000 m MSL; attractive flower; resistant to bacterial spot
-	*P. cincinnata*, *P. amethystine*	Wild species.

Varieties:

- Purple passion fruit breeds true to type from seeds.It can be used in crossing program.
- Yellow passion fruit and its hybrids perform better in tropical climate.Yellow is resistant to leaf spot, root rot and has bigger fruit size.
- Purple form is superior to yellow in yield and quality of juice.
- Kaveri: Hybrid between (Purple x Golden) released by IIHR in 1978. Resistant to collar rot, wilt, brown leaf spot and nematodes.
- Hybrids of (Purple x Golden) are resistant to nematodes, Passion fruit Woodiness Virus (PMV) and fusarium wilt.
- Noel's Special: Large fruited yellow type from Hawaii. Orange coloured juice. Tolerant to alternaria leaf spot, precocious bearer and self incompatible.
- Trellising, Purple Gold (syn. Day's Special), Black Beauty, Lacey, E-23 (*P. edulis* x *P. edulis* var. flavicarpa; self pollinating type, Sel-3-1 (Redland Triangular), Sel-3-26 (Redland Pink) are other hybrid varieties from Australia.
- Transgenic varieties: Flavicarpa, Degener.
- Reniform nematode: Vine show leaf yellowing & wilting.

Inheritance of characters:

- Fruit weight, juice volume, sugar percentage: Positively correlated with number of seeds/ fruit.

Characters	Inheritance pattern
Fusarium wilt resistance	Yellow form dominant to purple.
Fruit skin colour	Controlled by single pair of genes with no dominance

Pests and diseases:

- Queensland fruit fly (*Dacus tryoni*):
- California red scale (*Aonidiella aurantii*):
- Mealy bug (*Planococcus pacificus*): Controlled by lady bird beetle (*Cryptolaemus montrouzieri*), wasp parasites, lace wing larvae.
- Mite (*Brevipalpus phoenicis*):
- Reniform nematode (*Rotylenchulus reniformis*): Vines show yellowing and wilting symptoms.

- Septoria spot (*Septoria passiflorae*):
- Bacterial blight (*X. campestris* pv. *passiflorae*):
- Collar rot (*Rhizoctonia solani*):
- Woodiness virus. Aphid transmitted and through pruning implements.
- Anthracnose (*Colletotrichum gleosporioides*):
- Brown spot (*Alternaria alternata*):
- Phytophthora root rot or crown rot:
- Woodiness: Caused by potivirus. Sanitized nursery management & ELISA technique.

34. PHYLLANTHACEAE (EUPHORBIACEAE)

34.1 Aonla

- Eulogized as 'Indian goose berry or Fruit of 21st century or *Amla* or *Amritphal* or Sacred tree or Natural capsule of ascorbic acid or Star gooseberry'.
- Word *Phyllanthus* in Greek language denotes 'leaf flower'.
- Evergreen in tropics and deciduous in sub-tropics with sparse foliage.
- Ideal plant for arid and semi-arid region due to deep root system, reduced foliage and dormancy for fertilized fruitlets.
- Tree is common in mixed deciduous forest of India.
- Popular as backyard fruit throughout the country.
- Potential crop for afforestation of waste land & degraded areas.
- Insensitive to acidic and saline soils (pH 6.5-9.5).
- Pricking process is related to aonla.
- Ideal plant (amicable) for 2 to 3 tier cropping system.
- Fruits have maximum life on tree before ripening.
- Aonla contains 6 seeds/ fruit.
- Seed yields 16% fixed oil.
- Fruits, leaves, bark and seeds are used for various purposes.
- Medicinal value of fruits: Cooling, refrigerant, diuretic, laxative, anti-biotic treating jaundice Hepatitis B, cough, bronchitis, diabetes, haemorrhages, diarrhea, anaemia, dyspepsia, chronic dysentery and in tanning, dyeing industry (hair oils, hair dyes & ink preparation), vitality restorer and avoids scurvey disease.
- Only astringent fruits are used in Ayurvedic medicine.
- Active principle: Phyllanthin.
- Ascorbic acid in pulp: 600 mg/ 100g.
- Stability of ascorbic acid is maintained in dried fruits is due to presence of polyphenols or leucoanthocyanins.
- Anti-oxidant effect: Gallic acid.

- Phyllanthoid branching habit: Determinate (short & fruit bearing shoot) and indeterminate (long) shoots.
- Tree sheds determinate shoots from December onwards resulting indeterminate shoot devoid of foliage up to mid January. New shoots appear in February.
- Number of flowers/ cluster: 8-34.
- Number of clusters/ branchlet: 18-27.
- Average number of female flowers/ branchlet: 2 to 10.8
- Sex ratio (ratio of female to male flowers on tree): 1: 29 to 1: 36.
- Fruit set: 12-18%.
- Mature tree tolerates freezing temperature as well as high (46^{0}C) temperature.
- Warm temperature and ample humidity is conducive for initiation of dormant floral buds.
- Dormancy period: April-June and resume growth i.e. fruit bud differentiation (FBD): July-August.
- Two cropping seasons: July-August and April-May.
- Global warming cause off season flowering during November-December.
- Off season flowering is noticed in higher intensity in NA-7 and Chakaiya compared to Kanchan and Krishna.
- Flower bud differentiation noticed in 1st week of March.
- Flowers are borne in axils of leaves on determinate shoots.
- Inflorescence type: Racemose.
- Female flowers open in stages and take 72 h to open completely.
- Stigma receptivity: On 2nd to 5th day of anthesis.
- Pollination agents: Wind, honey bees and by gravity.
- Anthesis of male flowers: 8.30 to11.30 AM and 3.30 to 6.30 PM.
- Zygote formation occurs within 24-36 h of pollination.
- After fruit set, ovary remains in dormant condition up to 4-4.5 months and begins to swell by end of July to mid August.
- Maximum fruit growth (in dia. & volume) by November.
- Growth of fruit is due to enlargement of cells of mesocarp.
- Endocarp cells form the hard stone cells (Bajpai, 1968).
- Fruit type: Modified berry comprising edible part of epicarp & mesocarp while endocarp forms hard stone and contains average 6 seeds/ fruit.
- About 300-500 seeds weigh about 10 gram.
- Growth of fruit is due to enlargement of cells of mesocarp while endocarp cells form hard stone cells.
- Seed contains only one embryo.
- Seed viability: 1 year.

- Seed to pulp ratio: 1: 15 to 22 in different varieties.
- One year old seeds give better germination and March is adequate sowing time.
- Commercial propagation: Patch budding during May-September (maximum 60-100% success) and cleft grafting.
- Budding time: June to September.
- *In vivo* micrografting: Two and half month rootstock is grafted by micro-bud (1-1.5 cm length and 2-3 mm width) in 'V' notch made on terminal new growth in January giving 100% success.
- Top working to rejuvenate old trees of inferior types by heading back during March.
- Rejuvenation of old/ unproductive/ inferior orchard preferred budding: 'T' budding and top working.
- Planting time: February to March.
- Seed germination is enhanced by GA_3@ 500 ppm for 24 h.
- Systems of planting: Square, cluster, paired, hedge row, double hedge row (260 plants/ha) in rainfed areas.
- Ideal filler plants: Ber, guava and lemon.
- Recent problems: Self incompatibility and unfruitfulness (non-bearing condition).
- Planting of 3 different varieties in 2:2:1 ratio needs to be adopted.
- Training system: Single stem system and modified central leader system.
- Pruning: Removal of 50% of erect growing shoots each year after termination of crop.
- Irrigation period: April-June at biweekly interval.
- Irrigation should be avoided during flowering (mid March-mid April).
- Method of irrigation: Basin system.
- Mulching with organic wastes is very effective in salt affected soils.
- Fertilization schedule: September-October and April-May.
- Harvesting time: November to December.
- Harvesting method: Hand picking of individual fruits by bending smaller twigs or shaking the twigs.
- Maturity indices:
  - Period from flowering to fruiting: 8 months.
  - Period from fruit set to maturity: 140-150 days (18-20 weeks).
  - Specific gravity (1.07-1.10)
  - TSS: acid ratio (5 to 6).
  - Colour of fruit surface (dull greenish yellow to translucent).
  - Fibre (appear on seed cover)
  - Change seed colour from creamy white to brown.
- Marketing grades: Bold, (large), medium and small sized fruits.

- Large sized grades used for candy and preserve (*murabba*).
- Small sized grades used for *chavanprash* and *triphala churna* preparations.
- Yield starts at 4-5 years after planting.
- Yield: 100-150 kg/tree and 15-20 t/ha (high productivity/ unit area).
- Three stages of fruit drop:
  a) Heavy drop (70%): within 3 weeks of flowering due to degeneration of egg and lack of pollination.
  b) 2nd drop from June-September due to lack of pollination & fertilization.
  c) 3rd drop from August-October due to embryological & physiological factors.
- Fruits can be stored for 6-9 days at ambient temperature.
- In salt solution, fruits can be stored up to 7 days.
- Value added products: Sauce, dried chips, pickles, jelly, powder, juice, tablets, tophies.
- Aonla powder is superior to synthetic vit. C in treating deficiencies.

Species:

- Otaheite gooseberry or Country gooseberry or West Indian gooseberry or Malaya gooseberry or Tahitian gooseberry: *Phyllanthus acidus* (syn. *P. distichus*, 2n=28). It bears throughout year and have ornamental foliage and used for pickling.
- *Emblica officinalis* (syn. *Phyllanthus emblica, P. amarus*):
- *P. fischeri*, *P. longiflorus*: Used for pickling.

Varieties:

- NA-series of aonla are released from NDUA&T, Faizabad.
- Laxmi-52: Selection from cv. Francis. Good for *murabba* and candy making.
- CISH-A-33: Seedling selection, large-sized fruits (32-35 g), yield (55.45 kg/tree), rich in neutraceuticals (ascorbic acid 490.13 mg/100 g).

Name	Breeding method	Features
Early maturing (mid-Oct to mid-Nov)		
Banarasi	Local selection	Early maturing; shy bearer; prone to heavy dropping of fruits; seed to pulp ratio 1:21; tolerant to offseason flowering; best for *murabba*.
NA-5 (Krishna)	Chance seedling of Banarasi	Best for candy & juice purpose
NA-9	Chance seedling of Banarasi	Suitable for preserve & candy making; susceptible to internal necrosis
NA-10 (Balwant/ Agra Bold)	Chance seedling of Banarasi	Fruits skin yellowish with pink tinge; suitable for dehydration
Mid season (mid-Nov to mid-Dec)		
Francis (Hathi Jhool)	Local selection	Prolific bearer; seed to pulp ratio 1:22; tolerant to offseason flowering; highly susceptible to internal necrosis

NA-4 (Kanchan)	Chance seedling of Chakaiya	Heavy & regular bearer; suitable for pulp extraction
NA-6 (Amrit)	Selection from Chakaiya	Ideal for preserve, pickle & candy; alternate bearer; resistant to internal necrosis
NA-7 (Neelum)	Selection from Francis	Free from necrosis, precocious bearing & ideal for preparation of *chavanprash*, chutney, squash; resistant to internal necrosis
Late maturing (mid-Dec to mid-Jan)		
Chakaiya	Local selection	Alternate bearer;small fruits; seed to pulp ratio 1:17; ideal for making pickles; low yield; resistant to internal necrosis
Bhawanisagar (BSR-1) 1995	Selection from Thimbam local of Tamil Nadu	High yield (45 kg fruits/ tree/ year); fruit wt. 30 g; more ascorbic acid (610 mg/100 g); TSS 18.1^0 Brix
CIAH, Bikaner (CHES, Godhra)		
Goma Aishwarya (2007)	Clonal selection from NA-7	Early variety; fruit wt. 45.17 g; 47% juice; TSS 10.34^{0}Brix; ascorbic acid (554.78 mg/ 100 g); low in fibre content; drought tolerant; high yielding than 'NA-7'; yield 105 kg/ tree; suitable for processing & export
AAU, Anand		
Anand-1 (syn. Gujarat Aonla-1) 1994	Selection	Hard flesh; yield (100-140 kg/tree/year; bigger size (43 g); high pulp to stone ratio 1.98:1; TSS (16.33^0 Brix); vit. C (815 mg/100 g) & acidity (1.90 %)
Anand-2	Selection	Tall & upright growing; fruit wt. 45 g; vit. C 775 mg/ 100 g; yield 100-125 kg/ tree; moderate keeping quality
Anand-3	Selection	-
CIMAP, Lucknow		
Navyakriti	Selection	High yield

Pests, diseases and disorder:

- Ring rust (*Ravenelia emblica*): Major disease. It is controlled by spray of 2% Chlorothalonil.
- Blue mold rot (*Penicillium islandicum*): Spray NaCl @ 2% solution.
- Bark-eating caterpillar (*Indarbela tetraonis*): Major pest.
- Gall maker (*Betousa stylophora*): Spray neem oil 0.15%.
- Fruit borer [*Deudorix* (*Viracola*) *isocrates*]: Attack starts in August till November.
- Internal necrosis (browning of mesocarp and endocarp): 'B' deficiency. Combined spray of $ZnSO_4$ @ 0.4% + $CuSO_4$ @ 0.4% + Borax @ 0.4% during September-October.
- Off season flowering: Due to global warming or alteration in tree physiology.

35. PROTEACEAE

35.1 Macadamia nut

- Eulogized as 'Queensland nut or Australian nut or Tropical nut of the world or World's finest dessert nut or Most expensive nut in the world'.

- Evergreen tree, introduced from Australia.
- Major cash fruit in Hawaii, California, South Africa and Australia.
- Thrives well in sub-tropical conditions with high summer and low winter temperature.
- It is commercially grown in Kerala, TN, Karnataka and Odisha.
- Fruit comprises spherical, brown coloured shell (seed coat) surrounded by green husk (pericarp).
- Edible part: White cream coloured kernel (embryo) which are 2.5-3 cm long.
- On an average fruit weighs 20 g has 10 g seed and 3 g kernel.
- Kernels are also rich source of Ca, P and Fe.
- Kernel/ nut quality is related to its oil content (unsaturated fatty acid) and composition.
- Nuts are more oily in nature and globular in shape.
- Kernels contain 4% sugar, 10% protein, 80% fat (75-80 g/100 g).
- It has highest monosaturated fat content.
- Majority of fat is 100% cholesterol free and contains palmitoleic acid, which can improve metabolism and help our body to maintain healthy levels of insulin.
- Nuts have crunchy nature, delicate flavour and creamy colour.
- Kernels are consumed after roasting and salting.
- Raw kernels used in confectionary, ice creams, desserts and processed foods.
- Frost free regions with annual rainfall of 120 cm are well suited.
- Optimum soil pH: 5.5-7.5.
- Dichogamy is major problem.
- Trees have to be protected from frost and strong winds.
- Temperature influences vegetative flushes, flower initiation and nut development.
- For optimum tree growth, 25^{0}C temperature and long days are favorable.
- Flower initiation: 11-15^{0}C night temperature in short days.
- Pollination agent: Honey bee.
- Sclerophyllous (hard evergreen with waxy cuticle or oily compounds which retard water loss from exposed surface) nature of leaves is associated with adaptation to periodic drought.
- Proteoid roots: Dense cluster of rootlets.
- Propagation method: Seed (reproduce variability) and vegetative methods (cutting, layering, wedge grafting, *in situ* grafting) on seedling rootstock.
- Grafted tree produce 3-4 times more nuts and higher (15%) kernel yield.
- Latent incompatibility develops between *tetraphylla* rootstock and *integrifolia* as scion.
- Planting distance: 10 m x 5 m and HDP: 5 m x 3 m.
- Training system: Trained on single stem system to form bush type growth.

- Hedge row planting is adopted for mechanized operations.
- Pruning: Only remedial pruning is necessary.
- Floral buds remain dormant for 50-96 days.
- Floral initiation to anthesis: 137 to 152 days.
- Flowering season: December-January.
- Tree starts late bearing, after 7th year and 20 year old ones give full yield and continue to yield for about 40-60 years.
- Though it is self pollinated, need planting atleast two cvs. in orchard is better.
- Tree bear tassels of whitish flowers followed by strings of small, hard, roundish, pointed nuts in grayish-green husk.
- Nut growth increases rapidly between 8 and 12 weeks after anthesis.
- Oil accumulates 13 and 24 weeks after anthesis.
- Number of leaves required for formation of one fruit: 50.
- Seedling trees have long juvenile phase, produce bitter nuts with low oil content.
- Bearing behaviour: Cluster bearing.
- Period from flowering to fruit maturity: 30-33 weeks (7-8 months).
- Huge flower drop 5-6 weeks after anthesis.
- Three phases of fruit drop: 2, 6-7 and 10 weeks of post anthesis.
- Natural fruit set: < 1 to 4%.
- Shell hardens at 13th week and oil lay down between 13-17th weeks.
- Harvesting season: July-August.
- Maturity index: Husk begins to dry and splits, exposing inner brownish nut.
- Manual/ mechanized harvesting by using suspended nets is followed.
- After harvesting of fruits, dehusking and drying is done immediately.
- Third grade kernels (specific gravity >1.025) are unacceptable.
- Roasted kernels with specific gravity <1.0 are accepted for eating and processing.
- Hard shell is cracked and raw kernels are dried to 1.5% moisture and can be stored for about a year.
- Kernels are deep fried in oil for 15 min at 135^{0}C and used in various ways.
- Nut's maturity: Kernels accumulating 70% or more oil.
- Yield: 80-90 kg/ tree after 20 years or 3.2 to 3.5 T/ha.

Botanical name	**Shell type**	**Features**
M. integrifolia	Smooth shelled	Commercially important; sweet kernel; highly palatable; spherical & smooth seed shape; seed size (12-32 mm); adapted to sub-tropical climate
M. tetraphylla	Rough shelled	Sweet kernel & highly palatable; elliptical or spindle shaped kernels with pebbled surface; adapted to temperate climate
M. ternifolia	-	Inedible & bitter kernels

Varieties:

- *M. tetraphylla*: Renown, Nutty Glen (Hawaiian selections); Own Choice, Hinde, Daddow (Australian selections), Mammoth, Aramour, Sewell, Greber.
- *M. integrifolia*: Keauhou, Kakea, Ikaika, Keaau, Kau, Mauka, Makai, Purvis (All are Hawaiian selections).
- Both species are intercrossable and prominent hybrids belong to *M. tetraphylla* are Beaumont, Nelmark-1, Nelmark-2.

Inheritance of characters:

- Phyllotaxy and leaf attachment: Single pair of genes.
- Number of marginal serrations and colour of young flush: Complementary interaction.
- Numerous serrations and red colour of young leaves: Dominant.
- Thick shell: Dominant.
- Strong correlation between nut and kernel mass.

36. PUNICACEAE (LYTHRACEAE) LOOSESTRIFE FAMILY

36.1 Pomegranate

- Eulogized as 'Fruit of paradise or Fruit of love or *Anar* or Dollar Earner crop or Apple of Carthage'.
- Name pomegranate follows a Latin name of the fruit '*Malum granatum*' which means 'Grain apple'.
- National fruit of Azerbaijan.
- Pomegranate festival is celebrated annually in Tehran during 14-22 November.
- Photographs of 'Solapur pomegranate' have appeared on special cover and postage stamp by Indian Post's & Telegraph, Govt. of India released during 2021.
- World's largest pomegranate germplasm collection is maintained at Turkmenistan.
- Extensively grown in Spain, Morocco, Egypt, Iran, Afghanistan, Burma, Baluchistan, China, Japan, USA, USSR and India.
- In India, during 2020-21, area under cultivation (>2.61 lakh ha), production (25.67 lakh tones) and productivity of 12.56 tonnes/ ha.
- In India, area has increased by 152.7% while total production by 312.7% during 2011-12 to 2019-20.
- Assumed an important place in Indian economy.
- India ranks 1st in production of pomegranate in the world.
- India's share in world's production: 40-45%.
- India's share in global export: 2.26% compared to Israel (> 50%), Spain (22%) and Iran (8%).

- Export destinations: Arabian countries, Sri Lanka, Bangladesh & East Asian countries.
- Maharashtra is leading state in cultivation (1578 lakh metric tonnes from 1.32 lakh ha area).
- Pomegranate basket of India: Maharashtra.
- 1st crop in value chain management in Public Private Partnership (PPP) mode.
- Peak period of Indian exports: December to June.
- Fruits are widely used in medicinal and cosmetic industry.
- Highest nutritive value: Protein (1.6%), -CHO (14.5%), fibers (5.1%), minerals (0.7%) followed by guava, mango, etc. Hence, called as 'super fruit'.
- Fruits are rich source of phenolics and anti-oxidants.
- Fruit juice: Valuable medicine for leprosy patients.
- Anti-diabetic microcapsules: Prepared from pomegranate juice in Mexico.
- Powder is also prepared from juice and used for treating anti-diabetic & high blood pressure.
- Pomegrante taste is due to TSS: acid ratio.
- All plant parts contain tannin.
- Highly drought tolerant and winter hardy.
- Calorific value: 83 Kcal/100g.
- Nutrition score: 51.
- Red coloured arils: Anthocyanins.
- Peel of fruit is used to develop polyphenol rich functional foods. It helps in prevention of myocardial infarction by modulating nitric oxide signaling pathway.
- Grown in variety of climate ranging from temperate to tropical i.e. -12 to 44^{0}C temperature.
- Time span between flower bud differentiation and anthesis is 14-28 days.
- Flowers are male, hermaphrodite, intermediate type.
- Anthesis time: 11 AM to 2 PM.
- Pollen stored at 9^{0}C remained viable for 92 days.
- Stigma receptivity: From one day before anthesis to 5 days after anthesis.
- Pollination agent: Honey bee.
- Both self and cross pollination is observed.
- Edible portion: Aril (sarcotesta).
- Predominant pollination: Cross pollination. Heterostyly is common.
- Hermaphrodite flowers usually homostylous or pin eyed and male flowers are thrum eyed.
- Fruits are borne terminally on short spurs from mature shoots.
- Seedlessness is due to lack of lignification of testa.
- Method of propagation:
  - Hardwood cuttings: Easy to multiply.

  - Wedge grafting: Benefits of rootstock can be exploited.
  - Air layering: High success rate.
  - *In vitro* propagation: Disease free planting material.
- *In situ* budding technique: Patch budding.
- Branching pattern: Syllaptic.
- Double flower type ornamental part: Modification of stamens into petals look like rose flower.
- Training system: Multiple stems (3-4) system is most prevalent in India.
- Optimum crop load: Ganesh (50-60 fruits/tree).
- Maximum growth rate (2.09 g/ day) of fruit is attained between 60-120 days.
- Maximum concentration of total phenols is at marble stage (25-30 days old fruits) and lowest at harvesting stage (170-180 days old fruits).
- Use of fertigation technique saves water by 50-55%, fertilizer nutrients by 25-30% and increased yield and quality by 30-35%.
- Maturity indices:
  - Days from flowering to maturity: 150-180.
  - Days from fruit set: 120-135 in cv. Ganesh, Phule Arakta & 170-185 days in cv. Bhagwa.
  - Closure of calyx at distal end of fruit.
  - Change in colour from light green to yellowish pink or red, blood red as per cultivar.
  - Ripe fruits give distinct cracking sound of inside grains when slightly pressed from outside.
  - Fruit gets suppressed on sides.
- Motorized aril extractor is developed for pomegranate.
- Root treatment with 3,000 ppm IBA gives maximum survival.
- Diffuser technology of irrigation saves 60% water compared to drip.
- Anti-transpirants such as 10% kaolin, 10^{-5}M phenylmercuric acetate, 1.5% power oil, 1% liquid paraffin is beneficial for increasing productivity.
- Estimation of seed mellowness by quantitative method (kg/cm^2 with tablet hardness tester) is more accurate than crushing under teeth.
- Fruit bagging with white cellulose-based bags/ butter paper atleast 85-90 days before harvesting reduce cracking, scratches, retain peel and aril colour, thrips control and development of bacterial spots with reduced incidence of sun burning.
- Major problem for exporting pomegranate to European countries: Phosphonic acid residue.
- Cold storage temperature: 5^{0}C upto 56 days.
- Requirements for getting phytosanitory certificate: Farm registration under AnarNet, global GAP certificate, packhouse recommended by APEDA, certificate of free from insecticide residues, free from bacteria, insects, etc.

- Global GAP certificate is issued by autonomous apex body MSAMB.
- Adoption of pure organic farming is possible.
- Ready-to-eat and frozen arils packed in punnet has tremendrous demand in supermarkets of Europe and America.
- At world level, it is used as a table fruit & processed for making juice & RTS beverages.
- Value added products:
  - Soft gel capsules are prepared from seed oil.Using spray drying technique, dried powder and soft gel capsules are prepared.
  - Concentrate:
  - Grenadine:Light syrup prepared by mixing juice and sugar in 60:40 ratio and can be stored up to 60 days at 5-8^{0}C & for 20 days at room temperature 25-26^{0}C.
  - Jelly: Prepared by mixing juice and sugars in 2: 1 ratio and can be stored for 180 days at 8-10^{0}C & 60-75 days at room temperature.
  - Jam (known as Anar-rub in Iran): Having thick consistency (70-75^0 Brix).
  - Syrup: Having 60^0 Brix & 1.5% acidity as citric acid. It can be preserved by pasteurization or adding sodium benzoate.
  - Wine: Sweet table wine from fermented juice with starter yeast. Wine is flash pasteurized at 60^{0}C.
  - Juice: Recovery with low tannins (0.12%) content varies with methods:
    - From whole fruits/ arils by cloth hydraulic press- 42%.
    - Spiral type screw press- 50%.
    - Basket press- 70%.
    - Sodium benzoate (600 ppm) is added as preservative.
    - Pomegranate juice can be stored upto 4 days under room temperature and upto 10 days at low temperature without any changes in quality.
  - Beverages: Bentonite @ 1-1.5 g/lit and gelatin @ 0.05% as clarifying agent is recommended.
  - Anardana and its powder:

    a) Acidulant product used in souring and culinary preparation as condiment. It is prepared from sour type of wild pomegranate or cv. Daru with high acidity (7.8-15.4%) by dehydration of arils. Acidity is adjusted to 4.17%.

    b) It is rich in vit. C (36.6 mg/100g), moist. 10-12% & contains 2.57% proteins.
  - Waste utilization: Rind, leaves & flowers can be processed into value added products having medicinal, industrial & cosmetic value.

    a) Rind powder recovery: 15.5% on whole fruit basis and 34% on rind weight basis.

    b) Rind powder has potential use in medicines, leather & dying industry & in tooth powder.

Species:

- *Punica protopunica*: Resistant to disease and used as rootstock.
- Species suitable for pot culture: Dwarf pomegranate (*P. granatum* var. *nana*).
- Nana or dwarf type: Bonsai pomegranate: Exclusively for ornamental purpose.
- Two sub-species in *P. granatum*: *P. granatum* ssp. *chlorocarpa* and *P. granatum* ssp. *porphyrocarpa*.

Crop regulation:

- Problems in cultivation: Monoculture practice of growing pomegranate variety has caused biotic stress & bacterial blight is major threat.
- Summer crop maximum demand.
- Wood younger than 6 months and older than 18 months is unsuitable for cutting.
- Behaviour: Under tropical condition evergreen and sub-tropical condition deciduous.
- At national level, 50% area is under *mrig bahar* followed by 25% under *hasta bahar* & 25% under *ambia bahar*.
- *Bahar* treatment or flower regulation is followed for higher productivity.
- Best quality fruits are produced in cool winter and hot dry summer.
  - *Ambia bahar*: January to February flowering- most common favoured by farmers. Best quality fruits.
  - *Mrig bahar*: June to July flowering. Preferred in arid region. More prone to fruit cracking.
  - *Hasta bahar*: September to October flowering. Poorest quality fruits.
  - In temperate areas, flowering takes place in middle of April.

Varieties:

- Breeding methods followed: Introduction, seedling and clonal selections, hybridization and mutation.
- Varieties bred through single plant selection method in China (Liang & Cheng, 1991).
  a) Duo Hong-1 (green fruited skin).
  b) Duo King (yellow fruited skin).
  c) Duo Bai-24 (having good storage & transport qualities).
- Two ornamental types viz. a) Japanese Dwarf b) Double Flower type having red, white & yellow flowers are planted in ornamental gardens.
- Soft seeded varieties developed through mutation (γ-ray dose @ 10-20 kR) in Russia: Super Early (Sverkhrannii), Karabakh, Hongyushizi.
- Breeding work was started in 1905 in India and at GFES, Pune in 1962.
- 'Ganesh' was developed by Dr. G.S. Cheema.
- Echen: Grown in China: and have 2n=4x=32.
- 'Double Flower' and 'A.K. Anar' has 2n=18.

- Dholka, Ganesh, Kandhari, Muscat White and Patiala have 2n=16.
- 'Jodhpur Red' has maximum aril.
- Jalore Seedless: Tolerant to fruit cracking. Recommended for cultivation in Rajasthan.
- Bedana Bosec: Resistant to fruit borer and tolerant to fruit cracking.
- Nana: Donor for bacterial blight resistance.
- Daru: Commonly found in Himalayan region: Long productive cycle and resistant against bacterial blight. Used in breeding for anardana.
- Kandhari, Alandi: Hard seeded.
- Aasuti, Baladi, Manafaluty: Grown in Egypt.
- Wonderful: Introduced from USA.
- Rosh Hapered, Acco, Wonderful, Pomo Wonder (suitable for wine making): Popular in Israel.
- Hicanazar: Popular in Turkey.
- Purple Queen, Malta, Mollar de Elche, Meli, MR-100, Kingdom: Grown in Spain.
- Gul-e-Shah Red imparts dark red aril colour.

Varieties	Breeding method	Features
MPKV, Rahuri		
Ganesh (1954)	Clonal selection from Alandi	Soft seeded; pink arils; fruit wt. 234 g; yield 12.2 kg/tree; TSS 15.5^0 Brix; revolutionized production in country
G-137 (1984)	Clonal selection from Ganesh	Fruit wt. 290 g; dark pink arils; TSS 16^0 Brix; yield 12 kg/ tree
Mridula (1994)	Ganesh x Gul-e-Shah Red	Blood red aril & soft seeded; fruit wt. 178 g; TSS 15.28^{0}Brix; yield 14.36 kg/ tree
Phule Arakta (2003)	Ganesh x Gul-e-Shah Red	Dark red aril; fruit wt. 182 g; TSS 15.97^0 Brix; yield 29.83 kg/ tree
Bhagwa (2003)	Clonal selection	Popular Indian variety;saffron coloured; semi-hard seeded variety; maturing in 180 days; dark red aril; fruit wt. 405 g; TSS 15.4^0 Brix; yield 30.38 kg/ tree
Phule Bhagwa Super (2006)	Clonal selection from Bhagwa	Red arils; saffron coloured; semi-hard seeded variety; maturing in 180 days; dark red aril; fruit wt. 400 g; TSS 15.6^0 Brix; yield 29.30 kg/ tree
Phule Anardana (2015)	Selection	Seeds acidic (mellowness- 1.51 kg/cm^2) & blood red coloured arils; fruits acidic (4.18%); TSS 14.55%; yield (22 kg/tree; 16 t/ha); seed recovery 14%
UAS, Dharwad		
Jyothi (1985)	Selection from (Bassein Seedless x Dholka)	Soft seeded; pink arils; sweet fruit; moderate yielder; resistant to fruit borer
IIHR, Bengaluru		
Amlidana (1999)	Ganesh x Nana	Dwarf ornamental miniature, suitable for HDP, TSS-12.6^{0}Brix; highly acidic arils (4.8%); suitable for dehydration (anardana) preparation; field tolerance to bacterial nodal blight

Ruby (1997)	(Ganesh x Kabul) x Yercaud (Ganesh x Gul-e-Shah Rose Pink)	Dark red aril & soft seeded; fruit wt. 270 g; TSS 16⁰ Brix; yield 16-18 t/ha
CIAH, Bikaner		
Goma Khatta (2010)	Selection	Yield 6.59 kg/ plant; anardana yield 1.18 kg/plant; TSS 14.5⁰ Brix; acidity 7.3%; suitable for dehydration (anardana) preparation
NRCP, Solapur		
Solapur Lal (NR CP-H-06) 2017	Bhagwa x [(Ganesh x Nana) x Daru]	Bio-fortified variety [high Fe (61 mg), Zn (6.9 mg), TSS-17.6⁰ Brix, anthocyanin- 390 mg/100g]; vit. C (19.4 -19.8 mg/100 g); precocious bearer (165 days); yield (23-27 t/ha); suitable for table purpose; 35% more yield than Bhagwa
Solapur Anardana (NRCP-H-12)	Bhagwa x [(Ganesh x Nana) x Daru]	Suitable for processing; high acidity (4.8%); anardana recovery (21.3%)
TNAU, Coimbatore		
CO.1 (1983)	Clonal selection	Higher pulp & sweet taste; fruit wt. 340 g; soft seeded; pink arils; TSS 16⁰ Brix
Yercaud-1 (1985)	Clonal selection from Acc. No. 455	Easily peelable rind; fruit wt. 350-400 g; soft seeded; deep purple arils; TSS 15.2⁰ Brix
Other varieties: Muscat Red, Paper Shell, Bedana Seedless, Spanish Ruby, Jodhpur Local, Kabul, Vellodu		
Shirin Anar	Exotic	Resistant to bacterial leaf spot
Hyti	-	Red arils
P-26	Seedling selection from Muscat	Pink arils, hard seeds

Grading system:

- 12 A grade is preferred in northern and southern India.
- 12 B grade: Fruits weighing between 250-300 g with some spots.

Size of fruit	Fruit wt. (g)	Size of CFB box	Number of fruits
Extra large/ Super	>750	13" x 9" x 4"	6
Large/ King	500-750	15" x 11" x 4"	6-7
Medium/ Queen	400-500	15" x 10" x 4"	12
Small/ Prince	300-400	14" x 10" x 4"	12
12 A, 12 B	250-300	14" x 10" x 4"	24 & above

Pests, diseases and disorders:

- Anar butterfly or fruit borer (*Virachola isocrates*, *Deudorix isocrates*, *D. epijarbas*): Serious pest & maximum incidence in *mrig bahar*. It can be managed spraying NSKE @ 0.5% or bagging of fruits with muslin cloth or by insect *Trichogramma chilonis*. Cv. G-137, Muskat are less susceptible and cvs. Jalore Seedless, Achik Dana highly susceptible.
- Fruit sucking/ piercing moth (*Eudocima*/*Othreis materna*): 1st recorded in India by Lefroy in 1909. Cause 50-90% damage during night in August-October. Severe

during rainy season. Use of repellents (Citronella oil/ poison baits 0.2% zinc phosphite) is recommended.

- Bark eating caterpillar (*Inderbela quadrinotata*): Serious in June- April. Spot application of fungus *Beauveria bassiana* @ 3.6 x 10^{10} is economical.
- Shot hole borer (*Euwallacea/ Xyleborus fornicatus*): Original pest of tea & coffee plantations in Sri Lanka & now serious pest in Maharashtra & Karnataka since 1981. Apply Lindane paste @ 0.05% on trunks of plants or soil drench.
- Root knot nematodes (*Meloidogyne incognita*):
- Aphids, thrips, mealy bugs, scale insects and white fly: Major pests.
- Bacterial blight/ Nodal blight/ Black spot (*Xanthomonas axonopodis* pv. *punicae*): Serious multifactorial disease. Cause huge losses. Sprays of bact-Nashak @ 500 ppm after total harvest of earlier bahar fruits.
- Wilting/ declining (*Fusarium oxysporum*): Complex disease in heavy & ill drained soils pose more threat.
- Alternaria leaf & fruit spots (*Alternaria alternata*):
- Colletotrichum leaf & fruit spots (*Colletotrichum gloeosporioides*):
- Cercospora leaf & fruit spot (*Cercospora punica*).
- Fruit rot (*Aspergillus niger*):
- Internal breakdown/ Aril browning/ Blackening of arils: Disintegration of arils in matured fruits.
  - It is more in *ambia bahar*.
  - Infection of Alternaria fungus during pollination.
  - It is due to deficiency of Ca, B and K.
  - Catalytical enzyme activity in blackened arils.
  - Soil moisture imbalance.
  - Sudden fluctuation of day and night temperature.
  - Fruit maturing in hot weather (50-55^{0}C) season.
  - Harvest the fruits which are 130-135 days old.
- Fruit cracking (most common and serious): Due to 'B' deficiency and sudden application of water after *bahar* treatment. Gul-e-Shah, Khog, Sur-Anar, Francis, Shirvan, Krasnyl, Kazaki are tolerant varieties. Spray GA_3 @ 40 ppm, maintain soil moisture.
- Hardening peels is due to prolonged drought condition.
- Sun Scald: Maintain proper canopy architecture, spray kaolin @ 2.5% at 15 days interval, bagging of fruits with butter paper covers.

Inheritance of characters:

- Heterosis for juice weight/ fruit & rind thickness has been reported.

- Male parents contribute higher than females for almost all traits.
- L x T technique is most suitable to identify parents suitable for qualitative and quantitative development in hybrids.

Character	Number of genes	Inheritance pattern
Young foliage, flower & fruit colour	Monogenic	Pink flower colour dominant to yellow
Flower type	Monogenic	Double flower dominant to single
Fruit rind (skin) colour	Polygenic	Sensitive to sunlight
Aril colour	Polygenic with presence of modifier genes	Red/ pink dominant to white/ light pink; highly sensitive to temperature
Fruit size	Monogenic	Big dominant to small
Rosette plant type	Monogenic recessive	-
Bacterial blight resistance	Recessive	
Seed mellowness	Polygenic	Hard seediness dominant to soft; transgressive segregation observed

37. RHAMNACEAE (BUCK THORN FAMILY)

37.1 Ber

- Eulogized as 'King of arid fruits or Poor man's fruit or Poor man's apple or Crop of 21st century or Chinese date or Chinese fig or Apple of desert'.
- Ber is extremely drought hardy and ideal tree for arid and semi-arid culture.
- National field repository has been developed as CIAH, Bikaner.
- Tolerates as low as -20°C and as high as 48°C.
- Fruits have higher calorific value and vit. C than oranges.
- Branching pattern in *Zizyphus mauritiana*: Sylleptic.
- Flower colour: Greenish to yellow.
- Inflorescence type: Axillary cyme emerging from mature and current season growth.
- Ber also shows strong gametophytic SI. Pollen sterility is major problem.
- Reason for self incompatibility: High ploidy level.
- Major problems in breeding: High pollen sterility and self incompatibility.
- Seed viability: 2 years.
- Commercial propagation: T-budding- easier to adopt and convenient.
- Highly suitable for arid conditions: *In situ* budding (July to September).
- Irrigation during October causes flower shedding and that during March-April causes fruit spoilage and delays ripening.
- Caducous i.e. become dormant during summer.
- Time of pruning in Maharashtra: During hot and dry season between April end to May end i.e spring.
- Best time of pruning in northern India: mid May to mid June.

- Planting distance: 6 m x 6 m and for HDP: 5m x 5m i.e. 160 plants/ acre.
- Flowering time in north India: September-October and in mid-India (August to November).
- Anthesis time: 7.30-8.30 AM in Illaichi, 12-1 pm in Gola, 5.30-6.30 AM in Umran.
- Anther dehiscence: Within 1-2 h and continued for 4-6 h.
- Stigma receptivity: 4 h prior to anthesis and continues for 12 h afterwards.
- Pollens are sticky and not transferred by wind.
- Pollination agents: Honey bee, house fly, yellow wasp.
- Maturity indices:
    - o Days from fruit set: 125-150.
    - o Change in fruit colour- immature fruits green which turns yellowish, golden yellow to brownish at proper ripeness.
    - o Specific gravity: < 1.0 (Umran-0.81), (Gola-0.93), (Kaithali-0.88).
    - o Drying of fruit stalk and yellow colour develops near shoulders.
    - o An aromatic odour develops from ripened fruits.
    - o TSS : acid ratio
- Harvesting period: November to March.
- Yield: 80-200 kg/tree under irrigated condition. Under rainfed condition 50-80 kg/ tree.
- Value added products: Preserve, pulp, osmo-air dried products, squh, jam, beverages, nectar, leather, etc.
- Storage temperature: 3^0C + 85-90% R.H.
- Prevention of fruit drop: Spray 1.5% potassium sulphate and 20 ppm NAA at fruit set.
- Spraying of 3% thiourea or KNO_3, once in 2 days before pruning induces bud sprouting maximum number of nodes.
- Pre-harvest spray of ethephon @ 50 ppm at colour turning stage induces early maturity.
- Best intercrop: Ground nut.
- Anti-transpirants (power oil 0.1% + Kaolin 7.5%) are used to reduce water loss.

Species:

- *Zizyphus mauritiana* var. Tikdi: Vigorous growth & used as rootstock.
- *Z. mauritiana* var. Shukhawani: Vigorous growth & used as rootstock.
- *Zizyphus mauritiana* var. Rotundifolia: Vigorous growth & used as rootstock.

Name	Botanical name	Features
Indian ber	*Z. mauritiana*	Tetraploid; evergreen, spreading habit; first order sylleptic branches are usually observed; tolerates high temperature
Chinese ber	*Z. jujuba*	Deciduous, diploid; upright, highly resistant to frost; excellent dehydration quality; high vit. C & P content in fruit
Jhar ber/ Boradi	*Z. nummularia* (syn *Z. rotundifolia*)	Tetraploid & octaploid; most vigorous; dwarf, drought & salt tolerant rootstock; best rootstock for budding; incompatible with most of varieties; bark used for tanning & leaves as fodder; marginal timber
-	*Z. sativa*	Progenitor of cultivated jujube, tolerates stoney & infertile soils
Suran ber	*Z. rugosa*	Deciduous, edible fruits in April-May
Kat ber	*Z. xylopyrus*	Host for bacterial canker; used for tanning; host for rearing lac insects
-	*Z. fumiculosa*	Deciduous
-	*Z. spinachristi*	Deciduous; used as rootstock & give less vigour to scion
Makoh	*Z. oenoplia*	Bark for tanning; edible fruits
-	*Z. mistol*	Resistant to frost
-	*Z. lotus*	Dwarf; extensive rooting; early fruiting

Varieties:

- Indian jujube cultivars show polyploidy (diploid to octaploid) nature.
- Resistant to PM: Darakhi No. 1, No. 2, Guli, Seedless, Villati.
- Resistant to *Isariopsis* leaf spot: Safed Rohtak, Banarasi, Kadaka, Mundia, Murhara.
- Self incompatible: Umran, Illaichi, Safeda, Katha phal, Reshmi, Banarasi Karaka, Kaithali, Sandhura Narnaul, Safeda Selected, Kakrola Gola, Muria Murhara.
- Katha Phal: Fruit resembles in shape and colour with apple.
- Seb, Dodhia: Resistant to fruit fly.
- Tikadi: Minimum pulp: seed ratio, resistant to fruit fly.
- AM type (anthesis between 6-8 AM) e.g. Illaichi, Kathaphal, Rashmi, Sandhura Narnaul.
- PM type (anthesis between 12.30-1 PM) e.g. Umran, Banarasi, Kadaka, Kaithali, Kakrola, Gola, Safeda Selection, Muria Murhara.
- Single sigmoid growth curve (stone attains maximum size much earlier than fruit) observed in cvs. Gola, Umran, Kaithali and stone attains maximum size much earlier than fruit.
- Double sigmoid growth observed in cvs. ZG-2, Jogia, Thornless, Sandhura Namaul, Banarasi Pewandi/ Kadaka.

Name	Breeding method	Features
CIAH, Bikaner & CHES, Godhra		
CIAH Ber S-15	Chance seedling	-
CIAH selection-1	Selection from local germplasm	TSS- 23%; ascorbic acid (60 mg/ 100g fruit wt.)
Thar Sevika (2007)	Seb x Katha	Precocious & prolific bearer; early maturing; TSS 24.3%; ascorbic acid (88 mg/ 100g); free from PM disease
Thar Bhubhraj (2007)	Selection from Bhusavar area of Bharatpur district of Rajasthan	Early, high yielding & free from PM disease
Thar Malti	Selection	Fruit wt. (20.3 g); TSS (18.6^0 Brix); acidity (0.46%); vit. C (126.7 mg/ 100g); total flavonoids (2.49 mg/g); yield (65-70 kg/plant); tolerant to low temperature; suitable for table & processing purpose
Goma Kirti (1997)	Clonal selection from Umran	Early maturing; pulp to stone ratio (9.90); escapes from attack of fruit borer
MPKV, Rahuri		
Phule Shabari (2019)	Selection from local germplasm	Yield 25 kg/tree under rainfed condition; vit C. 275 mg/100g; good TSS: acid ratio; tolerant to fruit borer & PM
Other cultivars:		Maharwali, Narikeli, Narma, Nimaj, Sanur-2, 3, Mirchia, Madhuri, Vikas-2, Safed Rohatak, Ponda (largest fruits), Pathani, Chhuhara
Gola	Selection	Suitable for extremely dry area; earliest in maturity; pulp to stone ratio (8:7); tolerant to salinity & alkalinity, resistant to fruit borer
Illaichi	Selection	Octaploid (2n=96); seedless, 100% male sterility with aromatic flavour; maximum pulp: seed ratio (9.0); resistant to fruit fly
Umran (syn. Chameli)	Selection	Tetraploid (2n=4x=48); late maturing; originate from Rajasthan; processed & used as '*chhuhara*'; highest number of hermaphrodite flowers (22.2%); pulp to stone ratio (14.3)
Mehrun	Selection	Resistant to fruit fly

Pests, diseases and physoiological disorder:

- Fruit fly (*Carpomiya vesuviana*): Major pest in cultivation.
- Fruit borer (*Meridarches scyrodes*).
- Leaf eating caterpillars, beetles, leaf folders and webers.
- Powdery mildew (*Oidium* spp.): Major disease in cultivation.
- Stylar end browning: Due to high boron accumulation coupled with high temperature and evapo-transpiration.
- Fruit cracking: Due to soil moisture imbalance, low R.H. and fluctuation in day and night temperature. Spray NAA or GA_3 @ 20 ppm and boric acid @ 2 g/litre.
- Fruit drop: Due to hormonal imbalance, abortion of embryo, and inclement weather. Spray NAA @ 20 ppm in mid-October.

- Inverted bottle neck: Due to graft incompatibility, when ber is grafted on *Z. nummularia*.

38. ROSACEAE

Temperate fruits

- Temperate fruits are popularly known in India as hill fruits or cold region fruits.
- Temperate fruit production is growing rapidly in sub-tropical regions.
- Best time of planting: December-January.
- Best time of grafting: January- February or February-March.
- In pome fruit species, short shoots are named 'dards' when they are strictly vegetative.
- Bud wood of temperate fruits is stored as 32^0F.
- Term 'chilling hours' was coined by Weinberger.
- Temperate fruit crops are more susceptible to frost injury.
- Temperate berries originated from North America.
- Among deciduous fruits, alternate bearing reported in apple, pear, plum, prune, apricot, cranberry and blueberry.
- Chilling requirement: Almond> Apricot> Peach> Japanese plum> Pear> Apple> European plum> Cherry.
- Prolepsis: Development of lateral from terminal meristem to establish a shoot with some intervening period of rest of lateral meristem and the branches so formed are referred as 'prolleptic branches' e.g. Temperate fruit crops.

38.1 Apple

- Eulogized as 'King of temperate fruits or Premier fruit of world orSymbol of health or Cryophyllus crop or Prime fruit or Fruit basket of India'.
- A proverb 'An apple a day keeps the doctor away' was quoted by Benjamin Franklin.
- Most widely grown temperate fruit in the world.
- National fruit of Germany.
- The book entitled 'The History and the Romance of Apple' was written by Janick and Torre.
- Can be cultivated above 1500 m to 2400 m MSL altitude.
- Staple fresh fruit in temperate regions of the world.
- Sub-family: Pomoideae.
- Cultivation of temperate fruits is confined to North-Western Himalaya.
- Largest collection of apple germplasm is held at New York.

- China: Largest producer of apple in the world followed by USA.
- India ranks 3rd in world apple production.
- Fruit bowl of apples in India: Himachal Pradesh.
- Maximum production in India: Jammu and Kashmir followed by Himachal Pradesh.
- Among the fruits, apple has longest storage life.
- Apple can float in water.
- In pome fruits, short shoots are named 'spurs' when they are usually floral.Flower buds are mostly formed on spurs.
- Long day plant.
- Dry temperate region: Most suitable for cultivation in India.
- Place suitable in case of non availability of irrigation: Northern.
- Stone cells are absent in the flesh.
- Major sugar (predominant photo assimilate): Sorbitol.
- Critical leaf: fruit ratio to form flower bud in Delicious apple: 10 and < 5 flower bud is not formed.
- Average productivity of apple: 10 t/ ha.
- In apples, concept of effective pollination period (EPP) was developed by Williams in 1965.
- Optimum temperature for pollen germination and fruit setting is 21.1 -26.7^{0}C.
- Chilling requirement: An amount of cold needed by a plant to resume normal spring growth following the winter period.
- Cumulative chill units' requirements of apple for Kullu (Bajaura) and Shimla (CPRI-Shimla) regions were calculated by using Ashcroft *et al.* (1997) method and Utah model (Byrne and Bacon, 1992). The Ashcroft model uses only average temperature of coldest months, whereas, the Utah model uses daily maximum and minimum temperature.
- Prior to 1970, the most commonly used chilling model was based on hours under 45^{0}F (1 hour below 45^{0}F is a "chill hour"). The "Modified Chill Hour" model measures chilling as 1 hour at or below 45^{0}F.
- Utah chilling model: Each hour of the day was given positive, negative, or no chilling units based on the temperature in that hour. The Utah model works well in temperate growing regions of the world.
- Dynamic chilling model: The Dynamic Model measures chilling in units called chilling portions (CP). Best chilling model. One portion equals 28 hours at 6^{0}C (43^{0}F), or more than 28 hours at somewhat less effective temperatures (44^{0}F to 55^{0}F). The Dynamic Model accumulates fewer chilling units (called portions) for the same site compared to the other models.
- Shimla chilling model: Location specific and not applicable to all apple growing areas.

- Almost all varieties have a chilling requirement of 500-1000 hours at or below 7.2°C temperature.
- Low chilling varieties require < 300 h below 7°C e.g. Dorsett Golden (250 h); Anna and Tropic Man (300 h), Tropic Beauty, Gordon, Beverly Hills, Ein Sheimer.
- Insufficient winter chilling of tree results in abnormalities like smaller flowers, leaves and fruit size; small anthers with less pollens, low fruit set and flat fruit development.
- Length of light period rather than intensity has greatest influence on productivity.
- Average summer temperature during active growth period: 21-24°C.
- Critical day/ night temperature for colour development: 15°C (day) and 8°C (night).
- Severity of alternate bearing is calculated by formula by Monselise and Goldschmidt (1982).
  - Formula 1: Alternate bearing index (I) = (year 1 yield) - (year 2 yield) ÷ (year 1 yield + year 2 yield), where I = 0 is regular bearer and I = 1.0 is complete alternate bearing; and
  - Formula 2: Alternate bearing = (current year's yield) - (5-year running average yield)/5-year running average yield; when the current yield is 20% greater than the 5-year average yield, it is an on-crop and when the current yield is 20% less than the 5-year average, it is an off-crop.
- Best temperature for root growth: 18°C and pH 6.5-6.7.
- Polyhouse technology is employed commercially for production of apple nursery in cold desert valley.
- Bending of branches at 90° angle is practiced for high bearing potentials.
- Seed viability: 1 month.
- Seed stratification is done in moist sand at 4-7°C for 60-90 days.
- Tongue grafting: Ideal method of grafting.
- Common method of propagation of clonal rootstock: Stooling or mound layering.
- Rejuvenation of senile orchards: Top grafting.
- Scions cannot be used for grafting in their active stage of growth.
- Training system under HDP: Multiple hedge row system.
- Pruning in apple is essential to maintain balance between vegetative growth and spur development.
- Single axis or vertical axis architecture: Vertical space harvesting plant architecture.
- Spindle bush plant architecture: Modification of central leader training system.
- Spindle bush system of training accommodates 2,000 plants/ ha. Suitable for HDP.
- Super high density planting or meadow orchard: 20,000-70,000 plants/ha. Popular in European countries.
- Espalier plant architecture (EPA) is a type of kniffin training system in which 10 scaffold branches are trained on galvanized wire.

- Cordon plant architecture: Highly precocious system suitable for planting germplasm in gene banks at 0.75 x 1.5 m distance on M-9 rootstocks at inclined 45^0 angle position system.
- Head and spread plant architecture: Two tier training system suitable for cvs. raised on dwarf, semi-dwarf and vigorous rootstock.

Variety	Rootstock	Vigour of tree	Planting distance (m)	Number of plants/ha
Non-spur type	Seedling	Vigorous	7.5	178
Non-spur type	MM-111, MM-109	Semi-vigorous	6.0	278
Non-spur type	MM-106, M-7	Semi-vigorous	4.5	494
Non-spur type	M-9	Ultra dwarf	1.5	4444
Spur type	Seedling	Semi-vigorous	5.0	400
Spur type	MM-111, MM-109	Semi-dwarf	3.5	816
Spur type	MM-106, M-7	Dwarf	3.0	1111

- Most critical period of irrigation: April-August.
- Pigmentation of exposed fruits: UV radiation.
- Anthocyanin pigment in apple: Cyanidin-3-glucoside.
- 50-60% full sunlight exposure is required to develop maximum red colour.
- Best time for propagation: December-January.
- Most common method of planting: Square system
- Clean basin management: Common practice of floor management.
- In 1870, A.A. Lee introduced apple in Kullu, Himachal Pradesh.
- In India, apple was 1st introduced at RRS, Kodaikanal, Ooty by Alexander Coutt in 1889.
- 'Hillock Head' orchard was established by Alexander Coutt is situated in Mashobra.
- 'Mashobra' is apple research station.
- MI (Merton Immune) series released from East Malling Research Station, Kent, England.
- MM (Malling Merton) series released from John Innes Institute, England. It is cross between Malling series with woolly aphid resistant variety 'Northern Spy'.
- 1st research station on apple was established at East Malling Research Station (EMRS), Kent, England in 1917.
- 2nd research station on apple: The John Innes Centre of Merton, London.
- Largest collection of genotypes is maintained at Plant Genetics Resource Unit, Cornell University, New York.
- In India, recommended pollinizer trees for regular cropping: 11-33%.
- Ratio of pollinizer and main crop in orchard: 1:6.
- Pollination agent: Honey bee (*Apis mellifera*).

- Pollination techniques: Top working with pollinizers, flower bouquet placement, pollen dispenser and use of pollinators and 2-3 bee hives/ ha.
- Traditional pollinizers: Red Gold, Golden Delicious.
- Top working of Crab pollinizers (Manchurian Crab, Snow Drift Crab, Golden Hornet, Golden Spur, Summer Queen, King Pippin) results in flowering in same season.
- Fruit bud differentiation (FBD) occurs in terminal fruiting spurs (short shoots) and on or terminal / laterally on long shoots in early summer (early- mid May).
- Entire differentiation period: 4-13 weeks.
- Time between commencement of FBD and blossoming: 8-10 weeks.
- Major problem: Alternate bearing.
- Ringing is practiced 1 or 2 weeks after full bloom to reduce vegetative growth.
- Maximum number of seeds in fruit: 10.
- Maturity indices:
  - Days from full bloom.
  - Separation from spurs.
  - 'T' stage and starch index should be 1-2.
  - Seeds turn brown at maturity.
  - Attainment of full size of fruit skin.
  - Change in ground colour: from green to yellow.
  - Flesh firmness (kg/ sq.cm): varies from 6.8 (McIntosh) to 8.7 (Grenny Smith).
  - TSS: 11 to 13.5%.
- Non-destructive method of measuring harvest: Harvest window technique.
- Destructive measurements of maturity: De Jager Index (PFW-1), FARS Index & Streif Index.
- The SPI (Starch Pattern Index) for harvesting of apples: 4.5/10 (delicious apple) and 4.0/10 (Golden Delicious).
- The DFFB, a maturity index used commercially for Delicious group apples under Indian conditions is 126±4 days.
- Red Delicious and Golden Delicious apples, showed a significant increase in firmness immediately after storage at 38°C for 4 days.
- Chaubattia/ mashobra paste: Red lead + $CuCO_3$+ linseed oil in 4: 4: 5ratio to check microbial infection after pruning.
- Pre-harvest fruit bagging in Royal Delicious influenced fruit colour, texture, quality and reduced occurrence of cork pit, brown core and bitter pit incidence.
- Apples covered with red or yellow coloured bags produced apples of intense red colour and low incidence of bitter pit (nearly 2%) during storage.
- Fruit colour development in warmer and lower (below 1800 m) elevations is generally poor.

- Most commonly used fumigant: 1-MCP.
- Chemical used for vigour control: SADH.
- Best chemical thinner: Benzyl adenine.
- Embryonic dormancy: GA_4 and GA_7 in apple seeds causes inhibitory effect.
- In apples, the screw in plunger used in pressure tester is 1.1 cm.
- Term 'half produced' (i.e. half finished) is used to denote nursery trees which are lifted early when insufficiently developed for transplanting into orchard.
- Biennial cropping is achieved in tropics where no chilling receives.
- After harvest, 5% urea application improves fruit setting.
- Deficiency of N (0.5-1% urea), K (0.5-0.8% K_2SO_4), Ca (0.5% $CaCl_2$), B (0.1% boric acid) can be corrected through foliar sprays.
- Loss of fruit firmness during storage: Increased activity of â-galactosidasse enzyme.
- Ethrel is commercially used for colour development in lower hills.
- Apple colour development is more intense at higher hills.
- VENTEM (*Venturia inaequalis*), PODEM (*Podospora leuchotricha*) and NECTEM (*Nectaria gelligiana*) are disease forecasting system for apple scab, powdery mildew and apple canker.
- 'EPIVEN' and 'Mills infection periods i.e Mills criteria or Table' are meant for disease forecasting of apple scab.
- 'Host-physio-epidemiological model' is developed to predict outbreak of premature leaf fall disease.
- CA storage conditions: 0-5^{0}C at 1-2% O_2, 0-3% CO_2.
- Chilling sensitive apples are stored at -1 to 0^{0}C at 85-90% R.H; storage period: 4-8 months.

Species:

- Genus *Malus* contains about 25-30 species.
- Progenitor or ancestor of cultivated apple: *Malus sylvestris* (derived from *M. sieversii*)
- Domesticated apple (*Malus* x *domestica* syn. *M. pumila*, *Pyrus malus*):
- Flowering crab (*M. floribunda*): Small fruited spp. and resistant to scab. Good pollinizer.
- *M. sieversii*: Sucker free spp.
- Apomictic spp.: *M. sikkimiensis*, *M. toringoides* & *M. hupehensis*.
- *M. sieboldii*: Apomictic species and require minimum chilling hours. Occur in diploid, triploid, tetraploid and pentaploid forms.
- Indigenous to Himalaya: *M. baccata* var. *himalacia* (crab apple), *M. sikkimmensis*.

- Crab apple: Seedling origin. Cultivated as ornamental tree for attractive flowers and fruits. It is also good source of disease resistance and pollination. Used as rootstock; resistant to collar rot, root rot and woolly aphids.
- Resistant to scab: *M. atrosanguinea*: Single dominant gene and partially polygenic.
- Resistant to powdery mildew and Codling moth: *M. zumi* (*Pl-2*): Single dominant gene.
- Resistant to powdery mildew and fire blight: *M. robusta*.
- Resistant to Codling moth: *Malus* x *Pyrus* progenies.
- Resistant to woolly aphid: *M. hupehensis*.
- Resistant to bitter pit: Co-op-11, Co-op-12.

Fruit drop:

- May drop/ Early post blossom drop: Defective pollination and fruit competition. Very severe.
- June drop : Environmental factors i.e. moisture stress.
- Pre-harvest drop: Most serious economical losses; Remedy: NAA @ 10 ppm.
- Fruit thinning agent: Carbaryl or Sevin @ 750-1000 ppm or NAA @ 10-20 ppm.
- Early varieties experience 40-60% loss.

Varieties:

- In 1912, Ronald Hatton initiated the work of classification, testing and standardization of apple rootstocks. He developed Malling series of rootstocks.
- Apple production in world is dominated by Delicious apple (discovered in Iowa in 1872) and Golden Delicious (selected at West Virginia in 1905).
- 'Delicious' varieties were introduced in India by S.N. Stoke during 1918.
- Thomas A. Knight produced 1st apple cultivar of known parentage.
- Apple scab resistant varieties were developed by L. F. Hough.
- Virus free planting material was developed by IHBT, Palampur.
- Apple improvement work was initiated in Jammu and Kashmir in 1956.
- First ever exotic introduction of apple was made at Ooty in 1820.
- Golden Haidegg and Lysgolden: Radiation induced mutants of 'Golden Delicious'.
- Golden Delicious was transformed to produce transgenic Arctic apples which are non-browning.
- 'Modi' (Liberty x Gala): Developed by Consorzio Italiano Vivaisti- a group of specialist plant breeders, Italy in 2007.
- Black Diamond: Rare breed from the family of Hua Niu apples that is cultivated in the Tibetan region of Nyingchi. It has dark purple skin with white pulp due to high altitude.

- Apple varieties belonging to Delicious group are self unfruitful due to self incompatibility.
- English group of varieties are self pollinated, act as pollinizer for Delicious group.
- For Early Shanbury: Winter Banana and Rome Beauty are best pollinizers.
- For Red Delicious: Jonathan, Summer Queen and Yellow Delicious are best pollinizers.
- Red Gold and Golden Delicious: Pollinizer for Red Delicious and Starking Delicious.
- Polish apple rootstocks (P-series), American apple rootstocks (MAC- series) and Canadian apple rootstocks (Ottawa series).
- Irish Peach: Early variety grown in Uttar Pradesh.
- Ottawa: Resistant to fire blight.
- Grenny Smith is OP seedling of cv. French Crab. It takes 6-7 months for maturity and good pollinizer. Require maximum chilling hours.
- Anna: Developed by A. Stein in Israel. It is extensively grown in areas with limited chilling (300 h).
- Coloured sport of apple: Jonagold, Supreme.
- Spur require atleast 30% of full sun to form flower bud.
- HRMN-99: Farmer's selection. No chilling requirement, resistant to scab; can be grown in tropics; fruit wt. 250-300 g.
- Lod, Rymer: Indigenous variety grown in Kashmir.
- Liberty: Resistant to all fungal diseases.
- Shamrock: Green coloured.
- Bhura Delicious: Farmer's variety.
- Diploid varieties have plenty good pollen, self fruitful whereas triploids are self unfruitful and become productive only when pollinated by diploid group.
- Yellow Newton: Good seed viability.
- Yellow Newton, Spartan, Gravenstein: Most susceptible to bitter pit.

***Exotic*:**

Country	Table purpose	Processing purpose	Dual purpose
Italy	Braeburn, Mongendy, Lonas Gold, Gloster, Jonathan, Fuji, Red Delicious, Grenny	Spackle Geala	-
USA	Golden Delicious, Grenny Smith, Gala Gales, Fuji. Washington, Red Delicious, Empire Liberty, Jonathan, Red Delicious, Starking Delicious	Delicious, Rome Beauty, York, Imperial, Stayman Winsap, Northern Spy, Rhode Island, Greening, Prize, Freedom, Red Free	McIntosh, Cortland, Grenny Smith, Red Free
Hungary	-	-	Delicious, Golden Li. Well Spur

Germany	-	-	Gloster, Fonagold
France	Colapters, Cabarett, Rainette, De Flandres	-	-
China	-	-	Bolero, Maypole, Polka, Walts
UK	McIntosh, Empire		
Australia	Pink Lady		-
Japan	Fuji	-	-
New Zealand	Gala	-	-
Canada	McIntosh	-	-

Varieties	Features
Scarlet Gala, Red Fuzi, Royal Delicious	High yielding
Honey Crisp	Flavour rich variety, resistant to scab
Empire, Jonagold, Priscilla, Sir Prize, Freedom, Red Free, Delfloga, Deltana	Scab resistant
Red Chief, Red Spur Delicious, Golden Spur Delicious	Spur type varieties & high yielding
Varad, Tropical Beauty, Michael, Schlomit, Anna, Tamma, Neomi	Low chilling & table purpose
Yandik-Ovskoe, Papisovka Canniaga	Early maturing
Mutsu, Bramlay's Seedling, Gravenstein, Winesap	Triploid varieties
Red Elstar	Natural mutant
Perlin's Beauty	Low chilling& processing purpose
Winter Banana	Low chilling requirement
Aotea-1, Robusta-5	Resistant to woolly aphid but highly susceptible to bitter pit
Top Red, Skyline Supreme, Hardiman, Vance, Delicious	Standard colour mutants of Delicious apple
Yellow Newton	Internal browning
Ariane	Scab resistant; developed at National Institute of Agricultural Research, France
Aurora Golden Gala	Dessert apple; very long storage life
Autumn Glory (Fuji x Golden Delicious)	Red over golden background; very sweet with cinnamon flavour
Envy	Late browning
Ontario, Champagner Renette	Free from russeting
Delicious	Annual bearing habit
Baldwin, Early McIntosh	Biennial bearing habit
Gala, Splendour	Off season; susceptible to rubbery wood disease

Variety	Breeding method	Features
Florina	Introduced from France	Scab resistant
Mollies Delicious	Introduced from USA	Susceptible to PM
Brina, Golden Mira, Red Earlib, E, Nova	-	Resistant to scab & PM

Pink Lady (1973)	Golden Delicious x Lady William	-
Red Delicious (1918)	Chance seedling in USA	Introduced at Himachal Pradesh; most important variety in India; biennial bearing; long conical shape
Red Spur Delicious (1954)	Tree variant (whole tree mutation i.e. chance seedling) in Starking Delicious orchard	Selected at Yokima
Golden Delicious	Chance seedling	Commercial cv. of Europe; biennial bearing habit; good seed viability; susceptible to bitter pit & most widely grown in world; used as pollinizer for Delicious; suitable for processing; free from russetting
Gold Spur Delicious	Bud mutant of Golden Delicious	-
Starking Delicious (1921)	Bud sport of Red Delicious	Large, conical shape, skin yellow with red strips; spur type of Delicious; deep red colour;
Oregon Spur	Bud sport of Delicious	Large number of spur bearing branches
Rich-a-Red	-	Delicious strain
Red Gold	-	Used as pollinizer for Red Delicious & Starking Delicious; regular & heavy cropper
Red Chief	Bud sport of Delicious	-
Red Elstar	Bud sport of 'Elstar'	-
Junami	Idear Red x Mygold x Elstar	Popular in Switzerland, Netherlands, England
Top Red	Bud sport of 'Shot Well Delicious'	Mid season
Baldwin	Triploid	Self fruitful; biennial bearer; sour taste; susceptible to bitter pit; good keeping quality
Prima	*M. floribunda* x Rome Beauty	1st scab resistant variety
McIntosh	Leadingcv. of Canada	Annual bearing; free from russeting; good seed viability
Ambri	Indigenous cv. of Kashmir developed as chance seedling	Late season; cultivated only in J & K because of chilling requirement; long keeping quality; white pulp; irregular bearer, excellent taste and aroma
CITH, Srinagar		
Shalimar Apple 1	Sunehari x Prima	Resistant to scab, green aphids, red spider mite
Shalimar Apple 2	Red Delicious x Ambri	High yield potential (25-28 t/ha)
CITH Lodh	-	Regular bearer, red coloured fruits
IARI, New Delhi		
Pusa Gold (2016)	Golden Delicious x Tydemans Early Worcestor	Golden fruits with red blush, early maturity
Pusa Amartara Pride (2017)	Royal Delicious x Prima	Large fruit size, more TSS
SKUAST, Srinagar		
Lal Ambri (1973)	Red Delicious x Ambri	TSS 16.2^0 Brix, susceptible to scab, alternaria leaf spot

Sunehari (1973)	Ambri x Golden Delicious	Upright tree; free from scab; pollinizer for 'Shalimar Apple 2'
Firdous (1995)	Golden Delicious x Rome Beauty x *M. floribunda*	Yield 7.20 t/ha; resistant to scab, powdery mildew (PM), alternaria
Shireen (1995)	Lord Lam bourne x Melba XR-1274078	Mid-season crop; resistant to scab, alternaria & PM
Akber (2001)	Ambri x Cox's Orange Pippin	Tolerant to scab, PM, green aphid, tortrix moth; resistant to San Jose Scale & red spider mite
Dr YSPUHF, Solan		
Ambred (1978)	Red Delicious x Ambri-157	Good keeping quality; low incidence of PM, scab & sooty blotch; need Red Gold & Golden Delicious pollinizers
Ambstarking (1978)	Starking Delicious x Ambri-81	Red streaks over chrome yellow; crisp & juicy; tolerant to scab
Ambroyal (1986)	Starking Delicious x Ambri-84	Semi-dwarf; late maturity;
Ambrich (1978)	Rich-a Red x Ambri-15	Semi-dwarf; fruit shape round; mod. susceptible to PM & tolerant to scab
Directorate of Horticulture and Food Processing, Chaubattia, Uttarakhand		
Chaubattia Princess (1984)	Early Shanbury x Red Delicious	Early ripening variety; deep red straks on pale background; good keeping quality
Chaubattia Anupam (1984)	Early Shanbury x Red Delicious	Vigorous, conical shaped fruit; bright red streaks on pale ground colour; good keeping quality
Chaubattia Swarnima (1984)	Benoni x Red Delicious	Fruit mature in 2nd week of July; juicy & slightly tart in taste; good keeping quality
Chaubattia Alankar (1984)	Fanny x Red Delicious	Fruit mature in 2nd week of July; round shape; juicy & slightly tart in taste; good keeping quality
Chaubattia Anurag (1984)	Esopus Spitzenberg x Red Delicious	Fruit mature in 2nd week of July; conical shape; juicy & sweet in taste; fruit bright red colour
Chaubattia Agrim (1984)	X-ray mutant of 'Early Shanburry'	Fruit mature in 2nd week of July; conical shape; juicy & sweet in taste; fruit yellow with slight red tinge
TNAU, Coimbatore		
Kodaikanal Beauty (KKL-1) 1987	Clonal selection from 'Parlin's Beauty'	Yield 22 t/ha; mid-season variety; TSS 13^0 Brix
Pamapples	1st successful pear x apple hybrid	Developed by E. Marks (1952) in John Innes Centre, UK

Use of rootstocks:

- Dwarfing rootstock contain more phenolic compounds (phloridzin) than non-dwarfing one.
- Pusa Apple Rootstock-101: Selection of *M. baccata* (Shillong). It is resistant to powdery mildew, apple scab, woolly aphids, white root rot.
- Pusa Seb Moolvrint-1 (PSM-1): Selection of *M. baccata* (Shillong): 1st indigenous rootstock with high grafting success, easy propagation and resistance to root rot, powdery mildew and woolly aphid.

- Propagation of Malling rootstocks: Stooling
- Rootstock resistant to fire blight: Robusta-5.
- Pajam-1, Pajam-2: Selected in France.
- Jork-9, Burmenger 984, Supporter 1,2,3,4: Promoted in Germany.
- Clone NAKBT 337 was developed in the Netherlands.
- Rootstocks developed from Geneva rootstock breeding program: G.16, G.41, G.202, G. 935.
- East Malling Long Ashton (EMLA) series of rootstock are resistant to woolly aphid and viruses e.g. EMLA-111 less susceptible to apple russeting.
- Major problem in clonal rootstocks: Root suckering.

Seedling & clonal rootstock	**Features**
Crab apple (*M. baccata* var. Himaliaca)	Suitable for HDP; resistant to woolly aphid
M-3	Produce root suckers prolifically
M-4	Semi-dwarf; control tree size; suitable for HDP; resistant to woolly aphid; produce root suckers prolifically
M-5	Produce root suckers prolifically
M-7	Semi-dwarf; control tree size; earliest; suitable for HDP; resistant to woolly aphid
M-9	Dwarf; most widely used; suitable for HDP in flat and irrigated areas only; resistant to collar rot & susceptible to drought
M-11, M-16	Impart winter hardiness, vigorous & propagated by trench layering
M-12	Very vigorous; earliest & tallest; resistant to woolly aphid & collar rot
M-13	Vigorous; resistant to woolly aphid & collar rot
M-16	Vigorous; resistant to woolly aphid & collar rot
M-21	Suitable for HDP; resistant to woolly aphid
M-24	Suitable for HDP; resistant to woolly aphid
M-25	Very vigorous & propagated by trench layering; resistant to woolly aphid & collar rot
M-26	Precocious bearer; suitable for HDP; resistant to woolly aphid, collar rot, drought; suitable to all kinds of soil
M-27 (M-13 x M-9)	Developed by Mark Tydeman (1929); ultra dwarf, suitable for HDP; tolerant to drought
Merton-793	Very vigorous; 1st woolly aphid resistant variety developed in 1930; resistant to collar rot
MM-7	Tolerant to drought
MM-104	Semi-vigorous; most winter hardy; resistant to drought, woolly aphid; susceptible to collar rot
MM-106	Semi-dwarf; control tree size; suitable for HDP; susceptible to heavy & wet soils, collar rot; precocious bearer; resistant to woolly aphid; tolerant to drought; produce root suckers prolifically
MM-109	Resistant to woolly aphid
MM -111 (Northern Spy x Merton-793)	Semi-vigorous; dwarf; suitable in case of replant situation; tolerant to drought & woolly aphid

G. 41 (Malling 27 x Robusta 5)	Dwarf; highly resistant to fire blight & phytophthora
G. 16 (Ottawa 3 x *M. floribunda*)	Dwarf; highly resistant to fire blight
G. 202 (Malling 27 x Robusta 5)	Resistant to fire blight; good resistance to wooly apple aphid
G. 935 (Ottawa 3 x Robusta 5)	Winter hardy, highly resistant to fire blight & phytophthora
P-22	Ultra dwarf; suitable for HDP; resistant to cold
Northern Spy	Good seed viability; resistant to woolly aphid but susceptible to bitter pit
Bramley's Seedling	Cooking apple

Grading system:

- Six grades in international market: AAA, AA, A, Extra fancy, fancy class I and Fancy class II.
- HPMC standards: Super large (>85 mm equatorial dia.), Extra Large (80 mm), Large (75 mm), Medium (70 mm), Small (65 mm), Extra small (60 mm) and Pittoo (<45 mm).
- Wooden box size: 45.7 cm x 30.5 cm x 25.4 to 30.5 cm.
- CFB carton size: 50.4 cm x 30.3 cm x 28 cm.
- Packaging capacity 16-18 kg.

Inheritance of characters:

- Cv. Baskatong possesses a dominant gene for red leaf colour and used as pollinizer.
- Positive correlation between sugar (oligosaccharides) content and frost hardiness.

Characters	Inheritance pattern
Fruit size, fruit shape, russetting of skin, fruit surface, skin pigmentation, Acidity, sweetness, sourness	Polygenic
Compact growth & cold hardiness	Polygenic
Anthocyanin (red) colour of shoot	Dominant
Anthocyanin strips on skin	Monogenic dominant
Flower colour (white to pink)	Three independent genes *A, B, C*
Fruit colour	Yellow- Dominant genes; Red- 2 dominant genes; Green- recessive genes
Cream yellow flesh colour	Single dominant gene
Presence of anthocyanin strips	Single dominant gene
Mildew resistance	Polygenic (*Pl-1*, *Pl-2* from *M. zumi* & *M. robusta*)
Scab resistance (derived from Siberian crab apple Hansen's baccata #2)	*Vf* gene from *M. floribunda* 821

Pests, diseases and disorders:

- San Jose scale got its entry into India in Kashmir from France in 1906. Suck sap from twigs/ branches.

- Codling moth: Serious problem in Leh (J & K). Damaging stage- Adult.
- Woolly aphid of apple got its entry into India from England.
- European red mite cause 30% loss. Spread through infested nursery and bud wood.
- Rubbery wood disease: Caused by virus. Abnormally flexible (rubber-like) branches. Widespread in New Zealand.
- Bio-control of Cottony cushion scale: *(Rodolia cardinalis)*:
- Bio-control of mealy bug: *Cryptolaemus montrouzieri*.
- Leafy mistletoes and lichens: Use Caustic soda @ 10 g/litre after leaf fall.
- Major flowering parasites with 8-12% incidence and yield loss upto 15-20%.
- Parasitic plants: Leafy mistletoes and lichens in neglected and poorly managed orchards: Pruning or ethephon spray @ 5% to control in dormant host trees and spray Caustic soda @ 10 g/litre, respectively.
- Wetting period for apple scab infection: 17.2 to 23.9^{0}C for 9 h.
- Fire blight: Introduced in India from England in 1940. 1st discovered bacterial disease of plants.
- The bio-agents were 1st time used for controlling post harvest diseases.
- Split pit and gumming is common in pome type fruits.
- Fruit size and colour are positively correlated with leaf potassium.
- Zinc influenced degree of cold hardiness of trees.
- Burrknot formation: Tree disorder caused by adventitious root primordia formation at node.

Common name	Casual organism	Management
San Jose scale	*Quadraspidiotus perniciosus*	Use parasitoid: American strain of *Prosopaltella perniciosus* or *Encarsia perniciosi* @ 2000 adults/ infected tree once in spring
Woolly aphid	*Eriosoma lanigerum*	Use parasitoid: *Aphelinus mali* @ 1000 adults or mummies/ tree
Blossom thrips	*Thrips flaves*	-
Stem borer	*Apriona cinerea*	-
European red mite	*Panonychus ulmi*	Biocontrol agent: *Typholodromous* spp.
Leafy mistletoes	-	Seedling stage is highly susceptible; spray chaubattia paste + ethephon 5%
Tent caterpillar	*Malacosoma indicum*	Voracious defoliator
Root borer	*Dorysthenes hugelii*	Kill grub by intercultural operations
Collar zone weevil	*Dyscerus fletcheri*	-
Defoliating beetle	*Anomala* spp.	Nocturnal pest
Fruit eating beetle	*Holotrichia* spp.	Nocturnal pest
Apple scab	*Venturia inaequalis*	Crop loss up to 70-80%; Spray urea; plant resistant varieties
Fire blight	*Erwinia carotovora* (syn. *E. amylovora*)	-

Powdery mildew	*Podosphaera leucotricha*	-
Apple Replant Disease (ARD) or Sick soil syndrome	*Phytophthora infestans* (syn. *P. cactorum*): Presence of phenolic acid	-
Jonathan spot	Water deficiency	Seen on late harvested apples
Lenticel spot	Delayed cooling of harvested fruits; High storage temperature; Exposure to UV light	-
Interveinal chlorosis	Mg deficiency	Spray $MgSO_4$ @ 1 g/litre
Cork spot	Ca deficiency	Spray pro-hexadione calcium at 15 days interval
Bitter pit	Mineral imbalance & low level of Ca	Spray Calcium chloride (1%) as aqueous solution 15 days prior to harvest
Die back	Ca deficiency	Use Chaubatia paste
Fuji stain	Storage disorder of Fuji apples	-
Premature leaf fall	N deficiency	-
Black heart	Low temperature	-
Brown heart	CO_2 injury during storage	-
Blue mold	*Penicillium expansum*	-
Scald	Storage disorder	-
Brown core/ Brown heart/ Core flush	Storage temperature at -0.5 to 3.5^{0}C	-
Collar rot	*Phytophthora cactorum*	Poorly drained soils
White root rot	*Dematophora necatrix*	-
Water core	Delayed harvesting (formation of ice crystal & deposition of sorbitol)	Harvest at proper time
Crown gall	*Agrobacterium tumefaciens*	Destroy affected plant parts
Russeting/ cork cambium	*Fluctuating weather conditions especially frost at the blooming time; *High humidity & precipitation during 5-20 days after bloom,; *Low temperature during fruit set; *Pesticide application at high temperature; *Incompatible pesticide mixtures	Gale Gala is highly susceptible; Follow INM practices
Pre harvest fruit drop	-	Spray NAA @ 20 ppm
Premature defoliation/ Marssonina blotch	*Marssonina coronaria* (syn. *M. mali*)	-

38.2 Pear

- Eulogized as 'Gift of God'.
- Most tolerant to wet soils but less tolerant to drought than apple.
- Italy is largest producer of pear.
- Browning of cut pear fruit is due to polygalacturonase activity.
- Major acid: Malic acid.

- Flower colour: White.
- Inflorescence type: Corymbose.
- Flower consists of 5 petals and 20-30 stamens.
- Ovary has 5 locules with 2 ovules per locule.
- Pear genome sequencing was done by China in 2012.
- Sequenced spp.: *P. bretschneideri* (Asian pear group).
- Most of cultivars require chilling at < 7^{0}C for 1200-1500 h.
- Chilling requirement of *P. communis* is more than *P. pyrifolia*.
- Prunacin: Organic compound.
- Spring frosts are detrimental to pear production and temperature at -3 to 3°C or below kills the open blossoms.
- Critical temperature for flowering is 8^{0}C.
- Lowest mean daily temperature to start flowering: 9^{0}C.
- Parthnocarpic fruits lack flavour.
- Presence of gritt cells.
- Commercial propagation : 'T' budding or tongue grafting.
- Optimum soil pH: 6 to 7.5.
- Planting time: June-July to October-November.
- High density planting: 600-2000 trees/ha.
- Planting to be done at every 4th tree in every 4th row as pollinizers are adequate.
- For active growth of pear, soil depth should be 180 cm.
- Training system: Modified central leader.
- Flowering season: February-March.
- Most of the varieties are self sterile (due to gametophytic SI).
- Cultivars grown in hills are partially self fruitful.
- Exhibit vegetative parthenocarpy & produce seedless fruits.
- Maturity index: 135-150 days after full bloom, seed colour and loosening of fruit at the abscission zone.
- Post set availability of more heat units leads to faster rates of development and maturation of temperate fruits under sub-tropical regions.
- Harvesting stage for canning and distant market: Fully mature but firm and green.
- Harvesting time for sub-tropical pear: June-July.
- High N_2 is not suitable: Because incidence of pear psylla and fire blight is more.
- Premature ripening: Pink colouration near blossom end. It is due to night temperature < 7.1 ^{0}C and day temperature < 21^{0}C.
- Cyclohexamide: Prevents ripening in pear.
- Browning is due to presence of polyphenolase.
- Highest lenticels among temperate fruits.

Species:

- Drought of tolerant: *P. elaeagrifolia*, *P. korshinskyi*, *P. syriaca*, *P. heterophylla*.

Name	Botanical name	Derived from and features
Common/ European/ French/ English/ Soft pear	*P. communis*	*P. causasia*; cultivated; flower white & rarely pink; cluster of 4-12; fruits pyriform; resistant to oak root fungus; highly susceptible to fire blight
Japanese/ Oriental/Asian/ Hard pear/ Naspati	*P. pyrifolia* (syn. *P. serotina*)	*P. ussuriensis*; cultivated; poor fruit quality; used for hybridization purpose; commonly grown rootstock in south India; more vigorous rootstock for Bartlett pear than *P. pashia* and *P. pashia* kumaonii; resistant to fire blight, collar rot & powdery mildew (PM)
Chinese/ Pineapple/ Sand pear	*P. sinensis*	Cultivated; fruit has deciduous calyx; greety hard flesh; grown in north Indian plains; used for hybridization & grafting
Wild pear/ Kainth/ Mahal/ Afghan pear	*P. pashia*	Grown as vigorous & woolly aphid resistant rootstock used widely in north India; susceptible to fire blight, collar rot & PM
Snow pear/ Perry pear	*P. nivalis*	Suitable for perry preparation
-	*P. calleryana*	High yielding rootstock for Bartlett pear; resistant to fire blight
Willow leaf pear	*P. salicifolia*	Frost, drought & salt resistant
-	*P. koehnei*	Evergreen
Chinese white pear	*P.* x *bretschneideri*	-
Shiara/ Jarainth	*P. kumaonii*	Large sized fruits; resistant to PM but susceptible to fire blight
Besar	*P. jacquimontiana*	Small roundish brown fruits
Deingloporam	*P. polycarpa*	Small globose fruits; very good rootstock for pear; free from PM & fire blight
-	*P. ussuriensis*	Resistant to cold hardiness

Use of rootstocks:

- Most commonly used clonal rootstock for ultra-dwarfing: EMLA-9, Quince A and Quince C (*Cydonia oblonga*).
- Grafting 'Bartlett' pear on 'Quince' dwarfing rootstock is mostly incompatible: 'Old Home' is better interstock for compatibility.
- Graft incompatibility is overcome by double grafting (i.e. double working) with 'Old Home' or 'Hardy' pear varieties as compatible interstocks.
- Lavi-1 (*P. betulifolia*): Most vigorous & suitable for high temperature.
- D-4 (*P. calleryana*): Most vigorous.
- Old Home (OH) x Farmindale (F333) i.e. OHF series (OHF 87, OHF 97); Pyrodwarf, Pyro-2-33: Semi-dwarf & fire blight resistant

Varieties:

- Most of varieties grown in India were introduced during 1930.
- Patharnakh, Gola: Asian type pear, self fruitful and low chilling (150 chilling h < 7^0C) varieties. Most popular in north India and grown in sub-montainous regions of India. Heavy bearer (150 kg/ tree) with excellent shelf life of 3 weeks at ambient conditions.
- Conference: Require high chilling hours, pyriform shape, late but regular bearer and highly prone to cracking. Recommended for Uttarakhand.
- Jargonella: Triploid.
- Bud sports: 'Starkrimson' from 'Clapp's Favorite'; 'Red Anjou' from 'Anjou' and 'Eldorado' from 'Bartlett'.
- To get early bearing varieties and resistant to fungus and bacterial diseases, follow hybridization in *P. serotina* x *P. betulaefolia*.
- To get hardy varieties, follow hybridization in *P. serotina* x *P. ussuriensis*.

Name	Breeding method	Features
Kieffer	American cv. (French pear x Oriental pear)	Self fruitful; low chilling hours requirement; fruits large; prolific bearer; most popular in Tamil Nadu
Le-Conte	European pear x Oriental pear	Low chilling hours requirement; most popular in Tamil Nadu
Bartlett/ William Bartlett	-	European cv.; most popular all over the world; high chilling hours requirement (1200-1500 h < 7^0C); famous for dry pear slices & canning industry
Max Red Bartlett	Bud sport from 'Bartlett'	Very large fruits; high sugar (8.45%); TSS 14%; most popular in temperate regions (Europe)
Flemish Beauty	-	Extra large fruits; conical shape; self-fertile;TSS 13.5%, aromatic; free from gritt cells; high keeping quality; require high chilling hours; used as pollinizer
GBPUA & T, Pantnagar		
Pant Pear-3 (2000)	Clonal selection	Tree medium sized; pyriform; TSS 15%, thin skin; soft flesh
Pant Pear-17 (2000)	Clonal selection	Tree medium sized; pyriform; TSS 14.5%, thin skin; soft flesh
Pant Pear-18 (2002)	Clonal selection	Early maturing; large round fruits; TSS 13%; juicy flesh
PAU, Ludhiana		
Punjab Nector	Selection	Low chilling; soft flesh; fruit wt. 136 g; yield 80 kg/ tree
Punjab Gold	Selection	Low chilling; soft flesh; fruit wt. 168 g; yield 80 kg/ tree; TSS 14.5%
Punjab Soft	Selection	Soft flesh; fruit wt. 128 g; yield 86 kg/ tree
Punjab Beauty	Selection	Precocious & regular bearer; low chilling; fruit wt. 125 g; TSS 14%; 0.30% acidity; yield 100 kg/ tree

Varieties	Features
Baghu Gosha, Smith & William	Low chilling varieties; irregular & shy bearer; soft fruits; pulp white, sweet & gritty; yield 100 kg/ tree
Pineapple, Hood	Medium chilling varieties
Red Blush	Soft fleshed selection
Early China	Most popular in temperate regions (Europe)
Starkrimson, Clapp's Favorite (red coloured)	Spontaneous mutant
Starkrimson Delicious	Red colour & flavoured variety
Waite, Magness	Pollen sterile cultivars; free from gritt cells
Winter Nellis	Belgian variety; flesh delicious, juicy; regular bearer; better keeping quality; good pollinizer
Thompsons	Yellow skin, fine grained flesh, melting with good aroma; good cropping
Anjou	Introduced from Europe; require high chilling hours; free from storage disorder
Gold Nijisseiki	Gamma irradiated cv. of Asiatic pear 'Nijisseiki'; brown flesh; high resistant to black spot (*Alternaria alternata*); self compatible & eliminate need of pollinator

Intergeneric sterile hybrids:

- Mule: Troth Early Peach x Wild Goose Plum.
- Kamdesa: Peach x Sand Cherry.
- Pyronia: Pear x Quince.

Grading:

Grade	Size (cm)	Wt. (gram)
A	7.2 x 7.2	> 210
B	6.6 x 6.6	> 125
C	6.6 x 6.5	< 122

Diseases and pests:

- Fire blight (*Erwinia amylovora*): Most serious disease caused by bacteria.
- European pear is highly susceptible to fire blight than Oriental pear.
- Oak root fungus (*Armillaria mellea*).
- Pear decline/ Quick decline/ Tree collapse: MLOs. It is transmitted by pear psylla. Occurs due to little leaf. Necrosis of sieve tubes immediately below bud union. Antibiotic solution is infused into tree trunk after harvest & Oxytetracycline hydrochloride is suggested. Use of tolerant rootstock e.g. *P. communis* or *P. beautifolia* is recommended.
- Root rot: Soil borne.
- Crown gall: Clean nursery stock.
- Plum hairy caterpillar: Disfigured fruits.

- Bark eating caterpillar: Nocturnal pest.
- Pear aphids:

Physiological disorders:

- Corky tissue, calyx end rot and blossom blast: B deficiency.
- Black end and cork spot: Ca deficiency.
- Core break down and scald: Storage disorders.
- Core break down or brown heart: Abnormal cool season.
- Pink calyx end/ Pink end: Abnormal cool season preceding harvest.
- White hard end: Unfavorable water conditions/ drought. Caused by *P. pyrifolia* and *P. ussuriensis* rootstocks.
- Christmas tree appearance: Fe deficiency.
- Pear scald: Storage disorder. Due to prolonged holding of fruits in storage and mre common in cv. Conference.

38.3 Peach

- Major producers: Italy, USA, Spain, China, France, Greece, USSR, Japan.
- Most widely adapted temperate fruit to warmer climate.
- Require warmest climate and earliest in flowering among temperate fruits.
- Introduced in India during latter half of 19th century.
- Fruit skin colour yellow orange (xanthophyll); red blush (anthocyanin) and yellow (carotenoid).
- Carotenoid content: White flesh (0.19 to 0.53%), yellow flesh (0.75 to 0.79%).
- Rich in proteins, sugar, minerals and vitamins.
- Predominant acid: Malic acid followed by citric acid and quinic acid.
- Sugar and acid profiles in fruit flesh: Useful in characterizing peach and apricot cultivars.
- Amygdalin: Glycoside present in kernels gives bitter taste.
- Prunacin: Principle cyanogenic glucoside present in pulp.
- Kernel may be sweet or bitter in taste.
- *Prunus* have TSS about 8-13^{0}Brix.
- Oil content in peach seed: 40-50%.
- Kernel contains: Fat (39-55%); protein (23-30%); crude fibre (14.8%), minerals (2.7%).
- Commercial propagation: Tongue or cleft grafting and 'T' or ring budding.
- 'T' budding is done during May-June.

- In plains, grafting is performed during November-January and budding during April-June and September.
- In hills, tongue grafting is done during January-February.
- 'GF' (Grande Ferrade) series of root stocks was developed by Bernhard (1965) by crossing peach and almond.
- Common training system: Vase or open centre in hills.
- Oldest method of training followed: Open centre. If sun light is a limiting factor, plants are trained to open centre.
- High water table is limiting factor for cultivation.
- Acidic and saline soils are unfit for cultivation.
- Preferable soil pH: 5.8 to 6.8.
- Under rainfed conditions, apply fertilizers in one lot 15 days before bud break.
- Peach is very susceptible to Fe deficiency.
- Application of chelated Fe (Fe-EDTA) @ 50 to 250 g around the tree in small holes/ foliar sprays of 0.5-1% $FeSO_4$ trunk injection of 1% Ferrous sulphate or ferric citrate is beneficial.
- Swelling buds injured at -6.5^{0}C due to frost or chilling injury.
- Lowest chilling hours requirement among temperate fruits i.e. Grown at even below -25^{0}C.
- Chilling requirement of sub-tropical (low chilling) peaches: < 500 h i.e. 250-400 h.

Name & chilling hours required (h)	Name & chilling hours required (h)
* Okinawa, Red Ceylon (50);	* Flordasun, Early Amber (310);
* Flordagrande, UF Sun (100);	* Desert Gold, Jewel (350);
* Flordabelle, Flordared (110);	* Gulf Crimson, Gulf Prince, Flordahome, Sunripe (400);
* Flordaprince, Flordaglo, Tropic Beauty (150);	* Sunfire, Ventura (500);
* Spring Time, June Gold (650)	* Flordaqueen, Sun Gold (540)

Nectarine (*P. persica* var. nucipersica): Sunbest (225), UF Royal, UF Queen (250), Sunmist (275), Sundollar (350), Suncoat (375).

- Low chilling peaches are grown in sub-mountaineous regions in Punjab, Haryana and western Uttar Pradesh.
- There is no relationship between inhibitors level (ABA) in dormant floral buds and chilling requirement.
- Training systems: Modified leader, V-shaped Tatura Trellis, High density vase, Pillar, Bengium fench and Two scaffold vase.
- Requires heavy and regular pruning since fruiting occurs laterally.
- In heavy pruning, 3/4th heading back + 40% thinning out is recommended.
- Under temperate conditions, annual growth of 25 to 50% is essential for optimum productivity.

- Components of pruning: Thinning out and heading back of shoots.
- Best time for pruning in hills: Mid winter i.e. mid-December to January end.
- In Julie Elberta, 40 fruiting shoots are retained and each shoot is headed back to 15th node.
- Light pruning i.e. removal of 20-30% linear growth in early years of bearing.
- After 7-8 years, corrective pruning i.e. 3/4th heading back (removal of 70-80% linear expansion growth) followed by selective pruning (heading back of 20-30% linear growth) of 50% fruiting shoots in alternate years.
- Nectarine (*P. persica* var. *nucipersica*): It is genetic variant of common peach from China. It is smooth skinned peach, smaller in size having firm flesh. It is self fertile and short lived tree. They are low in fat, sodium, potassium, niacin, riboflavin, rich in vit. A & C and cholesterol free. It is used as rootstock for peach. In Peru, nectarine is considered as civilized fruit for eating at dinner table due to vinous flavour and aroma.
- Nectarine is 'fuzz-less' (non-pubescent) mutant i.e. arisen spontaneously as bud sport. The expression of a single recessive allele is thought to be responsible for the smooth peel of nectarine fruits. 1st mentioned in America in 1720.
- Kashmir valley: Ideal place for nectarine production.
- Peach is shallow rooted crop.
- Critical stage of irrigation: Fruit development stage.
- Flower colour: Pink.
- Flesh colour shows little influence on sweet/ sour balance.
- Fruit consists of outer portion/ skin, middle portion of ovary wall which becomes fleshy and inner portion which becomes hard and forms stone containing the seed.
- Fleshy mesocarp adhere to stone (cling stone) or separate from it (free stone).
- Mesocarp of melting flesh peaches undergo softening at last stage of ripening.
- Stones from ripe fruits are extracted within 2-3 days of picking.
- Long storage of stones in pulp damages seed/ kernel, making it unfit for germination.
- Stones are stored for 3 months in gunny bags to complete ripening period of embryo for better germination.
- Seed require after ripening process for germination.
- Seed stratification (with moist chilling at 4^{0}C for 2-3 months / thiourea chemical) breaks the seed dormancy.
- Seed viability decreases with each year of storage.
- Seed mature during lag phase of fruit growth.
- Planting distance: 4m x 4m.
- Training systems for HDP: Hedge row (519-889 plants/ha); Tatura trellies (5 m x 1 m= 2,000 plants/ha).
- HDP (5m x 1 m) was developed by Chalmers & Vanden Eude.
- Meadow system: 2m x 1m (5,000 plants/ha).

- To avoid frost/ freeze injuries, blooming period can be delayed by sprays of GA_3/ ethephon @ 200 ppm before leaf fall in spring season.
- About 5% of flowers set and develop fruits to full maturity.
- Excessive fruiting/ cropping cause small sized fruits in prolific bearing varieties.
- For optimum fruit thinning, spray of ethephon @ 300 ppm at petal fall stage is recommended in 'Julie Elberta'.
- In cv. Redhaven peach, ethephon @ 600 ppm is used for fruit thinning 20-30 days after fruit set when fruitlets are 20-25 mm in diameter.
- Hand thinning of fruits at pit hardening stage is equally effective.
- Leaf to fruit ratio of 40:1 and 50:1 coupled with girdling half the bark were found to improve the quality of nectarine.
- Micropropagation: Both scion and stock can be raised by this method.
- *In vitro* propagation from axillary shoots and embryo culture is successful.
- Crop regulation: Criteria for fruit thinning is based on leaf to fruit ratio.
  - 30-40 leaves per fruit is appropriate.
  - Hand thinning at 5-7.5 cm fruit spacing is effective.
  - Flower and fruit thinning is done by hand/ mechanical or chemical means.
  - Chemical thinners used are- CEPA or Ethephon, DNOC, NAA, 2,4,5-T, GA_3 and Thiourea.
- Maturity indices:
  - All peach fruits do not mature simultaneously and harvested in 3-4 pickings.
  - Peak harvesting period for different cvs. in hills is mid-May (Shan-e-Punjab) to mid July (Julie Elberta, Shimizu Hakuto).
  - Days from full bloom to fruit maturity vary (78-127 days); early ripening take 60-70 days, mid-ripening take 80-90 days and late varieties take 100-105 days after fruit set to maturity. E.g. Alexander (86 days), Babcock (122 days), Julie Elberta (101 days), Prabhat and Flordasun (60-70 days).
  - Fruit firmness (measured at shoulder by pressure tester): Pressure value ranges from 8-15 lbs/ sq. inch depending on variety e.g. Early Granade (10.9 lbs/ sq. inch) to Pratap (15 lbs/ sq. inch).
  - Freeness of pit;
  - Ground colour: in yellow fleshed peach, ground colour changes from green to yellow; white fleshed cvs. develop creamy ground colour on maturity.
  - Pit discolouration;
  - TSS : acid ratio.
  - Pulp to stone ratio varies from 12 to 16 in different varieties.
- Yield: 50 to 125 kg (hills). In conventional plantations 7-10 t/ha & in Tatura trellis 23 t/ha.

- Peaches ripen with good flavour and aroma at > 15^{0}C, develops undesirable flavour at 10^{0}C and internal breakdown at very low temperature (4.4^{0}C).
- Alar and ethrel enhances ripening and improve flesh colour.
- Fruits are hydrocooled with water at 10^{0}C.
- Peaches have shorter storage life than most other temperate fruits.
- In cold storage (0-3^{0}C & 80-85% R.H.) free stoned peaches and nectarines can be kept for 2 weeks and cling stone types for 4 weeks.
- Pre-cooled fruits stored at 0^{0}C with 85-90% R.H. for 28-36 days.
- Peaches are freezed in cold storage at -0.9^{0}C.
- In CA storage (5% CO_2 + 1-2% O_2 at 0^{0}C) peaches can be stored up to 42 days.
- Ventilated CFB box size: 28 cm x 20 cm x 5 cm for 2 kg fruits.
- Post harvest application of 1.5% calcium nitrate increases storage life for 6-9 days.
- Weed management: Use of Diuron @ 2-2.5 kg/ha as pre-emergent and Glyphosate @ 1.5 kg/ha as post-emergent herbicide during February-March.

Varieties:

- Prolific bearers: Julie Elberta, Redhaven, Sunhaven, Kanto-5 and Shimizu Hakuto.
- Suncrest, Glo Haven: Developed through clonal selection.
- Stark Earlygo, Stark Early, White Giant, Starking Delicious and Candor: Suitable for mid-hills of Himachal Pradesh.
- Saharanpur, Dawn Rambler, Dawn Rose: Suitable for sub-tropical regions of north India.
- Safeda, Early Cream, SRE-6: Suitable for Tarai regions of Uttar Pradesh.
- Praire Dawn, Praire Rambler and Praire Rose: Suitable for cold areas of dry temperate regions.
- Nectarines: Early Rivers, John Rivers, Lord Napier (white fleshed); Early Bearing, While Eiurge, Pineapple (late bearing); May Fire (cling stone type), Snow Queen (free stone type), Silver Queen, Silver King
- Early Red, Haven: Cold resistant.
- Early Crest, May Crest, Frederica: Most frost hardy.
- Late Red, Summer Red, Nectarine Red Prolific: Suitable for HDP.
- Safeda: Low chilling type; very sweet taste.
- Chinese Cling:
- Minolta 'b' values (indicating yellowness) are lower for white fleshed cultivars.
- Pant Peach-1: Chance seedling selection from population of 'Sharbati'. Red pigmentation on surface; semi-cling stone type.
- Australian Dwarf: Dwarf.
- Male sterile/ self sterile/ self unfruitful varieties: J.H. Hale, Julie Elberta, Halberta.

Varieties	Features
Annaqueen, Charokee, Late Le Grand, Nectared, Sungrand, Sunlite, Sunred (free stone type), Sunrise (cling stone type), Sunripe, Red Gold (syn. Red Nectarine)	Nectarine cvs. suitable for table purpose
Alexander, Babcock, Baifeng, Candor, J.H.Hale, Julie Elberta, Halberta, Cardinal, Red Top, Red Haven, Red Globe, Dixigem	Yellow flesh; free-stone type; suitable for table purpose
Early Grande (introduced from USA), Asahriya	Mid-season variety; low chilling cv.; popular in Uttarakhand; yellow flesh; semi-free stone type; fruit wt. 91 g; fruits ripen in 1st week of May & excellent shipping quality
Flordaprince	Early ripening (60-70 days); yellow flesh; semi-cling stone type; suitable for sub-tropical conditions; yield 100 kg/tree
Alton	Earliest ripening
Early Amber, Flordabelle, Flordared (white flesh & free stone type), Flordagold, Flordaglobe, Flordaking, Flordaqueen, Maravilha, San Pedro, Sungold, Rio Grande, May Gold (cling stone type)	Low chilling varieties & suitable for sub-tropical condition
Flordasun, Shan-e-Punjab	Yellow flesh;freestone type; early ripening; low chilling requirement; suitable for table & canning purpose; suitable for sub-tropical conditions
Sharbati (chance seedling from 'Saharanpur')	White flesh; cling stone type; suitable for dehydration purpose
Partap (TA-170 introduced from USA)	Yellow flesh; fruit wt. 66 g; require low chilling hours; good keeping quality; suitable for sub-tropical conditions
Arm King	Nectarine, yellow flesh & cling stone type; require low chilling hours; self sterile
Elberta, Cresthaven, Junegold, Loring, Camden.	Yellow flesh; cold resistant
Starlite, Scarlet Pearl, Nectar, White Star, Stonyhard, Belle of Georgia	White soft juicy flesh
Khurmani	White soft juicy flesh; cling stone type; suitable for sub-tropical conditions
Red June	Early maturing; popular in Uttarakhand
Paradelux	Late maturing; popular in Uttarakhand
Certex, Halford, Fortuna, Golden Bush, Steuart, Vivian, Veteran	White flesh, sweet & free-stone type; suitable for dehydration purpose

Use of rootstocks:

- Seedling rootstock- Wild Apricot
- *P. davidiana*: Resistant to cold hardiness.
- *P. armeniaca*: Highly resistant to root knot nematode.
- *P. amygdalus*, *P. besseyi*, *P. tomentosa*: Dwarf.
- *P. salicina*: Medium to large sized tree.

Name	Breeding method	Features
GF-557, GF-677, GF 8-1, Cadaman, Barrier 1	Natural hybrid of almond and peach	Widely used rootstocks for peach & almond; resistant to calcareous soils
Behmi (*P. mira*)	Natural hybrid of almond and peach	Cold hardy. Used as rootstock for peach, almond & plum
Sloh	Natural hybrid of almond and peach	Self fertile
Reglindis	Antonovka x *M. floribunda*	Highly resistant to scab, red mite; used for juice purpose
Remo	James Grieve x *M. floribunda*	Highly resistant to scab, PM, fire blight; suitable for juice purpose
Myran	*P. belsiana* x Yunnan	Tolerant to drought, root knot nematode, Verticillium & Armilaria disease
Myrobalan B	-	Resistant to cold, collar rot & nematode
Nemaguard	*P. persica* x *P. davidiana*	Widely used nematode resistant rootstock
Nemared, Flordaguard, Guardian, Shalin, Yunnan		Resistant to root knot nematode
Julior, Penta, Tetra, Rubira	-	Semi-dwarf; tolerant to water logged soil
Titan hybrid	-	Highly vigorous, root knot nematode resistance tolerant of calcareous soils
Redhar	Halehaven x Kalhaven	Bred at USA;
Regal	Harvester x Sure Crop	Self fertile; semi-free stone; yellow flesh; round fruits; resistant to cold & bacterial spot disease
Gala	OP seedling of 'Harvester'	Fruits oval to round shape; yellow flesh & semi-free stone
Glory	La Premiera x L-61-3-5	Self fertile; round shape; yellow flesh & free stone fruits
Prabhat	Sharbati x Flordasun	Very sweet; early maturing; white flesh; semi-cling stone type; low chilling requirement (550 chilling hours.); suitable for sub-tropical condition & dehydration purpose
Sharpe	-	Tolerant to *Armillaia* fungus
Pamirskij-5	-	Resistant to PM

Inheritance of characters:

- Breeding systems followed: Outcrossing, inbreeding and back crossing.

Character (s)	Inheritance pattern
Small fruit, flattened fruit shape, round fruit, low yield	Dominant gene
Flesh colour, fruit size, juicyness, acidity, cold hardiness, chilling, fruit maturity, red colour, fruit firmness & flavour	Polygenic
Flesh colour	White dominant over yellow
Fuzziness of nectarine fruits	Single recessive gene
Powdery mildew	Single dominant gene (*Vr2*)

Pests, diseases and disorders:

- Splitting of fruits: At dorsal and ventral sides at time of pit hardening stage and gum exudes from fruits and becomes unfit for consumption. Heavy rains after long dry spells is one of the cause of this problem.

Name	Causal organism	Cause	Remedy	Remarks
Peach leaf curl/ leaf blister	*Taphrina deformans*	High temperature & high humidity (Wet weather during bud beak & leaf emergence is favorable)	Spray Bordeaux mixture (12:12:100)	Serious fungal disease occurs all over the world
Peach leaf curl aphid	*Brachycadus helichnsyi*		Spray systemic insecticide	Most serious
Fruit fly	*Dacus* spp.	-	Use traps	Destructive pest
Stem borer	*Sphenoptera lafertei*	-	Collection & destruction	-
Twig borer	*Anarsia lineatella*	-	-	-
Root knot nematode	*Meloidogyne incognita*	-	-	-
Root lesion nematode	*Pratylenchus* spp.	-	-	-
Ring nematode	*Criconemella xenoplax*	-	-	-
Dagger nematode	*Xiphinema*	Transmit tomato ring spot & peach rosette viruses	-	-
Peach Short Life Syndrome (PSLS)	Ring nematode	-	Use resistant rootstock e.g. Nemaguard, Nemared, Shalil, Okinawa	-
Wisker's rot	*Rhizopus stolonifer*	Bacterial disease	-	-

Peach-X diesase	i.e. Western X/ Little cherry/ Western X red leaf/ Wilt & decline/ Red leaf/ Peach leaf casting yellow/ Cherry buchskin / Peach yellow leaf fall/ Small bitter cherry	Bacteria & phyto-plasma & transmitted through budding, grafting or leaf hoppers	Inject Oxytetracycline hydrochloride @ 1-2 g/plant in trunk of infected plalnts after fruit harvest and in middle of leaf fall stage	Serious threat; fruit taste is bitter & become unmarketable
Gummosis/ bud blast/ blossom blast/ spur blight/ die back/ twig blight	*Pseudomonas syringae* pv. *syringae*	Bacterial disease	Use Mashobra paste	-
Bacterial spots	*Xanthomonas campestris* pv. *pruni*	Bacterial disease	Spray Tetramycin	All parts affected
Sunscald	Tree trunk & scafflold bracnhes are affected	Very hot summer (temperature >40-45^{0}C) prevailing for 2-3 weeks during May-June	-	Major physiological disorder
Crown gall	Soil borne			Very severe in nursery
Brown rot	*Monilinia* spp.	-	-	All parts affected
Silver leaf	*Stereum purfureum*	-	Uproot & burn	Serious
Woolliness	-	Physiological disorder due to chilling injury	’	-

38.4 Plum

- World leading producer: China.
- European and Japanese plums were introduced in Himachal Pradesh in 1870.
- Prunes: Dried plums having high sugar content without any fermentation at pit.
- World production of prunes is relatively larger than plums.
- Plums stimulate bowl movement.
- Plums contain low Na and high K.
- Prunes juice reduces plasma low density lipoprotein cholesterol significantly compared to grape juice.
- Chilling hours required to break rest period: 700-1000 h <7^{0}C (Japanese plum) and 1000-1200 h < 7^{0}C (European plum).
- Ploidy level of European plum: Hexaploid.
- Commercial propagation: 'T' budding or Tongue grafting on seedling rootstock of peach, plum and apricot. Takes 2 years to produce plants of saleable size.

- Quickest method of propagation: Stenting (scion is grafted on cuttings of non-rooted rootstock).
- Suitable month for tongue grafting (February); Bench grafting (December); Shield budding (May to June).
- Flower colour: Greenish white.
- Anthesis time: 12 noon to 2 PM.
- Anther dehiscence: On day of flower opening & continuous upto next day.
- Peak anther dehiscence time: 11 AM to 10 PM.
- Self fruitful: It should exhibit average 30% fruit setting for commercial fruit production.
- Self-unfruitful varieties set only 1-2% fruit which is insufficient and need pollinizers.
- Japanese varieties are mostly self unfruitful and require pollination.
- It is recommended to plant every 3rd tree in every 3rd row with pollinizers.
- Fruit set can be improved with GA_3 @ 50-100 ppm on 10th day after full bloom.
- Extent of natural cross pollination: 3-16.6%.
- Pollination agents: Honey bees and insects.
- Pollen fertility: 56.2 to 83.2%.
- Pollen germination: 4.3 to 70.2%.
- Planting time: December to January.
- Training system for Japanese plums: Open centre system- an oldest system.
- Modified central system: Most commonly followed in India for upright growing.
- Pruning: Spur pruning, light pruning with heading back of branches or pinching during dormant season.
- Fruit thinning agents: NAA @ 25-75 ppm (Japanese plum), Ethephon (200 ppm) and Carbaryl (100 ppm), DNOC, 3-CPA.
- Japanese plum needs frequent pruning and fruit thinning (25-40% fruits) due to heavy crop.
- Maturity indices:
  - Colour development;
  - Flesh colour changes in prunes (yellow green to amber);
  - Flesh firmness (varies from 5.7 to 6.5 kg);
  - Days from full bloom (reliable index);
  - TSS at maturity: 12.5° Brix (European) and 17° Brix (Italian).
- Brix (22°) and pulp consistency (without skin): Best indicators of fruit maturity for drying.
- Fruits are harvested with stalk intact.
- Yield: 60-70 kg/ tree.

- Storage: 2-4 weeks at 0^0C with 85-90% R.H.
- Clean basin + permanent sod in orchard: Most common practice of floor management.
- Self incompatibility in plum is governed by polygenes.

Grading systems per AGMARK:

Grade	Fruit size (mm)	No.of layers	No.of fruits/layer	Box size (cm)
Special	42 and above	3	28-32	37 x 16.5 x 16.5
Grade I	36-42	4	38-43	37 x 16.5 x 16.5
Grade II	Below 36	4	50-56	37 x 16.5 x 16.5

Species:

- Most of European/ cultivated plums belong to *Prunus domestica* (*P. cerasifera* x *P. spinosa*).
- Most of the varieties grown in India belong to *P. salicina* (Japanese) group.
- Section *Euprunus* e.g. *P. domestica*, *P. insititia*, *P. cerasifera*, *P. spinosa*.
- Section *Prunocerasus* e.g. *P. americana*. *P. nigra*, *P. hortulana*, *P. munsoniana*, *P. maritima*, *P. subcordata*, *P. besseyi*.
- Easy crossability between all plum groups and many wild species.

Name	Botanical name	Origin & use
European plum	*P. domestica*	Europe; hexaploid (2n=6x=48)
Damson plum	*P. insititia*	Europe &Western Asia; used as rootstock
Cherry or Myrobalan plum	*P. cerasifera*	Europe &Western Asia; most commonly used as rootstock in India
Japanese plum	*P. salicina*	China; diploid (2n=2x=16)
American plum	*P. americana*	North America; used as rootstock
Simon plum	*P. simony*	North America; used as rootstock

Distinguishable characters:

European plum	Japanese plum
Tree bark smooth & grey	Rough even in young
Leaves- thick, glossy green & pale green underneath have pubescence	Free of pubescence
Leaves have coarsely serrated margin with notched or saw tooth fashion	Medium sized & sharp pointed leaves

Use of rootstocks:

- Recommended rootstock in India: Wild apricot seedlings called '*Zardalu*' (*chuli*) (for sandy loam soils), Kabul Green Guage (for heavy soils).
- Recommended clonal rootstocks for plums: Myrobalan B (more graft success with Satsuma and Santa Rosa cultivars than *P. salicina* and *P. americana*).

- Myrobalan 5-2: Drought tolerant rootstock.
- *P. japonica*: Standardized as a dwarfing rootstock for apricot, peach, plum, almond.
- Ultra dwarfing rootstock: *P. subordata* e.g. Pixy.

Name	Breeding method	Features
Marianna	*P. domestica* x *P. munsoniana*	Better rootstock for heavy soil; resistant to nematodes
Marianna-2624	OP seedling of 'Marianna'	Drought tolerant rootstock
St. Julien	*P. insititia*	Most versatile rootstock
Pixy	Selection from St. Julien	Ultra dwarf rootstock
Damas (GF-1809)	*P. domestica* x *P. spinosa*	Better rootstock for heavy soil

Varieties:

- Luther Burbank: Famous plum breeder.
- Fast track plum breeding started to reduce juvenile period.
- Most of varieties grown in India are partially self fruitful.
- 'Suppressed climacteric' varieties are found in plum.
- More sucker producing cvs.: Ackermann, Nancy-64, Nancy-104.
- Satsuma: Mid-season hybrid.
- EC-34052: Introduction from Kenya and had prolific bearing.
- Honey Sweet: Transgenic.
- Californian SI cvs.: Black Star, Black Gold, Black Diamond, Angeleno.
- Titron: Self fruitful, fruits medium sized with deep purple colour & very thin skin, yield 25-30 kg/ tree. Yield improves if pollinated with 'Alucha Early Round'.
- Pant Plum-1: Seedling selection from GBPUA & T, Pantnagar in 1993. Dwarf, yellow coloured, sub-acidic fruits and dwarfing rootstock.
- Alu Bokhara: Self unfruitful with 'Howe' as pollinizer. Fruits large, yellow coloured, sweet taste.
- Alu Bokhara Peshawari: Selection. Large fruits of 23.5 g; TSS: acid ratio 11.08; free-stone type; pink coloured flesh; TSS 13.3^0 Brix; free from sourness near pit.
- Kala Amritsari: Popular in Punjab. Fruits medium weighing 13 g; round, dark brown at maturity. Pulp is yellow mod. Juicy & excellent for jam making. Self pollinated but improves yield if pollinated with 'Titron'.
- Sutlej Purple: Earliest in market. Self incompatible & must be interplanted with 'Kala Amritsari' as pollinizer. Fruits big (28 g), crimson coloured; thick pulp; yield 30 kg/tree with excellent shipping quality.
- Damson plum: Fruits medium sized, thick skin, yellow coloured & very juicy. Yield 40 kg/ tree.
- Alucha Black: Fruits small sized, dark purple coloured & late ripening. Self incompatible & interplanted with 'Titron'.

- Howe: Fruits large, round, sweet & juicy. Yield 35 kg/ tree.
- Kataru Chak: Partially self-fruitful. Fruits large sized, purplish with creamy flesh; suitable for jam & squash making. 'Kala Amritsari' is used as pollinizer.
- Jamuni Meeruti: Fruits small sized, dull yellow, thin skinned with soft melting flesh; yield 28 kg/tree.
- Peshawari Kala: Shy bearer, Fruits black coloured with thin skin.
- Late Yellow: Fruits round shaped, sweet & juicy. Yield 25 kg/ tree.
- Fla-12: Seedling selection in 1999. Exotic type. large fruits; Ripen one week after Titron or Jamuni.

Suitable for	Varieties
For mid-hills of north-western Himalaya	Santa Rosa (Japanese plum hybrid; self fruitful), Au Amber, Red Stce
European plums	President, Victoria, Kabul Green Guage (self unfruitful)
Japanese plums	Beauty, Mariposa
Sub-tropical plums	Jamuni, Meeruti, Kataru Chak, Alubukhara, Alpha
Self fruitful/ pollinizers	Beauty, Mariposa
Self unfruitful	Kelsey, Eldorado, Wickson, Larado, Formosa

Interspecific hybrids:

- Plumcots/ Apriplums (Plum x Apricot): 1st generation hybrids. Name was given by Luther Burbank.
- Plouts (Plum x Apricot x Plum): Later generations of hybrid those are genetically ¼th (25%) apricot and ¾th (75%) plum. They were developed in the late 20th century by F. Zaiger.
- Apriums (Apricot x Plum x Apricot): These are genetically ¼th plum and ¾th apricot.
- Santa Rosa (*P. salicina* x *P. simonii* or *P. americana*):
- Au Rosa (Santa Rosa x Starcher): Self incompatible, highly resistant to bacterial wilt, almond leaf scorch, bacterial canker and black knot of cherry. Suitable for mid-hills of north-western Himalaya.
- Queens land Bellerosa (Burbank x Santa Rosa): Resistant to bacterial spot of peach (*Xanthomonas campestris* pv. *pruni*).

Complex hybrids	Varieties
Plumcots	Dinosaur Egg, Eagle Egg, Amigo, Tropical Plumana, Crimson Sweet, Sweet Treat, Summer Punch, Tropical Sunrise, King Kong
Plouts	Emerald Drop, Flavor Delight, Flavor Fall, Flavor Finale, Flavor Heart, Flavor Jewel, Flavor King, Flavor Prince, Flavor Queen, Flavor Rich, Flavor Rosa, Flavor Royal, Raspberry Jewel, Red Ray, Splash
Apriums	Cot-N-Candy, Tasty Rich Apriums

Pests, diseases and disorders:

- Leaf curl aphid (*Brachycaudus helichrysi*):
- San Jose Scale (*Quadrapidiotus perniciosus*):
- Plum scale (*Eulecanium* spp.):
- American plum weevil/ Plum curculio (Conotrachelus nenuphar): Cause irreparable damage to a fruit. Most active during spring time.
- Defoliating and fruit eating beetles:
- Bark eating caterpillar:
- Brown rot (*Monolinia* spp.)
- Powdery mildew (*Podosphaera pxycanthae*):
- Black knot of cherry (*Apiosporina morbosa*):
- Almond leaf scorch (*Xylella fastidiosa*):
- Bacterial canker (*Pseudomonas syringae*):
- Leaf canker (*Chandroetoreum purpureum*):
- White root rot (*Rosellinia necatrix*):
- Whisker's rot (*Rhizopus stolonifer*):
- Major problem in temperate cultivars: Plum pox virus and heavy bearing.
- Major problem in tropical cultivars: Sun burn.
- Misshapen fruits: B deficiency.
- Sourness near the pit: Serious drawback of Indian plums.

38.5 Cherry

- Cultivated globally.
- Sour cherry is known to Greek and Romans in 300 BC.
- Cherry growers in the world: Turkey, USA and Iran with production levels of 8.23, 4.47 and 3.03 lakhs metric tonnes, respectively in 2018.
- India ranks 34th in world cherry production.
- India's production ranges around 10-15 thousand mt.
- It is grown under rainfed conditions in India.
- J & K, H.P. and U.P. contribute significant part in production.
- Medicinal value: Reduce inflammation, blood pressure, uric acid levels and various infections.
- World's leading breeding institute: John Innes Horticultural Institution, Merton.
- Sour cherry is long lived, deciduous and self fertile tree grows upto 8 m height.
- Sweet cherry is long lives, deciduous, tall (10 m height) & intersterile.

- Fruits of sour cherry are 2 cm in size, with short stalk, deep crimson to balck coloured, more acidic in taste with slightly sweet flavour & rich in vit. A.
- Sour cherry fruits are useful for culinary purposes & to make pies, tarts, jams and cakes.
- Sweet cherry fruits are spherical, 2 cm in size, hang in groups along fruiting branches.
- Sensitive to frost and waterlogging.
- Grows best in coolest climate at altitude of 2000-2700 m MSL.
- Highest chilling requirement (1000-1500 h) among temperate fruits.
- Blossom is very sensitive to spring frost.
- High rainfall during flowering results in heavy blossom wilt.
- Heavy rains at time of fruit ripening causes fruit cracking.
- Optimum soil pH for cultivation: 6.5-7.0.
- It has more calorific value than apple.
- Fruits are low in calories and high in anti-oxidants.
- Fruits are earlist in market and highly perishable among temperate fruits.
- Can be grown near walnut, owing to its tolerance to juglone toxicity.
- Sour cherry is grown as companion crop with sweet cherries.
- Cherry seeds have great satanic power.
- Flavour of cherry juice: Methyl anthranilate and methyl salicylate.
- Colouring compound of cherry skin: Keracyanin chloride.
- Bitter taste: Amygdalin.
- Type of SI: Gametophytic.
- Most varieties are intersterile i.e. self as well as cross incompatibility is reported.
- Pollination problem in sweet cherry is very complex.
- Most of the sour cherries are self compatible while most sweet cherries are self sterile as well as cross incompatible.
- Varieties with same sterility allele if planted together will not set fruits and need another variety having different sterility allele for better fruit set.
- Sweet cherries have mixed parentage due to continuous selection and cross breeding.
- Duke cherry is self incompatible but cross pollination with sweet/ sour cherry improves fruit set.
- *S*-allele genotypes of sweet cherry cv. Lambert are S_3S_4.
- For better pollination, 2-3 bee hives/ ha is recommended.
- Propagation methods: Layering, cutting, grafting.
- Seedling rootstocks used for sweet cherry in India.
- Common method of clonal rootstock multiplication: Mound or stool layering.
- Tongue (whip) grafting time: February-March gives 90% success.

- Scion wood is dormant in winter and can be stored at 2-4^{0}C.
- Planting system: Contour or terrace system of planting in hilly areas and square system in valley areas.
- Planting distance: 4m x 4m to 6m x 6m. Rectangular system. Sweet cherry (10m x 14m) and Sour cherry (7m x 10m). On 'Colt' rootstock 4m x 4m in H.P.
- Planting season: December-January.
- Common training system: Modifed leader system i.e. fan like structure.
- Fruits are borne laterally on spurs of 1 year old shoots.
- Cherry need corrective pruning rather than too much heading back.
- Spur renewal pruning is adopted.
- Reckless pruning encourages gumming.
- Vegetative growth and fruit development occurs simultaneously.
- Sour cherries are more tolerant to poor drainage than sweet cherries.
- Avoid heavy soils as cherry plants are sensitive to water stagnation/ logging.
- Weeding: Diuron @ 4 kg/ ha as pre-emergence & Paraquat @ 0.5% as post emergent herbicide is recommended.
- Clean basin management with sod culture is required.
- Green manuring crops are grown to improve soil texture and fertility.
- Sod culture is most important cultural operation.
- Most commonly used sod crops: Rye, Vetch, Buckwheat, Oats and millets.
- Harvesting season: Spring (mid May to 1st week of July) under Indian conditions.
- Harvesting:
  - Early harvesting results in falt fruit with less yields.
  - Delayed or harvesting of over ripened cherries results in loss in weight, volume and quality.
  - Colour development, TSS and flavour are maturity indices for harvesting of fruits.
- Yield: 15-20 kg/ tree.
- Fruits are packed in 5 kg CFB boxes.
- Storage: Room temperature (17-23^{0}C) for 4 days and at 0^{0}C for 14 days.
- Cherry wine: Kirschwasser.
- Cherry cordial: Maraschinos.

Species:

Name	Botanical name	Uses
Mazzard cherry	*Prunus avium*	Putative ancestor; best & commercial rootstock for sweet cherry; dwarf; very difficult to root under *in vivo* condition; bear large sized & rich flavoured black fruits; popular in Europe & America;

Sweet cherry/ Gean/ Bird cherry	*P. avium*	Valuable fruit in central Europe & used for liqueurs; mostly used for table purpose; more sensitive to heat & cold than sour type
Sour or Morello cherry	*P. cerasus* syn. *P. acida* (*P. avium* x *P. fruticosa*)	Mostly used for canning or cooking
Duke or Royal cherry	*P. gudouini* (*P. avium* x *P. cerasus*)	Tetraploid (2n=4x=32) cherry hybrid; more hardy having sour cherry (Morllo) blood; fruits round to oblong, highly acidic; self compatible but cross pollination with sweet/sour cherry improves fruits set; intermediate in both tree & fruit characteristics
Mahaleb/ Perfumed cherry/ St. Lucie Cherry	*P. mahaleb*	Most drought tolerant rootstock; suited to deep & well drained loams; popular in Europe & America
Wild bird cherry	*P. padus*	Used as rootstock; fruits for culinary purpose & as ornamental
Paja	*P. cerasoides*	Mostly commonly used rootstock for sweet cherry; show symptoms of delayed incompatibility
Bush cherry	*P. japonica*	Dwarfing rootstock for apricot, peach, plum, almond, cherry
-	*P. cornuta*	Better rootstock of cherry than 'Paja'

Use of rootstocks:

- Seeds of 'Paja' don't require chilling treatment to break dormancy.
- Seeds of Mahaleb and Mazzard require stratification before sowing. Seeds soaked in 500 ppm GA_3 for 24 h and stratified at 2-4^{0}C for 80-120 days for 'Mahaleb' and 120-150 days for 'Mazzard' to break seed dormancy. As embryonic roots comes out from seed coat, seedlings are transplanted in nursery beds at 10-15 cm x 20-25 cm spacing.
- Meristem cultured on MS medium with concentrated BAP and IBA gives good multiplication and rooting, respectively.
- *P. besseyi*, *P. pumila*, *P. pennsylvanica*: Rootstock purpose and fruits used as ornamental.
- *P. tomentosa*, *P. pseudo-cerasus*: Fruits used as ornamental. Rootstock used in Japan and Asian countries.

***Clonal rootstocks*:**

Name	Features
GiSel-A-5, GiSel-A-6	Dwarf; cold hardy
Colt (*P. avium* x *P. pseudocerasus*)	Originated from UK; semi-dwarf; compatible; easy to root; can be multiplied by cuttings; resistant to gummosis, crown rot, stem pitting,root rot, bacterial canker & viruses; highly susceptible to oak root fungus
Charger	Semi-dwarf; resistant to root rot & canker
Mazzard F-12/1	Originated from UK; semi-vigorous but difficult to root; tolerant to canker, recommended for H.P.
SL-64 (Sainte Lucie)	Originated from France known as Mahaleb;
Weiroot-10	Vigorous

Varieties:

- Incompatible group of varieties: Bedford Prolific, Black Downton, Black Eagle, Black Tartarian, Black Rivers.
- 1st commercial self-fertile sweet cherry: Stella which require 200-250 chilling h. having dark red fruits.
- Gean type ahs softer flesh & variety called 'Bigarreau' has crisp texture.
- Sweet cherry varieties are divided into two groups:
    1. Heart group: Heart shaped fruit having soft & tender flesh, colour of fruits varies from dark with reddish juice to light coloured with colourless juice.
    2. Bigarreau group: Fruits roundish, colour of fruit & juice varies from dark to light red.
- Planting of universal donor pollinizers (Stella, Vista, Vic, Seneca and Vega) gives fruit set provided their flowering period overlaps.
- New introductions as pollinizers: Bing, Lapinus.
- CITH-Cherry-03 [selection from Double (Bigarreau Napolean)], CITH-Cherry-05 [selection from Misri (Bigarreau Noir Grossa)], CITH-Cherry-07 (Clonal selection from Misri).
- Merton (Very late flowering); Morello (Good pollinizer).
- Several varieties in colours ranging from yellowish pink to dark red are grown.
- Sweet cherry varieties grown in J & K, H.P. and U.P.: Bedford Prolific, Black Heart, Black Tertarian, Black Republican, Chico Beauty, Early Purple, Early Rivers, Ebony, Flogmore Early, Governor's Wood, Pink Early, Royal Ann (most popular), Sue (resistant to fruit cracking), Victor, Waterloo, White Heart, Yellow Spanish.
- Sour cherry:
    - Light coloured: Early Richmond, Montmorency.
    - Dark coloured: English Morello, Flemish Red, Louis Phillipe.
- Sour cherry varieties viz. Red Morello, Amarelle, Kentish Red and Flemish were grown before 2nd World war.
- Duke cherries: Ronald's Late Duke, Royal Duke, May Duke, Arch Duke (Very early, fruits ripen before longest days), Arch Duke.
- Popular varieties propounded by NAFED: Makhmalli and Mishri.
- Self fruitful: Early Richmond, Montmorency, Wilson Delicious, Compact Lambert.
- Resistant to fruit cracking: Windsor, Victor, Van (pollinizer).
- New varieties: Sam (resistant to fruit cracking), Summit, Sunburst, Compact Stella, Lapins.

Pests, diseases and physiological disorder:

- Cherry black fly (*Myzus cerasi*):

- Fruit fly (*Rhagoletis cerasi*): Use of lures or traps. Spray contact insecticide.
- Leaf spot: Most serious in sour cherry.
- Brown rot: Hot and humid conditions.
- Bacterial canker:
- Blossom of cherry is very much susceptible to frost and wind.
- Heavy rainfall during flowering causes: Blossom wilt.
- Most common deficiency: Abnormal reduction in fruit size (Zn); intervenial chlorosis (Mg).
- Dormant bud blast.
- Fruit cracking: B deficiency.

38.6 Apricot

- Eulogized as 'Coppery or Brass coloured fruit or Khubani or Armenian plum or *Zardalu'*.
- Productivity: Austria (28 T/ha), Slovenia (17 T/ha), USA (15 T/ha), India (4.16 T/ha).
- Highly perishable fruit.
- Planting density and cultivars play an important role in productivity.
- Commercially grown at varying elevations in warmer regions of India.
- Suitable crop for cold desert of cold arid zone.
- Hardy, drought resistant, salt tolerant, self pollinated temperate fruit.
- Most delicious and highly perishable among temperate fruits.
- Laetrile, a purported alternative treatment for cancer is extracted from apricot seeds.
- Used for treatment of tumors and ulcers.
- Fruit contains 84% flesh and 16% stone.
- Low temperature is limiting factor for proper flowering and fruiting.
- Minimum temperature require for flowering: 6°C.
- Chilling requirement: <7°C for 300-900 h.
- Total duration of flowering: 28 days.
- Fruiting intensity: 0 to 43.9 fruits/ meter length of shoot.
- It is rich source of protein and kernel oils (40-45%).
- Kernel oil: Rich in linolenic and linoleic acid.
- Seed fibre content: 350-815 mg/100 g.
- Vitamin A: 3600 IU and thiamine: 217 mg/ 100g.
- Wild apricot or *zardalu* is originated from India.
- Edible portion: Mesocarp and endocarp.
- Training systems: Open vase system.

- Apricot bears on spurs and laterally on 1 year old shoots.
- Apricot spurs life: 3-4 years.
- Ideal thinning agent: NAA @ 25-50 ppm 20 days after fruit set.
- Commercial propagation: T-budding.
- Rootstock used: Plum (for light soil); Peach (for heavy and wet soil).
- Training system: Modified central leader.
- Planting distance: 3.5m x 3.5 m or 5m x 5m.
- Highly sensitive to waterlogging.
- Maturity month: May to June.
- Ideal stage for freezing, canning and drying: Fully ripe fruits.
- Destoned fruits are treated with lye treatment (i.e. 0.2% NaOH for 2 min.) followed by dipping in clean water for 5 min.
- Post harvest losses: 60%.

Species:

- *P. mune, P. brigantica.*
- Black or purple apricot (*P. dasicarpa*): Genetic hybrid between Apricot (*P. cerasifera*) x plum (*P. armeniaca*); self sterile. Grown in Kashmir valley.
- Chulli or Wild apricot (*P. armeniaca*): Smooth skinned. Commercially used as rootstock for apricot and plum.

Varieties:

- Hybridization breeding program was started in 1969 at Chaubattia.
- Moor Park: One of the best apricot for outdoor cultivation in small garden.
- Cebasred, Primorosa: Self compatible, resistant to Plum Pox virus and very early ripening.
- Jojo: 1st completely Plum Pox virus resistant cv. of *P. domestica*obtained by conventional breeding from Germany.
- Late maturing varieties from New Zealand: Cluthaster, Cluthalate.
- Less chilling (sub-tropical) requirement varieties: New Castle, Early Shipley, St. Ambroise, Kaisha, Shakarpara, Raktchey Karpu.
- For kitchen garden purpose: Nugget, Farmingdale, Royal.
- For processing and value added products: Khantey (dehydrated), Raktchey Karpu (max. ascorbic acid 11.2 mg/ 100g), Afghani (beverage), Nari (sweetest i.e. TSS 29.8^{0}Brix & best for beverage making), Australian, Charmagz (kitchen garden purpose), Halman (low chilling requirement; best dried product & rich in carotenoid 8.56 mg/ 100g), CITH Apricot-D1, CITH Apricot-D2, CITH Apricot-D3, Turkey, Harcot, Erani.

Name	Breeding method	Features
Benazir	Introduced from Pakistan	Prolific bearer; fruits ripen in first fortnight of May
Flavor Cot	-	New variety developed in USA
Nugget	Hybrid	-
Zardalu (syn. wild apricot)	Selection	Indigenous to India; widely cultivated for oil; used for culinary purposes
Directorate of Horticulture & Food Processing, Chaubattia, Uttarakhand		
Chaubatia Alankar (1984)	(Kaishu x Charmagz) bud wood irradiation with gamma rays	Low chilling required; regular bearer; early ripening; good keeping quality
Chaubatia Madhu (1984)	(Turkey x Charmagz) bud wood irradiation with gamma rays	Early ripening; Low chilling required; regular bearer
Chaubatia Kasri (1984)	(St. Ambroise x Charmagz) bud wood irradiation with gamma rays	Early ripening; Low chilling required; mid-season ripening; regular bearer

Diseases and disorders:

- Black heart/ Verticillium wilt (*Verticillium lecanii*): Fungal disease.
- Brown rot (*Monilinia fructicola*) in apricot is more in areas with high R.H.
- Sharka: Plum Pox Poty virus. Severe threat to apricot industry in France.
- Dormant bud blast.
- Pit burn: Exposure to high temperature before harvest.
- Gel breakdown: Chilling injury.
- Apoplexy: Due to low temperature.

38.7 Almond

- Largest producer: USA, Spain, Syria.
- India's productivity: 0.73 T/ha.
- Cultivation restricted between countries lying 30^0N and 45^0S of equator.
- Highest calorific value: 597 Cal/ 100 g.
- Contains oleic acid 62%, linoleic acid 24% and palmitic acid 6%.
- Edible portion: Kernel or cotyledon.
- Kernel contains 20.8% protein, 59.8% fat and 10.5% carbohydrates &rich source of vit. E.
- Its use in diet increases high density lipo-proteins.
- Taste of kernels (sweet or bitter): Qualitative trait.

- Bitter taste of almond: High amygdalin glycoside ($C_{20}H_{27}O_{11}N$) content of 2.5 to 3.5%.
- On enzymatic hydrolysis, amygdalin releases hydrocyanic acid, which is poisonous & render bitter kernels unfit for consumption.
- It contains 49% oil.
- Oil extracted from bitter kernels is used in pharmaceutical and cosmetic industry.
- Type of fruit: Drupe (fleshy, one seeded, indehiscent fruit with seed enclosed in stony endocarp) with a leathery peri-mesocarp (called as hull) that encloses the hard endocarp.
- Peri-mesocarp splits on one side & exposes the endocarp at maturity.
- Major constraint in cultivation: Damage to blossom due to early spring frosts.
- Lowest chilling hours (<5°C for 90-427 h) requirement among temperate fruits e.g. Achak (266 h), Ramillete (326 h), Marcona (435 h).
- Almond can withstand temperature of -2.2 to -3.0°C for short time.
- Abrupt rise in day temperature by 3-5°C and gusty winds in February-March results in gynoecial abnormalities and very poor fruit set in almonds, high chill varieties of plum and Baghugosha variety of pear in Ludhiana.
- Pollination agents: Honey bees and bumble bees.
- Best flower stage for emasculation: Popcorn stage.
- Planting systems: Square or hexagonal.
- Planting distance: 4m x 4m (HDP) accommodates 400 plants/ha.
- Every 3rd row is planted with pollinizer variety or accession.
- For better fruit set, blooming time of pollinizers must coincide with blooming time of main varieties.
- Recommended bee hives for effective pollination: 5-8.
- Flowering: a) Early bloomers (flowering in 1st week of March); b) Late bloomers (flowering in 2nd week of April); c) Mid bloomers (flowering in between above two extremes).
- Cultivated almond is self sterile due to gametophytic SI.
- Self sterility make the cross pollination pre-requisite for fruit set.
- It is self as well as cross incompatible.
- Cross incompatible combinations: Jordanella x Nonpareil; Nonpareil x IXL.
- Sweet almond scions can be successfully grafted on bitter almond and peach.
- Whip/ tongue grafting: Performed to convert senile trees into productive one during February-March.
- 'T' or Shield budding time: July to August.
- Training system: Central modified leader system.
- Bears fruits on short spurs which remains fruitful for 5-6 years.

- Pruning: is done to replace 1/5th of fruiting wood every year & new spur growth is generated.
- Less vigorous & older trees need severe pruning by heading back large lateral limbs & thinning out of smaller & weak wood.
- Unwanted water sprouts & suckers from rootstocks need to be removed annually.
- Split application of nutrients, 3 weeks after fruit set & during fruit development stage in June-July is essential.
- Pollen viability: 30.5-73%.
- Harvesting: July-August and at higher elevations in September.
- Fruit shedding by blowing winds is severe problem.
- Maturity index: Hull colour change from green to yellowish with splitting of suture from pedicel end.
- Nuts are harvested by knocking the limbs with long wooden poles.
- Green unripe fruits are used for pickling, cooking or for direct consumption.
- Hull remains tight in prematured nuts & require more energy to dislodge the nuts.
- Hull: Leathery peri-mesocarp that encloses hard endocarp.
- Term 'dehulling' is related to almond.
- Almonds are categorized into 'Ment and Huller'.

Varieties:

- Cultivated almond/ bitter almond (*P. amygdalus*): Natural hybrid of *P. fenzaliana* x *P. bucharica*.
- Sweet kernels originated in these plants by mutation.
- Almond hybridization program was started at PAU, Ludhiana in 1970 to evolve cultivars for sub-tropical condition.
- Two types:
  - Bitter: Grown in Kashmir.
  - Sweet: Imported in India from Afghanistan.
- Suitable for high hills in India: California Paper Shell (introduced, bold nuts of 2.1 g, yield 3.8 kg/tree), Pethick's Wonder (introduced, bold nuts of 2.5 g, yield 3.7 kg/tree), Drake, Fritz (polyembryonic), JK-39, JK-55 (selection, earliest ripening, yield 3.5 kg/tree), JK-57, Monterey,NB-258, Primorskij, Ruby, Sonora (polyembryonic).
- Polyembryonic: Price, Carmel, Padre, Butte.

Name	Breeding method	Features
SKUAST, Srinagar		
Mukhdoom (1995)	Clonal selection	Medium nut; semi-soft shelled; regular bearer; plumpy; shelling 38-40%; shell yield 5 q/ha; popular in India; suitable for J & K and high hills

Parbat (1995)	Clonal selection	Mid-bloomer; shelling 49%; shell yield 5 q/ha; popular in India; suitable for J & K and high hills
Waris (1995)	Clonal selection	Mid-bloomer; regular bearer; soft shelled; shell yield 6-7 q/ha; popular in India; suitable for J & K and high hills
Shalimar (1995)	Clonal selection	Mid-bloomer; regular bearer; white nuts; high shelling ability; shell yield 6-7 q/ha; suitable for export; popular in India; suitable for J & K & high hills
IXL	Introduction	Regular bearer, high shelling %; popular in India; suitable for J & K and high hills
Nonpareil	Introduction	Polyembryonic, possess thin outer shell, smooth skin, easy to blanch, high kernel quality, best & widely adapted, 3-5 t/ha; popular in India; suitable for J & K and high hills
Pranyaj	Introduction	Regular bearer, suitable for HDP in India
Texas (syn. Mission)	Introduction	Polyembryonic & late blooming; suitable for dry temperate zone
Merced	Introduction	Thin outer shell; popular in India; suitable for J & K & high hills
Jordanolo	Introduction	Popular in India; suitable for J & K and high hills
PAU, Ludhiana		
Almond Hybrid-15	Pedigree selection from 'Thin Shelled x Sloh'	Bold nuts; nut wt. 1.7 g; yield 3.7 kg/ tree.
Hybrid H-258	Pedigree selection from'Tethick's Wonder x Sloh'	Self compatible
Hybrid-98	Pedigree selection from'Bruce x Sloh'	High yield & good kernel quality
Other varieties		
Peerless	,	Polyembryonic; suitable for lower hills
Ne-Plus Ultra	-	Most popular & used as pollinizer; popular in India; suitable for dry temperate zone
Supernova	Mutant	Bred in Italy; late flowering & self compatible
Katha, Dhebar, Drake	-	Self fruitful & used as pollinizer; suitable for lower hills

Use of rootstocks:

- Rootstock used: Kabul Green Gauge (dwarf).
- Nemaguard, Bitter almond, Marianna 2624: Most widely used.
- Peach-almond hybrids- Titan, Hansen
- Complex hybrids- Viking.

Grades:

- Shelling % = Weight of nut ÷ Wt. of kernel x 100.

On the basis of shell thickness-

- Papper shelled: Can be shelled by hand. 33-56% shelling.
- Thin shelled: Shelled by light stroke. 22-42% shelling.
- Thick shelled: Required repeated hammering. 18-39% shelling.

- **On the basis of unmarketable nuts:**
- Katha: Thick shelled (0.20-0.30 cm) nuts.
- Teeth: Bitter nuts.
- Ralla: Mixture of several nut types.

Inheritance pattern:

- Blooming time: Polygenic trait with heritability factor of 0.83.
- Self incompatibility: Dominant gene.
- Self fertility: Recessive.
- Bitterness: Monogenic recessive.
- Sweetness: Monogenic dominant.

Pests, diseases and disorders:

- Root knot nematode (*Meloidogyne incognita*): Cause root knot, defoliation & drying of trees.
- Leaf curling (*Brachycaudus belichryis*): Caused due to aphid.
- Green peach aphid (*Myzus persicae*): Attack on tender leaves & floral buds. Deformed flowers cause no fruit set or set fruit drop off prematurely.
- Stem borer (*Aeolestathus sarta*) andShot hole borer (*Scolytoplatypus* spp.): Common pest make big holes (3.5 cm dia.) on stem & pin heads hoies on branches results in die back.
- Twig borer (*Anarsia lineatella*):
- Indian meal moth (*Plodia interpunctata*): Noxious pest of stored nuts and shelled out kernels.
- Shot hole (*Coryneum beijerinkii* or *Clasterosporium carpophilum*): Fungal disease affects leaves & reduce photosynthetic efficiency and affect nut yield.
- Non-infectious bud failure or Mule tail or Crazy top: Genetic disorder transmitted by vegetative propagation and through seeds. This disorder results in failure of vegetative buds.
- Gummosis on fruits: Gum deposit on perimesocarp makes dehulling difficult, spoil taste of kernels. Due to Mo deficiency.

38.8 Strawberry

- Known as 'Artificial or Man made fruit hybrid'.
- Major production centres: Florida and Poland.
- Monoecious, short day and quick growing fruit.
- It has unique place among the cultivated berry fruits.
- Low, perennial, acaulescent (stemless) herb.
- Highly perishable fruit and shipped only under refrigeration.
- 1st fruit crop on which micropropagation was studied.

- In India, strawberry was first introduced by NBPGR in early 1960s.
- Photographs of strawberries cultivated in Mahabaleshwar region of Satara district of Maharashtra have appeared on special envelops by Indian Post's & Telegraph,Govt. of India released during 2021.
- Desirable level of CO_2 in green house for strawberry: 750 ppm.
- Complete fruit with 98% edible portion.
- Edible portion: Succulent thalamus and numerous achenes.
- The hard, indehiscent fruit is called as 'achene' is true fruit and is referred to as seed.
- Fruit type: Etaerio of achenes.
- The edible fleshy berry consists of an enlarged and ripened receptacle around the seed.
- When achenes are removed from area of receptacle, the growth ceases in that area.
- 'A' is the donor genome identified as *F. vesca*.
- Fruit contain pectin as Calcium pectate (0.54%).
- Fruits are rich in vit. C & Fe and consumed as fresh & jam & syrup are also prepared.
- Ellagic acid: Naturally occurring phenolic constituent and anti-cancerous property.
- Major acid present: Citric acid and Malic acid.
- Flavour of strawberry (major volatile compounds): Ethyl butanoate and ethyl hexanoate.
- Highly tolerant to water logging.
- Best suited for acidic soil (5.8-6.5 pH). It is resistant to Mn deficiency.
- Unique place among cultivated berry fruits.
- Anthesis time: 9-11 AM.
- Inflorescence type: Dichotomic raceme.
- Most strawberry cultivars produce hermaphrodite flowers and are self fertile.
- Flower type: Protogynous.
- Flowers are borne in small clusters consisting of primary, secondary and tertiary flowers and are white in colour.
- There is a definite order of blooming in a cluster.
- Sepal number varies with flower type viz. 7-8 (primary flowers), 6 (secondary) and 5 in tertiary flowers.
- Maximum number of fruits: Produced by tertiary flowers.
- Plant does not produce flowers in day lengths > 12 h.
- Flower initiation is stimulated by short days and inflorescence development by long days.

- Stamen length has relationship with achene development with primary and secondary flowers.
- Low temperature and short day results in poor pollination.
- Early maturing flowers are less fertile than late maturing.
- Types of fruiting habits: Single crop or June bearer, ever-bearer and day neutral.
- Seeds are borne outside the fruit.
- Developing seeds have influence on fruit growth.
- Seed dormancy: 2-3 months.
- Very small seeds need stratification before sowing.
- Seeds germinate within 8 days and seedlings are transplanted within 3-4 months.
- On an average strawberry contains 200 seeds.
- Propagation method: 1 year old runners or stolons of old plants.
- Single plant produces 7-15 runners/ plant.
- Propagation through division of crowns (3-5 plants/ crown) is avoided since it is tedious and more expensive.
- Leaf grafting: Technique used in China to identify virus free varieties.
- For runner production, strawberry should be planted at 1.2 x 1.2 m or 1.8 x 1.8 m.
- Commerical propagation: Tissue culture (meristem culture, anther culture, petiole segment, flower buds, leaf lamina and runners).
- More than 1 million plants/ year can be obtained by meristem culture.
- Embryo rescue technique can be used to generate more seedlings from achenes or poorly germinating hybrid crosses.
- Virus free plants are obtained by anther culture and produced by runner propagation.
- Removal of flower clusters increases runner formation.
- In ever-bearing varieties, runner production is very low.
- Planting density: 55,000- 60,000/ha.
- Planting distance: 30 cm x 20 cm.
- Systems of planting:
  1. Matted row: Commercially followed in India. It is simplest and least expensive. Runners planted at 90 cm x 45 cm. More number of plants/ unit area is accommodated.
  2. Spaced row/ beds: Runners planted at 90-100 cm x 30-50 cm. It is suitable to get desired number of daughter plants from mother plants.
  3. Hill system/ rows: Runners planted at 90 cm x 30 cm. It is adopted for cultivars developing few runners.
  4. Plastic mulch: Green/ black plastic mulch reduces rot & mold infection.
- Trickle irrigation: Saves 30% water & energy, less disruption of picking schedule, better water supply during winter, less rotting of fruits.

- Sprinkler irrigation is valuable in heat stress areas and need for frost control.
- Excess irrigation encourages more vegetative growth and incidence of botrytis rot increases.
- Water stress leads to defoliation, growth suppression and delayed fruiting.
- Removal of flower stem helps early establishment (plant set), aids in heat & drought tolerance & increases number of runners/ plant.
- Cutting of runners & removal of surplus plants is suggested.
- Emergence of weeds during fruiting season affects pollination.
- Type of pollination: Self and cross.
- Nicolas Longworth: 1st reported self unfruitfulness.
- Pollination agents: Honey bee (*Andrena nasonii*, *Apis mellifera*) and wind.
- Interplanting of perfect or pollinating variety at 1:5 ratio is recommended for fruit set.
- Natural self pollination results in lesser fruit set (53%) than natural open pollination (91%).
- Fruit development exhibit double sigmoid growth: 1st peak in fruit growth during rapid achene growth after fertilization and 2nd during accumulation of assimilates in receptacle.
- Fruit buds are formed chiefly under low temperature.
- Fall bearing types are long day plants.
- Ideal planting time in hilly region: Runners/ crowns in September to October.
- Very late planting causes more development of runners in March and results in low yields and quality of fruits.
- Flowering starts after 45-50 days of planting.
- Flower bud differentiation (FBD) in north Indian condition: November.
- Time required for FBD: 30-35 days.
- More than 20 short day cycles (11 h or less light) are essential for FBD.
- Minimum and maximum days required from bloom to ripe berries in any cultivar: 18 to 41.
- Ideal temperature for flower bud initiation: 14-18^{0}C.
- Fruit size is greater at 18^{0}C than that at 13^{0}C or 21^{0}C.
- Temperature > 28^{0}C inhibits flower bud initiation in all commercial varieties.
- Soil temperature < 25^{0}C increases reproductive development.
- High temperature increases rate of maturity but reduces fruit size.
- Fruits ripen slowly in fall season, but are larger in size and of higher quality with regularity in shape.
- Spring berries have irregular shapes when temperature is low but ripen much sooner (in about 30 days).
- The cultivars that flower and fruit once over a year are called as single croppers or June bearers or non-ever bearing or short day cultivars.

- Ever-bearing cultivars also called re-bloomers or perpetual or day neutral cultivars, characteristically bear more than once a year.
- Harvesting starts 20-25 days after flowering.
- Fruit ripens in 4-6 weeks after fertilization. Harvesting continues up to 4-4 ½ months.
- Harvesting stage:
  - 50-75% skin develops colour i.e. colour break.
  - Picking duration differs from cultivar to cultivar e.g. 53 days (Tioga); 43 days (Torry) during 1st year.
- Runner plants (or daughter plants) are produced in cycles.
- The earlier cycle runners are more developed, having thicker crowns and well developed root system, leaves and flower buds.
- Runner production occurs in environment of long days and high temperature.
- Red colour: Anthocyanin pigment (pelargonidin-3-monoglucoside).
- Anthocyanin pigment develops 28-35 days after petal fall.
- Mulching is important cultural operation.
- Waiting-bed (WB) system has potential to increase length of strawberry production season.
- In WB system, plants are deblossomed and runners are removed to stimulate production of multiple crowned plant.
- At senescence stage, fruit looses almost all their insoluble pectin polysaccharides and become incipid in taste.
- Strawberry pollen can be stored at 4^{0}C under low humidity and seeds can be stored at 1-4^{0}C.
- Pre-harvest foliar application of *Pseudomonas fluorescens* at flower initiation stage reduced the incidence of post harvest diseases of fruits during one week storage at room temperature (26 ± 2^{0}C and 55% R.H.).
- VAM fungi (*Glomus mosseae*) is effective in shoot growth.
- Foliar application of polyamine putrescine @ 100 ml/ litre at flower initiation stage reduced occurrence of misshapen fruit up to 18%.
- Guttation in leaves: Used as indicator of water status for scheduling irrigation.
- Specially designed plastic punnets are used for packaging.
- Decapping of fruits is necessary before processing.
- Precooling temperature: 4^{0}C within 4 h after harvest to enhance shelf life upto 4 days.
- Induction of runner formation: IBA @ 100 ppm and Morphectin @ 50 ppm at 10 days before flowering.
- Application of GA_3 @ 50-100 ppm increases runner production and inhibits flowering.
- Sprays of GA_3 @ 50 ppm or MH @ 0.1-0.3%, 4 days after flowering increases yields upto 31-41%.

- 'Come On Charlie': New brand of strawberry red wine from cv. Charlie.
- Fruits can be stored for 10 days in cold storage at 4^0C.
- CA storage of fruits: CO_2 15% + O_2 18%.
- Fruits can be frozen for processed products or as dessert.
- Use of GI tag and QR code is necessary for digitized marketing of strawberries.

Species:

- Antoine Nicholas Duchesne (1966), the Father of modern strawberry and was 1st to recognize separate sexes in strawberry.
- Basic chromosome number of genus is X=7 and occurs as polyploid series from 2n=14 to 2n=56.
- All the cultivated varieties of modern garden strawberry are allooctaploid (2n=8x=56).
- Wild species found 1st in Europe in 1360 AD.
- Hermaphroditism is more common in *F. virginiana*.
- Genus *Fragaria* constitute polyploid series and is composed of 9 diploids, 3 tetraploids, 1 pentaploid, 1 hexaploid and 4 octaploids.
- Tetraploid spp. (2n=4x=28): Spontaneous tetraploids from crosses between *viridis* x *vesca*.
- Hexaploid spp. (2n=6x=42): Originated from natural crosses of *vesca* x *viridis* with unreduced pollen or eggs of one parent.
- Octaploid spp. (2n=8x=56): Developed by doubling and redoubling of Alpine *vesca* using colchicine. They belong to facultative short day plants.

Common name	Botanical name	Features
Wild strawberry	*Fragaria nubicola*	Diploid (2n=14); fruits small, mild taste & sweet flavour
Wood strawberry/ Indian wild strawberry	*F. vesca*	Natural diploid species; hermaphrodite flowers; self pollinated; aromatic fruits; indicator plant to test presence of virus by grafting of runner of commercial variety on this species
-	*F. viridis*	Diploid; hermaphrodite flowers
-	*F. nilgerrensis*	Diploid; vigorous; strong spreading runners
-	*F. daltoniana*	Diploid; native to Sikkim; vigorous; flavourless
-	*F. nubicola*	Diploid; native to temperate Himalaya; dioecious
-	*F. iinumae*	Diploid; native to Alpine areas of Japan; yellow achene
-	*F. yezoensis*	Diploid; dioecious;native to north Japan; dormant during winter
-	*F. nipponica* & *F. mandschurica*	Diploid; native of Manchuria
-	*F. orientalis*	Tetraploid; found in Siberia; soft fruits; hermaphrodite flowers; slightly aromatic
-	*F. moupinensis*	Tetraploid; native to S-W China
-	*F. corymbosa*	Tetraploid;

-	*F. bringhurstii*	Pentaploid;
-	*F. moschata*	Hexaploid; Found in central Europe; dioecious; musky flavour
Cultivated strawberry	*F.* x *ananassa* (Natural hybrid of *F*. chiloensis (Chilean pine) x *F. virginiana* (scarlet strawberry)	Artificial hybrid was made in 19th century; octaploid; 1st developed in France; heavy yielder; introduced to Europe in 1712 & grown commercially as 'Little Scarlet' for jam making
-	*F. chiloensis*	Octaploid; progenitor of cultivated strawberry; vigorous; more drought tolerant than *F. virginiana*; tolerates very high salt levels (>1200 ppm) as compared to *F. vesca*
-	*F. virginiana ssp. glauca*	Octaploid; progenitor of cultivated strawberry; dioecious; produce profuse runners; best donor parent for developing cultivars with short rest period requirement; rich source of genes for crown production & stolon formation
-	*F. iturupensis*	Octaploid; spherical fruits
Alpine strawberry	*F. vesca* var. *semperflorens*	Native of Europe; miniature version of garden strawberry; differ from garden strawberry in two distinct ways- fruits & plants are smaller, do not form runners; self fertile; grown from seeds & need bottom heat technique (15°C); yellow & white fruited forms are available
Perpetual. (Remontant strawberry)	-	Self fertile; similar to summer strawberry & set early crop before summer varieties; continuous fruiting during autumn; it has *F. vesca* ancestry & are mixed hybrids; popular in Europe than in America or UK; cultivated in window garden

Varieties:

- 1st systematic strawberry breeding project was started in England in 1817 using *F. chiloensis* clones.
- In USA, breeding work was started in 1920.
- Day neutral varieties are ever-bearers, early and high yielders e.g. Brighton, Mrak, Yolo.
- German cvs. Fratina, Fecunda: Suitable for mechanical harvesting and resistant to botrytis.
- Phenomenal: Cultivated in Nilgiri hills of south India.
- Fort Laramie: American cv. extremely winter hardy.
- Kalimpong Local: Originated in West Bengal and ever-bearing.
- Suitable for canning (jam making): Cambridge, Talisman, Red Gauntlet, Huxley Giant, Royal Sovereign (popular in Europe, introduced in 1892).
- Tolerant to virus: Surprise, Huxley, Cambridge Rare Guard, Cambridge Premier, Talisman.

- Resistant to red stele: Surecrop, Midway, Sunrise, Guardian, Early Glow Scott, All Star, Lester, Late Glow, Hood, Benton, Sileth.

Varieties	Features
Torrey, Elista, Shasta, Douglas, Fair Fax, Sweet Charlie, Oso Grande, Camarosa, Winter Dawn, R-1, R-2	Introduction from Florida; grown in Mahabaleshwar area of Maharashtra
Temple	1st cv. bred in 1943 with resistant to red stele disease.
Blackmore	1st firm fruited variety
Tristar, Tribute (1981)	1st day neutral cvs.; flower in different times of the year; multiple resistance to red stele
Cambridge Favorite	Suitable for canning; tolerant to virus, mildew & verticillium wilt
Cambridge Vigour	Early & commercial cv. in Europe; resistant to strains of red core, virus; suitable for processing
Cardinal	Large fruits; suitable for processing & mechanical harvesting; resistant to leaf spot, leaf scorch & PM
Early Glow	Suitable for freezing; resistant to red core & verticillium wilt
Rking (Cardinal x Ark-5431)	Late maturity; heavy cropping; resistant to leaf spot, leaf scorch & PM
Belrubi (Pocahantas x Red Coat)	Tolerates high soil pH; susceptible to PM, gray mold; firm fruits & suitable for processing
Centinnial (Twentieth Century x Gem seedling)	Produce June & autumn crop; resistant to verticillium wilt; black spot, PM
Chambley (Sparkle x Honeoye)	1st June bearing cv.; 4-6 inflorescences/ plant; tolerates -25^{0}C winter temperature
Elista (Jacunda x self) x V.S. 3763	-
Red Gaunlet	Tall plants; heavy cropper; suitable for processing; resistant to several races of red core, PM & gray mold
Rindamore (Aiberry x Hokowase)	Early fruit bud differentiation; ever bearing; excellent taste
Senga Sengana (Markee x Sieger)	Easily detachable calyx; excellent freezing quality; suitable varieties for hydroponic culture; drought resistant; adapted to Septentrional culture (short days in autumn & hard winter)
Tioga	American cv.; suitable for meridional regions (long days in autumn & moderate winter); flower buds are formed under long days; excellent dessert & processing quality; tolerant to virus; yield 97 q/ha
Rainier	American cv.; good shelf life
Gorella	Dutch cv.; widely grown in France; short day; adapted to Septentrional culture (short days in autumn & hard winter) & suitable for hydroponic culture; resistant to drought
Guardian	Highly resistant to red stele races & verticillium wilt
Tenira	Russian cv.; large fruit & tolerant to fruit rot, wilt & red core
Red Gaunlet	Short day; adapted to Septentrional culture (short days in autumn & hard winter); resistant to PM, verticillium wilt, botrytis rot

Fern, Muir, Hecker	Day neutral, ever bearing, fruit wt. 20-25g
Silva	Day neutral & off season variety; fruit wt. 15-18g
Midway, Midland, Hood, Red Chief, Beauty	Suitable for processing; produce more suckers
Olympus, Hood, Shuksan (high flavour & bright red colour)	Suitable for ice cream making
Torrey	Produces numerous runners, tolerant to virus; yield 48 q/ha
Pusa Early Dwarf, Katrain Sweet, Jutogh Special, Shimla Delicious	Released from IARI; early fruiting
Pajaro	Suitable in summer cultivation; tolerant to virus
Chandler	Introduced from Florida; commercially grown in sub-tropical plains; high dessert quality, outstanding colour & flavour; suitable for processing
Fare Fax	Best parent for incorporating flavour
Howard 17	Used as parent in breeding programme
Barak	Grown in Israel; TSS- 9^0Brix; more post harvest life; deep red colour; sweet scented
Late Glow	Highly resistant to verticillium wilt
Delite	Resistant to both leaf spot & leaf blight
Sunrise	Useful parent for adding character like simultaneous fruit ripening
Hood, Benton	Parents for semi-erect growth & early capping types
Cavalier, Red Coat (Sparkle x Valentine)	-
Totem (1971)	Virus tolerant; winter hardy; resistant to phytophthora
Sumas, Tyee (1980)	Winter hardy
Beaver Early, Beaver Sweet, Beaver Ruby, Beaver Bells (1989)	Grown in temperature as low as -40^{0}C.
Shuswap (1990)	Winter hardy, virus tolerant & high yield
SO_1 colchicine treated seed of tetraploid hybrid of (*F. moschata* x *F. nubicola*)	Synthetic octaploid selection
SO_2 colchicine treated seed of tetraploid hybrid of (*F. vesca* x *F. alpina*) x (*F. viridis* x *F. moupinensis*)	Synthetic octaploid selection
Horticulture Research International, East Malling, UK	
Pegasus (Redgauntlet x Gorella) 1990	Self fertile; purple red fruits; suitable for fresh consumption; pick-your-own cultivation; resistant to verticillium wilt
Pandora (1988)	Firm & regular shaped berries; mod. resistant to verticillium wilt & gray mold
EMR-25, EMR-28	Resistant to PM, aphids

Other varieties: Red Coat, Royal Sovereign, Premier, Dil Pasand, Seascape, Catskill; (yield 48 q/ha)

Inheritance of characters:

- Enzyme used as a biochemical marker for ripening: Phenyl Alanine Ammonia-lyase (PAL) i.e. Ascorbic oxidase.
- Non-runnering is closely related with ever-bearing character.
- High TSS dominant while low titratable acidity is partially dominant.

- Cytoplasmic control accounts for variegation character.
- Heterosis is observed in flowering time, ripening time and rate of fruit development.
- In *F. vesca*, non-runnering (*r/r*) and ever-bearing habit (*j/j*) and arborea (long internode, runner forming, non-crown forming) types (*arb/arb*) are homozygous recessive mutants.

Name	Number of genes	Inheritance pattern
Fruit colour	Monogenic	Red dominant to white
Fruit softness, fruit size, ever bearing nature	Polygenic	-
Disease resistance	Polygenic	Partially dominant
Appressed stem pedicel pubescence	Monogenic	Appressed recessive to spreading

Diseases, pests and disorders:

- Blossom sterility: Due to lack of stamens or abortive stamens.

Name	Causal organism	Remedy & remarks
Gray mold or fruit rot	*Botrytis cinerea*	Serious disease in field and storage
Verticillium wilt	*Verticillium albo-atrum*	Soil borne
Red core/ Red stele	*Phytophthora fragariae*	Most serious soil borne disease; Use disease free runners
Anthracnose crown rot	*Colletotrichum acutatum*	Use resistant cultivars
Powdery mildew	*Sphaerotheca macularis* f.sp. *fragariae*	Use resistant cultivars
Leaf scorch	*Diplocarpon earliana*	-
Thrips	*Thrips atratus*	Use predator *Amblyseius barkeri*
Spotted red spider mite	*Tetranychus urticae*	Release predator *Phytoseiulus persimilis*
Aphid	*Myzus ascalonicus* & *Chaetosiphon fragaefolii*	-
Blossom weevil	*Anthonomus rubi*	Cause withering of flowers
Leaf roller	*Clenopsenstis obliquana*	-
Nematodes	-	-
Wingless weevil	-	-
Albinism	Lack of red fruit colour during ripening	-
Phyllody	MLO	-
Black eye	Winter injury	-
Winter flowering	Abnormal weather conditions	-
Leaf tip burn	High nutrients in soil and type of runner production	-
Blossom sterility	Lack of stamens or abortive stamens	-
Irregular fruit shape	Insufficient pollination of pistils i.e. Pistil sterility	-
Cat face	B deficiency	-

38.9 Loquat

- Eulogized as 'Japanese plum'.
- Commercially cultivated in China, Japan, Korea and Taiwan.
- Largest producer: Spain.
- Evergreen and strictly sub-tropical fruit, used as ornamental purpose.
- Commercially cultivated in U.P., Punjab and H.P.
- It was introduced in India under the name of 'Japanese Medlar'.
- Word '*Eriobotrya*' derived from two Greek words, *Erion* (wool) and *botrys* (cluster) is implied to woolly inflorescence.
- Sub-family: Pomoideae.
- *E. dubia*: Found in Eastern Himalaya and bear edible fruits.
- *E. angustissima*: Evergreen shrub from Assam.
- Upper half of leaf blade is bent upon the lower leaf i.e. reclinate.
- Development of edible portion consists of uniform growth of receptacle.
- Edible portion: Toral (pith and cortical area).
- Toral cells of mature fruits are large, thin walled and very juicy.
- Fruits are orange coloured & pear shaped with one or more big, brown-black seeds & sweet, acidic, chewy pulp.
- Fruit consists of 60-70% pulp and 15-20% seed.
- Nutrition composition/ 100 g edible portion: Water (87.4%), -CHO (10.2%), protein (0.7%), fibre (0.9%) fat (0.3%), vit. A: 500-2300 IU, 0.5% minerals (Ca, P, Fe, K, Mn).
- Seed viability: 6 months (92%)
- Seeds & peel contain amygdalin which is converted to HCN cause toxicity in children.
- Limiting factor in cultivation: Frost.
- Does not perform well in graveled soil, hard pan or excessive lime.
- Self unfruitfulness is noticed. Hence, pollinizer variety should be planted along with main variety.
- Type of SI: Gametophytic.
- Planting distance: 6-8 m and planted in mid-August or mid-February.
- Grafting methods followed: Inarching, top graft, root graft, cleft graft in Japan.
- Suitable month for shield and ring budding: January-February.
- Bark grafting: Employed as method of top working.
- Best method of propagation: Air layering. Three months old ringed shoots treated with 2500 ppm IBA or 3% NAA.
- Commercial method of propagation: Inarching.
- Rootstocks used: Mespilus, Quince, Pear, Apple.

- Quince: Dwarfing rootstock, rich source of pectin, tolerant to pests and diseases. Widely used in Europe, Japan, Australia and California.
- Training system: Central leader or Open centre.
- Pollination agent: Honey bee.
- Seeds are located in central region of fruit.
- Flower buds are produced at terminal end of branches.
- Bear flowers on current season's growth.
  - 1st flush of flowering: August-September but no fruit set due to non-viable pollen grains.
  - 2nd flush of flowering: October-November set maximum fruits.
  - 3rd flush of flowering: December-January: Reduction in fruit size due to hot dessicating winds.
- Seedless/ parthenocarpy: / parthenocarpic fruit development Due to triploidy. Spray GA_3 @ 100-200 ppm.
- Application of paclobutrazol @ 500 ppm around trunk: Increase in fruit size.
- Special horticultural practices: Fruit thinning and girdling.
- Thinning out of few fruits is impracticable because fruiting takes place in clusters.
- Terminal end of branches are clipped to avoid overcrowding of fruits.
- Thinning is practiced early in fruiting season.
- Fruits are susceptible to sun burn or purple spot.
- Days required for maturity: 70 days after fruit set.
- Harvesting method: Whole cluster.
- Harvesting of mature fruit bunch is a kind of pruning and encourages new growth.
- Maturity index: Fully matured and maximum sugar is developed.
- Cvs. California Advance, Golden Yellow, Thames Pride should be harvested at 11% TSS.
- Yield: 16-20 kg/tree.
- Spray of 2,4,5-T @ 20 and 40 ppm reduced fruit drop and hastens fruit maturity.
- Clean cultivation is preferred over other methods of orchard management.
- Value added products: Dessert purpose, jam, jelly, preserve, canning, chutney.

Varieties:

- Breeding work in India was started at HRS, Saharanpur in 1953.
- Two groups on the basis of origin and time of maturity:
  a) Chinese group: Fruits large, pyriform and deep orange colour.
  b) Japanese group: Fruits small, slender and light colour.

Early (ripen from mid March)	Mid-season (last week of March)	Late season (mid April)
Golden Yellow, Improved Golden Yellow, Large Round, Thames Pride, Pale Yellow	Fire Ball, Improved Pale Yellow, Large Agra, Mammoth, Matchless, Safeda	California Advance, Tanaka

- Kibou: 1st triploid variety.
- California Advance: Introduced from Australia. Good keeping quality. Partially fertile. Best pollinizer for Improved Golden Yellow, Tanaka.
- Thames Pride: Introduced from Australia. Heavy fruiting. Partially self incompatible.
- Best combination for better fruiting: Pale Yellow and Golden Yellow.
- Partially self incompatible: Large Round, Fire Ball, California Pride, Tanaka.
- Hybrid no.6/2 (Tanaka x California Advance) and 8/2, 8/4 (Tanaka x Golden Yellow) are promising for fruit size, taste, flavour and TSS content.
- Algerie: Commercially grown in Spain.

Pest and disease:

- Bark eating caterpillar: Common pest.
- Collar rot (*Diplodia natalensis*): Cause heavy loss.

38.10 Quince

- Eulogized as 'Bihi or Bamchount' in Kashmir valley.
- Commercially grown in Portugal and Spain.
- Mostly grown in Jammu and Kashmir, Himachal Pradesh as court yards.
- Odour is due to ionone glycosides.
- Rich in pectin content among rosaceous fruits.
- Mucilage in seeds is used as medicine for curing cystitis.
- Major water soluble polysaccharide present in seed: Gluconic acid.
- Monotypic, deciduous, self fertile, hardy& long lived, small bushy tree.
- Fruit (7 x 15 cm in size) golden coloured, fragrant, pear and round shaped with off white fealthy hairs on skin.
- Fruits are excellent room perfumes and can be used as base for pomanders.
- Quices can be made into aromatic clear jelly, jam or pulpy cheese.
- Flowers pink & white coloured, appear singly on short shoots (12-15 cm long).
- Propagation methods: Seed, suckers and stool layering.
- Commercial propagation method: Cuttings.
- Used as rootstock for pear.
- Planted as ornamental tree for flowers and leaves.
- Planting distance: 3m x 3m.
- Plant need staking during initial years of growth.
- Sour and astringent fruits are inedible when raw and develop pink colour upon cooking.

- Remedial pruning is required to remove dead, diseased and criss-crossing branches.
- Matured fruits are harvested in autumn season before they drop down.
- Fruits are not stored with apples or pears or vegetables as they may taint.

Species:

- Janonica quince (*Chaenomeles japonica*): Self fertile, thorny, bears round & greenish red or yellow coloured fruits in early spring. Fruits can be used for tart, baked, stewed or made into cheese or jelly.

Varieties:

- Portuguese: Pear shaped, vigorous & slow to bear a crop.
- Champion: Rounder & mild flavoured.
- Vranja: Famour in Serbia. Large fruits, pear shaped & with erect growth.
- Ispahan: Popular in Persia.
- Maliformis: Apple shaped & popular in Turkestan.
- Orange, Pineapplem Smyrna: Commercially grown in USA.
- Van Deman, Bencikli.

38.11 Raspberry

- Popularly known as 'Caneberry'.
- Largest producer: USA.
- Grown under protected cultivation (controlled condition) in European countries.
- LED lamps are widely used for heating (generates temperature) and light intensity which reduces humidty inside the protected cultivation.
- For artificial lightening, parabolic aluminized reflector (PAR) bulbs are widely used.
- Possible to grow in winter season by utilizing artificial lightening under green house conditions.
- Total sugar content: 8-9%.
- Ascorbic acid: 39 mg/100 gram.
- Major organic acid: Citric acid.
- Aroma: 4-p-hydroxyphenyl-1-2-buanone, ketones, carbonyls, linalool and geraniol.
- Phenolics in juice (anti-carcinogenic perperty): Quercetin and Ellagic acid.
- Highest ellagic acid concentration then strawberry and blackberry.
- Seed germination: Photoblastic.
- Planting system: Hill (stool) system and hedge row.
- Maturity indices: Fruit colour change.
- Yield: Positively correlated with can density and cane length.
- Biennial cropping system yields higher yield due to increase in can enumber and cropping nodes.

- Value added products: Jam, jelly, syrup, yoghurt, dessert tartes, vinegar, puddings, ice creams, bakery products, milk drinks, flavoured water and frozen products.

Species

Name	Salient features
Rubus idaeus	Red raspberry; ancestor of cultivated raspberry; self incompatible
R. strigosus	Light red fruits; self compatible; used as parent in development of American varieties
R. occidentalis	Black raspberry indigenous to N. America; self compatible
R. ellipticus	Yellow raspberry; used for fresh consumption & jam making
R. hirsutus	1-3 g fragrant sweet red fruits, 70-82% juice extraction rate, easily produce suckers; good flavour & colour to mix juice & jelly products
R. chingii	2-4 g red fruits; high yielder
R. corchorifolius	1 g red or orange fruits, 60% juice extraction rate
R. lambertianus	0.5 g red fruits; rich in stable anthocyanin
R. spectabilis	Salmon berry
R. phoenicolasius	Wine berry

Varieties:

- Present cvs. developed from *R. idaeus* var. *strigosus* x *R. occidentalis*.
- Lagorai, Squanza: Preferred for green house cultivation. These yielded 2-3.5 kg fruits/ sq.m due to non uniformity in age and size of plants.
- Aura (*R. articus* x *R. articus ssp. stellatus*): Taller, high yielder.
- Purple raspberry (*R. neglectus*): (*R. occidentalis* x *R. idaeus* var. *strigosus*).
- Balder (Norna x Malling Jewel): Winter hardy, high yielder.
- Glen Isla: Firm fruits.
- Glen Moy: 4th generation backcross hybrid. Resistant to spur blight, cane botrytis, and anthracnose.
- Glen Clova: Winter hardy, good flavour.
- Malling Admiral:
- Malling Jewel:
- Malling Promise: Frost hardy.
- Malling Exploit: Frost hardy.
- Comox (Skeena x BC 6-9-81): Self fertile, firm fruits.
- Double Delight (Fall Red x native spp.): Very hardy, good flavour.
- Heritage (Milton x Cuthbert) x Durham: Firm fruits.
- Willamette: Early flowering, large berry. Suitable for juice and processing.
- Meeker: Bright red fruits, excellent flavour; preferred as freezing berry.
- Boyne: Suitable for processing.
- Fairview: Early flowering, least vigorous, largest fruits.
- Veten: Largest fruit size.
- Vene: Very glossy fruit and best taste.
- Ville (Ottawa x Wild Finnish): Winter hardy, aromatic fruits.

- Pima (Mesma x Mespi).
- Zeva-1: Frost hardy.
- Royalty, Chilcotin, Puyallup, Mallis, Admiral: Resistant to cane disease, spur blight and gray mold.

Pests, diseases and disorder:

- Beetle (*Byturus tomentosus*): Severe damage to buds and blossoms.
- Cane borer (*Resseliella theobaldi*): Plant cv. Glea Clova because it produce non-splitting canes in 2nd flush.
- Sawfly (*Monophadnoides geniculatus*):
- Weevil (*Otiorhynchus singularis*): Nocturnal pest.
- Nematodes:
- Anthracnose (*Leptosphaerica coniothyrium*)
- Cane spot (*Elsinoe veneta*):
- Spur blight (*Didymella applanata*):
- Gray mold (*Botrytis cinerea*):
- Yellow rust (*Phragmidium rubi-idaei*):
- Root rot (*Phytophthora erythroseptica*): Resistant cvs. WSU-585, Cherokee, Durham, MN-646, Sunrise, Lathan, Pathfinder.
- Septoria leaf spot (*Septoria rubi*)
- Black Raspberry Necrosis virus (BRNV): Vector- Aphid.
- Raspberry Leaf Mottle virus (RLMV): Vector- Aphid.
- Raspberry Leaf Spot virus (RLSV): Vector- Aphid.
- Raspberry Vein Chlorosis virus (RVSV): Vector- Aphid.
- Raspberry Ring Spot virus (RRV): Vector- Nematode.
- Tomato Black Ring virus (TBRV): Vector- Nematode.
- Arabis Mosaic virus (AMV): Vector- Nematode.
- Strawberry Latent Ring virus (SLRV): Vector- Nematode.
- Raspberry Bushy Dwarf virus (RBDV): Vector- Pollen grains.
- White drupelet: Due to high temperature and solar radiation. Cover plant with black fabric. White polyester 1-3 weeks before harvesting.

39. RUBIACEAE

39.1 Noni

- Eulogized as 'Hog apple or Indian mulberry'.
- Sacred plant in Ayurveda and mentioned in ancient text as Ashyaki means longevity in Sanskrit language.
- Underutilized medicinal fruit plant.

- Highly useful from Therapeutic and nutraceutical values.
- Chemical constituents of fruits are useful against high blood pressure, respiratory problems and immune deficiencies.
- Active ingredient in fruit: Xeronines and Proxeronine.
- Fragrant flowers are used to worship Lord Ganesha.
- Seeds triangular shaped, whitish brown coloured with air sac attached to one end makes seed buoyant.
- Crops grows well in tropical and deciduous forest and found in Western Ghats.
- Tolerant to wet, dry, acidic, alkaline and saline soils.
- Most costliest drink among non-alcoholic beverages.
- Health amrut: Beverage of noni fruit extracts with pure honey (Brand name- Dancing Heart).
- Tree height: 20 ft.
- Fruit set does not take place < 10^0C.
- Seed wt/ fruit ranges from 25 to 40 g.
- TSS and pH of fruit juice varies from 8.0-12.5^0 Brix and 4.25-5.0, respectively.
- Fruit colour: Brownish black upon ripening.
- Yield: 1 q/ plant.
- Life expentancy: 50 years.
- Byproducts: Noni drink, Noni cookies.
- **Varieties (dwarf)**: CARI-Sanjivi, CARI-Samridhi, CARI-Sampada, CARI- Rakshak.

40. RUTACEAE (ORANGE FAMILY)

Citrus

- Word '*Citrus*' is derived from Greek word meaning 'Fruits of the Godly Trees'.
- Most wide genetic diversity.
- More sensitive to salinity stress.
- International Society of Citriculture was established in 1968.
- Indian Society of Citriculture was established in 1983.
- Citrus occupies about 9% of total land under various fruits of country.
- 1st citrus breeding programme: Swingle and Webber in 1893 by USDA, Florida.
- Globally, 33 genera and 224 species of *Citrus* are reported.
- Cultivation lies between latitude 40^0N also 40^0S.
- Citrus fruits ranks 1st in international trade in terms of value.
- Major citrus producing countries: USA, Spain, India, Italy, Japan, Brazil, Argentina, Mexico, Morocco, Algeria, Greece, South Africa, Australia, Iarael, Egypt, Jamaica.
- USA: Largest producer in the world (35-40% of world's total production).
- India: 3rd largest producer.
- Orange revolution: Citrus group.

- Maharashtra is major citrus growing state and accounts for 40.9% area and 21.61% of country's production with average productivity of 5.5 metric tones/ ha.
- Orange city of India: Nagpur district of Maharashtra.
- Tetraploid citrus rootstock has been developed for salt tolerance.
- Production trends indicate that oranges constitute about (60%), mandarins (20%), lemons and limes (11-12%) and grapefruit and pummelos (5-6%).
- North-East India, south China and north Myanmar are accalaimed to be primitive centres of origin of contemporary *Citrus* species.
- Most primitive species: *C. medica*. It has definite involvement in ancestry of *C. limon*.
- NBPGR established gene sanctuary for conservation of *C. indica*: Tanga range in Garo hills of Meghalaya.
- 1st gene sanctuary in world for conservation of endanged *Citrus* species: Meghalaya.
- Citrus tristeza virus was introduced from USA.
- Lemon results bitterness on oxidation.
- Scientist 'Swingle' is known as 'Lumper'.
- Swingle (1943) was 1st citrus taxonomist to propose the use of biochemical markers (glycosides) for taxonomy.
- Modern system of citrus classification: Swingle (USA) and Tanaka (Japan) system (1945).
- Most accepted system of classification: Ranjit Singh (1967).
- Major 36 species are most conveniently separated based on Hodgson's system (1968).
- Citrus classification based on chemotaxonomy: Barret and Rhodes (1975) and Scora and Kumamoto (1983) and have only 3 true species viz. citron, mandarin and pummelo.
- Smith (1976) classified based on organic or biochemical basis.
- Singh and Nath (1969) reported 31 species.
- Bhattacharya and Dutta (1956) reported 17 species.
- Mabberley (1997, 2004) was 1st taxonomist to try to integrate new phylogenetic knowledge into the citurs classification. He proposed 3 main species for commercial fruits for citrus: *C. medica*, *C. reticulata* and *C. maxima*.
- Three most closely related genera: *Citrus*, *Fortunella* and *Poncirus*.
- Genus *Citrus* has two sub-genera: *Papeda* and *Eucitrus*.

Sub-genus *Papeda* comprises true wild spp. of citrus	**Sub-genus *Eucitrus***
Fruits are inedible	Edible fruits
Presence of numerous droplets & acrid oil in juice sacs	Widely cultivated
C. ichangensis, C. indica, C. latipes, C. micrantha, C. celebica, C. macroptera, C. hystrix	*C. medica, C. limon, C. aurantifolia, C. aurantium, C. sinensis, C. reticulata, C. grandis, C. paradisi, C. tachibana*

- *Poncirus* (the Kumquat) is from Central and North China, sheds its leaves in winter.
- *Fortunella* (from Southern China) is evergreen but owes its hardiness to prolonged winter dormancy.
- *Ermocitrus* is highly drought resistant.
- True citrus trees are grouped into 6 genera (*Citrus, Eremocitrus, Fortunella, Clymenia, Microcitrus* and *Poncirus*). *Eremocitrus* and *Microcitrus* are originated in Australia; *Clymenia* in New Guinea; *Poncirus* and *Fortunella* in China and *Citrus* in India, Myanmar, Malaysia and China.
- Eremocitrus: Most suitable for xerophyic condition.
- Biochemical basis of drought tolerance: Accumulation of proline in leaves.
- Morphological markers used in citrus hybridization: Trifoliate leaf of Poncirus, purple anthocyanin in lemon leaves and winged petiole.
- Among citrus fruits, 8 are edible.
- Citrus are rich in vitamin 'P'.
- Citrus fruits have high amount of K (100-350 mg/100 g edible portion) and low Na (1-10 mg/ 100 g). Ash content in citrus fruits (0.4%) is highest in immature fruit and gradually decrease as fruit mature.
- Largest producer of citrus: USA.
- Spain is largest exporter of citrus.
- India is 6th largest producer of citrus fruits and contributes 4.7% of world's citrus production.
- Among citrus fruits, mandarin occupies maximum area followed by sweet orange, lime and lemons.
- India is largest producer of lime in the world.
- Italy is largest producer of lemon in the world.
- Japan is largest producer of mandarin in the world
- In the world scenario, almost 54% of drip irrigation is applied.
- Citrus is micronutrient loving plant.
- Citrus is rarely pruned except lemon.
- Citrus fruits have a special kind of fruit skin referred as 'Leathery rind'.
- Khasi mandarins and Kachai lemon juices are used for the preparation of different beverages, juice concentrates.
- In north India, fruit bud and flowering occurs during early spring (February-March).
- In north India, sweet orange and mandarins flower twice in a year in February-March and June-July.
- In citrus, fruit bud differentiation is just little before flowering.
- In citrus, vegetative growth occurs in definite cycles.
- Three growth flushes: Spring, Summer and Autumn.

- Odd season vegetative growth flush also occurs in acid limes (5 times), lemons (4 times) and sweet orange (6 times).
- Most of the *Citrus* species take 6-8 months from flowering to fruit ripening.
- Cell division and elongation in citrus rind continues till ripening.
- Pink grapefruit (e.g. Ruby Red) are "sports or somatic mutations".
- Bizzare orange: A graft chimera of orange evolved in Italy in 1641 when sour orange was grafted on citron. It has a core of citron and outer layers of sour orange.
- Term 'chimera' does not apply to budded and grafted plants.
- Acidless orange cultivars are aid to be chimeral nature.
- Less sugar citrus fruit: Grape fruit and sour orange.
- High citric acid content fruit: Sour orange (1.5-3%).
- 1st edible processed product of citrus, orange marmalade was obtained from Sour orange.
- TSS of most of the citrus group: 8-12%.
- TSS: acid ratio for marketable fruits: Oranges and mandarins (8:1), Grape fruit (6:1).
- Smell of citrus fruit: Hesperidin (flavonoids).
- Temperature < 25^0C is required for flower bud initiation in significant quantities. Also a drought period longer than 30 days is required.
- Low temperature (20-25^0F) is injurious to young trees & 12-16^0F is injurious to mature plants.
- Over irrigation cause decline of orchards.
- Sensitive to salinity (> 1000 ppm).
- About 60-80% root activity is confined to first 60 cm top soil and roots spread beyond the vegetative spread of tree.
- Two sexes in citrus: 1) Hermaphrodite (perfect pistil) 2) Staminate (rudimentary pistil).
- Fruit growth pattern: Sigmoid (Kinnow) & linear (Sweet orange).
- Flowering in citrus takes place in February-April.
- Anthesis time: 9-12 AM.
- Anther dehiscence time: In lemon- before anthesis; in sweet lime and sweet orange- after anthesis.
- Stigma receptivity: Starts 2-3 days earlier to 4 days after anthesis.
- Pollen storage upto 3 years.
- Pollens can be stored in silica gel at -20^0C.
- Lemons and oranges produce low amount of pollen while grapefruit produce large amount of pollens.
- Degree of seediness: 1) Seedless (with no seed) 2) Commercially seedless (0-10 seeds/ fruit) 3) Seedy (numerous seeds).

- Cross pollination increases seediness in citrus varieties viz. Shamouti orange, Clementine mandarin and Mineola tangelo.
- Different degree of seediness is due to both 1) Male sterility (Washington Navel, Satsuma), and female sterility (Marsh grapefruit, Eureka & Lisbon lemons) 2) Partial self incompatibility 3) Normal male and female fertility.
- Pollen grains from mature buds of *C. medica* has higher germination potential than dehisced one.
- Oil content in citrus peel: 0.46-0.59%.
- Development of colour: < 13^0C.
- Candied citrus fruit: Kumquat.
- Deciduous *Citrus* spp.: Trifoliate orange.
- Kumquat, Trifoliate orange and other citrus hybridize freely to produce natural hybrids.
- Important characters of nucellar seedlings: Thornyness along with high tree vigour, free from viral diseases and high yield.
- Cold hardiness: Major breeding objective in Japan and Russia.
- Highly polyembryonic (6 or more seedlings): Mandarin orange, Sweet orange, Grape fruit.
- Monoembryonic cultivars viz. Meyer (Lemon), Temple (Mandarin), Clementine (Mandarin) and Chandler (Pummelo) can give 10-15 embryos from nucellus *in vitro* techniques, which develop into complete seedlings.
- In citrus, pollen germination is tested by hanging drop method or modified cellophane method.
- Citrus seeds do not have dormancy, so they should be sown immediately after extraction.
- Bearss lime, Satsuma and Washington Naval mandarin oranges are pollen/ self sterile type and produce parthenocarpic seedless fruits.
- Cross pollination increases seediness in Shamouti orange, Clementine mandarins and Mineola Tangelo.
- Hazara (*C. madurensis*): Ornamental citrus.
- *C. megalaxycarpa*: Most acidic fruits.
- *C. microcarpa*: Ornamental purpose.
- *C. maxima*: Almost thornless.
- *C. aurantium* or bitter orange used for marmalade and liquor.
- *C. rugulosa*: Commonly known as '*athanni*' or '*chawanni*'. Grown in Uttarakhand.
- *C. lemon*: Satellite species.
- Monkey fruit (*C. latipes*): Non-edible and non-valid species of citrus.
- Large petiole wings: Grape fruit and Pummelo.
- Small petiole wings: Sweet orange and acid lime.

- In citrus fruits, the pericarp (rind or peel) is divided into exocarp (flavedo) and white spongy portion i.e. mesocarp (albedo) and endocarp (edible portion).
- Flavedo is outermost coloured layer contain carotene pigments, pectin and essential oil, whereas albedo in innermost colourless white layer contain cellulose.
- *In vitro* regeneration protocols have been standardized for *Citrus macrophylla*, Troyer citrange & Rangpur lime.
- Can be propagated by budding owing to high intensity of polyembryony (90-100%).
- For raising seedlings, almost 20-22 months period is required.
- Microbudding: New propagation technique standardized by NRCC, Nagpur. This technique revolutionized propagation of citrus crops.
- Microbudding can be performed on 6 month's old rootstock (Rangpur lime/ Jamberi/ Almo).
- Marketable buddlings can be produced 6-8 months earlier compared to conventional budding.
- Fast and year round multiplication of planting material is possible.
- Success of microbudding is at par with conventional budding (70-80%).
- Rootstocks are given wedge shaped cut & tender scion bud is inserted inside the wedge cut.
- It is converted with micro-tip for proper union.
- Days for bud sprouting is 13-15 days compared to 26-37 days in conventional budding.
- Micro tips are removed after sprouting of scion.
- Microbudding technology developed by Dr. Vijayakumari Narkulla from NRCC, Nagpur.
- Size of shoot tip scion in micro-budding: 0.1-0.3 mm.
- Shoot tip grafting on decapitated rootstock using inverted 'T' incision gives virus free plants.
- Biological indexing: Used to detect greening infection. Seedlings of indicator plants are inoculated with side grafts/ bud of a given source tree and symptoms are developed under 20-30^{0}C temperature.
- Recommended indicator plants of virus: Sweet orange (Mosambi, Malta, Pineapple or Valencia).
- Short-term indexing for exocortis, greening and psorosis.
- Long-term indexing for xyloporosis.
- Flower colour: White (most of species); purple (lemon and citron).
- Bitter glucoside 'naringenin' provides prevention of malaria.
- Ultra dwarf rootstock of citrus: Flying Dragon.
- Weeping Dragon: Ornamental citrus resulted from Flying Dragon (trifoliate orange) x Cipo (sweet orange).
- Maturity index: Juice content (50%).

- TSS: acid ratio: Good index of maturity in most citrus fruits.
- Optimum TSS: acid ratio at maturity: 8:1 (oranges & mandarins); (12:1 to 14:1) Kinnow; 6:1 (grape fruit).
- Monotypic genus: *Poncirus*: Highly resistant to cold.
- Ermocitrus: Highly drought tolerant.
- Acidless lime: Sweet lime, Persian Mitha.
- Sikkim is the only place where mandarins are packed in wooden boxes.
- Osage: Oranges used to repell cockroaches.
- 'Bergamot' orange is derived from *C. aurantium* x *C. medica*.
- *Citrus* genus '*Atalantia'* is used as dye.
- *Fortunella hindsii* and *Triphasis*: Natural tetraploids.
- Most suitable intercrop: Papaya.
- Best maturity index for orange: Acid: brix ratio.
- Aurantemanin glycoside is present in sour orange.
- Off-flavour in citrus: Ferulic acid.
- Citrus peel: Extraction of essential oil.
- IARI has developed technology to mitigate (salinity) NaCl stress in citrus through paclobutrazol at 125-250 ppm.
- Relative salt tolerance of rootstocks: Cleopatra mandarin < sour orange < *C. amblycarpa* < *C. volkameriana* < Rangapur lime.
- *C. volkameriana*, Cleopatra mandarin, Swingle, Carrizo citrange and Sacaton citrumelons are most suitable rootstocks for Valencia orange in high altitude valleys.
- Tangor cv. Ellendale is self compatible.
- Use of biphenyl is used by exporters to control blue and green molds.
- Citrus viroid 3 is used for dwarfing.
- RNA content in leaves serve as guide to test virus infected v/s healthy plants. It is more in infected tissue.
- Pummelos are the largest citrus fruits in terms of fruit weight and diameter while kumquats are the smallest.
- 1st fruit crop in which antisense plants showed dwarfness.
- 1st homozygous line developed through androgenesis.
- Plants arising from embryogenesis of nucellus *in vitro* are found free from viruses.
- Bud wood certification program for virus: Identification of disease free mother trees for scion wood in nursery.
- In citrus, *in vitro* raised etiolated seedlings are used as rootstock for micrografting.
- Micrografting technique described by Tusa *et al*. (1979) with 25-100% success.

- Requirements for getting phytosanitory certificate: Farm registration under CitrusNet, global GAP certificate, packhouse recommended by APEDA, certificate of free from insecticide residues, free from citrus psylla, tristeza virus, etc.
- MAHAORANGE: Plays role in grading & wax coating of mandarin fruits.
- Citrus estates actively involved in preparing concentrates from mandarin orange juice & in assembling of fruits for marketing chain.
- For processing industry, mechanical harvesting systems consisting of abscission chemicals, shakers, windrover & pick up machines are used in Europen countries.
- Post harvest handling comprises washing with fungicidal cleaning solutions (0.5-1.0% soap + 2% soda) or dipping fruits for 4-5 min. in 0.5-1.0% sodium-o-phenyl phenate solution.
- Of the total production, 60-70% fruits are packed in corrugated fibre board boxes & 30-40% for processing purpose.

Grade	Size	Diameter of fruits (cm)	Number of fruits/ box
Jumbo	Very big	7.31-8.0	96-104
A-1	Big	6.71-7.30	112-120
A-2	Medium	6.11-6.70	140-175
A-3	Small	5.50-6.10	200-220
A-4	Very small	4.70-5.49	225-250

- Standard orange boxes measure in: Florida (12 x 12 x 12 inches); California (11.5 x 11.5 x 24 inches); Australia (18 x 10.5 x 11.5 inches).
- Ventilation holes must be at bottom & top of container, not at sides.
- Shrink films are used to control moisture loss from fruits.
- Individual wrapping of fruits in polymeric films, 0.5-1.0 mm in thickness & then shrinking the film to fruit shape with heat is followed.
- **Chemical treatments to extend storage life:**
  - Wax coating for Kinnow mandarins.
  - Ethrel @ 1000 ppm & storage at 24 to 28^{0}C in 68% R.H. for mandarins.
  - Aureofungin @ 100 ppm + Bavistin 0.2% for sweet orange.
  - 2,4-D & 2,4,5-T in wax emultion for Eureka lemon & Persian limes.
  - MH treatment for kagzi limes.
- Recommended transit & storage temperature for citrus fruits.

Type	Temperature (^{0}C)	
	Transit	Storage
Oranges	10.0	0-1.1
Grape fruit	10-15.5	10-15.5
Lemons, limes	10	10
Mandarins	10	4.4

Oranges

Name	Botanical name	Features
Sweet orange	*C. sinensis*	Tight skin with solid central core; polyembryonic
Mandarin orange	*C. reticulata*	Easily or loose peeling skin; polyembryonic; hardier than sweet orange, leaves small, pointed & green cotyledons
Sour orange	*C. aurantium*	Bitter taste; polyembryonic; used for pickling purpose; tolerant to xyloporosis, exocortis & gummosis, phytophthora root rot; tolerant to calcarious and heavy soil & susceptible to tristeza virus
Multiple leaf orange	*C. multiflora*	-
Indian wild orange	*C. indica*	Most primitive species
Trifoliate orange	*Poncirus trifoliata*	Dwarf; sessile & claw like flowers present in leaf axil in previous season growth; cold hardy, tolerant to greening, phytophthora, tristeza, xyloporosis, exocortis, gummosis, cold and drought hardiness & root knot nematode but susceptible to iron chlorosis; high productivity per unit canopy. adaptable to heavy soils
cv. Flying Dragon	*P. trifoliata* var. *monstrosa*	Most dwarfing to sweet orange; tolerant to greening, tristeza
Ketas-shupfu	*C. ichangensis*	Non-edible; grows at higher elevation
Hatkora/ Satkara	*C. macroptera*	Non-edible; indigenous to India; fleshy mesocarp is used fo pickle making & fruit rind is rich in essential oil

40.1 Mandarin orange

- Tangerine/ Loose skinned/ Jacket orange.
- Mandarins and tangerines are names used more or less interchangeably to designate whole mandarin group.
- Tangerine is used to designate varieties producing deep orange or scarlet fruits.
- Highly polymorphic species.
- It is mostly grown in rainfed conditions in India and highly susceptible to water logging.
- Mandarin oranges occupy > 50% share under divergent citrus crops grown across the globe.
- Orange production in developed countries is growing @ 0.6% annually and in developing countries @ 0.8% annually.
- In India, oranges account for 12.03% and 6.40% share under total acreage and production, respectively in fruits.
- Mandarin orange occupies 50% area among citrus fruits and grown in 15 states.
- Area under citrus crops in vidharbha region of Maharashtra: 1.34 lakh ha.
- Average productivity in India: 8-10 t/ha while of Spain 80 t/ha.
- Productivity of Kinnow in Punjab (23.4 t/ha); mandarin orange in MP (17.37 t/ha); Nagpur Santra in MH (7.3 t/ha).

- Mandarin festival celebrated in China.
- Nutrition score: 67.
- Mandarin contains 25-30% peel, 15-20% pomace, 5-7% seeds.
- Oranges have natural wax coating over the peel.
- Protective coating reduces weight loss by 30-40%.
- Wax coating must be approved food grade.
- Pigments found: Deep orange pulp (Cryptoxanthin).
- Pulp contains violaxanthin, cryptoxanthin and neoxanthin.
- Development of carotenoids is favoured by cool temperature of day and night and soil.
- When night temperature remains warm at time of fruit maturity, chlorophyll synthesis continues on and unmasking of carotenoids does not take piae. This type of situation renders greenness to oranges although fruits are ripe.
- Commercially propagated by 'T' budding (Kinnow and Nagpur mandarin).
- Shoot Tip Grafting (STG): Precocious planting material e.g. Mandarin and Sweet orange.
- Softwood grafting: Novel and rapid multiplication technique.
- Desirable horticultural attribute for fresh fruit marketing and processing: Seedlessness.
- Glycoside responsible for bitter taste of mandarin fruit juice: Limonin.
- Irrigation requirement is much higher than other *Citrus* species.
- Best time for pruning: Late winter or early spring.
- Weeds are serious problem in nursery.
- Bromocil: Effective herbicide in controlling monocot and dicot weeds.
- Harvesting period in Nilgiri hills: August-October.
- Maturity indices of Nagpur mandarins:
  - Days from anthesis: 240
  - Peel colour: Greenish yellow
  - TSS (12-14^0 Brix).
  - TSS : acid ratio: 14
  - Juice content: 35-50%.
- Seed viability: 4 years (88%).
- Fruit drop during winter: Serious problem in Valencia Late Orange.
- Fruit drop can be reduced by 40% by spraying 2,4-D @ 50 ppm.
- Pre-harvest fruit drop: Spray 10 ppm NAA.
- Mandarins are individually wrapped in cling films or plastic mesh or trays of molded pulp or paper board of foamed paper.

- Mandarin fruits are packed in layers using 3-ply CFB separators as cushioning material between the layers.
- Growth flushes: Spring (Feb-March), pre-monsoon (May-June) and post-monsoon (Sept-October).
- Highest storage life (weeks) at optimum temperature among citrus fruits.
- Storage temperature for Nagpur mandarins: 5.2-6.8^{0}C @ 85-90 % R.H.
- Storage temperature at 3-4^{0}C results in chilling injury.
- Optimum conditions for CA storage for Satsuma mandarin: 8-12% O_2, 0-2% CO_2 at 1-4^{0}C and 83-90% R.H.
- Walk-in-type evaporation cool chamber developed by NRCC, Nagpur- inside dimensions of chamber 255 cm (L) x 180 cm (W) x 210 cm (H) can store 1.5 t mandarins, limes and sweet orange fruits upto 21, 30 and 40 days, respectively.
- Degreening of fruits is done in chambers with ethylene treatment of 5 ± 2 ppm by trickle method.
- Remote sensing technique is used in identification of healthy and declining mandarin trees.
- One kg fresh fruits yield 60% juice, 40% skin + seeds + extract of pulp.
- For production of dehydrated santra powder, juice is processed under microwave technology (refractive window drying) to obtain hygienic product and packed in HDPE pouches upto 3 months.
- Approximately 100 g powder can be obtained from 4-5 kg fresh fruits.
- Powder can be used for ready to eat, ice cream, cookies, chocolate, burfy preparations & as flavouring agent.
- Minimum chemical parameters for export of mandarin orange to European countries:
  - Juice content- 38-40%;
  - TSS- 10-12%;
  - Sweetness- ratio of sweetness to sourness- 5: 1 to 7: 1;
  - Carbendazim- limit of 5 ppm;
  - Monocrotophos- 0.2 ppm and Quinolphos 0.25 ppm.

Grading system for Nagpur mandains:

- Size of CFB boxes: 50 cm x 30 cm x 30 cm.
- Size determination by maximum diameter at equatorial section of fruits as

a) Size code 0-92 to 110 mm diameter.

b) Code 1-87 to 100 mm diameter.

c) Code 13-53 to 60 mm diameter.

Grade	Size group	Fruit diameter (cm)
A/ Extra class	Big/ large	6.71-7.30
B/ Class I	Medium	6.22-6.70
C/ Class II	Small	5.50-6.10

- Size code determination for Satsuma, Clementine and other hybrids as-
  a) Size code XXX-78 mm diameter.
  b) Size code 2-58 to 69 mm diameter.
  c) Size code 3-54 to 64 mm diameter.
  d) Size code 4-50 to 60 mm diameter.

In international markets, Mandarin fruits are demanded as per-

Size (cm)	Number of fruits/ 10 kg box	Demanding country
5.5-5.9	100-105	European
6.5-6.9	68-71	Singapore
7.5-7.9	53-60	Hong Kong

Species:

- Webber (1948) separated mandarin oranges into King group, Satsuma group, mandarin group, Tangerine group, Lime group and Mitis group.
- Apart from *C. reticulata* other types of mandarins are designated as separate species or their hybrids as—

Common name	Features
Japanese Satsuma mandarin (*C. unshiu*)	Finest variety in world; introduced to Florida in 1876; polyembryonic; frost tolerant & seedless, thornless; resistant to canker, gummosis, scaly bark & melanose; cvs. Owaki, Kara, Silver Hill, Wanmi
King mandarin (*C. nobilis*)	Known as King of USA or Kunembo of Japan; native to India; Swingle believed it as a tangor; prolific bearer, frost resistant
Calamondin (*C. madurensis*)	Very cold resistant; loose skinned
Clementine (Algerian tangerine) from USA (*C. taagerina*)	(Mandarine x sour orange); early variety
Willow leaf mandarin (*C. deliciosa*)	Almost thorneless; highly polyembryonic; fruits seedy & borne singly at the tip of branch; wrinkled & thin rind
Temple mandarin	Tangerin x sweet orange; highly flavoured fruit& orange pulp; late in maturity
Cleopatra mandarin (*C. reshni*)	Originated in China; thornless with dense top; highly suitable rootstock for cv. Blood Red; tolerant to tristeza virus, root rot, xyloporosis, exocortis, phytophthora, gummosis, greening; tolerant to salts, drought, cold; susceptible to citrus nematode & burrowing nematode

Kokni/ Monkey mandarin (*C. lycopersicaeformis*)	Fruit very small; moderately loose rind; deep orange coloured
Tangerine orange	*C. tangerine* (Trifoliate orange x Mandarin) cv. Dancy Tangerine of Florida; Highly prized of all mandarin oranges; thornless & late
Tangerine	*C. reticulata* x *C. aurantium* (Dancy mandarin & Clementine)
Kumquat	*Fortunella spp.* (ornamental spp.) cv. Calamondin; tolerant to spring frost/ due to winter dormancy; * *F. margarita*: Nagami kumquat; * *F. japonica*: Marumi kumquat; * *F. crassifolia*: Meiwa kumquat; * *F. hindsii*: Hong Kong wild kumquat
Alemow /Phillippine lemon (*C. macrophylla*)	Released by NRCC, Nagpur; rootstock for mandarin & acid lime; resistant to tristeza, phytophthoraroot rot; tolerant to boron deficiency, soluble salts & lime soils

Rootstocks:

- Breeding for improvement of citrus rootstock was intiated in 1972 at CHES, Chettalli using Trifoliate orange as donor source for phytophthora and citrus nematode resistance. Resultant hybrids viz. CRH-3, CRH-5, CRH-41 were evolved.
- Hybrids between Rangpur lime and Trifoliate orange (Australia) have high resistance to nematode and phytophthora root rot, highly polyembryonic is being tested as rootstock for mandarins and sweet oranges.
- Troyer citrange, *Karna khatta* and *Sohsarkar* have recommended as dwarfing, semi-vigorous and vigorous rootstocks for kinnow.
- Troyer citrange and Carrizo citrange: Rootstock for HDP (1.8 m x 1.8 m).Worldwide uses and tolerant to phytophthora, tristeza, exocortis and greening. More vigorous than trifoliate, hardy and cold tolerant. Most promising for dwarfing Nagpur & Kinnow mandarin in India.
- *P. trifoliata* 'tetraploid No. 1' was found to exhibit more dwarfing and lower fruit quality than diploid forms.
- Adajamir (*C. assamensis*): Resistant to greening and have ginger-eucalyptus aroma.
- Karna Khatta (*C. karna*): Polyembryonic. Both *C. jambhiri* and *C. aurantium* are involved in parentage of *C. karna*. Suitable for heavy soils; semi-vigorous for Kinnow mandarin.
- Sour orange and RLC-6 Attani: Salt tolerant rootstock.
- Box orange or box thorn (*Severinia buxifolia*), Suki mandarin: Tolerant to salt, tristeza, boron and chloride.
- Kinnow is grafted on Carrizo (*C. carrizo*). Very hardy and vigorous than trifoliate. Tolerant to tristeza, root rot, greening and cold.
- Kodakithuli: Tolerant to many viruses, resistant to root rot.
- *Sohsarkar*: Vigorous for Kinnow in India.

- Most promising rootstock for acid lime: Gajanimma (*C. pennivesiculata*) followed by rough lemon.
- Etrong: Indicator for citrus exocortis.
- Wood apple: Highly dwarfing rootstock but not recommended due to short life of grafted plants.
- US-852 (*C. reticulata* x *P. trifoliata*), US-802, US-812, US-897: Tolerant to phytophthora.
- Forner Alcaide (F & A series): Developed in Spain.
- X-639 (Cleopatra mandarin x Trifoliate orange): Developed in South Africa in 1950; used in salinity prone area.
- C-35 citrange (Ruby orange x Webber-Fawcett trifoliate): Developed in 1951 & released in 1986.

Varieties and hybrids:

- Nagpur mandarin (Ponkan of China) was introduced in India in 1894 by Shuji Raja Bhosle. It is national variety and finest mandarin grown in the world. Grown in Satpuda hills in Maharashtra. It has received global GAP certificate.
- Pigment present in Nagpur mandarin: Crytoxanthin.
- Developments are faster in Kinnow-growing areas compared to 'Nagpur' mandarin.
- Satsuma cv. Silverhill produce > 60% sterile fruits.
- 'Darjeeling' santra: From West Bengal.
- Orlando: Indicator plant for Xyloporosis. Self incompatible.
- Nagpur mandarin: 6m x 6m.
- Kinnow can be grown in HDP by using 'Troyer citrange' as a rootstock by spacing the plants at 1.8 m x 1.8 m (3,000 plants/ha).
- High temperature during maturity period cause poor fruit development and fruits remain green.
- Ohta: Transgenic variety.
- Laddu:

Name	Breeding method	Features
Coorg mandarin	Selection	Most commercial variety in South India
Khasi orange (syn. Sikkim or Kamala mandarin)	Selection	Commercially grown in Assam
Desi orange (syn. Pathankot)	Selection	Spineless; grown in hill tracts of Punjab and Himachal Pradesh
Emperor, Fuetrelles	Introduced from Australia	-
Sutwal	Introduced from Nepal	-

Satsuma	-	Seedless; thornless; non-viable pollen; resistant to canker, gummosis, scaly bark, melanose; commercial cv. of Japan
Daisy Seedless	Irradiation to bud of cv. Daisy	-
Mutkhed Seedless	Bud mutant of Nagpur mandarin	-
Kiyomi	Satsuma x Trovita Orange	Seedless & cold hardy
Kinnow (1915)	King x Willow leaf	Bred by H.B. frost in USA; released for commercial cultivation in USA during 1935, introduced in India (Punjab) in 1959 & in south India during 1958; popular in semi-arid irrigated zone of Punjab; excellent in quality when grown in sub-tropical climate; No. of seeds (14-19); TSS: acid ratio (12.1-14.1)
University of California		
Gold Nugget	-	Diploid; late maturing; excellent productivity; outstanding storage; seedless
Tahoe Gold	-	Mid season; large fruits; skin deep orange coloured; seedless; rich fruit flavour
Shasta Gold	-	Triploid; late maturing; large fruits; skin deep orange; seedless; rich fruit flavour
Yosemite Gold	-	Triploid; late maturing; large fruits; skin deep orange; seedless
Dazy	-	Very early in market
NRCC, Nagpur		
NRCC Mandarin Seedless-4	-	2-3 seeds/fruit; TSS 10-11%; acidity 0.6-0.75%; yield 25-30 t/ha; good for processing; suitable for export
Dr PDKV, Akola		
Nagpur Santra (2003)	Selection	Self compatible & cross compatible except with grapefruit; suitable for Vidarbha region; more yield; fruits big
PDKV Mandarin-5 (2017)	Selection	Apricot-orange colour; Fruit wt. 142-149 g; 50% juice; yield 25-27 t/ha; TSS: acid ratio (14.85: 1)
Nagpur Seedless-182 (2003)	Selection	85% fruits are seedless with best sugar-acid blend. Contain 1.44 seed/fruit; yield 17-18 t/ha

Parents	**Name of hybrids**
Orlando x Clementine	Robinson, Lee, Osceola & Nova
Clementine x Orlando	Ambersweet, Bower
Minneola x Clementine	Page
Bower x Temple	Fallglo
Clementine x Tangelo	Fairchild
Willow leaf x King	Wilking (1935)
King x Willow leaf	Encore; peel tough & leathery
Weizhou Stasmuma Satsuma x *C. sinensis* cv. S_8	Wanmi
Miho x Comune	Desiderio
Okitsu x Carvalhais	Bellezza
King x Satsuma	Kara

Crop regulation:

- Root pruning is practiced in central and southern India to regulate flowering while it is not recommended practice in Uttar Pradesh.
- Resting or root exposure practiced in Deccan Plateau.
- Blooming thrice a year (a) February flowering: *Ambia bahar* (b) June flowering: *Mrig bahar*; (c) October flowering: *Hasta bahar*. Very economic and important.

40.2 Sweet orange

- Best time for pruning: Late winter or early spring.
- Pruning has little effect on time and amount of bloom.
- Availability period: December-April.
- Sweet orange is susceptible to water logging and phytopthora rot, so water stagnation in orchard should be avoided.
- Double ring method: Best for irrigation.
- Seedlessness in sweet orange is due to pollen and embryo sac (ovule) sterility.
- Maturity index: TSS (12-13^{0}Brix).
- Zn deficiency along with N is major nutritional problem of sweet orange.
- Highly susceptible to malda goma foot rot.
- Storage temperature: 0-1.1^{0}C.
- In trickle method of degreening, it is completely degreened in 48 h at 26-30^{0}C.

Rootstock:

- *C. pectinifera* (*C. depressa*), Rangpur Lime: Most promising rootstock for Mosambi, Sathgudi and Jaffa.
- Bud union crease is a problem in all citrus species budded on Jatti Khatti.
- Karna Khatta, Jatti Khatti: Suitable for Blood Red.
- Rough lime: Suitable for Sathgudi.
- Jatti Khatti: Suitable for arid region.

Varieties:

- URS Campestre: Seedless.

Name	Breeding method	Features
Spanish orange group		
Mosambi	Originated in Mozambique	Most popular in Maharashtra. Early, minimum acid content & high TSS (10%), 15-25 seeds
Pera, Hamlin	Introduced from Brazil	Early variety; chance seedling from Florida; seedless or 1-5 seeds; suitable for juice & processing purpose
Sathgudi/ Chini/ Chinese orange	Origined in 'Sathgur' place in Tamil Nadu	Susceptible to granulation. TSS 6.4%, ascorbic acid 44 mg/ 100 g; most popular in Telangana, Andhra Pradesh

Shamouti	Originated in Palestine	Seedless
Batavin	Originated in Batavia	Grown in coastal districts of A.P.
Blood orange group		
Malta		Seedy (20-30)
Blood Red Malta		Grown in Punjab, Haryana, Rajasthan, U.P.
Yuvaraj Blood Red	Clonal selection from 'Blood Red' orange	Seedless; early maturing
Mediterranean orange group		
Jaffa	Originated in Palestine	Mid season variety, suitable for arid region; few seeds (8-10)
Pineapple	Originated as a seedling in Citra, Florida	Flavour like pineapple; mid season; indicator of citrus greening
Valencia	Introduced from America	Late season variety; indicator of citrus greening
Valencia Late	Originated in China	-
Cuter Valencia	Introduced from California	Juice 52-53%; TSS (12-13%); acidity (0.7%); soft yellow segments; fruit wt. 200-230 g; mature in December; yield 21-30 t/ha; suitable for processing; keeping quality 1 to 1.5 month
Naval Orange group		
Navel orange		Navel is present in styler end
Washington Navel orange	Originated in Brazil	Introduced to Washington during 1870s; seedless; cultivated in A.P. & produces non-viable pollen; contain secondary rudimentary fruit embedded in fruit apex
Autumn Gold	Spontaneous mutants of Washington Navel orange	-
Powell Summer	Spontaneous mutants of Washington Navel orange	-
Waller Red	Spontaneous mutants of Washington Navel orange	-
Other varieties		
Pera, Natal, Westin	Introduced from Brazil	-
IARI, New Delhi		
Pusa Sharad (2013)	Selection	Big fruits (227 g); juice 50%; high TSS (9.2%) & free from granulation
Pusa Round (2014)	Selection	Big fruits (269 g); juice 48%; high TSS (10%) & free from granulation
Dr PDKV, Akola		
Katol Gold (2005)	Selection	Yield 8-10 t/ha; juice content 47.32%; TSS: acid ratio 13.89
MPKV, Rahuri		
Phule Mosambi	Clonal selection from Nucellar Mosambi	Yield: 18-20 t/ha; high juice (47.37%) with lower acidity (0.40 %) & high TSS (9.66^0 B)

Major problems:

- Fruit sucking moth in south India and granulation in north India.
- Phosphorus deficiency and granulation are most common problems in north India.

Granulation:

- Term 'granulation' was 1st given by Bortholomew in 1934.
- Drying of juicy sacs, insipid tastedue to high pectin & polysaccharide content.
- Lignification of juice cells lead to formation of sclerenchyma.
- Major pre-harvest physiological disorder. 1st reported in California.
- Cause: High temperature, high R.H., age, vigour of tree, nutritional status.
- Remedy: Spray 2, 4-D @ 12 ppm and Zn+Cu+K @ 0.5% or spray lead acetate or lead arsenate orspray of GA_3 @ 15 ppm & NAA @ 200 ppm.

Pre-harvest fruit drop:

- It is due to a) Physiological factors b) Pathological factors.
- Remedy: Spray 2,4-D @ 20 ppm.
- Most prone variety Mosambi and Malta Blood Red.

40.3 Lime and Lemons

- Mexico: Largest producer and processer in the world.
- India ranks 5th among major lime and lemon producing country in the world
- Limes and lemons are generally grouped together and contribute nearly 32% of total citrus production in India.
- These fruits rank 3rd after mandarins and sweet oranges.
- Andhra Pradesh is leading producer followed by Gujarat, Karnataka, Odisha, Maharashtra.
- Production of lemons is very limited and grown mostly in homestead gardens.
- Commercial cultivation of lemons is restricted to Punjab. Himachal Pradesh, Uttar Pradesh Assam and N-E states.
- In coastal climate, lemons continue to flower through out year.
- Limes and lemons are commercially propagated through seeds.
- Kagzi lime seeds inoculated with *Aspergillus brasilense* and soil inoculation with AM (*Glomus fasciculatum*, *G. mosseae*) fungi gives vigorous seedlings in nursery.
- Verdeli: Summer production of flower following water stress associated with lemon.
- Endoxerosis: Disorder associated with water deficiency.
- Acid limes are grown in India while sweet lemons are grown in Egypt and South America.

Limes	Lemons
Thinner peel, more acidic (7-8%), smaller in size; juice content (50-55%)	Thicker peel, hardy; less acidic (3-5%), larger in size
Flower colour- white	Flower colour- purple tinged
Apex region of fruit- abruptly round/ slightly nippled	Nipple is prominent
Petiolar wing- not much well developed	Petiolar wing- narrow & prominent
Excellent quality in arid regions	Excellent quality in semi-arid irrigated & coastal areas
Less hardy	More hardy
Less prone to cracking	More prone to cracking
Susceptible to canker	Resistant to canker & die back

- Anamalous, Sweet lemon are groups of lemon.
- Lemons are highly frost tolerant.
- Seedlessness in lemon is due to triploidy.
- Citrus canker: Most serious disease of acid lime.
- Seed viability: 6-8 days (normal) and 6 months (max.).
- Sweet lime contains non-acid juice and high malic acid.
- Only citrus fruit containing malic acid.
- Sweet lime is resistant to greening.
- Most common used system of planting: Square.
- Training system: Single stem.
- Offseason fruiting time for acid lime: November to December.
- Verdelli practice (withholding water in summer until the tree begins to wilt). Common practice for inducing out-of-season bloom in lemon.
- Enhancement of shelf life: 2, 4-D and 2, 4, 5-T.
- Storage temperature: 8-10^{0}C.
- Number of leaves required to form single fruit: 40.
- Increase in fruit set or reduce fruit drop: 2,4-D @ 20 ppm.
- Acid lime budded on trifoliate orange is more tolerant to canker than on Karna khatta.
- Cross protection technique (against tristeza) is done in acid lime. Mild strain of virus is injected to tolerate infection of severe viral strain. Tristeza is phloem localized systemic virus.
- Cross protection is possible in stem pitting virus on grape fruit in Australia & on Galengo lime in Brazil.
- 6-9 months old kagzi lime seedlings are inoculated by means of bark patch grafting.
- Cross protection principle is used to rebuild lime industry by supplying pre-immunized acid lime seedlings to farmers.
- Low fruit set in acid limes in spring is attributed to more number of male flowers.

- Flowering age of shoot varies from 3-13 months i.e. irrespective of age, shoot flowers.
- Henry Perrine is credited with introducing the 'Key lime to Florida'.
- Assam lemon, Coorg lemon, Seedless lemon and Hill lemon are close o true lemons.
- Nepali Oblong, Italian Round and Dominica Spineless have close affinity with *C. medica* and treated as cvs. of Citron.

Common name	Botanical name	Features
Sweet lime	*C. limettoides*	Self incompatible; non-acidic fruits; highly polyembryonic; it has close affinity with *C. aurantifolia*
Tahiti lime/ Persian lime	*C. latifolia* (hybrid between lime & lemon)	Monoembryonic; plants thornless; seedless, fruits large, autotriploid (pollens non-viable) & tolerant to cold
Rangpur lime/ Marmalade orange	*C. limonia*	Polyembryonic, hardy, very vigorous, ornamental species; small seeds; loose rind; easily separable segments; tolerant to calcareous soils; excludes chlorine; rootstock for mandarin & sweet orange; tolerant to tristeza, gummosis but susceptible to xyloporosis, exocortis, citrus nematode & burrowing nematode; tolerant to drought; suitable for heavy soil; best rootstock in central & south India
Acid lime/ Mexican lime/ West Indian lime/ Sour lime/ Kagzi lime	*C. aurantifolia*	Tropical & tenderest species; polyembryonic; indicator plant for tristeza virus; small fruifed & seeded; trees susceptible to frost damage; profuse bearing
Key lime (of Florida)	*C.* x *aurantifolia* (*C. micrantha* x *C. medica*)	Fruits spherical; 2.5-5 cm in dia.; small fruits; higher acidity, stronger aroma & thinner rind
Lemon	*C. limon*	Purple flower colour; polyembryonic
Rough lemon	*C. jambhiri*	Polyembryonic; highly vigorous; heavy bearer, tolerant to phytophthora root rot, tristeza, xyloporosis, exocortis, greening, chlorosis but susceptible to gummosis, citrus nematode and burrowing nematode; tolerant to saline and calcareous soil;suitable for deep sandy soils; most preferred in India
Bush lemon	Lemon x Citron	Natural hybrid
Citron or Persian Lime	*C. medica*	Monoembryonic; commonly used for pickling; highly resistant to citrus canker
Buddha's hand or Fingered citron	*C. medica* var. *sarcodactylis*	Oldest citrus fruit having finger like sections; originated in lower Himalaya
C. limetta	Lime x Lemon	-
-	*Limonia aeidissima*	Used for pickle purpose
-	*C. myrtifolia*	Bud mutant of *C. aurantium*
Lemons		
Eureka lemon	Seedling selection of Sicilian lemon	Thornless, tip bearing tendency; fruits necked; 9-14 segments; highly juice & acidic; seeds 0-6.
Lisbon lemon	-	Thorny; neck prominent; 7-10 segments; very acidic; seeds few to 10; female sterile; resistant to heat, frost & high wind velocity
Hill lemon/ Galgal	*C. pseudolimon*	Indigenous to sub-Himalayan region; apex & base nipped, seeds 25-50; segments 8-10; TSS (6.8-8.4^0 brix), acidity (4.25-6.6%);

		used for pickle, candy & squash purpose
Nepali Oblong (syn. Assam Lemon)	*C. limon*	Hardy; irregular crown; seedless;
Nepali Round	-	Fruits with less prominent nipple
Villa Franca	Belongs to Eureka group	Introduced to Florida from Europe in 1875; thorny, juice colourless; seeds 25-30; 10-12 segments; acidic juice
Meyer lemon	-	Semi-dwarf; thornless, cold resistant, thin rind
Lucknow Seedless	-	Seeds usually absent
Kagzi Kalan	-	Released from IARI; hardy; acidic
Pant Lemon-1 (Seville)	-	Selection from Kagzi Kalan; seedless, self incompatible, tolerant to canker, scab & gummosis
Malta Lemon	-	Dwarf, compact. Grown in southern states of India
Ermioni	-	Resistant to mal secco disease
-	*C. taiwanica*	Tolerant to tristeza, gummosis, salt
Volk or Volkamer lemon	*C. volkameriana*	Suitable for naval orange, Valencia orange & grape fruit

Acid lime/ Sour lime/ Mexican lime varieties: 40-60% juice with solid core, papery thin skin & shinning.

- Kagzi: Main variety of India due to its thin peel.
- Petlur Selection 21, 25: Moderately resistant to canker.
- Persian lime, Sweet lime: Acidless lime.
- Every year Kachai lime festival is held in Manipur.
- Mexican lime seedling: Transgenic variety.
- ALH-77 (Kagzi Lime x Nepali Round Lemon): Canker resistant.
- ARL-1: Selection from Arunachal Pradesh.
- **Sweet lime varieties**: Mitha Chikna, Mithora, NRCC Sweet Lime-1 (seedling selection; yellow fruits; fruit wt. 162 g; TSS 10.2%; acidity 0.24%).

Name	Breeding method	Features
IIHR, Bengaluru		
Rasraj (1998)	Interspecific hybrid of [Kagzi lime (*C. aurantifolia*) x Nepali Oblong (*C. limon*)]	Fruit wt. 55g; 6% acidity; TSS 8^0 Brix; juice 70%; tolerant to bacterial canker
Tenali	-	Tolerant to salts (up to 4.6 dS/m);
IARI, New Delhi		
Pusa Udit	Clonal selection	Tolerant to canker
Pusa Abhinav	Clonal selection	Year round flowering; susceptible to canker
NRCC, Nagpur		
NRCC Acid lime-7	Clonal selection	Fruits single; juice 50.5%; fruit wt. 48 g; yield (4069 fruits/ tree; 54 t/ha)
NRCC Acid lime-8	Clonal selection	Fruits in bunches; juice 51.5%; fruit wt. 50 g; yield (4237 fruits/tree; 59 t/ha)

VNMKV, Parbhani		
Pramalini (1998)	Selection from local Kagzi lime	Cluster bearing; fruit wt. 47 g; high juice (57.72%); off season bearing; cankar & phytophthora tolerant
Vikram (1996)	Selection from local Kagzi lime	Off-season (2 crops in a year) & cluster bearing (5-10 fruits/ cluster); fruit wt. 46 g
MPKV, Rahuri		
Sai Sarbati (syn. Selection-49)1993	Selection from local germplasm	1000-1200 fruits/ha; tolerant to tristeza, cankar & phytophthora
Phule Sarbati (2017)	Seedling selection from natural clonal population	Yield: 45-50 t/ha; high summer cropping (25.42 %); high juice content (52.5 %) over check (48.05% in Sai Sarbati)
Dr PDKV, Akola		
PDKV Trupti (Akola Lime-3) 2017	Selection	Highly polyembryonic; fruit wt. 55-60 g; seeds 9-10; rag percentage 28.73%; highly acidic 5.55%; yield 25-27 t/ha; suitable for pickle making
PDKV Lime (2004)	Clone of Kagzi lime	Yield 18-20 kg/tree (35% higher yield over Vikram); best marketable quality due to the round shape, thin peel & luster on peel
PDKV Bahar (2014)	Selection	Cluster bearing; acidity 6.18%; peel thickness 1.62 mm; 53% juice; ascorbic acid 31.47%; yield (30-35 t/ha); minimum incidence of canker
PDKV Chakradhar (2014)	Selection	Seedless & thornless; cluster bearing; peel thickness 1.02 mm; acidity 5.9%; high in vit. C (30.3 mg); high juice (60-65%); yield (18-20 t/ha)
Hybrid No. 2	Kigzi lime x Seedless Lemon	Resistant to bacterial canker
Hybrid No. 4	Kigzi lime x Seedless Lemon	Resistant to bacterial canker
NS-52	Kigzi lime x Seedless Lemon	Resistant to bacterial canker
Dr BSKKV, Dapoli		
Konkan Lemon (2007)	Selection	Seedless; yield 23.52 kg/ tree; thick peel & good for pickle making
ANGRAU, Hyderabad (AICRP on Citrus, Tirupati)		
Balaji	Pure line selection from 'Tenali'	Yield 57 t/ha; resistant to canker, immune to bark eruptions & mod. resistant to dry root rot (*F. solani*); recommended for A.P. & Telangana
TNAU, Coimbatore (HC & RI, Periyakulum)		
Jai Devi (syn. PKM-1) 1990	Selection from Kadayam type of Thirunelveli district	Big fruits (52 g); high ascorbic acid (34.29 mg/ 100 g fruit juice); juicy (52%); pleasant aroma; heavy yielder; less susceptible to leaf miner & citrus butter fly
Kachai lime	Identified in Kachai village of Manipur	1000-3000 fruits/ tree; highest ascorbic acid; juicy (51%); fruit weight 70-100 g
SKRAU, Sriganganagar		
Gangangar Acid Lime-1	Selection	-

Other varieties: ALC-2, Baramasi lemon, (seedless & not require bahar treatment)

40.4 Pummelo

- Eulogized as 'Shaddock'.
- Ancestor of pummelo is grape fruit.
- Sour orange (*C. megaloxycarpa*): Highly acidic, indigenous to India & bold seeds.
- Largest fruit size among citrus fruits.
- Mainly 2 types: White fleshed and red fleshed.
- Propagation method: Air layering.
- Self incompatible.
- Pummelo produce large amount of functional pollens.
- Seeds are monoembryonic.
- Seed viability: 8 months.
- Fruit growth and development peaks from 44 to 60 days after pollination.
- Interspecific crosses with pummelo are usually of higher vigour.

Varieties

- Chandler (resistant to Citrus Tristeza Virus), Chakaiya, Kopjar (pink flesh), Nagpur Chakotra, NRCC Galgal-1 (cluster bearing; fruit wt. 325 g; TSS 7.5%; 5.9% acidity), Kao Phuang (white fleshed)
- Hayasaki (Matou Buntan x Hirado Buntan): It has oblate to pyriform fruits weighing 600-1000 g with light yellow rind and greenish yellow flesh with 12-15% TSS.

Name	Breeding method	Features
Pummelo US-145	Introduced from California	10% sugar; 32% juice, less astringent, rich in anti-oxidants
Flamingo	Red pummelo [(Chandler Pummelo x (Shamouti Orange x Clementine)]	Developed in Isreal; 14% sugar, seedless, presence of lycopene, red pigment
Hanna	White pummelo (Tahitian x Chandler Pummelo)	Developed in Isreal; white flesh, sweet, 12.6% sugar, seedless
IARI, New Delhi		
Pusa Seedless Pummelo-1 (2017)	-	India's 1st seedless white fleshed mutant; high juice recovery (41.13%)
NRCC, Nagpur		
NRCC Pummelo-1	Selection from seedling of OP seeds	Seedless; 2-5 fruits/cluster; fruit wt. 400 g; red flesh; 39% juice; 14 segments/fruit; TSS 11-12%; acidity 0.85%; very good for juice purpose
NRCC Pummelo-2	Selection from land races of NEH regions	Round fruits; fruit wt. 700 g; red flesh; TSS 10.2%; acidity 1.08%
NRCC Pummelo-3	Seedling selection	Round fruits; seedy; fruit wt. 1.25 kg; red flesh; TSS 10-11%; acidity 0.95%
NRCC Pummelo-4	Chance seedling	Yellow fruits with light yellow flesh; pleasant sweet flavour; TSS 11.5%; acidity 0.82%

NRCC Pummelo-5	Clonal selection	Yellow fruits with red flesh; TSS 11-13%; acidity 1.07%; fruit wt. 815 g; good for table purpose
NRCC Pummelo-7	Clonal selection	Yellow fruits with light pink coloured very tender segments; TSS 11%; good for table purpose
Pummelo-US-145	Introduced from USA	-
IIHR, Bengaluru		
Arka Ananta (2019)	Clonal variant of pummelo accession-25	Bears fruit in 2 season in a year; fruit wt. 1.2 kg; oblique fruit shape; pink pulp; TSS (11-12^0 brix); 1.2% acidity; low naringenin (160.6 ng/ ml); suitable for fresh consumption; yield 80-90 fruits/ plant/season
Arka Chandra (2019)	Clonal variant of pummelo accession-18	Bears fruit in 2 season in a year; fruit wt. 1 kg; spheroid fruit shape; white pulp; TSS (11-12^0 brix); 0.89% acidity; low naringenin (344.75 ng/ ml); suitable for fresh consumption; yield 35-40 fruits/ plant/season

40.5 Grape fruit

- Eulogized as 'Forbidden fruit or Break fast fruit'.
- It is from New World.
- The first record of the name 'grape fruit' in Jamaica was in 1814.
- By 1910, grape fruit became a commercial crop in California.
- Indian grape fruit: *C. rugulosa*.
- It is a cross between pummel and sweet/ bitter orange.
- The name grape fruit has been derived from habit of bearing the fruits in clusters like grapes.
- Japan: Largest producer of grapefruit.
- Nomillin: Bitter component which inhibits certain forms of cancer. Bitterness is due to oxidation.
- Grape fruit is used for preparation of dry and fortified wines.
- It is chance hybridization of pummelo and sweet orange: Unique interspecific hybrid.
- Naringenin: Bitterness (flavonoid compound) in juice.
- Vivipary is observed.
- Seed viability: 12 months (88%).
- Pink grape fruit is rich in anti-oxidant.
- Red grape fruit provides lycopene.
- Storage temperature: 10-15^{0}C.

Varieties

- Pigmented varieties: Foster, Thompson & Burgundy are periclinal chimeras by somatic mutations.

- NRCC Grapefruit-6: Chance seedling; very juicy, cluster bearing, red fleshed, TSS 10.2%, fruit wt. 358 g.

Name	Breeding method	Features
White fleshed		
Duncan	Chance seedling from Florida	Parthenocarpic seedless; pulp light yellow; abundant juice; juice acidic & bitter; pleasing aroma
Marsh Seedless	Bud sport of 'Marsh'	12-14 segments; abundant juice; female sterile; seeds few (2 seeds/fruit) & large; light yellow coloured fruits; suitable for close density planting
Walter	-	-
Red fleshed		
Star Ruby (1970)	Mutant of 'Hudson' using thermal neutrons	1st cv. from mutation breeding; dark red seedless flesh; large fruit of 425 g; high seed content; heavy bearer
Foster	Bud sport of 'Walter'	Very less juice; yellow pink flesh; 12-16 segments; 30-60 seeds/ fruit; abundant juice; acidic juice
Foster Pink	Bud sport of 'Foster'	Pink & seedy
Hudson	Bud sport of 'Foster'	Red seedy flesh
Thompson (syn. Pink Marsh)	Bud sport of 'Marsh Seedless'	Early; pink flesh & seedless
Einat- Pink Grape fruit	Hudson Tetra Fluoride x Pummelo	Sourless; pink flesh; sugar 11.5%; seedless segments
Aliza Grape fruit	Chandler Pummelo x Ora	16% sugar; sweet; seedless; dominate in global market
Red Blush	-	Dark red flesh colour; nealy seedless; highly acidic; fruit wt. 320 g
Flame	-	Seedless; suitable for HDP at 4m x 4m; fruit wt. 350-400 g; yield 25 t/ha
Triumph	-	-
Shaharanpur Special	-	Round to oblate fruits; 12-14 segments; pale yellow pulp; sweet-sour taste; numerous seeds
Ruby Red (1929)	Bud sport of 'Thompson'	1st citrus fruit variety patented; 1st variety with red pigmentation & seedless
Rio Red (1984)	Mutant of 'Star Ruby'	Red flesh, seedless and preferred in Texas

Artificial hybrids

Name	Parents involved	Remarks & name of hybrids
Intergeneric		
Citrange	*P. trifoliata* x *C. sinensis*	Used as dwarfing rootstock for grapefruit, Satsuma, Sweet orange & Lemon.Cvs. Troyer, Morton, Benton, Coleman, Rusk, Cunningham, Rustic, Sanford. Etonia, Savage, Carrizo.
Citrumelo	Citrange x *C. paradisi*	Swingle; resistant to tristeza
Citrangequat	Citrange x Kumquat (*Fourtunella marginata*)	Trigeneric; ornamental spp. & used for candying cvs. Telfair, Sinton
Citradia	*P. trifoliata* x Sour orange	-
Limequat	*C. aurantifolia* x *F. japonica*	Cvs. Lakehand, Eustris

Citrumquats	*P. trifoliata* x *F. japonica* or *F. margarita*	Very difficult hybrid to breed
Citrangor	Citrange x *C. sinensis*	Trigeneric back cross hybrid
Cicitrange	Citrange x *P. trifoliata*	
Citrandarin	*P. trifoliata* x *C. reticulata*	-
Citremon	*P. trifoliata* x *C.limon*	-
Poncimequat	(*F. japonica* x *C. aurantifolia*) x *F. hindisii*	-
Orangequats	*C. reticulata* cv. Satsuma x *F. japonica* x *F. margarita* cv. Meiwa	-
Citrumuats	*Poncirus* x *Fortunella*	-
Interspecific/ intrageneric hybrids		
Tangerin	Robinson x Osceola	Cvs. Sunburst, Dancy, Honey
Tangelo	*C. reticulata* x *C. paradisi* (Dancy x Ordinary grapefruit)	Cvs. Sampson, Seminole, Thornton, William
	Imperial grape fruit x Willowleaf	Cvs. Pear Tangelo, Allspice, Pearl
	Dancy x Duncan	Cvs. Orlando, Minneola, Sunshine
Tangor	*C. reticulata* x *C. sinensis*	Mostly monoembryonic cvs. Temple, Clementine, Monreal, Umatilla, Ariake, Murcott, Afourer, Dweet, Ambersweet, Ellendale
	C. unshiu cv. Kiyomi x *C. sinensis* cv. Okitsu	Cvs. Tsuno Kaori
Lemonime	*C. limon* x *C. aurantifolia*	Cv. Parrine
Lemonnage	*C. limon* x *C. sinensis*	-
Lemandarin	*C. limon* x *C. reticulata*	-
Orangelo	Orange x Grape fruit	-
Citrangedin	Citrange x Calamondin (*C. mitis*)	Trispecific hybrid
Pummelo hybrids	Ruby Orange (*C. grandis*) x King Tangore (*C. paradisi*)	Triploid & seedless cvs. Melogold & Oroblanco

Mutation breeding

Crop	Original cultivar	Nature of mutation	Mutant cultivar
Navel orange	Bahia	Limb sport	Baianinha
	Washington	Limb sport	Naveline, Navellate, Marrs, Autumn Gold, Powell Summer, Weller Red
Mandarin	Owari	Bud sport	Clausellin
	Pongan	Bud sport	Pongan 86-1
Grapefruit	Walters (white flesh)	Limb sport	Foster (pink flesh)
	Foster (pink flesh)	Bud sport	Hudson (deep red flesh)
	Hudson (deep red flesh)	Limb sport	Star Ruby (deepest red peel)
	Thompson (light pink flesh & peel)	Bud sport	Redblush (deep red flesh)
	-	-	Flame
	Apomictic seeds	Thermal neutron	Star Ruby
Pummelo	A local cv. of *C. maxima*	Bud sport	Wuheputaoyou
Seedless lemon	Bud wood	Irradiation	Rio Red

Incompatibility in citrus:

- Self incompatibility: Seedless lemon, Sweet lime, Clementine mandarin, Siamese pummelo, Italian Nepali Oblong, Lucknow Seedless lemon, Orlando tangelo and Grape fruit hybrids.
- Self as well as cross incompatibility exists in grape fruit, lemon, sweet orange and mandarins.
- Nagpur Orange is cross and self compatible except with grape fruit.
- Mosambi on Trifoliate orange and *C. maxima*.
- Kazgi lime on Karna Khatta and Trifoliate orange.
- Troyer citrange on Lemon var. Eureka.
- Karna Khatta on sweet orange var. Blood Red Malta.
- *Citrus taiwanica* on lemons.
- Nagpur mandarin onTrifoliate orange.

Harvesting stages

- Mandarin: Colour change from green to orange.
- Sweet orange: Colour change from green to yellow.
- Lime and lemon: Mature green.

Diseases and pests

- Citrus decline or Dieback or Reclamation disease: Complex of many disorders. Mostly due to Copper deficiency. Most susceptible crop- Mandarin.
- Sour rot (*Geotrichun candidum*): Severe in mandarins. Major during handling and transportation. Spray Guazatine fungicide.
- Greening is 1st reported in India. It can be identified through spectroscopy technique FTIR-ATR (Forier Transformed Infra Red-Attenulated Total Reflection). Chromatographic technique can confirm mycoplasma incidence.
- Citrus canker (Xanthomonas citri): Introduced in India from USA and was 1st observed at Dehradun during 1831. Spray Streptomycin @ 1% on emerging flush. Citron: Canker resistant.
- Specific symptoms of trizteza virus: Honey combing, stem pitting and vein flecking.
- Ring spot disease in kinnow cause 100% loss in Punjab.
- Phytophthora rot/ Collar rot/ Foot rot/ Crown rot/ Brown rot/ Gummosis (*Phytophthora parasitica*): Drench with Ridomil MZ with spray of Allitte. Rootstocks like sour orange, Cleopatra mandarin, trifoliate orange, rangpur lime are tolerant.
- Powdery milew (*Oidium tingtanium*): Dust sulphur 200-250 mesh.
- Pink disease (*Corticium salmonicolor*): Spray Blitox @ 0.2%.

- Scab (*Elsinoe fawcetti*): Spray Bordeaux mixture @ 0.3%.
- Felt disease (*Septobasidium pseudopedicellatum*): Clean cultivation & Bordeaux mixture spray.
- Lemon butterfly (*Papilio demoleus*): Larva defoliate branches.
- Citrus rust mite (*Phyllocoptruta oleivora*):
- California red scale (*Aonidiella aurantii*):
- Citrus white fly: Sooty mold develop & leaves turn pale. Use parasite *Eretmocerus* spp. and predator *Scymmus* spp.
- Oriental fruit fly (*Dacus dorsalis*): Cause premature fruit fall.
- Fruit sucking moth (*Eudocima aurantia*): Nocturnal pest and damages crop in adult stage.
- Citrus black fly (nymphal stage) was most critical & managed by 0.05% Monocrotophos followed by 1% neem oil.
- Trifoliate orange and its hybrids: Tolerant to tristeza, xyloporosis, gummosis, citrus nematode (*Tylenchulus semipenetrans*) but susceptible to exocortis, and burrowing nematode.
- Fungal parasite *Paecilomyces lilacinus* (8 g) on infected grains reduce nematode population.
- Citrus psylla (*Diaphorina citri*): Vector for greening MLO disease. Predatory lady bird beetle restricts infestation.Tree injection of tetracycline has been standardized.
- Bio-control of psylla: *Mallada boninensis* @ 30 larvae/tree and *Tamarixia radiata* @ 40 larvae /tree.
- Leaf miner (*Phyllocnistis citrella*): Serious in nursery, young/ old orchard.
- Parasitoids for citrus leaf miner: *Citrostichus phyllocnistoides*, *Cirrospilus ingenuus*, *Quadrastichus citrella*, *Asecodes delucchi*, *Sympiesis striatipes*, *Elasmus pantnagerensis*, *Closterocerus citrella*.
- Bark borer (*Inderbella* spp.) and trunk borer: Damaging pest.
- Orange trunk borer (*Anoplophora versteegi*): Damaging stage- Grub. Plug cotton soaked in Monocrotophos @ 5 ml/ 1 lit.

Disease	**Causal organism**	**Vector**	**Indicator plant (s)**
Exocortis/ Scaly butt	Virus	Mechanical tools & infected bud wood	Mexican lime & symptomless in sweet orange, mandarin orange, grape fruit, rough lemon
Tristeza/ Quick decline	Phloem localized systematic virus	Tissue grafts & Oriental citrus aphid (*Toxoptera citricida*)	Kagzi lime, Mexican lime
Spreading decline	Nematode	-	-
Psorosis/ California	Virus	Seeds i.e. no insect vector	Mexican lime, sour orange.

scaly butt/ Cachexia			sweet orange & mandarins, Mexican lime
Greening/ Yellow shoot tip	MLO & bacteria (*Spiroplasma citri*)	Citrus psylla	Sweet orange cv. Valencia, Pineapple, Naval orange
Xyloporosis	Virus	Mechanical tools & bud transmitted	Sweet lime
Canker	Bacteria (*X. campestris* pv. *citri*)	Leaf miner (*Phyllocnitis citrella*)	Acid lime
Gummosis	*Phytophthora* spp.	-	-
Green mold	*Penicillium digitatum*	-	-
Blue mold	*Penicillium italicum*	-	-
Gray mold	*Botrytis cinerea*	-	-
Mal secco	*Phoma tracheiphila*	-	-
Huanglongbing (Yellow dragon disease or citrus greening)	Bacteria (*Candidatusliberi-bacter asiaticus*)	Citrus psylla	Cannot be multiplied in laboratory; confirmed through chromatographic technique

Physiological disorders:

- Granulated juice sacs contain excess of Ca, Mg, Na, K, cellulose, hemicellulose, pectin, starch and lignins.
- Granulation is ripening disorder and can be indexed from changes in peel.
- Tree grafted on grapefruit are more susceptible to Mo deficiency.
- Zinc is absorbed by leaves at any time during year, while soil application of Zn is not effective.
- Excess K application increase acidity in fruit juice & induces Mn, Mg, Zn disorder.
- Nitrogen from nitrates is quickly available to plants.
- Continuous application of ammonium sulphate increases sub-soil acidity.
- In acidic soils, rock phosphate is used as a source of phosphorous.
- Seeded varieties are more prone to Mg deficiency & trees become more cold susceptible. Foliar spray of $MgNO_3$ or soil application of dolomite is recommended.

Name	**Cause (s)**	**Remedy**
Fruit drop	Temperature fluctuation & nutritional imbalance	Spray NAA or 2,4-D @ 20 ppm in September
Granulation/ Crystallization/ Dry end (serious in north India)	Luxuriant growth, rootstock, variety, frequent irrigation, mineral constituents in plant tissue, time of harvest, exposure to sunlight	Spray GA_3 @ 15 ppm followed by NAA 300ppm in October
Fruit cracking and splitting	Changes in atmosphere	-
Frenching/ Mottled leaf/ Foliocellosis	Zn deficiency	Spray $ZnSO_4$ & spray Ca Cl_2 % 0.5%
Little leaf& die back	Zn deficiency	Spray $CaCl_2$ @ 0.5%
Membranosis	Long term storage of lemon at low temperature (>13^{0}C) cause chilling injury	-

Lime induced chlorosis	Fe deficiency	Spray $FeSO_4$ @ 0.5%
Exanthema	Cu deficiency	Spray $CuSO_4$ @ 0.1%
Coarse & thicker rind	P deficiency	Apply P fertilizer
Die back	Ca deficiency	Apply lime or gypsum
Internal decline (Endo xerosis)	Moisture i.e. loss of water from internal tissue (water stress disorder in lemons)	-
Oleocellosis (Oil spotting)	Harvesting of wet fruits	-
Puffing in mandarins	Over maturity	-
Creasing of rind	Common in Naval orange	-
Crazy top	Trees grown in alkali soils	-
Blastomaenia (serious in Nagpur mandarin orange)	Viral disease (bud transmissible)	Adopt shoot-tip grafting
Foam (serious on Khasi orange)	Imbalance in sugar metabolism leads to bark splitting	-

Inheritance of characters

- Positive correlation of leaf phosphorous status with fruit yield.
- Fruit shape and presence of thorn: Polygenic.
- Rind texture: Monogenic.
- Nucellar embryony: One or twodominant genes. Simple inheritance.
- Polyembryony: Dominant gene having heterozygous allele (*Pp*) while homozygous recessive gene (*pp*) is present in monoembryony.
- Purple colour in young leaves in lemon: Dominant gene.
- Small fruit size, seediness, paleness of fruit colour: Dominant.
- Presence of thorns, pubescence, oil glands: Dominant.
- Resistance to citrus tristeza clostro virus (CTV): Single dominant gene.
- Trifoliate leaf character in *Poncirus*: Dominant.
- Curved thorns and twisted trunk: Pleiotropic effect of dwarfing gene.
- Bitter principle: Dominant-multiple genes.
- Yellow rind colour: Recessive.
- Seedlessness: Recessive, oligogenes.
- Dwarfness in 'Flying Dragon' rootstock: Single dominant gene.

40.6 Bael

- Eulogized as 'Bengal quince or Indian quince or Golden apple or Climate purifier or Symbol of Lord Shiva'.
- Generic name *Aegle* is Greek origin and species name *marmelos* is Portuguese one.
- Leaves are used to offer 'Lord Shiva'.

- Useful medicinal plant of India.
- Indigenous fruit tree of India.
- Deciduous tree with trifoliate aromatic leaves. Potential for processing and not popular as dessert fruit.
- Unripe or half ripe fruit contains 31.3-31.8% carbohydrates, 1.8% proteins and 2.9% fibre.
- Rich source of riboflavin (1.19 mg/100 g).
- Most widely used for preserve making.
- Ripe fruit is laxative and good for heart and brain while unripe fruits are prescribed for diarrhea and dysentery.
- Act as a sink for commercial pollution as it absorb poisonous gases from atmosphere.
- Fruit pulp has detergent action.
- Pulp is used as base of various fruit products like squash, jam, slab, toffee, powder, nectar, RTS, etc.
- Unripe/ half ripe fruit regarded as astringent, digestive stomachic, in chronic diarrhea, dysentery and tonic for heart and brain.
- Roots and bark used in form of decoction.
- Fruit rind nd bark in dyeing and tanning industry and yellow dye is extracted.
- The alkaloid Aegelin present in leaves is used for treating asthma.
- Indicator plant for tracing underground water.
- Commonly planted in agroforestry due to hardy nature.
- Susceptible to waterlogging.
- Most useful medicinal plant of India.
- It has very high phenolic (flavonoids) content. It is ideal for radical scavenging activity.
- Marmelosin: Active ingredient present in bael (0.03-0.37%), extracted from mucilaginous pulp. It is colourless, crystalline compound.
- Tanin content in pulp (9%) and rind (20%).
- Seed oil 11.9% and bitter in taste.
- Seeds contain 62% proteins (2% water soluble & 60% insoluble).
- High penolics (3000 to 17500 mg/100 g) contribute to its astringent taste.
- Alkaloids, coumarins, steroids and essential oils extracted from leaves, wood bark and roots.
- Gum is used as adhesive, water proofing and oil emulsion coating.
- Mucilage: 12.78-19.57%.
- TSS for bael pulp: 31-35.5%.

- It can withstand sodicity up to 30 ESP and salinity up to 9 dS/m and pH 5 to 10.
- Tree tolerates low temperature up to -7^{0}C.
- Branching habit: Dimorphic.
- Planting time: July-August and February-March.
- Fruit: Hard shelled berry.
- Edible portion: Succulent placenta.
- Training system: Modified leader system.
- Pruning month: Only dead, weak and criss crossed branches are removed in March-April during leafless condition. Suckers appearing from seedling rootstocks are removed periodically.
- Flowering month: April-May.
- Anthesis time: 6-8 AM.
- Anther dehiscence: 6.30-8.30 AM.
- Propagation methods: Seed, 'T' budding (July-October), chip budding (March-June), patch budding (June-July, 90% success) and Top working.
- Veneer grafting gives 80% success in June-July.
- Seed viability: 6 months
- Commercial propagation: Patch budding and soft-wood grafting.
- Hard-wood cutting (15-20 cm length & 2-3 cm thickness) obtained from prolific bearing mother plant and treated with IBA 4000 ppm gives good rooting within 15-20 days in controlled atmosphere.
- *In situ* patch budding in May-June with 1 to 1.5 month old scion shoot is best.
- *Aegle fraeglegabonensis*, *Aeglopsis chevalieri*: Used as rootstock for grafting.
- Spacing: 8m x 8m (budded plant) and 10m x 10m (seedlings).
- HDP: 5m x 5 m (400 plants/ha).
- Basin system of irrigation provides uniform distribution of water.
- Seedling trees require 8 years to bear fruits while budded plants starts 5 years after planting.
- Fruits become fully mature 8 months after fruit set.
- Bael takes 11 months from fruit set to ripen on tree.
- Mature green fruits are ideal for harvesting and have 15 days shelf life.
- Fruits harvested at ripe (greenish yellow rind colour) stage can be stored for a week.
- Fruit ripening can be advanced by 45 days with preharvest treatment of Ethephon @ 1000 ppm in February (or 9 months after fruit set).
- Off season availability of ripened fruits could be made by ethrel application coupled with storing at 30^{0}C.

- Yield: Budded plant at age of 10 years 100-150 fruits/tree or 18-20 t/ha and seedling trees bear 200-300 fruits/ tree or 20-30 t/ha at 12 years age.
- Astringent pulp contains 10-15 rectangular shaped seeds.
- For preserve making, mature green fruits are ideal for harvesting.
- Ripe fruits are used for beverage making.
- Main hindrance in processing: Extraction of pulp from fruit.
- Value added products: Preserve, RTS, Beverage, Nectar, Squash, Cider, Jam, Toffee, pulp powder, Syrup and Sharbat are made from pulp.
- Storage temperature of fruits in cold storage: 9^0C + 85-90% R.H.
- Chilling injury (appearance of brown spots on fruit surface) develops during storage of fruits below 9^0C.
- Use of PGRs viz. GA_3, 2, 4-D, 2,4,5-T can check fruit drop to reasonable extent.
- Significant correlations of fruit weight, fruit length and diameter; pulp weight vs. length and diameter indicates selection as best method for improvement.

Varieties

- Popular types: Mirzapuri, Kagzi Gonda, Kagzi Etawah, Kagzi Banarasi, PBN-7, Latur-5, OBD-5, OBD-7, Darogaji, Ojha, Rampure, Azamati, VN-DP 5/9, VN-DP 5/12, VN-DP 5/14, VN-DP 5/27, VN-DP 5/33.

Variety	Breeding method	Features
CIAH, Bikaner (CHES, Godhra)		
Goma Yashi (2010)	Selection from Jodhpur area	Dwarf, spineless, prolific bearer, early maturing, suitable for HDP; shell wt. 180 g; pulp TSS (35-39^0 Brix); 68-72% pulp; acidity 0.26-0.32%; ascorbic acid 22 mg/ 100 g; resistant to fruit drop & splitting
Thar Divya	Local selection from Badalpatti, Jaunpur	Early maturing; fruit wt. (1.51 kg); pulp TSS (37^0 Brix); vit. C (19.8 mg/100 g); acidity (0.3%); yield (85.2 kg/tree); suitable for table & processing purpose
Thar Neelkanth (2015)	Selection from Jaunpur area	Drought hardy; high pulp (71.3%); less acidity (0.29%); number of seeds (83); pulp TSS (41.2^0 Brix); yield (75 kg/tree)
CISH, Lucknow		
CISH-B-1	Selection from OP seedling	Precocious & prolific bearer; oval to spherical shaped fruits; fruit wt. 0.8-1.4 kg; pulp TSS 42^0Brix; fruit yield (58-60 kg/tree); excellent for processing
CISH-B-2	Selection from OP seedling	Dwarf; thin shell; orange yellow pulp; fruit wt. (1.7-2.6kg); pulp TSS (31^0 Brix); tannin 2.45%; fruit yield (58.90 kg/tree); titrable acidity 0.41%; good flavor & taste

GBPUA & T, Pantnagar		
Pant Shivani	Seedling selection	Tall; early mid-season, precocious & heavy-bearer. Fruit weight 2-2.4 kg; yield (52.0 kg/ tree); fruit shape ovoid; pulp TSS 36^0 Brix; ascorbic acid (19.55 mg/100g); taste & storage quality is very good
Pant Urvashi	Seedling selection	Tall, vigorous, precocious & heavy bearer. Fruit weight 1.5-2.50 kg; yield (45.65 kg/tree); pulp TSS 33^0 Brix in pulp & ascorbic acid 17.15 mg/ 100g pulp.
Pant Sujata	Seedling selection	Dwarf; precocious & heavy-bearer; fruit globose; fruit weight 1.12 to 1.40 kg; storage life better; thin rind; mucilage & fibre low; pleasant flavour; pulp TSS 32^0 brix; ascorbic acid 17.10 mg/100 g of flesh. Yield (78.59 kg/plant)
Pant Aparna	Seedling selection	Dwarf; almost thornless, precocious & heavy-bearer. Fruit globose; fruit weight 0.8-1.25 kg;pulp TSS 34^0 Brix & ascorbic acid 17.15 mg/100 g of pulp; yield (40.25 kg/ plant) at 6 years age.
NDUA&T, Faizabad		
Narendra Bael-1	Seedling selection	Medium oblong shaped fruits; mild fragrance; sweet taste with mild acidity; few seeds
Narendra Bael-2	Seedling selection	Spherical shaped fruits
Narendra Bael-4	Seedling selection	Excellent fruit quality & heavy bearer; fruits medium sized (775 g); yellow colour at maturity
Narendra Bael-5	Seedling selection	Precocious bearing; fruits medium sized; round smooth surface, very thin rind, rind yellow at maturity; low mucilage moderately fibrous; pulp TSS 33^{0}Brix; ascorbic acid 18.63 mg/100 g; more fruit set (28 kg/tree)
Narendra Bael-6	Seedling selection	Medium fruits; round shape; skull thin; mild acidic; low mucilage; soft flesh
Narendra Bael-7	Seedling selection	Tall; sparse bearing; fruit wt. 850 g; roundish oval, smooth surface & thin rind; fruits deep orange at maturity; pulp TSS 30^{0}Brix; ascorbic acid 19.78 mg/100 g
Narendra Bael-9	Seedling selection	Vigorous growth; fruits large (1.29 kg); roundish oblong, surface smooth & yellowish green at maturity; thick rind; pulp TSS 38^{0}Brix; ascorbic acid 19.20 mg/100 g; less seeds; yield 56 kg at 6th year age
Narendra Bael-16	Seedling selection	-
Narendra Bael-17	Seedling selection	-

Pests and diseases

- Bacterial leaf spot/ Bacterial shot hole/ Fruit canker (*Xanthomonas compestris* pv. *bilvae*) : Serious disease.
- Fungal leaf spot (*Alternaria* spp.).

- Fruit rot (*Aspergillus nidulans*) : Storage disease.
- Fruit and leaf anthracnose (*Colletotrichum* spp.)
- Gummosis.
- Wilt.
- Powdery mildew (*Oidium* spp.)

Physiological disorders

- Fruit drop : Due to embryo abortion, fruit borer attack, fruit rotting, fruit cracking. Spray NAA @ 20 ppm & Borax @ 1%.
- Fruit splitting/ cracking : Occurs just before ripening.
- Sunscald :

40.7 Woodapple

- Monotypic genus.
- Versatile adaptability, deciduous and hardy nature, low maintenance and high medicinal value.
- Spiny deciduous tree.
- Flower colour : Dull red.
- Fruit: Hard shelled, many seeded berry with pinkish edible pulp.
- Grown in light to heavy black cotton soils.
- Does not grow above 1500 m MSL.
- Fruit composition: TSS (9.4-16^0 Brix), vit. C (1.68-3.40 mg/ 100 g), titratable acidty (0.83-2.76%), total sugar (4.08-4.47%), protein (6.3 g/100 g); -CHO (15.6 g/100 g), total phenol (235 mg/ 100g), P (0.037-0.078%), K (1.29-1.86%), Ca (0.11-0.39%), pectin (1.39-1.65).
- Pulp represents 36% of the whole fruit.
- Propagation methods: Seed, budding, micrografting.
- Polyembryony upto 60% is reported.
- *In situ* budding under arid conditions.
- Budding and inarch grafting give 70% success.
- Micrografting gives 90% success when done on 3 months old rootstock in April-May.
- Planting distance : 8 m x 8 m.
- Training system: Central leader.
- Flowering season: February-May and fruits available in winter.
- Fruiting season: October-January.
- Yield : 200-250 fruits/ year.
- Grading : On the basis of size.
- Harvest index : Bouncing stage.

Varieties

Elite accessions/ superior genotypes No. 5, 9, 10, 15 (from MPKV, Rahuri), PNB-11, PNB-15, CHES-2, CHES-10, CHES-11, CHES-WA-18.

Name	Breeding method	Features
CIAH, Bikaner		
Thar Gaurav	Selection	Precocious bearer; fruit wt. (452 g); pulp (50.9%); TSS (14.12^0 Brix); acidity (3.85%); total sugar (3.07%); pectin (1.76%); protein (pulp 18.13%; seed 24.38%); K (1.73%); Ca (0.3%); yield (58.6 kg/plant); suitable for table purpose
CHESW-1	-	Fruit wt. 239 g; pulp 43.95%; TSS 15.6^{0}Brix; yield 50 kg/tree
CHESW-2	-	Fruit wt. 392 g; pulp 51.3%; TSS 18^{0}Brix; yield 108 kg/tree
CHESW-3	-	Fruit wt. 312 g; pulp 46.9%; TSS 12^{0}Brix; yield 58 kg/tree
CHESW-5	-	Fruit wt. 276 g; pulp 51%; TSS 14.6^{0}Brix; yield 68 kg/tree
CHESW-6	-	Fruit wt. 385 g; pulp 58.27%; TSS 20.3^{0}Brix; yield 148 kg/tree
CHESW-10	-	Fruit wt. 350 g; pulp 55.62%; TSS 18.6^{0}Brix; yield 105 kg/tree
VNMKV, Parbhani		
Ellora (HB-10)	Selection through survey	Fruit wt. 300-850 g; yield 200-250 fruits/ tree

41. SAPINDACEAE

41.1 Litchi (syn. Lychee)

- Eulogized as 'Queen of sub-tropical fruits or Fruit of high commerce or Fruit of summer and winter season'.
- Sapindaceae family is also known as 'Soap berry family' due to presence of saponin in fruits.
- Spanish name '*Melicoccus bijugatus*' belong to Sapindaceae family.
- Largely grown in tropics and sub-tropics between 13^{0}N and 6-29^{0}S.
- 1st introduced in India at Bengal during 16th century via Burma.
- State with largest producer of lychee and Mesta in India: Bihar.
- Land of litchi: Muzaffarpur.
- 1st monograph was written in 1059 AD by Ts'ai Hsiang was 1st publication in the world.
- Table fruit in India (litchi nut) while fresh, dried & canned in China and Japan.
- Evergreen precocious tree.
- Slow growing deep rooted tree.
- Highly perishable fruit.
- Largest producer in the world: China.
- Thailand is major exporter of litchi along with longan.
- Highest area, production and productivity: Bihar.

- Litchi plants grow commercially in Choota Nagpur area.
- Red colour of fruit pericarp: Anthocyanin.
- Fruits sprayed with Ethrel @ 250 ppm increase anthocyanin content.
- Major organic acid: Malic acid (80%).
- Toxic substance present in seed: Methylene cyclopropyl glycine.
- Fruit is rich in vit. C: 40-90 mg/100g and calcium.
- Fruit compostion: 60% juice, 8% rag, 19% seed and 13% skin.
- Fruits also contain 0.7% protein, 0.3% fat and 0.7% minerals.
- Food value (range of sugar content) of fruit: 6.74 to 18%.
- Pulp is out growth of the litchi seed.
- 'Chicken-tongue' refers to shriveled seeds with rudimentary embryo which is due to stenospermocarpy.
- Dried litchi is known as 'litchi nut' (dried flesh and seed rattle inside hard shell).
- Moisture content of litchi nut: 10-15%.
- Limiting factors in cultivation: Frost and dry heat.
- Requires high R.H. and high lime in soil.
- Seed viability: 4-5 days (max. 1 week) after extraction (ambient condition) and max. 3-4 weeks (8%) in intact fruit and 2 months in moist sphagnum moss mixed with charcoal powder.
- Symbiotic growth relation between mycorrhiza fungi (form nodules on roots) and plant.
- VAM association with roots improves water and nutrient uptake efficiency.
- Branching pattern: Hepaxanthic.
- 3 sex forms: Staminate i.e. male type (MT); functional female (FF)- imperfect hermaphrodite with non-dehiscent anthers; functional male (FM)- imperfect hermaphrodite with abortive ovary i.e. pseudohermaphrodite.
- Flowers of different sexes on panicle do not open simultaneously but open in different flushes.
- Sequence of flower opening: Male (phase I), hermaphrodite (phase II), pseudohermaphrodite (phase III).
- Inflorescence type: Branched panicle.
- Flowers are petal-less, small, greenish/ yellowish white.
- Less number of female flowers results in lowest fruit set.
- Bearing starts after 6th year onwards.
- Temperature directly influences floral initiation than photoperiod.
- Temperature < 20^0C induce flowering and fruit setting.
- At higher temperature flowering is irregular.

- Photoperiod duration is not vital for fruiting.
- Fruit bud differentiation (FBD) between November and March in Northern hemisphere while between June and September in Southern hemisphere.
- Anthesis time: Throughout day and night and maximum in afternoon on current season's growth.
- Duration of anthesis: 26-35 days.
- Maximum anther dehiscence: 10 AM.
- Stigma receptivity: On one day after anthesis.
- Pollination agents: Honey bees (*Apis* & *Melipona* species), Screw worm fly, ants, wasps.
- Failure to fruit set & higher fruit drop: Lack of fertilization & embryo abortion. Bats and birds cause considerable fruit loss.
- Reduction of fruit drop: Spray $ZnSO_4$ @ 1% combined with NAA 10 ppm or 2,4-D @ 15 ppm and wind breaks.
- Number of bee hives for effective pollination: 10-15/ ha.
- Fruiting season: April-May.
- Development of floral parts takes place in an acropetal succession.
- Calyx primordial appears first followed by primordia of stamens and carpels.
- Fruit type: Single seeded nut.
- HDP system: Double hedge row.
- Rejuvenation height in litchi: 2.5 m.
- Best source of nitrogen: Ammonium sulphate which shows greater cold tolerance.
- Training system: Modified leader and snipping of old branches.
- Regular yearly pruning is not required.
- Edible portion: Aril (60-83%).
- Growth curves of pericarp, seed and aril is sigmoidal.
- Propagation method: Air layering from 1 year old shoot during June-August with 5000 ppm IBA (most common, easiest & commercial).
- Off season air layering during spring (February-March) on non-flowering shoots with IBA 5000 ppm gives 90% success and highest B: C ratio of 3.52 : 1.
- July-October is most appropriate time for propagation.
- Soft wood cutting from April-May flush & made to root with bottom heat technique.
- Splice grafting on 18 months old stock.
- Inarching gives 30% success on longan rootstock.
- Rootstocks: Longan and Rambutan.
- 'Wai Chee': Rootstock preferred in Hong Kong.
- Critical part of crop cycle: Fruit setting.

- Critical period for irrigation: January end to the onset of monsoon.
- Make good growth on slightly acidic soil than neutral or alkaline soils.
- Ideal temperature for growth: < 40.5^{0}C in summer & below freezing point in winter with 70-85% R.H.
- Wet spring, dry summer and light winter are desirable conditions for fruiting in litchi.
- Red colour of fruit: 4 monomeric anthocyanin pigments cyanidin-3-glucoside, cyanidin-3-rutinoside, malvidin-3-glucoside, quercetin-3-rutinoside).
- Spacing: 10m x 10m, 8m x 8m, 6m x 6m.
- Number of fruits/ bunch: 10-15.
- Yield: 80-150 kg/ tree/ year.
- Fruit wt.: 20-25 g.
- Harvesting period: In bunches along with portion of branch & few leaves during May to June.
- Time required from fruit set to maturity: 50-60 days.
- Trunk or branch girdling or cincturingin September-October increases flowering & fruiting.
- Maturity indices:
  - Colour change (deep red) of fruits;
  - Flatnessof tubercles;
  - Smoothness of epicarp;
  - Chemical changes in fruits.
  - Develop full flavour.
  - TSS: acid ratio: Most commonly employed harvesting index at international platform.
- Fruits are harvested in bunches along with few leaves to avoid rupturing.
- Early varieties are more prone to cracking compared to late cultivars.
- NAA @ 100 ppm or 0.2% borax during fruit development stage is effective in fruit cracking.
- Mulching + 2,4, 5-T or NAA @ 35-100 ppm controls fruit splitting.
- Bagging of litchi bunches is widely practiced.
- Off season production: Low temperature triggers FBD and flowering in August-September at 1900 m MSL and June- August at < 20^{0}C and crop maturity in December-January.
- Litchi can be brought to flower by applying 400 ppm paclobutrazol and 40 ppm KH_2PO_4 during winter.
- Fruits having 2.5-4 cm long are suitable for export.
- Pulp to seed ratio is 4.3 to 6.3 in seeded and 12-28 in seedless varieties.
- CaO is essential for better crop.

- Spray of KNO_3 (1%) and ethrel @ 400 ppm was effective in advancing the flowering by 3 days and improvement in other physico-chemical characters.
- Major concerns processing industry: Seasonal availability (15-30 days) of fruits, short storage life (24-30 h), browning of fresh fruits.
- During sulphitation, tolerance limit of Sulphur residue in pulp is 10 ppm and in skin is 250 ppm.
- In precooling, it is preferable to use forced air cooling than hydrocooling.
- Litchi drying in sun or in a drier is very popular in China and exported all over the world.
- During packing, approximately 5% side area ventilation is adequate.
- Cold storage temperature: 3-5^{0}C for 30 days.
- MA storage: 3-5% O_2 and CO_2 concentration is optimum.
- Pericarp browning in litchi is delayed by MA packaging, 1-MCP fumigation and weak acid treatment.
- Freezing temperature: -25^{0}C.
- Main hurdle in canning: Discoloration of canned fruit.
- Pre-emergence herbicide: Diuron or Atrazine @ 2 kg a.i./acre.
- Value added products: Wine, pickle, squash, RTS, dehydrated pulp, canned fruits.
- Fruits are preserved by sun drying.

Species

- Progenitor of cultivated litchi: Mountain litchi (Shan chih). It is used as rootstock.
- Genus comprises two species:
  - *Litchi chinensis* (syn. *Nephelium litchi*): Leaves with 4-8 leaflets of horticultural importance.
  - *L. philippinensis*: Wild plant and used as rootstock in Philippines.
- Three sub-species of *L. chinensis* based on twig thickness, flower arrangement, stamen number and fruit characters (Menzel, 1991):
  - *Litchi chinensis ssp. chinensis*: Leaves with 4-8 leaflets.
  - *L. chinensis ssp. philippinensis*: Slender twigs, leaves with 2-4 leaflets, flowers in lax cymules, stamens 6-7 and fruit with pyramidal warts up to 3 mm high, smallest pollen. Rarely cultivated.
  - *L. chinensis ssp. javanensis*: Thick twigs, flowers in sessile clusters, stamens seven to eleven and fruits smooth or with pyramidal warts up to 1 mm high. Known only in West Java.

Varieties

- Varieties are classified as regular, irregular and shy bearers.

- Variety 'Seedless' is deceptive name where seeds are shriveled & pulp portion is relatively high.
- Seedless varieties are self sterile & cross sterile.
- Tejpur: Flowers in February, keeping quality 3 days, yield is 1600 kg/ha.
- Kasailiya: Least fruit cracking.
- Seedless Litchi: Farmer's selection done in Australia having pineapple flavour.

Name	Breeding method	Features
Haak Yip, Macclean, Mauritius (Tai So), Waichee, Bengal	Introduction From Thailand	-
Non Mei Chee	Introduction from China	Best Chinese variety
Sun Yit Hoong	-	Earliest cv. in China with large seed and thin flesh
Groff	Seedling selection of 'HakYip'	Chinese variety
CHES, Ranchi		
Swarna Roopa (1996)	Clonal selection of local type	1st variety developed in India;seedless, early maturing; TSS 19^0 Brix; yield 80-100 kg/tree; highly resistant to fruit cracking
CHES-2	Selection from 'Bombaia'	Late maturing; free from sun burn & fruit cracking;
BAU, Sabour		
Sabour Madhu (H-105) 1997	Purbi x Bedana	High fruits/ panicle (24); late maturing; fruit resembles 'Purbi'
Sabour Priya (H-73) 1997	Purbi x Bedana	High fruits/ panicle; late maturing, high fruit wt. & better than 'Purbi'
GBPUA & T, Pantnagar		
Saharanpur Selection (1980)	Chance seedling	Late mature; TSS 19.8%; fruit wt. 17.6 g; very low percentage of fruit cracking (2%)
Other varieties		
Kalkattia (syn. Calcutta)	Selection	Pulp to seed ratio 4.34:1; tolerant to hot & desiccating winds; less susceptible to sun burn & cracking; suitable for canning; fruits in bunches; best among all varieties
Late Seedless (syn. Late Bedana)	Selection	Pulp to seed ratio 28.09 :1; resistant to hot & desiccating winds
Brewster	Selection from 'Chen family Purple'	Introduced in Florida in 1906 by W.N. Brewster; require severe winter (7^0C) to initiate flowers; fragrant
Bombaia	Selection	Pulp to seed ratio 4.5: 1; suitable for canning & commercially grown in West Bengal; ripens in May; each developed fruit has another tiny under-developed fruit attached to fruit stalk

VNSDASU 1	Clonal selection	-
Early Seedless (syn. Early Bedana)	Selection	Suitable for table & processing purpose
Gulabi (syn. Sre No. 4)	Selection	Table purpose & late season; regular bearer; TSS 18.2%; pulp recovery 65%
Shahi (2001)	Selection through germplasm	Regular bearing; late maturity; TSS 20.4^0 brix; yield 100-120 kg/ tree
Dehradun (syn. Dehra Rose)	Selection	Late season; table purpose; pulp to seed ratio 3.75:1; highly susceptible to sunburn &fruit cracking
Rose Scented	Selection	Reagular bearing; distinct rose aroma; TSS 20%; 65-70% pulp recovery; pulp to seed ratio 6.40:1; high proportion of chicken tongue seed character
China (syn. Purbi)	Selection	Semi-dwarf; pulp to seed ratio 14.1: 1; alternate bearing; table purpose & suitable for canning
Elaichi	Introduction	Conical fruits; table purpose; pulp to seed ratio 6.91:1; susceptible to sun burn & cracking
Early seedless	Selection	High proportion of chicken tongue seed character
Sarguja-1, 2	Selection	Fruit pink colour
Gandaki Sampada	Selection	High pulp recovery; highly adaptive to Indo-Gangetic plain; late maturing & ripens during mid. June
Gandaki Yogita	Selection	Dwarf; late maturing; tolerant to fruit borer, fruit cracking; suitable for HDP; yield 70-80 kg/tree
Gandaki Lalima	Selection	High yielding (130-140 kg/ tree); fruit wt. 28-32 g; fruits ripen during second week of June
Late Large Red (syn. Muzzaffarpur)	Selection	Regular bearer; TSS 20.3%; pulp recovery 70%; pulp to seed ratio 4.78:1
Logan	Selection from Thailand clone	More storage life; fruits in August-Sept.
Ajhauli	-	Early maturing; vit. C 59.3 mg/100 g
Bengal	Seedling selection of 'Purbi' but selected in Florida	Large seeds; poor flesh recovery

Other varieties: Kasba, Khatti (syn. Sre No.1), Longiya, Mandraji, Green, Dehra Rose, Piyazi, Trikolia, Kaselia

Pests, diseases and disorders

- Eriophyid mite (*Aceria litchi*): Serious pest of foliage. Spray wettable Sulphur @ 0.15% before bud break in January.
- Litchi looper (*Perixera illepidaria*): Defoliates new shoots.
- Litchi stink bug (*Tessaratoma javanica* or *T. papillosa*): Major destructive pest.

- Bag worm (*Eumeta crameri*): Larva infests older leaves. Use of biological suppression and biorational approaches i.e. Neem based formulations.
- Red weevil (*Anoderus blandus*). Severe damage to new shoots.
- Fruit and seed borer (*Conopomorpha cramerella*): Become national problem and damage up to 32%. Spray 0.02% Cypermethrin.
- Bark eating caterpillar (*Inderbela tetraonis*): Major pest. Inject petrol in bark holes or DDVP in holes @ 1% solution. Spray Chlorpyrifos 20 EC @ 2.5 ml/l.
- Asian grey weevil:
- Leaf roller (*Dudua aprobola*)
- Red rust (*Cephaleuros virescens*): Most damage. Algal disease of litchi.
- Control of post harvest disease: Dip in solution (0.5g benlate/litre) or hot water treatment (52^0C for 2 min).
- Leaf blight (*Alternaria alternata*): Prominent nursery disease.
- Anthracnose (*Colletotrichum gloeosporioides*):
- Major problem: Fruit drop, alternate bearing.
- Fruit drop: Most serious.
- Cause: Failure of fertilization, embryo abortion, high temperature, low humidity, nutritional and moisture stress.
- Remedy: Spray IAA @ 40 ppm and NAA @ 20 ppm.
- Leaf bronzing and little leaf: Zn deficiency.
- Chicken tongue: Fruits having aborted embryo. Due to faulty pollination, fruits become shriveled. These fruits have high flesh to seed ratio.
- No blooming: Mg deficiency.
- Red rot: Managed by spray of lime and sulphur.
- Fruit cracking: Major problem in world due to 'B' deficiency.
- Sun burning: High temperature, low soil moisture during fruit development. Spray 0.4% boron. NAA @ 20 ppm or GA_3 @ 50 ppm 3 weeks of expected harvesting, 2,4-D @ 10 ppm.
- Pericarp necrosis (browning) and fruit rot by fungi: Post harvest problem.
- Pericarp browning: Due to degradation of anthocynin.
- Browning of mesocarp cells of pericarp: Non enzymatic reactions.
- Desiccation of peel: SO_2 fumigation (100 g/ m^3 area).
- Ball skin vs Bladder theory is related to fruit cracking.

Inheritance of characters

- Abortion of seeds: Recessive.
- Chiken tongue character is heritable.
- Crosses between litchi and longan indicate, small fruit size is dominant character.
- Positive correlation with between sex ratio and fruit set.

41.2 Rambutan/ Ramtum

- Eulogized as 'Hairy litchi' as it possess hairs on fruit skin (rind).
- Malaya word 'rambut' means 'hairs'.
- Commercial cultivation is confined to South-East Asia particularly Indonesia, Malaysia and Thailand.
- Fruit is source of anti-hyperglycemic agent.
- Fruits are good source of sugars, vit. C and minerals like Cu, Zn, Fe & P.
- Fruit composition : 47.5% skin, 46.1% aril, 6.3% seed, vit. C (185-225 mg/ 100 g) and TSS 18^0 Brix.
- Seed oil is used in soap making.
- Strictly humid tropical zone evergreen fruit crop i.e. high temperature loving tree, growing up to 12-15 m height.
- Preforms better at an altitude 30-500 m MSL.
- For successful cultivation, temperature of $20\text{-}30^0$C, R.H. 60-82% and rainfall of 200 cm (90-150 rainy days) for 3-4 months in a year is required.
- Dry winds affect tree growth and leads to browning of leaf margins.
- Higher soil pH results in chlorosis and leaf yellowing.
- Optimum soil pH: 4.5 to 6.5.
- Anthesis time: 6.30 AM and stigma is receptive at the time of anthesis.
- Inflorescence develops from terminal buds on past season's growth.
- Inflorescence: Panicle containing male, female and bisexual flowers.
- Highly cross pollinated crop.
- Most varieties are monoecious, highly heterozygous and cross pollinated.
- Sex type: Androdioecious.
- Large, spreading, evergreen tree bears clusters of 15-20 fruits.
- Fruits resemble like litchi, weigh 40-50 g each and bear long, thick soft hairs/ spines like tentacles on surface.
- Red and yellow coloured hairy outgrowth imparts distinctive exotic appearance to fruits.
- Edible portion: Pearly white, gelatinous, juicy pulp (aril) surrounding a single, large, inedible, brown seed.
- Fruits are eaten as fresh dessert purpose and pulp can be preserved in syrup or used in several conserves.
- Thin, leathery fruit skin is easily peeled away.
- Translucent pulp is sweet or sub-acid in taste and akin to litchi pulp.
- Propagation methods: Seeds, modified forkert (patch budding), approach grafting and air layering.
- Seed germinate within a fortnight.

- Seed propagation is discouraged due to long juvenile phase, uncertain performance and may show dioecious nature.
- It is self infertile crop because of dioecious nature.
- Genetic integrity of varieties is maintained through vegetative propagation only.
- For rootstock raising, fresh seeds are planted in nursery.
- One year old seedlings with stem dia. of 15 mm are used as rootstock for budding or grafting.
- Planting distance: 7m x 10m or 10m x 10m with planting of pollinizers.
- Parthenocarpic fruit set occurs.
- Training method: Modified leader.
- Fruits are produced near the periphery of the crown and hence rambutan trees need minimum pruning.
- Seedling trees take more than 6-7 years to bear a crop.
- Long dry season induces flower and fruit drop.
- Season of harvesting: July to September (120-150 days after flowering) & Dec.-Feb.
- Maturity indices:
    - Epidermal hairs disappear or their number is reduced.
    - Thin, leathery fruit skin is easily peeled away.
    - Fruit colour.
    - TSS: acid ratio.
    - All the fruits in a cluster mature at the same time and whole cluster is harvested.
- Yield: 150 kg fruits/ tree.
- Fruits are graded based on size & degree of ripeness.
- Keeping quality of fruits: Up to 21 days from harvesting.
- For edible purpose: Up to 8-10 days after harvesting.
- One kg accommodates about 30-35 fruits.
- For distant markets, fruits are packed in ventilated CFB boxes of 60 cm x 28 cm x 28 cm size.
- Pulp can be preserved in heavy syrup or used in several conserves.
- Value added products: Jam, jelly, cocktails, sweets used for pie (as raisin), ice cream, fruit ice and canned arils.
- In value added/ canned products, flavor of fresh fruit is lost.

Species:

- *Nephelium mutabilechryseum*: The Pulassan is native of Java. Fruits similar to Rambutan, but covered with warts instead of tentacles.
- *N. longana*: Popular in southern China. Fruits are smaller, brownish yellow & smooth skinned with chewy flesh.

Varieties:

- Bingjai: Indonesian cv. having dig fruits, sweet pulp, long soft hairs on fruit skin.
- Lebak Bulus: Indonesian cv. possessing sub-acidic pulp.
- Rapiah: Indonesian cv. Fruits small with very sweet pulp.
- Azimal: Malaysian cv. Thick aril & sweet to sub-acidic pulp.
- Kelip: Malaysian cv. Thick aril & very sweet taste.
- Singapura: Malaysian cv. Thin aril & very sweet taste.
- Rongrien & Chompu (both have crispy aril, suitable for canning & fresh consumption; popular in Thailand), Jitlee, Hainana, Thai rambutan, Seematajan, Lebakboeloos.

Name	Breeding method	Features
IIHR, Bengaluru (CHES, Chettalli)		
Arka Coorg Arun	Selection	Semi-spreading; early maturing; fruits-dark red coloured; ripen in September-October; fruit wt. 40-45 g; free stone; aril white coloured, thick, firm, dry & sweet (TSS 20^0 Brix), not attached to testa; yield (750 to 1000 fruits/ tree)
Arka Coorg Peetabh	Selection	Semi-spreading; regular bearer; mid-season variety; fruits yellow coloured; ripen in October; fruit wt. 25-30 g; aril white, juicy & sweet (TSS 21^0 Brix); yield (1200 to 1500 fruits/tree)
CHES-14	Selection	Semi-spreading; regular bearer; fruits yellow coloured; ripen in October; fruit wt. 45-50 g; free stone; aril: white, juicy & sweet (TSS 19.5^0 Brix)
CHES-26	Selection	Semi-spreading; regular bearer; fruits dark red coloured; ripen in October; fruit wt. 35-40 g; fruits cling stone & aril attached to testa, white, juicy & sweet (TSS 19^0 Brix)

Pests, diseases and disorders

- Mealy bugs (*Planococcus citri*): Release lady bird beetle (*Cryptolaemus montrouzieri*) after fruit setting.
- Red twig (*Zeuzera neitner*): Serious pest.
- Bostrichid beetle/ Auger beetle (*Sinoxylon* sp.)
- Fruit fly (*Bactrocera dorsalis* & *B. carueaea*): Follow IPM with sanitation.
- Litchi sting bug.
- Bark borer.
- Downy mildew, fruit anthracnose, wilt.
- Alternate bearing:
- Fruit cracking:
- Chlorosis: Fe deficiency.

41.3 Longan

- Eulogized as 'Dragon's eye or Little brother of litchi'.
- Species: *Dimocarpus longan* (syn. *Euphoria longana*).

- Developed from cross of 'Blackberry x Raspberry'.
- Commercially grown in Australia, China, Thailand, Taiwan, US and Vietnam.
- In India, commercially grown in Bihar and adjoining eastern states.
- Heartwood is red coloured.
- Fruit grows in drooping cluster.
- Planting distance: 8m x 8m.
- Bearing starts after 3-4 years.
- Fruiting period: August-September.
- Pollination agent: Honey bee, Soldier beetles, flies, native bees.
- Propagation methods: Seed, cutting, air layering (Commercial method) and grafting.
- Planting distance: 6m x 5m.
- Main sugars: Sucrose, fructose and glucose.
- Energy value: 485 KJ/ 100 g.
- Organic acids: Succinic acid, malic acid and citric acid (10:5:1).
- Flowering duration: 6-8 weeks.
- Three distinct pattern of vegetative flush:

1. Spring flush (in non-fruiting terminals),
2. Mid-summer flush
3. Autumn flush.

   And panicles may form on any of vegetative flushes, mostly on mid summer.

- Cycle of flowering: Staminate-bisexual with functional female-bisexual with functional male.
- Breaking of apical dominance is must.
- Ratio of endogenous polyamines is low during female flower differentiation.
- Measures to overcome alternate bearing: Thinning of empty panicles, flowers and fruits.
- Harvesting method: Whole bunch/cluster along with 1-2 leaves.
- Yield: 40-50 kg/ tree/ year.
- Storage: 1-5^{0}C for 30 days.
- Canned longans are more acceptable than canned litchi.
- Main exportable form of longan from Thailand: Dried form.
- **Varieties:** Dawuyuan, Guangyan, Chuliang, Wuyuan, Shuguan, Lucky Eye, Black Dragon Peak, Black Round, Youyi 106, Minjiao No.1, No.2, No.3, No.4, No.5 (China); Kohala, Biew Kiew, Chom Poo, Homestead No.1, Haew, Dang, Daw, Baidum (Thailand), Qingke Baoyuan, Songfengben, Quingshan, Lidongben (Malaysia).

Pests, diseases and disorders

- Scales
- Aphids
- Leaf eating beetles
- Flower caterpillars

- Mealy bugs
- Stink bug
- Fruit fly
- Fly foxes
- Black mildew
- Fruit spotting bug
- Fruit sucking moth
- Birds
- Witches broom
- Fruit cracking.

Inheritance of characters

- Shrivelled/ wrinkled seeds: Inherited phenomenon.

42. SAPOTACEAE

42.1 Sapota

- Eulogized as 'Chikku or Sapodilla'.
- Term sapodilla is derived from Spanish word *Zapotilla* meaning 'small sapote'.
- Naseberry (sapodilla) is national fruit of Jamaica.
- Drought tolerant, slow growing and long lived tree.
- Leading state in production and productivity: Maharashtra.
- Cultivation was taken up for the 1st time in Maharashtra in 1898 in Gholwad village of Thane district.
- Chickle/ *Gutta percha*: Commercial leatheryor gum resin product which forms base of the manufacture of chewing gum.Derived from latex of trees in Malaysia and South America.
- Chicklet/ Balata/ gutta gum is derived from the latex of *Manilkara bidentata*.
- Astringency of unripe sapota fruit is due to flavin (Leucodelphinidin).
- Fruit contains 12-18% sugar.
- 100 g edible portion of fruit contains maximum energy (100 IU).
- 100 g edible portion of fruit contains maximum protein (9.8 g) than other fruits.
- It has long pre-bearing age.
- Fruit type: Berry
- Edible portion: Mesocarp.
- Enhanced germination of khirni seeds: 1 % KNO_3 or 200 ppm GA_3.
- Commercial propagation: Inarching or approach grafting.
- Softwood grafting: Efficient and best technique (93% success). Practiced in West Bengal during mid-monsoon.
- Rootstock used: Adam's apple (*Manilkara kauki*), Star apple (*Chrysophyllum cainito* syn. *C. lanceolatum*,wider soil adaptability), Mee tree (*Bassia latifolia*, deciduous), Mahua (*Madhuca latifolia*).
- Sapota on *B. longifolia* exhibits incompatibility by overgrowing scion.

- Pala/ Khirni (*Manilkara hexandra*), Rayan (*Mimusops hexandra*): Commercially used rootstock and tolerant to drought.
- Rayan rootstock is the best in respect of plant vigour, productivity and longevity.
- Genera related to sapotaceae: Green sapota (*Calocarpum viride*),
- Planting distance: 8 m x 8 m (HDP: 5 m x 5 m).
- Training system: Single stem i.e. Central leader.
- Suitable intercrop: Papaya, banana, short duration vegetable crops.
- Flowering months: February-March and September-October.
- Anthesis time: 4-7 AM with maximum stigma receptivity on anthesis day.
- Anther dehiscence time: 8-11 AM.
- Fruit set, fruit size, fruit weight, number of seeds/ fruit, skin colour and scurf and maturity are influenced by pollination.
- Pollination agent: Wind
- Fruit set under open pollinated condition: 1.0 (Oval) to 23.7% (Cricket Ball).
- Natural fruit set: 10-12%.
- Fruit set percentage: 10-27% (own pollen); 3-12% (different pollen).
- Controlled cross pollination results in higher fruit set of 78%.
- Cv. Oval is good pollinizer for Kalipatti and Cricket Ball.
- Cv. Calcutta Round is fatal pollinizer (one way incompatibility) for Kalipatti.
- Fruit size is larger when pollen source is Oval, Kalipatti, Calcutta Round & Cricket Ball.
- Shape index: Oval (1.53) and round (1.11).
- Fruit shape is governed by pattern of distribution of seeds around placenta.
- In round fruits, seeds are more uniformly located around placenta compared to oval fruits.
- Round fruits contain heavier (100 g) than oval (70 g) and more number of seeds (4) than oval (2).
- Number of seeds/ fruit: 0-12 (3-5 most common).
- Temperature >43^{0}C during summer causes flower drop and fruit drop and fruit setting is problem.
- Control of fruit drop: Spray NAA @ 100-300 ppm during flowering.
- Metaxenia is reported in spaota w.r.t. fruit set, maturity, seed number, weight, size, TSS, shape, colour and appearance of fruit.
- Suitable temperature for fruit ripening: 12-14^{0}C.
- Days required for fruit ripening: 5 days (at room temperature).
- For ripening: Ethrel @ 1000 ppm with NaOH at 20-25^{0}C.
- Cold storage temperature: 12-16^{0}C for 14-21 days.
- Maturity indices:

- o East with brown scruff gets off on the surface;
- o No green tissue and milky latex;
- o Days taken flowering to fruit maturity: 7-10 ½ months and from fruit set to harvest (300 days).
- o Spine like stigma when dried or spineless stigma.

- Fruits are dipped in GA @ 300 ppm + Bavistin 1000 ppm at prepacking stage to extent shelf-life and avoid storage loss.
- Application of 2, 4, 5- Trichloro phenoxy propionic acid @ 25 ppm results in increased fruit size, weight and improved quality.
- Addition of 5-10% CO_2 & removal of ethylene from storage atmosphere enhances storage life.
- New growth and flowering occur sinultaneously & it is, a mixed type of bearing habit.
- Pruning of branches should not be done.
- Insufficient irrigation leads to yield loss up to 40%.

Varieties

- Exotic: Alano, Hassia, Makok, Molix, Prolific, Dwarapudi, Brown Sugar (from Florida).
- Tikal: Early maturing, fruit wt. 120 g, smooth texture.
- Ayyangar: Rose scented.

Varieties	Breeding method	Features
TNAU, Coimbatore (HC & RI, Periyakulum)		
CO.1	Cricket Ball x Oval	Oval fruit, 18% TSS; resistant to leaf spot
CO.2	Clonal selection from 'Baramasi'	Obivate fruits, 23% TSS; resistant to leaf spot
CO.3	Cricket Ball x Vavivalasa	Suitable for HDP, 40% high yielder
PKM-1 (1981)	Clonal selection from 'Guthi'	Dwarf; fruits oblong; bearing throughout year; yield 3547 fruits/ tree/ year; fruit wt. 100 g
PKM-2 (1992)	Guthi x Kirtibarthi	Oblong fruits; 26% TSS; fruit wt. 95 g; fruit yield 80 kg/ tree
PKM-3 (1994)	Guthi x Cricket Ball	Erect growing; suitable for HDP, cluster bearing habit; fruit yield 14 t/ha; tolerant to leaf spot & leaf webber
PKM-4 (2003)	Clonal selection from PKM-1	Spindle shape fruits, suitable for dry flakes production; high yield 21 t/ha; TSS 24-25^0 Brix
PKM-5 (2007)	Clonal selection from private orchard at Virudhunagar of Tamil Nadu	Off season bearing; yield 18 T/ha; High TSSS 25.5^0 Brix; suitable for dry flakes, milk shake powder, fruit jam production; retains coppery brown colour
UAS, Dharwad		
DHS-1 (Hybrid 10-17)	Kalipatti x Cricket Ball	Round fruits; 23% TSS
DHS-2 (Hybrid 10-25)	Kalipatti x Cricket Ball	Oblong fruits; 26% TSS

DHS-1-2/1	Selection from DHS-1	-
Other varieties: Chhatri, Guthi, Calcutta Special Round, Gavarayya, Baramasi		
Kalipatti	Local selection	Popular in Maharashtra, excellent quality; self incompatible; producing both oval & round shaped fruits on same tree; resistant to leaf spot
Pillipatti	Local selection	Suitable for HDP
Murabba	Selection	Popular in Maharashtra
Cricket Ball (syn. Calcutta Large)	Selection	Produce round & oval shaped fruits on same tree; popular in West Bengal, Tamil Nadu; resistant to leaf spot; show one way cross incompatibility with 'Kalipatti'
Pala	Selection	Fruits in clusters; popular in A.P. & T.N.
Kirthabharthi	Local selection	Good transport value; popular in A.P.
Dwarapudi, Jonnavalasa Round	-	Popular in A.P.

Pests, diseases and disorders

- Chiku moth or leaf webber (*Nephopteryx eugraphella*): Most destructive pest.
- Leaf spot (*Phavophelospora indica*) is most serious disease in India.
- Heart rot (*Phytophthora parasitica*):
- *Bacillus thuringiensis* reduce population of bud borer & pheromone traps was effective in monitoring fruit fly.
- Wilt or die-back is common problem in sapota due to anaerobic conditions in pre and post monsoon sessions.
- Orchard decline is a major problem in 8-10 old trees.
- Fasciation or flattening of branches: Fungus (*Botryodiplodia theobromae*).
- Abnormal fruit shape: Due to number of seeds in fruits. High temperature and rainfall during flowering.
- Cock's comb:

Inheritance of characters

- Positive correlation between number of seeds and fruit weight.
- Negative correlation between shape index and seed number per fruit.

Character	Inheritance pattern
Fruit size, fruit shape, skin thickness, flesh quality, seed size and number, fruit flavour	Polygenic
Fruit shape	Oval shape dominant over round

42.2 Khirni

- Multipurpose tree of economic importance.
- Common in Rajasthan.

- Peak period of flowering: December.
- Propagation method: Seed and Softwood grafting.
- Fruit maturity: Mid May.

Varieties:

Varieties	Breeding method	Features
NAU, Navsari		
Gujarat Khirni-1	Selection from Kharsalia village	Peak flowering in November; fruit ripening 1st week of March; fruit wt. 5.66 g; pulp wt. 4.93 g; TSS 21.1%; carotene 4.30 g/ 100 g; vit. C 16.2 mg/ 100 g.
Gujarat Khirni-10	Selection from Parwadi village	Peak flowering in December; fruit ripening 3rd week of May; fruit wt. 6.64 g; pulp wt. 5.71 g; TSS 26.4%; carotene 6.06 g/ 100 g; vit. C 24.25 mg/ 100 g.
CISH, Lucknow		
CISH K-10	-	28% TSS; 89.2 pulp %; anti-oxidant 189.79 g/ ml AEAC units
CIAH, Bikaner (CHES, Godhra)		
Thar Rituraj (2015)	Selection	Regular bearer; peak flowering in 1st week of December; fruit ripening 3rd week of May; fruit wt. 5.2 g; pulp wt. 5.71 g; TSS 24.7%; total sugar 17.8%; vit. C 28.3 mg/ 100 g; yield 13 kg/plant

42.3 Mahua

- Eulogized as 'Indian Butter tree or *Moha* or *Madhuka*'.
- Indigenous tree of high economic value.
- Important fruit crop for tribal farmers in Gujarat.
- Do not survive under waterlogged condition.
- Tree of dry regions- deciduous & withstands drought.
- Fruits contain 55-65% husk and 10-15% sugars.
- Cream coloured highly scented fleshy corolla, commonly called 'mahua flower' is rich source of sugars (20-25% total sugars), vit. A (528-890 IU) & vit. C (30-60 mg/ 100 g) and minerals (0.8-1.5%).
- Time of anthesis: Mid night till morning.
- Anther dehiscence: 2-4 days before time of anthesis.
- Training: Central leader system.
- Flowering period: March-April.
- Ripening span in different genotypes varies from 2nd week of May to 1st week of June.
- Fruit maturity: May-June & ripened fruits shed from trees during June-July.
- Seed propagated trees have long gestation period (15-20 years).

- Seeds have no dormancy but large variability.
- Seed germination: 13-47%.
- Fresh seeds after storage of 5-6 days at room temperature show 80% germination within 10-15 days.
- Propagation methods: Seed, stumps (66% success), veneer grafting (90% success in June).
- Fruit type: Berry.
- Polyembryony is reported in seeds and 15-20% seeds produce nuceller seedlings.
- Alternate bearing is observed.
- Edible parts: Flowers, fruits, seed oil.
- Seed kernel contains 51% oil and recognized as 'mahua oil or mahua butter'.
- Major unsaturated fatty acid present in oil: Linoleic acid.
- Seed is good source of oil and highly useful for heart patients since it reduces cholesterol content in blood serum.
- Seed oil is also used for manufacture of vanaspati, soap, greases & cosmetics.
- Seed yield contains saponin having industrial & commercial application.
- Dry fruit husk: Source of absolute alcohol.
- About 90% of flowers are used to prepare distilled liquors, alcohol & portable sprits.
- 1 tonne of dry husk yield 130 liters of absolute alcohol.
- Defatted seed flour is used in bakery products.
- Mahua cake is used as manure & has insecticide properties.
- Flowers and spent flowers (after fermentation) used as livestock feed.
- Value added products from flowers: Cake, jam, vinegar, syrup& honey.
- Fruit pulp is used as a source of sugar for alcoholic fermentation.
- Fruits are stored in hips for seed extraction.
- Dry flower yield: 100-150 kg & kernel yield 60-80 kg/tree/year.
- Fruit yield: 35-82 kg/ tree.
- Seeds are shelled within a week, otherwise they germinate.
- Germinated seeds are unfit for oil extraction.
- Kernels are dried upto moisture content of 8% to avoid fungal attack.
- Mahua Nutri beverage in 6 different fruit flavours in being prepared in joint collaboration of Trifid (Tribal Federation) and IIT, New Delhi. This beverage will contain < 5% alcohol.
- Canopy management: Follow canopy architecture practices. Young plants are allowed to 3-5 well spaced branches to develop main scafflold structure. Framework of branches is allowed to develop above 60-100 cm from ground level.

Species:

- *Madhuca indica* (syn. *Bassia latifolia*)- Deciduous. Bear flowers, rich in sugar & seeds rich in quality oil.
- *M. longifolia*- Evergreen.Bear flowers, rich in sugar & seeds rich in quality oil.
- *B. butyracea*: Found in Western Ghats & Himalayas at higher altitudes (4500 m).
- *B. malabarica*: Found in Western Ghats & Himalayas at higher altitudes (4500 m).

Varieties:

- Early flowering in 1st week of March was noted in MH-1, MH-4, MH-5.
- Late flowering in 2nd week of April in MH-6.
- Highest number of flowers (45) and fruits (8) per panicle in MH-2.

Varieties	Breeding method	Features
NDUA &T, Faizabad		
Narendra Mahua-2, NM-4, NM-5, NM-7, NM-8, NM-9	Seedling selections	-
CISH, Lucknow		
CISH M-8	-	Elite accession
CIAH, Bikaner (CHES, Godhra)		
Thar Madhu (2015)	Selection	Regular & precocious bearer; flowering in March; ripening in June; flower wt. 2.3 g; fruit wt. 29 g; juice 65.43%; TSS 26.63^{0}Brix (flower); & 26.63^{0}Brix (fruit); vit C. 58.61 mg/ 100 g (flower) & 48.38 mg/ 100 g (fruit); flower acidity 1.03%; fruit acidity 0.1%; fruit yield 20 kg/ tree
Mahua-10	Selection	Peak flowering in 2nd week of March; flower wt. 2.29 g, 65% juice & 26.37% TSS; fruit ripen in 2nd week of May; fruit wt. 30.5 g; see wt. 13.5 g; kernel wt. 11 g.
Mahua-14	Selection	Peak flowering in 2nd week of March; flower wt. 2.29 g, 65% juice & 26.37% TSS; fruit ripen in 2nd week of May; fruit wt. 29 g; seed wt. 12.7 g; kernel wt. 9.53 g.
Mahua-35	Selection	Peak flowering in 2nd week of March; flower wt. 2.13 g, 64% juice & 24.9% TSS; fruit ripen in 3rd week of June; fruit wt. 28.5 g; seed wt. 12.2 g; kernel wt. 10.08 g.
Mahua-63	Selection	Peak flowering in 4th week of March; flower wt. 2.5 g, 68% juice & 24.37% TSS; fruit ripen in 4th week of May; fruit wt. 23.5 g

Pests:

- Bark eating caterpillar (*Inderbela* spp.): Foliar spray with Dimethoate @ 0.05%.
- Mahua leaf roller (*Polychorosis cellifera*): Foliar spray with Chloropyriphos @ 2 ml/ litre.

42.4 Egg fruit

- Eulogized as 'Canisetel or Yellow sapote'.

- Egg fruit (*Pouteria campechiana* syn. *Lucuma nervosa*): Grown in homesteads of south Indian states.
- Mammey Sapota/ Marmalade plum (*Pouteria sapota*): Fruit has maximum life on tree before ripening. Pumpkin flavoured used in dessert and drinks.
- Yellow star apple (*P. caimito*): Used for fresh consumption in Brazil.
- Flesh is yellowish resembling boiled egg yolk and contains single large seed.
- Leaf infusion is used against abdominal disorders and heated leaf is appied as poultice.
- Commercially cultivated in Central America, southern Mexico, Guatemala, West Indies.
- Found in Western Ghats of south India, particularly in Kerala, tropical regions of South East Asia.
- Evergreen, abundantly branched and bushy nature. Branches contain gummy latex.
- Tree flourishes well in frost free & dry climate with moderate rainfall.
- Plants can tolerate saline soil conditions.
- Plants can tolerate salinity and iron deficiency.
- Fruit is rich source of vit. A (2000 IU/ 100 g), protein (2.5%) and vit. C (43 mg/100 g).
- Inflorescence: Terminal & axillary.
- Fruiting occurs during winter months and in spring season.
- Fruits resemble the size and shape of an egg, yellowish to orange coloured with mealy pulp having strong musky flavour.
- Flesh is yellowish resembling boiled egg yolk and contains single large seed.
- Propagation methods: Seed, veneer grafting, chip budding and air layering.
- Commercial propagation: Seeds.
- Seed germinate within 2 weeks and transplanted in polybags when they have 4-5 leaves.
- Seedlings are field planted after 6-8 months old.
- Side/ veneer grafting & chip budding is done on vigorous seedlings having 1 cm stem dia.
- Tree takes 3-4 years to bear fruits.
- Planting distance: 8m x 8m (156 plants/ ha).
- Symmetrical tree with an open canopy is desirable.
- Only remedial pruning is required.
- Peak season of fruiting: June-July.
- Epidermis of fruits is delicate and need careful harvesting & handling.
- Yield: 300-400 fruits/ tree/ year.
- Fruits ripen in a week's time after harvesting.

- Ethylene induces quick and uniform ripening.
- Fresh fruits are eaten without removing skin or after peeling & slicing.
- Pulp has consistency of hard boiled egg yolk and used in cudtards, pies, milk shakes & other desserts.
- Value added products: Jam, jelly.
- Specific varieties do not exists.

43. SOLANACEAE

43.1 Cape gooseberry

- Short cycled annual crop grown for edible fruits.
- Rich in vit. A, B, C and polyphenols.
- TSS: 16-18%.
- Uses: Control of asthama, bacterial infection, diabetes, earaches, hepatitis, jaundice, liver problems, rheumatism, skin disease, blood cleaning, worms, etc.
- Optimum temperature: 5 to 35^{0}C.
- Propagation: Seed and shoot cuttings.
- Seed rate: 5000-8000 seeds/ acre.
- Flowering time: November-December.
- Anthesis time: Morning hours.
- Maturity indices: 3-6 months after transplanting (55 days after anthesis) and colour change from green to yellow.
- Harvesting season: February.
- Staking after 3 weeks of planting is required.
- Require full sun and does not flourish in shady place.
- Yield: 3-5 kg/ plant.

Species

- *Physalis peruviana*: Cape gooseberry.
- *P. pruinosa*: Ground cherry, husk tomato.
- *P. alkekengi*: Chinese lantern. Used as ornamental.
- *P. pubescens*: Strawberry tomato.
- *P. minima*: Produce edible fruits.

Varieties:

- Giallo Grosso, Giant Giant, Poha Berry, Golden Berry, Long Aston.

Varieties	Breeding method	Features
CIAH, Bikaner (CHES, Godhra)		
CHESC-1	Selection through survery from Bihar region	Fruits ripen in Jan-Feb; fruit wt. 11.5 g; TSS 12%; acidity 1.64%; total sugar 7.5%; vit C. 220.10 mg/100 g
CHESC-2	Selection through survery from Bihar region	Fruits ripen in Jan-Feb; fruit wt. 10.75 g; TSS 11.2%; acidity 1.7%; total sugar 7.25%; vit C. 190.22 mg/100 g
CHESC-4	-	-

44. TILIACEAE (BASSWOOD FAMILY)

44.1 Phalsa

- Eulogized as '*Dhamani* or Star apple'.
- Hardy drought tolerant and 'Woody perennial' arid zone fruit crop.
- Important role in crop diversification due to bushy habit and small stature.
- 1st reported to be seen in India in 1793.
- Species: *Grewia subinaequalis* (syn. *G. asiatica*).
- Suitable for multistoried cropping.
- Most perishable fruit.
- Fruits are sub-acidic and good source of vit. A, ascorbic acid (2-2.5%), sugars (10-11%), rich in nutrients and juice (54-60%).
- Suitable for intercropping in established mango orchard.
- Main problem in cultivation: Non-synchronized ripening and poor keeping quality.
- Inflorescence: Cyme and fruit is berry.
- Flowering season: February-March.
- Flowering through cuttings starts during 2nd year of planting.
- Flowering and fruiting is confined to 15-20 nodes from base.
- Fruits borne on current season's growth.
- Highly cross pollinated.
- Pollination agent: Honey bee.
- Tolerable temperature >45^{0}C.
- High temperature favours fruit ripening and quality development.
- Rains at flowering time affect fruit setting.
- Tolerable pH: 6 to 8.5.
- Leaf extract has anti-bacterial activity against *E. coli* and *Staphylococcus aureus*.
- Days required for seed germination: 15-20 days.
- Seedlings of 8-12 months age are good for transplanting.

- Commercial propagation: Hardwood cuttings with 1000 ppm IBA in July-August (70% rooting); air layering with IBA + NAA @ 1500 ppm (85% success); softwood grafting on 1 year stock (100% success), ground layering (50% success).
- Plants complete flowering and fruiting within 4-5 months.
- Planting distance Spacing: 5m x 5m.
- Planting density: 1100-1500/ ha by paired row planting(number of plants/ area is doubled): 2 plants/ hill at 0.6m and 2nd pair at 3m from 1st pair and distance between 2 rows is 3m. Yield is increased by 20-30%.
- Pruning height: 0.9-1.25 m.
- In north India, heavy pruning is done during December to January.
- Severe pruning produces longer shoots with maximum nodes and fruits.
- 'Fe' deficiency is main problem in calcareous soil.
- Increase in fruit size and juice content: $ZnSO_4$ and $FeSO_4$ @ 0.4% at prebloom stage and faster berry set.
- GA_3 @ 20 ppm and 2,4,5-T @ 5 ppm improved fruit retention, fruit size, fruit wt., fruit yield and quality.
- Maturity indices:
  - Days from fruit set: 55.
  - Maturity is judged by colour (greenish to red).
  - Ripe fruits are collected daily from each plant.
- Grading is not practiced.
- Seed viability: 3-4 months.
- Cold storage conditions: 5-7^{0}C at turning stage fruits extends storage life up to 7 days.
- Value added products: RTS, juice, squash.

Varieties:

Name	Breeding method	Features
CIAH, Bikaner		
Thar Pragati (2016)	Selection	Spreading type; regular bearer; 90% pulp; TSS 20.12^0 brix; yield 3.6 kg/ plant
Other variety		
Sharbati	Selection	

Pests and diseases:

- Fruit fly: Serious at ripening stage. Erect 10 traps/ acre.
- Bark eating caterpillar (*Inderbella* spp.): Serious pest.
- Brown beetle (*Anomala* spp.): Damage foliage.
- Brown leaf spot (*Cercospora grewiae*): Serious in rainy season. Spray Benomyl @ 600 ppm.

44.2 Jamaica cherry

- Eulogized as 'Tropical cherry or Bird's eye cherry'.
- Fairly drought tolerant tree.
- Cutlivated as ornamental plant.
- Decoction of leaves is used as tea, flowers for incipient cold and headache.
- Fruit have many small seeds embedded in juicy pulp.
- Pulp has 24.6% total soilids, 1.98% protein, 8.1% reducing sugars.
- Propagation method: Semi-hardwood cutting.

45. VITACEAE

45.1 Grape

- Sophisticated fruit crop but deciduous climber.
- Originally grape belongs to temperate region but well adapted in tropical conditions. So behaves both as deciduous and evergreen.
- GIS technology developed by NRCG, Pune for selection of site for grape cultivation.
- National Referal Laboratory was established at NRCG, Pune in 2004 for testing minimum residue level (mg/kg) of pesticides in export oriented grapes to European countries. Use of 'Annexure 5' is compulsory.
- Grape park: Established by MTDC near Gangapur dam in Nashik district of Maharashtra.
- 'GrapeNet' integrates supply chain of grape export.
- 1st commodity in which grading and marketing rules were framed.
- Red wine is anti-carcinogenic property.
- Chile: Largest exporter of fresh grapes.
- Major competitors for export: South Africa and Israel.
- In the world, grape is largely utilized in form of wine (88%) followed by table grapes (8%) and raisin (4%).
- In India, grape is utilized for table purpose (80%), raisin (18%), wine and juice (2%).
- Area under cultivation in India: 1.40 lakh ha.
- India ranked 7th in world's production.
- Average productivity in India (16.95 T/ha) which is highest in the world.
- Fresh grapes are largely exported from India.
- India's share in export of table grapes: 3.5%.
- Indian grapes are exported to European countries during February-March/ April.
- Importers of Indian grapes: EU, Russia, Indonesia, Jordan, Sri Lanka, Mauritious, Taiwan, Canada.
- Turkey, Iran, China, USA, Australia: Largest exporters of raisins.

- Average productivity of wine grape: < 10 T/ha.
- Italy: Largest producer and exporter of wine.
- France, Italy and Spain: Leading wine producer in world.
- Total export of wine: 24% of total global production.
- In India, wine sector is growing @ 20%.
- American grapes are originated in North America.
- Cutin: Skin of grape covered with waxy layer.
- Ampelography: Cultivation of vine crops.
- Viticulture: Cultivation of grapes.
- Major sugar: Dextrose (glucose 8-13%) and levulose (fructose 7-12%).
- Cultivation of vine crops: Ampilography.
- Absense of seeds: Apireny.
- Life span of grape vine in tropical climate: 10-15 years.
- Extensive research on nature and cause of seedlessness in grapes was done by E.B. Babcock and F.T.Bioletii.
- Grape culture 1st began in Asia Minor.
- Grape introduced to India by Muslim invaders from Iran, Persia and Afghanistan in 1300 A.D.
- Dissecting microsope is widely used to distinguish vegetative and reproductive buds.
- Dr. Khanduja S.D. developed a method to forecast yield by microscopic examination of buds.
- In 1832, Christian missionaries introduced grapes from France to south India.
- 90% cultivation in India is grown inpeninsular India.
- Tartaric acid is commercially extracted from grapes.
- Manuka/ Manakka: Raisins prepared from white or greenseeded grapes.
- Bedana: Raisins prepared from white/ green seedless grapes.
- Kishmish: Raisins prepared from black seedless grapes.
- Metal ions associated with shift in colour pigments in grapes: Al, Cu and Fe.
- Branching pattern: Helicoïd or scorpioid sympodial.
- Inflorescence type: Panicle. Flower cluster consists of many small greenish coloured individual flowers which may be perfect, pistillate (reflexed stamens) or staminate.
- Length of inflorescence: 10-30 cm.
- Edible portion: Pericarp and placenta.
- Congenial temperature for development of all parts of vines: 28-32^{0}C.
- Required light intensity for photosynthesis; 30 Klux.
- Optimum leaf temperature for photosynthesis: 25^{0}C.
- Summer temperature should not exceed 35^{0}C for its cultivation.

- Temperature range for flowering: 18-21^{0}C.
- Congenial temperature for bud swelling and growth: 10-15^{0}C.
- Anthesis time: 8 AM to 9 AM.
- Anther dehiscence: Immediately after anthesis.
- Stigma receptivity: 1 day prior to anthesis upto 1 day after anthesis.
- Pollen viability: 10-25 days (ambient condition), 14 months (deep freeze at 0% R.H.)
- Critical stage of irrigation: Fruit set to maturity.
- Active root zone: 30-40 cm deep.
- Congenial climate for coloured grapes: Cool nights and short days.
- Critical day and night temperature inhibiting anthocyanin formation in coloured grapes: 28/26^{0}C.
- Higher night temperature (> 25^{0}C) requires for fruit ripening and colour development.
- Upper salt tolerance limit: 0.3%.
- Grape vine has axillary and compound bud often known as 'eye'.
- Fastening of grape vine to upright support is known as: Single stake.
- For root studies, P^{32} isotope is used.
- Bleeding of grapes is due to excess moisture during rest period of summer.
- Formation of pink pigments in green grapes: Difference in day and night temperature exceeds 20^{0}C during ripening.
- Grape requires long warm to dry summer and cool winter in temperate regions.
- Under Maharashtra condition, fruit bud differentiation takes place during April.
- Chilling temperature (< 7^{0}C) of varieties varies from < 100 to > 1500 h.
- DRIS norms on petiole nutrient content are developed.
- P/N, K/N, P/Zn play physiological role during flowering stage.
- N/P, N/K: Critical during bud differentiation stage.
- One leaf (150-160 cm^2 leaf area) can feed 8 berries.
- For 100-120 berries per bunch, 15-16 leaves are necessary.
- Fruitfulness in Thompson Seedless at light intensity of 3600 ft. candles at 35^{0}C is required for 12 h.
- In Tamil Nadu especially in district Theni: 5 crops of in two years can be taken against only one crop in other parts of India.
- Grape founder 'Sardar Bahadur Lal Singh' is known as father of north Indian grapes.
- Grape founder 'R. Shanker Pillay' is known as father of south Indian grapes.
- Ideal TSS: For processing purpose (15^0 Brix); for raisin purpose (22-24^0 Brix).
- Degree days required for early varieties to come to ripe stage: 1600-2000 h.
- Degree days required for late varieties to come to ripe stage: 3000-3500 h.
- Rains during berry ripening cause berry cracking and rotting.

- Raisins prepared by pre-treatment with pectinase enzyme are superior over to those prepared by golden bleach or cold dip methods.
- Codex quality specifications are related to raisin.
- Most common method of raisin preparation in India: Dipping berries in soda oil containing ethyl oleate + K_2CO_3 and shade drying.
- In modified Australian cold dip drying technology for raisin making, dipping oil is used as drying treatment.
- Full bloom stage/ condition: When 50% calyptras or caps fall from flowers.
- When calyptras fall, the pollen grains are released and fall on stigma.
- Seeds are rich source of resveratrol.
- 'Resveratrol' (a type of natural polyphenol & phytoalexin) has anti-oxidant and anti-carcinogenic property found in red wine and red grape.
- Seed oil: 8-9% of seed weight.
- LD_{50} to rooted cuttings: 2000 rads and beyond 3 kR no survival.
- Widely used chemical mutagen: NMU (0.04%), EMS.
- Dehydration temperature: 67-71^{0}C.
- Genome of reflexed stamen grape: S^OS^P/ S^OS^P.
- Polyethylene covered technique of cultivation is followed in 'Pimpalgaon Baswant' area of Maharashtra.
- Use mulch and anti-stress (Acrylic polymer) in combination after foundation pruning and 30-60 after fruit pruning is recommended.
- Sub-surface irrigation is an efficient water use technology widely followed.
- Pollen viability: 10-25 days at ambient temperature and upto 14 months under deep freeze at 0% R.H.
- Paper wrapping to grape bunches is a new practice.
- Principle product of grapes: Wine.
- Study of wine from grapes: Viriculture.
- Science of wine making: Enology.
- Wine capital or wine city of India: Nashik, Maharashtra.
- Wine produced in India with French collaboration by some private industries.
- Wine grapes: Varieties which produce satisfactory wine.
- Types of wines: Red wine, White wine, Rose wine, Fortified wine, Concentrated wine, Sparkling wine, Dessert wine, Blush and Sherry.
- Dessert/ Sweet wine: Prepared from grapes having high sugar and moderately low acid content. It contains 17-20% alcohol and some amount of unfermented sugars.
- Table/ Dry wine: Prepared from grapes having moderately low sugar and high acid content. It contains 14% alcohol and little or no unfermented sugar.

- Winery byproducts: 1) Tartrates (cream of tartar) 2) Argols (wine stones). These settle on wall and base of wine tank. These are purified as 'Rochelle salt' 3) Oil from seeds: Used as salad oil and in cosmetic industry 4) Tannins: This can also be purified.
- Word 'Must' in grape industry refers to crushed grape.
- Wines made from high acid grapes with *Schizosaccharomyces pombe* had considerable reduction in acidity as compared to wines made from same grapes with *Saccharomyces cerevisiae*.
- Composition of berry of total berry wt.: Skin (5-10%), pulp (80-90%), & seeds (0-10%).
- Grape seeds are rich in tannins (5-8%) and oil (10-20% of seed weight).
- Oil content in Anab-e-Shahi and Kali Sahebi: 10-13%.
- Juice content: 80-90% of the crushed grapes.
- Seed content in crushed grapes (must): 0-5%.
- Number of seeds/ berry: 4 (2 in each ovule) or even nil depending upon abortion of ovules.
- A tonn of grapes produce about 681-738 litres of wine.
- Pigments are found only in berry skin.
- Skin is covered with wax like layer known as 'cutin or bloom and constitutes 1-2% of total skin weight.
- Tannins in wine stabilize the colour and aid in fining.
- Inverse relation between intensity of juice colour and seed number.
- Venifera grape contain smaller amount of pectin compared to American grape which form stable jelly.
- Tannins in grape berry influence astringency.
- Enzyme responsible for late ripening: Polyphenol oxidase confined to skin.
- Enzyme responsible for early ripening: Catalase.
- Colour pigments are found only in skin: Anthocyanidin (red, blue, purple, black); yellow pigment (of both white and red grape) is flavones compound 'quercetin & quercitron'.
- Anthocyanin content (0 to 2500-3000 mg/kg in var. Alicante Bouschet (both skin & pulp/ juice is red coloured).
- Calyptra stage (cap like structure): Fusion of sepals and petals that detaches at the time of anthesis.
- Anlagen: It is closely related with tendril. It produces bunches, tendrils or second crop.
- Sex linked chromosome is observed only in Anab-e-Shahi.
- Morphological markers for *V. vinifera*: Forked tendril, shedding bark, diaphragm at node and elongated berries.

- Degree of seedlessness is determined on the basis of stage at which ovule development is arrested relative to berry development stage.
- Precooling: 1-2^{0}C within 6 h of harvest and storage at 0^{0}C with 95% R.H. is prerequisite.
- AGMARK certification- Extra class, Class-I and Class-II for quality assessment and gradation.
- New cluster for raisin making: Pandharpur, South Solapur, Barshi, Mohol tahsils of Solapur district of Maharashtra.
- Requirements for getting phytosanitory certificate: Farm registration, global GAP certificate, packhouse recommended by APEDA, certificate of free from insecticide residues, cold treatment, free from fruit fly, thrips, bacteria, virus, etc.

Species:

- Halfacre and Barden (1979) recognized 4 distinct types: European grape (*V. vinifera*), American grape (*V. labrusca*), French hybrids (*V. vinifera* x wild American species) and Muscadine grape (*V. rotundifolia*).
- Himalayan region: secondary centre of origin.
- True grape belongs to sub-genera *Euvitis*.
- *Muscadinia* has been given generic status (Olmo, 1976) and includes 3 spp. viz. *M. rotundifolia*, *M. munsonina* and *M. popenoeifennel*.
- Muscadine grapes (*V. rotundifolia*) bear berries that ripen over a period and harvested as individual berries.
- Muscadinia group have 2n=2x=40 (unified tendril, tight bark, lenticels present, beak absent in seed, dimorphism absent) while Euvitis have 2n=2x=38 (forked tendril, loose bark, lenticels absent, pyriform & beaked seed shape, dimorphism present).
- Euvitis or Bunch grapes bear berries that ripen uniformly in a bunch and thus are harvested in clusters.
- *V. assamica* have 2n=48 while *V. himalayana* have 2n=40. Both are incompatible with *V. vinifera*, but reciprocally cross with *V. assamica*.
- Triploid grapes are highly sterile & potential for using as vigorous rootstocks.
- Tetraplpoid grapes have empty seed & ripen earlier than diploids.
- Allotetraploids are more promising than autotetraploids.
- Autotetraploids have poor cultural characters, less fruitfulness, irregular berry size, more fragile & poor root system.
- In grape breeding, varieties having high seed index (ratio of berry weight to seed weight) are used as female parents to induce seedlessness in progeny.
- Genus *Vitis* is sub-dioecious.
- Wild species are polygamous-dioecious.

- About 90% of world's grape belongs to *V. vinifera* and its hybrids.
- *V. vinifera* cvs. tolerate vary high temperature (46^{0}C) in India but berry size and sugar content is reduced and thicker skin is induced.
- In terms of food value, vinifera cultivars are used in wine production and eaten fresh (table grapes), canned and preserved into juice or raisins.
- Cultivated grape (*V. vinifera*) is hybrid of *V. vulpina* x *V. labrusca*.
- Commercial cultivar of American grapes is originated from *V. labrusca* x *V. rotundifolia*.
- Cvs. Delware, Herbemont and Denoir developed by crossing *V. aestivalis* x *V. vinifera*.
- Cross between *Muscadine* female and *Euvitis* male is sterile.
- True representative varieties of *V. labrusca*: Concord (blue black table grape), Isabella and Rogers.
- *Vinifera* grapes contains smaller amount of pectin compared to American grapes which form stable jelly.
- Species reported in India: *V. barbata*, *V. rugosa*, *V. rumicisperma* and *V. parviflora*.
- *V. labrusca*, *V. riparia* and *V. amurensis*: Potential sources for PM and DM resistance breeding.
- Species found in various regions of world (Olmo, 1976).

Name	Botanical name	Features
Genus *Vitis*		
Wine grape	*Vitis vinifera ssp. sylvestris*	Progenitor of grape
European grape/ Table grape/ Old World Grape	*V. vinifera*	Natural origin from *V. labrusca*;behaves as both deciduous in temperate region & evergreen in sub-tropical regions; highly self pollinated; susceptible to phylloxera
New world Grape/ American grape/ Concord	*V. labrusca* cv. Delaware	Cold hardy; thick skin of fruit & slips from pulp at maturity; used for sweet grape juice, jam, jelly, preserve.
Sand Grape	*V. labrusca*	Suitable for sweet preparation (jam, jelly); resistant to *Phylloxera vitifolia*; used as rootstock
Muscadine Grape	*V. rotundifolia*	Dioecious; highly vigorous; bears functionally male & female flowers; resistant to PM & hot conditions; does not have seedless varieties; used extensively for making wine, Champagne & brandy
Summer Grape/ Pigeon Grape	*V. aestivalis*	Fruit size very small; susceptible to phylloxera; tolerant to hot conditions; high fungal disease (PM) resistant
Spanish Grape/ Winter Grape	*V. berlandieri*	Tolerant to high soil pH & phylloxera
Fox Grape	*V. rupestris*	Suitable for sweet preparation (jam, jelly); Resistant to *Phylloxera vitifolia* & anthracnose
River bank/ Frost Grape	*V. riparia* (syn. *V. vulpina*)	Cold hardy; most precocious; rootstock resistant to anthracnose, salinity

Desert wild Grape	*V. girdiana*	-
Silverleaf Grape	*V. argentifolia*	-
Canyon Grape	*V. arizonica*	Resistant to drought
Pacific Grape	*V. californica*	-
Calcarie Grape	*V. champini*	Used as rootstock for salinity, nematodes tolerance
Grayback Grape	*V. cinerea*	Resistant to aphids
-	*V. candicans*	Resistant to DM
-	*V. cordifolia*	-
-	*V. doaniana*	Resistant to nematode
Round Leaf Grape	*V. helleri*	
Florida Blue Grape	*V. gigas*	-
Bush Grape	*V. longii*	Used as rootstock
Sweet Mountain Grape	*V. monticola*	Resistant to lime & drought
Pilgrim Grape	*V. movae-angliae*	-
Cat Grape	*V. palmata*	-
Current Grape	*V. simpsoni*	Resistant to Pierce's disease
Fig leaf Grape	*V. smalliana*	Resistant to Pierce's disease
-	*V. parviflora*	Matures very early, reflexed stamen & resistant to anthracnose
-	*V. amurensis*	Resistant to DM, cold & frost
Genus *Muscadinia*		
Muscadine Grape	*M. rotundifolia*	-
Simpsory/ Little Muscadine grape/ Mustang Grape	*M. munsoniana* (syn.) *V. mustangensis*)	
Mexican Muscadine Grape	*M. popenoeifennel*	-

Special horticultural practices:

- Dr. A.J. Winkler an outstanding viticulturist developed many varieties, standardized pruning and agro-techniques.
- General viticulture: Internationally read and referred book by Winkler *et al*. (1974).
- Trellies system of training is considered most important.
- Vine is allowed to grow single stem without allowing side shoots upto certain height and growing point is cut back upto desired height.
- Most widely adopted: Bower system.
- Pendal system is most popular and adopted for export purpose.
- Head system of training is popular in Punjab.
- Kniffin system: Cheaper as compared to bower system. Mostly confined to research institute & not popular among farmers e.g. Beauty Seedless, Perlette, Bhokri, Delight, Early Muscat, and Banqui Abyad.
- Height of grape vine kept under head system of training: 1.2 m.
- Pergola system of training is popular in Tamil Nadu.
- Highest mean bunch weight + Berry weight is obtained under bower system of training.

- Highest Cost: benefit (1: 2.90): Bower/ Pergola/ Arbour/ Pandal system.
- For Thompson Seedless, spacing of 1.8 m x 2.5 m is ideal for bower system.
- For Thompson Seedless, spacing of 1.8 m x 3.0 m is ideal for 'Y' trellies system.
- Double stem better than single stem under flat roof gable system of training in 'Tas-A-Ganesh' grafted on 'Dogridge' rootstock.
- Retention upto 50 bunches per vine spaced at 10 x 6 feet is ideal for 'Sharad Seedless' grafted on 'Dodridge' rootstock.
- Double cordon with horizontal placement, harvest more berries.
- Vertical shoot position is recommended for better fruitfulness and for photosynthesis compared to horizontal position in Tas-A-Ganesh.
- HDP: 10 x 6 feet (1815 plants/ ha), 9 x 6 feet (2017 plants/ha).
- In India, double pruning and double cropping system is practiced in mild tropical region e.g. cv. Gulabi, Arka Vathi, Bhokari, Bangalore Blue.
- Ready to harvest: 35-50 days after pruning.
- Bud break to blooming: 47-70 days.
- Trunk and arms form permanent frame work of the vine.
- Arms have different units of pruning such as fruting spur, fruiting canes, renewal spurs & replacement spurs.
- Trunk: Permanent stem of grape vine; tendril is modified shoot.
- Shoot: Young leafy growth of current season
- Cane: Shoot after maturity.
- Spur: Basal portion of the cane left after pruning.It is intended to bear fruit.
- Renewal spur: Cane or spur cut back to 1-2 buds to produce fruiting wood for next year.
- Fruiting cane/ long cane is basal part of mature cane with 8-12 buds left after pruning to produce fruit.
- Fruiting spur/ short cane has normally 2-4 buds left after pruning and bear heavy fruiting.
- Replacement spur: Any water sprout sucker arising from arm is chosen as replacement spur which will produce growth for following year.
- Stem girdling: Removal of 5mm wide ring at full bloom stage.
- Nipping is done at terminal buds at 12-15 node stage.
- Purpose of nipping: To avoid staggered growth of berries.
- Cluster or berry thinning: GA_3 @ 50 ppm at calyptra stage.
- Pre-anthesis application of GA_3 is practiced for improving berry size, bunch weight and quality.
- Purpose of thinning: To improve colour, reduce uneven ripening, berry quality, reduce acidity, increase sugar contentand advances ripening.

- Uniform ripening: Ethrel @ 250-500 ppm at berry starts ripening stage.
- Flowering in north India: March-April and in south and western India (June-July) after April pruning and (November-December) after October pruning.
- Pruning consists of mainly thinning out & heading back.

Spur pruned varieties (canes are headed back to 2-3 or 4-5 buds)	Perlette, Beauty Seedless, Delight, Bangalore Blue, Bhokri, Gold, Early Muscat
Cane pruned varieties (canes are headed back to 8-12 buds)	Pusa Seedless, Thompson Seedless, Kishmish Chorni, Gulabi

- Pruning in sub-tropical regions (Punjab, Haryana, Delhi, Uttar Pradesh): Single pruning (Dec.-Jan.)- Single cropping.
- Pruning in hot tropical regions (Maharastra, Karnataka in Thompson Seedless): Double pruning (March and Sept.)- Single cropping.
- Pruning in mild tropical regions (Andhra Pradesh, Karnataka, Tamil Nadu in Anab-e-Shahi): Double pruning (March and Sept.)- Double cropping.
- Pruning in temperate regions (J & K, Himachal Pradesh): Single pruning- single cropping.
- Summer or back or foundation pruning: Twice: March to April.
- Pruning intensity is lightest (3-4 bud) in Bangalore Blue and Bhokari.
- Pruning intensity highest (10-14 bud) in Thompson Seedless.
- Sub-cane and sub-sub-cane pruning are followed in adverse condition in Maharashtra.
- October or forward or fruit pruning: Done in Maharashtra, Andhra Pradesh, Karnataka.
- Staggered pruning cultivar: Bangalore Blue.
- Air pruning technique is followed in bench grafting on Dogridge through machine. Adopted in Solapur area of Maharashtra which saves time in nursery.

Pruning practices considering climate change and market availability:

Pruning for fruting	Fruit availability period
June-July	October-November
July- August	November-December
August-September	January-February
October	March-April
November	May-June

- Trunk girdling improves berry set, berry retention, yield and quality.
- Inverse relationship between quality and resistance to biotic and abiotic stresses.
- Growth regulators commercially used: GA_3, Hydrogen cyanamide & CCC.
- Dormancy breaking chemical: Dormex contain hydrogen cyanamide @ 1 to 1.5%.
- Enlargement of panicle growth: GA_3 @ 10-40 ppm.

- Loose bunch with bold berries: GA @ 10 ppm at 5 leaf stage; 15 ppm at 8 leaf stage and 40 ppm at 75% bloom.
- Berry elongation: GA_3 @ 30-40 ppm + 2 ppm CPPU.
- Foliar spray of boron @ 0.2% at bloom and pre-bloom stage improves quality.
- $FeSO_4$ @ 0.05% enhances TSS.
- $ZnSO_4$ @ 0.2% improves berry set & yield.
- Suppressing vigour of vine and increase bud fruitfulness: CCC.
- Bud breaking in north India: Hydrogen cyanamide (HCN) 1.5-4%. It induces uniform and early bud sprout.
- Bud breaking in south India: Thiourea @ 4%.
- Thiourea hastens termination of dormancy by 10-15 days and increased bud burst 12-16%.
- For introduction of male sterility: Maleic hydrazide
- Golden bleached raisin: NaOH @ 0.2-0.3%.
- Wet drop: Berry is pulled out due to strain and stress in handling.
- Dry drop: Formation of abscission layer.
- Inception of berry ripening (berries begin to show colour & soften): Veraison stage.
- Under ordinary conditions grapes can be easily stored for 4-5 days.
- Cold storage conditions: 0-2^{0}C at 85-95% R.H, grapes can be stored for 4-10 weeks.
- Ripeness of individual bunch is judged by observing the berries at distal end of cluster which are last to ripe.
- TSS is used to determine the maturity as it has high correlation with palatibility.
- Fruit harvest period: November to May in south India and June-July in northern states.
- Seed matures prior to onset of berry quality.
- Maturity indices:
  - Heat unit concepts e.g. 3200-3600 photo-thermal units;
  - Appearance of bloom on the berries;
  - Colour and condition of stem cluster;
  - TSS: acid ratio 30-35(since relative ammounts of acidity & TSS effect taste);
  - TSS: Anab-e-Shahi (14-16^0 brix), Thompson Seedless (18-22^0 brix), Bangalore Blue (12-14^0 brix);
  - Composition of juice, thick and consistent with 18-22^0 TSS;
  - For raisins TSS should be 24-28^0 and moisture should not more than 17%;
  - Compact clusters for table purpose e.g. Thompson Seedless.
- Selection criteria for harvesting:
  - White wine: Brix 15-23^0; acidity >0.7%, juice pH >3.3.

- ° Red wine: Brix 20.5-23.5°; acidity >0.65%, juice pH >3.4.
- Output ratio of raisin: 4:1.

Propagation

- Sexual: Evolve new varieties through hybridization.
- Commercial propagation: Hardwood cutting (4 inch long, 4 buds and 8-10 mm dia.) with 3-4 nodes prepared from dormant canes during pruningand treated with 500 ppm IBA give 70-75% success.
- IBA @ 2000 ppm by quick dip method (10 sec.) is ideal for rooting of cuttings in September-October.
- Best grafting: Wedge grafting.
- Chip budding in April & T-budding in June (66-77% success).
- Layering: Difficult to root & as a quick method of gap filling in vineyards.
- *In vitro* propagation: Use of leaf blades, axillary buds, shoot apices as explants.
- Highly suitable explants for faster and disease free production: Shoot tip and micro-cuttings.
- Embryo rescue allows seedless x seedless progeny through ovule culture prior to devemental arrest.
- Embryo rescue done at 14-20 days after pollination in sub-tropical regions & 40-60 days after pollination in temperate regions produce more embryos.
- Genetic engineering is accomplished only in *V. rupestris*.

Rootstocks:

- Rootstock influences on viticultural traits viz. days taken for bud burst, cane fruitfulness, berry diameter, yield per vine and vegetative vigour i.e. shoot diameter and length of shoot.
- Muscadine grape commercially propagated by serpentine layering.
- October: Ideal time for plantingrootstock.
- Vines grafted on St. George rootstock exhibit more severe 'K' symptoms.
- Drought tolerant: 1103-P >Dogridge> Salt Creek > 1613 > 1616 >110-R, Ruggeri.
- Na^+/ H^+ anti-porter genes in different rootstocks in the response to salinity and water stress shows differential expression.

Name	Features
Dogridge	Cv. of *V. champini*; introduced from USA; resistant to nematode, drought, salinity prone areas. Compatible with Thompson Seedless, Tas-A-Ganesh, Flame Seedless and Sharad Seedless. Revolutionized grape industry in India
1613	Cross of *V. solonis* x Othello; imparts moderate vigour in Anab-e-Shahi; tolerant to salinity, drought & nematodes

1616	Cross of *V. solonis* x *V. riparia*; Tolerant to salinity, drought & nematodes
110-R	Increases water use efficiency of Thompson Seedless and restrict uptake sodium ions from soil. Compatible with Thompson Seedless, Tas-A-Ganesh, Flame Seedless and Sharad Seedless; tolerant to salinity & drought
99-R (syn. Richter 99)	Hybrid of *V. berlandieri* x *V. rupestris*; tolerant to salinity, drought & phylloxera
Degrasset	Clone of *V. champini*; rootstock for saline and drought conditions and more compatible with Thompson Seedless
Temple	Used against resistance to Pierce's disease
Frumoasa Alba	Tolerant to DM, PM
Marquis	Tolerant to PM
H-516, H-1204	Impart low vigour & delayed compatibility with Thompson Seedless
Jawahar	Impart low vigour & delayed compatibility with Thompson Seedless; high intensity of suckering, salt resistant
St. George	cv. of *V. rupestris*; high intensity of suckering; resistant to salt & phylloxera
Salt Creek (syn. Ramsey)	Tolerant to salinity, drought & nematodes
Freedom, Harmony	Resistant to root knot nematodes & salt tolerant
Teleki 5-A	Cross of *V. berlandieri* x *V. riparia* 5-A; tolerant to nematodes & phylloxera
1202	Hybrid of Mataro x *V. rupestris*; resistant to phylloxera
Couderc 1202	Cross of Mourvedra x Rupestris No. 1; tolerant to phylloxera
Selection Oppenheim No. 4	Tolerant to phylloxera
3306, 3309	Tolerant to phylloxera
Riparia Glorie de Montpellier	Seedling selection of *V. riparia*; tolerant to phylloxera
A x R-1 (syn. Ganzin No.1)	Hybrid of *V. vinifera* cv. Aramon x *V. rupestris* cv. Ganzin; tolerant to phylloxera
39-16	Cross of Almeria x *V. rotundifolia*; resistant to nematodes
43-43, 44-4	Hybrid of Hunisia x *V. rotundifolia*; resistant to nematodes
176-6	Hybrid of V. rofotomentosa x cv. Colombard; resistant to nematodes
Farcal	An INRA hybrid rootstock (V. berlandieri x V. vinifera cv. Colombard No. 1 x 333 EM); highly resistant to phylloxera; fairly resistant to nematode & resistant to chlorosis induced by calcareous soil

Varieties:

- International grape breeder and geneticist: Dr. H.P. Olmo. He evolved 'Delight' and 'Perlette' varieties at USA.
- Tetraploid grapes produced in California have larger fruits and fewer seeds per berry than diploids.
- In India, introduction of grape varieties was started as early as 1838.
- Sardar Bahadur Lal Singh: Father of grape development in north India.
- Rangspay, Sholtu White, Sholtu Red: Indigenous varieties found in Kalpa district of Himachal Pradesh.
- Monograph of grape varieties was prepared by Chadha and Randhawa (1974).
- Reflexed stamen grape should be used as female parent in hybridization to avoid task of emasculation and pollen fails to germinate due to lack of germpore resulting into seedless progeny.

- Discovery of 'Anab-e-Shahi' by R. Shankar Pillay in the home garden in 1930. It was introduced in India from Middle-East in 1890.
- Muhammed Bin Tughlaq introduced Bhokri, Fakhri and Sahebi cultivars in Aurangabad (Daulatabad). He discouraged practice of grape wine making.
- Grape improvement work was started at IARI in 1958.
- 1st cv. in which whole genome sequence was deciphered: Pinot Noir.
- Introductions:
  - Most of varieties grown in India are introduced from USA, USSR, California, Yugoslavia and Australia.
  - During 1994-96, Dr. Arve brought few rootstocks from USA.
  - Kishmish Beli, Kishmish Charni, Surnak Kitabiskij- From USSR.
  - Ruby Seedless, Gordo Blano, Wortly Hall hybrids- From Australia.
  - Totlocha from Brazil.
  - Iniyaone from South Africa: Black coloured, does not require growth regulators, no cracking with storage life of 90 days with 22^0 brix.
  - Black coloured table grape varieties: Aara-27, Aara-32, Aara-A/4.
  - Aara-15 from California: Black coloured.Export oriented.
  - Aara-32 from California: Black coloured. Tolerant to biotic and abiotic stresses. TSS 18^0 Brix; berry size 24-25 mm; bunch no. 40-42; productivity 36 t/ha.Export oriented.
  - Sahyadri Farmers Producer Company, Nashik imported 5 varieties viz. Ivory (greenish white colour), Timko (red colour), Melody (black colour), Timsun (whitish green colour), Aalisun (red colour) having big berry size, juicy, sweet, excellent shipping quality, uniform ripening, excellent keeping quality and disease resistant.
  - Special New Fruit Licening (SNFL) Company, Spain breeds patient varieties.
- Leading raisin grape variety in world: Thompson Seedless.
- Rubi Roman: Costliest grape in the world.
- Commercially variety used for 'Champagne' making in the world: White Riesling.
- Pink berry formation is common problem in Thompson Seedless and its clones.
- Queen's of Vineyard, Pusa Seedless: Used as male parent to transmit seedlessness in progeny.
- New Perlette (Loose Perlette): Self thinning (due to meiotic irregularity of chromosomal transversion). X-ray (2.5 kR) mutant from 'Perlette'.
- Japanese tetraploid grape variety having maximum berry size: Kyoho.
- Functionally female (reflexed stamen) varieties: Hur, Angoor Kalan, Banqui Abyad, Pandhari Sahebi, Katta Kurghan, Hybrid No. 1613, *V. parviflora*, *V. champini*.

- Interspecific hybrids: Tarheel, South Land, Magron, Regale, Sterling, Triumph, Telki5-A and Harmony.
- Cv. 'Hur' does not need emasculation when used as a female parent.
- Teintuier (French language): Term used for variety having red coloured skin and flesh e.g. Pusa Navrang.
- Cane pruned varieties: Thompson Seedless, Pusa Seedless, Kishmish Charni, Gulabi.
- Spur pruned varieties: Perlette, Beauty Seedless, Bangalore Blue, Delight, Early Muscat.
- Induced mutants: Red Niagara (from Niagara), Robin Cardinal (from Cardinal), Catawa, Concord, Emperor, Habsi, Muscat of Alexandria.
- Tetraploids: Pusa Seedless, Black Champa, Marvel Seedless (from Delight), Black King (from Campbell), Early Giant (from Campbell), Muscat, Case (from Sultana), Wallis Giant (from Concord), Centennial and Metcalf (from Waltham), Muscat Common Hall andSweeney (from Muscat of Alexandria).
- Variety having strong Muscat flavor: Cardinal.
- Grape varieties having non-acylated anthocyanin: Yan 73, Neronet & Pinot Noir.
- Table grape having black colour: Nana Purple, Krishna, 1813.
- Cheema Sahebi (syn. Selection-7): Clonal selection of 'Pandhari Sahebi'. Suitable for juice purpose.
- Rao Sahebi: Clonal selection from 'Cheema Sahebi' made by Shri. R.S. Kadlag.
- Manik Chaman: Seedless selection made by Shri. T.R.Dabhade.
- Monika: Selection made by Shri. A.G.Meher.
- Dilkhush: Seeded clonal selection of Anab-e-Shahi made by Shri. L. Venkataratnam.
- DaNaKa Seedless: Selection made by Shri. **Da**dasaheb **Na**nasaheb**Ka**le.
- King Sonaka Delux: Selection made by Shri. **Da**dasaheb **Na**nasaheb **Ka**le. Green coloured, 45-50 cm berry length and 24-25 mm dia., require less thinning, crunchier, yield 12-13 t/ acre.
- Manas Seedless: Selection from 'Sonaka'.
- 'Sudhakar Seedless', a variant of Thompson Seedless, having sweet berries, tolerant to water stress, less berry shedding and berry rotting was registered under PPVFRA.
- Raisin purpose export oriented varieties: Black Corianth, Gold, Kishmish Beli (seedless with high sugar & outstanding raisin cv.), Manik Chaman, Sree Ganesh, Clone-2A, Muscat of Alexandria.
- Seedless black grapes for export purpose: Nanasaheb Purple, Krishna Seedless, Sarita Seedless.
- Juice/ canning purpose: White and purple coloured with strong muscat flavoured varieties viz. Aramon, Carignane, Chasselas, Champion, Concord, Early Muscat, E 12-2, Gulabi, Kishmish Beli, Medika, Pusa Seedless, Seedless White Round, White Riesling.

- Wine purpose: Anab-e-Shahi, Bhokari, Carignane, Convent Large Black, Char Donnay, Chenin Blanc, Early Muscat, Muscat Canelli, Perlette, Pinot Noir, Tinta Madeira, White Riesling.
- Angoori: Indigenous varieties locally used to make wine.
- Sweet/ Dessert (red wine) purpose: Grapes with high sugar and moderate-low acid content are suitable e.g. Black Muscat, Convent Large Black, Rubi Red.
- Dry red table (wine) purpose: Grapes of high acidity and low sugar are suitable e.g. Cabernet Sauvignon, Carignan, Chardonnay, Fanteasca Neagre, Malvasia, Merlot, Muscat Canelli, Pinot Noir, Sapervi, Shiraz, Tievosa, Tinta Madeira, Zinfandel.
- Dry white table (wine) purpose: Alba Rekatsetali, Bayan Shirei, Chenin Blanc, Excelsior, Fanteasca, Ova Pagola, Sauvignon Blanc, White Riesling, Shiredon.
- Wines made from heat treated must have higher tannin content.
- Wines made from high acid grapes with *Schizosaccharomyces pombe* reduces acidity than with *Saccharomyces cerevisiae*.
- Red coloured seedless: Fantasy Seedless, Crimson Seedless (Sweet taste, pink berries, more crunchy), Krishna, Nana Purple, Flame Seedless (Tough berries, crunchier), Ruby Seedless (dark red berries, juicier, crunchier & sweet taste), Sweet Celebration, Timko, Red Globe (Pink to light red berries, tough & crunchy pulp).
- Blue/ Black coloured seedless: Summer Royal, Melody, Autumn Royal, Sable Seedless.
- Green/white skinned seedless varieties: Regal Seedless, Santenial Seedless, Autumn Crisp, Cotton Candy (smell of coffee/caramel), Sweet Globe (less acidic, crunchier), Sugra One.
- Premium wine grapes from USA: Norton, Cynthiana, Viginia Seedling.
- Premium wine grapes from Venezuela: French Coloumbar, Ruby Cabernet.
- Donia: Resistant to *A. tumefaciens*, PM, DM, botrytis, frost and phylloxera.
- Criollas: New race resulted due to spontaneous hybridization within *V. vinifera* in Venezuala.
- Bargron, Strangron, Shungron: Seedless cvs. Grown in Ladakh area.
- In grape breeding, seedlessness is achieved by doubling of chromosomes.
- Powdery mildew resistant: Chardonnay.
- Downy mildew resistant: Maroo Seedless, Madhu Angoor, Carolina Black Rose, Khalili.
- In French language, '*Blanc*' means white.
- Punjab Purple: Cattawa x Beauty Seedless.
- Perle: Cold hardy, polyploid variety commercially grown in Germany.
- Marble Seedless: Mutant of 'Delight'.

Varieties	Breeding method	Features
Seedless cultivars		
Crimson Seedless (2002)	Introduction from USA	Mature in 130-135 days; Naturally bold & coloured; no need of GA_3 to increase berry size; 18-19 mm berry; require less water for growth; export oriented; tolerate rains stored for longer period
Beauty Seedless (1964)	Introduction from California (Queen's of Vineyards x Black Kishmish)	Black coloured; table, juice& wine variety; salt resistant
Blush Seedless	Emperor x Z-4-87	Good for table & raisin making
Autumn Royal	-	Late maturing; no need of girdling
Autumn Seedless	Calimeria x (Muscat of Alexandria x Sultana)	White; good for table & raisin making
Merkis	Athens x Emrold Seedless	Good for processing; tolerant to DM, PM & black rot
Diamond, Summer Muscat, Sunglow	-	Early maturity; no fruit cracking in rainy season; grown in Australia
Hongju	Italia x Perlon	Red berry; non slip skin & slight muscat flavour
Thompson Seedless (syn. Australian Seedless, Sultana, Oval Kishmish) 1936	Origin from Asia Minor, named in USA & introduced from Australia	Green/white skinned; Multiple uses (table purpose, raisin, wine making); suitable for export purpose
Perlette (1969)	Introduction from USA (Hungarian x Sultania Marble)	Tetraploid; early ripening; prolific bearer; commonly grown in north India; shot berry is acute problem
Delight (1936)	Sister seedling of 'Perlette'	Good eating & shipping quality
Sharad Seedless (1990)	Clonal selection of 'Kishmish Chorni'	Red coloured berries; suitable for table & raisin purpose
Sonaka (1980)	Bud sport of 'Thompson Seedless'& selection made by Shri. Nana Saheb Kale	Green/ white skinned; suitable for table & raisin purpose
Tas-A-Ganesh	Bud sport of 'Thompson Seedless'	Green/ white skinned; Elongted berries, suitable for table & raisin purpose
Kishmish Rozavis (KR) White	Clonal mutant selection of red 'Kishmish Rozavis' from Russia	Genetically modified; white bold berries; suitable for raisin making & table purpose; TSS 23-24^0 Brix
Kishmish Beli	Introduction from USSR	Table & raisin purpose
Kishmish Chernyi (1964)	Introduction from Erstwhile USSR (Uzbekistan)	Black colour; table & raisin purpose
Flame Seedless (1993)	Origin from USA but introduction from Australia	Short duration (90-110 days) variety recommended for north India; suitable for juice production

Fantasy Seedless	Introduction	Black colour; berries are loosely filled in bunch; mature in 130-135 days; TSS 18-20^0 Brix; no need of plant growth regulators; good fruit taste & more shelf life
Early Sweet, Aara	Introduction from California	TSS 19-20^0 Brix; 22-42 mm berry; tolerant to abiotic stress; suitable for tropical &dessert areas; available in red, white and black colours
NRCG, Pune		
Manjari Naveen (2008)	Clonal selection of 'Centennial Seedless'	White berries, firm pulp & mild Vanessa flavor; self thinning; berry size 18-20 mm; scented; matures earlier than Thompson Seedless; tolerant to DM & anthracnose; suitable for export
Manjari Shyama (A-18/3) 2019	OP seedling selection from 'Black Champa x Thompson Seedless'	Early harvest; bold black berries; thick pulp; loose bunches; TSS (18-20^0 Brix); yield 18.34 kg/vine; suitable for table purpose; tolerant to mildews
Manjari Kishmish (2020)	Clonal selection from 'Kishmish Rozavis'	Green colour; harvest in 135-140 days;bunch wt. 34 kg; raisin recovery 26.5%; TSS 22.7^0 Brix; yield 32-35 t/ha; mod. resistant to PM
IARI, New Delhi		
Pusa Urvashi (1997)	Banqui Abyad x Perlette	Suited to 4 bud pruning; prolific bearer; TSS (22-23%); table & raisin purpose, resistant to anthracnose
Pusa Navrang (1997)	Madeline Angenine x Rubi Red (Alicante Ganzin x Tintocao)	Teinturier dark red (colour in berry peel & pulp) grape variety; TSS (17-18%); juice & coloured wine purpose & as a colour additive for coloured fruit beverages; resistant to anthracnose
Pusa Aditi (2017)	Banqui Abyad x Perlette	Early, seedless; tolerant to anthracnose & PM
Pusa Trishar (2013)	(Hur x Bharat Early) x Beauty Seedless	Tolerant to anthracnose & PM
Pusa Seedless (1970)	Clonal selection from unknown origin	Bold attractive bunches; uniform ripening; used as table & raisin purpose
R2P36	Pearl of Casaba x Beauty Seedless	Extra early maturing; black colour & TSS 22.2^0 Brix.
Pusa Swarnika (Hybrid 76-1) 2018	Hur x Cardinal	Suitable for sub-tropical climate; self thinning type; tolerant to anthracnose, PM, termite
Pusa Purple Seedless (2020)	-	Raised through embryo rescue; extra-early berry ripening variety (75-80 DAFB) under sub-tropical region
IIHR, Bengaluru		
Arka Vathi (1980)	Black Champa x Thompson Seedless	1st hybrid developed in India; yellowish green berries; suitable for table, raisin making & table wine purpose; suitable for double cropping
Arka Neelmani (1991)	Black Champa x Thompson Seedless	Suitable for table, red dessert wine purpose; dark red to black berries; tolerant to anthracnose
Arka Shweta (syn. Shweta Seedless) 1994	Anab-e-Shahi x Thompson Seedless	Greenish yellow berries; suitable for table & raisin making
Arka Krishna (1994)	Black Champa x Thompson Seedless	Dark coloured; suitable for beverage industry
Seeded cultivars		

Anab-e-Shahi (syn. Malta)	Introduction from Middle East in 1890	Bold size; lack stenospermocarpy; popular cultivar throughout India; susceptible to mildew, anthracnose & fruit rot
Bhokri (syn. Nasik, Pacha Draksha, Green Grape)	Introduction from Russia in 1838	High yield; strong muscat flavor; suitable for double cropping; best adopted to tropical climate of Tamil Nadu
Himrod (1928)	Ontario (American type) x Sultanina (Thompson Seedless)	Introduced from New York; thick skin; resistant to pests & diseases
Early Muscat	Introduction from USA	Tetraploid of Muscat of Alexandria, uneven ripening, juice highly flavoured
Bangalore Blue (syn. Bangalore Purple)	*V. vinifera* x *V. labrusca*	Table grape; very acidic, foxy flavor; suitable for double cropping, juice & wine making; tolerant to DM; resistant to anthracnose; highly susceptible to root knot nematode
Gulabi (syn. Paneer Draksha, Muscat, Karachi, Black Prince, Muscat of Hamburg) 1936	Origin from England but introduced from Australia	Suitable for head system & double cropping; muscat flavor; tolerant to DM, PM & anthracnose; highly susceptible to root knot nematode
Red Globe (1985)	Introduction from USA	Late ripening; red coloured, round shaped, bold berries (22-28 mm), TSS (18-20^0 Brix); good storage (4-5 months in cold); tolerant to PM & all sucking pests; free from cracking syndrome; seeds have ani-cancer properties; yield (11-12 t/ acre;)export oriented
Champian	Introduction	Juice highly flavoured
Black Champa	Introduction	Suitable for table, juice & red dessert wine purpose
Bharat Early	Introduction	Small bunches, uniform ripening
Banqui Abyad	Introduction	Reflexed stamen, cracking of berries, very sweet
Kali Sahebi	Introduced in India under name 'Habshi' from California	Large black berries
Pandhari Sahebi	Introduced under name 'Sahebi'	Best table variety; self sterile
Gold	Introduction	Muscat flavor; panicle drying is serious problem
Pearl of Casaba	Introduction	Earliest maturing variety of north India; very sweet; small bunch; high seed content
Cardinal	Tokay x Ribier	Bright red & spherical berries, table purpose
NRCG, Pune		
Manjari Medika (A-27/1) 2017	Pusa Navrang x Flame Seedless	Teinturier variety; soft seeded; multipurpose varietyi.e. red coloured juice, manuka & table purpose; high anti-oxidant level; TSS 21-22^0 brix; acidity 0.58%; anthocyanin (4 g/kg); mod. susceptible to PM, DM
IIHR, Bengaluru		
Arka Majestic (1994)	Angur Kalan x Black Champa	Very vigorous & table purpose variety; suitable for head system of training; tolerant to anthracnose, berry deep tan coloured
Arka Soma (1994)	Sister seedling of	Muscat flavor; suitable for white dessert wine

	Arka Kanchan	making; tolerant to anthracnose, PM, DM; gives 2 crops in a year
Arka Trishna (1994)	Bangalore Blue x Convent Large Black	Male sterile hybrid; deep tan coloured; suitable for juice & red dessert wine making (high sugar & low acid content); resistant to anthracnose, DM
Arka Kanchan (1980)	Anab-e-Shahi x Queen's of Vineyards	Late maturing; golden yellow berries; suitable for table & dessert wine purpose; Muscat flavour
Arka Shyam (1980)	Bangalore Blue x Black Champa	Mild foxy flavor; bluish black berries; TSS 20-22^0 Brix; suitable for table, juice & dessert wine making; resistant to anthracnose
Arka Hans (1980)	Bangalore Blue x Anab-e-Shahi	Yellowish green berries; suitable for quality wine making; foxy flavor, resistant to anthracnose
Arka Chitra (1994)	Angur Kalan x Anab-e-Shahi	Table variety; tolerant to PM; all buds are fruitful; gives 2 crops in a year
Agharkar Research Institute, Pune, Maharashtra		
ARI-516	*V. labrusca* (Catawba) x *V. vinifera* (Beauty Seedless)	Bluish black berries; ready in 110 days after Oct. pruning; suitable for table, raisin & wine purpose; resistant to rain, PM, DM & anthracnose; yield 20 T/ ha; pleasant aroma, high juice recovery (70%), suitable for processing; TSS-18^0 Brix & acidity 0.4-0.5%
ARI-27	Diamond Jubilee x Rubi Red	-
ARI-144	Cheema Sahebi x Catawba	-
ARI-302	Mutant of Anab-e-Shahi	Seedless
Other outstanding varieties		
Lake Emerald	*V. simpsoni* cv. Pixiola x *V. vinifera* cv. Golden Muscat	Resistant to Pierce's disease
Amur hybrid	*V. vinifera* x *V. amurensis*	Cold & PM resistant
Delaware	*V. labrusca* x *V. aestivalis* var. bourquiniana x *V. vinifera*	-
Tarheel	*V. rotundifolia* x *V. munsoniana*	Self fertile
Regale	-	Produce bronze coloured berry & resistant to Pierce's disease
Sterling	-	Cold hardy & bronze coloured berry
Triumph	-	Bronze coloured berry with very big berries
Italia (2002)	Introduction from USA	Greenish white; pleasant muscat flavour
Cabernet Sauvignon (1982)	Introduction from France	Small bunches with black purple berries & suitable for wine making
Chenin Blanc (1987)	Introduction from France	Round bunches with white berries
Sauvignon Blanc (1987)	Introduction from Blanc	White seeded small berry; sutiable for table & wine making

Shiraz (1993)	Introduction from France & Australia	Cylindrical bunch; suitable for rose wine or blending to provide colour
Zinfandel (1995)	Introduction from France	Bunch compact, dark purple berries; suited for rose wines
Malbec (1995)	Introduction from France	Red wine variety; berries small spherical
Ugni Blanc (1995)	Introduction from France	White wine variety used for blending with other varieties
Chardony	-	White wine variety popular worldwide
Grenache (1995)	Introduction from France	Red wine variety used for blending
Centennial Seedless (1985)	Introduction from USA & Australia	White seedless variety
Fantasy Seedless (2001)	Introduction from USA	Dark bluish black seedless; neutral flavour

Farmer's selections: Nanasaheb Purple Seedless (2004), Sarita Seedless (2004)

Grading system:

- Grape guard: Technique developed by Dr. Nelson of USA. Major achievement in handling & marketing.
- Grape guard: A craft paper coated with KMS, citric acid and plastic polymer. It releases SO_2 for fumigation under high humidity. It controls post harvest fungal diseases.
- Grapes can be economically stored up to 40-45 days in cold storage using grape guard.
- Size of CFB carton accommodating 4 kg grape: 37 cm x 25.5 cm x 11.5 cm.
- Berry size 16 mm and above are only fit for export.
- Individual berry wt. 3.5-5.0 g

Size group/ class	Large berries bunch weight (g)	Small berries bunch weight (g)
Extra	200	150
I	150	100
II	100	75
III	75	75

Inheritance of characters:

- Sodium carrier gene has been identified for salt tolerance in grapes.

Character	Inheritance pattern
Seedlessness	Polygenic recessive
Berry size	Recessive
Berry shape (Round), bunch shape and size, TSS, bunch compactness, seed content, number of bunches, yield, purple pigmentation in new emerging leaves, drooping habit of vine, pentagonal leaf shape, shorter maturity period, black berry, oval shape of seed	Dominant

Yield; no. of berries/ bunch; berry weight; no. of bunches/ vine; bunch weight; volume of bunch	Polygenes
Muscat aroma	Monogenic
Berry colour	Black dominant to red & white; red dominant to white
Hermaphrodite flower	Dominant
Reflexed stamen	Monogenic recessive
Maleness	Dominant
Femaleness	Recessive
Frost resistance	Polygenes
DM & PM disease resistance	Monogenic dominant
Pierce's disease resistance	3 independent dominant genes
Bacterial blight resistance	Recessive
Leaf size, main vein length, petiole length, short stiff hairs on lower surface of leaf	Pleiotropic

Diseases and pests:

- Model 'NRCG-SKAI PMExpert' is developed for forecasting of powdery mildew disease.
- Model 'Metwin 2' is developed for forecasting of downy mildew and anthracnose disease.
- Anthracnose (*Elsinoe ampelina*): All parts are affected.
- Black Prince, Pusa Navrang, Chardonny: Good donor parents for anthracnose tolerance.
- Grape fan leaf virus is transmitted by dagger nematode (*Xiphinema americanum*).
- Downy mildew (*Plasmopera viticola*): Most serious disease due to high temperature and high humidity.
- Powdery mildew (*Erysiphe necator*): Controlled by spray of Sulfex.Milastin K: A *Bacillus subtilis* formulation control PM @ 2 ml/ lit.
- Leaf roll virus came along with imported grape varieties.
- Dead arm (*Phomopsis viticola*):
- Rust (*Phakopsis vitis*):
- Botrytis fungus mostly grows on grapes.
- Berry rot: Controlled by wild yeast. It does not interfere with wine production.
- Udadya beetle/ Flea betle (*Scelodonta strigicola*): Damages sprouting buds.
- Mealy bug (*Maconellicoccus hirsutus*): 1st reported in Andhra Pradesh in 1974. Natural predators (*Anagyrus dactylopii* and *Scymnus coccivora*). Spray Chlorpyrifos @ 0.05%.
- Stem girdling beetle (*Sthenias grisator*):
- Bud eating caterpillar (*Spodoptera litura*):
- Thrips (*Thpiphorothrips cruentatus*): Suck cell sap.

- Chaffer beetle (*Adoratus* spp.):
- Pierce's disease (*Xylella fastidiosa*):
- *Phylloxera vitifolia* feed on roots.
- Bird eye spot (*Elsinoe ampelina*):
- Spray *Trichoderma* to manage pre-harvest infection of berries and post harvest rots by various fungi.

Physiological disorders:

- Mg deficiency: Universal problem in cultivation.
- Fe deficiency is very common in black soil.
- Inverted bottle neck: Disorder due to graft incompatibility, when Thompson Seedless is grafted on Dogridge rootstock.
- Uneven ripening: Presence of green berries in ripe bunch of coloured grape.
- Cane drying: Serious problem in cv. Gold.

Name	Cause(s) & susceptible cultivars	Remedy & remarks
Flower or bud drop	Improper pollination, fertilization, ambient temperature, heavy crop load	0.5 cm wide girdle from the trunk about 10 days before full bloom. Spray 500 ppm ethrel at veraison stage
Blossom end rot	Ca deficiency	Spray 1 % Calcium nitrate
Interveinal Chlorosis	Mg, Zn, Fe deficiency	Spray 0.2% $FeSO_4$
Uneven ripening	Bangalore Blue, Gulabi, Beauty Seedless, Thompson Seedless	Ethephon @ 250 ppm at colour break stage
Post harvest berry drop	Anab-e-Shahi, Beauty Seedless, Bangalore Blue, Cheema Sahebi	NAA @ 50 ppm
Pink berry/ Pigment syndrome	Observed only in India in white seedless grapes viz. Thompson Seedless, Tas-A-Ganesh, Bangalore Blue	Spray ascorbic acid @ 0.2% + 0.25% sodium diethyl dithiocarbamate; cover bunches with Tyvek paper at or before 75 days after fruit pruning.
Millerandage or Hen and Chicken	Bad weather, B deficiency, poor pollination (presence of different sized berries), heavy crop load e.g. Perlette	Ethephon 25 ppm + Sevin 2000 ppm for 1 min. and spray 0.2 % boric acid before bloom
Green berries	-	Ethrel spray
Coulure (failure of blossom to set fruits)	B deficiency	Serious in Beauty Seedless & Himrod; spray boron @ 0.05%
Water berry or mummification	B deficiency	Serious in Thompson Seedless & clones

Bunch stem necrosis	Heavy load of bunches & occurs during version stage of berry; Ca & Mg deficiency	Ideal canopy management; pre & post bloom sprays of salts @ 0.5%
Stalk necrosis	Ca deficiency	-
Red cane	Low carbohydrate	Sufficient nutrition
Shot berries	B deficiency (development of small seedless berries due to poor pollination)	Apply micronutrients
Little leaf	Zn deficiency	Spray $ZnSO_4$
Straggly cluster	Zn deficiency	Spray $ZnSO_4$
Spring fever	K deficiency	-
Inward leaf curling/ cupping	Commonly occurring disorder	-
Red vein necrosis	K deficiency in Thompson Seedless & its mutants	Apply K fertilizers
Tylose	Serious threat to Thompson Seedless resulting water berries; imbalance of nutrients	Spray micronutrients
Bud killing	Use of excess N application	Girdling & auxin spray

46. PROTECTED CULTIVATION OF FRUIT CROPS:

- High production in protected cultivation due to high photosynthetic efficiency.
- Largest producer of banana under green house: Morocco and Spain.
- Fruit crops suitable for protected cultivation: Apricot, Banana (cv. Grand Naine), Grape, Strawberry, Raspberry, Blueberry, Papaya, Peach, Pineapple, Pomegranate, Loquat, Mango, Nectarines, etc.
- Apricot variety 'Gold Sun' and grape variety 'Kyoho' are grown under protected cultivation in China.
- Fruit crop mostly cultivated under protected cultivation: Strawberry.
- Plastic houses are suitable for cherry cultivation.
- Polytunnel is suitable for raising apple nursery under cold arid temperate conditions.

46. OTHER UNDERUTILIZED FRUIT CROPS:

- Those species whose potential has not been fully realized.
- Miracle berry (*Synsepalum dulcificum*) when eaten, causes sour foods to taste sweet. The effect is due to 'miraculin'.
- Jojoba (*Simmondsia chinensis*): Dioecious and seed is rich in oil (45-55%) content.

Family	Common name
Anacardiaceae	Hog plum/ ciruela/ yellow mombin (*Spondias mombin*), Ker (*Capparis decidua*), Jamaica plum (*Spondias purpurea*)
Arecaceae	Salak (*Salacca edulis*)
Berberidaceae	Indian barberry/ Kingoda/ Kilmora (*Berberis aristata*)
Burseraceae	Pilinut (*Canarium ovatum*)
Cactaceae	Indian fig (*Opuntia ficus-indica*)
Clusiaceae	Gamboge tree (*Garcinia cambogia*), Cowphal (*Garcinia cowa*), Manney apple (*Mammea americana*)
Dilleniaceae	Elephant apple (*Dillenia indica*)
Ebenaceae	Tendu (*Diospyros melanoxylon*), Black sapote (*Diospyrous digyra*; not true sapote)
Elaegnaceae	Gewain/ silver berry (*Elaeagnus latifolia*)
Elaeocarpaceae	Ceylon olive (*Elaeocarpus serratus*)
Euphorbiaceae	Latka (*Baccaurea samiflora*)
Fabaceae	Locust bean (*Ceratonia siliqua*)
Juglandaceae	Wing nut (*Pterocarya pterocarpa*)
Lecythidaceae	Para nut/ Brazil nut (*Berthollctia excelsa*)
Meliaceae	Langsat (*Lansium domesticum*)
Moraceae	Timla (*Ficus auriculata*), Wild Himalayan fig/ bedu (*Ficus palmata*)
Myrtaceae	Surinam cherry/ Brazil cherry (*Eugenia uniflora*), Jaboticaba (*Myrciaria cauliflora*syn. *Plinia cauliflora*)
Passifloraceae	Giant granadilla (*Passiflora quadrangularis*)
Pinaceae	Chilgoza nut (*Pinus gerardiana*, not belong to angiosperms)& evergreen fruit
Rosaceae	Sohiong khasi cherry (*Prunus nepalensis*), Yellow Himalayan raspberry (*Rubes ellipticus*), European raspberry (*Rubus idaeus*), Black thorn sloe (*Prunus spinosa*), Indian hawthorn or Nepalese firrthorn or Ghingharu (*Pyracantha crenulata*)
Rubiaceae	Marmalade box (*Genipa americana*)
Rutaceae	Kichili (*Citrus maderaspatana*)
Salicaceae	Governor's plum (*Flacourtia ramontchi*),
Salvadoraceae	Grape of the desert/ Tooth brush tree (*Salvadora oleoides* or *S. persica*)
Sapindaceae	Spanish lime (*Melicoccus bijugatus*)
Sapotaceae	Indian butter tree (*Diploknema butyracea*), Molsari (*Mimusops elengi*), Star apple (*Chrysophyllum cainito*), Yellow star apple/ Abiu (*Pouteria caimito*), Green sapota (*Calocarpum virideae*), White sapota (*Casimiroa edulis*)
Saxifragaceae	Blackcurrants (*Ribes nigrum*), Red currants (*R. rubrum*), American gooseberry (*R. hirtellum*)

3

VEGETABLE SCIENCE

1. GENERAL OLERICULTURE

- Olericulture is Latin term '*Olerus*' meaning 'pot herb' and 'Cultra' meaning 'cultivation'.
- Definition: Vegetables are those plants wherein parts such as leaf, stem or root can be used for food.
- Herbs: Are those plants that are used for food, medicine, scent or flavour.
- Vegetables are called as 'Health capsules' or 'Protective food' because of high vitamin and mineral content.
- Vegetables are source of nutritional security, crop diversification and high income generation.
- China, India, USA, Turkey and Italy: Major vegetable producers.
- About 600 species contribute to global diversity in vegetable crops and only 1/4th is utilized as major group and remaining are named as minor or underutilized vegetable crops.
- Average productivity (in metric tons per ha) of different vegetable crops at world level: Potato (10.5), tomato (20.9), dry onion (12.9), cabbage (21.9), carrot (22.0), green pepper (7.7), snap bean (6.2), cucumber/ gherkins (13.3), musk melon (13.9), water melon (12.7), garlic (6.1), egg plant (13.9), pumpkins (9.8), green peas (4.8) and green onion/ shallots (14).
- Indian sub-continent has 80 species of major and minor vegetables apart from several wild species consumed as vegetable.
- About 175 different types of vegetables are grown in India, includes 82 leafy vegetables and 41 root (tuber and bulb) crops.
- Cucurbits, taros, yams, brinjal and okra have rich diversity in Indian gene centre.
- Germany leads in import of preserved onion, green pepper in brine and dehydrated onion flakes/ powder.
- Singapore leads in import of dried asparagus; Japan in dehydrated garlic flakes; UAE in dehydrated garlic powder; Bangladesh in peas and Switzerland in dried mushrooms including morels.
- FAO launched the Special Programme for Food Security (SPFS) in 1994.

- The SPFS started its programme in Low-income Food Deficit Countries (LIFDCs) to empower small farmers, as well as poor families in urban areas.
- West Bengal stands 1st in production of vegetables (14.1%), followed by Uttar Pradesh (11.4%), Bihar (9.3%), Madhya Pradesh (8.0%) and Gujarat (7.1%).
- India ranks 1st in productivity of cassava, ginger, okra and peas and 2nd in brinjal, cabbage, cauliflower, pea, potato, onion and tomato.
- India is 2nd largest producer of vegetables after China.
- India's share is 13.38% of world's and 3rd in vegetable production.
- Area under vegetables in India: 9.8 million ha (15.74% of world's area).
- Production of vegetables in India: 171 million tones.
- Avg. productivity of vegetables in India (17.4 T/ha), China (23.34 T/ha), USA (32.54 T/ha).
- Countries having highest per capita consumption of vegetables i) Greece (377 kg/year) and ii) Turkey (327 kg/year).
- Vegetable crops in India occupy only 6 % of total cropped (cultivated) area.
- Contribution of vegetables in horticulture sector in India: 59-61%.
- Production share of vegetables: Potato (27%), Tomato (12%), Onion (11%), Brinjal (8.0%), Cabbage (5%), Cauliflower (4.7%), Okra (4.0%), Others (28.3%).
- Vegetables consume about 22% of total pesticides used in India.
- Most of the vegetables are alkaline in nature.
- Vegetables supply fair amount of carbohydrates, proteins (6%), and calories (10%), leafy greens are rich source of calcium, phosphorous and iron than other nutrients.
- Karnataka state is called as'Seed capital of country'.
- Traditional vegetables: Onion, Potato, Okra, Bitter gourd, Chilli, Tomato, Beans.
- Seed coat dormancy (chemical dormancy phenols, coumarin & abscissic acid) is found in cucurbits and tomato.
- **Exotic vegetables**: Asparagus, Baby carrot, Baby corn, Broccoli, Celery, Cherry tomato, Chive, Cucumber, Endive, Gherkin, Globe Artichoke, Kale, Leek, Lettuce, Parsley, Pakchoi, Red cabbage, Shallot, Sweet pepper, Sweet corn, Zucchini, etc.
- Green leafy vegetables (GLV): Known as 'Nature's anti-aging wonders'.
- Probiotics: Food that provides health benefits beyond vitamins and minerals.
- Tuber crops are beckons of fsood basket of our country.
- From 1849 to 1857, cultivation of vegetables on systematic lines was done 1st at Govt. Botanical Garden, Ootacamund, Tamil Nadu.
- In 1860, vegetables seeds in India were supplied mostly by M/s. Sutton and Sons of London.
- Production of temperate vegetableswas started at Quetta (Baluchistan) in 1942-43.
- The South Asian Vegetable Research Network (SAVERNET): Sub-regional framework for cooperation composed of South Asian countries.

- Plant introduction scheme was sanctioned in 1947 at IARI.
- 1st Central Vegetable Breeding Station was established at Kullu Valley (Katrain), Himachal Pradesh in 1949.
- All India Coordinated Research Improvement Project (AICRIP) on vegetables was started during 4th five year plan in 1970-71.
- Indian Society of Vegetable Science established in 1973.
- Journal 'Vegetable Science' was 1st published in 1974.
- Project Directorate of Vegetable Research (PDVR) was started at IARI in 1986.
- Head Quarter of PDVR was shifted to Varanasi in 1992.
- PDVR was upgraded to Indian Institute of Vegetable Research (IIVR) in 1999.
- 1st Project Co-ordinator of AICRP on vegetables: Dr. Vishnu Swaroop.
- 1st Project Director of IIVR: Dr. G. Kalloo.
- Head Quarter of AICRIP on tuber crops is located at Tiruvanantapuram, Kerala.
- Central Potato Research Institute (CPRI) was started at Patna in 1949 and later its head quarter was shifted to Shimla in 1956.
- Earliest hybrid researcher in world: Hayes and Jones (1916).
- 1st mention of hybrid seeds in seed catalogue was mentioned in 1945, USA
- 1st vegetable seed testing station was established in IARI during 1958.
- In India, share of F_1 hybrids is maximum in tomato (34.4%) followed by cabbage (31.5%).
- National Horticultural Research and Development Foundation (NHRDF), Nashik was established by National Agricultural Co-operative Marketing Federation of India Ltd. (NAFED) and its Associate Shippers of Onion in 3rd November, 1977.
- Aluminium foil pouches are used for packing vegetable seeds.
- IIVR, Varanasi is credited with producing world's 1st green chilli powder technology.
- High temperature leads to bolting and seed formation in spinach andlettuce.
- "Pot herbs" are generally cool season crops.
- 'Pot herbs' (foliage + immature stems) are also called as green or leafy vegetables e.g. palak, amaranths, spinach, basella.
- Vegetable scientist received 'Padmashri' in 2014: Dr. Brahma Singh.
- Fruit of portulaca: Capsule.
- Maturity index for leafy vegetables: Solidity.
- Grubbin (1968) proposed the average nutritive value (ANV) of vegetables. As per him, cassava leaves have maximum ANV followed by hyacinth bean, amaranth.
- Calorie requirement of an adult individual of sedentary work is 2400 Kcal and regarded as 1 Adult Consumption Unit (ACU).
- Anti-oxidant capacity of vegetables: Kale> Amaranth> Chenopod> Spinach> Palak>Fenugreek >Sarson sag.

- Anti-oxidant capacity of cole crops: Kale>Broccoli> Brussels sprouts> Cabbage> Cauliflower.
- Flavonoid capacity of vegetables: Kale> Spinach> Broccoli>Brussels sprouts>Beet root.
- Limiting amino acid in green vegetables: Methionine.
- Cellars storage: Storage structure of cabbage, onions and potatoes during winter.
- In cole crops and lettuce, prickling (method of raising secondary nursery of crop) is done when 1st pair of true leaves develop.
- Thermosensitive vegetable crops: Potato, Tomato, Cabbage, Cauliflower.
- Steckling raising is practiced in radish, carrot, turnip, garden beet, and chicory for seed production in root-to-seed method.
- 'Save and Grow' term associated with tuber crops for sustainable production intensification campaign launched by FAO in 2011.
- Vegetable chocolate bars are prepared using peas, carrot, tapioca, corn which are free from gluten content.
- Garlic-Onion gravy wrestling championship: Held every year in 'Bacup' town of England.
- Anthocyanin is measured in mg/100 ml of juice.
- Use of gametocides: MH and GA in tomato, onion, cucurbits; GA in onion and lettuce; NAA in cucurbits; FW450 in tomato, sugar beet; ethrel in sugar beet.
- Absolute growth rate is important in leafy vegetables. In this case, biological yield and ecomonic yield is same.
- Purslane (*Portulaca oleracea*): contain highest Omega-3-fatty acid among leafy vegetables.
- Umami/ Savory fifth taste: Associated with ripe tomatoes, Chinese cabbage, celery, spinach.
- Yield increase through microirrigation system was 50% in tomato, 45% in chilli and 88% in water melon.
- Epigeal germination: Tomato, beans, gourds, etc.
- Hypogeal germination: Peas.
- Seeds of many vegetable crops show orthodox seed storage except Chow-chow.
- Free radical is a molecule with an unpaired electron. Hence, they are unstable and quite reactive e.g. super oxide (O_2^-), hydroxyl (OH-), hydro-peroxyl (HOO), alkyl peroxyl (ROO), etc.
- Yield of vegetables can be reduced by 5-15% when daily ozone concentrations >50 ppb.
- India is approaching towards 'Yellow Revolution'- growing *Brassica juncea*, having 40% oil & 36% proteins while soybean contains 18% oil.

2. VEGETABLE GARDENING:

- 200 m^2 area sufficient to supply adequate vegetables for fivemembers family.
- All India Kitchen Garden Association (AIKGA) launched in 1967 in memory of late Prime Minister L.B. Shastry.
- Sandy loam soil: Best suited for vegetable crops.
- Home/ Kitchen/ Nutritional garden: Most ancient type of garden.
- Market garden: Supply vegetables for local market and very intensive method of cultivation. Highest crop intensity.
- Truck garden: Supply vegetables for distant market and very extensive method of cultivation.
- In floating garden of Dal Lake (Jammu and Kashmir) shallow rooted vegetables are grown.
- Base of floating garden are made of typha grass.
- Processing vegetable garden: Specialized cultivation practices are followed. Mainly grown on contract basis.
- Vegetable garden for seed production- special type of vegetable are grown on contract cultivation.
- Roof Garden: Leafy vegetables and vine crops are grown.
- Vegetable forcing: Growing of vegetables in offseason e.g. Tomato, Capsicum.
- Vegetable forcing is commercially practiced in England and other European countries.
- Diara cultivation:Vegetable gardening in river beds e.g. Cucurbits.
- In Isreal, indoor plants are grown in 'Growtainer'. It is a container which is automatically controlled by computer.
- World's biggest terrace garden is located in Montreal, Canada. Green house cultivation of cherry tomato and brinjal is practiced.

2.1 Vertical farming/ Urban farming

- Concept was putforth by Dickson Despommier, professor emeritus at Columbia University during 1915.
- He wrote a book entitled 'The Vertical Farm: Feeding the World in the 21st Century'.
- It is a method of producing vegetables (spinach, amaranth, mint, lettuce, kale, basil, coriander, fenugreek) and non-tree fruits (tomato, brinjal, strawberry) where there is no available arable land.
- Grown in vertically stacked layers of PVC pipes resembling multi-storied cropping system.
- 1st underground vertical farming is located at London.
- Australia has developed fully automated vertical farming model.

Advantages:

- Ability to produce year round.
- Very high productive farming (70-80% more harvest/ area)
  - 1000 sq. ft. area is sufficient (= 3000-4000 sq. ft. plot).
  - Reduce water usage by 95%.
  - Crop cycle is 3-4 times a year.
- Substantial profit compared to traditional farming.
- Help to grow pesticide free vegetables using 95% less water.
- Clean & hygienic environment.
- User can be assured of consuming quality vegetables.
- Cut down cost of transport.
- Retain freshness of produce.
- Reduced susceptibility to weather extremes.
- Reduction in carbon foot prints (more efficient use of fossil fuel resources).
- Local production of local crops-vertical farmers often make use of old warehouses and factories in urban locations.
- The limited use of land-allows expansion of production, without increased risk of soil degradation.
- Increased potential of automation and use of SMART data and technology.

Disadvantages:

- Never take over traditional farming.
- Can not substitute for tree produce or cereals like rice, wheat, dals, etc.
- Capital intensive-lighting can account for up to 50% of capital expenditure.
- High production costs.
- High use of energy.
- Limited range of crops (salads & greens).

2.2 Micro-green vegetables

- Micro-greens or micro-green vegetables, are tiny form of young edible greens produced from various kinds of vegetables, herbs and plants. They are called as new generation smart foods. They belong to family Amaranthaceae, Chenopodiaceae, Cruciferae and Apiaceae.
  - Demand is increasing at faster rate.
  - They are rich in nutrients and anti-oxidants.
  - Can be cultivated on home scale in plastic trays containing soil/ coco peat/ perlite as growing media.

- Yield large quantity of edible leaves and roots are not eaten.
- Require sunlight for good growth of micro-greens.
- NASA & European Aviation Research Institute have developed special kits for continuous supply of fresh micro-greens.

- Sprouting broccoli microgreens are in great demand world over.
- Micro-greens are usually harvested 7-14 days after germination in tropical climate and slightly longer (14-28 days) in cold weather.

3. PROTECTED CULTIVATION OF VEGETABLE CROPS:

- Primary objectives of greenhouse cultivation: Off season cultivation.
- Growing of off-season cucumbers under transparent stone for Emperor Tiberius in the 1st century, is the earliest reported protected agriculture.
- Most common cucurbit grown under greenhouse: Cucumber.
- In Japan, primitive methods using oil-paper and straw mats to protect crops from the severe natural environment were used as long ago the early 1960s.
- The 1st greenhouse in the 1700s used glass on one side only as a sloping roof.
- The 1st use of polyethylene as a greenhouse cover was in 1948, when professor Emery Myers Emmert, at the University of Kentucky, used the less expensive material in place of more expensive glass.
- Vegetables suitable for protected cultivation: Asparagus, Bitter gourd, Celery, Coloured capsicum, Cherry tomato, Chive, Endive, Gherkins, Globe artichoke, Kale, Leek, Lettuce, Okra, Parsley, Pakchoi, Potato, Red cabbage, Shallot, Sprouting broccoli, Summer Squash, Tomato, Zucchini, etc.
- For green house production of vegetable crops, NFT pipe echnique is widely adopted.
- Greenhouse is now better understood as a system of Controlled Environment Agriculture (CEA)= Greenhouse Vegetable Industry. Principal crops produced under CEA:-

  a) Lettuce: Loose leaf types and Butter head types which have short season.

  b) Cucumber: European types (Gynoecious & parthenocarpic) are more important in CEA. The fruits of these have edible skin and are seedless.

  c) Tomato: Cultivars used in CEA are primarily 'beefsteak' types. Their fruits are large & yields are equal to or above those of standard fresh market tomatoes. Plants are strongly indeterminate in growth habit and fruits are harvested over an extended periods.

  d) Other crops grown in CEA:

     i) Various salad green (Water spinach, Water cress & Dandelion).

     ii) Green peppers

     iii) Egg plants

iv) Assorted herbs (basil, mint, rosemary, thyme, chive, sage, parsley & Terragon).

e) The main environmental factors relevant to CEA for plant growth include temperature, humidity, radiation and ambient CO_2 concentration.

Optimum growing temperature for greenhouse crops:

Crop	Day temperature (^0C)	Night temperature (^0C)
Cucumbers	70-80	70
Lettuce	60-70	45-55
Tomatoes	65-75	60-65

- Production guidelines (Wilcox, 1981) for green house lettuce growing in a nutrient film system recommended are air day temperature of 60-65^{0}C, night temperature of 45-50^{0}C and root zone temperature of 60-75^{0}C.
- Cabbage, cauliflower, broccoli and spinach are also grown in most intensive type of CEA in USA.
- Growing systems used in CEA are divided into 2 broad categories as-

A. Substrate culture:

i) Substrate culture comprises use of natural substrates viz. sand, gravel, peat, saw dust, pine bark and soil.

ii) Artificial substrates include perlite, vermiculite, rock wool and polystyrene.

B. Solution culture or Water culture or Hydro-culture includes 3 cultural systems as:

i) Aeroponics (misting roots) is used for lettuce than tomato or cucumber.

ii) NFT (Nutrient Film Technique): Developed by Green house Research Institute in England in 1970s and used extensively for commercial production of tomatoes, lettuce and cucumber.

iii) DFT (Deep Flow Technique): Comprises use of root holding structures like plastic containers, troughs, etc.

iv) All 3 systems are characterized by bare rooted plants.

- Hydroponics, term coined in early 1930s is classified as either:

a) Open system (drip irrigation method is used to apply fertilizers).

b) Closed system (nutrient solution is reused by recirculation i.e. soil less system).

- Zero energy naturally ventilated greenhouse is remunerative for cultivation of three crops of parthenocarpic cucumber with a production of 10 tones/1000 m^2 and a C: B ratio of 1:2.25 to 2.50.
- Insect proof net house is suitable for virus free hybrid seed production in bitter gourd.

- Walk-in-Tunnels and plastic low tunnels are remunerative for off-season Summer Squash cultivation during winter months (October–February) under northern plains of India.
- Propagation by seed takes 6-8 weeks while cuttings ready in 2 weeks.
- New technology of vegetative propagation: Stem cutting e.g. Capsicum, Tomato, Cucumber.
- Use tender and succulent cuttings (8-10 cm long) by retaining one set of true leaves.
- Field performance reveals that crop raised through cuttings produce same yield as that raised from seed.
- Most effective method to control nematodes: Formalin fumigation.

1. Tomato:

- Training system followed: Single stem.
- Cluster thinning is important for green house tomatoes.
- Perfect pollinators: Bumble bees.
- Suitable plant type: Indeterminate varieties.
- Ideal temperature for colour development: 18^{0}C.
- Optimum night temperature for fruit setting: 16-22^{0}C.

2. Cucumber: Varieties should be gynoecious and parthenocarpic.
3. Summer Squash: Bush type.
4. Musk melon: Andromonoecious type.
5. Beans:

- Pole type character is exploited for polyhouse cultivation.

Varieties:

Crop	Specific type	Varieties
Tomato	Beefsteak varieties	Trust, Match
	Big fruit varieties	Daniela, FA-179, FA-189, Badshah, Shansha, GS-600
	Cherry tomatoes	BR-124, HA-818, T-56, Phule Jayashree, Cherry Belle, Gardener's Delight, Super Beefsteak, Shirley, Trumbler.
	Indian varieties	* Arka Vardan, Arka Vishal, Naveen. Pant Polyhouse Tomato-1, 2. * Tropic, Dombello, Cobra, Stresa, Capello, Trust, Caruso, Belmondo, Tuckcross-520.
Capsicum	-	* Red: Bomby, Triple Star, Natasha, Inspiration, Pusa Deepti. * Yellow: Orobelle, Swarna, Sunnyez, Golden Summer, Larrio, Kanak, Bacchata. * Green: Indra, Bharat, Palodina, Pasarella, Asha.
Cucumber	Gynoecious varieties	Dinar, Hasan, Multistar, Shinny, Shinefit, Falconstar, MX-122, Improved Noori, Malini, Aviva, Infinity, Kian, Kafka, Damini, 005.
Musk melon	-	Arava
Summer Squash	-	Australian Green, Pusa Alankar, Goldy
Beans	Pole type	Kentucky Wonder, Canadian Wonder

4. VEGETABLE GRAFTING:

- Primary objective of grafting is to avoid damage caused by soil borne pathogens and to enhance tolerance to abiotic stresses such as soil salinity, organic pollutants, toxicity of heavy metals, drought, thermal and waterlogging.
- Problems associated with grafting: Additional cost and graft incompatibility that may appear in some cases causing physiological disorders and possible reduction in yield, and fruit quality.
- Vegetative propagation (through stem cuttings) in capsicum, tomato & cucumber can be alternative for multiplication of promising planting materials.Cuttings are ready in 2 weeks.
- Robot grafted seedling production.
- 1st commercial model of a grafting robot (GR800 series; Iseki & Co. Ltd., Matsuyama, Japan.) became available for cucurbits in 1993.
- Fully automated grafting robot (AG1000) was introduced by Yanmar Agricultural Equipment Co. (Osaka, Japan) in 1994 achieving a speed of 1200 grafts/ hour.
- Grafting is done by using specially produced robot G892 and G2.
- Robot produces 815 plants/ hour at the successs rate of 97.1%.
- 1st record of vegetable grafting as a yield increase and pest/disease control strategy was for water melon (*C. lanatus*), using a squash rootstock (*C. moschata*).
- In Solanaceae, 1st record was of brinjal (*S. melongena*) grafted on scarlet brinjal (*S. integrifolium*) in 1950s. Grafting tomato (*S. lycopersicum*) was introduced commercially in the 1960s.
- Use of grafted seedlings in commercial vegetable production occurred in 1930s in Japan for water melon grafted on *Lagenaria siceraria*.
- Research in grafting cucumber also started in late 1920s.
- Adoption of vegetable grafting in the Western world (American, European, Middle East countries) has increased since banning of fumigant methyl bromide in 2005 by the Montreal Protocol.
- Three primary techniques used for grafting: Tongue, Approach, Cleft and Tube grafting.
- Intergeneric grafts via splice/ side grafting and patch budding is possible in *Solanum*, *Capsicum* and *Lycopersicon*.
- Cleft grafting-(CG i.e. apical wedge grafting) and splice grafting (SG) are most commonly practiced in India.
- Four to five weeks old seedlings of egg plant are used as rootstocks whereas 25-30 days old tomato seedlings as scions.
- CG is much convenient, very simple and easy for tomato grafting than SG.
- The successful union of the graft is evaluated by using 'Thermal camera'.

- Recommended light level for graft acclimatization: 3-5 Klux.
- Leading grafted vegetable in world: Water melon, cucumber, musk melon due to endemic nature of several soil borne diseases.
- Grafted vegetables popular in Japan (81%) and Korea (54%).
- Grafted seedlings of water melon, cucumber and musk melons account for 57% production in open and 70% production in greenhouses.
- Japan is growing 32% tomato, 50% brinjal, 93% water melon and 7.2% cucumber as grafted plants.
- Tomato hybrids are popular as egg plant rootstocks in Europe.
- Interspecific grafting is popular in brinjal.
- Commercial rootstocks for brinjal: *Solanum integrifolium* and *S. torvum* (resistant to verticillium wilt and fusarium wilt).
- Scion of tomato produces poisonous fruits if grafted on datura (*Datura stramonium*).
- Future wonder plant: Pomato (i.e. Tomato tongue grafted on potato).
- Company 'Thompson and Morgan' sells grafted pomato under brand name 'TomTato'.
- Uniform seed germination is major problem in cultivation.

Tomato:

- Purpose of grafting:
  - Egg plant rootstock for flooded/ saturated or waterlogged soils.
  - To extend harvest season in greenhouse production.
  - To take advantage of increased vigour.
  - Organic production of heirloom tomatoes.
- Breeding lines using *S. pennelli* and *S. pimpinellifolium* have been developed for heat tolerance in tomato and sweet pepper.
- Major limitation to grafting tomato: ToMV resistance in rootstock and scion must be compatible a) Resistance to ToMV is derived from *Tm-1* or *Tm-2* alleles b) *Tm-1* carries symptomless response/ tolerance in host c) *Tm-2*confer hyper sensitive response d) It rootstock carries *Tm-1* resistance & scion carries *Tm-2* resistance, then rootstock may transmit virus to scion inducing systemic necrosis.
- Bacterial wilt resistant rootstocks in tomato: Cheong Gang, RST-04-106-T, BHN-998, BHN-1054, Hawaii-7996, Hawaii-7998.
- Salt tolerant (2009 mM NaCl) rootstocks in tomato: Radja and Pera.
- IIVR, Varanasi has made successful attempt to produce Brimato, an interspecific grafted plant (top working/ tip grafting/ joint grafting) which yields both tomato and brinjal on a single plant.

- In Brimato, scion of 'Kashi Sandesh' and rootstock is 'IC-111056' was used for grafting. This rootstock has 5% ability to develop two vigorous branches simultaneously.
- Age of scion stick: Brinjal 25-30 days and tomato 22-25 days old.
- Grafts were initially raised under controlled conditions in green houses and then transferred to main fields after 15-18 days of grafting.
- After grafting, fruit setting initiated after 60-70 days in both the scion sticks.
- Average yield of fruits from double interspecific graft: Tomato-36 fruits (2.383 kg) and brinjal-9.2 fruits (2.684 kg/ graft).
- The new technique is highly useful for vertical farming and/ or pot culture.
- This wonder double grafting plant Brimato (i.e. Brinjal & tomato grafted on brinjal) is similar to Pomato (i.e. tomato grafted on potato).

Cucumber:

- Purpose of grafting:
  - Cucurbita interspecific hybrid rootstocks increases heat tolerance.
  - Protection from cold along with durable fusarium resistance.
  - Fig leaf gourd rootstock imparts cold tolerance & resistance to fusarium wilt & has high affinity for cucumber.
  - Cucurbita interspecfic hybrid (CIH) rootstock imparts heat tolerance; protection from cold along with durable fusarium resistance.
  - *C. moschata* rootstock cause bloomless (wax free) fruits & longer shelf life.
- Cucumber can be successfully grafted onto *Cucumis* spp., *Cucurbita* spp., Fig leaf gourd, Wax gourd, *Luffa*, bottle gourd & Cucurbita interspecfic hybrid (CIH).
- Intergeneric or interspecific grafting is effective in cucurbits and solanaceous crops for biotic and abiotic stress tolerance.
- Interspecific grafting of wild *Cucurbita* spp. to Summer Squash induce early flowering.
- *Cucurbita ficifolia* (very late flowering) accessions are grown commercially as rootstocks for cucumber for early flowering during field pollination.
- Cucumber cv. Prachi and musk melon cv. Golden Lady are grown in polyhouse using squash rootstock.
- Cucumber cv. Jinchun No. 2 grafted on bottle gourd rootstock 'Chaofeng 8848' alleviated negative effect of salinity on shoot dry weight.
- Cucumber cv. cv. Jinchun No. 2 grafted on *C. ficifolia* and Chaofeng Kangshengwang (*L. siceraria*) resulted in higher fruit number and marketable fruit yield.

Other melons:

- Melons are grafted on same species but very rarely on white gourd and pumpkins.
- Musk melon is grafted on ash gourd in wilt affected areas.
- Water melons are generally grafted on bottle gourd and rarely on pumpkins.
- Water melon cv. Fantasy grafted on 'Strongtosa' rootstock (*C. maxima* x *C. moschata*) reduced the decrease of shoot weight and leaf area due to increase of salinity.
- Water melon cv. Crimson Tide grafted on *C. maxima* and two *Lagenaria siceraria* rootstocks has higher plant growth.
- Pumpkin is used as rootstock for cucumber against fusarium and water melon in Japan.
- 'Shintozwa' (*C. maxima* x *C. moschata*): Most widely used rootstock resistant to fusarium wilt for cucumber, water melon and other melons.
- Bottle gourd is used as rootstock for grafting water melon.
- Ash gourd (*Benincasa cerifera*) and fig leaf gourd (*Cucurbita ficifolia*) are graft compatible with musk melon scion because it shows resistance to wilt.
- In Japan, genotypes of *C. moschata* as rootstock cause bloomless (i.e. wax free) cucumber fruits along with longer shelf life & high consumer's preference.
- Hybrid RS-814 is a rootstock for water melon.

Brinjal:

- Brinjal is known fairly tolerant to waterlogging situation.
- 'Surya': Waterlogged and saturated soil tolerant rootstock for brinjal.
- Saline soils tolerant rootstocks for brinjal: Suqiqie and Torvum Vigor.
- Egg plant grafted on *S. torvum* reduced the Cadmium concentration in fruits.

Red pepper:

- Grafting induces genetic variation in red pepper viz. fruit shape, fruit colour and capsaicinoid content in fruits. These genetic changes are attributed to direct DNA uptake through the vascular system.
- Sweet pepper scions grafted on sweet pepper and hot pepper minimizes problems caused by flooding and soil borne diseases including bacterial wilt, phytophthora blight and nematodes.
- Most chillies can be grafted successfully with sweet pepper lines and seedlings may be grafted after developing 2-3 true leaves.

Scion	Rootstocks	Purpose
Tomato	*Solanum lycopersicum*, *S. pimpinellifolium*, *S. habrochaites*, *S. melongena*, *S. torvum*, interspecific hybrid (*S. lycopersicum* x *S. habrochaites*)	Maintain 2 stems on grafted plants, tolerance to bacterial wilt, fusarium wilt, root knot nematode, verticillium wilt, corky root, waterlogging, drought, extended fruiting period; reduction in seed cost of rootstocks
Brinjal	*S. torvum*, *S. integrifolium*, *S. melongena*	Plant vigour, tolerance to bacterial wilt, verticillium wilt, fusarium wilt, low temperature, root knot nematode
Water melon	*Lagenaria siceraria*, *Cucurbita moschata,* interspecific hybrid squash (*C. maxima* x *C. moschata*), *Benincasa hispida*	Vigorous root system, tolerance to fusarium wilt, wilting due to physiological disorders, low and high temperature, *B. hispida* for multiple disease tolerance
Musk melon	*Curucrbita moschata, C. pepo,* interspecific hybrid squash (*C. maxima* x *C. moschata*), *Cucumis melo*, *Cucumis metulifer*	Vigorous root system, tolerance to fusarium wilt, low & high temperature, *Phytophthora* disease, high soil moisture, nematode, fruit quality
Cucumber	*Cucurbita moschata*, *C. ficifolia*, *C. maxima*, *C. foetidissima*, *Sicyos angulatus*, Bottle gourd, AH cucumber	Vigorous root system, tolerance to fusarium wilt, low temperature, *Phytophthora* disease, high soil moisture, nematode, drought, cold & heat

5. CLASSIFICATION OF VEGETABLE CROPS:

5.1 Based on botany:

Family	Common name	Botanical name	Origin	Edible part	2n=
		Monocots			
Alliaceae	Onion	*Allium cepa*	Central Asia	Bulb (modified stem) & leaves	16 (2x)
	Tree onion	*A. cepa* var. *viviparum*	Canada	Roots & bulbils	16
	Welsh onion	*A. fistulosum*	Siberia	Enlarged stem & leaves	16
	Garlic	*A. sativum*	Central Asia	Cloves & leaves	16
	Leek	*A. ampeloprasum var. porrum*	Southern Europe	Blanched stem & leaves	32 (4x)
	Shallot	*A. cepa* var. *aggregatum*	-	Young bulb & leaves	16
	Chive	*A. schoenoprasum*	-	Enlarged stem & leaves	24 (3x)
	Rakkyo	*A. chinense*	-	-	-
Araceae	Elephant foot yam/ Suran	*Amorphophallus campanulatus*	India	Corms	28 (2x)
	Taro	*Colocasia esculenta*	South East-Asia & China	Corms	28 (2x), (42 3x)
	Tannia	*Xanthosoma sagittifoilium*	South America	Corms, cormels & leaves	26 (2x)
Dioscoreaceae	Yam	*Dioscorea* spp.	South West Asia	Tubers	30 (2x)-80 (2x)
Liliaceae	Asparagus	*Asparagus officinalis*	-	Spears/ Modified stem	20
Marantaceae	Queensland arrow root	*Canna edulis*	Tropical America	Rhizomes	27 (3x)
	West Indian arrow root	*Maranta arundinacea*	-	Corms/ tubers	48 (2x)
		Dicots			
Amaranthaceae	Amaranths	*Amaranths* spp.	India	Leaves & stems	32/ 34 (2x)/ 64 (4x)
Apiaceae	Carrot	*Daucus carotav* ar. *sativus*	S-W Asia (Afghanistan)	Tap root, leaves as fodder	18
	Celery	*Apium graveolens* var. *dulce*	S. Europe	Fleshy leaf stalk & leaf	22
	Celeriac	*Apium graveolens* var. *rapaceum*	-	-	-
	Parsley	*Petroselinum crispum*	Mediterranean region	Leaves	22
	Parsnip	*Pastinaca sativa*	Europe & Asia	Tap root	22
	Turnip rooted parsley	*Petroselinum crispum* var. *tuberosum*	-	-	-

	Turnip rooted chervil	*Chaerophyllum bulbosum* (syn. *Anthriscus cerefolium*)	-	Swollen root	32
	Skirret	*Sium sisarum*	China	Roots	12
	Coriander	*Coriandrum sativum*	Mediterranean region	Leaves	22
Asteraceae	Lettuce	*Lactuca sativa*	Mediterranean region	Leaves	10, 16, 18, 32, 34, 36, 38
	Chicory, Radicchio	*Chichorium intybus*	Europe	Leaves	18
	Endive, Escarole	*Chichorium endivia*	-	-	-
	Globe Artichoke	*Cynaria scolymus*	Mediterranean region	Flower heads or buds	34
	Cardoon	*Cynara cardunculus*	-	-	-
	Jerusalem artichoke	*Helianthus tuberosus*	N. America	Root tuber	102 (6x)
	Terragon	*Artemisia dracunculus*	-		-
	Dandelion	*Taraxacum officinales*	-	-	-
	Salsify	*Tragopogon porrifolius*	-	-	-
Basellaceae	Malabar spinach	*Basella rubra*	India	Fleshy stem &leaves	44 (2x)
		B. alba	India	Fleshy stem &leaves	48 (2x)
Chenopodiaceae	Garden beet/ Beet root	*Beta vulgaris* ssp. *crassa*	Mediterranean region (Europe, North Africa & West Asia)	Roots	18 (2x)
	Palak	*B. vulgaris* var. *bengalensis*	Indo-China	Leaves & leaf stalk	18
	Chard/ Swiss chard	*B. vulgaris* ssp. *cicla*	Italy	Leaves & leaf stalk	18
	Spinach	*Spinacia oleracea*	Iran	Rosette leaves	12 (2x)
	French spinach	*Atriplex hortensis*	-	Leaves & twigs	12
	Bathua	*Chenopodium album*	India	Leaves & twigs	36 (4x),54 (6x)
	Ceylon spinach	*Talinum triangulare*	South Asia	Tender stems	48 (2x), 72 (3x)
Convolvulaceae	Sweet potato	*Ipomoea batatas*	S. America	Tuber (modified root)	30 (2x); 40 (4x); 90 (6x)
	Water spinach	*I. aquatica* (*I.reptans*)	S. America	Terminal shoots	30
Cruciferae	Cabbage (white cabbage)	*Brassica oleracea* var. *capitata*	West Europe	Head (modified terminal bud)	18 (2x)
	Cauliflower	*B. oleracea* var. *botrytis*	Italy	Curd/ Prefloral apical meristem	18

	Brussels sprout	*B. oleracea* var. *gemmifera*	S.America	Swollen axillary heads (buds)	18
	Sprouting broccoli	*B. oleracea* var. *italica*	S. America	Flower head	18
	Knol khol/ kohlrabi	*B. oleracea* var. *gongyloides*	S.America	Knob/ young swollen stem	18
	Kale/ Collard/ Tree kale	*B. oleracea* var. *acephala*	S.America	Leaves & shoots	18
	Chinese kale	*B. oleracea* var. *alboglabra*	China	Tender leaves & petioles	20 (2x)
	Tronchuda cabbage	*B. oleracea* var. *tronchuda*	China	-	
	Chinese cabbage	*B. rapa* var. *pekinensis* (*B. chinensis*)	China	Leafy heads, fleshy petioles & leaf	20
	Turnip	*B. campestris* ssp. *rapifera* (syn. *B. rapa* var. *rapifera*)	Indo-China	Swollen hypocotyl	20
	Rutabaga (Swede)	*B. napus ssp.napobrassica*	Sweden	Enlarged & elongated tap root	38 (4x)
	Radish	*Raphanus sativus*	Mediterranean	Fleshy swollen & roots	18
	Water cress (Brahmi sag)	*Nasturtium officinales* (syn. *Rorippa nasturtium*)	-	Tender tops & leaves	32 (4x)
	Garden cress	*Lepidium sativum*	-	Leaves	16(2x), 32(4x)
	Horse radish	*Armoracia rusticana* (syn. *A. lapathifolia*)	Southern Europe & Western Asia	Roots	32 (4x)
	Spinach mustard	*B. rapa* var. *perviridis*	-	-	-
	Broccoli raab	*B. rapa* var. *revo*	-	-	-
Cucurbitaceae	Cucumber	*Cucumis sativus* var. *hardwickii*	India	Immature fruits (mesocarp, endocarp & placenta)	14 (2x)
	Gherkin	*C. anguria* var. *anguria*	West Africa	Whole fruit	24 (2x)
	Musk melon	*C. melo*	Tropical Africa	Ripe fruit (mesocarp & pericarp)	24 (2x)
	Water melon	*Citrullus lanatus*	Tropical Africa	Endocarp (placenta)	22 (2x)
	Round melon	*C. lanatus* var. *fistulosus*	India	Immature fruit	12 (2x)
	Long melon	*C. melo* var. *utilissimus*	India	Immature fruit	24
	Snap melon	*C. melo* var. *momordica*	India	Immature fruit	24
	Pumpkin	*Cucurbita moschata*	Mexico	Ripe fruit (mesocarp & pericarp)	40 (2x)

	Summer Squash	*C. pepo*	Mexico	Immature fruits	40
	Winter Squash	*C. maxima*	S. Mexico	Ripe fruits	40
	Buffalo gourd	*C. foetidissima*	S. Mexico	Fruits	40
	Bottle gourd	*Lagenaria siceraria*	S. Africa	Immature fruits	22 (2x)
	Bitter gourd	*Momordica charantia*	Indo-Burma	Immature fruits	22
	Balsam apple	*M. balsamina*	America	Immature fruits	22
	Sweet gourd	*M. cochinchinensis*	India	Immature fruits	28 (2x)
	Ridge gourd	*Luffa acutangula*	Asia	Immature fruits (endocarp)	26 (2x)
	Sponge gourd/ Smooth gourd	*L. cylindrica*	Asia	Immature fruits (endocarp)	26
	Pointed gourd	*Trichosanthes dioica*	India	Immature fruits	22
	Snake gourd	*T. anguina*	India	Immature fruits	22
	Ash gourd	*Benincasa hispida*	Japan	Immature fruits (endocarp)	24 (2x)
	Ivy gourd	*Coccinia indica*	India	Immature fruits	24
	Chow-chow	*Sechium edule*	Mexico	Single seeded fruits	24
	Meetha Karela	*Cyclanthera pedata*	-	Immature fruits	32
	Fig leaf gourd	*Cucurbita ficifolia*	Mexico	-	40 (2x)
Euphorbiaceae	Cassava	*Manihot esculenta*	Guatemala & Mexico	Tuberous roots	36 (2x), 54 (3x), 72 (4x)
	Chekkurmanis	*Sauropus androgynus*	Indo-Burma region	Green leaves	-
Fabaceae	Fenugreek	*Trigonella foenum-graceum*	Egypt	Tender leaves	16
	Agathi	*Sesbania gradiflora*	Malaysia	Leaves & flowers	24
Labiatae	Chinese potato/ Coleus	*Coleus parviflorus* (syn. *Solenostemon rotundifolius*	Africa	Adventitious root	48 (4x), 72 (6x)
	Chinese artichoke	*Stachys sieboldii*	China	Long slender roots	66-70
Leguminosae	Garden pea	*Pisum sativum*	C. Asia	Tender seeds	14 (2z)
	French bean	*Phaseolus vulgaris*	Mexico	Tender pod & seeds	22 (2x)
	Lima bean	*Phaseolus lunatus* (*syn. p. imensis*)	Guatemala	Tender pods	22
	Dolichos bean	*Lablab purpureus*	India	Tender pods	22 (2x), 24 (2x)
	Cluster bean	*Cyamopsis tetragonolobus*	India	Tender pods	14

	Winged bean	*Psophocarpus tetragonolobus*	New Guinea	Green pods, seeds, flowers	18 (2x), 22 (2x)
	Broad bean	*Vicia faba (syn. Faba vulgaris)*	Europe & Asia	Green pods	12 (2x), 14 (2x)
	Cowpea	*Vigna unguiculata*	Africa	Tender pods	22
	Yam bean	*Pachyrrhizus erosus*	S. America	Root tubers	22
	Soybean	*Glycine max*	China	Pods	40 (2x)
	Sword bean	*Canavalia gladiata*	India	Pods	22 (2x), 44 (4x)
	Jack bean	*Canavalia ensiformis*	West Indies	Pods	22 (2x)
Malvaceae	Okra	*Abelmoschus esculentus*	Tropical Africa	Tender fruits	130 (2x)
Moringaceae	Drumstick	*Moringa oleifera*	India	Green pod & leaves	28 (2x)
Poaceae (Gramineae)	Sweet corn	*Zea mays* var. *rugosa*	North America	Ears & kernels	20 (2x)
Polygonaceae	Rhubarb	*Rheum rhabarbarum* (syn. *R. rhaponticum*)	Siberia	Thick leaf stalks	44 (4x)
	Sorrel	*Rumex vesicarius* (syn. *R. acetosa*)	Europe	Leaves	14 (2x)
Portulacaceae	Portulaca	*Portulaca oleracea*	India	Leaves & young shoots	54 (2x)
Solanaceae/Night Shade family	Potato	*Solanum tuberosum*	S. America	Tubers (modified stem)	48 (4x)
	Brinjal	*S. melongena*	Indo-Burma	Fruits	24 (2x)
	Tomato	*S. lycopersicum*	S. America	Fruits	24
	Currant tomato	*S. pimpinellifolium*	S. America	Fruits	24
	Hot chilli	*Capsicum annuum*	Mexico	Fruits	24
	Sweet pepper	*C. annuum* var. *grossum*	Mexico	Fruits	24
	Tomatillo	*Physalis ixocarpa*	Mexico	Fruit	24 (2x)
Tetragoniaceae (Aizoaceae)	New Zealand spinach	*Tetragonia tetragonioides*	New Zealand	Tender leaves & tops	32
Trapaceae	Chinese water chestnut	*Eleocharis dulcis* (*Trapanatans* var. *bispinosa*)	-	-	18 (2x)
Valerianaceae	Corn salad	*Valerianella locusta*	-	-	-
Other minor vegetables					
Onocleaceae	Fiddlehead fern	*Matteuccia struthiopteris*	-	Fronds	40 (2x)

5.2 Based on life cycle

Perennial	Asparagus, Chichory, Chive, Dandelion, Egg plant, Garlic, Globe artichoke, Horse radish, Lima bean, Pepper, Potato, Rhubarb, Sweet potato, Tomato, Watercress
Biennial	Beet, Broccoli, Brussels sprout, Cabbage, Carrot, Cauliflower, Celery, Chard, Chinese cabbage, Collard, Kale, Kohlrabi, Leek, Onion, Parsley, Parsnip, Rutabaga, Turnip
Annual	Broccoli, Cauliflower, Cowpea, Cucumber, Endive, Lettuce, Lime bean, Musk melon, Mustard, New Zealand spinach, Okra, Pea, Potato, Pumpkin, Snap bean, Soybean, Spinach, Squash, Sweet corn, Water melon.

5.3 Based on transplanting age:

Age in weeks	Crops
6-8 weeks	Onion, Brussels sprout, Celery
4-5 weeks	Lettuce, Cabbage
3-4 weeks	Tomato, Brinjal, Cauliflower, Sprouting broccoli, Chilli

5.4 Based on photoperiod in relation to flowering, bulbing and tuberization:

Long day plants i.e. short night of 8-10 h (require a day longer than its critical day length for flowering)	Short day (long night of 10-14 h) plants	Day neutral plants i.e. photo-insensitive (flowering not influenced by day length)
Potato, Onion, Garlic, Cabbage, Chinese cabbage, Cauliflower, Celery, Radish, Lettuce (Grand Rapids types), Spinach, Palak, Cowpea, Swiss chard, Parsnips	Potato, Sweet potato, Pea, Cucumber, Indian spinach, Dolichos bean, Cluster bean, Winged bean, Hyacinth bean, Basella, Chayote, Yam, Cassava, Basella	Tomato, Brinjal, Chilli, Carrot, Beet, Okra, other cucurbits, Amaranths, French bean, Cowpea, Sweet pepper, Sweet corn, Asparagus, Potato, Onion, Turnip, Radish, Kohlrabi, Lettuce (Great Lakes types), Lima bean

5.5 Formation of underground strage organs in response to photoperiod:

Day neutral	Carrot, Beet, Turnip, Radish
Long day	Onion, Garlic
Short day	Potato, Sweet potato, Yam, Cassava

5.6 Based on flowering response of vegetables to vernalization:

No exposure needed to induce flowering	Snap bean, Lima bean, Sweet corn, Irish potato, Tomato, Peppers, Cucumber, Musk melon, Water melon, Pumpkin, Squash, Sweet potato, Egg plant, Garden pea
Quantitative (preferential)	Cauliflower, Sprouting broccoli, Lettuce, Radish, Spinach, Chinese cabbage, Kohlrabi, Turnip, Garden pea, Endive, Chicory
Qualitative (obligate)	Beet, Cabbage, Carrot, Celery, Swiss chard, Collard, Kale, Leek, Onion, Parsley, Parsnips, Rutabaga, Brussels sprout, Chicory

5.7 Based on temperature requirement and hardiness:

Cool season crops		Warm season crops	
Hardy	**Half-hardy**	**Tender**	**Very tender**
Asparagus, Broccoli, Brussels sprout, Cabbage, Chive, Collard, Dandelions, Garlic, Horse radish, Kale, Kohlrabi, Leek, Musatrd, Onion, Parsley, Pea, Radish, Rhubarb, Rutabaga, Spinach, Turnip	Beet, Carrot, Cauliflower, Celery, Chard, Chinese cabbage, Chicory, Globe artichoke, Endive, Lettuce, Parsnip, Potato, Salsify	Cowpea, New Zealand spinach, Snap bean, Soybean, Sweet corn, Tomato	Cucumber, Egg plant, Lima bean, Musk melon, Okra, Pepper, Pumpkin, Squash, Sweet potato, Water melon

5.8 Based on inflorescence type:

Inflorescence type	Crops
Racemose	Cole crops, Cucurbits, Radish, Sword bean
Cymose	Spinach, Sweet potato, Broccoli, Brinjal, Tomato, Potato
Panicle	Moringa, Palak, curry leaf
Spike	Beet root
Compound umbel	Carrot, Coriander
Capitulum	Lettuce

5.9 Based on soil acidity/soil reaction (pH) tolerance:

Less tolerant (pH: 6.8-6.0)	Moderate (pH: 6.0-5.5)	Highly tolerant (pH: 5.5-5.0)
Cole crops, Chinese cabbage, Okra, Musk melon, Onion, Lettuce, Celery, Palak, Cowpea, Asparagus, Beet, Broccoli, Leek, New Zealand spinach, Spinach	Brinjal, Chilli, Tomato, Radish, Carrot, Summer Squash, Winter Squash, beans, Turnip, Pea, Pumpkin, Garlic, Turnip, Kohlrabi, Cucumber, Parsely, Pumpkin, Turnip, pepper	Potato, Sweet Potato, Water melon, Rhubarb, Chicory

5.10 Based on soil salinity/ salt tolerance:

Less tolerant	Moderately tolerant	Highly tolerant
Sweet pepper, Tomato, Potato, Sweet potato, Brinjal, Radish, Pea, Snake gourd, Beans	Chilli, Cole crops, Onion, Water melon, Musk melon, Cucumber, Summer Squash, Bottle gourd,	Bitter gourd, Ash gourd, Ridge gourd, Palak, Turnip, Lettuce, Sugar beet, French bean, Kale, Asparagus, Spinach

5.11 Based on frost hardiness:

Hardy	Asparagus, Broccoli, Brussels sprout, Cabbage, Chive, Collard, Garlic, Kale, Knol khol, Leek, Onion, Pea, Parsley, Radish, Rhubarb, Spinach, Turnip.
Semi-hardy	Beet, Carrot, Cauliflower, Celery, Lettuce, Globe artichoke, Palak, Potato
Tender	Okra, Tomato, Brinjal, Chilli, All cucurbits, Cowpea, Cluster bean, Amaranth, Taro, Sweet potato, Cassava, Yam, Drumstick, Elephant foot yam.

5.12 Based on water requirement:

Water requirement level	Crops
High	Sweet pepper, Cole crops, Radish, Ridge gourd, Turnip, Beet root, Palak, Onion, Amaranths, Lettuce, Celery, Rutabaga
Moderate	Brinjal, Chilli, Tomato, Potato, Cucumber,Carrot
Low	Peas & Beans, Watermelon, Asparagus, Rhubarb, Horseradish, Beet, Ridge gourd
Very low	Muskmelon, Pumpkin, Ash gourd/ Wax gourd

5.13 Based on average feeder root depth (Fulton, 1986)

Shallow rooting (<0.67 m)	Medium rooting (0.68 to 1.0 m)	Deep rooting (1 to 2.0 m or more)
Broccoli, Beans, Artichoke, Brussels sprout, Beet, Asparagus, Cabbage, Carrot, Lima bean, Cauliflower, Chard, Muskmelon	Celery, Cucumber, Pumpkin, Chinese cabbage, Brinjal, Winter Squash, Garlic, Mustard, Sweet potato, Leek, Pea	Tomato, Lettuce, Chilli, Watermelon, Onion, Summer Squash, Potato, Turnip, Radish, Spinach, Sweet corn

5.14 Based on rooting depth and amount of irrigation water needed:

Rooting depth	Water needed for crop (inch)			
	12	12-17	18-24	30-40
Shallow (< 2 ft.)	Lettuce, Spinach	Broccoli, Brussels sprout, Cabbage, Cauliflower, Onion	Lettuce, Potato, Onion, Sweet corn	Celery, Potato
Medium (2-4 ft.)	Pea	Cucumber, Pole bean, Snap bean, Turnip	Beet, Carrot, Egg plant, Pepper, Summer squash	-
Deep (4 ft. & above)	-	Artichoke, Lima bean, Watermelon	Asparagus, Muskmelon, Parsnip, Pumpkin, Winter squash, Sweet potato, Tomato	-

5.15 Based on respiratory activity:

Level	Respiration rate (mg of CO_2/ kg/ h)	Crops
Low	< 40	Cabbage, Cucumber, Onion, Potato, Turnip
Moderate	40-80	Beet, Carrot, Chilli, Sweet pepper, Sweet potato, Tomato
High	80-120	Radish, Lettuce, Lima bean, Hyacinth bean
Very high	> 120	Asparagus, Broccoli, Brussels sprout, Cauliflower, French bean, Green onion, Indian bean, leafy vegetables, Mushroom, Muskmelon, Okra, Pea, Spinach, Sweet corn, Watermelon

5.16 Based on climacteric peak:

Climacteric	Non-climacteric
Tomato, Brinjal, Muskmelon, Watermelon	Pumpkin, Cucumber, Pointed gourd, Chilli, Capsicum, Tamarillo

5.17 Based on storage life:

Storage life	Crops
Highly perishable (0-4 weeks)	Asparagus, Bean, Broccoli, Brussels sprout, Cauliflower, Cucumber, Lettuce, Pea, Rhubarb, Spinach, Sweet corn, Tomato, Mushroom
Moderately perishable (4-8 weeks)	Cabbage
Perishable (6-12 weeks)	Celery, Leek, Marrow
Low perishable (> 12 weeks)	Beet root, Carrot, Onion, Parsnip, Pumpkin, Potato, Sweet potato, Swede, Turnip

5.18 Based on seed storability under cold conditions:

Group	Period (years)	Crops
Poor storer	1	Onion, Pea
Intermediate	2	Chilli, Pea, Carrot, Okra, French bean
Moderate	3	Asparagus, Bean, Carrot, Leek, Pepper, Cucurbits, Radish
High	4	Beet, Swiss chard, Mustard, Pumpkin, Tomato
Very high	5	Cole crops, Brinjal, Lettuce, Musk melon, Radish, Turnip, Spinach, Water melon

5.19 Based on useful compounds:

Vegetables	Compound	Role in disease/ disorder prevention
Onion, Garlic	Sulphur	Reduce blood cholesterol
Onion, Garlic	Quercetin (flavonoid- an anti-oxidant)	Prevent cancer & heart disease
Onion	Diphenyl amine	Effective against diabetes
Onion	Allicin	Anti-bacterial activity
Cole crops	Indoles & dithiolthiones	Prevent cancer
Cabbage	Indole-3-carbinol	Against bowl cancer
Bitter gourd	Cheratin	Effective against diabetes
Celery	3-n-butyl aldehyde	Effective against hypertension
Yams	Diosgenin	Manufacture of contraceptive drugs
Lettuce	Lutein	Nutritional anti-oxidant
Broccoli	Sulphoraphane & Glucoraphinanin	Anti-cancer activity
French bean, Broccoli	Kaemferol	Anti-cancer & cardiovascular disease
Brinjal	Nasunin (Anthocyanin)	Anti-cancer activity

5.20 Based on anti-nutritional factor (toxic substance) present:

Toxic substance	Crops
Trypsin inhibitors	Raw soybean, French bean, Sweet potato
Phytic acid (inositol hexa-phosphoric acid)	Peas & beans
Oxalic acid & oxalates	Amaranth, Portulaca, Celosia, Basella, Colocasia
Calcium oxalate crystals (acridity)	Elephant-foot yam, Colocasia, Taro & Tannia
Hydrocyanic acid	Tapioca (leaves)

Dioscorine alkaloid	Yam
Solanin	Potato
Solasodine	Brinjal
Serotonin	Water melon
Choline esterase	Pumpkin
Sinigrin	Cole crops
Saponine	Spinach, Asparagus, Tomato
Cucurbitacin	Cucurbits
Apiin	Celery
Haemaglutin	French bean
Vicin & covicine	Broad bean
Tomatine	Tomato
Cyanoglucosides (HCN-bitter principle)	Cassava
Sapotoxin (water soluble)	Sword bean
Rotenone	Yam bean

5.21 Based on edible colour rich varieties in India:

- Chemical composition of lycopene ($C_{40}H_{56}$) is same as that of carotene.

Colour	Pigment	Vegetable
Red	Lycopene	Tomato, Water melon
Red	Betacyanins	Beet roots
Red	Capsanthin & Capsorubin	Paprika
Orange	β-carotene	Carrots, Cantaloupe, Pumpkins & Sweet potato
Blue/ purple	Anthocyanin	Egg plant, Amaranth
Yellow	Leutin	Yellow corn
Green	Chlorophyll	Leafy greens, Broccoli, Kale, Spinach, Cabbage, Asparagus
Black	Anthocyanins	Black carrot

5.22 Based on optimum soil moisture range:

Crop	Optimum soil tension	Soil depth (cm)
Potato	30%	15
Tomato	40-50%	30
Brinjal	20-40%	30
Onion	50-65%	10
Chilli	20-40%	30
Cauliflower	25-30%	15

5.23 Aroma containing compounds

a) Cucumber: 2, 6- Nonadienal (raw) & Dimethyl disulphide (cooked).

b) Melons: Ester of acetic acid.

c) Soybean: 2-acetyl-1-pyrroline (2AP) emits special fragrance.

d) Cabbage: (a) Raw-Allyl isothiocynates; (b) Cooked-Dimethyl disulphide.

e) Cauliflower curd: Nitriles and isothiocyanates.

f) Potato: 2-Methoxy-3-ethyl pyrazine and 2,5-Dimethyl pyrazine.

g) Radish: 4- Methylthio-trans-3- butenyl isothiocynate.

h) Onion: Allyl propyl disulphide ($C_6H_{12}S_2$).

i) Garlic: Diallyl disulphide.

j) Mushroom: 1-octen-3-01, lenthionine.

k) Carrot: Harsh flvour (volatile terpenoids).

l) Bell & Jalapeno pepper: 2-isobutyl-3-methoxyprazine.

5.24 Based on photosynthesis pathway:

a) C_4 plant: Amaranths, Globe Artichoke, Basella, Ivy gourd.

b) C_3 plant: Lettuce, Carrot, Potato, Cassava, Sweet Potato, Tomato, Sugarbeet, Beans, Spinach, Cucurbits, Water melon, Soybean.

5.25 Based on acid present:

1. Citric acid: Tomato, Beet root, Leafy vegetables, Legumes, Potato, Water melon, Musk melon.
2. Malic acid: Carrot, Celery, Lettuce, Onion, Broccoli.
3. Oxalic acid: Basella, Amaranths, Portulaca, Celosia.

5.26 Based on pollination mechanism:

Extent of natural cross pollination

Type	Extent of cross pollination	Crops
Self pollinated	0-5%	Tomato, Pea and beans, Lettuce, Cowpea, Fenugreek
Often-cross pollinated	5-12%	Brinjal, Capsicum, Chilli, Okra, Lima bean, Sweet pepper, Potato, Celery
Cross pollinated	> 12%	Cole crops, Cucurbits, Amaranths, Asparagus, Spinach, Palak, Onion, Sweet corn, Drumstick, Sweet potato, Carrot, Parsnip

5.26.1 Autogamy:

- Cleistogamy (flowers remain closed at time of pollination & favours self pollination): True cleistogamy is not found.
- Chasmogamy (pollination follows opening of flowers & favours self pollination): Tomato, brinjal, chilli, sweet pepper, okra, peas, French bean, hyacinth bean, cluster bean, runner bean, lettuce, etc.

5.26.2 Allogamy:

- Sex forms and inherent mechanisms favour cross pollination.
- Monoecy: Cucurbits, Amarnaths, Sweet corn, Tapioca, Musk melon.
- Dioecy: Pointed gourd, Scarlet gourd (Bankunari i.e. *Solena amplexicaulis*), Ivy gourd, Giant spine gourd, Sweet gourd, Asparagus, Spinach, Yams, Beet root.
- Heterostyly: Brinjal.
- Protandry: Onion, Carrot, Beet, Leek, Celery, Parsley, Musk melon, Pointed gourd, Rhubarb, Swiss chard.
- Protogyny: Okra, Chilli, Elephant foot yam, Cabbage, Cassava, Amarnathus, Taro, Chekkurmanis.
- Gametophytic self incompatibility (SI): SI reaction is controlled by single locus 'S' with multiple alleles and is determined by genotype of pollen itself. Pollen tube growth is inhibited in style and does nit reach to ovaries. Observed in Solanaceae, Compositae, Leguminosae, Rosaceae, Cruciferae.
- Sporophytic SI: SI reaction is controlled by multiple 'S' alleles for a single locus (homomorphic) viz. Cauliflower, Cabbage, Sprouting broccoli, Brussels sprout, Kale, Radish, Turnip, Beet, Sweet potato, Broccoli.
- Male sterility: Tomato, Brinjal, Chilli, Onion, Carrot, Sweet potato. Musk melon, Sprouting broccoli, Brussles sprout.

5.27 Floral biology of vegetable crops

Crop	Time of		Duration of		Place of report
	Anthesis	Dehiscence	Pollen fertility	Stigma receptivity	
Tomato	7.0-8.0 h	9.0-11.0 h	On the day of anthesis	16 h before anthesis to the days of anthesis	Hisar, India
Potato	5.0-6.0 h	5.30-7.0 h	On the day of anthesis to next day early morning	On the day of anthesis to next day afternoon	Connecticut, US
Chilli	5.0-6.0 h	8.0-11.0 h	On the day of anthesis	On the day of anthesis	Ludhiana, India
Brinjal	6.0-11.30 h	4.15-11.0 h	On the day of anthesis to 2 days after anthesis	2-3 h before anthesis to 2 days after anthesis	New Delhi
	7.0-14.0 h	7.15-14.0 h	On the day of anthesis	One day before to 2 days after anthesis	Bihar
Okra	8.0-10.30 h	6.0-11.0 h	6.0-12.0 h	One day before to day of anthesis	Jaipur
Pea	5.45-6.30 h	5.45-7.30 h	On the day of anthesis to 24 h thereafter	48 h before and 24 h after anthesis	Bangalore

Lab-lab	9.0-17.0 h	5.0-14.0 h	On the day of anthesis	On the day of anthesis	Nagpur
French bean	5.0-7.0 h	5.30-7.30 h	On the day of anthesis	On the day of anthesis with peak between 7-8 h	Jaipur
Cluster bean	9.0-16.0 h	1-2 h before anthesis	2 h before to 11 hr after anthesis	On the day of anthesis	Hisar
Cowpea	Early morning	Shortly before anthesis	On the day of anthesis	1 h before anthesis	Texas, USA
Lettuce	7.0-8.0 h	6.30-8.0 h	-	For few hours	Virginia, US
Celery	Early morning	Few hours before anthesis	On the day of anthesis	5th-8th day after anthesis	California, USA
Sweet potato	4.0-14.0 h	Simultaneously or 2 h after anthesis	On the day of anthesis	On the day of anthesis	New Delhi
Radish	9.0-10.0 h	8.0-10.30 h	On the day of anthesis	At the time of anthesis	Palampur
Musk melon	5.30-6.30 h	5.0-6.0 h	5.0-14.0 h	2 h before to 2-3 h after anthesis	Ludhiana
Water melon	6.0-7.30 h	5.0-6.30 h	5.0-11.0 h	2 h before to 3 h after anthesis	Rajasthan
Bottle gourd	17.0-20.0 h	13.0-14.30 h	On the day of anthesis till next morning	36 hr before to 60 h after anthesis	Ludhiana
Bitter gourd	9.0-10.30 h	7.0-8.0 h	5.0-12.0 h	One day before and one day after anthesis	-
Snake gourd	18.0-21.0 h	Shortly before anthesis	10 h before to 49 h after dehiscence	7 h before to 51 h after anthesis	-
Ridge gourd	17.0-20.0 h	17.0-20.0 h	On the day of anthesis to 2-3 days after anthesis	6 hr before to 84 h after anthesis	-
Sponge gourd	4.0-8.0 h	4.0-8.0 h	On the day of anthesis	10 h before to 120 h after anthesis	Sharanpur
Ash gourd	6.0-7.0 h	3.0-4.0 h	7.0-16.0 h	12 h before to 36 h after anthesis	Ludhiana
Cucumber	5.30-7.0 h	4.30-5.0 h	Up to 14 h	12 h before to 6-7 h after anthesis	New Delhi
Summer Squash	3.30-6.0 h	21-3 h	16 h after anthesis	2 h before and 10 h after anthesis	Ludhiana
	2.20-3.45 h	-	-	Throughout open period	Mysore

5.28 Based on inbreeding (production of offspring by closely related parents) depression:

- Loss of vigour and vitality due to selfing.

Level of inbreeding depression	Crops	Extent of inbreeding
Very high	Carrot	2 years
High	Onion	2-3 years
Moderately high	Cabbage, Indian cauliflower, Broccoli, Brussels sprout, Turnip, Sweet corn, Radish	3-4 years
Very low/ insignificant	Snowball group of cauliflower	4-5 years
Nil	All cucurbits, Tomato, Peas, Beans, Brinjal, Lettuce	

5.29 Based on male sterility (MS) systems:

- Kaul (1988) classified male sterility in to two major groups *viz.*, genetic i.e. inherited (spontaneous or induced) and non-genetic (induced).
- On genotypic basis genetic male sterility was grouped as genic, cytoplasmic and gene-cytoplasmic male sterility.
- Male sterility has been reported in several vegetable crops and it is of different kinds.
- All the transgenic MS lines developed till date are GMS.
- Functionally sterile MS mutants: Certain mutants which which produce functional pollen but fail to self fertilize due to non-dehiscence of pollen or special flower morphology e.g. Exerted stigma in tomato, brinjal and other crops.
- Environment sensitive genetic MS (EGMS): Expression occurs within specified range of temperature and photoperiod regimes e.g. Cabbage, Brussels sprout, Broccoli, Pepper, Carrot, Tomato.

Type of male sterility	Inheritance pattern	Crops
1. Pollen sterility		
Cytoplasmic male sterility (CMS)	Caused by cytoplasmic genes	Onion, carrot, radish, beet, chilli
Genic male sterility (GMS)	Single gene, recessive (*ms*)	Tomato, Brinjal, Pea, Musk melon, Water melon, Chilli, Lima bean, Pumpkin, Cucumber, Cabbage, Summer Squash, Brussels sprout, Cauliflower
	Duplicate dominant	Cauliflower
Cytoplasmic-Genic (CGMS)	Single gene, recessive (*ms*)	Radish, Sweet pepper, Cole crops & Turnip
	Two recessive genes	Sugar beet, Onion, Carrot
	Single dominant	Carrot
2. Staminal male sterility (*sl*)		
Stamenless	Single recessive gene (*ms*)	Tomato
3. Structural/ Functional male sterility		
Short styled positional sterility (*ps*)	Single recessive gene	Tomato, Brinjal, Sweet pepper
Exserted stigma sterility (*ex*)	Single recessive gene	Tomato

a) Nuclear or Genic male sterility (GMS):

- It is result of mutation in any gene(s) both controlling microsporogenesis, stamen development.

Crop	Gene	Commercially utilized	Varieties
Tomato	Single recessive	*ps-2* gene	-
Chilli	Single recessive	*ms-12* & *ms-3* gene	CH-1, CH-3
Musk melon	Single recessive	*ms-1* gene	Punjab Hybrid

b) CGMS (cytogenetic male sterility):

Crop	Gene	Commercially utilized	Varieties
Onion	Single recessive	-	Arka Kirthiman, Arka Lalima, Arka Pitambar
Chilli	Single recessive	*ms-2 gene*	Arka Meghana, Arka Sweta, Arka Harita, Kashi Surkh
Carrot	Single recessive	-	Pusa Nayanjyoti, Pusa Vasudha

c) GCMS (genic cytoplasmic male sterility):

Crop	Types	Commercially utilized
Onion	S and T cytoplasm	S-cytoplasm type
Carrot	Petaloid (*pt*), brown anther (*ba*) & gummifer (*gu*)	Petaloid type
Cauliflower	-	Ogura cytoplasm
Cabbage	-	Ogura cytoplasm
Brussels sprout	-	Ogura cytoplasm
Sprouting broccoli	-	Ogura cytoplasm

5.30 Morphological markers for functional type male sterility identification and production of hybrid seed

Markers	Crops
Potato leaf shape, green stem colour (recessive marker gene), anthocyaninless stem, Antherless, closed anther mutant, parthenocarpic fruit, enzyme marker	Tomato cv. Meeruti
Closed anther mutant (single recessive gene)	Brinjal cv. John Baer
Blue anthers	Chilli
Glabrous seedling	Musk melon
Non-lobed leaf (at seedling stage, single recessive gene), glabrous leaf, delayed green seedling	Water melon
Glossy foliage & partial chlorosis (recessive marker gene)	Brussels sprout
Purple stem pigmentation (single dominant marker gene)	Cabbage cv. Wase Zenku
Brown seed coat colour	Onion
Bright green hypocotyls	Broccoli
Brown anther type (shrivel before anthesis), petaloid type (anthers modified into petaloid like filaments)	Carrot
Basal stem colour (red stalk) in identification of haploid seedlings	Asparagus
Anthocyanin shades & leaf shape in F_1 hybrids	Lettuce

5.31 Estimation of combining ability:

Combining ability	Mating design used
General combining ability (GCA)	Top cross, Poly cross
Specific combining ability (SCA)	Single cross, Pair cross
GCA & SCA	Diallel cross, L x T design

5.32 Based on genetic mechanism for hybrid seed development in cucurbits:

Mechanism	Name of cucurbits	Remarks
Hand pollination without emasculation	Pumpkins	Commercial
Emasculation & hand pollination	Musk melon	Due to andromonoecious nature
Pinching of male flowers & allow to open pollination	Bottle gourd	Commercial
	Pumpkin, Squash	Suitable due to long pedicel of male flowers
Use of gynoecious lines	Cucumber, Musk melon	
Use of monoecious lines	Musk melon	Problem due to uneven fruit shape
Use of GMS system	Musk melon	
Use of marker genes	Water melon	Non-lobing leaf
	Pumpkin	Yellow spot on upper surface of leaves
Defloration	Cucumber	Old strategy

5.33 Based on tendril types in cucurbits:

Simple	Branched
Cucumber, Ash gourd, Bitter gourd, Musk melon, Long melon, Snap melon	Water melon, Round melon, Bottle gourd, Snake gourd, Ridge gourd, Sponge gourd

5.34 Based on derivation of vegetable from plant tissue:

- Swollen inflorescence: Broccoli
- Stem sprout: Asparagus, Kohlrabi
- Main leaf bud: Lettuce, Brussels sprouts, Cabbage.
- Axillary bud: Brussels sprout
- Leaf petiole: Celery, Rhubarb
- Swollen leaf base: Leek.
- Leaf blade: Spinach, Beet, Cabbage, Lettuce, Swiss chard, Endive.
- Corm: Colocais, Amorphophallus.
- Modified stem: Knol khol.
- Swollen tap root: Carrot, Chicory, Celeriac

- Swollen hypocotyl: Beet root, Turnip, Radish.
- Stem tuber: Potato, Jerusalem artichoke
- Root tuber: Sweet potato, Cassava, Yams.
- Bulb: Onion, Garlic.
- Flower: Cauliflower, Broccoli.
- Flower bud: Globe artichoke
- Placental intralocular tissue: Tomato
- Fleshy immature fruits: Legumes, Tomato, Brinjal, Okra, Cucurbits, Rat tail radish, Green peppers, Summer squash.
- Non-fleshy immature fruits: Snap beans, Lima beans, Fava beans, Peas, Sweet corn, Okra, Cowpea.
- Fleshy mature fruits: Tomatoes, Red peppers, Pumpkins, White squash, Water melons.
- Non-fleshy mature fruits: Dry peans, Dry beans.
- Seed: Peas, Lima bean, Dolichos bean.

5.35 Based on edible part:

Root	Beet, Carrot, Cassava, Celeriac, Horse radish, Parsnip, Radish, Rutabaga, Salsify, Sweet potato, Turnip
Stem	Asparagus, Kohlrabi, Jerusalem artichoke, Potato & Yam (tuber)
Leaf	Brussels sprout (buds), Cabbage, Celery (petioles), Chard, Chicory, Chinese cabbage, Chive, Collard, Dandelion, Endive, Garlic (bulb), Kale, Leek (leaf base), Lettuce, Mustard, New Zealand spinach, Onion (bulb), Parsley, Rhubarb (petiole), Spinach, Turnip, Watercress
Immature flower part	Broccoli, Cauliflower, Globe artichoke
Immature fruit	Cowpea (seed), Cucumber, Egg plant, Lima bean, Okra, Peas, Podded pea, Snap bean, Soybean, Summer squash, Sweet corn (seed)
Mature fruit	Musk melon, Pepper, Pumpkin, Tomato, Water melon, Winter squash

5.36 Effect of ethylene:

Crop	Effect
Lettuce	Russet sprouting, discolouration
Carrot, Beet	Bitterness
Celery	Blanching
Cabbage	Leaf abscission, undesirable flavor
Asparagus	Fibrousness
Cucumber	Degreening
Pea	Toxin pisatin formation
Sweet potato	Hard core, production of phenolics
Tomato	Increased lycopene & carotene

5.37 Critical moisture period and impact of water deficit on vegetable crops (Fulton, 1986):

- Vegetables contain large quantity of water (80-85%).
- Most vegetables are shallow rooted; short period of 2-3 days of moisture stess reduce yields.
- Yield and quality suffers rapidly under water stress.
- Drip irrigation always maintains crop rhizophere almost at field capacity; crop never experiences water stress at any stage.

Crop	Critical moisture period	Major defects caused by water deficit
Broccoli	Heads development	Strong flavour, ricey curd & premature bolting
Brinjal	Flowering & fruit development	Reduced yield, blossom end rot, misshapen fruit, poor fruit colour
Cabbage	Head formation & enlargement	Growth cracks & tough leaf; tip burning, browning & buttoning of heads
Cauliflower	Curd formation & enlargement	Ricey curd & buttoning
Carrot, Beet	Root enlargement	Growth cracks, misshapen roots; strong & pungent odour, accumulation of nitrates in roots
Radish	Root enlargement	Pithy & distorted roots, accumulation of nitrates; strong pungent odour
Cucumber	Flowering & fruit development	Pointed and cracked fruits with bitterness; non-viable pollen grains
Chilli & capsicum	Flowering & fruit development	Flower shedding, Low fruit set, shriveled fruits, blossom end rot; reduction in dry matter
Tomato	Flowering & fruit development	Flower shedding, lack of fertilization, reduced fruit size, blossom end rot & fruit cracking
Peas	Flowering & pod filling	Poor pod filling & shriveled grains; reduction in root nodulation; reduction in root nodulation
Onion	Bulb formation & bulb enlargement	Poor sized bulbs & early bolting; splitting & doubling of bulbs
Okra	Flowering & pod development	Toughness & fibre development in pods
French bean	Pod setting & pod enlargement	Poor pod filling with pithy pods
Water melon	Flowering & fruit development	Blossom end rot leading to reduced marketable yield
Potato	Tuberization, tuber enlargement	Poor tuber growth, yield, splitting
Leafy vegetables	Entire crop duration	Toughness in leaves; tip burning; poor foliage growth & accumulation of nitrates
Potato	Tuberization & tuber enlargement	Poor tuber growth, yield & splitting
Turnip	Root enlargement	Strong & pungent odour accumulation of harmful nitrates
Lettuce	Consistently throughout development	Toughness of leaves; tip burning
Melons	Floweing & fruit development	Poor quality in musk melons; increased nitrate content in water melons
Vegetable soybean	Flowering & seed filling	Flower & pod drop, poor bean development, poor quality & yield
Sweet corn	Tasseling and ear development	Undeveloped ear development

5.38 Sufficient and critical level of nutrients in leaf tissue

Nutrient	Sufficient level	Critical level*
Nitrogen (%)	1.50-4.00	1.00-1.50
Phosphorous (%)	0.25-0.80	0.20-0.25
Potassium (%)	2.00-9.00	1.50-2.00
Calcium (%)	0.35-2.00	0.35-0.80
Magnesium (%)	0.25-1.00	0.20-0.25
Sulphur (%)	0.16-0.50	0.10-0.16
Manganese (ppm)	30-200	30-50
Iron (ppm)	50-250	50-80
Zinc (ppm)	30-100	20-30
Boron (ppm)	30-60	20-30
Copper (ppm)	8-20	4-8
Molybdenum (ppm)	0.5-5.0	0.2-0.5

* Below critical level of nutrients, deficiency symptom may occur.

- Soil containing 0.1 per cent potassium means 1 g potassium per kg of soil.

5.39 Removal of primary nutrients from the soil

Crop	Yield (T/ha)	Nutrient removal (kg/ha)		
		N	P	K
Potato	40	175	80	310
Tomato	50	140	65	190
Brinjal	60	175	40	300
Cabbage	70	370	85	480
Cauliflower	50	250	100	350
Knol khol	20	100	84	170
Carrot	30	125	55	200
Radish	30	120	60	120
Beet	25	60	40	112
Onion	35	120	50	160
Leek	30	102	50	160
Cucumber	40	70	50	120
Pumpkin	50	90	70	160
Musk melon	15	54	16	97
Pea	9	124	44	88
Beans	15	130	40	160
Okra	20	60	25	90
Celery	30	200	80	300
Lettuce	30	90	35	160
Spinach	25	120	45	200
Asparagus	5	120	60	150
Cassava	40	150	70	350
Sweet potato	40	190	75	340
Elephant foot yam	50	170	40	245
Yam	14	80	20	86

5.40 Biochemical basis of disease/ pest resistance

- Preinfectional barriers: Catechol, Proatechuic acid, Phenols, Terpentines, Flavonoid, Tomatine.
- Presence of toxic compounds: Sinigrin, Gossypol, Solanine, Chlorogenic acid, Coumarin, Eugenol, L-Pinene, Quercetin, Tannin, Thymol and Vanillin.

Crop	Prohibitins
Carrot	Chlorogenic acid, Caffecia acid, gallic acid, benzoic acid, N'-oxybenzoic acid
Radish	Raphanin
Potato	Saponin, solanine, demissine, tomatine, digitonin, chaconie
Tomato	Solanine, tomatine
Pea	Amino-y-butyr lactone
Onion	Protcatechnic acid, S-methyl & S-propyl, cysteine sulfoxides
Sweet potato	Caffecia acid, chlorogenic acid, iso-chlorgenic acid

5.41 Provision of primary type of nutrients

Nutrients	Vegetables
Carbohydrates	Potato, Sweet potato, Dry beans, Elephant foot yam, Taro, Cassava, Sweet corn
Protein	Peas, Beans, Leafy crucifers, Sweet corn
Fat	Mature seeds of few Legumes & Cucurbits
β- carotene Pro-vitamin A	Carrot, Pumpkin, Pepper, Green peas & beans, Green leafy vegetables
Vitamin C	Bitter gourd, Sweet pepper, Hot pepper, Cabbage, Sprouting broccoli, Leafy vegetables, Melons, Tomato, Immature bean seed, Bean sprouts, etc.
Minerals	Most leafy vegetables, Cole crops
Vitamin E	Green leafy vegetables

5.42 Centers conserving crop germplasm in medium and long term storage units

Country/ acronym	Center	Major crops	Seed storage conditions
AVRDC	Asian Vegetable Research and Development Center, Taiwan	Large collection of Asiatic land races, advanced cvs., breeding lines of Amaranths, Chinese cabbage, other brassicas, soybean, sweet potato & tomato	Stored at laminated aluminum foil packets at 5-8^{0}C
Belgium	Faculte des Sciences Agromiques de l'Etat a Gembloux	Large number of wild spp. of *Phaseolus*, *Vigna* & related genera	Seeds with moisture content of 6-7% stored in laminated aluminum foil at -20^{0}C
Bulgaria	Institute of Introduction and Plant Resources	Collection of brassicas, capsicum, cowpea, cucurbits, faba bean, legumes, onion, pea, potato, soybean, tomato	Seed stored in plastic at -18^{0}C
Chile	Bance de Genes, Instituto de Production y Sanidad Vegetal, Universidad Austral de Chile	Collection of land races & wild species of potato	Seeds stored in plastic at -18^{0}C
CIP	Centro Internacional de la Papa, Lima, Peru	Collection of indigenous Central and South American land races, wild spp., advanced cvs. of potato	Seeds with moisture content of 5-6% stored in aluminum foil at 0 to -10^{0}C
Colombia	Instituto Colombiana Agropecuaria, Bogota	Large collection of *Allium*, *Capsicum*, cucurbits, maize, *Phaseolus*, tuber bearing *Solanum*, tomato	Seed stored in laminated aluminum foil packets at 3^{0}C
Ethiopia	Plant Genetic Resources Center, Addis Ababa	Collection of indigenous brassicas, cucurbits, faba bean, capsicum, pea, *Phaseolus*	Seeds stored in cans and aluminum foil packets at 4 & -10^{0}C
France	INRA Station d'Amelioration des Plantes Maraichares, Montfavet to Avignon	Collection of introduced land races of Capsicum, Brinjal, melon, breeding lines of tomato	Seed stored at 3^{0}C
German Federal Republic	Institut fur pflanzenbau und Pflanzenzuchtung, Braunschweig	Large collections of land races & advanced cultivars of beet, brassicas, faba bean, tomato	Seed stored in sealed cans at 30% RH & 3-4^{0}C
Hungary	Research Center for Agrobotany, Institute for plant Production and Qualification, Tapiooszele	Beet, brassicas, capsicum, cucurbits, faba bean, legumes, lupin, pea, Phaseolus, sorghum, soybean, lettuce, maize, onion, tomato	Seeds with moisture content of 5-8% stored in glass jars at 4^{0}C

Isreal	Agricultural Research organization, Bet Dagan	*Brassicas*, melon, onion, pea, *Phaseolus*, water melon	Seeds stored at 12% in cans at -10^{0}C
Italy	Instituto del Germoplasma, CNR, Bari	Faba bean, legumes, pea, tomato	Seeds stored in laminated aluminum foil packets at 0^{0}C
The Netherlands	Institute of Horticultural Plant Breeding, Wageningen	Brassicas, *Capsicum*, Brinjal, lettuce, melon, pea, *Phaseolus*	Seeds stored at -18^{0}C
Nigeria	National Horticultural Research Institute, Ibadan	*Amaranths*, *Capsicum*, Cucurbits, tomato	Seed stored at -20^{0}C
Philippines	Institute of Plant Breeding, University of the Philippines, Los Banos	*Capsicum,* cowpea, cucurbits, eggplant, mung bean, okra, soybean, tomato, winged bean	Seeds with 5% moisture stored in aluminum foil packets at -15^{0}C
South Africa	Division of Plant and Seed Control, Pretoria	*Brassicas*, cowpea, cucurbits, onion, *Phaseolus*, soybean, tomato	Seeds stored in aluminum foil at -20^{0}C
Turkey	Aegean Regional Agricultural Research Institute, Izmir	*Brassica, Capsicum, Phaseolus*, okra, onion, spinach, beet, legumes, maize,	Seed with moisture of 6-8% in sealed cans at 10^{0}C
UK	National Vegetable Research Station, Wellesbourne	*Brassica*, beet, carrot, faba bean, lettuce, radish	Seed stored in aluminum packets at -20^{0}C
USA	National Seed Storage Laboratory, Colorado	*Brassica, Capsicum, Phaseolus*, cowpea, cucurbits, legumes, maize, okra, onion, pea, potato, soybean, tomato	Seed stored in laminted aluminum foil packets at -14^{0}C and -20^{0}C
USA	Southern Region Plant Introduction Station, Experiment, Georgia	*Capsicum*, cucurbits, Brinjal, okra	Seed stored at 4^{0}C and 40% R.H.
USA	North Eastern Region Pant Introduction Station, Geneva, New York	Wildrelatives of *Brassica*, celery, legumes, onion, pea, pumpkin	Seed stored in aluminum packets at -14^{0}C and -20^{0}C.
	USDA, Vegetable Production Research Unit, Salinas, California	*Brassicas*, chicory, lettuce	Seed stored at -18^{0}C
	North Central Region Plant Introduction Station, Ames, Iowa	*Amaranths, brassicas*, beet, carrot, *Cucurbita*, cucumber, radish, spinach, tomato	Seeds stored at 35-40% R.H. and 3^{0}C
	Western Region Plant Introduction Station, Pullman, Washington	*Allium, Brassicas*, faba bean, lettuce, *Phaseolus*	Seed stored at 38% R.H. and 3^{0}C

6. BREEDING METHODS FOLLOWED IN VEGETABLE CROPS:

6.1 General information:

- Number of gametes in a genotype = 2^n, where n= number of heterozygous position of gene.
- Jumping genes were discovered by Barbara McClintock (1950) in Maize.
- Camerarius (1694): 1st to demonstrate sex in plants. Suggested crossing as a method to get new types. Worked with mulberry and maize.
- Hannig (1904): Contributed to the idea of embryo culture.
- Harland and Pope (1920): Describeα backcross breeding technique.
- Genic balance theory of sex determination: C.B. Bridges.
- Holokinetic: A chromosome with diffused centromere.
- Polytene/ Giant/ Salivary gland chromosomes: 1st discovered in salivary glands of dipterian insect by Balbini (1881).
- Puffs/ Balbini rings are found in polytene chromosomes and are sites of DNA sysnthesis.
- Translocation homozygotes lead to alteration in linkage map.
- Duplication leads to addition of one or more genes to chromosomes.
- Pseudo-dominance is associated with deletions.
- Euploidy refers to change in entire genome while aneuploidy refers to change in one or few chromosomes of genome.
- Epistasis leads to modification of normal segregation ratio in F_2 generation.
- Coupling and repulsion phases of linkage were given by Bateson and Punnett (1906). Haldane (1942) used the terms cis and trans for coupling and repulsion, respectively.
- Morgan and Cattell (1912) first used term crossing over and it occurs at pachytene stage.
- Value of recombinants varies from 0-50%.
- Chiasma was first discovered by Janssens (1909).
- 1st case of cytoplasmic inheritance: Correns (1909) in *Mirabilis jalapa* for leaf colour.
- Cytoplasmic inheritance is also known as extra nuclear/ extra chromosomal/ non Mendelian/ organellar/ uniparental inheritance. It exhibits maternal effects.
- Mapping of plasma genes (genes associated with chloroplast DNA or mitochondrial DNA) is more difficult than nuclear genes.
- Term polygene: Mather (1941).
- Polygenic/ quantitative characters exhibit continuous variation and highly sensitive to environmental changes.
- Transgression is only possible in case of polygenic characters.
- Reverse transcription was first reported by Temin and Baltimore (1970).

- Frameshift mutation: Mutations arise due to addition or deletion of nucleotides in mRNA.
- DNA probe: Small sequences of DNA with known base sequences, origin and function.
- Vertical resistance is governed by oligogenes while horizontal resistance is governed by polygenes.
- Term 'Genetics of disaster' used by J.R. Harlan in 1972.
- Functional unit of a gene: Cistron.
- Functional unit of recombination: Recon.
- Functional unit of mutation: Muton.
- Linkage drag: Presence of undesirable traits in crop wild relatives.
- Genetic erosion and genetic shifts, risks loss of independence for egg plant seed market.

6.2 Quantitative genetics:

- Fisher (1918) divided genetic variance into additive, dominance and epistatic components.
- Term 'Diallel' coined by Yates (1947).
- Concept of Partial diallel andLine x Tester cross (modified form of top cross): Kempthorne (1957).
- Concept of quadriallel cross: Rawlings and Cokerham (1962).
- Concept of triallel cross: Kearsey and Jinks (1968).
- Concept of test cross: Bridges (1934).
- Concept of D^2 analysis was originally developed by P.C. Mahalanobis (1928).
- Concept of Generation Mean Analysis was developed by Haymand and Jinks and Jones (1958).
- Concept of Metroglyph analysis: Anderson (1957).
- Concept of path analysis: Sewall Wright (1921).
- Concept of bi-parental mating design: Comstock and Robinson (1948).
- Application of D^2 statistics for assessing genetic diversity: C.R. Rao (1952).
- Graphical approach of diallel analysis: Hayman (1954).
- Numerical approach of diallel analysis: Griffing (1956).
- Path coefficient analysis: 1st used by Dewey and Lu (1959).
- Joint Scaling Test: Cavalli (1952).
- Test cross ratio in case of duplicate gene is 3:1.
- Multiple effect of a single gene is known as pleiotropy.
- Cell linkage theory was proposed by Virchow.

- Bio-genetic law: Ernst Haeckel.
- Breeding methods for self-pollinated crops: Pure line selection, Mass Selection, Progeny selection, Bulk method, Pedigree method, single seed descent method, Back cross method.

6.3 Self incompatibility (SI):

- It is genetically controlled physiological hindrance to self fertilization. It is governed by oppositional factor hypothesis.
- Term 'self incompatibililty' is coined by Stout (1917).
- J.G. Koelreuter, 1st reported SI in Purple mullein (*Verbascum phoeniceum*).
- Gametophytic SI: 1st discovered by East and Mangelsdorf (1925) in flowering tobacco (*Nicotiana sanderae*).
- Sporophytic SI: 1st discovered by Hughes and Babcook (1950) in *Crepis foetida* and Gerstel in *Parthenium argentatum*.
- In cole crops, self incompatibility was 1st reported by Bateman (1954).
- In gametophytic SI, the pollen-pistil interaction is genetically controlled by haploid genome of each pollen grain and diploid genome of pistil tissue e.g. *Nicotiana*, *Lycopersicon*, *Solanum*.
- In sporophytic SI, it is controlled by genome of somatic tissue (sporophyte) in which pollen grain is formed.
- Sporophytic SI is genetically controlled and governed by oppositional factor hypothesis. In Broccoli, Brussels sprout and Knol khol it is, controlled by single locus with multiple alleles (50-70) known as *S*-alleles.
- S-alleles are active in stigma in flowering stage but remain inactive in bud stage i.e. 2-4 days before its opening.
- Glycoproteins present in stigma, hinders pollen grain germination and penetration.
- *S* allele collection started in 1968. They are maintained at Horticultural Research International, Wellesbourne, Warwick, UK.
- SI mechanism: Strongest in 'Kale' followed by broccoli, kohlrabi, calabrese, cabbage, cauliflower in Europe (Early Indian types) and Brussels sprout.
- Self incompatibility in broccoli, Brussels sprout and Knol khol can be studied by counting seed set a few weeks after self pollination or by counting pollen tubes in the style after 24 h of pollination. The latter involves macerating style with sodium hydroxide, staining with aniline blue and observing pollen tubes with fluorescence microscope.
- SI level is influenced by temperature, humidity, age of flower and plant.
- SI is used in development of hybrid varieties.
- Lines having higher degree of SI should be developed.

- A line should have only one type of S-allele which on crossing with other line having different allele will give only hybrid (crossed) seed.
- Cytodeme: A gene pool of a cultivated species (sharing a same chromosome number & intercrossable).
- Cytodeme of *B. oleraceae* consists of 6 cultivated vegetables and 9 wild relatives.

***Mechanism of SI can be grouped into 3 categories as*:**

1. Pollen-stigma interaction:
   a) Homomorphic system of incompatibility: Difference in stigmatic surface prevents pollen germination.
   b) In gametophytic SI: stigmatic surface is plumose (wet stigma) and pollen grain determine reaching the stigma and incompatibility occurs at later stage.
   c) In sporophytic SI: stigma is papillate and dry and covered with hydrated layer of protein known as pellicle, which is involved in incompatibility reaction. After reaching the stigmatic surface, pollen release exine exudates (either protein or glycero-protein) and this reacts with pellicle and induces callosus formation and prevents growth of pollen tube.
2. Pollen tube-style interaction:
   a) Pollen grain germination and pollen tube penetrates stigmatic surface. But in compatible combinations, the growth of pollen tube is retarded within style (as in petunia, lycopersicon, lilium). Protein and polysaccharide synthesis in pollen tube stops, resulting in bursting of pollen tube leading to death of nuclei.
3. Pollen tube-ovule interaction:
   a) In cocoa, pollen tube reaches the ovule and fertilization occurs but embryo degerates later due to some biochemical reaction.

***Breakdown of SI*:**

- Genetical factors like modified genes, less active *S*-alleles and competitive interaction between *S*-alleles cause breakdown of SI.
- SI may be partially or wholly broken down by genetical, environmental (extrinsic) and physiological (intrinsic) factors.
- Extrinsic factors like high temperature, high humidity and high concentration of CO_2 can lead to breakdown SI.
- Flowering age and stage of flowering are intrinsic factors.
- Incompatibility is not successful in Chinese cabbage, which generally breaks at high temperature.

***Methods to overcome SI*:**

- Application of mature pollen to immature stigma e.g. Brassica.

- Application of irradiatedpollen (at low doses 0.1 to 2 Krad) on stigma.
- Pollination of SI pollen grains after irradiated self compatible pollen (dead pollen) as in apple and in peach (mentor pollen technique).
- Bud pollination or Spray of 3% NaCl at ½ to 1 hr after pollination to produce self seeds.
- Application of NAA/ IAA on flowers for production of selfed seeds.
- Surgical technique: Removal of stigmatic surface e.g. Brassica or by removal of styles e.g. Petunia.
- End of season pollination: SI is reduced towards end of flowering season.
- Heat treatment of pistil upto 55-60^{0}C may induce pseudo-fertility.
- Allopolyploidy
- Doubling of chromosome number of diploids to tetraploids.
- SI alleles can be mutated by physical and chemical means.
- Transfer of self compatible allels in self incompatible plants.
- Use of electric aided pollination.
- Application of glutamic acid, folic acid and nicotinic acid (50 mg/l).
- Double i.e. repeated pollination of mixture of incompatible + compatible pollen grains.
- In green house, 3-5% CO_2 treatment for 8-24 h at 100% R.H. and spraying the crop at full bloom stage with sodium chloride (3-5%) removes inhibitor from stigma and permits self pollination.
- These methods are used for the multiplication of inbred lines in cole crops.
- Roggen (1979) reported use of liquid paraffin at flowering helps in overcoming SI and gives better seed set than hand pollination.
- Grafting of compatible branch onto incompatible plants.

6.4 Male sterility:

- Presence of male sterility eliminates emasculation.
- Koelreuter (1763) reported male sterility in flowering plants.
- CMS was 1st discovered by Jones and Clarke (1925) in onion cv. Italian Red.
- In cucumber, male sterility is associated with glabrous seedlings and determinate growth habit.
- CMS is best suited for hybrid seed production in vegetatively propagated crops.
- Male sterility is characterizedby absence of functional pollen grains (male gamate) but female gametes are normal and functional.
- Genic male sterility (GMS): Cole (1959) and Brocher (1966) reported genic male sterility in purple heading broccoli and calabrese and in Brussels sprout by Johnson (1958).

- Useful for making F_1 hybrids since it avoids tedious & costly hand emasculation of individual flowers.
- Limited use of GMS is done to produe F_1 hybrids of peppers in France, Bulgaria & Yugoslavia.
- Genic male sterility is governed by recessive male sterility gene (*ms*) mutated from male fertile gene.
- In broccoli, several male sterile genes *ms1*, *ms2*, *ms4*, *ms5*, *ms6* have been identified, which are not allelic.
- Cytoplasmic male sterility (CMS): It has not been found apparently in *B. oleracea.*
- It was transferred into *B. oleracea* from *B. nigra* by Pearson through repeated back crosses and embryo rescue technique. It was also transferred from Japanese radish Ogura type to *B. oleracea* through back crosses, embryo rescue technique and protoplast fusion.
- Both GMS and CMS can be used in development of F_1 hybrid cultivars.
- Male sterility has been reported in cucumber.

Nuclear male sterility in vegetable crops:

Crops	Salient features of male sterility
Tomato	More than 55 recessive genes have been reported; *sl-2*, *ms-13* and *ms-15* are temperature sensitive and *ps-2* gene has been exploited at commercial scale
Egg plant	Monogenic recessive gene has been reported, and monogenic recessive functional sterility is available
Hot pepper & sweet pepper	More than 12 recessive genes have been reported, MS-12 (*ms-509/ms-10*) and *ms-3* genes are commercially utilized in India and Hungary, respectively. The *ms-10* gene is linked with taller plant height, erect growth and dark purple anther.
Cauliflower	Both recessive and dominant genes have been reported
Cabbage	Both recessive and dominant genes have been reported
Brussels sprout	Recessive male-sterile mutant has been reported.
Broccoli	Six recessive non-allelic genes have been reported; linkage of ms gene with bright green hypocotyls
Water melon	Recessive mutants have been reported; linkage for *ms* gene with delayed-green (*dg*) seedling marker gene
Musk melon	Five recessive non-alleleic genes have been reported and *ms-1* is commercially utilized in India
Cucumber	Monogenic recessive gene has been reported and limited scope of utilization because of availability of gynoecious lines
Summer squash	Monogenic recessive gene has been reported and very limited scope of utilization because of availability of sex regulating mechanism using plant growth regulator, particularly ethephon
Onion	Monogenic recessive gene has been reported but not utilized commercially because of availability of CGMS lines
Carrot	Recessive male sterile genes have been reported but not utilized at commercial scale because of availability of CMS lines
Radish	Three recessive mutants have been reported but commercially not utilized.

Nuclear-cytoplasmic male sterility in vegetable crops:

Crop	Salient features of male sterility
Tomato	Sterile cytoplasm has been derived from the distant species through protoplasm fusion, and restorer gene (*Rf*) is not available
Hot pepper and sweet pepper	First reported in an Indian accession, most of the lines are temperature sensitive and occurrence of *Rf* allele is common in small-fruited (hot pepper) and *rf* in large fruited (sweet pepper) lines.
Cauliflower, Cabbage, Brussels sprout, Broccoli	In cole crops, sterile cytoplasm is derived from *B. nigra* and *R. sativus* (Ogura type). Problem of seedling yellowing at low temperature associated with Ogura based CGMS lines of broccoli, cauliflower, cabbage and Brussels sprout has been solved using protoplast fusion. Hybrid lines of cabbage and cauliflower are being utilized by seed companies in France and protoplast fusion has been utilized to transfer Ogura cytoplasm from broccoli into cabbage.
Onion	Two types of sterile cytoplasms viz. *S* and *T* have been reported and *S*-cytoplasm is most widely exploited commercially.
Carrot	Two types (petaloid and brown anthers) of male sterile lines are available and genetics of fertility restoration is complex because structural variants of mt-DNA are numerous
Radish	Sterile cytoplasm is widely distributed in wild radish and the occurrence of *Rf* allele is frequent is European and Chinese cultivars and *rf* in Japanese cultivars.

6.5 Selection:

- Oldest method.
- Oldest method of selection: Mass selection.
- Hopkins (1899) developed concept of ear-to-row selection method in cross pollinated crops.
- Pure line selection method was 1st employed by W.L. Johannsen (1903) to improve seed weight of French bean cv. Princess. He coined the term 'gene' to the Mendelian factor.
- Progeny test (Vilmorin principle) was developed by Louis de Vilmorin.
- Progeny test is also known as Vilmorin isolation principle.
- Jensen proposed idea of Multiline in 1952 for use in cereals.
- Stratified Mass selection was proposed by C.O. Gardener (1961).
- Name 'Mass pedigree method' was given by S.S. Rajan.
- Grid method of mass selection was suggested by Gardener (1962).
- Mass pedigree method was proposed by Harrington (1937).
- Single Seed Descent (SSD) method: Modification of bulk method.
- SSD method was suggested by Goulden (1939) and applied for 1st time in 'oat' by Graphius in 1965.
- Concept of SSD method: C.A. Brim (1966).
- SSD method is quite effective in brinjal & tomato to evolve lines resistant to bacterial wilt.

- Concept of Bulk breeding method: Nilsson Ehle (1908).
- Concept of Parallel Variation (law of homologous series of variation): Vavilov (1951).
- The procedure of recurrent selection was described by Jenkins (1940).
- The initial idea about recurrent selection was independently given by Hayes and Garber (1919) and East and Jones (1920).
- Term 'Recurrent selection' was coined by Hull (1945).
- Reciprocal selection for SCA was proposed by F.H. Hull (1945) in corn.
- Reciprocal selection for GCA was proposed by Jenkins (1945).
- Reciprocal (half sib) recurrent selection proposed by R.E. Comstock, H.F. Robinson and P.H. Harvey (1949).
- A multiline variety is a mixture of several pure lines.
- The concept of disruptive mating and selection: Mather (1953) and Thody (1958).
- The concept of diallel selective mating system: Jonsen in 1970.

6.6 Heterosis:

- Epistasis is term originally proposed by Bateson (1909).
- Hybrid vigour is at its maximum in F_1 hybrids e.g. Onion.
- Term 'Heterosis' was coined by G.H. Shull (1909).
- Term 'Heterobeltiosis' was coined by Fonseca and Patterson (1968). It is estimated over better parent.
- Term 'Useful heterosis' was used by Meredith and Bridge (1972).
- Term 'Overdominance' was coined by Hull (1945) in corn.
- Heterosis in vegetable crops is manifested in different ways like 1) high yield/ increased number of fruits 2) uniformity in size 3) early maturity 4) large number of marketable heads/ bulbs per unit area 5) better fruit quality 6) combination of resistance to biotic (diseases, insect pest) and abiotic (temperature, humidity, water, herbicide, etc.) stresses.
- Heterosis breeding is useful for overall improvement of all characters in onion, cabbage, tomato, chilli, etc.
- In pumpkin, heterosis is more pronounced when parents differed considerably in their observed characteristics than when parents are closely related.
- In tomato, there is general absence of heterosis for all the characters when parents with high level of expression are involved.
- Hybrid vigour in tomato not much in increased fruit size but in production of large number of fruits.
- Heterosis utilizes mainly dominance variance.
- Complementary hypothesis was proposed by Bateman (1952).

- Overdominance theory was proposed by G.H. Shull and E.M. East (1908).
- Dominance theory was proposed by C.B. Davenport (1908), A.B. Bruce, F. Keeble and C. Pellew (1910).
- Shull was the 1st scientist to produce a single cross hybrid in maize.
- Single cross hybrid method: Shull G.H.
- Double cross hybrid method: Jones D.F.
- Top cross method: Cross of an inbred line with an OP variety was suggested by Davis (1927).
- Double top cross: Cross between single cross and OP variety i.e. (A x B) x OP.
- Double cross programme of hybrid seed production in cabbage was proposed by Odland and Nole (1950).
- Double cross involves 4 lines with different S alleles.
- Double cross is used for getting increased yields of hybrid seeds.
- Double cross was proposed in 'Marrow Stem Kale' for producing hybrid seeds.
- Triple cross was suggested by Thompson to produce large quantity of seeds in Kale.
- Distant/ wide hybridization: Crosses are made between two different species or genera.
- Thomas Fairchild (1717) 1st to do distant hybridization in *D. caryophyllus* x *D. barbatus*.
- Distant hybridization is associated with hybrid sterility/ hybrid inviability/ hybrid breakdown.
- Distant hybridization is used to develop desirable recombinants as source of genes for a particular trait is not available within species / wild species
- Trait specific distant hybridization is followed in plantation crops.
- Backcrossing for incorporation of disease resistance: Harlan and Pope (1922).
- Double backcross method is adopted in tomato.

6.7 Intergeneric hybridization:

- Rimpu (1890) made 1st intergeneric hybridization between Bread wheat and Rye.
- In Russia, Karpechenko (1927) developed 1st intergeneric hybrid (Raphanobrassica) between radish and cabbage.
- English rocket (*Eruca sativa*) x mustard (*B. juncea*): Erussica.

6.8 Interspecific hybridization:

- Interspecific hybridization is resorted to generate useful variability.
- Interspecific hybridization through somatic cell hybridization in brinjal by utilizing *S. incanum*, *S. sisymbriifolium* and *S. macrocarpon* for transferring resistance against fruit borer and nematodes.

- Other interspecific crosses:
  - o Kale x Turnip: Nabicol.
  - o Cabbage x Cauliflower: Caulicob.
  - o Turnip (*B. campestris ssp. rapifera*) x Cabbage (*B. oleracea*): Rutabaga/ Swede (a man made vegetable).
  - o *B. nigra* x *B. oleracea*: *B. carinata*. Used as leafy vegetable.
  - o Cross between *Cucurbita maxima* x *C. moschata*: Sterile F_1 hybrids.
  - o Cross between cv. Butternut (*C. moschata*) x cv. Buttercup (*C. maxima*): Highly sterile F_1 hybrid.
  - o Cross between *C. ecuadorensis* x *C. moschata* yield squash resistant to multiple viruses.

6.9 Special breeding techniques:

- Different breeding procedures involve gene pyramiding, multiline, horizontal resistance, deployment of resistance gene are suggested.
- Concept of 'Biparental mating' was originally developed by Comstock and Robinson (1948, 1952).
- Term 'Ideotype' was proposed by Donald (1968).
- Term 'Homeostasis' was coined by Lerner (1954).
- Vander Plank J.E. (1963) developed concept of vertical and horizontal resistance.
- Nishi (1967) suggested bud pollination in Chinese cabbage to maintain & increase self incompatible lines.
- Muller (1921) observed the mutagenic effects of X-rays on the insect drosophilla.
- Recurrent or reciprocal selection methods are used in improving simultaneously horticultural characters while incorporating disease resistance.
- Bulk Segregant Analysis (BSA): Technique used to identify genetic markers associated with a mutant phenotype. This allows discoveryofgenes conferring disease resistance or susceptibility.
- Method adopted to develop synthetic variety: Additive genetic variance.
- Hayes and Garber (1919): 1st to suggest 'use of synthetic varieties' in maize for commercial cultivation.
- Basic concept in the development of synthetic varieties: Exploitation of hybrid vigour.
- Synthetic variety: Developed from-inbreeds, clones and open pollinated (OP) varieties.
- Inbred lines (4-6) which show good GCA are used in development of synthetic varieties.

- Complete genetic heterozygosity and heterogeneity is observed.
- Synthetic varieties are maintained by open pollination. These varieties require reconstitution after 5 years.

Type of gene action	Breeding procedure followed
	Self pollinated crops
Additive	Pureline, mass, progeny testing and hybrization and selection with pedigree breeding
Non-additive	Heterosis breeding and recombination breeding
	Cross pollinated crops
Additive	Synthetic breeding, composite & population improvement by recurrent selection for GCA
Non-additive	Heterosis breeding & population improvement by recurrent selection for SCA
Both additive & non-additive	Population improvement by reciprocal recurrent selection

***Purposes & Use of bridging species*:**

- To overcome sterility in interspecific crosses.
- To transfer disease resistance & other desirable genes from wild to cultivated species.
- Bridge crosses could be attempted to overcome distant hybridization barriers.
- Rootstock breeding in genus *Cucurbita* by utilizing *C. ficifolia* or *C. lundelliana* as bridge species.
- *C. edatifolia* is used as bridging species between xerophytic and mesophytic species.
- *C. moschata* is used as bridge to transfer disease resistance (PM, CMV) from *C. martinezii* to *C. pepo*.
- Difficult to cross between *C. pepo* x *C. martinezii* but can be accomplished with aid of embryo culture & this cross is facilitated by using *C. moschata* as bridge spp.
- *C. martinezii* x *C. moschata* cv. Butternut can be easily made with *C. pepo* cv. Scallop to produce three way cross which exhibit extraordinary degree of heterosis.

6.10 Mutation breeding:

- Majority of induced qualitative mutants are recessive and deleterious.
- Only few crops are highly sensitive to radiation and chemical mutagens e.g. potato, pea, tomato.
- In potato, tubers irradiated at beginning of germination yield 6 times more mutations than irradiated at dormant stage.
- In tomato, vegetative apex of *L. pimpinellifolium* express greater sensitivity to chronic irradiation than that of *L. esculentum*.
- In tomato, irradiation of gamete after pollination yield higher frequency of mutation.
- In tomato, EMS produce more chimeras than X-rays.

- In chilli, cotyledon stage is more radiosensitive among different stage.
- In chilli, ethylene imine (EI) superior to NMV and DES.
- In chilli, X-rays and γ -rays are found best.
- In pea, EMS produces higher frequency than DES.
- In French bean, EMS is more effective for producing resistant plants.

Crop	Dose (Krad)	Crop	Dose (Krad)	Crop	Dose (Krad)
Potato	5-6	Pea	15-25	Cucumber	25-40
Sweet potato	3-15	French bean	10-25	Carrot	30-50
Tomato	15-25	Broad bean	10-20	*Brassica* spp.	60-80
Brinjal	20-30	Onion	10-15	Radish	70-80
Chilli	10-20	Bhendi	30-60		

- Single seed descent or plant to row method is favoured to identify mutant.
- Chimera: Mixture of mutated and unmutated cells. Adventitious buds are used to present chimera in mutation breeding of potato.
- In chilli, male sterile gene mutant is used in seed production.
- In cluster bean, anthers of induced male sterile mutant differ in colour from fertile anthers.

Mutation with changed quality traits:

Crop	Mutagen	Remarks
Tomato	Gamma rays	High dry matter & sugar, uniform ripening
	Spontaneous	Increased β- carotene content
Chilli	Various mutagens	Increased capsaicin & reduced pigmentation
	Gamma rays	High capsaicin content
	Irradiation	High protein
	EMS	20-60% higher capsaicin
Sweet pepper	NEU, EI, DES	High dry matter content & high photosynthetic rate
French bean	X-rays	From yellow to green podded
	EI & DMS	Increased protein content in cv. Moskovsky from USSR
Cluster bean	Spontaneous	Green seed coat mutant
Broad bean	Spontaneous	Increased protein content
Sweet potato	Gamma rays	Change in tuber colour & variation in sugar content
Bhendi	Gamma rays	Increased starch content
Pea	Spontaneous	High protein content
B. oleracea (Botrytis group)	Spontaneous	Orange curd
B. pekinensis	EI & DMS	Increased ascorbic acid content
Fenugreek	MMS	Increased crude oil content

6.11 Polyploidy breeding:

A. **Euploidy**:

a) In Greek, eu means 'true or even' & ploidy means 'unit'.

b) Euploidy involves variation of whole set of chromosomes.

c) Euploids include 2n, 3n, 4n or even higher degree of polyploidy.

B. **Aneuploidy**:

a) In Greek, aneu means 'uneven'.

b) In aneuploidy, single chromosome within a set varies.

c) This variation may be either increase or decrease in the chromosome numbers.

C. **Polyploidy**:

a) Involves more than two genomes and is genometric mutation involving increase in the dose of whole genome.

Types	Number	Description
Euploids		
Monoploids	n	Genetically hemizygous
Diploids	2n	Two homologous sets
Polyploids		
Triploids	3n	Three homologous sets
Tetraploids	4n	Four homologous sets
Hexaploid	6n	Six homologous sets
Aneuploids		
Hypoploids	2n-x	Loss of one or more chromosomes
Nullisomics	2n-2	Loss of homologous pair
Monosomic	2n-1	Loss of one member of a pair
Double monosomic	2n-1-1	Loss of two non-homologous chromosomes
Hyperploids	2n+x	Addition of one or more chromosomes
Trisomic	2n+1	Addition of one chromosome of a pair
Tetrasomic	2n+2	Addition of two chromosomes of a pair
Double tetrasomic	2n+2+2	Addition of two chromosomes of two separate pair

1. **Haploids**: Produced by interspecific hybridization (e.g. use of *S. phureja* as male parent in potato); polyembryonic seeds (e.g. *Capsicum frutescens*, asparagus, *Beta vulgaris*); pollination with gamma ray irradiated pollen (e.g. potato, water melon, beet root); use of chemicals like laughing gas (e.g. potato, tomato, chilli, beet root); high and low temperature and anther culture (e.g. carrot, potato, pepper, asparagus).

   - Haploids can be identified/ distinguished by chloroplast number in guard cells.
   - Useful for production of homozygous plants; elimination of potato virus diseases which is not seed transmitted.

2. **Triploids**: Three identical genomes of which male and female gametes are non functional e.g. potato, water melon, beet root.
   - Poor seed germination; nursery sowing & transplanting required; late maturity; irregular fruit shape and size.
   - Triploids are highly sterile and do not produce any seeds.
3. **Autotetraploids**: Four identical genomes e.g. tomato, potato, cucumber, lettuce, carrot, turnip, musk melon, water melon, radish, cabbage, spinach, Chinese cabbage and onion.

Morphological features of autotetraploids-

Crop	**Characteristics**
Potato	Increase in yield in tetraploid form of diploid wild species
Tomato	Increased fruit size & prolonged flowering period
Brinjal	Resistance to insect & drought
Chilli	Increase in fruit size & reduction in fertility & yield
French bean	Late in flowering & bolder seeds
Bhendi	Smaller thicker darker leaves, inhibited growth, flowering, smaller fruits
Musk melon	Increase in fruit size
Water melon	Stronger fruit fibers, late maturing, reduced fertility; thicker & heavier fibers; reduced seed fertility; smaller fruits & lesser seeds; larger pollen grains, reduced pollen fertility; increased adaptation
Spinach	Increased fresh and dry weight; increased iron & total mineral content but reduced content of protein, cellulose, carotene & calcium
Radish	Higher yield & lesser bolting; improved root shape
Turnip	Increased yield; increased growth rate of root
Brassica oleracea (Botrytis group)	Reduced fertility
Brassica oleracea (Capitata group)	Larger compact head & shorter stalks
Yams	More vigour, increased tolerance to abiotic and biotic stress, high tuber yield

4. **Allopolyploids**: Originate through interspecific hybridization of two species, diverse in nature e.g. bhendi, onion, cabbage, cucurbits and turnip.
5. **Aneuploids**:
   - Primary trisomics: Tomato, beet root, spinach. Distinct morphological features, slower growth.
   - Secondary trisomics: *Solanum chacoense*. Dwarf, compact & slow growing.
   - Tertiary trisomics: Pea, tomato. Reduced height, yellow leaves, late flowering and maturity.
   - Compensating trisomics: Tomato.
   - Telotrisomics: Tomato.
   - Monosomics: Tomato, French bean.

6.12 Bio-technological applications:

- Conventional breeding may take support of molecular breeding approaches to tackle major biotic stresses in vegetable crops.
- Protoplast fusion to produce somatic hybrids have been utilized in number of vegetables.
- Anthers of capsicum variety 'Arka Gaurav' and tomato hybrid 'Avinash-2' respond to culture with embryogenic response without intervening callus phase.
- Triploid watermelon can be salvaged through embryo culture by using immaure fruits/ seeds.
- Marker Assisted Selections (MAS) are extremely important to shorten the breeding programmes.
- Molecular markers is important tool in understanding genetic diversity, evolutionay patterns, characterization of genotypes, identification of mutants, conformity of hybridity, identification of useful gene resources, setting of disputes/ claims on genetic material under patent regime, precision breeding, MAS, fingerprinting of genes, gene pyramiding, biotic/ abiotic resistance breeding in brinjal, tomato (leaf curl), cauliflower (fruit borer), cabbage (diamond back moth), potato (virus Y), and improved shelf life and quality traits, etc.
- Plant regeneration:

Crop	Explants	Crops	Explants
Solanum lycopersicoides	Leaf	*Ipomoea batatas*	Shoot buds, leaf, shoot tip, root
S. tuberosum	Shoot buds, roots	*Zinziber officinale*	Rhizome buds
S. melongena	Hypocotyl, embryos, ,plantlets	*Dioscorea alata*	Shoot buds, nodal segments
S. sisymbriifolium	Parenchymatous cell	*Solanum lycopersicum*	Cotyledon, stem internode, leaf, shoot apical meristem
Capsicum annum	Hypocotyl, cotyledon, shoot tips	*Asparagus officinales*	Stem segments, shoot apex, plantlets
Pisum sativum	Shoot apices, epicotyl segments	*Phaseolus vulgaris*	Root, hypocotyl, cotyledon
Vicia faba	Apex, root, cotyledon	*Vigna unguiculata*	Shoot buds, axillary buds
Lactuca sativa	Apical segments	*Allium cepa*	Axillary & adventitious shoots
Allium sativum	Shoot buds & plantlets	*Brassica oleracea* (Gemmifera group)	Stem section containing axillary buds
B. oleracea (Botrytis group)	Curd, leaf, leaf vein	*B. oleracea* (Capitata group)	Shoot buds, meristem tip seedlings
Cichorium endivia	Suspended cell	*Cucurbita foetidissima*	Apical shoot tips & axillary buds
Citrullus lanatus	Cotyledon	*Cucumis sativus*	Main & lateral apices
Cucumis melo	Cotyledon	-	-

7. AMARANTHACEAE

7.1 Amaranths

- Eulogized as 'Poor man's leafy vegetable'.
- Classified as 'pseudo-cereal'.
- It is C_4 plant.
- Consist of grain, leaf, forage and ornamental types.
- A multilingual, multiscript amaranth name database is given by Porcher Michel *et al.* (1999).
- Rodale Research Centre (RRC) and American Amaranth Institute (AAI) are leaders in amaranth research.
- Short duration crop and yield high edible matter/ unit area.
- Warm season crop (most common vegetable grown in summer and rainy season).
- Valuable vegetable for malnutrition in India.
- Rich in vit. A (β-carotene 9200 IU/ 100g), vit. C (99 mg/ 100g), Ca (397 mg/ 100g), Mg (247 mg/ 100g) and iron (38.5 mg/100g).
- Anti-nutritional factors: Leaves have high nitrate (0.29 to 0.89%), oxalate (0.8 to 1.9%) and crude protein (20-32%) on dry wt. basis.
- Seeds rich in protein (15.9%).
- Dry matter content in leaves: 8-21%.
- Grain type contains crude protein and lysine.
- All green types (*A. viridis*) has low oxalate content than red and green-red types.
- Interspecific barrier exists in *A. cruentus*, *A. hypochondriacus* and *A. hybridus*.
- Susceptible to water logging.
- It can be grown in ideal soil pH 5.5 to 7.5 and upto as high as 10.
- Type of fruit: Urticle.
- Seeds have no dormancy period and no need for vernalization.
- Seed rate: 2-2.5 kg/ha for direct seeding and 0.5-1 kg/ha for transplanted crop.
- Seeds sowing depth: 1.0-1.5 cm.
- Foliar application of 1% Urea is practiced for higher yield.
- Optimum leaf/ stem ratio should be > 1.
- Pollination agent: Wind.
- Flower: Protogynous.
- Anther dehiscence: 11 AM to 1 PM.
- Basic unit of inflorescence: Glomerule.
- Each glomerule consists of male flower and number of female flowers.

- Percentage of male flowers in glomerule is 0.5 in grain type and 10.25 in leaf type.
- Monocliny and dicliny lead to cross pollination.
- Male plants bloom early and are poor yielders.
- Male flowers with 2-3 stamen and female flowers with 2-3 styles and stigma.
- Flowers mature from bottom to top.
- Arrangement and sequence of anthesis favours combination of self and cross pollination.
- Leaf amaranths are self pollinated due to presence of large number of male flowers/ glomerule.
- In grain types, crossing between *A. cruentus* and other two grain species is unsuccessful.
- Grain type amaranth is widely grown in Gujarat and Maharashtra.
- Grain storage protein amaranth contains 2-4 times more essential amino acids than normal amaranth plants.
- Bolting is serious due to planting of short day varieties in Nov-Dec., deficit N, poor soil aeration and extreme high temperature during growth.
- Height of cutting is important in bolting.
- 1st cutting: 3-4 weeks after sowing.
- Chhoti chauli gives 6 cuttings.
- Leaf to stem ratio in vegetable types varies from 0.93 to 2.48.
- Crop used for leaf production is not used for seed production.
- Isolation distance for seed production: 400 m.
- Seed yield: 450-500 kg/ha.
- Optimum stage of harvest: 25-30 days after sowing.
- Harvesting of grain amaranth: When dry matter comprises atleast 65%.

Species:

- *Amaranths hybridus* (syn. *A. quitensis*): Common ancestor for all three cultivated grain species. Weedy species. Red stemmed varieties as ornamental & green stemmed as vegetable.
- Characteristic feature of species: Pollen types.
  1. Type A: Pollens are micrograined.
  2. Type B: Pollen grains with small pores e.g. Hybrids of *A. spinosus* and *A. dubius*.
  3. Type C: Pollen grains with large pores e.g. *A. spinosus*.
- Section *Blitopsis*: Include leafy types and flowers are borne in cluster in leaf axils e.g. *A. tricolor*, *A. lividis*, *A. viridis*.

- Section *Amaranth*: Include grain types where inflorescence is terminal e.g. *A. spinosus*, *A. dubius*, *A. hypochondriacus*, *A. cruentus*, *A. caudatus*.
- Leafy type species: Day neutral and need frequent irrigation e.g. *A. tricolor* (n=17), *A.blitum* (n=17), *A. spinosus* (n=17), *A. dubius*, *A. viridis* (n=17), *A. cruentus* (n=16).
- Grain type species: Short day and drought tolerant e.g. *A. hybridus*, *A. caudatus*, *A. retroflexus*, *A.albus*, *A. graecizens*, *A. hypochondriacus*.
- Multi-cut responding species: *A. tristis*, *A. blitum* from which 6-10 clippings within 60-70 days duration.
- Crossing between *A. tricolor*, *A. cruentus* and *A. dubius* is not possible.

Botanical name	Features
A. tricolor (syn. *A. gangeticus*, *A. tristis*, *A. mangostanus*)	Best & major cultivated vegetable species (2n=32/34)
A. blitum (syn. *A. lividus*)	Bush shaped plants; (2n=32/34); very early flowering
A. cruentus (syn. *A. paniculatus*; Blood amaranth)	Short day (2n=32/34); grain & leafy vegetable type; high dry matter content; flowers under long day conditions
A. hypochondriacus (*A. leucocarpus*, *A. flavus*)	Day neutral (2n=32); white seeded called as '*rajgeera*' i.e. the king of grains); used for making *laddoo* & for ornamental purpose
A. caudatus (syn. *A. edulis*, *A. mantegacianus*)	Short day & ornamental species (2n=32) & grain type
A. dubius	Tetraploid species (2n=4x=64); occurred due to repeated hybridization with *A. spinosus* & considered as morphological variation; resistant to leaf blight; green vegetable type; superior among species for carotene content (15.4 mg/ g) & low oxalate content.
A. spinosus	Prickly/ spiny/ thorny amaranth; noxious weed & used as vegetable
A. viridis (syn. *A. gracillis*)	Green amaranth; 2n=32/34; plants cone shaped
A. polygonoides	Cultivated leafy type; 2n=32/ 34
A. hybridus	2n=32
A. graecizans	2n=32 or 34

Varieties:

- A Surinam variety 'Klaroen' showed tolerance to wet rot (*Choanephora* spp.).
- Species of 3 tepal group are more resistant to stem borer than 5 tepal type.
- Height of cutting of amaranths would appear to be important in bolting.
- Kannara Local: Short day responsive red type.
- *A. caudatus* cvs. Oscar Blanco, Noel Viet Meyer, Alan Garcia are grown commercially in Peru.

Name	Belong to group & method of breeding	Features
IIHR, Bengaluru		
Arka Samraksha (2019)	Hybridization followed by selection (*A. tricolor*)	Pulling type; high yielding; high anti-oxidant 499mg (AEAC units) & minimum nitrate content of 27.3 mg & 1.34 g of oxalates/ 100 g leaves; yield 10.9 t/ha in 30-35 days
Arka Varna (2019)	Hybridization followed by selection (*A. tricolor*)	Pulling type; high yielding & high anti-oxidant (499mg (AEAC units); minimum nitrate content of 27.3 mg & 1.34 g of oxalates/ 100 g leaves; yield 10.9 t/ha in 30-35 days
Arka Suguna (1996)	Pure line selection from Taiwanese introduction IIHR Acc. No.13560 (*A. tricolor*)	Pulling type, multicuttype without becoming fibrous & regenerate at faster rate; grown in kharif & rabi season; ready for 1st picking within 25 days after sowing & continues upto 90 days; succulent stems along with broad & green leaves; yield 27 t/ha; mod. resistant white rust; rich in Ca & Fe
Arka Arunima (1998)	Pure line selection from IIHR Acc. No.18384 (*A. tricolor*)	Multicut variety, brown-dark purple leaves; grown in kharif & rabi season; yield 27 t/ha; rich in Ca & Fe but low in anti-nutritional factors & resistant to white rust
IARI, New Delhi		
Pusa Badi Chaulai	Selection from indigenous material of *A. tricolor*	Suitable for summer &kharif season; green leaves with thick stems; response to cutting
Pusa Chhoti Chaulai	Selection from indigenous material of *A. blitum*	Dwarf; suitable for spring, summer& rainy season; highly palatable vegetable type; responds to multicut; widely eaten in Greece, Taiwan & Madhya Pradesh
Pusa Kiran (1990)	Natural hybrid of *A. tricolor* x *A. tristis*	Glossy green leaves; suited for kharif; best for rainy season; 1st cutting in 21 days & continue for 75 days; leaves soft green & wide; stem to leaf ratio 1: 4.6
Pusa Kirti	Selection from indigenous material of *A. blitum*	Green leaves; suitable for summer season; stems and leaves green & soft; stem to leaf ratio 1: 8.4; ready for harvesting after 30 days
Pusa Lal Chaulai	Selection from indigenous material of *A. tricolor*	Upper surface of leaves deep red or magenta &lower surface purplish-red; stemdeep red colour, red dye extraction; suitable for kharif & summer season; suitable for kitchen gardening & ornamental variety; high carotenoids (69.4 mg/100 g); GAE 113.4 µg; pigments for natural dyes, food additives; yield 46 t/ha
Amt-105	*A. tricolor*	Rich in carotene & protein
Amt-237	*A. tricolor*	-
ICAR Research Complex for Eastern Region, Patna (HARP, Ranchi)		
Swarna Raktim (2015)	Selection	High yield; resistant to pests & diseases

IIVR, Varanasi		
Kashi Suhaavani (2018)	Selection	Soft succulent green leaf; yield 30-33 t/ha; suitable for growing during summer & rainy season
TNAU, Coimbatore		
CO.1 (1968)	Mass selection from *A. dubius*	Grown throughout year; seeds black & small; leaf yield 7 t/ha; suitable for late harvesting; resistant to leaf webber, leaf spot & green type
CO.2 (1976)	Mass selection from *A. tricolor*	Tender green leaves; seeds black & bold; leaf : stem ratio 1: 8; early germination; suitable for early harvest; leafyield 11 t/ha; resistant to rhizoctonia leaf blight
CO.3 (1981)	Mass selection from *A. tristis*	Clipping purpose; seeds black; 10 clippings spread over 3 months; enhances palatability of cooked vegetables; yield (7 t/ha green leaves &3 t/hagrain)
CO.4 (1989)	Mass selection from *A. hypochondriacus*	Grain type; leaves, stems & inflorescence green coloured; seeds pale yellow & medium sized&rich in protein(19.55%) & lysine (7.5 mg/100 g);suitable forgreen leaf cum grain type; popping rate of grains about 2.5 times by volume; yield (8 t/ha green leaves&3 t/hagrain)
CO.5 (1998)	*A. tricolor* (single plant selection from A-166-1)	Induced tetraploid & very vigorous in vegetative growth; high biomass; double coloured type with dual purpose; suitable for container cultivation
Sirukeerai	Traditional cv. belongs to *A. polygonoid*	Suited for uprooting
PLR-1	Selection from Thiruvannamalai local Sirukeerai type	Early; mod. resistant to white rust; yield 80-90 q/ha (greens) & 200 kg/ha (seeds)
KAU, Thrissur		
Arun (1992)	Selection from Palapur local	-
Renusree (2006)	Selection	Green leaves, purple stem with low anti-nutritional factor
Krishnasree (2006)	Selection	Red amaranth with high nutritive value & low antinutrional factor
Annapurna	Pure line selection from *A. hypochondriacus*	Resistant to lodging, drought, leaf spot, alternaria & frost injury
ANGRAU, Hyderabad		
RNA-1	Selection	Pulling type; thick stem & broad green leaves
OUAT, Bhubaneshwar		
Utkal Mayuri	Selection	Highly branched; leaves multicoloured; suitable for kharif & summer season
Utkal Cheka leutia	Selection	Dwarf & spreading type; suitable for kharif & summer season
Other varieties		
Konkan Durangi (2002)	*A. tricolor* (local selection from Shirgaon area)	Upper leaf surface green coloured; lower leaf surface, pedicel red coloured red stem; leaves with petiole are used as vegetable; enriched with proteins & vitamins; yield 22 t/ha
Green shan	*A. viridis*	Tolerant to partial shade (coconut & 50% shade) &rains in Andamans
Lal Marsha	*A. viridis*	Tolerant to partial shade (coconut & 50% shade)

Inheritance of characters:

- Red pigmentation (*RR*) is monogenic dominant to green (*rr*).
- Spineness is dominant to non-spiny.
- Nitrate content: Quantitative inheritance.

Trait	Gene	Source
Male fertile/ sterile	$Ms_1 ms1$	*A. hypochondriacus*
Leaf blade red/green	*R/r*	*A. tricolor*
Stem red/ green	*A/a*	*A. tricolor*
Stem green/ white	*B/b*	*A. tricolor*
Seed coat black/ pale	*P/p*	*A. hypochondriacus*
Tall/ dwarf	*Dw/dw*	*A. caudatus*

Pests and diseases:

- Amaranth is susceptible to number of insects.
- White rust: Major disease.
- Leaf blight (*Rhizoctonia* spp.)

8. ALLIACEAE

8.1 Onion

- Eulogized as 'Queen of kitchen' by Germans.
- *Allium* is a Greek word.
- Onion is mentioned in Bible and in early Greek literature and pictures of it have been found on ancient Egyptians monuments.
- Consumed in the form of fresh, frozen & dehydrated bulbs & green bunching onions.
- Some species are grown for food and many are used for ornamental purposes.
- In India, there are reports of onion in writing from 6th century BC.
- Grown in Chinese gardens as early as 5,000 years ago.
- Introduced in India from central Asia.
- Leading countries for production of dry onion: China, India, USA, USSR, Japan, Spain, Turkey, Brazil, Italy and Egypt.
- In 2015-16, India's ranks 2nd in area (13.20 lakh ha) and production (209.31 lakh tones) after China.
- Productivity of Republic of Korea (66.5 t/ha), China (22 t/ha), Netherlands (39 t/ ha), Austria (64.1 t/ha), USA (55.9 t/ha) and India 16.1 t/ha.
- Production by season: Kharif (Oct-Nov): 15-20%; *rangada* (Jan-Feb): 20%; rabi (Apr-May): 60-65%.
- Maharashtra: Leading state in India with 23.4% area, 27.5% production.
- Productivity in India: Kharif (8 t/ha), rabi (16.1 t/ha).

- Productivity in India: Gujarat (20.0 t/ha) followed by Haryana (19.69 t/ha).
- Among 142 onion growing countries, India stands at 88th position in terms of productivity.
- Causes of low productivity in India: Cultivated under short day tropical conditions; use of farmer's own seeds and/or seeds of OP varieties; Indian varieties mature in 90-120 days while European varieties mature in 160-180 days; less production in kharif season while production of *rangada* season onion has many problems.
- Market share of onion hybrids in India: < 5%.
- 'MAHAONION': Organization formed by NAFED and MAHAFPC for export of onion.
- Due to NHRDF technology,
  - Area of onion has increased by 75% and garlic by 98%.
  - Overall 123% increase in onion production and 158% in garlic.
  - Per capita availability of onion increased by 97% and garlic by 127%.
  - Productivity of onion increased by 28% and garlic by 31%.
  - Growth of exports on onion rose to 539% and that of garlic by 580%.
  - Onion accounts for >70% of total foreign exchange earned from fresh vegetables.
- Pink revolution: Promotion of onion production.
- Largest exporter of onion in the world: The Netherlands.
- India's ranks 9th in export in the world (12% of global exports).
- Export of onion during 2016-17: 30.68 lakh tones worth Rs. 4,195 crore.
- Onion accounts for 77% of total foreign exchange earning among fresh vegetables.
- Onion export both in terms of volume (80-84%) and in value (75-80%) of total fresh vegetable exports from country.
- It accounts for only 6-7% of total production of vegetables in country.
- Lasalgaon (Nashik, Maharashtra) area is the biggest onion market in India followed by Solapur (Maharashtra).
- Consumption in India: 12 kg/head/year.
- Nutrition score of green onion: 65.
- Calorific value: 27 Kcal/100g.
- Low salt tolerant crop.
- Rich source of vit. B.
- Shallow rooted vegetable.
- Each bulb is composed of a photosynthetic leaf blade and non-photosynthetic storage leaf base (scale).
- Onion is heat tolerant due to cylindrical leaf shape.
- Edible portion: Bulb (modified stem i.e. leaf bases).
- Bulbs are stem bases with true roots below the stem plate.

- These are biennial monocots that are cultivated for bulbs as annuals.
- Yellow colour of outer skin is due to pigment 'quercetin'.
- Anti-fungal factor in onion is phenolic compound known as 'catechol'.
- Medicinal property: Thiosulfinate and Thiosulfonates.
- Tear inducing action of onion: Lachrymator factor: 1-Propenyl sulfonic acid (C_3H_6SO a volatile compound when comes in contact with eye, a small amount reacts to form sulfuric acid, causing burning and itching sensation that accompany the tears).
- Pungency: Allyl propyl disulphide. Present in small quantity (0.0005%).
- Red coloured and long day onions are more pungent than white onion.
- Alliin: Colourless, odourless, water soluble amino acid present in bulbs.
- Diallyl thiosulphinate (Allicin): Sulphur containing compound gives typical odour to fresh onion.
- Allinase: Enzyme present in onion.
- Fructan: Soluble carbohydrate present in onion. It is associated with lower rate of colorectal cancer.
- High fructan concentration is associated with higher pungency and lower dormancy.
- Food storage in matured bulb consist primarily of sucrose.
- Vanadium accumulation in root cells is useful against sun stroke and cholera.
- Rainy season cultivation meets the demand of fresh bulbs in off season.
- Onion is predominantly rabi season crop (60% production), but kharif and late kharif or early rabi season i.e. *rangada* crop accounts for 40% of total production.
- *Rangada* onion produces inferior quality bulbs and shows poor keeping quality in storage.
- Kharif onion is most crucial in controlling market prices.
- Photo-thermo sensitive crop.
- Optimum temperature for seed germination: 20-25^{0}C.
- Optimum temperature for bulb development: 15.5-21^{0}C.
- To initiate flowering, plants must have 4 or more leaves & attained dia. of 1/3rd inch before subjected to temperature below 7-10^{0}C (45-50^{0}F) for flower initiation. It is not induced by photoperiod.
- Bolting: Premature production of seed stalks.
- White coloured onions are more susceptible to bolting.
- Rabi onion starts bolting at 20-25^{0}C.
- Early and late transplanting (use of over aged seedlings) induces bolting in kharif and rabi onion, respectively.
- Temperature is more important than day length in seed production while day length is more important for bulb production.
- Short day cvs. are adapted to south of 30^{0}N; medium day length adapted to 30^{0}N latitude to 38^{0}N and long day cvs. are adapted for spring seson & long term storage.

- Short day onions form bulbs when day length exceeds approximately 11.5 h.
- Long day types require 14 h or more day length to form bulbs.
- Onion cultivars grown in plains of India are short day types.
- Long day types are more useful in hilly areas than short day types.
- Optimum soil pH for growth: 5.8-8; for muck soil (5.3-6.5); for mineral soil (6.2-6.8).
- Scale leaf differentiation is controlled by long photoperiod.
- Flower colour: White or bluish.
- Highly cross pollinated due to protandry.
- Pollination agents: Honey bees, rock bees and blow flies (excellent pollinator).
- Inflorescence: Few to > 2000 flowers/ umbel.
- Flower stalk (scape or seed stem) bears umbel consisting of spath & flowers.
- Flowering lasts for 2 or more weeks.
- Individual flower consist of 6 stamens (3 inner & 3 outer) + 3 carpels untied with 1 pistil + 6 perianth segments.
- Pistil has 3 locules & each containing 2 ovules.
- Plants grown from seeds, usually produce only one seed stem or flower stalk.
- Anthesis time: 5-9 AM.
- Fruit: Black, three celled capsule & 2 seeds in each locule of the capsule.
- Pollen grains can be stored for short term at 5^{0}C and 20^{0}C in silica gel and cryopreserved for long term storage (up to 11 years).
- The most and recent systematic survey of crossability in cultivated *Alliums* reported by Raamdonk *et al.* (2003).
- Commercially utilized taxonomic classification: Hanelt (1990).
- Systematic R & D programmes were started in 1960 at Pimpalgaon Baswant, Nashik, Maharashtra.
- Hybrid onion programme was originated in 1925.
- Multiplasms: Term coined by Grogen (1971).
- Gene pool concept was given by Harlan and de Wet (1971).
- Selfing and mass breeding technique: Developed by Jones and Mann in 1963.
- Male sterility (MS) is observed in long day cultivars.
- MS mechanism involves both, genetic and cytoplasmic factors.
- Most widely used source of CMS: ‘S’ cytoplasm.
- CMS is due to incompatibility between mitochondrial and nuclear genomes.
- Onion chloroplast genome inherited through maternal inheritance.
- Mitochondrial gene mutations lead to male sterility.
- Male sterility is maintained only when: (a) Female line is homozygous for Sms/ms and (b) Male line is homozygous for Mms/ms and acts as maintainer.

- Historical pedigree number of male sterility is identified as 13-53 (cv. Italian Red). In this cv. bulbils are produced among florets instead of seeds.
- In onion, 2 types of male sterility systems viz. CMS-S (Jones and Emsweller, 1936) and CMS-T (Berninger, 1965) have been utilized for F_1 hybrid cultivars.
- 1st source of CMS (S cytoplasm) was indentified in cv. Italian Red grown in California and propagated from bulbils by Dr. H.A. Jones and Clarke (1925). It is widely used in seed production.
- 2nd source of CMS (T-cytoplasm) was discovered in French cv. Jaune Paille Des Venus which is different than that from 'Italian Red'.
- CMS discovered in French onion is difficult to use due to its complex inheritance.
- From India, male sterility was identified in cv. Nashik White Globe.
- A single restorer-of fertility locus (*Ms*) is involved in fertility restoration of the CMS-S system (Jones and Clarke, 1943), whereas three independent loci control fertility restoration of male sterility in CMS-T cytoplasm (Schweisguth, 1973).
- De Courcel *et al.* (1989) showed via molecular marker analysis that there are 2 groups of cytoplasms namely S and M group.
- Presently, CGMS is used worldwide for commercial exploitation of heterosis.
- In USA, several F_1 hybrids developed by Dr. Jones (1956) using MS lines e.g. Abundance, Aristocrat, Bonanza, Champion, Contender, Elite, Epoch, Encore, Surprise and White Granex.
- Dr. Jones (spent his life for productive research with onion) was nick named as 'Mr. Onion'.
- In onion, male sterile line has been isolated in cv. Pusa Red at IARI, New Delhi.
- Brown seeded MS lines and black seeded pollen parent can be used for producing F_1 hybrid seeds.
- Maleic hydrazide @ 0.1% is recommended for induction of male sterility.
- Ethephon 4,000 ppm or cycocel 2,000 ppm sprayed 85 days after transplanting gives more yield with minimum premature bolting in kharif onion.
- Diploid apogamia is reported in onion.
- Common onion is commercially propagated by seed.
- Best planting density for cultivation: 15 cm x 10 cm.
- Seed rate: Kharif (12-15 kg/ha); Rabi (10-12 kg/ha) and 750 kg bulbs/ ha.
- About 5-8 kg seeds are required to raise small bulbs called 'sets' in 200 m^2 area.
- For production of better quality 'sets', sowing of onion seed @ 15 g/ sq.m. in last week of December is suggested.
- About 12-15 quintals onion 'sets' of 1.5-2.0 cm dia. are required for planting 1 ha area.
- Sets are planted in mid-August to get crop by mid-November.

- Onion grown through 'sets' shows better performance (mature 3-4 weeks earlier & give higher yield) over seedling raised crop.
- Kharif onion production through 'sets' is most economical.
- Smaller sets (< 0.4 inch dia.) are used for dry bulb onion and larger sets (> 0.75 inch dia.) are more suitable for green onion.
- Very small sized sets results in more splits, doubles and bolters.
- Short day cultivars are grown to regions of 28^0 latitude and long day cultivars to $>35^0$ latitude while intermediate types are grown to regions between $32\text{-}40^0$ latitude.
- Mechanization reduces cost of cultivation up to 35%.
- Crop can be successfully grown with sprinkler/ drip irrigation.
- In onion, irrigation should be stopped 3 weeks before harvest to ensure better quality.
- Harvesting stage: Neck fall (25-50%) and drying of tops.
- Harvesting period: Kharif (Oct-Dec); late kharif (Jan-March); rabi i.e. summer crop (April-June).
- Harvesting stage of seed heads: Seeds inside capsules become black and 20-25% black seeds are exposed.
- Onion crop raised through 'sets' takes 90-110 days for maturity and through seeds require 150-180 days for bulb maturity.
- Long day onion bulbs take 150 days for bulb maturity.
- Lean period for onion: July-Sept.
- Premature harvest forms a thick neck bulb. Bulbs with thick neck do not store well.
- Buds developed in the axils of leaf bases if stimulated into growth, forms double bulbs.
- Early harvest results in sprouting of bulbs while late larvest results in formation of secondary roots during storage.
- Pre-emergent herbicide: Pendimethalin 30 EC @ 3.5 l/ha or Oxyflurofan 0.15 EC @ 0.25 kg/ha.
- Critical period of crop: Weed competition 30-60 days after planting.
- Yield reduction due to weeds: 72%.
- Flower induction: GA_3 @ 300 ppm.
- GA_3 at 40 ppm is recommended for increasing bulb yield. Six weeks old seedlings are dipped for 24 h before transplanting.
- Zinc application @ 1-3 ppm increases yield and improves quality.
- TSS and polar diameter: Important traits in breeding for high keeping quality.
- Long day onions are primarily storage onions while short day onions are for fresh markets.
- Red skin varieties have good storage capacity while yellow and white skinned varieties are difficult to store and storage losses are up to 80-100%.
- Kharif or late kharif crop does not store well while onion from rabi crop is store worthy.

- Twisted neck bulbs are good for storage.
- Post harvest storage losses in onion: 40-50%.
- Rabi onion post harvest losses: 30-70% (sprouting-17%, rotting-25%, desiccation-28%).
- Sprouting and rotting is lower in *rangada* onion.
- Growth regulator for inhibiting excess growth: Chloromequat chloride @ 6ml/lit.
- Reduction of sprouting: Gamma rays @ 60 Gy.
- Quality of onion and garlic cannot be improved after harvesting.
- Curing period in onion and garlic: 2-3 weeks.
- Curing aids in development of skin colour, strengthen skin and practiced to reduce misture content and remove field heat before storage.
- Field curing by window method (shade curing) along with tops for 10-15 days and 2.5 cm neck are effective in reducing storage losses.
- Maximum safe temperature for curing at field: 37.8^{0}C for 3-5 days.
- In low temperature areas, bulbs are cured artificially by passing hot air at 47^{0}C for 16 h.
- If onion stored along with leaves, it retains more shelf life.
- Storage structures are called *'chawl'*.
- Two tier/ three tier structures were developed by NHRDF at Pimpalgaon.
- Multistoried structure for commercial purpose. In one rack, 20 tons onion can be stored for 4 months.
- Within 4 months storage, less than 15% losses occur.
- Ambient storage conditions in storage structure: 30-35^{0}C at 65-70% R.H.
- Cold storage conditions: 0-2^{0}C at 65-75% R.H.
- CA storage conditions: 0-5^{0}C at 1-2% O_2, 0-10% CO_2.
- Dampness in storage causes rot and mold growth. High moisture and temperature may induce new growth.
- Bermuda types have poor keeping qualities and can be stored for no longer than 2 months.
- Spanish types can keep for 4-5 months.
- Late maturing, pungent types having more bulb dry matter, can be stored upto 8 months.
- Bulbs started from sets do not store well and are used soon after harvest.
- Bulbs are dormant at harvest for a period of 6-8 weeks.
- Green bunching onions are highly perishable and if held at 0^{0}C and packed in polyethylene film may be stored upto 3-4 weeks.
- Seed viability: 1-2 year.
- Seed viability remains high for longer period (5 years) at 5% seed moisture.

- Storage in liquid nitrogen retains seed vigour in absence of cold storage facility.
- *A. cepa* seeds can be stored in liquid nitrogen for 10 years and *Allium* spp. for 3 years without loss of viability.
- Seeds exhibit orthodox storage behaviour.
- Largest cultivated onion: Orange and yellow skinned.
- Red & yellow skinned varieties are less suited for processing due to presence pf anthocyanin and quercetin, respectively.
- White onion varieties are suitable for dehydration and used in Ayurvedic medicines.
- Quality parameter for export of dehydrated onion: White colour, small neck, high TSS (18-21%), high insoluble solid content (not <1%), low reducing sugar and low pungency.
- Desirable drying ratio for onion: 6:1.
- Indian varieties have drying ratio: 10:1.
- Maximum pungency is at just before the tops begin to fall over.
- Punguncy is estimated by measuring pyruvic acid concentration in juice using Schwimmer and Weston (1960) method and expressed in μmoles/ ml.
- Ideal pyruvic acid for dehydration industry: 0.50-0.70 %.
- Seed are dried to 6% moisture level.
- In Sudan, onions are stored in palm leaf barns called '*rakubas*'.
- Plastic woven ventilated bags of 25 kg capacity are used for onion packing.
- Onion packing in jute bags having 9 x 10 mesh per sq. inch helps in minimize loss.
- The cost of production per unit of Indian onion is quite higher as compared to other countries.
- Onion grown for bulb production is more remunerative than seed production.
- Importance of silicon: Increase chlorophyll content, bulb size, bulb weight and production upto 31%. Silicon spray during storage helps in preventing fungal rot, reduction in weight loss, retain colour and increases shelf life.
- Frequently used method for haploid induction: *In vitro* gynogenesis using isolated flower bud culture.
- Specific requirements for export purpose: Light to dark red, globose, 4-6 cm size and strongly pungent (for Bangladesh, South-East Asia and Gulf countries); yellow or brown, globose and 4-6 cm in size (for European and Japan market).
- Value added products: Onion flakes, powder, paste, pickles.

Species:

- Onions are divided into 3 groups & each reflect different growth characters (Jones and Mann, 1963) viz.

a) Common onion: Bulb form single plant, propagated from true seeds, inflorescence does not form bulblets, exist extremens of bulb shapes, dry scale colour & pungency e.g. different onion cvs. belong to this group.
b) Aggregatum group: Plants form many lateral bulbs or shoots, inflorescence lacks bulblets, sterile seed production and propagated by vegetative means e.g. potato or multiplier onions, ever-ready onion and shallots.
c) Proliferous group: Ground bulbs are poorly developed, inflorescence bears bulblets, true seed is usually lacking, reproduced by vegetative inflorescence & bulblets e.g. tree onion, top-set onions & Egyptian onions.

- Central Asia: Primary centre of origin.
- Central Asian spp.: *Allium vavilovii*, *A. oschaninii*, *A. galanthum* are crossable with *A. cepa* but interspecific hybrids are highly infertile.
- *A. galanthum*, *A. vavilovii*, *A. oschaninnii* and *A. pskemense* cross with *A. cepa* but hybrids have low fertility.
- *A. cepa* crossable with welse onion.
- Pran (*Allium* x *cornutum*) is triploid (2n=3x=24): *A. cepa* x *A. fistulosum*.
- *A. cepa* and *A. fistulosum* show sterility barrier.
- Longest genome: *A. roylei* (63.44 Mbp); shortest genome *A. cepa* (56.18 Mbp).

Important groups:

Botanical name	Common name	Features
A. vavilovii	-	Ancestor of onion
A. cepa	Common bulb-type onion	Bulbing onion under long or short day conditions; produce single bulb; produce seed & no bulbils; several bulb shapes & colours; mild to very pungent; soluble solids vary from 4-25%; important in commercial trade; low in calories & 110 g bulb yields approximate 40 calories.
A. cepa var. *aggregatum*	Potato onion/Underground onion/ Multiplier onion/ Egyptian onion/Sambhar onion	Described as 'garden onion'; small bulbs; produce multiple tops, each of which produces small onion bulbs in clumps; may or may not flower; do not produce seed; propagated by bulb division
A. cepa var. *cepiformae*	Shallot/ Perennial onion	Commercially important in Europe & USA; they form into single bulbs following division & their tops die down indicating maturity; go into dormancy like common onion; propagated asexually; cross freely with common onion & produce fertile progeny
A. cepa var. *viviparum* or *A. cepa* var. *proliferum*	Tree onion/ Top onion/ Egyptian tree onion	Produces bulblets at the tops of the stalks instead of flowering
-	Ever-ready onion	Similar to multiplier onion but has smaller bulbs; Stearn (1943) described it as perennial home garden cv. giving rise to numerous bulbs each year; rarely flowers & reproduce by division
A. schubertii	Tumbleweed onion	Used as cut flowers, potted plants & in dry bouquets
A. fistulosum	Japanese bunching	Popular garden onion of China & Japan; cultivated round the

	onion or Welsh onion/Cibol	year; non-flowering look similar to *A. cepa*; never produce enlarged bulbs; shape of seed stem is distinguishing feature; hybrids have been successfully made with *A. cepa* resulting bunching type cv. Beltsville Bunching; hybrids are sterile; propagated by basal tillers & division of clumps; resistant to smut, pink rot, neck rot, onion fly, thrips e.g. Belts-Ville Bunching (sterile hybrid developed by crossing with *A. cepa*)
A. caeruleum (syn. *A. azureum*)	Blue globe onion	Three angled leaves with 30-60 cm long scape; used on borders and beds, as a cut flower, forcing & in dry bouquets
A. giganteum	Giant onion	Cricket ball sized head, tightly packed with hundreds of flowers set on a 120 cm or taller stem; as a cut flower, it can be stored in good condition for 3 weeks
A. goodingii	Goodding onion	-
A. cernum	Pink onion	-
A. wakegi	Wakegi onion	-
A. schoenoprasum	Chive	Known as wild type in North America, Europe, Asia; most variable type & difficult to classify; flowers purple coloured, opens basipetal; free flowering; slender leaves; very rapid vegetative multiplication & forms dense clumps; extremely cold hardy, winter dormant & can grow in high altitudes
A. tuberosum	Chinese Chive/ Garlic Chive	Widely cultivated in China & Japan for edible leaves & young flowers; produce enlarged rhizome but not used for food; propagated by division of clumps of rhizomes; resistant to leek moth & fusarium wilt
A. chinense	Rakkyo	Native to China & eastern Asia; grown in home gardens; when mature, leaves die down; seed stems are solid but leaf blades are hollow; flowers purple coloured & do not set seeds due to tetraploids (Kurita, 1952).
A. ampeloprasum	Kurrat	-
A. ampeloprasum var. *porrum*	Great headed garlic/ Leek	Ancestor of leek & kurrat; extremely variable; bulbs oval shaped to non-bulb forming type, bladeless & called as 'cloves'; umbels produce seeds & this spp. rarely produce bulbils, which is common in true garlic; seed propagated
A. christophii	Stars of Persia	Bears 8-inch inflorescence of loose, shaggy, metallic blue-violet florets; dried flowers are popular in market
A. flavum	-	Highly fragrant yellow pendulous inflorescence
A. galanthum		New source of S-type CMS;induces male sterility in *A. cepa* & *A. fistulosum*
A. karataviense	-	Used for growing on rock garden
A. komarovianum	-	New *Allium* vegetable commercially grown in North Korea
A. roylei	-	Resistant to DM& leaf blight; used as a bridging species to introgress genes from *A. fistulosum* into onion
A. sphaerocephalon	Drumstick allium/ Round-headed garlic	Flowers are deep pink to purple in colour or brown-red; used as a cut flower as well as a dried
A. victorialis	-	Novel source of flavonoids (quercetin & kaemferol)
A. ledebourinum	Asatsuki	-
A. nipponicum	French Sevat	-
A. ursinum	Ramsons/ Wild garlic	-
A. vineale, *A. triquetrum*	-	Noxious weeds in some parts of world
-	Pickling or Pearl onion	Small bulbs which are pickled & used as condiments

Varieties:

- Time required for an inbred development: 11-12 years.
- Sen and Srivastava (1957) were the 1st to attempt developing F_1 hybrids in 1948 using exotic MS lines with Indian local male stocks and 1st hybrid 'VL Piaz 67' was released for Uttarakhand (hills) in 1973.
- Small onion type: Banglore Rose, Podisu, Mutlore, Nattu, Krishnapuram.
- White skinned type: Alibagh Local, Junagarh White Local, JWOL-85.
- White onion has low TSS (10-14%) while multiplier onion has high TSS.
- Suitable for export: Red Creole, Granex, Bombay Red, Bermuda Yellow, Patna Red.
- RO-1: Recommended for Rajasthan. Resistant to purple blotch, stem blight.
- Suitable for dehydration: White Imperial Spanish, Rivrina, Late Brown, Country Queen, Verma Giant, Dehydrator No.8, Dehydrator No. 106.
- Produces bulbs under short day conditions: Texas, Grano, Early Cape Flats, Beta Alpha.
- Local types maintained by farmers: Nashik Red, Poona Red, Patna Red and Bellary Red.
- Sandeep Pyaz: Selection from 'Poona Fursungi' & developed by Mr. Sandeep Ghole. Crop duration 120 days; tolerant to white fly, leaf blight, purple blotch, sweet-pungent taste.
- Yellow onion varieties suitable for export to European countries and Japan: Tana F_1, Arad-H, Suprex, Granex-55, Granex-429 and HA-60.
- Sweet Spanish types require long day length to bulb while Bermuda onions require short days of winter.
- Intermediate and short day cultivars require long growing season (upto 180 days).

Name	Breeding method	Features
Cougar, Bermuda Yellow, Linda Vista, Mercedes	Introduction from USA	Bulbs yellow coloured; mild flavour; suitable for fresh consumption
Sweet Sandwich	Introduction from USA	Suitable for dehydration
White Spanish, Early Lockyer Brown	Introduction	Suitable for hilly region; long day types
Italian Red, Local Brazilian	Introduction	Resistant to purple blotch disease
Granex, Excel-35	Introduction	Short day cv.; bulbs yellow coloured; resistant to pink root disease
Cream Gold	Australian introduction	Can be grown at 30-35°Nlatitude; long day type; suitable for hilly region
IARI, New Delhi		
Early Grano (1975)	Introduction from USA at RS, Katrain	Bulbs yellow coloured; long day type; TSS 6-7%; yield 50-60 t/ha; suitable for salad purpose & green onion

Brown Spanish (1975)	Introduction from USA at RS, Katrain	Bulbs brown coloured & mild pungent; long day type; TSS 13-14%; yield 50-60 t/ha
Pusa Riddhi (2012)	Selection from local material from Nashik	High anti-oxidant (107.47 mg/100g)
Pusa White Flat (1975)	Local selection	Suitable for dehydration & flakes; bulbs white coloured; TSS (12-14%); yield 30-32 t/ha
Pusa White Round (1975)	Local selection	Suitable for dehydration & flakes; bulbs white coloured; TSS (12-13%)
Pusa Red (1975)	Mass selection from indigenous collection	Bulbs red coloured; less pungent, less bolting; good for storage; TSS 12-13%; yield 25-30 t/ha
Pusa Madhvi (1987)	Selection from 'Muzaffarnagar'	Selfing variety; bulbs red coloured; suitable for kharif season; yield 30-32 t/ha
Sel. 126 (2011)		Bulbs brown coloured; TSS 17±2^0 Brix; suitable for storage, drying, processing and export; yield 25 t/ha
Pusa Ratnar (1975)	Single plant selection	Bulbs bronze deep red coloured; more exposed (above ground at maturity; TSS 12%; yield 32-35 t/ha; less pungent; resistant to thrips
Pusa Sona (2019)	-	Globular;bulbscreamish-yellow coloured; TSS 10±2^0 Brix; pungency medium (5.0 pyruvic acid μmol/g); bulbwt. 70-135g, yield (33-35 t/ha); most suitable for slicing & table purpose; suitable for rabi; suitable for export to Europe & USA
Pusa Shobha (2019)	-	Bulbs brown coloured; TSS 17 ±2^{0}Brix; pungency medium (5.09 pyruvic acid μmol/g); bulb wt. 70-100g, yield (25 t/ha); suitable for storage, drying, processing & export; suitable for rabi
IIHR, Bengaluru		
Arka Vishwas (2011)	Selection	Small dark red colouredbulbs having dia. (3-4 cm); bulb wt. 40 g, TSS (16^{0}Brix); yield (30 t/ha); suitable for rabi season & suitable for export
Arka Swadista (2010)	Pedigree selection	Bulbs white coloured; oval-globe shaped; TSS 18-20%; bulb wt. 35-40 g, small sized (3-3.5 cm); yield 16-18 t/ha; suitable for fermented or bottle preservation & export
Arka Sona (2011)	Pedigree selection	Bulbs yellow coloured; globe-shaped; bulb wt. 140 g; TSS 10^0 Brix; bulb dia. 6.5-7 cm; yield 45 t/ha; suitable for growing in rabi season & suitable for export to Asian countries
Arka Pitambar (1996)	Pedigree selection from (UD-102 (white) x IIHR 396 (red)	Short day; bulbs yellow coloured; globe-shaped; weight 80 g; suitable for kharif & rabi season; tolerant to purple blotch, basal rot & thrips; suitable for dehydration; suitable for export to Europe, Japan & USA; yield 35 t/ha
Arka Lalima (1996)	F_1 hybrid of (MS-48 x Sel-14-1-1)	Developed by CMS line; bulbs red coloured; tolerant to purple blotch, basal rot & thrips; free from splits & bolting; yield 45-50 t/ha; TSS 12%;
Arka Kirthiman (1996)	F_1 hybrid of (MS-65 x Sel-13-1-1)	Developed by CMS line; bulb red coloured; free from splits & bolters; resistant to to purple blotch, basal rot & thrips; yield 45 t/ha; TSS 10%; shelf life 5 months
Arka Kalyan (1987)	Mass selection from local collection	Suitable for kharif season; bulbs red coloured; resistant to purple blotch; TSS 11-13%; yield 35 t/ha

	IIHR-145from 'Kalwan' tehsil (Nashik) of Maharashtra	
Arka Bheem (2011)	Tri-parental synthetic variety	Bulbs red coloured, globe-shaped; bulb wt. 120 g; yield 47 t/ha
Arka Akshay (2011)	Tri-parental synthetic variety	Dark red coloured globe-shaped bulbs; bulb wt. 115 g; yield 45 t/ha
Arka Niketan (1987)	Mass selection from 'IIHR 153'	Suitable for kharif & rabi season; bulbs red coloured; TSS 12-14%; excellent keeping quality (3-4 months); yield 37 t/ha; suitable for export to Gulf & Asian countries; tolerant to thrips
Arka Bindu (1994)	Mass selection from 'IIHR 402'	Small, bulbs red coloured; suitable for export to Singapore, Malaysia, Sri Lanka & Bangladesh
Arka Yogith (2019)	-	Bulbs white coloured; TSS 18-20%; bulb wt. 60-80 g; yield 25-30 t/ha; suitable for dehydration
Arka Pragati (1984)	Mass selection from 'IIHR-149' from Nashik	Bulbs red coloured; suitable for rabi; thick neck; yield 20 t/ha
MPKV, Rahuri & Dept. of Agri. (M.S)		
Phule Safed (1994)	Selection from germplasm	Bulbs white coloured; TSS 13-14%; suitable for dehydration & salt preservation; yield 25-30 t/ha
Phule Suvarna (2001)	Selection from local	Bulbs yellow coloured; suitable for export;TSS 11.5%; yield 24 t/ha
Phule Samarth (2006)	Selection from local	Suitable for kharif; bulbs dark red coloured; yield 20-25 t/ha
N-53 (1960)	Selection from local	Bulbs red coloured; short day type; resistant to thrips; revolutionized onion cultivation; suitable for kharif; TSS 11-12%; yield 15-20 t/ha
Baswant 780 (1989)	Selection from N-53	Good for kharif season; bulbs red coloured; TSS 11-12%; yield 78 t/ha; less bolting & twins
N-2-4-1 (1985)	Selection from local	Good for kharif season; bulb brick red coloured; globose shaped; yield 25-30 t/ha
N-257-9-1 (1985)	Selection from local	Bulbs white coloured; suitable for rabi season
Kagal Red	Selection from Kagal tehsil of Kolhapur area	Bulbs red coloured
DOG, Rajgurunagar, Pune		
Bhima Raj (2007)	Selection from 'B-780'	Bulbs red coloured; suitable for kharif & late kharif; bulb wt. 60-70g; TSS 10-11^0 Brix; yield 24-26t/ha; resistant to anthracnose
Bhima Shweta (2010)	Selection	Bulbs white coloured; suitable for rabi; bulb wt. 60-70 g; TSS 11-12^{0}Brix; yield 36 t/ha; tolerant to thrips; resistant to anthracnose; suitable for dehydration & table purpose
Bhima Shubra (2010)	Selection	Bulbs white coloured; suitable for kharif season; bulb wt. 70-80 g; TSS 10-12^0 Brix; capacity to tolerate environmental fluctuation; yield 18-20 t/ha
Bhima Safed (2014)	Selection	Bulbs white coloured; recommended for kharif; bulb wt. 70-80 g; TSS 11-12^0 Brix; yield 18-20 t/ha; mod. tolerant

		to thrips & foliar disease; suitable for table & processing purpose
Bhima Kiran (2010)	Selection	Bulbs light red coloured; bulb wt. 60-70 g; TSS 11.5-12.5^0 Brix; yield 32 t/ha; tolerant to thrips & foliar diseases
W-448	Selection	Bulbs white coloured with high TSS
Bhima Super (2006)	Selection from 'B-780'	Bulbs crimson-red coloured;bulb wt. 70-80 g; TSS 11-12^0 Brix; yield 40-45 t/ha; suitable for *rangada* season; tolerant to thrips & foliar diseases; suitable for making dehydrated rings & salad
Bhima Red (2007)	Selection from 'B-780'	Bulbs red coloured; bulb wt. 70-80 g; TSS 10.5-11.5^0 Brix; yield 48-52 t/ha; suitable for *rangada* season; stored up to 4 months; tolerant to thrips & foliar diseases
Bhima Dark Red (2012)	Selection	Bulbs deep red coloured; bulb wt. 60-70 g; TSS 11-12^{0}Brix; yield 40-45 t/ha; suitable for *rangada* season; tolerant to thrips & foliar diseases
Bhima Light Red (2015)	Selection	Bulbs light red coloured; bulb wt. 70 g; TSS 12-14^0 Brix; suitable for rabi season; yield 36-40 t/ha
Bhima Shakti (2010)	Selection	Bulbs red coloured; TSS 12-13^0 Brix; mature 125-135 days after transplanting;bulb wt. 60-80 g; yield 32-36 t/ha; tolerant to thrips & foliar diseases
NHRDF, Nashik		
Agrifound Dark Red (1996)	Mass selection	Suitable for kharif; bulbs dark red coloured; TSS 12-13^0 Brix; pyruvic acid 10.07 µmol/g; yield 30 t/ha
Agrifound Light Red (1988)	Mass selection from 'Dindori area' of Nashik	Bulbs light red coloured; suitable for rabi; TSS 13-14^0 Brix; pyruvic acid 12.20 µmol/g; yield 30-32 t/ha
NHRDF-Red-1 (L-28) 2006	Mass selection from germplasm from Punjab	Bulbs dark red coloured; TSS 13-14^0 Brix; very popular among farmers; yield 25-30 t/ha.
NHRDF Red-2 (L-355)	Selection	Bulbs light red coloured; mod. resistant to stemphylium blight; yield 30-35 t/ha
Agrifound White (1994)	Selection from 'Nimad area' of Madhya Pradesh	TSS >15^0 Brix; pyruvic acid 12 µmol/g; yield 25-30 t/ha; suitable for late kharif and rabi seasons
Agrifound Rose (1987)	Selection from 'Chickbalapur' area of Karnataka	Small bulbs (2.5-3.5 cm); TSS 16-18%; pyruvic acid 10.27 µmol/g; yield 19-20 t/ha; suitable for pickling & export
NHRDF Fursungi (2019)	Selection	Bulbs red coloured
NHO-920 (2020)	-	Suitable for late rainy season, yield 35-40 t/ha; not suitable for high temperature areas
Dr PDKV, Akola		
Akola Safed (2005)	Selection	TSS- 11.5^0 Brix; bulb wt. 128 g; yield 30-35 t/ha; field tolerant to pests & diseases
CCSHAU, Hisar		
Hisar-2 (1976)	Mass selection from local	Bulbs red coloured; TSS 11.5 to 13.5^0 Brix; yield 20-25 t/ha; tolerant to drought & salinity
Hisar Onion Selection-1 (2006)	Selection	Bulbs red coloured; less bolting; good storage life; yield 32-35 t/ha

RAU, Udaipur		
Udaipur-101	Selection from local	Bulbs dark red coloured; suitable for salad purpose; suitable for dehydration
Udaipur-102	Selection from local	Bulbs white coloured; TSS 12^0 Brix; yield 30-50 t/ha; suitable for dehydration
Udaipur-103	Selection from local	Bulbs red coloured; TSS 12-14^0 Brix; yield 20-30 t/ha
PAU, Ludhiana		
Punjab Selection (1975)	Selection from local	Bulbs red coloured; tolerant to thrips; TSS 14^0 Brix; yield 20 t/ha; recommended for rabi
Punjab Red Round (1993)	Selection from local	Bulbs red coloured; TSS 12-14^0 Brix; yield 20-25 t/ha; suitable for rabi
Punjab-48 (1975)	Selection from local	Bulbs white coloured; TSS 14.6%; yield 30 t/ha; recommended for rabi season; most suitable for dehydration
Punjab Naroya (1996)	Selection from local	Bulbs red coloured; resistant to purple blotch; suitable for rabi; yield 15 t/ha
Punjab White (1998)	Selection from local	Bulbs white coloured; suitable for rabi
CSAUA &T, Kanpur		
Kalyanpur Red Round (1983)	Selection from local	Bulbs red coloured; globular shape; TSS 13-14^0 Brix; yield 25-30 t/ha; suitable for rabi
Dr YSPUH & F, Solan		
Solan Red	AFLR x Punjab Red x Pusa Red	-
VPKAS, Almora		
VL Piaz-67 (1973)	Hybrid of (BYG 2207A x Shajahanpur local	Bulbs red coloured; bulb wt. 80-150 g
VL Piaz-3 (1990)	Pedigree selection of (MS BYG 2207A x local line from Uttar Pradesh hills)	Bulbs light red coloured; TSS 12^0 Brix; yield 20-25 t/ha
CSKHPKV, Palampur		
Palam White (2013)	-	High yield
TNAU, Coimbatore		
CO.4	Pedigree selection from (AC-863 x CO.3)	-

Private sector hybrids: L-819, Lal-4, L-744, China King, Ellora Wonder, Ellora Rose, etc.

Grading system:

Size group	Bulb dia. (mm)
A	10-20
B	21-40
C	41-70
D	> 71

Seed production:

- Between 35 to 40^{0}N latitude, onion is biennial in seed production and requires >14 h day lengths for bulb production.
- It is a long day plant but seed production is day neutral.
- In sub-tropical and tropical parts of India between 12 to 25^{0}N latitude, it is biennial but able to produce bulbs under comparatively shorter photoperiod (11-11.5 h.) during winter season.
- Seed production of kharif onion is by annual method while that of light-red coloured rabi varieties by biennial method.
- Bulbs required for seed production: 1500 kg/ha (2.5-3 cm dia.)
- Total seed production by public sector: 10 %.
- Seed to seed production- is method of forcing an immature plant into flowering without producing bulbs.
- Merits of seed to seed production: Low cost of production, higher seed yield, early maturity, no need of storage.
- Demerits of seed to seed production: Low seed yield and quality, impossible to select true-to-type bulbs. Undesirable for nucleus or breeder seed production.
- Merits of bulb to seed production: Annual method (require 1 year for seed production). Best quality, high yield and commercially followed.
- Demerits of bulb to seed production: More time, loss of bulbs during storage and more cost.
- Seed yield: 800-850 kg/ha.

Genetics of characters:

- Single centred onions produce round shaped bulbs with complete rings & are important for processing & better storage. This trait is conditioned by additive gene effects &may drift to types with multi-center onions.
- Heterosis is exploited all over the world in long day and short day types.
- Heterosis is manifested in maturity, bulb size & shape, storage quality and dry matter content.
- Close correlation exists between flowering & maturity i.e. early maturing cultivars flower early.
- Bulb yield is positively correlated with leaf length and early leaf collaps and negatively correlated with short leaves, dry matter production and late maturity.
- Bulb weight is positively correlated with neck thickness and bulb diameter. Highly heritable character.
- Yield loss is positively correlated with neck thickness, bulb diameter, sprouting, rotting and physiological weight loss.
- Negative correlation exists between TSS and polar diameter.

- Coloured bulbs are more resistant to mold than white ones.
- Yellow red colour of bulb is linked with *Colletotrichum arienans* resistance.
- Glossy foliage plants are more resistant to thrips than non-glossy (Jones *et al.*, 1934 and Peterson, 1947).
- Waxy foliage and seed stems are more resistant to purple blotch.
- Two genes control wax production in foliage and scape.

Character	Number of genes	Type of gene action
Male sterility	Chromogene-one (*msms*)	Recessive to fertility
	Plasmagene-one (*S*)	Maternal inheritance, expressed as in female parent
Seed coat colour	Monogenic (*BB*)	Black dominant to brown
Bulb colour	Pentagenic (*ICGLR*) & existence of complementary & additive genes modify colour	* Increasing intensity from light to dark colour is due to accumulation of microgenes each with a small quantitative effect: (*ll*- white; *ii*- yellow red; *li*- between pure white & coloured); yellow x yellow cross produce pink coloured bulbs; homozygous *II* produce white bulbs; heterozygous *Ii* produce off-white or buff coloured bulbs. * 2 additional genes *G* & *L* are responsible for variation in bulb colour (El-Shafie and Davis, 1967).
Bulb shape, bulb size, bulb diameter, bulb neck thickness, bulb firmness, bulb dormancy, foliage colour, TSS content, bulb storability, pungency & high percentage of dry matter, bolting resistance	Polygenic	Additive
Downy mildew resistance	Monogenic	Resistance dominant to susceptibility
Yellow stripe virus resistance	Monogenic	Resistance recessive to susceptibility
Resistance to Pink root disease	Monogenic (*prpr*)	Resistance recessive to susceptibility (Jones & Perry, 1956)
Resistance to thrips	Monogenic (*glgl*)	Resistance recessive to susceptibility
Foliage colour, foliage morphology, disease & insect resistance	Polygenic	(Pike, 1986)

- Homozygous *II* produce white bulbs regardless of other genes & known as colour inhibiting genes;

- Heterozygous *Ii* produce off-white or buff coloured bulbs;
- Homozygous *ii*, other coloured gene's *C*/- or *R*/- in homozygous or heterozygous state produce yellow/ red coloured bulbs;yellow x yellow cross produce pink coloured bulbs.
- Existance of complementary & additive genes modify bulb colour.

Onion trait	Genetic condition	Onion trait	Genetic condition
Albino seedling	*a/a*	Bulb colour	
Yellow seedling linked with glossy	*y1/y1*	Homozygous red	*i/i, C/C, R/R*
Yellow seedling not linked with glossy	*y2/y2*	Heterozygous red	*i/i, C/c, R/R*
Pale green seedling	*pg/pg*	Heterozygous red	*i/i, C/C, R/r*
Virescent seedling	*v/v*	Heterozygous red	*i/i, C/c, R/r*
Glossy foliage	*gl/gl*	Homozygous yellow	*i/i, C/C, r/r*
Exposed anther	*ea/ea*	Heterozygous yellow	*i/i, C/c, r/r*
Yellow anther	*ya/ya*	Homozygous recessive white	*i/i, c/c, R/R*
Pink root resistance	*pr/pr*	Homozygous recessive white	*i/i, c/c, R/r*
Male sterility	*ms/ms*	Homozygous recessive white	*i/i, c/c, r/r*
-		Homozygous dominant white	*I/I, -, -*
-		Homozygous dominant white (buff)	*I/I, -, -*

Diseases and pests:

- Most important storage disease in India: *Aspergillus* spp. and *Penicillim* spp. Rot.
- Onion smut (*Urosystic sepulae*): Outbreaks at temperature < 30^{0}C.
- Smut is avoided by seed treatment with captan.
- Most favorable temperature and R.H.for purple blotch disease: 28-30^{0}C and 90% R.H.
- Management of purple blotch: Spray Mancozeb @ 0.25% or Hexaconazole @ 0.1% or Tricyclazole @ 0.2% at 15 days interval.
- Yellow dwarf (poty virus, insect vector aphid) and Aster yellow, Irish yellow spot, TOSPO virus are viral diseases.
- Silver top or White blast: Thrips damage.
- Thrips (*Thrips tabaci*): Most destructive pest in India. Lady bird beetle is a natural predator.
- Irish yellow spot virus (known as Straw Bleaching in Isreal): Major threat to onion seed production in India.

Diseases & pests	Casual organism	Features
Purple blotch	*Alternaria porri*	Seed borne, very serious foliar disease; 38-62% losses due to this disease
Basal rot/ Bottom rot/ Plate rot	*Fusarium oxysporum f.sp. cepae*	Seed borne
Black mold	*Aspergillus niger*	Most common post harvest storage disease
Onion Yellow dwarf	Viral	Vector: Aphid or mechanical

Stemphylium blight	*Stemphylium vesicarium*	Major field problem & foliar disease
Anthracnose	*Colletotrichum gloeosporiodes*	1st reported in India in 1981; major constraint in kharif production
Downy mildew	*Perenospora destructor*	Serious disease in temperate regions
Smut	*Urocystis capsulae*	Soil borne
Thrips	*Thrips tabaci*	Global pest & most injurious
Onion bulb and stem nematode	*Ditylenchus dipsaci*	Through soil infestation
Twister	*Glomerella cingulata*	Acute chlorosis, leaves curled several times
White rot/ Sclerotium rot	*Sclerotium cepivorum*	Root rot
Pink root	*Pyrenochaeta terrestris*	Root become yellow, shrivel & die

8.2 Garlic

- Eulogized as 'Nector of life'.
- Frost hardy perennial crop used as spice or condiment.
- It is sexually sterile i.e. non flowering bulb, diploid (2n=2x=16).
- Garlic oil is used as flavouring agent, insecticide and bio-fungicide.
- Garlic has highest nutritive value than any other bulbous crops.
- Ascorbic acid content is very high in green garlic.
- It is good against patients of high blood pressure.
- Consumed as culinary, medicinal and anti-microbial purposes.
- Possess anti-bacterial, anti-biotic, anti-tumor, anti-fungal, anti-viral, anti-micotic, anti-thrombotic properties.
- Powerful drug against amoebic dysentery.
- Netherland leads world's ornamental *Allium* market followed by Israel, France and Japan.
- China: Ranks 1st in area, production, consumer and exporter in the world.
- Per capita availability: Highest in Republic of Korea (11.14 kg/ year) while in India (0.34 kg/ year).
- India's ranks 2nd in area and 3rd in production.
- Egypt ranks 1st in productivity (21.5 T/ha) followed by USA (18.6 T/ha).
- India's productivity: 5.43 T/ha which is far low compared to China (14.53), Republic of Korea (11.25%) and Spain (7.5%).
- Madhya Pradesh have area (22.2%) and production (24.4%) with (25.96% share) while Gujarat has 28.98% share in production.
- Highest productivity: Gujarat.
- Garlic fertile clones were discovered by Etoh (1986).
- Taste parameters: Sweet, salty, botter and pungent.
- Alliin: Colourless, odourless, water soluble amino acid present in uninjured garlic.
- Di-allyl disulphide (Allicin): Anti-bacterial sub stance and sulphur compound impartstrue garlic odour/ flavor & pungency.

- Garlic oil: A product of commerce.
- Fresh garlic bulb contains 0.1 to 0.4% volatile oil by steam distillation and chief constituent (60%) is Di-allyl-disulphide.
- Whole plant on steam distillation yields 0.05-0.9% essential oil.
- Red-purple coloured varieties are more pungent.
- Curing (an additional process of drying) is done to remove excess moisture, allows bulbs to become compact and go into dormant stage.
- Artificial curing by hot air blow at 27-35^{0}C take 48 h.
- Differs from onion i.e. bulb is a compound structure composed of several small bulblets called 'cloves'.
- Each clove consists of 2 mature leaves and vegetative bud.
- Outer leaf forms thin protective covering or sheath around clove and become dry and papery at maturity.
- Inner leaf has thickened base and forms total mass of clove.
- Commercial propagation: Cloves and inflorescence bulbils in some cases.
- Bulb (modified stem) type: Multiple bulbs usually 10-32 cloves.
- Cloves are well developed axillary buds within the thin foliage leaves and dry scale enclose the cloves stored food.
- Cloves are covered with white or pinkish parchment like membrane or sheath.
- Highly alkaline/ saline soils are unsuitable for cultivation.
- Seed rate/ha: 500 kg cloves (of 8-10 mm dia.).
- Methods of planting: Dibbling, furrows, broadcasting and seed drill.
- Planting depth: 1½ -3 times the polar diameter of bulb.
- Long, slender cloves present in centre should not be used for planting. Such cloves give poorly developed bulbs.
- Garlic is planted only in winter season on flat beds at 10 cm x 8 cm during 2nd week of October.
- Late planting result in harvest maturity without physiological maturity.
- Spacing for exportable bulbs: 12.5 cm x 7.5 cm.
- Bulbing is good when cloves are exposed to 20^{0}C or lower temperature for 1-2 months.
- Most of the garlic types do not bolt naturally.
- Many cvs. of have arisen as vegetative mutations during cultivation.
- In India, mostly short day types are grown.
- Short day conditions and cool temperature promotes vegetative growth.
- In bigger cloved type, seed production is possible only in areas having 12 h day length.
- Longer the day length, higher will be the yield.

- Optimum planting time: When index of visual dormancy break in cloves reach 75%.
- Optimum temperature for clove germination: 7.2-15.5^{0}C.
- Bulbing occurs in long days and temperature upto 25^{0}C.
- Under short days and high temperature, bulbs are not formed.
- Optimum soil pH: 6-7.
- Bulbs stored without stalks at 15^{0}C tend to break dormancy earlier than those stored at ambient temperature.
- Exposure of dormant cloves/ young plants around 20^{0}C or lower for 1-2 months hastens subsequent bulbing.
- Black garlic results from fermentation. Due to release of sugar and amino acid.
- Recovery of cloves in garlic bulbs ranges from 86-96%.
- Specific requirements for export purpose: 40-60 mm dia., with 10-15 cloves in each bulb.
- Irrigation intervals: During vegetative growth 8 days & 10-15 days during maturation.
- Irrigation should be stopped 3 weeks before harvest to ensure better quality.
- Garlic freezes at -4^{0}C.
- Micronutrient sprays (0.1% $MnSO_4$, 0.2% Boric acid, 0.02% $CuSO_4$/ $ZnSO_4$) stimulates dry matter accumulation in the cloves.
- Borax @ 10 kg/ha increases bulb size and yield.
- Sulphur application @ 30-50 kg/ha is recommended.
- Harvesting stage: Leaves start yellowing or browning and 100% neckfall.
- Harvesting months: March-April.
- Yield: 8-10 T/ha.
- Crop duration: 170-180 days.
- Garlic splitting is due to delaying of harvest.
- Losses due to sprouting are not more than 0.5%.
- Stored in ventilated place at 28-30^{0}C, 60-65% R.H., along with leaves for 6-8 months.
- Optimum cold storage temperature: 0-3^{0}C at 78-80% R.H.
- Cloves start sprouting at 4-18^{0}C.
- High R.H. (>70%) during storage develop mold and start root growth.
- Gamma irradiation with 2-6 Krad (250-500 Gy) of Cobalt 60 dose, given within 8 weeks of harvesting inhibit sprouting, reduce weight loss and prolong storage life for 1 year.
- MH spray @ 1500-3000 ppm 3 weeks before harvest improves storage life, checks sprouting in storage when tops are green and before neckfall.
- Top cutting/ neck cutting: About 2-2.5 cm tops above bulb should be left while cutting tops so as to have tight neck and avoid storage loss.

- Bulbs are cured for 7-8 days in shade with tops or after cutting tops leaving 2.5 cm stalk.
- Gradual decrease in garlic weight as period of storage advances.
- For long day varieties, seed material is produced at higher altitude of 30^0N.
- Total seed production of garlic: Only 0.8% of total requirement.
- Garlic is dried to 6.5% moisture and sold as powder or granules or sliced form.
- 2.2 to 2.6 kg of sliced fresh garlic yield 1 kg of dry garlic.
- 3.2 to 4.5 kg of garlic bulbs weigh 1 kg of dried product.
- Dehydrated products are packed in polybags 750 gauge thickness or in foil pouch.
- Dehydration is done by solar drier (for 2-3 days) or mechanical tray drier (55^0C for 7-8 h).
- Total production of garlic seed is only 0.8% of total requirement.

Species:

- Wild ancestor of garlic: *Allium longicuspis*.
- Chinese garlic (*A. macrostemon*): Long day varieties producing bigger bulbs.
- Crow garlic/ Wild garlic (*A. vineale*):
- *A. ascalonicum*: Most commonly used local variety in India known as 'onion of sambhar'. In N-E hilly region of India, it's key ingredient for making '*momo*'.
- Field garlic (*A. oleraceum*):
- Non-bolting garlic (*A. sativum* var. *sativum*):
- Bolting garlic (*A. sativum* var. *ophiosorodon*):
- Meadow garlic (*A. canadense*):
- Elephant garlic (*A. ampeloprasum*): Resistant to white rot, leek yellow stripe virus & leek rust.
- *A. giganteum, A. aflatunense*: Attractive coloured multiflowered inflorescence.
- *A. cyrilli*: Possess sweet odour.
- *A. macleanii*: Possess spectacular leaves.
- *A. hollandicum*: Persian alliums or commonly called as big-headed alliums.

Varieties:

- Ukrainian farm "MR ***Garlic***" has developed black garlic by special process (acidification) which releases sugar and amino acids.
- Fawari, Rajalle Gaddi, Jamnagar, Madrasi, G-50: Local types.
- Japanese Local, Solan: Largest bulb size.
- Exotic varieties: Creole, Italian, Tabiti, California Early, California Late, Extra Sweet.

Name	Breeding method	Features
IARI, New Delhi		
Pusa Selection-10	Clonal selection	Suitable for rabi
NHRDF, Nashik		
Agrifound White (G-41) 1989	Mass selection from local collection from Bihar Sharif area in Bihar	Small cloves& silvery white skin; bulb dia. 3.5-4.5 cm; dry matter 43%; TSS-41%; size index 12-15 cm^2; susceptible to purple blotch & stemphylium blight; yield 13 t/ha
Agrifound Parvati (G-313) 1992	Selection from exotic collection from Hong Kong market	Long day type; big cloves (5-6 cm dia.); creamy white with pinkish tinge; size index 16-72 cm^2; TSS- 38-42%; 10-16 cloves/bulb; tolerant to purple blotch; suitable for export; suitable for hills & north India
Yamuna Safed-1 (G-1) (1991)	Mass selection from local collection from Delhi Azadpur market	Big cloves with silvery white skin with 25-30 sickle shaped cloves; bulb dia. 4-4.5 cm; size index 12-15 cm^2; TSS (38-40%); dry matter 39.5%; tolerant to thrips, purple blotch & stemphylium blight; yield 15-17 t/ha; cultivated all over India
Yamuna Safed-2 (G-50) 1996	Mass selection from local material from Karnal	Compact bulbs & small cloves; 35-40 cloves/ bulb; bulb dia. 3.5-4 cm; size index 11-12 cm^2;TSS 38-40%; dry matter 40-41%; yield 15-20 t/ha
Yamuna Safed-3 (G-282)1980	Mass selection from local material from Dindigul area of Tamil Nadu	Big cloves; earliest maturity; size index 27-29 cm^2; TSS 38-42%; 15-16 cloves/ bulb; yield18-20 t/ha; suitable for export
Yamuna Safed-4 (G-323) 1990	Mass selection from Uttar Pradesh	Bulbs silver white; TSS 40-42%; yield 18-20 t/ha
Yamuna Safed-5 (G-189)	Mass selection	TSS 39%; tolerant to stemphylium blight, purple blotch & thrips; yield 15-16 t/ha
Yamuna Safed-8	Clonal selection	Bulb dia. 5 cm; suitable for table & processing; tolerant to purple blotch, stemphylium blight
Yamuna Purple-10 (G-404) 2019	Mass selection	Short duration; purple coloured; bulb size 4.5-5 cm; yield 17-20t/ha
MPKV, Rahuri		
Godavari (1987)	Clonal selection from 'Jamnagar'	Short day; pinkish white bulb; 22-25 cloves/bulb
Shweta (1987)	Clonal selection from Gujarat	Short day; small cloved; white bulbs; 25-26 cloves/ bulb
Phule Nilima (Sel-10-3)	Selection from local	High yield; purple cloves; resistant to pests
Phule Basawant (2007)	Clonal selection from local	Purple coloured bulbs; suitable for rabi
Godavari Safed	-	-
Godavari Gulab	-	-
TNAU, Coimbatore		
CO.2	Selection	Small cloved & white bulbs
Ooty-1	Mass selection	Bigger bulbs weighs 30-40 g each; yield 17 t/ha

DOGR, Pune		
Bhima Omkar	Selection from germplasm collected from Bihar	Soft neck & short day type; white bulbs, TSS- 41.2%; yield: 10-12 t/ha; storability of 6-8 months
Bhima Purple	Selection from germplasm collected from Odisha	Short day type; purple coloured bulbs, TSS- 33.6% yield (6-8 t/ha); storability of 6-8 months
VPKAS, Almora		
V-Lahsun-2 (VGP-5)	Selection from germplasm	Long day; bulb weight (40- 70 g/bulbs); TSS (37.3 Brix); resistant to purple blotch & stemphylium blight; yield 15-24 t/ha.
V-Lahsun-6	Clonal selection from germplasm	White bulbs; suitable for rabi
V-Lahsun-7 (2004)	Clonal selection from EC 158250	White bulbs; suitable for rabi
GBPUA & T, Pantnagar		
Pant Lohit	-	Mod. resistant to purple blotch; 15-18 cloves/ bulb having light purple colour; yield 12-13t/ha
UHS, Bagalkot		
AAS-2 (2016)	Selection from 'Vannur local'	-
CCSHAU, Hisar		
HG-1	Clonal selection	White bulbs; suitable for rabi
HG-2	Clonal selection	White bulbs; suitable for rabi
HG-6	Clonal selection	White bulbs; suitable for rabi
HG-17	Clonal selection	Least incidence of purple blotch disease; yield 12-13 t/ha
HG-19	Clonal selection	White bulbs; suitable for rabi
CSKHPKV, Palampur		
Great Headed	-	-
PAU, Ludhiana		
Punjab Garlic-1 (1993)	Clonal selection	White bulbs; resistant to purple blotch; suitable for rabi; yield 38 q/ha
Garlic 56-4	Selection from local	White bulbs; 25-34 cloves/ bulb; yield 15-20 t/ha
GAU, Gujarat		
GG-1	Clonal selection	-
GG-2	Clonal selection	-
GG-10	Clonal selection	-
DIBER, Pithoragarh		
DARL-52	Clonal selection	-

Grades:

- Grading and packing done in 18 kg, 25 kg and 50 kg.
- Export standards: 18 kg and 25 kg packing in perforated 10 ply CFB.

Size (mm dia.)	Nashik garlic	Madurai plain garlic	Madurai hill garlic	Jamnagar garlic
Big	30	20	35	35
Medium	25	15	25	25
Small	10	10	10	12

Diseases, pests and disorders:

- Stemphylium and purple blotch: Very serious diseases (20-60% loss).
- Blue mold:
- Fusarium rot:
- Bacterial rot:
- Mites:
- Rubberification of bulbs: Due to over irrigation or over fertilization. Zn and Mo deficiency.
- Thick neck and Pre-mature sprouting of bulbs before harvest: Due to excess N and soil moisture.

8.3 Leek

- It is closely related to wild variety of Great headed garlic or Sand leek or Kurrat (*A. ampeloprasum* var. *porrum*) which grows wild in Southern Europe.
- *A. commutatum*: Potential donor of leek rust tolerance and most promising crossable species.
- It was held as sacred plant in Egypt.
- Giant leek contest is held every year in England since 1880s.
- Alongside the daffodil, the leek is national symbol of Wales.
- Major producing countries: France, Belgium, Netherlands, UK, Spain, Germany, Greece and Italy.
- Hardy, biennial but grown as annual, tetraploid (2n=4x=32), monocotyledonous, and more hardy than onion.
- Plant is larger than onion but does not produce hard bulb.
- It is grown for blanched leaf bases and good replacement for green onion.
- Nutritive value is better than other *Allium* spp.
- Contain good amount of K, Fe and high Ca, low amount of β-carotene, & vit. C content.
- Edible part: Leaf bases and green leaves.
- Favourite vegetable in kitchen garden with economic part: Blanched stem and leaves.
- Summer leek: Yellow green and green blue coloured.
- Winter leek: Blue and blue grey coloured.
- Flourishes well in sunny and in shadow sites.
- Optimum soil pH: Neutral to slightly acidic.

- Propagation method: Seeds or tillers.
- Leek clones can be propagated by top sets or *in vitro* using basal plate, the floral stem.
- Optimum tep for seed germination: 7^{0}C.
- For indoor cultivation, 13-16^{0}C temperature is essential.
- One gram contains 300-400 seeds.
- Seed rate: 5-7 kg/ ha.
- Seedlings of 15-20 cm or 12 weeks duration and pencil size thick are transplanted.
- Transplanted into 15-22 cm deep planting holes at 12 x 50 or 10-65 cm spacing.
- Planting distance: 15 cm x 30 cm.
- Planting at 7.5-10 cm apart in rows give high yield of slim leeks.
- Deeply planted (7.5 cm) leeks are more drought resistant.
- Earthing up is essential practice.
- Harvesting season: Mid season types in early to mid winter. Late types in early to mid spring.
- Leek does not have dormancy period and not influenced by photoperiod.
- Need vernalization for flower induction and blooms in Europe during mid-summer.
- Removing sterile male flowers or wounding young flower buds can induce top-set formation.
- Blanching is important practice.
- Day temperature > 24^{0}C cause retarded growth.
- Suitable intercrop: Lettuce variety Tom Thumb.

Crossability:

- Methods of crop improvement: Family selection using system of half-sib families.
- New technique of breeding: Anther culture, seed grading using specific gravity method.
- Onion, leek and kurrat are interfertile.
- Leek is outbreeding species (due to heteromorphism & male sterility) with upto 24% self fertilization (i.e. self compatible).
- Suffers from strong inbreeding depression (40%) from F_2 generation onwards.

Varieties:

- Turkish and Bulgarian types have long thin pseudostem and Western Europe types have shorter, thicker pseudostem.
- London Flag and American Flag: Mature in 105-135 days and yield 250-300 q/ha.
- Yarana and Titan: Suitable for frost free regions. Resistant to rust.
- King Richard, Pancho: High yield, mild taste, early with long shank & suitable for mild winter regions for mini leeks.
- Prelina: Harvested in early autumn with moderate length shank.

- Autumn Giant Cobra: Mid to late in harvest, medium length shank & resistant to bolting.
- Cortina: Harvested throughout winter & moderate yielder.
- Autumn Mammoth-2, Argentina, Goliath: Mature in late autumn, high yielding with medium shank length & thick stems.
- Large American Flag, Giant Musselburgh, Arkanas: Suitable for cold winter regions.
- Carlton F_1: 1st commercial hybrid.
- Palam Paushtik: 1st indigenous variety.
- Miner: Pedigree selection from 'St. George'.
- Splendid: Pedigree seletion. Cultivated throughout year. Resistant to rust.
- Renova: Pedigree selection from 'Regions'; less tendency to form bulbs.
- Special 050: Pedigree seletion. Suitable for forcing.
- Regius 930/57 (St. George x Special): Good cropper.
- Resistant to bolting: Borde Pearl, Bluevetia Early.
- Resistant to Leek Stripe virus: Siegfried, Deverrieres, Autumn Giant, Trimphatur, Ligina, Winto, Siegfried Frost.

Diseases and pest:

- White tip (*Phytophthora porri*): Spray Carbendazim @ 2 g/litre. Winter leek cvs. Alaska (developed by mass selection), Carina, Titan, Pize Taker, Pancho, Musselburgh are resistant.
- Rust: Cause severe damage. Feed with potash fertilizers & grow partially resistant verielties.
- Purple blotch (*Alternaria porri*): Spray Dithane N-45 @ 2 g/litre at 15 days interval.
- Thrips: Spray systemic insecticide @ 1 ml/litre + sticker @ 1 ml/litre at 15 days interval.

Inheritance of characters:

- Many genes are inherited as tightly linked supergenes or gene blocks.
- Male sterility trait (shrunken anthers/ sterile anthers): Monogenic.
- Resistance to white tip: Dominant or additive polygenes.

8.4 Chive

- Popular crop for home gardens.
- Grass like slender leaves of plants are eaten and valued for onion-like flavour.
- Only member of onion group found wild in Europe, Australia and North America.
- Extremely wide spread in Eurasia and North America since 16th century.
- They are favorite in China as long as 3000 BC.

- During middle ages, chive was known as rush leek. In Greek language, 'schoinos' meaning 'rush' and 'parson' meaning 'leek'.
- It is cross between tetraploid giant form of *A. schoenoprasum* (2n=4x=32) x common diploid chive (2n=2x=16) gave a triploid (2n=3x=24).
- Production is confined to China and Japan.
- Used as fresh or dried with other vegetables.
- Cool season, hardy, perennial plant grows up to 30 cm height.
- Leaves are delicious mild onion flavour and used as antidote to poison & to stop bleeding.
- Flowers: Usually purple, open first at top of umbel, then successively towards the base, which is opposite to flowering habit of other *Alliums*.
- It is composed of clumps of small plants with smaller bulblets.
- Plants grow by means of tillering (development of new shoots from the base of the original plant).
- Grown in moist soils in damp meadows.
- It is rhizomatous, posses thin leaves with hollow solid scape.
- Leaves flat, grass like and keeled.
- Flowering period: May-June.
- Pollens shed within 24 to 36 h of anthesis.
- Anther dehiscence time: 9 AM to 5 PM.
- Capsular fruit contain small black seeds.
- Propagation method: Seed and division of clumps (6-10 bulbs) either in early spring or in fall season.
- Need 19^{0}C for germination and growth of seedlings.
- Plant 10-15 seeds / 3 cm cell.
- Harvesting: Leaves are harvested sequentially in several cuttings after every 4-6 weeks.
- Cutting of leaves stimulate multiplication of plants.
- Yield: 33,000 kg/ha.
- Succulent fresh leaves are sealed in polybags and kept in refrigerator retain crispiness for 7 days.
- Fully opened flowers are used in salads and sauces.
- Male sterility is conditioned by genic male sterility controlled by single nuclear gene.

Species:

Botanical name	Common name	Features
A. schoenoprasum	Ordinary chive	Hardy perennial, height 30 cm; cylindrical green leaves; flowers purple coloured; used for culinary purpose
A. schoenoprasum	Extra fine leaved chive	Hardy perennial, height 20 cm; very narrow cylindrical green leaves; flowers purple coloured; used for culinary purpose
A. schoenoprasum	White chive	Hardy perennial, height 20 cm; narrow cylindrical green leaves; flowers white coloured
A. schoenoprasum-Forescate	Pink chive	Hardy perennial, height 20 cm; narrow cylindrical green leaves; flowers pink coloured; used in flower arrangement
A. tuberosum	Garlic chive/ Chinese chive	Hardy perennial, height 40 cm; young leaf mid-green, flat, solid with sweet garlic flavoured. Old leaf tougher & coarser in taste; flowers white coloured

8.5 Shallot (syn. Aggregatum onion, Multiplier onion)

- Eulogized as 'Country onion or Potato onion or Underground onion or Sambar onion'.
- Messian *et al.* (1993) named shallot as *A. cepa* var. *aggregatum*.
- The series of shallot monosomic addition lines developed by Shigyo *et al.* (1996).
- They have delicate onion-like flavour and used in same manner as green onion or grown for their dry bulbs.
- Noted for its hardiness & early ripening than common onion.
- Produces closely packed clusters of bulb underground.
- Perennial onion which rarely produces flowers and seeds.
- Produces top-sets or 2 to 15 bulblets in flower cluster.
- Perpetuated each year by replanting some of bulbs which form a cluster on the soil surface.
- Amphidiploids (2n=2x=16) are resistant to pink root disease and suitable for green onion production.
- Tropical and sub-tropical shallots are tolerant to hot and humid climate, better tolerance to pests and diseases and longer storage life.
- Warmer temperature and long photoperiod favour bulbing.
- Seeds of tropical shallot are smaller than those of bulb onion.
- Major disadvantages in vegetative propagation: Low rate of propagation, large amount of storage space requirement, losses during storage due to decay and sprouting, perpetuation of soil borne diseases; need for labour prior to and at planting.
- There is gradual or fast increase in virus contamination with subsequent decrease in yield.
- Viruses can be elimated by meristem tip culture.
- 1000 seed wt.: 2-4 gram.
- Seeds have no dormancy.

- Shallot grown for green onions are pulled when their tops are 6-8 inch long and after they have obtained a minimum dia. of 0.25 inch.
- Shallot branching results from loss of apical dominance.
- Habit of branching differs from that of bulb onion.
- Water stress has no effect on the number of bulbils per plant.
- High density bulbing promotes earliness compared to less crowded plants.
- In field, shallot suffers from high light intensity, saline condition, high temperature, water stress, mechanical damage to foliage.
- Curing is practiced for small & multiplier onion.
- Specific requirements for export purpose: Bigger cloved bulb of bright red colour.

Varieties:

- Development of varieties was done by TNAU, Coimbatore.
- It crosses freely with common onion and produces fertile progeny.
- Delta Giant: *A. cepa* x *A. fistulosum*. Triploid. Propagated vegetatively and cultivated in small scale in USA.
- Lousiana Pearl: Tolerant to pink root.
- Half Long Jersey: French cv.
- Short day varieties: Tropix, Rox, RAM-7411, RAM-7419.

Name	Breeding method	Features
TNAU, Coimbatore		
CO.1 (1965)	Selection from local	Multiplier onion; bulbs red coloured; fairly pungent with medium TSS; yield 10 t/ha; suitable for kharif & rabi; vegetatively propagated
CO.2 (1972)	Selection from local	Bulbs crimson coloured; yield 12 t/ha; mod. resis. tothrips & alternaria blight; vegetatively propagated
CO.3 (1988)	Selection from local	Bulbs pinkish; TSS 13%; yield 16 t/ha; mod. resis. tothrips;vegetatively propagated
CO.4 (1984)	Selection from local	Bulbs light brown; yield 18 t/ha; mod. resis. to thrips; vegetatively propagated
CO.5 (1982)	Mass selection	Bulbs pinkish; yield 19 t/ha; vegetatively propagated
MDU-1 (1982)	Selection from local	Bulbs bright red; yield 15 t/ha; tolerant to lodgingdue to thick erect leaves; vegetatively propagated
NHRDF, Nashik		
Agrifound Red (1987)	Selection from 'Dindigul area' of Tamil Nadu	TSS 17-19^0 Brix; pyruvic acid 10.13 μmol/g; yield 18-20 t/ha; suitable for kharif & rabi
IIHR, Bengaluru		
Arka Ujjwal (2010)	Pedigree breeding	Bright dark red bulb color; suitable for export market; TSS 18^0 Brix; yield: 30 t/ha; bulb size 4-5 cm, 3-5 bulblets/ bulb; bulb wt. 40-45 g; dry matter 14-16%

8.6 Welsh onion

- Eulogized as 'Cibol or Japanese bunching onion or Japanese leek'.
- Extensively grown in Japan and China.
- Name 'Welsh' comes from walsch meaning 'foreign'.
- Evergreen, hardy perennial and 60-90 cm height.
- Leaves green, hollow & cylindrical.
- Small greenish yellow flowers appear in early summer.
- Nutrition composition/ 100 g edible portion: Fibre (2.6 g), vit. A (997 IU), calories (31).
- Leaves have strong onion flavour.
- Non-bulb forming species and possess hollow leaves (fistulosum means hollow).
- Pollination agent: Honey bee.
- Propagation method: Division of clumps or seed.
- Seed loses its viability within 2 years.
- Bottom heat technique between 15-21^{0}C gives high germination.
- Planting distance: 15 cm x 10 cm or 25 cm x 15 cm.
- It has high dry matter content is more pungent and winter hardy.
- Temperature for bolting: 10-15^{0}C.
- Harvesting: 1st harvesting 60 day after transplanting.
- Yield: 27 t/ha.
- Seed yield: 7-9 q/ha.
- Virtually resistant to all pests, onion fly, smut and pink rot disease.
- Carries resistant genes against onion leaf blight, pink root anthracnose, smut & onion yellow dwarf virus (OYDV).

Variety:

Name	Breeding method	Features
Pusa Soumya (2012)	-	1st bunching type onion for leafy vegetable & year round cultivation; multiplied by seed & division of clumps; can tolerate both cold & high temperature

8.7. Tree onion

- Eulogized as 'Egytian tree onion or Top onion or Lazy Man's onion.
- It is hardy, viviparous plant that grows as a perennial up to 90-150 cm height.
- Small, greenish-white flowers appear in early summer.
- It produces bulb underground and then at the end of flowering season, bears bulbs in air.

- Unusual type of onion that produce bulblets (2-16) at top of stem in place of inflorescence which are green and turn into brownish red coloured stems,
- Bulbs are very spicy hot.
- It is not propagated from seeds.
- Easy to propagate through underground bulbs.
- Air growing bulbils have small root system and each one is capable to reproduce another plant.
- Planting distance: 30-45 cm and in following year, it produces masses of small onions.
- Little tree onions are harvested along with stems and stored in cool place with ventilation.
- Resistant to all known pests and diseases of onion.

8.8 Rakkyo

- Grassy appearance.
- Hollow leaves emit onion like odour.
- Bulbs white, small, 3 cm in diameter.
- Each plant has several bulbs clustered at base.
- Propagated through seeds and division of bulbs.

9. APIACEAE/ (UMBELLIFERAE)

9.1 Carrot

- Eulogized as 'Poor man's ginseng'.
- Introduced in India from Persia in 13th or 14th century.
- Major producing countries: China, USA, USSR, Japan, Poland and France.
- China produces 34% of world's carrot followed by Russia and USA (each 7% of world output).
- Historically, carrots were used primarily for medicinal purposes.
- Carrots use as food crop was started only in 16th century.
- Grown for use both as fresh & processed form.
- Carrots are grown commercially in Europe for both fresh market (68%) and processing (32%) and extensively grown in home gardens.
- Crop is produced year round in USA as summer production (25%), fall production (35%), winter production (20%), and spring production (20%).
- Carrot roots are rich in sucrose: 10 times more than glucose and fructose.
- Main forms for storage compounds: Soluble sugars (34-70% of dry wt.).
- Fresh carrot contains 8.17% free sugar, constituting 3.39% sucrose, 1.05% fructose, 1.89% β-glucose and 1.45% α-glucose, 88% water, 1-2% fibres, 0.7-1.2 % proteins, 1% ash, 0.3% fat.

- 100 g fresh carrot contains approximately 3150 IUvit. A.
- Calorific value: 36 Kcal/ 100g.
- Nutrition score: 51.
- Anti-nutritional factor: Nitrates.
- Carrot extract is added to poultry feed to intensify skin and egg yolk colour.
- Carrot taste: Glutamic acid.
- Fresh carrot flavour: Volatile terpenoids (mono and sesquiterpenes) and sugars (invertase).
- Desirable level of volatile terpenoid (20-50 ppm).
- Low levels give bland flavour (i.e. lack desirable flavour) but roots are edible.
- Harsh flavour: High level of volatile terpenoid (> 50 ppm) and roots become inedible.
- Bitterness or off flavour: Isocoumarin (group of compounds called polyacetylenes which ranges from 20-100 mg/ kg of fresh wt.). It is due to prolonged cold storage in presence of ethylene and is quantitative trait.
- Edible portion: Enlarged fleshy tap root.
- Roots develop from secondary thickening of hypocotyls and tap root.
- Cool season root vegetable cultivated in temperatre countries during spring & summer season while in tropical regions during winter season.
- Tropical carrots are used to make sweet dish called '*Gajar halwa*'.
- Kanji: Fermented spiced beverage (juice) prepared from purple-black carrot.
- Seeds are aromatic, stimulant and carminative, useful in kidney diseases and in dropsy.
- Carrot seed oil is commercially used in France to flavour liquors and food seasonings.
- Steckling roots are observed.
- Edible root is actually an enlarged tap root that includes stem, hypocotyl and root tissue.
- For high edible quality, fleshy tap root should have minimum core (xylem) and maximum cortex (phloem) and core should be deeply pigmented.
- Outer core consist of thin periderm (cork & secondary phloem) and in this region only sugar is stored.

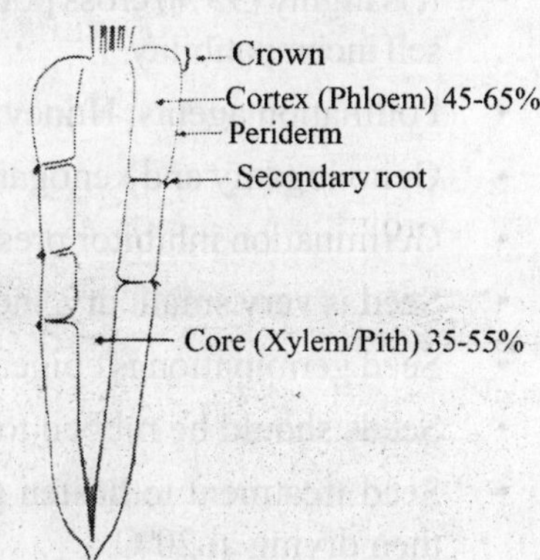

- Inner core has secondary xylem and pith.
- Coreless carrot: Core is small and deeply pigmented so that cortex and core are evenly coloured.
- Carotene is highest in cortex during initial development.
- Phloem tissue contains 30% more pigments than xylem.
- Conversion of glucose to sucrose form results increase in sweetness with age.
- It needs earthing up during root formation.
- Purple or red Asiatic carrots are rich source of anti-oxidants such as β-carotene, lycopene and anthocyanin.
- Good source of calcium pectate.
- Crown of root exposed to light causes 'greening' and lowers quality.
- Carrot gives high protein recovery per unit area.
- Inflorescence type: Compound umbel consisting small, white bisexual flowers.
- Flower position: Epigynous.
- Anthesis is centripetal and completed within 7-9 days.
- The 1st, 2nd and other umbels flower at an interval of 8-12 days from each other.
- Stigma receptivity: 5th day after anthesis and for 8 days.
- Fruit type: Bilocular schizocarp, which develops from two loculed ovary.
- Fruit dries & splits upon maturity to yield two mericarps (achenes) with one seed each.
- Flowering period: > 1 month.
- Primary umbel contains over 1000 flowers at maturity, secondary/ tertiary/ quaternary umbels bear successively fewer flowers.
- It is highly (95%) cross pollinated due to andromonoecy, protandry, male sterility and self incompatibility.
- Pollination agents: Honey bees and wild bees.
- Geitonogamy and xenogamy is also observed.
- Germination inhibitor present in seed: Carrotal.
- Seed is very small, dry, indehiscent one sided fruit.
- Seed germination is epigeal.
- Seeds should be rubbed to remove fine hairs before sowing.
- Seed treatment to hasten germination: Seed soaking at 20^{0}C in water for 12-24 h then drying at 20^{0}C.
- Osmotic priming increases speed and uniformity of germination and polyethylene glycol (PEG) 6000 g/litre.
- Seed rate: 5-6 kg/ha (European carrot); 7-8 kg/ha (Desi carrot).

- Sowing depth: 1.5-2 cm.
- Days required for seed germination: 10-20 days.
- Optimum temperature for bolting of European carrot: 5-8^{0}C for 40-60 days.
- Optimum temperature for seed germination and root formation: 18-22^{0}C.
- At 4-10^{0}C, very little enlargement of roots and very little top growth.
- High temperature (24-25^{0}C) causes thicker, shorter with reduced top growth and less flavoured roots.
- Asiatic types can form root even at high temperature of 25^{0}C.
- Top growth is reduced at mean temperature of 28^{0}C.
- Temperature < 15^{0}C causes slender roots with poor colour development, which is problem in winter grown carrots.
- Prolonged high temperatures bring strong flavour and coarse roots.
- Best temperature for orange colour development: 15.6-21.1^{0}C.
- Day length of 9-14 h has no effect on development of root colour.
- Best soil pH: 6.6-7.1.
- Carrots grown on heavy soils are likely to produce abundant leaf growth and more forked and rough and coarse roots.
- Sowing in north India: August- early October (Asiatic), October-December (European).
- Sowing in south India: January-February (Asiatic), October-November (European).
- Widely accepted method of planting: Ridges and furrows.
- Planting distance: 45 cm x 45 cm (Asiatic) and 30 cm x 30 cm (European).
- Over-crowding of seedlings leads to deformed roots.
- Seedlings do not tolerate soil crusting.
- Excess N affects sugars, dry matter, vit. C, carotene content and storage quality.
- Top dressing along with earthing up is essential after 45 days of sowing for proper shape and size of roots.
- Potassium is most abundant mineral in carrot which ranges from 443-758 mg/ 100 g fresh wt.
- Carrot grown on heavy soils is rough and coarse than on light soils.
- Hispid branches produced from 2nd year.
- Critical stage of irrigation: Root enlargement.
- Water deficit causes root cracks and misshapen roots and develops strong and pungent flavour.
- Excess irrigation after drought results white corky outgrowth (side root development).

- High temperature and irregular water supply: Cause deep depression on roots and rough root surface.
- Weed control: Stomp @ 3.3 litre/ha immediately after ridge preparation.
- Polycross technique: Highly effective in increasing keeping quality of roots.
- Roots with colour in the tap roots are referred as 'red tails'.
- Baby carrot (Cut and peel carrots): Bred for supermarket as a leading vegetable snack item e.g. Paris Market.
- Baby carrot: A minimally processed value added product.
- Harvesting stage: Root shoulders become visible above ground (3-3.5 months after sowing). It should be 2.5-4 cm at upper end (Asiatic); 3-4 cm root dia. (European).
- Average days to harvest range from 70 days (for fresh market) to over 100 days (for processing).
- Delay in harvest results in more root firmness and splitting of roots.
- Bunch carrots means roots harvested with tops and bulk carrots means roots harvested without tops.
- Root yield: 25-40 T/ha (Asiatic), 10-15 T/ha (European).
- Cold storage for 6 months at 0-4.5^{0}C with 93-98% R.H.
- CA storage is not successful.
- Matured topped carrots can be stored upto 7-9 months.
- Immature bunched carrots can be stored no more than 2-3 weeks.
- Immature topped carrots can be held for 4-6 weeks if hydro-cooled and packed in polyethylene bags.
- Plant regeneration by somatic embryogenesis: 1st reported by Steward *et al.* (1958).
- Cell culture: Rapid callus, protoplast regeneration technique.
- URP markers can be used successfully in genetic diversity analysis of tropical carrots.
- Round the year cultivation technology has been developed and found lucrative.
- Dehydrated products: Chips, flakes, and powder.

Species:

- Almost all species are diploid and basic number varies from X=9 to 11.
- Afghanistan: Primary centre of genetic diversity of purple colour (anthocyanin) carrot.
- Genus contains 2 sub-genera:
  1. *Eucarota*: *D. carota*, *D. maritimus*, *D. major*, *D. sativus*, *D. maximus*.
  2. *Gummiferea*: *D. cumutalis*, *D. hispanicus*, *D. fontanesii*, *D. boeconiel*, *D. gummifer*.
- Albino carrot (*Daucus carota*) and *D. sativus* are only cultivated species.

- Wild carrot (*D. carota ssp. carota*): Annual, known as 'Queen Anne's Lace' have winter annual life cycle. They are found in Asia Minor, Japan, Asia and USA and have same chromosome number 2n=2x=18.This is readily crosses with cultivated carrot.
- Wild carrot *ssp. hispicanus* is a source of gene for resistance to *M. hapla.*
- Cultivated spp. *D. carota* ssp. *sativus* is developed by spontaneous mutation and selection from wild species *D. carota* ssp. *carota.* It is biennial and requires higher cold temperature for vernalization.
- Cultivated carrot intercrosses freely with almost all of its wild forms and no incompatibility is observed.
- Both wild and cultivated forms of carrot are andromonoecious and protandrous.
- Green carrot/ Carrot fly resistance source from North Africa: *D. capillifolius* (2n=18). It is Southern Mediterranean species readily crosses with *D. carota.*
- Resistant to powdery mildew: *D. carota* ssp. *siculus*, *D. carota* ssp. *maximus*, *D. carota* ssp. *dentatus.*
- Western carotene carrot was originated or derived from eastern anthocyanin carrot as a mutant from ancestor *D. carota* ssp. *carota.*
- Modern orange carrots have narrow genetic base and have been derived from 18th century Dutch carrots.
- Neither polyploidy nor structural changes in chromosomes played any role in species differentiation.

Two major groups:

a) Annual/ Asiatic/ Oriental/ Tropical type: For root and seed production.

b) Biennial/ Temperate type: For seed production.

Asiatic/ Red colour/ Desi carrot	European/ Orange colour carrot
Syn. Tropical/ Eastern/ Anthocyanin carrot	**Syn**. Western/ Temperate/ Carotene carrot
Sown from August-January in N. India	Sown from September-March
High temperature tolerant	Cold temperature tolerant
Cultivated in short day conditions	Cultivated in long day conditions
Scarlet to dark scarlet coloured, coarse flesh	Bright orange coloured, crisp flesh
High yielding, low in quality, carotene but rich in anthocyanin	Rich in carotene
Produce seed under tropical condition in plains	Produce seed only in temperate region
Annual for root and seed production &do not require low temperature exposure for flowering and seed set in long day conditions in spring	Biennial for seed production & need vernalization (6-8 weeks at 4.8-10^{0}C) after full root development stage
Core is distinct with different colour	Core is indistinct with self colour, stumpy&blunt end
E.g. Pusa Kesar, Pusa Meghali, Pusa Vrishti	E.g. Pusa Yamdagni & Early Nantes

Use of male sterility:

- Male sterility (MS): It is cytoplasmic-genic in nature, determined by interaction of cytoplasmic factor (N for normal cytoplasm & S for sterile cytoplasm) andnuclear gene (dominant gene *Ms* for male sterility & recessive gene *ms* for fertility).
- The MS line has genetic constitution *SMsMs* or *SMsms* & male fertile are *NMsMs*, *NMsms* or *Nmsms*.
- 1st report on heterosis by crossing 2 inbred lines is reported by Poole (1937).
- Male sterile forms produce more heterosis (20-22% more) than using without CMS form.
- Hybrids obtained from MS forms yield 34-45% more, contain high dry matter & sugars, good root formation, high carotene content and possess high quality.
- Hybrids exhibit heterosis for carotene content, leaf and root weight (increased dia., than root length).
- Inbreeding depression is severe in carrot since genetic variability is consequence of allogamy.
- Male sterility is confined to 2 primary umbels.
- Dr. Pritam Kalia established CMS system in tropical carrot.
- Recurrent selection strategy used for trait improvement: Family breeding.
- There are 2 distinct types of male sterile flowers depending on the source of sterility inducing cytoplasm:
  a) Brown anther (*ba*) type
  b) Petaloid stamen (*pt*) type
- Brown anther type CMS (anthers degenerate, shriveled & brown, without any viable pollen) was 1st reported in cv. 'Tender Sweet' by Welch J.E. and Grimball E.L. (1947) in USA.
- Hanche and Gabelman (1963) reported digenic control of brown anther type sterility with either of two genes, dominant (*Ms4*) or recessive (*ms5*), produce sterility interacting with cytoplasm from cv. Tender Sweet (& produce 15 sterile: 1 fertile in F_2).
- Sources of male sterility genes viz. *Ms1*, *Ms2*, *Ms3*, *Ms4* & *Ms5* in the cvs. Tender Sweet, Imperato-58 & PI-169486.
- Brown anther type MS is present in all cultivated orange coloured open pollinated varieties e.g. Amsterdam Forcing, Flakee, Nantes, Vertau, Grelot, Parisienne.
- The petaloid cytoplasm known as 'Cornell Petaloid' was 1st discovered by H.M.Munger in 1953 in wild form of *D. carota* cv. 'Cornell Wild'.
- Petaloid type male sterile flowers, in which stamens are replaced by 5 petals & exhibit range of morphological structures (Eisa and Wallace, 1969).
- Petaloid sterility in wild carrot cv. Wisconsin was reported by Morelock T.E. (1970).

- Petaloid anther type CMS (5 additional petals replace anthers) in wild carrot is based on S-cytoplasm and 2 dominant nuclear genes with complimentary action (15 fertile: 1 sterile in F_2) (Morelock, 1971).
- Genetic constitution of petaloid MS plant: *SMsMs* and of brown anther MS plant: *Smsms*.
- Recent Petaloid type is 'Guelph Petaloid' was identified in cv. Ontario Canada by Wolyn and Chahal (1998).
- Commonly used CMS for hybrid seed production: Petaloid anther type because of higher seed yield.
- In USA, majority of hybrids are produced using Cornell cytoplasm.
- Gummifer male sterility(total reduction of anthers & petals in orange coloured carrots) is derived from wild spp. *D. gummifer* (single recessive gene) discovered by T. Nothangel (1992).

Seed production:

- Small or stock roots (stecklings) are stored for 6-8 weeks at 2.5^{0}C before replanting.
- For greenhouse seed production, vernalization of stecklings during storage is done for 8-10 weeks at < 5^{0}C.
- Roots are planted with crowns about 1 inch below soil surface.
- Half cut roots gives higher seed yield (897.15 Kg/ha).
- F_1 hybrid seed production: 4 rows of MS seed parent are planted alternatively with 2 rows of pollinator lines in isolated field.

  a) Seed to seed: More seed yield and certified seed production.

  b) Root to seed: More advantageous over seed-to-seed method due to a) Less requirement of stock roots; b) To maintain high genetic uniformity in hybrid cvs.; c) In hybrid seed production, female to male ratio of 4: 1 to 8: 2 is maintained. High quality seed production of nucleus seed and seeds of parental lines.

  - Steckling at 8-10 plants/m^2 is ideal.
  - For biennial cvs. Vernalization is essential for bolting.
  - Oriental types are sown during August-September in plains.

- Seed quality of main and 1st order umbel (7.5 g/ umbel) is better than that of 2nd order (3.8 g/ umbel) and 3rd order umbel (0.3 g/ umbel).
- Average contribution to total seed yield by main umbel, 1st order and 2nd order umbel: 21, 67 and 12%, respectively.
- Carrot seeds produced from primary umbel are more mature, heavier and high quality.
- Seed shattering occur to some extent.

- GA_3 @ 250 ppm at 8-10 leaf stage hastens bolting, flowering, seed maturity and increase in seed yield.
- Carrot has high reproduction potential upto 50,000 seeds/ plant.
- Seeds are flat, ribbed and spiny.
- Single pollination gives 1 or 2 seeds.
- Seed producers use colonies of bees (*Apis mellifera*) during seed production.
- Number of seeds/ gram; 500-1000.
- Seed crop matures in 12-13 months.
- Seed yield: 500-600 kg/ha.
- Seed storage: 10^0C at 50% R.H.

Pigments in root colour:

- Purple and yellow coloured forms were cultivated in Europe in 11th century.
- In India, red/ purple carrots introduced from Persia during 13th century and orange forms during British period.
- Main phenolic compound: Chlorogenic acid which contributes to organoleptic property. It is maximum in purple coloured carrots followed by orange, white and yellow carrot.
- Presence of total carotenoids determine visual colour of roots viz. white, yellow, purple, pink, reddish orange and orange.
- Maximum carotene in carrot is recorded at 90-130 days after planting.
- High carotene mass varieties have high carotene content (> 500 µg/g) and rich in thiamin & riboflavin.
- Lutein is important in eye health.
- Lycopene: High anti-oxidant activity and gives protection from cancer.
- White carrot: No pigment accumulates in root.
- Red (lycopene 50-100 ppm).
- Orange (α-carotene 10-40% and β-carotene 60-80% of carotenoids i.e. concentration of 530-35833 µg/ 100g fresh wt. & 1161-64350 µg/100 g fresh wt., respectively).
- Purple and black (anthocyanin) with white core contains low carotene 4-6 ppm.
- Yellow (carotenoid-lutein/ zeaxanthin 1-5 ppm (256 µg/ 100 g fresh wt.).
- Carotene content of most widely grown carrot cvs.: 60-120 µg/ g fresh wt.
- Carotene content in purple-orange cvs.: 38-130 ppm.
- Total carotenoid content in edible portion in roots: 60-540 ppm.
- Anthocyanin content in black (dark purple) carrot: 350-1750 mg/100 g.

Root colour	Carotene		Carotenoids
	α	β	
White	-	-	3.2
Yellow	0.5	2.5	2.5
Light orange	15.5	35.6	50.6
Orange	25.4	50.5	95.2
Deep orange	45.2	68.2	120.5

- Yellow and purple cvs. contain anthochlor and anthocyanin, respectively.
- Yellow coloured forms are mutants of anthocyanin coloured carrots.
- Orange forms are developed from yellow types by mutation.
- White and orange (carotene) carrots are probably mutations of yellow form.
- Carotenoids are accumulated in chromoplast and in older cells of phloem.

Varieties:

- McCollum (1975) attempted interspecific hybridization between *D. carota* x *D. capillifolius*.
- Hybrid cvs. began to appear in early 1960s.
- Takii Seed Company, Japan developed 1st hybrid in 1982 using CMS.
- Flyaway: 1st carrot fly resistant varietydeveloped by Single Seed Descent method in 1993.
- Kashmir Beauty and Golden Heart.
- Jatti Local.
- White orange carrots are probably mutants of yellow form.
- Virginia Savoy: Resistant to CMV.
- Beta III: High carotene content and used in human nutrition programme in India.
- Long Orange and Horn types were bred during 17th century in Europe.
- Brasilia: Resistant to nematodes *M. incognita* and *M. javanica*.
- Asian and Brazilian cultivars are source of resistance to *M. javanica* and European OP cultivars for *M. hapla*.
- Male sterile cvs.: Sansun, Kuroda.

Different root shapes: Cultivars are grouped by shape and length fall into categories as-

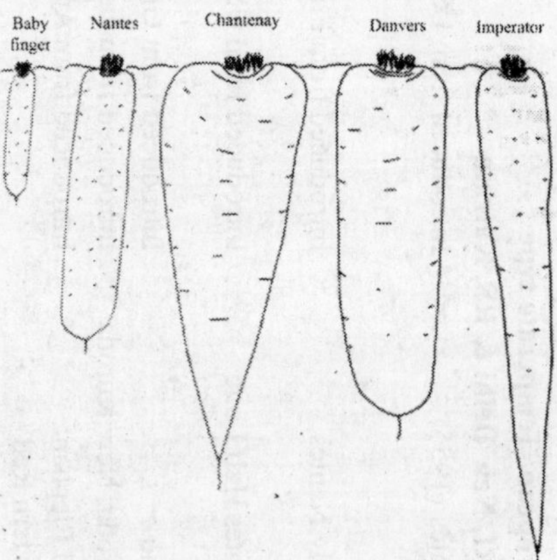

Name	Breeding method	Features
European/ Temperate type		
IARI, New Delhi & RS, Katrain		
Nantes (1955)	Introduced from USA	Best eating quality; cylindrical roots with straight or sloppy shoulder; self coloured orange core; yield 12 t/ha; resistant to pythium & tip burn; vulnerable to longitudinal cracking; suitable for processing
Early Nantes	Introduced from France	Cylindrical roots terminating abruptly in small thin tail; 12-15 cm long; orange colour with self coloured core
Nantes Half Long	Introduced from USA	Roots cylindrical, stumpy with abrupt tail; suitable for growing in winter; orange scarlet with self coloured core; take 110-120 days for root formation
Zeno	Introduced from Germany	Roots deep orange with self coloured core; suitable for Nilgiri region of Tamil Nadu
Kuroda, New Kuroda	Introduced from Japan	Deep orange & stumped root; heat tolerant
Red Elephant, Western Red	Introduced from Australia	Processing purpose
Spring Market Improved, Akaroa Long Red	Introduced from New Zealand	Processing purpose
Scarlet	-	Resistant to tip burn
Early ScarletHorn	Introduced from Holland	Oval shaped; short stump rooted type; can be grown in heavy soils; famous for earliness & for tender, mild flavoured roots
Chantaney	Introduced from USA	Root 11-15 cm long, 3-5 cm broad with tapering to blunt end; orange coloured & self coloured core; excellent for canning & storage
Royal Chantaney	Introduced from USA	Roots 15-16 cm long; 3-5 cm dia., with tapering to blunt end; deep orange cortex & core; grown for processing (canning & freezing); suitable for home garden
Danvers	Introduced from USA	Roots have deep orange cortex & yellow core; suitable for both fresh consumption & processing; resistant to pythium
Oxheart	-	Heart shaped cultivar; suitable for heavy soils & orange flesh & distinct core
Texas Gold Spike	OP selection from (Pioneer x WI 33)	Orange coloured; high carotene content
Imperator	Nantes x Chantaney	Grown for fresh market; deep orange cortex & less pigmented core
Early Gem Imperator	Nantes x Chantaney	Orange scarlet with self coloured core; mid season to late maturing; resistant to pythium
Long Imperator-58	-	Best hybrid; suitable for fresh market

Spartan Binus	Three way cross hybrid	-
Bonus	Three way hybrid	Developed by GCMS technique; resistant to cercospora & *Alternaria*.
Pusa Yamdagni (Selection-5) 1986	Pedigree selection of [EC-9981 (early) x Nantes]	Fast growing temperate type; roots 15 cm long; orange flesh & self coloured core; yield 10 t/ha
Pusa Nayan Jyoti	F_1 hybrid through CMS	1st temperate hybrid; high β-carotene content; orange self coloured root with no core; yield 35-45 t/ha
IIHR, Bengaluru		
Arka Suraj (2007)	Pedigree selection of (Nantes x IIHR-253)	Smooth surface; TSS 8-10%; tolerant to PM & nematode; set seeds under tropical condition
Dr YSPUH & F, Solan		
Solan Rachna	OP selection	Long, smooth, orange colour, self-core, stumpy to semi-stumpy roots; rich in β-carotene; yield 25 t/ha
SKUAT, Srinagar		
Chaman	Selection	-
TNAU, Coimbatore		
Ooty-1 (1997)	Selection from half-sib progeny	Long roots; root deep orange with self coloured core; free from premature bolting; resistant to PM; yield 49 t/ha
Asiatic/ Tropical type		
IARI, New Delhi		
Pusa Kesar (1963)	Selection from cross of (Local Red x Nantes Half Long)	Highest carotene (7753 IU/100 g); scarlet coloured roots with red coloured core; tolerant to high temperature; yield 25 t/ha
Pusa Meghali (1985)	Selection from cross of (Pusa Kesar x Nantes)	Rich in carotene (11571 IU/100 g), orange colour with self coloured core; suitable for dehydration, shreds & pickles; yield 25-26 t/ha
Pusa Vasudha (2012)	F_1 hybrid through CMS	1st public sector tropical hybrid; red roots with self coloured core
Pusa Asita (2008)	OP selection from exotic lines	1st black coloured variety in India (anthocyanin 520 mg/100 g fresh wt.); 30% higher yield than 'P. Kesar'; yield 30 t/ha
Pusa Vrishti (2009)	OP selection from exotic lines	Obtriangular shape of roots with purple pigmentation on shoulders; heat and humidity tolerant & suitable for kharif sowing (off season) i.e. tolerant to rainy season & pink coloured; yield 25 t/ha
Pusa Rudhira (2008)	-	Red coloured self core variety i.e. coreless; delayed bolting; yield 33 t/ha
Pusa Payasa	OP selection from exotic lines	1st mustard coloured variety
Pusa Kulfi	OP selection from exotic lines	1st whitish (pale mustard colour) variety

Imperial Long Scarlet	-	Resistant to alternaria blight
IIVR, Varansi		
Kashi Krishna (2019)	Mass selection	Annual; black coloured; danvers (triangular) type root shape; self coloured; roots 22-25 cm long; root wt. 110-120 g; shoulder dia., 3.2-3.5 cm; tolerant to bolting; yield 21-23 t/ha; excellent source of anti-oxidative phytochemical; suitable for salad/ juice/ *halwa*/ drink/ *kanji*/ pharmaceutical/ nutraceutical uses; anthocyanin content (285 mg/100 g)
CCSHAU, Hisar		
Hisar Gairic (1993)	Mass selection	Long roots; less fibre & forking; self cored, high carotene (96.2 mg/ 100 g), roots longer than Pusa Kesar; yield 30 T/ha.
PAU, Ludhiana		
Selection No. 29	Selection from local material	Quick growing & long tapering, thin & light red coloured roots, core thin
Selection No. 21	Selection	TSS 11%; carotene (6.45 mg/100 g); excellent for candy, pickle & spiced juice making
Selection No. 233 (1978)	Pedigree selection of (Nantes x No. 29)	Roots semi-cylindrical; orange coloured & self coloured core & 15 cm long; less cracking & forking; take 90-100 days for root formation

Private sector hybrid: Hybrid No.1 (deep orange root; suitable for processing & fresh marketing)

Inheritance of characters:

- Genic male sterility is controlled by plasmagene '*S*' and chromogenes *a* and *B* with duplicate gene action.
- External greening is positively correlated with root weight, root length, root diameter and root shape index.
- Mild flavour is incompletely dominant & quantitatively inherited.
- Positive correlation between colour intensity and total carotenoids content.
- Sugar content is correlated with sweeter carrot.
- Inheritance of nitrate content is complex with complete dominance.
- All genes that enhance carotene are recessive. Variety with high carotene content is recessive for 7-9 carotene genes.
- Two recessive gene model for *M. hapla* and single dominant gene to *M. javanica* & *M. incognita*.
- Total dissolved solids (TDS) and percent dry wt. show high correlation.
- Sugar quantity, TDS and percentage of dry wt. show quantitative inheritance.

Character	Number of genes	Type of gene action
Growth habit	Monogenic	Annual dominant over biennial
Flavour	-	Incomplete dominance for mild flavour & low terpenoid level
Leaf stalk	Monogenic dominant (*Pr*)	-
Root colour	Digenic (*P-Y-*) two modifiers (*E-I-*) * Deep purple (*iiPPYYEE*) * Purple (*iiPPYYee*) * Diffused purple (*iiPPyyee*) * Yellow (*IippYYee*) * Red (*iiIIyyEE*) * Light red/orange (*Iippyyee*) * White/ non pigmented (*YYY2Y2*) * Orange (*yyy2y2*)	* White root colour dominant to yellow, orange and light orange; * Light orange dominant over orange; * Lemon colour dominant over light orange.
	Polygenic	Light colour dominant over dark
	Monogenic dominant (*P1*)	Purple dominant to non-purple; gene *P2* is epistatic to *P1* & conditions purple pigmentation in aerial parts.
Root shape	Trigenic (*D*, *N*, *P*)	* Long/ desi type (root long and tapering *D-N-P-*) e.g. Pusa Desi. * Cylindrical type (cylindrical root *ddnnP-*) e.g. Nantes. * Chantenay type (root obovate/ cuneate genotype *ddN-P-*) e.g. Chantenay. * Round type (root round *ddN-pp*) e.g. European types.
Root tip	Monogenic (*S-*)	Blunt end incompletely dominant to pointed end
Root cracking	Monogenic dominant (*Cr*)	Root cracking dominant to cracking; 3 dominant alleles *Y*, *Y1* & *Y2* prevent formation of orange colour in root

		xylem tissue; lack of pigmentation *Y* allele dominant to orange
Longitudinal cracking in cv. Touchon	Monogenic dominant	Cracking (*Cr*) dominant to non-cracking
Flower colour	2 complementary genes	-
Presence of sugars	Monogenic dominant (*Rs*)	Sucrose dominant over reducing sugar; in dominant condition, root accumulates reducing sugars (fructose and glucose) & in recessive alleles condition (*rsrs*), roots accumulate primarily sucrose
Glabrousness of seed stalk	Monogenic dominant (*Gls*)	-
Vernalization requirement	Digenic (*VrnA*, *VrnB*)	-
Harsh flavour	Polygenic	-
Root knot nematode resistance	2 different homozygous recessive genes	-
Petaloid male sterility	-	Dominant alleles of each of the three duplicate nuclear genes (*Ms1*, *Ms2* and *Ms3*)
Cercopsora leaf spot & PM resistance	Monogenic dominant	-

Diseases, pests and disorders:

- Aster yellow (referred as carrot yellow): MLO disorder transmitted through 6 spotted leaf hopper (*Macrosteles fascifrons*). Infected plants show heavy concentration of very fine rootlets on tap root. Most destructive in temperate parts of the world and European OP cultivars serve as source of resistance.
- Water soft rot/ white mold (*Sclerotinia sclerotiorum*): Cause roots to rot.
- Root die back (*Pythium ultimum / P. irregulare*): Soil borne. It kills young tap root to become forked and stubby and roots become unmarketable.
- Cercospora leaf spot/ blight (*Cercospora carotae*): Soil borne fungal disease gives scorched appearance to maturing crop.
- Powdery mildew (*Erysiphe polygoni*): Serious disease. 1st reported in California in 1976.
- Alternaria leaf spot (*Alternaria dauci*): Serious foliar disease. Genetics of resistance is conditioned by polygenes with varying levels of dominance. Source of resistance is Asian and Brazilian cvs.viz. Kokubu, Sai Nai, Imperial Long Scarlet.
- Hot water seed treatment is alternative to fungicide to eradicate seed borne pathogens.
- Bacterial blight: Hot water treatment to seed @ 51^{0}C for 15 min.
- Carrot little dwarf: Induced by 2 viruses- carrot mottle & carrot red leaf. Transmitted by Willow aphid (*Cavariella aegopodii*). Common disease in UK, USA & Australia.

- Brown rot or Rusty rot (*Pythium* spp.): Most destructive post harvest disease.
- Crown rot (*Rhizoctonia solani*): Minor disease.
- Cavity spot (*Clostridium* spp./ *Pythium viole*) in cortex and pitted lesion spot: Soil borne fungal disease favoured by cool soil temperature. Cause severe rotting of roots. Type of root defect and Ca deficiency due to excess application of K fertilizer and change in soil moisture.
- Wire worm: Most important pest.
- Carrot weevil bores through shoulders of young roots.
- Rust fly or Carrot fly (*Psila rosae*): Larvae bore into young seedling roots & feeds on root.
- Turnip moth (*Agrostis segetum*):
- Northern root knot nematode (*M. hapla*) severe in temperate regions and *M. javanica* and *M. incognita* in warmer regions. Controlled by soil fumigation.
- Lygus bug (*L. hesprerus* or *L. elisus*): Serious pest of seed crop& cause reduction in seed quality. Immature seeds attacked by bug don't develop embryo & difficult to separate from normal seeds in milling process. Cv. Imperida is resistant.
- Physiological disorders mostly observed in processing carrots & such roots are unacceptable to trade viz. Cottony xylem, hollow heart and spongy phloem. These defects develop in winter carrots subjected to low temperature in moist soils (i.e. crop planted in Sept-Oct. & harvested in Feb.-March).
- Growth cracks appear in processing cultivars when harvesting is delayed after root maturity.
- Longitudinal cracks/ Harvest cracks/ shatter cracks: Terms used for processing & fresh market carrots. This occurs when turgid roots are subjected to mechanical abuse at harvest. It occurs during field storage during autumn months.
- Carrot splitting: Fluctuation in soil moisture + excess ammonical N fertilizer + B deficiency. Large root size and wider spacing results in greater amount of splitting.
- Bitterness: High ethylene production. Hence, it should not be stored with fruits that emit ethylene.
- Branching or misshapen roots or root forking: Hard soil pan and undecaying manures.
- Cracking: Ca deficiency.
- Stocky or spindle shaped roots: Cu deficiency and high temperature.
- Black spots on roots: B deficiency.
- Greening: Exposure to direct sunlight. Apply Borax (10 kg/ha) & avoid cultivation in alkaline soils.

9.2 Parsley

- Also known as 'Common parsley/ Garden parsley/ Rock parsley'.
- Most popular garden herb grown in western countries on commercial scale.

- Herbaceous biennial crop with long tap root, branched, striated cylindrical stem and cultivated for root.
- Used as salad and for flavouring and garnishing purpose.
- Fresh leaves have strong culinary odour and commonly used for garnishing and seasoning.
- It is eaten fresh, incorporated in salads and used as ingredient of soups, stews and sauces.
- Rich source of vit. A, C, thiamin, riboflavin, Fe and Ca.
- Grown in limited area in H.P., Punjab, Haryana, U.P. and high altitude of southern India.
- Herb is reported to possess diuretic, carminative and anti-pyretic and expectorant properties and has long been used for urinary troubles.
- It increases mother's milk and tones the uterine muscles. It is well known breath freshner and is used as poultice as an antiseptic dressings for sprains, wounds and insect bites.
- Calorific value: 292 Kcal/ 100g.
- Nutrition score: 69.
- It is cool season hardy crop, flourishes well in temperate and tropical climate.
- Optimum temperature for growth: 15-20^{0}C.
- Can be grown in greenhouse or polyhouse.
- Optimum soil pH: 5.5-7.0.
- Leaves are three, pinnate with oval lobes with round incised margin.
- Basal leaves are narrower than the apical.
- Flowers are grouped into compound umbels of ray florets.
- Fruit is ovoid, small, ribbed diachemium.
- Requires little shaded, moist, deep loamy soils for cultivation.
- Plants are thinned to 15-20 cm apart.
- Flowering stem arises in second season is removed for more vegetative growth.
- Edible part: Leafy stalks and petioles.
- Rich source of Fe and vit. C (281 mg/ 100g).
- Essential oil content: 0.15%.
- Characteristic flavour and green colour of leaf can be retained, if dried rapidly at 120^{0}C in oven.
- Propagation method: Seed.
- Seedlings are raised in nursery beds.
- Fresh seeds are sown 25 cm apart in early summer.
- Seed rate: 3-3.5 kg/ha (direct sowing); 250-300 g/ha (transplanting).
- Overnight soaking in warm water helps in early germination.

- Days taken for seed germination: 18-24 without bottom heat and 2-3 weeks with propagator.
- Sowing season: February-March or September-October and seedlings in nursery are thinned to 6 inches apart.
- Transplanting stage: 6-8 weeks old seedlings at 45 cm x 15 cm.
- Harvesting method: It requires 60-75 days from planting to first harvesting.
- Harvesting stage: Outer and larger leaves are harvested first. Green and tender leaves are harvested and tied into bunches for market. Entire plants are harvested at end of cropping cycle.
- Remove flower heads in initial stages (from 2nd year plants) to encourage new growth.
- Placing ice blocks in basket prevents heating and decay of leaves during transit.
- Yield: 110-125 q/ha of leaves.
- Seed viability: 3 years.
- Seed count: 650-1000 seeds/ gram.

Species:

- **Curly-leaved/ Common parsley** (*Petroselinum crispum* syn. *P. hortense* var. *crispum*): The leaves are dark green and finely cut with toothed-leaf edge. Plants are dwarf, compact and bushy (30-40 cm). This is the most common variety that is used as a garnish and dried or dehydrated in food products. It requires 60-75 days to harvest. Curled leaved types are mostly grown in India.
- **Flat/ Plain leaved or Italian parsley** (*P. crispum* var. *neapolitanum*): The leaves are dark green, flat, less finely cut and fleshy roots. Plants are tall, coarse with tough stem. Mainly grown for both its leaves and roots that are used for flavouring soups and stews. This variety has a stronger flavor and easier to work than curly-leaf parsley. It requires 60-75 days to harvest.
- **Hamburg parsley or Turnip-rooted parsley or Parsley root** (*P. crispum* var. *tuberosum*): It is dual purpose vegetable. It has flat leaves, but is grown for its enlarged, edible root and is popular in specialized markets. Tapering white root can be eaten cooked or raw. Roots contain starch, sugar, leaves are rich in beta carotene, vit. C, and iron. It is very hardy and can withstand a moderate freeze or cold in the open. It grows in partial shade, is very hardy and an ideal winter vegetable. Plants may be left in the ground until marketing, or may be dug and stored in trenches or a root cellar until marketing. Spreading hay over the crop in the field has been used to improve tolerance to severe freezing temperatures. This is grown in the vicinity of the large cities where it is utilized mainly by the foreign population and in five star hotels. For vertical / kitchen garden, leafy varieties of parsley such as curly and flat leaf work best.

Varieties:

- CITH-P-4 (curly leaf type), Festival 68, Hybrid No. 41, Hybrid No. 42.

Name	Leaf type	Features
Smooth Italian Giant	Plain/ Flat leaf type	Dwarf; mature in 80-85 days; leaves dark green, 2-3 feet tall, more flavoured than curled type; excellent for seasoning & cooking
Moss Curled	Curly leaf type	Dwarf, compact; mature in 80-85 days; leaves dark green with exceedingly fine cuts, serrated & deeply curled. Frilled leaves are perfect for garnishing and decorative purpose
Champion Moss Curled	Curly leaf type	Very robust & quick growing; densely curled dark green leaves; mature in 70-75 days
Extra Triple Curled	Curly leaf type	Plants 30 cm tall, vigorous & compact; mature in 70-75 days; leaves very dark green, finely cut & deeply curled; excellent for garnishing, seasoning & culinary decoration;
Paramount	Curly leaf type	Uniformly triple curled with dark green leaves; tall stout stem; mature in 85-90 days
Extra Curled Dwarf (syn. Emerald)	Curly leaf type	Compact plants with finely curled, dark green, moss like leaves; mature in 80-85 days
Double curled	Curly leaf type	Dark green leaves with fine cuts, serrated & deeply curled

Pests and diseases:

- Carrot fly:
- Celery fly:
- Nematodes: Causes leaf yellowing.
- Aphids, green caterpillars, Army worms, mole cricket: Common pests.
- Damping off: Treat nursery beds with Formaldehyde solution 1: 50 to depth of 10 cm before sowing.
- Leaf spot (*Cercospora* spp.): Seed treatment with hot water at 59^{0}C for 30 min and spray Blitox @ 3 g/litre.
- Septoria leaf spot (*Septoria apiicola*): Seed treatment with hot water at 50^{0}C for 30 min and spray Dithane Z-78 @ 2 g/litre.
- Parsley mosaic: Removal of infected leaves and spray Metasystox @ 2 ml/ litre.

9.3 Celery

- 2nd important salad crop after lettuce.
- It was 1st mentioned as a cultivated crop in France in 1623, later used as a medicinal plant centuries before it was used as a food. It was brought to USA in 1806.
- In USA, California (72%) and Florida (16%) followed by Michigan, New York, Ohio are leading states in celery production in winter, spring & summer seasons.
- Commercial cultivation is done on limited scale in India in UP, HP, TN, Punjab, Karnataka, Kerala.
- Grown for long, fleshy petioles which are valued for their flavour and texture.
- Fresh product contains approximately 94% water and 6% fibres.

- Inflorescence: Compound umbel consists ofvery small greenish white protandrous flowers.
- Used for flavouring vegetable juices & soups.
- Crop of cool temperate regions.
- Shallow rooted and moisture loving plant.
- Fruit: Two united carpels & each produce single seed.
- Seeds small (1-2 mm length), oval shaped & greenish brown in colour.
- Seed used as condiments, spices as well as medicines. It has stimulant & carminative property.
- Fatty acid from seeds is anti-spasmodic & nerve stimulant.
- Seed contains 2-3% volatile oil.
- Seed oil contains selinene, d-limonene, sadanolide & sesquiterpenes.
- Seed oil is used to treat asthama, bronchitis, for seasoning & flavouring of purees & sauces.
- Leaves contain glucoside 'apiin'.
- Seeds very small, dark brown & emit peculiar odour with pungent taste.
- Contains '3-n-butyl pthalide' effective against hypertension.
- Propagation method: Seeds.
- Gel seedling is used to enhance seed germination.
- Seed germinate in light, above field capacity and at15-35^{0}C.
- Classified as halophyte (saline marshy habitat) and grows well at salinity EC <11 dS/m.
- Sensitive to acidic soils and optimum soil pH for growth is 5.5-6.6.
- Plant growth, development and flowering:
  - It is biennial but grown as annual and slow growing crop.
  - During 1st year, stem develops as a short compact, lens-shaped plate, which forms rosette of leaves with thick petioles.
  - Older petioles develop on outside, while young ones form on inside and comprise the heart of plant.
  - During 2nd year, following exposure to low temperatures, the stem elongates to produce flower stalk.
  - The plant bears compound clusters of small, white flowers which produce seeds towards end of flowering season.
  - Premature flowering and seed stalk formation may occur if plants are exposed to temperature < 50^{0}C or 10 or more days.
  - After seed stalk formation, celery is no longer marketable.
  - It is grown for its thickened petioles or leafstalks that originate from a compact stem plate.

- o The leafstalks are prominently ribbed along their abaxial (outer) length, with considerable differences among cultivars.
- o Thin walled parenchyma tissue makes up the bulk of interior of leafstalk, while out ribs are composed of thick walled collenchyma cells.
- o Both these cells comprise mechanically strong tissue and are mainly responsible for its characteristics stringiness.

- 1 gram contains 2,470 seeds.
- Seed rate: 100-125 g to raise seedlings for 1 ha area.
- Seed rate for seed production: 1 kg/ha.
- Sowing months: March-April (temperate region) and August-September (plains).
- Days for seed germination: 30 days (slow germinating crop).
- Low germination rate can be improved by fluid sowing.
- Diffuse light and diurnal temperature fluctuation of 29.4^{0}C day and 15.5^{0}C night can be used to increase germination.
- Propagated in green house at 13-16^{0}C.
- Direct seed sowing is cheaper and high plant population is economically feasible or seedlings can be later thinned to about 6-8 inches between plants when seedlings have 4-6 true leaves.
- Flowers during March & sets fruits in April.
- Hardening of seedling is necessary before transplanting.
- At transplanting stage, plants should have 3-6 true leaves.
- Use of transplanting helps in easier establishment, earlier maturity and low incidence of bolting in early plantings.
- Planting distance: 60 x 10-20 cm (vegetable purpose) & 40 cm x 15 cm (seed purpose).
- Close spacing and crowding of plants inhibit colour development in stalk.
- Double bed system of planting is adopted.
- Planting methods are different fro trench celery and self-blanching types.
- Critical stage of irrigation: Being moisture loving plant, throughout the whole vegetative period at field capacity.
- Sensitive to water logging.
- Topping is practiced during hot periods and dispensed with during cool cycle.
- Vernalization initiate at 17-20 leaves including leaf primordia e.g. in cv. Celebrity, first 17 leaves require 42 degree days (above a base temperature of 3^{0}C) for initiation.
- Exposure to high temperature: Bitterness in leaves.
- Optimum temperature for cultivation: 15-21^{0}C.
- Celery crop bolts when temperature falls < 15^{0}C.
- Grown as winter annual for seed crop in Punjab.

- Harvesting stage: 100-150 days after transplanting and seeds starts browning.
- Celery stalks are topped at 40 cm to accommodate shipping containers.
- Celery is easier to blanch when planted in single row at 30-45 cm apart.
- Blanch by earthing up plants when 30 cm high.
- Trench celery denotes the method used for blanching the stems.
- Blanching is a process of excluding light from the leaf stalk which checks the development of chlorophyll by wrapping of leaf petioles with dark brown paper or news paper.
- Blanching is done to make the crop crisper, reduce acrid flavour, increases good flavour and tenderness.
- For blanching purpose, strips of thick paper-news paper, corrugated cardboard, brown wrapping paper or thick black polyethylene can be used.
- Methods of covering leaf petioles:
  - Hilling the plants with soil.
  - Shading the plant rows with black plastic or shade cloth.
  - Stalks can be blanched while they are in storage.
  - Self blanching cultivars have been developed to reduce the labour cost.
  - Blanching was popular in the past and is no longer a common practice due to increasing demand for green celery.
- Harvesting: Crop is hand harvested by cutting with knife just below the stem, trimmed to uniform length and packed into crates in the field. Tender leaves along with stalks in May in plains & during November & April-May in hills.
- It is harvested regularly from 5th week after planting.
- Yield: 330-560 q/ha (vegetable); 1.4 t/ha (seed).
- 6-BA @ 10 ppm enhances shelf life.
- GA_3 @ 25 or 50 ppm enhanced growth.
- Pithiness: Major source of quality loss and decreased shelf life.
- Storage temperature has major impact on development of pithiness.
- Cold storage: 0^0C at 95-98% R.H. for 2 months period.
- Cut celery is hydro or vacuum cooled at 0.5^0C & stored at 100 % R.H.
- Paper cartons are used with celery for vacuum cooling.
- Seed crop is harvested when 80% of umbels begin to turn light/dark brown in colour.
- Seed shattering is major problem.
- Celery absorbs foreign flavour during storage so it should be stored in an isolated place.

Botanical varieties:

- *Apium* refers to its flavoured water habitat (marshy ground) and *graveolens* means its heavily scented aroma.

- Stems of wild plants are very bitter and differ from variety *dulce* meaning sweet or pleasant flavour.
- *Apium graveolens* var. *rapaceum*: Celeriac/ Knob/Root celery. Development of enlarged hypocotyl and root tissue. Strong flavour and consumed mostly cooked. This swollen stemmed celery is widely grown in Northern and Eastern Europe. Lowest part of stem known as bulb is eaten and roots that grow below are removed.
- *A. graveolens* var. *secalinum*: Leaf type. Slender, leafy with hollow petioles. Mostly used for their leaves as condiment garnish and medicinal purpose.
- *A. graveolens* var. *dulce*: Blanched type. Solid petioles which are consumed mostly raw in salads and often cooked in soups and stews. Widely grown in Europe and America.

Types:

I. **Self blanching or golden (yellow) leaved varieties**: Golden coloured foliage, earlier, less vigorous, thinner petioles, but more sharply ribbed and rich in 'vit. A' than green leaved varieties e.g. Golden, Florida Golden, Supreme Golden, Golden Detroit, Golden Plume, Golden Self-Blanching (compact, firm golden yellow hearts & do not become stringy), Cornell 19, Cornell 619, Celebrity (early maturing, long stems, nutty flavoured & bolting resistant), Latham Self-Blanching (vigorous, early with crisp stems), Michigan Improved Golden, Green Sleeves (produce green sleeves), Ivory Tower (long, white stringless stems), Tall Utah Triumph (long, succulent tender green stems).

II. **Green leaved varieties**: Preferred in Indian market for green foliage, large number of well overlapped petioles, salad purpose with excellent eating quality and resistant to fusarium yellow. Green celery cvs. are grouped as-

   A. ***The Utah type***:

      i) Predominant because they have large number of well, overlapped petioles and well developed heart.

      ii) Many selections/ strains have been developed which differ in green colour, number of petioles and length of petioles, days to maturity and susceptibility for bolting, etc.

   B. ***Summer Pascal type***: They have excellent eating quality but lack compactness and have few petioles and poor heart development.

   C. ***Slow bolting types*** are less affected by cold temperatures and less likely to bolt in early plantings. Other varieties belonging to green leaved type are Wright Grove Giant (tall, large white stalks of fine quality), Ford Hook Emperor (late, dwarf, broad & tender leaves), Giant Pascal, Giant Pink (hardy, pale pink stalks & blanch easily), Giant Red (hardy & vigorous), Giant White (tall & white coloured), Summer Pascal (resistant to brown spot), Emerson Pascal, Ooty-1, Utah 52-70, Utah52-70 R,Utah52-70 HK, Florida 683, Tall Green Light, Tendercrisp, Slow Bolting Green No. 12, Slow Bolting Green No. 96.

III. **Leaf, cutting or soup celery**: Produces leaves and stems for longer period and very hardy e.g. French Dinant (excellent for drying & full of flavour), Soup Celery d' Amsterdam (very aromatic, prolific, produce thin stems).

Varieties:

- Japan developed 1st F_1 hybrid using CMS: Green Giant (1982) by Takii Seed Company.
- Celery Paris: Resistant to heat and rain.
- Standard Beared: Developed by IARI. Early, semi-tall, light pink stem, green leaved, used for salad purpose.
- Trench celery: Giant Pink (very hardy, crisp, pale pink stalks blanch easily), Giant Red (hardy & vigorous), Giant White (tall, white, stems solid & flavoured), Hopkins Fenlander (late maturing, green with good flavour).
- Cvs. of Celeriac: Iram, Ball, Blader, Brilliant, Monarch, Tellus.
- Punjab Celery-1: 20% oil content.
- RRL-85-1: Developed by RRL, Jammu. 2-3% volatile oil and 16-20% fatty oil.
- NRCSS-Ajmer Cel-7: Seed purpose. Salinity tolerant.
- Ajmer Celery-1: Seed yield 8-10 q/ha. Essential oil: 2.4%.

Disease and physiological disorders:

- Aster yellow: Viral disease.Spread by leaf hoppers.
- Early blight (*Cercospora apii*): Hot water seed treatment (48^{0}C for 30 min) is recommended.
- Late blight (*Septoria apiigraveolentis*):
- Damping off (*Pythium* spp.): Drench with Captan @ 2 g/litre.
- Fusarium yellow (*F. oxysporum* f.sp. *apii*):
- Bacterial rot (*Erwinia carotovora*):
- Bacterial leaf spot (*Pseudomonas apii*):
- Western Celery mosaic virus:Viral disease spread by aphids.
- Blackheart: Tip burn on young leaves. B & Mn deficiency.
- Brown inner tissue/ Brown checking/ Cat scratches/ Cracked stem: B deficiency. High rates of N and K. Cv. Tall Utah 52-70 R is tolerant.
- Pencil strip: Excess application of P.
- Chlorosis: Mg deficiency. Deterioratiion in quality.
- Freezing injury: Below 0.5^{0}C.
- Pithiness: Due to high nitrogen rate.

10. ARACEAE

10.1 Elephant foot yam

- Eulogized as '*Suran* or *zimikand*'.

- Grown as vegetable in tropical and sub-tropical regions in many countries and for processed food in Korea, Japan, China, S. America and South-East Asia.
- Commercially grown in India, Thailand, Sri Lanka, Indonesia and Malaysia.
- Buds are spread all over the periderm (body surface) of yam tuber.
- Perennial plant having underground saucer shaped stem tuber/rhizome.
- Paste of this yam is used to reduce pain.
- Recommended for recovery of piles and dysentery and as blood purifier.
- Odour: Dimethyl oligosulphides.
- Most successful intercrop in banana.
- Can be cultivated under rainfed and irrigated conditions.
- Irrigated variety is called as '*Thiya kanda*' and upland is called as '*Dorada kanda*', which is more acrid in taste.
- Cheapest source of –CHO, rich in minerals, vit. A and B.
- Mature corm contains 24% starch and 1% protein.
- Economic yield is obtained from corm and cormels.
- Multiplication ratio: 1: 2 or 1:4 (traditional).
- Anti-nutritional factor: Due to calcium oxalate crystals causing acridity or irritancy.
- Smooth corm types grown in south India is of good quality and commercially acceptable. It do not produe daughter corms for rapid multiplication.
- Neutral pH (6-7) is ideal for crop.
- Cannot tolerate frost and growth is affected at temperature below 20^0C.
- Inflorescence: Extremely protogynous.
- Stigma receptivity: 24-78 h before anthesis.
- Anthesis time: 6 PM or 24 h before pollen dehiscence.
- Fruit maturity: 8 months.
- Fruitlets contain 1-3 seeds.
- Propagation method: By tubers (corm).
- Time of planting: February-April.
- Crop is grown on flat beds or broad ridges (practiced in high rainfall area) or by making holes (50 x 50 x 30 cm) according to seed corm wt.
- Planting of 0.5 kg corms with crop density of 90,000 plants/ha is recommended for *A. konjac*.
- Higher plant density increases leaf area index, crop growth rate, net assimilation rate, dry matter accumulation in different parts and total dry matter production.
- Corm setts weighing 750-1000 g are conventional size of planting material.
- In minisett technique, small corm pieces of 75-100 g weight are used as planting material for seed production, enhanced multiplication ratio (1:15).
- About 15 minisetts could be made from corm weighing 1.5 kg.
- Seed rate of minisetts/ha: 37,000 @ 60 cm x 45 cm.

- Reducing size of minisetts to 30 g, multiplication ratio of 1: 24 could be obtained.
- Raising of minisetts in nursery is not required.
- Fertilization: High dose of FYM 25 T + NPK (80 + 60 + 100 kg/ ha).
- Application of *Azotobacter* @ 2% solution as corm dipping and soil application @ 9 kg/ha at 35 days after planting improves nitrogen use efficiency.
- Number of irrigations required: 8-10.
- Cleavage of polyembryony has also been observed in elephant foot yam.
- By removing central apical bud, drying the corms and exposure to smoke for 6 h/ day for 4 weeks gives cent percent sprouting at 16 days after planting.
- Heat treatment (35, 40, 45^{0}C) induces early sprouting.
- Corm treated with thiourea is most effective in breaking dormancy with 92% sprouting in 75 days.
- Long dormancy period can be broken by storage in diffused light and treating corms with thiourea, GA_3 and ethrel (0.1% each).
- Mulching the pits with black polyethylene film or leaf litter, immediately after planting gives better sprouting, conservation of moisture, reduction of temperature around corms and increases yield and size of individual corms.
- Trailing of vines enhances tuber yield by 20%.
- Harvesting period: 7-8 months after planting and corm become 3-5 kg.
- Signs of maturity: Yellowing and drooping of leaves.
- Corms can be retained in soil even after full maturity.
- Yield: 50-100 t/ha.
- This corm has better shelf life compared to other tropical tubers and can be stored for several months in well ventilated rooms without any damage.
- Corms loose weight during prolonged storage but without quality deterioration.
- Traditionally, corms are stored in heaps under well ventilated sheds.
- Storage temperature: 10^{0}C.
- To lengthen shelf life of seed corms in storage, use of dry ash, sand, rice bran, saw dust and dry soil is highly useful and checks moisture loss.
- Moisture loss in storage for first 4 days is about 3-4% per day and extends to >25% in 1st month of storage.
- Use of maleic hydrazide lowers rotting or corms in storage.
- *In vitro* storage of cuttings of adventitious buds (0.5 to 1.5 cm length) is possible at 4^{0}C for 180 days.
- *In vitro* culture using modified MS medium is used for edible varieties of *A. paeoniifolius*.
- Tissue culture of corms of *A. konjac* yields planting material on large scale in short time.
- Plant regeneration from explants of tubers of *A. konjac* is directly achieved via multishoot formation after 5-6 weeks in culture.

- Organic farming is promising due to highest corm yield, higher dry matter and starch content and lower oxalate content.
- Zimikand Growers Society under Societies Registered Act.
- Progressive farmer Mr. Shyam Lal Thakur received National award and Kisan Doot award in 2003.

Species:

- *Amorphophallus paeoniifolius* (syn. *A. companulatus*), *A. kiusianus*: Edible Taiwanian species.
- *A. paenoiifolius* var. *paenoiifolius*: Wild ancestor and thorny.
- *A. titanium*: Produce tuber weighing >100 kg.
- *A. konjac* (*A. rivirei*): Widely used for food, medicine, cultural symbols, animal fodder, gum or wine making. Corm flour is used for improper lipid metabolism. Cultivated in Japan, China.
- *A. dubius*: Medicinal purpose.
- *A. henryi*, *A. hirtus*: Endemic Taiwanian species.
- *A. zengianus*: Chinese spp. Erect, boat shaped spathe, sterile and pleasant flavour.
- African spp., *A. richardsiae* (from Zambia), *A. abyssinicus* ssp. *akeassii* (from Ghana, Nigeria), *A. calabaricus* ssp. *mayoi* (from Zaire, Uganda and Kenya)
- *A. concophyllus*, *A. variabilis* and *A. rivieri*: Produce small, non-edible tubers.
- Two forms:
  1. *f. sylvestris* (scabrous petiole, acrid tuber)
  2. *f. hotensis* (smooth petiole, non-acrid tuber).

Varieties:

- Myougiyutaka (*A. konjac*): Japanese cv., very high yielding and resistant to leaf blight and root rot. High flour yield and flour viscosity.
- Shina-Shu and Harunakuro: Promising Japanese genotypes.
- Karuna Kilangu: Popular in Tamil Nadu.
- S-5: Superior seedling selection.
- AM-42: 1st hybrid.

Name	Breeding method	Features
CTCRI, Thiruvanantpuram		
Sree Padma (1998)	Clonal selection from local (AM-15) germplasm	Non-acrid; cultivated under tree shade; duration 8-9 months; yield 42 t/ha
Sree Athira (2006)	Hybrid of (Sree Padma x AM-45)	1st genetically improved variety in world with no acridity or sliminess; cultivated under tree shade; yield (41 t/ha); cropduration 9-10 months
NDA-9	-	Total starch: 17.2 %; calcium oxalate (dry wt.): 0.9

		%; yield 38-85 t/ha; tolerant to collar rot but susceptible to mosaic
AM-6, AM-7, AM-8, AM-15, AM-16	-	High yielding
CSKHPKV, Palampur		
Palam Zimikand-1 (2013)	Selection	White flesh; solid, round, densely spotted pseudo-stem; ready to harvest in 170-180 days; yield from 100 g cormlets (200-250 q/ha)
BCKV, Kalyani		
Bidhan Kusum (1999)	Clonal selection from 'Kovur'	Commercial cv.; vigorous; creamy flesh; no daughter corms; yield 100 t/ha; non irritant; smooth corm; tolerant to sclerotium rot, leaf spot and mosaic
NDUA & T, Faizabad		
Narendra Asha (2006)	Clonal selection	Yield 65 t/ha
ANGRAU, Hyderabad		
Gajendra (syn. Kovur) 1991	Selection from Kovvur region	Non-acrid/ non-irritant; white flesh; smooth corms with no cormels; yield 100 t/ha; popular in Andhra Pradesh, Bihar, West Bengal
Santragachi	Selection	Several rough daughter corms; flesh light cream with slight acridity; popular in eastern India

10.2 Taro

- Eulogized as 'Arvi or Colocasia or Cocoyam or *Dasheen* or Elephant's ear or West Indian kale'.
- Crops of 3rd world countries and grown in Africa and Asia.
- It is traditional and popular staple food in Japan.
- Africa rank 1st in area and production.
- Genus nameColocasia is derived from Egyptian word 'Colcas or Qulquas'.
- Sub-family: Colocasiodeae.
- Global productivity: 6.1 T/ha.
- Highest productivity: Egypt (31.3 T/ha).
- Asia's productivity: 14.6 T/ha.
- Three phases of growth:
    - Phase I (up to 8 weeks): Regeneration of mother corm by emergence of roots and leaves.
    - Phase II (2-6 months): Grand growth period for rapid vegetative growth. Plant produces 20-35 leaves. Leaf area index is 3.0.
    - Phase III: Crop maturity and duration varies with cultivar and growing conditions.
- Leaf number and LAI in low land taro is always more than upland and rainfed taro due to higher rate of leaf production, longer leaf life and more number of suckers.

- Morphologically, corm is stem while stolons & cormels are lateral branches of stem.
- Leaves, petioles, corms, cormels and cormlets are edible.
- Corms are high in starch (18-28% amylose), carbohydrate (17-27%), crude protein (0.6-3.3 %) and low in fat.
- Leaves are good source of protein, β-carotene (10278 mg), Ca (227 mg/ 100 g).
- Energy: 293-599 KJ/ 100 g.
- Underground parts consist of one or more edible central corms & large number of cormels (lateral tubers).
- Alocasia is an eye-catching foliage plant.
- Taro can tolerate water logged conditions due to presence of parenchyma cells inside leaves, stolons and gas flow inside plant tissues for root respiration.
- Colocasia and Xanthosoma are together known as 'Cocoyam'.
- Nutrient composition/ 100 g edible portion of cocoyam:

Plant part	Ca (mg)	P (mg)	Fe (mg)	Vit. A (IU)	Thiamine (mg)	Riboflavin (mg)	Niacin (mg)	Ascorbic acid (mg)
Corms	51	88	1.2	Trace	0.10	0.03	08	8
Leaf stalks	49	25	0.9	180	0.02	0.04	0.4	13

- Anti-nutritional factor: Acridity due to calcium oxalate crystals.
- Taro recommended for gastric patients.
- Natural cultivars are fertile diploids and sterile triploids (2n=3x=42).
- Crop cannot stand cool climate/ frost conditions.
- Under sub-tropical conditions, crop grows luxuriantly around 21°C.
- Temperature < 10°C is detrimental for growth.
- Flowering is promoted by long days.
- Crop performance is better on puddle lands, on ridges and furrows and in beds.
- Flat planting followed by earthing up at 60-70 days after planting imparts better soil coverage to developing cormels and better support to crop.
- Optimum soil pH: 5.5-7.0.
- Some cultivars are tolerant to salinity.
- Planting time: April-June under rainfed conditions.
- Crop duration: 12-18 months.
- Number of leaves produced/ plant in one crop cycle: 20-35.
- Plant retains 4-7 leaves at a time with longevity of 30-35 days.
- Propagation methods: Corms, cormels, suckers, shoot tips.
- Taro possess smallest grained (1-5 microns in dia.) starch in plant kingdom.
- Blue colour rhizomes give higher starch yield than yellow coloured.

- Human digestivity of starch: 97 %.
- Tuber contains mucilage (0.9%).
- Seed rate: 37,000 cormels/ ha at 60 cm x 45 cm.
- Plant at 3 months age forms corms.
- Tuber bulking is long duration & at lower rate in late maturing types than in early maturing ones and in long days than in short days.
- Leaves are large, peltate with long petiole clasping the base.
- Cultivated types rarely flower and true flowers are enclosed within larger spathe.
- Inflorescence: Spadix.
- Inflorescence consists of 20-40 cm long, rolled spathe & 5-8 cm long cylindrical golden yellow spadix inside.
- Spadix is cylindrical with basal female flowers, above which section of aborted flowers compressed by neck of spathe, large section of male flowers and short sterile appendages at apex.
- Corms cylindrical with short internodes and few side tubers.
- Root system is shallow and fibrous.
- Flower type: Protogynous, fragrant.
- Pollination agents: Flies.
- It requires pollination one day before spadix anthesis.
- Type of fruit: Berry.
- Huli: Means 1 cm corm tip with 15-20 cm petiole is used as planting material in Hawaii.
- Huli yields higher than corms.
- Cormels are preferred in places where winter is severe.
- Large sized cormels (55-70 g) are better than corms.
- Ideal planting material: Cormel weight 20-25 g.
- Inherent multiplication ratio is higher being 1:20 compared to other tuber crops.
- By adopting minisett technique, multiplication ratio can be enhanced to 1: 120 in taro.
- Raising minisetts in nursery is not required.
- Minisett weight for taro: 10 g.
- Microsetts weighing 2 g from top, middle and bottom can be used.
- Planting depth: 5-7 cm.
- Planting distance: 60 cm x 45 cm (India); 90 cm x 30 cm (Cuba); 60 cm x 100 cm (Japan).
- Plant population: Upto 54000 plants/ ha in flat culture at 60 cm flat row spacing and upto 3600 plants/ ha on ridges at 60 cm x 90 cm spacing.

- HDP of 6.7 plants/ sq. m produces higher cormels yield (42 t/ha) compared to 28, 30, and 38 t/ha at 2.7, 3.3 and 4.4 plants/ sq.m.
- Mulching with dried leaves or polyethylene sheet or straw gives early sprouting, maintain soil temperature, higher yield (30% more) and good weed control.
- Best herbicide: Paraquat.
- Type of parthenocarpy: Vegetative.
- Two botanical varieties based on arrangements of corms and cormels:
  a) Eddoe- Arvi (*C. esculenta* var. *antiquorum*). It is different from single-tubered dasheen. Corm edible with 5-20 cormels attached with mother tubers. Bear bigger cormels than mother corms. Central tuber is surrounded by clusters of small tubers which are harvested. Brown, hairy tubers weigh upto 2.2 kg and have yellow, pink or orange flesh and contain calcium oxalate crystals. This group has 42 chromosomes. Rich in starch, Mg, K & vit. C. Amylase content is lowest. Eddoe type is most prevalent as vegetable. Takes 5-6 months to mature.
  b) Dasheen- Bunda (*C. esculenta* var. *esculenta/ globulifera*). Central corm is large, cylindrical (used for food) with fibrous roots and 2-3 small cormels (used for planting). Upright stems are topped with large, heart shaped leaves with prominent ribs on underside. This group has 28 chromosomes. Non-acrid taste. Cultivated types are grouped by the colour of flesh ranging from pink to yellow and leaf stems of green, pinkish purple to almost black.
- Other botanical varieties which vary in colour of leaves and petioles and shape of corms and cormels are: var. *nymphaefolia*, var. *globulifera*, var. *aquatilis*, var. *antiquoram*, var. *euchlora*, var. *fontanesii* and var. *illustris*.
- Mother corms are marketed in 'Dasheen' type while cormels (smaller than mother corms) in 'Eddoe' type.
- Green manuring of Leucaena leucocephala is recommended for vigorous growth, high yield, formation of large corms & higher total corms yield and marketability.
- Application of 350 kg N fertilizer in equal parts at planting and at 70, 100 and 130 days after planting gives more economic returns.
- Crop can sustain itself upto 6th leaf stage from nutrients stored in corms.
- Crop requires more K than N and P for increased starch content and higher corm yield.
- Harvesting stage: At senescence stage (yellowing of leaves) 7-9 months after planting. Crop is harvested by pulling the plants out of soil with the help of hoes or spades.
- Side harvesting or partial harvesting is practiced in India.
- Yield: 16-26 t/ha.
- Seed viability: 4 months.
- Seed very small (1 mm), hard and pale yellow in colour.

- Taro is tropical crops and prefers abundant supply of water/ flooded conditions and tolerant to water logged conditions.
- Critical stage for irrigation: Tuber bulking.
- About 450 g water is needed to produce 1 g dry matter.
- Moisture stress adversely affects canopy development, dry matter production and tuber yield which results in dumbbell shaped and poor quality corms.
- Corms remain in ground for 3 months after maturity without any deterioration.
- Viability of taro corm is extremely low (<15 days).
- Tubers can be stored for several weeks under dry and well ventilated conditions.
- Corm paste prepared from cooked taro known as 'fufu' in West Africa.
- Pressure cooked taro corms are used for fermented acidic product called 'Poi'.
- White cassava is sweet, soft and usually grown as vegetable.
- In recent selections of sweet varieties, most of toxin is in the skin and tubers are edible after simple cooking.
- Cassava chips known as 'Singkong' are thin crispy wafers.
- Cassava is source of starch for manufacture of plywood, textiles, adhesives and paper.
- Tapioca flour is made from ground chips.
- Industrial applications of starch: Preparation of high fructose syrup and alcohol, talcum powder, aerosols, bio-degradable plastic, bakery flour, etc.
- Flour (from pre-cooked & peeled tubers) is used to prepare soups, biscuits, bread, infant foods, puddings, beverages & cosmetics.
- Tubers of cv. CM-17 are suitable for production of chips because a) it retains quality even after 180 days of storage 2) contains low phenols and sugars 3) high dry matter and starch content.
- It is used as speciality food in management of gluten allergy in infants.
- *In vitro* propagation of xanthosoma and colocasia has been well perfected.
- Zygotic embryo culture of taro on LS medium has been successful and developed into mature plants only in presence of endosperm tissue.
- Meristem from apical/ lateral buds can be grown in tissue culture.
- Dasheen mosaic free plants were developed by 'cormel tip' culture at CTCRI.
- On the basis of peroxidase and esterage isoenzyme patterns, grouping and identification of duplicate varieties/ land races has been successfully attempted.
- On the basis of karyo-morphology, taxonomic separation of diploid taro morphotypes has been successfully attempted.
- Transgenic plants have been developed by using high velocity particle bombardment system.

- Highly generative callus is obtained by apical meristem.
- Transformants are confirmed by amplification of *GUS* gene and southern hybridization.

Species:

- Different popular forms viz. Nandeeba (quick to mature) & Macapera (used for boiling) are widely cultivated in Brazil.
- Comprises 3 edible spp.
  - Taro (*Colocasia esculenta*): Important crop in Hawaii and more common in India.
  - Tannia (*Xanthomonas* spp.):
  - Giant taro (*Alocasia* spp.): In Hawaii, giant taro is called as 'Ape' and also referred as 'Wild taro'.
- Giant swam taro (*Cryptosperma chamissionis*): Largest taro. Serves as famine food in food scarcity. Leaves used as food wrappings/ plates and stem, tuber is cooked and eaten.
- Giant taro (*Alocasia macrorrhiza*, *A. indica*): Primitive spp. and edible. Economic part: Corms and cormels. Known as elephant ears. Corm and leaf juice used for medicinal purpose.
- Chinese taro (*A. cucullata*): Cultivated and edible spp. Possess small elephant earlike thick, shiny green, heart shaped leaves. Flower spathe is hooded.
- Three morphotypes (diploids 2n=28) are available as-
  a) Purple leaved (inedible corms, long, thin stolons).
  b) Green leaved (edible corms).
  c) Green leaved with purple vein junction on lamina (edible corms). Flowers of such types produce fertile pollens and spathes and spadix are extremely long (40 cm).

Varieties:

- Both seed and pollen parents serve as double genome donors of the triploids.
- Taro cvs. are grown by tribal people by jhum cultivation.
- On the basis of shape of corms, cvs. are named as- 'Panch mukhi' in Assam, 'Sahastra mukhi' in Kerala, 'Tamarakannan' in Meghalaya, 'Kovvur' in Andhra Pradesh. All these varieties have good culinary qualities.
- For hydroponic culture, cv. Bun Long, Lila, Blanca are recommended. Crop is grown for 9 months. Plant spacing adopted 90 cm x 30 cm and 90 cm x 60 cm. 14-3-13 NPK commercial mixture is used.
- PSB-G2, Toantal, Thailand, Sushi, Gilin, Kugfel, Oglang, Pastora: Resistant to leaf blight. They are rated for taste and dry weight.

- White Guariya (dwarf, all plant parts edible; free from acridity).
- KCS-3.

Name	Breeding method	Features
CTCRI, Thiruvanantpuram		
Sree Kiran (2004)	Hybrid of (C. 303 x C. 383)	1st genetically improved variety; yield 18 t/ha
Sree Rashmi (1987)	Clonal selection from local germplasm	Natural triploid; eddoe type; resistant to nematode; cultivated under tree shade; all plant parts non-acrid; 15% starch; 2.5% proteins; mature in 210-250 days; excellent cooking quality; yield 18 t/ha
Sree Pallavi (1987)	Clonal selection from Meghalaya	Eddoe type; triploid; corms big; 20-25 corms/ plant & club shaped; mature in 200-210 days; yield 16 t/ha
Sree Padma	Selection from indigenous germplasm	-
Sree Padmanabha	Selection from exotic collection	Mosaic & CMD resistant
Muktakeshi (2002)	Selection from indigenous germplasm	Tolerant to leaf blight; cultivated under tree shade
Pani Saru-1	Clonal selection	Suitable for water logged condition & tolerant to leaf blight; cultivated in Odisha
Pani Saru-2	Clonal selection	Suitable for water logged condition & tolerant to leaf blight; cultivated in Odisha
C-9	Selection	Good culinary qualities; starch 16.5%; yield 20 t/ha
C-266	Selection	Yield 10-12 t/ha
C-135	Selection	-
C-149	Selection	-
CTCRI Regional centre, Bhubaneswar		
Bhu Kripa (Jhankri) 2013	Clonal selection	Brown skin with white flesh; yield 12-18 t/ha; tolerant to submergence, drought, salinity & phytophthora leaf blight
Bhu Sree (Sonajuli) 2013	Clonal selection	Brown skin with white flesh; yield 12-18 t/ha; tolerant to drought, salinity & phytophthora leaf blight
ICAR Research Complex for NEH region, Meghalaya		
Megha Taro-2	-	-
BCKV, Kalyani		
Bidhan Chaitanya (1997)	Clonal selection from 'BCC-1'	Tubers non-irritant; non-aromatic; yield 15 t/ha
Bidhan Joydeb (1997)	Clonal selection from 'BCC-2'	Tubers non-irritant; non-aromatic; yield 12 t/ha
AAU, Jorhat		
Panchamukhi	Clonal selection	Eddoe type; promising variety of N-E hilly regions of India; non-flowering; 5 tubers attached together; 130-160 days formaturity; good keeping quality; yield 25-40 t/ha; tuber can be kept more than a year after harvest
Satamukhi	Clonal selection	Promising variety of N-E hilly regions of India
Sahastramukhi	Clonal selection	Promising variety of N-E hilly regions of India
Koni Kachu	Clonal selection	Eddoe type; many daughter tubers similar to poultry

		eggs;mature in 130-170 days; yield 17-25 t/ha; good cooking quality
Kaka Kachu	Clonal selection	Dasheen type; large corms, better taste; mature in 140-250 days; yield 22-40 t/ha; susceptible to phytophthora blight
Munshi Kuntia Kachu	Clonal selection	Dasheen type; corm is like wooden peg in shape and size; highly palatable, very soft; contain calcium oxalate; mature in 140-270 days; yield 20-35 t/ha
Naga Kaju	Clonal selection	Eddoe type; suitable for N-E hilly region of India; bigger sized mother tubers & very small daughter tubers; mature in 130-150 days; yield 12-25 t/ha
RAU, Ranchi		
Kadma Arvi (2006)	Clonal selection	18 cormels/plant; resistant to leaf blight, virus & pests
AAU, Jorhat		
Ahina Katchu (2004)	Clonal selection	High yield 17 t/ha
KAU, Vellanikkara		
Sonajuli	Selection from indigenous germplasm	-
Thamara Kannan	Local germplasm collection from Kerala	Mutant & triploid; immune to root knot nematode; good cooking quality
NDUA & T, Faizabad		
PKS-1 (2006)	Clocal selection	Good for chips making; yield 20-31 t/ha
Narendra Bunda-1 (2001)	Clonal selection	Cylindrical corm; resistant to lodging; suitable for table purpose; yield 30-40 t/ha
NDB-21 (2006)	Clonal selection	Early; corm cook easily; yield 45-50 t/ha
NDB-03 (2006)	Clonal selection	Corm cook fast; yield 35-40 t/ha
CSAUA &T, Kanpur		
Azad Arvi-1	Clonal selection	Edible corms ready for picking in 135 days
ANGRAU, Hyderabad		
RNCA-1 (2006)	Clonal selection	Medium duration; yield 14-18 t/ha
IGKVV, Raipur		
Indira Arvi-1 (2003)	Clonal selection	Higher number of main cormels; tolerant to water logging condition; yield 22 t/ha
SVBPUA & T, Meerut		
Vallabh Nikki (2007)	Selection from germplasm	Resistant to leaf blight; suitable for plains
PAU, Ludhiana		
Punjab Arvi-1	Selection	Tall, mature in 176 days; yield 23 t/ha
ML-1, 2		Suitable for N-E-hilly regions of India; tolerant to leaf blight
UHS, Bagalkot (HRS, Sirsi)		
Sirsi Colocasia-1 (2008)	Selection	-

Diseases, pests and disorders:

- Acts as alternate host for banana bunchy top virus.
- Leaf blight (*Phytophthora colocasiae*): Most destructive.

- Leaf rot (*Rhizoctonia* sp.)
- Dasheen mosaic disease: Most serious.
- Storage rot: Dip the corms in 500 ppm Carbendazim before storing in soil pits.
- Root knot nematode: Serious pest.
- Leaf eaters: Feed on leaves.
- Metsubre: Ca deficiency. Use lime.

Inheritance of characters:

- Number of cormels/ plant and mean cormel weight and yield per plant has positive correlation with high yield.

10.3 Tannia

- Economic part: Corms, cormels and leaves.
- Ideal planting material: Cormel weight 60 g.
- Inherent multiplication ratio is 1:10 compared to other tuber crops.
- By adopting minisett technique, multiplication ratio can be enhanced to 1: 80.
- Ideal minisett weight: 15 g.
- Viability of planting material: About a month.
- Nutrient composition/ 100 g edible portion:

Plant part	Ca (mg)	P (mg)	Fe (mg)	Vit. A (IU)	Thiamine (mg)	Riboflavin (mg)	Niacin (mg)	Ascorbic acid (mg)
Corms	20	47	1	Trace	0.1	0.03	0.5	10
Leaves	95	388	2	3300	Nil	Nil	Nil	37
Shoots	49	80	0.3	Nil	Nil	Nil	Nil	82

- Growth period: 9-12 months.
- Central corm is not eaten & cormels form the crop.
- Cormels are harvested & stored upto 6 months.
- Weight loss & quality deterioration occurs 8 week's after storage under ambient condition.
- Anti-nutritional factor: Acridity (irritant effect) of tubers is undesirable trait.

Species:

- *Xanthosoma violaceum*: Possess violet petiole and leaves and pink fleshed edible tubers and foliage as vegetable.
- *X. artovirens*: Yellow fleshed edible tubers.
- *X. caracu*: White fleshed edible tubers.

- *X. brasiliense*: Mainly grown for its leaves as salad and not tuber purpose.
- *X. belophyllum*: Edible.
- *X. jacquini*: Edible.
- *X. mafaffa*: Edible.
- *X. sagittifolium*: Edible.

Varieties:

- Xa-31, Xa-33, Xa-40, Xa-41: Promising and high yielding selections developed by CTCRI.

Name	Breeding method	Features
Dr BSKKV, Dapoli		
Konkan Haritparni (2000)	Selection from 'Sakhloli'	6 months duration; less acrid; yield 25 t/ha

11. ASTERACEAE

11.1 Lettuce

- Earliest existence (about 4500 BC) was recorded in tomb paintings in Egypt, showed plants with narrow pointed leaves (now called Asparagus lettuce). It is similar to the modern form balady (meaning local) found in Egypt as early as 4500 BC.
- It was brought to the New World by Spanish explorers and by the 18th century it was widely used in the Americas.
- USA leads in area, production and consumption followed by Europe.
- Annual to biennial, grows upto 20 cm height.
- As a staple food, ranks 4th after tomato, orange and potato.
- Primarily a salad vegetable and common ingredient of sandwiches in North America.
- It ranks 26th on the list of commercial vegetables arranged in order of nutritional value in unit terms (IU or mg/ 100 g tissue).
- Leaves are rich in vit. A (900 mg), vit. C (10 mg), choline (178 mg), Ca (50 mg) and P (28 mg), if cooked, most of vit. C is lost.
- A cigarette containing no nicotine is made from leaves.
- Seeds of primitive forms of lettuce in Egypt are used as source of edible oils.
- Latex from wild lettuce relative (*L. virosa*) is used inmanufacture of sleep inducing medicine.
- Used as pilot plant in comparative physiological investigations on cadmium uptake and distribution.
- Lettuce contain highest amount of 'Na'.
- Lutein rich vegetable.

- Leaf shape is a function of length, width and marginal folding and undulation.
- Sensitive to highly acidic soils.
- Optimum soil pH: 5.8 to 6.6.
- Shallow rooted vegetable.
- Cool season crop. Performs well under sub-tropical & temperate (12-15^{0}C) conditions.
- Cultivated lettuce prospers in cool environment and tolerates short period of freezing temperature.
- Mulching is recommended practice.
- Seed rate: 400-500 g/ha.
- Planting distance: 30-45 cm x 20-25 cm.
- Recommended CO_2 in green housecultivation: 1000-1500 ppm.
- Seeds have period of dormancy.
- Chilling treatment given to seeds in refrigerator or seeds kept in moist sand/ cloth at 4-6^{0}C for 3-5 days breaks its dormancy.
- Both, lower and high temperature affects itsseed germination.
- Seed germination is poor, if soil temperature is > 30^{0}C.
- Photoblastism (i.e. light-induced seed germination) is common.
- Seed germinate within 4-5 days and is promoted by red light (680 nm) and inhibited by infra-red light (730 nm) and blue light (450 nm).
- Sowing is done in nursery beds and 4 to 6 weeks old seedlings are transplanted.
- Fruit type: Greyish coloured achene (one seeded dry fruit that remains closed at maturity), 6-8 mm, obovate, narrow & finely muricate at apex.
- Growth occurs in 2 stages:
  1. Vegetative growth i.e. formation of rosette of leaves or a head.
  2. Seed stalk elongation and flowering: Seed stalk formation is agriculturally important event. undesirable event and indicates end of marketability of crop but is essential to produce seed crop.
- High temperature as well as lack of adequate soil moisture favours seed stalk elongation & induces bolting of plants.
- Temperature >22^{0}C, causes bitter taste of leaves.
- Long days essential for flowering.
- High temperature & increased light speed up the process.
- Highly self pollinated crop.
- Flower open only once & take 1-2 h for anthesis.

- Inflorescence type: Capitulum (dense corymbose, flat topped panicle).
- Elongating seed stalk produces single terminal capitulum (composite flower) & series of branches with many capitula forming panicle.
- Each capitulum comprises several (10 or > 20) florets.
- Each floret consists of ligulate (strap shaped) yellow corolla enclosing sexual parts.
- Flowers open in morning & expose the stamens.
- Stamens are fused & form tube.
- Anthers shed pollens at inside surface.
- Pollen is sticky & not easily wind blown.
- Style has two stigmatic lobes.
- Structure of flower obligates self fertilization.
- Bolting resistance is a quality trait.
- Crosses can be easily made in green houses/ outdoors.
- Critical stage of irrigation: Head formation.
- Salt accumulation in soil hampers production of leaves.
- At E.C.13 dS/m and above, lettuce cannot be grown i.e. salt accumulation in soils limit the production of lettuce.
- Lettuce matures non-uniformly and requires 3 or more harvests.
- It is better to avoid harvesting when there is rainfall/ dew, because leaves become very crisp & break easily on handling.
- Head type is harvested in 60-70 days when the heads are well formed, solid and of good size.
- Leafy type is harvested in 50-60 days when leaves are tender and immature but large enough to use.
- Yield: Head type (100-140 q/ha); leafy types give comparatively higher yields.
- Component of yield: Uniform maturity.
- Yield is measured in unit terms as 1 Carton= 24 lettuce heads.
- Seed yield: Leaf type (500-600 kg/ha), head type (100-125 kg/ha).
- Lettuce can be stored for 3-4 weeks under refrigerated conditions.
- Pre and post-harvest spray of BA @ 5-10 ppm delay senescence in storage and improves shelf life.
- Lettuce grown in soilless culture is bitterer than grown in soil.
- Uniform maturity is a component of yield.
- Wrapper leaves: Leaves surrounding the head.

- Leaf shape is the function of length, width, marginal folding and undulation.
- Wrapper leaves = leaves surrounding the head.
- Firmess or head density for harvest maturity is assessed by passing X-rays or gamma rays through head.
- In lettuce, genes for anthocyanin, shades of green & leaf shapes are useful as markers.
- Specific requirement for export purpose: Round, medium to large head (750 g to 1 kg) with wrinkled and green non-wraper leaves, brittle textured and tight folded.

Species:

- Seven levels of chromosomes in genus *Lactuca*: 2n= 10, 16, 18, 32, 34, 36 & 48.
- Garden lettuce, referred in generic sense as leaf lettuce, which differs from stem lettuce or Celtuce (*L. sativa* var. *augustana*).
- Indian lettuce (*Lactuca indica* syn. *L. sativa* 2n=2x=18): Cultivated; obligate self pollinating; involucre bracts erect when mature; cauline leaves not held vertically; flat or round inflorescence; achenes black/ white/ yellow/ brown & non-spiny; rosette more upright & only one stem at bolting.
- Wild/ Prickly lettuce (*L. serriola* 2n=2x=18): Probabale progenitor of cultivated lettuce. Obligate self pollinating. Cultivated; involucre bracts reflexed when mature, cauline wider leaves held vertically; inflorescence pyramidal panicle; spiny; forms rosette before bolting; possess multiple stems; achenes black & smaller; resistant to DM, Lettuce Mosaic virus and cabbage looper.
- Primitive forms: *L. altaica*, *L. augustana*: Both have large seeds & single stems; may or may not have spines; have erect involucres when mature; leaves may not be held vertically; panicles are corymbose and flat topped and forms flat rosette.
- *L. virosa* (2n=2x=18): Wild relative of lettuce; obligate self pollinating; resistant to DM, lettuce aphid and Lettuce mosaic virus. Latex is used to manufacture sleep inducing medicine.
- *L. saligna* (2n=2x=18): Wild relative of lettuce; obligate self pollinating; narrow & linear stem leaves; spike like panicle with sessile flowers; resistant to leaf spot, DM and cabbage looper.
- *L.dentata*, *L. perennis*: Resistant to basal drop.

Crossability:

- Primitive forms like *L. sativa* and *L. serriola* cross freely with each other despite of morphological differences.
- *L. saligna* when used as female parent only can cross with *L. sativa* or *L. serriola* & hybrids are fertile.

- *L. virosa* can cross with *L. sativa* & *L. serriola* in both the directions & hybrids are sterile. Hybrids can be made fertile by chromosome doubling.
- *L. altaica*, *L. augustana* cross readily with each other & with *L. sativa* and *L. serriola*.
- *L. saligna* & *L. virosa* are cross incompatible either way.

Varieties:

- Lettuce cultivation and breeding is done at Green house Crop Research Institute, Littlehampton, England.
- Crosses between Butter head & Crisp head types are easily distinguished by degree of colour, leaf shape, texture & modified growth.
- Alaska: Resistant to anthracnose.
- Valverde: Released by Whitkar & Leeper in 1959. Wider adaptability. Resistant to DM, brown blight, tip burn, big vein & Lettuce Mosaic virus.
- Padma: Attractive green and crispy leaves; mod. resistant to DM, aphids & cut worms.
- Thompson, Sea Green: Multiple disease resistant (DM, corky root rot, infectious yellow & root aphids).
- Crisp head type: Climax, Empire, Merit, Winter Heaven, Moranguard. These have wider adaptability and grown year round in USA.
- Butter head type: Bibb, Butter Crunch, Dark green Boston, Summer Bibb, White Boston.
- Cos type: Green Tower, Valmaine.
- Bunching type: Black seeded Simpson cv., Grand Rapids, Oak Leaf, Red Salad Bowl, Ruby Red, salad Bowl, Waldmann's Green.

Six morphological types:

Name	Breeding method	Features
Crisp head or Iceberg type (var. *capitata*): Most commonly grown (>30%) in USA; heading type with wrinkled, non-wrapper leaves, brittle textured; tight buds; prominent veins & mid-ribs; outer leaves are larger & dark green while inner leaves are light coloured & tightly folded; very sensitive to heat & excellent shipping and handling ability. Food value/ 100 g of tissue: vit. A (330 IU), Ca (20 mg), ascorbic acid (6 mg)		
Punjab Lettuce No.1	-	Non-bunching; bears loose leaves
Great Lakes-118, 659	Back cross pedigree method	Large head; bright green leaves with wavy margin; very crispy; butt whitish with prominent ribs; resistant to tip burn & Lettuce Mosaic virus; wider adaptability; recommended for cultivation in India
Imperial-859	-	Medium head; light green leaves with soft texture with serrated or wavy margin; varied in butt colour & ribiness; resistant to tip burn
Imperial-850	-	Resistant to PM
Imperial-410	-	Resistant to brown blight & DM
Imperial-44, 456	-	Resistant to brown blight & DM
LS-2, Iceberg	Introduction	Resistant to PM
Vanguard (1958)	Cross between [PI-125130 (*L. virosa*) x Complex line of (*L. sativa* x *L. serriola*) & F_1 hyrbid is back crossed to domestic lettuce *L. sativa*	Principal cv. grown in California & Arizona; creamy to yellow interior colour; spherical head; soft pliable leaves; leaf margin wavy & not serrated; butt green & flat ribs; extensive root system; less tendency towards bitterness & superior flavour; resistant to tip burn
Vanguard-75	Back cross & mass selection	Grown for late winter season in California & Arizona districts; dull green outer leaves & creamy yellow inner leaves; spherical head shape; 1st cv. resistant to Lettuce Mosaic virus; resistant to tip burn
Empire	-	Grown all the year round in US; Light green leaves which are deeply serrated; very crispy; heads conical shaped; butt whitish with flat ribs; resistant to bolting & salts
Calmar	Back cross pedigree method	Resistant to DM, brown blight, tip burn, big vein & Lettuce Mosaic virus
Salinas (1975)	Pedigree selection from cross of 'Calmar (crisp head type) x No. 8830 (*L. virosa* derived breeding line)'	Resistant to tip burn, Lettuce Mosaic virus, DM; grown year round in California

Francisco (1962)	Inbreeding	Principal cv. produced in USA
Monterey (1972)	Hybridization & pedigree selection	Resistant to tip burn
Butter head or Bibb lettuce or loose leaftype(var. *crispa*): Cultivated in green house & mostly favoured in England, France, Holland & western European countries. It has small, loose heads having oily, soft textured leaves. Leaves bruise & tear easily. Veins, mid-ribs & stem are not prominent; better table quality & more delicate flavour than crisp type; require care in handling & shipping. Food value/ 100 g tissue: vit. A (970 I.U), Ca (35 mg), ascorbic acid (8 mg)		
Reskia Wonder	-	-
Van Voorfing	-	-
Mary King	-	-
White Boston	-	Soft solid heads & inner leaves have oily, soft, greasy texture
Big Boston	-	-
Midas	-	-
Leaf or bunching type: Highly favoured in England, France, Holland & western European countries. Non-heading or leaf type lettuce produce rosette of leaves.They are early, easy to grow & popular for home garden; not adapted for long distance shipment & its market life is short; grown primarily in green house in winter.		
Slow Bolt	-	Leaf is broad, frilled & slightly yellowish green; very late bolting; resistant to tip burn; recommended for cultivation in India
Chinese Yellow	-	Early; light green crisp & tender leaves; resistant to tip burn; recommended for cultivation in India
Grand Rapids	-	Resistant to DM; very sensitive to far-red light dormancy
Solan Kriti	OP selection	Long leaves, soft & dark green colored; rich in β-carotene (5.59 µg/100g), Fe (1.63 mg/100g), Ca (58.07 mg/100g); yield 25 t/ha
Stem type (var. *asparagina*): Grown in Orient & Egypt. Perennial, produce thick stems, which are eaten rawafter peeling. Usually cooked for use in stewed & creamed dishes; not extensively grown; Most commonly found in home gardens.		
Celtuce	-	Thick stem is eaten after peeling
Romaine or cos type (var. *longifolia*): Commercially grown in Mediterranean region. It has greater proportion of green tissue, upright growth habit, elongated leaves form loaf-shaped head. More tolerant to unfavorable weather conditions; best adapted for local & export market. Food value/ 100 g tissue: vit. A (1900 IU), Ca (68 mg), ascorbic acid (18 mg)		
Dark Green	-	It has narrow leaves with elongated upright heads
Florida 83, Florida-1974, Floribibb	Selection from germplasm	Resistant to Lettuce mosaic virus, corky root rot & Bidens Mottle virus (viral disease found in Florida)
Parris Island	-	Very popular
Latin type: Grown extensively in South America & Mediterranean region		

Pests, diseases and disorders:

- Lettuce green peach aphid (*Nasonovia nibisnigri*): Spray systemic insecticide.
- Cabbage looper (*Trichoplusia ni*): Serious pest in desert districts in USA. Resistance based on antixenosis (oviposition & larval non-preference in *L. saligna*) & antibiosis (oviposition non-preference in *L. serriola*) have been identified.
- Infectious yellow: Caused by root aphids.
- Corky root rot:
- Brown blight (*Septoria lactucae*): Most serious disease 1st reported by I.C. Jagger (1926).
- Downy mildew (*Bremia lactucae*): Major problem Western Europe. Cvs. Montemar, Cal-K-60, Portage, Mesa-659, Valmine, Valtemp are resistant while, Empire, Ithaca, White Boston are highly susceptible. Spray Dithane M-45 @ 1.5 g/litre.
- Powdery mildew (*Erysiphe cichoracearum*):
- Verticillium wilt (*Verticillium dahliae*):
- Basal drop (*Sclerotinia minor, S. sclerotiorum*): Severe wilting of maturing plants. Common in muck soils during cool period. Crop rotation of onion, spinach and small grains is recommended.
- Bottom rot (*Rhizoctonia solani*): Prevalent during wet weather. Crop rotation of onion and sweet corn is practiced.
- Most serious post harvest diseases in green head lettuce: Botrytis rot and slimy soft rot (*Erwinia carotovora*).
- Slimy soft rot: Early removal of heads and keep soil surface relatively dry.
- Lettuce Mosaic virus: World wide disease problem since 1950. Seed borne and Green peach aphid transmitted. Chronic problem in most lettuce growing areas of the world in 1950. Transmitted @ 1-3%. Vein clearing followed by mottling. Mature plants become yellow, stunted and not harvestable. Crisp head cvs. are highly susceptible. Use virus free seed. Cv. Monterey is resistant.
- Big Vein: Virus like characteristics of vein clearing & stiffening of leaves causing delayed or prevention of heading. Caused by virus like agent introduced into the plants by root feeding fungus (*Olpidium brassicae* or *O. lpidium*). Cvs. Sea Green, Calmer and Thompson are resistant.
- Tip burn: Burning/ scorching of lateral margins of inner leaves. Due to high light intensity, high temperature and duration causing heavy economic loss. Ca, Mn, B deficiency, excess N, high IAA; soil moisture content and ontogenic age of plant. Application of Calcium chloride can reduce the incidence.
- Russet spotting: Ethylene injury >0.1 ppm combined with high storage temperature (5^0C).
- Bolting: Plants exposed to hot and dry weather (> 29^0C) and long days may induce pre-mature flowering and seed stalk formation. Crisp head cvs. are more resistant.

- Brown stain: CA storage with excessive CO_2 concentration develops dark water soaked lesions near leaf base & mid-ribs. Usually intensified when O_2 levels are around 3%.
- Pink rib: Pink discoloration along mid-rib of outer leaves is most severe under high transit temperature and low O_2 atmosphere.
- Aster yellow (MLO): Spread by leaf hoppers.Affected plants show yellowing & curling or twisting of young leaves.

Inheritance of characters:

- Rate of bolting is positively correlated with earliness.Bolting resistance = slow seed stalk formation.
- Coupling linkage is observed between indeterminate growth habit and photoperiodic response.
- Resistance to root aphid. Controlled by extra nuclear factors & involves modifying genes.
- Male sterility (MS) was 1st identified by Lindqvist (1960) & it is controlled by 3 complimentary recessive genes.
- MS is controlled by dominant-recessive epistasis (Ryder, 1963) or by single recessive gene (Ryder, 1967) or by single dominant gene (Ryder, 1971) & none have cytoplasmic basis. It is not cost effective in hybrid seed production.
- Seedling marker genes:
  a) In F_1 and selfed progeny are available.
  b) Genes for anthocyanin, shades of green and leaf shape are used as markers.
  c) Selfed show recessive gene for anthocyanin content and
  d) Hybrids show dominant trait if male is dominant.

Character	Number of genes	Type of gene action
Anthocyanin	-	Complementary *CCGG* results in anthocyanin formation & give red colour
Anthocyanin distribution pattern	-	*R*- Full red; R^s- spotted; R^{bs}- red brown spotting; R^t- tinged with red.
Leaf lobing	Monogenic (*UU*)	Non-lobed (*UU*) dominant to lobed (*uu*) & oak leaf (u^o)
Seed colour	Monogenic (*WW*)	* Black (*WW*) seed dominant to white (*ww*); * White seed epistatic to yellow (*yy*)
Resistance to DM	Monogenic (*RR*)	Resistance dominant to susceptibility
Resistance to Lettuce Mosaic virus	Monogenic recessive	Resistance recessive to susceptibility
Resistance to leaf aphid	Monogenic (*Nr*)	Resistance dominant to susceptibility
Male sterility	-	*ms-4, ms-5, ms-6*

11.2 Globe artichoke/ French artichoke/ Green artichoke

- Eulogized as 'Food for rich'.
- Crop was grown by Romans and Greeks as delicacy.
- Introduced to France in 16th century.
- Plant was brought to US by French settlers in Louisiana and by Spanish and Italians in California.
- Common name comes from Italian 'articoclos' meaning 'pine cone like appearance of flower bud'.
- Worldwide, the major producers are USA, Italy, Spain, France.
- USA production accounts for 4% of world supply.
- Herbaceous perennial exotic vegetable grown in temperate regions as annual.
- It has high medicinal and nutritional values.
- Used in folk medicine as contraceptive & aphrodisiac. Aids in liver detoxification and regeneration. Stimulates gall bladder and fat metabolism. Used to treat hepatitis and jaundice.
- Leaves are bitter and useful in dropsy and rheumatism.
- Lowers sugar in body, cholesterol, cure migraine caused by toxins in blood, diuretic and improve lust of skin.
- In Italy, its bitter principle is used as vermouth.
- Comprises 85% water, half carbohydrate indigestible inulin, turning to fructose in storage. Moderate in iodine and iron content.
- Leaves are thistle-like, giving the plants a coarse appearance.
- Edible part: Fleshy involucural bracts (i.e. immature flower buds) and the base (i.e. thick receptacle known as 'heart' is used for canning. The mass of immature florets in centre of bud is called the 'choke'.
- When artichokes are grown from seed, they can be grown as annual.
- Highly sensitive to frost.
- Optimum soil pH: 6-7.5.
- Planting time: February-March.
- Commercial propagation: Root suckers/ Offshoots (30-45 cm height from older/ established plants in November) or Division of old crowns with stem portion of original plant.
- Planting distance: 1.8-2 m x 0.6 m.
- Optimum temperature for growth: 12-18^{0}C.
- Temperature > 25^{0}C results in tough buds and plant shows tendency to spread.
- Roots can tolerate freezing temperature (-2 to 1^{0}C) but kills buds and above ground growth is injured and delayed harvest by 6-8 weeks.

- Frost cause blistered appearance and affect marketability.
- Head diameter: 2.5 to 10 cm.
- Progenitor: Cardoon (*Cynara candunculus*).
- Cross pollinated crop by insects.
- Slashing and stumping: Techniques necessary in perennial types for manipulation of growth cycle to enhance availability period.
- Slashing: Plants are cut at 20 cm above ground.
- Stumping: Plants are cut below 5 cm of ground level. It helps more regeneration than slashing.
- Harvesting season: September-October.
- Harvesting:
  - Each flowering stem produces one large artichoke at the tip and several smaller ones below.
  - Harvest when scales are tightly closed.
  - Remove the terminal bud first with 5-7.5 cm of stem and remaining side buds when grow large enough.
  - Remove the lower buds for eating when about 4 cm long.
  - Once scales bein to open, globe artichoke become inedible.
- Yield: Buds of 10-12 t/ha.
- Buds are graded for size and quality and then packed in paperboard cartons containing 48-125 buds.
- Storage: Buds are stored for 3-4 weeks at 0.5^0C and 90% R.H.

Varieties:

- Head green colour, big sized: Camsude Bretagne, Castel, Green Globe (large heads with thick fleshy scales).
- Head green colour, medium sized: Argentina, Espanola, Sakiz, Bayrampsha, Bianco, Tarantino, Purple Sicilian (small, deep purple coloured artichoke excellent for eating raw. Susceptible to frost).
- Head purple colour, big sized: Romanesco, C_3, Purple Globe (hardier than green forms but not tasty).
- Head purple colour, medium sized: Brindisina, Catanese, Baladi, Criolla.
- Gros Camus de Bretagne: Suitable for warm climate, large, well flavoured heads.

Pests and diseases:

- Aphids: Cause damage by sucking sap from underside of leaves.

- Plume moth: Larvae cause serious looses by feeding on blossom buds.
- Fusarium root rot and botrytis rot: Most severe during the period of warm and wet weather.
- Black tip: Severe under moisture stress condition.

11.3 Jerusalem artichoke/ Girasole/ Sunchoke

- It is not related to globe artichoke nor does it bear any relationship to Jerusalem.
- Erect, hardy, tuberous cool season perennial but cultivated as annual.
- In 1920, it was invented that Jerusalem artichoke is commercial source of fructose and can replace beet and can as a source of sugar.
- Grown for their potato like fleshy, oblong tubers i.e. young rhizomes (3-4 inches long).
- Tubers contain inulin (storage polysaccharide $C_6H_{10}O_5$ that is difficult to digest & turning to fructose in storage) in lieu of glucose.
- Considered as equal to potato in food value.
- Nutrient composition/ 100 g edible portion: Moisture (71.4-84.2%), protein (0.9-3.3%), ash (0.9-2.5%), crude fibre (0.3-3%), fat (0.1-2.5%), -CHO (8-19%) and low in calories.
- Nutritive value of tuber: Digestible protein (1.2%), digestible nutrients (15.9%), nutritive ratio (12.3%).
- Principal –CHO in tubers: Levulose, glucose, & whole series of gluco-fructosans from sucrose to inulides.
- It is commercial source of levulose, used as sweetening agent by diabetic patients.
- Nutty flavoured tubers contain a carbohydrate which causes flatulence.
- Tubers may be eaten raw or boiled, pickled, made into chips or ground to flour, industrial alcohol and beer like beverages are prepared from it.
- Green tops and stems and stakes of young plants yield 20% pulp, which is suitable for papar making.
- Tubers are knobby and range in colour from white to yellow and from red to blue.
- It is frost hardy, grows 4-5 feet in height and resembles sunflowers.
- Planting distance: 2-3 inches deep, 2-3 feet apart in rows 3-4 feet apart.
- Planting season: March-May (plains), February-April (hills).
- Propagation method: Optimum size of seed tubers/ small setts of 50 g with 2-3 eye buds.
- Tuberization occurs in late summer when day length decreases.
- Harvesting: About 5 months after planting when top growth is killed by frost.
- Prior to harvest, the tops should be removed.

- Higher yield obtained under long day conditions.
- Yield of tuber is greatly reduced by early cuttings of tops.
- Optimum temperature for cultivation: 18-26^{0}C.
- Crop requires 125 frost-free days for yield.
- In colder regions, tubers are dug before the soil freezes and stored at 0^{0}C and 90-95% R.H. upto 4-5 months.
- Unharvested tubers resume growth in late winter or early spring and may become weed problem.
- Tubers are field stored without any deterioration in quality or flavour.
- Tuber quality is not deteriorated in soil.

Pests and diseases:

- Slugs tend to hollow out tubers. Use aluminium sulphate traps.
- Sclerotinia rot: Stem bases are covered with white mold.
- Cut worms cause damage to stems at ground level.

11.4 Chichory/ Endive

- Eulogized as 'Belgian endive or French endive or Italian dandelion or Wit loof chicory.
- Very old vegetable was known to Egyptians & discovered as early as 1806 and grown in home gardens exclusively in USA and Canada.
- Herbaceous annual or biennial or perennial herb produces continuous rosette of leaves.
- Leafy salad vegetable.
- Responds to day length and high temperature to bolting.
- When plant bolts, it produces elongated, sparsely foliated stem and bears perfect, self compatible/ self pollinated, purple/ white coloured flowers that open in the morning h only.
- Types of leaf characteristics of escarole group:
  1. Smooth/ slightly crumpled leaved, more broadened or deeply toothed with white mid-rib.
  2. Crinkly leaved or heavily curled and deeply toothed leaves.
  3. Either type of leaf encloses loose head which is creamy in interior parts.
- Both types are grown for their dried roots, which are grown and used as coffee substitute.
- Seeds are naked achenes.
- Optimum temperature for growth: 15-18^{0}C.
- Production season: November- May.

- Optimum soil pH: 6-7.5.
- **Species**: *Cichorium endivia* (syn. *C. endivia* var. *crispa*).
- **Varieties**: Sugar Hat, Radicchio, Hybrid Zoom, Salad King, Grower's Giant, Deep Heart Fringed.

Composition:

Parameters	Endive raw	Chichory (wit loof)	Chichory green
Ca (mg)	81	18	86
P (mg)	54	21	40
Fe (mg)	1.7	0.5	0.9
Na (mg)	14	7	Nil
K (mg)	294	182	420
Vit A (IU)	3300	Trace	4000
Thiamine (mg)	0.07	Nil	0.06
Riboflavin (mg)	0.14	Nil	0.10
Niacin (mg)	0.5	Nil	0.5
Ascorbic acid (mg)	10	Nil	22

12. BASELLACEAE

12.1 Basella

- Eulogized as 'Indian spinach or Malabar spinach or Malabar night shade or Vinespinachor Climbing spinach or Chinese spinach or East Indian spinach or Poi'.
- Nutrition composition/ 100 g edible portion: -CHO (6.5 g), dietary fiber (0.7 g), fat (0.8 g), protein (3.4 g), vit. A (1759 µg or 3250 IU), vit. C (70 mg), Ca (380 mg), Fe (16.2 mg), P (30 mg) and energy (46 Kcal).
- Short day, twinning, much branched, perennial leafy vegetable.
- C_4 cycle photosynthetic pathway.
- Long day promotes flowering and extremely heat tolerant.
- *Basella alba* (Dark green and heart shaped, thick fleshy leaves): 2n=2x=48.
- *B. rubra* (Red Ceylon spinach): 2n=2x=44. Red stem and red, oval round leaves. Grown as edible and ornamental purpose. Highly susceptible to root knot nematode. Not affected by insects.
- Other botanical forms: *B. nigra*, *B. saponica*, *B. cannifolia*.
- In Thailand, flower spikes are sold as vegetables.
- Colours obtained from leaves, stems and ripe fruit of red cultivars are used for colouring food, dying fabrics and in paintings in North-Eastern hilly regions of India particularly Manipur.
- Juice of leaves is prescribed against constipation for children and pregnant women in China, bright red juice is stored in the form of powder called '*gintjoo*'.

- Leaves are stems are used as poultice to treat boils.
- Flowers are used as antidote to poison.
- Grows well in hot and humid climate.
- Low temperature inhibits growth rate and results in smaller leaves.
- Partial shade produces larger leaves than under full sunlight.
- At high altitudes (> 500 m MSL) growth is limited.
- Optimum soil pH: 5.5-7.5.
- Seedlings are thinned at 2-3 true leaf stage.
- Seedlings are transplanted at 5th true leaf stage.
- Plants are trained on support when start trailing.
- Water stress induces early flowering and lead to thin stems and smaller leaves.
- Edible part: Succulent mucilaginous leaves along with petiole.
- Optimum temperature for growth: 25-33°C.
- Flowers: Sessile, bisexual and yellowish white or rose pink coloured.
- Flowering does not occur in day length > 13 h.
- Type of fruit: Single seeded berry.
- Ideal soil pH: 5.5 to 6.8.
- Crop duration: 120-150 days.
- Commercially propagation: Seed, stem or root cuttings.
- Seed rate: 12-15 kg/ha.
- Produce seeds freely in spring (N. India)/ winter (S. India).
- Harvesting stage: 8-10 weeks after seed sowing & 6-8 weeks from root/stem cuttings.
- Yield: 10-50 t/ha.

Varieties:

Name	Breeding method	Features
CARI, Port Blair		
CARI Poi Red	-	Multicut type
CARI Poi Red Shaan	-	Fast growth
IIVR, Varanasi		
Kashi Poi-1	-	Soft, lush green shoots; early picking with delayed flowering; tolerant to water lodging; excellent source of anti-oxidant with low oxalate content; yield 51 t/ha
Kashi Poi-2	-	Fast growing bush type; green stems and leaves; suitable for making saag, pakode, soup; excellent source of anti-oxidant with slightly lower oxalate content; yield 63.5 t/ha
Kashi Poi-3	-	Fast growing; twinning growth habit; high betalain content, suitable for year round cultivation; rich source of carotenoids with lower oxalate content; yield 61.3 t/ha

13. CHENOPODIACEAE (GOOSEFOOT FAMILY)

13.1 Garden beet/ Beet root

- Introduced in USA in 1800 and become known as 'garden beet'.
- The 1st extensive records of beet culture are available from the 16th century.
- The Garmans and French became interested in beet culture around year 1800 and since then many improved varieties / types have been developed.
- 1st domesticated as leafy vegetable then as root crop and finally as source of sugar.
- It is herbaceous, dicotyledonous biennial plant and cultivated as annual for sugar production.
- It is grown in 45 countries and provide > 25% of world's sugar requirement.
- World's 40-45% sugar is manufactured from sugar beet.
- Major producers: USA, UK, Russia, Egypt, Turkey, Germany, China, France and Ukraine.
- Introduced into India as a commercial sugar crop with most of exotic varieties.
- In India, it was 1st grown in Punjab in 1914 and in 1968, beet sugar was prepared at Sri Ganganagar, Rajasthan.
- It is one of the efficient converter of solar energy into stored energy.
- Calorific value: 22 Kcal/ 100g.
- Nutrition score: 70.
- Parts used: Root and leaves (vegetables) and sugar industry.
- Roots of table beet can be served in salads and boiled or pickled. Tops can be used as leafy green or salads or boiled.
- It is a 6-7 months crop and yields sugar almost as 12 months.
- Stem: Short and plate like.
- Leaves: (Dark green to red coloured), simple and arranged in a closed spiral on a part of stem called 'crown'.
- In 2nd year, plate-like stem elongates and flowers and seeds are produced.
- Betanin: Act as anti-depressant.
- Tyrosine: Boost L-Dopa (dopamine) production.
- Rich source of folic acid, essential for pregnant women to reduce risk of *spina bifida*.
- Beet greens (leaves) rich in Fe and vit. A (21000 IU).
- Initial sucrose content is 7.5% and was increased to 13-17% and thereafter sugar beet was used in sugar manufacturing.
- Industrial uses: Manufacture of citric acid, yeast, anti-biotics and other products of fermentation industry.

- Nine tonnes of sugar beet produces 50 kg dried and 300 kg wet pulp.
- Dry pulp contains 60% -CHO and 5% crude proteins.
- Lactic acid and vit.Bis extracted from beet molasses.
- The mature root is divided into 3 parts: a) the crown is convex cone b) just below is neck, which is broadest part of beet c) lower most part is root, which terminates into a long tap root.
- Colour development is due to betaine, which is suppressed at high temperatures and results in marked increase in zoning under hot weather.
- Colour of root is due to presence of –
  - Red-violet pigment : β-cyanins.
  - Yellow pigment: β-xanthin.
- Range of betaine: 426-691 mg/kg fresh weight.
- Upper portion of root develops from hypocotyls and lower portion from tap root.
- Enlargement of hypocotyls is due to growth of several concentric vascular rings.
- Concentric rings are result of alternate formation of vascular tissue and storage parenchyma tissue during development of fleshy root.
- Plant forms large storage root + leafy top.
- Edible part: Alternate circular bands of conduting and storage tissues.
- Bands of storage tissues are relatively broad and dark, while those of conducting tissues are narrow and light.
- Contrast in colour between alternating bands is known as 'zoning' which varies between cultivars and within a cultivar.
- Zoning consist of alternating bands of storage and conducting tissues.
- Cool season crop and tolerates mild frost and light freezing temperatures.
- Inflorescence type: Large spike which normally develops in 2nd year.
- Pollination agent: Wind (anemophilous).
- Indicator plant for sodium deficiency.
- Earthing up is essential to prevent greening of roots.
- Propagation method: Seed.
- Type of fruit: Capsule i.e. dry cork like body containing seed ball (aggregates of two or more fruits).
- Seed ball (glomule) type: Monogerm (uniloculari.e. one seed per seed ball & highly desirable for precision planting) and Multigerm (i.e. multilocular).
- Seed ball contains 2-6 seeds.
- 1 g seed-ball contains 50 seeds.
- True seeds are small, kidney shaped and brown coloured.

- Seed viability under normal storage condition: 5-6 years.
- Seed rate: 5-6 kg/ha (for monogerm) and 8-10 kg/ha (for multigerm).
- Seeds are covered with thick hard layer.
- Optimum temperature for seed germination: 18-24^{0}C.
- Seed soaking in water for 2-4 hours is practiced to remove germination inhibitor.
- Seedlings are raised under green house on hot beds or cold frames.
- Seedlings are hardened for 15-20 days.
- Seed balls are usually planted, 0.5-1.0 inch deep, in rows 12-24 inches apart @ 8-10 lbs/ acre for fresh market beets to 15-25 lbs of seeds/ acre for processing beets.
- Staggered sowing at 2 weeks interval is commonly recommended for beet root.
- Sowing time: September-November (plains); March-April or June- August (valley).
- Planting distance: 45 cm x 8 cm (accomodates 80,000-1,00,000 plants/ ha).
- Plant population significantly affects shape and size of beet root.
- Thinning at 5-10 cm is practiced in multigerm seeds for uniform shape and size of roots.
- Tops of the beet roots after attaining fair size can be pruned or thinned to be used as greens.
- Transplanted seedlings develop malformed or fangy root with less weight.
- Vernalization temperature for premature bolting: 4-10^{0}C for 2-3 weeks.
- Ideal temperature for proper growth of plants and sugar accumulation: 20-22^{0}C.
- In cool temperature (13-21^{0}C) growth is rapid and uninterrupted, zoning is reduced, and sugars are relatively high.
- Temperatures > 26^{0}C can make roots tough and low sugar content.
- Sugar accumulation retards at >30^{0}C temperature.
- High temperature produce roots with coarse and woody flesh with dull colour.
- Low sugar content is associated with poor colour.
- Under unfavorable conditions, beet shows alternate white and coloured circles when sliced.
- Crop is very sensitive to acidic soils.
- Thrives well in alkaline soils (pH 9-10).
- Optimum soil pH: 6.5 to 8.0.
- Rich loam soil is desirable for producing shapely roots, lighter soils for early crop and muck soil is excellent for late beet, since it is loose and moist.
- For fresh market, it is harvested when it attain a diameter of 5-7cm and 55-80 days after planting.
- For processing, it is harvested 90-110 days after planting and when 60% roots are less than 2 inch in diameter and 40% are over 2 inch diameter.

- Beets for bulk marketing or canning are topped in the field when attain dia. of 6.5 to 8 cm.
- Deterioration starts if roots are left for more than 10 days after attaining full size.
- Fresh market beets are marketed with tops on.
- Topped beets can be stored for 4-6 months at 0^0C at 90-100% R.H.
- Bunched beets (3-6 roots/ bunch) are kept for about 10-14 days.
- Sugar beet produces about 35-50 tonnes roots/ ha with sugar content of 15-16% amd 10-12% sugar recovery.
- From healthy crop, 8-10 tonnes of sugar/ ha is produced.
- Seed maturity starts from base of inflorescence.
- Cross pollination is due to self incompatibility.
- Self sterility can be overcome by sib-matings.
- CMS was discovered by Owen (1945).
- Seed production in India: Only in hills.
- For producing elite seeds, stecklings are selected and replanted.
- In root-to-seed method, planting of whole root is recommended.
- About 1/3rd bottom root length is cut off. These are sown in August-September. Seed crop mature in 12 months.
- Seed yield: 800 kg/ha.
- Roots of triploid sugar beets are larger in size than diploids but they maintain sugar content of diploid and hence yield more sugar/ unit area. Triploids are highly sterile and do not produce any seeds.
- Triploids are produced by interplanting diploids and tetraploids.

Species:

- Beet root, sugar beet and palak are cross compatible.
- Non-horticultural form of beet root: Sugar beet, mangels and fodder beet, but belong to same species as garden beets.
- Garden beet originated from *Beta vulgaris ssp. maritima* by hybridization with *B. patula* (closely related spp.)
- Ancestor of garden beet root: Sea beet or Fodder beet (*B. vulgaris ssp. maritima*): Indigenous to southern Europe.
- Leaf beet chard: *B. vulgaris ssp. cicla.* Grown as leafy vegetable.
- Garden/ Sugar beet/ Table beet/ Red beet: *B. vulgaris ssp. crassa.*
- Spinach beet: *B. vulgaris ssp. benghalensis.*
- *B. vulgaris ssp.maritima* and *B. macrocarpa*: Resistant to phytophthora root rot.

Classification based on root shape:

1. Flat type: Flattened at top & bottom with rounded sides and conical/ tapered base e.g. Flat Egyptian.
2. Round/ globular type: Root shape round or globular e.g. Detroit and Crimson Globe.
3. Half long: Length is shorter than long types e.g. Half Long Blood, Winter Keeper.
4. Long type: Long roots (40 cm) and popular in Europe e.g. Long Dark Blood.

Classification based on the edible part:

1. Grown for their fleshy roots belong to Crassa or Garden group and include yellow beets, sugar beets and the common table or red beets.
2. Those kinds grown as leafy vegetables belong to the Cicla group and include leafy beets and Swiss chard.

Varieties:

- In beet root, tropical or Asiatic or annual types are unavailable.
- All cultivars are temperate biennial types.
- Exotic varieties and early maturing: Crosby Egyptian, Early Wonder (dark red skin, roots globe shape).
- Danish polyploidy multigerm cvs.: Maribo Magnapoly, Marcopoly.
- Bristish cv. Avon Early: Resistant to bolting & DM (*Peronospora farinose* f. sp. *betae*).
- Russian cv. Khavskaya: Mid season and monogerm; Ramonskaya: Diploid and multigerm. 14-16% sucrose, sensitive to leaf spot.
- Ohio Canner: Developed through sib-mating.
- Joniai (Russian cv. x Dutch cv.): Universal mid-early variety.
- Suitable for canning: New York, Washington & Detroit Dark Red.
- Poor colour development is due to high temperature
- IISR Composite-1: Developed at Lucknow is diploid multigerm. Self fertile, 14-18% sucrose and 7.25-9 t/ha, suitable for saline soils.
- Ooty-1 (selection from local type; used as salad). Duration 120-130 days.
- Pant S-10: Selection from genetically broad based population, semi-spreading, spindle shaped roots, yield 50-55 t/ha with sucrose content 14.5-15%. Suitable for saline soils. Tolerant to cercospora leaf spot and sclerotium root rot.
- For saline soils, Pant-S-1, IISR Composite-2 are recommended.
- Private sector: Madhur, Ruby Red.

Cultivar	Days to maturity	Root		Comments
		Shape	Colour	
Cardinal	60	Globe	Bright red	Processing; roots hold shape
Crosby Green Top	58	Oval	Dark red	Home garden, bunching; distinctly zoned
Detroit Dark Red	60	Globe	Dark red	Processing, market, home garden; main season crop
Early Wonder Green Top	58	Oval	Purple-red	Bunching, greens; tops hold colour
Gladiator	54	Globe	Bright red	Early; processing
Redpack	68	Globe	Dark red	Processing; little interior zoning
Ruby Queen	55	Round	Bright red	Processing, market; home garden; holds shape

Diseases, pests and disorders:

- Phytophthora root rot (*Phytophthora drechsleri*):
- Beet mosaic yellow virus: Transmitted by aphids.
- Curly tip virus: Transmitted by hoppers.
- 'Zoning' (appearance of alternate light and dark red concentric rings in root): Due to high warm weather.
- Internal black spot/ Brown heart/ Heart rot/ Crown rot/ Canker: 'B' deficiency in alkaline soils. Irregular black spots through out the ineterior of roots. Dead areas and cavities form along the cambium rings within fleshy roots.
- Boron deficiency is common in alkaline soils & overcome by liming.
- High N fertilization causes increased glutamine in leaves and gives off flavour.
- Speckled yellow: Mn deficiency.
- Sodium is essential nutrient.

Inheritance of characters:

- Green leaf yield is positively correlated with leaf length and leaf width.
- Red colour (*RRYY*) of root dominant to yellow (*rryy*) or white (*Rryy*).
- Intensity of red root colour is influenced by minor polygenes.

13.2 Palak

- Eulogized as 'Indian spinach beet or spinach beet or Beet leaf'.
- Palak is closely related beet root, sugar beet and swiss chard (2n=2x=18).
- Palak produces hermaphrodite bisexual flowers.
- Most common leafy vegetable of tropical and sub-tropical region.

- Winter season crop.
- Tolerates frost than other vegetables.
- High temperature leads to premature bolting.
- Temperature above 25^0C coupled with long day condition leads to bolting.
- Anthesis time: 9 AM to 5 PM with peak 11 AM to 1 PM.
- Pollination agent: Wind.
- It requires more 'N' for growth.
- Temperature above 25^0C coupled with long day condition leads to bolting.
- Bud development phase takes 35 days to come to bloom.
- Nutrient composition/ 100 g edible portion: vit. A (9770 IU), vit. C (70 mg) and Ca (380 mg).
- Palak contains 9.5% oxalate. Varieties with less oxalate content (<780 mg/100 g) have been developed in University of Arkansas, California.
- Palak is tolerant to saline soils (pH 7.0).
- Seed rate: 25-30 kg/ha (summer crop) and 10-15 kg/ha (winter crop).
- Line sowing facilitates weeding, hoeing and harvesting.
- Seed germinate after 8-10 days of sowing.
- Spinach beet is herbaceous annual for edible leaf production and biennial for seed production.
- It crosses readily with Swiss chard and beet root and cross incompatible with spinach.
- Seed viability: 3-4 years.
- Seed is monogerm or multigerm (2-3 seeds/fruit) in spinach beet.
- Fruit is seed ball.
- Harvesting: 1st cutting after 35-40 days after sowing.
- Average leaf cuttings: 4-6.
- Crop bolts about 75 days after sowing and seeds mature in 150-180 days.
- Seed yield: 600 kg/ha.

Two groups:

1. Cultivars with reddish midrib and leaf veins.
2. Cultivars with green midrib and leaf veins.

Varieties:

Name	Breeding method	Features
IARI, New Delhi & regional station, Katrain		
All Green	Inbred selection from indigenious source	Uniform green tender leaves
Pusa Bharati	Polyploid breeding	Leaves 25 cm long & 14 cm breadth; high vit. C & β-carotene; yield 50 t/ha
Pusa Palak	Hybridization of 'Swiss Chard x Local Palak'	Late bolting
Pusa Harit	Hybridization of 'Sugarbeet x Local Palak'	Thick, green, very large & slightly crinkled leaves; very late bolting & does not bolt in plains; yield 26 t/ha; suitable for hills; tolerant to alkaline soils
Pusa Jyoti	Induced mutant of cv. 'All Green'	Polyploid cv; leaves very big, crisp, dark green; 6-8 cuttings; grown throughout year; yield 43 t/ha
IIHR, Bengaluru		
Arka Anupama (2001)	Pedigree selection from 'IIHR 10 x IIHR 8' upto F_7 generation	Late bolter; multicut type; low in oxalates; resistant to cercospora leaf spot & excellent cooking type
CIAH, Bikaner		
Thar Hariparna (2018)	Selection over native population	7-9 pickings from Nov.-March; leaf length (9.81–12.54 cm); leaf width (5.72–8.11 cm); leaf width (1.748–1.838 g); wt. of 100 leaves (174.8–183.8 g)
RAU, Jobner		
Jobner Green	Selection from spontaneous mutation from local collection 'sel. No.5'	Leaves large, green, thick, strong flavour with entire margin; yield 30 t/ha; tolerate high soil pH upto 10.5
PAU, Ludhiana		
Punjab Green (1990)	Selection from local germplasm	Purple pigment on stem; slow bolter; 1st cutting at 30 days after sowing; free from sourness
Punjab Selection	Selection from local germplasm	Thick leaves, low oxalic acid content
HS-23	Mass selection	Quick growing; dark green leaves
GBPUA & T, Pantnagar		
Pant Composite-1	Composite breeding	Tolerant to cercospora leaf spot
BCKV, Kalyani		
Banerjee's Giant	Hybridization of 'Local Palak x Beet root'	Very succulent stem
TNAU, Coimbatore		
Ooty-1 (1995)	Selection from introduced material from Himachal Pradesh	Leaves vey large; higher in vit. A & carotene in content; grown throughout year
Other varieties		
Palak No.51-16	Selection from local germplasm	Several cutting & late bolter
AHLP-1 (2019)	Selection	First harvesting of leaves at 34.2 days with October sowing & 100 leaves wt. 178.35 g

13.3 Spinach

- Eulogized as 'Vilayati palak or *Chukka*' or *Pahari palak*' and classified as pot herb.
- First cultivated by the Arabs, who later introduced it into north Africa. From there it was brought to Western Europe through Spain around the year 1100 AD and spread to rest of the Europe by 15th century.
- Most important vegetable greens grown in USA.
- Texas and California are leading states for fresh market (75%) and processing spinach (50%) production.
- It is cooked alone or with other vegetables.
- Spinach is highly nutritious among all leafy salad vegetables.
- Leaves contain high oxalic acid.
- Dioecious annual that grows to maturity in about 30-50 days.
- Good source of Omega-3-fatty acid, carotenoids.
- Nutrient composition/ 100 g edible portion: -CHO (2.9 g), protein (2 g), vit. A (7045 IU), vit. C (28 mg), folic acid (132 mg), Ca (107 mg), K (605 mg), Na (110 mg), Mg (92 mg), P (70 mg) and energy (23 Kcal).
- It is temperate crop and extensively cultivated in Europe, USA and Canada.
- Hardy and cool season crop.
- It is a long day plant w.r.t. flowering and critical day length ranges from 12-15 h.
- The change from vegetative to reproductive growth is conditioned by temperature and is usually accelerated by exposure to cold temperatures followed by high temperatures.
- Exposure of plants to 10-15^{0}C for a month can induce flowering in short day condition.
- Long days coupled with warm weather (>25^{0}C) are favorable for seed stalk formation.
- Under high humid conditions, leaves become more succulent and tender.
- Photoperiodic response can be altered by low temperature treatment.
- Crop is very susceptible to air pollution including ozone and SO_2 emittants, which cause speckling and marginal necrosis on leaves.
- In plains, desi types are sown during June-November whereas exotic types from October-December.
- In hills, desi types can be sown in March-may, whereras exotic types from October-December.
- Edible part: Compact rosette leaves with lobbed leaf margin.
- Sensitive to acidic soils (pH <6 causes poor growth) but has high tolerance to saline conditions.
- Optimum soil pH: 6-7.
- Seed of spinach is prickly.

- Prickly seeded variety is best suited for autumn /winter crop in the hills.
- Smooth leaved and round seeded variety is best suited for spring (Sept-Oct.)/ summer crop in the plains.
- Spinach tolerates frost better than most other vegetables.
- Pollination agent: Wind.
- Photoperiodic response can be altered by low temperature treatment.
- Optimum temperature: Seed germination (10-15^{0}C) and growth and development (15-25^{0}C).
- As soil temperature decreases, the percentage of seed germination increases, but seedling emergence is delayed.
- It has very high respiration rate and large leaf surface to weight ratio.
- Number of flowers/ cluster: 6 to 12.
- Multigerm plant is reduced to one by a process called 'singling'.
- Multigerm seeds occur as a cluster of seed fused together and produces more than one plant when it germinates.
- Asian types are mostly prickly seeded and have triangular shaped leaves.
- Plant passes through two stages of development viz. vegetative stage and reproductive stage.
- In vegetative or rosette stage: (a) the plant has single stem in which the internodes are extremely short (b) smooth or savoyed leaves arise in a whorl around the stem, forming a rosette of foliage.
- The reproductive stage is initiated by elongation of stem, which breaks apart the rosette and forms a branching flower-seed stalk.
- Reproductive stage is usually in response to long days and warm temperatures and marks the end of its marketable life.
- Rosa (1925) described 4 sex forms (i.e. multisex) viz.
  1. Extreme males:Small with little vegetative development and poor yielders. Seed stalk bear smaller leaves and staminate flowers and early bolting nature than vegetative males and female plants. They are not preferred due to their small sized leaves and early bolting nature.
  2. Vegetative males: Plants larger in size than extreme males and remain vegetative for longer period. Produce more foliage due to longer vegetative phase, give fairly high yield and are preferred plant types for commercial production.
  3. Females: Plants larger in size, remain vegetative for longer period & bear only pistillate flower.
  4. Monoecious: Rarely few plants bear varying proportions of staminate and pistillate flowersin certain cultivars. Most desirable for market and seed production. These are true breeding plants.
- Male flowers in cluster on spike whereas female flowers borne in clusters in leaf axil.

- Extreme males and vegetative males do not bear any seed.
- Male and female plants appear in almost equal proportion.
- Female and monoecious plants are used for edible purpose, breeding purpose and production of F_1 seeds.
- Monoecious and male plants are uprooted as and when noticed in hybrid seed production.
- Seed rate: 37-45 kg/ha, due to 50% male plants with poor growth and forms seed stalk.
- Time of sowing depends on varieties and place of cultivation.
- It is planted in such a way that plants will grow and mature in cool season.
- Using ammonical fertilizer can result in lower nitrate concentration in leaves than with nitrate sources.
- Fertilization regimes using nitrification inhibitors such as Nitrapyrin (2-chloro-6-trichloro methyl pyridine) in combination with ammonium fertilizers have been used to lessen nitrate accumulation in spinach.
- Crop requires around 9-12 inches of water and pre-sowing irrigation is advised.
- Between emergence and harvest, 3-4 irrigations are required at 4-5 days interval.
- Seed stalk is produced in 65 days after planting and seeds can be harvested in 180 days.
- Harvesting: Crop is ready for 1st trimming in 4 weeks after sowing.
- Average number of cuttings: 3-4/ season at 15-20 days interval depending on variety and season.
- Harvesting is done in evening because leaves become crisp due to dew and easily break in morning.
- Under short day conditions, multiple harvests can be made from plants that have been cut above the growing point.
- Trimming is done in field or in packing sheds.
- Plants harvested for fresh market are allowed to wilt slightly before handling and hauled in order to minimize the breakage of leaves.
- After harvesting, diseased and damaged leaves are removed and bundled into bunches of about 10-20 leaves for convenience in handling and marketing.
- Yield: 8-10 t/ha.
- It is highly perishable and leaves can be stored only for about 24 hrs after harvesting under ambient conditions.
- Cold stored at 0^0C and 90-95% R.H. for 10-14 days.
- Crushed ice, hydrocooling and vacuum cooling are satisfactory methods for cooling.
- Precooled by vacuum cooling to prevent wilting and weight loss.
- CA storage: CO_2 (10-40%), O_2 (10%) reduce yellowing and improve quality.
- Spinach for market is packed in bushel baskets, hampers and crates.

- For long distance markets, crop is transported by refrigerated trucks.
- The sealed transparent packages prevent wilting and allows gaseous exchange for maintenance and quality.
- Heterosis can be exploited for practical purposes.
- Spray of GA_3 @ 10 ppm + 1% urea increases yield.
- Seed shattering is major problem.

Varieties:

- Five groups:
  1. Prickly seeded types:
  2. Smooth seeded types:
  3. Savoyleaved: Plants produce large leaf blades, dark green, wrinkled and curled leaves, enhanced appearance and mostly grown for fresh market as well as long distance shipment, by reducing losses due to anaerobic respiration. Low night temperature tends to cause savoy form of leaves.
  4. Flat or smooth leaved: Plants produce broad, smooth leaves, easier to wash and suited for processing and machine harvest.
  5. Semi-savoyed type: Hybrid variety produces slightly wrinkled leaves and grown for fresh market and processing into frozen packs.
- For mechanical harvesting, erect growth formed cultivars are preferred.
- Cultivars vary in their resistance to bolting and length of time they remain in vegetative stage after reaching market maturity. This characteristic is known as 'long standing'.
- On the basis of growth habit varieties are classified as prostate, semi-erect and upright.
- Seed type in spinach does not indicate whether it is smooth leaved or savoy type.
- Asian types are mostly prickly seeded and have triangular shaped leaves.
- Prickly seeded cvs. (Virginia Savoy) perform well in hilly areas and round/ smooth seeded cv. (Early Smooth Leaf) in plains.
- Smooth seeded: Blistered large dark green leaves with round tip.
- Popular desi types: Khara Lucknow, Khara Palak, Banarasi (Katvi palak), Banerjee's Giant.
- Early Hybrid 7, Early Hybrid 10: Disease resistant from Texas Agri. Expt. Station.
- Pusa Vilayati Palak: Short duration, two cuttings, yield 12 t/ha. Contains high ascorbic acid, iron and calcium (65, 8 and 186 mg/100 g, respectively).
- Lal Palak (syn. USDA Red): Developed at Plant Development and Protection Research Centre, California. It is having red leaf veins (presence of β-cyanin), more nutritious, high anti-oxidants (42-53% more) than any other prickly, red leaved varieties. Leaf veins are rich in β-carotene, folic acid, and minerals like iron, calcium & phosphorus. Resistant to bolting & cancer. Used for salad purpose. Releases stress in canver patients.

- **Important characteristics of selected cultivars of spinach.**

Cultivar	Chief use	Season (days)	Long standing	Leaf type	Resistance to			
					Heat	Cold	Mosaic	Mildew
Bloomsdale Dark green	H,M,S,C,F	40	Med.	Savoy	No	Med.	No	No
Bloomsdale Long Standing	H,M,S,C,F	42	Yes	Heavy savoy	Fair	Med.	No	No
Bounty	M	42	Yes	Semi-savoy	-	-	-	Yes
Chesapeake Hybrid	F	40	No	Semi-savoy	No	Good	Yes	No
Dixie Market	M, C, F	37	Med.	Savoy	-	Med.	Yes	Yes
Hybrid 7	H, M, S, C, F	39	No	Semi-savoy	No	Med.	Yes	Yes
Hybrid 424	H	38	Med.	Smooth	-	Med.	-	Yes
Hybrid 612	M	43	No	Savoy	-	Med.	Yes	Yes
Hybrid 621	H, M, C, F	40	No	Savoy	-	Good	Yes	Yes
Melody	H, M	45	Yes	Semi-savoy	Fair	Med.	Yes	Yes
Packer	M, C	39	Yes	Savoy	-	Good	-	Yes
Seven R Hybrid	C, F	37	No	Semi-savoy	No	Exc.	Yes	Yes
Viking	S, C, F	45	Yes	Smooth	Fair	Med.	No	Yes
Virginia Savoy	M, S, C, F	39	No	Savoy	No	Med.	Yes	Yes

H (home), M (market), S (shipping), C (canning), F (freezing).

Diseases and pests:

- White rust (*Albigo occidentalis*): Major foliar disease of winter grown fresh market spinach.
- Downy mildew or Blue mold (*Perenopsora effusa*):
- Anthacnose (*Colletotrichum spinaciae*):
- Cercospora leaf spot (*Cercospora veticola*):
- Leaf spot (*Heterosporium* spp.): Widely distributed & most severe in winter.
- Fusarium decline: Air temperature above 22.2^{0}C or soil temperature > 21^{0}C are conducive to develop disease. Use of crop rotation.
- Mosaic or blight: Due to Cucumber mosaic virus.
- Wilt
- Tobacco ring spot virus.
- Beet curly top virus: Transmitted by leaf hopper.
- Aphids (*Myzus persicae*): Spray systemic insecticide.
- Spinachleaf miner (*Pegomyia hyoscyami*): Feed between leaf surfaces.
- Seed corn maggot, cut worms, grass hoppers, flea beetles: Other pests.

Inheritance of characters:

- Sex determination-
  - Gene *A* or *a* for maleness.
  - Gene *G* or *g* for femaleness.
  - Heterozygote *AG*/ *ag* for intersex.
- X-Y system involved in expression of sex.
- Presence of Y chromosome, controls maleness (XX- pistillate; X^mX, X^mX^m; XY, X^mY- staminate).
- In addition to X/Y mechanism-
  - *zz*- male determining.
  - *ZZ*- female determining.
  - *Zz*- intersex.

13.4 French spinach

- Eulogized as 'Orach or *Chakwat* or Mountain French spinach or Wonder plant'.
- Strong flavour than spinach.
- Crop is grown for its large, ovate leaves that develop on the upper portions of its tall stalks (6-8 feet high) throughout the season.
- It is drought resistant and easily grown.
- Seed dormancy period: December-February.
- Leaves contain sulphated flavonoids.
- Winter season vegetable grown as a substitute for spinach.
- It can be grown during times when spinach readily bolts.
- Four types of seeds: Black or yellowish brown in colour and with or without bracts.
- Black seeds require nitric acid treatment for germination.
- Pollination agent: Wind
- Propagation method: Seed.
- Seed rate: 5 kg/ha.
- Planting distance: 60-90 cm x 45-60 cm.
- Optimum soil pH: 6-7.
- Harvesting stage: Tender leaves after 4-5 weeks after sowing.
- Yield: 70 q/ha.
- Variety: Chakwat No. 11.

13.5 Bathua

- Eulogized as 'Pig weed or Lamb's Quarters'.
- Winter season wild weed.
- Tender leaves and stems are rich in carotene, iron and calcium.

- Leaves are dull green, with pale pink centre with waxy coating and wavy margins.
- Nutrient composition/ 100 g edible portion: 2.9 g carbohydrates, 3.7 g proteins, 0.4 g fat, 0.8 g fibre and vit. A_1, B_2, B_3 and C, 150 mg Ca, 80 mg phosphorous.
- Propagation: Seeds (smaller than mustard).
- Brown seed germinate rapidly while black seeds take longer time.
- Seedlings of 35-40 days are uprooted or clipped near ground and used as greens.
- Yield: 30 t/ha in 50-60 days.
- CURAC: It has Cupric iron reducing anti-oxidant capacity (CURAC).

Varieties:

Name	Breeding method	Features
IARI, New Delhi		
Pusa Bathua-1	Selection	Multi-cut variety; large size and dark green leaves; 2-2.5 m tall; ascorbic acid 23 mg/100 g; yield 30 t/ha
Pusa Bathua-2	-	-
Pusa Green	Selection	Multi-cut variety; carotenoids (91.31 mg), iron (7.6 mg), ascorbid acid (50 mg); 2-2.5 m tall; yield 37 t/ha
IIVR, Varanasi		
Kashi Bathua-2	-	Upright growth, green leaves; excellent source of vit. A, vit. C, phenolics & anti-oxidants; yield 37 t/ha
Kashi Bathua-4	-	Upright growth, purple green leaves; excellent source of vit. A, vit. C, phenolics & anti-oxidants; yield 35 t/ha
TNAU, Coimbatore		
Ooty-1	-	-

13.6 Ceylon spinach

- Eulogized as 'Water leaf'.
- Species in which leaves are eaten: *Talinum crassifolium, T. cuneifolium, T. portulecefolium, T. indicum, T. patens, T. arnotti, T. cuffurum*.
- Edible portion: Tender stem and leaves.
- High oxalate content of leaf makes its consumption limited.
- It is a warm season, soft mucilaginous leafy vegetable.
- Short day favours flowering & fruiting.
- It is a shade loving vegetable.
- Highly self pollinated.
- Propagation method: Seeds or herbaceous cuttings.
- Spacing: 30 cm x 30 cm.
- Harvesting stage: 15-20 cm length shoots.
- Yield/ ha: 4000-6000 kg cut green.
- 1st harvest in 45 days after sowing.
- Purple flower colour is incompletely dominant to white flower colour.

13.7 Swiss chard

- Also known as Leaf beet or Seakale beet or Silver beet or Spinach beet or Chard'.
- Closely related to beet but grown for its of foliage instead of roots.
- Plant develops large, fleshy leaf stalks which may be white, green, pink or red.
- Nutritional values/ 100 g edible portion: Vit. A (6500 IU), Ascorbic acid (32 mg), Ca (88 mg), P (39 mg), Fe (3.2 mg), Na (147 mg), K (650 mg), Thiamine (0.06 mg), Riboflavin (0.17 mg), and Niacin (0.5 mg).
- Broad leaf blades are used for fresh salad purpose and mid-ribs or stalks are cooked.
- Cool season herbaceous biennial that tolerates hot temperature.
- Field planting can be done from transplants or from direct seeding.
- Plants grow larger in size and need to be thinned to at least 4-6 inches apart in row.
- Harvesting: It is hand harvested usually by removing only the outer, larger petioles after 50-60 days after planting.
- It is highly vegetative plant, new heart growth occurs and outer petioles successively mature for continuous harvest.
- Outer leaves are harvested without injuring growing point.
- Stalks that are bright and blemish free are bundled together in bunches & quickly cooled to remove field heat and to reduce the rate of respiration.
- Harvesting period: Several weeks to 2 months.
- It is stored up to 10 days at 0^0C and high R.H. of 90-95%.
- Constant top icing is necessary to maintain shelf life.

Varieties:

- The ancient Greeks (350 BC.) recognized the Red chard, the White (called Sicula) and the Black (so named for its intense deep green colour).
- Lucullus: A yellowish-white petioled chard is most important cv.
- Cultivars are distinguished primarily by mid-rib colour ranging from white to burgundy red.
- There are many highly coloured ones such as Dark Green Lucullus, Ford Hook Giant, Large Rib, Rhubarb Giant, Rhubarb Chard, Ruby Red and Dark Green White Bibbed.
- Dark Green Lucullus, Ford Hook Giant, Large Rib, Rhubarb Giant.

13.8 Some spinach-like vegetables

Common name	Species	Origin & current distribution
Tender green mustard	*Brassica campestris*var. *viridis*	Chinese; South-East Asia, North America
Abyssinian mustard	*B. carinata*	Ethiopia; North America and Britain

14. CONVOLVULACEAE/ (MORNING GLORY FAMILY)

14.1 Sweet potato

- Eulogized as 'Irish potato or White potatoor Spanish potato or Louisiana yam'.
- Only food crop in morning glory family.
- Introduced to China and India by the Portuguese.
- It is world's 7th largest food crop.
- Chosen as one of 8 crops to be grown for long term space mission by NASA.
- Grown as starchy food crop in the world after potato.
- In USA, it is referred commercially as a 'yam'.
- Largest grower in the world: China representing 88.9% of world production.
- In USA, 60-70% of sweet potato is utilized for human food.
- India is largest producer in South East Asia and 6th largest in the world.
- In India, sweet potato is generally cultivated as rainfed crop with a productivity of 8.3 T/ha as against world's 13 T/ha.
- Maximum area under cultivation in India: Odisha (42,000 ha).
- Every year sweet potato festival is organized in England by Scot Farm International.
- Leaves are rich source of nutraceuticals.
- Vines and roots are fed to livestock. It has potential for fuel alcohol conversion and successfully tried in many countries.
- Source of industrial starch in Japan.
- Fresh produce has superior taste than to processed products.
- Anti-nutritional factor: Trypsin (Protease) inhibitor, oxalic acid.
- Anti-mutagenic activity of purple fleshed sweet potato: Cyanidin type anthocyanin.
- Lipids present in roots give off-flavour during storage of processed products like flakes and chips.
- Cultivars differ for ploidy level.
- Sweet potato is short day plant.
- Drought hardy crop.
- Dicot, vining or rosette herbaceous perennial in tropical and sub-tropical climate but cultivated as annual in temperate region and not found in wild state.
- Grown throughout the world from 40^0 N to 30^0S latitude, under highly contrasting production systems.
- Cultivated in latitudes between 40^0N and 40^0S and altitude of 2000 m MSL.
- It is tolerant to saline soil conditions.

- Average dry matter content: 27-30% of which 75-90% is –CHO and 0.4% fat.
- Fresh sweet potatoes provide about 50% more calories than Irish potatoes.
- High calorie diet and cheapest source of calories (152 Mega Joules/ha/day).
- Calories per 100 g edible portion are between 95-117 for dehydrated product.
- Richest source of vit. A (14190 μg/100 g) of edible portion. Watt *et al.* (1963) reported that vit. A content varies as (i) Firm fleshed-Jersey types (9200 IU), (ii) soft fleshed-Puerto Rico types (8700 IU) and (iii) In dehydrated sweet potatoes (12000 IU).
- β-carotene content: 5.4-30 mg/100 g.
- Total sugar content: 0.4 to 0.6% on fresh wt. basis.
- Fibre content- about 7% and pectin content (5% on fresh wt. basis).
- Root storage protein 'sporamin' accounts for 75-80% of total protein in roots.
- Anthocyanins have medicinal properties like anti-oxidant and anti-hypertensive effects.
- Botanically, tuber is fleshy sub-terranean stem or root.
- Plant arises from adventitious buds on fleshy roots.
- Plant may develops 4 to 10 tuberous roots which vary from fusiform (tapering to both ends) to globular in shape and may be smooth or ridged.
- Fleshy roots produce adventitious shoots called 'slips'.
- The slips develop adventitious roots of their own and become small plants attached to the original root. These are used as commercially as propagating material.
- Three types of adventitious roots: Storage (arise from nodes), primary fibrous (arise from internodal region) and pencil (greater in dia. compared to fibrous roots but smaller than storage roots).
- Moisture shortage delays harvesting and excess soil moisture encourages tuber cracking.
- Excessive rainfall and long photoperiod encourage vine growth but reduce tuber yield.
- Ridge and furrow: Best for raising crop.
- Optimum row to row spacing: 60 cm.
- Optimum soil pH: 5.8 to 6.7 and sensitive to alkaline and saline conditions.
- Better quality roots are produced when soybeans or other legumes are followed in rotation.
- High soil pH invites pox and scurf diseases,
- Compact soil checks development of tubers and highly sandy soil encourages long cylindrical pencil like tubers.

- Regular removal of secondary branches is practiced for better development of roots.
- Optimum temperature for growth (>24^{0}C) and for tuber formation (20-30^{0}C).
- Crop growth ceases < 15^{0}C & chilling injury and set back occurs at 10^{0}C.
- Required light intensity for tuber formation: 18,000-40,000 lux.
- Ideal day length for flowering: 11.5 h.
- Long photoperiod encourages vine growth and reduces tuber yield.
- Tubers contain starch 16% (15-28%), 3-6% sugar. It is composed of 1/3rd of amylase and 2/3rd of amylopectin.
- During cooking, starch is converted into maltose which gives sweet taste.
- Anthesis time: 4-5 AM and closes by 9-11 AM.
- Inflorescence type: Cymose.
- Flowers funnel shaped, bisexual, occur in axillary inflorescence of 1 to 22 buds.
- Flower opens in group of 2 or more in morning & fade by noon.
- Flower colour: White to purple and funnel shaped.
- Type of fruit: Capsule containing 1-4 glabrous or pubescent, flat & hard coated seeds.
- Mature seed are dark brown/ black coloured and flat on two sides and round on other points.
- 100 seeds weigh 2 gram.
- Seed diameter: 3-5 mm.
- Seed coat is hard and requires soaking in H_2SO_4 for 20-40 min and mechanical scarification for germination.
- Seed viability: 20 years or more.
- Pollination agents: Honey bee and bumble bee.
- Sporophytic SI is observed.
- Seed germination: Very irregular & require mechanical/ chemical scarification.
- Sexual seedlings are highly variable.
- Modes of propagation: Seed propagation is followed in breeding for improved cultivars.
- Vegetative propagation either by transplants called 'slips' (most common in sub-tropical & temperate zones) or by vine cuttings of 2/4/6 node stems avoids transmission of nematodes or root borne diseases & produce higher yields.
- Commercially propagation: Vine cuttings (40,000-50,000 cuttings/ha) prepared from upper portion than basal or middle portions.
- In nursery, seed tuber planting @ 1.5 kg/100 m^2 at 25 x 60 cm is ideal for field planting for 1 ha area.

- Weight of cuttings required for hectare planting: 10-12 q.
- Optimum size of cuttings: 20-30 cm long.
- For having 4-5 sound (healthy) buds, the minimum length of cutting should be 30 cm.
- By forcing of tuberous roots, the sprouts/ draws/ shoots formed are stripped and planted in hot beds. When they have 6-8 leaves and good root system are used for field planting.
- Upto 15 slips can be produced from each parent root.
- Tuberous roots are sliced in sections and planted after suberization.
- Micropropagation: Tissue culturing of meristematic tissue.
- About 450-675 kg of tuberous roots/ ha or 29,786 plants/ ha are required.
- Planting by hand or with single/ multi-rowed transplanters is practiced.
- Ideal planting period: May-July. October to November when assured irrigation is available and January-February in summer.
- Primary nursery: 100 sq.m area/ha. Plant at 60 cm x 30 cm. Tuber wt. 100-150 g add 1.5 kg Urea duting planting.
- Secondary nursery: 500 sq.m. Plant terminal cuttings at 60 cm x 30 cm. Apply Urea @ 5 kg after 15 and 30 days after planting.
- No. of irrigation cycles required: 4 to 8 irrigations or 45-60 cm of water.
- Over irrigation results in over growth of vines and leads to over sized and misshapen or cracked roots.
- Irrigation is withheld during last 3-4 weeks before harvest.
- Black plastic mulching (2mm) over the sprouting tuberous roots induces early establishment of plants.
- Turning of vine practiced at early growth stage to increase tuber yield.
- Harvesting stage: 4-5 months after planting.
- Correct stage of maturity: Latex remains whitish in colour after cut; leaves turn yellow and drop down.
- By cutting tubers and verifying that latex dries up without turning black indicates its maturity.
- Harvesting of small sized roots (prior to maximum root development) results in maxium bulk yield.
- Highly perishable & very susceptible to fungal rots.
- After harvest, tubers are cured in partial shade.
- Curing of roots promotes rapid healing injury i.e. suberization, forms new corky layers and reduces further decay in storage (prevents microorganism invasion & undue water loss).

- Best curing temperature for suberization: 27-30^{0}C and 80-85% R.H. for 4-7 days.
- Cured and stored roots remain edible for 6-7 months at 13-15^{0}C and 85-90% R.H.
- Cannot be stored for longer period at ambient conditions.
- Pit storage method increases shelf life of tubers upto 6 months.
- Storage temperature >30^{0}C can stimulate the development of sprouts and increase in pithiness of tubers.
- Storage temperature < 10^{0}C causes chilling injury and results in discolouration of flesh, internal breakdown, increased decay susceptibility, losses in vitamin content and off-flavour when cooked.
- During curing, weight loss may occurs upto 5%.
- Shrinkage of tubers (weightloss of about 2%) is also recorded due to dehydration as well as some transformation of starch to sugars.
- During curing & storage period, starch is converted to sugars & dextrins.
- PGR for reducing sprouting: Isopropyl-N- (3-chlorophenyl carbamate).
- Reduction in starch and increase in reducing sugar leads to poor quality.
- Difficulties in production of pure white starch: Polyphenolic compounds, ascorbic acid, and carotene present in tuber.
- Starch can be converted into glucose by acid or enzyme hydrolysis.
- Periderm acts as formidable barrier to insect.
- CCC (500-1000 ppm) and SADH are the best PGRs used for tuber yield.
- Yellow fleshed cultivars contain carotene and red fleshed contain anthocyanin.
- Yellow types are not as sweet as white cultivars but have good flavour and cooking qualities.
- Orange fleshed varieties with high dry matter content are suitable for making chips & French fries.
- High levels of phenols lead to discoloration in processed products.
- ‘Fermented n-butyl’ alcohol is manufactured from sweet potato.
- Sweet potato is easy to micropropagate but recalcitrant to regenerate.
- Artificial seeds of cv. White Star, encapsulated in genes have been produced in Univ. of Florida.
- Incorporation of mycorrhiza long with ‘P’ sources increases sugar content.
- Root yield sharply decreases under coconut shade.
- Short duration and early bulking cultivars escape weevil infestation.
- Tissue culture is used for production of foundation stock.
- Lack of stability in tuber production is major problem in cultivation.

- Value added stable products: Jam, pickle, puree, soft drinks, instant gulab jamun mix.
- Uses:
    - Industrial starch, syrup and alcohol.
    - Roots are eaten boiled or baked, candied with syrup or pureed.
    - Roots can be used for canning, dehydrating, flour manufacturing.
    - They can be used as source of starch, glucose, syrup and alcohol.
    - Tuberous roots/ older vines can be used as feed. Fodder for livestock.
    - Because of vining growth habit, some cultivars have ornamental value as ground cover or in hanging basket and planters.
- Starch extracted from tubers is used in textiles, paper, food manufacturing industries and preparation of glucose, adhesives & production of ethyl alcohol.
- Tubers are processed into frozen, canned or flaked products.

Grading of roots for baking purpose (US standards):

1. Standard grade # 1: 2-3" dia. & 3-9" length.
2. Canner roots: 1-2" dia. & 2-7" length.
3. Jumbo or over-sized roots: Exceed the standard grade # 1 in dia. & length.
4. Cull roots: 1" or large in dia. & mis-shapened/ cracked/ unattractive.

Species:

- Most probable ancestor: : *Ipomoea trifida* consisting 2x, 3x, 4x and 6x cytotypes.
- Name 'batatas' was used by the native American Indians in referring to this vegetable.
- *Ipomoea batatas* (syn. *Batatas edulis*) is allohexaploid (2n=6x=90) with B genome and highly heterozygous crop.
- *I. mauritiana*, *I. alba*, *I. digitata*, *I. marginana*, *I. campanulata*: Medicinal value.
- Suitable rootstock cultivar for flowering and seed set inducer (*I. carnea ssp. fistulosa*).
- Taxonomic classification is reported by Robbins (1931).

Varieties:

- Cultivars are very heterozygous and genetically unstable.
- Kind of variability is attributed to mutations which occur with different frequencies for different traits.
- Yellow and red skinned potatoes may occur on the same plant.
- Soft fleshed, gelatinous and sweeter types actually contain less water than the firm type.
- Methods of breeding: Polycross and mass selection (widely adapted method).

- Ayamurasaki: Japanese variety of deep violet coloured is commercially used for extraction of pigments.
- Bio-fortified (carotene rich) varieties: Kala, Karoti Dar, Resisto, Simama, SPK 004-Kakamega, Tainung, Zapallo.
- Verde, Kalmegh are sweet potato varieties.
- Carver: Resistant to fusarium wilt and flea beetle.
- Pope, Travis: Resistant to internal cork, fusarium wilt, southern root knot and flea beetle.
- Maryland Golden, Ruby, Heart-a-Gold, Nema Gold: Resistant to root knot nematode.
- ST-13, CIP-SWA-2.
- Promising cvs. grown in USA: Georgia Jet, Oklamex Red, Caromex, Pope, Carver.
- Firm fleshed cvs.: Nugget, Red & Yellow Jersey strains.
- Leading non-food cvs. are White Star and Pelican Processor.

Name	Breeding method	Features
Unit-I, Cleitt Buneh, Puerto Blanco, Nancy Hall, Ranger, Early Port, Georgia Red	Exotic	Soft fleshed
Centennial	Exotic	Soft flesh; large tapered roots; vigorous; good keeper; resistant to hard core disorder
Puerto Rico	Exotic	Purple stain at base of leaves; light rose to rose skin colour; Soft flesh; disease susceptible; resistant to hard core disorder; widely adapted
Nemagold	Exotic	Soft flesh; tubers yellow; deep orange flesh, high in carotene; resistant to black rot & root knot nematodes
All Gold	Exotic	Purple stem, golden skin; high in ascorbic acid content; resistant to wilt & black spots
Nancy Gold	Exotic	Buff skin colour & deep orange flesh
Tipian, Red Gold, Orlis, Jersey Orange, Rod,	Exotic	Firm flesh & resistant to fusarium wilt
White Star	Exotic	Heavy yielder; light fleshed; white skinned, feed & industrial use; tolerant to stem rot
Yellow Jersey	Exotic	Yellow firm flesh; russet skin; green leaves without purple stain on leaf base; resistant to fusarium wilt
Gold Rush	Exotic	Deep orange flesh, light copper skin, resistant to fusarium wilt
Canner, Triumph	Introduction from Australia	-
Jewel (NC-240) 1971	-	Commercial cv. of America; soft flesh: multiple pest resistant; resistant to fusarium wilt, flea beetle, southern root knot nematode & internal cork; good baking & canning quality

Jasper, Eureca, Rojo Blanco, Painter, Vardaman	-	Released by North Carolina Expt. Station & commercial cvs. of America; soft fleshed; resistant to soil rot infected areas
Liberty	-	Commercial cv. of America; nematode and fusarium wilt resistance; skin red colour & flesh cream coloured
Boneto	-	Grown in USA; less sweetness; used either as cooked or fried or to make curry
Charleston Scarlet	-	Grown in USA; orange flesh with multiple pest resistance
B-4004	American type	White skin with red/purple streaks & cream coloured flesh
Tai Nong-57	Exotic	Resistant to leaf eating caterpillar (due to sporamine content)
CTCRI, Thiruvananthapuram		
H-41 (1971)	Hybrid of (Japanese cv. Norin x Indigeous cv.)	Duration 120-130 days; sweet low fibre content; red skin & white flesh; suitable for Karnataka
H-42 (1971)	Hybrid of (Indigenous cv. Vella Damph x American cv. Triumph)	Duration 120-130 days; sweet; low fibre content, pink tubers; suitable for Karnataka
H-635	-	-
H-620	-	Resistant to weevil
Sree Nandini (1987)	Seedling selection from OP progeny	Drought tolerant; cream coloured tubers; yield 20-25 t/ha; skin & flesh white; suitable for paddy fields as catch crop
Sree Vardhini (1987)	Seedling selection from OP progeny	Pink skin & orange flesh; β-carotene rich (1200 IU/100 mg) & dual purpose variety (tubers & for animal feed-vines); tolerant to feathery mottled virus; highly resistant to root knot nematode
Sree Bhadra (1996)	Selection from seeds introduced from IITA, Nigeria	Early maturing (90 days); creamy flesh & light pink skin; excellent trap crop for root knot nematode
Sree Rethna (1996)	Hybrid of (S-187 x Vardhini)	Early maturing; purple skin & orange flesh (3200-3500 IU/ 100 g)
Sree Kanaka (2004)	Hybrid of (S.187 x H.633)	Short duration; bio-fortified (β-carotene rich) (8.8-10 mg/ 100 g); good flavour; useful for preparing baby food; yield 13 t/ha
Sree Arun (2002)	Seedling selection from OP	Pink skin & cream flesh; yield 20-28 t/ha
Sree Varun (2002)	Seedling selection f.om CIP, Peru	Cream skin & cream flesh; yield 20-28 tha
Sree Varsha (H-268) 1966	Double hybrid between two exotic & two indigenous cvs.	Late group, red skin & light yellow flesh; drought tolerant; suitable for Konkan region; yield 20-22 t/ha
Sankar (1998)	Hybrid of (H-219 x H-73)	Yield 14 t/ha
Gouri (1998)	Hybrid of (H-219 x H-42)	Purple skin & orange flesh; yield 19 t/ha

Kalinga (2004)	Seedling selection from OP progeny	Red skin; high starch (29-30%); suitable for black sandy soils; sweet taste; yield 17 t/ha
Goutam (2005)	Seedling selection from OP progeny	White skinned & creamy white flesh; for upland & hilly areas; yield 19 t/ha
Kishan (2005)	Seedling selection from OP progeny	Red skin; high starch (29-30%); suitable for black sandy soils; sweet taste; yield 17 t/ha
Sourin (2005)	Seedling selection from OP progeny	Mid-season; tolerant to drought; yield 16 t/ha
Kiran (1994)	Seedling selection	Yield 22 t/ha
Kamal Sundari	Selection	Skin and flesh orange coloured; β-carotene rich variety; resistant to weevil
CTCRI Regional centre, Bhubaneswar		
Bhu Sona (ST-14) 2017	Pure line selection from exotic germplasm	Nutritionally fortified; rich in anti-oxidants; β carotene rich (14 mg/ 100g), white skin & white flesh; starch (19-20%); total sugar (2-2.4%); yield (20 t/ha) & tolerant to salinity (6-8 dS/m)
Bhu Krishna (ST-13) 2017	Pure line selection from exotic germplasm	Nutritionally fortified; starch (19.5%); purple flesh; anthocyanin rich (90 mg/ 100g); total sugar (1.9-2.2%); yield (18 t/ha); tolerant to salinity (6-8 dS/m)
Bhu Swami (ST-10) 2013	Pure line selection from exotic germplasm	White flesh; suitable for food & processing industries; tolerant to mid-season drought
Bhu Kanti (CIP-440127)	Pure line selection from exotic germplasm	Orange or golden flesh; β carotene rich (6.5 mg/ 100g); total sugar 1.9-2.2%; yield (20 t/ha); good cooking quality
Bhu Ja (CIPSWA-2) 2013	Pure line selection from exotic germplasm	Orange flesh; β carotene (5.5-6.4 mg/100g); total sugar (2.4-3%); yield (22 t/ha); good cooking quality
Central Island Agricultural Research Institute, Port Blair		
CARI-Swarna (SP-1)	Selection	Tubers light pink, orange fleshed; crop duration 110-120 days; yield 21 t/ha; resistant to weevil & suited to island conditions
CARI- Aparna (SP-2)	Selection	Tuberslight pink, orange fleshed; crop duration 110-120 days; yield 21 t/ha
IARI, New Delhi		
Pusa Sunheri	Selection from American complex cross (Porto Blanco Wannop x Australian Canner)	Brown skin; flesh light orange coloured, rich in carotene (24.8 ppm)
Pusa Safed	Single plant selection from China cv. FA 17 White	White skin & white flesh; excellent keeping quality; yield 30 t/ha
Pusa Lal	Selection from Japanese cv. Norin	Skin red & light orange flesh

RAU, Dholi		
Rajendra Sakarkand-5 (1985)	H-4 (commercial cv. of Bihar; susceptible to weevil) x H-5 (red coloured; highly resistant to weevil)	Tubers cylindrical with long neck; mature in 105-120 days; both skin & flesh white; yield 24-30 t/ha; suitable for flood prone area of north Bihar; resistant to fusarium wilt & cercospora leaf spot
Rajendra Sakarkand-35	-	Cylindrical fusiform tubers; skin white & flesh white; tuberization is non-clustering; mature in 105-110 days; yield 25-30 t/ha; mod. tolerant to weevil & cercospora leaf spot
Rajendra Sakarkand-43	-	Skin brown & flesh white; mature in 110-120 days; yield 20-23 t/ha; resistant to cercospora leaf spot & tolerant to weevil
Rajendra Sakarkand-47	-	Late harvesting; skin red & flesh white; yield 25-32 t/ha; tolerant to cercospora leaf spot & weevil
Rajendra Sakarkand-92 (2001)	Seedling selection	Red skin & white flesh; suitable for flood prone area of north Bihar; yield 25 t/ha
Kalmegh	Selection	Short duration (90 days); Round, light brown tubers with white flesh; mature in 90-105 days; yield 26-32 t/ha
APAU, Hyderabad		
Samrat	Clonal selection	Photo-insensitive (can be grown under diffused sunlight (40-60%); skin & flesh brown coloured; yield 18-25 t/ha; drought & salt tolerant; shallow bulking type
Dr BSKKV, Dapoli		
Konkan Ashwini (2000)	Selection from Varor village	Dual season; yield 19 t/ha; long tubers with dark purple colour
BCKV, Kalyani		
Bidhan Jagannath (2004)	Clonal selection	High carotenoid; yield 21-24 t/ha
BAU, Ranchi		
Birsa Sakharkand (2004)	Clonal selection	High carotenoid; yield 28 t/ha
IGKVV, Raipur		
Indira Madhur (2006)	Selection from CIP collection	Orange flesh; yield 22 t/ha
IGSP-4 (2004)	Clonal selection	Short duration; yield 25 t/ha
IGSP-15 (2006)	Clonal selection	Medium duration; yield 28 t/ha
IGSP-22	Clonal selection	White flesh, yield 30 t/ha
IGSP-10-6	Clonal selection	White flesh, yield 27 t/ha
CIP-440127	Clonal selection	Salt tolerant
NDUAT, Faizabad		
Narendra Sakharkand-9 (2004)	Clonal selection	Yield 26 t/ha
Narendra Sakharkand-10 (2004)	Clonal selection	Yield 22 t/ha

ANGRAU, Rajendranagar		
RNSP-1 (1999)	Selection from OP progeny	Yield 22 t/ha
RNSP-3 (2006)	Clonal selection	Yield 15 t/ha
TNAU, Coimbatore		
CO. 1 (1976)	Selection	Orange flesh, high β-carotene rich variety; yield 28 t/ha
CO. 2 (1980)	Clonal selection from OP progeny	Short duration & high starch (29.5%), β-carotene (3.2 mg/ 100 g); yield 32 t/ha
CO. 3 (1982)	Selection	Deep orange flesh; red skin; 3% root weevil incidence
CO.4	Selection	White flesh
CO. CIP-1 (1999)	Clonal selection	Yield 32 t/ha; tolerant to weevil incidence; pink skin; suitable for RTS, cutlet & chips making
VPKAS, Almora		
VL Sakarkand - 6 (1974)	Introduction from USA	Skin purple, flesh light yellow; mature in 120-135 dyas; yield 20 t/ha; suitable for Uttar Pradesh hills
VL Sakarkand-19 (1974)	Introduction from USA	Red, roundish; resistant to fruit rot; susceptible to late blight
KAU, Trissur		
Kanchangad Local	Selection	Early, spindle shaped roots; purple skin with yellow flesh; tolerant to shade; resistant to weevil

Other varieties: Badrakali Chuvala, Chakkaravalli, Anakomban, Kottaram Chuvala, Kalmegh

Inheritance of characters:

- Leaf shape is important character for identifying clones.
- Flower sterility of different intensities is due to allo-hexaploidy.
- Non-flowering trait perpetuates in subsequent generation.
- Positive correlation between:
  1. White or light flesh colour & high dry matter content;
  2. Orange & dark orange types & high specific gravity (1.04-1.06) or dry matter content.

Character	Number of genes	Type of gene action
Stem colour	Monogenic	Red stem dominant to green stem
Tuber skin colour	Digenic	Red skin dominant to green skin
Tuber flesh colour	Digenic	Red flesh dominant to white
Internode length	Monogenic	Long dominant to short
Floral fertility	Monogenic (S_1S_1)	Self fertility is dominant to self sterility
Day length	Monogenic	Short day condition characteristics dominant over long day

Pests, diseases and disorder:

- Root knot nematode (*Meloidogyne incognita*).
- Reniform nematode (*Rotylenchulus reniformis*).

- Sweet potato weevil (*Cylas formicarius*): World wide serious pest. Severe damage up to 20-55% in summer crop.
- Seed weevil (*Megacerus impiger*): Serious pest in field or in storage.
- Flea beetle:
- Sweet potato sphinx attacks mainly on leaves.
- Tortoise beetle feed on foliage and make holes on leaves.
- Soil and insect v.ire worms cause great damage.
- Convolvulus hawk moth: Cause defoliation of plants.
- Spotted tortoise beetle.
- Soft rot/ Rhizopus rot (*Rhizopus stolonifer*): Storage disease.
- Fusarium wilt (*F. oxysporum* f.sp. *batatas*) is major disease in nursery.
- Java black rot (*Ceratocystis fimbriata* or *Diplodia tubericola*): Major disease.
- Cercospora leaf spot: 1st reported in Africa.
- Stem rot: Major field disease. Follow crop rotation.
- Charcoal rot (*Macrophomina phaseolii*): Storage disesase.
- Hard core: Chilling of roots during storage < 5^0C.
- Internal cork: Most prevalent virus disease spread by aphids.
- Russet crack: Caused by Sweet potato Feathery Mottle Virus (SPFMV). Vector- Green peach aphid.
- Pox and scurf: Severe disease in neutral and high pH.
- Growth crack: Moisture imbalance.
- Failure of tuber formation: B deficiency.
- Excess N leads to production of very rough, irregular and tender tubers and increased weight loss during storage.
- Chilling injury causing internal breakdown: < 13^0C.

14.2 Water spinach

- In Thailand and Malysia, it is 2nd most widely grown vegetable after pakchoi.
- Popular in eastern states of India.
- Semi-aquatic tropical vegetable grown prolifically throughout Asia.
- It grows well in rainy season in ponds, lakes and other water bodies.
- Young tops are cooked and fried.
- Two common cultivars/ types:

1. Up-land grown: var. *reptans*. On dry/marshy lands. It has long narrow leaves with pointed ends and bears white flowers. Succulent foliage and stem tips are light green coloured. Propagated by seeds and cuttings.

2. Grows in water: var. *aquatica*. Propagated by cuttings and grows in wild or cultivated form in fish ponds/ water courses/ in beds with plenty of moisture.

- Fruit type: Seed bearing pods.
- Edible part: Practically all parts of young plant eaten raw as salad.
- Roots cure haemorrhoids.
- Due to its high iron content (1.67 mg/ 100 g), it is recommended to cure anaemia.
- Rich in vit. A, B_1, B_2 and C.
- Nutrient composition/ 100 g edible portion: Protein (2.6 g), -CHO (3.14 g), fat (0.3 g), dietary fibre (2.1 g), Ca (77 mg), P (39 mg), vit. C (28 mg) and energy (19 Kcal) of young shoots and leaves.
- Optimum soil pH: 5.5-7.0.
- Optimum temperature: 24-30^{0}C with atleast 760 mm rainfall per year.
- Crop is harvested several times as regrowth of shoots readily occurs.
- Harvesting time: 4-5 weeks after planting.
- Yield: 10-15 t/ha.

15. CRUCIFERAE

COLE CROPS/ VEGETABLE BRASSICAS

- Word 'cole' is abbreviated derived from Latin word '*Caulis*' means 'stem or stalk'.
- Family name 'Cruciferae' in Latin means 'cross bearers'.
- Latin name 'Brassica' is derived from Celtic word 'bresic' meaning 'Cabbage'.
- They belong to family 'Cruciferae' under order 'Papaverales'.
- Broccoli has smaller sized flowers than Brussels sprout, knolkhol and cabbage.
- Petal colour is cream-yellow to yellow.
- Flowers have 4 sepals, 4 petals, 6 stamens and superior ovary having 2 carpels.
- 'Tetra-dynamous' (six stamens i.e. 2 short & 4 long stamens) is the special anther type feature of cole crops.
- Two functional pistils are situated between the bases of two short stamens and ovary.
- Pollen grains size: 30-40 μ in dia. and have 3 germination pores.
- A protogynous flower, in which stigma remains receptive 3-5 days before and 4 days after anthesis.
- Ideal temperature for fertilization: 12-18^{0}C.
- Time required from pollination to fertilization: 24-48 h.
- They are highly heterozygous and heterogeneous in nature due to protogyny and sporophytic self incompatibility.

- Highly cross pollinated: Broccoii (95%), Knol khol (91%), Cabbage (73%) and Brussels sprout (72%).
- Pollination agents: Honey bees (*Apis* sp.) and blow flies (*Calliphora erythrocephala*).
- Fruit of cole crops: Siliqua i.e. bicarpellary pod containing 10-30 seeds. Siliqua is 4-5 mm wide and 10 cm long with 2 rows of seeds lying along edges of replum.
- Male sterility has been reported in cole crops but due to unstability, it is not used for commercial F_1 hybrid seed production.
- Male sterility can be induced by GA.
- Gibberellic acid (GA_{417-}) as a gametocide (induces complete sterility) for cabbage, cauliflower and Brussels sprout was proposed by Meer *et al.* (1979).
- Brassica's "Triangle of U" diagram proposed by 'Nagaharu U' (1935) shows genetic relationships of six species in the genus *Brassica.*
- Estimation of sibs in F_1 hybrids in cabbage and Brussles sprout is possible by analysis of acid phosphatase isoenzymes in seeds and seedlings (Will and Wiseman, 1980).
- Hegi (1919) reported all cole crops have originated from single wild cabbage or Cliff cabbage or Colewort (*B. oleracea* var. *sylvestris*).
- The species *B. oleracea* is triple tetrasomic with 6 basic genomes and genomic formula is *AABBCCDEF*.
- Genomic constitution of European mustard (*B. carinata*) is BBCC. It is resulted from crossing *B. nigra* x *B. oleracea*. It is cultivated as oil seed crop in Ethiopia.
- All these species have 'C' genome contain same number of chromosome and readily cross with each other.

Designation of cytoplasmic and nuclear genomes:

Species	ssp or var.	Cytoplasm	2n genome descriptor	Common name
B. nigra	-	B	*bb*	Black mustard (2n=16)
B. oleracea	-	C	*cc*	Cole crops (2n=18)
B. campestris	-	A	*aa*	-
-	*chinensis*	-	*aa.c*	Pak-choi
-	*nipposinica*	-	*aa.n*	-
-	*oleifera*	-	*aa.o*	Turnip rape (2n=20)
-	*parachinensis*	-	*aa.pa*	Choy sum
-	*pekinensis*	-	*aa.p*	Chinese cabbage (2n=20), pet-sai
-	*rapifera*	-	*aa.r*	Turnip (2n=20)
-	*trilocularis*	-	*aa.t*	Sarson
B. carinata	-	BC	*bbcc*	Ethiopian mustard (2n=16)
B. juncea	-	AB	*aabb*	Brown mustard (2n=36)
B. napus	-	AC	*aacc*	Fodder and oil rape, swede (2n=38)
	napobrassica	-	-	Swedish turnip/ Rutabaga (2n=38)
B. sativus	-	R	*rr*	Radish, daikon

- Vernalization (specific cold temperature treatment i.e 4-7^{0}C for 6-8 weeks) is prerequisite for bolting in cole crops.
- Plants of 3-5 months are easily vernalized and induce flowers.
- Chinese kale, broccoli, and early summer cauliflower need no vernalization even grown at 27^{0}C.
- Winter hardy kales and Brussels sprouts require 4-6 weeks of vernalization below 10^{0}C.

Crops	Chilling temperature	Weeks
Cabbage	4-10^{0}C	6-8
Brussels sprout	4-10^{0}C	4-6
Knol khol	7-10^{0}C	5-7

Species:

Cabbage	*Brassica oleracea* var. *capitata*
Cauliflower	*B. oleracea* var. *botrytis*
Brussels sprout	*B. oleracea* var. *gemmifera*
Sprouting broccoli	*B. oleracea* var. *italica*
Knol khol/ kohlrabi	*B. oleracea* var. *gongyloides*
Kale/ Tree Kale/ Collard	*B. oleracea* var. *acephala*

- Brussels sprout and Knol khol are typically biennial crops while broccoli comprises of both annual and biennial types.
- All biennials require low temperature (<10^{0}C for 6-8 leaves) for transformation from vegetative to generative stage i.e. initiation to flowers.
- Cauliflower is only crop in which intermediate stage of curding lies between vegetative and reproductive stage.
- Excessive use of cole crops induces swelling of thyroid glands and goiter disease.
- Highest vit. A: Kale (20,000 IU./ 100 g), Sprouting broccoli (9,000 IU./ 100 g).
- Highest vit. C: Kale (187 mg/ 100 g), Brussels sprout (185 mg/ 100 g).
- Browning of cabbage: Enzyme catalase.
- Cole crops are biennial for seed production and annual for consumptive use.
- Cole crops are calcicole or calciphyte or calciphile (thrives in lime rich soils).
- Father of cole crops in India: Dr. Pritam Kalia.
- Nieuwhof (1959) proposed family selection method (> 1 cycle of selection) and mass pedigree method of cabbage improvement.
- Book 'Cole crops' was written by Nieuwhof (1969).
- *Brassica* spp. has higher glucosinulates (stable precursor of isothiocyanates & stable water soluble compound) in seeds.

- Toxin 'thiocyanate' is more in kale and cauliflower.
- New vegetable 'Hakuran' is:-
  - Derived from interspecific hybridization between Cabbage and Chinese cabbage by embryo culture.
  - Resistant to bacterial soft rot, drought and heat.
  - Most commercially used in Japan.
- Matromorphy is nothing but diploid parthenogenesis and resultant plant is called as matromorphic plant.
- Matromorphy is obtained after intergeneric or interspecific crosses of using foreign pollen.
- Matromorphic plants developed from diploid embryos are largely heterozygous.
- GA application increases matromorphic seeds.
- *Brasscia* species require embryo culture to obtain F_1 plants after interspecific hybridization.
- *B. oleracea* is used only as a pollen parent in crossing program.

15.1 Cabbage

- For more than 3000 years, cabbage has been used as food crop.
- The ancient Greeks have utilized it more for medicinal purposes.
- Grown of its fleshy leaves, which are served boiled, raw (cole slaw) or fermented (sauerkraut).
- It is leading vegetable crop both for fresh market and processing.
- Cabbage covers 4% of total area under vegetables.
- Thermosensitive crop, hardier than cauliflower and can withstand frost and extreme cold weather.
- Because of its waxy leaf surface, cabbage is drought tolerant.
- India ranks 1st in cabbage production.
- Indole-3-carbinal: Anti-cancerous property to cure bowel cancer.
- Pungent flavour of leaves: Sinigrin glucoside, which contains sulphur.
- Glucosinolates content: 40-90 mg (white cabbage); 30-95 mg (red cabbage); 60-200 mg/100g (savoy cabbage).
- Cabbage juice: Remedy against poisonous mushrooms.
- Main source of vitamin B.
- Inflorescence: Raceme.
- Anthesis time: 8-10 AM.
- Stigma receptivity: 2-3 days before anthesis.

- Pollens are sticky and not wind blown.
- It is responsive to photoperiod i.e. large heads are developed under long summer days and smaller heads under short days.
- Chilling temperature (-3 to -8^{0}C) available at head maturity for overwintering helps the initiation of flower primordia.
- Copenhagen types exhibit more bolting than the Wakefield types.
- Cvs. adapted to over-wintering (viz. Round Dutch, Greenback, Rio-Verde, Superette) are bolting resistant & require long cold period to induce flowering. They are slightly savoyed or have blistered leaves.
- 1st recessive genic male sterility was reported by Cole (1959) and Sampson (1966).
- Sessile fleshy
- Head consists of short, compressed stem surrounded by growing leaves and resembles an enlarged terminal vegetative bud.
- Head compactness is determined by Pearson formula (1931): Z = (C/ W^3 x 100) (where Z= an index of compactness; C= average wt. of cabbage head (g); W= diameter of cabbage head).
- Head shape index: A head character of cabbage and Chinese cabbage. It is ratio of mean head length with mean head width (polar to equatorial diameter) and expressed in centimeter or head shape is expressed in terms of polar and equatorial diameter of head and their ratio.
- Head shape index: Normal or spherical head (0.8 to 1.0); Drum head (< 0.5) and Conical head (> 1.0).
- Optimum temperature: 12-16^{0}C (seed germination) and 15-20^{0}C (growth and head formation).
- Minimum temperature for growth: Just above 0^{0}C.
- Young and well hardened plants can tolerate cold and hot temperature extremes.
- Cabbage is heavy feeder of nitrogen and potassium.
- Optimum pH: 6-6.5 and sensitive to soil acidity & salinity.
- Seed rate/ha: Early variety (500 g) and late variety (375 g).
- Closer in-row spacings tend to produce smaller heads.
- Crop requires 15-25 inches of water per season.
- Furrow or sub-surface irrigation is practiced, since sprinker irrigation will wet leaf surfaces which is conducive to spread of diseases.
- Spray of CCC or SADH 2500-5000 ppm increases low temperature resistance.
- Cabbage is not observed in *in vitro* repository.
- Desirable traits in cabbage:
    - Exclusive round head shape;

- Narrow core width is desirable;
- Short core length less than 25% of head diameter;
- For processing purpose, soft core is desirable over tough core (which results woodiness in processed products).
- Fresh market cvs. have smaller frames than processing types.

- Undesirable traits in cabbage:
  - Tall & long stem falls due to weight of cabbage head;
  - Axillary heading cause loose heads & difficulty in harvesting of crop;
  - Eating quality of very late maturing cultivars is inferior because leaves become hard & tough.
- Maturity indices:
  - Dry matter reaches a plateau & density measurement by water displaced method;
  - Density measurement by water displaced method is helpful and close to unity;
  - Closer to unity = ratio of head weight to weight of water displaced;
  - Closer to unity indicates denser & matured heads;
  - Cabbage for fresh market should be green.
  - Dry matter is positively correlated with late maturity;
  - Dry matter is correlated with soluble solids (%);
- Cabbage heads having high dry matter are used for seed production and head forms knots at the base of its core.
- High dry matter indicates better storage ability.
- Late, slow growing Dutch hybrids have high storage ability.
- Cultivars belonging to Danish class generally store best.
- Late cultivars can be stored for 5-6 months and early cultivars for 1-2 months.
- Storage temperature: 0^0C and 90-95% R.H. for 2-3 months.
- CA storage up to 6 months conditions: $0-5^0$C at 2-3% O_2, 3-6%CO_2.
- Pre and post harvest losses by different factors: 37%.
- Cabbages should not be stored with frutis since ethylene concentrations of 10-100 ppm causes loss of green colour and leaf abscission.
- *Kraut* is convenient means of conserving surplus cabbage during period of temporary overproduction.
- Sauerkraut: Value added product of shredded or white cabbage leaves fermented under pressure. It is effective against scurvey disease. Cabbages for this purpose are primarily produced in USA.
- Desirable characters for sauerkraut:
  - Solidity, small ribs, white internal head colour;

- ° High percentage of dry matter;
- ° Short & narrow core length (25% or less of head dia.);
- ° Soft core & cracking resistance.

- Cabbage used for 'Cole slaw' (for processing) should be white, less juicy, eaten as fresh. It is major stored product in USA.
- Almost all cabbages for processing as kraut or for immediate use in cole slaw are machine harvested.
- Head splitting: Large cored cvs. (Hy. Round Up) usually split at top of head, while short cored cvs. split at the base (Chiang, 1972).
- Heads exhibit storage breakdown due to Turnip Mosaic virus (TuMV) or bacterial speck.
- CMS in *B. oleraceae* is petaloid type.
- The R cytoplasm of male sterile radish has been combined with *B. campestris* & *B. napus* to obtain CMS in these species.
- Specific requirement for export purpose: Round to flat round head with dark green, smooth outer leaves, solid, short core.

Species:

- Cultivated forms of cabbage, based on size, shape, colour and texture of leaves and heads (Nieuwhof, 1969).
- Salt index (C-index) is a measure of the salt concentration as number of grams of NaCl per litre of soil moisture.
- At C_8, there may be reduction of 40% in yield.

Name/ Types	Botanical name	Salt index
White cabbage (head forms by unfolding of leaves, externally green, internally white i.e. cabbage of commerce)	*B. oleracea* var. *capitata* f. *alba*	C_6
Red cabbage (head is internally reddish white coloured)	*B. oleracea* var. *capitata* f. *rubra*	C_4
Savoy cabbage (loose headed; foliage highly wrinkled; highly attractive in appearance; green or yellow coloured; better flavoured than smooth leaved; less gas producing than smooth-leaved cvs.; used as ornamentals in landscaping; highest in soluble solids or dry matter content (9-10%) of all cabbages; leaves edible even after > 40 days of maturity)	*B. oleracea* var. *sabauda*	C_6

Varieties:

- Major centers of breeding: Hommand and Japan.
- Cultivars are grouped into "types or classes" based on a classification established in 1915 and still in use today.

Type	Features
Wakefield (pointed)	Small, pointed heads; early maturing; cold tolerant; resistant to bolting e.g. Jersey Wakefield
Copenhagen Market (domestic)	Round, medium-large compact head having few outer leaves with small core; early maturing; prone to bolting from cold temperature; also used for main season & fall crops
Flat Dutch (domestic)	Large, flat, very solid heads; cultivars vary in resistance to bolting & days to maturity
Danish Ballhead (Danish)	Round-oval, medium sized head; relatively late maturing; intolerant of cold temperature; excellent for storage
Savoy	Medium-large; flat-globe-shaped heads; crinkly leaves; superior fresh market quality
Red	Round, medium-sized heads; reddish-purple leaf colour
Alpha (domestic)	Round, very small heads; early maturing
Volga (domestic)	Flat-globe shaped; medium sized heads; late maturing; thick & blue coloured leaves

- Modern hard-head cabbage cvs. are developed in N. Europe. These are descended from wild non-heading *Brassicas* originated in eastern Mediterranean region and Asia Minor.
- Loose-heading, heat resistant types are developed in Southern Europe.
- Round headed types are older than flat or egg shaped cultivars.
- White and round type cabbages are grown commercially in India.
- Synthetic varieties of cabbage have been developed in India.
- Hybrids occupy 85% of the total area under crop.
- Cultivars are divided into 3 groups on the basis of maturity of heads after transplanting viz. early group (round head type: 55-70 days), late group (flat head type: 85-130 days) and mid-season (conical type: in between days).
- Allen (1914) classified cabbage based on size and shape of head (round, conical, oblong, drum head, flat or savoyed depending on variety).
- Myers (1915) classified cabbage depending on maturity size, shape and colour of head into 8 distinct groups.
- Popularity of F_1 hybrids is due to easier and cheaper method of hybrid seed production.
- Cole Wrap: Mild fragrant and suitable for sandwich making.
- Nagaoka Kohai No.1: 1st hybrid developed in world using two SI inbred lines in 1951 by Takii Seed Company, Japan.
- Hybrid cv. Round Up has very tough core & results in woodiness in processed products.
- Generally thick and waxy leaved varieties are suitable for high temperature.
- Tropical hybrids are produced for southern India and temperate hybrids for northern India.

- Tropical (low chilling requirement) lines 'Selection 505-4', 'Selection-528', 'Selection-507-22' with acceptable head quality were developed at IARI for seed production.
- Cultivars K-K cross, K-Y cross, Summer King, Green Express: Tolerant to high temperature and possible to grow cabbage in non-traditional areas.
- Globelle: Resistant to fusarium yellow, internal tip burn, PM, damping off, TuMV race-1 & 2.
- Hybelle (Badger inbred 12 x Globelle): Resistant to yellow tip burn, PM, mosaic,rhizoctonia.
- Sanibel (Badger inbred 13 x Globelle): Resistant to yellow tip burn, PM, mosaic, rhizoctonia.
- Jery Queen, Badger Shipper: Resistant to club root races 1, 3, 5 & 6.
- Two self incompatible lines 'H-44 & H-64' were developed by using CMS.
- Suitable for canning: Lucknow Local, Infusion of Glory.
- Baby Cabbage: 300 gram head after 60 days. Strong tolerance to bolting having green exterior and yellow interior.

Name	**Breeding method**	**Features**
Glory of Enkhuizen	Introduction from Germany	Drum Head group; popular in Nilgiri hills
Drum Head Savoy	-	Blistered or wrinkled leaf type
September	Introduction from Germany	Large frame; bluish-green foliage; head very compact, oblong weighing 4-6 kg each; 110-120 days for maturity; yield 40-50 t/ha
IARI, New Delhi and IARI, regional station, Katrain		
Early Drum Head (1978)	Introduction	Early; flat head; yield 20 t/ha
Late Large Drum Head	Introduction	Wide frame (plant spread); large flat head which are loose; maturity period 115-120 days
Pusa Drum Head (1970)	Single plant selection from EC-6774 of Drum Head group	Flat head type; resistant to black leg & largest head (3-4 kg); yield 21-22 t/ha; suitable for canning
Pusa Mukta (1989)	Pedigree selection from (EC-24855 x EC-10109)	Resistant to black rot; yield 20-22 t/ha
Pusa Ageti (2000)	Recurrent selection from 'TKCBH-28' from Taiwan	1st tropical variety (grows and form marketable head at 15-30^{0}C) & does not require vernalization for seed stalk emergence; produce seeds in sub-tropical condition i.e. north Indian plains; tolerant to heat; yield 11-33 t/ha
Pusa Sambandh	Synthetic variety from 'Pusa Synthetic'	Round & compact heads with narrow frame; wider adaptability & early maturing; suitable for HDP
Pusa Cabbage Hybrid 1	-	-
Golden Acre (1970)	Selection from 'Copenhagen Market'	Solid, small & round head type; head wt. 1-1.5. kg with few outer cup shaped leaves; harvested immediately after

		head formation; mature in 60-65 days; yield 18-20 t/ha; suitable for canning
KGMR-1	83-1-621 x GA-111	Better staying capacity in field; yield 35-40 t/ha
Copenhagen Market (1978)	Introduction from UK	Early &round head type; head wt. 1.5-3 kg; 75-85 days for head formation; popular in West Bengal; yield 18-20 t/ha; highly susceptible to fusarium yellow disease
BRH-5	Sel.8 x AC.204	1st hybrid in India
H-113	Sel. 8 x 83-6	Compact head & waxy leaves
Pusa Hybrid -81 (2018)	-	-
KTCBH-81	-	Dark green, round head type; yield 40-45 T/ha
KTCBH-822	-	Yield 40 t/ha
DIBER, Pithoragarh		
DARL-801	-	Early maturing; vigorous growth with compact head; tolerant to black rot
Dr YSPUH & F, Solan		
Pride of India (1973)	Selection from 'Copenhagen Market'	Early & round headed type; head wt. 1.5-2 kg; yield 22-24 t/ha; suitable for canning
Kinner Red (1999)	Mass selection	Red cabbage type; high in anthocyanin; yield 25-28 t/ha
CSKHPKV, Palampur		
Palampur Green (1996)	Mass selection	Yield 38-40 t/ha
Red Acre, Primero	Introduction	Red cabbage type
Chieftain	Introduction	Savoy cabbage type
CCSHAU, Hisar		
Hisar-1	Single plant selection	-

Private sector hybrids: Quisto, Sri Ganesh Gol (Mahyco), Stone Head, Green Challenger, Green Cornet, Green Express (suitable for tropical conditions), Hari Rani, Kranti, Meenakshi, Nath Laxmi 401 (Nath seeds), Uttam, Bajrang, Sudha (fusarium wilt resistant), Swarna, BSS-44 (fusarium wilt resistant), BSS-50 (Beejo Sheetal), Vishesh, Kinner Red, Konark.

Seed production:

- Flower stalk arises from leaf axils of upper stem part just below the head.
- Summer cabbage matures early and produces seed stalks soon after splitting.
- Asexual propagation (lateral buds from supporting stump) are excised, rooted, vernalized & allowed to bloom in small pots (2-4 inch dia.)

- Axillary heading is undesirable & can be best assessed by splitting the head vertically through core.
- A long and tall stem is undesirable & will fall due to weight of cabbage head.
- Seed production is taken in hills.
- Biennial crop for seed production.
- Chilling (-3 to -8^{0}C for 40-60 days) is necessary to enter into reproductive phase after 6 weeks period of vegetative phase.

- York (1957) exploited self incompatibility for commercial production of F_1 hybrid seeds in cabbage.
- Single cross method is widely used in USA for commercial F_1 hybrid seed production (York *et al.*, 1957).
- Beheaded portion is called as 'stump'.
- Seed to seed method (*in situ*): Practiced for production of foundation and certified seed; August-September best time for seed sowing; 4-6th true leaf stage is important.
- Head to seed method: Used for nucleus and breeder seed production.
  - Suitable time: Last week of November.
  - Head intact method.
  - Stump method: Higher seed yield.
  - Stump with central core intact method.
- Late planting method: For certified seed production.
- Cabbage seeds mature 60 days after pollination.
- Boric acid spray @ 50 ppm at flowering enhances seed yield.
- Seed yield: 635-650 kg/ha.
- Plant with large heads yield 54-76 g seed/ plant.
- National Vegetable Research Station, Wellesbourne, England has collection of all known *S* allele genotypes (inbred lines that can be used as parents in producing seed of hybrid cabbage cvs.).

Diseases, pests and disorders:

- In cole crops, waxy coating on leaves interfere with insect attack.
- Damping off (*Pythium* spp.): Destructive disease in nursery. Treat seeds with hot water @ 50^{0}C for 30 min. or with captan or Thiram @ 2.5 g/kg seed before sowing.
- Cabbage yellow/Fusarium yellow (*Fusarium oxysporum* f.sp. *conglutianus*): Soil borne. Most severe under high temperatures. Plants have sickly dwarf appearance and discolouration of vascular tissue. It is a classic example of stable resistance controlled by single gene.
- Powdery mildew (*Erysiphe polygoni*):
- Downy mildew (*Perenospora parasitica*): Soil borne & serious in young plants. Chinese cabbage, cabbage, broccoli and kale are resistant.
- Black leg/ Dry rot (*Phoma lingum*): Attacks stem of young plants and cause dark, sunken areas. More common in saline soil. Seed soaking in hot water at 50^{0}C for 30 min is practiced.
- Black rot (*Xanthomonas campestris* pv. *campestris*): Seed borne, chlorosis and 'V' shape lesion in leaf. It is managed by seed soaking in hot water at 50^{0}C for 30 min. *Gobhi Sarson* 'BN-2' and 'Early Fuji' has novel resistance.

- Club root (*Plasmodiophora brassicae*): Soil borne. Most prevalent in acidic soils. Warm temperature & high field moisture are also responsible. Follow long crop rotation with non-cruciferous crops. Kale, Swede, Chinese cabbage and Rutabaga are resistant while cvs. Jersey Queen, Badger Shipper, Laurentian are resistant.
- Stalk rot (*Sclerotinia scleratium*): Major problem in seed production.
- Bottom rot (*Rhizoctonia solani*): Soil borne.
- Diamond back moth i.e. DBM (*Plutella xylostella*): Cause damage by chewing holes in leaves and heads. Pre-heading condition is critical stage for attack of DBM. Resistant source is development of *Bt* cabbage. Use neem seed pellets.
- Entomopathogenic fungus for management of DBM: *Beauveria bassiana*.
- Trap crop for DBM: Chinese cabbage and mustard.
- Parasitoids for management of DBM: *Cotesia plutellae* and *Diadegma semiclausum*.
- Cabbage aphids (*Brevicorne brassicae, Myzus persicae*): Transmit Turnip and Cauliflower mosaic virus. *Coccinella septempunctata* is very commonly used against it.
- Cabbage web worm (*Pieris rapae*):
- Cabbage butterfly/ Cabbage white (*Pieris brassicae*):
- Hairy caterpillar (*Spilosoma obliqua*):
- Stem borer (*Hellula undalis*):
- Thrips (*Caliothrips indicus*):
- Resistance to cabbage aphid is related to low sinigrin content in leaves.
- Black petiole/ Black mid-rib: Complex physiological disorder.
- Black spot on outer leaves of head can be reduced by excessive application of K.
- Heart rot: 'Mo' deficiency.
- Internal tip burn/ Internal breakdown: Breakdown of tissue near centre of head. Affected tissue become dry and papery and turn brown or black. Poor drainage and 'Ca' deficiency.Cvs. Green Boy, Rio-Verde, Titanic, Round Up, Super Boy are susceptible.
- Cabbage head splitting/ head burst/ head cracking: Occurs at top or along one side of head. Heavy irrigation after head development or delayed harvest causes bursting/ splitting within 24 h.

Inheritance of characters:

- Use of dominant marker gene (*Wase Zenku*) for purple stem pigmentation facilitates identification of F_1 hybrid seedlings before transplanting during seed production (Swarup and Gill, 1964).

- Recessive genes controlling glossy foliage and partial chlorosis is also exploited for F_1 hybrid seed production in cole crops.
- Naturally occurring compounds like glucosinolates, pipecolic acid, and β-nitroprionic acid are responsible for resistance to cabbage looper and imported cabbage worm.

Character	Number of gene (s)	Inheritance pattern
Plant height	Monogenic (*TT*)	Tall & long stem dominant to short
Growth habit	Monogenic	Annual habit dominant to biennial
Maturity	Monogenic	Early dominant to late
Head shape	Polygenic	Pointed head dominant to round
Head formation	2 or more genes (*n1*, *n2*)	Heading recessive to non-heading
Axillary heading	Monogenic + modifier gene	Precocious axillary heading recessive
Head leaves	Monogenic	Few wrapper leaves dominant to many wrapped
Head size	-	Quantitative trait & related to hybrid vigour
Head splitting	Trigenic	Additive with partial dominance for early splitting
Head compactness	More than 1 gene	Solid curd recessive to soft curd.
Loose head of savoy cabbage	-	Loose head recessive to hard head of smooth leaf
Savoy leaf texture	Trigenic	-
Core width	Monogenic	Wide core dominant to narrow
Core length	Digenic	Incompletely dominant for short core length
Anthocyanin colour of red cabbage	Polygenic	Quantitatively inherited (*M*- magenta; S- purple on upper side of leaf)
Dry matter/ Soluble solids	-	Quantitatively inherited with low dry matter (6%) is recessive & present in early cvs.; high dry matter (9-10%) occur in late winter storage cvs. & savoy cabbage
Club root resistance	Polygenic recessive & monogenic	Resistance dominant to susceptibility
Powdery mildew resistance	Monogenic	Resistance dominant to susceptibility
Black rot resistance	Monogenic recessive (*ff*)	Two modifier genes (one dominant & one recessive)
Cabbage yellow or fusarium yellow	-	Type A resistance (monogenic dominant, permanent nature & not influenced by temperature); Type B resistance (several genes & breaks down at > 22^{0}C)
Bottom rot resistance	Monogenic	Resistance dominant to susceptibility
Tip burn	Digenic & trigenic	Susceptibility dominant to resistance
Lepidopteran worm resistance	-	Resistance recessive to susceptibility; resistance is due to antibiosis (i.e. larve don't grow as healthy on resistant lines)
Genic male sterility	Dominant	-

15.2 Cauliflower (syn. Heading broccoli)

- Term 'cauliflower' is derived from two Latin words '*Caulis*' means 'stem' or '*Floris*' means 'flower'.
- Grown in all continents of the world at 45-65^0 N latitudes.
- It is introduced to India (Saharanpur, U.P.) from Kew Garden, England by Dr. Jemson in 1822.
- Improvement of Indian cauliflower started at IARI in 1965 by Swarup and Chatterjee.
- India is largest producer in world.
- Thermosensitive crop for curd initiation and development.
- Frozen cauliflowers are available in Indian markets.
- Originated from *B. cretica*.
- It has descended through mutation and selection from common ancestor, wild cabbage *B. oleracea* var. *sylvestris*.
- Many types of cauliflowers were developed in Europe in 16th to 17th century.
- Cauliflowers grown in Europe are either temperate annuals (viz. Cornish (in England), Alpha, Prfurt (in Germany), Danish, Lecerf) or biennial types with winter hardy and require vernalization for flowering (viz. Roscoff, Angers, Walcheran (in France), Old English).
- Cornish types of cauliflower were 1st introduced in India in 1822 from England.
- Tropical or Asian or Australian or Indian cauliflowers are developed as results of natural crossing between European annual and biennial types.
- Four maturity groups are recognized under tropical cauliflower group viz.
  1. September or Kunwari (early);
  2. October or Kataki (mid-early);
  3. November or Agahani (mid-late) and
  4. December or '*Poosi* and/ or *Maghi*' (late).
- Snowball cauliflowers are late type, genetically less diverse and have less hybrid vigour having pigmented stem.
- Indian cauliflowers are capable for giving high hybrid vigour since genetically diverse varieties are available.
- Somatic hybrids were produced between radish and cauliflower by electrofusion of protoplast from hypocotyls.
- Initial introduction was developed from Cornish (biennial) type from England.
- Cauliflower is monogenomic species with genomic constitution of '*C*' and n=9.
- High source of glucosinolates (40-80 mg/ 100 g fresh wt.) containing sinigrin and glucobrassicin having anti-carcinogenic property.
- Indicator plant for browning disorder and whip tail disorder.

- Difference between cauliflower and Sprouting broccoli: Cauliflower lacks axillary branching habit.
- Seed rate: 500-650 g/ha.
- About 50-75 m^2 area is enough to raise nursery for 1 ha.
- Temperate annual type cauliflower is known as 'Erfurt' or 'Snowball' type.
- Early cauliflower and Sprouting broccoli are annual in nature.
- Cultivated cauliflower has biennial habit with yellow flowered racemose inflorescence.
- Blanching: Practice to protect curd from light, heat and to obtain clean white colour.
- Self blanching: Inner leaf whorls fold to cover the curd.
- Late maturing (Snowball) types are usually self blanching in nature and early maturing type lacks this character.
- Late cauliflower does not set seed in plains due to absence of short days and low temperature.
- Number of leaves during curding stage: 18-50.
- Botanically, curd is a prefloral fleshy apical meristem.
- Estimation of curd size index: Equatorial diameter x polar diameter of curd.
- Any check in growth at any stage results in buttoning.
- Optimum temperature for curd initiation: 12-27^{0}C (tropical type); 10-16^{0}C (temperate type).
- Optimum temperature for curd formation: 20-25^{0}C (tropical type); 16-20^{0}C (temperate type).
- High temperature (>25^{0}C) results in small, hard and loose curds with yellow or creamish colour, leafy and ricey.
- Out of total area under cauliflower, about 40% is under hot tropical type.
- Colour of curd is yellowish (early varieties); off-white (mid-season) and milky white (late varieties).
- Curd colour is influenced by self blanching habit of variety and growing temperature.
- Optimum spacing for late sown cauliflower: 60cm x 45 cm.
- It requires 5-8 irrigation during growth.
- Common herbicide: Basalin.
- Early cauliflower types are grown in saline soils having salt index-1 within C_2-C_4 but late types have high salt tolerance.
- Cauliflower crop crossability: Intravarietal crossing and also with other members of cole group.
- Most of heat tolerant and early Indian cauliflower and winter cauliflower (European) shows high level of self incompatibility while late maturing types are more self compatible.

- Male sterility was introduced by Pearson (1972) by crossing *B. nigra* (wild mustard) x *B. oleracea* var. *italica* (Sprouting broccoli).
- Two types of male sterility-
  1. Anthers not fully developed and infertile pollen i.e. poorly developed stamens with sterile pollen.
  2. Stigma protrudes from bud but not self pollinated although pollens are fertile.
- CMS, NKC-A has been also identified in cauliflower.
- GMS has been reported in cauliflower by Nieuwhof (1961) and in purple cauliflower by Brochers (1966).
- Dr. Pritam Kalia established CMS system in Indian cauliflower for F_1 hybrid breeding.
- Two types of CMS: Ogura type & McCollum type.
- Ogura type CMS of radish is most important source of sterile cytoplasm used in cauliflower in different parts of the world. It was transferred into cauliflower by Jourdan *et al*. (1989).
- Ogura type is associated with low seed set and poor curd quality.
- Atrazine resistant cauliflower obtained by somatic hybridization between *B. oleracea* and *B. napus*.
- Dehydrated cauliflower segments can be marketed- blanched for 4-5 min and stepped in 0.5% SO_2 solution for 1 hr and dried 60^0C for 12 h.
- Value added products: Boiled cauliflower, dehydrated cauliflower, frozen cauliflower, grated cauliflower and pickles.

Tropical/ Asian/ Indian type	**Temperate/ European type**
Plants short & long stalked	Plants dwarf
Cvs. of maturity group I (early), II (mid-early), III (mid-late) belongs to tropical cauliflower	-
Annual	Biennial; temperate annual or summer type
Tolerant to heat	Not tolerant to heat
Curd formation at and >20^0C	Form curd at 16-20^0C & grown as late variety (Maghi group)
Curd flat, loose, yellow to creamy & highly flavoured	Curd solid, knobby, bright white, mild or no flavoured, high quality & less sensitive to riceyness
Early	Late
Short juvenile phase	Long juvenile phase
Leaves loosely arranaged, broad & wavy	Leaves short, green, erect or spreading
Predominant SI	SI is more common
No need of vernalization but needs cold treatment at 10-13^0C for 6 weeks for seed production	Need vernalization at 7^0C for 8-10 weeks for seed production

Varieties:

- Green curd cauliflower has been reported from Italy.
- Glossy leaved cauliflower from Australia CI-234599 is highly resistant to DBM and both traits are closely linked.
- Takii 2: Suitable for cold storage.
- Neptune F_1: Suitable for canning and fresh use.
- Snowball A: Resistant to striped flea-beetle.
- Early Patna: Resistant to Cabbage head borer.
- Economically useful genes like *trypsin inhibitors*, *CaMe capsid*, anti-sense *CaMv* gene VI, and anther specific *BcP1* genes were explored in gene transformation.

Early varieties		Mid-early varieties	Mid-late varieties	Late varieties
Sowing time: Mid-May		July end	August end	September end
Harvesting time: July end		September end	September end	October end
Curd initiation temperature				
Early I (20-27^{0}C)	Early II (20-25^{0}C)	16-20^{0}C	12-16^{0}C	10-16^{0}C
Pusa Early Synthetic (1990)	Pusa Deepali	Pusa Hybrid-2	Pusa Synthetic	Pusa Snowball-1
Pusa Meghana	Pusa Kataki	Pusa Sharad	Pusa Himjyoti	Pusa Snowball-2
Kashi Kunwari		Improved Japanese	Pusa Shubhra	Pusa Snowball Kt-1
		Pant Gobhi-4	Pusa Paushija	Pusa Snowball-16
			Pusa Shakti	Ooty-1

Variety	Method of breeding	Features
IARI, New Delhi & regional station, Katrain		
Pusa Kataki (1970)	Mass selection from local germplasm	Early; waxy leaves; curd creamy-white; highly resistant to black rot & free from riceyness; yield 13-14 t/ha
Pusa Hybrid-2 (1993)	Heterosis breeding of 'CC-35 x sel. 1-3-18-19'	1st hybrid released by public sector using SI mechanism; curd white; resistant to DM; yield 25-27 t/ha
Pusa Kartik Sankar (2002)	Heterosis breeding of 'CC-14 x 41-5'	1st hybrid developed; early; curd white; curd wt. 450 g; mature in Sept.; temperature requirement for curd formation is 22-25^{0}C; resistant to DM; yield 16 t/ha
Pusa Shubhra (1985)	Selection from triple cross of 'MGS-2-3 x 15-1-1 x D-96' by back cross method	Curd compact & white; highly resistant to black rot, curd inflorescence blight & riceyness; yield 25-30 t/ha
Pusa Snowball K-1 (1988)	Selection of exotic line 'EC-12012'	Curd white; resistant to black rot, curd inflorescence blight & riceyness; suitable for dehydration & pickling; yield 20-22 t/ha
Pusa Snowball K-2	-	Curd snow white & field resistant to black rot
Pusa Snowball K-25	Selection from (EC-103576 x Pusa Snowball K-1)	Self blanching type; curd white; tolerant to black rot; resistant to sclerotiana rot;very late maturing; yield 30 t/ha

Pusa Snowball-1 (1978)	Mass pedigree selection of Snowball type cross between 'EC 12013 x EC 12012'	Self blanching habit with inner leaves covering the curd tightly; curd white; yield 14-16 t/ha
Pusa Snowball-2 (1975)	Inbred selection from 'EC 12012'	Upright leaves cover curd tightly; poor seeding ability; yield 17-19 t/ha
Pusa Snowball-16 (1970)	Mass pedigree selection from exotic collection from Holland (EC-12013)	Curd white; self blanched; yield 15-20 t/ha
Pusa Meghna (2004)	OP selection from indigenous material	Curd wt. 400 g; white, compact curd; yield 12-15 t/ha
Pusa Sharad (2004)	Recurrent selection	Mature in Sept. end; curd white; curd wt. 900 g; yield 26-28 t/ha
Pusa Beta Kesari (2015)	Pure line selection	1st ever indigeneously bred bio-fortified rich variety [β-carotene 8-10 ppm (800-1000 μg/100 g)]; yield 40-50 t/ha
Pusa Deepali (1978)	Mass selection from local germplasm	Self blanching; early maturing; yield 15-17 t/ha; riceyness absent
Pusa Himjyoti (1986)	Recurrent selection from MGS-2-4 from 'Ganganagar'	'November maturity' group of Indian cauliflower; self blanched & off season (April to July in hills above 1000 m MSL) variety having bluish green foliage for hilly area; curd white; yield 16 t/ha
Pusa Synthetic (1975)	Synthetic variety from 7 inbred lines	Curd creamy white; tolerant to curd & inflorescence blight
Pusa Early Synthetic (1993)	Synthetic variety from 6 inbred lines	Thermo-insensitive; curd yellowish-white; resistant to riceyness & grown in tropical warm climate; yield 12-15 t/ha
Improved Japanese	Introduced from Israel	Curd white; mid-season group; susceptible to heat; yield 11-12 t/ha
Pusa Paushija (DC-76) 2008	-	Curd white; yield 40 t/ha; suitable for north Indian plains
Pusa Shukti (2011)	-	Curd compact & white; tolerant to DM & black rot; yield 44 t/ha; suitable for north Indian plains
Pusa Ashwini (DC-31)	-	Early maturing; curds compact, white coloured; curd wt. 500-600 g; yield 16-18 t/ha
Pusa Moti (DC-5)	-	Mid-late maturity; curd compact & white; yield 30-33 t/ha; tolerant to low frost temperature
KTH-27		1st CMS based F_1 hybrid & tolerant to black rot
Pusa Hybrid-301 (KTH-301) 2019	-	Suitable for cultivation in mid-season; yield 39 t/ha
Pusa Snowball Hybrid-2 (KTH-DH-1) 2020	-	1st double haploid based F_1 hybrid; more uniformity
Pusa Purple Cauliflower (KTP-CF-1) 2020	-	Curd intense purple; pigmentation is present deep inside the bracts below the curd; anthocyanin concentration (43.7 mg/ 100 g); curd weight 0.76 kg
D-96	Introduced from Israel	Susceptible to several diseases
Selection 12 (EC 12012)	Hybridization of 'Tropical line Sn 445 x Pusa Snowball-1'	Resistant to black rot
DC-31 (2014)	-	Curd initiation & development at 22°C-27°C; curd compact & white; curd wt. 500-600 g; yield 16-18 t/ha

IIVR, Varanasi		
Kashi Agahani	Selection from gene pool	Tolerant to high temperature & mod. resistant to DM
Kashi Kunwari (2006)	Mass selection	Tolerate high rainfall during vegetative growth; curds semi-dome type, compact & white; yield 30-35 t/ha
Kashi Gobhi-25 (VRCF-50), 2018	-	Tropical cauliflower; curd compact & white; yield 25-28 t/ha; β-carotene content (0.75-1.50 mg/100 g)
IIHR, Benguluru		
Arka Kanti (IIHR-250)	Selection fom local cv. from Hazipur, Bihar	Tropical type; curd compact & white; duration 60 days; yield 22-25 t/ha
Arka Spoorthi	Mass pedigree selection of (IIHR Acc.No.21957)	Curd compact & white; good seed set under tropical conditions; yield 15-16 t/ha; mod. resistant to DM & alternaria leaf spot
Arka Vimal	Mass pedigree selection of (IIHR Acc.No.21250)	Curd compact & creamy white; good seed set under tropical conditions; yield 17-18 t/ha; mod. resistant to DM & alternaria leaf spot
IIHR-142, IIHR-217	-	Indian cauliflower lines resistant to curd blight
GBPUA & T, Pantnagar		
Pant Shubhra	Recurrent selection	Thermo-insensitive; mature in Dec-Jan; curd creamy white; yield 25 t/ha; curds do not fade even delayed harvesting & storage
Pant Gobhi-2	Synthetic variety	Mature in Nov-Dec; yield 10 t/ha
Pant Gobhi-3	Synthetic variety from 8 inbred lines	Stem long; curd compact & creamy white; yield 15 t/ha
Pant Gobhi-4 (1995)	Recurrent selection in local cv. Agahani	Curd creamy white; non-ricey curd; yield 15-17 t/ha
CSK HPKV, Palampur		
Palam Uphar	-	Curd white
PAU, Ludhiana		
Punjab Giant-26 (1978)	Selection	Tall spreading; curd big & yellow-white; yield 11 t/ha
Punjab Giant-35	Selection	Vigorous growth; medium sized; curd compact & creamy white
Early Kunwari (1973)	Selection from local germplasm	Curd yellow; mature in mid-Sept.; yield 16-18 t/ha
Punjab Kunwari	Selection	More sensitive to riceyness
CCSHAU, Hisar		
Hisar-1 (1976)	Mass selection	Curd compact & white; tolerant to salts; yield 25 t/ha
TNAU, Coimbatore		
Ooty-1 (1998)	OP selection	Curd compact & white; yield 47 t/ha
SKN college of Agriculture, Jobner		
RC-JOB-1	Selection	High yielding; resistant to stress & caterpillars
BAU, Sabour, Bihar		
Sabour Agrim (2014)	OP selection	Curd wt. 450-480 g; yield 17-19 t/ha
Other varieties		
Dania	Exotic collection developed at Kalimpong	Snowball type; Curd compact & white; curd formation during Jan-Feb

Private sector hybrids: Candid Charm, Carotena, Cash More, Early Himlata, Himani, Nath Ujwala, Nath Shweta, Swathi, White Flesh

Seed production:

- Methods of hybrid seed production: Single cross, double cross, top cross and triple cross.
- Blow flies (*Calliphora erythrocephala*): Effective pollinator instead of honey bees (*Apis* spp.).
- Contact, solid curd gives low seed yield due to less number of bolters.
- Scooping (removal of central portion of curd): Special operation for initiation of more number flower stalk widely practiced in Darjeeling hills of West Bengal.It is effective in increasing seed yield.
- GA_3 sprays @ 50-100 ppm at curd development and bolting stage gives higher seed yield.
- Harvesting stage: Pod colour of 60-70% pods turn brown (55-60 days after anthesis is best).
- Delay in pod harvesting results into seed shattering.
- Seeds of snow type are harvested in June and early types in February-March and mid-maturity group in March-April.
- Seed lot is dried at 40^0C.
- Seed yield: 500-600 kg/ha (Indian cauliflower), 300-400 kg/ha (Snowball type).
- Chlorophyll Fluorescence (CF) as a non-destructive marker is used to test seed maturity and seed performance.

Inheritance of characters:

- Cauliflower curd formation is due to 2 mutant genes: *BoAP1-a* and *BoCAL-a*. Plays key role in determining formation of cauliflower quality i.e. bracting and riceyness.
- Looseness and riceyness of curd are highly heritable and difficult to eliminate completely.
- Glossiness of leaves (desirable character) is associated with small sized plant having poor curd quality.
- Orange cauliflower: Rich in β-carotene (*Or*-gene).
- Negative correlation between curd firmness and seed yield.
- Two types of male sterility is governed by recessive nuclear genes:
  I. Anthers not fully developed and pollens are not fertile
  II. Stigma protrudes from bud and does not get any chance for self pollination, although pollens are fertile.

Character	Number of genes	Type of gene action
Plant height, leaf size	Polygenic	-
Plant type	Monogenic (*EE*)	-
	3 major genes	Additive & dominance & epistasis
Stalk length	Monogenic (*St*)	Long dominant to short
Number of leaves	Polygenic	
Leaf length	Monogenic	-
Leaf petiole	Monogenic (*PET*)	Presence dominant to absence
Leaf apex	Monogenit (*RO*)	Round apex dominant to plain
Leaf margin	Monogenic (*WY*)	Wavy dominant to non-wavy
Leaf arrangement around curd	Digenic (Bl_1, Bl_2)	Dominant for semi-blanched
Leaf in curd	Monogenic (*LL*)	Absence of leaf in curd is dominant to presence of leaf
Leaf glossiness (wax layer)	Digenic	Normal dominant to glossy (monogenic recessive) & used as a marker gene at seedling stage
Stem pigmentation	Monogenic	Purple dominant to green; used as a marker gene at seedling stage
Late maturity	-	Recessive polygenes
Cotyledon size	Monogenic (*LcLc*)	Large dominant to small
Puffiness of bud	Monogenic (*pbpb*)	Non-puffy bud dominant to puffy bud
Blindness	Monogenic (*bcbc*)	Presence of curd dominant to absence
Flower colour (white, yellow, cream)	2 independent genes	Dominance epistatic interaction with few modifiers
Curd maturity	-	Dominant & epistasis
Curd colour	-	Orange (monogenic), green (digenic), retentive white (three genes for bleaching controlling peroxidase activity)
Curd weight	Polygenic	Additive & dominant; dominant & epistasis
Curd to plant ratio	-	Partial dominant
Curd diameter	-	Dominant
Curd size index	Polygenic	Additive & dominant; partial dominant; dominance & epistasis
Curd angle	-	Additive & dominant
Curd compactness/ solidity	Polygenic	Additive & dominant
Curd shape, Curd depth	Polygenic	-
Black rot & curd blight resistance	Polygenic	Resistance dominant over susceptibility
Loose bracted & ricey defects in curd	Polygenic	Influenced by environment;
Male sterility & siliqua size	Monogenic	Fertility dominant to sterility

Pests, diseases and disorders:

- Important pests: Cabbage aphid, Turnip aphid, Cabbage head borer, Diamond back moth, Green peach aphid. Cause severe damage to seedlings and at curd formation to seed setting stage.
- Yellowing: Serious fungal disease attack seedlings through rootlets. Seed treatment with *Trichoderma viride* @ 5 g/kg of seeds.
- Soft rot/ Bacterial rot occurs after occurance of black rot or after mechanical injury to mature curd. Spray Copper oxychloride @ 0.3% + Streptomycin sulphate @ 100 ppm.
- Among all cruciferous crops, cauliflower is most sensitive to 'B' deficiency.

Name	Cause (s)
Riceyness (premature initiation of floral buds at upper surface of curd due to which curd become velvety & unfit for marketing)	Excess N; fluctuation in temperature & high humidity; poor seed stock
Fuzziness	Crop cultivation in abnormal time
Blindness (full development of plant without flower)	Frost or low temperature injury or injury caused by insects or damage to growing point at early stage of plant growth; planting of late varieties in early season
Leafyness	High temperature
Buttoning (bunch of many small flowers)	Low N; planting of over aged seedlings; high temperature; exposure of seedlings to poor light condition; planting of early varieties in late season
Hollow stem	Excess N
Whip tail	Mo deficiency, common in acidic soil (pH <5.5); cvs. Lecerf, M16/1 are resistant
Chlorosis	Mg deficiency
Hollow heart/ Browning/ Red rot/ Brown rot of heads	B deficiency; common in alkaline soil & affected curd is bitter in taste
Leaf tip hooking	Ca deficiency

Varieties resistant to parasitic and non-parasitic diseases:

Disease	Resistant varieties	Mode of inheritance
Tip burn (non-parasitic)	Wisconsin, Copenhagen, Bonanza	Dominant
Black leaf spot/ Inflorescence blight (*Alternaria brassicola*)	Snowball KT-9, MGS-2-3	Dominant & polygenic
Damping off (*Rhizoctonia solani*)	South Specific	-
Powdery mildew (*Mycosphaerella brassicola*)	Louisiana	Monogenic dominant
Downy mildew (*Peronospora parasitica*) an obligate parasite	January King, Pusa Hybrid-2, 3-5-1-1, 1-6-1-2, BR-2, CC, First Early, Laxmi, Kunwari-4, Kunwari-7, Kunwari-8	Polygenic dominant

Black rot (*Xanthomonas campestris* pv. *campestris*)	Louisiana, CBR-6, CBR-7, Sn-445, MGS-2-3, *Brassica napus* 'BN-2', Quakea from Hawaii	Dominant & polygenic
Sclerotia rot/ White rot (disease of seed crop)	Beet Malika, Suryamukhi, Pusa Himkiran, Kataki-6, Kataki-13, Patna Kataki	Recessive & polygenic
Soft rot/ bacterial rot/ Curd rot (*Erwinia carotovora*)- most destructive during storage	-	-
Mosaic (viruses)	Badger Ball Head	-
Yellowing (*Fusarium oxysporum*)	Wisconsin Ball Head, Marion Market	Monogenic dominant
Club root (*Plasmodiophora brassica*)	Miher, Late Moscow	Polygenic, recessive

15.3 Sprouting broccoli/ Broccoli

- Eulogized as 'Jewel of nutrition' 'Italian broccoli' or 'Top power house of nutrient density'.
- Broccoli is an Italian plural of '*Brachilum*' means an arm or branch which refers to 'flowering top of a cabbage'.
- In Gardener's dictionary of Philip Miller (1724), it is mentioned as sprout cauliflower or Italian asparagus.
- Winter vegetable produces succession of small flower heads over long season from early winter to late spring.
- Calabrese was introduced to France in 1560 and spread from there to rest of Europe. It is also known as 'American/ Italian/ Green sprouting broccoli'.
- Calabrese produces large central flower head surrounded by smaller side shoots, which develop after main head is harvested.
- Broccoli refers to young floral shoots of several brassica crops.
- Asparagus broccoli has a large number of heads with many thin stalks.
- Largest producer in world: USA followed by Italy and northern Europe.
- In India, it is mostly cultivated in hilly areas of H.P., U.P., J & K, Nilgiri hills and northern plains.
- Calorific value: 141 KJ (34 Kcal).
- Heading type broccoli is more akin to winter cauliflower.
- In the world market, about 40% is marketed as fresh and remaining 60% as frozen.
- Head and spears (long slender smaller heads) are used in fresh form.
- It is used as salad, cooked in curries, boiled and also processed.
- It has anti-cancerous properties and has been found useful for number of other diseases.

- Stalk has as much nutrition as curd/ florets.
- It is widely grown in Himachal Pradesh during winter season.
- Not suitable for protected cultivation.
- Broccoli improvement was carried out by Dr. Pritam Kalia.
- Broccoli possess glucosinolates (Sulphur containing compound) having anti-cancerous and anti-oxidant properties.
- Dominant glucosinolates: Glucoraphanin (in *Brassica villosa*), glucorapin, glucobrassicin and sinigrin.
- Sulphoraphane glucosinolates: Strong anti-oxidant having anti-cancerous property.
- Dark green colour: Carotene.
- Quercetin: Flavonal glucoside (65 mg/ kg).
- Contains compound isothiocyanates (Indole carbinol) which selectively binds to mutated *P53* gene, causing cancer cell death (breast cancer cells).
- Most nutritious and remunerative vegetable among cole group.
- High in β-carotene, vit. C, folic acid, iron and Ca.
- It is a rich source of vitamins and minerals and has about 14 times more β-carotene than commonly cultivated cabbage.
- It has 130 times more vit. A than cauliflower and 22 times more than cabbage.
- Nutrition score: 50.
- Inflorescence type: Cymose.
- Flowers have 4 sepals, 4 petals, 2 short and 4 long stamens and superior ovary with 2 carpels.
- Optimum temperature for seed germination: 12-16^{0}C.
- Optimum temperature for fertilization: 12-18^{0}C.
- Optimum temperature for head development (Heading stage): 15-20^{0}C.
- Vernalization is required for development of head and initiation of flowering stalk.
- Heads become loose in warm weather condition.
- Water requirement: 322 to 426 mm.
- Water deficit causes strong flavour, ricey curd and premature bolting.
- Optimum soil pH: 5.5 to 6.5.
- Excess N cause hollow stem.
- Seed rate: 400-500 g/ha.
- Planting distance: 50 cm x 40 cm.
- In dry condition, crop becomes fibrous.
- Harvesting stage of sprouting broccoli:

- º Inflorescence or bud clusters are green or still immature & compact & before individual flower heads open.
- º Over matured heads develop tough, woody fibres in the stems and bud clusters become loose, which makes the product unmarketable.
- º The central bud cluster or head matures first.
- º Heads having 10-15 cm stems should beharvested with a sharp knife.
- º The present cultivars donot mature uniformly.
- º Growth of lateral shoots is promoted in leaf axils & these sprouts/ secondary heads may attain dia. of 3-10 cm over 1 or 2 months period. This condition may necessitate 4 to 6 cuttings and thus harvesting is prolonged for several weeks.
- º Secondary heads are harvested if cost effective.

- Harvesting of calabrese:
  - º Harvest the firm and matured central head with sharp knife.
  - º This encourages growth of side shots with 2-3 weeks.
- Yield/ ha: 10-15 Tonnes.
- High rate of respiration results in deterioration of its quality.
- Hydrocooled immediately after harvest 4.4^{0}C & then packed with ice in crates & stored in refrigerators at 4^{0}C for 7-10 days.
- Storage period should be as brief as possible to maintain its deep green colour and firmness.
- Broccoli can also be preserved in glass jars after lactic acid fermentation.
- CA storage conditions: 0-5^{0}C at 1-2% O_2, 5-10%CO_2.
- LDPE packaging keep heads more fresh and green.
- Annuals are sensitive to frost while late type cultivars need vernalization.
- Yellowing of broccoli is a problem in storage. It can be delayed by 1-MCP.
- Use of GMS in green Sprouting broccoli is reported by Cole (1959).

Varieties:

- Mass selection is most common method used in cross pollinated crop for the improvement of qualitative characters governed by single or few genes.
- Back cross method is used to transfer resistance governed by one or few dominant or recessive genes.
- Ancestor of broccoli: *B. cretica ssp. nivea.*
- In India, it is commonly known as 'calabrese (*Cavolo broccoli di Calabria*)/ green cauliflower' named after Calabrian region in Italy. These are popular for fresh consumption and processing.

- Cvs. of Calebrese: Broccoletto (quick maturing & sweet with single head); Citation (early, blue-green heads, resistant to DM but prone to hollow stem & flower prematurely); Green Comet (early with large dark green flower head & masses of side shoots); Mercedes (mature rapidly, produce high quality blue-green stems with large flat heads); Ramoso (syn. DeCicco- An Italian variety for spring/ autumn crop, heads are tasty & freezes well); Romanesco (very tender with excellent flavourt & lime-green heads).
- All heading broccoli introductions are resistant.
- Broccoli is of two types-
  A. Heading type broccoli forms curds like cauliflower.
  B. Sprouting broccoli contains group of green/ purple buds and thick fleshy flower stalk forming a head. It is more popular in India and mostly early and mid types are cultivated.

  There is more demand for green sprouting broccoli having green, firm and compact crown heads. The side shoots or heads are less preferred in Indian market.
- Two types:
  1. Green headed types: Most commonly grown, early type, biennials and more nutritive than white coloured broccoli e.g. Green Bud, Spartan Early, De Cicco, Palam Samridhi, White Sprouting Late, White Sprouting Early.
  2. Purple headed types: More hardy than white type, better taste, crop later but less productive, withstand frost and harvested in winter e.g. DOG PPB-1, Purple Sicilian broccoli (syn. Purple cauliflower), Purple Sprouting Late, Purple Sprouting Early, Christmas Purple Sprouting.
- On the basis of maturity, broccoli may be divided into early types (40-50 days), mid (60-90 days) and late types (100 or more days).
- Early types are annual while late types are biennial in nature.
- Early types matures in 40-45 days, mid-group in 60-100 days and late group in >100 days of transplanting.
- 'Bronzio': Purple heading type with large head (300-400 g).
- Nine Star: Old variety of perennial broccoli. It is multi-headed variety with small white heads.
- Heading broccoli 'EC 103576': Resistant to black rot and sclerotinia rot.
- 5 more heading broccoli viz. EC 131592, Janavon, Early Winter Adam's White Head, EC 177283 and KN-81 possess resistance to sclerotinia rot.

Name	Method of breeding	Features
IARI, regional station, Katrain		
Pusa Broccoli Kt-S-1 (1996)	Selection	Head compact with 250-400 g wt., light green with small buds; waxy foliage; mature in 90-105 days in temperate climate while 5-10 days earlier in tropical plains; yield 13-16 t/ha; resistant to mild frost & snowfall
CSKHPKV, Palampur		
Palam Samridhi (1997)	Mass selection from exotic material	Compact, head green; head wt. 300-400 g; head free from yellow eyes, bracts; mature in 85-90 days; suitable for sub-tropical conditions; yield 15-18 t/ha
Palam Kanchan (2005)	Mass selection	Head yellowish green; yield 25-27 t/ha
Palam Vichitra(2005)	Mass selection	Head purple; rich in nutrients; yield 23-26 t/ha
Palam Haritika (2003)	Mass selection	Late maturing; head green; yield 23-25 t/ha
YSPUH & F, Solan		
Italian Green	-	-
Green Head	-	Compact, dark green heads composed of small buds; branched plant habit; head wt. 200-250 g; mature in 95-100 days; yield 12-15 t/ha
MPKV, Rahuri		
Phule Ganesh Broccoli	-	Tolerant to DM & bacterial blight; suitable for rabi; yield 65 q/ha
PAU, Ludhiana		
Punjab Broccoli-1 (1993)	Selection	Dark green foliage; smooth leaf surface having bluish tinge; branched plants; less compact head; heat wt. 150-200 g; mature in 60-70 days; sprouts compact, succulent; yield 60-70 q/ha

Private sector hybrids: Atlantic, Besty, Clipper Laser, Coastal, Cruisesr, Everest (Sandoz), Excaliber, Fiesta (Bejo Sheetal); Green Mountain, Green Surf,Late Corona, Lucky, Packman and Pirate (Indo-American), Premium Crop, Solohead, Southern Comet.

Pest:

- Nematodes: Drench neem soap and bio-pesticides (*Trichoderma viride* + *Pseudomonas fluorescens* + *Pochonia chlamydosporia*).

15.4 Radish

- Common name radish is derived from Latin '*radix*' meaning 'root'.
- Greek name of genus *Raphanus* means quickly appearing and refers to rapid germination of these plants.
- The Night of the Radishes: An annual event held in Mexico, dedicated to the carving of oversized radishes to create scenes.
- Cultivated in Egypt long back to about 2000 BC.
- Grown as annual for its enlarged fleshy tap root which also consist some stem tissue.

- Absorbing roots are 2-8 inch long.
- Leaves are good source for protein extraction.
- Useful for curing liver and gall bladder problem.
- Bigger sized Oriental radish are called as 'diakens'.
- Radish root develops from both primary root and hypocotyl.
- Edible root-cum-leafy vegetable.
- The fleshy radish is modified form of radish root known as 'fusiform' (swollen in middle & gradually tappers towards apex and base).
- Sinki: Fermented radish tap root product.
- Radish is good source of vit. C (15-103 mg/100g).
- Vitamin C content is influenced by blue light and phosphatic fertilizer.
- Major sugar present in radish: Glucose.
- Famous Japanese radish pickle: Takoan.
- Indigenous types are more pungent than European types.
- Pungency is due to glucosinolates (GSLS). Major is isothiocyanates (tran-4-methyl-thiobutnyl isothiocynate) present in leaves.
- Glucosinolates content: 10-70 mg/100g fresh wt.
- A gram of pod counts about 125 seeds.
- Seed rate: Tropical: 8-10 kg/ha and temperate: 10-12 kg/ha.
- Seed drilling or broadcasting is done in mid-June and mid-July for fall crop, so roots mature in cool temperatures.
- In tropical climate, best quality roots are produced from November-December sowing.
- Temperate varieties are given closer spacing compared with tropical types.
- Staggered planting (at 7-10 days interval) is followed in European countries to obtain successive harvests.
- Planting of two varieties alternatively in concentric circles produce up to 90% hybrid seeds which give 30-60% more yield of roots.
- Shallow weeding helps proper root development.
- It is suitable as intercrop and companion plantings.
- Long photoperiod and warm temperature favours early bolting.
- Pithiness determines the edible quality of roots.
- Degree of pithiness is greater in summer and with delayed harvesting, increase in fertilizer dose and decreased soil moisture content.
- Vernalized radish flowers in total darkness even under short day condition.

- Types:
- Cultivated forms of European types are grouped into 2 types:
  1. Spring radishes: Annual, grow quickly and mature in short time (20-30 days). Roots are small and mildly pungent.
  2. Winter radishes: Biennial, grows slower (50-90 days), have large roots, very strong flavour and store better than spring types.

Temperate/ European/ Oriental type	Tropical/ Asiatic/Occidental type
More sensitive to temperature than day length for bolting & flowering	More resistant to temperature than day length for bolting & flowering
Quick growing & short duration (25-30 days)	Slow growing & long duration
Biennial, require chilling for bolting, no seed setting under tropical conditions, quick growing, short duration, less pungent & small size	More pungent and have large roots than temperate types
Produce seeds in temperate regions	Produce seeds both in tropical & temperate region of India
Seed to seed method is useful for European varieties	Root to seed method of seed production useful to Asiatic varieties

- Pink, red, purple colour (Anthocyanin); Purple (Cyanidin); Red (Pelargonidin (raphanusin).
- Red fleshed winter cvs. Have anthocyanins ranges from 12.2 to 53 mg/100g.
- Pink skinned radish is generally rich source of ascorbic acid.
- Automatic Self Pollination Ability (ASPA) is closely associated with flower morphology.
- Inflorescence type: Terminal raceme with white flowers.
- Stigma receptivity : Upto 4 days of anthesis.
- Fruit type : Indehiscent pod i.e. siliqua.
- No problem of seed shattering.
- Roots develop best flavor, texture and size at 10-15^{0}C.
- Temperature > 25^{0}C favours more foliage growth on European varieties than Asiatic ones.
- Normally plants bolt when days are 8-10 hours long.
- Root become tougher, pithy and develops pungency under hot weather.
- Long photoperiod and high temperatures favour early bolting even to proper development of roots.
- Maturity of European cultivars is early (25-30 days) compared to Asiatic types (45-60 days).
- Harvested roots are cooled quickly to 0^{0}C or below and hydro-ccoling is effective.
- About 3-6 roots are tied in a bunch depending on size of roots.

- Roots can be stored upto 2 months in cold storage at 0^0C at 90-95% R.H.
- Nearly all spring radishes are topped and pre-packed in plastic bags for retail sale.
- Seed viability: 4-5 years.
- Seeds are recalcitrant in nature.
- Radish CMS systems: 1. Ogura type 2. Kosena type.
- Ogura (1968) was 1st reported CMS in Japanese gynodioecious wild radish cultivar.
- Ogura system of CMS is commercially utilized for hybrid seed production. It has been transferred in cvs. Japanese White, Pusa Chetki and Pusa Desi.
- *Orf-138* (Ogura-CMS) is mitochondrial gene responsible in wild radish.
- Two dominant restorer genes control Ogura-CMS in radish.
- In Kosena CMS radish, fertility restorer gene *orf* 687 has been cloned.
- Kosena CMS associated gene *orf* 125 and Ogura *orf* 138 gene are almost identifical.
- The 'Won Back-CMS' line from China is different from 'Ogura-CMS'.
- NWB CMS line is from South Korea.
- Pseudo-self incompatibility is observed in radish.
- Stout (1920) was 1st to present evidence of sporophytic SI.
- Incompatibility is controlled by multi-oppositional alleles at one locus (Sampson, 1957).
- Bud pollination is effective in F_1 hybrid seed production.
- Shows considerable inbreeding depression on selfing.
- *Raphanus* genome has 1.1 x 10^9 bp.
- ¾ size steckling (15 cm long) is ideal for seed production.
- Stecklings are prepared by cutting lower 2/3rd portion of roots and trimming of tops in the same preparation.
- Pollination agent: Honey bees, beetles, flies and bumble bees.
- Late sowing (after November) cause earlier bolting.
- Seed yield: 500-600 kg/ha (European) and 500-1000 kg/ha for Asiatic type.
- For nucleus seed production, root to seed method is followed.
- Root bulging is common process.
- Black spot is reduced by washing in chlorinated water.
- Value added products: Radish ministicks which is low calorie and fresh cut product and highly sensitive to ethylene and stored at $0\text{-}2^0C$.

Species:

- Banga (1976): Classified radish types based on morphology.
- Asiatic radish originated from *Raphanus sativus* f. *raphanistroides* grown at high temperature.

- European radish originated from wild species namely *R. raphanistrum, R. maritimus, R. laundra* and *R. rostratus*.
- Small radish (*R. sativus* var. *sativus*):
- Garden/ European/ Small cool season radish (*R. sativus* var. *radicula*): Globular forms of salad radish.
- Oilseed / Leaf radish/ Fodder radish (*R. sativus* var. *oleiformis*):
- Rat-tail/ Mougri radish (*R. sativus* var. *caudatus*): Long thin edible immature green or purple pods used as vegetable in India. Edible portion- leaves & young seed pods. Does not produce fleshy roots i.e. non-tuber forming. Pods contain 1.3% protein, 1.1% fibre.
- Large radish/ Black/ Spanish radish (*R. sativus* var. *niger*):
- Japanese/ Chinese/ winter radish (*R. sativus* var. *raphanistroides*): Intermediate to Indian and European types. Turnip shaped giant radish cultivated in Sakurjuna regions of Japan.
- Indian radish (*R. indicus*): Frost tolerant, pungent and used for pickle making.
- Spring/ Summer radish (*R. sativus* var. *longipinnatus*):
- Horseradish (*Armoracia rusticana*):
- All botanical varieties are intercrossable.
- Radish is crossable with some members of Brassica family namely turnip, Chinese cabbage and mustard.

Varieties:

- Frost (1923): 1st to develop hybrid seedling radish by heterosis.
- Sakurajuma: Japansese variety.
- Globular or round varieties: Rapid Red White Tipped (RRWT), French Break Fast.
- Kvarta: Short duration tetraploid variety having bright red colour, suitable for protected cultivation. Harvest maturity within 24-30 days after emergence.
- Hill Queen: Popular variety in north India.
- Round shaped variety: Reggae.
- Ramgo: Resistant to *M. incognita*.
- Taichung No. 2: Heat tolerant.

Name	Breeding method	Features
A) Asiatic varieties		
Pusa Chetki (1988)	Selfing & massing from Denmark collection	Suitable for high temperature; shortest duration variety & less pungent; 40-45 days crop duration; yield 20-25 t/ha
Pusa Desi (1965)	Mass selection from indigenous type	1st variety released by IARI; resistant to alternaria blight; yield 30 t/ha
Pusa Reshmi	Selection from local germplasm	Tolerant to high temperature; mild pungent; yield 35 t/ha
Pusa Gulabi (2012)	-	1st entire pink fleshed unique trait nutritional rich radish variety; roots cylindrical; high in total carotenoids, anthocyanins & ascorbic acid.
Pusa Shweta	Selection from P. Chetki	Staight long tapering with pointed tip
Pusa Mridula (2005)	-	Roots globular with bright red coloured; mildly pungent; suitable for growing in kitchen garden & container garden; yield 13 t/ha
Pusa Vidhu	-	Long staying capacity; roots white coloured
Pusa Jamuni (2012)	-	1st purple coloured roots; nutritionally rich (higher anthocyanins & ascorbic acid)
Pusa Sagarika	-	Roots purple coloured
Pusa Shuka	-	Green shoulder (necked) variety
Arka Nishant (1991)	Mass selection from IIHR-72 (material from Singapore)	Mild pungent; resistant to white rust, pithiness, premature bolting, root branching & forking; multiple disease resistant; set seeds in plains; yield 35-40 t/ha
Phule Ganesh Synthetic	-	Mild pungent & ready for harvest within 30-40 days
Japanese White (1973)	Introduction from Japan	Thick roots; 20-30 cm long; 5 cm dia.
Punjab Safed (1975)	Hybrid of 'White-5 x Japanese White'	Maturity within 40 days; resistant to leaf spot; free from forking; roots remain edible for 10 days after attaining full size
Punjab Pasand (1997)	Selection from 'Pusa Chetki'	Roots long, pure white coloured; free from hairs
Punjab Ageti (1986)	Selection from local material	Roots red coloured at top & white at lower half
Jaunpuri (syn. Giant radish or Newari)	Selection from Uttar Pradesh	Roots >1m long; wt. 5-15 kg; popular in Uttar Pradesh; set seeds in plains
Kalyani White	Hybrid of 'Pusa Chetki x Japanese White'	-
B) European varieties		
Bombay Red	Introduction	-

Chinese Pink	Introduction	Globe shape & dual season variety
Chinese Rose	Introduction	-
Rapid Red	Introduction	Non-table variety; round roots; roots red coloured at top and white at lower half; become edible in 30 days
Contai	Introduction	-
French Breakfast	Introduction	Roots red coloured with white tip
Pusa Himani	Hybrid of (Black x Japanese White)	Only variety that can be grown throughout year; high in vit. C (192 mg/ 100g); mildly pungent; yield 33 t/ha
Scarlet Long	Introduction	Roots white, crispy; 15-20 cm long
Scarlet Globe	Introduction	Requires 25-30 days from sowing to root formation; roots globular or round shape
Scarlet Red	Introduction	Roots long, tapering to point; roots red coloured & crispy
White Icicle	Introduction	Tender variety; sweet flavoured, crisp & juicy
White Tipped	Introduction	Table variety; round roots; globular; roots red coloured with white tip
Kashi Hans	Selection	Yield 43-45 t/ha
Kashi Sweta	Selection from 'Pusa Chetki'	25-30 cm long roots; 3-4 cm dia.; yield 45-47 t/ha
Kashi Ganga	Selection from local material	Late in pithiness & suitable for delayed harvesting; soft & smooth foliage
Kashi Mooli-40 (2018)	-	Tolerant to high temperature (35-42^{0}C); suitable for summer cultivation, delayed bolting, less pithiness, roots white coloured with iciclicle shaped; root yield 30-35 t/ha (normal season) & 20- 23 t/ha (summer season)
Kashi Lohit (2018)	-	Roots red coloured with iciclicle shaped; suitable for salad dressing, rich in anti-oxidants (80- 100% higher than white radish), good source of anthocyanin & phenolics; tolerant to pithiness; yield 40-45.0 t/ha
Kashi Aardra (2019)	-	Roots white coloured with long and icicle shaped; yield 24-40 t/ha
Palam Hriday (2003)	Selection from exotic source	Early maturing; roots pink coloured, late bolting, oblong root shape & free from pithiness
Kalyanpur No.1	Selection from local material of Uttar Pradesh	Roots 22-25 cm long; white & tapering; crispy; free from mustard fly, aphids & white rust
CO.1 (1981)	Selection from 'RS 44-2-1'	Long roots; less pungent; susceptible to rust & aphid; yield 22 t/ha
Hisar Sel.1	Selection	Yield 30-32 t/ha

Genetics of characters:

- Crossing varieties contrasting in photoperiodic response exhibit high heterosis.
- Root yield is positively correlated with root length, root width, skin width, root weight, leaf number, foliage weight, foliage height and root top ratio.
- Early maturity is positively correlated with abundant foliage.
- Early yield is positively correlated with low number of leaves, low weight of leaves, small leaf area and high root-top weight ratio.
- Resistance to white rust race-I is governed by dominant gene (*Ac1*) and pink pigmentation by gene (*Pi*). Both are linked.
- Genic male sterility in Japanese radish is governed by interaction of recessive gene *ms* and *S*-cytoplasm.
- CGMS is determined by cytoplasm and two genes in nucleus.
- Belt and Lydiate (2003) developed 1st genetic map of *Raphanus* genome based on meiosis in hybrid between *R. sativus* (cultivated) and *R. raphanistrum* (wild).

Character	Number of genes	Type of gene action
Early maturity	Polygenic	-
Plant colour	Monogenic (*Pi*)	Pink dominant to white
Leaf lobbing	Monogenic	Lobbed leaf dominant to simple
Leaf hairiness	Monogenic	Hairy leaf dominant to glabrous
Leaf colour	Monogenic (*YgYg*)	Dark green leaf colour dominant to yellow green
Ivanova leaf shape	Monogenic	Lyrate leaves dominant over entire leaves
Green flecking on leaves	Monogenic (*gf1*, *gf2*)	Recessive
White petal colour	Monogenic	-
Stem colour	Monogenic	Red stem dominant
Hypocotyl length	Polygenic	Dominance of long hypocotyl
Root shape	Monogenic	Long dominant to round
Root texture	Monogenic	Corky dominant to smooth
Root colour	Digenic (1 for presence/ absence of colour) & other for type of colour	• Red- $R_2r_2R_3r_3cc$; • White- $r_2r_2r_3r_3CC$; • Purple- $r_2r_2R_3r_3cc$; (red, purple, yellow dominant to white)
Seed coat colour	Monogenic	Brown dominant
Siliqua colour	Monogenic	Purple dominant
Pollen colour	Monogenic	Bright yellow dominant to cream
Fusarium yellow resistance	Polygenic	-

Pests, diseases and disorders:

- Aphids: Serious & most commonpest.
- Radish mosaic virus: Aphid transmitted.

- Radish phyllody: Transmitted by Jassids. Floral parts become leafy.
- Mustard saw fly (*Athalia lugens-proxia*): Most common pest. Attacks in vegetative and flowering stage.
- White rust (*Albugo candida*): Most common in acidic soils. It is controlled by soil application of lime.
- Alternaria blight: Fungal disease of seed crop.
- Pithiness/ Bitterness of roots: Delayed harvesting. It is more in summer crop and is due to excess NPK and soil moisture stress.
- Hollow root: Due to high temperature intercellular spaces develop during 16-30 days of sowing and results hollow root formation.
- Wart: Soil moisture deficit, inner root tissue splits in skin.
- Brown heart/ Akashin disorder: B deficiency, high day and night temperature (30/20^{0}C).
- Downward cupping: Mo deficiency.
- Internal browning: High temperature condition.

15.5 Knol khol/ Kohlrabi

- Kohlrabi is a German name for cabbage turnip and belongs to botanical variety 'Gongyloides'.
- Progenitor: Wild cabbage (*B. oleracea* var. *sylvestris*).
- Grown for its turnip like enlargement of lower stem that may be eaten either raw or cooked.
- An excellent vegetable having mild taste similar to turnip.
- Most common in Europe & used for human consumption as well as stock feed.
- Makes best growth between 15.5-21^{0}C and subject to vernalization & bolting at temperature < 7.22^{0}C.
- High temperature checks growth causing the stem to become tough and stringy.
- Edible part is above 'ground tuber' formed by thickening of stem tissues above cotyledon.
- It is biennial and plants bolts at low temperature.
- Rich source of Ca, Mg, K, P, B, Na and S.
- It is more popular in Kashmir
- Inflorescence type: Racemose.
- Best time for planting: October.
- Kohlrabi is quick growing crop (55 days from seeding to harvest).
- Edible maturity of knob: 6-8 cm dia. In early, 10-20 cm in late maturity varieties.

- Harvested when swollen stem is 2-3 inches in diameter and before it becomes tough and woody.
- Stem can be cut just above the ground or can easily be pulled by hand.
- When prepared for market, the roots are cut off and plants are tied in bunches with leaves still attached.
- Seed rate: 800-1000 g/ha.
- Storage temperature: 0^0C, 95-100% R.H. for 25-30 days.

Varieties:

- The 1st hybrid was developed by the private firm 'Roggli'.
- Introduced: King of North, King of Market, Large Green, Golith White, Sutton's Earliest Purple, Purple Speck, Korist, Kolibri.
- Knol khol (a) for seed production- Annual (b) for flowering, fruiting- Biennial.
- Purple/ Early varieties are more susceptible to premature bolting.

Name	Breeding method	Features
IARI, New Delhi & RS, Katrain		
White Vienna (1975)	Introduction	Early maturity; yield 18-20 t/ha
Purple Vienna (1975)	Introduction	Late maturity; yield 18-20 t/ha
Large Green (1975)	Inroduction	Tops tender; yield 23-25 t/ha
Yellow Vienna	-	-
Early White Vienna	-	Early; dwarf; short tops & green leaves; knobs globular round shaped; mature in 50-60 days
Early Purple Vienna	-	Early; purple foliage colour; knobs globular round shaped; mature in 55-60 days
Pusa Virat	OP selection	It does not form fibre even few days after ready for harvesting
CSKHPKV, Palampur		
Palam Tenderknob (2005)	Mass selection	Turnip-shaped knobs; yield 25-27 t/ha

15.6. Turnip

- Fleshy thickened underground portion i.e. modified root (napiform) is actually swollen hypocotyls (an edible portion of turnip).
- European types are relatively sweeter and more palatable.
- Young leaves are rich source of ascorbid acid, iron and vit. A (15669 IU.).
- Higher the light intensity (up to 500 foot candles), greater the content of ascorbic acid.
- Extra seedlings from thinning are often used as 'greens'.
- Roots become woody, tough and bitter in taste in hot weather.
- Tolerant to frost and freezing temperature.

- It can be grown at an elevation of 1500 MSL or above but it is not suitable for growing in low lands of wet tropics.
- Pollination agent: Flies.
- It has strong sporophytic self incompatibility.
- It is cross compatible with radish, rutabaga and cabbage.
- Pollen sterile lines and SI lines are used in hybrid seed production.
- Bud pollination and Sodium chloride @ 3% and CO_2 used to overcome self incompatibility.
- Thinning is important to maintain optimum plant to plant spacing and required population.
- Turnip is closely related to Swede (*B. napus* var. *napobrassica*; *B. carinata* 2n=16).
- Swede or Rutabaga or Sweet turnip or Swedish turnip: Amphidiploid (2n=38; AACC genome).
- Natural cross between *B. campestris* (2n=20, AA) x *B. oleracea* (2n=18, CC).
- Turnip classification is given by Shoemaker (1949).
- Inflorescence type: Terminal raceme.
- Elongation of hypocotyl stops at 6th leaf stage.
- Dry matter content of turnip should be 8-9%.
- Most favorable temperature for root formation 10-13^{0}C and 18-23^{0}C soil temperature.
- Edible maturity: Within 40-60 days.
- Temperature <10^{0}C induces flowering.
- Under shade conditions, foliage grows at the expense of root development.
- Long days and high temperature induces early bolting.
- 1 gram of seed contains 460-500 seeds.
- Type of fruit: Pod.
- Seed rate: 3-4 kg/ha.
- Sowing depth of seed: 2-3 cm.
- Days for seed germination: 4-6.
- Seed yield: 550 kg/ha.
- Seed viability: 5-6 years.
- Fleshy roots reach edible maturity in 40-60 days after sowing.
- Micronutrient (B, Ca & Mo) spray helps to control hollow stem, pith formation and brown heart.
- Major problem in seed production: Phyllody disease.
- Storage temperature: 0^{0}C at 85-95% R.H.
- Shattering: Serious problem in fully dried seed crops.

- Asiatic types produce seeds in plains while European types in hills only.
- Seed pods are harvested at light yellow colour before shattering.

Varieties:

- Method of crop improvement: Mass selection.
- Early Milan Red Top: Extra early and high yielding cultivar and matures in 45 days.
- Foliage cultivars: Seven Top, Flat Japan.
- Resistant to club root: Manga (from New Zealand), Dutch Half Long, Date Hybrid and Yellow May.
- Resistant to cold, wind and bolting: Charleston.
- Improved Golden Ball; Mass selection from Golden Ball.
- Two types:
  - Asiatic/ Annual/ Oriental/ Tropical: Ludhiana White.
  - European/ Biennial/ Temperate: Rich in dry matter and carotene content than Asiatic types e.g. Snow White.

Annual/ Asiatic/ Oriental/ Tropical type		European/ Temperate type	
Name	**Root colour & features**	**Name**	**Root colour**
Pusa Kanchan [Local Red Round (Asiatic) x Golden Ball (European)] 1960	Skin red & flesh creamy yellow; set seeds in plains; resistant to pithiness	Pusa Swarnima [Japanese White (Asiatic) x Golden Ball (European)]	Creamy yellow skin & amber colour flesh; flat round roots; less susceptible to malformation
Punjab Safed-4	Pure white	Pusa Chandrima (Snow Ball x Japanese White)	Pure white skin; doesn't produce seeds in plains
White-4	-	Snowball	White skin & light yellow flesh
Red-4	-	Golden Ball	Bright creamy yellow skin & amber coloured flesh
Pusa Swati (single plant selection from indigenous germ plasm) 1976	Mature in 45-50 days; white & off season variety	Purple Top White Globe (1975)	Purple on top & lower half white; large rooted; resistant to cold & aphids
Turnip L-1	Round, pure white roots	Early Milan Red Top	Purplish red at top & white at lower portion

Pests, diseases and disorders:

- Turnip Yellow Mosaic virus (TYMV): Transmitted by flea beetle. Alternate host cabbage.
- Turnip Crinkle: Viral disease.
- Turnip phyllody: Caused by MLOs.
- Brown heart/ Water core: B deficiency.

Genetics of characters:

- Linkage between gene controlling leaf shape and root colour was observed.
- Seed coat colour is controlled by pleiotropic effect (brown seeds *Pp* and creamy seeds *pp*).

Character	Number of genes	Type of gene action
Skin colour	Digenic (*R-P-*)	• *R-PP*-Red; • *rrP*- Purple; • *R-P*- Deep red; • *rrPP*- White
Cream corolla	Monogenic recessive	-
Root shape	Monogenic	Round incompletely dominant to flat root
Leaf type	Monogenic (*CC*)	Compound leaf dominant to simple leaf
Petal margin	Monogenic	Rolled margin dominant to wavy
Club root resistance	3 independent dominant genes	-
Powdery mildew resistance	Partially recessive	-
Turnip mosaic virus resistance	Monogenic	Resistance dominant to susceptibility

15.7 Brussels sprout

- Eulogized as 'Miniature cabbage or Sprouts or Buttons'.
- Mostly grown in European countries and USA. It is grown in the city of Brussels in Belgium since 13th century.
- Spontaneous sport (non-heading cabbage of rosette form) from cabbage found in Belgium in 1750.
- The plant produces a series of lateral buds or sprouts in the form of miniature heads in axil of leaves along the single unbranched stem, usually 2-3 feet tall.
- Cool climate winter vegetable and frost resistant crop.
- Among crucifers, glucosinolates is highest (160-250 mg/100g) in Brussels sprout.
- In Europe, it is grown mainly for fresh market while in California, it is grown for freezing.
- Inflorescence type: Racemose.
- Edible part: Swollen axillary buds.
- Stem of crop makes normal longitudinal growth.
- Sib-incompatibility is very much prevalent.
- Frost resistant and late cultivars withstand temperature as low as -10^{0}C and grow even at 0^{0}C.
- Ideal soil pH: 6-6.5.
- It is salt tolerant (C_4 to C_8) but plant remains dwarf.
- Sowing time: August-September (plains) and transplanting time: September-October.
- Temperature for seed germination: 12-16^{0}C.
- Optimum temperature for growth: 16-20^{0}C.

- Topping is done to increase harvesting time.
- Loose sprouts marketed as a 'blowers'.
- Seed rate: 300-400 g/ha (hybrid cvs.)
- Planting distance: 60 cm x 60 cm or 90 cm x 90 cm or 70 cm x 45 cm.
- One gram seed produce 100 seedlings.
- Single cross (Avan cross) using SI mechanism is used for production of F_1 hybrid seeds (Johnson, 1966).
- Crop has 2 distinctive phases: a) Vegetative (form sprouts), b) generative (form flowers & seeds) after exposing to chilling temperature 5-8^{0}C for a period of 6-8 weeks.
- For single mechanical harvesting, close spacing between plants is followed.
- Harvesting method: Firm, solid, upper leaves folded closely, uniform size & dark green in colour, 3-5 pickings are done.
- Harvesting period: January-February (plains) and November-March (hills).
- Topping and removal of growing point promotes the maturity of small sprouts at top of stem. This should be done when lower sprouts are 0.5 inch in diameter. In this way, full stem is uniform sprouts develops in about 4 weeks.
- Yield: 3-5 T/ha.
- Freezing industry require sprouts less than 3 cm diameter.
- Packing: Packed only in ceramic film (0.0013 mm thick) store well for 16 weeks at 0^{0}C.
- Excess application of potash imparts bitter taste to spouts while excess N cause development of loose spout.
- CA storage: Good appearance for 4 weeks at 2.5^{0}C
- MA storage: 2-5% CO_2, 14.5-16.8% O_2 at 0-1^{0}C.
- Brussels sprout should not be stored with fruits that emit ethylene, which can cause yellowing and abscission.
- Internal browning: Ca deficiency.
- Genic MS has been reported by Johnson (1958) and Nieuwhof (1961).
- A recessive marker gene for glossy foliage is being used for production of F_1 hybrid seeds (North and Priestly, 1962).

Varieties:

- In Europe, cultivars are selected through mass selection by growers themselves.
- Hybrids have wider adaptability, uniformity in maturity and sprout shape is suitable for machine harvesting.
- Two distinct type of cultivars:
  1. Dwarf- short stem (< 50 cm length), sprouts are small and crowded on stem. These are mostly early cropper and most suitable for areas at short growing

season e.g. Catskill, Early Dwarf, Dwarf Gem, Dwarf Improved and Improved Long Island.

2. Tall-Grown in areas where growing season is longer e.g. Amager Market, Danish Prize, Red Vein, Rubine, Eveshan, Oliver, Rampart, Cambridge No. 1, 3 & 5.

- Late and hardier cvs.- Hilds Ideal, Red Vein, Amazer, De Rosny.
- Hilds Ideal: OP cv. introduced by IARI. Tall (60-65 cm) having 45-55 sprouts/ plant, measuring 7-8 cm across of 7-8 gram each. Sprouts lighter green, globular and solid, takes 110-120 days for 1st picking after transplanting. Yield/ plant: 250-450 g in 4-5 pickings; hardierandsuitable to northern plains and hills. Yield 16 t/ha.
- Hybrids marketed by seed companies of Japan and Europe are Jade Cross (F_1 hybrid of Japan), Pearl Crystal, Doreman, Predora, Rovoka, Sonara, Ladosa, Oliver, Valiant, Rogor, Rider, Boxer, Asgard, Royal Marvel, Rasmunda, Kundry and Stephan.

Disease and pest:

- Damping off in nursery is serious.
- Hairy caterpillar: Spray systemic insecticide.

15.8 Kale

- Kale grown in Kashmir known as 'Karamsag'.
- Resembling non-heading or loose leaf type of cabbage.
- It has short season and require 40-50 days from seeding to harvest.
- Requires chilling for flowering.
- Cultivars differ in curling of leaves and winter hardiness.
- Chinese kale is adapted to tropical conditions and can be grown at high temperature (18-20^{0}C).
- Hardiest crop, can withstand 10-15^{0}C, heat and tolerant to salt.
- Contain highest anti-oxidants among cole crops.
- Kale: Lutein rich leafy green vegetable (9.8-13.4 mg/ 100 g of fresh wt.).
- Origin of Chinese kale: China.
- Progenitor of Chinese kale: *B. cretica ssp. nivea.*
- Glucosinolates content: 65-151 mg/100g.
- Edible portion: Cluster of numerous tender leaves at its top.
- Most forms bear cluster of leaves at tip of stem which is harvested and used as leaf vegetable.
- Leaves are harvested one by one from bottom for fresh market before they become tough and woody.
- Planting distance: 40cm x 50 cm.
- Harvesting: Either the entire plant can be cut at ground level or selected outer leaves are harvested. In later method, inner leaves and growing points should be left to allow for additional harvests.

- Yield: 10-25 t/ha.
- Hydro cooling or vacuum cooling or crushed ice is used for cooling the produce for shipment. At 0^{0}C and 95-100% R.H. kale can be stored in cold storage for no longer than 2 weeks.

Different form:

Curly kale	*B. oleracea* var. *acephala* sub-var. *lacinata*; highly curled foliage; more common
Smooth leaved kale	*B. oleracea* var. *acephala* sub-var. *plana*; smooth rosette type
Thousand headed kale	*B. oleracea* var. *acephala* sub-var. *mellicapitata* (syn. *B. oleracea* var. *fruiticosa*); produce whorls of young shoots
Tree kale	*B. oleracea* var. *acephala* sub-var. *palmiflora*; tall > 2m
Marrow stem kale	*B. oleracea* var. *acephala* sub-var. *medullosa*; long thicked stems
Chinese kale	*B. oleracea* var. *alboglabra*
Collard	*B. oleracea* var. *sabellica*
Kitchen kale	*B. oleracea* var. *fimbriata*

Varieties:

- Scotch type: Much curled and crumpled foliage of grayish green colour.
- Siberian type: Less crinkled, bluish green and suitable for temperate region.
- Pusa-64 (syn. KTK-64), VRKALE-1 (did not require vernalization), Dwarf Green, Dwarf Moss, Dwarf Blue, Moss Curled, Curled Scotch, Tall Curled Scotch, Hamburger Market, Georgia, Blue Max, Heading, Morris, Heavier Crop, Top Bunch.

15.9 Collard

- Non-heading form or loose leaf type of cabbage grown for their fleshy leaves.
- Plants are biennials although grown as annuals.
- Plant forms rosettes of smooth thick, bluish green leaves that can be boiled or fried.
- Crop is very popular in South America where they are used as winter green.
- Plants grow to a height of 2-4 feet and are hardier than cabbage to cold and heat.
- Grown year-round but it is essentially a cool season crop.
- Culture is similar to that of cabbage.
- Field planting can be done form transplants or from direct seeding.
- Plants are spaced 12-14 inches apart and in rows 3-4 feet apart.
- Leaves are harvested sequentially as they approach full size but before they become tough and woody.
- Harvesting of leaves is done usually 75-90 days after seeding. This results in tall bare stalk with tuft of succulent leaves at the top.
- Staking is frequently necessary to hold the older plants in upright position.
- Collards can also be harvested when the plants are younger (6-12 inches tall) by cutting off the whole rosettes at ground level.

15.10 Chinese cabbage

- Also known as 'Chinese leaves or Celery cabbage'.
- Non heading strain of cabbage.
- Originated from spontaneous hybridization between turnip (*B. campestris ssp. rapifera*) and Pak-Choi (*B. campestris ssp. chinensis*).
- Tender and succulent leaves are used as sag (vegetable).
- Grown as annual for edible leaves, stems and flowering shoots.
- Moderate in folic acid and vit. C.
- Cultivated in China since 5th century.
- 1st large scale commercial cultivation was taken by Israelis in 1970.
- It was marketed as Napa cabbage in USA.
- It is resistant to all 4 strains of Turnip Mosaic virus.
- Photoperiods of 15-16 h or more for 4-5 weeks cause flowering in crop.
- Cool season crop thrives best from 16-22^{0}C.
- Optimum soil pH: 6-7.5.
- Seed rate: 500 g for transplanting and 2.5 kg/ha for direct seedlings.
- Planting distance: 60 cm x 45 cm (early maturing-37,000 plants/ha); 70 cm x 50 cm (medium maturing-28,000 plants/ha).
- Most common sowing method: Direct sowing.
- Thinning (5-6 leaf stage) is very important operation.
- Low O_2 (2%) in combination with CO_2 (2%) improved shelf life of Chinese cabbage.
- Mulching is recommended in Chinese cabbage.
- Harvesting method: Heading types are harvested by cutting off the entire head at ground level and removing outer leaves whereas in non-heading type, whole plant is cut at base and trimmed by hand when matured 60-100 days after field planting.
- Harvesting stage: Head must be firm & outer leaves bright coloured.
- Days taken for harvesting: 65-100 days (heading type), 35-60 days (non-heading type).
- CA storage: 0^{0}C, 2% O_2, 2-5% CO_2 and 95% R.H.
- Hybrids between Chinese cabbage and pak-choi were produced by double cross system by Tateo and Kanji (1931).
- Bud pollination is practiced for F_1 hybrid seed production.
- **Species**: Two most common types used as salad or cooked vegetables.
  1. Heading type is *Pe-tsai* (*B. rapa* var. *pekinensis*): Forms erect, moderately compact and usually cylindrical heads.Cultivars include the traditional Michihli (elongated head), Wong Bok (shorter head) and the newer F_1 hybrids Jade Pagoda (tall head), Spring Time, Summer Time, Winter Time (all three have short, compact heads).

2. Non-heading type is *Pak-choi* (*B. campestris ssp. chinensis*): Develops cluster of long, dark green, oval or oblong succulent leaves with forming head. It is closely related to mustard and is also known as 'Mustard cabbage or Chinese mustard'. Standard cultivars of leafy types are 'Crispy Choy', 'Pac Choy' and the slow bolting 'Lei Choy'.

- Four types:
  1. **Loose leaved variety (var. *dissoluta*):** Terminal bud under developed, forming no leaf bud; rosette leaves oblanceolate, spreading or erect & usually grown in spring and summer in all parts of China.
  2. **Semi heading variety (var. *imfareta*):** Terminal bud with its outer layer of leaves fairly well developed, forming head with a hollow centre; plants large & tall. Usually grown in autumn.
  3. **Fluffy topped heading variety (var. *laxa*):** Terminal bud well developed forming rather a solid head with its leaf tips curling upwards & forming a fluffy top; plants small, rosette leaves obovate and spreading. Usually grown in late summer & autumn and
  4. **Heading type:** It is further classified into 3 types – (a) Ovate type (f. *ovata*) (b) Flat topped type (f. *depressa*) (c) Cylindrical (f. *cylindrica*).
- Three major groups:

A. Tall cylindrical type:

i) Has long upright leaves and forms compact head.

ii) It is slow growing, takes about 70 days from sowing to harvest.

iii) Most susceptible to bolting

iv) Sweet type & stores well.

v) Cv. Jade Pagoda: Cylindrical with form crisp head, takes 65 days to mature & cold tolerant.

B. Hearted type or barrel shaped:

i) Has compact, barrel shaped heads with tightly wrapped leaves & dense heart.

ii) Mature after 55 days and slow to bolt.

iii) Cv. Kasumi: compact head & resistant to bolting.

iv) Cv. Nerva: matures quickly, has dark green leaves with dense head.

v) Cv. Ruffles: Early maturing with pale green heads & creamy white heart, liable to bolt.

C. Loose headed type:

i) Are lax & open headed with creamy centres and textured leaves.

ii) Self blanching type & less liable to bolt.

iii) Cv. Santo Serrated Leaved: Loose headed, has serrated leaves & cold resistant.

iv) Cv. Shantung: Spreading habit with tender light green leaves & dense heart.

v) Cv. Tip Top: Early type for spring planting, harvested in 70 days, produce good sized heads.

Varieties:

- Crop improvement by utilizing self incompatibility began in mid 20th century.
- Breeding methods: Single cross, double cross and tree way cross.
- Embryo culture and wide hybridization methods are used.
- Nowadays F_1 hybrids are developed in China, Korea, Japan.
- Scientists from World Vegetable Centre, Taiwan identified heat tolerant lines.
- Wong Bok (heading type): It has elongated, compact, large sized head & thickly veined, green, slightly wrinkled leaves with light green & broad mid-rib. Plants are short and chunky.
- Pusa Sag-1: Wong Bok x Turnip.
- UHFVR12-1, UHFVR12-2.
- Chini Sarson No.1: Non-heading type and field resistance to alternaria leaf spot.
- CITH- CC-3.
- Chihili: Tall growing, large sized, cylindrical, compact head & thickly veined leaves with prominent mid-rib.
- Tianjin Qingmaye: Chinese variety, low cellulose content.

Diseases and pests:

- Downy mildew (*Perenospora parasitica*): Seed treatment with Metalaxyl @ 0.3 to 0.6 g/ kg.
- Damping off (*Rhizoctonia solani*): Serious in nursery. Treat the nursery bed with formalin (1 part formalin in 7-10 parts water). Seed treatment with Carbendazim @ 0.3%.
- Black spot (*Alternaria brassicae*): Spray Dithane M-45 @ 1 g/ litre.
- Black leg: Hot water treatment (50^{0}C for 30 min) to seeds. Seed treatment with Thiram or Carbendazim @ 2-3 g/ kg.
- Sclerotia rot (*Sclerotinia sclerotiorum*): Follow crop rotation with monocots and alternate sprays of Dithane M-45 @ 2 g/litre and Carbendazim @ 1 g/litre at 10-15 days interval.
- Diamond back moth (*Plutella xylostella*): Serious pest.
- Aphids: Common during early spring and summer season. Spray systemic insecticide like Imidacloprid @ 1 ml/litre

Inheritance of characters:

- Fibre content: Atleast 3 pairs of genes.
- Sugar & protein content: Single pair of genes.

15.11 Horseradish

- English name came from adaptation of its German name 'meerrettich' which is translated 'mareradish'.
- Romans referred to it as amoracia.
- It is highly specialized and relatively expensive crop to produce.
- In USA, > 80% of the produce goes directly to the processing for grating and grinding.
- It shares prime place at nations dinner table in European countries as appetizer condiment.
- Cool season hardy perennial crop having large dark green leaves which are wavy. Cylindrical tap root which branches profusely at its terminal.
- Although it is perennial, but grown as annual with roots harvested every year.
- When grown as annual, smaller roots are harvested in late winter.
- Optimum soil pH: 6-7.5.
- Credited with digestive and anti-scorbitic properties due to high vit. C. content.
- Nutrition value/ 100 g: Raw horseradish is high in K (554 mg), Ca (140 mg) and vit. C (81 mg).
- Leaves and roots are used for food, condiments and originally for medicinal purposes.
- It is grown for its enlarged tap root which is used as appetizing condiment for meats and fish.
- It is infact large/ strong or coarse radish.
- Large whorl of coarse-textured leaves arise from the crown.
- Root penetrate deeply into soil or lateral roots spread in upper soil area.
- Tap root is white/ buff coloured, relatively smooth, 30 cm long and 12-18 mm thick with several swollen roots branching out from it at different angles.
- Roots exhibit distinct polarity.
- Small, branched roots/sets arise from the distal end of taproot and are used as propagating material for next year's crop.
- Edible part: Roots which emit highly pungent odour.
- Pungency is due to sulphur compound 'allyl butyl isothiocyanate'.
- Propagation method: Vegetatively from sets or 1 year old secondary roots (small branch roots) from previous year's growth.

- Sets should be 6-18 inches long, 0.5-0.75 inch in dia., and fairly straight. They are stored over winter in pits or cold cellars.
- Flowers small, white, borne on stalk, numerous and aromatic.
- Fruit pods are short, oblong and crinkled, fail to mature but contains viable seeds.
- Plants rarely flowers and produce seeds.
- If exposed to air or stored improperly, horse radish loses its pungency rapidly after it has been ground or processed.
- Sets are placed in furrows, 4-5 inches deep and at 18-24 inches apart.
- Furrow spacing vary from 30 to 36 inches apart and accommodate 7200-11600 plant/ acre.
- Prior to planting, sets are given slanting cut at bottom ends & square cut at top or crown ends for proper root placement.
- Sets are best planted with top ends slightly higher at 45^0 angle than bottom ends.
- Irrigation is given during August-September.
- Water stress causes underdeveloped and small roots.
- In order to obtain straight roots with few side shoots lifting procedure is used. This involves lifting the top or crown end of main root out of soil, stripping off the side roots and all main crown leaves and then replacing root & covering it with soil. This is usually done twice during the season when leaves are 6-10 inches tall and again about 6 weeks later.
- Excess N fertilizer results in too much top growth and highly branched irregular roots. It has high requirement for boron.
- Crop is harvested after the tops have been killed by frost.
- Roots are lifted from soil with modified potato diggers or heavy plough.
- To facilitate harvest, killed tops are mowed down about 7-10 days before roots are dug.
- Harvested roots are placed in plastic bags & stored over winter in pits/ barns/ cool cellers or left in ground over winter & harvested in early spring.
- Storage: Roots are cold stored at -1.1 to 0^0C and 98-100% R.H. to prevent drying out & store well for 10-12 months and for summer use or for fresh marketing and processing.
- If exposed to light, roots become green.
- It is cut into small thin chips and dried for use during time of scarcity of other vegetables.
- Recovery percent on drying: 20.
- Value added products: Peeled roots are mixed with vinegar solution & used to blend whipped cream, sour cream and in yogurt. Pickles also prepared.

Varieties:

- Two types (Shoemaker, 1953):
  1. Common type: Widely cultivated having broad, brown crinkled leaves & hollow petioles, having high quality roots. Roots are corky tan on surface & white within. Very susceptible to Turnip Mosaic virus & white rust.
  2. Bohemian type: Narrow, smooth edged leaves & solid petiole, having inferior quality roots. Resistant to white rust & mosaic.
- Bip Top Western: Large, upright, smooth leaves. Resistant to white rust & tolerant to Turnip Mosaic virus.
- Swiss: Smooth leaves, susceptible to white rust & TMV.
- Maliner: Crinkled leaf type.

Pests and diseases:

- Flea beetle and Beet leaf hoppers: Most serious & cause injury to young shoots.
- White rust (*Albugo candida*):
- Turnip Mosaic virus (TMV): Cause extensive leaf damage which prevents normal root growth & reduced yields.
- Brittle root (*Spiroplasma citri*): Transmitted by beet leaf hopper and cause internal browning of vascular tissue of roots. Starch accumulates in the roots which snap easily when bent.
- Curly top virus: Spread by leaf hoppers.
- Verticillium wilt: Serious.
- Root knot nematode: Serious.

15.12 Rutabaga

- Eulogized as 'Lapland turnip or Turnip rooted cabbage'.
- Flesh is solid and its colour remains after cooking.
- Higher temperature (>25^{0}C) cause growth cracks.
- Highly sensitive to herbicide triazine or trifluralin derivatives.
- Storage: 0^{0}C with 90% R.H.
- Hot wax treatment maintains longer shelf life.
- **Varieties**: American Purple Top, Laurentian, York, Fortune, Canola.

Pests, diseases, disorders:

- Cabbage maggot: Severe damage.
- Flea beetle: Destructive pest.
- Irregular size: Lack of seed sizing before planting.
- Water core or brown heart: B deficiency & soil pH > 6.5.

16. CUCURBITACEAE (GOURD FAMILY)

CUCURBITS

- Term 'Cucurbits' is coined by Dr. Bailey.
- Today, cucumbers are grown all over the world for pickling (pickles) and fresh markets (slices).
- Share of cucurbits: 5-6% of total vegetable production of India.
- Trend of evolution in *Luffa* as given by Dutt and Roy (1971).
- Unfruitfulness is associated with dioecious nature.
- Seeds valued for high oil and protein content.
- Seed protein of cucurbits is generally richer in methionine than the legumes.
- Cucurbits do not withstand root disturbance.
- *Cucumis* and Cucurbits have usually unsaturated acids like oleic acid and linoleic acid.
- Cucumber and melons are separate and unrelated species.
- Vegetatively propagated and tendriless cucurbits: Parwal (pointed gourd), Chow-chow, Ivy gourd.
- Bitter gourd rich in vit. C (96 mg/100 g); pumpkin contain high carotenoid; kakarol is high in protein (3.1%), Chow-chow high in calcium (140 mg/ 100g).
- Metaxenia is high in cucumber and bottle gourd.
- Bitter principle is due to cucurbitacin. It prevents spoilage in cucurbits. Attractant for cucumber beetles.
- Temperature > 33^0C increases bitterness in fruits.
- Bitterness is common problem in oriental pickling melon, cucumber and bottle gourd.
- High concentration of cucurbitacins is in fruits, roots, pollens and less in leaves.
- Flavour is due to terpenes.
- Non-dessert melons used as vegetables: Round melon and Long melon.
- Long melon can easily cross with musk melon and snap melon.
- Flowering in cucurbits generally starts 40-45 days after sowing.
- Early planting in November escapes attack of red pumpkin beetle.
- Robinson *et al*. (1976): Gene nomenclature for cucurbit crops.
- Cucurbits depend solely on insect pollinators on account of monoecy or dioecy.
- Economic sex ratio in cucurbits: 25-30:1 or 15:1.
- Seven types of sex forms exists in cucurbits: Monoecious, Androecious, Andromonoecious, Trimonoecious (rare), Gynoecious, Gynomonoecious.
- Primitive sex form in cucurbits: Hermaphrodite.
- Predominant/Advanced sex form: Monoecious.

- Highly unstable and not breeding true: Trimonoecious (androgynomonoecious).
- Trimonoecious cucurbits: Cucumber, musk melon and ridge gourd.
- Andromonoecious cucurbits: Musk melon, bottle gourd, bitter gourd, sponge gourd, snake gourd and rare in water melon, smooth gourd, ridge gourd and cucumber.
- Pistillate and hermaphrodite flowers borne solitary and staminate flowers in clusters.
- In cucurbits, long day (16 h) and high temperature promotes male flower development.
- Short day treatment for 9 h, low temperature and high R.H. stimulate development of female flowers.
- Fruits turn to lighter in colour on maturity in different cucurbits.
- First 4-6 nodes bear male flower then female in cucurbits.
- Staminate flower appear 7 days earlier than pistillate.
- Sex differentiation occurs at 2 and 4 true leaf stage. This stage is most responsive for sex modification with growth regulators.
- NAA, Ethylene (250-300 ppm), acetone induces femaleness.
- Pollination agents: Honey bees, bumble bees, beetles.
- Family Cucurbitaceae is taxonomically recognized by berry-like pepo fruit due to hard rind when mature.
- In all cucubits, seeds exhibits parietal placentation.
- Leaves of melons simple, 3-5 lobed, palmate, simple and rarely pinnataly lobed (*Citrullus* spp.) and more or less rounded.
- Formation of abscission layer is the maturity index for melons.
- In cucurbits, seeds continue to mature in fruit even after harvest.
- 'Shrivelling and browning' of androecium in *C. pepo* is controlled by single recessive gene: Marker gene.
- Common summer squashes and winter squashes have been derived from Chilean varieties.
- Bitter and non-bitter forms are known in *Lageneria* as *Cucumis*, *Cucurbita* and *Citrullus*.
- Axillary buds/ cotyledons/ hypocotyls and apical shoot tips have been used for regeneration.
- All cucurbits are called as 'sulphur shy' plants.
- BHC insecticide is phytotoxic to cucurbits.
- Seed should be dried to 7% moisture before storage.

16.1 Cucumber

- Oldest cultivated vegetable crop.
- It has been cultivated in western Asia for 3000 years.

- From India, it spread to Greece-Italy and later into China.
- Often regarded as health food due to low calorie content.
- Model plant for sex determination studies and plant vascular biology.
- USA is leading importer of cucumber and gherkins, assorted canned vegetables and other dehydrated vegetables from India.
- Commercial production includes i) Processing type for pickling ii) Fresh market types for slicing.
- Largest producer: Sri Lanka.
- 2nd most widely cultivated cucurbit after water melon.
- 3rd most cultivated vegetable after tomato and water melon.
- 1st sequenced vegetable crop (old cultigens from Asia) consumed in salad, cooked and pickle form.
- Average productivity in India (6.67 T/ha) and world (16.53 T/ha).
- In temperate countries, grown extensively in glasshouses.
- Introduced into New World during 'Slave trade'.
- Fruits from river bed cultivation are available 30-50 days before than normal field sown crop.
- Presence of minerals especially Mg, K and Si are used in skin cream, face mask, etc.
- Genome size of cucumber: 4.25×10^8 bp and total length of assembled genome is 243.5 Mb.
- Day neutral, frost susceptible and thermophilic crop.
- Growth and development are favoured at > 20^0C.
- Tolerates cooler weather than melons.
- It has narrow genetic base (3-8% polymorphism).
- Seed oil is used as anti-pyretic.
- Monoecious, annual, trailing/ climbing vine.
- Cucumbers have hirsute (scabrous) stems.
- Fruit parts: Exocarp (tough or tender skin) + mesocarp (carpel walls) + endocarp (seed cavity or locule size).
- Slender fruits (larger L/D) have greater diameter in mesocarp & exocarp than in endocarp.
- Fruits with lesser L/D have proportionally larger endocarp areas.
- Major carotene present in peel and flesh: β-carotene.
- Dark green peel contains 25-45 ppm carotene while pale green contains 8-15 ppm carotene.

- Optimum temperature for growth: 26.4^{0}C.
- Optimum soil pH: 6-7.
- Planting density: a) For slicers by hand picked (7,000-20,000 plants/ acre); b) By machine harvested (30,000 to 60,000 plants/ acre).
- Wider spacing is used for fresh market slicers.
- In Europe, high density cultural systems (> 50,000 plants/ acre) is adopted in pickling cucumber industry over single row spacing (15,000-20,000 plants/ acre).
- Single row spacing is used for multiple harvests.
- Increase in plant density results in-
  a) Decrease in number of fruits/ plant
  b) Reduction in fruit quality (decrease in fuirt firmness & colour)
  c) Reduction in fruit number/ plant
  d) Increased incidence of fruit rots
  e) Decrease in stability of gynoecious character.
- In gynoecious cucumber, pollination is done by blending seed of monoecious cultivar in field. Most of times, its 88% gynoecious and 12% monoecious.
- When cucumber set fruit without pollination, the fruits are seedless. The fruits contain soft white seed coats. This type of fruit set usually happens in low light & cool night conditions. Green house plants are parthenocarpic (facultative parthenocarpy).
- Open pollinated cultivars of cucumber are monoecious (most common).
- No need of pollination for seedless cucumbers.
- Chemically 'cucurbitacin' is tetracyclic triterpenes compounds responsible for bitter taste and flavour.
- Chilling injury is physiological disorder when fruits exposed <15^{0}C.
- Economic sex ratio of cucumber: 15 male: 1 female.
- Pollination agents: Honey bees.
- Monoecious and hybrid "PF" types require one hive per acre and gynoecious types require 3-4 hives or 10-15% planting of male plants acts as seed pollinators.
- Flowers open for only one day.
- Cucumber is diclinous in nature.
- Basic sex forms: Androecious, monoecious, gynoecious & hermaphrodite.

The phenotypes and genotypes of basic sex types in cucumber:

- Sex expression in cucumber is controlled by 3 major loci.
  a) m^+,m- develops staminate & pistillate flowers.m^+/- genotypes are strictly diclinus.
  b) F^+,F- controls degree of female tendency. F allele is partially dominant & intensifies female expression.

c) a^+,a- homozygous 'a' allele intensify male tendency.

d) Genotypes $m^+/-$, F^+/F^+, a/a & m/m, F^+/F^+, a/a are typically androecious.

Phenotype	Genotype, locus		
	m	***F***	***a***
Androecious	-/-	F^+/F^+	a/a
Monoecious	m^+/m^+	F^+/F^+	-/-
Hermaphroditic	m/m	F/F	-/-
Gynoecious	m^+/m^+	F/F	-/-

- Only staminate (male) flowers are produced on main stem of monoecious cucumber and later and lateral shoots produce pistillate (female) flowers.
- Staminate flowers borne either singly or in clusters of 3 to 5.
- Pistillate flowers are solitary in leaf axils and have shorter pedicels than staminate flowers. It is recognized by presence of miniature fruit at base of flower.
- In gynoecious cucumbers, only female flowers are produced and often referred to as 'all female'.
- Similar to gynoecious, "PF" (predominantly female) cultivars are available.
- Light intensity and day length influence anthesis than temperature. Temperature influences anther dehiscence and pollen fertility.
- Optimum temperature for anthesis and dehiscence: 13-18^{0}C.
- Anthesis time: 5.30-7 AM.
- Pollens are more sticky and no wind dessimination of pollens.
- Pistillate flowers are receptive in morning (to mid-day) on day of anthesis.
- Hot day condition reduces pistil receptivity and pollen viability.
- All cucumbers are day neutrals except *C. sativus* var. *hardwickii*.
- Gynoecious type produce pistillate flowers under both SD and LD conditions.
- In gynomonoecious, short day condition increases pistillate flowers and reduces staminate flowers.
- Nowadays, tropical gynoecious i.e. parthenocarpic lines are more commonly cultivated in green house. These are developed by Dr. V.S. Sheshadri and Dr. T.A. More in 1980.
- Gynoecious lines can be commercially exploited for heterosis of economic characters.
- Fruits of parthenocarpic cucumber are mild in flavor, seedless, thin edible skin that require no peeling, 25-35 cm in length and 500 g in weight.
- Gynoecious cucumber hybrids are earlier, more productive, more uniform and adaptable to machine harvests than monoecious types.

- Induction of parthenocarpic fruit setin cucumber: Morphactin (Chlorfluorenol).
- Growth and development of cucumber is favoured by > 20^{0}C.
- Higher temperature and long photoperiod (long day) induces maleness whereas short days & lower temperature promote femaleness.
- 1st report on alteration of sex expression via exogenous chemicals was in 1945.
- Auxin application shifts sex expression in cucumber towards femaleness (Laibach & Kribben, 1949).
- Abiotic stress increases male flowering in "PF" types and also in gynoecious lines.
- GA_3, GA_4 and GA_7 promotes male flowers in monoecious cvs. but increases bitterness of stems.
- Parthenocarpic lines are maintained by Silver nitrate and GA_3.
- GA_3 (15 ppm) and $AgNO_3$ (50-100 ppm) or Silver thiosulphate i.e. $[Ag(S_2O_3)_2]$ (500-2000 ppm) or Aminoethoxyvinylglycine (AVG) at 2 and 4 true leaf stage are used to enhance male flowers on gynoecious cucumber.
- $AgNO_3$ induces sufficient pollen production for gynoecious lines to serve as male parent in gynoecious x gynoecious hybrids.
- Ethylene and acetylene are potent promoters of femaleness.
- Ethrel @ 250-500 ppm helps in increasing early femaleness (modify sex expression) in andromonoecious, gynomonoecious and monoecious varieties.
- Parthenocarpic cultivars are sprayed with Chlorflurenol to obtain normal fruit growth and development.
- Pinching of male bud can be commercially exploited for hybrid seed production in cucumber.
- Cucumber fruit yield reduction is due to crown fruit inhibition or 1st fruit inhibition.
- Xenia: Effect of genes from male parent in development of fruit or seeds.
- Metaxenia: Effect of pollen on fruit shape and other characteristics. Bitter pollen or foreign pollen fertilizes the non-bitter or normal ovule causes 'bitter fruit'.
- Fruit shape in relation to flower type:
  1. Epigynous and perigynous flowers develop into differing fruit shape.
  2. Elongated/ longer fruits are associated with epigynous flowers.
  3. Fruits from perigynous flowers are more rounded and have pronounced scar after shedding of receptacles.
- A developing fruit set at lower node inhibit or delays fruit setting at subsequent nodes.
- Size and shape of fruit is related to number of seeds produced by pollination.
- Poor pollination causes fruit abortion/ misshapen fruits/ poor fruit set.
- Optimum temperature for seed germination: 27-29^{0}C.

- Most herbicides are extremely phytotoxic to cucumber.
- Sulphur causes phytotoxicity when applied or sprayed on foliage.
- Maturity indices: Fruit size, skin colour, wax deposit on fruit surface.
- Instrument used for measuring fruit firmness: Magness Taylor Fruit Pressure Tester.
- Pressure test readings or brine solution indicate/ measure fruit firmness.
- Quality parameter of fruits: Flesh firmness & skin tenderness.
- Fruit firmness is related to both flesh firmness and seed cavity or locule size.
- Seed cavity is measured as ratio of cavity diameter to fruit diameter.
- As seed cavity diameter increases, the fruit becomes less firm.
- Slender fruits have more mesocarp (carpel walls) and exocarp (skin) than endocarp (seed cavity).
- Internal harvest index of maturity: Jelly formation in seed cavity, small immature seeds and crisp texture.
- Harvesting stage: 6-7 days after anthesis.
- Harvest index for gynoecious and parthenocarpic cultivars: Acidity of fruit pulp.
- Sign of over maturity: Fruits turn yellow and show carpel separation in cross-section.
- Yield: 15-20 t/ha (monoecious); 200 t/ha (gynoecious F_1 hybrids).
- In European countries, pickling cucumbers and gynoecious types are mechanically harvested while slicing types are hand harvested.
- USDA marketing grade of slicing cucumber: Fancy grade fetches high price.
- Fruit grades as per Michigan State University:
  - U.S. Fancy, U.S. Extra No.1, U.S. No.1, U.S. No. 1 Large, U.S. No. 1 Small, U.S. No. 2.
  - Pickling cucumbers are graded by fruit diameter into No. 1(upto 1.06 inch), No. 2 (upto 1.06-1.5 inch), No. 3 (upto 1.5- 2.0 inch).
- Cucumbers are hydrocooled to remove field heat.
- Fruits ripen at > 10^{0}C and colour changes from green to yellow.
- Optimum temperature for storage and transport: 10^{0}C, below this results in chilling injury.
- Fruits can be held 10-14 days at 10-13^{0}C and 95% R.H.
- Cucumbers should not be stored with fruits that emit ethylene, which accelerates yellowing.
- Slicers for fresh market are usually waxed to reduce moisture loss and packed in water proof cardboard cartons.
- Seeds attain optimum maturity/ quality 60 days after pollination.
- About 100 to > 200 seeds is common during hand pollination.

- Male sterile lines are developed through gamma rays.
- Genic male sterility *ms-1* and *ms-2* cause abortion of staminate flowers (Robinson *et al.*, 1976).
- CMS is absent in *C. sativus*.
- Peterson and Weigle (1958) advocated use of gynomonoecious lines for production of hybrid seeds.
- Peterson and Anhder (1960) suggested use of monoecious lines for production of hybrid seeds.
- 'Lemon cucumber': Intergeneric hybrid between cucumber x orange was obtained by Fullerton in 1910.

Species:

- Native to India or Southern Asia.
- India is treasure house of cucumber diversity.
- Tapley *et al.* (1935) written an excellent treatise on cucumber classification.
- *Cucumis* x *hytivus* (2n=38): New synthetic man-made species derived from *C. hystrix* x *C. sativus* and chromosome doubling. It was proposed by Chen and Kirkbride (2000).
- Cucumber is distinct from other *Cucumis* spp and has 7 pairs of chromosomes (2n=2x=14).
- Other *Cucumis* spp. have 12 pairs or multiples of 12 i.e. (2n=2x=24, 48, etc.).
- Other uncultivated *Cucumis* spp. are more genetically similar to musk melons/ cantaloupes than to cucumber.
- Wild *Cucumis* spp. from S. Africa *C. anguria* var. *longipes* has many morphological features common with var. *anguria* and is cross compatible.
- Var. *anguria* is non-bitter variant of var. *longipes* that has reached New World in 17th century through slave trade.
- Cucumber is known only as cultivated plant.
- Another *Cucumis* form *C. sativus* var. *hardwickii* is cross compatible with cucumber & sets fruits with plump seeds from reciprocal crosses. Var. *hardwickii* has ability to set large number of seeded fruits/ plant in sequential fashion.
- In *C. sativus*, fruits with developing seeds inhibit development of lateral fertilized flowers.
- Interspecific hybridization between cucumber and musk melon is successful but embryo does not develop.
- Cucumber is readily crossable with ridge gourd.
- Common cucumber is green/white fleshed is low in nutritional quality.

- Orange fleshed cucumber is derived from landrace Xishuangbanna gourd from south west China. It contains 10 times more carotenoids.
- 'Arya' (Snake) cucumber: *Cucumber melo* var. *flexuosus*.

Name	Features
C. sativus var. *hardwickii* (2n=2x=14)	Progenitor form of cultivated cucumber *C. sativus* (De Candolle, 1886); smooth surface & extremely bitter flesh; sequential fruiting; resistant to DM & root knot nematode; objectionable weed; cross compatible with *C. sativus*.
C. metulliferus (2n=24)	African horned cucumber; root knot nematode resistant
C. dispaceus (2n=24)	Hedge hog or Teasal gourd
C. hystrix (2n=24) (syn. *C. muriculatus*)	Native of Asia; used as bridging species between *C. sativus* & *C.melo*; resistant to DM, gummy stem blight, virus & nematode
C. trigonus (2n=14)	Source of resistance to fruit fly; crosses freely with cultivated form; multiple fruiting & branching habit
C. hirsutus	Perennial & dioecious
C. sativus var. *xishuang bannaenesis* (Xishuangbanna gourd)	Fruit shape long & narrow column like & round with length-dia.; ratio of 3:1 in all these types; orange fleshed cucumber from China (source of β-carotene 700 I.U/ 100 g)
*C. ficifolia*or *C. lundelliana* (2n=42)	Used as bridging species/ grafting purpose; resistant to root knot nematode, PM; widest natural distribution among cultivated *Cucurbita* spp.
C. longipers, *C. heptadactylus* (2n=42), *C. zeyheri*	Resistant to root knot nematode

Varieties:

- Green cucumber with white to green mesocarp is used as salad crop.
- Temperate gynoecious lines are unsuitable for gynoecy under high temperature and long photoperiod condition.
- Orange fleshed cucumber contains >10 times carotenoids compared to green/ white cucumber.
- In Japan, the hybrid cucumbers were 1st available in 1935.
- Spartan Dawn: 1st hybrid cucumber for processing purpose.
- In America, about 12% seedless cucumbers are usedin pickle and processing industry.
- White spined cultivars are slower in rate of development than black spined fruits.

Three types:

- In black spined types of pickling cucumbers, exterior of fruit turns yellow/ orange or bronze as they increase in size & approach maturation.

Slicing type	Commonly called 'fresh market' varieties. Grown in home garden. Fruits have white spines, possess dark green exterior colour and larger than pickling type. Fruit length varies from 6-10 inch & dia. 1.5- 3 inch. Slicers are thicker skinned & have L/D ratio > 4.0. Fruits are cylindrical with rounded ends & taper from stem to blossom end. White spine colour is an indication for edible maturity in slicing cucumber. Varieties with white spines have better acceptability than black spines. Marketing is subjected to USDA market standards and grades in terms of 'Bushels'. Fruits are harvested 50 days after planting and Monoecious cultivars 65 days after planting.
Pickling type	Grown under glass; develop shorter vines, more prolific, fruits with small seed cavity and thin skin. Possess smaller length/ diameter ratio than slicers. L/ D ratio ranges from 2.8 to 3.2. L/D is influenced by plant density i.e. increased plant density cause shorter fruits and lower L/D. Fruits at base or crown of plant have smaller L/D than borne on laterals or on upper portions of plant. Fruits have lighter green coloured skin with more pronounced warts (tubercles) at immature stage. Cylindrical shaped fruits are preferred for chipping/ stripping of processed fruits. Fruits are either black or white spined. Black spine colour is an indication for edible maturity in pickling cucumber. Pickling types are fresh processed (quick pasteurization) or brined & then processed. Processed cucumbers are available in several sizes and different forms (whole, half strips, chips, cubed, diced) & favour (dill, garlic, sweet & sour). Yield is based on weight and fruit diameter. Yield is greater/ acre. Fruits are harvested 5-12 days after anthesis or 32-36 days after planting.
Parthenocarpic slicing type	Bred for green house cultivation. Fruit set and development without pollination. Fruits are seedless, mild in flavor, no bitterness & thin edible skin that require no peeling. Fruit length > 12 inches (25-35 cm long & 500 g wt.) & have tender, smooth, uniform green coloured skin.

Fresh market and processing cucumber cultivars:

Market type	Flowering type	Cultivar	Disease tolerance	Comments
Slicers	F_1- Gynoecious	Centurian	-	Very early
		Dasher II	1,2,3,4,5,6	Early, uniformly dark green
		Gemini	1,2,3,4,5,6	Early; short fruit
		Raider	2,5	Early
		Slicemaster	1,2,3,4,5,6	Early; commercial, market, home garden
		Sprint 440	1,2,3,4,5	Early; large; dark green
		Victory	1,2,3,4,5,6	Early; mod. long fruit
	Monoecious	Pacer	2,5	F_1; medium maturity; deep green; need spray program
		Poinsett	1,3,4,6	Medium maturity; long time standard
		Poinsett 76	1,2,3,4,5,6	Medium maturity
		Marketmore 76	2,3,4,5	Late maturity; dark green
		High Mark II	2,3,5	F_1; medium maturity; green house use
		Sweet Slice	2,5	F_1; medium maturity; market, home garden
Pickles	F_1-Gynoecious	Bounty	1,2,3,4,5,6	Black spine; long fruit; excellent for brining
		Calypso	1,2,3,4,5	White spine; dark green; mod. long

Carolina	1,2,3,4,5,6	White spine; med. Green; widely adapted
Flurry	1,2,3,4,5,6	White spine
Earlipik	2,5	White spine
Peto Triple Mec	1,2,3,4,5	White spine; widely adapted; strongly Gynoecious
Pioneer	2,5	Black spine; hand harvest
Premier	1,2,3,4,5,6	White spine; widely adapted; med. Green
Score	1,2,3,5,6	White spine; medium-dark green

1. Angular leaf spot; 2. Cucumber mosaic virus; 3. Downy mildew; 4. Powdery mildew; 5. Scab; 6. Anthracnose.

- Little leaf: New morphotype is reported in Pickling type cucumber by Goode *et al.* (1980).
- 1st gynoecious line: MSU 71305 i.e. Wisconsin 998 [Shogoin (Korean variety P. I220860 & gynoecious) x Wisconsin SMR18; pickling variety) developed by C.E. Peterson (1983).
- Var. hardwickii line LJ-90430 is used in breeding programs because of short day plant, bitter fruited, seeds are 1/6th size of seeds of cucumber and average 80 mature fruits/ plant.
- Parthenocarpic cvs.popular in world: Kalunga, Bellissma, Millagon, Discover, Marianna, Fitness, Aramon, Sweet Success, Country Fair, Bush Crop, Space master, Fan Spot, Sweet Slice.
- Resistant to Powdery mildew: Polaris, Sparton Salad, Ambra, Yamaki.
- Resistant to Angular leaf spot: Dixie Gemin.
- Resistant to downy mildew: Palmetto, Ashley, Chinese Long, PR-27, Wantee and Palomar.
- Resistant to Water melon mosaic virus: Chinese Long, Tokyo Long Green, Shamrock Ilima, Ohio MR-200, Ohio MR-17, Surinam.
- Resistant to Cucumber mosaic virus: Tokyo Long Green, Chinese Long, Wins Crimson, Table Green, Eprix pickling cucumber (resistant to nematode).
- Virus resistant: Poinsett 83, Balam, RKS-284.
- Scab & CMV resistant: Wisconsin SMR-9, Wisconsin SMR-12, Wisconsin SMR-15, Wisconsin SMR-18.
- For processing purpose: Green Spear 14, Pioneer, Lucky Strike.
- IC-420405 and IC-420422: Orange flesh colour lines identified in Mizoram.
- PI-197087: Line resistant to anthracnose.
- Tropical gynoecious lines viz., Gyc-1 (87-304), Gyc-2 (87-319), Gyc-3 (87-338) by IARI, New Delhi and Gyc-4 (PKG-1) by MPKV, Rahuri were developed for polyhouse cultivation.
- Cvs. All Season, Improved Long Green, GY-604, GY-598: Less susceptible to red pumpkin beetle.

Name	Breeding method	Features
Moviri	F_1 hybrid from Moscow	Suitable for growing under glass or plastic; resistant to bacterial disease, CMV & scab (*Cladosporium cucumerium*).
Askon	F_1 hybrid from Russia	Gynoecious type with high degree of parthenocarpy without insect pollination
Kid	F_1 hybrid from Russia	Suitable for pickling; resistant to DM
Guloi 82	F_1 hybrid from Korea	Suitable under different systems of cultivation
Martina	F_1 hybrid from Bulgeria	Small fruits; suitable for canning; resistant to PM
Renesansa	F_1 hybrid from Yugoslavia	Salad type;gynoecious; suitable for protected condition
Jinyou-2	F_1 hybrid from China	Highly resistant to PM & DM
Jinlu-4	F_1 hybrid from China	Highly resistant to DM, PM & fusarium wilt; tolerant to heat; grows well at 34-36^{0}C
Poinsett, Ashby	Introduced from USA by NSC	Resistant to multiple diseases (PM, DM, anthracnose, angular leaf spot)
IARI, New Delhi		
Japanese Long Green (1975)	Introduced from Japan	Restricted to temperate region; light green & crisp flesh; need staking; yield 15-28 t/ha
Straight Eight	Introduced from USA	Restricted to temperate region; fruits straight, long, flesh crisp
Pusa Uday (2005)	Selection from indigenous material	Suitable for spring-summer & kharif; yield 15 t/ha; non-prickled fruits
Pusa Barkha	Selfing & individual plant selection from local material from West Bengal	1st extra early (40-45 days after sowing); tolerant to high temperature, high humidity & downy mildew
Pusa Seedless Cucumber 6 (2018)	Developed fromcommercial hybrid through reverse breeding	1st extra early parthenocarpic gynoecious variety for protected cultivation; yield 120 t/ha (1,260 kg/ 100 m^2)
Pusa Pickling Cucumber-8 (DG-8) 2020	-	Suitable for off season production (Nov-March) in polyhouse; yield 80-85 t/ha
Pusa Sanyog (1972)	Heterosis breeding of 'Japanese gynoecious line (EC-5082) x Green Long Naples (Italian introduction)	1st gynoecious hybrid developed in India; restricted to temperate region; early & high yield 20 t/ha; cylindrical fruits, dark green skin with yellow spines

Pusa Alankar	F_1 hybrid (Austalian Green x Yellow Prolific)	Very early & high yield; delicious flesh
DGC-102	-	Light green skin colour with greenish white stripes, cylindrical (12-15 cm) smooth skin and tender and crispy flesh
DCH-1, DCH-2	Hybrids by using tropical Gynoecious hybrid as female parents	-
KTCH-11	F_1 hybrid	Gynoecious; long fruits; smooth, sweet with brown spines; crispy flesh
KTCH-8	Poinsett x LC-3	Dark green fruits; white spines
PH-9	Hybrid of 'GYC-2 x Phule Shubhangi'	Gynoecious line based hybrid; fruits green; yield 49 t/ha
PH-18	Hybrid of 'GYC-4 x Poona Khira'	Gynoecious line based hybrid; fruits yellow; yield 49 t/ha
ICAR Research Complex for Eastern Region, Patna (HARP, Ranchi)		
Swarna Ageti (2006)	Mutation	Fruits cylindrical long;fruit wt. (200 g); green colour without placental hollowness; tolerant to PM; yield 30-32 t/ha
Swarna Sheetal (2006)	Hybridization followed by recurrent selection of 'Hot Season x Long Green'	Fruits cylindrical long; fruit wt. (250 g); greenish white in colour without placental hollowness; slicing type; yield 25-30 t/ha; tolerant to PM
Swarna Poorna (2004)	Pure line selection	Fruits cylindrical long; fruit wt. (300 g); greenish white in colour with no placental hollowness; slicing type; tolerant to PM; yield 31-33 t/ha
IIVR, Varanasi		
Kashi Nutan (2018)	Hybrid	Fruit cylindrical long, dark green; fruit wt. 200-225 g; yield 17-18 t/ha
DIBER, Pithoragarh		
DARL-101	-	Specially suited to microclimatic conditions of hilly region; tolerant to PM
DARL-102	-	Excellent for hills in open and protected conditions. Field tolerant to PM & fruit fly
CIAH, Bikaner		
AHC-2	-	High yield; long fruits
AHC-13	-	Small fruits; drought hardy; bear fruits under high temperature
MPKV, Rahuri		
Himangi (1992)	Pedigree seletion of (Poinsett x Kalyanpur Ageti)	Fruits white coloured; resistant to bronzing; yield 18 t/ha

Phule Shubhangi (2001)	Sister line of cv. Himangi through pedigree selection	Straight & green fruits; resistant to bronzing, tolerant to PM; yield 19 t/ha
Phule Prachi	1st gynoecious F_1 hybrid by exploiting parthenocarpic tropical gynoecious female parent	Yellow coloured; suitable for year round cultivation
Phule Champa	Gynoecious F_1 hybrid	Green & suitable for year round cultivation
Phule Priyanka	Hybrid of (RHRB-5 x RHRBG-4)	Fruits dark green; highly prickled; tolerant to DM; yield 28 t/ha
Gyn-4 (PKV-1)	-	Tropical gynoecious line having parthenocarpic gene in it
Dr BSKKV, Dapoli		
Sheetal (1984)	Local selection from Pen area of Konkan	Fruit length 20 cm; fruit wt. 225-300 g; summer & kharif season; 24 fruits/ vine; yield 38-40 t/ha (rainy) & 20-23 t/ha (summer)
Konkan Kakdi (2019)	-	-
GBPUA & T, Pantnagar		
Pant Khira-1 (2006)	Selection from local germplasm	Fruit 20 cm; seed rate 4 kg/ha; yield 13-15 t/ha
Pant Khira-2	Heterosis	Parthenocarpic; suitable for polyhouse cultivation; 551 female flowers/vine; yield 21 t/ha
Pant Khira-3	Heterosis	Parthenocarpic; suitable for polyhouse cultivation; 465 female flowers/ vine; yield 20 t/ha
Pant Sankar Khira-1 (2005)	Heterosis breeding of (PCUC-28 x PCUC-8)	20 cm long; cylindrical fruit; yield 20 t/ha; resistant to PM & DM
Pant Parthenocarpic Cucumber -1	-	-
Pant Parthenocarpic Cucumber -2	-	Bears only female flowers; seedless fruits; fruit wt. 630 g; yield 14.5 t/ha
Pant Parthenocarpic Cucumber -3	-	Bears only female flowers; seedless fruits; fruit wt. 415 g; yield 16 t/ha
Dr YSPUH & F, Solan		
Solan Green (1975)	Selection	Fruits light green; yield 15-19 t/ha
Solan Srijan	Hybrid	Fruits cylindrical, crispy & green; fruit length 18-22 cm; fruit wt. 255-265 g; 10-15 fruits/plant; yield 20-22 t/ha
Khira-75	Selection	High yield
Khira-90	Local selection	Fruits smooth; light green; cylindrical shaped; 15-20 cm long; picking starts after 90 days

CSAUA& T, Kanpur		
Kalyanpur Green (1983)	Selection	Fruits thick, green; yield 10-12 t/ha
TNAU, Coimbatore		
CO.1 (1989)	Selection from Kanyakumari district	Fruits long with narrow neck; yield 25-28 t/ha; good consumer appeal
AAU, Anand		
Gujarat Cucumber-1 (2006)	Selection	Fruits long; long shelf life; yield 24-26 t/ha
AAU, Jorhat		
AAUC-2	Selection	Fruits long, whitish green coloured
KAU, Thrissur		
KPCH-1	Hybrid	Parthenocarpic; suitable for polyhouse cultivation; early maturing; long dark green fruits; yield 1149 kg/100 m^2
Heera	Selection	Light green fruit (15.5 cm long; fruit wt. 260; yield 73 t/ha; suitable for open & rain shelter cultivation
Shubhra	Selection	Greenish white fruit (15.5 cm long; fruit wt. 275 g; yield 60 t/ha; suitable for open & rain shelter cultivation
Other hybrids		
Rodnichok	F_1 hybrid	Resistant to PM, *Pseudomonas*, *Ascochyta*, *Colletotrichum*, *Cladosporium*
Burpee	Hybrid	All purpose variety; resistant to DM, mosaic
Priya	Hybrid of IAHS, Bengaluru	Bitter-free & slicing type; tolerant to mildew
Gemini	Hybrid of IAHS, Bengaluru	Suitable for salad; angular leaf spot resistant

Inheritance of characters:

- Recurrent selection method used for improvement of quantitative traits.
- Yield of pickling cucumber is complex character and has narrow sense of heritability (< 20%).
- Cucumber beetle resistance is associated with low cucurbitacin content.
- Higher concentration of D-glucose in fruits, more resistance to pickleworm moth.
- Mechanical & nutritive factors are associated with resistance to squash vine borer i.e. hard, woody stem shows resistance to borer.
- Non-bitter gene *bi* suppress development of cucurbitacin (bitter terpenoid compound).
- Hayes and Jones (1916) were 1st to report heterosis in cucumber.
- Spine colour and disease resistance are commonly associated and resistance to scab & CMV are developed in black spined cultivars.
- Gynoecious lines along with parthenocarpic genes are being used to produce commercial hybrids.
- Seed protein content is negatively correlated with yield.
- Flesh firmness and seed cavity are negatively correlated with fruit firmness.
- Exocarp and mesocarp structure affect fruit texture.
- Determinate (*de/de*) and compact (*cp/cp*) plant types have pleiotropic effect on sex expression (Prend and John, 1976).
- In gynoecious plant types, genes *de* and *cp* reduce the size of plant frame & reduce male/ staminate expression.
- Glabrous (*gl*) character limits fruit infestation due to lack of trichomes and eliminate oviposiiton site of adult pickleworm moth.
- Expression of different sex forms (Yamasaki *et al*., 2002) is controlled by series of multiple alleles at the "*F/M*" locus interacting with genes controlling photoperiodic reaction i.e. (gynoecious-*MMFF;* monoecious-*MMff;* andromonoecious-*mmff*). Gene '*F/f*' in dominant condition shifts monoecious sex pattern downwards & promotes femaleness (by higher level of ethylene in plants); gene '*M/m*' in dominant condition, suppress stamen development & leads to female flower; flowers of *M*' plants are unisexual and flowers of *mm* plants may be hermaphrodite.

Character	Number of genes	Type of gene action
Growth habit	Monogenic (*De*)	Determinate dominant to indeterminate
Spine colour	Monogenic (*BB*)	Black or brown spines dominant to white
Spine number/ frequency	Monogenic (*SS*)	A few spines dominant to many
Spine surface	Monogenic (*FF*)	Coarse or intermediate dominant to fine
Skin colour	Monogenic	Dull skin dominant to glossy
Netting on fruit surface	Monogenic (*HH*)	Heavy netting dominant to no netting
Fruit skin	Monogenic	Tender & thin skin of European cvs. recessive to tough & thin skin of American cvs.
Parthenocarpy	Incomplete dominant gene *Pc* or multiple genes	• *Pc* produce parthenocarpic fruits; • *cP* produce short intermodal length; • *PP* produce parthenocarpic fruits early with first develops at 5th node; • *pp* produce no parthenocarpic fruits; • *Pp* produce parthenocarpic fruits later & few in number;
Gynoecious nature	Monogenic (*F/Acr*)	
Fruit colour	Digenic (*R,C*)	• Uniform immature dominant to mottled/ stripped colour. • White recessive to green. • Red- RRCC • Orange- RrCC • Yellow- rrCC • Cream- rrcc
Flesh colour	Digenic (*V, W*)	Dirty white-V-W- Intense white-V-ww Intense yellow-vv WW Orange-vvww
Vine length	Monogenic (*Tt*)	More vine length dominant to less vine length
Leaf colour	Monogenic (*Vv*)	Normal leaf colour dominant to virescent
Corolla colour	Monogenic	Orange dominant to yellow
Cluster flowering	Monogenic (*Cl*)	Solitary dominant to cluster habit
Multiple pistillate flowers per node	Monogenic recessive	-
Fragrance	Monogenic recessive (*fgr*)	-
Male sterility	Monogenic (MS_2ms_2)	Fertility dominant to sterility
PM resistance	2 pairs of duplicate genes	-
DM resistance	More than 1 dominant gene	-
Angular leaf spot	Polygenic (*pl*)	-
Trimonoecious sex form	Monogenic (*Tr*)	-
Water melon mosaic virus resistance	2 recessive genes (*wmv1-1*)	Resistance dominant to susceptibility
Cucurbit leaf crumple virus resistance	Monogenic recessive	-
Resistance to CMV	Monogenic	Resistance dominant to susceptibility

Genes isolated:

Gene	Phenotype
a	Androecious
Acr	Female, high degree of female sex expression
Gy	Gynoecious fruit habit
Pc	Parthenocarpic
Dm	Scab resistant gene
Cmv	Cucumber mosaic resistant gene
p	Downy mildew
pl	Angular leaf spot
Cgm	Cucumber green mottle virus
de, cp	Reduced size of plant frame & reduced staminate expression in gynoecious hybrids
gl	Avoid damage to fruits caused due to pickleworm

Pests, diseases and disorders:

- Fruit fly (*Bactrocera cucumis*): Very serious pest of most of cucurbits.
- Trap used to attract male fruit fly: Cue-lure [4-(p-acetoxyphenyl)-2-butanone] trap.
- Pickleworm moth (*Diaphania nitidalis, Diabrotica nitidalis*):
- Bacterial wilt (*Erwinia tracheiphila*) is transmitted by striped cucumber beetle.
- Powdery mildew(*Sphaerotheca fuliginea* syn. *Golovinomyces cichoracearum*): Spray Dinocap or Chlorothalonil.
- Downy mildew (*Pseudoperonospora cubensis*):
- Angular leaf spot (*Pseudomonas lachrymans*):
- Cucumber mosaic virus is transmitted by aphids and seeds.
- Scab (*Cladosporium cucumerinum*) resistant varieties: Stono, SMR-12, Ashe Fletcher.
- 'Pillow' is fruit disorder: Ca deficiency.
- Fruit twisting and scarring: B deficiency.
- Bloating: Production of excess CO_2 in cucumber tissue.
- Cucurbit leaf crumple virus: Transmitted by sweet potato white fly (*Bemesia tabaci*).
- Crooked neck shaped fruits: Imperfect pollination and fertilization and fruit fly attack.
- Bronzing process is associated with black spined cvs. & renders fruits unsuitable for processing.
- Physiological aging process also occurs in white spined cultivars but they remain light green or cream colour.

16.2 Gherkin

- Eulogized as 'horned cucumbers' or 'crumplings'.
- Small sized cucumbers used for pickling purpose.

- Largest consumer: USA, France, Spain, UK, Holland, Belgium.
- Karnataka state is world leader in production and export of gherkins.
- Cultivation, processing and export were started in India during 1990s.
- Exported in ready-to-eat jars.
- Preserved in natural vinegar and acetic acid.
- Cultivated on contract farming basis.
- Harvesting stage: Very small fruits (4-6 g) after 4-5 days of anthesis & without fruit stalk.
- Marketing unit in USA: 1 bushel (= 24 kg).
- Seed count: 50 seeds/ gram.
- Specific requirements for export purpose: Green, small sized having 160-300 fruits/ kg in premium grade.

Species:

Name	Features
C. anguria var. *anguria* (2n=24)	West Indian gherkin or Burr cucumber; non-bitter variant of var. *longipes* brought to New World in 17th century. Oval oblong fruits; 4-5 cm long; cultivated in Brazil & west Indies; used for eating, pickles & cooked vegetable; resistant to root knot nematode; not cross compatible with *C. sativus*
C. anguria var. *longipes*	Wild *Cucumis* spp.; cross compatible with gherkin

Varieties:

- Different types of gherkins:
  - American processing and fresh market class.
  - European gherkins and glass house types.
  - The German Schalgurken.
  - The Mideast Beit Alpha form.
  - Oriental trellies (burpless) varieties.
- Pickling purpose: Calypso, Ajax, Mincu.
- Chandini: Tolerant to DM and CMV.

Grades of gherkins:

- In Europe- small size less than 1.0625 inch dia.
- In America, 2A/B- 1.0625 to 1.6 inch dia.; 3A/B- 1.5 to 2.0 inch dia.
- 1-3 cm/ 160 fruits/ kg.
- 4-7 cm/ 100 fruits/ kg.

- 6-9 cm/ 60 fruits/ kg.
- 9-12 cm/ 30 fruits/ kg.
- >12 cm/ <30 fruits/ kg.

16.3 Water melon

- Eulogized as 'Fruit of 22nd century or Common man's fruit'.
- Mexico: Highest exporter in world by volume.
- China: World leader in production with 17.75% share.
- Used as fresh dessert fruit in America.
- In Soviet Union, it is used to prepare beer or heavy sweet syrup is made from boiled juice.
- Richest source of iron among cucurbits.
- Fruit contains water (95%), -CHO (3.3%), proteins (0.2%), minerals (0.3%), potassium (160 mg) per 100 g of fresh weight.
- Seeds contain linoleic acid, 26-28% protein, 30-40% oil.
- Stigma is of 'wet type'.
- Highly cross pollinated due to monoecious and andromonoecious nature.
- Taxonomy indicates that water melon is trailing vine.
- Main bitter substance: Cucurbitacin E (Tetracyclic triterpenes).
- Does not have flowering peaks or fruiting cycle unlike cucurbits (Porter D.R. 1933).
- Pistillate/ hermaphrodite flowers normally occur in every 7th leaf axil and intervening axils by staminate flowers.
- Flowers are smaller & less showy than most other spp. of cultivated cucurbitaceae.
- Corolla: Greenish yellow, united in tube & deeply five lobes, 3 stamens at base of corolla & inferior ovary.
- Flower ratio of typical water melon: 7 (staminate): 1 (pistillate).
- Sex ratio: 4-15 males : 1 female.
- Large amount of self pollination & sibling occurs normally.
- Pollination agent: Honey bee.
- Time of anthesis: Shortly after sunrise & remain open for one day only.
- Stigma receptivity: Throughout the day.
- Fruit setting frequency is more during morning h 6-9 AM.
- High atmospheric humidity favours fruit setting.
- Fruits already set, inhibits further fruit setting.
- Optimum soil pH: 5.5-6.8.
- Melons require high temperature (35-40°C) during fruit development.

- For seedless water melons, the temperatures should be 10^0 warmer.
- In hot arid region, it is grown as summer and rainy season crop.
- Pigments present: Anthocyanin + lycopene.
- Highest concentration of lycopene (4.1 mg/100g) of any fresh fruit or vegetable.
- Amino acid: Citrulline and arginine.
- Soluble solids reflect sweetness of melons.
- TSS: 8-13%. It assists in verification of fruit maturity.
- Sugar content is major component of flavour.
- Sweetness in water melon: Glucose, fructose and sucrose.
- Excess moisture during fruit development cause cracking even before maturity.
- Training system practiced: Archway, Inclined cordon, Vertical cordon.
- Archway system of training accommodates 9,500 plants/ ha.
- Vertical cordon system: 12,000 plants/ ha.
- Parthenocarpy does not occur naturally in water melon.
- Type of parthenocarpy: Stimulative (pollination with normal diploid pollens).
- Tetraploid females are hand pollinated with diploid pollen.
- Cross of tetraploid 4x (female) x diploid 2x (male) results seeds containing triploid embryo.
- Triploid fruits are triangular in shape compared to round in 4x X 2x plants.
- Reciprocal cross using diploid as female results in sterile empty seeds.
- Seedless fruits: Due to embryo abortion and false rudimentary seed.
- Triploid seeds are difficult to germinate; removal of part of seed coat facilitates germination.
- Triploid hybrid is female sterile and ovules develop into hardened seed coats called 'ex-embryonate of false seeds'.
- Major problems in production of seedless fruits: Maintenance of tetraploid lines is expensive (much smaller number of seeds than diploids), poor seed germination (seeds need to germinate at 86^0F in hot beds/ green houses), late maturity of triploids ultimately increases production cost.
- For seed production of seedless triploid hybrid, tetraploid line must be used as female parent. and diploid should be interplanted with seedless hybrid.
- Triploids require some diploids in near vicinity for pollination and fruit set.
- Triploids are very vigorous and have only a few hollow seeds.
- Tetraploids with less than 150-200 seeds/ fruit make seed production expensive.

- Cultivars with bitter fruit are cultivated in Africa for edible seeds.
- Seed type: Egusi seed (seeds covered with fleshy pericarp).
- Seed is eaten as snack after roasting and shelling.
- Edible and non-edible flesh thickness: 14 to 16 cm and 1.35 to 1.62 cm, respectively.
- Edible flesh is derived from placenta and pericarp is hard outer rind.
- Flesh texture varies from fine grained & melting to firm, coarse & fibrous.
- Seed rate: 3-5 kg/ha.
- *In situ* sowing is practiced or can be transplanted at 2 true leaf stage.
- Days for seed germination: 2-4.
- Days required from anthesis to harvesting: 40-45.
- Days required from fruit setting to maturity: 30-35.
- Fruits of early maturing cvs. requires 26 days to mature (cv. Petite Sweet & limited vine growth); late maturing 45 days (cv. Super Sweet) while very late maturing (cv. White Mountain, New Hampshire Midget) require 65 days to mature.
- Glabrous male sterile mutants and Chinese male sterile mutants are useful for hybrid seed production.
- Seed colours: White, tan, brown, black, red, green and mottled black.
- Use of plastic mulch is very common. Melons respond faster to the extra heat generated by this mulch, resulting in more prolific early growth, greater productivity, earlier harvest and larger fruits.
- Quantity of seed and seed size are heritable traits.
- Large number of large sized seeds results in low percentage of edible flesh which is undesirable trait.
- Seed maturity and edible maturity of fruit coincide with each other.
- Black seeds intensify red flesh colour, while white seed colour is associated with melon immaturity.
- In cv. Royal Golden, rind colour changes from green to orange indicates good maturity.
- Use of colchicine to induce polyploidy: O.J. Eigsti (1938).
- Production of tetraploid plants: 0.2-0.4% colchicine treatment to diploid seedlings at 1 or 2 true leaf stages.
- Two sprays of 'FW 450' (i.e. Sodium alpha beta dichloro isobutyrate) @ 0.3% is used to suppress male flowers (functional male sterility) in female parent lines.
- CPPU @ 200 ppm promotes fruit set and seedlessness without adverting fruit quality.
- Yield losses up to 30% have been observed due to weeds.
- NAA @ 100 ppm or MH @ 200 ppm results in heavier and large fruits.

- Maturity indices:
  - 30-40 days after anthesis;
  - Size of fruits and colour of skin are not good indicators to know proper stage;
  - Browning or withe^r^ing of tendrils at fruit axil;
  - Dull sound when fruit is thumped in contrast to metallic sound;
  - Ground spot turning yellow (i.e. colour change on belly of fruit);
  - Rind of ripe melon yields to pressure;
  - Colour of flesh has no relationship with degree of sweetness.
  - Specific gravity.
- Storage: 2-2-4.4^{0}C at 80% R.H. for 2-3 weeks.
- Water melon cannot be stored for more than 2-3 weeks.
- CA storage: At 7.2^{0}C with 85-90% R.H.
- Flesh firmness is important factor in durability to rough handling.
- Rind firmness is determined by pressure tester with 5/32 inch.probe.
- Flesh firmnessis determined by pressure tester with 23/32 inch.probe.
- Seed viability: 5-6 years.
- Seed yield: 200 kg/ha.
- Number of seeds/ fruit: 50- 700.
- 100 seed wt.: 3 gram.
- 1000 seed wt.: 70-110 grams.
- Due to insufficient genetic information, mapping of the water melon chromosomes is not possible.
- Reference genomes have been identified for development of new varieties.
- Long Rid Sequencing Technology has been developed in 2013.
- Genome sequencing and utilization:
  - Using *C. amarus* (progenitor of cultivated water melon) and 2 wild spp. C. *mucosospermus*, *C. colocynthis*, scientists have developed varieties resistant to fusarium wilt, PM, root knot nematodes & tolerant to drought.
  - Quality parameters viz. big sized fruits, higher sweetness, intense red colour and more crunchy pulp has been incorporated by using above mentioned species.

Species:

- Genetic diversity is due to mutations and chromosomal rearrangements.
- Thieret (1963) gave correct name as *C. lanatus*.
- *Citrullus* species (explored by Shimotsuma, 1963) & all originated in Africa & all 4 spp. have 2n=22 chromosomes.
- Both bitter & sweet melons grow together as wild in Africa.

- *C. colocynthis*, *C. lanatus*, *C. ecirrhosus* and *C. naudinianus* are cross compatible with each other. All these species have different geographical isolations, differences in morphological (flowering habit) and cytogenetic (genetic differences & structural changes in chromosomes) factors contribute to their identity.
- *C. fistulosus* does not hybridize with other 4 species.

Common name	Botanical name	Features
Citron melon/ Tsamma melon/ Large water melon/ Preserving melon	*Citrullus amarus* (*Citrullus lanatus* var. *citroides*)	Proginator of cultivated water melon; intermediate stage between primitive bitter form & cultivated sweet form; hard inedible flesh; fruits bitter; small seeds with greenish and tan coloured; rind used as preservative for pickles
-	*C. vulgaris*	Cultivated water melon originated in Japan; annual & 2n=22; with cucurbitacin E as main bitter substance
Water melon	*C. lanatus* var. *lanatus* (syn. *C. vulgaris* var. *lanatus*)	Only cultivated species; annual; large sized fruits; globular to elongated fruit shape; thick rind, crispy & solid flesh; flesh red, yellow, orange coloured & high water content; no seed cavity; TSS 14^0Brix; fruit wt. 2-10 kg; widely distributed in Egypt & in Southern, Western & Central Asia
Round melon	*C. vulgaris* var. *fistulosus*	Rich in cucurbitacin E
-	*C. colocynthis*	Progenitor (ancestor) of water melon (2n=22); originated in Morocco; perennial, xerophytic (potential crop for arid lands); fruits small, round (3 inch dia.), spongy flesh, highly bitterin taste with small seeds; fruits used for medicinal purpose (cures ulcers, jaundice, anaemia, constipation & bronchitis); fruits round with 5 cm dia.; spongy flesh is always bitter/ pungent taste with cucurbitacin E as main bitter substance; highly resistant to WBNV;
-	*C. ecirrhosus*	Originated in S-W Africa; perennial (2n=22); xerophytic; pungent & without tendrils; leaves more divided & covered with dense fine hairs; white fleshed, square fruits; rich in cucurbitacin B & E with cucurbitacin E as main bitter substance
-	*C. naudinianus*	Originated in S-W Africa; perennial (2n=22); dioecious; xerophytic; leaves deeply palmatified & covered with dense hairs; fruit has thin rind & soft juicy flesh white seeds; rich in cucurbitacin B & E; immune to anthracnose & fusarium wilt
Egusi water melon	*C. mucosospermus*	Wild & cultivated forms, cross readily with *C. lanatus*
-	*C. fistulosus*	Originated in India; annual; 2n=24; does not hybridize with *Citrullus* spp.

Varieties:

- Inbreeding does not reduce vigour/ productivity and produce uniformity in many horticultural traits (Porter, 1933).

- Dwarf types are suitable for garden culture & machine harvesting.
- Improvement of small water melon: J.M. Crall (1986) bred varieties- Minilee, Mickylee.
- 1st true mini water melon cultivar: New Hampshire Midget: Developed by A.F. Yeager (1951) in USA weighing 1.5-2 kg and require 65 days to mature. Limited vine growth.
- Shimotsuma (1968) developed reciprocal translocation stocks for production of seedless fruits.
- Personal size seedless cv. 'Pure Heart' was developed in 21st century.
- Most sensational F_1 hybrid among cucurbits is 'seedless triploid water melon'. It was developed by Japanese scientist Dr. Kihara in 1951.
- Mini water melon (2-4 kg): Popular in India.
- 'Icebox' variety (4.5-5.0 kg): Suitable for city, hotel and processing industry.
- Bush Baby: Dwarf, mutant.
- Thin and explosive rind: Yellow Baby (yellow flesh), Carnival, Red Glory.
- Thick and tough rind for long distance transport: Peacock, Crimson Sweet.
- Popular tetraploid cv.: Tri-X 313.
- USDA developed stable tetraploid lines Tetra-1,2,3,4 for production of seedless water melon seeds.
- Alena: Tetraploid cv. from diploid 'Sugar Baby'.
- Resistant to anthracnose: Congo, Fairfax, Crimson Sweet, Graybelle.
- 1st USDA scientist W.A. Orton (1907) initiated plant breeding program with disease resistance as goal.
- Conqueror: 1st fusarium wilt resistant hybrid among cucurbits was developed by W.A. Orton in 1911 using Citron stock.
- Fusarium wilt resistant hybrids bred at ARC, Leesburg, under Florida Water melon breeding program: Summit, Shipper, White Hope, Sugarlee, Dixielee, Smokylee, Verons, Calhoun Gray.
- Cv. Summit: Possess one major dominant gene for fusarium wilt resistance (Henderson *et al.*, 1970).
- Peacock-132: Source of intense red colour, firm flesh, tough rind & resistant to wilt.
- Fruit rind is extremely hard in cv. Peacock and very soft in cv. Calhoun Sweet.
- Dixie Queen: Resistant to *Meloidogyne javanica*.
- *C. moschata* var. Jaipuri: Resistant to *M. incognita*.
- Mateera: Indigenous type of water melon grown in rainy season in Bikaner, Rajasthan. It is tolerant to high temperature and drought conditions.
- Jobner-21, Jobner-18-1: Can be grown in higher pH of soil (>7.0).

- Dwarf hybrid cvs. Kengarden (designated as home garden cv.), Kentucky & New Hampshire Midget were released by The Kentucky Water melon Breeding Program, Lexingtonusing advance line 'W-5':
- Desert King. It is yellow fleshed, yellow rind but very late maturity & disease susceptible.
- Nigerian varieties grown for seed purpose: Bara, Serewe, Sofin.
- High degree of resistance to red pumpkin beetle: Selection No. 120, Sel. 98 and Afghan line.
- Local land races grown in Uttar Pradesh: Farukabadi, Moradabadi.
- Cv. Kategolan from Jamuna river bed, whose flesh not sweet but keeping quality is 2-3 months at ambient temperature, flesh becomes dry and fibrous.

Name	**Breeding method**	**Features**
Dixie Cream, Fuken, Dixie Ice,	Introduced from USA	Suitable for home garden
Charleston Gray (1975)	Introduced from USA	Vigorous long vines (up to 20 ft.); suitable for home garden
Improved Shipper (1978)	Introduced from USA	Fruits big & dark green; fruit wt. 8-9 Kg; TSS 8-9%; suitable for home garden
Shinasahi	Asahi Yamoto x Miyako	Early; disease resis2tant & transport ability
Smokylee	Intervariety hybrid of '[Texas-W-5 (fusarium resistant) x Charleston Gray (anthracnose resistant)]'	Resistant to fusarium wilt
Dixielee (Florida 75-1)	Combination of 3 different backcrosses by using Texas W-5 resistant breeding line viz. (W-5 x Peacock-132) x (W-5 x Fairfax) & (W-5 x Summit)	Flesh firm with intense red coloured; resistant to fusarium wilt, anthracnose
IARI, New Delhi		
Sugar Baby (1975)	Introduced from USA	Deep red flesh; 11-13% TSS; resistant to drought; yield 15-17 t/ha; brown small seeds
Asahi Yamoto	Introduced from Japan	Flesh deep pink; fruit wt. 6-7 kg; TSS 9-11%; yield 20 t/ha
Pusa Bedana (1972)	Polyploidy breeding of [Tetra 2 (4x) x Pusa Rasaal (2x)]	1st seedless variety; triploid; TSS 12-13%; yield 20-25 t/ha
IIHR, Bengaluru		
Arka Muthu	Selection from (IIHR-81-1-1)	Short vine (1.2 m); early maturing (75-80 days); 12-13^0 brix, yield 70-75 t/ha
Arka Akash	F_1 hybrid of 'IIHR-60-1 x *Arka* Manik'	Oblong shape; red flesh; TSS 12-13%; fruit wt. 6.5 kg with 1 fruit/ vine; duration 90-95 days; yield 65-70 t/ha
Arka Aiswarya	F_1 hybrid	Oval fruits; red flesh; TSS 13-14%; fruit wt. 7.5 kg

		with 1-2 fruit/vine; duration 95-100 days; yield 75-80 t/ha
Arka Manik (1990)	Modified back cross method of selection between 'IIHR 21 x Crimson Sweet'	Green rind & dull green stripes; very few seeds; resistant to anthracnose, DM, PM & blossom end rot; TSS 12-15%; yield 60 t/ha; suitable for long distance transport
Arka Jyoti (1986)	Heterosis breeding of (IIHR 20 x Crimson Sweet)	Excellent quality, less seeds; angular stripes; TSS 12-13%; yield 70-72 t/ha
Arka Madhura	Polyploidy breeding of [IIHR Tetra-1 (4x) x Arka Manik (2x)]	Triploid & seedless; suitable for year round production under protected condition; 60 t/ha; TSS 14%
Arka Shyama (2020)	OP seedling selection	Oblong shape; belong to icebox segment; TSS 12%; fruit wt. 3-4 kg; dark red pulp; suitable for long distance transport; suitable for export
RAU, Rajasthan (RARS, Durgapura)		
Durgapura Meetha (1978)	Selection from local material	Andromonoecious; dark red flesh; fruit wt. 7-8 kg; TSS 11%: yield 48-50 t/ha; seeds have black line at tip & margin; suitable for long distance transport
Durgapura Kesar (1978)	Selection from (Red Local x Yellow Local)	Monoecious; late type; skin green with stripes, yellow flesh; seeds very large; fruit wt. 4-5 kg; yield 40-45 t/ha
Durgapura Lal (RW 177-3) 2002	Heterosis breeding of (Sugar Baby x Russian germplasm K-3566)	Simple unlobed leaf (marker gene); TSS 10-11%; fruit wt. 4-5 kg; resistant to blight & bud necrosis; yield 43-45 t/ha
PAU, Ludhiana		
Shipper (1978)	Introduction from USA	Fruits 6-10 kg; 8-9% TSS: thick rind; yield 30-32 t/ha
Special No. 1	Selection	Early mature; small, round fruits with red flesh & red seeds
CIAH, Bikaner		
AHW-19 (1998)	Selection from local germplasm	Early-mid maturing mateera; 3-4 fruits/vine; TSS 8-8.4%; tolerate high temperature
AHW-65 (1998)	Selection from local germplasm	Early-mid maturing mateera; flesh dark pink, stripped fruits; TSS 8-8.5%
Thar Manak (2007)	AHW-19 x Sugar Baby (selection in F_6 generation)	Very early maturity mateera; 3-4 fruits/vine; TSS 9.5-11.2%; seed oil 30-40%; devoid of fruit cracking; suitable for summer & rainy season
TNAU, Coimbatore (HC & RI, Periyakulum)		
PKM-1 (1993)	Selection from local germplasm	Suitable for arid, semi-arid, irrigated conditions, pulp pink coloured; yield 37 t/ha
KAU, Thrissur		
Shonima	Polyploid breeding	Red flesh; seedless, high TSS, yield 19 t/ha
Swarna	Polyploid breeding	1st yellow fleshed seedless water melon in India; high citrulline 5.1 mg/g; fruit wt. 3.08 kg; yield 11 t/ha
KAU-CL-Tetra-1	Polyploid breeding	-

Private sector hybrids: Madhur, Max, Milan, Sangria, Swapnil, Mohini, Samptrupti, Amruth, Suruchi, Century-2 (resistant to wilt), Sugar Queen (Syngenta); Vishala, Aarohi, Anmol, Saraswati, Mannat (Taiwan F_1 hybrids from Known-You Seed Company; 70-75 days for harvest, 2.5-3.5 kg fruit; 12% sugar content); Sugar Dew, Mukasa, Red Velvet; NS Joy (Namdhari Seeds)

Inheritance of characters:

- Probable linkages in water melon were published by Poole (1944).
- Early maturity and early flowering nature: Pleiotropic gene action.
- Watts (1962) suggested spontaneous mutation induced variations such as non-lobed leaves, glabrous leaves and stems and male sterility are used in F_1 hybrid seed production.
- Use of non-lobed (entire) leaf shape character as a single recessive marker gene for producing hybrid seeds was suggested by Mohr *et al.* (1955). This character can be used to distinguish at seedling stage. F_1 hybrid progeny (possess normal leaf) while progeny from self pollination bear non-lobed type leaves and can be thinned out.
- Bitterness is undesirable trait inherited from *C. colocynthis*.
- False seed or ex-embryonate seeds: Triploids are sterile because unequal chromosome distribution causes pollen and ovular abortion. But few ovules may develop into hardened seed coat.
- Short internode character has been utilized for improvement of plant ideotype.
- Fruit shape related to cotyledon shape at seedling stage i.e. plants with elongate fruits have elongate cotyledon and round with round cotyledons.
- Elongated cvs. have tendency to produce gourd neck fruit called as 'culls'.
- Round fruited cvs. are susceptible to hollow heart defects.
- Parris G.K. (1949) proposed inheritance of fusarium wilt as recessive or dominant gene depending on source of resistance.

Character	Number of genes	Type of gene action
Inheritance of sex/ sex expression	Monogenic (*AA*)	Monoecy dominant to andromonoecy (both sex forms have fixed ratio of 6 staminate : 1 pistillate flower) (Rosa J.T. 1980)
Leaf shape	Monogenic	Lobed leaf incompletely dominant over non-lobed
Plant habit	Digenic (*dw1, dw2*)	Spreading/multiple branching dominant to dwarfness (bush nature)
Male sterility & glabrous leaf	Monogenic (*gms gms*)	Male sterility & glabrous leaf are pleiotropic & governed by recessive gene
Seed number	Monogenic (*Ns*)	High seed number dominant to low number
Rind toughness/ thickness	Digenic (*Tr1, Tr2*)	Toughness incompletely dominant to lesser toughness
Fruit rind colour	Monogenic (*GG*)	Dark green dominant to light green (called gray) (Weetman L.M., 1937)
Striping on skin	Monogenic	* Recessive to solid dark green * Inherited independently of dark green colour * Non-striped recessive to striped * Dark green faintly stripped rind colour in diploid is incompletely dominant over slight green stripped rind of tetraploid parent
Fruit size	Polygenic	25 genes involved (Poole and Grimball, 1945)
Fruit surface	Monogenic (*SS*)	Smooth surface dominant over furrowed or grooved

Fruit shape	Monogenic (*OO*)	Oval/ elongated/ melon shape incompletely dominant over round/ spherical (Weetman, 1937 & Porter, 1937)
Flesh colour	Monogenic	* Coral red (*YY*) dominant to orange (*Yy*) which is dominant to salmon yellow (*yy*); * Deep pink dominant over pale pink and pink; * White (*Wf*) dominant to red in *C. colocynthis.* * Red dominant over yellow (*y*); * Canary yellow (*CC*) dominant over non-canary yellow (*cc*) and pink (Shimotsuma, 1963)
Flavour (free from bitterness)	Monogenic	Bitter flavour dominant over non-bitter
Fruit maturity	Monogenic	(Barham, 1956)
Seed size	Digenic	* Small seed dominant to large seed; * Medium seed size dominant to large; * Short seed epistatic to long seed.
Seed colour	Digenic	Black dominant over white
Seed coat	-	Red recessive to tan
Furrowing/ grooving of rind	Monogenic	Recessive to smooth surface & has no practical value
Resistance to red pumpkin beetle	Monogenic (*Af*)	Resistance dominant to susceptible
Resistance to anthracnose	Monogenic (*Ar*)	Resistance dominant to susceptible
Resistance to cotton aphid	Monogenic	Resistance dominant to susceptible
Resistance to Zucchini Yellow Mosaic virus	Monogenic	Resistance recessive to susceptible
Papaya Ring Spot Virus- water melon strain resistance	Monogenic recessive (*prv*)	Resistance recessive to susceptible
Resistance to leaf miner	Monogenic (*Ls*)	Resistance dominant to susceptible
Resistance to fruit fly	Monogenic (*FF*)	Resistance dominant to susceptible
Resistance to fusarium wilt	Monogenic & polygenic recessive	Resistance dominant to susceptible

Diseases, pests and physiological disorders:

- Anthracnose (*Colletotrichum lagenarium* syn. *Glomerella cingulata* var. *orbiculare*): Air borne. Fruit pedicle dries. Very destructive in water melon, snake gourd, cucumber and bottle gourd.
- Alternaria blight and fruit rot: Use disease free seed material, crop rotation, and proper drainage is necessary.
- Powdery mildew (*Sphaerotheca fuliginea*): Do seed treatment and soil drenching with systemic fungicide.
- Downy mildew (*Pseudoperonospora cubensis*): Affects ridge gourd, bottle gourd, cucumber and musk melon.
- Gummy stem blight (*Didymella bryoniae, Mycosphaerella citrullina*): Seed and water borne fungal disease serious in south India. Attack fruits, seedlings, leaves,

cotyledons & stem. Spray Metiram-pyroclostrobin (3g/lit). Wild Citron types are resistant.

- Water melon mosaic virus: Vector- Aphid.
- Fusarium wilt (*F. oxysporum* f.sp. *nivenum*): Soil inhibiting fungus invades roots and cause brown discoloration of vascular system. Disease difficult to control by chemicals.
- Rhizoctonia root rot:
- Fruit fly (*Bactrocera cucurbitae*):
- Red pumpkin beetle (*Aulacophora foveicollis*):
- Leaf miner (*Liriomyza sativae*):
- Bud necrosis: Viral disease (TOSPO virus group). Transmitted by thrips causing 80-100% yield losses. Apply Thimet/ carbofuran 10G @ 15 kg a.i/ha followed by Rogor @ 0.05%.
- Yellowing: Vector is white fly. Soil incorporation of carbofuran at time of planting.
- Blossom end rot: Due to high temperature, fluctuation in irrigation & 'Ca' deficiency. Spray $CaCl_2$ @ 0.5% at fruit development stage.
- White heart: Commonly found in Indian varieties.
- Hollow heart and fibrous heart: Signify over maturity.

16.3 Musk melon

- Eulogized as 'Wholesome fruit of Sahara desert or Cantaloupe or Melon casaba or Winter melon'.
- The name describes aroma (musk or perfume) of ripe fruit, granular texture and low in soluble solids.
- Introduced in India by Arabs in Mughal period (around 14th century) from Central Asia region.
- Most suitable for diara (river bed) cultivation.
- Nutrient composition/ 100 g edible portion: 90% water, 10% -CHO.
- Nutrition score: 50.
- Calorific value: 34 Kcal/100g.
- Highly polymorphic and frost sensitive species valued as summer fruit.
- Cantaloupe: Cultivars those are highly uniform in netting with relatively indistinct vein tract. It is polyploid with 2n=48. They are most popular in USA and Europe since Roman times. It contains more β-carotene and vit. C (45 mg/100 g) than other melons. Edible part is pericarp.
- 1st horticultural classification of melons: Naudin (1859) & modified by Munger and Robinson (1991).
- Cucurbits Genomics Database, Institute of Vegetables and Flowers, Beijing, China.

- Musk melon is cross incompatible with cucumber, water melon and round melon.
- Musk melon, snap melon and long melon easily cross with each other because they belong to same species and heterosis for seed germination is evidenced but none of them crosses with round melon (2n=24).
- Fruit set is higher when musk melon is used as pollen parent.
- Pre-fertilization barrier is involved in failure of interspecific hybridization in *Cucumis*.
- Inbreeding depression is not observed upto 25 generations.
- Techniques involved in interspecific hybridization: Mentor pollination, use of BA growth regulator and organic solvent (n-hexane).
- Gynoecious line 'MSU-IG' is being used for hybrid seed production.
- F_1 hybrids are produced using gynoecious lines as maternal lines.
- Silver thiosulphate @ 300-400 ppm induces maleness in gynoecious lines.
- AVG (50 ppm), silver nitrate (100 ppm) are used to induce prefect flowers in monoecious lines for its maintenance.
- Ethephon (300-500 ppm) induces female flowers and is used for F_1 hybrid seed production in monoecious lines.
- Maximum numbers of fruits with highest TSS are produced between 9th and 12th (bud) nodes on main stem.
- Pollination agent: Honey bees.
- Anthesis takes place at 5.30-6.30 AM at temperature of 22-29^{0}C.
- Anther dehiscence takes place before anthesis.
- Prominent sex form: Andromonoecious (bisexual flowers and staminate flowers on separate nodes).
- Andromonoecious flowering habit is predominant in dessert types and monoecious in non-dessert types.
- Fruit set in monoecious lines of *C. melo* is 29-42%.
- Calcium 20-30 ppm & boron 10 ppm promotes growth and increases fruit and seed yield.
- Transplanted crop matures earlier than direct seeded one.
- Musk melon is slightly more tolerant to soil acidity.
- Musk melon is used in ice cream industry in western countries.
- Ideal conditions for sugar accumulation: Cool nights and warm weather.
- High temperature along with dry climate at fruit maturity and ripening increases sweetness.
- Maximum number of fruits with high TSS: 9-12 nodes.
- Oil content in seed (on whole seed basis): 12.5-39.1%.
- Seed kernels are edible, tasty and nutritious.

- Over half of the final concentration of sugars in the fruit is accumulated during last 2 weeks of fruit ripening.
- Since no starch reserves in the fruits, there is no increase in sugar content of fruits after harvest.
- Melons in reticulates group develop clear abscission layer between pedicel and fruit during maturation.
- Determination of maturity is more difficult in melons belonging to inodorus group.
- Ethylene treatment @ 1000 ppm for 18-24 h given to Honey Dew melons to complete ripening process.
- TSS content in most of varieties: 11-17%.
- Minimum standard TSS: 10%.
- High sugar containing variety has 17% TSS.
- Harvesting stage: Full slip stage (automatic separation of fruit from vine leaving a clean stem cavity). This stage contains maximum sugar.
- Half slip stage: Fruits are to be separated with a slight force.
- In USA, fruit maturity is judged by electronic sensors.
- Long distance transport: ¾th slip stage.
- Post harvest life of a healthy melon is a function of temperature. Hence, cooling to 0^{0}C is an important part of handling melons.
- Cooling methods used: Hydro-cooling, forced air cooling, top icing or package icing.
- Optimum temperature for seed germination: 35^{0}C.
- Seed does not germinate at temperature $< 18^{0}$C.
- Seed rate: 5-6 kg/ha.
- Fresh seeds show dormancy and after ripening period is required at all stages of seed development.
- Position of fruits on vine influences seed quality.
- Male sterility is used in exploitation of heterosis.
- Male sterility gene '*MS1*' was discovered in a cross 'Georgia 47 x Smith Perfection'.
- Seed set in hybrids is very low (15-20%).
- Fungicide 'Ridomil' is used to control downy mildew.

Species:

- Cucumber Green Mottled Mosaic Virus (CGMMV) resistant: *C. figarei, C. ficifolia, C. meeusii, C. zeyheri*-2.
- Nematode resistant: *C. auguria, C. ficifolius, C. metaliferus*.
- 1st recorded attempt to cross musk melon with other species: Naudin (1859).
- Sarda melon is grown in Afghanistan and is available in India in October-November.

Name	Common name	Features
C. melo var. *reticulatus*	Netted musk melon/ Rough skinned melon/ American cantaloupe/ Persian melon	Fruits small with ribbed & netted surface; thick orange flesh, musky fragrant odour, sweet taste, stem separates from fruit at full maturity; mature 110-115 days from planting e.g. Punjab Rasila, Punjab Sunehari
C. melo var. *inodorus*	Smooth skinned melon/ Winter melons of USA/ Honey Dew melon/ Canary melon	Fruits with smooth surface, white or green flesh; skin bright coloured; hard rind; stem does not separate easily from fruit; difficult to determinate maturity; fruit wt. 1.5-3 kg; mature 110-115 days from planting susceptible to foliar diseases e.g. Honey Dew, Casabas, Canaries
-	Casaba melon	Globular fruits with pointed stem end; fruit colour golden yellow; fruit surface hard & covered with longitudinal wrinkles; white flesh; no abscission layer forms between stem & fruit; maturity takes from 110-125 days; susceptible to foliar diseases
-	Crenshaw melon	Fruits very large, fig shaped weighing 3.5-4 kg; smooth skinned with orange flesh; very hollow (greater seed cavity) & matures within 110-125 days; highly susceptible to various diseases
C. melo var. *cantaloupensis*	Cantaloupe of Europe	Fruits rough-warty rind, scaly, rough & hard rinds; 2n=48; andromonoecious; netting absent; cultivated in Europe e.g. Hara Madhu
C. melo var. *momordica* (syn. *C. trigonus*, *C. melo* var. *callosus*)	Small gourd/ Wild musk melon/ *Kachri*	Most drought hardy, bitter taste; resistant to fruit fly (*Dacus cucurbitae*), DM & fusarium wilt; ripe fruits are dried/ sliced e.g. AHK-119, AHK-200
C. melo var. *acidulus*	-	Sour taste
C. melo var. *flexuosus*	Snake or serpent melon	Fruits long, slender, 2-8 cm dia.; use to some extent for preserve making
C. myriocarbus	Gooseberry gourd	
C. metulifer	-	Used as salad; resistant to PM, fruit fly, Water melonMosaic virus & nematode
C. africanus	-	Resistant to fruit fly & CGMMV
C. melo var. *agrestis*	-	Inedible fruits
C. melo var. *conomom*	Oriental pickling melon/ Chinese (white cucumber)	Pickling melon without musky odour
C. melo var. *dudain*	Mango melon/ Pomegranate melon	Fruits small, very fragrant; grown for ornamental purpose & strong scent; pickling type
C. melo var. *chito*	Mango lemon/ Lemon cucumber/ Orange melon/ Vegetable orange/ Melon apple	Fruits small, used for making preserve
C. melo var. *rigidus*	-	Melons growing in hot dry regions (Central Asia & Iran)
C. melo var. *orientale*	-	Melons growing in hot & humid regions (Asia minor)
C. melo var. *europees*	-	Melons growing in cool dry regions (Asia minor)

Varieties:

- 1st F_1 hybrid (Punjab Hybrid-*ms* based) was released at national level in 1984.
- 1st monoecious line in musk melon developed by Peterson (1983).
- 1st report of heterosis in musk melon: Munger (1942).
- Resistant to alternaria leaf spot: Purduee-44.
- Cantaloupe (from California), Jumbo, Seminole and PMR-6, PMR-7, PMR-45: Resistant to PM developed by L.C. Jagger and G.W. Scott (1937).
- Gynoecious sex form WI 998 has been isolated in stable condition in USA.
- Polyploidy induction was attempted in 1953 by using colchicine.
- 'Texas Resistant': Resistant to DM and aphids.
- Resistant to fusarium wilt (*F. oxysporum* f.sp. *melonis*): Golden Gopher, Iriquois, Minnesota Midget, Harvest Queen, Delicious 51.
- Tolerant to root knot nematode: Edisto, Pewlita, Vardae.
- Resistant to gummy stem blight: Shiro-2, Korea 11, Early Forcing, Chilton, Gulf Coast.
- Honey Dew and Casaba: Do not separate easily from plants.

Name	Breeding method	Remarks
Campo, Jacumba, Gulf Stream, Perlita	Pedigree	Resistant to powdery mildew (PM)
Georgia 47, Home Garden, Planters Jumbo, Edisto 47	Pedigree	Resistant to downy mildew (DM)
IIHR, Bengaluru		
Arka Jeet (1986)	Single plant selection from 'Prati' strain of Uttar Pradesh	Dwarf & very early (90 days); fruits flat, small, weighing 300-500 g; orange to orange brown skin; white flesh; high TSS13-16% & vit. C (41.6 mg/100 g); big seed cavity; resistant to PM, DM; yield 15-17 at t/ha
Arka Rajhans (1986)	Single plant selection from local collection from Rajasthan	Resistant to PM; flesh white; sweet; fruit wt. 1 kg; fine netting on skin; excellent keeping quality; 11-14% TSS: yield 25 t/ha
Arka Siri (2019)	Selection	Tuscan Cantaloupe background; fruits elongated globe shaped with brownish yellow rind, medium netting, dark orange flesh; TSS 12-13%; yield 25 t/ha
IARI, New Delhi		
Pusa Madhuras	Selection from germplasm collected from Rajasthan	Early variety; TSS 12-14%; orange juicy flesh & green stripes on skin, orange flesh; poor keeping quality; yield 15-17 t/ha
Pusa Sharbati (1978)	Pedigree selection of [Kutana (Indian) x American Cantaloupe (PM resistant No.6 from USA)]	Fruits round with green stripes on moderately netted skin; fruit wt. 1 kg; flesh bright orange with narrow seed cavity, cantaloupe flavour; 3-4 fruits/ vine; TSS 10-12%; yield 16 t/ha
Pusa Rasraj (1993)	Heterosis breeding of (Monoecious-3 x Durgapur Madhu)	Fruits without netting; fruit wt. 1 kg; 12-14% TSS; yield 23 kg/ha

Pusa Sarda (2015)	-	1st variety of sarda melon grown in net house under N.I. plains. Golden yellow coloured fruits; TSS 13.6^0 Brix
Pusa Madhurima (2015)	-	Unique shape; ready to harvest in 80 days; TSS 12% brix; yield 22.5 t/ha
DMDR-2	Recurrent selection	Resistant to Cucumber Green Mottle Mosaic virus (CGMMV) & DM
Pusa Suneheri (2020)	-	1st orange fleshed sarda melon suitable for protected cultivation
IIVR, Varanasi		
Kashi Madhu (2006)	Selection from Mau melon	TSS 13-14%; seeds loosely packed in seed cavity; long post-harvest life; tolerant to PM, DM & mosaic virus; yield 25-27 t/ha
CIAH, Bikaner		
AHK-119		Small gourd/ kachri; fruit wt. 50-60 g; 22 fruits/ vine; yield 9.5-10 t/ha
AHK-200	-	Small gourd/ kachri; fruit wt. 100-120 g; yield 12 t/ha; fruits suitable for garnishing vegetables & salad.
PAU, Ludhiana		
Punjab Hybrid-1 (1987)	Heterosis breeding of (MS-1 x Hara Madhu)	1st F_1 hybrid using MS line; fruit wt. 800 g; flesh thick, orange; 12% TSS; yield 16-18 t/ha; resistant to PM & fruit fly; suitable for distant transport
Punjab Sunehri (1978)	Pedigree selection of [Hara Madhu x Edisto (American introduction)]	Orange flesh; dull yellow rind; fruit wt. 1 kg; 11% TSS; long post harvest life; yield 16-18 t/ha; male sterile & resistant to fusarium wilt
Punjab Rasila (1996)	Pedigree selection of (WMR- 29 (American) x Hara Madhu)	Green sutured; green flesh; fruit wt. 500 g; TSS-10-11%; yield 18 t/ha; resistant to DM, PM.
Hara Madhu (1970)	Selection from local type from Haryana	Late; globose fruit shape; no slip stage at maturity; fruit wt. 1 kg; light green flesh; pale yellow rind; very sweet; TSS 12-15%; yield 13-15 t/ha
Lucknow Safeda (1975)	Selection	Very early; fruit wt. 300 g; yield 11-13 t/ha
MH-10 (1996)	Heterosis breeding of [WI-998 (monoecious line) x Punjab Sunehri)]	Early; fruit wt. 915 g; TSS 9-10%; netted rind; suitable for distant transport; yield 24-25 t/ha
Kutana Selection	-	-
GAU, Anand		
Gujarat Musk melon-1 (1984)	Selection from Sabarkantha district	5-6 fruits/plant; fruit wt. 1 kg; yield 14-17 t/ha
Gujarat Musk melon-2 (1984)	Selection from Nagpur area	4-5 fruits/plant; fruit wt. 1.3 kg; yield 12-15 t/ha
Gujarat Musk melon-3 (2006)	Selection from local germplasm	Fruits oblong shaped; good aroma; TSS 12%; yield 13 t/ha
CCSHAU, Hisar		
Hisar Madhur	Pusa Sharbati x 75-34	Early & tolerant to DM
RAU, Rajasthan (RARS, Durgapur)		
MHY-1	Single plant selection	-
MHY-3 (1999)	Pedigree selection from (Durgapur	Light green sweet flesh; 13-16% TSS; yield 18-20 t/ha

	Madhu x Pusa Madhuras)	
MHY-5 (2004)	Pedigree selection of (Durgapur Madhu x Hara Madhu)	Fruit taper at stem end; light green flesh; TSS 13-16%; yield 18-20 t/ha; mod. resistant to root rot, PM, DM & viruses
MHY-9	-	-
MHY-10	Gynoecious line W 1998 x Indian cv. Punjab Sunehri	Monoecious; good shelf life; netted rind; early maturity; orange flesh; non sutured
MHY-25	Gynoecious line W 1998 x Indian cv. Punjab Sunehri	Monoecious; good shelf life; netted rind; early maturity; orange flesh; non sutured
NS 7455	-	Deep saffron flesh; TSS 13-15%; non sutured
MM-28	MHC-11 x Linco	Orange flesh; TSS 11-13%
Durgapur Madhu (1974)	Selection	Fruits oblong; fruit wt. 500-600 g; TSS 14%; yield 13-15 t/ha
RM-43 (1997)	Selection from local germplasm	Oblong fruits; TSS 10-12%; good keeping quality; yield 20-22 t/ha
RM-50 (2004)	Pedigree selection from (Durgapur Madhu x Sel.1)	Fruits pale green; TSS 13-16%; fruit wt. 500 g; yield 18-20 t/ha
NDUA & T, Faizabad		
Narendra Musk melon-1 (2006)	Selection from local germplasm	Round fruits; TSS 9-11%; fruit wt. 700-900 g; yield 12-15 t/ha
NDM-2	-	-
NDM-5	-	-
NDM-9	-	-

Private sector hybrids: Sweta, Swarna, Manjeet, Kundan, Khushbu, Patasha, MHC-2,5,6, NS Sunny Plus, NS Joy

Inheritance of characters:

- Yield is positively correlated with number of fruits, fruit weight, node at which first hermaphrodite flower appeared, number of branches and vine length.
- Fruit weight is positively correlated with fruit length, fruit girth, flesh thickness and length and width of cavity.
- 1st recessive male sterile line gene *ms-1* in musk melon: Bohn and Whittaker (1949).
- Gene for flesh colour: '*Or*'.
- Gynoecious sex: Multiple modifying genes in addition to major genotype *A-gg* and is unstable.
- Non-lobed leaves: Marker gene.
- Biparental mating and recurrent selection are best to improve ascorbic acid content.
- High TSS: Large number of dominant genes.
- Significant correlation between TSS and β-carotene content.

Character	Number of genes	Inheritance pattern
Earliness	-	Earliness partially dominant to lateness
Sex form	Digenic (*A* & *G*)	* Monoecious (*AAGG*) dominant over gynomoecious (*Aagg*), hermaphrodite (*aagg*) & andromonoecious (*aaGG*); * Andromonoecious recessive to monoecious; * Hermaphrodite double recessive to monoecious
Number of fruits/vine	-	Partially dominance & additive gene action
Fruit weight		Small fruited partially dominant to large fruited
Red pumpkin beetle resistance	Monogenic	Resistance dominant to susceptible
PM resistance	Monogenic (*Pm1*)	Resistance dominant to susceptible
DM resistance	Two incompletely dominant genes	-
Water melon mosaic resistance	Monogenic (*Wmv*)	Resistance dominant to susceptible
Resistance to CGMMV	Polygenes with recessive nature	-
Resistance to fusarium wilt	*Fom 1*, *Fom 2*, *Fom 3*, *Fom 4*	-
Resistance to fruit fly	-	2 complementary dominant genes
Skin/ rind colour	Monogenic	* Yellow partially dominant to cream; * Dark green dominant to green; * Greenish grey dominant to light green; * Stripped & mottled pericarp dominant to white * Green dominant to yellow.
Flesh colour	Monogenic	* Orange dominant to light green; * White dominant to green; White recessive to orange; Green recessive to salmon.
Flesh thickness	Monogenic	Thinner partially dominant to thicker
Stripes on rind	Monogenic recessive (*ht*)	Inheritance is independent of nature of rind whether netted or smooth
Fruit shape		* Oblong dominant over round; * Oblong incompletely dominant over flat; Oval dominant to round; Spherical recessive to obtuse.
Netting on fruit	Digenic	*N*-netting & *n*-smoothness * (Netting dominant to smoothness); * *N*-epistatic over S and so far *n* or *s*)
Seed coat colour	Monogenic	White dominant to yellow or tan.
Ascorbic acid content	Additive & dominant	-
β-carotene content	Digenic (green flesh (*gf*) & white flesh (*wf*)	Dominant form *Wf* gene responsible for orange flesh & epistatic interaction of *gf* & *wf* create orange, white & green colour.
Juicyness	Monogenic	Less juicyness dominant to juicyness
Fruit slipping	Monogenic	Slipping dominant to non-slipping
Rind cracking	Digenic	Complementary & supplementary gene action
Ribbing	Monogenic	Regular dominant to non-ribbing
Sutures	Monogenic	Sutureless dominant to sutured

16.4 Round melon (syn. *Praecitrullus fistulosus*, *C. fistulosus*)

- Eulogized as 'Squash melon or Indian squash or*Tinda* or Round gourd'.
- Monospecific genus confined to drier regions of South Asia.
- Anthesis: 5-7 AM.
- It has higher nutritive qualities than most of other cucurbits.
- It has cooling effect on human body and contains vitamin A.
- Fruit juice is given during Typhus fever, hepatitis, infections of urinary organs.
- Require maximum irrigation among cucurbits.
- Useful for cough and improve blood circulation.
- Optimum temperature for seed germination: 27^0C.
- Optimum temperature for fruit setting: 30-35^0C.
- MH (50 ppm): Most effective growth regulator for inducing femaleness.
- Harvesting stage: Tender stage before seed becomes hard.
- Used for pickles and preserve making.

Varieties:

Name	Breeding method	Remarks
IIHR, Bengaluru		
Arka Tinda (1986)	Pedigree selection of (T-3-4 x T-8-2)	1st improved variety in country & tolerant to fruit fly; very tender fruits; yield 10 t/ha
IARI, New Delhi		
Pusa Raunak (2016)	-	1st early maturing variety for spring and summer season; 55-60 days for maturity; 8-10 fruits/vine; flesh white, yield 8 t/ha
PAU, Ludhiana		
Punjab Tinda (1978)	Selection from local material	Flesh white; good cooking quality; yield 45-50 t/ha
TNAU, Coimbatore		
Annamalai Selection	-	-
CCSHAU, Hisar		
Hisar Tinda-10 (2006)	Selection from local germplasm	Semi-spreading; tolerant to DM & root rot wilt; yield 7.5-10 t/ha
Other varieties		
Mahyco Tinda	-	-
White Green Tinda	-	-

16.5 Long melon/ *Kakri*

- Eulogized as 'Serpent melon or Snake melon or Opp squash or *Thar kakri*'.
- *C. melo* var. *utilissimus* (syn. *C. melo* var. *flexuosus*).

- Popular as summer salad or pickled.
- Plants are monoecious.
- Oriental pickling melon or Chinese white cucumber (*C. melo* var. *conomon*): Used in East Asia for pickling.
- Oriental pickling melon is resistant to musk melon mosaic.
- Optimum temperature for growth and development: 25-35^{0}C.
- Fruits ready to harvest 7-9 days after setting.
- Harvesting stage: Very tender and half grown stage.
- Green types are good for transport.

Varieties:

Name	Breeding method	Remarks
IIHR, Bengaluru		
Arka Sheetal (1986)	Pure line selection	Free from bitter principle; shallow ridges; fruit wt. 90-100 g; yield 21-25 t/ha
IIHR-4	-	
IARI, New Delhi		
Pusa Utkarsh (2015)	-	1st early maturing variety for spring & summer season; fruit wt. 135-140 g; fruits sets ready for first harvest in 45-50 days after sowing; yield 29 t/ha
IIVR, Varanasi		
Kashi Santushti	-	-
CCSHAU, Hisar		
Karnal Selection	Selection	Prolific bearer; yield 9-10 t/ha
CIAH, Bikaner		
Thar Sheetal (2018)	Selection	Tolerant to high temperature (upto 42^{0}C); best adapted to tunnel cultivation where the crop is sown during Dec-Jan.; fruit length (25.83-29.67 cm); prolific bearer; yield (18-22 fruits/ plant)
AHC-2 (1998)	Selection	Very early maturing; fruits have light green skin; fruit wt. 2.75-3.3 Kg; yield 18-20 t/ha
AHC-13 (1998)	Selection	Very early maturing; fruits have light green skin; fruit wt. 2.15 kg; yield 85-125 q/ha; high heat tolerant
GBPUA &T, Pantnagar		
Pant Kakri-1	Selection	Seed to seed stage is about 90 days; yield 30 t/ha
PAU, Ludhiana		
Punjab Long melon-1 (1996)	Selection from local germplasm	Long, thin & light green fruits; yield 20-22 t/ha
CSAUA & T, Kanpur		
Lucknow Early	-	

16.6 Snap melon/ *Phoot/ Kakadia*

- Mature but unripe fruits are used to prepare *rayta* or pickle.
- Ripe fruits are used as dessert or salad.
- Fruit skin cracks on maturity.
- Optimum temperature for growth: 18-38°C.
- Keeping quality is very poor.

Varieties:

Name	Breeding method	Features
IARI, New Delhi		
Pusa Shandar (2004)	Selection from indigenous material	Fruit wt. 700 g; resistant to DM, PM & CGMMV; yield 40-42 t/ha
CIAH, Bikaner		
AHS- 10 (1998)	Selection from local germplasm	Flesh white pink & sweet; TSS 4.5-5^0 brix; oblong fruits; resistant to DM, PM & CGMMV; drought hardy; yield 22-23 t/ha
AHS- 82 (1998)	Selection from local germplasm	Flesh light pink & sweet; TSS 4.5-5^0 brix; oblong fruits; resistant to DM, PM & CGMMV; drought hardy; yield 24-25 t/ha
Dr BSKKV, Dapoli		
Konkan Madhur (DPLSM-2) 2014	Mass selection from local germplasm	Suitable for high rainfall area in kharif season; yield 15-31 t/ha; prone to ha; less cracking

16.7 Other minor melons

- Horticulturally important groups of melons based on fruit characteristics and uses rather than phylogeny.

Common name	Botanical name
Nutmeg melon/ Netted melon (Aromatic/ Persian melon)	*C. melo* var. *reticulatus*
New melon	*C. melo* var. *albida*
Lemon melon	*C. melo* var. *chito*
Orange melon	*C. melo* var. *hime*
Pineapple melon	*C. melo* var. *saccharinus*
Rock/ Cantaloupe melon	*C. melo* var. *cantaloupensis*
Weed melon	*C. melo* var. *argrestis*
Sour melon	*C. melo* var. *acidulus*
Egg melon	*C. melo* var. *tomago*

16.8 Bottle gourd (syn. *L. vulgaris, L. leucantha*)

- Eulogized as 'White flower gourd or Calabaza (Spanish word came from Arabic "dry gourd") or Zucca melon or Trumpet gourd'.
- Term gourd refers to 'hard tough rind'.

- Cultivated in both, New and Old world since early times.
- Wild, perennial and dioecious: *Lagenaria abyssinica*, *L. leucantha* and *L. brasifolia*.
- Used as rootstock for various cucurbits.
- Bower system training is practiced in Maharashtra.
- It is highly photosensitive.
- Flower colour: White.
- Bitterness: Cucurbitacin.
- Dry hard shell is used for preparation of musical instruments.
- Tender fruits, seeds and seed oil are edible.
- Widely used in indigenous system of medicine; cardiotonic and diuretic.
- Processed product: Tooty-fruity.
- 'Kofta': Most popular preparation from bottle gourd.
- Fruit pulp is very good source of fibre free carbohydrates.
- Good for heart patients and used in weight loss programme.
- Anthesis takes place in evening/ night hours (5-8 PM).
- Stigma receptivity: 36 h before anthesis to 60 h after anthesis.
- Temperature for seed germination: 25-30^{0}C and affected below 15^{0}C.
- Brownish or whitish brown seeds germination well.
- Ratio of male and female flowers: 6:1 to 25:1.
- Short day and humid climate promotes femaleness.
- High temperature and high N induce maleness and wider sex ratio.
- Heterosis is present throughout its life cycle at all stages.
- Heterosis is reported by I.D. Tyagi (1973).
- Pinching of male flowers on female plant is commercially practiced in hybrid seed production.
- MH @ 200-300 ppm promotes female flower production and increase fruit set.
- For higher female to male ratio, spray boron @ 3 ppm at 2nd and 4thleaf stage.
- Seed rate: 6-8 kg/ha.
- Mulching with polythene sheet gives increased yields (50-95%).
- Fruits are picked at 12-15 days after fruit set.
- Physiological maturity of seed: 65 days after anthesis.
- Number of seeds/ fruit: 400-700.
- Seed weight: 10-15 g/ 100 seeds.
- Specific requirement for export purpose: Green, tender, cylindrical, 20-25 cm with soft hairs.

Varieties:

- In India, Choudhary and Singh (1971) developed 1st hybrid.

Name	Breeding method	Features
IARI, New Delhi		
Pusa Summer Prolific Long (1975)	Selection from local germplasm	Suitable for both summer & kharif season; long fruits (40-45 cm); yield 25-30 t/ha
Pusa Summer Prolific Round (1975)	Selection from local germplasm	Suitable for both summer & kharif season; round fruits
Pusa Samridhi (2005)	Selection from indigenous germplasm	Non-crook neck variety; superior in nutritional qualities; yield 31t/ha
Pusa Santushti (2008)	Single plant selection from OP land race (Sel.P-6)	Pear shaped fruits with neck; suitable for throughout year cultivation, set fruits under low temperature (10-12^{0}C) & high temperature (35-40^{0}C); yield 26 t/ha.
Pusa Sandesh (1989)	Selection from indigenous germplasm	Round green fruits; fruit wt. 600 g; suitable for summer & kharif; fruit wt. 600 g; yield 32 t/ha.
Pusa Naveen (1992)	Selection from indigenous germplasm	Fruits cylindrical & free from crook necked fruits; suitable for packing for long distance transport; Yield 32 t/ha
Pusa Meghdoot	Heterosis breeding of (PSPL x Sel. 2)	1st F_1 hybrid by public sector in 1971; suitable for summer & kharif; oblong fruited
Pusa Manjari	Heterosis breeding of (PSPR x Sel. 11)	1st F_1 hybrid by public sector in 1971; suitable for summer & kharif season; round fruits
Pusa Hybrid-3 (1998)	Heterosis breeding of (Pusa Naveen x Sel. P-8)	Suitable for easy packing & long distance transport; club shaped fruits; yield 43 t/ha
IIHR, Bengaluru		
Arka Bahar (1984)	Pure line selection from indigenous flora from Karnataka	Non-crooked neck variety; tolerant to blossom end rot; yield 40-45 t/ha
Arka Shreyas (2019)	Modified back cross breeding & selection from (IIHR-21 x Crimson Sweet)	Early flowering; female flower appear at 15th node; 60 days for first picking; yield 48 t/ha; resistant to gummy stem blight
Arka Nutan (2019)	Modified back cross breeding & selection from (IIHR-21 x Crimson Sweet)	Early flowering; female flower appear at 9th node; 56 days for first picking; yield 46 t/ha & resistant to gummy stem blight

Arka Ganga (2019)	-	Early flowering; female flower appear at 12th node; 56 days for first picking; yield 60 t/ha & resistant to gummy stem blight
IIVR, Varanasi		
Kashi Ganga (2006)	Pedigree selection (IC 92465 x DVBG-151)	Cylindrical shaped fruits; fruit yield 48-55 t/ha; tolerant to anthracnose
Kashi Bahar (2006)	Heterosis breeding	Cylindrical shaped fruits; fruit yield 50-52 t/ha; tolerant to anthracnose, DM & cercospora leaf spot
Kashi Komal	-	-
Kashi Kirti (2018)	-	Fruits green, small, cylindrical shape (Gutka type); resistant to DM; suitable for distant market; yield (45 t/ha)
Kashi Kundal (2018)	-	Pear shaped green fruits; suitable for July-Sept. sowing; 12-14 fruits with fruit weight of 1.3 to 1.5 kg; resistant to DM; yield (47.5 t/ha)
Kashi Kiran (2018)	-	Light green attractive round fruits, tolerant to DM; fruit wt. 600-700 g; fruits 13-14/ plant; yield 45-48 t/ha
CIAH, Bikaner		
Thar Samridhi (2007)	Hybridization of 'Banaswara Local x Gujarat Local-1'	Fruit wt. 450-700 g; yield (3.82-5.82 kg/plant) & 24-30 t/ha
ICAR Research Complex for Eastern Region, Patna (HARP, Ranchi)		
Swarna Sneha (2013)	Pure line selection from IC-284939	Suitable for summer & rainy season crop; yield 50-55 t/ha; tolerant to PM & DM
Krishidhan Vegetable Seeds India Pvt. Ltd, Pune		
Santosh 20 (KBGH 20)	KVBG 53 x KVBG 11	Fruit wt. 500-550 g; tolerant to PM, DM; yield 35-40 t/ha.
MPKV, Rahuri		
Samrat (1992)	Local selectionfrom Dahanu area	Long & slender (30-40 cm); cylindrical; non-crooked neck variety; yield 40 t/ha; suitable for box packing
PAU, Ludhiana		
Punjab Komal (1988)	LC 11 x LC 5	Light green fruits; tolerant to CMV; yield 20-22 t/ha
Punjab Round (1978)	Selection	Prolific bearer; round fruits; yield 35-37 t/ha
Punjab Long (1999)	Selection from local germplasm	Long fruits, tender green

CCSHAU, Hisar		
GH-22	-	Long, green color fruits; stem-end with round bottom and slight bending at neck
HBGH-35	-	Fruit medium, long cylindrical green colour; stem-end with bit flat
CSAUA & T, Kanpur		
Azad Nutan (2000)	-	Long, green; neck free; yield 35-40 t/ha
Kalyanpur Long Green (1983)	Selection	Long fruited; yield 28-30 t/ha
Lauki Azad Sankar-1 (2006)	Heterosis breeding	Yield 58-60 t/ha
KBG-16	-	Long fruited
GBPUA & T, Pantnagar		
PBOG-1	-	Long fruited
Pant Sankar Lauki-1 (1991)	Heterosis breeding of 'PBOG-22 x PBOG-40'	Long fruit, light green colour, suitable for planting in plains & in hills; yield 40t/ha
Pant Sankar Lauki-2 (2001)	Heterosis breeding of 'PBOG-22 x PBOG-61'	Fruits 40 cm long; suitable for plains & hills; yield 40-42 t/ha
Pant Sankar Lauki-3 (2006)	Selection	Fruits 40 cm long; suitable for plains & hills; yield 35-37 t/ha
Pant Lauki-4	-	High yielding; long fruits (40 cm) of light green colour with light strips having hairs; yield 30 t/ha
AAU, Anand		
Anand Bottle gourd -1	Selection from germplasm 'BGM-9' collected from local	Indeterminate; fruit wt. 50 g; fruit skin smooth, non-hairy & long shelf life;yield 24 t/ha
Anand Bottlegourd hybrid-1	F_1 hybrid	Low incidence of mosaic & DM; yield 28t/ha
RAU, Pusa		
Rajendra Chamatkar (1984)	Selection	Prolific bearer; cylindrical shape; yield 18-20 t/ha
NDUA & T, Faizabad		
Narendra Sankar Lauki-4 (NDBGH-4) 2006	Hybrid	Prolific bearer; yield 70 t/ha in summer, 100 t/ha in rainy

Narendra Rashmi (2006)	Selection from local germplasm	Suitable for summer & rainy season cultivation; mod. resisn to PM, DM; early mature (60 days); yield 35-40 t/ha
Narendra Pooja (NDBG-10)	Selection	Near cylindrical shape
Narendra Dharidar (NDBG-208-1) 2006	Selection from 'NDBG-208'	Suitable for summer season; yield 35 t/ha
Narendra Jyoti (NDBG-104) 2006	Selection	Fruits long slender; yield 40 t/ha (summer) & 60 t/ha (rainy)
Narendra Shishir (NDBG-202)	Selection	Winter type round fruited variety & has peculiar multifid/ pedate leaf shape; resistance against anthracnose, DM, PM & viral disease complex; yield 8.5 t/ha
Narendra Madhuri (NDBG-505)	Selection	Fruits round; highly palatable cooked vegetable; yield 100 t/ha
Narendra Shivani (NDBG- 403)	Selection	Winter type prolific bearer; very long slender fruits fit for kitchen garden purpose; yield 13 t/ha
Narendra Bottle gourd (NDBG-132)	Selection	Fruits long slender shaped; early maturing; yield 30 t/ha
Narendra Prabha (NDBG-619)	Selection	Fruits cylindrical in shape, early maturing (55 days); yield 30 t/ha
TNAU, Coimbatore		
CO. 1 (1981)	Selection	Fruits round at base bottle neck at the top (pot shaped); light green coloured; yield 36 t/ha
TNAU Bottlegourd Hybrid CO. 1	F_1 hybrid of 'IC418246 x IC393752'	Fruits cylindrical, without crook neck, medium sized (0.95-1.00 kg); suitable for bower system cultivation; yield 60 t/ha
PLR-1	Selection from Palur local type	Fruits good taste & suited for salad; yield 31 t/ha.
PLR-2	Selection from Uchimedu	Round fruit; no bottle neck; very appealing light green fruits; fruit wt. 975 g; yield 41 t/ha
OUAT, Bhubaneswar		
Utkal Shobha	-	-

Inheritance of characters:

- Single gene pair determines patchy vs. white colour in *L. leucantha*.

Character	Number of genes	Inheritance pattern
Fruit colour	Monogenic	* Green dominant to light green; * Yellow dominant to green.
Stem colour	Monogenic	Dark green dominant to light green
Bush habit	Monogenic	Short internodes dominant tovine habit
Fruit shape	Monogenic (*Di*)	Long & disc dominant to round & bottle or spherical shape
Rind thickness	Monogenic	Hard dominant to soft
Corolla colour	Monogenic	Light yellow recessive to orange yellow
Flesh colour	Monogenic	White dominant to cream
Segmented leaf shape	Monogenic	Dominant
Days to maturity	Polygenic	-
Seed size	Polygenic	-
Seed colour	Monogenic	Dark brown dominant to white
Resistance to red pumpkin beetle	Monogenic (*Af*)	Resistance dominant to susceptibility
Resistance to powdery mildew (PM)	Monogenic	Recessive
Resistance to zucchini yellow mosaic virus (ZYMV)	Monogenic	Dominant
Bitterness in *L. leucantha*	Monogenic	Bitterness dominant to non-bitterness
Monoecious nature	Monogenic	Monoecious dominant to andromonoecious

Physiological disorders:

- Preponderance of staminate flowers: Excess N application, high temperature, long days.
- Bitterness: Prevalent under cool weather and at higher elevations and triggered by environmental stress.
- Brown end: Blossom end of fruit turn brown and hard.
- Light belly colour: Side of fruit touching ground turns whitish yellow. Use mulch, turning of fruits time to time and training on trellies.

16.9 Bitter gourd

- Eulogized as 'Bitter melon or Bitter cucumber or Balsam pear or Insulin plant'.
- Major importers of Indian bitter gourd: EU, UAE, etc.
- Rich source of iron (2 mg/ 100g) among cucurbits.
- Bitter principle: Momordicine.
- Bitterness increases during maturation and lost during ripening process.

- It has anti-microbial, anti-fertility, anti-viral, anti-ulcerogenic activity.
- Cheratin: Hypoglycemic ingredient having anti-diabitic properties.
- It has got heating and wormicidal effect on the human body.
- Contain protein similar to bovine insulin referred to as 'P-insulin or polypeptide-p'.
- Principal chloroplast & chromoplast present in ripe fruit: Cryptoxanthin.
- Carotene in ripe seed coat: Lycopene.
- In Vietnam and China, the ripe fruit of sweet gourd arils are used to prepare '*xoi gac*' with red glutinous rice.
- Seed rate: 4.5-6 kg/ha.
- If temperature goes above 40^0C, induces maleness.
- Day neutral crop.
- Seed germination enhanced by GA_3 @ 25-50 ppm.
- Flowering starts 40-45 days after sowing.
- Sequence of flowering follows pattern as 1) male phase 2) mixed phase 3) female phase.
- Anthesis time: 4 AM to 9 AM.
- Anther dehiscence: 5 AM to 7.30 AM.
- Stigma receptivity: 24 h before and 24 h after anthesis.
- Average ratio of male to female flowers in monoecious type: 9:1 to 48:1 (5: 1 to 40: 1).
- Pollination agent: Honey bees (*Apis flora*, *A. dorsata*, *A. cerana*)
- 1st pistillate flower at lower node is indication of earliness of variety.
- For enhancing female: male ratio: MH @ 50-150 ppm and CCC @ 50-100 ppm.
- For induction of hermaphrodite flower: Spray $AgNO_3$ @ 200-300 ppm at pre-floweing stage.
- Heterosis in bitter gourd was 1st studied by Pal and Singh (1946).
- Gynoecious lines viz. DBGy-201 and DBGy-202 were developed by Dr. Behara, IARI during 2009.
- In South India, it is trained on bower system.
- Fruits are ready for harvest: 60-70 days.
- Used in chips preparation.
- Immature, tender fruits are harvested as vegetable and for pickling.
- Maturity indices: Change in fruit colour, increased exocarp development and change in seed colour.
- Seed protein (ricine) inhibited growth of immune virus (HIV) in human cell culture.
- Seed yield: 250-300 kg/ha.

- Number of seeds/ gram: 5-7.
- 100 seed wt.: 23 gram.
- Requirements for getting phytosanitory certificate: Farm registration under VegNet, global GAP certificate, packhouse recommended by APEDA, certificate of free from insecticide residues, free from fruit fly, thrips, virus, treatment with vapour heat treatment (VHT), etc.
- Specific requirement for export purpose: Complete green, lustrous, more prickly, medium long and spindle shaped.

Species:

- Bitter gourd is incompatible with *M. dioica* and *M. balsamina*.
- *Thladiantha cordifolia*: Wild bitter gourd. 1st to be used as fruit vegetable in India.

Botanical name	Features
Momordica charantia var. *abbrevita*	Progenitor of bitter gourd
M. balsamina	2n=22; annual, bitter fruits; monoecious African spp. with medicinal properties & potential as ornamental; highly tolerant to cucurbit diseases & pests
M. charantia var. *muricata*	Small fruits; highly tolerant to fruit fly, root knot nematode & pumpkin caterpillar
M. charantia var. *charantia*	2n=22; large & bitter fruited
M. sahyadrica	Dioecious, perennial, large fruits
M. subangulata	Dioecious with adventitious tubers
M. suboica	Good for interspecific hybridization
Teasle gourd/ Gantola (*M. subangulata* ssp. *reningera*)	2n=4x=56: segmented autopolyploid (Spine gourd x Sweet gourd)
M. foetida, *M. rostrata*	Insect repellent properties and used in resistance breeding

Varieties:

- NHBI-2009:
- Suitable for canning: BG-14, C-96.

Name	Breeding method	Remarks
IARI, New Delhi		
Pusa Do Mausami (1975)	Selection from indigenous material	Suitable for spring-summer & rainy season; yield 15 t/ha
Pusa Vishesh (1987)	Selection from local variety	Dwarf; suitable for high density planting, pickling & dehydration; yield 15 t/ha
Pusa Hybrid-1 (1995)	Heterosis breeding of (Pusa Do Mausami x Pusa Vishesh)	Suitable for spring-summer season, pickling & dehydration; yield 20 t/ha
Pusa Hybrid-2 (2006)	Hybridization of 'S-63 x Pusa Do Mausami'	Suitable for pickling & dehydration; yield 19-21 t/ha
Pusa Hybrid-4 (2018)	-	1st monoecious hybrid; high female: male ratio (2:1); fruit length 16 cm; fruit wt. 60 g; yield 22 t/ha
Pusa Aushadhi	Backcross & single plant selection (DBGy-201 x Pusa Do Mausami)	-
Pusa Rasdar (2016)	-	Suitable for protected cultivation; extra early
Pusa Meghdoot	-	-
Pusa Purvi (2016)	-	1st small fruit variety; rich in anti-oxidants &minerals
IIHR, Bengaluru (CHES, Chettalli & CHES, Bhubaneshwar)		
Arka Harit (1984)	Pure line selection from local strain of Rajasthan	Suitable for stuffing purpose; small spindle shaped fruits, green colour; moderate bitterness with less seeds; yield 12 t/ha
Arka Sumeet	-	-
Arka Sujata	-	-
Arka Bharath	Selection	Vigorous; fruits dark green; long, oval; fruit wt. 100 g; yield 10 t/ha; suitable for high altitude area
IIVR, Varanasi		
Kashi Urvasi	IC-85650B x IC-44435A	Fruit wt. 90-110 g & yield 20-22 t/ha
Kashi Mayuri (2018)	-	Medium maturity, green fruits of 15-18 cm long; tolerant to anthracnose, DM & mosaic; yield 19 t/ha
DVBTG-1	-	-
DVBTG-12	-	-

ICAR Research Complex for Eastern Region, Patna (HARP, Ranchi)		
Swarna Yamini (2013)	Hybridization followed by pedigree selection	Fruit wt. 70 g; yield 20 t/ha; suitable for summer & rainy season; tolerant to PM & DM
DIBER, Pithoragarh		
DARL-305	-	Early, determinate, very high yielding; suitable for both fresh market & processing
GBPUA & T, Pantnagar		
Pant Karela-1 (1996)	Pure line selection	Suitable for planting in the hills; yield 15t/ha; highly resistant to red pumpkin beetle
Pant Karela-2 (2006)	Selection from 'PBIG-1'	Yield 15-16 t/ha
Pant Karela-3	-	Early maturing, dark green
MPKV, Rahuri		
Hirkani (1991)	Selection from local germplasm	Dark green fruits with prickles; fruit length 15-20 cm; yield 14 t/ha
Phule Priyanka (2001)	F_1 hybrid of 'RHR-5 x RHR-4'	Dark green; highly prickled fruits; suitable for kharif & summer season; tolerant to DM; response to bower system; yield 20-25 t/ha
Phule Ujwala	Selection	Prickled fruits; fruit wt. 84 g; fruit length 18 cm; yield 18 t/ha
Phule Green Gold (1996)	Pedigree selection of 'Green Long x Deshi Local'	Fruit dark green; fruit length 25-30 cm; suitable for kharif & summer season; yield 23 t/ha; tolerant to DM
Dr BSKKV, Dapoli		
Konkan Tara (1993)	Selection from Tarapur village of Konkan	Long (15 cm) green fruits, prickly, spindle shaped; fruit wt. 45 g; with more shelf life (7-8 days) & export quality; yield 15-20 t/ha
Konkan Karli (2019)	Selection from local type	-
TNAU, Coimbatore		
CBM-12	-	Anti-diabetic property
MDU-1 (1984)	γ- irradiation to local cv. MC-103	Earliest flowering; white colour; fruit wt. 410 g; high sex ratio (20:1); 17 fruits/ plant; yield 30-33 t/ha
MC-23	-	-
CO.1 (1978)	Selection from local type	Fruits green, 30-35 cm long; fruit wt. 100-120 g; yield 14 t/ha
CO-BgH-1 (2000)	F_1 hybrid of (MC 84 x MDU-1)	Fruits creamy white & weighs 390 each; yield 51 t/ha
Coimbatore LongWhite	Selection by NSC	Tender white fruits; suitable for processing

Coimbatore Long Green	Selection from local germplasm	Long dark green fruits
BTH-7	VRBT-3A x VRBT-82-1	Long green fruits; tolerant to DM, PM
BTH-165	KB-1 x VRBT-36	Long green fruits; tolerant to DM, PM
KAU, Thrissur		
Priya (1976)	Selection from 'Kannur' local	Fruit length 40 cm; length; 40-50 fruits/ vine
Priyanka (1996)	Selection from local germplasm	Fruits green coloured, 40 cm long, weigh 300 g; yield 28 t/ha
Preethi (1998)	Selection from 'MC-84'	Fruits white & spindle shaped & spiny; fruit wt. 70 g; fruit length 30-40 cm; yield 14-15 t/ha
MC-84	Selection	-
VK-1	Selection	High yield
CSAUA & T, Kanpur		
Kalyanpur Baramasi (1983)	Selection	Tolerant to fruit fly & mosaic virus; yield 20-22 t/ha
Kalyanpur Sona (1996)	Selection from local germplasm	Yield 12-13 t/ha
Kalyanpur Priya	-	-
PAU, Ludhiana		
Punjab-BG-6	-	-
Punjab-14 (1987)	Selection from local germplasm	Fruits light green & small sized; yield 12 t/ha; suitable for spring, summer & rainy season
Punjab Karela-1	-	Fruits green; fruit wt. 50 g; yield 7 t/ acre
CCSHAU, Hisar		
HK-127 (2019)	-	-
NDUA & T, Faizabad		
NDB-1	-	-
IGKVV, Raipur		
Indira Kankoda-1	-	-
Indira Kankoda-2	-	-
Chhattisgarh Kankoda-2	-	-

Private sector hybrids: Pia (launched in T.N)

Inheritance of characters:

- White pericarp monogenic recessive (*ww*) to green.
- Negative correlation between fruit quality and fruit fly resistance.
- 1st genetic linkage map of bitter melon by Kole *et al.* (2012). Total distance of 3060.7 cM.

Character	Number of genes	Inheritance pattern
Fruit colour & surface	Monogenic	Green dominant to white
Seed coat colour	Monogenic	Dark brown dominant to light brown
Seed size	Monogenic	Small seed dominant to large
Gynoecious nature	Monogenic (*gy-1*)	Gynoecy recessive to monoecy (Ram *et al.*, 2006)
Bitterness	Monogenic	More bitterness dominant to less
Maturity time	Polygenic	-
Fruit length	Polygenic	Incompletely dominant
Fruit shape	Monogenic	Long dominant to round
Fruit colour	Digenic	Green dominant to white
Spiny fruit (triangular tubercles)	Monogenic	Spiny dominant to smooth
Ridges on fruits	Monogenic	Broken ridges dominant to unbroken ridge
Pericarp	Monogenic (*W*)	Green dominant to white
Resistance to fruit fly	-	Dominant

16.10 Sweet gourd/ *Kakrol*

- Perennial with ratoon potential.
- Due to dioecious nature, tuberous roots of male and female plants are collected separately.
- 10% male plants should be planted for good fruit set.
- Tubers or stem of male and female plants can be recognized by seeing flowers and fruits.
- Propagation methods: Mode of propagation: Tuberous roots (125-150 kg/ha), seeds, stem cuttings (two node), apical shoots.
- Nutrient composition/ 100 g edible portion: Protein (2.61 g), fat (0.66 g), -CHO (5.69 g), crude fibre (5.93 g), minerals (1.02 g), calcium (21 mg), phosphorous (148 mg), iron (2.59 mg), moisture (84.09 g).
- Fruits are low in vitamins but seeds are rich in fatty acid (oleostearic acid).
- Fruits are cooked after removing soft thorns present on fruit surface.
- Plant starts fruiting 55-65 days after planting of roots.
- Plants remain dormant in winter.
- Optimum temperature for growth: 32-40^{0}C.
- Anthesis time: 6-7 PM.
- Fruits attain marketable size in 11-12 days after anthesis.

- Seed propagation is avoided because seeds long dormancy period (8-9 months), low germination, show 50:50 male/ female population and viable for 1 year only.
- Seed oil is used as illuminant.
- Sex form is controlled by single factor. Male being heterozygous and female being homozygous recessive.
- Sweet gourd: *Momordica cochinchinensis* (2n=28): Rich in β-carotene, vit. C. Tolerate soil salinity upto 4 dS/m.

Characters	Sweet gourd	Spine gourd
Root develops	Big tubers	Small tubers
Leaves	Big	Small
Flowers	Large & white to light yellow coloured	Small & yellow in colour
Glands in lamina	Umblicate glands in lamina base of leaves	-
Glands in petiole	1-5 glands	-
Dots on base of petals	3 small deep black or blue circular dots	No circular dots
Anthesis time	Early morning	During evening
Time required for flower opening	72 minutes	7 to 22 minutes
Pollen viability	For 36 h	For 36 h
Stigma receptivity	Upto 18 h	Upto 18 h
Flower shape	Abnormmaly large & oblong	Round to oval
Individual fruit weight	60-80 g & can attain upto 500 g	10-15 g & can attain 30 g
Fruit ripening	From periphery to inside	From inside to periphery
Fruit colour	Light green to light yellow	Dark green
Spines	Tough spines on fruit	Smooth & false spines
Days for edible maturity	26 days	20 days
Flowering & fruiting period	Continue for short period	Continue for longer period
Yield/ plant	45-50 fruits	80-100 fruits

Varieties:

- C-8, C-20

Name	Breeding method	Features
IIHR, Bengaluru (CHES, Bhubaneshwar)		
Arka Neelachal Gaurav	Selection	Teasel gourd variety; high yield; soft seed; high market preference; tolerant to DM & anthracnose; yield 18-20 t/ha
Arka Neelachal Arakta	Selection	Sweet gourd variety; rich in carotenoids & lycopene; fruit wt. 500-900 g.; fruits length 15 cm; long; fruits fleshy & reddish

Pests:

- Epilachna beetle:
- Fruit fly:

16.11 Spine gourd/ *Kartoli*

- Spine gourd/ Kartoli/ Bitterless bitter gourd: *M. dioica* (2n=28):
- Considered as wild type crop.
- Rest period of crop: January-May.
- Great scope for value additions.
- Project on kartoli has been initiated by Custard Apple Grower's Association.
- It can be taken as intercrop in custard apple.
- Tissue cultured plantlets are available.
- Anthesis takes place in evening hours.
- Perennial dioecious climber with thicker tuberous roots.
- Roots of female plants are preferred for paste preparation and applied over body during high fever.
- Preferable soil pH: 6-7.

Varieties:

Name	Breeding method	Features
IIHR, Bengaluru (CHES, Bhubaneshwar)		
Arka Neelachal Shree	Selection	High yield; good appearance; high market preference
Arka Neelachal Shanti	Natural pollination between 'Spine gourd x Teasel gourd'	Flower morphology similar to teasel gourd; mod. tolerant to fruit borer, anthracnose & DM; yield 8-9 t/ha

16.12 Snake gourd (syn. *T. anguina*)

- Eulogized as 'Cucumber of the southern barbarians or *Chinchida* or *Pallakaya*'.
- Roots and seeds are used in treatment of diarrhoea, bronchitis and fever.
- Bower or arbour system of training is best.
- 'Trichosanthin' compound used for anti-HIV activity.
- Flower diclinus, flower colour white, large and fringed.
- Ratio of male to female flower: 31:1 to 225:1.
- Tendriller flower: Common in snake gourd.
- High humidity favour growth and development and fruit formation.
- Anthesis time: 5 to 9 PM.
- Anther dehiscence: Before anthesis.
- Stigma receptivity: 7 h before anthesis to 51 h after anthesis.
- Seed yield: 200-300 kg/ha.
- 100 seed wt.: 22 gram.

- Preference for export market: Small fruit having 50-70 cm length and light green fruit colour.

Species:

- *Trichosanthes*: Largest genus in cucurbitaceae family.
- Progenitor of snake gourd: *T. cucumarina* (2n=22, 24)
- Japan's snake gourd: *T. origera*.
- Chinese snake gourd: *T. kirilowii*.
- Cultivated species: *T. anguina*, *T. cucurmerina*, *T. dioica*.
- Objectionable weeds: *T. palmata*, *T. labata*.

Varieties:

Name	Breeding method	Features
MPKV, Rahuri		
Phule Vaibhav	Pure line selection from germplasm collected from Solapur	Fruits white, 90-100 cm long; tolerant to PM, DM; yield 29 t/ha
Dr BSKKV, Dapoli		
Konkan Shweta (1992)	Selection from Mahim area of Konkan	Suitable for cultivation in kharif & summer; fruitslong 110 cm; white in colour; yield 15-20 t/ha
TNAU, Coimbatore		
CO.1 (1976)	Single plant selection	Fruit wt. 50-75 g; yield 18-19 t/ha
CO.2 (1986)	Pure line selection from local germplasm	Vines less spreading; fruit wt. 400-600 g; yield 35-37 t/ha
CO.4	-	Early maturing; dark green fruits
CO.H-1	F_1 hybrid of (IC 622556) x IC0599591)	Fruits white; 55 fruits/plant; yield 70 t/ha
MDU-1 (1981)	Heterosis breeding of 'Pannipudal x Selection-1'	Sex ratio of 1: 38; yield 32 t/ha; fruit wt. 55 g
PKM-1 (1979)	Mutant using gamma irradiation to cv. H-375	Fruit wt. 700 g; yield 25-27 t/ha
KAU, Vellanikkara		
Kaumudi (1996)	Local selection	100 cm long; white fruits with acute tip; fruit wt. 1.34 kg.
Baby (2006)	Selection	Small white fruits; fruit wt. 474 g.
Manushree (2006)	Selection	Long white fruits (68 cm); fruit wt. 775 g
Harithasree	Selection	High yielding variety having green fruits with white stripes
TA-19	Selecction	High yield
APAU, Telangana		
Swetha	Selection	Fruits long with green stripes

Inheritance of characters:

- White fruit colour (*WW*) dominant over green white stripe (*ww*).
- Deep green pericarp was dominant over pale green, yellow and white; pale green dominant over yellow and yellow dominant over white.
- Fruit yield, days to 1st female flowers, fruits/ plant, fruit weight are governed by polygenes.

16.13 Pointed gourd

- Eulogized as 'King of gourds or *Parwal*'.
- Unique heter ochromosomes and true diploid (2n=2x=22).
- Dioecious and perennial crop.
- Immature fruits are used as vegetable and for pickling.
- Protein content in fruits is 10 times that of bottle gourd, and 4 times that of snake gourd, ridge gourd and wax gourd.
- Provitamin A and vitamin C content is higher than any other cucurbits.
- Minerals, fiber and calcium content of leaves are highest among all the cucurbits and provide high energy of about 55 Kcal.
- Parwal is good crop for diara (river bed upland) cultivation.
- Methods of vine planting in eastern India: Ring, lunda or lachhi (figure of eight), moist lump or straight vine.
- Layering and tissue culture is also practiced.
- Preferred training system: Vertical staking or bower system.
- Crop remains dormant during winter and again sprouts in summer season.
- Commercial mode of propagation: Vine cuttings having 10-15 nodes from basal portion of female plants @ 2000-2500 cuttings/ha.
- Least expensive method of propagation: Root sucker cutting.
- Ratoon cropping is generally practiced.
- Planting distance: 2m x 0.6 m accommodating 9,000 plants/ ha.
- Best time of planting: October.
- Optimum temperature for growth: 25-35^{0}C.
- Long duration crop of 8 months.
- Pollination agent: Red brown beetle (*Carpophicus dimidiatus*).
- Hand pollination in early morning h (5-5.30 AM) increases higher fruit set than natural pollination.
- Pollen from single flower are sufficient to pollinate 7-8 female flowers simply by touching stigma.

- 2% male plants are necessary to get high yield.
- Alar @ 1000 ppm produces higher number of fruits/ plant.
- Pollen grain germination peak period at 9-9.30 PM.
- Flower colour: White.
- Fruits are particularly recommended during convalescence (regains health after illness).
- Anthesis and anther dehiscence tend to go together.
- Staminate flower takes 16-19 days and pistillate flowers 10-14 days from initiation to anthesis.
- Male flowers are wooly outside and not racemed.
- Widely used method of crop improvement: Single plant selection.
- Parthenocarpic fruit set may occur naturally or can be induced by NAA @ 100-500 ppm.
- Seed propagation leads to segregated seedlings.
- Mature seeds fail to germinate even after scarification.
- Harvesting starts 90-100 days after planting.
- Immature, tender fruits with soft seeds inside are harvested or 7-15 days after fruit set.
- Show non-climacteric respiratory behaviour.
- Salicylic acid enhances post-harvest life of fruits.
- Storage in ZECC (27-31^{0}C, 94-96% R.H.) increases shelf life by 4 days.
- Seeds exhibit recalcitrant storage behaviour.
- No marker characters are available to predict sex form in the crop.

Varieties:

- Bihar Sherif, FP 1, 3 and 4, Damodar, Kazil Bombay, CHPG-11, CHPG-16.
- Genotypes FP-4, FP-152, FP-260, FP-304, FP-305 and FP-316 are superior for making different sweets.

Name	Breeding method	Features
ICAR Research Complex for Eastern Region, Patna (HARP, Ranchi)		
Swarna Alaukik (2006)	Clonal selection	Elongatedfruits light greenish in colour with blunt ends; suitable for table & sweet preparation; yield 20-25t/ha
Swarna Rekha (2006)	Clonal selection	Striped green fruits with soft seeds; yield 20-23 t/ha
Swarna Suruchi (2011)	Clonal selection	Fruits oval, light green coloured; yield 25-30 t/ha; suitable for table & sweet preparation
CHES Hybrid-1	Hybrid	1st hybrid developed in the country; solid, green striped fruits wt. 30-35 g each; yield 28-32 t/ha; resistant to fruit fly

CHES Hybrid-2	Hybrid	Dark green striped fruits; fruit wt. 25-30 g; yield 30-40 t/ha
IIVR, Varanasi		
Kashi Alankar (VRPG-1)	Clonal selection	Light green spindle shaped fruits with some strips at distal end; 100-130 fruits/plant; yield 30-38 t/ha
Kashi Amulya (2018)	Clonal selection	Light green fruits; less seeded (5-8 seeds/fruit); suitable for culinary, stuffing & confectionary purpose. Fruit length 7-7.5 cm; fruit dia. 3 cm; yield 26-29 t/ha
Kashi Suphal (VRPG-2) 2018	Clonal selection	Light green fruits; fruiting starts from 4th to 6th node onward; capable of fruiting even temperature goes beyond 40^{0}C; yield 28-30 t/ha; suitable for cultivation in garden land & river bed
IIHR, Bengaluru (CHES, Bhubaneswar)		
Arka Neelachal Kirti	Selection	Fruits spindle shaped, dark green; 40-45 g with solid core; yield 15 t/ha
CHES Hybrid -1	Hybrid	1st hybrid developed in country; resistant to fruit fly
RAU, Sabour, Bihar		
Rajendra Parwal-1 (1994)	Clonal selection	Suitable for diara cultivation & long distance transport; yield 18-19 t/ha; tolerant to fruit fly
Rajendra Parwal-2 (1994)	Clonal selection	Suitable for diara cultivation & long distance transport; yield 19-20 t/ha; tolerant to fruit fly
NDUA & T, Faizabad		
Faizabad Parwal-3	Clonal selection	Fruits spindle shaped, green, less striped; excellent for culinary purpose; yield of 13-15 t/ha
Faizabad Parwal-4	Clonal selection	Fruits spindle shaped, green with tapering ends; recommended for bower system & sodic soils
Narendra Parwal-260	Clonal selection	Fruits light green, striped, 13-15 cm long with thick flesh; yield 22.5 t/ha; tolerant to wilt
Narendra Parwal-307	Clonal selection	Fruits small, round shaped, dark green with strips; yield 22.5 t/ha; good shelf life
Narendra Parwal-604	Clonal selection	Fruits light green, without stripes; yield 22.5 t/ha
BCKV, Kalyani		
BCPG-3	Selection from local germplasm	Early; fruit light green with white alternate stripes; fruit length 7.30 cm, girth 3.5 cm & fruit wt. 34 g; yield 62 t/ha
BCPG-4	Selection from local germplasm	Early; fruit light green with white alternate stripes; fruit length 8.78 cm, girth 3.5 cm & fruit wt. 44 g; yield 60 t/ha
BCPG-5	Selection from local germplasm	Early; fruit light green with white alternate stripes; fruit length 9.5 cm, girth 3.5 cm & fruit wt. 46 g; yield 58 t/ha
Other varieties		
Dandali	Selection	Fruits medium-sized (6.84 cm x 3.89 cm), egg-shaped, light green, stock end dispersed, striped & slightly grooved towards distal end
Hilli	Selection	Fruits oblong (9.65 cm x 3.08 cm), greenish white, white striped & tapering towards distal end with dispersed neck
Shankolia	Selection	Fruits medium long (7.56 cm x 2.94 cm), resembling to those of "shankh or shell"; taper towards ends, greenish with white stripes, slightly beaked towards distal end & bulged towards stalk

Inheritance of characters:

- Stem pubescence (*sst*), stem shape (*rst*), tendril coiling (*stl*), tendril branching (*utc*), and pubescence (*plf*) are governed by single gene.
- Femaleness is due to lethal/ sub-lethal genes linked to female determining locus.
- Cytology of sex expression: Y chromosome plays strong role in determination of maleness.

Pests and diseases:

- Red brown beetle (*Carpophilus dimidiatus*) contributes appreciably to flower pollination.
- Fruit fly (*Dacus dorsalis*): Most destructive pest.
- Shoot and fruit rot: Soil borne fungi.
- CGMMV and CMV cause mosaic mottling on crop which is forced during winter months (November-February) in diara land.

16.14 Ash gourd

- Eulogized as 'White gourd or Wax gourd or Hairy melon or Winter melon or White pumpkin or Chinese preserving melon or Chinese water melon or Ash pumpkin'.
- Monoecious annual climber.
- Longest storage life, among cucurbits.
- Introduction to India from Japan and occurs in wild state in Indonesia (Java).
- Juice, seed oil and fruit rind has medicinal uses.
- It is good for people suffering from weak nervous system and debility.
- Tender leaves and buds are used as vegetable.
- Optimum soil pH: 5-7.5.
- Optimum temperature for growth and development: 24-30^{0}C.
- Short days, low night temperatures and humid climate are good for production of female flowers.
- Flowering starts 60-80 days after planting.
- Crop maturity period: 90-140 days.
- Immature fruits are harvested in a week after anthesis while mature fruits are harvested 30-40 days after anthesis.
- Resistant to water loss but susceptible to frost.
- Graft compatible with musk melon scion.
- Produce more pistillate flowers under short day, low night temperature conditions.
- An Ayurvedic medicine '*Kooshmanda rasayan*' is prepared from ash gourd.

- Sugar candy i.e. *Petha*: Famous sweet dried product prepared from young and mature fruit.
- Used in production of *cheddar* cheese.
- Two types: Purple green and green coloured.
- Pollination agent: Bees.
- Flower sex ratio (staminate to pistillate): 20:1 to 33:1.
- Anthesis time: 4.30-7.30 AM and closes at 5.30 PM.
- Anther dehiscence time: 3 to 5 PM.
- Seed rate: 5-7 kg/ha (5000 to 6000 plants/ha).
- Fruits at maturity have white flesh (generally spongy) with waxy ash surface.
- Annual hispid (rough) with bristle like hairs.
- Crop maturity: 90-140 days after sowing.
- Fruit set after hand pollination: 60-70%.
- Seed yield: 175 kg/ha.
- 100 seed wt.: 5 gram.
- Botanical varieties:
  1. Typical
  2. Emarginate
- Emarginate fruits lack the velvet testa and marginal band around the seed in typical form.

Varieties:

- Okinawa No. 1 and Kurokawa Early: Popular in Japan.
- Eklavya: Farmer's selection, resistant to yellow mosaic virus.
- Thudiyalur: Popular in Maharashtra.

Name	Breeding method	Remarks
IARI, New Delhi		
Pusa Urmi (2013)	Hybrid	Fruits oblong; yield 48 t/ha; suitable for canning (*petha* preparation)
Pusa Urmani	-	Suitable for canning (*petha* preparation)
Pusa Shreyali (2013)	Hybrid	Fruits cylindrical; yield (52 t/ha); suitable for canning (*petha* preparation)
Pusa Ujwal (2007)	Selection from indigenous material 'DAG-1'	1st improved variety; ideal for canning (*petha* preparation); yield 48-50 t/ha (kharif) & 41-42 t/ha (summer)
Pusa Shakti	-	Oblong fruits; suitable for canning (*petha* preparation)
Pusa Sabzipetha (2014)	-	Fruits cylindrical; yield (36.5 t/ha); suitable for kharif season

GBPUA & T, Pantnagar		
Pant Petha-1	-	-
IIVR, Varanasi		
Kashi Dhawal (2006)	Selection from local germplasm	Fruit wt. 11-12 kg; yield; 58-60 t/ha; suitable for *petha* making
Kashi Ujwal (2006)	Selection from local germplasm	Less seeds; suitable for canning (*petha* making); yield 60-61 t/ha
Kashi Surbhi	Distant hybridization	Suitable for canning
TNAU, Coimbatore		
CO.1 (1971)	Selection from local germplasm	Narrow sex ratio; crop period 140 days; fruit weight 6-8 kg; 6-8 fruits/vine; yield 25 t/ha; low seediness
CO.2 (1984)	Selection from local germplasm	Early maturing (120 days); light green flesh; small oval fruits weighing 2-3 kg; yield 20 t/ha; less seeds (200-300)
TNAU Ash gourd Hybrid-1	PAG -3 x CO. 2	Fruits are oblong & medium sized; yield 90 t/ha
Mudlier	-	Fruits pale green coloured
KAU, Vellanikara		
Indu (2001)	Mass selection from 'AG-1'	Round fruits; fruit wt. 4-5 kg; tolerant to mosaic
KAU Local (2000)	Single plant selection	Oval-oblong fruits; fruit length 45-55 cm; fruit wt. 6-8 kg
Thara	-	Small fruited; fruit wt. 2.5-2.7 kg; fruit length 25-28 cm, fruit width 13-15 cm; flesh thickness 3.1-3.3 cm; yield 18 t/ha
APAU, Hyderabad		
APAU Shakthi	Local selection	Long, cylindrical fruits
Other varieties		
Karikumbala	Local selection	Dark green fruits without ashy coat
Boodikumbala	Local selection	Dark green fruits with ashy coat

Diseases and pests:

- Fruit rot (*Fusarium semitectum* or *F. equiesti*):
- Fusarium wilt (*F. oxysporum*): Most serious.
- Anthracnose (*Colletotrichum lagenarium*): Serious and seed borne disease.
- Powdery mildew (*Sphaerotheca fuliginea* & *Erysiphe cichoracearum*)
- Downy mildew (*Pseudoperonospora cubensis*)
- Fruit fly and red pumpkin beetle: Polyphagous pest.

16.15 Ridge gourd

- Eulogized as 'Ribbed gourd or Angled loofah or Four angled gourd or Low cost vegetable.

- Trend of evolution in *Luffa* as given by Dutt and Roy (1971).
- Progenitor of cultivated smooth and ridge gourd spp.: Monoecious wild spp. *L. graveolens*.
- *L. hermaphrodita* originated from *L. graveolens*.
- All species are monoecious except *L. echinata* which is dioecious arose directly from *L. graveolens*.
- Both ridge gourd and sponge gourd are intercrossable.
- Gelatinous compound present in *Luffa* fruits is called as 'Luffein'.
- Contains 0.5% protein, 3-4% carbohydrate, 37 mg β-carotene, 18 mg vit. C/ 100 g edible portion.
- Commercially trained on kniffin system.
- Used in bathing sponge.
- Flower colour: Pale yellow.
- Anthesis time: Evening at 5-8 PM.
- Stigma receptivity: 6 h before to 84 h after anthesis.
- Bears only hermaphrodite flowers in cluster (5-6 fruits/ cluster).
- Node at which 1st hermaphrodite flower appear: 9th.
- Ratio of male to female flowers: 40:1.
- Seed rate: 4-5 kg/ha.
- Seed colour: Black.
- Both ridge gourd and sponge gourd are intercrossable.
- Optimum soil pH: 6-7.5.
- Optimum temperature for growth and flowering: 25-27^{0}C.
- NAA @ 200 ppm, ethrel @ 250 ppm increases female flower production.
- Fruits attain marketable maturity about 5-7 days after anthesis of female flower.
- Tenderness decides the edible maturity and not fruit size.

Characters	Ridge gourd	Smooth gourd
Sex form	Six [Monoecious (*AG*), androecious (*aG*), andromonoecious (A'*G*), trimonoecious (*ag*), gynomonoecious (*Ag'*), hermaphrodite (*ag, a'g, a'g', ag'*)]	Monoecious
Leaf	Shallowly lobed & larger in size. No white patches on leaf	Deeply lobed & comparatively smaller in size; white patches on leaf
Staminate flower	Smaller in size	Comparatively larger in size
Ovary shape	Disc shaped & not tomentose	Cylindrical & tomentose
Fruit shape	Angled & 10-ribbed	Smooth surfaced
Seed colour & shape	Black & pitted	Black, white flat & not pitted
Anthesis time	Afternoon	Early morning

Varieties:

Name	Breeding method	Remarks
IARI, New Delhi		
Pusa Nasdar	Selection from Madhya Pradesh	Early maturing; club shaped fruits; flowering starts in 60 days; more suited for rainy season; 15-20 fruits/ vine
Pusa Nutan	-	Fruits long (25-30 cm), straight; suitable for spring summer & kharif; yield 16 t/ha
Satputia	Cv. of Bihar	Hermaphrodite; fruits small, pale green & born in clusterof 5-7.
IIHR, Bengaluru		
Arka Sujata (1996)	Pedigree selection of (IIHR-54 x IIHR-18)	Resistant to DM; good transport value; yield 63-64 t/ha
Arka Sumeet (2001)	Pedigree selection of (IIHR-54 x IIHR-18)	Fruit wt. 38 g; slow seed maturity; yield 20-25 t/ha; suitable for year round cultivation
Arka Prasan	OP (inbred selection from IIHR-53)	Early (45 days for 1st picking), green; yield 26 t/ha
Arka Vikram	IIHR-6-1-1 x IIHR 53-1-3	Green, long; rich in anti-oxidants; yield 34 t/ha
IIHR-8	-	Round, green coloured fruits; fruit wt. 100 g; 45 fruits/vine; mod. resis. to DM; good for stuffing purpose
CIAH, Bikaner		
Thar Karni (2007)	Selection	Non-bitter; cylindrical fruits; fruit wt. 95 g; yield 14-15 t/ha; resistant to mosaic & melon fruit fly
IIVR, Varanasi		
Kashi Shivani	-	Yield 18-20 t/ha; mod. resistant to DM
Kashi Khushi	Single plant selection (OP landrace from kushinagar)	Hermaphrodite flower, cluster bearing, early maturing with light green fruit & ten dark superficial & continuous longitudinal ridges, yield (12.7 t/ha); highly suitable for spring, summer & kharif season; tolerant to DM & mosaic
ICAR Research Complex for Eastern Region, Patna (HARP, Ranchi)		
Swarna Sawani (2013)	Pure line selection from local germplasm	Satputia type; suitable for rainy season; fruit wt. 35-45 g; yield 20-25 t/ha; tolerant to PM & DM
Swarna Manjari (2006)	Hybridization followed by selection	Elongated; fruit wt. (175 g), highly ridged, greenish colour, pulp soft & contain less fibre; tolerant to PM; yield 18-20 t/ha
Swarna Uphar (2006)	Hybridization followed by pedigree selection	Elongated; fruit wt. (200 g), highly ridged, greenish colour, pulp soft & contain less fibre; yield 28-31 t/ha
Dr BSKKV, Dapoli		

Konkan Harita (1993)	Local selection from Panvel area of Maharashtra	Dark green fruits; 30-45 cm long; tapering at both the ends; fruit harvest at 45 days after planting; yield 15-20 t/ha
MPKV, Rahuri		
Phule Sucheta	Pure line selection	Fruits green; 33 cm long; yield 12 t/ha; fruit wt. 118 g; suitable for kharif & rabi; tolerant to DM
PAU, Ludhiana		
Punjab Sadabahar	Selection from 'Tori Jhing Dharidar'	Fruits long, 3-5 cm thick; green; ridged & slightly curved; rich in protein content
UAS, Dharwad		
DMRG-1	-	-
GBPUA & T, Pantnagar		
Pant Torai-1 (1999)	Pure line selection	Club shaped fruits; suitable for rainy season; yield 10 t/ha
TNAU, Coimbatore		
PKM-1 (1980)	Induced mutant to 'H-160'	Dark green fruits; fruit wt. 300 g; tolerant to red pumpkin beetle, fruit fly & PM; yield 28 t/ha
CO.1 (1976)	Selection from local germplasm	Fruits long (60-75 cm) ; 1st harvest 55 days after sowing; fruit wt. 300 g each; yield 25t/ha
CO.2 (1984)	Selection from local germplasm	Fruits very long (1 m) ; yield 25 t/ha
CO.H-1	F_1 hybrid	Very early to harvest (30-35 days); fruit green with soft pulp; fruit wt. 370-380 g; yield (35 t/ha)
CCSHAU, Hisar		
Hisar Kalitori (1995)	Selection	Tolerant to PM, suitable for rainfed areas; yield 8-10 t/ha
AAU, Anand		
GJRGH-1	-	Suitable for kharif season; yield 13 t/ha
Gujarat Anand Ridge Gourd-1	-	Less mosaic & DM incidence; yield 15 t/ha
JAU, Junagarh		
Gujarat Junagarh Ridge gourd hybrid-1	-	-
KAU, Vellanikkara		
Haritham (2001)	Local germplasm selection	-
Deepthi (2006)	Local germplasm selection	Fruit wt. 165 g; resistant to mosaic & DM; yield 30-33 t/ha
Surekha	-	-
CSAUA & T, Kanpur		
Kalyanpur Dharidar	-	-

Inheritance of characters:

- Roy and Dutt (1977) explained genetic mechanism of sex expression on the basis of 2 genes, *A* and *G* with multiple alleles. The genes *A, a, a'* and *G, g', g* control appearance of male and femaleness in the manner of *A-a'-a* and *G-g'-g*.

Character	Number of genes	Type of gene action
Seed surface	Monogenic (*PP*)	Pitted dominant to smooth
Flower node colour	Monogenic (*NN*)	Blue dominant to green
Sex form	2 independent suppresser genes	*A* (suppress male flower) & *G* (suppress female flower); Monoecious dominant to andromonoecious & hermaphrodite
Fruit bearing habit	Monogenic	Non-clustering habit is dominant over clustering habit
Bitterness	Monogenic	Dominant
Corolla colour	Monogenic(*YY*)	Orange yellow dominant over lemon yellow
Fruit surface	Monogenic (*RR*)	Ridged surface dominant over smooth
Fruit taste	Monogenic (*BB*)	Bitterness dominant over non-bitterness
Stamen type	Monogenic (*FF*)	Partially fuse stamen dominant over free
Fruit number	-	Additive
Fruit length	-	Additive & non additive
Fruit girth	-	Non additive
Tomato leaf curl virus resistance	Monogenic	Resistance dominant to susceptible
Cytoplasmic male sterility	2 dominant genes	-

Pests and diseases:

- Red pumpkin beetle: Major problem at cotyledon stage to 2nd leaf stage.
- Mosaic virus.

16.16 Sponge gourd (syn. *L. aegyptiaca*)

- Eulogized as 'Towel gourd or Vegetable sponge or Smooth loofah or Dishcloth gourd or Rag gourd'.
- Sponge gourd contains higher protein and carotene than ridge gourd.
- Fibrous sponge has industrial uses (filters in oil engine, insoles of sandles, door mats, insulator in helmet, bath sponge).
- Renewable source of bio-diesel.
- Fruits are harvested at tender stage.
- Fruit is fleshy and many seeded 'pepo'.
- Flower colour: Deep yellow.
- Strictly monoecious crop.
- Female flowers borne single while male flowers appear in cluster and one male flower open at one time.

- Anthesis time: Morning hours (4-8 AM).
- Ratio of male to female flowers: 25: 1.
- Seeds are white and flat.
- Seed rate: 2.5-3.5 kg/ha.

Varieties:

Name	Breeding method	Features
IARI, New Delhi		
Pusa Chikni (1975)	Selection from Bihar collection	15-17 fruits/ vine; yield 20-23 t/ha
Pusa Supriya (1997)	Selection from indigenous material	Fruits pale-green; 10-12 fruits/vine; fruit wt. 110 g; yield 13-14 t/ha; suitable for kharif & summer season
Pusa Sneha (2004)	Selection from indigenous material	Suitable for long distance; yield 20-23 t/ha
Pusa Shrestha (2018)	-	-
IIVR, Varanasi		
Kashi Divya	Selection from local landrace	Tolerant to high temperature, leaf miner, fruit fly & red pumpkin beetle; high TSS; yield 25 t/ha
Kashi Saumya (2018)	Hybrid	Fruits green, long straight (20-25 cm); yield 18-20 t/ha; resistant to Sponge Gourd Mosaic Virus & tolerant to DM & PM
Kashi Jyoti (2018)	Hybridization followed by selection	First male and female flower appear at node number 5-10 and 14-20; fruits light green, long straight; yield 14-18 t/ha; resistant to Sponge Gourd Mosaic Virus; tolerant to DM & PM.
Kashi Rakshita (VRSGH-1) 2018	Hybrid	Fruits dark green, long straight (20-25 cm); yield 20-25 t/ha; resistant to Sponge Gourd Mosaic Virus & DM.
Kashi Shreya (VRSG-194) 2018	Selection from germplasm of eastern Uttar Pradesh	Fruits dark green, long straight (20-25 cm); Fruits are harvested in 50-55 days after sowing; yield 15-20 t/ha; resistant to Sponge Gourd Mosaic Virus & DM.
VRSG-1-17 (2019)	-	Possess typical aroma of 'basmati rice' in plant parts & retains its special aroma even after cooking; yield (1.375 kg / plant); tolerant to DM, Sponge Gourd Mosaic Virus; melon weevil & leaf miner
CIAH, Bikaner		
Thar Tapish (2018)	Hybrid of 'AHSG-4 x AHSG-16'	Dark green fruits; yield (9-13 fruits/plant & 14-15 t/ha)
ICAR Research Complex for Eastern Region, Patna (HARP, Ranchi)		
Swarna Prabha (2006)	Pure line selection	Fruit wt. 150-200 g; tolerant to PM, DM & resistant to leaf miner; yield 20-25 t/ha
MPKV, Rahuri		
Phule Prajakta (1999)	Selection from local germplasm	Fruits green, straight, flesh white & dark green sutures; yield 13-15 t/ha

Phule Komal	Selection	Green, cylindrical fruits; fruit wt. 110 g; mod. resistant to PM, DM, fruit fly, leaf miner, white fly & thrips
Dr BSKKV, Dapoli		
Konkan Ghosali (2016)	-	-
CSAUA & T, Kanpur		
Azad Toria Chikni-1 (2006)	Selection	Profuse fruiting; yield 18-20 t/ha
Azad Toria Chikni-2	Selection	Yield 14-16 t/ha
Kalyanpur Hari Chikni (1983)	Selection	Early; suitable for rainy season; yield 18-20 t/ha
Rajendra Nenua-1	-	-
VR-01	-	-
AAU, Anand		
Gujarat Sponge Gourd-1 (2005)	Selection	Mod. Tolerant to DM & leaf miner; yield 12-14 t/ha

Inheritance of characters:

- Resistance to yellow mosaic virus: Monogenic dominant.

16.17 Pumpkin

- Eulogized as 'National vegetable of India or White Squash or Winter crook neck squash or Vegetable of immense value or Field pumpkin or Tropical pumpkin or *Lal kaddu* or *Kashiphal*'.
- The botanical characteristics of the pumpkin and squash species are not followed in distinguishing pumpkins and squashes.
- Pumpkins and squashes are annuals and trailing vines with tendrils.
- Annual per capita consumption of squashes & pumpkins in USA is 0.22 kg (for processed products only).
- Introduced from South America.
- World Pumpkin Day: 29th September.
- European festival 'Halloween' is celebrated annually with pumpkins only.
- Nutritive value of pumpkin (2.68) is higher than brinjal (2.41), tomato (2.09) and cucumber (1.69) because of stored carbohydrates and carotenoids.
- Nutrition score: 84.
- Vitamin A: 1600 IU
- Pumpkin contain highest amount of iron (15 mg/100g).
- Flowers are more mutritious than fruits.
- Flowers contain vit. C, folic acid, and calcium and hence used for vegetable purpose.
- Fruits have diuretic and vermicidal action and effective against diabetes.

- Its leaves, tender stems are also cookied and consumed.
- Yellow or orange flesh is delicious and used in preparing sweets, candy or fermented into beverages.
- All squash and pumpkin seeds are edible & nutritious (they are rich in proteins & oils).
- Calorific value of seeds: 559 Kcal/ 100g.
- Pumpkins have high storage carbohydrate mainly glucose and carotenoids (74% β-carotene).
- Varieties of musical instruments are prepared using variable sizes of fruits.
- Pumpkin festival celebrated at Ludwigsburg palace, Stuttgart, Germany for preparation of human's facial structures.
- On each 31st October, in European countries (Britain and Ireland), 'Halloween' festival is celebrated by preparing variety of products
- 'Giant pumpkin regatta' is annual water race held every year in October in West Coast, USA and Nova Scotia, Canada.
- Odisha state contributes 85% area and 90% production.
- Day neutral and frost tolerant cucurbit.
- Monoecious climber with hard and tough rind and smooth surface.
- Pumpkin is edible fruit of any species of *Cucurbita*, used when ripe as table vegetable or in pies.
- Squash indicates fruit eaten as raw as immature fruit or consumed for mature seeds or for baking products.
- Squash crop do not tolerate below freezing temperature.
- Gynodioecism is artificially synthesized in buffalo gourd.
- No inbreeding depression is observed.
- Source of CMS has not been found in *Cucurbita*.
- Male sterility eliminates need for emasculation.
- Self pollination is possible in *Cucurbita*.
- Male flowers are large, showy, yellow coloured, and less in number compared to other cucurbits.
- 'Channel and hill' system of cultivation is most useful for higher yield.
- Cloudiness favours production of pistillate flowers.
- Pollination agent: Honey bee.
- Anthesis and anther dehiscence starts at 4 AM & complete by 5-6 AM.
- Flower remains open up to forenoon only and close by noon.

- Stigma receptivity: On day of anthesis.
- Retention of only one fruit/ vine shows superior performance.
- Male to female flower ratio: 5: 1 to 20: 1.
- Seed rate for zaid crop: 4-5 kg/ha.
- Short day, low temperatures (18-300C), high humidity are ideal for cultivation.
- High nitrogen under high temperature conditions promotes maleness in flowering resulting in low fruit set and low yield.
- Optimum soil pH: 5.5-6.8.
- Optimum soil temperature for seed germination: 30-35^{0}C.
- Days taken for seed emergence: 5-10.
- For off season cultivation (late winter & early spring season) in plains, nursery is raised in polyhouse during winter.
- Isolation distance: Foundation (1500 m), certified (1000 m).
- Male and female parent can be grown in 1: 3 ratio.
- One bee hive / acre is placed when female flowers appear.
- Yerusseri or Erissery: Traditional recipe of Kerala is made from immature fruits.
- Sweet pie (*pumpkin halwa*) and pumpkin ketchup are made with mature fruits.
- Seed kernel (*magaz*) widely used in confectionary.
- Seed treatment with boron @ 4 ppm for 20 h increases fruit carotenoids and ascorbic acid content.
- Ethrel @ 250 ppm increases female flower production.
- Fruits reach maturity 75-180 days after sowing depending on variety and season.
- Single fruit produce 40-50 kg seeds and about 1600 fruits are harvested per acre.
- Number of fruits/ plant: 1-6.
- Average fruit wt. 1.5 to 40 kg.
- Seed produced from 1 ha is sufficient for cultivation of 70-80 ha.
- Seed yield: 250 kg/ha.
- 100 seed wt.: 12 gram.
- Fruits can be stored for 4-6 months in ventilated chambers.
- Fruits are cured for 10 days at 26.6-29.4^{0}C and 80% R.H.
- Pumpkins and winter squashes require warm temperature and dry conditions during storage.

Species:

- Most *Cucurbita* species are originated in Mexico.
- Xerophytic spp.: *C. digitata* (black coloured seeds), *C. palmata*, *C. cylindiata*.

- Mesophytic spp.: *C. ficifolia, C. sororia*.
- Both wild and cultivated species have same chromosome number (2n=40).
- Squashes and pumpkins can be crossed with musk melons, water melons and cucumbers.
- *C. lundelliana* is cross compatible with all species of genus *Cucurbita*.
- *C. moschata*, *C. pepo*, *C. maxima*, *C. mixta*, *C. ficifolia* are cross compatible with each other.
- Cross incompatibility is present between *C. foetidissima* & *C. maxima*, *C. pepo* and *C. moschata*.
- Colchicine amphidiploidy is used to combat sterility in the crosses between *C. maxima* x *C. moschata*.
- Genes for good fruit quality/ other desirable traits & insect resistance of *C. moschata* can also be transferred to *C. pepo* by three way cross.
- Crosses with *C. moschata* cv. Butternut can be easily made with *C. pepo* cv. Scallop.
- Embryo culture: Interspecific hybrids have been developed in crosses *C. moschata* x *C. pepo* (Wall, 1954); *C. pepo* x *C. ecuadorensis* (Washek, 1982); *C. pepo* x *C. martinezii*.
- Pearson *et al.* (1951) used colchicine induced amphidiploidy to combat the problem of sterility in crosses of *C. maxima* x *C. moschata*.
- Interspecific hybrids between *C. moschata* (cv. Butternut) x *C. maxima* (cv. Buttercup) show heterosis for female sex expression & yield.
- Resistance to bacterial wilt is more common in genus *Cucurbita* than in other genera of Cucurbitaceae.

Variation of fruit character in *Cucurbita*:

Fruit	Cultivated species	Wild species
Size	Large (0.45-146.5 kg)	Small (0.17- 0.25 kg)
Shape	Globular, oval, bell, pyriform	Round, oval, pyriform
Exterior	Usually grooved	Smooth
Shell	Moderately hard at maturity, non-durable	Hard at maturity
Skin colour	Various, mostly solid colours	Usually green with stripes or mottling, yellowish at maturity
Flesh	Non-stringy; orange, white or creamy white	Stringy, white, yellowish or greenish
Taste	Non-bitter	Bitter
Seeds	Large (comparatively few)	Small, many

Common name	Botanical name	Features
Fig leaf gourd/ Malabar gourd	*Cucurbita ficifolia*	Cultivated; perennial; monoecious; photosensitive; very late to flower; requires short days for flowering; widest natural distribution among all cultivated *Cucurbita* spp.; black seeds; cold tolerant; grows best in temperate climate; used as commercial rootstock for cucumber for field pollination; resistant to bacterial wilt
Field pumpkin	*C. moschata*	Cultivated; amphidiploid (2n=4x=40); trailing habit; long internodes; edible fruit of any species of *Cucurbita* utilized when ripe as table vegetable; used as bridging species between wild & cultivated species; eaten as mature & immature fruit; fruits 3-5 ridged; resistant to Squash bug & Squash Vine borer
Summer squash	*C. pepo*	Cultivated; growth bush type; eaten as immature fruit; short internodes; fruits 5-8 ridged; resistant to bacterial wilt, squash bug
Winter squash	*C. maxima*	Cultivated; growth trailing type; long internodes; fruits round, eaten as mature & immature fruit;resistant to fruit fly, bacterial wilt but highly susceptible to squash bug & Squash Vine borer
Buffalo gourd	*C. foetidissima*	Xerophytic; perennial; rich in protein& oils; its large storage roots is good source of carbohydrates; useful for development of gynoecious line;grows wild in arid dessert; produce abundant seeds; highly resistant to drought, PM & viruses (WMV-1, WMV-2 & CMV)
Peten gourd	*C. lundelliana*	Xerophytic; perennial; wild & found in Mexico; resistant to PM, bacterial wilt; used as bridging species in interspecific gene transfer involving *C. pepo*, *C. maxima*, *C. mixta*, *C. moschata*.
-	*C. okechobeensis* (syn. *C. martinezii*)	Xerophytic; annual; closely related to cultivated spp.; highly resistant to PM, CMV, BYMV
-	*C. ecuadorensis*	Used for development of disease resistance to viruses (WMV-1, WMV-2, CMV & BYMV)

Varieties:

- Butternut: Selection from population of Canadian crookneck developed by private seed company in Boston in 1936. It is used as a bridge, to transfer PM & CMV disease resistant genes from *C. martinezii* to *C. pepo* by three way cross (Munger, 1981.)
- Butternut No. 23: Resistant to pickleworm. Fruits contain more galacturonic acid which imparts resistance.
- Exotic cultivars: Large Cheese, Sugar Cheese, African Belt, Crown, Cushaw, Baby Delica, Blue Kierj.

Name	Breeding method	Features
IIHR, Bengaluru		
Arka Chandan (1990)	Selection from local material 'IIHR-105-1-1'	Pleasant aroma; highest β-carotene content (3331 IU/100 g); yield 33 t/ha
Arka Suryamukhi (1984)	Selection from local collection	Fruit round with flat end; flesh orange-yellow; fruit wt. 1 kg; 1st variety resistant to fruit fly; yield 34 t/ha
IARI, New Delhi		
Pusa Biswas (1990)	Local selection from line 'SM-107'	Light brown fruit, deep golden yellow flesh & 5 kg wt.; yield 40-42 t/ha
Pusa Vikas (1985)	Selection from local germplasm	Dwarf; rich in vit. A; suitable for spring summer season; yield 30 t/ha
Pusa Hybrid-1 (1996)	Heterosis breeding of 'Sel. 107 x Sel. 124'	1st hybrid available for commercial cultivation; flesh deep golden yellow & ready for picking in 100 days; yield 52 t/ha
Sel. 124	Individual plant selection	Suitable for home gardening
IIVR, Varanasi		
Kashi Harit (2006)	Pedigree selection from (NDPK-24 x PKM)	Green fruit production during kharif & rabi season; highest β-carotene content (3.14 mg/100g); takes 85-92 days from seed sowing to seed maturity; seed yield 30-35 t/ha
Kashi Shishir (2018)	Hybrid	Crop duration 100 days; fruit colour mottled green; flat round shape, size small (2-2.25 kg); yield 40-45 t/ha
CIAH, Bikaner		
Thar Kavi	Hybridization followed by selection of (CM16 x CM19)	Fruit wt. 900 g; yield 7-8 kg/ plant; suited for rainfed, semi-arid situation; mod. resistant to fruit fly, PM, pumpkin mosaic virus
ICAR Research Complex for Eastern Region, Patna (HARP, Ranchi)		
Swarna Amrit (2009)	Pure line selection	Dark green fruits; fruit wt. (2.5-3.0 kg); yield 50-60 t/ha
AAU, Anand		
Anand Pumpkin-1	Selection from local area	High TSS; flesh deep yellow coloured; yield 25 t/ha
NDUA & T, Faizabad		
Narendra Agrim (2006)	Selection	Suitable for summer crop; mature in 55 days; yield 30-40 t/ha
Narendra Amrit (2006)	Selection	Suitable for summer crop, mature fruit weight 5-6 kg
Narendra Abhooshan	Selection	Yield 70 t/ha
NDPK-224	Selection	-
TNAU, Coimbatore		
CO.1 (1971)	Selection from local germplasm	Fruits globular, large sized (8-10 kg); yield 30 t/ha
CO.2 (1978)	Selection from local germplasm	Fruits small (1.5 kg); TSS 3.4%; suitable for HDP; yield 45-47 t/ha
KAU, Vellanikkara		
CM-14 (1987)	Selection from local germplasm	Flat round shape; green colour; high yield

Ambili (1988)	Selection from local germplasm	Spreading habit; leaves have white spots on upper surface of lamina; fruit wt. 6 kg each; yield 34-36 t/ha
Suvarna (1998)	Single plant selection from 'CM-349'	Medium sized flattended fruits; orange coloured thick flesh; yield 37 t/ha
Sooraj (2003)	Selection	Thick flesh; yield 35-40 t/ha
Saras (2006)	Selection from local germplasm	Fruits orange fleshed; fruit wt. 3 kg; yield 35-40 t/ha
CSAUA & T, Kanpur		
Azad Pumpkin-1 (2006)	Selection	Less seeds; yield 42-45 t/ha
Dr YSPUH & F, Solan		
Solan Badami	-	Early & prolific bearer; fruits orange coloured & yellow flesh; fruit wt. 2-4 kg; good keeping quality; fruiting starts 100-120 days

Disease and disorder:

- Pumpkin mosaic virus: Transmitted by mechanical means, grafting and aphids.
- Sunscald: Due to hot and dry winds.
- Downy mildew: Spray Mancozeb @ 1 g/liter or Saaf @ 0.5 g/litre.
- Powdery mildew (*Sphaerotheca fuliginea*): Spray Karathane @ 0.5 g/litre or Difenoconazole @ 0.5 g/litre.
- Cucumber mosaic virus:
- Bacterial wilt (*Erwinia tracheiphila*):

Inheritance of characters:

- Non-additive gene action for vine length, number of laterals, nodes of first staminate and pistillate flowers, days to 1st staminate and pistillate flower, number of seeds/ fruits, 100 seed weight and seed size index.
- Over dominance and dominance for fruit weight.
- Over dominance for vine length, fruit number/ plant, flesh thickness, fruit shape index and fruit yield/ plant.
- Over dominance gene action for all nutritional traits i.e. TSS, carotenoids, ascorbic acid, Ca and Fe content.
- Sex forms in cucurbits:
  a) Ubiquitously monoecious.
  b) Gynoecious sex form in *C. pepo* and *C. maxima*.
  c) Single dominant gene controlling monoceious sex expression in *C. foetidissma*.
- Back cross method is mainly followed for resistance breeding.
- Positive correlation between flesh thickness and weight of fruit.

- Positive correlation between β-carotene and fruit diameter and vit. C and dry matter content of fruit.
- No inbreeding depression is observed.
- Eisa and Munger (1966) discovered inheritance of male sterility in cv. Eskandarang introduced from Egypt in 1962.
- Plants with silver leaf escape virus infection.

Character	Number of genes	Type of gene action
Naked kernel (absence of tough seed coat)	Pair of recessive genes	-
Fruit colour	Monogenic (*M*/*dg*)	Mottled light dominant over dark green
Silver leaf mottling	Partially dominant gene; conditioned by 2 genes or single gene *M*	Dominant over non-mottled leaf & modified genes affected its expression
White fly induced silver leaf disorder	Monogenic dominant	-
Fruit fly resistance	Monogenic (*F*)	Resistance dominant over susceptibility
YVMV resistance	Monogenic	
Zucchini Yellow Mosaic virus resistance	Monogenic (*Zym*) or 2 closely linked genes	Dminant with additive gene action
Water melon Mosaic virus (WMV) resistance	Monogenic (*Wmv*)	Resistant dominant over susceptible
Cucumber Mosaic virus (CMV) resistance	Monogenic (*Cmv*)	Resistant dominant over susceptible
CMV resistance in *C. pepo*	Digenic	Unlinked recessive genes
Papaya Ring Spot virus (PRSV) resistance	Monogenic recessive (*prv*)	-
PRSV resistance in *C. ecuadorensis*	Polygenic	With additive gene action
Pumpkin Mosaic virus resistance	Monogenic recessive	
Yellow Vein Mosaic resistance	Monogenic	Resistant dominant over susceptible
Powdery mildew (PM) resistance in *C.lundelliana*	Monogenic	Resistant dominant over susceptible
PM resistance in *C. martinezii*	Monogenic	Major gene showing partial dominance & influence of a modifier minor gene
Herbicide (Trifluralin) tolerance	Dominant (*TT*)	-
Male sterility	Monogenic recessive	-

16.18 Summer squash/ Zucchini

- Eulogized as 'Bushy gourd or Bushy cucurbit or Bush squash or Ornamental cucurbit or Vegetable marrow or *Chappan kaddu*'.
- Terminology of summer squash and winter squash bears no relation to the season when they are grown but rather to the state of maturity of fruit when utilized.
- Develops bushy plants, shorter internodes and tendrils are absent.

- Squashes and pumpkins are difficult to transplant and crops are direct seeded.
- Ancient crop of America.
- World leaders in production: USA, China, Russia, Italy.
- Fruits used for cotrolling hypertension.
- Fruits are eaten in immature stages when the rinds are very soft.
- Growing tips and flowers are also consumed.
- Popular group: Zucchini (USA and Italy) and Courgettes (UK).
- Cultivated species can be distinguished on the basis of trichomes, stem & peduncle characters.
- Six types on the basis of colours & shapes:
  1. Green zucchini: Most popular in market. Cylindrical shaped, light green to dark green coloured fruits similar to cucumber. More demand in hotels than yellow coloured
  2. Yellow/ Golden zucchini: Golden coloured cylindrical shaped fruits, soft &sweeter in taste.
  3. Rounded zucchini: More popular in European market due to unusual round shaped fruit.
  4. Costato Romenesco zucchini: Famous in Italy. Lighter pink or brownish green coloured fruits; thin & soft skin.
  5. Crook necked zucchini: Oldest cv. among yellow squash, contain more carotenoids.
  6. Zephyr squash: Hybrid crook necked type is easily idenfiable due to its bicoloured nature with softest stalk end than Summer Squash.
- Progenitor of Summer Squash: *C. fratena.*
- Earliest summer vegetable appears in market.
- Crop duration: 90-95 days.
- Nowadays, they have been specially bred to be harvested at 10 cm long.
- Fruits do not store well and perishable in nature.
- Edible portion: Pericarp.
- Mature fruits become very hard and unfit for consumption.
- Main bitter substance: Cucurbitacin E (Tetracyclic triterpenes).
- Can withstand lower temperature than other *Cucurbita* spp.
- Optimum soil pH for growth: 5.5-6.7.
- Anthesis time: 3.30-4.0 AM.
- Anther dehiscence: 9 pm to 3 AM.
- Pollination agent: Honey bee, gourd or squash bees (*Peponapis* spp. & *Xenoglossa* spp.).
- Seed rate: 1.5-2 kg/ha.

- Vine tip cutting for green house propagation.
- Planting distance: 3-5 feet (bush type); 5-8 feet (vine type).
- High or low N fertilization increases percentage of male flowers.
- Planting season: June-July (kharif), October-November (rabi).
- Seed sowing depth: 1.5-2.5 cm.
- Seedlings raised in plastic trays perform better than dibbling of seeds.
- Planting of maize/ marigold around zucchini is recommended.
- Green house production is better for off season planting.
- Optimum temperature for growth: 25-35^{0}C and soil temperatureis 21^{0}C.
- Optimum temperature for seed germination: 21-35^{0}C with minimum of 15.5^{0}C and maximum of 37.7^{0}C.
- High cool temperature during sowing affects seed germination.
- Planting to harvest time: 12-14 weeks.
- Harvesting stage:
  - Usually 2-8 days after anthesis (40-60 days after planting);
  - When fruits are immature and rinds are soft.
  - At 1/3rd maturity or 6-8 inch length (green); 4-6 inch length (yellow).
  - Elongated fruits are harvested when they are 4-8 inch long & 2 inch in diameter.
  - Scallop squashes are harvested when 3-4 inch in diameter.
- Crop requires multiple harvesting.
- Yield: 30-40 fruits/ plant; 8-15 t/ acre; 20 t/acre (green house production).
- Fruits do not store well.
- Number of seeds/ 100 g: 600.
- Seeds continue to mature in fruit even after harvest.
- Sensitive to stagnant water.
- MH (100 ppm) suppresses male flowers in female parent lines.
- Ethephon @ 250 ppm or 2 application of 400-600 ppm promote pistillate flowers.
- L.C. Curtis (1939) proposed manual defloration (i.e. removal of male buds by hand from female parent of hybrid) to permit use of open pollination method for seed production.
- Marrow seeds show certain amount of dormancy which can be eliminated after ripening of seeds for 1-2 months.
- Inbreeding depression cause reduced seed yield.
- Ethephon @ 400-600 ppm is used in hybrid seed production, which prevents development of male flowers.
- Seeds of squash cultivars are preserved in National Seed Storage Laboratory, Fort Collins, Colorado.

Varieties:

- These types include Yellow summer squash (crook necks & straight necks), Scallop squash and zucchini.
- In few varieties, 1st fruit is either deformed or black coloured.
- Bush type growth: Table Ace, Table King.
- For edible seeds: Emerald, Lady Godiva, Eat All.
- Free from crookneck rogue: Waltham Butternut, New Hampshire Butternut, Butternut Ponca.
- Golden Delicious: Rich in β-carotene content.
- Kitchenette Hubbard: Inbred selection from Hubbard Squash.
- Black Zucchini: High cucurbitacin content than cv. Early Golden Bush Scallop (Shanma and Hall, 1971).

Name	Breeding method	Features
IARI Regional station, Katrain		
Early Yellow Prolific (1975)	Introduction	Early maturing, bushy; dark green fruits; highly productive; yield 25-27 t/ha
Australian Green	Introduction from Australia	Fruits 25-30 cm long, very tender & delicious; suitable for late Jan-Feb
Pusa Alankar	Heterosis breeding of (Austalian Green x Yellow Prolific)	Earliest to come to market; dark green fruits; taper towards stem end; fruits 20 cm long
Pusa Pasand	-	-
Pusa Shreyash (DS-17) 2020	-	Yield 20-22 t/ha in winter season under polyhouse
IIHR, Bengaluru		
Patty Pan (1986)	Introduction from USA	Short duration; bush type, white disc shaped fruits; yield 55-57 t/ha; perform well in river bed (70 t/ha) & field (50 t/ ha)
Green Hubbard	Introduction from USA	Bush type, white disc shaped fruits
Golden Hubbard	Introduction from USA	Bush type, white disc shaped fruits
IIVR, Varanasi		
Kashi Shubhangi (2018)	Hybrid	Medium maturing; bushy; fruit colour dark green, elongated shape; size medium (800-900 g); yield 600-650 q/ha
PAU, Ludhiana		
Punjab Chappan Kaddu-1 (1983)	Inbred selection from segregating material	Resistant to DM, red pumpkin beetle & tolerant to CMV; yield 30-32 t/ha
CCSHAU, Hisar		
Hisar Selection	-	-
Other varieties		
Freedom	Transgenic	Yellow crook-neck; resistant to watermelon mosaic virus-2 & zucchini yellow mosaic virus
Yankee	Hybrid	Double number of fruits & 3 times more wt. than either parents

Inheritance of characters:

- Inbreeding depression for seed yield is reported.
- Gynoecious sex expression by gene *G* in *C. foetidissima*.
- Naked seed: Monogenic recessive (*nn*).
- Bi-coloured gourd (*C. pepo* var. *ovifera*): Gene *B* produces deep golden fruit colour.Gene *B* controls bicolour in flesh and in presence of *B* in different backgrounds reduces fruit size and rind hardiness.

Character	Number of genes	Mode of inheritance
Andromonoecious condition	Monogenic	Recessive (Kubicki, 1970)
Male sterility in *C. pepo*	Monogenic	Recessive (Eisa and Munger, 1968)
Male sterility in *C. maxima*	Monogenic	Recessive (Scott and Riner, 1946)
Bush habit	Monogenic (*Bu*)	Incompletely dominant to vine habit
Silvering of leaves	Monogenic (*M*)	Modifier genes
Resistance to PM	Monogenic	Resistance dominant to susceptibility
Presence of band on inner side of petal base	Monogenic (*Gb*)	Green band dominant to non-band
Placenta colour	Monogenic (*Ygp*)	Yellow green dominant to yellow
Fruit surface	Monogenic (*Wt*)	Warty dominant to smooth
Resistance to Squash bug	Trigenic	-
Resistance to Striped cucumber beetle (*Acalymma vittatum*)	Polygenic	Partially dominant over susceptibility
Resistance to Spotted cucumber beetle (*Diabrotica undecimpunctata*)	Dominant/ Polygenic	But not simply inherited
Total sugar content of squash cotyledons	Polygenic	-

16.19 Winter Squash (syn. *C. angyrosperma, C. maxima*)

- Eulogized as 'Turbon squash marrow or *Vilayati kaddu*'.
- They have flesh of mild flavour and fine texture and are suitable for baking.
- Used as table vegetable or as ingredient in pies.
- Mature fruits, flowers and leaves are used as vegetable.
- Grown mostly in hills and have vine growth habit.
- Monoecious, annual climber commonly grown in hills.
- Type of fruit: Inferior berry.
- Harvested in mature fruit stage when the rinds are hard (80-140 days after planting).
- They store well for use throughout the winter due to hard shell.
- Male sterility is used in hybrid seed production.

Varieties:

- Widely used for processing.
- Pink Banana: Selection from foreign introduction; resistant to fruit fly.
- Golden Delicious: Rich in carotene (11.5 mg/100g).
- Interspecific hybrids between (*C. maxima* x *C. moschata*): Alguri, Kikusui, Tetsakabuto.
- Emerald: Bush type & widely grown.
- Hard shelled types: Hubbard Squash, Butter Cup, Banana, Acron, Orange Marrow, Delicious.

Diseases and pests:

Name	Causal organism	Vector	Affected crop
Powdery mildew	*Erysiphe cichoracearum*	-	All cucurbits
Downy mildew	*Pseudoperanospora cubensis*	-	All cucurbits
Witches broom	MLOs	Leaf hopper	Bottle gourd
Green Mottle Mosaicvirus	Virus	Seeds	Cucumber
Bud necrosis	Virus	Thrips	Water melon
Fruit fly/ Melon fly	*Bactrocera cucurbitae*	-	Young plants
Red pumpkin beetle	*Aulacophora foveicollis*	-	Cotyledony leaf stage

Inheritance of character:

- Two or more genes determine growth habits, days from sowing to flowering, fruit colour, fruit weight & total solids in fruits (Singh, 1949).
- Resistance to fruit fly is not influenced by maternal effects. Resistance is dominant to susceptibility.

16.20 Chow chow

- Eulogized as 'Chayote or Poor man's vegetable or *Christophine* or *Choko*'.
- Introduced by Western missionaries.
- Columbus introduced this crop to West Indies Island and hence called '*Christophine*'.
- Monoecious, perennial spreading climber with large tuber roots.
- Holds promise in shifting/ *jhum* cultivation.
- Cultivated in hilly terrain having 100% slope, where no other crop cultivation is possible.
- Leading states in cultivation: Mizoram, Meghalaya.
- Iskut Growers Association in Mizoram manages marketing of Chow chow.
- Immense food and feed value for pigs in Mizoram.
- Fruits and seeds are rich in almost all amino acids.

- Starch from roots used in textile industry and making bio-degradable plastics.
- Only cultivated cucurbit in sub-family Sicyoideae.
- Wild form: *S. compositum*.
- Highest nutritive value among cucurbits in carbohydrates (6.3%) and low calorific value.
- Fruits contain TSS (2.4-6.2%), acidity (0.06-1.66%), ascorbic acid (9.36 to 24.68 mg/ 100 g), calcium (17-140 mg/ 100 g).
- Leaves: Large and shallow lobed.
- Unripe fruits, tender shoots and tendrils, young leaves, seeds and tuberous roots (starchy) are used as vegetables.
- Fruits can be used to supplement potatoes for diabetic patients. It is good for stomach ulcers.
- This versatile vegetable can be made into soups, boiled, candied, pureed or added to stews, curries and chutneys.
- Flesh stays firm after cooking. Seeds can be cooked in butter and tuber is eaten when tender.
- Flower light to cream-yellow in colour.
- Inflorescence is axillary racemose.
- Day length of 12 just over 12 hours for flowering.
- Both male and female flowers are produced in same leaf axil.
- Male flowers are peduncled in cluster (usually 4) and female flowers solitary.
- Vine starts flowering in about 3-4 months and production is continuous.
- Single seed is located near the broad end of pear shaped fruit.
- Fruit wt. (200-400 g), diameter (5-11 cm), length (10-20 cm).
- Fruit shape: Round to pear shaped, corrugated (with shallow longitudinal furrows), surface covered with or without soft spines.
- Fruit colour: Light yellow to dark green.
- Predominantly cross pollinated but self compatible.
- Pollination agent: Honey bee.
- Propagation method: By whole fruit is planted with narrow end protruding from soil.
- Single large seeded, flat (5 cm x 3 cm) fruit with viviparous germination.
- Planting is done in pits or basin at 1.8 m x 2.4 m.
- For true to type plants, stem cuttings (15-20 cm long) are used those are planted at 18^0C.

- Grown on mounds (30-40 cm high) and 90 x 90 cm apart.
- Optimum soil pH: 5.5-6.5.
- Highly sensitive to frost.
- Vines trained on permanent bower system, poles and trellis or 15 cm mesh netting.
- Pruning is practiced to improve light penetration.
- Fruit availability period: July-December (preferably during October-November).
- Tuberous roots available from 2nd year old crop during January-March.
- Duration of productive cycle: 5-8 years.
- Fruit reaches its maximum size 25-30 days after fruit set. I ı tropical climate, plants last for several years.
- Fruits ready for harvest 120 days after planting.
- 1 year plant may yield 500-600 fruits/ year.
- Storage: For a month at 10-15^{0}C with 85-90% R.H.
- Seeds show recalcitrant storage behaviour.
- Green rind (*Gr*) monogenic dominant to buff skin of mature fruit.
- **Varieties**: Ivory White, Round White, Long White, Pointed Green, Broad Green, Oval Green.

Pests and diseases:

- Root knot nematode:
- Red spider mite:
- Powdery mildew:
- **Genetics of characters**:
- Green rind (Gr) dominant to buff skin of mature fruit.

16.21 Ivy gourd (syn. *C. cordifolia*, *C. grandis*, *Ciphlandra indica*)

- Eulogized as 'Little gourd or Baby water melon or Scarlet gourd or *Tondli* or *Kundru*'.
- C_4 plant, semi-perennial, dioecious creeper with angular and lobed leaves.
- Tender leaves are used for making soup and curry.
- It controls skin disorders, bronchitis, fever and as trauma aid by villagers.
- Effective for lowering sugar content of diabetic patients.
- Immature fruits and tender shoots are used as vegetables.
- Flowers and fruits are formed abundantly during summer.

- Flower colour: White and open during night hours.
- Semi-hardwood cuttings (5-20 cm length and 1.5 cm dia.) from female vines are used.
- About 10% male plants should be planted for good fruit set.
- Vegetative parthenocarpy is noticed.
- In winter months, vines are pruned back.
- Pollen of pointed gourd (*Trichosanthes dioica*) induce greater fruit set (84%) in *Coccinia* than its own pollen.
- Survives best in calcareous soils having pH 8.5.
- Intergeneric cross between *C. indica* and *L. acutangula* is possible.

Varieties:

Name	Breeding method	Features
IIHR, Bengaluru (CHES, Bhubaneswar)		
Arka Neelachal Sabuja	Selection	Hardy; tolerant to bruising; high biomass; dark green with fractured stripe and conical in shape; 70-80 harvest per season (10-11 months); yield 20-25t/ha (30-35 kg/plant)
Arka Neelachal Khunkhi	Selection	Extra large fruits; soft texture; dual-purpose (salad & cooked); fruit wt. 15-20 g; yield 20-25 t/ha; 800 fruits/ plant/ season
IIVR, Varanasi		
VRK-20	Clonal selection	Very early bearing; light green striped fruits (6.0 cm length x 2.7 cm dia.); fruit wt. 20 g
VRK-31	Clonal selection	Fruits swollen in middle but pointed at upper portion; fruit wt. 25-30 g
VRK-35	Clonal selection	Highly striped fruits; fruit wt. 15-18 g
VRK-37	Clonal selection	Oval shaped fruits; fruit wt. 16 g
VRK-49	Clonal selection	Oval shaped fruits; fruit wt. 15 g
IIVRK-1	Clonal selection	Early maturing; fruits long striped; yield 25-30 t/ha
CIAH, Bikaner		
Thar Sundari (2018)	Clonal selection from local germplasm	Gynoecious & parthenocarpic; fruits ready in 6.28-8.42 days from opening of female flowers; yield 25-35 t/ha.
AHIG-1 (2019)	Selection	Parthenocarpic fruits; prolific bearer; yield 2.18-3.23 kg/plant/ season
IGKVV, Raipur		
Indira Kundru-05 (2006)	Clonal selection	Fruiting round the year; picking starts 75-85 days of vine cutting; suitable for table purpose; yield 102 t/ha; tolerant to stem borer, PM, frost & drought
Indira Kundru-35 (2006)	Clonal selection	Fruiting round the year; picking starts 75-85 days of vine cutting; suitable for table purpose; yield 94 t/ha; tolerant to stem borer, PM, frost & drought
Ac. No. 51	Clonal selection	Fruits light green, oval shaped; yield (21.20 kg/plant)

KAU, Vellanikara		
Sulabha (2006)	Clonal selection from local germplasm	Takes 37 days from planting to flowering; 1st harvest in 45-50 days after planting; long fruits & more than 20 g fruit wt.; yield 40-43 t/ha
TNAU, Coimbatore		
TNAU Coccinia CO.1	Clonal selection from 'Annaikatti'	Fruits less seeded; sweet taste; suitable for culinary purpose & salad; yield 50 t/ha

Inheritance of characters:

- 1st report on sex mechanism and sex chromosome was made by Kumar and Deodikar (1940), Chakravarty (1948) amd Kumar and Visweswariah (1952).
- Sex forms are due to presence of distinct sex chromosomes. Y-chromosomes influences expression of maleness.
- Fruit coat colour: Deep green dominant over green, yellow and white; green dominant over yellow and white; yellow dominant over white.

16.22 *Meetha karela*

- Eulogized as 'Stuffing cucumber or *Pahari karela*'.
- Annual and introduced from South Africa.
- Fruits bitterless.
- Monoecious, tolerant to frost.
- Fruits rich in Ca (14 mg) and P (14 mg).
- 8-10 seeds/ fruit.
- 4-6 green pickings possible.

Variety: UHF Meetha Karela-1.

17. DIOSCOREACEAE

17.1 Yam

- Minor tuber crops very oftenly grown as wild in Asian and African countries.
- West Africa is largest producer, accounting for 95% of total world production.
- Tuber is used for curing leprosy, piles and gynorrhea.
- Itchiness in tuber: Cells containing bundles of crystals (raphides).It can be reduced by slicing and boiling.
- Contain alkaloids, tannins & steroids which have pharmaceutical value.
- Anti-nutritional factors: Terpenoid, Calcium oxalates, Diosgenin, Stigma sterol, etc.
- Yams are rich in starch (18-20%) but poor in protein (1-2% of fresh wt.) content.
- Sugar present in yams: Sucrose.
- Calorific value: 182 MJ/ha/day (i.e. 87 MJ/ 100 g).

- Erratic flowering leads to non-synchrony of sexes and prevalence of polyploidy.
- Flowering season: Mid-September-end of November.
- Flowering duration: 12-20 days (within individual male clones); 5-10 days (within individual female clones).
- There are more male than female plants and also more male inflorescences.
- Male flowers are very small (2-4 mm dia.), inconspicuous, white, creamish to greenish in shade than female flowers. They are borne on axillary spikes/ panicles, contain more number of individual florets and droop downwards.
- Number of stamens: 6 in 2 whorls.
- Anthers are basifixed on short filaments.
- Pollen grains: Small & sticky.
- Anthesis & anther dehiscence in male flowers: Simultaneously at 12.30 h.
- Anthesis & anther dehiscence in female flowers: Simultaneously at 13.00-14.30 h.
- Male and female flowers emit strong scent upon anthesis.
- Stigma receptivity: Upto 6-7 days after anthesis.
- Ovary inferior, trilocular with 2 ovules in each locule and dehisce along with septum.
- Type of placentation: Axile.
- Seeds are small, light in weight, flat and winged to aid in wind dispersal.
- Stems in many species are armed with spines which protect them from wild animals and also assist in supporting on host plant.
- Simple leaf is typical to the genus but in *D. dumetorum* and *D. hispida* possess compound leaves having 3 or more leaflets and leaf lamina size varies from 50-200 cm^2.
- Flesh colours: White, cream, pink red or purple.
- True seeds and sexual progeny of *D. alata* exhibit wide range of variation in all characters and show enhanced flowering frequency and high sexual fertility.
- High rainfall is essential for maximum production.
- Better growth promotion at 26-31^{0}C and growth is restricted < 20^{0}C.
- Long day (>12 h) during initial stage favours vine growth while short day during later part of growing season favours bulbil production.
- Propagation by vine cuttings results in slow tuber production.
- Whole tuber is cut into seed pieces consisting of top (proximal, middle), and bottom (distal) part.
- Tops are preferred for earliness and uniform sprouting.

- Planting time: March-June.
- Planting distance and density: Greater yam (90 cm x 90 cm); Lesser yam & White yam (75 cm x 75 cm) with optimum density of 18,000 plants/ ha.
- Economic parts: Tuber, bulbils or rhizomes.
- Bulbils / tubercles (small aerial tuber) are small, round and have swellings in leaf axil i.e. bulbil originate from leaf axil. It is considered as an arrested state of tuber development.
- Size of bulbil: As large as 2 kg.
- Bulbils (main storage organ): Used as setts in cultivation.
- Minisett technology is standardized by CTCRI.
- Minisett: Tubers are cut into small cylindrical pieces of 5 cm length. From these, minisetts of 30 g weight are preferred.
- Ideal stage for transplanting minisetts: 3-4 leaves.
- Multiplication ratio by minisett technique: 1: 24 & that of traditional is 1: 4-6.
- Seed rate of minisetts/ ha: 34,000 @ 60 cm x 45 cm.
- Dry matter in peeled roots varies from 16-26% in different species.
- NPK @ 80:60:80 kg/ha is optimum for *D. esculenta*, *D. alata* and 120:60:80 kg/ha for *D. rotundata*.
- Yam flour is used for human consumption as 'kokonte' in West Africa.
- Yam tuber grows from a small corm structure located at base of stem and referred to primary nodal complex.
- In all edible yams, tubers are renewed annually.
- Bulkiness of tuber, high moisture content makes post-harvest handling more difficult.
- Trailing (staking) of vines is essential practice for higher yield.
- Tuber dormancy: Due to endogenous phenolic growth regulator.
- Tubers have long dormancy period (2-3 months), necessary for maximum yield.
- Longest storability after harvest (4-6 months).
- Gamma irradiation @ 7.5 Krad prolongs storage life for 6-8 months.
- Polarity influences sprouting.
- Ethylene chlorohydrine (4-8%) is used for enhancing early sprouting and taking crop earlier than normal season.
- NAA helps in sprouting while GA_3 inhibit sprouting.
- Soaking of yam in 0.1% (1000 ppm) Maleic hydrazide for 10 h delays sprouting in storage.

- Yam takes 30-40 days for sprouting and another 2 months to develop vegetative cover on ground.
- *In vitro* production of micro-bulbils from nodal segements is developed.
- In lesser yam, tuber grows from massive corm like structure located as base of vine.
- Yam tuber is neither a root structure nor stem structure but it originated as hypocotyl.
- Ideal seed (whole tuber) weight for optimum production: Greater yam (200-250 g setts); Lesser yam (100-125 g setts).
- Major constraints in breeding: Occurrence of different ploidy level, high sexual sterility; scarcity of flowering, non-synchrony in flowering of male and female phase, shy flowering, poor seed set, lack of seed production, vegetative propagation leading to less genetic variation, and stickiness of pollens.
- Bulkness of tubers and high moisture content make post-harvest handling more difficult.
- Curing of tubers minimizes storage losses.
- Tubers stored below 16^{0}C cause chilling injury.
- Mignouna *et al.* (2002) constructed genetic linkage map of white yam. Total map length 1.233 cM.

***Harvesting, handling & storage*:**

- Delayed harvesting up to 2 months does not affect yield.
    - Single harvesting: Harvesting done at any time. Practiced in India.
    - Double harvesting: Yams are amenable for double harvesting (removal of mother tubers after 2 months of growth & allowing for subsequent production of side tubers). 1st hearvesting done at mid season, about 4-5 months after emergence. Tuber is removed and soil is placed on roots. Plant forms 'retuberization' around the scar left left after 1st harvesting. When plant attains maturity at end of season, then 2nd harvest is done. Double harvesting is not economical compared to single harvesting. Practiced in African countries.

1. ***Greater yam*:**
    - Harvesting stage: 9-10 months after planting.
    - Tubers of greater yam can be stored for 4-6 months under ambient conditions.
    - Processed products of greater yam: Yam flakes, yam powder are popular in Africa. Fried chips & French fries can be prepared.
2. ***Lesser yam*:**
    - Harvesting stage: 6-7 months after planting.

- Tubers thin skinned & succulent & easily damaged during harvesting.
- Tubers can be stored for several weeks under ambient conditions (upto 4 months) without significant changes in biochemical constituents.
- Problems encountered on prolonged storage: Sprouting & weight loss (excessive dessication).

3. ***White yam***:
   - Harvesting stage: 7-8 months after planting.
   - One plant bears single tuber (2-5 kg. wt.)
   - Tuber skin: Brown & thick & flesh is white.
   - Storage upto 4 months under ambient conditions.
   - Fufu: Traditional yam food can be prepared.

Species:

- All *Dioscorea* species are perennial, dioecious & deciduous vines.
- Species in sections: *Lasiophyton* (*D. dumetorium*, *D. hispida*), *Opsophyton* (*D. bulbifera*), *Combilium* (*D. esculenta*), *Macrogynodium* (*D. trifida*).
- *D. villosa*: Wild yam.
- *D. bulbifera* (X=10 and 2n=80): Only edible species native to both Asia and Africa.
- West African varieties of *D. bulbifera* multiples of nine or ten i.e. 2n=36, 40, 54, 60.
- Temperate yam species: *D. deltoidea*, *D. japonica*, *D. opposita*.
- Three food yams of the world: *D. alata*, *D. esculenta*, *D. rotundata*.
- Bulbil bearing tropical yams: *D. alata*, *D. bulbifera*. Setts of these are used in cultivation.
- *D. esculenta*, *D. dumetorum*: Smaller starch grains than most of the yams.
- *D. esculenta* is sexually sterile and improvement is through introduction and selection.
- *D. esculenta* var. *spinosa*: More thorny.
- *D. esculenta* var. *fasiculata*: Less thorny.
- *D.composita*, *D. floribunda*, *D. purpurea*, *D. lanata*: Used for extraction of diosgenin drug on commercial basis. This drug is used for preparing oral contraceptives.
- Hybrids between wild and cultivated species are spontaneously formed.

Botanical name	Common name	Features
D. alata	Greater yam or True yam or Tropical yam or Chinese yam or Lisbon yam or Winged yam or Water yam or Larger yam or Ghorkand or White yam or *Ratalu* (allotetraploid i.e. male tetraploid (2n=40) & female 2n=60 & 80)	Monoecious; polymorphic & no wild forms;non-spiny stem; stem twines to right; tuber cylindrical; tuber skin black or brown; flesh white/ yellow/ purplish; each plant may produce 1-3 tubers; bears bulbils which is minor storage organ; most widely distributed species globally & main species grown in India. Purple pigmentation on stem & leaves are used to distinguish cultivars; flowering is erratic (overlapping male & female phases); female flowers earlier than male; male flowers borne in terminal and axillary panicles; susceptible to anthracnose
D. esculenta (syn. *D.fasciculata*)	Asiatic yam or Lesser yam or Sweet yam or Kangar	Early maturing & sweeterthan other species; tubershave smooth yellow-brownish skin with white flesh &borne in cluster of 15-35(small & spindle shaped tubers with round ends); white flesh
D. rotundata	White yam or African yam or Guinea yam (allotetraploid 2n=4x=40)	Stem twines to right direction without support; cylindrical tubers; white flesh; resistant to anthracnose
D. bulbifera	Air potato or Aerial yam or Potato yam or Turkey liver yam or Bulbil bearing yam	Single tuber; produce large number of bulbils which is main storage organ; used as wild vegetable in Konkan region & Western Ghats by tribal people during fasting days
D. nummularia	Pacific yam or Hard yam or Spiny yam or Wild yam	-
D. trifida (syn. *D. praehensilis*)	Cush-cush yam orAmerican yam or Yampi yam	Vine twines to left; small tubers; white flesh
D. cayanensis	Yellow guinea yam	Yellow flesh; rich in carotenoids
D. deltoidea	Nepal/ Indian yam	Found in forests of Jammu & Kashmir, Himachal Pradesh, Uttar Pradesh
D. pentaphylla var. *jacquemontii*	Five leaved yam or Mountain yam or Prickly yam or Fiji yam	Tender branches; flowers used as vegetable purpose
D. mexicana	-	Non-edible species; used in pharmaceutical industry
D. batatas (syn. *D. opposita*, *D. japonica*)	Cinnamon yam or Chinese yam or Japanese yam	Hardiest yam with heart shaped leaves; rich in carotenoids; vine twines to right; used for food & medicine; tolerate cold climate
D. hispida	Asiatic bitter yam or Intoxicating yam	Wild species; possess single tuber

Varieties:

- Widely adopted crop improvement method: Clonal selection.

Greater yam:

Name	Breeding method	Salient features
CTCRI, Thiruvananthapuram		
Sree Keerthi (1987)	Clonal selection from germplasm	Compact tuber shape & good cooking quality; stem & petiole colour of male clone is green coloured; tuber skin brown; flesh white; crop duration 280-300 days; yield 25-30 t/ha; highly resistant to root knot nematode
Sree Karthika (2004)	Clonal selection from germplasm	Yield 30 t/ha
Sree Roopa (1987)	Clonal selection from germplasm	Vigorous & purple stem; female clone produces 2-3 digitate smooth tubers; skin black & flesh white; 9 months duration; excellent cooking quality; yield 25-30 t/ha
Sree Shilpa (1998)	Intervarietal hybrid	1st & only hybrid variety; oval shaped tubers; white flesh early mature; 8 months duration; excellent cooking quality; yield 28 t/ha
Sree Swathy	Clonal selection from germplasm	White flesh; yield 30-40 t/ha; tolerant to drought & anthracnose
Sree Neelima	Clonal selection from germplasm	Purple flesh colour; bio-fortified variety
CTCRI Regional centre, Bhubaneshwar		
Bhu Swar (Da-25) 2013	OP Selection	Good cooking quality; starch (18.0-20.0%); total sugar (1.0-1.5%); yield 20-25 t/ha
CIARI, Port Blair		
Yamini	Clonal selection	Yield 45-50 t/ha; ideal as intercrop in the coconut & arecanut plantations; mod. tolerant to anthracnose & leaf spot diseases
KAU, Thrissur		
Indu (1998)	Clonal selection from 'TCR-5'	High yielding
Dr BSKKV, Dapoli		
Konkan Ghorkand (2002)	Selection from Konsai village	Erect growing; purple green colour stem; snow white tubers with purple tinge; yield 17.4 t/ha
OUAT, Bhubaneshwar		
Orissa Elite (2005)	Clonal selection	Tolerant to virus, leaf spot, scale insect, mealy bugs, cultivated under tree shade; yield 25 t/ha
Konuvari Aloo	Selection	-
TNAU, Coimbatore		
CO.1 (1999)	Clonal selection	Yield 45 t/ha; big with white flesh; tubers rich in carbohydrates

Lesser yam:

Name	Breeding method	Salient features
CTCRI, Thiruvananthapuram		
Sree Latha (1983)	Clonal selection (DE-11)	Crop duration 8 months; released 1st time in India; grayish brown skin; stem partially hairy; excellent cooking quality; used as snack; crop duration 220-240 days; yield 25 t/ha; highly resistant to root knot nematode
Sree Kala (1993)	Selection from African exotic collection	Early maturing (7 months); stem hairy with purple colour; brown skin; white flesh; crop duration 240-270 days; excellent cooking quality; yield 20 t/ha
Dr BSKKV, Dapoli		
Konkan Kanchan (1984)	Clonal selection	Tubers elongated; white & sweet taste; crop duration 110-210 days; yield 18 t/ha
OUAT, Bhubaneshwar		
Moa Aloo	Clonal selection	Excellent culinary quality

White yam:

- Da-11, Da-68: Field tolerance to anthracnose disease.
- Da- 119: Good tuber shape and excellent cooking quality.

Name	Breeding method	Salient features
CTCRI, Thiruvananthapuram		
Sree Shubhra (1987)	Selection from OP seeds of African cv. Iwo	Drought tolerant; 1-2 cylindrical tubers which are partly hairy; 9 months duration; excellent cooking quality; yield 35 t/ha
Sree Priya (1987)	Clonal selection from African cv. Umidika	2-3 tubers; leaf with wavy margin; 9 months duration; suitable as inter crop in coconut, rubber & banana gardens; yield 35 t/ha
Sree Dhanya (1993)	Clonal selection from African cv. I-184	Dwarf, bushy (30-50 cm height) male clone; no need of staking; male clone with cylindrical shape; brown skin & white flesh; yield 20 t/ha
CTCRI Regional centre, Bhubaneswar		
Drd. 657	Clonal selection	Good culinary quality
Drd 1038	Clonal selection	Dwarf; 51.70 t/ha
Drd-1157	Clonal selection	Highest tuber yield (73.20 t/ ha)
Drd-1118	Clonal selection	Yield (51.10 t/ha)
Drd-1095	Clonal selection	Yield (39.50 t/ ha)
Drd-9495	Clonal selection	Better cooking quality
Drd-1060	Clonal selection	Better cooking quality
Sd-15	Clonal selection	High yield coupled with excellent culinary quality

Genetics of characters:

- In *D. sinaata*, femaleness is controlled by 2A+ 2x and male by 2A+ x.
- Strong 'Y' chromosome is involved in sex determination.

Pests anddiseases:

- Scale insect (*Aspidiella hartii*) is important and serious pest in India. *D. hispida* and *D. bulbifera* are free from attack.
- Sucking pests are major problem in cultivation.
- Arecanut beetle: Storage pest.
- White spotted beetle (*Monolepta signata*):
- Yam tuber beetle (*Heteroligusbicolor* or *Galerucida bicolor*) and *Lema lacordairei*: Major pests that feed on leaves and shoot tips.
- White grubs (*Leucopholis coneophora*) attack roots and tubers.
- Root knot nematode causes malformation and reduction in tuber size.
- Dry rot: Due to nematode infestation.
- Anthracnose (*Colletotrichum gloeosporioides*): Most devastating disease of greater yam causing upto 70-80% loss.
- Growing maize as an intercrop reduces anthracnose incidence by 57-62%.
- Leaf spot (*Cercospora* spp.):
- Yellow mosaic virus.

18. EUPHORBIACEAE/ SPURGE FAMILY

- Tropical tuber crops are known as energy reservoirs of nature. They are called as 'crops of adversity'.
- Recognized as most efficient converters of solar energy into carbohydrates.
- As cheap energy producers, tuber crops meet food and nutritional security in warm humid tropics.
- 3rd most important food crops after cerelas & grain legumes.
- They form staple food of 1/5th of world population.
- Roots and tubers form staple food over 1 million people in developing world.
- CTCRI is recognized as national active germplasm site for tuber crops.
- Root and tuber crops can tolerate water logged conditions for 5 days.
- Root and tuber crops have high potential to trap atmospheric CO_2 and convert to dry matter.
- Root and tuber crops have highest rate of dry matter production per day.
- Important as vegetable & raw materials for industries like starch, sago, animal feed etc. and find application in food industry.

18.1 Cassava

- Eulogized as 'Tapioca or Yuca or Manioc or Mandioca or Poor man's food'.
- Believed to have been cultivated since at least 2500 BC.
- Term 'cassava' denotes roots of cassava plants.
- Term 'tapioca' denotes baked products of cassava flour.
- Major starchy root crop of tropics.
- Crop adaptability: Between 30^0N and 30^0S.
- It was introduced in India by Portuguese during 17th century at Kerala and popularized as 'subsidiary food crop'.
- Nigeria: Major country growing cassava 20% of world area and 20% of world production.
- Brazil is largest producer followed by Thailand, Nigeria, Zaire & Indonesia.
- India is 9th largest producer.
- Kerala (50%), Tamil Nadu (35%) and Andhra Pradesh (9%) contribute 93% area and 98% production in India.
- Average productivity of world: 12.84 T/ha.
- Average productivity in India: 27.92 T/ha (highest in the world).
- Maximum productivity: Kerala (38 T/ha).
- Thailand and India are main exporters of cassava starch in international market.
- Thailand & Indonesia: World's largest exporters of cassava pellets for livestock feeding.
- Commercial cassava industries are located in Salem (Tamil Nadu) and Smalkot areas (Andhra Pradesh).
- It is grown as rainfed crop in Kerala and Andhra Pradesh while as irrigated crop in Tamil Nadu.
- It is diploid (2n=36) but triploids (2n=54) and tetraploids (2n=72) are also available.
- Tetraploids contain higher proteins in tubers than in diploids.
- Drought tolerant crop and shed leaves during dormancy.
- Serve as insurance crop during times of food scarcity.
- Photosynthesis is combination of C_3 and C_4.
- Being photo-insensitive crop, it can be cultivated throughout year.
- Short day plant and longer light period inhibits starch storage.
- Long day condition favours induction of more flowering.
- Photosynthetic rate is highest at 30-35^{0}C.
- It is perennial monoecious shrub, produce 5-10 cylindrical tubers/ plant.
- Energy is obtained from cassava: 121 Mega joules /ha/day.

- Cassava provides energy (150 Kcal/ 100 g), fibre content (1.4%) and fat (0.3%).
- Highest stipulated yield: Leaf area of 500 cm^2/ plant.
- It cannot withstand frost.
- Growth ceases temperature below 10-12^{0}C.
- Flowering may commence 6-7 weeks after planting.
- Each flower has 5 united sepals with or without red/ yellow tinge and no petals.
- Inflorescence type: Racemose.
- Male flowers at terminal while few female flowers close to base of panicle.
- Female flowers are usually larger in size than males.
- Male flower has 10 stamens arranged in 2 whorls of five each.
- Anthers are small in size and filaments are free.
- Female flower has ovary mounted on 10 lobed glandular disc.
- Ovary has 3 lobes which unite to form a single style.
- Highly cross pollinated due to protogyny (female flower open 10 days before male phase).
- Highly heterozygous and exhibit high degree of genetic variability.
- Stigma receptivity: 6 AM to 2.30 PM.
- Period from pollination to fruit maturity: 3-5 months.
- Fruit type: Trilocular capsule.
- Foliar application of IAA/ NAA/ ascorbic acid @ 50 ppm increases intensity of female flowers.
- Optimum soil pH: 5.5-7.0 or upto 8.
- Time of planting: Rainfed (April-May or August-September), irrigated (throughout year).
- Two distinct plant types: 1) Erect with or without branching at top 2) Spreading type.
- Planting distance: Non-branching type (75cm x 75 cm); branching and semi-branching type (90 cm x 90 cm).
- Number of plants/ ha: 10,000-15,000.
- Commercial propagation: Stem cuttings which are also known as 'stakes or setts' obtained from bottom and middle portion of stem.
- Stakes for planting: 8-10 months maturity, 15-20 cm long, 2.5-3.5 cm thick with 10-12 buds.
- Planting method: 1 stake per hill.
- About 5% stakes are planted in nursery at 4 cm x 4 cm for gap filling in 1 sq. m. area.
- Polarity of cuttings is essential for its establishment.

- Remove excess sprouts from top portion of plant and retain 2 sprouts per plant in opposite side.
- Storage of stem cuttings beyond 60 days results in loss of viability.
- Multiplication ratio: 1:10 (traditional) and enhanced to 1:70 (minisett).
- Two node minisett is standardized as optimum size for rapid production.
- Setts treated with 0.5% KCl + phosphate slurry (30 g SSP + 30 g red soil in 60 litres of water) effectively tolerate water stress.
- Optimum area for producing minisetts for 1 ha area: Nursery bed of 45 m^2& 35% shade.
- Number of minisetts/ ha: 50,000.
- Raise setts in raised beds by planting very close (400 setts/ m^2).
- Ideal stage of minisett for transplanting: 2-3 leaf stage.
- Plant matures in 7-9 months using minisett technique.
- Stems from minisetts can be safely stored for over 3 months in zero energy cool chamber (ZECC).
- Commercial cultivation: Clonal material and also amenable to hybridization.
- Meristem tip culture: Production of virus free plants.
- Polyploidy breeding: Unique advantages as plant exhibit gigas character.
- Clonally multiplied tetraploids are at par with diploids.
- Yellow flesh colour: β-carotene.
- Effective fumigants for disinfection of chips in storage: Aluminium phosphide and methyl bromide.
- Latex is present in leaf and stem.
- Root contains essential oil, saponin and glucosides.
- Tap root and 1 or 2 secondary roots develop into tuber by storing carbohydrates.
- Colour of cortex (known as peel or rind): Cream or pink.
- Fresh roots contain 30% starch (25-40% of fresh wt.) and leaf contains 26-39% protein on dry weight basis.
- Globally, 60% cassava production is used for human food.
- Starch is also used as industrial raw material for production of alcohol and bio-degradable plastics.
- CTCRI, Thiruvananthapuram has patented technology for bio-ethanol production.
- Each metric ton of tubers, yield about 170 litres of alcohol.
- Par-boiled chips are harder than plain sun dried chips due to partial gelatinization.
- Recovery of chips: 20-40%.
- Degree of sweetness or bitterness is based on HCN content.

- Bitter principle: Cyanogenic glucoside called 'linamarin' which is converted to toxic compound HCN (pruslic acid).
- Bitter principle is found in roots (i.e. root peel), branches and leaves except seeds.
- Drought and potassium deficiency increases HCN content.
- All plant parts contain cyanogenic glucoside called 'Phaseolunatin' with leaves having higher concentration.
- Cyanogenic glucoside content in different cassava cvs.: 0.2-62.4 mg HCN/ 100g.
- Cyanogenic glucoside content in sweet type cvs.: 20-50 mg HCN/ kg of fresh roots.
- Prusic acid in flesh: 41 mg/ kg.
- In sweet varieties, Prussic acid located in skin & in exterior cortical layer while in bitter types, acid uniformly distributed in all parts of roots.
- Morphological character of bitter type: Presence of winged seed.
- Bitter ones are cultivated for industrial market.
- Cassava grown from seeds develops tap root system.
- Adventitious roots arise from stem cuttings may differentiate into tubers.
- Mature tubers can be easily differentiated into thin periderm followed by cortex and massive flesh.
- Mukibat system: Replacement of tapioca upper canopy with grafts or buds of Cera rubber (*Manihot glaziovii*) which improves productivity.
- This system is gaining popularity in East Java and Indonesia.
- Mean growth rate: 11 g/m^2/ day for annual production of 41 T/ha.
- Crop growth ceases at 10^{0}C.
- Ideal temperature for cassava stems sprouting: 28-30^{0}C.
- It produces 250000 calories of energy per hectare.
- True Cassava Seeds (TCS) technology has been developed at CTCRI.
- Seed rate of TCS: 1.5 kg/ha.
- Viability of cassava seeds: 8 months.
- Seed dormancy: 3-4 months.
- Tubers are highly perishable and can not be stored for more than 2-3 days after harvesting.
- Plants are 'topped' before harvesting for pulling out plants from soil.
- Staggered harvesting practiced in cassava.
- Harvesting: For food (at any age < 12 months); for starch (18-20 months).
- Harvest index: Root wt. / total plant wt. It should be in range of 0.5 to 0.7.
- Harvesting begins after 8 months after planting. It will take 18 or more months to produce crop under adverse conditions.

- Delayed lifting of roots cause root ageing, sprouting, central portion become woody & drastic fall in starch content.
- Roots begin to deteriorate within 48 h after harvest.
- The day before harvest, plants are topped i.e. stalks are cut off 40-60 cm above ground.
- Mechanical harvesting is adopted in Brazil.
- Mechanical injury to tubers leads to biochemical and physiological processes called 'vascular blue lining or vascular streaking' along the periphery of cortex.
- 'Blue lines' spoils tuber and makes unfit for consumption and industrial use.
- Dipping of roots in wax or storing in plastic bags reduces incidence of vascular streaking & extends shelf-life to 3-4 weeks.
- Roots can be peeled and frozen.
- Tubers are harvested 9-12 months after planting.
- Delayed harvesting- tubers become fibrous & quality deteriorates.
- Tubers can be stored without spoilage only for 2-3 days.
- Deterioration during storage due to physiological & due to microorganisms (i.e. internal rotting).
- Traditional storage practice: Under soil in pits upto 2 months.
- Best storage temperature: Cold storage at 3^0C for 2 weeks.
- Yield: 30-40 t/ha.
- In world trade, starch produced from tubers is known as 'tapioca flour'.
- Value added products: Sweet fries, fried chips, sago (*saboo dana*), pakkawada, pasta, vermicelli, cakes, cookies, and bakery products. Tubers are processed into silage.Unpeeled roots & leaves are used as animal feed.
- Stable products: Rava, flour, texcool (cold water soluble starch).
- Cassava fibrous waste or *thippi* contains about 50-55% unextracted starch.
- Cassava starch is used as filler material in paints, medicine and health drinks.
- Starch: Major industrial product has application in soap, detergent, laundry starch, cosmetics, pharmaceutical & explosives.
- Fermented form of cassava preparation: Gari/ farinha de manioc popular in African countries.

Species

- Ancestors: Brazilian wild spp. *M. esculentassp. flabellifolia* and *M. esculentassp. peruviana*.
- Clones sweet in taste belong to *M. esculenta*.
- Maximum genetic diversity: Brazil and Columbia.

Name	Features
M. alutecea, M. anisophylla	Resistant to low temperature
M. glaziovii	Source of Cassava mosaic disease resistance
M. anomala	Tuber bearing with high leaf retention
M. caerulescens	Resistant to drought & excessive soil toxicity
M. tristi, M. oligantha	Improve protein content; low HCN content & high root production
M. falcata	Limited vegetative growth
M. neusana	Evergreen; tolerant to low temperature & stem borer
M. melanobasis	Good source of root protein
M. ultissima, M. aipi	Edible species

Varieties:

- Major hindrance in breeding: Long gestation period.
- Clones are often classified by taste as sweet (*M. esculenta* syn. *M. utilissima*) or bitter (*M. dulcis*).
- Natural hybridization results in polyploids viz. triploids (2n=54) and tetraploids (2n=72).
- Triploids grow and yield better than tetraploids.
- Triploidy breeding have produced superior varieties with higher dry matter and starch content.
- Ichapuram Local: Promising cv. of Andhra Pradesh.
- Ullichuvala: 8-9 months for maturity; popular in Kerala.
- Mnga-1: Field tolerant to Cassava Mosaic virus (CMV).
- Tapioca Yethapur-1.
- San Pedro Preto: Cv. from Ghana & excellent for starch production.

Name	Breeding method	Features
KAU, Thrissur		
Cassava Malaya-4 (M-4)	Introduction from Malaysia	Leading variety of Kerala; non-branching; good keeping quality; purple colour on rind; tolerant to CMV
Nidhi (1996)	Clonal selection	Tall, erect branching; suitable for sandy loam areas; short duration (6 months); yield 25 t/ha; tolerant to CMV
KMC-1- Kalpaka (1996)	Clonal selection from locally cultivated var. Ramanthala	Erect, non-branching & short duration (6 months); tuber rind pink coloured; cream rind & white flesh; starch content 31.4%; excellent cooking quality; suitable for intercropping in coconut
Vellayani Hirswa	Selection	Short duration (5-6 months for maturity), pink tuber rind, excellent cooking quality & popular in Kerala
Uthama (2018)	Selection	Cylindrical tubers; light brown skin, white flesh; yield 3.97 kg/plant; HCN 42 ppm; starch 22.52%; fibre 1.05%; good cooking quality; yield 56 t/ha
CTCRI, Thiruvanantpuram		
Kalikalan	Local cultivar	Highly susceptible to CMV; yield reduction upto 80%
H-7	Hybridization	Industrial variety (starch & sago production)
H-96	Hybridization	-
H-97 (1971)	Hybrid of [Manjavella (local cv.) x Brazilian acc. No. 300 (Brazilian seedling selection)]	Semi-branching; brown coloured tubers; 10 months duration; 27-31 % starch on fruit wt. basis; tolerant to CMV, spider mite & scale insect; drought tolerant
H-165 (1971)	Hybrid of local types (Chadayamanagalam Vella x Kalikalan)	Mukibat hybrid; diploid; non-branching; early (8 months) duration; golden brown tubers & cream coloured rind; flesh creamy; 23-25% starch on fresh wt. basis; popular industrial variety (starch & sago production); drought tolerant; resistant to CMV, scale & red mites
Sree Haritha (H-226) 1971	Hybrid of [Local cv. Ethakkakaruppan x M-4 (introduced from Malaysia]	Mukibat hybrid: erect with branching type; creamish tubers with purplish patches; rind light purple & white flesh; duration 10 months; most preferred for starch & sago production by industry; starch content (28-30%); drought tolerant; CMV resistant
Sree Athulya	Polyploidy breeding	Triploid; starch 30.2%; yield 38-54 t/ha; tolerant to Cercospora leaf spot, resistant to spider mite & scale insects

Sree Apporva	Polyploidy breeding	Triploid; starch content (33.3%); 10 months for maturity; ideal for cassava based industries; cynogen (85-93 ppm); yield 60 t/ha; tolerant to Cercospora leaf spot & resistant to spider mite & scale insects
Sree Visakham (H-1687) 1977	Hybrid of (Local cv. Cheenikappa x Madagascar var.)	Erect, sparsely branched; table variety; 25-27% starch; β-carotene rich variety (466 IU/ 100 g), ideal for making *rawa*, low cynogen (< 100 ppm) & excellent to cook; field resistant to mosaic
Sree Sahya (H-2304) 1977	Multiple hybrid involving 5 parents of which 2 are exotic (acc. No. 468, 174, 3027, 1310, 82, 3939, 3588 & M-4)	Table variety; diploid; non-branching type; tubers long necked; tuber light brown with cream coloured rind; high starch content (38-41%), low cynogen (<100 ppm); drought tolerant; field resistant to mosaic; excellent cooking quality
Sree Harsha (1996)	Triploid clone by crossing [OP-4 (2x) x H-2304 (4x)]	Erect & non-branching type; skin light brown with cream rind, white flesh; excellent cooking quality; highest starch content (36-40%); crop duration 7-8 months; high yield 60 T/ha
Sree Jaya (CI-649) 1998	Clonal selection from indigenous germplasm	Erect, branching type; brown tuber skin with purple rind & white flesh; short duration of 6 months (as rotation crop in paddy based cropping system); 23-27% starch; good cooking quality; cultivated under tree shade (diffused sunlight); drought tolerant
Sree Vijaya (1998)	Clonal selection from indigenous germplasm	Erect, branching type; short duration of 6 months (as rotation crop in paddy based cropping system); good cooking quality; conical shaped tubers with brown stem, cream coloured rind & light yellow flesh; high carotene content; cultivated under tree shade (diffused sunlight); drought tolerant
Sree Prakash (1987)	Clonal selection from indigenous germplasm (S-856)	Short statured & non-branching type; short duration of 6-8 months (as rotation crop in paddy based cropping system); 30% starch; very shy flowering; resistant to cercospora leaf spot & tolerant to drought
Sree Rekha (2000)	Top cross hybrid (TMS 63198- R_1S_1-2; R_1S_1-2; x H-1687)	Starch 27-31%; suitable for upland and low land areas; field tolerant to leaf spot, spider mite & scales
Sree Prabha (2000)	Top cross hybrid (TMS 63198- R_1S_1-2; R_1S_1-2; x H-1687)	Starch 26-29%; yield 40 t/ha; excellent cooking quality; cynogen (50-85 mg/g)
Sree Padmanabha (2006)	Introduction from IITA, Nigeria	Starch 26%; cynogen (38-45 ppm); yield 38-46 T/ha; tolerant to drought & 1st variety resistant to Cassava mosaic virus (CMV) disease; yield 38 t/ha
Sree Pavithra	Clonal selection	High K-use efficiency; excellent cooking quality; low cynogenic glucoside (25.8 µg/g)
Sree Sakthi (2018)	Clonal selection	Non-branching; crop duration 9-10 months; cylindrical tubers with brown skin, cream rind & white flesh; starch 29%; yield 43 t/ha; resistant to CMD

Sree Swarna (2018)	Clonal selection	Non-branching; crop duration 7 months; cylindrical tubers with brown skin, cream rind & white flesh; starch 27%; low cynogen 45 ppm; yield 38 t/ha; resistant to CMD
TNAU, Coimbatore & state Dept. of Hort, Tamil Nadu		
CO.1 (ME-7) 1977	Clonal selection from local type	8-9 month duration; 35% starch; creamy rind; white flesh; non-bitter taste; 8-12 tubers/plant; tolerant to CMV & scale insects; non-bitter type; low HCN content
CO.2 (ME-164) 1984	Clonal selection from OP seedling progeny of Thiruvarur	Highly branched; very compactly arranged tubers; 8-9 months duration; starch 34.6%; suitable for starch industry; brown skin, white rind, flesh white; tolerant to CMV; low HCN content
CO.3 (ME-120-1) 1993	Clonal selection from OP seedling progeny from IITA, Nigeria	Branching habit; 8-9 months duration; brown skin & creamy white flesh; resistant to CMV; high starch (35.6%) & low HCN content; suitable for rainfed & irrigated condition
CO.4 (2002)	Clonal selection	Suitable for rainfed & irrigated conditions
CMR-1	Selection from 'Sree Padmanabha'	Resistant to CMD; high starch & high yield
CMR-129	-	High starch & high yield
CMR-70, 73, 106, 109, 120		Resistant to CMD.
MVD-1 (1983)	Selection	Suitable for staple food & industrial uses

Diseases, pest, disorders:

- Cercospora leaf spot (*Cercospora carbonaceae, C. dioscoreaceae*):
- Curvularia leaf spot/ Brown leaf spot (*Curvularia eragostidis*): Severe in warm humid regions and high rainfall areas.
- Cassava mosaic virus (CMV) disease: Transmitted by white fly (*Bemisia tabaci*).
- African mosaic.
- Tuber rot (*Phytophthora dreschleri*): Serious in ill drained soils. Use *Trichoderma*.
- Witches broom: Due to MLO.
- Rotting of tubers due to *Bacillus*, *Rhizophus*, *Penicillium* and yeast species.
- Papaya mealy bug (*Paracoccus marginatus*): Polyphagus pest.
- Cassava white fly (*Bemisia tabaci*): Noxious pest cause damage upto 6-30%. Major vector of CMV. Abundant throughout the year. Use pupal parasite *Prospaltella flava* which regulates the population up to 6.8-30% in field.
- Spiral white fly (*Aleurodicus disperses*): Major pest.
- Cassava scale (*Aonidomytilus albus*):
- White grub (*Leucopholis coneophora*): Serious pest.
- Termite: 20-40% seedling mortality.
- Spider mite: Foliage feeding pest cause chlorophyll depletion, bronzing and rusted leathery appearance.
- Thrips (*Retithrips syriacus*): Severe foliage pest.
- Stored chips are affected by lesser grain borer (*Rhyzopertha dominica*) and rice weevil (*Sitophilus oryzae*).
- Locust beetles; ants, rats, wild pigs: Troblesome pests.

Inheriance of characters:

- Triploidy is correlated with vigour, increased starch content and high tuber yield.

18.2 Chekkurmanis (*Madura keera*)

- Eulogized as 'Vegetable of 21st century or Multivitamin Green or Multimineral packed leafy vegetable'.
- Species: *S. albicans*, *S. gardnerianes*, *S. zeylanicus*, *S. indicus*, *S. assimilis*, *S. quadrangularis*, *S. rigidus*.
- Introduced from Malaysia in 1953.
- Leaf juice is used against eye troubles.
- Found in hills upto 1200 m MSL.
- Edible part: Tender shoots and leaves.
- Apex of plant is nipped off to putforth new branches.

- Drought tolerant.
- Origin: India.
- Perennial leafy vegetable grown wild in evergreen forest.
- Vitamin A: 9,510 IU/100 g leaves.
- Vitamin C: 247 mg/100 g.
- Succulent shoots and leaves are rich in carbohydrates (11.6 g/100 g), proteins (6.8-7.4 mg/100 g).
- Grounded roots and leaves used as poultice for ulcers in nose and against fever.
- Pollination agent: Insects, due to protogyny and monoecy.
- Propagation method: Stem cuttings (6-12 months old) and seeds.
- Planting density: 1 lakh stem cuttings/ ha.
- Plants are trimmed to encourage fleshy growth.
- Tuber (15-20 g) planted on ridges in nursery.
- Nursery area 500 m^2 to produce vines/ ha area.
- Harvest period: 3-4 months after planting.
- Yield: 1-3 kg leaves/ plant/ year or 30-50 t/ha.

Pest:

- Root knot nematode: Serious pest.

19. FABACEAE

19.1 Fenugreek

- It is both tropical and temperate crop.
- Used as condiment for flavouring of foods as well as medicinal purpose.
- Maximum area and 80% production: Rajasthan.
- It is 3rd largest seed spice in India after coriander and cumin and valued as food, flavouring agent and medicine.
- India is major producer and exporter of this spice.
- Tolerant to frost and freezing weather.
- Annual herb and leaves are pinnately trifoliate.
- Cultivated forms are diploid (2n=16) and steriles are hexaploid (2n=44) and tetraploids are mixoploids with chromosome between 22 and 44.
- Seeds are carminative, tonic and aphrodisiac.
- Seeds of tetraploid are larger but seed sterility is very high.
- Highly self pollinated due to cleistogamous flowers.

- Each pod contains 10-20 small, hard and yellowish brown seeds of about 3 mm long, which are smooth, oblong and grooved across one another giving a hooked appearance.
- Flowers: Papilionaceous.
- Endospermic dicot seed.
- Seeds contain 45-60% carbohydrates (mucilaginous fibre galactomannan), 20-30% proteins (high in lysine & tryptophan) and 5-10% lipids.
- Crop duration: 120-135 days.
- Calcium content: 395 mg / 100 g of edible portion.
- Bitter principle: Choline (present in leaf) and alkaloid Trigonelline (present in seed).
- Volatile oil content: 0.02% and fixed oil 5-7%.
- Anthesis time: 9 AM to 6 PM with peak at 11.30 AM to 12.30 PM.
- Plant flowers in 30-37 days after sowing.
- Flowering duration: 7-18 days.
- Pollen fertility: 95-98% in unopened flower buds and 67-80% in opened flowers.
- Pods mature within 60-70 days of sowing.
- Water requirement through surface irrigation: 300-350 mm.
- Critical stages of irrigation: Early vegetative growth and grain formation stage.
- Crop is thinned 20-30 days after sowing.
- Optimum soil pH: 6-7.
- Can be grown on sodic soils having 20-30 ESP.
- As leaf crop grown throughout year and for grain crop June-July and September-December are two distinct seasons.
- Fenugreek seed removes NPK in the ratio of 2:1:2 from soil.
- Seed rate: 20-25 kg/ha
- Objectionable weed: *Melilotus*.
- Seed treatment with *Rhizobium melilotti*.
- Thinning is necessary for fenugreek cultivation.
- Fenugreek seed contains 'Diosgenin' (0.4-1.26%), the precursor of steroids of sex hormones and oral contraceptive pills.
- Algerian and Morocco types contain higher level of diosgenin.
- Useful for nematode control.
- Harvesting: 20-25 days after sowing (vegetable purpose).
- Two pickings are taken at 50-80 days of sowing which does not affect seed yield.
- Picking of young shoots is done after 10-30 days after sowing.
- Yield: 10-11 q/ha.

- Sprays of ascorbic acid @ 250-450 ppm improves plant growth, enhances flowering, seed number and seed size.
- GA_3 @ 10-100 ppm enhances shoot length, plant height, number of leaves and induces early flowering.
- Spray of 0.05% sodium-2,-3 isobutyrate just before flowering decreases pollen sterility and improves seed yield.
- LD_{50} for dry seeds: 25 Kr and for soaked seeds: 20 Kr.
- Critical moisture level for seed storage: 7-8%.
- Objectionable weed in seed spice: Melitotus (senji).

Species:

- '*Trigonella*' refers to angular seeds.
- Common/ Deshi methi (*Trigonella foenum-graecum*):Plant bears 10-15 twigs, white or light violet coloured flowers, long, slender straight 100-200 pods with a prominent beak.
- Champa methi/ Kasuri methi/ Marwari methi (*T. corniculata*): Slow growing, scented type, bright orange or yellow flowers and curved/ sickle shaped pods and multiple cutting. Remains in rosette condition during most of vegetative growth period.
- *T. coerulea*: Blue fenugreek and cultivated in Europe.

Varieties:

Name	Breeding method	Features
TNAU, Coimbatore		
CO.1 (1982)	Selection from germplasm 'TG-2336'	Dual purpose, early maturing variety (85-90 days); leaf yield (9 t/ha); grain yield (68q/ha); suits well for intercropping & relay cropping; seeds contain 20-22% protein & leaf contain 15.9% protein
CO.2 (1999)	Selection from germplasm ' CF-390'	Dual purpose, early maturing variety; grain yield (482 kg/ ha); tolerant to root rot
IARI, New Delhi		
Pusa Early Bunching	Selection	Early maturing champa methi; useful for multi-cut purpose; 1st cutting in 25-30 days; non-scented type; suitable for leaf & seed purpose; resistant to DM, rots
Pusa Kasuri	Selection	Early maturing champa methi; small seeded Kasuri type; scented; mainly for leaf purpose; takes 150-155 days for seed maturity; useful for multi-cut purpose (5-7 cuttings & 1st cutting in 25-30 days); suitable for dehydration
NRCSS, Ajmer		
NRCSS AM-1 (2006)	Pure line selection	Small seeds; seed yield 27 q/ha; exclusively for leaf purpose
NRCSS AM-2 (2006)	Pure line selection	Bold seeds; yield 18 q/ha; exclusively for leaf purpose

Ajmer Fenugreek-1	Pure line selection	Seeds bold, seed yield 27 q/ha
Ajmer Fenugreek-2	Pure line selection	16-18 seeds/pod; seed yield 18 q/ha
Ajmer Fenugreek-3	Pure line selection	Mod. resistant to PM, root knot nematode
Ajmer Fenugreek-5	Pure line selection	High anti-oxidant content; suitable for green leaf production under shade
SDAU, Jagudan		
Gujarat Methi-1 (1999)	Recurrent selection based on pure line selection from 'J. Fenu 102'	Dwarf; seed yield 18.6 q/ha
CCSHAU, Hisar		
Hisar Sonali (1993)	Pure line selection from local type	Mod. tolerant to leaf spot, root rot & aphids; grain yield (17 q/ha)
Hisar Suvarna (HM-103) 2001	Pure line selection from local type	Dual purpose; yield 19 q/ha; resistant to PM & Cercospora leaf spot; suitable for cultivation throughout India
Hisar Mukta (HM-350) 2001	Pure line natural green seed coated mutant line from U.P	Highest salinity tolerant cv.; mod. resistant to DM & PM; seed yield (20q/ha);
Hisar Madhavi (HM-348) 2001	Pure line selection from local germplasm of U.P.	Mod. resistant to DM & PM; suitable for rainfed & irrigated condition; dual purpose; seed yield (20q/ha);
Hisar Manohar (HM-346)	Pure line selection	Light green narrowed leaves; unique green seed colour resistant to DM
HM-425	Selection	High yield (20-22 q/ha); PM & DM resistant
RAU, Bihar (Trihut College of Agriculture, Dholi)		
Rajendra Kanti (1988)	Pure line selection from Raghunathpur collection	Bushy; suitable for sole crop & intercropping; seed yield 13 q/ha; mod. resistant to PM, caterpillars, aphids
Rajendra Abha	-	Kasuri methi;
Rajendra Khushba	-	-
RAU, Jobner		
(Rajasthan Methi-1) Rmt-1 (1990)	Pure line selection from Nagpur local	Seed protein 2.1%; seed yield (15 q/ha); resistant to root rot, root knot nematode, PM & aphids
Rmt-143 (1997)	Pure line selection from local	Mod. resis. to PM; suitable for heavier soils of Jodhpur; seed yield (16.5q/ha)
Rmt-303 (1999)	Mutation breeding fiom 'Rmt-1'	Bold seeds; less susceptible to PM; grain yield (19 q/ha)
Rmt-305 (Udaipur Methi) 1995	-	1st determinate type variety; resistant to PM, root knot nematode; 21.7% protein; seed yield (18q/ha);
Rmt-354	-	Resistant to PM & DM
Rmt-361	-	Suitable for fenugreek growing areas

MPKV, Rahuri		
Phule Kasturi (2019)	Selection	Reddish colour at leaf blade; yield 110 q/ha; mod. resis. to damping off
NDUA & T, Faizabad		
Narendra Methi-2	-	Mod. resistant to cercospora leaf spot & DM; salinity tolerant
Narendra Richa	-	Dual purpose; alkaline tolerant; mod. resistant to PM
CSAUA & T, Kanpur		
Kalyanpur Selection	-	More tolerant to sodicity. Produce more biomass & seed yield
SVPUA & T, Meerut		
Vallabh Chinki	-	-
ANGRAU, Hyderabad (RARS, Guntur)		
Lam Selection-1 (1992)	Selection from germplasm	Dual purpose; more branches; leaf yield 12 t/ha; grain yield (740 kg/ha); seed protein (5.3%)
Lam Sonali	Selection	-
Lam Methi-3	Selection	Medium diosgenin content (0.31 %)
GBPUA & T, Pantnagar		
Pant Ragini (2001)	Selection from local germplasm	Dual purpose; bushy; resistant to DM, root rot; 2.5% essential oil; seed yield (15 q/ha);
CSK HPKV, Palampur		
Palam Soumya	Selection	-
Palam Kasuri	Selection	-
Other varieties		
Sindhu	-	Tolerant to wilt & resistant to aphids
Methi No. 47	Improved variety from Maharashtra	Broad & succulent leaves; rich in vit. C

Diseases and pests:

- Root rot (*Rhizoctonia solani*): Serious soil borne disease.
- Powdery mildew: Serious at pod formation stage and temperature between 15-25^{0}C and R.H. of 60-70%.
- Downy mildew (*Peronospora trigonellae*): Serious in February-March.
- Leaf blight (*Alternaria alternata*): 3 foliar application of Propiconazole (0.05%) or Difenoconazole (0.05%) at 15 days interval.
- Aphids: Serious during December-March.
- Jassids: More serious during seedling stage.
- Leaf miner:

Inheritance of characters:

- Diosgenin content is negatively correlated with grain yield.
- Number of branches and pods per plant exhibit maximum correlation with grain yield.

19.2 Agathi/ *Hadga*

- Eulogized as 'Humming bird tree'.
- Perennial, tropical, quick growing and soft wooded tree.
- Two forms: 1) Red flower type 2) White flower type (suitable for kitchen garden).
- Tree is used as standard for betel vine and black pepper and as wind break and shade plant for banana and coconut.
- It has ornamental, food and fodder values.
- Edible part: Leaves and flowers.
- Nutrient composition/ per 100 g edible portion:Leaves rich in protein (8.4 g), vit. A (9000 IU), vit. C (169 mg), fibre (2.2 g) and minerals like Ca (1.13 g), P (80 mg), Fe (3.9 mg).
- Propagation method: Seeds.
- Tender leaves produced throughout the year are harvested periodically and used as green pot herb.
- Flowering time: September-December.
- Fruiting season: During summer.
- 1st harvest: 2-4 months after planting.
- Yield: 4.5-9 kg leaves/ plant/ year.
- Disease: Seedling blight.

20. LABIATAE

20.1 Coleus (Chinese potato/ *koorka*)

- Eulogized as 'Poorman's potato or Country potato'.
- Bushy, annual herb, producing a cluster of dark brownish, round to oval tubers.
- Tropical tuber crop.
- Tubers dark-brown coloured, heteromorphous (small sized & round to oval shaped), bear aromatic flavor & found at base of stem.
- Deserves to be popularized as a vegetable.
- Its nutritive status compares favorably wuth that of major tuber crops.
- Tubers are used as vegetable in boiled/ baked/ or fried forms.
- Grown as vegetable in homestead gardens in Tamil Nadu, Kerala, Karnataka and tribals from N-E states.
- Bushy, annual, herbaceous crop grows to height of 20-25 cm.
- Leaves thick, succulent with aromatic smell.
- Possess anti-oxidant and anti-tumor properties.
- Hot humid/ sub-tropical to hot temperate climate is ideal for its cultivation.

- Crop is susceptible to to cold & cannot withstand frost as well as drought conditions.
- Essential oil compound: β-thujone and α-farnesene.
- Highly irregular meiosis and occurrence of desynapsis leads to sterility.
- Complete pollen sterility, hence seed setting is absent.
- Polyploid with 2n=6x=72.
- Optimum soil pH: 6.5-7.0.
- Propagation methods: Suckers, Stem cuttings-15-20 cm length (from suckers/ sprouted tubers) or small sized seed tubers.
- Vine cuttings obtained from sprouted tubers after 2 weeks.
- Tubers (400-1200 kg) planted in 0.2 ha nursery to produce suckers for 1 ha crop.
- Tubers sprout after 15 days & grow up to 15-20 cm long after 3 weeks.
- Seed tubers of 50 kg generate planting material for 1 ha crop area within 2 months for staggered planting.
- Best fitted for multiple cropping system.
- Seed rate: 170-200 kg/ha.
- Planting time: 1st week of October gives higher yields.
- Planting methods:
  a) Coiled stem cuttings 22 cm long with 5 leaves are planted on ridges at 15-20 cm spacing give higher tuber yield.
  b) In horizontal planting method, 2 pieces of stem cuttings are planted on ridges in opposite directions at 7-10 cm apart.
  c) Dense planting produces smaller sized tubers.
- Earthing up and split application of fertilizers is beneficial.
- Difficulty in peeling and no fixed tuber shape are drawbacks of this vegetable.
- Edible portion: Tuber and matures in 135-150 days.
- Increase starch content of tubers: Spray cycocel and ethrel.
- Harvesting stage: Withering and yellowing of leaves and vines (5-8 months after planting).
- Matured tubers deteriorate rapidly in the soil.
- Three foliar sprays of Cycocel @ 100-150 ppm enhances tuber yield 3 times more.
- Crop duration: 4-6 months.
- Matured tubers start quick decay in quality if left in field.
- Yield: 7 t/ha (rainfed) to 15 t/ha (irrigated).
- Complementary factors of yield: Level of N and mean leaf area.
- *In vitro* shoot regeneration is reported.
- About 85% growth recovery results after cryopreservation.

Species:

- *Coleus parviflorus* (syn. *Solenostemon rotundifolius*),
- *C. tuberosus*, *C. rotundifolius*, *C. dysentericus*.

Varieties:

Name	Breeding method	Features
CTCRI, Thiruvananthapuram		
Sree Dhara (1993)	Clonal selection from indigenous germplasm	1st variety grown in Kerala; matures in 5 months; susceptible to root knot nematode
KAU, Thrissur		
Nidhi (2001)	Clonal selection from NBPGR acc. CP-79	-
Suphala (2006)	Tissue culture mutant from local cultivar	Cultivated year round; yield 16 t/ha
TNAU, Coimbatore		
CO.1 (1991)	Clonal selection from local germplasm	Yield 32 t/ha; tubers have 21.5% starch; cooked tubers tasty & less soil odour

Pests:

- Leaf folder (*Pycnarmon cribrata*): Serious pest. Use endoparasitoid *Choeras psarae*.
- Top shoot borer (*Phostria piasusalis*): Controlled by natural enemy *Leptobatopsis indica*.
- Tingid bug (*Monantha globulifera*):
- Spike borer (*Helicoverpa armigera*): Cause economic loss.

Inheritance of character:

- Heritability for economically important traits are less, hence selection is not recommended
- Shoot characters have no relevance compared to tuber characters in determining yield.

21. LEGUMINOSAE

- Genome size: *Lablab niger* (370 Mbp), *Vicia faba* (13000 Mbp).
- Cowpea, common bean, mung bean, chick pea, clover: Haploid genomes <1000 Mbp.
- Favourable conditions for hybridization: 22-25^{0}C, 65-75% R.H, 15 lux intensity/m^2 and 10-12 h photoperiod.
- Epicotyl/ shoot apical meristem is best to regenerate whole plant.

- Anti-nutritional factors are associated with seed coatand heat liable. Therefore, become harmless after cooking.
- All beans except lima bean contain cyanide in safe limit i.e. 10-20 mg/100 g.
- Winged bean contains large amount of inhibitors which is destroyed during cooking even in pressure cooking at 120^{0}C for 20 min.
- All legume vegetables are self pollinated due to cleistogamy.
- CA storage conditions: 5-10^{0}C at 2-3% O_2, 4-7%CO_2.

21.1 Garden pea/ vegetable pea

- Eulogized as 'Queen of pulses'.
- Edible legume or pulse crop.
- Per capita consumption in USA: 6.45 lbs as canned, 4.23 lbs as frozen & 0.35 lbs as dry field peas.
- Among the pulses, pea occupies 3rd position in production and 7th place in area.
- Highly nutritive and rich source of digestive protein (15.5-39.7%) along with –CHO (56.6% of seed wt.) and vitamins.
- Nutrition score: 67.
- Calorific value: 77 Kcal/ 100g.
- Composition of matured seed (Blixt, 1975): a) Partly developed embryo (1-3% of total seed wt.) b) Two cotyledons (90% of seed wt.) c) Testa (7-9% of wt.).
- Chemical composition of seed: -CHO (34-46%), protein (20%), lipid (2%).
- Seed shapes: Round, dimpled/ wrinkled.
- Seed colours: Green, cream or yellow.
- Soil binding crop.
- Geneticist done great work on germplasm collection: Herbert Lamprecht and Stig Blixt.
- Pea germplasm is maintained at Nordeic Gene Bank, Lund, Sweden.
- Double cropping technique for off season production: CITH, Srinagar.
- Both, indeterminate (vining/ tall type) and determinate (bush/ short) types are available.
- Determinate bear the concentrated (bunch) pod set, while indeterminate types set the pods along a long main stem over extended period of time.
- Determinate types produce 2 or more pods at each flower node and have high ratio of pods to vine weight, tend to be earlier and produce pods over a shorter period of time.
- Indeterminate types tend to be single podded.
- Inflorescence: Raceme arises from leaf axil.
- Stigma receptivity: Prior to anthesis.

- Anthesis and anther dehiscence: In morning hours.
- Diadelphous stamen condition is present.
- Gynoecium: Monocarpellery with ovules upto 13.
- Fruit: Pod or legume, derived from superior ovary, which contains two rows of ovules that develops into seeds.
- Garden pea was model system used by G. J. Mendel to formulate laws of inheritance.
- F_1 hybrid seed production is almost restricted due to more number of seeds per pod.
- 98% pea consumed as fresh vegetable.
- Dried pea flour contains 343 calories.
- Highest area: Uttar Pradesh.
- Thomas A. Knight: Pioneer in producing garden pea varieties.
- Growth pattern, pod thickness, pod length and seed diameter: Simple sigmoid growth curve.
- Peas and beans are self pollinated due to presence of 'keel'.
- The node at which flower initiation occurs is constant for genotype and environment.
- Early pea varieties produce 1st flower at 5-11th node while late varieties at 13-15th node.
- Early varieties have single flower while late varieties have double or triple flowers.
- Mutant of pea in which all the leaves are converted into tendril.
- Anti-nutritional factors: Cyanide containing compounds.
- Seeds contain trypsin and chymotrypsin which is used for contraceptive, fungistatic and spermicide.
- Vegetable pea (wrinkled seeded) contains 10-13% total sugar, 33% starch, 24-33% proteins.
- Field pea (smooth/ round seeded) contains 6-7% total sugar, 46% starch, 23-31% proteins.
- Smooth seeded varieties are more hardy, high in starch (amylopectin), lower in sugar/ starch ratio whereas wrinkled seeded are low in starch and contain more amylase (34%).
- Immature peas have higher sugar content and eaten as green vegetable.
- Flowers: Zygomorphic (can be divided into two symmetrical parts).
- Stigma receptivity: Several days prior to anthesis.
- Anthesis begins at lowest floral node & proceeds upward.
- Pollination occurs one day before anthesis.
- Number of vegetative nodes before 1st inflorescence vary from 4 (for earliest) to 25 (for latest).

- Late cvs. starts flowering at 13-15 nodes.
- Seed germination: Hypogeal.
- Maturity indices:
  - Heat units during fruit devclopment.
  - Size of the peas for taste sampling.
  - Quantitatively by tenderness (determined by tenderometer).
- Early types mature within 55-60 days and late types up to 80 days.
- Edible podded types are picked when pods have reached full length and seeds are just developing.
- Pod quality depends on tenderness and sugar content of seeds.
- Base/threshold temperature (minimum temperature for pea germination & growth) for computing heat units is 40^0 For 4.4^0C.
- Heat unit system: Commonly used for determine the maturity of pods.
- Heat units required: Early cvs. (1150-1200^0F); late cvs. 1550^0 F.
- Glaman *et al.* (1989) gave heat sums for various maturity groups-
  - Early 870-980^0 F (60-70 days);
  - Mid early 980-1060^0 F (70-75 days);
  - Mid late 1060-1170^0 F(75-80 days);
  - Late >1170^0 F (>80 days).
- As the peas increase in size during maturation, the seed coats and cotyledons become tougher and the percent of sugar decreases while starch and proteins increase.
- Wrinkled seeded cultivars are more sensitive to high temperature (30^0C) than round seeded.
- Peas are free from goiter causing 'goitrogens'.
- Seed crop mature in 130-140 days after sowing.
- To test the maturity, seeds are squeezed between fingers.
- AIS (Alcohol Insoluble Solids) indicate sugar/ starch content of peas.
- FMC Texture meter: Measures the quality of peas and indicates higher quality above at a reading of 34-36 kg/ 6.45 cm^2 pressure.
- Measurement of seed toughness/ pea maturity: Tenderometer for processing purpose. Low readings offer high price.
- A tenderometer unit is a direct measure of the maturity and quality of the raw product.
  a) High readings indicate overmaturity & increase in starch.
  b) Lower readings indicate more sugars & tenderness.
  c) In overmaturity indicates rapid decrease in quality.
- Martin (1937) developed tenderometer.
- Tendrometer pressure reading: Gain in weight at tendrometer reading between 43 & 50 kg indicates pea maturity is complete and gets higher prices.

- Tenderometer reading beyond 95-110 optimum reflects reducing percentage of quality peas.
- Peas in 130 level on tenderometer indicate by-pass status.
- For drying purpose, tenderometer reading should be at least 85-95psi.
- For canning purpose, tenderometer reading should be 120 psi.
- For freezing purpose, tenderometer reading should be 105 psi.
- OTMS (Ottawa Texture meter system): Provides best objective measurer of pea quality.
- Peas should be blanched in hot water at 95^{0}C to prevent enzymatic activity to minimize development of undesirable flavour.
- Peas with split open on boiling are preferred for dehydration.
- For canning, alcohol insoluble solids should be 11-16%.
- Vacuum cooling ensures rapid cooling of pods.
- For longer storage, pea seed is stored in seed container at 10% moisture content and in air cooled rooms.
- Edible podded peas originated from spontaneous mutation.
- Father of pea breeding: S. Blixt.
- Legumes are low in methionine and good source of lysine amino acid.
- Peas if sown earlier, suffer from wilt and if sown later then suffer from mildew attack.
- Best soil pH: 5.5-6.0
- Peas does not tolerate excess soil acidity and affects germination.
- Soil with pH >7.5 cause wilting by fusarium attack.
- Tolerates frost upto -20^{0}C in seedling stage.
- Winter hardy pea can withstand -10^{0}C to -40^{0}C.
- Optimum temperature for seed germination: 22^{0}C.
- Optimum temperature: 16-21^{0}C (vegetative growth) & 10-16^{0}C (reproductive growth).
- High temperature (>25^{0}C) hastens maturity but lowers pod set and adversely affect pod quality. It increases pod fibre content and seed starch content and yields drop off rapidly.
- During maturity, sugar content decreases and polysaccharides and protein content increases.
- Removal of field heat is essential to prevent loss of quality.
- Green peas lose much of their sugar content unless promptly cooled at 0^{0}C.
- Hydro-cooling is preferred method for pre-cooling.
- Green peas can be stored for 1-2 weeks at 0^{0}C and 95-98% R.H.
- Pollengrains can be maintained for more than half year at -5^{0}C at 35-40% R.H.
- Pollen storage: Vacuum drying & storage at -25^{0}C extend viability to 1 year.

- Seed rate: 100-120 kg/ha.
- For processing purpose, determinate types and higher plant population (4,00,000 to 7,00,000 plants/ acre) is preferred.
- Seed yield: 1500-2000 kg/ha.
- Seed viability: 2-3 years.
- Weight of 100 seeds: 20 gram.
- Shelling percentage of pea: 35-45%.
- Shelled peas of canning cvs. are light green coloured & resistant to leaching of chlorophyll into sugar-salt liquid in can.
- Freezers are characterized by dark green shelled peas (called berry).
- Moisture percentage should not be more than 9 % of seeds.
- Foliar spray of chloromequat (3-6 kg/ha) and soil application (6 kg/ha) before flower bud differentiation improves drought tolerance.
- '*Pisum* genetics' newsletter published from John Innes Centre, England, 1994.
- Peas are processed as canned/ frozen/ dehydrated for consumption in off season.
- Foliar application of 0.1% ammonium molybdate increases number of root nodules, TSS and number of seeds/pod.
- Seed crop gives more remuneration than green pod purpose.

Species:

- Monograph of genus *Pisum* prepared by Lamprecht H. (1974)
- All *Pisum* species are self pollinated diploids and they intercross freely.
- Linnaeus distinguished two spp. as *P. arvense* (coloured flower field pea), *P. sativum* (white flowered horticultural or garden pea).
- Cultivated pea arose from wild field pea (*Pisum arvense*) or related wild spp. *P. elatius*.
- Based on genetic diversity, there are 4 centres of origin viz., Central Asia, Near East, Abyssinia and Mediterranean region.
- Primary centre of origin: China or Central Asia.

Traits modified as a part of domestication syndrome-

Wild type phenotype	Cultivated phenotype
Dehiscent pods	Indehiscent pods
Dormancy present	Dormancy lacking
Tall	Dwarf
Many basal branches	Few basal branches
Small seeds	Large seeds
Poor seed quality	Good seed quality
Long day flowering	Day neutral flowering

Garden pea/ Horticultural pea	Field pea
P. sativum ssp. *hortense*	*P. sativum* ssp. *arvense*
Table & canning purpose (green immature seeds or immature pods)	Ripe, mature seeds for pulse & forage or green manure; consumed as dry seeds
Seeds bold & wrinkled	Round, less sweet & angular
Plants with big white flowers	Small, pale lilac/ lavender coloured flowers
Leaf axils- green	Leaf axils- pigmented
Seeds are yellow-whitish/ bluish green	Seeds are grayish green/ grayish brown/ grayish yellow or pigmented
Pods fibrous	Pods fibrous
Viny dwarf plants with long internodes	Bushy, indeterminate growth habit, grown primarily for feeding livestock

Edible podded peas are 2 types:

1. Snap pea/ Sugar snap pea (*P. sativum* var. *saccharatum*): Snap peas were developed by crossing standard pod pea (garden pea) with a mutant snow pea. These are characterized by slow development of seeds and pod fiber. Difficult to grow than standard green peas. Very sensitive to adverse environmental conditions. These lack pod parchment layer or fibre and have thick pod walls. These are crunchy, delicious, plumpy pods, and fully grown large seeds. Cultivars have wrinkled seeds with green cotyledons, white flower and short internodes and known as 'Butter sugar peas or Sugar snap peas'. Varieties can be used as such for consumption. Term 'Snap pea' was used by Gallatin Seed Company, USA.Very sensitive to over-ripeness and must be harvested within 12-24 h of maturity. They are harvested before the seed enlarges and pod becomes fibrous.Very susceptible to PM and fungal leaf spot diseases.
2. Snow pea (Mange-tout type)/ China pea (*P. sativum* var. *macrocarpon*): Snow pea plant is a vine and grows up to 60-200 cm. Lack of parchment layer, thin pod walls. Flat tender pods with small undeveloped peas inside. Endocarp remain soft & succulent compared to shelling types. Snow peas have flat pods and are eaten before its seeds are properly formed. Therefore, both the immature pods and seeds can be consumed whole. Seeds may be pigmented when mature. It can be stored for 1-2 weeks at 0-2^{0}C with 90-95% R.H.

Three main groups:

1. Red yellow pea (*P. fulvum*): Resistant to powdery mildew.
2. Abyssinian pea/ Afghanistan pea (*P. abyssinicum*): It is a primitive, land race display several traits viz. indehiscent pods, smooth pods and thin testa.
3. Wild group: All other species of *Pisum* including *P. humile* (dwarf pea) and *P. elatus*.
   - Perennial pea (*P. formosum*) and *P. aucheri*: Tuber forming perennials & are synonymous & do not cross with *Pisum*.

- Tufted/ crowned pea: Pods clustered at the top of the plant rather than in middle, due to strong expression of apical fasciation.
- *P. coccineus*: Resistant to bacterial wilt, root rot and Bean Common Mosaic virus.
- *P. acutifolius*: Resistant to bacterial blight, bacterial wilt.
- Leafless type peas (*afila*): Tolerant to waterlogging and suitable for mechanical harvesting.
- Sexual hybridization of pea with other genera of Vicieae is unsuccessful.
- In cross between *Pisum* (female) with *Vicia faba* (male), the hybrid embryo degenerates.

Varieties:

- 1st edible podded variety 'Sugar Pea' was developed in Holland in 16th century.
- Snow pea varieties: Snowman, Snowflake, Prolific, Sweet Pod, Mammoth Melting Sugar.
- Snap pea varieties: Cascadia, Sugar Anne, Sugar Bon, Sugar Daddy, Sugar Lady, Sugar Stick, Sugar Snap.
- Mutant varieties: Barton, Filby, Wemsum.
- Near wilt resistant: Delwiche Commando, New Era.
- Fusarium wilt resistant: Alaska, Surprise, JM-1, JM-2, Kala Nagin.
- Better quality pods, bigger and sweet seeds and resistant to PM: Stratigen, CVTHEP-6, Rachana, Kinnauri, FC-1, Giant Sugar, American Wonder,GS-10, NDVP-4, Xucai-1, DPP-9411, JP-71, JP-83, JP-4, PRS-4.
- JP-9: Resistant to PM and bruchus.
- JP-501 A/2: Resistant to fusarium wilt, bruchus and PM.
- JP Batri Brown-3, JP Batri Brown-4: Resistant to rust and bruchus.
- JP-179: Resistant to PM, fusarium wilt, bruchus and leaf miner and tolerant to rust.
- PC-55-11-1-2: 1st aluminium tolerant line for acidic soils.
- GC-14 (T-19 x Greater Progress): Plants bushy, erect, pods 8.7 cm long, wrinkled & 7 seeded; picking starts from 90 days.
- GC-195 (7.19 x Little Marvel): Plants 45 cm tall, 7.1 cm pods, 8 seds/ pod, picking starts from 75 days.
- Resistant source of aphid: Feltham First.
- Tolerant to salinity: Market Prize and Duke of Albany.
- Smooth seeded: Asauiji.
- Wrinkle seeded: Early December, NP-291.
- Most popular variety of Madhya Pradesh & Maharashtra: Khaper Kheda. It has double pods, wrinkled seeds; yield 5-6 t/ha.

- Branching habit variety: Wando.
- Early varieties: Surprise, Thomas Laxton.
- Suitable for canning: Abundance, Advance, Admiral,Al Sweet, American Wonder, Alaska, Canners, Champ, Charger, Dawn,Delwiche Commando, Early Perfection, Early Crop, Early Giant, Early Sweet, Frosty, Green Giant, Gregory's Surprise, Marrow Fat, Model, NP-291, Perfection,Pride of Wales, Sutton, S-537, Telephone, Trend, Troja, William Wonder, Yates.
- Suitable for dehydration: Duke of Albany, Selection-2, Varanasi Sweet, Morris.
- Suitable for freezing: Abador, Beacon, Coronet, Dark Skin, Ivy Spring, Sprite, Rigo, Mars, Trumpet, Venus.

Name	Breeding method	Features
Perfection, New Line	Introduction from USA	Popular in India; yield 10 t/ha; resistant to septoria leaf blotch; tolerant to salinity; suitable for canning
Alderman		Early; double pods; suitable for dehydration
Little Marvel		Wrinkled seeds; suitable for dehydration; tolerant to heat, drought, fusarium wilt
Sylvia	Introduced from Sweden	Whole edible snap pea having soft pods & without parchment layer; suitable for kitchen garden
Early Superb	Introduction from UK	Popular in India
IARI, New Delhi		
NP-29	-	Blossom appear at 14-16th node; double pods; 50% shelling; 6-7 seeds/pod; suitable for dehydration
Bonneville (1975) yield 10-12 t/ha	Introduction from USA	Double pods; wrinkled seeds; suitable for dehydration;
Lincoln (1987)	Introduction from USA	Double pods; sickle shaped; branching habit; 46% shelling; suitable for canning & dehydration; yield 7-10 t/ha
Arkel (1975)	Introduction from England	Wrinkled seed; resistant to PM & rust; suitable for dehydration; yield 10-12 t/ha
Early Badger (1975)	Introduction from USA	Dwarf; wrinkled seed; suitable for canning; yield 5-6 t/ha
Meteor (1972)	Introduction from UK	Dwarf; smooth seeds; resistant to PM, rust & aphids; suitable for dehydration; yield 9-10 t/ha
Pusa Pragati (1987)	Introduction from Germany in 1983	Long pods; resistant to PM & suitable for frozen peas; yield 7 t/ha
Pusa Shree	-	Resistant to fusarium wilt
Pusa Prabal (2018)	-	Medium maturing; 7-9 seeds/ pod; yield 10-13 t/ha; PM & fusarium wilt resistant
IIHR, New Delhi		
Arka Ajit (1993)	Back cross & pedigree selection of (Bonneville, Freezer 656 Erygel x IIHR 209)	Resistant to PM & rust; 55% shelling; yield 10 T/ha
Arka Karthik (2001)	Pedigree selection of (Arka Ajit x IIHR-554)	Bushy; mid-season type; pods 11 cm long; resistant to rust & PM; yield 11 t/ha
Arka Sampoorna (2001)	Back cross & pedigree selection of (Bonneville, Freezer 656 Manoa Sugar x IIHR 209)	Whole pod edible; mid-season type; resistant to rust & PM; yield 8 t/ha

Arka Nirmal	Pedigree selection of (IIHR 103 x Arka Pramodh)	Dwarf; 60% shelling; sweet seeds; yield 8.5 t/ha; suitable for kharif & rabi
Arka Harini	Pedigree selection of (IIHR 103 x Arka Pramodh)	Dwarf, early; shelling percentage (60%), sweet seeds; suitable for kharif & rabi; yield 8 t/ha
Arka Mayur	Pedigree selection of (IIHR 105 x Arka Pramodh) x Oregon Sugar)	Dwarf, shelling percentage (60%), sweet seeds; suitable for kharif & rabi; yield 8 t/ha
Arka Tapas	Pedigree selection of (Arka Pramodh x Oregon Sugar) x Arka Priya)	Oval round pods; tolerant to high temperature (up to 35^{0}C); yield 6 t/ha
Arka Uttam	Pedigree selection of (Arka Ajit x Arka Sampoorna) x (Arka Pramodh x Oregon Sugar)	Oval round pods; seeds dark gree; suitable for summer cultivation (up to 35^{0}C); yield 7 t/ha
Arka Chaitra	Pedigree selection of (Arka Ajit x Arka Sampoorna) x (Arka Pramodh x Oregon Sugar)	Tall, maturing in mid season; tolerant to high temperature (up to 35^{0}C); yield 7 t/ha
Arka Priya	Pedigree selection of (Arka Ajit x IIHR 562)	Mid-season variety; seeds very sweet & bold; yield 12 t/ha; resistant to PM& rust
Arka Apoorva	Pedigree selection of (Oregon Sugar Pod x IIHR 18)	Dual purpose variety; whole pod edible; TSS 12%; yield 11 t/ ha; resistant to PM & rust
Arka Pramodh	Pedigree selection of (Arka Ajit x IIHR 562) x CHPMR-1)	Mid-season variety; seeds bold, round; resistant to PM & rust; yield 12 t/ha
UN 53-(6)	-	Snap pea line (whole pod edible)
ICAR Research complex for Eastern Region, Patna (HARP, Ranchi)		
Swarna Amar (2004)	Pure line selection	Dark green pods; pod yield 20-25 t/ha; shelling 50%; tolerant to PM; wrinkled seeds
Swarna Mukti (2006)	Hybridization followed by pedigree selection	Sweet taste with very good cooking quality; yield 20-25 t/ha; resistant to PM
Swarna Tripti (2008)	Hybridization followed by pedigree selection	Snow pea type; fibreless, flat, green pods (7-10 cm); yield 24-28 t/ha; suitable for direct use as sweet salad & cooked vegetable; resistant to PM
IIVR, Varanasi		
Kashi Nandini (2006)	Pedigree selection from (P 1542 x VT-2-1)	Determinate; earliest in seed chain of country; 7-8 seeds/ pod; 9-10 pods/ plant; 11-12 t/ha; tolerant to leaf miner & pod borer
Kashi Udai (2006)	Pedigree selection from (Arkel x FC-1)	Determinate; curved pods; 7-9 seeds/pod; 8-10 pods/ plant; yield 11 t/ha
Kashi Mukti (2006)	Pedigree selection from (No.7 x PM-5)	Determinate; 8-9 seeds/pod; 9-10 pods/plant; resistant to PM; yield 11-12 t/ha
Kashi Shakti (2006)	Pedigree selection from (Hara Bona x NDVP-8)	Semi-determinate; 7-8 seeds/pod; 10-12 pods/plant; resistant to PM; yield 14-16 t/ha
Kashi Samridhi (VRPMR-11)	Pedigree selection from (FC-1 x PM-5)	Semi-determinate; 7-8 seeds/pod; 13-15 pods/plant; yield 10-13 t/ha; resistant to PM, leaf miner, pod borer & shattering

Kashi Samarth	-	Late maturing; suitable for late sowing; PM resistant
Kashi Ageti	Pedigree selection from (PM-5 x MG)	Early, long green pods, very sweet; 50% shelling; yield 9-10 t/ha
Kashi Kanak (VRP-2)	Selection	Determinate, green & straight pods, 7-8 seeds/pod; 8-9 pods/plant; yield 10 t/ha
Kashi Arati (VRP-3)	Selection	Determinate, green pods, 7-8 seeds/pod; 8-9 pods/plant; yield 8 t/ha
CSAUA & T, Kanpur		
Azad Pea-1	Pure line selection	45 days to flowering; yield 8-9 t/ha; susceptible to PM & rust
Azad Pea-2	Selection from cross 'Bonneville x 6587'	Tall; 8-10 seeds/ pod; 30-40 pods/plant; shelling 55%; resistant to PM; yield 12t/ha
Azad Pea-3	Pure line selection	Early; resistant to PM; yield 8 t/ha
Azad Pea-4	Pure line selection	Resistant to PM; yield 8-9 t/ha
Azad Pea-5	Pure line selection	Resistant to PM; yield 9-10 t/ha
PAU, Ludhiana		
Mithi Phali		Edible pods; tolerant to PM
Matar Ageta 6	Pure line selection from Australian cv. Massey Gem x Local cv. Hara Bona	Dwarf; early; gives 50% produce during 1st picking with 44% shelling; edible pods; seeds smooth, sweet, dented; yield 6 t/ha; tolerant to high soil temperature; suitable for processing
Matar Ageta-7 (2020)	-	-
Punjab-87	-	Pod length 9.3 cm; bold & wrinkled seeds; 7.6 seeds/ pod; yield 10-12 t/ha
Punjab-88 (1980)	Pedigree selection of (Pusa-2 x Morrasis-55)	Long pods; 47% shelling; yield 10-12 t/ha; highly susceptible to PM
Punjab-89	-	Double pods; 55% shelling; yield 15 t/ha
Hara Bona	-	Early; 7-8 cm pods; 5-6 seeds/pod; escapes PM &rust
Punjab-8 (1985)	-	7-8 seeds/pod; 47% shelling; less sweet; susceptible to PM
PC-531		Mid-season variety; 8-9 cm long; 50% shelling; yield 10 t/ha
CSKHPKV, Palampur		
DPP-9411 (2002)	Recombination breeding	Pods light green; 7-8 grains/pod; TSS 16.5^0 Brix; yield 10-11 t/ha; resistant to PM
DPP-62	-	Resistant to PM
DPP-4		Resistant to PM
Palam Priya (2001)	Pedigree selection from (Bonneville x P. 388)	Double pod type; self staking; 7-8 seeds/pod; 60% shelling; TSS 15%; yield 12-15 t/ha; resistant to PM, tolerant to leaf miner
Palam Triloki (2013)	Selection	Early maturing; wrinkled seeded; yield 70-75 q/ha; 50% shelling
Palam Sumool (2013)	Selection	Yield 7 t/ha
GBPUA & T, Pantnagar		
Pant Uphar (1985)	Selection from indigenous germplasm	Pods at 11th node; 52% shelling; tolerant to stem fly; susceptible to PM; yield 9-10 t/ha
Pant Matar-2 (1989)	Pedigree selection of 'Early Badger x Pant Uphar'	Early variety; susceptible to PM
Pant Sabji Matar-2	Pedigree selection from (Early Badger x Pant Uphar)	Fruit set start from 6th node; 6-8 sweet wrinkled seeds; pod yield 7-8 t/ha

Pant Sabji Matar-3 (1996)	Pedigree selection from (Arkel x GC-14)	Dwarf; 8-10 seeds/pod; yield 9-10 t/ha
Pant Sabji Matar-4 (2001)	Hybrid of 'Arkel x HFP-4'	Early; leafless type; resistant to PM; yield 9 t/ha
Pant Sabji Matar-5	Pedigree selection from (Bonnevile x P. 388)	Early; suitable for polyhouse cultivation; 7-8 fruits/ bunch; fruit wt. 260 g; yield 9-10 t/ha; resistant to PM
Pant Sabji Matar-6	-	Early maturing; yield 11 t/ha; resistant to PM
Pant Pea-5	-	Early & dwarf; resistant to PM
AAU, Anand		
GC-14	T-19 x Greater Progress	-
GC 195	T-19 x Little Marvel	-
PH-1	Bonneville x P-23	-
VPKAS, Almora		
Vivek Matar-3 (1989)	Pedigree selection of (Old Sugar x Early Wrinkled Dwarf 2-2-1)	Mid-season variety; determinate; 5 seeds/pod; 46% shelling; yield 10-11 t/ha; susceptible to PM but resistant to wilt; suitable for vegetable & pulse purpose
Vivek Matar-6 (1997)	Pedigree selection of (Pant Uphar x VL-Matar-3)	Dwarf; 6 seeds/pod; yield 10-11 t/ha; mod. tolerant to PM, cold & moisture stress
VL Ageti Matar-7 (1993)	Pedigree selection of (IP-3 x Arkel)	Longer shelf life; escapes PM due to earliness; longer shelf life
Vivek Matar-8 (1997)	Pedigree selection of (Perfection x Bonneville)	Mod. Resistant to PM, White rot, alternaria blight, cold & moisture stress condition; yield 11-12 t/ha
Vivek Matar-9 (2006)	Pedigree selection of (VP 8591 x P-185)	Yield 9-11 t/ha; tolerant to PM & white rot;
Vivek Matar-10 (2008)	Pedigree selection of (Azad Pea x PRS-18-6-4-5-1)	Resistant to root rot, wilt, leaf blight, PM & tolerant to pod borer; off season production; yield 9-10 t/ha
Vivek Matar-11 (2010)	Hybrid of 'Azad Pea-1 x PRS-18-6-4-5-1'	Double pods; resistant to PM & tolerant to pod borer; off season production; yield 9-10 t/ha
VL Sabji Matar-13 (2018)	-	Early; suitable for August (off-season); 8-10 seeds/ pod; 48-50% shelling; yield 11 t/ha
VL Sabji Matar-15	-	8-10 seeds/ pod; shelling% 50-55; yield 12 t/ha; resistant to PM
TNAU, Coimbatore		
Ooty-1 (2000)	Pure line selection	Dwarf; high protein in seed (19.94%); tolerant to white fly & resistant to fruit fly; yield 12 t/ha
Ooty-2	Pure line selection	Pole type; yield 33 t/ha
JNKVV, Jabalpur		
Jawahar Matar-1 (1984)	Pedigree selection of (Type 19 x Greater Progress)	Mid-season variety; straight pods; sweet & wrinkled seeds; 52% shelling; yield 10-12 t/ha
Jawahar Matar-2 (1985)	Pedigree selection of (Russian-2 x Greater Progress)	Mid-season variety; 8-10 seeds/ pod; susceptible to PM
Jawahar Matar-3 (1983)	Pedigree selection of (T-19 x Early Badger)	Early season; tolerant to fusarium wilt & PM
Jawahar Matar-4	Pedigree selection of (T-19 x Little Marvel)	50% shelling; yield 12 t/ha
Jawahar Matar-5 (1983)	Bulk of 3 selections (6588-1, 6587-1, API)	Highly resistant to PM

Jawahar Matar-15	Selection from triple cross '(JMI x R-98-B) x JP-501 A/2'	Dwarf (50 cm); 8 seeds/pod; yield 13 t/ha
Jawahar Peas-4	Selection from cross of [(Local Yellow Batri) x (6588 x 46c)]	Medium sized pods; 5-6 bigger sized green seeds
Jawahar Peas-54	Selection from double cross of [(Arkel x JM-5) x (46c x JP 501)]	8-9 seeds/pod; wrinkled seeds; yield 7 t/ha; resistant to PM
Jawahar Peas-71	Selection from double cross of [(Arkel x JP-829) x (JP-501 x JM-1)]	50 cm height; mid-season; big & wrinkled seeds; 6-7 seeds/pod; yield 12 t/ha; resistant to PM
Jawahar Peas-83	Selection from double cross of [(Arkel x JP-829) x (46c x JP-501)]	Dwarf; pods very large; 8 seeds/pod; yield 12 t/ha; resistant to PM
Jawahar Peas-19	-	Dwarf & erect; whole pods edible; yield (green pod 11 q/ha & seed 9 q/ha); resistant to PM
Jawahar Peas-179	-	Edible pods; resistant to fusarium wilt, PM, tolerant to rust, leaf miner, bruchus
Jawahar Peas-220	-	Edible pods
Jawahar peas-501	Pedigree selection of 'JM-2 x JM-5'	Sickle shaped pods; wrinkled seeds; highly resistant to PM
Harbhajan	Single plant selection	Extra early variety; highly susceptible to PM
MPKV, Rahuri		
Phule Priya	Selection	Suitable for rabi season; tolerant to pod borer & PM; yield 10-11 t/ha
CCSHAU, Hisar		
Hisar Harit	Bulk pedigree method of selection of 'Bonneville x P-23'	Seed remain round & green after drying; pod length 6.8 cm; yield 10 t/ha
NDAU & T, Faizabad		
Narendra Sabji Matar-2	-	Height 75 cm; mod. tolerant to rust, PM & pests
Narendra Sabji Matar-4	-	Height 75 cm; 7-9 seeds/pod; yield 10-11 t/ha
Narendra Sabji Matar-6 (2006)	Pedigree selection of 'CKS-123 x Arkel'	Tall, early, 7-8 seeds/pod; yield 9-10 t/ha
Other varieties		
Sarla	Mutant	-
Stral-art	Presoaked seed irradiated with 15 krad X-rays to cv. Kloster	Vigorous, 2-6% high seed yield, high generative capacity & stable yield
Wasata	X-ray mutant	Early, high yield, lodging resistant
PMR-21	-	Tendril type; resistant to PM
Taichung 13	Sugar Snap x Knight	Tolerant to fusarium wilt

Inheritance of characters:

- Heterosis for dry seed yield: 56%.
- Change from string bean to snap bean denotes elimination of strings from pods.
- Non-shedding: Recessive genes.

- Low ascorbic acid: Partially dominant with additive effect.
- High sugar content: Recessive genes.
- Overdominance is responsible for manifestation of all yield components.
- Green pods, inflated form of ripe pods and long axis are dominant characters.
- Highly heritable quantitative characters: Polygenes.
- Linkage in peas: 1st described by Vilmorin and Bateson (1912).
- 1st pea linkage map was computed by Wellensick (1925) and established 6 linkage groups.
- Freezer cvs. are wrinkled seeded due to recessive genes at *R* locus (*r/r*, *Rb/Rb*).

Characteristics	Genes involved & inheritance pattern
Plant height	1. Length of internode: *Coe, Cob, Cona, Cry, H. La, Le, Lm, Min, Prae*; high heritability & high genetic advance 2. Number of internodes: *Mie, Mier, Mine, Miu*
Number of days from sowing to end of flowering	*E, Hr, Lf, Sn*; non-additive gene action
Earliness	Dominant & high heritability
Number of basal branches at beginning of maturity	*Fr, Fru*
Number of other branches at beginning of maturity	*Ram*
Development of leaflets & tendrils	Digenic AFILA (*AF*) & TENDRIL- LESS (*TL*): 1. Wild type (*AFAF TLTL*): with two or three pairs of leaflets and numerous tendrils; 2. 'Afila' (*afaf TLTL*), with tendrils only; 3. 'Clavicula' (*AFAF tltl*), with leaflets only; 4. 'Pleiofila' (*afaf tltl*), with rachids ending with small leaflets
Number of flowers on the plant	*Fn, Fma*
First node bearing flower	Dominant
Number of pods/ plant	High heritability; epistatic gene action; high genetic advance
Number of seeds/ pod & test wt.	High heritability; additive
Thick & fleshy pods of snap peas	Recessive *n* gene& recessive for *p* & *v* genes condition for fibre development in pods.
Round seeds	Dominant *R/R*, *Rb/Rb*
Cotyledon colour	Monogenic: Yellow (*II*) dominant to green (*ii*)
Seed colour	Monogenic; controlling presence or absence of chlorophyll in seed coat
Seeds/ plant	Epistatic gene action; additive, dominance & over dominance
Pod yield	Low heritability
Number of embryos in 5 pods	*B5*
Thousand grain weight	Sg^{-1}, Sg^{-2}
Cold resistance	Intermediate dominance; polygenic & many recessive genes

Diseases, pests and disorder:

- Powdery mildew: Air borne.
- Ascochyta blight: Serious disease causing huge loss.
- Resistance against foot rot is due to phenol content.
- Aphids, leaf miner, pod borer and stem fly: Most serious pests.
- Pea weevil (*Bruchus pisorum*):
- Pea beetle (*Sitona lineatus*): Serious pest.
- Stem fly (*Ophiomyia phaseoli*): Attack early sown crop.
- Root rot can be managed by fungi actinomycetes (*Streptomyces lydicus*).
- Number of leaves and trichome density avoids aphid incidence.
- Trichodorid (*Trichodorus* spp.) nematode transmits pea early browning virus.
- Fasciation is most common.
- Marsh spot: Mn deficiency.
- Formation of toxin 'Pisatin': Ethylene injury.
- Hollow heart: Pea seed disorder reduces pea seed vigour and associated with high temperature after seed set and due to starch deficiency in adaxial region of cotyledon.
- Afila: Leaflets are replaced by proliferation of tendrils & plants are called semi-leafless types. Due to homozygous recessive gene '*af*'.
- Fasciated trait: Gene '*Fa*'- this traits brings greater uniformity of shelled peas at harvest.
- Blanking: Heat or drought induced disorder cause reduced development of ovules within pods.

Diseases	Causal organism	Inheritance pattern
Powdery mildew	*Erysiphe polygoni* (*E. pisi*)	Two recessive gene (*er1* & *er2*) & one dominant gene (*Er3*)
Downy mildew	*Perenospora pisi*	Monogenic dominant
Bacterial blight	*Pseudomonas syringae* pv. *pisi*	Monogenic recessive (*er-2*)
Ascochyta blight	*Ascochyta pisi* (syn. *Mycosphaerella pinodes*)	Monogenic dominant & duplicate gene
Fusarium wilt	*Fusarium oxysporum* pv. *pisi*	Monogenic dominant (*Fw*)
Near wilt	*Fusarium oxysporum* pv. *pisi* (race-2)	Monogenic dominant (*Fnw*)
Brown root	*Fusarium solani* pv. *pisi*	Monogenic dominant
Rust	*Uromyces fabae*	Monogenic dominant (*Ruf*)
Root rot	*Macrophomina phaseoli* (*Aphanomyces euteiches*)	-
Bean yellow mosaic virus	-	Monogenic recessive (*mo*)

Top yellow virus; Pea leaf roll virus; Pea streak virus; Bean virus-2	-	Monogenic recessive
Pea seed borne mosaic virus	-	Monogenic recessive (*sbm*)
Pea mosaic virus	Seed transmitted & cause curling of tendrils into tight ball	Monogenic recessive (*pmv*)
Resistance to pea enation mosaic virus (PEMV)	Aphids (*Acrythosiphon pisum*)	Monogenic dominant (*En*)

21.2 French bean/ Snap bean

- Eulogized as 'Common bean or Garden bean or Dry bean or Kidney bean or Haricot bean or Rajma bean or Navy bean or Fresh bean or Farash bean or Pole bean or Dwarf bean or Wonder bean or String bean'.
- World's most important food legume vegetable.
- Consumed as tender pod, shelled green bean (i.e. large but still soft immature seeds) and dry shelled bean seed/ grain legume/ pulse crop.
- The navy bean got its current popular name because it was a staple food of the United States Navy in the early 20th century.
- Leading producers: Brazil, USA, Canada, China, Egypt, UK and Spain.
- In USA, it is grown for processing in large quantities.
- Snap beans: Stable component of vegetable diet of European & American (about 7 lbs/ capita).
- Snap bean seed is also used in dry state like dry bean types (Pinto, Kidney, Pink, Small red/ black, etc.).
- Dry beans account for 57% of the world's food legume production.
- Latin America produces nearly half of the supply of dry beans followed by Brazil, Mexico and Central America.
- Nearly 80% of dry bean production occurs in developing countries.
- Tall vine types are called 'Pole beans'& short vine types referred as 'Half-runner types/ bush types'.
- Canned & frozen uses have increased in European countries than fresh consumption.
- Most of the beans for processing viz. canned, frozen, freeze dried, are round podded types.
- Fresh market cvs. are flat or oval podded.
- Term 'snap bean' originated from the way fresh garden beans are snapped or broken into short segments by hand for cooking.
- High density culture (HDC): 174,200 plants/ acre is developed by Andy Duncan in mid. 1960s.

- HDC means narrow row with widely spaced plants within the row.
- Snap bean grown for seed production also responds to high density culture.
- Tap rooted with poor nodule formation.
- White seed varieties pods have more sugar content.
- It is sensitive to frost and very high temperature.
- Most of varieties are bushy, day neutral except semi-pole types which are short day types.
- Photo-insensitive varieties can be grown throughout year.
- Edible portion: 94% of the pods.
- Edible beans: Source of vit.A 221 IU/ 100 g and good source of amino acid.
- Copper content/100 g: 0.208 mg (canned) to 0.834 mg (raw mature seed). Median value is 0.37 mg.
- Alkaline and extremely acidic soils are unsuitable for beans.
- Seed rate: Bush type (65 kg/ha) while pole type (25-30 kg/ha).
- Seed sowing in summer season produce better quality pods.
- Higher plant density (43-65 plants/ m^2) give 20-38% increase in pod yield than at lower density (22-29 plants/m^2).
- Narrow spacing along with spray of ethrel @ 0.25 a.i./ha at 2nd true leaf stage give higher yields.
- Pole (climbing) type beans are spaced more between rows compared to narrow spacing of bush beans.
- Optimum pH for cultivation: 5.3-6.0.
- Optimum soil temperature: 13-20^{0}C.
- Optimum cultivation: Short day condition and 24-29^{0}C.
- High day temperature (>35^{0}C) reduce pollen production & pollen viability and cause blossom drop & ovule abortion.
- High temperature (27-32^{0}C) increases flower number but markedly decreases pod set.
- High temperature at seedling stage increases incidence of wilt and viral diseases.
- French bean plants fix 27 to 35 kg N/ha.
- Nitrogen fixation rate and node fresh weight in *P. vulgaris* cultivars 10 times higher in cool and high rainfall areas than at hot regions.
- Nodulation decreases with increase in N application and P application enhances nodulation.
- Nitrate and ammonium fertilizers are inhibitorier to nodulation than urea.
- In hydroponic culture, N fixation by bean nodules is strongly inhibited when $CaNO_3$ is present in medium.
- TVC: is attributed to seed coat permeability for proper germination and varies from 0-95% among bean cultivars.

- White seeded cultivars are more susuceptible to TVC because they imbibe water rapidly.
- Structural weakness along cell walls and low seed moisture content are attributed to TVC.
- Hard seed coat is essential for resistance to TVC and seed coat shattering.
- Bean cultivars resistant to this disorder show 60-80% germination, while susceptible ones show 20% or less germination.
- Flowers: Self fertile, axillary racemes & vary in colour from white to yellow to red or purple.
- Anthesis time: 5-7 AM.
- Anther dehiscence immediately after anthesis.
- Stigma receptivity: Peak on the day of anthesis at 7-8 AM.
- Pre-emergent herbicide: Fluchloralin @ 2 litre/ha.
- Days taken for seed germination under optimum conditions: 6.
- Below 0^0 and > 35^0C, germination does not occur.
- Seed rate: Bush type (65 kg/ha) while pole type (25-30 kg/ha).
- Seed sowing in summer season produce better quality pods.
- Seed moisture <12% enhances cracking of cotyledon.
- Commercial seeds contain about 7.7-13.7% moisture.
- Seeds containing 12% moisture give better germination than low moisture containing seeds when soil temperature is < 10^0C.
- Seed viability is lost within 9 months storage at 30^0C, if seeds contain > 6.7% moisture.
- With same moisture content, if seeds are stored at 20^0C, remain viable for 3 years with 85% germination.
- Osmotic priming with PEG-8000 gives better germination.
- Bush types are hardier than pole types.
- Staking is important operation in pole types.
- Pole (climbing) types have indeterminate inflorescence and long duration.
- Pole type character is exploited for polyhouse cultivation.
- Optimum storage and transit temperature: 3.32-5.56^{0}C.
- Anti-nutritional factor: Flatulence causing factor.
- When string bean matures, two halves of the pod split along the string and release the seeds.
- Stringless types do not split when mature.
- Stringiness types have deposition of fibres in the pod sidewalls and stringless type contain less fibres in sidewalls.
- Improved varieties are stringless type.
- Pod yield: 60-120 q/ha and seed yield: 1200-1800 kg/ha.
- Seed treatment with Mixtalol (Triacontanol) @ 2 g/kg seed increases seed yield.

- Water stress markedly influences pod length, pod yield, number of seeds, sieve size distribution, colour, firmness and sloughing (i.e. separation from epidermal cells during blanching). Pod malformation, fibre content of pods and weight/ seed increases by low irrigation.
- Hard seededness: Type of dormancy induced by the water impermeability of testa. It is a wild trait & cause difficulty in cooking.
- In canning, cut beans after blanching in acid or $CaCl_2$ are stored in cans filled with 2% brine solution.
- PCPA (2 ppm) and NAA (5-25 ppm) enhances fruit set and yield.
- Foliar sprays of GA_3 @ 50-200 ppm, CCC @ 400-500 ppm, SADH @ 1500 ppm promotes earlier flowering under both long day and short day conditions.
- Reliable maturity indices (Reddy and Sulladmath, 1975): Seed size, per cent seed, dry matter content, AIS (alcohol insoluble solids) and distribution of pods according to sieve size.
- Culpepper (1937) suggested percent by weight of seed sewed as an index of maturity of snap beans.
- Harvesting stage:
  - Full grown but immature and tender i.e. 40 days onwards after germination.
  - Crop takes 7-12 days after flowering for pods to be ready for picking.
  - Days taken for maturity: Bush type (45-65); pole type (55-75).
  - About 2-3 pickings for bush beans and 3-5 for pole beans are followed.
  - Loss of crispness during storage is due to loss of water and increase in water soluble pectins.
  - Seed weight is major indicator of green bean harvest maturity.
- Storage life is from 10-11 days.
- Hydro-cooling is preferred over vacuum cooling.
- Seed viability: 3-4 years at dry atmospheric conditions.
- Dry seeds with < 14% moisture, develop fine hairline cracks and affects germination.
- Seed index: [(seed wt. ÷ total pod weight)] x 100 x 10–seed length.
- Seed index is positively correlated with fibre development of sieved snap beans.
- Based on seed index, snap beans are graded as-
  - Extra fancy: 4% maximum seeds.
  - Fancy: 8% maximum seeds.
  - Extra standard: 12% maximum seeds.
  - Top standard: 16% maximum seeds.
  - Standard: 24.9% maximum seeds.
- CMS is used in F_1 hybrid seed production.
- Genetic transformation has been reported using *Agrobacterium*, particle bombardment and electroporation.

- RAPD marker OAM 10560 and *z* gene and marker mapped at a distance of 1.4 cM.
- Specific requirements for export purpose: Straight 10-12 cm long, round green pods in bush beans, flat beans having 12-13 cm length and pods are also in demand in European markets.

Species:

- Secondary centre of origin: Africa.
- Four cultivated species in the New World (Westphal, 1974): All species diploid (2n=2x=22), self pollinated (with small amount of cross pollination) except *P. coccineus*.
  1. *P. vulgaris*: The Common, American, Haircot, Navy, French or Snap bean.
  2. *P. coccineus*: The Runner or Scarlet runner or Multiflora bean.
  3. *P. lunatus*: The Lima bean (large seeded), Sieva bean (small seeded).
  4. *P. acutifolius* var. *latifolius*: The Tepary bean.
- Ancestor of French bean: *Phaseolus aborigineus*.
- *Phaseolus* is monophyletic genus.
- 1st interspecific hybrid between *P. vulgaris* and *P. coccineus* reported by Mendel (1865).
- *P. coccineus* and *P. acutifolius* are crossable with French bean.
- Three lobed kidney bean/ Pillipesara (*P. trilobus*): Indigenous to India.
- Runner bean: Not important for food value in USA, but precious for ornamental blossoms. In Europe, these beans are highly valued for their edible, immature pods much like snap beans. Grown during summer months in more temperate climate. Plant develops central twining vine that reaches > 10 feets. Resistant to bacterial diseases, bean yellow mosaic virus, root knot nematode & tolerant to cold climate. A white runner cv. Dutch Caseknife is popular for both its white, cream-coloured blossoms and its delicious, long, broad and slightly curved pods
- Potato bean/ Yam bean (*Pachyrrhizhus tuberosus*): Perennial, grown for its immature pods and tuberous roots. Tubers are used as vegetable. It is also green manure crop because of excessive nodulation.
- Thicket bean (*Phaseolus polystachyus*): Wild, perennial/ annual in growth.
- Year long bean (*P. polyanthus*): Outcrossing and green seed is preferred.
- Adzuki bean: *P. angularis*.
- Cold tolerant spp.: *P. filiformis* and *P. angustissimus*.
- Salinity tolerant spp.: *P. filiformis*.
- Drought resistant spp.: Gray Tepary bean (*P. acutifolius* var. *latifolius*) or Moth bean (*Vigna aconitifolia*): Outcrossing and dry seeds rich in protein and –CHO.
- Dry seed type varieties are called '*Rajmash*' in India.

Varieties:

- Breeding method to improve yield: Hybridization and mass sowing of individual selection (HIMSI).
- Hooking method of hybridization is better than rubbing method for better seed set.
- Qualities for canning purpose: Light or medium green, round, fleshy, stringless pods having white seeds.
- Thompson and Kelly (1957) classified cvs. as follows-
  - Snap beans: for vegetable pods.
  - Green- shelled beans: used in green-shelled condition.
  - Dry-shelled beans: used in dry state (field bean).
- Interspecific hybridization between (*P. vulgaris* x *P. acutifolius*) and (*P. vulgaris* x *P. coccineus*) fails due to embryo abortion and need embryo culture.
- Interspecific hybridization between *P. vulgaris* with *P. lunatus* fails due to distant phylogenetic relationships.
- 1st round podded cv. was released in 1865.
- 1st stringless cv. was released in 1870.
- Photographs of cv. *Waghaya Ghevada* have appeared on special postal packets issued by Indian Post's & Telegraph, Govt. of India released during 2021.
- Bio-fortified varieties viz. BIO-101, BIO-107 are rich in iron (83 ppm) and zinc (44 ppm) are cultivated in Columbia.
- Snap bean cv. Canyon: Lowest rate of N_2 fixation whereas cv. Viva Pink has highest rate of N_2 fixation.
- Cv. Haibushi was developed by Nakano *et al*. (1997) in Japan by pure line selection method from heat tolerant Malaysian accession (black seeded). This cv. shows tolerance to heat in both long and short day conditions and pod setting occurs at temperature range of 28-29.5^{0}C.
- 'Tender Crop' revolutionized snap bean improvement program. It is 1st high quality processing cv. with slender dark green coloured pods, concentrated (one time) pod maturity for mechanical harvesting for frozen bean processing industry developed by USDA scientist Prof. Bill Zaumeyer in 1958-59.
- Gallatin-50: Leading canning cv. is off-white seeded mutant of cv. Tender Crop.
- Scully *et al*. (1995) developed Beller snap and Tender Cream varieties resistant to root knot and cercospora leaf spot.
- Lines SP-6C, SP-377C, SP-17B, SP-61 and SP-180D have been developed which are resistant to BCM, BYM, CYV and BBW.
- Suitable for processing: Cascade, Selection No. 572, Blue Lake (pole type), Early Gallatin (white seeded).
- Accession PI 165426: Resistant to Rhizoctonia root rot & root knot nematodes.
- L-1: Small leafed compact bush type bean.

- Del Monte: Free from split set disorder.
- Great Northern-27 (Selection-1): Interspecific hybrid between (Tepary bean x Common bean). Highly resistant to common blight.
- Mel Anderson developed > 40 cvs. including Early Green, Early Wax, Slender Green, Slim Green, Improved Tender Green.
- Suitable for mechanical harvesting: Alba, Sanilac, Baymax, IcaTui.
- Seaway, Gratiot, Seefarer: X-ray mutant varieties from USA.
- Resistant to PM: Lady Washington Pinto, Long Kidney, Top Crop, Hungarian Yellow.
- Resistant to anthracnose: Cornell 49-242, Wells Red, Tweed Wonder, Seaway.
- Resistant to rust: Ricobaio 1014, West Ralius, Bush Blue Lake, Mountaineer White, Half Runner, Resisto, BARC-1, BBSR-130.
- Resistant to angular leaf spot: Alabama No.1, California, Small White, Epicure.
- Resistant to halo blight: Refugee, Extra Early, Valentine, Red Mexican, GN Nebraska, V 4604, Noorinbee.
- Resistant to *M. incognita*: Manoa Wonder.
- Resistant to Common Bean Mosaic virus (CBMV): Cranbury, Lady Washington, Pinto, Red Mexican, Morena, Niveo, Monviso.
- Resistant to CTV: Apollo, Blue Mountain, Gold Crop & Wonder Green.
- Resistant to brown spot: Epoch.
- Resistant to leaf hopper: Top Crop from USA.
- Taichung 1: Resistant to rust. Released from AVRDC, Taiwan.

Name	Breeding method	Features
IARI, New Delhi & RS, Katrain		
Contender (1960)	Introduced from USA	Bush type; pink flowers; light brown seeds; suitable for canning; tolerant to PM, mosaic & leaf hopper
Pencil Pod	Introduced from USA	Bush type;
Bountiful	Introduced from USA	Bush type; high seed protein content
Jampa, Watex	Introduced from USA	Bush type;
Pusa Parvati (1972)	X-ray mutant of yellow 'Wax Pod' line (EC-1906) from USA	Bush type; resistant to mosaic & PM; yield 22 t/ha
Pusa Himlata (1991)	Exotic introduction	Pole type; stringless pods; 14 cm long; white seeds; yield 20 t/ha; suitable for canning
Premier, Giant Stringless, BKW-74 (1978)	Introduced from Sweden	Bush type; high seed protein content
Universal	X-ray mutant of cv. Granda from USA	Bush type; resistant to *Colletotrichum*
Sanilac	X-ray mutant of cv. Michelite from USA	Bush type; resistant to races of *Colletotrichum* & BMV
Kentucky Wonder (1975)	Introduction from USA	Pole type; mostly commonly grown in India; long, flat, stringless pods; light brown seeds; ideal for polyhouse cultivation; resistant to halo blight

Canadian Wonder (1978)	Introduction from USA	Pole type; mostly commonly grown in India; long, flat, stringless pods; light brown seeds; ideal for polyhouse cultivation; resistant to halo blight
Wade, EC-29490, EC-24958, EC-30021	Introduced from Russia	-
IIHR, Bengaluru		
Arka Komal (1990)	Pure line selection from Australian collection 'IIHR-60'	Bush type; pods green, straight; photo-insensitive; brown seeds; resistant to anthracnose; yield 20 t/ha; 70 days for flowering; good for transportation & excellent cooking quality
Arka Sukomal	-	Pole type
Arka Suvidha (2006)	Pedigree selection of 'Blue Crop x Contender'	Bush type; photo-insensitive, resistant to rust; yield 19 t/ha
Arka Sharath (2010)	-	Bush type; photo-insensitive; smooth, stringless pods; pods crispy, fleshy with no parchment & perfectly round; suitable for kharif & rabi season; yield 19 t/ha; suitable for steamed beans
Arka Bold (1998)	Pure line selection from Hungarian cv. IIHR-220	Bush type; photo-insensitive, flat type; yield 15 t/ha; resistant to bacterial wilt
Arka Arjun	-	Bush type; photo-insensitive, yield 17.4 t/ha; stringless & resistant to MYMV
Arka Anoop (2007)	Pedigree selection of 'IIHR-220 x Arka Komal 91-17-2-1-4-12-3'	Bush type; photo-insensitive; flat pods, long; resistant to bacterial blight & rust; yield 20 t/ha
IIHR 220	Pure line selection	Bushy& resistant to rust
IIVR, Varanasi		
Kashi Param (2006)	Pure line selection	Determinate; yield 12-14 t/ha; leaves are dark green. Pods fleshy, length 14.7 cm, round, dark green.
Kashi Rajhans (2018)	-	-
Kashi Sampann (2018)	-	-
Kashi Baingani	-	-
ICAR Research complex for Eastern Region, Patna (HARP, Ranchi)		
Swarna Lata (2007)	Pure line selection	Pole type; pods round, fleshy & stringless with good cooking quality; yield 12-14 t/ha
Swarna Priya (2007)	Pure line selection	Bush type; pods flat, green, fleshy having good cooking quality; yield 12-14 t/ha; suitable for *rajma* preparation
GBPUA & T, Pantnagar		
Pant Anupama (1984)	Pure line selection from exotic germplasm	Bush type; dwarf; stringless & translucent pods; resistant to angular leaf spot, blight & common bean mosaic; yield 9 t/ha
Pant Bean-2 (1996)	Pedigree selection of 'Turkish Brown x Contender'	Bush type; mod. resis. to bean CBMV; yield 10 t/ha
CSKHPKV, Palampur		
Palam Mridula (2013)	Selection	Bush type; short duration; yield 40-45 pods/plant
MPKV, Rahuri		
Phule Surekha (2000)	Pure line selection from 'Jampa Improved'	Bush type; straight & flat pods; photo-thermo-insensitive; resistant to anthracnose, CBMV, wilt &

		leaf crinkle
Phule Suyash (2003)	Pedigree selection of 'Waghya x Shahapur local'	Bush type; suitable for kharif & rabi season; yield 17 t/ha
Muttha (HPR-35)	-	Days for maturity 70-80; yield 18-25 t/ha; resistant to wilt
Varun	-	
Phule Beans	-	
TNAU, Coimbatore		
YCD-1 (1994)	Pure line selection from local type	Resistant to root rot, rust, yellow mosaic & anthracnose; yield 6.3 t/ha; dual purpose for green pods & grains
TKD-1 (2001)	Pedigree selection from cross of 'Sel.1 x PV-118'	Pole type; yield 6 t/ha (green) & 3 t/ha (dry); low fibre
Ooty-1 (1999)	Pure line selection from PV. 26	Pole type; yield 33 t/ha; resistant to leaf spot, anthracnose & pod borer
Ooty-2 (2002)	Single line selection from PV 15-1	Dwarf; fiberless pods; highly suitable for cooking; yield 14 t/ha
Ooty-3	Pureline selection	Pole type, stringless pods; shelf life 7 days (hills) & 4 days (plains); yield 35 t/ha
KKL-1 Moringa bean	-	Pole type; seed white & flat; suitable for growing in hills; dual purpose
YED-1	-	Bush type; dual purpose; seeds dark purple; tolerant to root rot, rust, yellow mosaic virus & anthracnose
VPKAS, Almora		
VL-Lata Bean-12 (1973)	Introduction	Bush type; plants 110 cm tall; pods borne in cluster; picking starts after 65 days
VL-Lata Bean-17 (1973)	Introduction from USA as 'Kentuki Wonder'	Bush type; pods green & stringless; picking starts at 60-70 days
VL-Bauni Bean-1 (1985)	Pedigree selection	Dwarf, white flowers, stringless pods, long, round & fleshy; rust resistant; pod yield 8 t/ha
VL- Bean-2	Pedigree selection of '*P. vulgaris* x *P. multiflorus*'	Pole type; photo-insensitive; stringless pods; yield 12.5 t/ha
CSAUA & T, Kanpur		
Azad Rajmesh	-	Bush type; highly attractive, smooth pods, stringh less; yield 6.5-7 t/ha
DrYSPUH & F, Solan		
Lakshmi (P-37)	Pedigree selection of 'Contender x Local type (pole)'	Pole type; stringless pods; seed white with yellow scar; tolerant to angular leaf spot
Solan Naina	-	Bush type; green coloured stringless, straight pods; yield 10-12 t/ha
Other varieties		
Renus	-	Bears pod above leaves
SVM-1	Interspecific hybrid of '*P. vulgaris* var. Contender x *P. multiflorus* var. PBL-257'	Resistant to angular leaf spot

Genetics of characters:

- Seed yield is positively correlated with pods/ plant, seeds/ pod, 100 seed weight, days to flowering, plant height and number of productive nodes.
- Strong association between small leaf size & small pod size is reported.
- Days to flowering is positively correlated with days to maturity.
- Pod number and por weight are negatively correlated.
- Red or purple stem is always associated with red flower colour; pink stem with pink flowers and green stem can have all the coloured flowers.
- White flowered plants bear white seeds while darker coloured ones bear all types of coloured seeds.
- Seed coat colour: Complicated character comprising 8 genes, one basic gene *P* for coloured seed, white seeds homozygous recessive *pp* and black seed colour epistatic to all other seed colours.
- Five genes namely *t, z, I, Bip* and *i* control expression of partly seed coat patterns in common bean and give various seed coat patterns due to their complex interactions.
- Direct positive correlation exists between seed size and seedling size.

Character	Number of genes	Type of gene action
Growth habit	3 genes for pole & bush types; * *L* (long stem) >*l* (short stem); * *A* (indeterminate) > *a* (determinate); * *T* (viny)>*t* (non-viny)	Indeterminate or climbing habit dominant to determinate Pole type (*LLAATT*); Bush type (*llaatt*)
Earliness	Monogenic (*fd fd*)	Early flowering dominant to late
Dwarf plant	Duplicate gene (*dw1*, *dw2*)	-
Green hypocotyls	Recessive	One inhibitory gene
Unifoliate leaves	Monogenic (*Uni*)	-
Leaf variegation	-	Normal > variegated
Flower colour	Monogenic recessive (*wb*)	This phenotype produce white banner petal & pale-violetwings
Hard seeds	-	Few genes
Seed eye pattern	Monogenic	-
Pod stringness	Monogenic	Stringness dominant to stringlessness
Pod surface	Monogenic (*acc acc*)	Shiny node recessive to non-shiny
Pod shape	Monogenic	Round > flat; Large > short
Groove of pods	Monogenic	Non-grooved dominant to grooved
Pod number, pod wt., pod length, pod dia., days from sowing to flowering	-	Dominant or epistatic

Number of pods/ plant	1 or 2 dominant genes	Epistasis present
Foliage colour	Digenic	Green dominant to variegated, duplicate gene action
Hard seed	Monogenic	Soft seed dominant to hard seed
Resistance to root knot nematode	Trigenic	-
Anthracnose	Monogenic (*ARE*); *Mexique 2,* Maxicue 3	Resistance not simple
PM resistance	Monogenic	Resistance dominant over susceptible
Bean rust resistance	Monogenic	Resistance dominant or incompletely dominant
Angular leaf spot resistance	Monogenic gene of *P. coccineous*	Resistance recessive to susceptibility
Bacterial halo blight resistance	Monogenic (*ptpt*) for races 1 & 2	Resistance recessive to susceptibility
Fusarium yellows	-	Incomplete dominant gene
Bean virus resistance	Monogenic (*mo* & *ri*)	Resistance recessive to susceptibility
Common bean mosaic virus (CBMV) resistance	Monogenic (*II*)	Recessive race specific genes, *bc1, bc2, bc3*; most snap bean cvs. in USA carry this gene
Curly top virus (CTV) resistance	Two epistatic dominant genes	-
Fusarium root rot resistance	Polygenic	-

Diseases, pest and disorders:

- Ashy stem blight (*Macrophomina phaseoli*): Seed borne.
- Common blight (*Xanthomonas phaseoli*): Bacterial disease-seed and soil borne.
- Halo blight (*Pseudomonas phaseolicola*):
- Rust (*Uromyces phaseoli*):
- Root rot (*Fusarium solani* f. sp. *phaseoli*): Yield reduction up to 25-50%.
- Brown spot: Bacterial disease.
- Stem fly (*Ophiomyia phaseoli*): Polyphagus pest.
- Split set (i.e. expanded & uneven distribution of pod maturity): Is a problem for bean processors & bean seed producers (Farlow *et al.*, 1979). Due to high day temperature (> 35^{0}C) during flowering, pollen production and/or viabilty is drastically reduced.
- Transverse cotyledon cracking (TCC): Major physiological disorder among bean cultivars. It is enhanced when dry seeds are sown in wet soil. White seeded cultivars are more susceptible. Seed containing 12% moisture has better germination.
- Hypocotyl cracking or necrosis is germination disorder. It is due to low 'Ca' content in seed.

- High temperature at seedling stage increases incidence of viral diseases.
- Common bean mosaic virus: Most serious viral disease and transmitted by aphids.
- Curly top virus (CTV): Severe in desert regions and spread by beet leaf hopper.
- Low soil temperature (<15^0C) hinders seed germination.
- Pod abscission: Lack of pollination; high rate of ovule/ seed abortion, fewer pods/ plant, fewer seeds/pod & more crooked pods at low night temperature of 8.5^0C (Dickson and Boettger, 1981).
- Low protein in French bean: Ca and Mg deficiency.
- Bronzing: Ozone pollutants.

21.3 Cowpea

- Eulogized as 'Vegetable meat or Lobia or String bean or Indian pea or Catjang bean or Snake bean'.
- When grown for dry seeds, it is also known as black-eye pea, kaffir pea, China pea and Southern bean.
- The cultivars grown for their immature pods are variously known as Asparagus bean or Snake bean or Yard-long bean.
- Key dietery staple food in Africa, Latin America and Asia.
- Widely cultivated in Latin America, Africa, Southern Asia, and in southern USA.
- Cowpea is considered as sign for 'New Year's Good Luck' in USA.
- Earliest known name of cowpea in English is 'Callivance'.
- Edible products like soup, salad & cutlets prepared from pod vegetable cowpea are popular out the world and particularly in European and Arabian countries.
- 'Phalaphal' fermented spiced product is prepared from vegetable cowpea in Egypt.
- Excellent smoother crop in weed infested areas.
- Self pollinated, tap rooted and drought hardy vegetable.
- It is grown as cover crop, catch crop, cash crop, and erosion reducing crop.
- Suitable for sequential and intercropping system.
- Grown mostly as pulse crop in kharif and rabi season since, less demand as green pod vegetable.
- Grown throughout India for its long green pods as vegetable, seeds as pulse vegetable, foliage as fodder and green manure.
- Uses:
  - o As food at both green shell and dry tage.
  - o Grown for hay/ silage/ pasture as source of protein (especially lysine).
  - o Used at all stages of growth as a vegetable crop.
  - o Green/ dry mature seeds are boiled/ canned/ frozen.

- o Immature snapped pods as vegetable.
- o Tender green leaves are used as pot herb in Africa.
- o Seed is valued as nutritional supplement to cereals.
- Intercropped with okra in yellow vein mosaic virus management.
- In crop rotation controls sweet potato weevil.
- In USA, HDP of 100-400 thousand plants/ ha with snap pea is followed,
- Protein digestibility and reduced protein quality is due to trypsin and chymotrypsin inhibitor, cyanogenic glucosides and condensed tannins.
- Protein output of cowpea leaves is 15 times greater than seeds.
- Composition of green pods/ 100 g edible portion: Moisture (84.6 g), proteins (4.3 g), -CHO (8 g), fibre (2 g), minerals (0.9 g), fat (0.2 g), Ca (80 mg), P (74 mg), vit. C (13 mg), iron (2.5 mg), vit. B, vit. A (941 IU/100 g),
- Nutrient content of mature seed (Davis *et al*.,): Proteins (24.8%), fat (1.9%), fibre (6.3%), Thiamine (0.00074%), Riboflavin (0.00042%), Niacine (0.00281%), -CHO (63.6%).
- Protein concentration: 3-4% green leaf.
- Crude protein content in seeds: 24.6%.
- Calorific value: 46 Kcal/ 100g.
- Seeds are rich in essential amino acids viz. lysine, leucine, tryptophan & phenyl alanine.
- Low in anti-nutritional factor: Alpha-amylase.
- Highly sensitive to low temperature, frost, water logging and susceptible to 'Zn' deficiency.
- Varieties show varing response to temperature and day length i.e. rarely insensitive to photoperiod.
- Most varieties are quantitative short day plants but day neutral and long day cultivars also exist.
- High light intensity reduces plant height and delays flowering but promotes profuse flowering and pod set.
- Plant types are catagorized as erect, semi-erect, prostrate (trailing) or climbing.
- Growth habit ranges from indeterminate to determinate (non-vining) types.
- Seed coat is smooth or wrinkled and of various colours like white, cream, green, red, brown, black.
- Seeds may also be specked or mottled or blotchy or eyed where white coloured hilum is surrounded by another colour.
- Flowers are borne in multiple racemes on 8-20 inches flower stalks that arise from leaf axil.

- Pods/ peduncle are 2-4 pods and long peduncles is distinguishing feature.
- Anthesis time: 6.30 to 9 AM.
- Anther dehiscence time: 7 to 8 AM.
- Pollen viability: For 42 h at room temperature (28.5^{0}C at 91% R.H.).
- Stigma receptivity: 12 h before blooming to 6 h after blooming.
- Successful time for pollination: 5.45 AM to 7 AM.
- It rarely flowers or set seeds when temperature is <20^{0}C.
- Optimum temperature for flowering: 25-28^{0}C and 10-14.5 h day period is essential for flowering.
- Optimum soil temperature for seed germination: 18-25^{0}C.
- Optimum temperature for root nodulation: 24-33^{0}C.
- Temperature for growth and pod yield: 21-27^{0}C.
- Temperature >35^{0}C cause flower and pod shedding.
- Optimum soil pH: 5.5-6.5.
- Planting distance: 50-60 cm x 50-60 cm (bushy), 75 cm x 50 cm (indeterminate) types.
- Sowing seasons: Jan-Feb. (spring-summer season); May-June (summer-rainy season); July-August (rainy-autumn season); August-Sept (early autumn season).
- Application of calcium aids nodulation.
- International cowpea disease resistance breeding work is carried out at International Institute of Tropical Agriculture (IITA), Nigeria.
- Seed rate: 20-25 kg (bush cvs.) and 10-12 kg/ ha (pole/ vine cvs.) in rainy season.
- Phosphatic fertilizers: Important for better nodulation through rhizobium symbiosis.
- Spray of Borax @ 0.3% and 0.1% ammonium molybdate improves quality and pod yield.
- Pre-emergent herbicide: Trifluralin @ 1 kg/ha.
- Nipping of excess vegetative growth is commonly practiced to induce flowering and fruiting.
- Critical period of irrigation: Flowering and pod development.
- Cowpea shows both photo-sensitive and photo-insensitive characters.
- Storage protein 'vicillin' is responsible for bruchid resistance in cowpea.
- Crop duration: 125-160 days (pole type); 80-100 days (bush type).
- Days for flowering: 40-45 days from sowing.
- Harvesting of green pods (for vegetable purpose): 16-17 days after flowering (i.e. 2 weeks after pod setting).

- Harvesting stage: 60-65 days after sowing (bush type); 75-80 days (pole type).
- Maturity of seed crop: 125-135 days after sowing.
- Main problem in seed production: Seed shattering.
- Vegetable cultivars are less seed yielder than pulse types.
- Mechanical harvesting of green pods is effected in USA.
- Pods of asparagus bean harvest in tender stage and 30-50 cm long. Otherwise pod become tough and fibrous.
- Pod length and pod weight reaches maximum at 12 days after anthesis and is optimum harvest stage for vegetable use.
- Physiological maturity and optimum storage for use as seed: Medium pod length and harvested at 18 days after anthesis.
- High respiration and transpiration rate make pods leathery and unfit for marketing and consumption.
- Delay in harvest decreases quality, increases total yield.
- Number of pickings: 5-9 (pole type); 2-3 (bush type).
- Tender pod yield: 12-18 T/ha (pole type); 7-12 T/ha (bush type).
- Dry seed yield: 1.5-2 T/ha.
- Fresh green pods can be kept for 2 weeks at 0^0C and 90-95% R.H.
- About 8-9% seed moisture is best for safe storage of dry seed.
- Ratoon crop is practiced in Africa (cutting at 10 cm above soil surface) where 10-20% leaves are harvested before start of flowering with little detrimental effect on seed yield.
- MH @ 50-200 ppm before flowering improves pod set and yield.
- CCC sprays induce tolerance to mosaic disease.
- Green colour of pods is restored during blanching (100^0C for 5 min) in 0.5-1.5% $MgCO_3$ followed by dipping into 1% sodium sulphite solution for 10 min.
- Seeds are inoculated with Rhizobium culture @ 375-500 g/ ha.
- Esterage zymograms helps to evaluate accessions of cultivated cowpea (ssp. *unguiculata*, *biflora*, *sesquipedalis*) for variability.
- RFLP marker 'bg4D9b' is tightly linked to aphid resistance gene *Rac1* present opportunity for cloning this insect resistance gene.
- Genetic map consisting of 11 linkage groups spanning total of 2670 cM with an average distance of 6.43 cM between markers has been developed.
- AFLP marker linked to striga resistance provides stepping stone for marker assisted selection and genes encoding resistance to this noxious parasitic weed.
- cDNA library enriched for cowpea genes confirming drought tolerance has been prepared by SSH (Suppression Subtractive Hybridization) consist of 4160 individual clones.

- Novel value added products: Frozen and canned vegetable, replacement of milk protein with protein from cowpea and field pea flour in baking powder biscuits and as legume starch, baby foods, cakes, puddlings, dumplings are prepared as meat substitutes.
- Chilling tolerance during emergence of cowpea seedlings is associated with dehydrin and slow electrolyte leakage.
- In cowpea line 'VCR 1396-2-11', a '*dehydrin*' gene is involved in chilling tolerance during seedling stage.
- Electroporation and partile gun methods can be used to analyse genes that are responsive to drought.

Species:

- Typical cowpea has long and stringless pods with fleshy pericarp, with higher monosaccharide to polysaccharide ratio. Seeds oblong to globuse (0.5-1.0 cm long), black/ brown/ white/ pink in colour, hilum oblong, covered with white tissue and with blackish rim like aril. Germination is epigeal. Cotyledons are oblong or sickle shaped and thick. Flowers are cleistogamous and bisexual (favour self pollination) with polypetalous and irregular corolla. Inflorescence is unbranched, axillary or terminal false raceme, more than a foot long, bearing several flowers at terminal end or peduncles. Flower colour: white with shades of purple, pale violet or yellow. Gynoecium is monocarpellory and androecium is diadelphous consisting 10 (9+1) stamens. Flowers open only once, before dawn (4.30-5.30 AM) and shut by noon. Anther dehiscence between 8-10 PM.
- Several different types of beans belonging to *Vigna unguiculata* are grown and used as vegetables. These include-
  a) Cowpea or Southern pea (*V. unguiculata*): Plants tall, erect and twining. Pods 3-12 inches long, held on stalks above foliage. Bush types mature in about 55-75 days from planting. Pods may be picked as green shell beans or left on plant and used as dry beans. Resistant to heat and insects but more susceptible to cold weather.
     i) Various kinds of cowpeas are distinguished by pod type and colour and pattern of seed coat and these include:-
        1. Purple hull type (red to purple pods);
        2. Cream type (seeds are cream coloured when cooked);
        3. Black-eyed types (*V. unguiculata* ssp. *unguiculata*. Seed have coloured eye around hilum); used extensively as culinary vegetable and grown as field crop to supply dry seeds.
        4. Crowder type (seeds are tightly crowded in the pod).
  b) Asparagus bean or Yard-long bean (*V. unguiculata* ssp. *sesquipedalis*): Grown for edible, immature pods of extraordinary length (12-36 inches long). Considered

to be late maturing runner type of cowpea. Plant is an annual trailing vine. Pods are harvested as either green shell beans or dry beans. Seeds are kidney shaped and 0.25 to 0.5 inch long.

c) Catjang bean (*V. unguiculata* ssp. *cylindrica*): Preferred for semi-arid tropical conditions and are of limited commercial importance. Plants erect or semi-erect. Harvested for immature pods which contain small and spherical seeds.

- Ancestor/ progenitor of cowpea: *Vigna unguiculata* var. *mensensis* is an obligate outcrosser. Found in forest.
- Wild ancestral form in Africa: *V. unguiculata* ssp. *dekindtiana* in Savana zone of Africa and Ethiopia.
- Sampson (1936) classified under 3 groups as below: These variants merge with one another and also cross freely to produce intermediate types.

V. sinensis ssp. *unguiculata*	Common cowpea	Plants viny, erect with short pendent pods (20-30 cm long) & small seeds
V. catjang/ *V. cylindrica*	Catjung bean	Erect plants, small pods (7-13 long), seeds small (5-6 mm long), kidney shaped & thick
V. sesquipedalis/ (syn. *V. sinensis* var. *sesquipedalis*)	Asparagus bean or Yard long bean	Plants trailing; pods pendent; 30-90 cm long, fleshy & inflated to shrink when dry. Seeds elongated, kidney shaped, 8-12 mm long

- All above five ssp. are interfertile but cross incompatible with wild progenitors *V. luteola*, *V. marina*, *V. nilotica* (Faris, 1965).
- Three related species of cultivated cowpea:
  1. *Vigna luteola*: Source of resistance and improved in nutritive value but it is cross incompatible with other *Vigna* species.
  2. *V. nilotica*:
  3. *V. marina*:
- Interspecific hybrid between wild spp. *V. unguiculata* var. *mensensis* and *V. unguiculata* need to use embryo rescue or bridging species technique to transfer disease resistance to cowpea.
- *V. unguiculata*: Completely resistant to bruchid beetle.
- *V. vexillata* and *V. oblongifolia*: Resistant to aphids, pod borer.
- All the four cultivated and 2 wild sub-species of *V. unguiculata* are interfertile.
- Reasons for poor crossing:
  1. Pollen germination is poor at prefertilization stage;
  2. Greater genetic divergence between the parents, lesser is the crossing success.
- Gamble (1918) classified Indian cowpeas into *Phaseolus* and *Vigna* based on spiral or non-spiral keel petals.
- Purseglove (1968) classified all cultivated types in 3 groups as-

V. unguiculata ssp. *unguiculata*	-	Day neutral & grown for forage purpose
V. unguiculata ssp. *cylindrica*	Catjang bean	Evolved through selection from ssp. *unguiculata*; determinate, grown for forage purpose
V. unguiculata ssp. *sesquipedalis*	Yard long bean or Asparagus bean or vegetable cowpea	Evolved through selection from ssp. *unguiculata*; plant vigorous, annual, climbing, pod length >50 cm; pods hang in pair; grown for long pods & used as vegetable

- Cultigroup: An interspecific category below sub-species.
- Cowpea grown for pod as vegetable purpose are intermediate between cultigroups *unguiculata* (grain type), *sesquipedalis* (vegetable type) and *biflora* (fodder type).
- Verdcourt (1970) classified into five sub-species on the basis of length of calyx lobes.

Common name	**Botanical name**	**Features**
Common cowpea/ Bush or dwarf cowpea	*V. sinensis* ssp. *cylindrica*	Determinate growth
Asparagus bean	*V. sinensis* ssp. *sesquipedalis*	Plants vine/ pole type; pod length >50 cm; grown for immature green pod
Catjang bean	*V. sinensis* var. *dekindtiana*	Resistant to aphids
Black eye bean/ Kiffer bean/ China bean/ Southern bean	*V. unguiculata* var. *sem*	Grown for dry or immature seed
Long penduncled cowpea/ Fiber cowpea	*V. unguiculata* cv. *textilis*	
-	*V. unguiculata* var. *radiata*	Pulse type
-	*V. unguiculata* var. *cylindrica*	Dual (grain & fodder) purpose type
-	*V. unguiculata* cv. *biflora*	Resistant to pod borer

Varieties:

- Most common method of breeding: Pedigree method.
- Red cowpea is local type having reddish pink seed coat.
- New Era: Dwarf fodder cowpea. Green manure crop in rice lands.
- Macaibo: Resistant to CSMV of group Como virus. Resistance to this is governed by recessive genes.
- California Blackeye-27: Semi-dwarf, heat tolerant and resistant to root knot nematode and fusarium wilt.
- Asparagus bean var. Zhujiang No. 1 from China is highly resistant to wilt, tolerant to rust and low temperature.
- African cvs. CRSP Niebe and Lori Niebe: Resistant to seed and pod weevil, diseases and suitable for rainfed production.
- Striga resistant var. has been developed by IITA, Nigeria.

- Different cultivars respond differently to photoperiod, hence distinct cultivars for spring, summer and rainy season.
- Genotypes CNC-043, TVU-612, CE-315, BR-1, Poty: Resistant to Cowpea Golden Mosaic virus (CGMV).
- Mississippi, Silver, Victor K-798: Resistant to *Meloidogyne arenaria*.
- VITA-25: Erect type, mutant line carring male sterility genes (*ms2ms2*).
- Tender Cream: Resistant to cercospora, southern leaf blight, PM & root knot nematode.
- For F_1 hybrid production: Use protruded stigma types as females and male sterile lines.
- Bacterial blight resistant and photo-insensitive vegetable cowpea lines: No. 1552, No. 750, No. 754.
- Cowpea-88: Mutation breeding. Highly resis. To yellow mosaic virus, anthracnose.
- Ebony PR (syn. Line 4A): Diploid Australian hybrid derived from Bechuana White x Black eye-5. Spreading and forage type cv. has 16.6 seeds/ pod and 100 seed wt. 130 gram. Resistant to *Phytophthora vignae* races 3 & 4.
- Tender Cream: Derived from Flori Cream x Ala. 963.8 line (resistant to cowpea curculio). Pods slightly curved, 14-16 cm long containing 12-14 seeds. Cream coloured seeds are small (20 g/ 100 seeds), ovate to reniform with smooth testas.Highly suitable for canning and resistant to curculio, rust, PM, southern blight and root knot nematode.
- Selection 61B: Early maturing cv. from Maharashtra and suited for vegetable purpose.

Name	Breeding method	Features
Philippines Early	Introduced from Philippines	Spring (rainy) season
Vuli-1	Introduced from IITA, Nigeria	Multiple disease & pest resistant
Tvu 1889	-	Source of aphid (*Aphis craccivora*) resistance
Tvu- 908	-	Resistant to leaf beetles
Kamran	Iranian cv.	Resistant to cowpea weevil
IARI, New Delhi		
Pusa Barsati (1974)	Single plant selection from Phillipines	Suitable for rainy season; early maturing in 35 days; pods 26 cm long; large green seeds; yield 7.5 t/ha; suitable for vegetable purpose
Pusa Dofasli (1978)	Pedigree selection of 'Pusa Phalguni x cv. From Philippines	Photo-insensitive, bushy & suited for both spring-summer & rainy season; flowers in 40 days; pods 18 cm long; yield 8 t/ha; suitable for vegetable purpose
Pusa Phalguni (1974)	Selection from Canadian cv. 'Dolique Du Tonkin'	Dwarf; suited for spring season (Feb-March); pod 10-12 cm long; appear in two flushes; pods reay for harvesting in 60 days; yield 7.5 t/ha; suitable for vegetable purpose

Pusa Komal (1983)	Hybridization & selection of P-85-2 x P-426 (photosensitive & resistant to bacterial blight)	Photo-insensitive; earliest flowering, indeterminate; suited for both season; flowers in 40-45 days; pod length 22 cm long with synchronous bearing habit; suitable for canning; resistant to bacterial blight, rust, cercospora, PM, southern blight, root knot nematode, cowpea curculio weevil; yield 10-15 t/ha
Pusa Sukomal	-	Highly resistant to golden yellow mosaic virus & leaf spot disease; yield 6-6.5 t/ha during summer & kharif season, respectively.
Pusa Rituraj	Selection	Photo-thermo-insensitive; bushy; pods and red seeds suitable for vegetable & fodder purpose i.e. dual purpose
Pusa Dharni (2019)	-	-
IIHR, Bengaluru		
Arka Garima (1990)	Back cross method (IITA Tvu 762 x *V. unguiculata* ssp. *sesquipedalis*)	Vine type; photo-insensitive; pods stringless; suitable for vegetable purpose; tolerant to heat & low moisture stress; resistant to CGMV; yield 18 t/ha
IIHR Selection-16	Pedigree selection of 'Arka Garima x Pusa Komal'	Bushy, photo-insensitive; rust resistant
Arka Suman (IIHR-selection-11) 2006	Pedigree selection of 'Pusa Komal x Arka Garima'	Bushy; photo-insensitive; rust resistant
Arka Samrudhi (IIHR selection-16) 1998	Pedigree selection of 'Arka Garima x Pusa Komal'	Bushy; photo-insensitive; resistant to CGMV; yield 19 t/ha
Arka Mangala	Selection	Yard long bean variety; pole type; photo-insensitive; long pods (75 cm); stringless; 42 pods/ plant; pod yield 25 t/ha; suitable for kharif & rabi season
Arka Green	Selection	Long, thick & stringless pods; tolerant to heat & moisture stress; suitable for vegetable purpose
IIVR, Varanasi		
Kashi Sudha (2009)	Pedigree selection of 'Kashi Shyamal x NDCP-13'	Bushy, photo-insensitive, resistant to CGMV; free from parchment; yield 8.5-12 t/ha
Kashi Gauri (2006)	Pedigree selection of 'IIHR Sel. 16 x Sel. 2-1'	Bushy, photo-insensitive; resistant to CGMV; yield 10-12 t/ha
Kashi Gaurav	Pedigree selection	Bushy, photo-insensitive, resistant to CGMV & leaf spot
Kashi Shyamal (2006)	Pedigree selection	Dwarf & bushy; 10-12 seeds/pod; 35-40 pods/plant; pod length 30-33 cm; resistant to CGMV; yield 7-8 t/ha
Kashi Unnati	Pedigree selection	Bushy, dwarf; free from parchment; resistant to CGMV; pod yield 13-15 t/ha
Kashi Nidhi	Pedigree selection of 'Kashi Unnati x Cowpea-263'	Dwarf, bushy, early maturing, resistant to CGMV; free from parchment; grown in kharif & zaid season
Kashi Kanchan	Back cross pedigree selection	Bushy, resistant to CGMV & cercospora leaf spot; yield 15-20 t/ha

VRCP-6	Pedigree selection of 'Kashi Unnati x Cowpea-263'	Bushy, dwarf, resistant to CGMV
ICAR Research Complex for Eastern Region, Patna (HARP, Ranchi)		
Swarna Harita (2008)	Pure line selection	Pole type; pods straight, round & fleshy having excellent cooking quality; yield 30-35 t/ha; tolerant to mosaic viruses & rust
Swarna Sweta (2004)	Pure line selection	Pole type; pods white, straight, round & fleshy pods having very good cooking quality; yield 25-30 t/ha; resistant to mosaic viruses, rust & tolerant to pod borer
Swarna Suphala (2006)	Introduction & direct use of NBPGR germplasm line	Pole type; long green pods; seed bicoloured; yield 25-30 t/ha; resistant to rust & CGMV; tolerant to pod borer
Swarna Mukut (2011)	Hybridization followed by pedigree selection	Straight round, light green pod (20-25cm) ; yield 12-15 t/ha; tolerant to CMV & pod borer
Dr BSKKV, Dapoli		
Konkan Wali (2000)	Selection from Sindhudurg area of Konkan	Yard long bean variety; light green pods suitable for vegetable; pod length 35-40 cm; yield 6-7 t/ha
Konkan Sadabahar (1991)	Selection from (V-16 x CM-11)	Dwarf, determinate; Yield 10-11 t/ha
Konkan Safed (1991)	Selection from 'C-152 x JC-10-2-5'	Dwarf; brown grains; yield 9-10 t/ha; resistant to yellow mosaic virus
PAU, Ludhiana		
Sel. 263	-	Early maturing; dwarf; photo-insensitive; popular & cultivated across the country; resistant to bacterial blight, anthracnose, mosaic & CGMV
CSKHPKV, Palampur		
Palam Long Bean (2013)	Selection	Indeterminate; ready for harvest in 55 days; pods very long & profuse pod bearing; green, tender, juicy & stringless; yield 11 t/ha
GBPUA & T, Pantnagar		
Pant Lobia-1 (2008)	-	White seeds; rich in Zn 40 ppm; yield 15t/ha
Pant Lobia-2 (2010)	-	Red seeds; rich in Fe 100 ppm; yield 15 t/ha
Pant Lobia-3 (2013)	-	Fe 67 ppm; Zn 38 ppm; yield 15 t/ha
Pant Lobia-4 (2014)	-	Fe 51 ppm; Zn 36 ppm; yield 17 t/ha
NDUA & T, Faizabad		
Narendra Lobia-1 (1993)	Pedigree selection of (Pusa Komal x Varanasi Local)	Photo-insensitive; yield 9 t/ha; susceptible to cercospora leaf spot
NDCP-3	-	Resistant to CGMV
MPKV, Rahuri		
Phule Pandhari (2006)	Pedigree selection of (VCM-8 x V-585)	Indeterminate; days for maturity 115; red seeded; yield 10-12 t/ha; low stringiness; suitable for irrigated & dry land conditions; mod. resistant to YVMV & PM
Phule Rakhumai (2015)	Pedigree selection of (Pusa Dofasli x VCM-8)	Mod. resistant to cercospora leaf spot & CMV; yield 10 t/ha

Phule Vithaai (2015)	Pedigree selection of (VCM-8 x Konkan Safed)	Determinate; early; resistant to CMV; yield 12 t/ha
Phule Sonali (PBP-1123) 2019	Pedigree selection of (RC-101 x Phule Vithai)	Early; dwarf; determinate; white seeded with brown eye; mod. resistant to YVMV, wilt; yield 13 t/ha
UAS, Bengaluru		
PKB-6 (2007)	Pedigree selection of (Pusa Komal x APC 729)	Bushy; low stringiness; yield 10-12 t/ha; suitable for late kharif & summer season
PKB-4 (2010)	Pedigree selection of (Pusa Komal x APC 729)	Bushy; low stringiness; yield 10-12 t/ha; suitable for late kharif season
TNAU, Coimbatore		
PKM-1	Pure line selection	Semi-training; pods long 40-45 cm; cluster bearing; yield 25 t/ha
CO.1 (1970)	Selection from local germplasm	-
CO.2	Pure line selection	Semi-spreading; long pods; less fibre
CO.3	Selection from C-152	Semi-erect; mature in 80-85 days.
CO.6	Pure line selection	Suitable for drought prone areas
CO. 7	Pure line selection	Suitable for drought prone areas
KAU, Thrissur		
KMV-1 (1996)	Selection from 'Manjari Red Plain'	Trailing habit; black seeds; 20-22 seeds/ pod
Bhagyalakshmi (1975)	Selection	Photo-insensitive; early flowering; mottled seeds
Kanakamony (1977)	Selection from Kunnamkulam local	Semi-trailing; reddish brown seeds; 17 seeds/ pod; dual purpose
Krishnami (1991)	Hybrid of (Kanakamony x Kozhingipayar)	-
Pournami (1993)	Selection from KYM-1	-
Kairale	-	Resistant to mosaic; pink coloured pods
Anaswara	-	Semi-trailing; 19 seeds/ pod
Varun	-	Tolerant to mosaic; reddish brown seeds
AVCP-1		Yield 7 t/ha
Shreya (2010)	Selection	Purple pods, purple streaks at the base of petiole; seeds biscuit coloured; tolerant to leaf rust, aphids, pod borer & American serpentine leaf miner
Hridya (2010)	Selection	Tolerant to aphids, pod borer, rust & American serpentine leaf miner
Mallika (1992)	Single plant selection	-
Sharika (1993)	Selection from 'Valiyavila local'	Pole type; long pods with purple beak; crop duration 90-110 days; yield 10 t/ha
Lola (2001)	Pure line selection from 'Kerala local'	Yield 20 t/ha; trailing growth habit; black seeds; 20-22 seeds/ pod
Vaijayanthi (1998)	Pure line selection from 'Perumpadavam local'	Yield 20 t/ha; 20-22 seeds/ pod; susceptible to pod rot
Vellayani Jyothika (2006)	Selection from 'Sreekayyam local'	Yield 19 t/ha
VS-389	-	Superior variety

Githika	-	Long pods (50 cm); reddish brown seeds, tolerant to mosaic & pod borer; yield (28 t/ha)
Manjari	-	Ideal for intercropping; tolerant to mosaic, good culinary characteristics; pods light green with red seeds
Mithra	-	Trailing growth; long (40 cm) light green pods; deep brown seeds with white speck at one end; tolerant fusarium wilt & pythium rot; yield 21 t/ha
BCKV, Kalyani		
Bidhan Barbati-1 (2001)	Pedigree selection of 'EC 243954 x EC 305827'	Bushy; high yield; resistant to CMV & CGMV; resistant to root knot nematode
Bidhan Barbati-2 (2001)	Pedigree selection of 'V-70 x Sel. Tm-3'	Semi-determinate; non-viny; pods light green; resistant to root knot nematode; yield 16 t/ha
Bidhan Sadabahar		Early mature; determinate; pod yield 11 t/ha; resistant to Cowpea Aphid Borne mosaic virus
BC-244002	-	Resistant to CGMV
BAU, Birsa		
Birsa Shweta (1986)	-	Vine type
Gomti (1974)	Selection	Grown throughout year
IGKVV, Raipur		
Indira Barbati Lal	-	Early mature (within 50 days); purple poded; yield 55-77 q/ha

Diseases and pests:

- Anthracnose (*Colletotrichum lindemuthianum*): Seed transmitted.
- Ashy stem blight (*Macrophomina phaseolina*): Seed borne disease and kills vascular portions of roots. Seed dressing with Thiram @ 2 g/ kg.
- Common blight or Bacterial canker (*Xanthomonas phaseoli*):
- Halo blight (*Pseudomonas syringae* pv. *phaseolicola*): cv. Red Mexican is resistant.
- Bacterial blight (*Xanthomonas vegnicola*): Cvs. No. 779, 868, 1552 are resistant.
- Powdery mildew (*Erysiphe polygoni*): Spray wettable Sulphur @ 0.5%.
- Die back (*Colletotrichum capsici*): Cause pod shriveling, twigs and branches dry up. Use Copper based fungicides.
- Rust (*Uromyces phaseoli*):
- Angular leaf spot (*Isariopsis griseola*): PBL-257 (*P. coccineus*) acts as resistance source.
- Cercospora leaf spot (*Cercospora cruenta*):
- Pod rot (*Choanephora infundibufera*):
- Viral mosaic: Seed borne disease transmitted by aphids. Cv. Sugarcrowder, Sowanee, Taylor are resistant. Use systemic insecticide.
- Cowpea stunt disease: Caused by CMV.

- Black eye cowpea mosaic virus: Seed borne & aphid transmitted.
- Cowpea Golden mosaic virus (CGMV): Major disease.
- Bruchid beetle, spotted pod borer: Affects severely.
- Cowpea weevil/ Bruchid beetle/ Seed beetle (*Callosobruchu smaculatus*): Damage stored seeds. Cv. Kamran from Iran is tolerant.
- Cowpea curculio (*Chalcodermus aeneus*):
- Agromyzid fly and spotted pod borer (*Maruca vitrata*): Most serious pests. Resistance indicate anti-biosis (post digestive effects) and anti-xenosis (deterrence to boring into pods to feed) mechanism of resistance are involved.
- Galerucid beetle (*Madurasia obscurella*): Damage foliage during night hours. Apply granular insecticide Phorate @ 10-15 kg/ha.
- Pod borer (Adisura spp., *Heliothis armigera*): Serious pest.
- Bean weevil (*Bruchus* spp.): Infest seeds in storage and damage quality. Use of 1-2 tablets of Celphos/ Phosfume.
- Flower bud thrips (*Megalurothrips sjostedti*):
- Root knot nematode (*M. incognita*):
- Lygus bug: Serious pest stings on pods & cause pitting of seeds.
- Difference in fiber content of pod wall avoids pod borer incidence.

Genetics of characters:

- Yield is positively correlated with pods/plant, seeds/pod, seed weight, pod bunches/ plant, branches/plant and plant height.
- Seed yield is positively correlated with leaf area, pod number and 100 seed weight.
- No correlation between seed colour and total seed protein banding pattern.
- Generally, resistance to a number of diseases is monogenic.
- Genes *Cls-1* (completely dominant) and *Cls-2* (incompletely dominant) controlling resistance to cercospora leaf spot are unlinked to each other.
- Resistance to Tobacco Ring Spot virus is controlled by dominant gene and this is linked with CMV susceptibility in cv. Black.
- Insecticidal activity gene: Cowpea trypsin inhibitor gene (*CpTi*).
- Simply inherited qualitative characters: Axillary buds; peduncle; plant growth; leaf shape and size; colour of plant, petiole, inflorescence and flower; pod shape and colour; pod attachment; appearance and texture; seed colour, spotting, mottling and hilum.
- Characters conditioned by polygenes: Flowering and maturity; pod number/ plant; pod length, weight and girth; seed weight and shape; pod and seed protein content; nitrogen fixation; pod yield.

- Seed protein content: Conditioned by additive gene action is negatively coorelated with pod yield.

Character	Number of genes	Type of gene action
Day length	Pair of major genes	Short day dominant over day neutral
Viny character	Monogenic	Vine dominant to bushy
Pod colour	Monogenic (*GpGp*)	Green dominant to white; brown dominant to straw
Pod attachment	Monogenic	Erect pod dominant to drooping
Peduncle length	Monogenic	Long dominant to short
Pod length	Monogenic	Short partially dominant to long
Pod weight	Monogenic	Light pod partially dominant to heavy
Flower colour	Monogenic (*PfPf*)	Purple dominant to white
Standard petal colour	Monogenic (*Ystp Ystp*)	Yellow dominant to white
Grain length	Monogenic (*LgLg*)	Long dominant to short
Leaf shape	Oligogenic	Hastate leaves dominant to rhomboid
Leaf size	Monogenic	Small leaf recessive to large leaf; narrow leaf dominant to broad
Seed shape	Monogenic	Elongated & reniform shape dominant to shorter & cylindrical shape
Seed coat colour	-	Purple dominant overall other colours, black dominant over other colours except purple
Leaf foliation	Monogenic	Trifoliate dominant to unifoliate
Cotyledon colour	Monogenic	Purple dominant to green
Calyx colour	Monogenic	Brown dominant to green
Protein content	-	Maternal inheritance
Rust resistance	Polygenic with dominant & recessive resistance components	*RB 11*
	Cytoplasmic & monogenic dominant	-
PM resistance	Monogenic	Resistance recessive to susceptibility
Bacterial canker	Digenic with epistasis (*Bp1*, *Bp2*)	
Angular leaf spot resistance	Monogenic recessive	-
Cercospora leaf spot	Monogenic (*Cls-1*)	Resistance dominant to suscpetibility
Common blight resistance	Monogenic	Low heritable; resistance recessive to susceptibility
Rust resistance	Polygenic	Presence of dominant & recessive resistant components
Halo blight	Monogenic dominant	-
Bean Yellow Mosaic (BYM) virus	Monogenic (*by3*)	Resistance dominant to suscpetibility
Blackeye Cowpea Mosaic virus (BCMV)	Single dominant (*Bcm*)	-
Cowpea Aphid Borne Mosaic virus (CAMV)	One partially dominant gene	-

Cowpea Chlorotic Mottle virus (CCMV)	Monogenic recessive (*cc*)	-
Cucumber mosaic cucumovirus strain Y resistance	Monogenic dominant (*RR*)	-
Cowpea Severe mosaic virus (CSMV)	Recessive	-
Aphid resistance	Monogenic dominant (*Ag*)	1 or 2 loci & modifiers involved in expression
Root knot nematode resistance	Monogenic dominant (*Rk2*)	Complex nematode resistance locus
Curculio weevil resistance	-	Additive, dominant & maternal effect
Bruchid & thrips resistance	Digenic	Additive
Drought hardiness	40 independent genes	Dominant
Heat tolerance	Monogenic	Tolerant dominant to less tolerant
Adaxial stomatal frequency	-	Additive

21.4 Cluster bean

- Eulogized as 'Poor man's bean or Soybean of India or Guar or Dry bean'.
- Grown for green vegetable, dry seeds and as forage crop.
- Crop is used for soil improvemt and as medicine.
- Arab traders have introduced this crop to Asia via south India.
- Guar was introduced into USA from India in 1903.
- Crop is grown in India, Myanmar, Sri Lanka, Pakistan, and in arid zones of USA like Texas, Arizona and Oklahoma.
- Ancestor of guar: *Cyamopsis senegalensis*.
- Cultivated guar (syn. *C. psoraloides*).
- Nutrient composition/ 100 g edible portion: Moisture (81 g), Protein (3.2 g), fat (0.4 g), -CHO (10.8 g), vit. A (65.3 IU), thiamine (0.09 mg), niacin (0.6 mg), ascorbic acid (49 mg), Ca (57 mg), P (57 mg), Fe (5.7 mg) and energy (16 Kcal).
- 1st agricultural product to enter in commodity market.
- It is hardy, drought tolerant, grown up to pH 7.5-8.0 and withstands salinity and alkalinity.
- In heavy soils and at high salt concentration, bacterial nodulation is inhibited.
- Soil E.C. level of 10 dS/m is almost toxic and at E.C. level of 8.3 dS/m, 60% decline in dry matter and grain yield production is observed.
- Crop can withstand 30-40^{0}C during summer.
- Crop is grown round the year in south India and June to August in north India.

- Require long days for vegetative growth and short day for flowering.
- India is major producer and exporter (80% of world production) of guar gum.
- Major importer: USA, Germany and China.
- Two distinct forms:
  1. *Pardeshi* or exotic- Grown as vegetable;
  2. Sotia guar- Used as green manure, vegetable or shade crop.
- Deshi/ indigenous type: Grown as rainfed crop mostly for seed only.
- 'Tympanitics': Animal disease caused by feeding cluster bean.
- 'Hydrocyanic acid': Cause toxicity in animals.
- Shallow rooted crop with surface feeding nature.
- White or pink coloured flowers are small and borne on axillary raceme.
- Mostly self pollinated due to cleistogamy.
- Androecium: Monodelphous (10 stamens).
- Pods compressed, linear & clustered.
- Seeds 5-12 per pod, white to grey or black coloured, 5 mm long with weight of 0.06 g.
- Seed reach physiological maturity at 50 days after planting with 18-20% moisture content.
- Mature seeds (ground endosperm of seed) are crushed & turned into flour, known as 'guar gum'.
- Composition of guar seed: Hull (14-16%), endosperm (38-45%), germ (40-45%).
- Gum percentage in cluster beanseeds: 30-33%.
- Endosperm contains galactomannan gum.
- Composition of guar gum: Galacto-mannan-a mucilaginous substance (80%), water (12%), proteins (5%), acid insoluble ash (2%), fat (0.7%), ash (0.7%).
- Gum is a polysaccharide containing hexose sugar, mannose & galactose.
- Guar gum is composed of D-Galactopyranose and D-Mannopyranose.
- It is compatible with starch, alginate and agar, etc.
- Gum remains stable in pH 5-7
- Gum has high viscocity, capacity of water binding, compatible with many hydrocolloids used in food formulations.
- Gum is useful absorbant for explosives.
- *Guar meal* (dry seeds) contains about 33.3% protein.
- Gum has 8 times thickening power than of corn starch.
- Industrial applications of guar gum: Thickening and stabilizing agent in liquid oral, pharmaceutical industries, dairy products like ice cream & as a stabilizer in cheese, cold meat processing,textile, paper, cosmetic and crude oil extraction industries.

- Gum is used in sauces, dressings, baking mixes, paper manufacturing, texiles and printing.
- India's share is 80% of the world production. It is exported to America, China, Australia, France, Japan, Italy, Holland, Belgium, New Zealand, UK, Singapore and Germany.
- Seed protein content decreases due to degredation into amino acids by protease enzyme.
- Critical stages of irrigation: Seedling stage, branch initiation stage, grand growth period, pod formation and grain maturation period.
- Harvesting of cluster bean for forage purpose should be done after flowering.
- For green manure purpose, it is raised mostly from April onwards.
- Broad casting or line sowing at 25-30 cm is followed.
- Seed rate: 10-11 kg (vegetable purpose); 15-20 kg (grain purpose); 30-40 kg/ha (when raised for fodder or pod); 50-70 kg/ha (for green manuring).
- Seed yield increases with application of phosphorus up to 20 kg/ha.
- Flowering occurs at 55 DAS and pod formation at 75 DAS.
- Most sensitive stage for irrigation: Flowering.
- Single irrigation after sowing increases seed yield by 32%.
- Most critical period of crop-weed competition: 20-50 days after sowing.
- Most effective herbicide: Basalin and Nitrofen or 2, 4-D @ 2 kg/ha.
- Increased seed germination (8-26%) and seedling vigour index (32-83%) is obtained by foliar spray of 1.5% ammonium nitrate.
- Crop duration: 120 days.
- Harvesting stage: 10 days of leaf fall, 40 days afterwards.
- Yield: 5-6 t/ha (green pods) and 6-10 q/ha (seeds).
- Maintain seed moisture between 8-10%.
- Specific requirements for export purpose: Green, tender, 7-10 cm long.
- Seed production:
  - Seed rate for seed crop: 10-25 kg/ha.
  - Under dry land conditions, seed yield of 1 t/ha can be obtained.
  - Two cvs. should be sown 50 m apart to get pure seeds.

Varieties:

- Monopodial types (single stem) and dwarf types are more suitable for green pod production.
- Vegetable type cultivars grown in south India and grown for seed purpose in N-W India.

- Two well defined forms viz. Giant type-grown in Gujarat and dwarf types in Punjab and Uttar Pradesh.
- Two different dwarf forms viz. smooth (vegetable type) and hairy (fodder type).
- CP-78: Early bearing (60 days).
- HG-75: Highest yielder of seeds (1.4-1.46 t/ha); gum (0.4 t/ha); proteins (0.45-0.56 t/ha).
- Vankadia: Famous local variety from north Gujarat.
- Pardeshi: Vegetable type grown in Gujarat. Produces long (12-15 cm) pubescent pods.
- Santacruz: Cool season, sparsely branching, indeterminate andglabrous cv. of USA; adapted to high altitude.
- Gaur-34: Seed purpose and high gum content (30.9%). Mod. resistant to bacterial blight, leaf spot, powdery mildew.
- Suitable for guar gum extraction: HG-884, HGC-365, HGC-563, RG-1031, RGC-1002, RGC-1003, RGC-1017, RGC-1038, RGC-986, RGC-936, RGM-112.
- In breeding program, cross HFG-516 x HFG-590 is best combination for desirable characters.
- Naveen: Early maturing; 40-45 pods/ plant; seeds contain 36.8% gum; yield 11.7 t/ ha.

Name	Breeding method	Features
IARI, New Delhi		
Pusa Mausami (1960)	Selection from indigenous variety from North India	Suitable for rainy season, late podding type, densely branched
Pusa Sharadbahar	Single plant selection from 'IC-11704'collected from Maharashtra	Suitable for mild cold season; branching type; 12-15 branches with avg. 133 pods/ plant.
Pusa Sadabahar (1960)	Selection from local cv. Jaipuri	National variety; suitable for summer & rainy season; single stem with non-branching type
Pusa Navbahar (1965)	Pedigree selection of (Pusa Mausami x Pusa Sadabahar)	Single stem, non-branching variety; suitable for summer & rainy season
Maru Guar	Selection	Straight pods contain round, bold, grayish seeds; seeds contain 32% gum; high protein (31.7%); superior performance in arid regions of Jodhpur; resistant to bacterial blight & alternaria leaf sot
NBPGR, New Delhi		
P 28-1-1	Pusa Navbahar x IC-11521	Photo-insensitive; highly branched grown in summer & rainy season; yield 14-15 t/ha
IC-11388	Single plant selection from Kutch area of Gujarat	-

IC-11704	-	-
PLG 850	-	-
PAU, Ludhiana		
Punjab Guar No. 1	Selection	Bold & big seeds; medium duration & take 90 days for flowering
Punjab Guar No. 2	Selection	Highly drought resistant; sympodial growth & profuse branching; 25-30 t/ha.
Punjab Guar No. 3	Selection	Similar to Punjab Guar-2; short duration; 20-25 t/ha
Punjab Guar No. 4	Selection	Tall, hairy & robust; monopodial; 15-20 t/ha.
Punjab Guar No. 5	Selection	Vegetable variety.
FS-277 (1978)	Selection from local material	Recommended for entire guar growing areas
Agaita Guara-111 (1983)	Pedigree selection of (G-325 x FS-277)	Green fodder 23 t/ha;
Agaita Guara-112 (1983)	Pedigree selection of (G-326 x FS-277)	Early; hairy, unbranched; green fodder 30 t/ha;
Guara-80 (1973)	Pedigree selection of (FS-277 x Strain No. 119)	Green fodder yield 27 t/ha; suitable for N-W zones of India
IGFRI, Jhansi		
Bundel Guar-1 (1993)	Single plant selection from native accession B-5/54	Seed purpose; yield 35 t/ha (green fodder), 6.5 t/ha (dry matter), 1.5 t/ha (seed); lodging resistant; drought tolerant; non-shattering; mod. resistant to bacterial blight
Bundel Guar-2 (1995)	Selection	Superior for grain/ gum production; yield 30 t/ha; suitable for fodder purpose
Bundel Guar-3 (1999)	Selection from local accession	Superior for grain/ gum production; yield 35 t/ha; suitable for fodder purpose; mod. resistant to bacterial blight & PM
CIAH, Bikaner		
Thar Bhadavi (2010)	Selection from local germplasm	Yield (9 cluster/plant); pod yield 75 g/plant; first harvest 55-60 days after sowing; recommended for desert agroclimate
Selection 279-6	-	Early, flowers in 26 days with long pods
CHES, Godhra		
Goma Manjri (1998)	Selection from local germplasm	Erect single stem; resistant to PM, bacterial blight & leaf spot; yield 9-10 t/ha
CAZRI, Jodhpur		
Maru Guar (1986)	Selection from germplasm	Dual purpose; gum content (32.1%); green fodder yield 23 t/ha; suitable for arid region; resistant to alternaria leaf spot, bacterial blight
AAU, Anand		
Anand 301-26	-	Narrow podded with branching habit & flowers in 42 days of sowing
Selection-47	-	Clustered variety (10-12 pods of 8-10 cm length); useful as catch crop in orchards
Guar 160-1	-	Commonly grown in Gujarat

MPKV, Rahuri		
Phule Guar	Selection	Resistant to PM; pod length 6 cm; 50 pod wt. 41 g suitable for kharif & summer season
RAU, Rajasthan (ARS, Durgapur)		
Durgapur Safed (1980)	-	Branched; suitable for grain & fodder purpose; seed yield 15.5 t/ha
Durgapur Bahar (1985)	Pusa Navbahar x RGC-401	Photo-insensitive; unbranched; suitable for vegetable purpose; suitable for kharif & zaid season; recommended for whole country
Durga Jay (1980)	Selection from local landrace	Branched type; recommended for whole country
Guar Kranti (2005)	Cross of (RGC-936 x RGC-986-P-10)	Superior for grain/ gum production; yield 34 t/ha; suitable for fodder purpose
RGC-936 (1991)	EC-248 x RGC-401	Bushy; branched; photo-insensitive; recommended for drought prone areas
RGC-197 (1990)	Selection from landraces	Tolerant to drought; suitable for intercropping; recommended for whole country; yield 10-12 t/ha
RGC-471 (1991)	Selection from landrace	Seeds kidney shaped; resistant to PM & bacterial wilt
CCSHAU, Hisar		
FS-277 (1980)	Selection from landrace	Single stem variety; 28.4% gum; 43% protein; grain yield 15-16 t/ha
HG-75 (1982)	Selection	High yield & early flowering; resistant to bacterial wilt; recommended for whole country
HG-182 (1982)	Single plant selection	Ready to harvest in 110-125 days
HFG-119 (1982)	Selection	Green fodder yield 30 t/ha; highly drought tolerant, non-shattering; resistant to alternaria leaf spot
TNAU, Coimbatore		
MDU-1	Selection from 'IC 432117'	Erect growing; cluster bearing; fruits long attractive; yield 18 t/ha

Diseases and pests:

- Bacterial wilt: Most serious disease.
- Bacterial blight (*Xanthomonas cyamopsis*): Treat seeds in hot water (50^{0}C) for 10 min.
- Powdery mildew (*Leveillula taurica*):
- Anthracnose (*Colletotrichum capsici* f.sp. *cyamopsicola*).
- Root rot (*Pellicularia filamentosa*).
- Bihar hairy caterpillar (*Diacrisia obliqua*): Destroy foliage.
- Aphids (*Aphis crassivora*): Affect flowering and seed development.

Genetics of characters: Ray and Stafford (1985)

Character	Type of gene action	Gene symbol
Plant type	Normal (*BB*) dominant to bushy (*bb*)	*B*
Branching habit	Branched (*Br*) dominant to non-branched (*br*)	Duplicate recessive epistasis
Growth habit	Indeterminate (*De*) dominant over determinate (*de*)	*De*
Pubescence	Pubescent (*G*) dominant to glabrous (*g*); Hairy (*H*) dominant to non-hairy (*h*)	*G*
Leaf size/ shape	Narrow leaflet dominant to broad (normal) leaflet	*Ls*
Leaf colour	Green (*Y*) dominant to yellow (*y*)	*Y*
Leaf margin	Serrated dominant to smooth	-
Foliage colour	Dark green dominant to light green	
Flower colour	Purple dominant to white	-
Pod shape	Straight pod dominant to crescent pod	-
Seed shape	Flat dominant to round (*r*)	*R*
Seed size	Intermediate dominant to small	-
Raceme clustering habit	Cluster not at each node dominant over cluster at each node	*Cl*
	A bearing dominant to all node bearing	-
Male sterility	Male fertile dominant to male sterile	*Ms*
Asynapsis	Synapsis dominant to asynapsis	-

21.5 Dolichos bean

- Eulogized as 'Indian bean or Indian butter bean or Hyacinth bean or Lab-lab or Wal or Country bean or Bonavist bean or Sem or Field bean or Lubia bean or Egyptian kidney bean or Australian pea or Waby Salad bean or Garden bean or Creeper bean or Helmet bean'.
- Most ancient type of bean.
- Under-exploited tropical legume bean.
- It is rich in nutritive value than French bean.
- Lablab bean contains 26-30% proteins on dry weight basis.
- Albumins, globulin, prolamin and glutelin, respectively accounted for 20, 48, 1 and 31% of total seed proteins.
- Anti-nutritional factor: Trypsin inhibitor present in mature and dark coloured seeds.
- On heating trypsin broken down into toxic cyanogenic glucoside which is soluble in boiling water.
- Seeds contain water soluble polysaccharides: Rhamnose, Xylose, Arabinose, galactose, glucose, uronic acid and proteins.
- Indian bean is cool season, drought tolerant crop and resistant to weevils.

- Also grown as pulse vegetable, green manure, and cover crop.
- Grown throughout the country as field crop in Madhya Pradesh, Tamil Nadu and Maharashtra.
- Caruncle: An outgrowth near the hilum of seeds.
- Methionine: Most limiting amino acid.
- Anthesis time: 9 AM to 5 PM.
- Anther dehiscence time: 5 AM to 2 PM.
- Stigma receptivity: Only on day of anthesis.
- Spacing: Pole type (100-150 cm x 75-100 cm), Bush type (60-75 cm x 45-60 cm).
- Seed rate: 20-30 kg/ha.
- Yield: Bush type (40-60 q green pods/ha; 10-15 q seeds/ha). Pole type (80-120 q green pods/ha).
- Limiting factor for productivity: Flower drop. Only 10-20% flowers develop into mature pods.
- Spray of $CaCl_2$ @ 0.1% + NAA 100 ppm at 1st inflorescence increase fruit set.
- Range of heterobeltiosis for various characters: 44-250%.
- Isolation distance for seed production: 50 m (foundation), 25 m (certified).
- Polymorphism between species is higher than those within species or genera.
- Gene coding for lectins arose by duplication of common ancestral gene followed by limited divergence.
- Packing in 100 gauge polyethylene bags with 18-36 vents improve keeping quality.

Species:

- Origin of lablab bean is tropical Asia (India) and it was introduced to China, Sudan and Egypt.
- Verdcourt (1970) has placed hyacinth bean in separate genus Lablab from Dolichos and designated as *L. purpureus* (syn. *Dolichos lablab/ D. purpureus*). He classified *L. purpureus* into following subspecies and these races interbreed freely.
  a) ssp. *purpureus*- comprises common cultivated races of hyacinth bean.
  b) ssp. *uncinatus*- has more slender inflorescence with smaller pods (4 cm long and 1.5 cm wide).
  c) ssp. *bengalensis*- pods linear, similar to kidney bean but dissimilar to hyacinth beans.

Two botanical varieties: Cross compatible.

- *D. purpureus*: Ancestral species.
- Garden type/ Vegetable type: *D. lablab* var. *typicus* (seeds arranged parallel to suture). Possess earthy smell and slightly bitter in taste e.g. CO.3, CO.11, Avarai.

- Field type/ Pulse type: *D. lablab* var. *lignosus* (seeds arranged at right angle to suture). Seeds are mostly rounded with white brown on black coat. Possess sweet taste. It has more protein (20.9-29.2%) than var. typicus.
- *D. bracteatus*: Occurs in Konkan region and seeds are used as food.
- *D. falacatus*: Found in Khasi hills soley for green manuring. Roots have medicinal value.
- *D. hosei* (Craib or Sdarak bean): Introduced from Borneo; used as cover crop in tea and coffee estates.

Varieties:

- On the basis of growth habit cvs. are categorized as a) bushy field cvs. b) twining pole garden cvs.
- Ardhanari: Garden bean x Field bean. Grown in Tamil Nadu.
- Bhadrachalam: Grown in Andhra Pradesh. Spreading variety; purple flowers and purple seeds.
- Rajulu Chikkudu: Creeping variety grown in Andhra Pradesh. Seeds are used for preparing dishes during feasts and festivals.
- 'Rewa' variety has 25.11% protein.
- Generally pole types are photosensitive.
- Photo-insensitive varieties can be grown throughout year.

Name	Breeding method	Features
IARI, New Delhi		
Pusa Early Prolific (1970)	Selection from indigenous material	Pole type; born in bunches
Pusa Sem- 1	Selection from indigenous material	Pole type;
Pusa Sem-2 (1990)	Selection from indigenous material	Stringless pods; tolerant to viruses, anthracnose, aphids, jassid, pod borer & frost; yield 15 t/ha
Pusa Sem- 3 (1990)	Selection from indigenous material	Stringless pods; tolerant to viruses, anthracnose, aphids, jassid, pod borer & frost; yield 17t/ha
Pusa Garima	-	-
IIHR, Bengaluru		
Arka Sambhram	Pedigree selection from F_7 generation (Arka Jay x Arka Vijay) x Konkan Bhushan)	Pole type; photo-insensitive; yield 19 t/ha
Arka Soumya	Pedigree selection from F_7 generation (Arka Jay x Arka Vijay) x Konkan Bhushan)	Pole type; photo-insensitive; yield 19 t/ha

Arka Amogh	Pedigree selection from F_7 generation (Arka Jay x Arka Vijay) x Konkan Bhushan)	Pole type; photo-insensitive; pods wavy, green, medium long & ready for harvest in 55 days; yield 20 t/ha
Arka Swagath	Pureline selection from IC 556736	Pole type; photo-insensitive variety & suitable for round the year cultivation
Arka Visthar	Pedigree selection from F_7 generation involving (IIHR 178 x Arka Swagath)	Pole type; photo-insensitive; pods long, thick, very broad & dark green coloured; yield 37 t/ha
Arka Bhavani	Pedigree from selection F_7 generation involving (IIHR 178 x Arka Swagath)	Pole type; photo-insensitive; pods slender, wavy & dark green coloured; yield 32 t/ha
Arka Adarsh	Pedigree selection from F_7 generation involving (IIHR 178 x Arka Swagath)	Pole type; photo-insensitive; early variety; pods borne in clusters; dark green coloured; pods setting from base; yield 30 t/ha
Arka Krishna	Pedigree selection from F_7 generation involving (IIHR 178 x Arka Swagath)	Pole type; cluster bearing; pods setting from base; photo-insensitive; early: pods borne in clusters & dark green coloured; yield 30 t/ha
Arka Prasidhi	Pedigree selection from F_7 generation involving (IC 556824 IPS-2 x Arka Swagath)	Pole type; photo-insensitive; pods dark green, long, flat & slightly curved; rust resistant; yield 37 t/ha
Arka Pradhan	Pedigree selection from F_7 generation involving (IC 556824 IPS-2 x Arka Swagath)	Pole type; photo-insensitive; pods green, smooth & shiny with undulating surface; yield 35 t/ha
Arka Jay (IIHR selection-1) 1990	Back cross & selection of (Hebbal Avare x IIHR-93)	Bush type; photo-insensitive; suitable for vegetable purpose; tolerant to heat & drought; yield 12 t/ha excellent cooking quality
Arka Vijay (IIHR selection-2)1990	Back cross & pedigree selection of (EP x Hebbal Avare-3)	Bush type; photo-insensitive; suitable for dual purpose; tolerant to heat & drought; yield 12 t/ha; excellent cooking quality
Arka Supriya (2019)	-	-
Arka Neelachal Pushti	Pure line selection from local material	Pole type, round podded; pods rich in protein (4.61 g/ 100 g), iron 15 ppm, zinc 37 ppm; yield 24 t/ha
IIVR, Varanasi		
Kashi Haritima (VRSEM-8)	Pure line selection from local material	Pole type; yield 38 t/ha; mod. resistant to Dolichos Yellow mosaic virus (DYMV); tolerant to jassids, aphids & pod borer
Kashi Sheetal (VRSEM-11) 2018	Selection	Semi-pole type; tolerant to low temperature & DYMV; rich in protein (590.8 mg/g); low in total sugar (0.621 g/100g), yield 18-20 t/ha
Kashi Khushhal (VRSEM-3) 2018	Selection	Semi-pole type; cluster bearing; very early; pods dark green, slightly curved, glabrous, tolerant to high temperature & DY-

		MV, rich protein (635.6 mg/g), low total sugar, yield 40 t/ha
VRSEM-6	Selection	Pole type; yield 37 t/ha
VRSEM-186	Selection	Pole type; yield 34 t/ha
VRSEM-501	Individual plant selection	Pole type; yield 34 t/ha
VRSEM-894	-	Spreading; white flowers; pods small, flat; 60% fruit setting; 320-350 pods/ plant; creamy coloured seeds with white dots; 3-4 seeds/ pod
VRSEM-860	-	Spreading; pink flowers; 70% fruit setting; pods small, flat; 340-390 pods/ plant; creamy coloured seeds with white dots; 3-5 seeds/ pod; used for development of resistant to DYMV
VRSEM-887	-	Spreading; pink flowers; 57% fruit setting; pods small, flat; 210-260 pods/ plant; creamy coloured seeds with white dots; 4-6 seeds/ pod
VRBSEM-3	Hybridization & selection from [VRSEM-11 (pole type) x Arka Vijay (bush type)]	Bush type; pods light green 12.5-14.2 cm; yield 36 t/ha; protein (93.5 mg/g); carotenoid (0.212 mg/g); tolerant to DYMV
VRBSEM-9	Hybridization & selection from [VRSEM-11 (pole type) x Gomachi Green (bush type)]	Bush type; pod length 12.6 cm; pods green 10-12 cm; yield 35 t/ha; tolerant to DYMV
VRBUSHSEM-14	Hybridization & selection of [Kashi Sheetal (pole) x Konkan Bhushan (bush)]	Bush type; pod length 12.9 cm; protein 77.6 mg/g; phenol 1.36 mg/g; proline 1.42 ug/g; yield 21 t/ha; tolerant to DYMV
VRBSEM-18	Hybridization & selection of [Kashi Sheetal (pole) x Konkan Bhushan (bush)]	Bush type; pod length 12.6 cm; yield 25 t/ha; tolerant to DYMV
ICAR Research Complex for Eastern Region, Patna (HARP, Ranchi)		
Swarna Rituvar (2011)	Pure line selection	Pole type; photo-insensitive; flat creamy white pods; yield 13-15 t/ha; suitable for off-season cultivation in rainy season
Swarna Utkrisht (2006)	Pure line selection	Pole type; photo-insensitive; flat green pods; yield 35-40 t/ ha; tolerant to anthracnose, mosaic viruses & pod borer
CIAH, Bikaner		
Thar Kartiki (2010)	Selection	Pole type; pod yield (1.75 kg/ plant; 11 t/ha)
Thar Maghi (2010)	Selection	Pole type; pod yield (1.75 kg/ plant; 11 t/ha); suitable for commercial cultivation
TNAU, Coimbatore		
CO.1 (1980)	Pure line selection from local strain (var. *typicus* x var. *lignosus*)	Bush type; pods flat; crop duration 140 days; drought tolerant; dual purpose; high protein & fat content
CO.2 (DL 250) 1984	Hybrid of CO.8 x CO.1	Bush type; 5-6 branches; photo-insensitive, deep purple flowers; prolific bearer; pods 12 cm long, flat, green, tetra seeded; black seeds

CO.3 (DL 269)	Selection from *Yanaikathu Avarai*	Pole type; deep purple flowers; shy bearer; pods 12 cm long; black seeds
CO.4 (DL 453)	Selection from *Sivappa Avarai*	Pole type; purple flowers; grown round the year; flowers in 85-90 days
CO.5 (DL 692)	Selection from *Kozhikkal Avarai*	Pole type; white flowers; yellowish green pods with chocolate colour seeds; flowers in 110-120 days
CO.6 (DL-259)	Pedigree selection of 'DL-244 x DL-3196'	Bush type; white flowers; narrow pods; deep brown seeds
CO.7 (DL-244)	Pedigree selection of 'DL-3169 x CO.5'	Bush type; white flowers; semi-flat white pods with brown seeds
CO.8	Pedigree selection of 'CO.5 x DL-3169'	Bush type; 120 days duration
CO.9	Spontaneous mutant MS-98678	Bush type; dual purpose
CO.10	Gamma ray mutant of 'CO.6'	Dual purpose; white pods;
CO.11	Hybrid of (CO.9 x Yanaikathu)	Bush type;
CO.12	Hybrid of (CO.9 x CO.4)	Bush type;
CO.13	Hybrid of (CO.9 x Trailing type)	Bush type; pods long & green
KKL-1	Selection from local type	Pole type; pods in cluster; 11.6 cm long pods; 5-6 seeds; yield 3.5 t/ha.
DL-1428	Hybrid of (Garden bean x Field bean)	White seeds; white pods
DL-2542	-	Good for rainfed; crop duration 165 days; purple flowers & black coloured seeds
DL-231	-	Long duration; white flowers & buff coloured seeds
DL-269	-	Flat podded; purple flowers & black coloured seeds
DL-125-26	-	Bush type; purple ringed pods
CSAUA & T, Kanpur		
Kalyanpur type-1	-	Pole type;
Kalyanpur type-2	-	Pole type;
Azad Sem-1	-	Pole type;
Rajani	-	Pole type; pods narrow, ovate, 10 cm length & 1.2 cm width; cross section has bright shinning green colour; yield 7-8 t/ha in 200 days
KDB-403	-	Pole type; pods long (13 cm) & narrow (1.2 cm); shinning green colour; yield 5-6 t/ha
KDB-405	-	Pole type; pods medium (9.6 cm long), very narrow in breadth (1.3 cm); pods have dark green band in middle whiel border is light; yield 3-4 t/ha
Dr PDKV, Akola		
Dasara wal (1985)	-	Pole type; pods violet coloured with length (8-10 cm) & breadth (2-2.5 cm); seeds milky whte coloured; yield 10-12 t/ha
Dipali wal (1985)	-	Pole type; pods flat, cream coloured with length (12-15 cm) & breadth (3-3.5 cm); seeds red coloured; yield 12-15 t/ha

Dr BSKKV, Dapoli		
Konkan Wal-1 (1982)	Selection of 'Wal-2-K-2 x Wal-125-36'	Bush type; photo-insensitive; dual purpose; yield 9-10 q/ha; resistant to Yellow mosaic virus
Konkan Bhushan (1989)	Pedigree selection of (Hebbal Avare-3 x Wal-1)	Bush type; photo-insensitive; pods slightly curved, stringless; dual purpose; yield 12-15 t/ha
Konkan Wal-2 (1991)	Selection from 'Wal-21 x Konkan Wal-1'	Bush type; yield 9-10 t/ha; tolerant to Yellow mosaic virus
MPKV, Rahuri		
Phule Gouri	Pure line selection	Pole type; tolerant to pod borer, anthracnose, leaf spot & leaf miner
Phule Suruchi	Local selection from Kolhapur area	Pole type; photo-insensitive; straight pods
AAU, Anand		
AHDB-3	Single plant selection	Pole type;
AHDB-6	Single plant selection	Pole type;
CCSHAU, Hisar		
Hisar Kirti	-	Pole type;
JNKVV, Jabalpur		
JDL-79	-	Pole type; flat broad whitish green pods
JDL-53	-	Pole type; flat small narrow whitish green pods
IGKV, Raipur		
Chhattisgarh Sem-1	-	Early mature; yield 20 t/ha; resistant to Bean mosaic virus, rhizoctonia blight & insects
Chhattisgarh Purple Sem	-	Early mature; purple pods; yield 21 t/ha
UAS, Bengaluru		
Hebbal Avare-1	Pedigree selection of 'US-67 x 31'	Bush type; photo-insensitive
Hebbal Avare-3	-	Bush type; determinate type; photo-insensitive
Hebbal Avare-4	-	Bush type; photo-insensitive
KAU, Vellanikkara		
Hima (2006)	Selection from local germplasm	Pole type; yield 13 kg/plant
Grace (2006)	Selection from local germplasm	Pole type; yield 13 kg/plant

Inheritance of characters:

- Highly heritable characters: Pods/ plant; seeds/ pod and 100 seed wt.
- Negative correlation between seed protein and methionine content was reported.

Character	Number of genes	Type of gene action
Pod colour	Monogenic	Green dominant to light green
Pod character	Monogenic (*FpFp*)	Flat dominant to swollen
Seed colour	Monogenic	Chocolate dominant to brown
Pigmentation of vegetative parts & flower	Monogenic	Purple dominant to white

Genes isolated:

Gene	Phenotype
Are	Resistance to anthracnose
Da	Straight pods
Gas	Determinate plant growth
In	Causes both male & female sterility
Itor	Determinate growth *(fin)*
neu^{+}	Short day flowering response
Mo	Conditions resistance to bean virus
Uni	Unifoliate leaves
Tri	Produces three cotyledons

Diseases:

Name	Casual organism	Vector
Anthracnose	*Colletotrichum lindemuthianum*	-
Powdery mildew	*Erysiphe polygonii*	-
Ashy stem blight	*Macrophomina phaseolina*	Seed borne
Web blight	*Rhizoctonia solani*	-
Angular leaf spot	*Isariopsis griseola*	-
Floury leaf spot	*Ramlaria phaseoli*	-
Inflorescence blight/ pod rot	*Choanephora infundibulifera*	-
Dolichos yellow mosaic virus (DYMV)	Virus	White fly
Enation mosaic	Virus	Mechanical sap, spider mite
Yellow flecks	MLOs	White fly
Phyllody	MLOs	Leaf hopper
Golden mosaic	MLOs	White fly

21.6 Lima bean

- Eulogized as 'Double bean or Butter bean or or Big lima or Potato lima or Burma bean or Rangoon bean or Madagascar bean or Java bean or Hibbert bean or Sugar bean or Prolific bean or Civet bean or *Pavata*'.
- Cultivation evidence dates back to 7000 years.
- Introduced from USA.
- Highly nutritious legume.
- It is used to prepare wine.
- Anti-nutritional factor: Protease inhibitor.
- Cultivated primarily for their enlarged (but not fully mature) seeds and utilized for processing/ canning in USA.
- Utilization: Frozen products (50%), canning (30%), fresh utilized (20%), seeds (green or dried) are boiled/ steamed/ baked. Pods are not consumed.

- Require considerably longer growing period (60-110 days) than snap beans.
- Pods are curved, oblong and contain 2-6 seeds, ranging in size from 0.25-1".
- Seed coat colour: White, cream or light green & other colours (red, purple, brown) occur.
- Coloured ripe seeds contain cyanogenic glucoside (HCN).
- Optimum soil pH for cultivation: 6-7.
- Can stand alkalinity upto pH 8.0.
- Flower bracts are small, inconspicuous & pointed in *P. lunatus.*
- Predominantly self pollinated but cross pollinate upto 20%.
- Herkogamy is noticed.
- Cross incompatible with French bean.
- Seed germination occurs in 30 to 48 days at soil temperatures of 15-20^{0}C and at 25-30^{0}C, seed germinate within a week.
- Soil temperature < 10^{0}C and > 35^{0}C seed germination is extremely poor.
- It is extremely heat sensitive crop.
- High temperature (26-30^{0}C) and low humidity during blossoming drastically affects fruit set.
- Above 30^{0}C, and R.H. less than 65%, drastically affects fruit set in large seeded cultivars.
- Extremely damp and rainy weather also causes blossoms to drop and this severely limits production of these types to coastal areas.
- Harvesting:
  - Bush types mature earlier and are harvested in few pickings.
  - Lima bean harvesters remove pods from vines and shell the beans in one operation.
  - Pole types are not adapted to mechanical harvesting and are picked by hand.
- It is highly perishable and need rapid cooling after harvest to maintain quality.
- It is cooled by any one of 3 methods: Hydro-cooling, vacuum cooling and forced-air cooling.
- Hydro cooling is preferred since free water helps prevent wilting and shriveling.
- Lima beans are cold sensitive and occurs chilling at recommended storage temperature.
- Storage/ transport temperature below 2.7^{0}C causes severe chilling injury in shelled limas.
- Chilled beans develop russeting and surface pitting after removal to warm temperature.
- Dry beans are stored at 4.4-10^{0}C & R.H. of 40-50% and have storage life of 6-10 months.
- If beans have moisture content below 14%, the R.H. should be 70%. This increases seed moisture content and avoids seed coat cracking during storage and marketing.

Species and types:

- They are grouped into large and small seeded types.
    a) Large seeded lima (*P. limensis*): Perennial but grown as annual. Require more heat than small seeded. These contain 3 seeds/ pod as contrasted to 4-5 in smaller types.
    b) Bush form is classified as *P. limensis* var. *limenanus*.
    c) Small seeded or baby types are annual & belong to *P. lunatus*.
    d) Dwarf/ bush form of small seeded 'Sieva bean' is *P. lunatus* var. *lunonanus*.
- Cultivars are grouped according to growth habit (bush & pole type) & seed size (small & large).
- Dwarf/ bush types are used for processing.
- Bush types have increased earliness & better tolerance to weather stresses.
- Pole or climbing types are grown in home gardens.
- Large seeded lima beans are more robust than small-seeded limas but slower to form seeds in the pods and less tolerant to heat and humidity.
- Small seeded, red coloured types called 'sieva or butter bean' and used as pulse.

Varieties:

- Improved cultivars are day neutral type.
- Henderson Bush: Discovered in Virginia in 1939 by chance selection ffom dwarf plants. Small, erect bush, very small green seeds and used for canning.
- Fordhook: Discovered in California in 1903 by chance selection from Sieva pole beans. It is large seeded, dwarf plant type and sensitive to adverse weather conditions. Widely used for canning.

	Cultivars	Days to maturity	Uses	Seed colour
Bush types				
Large seeded	Fordhook 242	78	Fresh market, processing & garden	Light green
	Fordhook 169	75	Fresh market, processing & garden	Light green
Small seeded	Dixie Butterpea	75	Fresh market & garden	White
	Thaxter	70	Processing	Greenish-white
	Early Thorogreen	66	Processing	Green
	Henderson Bush	65	Fresh market & garden	Pale green
	Nemagreen	70	Processing	Green
	Bridgeton	70	Processing	Pale green
Pole type				
Large seeded	Challenger	90	Garden	Light green
	King of the Garden	88	Garden	Greenish-white
Small seeded	Sieva	80	Garden	White

- Pole type: Karolina Butter, Florida Butter, KKL-1.
- Bush type: Baby Potato, Baby Fordhook, (canning purpose), Handerson Bush (canning purpose), Burpee Bush.
- Semi-pole type: Wilbur, Hopi.
- Nemagreen: Resistant to nematodes.

Name	Breeding method	Features
ICAR Research Complex for Eastern Region, Patna (HARP, Ranchi)		
Swarna Poshan (2015)	-	High yield & resistant to many diseases
TNAU, Coimbatore		
CO.2 (1984)	CO.8 x CO.1	Photo-insensitive; tetra seeded pods
CO.6	-	-
CO.10	γ- ray irradiation of CO.6	-
MPKV, Rahuri		
Phule Suvarn	Selection	Green pods, yield 13.7 t/ha; mod. resis. to aphids
Dr PDKV, Akola		
Shakuntala (AKKLB-2)	-	Long green pods; attractive seed colour, palatable; yield 35-40 q/ha

21.7 Broad bean

- Eulogized as 'Faba bean or Winter bean or Horse bean or Bakla bean or Frost resistant bean or Field bean or Tick bean or Windsor bean'.
- This bean has been on man's food list since the Stone Age.
- Largest collection in world is maintained at International Centre for Agriculture Research in Dry Areas (ICARDA), Aleppo, Syria.
- Erect vigorous annual with well developed primary root.
- Only bean sown in autumn and grown as winter crop in high elevations.
- Cultivated in ancient Egypt, Greece, Rome and Israel.
- Popular vegetable in northern Europe, Canada, USA, Brazil and Mexico.
- Used as fresh tender bean or green shelled bean, frozen or dried product.
- Minor crop and planted as cover crop in orchards.
- Require long, cool to moderate warm growing season.
- Optimum temperature for growth: 15-18^{0}C & tolerate to low temperature (4^{0}C) but not higher than 24^{0}C.
- Tolerates drought and much cooler conditions.
- Highly susceptible to acidic soils.
- Stem is square in cross section and flowers pollinated by insects.
- Susceptible to acidic soils.
- Leaves: Pinnately compound & with age, broad bean leaves become blackish.

- Inflorescence: Axillary raceme of 2 to 6 white, self fertile flowers with wings marked by large black spot.
- 'Dancing style' of stigma is reported.
- Pods are borne in upright clusters of 5 or more in leaf axil.
- Pods 15 cm long, 2 cm wide with round in cross section.
- Pods contain 5-6 large seeds, which are used as green shell beans or dried for storage.
- Nutrient composition/ 100 g edible portion:
  - Fresh seeds: Proteins (7.1 g), Ca (38 mg), P (127 mg), Ascorbic acid (140 mg).
  - Dried seeds: Proteins (26.2 g), Ca (104 mg), P (34 mg), Fe (6.7 mg), Vit. A (130 IU), Thiamine (0.38 mg), Riboflavin (0.24 mg), Niacin (2.1 mg), Ascorbic acid (16 mg).
- Good source of L-Dopa (Dopamine).
- Anti-nutritional factor: Haemolytic anaemic factor causing '*favism*'.
- Favism: An illness in people caused by inhaling pollen or eating extremely small quantities of green pods.
- Tolerates more water stress due to higher protein accumulation.
- Protein content is maximum in black seeded varieties (25-30%) followed by yellow (23-27%), brown (23-28%).
- Seed rate: 70-100 kg/ha.
- Sown in autumn and grown as winter crop in higher elevations in tropical regions.
- Removal of side shoots and pinching of growing points encourages greater uniformity in pod setting and early swelling of pods.
- Harvested as an immature shelled product or as a seed crop.
- Days taken for maturity: 120 (as winter crop); 65-75 (summer crop).

Classification:

a) On the basis of seed colour-
  - White seeded: Less soft.
  - Green seeded: Soft and suitable for freezing.

b) On the basis of pod size-
  - Large podded: Plants tall, erect, pods long and borne in cluster.
  - Small podded: Plants small, erect, pods small, fleshy and borne in cluster.

Varieties:

- Long pod type: Red Epicure.
- Windsor type: Imperial Green Windsor, Imperial White Windsor, Giant Four Seeded Green Windsor.

- Selection BR-1: Black seeded.
- Selection BR-2: Yellow seeded.
- Jawahar Vicia-73-31: Dormant type grown in Madhya Pradesh.
- Warrior, Alabama 1984: Resistant to *M. incognita.*
- White seeded mutant through irradiation is resistant to southern cowpea weevil.

Name	Breeding method	Features
IARI, New Delhi		
Pusa Summet	-	1st high yielding protein rich variety for nutritional security; long pod type; pods in cluster; 10 branches/ plant; pod length 6 cm; pod wt. 1.75 g; 100 pods/ plant; mature in 70 days; yield 18 t/ha
Pusa Udit (2012)	-	Long pod type; pods are extra long, flattish and light green; dual purpose
ICAR Research Complex for Eastern Region, Patna (HARP, Ranchi)		
Swarna Safal	Selection	-
Swarna Suraksha (2019)	Selection	Semi bushy; early (110-115 days); drought tolerant; mod. resistant to major pest & diseases; pod length (4.0-4.5 cm); yield (2.5-3.1 t/ha); TSS 10.9%; low content of anti-nutritional factors tannin & phytate
Swarna Gaurav (2019)	Selection	Bushy; early (120-125 days); drought tolerant, mod. resistant to majorpest & diseases; pod length (4.0-4.5 cm); yield (3.5-4 t/ha); TSS 10.34%; low content of anti-nutritional factors tannin & phytate

Genetics of character:

- Seed yield is positively correlated with pods/plant, seeds/pod, clusters/plant, branches/plant and internode length while it is negatively correlated with flowering time, days to maturity nd plant height.
- Protein content is controlled by polygenes and influenced by environment.

Diseases and pests:

- Wide spread, seed borne and unique diseases are Broad bean Mottle virus, Broad bean Stain virus, Broad bean True mosaic virus, and Broad bean Vascular virus.

21.8 Winged bean

- Eulogized as 'Vegetable of 20th century or Four angled bean or God sent vegetable or Goa bean or Fox tail bean or Creeping bean or Supermarket on a stalk or Multiflorus bean or Asparagus pea or Princess pea or One Species Super market or Wonder vegetable or Manilla bean or Soya's rival'.
- International gene bank for winged bean: The Institute of Plant Breeding, University of Phillipines.

- Model crop for study of genetic modifications in legumes.
- An important legume for malnutrition in 3rd World countries.
- Introduced to India in 1799 at Kolkata.
- Grown in entire N-E states and Tamil Nadu, Goa, Maharashtra, Kerala, Karnataka and West Bengal.
- Herbaceous perennial grown asannual climber in north India with wiry stem having tendency for twinning.
- Used as cover crop to prevent soil erosion.
- Restorative fallow crop because of its nodulation.
- Possess many medicinal uses viz. leaf infusion to treat eye and ear infection and dyspepsia; leaf paste for boils and to treat small pox; seeds in treatment of veneral diseases; pods are diabetic diet and good for blood; tuber poultice to treat vertigo.
- Great potential to ease the problem of protein malnutrition.
- It is multi-vitamin and multi-mineral packed legume.
- Practically all parts are edible (tender pods, flowers, flower buds and green fruit rich in protein as vegetable, grain as pulse, edible tuber and foliage as fodder).
- Tuberous roots are pealed, baked or boiled and eaten as snacks in Myanmar, New Guinea.
- Tubers are cylindrical shaped with brown fibrous skin. Flesh is white & solid.
- Globulin protein fraction of seeds is high in lysine, arginine and leucine.
- The albumin fraction is high in cystine and methionine.
- Seeds contain 2.8 to 4.8% starch and 6.4 to 8.9% soluble sugars.
- Winged bean oil contains fatty acids (53.8 to 68.5%).
- Galactose (44 to 54.9%) is the main sugar.
- Polysaccharides are essentially non-starch polysaccharides, heterogeneous and insoluble.
- Tubers deteriorate rapidly.
- Small tubers are suitable for eating.
- Very high nitrogen fixing ability due to exceptionally large and numerous nodules, which was 1st quantified by Masefield (1957).
- Individual plant produces 440 nodules (Rhizonbia strain) with their fresh wt. upto 700 lbs/ acre and is capable of fixing 120-247 kg/ ha nitrogen.
- Nodule number is hghest in 45 days old plants and nodule dry weight in 75 days old plants.
- High nodulating strains viz. JCv44 (in West Bengal), TAL223 (in Hawaii), RRIM56 (in Malaysia) and LBNC3 (in Sri Lanka).
- Seed inoculation with *Rhizobium* increases weed yield by 6.2 to 23.6% in Nigerian winged bean.
- Seeds are not easily separated from pod.

- Trifoliate leaves and vary in shape from oval to ovate-lanceolate with entire margin.
- Inflorescence: Axillary raceme bearing many flowers.
- Flowers: Blue/ purple/ whie to reddish purple.
- Pods show 4 sides with wings protruding from angles and vary in shape and length.
- Seed: Vary from 5 to 40 per pod and are spherical and white/ tan/ dark brown/ black coloured.
- Self pollinated but cross pollination to extent of 7.6%.
- Pollination agent: Bumble bee.
- Tubers (storage roots) are small, irregular, spindle shaped and weigh around 50 g.
- Tuber contains 8.2 to 31.1% protein (Hildebrand *et al.*, 1982) while pods contain 1.2-2.9%.
- Tuberization occurs in many cultivars and is varietal characters.
- Typical short day plant.
- Day length of 11-13 h helps in vegetative phase.
- Photo-insensitive short day plant for flowering and fruiting.
- Short day planting results in flowering within 8-10 weeks.
- Critical day length for flowering and tuber initiation: 11.25 and 12.25 hours.
- Optimum temperature for flowering: 20-27^{0}C.
- Optimum temperature for tuber formation: 13-24^{0}C.
- Higher temperature (30/ 22^{0}C) promotes vegetative growth and affect tuber development.
- Tuber root formation is induced by short days and 20^{0}C long days.
- Photo-insensitive cvs. form tuberous roots under long and short days at 20 and 25^{0}C and at 30^{0}C under long days.
- Composition and nutritional quality of edible parts can be modified by day length and flower removal.
- Positive effect of rainfall is reported.
- Sandy and well drained soils favours seed germination.
- Seeds pre-soaked for 2 days before planting gives emergence of 83.4% in 5-6 days at 25^{0}C.
- Normally seeds take 10 days to germinate.
- Seeds are sown in flat beds. Ridges and furrow method of planting is recommended for flood areas.
- Optimum plant density: 20,000 plants/ ha for high yield of green pods and dry seeds.
- Planting distance: 60-75 cm x 45-60 cm.
- Seed rate: 50-60 kg/ha.
- Water requirement: 8 mm/day.
- Highly susceptible to water logging.

- Number of seeds/ pod: 5 to 40.
- Harvesting stage: Tender stage.
- Green pod harvesting: 10 weeks after sowing.
- Green pods are harvested 21-35 day after anthesis and after that, it is utilized as grain legume.
- Tubers are harvested 4-8 months after sowing.
- As size increases, tubers become more fibrous & have poor flavor as they mature.
- Yield: 7.3-8.1 t/ha (green pods); 2 t/ha (seed).
- Pods on drying shatter. Dry pods are harvested when they turn yellow.
- Seeds are hard to cook and hence should contain less tannins.
- Subabool (*Leucaena leucocephala*)/ bamboo/ wireareused as live stake for twining vine.
- 'Y' shaped trellis helps in easy harvesting of hanging pods and prevents pod rot infection.
- Support of T or A shaped frames gives early flowering (by 10 days), produce higher pod number, leaves, branches and quality seeds.
- Tuber yield is more in unsupported plants.
- Plants grown on supports accumulates higher leaf nitrogen at vegetative stages and seed nitrogen, total dry matter accumulation and seed yield compared with unsupported plants.
- Vines for green pod yield are not pruned.
- Removal of flowers and pruning increases tuber yield, early bulking (within 5 weeks) of tubers compared to unpruned vines (take 16-17 weeks for tuber bulkning).
- Mulching is beneficial when it is grown for tuber production.
- Application of mixed fertilizers @ 250 kg/ha is recommended.
- TIBA @ 30 or 45 ppm; NOA @ 50 or 75 ppm; CCC @ 50 or 75 pp to foliage at 2-4 and 5 elaf stage increases number and yield of fresh pods.
- Gamma rays @ 10-20 Krad or EMS @ 0.05-0.2% with longer treatment of 1-12 h is beneficial to evolve mutations having dwarf (bush) type growth and low tannin content in seeds.
- Explant used for tissue culture: Leaf.
- Somatic embryogenesis: Attempted in cvs. Tpt-1, Tpt-2, UPS-122.
- Molecular biology studies have been reported for Chymotrypsin inhibitor (WCI) in seeds, stems, and tuberous roots.

Species:

- *Psophocarpus tetragonolobus*: Cultivated, 2n=18, grown in almost all parts of world for immature pods used as vegetable.
- *P. palmettorum*: 2n=20, grown as wild in tropical Africa & sometimes grown for edible pods.

Varieties:

Name	Breeding method	Features
Gui Ai	-	Developed in China; natural dwarf mutant line KUS-101 (climbing habit); many root nodules; vigorous branching; determinate growth; yield high quality pods & seeds
Bogor, TPT-2, UPS-53	-	Day neutral type developed in Zambia
Puttalam	-	Developed in Sri Lanka; grown for tubers
Colombo	-	Developed in Sri Lanka; grown for tubers & seeds
Karaliyadde	-	Developed in Sri Lanka; grown for seeds
UPS-122	-	Developed in New Guinea; grown for tubers & seeds
UPS-121, 62, 47	-	Developed in New Guinea; grown for tubers
IIHR, Bengaluru		
IIHR selections-21	Selection	-
IIHR selections-60	Selection	-
IIHR selections-71	Selection	-
NE Parvatiya Anusandhan Kendra, Meghalaya		
WBC-2	-	-
KAU, Thrissur		
Revathy	-	Pole type; long green pods with black seeds; crop duration 120 days; yield 10-12 t/ha; suitable for growing in August-September
IGKVV, Raipur		
Indira Winged Bean-2	-	-
CCSHAU, Hisar		
GRWB-24, GRWB-10B	-	High pod yield
GRWB-26	-	Day neutral type
GRWB-25, IC-14981	-	High tuber yield

Genetics of characters:

- Shelling percentage is positively correlated with seed yield.
- Pod yield is positively correlated with pod number but not with nodule weight/ plant.

Character	Number of genes	Type of gene action
Pod colour	Monogenic	Purple dominant over green
Pod length	Polygenic	Partial dominance to complete dominance
Pod shape	Monogenic	Rectangular pod dominant over flat pods
Pod weight, seed size, seed weight, seeds/ pod, leaf size, time from flowering to maturity	Polygenic	Additive
Shelling (%)	Polygenic	Dominance
Earliness	Polygenic	Partial dominance
Tuber production	Polygenic	-
Flowering & green pod yield	-	Additive genes

21.9 Yam bean

- Eulogized as 'Mexican turnip or Potato bean or Mishri kand or Soya's rival'.
- Cultivated in central and South America, Philippines, Vietnam, Indonesia, Tropical Africa, South Pacific Islands, China, Thailand, Singapur, Hawaii and India.
- Crop is adapted in sub-tropical to humid, hot, temperate zones.
- Heavy rainfall & water logged condition are unfavorable for cultivation.
- Optimum soil pH: 6-7.
- Largest state producing yam bean in India: Bihar.
- It is perennial when underground tubers are concerned and an annual with respect to aerial portion.
- Require hot humid climate and wet climate is unfavorable.
- Excess rainfall results in low yields and tuber rot.
- Yields starchy, conical shaped, fleshy and sweet tubers.
- They are twining herbs with pinnate leaves, trifoliate, and leaflets often angular/ sinuately lobed.
- Inflorescence: Long stalked racemes.
- Flowers: Violet-blue in clusters on large grandular swellings.
- Tuber bulking stops at time of flower and pod development.
- Young tubers have crispy, juicy and refreshing flesh and are eaten raw in salad or cooked or in chutney & pickles.
- Tubers can be sliced and made into chips.
- Mature dried roots are used in fever as cooling agent.
- Self pollinated leguminous tuber crop.
- Short days & low temperature promote flowering and better tuberization while long days (14-15 h) promote shoot growth at the cost of root growth.
- Shorter photoperiod results in high yield of tubers.
- Dry matter of stem increases at the cost of tubers, pods and nodules.
- Prolonged vegetative growth period delays tuberization.
- Tubers: 10-15 cm in dia., weigh 2-2.5 Kg, have creamy surface & white (watery) flesh.
- Tubers contain adenine, arginine, choline and phytin.
- Peeled tubers flesh contains 82.38% moistur e, 9.72% starch, 1.47% proteins, 0.64% fibres, 16 mg Ca and 14 mg ascorbic acid per 100 gram.
- Edible portion (90%) of young pods contains moisture (86.4%), proteins (2.6%), -CHO (10.8%), fibres (2.9%), vit. A (575 IU), Ca (221 mg), P (39 mg) per 100 gram.

- Yam bean seeds contain high oil (20-28%), protein (23-34%), starch (2.8-4.8%) and fatty acids (53-68.5%).
- Seed oil contains high concentration of palmitic (25-30%), oleic (21-29%) and linoleic acid (35-40%).
- Glutelins constitute highest protein fractions followed by globulins.
- Flower buds, flowers and pods appear respectively in *P. tuberosus* (at 120, > 120, >>120 DAS), *P. ahipa* (at 40, 60 and 75 DAS), *P. erosus* (at 75, 90 and 110 DAS).
- Dry matter content of roots is 18%, 30% and 20% at 45 DAS and highest fresh weight at 120 DAS in three species, respectively.
- Anti-nutritional factor: Tannins and trypsin inhibitors.
- Juicy flesh of tuber has anti-scorbutic action on rats.
- Propagation method: Tubers or seeds or *in vitro* propagation.
- Commercial propagation: Seed and sprouted roots from previous crop.
- Seed pods 7-15 cm long containing 8-10 seeds.
- Seeds almost square, flat 5-10 mm dia., yellow, brown or red in colour.
- Seed rate: 20-60 kg/ ha.
- Planting method i.e. transplanting or direct sowing influences root growth in *P. erosus*.
- Root diameter is greater in direct sown crop at 26 and 45 weeks after sowing/ planting.
- Planting distance: 30 cm x 30 cm to depth of 2 cm.
- Seeds @ 3-5 per hill are sown at 0.75 x 1 m during June to September.
- Days for seed germination: 7 days.
- Flowering starts 60-75 days after sowing.
- Non-flowering plant produces best quality tubers.
- Weight of 100 seeds: 20 gram.
- Can be conserved through true seeds.
- Yam bean produces single tuber.
- Harvesting stage of tubers: 5-8 months after sowing.
- Delayed harvesting results in more fibre content, cracking of tubers, increased damage from rats and termites making unfit for consumption.
- Plants allowed for flower and fruit formation are normally harvested after ripening of pods.
- High dry matter production of vines and more amount of tuber formation within 45 days is obtained from September sowing.
- Yam bean is intercropped with maize for trailing.
- Critical stage for irrigation: Tuber formation.
- Irrigations at 45, 75 and 105 days after sowing promotes tuber development, increase in tuber yield, dry matter (by 13.4%) and total sugars (by 3.5%) of tubers.

- Frequent irrigation makes tubers more succulent and reduces keeping quality.
- Straw mulching is widely practiced but earthing up is not essential like other tuber crops.
- Tubers produced from late sown (September) crop are free from cracking.
- Proper soil moisture during 45-90 days crop growth checks cracking.
- Application of K and Mg increases nodule dry matter production.
- Nitrogen fixation nodulation (75%) is due to *Bradyrhizobium* and 25% due to *Rhizobium*.
- Percent N derived from atmosphere (Ndfa) ranges from 55 to 69% got *P. ahipa* (i.e. N fixation ranges from 74-95 kg N/ha) and 68-77% for *P. erosus* (i.e. N fixation ranges from 172-190 kg N/ha).
- Application of K & delayed harvesting reduces cracking.
- Crop is harvested with small sized tubers after 100 days.
- Top vegetative part is removed & tubers are dug manually.
- Plants are pruned once or twice after 2 months to restrict vegetative growth and encourage tuber development.
- Reproductive pruning (removal of flowers) is practiced to symbiotic nitrogen fixation, increase tuber yield (by 51.5%), biomass production and sugar content by diverting photosynthates from flowers to roots.
- Seed crop is harvested after 240 days during March-April.
- Yield: 30-40 t/ha fresh tubers.
- Tuber yield is drastically reduced if flowers are allowed to develop and form pods.
- Seed flour has good *in vitro* digestibility and rich in essential amino acids.
- High grade flour is produced from *P. erosus* tubers in India.
- Tubers are also used as fodder and superior quality starch is obtained from mature tubers.
- Tender fresh tubers impart sweet taste due to high sugar content.
- Tubers are slightly dried to develop protective cork layers and tubers are stored in dry cool places for few weeks.
- Tubers can be stored for 3-5 days without any deterioration.
- Roots stored at 12.5^{0}C for > 4 weeks remain in excellent condition.
- Roots stored at 13^{0}C show fewer changes in internal quality over 5 months period but weight loss exceeds to 35%.
- Storage at 5^{0}C results in external decaying and greying of pulp.
- Storage at 10^{0}C does not affect external quality but severe internal discoloration occurs.
- Parafin wax treatment: Most effective control in reducing moisture loss.

- Wrapping with PVC film reduces 50% moisture loss and no losses due to decay.
- Roots remain more crunchy and juicy and sweeter with more aroma and flavour than paraffin coated roots.
- 2,4-D (50 ppm) at flower initiation stage induces flower thinning and increases tuber yield.
- Insecticidal toxic substance present in mature seeds: Rotenon ($C_{23}H_{22}O_6$).
- Powdered seeds are useful as insecticide (stomach poison) and fish poison in tropical countries and process has been patented.
- Canned tubers are marketed.

Developmental stages of genus *Pachyrrhizus*, based on morphology and physiological changes (Sorensen *et al.*, 1993)-

Stage	Description
Germination	Appearance of primary root
Emergence	Primary leaves and epicotyls emergence
Primary leaves totally opened	Primary leaves fully unfolded
First trifoliate leaf opens	Second trifoliate leaf appears
Third trifoliate leaf opens	Buds at lower nodes produce branches
Preflowering	First flower bud or reproductive shoot appears
Flowering	First flower opens
Pod formation and filling	At the end of this stage the pods feel hard
Post-pod growth	Pods filled and are hard
Physiological maturity	Leaves senesce and defoliate starts

Species:

- Three cultivated and edible tuber crop species are often termed as yam beans viz. Yam bean or Jicama (*Pachyrrhizus erosus*), Jacatupe bean (*P. tuberosus*), Andean yam bean (*P. ahipa* (non-climbing, cultivated in Bolivia).
- Interspecific crossing of *P. erosus* x *P. ahipa* and *P. erosus* x *P. tuberosus* and their respective reciprocal crosses yields fertile F_1 hybrids with desired characters.

Name	Origin	Features
P. erosus	Central America	Perennial herb; twining stem, leaflets angular & sharply toothed; flowers purple, 15-25 cm long; grown for edible tuberous roots which are consumed either raw or boiled
P. tuberosus	Tropical America	Twinning herb (3-6 m high); leaves entire; flowers purple in dense raceme; pods 20-25 cm long & used as beans; free from strings; seeds poisonous but roots are nutritious
P. palmatilibus	Tropical America	Climbing with glabrous/ hairy stem; leaves broadly ovate, leaflets lobed; flowers purplish in long stalked racemes

Varieties:

- Clonal selection and gamma irradiation (10, 20, 25 kR) to seeds or EMS treatment (0.5 to 1.25%) yields mutations with higher tuber yield, better quality, higher tuber protein and starch content.
- Mexican type: Tuber size large (500-700 g), less sweet, tendency to develop cracks on tubers, less preferred in Indian market.
- Local types: Smaller tubers (200-300 g), sweeter, white flesh with less fibres & no cracking.

Name	Breeding method	Features
Rajendra Mishrikand-1 (1999)	Seedling selection	Excellent quality; resistant to major pests & diseases; cultivated under tree shade; yield 40-55t/ha

Inheritance of characters:

- Negative correlation between tuber yield and pod formation; tuber weight and dry matter content.
- Positive correlation between soluble solids content and dry matter content.
- Tuber yield: Controlled by polygenes.

Pests, diseases and physiological disorder:

- Almost free from diseases and pests.
- Angular leaf spot (*Pseudomonas syringae* pv. *pachyrrhizus*): Serious in China.
- Cracking of tubers.

21.10 Soybean

- Eulogized as 'Miracle bean or Magic bean or Wonder bean'.
- Chinese gift to the world.
- China: Major importer in the world.
- It is golden bean + oil seed crop + pulse seed crop + cash crop.
- Genus *Glycine* contains 2 sub-genera: *Soja* and *Glycine.*
- Sub-genus *Soja* contains 2 annual species *Glycine max* (2n=4x=40 cultivated soybean) and *Glycine soja* (2n=4x=40 wild species).
- *G. soja*: Undesirable parent in crossing programme except transfer for particular gene.
- Chemical composition of seed: -CHO (14%), protein (37%), lipid (17%).
- Edible soybean is close relative of cowpea and looks similar to field-type soybean.
- Grown principally for shelling and eating in green seed stage.

- Short, downy pods contain 2-3 seeds which are rich in oil and proteins.
- Soybeans as a green vegetable is harvested when seeds are fully grown and still succulent but not hardened as in field-type.
- Young pods have nut like flavour.
- Foremost industrial crop of USA for preparing bio-diesel.
- Productivity of world: 2770 kg/ha
- Area under cultivation India: 113.99 lakh ha.
- Productivity in India: 865 kg/ha.
- In production, share of Madhya Pradesh is 45% followed by Maharashtra 40%.
- Broad base furrow technique of cultivation increases productivity.
- Substitute for pigeon pea.
- Short day plant and very sensitive to photoperiod.
- Temperature for seed germination: 15-32^{0}C.
- Optimum temperature for growth: 30-33^{0}C.
- Pollination agent: Insect.
- Beans contain brain building substance 'cephalin' in addition to 'lecithin'.
- 'Diadelphous stamen' condition is absent.
- Soybean protein has 5% lycine.
- Cake is rich in proteins (47% proteins from meal).
- Soya floor contain 20% fat.
- Crop yields 18-20% oil and 80% DOC (de-oiled cake) or soy-meal.
- Traditional soybean varieties yield 18-20% oil. With improved varieties, it is possible to get 20-24% oil.
- Raw oil of IGC (International Grains Council) and CBoT (Chicago Board of Trade) shows that:-
  a) Sale of soybean in the world is increasing at a faster rate during 2019-20 and 2020-21.
  b) Use of soybean oil for bio-diesel blending purpose is increasing throughout the world.
  c) Share of USA in world production of soybean is 30%.
- Seed rate: 65 kg/ha with plant population of 4.4-4.5 lakh/ha must be maintained.
- Seed treatment with rhizobium 25 g + PSB 25 g/ kg of seed is essential.
- Initial 15 to 40 days period from sowing is very critical and crop should be kept weed free. Otherwise weeds cause 50% reduction in yield.
- Seed production in summer season causes 40% reduction in yield compared to kharif.

- Irrigation method: Hanging sprinkler system.
- Seed germination: 85-90%.
- Basis of sale is by volume (Bushels) or weight.
- 1 bushel= 27.21 kg.
- Seed weight (100 seed wt.): Kharif (11-13 g), summer (8-10 g).
- SOPA (Soybean Processors Association of India).
- Value added products: Soya milk, soya paneer, soya butter, soya nuggets, soya flour, soya protein powder, soya lecithin, oil, Tofu, etc.
- Nutritional feed for birds and animals has increased demand at national and international markets.
- Indian soya meal products are highly demanded throughout the world.
- Environmental study reports from USA indicates that polluted air causes average reductions in yields in soybean by 3.8%.
- Pollution free air during periods from 1999 to 2019 has helped 20% increase in yield.

Varieties:

- C.A. Brim (1966) proposed modified pedigree method-single seed descent method for soybean improvement.
- Cross fertilization of *G. max* x *G. tomentella* is obtained using *in vitro* embryo rescue technique.
- Cross fertilization of *G. max* with other species in sub-genus *Glycine* are sterile or produce only immature pods.
- Mutant varieties: Tainung No. 1, Tainung No. 2, Raiden, Raiko.
- Resistant to frog eye leaf spot: Lincoln, Wabash, Kent, Mukden.
- Resistant to pea nut mottle virus: York, Shore, Dorman, Black Hawk, Arksoy.
- Resistant to soybean mosaic virus: Merit.
- Resistant to stem canker: Tracy.
- Black seeded varieties are rich in protein but low in oil.
- Yellow seeded varieties are rich in oil and poor in protein.
- "Lipoxygenase-2 free Soybean" with reduced off-flavour: NRC 109.
- Mrudgandh: Developed by farmers private Seed Company.
- HEFTY 457S- Highest yield (52 q/acre) achieved was by Georgia farmer Mr. Randy Dowoodi in 2019. Crop duration 150-160 days as compared to India 100-110 days. Yield is 5 times and 13 times more than world and Indian production, respectively.
- GM soybean 'HB-4' is cultivated on large scale in Brazil, America, and Canada since 2018. This has brought golden revolution in soybean production in European countries.
- Warpudkar Selection: Selection made by farmer.

Name	Breeding method	Features
Bragg, Clarke-63, Delmar, Delmon, Hutton, Hill, Hampton 266A, Lee-74, Lindarin, Wayne	Introduction	Resistant to bacterial pustules
Punjab-1, Alankar, Jawa 16, Hardee, Shivalik	-	-
Shilajeet	-	Dwarf; resistant to yellow mosaic
IARI, New Delhi		
Pusa-16	Pedigree selection of 'CNS x Lee'	Tall
Pusa-12 (2015)	-	Yield 23 q/ha; oil 19.6%; resistant to YMV
Pusa-20	Pedigree selection of 'Bragg x Lee'	Tall
Pusa-24	Pedigree selection of 'Shelby x Bragg'	Tall
PK-416	Pedigree selection of 'UPSM 534 x Ankur'	-
Pusa-97-12 (2009)	-	Yield 22.9%; oil 19.6%; resistant to YMV, charcoal rot
Pusa DS 97-12 (2005)	-	Non-shattering; oil 18%; yield 22-25 q/ha; resistant to YMV, stem fly
Pusa DS-98-14 (2006)	-	Yield (19-22 q/ha); oil 16.89%; resistant to YMV, SMV, pod blight & stem fly
ICAR Research Complex for Eastern Region, Patna (HARP, Ranchi)		
Swarna Vasundhara (2008)	-	Green pods; grey pubescence;resistant to rust under natural epiphytotic condition; yield 15-20 t/ha; cultivation was promoted by AVRDC in Jharkhand; recommended for processing & vegetable purpose
GBPUA & T, Pantnagar		
Pant Soybean 564	Pedigree selection of (UPSM 534 x Ankur) x Bragg)	-
PS-1347 (2006)	-	Yield 31 q/ha; oil 15.5%; resistant to YMV, rhizoctonia aerial blight, bacterial pustule, SMV & charcoal rot
PS-1225 (2007)	-	Yield 31 q/ha; oil 18%; shattering & lodgingresistant; multiple disease resistant to YMV, bacterial pustule, collar rot, anthracnose, pod blight & SMV
PS-19 (2010)	-	Yield 21.2 q/ha; resistant to foliar diseases, YMV, bacterial pustule & rhizoctonia aerial blight

MPUA & T, Udaipur		
Pratap Soya-1 (2007)	-	Yield 30-35 q/ha; oil 17.98%; resistant to girdle beetle, stem fly & defoliators.
Pratap Soya-2 (2007)	-	Yield 23 q/ha; oil 17.13%; mod. resistant to bacte ial pustule (BP), girdle beetle, leaf miner but susceptible torust
DrPDKV, Akola		
PDKV Yellow Gold (AMS-1001)	-	Mature in 97 days; oil 21.44%; trypsin inhibitor content is comparatively less (35.79%); pod shattering resistance up to 10 days from harvest maturity; resistant to root rot & viral disease; mod. resistant to girdle beetle & stem fly
AMS 2014-1	-	Bold seeds, resistant to yellow mosaic, root rot & stem rot; recommended for eastern states
AMS-98-21 (2007)	-	Yield 22-26 q/ha; oil content 18%; mod. resistant to rust, leaf spot & insects
AMS-100-39	-	Crop duration 97 days; high yield; resistant to root rot, fruit dly & beetle attack
Suvarna Soya (AMS-MS-5-18)	-	-
PDKV, Amba (AMS-100-39)	-	-
MPKV, Rahuri		
Phule Kalyani (DS-228), 2006	-	Mid-late maturity (95-100 days); yield 23.5 q/ha; oil 20.3%; protein 41.6%; less susceptible to rust
Phule Agrani (KDS-344), 2015	-	Mid-late maturity (95-100 days); yield 30-32 q/ha; tolerant to rust
Phule Sangam (KDS-726) 2019	-	Early maturity (90-95 days); 100 pods/plant; suitable for sole, inter-cropping & early as well as late sowing; drought tolerant & non shattering; resistant to rust, root rot, stem rot, stem fly; 18.42% oil; yield 25-30 q/ha
Phule Kimaya (KDS-753) 2020	-	-
KDS-992 (2020)	-	Big grain size; resistant to rust, leat eating caterpillar, grain spot & sustainable to climatic changes.
KS-103	-	-
Raj Soya (RVS-2002-4)	-	-
MAUS-725 (2021)	-	Local type; resistant to pests & diseases
VNMAU, Parbhani		
Parbhani Sona (MAUS-47)'	-	Very early
Parbhani Samruddhi (MAUS-71), 2002	-	Early mature (93-100 days); yellow seed with black hilum; yield 18-30 q/ha; oil 18.2%; protein 41.6%; tolerant to pest; resistant to pod shattering; tolerant to climate change
Parbhani Shakti (MAUS-81), 2009	-	Early mature (93-97 days); oil 20.6%; protein 42.4%; yield 23 q/ha; resistant to rhizoctonia root rot, aerial blight, collar rot, charcoal rot & stem fly; non-seed shattering
Parbhani Pratikar (MAUS-61), 2002	-	Mid-late maturity; yellow seed with brown hilum; 18.8% oil; yield 26-28 q/ha; resistant to Myrothecium leaf spot

Parbhani Pratistha (MAUS-61-2), 2002	-	Medium late (93-98 days); yellow seed with brown hilum; oil 19.7%; 3 grains/ pod; resistant to rust, leaf blight, pod blight, alternaria; tolerant to stem fly midge, pod borer & pod splitting
MAUS-162 (2012)	-	Late mature (100 days); yield 25-30 q/ha; oil 21.4%; protein 41.2%; less seed shattering, resistant to charcoal rot; suitable for machine harvest
ParbhaniPooja (MAUS-2), 2014	-	Yield 25-35 q/ha; oil 20%; resistant to bacterial pustule.
MAUS-158	-	Crop duration 93-98 days; yield 36-31 q/ha; tolerant to stem fly & pod splitting
MAUS-725	-	Suitable for dry areas; crop duration 95-100 days; yield 27-32 q/ha; 3-4 grains/pod; tolerant to climate change, pests & diseases
MAUS-731	-	Suitable for dry areas; crop duration 95-100 days; yield 27-32 q/ha; 3-4 grains/pod; tolerant to climate change, pests & diseases
MAUS-732	-	Suitable for dry areas; crop duration 95-100 days; yield 27-32 q/ha; 3-4 grains/pod; tolerant to climate change, pests & diseases
Agharkar Research Institute, Pune		
MACS- 13	Pedigree selection of (Hampton x EC-7034)	-
MACS-58	Pedigree selection of (JS-2 x Improved Pelican)	-
MACS-124	-	-
MACS-450	-	-
MACS-1188 (2013)	-	Oil 19%; non-shattering of seeds; highly suitable for wet condition; yield 25 q/ha; tolerant to bacterial leaf blight, charcoal rot & bacterial pustules, stem fly, leaf rolling caterpillar, leaf miner
MACS-1281 (2016)	-	-
Durga	Pedigree selection of 'EC 14437 x Bragg'	Resistant to bacterial pustules
Gaurav	Pedigree selection of 'D-60-9647 x EC 7034'	-
JNKVV, Jabalpur		
Jawahar (syn. JS-335) 1994	-	Early; maximum area under cultivation; resistant to bacterial spot; very popular among farmers
JS-93-05	-	Popular among farmers
JS-95-60 (2007)	-	Extra early; 4 seeds/pod; oil 16.6%; yield (18-20 q/ha); resistant to lodging, seed shattering, stem fly, defoliators, girdle & blue beetles, root rot, bacterial pustule, RAB, TLS
JS-97-52 (2008)	-	Yield 25-30 q/ha; oil 17.5 %; tolerant to excessive soil moisture; resistant to YMV, collar rot,rhizoctonia aerial blight & insects

JS-20-29 (2014)	-	Yield 21.3 q/ha; oil 21%; resistant to YMV
JS-20-34 (2014)	-	Yield 20.5 q/ha; oil 20.3%; extra early
JS-20-69 (2016)	-	-
JS-20-98 (2018)	-	-
JS-20-116	-	Photo sensititve; suitable for mechanical harvesting & bear pods in cluster; suitable for kharif season
IISR, Indore		
Aahilya-4 (NRC-137) 2001	-	Tolerant to major pests & diseases
Aahilya-6 (NRC-86) 2015	-	-
NRC-127	-	Tolerant to climate change
NRC-130	-	Very early bearers (90-95 days)
NRC-138	-	Very early bearers (90-95 days)
MSCS-1460	-	Very early bearers (90-95 days)
NRC-142	-	Without trypsin inhibitors; Soya flour can be prepared directly after boiling & drying of seeds
MASC-NRC-1667	-	Without trypsin inhibitors; Soya flour can be prepared directly after boiling & drying of seeds
NRC-147	-	Increase in oleic acid content & oil is free from off-flavour; recommended for western Maharashtra
PAU, Ludhiana		
SL-688 (2008)	-	Yield 25 q/ha; protein 40.3%; oil 20.5 %; resistant to YMV
SL-744 (2012)	-	Yield 18.4 q/ha; oil 21%
VPKAS, Almora		
VL-Soya 59 (2008)	-	Yield 26 q/ha; protein 39.15%; oil 20.4 %; resistant to pod blight & target leaf spot
VL-Soya 63 (2008)	-	Yield 27 q/ha; protein 41%; oil 20.2 %; resistant to pod blight, target leaf spot, frog eye leaf spot
VL-Soya 65 (2009)	-	Yield 15-18 q/ha; resistant to frog eye leaf spot, pod blight & leaf blight
UAS, Dharwad		
DSB-1 (2009)	-	Yield 25-30 q/ha; oil 18.2%; resistant to rust & pod shattering
DSB-21 (2015)	-	Yield 25-30 q/ha; oil 18.2%; resistant to rust
DSB-23 (2018)	-	-
DSB-228 (2007)	-	-
UAS, Bengaluru		
Karune (GC-00209-4-1-1), 2011	-	70-80 q green pods/ha; vegetable type
CSKHPKV, Palampur		
Palampur Early Soya-1	-	-

Diseases and pests:

- Yellow mosaic: Vector- White fly.
- Pod blight: Grain become shriveled and moldy.
- Seedling rot (*Aspergillus flavus*).
- Stem rot (*Phytophthora megasperma f.sp. glycinea*):
- Soybean rust (*Phakospora pachyrhizi*):
- Purple seed strain (*Cercospora kikvchii*):
- Bacterial blight (*Xanthomonas campestris* pv. *glycines*).
- Soybean mosaic virus: Seed borne and transmitted by aphids.
- Bean yellow mosaic virus: Transmitted by white fly (*Bemisia tabaci*).
- Soybean cyst nematode (*Heterodera glycine*):
- Root knot nematode.
- Trap crop for pod borer: Sunflower and castor.
- Stem fly (*Melanagromyza phaseoli*): Cause 15-30% yield loss. Use neem oil @ 5%. If damage level is >10% use Ethion 50 EC @ 1.5 ml/lit.
- Gridle beetle (*Obserea brevis*):
- Bihar hairy caterpillar.

Genetics of characters:

- Glabrous leaves: Monogenic dominant.
- Single dominant gene for disease resistance and hairy caterpillar resistance.
- Resistance to phytophthora depends upon *Rps* gene, race, light, temperature and wounding.
- Genic male sterility: Ten recessive genes.
- Determinate growth habit: Recessive gene *dt-1*.
- Three recessive genes (*rhg-1, rhg-2, rhg-3*) and 2 dominant genes (*Rhg-4, Rhg-5*) for cyst nematode.
- Identification of male sterile plants: Green plants with partially filled pods.
- Thermostability of cellular membranes: Polygenic with additive effect.
- Resistance to Mn toxicity: Polygenic with maternal effects.
- Cl exclusion from shoot: One dominant gene *Nel*.

21.11 Velvet bean

- Highly drought resistant.
- **Varieties**: Arka Dhanvantari, Arka Aswini.

21.12 Sword bean

- Mainly grown in North-East region of India.
- Drought resistant legume, perennial climber.

- Both sword bean and jack bean are grown as green manure, for young pods, forage, cover crop and immature seeds are used as food for human and animals.
- Natural introgression between two species is observed.
- Both species are intercrossable with each other and hybrids are fertile.
- Ancestor of sword bean: *C. gladiolata*.
- Sword bean (*Canavalia gladiata*): Native of South Asian or Africa. Cultivated on limited scale on N-E hilly regions of India for edible pods.
- Four species cultivated in India for edible pods:
  - *C. ensiformis* (jack bean) do not exhibit morphological variation.
  - *C. gladiata*: Exhibit variation in flower colour (white & pink), pod characters and seed size.
  - *C. maritima*.
  - *C.virosa*.
- Green pods are rich source of proteins (28.31%) and seeds contain 44.56% (-CHO).
- In Japan, young pods are sliced and pickled in soy sauce.
- In Philippines, matured seeds are used as salted dish (ginisa) and immature pods and immature leaves are used as vegetable salad dish (pinakbet/ lumpia/ gigataan) or as vegetable component of meat dish (sinigang/ nilaga).
- Seed colour: Scarlet.
- Tender pods contain 2.7% protein and 1.5% fibers.
- Toxic substance present in seed: Saponin.
- Pollination agent: Bees.
- Require support of trellies system for commercial cultivation.
- Days to flowering: 68-72 days of sowing.
- Days to harvesting: 90-95 days of sowing.
- Seed rate: 12-15 kg/ha.
- Yield: 2-2.5 kg pods/ plant.
- Mature seeds are not used as a cattle feed as it contain poisonous alkaloid.
- Used as green manure in Sudan.
- **Varieties**: AHSB-1.

Name	Breeding method	Features
CIAH, Bikaner		
Thar Mahi (2010)	Selection	Pod yield (1.73 kg/ plant & 56 q/ha);

21.13 Jack bean

- Annual, tropical and sub-tropical plant.
- Climbing form is called ‘sword bean’.
- Deep rooted plants with surface feeding nature.

- Dwarf, very hardy, drought resistant and high in protein (6.9%).
- Used as forage and cover crop.
- Mainly cultivated in North-East hilly regions of India, Japan, China and Indonesia.
- Immature pods and seeds contain moisture (75.2%), proteins (6.9%), -CHO (13.3%), fibres (3.3%), fats (0.5%), and ash (0.8%).
- Leaves: Cordate, large. True leaves are simple, ternate, alternate, spherical-elonagted.
- Inflorescence: Axillary racymes (about 10/ plant). Each raceme contains 30-40 bisexual flowers.
- Pods: large, 20-25 cm long, flat, broad and sword shaped and hooked.
- Pods are indehiscent and yellowish coloured.
- Seed: Large, kidney shaped, white coloured, 1-2 cm in dia., and scar upto 1 cm long and 8-18 per pod.
- Weight of 1000 seeds: 1000-2000 gram.
- Day length required: 10-12 hours.
- Optimum pH for cultivation: 5-7.
- Temperature for seed germination: 25-27^{0}C.
- These beans require adequate soil moisture during early vegetable stage and flowering.
- Terrace cultivation is preferred with 1 m x 75 cm spacing.
- Direct seed sowing in April-July in pits or seedlings raized in polybags are transplanted.
- Harvesting: Tender pods.
- Delayed harvesting cause fibrous pods and unfit for market.
- In early types, marketable pods are available from 68-74 days.
- In pole types, pods take 110 days for harvesting.
- For seed production, yellow coloured pods are harvested at full maturity and seeds are extracted manullay by breaking pods.
- Yield: 2.67-3.14 kg green pods/ plant (early); 2.93-3.5 kg/ green pods/ plant (pole type).

Pest:

- Hairy caterpillar (*Anisecta* spp.): Creates problem during early stage of growth. Spray Quinolphos @ 2 ml/ litre.

21.14 Other minor beans/ legume vegetables

- Grown for young pods and immature seeds for forage/ green manure.

Name	Botanical name
Gotani bean	*Canavalia plagosperma*
Yam bean	*Pachyrrhizus erosus*
African yam bean	*Sphentylis stenocarpa*
African locust bean	*Parkia clappertonia*
Ground bean	*Voandzeia subterranean*
Marama bean	*Tylosema esculentum* (*Bauhinia exculenta*)

22. LILIACEAE

22.1 Asparagus

- The Greeks gave the name to cultivated asparagus as a 'luxury vegetable' as early as 200 B.C.
- The Romans of 200 B.C. esteemed asparagus as a great delicacy and its culture is frequently described in Latin literature.
- In Spain and Greece, tender young spears (without spines) of spiny spp. *A.acutifolius* are preferred.
- Historically, it has been a high-value crop, popular for home gardens and bulk of the crop is grown for processing.
- The Greek word 'aspharagos' means 'to sprout' or shoot and English changed the name 'sparagrass' (sparrow grass).
- Asparagus was 1st noted for its medicinal properties and has been in cultivation for atleast 2000 years. Officinalis means 'medicinal'.
- Major producers of canned white asparagus: Taiwan (46% of world's production),Europe, Spain, Japan, Australia, Canada & Mexico.
- Potential export markets for canned white or bleached asparagus: Germany and USA.
- Per capita consumption of asparagus in all forms i.e. fresh (0.62 lbs), canned (0.98 lbs) & frozen (0.35 lbs) is highest in USA.
- In European countries, about 40% of asparagus is consumed as fresh, 50% canned and rest is frozen. The annual consumption per capita is about 380 g.
- Asparagus is recommended for athletic players as it contains minerals.
- Minerals and vitamin content/ 100 g edible portion: Ca (22 mg), P (62 mg), Fe (1 mg), Na (2 mg), K (278 mg), vit. A (900 IU), Thiamine (0.18 mg), Riboflavin (0.20 mg), Niacin (0.15 mg) and ascorbic acid (33 mg).
- Plant is valued for its edible spring shoots or spears which can be used in fresh, canned or frozen form.
- The whole spears or only green tips can be used.

- It can be served in salads, soups, hot dishes and in combination with various sauces.
- Crown Critical growth centre. Mass of branching rather than woody rhizomes with buds at the tip which give rise to edible shoots.
- Soft tender shoots called 'spears' (aerial shoots) arising from buds on rhizomes are used as vegetable.
- Tender shoots contain a white crystalline substance called 'asparagine' which is used in medicine for treatment of bee strings to heart trouble, toothache, as diuretic in cardiac dropsy and chronic gout.
- Soup is prepared from spears or they are canned and frozen to convert into pickles also.
- Spears are excellent source of vit. A and also contain significant amount of proteins, calcium, iron, phosphorous, riboflavin and vit. C.
- Medicinal uses: Treatment of bee stings to heart trouble, dropsy and toothache.
- Major cause for loss of production: Fusarium stem & crown rot disease.
- Male and female plants occur in equal number (Flory, 1932; Robbins and Jones, 1931).
- Crop growth is divided into 3 phases viz. crown development, spear development and fern development.
  a) Crown development:
    i) Underground portion of plant consist of network of rhizomes, (stem), fleshy roots (as storage organ & die after providing nourishment for next generation of spears) and fibrous roots (as absorption organ & die after each year's growth).
    ii) Together, the fleshy roots and rhizomes make up the crown, which is perennial portion of plant stores food material for growth of spears in following spring. The fibrous roots die back & new ones are developed.
  b) Spear development:
    i) Spears are edible stems containing nodes & internodes which arise from buds developed on the rhizomes in summer.
    ii) Nodes are marked by presence of small scale like leaves which overlap & from tip.
    iii) Rate of spear development is influenced by temperature.
    iv) In warm weather, rapid spear growth results & cool temperature increases fibre content of spear & causes excessive development of anthocyanin pigments, which give the spears an undesirable purple appearance.
    v) Desirable features of spear quality are large diameter, good length, compact tips and low fibre content.
  c) Fern development:
    I. Spears, if not cut for food, become the ferns of asparagus plant.

II. Unharvested spears elongate into ferns, 4-6 feet tall. This occurs when internodes in the tip begin to elongate and secondary branches develop in the axils of leaf scales. The secondary branches give rise to more side branches, which bear small, leaf like structures called 'cladophylls'. These impart fine or leathery texture to shoots & account for to its description as a fern.

III. True leaves are scale like structures that form at the tip of spear and down the stem.

IV. As the plant grows, scales give rise to cladophylls, which in turn give rise to flowers.

- Although 1-3 years are required to establish planting, once on production, can last upto 25 years.
- Difficulty in recognizing sex in one year old plant.
- Norton (1913) reported that hermaphrodite plants with predominance of normal male flowers plus few androgenous flowers with small but functional pistils i.e. andromonoecious plants (which are strongly male) are found to an extent of 2% only.
- Flowers: Borne on new shoots, 1-4 in axils of cladodes (or branches), campanulate, bell-shaped & yellowish green in colour. Reach anthesis before maturity of shoots.write after full stop but no bullet as

  Flowers form 1 to 9 seeded berry (3 carpels).
- Male plants flower more prolifically produce more spears and high yielder than females.
- Male plants flower in 210-235 days and female plants in 265-295 days after seed sowing in greenhouse.
- Female plants are less productive & short lived than male plants.
- Female plants produce seeds by taking energy and photosynthates away from crown.
- Spear of male plants are more numerous but are smaller in diameter than those on female plants whereas pistillate spears are heavier but new in number.
- Male flowers are yellowish green, more conspicuous, have rudimentary pistil and may set fruits with 1 or more seeds.
- Female flowers have vestigial stamens, white anthers and do not produce pollens.
- Type of fruit: Red coloured berry, ¼ to 3/8 inch size and 1-9 seeded.
- About 20,000-25,000 seeds weigh/ pound.
- Bears excellent crop during temperature range 15-24^{0}C.
- Spear initiation occurs at soil temperature >10^{0}C.
- Root and shoot development is reduced below 13^{0}C and above 29^{0}C.
- In warm weather, spear tips open prematurely and quality is reduced.
- Elevation >1000 m MSL is good for high yield.
- Optimum soil pH: 6.5 to 7.5.
- Most critical stage of irrigation: Fern development.
- Propagation methods: Crown division and seed.

- Crown division produce 5-10 new plants from single plant.
- Crown can be stored over winter at low temperature of 35-40^{0}F.
- Crown height 50-125 pounds/ 1000 and one year old crowns are better than two years old plant.
- Tissue culture (cloning): Efficient method to propagate vegetatively.
- Meristem or bud culture yield genetically stable plants.
- Seed rate: 2-2.5 kg/ha.
- Planting distance: 1.5-2 m x 45-60 cm.
- Seed diameter: 4 mm.
- Seedlings are raised in nursery bed for 12 months period.
- One year old crowns are good for commercial planting.
- It is not possible to recognize sex of plants in nursery and hence plants are selected accoding to root growth.
- The crowns (underground roots) having good growth and branching are male plants.
- Naturally cross pollinated by insect.
- Inbreeding brings depression of vigour and yield.
- Hybrid maleplants donot produce seedling weeds, which is a problem in dioecious field.
- Female plants yield larger spears than males.
- Application of common salt is beneficial in cultivation.
- Seed germinate in 12-14 days in warm house & take > 1 month in outdoors in spring.
- Low seed germination is common problem.Growth can be hastened by soaking seeds for 3-5 days at 85-90^{0}F. This effect is due to hastening the absorption of water rather than breaking dormancy.
- Green spears have more nutritive value and more popular than white (blanched).
- Green asparagus are mainly produced for fresh market while white or light green ones are used in processing.
- Blanched young spears are preferred for canning.
- Blanching an essential operationis done by mounding soil to a height of 25-30 cm over rows.
- Economic yield starts after 2-3 months after transplanting.
- Maturity index: Toughness.
- Harvesting season: In late April.
- Normal harvest period: 6-8 weeks from planting.
- Tender spears are harvested after 3rd year onwards during spring-summer and again in autumn season. Green coloured long 15-20 cm spears are cut by V-shaped blade knife near ground level including white butt (2 inches height above the crown) or snapped off by hand, avoiding injury to developed buds.
- In warm weather, tips open at shorter spear length. Hence, spears are cut daily at shorter height from crown.

- For processing purpose, asparagus is snapped rather than cut, which reduces harvesting cost and yields higher percentage of tender stalks.
- Harvesting is done when spears become slender and woody, cutting should be stopped to avoid excessive depletion of roots and reduction of yields.
- Yield: 40-50 q/ha after 4th year of planting and continues upto 15 years.
- Pollination of hermaphrodite flowers on male plants is by self pollination.
- Controlled pollination is achieved by either by hand or by use of honey bees.
- Ample seeds can be produced by hand pollination (100 fruits yield 300 seeds).
- Seeds from red ripe fruits (berry dia. 9 mm) is superior than from less matured bronze coloured fruits.
- In seed production, 1 male : 4 female ratio is maintained.
- Morning glory: Notorious weed in seed blocks.
- Weed control: Calcium cyanamide (22% nitrogen) is good nitrogen fertilizer and valuable weed killer. Broadcasted @ 200-400 lbs/acre or placed in bands 18 inches wide over the rows.
- Post harvest handling:
  - Asparagus has high rate of respiration even at low temperature and quickly looses quality.
  - At temperature > 40°F, sugars and vit. C are lost rapidly and coarse fibres develops.
  - Immediately after harvest, the spears are cooled at 32-36°F and low temperatures are maintained in transit.
- Removal of field heat by hydro-cooling and storage at 2-3°C minimize fibre development (i.e. Butt of spear are kept in water or rested on wet pad).
- Fibres start to develop, the moment the spear is cut.
- Vacuum cooling is also practiced.
- Storage temperature: 0-2 °C with 90-95% R.H.
- USDA standards for two grades:
  - US # 1: Fresh, tender, well trimmed & fairly straight spears having dia. of 0.5-1.0 inch from butt end and green colour not less than 2/3rd of stalk length.
  - US # 2: is alsobased on colour, spear diameter and appearance.
- Spear quality popular in trade:
  a) Narrow neck below the tip.
  b) Tender spears has white or pale green tip.
  c) Dark green spear colour with dark purple bracts and tip (this is original colour of Mary, Martha & Washington types spear colour & popular in trade).
  d) Long and fibre free spear is desirable.
- Spreas are bunched of ½ to 1 pound using rubber band.
- Packaging:

- Spears are packed either loosely or vertically in bunches in pyramid crates lined with moistened paper to preserve spear quality.
- In western countries, crates containing either sixteen 1.5 pound bunches or twelve 2 pound bunches are used.
- If spears are held for 24 h or longer or to be shipped, hydrocooling is most common method used to lower temperature below 40^{0}F.

- Box size: 10.5 inch deep x 9.5 inch wide at top x 10.5 inch wide at base and 17.5 inch long.
- Storage:
  - It is rarely stored. For storage of 10 days or less, 32^{0}F is best. For > 10 days holding period, temperature of 36^{0}F is recommended to avoid chilling injury.
  - For storage and transit, 95% R.H. is desirable.
  - Bacterial soft rot and grey mold rot are major diseases in storage.
- Spear grades: Measured with spear diameter gauge-
  a) Cull size- less than 3/8 inch diameter.
  b) Jumbo size- 5/8 inch diameter.
  c) Medium size- between 3/8 to 5/8 inch diameter.
- Telltale purple tip is associated with older spears.
- Brush (size of stalk) vigour is defined as number & diameter of stalk.
- Pollen grain viability: 6 months in domestic freezer.
- Pollens can be stored upto 60 weeks at -20^{0}C and 0% R.H. and viability diminish after 2 weeks at -20^{0}C and 75% R.H. or after 8 weeks at 1^{0}C and 75% R.H. or at -20^{0}C and 15% R.H.
- Advantages of male asparagus hybrids compared to dioecious asparagus:
  2. No seed to make seedling weeds in field.
  3. No seeds to compete with storage roots for photosynthate.
  4. No seeds for growers to save and ruin genetic quality.
- For seed production in field-
  a) Don't harvest the spears.
  b) Keep 2-4 bee hives per acre.
  c) Control asparagus beetle which ruins the seeds.
  d) Harvest only ripe berries since-
     i) Low germination is common problem.
     ii) Seeds from red ripe fruits (berry dia. 9 mm) is superior than from less matured bronze coloured fruits.
     iii) Poor germination in seeds harvested from Late brush (fern) v/s Early brush.
  e) Seed block spacing: 5 ft x 2 ft with 1 male: 4 female.
  f) Berries are washed in water to separate berry skin and pulp from seed.
  g) Treat seeds with Benomyl @ 5 g/ kg of seeds or Thirum @ 8 g/ kg of seeds.

Species:

- Bailey (1942) lists the asparagus as a large genus (about 150 spp.) of herbaceous perennials and tender woody shrubs & vines, grown mostly for ornamental foliage and *A. officinalis* for food.
- Closely related species of asparagus: Smilax (ornamental asparagus).
- Garden asparagus (*A. officinalis* var. *altilis* syn. *A. martimus*): Dioecious. Grown in gardens (trench planting) by Romans for large spears. Only cultivated species as monocot and herbaceous perennial vegetable. Cultivated for its tender shoots commonly known as 'spears'.
- *A. acutifolius*: Spiny species and grows wild in Mediterranean region but young spears have no spines.
- *A. springeri*: Highly resistant to fusarium but cross incompatible with *A. officinalis*.

Varieties:

- Most of cultivars from Europe are clonal hybrids (F_1 progenies from single cross).
- Dr. G.C. Hanna: Vegetable specialist, Univ. of California, Davis.
- Two male hybrid cvs. Jersey Giant and Greenwich are patented & released for commercial scale.Both have improved yields & field tolerance to rust & fusarium.
- Double cross hybrids: Diane, Junon, Minerve and Larac were released between 1974-77 in France by Corriols- Thevenin (1979).
- Hybrid male plants (super malesi.e. all male hybrids) are high yielder(3-5 times more), earlier and live longer than female plants. These are resistant to rust, fusarium crown rot. All-male plants do not produce seeds and avoid weed problem in commercial fields.

Asparagus hybrid cultivars and characteristics:

Hybrid cv.	Flowering type	Disease tolerance	Features
New Jersery Hybrids			
Jersey Giant	All male	Rust resistant, Fusarium tolerant	Extremely vigorous, high yields
Jersey Centennial	Dioecious	Rust resistant, Fusarium tolerant	Widely available; does not start producing maximum yields as quickly as others
Greenwich	All male	Rust resistant, Fusarium tolerant	High yields
Rutgers synthetic strains	Mixtures of dioecious hybrids or male hybrids	Rust resistant, Fusarium tolerant	Adapted for production in north-east
California Hybrids			
UC-157	Dioecious	Rust resistant	High yields, not recommended for colder climates

- Tissue cultured clonal hybrids: Aneto, Lesto, Bruneto, Steline were released by them in 1979.
- Male plant Washington (A7-83) transmits rust resistance, more seed wt., (heavy seeds) and greater seedling height.
- Female plant Martha (B-32-39) and Mary (A5-11) transmits rust resistance and developed by Sutton and Sons Company.

Name	Breeding method	Features
Perfection, Book's Special, New Jersey Queen, Mammoth White, Viking, Waltham Washington,	Introduction	-
Jersey Centennial	Clonal hybrid of No. 51 x No. 22	Dioecious, large spears, vigorous, high yield; rust resistant & fusarium tolerant
Jersey Giant	-	Rust resistant & fusarium tolerant
Mary Washington	F_1 hybrid of (A5-11 x A7-83)	Rust resistant; good productivity; wide adaptability
Martha Washington	F_1 hybrid of (B-32-39 x A7-83)	Rust resistant
California-500	Selection	Tighter heads; less purpleness; more uniform sized spears; rust resistant
Minnesota	4 way cross hybrid	Longer & heavier stalks
French Argenteuli, Palmetto	-	Rust resistant
CITH-A-1	-	-

Diseases, pest and disorder:

- Rust (*Puccinia asparagi*): 1st discovered in America in 1896 by B.D. Halstead. It is an obligate parasite, most serious in nursery and in field which cause premature defoliation. Spray Bavistin @ 2 g/litre. Use of resistant cvs. (New Jerser Selections) is recommended.
- Fusarium stem & crown rot (*Fusarium moniliforme)*: Major problem all over the world. Soil treatment with Formalin before planting is suggested.
- Wilt and root rot(*F. oxysporum* f.sp. *aspergi*): More harmful than rust.
- Stem and crown rot (*Fusarium moniliformae*): Drying and dwarfing of plants.More devastating than foot rot. Serious in poorly drained soils.
- Asparagus beetle (*Crioceris asparagi*)and Spotted asparagus beetle (*C. duodecimpuntato*): Major seed attacking pests.
- Asparagus aphid (*Brachycolus asparagi*): Chemical control is best.
- Grubs, wire worms & cut worms also cause damage to spears below ground.
- Fibrousness: Ethylene injury.
- High desert temperature causes the tips to open prematurely.

Inheritance of character:

- Bassett *et al*. (1971) developed recessive seedling marker gene (basal stem colour) to detect parthenogenesis in female plants.
- Rate of fibre development is positively correlated with temperature in which spear is kept.
- Positive correlations with male plants between crown weight and number and total weight of spears during first three cutting seasons.It is not found in female plants.
- Rust resistance: Phenotypic resistance.
- If andromonoecious male (M/m) is selfed, it yields 1 MM (super male): 2 Mm (normal male) : 1 mm (female).

Character	Number of genes	Type of gene action
Spear colour	Monogenic recessive (gg)	Persistent greenrecessive to normal green (GG); as a marker gene maintains dark green foliage and their foliage pigments and plants never turn yellow
Basal stem colour	Monogenic recessive (pp)	Red stalkrecessive to green or no anthocyanin stalk & is a marker for identification of haploid seedlings
Sex expression	Monogenic dominant (MM)	Male dominant to female (Rick & Hanna, 1943; Thuesen, 1960)

23. MALVACEAE

23.1 Okra

- Eulogized as 'Lady's finger or *Bhendi*'.
- Cultivated okra is of Old World origin.
- Arose as cultigens in Ethiopia.
- Early records of okra dates back to 12th century Egypt.
- India ranks 1st in world production (70% of total world production).
- After onion, it accounts 70% of the 30% exchange earnings from export of vegetables.
- Rich source of Iodine. Also rich source of calcium (66 mg/100 g), potassium (103 mg/ 100g) and vit. C (30 mg/ 100 g).
- Chromosome count is difficult due to small size and large numbers.
- Mucilage (roots and stems) is polysaccharides (galacturonic and glucoronic) used in clearing of juice in jaggary preparation.
- Seed is alternate source of greenish yellow edible vegetable oil 13-22% (e.g. Pusa Makhmali 17.3%) containing 20-25% protein and 40% fat.
- Oil content of seed: 40%. Oil is rich in unsaturated fatty acids viz. oleic acid and linoleic acid.
- Dry fruit shell and stem fibres are used to make strings and nets and in paper and card board industry.
- In Africa, ripe seeds are roasted, ground and used as substitute for coffee powder.

- Okra is useful against genitourinary disorders, spermatorrhoea and chronic dysentery, cures ulcer and relief from haemorrhoids.
- In soups, they impart a flavour & glutinous consistency known as 'gumbo'.
- Major breeding objective: Resistance to YVMV.
- Most effective gametocide to induce sterility: Maleic hydrazide.
- Okra is polyploidy with n=12 suggested by Charrier (1984).
- Okra is facultative autogamous.
- Flower numbers 2 to 4 are best pollen producers.
- Flower bud initiation: 22-26 days after sowing.
- 1st flowering occurs 20-22 days after initiation.
- Flower bud appears in leaf axil above 6-8 leaf depending upon cultivar.
- Flower bud takes 22-36 days from initition to full bloom.
- Type of dichogamy: Protogyny.
- Anthesis time: 8 to 10 AM.
- Anther dehiscence: Transverse and occur 15-20 minutes after anthesis.
- Pollen grains are polysiphonous (many tubes can develop from one pollen grain).
- Distant hybridization is used for transfer of quality traits like green colour.
- Hybrid vigour has been reported from India alone.
- No inbreeding depression is noticed.
- Okra cultivation during summer is problematic and less economic.
- Seed rate: Summer season (18-20 kg/ha) and rainy season (10-12 kg/ha).
- Seed viability: 2 years.
- Fruit is a capsule or pod and grows quickly after flowering.
- Greatest increase in pod size takes place during 4th to 6th day.
- Flowers structure combines hermaphroditism and self compatibility.
- Flower bud takes 22-26 days from initiation to full bloom.
- Flower open only once in morning and close after pollination.
- Attributes for dehydration: Less fiber, less mucilageneous substance, high protein, high dry matter and minerals.
- Attributes for canning and freezing: High chlorophyll, less crude fibre and mucilage substance, low dry matter, high proteins, vitamins and minerals.
- Export standard: 6-8 cm long fruits.
- Temperature >42°C cause flower bud drop.
- Optimum temperature for seed germination: 29.5°C.
- Optimum temperature for normal growth and development: 24-28°C.
- Okra cultivation during summer is problematic and less economic.
- Okra gives 300-500% crop land use efficiency as an intercrop in cassava and cucurbits.

- Tender fruits are used for fresh market.
- Fruits ready harvest 30-45 days after sowing or 6-7 days after flower opening.
- Post harvest treatment of CCC @ 100 ppm enhances shelf life.
- During seed production, initial 1-3 pods should be harvested for fresh pods to encourage growth and flower production.
- Most suitable season for seed production: Rainy season.
- Seed yield: 1200-1500 kg/ha.
- Seed shattering is major problem in seed production.
- Seed storage: Below 10% moisture at 1-5^{0}C.
- Recommended spacing for seed production: 24 x 12 inch (14 pods/plant).
- Pods required for producing 1 kg seed: 1.6 kg.
- Seed germination test: Floatation method.
- Seeds have hard seed coat and soaking seeds in hot water (43^{0}C) for 1-2 h prior to planting improves germination.
- Processed product for preservation and export: Dehydrated bhindi.
- For year round consumption, sun-dried, frozen & sterilized fruits are used.
- Specific requirement for export purpose: Green, tender, 6-8 cm, 4-5 ridges, slender and roundish with pointed tips.

Species:

- Wild species are indigenous to Africa.
- Wild species native to India: *A. tuberculatus*, *A. moschatus*, *A. ficulneus*.
- Genus *Abelmoschus* was 1st established by Medikus in 1787.
- Taxonomic revision is done by Borssum Waalkes (1966).
- Dr. Harbhajan Singh initiated systematic research work on okra improvement in India.
- Three species are cultivated: *A. esculentus*, *A. manihot*, *A. moschatus*.
- Cultivated okra *A. esculentus* (syn. *Hibiscus esculentus*) is natural amphidiploid (2n=130) and composed of two genomes (29 + 36).
- *A. manihot* types are leafy types from Solomon and Fiji islands and did not flower.
- There are 6 species on the basis of epicalyx, corolla, capsule and fruit characteristics viz., *A. moschatus*, *A. manihot*, *A. esculentus*, *A. ficulneus*, *A. crinitus*, *A. angulosus*.
- Other putative ancestors: *A. ficulneus* (2n=72, 78), wild *A. caillei* (2n=185 to 199).
- Species *A. caillei* (2n=196) and *A. tetraphyllus* have been utilized in okra improvement.
- Six truly wild species: *A. manihot*, *A. angulosus*, *A. manihot* var. *pungens*, *A. tuberculatus*, *A. tetraphyllus*, *A. moschatus*.

- Through interspecific hybridization, it is possible to transfer symptomless carrier type of tolerance to YVMV from *A. callei* (Parbhani Kranti, Punjab-7, Punjab Padmini) and *A. tetraphyllus* (Arka Anamica, A. Abhay) to the conventional varieties.
- Resistant to PM disease: *A. tetraphyllus*, *A. manihot*, *A. moschatus*.
- Crossability between different species (pre and post zygotic barriers):
  a) *A. esculentus* x *A. ficulneus*: Fail due to chromosomal difference.
  b) Formation of no bivalents and irregular gametes in *A. manihot*.
  c) Sterile hybrids between *A. esculentus* x *A. tetraphyllus*.
  d) Crosses between *A. esculentus* x *A. caillei* produce viable hybrids with strongly reduced fertility.
  e) Sterile hybrids in cross of *A. caillei* x *A. tetraphyllus*.
  f) *A. esculentus* x *A. moschatus*: Get fruit set but no seed set.
  g) Reciprocal crosses between *A. caillei* (2n=184) x *A. esculentus* (2n=130): 65 bivalents during meiosis of interspecific hybrids.

Botanical name	Features
A. tuberculatus (2n=58) Origin: North India	Progenitor & putative ancestor of cultivated okra; symptomless resistance to YVMV for limited period of time
A. manihot var. *pungens*, *A. crinitus* (2n=138), *A. panduraeformis*, *A. vitifolius*	True resistance to YVMV; but interspecific barriers occurs; used as leafy vegetable
A. caillei (Guinean okra/ West African okra) (2n=196)	Resistant to YVMV, ELCV, shoot and fruit borer, fusarium wilt, PM & microphomina blight
A. esculentus x *A. manihot*	Guinean okra is natural amphidiploid
EC 31830 (*A. manihot*) (2n=66)	Known as 'Ghana okra' (complex poly species); resistant to YVMV
A. manihot ssp. *manihot* (2n=194)	Highest chromosome; immune to YVMV; resistant to PM
A. manihot var. Ghana	Resistant to jassid
A. moschatus (Ambrette 2n=72)	Aromatic seeds & wild species
A. tuberculatus, cv. Narnaul Special (n=29)	Wild; tolerant to shoot and fruit borer
A. angulosus (2n=56)	Resistant to low temperature & frost
A. moschatus ssp. *moschatus* (2n=72)	Musk scented seeds
M. javanica	Highly resistant to nematode

Varieties:

- Hybrid vigour has been reported from India alone.
- Heterosis in okra is very moderate about 30% over the best OP variety.
- Suitable for canning: Dwarf Green Smooth, Vaishali Vadhu.
- White Snow, Red Round, Narnaul Special: <10% infestation of shoot and fruit borer.
- Red okra: Farmer's variety having 7-8" long fruits, 1-1.5 kg fruits/plant, cultivated throughout year.

Varieties	Breeding method	Features
Long Green Smooth	-	Resistant to root knot nematode
IC-8899, IIHR-21, AE-15	-	Resistant to jassids
Red Wonder-I, II, Long Green Smooth	-	Resistant to fruit & shoot borer
EC-32598	Introduction from Nigeria	Resistant to PM
EC-41292	Introduction from Nigeria	Resistant to cercospora leaf spot
IC-8248, IC-10238	-	Resistant to cercospora leaf spot
IARI, New Delhi		
Pusa Makhmali (1955)	Selection from local material from West Bengal	5 ridges on fruit; suitable for spring-summer season; resistant to fusarium wilt; susceptible to YVMV
Pusa Sawani (1958)	Pedigree selection from 'IC 1542 (resistant to YVMV) x Pusa Makhmali'	5 ridges on fruit; highly stable; tolerant to high pH & salinity; spineless, day neutral & resistant to virus, fusarium wilt; suitable for canning, dehydration & export
Pusa A-4	Pedigree selection of [*A. manihot ssp. manihot* Ghana x Pusa Sawani) x Parbhani Kranti)]	Tolerant to jassids, fruit & shoot borer & YVMV; suitable for export; respond to pruning & suitable as ratoon crop
Perkins Long Green	Introduction from USA	8 ridges on fruit; suitable for hills; <10% infestation of shoot & fruit borer
Clemon's Spineless	Introduction from USA	Suitable for hills; <10% infestation of shoot & fruit borer
Pusa Bhendi-5 (2018)	-	Dark green coloured 5 ridged fruits; yield 18 t/ha; resistant to YVMV
Selection 2-2	Pedigree selection of (Pusa Sawani x Best One) x (Pusa Sawani x IC 7194)	Tender fruits; 16-20 cm long fruits; 50 days for 1st harvesting; suitable for dehydration
IIHR, Bengaluru		
Arka Anamika (Sel. 10) 1990	Interspecific hybrid of (*A. esculentus* x wild spp. *A. manihot* ssp. *tetraphyllus*) followed by back cross	Resistant to YVMV, fruit borer; short internodes, less branching
Arka Abhay (Sel. 4) 1992	Sister line of 'Arka Anamika'	Resistant to YVMV & tolerant to fruit borer; suitable for ratoon crop
Arka Nikita	Pedigree selection of (GMS-4 x IIHR-299-14-11-585)	1st commercial GMS based F_1 hybrids from India and world; dark green fruits; yield 36 t/ha; rich in iodine (33.31 ìg/kg)
IIHR-21	-	Resistant to cotton jassids
IIVR, Varanasi		

Kashi Lila	Pedigree selection of [(NIC9305 x HRB9-2) x IIVR 50]	Early, resistant to YVMV, OLCV
Kashi Vibhuti (2006)	Pedigree selection of [(NIC 9303 x IC111547) x IIVR 20]	Dwarf; flowering starts on 4-5th node; yield 17-18 T/ha; resistant to YVMV, OLCV
Kashi Pragati (2006)	Pedigree selection of [(NIC 9303 x Parbhani Kranti) x IIVR- 20]	Tall, short internode; fruits 8-10 cm long; yield 18-19 t/ha; resistant to YVMV, OLCV
Kashi Satdhari (2006)	Pedigree selection of [(Parbhani Kranti x IC111547) x IIVR-20]	Tall, short internode; plant bears 18-25 fruits with seven ridges, fruit length 13-15 cm; yield 11-14 t/ha; resistant to YVMV, OLCV
Kashi Kranti	Pedigree selection of (VRO-6 x 67-10-02)	Medium tall; resistant to YVMV, OLCV
Kashi Bhairav (2006)	F_1 hybrid of (IIVR-19 x IIVR-50)	Medium tall; yield 16-18 t/ha; resistant to YVMV, OLCV
Kashi Mahima (2006)	F_1 hybrid of (IIVR-21 x IIVR-15)	Tall; yield 13-15 t/ha; resistant to YVMV, OLCV
Kashi Mohini	F_1 hybrid	Tall; yield 13-15 t/ha; flowers at 4-5 node during summer; resistant to YVMV, OLCV
Kashi Mangali	Pure line selection	Medium tall; yield 13-125 t/ha; resistant to YVMV, OLCV; withstand high temperature during summer
Kashi Lalima (2018)	Pedigree selection from (IC-93892 x VROR-150)	1st bio-fortified(reddish purple fruited) cv.; contain more anti-oxidants, iron, calcium; used for salad purpose due to less stickiness in fruits; tolerant to YVMV & ELCV; suitable for both summer &rainy season; yield 14-15 t/ha
Kashi Chaman (2018)	Pedigree selection from (Kashi Kranti x Punjab Padmini)	Free from YVMV & OELCV; flowering occurred 42-44 days after sowing; fruits dark green; fruit 12-15 cm; fruit dia. 1.4-1.5 cm; yield 15-16 t/ha;
Kasha Shristi (2018)	F_1 hybrid of (Kashi Kranti x VRO-10)	Fruits dark green, fruit length 12-15 cm & fruit dia. 1.4-1.5 cm; yield 18-19 t/ha; tolerant to YVMV
Shitla Uphar	F_1 hybrid	17-18 fruits/plant; resistant to YVMV, OLCV
Shitla Jyoti (2001)	F_1 hybrid of (PDIB-3 x PDIB-1)	17-18 fruits/plant; resistant to YVMV, OLCV
Dr YSPUH & F, Solan		
Harbhjan Bhendi (1984)	Secondary introduction from 'Perkin's Long Green'	Very long, tapered; spineless; mostly 8 ridged; resistant to YVMV
MPKV, Rahuri		
Phule Kirti	F_1 hybrid	Resistant to YVMV
Phule Utkarsha (2003)	F_1 hybrid	Suitable for kharif & summer; low incidence of YVMV; yield (23 t/ha)
Phule Vimukta (2018)	F_1 hybrid	Yield (20 t/ha); suitable for kharif & summer; low incidence of YVMV & tolerant to white fly, jassids & fruit borer

Dr BSKKV, Dapoli		
Konkan Bhendi	-	Tolerant to virus, suitable for kharif & high rainfall area; yield 13 t/ha; non-branching
Dr PDKV, Akola		
Akola Bahar (2005)	-	Fruits long, slender, yield 10-11 t/ha
PDKV Pragati (AKOV-107)	-	Morphological marker: one sided red spot at the base of the petals (inner side); yield 99 q/ha; resistant to YVMV
VNMKV, Parbhani		
Parbhani Kranti (PB-57) 1985	Interspecific hybrid of (*A. esculentus* cv. Pusa Sawani x *A. manihot*)	Resistant to YVMV, jassids, white fly, fruit borer & suitable for export
Parbhani Tillu	Induced mutant (40 kR gamma radiation)	Suitable for processing & export purpose
TNAU, Coimbatore		
CO.1 (1976)	Pure line selection of 'Red Wonder' from Hyderabad	Pods slender, smooth, dark purple coloured; Tolerant to YVMV but susceptible to fruit borer & PM
CO.2 (1987)	Heterosis breeding of 'AE-180 x Pusa Sawani'	Fruits fairly long; yield 17 t/ha; better consumer appeal
CO.3 (1991)	Heterosis breeding of 'Parbhani Kranti x MDU-1'	Resistant to YVMV & suitable for growing in kharif & summer
CO.4	IC-620618 x IC-620619	Resistant to YVMV; yield 25 t/ha
TN Hybrid 8	-	Resistant to YVMV
COBhH-1 (2007)	Heterosis breeding of 'Varsha Uphar x PA 4(T)'	Less fibrous & sparsely pubescent; resistant to YVMV; yield 23 t/ha
MDU-1 (1978)	Gamma ray mutant of 'Pusa Sawani'	Fruits light green with light purple pigmentation; fruits 20 cm long; 5 ridges
EMS-8	Mutant of 'Pusa Sawani' by 1% EMS	Fruit 5 ridged; resistant to YVMV & tolerant to fruit borer
PAU, Ludhiana		
Punjab Padmini (1982)	Pedigree selection of [*A. esculentus* cv. Reshmi x *A. manihot* ssp. *manihot* cv. Ghana Red] was hybridized with F_2 (OP) plant (of cross *A. esculentus* cv. Pusa Sawani x *A. manihot* ssp. *manihot* cv. Ghana Red) led to Ludhiana Sel. 1 in F_8 generation	Flowers 45-50 days & 1st picking on 55 days after sowing; fruits starts from 6th to 8th node; resistant to YVMV; tolerant to hoppers; fruit remain tender for long period; suitable for canning

Punjab-7 (1985)	(*A. esculentus* cv. Pusa Sawani x *A. manihot* ssp. *manihot* cv. Ghana Red) F_1 was backcrossed to Pusa Sawani 4 times & selection in F_8 generation	Resistant to YVMV; suitable for canning
Punjab-8 (syn. EMS-8) 1989	Induced mutant (1% EMS) of 'Pusa Sawani' in M_8generation	Resistant to YVMV & tolerant to fruit borer; 5 ridges, long thin, tender; suitable for canning
Punjab-13	-	Light green fruits; susceptible to mosaic
CCSHAU, Hisar		
Hisar Unnat	Pedigree selection of (Sel-2-2 x Parbhani Kranti)	Petiole base pigmented from inner side only; resistant to YVMV
Hisar Naveen	-	Tolerant to YVMV; yield 11-12 t/ha
Varsha Uphar (HRB-9-2) 1992	Pedigree selection of (Lam Selection-1 x Parbhani Kranti)	Resistant to YVMV, tolerant to leaf hopper & suitable for export
HBH-142	Hybridization	Fruiting start on ¾th node; tolerant to YVMV; yield 14-15 t/ha
CSAUA & T, Kanpur		
Azad Kranti	Selection	Five ridged with long beak; yield 12.5 t/ha; resistant to YVMV
Azad Ganga (Azad Bhindi-1)	-	Mod. resistant to YVMV; 10-12 t/ha.
Azad Bhendi-2	-	Mod. resistant to YVMV
Azad Krishna (Azad Bhendi-3)	Hybridization & pedigree selection	Mod. resistant to YVMV; red fruit suitable for both; yield 13-15 t/ha
CSK HPKV, Palampur		
Palam Komal	Pedigree selection of (DPO-P-20 x P-8)	High yield; resistant to YVM
AAU, Anand		
Gujarat Anand Okra-5	-	Fruits dark green; it has less YVMV & low population of sucking pest; yield 14 t/ha
Gujarat Bhendi-1 (1986)	Pure line selection from unknown bulk sample from IARI	Purple tinge on stem, leaf veins, 5 ridges on fruit
AOH-262	Hybrid	Tall plants; fruit wt. 11 g; yield 18 t/ha
AOH-263	Hybrid	Tall plants; yield 8-9 t/ha; resistant to YVMV
JAU, Junagarh		
Gujarat Okra-6 (2018)	-	-
KAU, Thrissur		

Kiran (1990)	Selection from 'Kilichundan Local'	Long, straight, yellowish green fruits; suitable for kharif, summer season; crop duration 100 days
Salkeerthi (1998)	Reselection from NBPGR No. 144	Purple pigmentation at base & terminal end of petiole; light green coloured; long (24-30 cm) & 5 ridges on fruit; yield 15 t/ha
Aruna (1998)	Selection from NBPGR No. 1343	Red coloured stems, leaves & fruits; fruits 7 ridged & long; crop duration 120 days; yield 15 t/ha
Anitha (2006)	Mutation breeding	Yield 14.6 t/ha; resistant to YVMV
Manjima (2006)	Heterosis breeding of 'Gowreesapattom Local x NBPGR- TCR-874'	Yield 16 t/ha; YVMV resistant
VPKAS, Almora		
VL Bhindi-1 (2003)	Hybrid of 'Pusa Sawani x PS-1'	Tall; yield 15 t/ha; tolerant to mosaic & spotted leaf disease
SKUAST, Jammu		
Jammu Okra-05	-	-
Other varieties		
Red Bhendi	-	Fruit 5 ridged; red, long & slender

Private sector hybrids: Panchali, Adhunik, Supriya, Varsha Uphar, Sonal, Sarika, Nath Sobha, Sungrow 35

Inheritance of characters:

- Fruit yield is positively correlated with fruits/plant, fruit length, plant height and branches/plant.
- Additive gene action is noticed in earliness, plant pigmentation, petiole and leaf character, corolla and calyx colour.
- Polygenic characters: Plant height, days to flower, days to marketable maturity, fruits/ plant, fruit length, fruit diameter, fruit weight, ridges on fruit, seed weight, seeds/ plant and yield.
- Transfer of resistance from wild relatives is hampered by sterility problems.

Character	Number of genes	Type of gene action
Plant height	Monogenic	Tall dominant to dwarf
Plant colour	Monogenic	Dark green dominant over light green; green recessive to greenish red
Leaf margin	Monogenic	Cut leaves dominant to lobed leaves
Leaf lobing	Monogenic	Incompletely dominant
Pod colour	Monogenic or digenic	* White dominant to green; * Deep green dominant over pale green
Pod shape	Oligogenic	Angular dominant over round & epistasis has been observed
Pod spininess	Monogenic	Spininess dominant to non-spininess
Pod hairiness	Monogenic	Fruit hairiness is incompletely dominant over non-hairiness
Stem colour	Monogenic	Purple stem colour dominant to green stem colour
Calyx colour & petal vein colour	-	Pleiotropic
Calyx pigmentation	Monogenic	Pigmentation dominant
Yellow corolla	Monogenic	Yellow dominant over cream
YVMV resistance	2 complementary dominant genes (*Yv1* & *Yv2*)	Resistance dominant to susceptible; Single dominant gene in *A. manihot* and *A. manihot* ssp. *manihot* cross polygenic with dominant- additive effects
	-	Polygenic with dominant- additive effect

Pests and diseases:

- Jassids (*Empoasca devastans*): Most serious pest.
- Shoot and fruit borer (*Earis vittella*): Most common occurring pest. Difficult to control with chemicals.
- Aphids (*Aphis gossypi*):
- Semi-looper (*Anomis flava*):
- Red spirder mite (*Tetranychus telarius*): Very serious during dry period.
- Spotted bollworm (*Earias fabia*).

- Red cotton bug (*Dysdercus koenigi*): Serious pest of seed crop.
- Cut worm (*Agrostis* spp.): Damage to young seedlings.
- Trap crop for root knot nematode: Pink and white periwinkle.
- Powdery mildew (*Erisiphe cichoraceraum*): Major problem in south India.
- Yellow vein mosaic virus (YVMV) and Enation Leaf Curl virus (ELCV): (Vector: White fly-*Bemisia tabaci*): Most devastating diseases. *A. pungens*, *A. crinitus*, *H. panduraeformis* are immune.
- Enation leaf curl: Viral disease (vector- white fly). It was 1st reported at IIHR in 1984.
- Damping off: *A. manihot* PI 379584 possess high resistance.

24. MARANTACEAE

24.1 Queensland arrow root

- Eulogized as 'Purple arrow root'.
- Stem purple.
- Rhizomes are fleshy, cylindrical & covered with regular scales.
- Word 'arrow root' derived from pointed shape of rhizome.
- Caribbean word '*araruta*' means' many roots'.
- Introduced to India in 1831 from Cape of Good Hope.
- Edible tubers (rhizome) used for starch.
- Starch-dry, white powder, very fine & easily digestible.
- Young shoots & petioles are used as fodder.
- Pollination agent: Insect.
- White coloured varieties: Creole, Banana.
- Major hurdle in breeding: Difficulty in seed setting.
- Small piece of rhizome (4-7 cm size with 2-4 nodes) known as bits are used for planting.
- Propagation method: Fleshy rhizomes treated with 10% $CuSO_4$ before planting.
- Planting distance: 60 cm x 60 cm.
- Seed rate: 2.5 t/ha.
- Tolerates partial shade and taken as intercrop in coconut.
- Harvesting: 10-12 months after planting (for starch purpose); 5 months after planting (cooking purpose).
- Maturity index: Yellowing and wilting of leaves.

- Once harvested, rhizomes deteriorate very rapidly & must be processed within 2-5 days.
- Delayed harvesting cause decline in starch content and increase in sugar content.
- Yield: 25-30 t/ha.
- Rhizomes are eaten in boiled or roasted forms.
- Starchy arrow root is used as an infant food & also in biscuits, cakes, puddings and substitute for agar.
- It is used for production of carbon-less paper for computer print.
- Cigar root (*Rosellinea bunodes*): Prevalent in high rainfall areas and due to poor drainage. It results in long thin rhizome with much fibre and little starch.

24.2 West Indian arrow root

- Eulogized as 'Bermuda arrow root'.
- *Maranta bicolor* and *M. leuconeura*: Ornamental purpose and possess variegated leaves.
- Commercially grown in Australia for starch production.
- Rhizome composition: Starch (27.8%), fibre (3%), sugars (2.1%), crude protein (1.6%), fat (0.2%), moisture (63.4%).
- Edible part: Young rhizome.
- Tops of plant and tubers used as fodder purpose.
- Leaves are used as packing material for fish and meat.
- Seed rate: 3000-3500 kg bits/ha.
- Flowers are nipped off as and when appear.
- Harvesting method: Rhizomes are harvested when leaves begin to wither and die in 10-11 months after planting.
- Yield: 4-7 t/ha (rhizome).

25. MORINGACEAE

25.1 Drumstick

- Eulogized as 'World's most useful tree or World's most nutritious plant or Multipurpose tree or Perennial vegetable moring or Horse radish tree or Radish tree or West Indian ben or Ben oil tree or Tree of life or Miracle tree or Wonder tree or Mother's best friend or Never die tree or Super foods on earth or Indespensible plant for health management'.
- Monogeneric family.

- Deciduous, tropical and drought tolerant crop.
- Exported to UAE, Malaysia and Singapore.
- Out of total export, 70% is from Nashik district of Maharashtra.
- Species: *Moringa oleifera* (syn. *M. pterygosperma*).
- Leaves are known as the 'World's Greatest Unknown Supplement'.
- Leaves contain 4 times vit. A than in carrot, 7 times vit. C in oranges, 4 times calcium in milk, 3 times potassium in banana and 2 times proteins in milk.
- Leaf powder is effective in lowering blood sugar level and increases milk in lactating mothers.
- Fruits (pods), leaves and flowers are equally useful for culinary purpose.
- KaSaMaDe i.e. Ka (Kalwan), Sa (Satara), Ma (Malegaon), De (Deolali) tehsils of Nashik are famous for cultivation.
- Cultivated extensively for truck gardens owing to consumer preference & industrial uses.
- Hypocholesterolomic effect of leaves, antifertility effects of roots, hypotensive, anti-tumor and anti-spasmodic activity of leaf extract, anti-ulceronic effect of flower buds have been established.
- Pods are rich in free amino acid 'Leucine'.
- Anthesis: Continuous throughout day.
- Optimum temperature for growth: 25-30^{0}C.
- Ideal soil pH: 6 to 7.5
- Pod contains 10-20 seeds.
- Average seed weight: 0.288 g and 10 g contains 35 seeds.
- Pod requires 3 months to attain its full length upto 20 inches.
- Seed contain yellow coloured oil called 'behen/ ben oil'.
- Oil percent in seed: 38-40%.
- Oil is non-drying, clear, odourless, edible & never become rancid.
- Oil is used for illumination, soap industry and highly priced for lubricating watches and computers.
- Wood yield blue dye & fibre.
- Flowering season: February-April.
- Drumstick oil cake is used as organic substitute for water purifying chemicals such as potassium aluminium sulphate (i.e alum).
- Highly cross pollinated due to heteromorphism and entomophilous (honey bee, carpenter bee).

- Flower colour: Creamy white
- Propagation method: Limb cuttings (perennial type) and seeds @ 650 g/ha (annual type).
- Stima receptivity: 1 day before anthesis.
- Anthesis time: 4.30-6.30 AM with peak at 5.30 am.
- Inflorescence carries 19-126 flowers.
- Harvesting starts 160-170 days after plaı ting.
- Normally, 2-3 fruits/ inflorescence are obtained.
- Fruit setting range: 1-2.8%.
- Fruit length varies from 25-100 cm.
- Spacing: 3 m x 3 m or 2.5 m x 2.5 m.
- Planting density: 1600 seedlings/ ha (640-650 seedlings/ha).
- Average yield: 25-50 pods/tree; 52 T/ha (i.e. 18-20 T/acre).
- Plant start bearing 4-5 months after heading back.
- 75 kg FYM + 370 g ammonium sulphate/ tree increase yield by 3-4 times.
- Highly susceptible to frost & high temperature.
- Pods are harvested before they develop fibre.
- Moringa pod pieces can be dried in solar drier.
- Drying ratio: 6.4: 1
- Important cultural operations: Nipping and pruning.
- Nipping of shoot tips at 50-75 cm height encourage side branching and higher pod number.
- Pollarding is necessary.
- Ratooning is practiced after harvest of all pods. Ratooned stems bear the pods within 4-5 months.
- Year round production: Withholding of water followed by pruning.
- Value added product: Moring energy bar, powder.

Varieties:

- ECHO (Educational Concerns for Hunger Organization, Florida) maintains seed bank.
- Chavakacheri, Murungai, Pal Murungai, Rohit-1, Deccan Odissi, Shaktiman, Vasanth, Siddhivinayaka (Farmers' selections).

Name	Breeding method	Features
TNAU, Coimbatore		
KM-1	Selection	Annual; developed at Annia farm, Kudumianmalai in Tamil Nadu; pod length 32-37 cm; pod wt. 65-82 g;
PKM-1 (1989)	Pure line selection	Annual; seed propagated; 70 cm long pods; attain edible maturity 65 days after flowering; yield (250-300 pods/ tree/ year); pod length 60-75 cm; 3 ratoon crops can be taken; revolutionized drumstick cultivation
PKM-2 (2000)	MP-31 x MP-28	Annual; starts flowering in 100-110 days & harvested in 170-180 days; pods less seeded; pod length (20-25 cm); yield (250 fruits/ tree/year); suitable for kitchen garden
CO.1	Selection	Long pods
CO.2	Selection	Long pods
CIAH, Bikaner		
Thar Harsha	Selection	Flowers in Dec-Jan.; 160-180 days for maturity; pod length (20-25 cm); 314 fruits/ tree; fruit wt. 155 g;protein (9.3 g/ 100 g); vit. C (246 mg/ 100 g); vit. A (9783 IU/ 100g)
UHS, Bagalkot		
Bhagya (syn. KDM-01)	-	Long pods upto 1 m length
UAS, Dharwad		
Dhanaraj	Selection	Dwarf (2-2.5 m); yield starts after 9-10 months of sowing; yield (250-300 pods/ year); pod length 35-40 cm; recommended as intercrop in coconut and mango garden; most suitable for homestead gardens
UAS, Bengaluru		
GKVK-1	Selection	Plant height 1.5 m; yield 250-300 pods; pod wt. 40 g; pod length 35-40 cm; most suitable for HDP
GKVK-2	Selection	Dwarf (1-1.5 m height); yield 300-400 pods/ year
GKVK-3	Selection	Dwarf (1-1.5 m height); pods long conical shaped; yield (250-300 pods/ year); most suited for HDP
Dr BSKKV, Dapoli		
Konkan Ruchira (1992)	Selection from Vasi village	Best quality; pod length 50-55 cm; 30-35 kg/plant; yield 30-35 t/ha; medium sized pods
KAU, Thrissur		
Anupama	Selection	Early bearing; protracted flowering; fruit length 65 cm; yield 50 t/ha
Other varieties:		
Chem Murungai	Local selection	Red pigmentation on tip of pod; flowers throughout year
Jaffna	Introduced from Jaffna	Extremely drought hardy; perennial; popular in south India; long pods (90-100 cm); soft flesh; yield (400 pods/ tree/ year); unpruned & allowed to grow as it is; propagated through limb cuttings; susceptible to hairy caterpillar
Moolanoor Murangai	Local selection	Perennial; commercially cultivated in Mulanoor of Erode district of Tamil Nadu; pod length 30-40 cm; yield (500-600 pods/ tree/ year); less pet & disase attack
Palmurungai	Ecotype of Jaffna	Flowers throughout year; yield (400-500 pods/ tree/ year)
Kodikal Murungai	Local selection	Cultivated in betelvine gardens of Tirunelveli, Tanjavar, Dharmpuri districts of Tamil Nadu; annual type; pod length 20-25 cm & thick fleshed
Palamedu Murungai	Local selection	Cultivated in Madurai district of Tamil Nadu; long pods (60-75 cm)

Pests and diseases:

- Hairy caterpillar causes defoliation which is managed by spraying fish oil resin soap.
- Aphids (*Aphis craccibora*):
- Scale (*Diaspidotus* spp.):
- Fruit fly (*Gitonia* spp.):
- Fruit borer (*Diaxenopsis apomecynoides*):
- Diplodia root rot:
- Brown spot:

26. ONOCLEACEAE

26.1 Fiddlehead fern

- Edible portion: Tightly coiled tender fronds.
- Nutrient composition per 100 g edible portion: Protein (4.6 g), Cu (0.32 mg), niacin (4.98 mg), ascorbic acid (26.6 mg), Mn (0.51 mg), Fe (1.31 mg).
- Found in shady and swampy places.

27. POACEAE (GRAMINEAE)

27.1 Sweet corn

- Eulogized as 'Maize dulce or Shiveled corn'.
- Sub-family- Panicoidae, tribe- Maydeae.
- Consumed as a fresh market & processed vegetable.
- Produced primarily in North America.
- Among vegetable crops, it ranks 2nd & 4th in farm value for processing & fresh market, respectively.
- It is most important vegetable crop in USA, valued for both fresh market (21%) and processing i.e. canning (57%) and freezing (43%).
- Per capita consumption of processed form in USA: 7 lbs.
- America, Brazil, Arjentina are major exporters while Asian countries are major importers of maize.
- In India, as much as 55% of maize production is utilized for poultry/ animal feed purposes and 15-20% for starch industry.
- It is a genetic rather than taxonomic entity.
- It is a single gene mutation in cultivated maize (2n=20).
- Sweet corn as a specific crop might have appeared in 1820.
- Crop was taken to Europe by Columbus in 1493.
- Sweet form of maize was cultivated in USA in 1780 and was recognized as major crop by 1820.
- 1st listing of sweet corn in seed catalogues of USA appeared in 1828.
- It is a source of bio-fuel production.

- As much as 30% of maize production in America is utilized for production of ethanol.
- Both self & cross pollinated.
- Cross pollination among different types results in undesirable starchy corn.
- Plant develops single dominant stem headed by male inflorescence (tassel).
- Female inflorescence (ear) is lateral flower stalk which terminates one of the side branches.
- Cob is receptacle, bearing the ovaries (future kernels) and the styles or silks. The husks are leaves, mostly sheath.
- Kernels are fruitlets in which the plant stores food primarily as sugar and starch.
- Each kernel develops from an individual flower.
- The silks are the stigmas and elongated styles of the individual fruitlets that develop into kernels.
- Initiation of tassel occurs 21 days after planting, when 7 leaves are visisble.
- Well developed tassel appears in whorl of leaves.
- Male flowers in tassel open and release the pollens, which are carried by air currents to silk over a period of 7 days.
- Pollination begins 3-4 days before silk appear (protandrous nature).
- About 50,000 pollen grains are available for each silk.
- Silk remain receptive to pollen for 9 days.
- Improper pollination results in failure of kernel development and incomplete tip fill.
- Following pollination, ear elongates and rapidly develops and sugars move into developing kernels from other plant parts.
- As the ear matures, kernels increase in size and pass through 4 stages of maturation i.e.
  1. Pre-milk stage: Kernels are small and their juice is clear and watery.
  2. Milk stage: Kernels become large and plumpy and juice becomes milky. Kernels are sweet since sugars are high.
  3. Early dough and
  4. Dough stage: Within a week, the kernels pass through these stages and pericarp becomes tough and sugars are changed to starch.
- Seed is composed of 3 principal parts as- Pericarp (protective surface layer of ovary wall); endosperm (bulk of seed and functions as source of food material for growing embryo) and embryo (comprises scutellum and main axis of plumule containing 4-5 embryonic leaves and coleoptile).
- Chemical composition of seed: -CHO (51-74%), protein (10%), lipid (5%).
- At higher temperature (4.4-32^{0}C), the growth is greater and short time is required to reach a particular stage of development.
- Cultivar planted in late summer take 60 days to reach maturity and has higher leaf count compared to winter planting (take 120 days for maturity).
- Plants flower earlier under short days than in long days.

- Optimum temperature for growth: 21-30^{0}C and requires frost free season of 65-110 days.
- Threshold temperature for growth is 10^{0}C.
- Cold night temperatures depress growth rate and take more time to reach maturity.
- Hot nights donot favour corn growth and reduces dry weight and increases respiration.
- Optimum soil pH: 6.0-6.8 for best yields and highest quality.
- It is directly seeded in the field and doesnot transplant well.
- HDP: 16000 (early cvs.) to 24000 (nid-season cvs.) plants/ acre is recommended.
- Seed germination: > 20 days in cool soil (10^{0}C) to 4 days in warm soil (24^{0}C).
- Shallow planting (2 cm depth) is recommended for better seed germination and early seedling emergence.
- In corn, heat unit concept plays important role on the rate of crop growth.
- Early planting of corn require more days to mature than late plantings; but both require same number of heat units to reach maturity.
- In corn, heat units are based on night temperature above 4.4^{0}C, day temperature >10^{0}C and maximum temperature of 30^{0}C.
- The shrunken, brittle & ADX hybrids are prortected from pollens produced by standard (*Su*) sweet corn hybrids as such cross pollination make the product starchy.
- Thicker the pericarp, kernels are less susceptible to damage & subsequent diseases.
- As sugar level increases, less storage polysaccharides are formed in the matured kernels.
- As a monoecious, it possesses staminate flowers in tassel & pistillate flowers on the ear shoots.
- Anthesis in tassel begins near the centre of spike & proceeds upwards & downwards, with the upper flower of the upper spikelet commencing the process first.
- Type of fruit: Single seeded fruit known as 'Caryopsis'.
- Kernels store sugar, starch and water soluble polysaccharides in the endosperm.
- Quality parameters of sweet corn: Sweetness, pericarp tenderness (primarily quality factor), creamy texture (due to accumulation of water soluble polysaccharides) and low starch content.
- Tenderness is measured with 'Microtome machine' in dry seed stage with Crystal Violet stain.
- As sugar level increases, less storage polysaccharides are formed in the mature kernels.
- Starch content is much lower than normal corn.
- Starch concentration (% of dry wt.) increases 20 days after pollination & then remains constant & again increases 30-40 days of post-pollination.
- Accumulaes more sugar than normal (*Su*) maize.
- Principal sugars in kernels: Sucrose & lesser amounts of glucose, fructose & maltose.

- As kernels pass from edible stage (20 days post pollination) to dry maturity stage, sugars are converted in to starch.
- Sugary cvs. have 10-15% sugar at harvest and in high-sugar type cvs. contain elevated sugar levels of 25-35%.
- Main effects associated with '*su*' is the accumulation of phytoglycogen to 25% or more of the kernel dry wt.

Character	Sweet corn	Field corn
Plant spacing or uneven germination	Critical influence on uniform maturity	Some influence
Maturity at harvest (% moisture)	68-78	13-18
Perishability	Extremely rapid	Rapid
Second ears contribute to yield	Partially	Fully
Shape of cob	Critically important	Un-important
Appearance of ear	Critically important	Un-important
Utilization of growing season	Partial	Full
Quality evaluation	Difficult to measure	Easy to evaluate
Adaptation to processing requirements	Many considerations	Few critical
Seed production	Difficult	Relatively routine

- Thicker the pericarp, kernels are less susceptible to damage & subsequent diseases.
- Kernel row number influences kernel shape.
- High row number is associated with narrower kernels which are preferred for processing & fresh market place.
- Use of CMS is needed to prevent detasselling.
- Use of plastic mulching enhances seed germination and speed up maturity of early plantings of sweet corn by 10-14 days.
- Requires 12-25 acre inches of water.
- Method of irrigation: Furrow or sprinkler system.
- Trizine herbicides (Atrazine, cyanazine) are widely used.
- Texas-type cytoplasm (cms-T) is used in seed production.
- In hybrid field corn seed production, close linkage of gene '*y*' (white cytoplasm) & ms (male sterile) is used to separate yellow kernels from white.
- Isolation distance of 250 feet minimizes cross pollination effect.
- Isolation can be provided by scheduling planting time of minimum 14 days between tasseling and silking dates of different cultivars.
- Maturity indices:
  1. Ears are harvested at milky stage i.e. around 18-21 days after first silking.
  2. Drying of silks and plump feeling of ears indicate the attainment of desired maturity for harvesting.
  3. When about 70% of ears reach the desired maturity and are filled out.
  4. Machine harvest of processing sweet corn is widely practiced.

5. After harvesting, eating quality of sweet corn decreases rapidly.
6. Changes of decrease in sugars and increase in starch content are directly proportional to temperature.
7. Loss of sugars is about 4 times as rapid at 86^0F as at 32^0F.
8. At 86^0F, about 60% sugars are converted to starch in one day as compared to only 6% at 32^0F.
9. Water loss from kernels through transpiration causes denting in kernels and pericarp becomes tough.

- Time required for maturity, ranges from 65 days in early cultivars to 110 days for late ones.
- Early cultivars produce small marketable ears while late cultivars produce larger ones and sometimes two ears/ plant.
- At optimum edible maturity, high quality sweet corn contains 70-75% moisture and high sugar concentration.
- Proper stage of ear maturity at harvest is critical to market quality.
- Cooling and storage:

1. Pre-ccoling to 32^0F slows down the respiration rate but flavour and texture of sweet corn is lost rapidly even at this temperature.
2. Hydro-cooling is traditionally preferred method to compensate for some water loss.
3. Vacuum cooling and slush ice is also used.
4. At 32^0F & 95-98% R.H., sweet corn can be stored for 5-8 days only.

Species:

- Wild ancestor: Perennial teosinte (*Z. diploperenis*, 2n=20).
- Cultivated sweet/ sugar/ pole corn: *Zea mays* var. *saccharata*. (*Z. mays* var. *rugosa*). It represents sugary form of maize.
- It is considered to be mutant of field/ dent corn in which sugary gene prevents/ retards normal conversion of sugar to starch, resulting in sweetish kernel at immature stage.
- Principal types of maize:

a) Flour or soft corn (var. *amylacea*): Kernels have soft starch throughout.

b) Flint corn (var. *indurata*): Kernels have hard starch endosperm and possesses good storage and germination quality.

c) Dent or field corn (var. *indentata*): Kernels has endosperm characteristics of above two. The centre is soft and floury, while sides of the kernel are flinty. Because of soft core, apex of kernel shrinks on drying, resulting in dented crown.

d) Pop corn (var. *everta*): Has small, pointed kernels with thick skin. Upon heating, steam is trapped until the kernel explodes, exposing the white endosperm.

Varieties:

- Development of OP cultivars progressed at rapid rate in late 19th century.
- More than 60 hybrids have been developed by one or more mutant endosperm genes other than or in addition to '*su*'.
- Mammoth Sweet, Stowell Late Evergreen.
- Stowells Evergreen: Hybrid between 'Menomy Sweet corn x Northern Sugar' was developed in 1851.
- 1st high sugar hybrid: Illini Super (Xtra) Sweet (based on *sh2* gene).
- Florida Sweet (based on *sh2* gene): High quality for fresh market.
- Florida Stay Sweet (based on *sh2* gene) by Wolf in 1978.
- Penn fresh ADX (based on *ae*, *du*, *wx* genes) by Garwood and Creech in 1979. This triple mutant combinations has improved eating quality & reduced rate of post harvest carbohydrate transformation.
- The brittle (*bt* & *bt2*) genes have been used by Brewbaker to develop OP corn cvs. Hawaiian Super Sweet # 6 & Hawaiian Super Sweet # 9 in 1977 and 1971, respectively. They have high sugar content & retain good quality at high temperature in tropics.
- Everlasting Heritage type is developed by genetic combination of *SeSe*, *susu*.
- Symphony: Bicoloured hybrid.
- Iochief (based on *su* gene) having high sugar content is a cross between lines 'Ia 5125 x IA 453'.
- Hybrids: Silver Queen, Mainliner, Tendertreat developed by selection.

Diseases and pests:

- On world basis, maize has large number of diseases & pests.
- Losses due to insect attack are >14% in tropical regions.
- Ear rot (*Diplodia* spp. & *Gibberlla zeae*):
- Fusarium kernel rot:
- Kernel crown spot: Bacterial disease attack before harvest maturity.
- Stalk rot: Complex disease caused by *Pythium*, *Fusarium*, *Diplodia*, *Gibberalla*.
- Leaf blight (*Helminthosporium turcicum*): Water soaked lesions on lower foliage. Follow crop rotation & use resistant varieties.
- Stewart's wilt or Bacterial wilt (*Erwinia stewartii*): Wilting and dieing of plants at silk formation stage. Seed borne and cucumber/ flea beetle act as vectors. Use resistant cultivars.
- Leaf rust (*Puccinia sorghi*): Late plantings are more susceptible to infection. Use resistant varieties and fungicidal infection.
- Common smut (*Ustilago maydis*): Hot and dry weather favours disease development. Use of field sanitization and tolerant cvs. is recommended.

- Head smut (*Sphacelotheca teiliana*): Seed borne.
- Maize Dwarf Mosaic (MDM) virus: Serious viral disease affects plants at any stage. Stunting of old plants and poor development of ear shoots. Vector is aphid. Use tolerant cvs.
- Corn ear-worm (*Heliothis zea*): More loss than any other insect. Spray systemic insecticides from silk emergence until 2 weeks later. Husk length & tightness are associated with ear-worm resistance. Greater husk number & husk length results greater resistance.
- European corn borer (*Ostrinia nubilolis*): Cause lodging & ear drop. Most wide spread and destructive pest on early plantings. Larvae feed on leaf surfaces, collars and whorls and bore into stems and ears.
- Corn root worm (*Diabrotica* spp.): Larvar feed on roots & adult feed on foliage, silks and pollens. Crop rotation and soil application of insecticides.

Inheritance of characters:

- Humans have tailored sweet corn & it occurred as recessive mutation of chromosome 4 at *Su* locus of cultivated corn, which affects endosperm chemistry.
- Normal sugary gene (*su*) and several other mutant genes impart high sugar levels in the kernels.
- High sugar corns have two genetic types- a) Sugary enhanced, called 'se corn' and b) Super sweets/ extra sweets called 'shrunken-2s'.
- Homozygous for recessive (*susu*) allele while filed/ dent corn & other non-sweet types are homozygous dominant (*SuSu*) for starchy allele.
- Biochemical effects associated with '*su*' locus involves alterations in kernel carbohydrate composition.
- Types of genes:
  1. In Standard sugary/ normal/ traditional cultivars viz. Gold Cup, NK-199, Silver Queen, Butter and Sugar:
     a) Kernels contain '*su*' gene which imparts moderate levels of sugars and creamy texture of kernels.
     b) Rapid conversion of sugars to starch results in rapid loss of quality in these cvs.
  2. In Sugary enhancer cultivars viz. Golden Sweet EH, Kandy Korn EH, Paramount, White Lightening:
     a) Elevated sucrose level is due to single recessive gene (sugar enhancer '*se'* gene) acting in combination with '*su'* gene and
     b) Genotype is abbreviated as 'suse' or commonly known as 'se'.
     c) These genotypes remain sweeter for a longer period after harvest than normal sweet corn and give kernels creamy texture.

3. In Super sweet/ Extra sweet corn cultivars viz. Illini, Xtra Sweet, Florida Stay Sweet, Sucro and Dinner Time:
   a) Shrunken-2 (*sh2*) gene has been identified, which contains more sugar than the standard cvs.
   b) This gene is called 'shrunken' since dry seed weight is light and has shriveled appearance and
   c) It is much slower in conversion of sugar to starch at maturity.
   d) Super sweet types single gene mutants containing '*sh2* gene' and not '*su*' gene.
   e) Seed coat of kernel is tough and has crispy texture.
   f) Kernels are less creamy and more watery than other sweet corns.
   g) These cultivars have poor seedling vigour and are less yielder than standard cvs.
4. In Augmented corns-
   a) Various genetic models of '*su*, *sh2* & *se*' genes have been developed.
   b) This modification may be partial occurring in about 25-44% of the '*su*' kernels or in all kernels.
   c) The taste sensation is sweeter than in standard sweet corn with little difference in texture.
   d) The hybrid seeds resemble & germinate similar to standard sweet corn seeds.
   e) Examples of Augmented corns
   i) In partial shrunken synergistic cultivars viz. Sugar Loaf, Honey Comb, Intrepid Synergistic and Sugar Time.
      a) Genetic types are full '*su*'& half *sh2*'.
      b) These are sweeter than standard, but less than full shrunken & generally crisp
   ii) In Augmented Sugary enhanced plus shrunken cultivars viz. Symphony
      a) Genetic types are full '*su*' & partial '*sh2* + *se*'.
      b) Corn cultivars are sweeter than standard & partial '*sh2* or *se*' but less than full '*sh2* or *se*'.
   iii) In Augmented full sugary enhanced corn cultivars viz. Miracle, Remarkable and Double Treat:7
      a) Genetic types are 'full su' & 'full se' (i.e. 100% modification).
      b) Corn cultivars are sweeter than standard, less than full shrunken but more creamy.
5. In addition of above, other mutant genes called brittle (*bt*) & gene combination called ADX have been used to make sweet corn more sweeter.
   i) In ADX type cultivars viz. Pennifresh ADX

a) High sugar levels are obtained through combined effects of 3 different genes: the 'amylase' extender gene (*ae*), the 'full gene (*du*) & 'waxy gene (*wx*) and no '*su*'.

b) Cultivars contain high sugar levels similar to full shrunken type.

ii) In brittle type cv. Hawaiian Super sweet.

a) Genetic type 'full *bt*' (no '*su*').

b) Other mutant gene brittle cvs. are sweeter than standard and similar to full sugary enchanced types.

- Snyder (1967) noted relationship of silk balling, husk length, husk tightness & blank tip to earworm & sap beetle resistance.
- Wann (1980) developed 'Composite 9E-79' earworm resistant corn by recurrent mass selection method.

Character	Number of genes	Mode of inheritance	Resistance source
Resistance to leaf blight	-	Resistance to race-T is cytoplasmically controlled; Resistance to race-O is polygenic or monogenic recessive	GF 440, Lady Finger Popcorn
Bacterial wilt	-	Resistance by 2 major & 1 minor dominant & independently inherited genes	Golden Cross Bantam
Leaf rust	-	Hypersensitive type resistance is controlled by single dominant gene *Rp* localized on chromosome 10	-
Common smut	Polygenic	-	-
Maize dwarf mosaic virus	-	-	Pa 405, B68, GA 209
High row number	Polygenic	-	-
European corn borer	-	-	Zapalote Chico, Antigua
Stalk rot	-	Quantitative	-

28. POLYGONACEAE (BUCKWHEAT FAMILY)

28.1 Rhubarb

- Eulogized as 'pie' plant because fleshy leaf petoles are most commonly used for preparation of pies, sauces and other desserts.
- Perennial vegetable that emerges from the same crown each year.
- Cold resistant or winter hardy plant and grown round the year in warm climate.
- Edible part: Thick leaf stalk or fleshy petiole having tart taste.
- Leaf blades contain oxalic acids, are poisonous and should not be eaten raw or cooked.
- Colour of leaf stalk: Crimson red-light pink to light green.
- Stem colour: Anthocyanin.
- Inflorescence type: Panicle consists of greenish-white flowers, protandrous nature.

- Self pollination within a flower does not take place.
- Crown consists of fleshy rhizome and buds.
- Dormant corms require cold temperature (<5^{0}C) for bud break and subsequent growth.
- At temperature < 3.3^{0}C vegetative parts of plant are killed.
- Summer temperature > 23.5^{0}C and winter temperature < 4.5^{0}C cause poor plant growth.
- Optimum temperature for development of stalks: 15.6^{0}C.
- During winter and spring seasons, excellent growth as temperatures rise above 7.2^{0}C.
- Summer-produced rhubarb is of low quality and plant exhibit dormancy.
- Hot weather results in seed-stalk growth and plant vigour is reduced.
- Rhubarb drug is used tonic and laxative which is derived from dried rhizome and roots.
- Propagation method: Division of crown.
- Collectively, divisions consist of roots and pieces of stem and rhizome.
- Each division of crown should have at least two large buds and a large piece of rhizome.
- Crowns are divided every 7-8 years, or otherwise plants become too thick and produce only slender stalks.
- Seed should not be used for propagation since plants from seeds take much longer time to mature and are highly variable.
- Tolerate pH as low as 5.0 but best growth at 6 to 6.8.
- Planting distance: 1.2-1.8 m x 0.6-1.2 m.
- Harvesting:
  - Starts from 2nd year after planting.
  - Leaf stalks are pulled out manually (by pulling the petioles from plant at soil line).
  - The best quality rhubarb petioles are deep red, long, thick and fleshy.
  - Length of harvest may last upto 8 weeks.
  - Leaf blades are removed leaving mid-ribs with interveining tissues and marketed.
  - In vigorous plant, second harvesting is done in late summer or early fall. Some leaves are left on plants to store food reserves in the crown for next year's growth.
  - Once a plant produces seed stalk, production of leaf stalks/ petioles declines.
  - Crowns are divided every 7-8 years or otherwise plants become too thick and produce only slender stalks.
  - Foliar growth declines during July and August and young shoots are susceptible to frost.

- Post harvest management:
    - After harvest, the petioles are sensitive to dehydration and wilt easily when exposed to high temperatures and low humidity.
    - Stalks can be stored 2-4 weeks at 0^0C and 95% R.H.
- Meristem tip: Rapid multiplication.
- Forcing of rhubarb:
    - Used as forcing crop to produce new leaf stalks.
    - Two year old crowns are dug after they become dormant and moved inside the green house/ cellars/ forcing beds/ suitable structure for forcing during winter.
    - Normally, no stalks are removed from crowns in the field that are later to be forced.
    - Crowns are forced at 13-18^0C in the dark, to avoid chlorophyll development in stalk.
    - Prior to forcing, low temperature < 4.4^0C or GA sprays on the crowns are used to break dormancy.
    - After production, the crowns are discarded since forcing substantially reduces their vigour.
    - All forced rhubarb is sold as fresh.

Varieties:

- Cultivars are grouped according to petiole colour and resistance to seed stalk formation.
- Red petiole types: Generally these are smaller than others. They produce relatively few seed stalks and are grown in warmer regions e.g. Canada Red, Cherry Red, Ruby, Valentine.
- Pink petiole type: e.g. McDonald.
- Green petiole type: e.g. Victoria.
- Strawberry, Sun Rise, Linnaeus,

Pests and disease:

- Curculio beetle: Bores into stalks, crowns and roots.
- Snout beetle:
- Potato stem borer: Rely on weeds as alternate host. Destroy grassy and large stemmed weeds.
- Phytophthora crown rot: Most serious.Use of disease free material and planting in well drained soils.
- Root knot nematode (*Meloidogyne* spp.): Highly susceptible.

28.2 Sorrel

- Eulogized as '*Khatta palak* or Bread & Cheese or Sour leaves or Tom Thumb or A thousand fingers or Sour sauce'.

- Genus name '*Rumex*' comes from Latin word 'rumo' meaning 'I suck'.
- Roman soldiers sucked the leaves to relieve thrist.
- The name 'sorrel' comes from old French word 'surelle' meaning 'sour'
- Cultivated for edible sour leaves having acid flavour.
- Useful in heart troubles, tumours, constipation, piles and bronchitis. It has bood cleansing and blood improving (haemoglobin content) qualities.
- Leaf is is used in poultice to treat skin complaints.
- Leaves rich in ascorbic, citric and tartaric acid.
- Its oxalic acid contain is harmful to health, if taken in excess.
- It is good dye plant & yellow or green dye is prepared from leaves.
- Juice of leaf is used to remove rust, mold and ink stains from silver, linen.
- Low growing pot plant can be made from variety 'Bucker Leaf sorrel'.
- Leaves are triangular-arrow shaped.
- Fruit type: Nut and brown in colour.
- Seed sowing is done in mid-spring.
- In summer season, flowers are removed to maintain leaf production & to prevent self seeding.
- Regular irrigation is essential to keep leaves succulent.
- Young leaves are harvested throughout growing season for fresh use.
- Propagation method: Seed.
- Seed germinates within 10-20 days.
- Seedlings are planted at 30 cm apart.
- Established plants are divided in autumn season for replanting.

Species:

Common name	Botanical name	Features
Sorrel/ Broad leafed/ Common sorrel/ Garden sorrel/ Meadow sorrel	*Rumex acetosa* (syn. *R. vesicarius*)	Hardy perennial; plant height 60-120 cm; spread 30 cm; flowers small, dull & inconspicuous, greenish & turn reddish brown as fruit ripen; mid-green leaves are lance shaped with 2 basal lobes pointing backwards
Sheep's sorrel	*R. acetosella*	Grows wild
French sorrel/ Buckler leaf sorrel	*R. scutatus*	Similar to common sorrel; mild green leaves are shaped like squat shields

29. PORTULACACEAE

29.1 Portulaca

- Annual succulent herb.
- Leaves and young shoots are used as green leafy vegetable.
- Plant bears fleshy oval leaves and yellow flowers.

- Rich in β-carotene, folic acid, vit. C and essential fatty acids.
- Propagation method: Seed.
- Sowing time: April-September (hills), March-June (plains).
- Maturity: Within a month after sowing.
- Seeds are sown at 15 days interval for continue supply of leaves.

30. SOLANACEAE

30.1 Tomato

- Eulogized as 'Wolf peach or Wolf Apple or Poor man's Orange or Love Apple or Amorous Apple or Apple of Peru or *Vilayati baigan*'.
- Universally treated as 'Protective food'.
- During 18th century, in Europe, it was considered as poisonous apple due to their strong odour and bright white, red & yellow berries and were grown only as ornamentals.
- No.1 processing vegetable in the world.
- 2nd largest cultivated crop after potato.
- Major suppliers of processed tomato products in world market: Italy, Spain, Greece.
- Most popular and widely grown vegetable in the world.
- Crop is exploited as classical experimental material for research.
- In India, it is cultivated over 7.8% of total area with 9.4% of total production.
- Largest processed vegetables (30%) in India.
- About 20-22% tomatoes wasted during transport to distant markets & during storage.
- India's production during 2018-19: 19.39 Million tones.
- National average yield: 17.7 t/ha while average yield in developed countries: 34 t/ha.
- Contractual farming is practiced in tomato.
- About 33% of total tomato growing area is covered by F_1 hybrid which is highest.
- Patromorphy i.e. diploid Androgenesis (refers to the situation in which male nucleus does not fertilize the egg cell but itself divides and form a haploid embryo) is observed.
- '*La Tomatina*': A festival of tomato takes place in Bunol city, Valencia, Spain during last Wednesday of August.
- Red revolution: Promotion of tomato production.
- Chromosome number of trisomic tomato: 2n=26.
- Introgression libraries (Ils) are developed by Eshed and Zamir (1994).
- Introgression lines or pre-bred stock are commonly used.
- 1st report of male sterility in tomato was published by Dr. C.M. Rick (1944).
- Tomato Genetic Resource Centre (TGRC) is a genebank of wild relatives, monogenic mutants and miscellaneous and Tomato Genetics Co-operative (TGC) were

established in 1951 and located at University of California, USA. It is a group of researchers who share and interest in tomato genetics and who have organized informally for the purpose of exchanging information, germplasm and genetic stocks.

- TGC was established by Dr. C.M. Rick in 1951.
- Greshof and Doy (1992) produced haploid plants.
- Heterosis for quality and yield was 1st reported in USA during 1908.
- 1st tomato linkage map published by Hendrick and Booth (1907).
- 1st high density map was constructed by Tanksley (1992) by crossing *L. esculentum* x *L. pennellii* (LA716). Total map length of 1.2 cM.
- AB-QTL (Advanced Backcross QTL analysis) was proposed by Tanksley and Nelson (1996).
- International Solanaceae Genome Project (SOL), Cornell University, USA.
- Dr. C.M. Rick (1976) suggested single cell culture and cell hybridization for tomato improvement.
- Father of tomato breeding: Dr. C.M. Rick, USA
- Father of tomato breeding in India: Dr. G. Kalloo.
- Book entitled 'Tomato' was written by Dr. G. Kalloo in 1986.
- Seed contain 24% oil. Oil is used in manufacture of margarine.
- Of the total 52% anti-oxidants, 48% lycopene, 43% ascorbic acid & 53% phenolics are located in epidermis of fruit.
- Ascorbic acid: Higher near skin and in locular tissue. More in small fruited varieties than large fruited and less in firm fruited types.
- Fruit colour is determined by colorimeter.
- Pigments: Yellow (carotenoid); red (lycopene); tangerine (prolycopene).
- β-carotene (Pro-vitamin A) content decreases rapidly after pink stage of ripeness.
- Deeper the red colour of fruits, higher is the yellow pigmentation of the fruit skin.
- Red spectrum light favours colour development.
- The content of betalins are more in improved varieties to extent of 60% than normal tomato.
- Steroidal glycoalkaloid present in tomato: Tomatine. It is higher in leaves and flowers than fruits.
- Tomatine content 300 mg/100g (small hard tomato) and 150 mg/100g (large green tomato).
- Contains vit. A. (900 I.U/ 100 g) and vit. C (23 mg/ 100g). Ripened tomato contains 94% water.
- Aroma of fruits is due to sulfonium.
- Crop completes its reproductive life cycle in 95-115 days.
- Inflorescence type: Forked racemose cyme.

- Inflorescence is borne at every 3rd node in indeterminate type while in determinate types only raceme is formed.
- Each compound inflorescence bears 4-8 flowers.
- Normal corolla colour is dark yellow to yellow brown.
- Single plant produces as many as 20 or more successive inflorescences during its life cycle.
- Number of stamens in Solanaceae: 5.
- Type of fruit: Berry (consisting of pericarp, a fleshy septa between locules, a placenta and central axis).
- Present day cultivars range from multiloculed to two loculed types.
- Locule in tomato fruit plays an important role in governing quality.
- Pear shaped and cherry tomato fruits have 2 locules while round shaped fruits have higher locules.
- Three types of flower position:
  - Flowers in which style and stigma are hidden in anther cone.
  - Stigmatic position at level of anther cone.
  - Style is elongated (exerted stigma) and latter two forms are suitable for hybrid production.
- Genetic or environmental modification of stigma position affects both fruit set & degree of cross fertilization.
- With discovery of 3 types of male sterility i.e. genetic, functional or closed anther & stamenless type, a new hybrid seed production has been developed.
- Closed anther type male sterility is best and most useful.
- Natural cross pollination rate in temperate regions: 0.5 to 4%.
- Self pollinated crop but small percentage of cross pollination also noted.
- Anthers are released from the pollens prior to elongation of style.
- In green house types, plants are vibrated for effective pollination and fruit set.
- Type of fruit: Multi seeded berry with fleshy mesocarp.
- Anthesis time: 6 AM to 12 noon.
- Anther dehiscence longitudinally from base to top from 6.30 to 11 AM.
- Pollination agents: Solitary bees and bumble bees.
- Seed germination is inhibited by caffic acid and ferulic acid.
- Tube and stick method of grafting: developed by AVRDC, Taiwan.
- Thermosensitive and typical day neutral plant.
- Optimum temperature for stigma receptivity: 18-25^{0}C.

- Temperature < 15^{0}C and > 35^{0}C hampers pollen release and cause imperfect ovulation and incomplete fertilization leading to cat-face disorder.
- Critical factors for fruit set: Optimum night temperature (15-20^{0}C).
- Optimum temperature for pollination: 21^{0}C.
- Excessive rains adversely affect its fruit set causing flower drop.
- From a single pollination, 200 or more seeds are obtained.
- Lycopene production is highest at 21-24^{0}C. Production of this pigment drops rapidly above 27^{0}C.
- Lycopene content: Fresh red fruit (3.8-7.7 mg/100 g), red fruit juice (7.83 mg/100 g) and ketchup (16.6 mg/100 g).
- High C/N ratio and optimum night temperature are the important factors for fruit setting.
- Reasons for failure to fruit set: a) day temperature > 38^{0}C and b) night temperature < 13^{0}C and > 21^{0}C.
- Hot set genotypes: Cultivars which set fruits above critical temperature e.g. All AVRDC lines set fruits at 20^{0}C night temperature.
- Cold set genotypes: Cultivars which set fruits below critical temperature (15^{0}C night).
- Pre-cooling temperature for tomato: 13^{0}C and best storage temperature: 12-15^{0}C.
- Optimum CO_2 concentration in green house: 4000 ppm.
- Varieties having high solids with low acidity are unsuitable for processing.
- Attributes for processing: TSS (6.5 to 7.5^0 Brix), high reducing sugars, firm, bright red (lycopene) pulp, acidic pH (<4.4) and low content of peel (easy peeling).
- Export quality tomato is produced in Nashik and Pune (Maharashtra) and Bengaluru (Karnataka).
- Training, staking and pruning are followed in indeterminate growth habit of tomato (single stem system).
- Determinate type: Inflorescence occurs at every internode.
- Indeterminate type: Inflorescence occurs at every 3rd internode.
- 'Self topping/ self pruning' term related to determinate growth habit. It results in more compact growth & more concentrated flowering essential for machine harvested cultivars.
- Cluster of flowers known as 'Truss'.
- Types of tomato grown in green house: Beefsteak, Truss (vine) and Cherry type.
- Application of 'P' fertilizer increases flower number.
- Seed treatment with 2, 4-D @ 2-5 ppm increases fruit set, earliness and parthenocarpy.
- Foliar spray of PCPA @ 20 ppm is very effective in increasing fruit set and yield.

- Reduce the incidence of leaf curl virus in tomato: CCC @ 250 ppm.
- Hardening of seedlings: CCC @ 200 ppm.
- To enhance ripening of fruits: Ethrel @ 1000 ppm.
- GA_3 induce parthenocarpy in tomato.
- Parthenocarpically developed fruits are seedless.
- Type of parthenocarpy: Facultative e.g. tomato mutants.
- Important micronutrients required for production for long distance market: B and Zn.
- Acid present in fruit: Citric acid.
- Maximum acidity (0.39 to 1.0%) is found at pink stage.
- For processing purpose pH of juice should be 4.5, 26^0 Brix and acidity 0.35 percent.
- Maturity index for very distant market: Mature green stage.
- Maturity index for long distance market: Breaker/turning stage (10% lycopene).
- Maturity index for local market: Pink stage.
- Maturity index for table or salad purpose or sale at farmer's field: Ripe stage.
- Maturity index for processing purpose: Over ripe stage.
- Assessment of fruit firmness: Durometer.
- Maleic hydrazide @ 100 ppm once or twice or 50 ppm twice, produces complete pollen sterility.
- Losses in 1st grade tomatoes can be reduced from 1.5 to 3% by using upright cone baskets together with dry grass as packing material.
- Packing of tomatoes in sealed unventilated polyethylene provides a modified atmosphere which extends storage life.
- Ripening mutant genes (*rin, nor, nr*) inhibit the changes that accompany ripening, colour development, fruit softening, ethylene production are non-climacteric fruits.
- *rin* C (ripening inhibitor) hybrids were more firm than normal cultivars but show low level of flavour & low in sensory tastes.
- In tomato, fruit maturity stage is not harvesting stage.
- Seed extraction: One day fermentation of seeds at >25^0C.
- Best method for seed extraction: By HCl (567 ml for 10 litre of pulp & seed mixture) method, very bright and clean seeds are produced.
- Seed extraction with 10% Sodium carbonate i.e. washing soda is not used commercially as it darkens seed testa.
- Seed yield: ton of fruit, produce 10 kg of seeds and 100-120 kg/ha.
- Safe temperature for seed drying: 35-40^0C with 90% germination.
- Inbreeding is deleterious in tomato.

- Stamenless mutant of tomato is sensitive to temperature.
- Hybrid tomatoes are produced by using closed anther parent as female.
- Genetically modified (GM) tomatoes are resistant to Alzheimer's disease.
- Plum tomatoes: Tomatoes grown for canning. These are elongated, 7-9 cm long, 4-5 cm dia.
- Cherry tomato is preferred for export in European countries.
- Tomato puree and tomato paste have great export demand.
- BIS has specified 4 grades: Super A, Super, Fancy and Commercial.
- Tomato has 5 forms based on growth habit and fruit characters: i) Cherry tomato ii) Pear tomato iii) Common tomato iv) Potato leaf type and v) Upright tomato.
- Recommended herbicide: Alachlor @ 2-2.5 kg a.i./ha.
- White polythene film mulching is recommended for weed control and resulting soil temperature.
- Pollen viability: 0-5^{0}C for 6 months.
- For seed production, ratio of seed parent to pollen parent: 3:5:1
- Crop Canopy Air Temperature Difference (CCATD) measurement by infrared thermometry can be used to screen tomato cultivars for tolerance to moisture stress.
- Division. of Vegetable Science, IARI, New Delhi is acting as a hot spot for ToLCNDV disease.
- CA storage conditions: 10-15^{0}C at 5% O_2, 2.5%CO_2.
- International tomato genome sequencing project: 10 countries involved. India is working under 5th chromosome.
- For ketchup, viscosity (or consistency) is primary quality attribute.
- For tomato paste, high TSS cultivars yield more per ton.
- Specific requirement for export purpose: Round, medium sized and red in colour.

Species:

- Jenkins worked on diversity and origin of tomato.
- Miller coined the name *Lycopersicon esculentum* to cultivated tomato.
- Botanically tomato was called *Solanum lycopersicon* (lycos- Wolf and persicon-peach). In 1978, cultivated tomato is renamed as *Lycopersicon esculentum* Mill.
- Muller (1940) divided genus *Lycopersicon* into 2 sub-genera--*Eulycopersicon* (red fruited with carotenoid pigmentation & self compatible) and *Eriopersicon* (green fruited with anthocyanin pigmentation & self incompatible).
- Botanical classification (Bailey, 1963 and Yamaguchi, 1983): Separation of sub-genera is based upon fruit colour as:

a) *Eulycopersicon* (Red fruited):

1. *S. esculentum*: Common tomato.
2. *S. pimpinellifolium*: Current tomato.

b) Eriopersicon (Green fruited):

1. *S. cheesmanii*: Wild type.
2. *S. chilense*: Wild type
3. *S. glandulosum*: Wild type.
4. *S. hirsutum*: Wild type.
5. *S. peruvianum*: Wild type.

- **Botanical varieties:**
  1. *S. esculentum* var. *commune*: Common tomato.
  2. *S. esculentum* var. *grandiflorum*: Large leaved/ potato leaved tomato.
  3. *S. esculentum* var. *validum*: Cherry tomato.
  4. *S. esculentum* var. *pyriforme*: Pear tomato.
- *Solanum lycopersicum* (new classification given by Peralta and Spooner, 2006).
- Dr. C.M. Rick (1976) divided genus *Lycopersicon* in two groups based on their compatibility i.e. ability to cross with cultivated tomato.
  - Esculentum complex (crossable with cultivated tomato) e.g. *L. esculentum*, *L.pimpinellifolium*, *L. cheesemanii*, *L. hirsutum*, *L. parviflorum*, *L. chmielewskii*, *L. pennellii*.
  - Peruvianum complex (not crossable with cultivated tomato) e.g. *L. peruvianum*, *L.chilense*, *L. gladulosum*.

Species	Common name	Somatic chromosome no.	Reproductive features
L. esculentum	Common tomato	24	SP
L. pimpinellifolium	Currant tomato	24	SP + CP
L. cheesmanii	Wild species	24	SP
L. parviflorum	Wild species	24	SP
L. chmielewskii	Wild species	24	CP
L. pennellii	Wild species	24	SI
L. hirsutum	Wild species	24	SF + SI
L. chinense	Wild species	24	SI
L. peruvianum	Wild species	24	SI

SP- Self pollinated; CP- Cross pollinated; SF- Self fertile; SI- Self incompatible

Survery of intra and interspecific breeding barriers

♀/♂	*L. esculentum*	*L. pimpinellifolium*	*L. hirsutum*	*L. chinense*	*L. peruvianum*
L. esculentum	+	+	+	EA	EA
L. pimpinellifolium	+	+	+	EA	EA
L. hirsutum	+, UI	+, UI	+, SI, UI	?	EA
L. chinense	UI	UI	?	SI	EA
L. peruvianum	UI	UI	UI	EA	SI

+- No serious barrier; SI- Self incompatibility; UI- Unilateral incompatibility; EA - Embryo abortion; ?- No research results known.

- Self incompatibility common in many wild species is also transmitted to interspecific hybrids.
- Cold Spring Harbor Laboratory, USA has revealed tomato genome sequence of *S. pimpinellifolium*.
- Based on growth habits and fruit characters, 5 forms of *L. esculentum* are identified- 1) Commune (common tomato) 2) Cerasiformae (small fruited cherry tomato) 3) Pyriformae (pear shaped tomato) 4) Grandifolium (potato leaved tomato) 5) Validum (erect and upright tomato).

Name	Features
Solanum lycopersicum var. *cerasiforme*	Progenitor (ancestor) of cultivated tomato/ Cherry tomato; self pollinated; tolerant to humidity, resistant to fungi, root rot, leaf mold, anthracnose, leaf spot, early blight & verticillium wilt
S. lycopersicum var. *commune*	Edible tomato or round fruited tomato
S. lycopersicum var. *validium*	Upright (erect) or Cherry tomato; dark & dense foliage
S. lycopersicum var. *grandiflorum*	Large leaved, or potato leaf type tomato
S. lycopersicum var. *pyriforme*	Pear shaped tomato
S. pimpinellifolium	Self pollinated but facultative autogamous;source of high ascorbic acid & carotene content; red fruits; resistant to bacterial wilt, bacterial speck, bacterial canker, fusarium wilt, early blight, late blight, leaf mold, leaf curl, grey leaf spot, cucumber mosaic virus, spotted wilt virus; tolerant to low temperature, collar rot, brown root rot; roots high in tomatine (>775 ppm)
S. hirsutum	Self pollinated & self incompatible; resistant to fusarium wilt, botrytis mold, bacterial canker, septoria leaf spot, fruit borer, leaf miner, tobacco flea beetle, tobacco horn worm, greenhouse white fly, carmine spider mite, two-spotted spider mite, pinworm & Colorado potato beetle
S. hirsutum f. sp. glabratum	Highly resistant to white fly, fruit borer, bacterial canker, leaf miner, spider mite, flea beetle, fusarium wilt, mosaic; self fertile & self incompatible (sporophytic & gametophytic); readily crossable with *S. lycopersicum*
S. peruvianum	Strictly self incompatible; higly polymorphic green fruited; source of high ascorbic acid; resistant to TOSPO virus (*Sw-5* gene), verticillium

	wilt, root knot nematode (*Mi*), corky root, cucumber mosaic virus, curly top virus, tobacco mosaic virus, tomato mosaic virus, big bud, groundnut bud necrosis virus; tomato yellow top virus & potato aphid
S. peruvianum var. *humifusum*	Resistant to curly top virus; resistant to green house white fly
S. peruvianum var. *dentatum*	Resistant to curly top virus
S. pennelli	Gametophytic self incompatible; resistant to leaf miner; tolerant to drought; high TSS content
S. galapagense	Yellow to orange fruits; tolerant to salt
S. cheesmanii	Jointless gene (*j-2*), β-carotene & thick pericarp; highly autogamous, fruits orange to yellow; high TSS & salinity tolerant; resistant to pinworm; set fruits at high temperature
S. chmielewskii	Cross pollinated; green fruits; salt tolerant & high sugar content (10%); fruits greenish white
S. neorickii	Resistant to bacterial disease
S. habrochaites f. sp. glabratum	Tolerance to cold & chilling; resistance to insects & diseases (TMV)
S. chilense	Gametophytic self incompatible; green fruits; resistant to drought & diseases (CMV, TMV, TLCV, curly top virus, groundnut bud necrosis virus)
Physalis pubescens (syn. *P. pruinosa*)	Husk tomato
S. sisymbriifolium	Rootstock to combat low temperature stress, drought & nematode infestation
S. incanum, S. macrocarpon	Fruit borer & nematode resistance
S. parviflorum	Genetically uniform, fruits 10-14 mm dia., highly autogamous
S. betaceum	Known as 'Tamarillo or tree tomato'
S. esculentum	Resistant to spider mite

Varieties:

- Tomato germplasm from all over the world is maintained at North Central Region Plant Introduction Station, Ames, Iowa.
- Hedrick and Booth 1st reported heterosis in tomato in 1908.
- Livingston (1870) Was 1st American initiated constructive breeding in tomato. He developed 13 cvs. by single plant selection method.
- Red Cherry, Red Pear, Trophy: Represent foundation upon which modern day cvs. are developed.
- Karnataka: 1st F_1 hybrid by Indo-American Hybrid Seed Company, Bengaluru in 1973.
- 1st machine-harvestable cv. was developed by Mr. G.C. Hanna.
- Pan American: 1st highly resistant cv. to fusarium wilt having red coloured fruits was developed by Prof. W.S. Porte and H.B. Walker (1941) using *L. pimpinellifolium*. This hybrid reflects the North and South American parentage in its pedigree. It is immune to fusarium race-1 & gene symbol *I-1*.
- Bailey (1941) was 1st to report root knot nematode resistance in *L. peruvianum* (PI-128657) through embryo culture.

- Embryo abortion occurs in crosses of *L. esculentum* x *L. peruvianum* & can be overcome by embryo culture (Smith, 1944) or by embryo callus culture (Thomas and Pratt, 1981).
- Schaible (1962) was 1st to show the fruit setting response of tomatoes to low & high night temperature.
- Dr. C.M. Rick (1960) and Wann and Johnson (1963) performed successful intergeneric crosses between *L.esculentum* & *S. lycopersicoides* and *S. pennellii.*
- E.V. Wann and K.W. Johnson (1963) performed intergeneric crosses between *L. esculentum* & *S. pennellii*.
- Interspecific hybridization with *L. pimpinellifolium* encourages increased TSS but reduces fruit size.
- Determinate/ Self topping type: Roma (suitable for canning), HS-101.
- Indeterminate type: Sweet 72.
- Heat tolerant: Kewalo, Saladette, NDTVR-60, Hot Set.
- Caro-Red, Caro-Rich: Distinctive red-orange colour containing 10 times higher β-carotene.
- Taichung Asveg 4: Highly resistant to TMV and set good seeds at high temperature.
- Resistant to tobacco mosaic virus: Moto Red, Florida MH-1, Virosa, Curabel, Linda, Maltino, Nemato, Nortona, Sonato, Santo, Lucky, Testa, Maritsa, Royal Red Cherry, Kristi, Karobeta.
- Improved Meeruti: Developed by single plant selection.
- A-408, A-276: Good donors for high TSS breeding.
- Red Cherry: Good donors for high TSS breeding; resistant to buck eye rot.
- Suitable for canning: Pearl Harbour (resistant to TOSPO virus), Marglobe, Kullu Valley, Italian Red Pear, Melka Shola, Melka, MTH-6, Monte Verde, Mountain Delight, Mountain Fresh, Mountain Gold, NDT-120, Red Rose, Red Top, Rupali and Sel-152.
- *L. esculenta* Russain cv. Severianin: Parthenocarpic & set fruits at low temperature.
- Cold Set, Montfavet 63-5, Montfavet 63-8, Precoce: Set fruits in winter at very low temperature.
- Suitable for mechanical harvesting: Pitomek, Raduga, Planta, Early Mech, Eva, Ranch, Elgen.
- Walter: Determinate, resistant to race 1 & 2 of fusarium and gene symbol *I-2*. Developed by Strobel *et al.* (1969).
- Resistant to bacterial wilt: BT-1, BT-10, BWR-1, BWR-5, LE-79.
- Resistant to fusarium wilt: Columbia, Homestead, Sel.28.

- Resistant to fusarium wilt & early blight: Floradade.
- Resistant to fusarium wilt & verticillium wilt: Rutgers, Pritchard, Tropic, Royal Red Cherry.
- Japanese cv. Tsueeze: Show broad spectrum resistance to TMV, fusarium and alternaria.
- Resistant to root knot nematode: Sel-124, Nematex, Nemared, Ronita, Monita, Nemacross, Small Fry, Cold Set-1, Rossol, Rutgers, Anahu, Atkinson, VNF-8, NT-3, NT-8, NT-12.
- Resistant to radial cracking, fusarium wilt and verticilium wilt: Manulucie.
- Black Galaxy: Developed by Seeds Technologies DM Ltd., Isreal. Semi-determinate, more vit. C, anti-oxidant, photosensitive and suitable for export.
- FLCR-1 and MLCR-2: Leaf curl virus resistant somaclonal lines derived from cv. CO.3.
- In 2012, genome of *S. lycopersicum* cv. Heinz 1706 has been decoded by Tomato Genomics Consortium an international collaboration between Argentina, Belgium, China, France, Germany, India, Israel, Italy, Japan, the Netherlands, South Korea, Spain, UK, USA and others.
- Avinash-2 has responded well to anther culture.
- Double Reach (cultivated tomato x *S. peruvianum*): Rich in vit.C (50 mg/100 g) from USA.
- Money Maker, Ailsa Craig and UC-82-B: Widely used in transformation studies via *Agrobacterium* as they possess good regeneration capacity.
- Cherry tomato: Cherry Belle, Gardener's Delight, Super Beefsteak, Shirley, Trumbler.

Name	Breeding method	Salient features
LaBonita, Marvel, Tip Top, Ageti, Rudger	Introduction from USA	Resistant to leaf mould; cercospora leaf spot
Anahu	From Hawaii	1st commercial type tomato with resistance to root knot nematode
Tropic	Exotic hybrid	Indeterminate; fruit wt. 226 g; resistant to verticillium wilt, fusarium wilt, stemphyllum leaf mould, TMV No. 1, alternaria stem canker
Dombello	Exotic hybrid	Indeterminate; fruit wt. 198-225 g; resistant to TMV, verticillium wilt, fusarium wilt, nematodes & silvering
Cobra	Exotic hybrid	Yield 3.72 kg/plant; resistant to TMV, verticillium, fusarium wilt races 1 & 2.
Stresa	Exotic hybrid	Yield 3.9 kg/plant; resistant to cladosporum leaf mould, root knot nematodes, verticillium, fusarium wilt races 1 & 2.
Capello	Exotic hybrid	Yield 3.8 kg/plant; resistant to cladosporum leaf mould, root knot nematodes, verticillium, fusarium wilt races 1 & 2.
Trust	Exotic hybrid	Yield 3.7 kg/plant; resistant to fusarium crown rot & root rot, verticillium
Caruso	Exotic hybrid	Yield 3.6 kg/plant; resistant to cladosporum leaf mould, root knot nematodes, verticillium, fusarium wilt races 1 & 2.
Belmondo	Exotic hybrid	Yield 3.9 kg/plant; resistant to cladosporum leaf mould, root knot nematodes, verticillium, fusarium wilt races 1 & 2.
Tuckcross-520	Exotic hybrid	Indeterminate; fruit wt. 200 g; oblate shaped fruits; resistant to fusarium wilt & alternaria stem canker
IARI, New Delhi		
Marglobe (1970)	Selection (introduction from USA)	Indeterminate; fruits round, deep scarlet coloured; solid & less seeded; yield (20-25 t/ha); fusarium wilt & verticillium wilt resistant; suitable for canning
Money Maker	Introduction from USA	Resistant to buck-eye rot
Sioux (1970)	Introduction from USA	Indeterminate; fruits uniform red, smooth & less seeded; yield (20-22 t/ha); suitable for canning; resistant to radial cracking
Best of All (1973)	Introduction from USA	Indeterminate; fruits borne in cluster & scarlet red coloured, smooth & less seeded; yield (30-32 t/ha);
Pusa Red Plum	*S. lycopersicum* x *L. pimpinellifolium*	Indeterminate; interspecific hybrid; indeterminate; borne in cluster of 6-8; very sweet fruits; rich in vit. C; resistant to virus
Pusa Sadabahar (2004)	Introduction & selection	Determinate; suitable for growing under wide temperature of 8-30^{0}C; ideal for distant marketing; yield (25-35 t/ha)

Pusa Ruby (1970)	F_1 hybrid of (Sioux x Improved Meeruti)	Indeterminate; best combiner & most famous variety; mild acidic; 4-5 locules/ fruit; suitable for dehydration; resistant to nematodes; yield 28-30 t/ha
Pusa Early Dwarf (1975)	F_1 hybrid of 'Improved Meeruti x Red Cloud'	Determinate; early maturing; fruits ribbed; 5-6 locules/ fruit; suitable for rainy season; yield 30-33 t/ha
Pusa Rohini (2004)	Introduction & selection	Determinate; highly suitable for long distance transport & processing & canning; TSS 6%; yield 41 t/ha
Pusa Gaurav (1993)	Pedigree selection from (Glamour x Watch)	Determinate; highly suitable for long distance transport & processing & canning; TSS 6%; yield 35-37 t/ha
Pusa Uphar (1999)	Selection	Indeterminate; high fruit setting under slightly adverse temperature; tolerant to fruit borer & suitable for processing; yield 37 t/ha
Pusa Divya (1997)	Heterosis breeding from (Long Style x Roma)	Developed using MS-line (antherless mutant); indeterminate; yield 35-45 t/ha
Pusa Sheetal (1987)	F_1 hybrid of [Balkan (Bulgarian cv.) x Jemnorrosuij (Russian cv.) both low temperature fruit set lines]	Determinate; suitable for temperate region & fruit set at night temperature of 8^0C i.e. cold set; fruits during March-April; yield (35 t/ha)
Pusa Lal Meeruti	Gamma ray mutant (30 Krad) of Improved Meeruti	Uniform fruit ripening
Pusa Hybrid-2 (1996)	Heterosis breeding from (Pusa-120 x Pusa Gaurav)	Semi-determinate; prolific bearing; highly tolerant to root knot nematode; yield 62 t/ha
Pusa Hybrid-4 (1996)	-	Determinate; fruits round, smooth, weighing 70-80 g; 3 locules, thick pericarp; resistant to root knot nematode; yield 43-45 t/ha; suitable for semi-arid areas
Pusa Hybrid-8 (2001)	-	Determinate; heavy fruit bearer; round fruits; 75-80 g; yield 43-45 t/ha
Pusa 120 (Sel-120) 1970	Individual plant selection from 'Anahou' from Hawaii	1st root knot nematode resistant variety; determinate; yield 30-32 t/ha; suitable for summer & winter season production; less seeded
Pusa Cherry Tomato -1	-	-

Pusa Rakshit (2020)	-	1st F_1 hybrid for polyhouse cultivation; fruit yield (15 kg/m²/plant); TSS (5.1° Brix); lycopene 6.0 mg/100 g
Katrain hybrid 1	-	Functional male sterile mutants; highest acidity
Katrain hybrid 2	-	
IIHR, Bengaluru		
Arka Vikas (1984)	Pure line selection from variable population of 'Tip Top' from USA	Indeterminate; suitable for cold & drought condition; deep red flesh; yield 40-42 t/ha; tolerant to mosaic
Arka Alok (DWR-5 (1992)	Pure line selection from IIHR 719-1-6 from AVRDC	Determinate; suitable for fresh market; resistant to bacterial wilt (BW); yield 46 t/ha
Arka Abha (DWR-1 (1990)	Pure line selection from line VC-8-1-2-1 from AVRDC	Semi-determinate; fruit wt. 75 g; yield 43 t/ha; resistant to BW
Arka Saurabh (1984)	Pure line selection from line 'V-685' from Canada	Semi-determinate; nipple tipped fruits; suitable for fresh market & processing; resistant to fruit cracking; yield 35 t/ha
Arka Ahuti (1990)	Pure line selection from 'Ottawa 60'	Thick fleshy fruits; 5.2% TSS; semi-determinate; tolerant to powdery mildew (PM); suitable for processing
Arka Ashish (1990)	Selection from line 'UC-82-B' from USA	Determinate; tolerant to PM & fruit cracking; yield 38 t/ha
Arka Vishal (1990)	Heterosis breeding of 'IIHR 837 x IIHR 932'	Indeterminate: tolerant to fruit cracking & suitable for fresh market; yield 75 t/ha
Arka Shreshta (1996)	Heterosis breeding of '15 SBSB x IIHR 1614'	Semi-determinate: suitable for rabi season; resistant to BW; yield 76 t/ha
Arka Ananya (2005)	F_1 hybrid of 'TLBR-6 x IIHR-2202'	Semi-determinate; fruits oblate-round, medium (65-70 g), deep red, medium firm fruit suitable for fresh market; resistant to ToLCV & BW; yield 65-70 t/ha
Arka Abhijit (1996)	F_1 hybrid of '15 SBSB x IIHR 1334'	Semi-determinate; suitable to fresh market & resistant to BW; yield 65 t/ha

Arka Vardan (1990)	Heterosis breeding of 'IIHR 550-3 x IIHR 932'	Indeterminate; resistant to nematode & BW; tolerant to cracking; yield 75 t/ha
Arka Rakshak (2010)	Hybrid of (line 12-21-43-1 x CLN-2498E)	India's 1st F_1 hybrid withtriple disease resistant (bacterial wilt, ToLCV, early blight); yield 18 kg/ plant; square round fruits; fruit wt. 90-100 g; yield 75-80 t/ha; suitable for processing
Arka Samrat (2015)	F_1hybrid of (IIHR-2835 x IIHR-2832)	Round fruits; fruit wt. 90-110 g; 1st F_1 hybrid withmultiple disease resistance (BW, ToLCV, early blight); yield 80-85t/ha
Arka Meghali (1996)	Pedigree selection of (Arka Vikas x IIHR- 554)	Semi-determinate; tolerant to water stress & heat; yield 27-29 t/ha
Arka Abhed (H-397) 2018	F_1 hybrid	Indeterminate; fruit wt. 90-100 g; TSS (4.2^{0}B), acidity (0.38%); yield 70-75 t/ha; resistant to 4 diseases [ToLCV (carry gene *Ty2*, *Ty3*), BW, early blight & late blight (*Ph2*, *Ph3*)]
Arka Aditya (H-331) 2020	F_1 hybrid	Semi-determinate; yield 60-65 t/ha; resistant to 3 diseases (ToLCV, EB, BW); suitable for fresh market
Arka Vishesh (H-391) 2019	F_1 hybrid of 'ITHR-2834 x ITHR-2917'	Determinate; TSS (4.6^{0}Brix), acidity (0.38%), lycopene (14.14 gm/100 g); yield (50-90t/ha); resistant to 3 diseases (ToLCV, BW, EB); suitable for machine harvesting & processing
Arka Apeksha (H-385) 2019	F_1 hybrid of 'ITHR-2834 x ITHR-2918'	Determinate; TSS (4.7^0 Brix); lycopene (14 mg/ 100 g fresh wt.); acidity (0.38%); yield (50-90 t/ha); resistant to 3 diseases (ToLCV, BW, EB); suitable for machine harvesting & processing
IIVR, Varanasi		
Kashi Vishesh (2006)	Back cross pedigree selection of (*L. esculentum* cv. Sel. 7 x *L. hirsutum* f. *glabratum* 'B-6013')	Determinate, round fruits; vit. C (25 mg/100g); resistant to ToLCV; yield 40-45 t/ha
Kashi Anupam (2006)	Back cross pedigree selection of (*L. esculentum* cv. Sel. 7 x *L. hirsutum* f. *glabratum* 'B-6013') i.e. sister line of 'Kashi Amrit'	Determinate; vit. C (24 mg/100g); resistant to ToLCV; yield 57-60 t/ha
Kashi Amrit (2006)	Back cross pedigree selection of (*L. esculentum* cv. Sel. 7 x *L. hirsutum* f.	Determinate; round fruits; vit. C (24 mg/100g); resistant to ToLCV; yield 62 t/ha

	glabratum 'B-6013')	
Kashi Hemant (2006)	Pedigree selection of (Sel. 18 x Flora Dade)	Determinate, spherical round fruits; vit. C (22 mg/100g); resistant to ToLCV; yield 42 t/ha
Kashi Sharad (2006)	Pedigree selection of (MTH-6 x Kalyani Eunish)	Indeterminate with broad potato type leaves; slightly oval fruits; fruit wt. 90 g; longer shelf life; vit. C (20 mg/100g); yield 48-50 t/ha
Kashi Adarsh (2016)	Pedigree selection	Semi-determinate with 80-115 g fruit wt.; yield 60 t/ha
Kashi Abhimaan (2011)	Heterosis breeding	Determinate; fruit wt. 75-95 g; TSS 4.2-4.6^{0}Brix; carries *Ty-2* gene; mod. resistant to ToLCV; yield 60-70 t/ha
Kashi Aman (2013)	Heterosis breeding	Determinate; resistant to ToLCV & early blight; fruit wt. 80-110 g; yield 50-60 t/ha
Kashi Hybrid-1 (VRTH-2)	Heterosis breeding	Determinate; short duration; yield 90 t/ha
Kashi Hybrid-2	Heterosis breeding	Short duration
Kashi Chayan (2020)	-	Indeterminate; resistant to ToLCV & early blight; carries *Ty3* gene; yield 60-70 t/ha
Kashi Amul (2016)	-	Semi-determinate; round fruits; pericarp thickness 0.6 cm; fruit wt. 90 g; yield 50-60 t/ha
ICAR Research Complex for Eastern Region, Patna (HARP, Ranchi)		
Swarna Anmol (2013)	Heterosis breeding	Indeterminate; fruits round, red & borne in clusters of 5-6; fruit wt. (60-70 g), TSS 4.5-5.0^{0}Brix; acidity 0.30-0.35% & ascorbic acid 40-42 mg/100 g; yield 180 t/ha; resistant to BW; suitable for protected cultivation & year round cultivation
Swarna Kanchan (2015)	Heterosis breeding	Suitable for processing
Swarna Ratan (2015)	Heterosis breeding	Suitable for table purpose
Swarna Lalima (2006)	Pure line selection	Fruits round;fruit wt. (120-125 g); TSS 4^0 Brix; resistant to BW; yield 60-70 t/ha
Swarna Vijaya (2008)	Heterosis breeding	Determinate; fruits in cluster; fruit wt. (80-90 g); TSS 4.5-5.0^0 Brix; yield 100 t/ha; resistant to BW & early blight
Swarna Naveen (2006)	Pure line selection	Fruits oblong; fruit wt. (40-50 g); TSS 5^{0}Brix; resistant to BW; yield 60-65 t/ha
Swarna Vaibhav (2004)	Heterosis breeding	Determinate; fruit wt. 140 g; suitable for long distance transportation & processing; resistant to BW; yield 90-100t/ha
Swarna Samridhi (2004)	Heterosis breeding	Indeterminate; fruits in cluster; fruit wt. 40-50 g; yield 100-105 t/ha; resistant to BW & early blight
Swarna Sampada (2006)	Heterosis breeding	Round, red; fruit wt. (70-80g); TSS 4.5-5.0^{0}Brix; resistant to BW & early blight; yield 100-105 t/ha
Swarna Deepti (2011)	Heterosis breeding	Fruits round; fruit wt. 120-130 g; yield 100 t/ha;suitable for table & processing; resistant to BW & early blight
ICAR, Research Complex for North-Eastern Hilly Region, Meghalaya		

Mani Leima (2006)	Selection	Determinate; for processing, good keeping, resistant to fruit cracking & tolerant to moisture stess; yield 63-65 t/ha
Mani Khamnu (2003)	Pedigree selection of 'EC 160193 x HS 101'	Resistant to fruit cracking; tolerant to moisture stress, leaf curl virus, mosaic stress
Mani Khamena-shinba-1	-	Mod. resistant to BW; free from fruit cracking; yield 43 t/ha
Mani Khamena-shinba-12	Progeny of 'Pusa Sheetal x Lima'	Fruits medium; round to oval shaped; TSS 5-7.3^{0}Brix; yield 41 t/ha
Mani Thoibi	-	Processing, tolerant to leaf curl
Megha Tomato-1	-	Tolerant to bacterial wilt & late blight
Megha Tomato-2	-	Ideal for rainy season in blight & wilt prone areas
Megha Tomato-3	Pedigree selection from 'Pusa Sheetal x Lima'	Indeterminate; fruits round, wt. 55-75 g; rich in lycopene, TSS, acidity & ascorbic acid; tolerant to bacterial wilt; yield 40-45 t/ha
CIAH, Bikaner		
Thar Anant	Mutation	High lycopene (7.9 mg/100 g); yield 54.5 t/ha; tolerant to heat stress & drought; suitable for semi-arid region
DIBER, Pithoragarh		
DARL-68 (2014)	-	Indeterminate; fruits long oval, red; suitable for long transit; TSS 6%; tolerant to PM; yield 32 t/ha; suitable for open field & protected cultivation
CCSHAU, Hisar		
HS-101 (1976)	Pedigree selection from (Sel. 2-3 x Exotic cv.)	Determinate; dwarf; suitable for winter season; yield 31-32 t/ha
HS- 102 (1977)	Pedigree selection from (S-12 x Pusa Early Dwarf)	Determinate; suitable for winter & summer season; yield 25-28 t/ha; very late maturing & heat tolerant
HS-110	Single plant selection from an exotic line	Determinate; potato leaf type; suitable for table & processing; resistant to fusarium wilt
Hisar Lalit (1993)	Pedigree selection of (HS 101 x Resistant Bangalore)	Semi-determinate; resistant to root knot nematode; yield 30-32 t/ha
Hisar Arun (Sel. 7) (1994)	Pedigree selection of (Pusa Early Dwarf x	Determinate, dwarf & bushy; 4-6 locules/fruit; high harvest index; fruit set at low temperature; yield 17-28 t/ha

	K-1)	
Hisar Lalima	Pedigree selection of (Pusa Early Dwarf x HS 101)	Determinate; round fruited; determinate; yield 28-30 t/ha
Hisar Anmol (H-24)	Pedigree selection of (*S. hirsutum* f. *glabratum* line B-6013 x Hisar Arun)	Determinate; flat-round fruits; resistant to ToLCV
Hisar Gaurav	-	Resistant to ToLCV
H-2, H-11, H-17, H-23, H-24	*S. hirsutum* x *S. glabratum*	Resistant to ToLCV
MPKV, Rahuri		
Bhagyashree (1992)	Selection	Fruits big (70-80 g); yield 52 t/ha; more lycopene, low seed content & suitable for processing
Dhanashree (1992)	Pedigree selection of (407D PDBK x LA-124)	Fruits 60-70 g; tolerant to spotted wilt virus & leaf curl; TSS 4.10%; cluster bearing; orange coloured fruits; yield 60-80 t/ha
Rajashree (1994)	Heterosis	Fruits 60-80 g; orange coloured fruit; yield 75 t/ha; suitable for distant market; tolerant to leaf curl
Vasundhara (2001)	Heterosis	Determinate; resistant to virus & blight; yield 50-52 t/ha
Phule Raja	M-1-2 x 85-1	Tolerant to leaf curl; yield 65 t/ha
Phule Keshari (2018)	Selection from local	Rich in β-carotene; oval shape
Phule Jayashree (2018)	Selection	Cherry tomato variety; fruit wt. 6.30 g; yield 53.31 t/ha; TSS 6.32%; orange red colour; round & juicy; suitable for growing under shade net
RHRTH-57	32-2 x 85-1	Oval fruits, red, stout, TSS 4.1%
RHRTH-92	Dhanashree x RHRT-1	Round fruits, orange red colour; TSS 3.9%
VNMKV, Parbhani		
Parbhani Yashasree (syn. Sel. 14) 2001	Hybrid of (*L. esculentum* x *L. hirsutum*) & back crossed to ATV-2	Semi-determinate; yield 60-62 t/ha; resistant to early blight & viruses; tolerant to virus & blight
Yashwant	-	Tolerant to buck-eye rot; suitable for processing
PBNT-5	Selection	-
ATV-1 (1985)	-	Determinate; fruit wt. 95 g; sphere shaped; blood red coloured; resistant to early blight; yield 40-50 t/ha
Devgiri (ATV-2)	-	Fruit wt. 90-95 g; resistant to early blight, leaf curl; yield 55 t/ha

Vasundhara (2000)	F_1 hybrid (PMSK-2 x Kalyanpur T-2)	Determinate; fruit wt. 70-75 g; resistant to early blight, spotted wilt virus; yield 55-60 t/ha
ATH-1	F_1 hybrid (ACC-2549 x Hawaii 7992)	Indeterminate; fruit wt. 110-120 g; resistant to early blight; TSS 7^0 Brix
Dr BSKKV, Dapoli		
Sonali (1986)	Hybrid of (VS-48-1 x Tami Chico-III)	Dwarf, determinate; oval shaped fruits; yield 20-25 t/ha; resistant to BW; suitable for processing
Konkan Vijay	-	Fruits round, smooth surface; uniform red colour; resistant to TLCV; excellent keeping quality
PAU, Ludhiana		
Punjab Selection No. 12 (1975)	Selection	Dwarf; yield 45-48 t/ha
Punjab Chhuhara (1981)	Pedigree selection from (EC 55055 x Punjab Tropic)	Determinate; pear shaped fruits; suitable for long distance transport; tolerant to high temperature & highly susceptible to ToLCV; yield (23-25 t/ha)
Punjab Tropic (1971)	Introduction from USA	Indeterminate; late fruit setting with slow development of fruit; suitable for table & juice purpose; yield 23-24 t/ha
Punjab Kesari (1987)	Pedigree selection from (EC-55055 x Punjab Tropic)	Determinate; oval fruits; good keeping quality; early & heat tolerant; yield 23 t/ha
Punjab NR-7 (1987)	Pedigree selection from (S-12 x NMR-1)	Determinate; excellent blend of TSS & acidity; require less water; fairly tolerant to sub-optimal temperature; yield 38-40 t/ha
TH-802	Heterosis breeding from (Healani x Castle Rock)	Determinate; round fruits; TSS 4.75%; yield 63 t/ha; resistant to root knot nematode
TH-2312	Heterosis breeding from (VFN-8x Punjab Chhuhara)	Determinate; dwarf; oval fruits; TSS 4.75%; yield 63 t/ha; resistant to root knot nematode
Punjab-2372 (2011)	-	Indeterminate; fruits flat-round; yield 45-55 t/ha
Punjab Varkh Bahar-1	-	Round, dark red coloured, resistant to ToLCV
Punjab Varkh Bahar-2	-	Round, dark red coloured, resistant to TLCV
Punjab Ratta (2014)	-	Determinate; oval shaped; TSS 6.43%; yield 56 t/ha; suitable for processing
Punjab Upma	-	Suitable for processing

S-12	Induced mutant of cv. Sioux.	Dwarf; juicy & acidic fruits
OUAT, Bhubaneshwar		
Utkal Pallavi (BT-1) 1992	Selection	Determinate; 6-12 fruits/ cluster; pear shaped fruits; good for saline soils; resistant to BW & nematode; yield 37-38 t/ha
Utkal Pragyan Mukthi (BT-19-1-1-1) 2019	-	Fruit wt. 70-80 g; tolerant to BW; yield 30 t/ha
Utkal Urvashi (BT-12) 1996	-	Indeterminate; thick skinned round shaped
Utkal Kumari (1998)	Selection from 'Selection 22 x BT-2	Indeterminate; round fruits; yield 40-41 t/ha; resistant to BW
Utkal Deepti (2002)	Selection	Resistant to BW
KAU, Vellanikkara		
Sakthi (1990)	Single seed descent method from North Carolina line 'LE-79'	Semi-determinate; fruit wt. 50-60 g; yield 32 t/ha; resistant to BW
Mukthi (1998)	Pure line selection from 'LE-79'	Determinate; fruit wt. 58 g; yield 43 t/ha; heat tolerant; resistant to BW & fruit cracking
Vellayani Vijai (2006)	Introduction & selection from 'CLN1621F' from AVRDC	High yield; resistant to BW & high temperature
Anagha	-	Semi-determinate; round fruits; resistant to BW & fruit cracking
Akshaya	-	Semi-determinate; fruit wt. (50-55g), oval shaped; resistant to bacterial wilt
Manuprabha	-	Fruit rounds; yield 1.88 kg/plant; fruit wt. 55-60 g; wilt resistant
AAU, Anand		
Gujarat Tomato-2 (2006)	Pedigree selection of (Angurlata x Punjab Chhuhara)	Determinate; tolerant to leaf curl virus & leaf blight; yield 33-35 t/ha
Gujarat Anand Tomato-3 (2002)	Selection from F_7 progeny of cross	Determinate; long shelf life; TSS 4.8%; fruit wt. 56 g; ascorbic acid 22 mg/ 100g; tolerant to ToLCV; yield 33 t/ha

	'Mahabaleshwar-2 x Sel.-7'	
Gujarat Anand Tomato-5 (2018)	OP selection	Determinate; circular shaped; good firmness; less infection of ToLCV, leaf miner damage & fruit borer; yield 40 t/ha
Gujarat Anand Cherry Tomato-1 (2014)	-	Red colour; ovoid shape & higher total soluble solids, lycopene & total soluble sugar; yield 35 t/ha
Anand Tomato-4 (2011)	-	Determinate; dark green shoulder on fruits at breaker stage; yield 35-40 t/ha; tolerant to ToLCV
ATL-8-21 (2016)	-	Determinate; round fruits; yield 45-50 t/ha
GAU, Junagarh		
Junagarh Ruby (1984)	Pedigree selection of (Big Silari x Pusa Ruby)	Fruits in cluster; yield 28-30 t/ha
Gujarat Tomato-6 (2018)	-	-
Gujarat Tomato-7 (2019)	-	-
UAS, Dharwad		
GPBI-8	Selection	-
GBPUA & T, Pantnagar		
Pant Bahar (1985)	Pure line selection from AC 238	Indeterminate; yield 25-27 t/ha; good for processing; resistant to verticillium wilt & fusarium wilt
Pant T-3 (1987)	Pure line selection from germplasm	Semi-determinate; good for processing; yield 32-35 t/ha
Pant T-10 (2009)	-	Determinate; TSS 6^0 Brix; yiled 35-45 t/ha; tolerant to blight
Pant polyhouse tomato-1	-	No. of fruits/ bunch are 5-6; fruit wt. 202 g; yield 140 t/ha; suitable for polyhouse cultivation
Pant polyhouse tomato-2 (2011)	-	Fruit wt. 100-105 g; thick pericarp 1 cm; 5-6 fruits/ cluster; yield 130 t/ha

Pant polyhouse tomato hybrid-1 (2011)	-	Fruit wt. 265 g; 7-8 fruits/cluster; yield 180 t/ha; suitable for polyhouse cultivation
TNAU, Coimbatore		
CO.1 (1969)	Pure line selection from American cv. 'Pearl Harbour'	Round fruits; more flesh content; susceptible to cracking; yield 36 t/ha
CO.2 (1974)	Pure line selection from Russain introduction	Semi-dwarf; 4-6 fruits/ cluster; yield 42 t/ ha
CO.3 (syn. Marutham) 1987	Mutant of CO.1 treated with EMS	Determinate; round fruits; high vit. C; yield 45-47 t/ha; crop duration 100 days; tolerant to early blight & leaf curl
Paiyur-1	F_1 hybrid of 'Pusa Ruby x Marutham'	Suited for long distance transport; early; suitable for rainfed condition; 10-12 pickings; yield 32 t/ha
COTH-1 (1998)	Heterosis breeding of (IHR 709 x LE 812)	Fruits born in clusters of 4-5; acidic fruits; TSS 4.43^0 Brix; yield 96 t/ha
COTH-2	LCR2 x CLN 2123	Resistant to leaf curl virus; yield 90 t/ha
TNAU Tomato Hybrid CO. 3	HN2 x CLN 2123	Resistant to leaf curl virus & root knot nematode; yield 95 t/ha
PKM-1 (1978)	Gamma ray mutant of local cv. Annaji	Determinate; green flesh type, flat-round fruits; suitable for long distance transport; yield 32 t/ha
COLCRH-3 (2006)	Heterosis breeding of (LCR-2 x CLN 2123 A)	Semi-determinate; resistant to leaf curl virus; suitable for HDP
Paiyur-1 (1988)	Pedigree selection of (Pusa Ruby x CO.3)	Extended harvest period of 10-12 pickings; suitable for long distance transport; low incidence of fruit borer, leaf spot & leaf curl virus
Kalinga Tomato-121	-	-
CTH-1 (2019)	-	Fruits thick round, thick pericarp; 10 days shelf life; yield 80-90 t/ha
CSAUA & T, Kanpur		
Azad T-2 (1985)	Pedigree selection of (HB-6 x Kuber)	Determinate; TSS 5.66%; 15 mg/100 g vit. C; lycopene 3.68 mg/g; mod. resis. to leaf curl virus; yield 33-35 t/ha
Azad T-5	-	Indeterminate; yield 40-45 t/ha.
Azad T-6 (2006)	Selection	Determinate; yield 25-27 t/ha.

Azad T-8	-	Mod. resistant to leaf curl mosaic, root knot nematode & alternaria blight; suitable for high density planting
Kalyanpur Angoorlata (1983)	Selection from local germplasm	Indeterminate; creeping nature; yield 48-50 t/ha; mod. resistant to leaf curl & root knot nematode
Kalyanpur T-1	-	-
Kalyanpur T-3	-	-
KTH-1	Hybrid	Yield 50-55 t/ha
KTH-2	Hybrid	Yield 55-60 t/ha
Dr YSPYH & F, Solan		
Solan Gola (1975)	Selection	Indeterminate; yield 38-39 t/ha; suitable for processing
Solan Sagun (1996)	Heterosis	Indeterminate; fruit wt. 65 g; suitable for long distance transport; tolerant to alternaria blight & buck-eye rot; yield 49-50 t/ha
Solan Vajr (1998)	Selection	Indeterminate; heart shaped; yield 45-47 t/ha
Solan Lalima	OP selection	Indeterminate; fruit wt. 70-80 g; yield 75-80 t/ha
Solan Garima	F_1 hybrid	Indeterminate; fruit wt. 80-85 g; 3-4 fruits /cluster; yield 66 t/ha
Solan Red Round	Selection	Indeterminate; cherry tomato type; fruit wt. 7-10 g; yield 30-35 t/ha
CSKHPKV, Palampur		
Palam Tomato Hybrid-1 (2013)	BWR-5 x Palam Pride	Resistant to BW; suitable for protected condition
Palam Pride	-	-
NDUAT, Faizabad		
NTDR-1 (1982)	Pedigree selection of (Bangalore x Kalyanpur Kuber)	Fruit wt. 40-50 g; suitable for processing; tolerant to root knot nematode; yield 35-38 t/ha
Narendra Tomato-2 (1996)	Selection from EC 119201	Determinate; fruit wt. 60-75 g; yield 44-45 t/ha
Narendra Tomato-5 (2006)	Selection	Indeterminate; fruit wt. 85-110 g; yield 40-45 t/ha
Narendra Tomato-6 (2006)	Pedigree selection of (Pusa Ruby x Kalyanpur Kuber)	Good keeping quality; yield 35-37 t/ha

VPKAS, Almora		
VL Tamatar-1 (2003)	Pedigree selection of [(Punjab Chhuhara x A2) x Punjab Chhuhara x Punjab Chhuhara]	Suitable for processing; resistant to fruit rot; susceptible to late blight; yield 20-25 t/ha
VL Tamatar-4	-	Mature in 60-70 days; suitable for poly house conditions; mod. resistant to fruit rot; yield 20-30 t/ha
VL Cherry Tomato-1 (2020)	-	-
AAU, Jorhat		
VC-48-1	Introduction	Determinate; high ascorbic acid; resistant to BW
BCKV, Kalyani		
BCTH-4	-	Semi-determinate; 14 fruits/kg; highly tolerant to leaf curl virus; suitable for West Bengal region
BCTH-62	-	Semi-determinate; Yield 50 t/ha; suitable for processing
Other popular hybrids		
Sel. 1	Pusa Early Dwarf x HS-101	-
Sel. 2	(HS- 101 x Punjab Tropic) x (H-14 c Punjab Tropic)	-
Sel. 7	Pusa Early Dwarf x K2	-
Sonali	Selection from exotic collection	Heat tolerant & resistant to bacterial wilt (BW)
S-12	X-ray (15-30 Kr) mutant of Sioux	Large number of fruit & high yield

Private sector hybrids: Naveen, Avinash, Meenakshi, Manisha, Krishna, Angur Lata, SUN-GROW-496, Madhuri, Megha, ARTH-3, ARTH-4, ARTHS-6, Gulmohar, Krishi Aman, Bhagya, Virang, US 440.

Grading system:

- As per BIS 4 grades: Super A, Super, Fancy, Commercial.

Size code	Fruit diameter (mm)	
	Minimum	Maximum
1	30	34
2	35	39
3	40	46
4	47	56
5	57	66
6	67	81
7	62	101
8	102	above

Diseases, pests and disorders:

- Models like 'TOMCAST', 'FAST-model' is developed for forecasting of early blight disease at Pennsylvania State University.
- Cross protection technique is adopted against Tomato Mosaic virus.
- In Punjab, only spring summer crop is taken due to heavy incidence of tomato leaf curl virus in autumn.
- 1st report of insect resistance: K.B. McKinney (1938).
- Glandular dense hairs (trichomes) works as defence against aphid attack.
- Capsidiol shows resistance against late blight.
- Anti-biotic factor in leaves hinders fruit borer attack acting as death trap.
- Entomopathogenic fungi for fruit borer: *Beauveria bassiana*.
- Root knot nematode: Use *Bacillus subtilis* 1% A.S and *B. amyloliquefaciens* @ 5 ml/ kg of substrate.

Diseases	Vector	Remarks
Tomato Spotted Wilt (TOSPO) virus	Thrips	*S. peruvianum* (*Sw-5* gene) resistant
Tomato Leaf Curl virus (ToLCV) syn. Bunchy top virus	White fly	Most serious disease (90% yield loss) & occur in autumn crop; highly curly leaves; *Ty-3* resistant gene incorporated in cv. Kashi Aman.
Tomato Yellow Leaf Curl virus (TYLCV)	White fly	*S. habrochaites* (*Ty-2* gene) commercially used in India.
Groundnut Bud Necrosis virus (GBNV)	Thrips	20% damage; black spots on tips of branches
Tobacco Mosaic virus (TMV)	Aphids	Leaf shape changes to fern leaf type & stunted plants
Tomato Chlorosis virus (TCV)	White fly	Leaves become chlorotic

Cucumber Mosaic virus (CMV)	Aphid	Shape of branches become shoe lace
Tomato Vein Distortion virus (TVDV)	Aphid	Vein become thick & change leaf shape
Fusarium wilt	*F. oxysporum* f. sp. *lycopersici*	Seed borne
Bacterial wilt	*Ralstonia solanacerum*	Serious disease in tropical humid climate
Bacterial canker	*Corynbacterium michiganense*	-
Leaf mold	*Cladosporium fulvum* (*Fulvia fulvum*)	-
Gray mold	*Botrytis cinerea*	Major post harvest disease
Pests:		
Fruit borer	*Helicoverpa armigera*	Ubiquitous pest; use marigold as trap crop & egg parasitoid *Trichogramma brasiliensis*
Fruit worm/ Corn earworm/ cotton boll worm/ soybean pod worm	*Heliothis zea*	*S. hirsutum* f. *glabratum*-PI 126449 resistant
White fly	*Bemisia tabaci*; *Trialeurodes vaporariorum*	Transmit tomato leaf curl virus; *S. hirsutum*- IVT 74453 & *S. pennellii*- IVT 72100 resistant
Serpentine leaf miner	*Liriomyza trifoli* & *Tuta absoluta*	-
Tobacco horn worm/ Horn moth/ hawk moth	*Manduca sexta* (*M. quinque-maculata*)	*S. hirsutum* f. *glabratum* resistant
South American tomato moth (Pin worm)	*Tuta absoluta*	Detected 1st at Nauni, Solan in 2015; *S. arcarnum*; *S. pennellii* & *S. coreliomulleri* resistant
Flea beetle	*Epiyrix hirtipennsis*	-
Potato aphid	*Macrosiphum euphorbiae*	-
Spider mite	*Tetranychus telarius*	cv. Anahu resistant
Carmine spider mite	*Tetranychus cinnabarinus*	Line-PI 134417 resistant
Colorado potato beetle	*Leptinotarsa decimlineata*	Line-PI 134417 resistant
Pinworm	*Keiferia lycopersicella*	Line-PI 127826 resistant

- Physiological disorders cause huge losses 15-20% in production.

- Radial cracking at ripe stage is more damaging than other (concentric, circular & burst) types of cracking.
- Bronzing is shock reaction due to spots with virus.
- Silvering: Exposure of plants to low temperature (<21^{0}C).
- Pithy stem: Both under and over irrigation.
- Oedema/ Dropsy: Over watering.
- Crease stem: High 'N' and water supply.
- Watery rot:
- Soft rot during storage: Excess N.
- Chilling injury: Storage disorder.

Name of disorder	Cause	Remedy
Fruit cracking	B deficiency; effect of soil temperature	1. Spray borax (0.25%) 2. Use resistant varieties
Blotchy ripening/ Greenback	K deficiency	Apply K fertilizer
Blossom end rot, black seed	1. Ca deficiency (major problem in green house). 2. Extreme fluctuations in moisture 3. Root pruning 4. Excessive nitrogen fertilization 5. High salinity 6. High K, Mg in soil	1. Spray $CaCl_2$ (0.5%) at fruit development stage. 2. Avoid excess application of N fertilizers particularly in ammonium form. 3. Application of lime or calcium based fertilizers (e.g. CAN @ 150 kg/ha) as basal dose
Puffiness or pocket (locules not filled with pulp, placenta & seeds)	Lack of fertilization/ embryo abortion (high nitrogen & low potassium)	1. Grow resistant varieties 2. Spray 0.3-0.4% borax at flowering & development stage 3. Use mulching
Sunscald	Excessive exposure to sun	1. Maintaining a continuous disease control program lessen foliage loss. 2. Plant staking 3. Hide fruits inside foliage 4. Cvs. with heavy foliage are less prone to this
Cat face (Distortion of blossom end of fruits)	Internal & external stress during tissue development	1. Grow resistant varieties 2. Clean sunlight & adjust date of planting.
Gold fleck (Tiny yellow spots around calyx & on fruit shoulder)	Low K: Ca ratio & excess calcium oxalate	1. High Mg & low P in nutrient solution with high EC (3.2 mS/cm^2). 2. Use of tolerant varieties. 3. In rockwool, the disorder is less than in soil.
Blotchy or slow ripening	N & K deficiency	Regulate light & temperature
Green back	Plants grown under glass; hard green patches appear near stalk caused by sun scorch & overheating	Apply potash & liquid fertilizers

Inheritance of characters:

- Three genes cause anthocyanin expression in fruit viz. a) Anthocyanin fruit (*Aft*) from *L. chilense* b) Aubergine (*Abg*) from *S. lycopersicoides* c) Atroviolacium (*atv*) from *L. cheesmanii.*
- Self incompatibility is of Nicotiana type, and conditioned by single locus.
- Many loci produce genetic male sterility (Rick and Butler, 1956).
- Larson and Pour (1948) reported functional male sterility.
- Expression of antherless plants is influenced by temperature.
- Long style is heritable character is barrier against self pollination (Butnaru, 1979).
- Fruit colour crimson gene *Og^c^* & high pigment gene (*hp*) enhance fruit colour. The *Og^c^* gene increases lycopene at the expense of β-carotene & results fruit with low vit. A level.
- Genes controlling dwarf (*d*) & brachytic (*br*) habit of growth are used for pot culture production.
- Mostly fungal disease resistance is conditioned by single dominant gene.
- Disease resistance is often inherited as dominant condition (Rick *et al.*, 1956).
- Tolerance to rhizoctonia fruit rot is associated with oblong fruit shape and mechanical puncturing of epidermis.
- Bacterial wilt has an unfavorable association with fruit size.

Character	Inheritance pattern & genes involved	Host resistance (species/ cvs.)
Plant height	Monogenic recessive (*sp*)	-
Flowers/ plant; percent fruit set, seed set, stigma exsertion	Polygenic	-
Fruit colour	Digenic	
Free neck	Monogenic recessive (*fn*)	-
Locule number	Monogenic recessive (*lc*)	-
Oval fruit shape	Monogenic recessive (*o*)	-
Pinkish red flesh	Recessive	-
β-carotene synthesis	Monogenic dominant (*BB*)	
Resistance to leaf curl virus	Monogenic dominant (*Tlc*)	Silvestra, PR 5
Resistance to root knot nematode	Monogenic dominant (*Mi*)	*L. peruvianum*, Nematex, Bangalore
Combined resistance to root knot nematode & bacterial wilt	Digenic	-
Closed anther/ Antherless condition/ Staminal sterility/ Stamenless condition/ Exerted stigma	Monogenic recessive (*sl-1*, *sl-2*, *ps*, *ps-2*)	-
Resistance to concentric cracking	Dominant to radial	-
Fruit firmness & longevity	Additive & partially dominant gene *rin*	Gene *rin* cause 20-30% increased shelf life

Parthenocarpic fruit set	Monogenic recessive (*pat-2*)	-
Dry matter content	Trigenic & additive	-
High acidity	Monogenic dominant	-
Anti-biotic factor in leaves	Recessive	-
Resistance to horn worm	3 recessive factors	-
Resistance to buck eye rot	Monogenic dominant(*Br*)	*L. pimpinellifolium*
Resistance to early blight	Monogenic dominant (*Ad*)	71B2
Resistance to collar rot	Monogenic dominant	*L. hirsutum*
Resistance to root rot	1 incomplete dominant gene	*L. esculentum* line from USA
Resistance to fusarium wilt	Monogenic dominant (*I*)	*L. pimpinellifolium*
Resistance to late blight	Monogenic semi-dominant (*Ph-l*)	*L. pimpinellifolium*
Resistance to soft rot	Polygeաic	Heinz 3,, MH1
Resistance to stem cancer	Monogenic dominant	6718VF
Resistance to verticillium wilt	Monogenic dominant (*Ve*)	-
Resistance to leaf mold	Monogenic (*Cf-1*to*Cf-24*)	-
Resistance to bacterial canker	Polygenic incomplete dominance	Okitsu Sozai-1
Resistance to bacterial wilt	Polygenic	PI 126408
Resistance to target leaf spot	Monogenic dominant (*Sm*)	PI 120265

- **Genes isolated**: For tomato improvement, following single genes have been useful.
- TLCV resistant *Ty-2* gene is found on chromosome number 6.

Trait	Gene symbol	Variety
High pigment	*hp*	Red Bush
Green stripes	*gs*	Tigerella
High β-carotene content	*B*	Caro Rich
Crimson colour	Og^c	Vermillion
Low total carotene	*r*	Snow Ball
Colourless peel	*y*	Traveller
Non-ripening	nor^A	Long Keeper
Uniform ripening	*u*	Heinz-1350
Parthenocarpic fruit	*pat-2*	Severianin
Self pruning/ determinate growth	*sp*	Many varieties
Brachytic	*br*	Red Blush
Dwarf	*d*	Epoch & Tiny Tim
Potato leaf	*c*	Geneva-11
Jointless pedicel	*j-1, j-2*	Penn Red & many varieties
Leaf mold (*Falvia fuisum*) resistance	*Cf-1*	Sterling Castle
	Cf-2	Vetamold
	Cf-3	V-121
	Cf-4	Purdue-135
Septoria resistance	*Se*	Targinnie Red
Late blight resistance	*Ph-1*	New Yorker
Nematode resistance	*Mi*	Rossoll, VFN-Bush

30.2 Brinjal

- Eulogized as 'Egg plant or Poor man's cup or Aubergine (French term) or Garden egg or Guinea squash'. or Bringall or Bringal'
- It is largest cultivated crop in Asia followed by Africa and Europe.
- Important vegetable crop widely cultivated in India, Bangladesh & Philippines.
- China (56% of world production) & India (26% of world production) are major producers.
- Among vegetables, brinjal has widest area and distribution in India.
- Covers 8.14% of total vegetable area and produces 90% of total vegetable production in India.
- It can withstand greater drought than most of vegetables.
- Major growing states: West Bengal > Odisha > Gujarat.
- Area under brinjal covered by hybrid varieties: 14%.
- Dry fruit contain goiterogenic principle.
- White brinjal is used for diabetic patients.
- De-cholestrolizing action is due to the presence of poly-unsaturated fatty acids (lanoleic & lanolenic) which are present in flesh and seeds (65.1%).
- Anti-cancerous property in brinjal: Nasunin.
- Pigment in purple coloured fruit: Anthocyanin.
- Vitamin A content: 124 IU
- Fruits are good source of vitamin-B group: B_1 (thiamin) and B_2 (riboflavin).
- Leaves contain more vit. C (38-104 mg/ 100g) than fruits. Vit. C content of fruits is affected by canning.
- Pigmented, dark purple coloured fruits have more vit. C than white coloured one.
- Fruits yield only 25 calories/ 100 g when raw and only 19 calories when cooked.
- Stimulates the intra-peptic metabolism of blood cholesterol.
- Toasting of fruits raises nicotinic acid at the expense of *Trigonellin* and 66.69% of it is converted into nicotinic acid during toasting.
- Anthocyanin pigment gives purple and violet colour to fruits.
- Colours of egg plant fruits: Purple (most popular in North America) to white or yellow (most popular in Europe) to ash coloured, green or brownish.
- Brown discolouration of fruits when cut open: Due to polyphenol oxidase.
- Bitter taste (toxic compound) and off flavour: Due to glycol-alkaloid solasodine.
- Glyco-alkaloid content in brinjal: 0.37 to 4.38 mg/ 100g.
- Earlier fruiting types begin flowering at 6th node while late maturing types don't begin flowering until 14 nodes have formed.

- Most favourable temperature for growth 21-29^{0}C (min 18^{0}C and max. 35^{0}C).
- Round fruited varieties set fruits at low temperature but are highly susceptible to fruit.
- Long fruited varieties set fruits at high temperature and show tolerance to frost.
- Brinjal is susceptible to severe frost.
- Optimum temperature for seed germination: 25^{0}C. most preferably 24-32^{0}C (min 15.5^{0}C and max. 35^{0}C).
- Plants need hardening at 18-21^{0}C.
- Seedlings are transplanted best when temperature is around 20^{0}C.
- Day temperature > 35^{0}C adversely affect fruit set and growth.
- In low temperature (< 10^{0}C) more short styled flowers produced, ovary in bud stage splits and deformed fruits develop. Besides, fruit pitting, surface bronzing, internal discolouration and browning of seeds are noticed. Chilled fruits are susceptible to alternaria decay.
- Flowers are pentamerous.
- Flowering: Extra-axillary & borne in 3 patterns i.e. solitary, cyme (in cluster) & mixed (both solitary & cyme).
- Flowering commences 70-75 days after transplanting.
- Anthesis time: 6-7.30 AM in summer and 11.15 AM in winter.
- Anther dehiscence: Immediately after anthesis.
- Pollen viability: 8-10 days at 20-22^{0}C with 50-55% R.H.
- Stigma receptivity: Day prior to anthesis to 4 days after anthesis.
- Fruit setting: 70-80%.
- Fruit is pendent, fleshy berry of oval/ round/ oblong shaped and 2-8 inch in diameter.
- Botanically, fruit is fleshy placenta, in which seeds are embedded in a mass of spondy tissue.
- Heterostyly (heteromorphic flower structure i.e. longi-style, peri-styly & brevi-styly) is common in multi-flower cymes except in bunchy type cultivars. Occasionally, parthenocarpic fruit set occurs as well.
- Longi-styly and peri-styly flowers are able to set fruits to the extent of 70-87% and 13-56%, respectively.
- Four types of styles (long, short, medium & pseudostyle) are reported. Among these only medium style (12 to 55%) and long style (70-80%) set fruits.
- Solitary flowers and basal flowers of cyme are long styled and functionally fertile. Clustered flowers are functionally sterile.
- Pseudo short styled and short styled flowers are functionally sterile.

- Ratio of short styles to long/ medium styled flowers in cluster is much high (3-4: 1).
- It is often cross pollinated (29%) or facultative cross pollination.
- High proportion of long styled flowers in summer (66%) than in winter (44%).
- Pollination agents used in green house: Bumble bee (*Bombus asiaticus*) and honey bee (*Apis mellifera*).
- Fruit set by insects (60-70%) and 30-40% by gravity (wind).
- Fertilization of flowers is due to both auto and allo-pollens.
- Artificial pollinated fruits contain less seeds than OP fruits.
- Insect pollination is essential for fruit and seed set as well as fruit growth (avg. 158% improvement).
- In solitary flowering types, flower drop is very low compared to clustered flowering type.
- 1st time artificial hybridization: Bailey and Munson (1891).
- 1st report of heterosis: Kakizaki (1931).
- 1st report on hybridization of brinjal varieties: Rao (1934).
- 1st molecular map: Nunome *et al*. (1998).
- 1st male sterility: Jasmin (1954).
- 1st functional male sterile line: UGA1-MS (cv. Florida High Bush), Pathak and Jaworski (1989).
- 1st report of hybrid vigour among some Japanese varieties: Nagai and Kida (1926).
- Heterosis %: 50-80.
- Seed rate: 300-400 g/ha (OP) and 150-200 g/ha (F_1 hybrid).
- Number of seeds in 1 gram: 250.
- Seed longevity: 4 years.
- At physiological maturity, white or green fruits turn yellow, whereas others turn brown.
- Processing cultivars should have high dry matter and low level of phenolics.
- 'Touch me Not' (*Mimosa pudica*) plants should be planted in vicinity of brinjal to enhance pollination.
- Sarkanda (*Erianthus arundinaceus*) grass is used as a mulch.
- Use of 2, 4-D @ 2 ppm at flowering induces parthenocarpy, increase fruit set, earliness and total yield.
- In brinjal, yield can be increased by 'Cu' application.

- Foliar spray of potassium nitrate (KNO_3 @ 2000 ppm), boron and zinc sulphate (500 ppm) increase yield of brinjal.
- Green brinjals have maximum (4 weeks) storage life.
- Storage: 7-10 days at 7.2^{0}C @ 85-95% R.H.
- Orobanche (root parasite): Serious weed.
- Yields are better when leaf area ranges from 11000 to 14000 sq. cm/ plant.
- Black and clear plastic mulch is extensively used ti increase yields and promotes earliness.
- Vegetative propagation can be achieved in November (96% success) with Seradix B.
- Seed extraction: HCl is added in pulp at 1: 4 ratio (25 ml per kg pulp).
- Induction of male sterility: MH (100 ppm), NAA (500 ppm), 2,4-D (20 ppm).
- Key documents on Bt brinjal are available on www.moef.gov.in
- Specific requirement for export purpose: Round, thornless, shiny purple with dark green calyx.

Species:

- Primary centre of origin for large fruited form (*S. melongena* var. *esculentum)* for large fruited types and secondary centre of origin in China for small fruited types.

Species	Features
S. melongena var. *incanum* (Sodom apple)	Progenitor of cultivated brinjal; small fruits; commercially important & included in the prickly group;resistant to bacterial wilt (BW)
S. melongena var. *serpentium* (snake brinjal)	Snake egg plant; bears extraordinary long & slender type fruits; leaf highly prickly
S. melongena var. *depressum* & *S. melongena* var. *bulsarensis*	Dwarf, early cvs.; small, purple & pear shaped fruits
S. melongena var. *esculentum*	Common egg or round shaped fruits
S. melongena var. *melongena*	Round egg shaped fruits
S. macrosperma	Resistant to phomopsis rot
S. integrifolium	Tolerant to drought
S. avivulares	Source of solasodine
S. khasianum	Source of solasodine & tolerant to shoot and fruit borer; resistant to phomopsis fruit rot
S. xanthocarpum, *S. nigrum*	Small, clustered acidic fruits; used as leafy vegetable in Tamil Nadu; immune to fruit rot (*Phomopsis vexanas*) & phomopsis blight; resistant to BW

S. indicum	Resistant to verticillium wilt & immune to root knot nematode
S. sisimbrifolium	Variegated leaves; resistant to little leaf, BW, phomopsis fruit rot; immune to fruit rot, root knot nematode, spider mite
S. viarum	Resistant to little leaf, shoot and fruit borer
S. habrochaites f. glabratum	Resistant to low temperature & insect resistance
S. auriculatum	Immune to little leaf
S. macrocarpon (African egg plant) syn.	(2n=36); cultivated in Africa for edible fruits & leaves;
S. integrifolium	tolerant to drought; resistant to shoot & fruit borer, little leaf, leaf hopper, nematodes & gall midge; susceptible to cercospora leaf spot; cross incompatible with *S. melongena*
S. aethiopicum	2n=24; cultivated in Africa for fruits & leaves; resistant to anthracnose
S. anomalum	Tolerant to drought & immune to shoot & fruit borer
S. gilo	Tolerant to drought & immune to shoot & fruit borer & resistant to little leaf, phomopsis fruit rot; cross incompatible with *S. melongena*
S. mammosum	Resistant to spotted *Epilachna* beetle
S. khasianum	Resistant to spotted *Epilachna* beetle & phomopsis fruit rot
S. torvum (Turkey berry/ Prickly Night shade)	Rootstock for grafting tomato & brinjal; resistant to bacterial wilt, immune to root knot nematode & resistant to spotted *Epilachna* beetle
S. pubescens	Non-prickly
S. toxicarium	Resistant to BW
S. torvum	Resistant to phomopsis fruit rot
S. testiculatum	Resistant to phomopsis fruit rot
S. incanum x *S. melongena*	Produce fertile hybrids
S. macrocarpon x *S. melongena*	Tolerant to biotic stresses like little leaf, leaf hopper, nematode & gall midge attack

- **Interspecific cross compatibility**: Crosses are compatible with group A or group B and vice versa but are otherwise incompatible.
  1. **Group A**: Comprises *S. melongena, S. incanum, S. macrocarpum.*
  2. **Group B**: Comprises *S. integrifolium, S. gilo, S. nodiflorum.*
  3. **Group C**: Comprises *S. indicum, S. mammosum, S. torvum, S. sisymbrifolium, S. toxicarium.*

Crossability with *S. melongena*:

- *S. capsicoides*: No seed germination.
- *S. mammosum*: Abnormal seeds.
- *S. viarum*, *S. grandiflorum*, *S. macranthum*, *S. hispidum*, *S. torvum*: Hybrid virtually sterile.
- *S. sisymbriifolium*: Death of hybrid seedlings.
- *S. strmonifolium*: No fruit set.
- Filov (1940) classified both cultivated and wild forms into 5 sub-species as-
  - *agrestis*: Form which bears extremely bitter & inedible fruits.
  - *occidentale*: Which arise in higher temperature and adequate humidty in western Asia minor.
  - *orientale*: Asiatic cultivars originated in Japan and China.
  - *palentinicum*: A hydrophytic plant adapted to withstand high temperature.
  - *arabico-italicum*: Has bitter fruits and has only ornamental value.

Varieties:

- 1st report of hybrid vigour in brinjal was given by Nagai and Kida (1926).
- Dr. H.B. Singh developed 'Pusa Purple Round' and 'Pusa Purple Long'.
- NDB-25: Soft joint and easy to harvest.
- Brinjal variety suitable for *bharta* making: BH-2
- Surya: Flooding and saturated soil resistant.
- Resistant to BW and phomopsis fruit rot: Florida Market, Florida Beauty, Black Beauty, Muktakesi, White Gih.
- Resistant to *Meloidogyne javanica*: Bhanta.
- Resistant to *M. incognita*: Vijaya.
- Highly resistant to fruit borer: White Long, Thorn Pendy, Black Pendy, Aushey.
- Resistant to spotted beetle: Apple Green Flesh, Pusa Purple Round.
- Resistant to bacterial wilt: Surya, BB-7, BWR-12, SM-6-7.
- Resistant to fusarium wilt and drought: BB-44.
- Functional male sterile (shriveled anthers devoid of pollen grains) lines: Blackie, UGA-1 MS.
- Genac, BSS-793: *Bt* brinjal varieties by Beejo Sheetal.
- Purple, oval fruited and large types: Black Magic, Black Beauty, Dusky, Epic.
- Oriental types (small, elongated & slender fruits): Long Tom, Tycoon, Ichiban.

Name	Breeding method	Features
IARI, New Delhi		
Pusa Purple	Cluster White x Muktakesi strain	Uniform attractive fruits
Pusa Purple Round (1970)	Selection from Punjab cv. 'Batia'	Yield 28-31 t/ha; fruits purple coloured; resistant to little leaf, shoot borer, jassids
Pusa Purple Long (1970)	Single plant selection from indigenous collection	Earliest; spineless; fruits long, purple coloured; suitable for ratooning; tolerant to shoot borer; yield 28-31 t/ha
Pusa Purple Cluster (1978)	Single plant selection from indigenous collection	Its stem & foliage colour is deep purple; spineless; resistant to little leaf, bacterial wilt (BW) & shoot and fruit borer
Pusa Anmol	Heterosis breeding of (Pusa Purple Long x Hyderpur)	Early & more yield; non spiny; dark purple fruits
Pusa Kranti (1977)	Pedigree breeding of (Pusa Purple Long x Hyderpur) x Wynad Giant	Fruits dark purple coloured; fruits oblong; less seeded; resistant to BW
Pusa Bhairav (1985)	Progeny selection of (Pusa Purple Long x No. 11a-12-2-1)	Non-spiny; fruits 12-15 cm long; resistant to phomopsis blight (*Phomopsis vexans*)
Pusa Anupam (1991)	Pusa Kranti x Pusa Purple Cluster	Fruits in cluster of 3-5; 30-35 frutis/plant; resistant to BW, phomopsis foot rot; suitable for pickles; yield 37 t/ ha
Pusa Hybrid-4	Heterosis breeding of (Pusa Purple Long x Hyderpur)	-
Pusa Hybrid-5 (1994)	Heterosis breeding of (Sel. NDB-25 x Sel. 129-5)	Plants non-spiny; dark purple coloured long fruits; yield 54 t/ha
Pusa Hybrid-6 (1993)	Heterosis breeding of (Sel. Br-112 x Sel. 91-2)	Plants non-spiny; violet purple coloured round fruits; yield 47 t/ha
Pusa Hybrid-9 (1997)	Heterosis breeding of (Sel 91-2-1 x Sel. 190-10-12)	Plants non-spiny; dark purple fruits with pigmented peduncle; yield 67 t/ha
Pusa Uttam (1997)	Progeny selection of (GR x Pant Rituraj)	Plants spineless; dark purple fruits; single fruit weight 250-300 g; yield 43-45 t/ha
Pusa Upkar (1997)	Progeny selection of (GR x PB-91-1)	Spineless; greenish purple leaves bearing 15 fruits; fruits dark purple & weighs 300 g each; yield 65-67 t/ha
Pusa Bindu (1997)	Progeny selection of (GR x Pant Rituraj)	Cluster bearing small fruited; fruit weighing 125 g; yield 25-30 t/ha
Pusa Ankur (1999)	Progeny selection of (GR x Pant Rituraj)	Fruits small, round, purple coloured; yield 56-58 t/ha

Pusa Shyamala	Pedigree selection of (Sel NDB-25-11 x Sel. HE-12-2)	Plants non-spiny; fruits dark purple; fruit wt. 80-90 g; yield 39 t/ha
Pusa Safed Baingan-1 (2019)	-	White oval round fruits; yield 35 t/ha; total phenol content (31.21 mg GAE/100 g); rich in anti-oxidant activity (3.48 CUPRAC mol trolox/g, 2.58 FRAP mol trolox/g)
Pusa Hara Baingan-1 (2019)	-	Green oval fruits; non-spiny calyx; yield 40-45 t/ha; high anti-oxidant activity (3.41 CUPRAC mol trolox /g, 3.07 FRAP mol tr olox /g)
Pusa Kausal (2016)	-	Fruits dark purple; yield 53 t/ha
Pusa Oishiki (2018)	-	Early; plants non-spiny; purple pigments on stem; fruits purple coloured with non-spiny, long (20 cm) &cylindrical; fruit wt. 100-125g
Pusa Vaibhav(2019)	-	Fruits round, shiny purple; non-spiny calyx; fruit wt. 250 g; yield 41 t/ha
DBL-02 (2010)	-	Plants non-spiny; fruits long, violet-purple; yield 37-39 t/ha
IIVR, Varanasi		
Kashi Sandesh (2006)	Heterosis breeding (F_1 hybrid)	Purple coloured oval-round fruits; 50-60 fruits/plant; yield 78 t/ha
Kashi Komal	Heterosis breeding (F_1 hybrid)	Long purple coloured fruits; 25-30 fruits/plant; yield 80 t/ha
Kashi Prakash (2006)	Mass selection	Oblong purple coloured fruits; spiny calyx; 14-17 fruits/plant; yield 70 t/ha
Kashi Taru (2006)	Mass selection	Long, dark purple coloured fruits; 20-25 fruits/plant; yield 75 t/ha
Kashi Himani (2018)	-	Shiny white fruits with less seeds; suitable for kharif; tolerant to fruit and shoot borer, moisture deficit & lodging; medicinal value for diabetic patients; yield 43 t/ha
Kashi Vijay	-	-
IVBL-23 (2019)	-	Fruits 14 cm long, crimson coloured; fruit wt. 150 g; yield 40 t/ha; tolerant to phomopsis blight, fusarium wilt
IIHR, Bengaluru & (CHES, Bhubaneshwar)		
Arka Navneet (1981)	Heterosis breeding from 'IIHR-22-1 x Supreme (from Australia)'	Indeterminate; 1st F_1 hybrid released by IIHR; highest yield (75 t/ha); round & oval shaped bright purple coloured fruits
Arka Kusumakar (1986)	Pure line selection from 'IIHR 193'	Cluster bearing of 5-7 fruits; skin light green colour; resistant to BW; 70-75 fruits/plant.
Arka Sheel (1986)	Pure line selection from 'IIHR 192'	Fruits medium long, skin deep purple; fruit wt. 100 g; 50-55 fruits/ plant; yield 38 t/ha; resistant to little leaf
Arka Nidhi (1990)	Pedigree selection of 'Dingrass Multiple Purple x Arka Sheel'	Resistant to BW; free from bitter principle; yield 49 t/ha

Arka Keshav (1990)	Pedigree selection of 'Dingrass Multiple Purple x Arka Sheel'	Red purple glossy fruit skin; free from bitter principle; resistant to BW; yield 47 t/ha
Arka Neelkanth (1990)	Pedigree selection of 'Dingrass Multiple Purple x Arka Sheel'	Resistant to BW; slow seed maturity; yield 45 t/ha
Arka Shirish (1986)	Pure line selection from 'IIHR 194-1'	Green coloured fruits & resistant to BW; half of fruit length towards stem has no seeds; yield 39 t/ha
Arka Harshitha (2016)	Pedigree selection of 'IIHR-108 and IIHR-3'	Green coloured fruits; yield 38-40 t/ha; resistant to BW, root knot nematode
Arka Unnathi (2016)	Pedigree selection of 'IIHR-108 and IIHR-3'	Green coloured fruits; yield 36-38 t/ha; resistant to BW
Arka Avinash (2016)	Pedigree selection of 'IIHR-108 and IIHR-3'	Green coloured fruits; yield 40-44 t/ha; resistant to BW
Arka Anand	Heterosis breeding of (IIHR-3 x SM6-6)	Fruits green; yield 60 t/ha; resistant to BW & suitable for kharif & rabi
Arka Vaibhav	-	Resistant to BW; yield 49 t/ha
BPLH-1	F_1 hybrid	Fruits purple long; suitable for kharif & rabi; yield 55 t/ha
Selection-2	Selection from 'IHR-500A x IIHR-571'	Dwarf; round fruits; yield 35 t/ha
Arka Neelachal Shyama	Mass selection	Round, light purple fruits; suitable for frying; mod. tolerant to phomopsis blight; yield 34 t/ha
Arka Neelachal Kranti	Mass selection	Oblong, green fruits
ICAR Research Complex for Eastern Region, Patna (HARP, Ranchi)		
Swarna Shree (2006)	Pure line selection	Fruits creamy white, round to oval, soft & preferred for *bharta* preparation; yield 55-60 t/ha; mod. resistant to BW
Swarna Mani (2004)	Hybridization followedby pedigree selection & back cross method	Round, purple coloured fruits; mod. resistant to BW; yield 60-65 t/ha
Swarna Shymal (2006)	Pure line selection	Fruits round, attractive green colour with white stripes & resistant to BW; yield 58 t/ha
Swarna Pratibha (2004)	Pure line selection	Long, purple coloured fruits; resistant to BW; yield 45-50 t/ha
Swarna Shobha (2006)	Hybridization followed by pedigree selection	Fruits round having milky white colour with purple tinge; yield 50-60 t/ha; tolerant to BW

Swarna Abhilamb (2007)	Pure line selection	Long, purple coloured fruits; yield 60-70 t/ha; resistant to BW & phomopsis blight
Swarna Shakti (2004)	Heterosis breeding	Oblong; light purple coloured fruits; yield 70-75 t/ha; mod. resistant to BW & phomopsis blight
Swarna Mohit (2008)	Heterosis breeding	Oblong; light purple coloured fruits; yield 65-75 t/ha; mod. resistant to BW & phomopsis blight
Swarna Ajay (2006)	Heterosis breeding	Oblong; light purple coloured fruits; yield 70-75 t/ha; mod. resistant to BW & phomopsis blight
Swarna Neelima (2008)	Heterosis breeding	Round; light purple coloured fruits; yield 70-75 t/ha; mod. resistant to BW & phomopsis blight;
HABR-21 (2013)	Pure line selection	Stems & leaves purple; fruits black; yield 55-60 t/ha
ICAR Research Complex for North-Eastern Hilly region, Meghalaya		
RCMDL		Deep purple coloured fruits & 3-4 fruits/cluster
RCMD-2		Tolerant to bacterial wilt
RCM-DHL-3		Purple long fruits of 25-30 cm
RCM-DHL-4		Pink coloured fruits with less seeds
ICAR Research Complex for Goa		
Goa Brinjal-1, 2, 3, 4	-	Purple fruit colour; resistant to bacterial wilt
CIAH, Bikaner		
Thar Rachit	-	Early; fruits oblong dark purple; fruit wt. 40-45 g; yield 3-4 kg/plant; suitable for arid zones
AHTB	-	Thorny; fruit length 6 cm & width 6.89 cm; suitable for high temperature condition
CCSHAU, Hisar		
Hisar Shyamal (syn. H-8) 1991	F_1 hybrid (Aushey x BR-112)	Plants non-spiny; dark purple fruits; tolerant to little leaf & resistant to BW; yield 32 t/ha
Hisar Jamuni (syn. H-9)	Pedigree selection of (Oro x R-34)	Dark purple fruits; thornless fruits; suitable for ratoon cropping; yield 28 t/ha
Hisar Pragati	F_1 hybrid of (R-34 x Sel.26)	Suitable for summer season, fruits long bright dark purplecoloured; yield 35 t/ha; tolerant to little leaf
H-4 (1976)	Pedigree selection of 'Hyderpur x Pusa Purple Long'	Deep purple coloured fruits; long fruits (15-20 cm); fruit wt. 125-150 g; yield 22-25 t/ha
BR-112	-	Fruits bright purple coloured & yield 25 t/ha
HLB-12	-	Indeterminate; fruits purple; tolerant to high temperature, shoot & fruit borer; yield 20 t/ha

HLB-25	-	Early, erect, semi-spreading; bushy; bright purple black colour fruits
NAU, Navsari		
GNRB-1	-	Presence of anthocyanin on stem & young purple green leaves with purple veins; fruits dark purple
JAU, Junagadh		
GJB-3	-	Suitable for late kharif; yield 39 t/ha
Junagarh Long (1984)	Selection	Plants non-spiny; free from collar rot; yield 30-35 t/ha
Gujarat Round Brinjal-5 (2018)	Selection	Plants non-spiny; round; yield 30-32 t/ha
AAU, Anand		
GBH-1 (1996)	Heterosis breeding of (M-2 x M-35)	Tolerant to shoot and fruit borer; yield 58 t/ha
GBH-3	F_1 hybrid	Fruits dark purple; medium spiny on leaves and calyx; mod. resistant to little leaf, jassids & whitefly; yield 62 t/ha
GA Oblong Brinjal-1	-	Fruits black in colour & shining; tolerant to leaf disease. Yield 47 t/ha
GA Oblong Brinjal-2	OP selection	Yield 45 t/ha
Anand BrinjalSmall Round-2	-	Fruits light pinkish, shiny with non-spiny calyx; yield 41 t/ha
AAU, Jorhat		
JC-1	-	Tolerant to BW, phomopsis blight, little leaf virus & borer; yield 34 t/ha
JC-2	-	Tolerant to BW, phomopsis blight, little leaf virus & borer; yield 35 t/ha
GBUA & T, Pantnagar		
Pant Samrat (1985)	Pure line selection from germplasm	Tolerant to shoot and fruit borer & resistant to BW, phomopsis blight; yield 39 t/ha
Pant Rituraj (1985)	Pedigree selection of (Type 3 x Pusa Purple Cluster)	Fruits round; field resistance to BW; yield 30 t/ha
Pant Brinjal Hybrid-1 (1994)	Heterosis breeding of (PB-129 x PB-225)	Resistance to BW, phomopsis blight, shoot & fruit borer; yield 60 t/ha
Pant Brinjal-4	Pedigree of cross (PB 129 x PB-7)	Fruits long, purple coloured; resistant to BW, phomopsis, alternaria leaf spot & shoot and fruit borer
Pant Brinjal-67 (2009)	-	Early maturity, resis. to bacterial wilt & phomopsis; yield 41 t/ha
Pant Brinjal-70 (2010)	-	Resis. to phomopsis blight, bacterial wilt & shoot and fruit borer, yield 40 t/ha
CSKHPKV, Palampur		
Palam Yellow (2013)	-	Semi-indeterminate; suitable for table purpose; resistant to bacterial wilt

MPKV, Rahuri & Agril. Dept. Maharashtra		
Manjari Gota (1965)	Local selection from 'Manjari' area	Spines on leaves, mid rib & peduncle; resistant to BW, little leaf & jassids; yield 25 t/ha
Krishna (1991)	F_1 hybrid of 'Poona Selection x Ruchira'	Hardy, egg shaped, spiny purple coloured fruits with white stripes; resistant to lodging; yield 48 t/ha
Phule Harit (2006)	Pure line selection	Fruits green with white patch at apical end; fruit wt. 190 g; 25 fruits/ plant; 18 pickings; suitable for roasting (*bharta* making) & culinary purpose; yield 20 t/ha
Phule Arjun	F_1 hybrid	Fruits green with purple-white stripes, oval shaped, spiny; fruit wt. 61 g; suitable for kharif & summer season; yield 45 t/ha
Vaishali (1985)	Pedigree selection of 'Manjari Gota x Arka Kusumakar'	Cluster bearing habit of 3-4 fruits; fruitsoval shaped,purple with white strips; yield 35 t/ha
Pragati (1988)	Pedigree selection of 'Vaishali x Manjari Gota'	Hardy, resistant to lodging; purple with white strips; cluster bearing; yield 35 t/ha
RHRBH-1	Heterosis breeding of (RHRB-1 x JB-16)	Fruits non-spiny; purple with white stripes; yield 57 t/ha
RHRBH-2	Heterosis breeding of (RHRB-1 x RB-25)	Fruits purple with white stripes; yield 41 t/ha
RHRBH-3	Heterosis breeding of (RHRB-1 x Vaishali)	Fruits spiny; purple with white stripes; yield 44 t/ha
PAU, Ludhiana		
Black Beauty (1975)	Introduction	Fruits roundish oblong; resistant to *Meloidogyne javanica*; yield 25-27 t/ha
Punjab Haryana Brinjal-4 (1976)	Pedigree selection of (Hyderpur x Pusa Purple Long)	Plants bushy; fruits dark purple coloured; yield 22-25 t/ha
Punjab Bahar (1978)	Selection	Plants tall; non-spiny; fruits purple, less seeded; suitable for bharta making; yield 27-30 t/ha
Punjab Neelum (1988)	Jamuni Gole x Pant Rituraj	Tolerant to fruit borer; yield 14 t/ha; tolerant to fruit borer
Punjab Chamkila (1978)	Selection	Suitable for summer & autumn season; fruits dark purple coloured; yield 43-45 t/ha
Punjab Barsati (1987)	Selection from (Pusa Purple Cluster x H-4)	Thornless; purple fruits; tolerant to fruit borer; yield 14 t/ha
Jamuni Gole Baigan (1986)	Selection from 'Selection-16'	Non-spiny; purple coloured fruits; excellent for bharta making
Punjab Sadabahar Baigan (1987)	Pedigree selection of 'Pusa Japanese Long x R-34'	Fruits long & blackish purple; thornless; tolerant to fruit & shoot borer; yield 13 t/ha

Punjab Moti (1993)	Selection	Small fruited; dark purple fruits; yield 12 t/ha
BH-1 (1996)	Heterosis breeding of 'Punjab Barsati x Jamuni Gola'	Plants thornless; purple fruits; tolerant to fruit borer; yield 52 t/ha
BH-2 (1996)	Heterosis breeding of 'Punjab Neelum x Punjab Barsati'	Thornless fruits; dark purple fruits; suitable for making *bharta*; tolerant to fruit borer; yield 52 t/ha
S-4	-	Cluster bearing habit; deep coloured fruits
PHBL-51 (2012)	-	Fruits medium-long, thin; deep purple; yield 55-65 t/ha
PBHL-52 (2014)	-	Fruits long, purple, borne in cluster; yield 68 t/ha
Punjab Raunak	-	-
PBL-232 (2019)	-	Early; long fruits; fruits long purple coloured; yield 36 t/ha
PBHSR-31 (2012)	-	Fruits small, oblong, purple coloured; yield 60-65 t/ha
ANGRAU, Hyderabad		
Bhagyamati (1982)	Selection	Purple shoots; purple coloured fruits; yield 15-18 t/ha
BCKV, Kalyani		
Bidhan Super (2019)	-	Round fruits with glossy blackish purple colour; yield 29 t/ha
Bidhan Supreme (2019)	-	High yield (29 t/ha); resistant to bacterial wilt
Dr BSKKV, Dapoli		
Konkan Prabha (2019)	-	Fruits 15-20 cm long with 4-6 cm dia.; fruits dark purple, soft & shiny; non-prickly plants bear fruits in cluster of 4-6; yield 30 t/ha; resistant to BW
Dr PDKV, Akola		
Aruna (1985)	Selection	Prolific bearing; small, violet coloured; yield (30-35 t/ha kharif) & 20-22 t/ha summer)
AKLB-9	-	Thorn-less; fruit colour pale green with white streaks; suitable for summer & rainy season
VNMKV, Parbhani		
Anuradha	Selection	Fruits in clusters, purple coloured white stripes, spiny
ABV-1 (1985)	-	Fruits round shaped; small with green purple stripes; yield 25 t/ha
NDUAT, Faizabad		
Narendra Baigan-1 (1996)	Selection	Fruits dark purple; less seeded; yield 30 t/ha
NDBH-1 (1995)	Heterosis breeding of (PBR-91-1 x K-202-14-90-110)	Resistant to little leaf; non-spiny & round purple fruits; yield 47 t/ha
NDBH-3 (2006)	Heterosis breeding	Fruits shiny purple coloured; yield 50 t/ha

NDBH-6	Heterosis breeding of (Narendra Hybrid T-3 x Pant Samrat)	Non spiny; long fruits; resistant to phomopsis blight, shoot borer & little leaf
TNAU, Coimbatore		
CO.1 (1978)	Pure line selection	Fruits light green with white base; mod. resistant to root knot & reniform nematode; yield 24-26 t/ha
CO.2 (1988)	Pure line selection from local cv. Varikkathiri	Fruits oblong with brown stripes; yield 35 t/ha
MDU-1 (1982)	Selection from Madurai local cv. Kallamp	Fruits round, bright purple; weight 280 g; yield 34 t/ha.
PKM-1 (1984)	Gamma ray mutant of local cv. Puzhuthi Kathiri	Drought tolerant & withstand long distance transport; fruits dark purple coloured; yield 34 t/ha
KKM-1 (1999)	Pure line selection from 'KulathurLocal'	Fruits egg shaped &milky-white coloured; yield 37 t/ha; suitable for diabetic patients
COBH-1 (2001)	Heterosis breeding of 'ED-45 x CO.2'	Fruits slightly oblong, glossy violet; high ascorbic acid (16.65 mg/100 g); yield 56 t/ha
COBH-2	EP65 x Pusa Uttam	Fruits medium in size; oblong in shape, dark violet; yield 60 t/ha
PPI-B-1 (2002)	Selection from 'Karungal local' type	Fruits oblong, pale green & mod. resis. to shoot & fruit borer & wilt; yield 45 t/ha
PLR-1 (1990)	Reselection from 'Nagpur' ecotype	Extended shelf life upto 10 days; fruits egg shaped & dark purple coloured
PLR (BR) 2	Selection from Sevanthampatti Local	Fruits oval; dark purple with pink tinge; yield 38 t/ha
TNAU Brinjal VRM 1	-	Fruits oval; glossy pink with green tinge; yield 45 t/ha
Annamalai (1985)	Selection	Aphid & BW resistant, tolerant to shoot & fruit borer
CSAUA&T, Kanpur		
Azad-B-2	F_1 hybrid of (Pusa Purple Round x Arka Sheel)	Fruits round, bright purple; rsistance to phomopsis fruit rot; yield 35-40 t/ha
Azad-B-3	-	Fruits long cylindrical, shining purple; yield 40-45 t/ha
Azad-B-4	-	Fruits round, light purple; yield 30-35 t/ha
Azad Hybrid	-	Fruits long, bright purple; yield 50-55 t/ha
Azad Kranti (1985)	Hybrid of (Pusa Purple Long x BGL)	Dark purple fruits; tolerant to fruit rot; resistant to little leaf blight & fruit rot; less seeded; yield 31-33 t/ha
Kalyanpur T-3 (1983)	Selection	Fruits round; purple & whitish end; yield 30-32 t/ha
Kalyanpur-2	Selection	Tolerant to jassids

OUAT, Bhubaneshwar		
Utkal Keshari (1998)	Pedigree selection of 'BB-11 x KJ-3-1'	Tolerant to BW & fusarium wilt; yield 35 t/ha
Utkal Tarini (1992)	Pedigree selection of 'Pusa Kranti x Gopa Local'	Oblong fruits; resistant to BW; yield 35 t/ha
Utkal Madhuri (1998)	Pedigree selection of 'PBR 125-5 x Pipili-4'	Resistant to drought & fusarium wilt; yield 33 t/ha
Utkal Jyoti (2004)	Pedigree selection of 'JT-4 x BB-11'	Tolerant to BW; yield 37 t/ha
IGKV, Raipur		
JC-1 (1998)	Selection	Free from phomopsis blight & little leaf; yield 42 t/ha
JC-2 (1998)	Selection	Free from wilt, phomopsis blight, fruit borer & little leaf; yield 49 t/ha
Chhattisgarh Safed Baigan-1	-	White; soft; long; yield 35 t/ha; tolerant to high temperature; resistant to phomopsisblight
KAU, Vellanikkara		
Surya (1990)	Selection from 'SM6-7'	Yield 35 t/ha; resistant to BW
Sweta (1996)	Selection from 'SM6-6'	Resistant to BW; yield 33 t/ha
Haritha (1998)	Selection from 'SM-141'	Resistant to BW; yield 35 t/ha
Neelima	Surya x SM-116	Round/ oval purple fruits; resistant to BW
Sonali	Selection from (VS-48-1 x Tami Chico III)	Resistant to BW
Ponny	-	Non-spiny stem; green long fruits, yield 32 t/ha; resistant to BW
Other hybrids		
Kachbachia, Annapurna, ARUZC	-	Tolerant to shoot & fruit borer

Private sector hybrids: Hindustan, Vardan, Nisha, Suphal, Shiva, Vaishali, Kopek, Anamika, Kalpataru, Shyamal, Ravaiyya.

Pests, diseases and physiological disorders:

- Of the total cost of production, 40% expenditure is on plant protection measures.
- Major pest: Shoot and fruit borer (*Leucinodes arbonalis*) causing yield loss up to 50-70%.
- Brinjal weevil (*Myllocerus subfasciatus*): Use *Bacillus* sp. and *Beauveria bassiana*.
- Root knot nematode: Serious problem. Plant marigold in 1:1 row ratio.
- Hadda beetle (*Epilachna vigintioctopunctata*):
- Phomopsis blight (*P. vexans*) causes severe fruit rot in seed production.
- Anthracnose (*Colletotrichum gloeosporioides*):
- Bacterial wilt is a serious vascular disease in West Bengal and Odisha.
- Fusarium wilt: Vascular disease.
- Damping off: Serious in nursery stage. Seed treatment with Thiram/ Ceresan @ 2 g/kg of seed before sowing.
- Little leaf is most serious disease caused by MLOs and transmitted by leaf hopper (*Cestius phycitis*)
- 1st report of little leaf disease in India: Thomas and Krishnaswamy (1939).
- Calyx withering: Physiological disorder.
- Thorny and deep purple coloured fruits: Less incidence of fruit borer.

Inheritance of characters:

Character/ trait	Number of genes	Type of gene action
Plant height	Monogenic	Tall dominant to dwarf
Fruit shape	3-4 genes	* Round shape partially dominant to oval long; * Elongated dominant to round;
Prickly (spines) nature	Monogenic	* Prickly nature dominant to non-prickly; * Purple spine dominant to green spine
Fruit clusterness	Monogenic	Clustering partially dominant to solitary nature
Fruit size	Monogenic	Large fruit size partially dominant to small fruit size
Fruit colour	Monogenic, digenic & trigenic	Purple dominant to green; Green dominant to white
Fruit flesh colour	Monogenic	Green dominant to white
Flower colour & hypocotyl colour	Monogenic	Violet/ purple dominant to green
Stem colour	Monogenic	Purple (stem, petioles & veins) dominant to green
Style erectness	Monogenic	Incurved dominant to straight
Male sterility	Monogenic (*ms1* & *ms2*)	-

Bacterial wilt resistance	Monogenic (*Rps*)	Resistant dominant to susceptibility
Anthracnose resistance	Monogenic	Resistant dominant to susceptibility
Phomopsis fruit rot/ blight	Polygenic	Recessive
Resistance to shoot & fruit borer	-	Susceptible dominant to resistant
Resistance to nematode	Polygenic	Recessive
Total phenol content	-	Additive
Protein content	-	Dominant
Sugar content of fruit	-	Additive & non-additive

30.3 Chilli

- Eulogized as 'Red pepper or Irritant spice'.
- By turn of 15th century, cultivation of chilli pepper started widely throughout the world.
- Word 'chilli' is derived from the Mexican word 'chile', which in Mexico & Central America means 'any pepper'.
- In Europe & USA, chilli refers to most pungent peppers, but not to non-pungent cultivars.
- The American Indian word pronounced 'ah-hee', meaning 'hot pepper' was recorded by Columbus in 1493.
- Peppers have been introduced into Spain by Columbus in 1493.
- As per Clifford Ranney (2000), capsicum spice is the dehydrated state of red and occasionally green capsicum peppers.
- Word 'Pimiento' is Spanish word for any pepper.
- The Portuguese carried Capsicum from Brazil to India prior to 1885.
- Term 'chilli' refers exclusively to smaller, hot type fruits of *Capsicum* species.
- Word 'capsicum' originated from Green word '*Capto*' which means bite i.e. biting sensation of hot chilli when consumed.
- Latin word '*Capsa*' meaning a 'box shape of fruit'.
- Portuguese brought capsicum from Brazil to India during 1584.
- China: Major capsicum (bell pepper) producing country.
- India is world's largest producer and exporter contributing 17% of world's total chilli production.
- Major importers of Indian chilli: Malaysia (30%), Bangladesh (20%), EU (18%), Sri Lanka (15%), USA (9%) and UAE (8%).
- In India, among the spices consumed per head, dried chillies contribute a major share.
- Major export is composed of chilli powder, dried chillies, pickled chillies and chilli oleoresin.

- Chilli festival of cv. Hathei is held in Manipur state every year.
- Chilli eating contest is held every year in China.
- Chilli tolerates extremes of climates than tomato and brinjal.
- Maximum production among all spices.
- State having highest productivity: Andhra Pradesh.
- Green chilli is rich in lutein (used to improve eye health) and Vitamin P.
- Giant chillies are richest source of thiamine, vitamin C and fiber (6.8 g/100 g).
- Quality characteristics: Pungency, vit. A and ascorbic acid.
- Green chilli retard cancer due to enzyme 'Asperginae'.
- Buttery *et al.* (1969) 1st identified flavour components of bell peppers.
- Haymon and Aurand (1971) identified 23 flavour compounds in Tabasco pepper.
- Thermal processing destroys flavour compounds.
- Processing increases the capsaicin content many times throughout the fruit.
- Pungency/bitterness: Due to capsaicinoids [capsaicin (more prevalent), dihydrocapsaicin and nordihydrocapsaicin].
- Pungency: Alkaloid capsaicin or capsiculin ($C_{18}H_{27}NO_3$). Maximum in core/septa walls, less in placenta and none in seeds.
- Capsaicinoid contentation is highest at between 20-40 days after flowering.
- Range of vit. C: 113-160 mg/ 100g (green chilli) to 210 mg/ 100g (immature ripe chillies).
- Higher day and night temperature is responsible for higher capsaicin content.
- Pungency in pods increases with increased environmental stress i.e. few hot days.
- Capsicum seeds are free of both capsaicin and colour constituents.
- Nelson in 1920 1st determined the structure of capsaicin (Vanillyl amide of isodecylamic acid).
- In food industries, chilli is used in the form of oleoresin which permits better distribution of colour and flavour.
- Generally, short fruited varieties have higher capsaicin content than long fruited ones.
- Capsaicinoid concentration was determined by High Performance Liquid Chromatography (HPLC).
- Oleoresins are dissolved total extracts.
- Shelf life of oleoresin: 1 year.
- Ethylene dichloride: Solvent for extraction of oleoresin.
- Red colour of chilli is due to capsanthin 30-60% ($C_{40}H_{56}O_3$) and capsorubin (16-18%) while yellow-orange colour is from β-carotene and violaxanthin; purple colour is due to anthocyanin.

- Percentage of capsanthin: 36%.
- Capsanthin is the condensation product of 3-hydroxy-4- methoxybenzylamine and decyclenic acid, which produces highly irritating vapour on heating.
- Major carotenoid pigments of capsicum oleoresin: Capsanthin, capsorubin, β-carotene, zeaxanthine, neoxanthine & lutein.
- Capsanthin & capsorubin are red pigments and high at ripe stages & others like β-carotene and allied pigments are orange to yellow in colour and are formed early.
- β-carotene are incorporated in poultry feed in USA & Mexico.
- Chilli has bidirectional root system.
- In the tropics, peppers are perennials and when grown in sub-tropical and temperate zones are annuals.
- Typical flowers of *Capsicum* spp.: Pentamerous, hermaphrodite, hypogynous.
- Flowers: Protogynous.
- Anthesis time: 5-9 AM.
- Anther dehiscence: Longitudinal and between 8-11 AM.
- Stigma receptivity: On day of anthesis.
- Cross pollination percentage in chilli: 63% (facultative cross pollinated).
- Pollination agents: Bees, ants and thrips.
- Days required from pollination to fruit maturity: 45.
- Natural crossing in field: 7.6 to 36.8% (avg. mean 16.5%).
- Fruit setting percentage: 40-50%.
- Severe fruit drop and poor fruit set occur when temperature beyond 40^{0}C.
- In chilli and sweet pepper, low night temperature (8-10^{0}C and 15^{0}C) increases fruit set and reduces pollen viability leading to development of parthenocarpic fruits (seedlessness).
- Productivity decreases if temperature goes down at 15^{0}C or below.
- Peppers are photoperiod insensitive.
- Long dry periods, high night temperature (>24^{0}C) and high day temperature (>30^{0}C) coupled with low light intensityleads to flower and fruit drop.
- Pollens from matured undehisced anthers can be stored at -5^{0}C at 97% R.H. for 10 days.
- Major chilli growing period in South India: June-October.
- NAA (Planofix) and Tricontinol (Vipul) is used to control flower and fruit drop.
- Type of fruit: Multiseeded berry.
- Seed rate: 400-500 g/ha.
- Seed viability: 2 years.

- Artificially red ripe fruit drying temperature by air blow drier: 54.4^{0}C for 2-3 days.
- If pods are not dried properly may loose colour, glossiness and pungency.
- Critical stages for irrigation: Flowering and fruit development stage.
- Fifteen irrigations are required for capsicum.
- Rains during November-December, results in powdery mildew incidence.
- Isolation distance for hybrid foundation seed production: 400 m.
- Variety with thin pericarp, few seeds and strong pedicle are suitable for drying.
- Three to ten days are required for sun drying to lower moisture from 80 to 10%.
- Ratio of green to dry chilli: 10: 1. While ratio of fresh red to dry chilli: 4: 1.
- Yield of fresh green chillies is 3-4 times higher than that of red-ripe chillies and 6-10 times that of dry chillies.
- Dry chilli generally contains about 6% stalks + 40% pericarp + 54% seeds
- Green chillies and capsicum should be stored between 7-10^{0}C at 90-95% R.H. to enhance shelf life upto 2-3 weeks.
- Storage temperature for dry chilli: 27^{0}C with 65% R.H.
- For whole dried chilli, pods are sliced and dried to 4-6% moisture content.
- Dehydrated peppers are preserved by spraying sulfite solution of 1000-2500 ppm.
- Destalkness in chilli is desirable trait in export.
- Nitrate form of nitrogen is preferred than ammonical form.
- High phenols show resistance to anthracnose.
- Application of paclobutrazol @ 25 mg/litre to soil significantly increased early yield, fruit weight and pericarp weight.
- Number of seed set/ pods is higher with hand pollination than natural pollination involving male sterile lines.
- Pollen grains can be stored for 2-3 days under ambient temperature.
- Pollen grain storage in sealed vial at -5^{0}C for 10 days.
- For export purpose, USA insists on ASTA cleanliness certification.
- Use of Azospirillum @ 2 kg (N_2 requirement) and AM fungus (*Glomus* spp.) @ 2 kg for 3 x 1 m bed size enhances the yield.
- Value added products: Dehydrated chilli, canned chilli, brined/ pickled chilli, fermented chilli.
- Requirements for getting phytosanitory certificate: Farm registration under VegNet, global GAP certificate, packhouse recommended by APEDA, certificate of free from insecticide residues, free from fruit borer, thrips, virus, etc.

Classification based on flower colour:

1. Purple flowered: *C. pubescence* and associated wild species *C. cardenasii*, *C. eximium*.
2. White flowered: *C. annuum*, *C. chinense*, *C. frutescens* (*C. annuum* group), [(*C. baccatum* var. *pendulum* (baccatum group)]. It is introduced to India.

Pungency level in dried red capsicum powder:

- ASTA uses the Scoville Units as measure of pungency.
- There is decrease in pungency from chillies to paprika.
- Pungency level of chillies: 0.1 to 1.4%.
- Bell and Paprika peppers have very low capsaicinoids (< 0.1%).
- Hotness is maximum in *C. chinense* followed by C. *frutescens* and *C. annuum.*
- Cv. Tezpur contains highest amount of capsaicin (4.28%) and dihydrocapsaicin (1.42%).
- Cvs. Tabasco and Greenleaf Tabasco are highly pungent belongs to *C. frutescens.*
- *C. pendulum* grown for pickling is mildly pungent immature yellow-green stage & sold under brand name 'Mild Italian'
- Hotness increases with maturity of fruit.
- Hotness/ pungency of chilli is measured organoleptically in terms of Scoville Heat Units (SHU).
  - Non-pungent bell peppers are rated- 0.
  - Anaheim chilli types are rated from 150-2500 Scovilles.
  - Cayenne and Jalapeno groups are rated from 10,000-18,000 Scovilles.
  - Pungency of Tabasco group is rated at about 40,000 Scovilles.
- SHU values also contains non-pungent phenolic compounds viz. epigenol & lutein.
- 1 ppm concentration of capsaicinoids is equal to 15 SHU.
- Hotness of pure capsaicin: 15,000,000-16,000,000 SHU.
- Hotness of 'Naga chilli (syn. King of chillies) and 'Bhut Jolokia' chilli (*C. chinense*): 10,01,304 SHU.
- Hotness of 'Trinidad Scorpian Bush Tailor' chilli: 14,63,700 SHU.
- Hotness of HP22-B chilli: 1.5 million SHU.

Species	Variety/ accession	Capsaicinoids (%)	SU (pungency scale in 1000's)
C. annuum	Long Red Cayenne	0.55	90
C. annuum	Fresno Chilli	0.32	52
C. annuum	Large Bell	0.06	10
C. frutescens	Tabasco	0.88	144
C. microcarpum	AC-1553	0.58	95
C. chacoense	AC-1256	0.35	57
C. pendulum	AC-1941	0.41	67
C. pubescens	Roja	0.65	107

Remarks:

1. Up to 10: no pungency detectable.
2. 11-30: Mildly pungent.
3. 31-80: Moderately pungent.
4. > 80: Highly pungent.

Heat units of major international chilli varieties

Chilli type	Scoville Heat Units (SHU)
Bell/ Sweet pepper	0-100
New Mexican	500-1,000
Espanola	1,000-1,500
Ancho & Pasilla	1,000-2,000
Cascabel & Cherry	1,000-2,500
Jalapeno & Mirasol	2,500-5,000
Serrano	5,000-15,000
De Arbol	15,000-30,000
Cayne & Tabasco	30,000-50,000
Chiltepin	50,000-1,00,000
Scotch Bonnet & Thai	1,00,000-3,50,000
Habanero	2,00,000-3,50,000
Nagahari (Assam)	>8,55,000

Use of male sterility:

- Chilli and capsicums can be grouped in often cross pollinated crops.
- GMS and CGMS have been commercially exploited for development of F_1 hybrids in chilli.
- Male sterility: A line- male sterile line and B line- maintainer line (male fertile).
- Genic male sterility was 1st reported by Martin and Crawford (1951) in *C. frutescens*.
- CGMS in chilli was 1st discovered by Peterson in 1958 in cv. PI-164835 from India.
- Peterson (1958), Shifriss and Franckle (1971) and Ohta (1973) grouped pepper cvs. as
  1. Male sterile gene (*ms*) cvs. viz. Yolo Wonder, Yolo Y, California Wonder, Delaware Bell, Liberty Bell, Pimento, Log Red Cayenne, Ojisi, Vinedale.
  2. Restorer gene (ms^+) cvs. viz. Floral Gem, Anaheim Chilli, California Chilli, Jalapeno, Puri Red, Serrano & Takanotsume.
- CMS in chilli is maintained through heterozygous pollinator.
- Male sterile (S-) cytoplasm has so far been most commonly used for commercial hybrid development in South Korea.
- Sterile cytoplasm in all capsicum CMS lines originated from 'Seungchon' except for CCA7231, which originated from 'Suwon'.

- Gametocide: FW 450 (0.3% sprayed 1-5 times).
- Male sterility may occur after interspecific hybridization due to chromosomal or Plasmon-genome incompatibility.
- Extensive studies on male sterility: Shifriss (1997).
- Male sterile line possessing '*ms-509*' gene (bell pepper type) (renamed as *ms-10*) was introduced in India.
- CGMS is mostly controlled by major recessive '*ms*' gene interacting with specific 'S'-plasma type.
- A dominant '*Ms*' allele is necessary to restore pollen fertility.

Species:

- The centre for morphological diversity for *C. annuum* is Mexico.
- Capsicums includes 22 wild species and 5 dometicated spp.
- Species having n=13 chromosomes: *C. ciliatum*, *C. scolnikinum*.
- All important peppers cultivars (hot and sweet) belong to the genus and species *C. annuum*.
- Today the most commonly used peppers for dehydration purposes are Cayenne, Chile and Pimiento types.
- Most comprehensive modern source book on genus *Capsicum*: Peppers: The Domesticated Capsicums by Jean Andrews (1984).
- Taxonomic characters of five cultivated species: Greenleaf (1986).
- Ohta (1962) prepared the ideogram of 6 species.
- Centre of origin: Mexico (*C. annuum*); Amazona (*C. chinensis* & *C. frutescens*); Peru and Bolivia (*C. pendulum* & *C. pubescens*).
- Wild forms exist in all but *C. pubescens* is known only in cultivation.
- Pepper types: Bell pepper, Paprika, Pimiento, Jalapeno, Cayenne, Small Yellow Pickling, Cherry, Cubanelle, Hot Banana, Tabasco, Sweet Banana, Small chili, Pepperoncini, Serrano.
- Horticultural classification of peppers in 14 groups: Dr. P.G. Smith (1950), University of California, Davis viz.

Group	Features
Bell pepper	Fruits large, smooth, blocky & blunt; thick fleshed; 3-4 lobed; square or rectangular; fruits greenish yellow, red, purple, white coloured; mostly non-pungent; red pepper fruits have greater concentration of vit. A & C as well as higher sugar content then green fruits; used for fresh market, salad, stuffing, pizza, meat loaf, dehydrated, processed meat & canning purpose shown in text. 1) Non-pungent-a) Green turning red e.g. California Wonder, Yolo Wonder, Florida VR-2, Early Calwonder, Ruby King, Bell Boy, Miss Belle, World Beater. b) Orange- turning red e.g. Golden California Wonder. c) Yellow-turning red e.g. Golden Bell, Rumanian. 2) Pungent-a) Green turning red e.g. Bull Nose Hot. b) Yellow- turning red e.g. Rumanian Hot.

Pimiento	Sub-group of bell pepper; fruits large, heart shaped; green turning red; thick walled; non-pungent; usually processed & used for fresh market, salad, soups, meat loaf, cheese processed meat, stuffed olives & canningfor their intense red colour e.g. Pimiento, Pimiento Perfection, Pimiento Truhart, Pimiento Select, Pimiento Bighart, Pimsan.
Jalapeno	Fruits elongated, round, cylindrical (bullet shaped); smooth with or without corky network on skin; thick flesh, green turning red; highly pungent; used as green pepper, canned, fresh market, sauce purpose e.g. various strains
Cayenne	Sub-group of Anaheim chile group; fruits more slender, thin flesh, wrinkled & irregular shaped, green turning red; highly pungent; used for fresh market, dried powder, hot sauce, pickling purpose, pungent spice shown in text. 1) Red coloured e.g. Cayenne Long Red, Cayenne Long Slim, Cayenne Long Thick. 2) Pasilla: Fruits long, glossy, turning chocolate brown at maturity with rich flavour; used as dried & toasted in sauces 3) Non-pungent form: Used as fresh in salads & culinary purpose e.g. Centinel, Doux Long des Landes
Cherry pepper	Fruits small, spherical having thick flesh, green turning red; used for pickling purpose& salad purpose 1) Pungent e.g. Red Cherry Large, Red Cherry Small. 2) Non-pungent e.g. Sweet Cherry.
Small hot	Fruits slender, thin walled, green turning red; used for fresh green, dried powder for sauces & seasoning purpose 1) Highly pungent e.g. Fresno chilli, Serrano chilli, Santaka and Hontaka chilli
Cuban	Fruits thin walled, irregular shape, yellow-green turning red; used for fresh market, salad, pickle & frying purpose 1) Mild pungent e.g. Cuban, Golden Greekm Cubanelle 2) Non-pungent e.g. Green Italian
Tabasco	Fruits very small & slender, yellow or green to red coloured; most pungent peppers e.g. Tabasco, Greenleaf Tabasco are grown for making Tabasco sauce from red ripe fruits & vinegar sauce from yellow-green immature peppers pickled in vinegar
Squash or Cheese	Fruits small to large; flat or semi-pointed; thick walled; green to yellow coloured; non-pungent; used for processing, canning, pickling, stuffing, culinary purpose e.g. Cheese, Yellow Cheese, Sunny Brook, Frommage, Gambo, Antibois, Rocotillo.
Long wax	Fruits yellow turning red, pointed or blunt; used for fresh, pickled, sauce, relish, canning purpose 1) Pungent e.g. Hungarian Yellow Wax 2) Non-pungent e.g. Sweet Banana, Hungarian Sweet Wax, Long Yellow Sweet.
Short wax	Fruits yellow turning orange-red, smooth, thick walled, tapering; used for fresh, pickled, sauce, processing, cooking purpose 1) Pungent e.g. Floral Gem, Cascabella, Caloro. 2) Non pungent e.g. Petite Yellow Sweet
Long Green Chile (Anaheim group)	Pods long, slender, thick flesh, dark-green turning red; moderately pungent to sweet; used for dehydrated whole pods, powder, canned, sauces & colour purpose. 1) Mod. pungent e.g. Floral Gem, Cascabella, Caloro. 2) Non-pungent e.g. Petite Yellow Sweet
Ancho group	Fruits large, heart shaped, thin walled, mildly pungent; used for dried whole or powdered or fresh, roasted & peeled purpose 1) Green turning to red e.g. Ancho, Mexican Chilli. 2) Green turning to brown-black e.g. Mulato
C. annuum	Fruits very slender, ¼-10 inch long; smooth, varying shades of green to yellow to red, orange, brown colours. 1) Pungent 2) Non-pungent

- Annuum complex consists of *C. annuum*, *C. frutescens* and *C. chinense* which are most commercial peppers in the world.
- Varieties of *C. frutescens* grown in India are still called as 'Bird pepper'.

Species	Features
Capsicum annuum var. *minimum*	Progenitor of chilli
C. annuum var. *annuum* (syn. *C. annuum* var. *longum*)	Chilli of commerce; herbaceous annual, 2 white flowers/ node; blue/ purple anthers; fruit vary in length, fruit colour (red, orange, yellow, brown, violet, black at maturity); pungent; seeds tan/ straw coloured; resistant to southern bacterial blight
*C. annuum*var. *abbreviatum*	Ornamental bush pepper
C. annuum var. *avicular*	Progenitor of bell pepper
C. annuum var. *grossum*	Called as 'Bell/ Sweet/ Bull nose pepper'; large fruits with thick flesh; less pungent, mild flavor; green when immature & different cvs. ripen to yellow, red, orange & black.
C. pubescens	Oldest domestic pepper; it is 'High land pepper' known as 'Rocoto'. Require cool climate (< 5^0C harmful); bushy but can attain tree like appearance; white/ purple petals; purple anthers; 1 flower/ node, fruit become red/ yellow at maturity; seeds black; highly pungent, fruits have thick pericarp & lot of moisture; resistant to PM
C. frutescens (syn.*C. pendulum*)	Called as 'Tabasco pepper'; biennial or perennial; bushy; small fruited & highly pungent; anther colour blue, pale greenish yellow corolla, 2-5 flowers/ node (usually 2), fruit become red at maturity; resistant to root knot nematode, anthracnose, phytophthora, CMV, leaf curl virus, Southern bacterial blight & PM
C. frutescens ssp. *cerasiforme*	Sikkim cherry pepper
C. baccatum	Self pollinated,; white flowers; anthers colour white before dehiscence & later turn brown; 1 flower/ node, prominent calyx teeth & yellow brown spots on corolla; fruits red, orange, yellow at maturity; seeds tan/ straw coloured; source of PM, anthracnose, fruit rot resistance.
C. eximum, *C. cardensii*	Purple flowers; self incompatible
C. angulosum	Found in Peru & south Brazil; resistant to *Verticillium albo-atrum*
C. microcarpum	Resistant to PM & cercospora leaf spot
C. chinense	Most commonly cultivated in S. America; plants have multiple stem, erect habit; fruits long, slender to short and obtuse; anthers blue coloured; white corolla, 2-5 flowers/ node (usually 3); leaves 4 inch long and wide; fruit become red, orange/ yellow/ white at maturity; seeds tan/ straw coloured; extremely pungent e.g. Habanero, Bhut Jolokia; resistant to anthracnose, TMV, leaf curl virus, verticillium wilt & Southern bacterial blight
C. chacoense	Resistant to tobacco mosaic virus, bacterial spot
C.fasciculatum	Resistant to *Verticillium albo-atrum*
C.flexuousum	Perennial; round fruits with cluster erect habit; immune to leaf curl virus
C. minimum (syn. *C. fastigiatum*)	Called as 'Bird's eye chilli'

C. annuum	*C. frutescens*
Include commercially important type viz. Nepal pepper, Cayenne pepper, Hot pepper, Bell/ Sweet/ Bull nose/ Red pepper, Paprika	Bird pepper, Perennial chilli, Pickling chilli, Tobasco pepper
Leaves small & narrow	Leaves large & broad
Flowers small, solitary, pendulous	Flowers large, in clusters & erect
Pedicel to fruit ratio <1	Pedicel to fruit ratio >1
Less pungent (0.1% of capsaicin)	Highly pungent (0.22% of capsaicin) & suitable for oleoresin extraction, sauce preparation
Diploids & polyploids are observed	Only diploids are observed (does not cross freely with other species)

Taxonomic characters of 5 major cultivated spp. of *Capsicum*:

Species	Corolla colour	Corolla throat spot	Corolla shape	Anther colour	Calyx teeth	Seed colour	Flowers/ node
C. annuum	White or purple	None	Rotate	Blue purple	Present	Tan	1
C. frutescens	Greenish white	None	Rotate	Blue	None	Tan	1-3
C. chinense	White to greenish white	None	Rotate	Blue	Present	Tan	1-5
C. baccatum	White	Green yellow	Rotate	Yellow	Present	Tan	1-2
C. pubescens	Purple	None	Rotate	Purple	Present	Black	1

Crossability of *Capsicum* species:

- *C. frutescens*, *C. pendulum* & *C. microcarpum* each have 3 similar karyotypes. Similarity in karyotype corresponds with their crossability.
- The extensive crossability studies done by Smith and Heiser (1957).
- Cross of *C. annuum* x *C. chinense* and *C. frutescens* x *C. pendulum* gives many seeds.
- *C. annuum*, *C. frutescens* and *C. chinense* are currently treated as species complex.
- Hybrids of *C. annuum* x *C. chinense* show higher values of capsaicin, oleoresin and colour.
- Cross between *C. annuum* and *C. frutescens* show one way incompatibility and existence of pre-fertilization barrier.
- Most of the wild species are self compatible.
- *C. cardensii*: Self incompatible.
- Unilateral incompatibility (expressed in stigma) is reported in capsicum.
- Both *C. eximium* and *C. pubescens* are bilaterally compatible.
- *C. annuum* x *C. chinense* and *C. annuum* x *C. frutescens* to develop interspecific hybrids.

Cross	Initial cross	F_1 seed	F_2 seed	Back cross seed
C. annuum x *C. frutescens*	-	-	-	-
C. annuum x *C. chinense*	+ +	+	E	E
C. annuum x *C. pubescens*	-	-	-	-
C. frutescens x *C. annuum*	+	+	+	+
C. frutescens x *C. chinense*	+	+	+	+
C. frutescens x *C. pendulum*	+ +	+ +	+	+
C. chinense x *C. annuum*	+	+	+	+
C. chinense x *C. pendulum*	+	+	-	-
C. chinense x *C. pubescens*	E	E	-	-
C. pendulum x *C. pubescens*	-	-	-	-

E = Seed germinated by embryo culture only; — = No viable seed
+ = Few viable seed; + + = Many viable seed

Barriers in interspecific hybridization:

1. Dwarfism i.e. termination of leaf emergence after bearing of several normal leaves. It is controlled by two complimentary dominant genes with AAbb genotypes in *C. annuum* and aaBB in *C. chinense* and *C. frutescens*. Single nuclear gene of *C. annuum* causes stunted growth in interactions with cytoplasm of *C. chinense*.
2. Abnormal growth i.e. female sterility and shrunken leaves by Virus Like Syndrome (VLS) in *C. frutescens* x *C. baccatum* & *C. chinense* x *C. baccatum*. VLS is due to interaction between cytoplasm of *C. chinense* & nuclear gene from *C. baccatum*.

Varieties:

- Improvement of chilli was started at Lam, Andhra Pradesh as early as 1928.
- At national level, 1st report of hybrid vigour in Chilli was reported by Dr. Deshpande from IARI in 1933.
- Chinese Giant, Spartan: Resistant to fruit rot.
- Tuzluf, Santaka, Mexico Pepper: Introduced from Israel. Resistant to root knot nematode.
- White Khandari, Antibois, Conic: Resistant to bacterial wilt.
- Chinese sweet pepper cv. Haihua-3: Developed by anther culture.
- Black Pearl: Black foliage with erect clusters of small round-red pigmented fruits.
- Bhivapuri (Nagpur)-Chilli has special features viz. late maturity (30-40 days late than others), red colour, non-pungent & storage life up to 1 year. These features are considered during GI ranking.
- DKC-8: Single Plant Selection from OP variety. Upright bearing, cluster bearing, resistant to fusarium wilt.
- Carolina Hot: Selection from cv. Cayenne grown for powder production. It has deciduous calyx, nematode resistant.
- Mississippi Nemahart: Pimiento type, highly pungent, root knot nematode resistant, fruit size not acceptable.

- Cayenne-16: Fruit size 20 cm long, fruit wt. 26 g; used for making sauce. Resistant to TEV, PMV.
- Promising parent for new ideotype: Truhart Pimiento (for fruit size & long pedicel); Rocotillo (for multi-fruitedness & disease resistance).
- Popular in Europe: Hungarian Yellow Wax Hot (grows in cool areas), Italian White Wax (pointed fruits & mild tasting), Jalapino (extremely hot & harvested over a long period), Large Red Cherry (extremely hot with flattended fruits, good for drying & ideal in curries, pickles & sauces), Ring of Fire (produce cayenne-type peppers), Serrano (extremely hot with orange red fruits, prolific yield & fruits can be dried).

Name	Breeding method	Features
Important indigenous cvs.		
Suryamukhi	Selection	Fruit green, 4-5 cm long with blunt apex; erect oriented; less pungent; high ascorbic acid
Bullet	Selection	Fruit short (3-4 cm), conical shape, lettuce green colour, pendent oriented; late maturing & high capsaicin content
Bird's Eye/ Dhani chilli/ African Devil chilli	Selection	Fruits tiny green & bright red coloured when mature; ASTA colour value-41.7; highly pungent; capsaicin 0.589%; grown in Mizoram
Guntur Sannam-S4 chilli	Selection	Fruits long with thick red skin; highly pungent; ASTA colour value-32.11; capsaicin 0.226%; grown in Guntur, Warangal, Khammam districts of Andhra Pradesh
Elaichipur Sannam-S4 chilli	Selection	Fruits dark red coloured when mature; highly pungent; capsaicin 0.2%; ASTA colour value-70.4; grown in Amaravathi, Maharashtra
Nagpur	Selection	Fruits red & pungent; grown in Bhimapur, Maharashtra
Nalchetti	Selection	Fruits red & highly pungent; ASTA colour value-77.03; capsaicin 0.12%; grown in Nagpur, Maharashtra
Jwala chilli	Selection	Fruits long, slender & green when unripe, turning red at ripe stage & highly pungent; capsaicin 0.4%; grown in Kheda, Mehsana, Gujarat
Kashmiri Mirch	Selection	Fruits smooth with shining skin, dark red colour at maturity
Kandhari chilli	Selection	Fruits small, ivory white coloured & highly pungent
Naga Jolokia/ Tezpur chilli/ Bhut Jolokia	Selection	Fruits borne singly, obtuse in shape, turn red at maturity; guiness book of world record confirmed it to be hottest pepper on earth (855,000-104,1427 SR); pesticidal value
Hindpur-S7	Selection	Fruits red, hot & highly pungent; ASTA colour value-33.00; capsaicin 0.24%; grown in Hindpur, Andhra Pradesh
Kandhari White	Selection	Short & ivory white coloured; highly pungent; capsaicin 0.504 %; ASTA colour value-2.96; grown in Kerala & Tamil Nadu
Kashmir chilli	Selection	Fruits long, deep red coloured; capsaicin 0.325%; ASTA colour value-54.10; grown in temperate regions such as H.P., J & K., etc.
Madhya Pradesh G.T. Sannam	Selection	Fruits red & pungent; grown in Indore, Malkapur areas of Madhya Pradesh

Madras Pari	Selection	Fruits pure red & hot; ASTA colour value-73.82; capsaicin 0.21%; grown in Nellore, Andhra Pradesh
Sattur-S4	Selection	Fruits red & highly pungent; ASTA colour value-59.01; capsaicin 0.24%; grown in Dindigul, Theni districts of Tamil Nadu
Scotch Bonnet	Introduction from Jamaica	Fruits short, round, yellowish; ASTA colour value-38.25; capsaicin 0.878%; grown in hilly regions of Kerala, Karnataka
IARI, New Delhi & Regional station, Katrain		
Pusa Jwala (1983)	Pedigree selection from (NP-46-A x Puri Red)	Solitary bearing habit; resistant to leaf curl; thrips, mites & aphids; yield 85 q/ha (green) &18 q/ha (dry)
Pusa Sadabahar (1993)	Pedigree selection from (Pusa Jwala x IC-31339 *C. frutescens*)	Perennial (2-3 years); fruit length 6-8 cm; resistant to CMV, TMV, leaf curl virus, thrips & mites; yield 95 q/ha (green) & 20 q/ha (dry); highly pungent
DH-76-6	Pedigree selection of 'Puri Red x Byadgi Local'	60% seed recovery; seed yield 1.2 q/ha; yield 20 q/ha (dry)
NP-46-A	Pure line selection from indigenous material	Dwarf; tolerant to virus & thrips; yield 75 q/ha (green)
IIHR, Bengaluru and CHES, Bhubaneshwar		
Arka Suphal (2002)	Pedigree selection of 'Pant C-1 x IIHR 517A'	Tolerant to powdery mildew (PM) & field tolerance to virus; yield 25 t/ha (green) & 3 t/ha (dry)
Arka Lohit (1990)	Pure line selection from local 'IIHR 324'	Tolerant to PM & highly pungent; highly pungent (capsaicin 0.71%); yield 25 t/ha (green) & 3 t/ha (dry)
Arka Sweta (2005)	Heterosis breeding using CGMS lines (MSH-149 x MSH-172)	Fruit length 12 cm; tolerant to virusesbutsusceptible to PM; yield 33 t/ha (green) & 5 t/ha (dry)
Arka Meghana (2006)	Hybrid developed by using CGMS line 'MSH-172'	Fruit length 10 cm; mature in 150-160 days; tolerant to PM & virus; yield 33.5 t/ha (green) & 5 t/ha (dry)
Arka Harita (2011)	Hybrid developed by using CGMS line 'MSH-96'	Suitable for stuffing purpose; tolerant to PM & virus; yield 38.2 t/ha (green) & 5.86 t/ha (dry)
Arka Khyati (2011)	Heterosis breeding using CGMS lines (MS-4 x IIHR-3315)	Fruit length 10-12 cm; tolerant to CMV; yield 40-45 t/ha (green) & 5-5.5 t/ha (dry)
Arka Gagan (H-30) 2020	CGMS system based F_1 hybrid	Fruits pendent; highly pungent (1-1.2 lakh SHU); yield of green chilli (10 t/ ha); tolerant to root knot nematode, root wilt & resistant to ChLCV
Arka Tanvi (H-45) 2020	CGMS system based F_1 hybrid	Fruits pendent; pungent (65,000 SHU); yield of dry chilli (10 t/ ha) & green chilli (30-35 t/ ha); tolerant to root knot nematode, PM & resistant to ChLCV
Arka Saanvi (H-19) 2020	CGMS system based F_1 hybrid	Fruits pendent; belong green & dry segment; pungent (60,000 SHU); yield of dry chilli (10 t/ ha) & green chilli (30-35 t/ ha); resistant to ChLCV
Arka Yashasvi (H-8) 2020	CGMS system based F_1 hybrid	Fruits pendent; pungent (50,000 SHU); yield of dry chilli (10 t/ ha) & green chilli (30-35 t/ ha); tolerant to PM, root knot nematode; resistant to ChLCV

Arka Tejasvi (H-41) 2020	CGMS system based F_1 hybrid	Fruits pendent; belong to teja segment; pungent (95,000 SHU); yield of dry chilli (10 t/ha) & green chilli (30-35 t/ha); resistant to PM & ChLCV
Arka Neelachal Prabha	Mass selection	High yield; upright growth; mod. tolerant to anthracnose
Arka Neelachal Agni	Mass selection	High yield
IIVR, Varanasi		
Kashi Surkh (2006)	Heterosis breeding using GMS line [CCA-4261 (non- dehiscent anthers) x Pusa Jwala]	Fruit length (10-12 cm); 85-90 fruits/plant; vit. C (23 mg/100g); 0.5% capsaicin suitable for green & dry fruit; yield 24 t/ha (green); tolerant to thrips, mites & viruses
Kashi Gaurav (2011)	Selection from local collection	Fruits 9-12 cm long; fruit wt. 11 g; tolerant to thrips, mites & anthracnose; yield 15 t/ha (green) & 95-99 q/ha(dry)
Kashi Anmol (2006)	Pure line selection from (K-2) - introduced -from Sri Lanka	Determinate; bushy; fruit length (5.5-7.5 cm); vit C. (40 mg/100g); 0.5% capsaicin; suitable for green fruit production; yield 20 t/ha (green)
Kashi Sindhuri (2009)	Introduction from AVRDC, Taiwan & Selection	Determinate; fruits pendent; non-pungent; high oleoresin content; tolerant to thrips & anthracnose; yield (131-155 q/ha)
Kashi Vishwanath	CMS based hybrid	Yield 20 t/ha; suitable for dry fruit production
Kashi Early	F_1 hybrid of (PBC-473 x KA-2)	Indeterminate; fruit length (9-10 cm); 100-125 fruits/ plant; vit C (45 mg/100g); 0.7% capsaicin; useful for green & dry fruit production; pendent fruits; yield 25 t/ha (red ripe)
VR-338	Mass selection	Indeterminate; fruit length (9-12 cm); 55-60 fruits/plant; vit C (40 mg/100g); 0.3% capsaicin
Kashi Tej (2018)	CMS based F_1 hybrid	Early maturing, mild pungent; tolerant to anthracnose, fruit rot & thrips; green fruit yield (15 t/ha)
Kashi Ratna (2018)	CMS based F_1 hybrid	Fruit contains 0.62% (93450 SHU) capsaicin; vit. C (175.6 mg/ 100 g); vit. C; tolerant to anthracnose & thrips; yield 22 t/ha (green)
Kashi Abha (VR-339) 2019	-	Fruits short stout with blunt apex & highly pungent; tolerant to biotic (anthracnose, CLCV, thrips, mites & abiotic stress (low and high temperature), yield 15 t/ha (green)
ICAR Research Complex for Eastern Region, Patna (HARP, Ranchi)		
Swarna Praphulya (2013)	Pure line selection from local germplasm	Yield 20-25 t/ha; resistant to BW; suitable for pickle purpose
Swarna Tejashwi (2015)	-	Suitable for pickle purpose
Dr BSKKV, Dapoli		
Konkan Kirti (1989)	Selection from 'NP-46-A x JCA-154'	Dwarf, compact; fruit length 7-8 cm; mild pungent; yield 10-12t/ha; suitable for export
VNMKV, Parbhani		
Parbhani Tejas (1992)	Pure line selection from local material	Suitable for rainfed condition; fruits long (22 cm), highly pungent; yield 18 t/ha
Dr PDKV, Akola		
Jayanti (1996)	Selection from 'AKC-86-39'	Yield 18-20 q/ha (red ripe)

Surakta	Pure line selection	Red fruits
AAU, Anand		
GAVCH-1	F_1 hybrid	Fruits elongated straight with pointed blossom end; semi-wrinkle & light green colour; yield 24 T/ha
GARG-1	OP selection	Fruits pungent, elongated, light green coloured; less infection of borer damage & anthracnose; yield 12 t/ha
Gujarat Veg. Chilli-111 (2006)	Selection from 'GVC-111'	Pungent; yield 11-12 t/ha
Gujarat Veg. Chilli-121 (2006)	Selection from 'ACS-97-2'	High ascorbic acid; yield 10-12 t/ha
ACH-30	Hybrid of 'S-5-5 x Punjab Guchechdar'	Fruit length 10.2 cm; 78 fruits/plant
ACH-15	Hybrid of 'S-49 x CDPS-120'	Fruit length 10.4 cm; 100 fruits/plant
ACS-06-2 (2011)	-	Fruits pungent, straight, compact; yield 13 t/ha (green)
MPKV, Rahuri		
Phule Surya-mukhi (1996)	Selection from germplasm	Fruits in clusters & upright, erect; tolerant to thrips & wilt; yield 19 t/ha (green), 22 q/ha (dry)
Agnirekha (1992)	Pedigree selection of 'Dondaicha x Jwala'	For green fruits; yield 25 t/ha
Musalwadi Selection (1991)	Pure line selection from 'Musalwadi Local'	Fruits dark green with black patches; tolerant to die back & PM; suitable for essence & oleoresin; yield 11-12 t/ha (green)
Phule Jyoti (1995)	Pure line selection from local germplasm	Tolerant to thrips, mites, wilt; yield- 250 q/ha (green) & 24 q/ha (dry)
Phule Sai	Pedigree selection of 'Pant C-1 x Kamandalow'	Suitable for rainfed condition; fruits retain colour in storage for 6-7 months; tolerant to thrips, anthracnose & wilt; yield 16 q/ha (dry)
Phule Mukta	Pure line selection	Resistant to PM, fusarium wilt, leaf curl, thrips, mites, lodging
RAU, Bihar		
Sabur Arun	Selection from local germplasm	Long fruits
IGKVV, Raipur		
Indira Mirch-1	-	Early mature; yield 9 t/ha; resistant to bacterial wilt
CSKHPKV, Palampur		
Palam Yellow (2013)	-	Low pungent; suitable for salad purpose
CSAUA & T, Kanpur		
Azad Mirch-1	-	Grown in summer & rainy season; fruits in bunches
Azad Achar Mirch-2	-	Suitable for pickle purpose & high yielding
APHU, Guntur (HRS, Lam)		
G-1 (1937)	Pure line selection from local type 'Nallapadu'	Lengthy pods; sickle shaped; resistant to thrips; yield 40 q/ha
G-2 (1954)	Pure line selection from NP-46A	Calyx cup-shaped; wide adaptability; yield 45 q/ha
G-3 (1962)	Pure line selection from NP-46A	Good retention of red colour; yield 30 q/ha

G-4 (Bhagya-lakshmi) 1968	Pure line selection from Sri Lankan cv. Thohian chilli	Cherry type fruit; tolerant to diseases & pests
G-5 (Andhra Jyoti) 1971	Pedigree selection from 'DG-2 x Bihar cv. B-31'	Cherry type fruit with conical shape; capsaicin (0.65 mg/g); yield 50 q/ha; thick pericarp; tolerant to thrips
CA-960 (Sindhur) 1977	Pure line selection from LIC-44 (Hot Portugal)	Thick pericarp; long pods; capsaicin (0.81 mg/g); mild pungent; seed content 38%; yield 60 q/ha (irrigated); highly suitable for pickle making
LCA-200 (Kiran) 1982	-	Pods long, thin; tolerant to aphids; suitable for rainfed condition; yield 45 q/ha
CA-1068 (Aparna) 1982	-	Leafless; light green fruits; highly pungent; tolerant to thrips & mites; yield 45 q/ha
LCA-235 (Bhaskar) 1985	Pedigree selection from 'G-4 x Yellow Anther Mutant'	Bushy; 45% seed content; yellow anther type; highly pungent; tolerant to mite, thrips & aphids; yield 70 q/ha
LCA-206 (Prakash) 1991	G-3 x Huntaka	Glossy red pods; mild pungent; yield 60 q/ha
LCA-334 (Prasanth) 2006	Selection from 'LCA 334'	Very good for export; pungent; tolerant to mite, thrips & aphids; yield 15-17 q/ha
LCA-305 (Lam-305) 1993	Selection from 'Lam 305'	Tolerant to leaf curl virus; yield 60 q/ha
LCA-625	-	High colour & high pungency (45000-50000 SHU); yield 65-70 q/ha; suitable for dry powder & oleoresins
LCH-111	-	yield 75-80 q/ha; high colour (70-80 ASTA), pungent (25000-30000 SHU)
X-197	G-3 x Assam chilli	Highly pungent; tolerant to thrips
TNAU, Coimbatore		
MDU-1 (1985)	Gamma ray mutant @ 30 Kr to 'K-1'	Dwarf; fruits borne in clusters of 4-9; capsaicin (0.72 mg/g); yield 2 t/ha (dry)
CO.1 (1982)	Pure line selection from local cv. Sattur Sambha	Seed content 55%, sambha type; high capsaicin content (0.72 mg/ g); yield 2 t/ha (dry); suitable for year round cultivation
CO.2 (1984)	Selection from 'Nambiyar local x Gundu type' Ramnad Mundu land race	Seed content 60%, cherry type fruits; capsaicin 0.56 mg/g; yield 2 t/ha (dry)
CO.3 (2001)	Selection from OP progeny from Sri Lankan type	Dwarf; suitable for export; yield 38 t/ha (green)
CO.4 (2000)	Single plant selection	Gundu type; less pungent & suitable for high density planting; yield 3 t/ha (dry)
K-1 (B-72-A) 1965	Pure line selection from Assam local cv. Sattur Sambha	Long sambha type; dark red on ripening; yield 2 t/ha (dry); mature in 210 days; tolerant to thrips; suitable for rainfed condition
K-2 (1985)	Pedigree selection from 'K-1 x Sattur Sambha'	Sambha type; high seed content; yield 12 q/ha (green) & 2 t/ha (dry); high capsaicin 0.49%; tolerant to thrips
PKM-1 (1991)	Pedigree selection of 'Acc. No. 1797 x CO.1'	Dwarf; suitable for irrigated condition; high capsaicin 0.36%; gundu type; yield 3 t/ha (dry)

PKM-2	Pedigree selection of Acc. No. 1797 x CO.1	204 pods/plant; 85 seeds/ fruit; yield 3 t/ha (dry)
KKM-1 (2006)	Pedigree selection from 'Acc. 240 x CO.3'	Dwarf; tolerant to mosaic; resistant to fruit rot
PLR-1 (1994)	Single plant selection from 'Kanchengadu Local'	Gundu type; yield 19 t/ha (green)
TNAU Chilli Hybrid Co 1	Selection 1 x CA97	0.58% capsaicin; mod. resis.to fruit rot; yield 28 t/ha (green) & 7 t/ha (dry)
OUAT, Bhubaneshwar		
Utkal Reshmi	-	Resistant to bacterial wilt
Utkal Ava (2004)	Selection from 'BC-14-2'	Resistant to bacterial wilt; yield 12-14 t/ha (green), 35-50 q/ha (dry)
Puri Red	Local selection	Resistant to mosaic disease
BCKV, Kalyani		
Bidhan Chilli-4	-	Early mature; yield 10 t/ha; suitable for dual purpose (green and dry chilli); resistant to PepLCV
GBPUA & T, Pantnagar		
Pant C-1 (1982)	Selection from 'NP-46-A x Local Kandhari (*C. frutescens*)'	Solitary & upright bearing habit; tolerant to mosaic, leaf curl virus & thrips, bacterial wilt, root knot nematode & suitable for essence & oleoresin; yield 75 q/ha (green); 15 q/ha (dry)
Pant C-2	Selection from 'NP-46-A x Local Kandhari (*C. frutescens*)'	Pendent fruit bearing; tolerant to leaf curl virus
Pant C-3 (2009)	-	Fruits long, tolerant to ToLCV, anthracnose, yield 18 t/ha (green)
PAU, Ludhiana		
Punjab Lal (1987)	Pedigree selection from 'Perennial x Long Red'	Rich in capsaicin; suitable for essence & oleoresin; yield 10-12 t/ha (green); tolerant to spodoptera leaf eating caterpillar, mites, aphids; resistant to CMV, TMV, LCV, wilt, die back, fruit rot & leaf curl.
Punjab Guchhedar (1996)	Selection	Suitable for drying & canning; yield 15-17 q/ha (dry)
Punjab Surakh (1996)	Selection from 'ELS-2'	Multiple disease resistant (leaf curl, TMV, wilt & die back); yield 20-25 q/ha (dry)
CH-1	Hybrid of 'ms-12 (ms-10) (male sterile gene from France (ms-509) x LLS'	Fruits highly pungent (0.83%); 200 fruits/ plant; tolerant to fruit rot & wet rot; suitable for processing purpose; yield 95 q/ha
CH-3	Hybrid of 'Ms-12 x S-2530'	Fruit length more than CH-1; 220 fruits/plant; yield 95 q/ha
CH-27 (2019)	-	Fruits 7.5 cm long; pungent (0.8% capsaicin), rich in colouring matter (242 ASTA units); resistant to CLCV, fruit rot & root knot nematodes; yield 15 t/ha (green)
CCSHAU, Hisar		
Hisar Shakti (H-44)	-	Tall, perennial; highly pungent; tolerant to leaf curl mosaic virus, fruit rot & PM; yield 17-19 t/ha
Hisar Vijay (H-28)	-	Highly pungent; born in cluster; tolerant to leaf curl mosaic virus, fruit rot; yield 15-17 t/ha

CSAUA & T, Kanpur		
Chanchal (1985)	Selection	Highly pungent; suitable for kitchen gardening; yield 15-20 q/ha (dry)
Kalyanpur Red	Selection	Resistant to mites & aphids
JNKVV, Jabalpur		
Jawahar Mirch-218 (1987)	Pedigree selection from 'Kalipeeth x Pusa Jwala'	Dwarf; tolerant to leaf curl & fruit rot; yield 90-100 q/ha (green) & 20-30 q/ha (dry)
Jawahar Mirch-283 (1999)	Selection from local type	Dwarf; yield 80-100 q/ha (green)
SKUA & T, Srinagar		
Kashmir Long-1 (2001)	Selection	Mod. resis. to fusarium wilt; yield 16-18 t/ha (dry)
HS-HP-154 (2009)	-	Fruits 6-7 cm; green chilli yield 15-20 t/ha;
UAS, Dharwad		
HCH-9646	-	Long fruits (10-11 cm); pungent; tolerant to leaf curl complex
KDC-1	Byadagi x *C. frutescens*	Deep red; semi-wrinkled fruits; low pungent; resistant to leaf curl
DC-1007	-	-
UAS, Bengaluru		
Sonia (KBCH-1)	-	-
UHS, Bagalkot		
Varada	-	-
KAU, Vellanikkara		
Jwala Sakthi (1987)	Pedigree selection of 'Vellanotchi x Pusa Jwala'	Low pungent; suitable for green chilli purpose; suitable for HDP; tolerant to leaf curl & leaf spot; ideal for culinary purpose
Jwalamukhi (1987)	Pedigree selection of 'Vellanotchi x P. Triala'	Dark green fruits; less pungent; suitable for HDP; resistant to virus; ideal for culinary purpose
Ujwala (1996)	Selection from 'CA 219-1-19-6'	Highly pungent; resistant to bacterial wilt; tolerant to mosaic & leaf curl virus
Vellayani Athulya (2006)	Selection from local	High yield; shade tolerant
Vellayani Samrudhi	-	Fruits creamy white; mod. pungent; shade tolerant; suitable for homestead cultivation; yield 30 t/ha
Vellayani Thejus	-	Belongs to *C. chinense*; highly pungent, perennial, shade tolerant, suitable for homestead cultivation; yield 30 t/ha
Anugraha (2006)	Hybrid of 'Jwala x Ujwala'	Indeterminate; fruit length 12 cm; fruit wt. 3.6 g; yield 30 t/ha; resistant to bacterial wilt; light green fruits
KAU Cluster	-	Green fruits
Keerthi	-	Medium sized, green long fruits; mild pungent; fruit length 10-12 cm; single fruit wt. 8 g; tolerant to mosaic; yield 11 t/ha
Manjari	-	Resistant to bacterial wilt; popular in Kerala

Private sector hybrids: Tejaswini, Champian, Gayatri, Agni, Delhi Hot, Skyline, Dushera, Fire, Laava, Teja-1, Teja-4, BSS-141, ARCH-236, BSS-138

Genetics of characters:

- Indeterminate varieties had solitary fruits and determinate varieties clustered fruits.
- Immature fruit colour is determined by duplicate gene factor hypothesis (Odland & Porter, 1936).
- Seven semi-recessive additive genes determine multi-fruitedness in *C. chinense*.
- Additive gene action: Capsaicin content, single fruit weight, 100 seed weight, number of fruits/ plant and fruit length.
- Smooth/ hairless (H_1) stem in *C. annuum* var. minimum dominant to hairy stem.
- Plant height, earliness, fruit yield, fruit length, fruit number, fruit wt., pungency: Quantitative characters governed by both additive and non-additive action of polygenes.

Character	Number of genes	Type of gene action
Plant habit	Monogenic	Tall dominant to dwarf
Plant spread	Monogenic	Spreading dominant to erect
Fruit bearing habit	Digenic	Solitary fruiting dominant over clustered fruiting
Fruit orientation/ position	Digenic (*up*)	Pendulous dominant to erect
Fruit colour	3 independent gene pairs (Y & Y^+, C_1 & C_1^+ and $^-C_2$&$^-C_2$)	* Red- Y^+C_1, * Salmon red- YC^+ * Pink- Y^+C_2 * Orange- YC^+ * Lemon yellow- yC^1 * Ivory- yC^2 * White- y
Beta carotene in fruits	Monogenic (*B*)	High expression following interaction with '*t*' gene
Anthocyanin content in leaf	Monogenic (*A*)	Purple colour in leaves, stem, flower & fruit is in completely dominant
High beta carotene	Monogenic (*t*)	Complementary with *B* gene
Brown fruit colour	Monogenic	* Presence of recessive chlorophyll retainer gene *cl*, which prevents complete degradation of chlorophyll; * Presence of chlorophyll with red pigment lycopene gene y^+ produce brown fruit colour
Pedicel length	Monogenic	Short dominant to long
	Polygenic (3 loci)	Long dominant to short
Pungency	Monogenic (*CC* or *Pun1*)	* Pungency dominant to non-pungency; * Modifier genes increase or decrease the contents
	Polygenic	Acting in cumulative manner
Fruit shape	Monogenic (*OO*)	Oblate or round dominant to elongate
Fruit apex	Monogenic (*PP*)	Pointed incompletely dominant to blunt
Flesh texture	Monogenic (*SS*)	Soft flesh, fruit easily separated from calyx is dominant to fruit attached tightly with apex
Fruit lobbing	Monogenic	Multilobed dominant to bilobed fruit
Ascorbic acid content	-	Dominant & additive effect
Multi-fruitedness	Trigenic	Double flowers & more genes to produce 3/4 flowers/ node.

Seedlessness	Monogenic	Seeded dominant to seedlessness
Complete sterility	Monogenic	Complete fertility dominant to sterility
Male sterility	Polygenic	Plasmon-genome nature
Female fertility	Monogenic	Female fertility dominant to sterility
Destalkness	Digenic	Recessive
TMV resistance	Monogenic dominant	Resistant dominant to susceptibility
Tobacco Etch virus (TEV) resistance	Monogenic dominant	Resistance dominant to susceptibility
CMV resistance	Monogenic dominant	
Leaf curl virus (LCV) resistance	Monogenic	Susceptible dominant to resistance
Potato virus X resistance	Monogenic recessive	-
Soft rot resistance	Oligogenic/ polygenic	-
Damping off resistance	Digenic	-
Anthracnose resistance	Polygenic recessive	-
Wilt resistance	Incomplete dominant	-
PM resistance	Trigenic	Resistance dominant to susceptibility
Phytophthora root rot resistance	Both monogenic recessive & dominant in *C. chinense* & *C. annuum* and polygenic in *C. annuum*	Resistance dominant to susceptibility
Bacterial wilt resistance	Monogenic	Resistance dominant to susceptibility
Bacterial leaf spot resistance	Monogenic & 2 recessive genes	Resistance dominant to susceptibility
Cercospora leaf spot resistance	Polygenic recessive	3 complementary genes with both additive & dominant effects
Pepper mottle virus resistance	Monogenic	Resistance recessive to susceptibility
Root knot nematode resistance	Monogenic	Resistance dominant to susceptibility
Pepper huasteco yellow vein virus (PHYVV)	Monogenic	Resistance recessive to susceptibility

Pests, diseases and disorders:

- Chilli is mostly affected by thrips.
- Corkiness in chilli: Due to waterlogging condition.
- Fruit cracking: Reduction in night transpiration.
- Most susceptible to wilt diseases.
- Phytophthora root rot (*Phytophthora capsici*):
- Bacterial wilt (*Ralstonia solanacearum*):
- Bacterial leaf spot (*Xanthomonas campestris* pv. *vesicatoria*):
- Southern bacterial blight (*Pseudomonas solanacearum*):
- Southern blight (*Sclerotium rolfsii*):

- Most harmful species of nematode: *Meloidogyne arenaria*. Drench with *Paecilomyces lilacinus*, *Pasteuria penetrans* and Arbuscular Mycorrhizal fungus (*Glomus fasciculatum*) @ 5 g/litre each.
- 'Fish mouth': A seed with under developed endosperm.
- PAN injury noticed in rapidly expanding leaves. Leaves become bronze, glazed and silvery appearance due to air pollution.
- Pepper mild mottle virus (PMMoV): Serious in green house cultivation.

Name	Casual organism & cause	Vector
Anthracnose/ Die back/ Fruit rot	*Colletotrichum capsici*	Seed borne
Frog eye leaf spot	*Cercospora capsici*	Most common nursery disease
Leaf curl virus (most destructive)	Virus	White fly
Mosaic	Virus	Aphids
Thrips	*Scirtothrips dorsalis*	Transmit chilli leaf curl disease
Blossom end rot	Excessive N + water stress	Non-parasitic cause

Varieties resistant to parasitic and non-parasitic diseases:

Disease	Resistant varieties
Blossom end rot	Avelam, Ikeda
Damping off	Kuban Early, Sal-gochu
Verticillium wilt	Podanok, Buketan
Soft rot, PM, Cercospora leaf spot	Jalapeno
Powdery mildew	Bull Nose, Midway, Spanish Long, World Beater Chilli Long
Bacterial wilt	Kandari, Pungent Pride, Cherry Red, Manjari, Ujjwala, Anugraha

30.4 Paprika

- Paprika or Hungarian paprika belongs to Anaheim chilli group (long green or long red chillies *C. annuum*).
- Paprika is a Hungarian name, used for mild, non-pungent varieties developed in Hungary.
- International spice traders use the term 'paprika' for non-pungent (sweet) red chilli powder.
- Chief producers of paprika: Zimbabwe, South Africa, Spain, Hungary, USA, MoroccoandYugoslavia.
- India exports capsicum colour as paprika oleoresin.
- Paprika contains < 0.1% of capsaicinoids.
- Spanish pimento is the mild or non-pungent variety of chilli or capsicums and dried red pods are valued chiefly for their brilliant red colour and mild capsaicinoid.
- Best paprika (Spanish paprika) contains pungent matter from 0 to 0.0003% capsaicinoid.
- One kg of paprika oleoresin of 100 colour unit = approx.30 kg of Spanish paprika.Most common method used to evaluate paprika colour: ASTA (American Spice Trade Association).

- Colour value ranges from 120 ASTA to 175 ASTA.
- 120 ASTA colour units: Brighter red colour.
- Range of pigment content in paprika powder: 0.1 to 0.8%.

Varieties:

- All condiment paprika cultivars belong to *C. annuum* co-var. *longum*.
- Single Seed Descent method is utilized to evolve high yielding and red coloured lines.
- Kt-8, Kt-18, KTPL-19, Aparna, Pachas Yellow.

Name	Breeding method	Features
Important indigenous cvs.		
Byadagi (Kaddi) chilli	Selection	Skin wrinkled & red coloured after drying; mild pungent & aromatic; capsaicin 0.2%; ASTA colour value- 156.9; grown in Dharwad, Karnataka
Guntur Sannam-S4 chilli	Selection	Fruits long with thick red skin; highly pungent; ASTA colour value-32.11; capsaicin 0.226%; grown in Guntur, Warangal, Khammam districts of Andhra Pradesh
Tomato chilli/ Warangal Chappatta chilli	Selection	Fruits short, dark red when dried; mild pungent; ASTA colour value-125.26; capsaicin 0.17%; grown in Warangal, Andhra Pradesh
IARI Regional station, Katrain		
Kt-PL-19 (1994)	Pure line selection from exotic material 'P-12' from USA	Highly coloured; low pungent (0.05% capsaicin); suitable for oleoresin & powder making; good for export
IIHR, Bengaluru		
Arka Abhir (1995)	Pure line selection from 'Dyavanur Dubba'	Suitable for oleoresin extraction
IIVR, Varanasi		
IVPBC-535	Selection from introduced population of AVRDC, Taiwan	Determinate; semi-dwarf; fruit length (11-12 cm); 50-55 fruits/plant; vit C. (43 mg/100g); non-pungent
APHU, Guntur (HRS, Lam)		
LCA-436	-	Erect and intermediate; fruits medium (6-8 cm); early, high colour (110-115 ASTA) & low pungent (13500-15500 SHU); yield 40 q/ha (dry).
LCA-424	-	Erect & intermediate; fruits are medium (6-8 cm); high colour (110-115 ASTA) & low pungent (15000-16000 SHU); yield 35-38 q/ha (dry).
LCA-620(2014)	-	Erect & intermediate; fruits are medium (6-8 cm); early, high colour (110-115 ASTA) & low pungency (13500-15500 SHU); yield 40 q/ha (dry); 14 t/ha (green)

30.5 Capsicum or pepper

- Eulogized as 'Bell pepper or Sweet pepper or *Shimla mirch*'.
- They were introduced to Spain in 1493, in England by 1548 and central Europe by 1585.
- They are plumpy, bell shaped vegetable, featuring either 3-4 lobes in the fruits (2-5 inches in dia., & 2-6 inches in length), thick flesh in inner cavity with edible seeds and white spongy coat.
- Important constituent of many foods, adding flavour, colour, vit. C and pungency.
- Fruits are glossy and have wide array of colours viz. green, orange, red, yellow, purple, brown to black.
- Main producers of sweet pepper: China followed by Turkey, Spain, Romania, Nigeria and Mexico.
- Warm season crop.
- Rich source of vit. C, vit. A, vit. B6, folic acid and minerals like Mo and Mn.
- Himachal Pradesh is leading supplier of capsicum in off season.
- Highly self pollinated and fruit set is problem during hot and dry season.
- Bell peppers are not hot as they contain recessive genes that inhibits accumulation of capsaicin.
- Anthesis time: 7.15 AM continues upto 11.15 AM.
- Anther dehiscence 30 min. after anthesis.
- Stigma receptivity: From day of anthesis upto 2 days.
- Pollen fertility: 96%.
- Extent of natural crossing: 7.6 to 36.8%.
- Optimum temperature for growth: 25-30^{0}C.
- Optimum temperature for fruit set: (day: 20-25^{0}C) and (night: 15-16^{0}C).
- Higher temperature (32^{0}C) results in flower abortion.
- Planting distance: 45 cm x 45 cm (50,000 plants/ha) and 60 cm x 30 cm (55,000 plants/ha).
- Short day conditions (9-10 h light) stimulates plant growth and increases productivity by 20-24% and quality.
- Flesh thick with non-pungent.
- Fruits blocky, 3-4 lobed, dark green skin colour and scarlet red or orange yellow on maturity.
- Dipping of seedlings in 1.5% single super phosphate solution before transplanting is advisable.
- Nitrate form of nitrogen is preferred.
- Water stressed plants produce more pungent fruits and blossom end rot.

- Preferable soil pH: 5.5-6.8.
- Parthenocarpic fruits are produced.
- Tipping of initial flowers is advocated for higher yield.
- Harvesting stage: Immature (green) stage.
- Fruit stored at 5-10^{0}C and 90-95% R.H. for 2-3 weeks and upto 40 days at 0^{0}C and 95-98% R.H.
- Dipping of harvested fruits in 1-2% potassium bicarbonate reduces decay and stimulates shelf life.
- Anther culture has been used in cv. Arka Gaurav.
- Use of solitary bee *(Osmia cornifrons)* as a pollinator of sweet pepper under green house condition gives more fruit set, enhanced seeds/ fruit, better fruit quality and higher fruit weight.

Varieties:

- Back cross breeding employed at IIHR to incorporate resistance to powdery mildew from *C. baccatum* var. *pendulum*.
- Bharat: 1st F_1 hybrid by Indo-American Hybrid Seed Company (IAHS), Bengaluru in 1973.
- Green Gold: F_1 hybrid by MAHYCO. 3-4 lobed, green coloured.
- Florida VR-4, USA JI-5: Resistant to Pepper Mottle virus, Tobacco Etch virus, PVY.
- Arka Mohini, Arka Gaurav were bred by Dr.D.P. Singh.
- Koral: Highly resistant to white fly.
- Sharp, California Wonder: Resistant to white fly, *M. javanica*.
- No. 82823, Tuzluf: cvs. from Isreal. Nematode resistant and suitable for organic cultivation.
- World Beater, Yolo Wonder, Ruby King, Resistant Giant: Resistant to tobacco mosaic virus, nematode and high yielding.
- Chinese Giant, Yolo Y, Hungarian Yellow Wax, Spartan Emerald: Resistant to anthranose fruit rot (*Colletotrichum capsici*).
- Merrimack Wonder: Resistant to cercospora leaf spot.
- Male sterile cvs.: Allbig, California Wonder.
- Bruinsma Wonder (California Wonder x Sweet Westland). Grown in green house.
- Big Bertha (largest fruits, 18 cm long & 10 cm wide), Calwonder Wonder Early (prolific yielder & grows well in short season), Gypsy (early with slightly tapered fruits), Red Skin (compact & ideal for pots & growbags), Sweet Chocolate (unusal chocolate brown coloured & good for frozen whole).

Name	Breeding method	Features
IARI, New Delhi and Regional station, Katrain		
California Wonder (1975)	Introduction from USA	3-4 lobed with thick flesh; dark green coloured fruits; yield 12-15 t/ha; tolerant to TMV; resistant to Cercospora leaf spot
World Beater, Golden Wonder	Introduction from USA	3-4 lobed with thick flesh; dark green coloured fruits; yield 12-15 t/ha; tolerant to TMV
Sweet Banana	Introduction from USA	Long & sweet fruited; Hungarian type; non-pungent; mod. resistant to bacterial wilt.
Emerald Giant	Selection from 'Keystone Resistant Giant'	-
Chinese Giant (1975)	Introduction from USA	3-4 lobed with thick flesh; dark green coloured fruits; yield 12-15 t/ha; tolerant to TMV
Bull Nose (1978)	Introduction from USA	3 lobed with thick flesh; scarlet red coloured fruits on maturity; yield 10-12t/ha;
Yolo Wonder	Introduction from USA	Vit. C (150 mg/ 100 g); tolerant to TMV & highly resistant to white fly
Pusa Deepti (Kt-1) 1997	Heterosis breeding of ' Yolo Wonder x Reunion Yellow'	Conical shape; cream coloured; tolerant to bacterial leaf spot & anthracnose; yield 25-30 t/ha
Kt-2	Heterosis breeding of 'Yolo Wonder x Russian Yellow'	Resistant to fruit rot
KTCPH-3(2005)	-	Blocky fruits; smooth green coloured; 80 g fruit wt.; flesh thick, sweet
KTCPH-5	Heterosis breeding of 'Yolo Wonder x EC 143570'	Blocky fruits; smooth green coloured; square shaped; fruit wt. 100 g
KTC-1 (2019)	-	Fruits green, fruit wt. 70 g; yield 20 t/ha
IIHR, Bengaluru		
Arka Basant (1986)	Mass selection from Hungarian cv. Soroksari	Creamish white coloured fruits; suitable for kharif & rabi; good export value; yield 15-20 T/ha
Arka Mohini (1986)	Pure line selection from USA cv. Titan	Red coloured fruits on maturity; fruits drooping; yield 18-25 t/ ha
Arka Gaurav (1986)	Pure line selection from 'Golden California Wonder' from USA	Dark green coloured fruits; orange-yellow coloured fruits on maturity; tolerant to bacterial wilt; yield 18-25 t/ ha
Arka Atuyla (2018)	F_1 hybrid	High yield (45-50 t/ha); fruit wt. (100-120 g); tolerant to PM

ICAR Research Complex for Eastern Region, Patna (HARP, Ranchi)		
Swarna Atulya (2013)	Pure line selection from EC-596749	Yellow coloured fruits; fruit wt. 120-130 g; yield 40-45 t/ha; tolerant to PM
DIBER, Pithoragarh		
DARL-70(2013)	-	Fruits green coloured; pendent bearing with 3-4 lobed; tolerant to fusarium wilt & PM; yield 20-22 t/ha
DARL-202 (2003)	-	18-20 fruits/ plant; yield 34-37 t/ha
Dr YSPUH & F, Solan		
Solan Hybrid-1 (2001)	Hybrid	Fruit lobed; bell shaped; yield 30-35 T/ha
Solan Bharpur	OP selection	Tolerant to Phytophthora fruit rot; fruit wt. 50-60 g; yield 30-35 t/ha
VPKAS, Almora		
VL Shimla Mirch-3	Selection	Mature in 70-100 days; suitable for poly house cultivation; 8-12 fruits/ plant; fruit wt. 80-120 g; yield 15-30 t/ha
SK UAS & T, Srinagar		
Nishat-1 (2001)	Selection from 'Capsicum Sel.2'	Indeterminate; yellow coloured fruits; bell shaped; yield 20-22 t/ha
SH-SP-5	-	-

Private sector hybrids- Asha (green), Bomby (red), Early Bounty, Hira, Indra (green), Natasha, Inspiration (red), Lario, Orobelle (yellow), Palodina, Pasarella, Triple Star.

Physiological disorders:

- Twisted fruits with black spots: Boron deficiency.
- Blossom end rot: Excess N and heavy irrigation. Also because of Ca deficiency.
- Skin cracking: Temperature fluctuation and humidity.
- Sunscald: Fruits exposed to long durations of intense sunlight.

30.6 Potato

- Eulogized as 'King of vegetables or Poor man's friend or Poor man's strength or Wholesome miracle food or Food for future or Second bread of the man or Cleaning crop or White Man's yam or European root'.
- World's 3rd major non-cereal food crop grown in >148 countries in the world.
- 4th major food of the world after rice, wheat and maize.
- It is staple food of Ireland.
- India is only country after Japan which has well established national seed production programme.
- Term 'Round revolution' is related with potato.
- Potato was tested as absorbant and reflector of wireless signals in Boeing aircraft in 2012.
- Year 2008: International Year of Potato declared by United Nations.
- CPRI, Shimla: National repository for potato germplasm collection in country.
- International DUS testing workshop was held on 11-12 June, 2018 at CPRI, Shimla.
- Premier Gene Bank of Potato: N.I. Vavilov Institute of Plant Industry at St. Petersburg, Russia.
- Commonwealth Potato Collection (CPC): A unique repository of potato germplasm maintained at Dundee, Scotland.
- About 90% of total potato area is located in sub-tropical plains, 6% in hills and 4% in plateau region of peninsular India.
- Cultivation is confined between 38^0N and 41^0S latitude with more species in southern hemisphere.
- Europe is the largest per capita consumer (86 Kg/year) followed by North America and Latin America and in Asian countries (14 Kg/year).
- Four Agri-Export Zones in India: Punjab, Uttar Pradesh, West Bengal, Madhya Pradesh.
- Major importers of fresh and frozen potatoes: Sri Lanka, Nepal, Maldives.
- Industrial uses: Starch, alcohol, dextrins and glucose.
- Uses: For both fresh market & processing-made into chips, dehydrated, canned, frozen and used for starch and flour.
- Used extensively around the world as livestock feed and in production of vodka, paste and dyes.

- Potatoes grown commercially in the world are marketed in processed form including frozen potato products (31%), chips (13%), dehydrated (8%) and canned (1%).
- Other uses include seed potatoes (7%) and livestock feed (1%). Shrinking and other losses amount to about 8%.
- Culled and surplus potatoes are fermented into ethyl alcohol and mixed with gasoline as a fuel alcohol source.
- Worldwide, the USSR leads in production (grows 28% of the crop), followed by China, Poland, USA, India, Germany and France.
- Important crop for higher population areas of Asia because it produces more dry matter food.
- Freeze dried processed potato 'chuno' is used in Peru to feed the troops and miners.
- Only 2-3% of world potato production is traded internationally.
- Asia's share is export and import of potato is only 9.8 and 11.6%, respectively.
- World's average productivity: 17.18 T/ha.
- Highest productivity: New Zealand (16.49 T/ha).
- India ranks 3rd in both, area and productivity of potato.
- India occupies 10% area and 12% production in the world.
- India tops the productivity, if it is expressed as production/ solar radiation hour/ ha.
- Per capita availability in India: 17.7 kg which is 1/3rd of world average.
- Highest area and production in Uttar Pradesh.
- India's average productivity: 22 T/ha and highest in Gujarat (25.4 T/ha).
- Physiological potential yield: 120 T/ha.
- India utilizes only 7.5% of the total production for processing as against 30-67% in leading potato-processing nations such as the USA, Canada and Europe.
- Maximum area under potato is in Indo-Gangetic plains i.e. alluvial soil.
- Main planting season in Indo-Gangetic plains: October-March.
- It contains practically all the essential dietary constituents, except fat-soluble nutrients.
- Produces more food, more edible energy and proteins per unit area and time than other crops.
- Potato supplies about 2 ½ times more calories than wheat and rice.
- Potato is a low energy food, but when it is fried, it becomes rich in energy (200 g boiled potato-138 Kcal; French fries- 597 Kcal and 50 g chips- 239 Kcal energy).
- Due to high protein-calorie ratio (17 g protein: 1000 Kcal) and short vegetative cycle, potato yield substantially more edible energy, protein, dry matter per unit area.
- Biological value of protein (71% of whole egg) is better than wheat (53%), pea (48%), beans (46%).
- Potato contains 22.6% -CHO, 1.4-2% protein, 0.3% fat, 17 mg/100 g vit. C, 568 mg/ 100 g potassium, and 1.1% crude fibre.

- It is very low in phytic acid content.
- Beta-carotene content in tubers: 111 µg /100 g fresh tuber weight.
- Starch percentage: 60-80% is primary storage of carbohydrate in tuber accumulating upto 70% dry matter.
- Enzyme responsible conversion of starch to sugar: Glucose-1-phosphate.
- Amylase content of starch is regulated by enzyme Granule Bound Starch Synthase-1 (GBSS-1).
- Dicot, thermosensitive and C_3 plant.
- Crop of temperate region and highly susceptible to frost.
- In tropics and sub-tropics, flowering and berry setting occurs only at high altitude (1500 m MSL).
- Potato is long day plant but cultivated as short day plant in India during winter and crop duration of 90-100 days.
- In Europe, it is grown in summer with long photoperiod and long duration of 140-180 days.
- In India, it is grown as summer crop in hills and winter crop in sub-tropical and tropical regions.
- 82% potatoes are grown in plains during winter (October-March), 10% in hills uder long day during summer (April-September) and rest 8% in south eastern peninsular India as rainfed crop (July-October).
- It was introduced from Europe to India in 17th century (1665) by Portuguese.
- It is grown in all states except Kerala.
- Research on potato was started at IARI in 1935.
- In potato based cropping system, 300 % cropping intensity can be achieved.
- Morphological (distinctive) parts of tuber: Periderm (bark/ skin), cortical tissue stores starch (cortex), pith (inner medulla), array of buds (apical & lateral eyes).
- Basically self pollinated but cross pollination occurs due to protruding stigma & self incompatibility and propagated by vegetative means.
- Pollination agent: Bumble bee (*Bombus* spp.) and honey bee (*Apis* spp.) and wind.
- Flower: Actinomorphic, hypogynous & consist of tubular or fused corolla with 5 lobes, together with whorl of 5 stamens alternating with corolla lobes and attached to tube.
- Flower has multi-ovular gynoecium.
- Flowering genotypes are male sterile.
- Inflorescence type: Flowers are initiated in clusters or cymes at the top of plant in leaf axil.
- Blossom colour ranges from white to purple or combination of colours.
- Anthesis time: 5-8 AM.
- Optimum pollen load is necessary for maximum seed set.

- Fruit: Berry with two chambers containing 50-200 small, flat, oval seeds.
- Periderm: Thin outer protective layer (skin) of tuber.
- Two types of stems are produced- aerial and under ground (stolon).
- Tuber arises as terminal enlargement of stolon and tuber enlarges after the stolon has ceased to grow.
- The bud end of tuber represents the growing point of original stolon.
- Flowering arrangement is determinate in character.
- Tubers contains lenticels (respiratory structures).
- Tubers are morphologically underground stem, which bears eyes/ buds and develop into haulms.
- Tubers are formed on distal end or tip of stolons (appearing from base of haulms or underground side shoots) & may occasionally develop along the stolon itself.
- Stolon: Lateral stem growing horizontally below ground from the buds of underground stem.
- Stolons arise from stem tissue, while true roots arise at the base of stem.
- Basal end or heel end: End of potato tuber attached to stolon.
- Opposite end: Called as apical/ rose/ distal end.
- As the plant grows, stolons thicken at their ends and produce new tubers.
- Initial thickening of tubers results from rapid cell division in the centre or pith.
- As tubers mature, periderm becomes tougher, starch content increases and water content decreases, resulting in increase in specific gravity (dry weight of tubers).
- At maturity, tubers go into rest period for 1-3 months.
- When tubers first emerge from rest period, eyes exhibit strong apical dominance.
- Aerial stems or haulms are angular, pubescent/ glabrous, green or purple in colour.
- The haulms may contain anthocyanin pigments in them when tuber is green coloured.
- Skin colours of potato: White-cream, yellow, orange, red and purple.
- Anthocyanin content: 508 mg/ 100 g fresh weight.
- Anthocyanin imparts red, pink, purple colour to skin and flesh.
- Red colour is due to acylated glycosides of pelargonidin.
- Purple tinge is due to acylated glycosides of pelargonidin with acylated glucosides of malvidin, petunidin, peonidin and delphinidin.
- Sugar free potato: Potato stored at 10-12^{0}C have low level of sugars. They are sold as 'Diet potato' and '*Pahari Aloo*'.
- Potato is alkaline yielding food.
- Tubers from light soils have shape and colour of the variety while tuber from heavy/ red soils have darker/ reddish tinge on their skin.
- Unique reproductive feature: Flowers only under long days.
- For best yield, potato needs long day conditions during growth and short day conditions during tuberization.

- Long day promote top growth & stolon growth and extend the period taken for tuber initiation.
- Effects of short days: Supression of vegetative growth, flowering, induction of earliness and profuse tuberization.
- Number of tubers per plant is higher at low temperatures but tuber size remains smaller.
- Crop is highly sensitive to high temperature.
- Optimum temperature for periderm formation (i.e. cork cambium develops new protective layer): 15-20^{0}C.
- Optimum temperature for tuberization: 20^{0}C.
- Optimum tuber production is obtained at 15.5-18.3^{0}C with maximum average temperature of 23.8^{0}C and minimum of 7.2^{0}C.
- Maximum tuber yield occurs at soil temperature of 15.5-23.8^{0}C.
- Soil temperature >28.8^{0}C leads to no tuber formation.
- High soil temperature during tuber enlargement period causes internal discoloration.
- High night temperatures are more detrimental to tuber yield than high day temperature.
- Generally potato is raised in India when maximum day temperature is <35^{0}C and maximum night temperature <20^{0}C.
- Most of varieties do not tuberize when night temperature is >23^{0}C.
- Potato sprouting is best at 22-34^{0}C.
- Water requirement per growing season: 350-550 mm i.e. 2.5 cm of water/ week.
- Critical stages of irrigation: Emergence, stolon formation, tuber bulking.
- Drip irrigation: Efficient method with 20-30% increase of tuber yield.
- Up to 25 days, weeds cause 20-70% tuber yield loss.
- Predominant weed: *Chenopodium album*.
- Optimum soil pH: 5.2 to 6.4 and for scab problems soil reaction should be near 5.0.
- Paired row planting is new practice.
- Earthing up is done up to 40 days after sowing when plant reaches 15-22 cm height.
- Excess N delayes tuber initiation, onset of linear phase of tuber growth & delays maturity.
- Calcium ammonium nitrate and Ammonium sulphate are good source of nitrogen.
- Single Super Phosphate and Di-Ammonium phosphate are best source of phosphate for tuber development.
- KCl @ 2% at 50 to 70 days after planting is highly effective.
- Potassium sulphate (K_2SO_4) is better than Muriate of potash (KCl) for quality improvement.
- Solanin: 5 mg/100 g.
- Potato is unfit for consumption, if solanin is greater than 20 mg/100g.

- Potato tuber dormancy: 8-10 weeks.
- To break tuber dormancy, seed can be dipped in 1-5 ppm postassium gibberelate solution for 5 min. This treatment increases CO_2 level inside the tubers, which promotes sprout growth.
- Planting of whole seed potatoes produce heavier set and small tubers than cut seed.
- Crop grown in ridged rows prevent sun greening of developing tubers.
- Ridging/ hilling on heavy soil also promote stolon growth, better tuber development and easy harvesting.
- Hills accounts for only 5% of area under potato.
- Most popular method of planting: Ridges and furrow at 60 cm x 20 cm.
- Quality for culinary purposes:
  - Dry matter content is important measure of quality for best utilization.
  - Measured (with hydrometer) by specific gravity or density of tubers.
  - Potato tubers with high specific gravity contain more dry matter & preferred for baking, chipping, dehydrating & making frozen products.
  - Potato tubers with low specific gravity are preferred for canning.
  - Tuber dry matter influences oil content of potato chips.
  - Higher the dry matter, lower the oil level in finished product.
  - Potatoes used for boiling are intermediate in specific gravity measurement.
- Primary flavor compound: Methinol.
- Major problem associated with potato processing: Loss of methinol.
- Indian processing industry consumes 4 % of potato for processing.
- Currently 7-8% of non-marketable potatoes go waste due to non-availability of indigenous technology for their utilization.
- Phenols causes brown colour to chips and forms carcinogenic compound 'acrylmide'.
- Requirement for processing (chips):
  - Uniform grade tubers (45-85 mm for chips & >75 mm for French fries).
  - High dry matter (> 20%);
  - Low reducing sugar for chips (<0.15% or <100 mg/100 g) & for French fries upper limit as high as 0.5%.
  - High amylase to amylopectin ratio. Otherwise colour of processed product becomes dull;
  - Low glycoalkaloid content (< 15 mg/100 g);
  - Specific gravity (> 1.080);
  - Long dormancy;
  - Acceptable chip and fry colour score (< 3).
  - For canning purpose, small sized potato containing 18-20% dry matter with waxy texture are preferred.

Quality requirement of potato for processing:

Character	Chips	French fries
Tuber shape	Round to oval	Long oval
Tuber size	45-90 mm	> 90 mm
Eyes	Shallow	Shallow
Specific gravity	> 1.080	> 1.080
Dry matter (%)	> 20	> 20
Reducing sugar at harvesting	< 0.1%	< 0.2%

Potato utilization characteristics:

Specific gravity	Total dry matter	Cooked texture	Best use
< 1.06	< 16%	Very soggy	Frying, salads
1.06-1.07	16-18%	Soggy to waxy	Frying, salads
1.07-1.08	18-20%	Waxy	Boiling
1.08-1.09	20-22%	Mealy	Baking, mashing
> 1.09	> 22%	Very mealy	Baking, French frying

- Seed tuber: Extreme genetic uniformity and ease of raising vigorous crop.
- Seed tuber constitutes >50% (1/3 to ½) of cost of cultivation.
- Development of sprouts from seed tuber meant for seed is called as 'Chitting'.
- Optimum size of seed tuber: 30-40 g (3-5 cm dia. having 2-3 spouts).
- Seed potato certification program was initiated in 1913 in the US and in 1914 in Canada.
- Breeder's seed production started at Shimla and Kufri during 1935. It is beginning of seed potato industry in country.
- Seed Plot Technique (SPT) was developed by Dr. Puskarnath (1965).
- SPT was developed for multiplication of seed tubers in low aphid period (free from viruses) in north Indian plains i.e. 1st week of October-January.
- Dehaulming (removal of aerial portion of plant i.e. haulm, when the plant turns yellow) is done so as to stop the plant's vegetative growth. It is done 10-12 days before harvesting (end of December to 1st week of January in hills and mid August in plains) to avoid aphid population reaches critical level (ETL) i.e. 20 aphids/ 100 compound leaves.
- Tubers are soaked in 1% thiourea + 1 ppm GA_3 for 1 hr to break tuber dormancy.
- Seeds extracted from berry are sexual seeds or botanical seeds or TPS.
- True Potato Seed (TPS) concept was putforth by Dr. S. Ramanujan (1st Director of CPRI).
- TPS is botanical seed produced through sexual reproduction (selfing and sibmating) e.g. HPS-1/13, TPS C-3 and 92-PT-27 are high yielding population of TPS.
- TPS is botanical seed produced through sexual reproduction (selfing and sibmating) e.g. HPS-1/13, TPS C-3 and 92-PT-27 are high yielding population of TPS.

- TPS offers cheap alternative to the costly seed tuber.
- In TPS technology, single plant produces 50-100 berries, containing 150-200 seeds/ berry.
- 1500-2000 seeds weigh 1 g TPS.
- Advantages of TPS technique:
  - Plants obtained from TPS seeds are genetically homozygous.
  - TPS offers cheap alternative to costly seed tuber.
  - Easy to store & transport.
  - Elimination of tuber borned diseases and pests.
  - TPS made possible by extending photoperiod by 4-5 h in sub-tropical plains, where potato normally does not flower.
  - TPS can be stored at ambient temperature and under low humidity for 2-3 years.
- Major hindrances in TPS technology:
  - Low germination,
  - Heterozygous nature of progenies,
  - Production of non-uniform tubers,
  - Long duration of transplanted crop (15-20 days more to mature),
  - Limited choice of hybrids,
  - TPS population and TPS based production technology is cumbersome.
- True seed form is maintained at 10-15^{0}C.
- Freshly extracted TPS has dormancy of 5-6 months.
- Breaking seed dormancy of TPS: Dip in 1500-2000 ppm GA_3 for 48 hours.
- Sibmating is resorted in diploid species which are self incompatible.
- Number of years taken from hybridization to release of variety: 10-12 years.
- Sugar % in table potatoes: 250 mg/100g.
- Potato is beset with problem of low seed multiplication rate (1:6) per generation.
- TPS seed rate: 100-120 g/ha.
- Seed rate: 800-1500 kg/ha of seed tubers.
- Aeroponic: Plants grown in closed environment by spraying roots with nutrient rich solution.
- CPRI, Shimla has developed aeroponic technique for seed production.
- Eyes are found in spiral pattern and concentrate towards apical end.
- 'Eyes' of potato tubers are stem buds and contain axillary buds.
- Best stage for planting: Multiple sprouting.
- Main obstacles of seed formation:
  - High degree of male sterility with no viable pollens;
  - Few sterile pollens and hence fruits/ berries are not formed;
  - Self incompatibility;

- o Low pollen production;
- o Bud and flower crop before or after fertilization.
- Selfing or inbreeding leads to loss of vigour in progenies and non-flowering.
- Pollen storage: Dried pollens can be stored in sealed glass or plastic vial at 0^0C for 1-2 months.
- Berry setting in successful crosses is in 5-7 days.
- Blocky seed pieces with one or more well developed eyes are used to propagate.
- Seed pieces can be cured to suberize (to form corky protective layer) and heal.
- Suberization: Process of sealing off wounds, cuts, and general skin damage that occurs during harvest.
- Suberization is accomplished by holding cut seed pieces at 12.7-18.3^0C for 3-5 days in atmosphere of 85% R.H. and good ventilation.
- Seed tuber: Extreme genetic uniformity and ease of raising vigorous crop.
- Presprouting increases physiological age of seed tuber and results in hastening of emergence.
- Seed tubers after removal from cold storage are kept in diffused light for 10-15 days for presprouting.
- Presprouts should be short, thick and green.
- Little tubers: Small sized (0.3-1.0 g) tubers produced on aged mother tubers.They are offer virus free, cost effective and alternative planting material. Little tubers can be planted directly in field at half the normal spacing (60 x 10 cm) with yield performance at par with that of normal seed potato tubers (40-60 g and 60 x 20 cm).
- Low temperature exposure at 2-4^0C and repeated desprouting (3 times) during storage at 18-20^0C for production of little tubers.
- About 12 little tubers (0.25-0.50 g or more) can be produced on a single mother tuber in more than 1 year.
- Time taken for little tuber production is more than 1 year.
- Little tubers show very long dormancy period (115-132 days) compared to normal (57-65 days).
- Microtuber: Miniature tubers developed under *in vitro* conditions.
- Microtubers planted at 50/m^2 in nursery used as breeder's seed production programme.
- Each microtuber yields 13 minitubers of 10 g average weight.
- Minitubers: Small tubers of 5-20 mm dia., produced *ex vitro* obtained by *in vitro* or microtuber.
- Microtuber production has been scaled up using bio-reactor technology in Hindustan Lever Ltd., Mumbai.
- Microtuber yield less than mini tubers or normal tubers.
- Yield of minitubers: 52,900 tubers from single plant in 3 years.

- Yield of traditional breeder's seed: 2250 tubers in 4 years.
- Both conventional and hi tech microtuber- minituber production system take 7 years to produce certified seeds.
- Three crops/ year can be taken in Nilgiri hills [spring (Mar-April sowing and July-August harvest); summer (February-March sowing & July-August harvest) and autumn (September sowing & December harvest)].
- Maturity index: Drying of foliage and specific gravity.
- Harvesting of potato: 10-15 days after haulm cutting when tubers become thick and firm.
- Harvesting of potato done at < 30^0C to avoid charcoal rot disease.
- Harvesting is completed by end of January in central and eastern plains and 15th February in western plains to avoid rotting of tubers due to high temperature.
- Potato harvesting in north hills: September-October.
- Delayed harvesting (beyond 3rd week of February) results in soft rot and charcoal rot disease.
- Specific gravity for harvesting: 0.98-1.02.
- In warehouse, potato is stored at 8-10^0C and 80% R.H.
- For processing purpose, potato is best stored at 7^0C.
- Seed treatment by dip in 2% boric acid for 15 min to protect against surface borne diseases.
- Desired diameter of tuber for chips making is 6-8 cm.
- For low sugar content, they are stored at 5-10^0C.
- For long storage, they are stored at 10-15^0C.
- Clamps (sand brick kiln soil): Traditional method of storing potatoes in India.
- Pieces of seed tubers can be directly planted or stored for 7-20 days at 15-22^0C with high R.H. to induce suberization (reduces decay after planting).
- Storage comprises 3 phases: Curing, holding and removal period.
- Curing, a post harvest treatment given to tubers helps in suberization of outer tissue.Initially tubers are held at 12.7-15.5^0C with high humidity and good ventilation for 2-3 weeks.
- Holding: Tubers for seed or table stock are held at 3.3-4.4^0C for extended storage. Potatoes for processing are held at high temperatures to prevent accumulation of reducing sugars. Tubers for chipping are held at 10-12.7^0C and for frozen or dehydration are stored at 5.5-7.2^0C with 92-95% R.H. and good ventilation to provide oxygen for respiring tubers.
- Removal period: Tubers are given warming treatment of 10-15.5^0C for 2-3 weeks before removal from storage to recondition of tubers i.e. reduce damage/ to reverse changes of starch to sugars due to holding period.

- Commonly used sprout suppressants: Maleic hydrazide, IPC (isopropyle-N-3-phenyle carbamate) or CIPC (chlorpropham i.e. Chloro Iso Propyle Phenyl Carbamate), tetra-chloro nitrobenzene alcohols, abscissic acid @ 25 mg a.i / kg of tubers.
- Maleic hydrazide (MH) is sprayed on green foliage 2-4 weeks before harvest.
- CIPC inhibits sprouts by interfering with spindle formation.It is applied after harvest in holding period during storage.
- CIPC is marketed in India by tradename 'Oorja' and its residual level prescribed by European Potato Association (EPA) is 30 ppm (i.e. 30 mg/ kg of tuber).
- Cold temperature at 2-4^{0}C also inhibits sprouting but not feasible in storage since conversion of starch to sugars reduces tuber quality for processing.
- 'Oorja' dose: 30-35 ml for fogging 1 ton of potatoes and safe for consumption 3-4 weeks after treatment.
- Water stress encourages secondary growh called knobbiness and it affects processing quality.
- Spray 2,4-D @ 250 ppm to control berry drop which is common in hybridization.
- New anti-sprouting agent contains modified alfa, beta unsaturated keytones.
- Printed plastic bags are used to reduce light transmission to potato tubers.
- Plastic woven ventilated bags of 50 kg capacity are used for potatoes.
- Pre-planting herbicides: Fluchloralin and Pendimethalin.
- Pre-emergent herbicides: 2,4-D, Alachlor, Atrazine, Simazine, Isoproturon.
- Post emergent herbicides: Paraquat and Propanil.
- Maintenance of germplasm: *In vivo* clonal propagation (*S. tuberosum* & *S. andigena* accessions are maintained and multiplied), *in vitro* clonal propagation, sexual.
- Genes of *S. demissum* have been incorporated into >50% of world's cultivars for resistance to late blight and PLRV.
- Pollen grains remain viable for 1 year at -24^{0}C and at 2.5^{0}C for 1 month.
- Shoot culture method is restrictd mainly to non-commercial dihaploid clones.
- Potato genome sequencing consortium (for late blight) deciphered the 727 Mbp long potato genome.
- Genes responsible for tuberization have been established.
- 1st report of *Agrobaterium* mediated gene transfer in plants in 1983.
- Information on potato genome sequence is available on www.potatogenome.net.
- Potato Yield Estimator: Tool uses radiation and temperature data.
- Potato Pest Manager: PC based tool identification and solution to problem.
- 3rd edition of Global Potato Conclave held at Gandhinagar, Gujarat on 28-31st Jan, 2020.

Species:

- Genetic structure is very complicated and contains 39,000 genes and about 2622 genes have been identified.
- Maximum species diversity is found in Andes, South America. Of 2,000 known species, only 235 produce tubers and only *S. tuberosum* is widely cultivated.
- Wild potato tubers are bitter in taste and contain toxic steroidal alkaloids.
- Wild potato typically occurs between 2000-4000 m MSL.
- Resistance against pest and disease problems is being studied in context of climate change.
- Probable ancestor of *S. tuberosum*: *S. stenotomum* (2n=24) which originated from wild. spp. *S. leptophyes* (syn. *S. brevieaule*).
- Other progenitors of present day cultivated potato: *S. sparsipilum* (2n=24), *S. acaule*, *S. megistacrolobum*.
- Commonly cultivated *S. tuberosum* is autotetraploid (2n=4x=48) or segmental allopolyploid. These varieties are highly heterozygous and pollen sterile.
- Ploidy level of tuber bearing species varies from (2n=2x=24) to (2n=6x=72) with 73% diploids, 15% tetraploids, 4% triploids, 2% pentaploids and 6% hexaploids.
- The species *S. tuberosum* and *S. andigenum* are crossable.
- Diploid and tetraploid species are highly tolerant to *Myzus persicae*.
- Hybrids between *S. commersoniana* & *S. chacoense* are immune to charcoal rot.
- Late blight resistant species spp. are found in Mexican genepool where this fungus reproduces sexually.

Name	Breeding utility
S. stenotomum	Diploid (2n=2x=24)
S. x *curtilobum*	Pentaploid (2n=5x=60); resistant to frost, PVX & root knot nematode
S. tuberosum var. *tuberosum*	Known as White/ Irish/ English potato; present day cultivated tetraploid spp. adapted to long days; selection from *S. tuberosum* ssp. *andigena*; grows at sea level; evidence show's that S. tuberosum is a man-made, synthetic species and it is not found wild.
S. tuberosum var. *andigena*	Wild spp from Peru; tetraploid spp.adapted to short days; resistant to PLRV, PVY, PVX, root knot nematode, cyst nematode, late blight & cold induced sweetening
S. demissum	Wild spp. from UK; hexaploid; resistant to late blight, PLRV, PVA, PVY, cold induced sweetening & Colorado beetle
S. bulbocastanum	Triploid; grows in very seasonal wet/ dry climate; resistant to late blight,dry rot, soft rot, aphid,heat & drought
S. antipoviczii	Triploid; resistant to late blight,dry rot, soft rot, aphid, heat & drought
S. stoloniferum	Tetraploid; wild donor resistant to late blight, PVA, PVY, PVX, frost, Colorado beetle & aphids
S. verrucosum	Diploid; resistant to late blight in India
S. anomalocalyx, *S. jamessi*, *S. saltense*	Resistant to early blight

S. microdontum	Resistant to bacterial blight, late blight, bacterial wilt, common scab, verticillium wilt, root knot nematode & heat
S. chacoense	Non-dormant; diploid wild species, tolerant to high temperature, resistant to bacterial blight, late blight, common scab, bacterial wilt, tuber moth, Colorado beetle, root knot nematode, PVA, PVX, PVY, charcoal rot
S. acaule	Tetraploid; resistant to wart, fusarium rot, PLRV, PVX, frost, root knot nematode, potato cyst nematode & spindle tuber viroid
S. spegazzinii	Wild species resistant to charcoal rot, late blight, tuber moth, PVA, PVY, root knot nematode, fusarium, wart & cyst nematode
S. vernei	Diploid; high starch content; resistant to potato cyst nematode & frost
S. berthaultii	Resistant todry rot; potato cyst nematode, wart, PLRV, PVX, aphid, Colorado beetle & spindle tuber viroid
S. buthaltii, S. jopetalum, S. guerreroense	Resistant to dry rot
S. hjertingii	Lack of tuber blackening & resistant to dry rot
S. maglia	Resistant to drought & heat
S. ajanhuiri	Diploid; resistant to frost
S. multidissectum	Resistant to 2 species of *Heterodera* nematode, aphid & frost
S. commersonii	Non-dormant; tolerant to high temperature; resistant to Colorado beetle & frost
S. albicans, S. jamesi	Resistant to cold induced sweetening; Colorado beetle
S. phureja	Diploid (2n=2x=24); non-dormant; high protein content; used as pollinator to develop dihaploids; contributes multiple crops per year; resistant to bacterial wilt, fusarium wilt, black scurf, root knot nematode, PVX & PVY
S. rybini	As bridging species with *S. tuberosum* & *S. demissum*
S. x *chaucha* (*S. tuberosum* ssp. *andigena* x *S. stenotomum*)	Triploid (2n=3x=36)
S. brachistotrichum	Resistant to *M. persicae*
S. simplicifolium	Used as bridging ssp. with *S. acaule* & *S. tuberosum*
S. polyadenium	Resistant to Colorado beetle
S. lignicattle, S. medians, S. marinaserse, S. infundibuliforme	Resistant to aphids
S. capsicibaccatum, S. gourlayi. S. boliviense, S. cardiophyllum, S. sucrense	Resistant to potato cyst nematode
S. sparsiphyllum	Resistant to root knot nematode, bacterial wilt & PVX
S. ajanhuiri, S. boliviense, S. brachistotrichum, S. brevidens, S. canasense, S. chomatophilum, S. raphanifolium , S. tolarapanum	Resistant to frost
S. megistacrolobum, S. papita, S. pinnatisectum	Resistant to late blight, heat & drought
S. tarijense	Resistant to heat, drought & PVX
S. colombianum	Grows in high altitude grassland
S. candolleanum	Grows in upland rain forest

Varieties:

- Potato breeding aims at short stolons.
- Generation raised from true seeds show high inbreeding depression and are highly variable & heterozygous.
- Pure line breeding is not practiced owing to heterozygosity and high degree of pollen sterility.
- Species hybridization depends largely on taxonomic nearness of species and is a measure of success of interspecific hybridization.
- Many interspecific crosses fail.
- 1st successful cv. from controlled cross by the USDA was 'Katahdin' released in 1932.
- For successful interspecific crosses, ratio of female EBN (endosperm balance number) to male EBN in endosperm should be 2 : 1.
- Symmetric fusion: Equal contribution of cytoplasm imparting resistance to erwinia and phytophthora in hybrids between *S. tuberosum* x *S. bresidess*.
- Asymmetric fusion: Unequal contribution of cytoplasm & nuclear genetic material forming cybrids e.g. *S. tuberosum* x *L. esculentum*.
- At Gwalior station, only quality potato seed production is taken.
- Apomixis is used to produce homozygous autodiploid and tetraploid lines from haploids and used to fix heterosis.
- A variety producing less acrylamide and bruising was developed by J.R. Simplot in 2014.

Varieties developed via hybridization using both parents of Indian origin: K. Sindhuri, K. Neelamani, K. Chandramukhi, K. Badshah, K. Megha, K. Jawahar, K. Sutlej, K. Anand.

Varieties developed via hybridization using only exotic parents: K. Kuber, K. Kumar, K. Kundan, K. Neela, K. Jyoti, K. Muthu, K. Lauvkar, K. Sherpa.

Varieties developed via hybridization using parents of Indian, exotic germplasm and wild species: K. Kisan, K. Red, K. Safed, K. Alankar, K. Chamatkar, K. Khasigaro, K. Naveen, K. Sheetman, K. Dewa, K. Bahar, K. Lalima, K. Swarna, K. Ashoka, K. Pukhraj, K. Giriraj, K. Chipsona-1, K. Chipsona-2, K. Kanchan.

Distinguishing characters	Early varieties	Late varieties
Period (sowing to harvest)	2 to 2.5 months	4.5 to 5.5 months
Stolon length	Short	Long
Stem	Hollow	Solid
Stolon number	Less	More
Tube colour	White	Coloured
Photoperiodism	Long days	Short days for tuber development
Varieties	Gola, Up-To-Date, K. Chandramukhi, K. Khasigaro, K. Chamatkar, K. Alankar	Phulwa, K. Kisan, K. Safed, K. Neela, K. Jeevan

- Worldover, example of bio-fortified potato developed by conventional breeding is 'INIA 321 Kawsay' variety with high iron and zinc content.
- Russet Burbank: Dark brown skin with few eyes.
- A russet type, its flesh is white, dry and mealy and is good for baking, mashing and French fries.
- Gola: Old Indian potato, probably introduced a long time back in India.
- Among 46 varieties, 40 varieties possess white or yellow skin and 5 varieties possess red tuber skin.
- Indian varieties popular in other countries: K. Chandramukhi (Afghanistan), K. Jyoti (typically day neutral & grown in Nepal, Bhutan), K. Sindhuri (Nepal, Bangladesh), Khrushi, and Sita (Sri Lanka), Montanosa and BSUP-04 (Philippines), Mailaka (Madagascar), India (Bolivia), Red Skin (Vietnam) and CCM-69.1 (Mexico).
- Long duration varieties: K. Badshah, K. Sindhuri, K. Jyoti are more responsive to nitrogen.
- Indian varieties resistant to late blight having exotic *S. demissum* gene: K. Jeevan, K. Jyoti, Khasigaro, K. Naveen, K. Neelmani, K. Muthu, K. Badshah, K. Megha, K. Jawahar.
- World's leading variety used for French fry: McCain.
- American varieties for chips and French fries: Frito Lay Hybrid 1533, Atlantic.
- Potato variety with low glycemic index: Karizma.
- 2001P-55: Red skinned hybrid.
- Innate: GM potato developed using RNA interference technology.
- Baby/ salad/ speciality potatoes: K. Phulwa, K. Himsona.
- FC-5: Developed by Pepsico Company for chips and sold under brand name 'Lays'.

Indigenous-Agra Red, Chamba Red, Coonoor White, Coonoor Red, Darjeling Red Round, Dhantauri, Desi, Gola Type A, B, C, Phulwa, Phulwa Purple Splashed, Red Long Kidney, Sathoo, Shan, Silbilati	**Salient features-**Heat and drought tolerant, tolerant to degenerative viruses, due to physiological advantages can be stored in country stores during hot Indian summers
Exotic- Ally, Arran Counsal, Ben Cruachan, Craig's Defiance, Dunbar Cavalier, Great Scott, Italian White Round, Late Carman, Magnum Bonum, Majestic, Northern Star, President, Raeburn's Gregor Cup, Red Rock, Royal Kidney, Up-to-Date	Long day adopted, suitable for Indian hills only, multiplication is characterized with progressive accumulation of degenerative viral diseases; physiological limitations on tuber storage & utilization in hot Indian summers

- 'Up-to-Date' is most popular variety in India (introduced from UK). Cross between 'Victoria's Blue x Don'.
- Phulwa, Surpomeera: Originated from Hungery; late blight resistant.
- Atzimba, Grata, Desiree, Dobrin, Kalyuga: Resistant to early blight.
- Omega, Certa: Resistant to black scurf.
- Snowdrop, Victoria, Regent, Champion, Maincrop, Abundance, Bruce: Resistant to wart disease.
- Earmak, Flora, Jubel, Saphir, Epicure, King Edward: Resistant to PVX.

- Loshitsa, Kandidat, Little Fire, Akkord: Resistant to PVY.
- Montana, Pentland Crown, Black Bird, Karaganda, Roza Poles: Resistant to leaf roll virus.
- Sowa, Pola: Resistant to spindle tuber virus.
- Craigs Defiance is an old cv. prone to internal brown spot.

Name	Breeding method	Features
CPRI, Shimla		
Kufri Himalini (2006)	Hybridization & clonal selection of [I-1062 x Bulk pollen of (Tollocan, LT-5, I-1039, K. Pukhraj)]	Mod. resistant to late blight; excellent cooking
K. Shailja (2005)	Hybridization & clonal selection of (K. Jyoti x EX/A 680-16)	Mod. resistant to late blight; excellent cooking
K. Kisan (1958)	Hybridization & clonal selection of (Up-To-Date x Sd.16)	Late bulking (>100 days); round, eyes deep; good keeping quality; flesh white
K-1241	Selection from Phulwa	-
K. Kundan (1958)	Hybridization & clonal selection of (Ekishrazu x Katahdin)	Short day variety; white skin & yellow flesh; excellent keeping quality; resistant to characoal rot
K. Kumar (1958)	Hybridization & clonal selection of (Lumbri x Katahdin)	Self incompatible; oblong tubers; immune to wart & resistant to charcoal rot, late blight
K. Jeevan (1968)	Hybridization & clonal selection of (M 109-3 x Sd- 698-D)	Flesh white; mod. resistant to late blight
K. Naveen (1968)	Hybridization & clonal selection of (3070 d x Sd. 692-D)	Mod. resistant to late blight & immune to wart
K. Chamatkar (1968)	Hybridization & clonal selection of (Ekishirazu x Phulwa)	Medium round; late; resistant to early blight & immune to wart
K. Girdhari (2008)	Hybridization & clonal selection of (SS/C-562 x Bulk pollen of 10 genotypes)	Highly resistant to late blight; white flesh
Kufri Kuber (1958)	Hybridization & clonal selection of [*S. curtilobum* x *S. tuberosum*) x *S. andigena*]	Resistant to black scurf, leaf roll, PLRV & immune to PVY
K. Chandramukhi (1968)	Hybridization & clonal selection of (Seedling 4485 x K. Kuber)	Early bulking (75-80 days); light red purple flowers; fleet (shallow) eyes; quantitative short day; self incompatible; white fleshed; high protein content; good keeping quality; suitable for little tuber production, flakes flour, chips, French fries, dehydrated products; susceptible to late blight; yield 20-25 t/ha
K. Jawahar (1996)	Hybridization & clonal selection of (K. Neelmani	Early bulking (80 days); white flowers; pale yellow flesh; mod. resistant to late blight; suitable for

	x K. Jyoti)	mechanized cultivation due to erect habit & compact foliage; immune to wart
K. Ashoka (1996)	Hybridization & clonal selection of (EM/C- 1021 x Allerfruheste Gelbe)	Early bulking (75-80 days); light red-purple flowers; very high yield; susceptible to late blight
K. Lauvkar(1972)	Hybridization & clonal selection of (Serkov x Adina)	Early bulking (75-80 days); tolerant to heat; suitable for flour, chips, flakes; yield 20-25 t/ha
K. Sheetman (1968)	Hybridization & clonal selection of (Craigs Defiance x Phulwa)	Resistant to frost; mod. resistant to charcoal rot
K. Surya (2006)	K. Lauvkar x LT-1	Most heat tolerant; resistant to leaf hoppers; pale yellowish flesh; suitable for processing into high quality French fries, chips; yield 30-35 t/ha.
K. Sutlej (1996)	Hybridization & clonal selection of (K. Bahar x K. Alankar)	White flesh; fleet eyes; white flowers; mod. resistant to late blight; immune to wart
K. Alankar (1968)	Hybridization & clonal selection of (Keenebee x ON-2090)	Immune to race *O* of late blight; very high bulking rate
K. Anand (1999)	Hybridization & clonal selection of (K. Ashoka x PH/ F-1045)	Suitable for making chips & French fries; resistant to late blight, tolerant to frost
K. Arun (2005)	Hybridization & clonal selection of (K. Lalima x MS/ 82-797)	Red skinned; 20% dry matter; resistant to late blight & tolerant to frost
K. Pukhraj (1998)	Hybridization & clonal selection of (Craigs Defiance x JEX/B-687)	Early bulking (75 days); yellow flesh; suitable for low soil fertility; mod. resistant to early blight & late blight; immune to wart
K. Pushkar (2005)	Hybridization & clonal selection of (QB/A 9-120 x Spatz)	Field resistant tophoma blight, late blight & early blight; immune to wart
K. Safed (1958)	Clonal selection from 'Phulwa'	Self incompatible; short day; flesh light-yellow
K. Red (1958)	Clonal selection from 'Darjeeling Red Round'	For dry matter; self incompatible; short day; red skinned & yellow flesh
K. Lalima (1982)	Hybridization & clonal selection of (K. Red x AG-14)	Red skin; white-purple tinged flowers; tubers round with deep eyes; resistant to early blight & PVX
K. Lalit (2014)	Hybridization & clonal selection of (85-P-670 x CP 3192)	Red skin with yellow flesh; resistant to late blight
K. Jyoti (1968)	Hybridization & clonal selection of [3069d(4) x 2814a(1)]	Day neutral; resistant to early blight, late blight, wart & viruses; tendency to crack in heavy soil & low temperature; suitable for dehydrated products; yield 30 t/ha
K. Kanchan (1999)	SLB/ Z-405 (a) x Pimpernel	Red skinned; field resistant to late blight, wart, very slow rate of degeneration
K. Giriraj (1998)	Hybridization & clonal selection of (SLB/ J-132 x EX/A 680-16)	Light purple flowers; white tubers; immune to wart & resistant to late blight

K. Sherpa (1983)	Hybridization & clonal selection of (Utimus x Adina)	Good for chips; immune to wart & resistant to late blight
K. Sindhuri (1967)	Hybridization & clonal selection of (K. Red x K. Kundan)	Red skinned & possess waxy coating; light red-purple flowers; suitable for dehydrated flakes & canning; resistant to early blight, PLRV, frost; qualitative short day; long tuber dormancy; yield 30-35 t/ha
K. Shakthi	Sister clone from (K. Red x K. Kundan)	Resistant to early blight, leaf rolling virus & frost
K. Badshah (1979)	Hybridization & clonal selection of (K. Jyoti x K. Alankar)	Late maturing; white flowers; fleet (shallow) eyes; white flesh; multiple disease resistant (late blight, early blight, frost & PVX); yield 30-35 t/ha
K. Bahar (1980)	Hybridization & clonal selection of (K. Red x Gineke)	White flesh; white flowers; fleet (shallow) eyes; table purpose; suitable for little tuber production; immune to wart
K. Sadabahar (2008)	Hybridization & clonal selection of (MS/81-145 x PH/ F-1545)	White flesh; resistant to late blight; tolerant to frost; suitable for French fries; high dry matter content
K. Dewa (1973)	Hybridization & clonal selection of (Craig's Defiance x Phulwa)	Resistant to cyst nematode & late blight; tolerant to frost
K. Neela (1963)	Hybridization & clonal selection of (Katahdin x Shamrock)	White tuber; flesh white; resistant to cyst nematodes
K. Neelima (2010)	E/ 79-15 x E/ 79-42	Resistant to cyst nematode & late blight
K. Neelmani (1968)	Hybridization & clonal selection of (K. Kundan x 134-D)	Mod. resistant to late blight
K. Neelkanth(2017)	-	Bio-fortified cv; light violet purple coloured tubers with yellow flesh; higher anti-oxidant content; resistant to late blight; yield 40-45 t/ha
K. Swarna (1985)	Hybridization & clonal selection of (K. Jyoti x $(VTn)^2$ 62.33.3)	Non-cracking; white flowers; resistant to early blight, late blight & cyst nematode
K. Frysona (2008)	MP/ 90-30 x MP/ 90-94	Dry matter 22%; low reducing sugars 30-80 mg/100 g; yield 30-35 t/ha; suitable for processing into French fries
K. Chipsona-1(1998)	Hybridization & clonal selection of (MEX. 750826 x MS/78-79)	White flowers; white tubers; dry matter 20-23%; reducing sugar 10-75 mg/100 g; excellent for chips & French fries; yield 30-35 t/ha; resistant to frost & late blight
K. Chipsona-2 (1998)	Hybridization & clonal selection of (F-6 x QB/B- 92-4)	Low phenol content; white flowers; white flesh; reducing sugars 30-100 mg/ 100 g; dry matter 22-24%; yield 30-32 t/ha; excellent for chips, French fries & flakes; resistant to frost & late blight
K. Chipsona-3 (2006)	Hybridization & clonal selection of (MP/91-86 x K. Chipsona-2)	Reducing sugar 10-100 mg/100 g; dry matter 20-23%; suitable for chips & French fries; resistant to late blight
K. Chipsona-4 (2010)	Hybridization & clonal selection of (Atlantic x MP/ 92-35)	Early maturing; round-ovoid shaped tubers; dry matter >20%; low reducing sugar 40-80 mg/100 g; yield 30-35 t/ha; resistant to late blight
K. FryoM (2019)	Progeny selection of	20% dry matter; low reducing sugar 50-90 mg/100 g;

	(Kufri Chipsona-1 × MP/92-35)	yield 30-35 t/ha; suitable for French fries; tubers do not show deformities like cracking or hollow heart; resistant to late blight
K. Surya (2004)	Hybridization & clonal selection of (K. Lauvkar x LT-1)	Early maturing; heat tolerant; hopper burn resistant & suitable for chips & French fries
K. Muthu (1971)	Hybridization & clonal selection of (3046 (1) x M109-3)	Self incompatible; resistant to late blight & immune to wart
K. Megha (1989)	Hybridization & clonal selection of (SLB/ K-37 x SLB/ Z-73)	Late maturing (145 days); highly resistant to late blight.
K. Himsona (2007)	Hybridization & clonal selection of (MP/92-35 x K. Chipsona-2)	1st processing variety for Himachal Pradesh; yield 15-20 t/ha; highly resistant to late blight & suitable for making chips & flakes
K. Khasigaro (1968)	Hybridization & clonal selection of (Taborky x Seedling 698-D)	Rapid bulking possesses short dormancy; mod. resistant to early blight, late blight & immune to wart
K. Khyati (2008)	Hybridization & clonal selection of (MS/ 82-638 x K. Pukhraj)	Early maturing; white tuber; mod. resistant to late blight
K. Garima (2012)	Hybridization & clonal selection of (PH/F 1045 x MS/82-638)	Yellow tubers; 18% dry matter; suitable for table purpose; yield 35-40 t/ha; resistant to late blight
K. Gaurav (2012)	Hybridization & clonal selection of (JE 812 x K. Jyoti)	-
K. Mohan (2015)	-	Pleasant flavour on cooking; table purpose; resistant to late blight
K. Moti	3046 x M 109-3	-
K. Manik (PS/06-88) 2018	-	Bio-fortified cv; rich in iron, zinc, carotenoids & anthocyanin; yield 23-25 t/ha; resistant to late blight, virus, common scab, black scurf
K. Thenmalai	-	Resistant to cyst nematode & late blight
K. Lima (2017)	-	1st CIP clone recommended for release in India; early bulking; white-cream flesh; low degeneration rate; tolerant to heat, hoppers & mite burn; resistant to PVX & PVY
K. Ganga (MS/6-1947) 2017	-	High tuber yield (35-40 t/ha); table purpose; resistant to late blight, good keeping & culinary quality; suitable for North-Indian plains
K. Karan (SM/00-42)	-	Yield 25 t/ha; dry matter 18%; multiple disease resistant
K. Sahayadri (2018)	-	Yield 32 t/ha; dry matter 18%; highly resistant to potato cyst nematode; suitable for Nilgiri hills & year round cultivation
Yusi Maap (CIP clone # 392797) 2019	-	Recommended for low, mid and high altitude potato growing areas
K. Thar-1	-	-
K. Thar-2	-	-
K. Thar-3	-	-
K. Sangam	-	-

Grades:

- Small: below 25 g (<25 mm).
- Medium: 25-60 g (25-35 mm).
- Large: 60-90 g (35-50 mm).
- Extra large: above 100 g (>50 mm).

Inheritance of characters:

- Cultivated potato show tetrasomic inheritance.
- Most of agronomic characters are polygenically controlled.
- Disease resistance is governed by recessive genes.
- Three alleles at *R* locus i.e. *R, Rpw*, and *r* with *Rpw* gives pink tubers & white flowers.

Character	Number of genes	Type of gene action
Skin colour	Digenic (*D-R-*)	Complimentary D-R-red, D-rr-white, ddR-white, ddrr-white
Position of eye	Monogenic	Flat eye is incompletely dominant to deep eye
Flesh colour	Monogenic	Deep yellow colour is incompletely dominant to white; the intermediate is pale yellow
Stolon length	Monogenic	Long stolon dominant to short '
Tuber shape	Monogenic	Long tuber axis dominant to short axis
Tuber dormancy	-	Additive
True seed & tuber dormancy	Polygenic	-
Violet corolla colour	*chi, chs, RDR*	-
Resistance to		
Aphids	Polygenic	Resistance dominant to susceptibility
Late blight	Series of major (*R*) & minor genes in *S. demissum*	Single dominant gene
Verticillium wilt	Monogenic	Single incompletely dominant
Fusarium solani	Monogenic	Resistance dominant over susceptible
Potato wart	Monogenic	Single dominant gene (*X*) or two complementary gene (*Y, Z*) or single dominant gene (*A*) inhibited by 3 complementary genes (*B,C,D*)
Bacterial wilt	3 independent genes in *S. phureja*	Few dominant major genes
Potato virus X	3 complex genes & single dominant	Monogenic dominant
Potato virus Y	Single dominant & 3 alleles	Monogenic dominant
Potato virus A	Digenic (*Natbr, Nctbr*)	-
Potato virus C	Monogenic (*Nc*)	-
Potato virus S	Monogenic recessive in cv. Saco	-
Potato leaf roll virus	Polygenic	-

Diseases and pests:

- Various concepts viz. Dutch rules, Beaumont's periods, Irish rules, moving days concept (Hyre, 1954), severity value accumulation (Wallin, 1926), negative prognosis (Ullrich and Schrodter, 1998), mathematical models have been developed for forecasting of late blight.
- JHULSACAST and BLITECAST: Disease forecasting model for late blight.
- Bio B5: Formulation for growing bacterial wilt disease free crops. Control soil borne diseases up to 80%.
- High O-diphenol level exhibit resistance to phytophthora.
- Irish potato famine during 1845 was due to late blight.
- Late blight of potato occurs every year in the hills but in plains only occasionally.
- 'Crinkle-A': Due to virus infection.
- Potato tuber moth is introduced in India from Italy through seed material.
- Cross protection technique is adapted against Potato Spindle Tuber Viroid.
- Domestic quarantine exist in India for potato eelworm.

Diseases	**Casual organism**	**Remarks**
Late blight	*Phytophthora infestans*	Most serious & epiphytotic disease of potato reproduces sexually
Early blight	*Alternaria solani*	Soil borne; serious disease in Deccan plateau during kharif
Wart	*Synchytrium endobioticum*	Soil borne disease endemic in Darjeeling hills in seed industry; introduced from Holland in 1952; affects both plants and tubers & cause heavy yield losses
Black scurf	*Rhizoctonia solani*	Fungal disease
Dry rot	*Fusarium solani* var. *coeruleum*	Storage disease; treat tubers with 3% boric acid for 30 min.
Bacterial soft rot/ Black leg	*Erwinia carotovora*	Storage disease
Bacterial ring rot	*Clavibacter michiganensis*	-
Bacterial wilt/ Brown rot	*Ralstonia solanacerum*	Soil borne bacterial disease carried through seed tubers
Charcoal rot	*Macrophomina phaseolina*	Storage disorder; soil & tuber borne; do surface disinfection with mercurial fungicide
Purple top wilt	MLOs	-
Common scab of potato	*Streptomyces scabis*	Soil borne; decrease market value of produce
Potato leaf roll virus (PLRV)	*Virus*	Aphids
Latent or faint mosaic	*PV-X* and *S*	Aphids
Severe mosaic	*Virus*	Aphids
Witches broom	MLOs	-
Silver Top	-	Thrips

Pests		
Green peach aphids	*Myzus persicae*	Vector of more than 100 potato virus
Cut worm	*Agrotis ipsilon*	-
Potato tuber moth	*Phthorimaea operculella*	30-70% damage in field &during storage; serious in warm regions of Maharashtra, Karnataka & Madhya Pradesh
Golden cyst nematode	*Globodera rostochinensis*, *G. pallid*	Introduced from Europe in 1960; serious problem in southern hills

Physiological disorders:

- Greening of tubers: Due to exposure of developing tuber either in field or in storage to sunlight. Green flesh is bitter & affects flavour of cooked tuber due to alkaloid compound 'Solanine'.
- Internal brown spot: Moisture deficiency.
- Darkening of potato: P deficiency.
- Leaf fall: B deficiency.
- Sprout failure and tip burn: Ca deficiency.
- Fern leaf/ little leaf: Zn deficiency.
- Black heart: Poor ventilation (storage of tuber at -1 to 0^0C).
- Hollow heart: Development of cavities of various sizes in centre of tubers due to irregular growth patterns. Wider spacing, excess fertigation of nitrogen, excess irrigation and high temperature during tuberization, common in large sized tubers.
- Black spot: Bruising of tubers rough handling results into this disorder. Small, numerous, discoloured areas beneath the tuber skin and no outward signs. Tubers having immature skin of early crop types harvested before maturity are most susceptible.
- Potato phyllody: Transmitted through tubers.
- Ecodormancy: Due to water stress.
- Chilling injury: Low temperature 0^0C.
- Freezing injury: Low temperature (-1 to -2^0C).

30.7 Tomatillo

- Glabrous annual herb.
- Fruit: Yellowish violet coloured berry like a big tomato.
- Eaten as raw/ salad/ jam/ pickle and soup.

31. TETRAGONIACEAE (AIZOACEAE)

31.1 New Zealand Spinach

- It is both, green and salad vegetable grown for its succulent leaves and branch tips mainly in home gardens.

- It is not true spinach and differs markedly in growth habit and climatic requirements.
- The chief similarity between the two plants is in flavour.
- It an annual, warm season crop and moderately tolerant to frost.
- Field planting can be done from transplants in late winter or from dirct seeding or sowing.
- Plants are spaced 1-2 feet apart and in rows 3-5 feet apart.
- Plants are ready for harvest when they are large enough and 3-4 inches long tender tips are harvested, which stimulates new growth.
- Harvesting can be continues until cool weather in fall season.
- The entire plants may be cut off about 2 inches above ground.

32. TRAPACEAE (CYPERACEAE)

32.1 Chinese water chestnut

- Eulogized as '*Shingada* or *Paniphal*'.
- Aquatic herbaceous annual, commonly found in marshes and swamps throughout world.
- Nutrient composition/ 100 g edible portion: Starch (7.3%), sucrose (6.4%), reducing sugar (1.9%), protein (1.5%), fibres (0.9%), fat (0.2%), water (77.3%).
- Calorific value: 97 Kcal/100g.
- Nutrition score: 50.
- It is sold in Calcutta under the name of "Singapuri Keysur".
- Edible part: Tuber.
- Propagation: Corm.
- Grow in rainy season in ponds and lakes.
- Optimum pH: 6.9-7.3
- Optimum soil temperature for corm germination: 14-15^{0}C.
- Planting distance: 75 cm x 75 cm.
- Triangular spacing of 45-60 x 45 cm is common in China.
- Accumulate heavy metals from polluted water bodies.
- Crop duration: 180-200 days.
- Harvesting season: September-October.
- Marvesting method: Clumps become brown & maturity is attained in 7-8 months.
- Yield: 20-40 t/ha.
- Types: Bhagwa shingada (20-25 g wt.); Red shingada (20 g wt.); Green shingada (20 g wt.).

33. USE OF PLANT GROWTH REGULATORS IN VEGETABLE CROPS:

Crop	PGR & rate of application	Effects	Remarks
Tomato	Tomatotone (4-CPA)	Enhance fruit set at high temperature 34/20^{0}C	Apply at flower cluster
	2,4-D @ 2-5 ppm	Increase fruit set, earliness & parthenocarpic fruits	Seed treatment
	p-chlorophenoxy acetic acid (PCPA) @ 50-100 ppm	Fruit set under high & low temperature conditions	-
	Cycocel @ 250 ppm	Resistance to virus, fruiting & yield	Seedling treatment
Brinjal	2,4-D @ 5 ppm; GA @ 50 ppm; 4 CPA @ 20 ppm	Improve fruit set, early yield	Spray at appearance of 1st flower
Chilli	NAA @ 40 ppm	Enhance flower and fruit set	-
	GA_3 @ 10-100 ppm	Enhance flower and fruit set	-
Okra	NAA @ 20 ppm; IAA & GA_3 @ 25, 50, 75 & 100 ppm	Enhance seed germination	Seed treatment
Bottle gourd	MH @ 50-150 ppm & 3 ppm boron	Induce more female flowers	2 & 4 leaf stage
	Ethephon @ 50-100 ppm	Increases number of fruits, fruit wt., fruit length & early appearance of female flowers	
Ridge gourd & sponge gourd	IAA @ 20-200 ppm	Induce more female flowers	
	NAA @ 25-100 ppm	Induce more female flowers	
Water melon	TIBA @ 25-50 ppm	Induce more female flowers	
Musk melon	Ethrel @ 250 ppm	Induce more female flowers; Increases fruit set	
Round melon	MH @ 50 ppm	More femaleness, more vegetative growth & increase in yield 50-60%.	
Musk melon (gynoecious line)	Silver thiosulphate @ 300-400 ppm	Induce more male flowers in gynoecious lines	
Cucumber	Ethrel @ 150-200 ppm	Increase more female flowers	
Cucumber (gynoecious line)	Silver nitrate @ 200-300 ppm	Induction of male and functional bisexual flowers	
	Silver thiosulphate	Induce male flowers in gynoecious lines	
	Amino ethoxyvinyl glycine (AVG) @ 50-100 ppm	Induction of male flowers	
	GA_3 @ 15-20 ppm	Induction of male flowers	
Bitter gourd	CCC @ 100-500 ppm	Increase female: male ratio	
	MH @ 150-200 ppm &	Increase female flowers	

	Ethrel @ 20 ppm		
Bitter gourd (gynoecious line)	Silver nitrate @ 200-300 ppm	Induce hermaphrodite flowers	
Snake gourd	Cycocel @ 200 ppm	Induction of female flowers	At vegetative stage
	Ethrel @ 150-200 ppm	More female flowers	
Summer Squash	Ethephon @ 250 ppm	Temporarily suppression of male flowers	1st true leaf stage & repeated upto 2-3 weeks
	Ethephon @ 600 ppm	Complete suppression of male flowers	2 & 4 leaf stage & 7-10 leaf stage later
Pumpkin	Ethephon @ 250 ppm	High female flowers; increased fruit set	
Garden pea	CCC @ 50 ppm	Increase yield & drought tolerance	
	GA_3 @ 50 ppm		Increase yield
Onion & garlic	MH @ 1500-2000 ppm	Sprout inhibition	Apply 2-3 weeks before harvest
Potato	GA_3 @ 10-15 ppm	Break tuber dormancy	10-20 min. dipping
	Thiourea @ 1%	Break tuber dormancy	-
	Maleic Hydrazide	Sprout inhibitor	-
	Chloropropham @ 25 mg/ T of tubers	Sprout inhibitor	Apply after curing of tubers
	Ethylene chlorohydrin @ 20 g	Break tuber dormancy	Vapour treatment

34. SEED PRODUCTION OF VEGETABLE CROPS:

- In Japan, 80-90% of total brinjal seed and 60-65% of cucumber seeds are of hybrid origin and about 50-90% of commercial varieties of different vegetable crops are F_1 hybrids.
- During 10th plan, ICAR launched ambitious 'Mega Seed Project' on seed production in agricultural crops and fishries.
- Organized production of quality seed at national level started in 1963.
- MAHYCO was established in 1964.
- Only 10% area of vegetables is under hybrids of which tomato has 36%, cabbage 30%, brinjal 18%, okra 7%, melons and gourds 5%, cauliflower 2% and chilli 1%.
- Share of hybrid seed is increasing at 8-10 % annually in most of crops.
- Leading hybrid vegetable seeds in India: Tomato (F_1 hybrids have 35% share & 60% area), Okra, Chilli.
- India's rank in world seed trade: 8th.
- Indian seed market is 5th largest in the worldaccounting for 4% of global seed market after USA (27%), China (20%), France (8%), and Brazil (6%).
- In India, vegtable seed industry is estimated around 1800 Cr (350 million USD).
- Seed production is concentrated in Karnataka, Maharashtra and Gujarat.

- Karnataka produces nearly 90% of total vegetable seeds.
- Total area under hybrid seed: 23,802 ha.
- Total production of hybrid seeds: 1,410 tones.
- Among the Asian countries, India is the 2nd largest producer of hand pollinated hybrid seeds in vegetables.
- During 2018, India imported 7.58 thousand MT of vegetable seeds worth of 90 million USD.
- During 2019-20, India exported 11.99 thousand MT of vegetable seeds worth of 109.22 million USD.
- Vegetable seed exports consist of 4% of total horticultural exports from India.
- NHRDF contributes 4-5% in onion seed production of total seed production in India.
- Seed replacement in vegetable crops is more than 80% as compared to nearly 10% in other food crops e.g. Tomato (99.3%); Brinjal (63.4%); Chilli (83.7%); Capsicum (95%); Cauliflower (86.4%); Cabbage (100%); Radish (96.5%); Onion (87.3%); Okra (92.4%);, Water melon (89.2%); Musk melon (7%); Cucumber (72.6%); Gourds (73.5%).
- Basic steps in hybrid seed production: Emasculation and pollination.
- In onion and carrot, emasculation is difficult due to arrangement of floral parts.
- The commonly employed mechanism for overcoming emasculation and pollination are sex expression, self incompatibility and male sterility.
- Seed replacement rate in vegetable crops: 78.0%.
- Optimum temperature for breaking dormancy for biennial vegetables: 4.4-10^{0}C.
- During flowering stage for pollination, fertilization and seed setting: 30^{0}C.
- Commercial seed production of Indian cauliflower done at North Indian plains.
- Snowball cauliflower does not need chilling requirement but its seed production is done in temperate regions in India.
- No significant difference in performance of onion seed produced through seed to seed and bulb to seed methods.
- Wind plays important role in seed production of turnip.
- Block method of seed production in pumpkin ensure higher genetic purity of hybrid seed.
- In tomato, female lines having exerted stigma are used for hybrid seed production.
- In tomato, a new outlook on hybrid seed production has been developed with discovery of some male sterile mutants.
- Dropcopter: A New York based Startup Company pitching precision pollination of fruits and vegetables by drone.
- Drone delivered soap bubbles could help pollinate flowers.

Requirement and availability of seeds:

Vegetable	Requirement (tones)	Seed availability (tones)	Replacement (%)	Seed multiplication ratio
Tomato	169.94	168.75	99.30	1: 400
Brinjal	239.54	151.87	63.40	1: 450
Cabbage	228.12	197.09	86.40	1: 433
Cauliflower	228.12	197.09	86.40	-
Cucumber	54.10	39.27	72.60	1: 200
Chilli	2046.35	1504.06	73.50	1: 240
Gourds	2046.35	1504.06	73.50	1: 40, 1: 99
Melons	423.37	377.65	69.20	1: 100, 1: 160
Onion	4849.37	4233.50	87.30	1: 171
Leafy vegetables	5530.0	2328.13	42.10	-
Okra	4645.81	4292.73	92.40	1: 100
Peas	17037.15	15929.74	93.50	1: 19
Radish	745.80	719.69	96.50	1: 100
Beans	11880.10	7983.43	67.20	1: 10, 1: 50
Others	37118.42	2699.57	72.60	-
Total	**51975.91**	**40986.59**	**78.86**	-

Websites:

- http://agricoop.nic.in/divisiontype/seeds
- https://seednet.gov.in
- https://commerce.gov.in/about-us/divisions/export-products-division/export-products-agriculure/#
- https://www.worldseed.org/resources/seed-statistics/
- https://nsai.co.in

Main classes of hydrolytic enzymes involved in the mobilization of the food reserves of seeds:

Reserve compound	Enzymes	Products of hydrolysis
Starch	α & β- amylase Maltase Phosphorylase	Maltose, glucose Glucose Glucose-1-phosphate
Hemicelluloses	Cytases	Hexoses, pentoses
Lipid	Lipases (esterases)	Fatty acids & glycerol
Protein	Proteinases Peptidases	Amino acids, peptides Amino acids
Phytin	Phytase	Inorganic phosphate & inositol
Ribonucleic acid	Ribonuclease	Ribonucleotides
Cellulose	Cellulose Cellobiase	Cellobiose Glucose

Hybrid seed production (male: female parent planting ratio):

- Tomato: 1:3 to 1:5
- Brinjal: 1: 5
- Chilli: 1: 5 (male sterile line as female parent)
- Hot pepper: 1: 2
- Carrot: 2: 8 or 1 : 4.
- Okra: 1: 4
- Musk melon: 1: 8
- Cucumber: 1: 5
- Water melon: 1: 6
- Summer Squash: 1: 5or 1: 2.
- Bottle gourd: 1: 2 or 1:3.
- Bitter gourd: 1: 4.
- Pumpkin: 1:3.
- Cabbage and Cauliflower: 1: 1 or 1: 2.
- Onion: 1: 4 or 1: 8.
- Radish: 1: 1.
- Spinach: 2: 6 or 2: 14.f
- Seed multiplication rate in potato seed production 1: 6 per generation.

Methods of hybrid seed production

Methods	Vegetables
Hand emasculation & manual pollination	Tomato, brinjal, sweet pepper, hot pepper, okra
Pinching of staminate flowers & hand pollination	Bitter gourd, bottle gourd, pumpkin
Removal of staminate flower + emasculation + hand pollination	Water melon, musk melon
Functional male sterility & hand pollination	Tomato, brinjal
GMS + bee pollination	Chilli
CMS + natural pollination	Capsicum, onion, cabbage, carrot, radish
Self incompatibility & natural pollination	Cauliflower, broccoli
Gynoecium & natural pollination	Cucumber
PGR & natural pollination	Squash's
Detasseling & wind pollination	Sweet corn, baby corn

Isolation distance of vegetable crops:

Name of crop		Isolation distance (m)	
		Foundation seed	Certified seed
Cole crops	Cabbage	1600	1000
	Cauliflower	1600	1000
	Chinese cabbage	1600	1000
	Khol khol	1600	1000
Fruit vegetables	Tomato	50	25
	Brinjal	200	100
	Chilli	400	200
	Okra	400	200
Bulb vegetables	Onion	1000	500
	Garlic	10	5
Root vegetables	Radish	1600	1000
	Carrot	1000	800
	Beetroot	1600	800
	Turnip	1600	1000
Tuber vegetables	Potato	10	5
	Sweet potato	10	5
Legume vegetables	Peas	10	5
	Cluster bean	50	25
	Cowpea	50	25
	French bean	50	25
	Indian bean	50	25
	Lima bean	50	25
Leafy vegetables	Amaranths	400	200
	Beet leaf	1600	1000
	Coriander	800	400
	Fenugreek	50	25
	Spinach	1600	1000
All cucurbits	-	1000	500

34.1 Seed Labeling, Testing, and Certification:

- Four seed quality parameters: Physical purity, Germinability, Seed health, Genetic purity.
- Seed certification in India: Voluntary.
- At present, seed act as well as seed certification in India are applicable to notified varieties (Notified under Section 5 of Seed Act).
- Indian Seed Act is essentially a truthful labeling act.
- National Seed project was launched in 1976.
- USA: Largest export market for Indian seeds.
- Indian Minimum Seed Certification Standards (IMSCS) were 1st published in 1971 and revised in 1998.
- India follows 3 generation system (breeder, foundation and certified seed).

- Seed coat hardness is due to sclerenchyma tissue.
- Nucleus seed (100% pure) is source of breeder's seed.
- Foundation seed is derived from Breeder's seed.
- Breeder seed: Golden brown tag
- Foundation seed: White tag
- Certified seed: Azure blue tag
- Labelled seed/ Truthful seed: Opal green tag.
- Orange certificate is issued by ISTA.
- Rapid method of seed testing: Tetrazolium (2,3,5- triphenyl tetrazolium chloride) test developed by Lakon in Germany in 1942. It gives red colour to viable seeds.
- Testing of mechanical damage of seeds: Ferric chloride test
- Seed vigour test: Brick gravel test (The Hiltner test).
- Testing of varietal purity: Grow OutTest (GOT).
- Germination %: Paper towel method.
- National Seed Corporation (NSC) was established in March, 1963.
- New Seed Policy: 1988.
- International Seed Testing Association (ISTA) founded in 1924, Geneva, Switzerland.
- Asia and Pacific Seed Association (APSA). Thailand, 1994.
- FAO of the UN declared the year 1961 as World Seed year.
- Seed Act was enacted in 1966.
- Seed rules notified in 1968.
- Central Seed Certification Board (CSCB): 1972.
- Seed Control Order: 1983. It was passed for voluntary seed certification.
- Seed Bill: 2004
- Central Seed Laboratory is located at New Delhi.
- Directorate of Seed Research (DSR) is located at Mau Nath Banjan, Uttar Pradesh.
- Genetic purity of seed crop is vitiated due to pollination by foreign pollen.
- Greater the isolation distances, lesser the chances of contamination.
- Lack of synchronization of flowering in parental lines not only reduces seed set but also increases chances of contamination.
- In hybrid seed plot, area under seed parent in relation to that of pollinator, determines yield of hybrid seed.
- IIHR, Bengaluru's portal for seed purchase: www.seed.iihr.res.in
- Physical purity (%) = Weight of pure seed ÷ total wt. of working sample x 100.
- Mobilization efficiency (%) = Increase in dry wt. of embryonic axes ÷ decrease in dry wt. of cotyledon x 100.

34.2 Seed storability in different vegetables

- Temperatures of 0 to 10°C are used for short to medium term storage and -20°C for long term storage.
- Fumigants used in seed storage: Ethylene dibromide or Malathion.
- Seed treatment with chemicals or pesticides are avoided during conservation.
- Vegetable seeds are packed with 5-7% moisture in sealed conditions.
- Container used: Cloth, jute, paper bags, polyethylene bags, metal cans and laminated aluminium foil pouches.
- Retention of seed viability is greater at -20°C than at 5°C storage.
- Modified atmosphere (MA) storage is effective for short-term preservation in absence of cold storage facility.
- Seeds preserved in CO_2 atmosphere: Garden peas, cluster bean, cowpea, pepper, bitter gourd, cucumber, French bean.
- Seeds preserved in nitrogen atmosphere: Musk melon, water melon, okra, onion.
- Seed coating: Process of applying precise amount of active ingredients directly to seed surface without obscuring its shape.
- Seed pelleting: Process of enclosing a seed which alters the size, shape and weight of seeds.

Name	Seed storage period (years)	
	Ambient condition	-20°C
Tomato	3	20
Brinjal	2	20
Chilli	1	20
Okra	2	25
Radish	1	25
Carrot	1	20
Onion	1	25
Amaranth	1	20
French bean	2	25
Garden pea	1	33
Broad bean	1	3
Hyacinth bean	2	5
Cluster bean	1	25
Cowpea	1	5
Musk melon	4	20
Water melon	7	25
Cucumber	2	20
Pumpkin	2	25
Winter Squash	2	20
Bottle gourd	2	15
Ash gourd	2	20
Ridge gourd	2	20

35. MUSHROOMS

- Eulogized as 'Delight of diabetic or Land saving husbandry or Queen of vegetables or Vegeterian meat or Meat of the vegetable kingdom'.
- Edible macro-fungi are known as mushrooms whereas toxic species are referred as toad stools.
- Only non-green horticultural crop grown in world for commerce.
- Non-traditional food resource.
- Used raw or sliced or whole in salads. Added in gravies, sauces, soups and casseroles, canned or freeze dried.
- Intensified cultivation made mushrooms a round-year crop.
- Use of mushrooms as human food dates back to antiquity.
- Indian, Roman and Greek culture find references of mushrooms.
- Name mushroom is derived from the Middle English Muscheron/ from old French Mouscheron or Mouseron.
- Technique of growing domesticated mushrooms was discovered by gardeners near Paris around 1650.
- Mushrooms do not require sunlight to make energy for themselves.
- Mushroom production has the capacity to double or triple the farmers' income within a year due to remarkably higher productivity than any other agriculture/horticulture.
- Contains anti-viral, anti-cancerous properties.
- Regular consumption increases immunity in human body.
- Mushroom cultivation is ecofriendly activity where agricultural/ industrial wastes are utilized & recycled.
- Total world production is increasing @ 7% per annum due to diversity of mushroom species under production.
- Mushrooms like wood ear, winter, and shiitake were cultivated in China on wood logs more than 1,000 years ago.
- Button mushrooms were cultivated in France about 4 centuries ago.
- World produces 61.16 lakh tones, out of which70% is produced in China.
- Global mushroom exporting countries: China, India and Indonesia.
- China: Major consumer in the world and consumes 20 kg of mushroom/ person/ year as against 6 kg of average world consumption.
- Of total world production, China share 40-45% and India 0.15%.
- Mushroom growing ranks 3rd in economic value of all horticultural crops.
- India produces about 60-70 thousand tones annually, out of which 60% is exported and 40% consumed within country.
- In India, present internal consumption is estimated to be about 250 tonnes/ annum which is expected to rise with increasing awareness about its high nutritive value.

- India ranks 14th in world's production.
- Rate of increase in mushroom production in India: 35-40%.
- Major export destinations from India: USA, UAE, Israel, Netherlands, Switzerland, Germany, Korea, Swden, Australia, Brazil, Denmark and Russia.
- World's two most popular mushrooms: White button mushroom and Shiitake.
- USA and EU are major producers of button mushrooms of preserved mushrooms.
- The Netherlands: Largest exporter of canned button mushrooms followed by China.
- Germany: Largest importer followed by Russia.
- Japan imports 'Cloud ear' mushrooms from China.
- Combined project on solar energy generation (about 4 thousand kilo watts energy) & cultivation of edible 'Cloud ear' mushrooms (40 t /year) is implemented in Tokyo.
- Kenya leads in shiitake mushroom production.
- Ranking in world production: Button (31%), Shiitake (24%), oyster (14%), black ear (9%), paddy straw (8%) and milky and others (rest).
- Ranking in India's production: 73% Button (*Agaricus bisporus*), 16% Oyster (*Pleurotus* spp.), 7% paddy straw (*Volvariella volvacea*, *V. diplasia*)and 3% milky mushroom (*Calocybe indica*).
- Mushroom production in India began in late 1960s in H.P. and J & K.
- Major mushroom growing states: Haryana, Uttar Pradesh, Tripura, Kerala, Maharashtra, Tamil Nadu, Karnataka and Punjab.
- Mushroom cultivation is an indoor activity and does not require cultivable land.
- Relative ease with mass multiplication on lignocelluloses wastes with minimal water requirement.
- Agro-Dutch Industries: It is the largest integrated mushroom growing and canning company in the world located in Punjab.
- Mushroom city: Solan, Himachal Pradesh.
- National Mushroom Day: 23rd December.
- Mushrooms are popular for their delicacy and flavour rather than food value.
- In India, for nutritional balance, consumption of 100-200 g in daily diet is recommended.
- Per capita consumption in India is 100 g per annum while in USA (2-3 Kg), Australia (3 kg), Belgium (3.3 kg), Mexico (4.8 to 7.5 kg) and Zimbabwe (1.8 kg).
- Nutrition composition: 85-95% moisture, 3-7% protein and 4% carbohydrate on fresh weight basis.
- Composition of cultivated mushrooms (per 100 g weight basis): Calories 16, moisture 91.1%, fat 0.3%, -CHO 4.4%, proteins (on dry wt. basis) 26.9%, tryptophan (3.94%) & lysine (Wooster, 1954).
- Highest producer of proteins per unit area (15,000 kg/ha) as against 5,000 kg/ha by conventional crops.

- Protein content of dry form: 77-80% and digestible protein is 72-83%.
- One pound (454 g) of fresh mushroom provides 120 Kcal energy.
- They are very rich in lysine and tryptophane.
- They are excellent source of copper.
- Flavouring compound: 1-octen-3-ol, lenthionine.
- Whiteness is more acceptable to consumers and fetch higher price.
- Production cycle: Occurs from 84 to 144 days and 4 cycles in a calendar year is the goal.
- Phases of preparation & production are summarized as follows:
  a) Phase-I: Composting 7-21 days.
  b) Phase-II: Pasteurization & final composting 5-14 days.
  c) Spawn run: 14 days.
  d) Casing: 14-21 days.
  e) Harvest: 8-12 days & flushes: 21-42 days.
- Export of mushrooms in 3 forms: 1) Collection from nature 2) Dried (including morels) 3) Processed/ preserved form.
- Most of mushrooms exported from India are in processed form (canned/ freeze dried) in cans/ glass bottles.
- Trade of fresh mushrooms is limited due to its perishable nature.
- Commercial cultivation of button mushroom in India has attained high-tech farming status.
- Oyster mushroom production is popular due to broader growing temperature range of 20-30^{0}C, ease method of cultivation and low technology infrastructure required.
- Casing: Vital factor towards successful mushroom production.
- Purpose of casing is to force mushroom mycelium to change from vegetative to fruiting stage.
- First flush of mushrooms occurs 8-10 days following casing.
- Spawn: Technically equivalent to seed of a plant. It is a pure mushroom mycelium growing on sterilized grain medium.
- Seeding process is generally termed as spawning.
- Spawn is sold on volumetric basis & 1 litre equals to 0.6 kg.
- Among different strains, mycelia culture of PS-1 strain is best spawn for commercial cultivation of paddy straw mushroom.
- Substrates for spawn: food grains, straw, saw dust + rice polish + $CaCO_3$.
- Best substrate for mushroom growth: Contains 2% N (dry wt. basis), no ammonia, 60-70% water, fibrous & has pH 7-7.5.

- For effective pasteurization of compost, steam is injected later to raise temperature to 57-59^{0}C.
- Fresh air is introduced to lower down compost temperature to 50-53^{0}C for conditioning & 25-28^{0}C for seeding.
- Peat moss is used as casing material in European countries because it is poor in nutrients, good water holding capacity, good aeration, pH 7-7.5 is maintained.
- Mushroom pinheads start appearing after 7-10 days of spawning & appear in flushes every 7-10 days.
- Temperature required for mycelium growth: 20-30^{0}C.
- Temperature required for fructification of button mushroom: 16-18^{0}C.
- Temperature required for paddy straw mushroom: Max. 35^{0}C
- Relative humidity for cropping: 70-90%.
- High CO_2 concentration is desirable until pinning.
- CO_2 requirement at different stages: During pinning (1000-2000 ppm); during enlargement of fruiting body (little increase by 500 ppm).
- 'Arka Mushroom Chutney Powder' has been prepared by oyster mushroom; Brahmi, moringa leaves, flax seeds, sesame seeds, ground nut and coconut.
- Value added products: Soup, powder, pickle, nuggets, biscuits.
- Poultry feed called 'Muril' is made from button mushroom. It increases resistance power.
- In Japan, for higher yield, mushrooms are cultivated in medium containing aluminium compound.
- 'Pure Taste' brand is famous in Colorado, USA for production of vegetable proteins.
- These proteins are mixed in roti 'Tartila' (prepared from Mexican corn) for fortification.
- Genome and Transcriptome studies have been conducted in cultivated wild types of button mushroom.
- About 12 genes are responsible for growth and development of edible part of mushroom.
- Grades of mushrooms: Grade A, Veil, Cup, Flat.
- 'Cambium Gold' brand of button mushroom is very popular throughout the world.
- As per International Trade standards, button mushrooms weighing 200 gram is packed in 53 μ plastic box for export purpose.
- International Mushroom school is located in Netherlands.

Parts of mushrooms:

a) Cap/ Pileus: Expanded portion of carpophores.

b) Gills/ Lamellae: Situated on underside of pileus from apex of stalk and radiate outwards the margins.

c) Veil: In young fruiting bodies, gills remain covered by tissue that extends from margin of cap to the stripe. This tissue is called as veil.

d) Stripe/ Stalk: Supports the pileus. Its presence or absence and its mode of attachment to cap is important character for identification of genera.

e) Volva (universal veil): Entire fruit body prior to differentiation is covered by universal veil. As carpophores extends, this veil breaks & remain as a cap volva surrounding the base of stripe.

Marks of identification:

1. In Agaricus- only annulus is present and volva is absent.
2. In Volvaiella- only volva is present and annulus is absent.
3. In Amanita- both annulus and volva are present.
4. Both are absent in common fairy ring (*Marasmius oreades*) mushroom.

Mushroom types:

- Edible varieties of mushroom belong to family Agaricaceae (Gill family) of the class Basidomycetes/ Ascomycetes.
- Sub-kingdom: Thyllophyta, to which mushrooms belong, includes algae, fungi & bacteria.
- Members of this kingdom lack true roots, stems or leaves and donot contain chlorophyll & cannot tak CO_2 from air to manufacture their own food.
- This group of fungi obtain their food from external sources and are placed in saprophytic group.
- Mushroom comprises above ground part (is reproductive or sporophore portion) & underground or vegetable part known as mycelium or spawn (are not roots at all).
- Mushooms doesnot flower or bear seeds but reproduces by spores generated by basidia located on the gills.
- By means of mycelium (spawn), mushrooms produce successive crops of fruiting bodies.
- Mushrooms are highly sensitive to temperature.
- Mushrooms = fruiting bodies of fleshy fungi.
- Three main groups: Edible mushroom (54%), medicinal purpose (38%), wild forms (8%).
- Wild mushrooms viz. *Morchella* spp. and *Pleurotus eryngii* have great export demand in Switzerland, Germany & France.
- *Flammulina velutipes* (Enoki mushroom) and *Hypsizygus marmoreus* (Elm mushroom) occupies 1st and 2nd position in world trade, respectively.
- New spp.: *Grifola frondosa* and *Pleurotus eryngii* are fast catching up.

- Edible mushrooms grown in China: *Pleurotus ostreatus*, *Lentinula edodes*, *Auricularia polytricha*, *Volvariella volvacea* and medicinal mushrooms (*Ganoderma lucidum*, *Flamulina velutips*, *Hericium erinaceus*).
- Oyster spp. under cultivation in India: *P. sajor-caju* (most popular & well adapted), *P. flabellatus*, *P. osteratus* (brown colour & found in high altitude areas), *P. florida*, *P. platypus*, *P. citrinopileatus* are popular in Uttaranchal.
- Three species of paddy straw mushroom: *V. volvacea*, *V. dysplasia* (most popular), *V. esculenta* are under cultivation.
- Marcella is collected from coniferous forests of Himachal Pradesh, Jammu and Kashmir, Uttarakhand by women workers.
- Mushroom types:
  - Temperate mushrooms: Black oyster mushroom (*Pleurotus ostreatus*, *P. eryngii*), *Volvariella bombycina*.
  - Sub-tropical mushroom: Grey oyster mushroom (*P. sajor-caju*),White oyster (*P. florida*), Pink oyster (*P. djamor*), Yellow oyster (*P. citrinopleatus*).
  - Tropical mushroom: Paddy straw mushroom.

Common name	Botanical name	Features
White button mushroom or Eurpean or Temperate button type	*Agaricus bisporus* (syn. *A. campestris*, *A. brunnescens*, *Psolliota campestris*)	90% of India's total production; widely accepted all over the world both in fresh & canned form; plays important role in carbon management of forest areas & cultivated round the year; temperature tolerant
	A. bitorquis	New species known as Town's/ street mushroom in Europe; grows at higher temperatures & high CO_2 concentration; fruit body is course with short stalk; cap silky white & little indented; better shelf life; resistant to die back & all known mushroom viruses & nematodes (*Apenchoides sacchari*)
Oyster mushroom or Wood fungus or Dhingri mushroom or King oyster	*Pleurotus eryngii* (syn. *P.ostreatus*)	Called as 'future mushroom of India'; 3rd most significant type & widely cultivated in western Europe (HUngery, Italy, France & west Germany); grows under natural conditions on trees, dead wood branches of trees, waste material of banana and arecanut as saprophytes & primary decomposers; used as fresh/ dehydrated form
Paddy straw mushroom or Warm mushroom or Chinese mushroom	*Volvariella volvacea*	1st edible mushroom cultivated in India; 10% of total production of world; fastest growing edible mushroom; growing at 32-34^{0}C hot & humid areas of peninsular India; grown in south India especially in Tamil Nadu & Karnataka; cultivated very easily on any kind of farm structures; completes life cycle in 30-40 days; very short shelf life; low productivity & low keeping quality
Wood ear or Black ear or Jew's ear or Rat's ear mushroom or Jelly fungi	*Auricularia polytricha*	Very common edible mushroom; ranks 5th among different cultivated mushorooms; highly priced in China for soups& curesthroat disorders, anaemia & digestive disorders (piles), stomach diseases, diabetes & anti-cancer; cartilaginous & purplish brown in colour;

		grown in wheat straw, cotton hull; ear like shape of fruiting body; widely grown in China, Japan & South Korea; require 22-28^{0}C for spawn run; remain on substrate up to 7-10 days after attaining maturity; yield 6-8 kg dry from 100 kg cotton seed hulls
Milky or Sweta mushroom	*Calocybe indica*	Grows in high temperature; high production in summer season; white coloured; excellent shelf life (4-5 days more than Dhingri) & shows no browning on long term storage; require casing for fructification
Shiitake mushroom	*Lentinus edodes*	2nd most important edible mushroom in the world having medicinal uses & account for 20% of world production; widely cultivated in N-E states of India & Japan; stimulates immune system against cancer; suitable wood is oak (by log method) or on saw dust (by bag method); grows more rapidly in dark; require 10-50 lux light (8-12 h/ day) for development of fruiting body
Giant mushroom	*Stropharia rugusa* var. *annulata*	Called as 'Gardens Giant' due to its giant size (60 g single fruiting body); pileus dia. varies from 5-40 cm; require pH of covering soil 5.7-6.0; takes 10-12 days for fruit body to reach full maturity; yield 16 kg/m^{2}; widely cultivated in the world; found in USA
Monkey cap mushroom	*Podaxis pistillaris*	Edible but not cultivated; large fruiting body; collected from forest in Himachal Pradesh
Wild edible mushroom	*Melanoleuca* spp.	-
Enoki mushroom	*Flammulina velutipes*	Occurs all over the world-in China, Asia Minor, Europe, Africa, South America, Japan, Australia & Siberia. Grows on tree trunks/ water logs or on saw dust from Autumn to early spring season; polypropylene bottles (800-1000 ml) are used as vessels for cultivation; takes 50-60 days from initial fruiting to crop; yields 100-140 g/ 800 ml bottle as 1st crop & 60-80 g in same bottle as 2nd crop.
Hallucinogenic or Poisonous mushroom	*Amanita muscaria*, *A. phalloides*, *Morchella taleciyosa*, *Boletus edulis*	Poisonous
Medicinal caterpillar mushroom	*Ophiocordyceps sinensis*	-
-	*Pestalotiopsis microspora*	Capable of eating plastic (contains chemical that break down polyurethane, the key ingredient in plastic & turns into organic matter)
-	*Pholiota nameko*	Important wood inhabiting or saw dust cultivated mushroom found in Japan; Nameko means 'Viscid mushroom'; it has viscid or glutinous pileus; grows on dead trunks/ stumps of deciduous trees; fungus is naturally collected in rainy season in Japan; it is hygrophilous fungus & need high moisture for fruiting compared to other mushrooms; fruiting bodies appear after 20 days & 4-5 flushes are harvested within 90 days.

Harvesting and post harvest technology:

- Harvested when cap is 2.5-7.5 cm or larger in dia., than base stem.

1. White button mushroom:
   - Harvested at proper stage; if allowed to grow further reveals pink gills due to rupture of veils. They further grow in size and become fully open or flat exposing the dark gills.
   - Cap size is 30-45 mm in dia. or when cap dia. is twice the length of stem.
   - Spray of 2% ascorbic acid improves colour by inhibiting polyphenol oxidase activity.
   - Short term preservation methods help to prolong shelf-life from 1 to 3 weeks.
   - Once the fruiting body matures & harvested, degradation process starts.
   - Deterioration changes associated with storage: Prolongation of stalks, opening of veils, toughness of texture & loss of whiteness.
2. Oyster mushroom:
   - Harvested when their fruit bodies have curled under edges with well formed gills i.e. wrinkled stage of umbrella.
   - Fully matured fruit bodies are fragile & difficult to handle.
   - With advanced maturity, fruit bodies lose water & shrinkage occurs.
   - Loss of turgidity is followed by darkening of colour & liquescent margins.
3. Paddy straw mushroom:
   - Harvested at button or egg sized stage i.e. when begins to differentiate into cap & stem stem growth inside the universal veil continues until differentiation completed.
   - Due to fast post harvest maturity, many changes occur as cap opens & gets the appearance of flattened umbrella and
   - Release of spores causes pink coloration of fruit bodies, causing off flavour & unmarketability.

a) Precooling:
   - Mushrooms are precooled immediately after harvest at 5^{0}C to check high respiration & deterioration at ambient temperature.
   - Mushrooms are preserved by quick freezing.

b) Disinfection:
   - To maintain whiteness of fresh button mushrooms, dip in dilute solution of hydrogen peroxide (1:3) & steeping in 0.25% citric acid solution + 500 ppm SO_2 or washing in 0.025% to 0.05% KMS solution.

c) Packaging:
   - Packed in 100 gauge polybags with 0.05% ventilation for refrigerated storage.
   - PVC packing creates MA storage (10% CO_2 + 2% O_2).

d) Storage:
   - Mushrooms cannot be stored at room temperature for more than 24 hours and/ or 1-2 weeks in refrigerated conditions.
   - Total sugars, soluble proteins & total phenol content decreases & polyphenol oxidase activity is enhanced.
   - *Pleurotus sajor-caju* could be kept up to 3 months in steeping solution (5% salt + 0.2% ascorbic acid & 0.1% KMS in glass bottles).

e) Irradiation:
   - With gamma rays (1-2 kGy dose) increases storage life for 9-10 days at 15^{0}C by delaying cap opening and stem elongation in button mushrooms.

f) Processing:
   - Pickling and sun drying: Economically viable methods of preservation.
   - Pickling is cheap method of preservation.
   - Low temperature or quick freezing is a process where temperature of mushrooms is brought to 0-3^{0}C in 30 minutes or less, stops microbial activity and retards enzyme activity.
   - Hermatic sealing is practiced all over the world.

g) Canning:
   - Button mushrooms are steeped in 0.5% solution of Methyl cellulose/ Carboxy methyl cellulose prior to canning increases yield by 5-9% without deterioration in quality.

h) Food additives:
   - Agar (0.125%) & pectin (0.5%) improved flavour of canned products.

i) Drying:
   - Removes free water (<0.7% of actual weight) & checks biochemical & microbial activity.

j) Fermentation:
   - It is a process of partial anaerobic condition of carbohydrates.
   - During fermentation, lactic acid is produced to prevent further spoilage during storage.

- For drying, milky mushrooms are cut as chips and dried on oven at 40-50^{0}C without change in colour.
- Spray drying technique: Powder form of mushroom.
- Solid state fermentation is widely used for raising mushrooms.
- Storage temperature: 3.5 to 4.0^{0}C.
- Storage life is from 17-20 days at 0^{0}C; 10-15 days at 3^{0}C; 7-10 days at 7^{0}C and 3-5 days at 12^{0}C.
- Use of washing solution- Potassium metabisulphite @ 0.05% improves colour.

- Storage life of white button mushrooms can be extended upto 21 days by use of $CaCl_2$ packets in punnet packaging (similar to grape packags).
- Before harvest, spray of Chlorine dioxide @ 200 ppm prevents bleaching and microbial infections and maintains white colour of buttons.
- Yield, quality and shelf life of button mushrooms increases by using $CaCl_2$ in irrigation waterand preharvest spray of 0.3% $CaCl_2$ or 125 ppm EDTA.
- CA storage is highly beneficial in mushroom production.

Varieties:

- Button mushroom: Ooty-1, 2 (good keeping quality), S-11, S-140, X-13 and hybrid strain U-3.
- 1st hybrid pink oyster mushroom in the country: AKP-1.
- Arka OM-2: Pink coloured oyster mushroom from IIHR, Bengaluru.
- Elm oyster mushroom: CO.2
- White button mushroom: DMR-Button-03, DMR-Button-06, NBS-1, NBS-5.
- Paddy straw mushroom: Strain DMRO-247, White strain DMRO-484.
- Milky mushroom: DMR-Milky-334.
- Shiitake mushroom: DMR-Shiitake- 38, DMR-Shiitake-388.
- 'Gucchi' from Jammu and Kashmir is India's costliest mushroom (Rs. 20,000/ kg). It has GI tag, medicinal and anti-inflammatory properties. It is found in temperate forests.

Diseases and pests:

- Cobweb disease (*Cladobotrym dendroides*): Major disease. Greyish white mycelium on casing & later on button cause decay and death.
- Dry bubble disease (*Verticilliumfungicola*): Infection produce light brown depressions on caps leading to blotching, drying and cracking.
- Wet bubble disease (*Mycogone perniciosa*): Leads to monstrous & distorted mushrooms. Brown droplets ooze out of decayed tissue with foul odour.
- Sciarid fly/ Forid fly/ Mushroom flies (*Bradysia tritici*, *Sciara* spp.): Feed on mycelium/ casing & disrupt attachment to pinheads, turn brown & die. Also enter into stripe & make mushrooms spongy and hollow
- Sesid fly: Feeds onknots developed in mycelium.
- Phorid (Dung flies): Larve feed into cap from gills.
- Spring tails: Feed mycelium. Button & oyster mushrooms are highly susceptible.
- Microphagus & Saprophagus bug: Feed on mycelium, attack on buttons.
- Viruses.
- Mites (*Tyrophagus* spp.): Produce brown rusted spots on caps & kill young buttons.

- Nematodes (*Aphelenchoides composticola*): Feed on mycelium & compost colour turns brown. Flushes become poor, delayed & yield declines. Management: Efficient pasteurization of compost & casing.
- Molds: Presence of ammonia in compost encourages growth of molds. Molds indicate inferior compost quality.
- Yellow mold (*Myceliophthora lutea*): Forms circular colonies in stroma & completely inhibits fructification.
- Green mold (*Trichoderma viride*): Form greenish growth on casing, spawn grains, caps & dead buttons.
- Brown plaster mold (*Populaspora byssina*): Forms white mycelial patches on casing & inhibits fructification.
- False truffle (*Diehliomyces microsporum*): Forms wrinkled brain like soild structures whic turn pink at maturity.
- Management of all diseases: Proper pasteurization of casing soil & hygiene.

Abnormalities:

- Rose comb: Gills on the top of mushroom fruit body is manifestation of rose comb. Malformed cap and gills forms on its upper surface. On top of cap, pink wart like outgrowths of malformed gills. It is a mis-shapen mushroom because of use of mineral oils, fumes in room and excessive application of BHC during fruiting.
- Scaly and cracked mushroom: Due to drought or cold air or less humidity in production room.
- Premature opening of caps: Due to high temperature and high CO_2 in production room.
- Stroma: White mycelial growth on casing soil makes compact structure of mycelium and hinders pin formation of the mushrooms of the house. Also due to less humidity and high CO_2. It is advised to recase the trays.
- Weepers: May be in form of leakers and stinkers. High humidity in casing or < 65% R.H. in compost media cause this disorder.
- Hollow & Brown stems: Cause weight loss. Creamy mushrooms are highly susceptible.
- Pink spunj: Knots appear on gills & become unmarketable. Pollution and smoke in surrounding areas leads to this disorder.
- Wrinkleness: Appear on caps and mushrooms become unmarketable. Less humidity, strong blowing winds are mainly responsible.
- Long stalked mushrooms: Improper ventilation i.e. more accumulation of CO_2 in incubation rooms cause slender, stalky growth with stunty/ small sized caps.
- Browny mushrooms: Pin head type incomplete growth cause drying & browning. High temperature, use of chlorinated water & high pressure during watering of beds cause this malady.

4

FLORICULTURE AND LANDSCAPE ARCHITECTURE

4

FLORICULTURE AND LANDSCAPE ARCHITECTURE

1. GENERAL FLORICULTURE

- USA ranks 17th in per capita cut flowers consumption.
- India ranks 2nd in flower cultivation next to China.
- India stands 14th in the world in exporting floricultural products, while the Netherlands and Columbia rank 1st and 2nd, respectively.
- The production of loose flowers almost tripled between the 8th Plan and the 11th Plan.
- The annual domestic demand is valued at around 60 billion USD.
- Annual growth rate of domestic trade of floriculture products: 25-30%.
- About 2,78,000 hectares across the country was used for floriculture, producing 21,84,000 metric tones (MT) of loose flowers and 528 million tons of cut flowers.
- India has imported 17,409 MT of floriculture products and exported 19,726 MT of floriculture products to the world for the worth of Rs. 548.74 crores in 2018-19.
- Export trend: Dried flowers and plant parts (45%), flowering plants (22%), fresh foliage (13%), fresh cut flowers (10%), live plants (7%) and bulbs and tubers (3%).
- Export of potted plants: Rs. 124,320 million.
- From India, foliage plants are exported to Middle East, USA, Europe.
- Major importers of potted plants: Germany, Sweden, France, Finland, Norway, etc.
- Most popular foliage plants exported from the Netherlands: *Ficus benjamina*, *Hedera*, *Dracena*, *Yucca*, *Schefflera*.
- **Major Export Destinations**: United States, United Kingdom, Germany, the Netherlands, Japan and United Arab Emirates.
- There are more than 300 flower export oriented units in India and more than 50% of floriculture units are based in Karnataka, Andhra Pradesh and Tamil Nadu.
- India's share in global floriculture trade- 0.6%.
- Share of floricultural products in total horticultural produce: 1.1%.
- Flowers domestic industry is growing at annual rate of 7-8% per annum.
- Leading flower producing states: Tamil Nadu (19%), Karnataka (13%) and West Bengal (12%).

- Maharashtra, Karnataka, Andhra Pradesh, Haryana, Tamil Nadu, Rajasthan and West Bengal: Major floriculture centers.
- Highest production of flowers in Tamil Nadu (416.63 thousand tones) followed by Karnataka (280.92 thousand tones).
- West Bengal emerged as the largest producer in cut flowers with 25,429 lakh pieces, followed by Karnataka and Maharashtra.
- The area under protected cultivation was 0.23% of the total area under horticulture.
- Division of Floriculture and Landscape Gardening was started at IIHR, Bengaluru in 1969.
- Division of Floriculture and Landscape Gardening was started it IARI, New Delhi in 1983.
- 'Development of Floriculture' was recommended by Dr. P.P. Trivedi committee.
- Milieu Project Sierteelt (MPS): Quality certification programme by Dutch Floriculture Industries and the auction houses for environmentally sound cultivation practices of flowers and plants.
- Flower Label Programme (FLP), Germany: Organisation that helps to make worldwide production of cut flowers more environmentally friendly, socially acceptable and economically sustainable.
- 'Transforming the lives and landscapes with trees' is the motto of ICRAF, Nairobi.
- Flower auction centres in world: Aalsmeer, Amsterdam (the Netherlands), Miami (USA), Bogota (Columbia), Tel Aviv (Isreal).
- Largest flower auction centre in the world: Aalsmeer Flower Auction (Bloemenveiling Aalsmeer).
- On 1st January, 2008 the auction centre merged with their biggest competitor Flora Holland.
- FloraHolland flower auction: International market leader in flower sales.
- In India, 1st international flower auction centre has been set up in Bengaluru (www.rosebazar.com) in 2003.
- Model Floriculture Centres (MFCs) were established in (Rajgurunagar) Maharashtra and Karnataka.
- National Floriculture Model Farm in Himachal Pradesh is situated at Chail.
- Floriculture Infrastructure Parks (FIPs) were established at Hosur, Tamil Nadu (TANFLORA) and Talegaon (Floriculture park), Maharashtra.
- Fragrance and Flavour Development Centre (FFDC), Kannauj, works under Ministry of Small Scale Industries and Agro & Rural Industries.
- Miraah solar project: Oman country.
- Largest importer of floriculture products from India: USA (27%).
- Leading flower product exporting country:The Netherlands (57%), Columbia (14%).

- Leading flower product importing country: Germany, USA.
- Leading cut green exporting country: Italy followed by The Netherlands.
- Largest loose flowers producing country: India.
- Lake Placcid: Caladium capital of the world.
- Flower capital of the world: California.
- Foliage capital of the world: Apopka, Florida.
- No. 1 foliage plant in global market: Dieffenbachia.
- No. 1 pot plant in global market: Hedera.
- No. 1 cut green plant in global market: Asparagus.
- *Raffelsia arnoldii*: Largest flower in the world. Flower diameter of 3-4 feet and weigh 10 kg. It is a parasite flower produce aerial roots to anchor/ grows on another tree and produces objectionable odour.
- Conifer 'Chir pine' is not used as cut green.
- New country started importing Indian flowers: Haiti.
- Titan arum (*Amorphophallus titanum*): Possess largest unbranched inflorescence have foul smell.
- State famous for growing rhododendrons: Mizoram.
- Plants valued for their ornamental bracts: Bougainvillea, Mussaenda, Poinsettia, Heliconia.
- Due to betalins, plants become resistant to gray mold.
- Betalins are widely used in strawberry yogurts and in medicine industry for L-Dopa production.
- Plants sensitive to Sulphur dioxide (SO_2): Sweet pea, Cosmos, *Hibiscus esculentus*, Zinnia.
- Plants resistant to SO_2: Thuja, Rhododendron, *Acer palmatum*.
- Plant sensitive to nitrous oxide (NO_2): Bougainvillea, Hibiscus, Oleander.
- Plant resistant to NO_2: Croton, Juniper.
- Dragon tree (*Dracaena marginata*): Removes xylene, trichloroethylene, toluene from air.
- English ivy (*Hedera helix*): Removes formaldehyde, benzene, airborne faecal matter.
- *Ficus* spp.: Adapt in clearing formaldehyde, good air purifier.
- Peace lily (*Spathiphyllum wallisii*): Removes variety of alcohols and chemical vapours including acetone, benezene, ammonia, formaldehyde, xylene and scores top among the plants tested for removing several toxins.
- Rubber plant (*Ficus elastica*): Removes formaldehyde.
- Snake plant (*Sansevieria trifasciata*): Clears smog, formaldehyde and trichloroethylene. Produces oxygen and removes CO_2.

- Spider plant (*Chlorophytum comosum*): Removes smog, benzene, formaldehyde and xylene found in auto exhaust, synthetic perfume and paints.
- Weeping fig (*Ficus benjamina*): Removes pollutants like formaldehyde, xylene and toluene.
- Plants such as iris, reed, sweet flag are able to recycle water through their root system.
- Edible flowers or Future nutrition capsule e.g. Rose, Antirrhinum, Chrysanthemum, Pansy, Balsam, Daffodil, Black elder (*Sambucus nigra*), Dandelion, Dianthus, Fuchsia, Marigold, Calendula, Hibiscus, Nasturtium.
- Acid soil loving plants: Rhododendron, Camellia, Hydrangea.
- Alkaline soil loving plants: Petunia, Rose, Zinnia.
- Bells of Ireland was earlier cultivated as vegetable but now used as cut flower.
- In enforced dormancy, seeds fail to germinate due to absence of light and low temperature.
- After ripening period in seeds is shorter under higher storage temperature and higher seed moisture content.
- International Cherry Blossom festival was held in Shillong, Meghalaya.
- Arunachal Pradesh is called as 'Cradle of flowering plants' and 'Bio-geographical gateway' of biological resources.
- Indian Nurserymen Association was established in 1987.
- Sigmoid growth curve: Easter lily, Chrysanthemum, Poinsettia.
- Design and drafting of a landscape design with the aid of computer is known as CAD.
- CAD technique was initiated in Massachusetts Institute of Technology (MIT) by Ivan Sutherland.
- Under SAGE program, the 1st sketchpad system was created.
- A 3D sketch helps the designer to imagine real garden.
- Two components of CAD are software and hardware.
- Widely used computer programs (CAD softwares) for architectural drafting in landscaping: AutoCAD, ArchiCAD, Advance Concrete, Advance Design, Advanced Steel, BRL-CAD, BricsCAD, ZACAD, CADbro, CADPOCKETS, iScape, Tekla, Revit, LANDCADD, etc.
- HIMFLORA: Computerized botanical database on wild ornamental plants of Himachal Himalayas contains detailed records of 250 wild ornamental plants (36 trees, 82 shrubs, 28 climbers, 56 herbaceous plants, 18 ferns, 11 orchids, 19 bulbous plants).
- Resurrection plant [*Selaginella lepidophylla* (syn. *Lycopodium lepidophyllum*] any poikilohydric plant that can survive extreme dehydration, even over months or years.

- Dew plant (*Drosera eloisiana*): Carnivorous plant.
- French mulberry (*Callicarpa tomentosa*, Verbenaceae): Called as Pandavas' torch.
- Duck's foot or Kaikomako (*Pennantia corymbosa*): World's lonliest/ rarest tree on earth.
- Speciality flowers means variety of ornamental flowers having vivid shapes and colours e.g. Bird of paradise, Heliconia, Torch lily, and Ginger lily, etc.
- Fillers like ornamental asparagus, acalypha and crotons can be taken as ointercrops in fruit orchards.
- Blue light is absorbed to its maximum in spectrum region of 430-450 nm.
- **Pinking**: Abnormal pink coloration of caladium leaves due to low temperature.
- **Antholyse**: Failure of a flowering sized tulip bulb to initiate a flower after forming a complete component of leaves (usually 3-5).
- **Blackout system**: A means of covering plants to shorten the photoperiod by means of black sheet.
- **Bypassing shoot**: In azaleas, vegetative shoot develops immediately below the flower bulb.
- **Corona**: A crown or trumpet shaped outgrowth of petals in daffodil flower.
- **Bulb finger**: An irritation resulting due to handling of tulip bulbs and cut flowers of alstroemeria, narcissus and tulip.
- **Bulb units**: Referring to the annual increments of bulb growth e.g. Narcissus.
- **Bypassing shoot**: In azaleas, vegetative shoot develops immediately below the flower bulb.
- **Controlled temperature forcing (CTF)**: It is a procedure for forcing Easter lily cvs. 'Ace' and 'Nellie White' where non-precooled bulbs are potted and then are placed in controlled temperature at 16-17^{0}C for 2-4 weeks and then at 2-4^{0}C for 6-7 weeks prior to being placed in the greenhouse.
- **Dropper (Diverticullum)**: It is an unusual plant organ, especially in tulips, a bulb being formed at distal end inside the lining of a hollow stolon.
- **Fasciated** The malformation with flattened stems looking as if many stems have joined together e.g. Amaranthus and Celosia.
- **Flat bulb**: Shape of daughter bulbs produced by bulbous plant e.g. Dutch iris & Narcissus.
- **Floral bud split**: Floral bud splits due to high temperature or aphid infestation e.g. Lilies.
- **Floater-sinker**: A method of separating healthy bulbs from those affected with basal rot which float with other debris.
- **Flore-pleno**: Flowers having abnormally high number of petals e.g. Carnation, narcissus and tulips.
- **Gooseneck**: Stage of flower development to cut daffodil.

- **Hose-in-hose**: Refers to mutation where calyx looks like a corolla, appearing as if one flower is sitting within another.
- **Limber neck (syn. stem topple, Wet stem)**: Toppling of the floral stock just below the neck of flower in certain Dutch irises, hyacinths, *Lilium* and tulip before or during flowering due to heavy flowers or imbalance of water or certain nutrients.
- **Pupation**: Formation of new corm from an old corm e.g. Freesia.
- **Scooping or De-eying**: A method of propagation in certain bulbs e.g. Caladium, *Hyacinthus*, in which apical dominance is terminated by scooping out the basal plate of the bulb to encourage more bulblet formation.

TOP TEN FLOWERS AND PLANTS IN THE WORLD:

Cut flowers	Annual flowers	Bedding plants	Pot plants
Rose	Marigold	Begonia	Ivy
Tulip	Geranium	Sweet pea	Kalanchoe
Chrysanthemum	Impatients	Busy lizzie	Ficus
Gerbera	Flowering tobacco	Geranium	African violet
Lily	Gerbera	Antirrhinum	Chrysanthemum
Alstroemeria	Sweet pea	Lobelia	Spathiphyllum
Freesia	Cosmos	Petunia	Hyacinth
Carnation	Morning glory	Rudbeckia	Dracaena
Iris	Sunflower	Californian poppy	Potted rose
Gypsophila	Zinnia	Cosmos	Primrose

NATIONAL FLOWERS OF DIFFERENT COUNTRIES:

Country	Flower	Country	Flower
Afghanistan	Tulip	Israel	Cyclamen
Argentina	Ceibo (*Erythrina crista-galli*)	Japan	Cherry Blossom (*Prunus cerasus*)
Australia	Golden Wattle (*Acacia pycnantha*)	Jordan	Black Iris
Austria	Edelweiss (*Leontopodium nivale*)	Malaysia	Hibiscus
Bangladesh	White Water Lily	Mexico	Dahlia
Barbados	Pride of Barbados (*Caesalpinia pulcherrima*)	Myanmar	Padauk (*Pterocarpus macrocarpus*)
Belgium	Red Poppy	The Netherlands	Tulip
Bermuda	*Sisyrinchium bermudiana*	New Zealand	Kowhai (*Sophora microphylla*)
Bhutan	Blue Poppy (*Meconopsis gakyidiana*)	Norway	Purple Heather (*Callunna vulgaris*)
Bolivia	Cantuta (*Cantua buxifolia*)	Pakistan	*Jasminum officinale*
Brazil	*Cattleya labiata*	Philippines	*Jasminum sambac*
Bulgaria	Rose	Poland	Corn poppy (*Papaver rhoeas*)
Chile	Copihue (*Lapageria rosea*)	Puerto Rico	Flor de Maga (*Thespesia grandiflora*)

Columbia	Cattleya Orchid	Romania	Dog rose (*Rosa canina*)
Cuba	Mariposa	Russia	Chamomile (*Matricaria recutita*)
Cyprus	Cyclamen	Scotland	Thistle (*Cirsium arvense*)
Denmark	Marguerite Daisy	Singapore	Vanda Miss Joaquim
Egypt	Lotus	South Africa	King Protea
England	Rose, Tudor Rose	South Korea	*Hibiscus syriacus*
Ethiopia	Calla lily	Spain	Carnation
Finland	Lily of the Valley	Sri Lanka	Blue Lily
France	Iris	Switzerland	Edelweiss
Germany	Cornflower (*Centaurea cyanus*)	Taiwan	Plum Blossom
Hungary	Tulip	Thailand	*Cassia fistula*
India	Lotus	USA	Rose
Indonesia	Pusapa Bangsa (*Jasminum sambac*)	Vietnam	Lotus
Iraq	Red Rose	Zimbabwe	Flame lily
Ireland	Shamrock (*Oxalis acetosella*)	-	

2. IMPROVEMENT OF FLOWERS THROUGH OUTCROSSING:

- 1st hybrid in ornamentals: 'Primma Donna' in *Begonia semperflorens* (1909) by Benery Seed Company, Germany.

2.1 Breeding methods followed in flower crops

- Selection: Amaryllis, Anthurium, Bougainvillea, China aster, Chrysanthemum, Crossandra, Dahlia, Gaillardia, Geranium, Gerbera, Gladiolus, Hibiscus, Hollyhock, Jasmine, Lotus, Marigold, Rose, Tuberose.
- Single seed descent method: Salvia.
- Heterosis is a function of specific combining ability of parental combinations and depends on genetic divergence of parents involved in cross.
- Heterosis in flower crops is manifested in plant height, length and width and leaf blade, days from emergence to maturity of leaves, leaf area, number of laterals/ plant, increased number of petals, flower size, ,time taken for first flowering, yield and vase life e.g. Balsam, Calendula, China aster, Geranium, Gladiolus, Hollyhock, Marigold, Pansy, Petunia, Zinnia.
- Intergeneric hybridization: Amaryllis, chrysanthemum, orchids.
- Inter sub-generic hybridization: Water lily.
- Interspecific hybridization: Ageratum, Amaryllis, Antirrhinum, Anthurium, Balsam, Bougainvillea, Calla lily, Carnation, Chrysanthemum, Geranium, Hibiscus, Marigold, Lilium, Orchids, Pansy, Periwinkle, Petunia, Phlox, Statice, Tuberose, Tulip, Verbena, Water lily, Zinnia.
- Intervarietal hybridization: Amaryllis, Anthurium, Balsam, Bougainvillea, China aster, Chrysanthemum, Crossandra, Dahlia, Geranium, Gerbera, Gladiolus, Hibiscus, Hollyhock, Lilium, Marigold, Rose, Tuberose, Water lily.
- Interploidy hybridization: Lilium, Marigold.

- Intersectional hybridization: Lilium.
- Introgressive breeding: Enables monitoring of presence/ absence of alienchromosomes or recombination between genomes in F_1 hybrids and back cross progenies e.g. Tulip.
- Double cross: Selection of inbred lines & development of F_1 hybrids using 4 inbred lines e.g. Christian Dior [(Independence x Happiness) x (Peach Happiness)], Super Star, Memorium of rose.
- Triple cross: Three parents are involved e.g. Little Darling, Charlestan of chrysanthemum.
- Backcross breeding: It is a system of breeding where by recurrent back crosses are made to one of the parents of hybrids and accompanied by selection for a specific character e.g. Amaryllis, Tulip, Verbena, Zinnia.
- Mutation breeding: Amaryllis, Antirrhinum, Bougainvillea, Chrysanthemum, Cosmos, Crossandra, Dahlia, Gladiolus, Jasmine, Periwinkle, Petunia, Rose, Tuberose, Tulip, Verbena, Zinnia.
- *In vitro* mutagenesis: Anthurium, Carnation, Chrysanthemum, Geranium, Water lily.
- Space mutagenesis: Salvia.
- Use of heavy ion beam (HIB) radiation: Verbena.
- Polyploidy breeding: Tetraploids possessed stronger petioles, thicker, larger and deeper green leaves, larger stomatal size and low stomatal density, thicker and longer lived spathes, large guard cells, higher number of chloroplasts e.g. Amaryllis, Antirrhinum, Balsam, Bougainvillea, Chrysanthemum, Carnation, Crossandra, Dahlia, French Marigold, Gerbera, Geranium, Hibiscus, Jasmine, Orchids, Phlox, Rose, Tulip, Water Lily, Zinnia.
- *In vitro* polyploidization: Anthurium, Rose, Statice.
- Genome breeding: Orchids, Anthurium (for enhanced resistance to bacterial leaf blight).
- Embryo rescue: Useful in rescuing embryos of sexual crosses that fail because hybrid embryo abort e.g. Cosmos, Tulip, Pelargonium, Rose, etc.

2.2 Species involved in cross breeding

Flower	Hybrid	Species involved in cross breeding
Antirrhinum	Dwarf Rock hybrids	*A. molle* x *A. glutinosum*
Annual chrysanthemum	*Chrysanthemum x spectabilis*	*C. carinatum* x *C. coronarium*
Bougainvillea	*B.* x *buttiana*	*B. peruviana* x *B. glabra*
	B. x *specto-peruviana*	*B. spectabilis* x *B. peruviana*
	B. x *specto-glabra*	*B. spectabilis* x *B. glabra*
Gerbera	Hybrids	*G. jamesonii*, *G. viridifolia*
Heliconia	Hybrids	*H. psittacorum* x *H. metallica* (red varieties), *H.*

		bihai, H. rostrata, H. humilis
Hippeastrum	Hybrids	*H. reginae* x *H. vittatum*
Lilium	LA hybrid	*L. longiflorum* x Asiatic
	LO hybrid	*L. longiflorum* x Oriental
	OT hybrid	Oriental x Trumpet
	OA hybrid	Oriental x Asiatic
	FA hybrid	*L. formolongi* x Asiatic
	FO hybrid	*L. formolongi* x Oriental
	OH hybrid	Oriental x *L. henryii*
	L. x *formolongi*	*L. formosanum* x *L. longiflorum*
Nymphaea	*N.* x *marliaca*	*N. alba* or
	N. x *laydekeri*	*N. tuberosum* x *N. mecicana*; *N. alba var. rubra* x *N. tetragona*
Pansy	*Viola* x *wittrockiana*	*Viola tricolor* x *lutea*, *V. altaica*
Pelargonium	Zonal/ Fish type geranium (*P.* x *hortorum*) for bedding purpose	*P. zonale* x *P. inquinans*
	Ivy leaved geranium (*P. peltatum*) for hanging basket purpose	*P. inquinans* x *P. peltatum*
	Regal geranium (*P.* x *domesticum*) for greenhouse purpose	*P. grandiflorum* x *P. cucullatum*
	Rose geranium (*P. graveolens*) for essential oil purpose	*P. radens* (2n=8x=88) x *P. capitatum* (2n=6x=66)
Petunia	*Petunia* x *hybrida*	*P. axillaris*, *P. inflata*, *P. inflora*, *P. violacea*, *P. platensis*
Statice	*Limonium barceoli*	*L. gibertii* x *L. boirae*

2.3 Flower breeders in India:

- Bougainvillea: T.N.Khoshoo, S.N. Zadoo, B.P. Pal.
- Carnation: Tejeswini, M.V. Dhananjaya
- China aster: S.S. Dumbre Patil, T. Janakiram, Rajeev Kumar, S.M. Katwate.
- Chrysanthemum: M.A.Kher, S.K. Dutta, M.N. Gupta, M.V. Dhananjay.
- Dahlia: Swami Vinayananda, P.K. Das, A.K. Dey.
- Gerbera, Crossandra: C. Aswath.
- Gladiolus: Bajrang Bahadur Singh Bhandari, R.L. Mishra, S.S.Negi, D. Mukherjee, T. Manjunath Rao, Manoj Nazir, etc.
- Hibiscus: R.N. Bhat, M. Virupaksha.
- Jasmine: S. Muthuswamy, Madhava Rao, Bhupal Rao, H.C. Srivastava, etc.
- Orchids: Foja Singh, Abraham.
- Rose: B.P.Pal, S.C. Dey, J.P. Agarwal, A.P. Singh, Tejeswini.
- Tuberose: Meenakshi Srinivas, S.M. Katwate.

3. CLASSIFICATION OF FLOWER CROPS

3.1 Based on botany:

Family	Common name	Botanical name	Origin	2n=
Monocots				
Agavaceae	Tuberose	*Polianthes tuberosa*	Mexico	60 (2x, single); 50 (2x, double)
Amaryllidaceae	Amaryllis	*Amaryllis* spp. (syn. *Hippeastrum* spp.)	S. America	22 (2x), 44 (4x)
	Daffodil	*Narcissus pseudonarcissus*	Spain	28 (2x)
	Day lily	*Hemerocallis fulva*	Asia	44 (4x)
Apocynaceae	Periwinkle	*Catharanthus roseus*	Madagascar	16 (2x), 32 (4x)
	Adenium	*Adenium obesum*	Africa	22 (2x)
Araceae	Anthurium	*Anthurium andreanum*	Columbia	30 (2x)
	Calla lily	*Zantedeschia aethiopica*	S. Africa	32 (2x)
Asteraceae (Compositae)	Dahlia	*Dahlia variabilis*	Mexico	16 (2x), 32 (4x)
Heliconiaceae	Heliconia	*Heliconia psittacorum*	Central America	24 (2x)
Iridaceae	Gladiolus	*Gladiolus hybridus*	South Africa & Asia Minor	30 (2x), 60 (4x)
	Iris	*Iris* x *germanica*	India	24 (2x), 48 (4x)
Liliaceae	Lilium	*Lilium* spp.	N. America & Europe	24(2x), 36(3x)
	Tulip	*Tulipa gesneriana*	Central Asia	24 (2x), 36 (3x), 48 (4x), 60 (5x)
Nelumbonaceae	Lotus	*Nelumbo lutea*; *N. nucifera*	America & India	16 (2x)
Nymphaeaceae	Water lily	*Nymphaea spp.*	India, Europe, S. America	28(2x), 42, 56, 84 to 224(16x).
Orchidaceae	Orchids	*Cattleya*, *Dendrobium*, etc.	India, S. America & C. America	36 (2x), 38 (2x), 40 (2x), 42 (2x)
Strelitziaceae	Bird of paradise	*Strelitzia reginae*	South Africa	22 (2x)
Dicots				
Acanthaceae	Crossandra	*Crossandra undulaefolia*	India, Malaysia, Sri Lanka, East Indies	20 (2x), 30 (3x), 40 (4x)

Alstroemeriaceae	Alstroemeria	*Alstroemeria* spp.	South America	16 (2x)
Amaranthaceae	Gomphrena	*Gomphrena globosa*	India	40 (2x)
Asteraceae (Compositae)	China aster	*Callisteohus chinensis*	China	18 (2x)
	Chrysanthemum	*Chrysanthemum* spp.	China	18 (2x), 36 (4x), 54 (6x)
	Cosmos	*Cosmos sulphureus*	Mexico	24 (2x)
	Gaillardia	*Gaillardia pulchella*	S. Ameica	36 (2x)
	Gerbera	*Gerbera jamesonii*	S. Africa	50 (2x)
	Marigold	*Tagetes erecta, T. patula*	S. America	24 (2x), 48 (4x)
	Pot marigold	*Calendula officinalis*	India	18 (2x)
	Zinnia	*Zinnia elegans*	Mexico	22 (2x), 24 (2x)
Balsaminaceae	Balsam	*Impatiens balsamina, I.wallerana*	India, North America	12 (2x), 16 (2x)
Caryophyllaceae	Carnation	*Dianthus caryophyllus*	Mediterranean region	30 (2x)
Cruciferae (Brassicaceae)	Stock	*Matthiola incana*	S-W Europe & West Asia	14 (2x)
Geraniaceae	Rose scented geranium	*Pelargonium graveolens*	South Africa	18 (2x), 44 (4x), 66 (6x), 88 (8x)
Labiatae	Salvia	*Salvia splendens*	Brazil, Western Asia & Mediterranean region	16 (2x), 32(4x)
Malvaceae	Hibiscus	*Hibiscus rosa-sinensis*	India, China	18 (2x)
	Hollyhock	*Althea rosea*	Central Asia	18 (2x), 27 (3x)
Nyctaginaceae	Bougainvillea	*Bougainvillea* spp.	Brazil	34 (2x), 51 (3x), 68 (4x)
Oleaceae	Jasmine	*Jasminum* spp.	Indo- Malaya region	26 (2x), 39 (3x), 52 (4x)
Plantaginaceae (Scrophulariaceae)	Snapdragon	*Antirrhinum majus*	Europe	16 (2x)
Plumbaginaceae	Statice	*Limonium sinuatum*	Europe	18 (2x), 36 (4x), 54 (6x), 72 (8x)
Polemoneaceae	Phlox	*Phlox cuspidata; P. drummondii*	N. America	14
Rosaceae	Rose	*Rosa hybrida*	Europe & N. America	14 (2x), 56 (8x)
Solanaceae	Petunia	*Petunia hybrida*	S. America	14 (2x)
Verbenaceae	Verbena	*Verbena hybrida*	South & Central America	14 (2x)
Violaceae	Pansy	*Viola tricolor*	S. America & Himalaya	24 (8x)

3.2 Based on pollination mechanism:

- Corona: Trumpet or cup of daffodil flower. This structure is also found in passion flower, Hippeastrum and Lilicaceae family.
- Brushing improves seed set in carnation and pansy.
- Single gene male sterility is transferred in 7-8 generations.
- Cindrella: Flower abnormality observed in begonia.
- The 'Twinkle' varieties with star-shaped petals in phlox: Results of gene mutation.
- *Pothos* spp. and *Vallisnaria*: Non-endospermic monocot seeds.

Type	Crops
Self pollinated	Aster, Balsam, Clianthus, Lupin, Pansy, Sweet pea, Salvia
Often-cross pollinated	Antirrhinum, Dahlia, Larkspur, Lineria, Phlox, Salvia, Wall flower
Cross pollinated	Arctotis, Calendula, Cineraria, Gazania, Stock, Sweet Alyssum, Zinnia

3.2.1 Autogamy:

- Cleistogamy (i.e. fertilization even before flower opening). The pollen is shed, and stigma becomes receptive even before anthesis e.g. *Viola pubescens, Viola odorata, Impatiens glandulifera*.
- Chasmogamy (i.e. act of fertilization at the time of flower opening) e.g. *Viola grypoceras*, *Clitorea ternatea*, Gerbera.
- Homogamy (i.e. anther, and stigmas of a bisexual flower mature at the same time e.g. Lupine, Aster, *Calendula*, Sweet pea (*Lathyrus odoratus*).
- Cleistogamy, and chasmogamy are the two flower modifications in hermaphrodite flowers leading to autogamy e.g. Aster, Antirrhinum, Balsam, Bells of Ireland, China aster, Clianthus, Crossandra, *Dianthus barbatus*, *D. chinensis, D. caryophyllus,* Gypsophila, Sweet pea, Lupine, *Primula vulgaris*, Salvia, Saponaria, Pansy.

3.2.2 Allogamy:

- Heteromorphism: Dissimilarity in the position and placement of floral parts.
  - Distyly: *J. grandiflorum*, *J. pubescence*, Primrose, *Primula vulgaris,* Salvia.
  - Tristyly: *Oxalis pes-caprae*, *Lythrum*.
  - Heterostyly: Antirrhinum, Primula, *J. auriculatum*, *J. grandiflorum*, *J. pubescence*, Pentas, *Primula obconica,* Salvia, Statice.
- Unisexuality / Decliny: Cross pollination takes place due to separation of sex.
  - Monoecious condition: Male and female flowers are separate, but seen in one plant e.g. Anthurium, Begonia, *Casuriana equisetifolia*, Gerbera, Rose, Marigold, Petunia, etc.

- Dioecious condition: Where male plant (androecious) & female plant (gynoecious-pistillate) are separate (e.g. *Polygonum cuspidatum*, Juniperus, Willow).

- Dichogamy: Difference in the time of maturity of male and female parts.
  - Protandry: Alstroemeria, Amaryllis, Chrysanthemum, Gladiolus, Hollyhock, Marigold, Pansy, Phlox, Salvia.
  - Protogyny: Anthurium, Antirrhinum, Begonia, *Casuriana equisetifolia*, Lotus, Petunia, Gerbera.
  - Geitonogamy: China aster, Periwinkle, Salvia, Hollyhock.
  - Xenogamy: Both autogamy and geitonogamy occur in flowers e.g. *Salvia miltiorrhiza*.
- Herkogamy: Spatial separation of anther and stigma in flowers e.g. *Arabidopsis thaliana*, Hollyhock, *Narcissus longispathus*, Peperomia, *Ruellia brevifolia* and Pansy.
- Geitonogamy: It is genetically equivalent to self pollination. When pollen grain of a flower falls on the stigmas of another flower, on the same plant, it is called as geitonogamy e.g. China aster, Hollyhock, Periwinkle, Salvia.
- Self incompatibility (SI):
  - Sporophytic self incompatibility (SSI): Pollen-pistil reaction where pollen reaction depends on the diploid pollen parent as well as the female parent e.g Ageratum, Antirrhinum, Bougainvillea, Chrysanthemum, Cosmos, Daisy, Dahlia, Gaillardia, Gerbera, Statice, Geranium and Zinnia.
  - Gametophytic self incompatibility (GSI): Pollen-pistil reaction depends on the pollen grain itself and pollen grain rejection is determined by the haploid genotype of the individual pollen grain e.g. Nemesia, Nicotiana, Easter lily, *Dendrobium* orchid, Geranium, Petunia, Phlox, Rose.
  - Plastome-genome incompatibility e.g. Calla lily.
  - Endosperm-embryo incompatibility e.g Orchids.
  - Heteromorphic diallelic self incompatibility: Pollen and floral dimorphism is noticed e.g. Statice.
- Male sterility:
  - Functional male sterility: Anthers do not dehisce, to release the pollen i.e. closed anther mutant e.g. Chrysanthemum, Pelargonium, Periwinkle, Verbena, Zinnia.
  - Structural male sterility: Absence of stamens e.g. Ageratum, Antirrhinum, Calceolaria,
  - Delphinium, *Impatiens*, Marigold, Petunia, Salvia, Zinnia. Cytoplasmic male sterility (CMS) e.g. Ageratum, *Impatiens*, Petunia, Sunflower.

- o Genic male sterility (GMS) e.g. Ageratum, Marigold, Zinnia, Calceolaria, *Nigella sativa*, *Pelargonium*, Periwinkle, Salvia, Verbena.
- o Cytogenetic male sterility (CGMS) e.g. Cosmos, Marigold, Petunia, Zinnia.

3.3 Based on photosynthetic pathway:

C_4 plant	C_3 plants	Both C_3 & C_4 plant	CAM plants
Carnation	Horse shoe pelargonium, African marigold, Petunia, Cock's comb, Alstroemeria, *Cymbidium* orchid	Gomphrena, Bougainvillea	Agave, *Phalaenopsis* orchid, cacti & succulents

3.4 Based on day length requirement:

Short day (long night of 10-14 h)	Long day (short night of 8-10 h)	Day neutral (flowering not influenced by day length)	Long short day	Short long day
Amaranthus, Azalea, Bougainvillea, *Cattleya trianae*, Chrysanthemum, China aster, Cosmos, Dahlia, *Euphorbia pulcherimma*, Kalanchoe, Morning glory (*Ipomoea hederacea*), Poinsettia, Rieger begonia (called as winter begonia & facultative), Salvia, Tuberous begonia (tuber formation is long night response), Zinnia (facultative)	Antirrhinum, Aster, Bryophyllum (plantlets form along the margins), Calceolaria, Carnation (facultative), Cineraria, Dahlia, Easter lily (height increases), Hollyhock, Petunia, Rudbeckia, Sweet William, Tuberous begonia	Balsam, Calceolaria, Cineraria, Coleus, Gomphrena, Jasmine, Orchids, Rose	Aloe	Campanula, Pelargonium (facultative), White clover

3.5 Based on seed storage behaviour:

- In general, 4-6% moisture content in seeds is optimum for longer storage.
- Insect-pest occurrence takes place at 8-9% moisture and fungal growth at 12-14% moisture.
- Ideal moisture for safe storage of seeds: 5-7%.
- Robert (1983) classified seeds as orthodox and recalcitrant.

Orthodox seeds	Recalcitrant seeds
Amaryllis, Begonia, Cactus, Calendula, Camellia, China aster, Chrysanthemum, Dahlia, Dianthus, English daisy, Gerbera, Gladiolus, Gypsophila, Lupin, Marigold, Orchids, Pelargonium, Petunia, Periwinkle, Rhododendron, Rose, Salvia, Zinnia	Anthurium, Begonia, Caladium, Delphinium, Lantana, Lotus, Palms, Primrose, Salix, Pansy, Verbena.

3.6 Based on endopsperm content

Endospermic seeds	Non-endospermic seeds
Delphinium, Cyclamen, Primula, Begonia, Petunia, Antirrhinum, Linaria, Penstemon, Nemesia, Lobelia, Kochia, Celosia, Gomphrena, Four O'Clock	Anchusa, Balsam, *Abutilon*, Lavendula, *Mathiola*, Marigold, Orchids, Pelargonium, Salvia, Verbena, Pansy

3.7 Based on type of inflorescence

Type	Flower crops
Racemose	Gaillardia, Gerbera
Cymose	Jasmine, Salvia, Periwinkle
Spadix	Anthurium, Calla lily
Corymb	Statice

3.8 Based on fruit type

Fruit type	Crops
Berry	Anthurium, Calla lily, Cactus & succulents, Jasmine
Capsule	Amaryllis, Antirrhinum, Carnation, Crossandra, Gladiolus, Hibiscus, Lilium, Orchid, Petunia, Statice, Tuberose, Tulip, Pansy
Schizocarp	Hollyhock, Salvia
Ribbed achene	Chrysanthemum
Follicle	Periwinkle

3.9 Based on type of carotenoids

Name of carotenoid	Characteristic colour	Occurrence
Lycopene	Red	E.g. Rose hips
α- Carotene	Yellow	Leaves
β- Carotene	Orange	Major carotene of all plants e.g. Osmanthus, Pot marigold, Narcissus, Coreopsis, Pansy, Golden rod, Tulip,
γ- Carotene	Red-orange	Traces in some plants
Lutein	Yellow	Major xanthophyll e.g. Marigold, Chrysanthemum, *Lilium*, Dandelion,
Violaxanthin	Yellow	Second major xanthophylls e.g. *Lilium*, *Oncidium*,
β- Cryptoxanthin	Orange	Found in few species e.g. Christamas bells,
Zeaxanthin	Yellow-orange	Found in many plants
Astaxanthin	Red	E.g. Summer pheasant's eye

3.10 Morphological markers for identification

Markers	Crops
Striated stem pigmentation	Salvia
Purple hypocotyls & pubescent leaves (30 days old)	Periwinkle
Pitcher type shape of flower buds in male sterile plants	Marigold

4. PROPAGATION OF ORNAMENTAL CROPS:

- In nursery production, a 'liner' refers to a rooted cutting or small seedling.
- Most difficult to root species like *Bougainvillea glabra*, *Clerodendron splendens*, *Jasminum pubescens* and *Petrea volubilis* contain salicylic acid.

4.1 Sexual propagation:

- Chemicals inhibiting seed germination: HCN, ammonia, ethylene.
- Require little moisture for germination: Portulaca, Eschscholtzia.
- Require light for germination: Flowering tobacco, Lobelia, Echium, Veronica, Ranunculus.
- Require dark for germination: Amaranthus, Carnation, Nigella, Phlox, Cineraria.

4.1.1 Methods of breaking seed dormancy

A. Scarification:

- o Mechanical: Gladiolus, Globe amaranth, Lilium, Clianthus.
- o H_2SO_4 add treatment: Balsam, Geranium, Lotus, Zinnia.

B. Stratification:

- o Low temperature: Lilium, Lotus, Petunia, Rose, Verbena, Clianthus.

C. Use of chemicals:

- o KNO_3: Pansy, Calendula,
- o $KMNO_4$: Gerbera.

D. Use of hormones:

- o GA_3: Balsam, Gaillardia, Pansy, Rose, Tulip,

E. Seed priming: Marigold, Pansy, Salvia, Statice, Water lily.

4.2 Asexual propagation:

- Hard wood cutting: Cuttings are usually prepared from dormant, mature stems in early spring or summer season growth e.g. Bougainvillea, English ivy, Boxwood, Thuja, Juniper, Rhododendron, Viburnum, Honeysuckle, Poplar, Hibiscus, Trumpet creeper.
- Soft wood cutting: Cuttings prepared from 4 to 6 months old spring growth e.g. Carnation, Chrysanthemum, Coleus, Crotons, French lilacs, Eranthemum, Foresythia, Graftophyllum, Magnolia, Maples, Nerium, Spiraea.
- Hebaceous stem cutting: Cuttings are taken from succulent herbaceous greenhouse plants e.g. Chrysanthemum, Coleus, Carnation, Geranium, Cactus and many foliage plants.
- Terminal/ Tip cutting: Carnation, Geranium.

- Cane cutting/ Node cutting: Dieffenbachia, Dracaena, Aglaonema. They are inserted horizontally in sand.
- Leaf cutting: In leaf cuttings, the leaf blade with or without petiole and axillary bud is usedfor starting new plants. Sand or sand and peat moss (1: 1) are satisfactory rooting media forleaf cuttings e.g. Begonia, African violets, Peperomia, Sansevieria.
- Leaf bud cutting: A leaf-bud cutting consists of a leaf blade, petiole and a short piece of stem e.g. Rhododendron, Poinsettia, Hydrangea, Geranium.
- Leaf vein/ lamina cutting: Rex begonia.
- Leaf petiole: With attached axillary bud of actively growing leaf e.g. African violet.
- Root cutting: Rose.
- Simple layering: Jasmine, Oleander.
- Mound or stool layering: *Cestrum* spp., Deutzias.
- Compound/ Serpentine layering: *Jasminum sambac*.
- Trench/ Continuous layering: *Hydrangea*, Carnation.
- Suckers: *Millingtonia hortensis, Holarrhena antidysenterica*.
- Inarch grafting: Rose, *Petrea volubilis, Allamanda violacea*.
- Side grafting: Camellia spp.
- Saddle grafting; Rhododendron, Lilac.
- Flat grafting: Scions for cactus *Cereus*, *Cephalocereus*.
- Cleft grafting: *Zygocactus*.

4.3 Vegetative propagation:

- Rhizome: Canna.
- Stolon: Term used to describe various types of horizontally growing stems that produce adventious roots when come in contact with the soil e.g. Bermuda grass, Mint, Ribbon plant.
- Offset: It is a short thickened horizontal branch growing out of the crown ending at the apex with a tuft of leaves and a cluster of leaves below e.g. Pistia, Agave, Water hyacinth, Cycas, Dracaena.
- Tuber: Thickened tuberous growth that functions as storage organs e.g. Begonia, Dahlia.
- Tunicated bulb: Amaryllis, Crinum lily, Daffodil, Tulip, Tuberose, Zephyranthes.
- Non-tunicated bulb: Lilium.
- Bulbil: Tiger lily, Narcissus.
- Slab: Narcissus.
- Corm: Modified stem in which food is stored in this compact stem, which has nodes and very short internodes and is wrapped up in dry, scaly leaves e.g. Gladiolus, Iris, Freesia.
- Pseudo-bulb: *Dendrobium* orchid.

Consumer preference for flowers in European countries

Country	Flowers	Colour/shades
U.K.	Carnation, Chrysanthemum	White
	Rose, Tulip, Narcissus	Pink, Pastal shades
France	Rose, Chrysanthemum	Soft colours & white
Netherlands	Chrysanthemum, Rose, Carnation, Freesia, Tulip	Soft shades
Switzerland	Rose, Chrysanthemum, Tulip, Gerbera, Freesia, Gladiolus	Red, Violet to soft shade & white
West Germany	Rose, Carnation, Tulip, Orchid, Chrysanthemum	Soft shades, pink & lilac

5. PRINCIPLES OF GARDENING:

- Garden is originated from the Latin term '*Gyrdan*' meaning 'to enclose'.
- Aesthetic refers to sense of beauty.
- 1st evidence of an ornamental tree, the pipal (*Ficus religiosa*) comes from Mohenjo-Daro.
- Hogarth course is also known as line of beauty.
- Lotus pond is used as the locket of the garland.
- Energy conservation landscaping is a new concept in field of landscape planning.
- Studies indicated that as much as 30% reduction in cooling and heating costs through careful landscape planning.
- Wind breaks reduces wind speed for a distance of as much as 30 times the windbreaks height.
- Use of trees, shrubs, climbers in landscape planning can efficiently modify micro-climate to reduce heat gains in summer and heat losses in winter.
- Plant species namely *Ficus religiosa*, *F. infectoria*, *Morus alba*, *Azadirachta indica* and *Alstonia scholaris* are efficient to modify micro-environment.
- 'Circle template': Landscape designer's tool for drawing circles on landscape plan.
- Components of beauty: Colour, shape, texture, pattern, line and point.
- Trophy: Arrangement of potted colourful plants / flowering shrubs / annuals, etc. around a tree or in water based solution.
- Tangible items: Objects that can be touched e.g. Water, Animals, Rocks, etc.
- Intangible items: Objects that cannot touched e.g. Sound of waterfall, Light, Colour, etc.
- Forced perspective: Technique of creating illusion of more space in garden.
- Interconnection: Visual components are physically linked together.
- Food can also be act as element in garden.
- Public/ Approach/ Front area: Portion of garden that can be viewed from street.

- Service area: Part of home landscape which provides room for necessities.
- Simplicity- can be achieved by-
  - Avoid too many species in small place.
  - Repetition of same species or similar form (silhouette), habit or colour and construction.
- Unity/ Harmony-
  - Overall effect of various features, styles and colours of total scene.
  - It is achieved by using mass planting and repetition.
- Balance-
  - Implies stability.
  - Illusion of equilibrium around central axis.
  - Used to maintain symmetry in garden.
- Size or Proportion- Refers to size relationship to each other and to design as whole.
- Rhythm/ mobility-
  - Brings feeling of continuity.
  - Also referred as movement in garden.
  - Repetition of same object at regular interval.
  - Progression of size
  - Change in leaf colour & movement of fish in pond.
  - Use of deciduous trees.
- Accent/ Emphasis/ Focalization-
  - Feature which attracts to eye first.
  - Used to stress most important item or thing.
- Line-
  - Related to eye movement or flow.
  - An imaginary line which divides garden into two parts.
- Form-
  - Related to size of an object or area or total mass of an object.
  - May be upright, oval, round, columnar, weeping, etc.
- Texture: Describes surface quality of an object.
- Vista- *3D view of an object.
  - Hidden focal point.
- Colour scheme:
  - Predominant colour in nature: Green.
  - Hue (characteristic of colour), Value (brightness/lightness) and Chroma (colour purity/saturation).

- A hue with white added is called as tint.
- A hue with black added is called as shade.
- Monochromatic: Use of single colour.
- Dichromatic: Use of two colour.
- Polychromatic: Use of more than three colours i.e. carnival like effect.
- Double split-complementary: Colour scheme that is adjacent to direct complement colours.
- Quadraplex is not recognized colour scheme from colour wheel.
- Complementary/ contrasting colour: Blue & Orange, Red & Green, Violet & Yellow.
- Analogous colour: 2 or 3 closely related or adjacent colours i.e. combination of blue & green, yellow & orange.
- Triads: Combination of Yellow, Blue and Red (YBR).
- Basic/ Primary colour: Yellow, Blue, Red (YBR).
- Secondary colour: Orange, Green, Violet (OGV).
- Hard/ Warm/ Bright colour: Red, Orange, Yellow (ROY).
- Soft/ Cool/ Light colour: Blue, Violet, Green (BVG).
- Neutral colour: White, Black, Grey, Silver (WBGS).

6. HISTORY OF GARDENS:

- The first few gardens in history recorded were those of the ancient cultures of Egypt and China.
- Egyptian gardens developed at the edge of deserts where the natural vegetation was sparse.
- Egyptians were among the earliest civilized men to cultivate plants for aesthetic values.
- Formalism reached its peak in the age of King Louis XIV.
- Founder of Indian Botanic Garden: Robert Kyd (1787).
- King George established Botanical Survey of India in 1890.
- Father of ornamental gardening in India: Dr. M.S. Randhawa.
- Garden of Eden (U.K.): Genesis of gardening.
- Hanging gardens of Babylon: One of the Seven Wonders of the World.
- In Asia, 1st the Chinese, then Koreans and late Japanese used plants within and surrounding their homes.
- Aryavarta: Country of lotus flowers.
- Art of Indian style of gardening reached 1st in China.

- Pipal (*Ficus religiosa*) and *F. benghalensis* are symbols of fertility during Harappan period.
- Lord Vishnu and Goddess Laxmi are associated with lotus; Lord Shiva with Semul (*Bombax ceiba*); Goddess Saraswati with Kachnar (*Bauhinia variegata*) and Goddess Kali is associated with Amranthus.
- Buddhist and Temple gardens were originated in India.
- Buddhist monksreached art of Indian style gardening to Japan.
- Birth of Lord Buddha was associated with Ashoka, Palash and Sal trees.
- The art of gardening and the kinds of gardens were described by Sarangdhara and Vatsyayana, respectively.
- Vatsyayana (300-400 AD) in his book 'Kamasutra' described four kinds of gardens i.e. Paramodyana (private garden of king and queen), Udyana (king spend their leisure time in playing chess and enjoying dance), Vrikshavatika (garden for ministers and courtiers) and Nandanvana (garden dedicated to Lord Krishna).
- Climber,*Parthenocissus tricuspidata* was used on the buildings to make a seamless change over between house and garden.
- Glasshouse is a feature of Lal Bagh Botanical garden, Bengaluru while it is not a feature of Government Botanical garden, Ootacamund.
- Queen Elizabeth: Not associated with redefining of English gardens from picturesque to natural style.
- Rashtrapati Bhavan Garden was laid out by Sir Edwin Lutyen (famous architect) on the advice of Lady Hardinge.
- Maharaja Sayajirao-III built Sayaji park at Baroda.
- King Bhupinder Singh and his son Yadvindra Singh built Baradari garden at Patiala.
- Garden at Amber fort near Jaipur was started by King Man Singh and completed by Jai Singh II.
- Dara Shikoh constructed Bijebehara garden.
- Raja Abhai Singh constructed Mandore garden near Jodhpur.
- Garden palace at Deeg, Rajasthan was founded by Suraj Mal.
- 'Garden of Five Senses' is situated at New Delhi.
- Double Decker Living Root Bridge, is located at Cherrapunjee, Meghalaya.
- Formal type gardens- Persian, Mughal, Moorish, Italian, French andAmerican.
- Informal type gardens- Chinese, Japanese and English.
- In 18th century, Britishers completely changed the idea of garden with nature.
- Hortus Kewensis: Catalogue of plants cultivated at Royal Botanical garden, Kew was published in 1789 AD.
- Dutch gardens: Dense atmosphere and efficient use of space.
- Mini Lalbagh i.e. Siri Horticulture Garden: Located in Ootacamund, Tamil Nadu.

- Every year 10th February to 15th March period is celebrated as 'Udyanostav' at Rashtrapati Bhavan.
- Varieties of ornamental and medicinal plants at Mughal garden, Spiritual garden, Herbal garden, Bonsai garden and Bio-diversity parks are attractions for visitor's at Rashtrapati bhavan.
- Micro-gardening: Practice of intensively food 'farming' in containers and well-designed, small urban spaces. It is designed to be highly productive, energy and space efficient.
- Xeriscaping: Use of plant materials and landscaping techniques to conserve soil moisture and to reduce water losses.
- Moon gardening: Garden created accommodating white flowering plants blooming during night.
- India's 1st digital garden: Kanakakunnu Palace, Thiruvananthapuram.
- 'Vasundhara Udyaan' to be established on 108 acres near Pune to conserve forest including *nakshtra* garden.
- *Ex-situ* conservatory of Ipomoea is located at Jawaharlal Nehru Tropical Botanic Garden and Research Institute, Thiruvananthapuram.

6.1 FORMAL TYPE:

- First plan is made on paper and then executed in field.

6.1.1. Mughal gardens-

- Maximum Mughal gardens were constructed by Firoz Tughlaq (1200 gardens).
- Babur introduced Persian rose in India.
- Gardensare bilaterally symmetrical.
- Garden style was an extended plan of '*Char bagh*' design of Persia, Iran.
- Garden shape: Rectangular or square.
- Crafted material, pierced marble stone and highly polished stones are used.
- Main concept of Persian garden: Naharas or flowing water canals (where cooling water flows).
- Pleasure garden and Tomb garden were common during Mughal period.
  - **Main features**: Terrace, Running water, High protecting walls, Big entrance gate, Baradari, Terminal building and Chabutras or stone platform.
  - Cypress tree (*Juniperus chineus*): Symbol of death and eternity.
  - Fruit trees: Symbol of life and mango tree: pride of garden.
  - Flowering trees: Symbol of renewal of life
  - White kachnar tree: Symbol of youth and life
  - Running water/ *Naharas*: Symbol of source of life

Famous Mughal gardens:

- 1st Islamic garden in India was developed by Feroz Shah.
- In 1526, 1st Mughal garden was laid by Babur at Agra called 'Ram bagh' (earlier Aaram bagh). It is an orchard garden and Zohra bagh at Agra; Bagh-e-Wafa and Bagh-e-Kalan at Kabul.
- 1st tomb garden made in India: Humayun's Tomb.
- Akbar made 1st garden at Fatehpur Sikri (Agra) and 2nd at Sikandra (Agra).
- Akbar established Nasim bagh, close to Dal Lake.
- Taj mahal, Mehtab bagh: Agra, (UP).
- Khusro bagh: Allahabad (UP).
- Humayun's tomb and Safdarjung's tomb are situated at New Delhi.
- Shalimar bagh, Nishat bagh are situated at Srinagar (J &K).
- Nishat bagh was constructed by Asaf Khan in 1632. It was built in 12 terraces.
- Jehangir built Shalimar, Achabal, Verinag gardens at Kashmir, Tomb garden at Itimud-ud-Daulah and Dilkhush garden at Lahore.
- Shah Jahan built gardens at Chasma Shahi (Srinagar), Taj mahal (Agra), Red fort (Delhi).
- Fadai Khan built Pinjore garden (Rajasthani-Mughal style) at Haryana.
- Hyder Ali and Tipu sultan built 'Lal bagh' at Bengaluru.
- Mir Alam bagh at Hydrabad was build by Nawab Salar Jung.
- Available Mughal gardens of Rashtrapati Bhavan: Spritual garden, Herbal garden, Bonsai garden, biodiversity park, Cacti garden and Floral carpets.

6.1.2. Roman/ Italian gardens-

- Eulogized as 'Heaven of Man'
- Use of heavy masonry features.
- Stone sculptures and statues.
- Steps, stair, lamp and balustrades are important features.

6.1.3. French gardens-

- Le Notre- a French garden architect emphasized on 'scale'. He taught "How to think big".
- Le Notre's 1st master piece was the garden at 'Vaux-le-Vicomte' for which he removed three villages.
- Gardens with tremendous length and width.
- Follows the principle of imposing order over nature.
- Important features: *Allee* (straight path often lined with trees), *Bosquet* (small group of trees), *Broderie* (very curling decorative pattern within a parterre), Parterre (planting bed having design with low closely clipped hedges).

6.2 INFORMAL TYPE:

- Plan is forced to fit the land for securing natural beauty.
- Terrace gardening: Very common feature of English and Japanese gardens.

6.2.1. Japanese gardens-

- Also known as Nature in miniature or Zen gardens.
- Famous in world for their naturality and immutability.
- Made by Zen-Buddhists for worship and meditation.
- Gardens of Kyoto is associated with Zen Buddhist.
- Origin: Era of Empress Suiko (592-628 AD).
- During Edo period, making of small gardens dominated.
- Features: Raking of sand and usage of pebbles, dry landscape, mountains, pagoda, pond, small bridges, standing water in lake or pond, rock arrangement, stone lanterns, trees, shrubs, streams, water fall and well.

  E.g. Buddha Jayanti garden (1990), Prime Minister's house and Swarna Jayanti garden, Mahavir Jayanti park, Garden of Five Senses (New Delhi), Kamla Nehru park (Mumbai), Residence of Poet Rabindranath Tagore.

Types-

1. Hill garden (*Tsukiyama sansui*): Means hill and water.
2. Tea garden: Area (200m^2), attached to tea house e.g. Heianji temple.
3. Flat garden (*Hira-niwa*): Represents mountain valley & devoid of hills, streams or ponds.
4. Sand garden: Totally devoid of plants e.g. Ryoanji garden, Kyoto, Japan.
5. Passage garden (*Roji-niwa*): Laid in narrow passages.
6. Fancy garden: Garden for guests.

6.2.2. English gardens-

- Formation of formalism and naturalism.
- Formation of botanical gardens.
- Most beautiful among European gardens.
- During 16th century, flower beds, topiaries and terrace gardens were introduced.
- 1st rock garden was demonstrated in 1859.
- Architects: William Kent, Humphrey Repton and Capability Brown.
- William Robinson invented herbaceous border but the term 'herbaceous border' was given by Gertrude Jekyell.
- Concept of Cottage garden was developed by Gertrude Jekyell.

- Hedge of Yew and topiary are common features of cottage gardens.
- Most amazing garden in world: The Lost Gardens of Heligan, UK.

  Features- Statue of beast, Herbaceous border, Lawn, Cottage garden, Botanical gardens and Rockery. E.g. Indian Horticultural Society, Kolkata, Royal Agri-Horticultural Society, Kolkata.

6.3 FREE TYPE:

- Combines both formal and informal style of gardening e.g. Rose garden, Ludhiana; Brindavan garden, Mysuru; Lal Bagh botanical garden, Bengaluru and Ajawa garden, Baroda.

Famous national gardens:

Name of garden & its feature	Year of establishment
Shalimar garden, Jammu and Kashmir	1619
Achabal garden, Kashmir	1620
Roshnara park, New Delhi (1st Japanese garden in India)	1650
Horticultural Research Institute, Saharanpur	1750
Lal bagh botanical garden, Bengaluru (Floral clock)	1760
The Indian botanical garden, Sibpur, Kolkata	1787
Sikandar bagh (NBRI), Lucknow	1789
The Agri-Horticultural Society garden, Kolkata	1825
Government botanical garden, Ootacamund	1848
Sim's Park, Coonoor, Tamil Nadu	1874
Lloyd botanical garden, Darjeeling (WB)	1878
Sayaji park, Baroda (Branching palm, *Hybaena thebaica*)	1879
Hanging garden, Mumbai (Feroze Shah Mehta garden)	1881
Rock garden/ Sculpture garden/ Nek Chand's rock garden, Chandigarh	1975
Botanical garden, Coimbatore	1908
Byrant park, Kodaikanal, Tamil Nadu	1909
Brindavan garden, Mysore (Biggest formal garden)	1927-1932
Rashtrapati Bhavan garden, New Delhi (Mughal + British style & Sunken garden)	1929
Botanical garden of Forest Research Institute, Dehradun	1934
Mandore garden, Jodhpur	1929-1943
Zakir Hussain rose garden, Chandigarh (Free type; biggest rose garden in Asia)	1967
Indira Gandhi Memorial Tulip garden (Asia's largest tulip garden, Kashmir)	2006-07
Pu La Deshpande garden, Pune (Pune-Okayama Friendship garden; Japanese garden)	2006
National Cactus and Succulent botanical garden and Research Centre (known as Cactus garden) Panchkula, Haryana	1987
Nehru Memorial Botanical Garden, Srinagar, Jammu and Kashmir	1969
Talkatora garden, New Delhi	1737
Jayantrao Tilak Rose garden, Pune	
Cactus garden, Kevadia, Gujarat	2018
Globe park: Lucknow	

Famous international gardens:

- There are about 1600 botanical gardens and arboreta in the world.
- 1st botanical garden in world was started at Padua, Venice, Italy in 1545 followed by Botanical garden at Oxford (1621), Royal botanical garden, Edinburgh (1670), Botanical garden, Amsterdam (1682), Botanical garden of Academy of Sciences, Leningrad (1712), Botanical garden, University of Austria (1754), University botanical garden, Cambridge (1762), Indian botanical garden, Howrah, India (1787), Royal botanical garden, Kew, UK (1841), and Leyden national park, the Netherlands (1840).
- In tropical region, the 1st botanical garden was created at Pamplemousses, Mauritius (1735), followed by Calcutta botanical garden in India (1787) and Royal botanical garden, Peradeniya in Sri Lanka (1821).
- Missouri botanical garden (Henry Shaw's garden) founded in 1859 was 1st botanic garden in USA.
- Botanical gardens play a leading part in achieving conservation of plant life.
- Botanical gardens can be called as living repository of plants arranged and maintained in some scientific basis.
- IABG: The International Association of Botanical Gardens is the official umbrella of more than 800 botanical gardens and arboreta all over the world.
- Oldest botanical garden in Europe is at Leydon situated at the Netherlands.
- International Rose garden of Kortrijk, Belgium.
- World's largest rose garden: Peggy Rockfeller Rose garden in New York botanical garden.
- World famous flower and tulip garden: Keukenhof gardens, Amsterdam.
- Moorish gardens were developed in Spain.
- Highline park of New York is wild type garden.
- Dubai's Miracle garden: World's largest natural flower garden featuring over 50 million flowers and 250 million plants spreading over 7,80,000 sq. ft.
- Dubai'sButterfly garden: World's largest and region's 1st indoor butterfly garden and sanctuary for over 15,000 butterflies from 26 species.
- Dubai's Palm Fountain at Jumeirah: World's largest fountain that spread over 14,000 ft.^{2} of sea water.
- Circular garden city 'Brondby Haveby' is a collection of houses nestled inside a grid of perfectly circular greenery is located at Copenhagen, Denmark.
- Atlanta botanical garden: Comprises Fuqua Orchid Center, mosaiculture exhibition including giant living sculptures made up of plants.

Name of garden	Year of establishment
Yuyuan garden, Shanghai, China	1577
Gardens of Versailles, France	1632
Singapore botanical garden, Singapore	1859
Brooklyn botanical garden, USA	1910
Botanical garden, Berlin	1910
Kirstenbosch National botanical garden, South Africa	1913
Montreal botanical garden, Canada	1931
Garden of cosmic speculation, Scotland	1931
Nong Nooch Tropical botanical garden, Thailand	1980
Banpo Bridge Rainbow Fountain, Seoul, South Korea	2019
Miracle garden, Dubai	2013

7. WATER GARDEN:

- Oldest reference comes from Budhist period.
- Rate of fish population in water garden: 2.5 cm long (excluding tail) for every 4.5 to 5 l of water.
- Problematic weed: Blanket weed.
- Management of blanket weed: Add $KMnO_4$ 30 g per 1,00,000 or 1,25,000 litres of water.
- Surface flowering plants: *Aponogeton distachyus* (Water hawthorn), *Nelumbo lutea* (American lotus), *Limnanthemum indica* (Water Snow flake), *Nelumbo nucifera* (Indian lotus), *Victoria regia* (Giant lily having largest leaves).
- Oxygenator plants: Plants maintain hygiene and balance. *Callitriche autumnalis*, *Ceratophyllum submersum*, *Elodea*, *Ranunculus aquatilis*, *Vallisneria spiralis*.
- Floating plants: *Azolla caroliniana*, *Eichhornia speciosa*, *Lemna gibba*, *Trapa natans*.
- Marginal plants: Plants grow with their roots in shallow water but raise their stems and flowers above the surface. Marginals are mostly hardy and coarser plants. *Acorus calamus varigatus*, *Calla palustris*, *Cyperus alternifolius*, *Iris laevigata*, *Sagittaria sagittifolia*, *Typha angustifolia*.

8. ROCK GARDEN:

- Ornamental gardening in rocky place or in areas on which rocks have been placed.
- Rocks should be well weathered of local origin and only one kind of rocks should be used.
- Naturalistic rock garden: Best used on natural slope.
- Moraine garden: Type of rock garden with or without rocks.
- Seree garden: Similar to moraine garden except inclusion of water beneath the surface.

- Alpine lawn garden: Modification of naturalistic rock garden.
- Wall garden: Most practicable form of rock garden.

  Famous rock gardens:
- Lal bagh botanical gardën, Bengaluru; Sim's park, Coonoor; Agri-Horticultural Society garden, Kolkata and Rock garden, Chandigarh.
- Ringing Rocks park: Pennsylvania

9. MARSH/ BOG GARDEN:

- Garden in stagnant acidic water.
- Garden shouid never exceed depth of 60 cm.
- E.g. Govt. Botanical garden, Ootacamund, Tamil Nadu.
- Suitable plants: *Acorus calamus* (sweet flag), *Asplenium*, *Calla palustris*, *Eriophorum* (cotton grass), *Hemerocallis fulva* (day lily), *Hosta glauca* (plantain lily), *Osmunda regalis* (royal fern), *Pandanus odoratissimus* (screwpine), sundew, butterworts, etc. can grow.

10. SUNKEN GARDEN:

- Garden laid below ground level.
- Existing ditch or dried out pond may be utilized.
- E.g. Byrant park, Kodaikanal.

11. TERRACE GARDEN:

- Raised space of ground constructed around dwelling house or at corner of garden.
- E.g. Byrant park, Kodaikanal semi-colon, Llyod botanical garden, Darjeeling.

12. VERTICAL GARDEN:

- The earliest example of vertical garden is hanging gardens of Babylon established in 6th B.C.
- Vertical gardens are also called as 'bio-walls or green walls or smart walls or vertical vegetated green walls'.
- Concept of gardening was developed in Switzerland.
- Single vertical garden should not have mixed planting i.e. sun and shade loving plants.
- Dr. Patric Blanc (father of vertical gardening), is a French botanist 1st to design the 'modern' pattern of green walls.
- These green walls lower the energy loss of building, prevent creation of urban dust and absorb heavy metal particulates from atmosphere.

- World's 1st vertical forest: Bosco Verticale in Milan.
- Kokedama: '*Koke*' meaning 'moss' and '*dama*' meaning 'ball'. Knows as 'Moss balls or string gardens'. It is a practice of taking root ball of plant and suspending it in a mud ball, coated with soft green moss.
- In moss, moisture will let out when humidity falls below (12 g/m^3) and when moisture goes up (17 g/m^3) it will absorb moisture.
- Moss act as air purifier through a system of roots called rhizoides.
- Suitable plants: Begonia, Calendula, Coleus, Dianthus, Geranium, Marigold, Pansy, Petunia, Periwinkle, Portulaca, Dwarf Snapdragons, Verbena, Strawberries, Sweet Alyssum.

13. TERRARIUM:

- Also called as 'bottle gardening'.
- Technique of growing tender, moisture loving plants inside transparent glass container to make complete ecosystem.

14. FLOWER ARRANGEMENT:

- 1st civilization to have professional floral designers: Greek.
- English/ Occidental/ British/ Western flower arrangement: Emphasize on mass flower arrangement.
- Ikebana/ Eastern/ Oriental/ Japanese flower arrangement: Emphasize on spiritual and religious background.
- Word Ikebana is derived from '*ikenobo*'.
- Ikenobo school based at Kyoto, was formed in 15th century by Buddhist monk Ikenobô Senkei.
- Establishment of 'Ikebana International' by Mrs. G. Ellen at Tokyoin 1955.
- In Ikebana, plant material never touches the base of vase.
- First and foremost requirement of ikebana: Look natural.
- Art of Ikebana developed and flourished with 3 schools in Japan: Ikenobo, Ohara and Sogetsu.
- Kuge: The earlist style of Ikebana which later evolved into 'Rikka'.
- Rikka means standing flowers developed in Ikenobo, the oldest school.
- Ikebana has 3 main axes: Shin (Heaven; always tallest stem), Soe (Man) and Hikae/ Tai (Earth).
- In Japanese language fillers are called as '*Jushi*'.
- Corsage: Decorating pockets and coat collars with a single flower e.g. Carnation.
- *Veni*: a special kind of flower arrangement widely used in *Bharat Natyam* dance.

- Floral foam: Most common to support stem used by florist.
- Cut branches of evergreen 20-30 inches long stem are called as boughs.
- In flower arrangement, stem height should be 1.5-2 times height of container.
- A floral piece commonly displayed at funerals: Standing spray.
- Typical length of florist wire: 18 inches.
- Wreaths are laid down to give respect to departed soul.
- Framework of floral design is created by lines.
- Most commonly used design for all-purpose vase arrangement and basket is symmetrical triangle.
- In symmetrical triangular floral arrangement, line/skeleton flowers are placed first.
- Piercing method of wiring is commonly used to wire flowers having large, thickened calyces e.g. carnation and roses.
- Hook method of wiring flowers is used for flat headed flowers.
- While making hand tied bouquets, the stems should be positioned in spiral manner.
- Transition in floral arrangement is changes through progression, sequence or gradation.
- World Association of Flower Arrangers (WAFA) was formed in 1981.

Types of ikebana:

a) Moribana/ Natural Ikebana: Piled flowers in shallow containers are used.

b) Jiyubana: Free flower arrangement (Moribana + Nagiere style)

c) Morimono: Fruits, vegetables, flowers are used (English flower arrangement).

d) Nagiere: Tall vases are used. Flowers are 1.5 times taller than vase (Western style)

e) Zeneika: Straight material with uneven height is used (Abstract style & does not simulate nature).

f) Zeneibana: Beautiful sculptures using wood, stone, rocks and metals (Depict any natural scenary).

g) Sogetsu: Japanese flower arrangement where all basic principles are used but students can use their creativity.

14.1 Dry flower technology:

- Leading dry flower products exporting country: The Netherlands, followed by Columbia, Mexico, India, Israel.
- Leading dry flower products importing country: U.K, Germany, Italy.
- Biggest market for dried flowers in the world: U.K.
- Largest importer of dried flowers from India: U.K.
- Share of dry flower products in India's total floricultural export: 60%.
- India's share in export of dried flowers in Europe: 4.80%.

- Indian dried flowers are exported to USA, Isreal, Hongkong, Singapore, west European countries.
- Dry flower industry was brought to India by British and prospered in Kolkata.
- Dry flower units are concentrated in Tuticorin, Tamil Nadu and West Bengal, Kolkata.
- Popular due to non-perishability & longer indoor life.
- Plant parts exported from India: Lotus pods, Pods of Arjun, Camellia, Dahlia, Jute flower, Wood rose, Marigold, Bell cups, Wild lilies, Helichrysum, Lady's lace, etc.
- Dried flowers are used in bouquets, flower arrangement, flower pictures, greeting cards, flower falls, festive decoration, pomenders, sweet smelling potpourri, wall plates, landscapes, etc.
- No. 1 dry flower in global market: Helichrysum.
- '*Potpourri*' is a French word meaning mixture of dried, sweet-scented plant parts including flowers, leaves & seeds, etc.
- Pioneer institute working on dehydration of flowers, foliage & floral crafts: NBRI.
- Dr. J.C. Bhutani standardized dehydration technology of flowers and foliage at NBRI, Lucknow.
- Technique consist of:- Procurement of flowers- first baked under direct sunlight till they loose their original colour- fumigate with acid & bleaching powder- dip in lime water & salt- dried & cut into desired shape by the artists.
- Flowers dried by water drying method: Hydrangea, Baby's breath, corn flower.
- Press dried flowers are used for making greeting cards e.g. Pansy.
- Daffodil is not suitable for press drying.
- Vein skeleton i.e. skeletonizing of leaves of *F. religiosa* by fermentation process has been standardized by NCL, Pune.
- Anaerobic fermentation with baker's yeast (*Saccharomyces cerevisiae*) @ 2% digest the chlorophyll content & other green cells of leaves and forms vein skeleton within 15 days.
- The pH of solution is 5.5.
- Processes like bleaching, softening, colouring is done over the skeleton leaves for decoration and beautification purposes.
- Flowers of arum lily, periwinkle, and Hybrid T roses can be dried/ preserved and processed to retain their beauty as well as everlasting value.
- Indian liquorice has beautiful natural dried seeds.
- **Methods of drying:**
  - Air drying/ Hanging method: Most common, simplestand cheapest method of drying.
  - Press drying: Drying between newspapers.

- º Embedding: Placing is silica gel or borax or sand.
- º Oven drying technique was developed at NBRI, Lucknow.
- º Microwave oven drying (300-700 Hz): Quickest method of drying.
- º Cryo-drying technique is followed in western countries for dehydration of carnation.

Air drying	Helipterum, Helichrysum, Statice
Press drying	Candytuft, Chrysanthemum, *Euphorbia leucocephala*, Lantana, *Ixora*, *Mussaenda*, *Galphimia nitida*, *Pentas carnea*, Rose, Verbena, Larkspur, Pansy, Grasses, Golden fern, Silver fern
Oven drying	Helipterum, Chrysanthemum, Candytuft, Gerbera, *Gomphrena globosa*, Straw flower, *Zinnia linearis*, Rose, Bougainvillea, Narcissus, Dahlia, Gladiolus, Marigold, *Nymphaea* spp.
Microwave drying	*Antirrhinum majus*, China aster, Chrysanthemum, Dahlia (pompon), Carnation, Bougainvillea, Gerbera, Gladiolus, *Lagerstroemia indica*, *Delphinium ajacis*, *Helichrysum bracteatum*, Phlox, *Helipterum roseum*, *Ixora coccinea*, *Nymphaea* spp.

- After dehydration, yellow flowers retain colour properly but white becomes off-white, red, blue & other bright colours become considerably dark.
- Most ideal temperature range for drying of ornamentals in hot air oven: 40-60^{0}C.
- Flowers are frozen upto -35^{0}C.
- Non-metallic containers are used for drying in microwave oven.
- Commonly used preservatives in dried ornamentals: Glycerol, Polyethylene glycol (PEG), KCl, Quaternary ammonium compounds.
- Glycerine method: Used for foliage preservation.
- Silica gel: Excellent desiccant (dehydrating agent). Fastest acting dessicant. It holds moisture by a phenomenon known as physical absorption and capillary condensation.
- Desiccant size: 0.02-0.2 mm.
- Setting time: 30-40 minutes.
- Silver fish, booklice, mice: Serious pests.
- *Aspergillus*, *Penicillium*, *Rhizopus*: Serious fungi.
- Drying of native flowers done with the help of resins known as resin encapsulation technique. This is permanent encapsulated technique in which dry flowers are locked inside resin permanently exhibiting eternal beauty forever.
- Value added products: Collages, flower balls, cards, pomanders, festive decorations, bouquets, wreathes, potpourries, etc.
- Value added products of epoxy resin encapsulation: Pendants, ear rings, rings, paper weights, wall paintings, key chain rings, table top covers etc.

Temperature and time required for drying of flower crops

Flower	Temperature (^{0}C)	Time (h)
Helipterum, Chrysanthemum, Candytuft, Gerbera, Dombeya, Strawflower, Gomphrena & Statice	45-49	48
China aster, Larkspur, Rose buds, Zinnia	40-44	48
Narcissus & Dahlia	35-39	72
Bougainvillea	35-39	48
Large flowered rose cultivars	40-44	96
Adiantum, Fern, Golden fern, Silver fern	40-44	24
French marigold	45-49	72
African marigold	45-49	96
Water lily	45-49	120

15. ANNUALS

- Definition: Group of herbaceous plants which grow from seeds, produce flowers, set seeds and complete life cycle in one season or in one year.
- Highly evolved family: Asteraceae.
- In India, annual flowers were introduced by Britishers in the end of 18th century.
- By 1912, the popularity of these flowers increased and many seed companies dominated flower seed business in India.
- Leading flower seed producing states: Punjab, Haryana, Himachal Pradesh, Tamil Nadu and Karnataka.
- IARI celebrated the year 2011-12 as 'Year of Seasonal Flowers'.
- Origined in India: Balsam, Gomphrena, Lady's lace.
- Some annuals are used as cut flower/ loose flowers.
- Annuals are transplanted at 4 leaf stage.
- Ideal sowing time of annuals: South India (September- October), Northern hills (March-April).
- Annuals like *Cosmos bipinnatus*, *Nicotiana* spp., and *Callistephus chinensis* are typical short-day plants for both vegetative growth and flowering.
- Annuals viz. *Dianthus barbatus*, *Nigella damascena* are typical long-day plants for vegetative growth and flowering.
- Some annuals require long days for flower initiation followed by short days for flower development.
- Salvia, candytuft and clarkia flower prematurely, if soil is deficient in N.
- Lupins, sunflower, African marigold and flowering tobacco flower prematurely if soil N level is high.
- Summer cypress (*Kochia scoparia* var. *tricophylla*) is summer foliage annual.
- Fragrance in lisianthus: Benzyl alcohol acetyl transferase (BEAT).
- The value of hybrid seed produced/ unit area is very high for petunia hybrid seeds.

- Planting distance: Dwarf (30 cm x 30 cm); medium (45 cm x 45 cm); Tall (60 cm x 60 cm).
- They thrive best in soil pH between 6.0-7.5.
- Almost all annuals can be propagated by seeds except marigold which can be propagated by cuttings also.
- Common purslane (*Portulaca oleracea*): Abode of omega-3-fatty acids.
- Annuals having bold seeds: Hollyhock, Morning glory, Lupin, Nasturtium, Sunflower, Sweet pea.
- Difficult to transplant (i.e. don't like to be transplanted): Butterfly weed, Californian poppy, Clarkia, Larkspur, Lineria, Lupin, Nasturtium, Poppy.
- For seed germination, temperature of propagation medium is 22-29^{0}C (75-85^{0}F).
- Maximum number of seeds/ gram: Petunia and Portulaca (>10,000).
- Minimum number of seeds/ gram: Sweet pea and sunflower (18-20).
- Growth retarding chemicals viz. CCC @ 1000-2000 ppm, B-nine @ 2000-5000 ppm and SADH @ 1000-3000 ppm control growth and flowering in Arctotis, Hollyhock, Sweet sultan, Coreopsis, Cosmos, Phlox and Pansy.
- GA_3 @ 100-400 ppm promote vegetative gorwht and flowering in African marigold, China aster and antirrhinum.
- Post harvest management is necessary to proong vase life if traded in national/ international markets.

15.1 Classification:

15.1.1 Based on height:

- Tall: Height > 0.75 m e.g. African marigold, Annual chrysanthemum, Sunflower, Sweet pea, Naturtium, Cosmos, Helichrysum, Heliotrope, Hollyhock, Coreopsis, Larkspur, Clarkia.
- Medium: Height vary from 0.45-0.75 m e.g. Antirrhinum, African marigold, Balsam, Calendula, Carnation, Celosia, China aster, Coreopsis, Cosmos, Cosmos, Gomphrena, Gypsophila, Lupin, Garden poppy, Salvia, Zinnia.
- Dwarf: Grows up to 0.45 m height e.g. Acroclinum, Ageratum, Calendula, Calceolaria, Candytuft, Daisy, Dianthus, Gazania, Ice plant (15-20 cm), Nasturtium, Pansy, Petunia, Phlox, Portulaca, Sweet Alyssum, Verbena, Wall flower.

15.1.2 Based on hardiness:

- Hardy annual: Digitalis, Rudbeckia, Pansy.
- Tender annual: Oxalis.

15.1.3 Based on colour:

- Blue: Corn flower, Blue larkspur, Ageratum, Anchusa, Lineria, Browallia.

- White: China aster. Dimorphotheca, Stock, Nigella, Phlox, Poppy, Zinnia, Stock, Sweet Alyssum.
- Yellow and orange: Coreopsis, Helichrysum, Marigold, Nasturtium, Pot marigold, Wall flower, Zinnia.
- Pink: Acroclinum, Candytuft.

15.1.4 Based on commercial value:

- Cut flower: Cut blooms are used as vase decoration e.g. China aster, Antirrhinum, Calendula, Carnation, Gypsophila, Sweet pea, Zinnia, etc.
- Loose flower: Flowers used for making garlands, veni, etc. e.g. Annual chrysanthemum, Marigold, Amaranthus, Gaillardia, Balsam, China aster, Sunflower, etc.

15.1.5 Based on purpose:

- Screening: Cineraria, Hollyhock, Nasturtium, Morning glory, Sweet pea, etc.
- Peculiar shape: Clianthus possess claw/beak shaped flowers.
- Climbing: Sweet pea, Nasturtium, *Clitoria ternatea*, *Cobaea scandens*, etc.
- Hanging basket: Ageratum, Daisy, French marigold, Lobelia, Nasturtium, Petunia, Phlox, Portulaca, Sweet Alyssum, Torenia, Verbena, Zinnia.
- Shady situation: Ageratum, Balsam, Calendula, Cineraria, Delphinium, Phlox, Verbena, Salvia, Sweet alyssum.
- Edging: Alyssum, Ageratum, Brachycome, Candytuft, French marigold, Lobelia, Pansy, Phlox, Portulaca, Sweet alyssum, Torenia.
- Rockery: Antirrhinum, Brachycome, Candytuft, Ice plant, Nasturtium, Pansy, Phlox, Portulaca, Sweet Alyssum, Verbena.
- Potted plant: Antirrhinum, Aster, Petunia, Sweet William.
- Carpet bedding: Antirrhinum (single), Candytuft, Dahlia, Ice plant, Marigold, Pansy, Petunia, Phlox, Salvia (dwarf), Sweet Alyssum, Sweet William, Verbena.
- Ornamental foliage: Amaranthus, Kochia, Nasturtium (variegated), etc.
- Window sill: Aster, Calendula, Candytuft, Nasturtium, Petunia, Phlox, Portulaca, Zinnia.
- Natural dry flower: Acroclinum, Cock's comb, Gomphrena, Helichrysum, Lady's Lace, Nigella, Statice.
- Fragrance: Jasmine tobacco, Lemon bergamot, Mignonette, Moonflower vine, Nasturtium, Sweet pea, Sweet William, Sweet Sultan, Sweet Alyssum, Stock.
- Pinching requirement: Marigold, Ageratum, Calendula, Chrysanthemum, Petunia, Phlox, Carnation, Antirrhinum, Verbena, Zinnia, etc.
- Filler material: Gypsophila, Statice, Candytuft, etc.

15.1.6 Based on soil requirement:

- For very poor soil: Cock's comb, Gaillardia, Godetia, Balsam, Portulaca, Petunia, Sweet Sultan, Sweet Alyssum, etc.
- For alkaline soil: Balsam, Phlox, Mignonette, Nasturtium, Poppy, Zinnia.
- For acidic soil: French marigold, Nasturtium, Periwinkle, Zinnia.

Common name	Other name	Botanical name	Family
Rainy season			
Cock's comb	Murgkesh	*Celosia cristata*	Amaranthaceae
Loves lies bleeding	Amaranthus	*Amaranthus caudatus*	Amaranthaceae
Bachlor's button	Globe amaranth	*Gomphrena globosa*	Amaranthaceae
Gaillardia	Blanket flower	*Gaillardia pulchella*	Asteraceae
Balsam	Gulmehendi	*Impatiens balsamina*	Balsaminaceae
Summer season			
Tithonia	Mexican sunflower	*Tithonia speciosa*	Asteraceae
Sunflower	Surajmukhi	*Helianthus annus*	Asteraceae
Zinnia	Youth and age	*Zinnia elegans*	Asteraceae
Indian angel balsam	-	*Impatiens latifolia*	Balsaminaceae
Kochia (Foliage annual)	Summer cypress/ Burning bush	*Kochia scoparia*	Chenopodiaceae
Tick weed	Asian spider flower	*Cleome viscosa*	Cleomaceae
Moss-rose purslane	Sunplant	*Portulaca grandiflora*	Portulacaceae
Winter season			
Ice plant	Living stone daisy/ Fig marigold	*Mesembryanthum criniflorum*	Aizoaceae
Acroclinum	Paper flower	*Acroclinum roseum*	Asteraceae
Ageratum	Floss flower	*Ageratum houstonianum*	Asteraceae
Anchusa	-	*Anchusa capensis*	Asteraceae
Annual chrysanthemum	Garland chrysanthemum	*Chrysanthemum coronarium*	Asteraceae
Arctotis	African daisy	*Arctotis stoechadifolia*	Asteraceae
Brachycome	Swan river daisy	*Brachycome iberidifolia*	Asteraceae
Calendula	Pot marigold	*Calendula officinalis*	Asteraceae
Cineraria	Florist's cineraria	*Senecio cruentus*	Asteraceae
Coreopsis	Tick seed	*Coreopsis tinctoria*	Asteraceae
Corn flower	Blue bottle	*Centauera cyanus*	Asteraceae
Cosmos	Mexican aster	*Cosmos bipinnatus*	Asteraceae
Cape marigold	White African daisy/ Cape daisy	*Dimorphotheca pluvialis*	Asteraceae
Gazania	Treasure flower	*Gazania splendens*	Asteraceae
Helichrysum	Everlasting / Straw/ Paper flower	*Helichrysum bracteatum*	Asteraceae
Rudbeckia	Cone flower	*Rudbeckia bicolor*	Asteraceae
Sweet Sultan	-	*Centaurea moschata*	Asteraceae
Marigold	African & French marigold	*Tagetes erecta, T. patula*	Asteraceae
Lobelia	-	*Lobelia erinus*	Campanulaceae
Gypsophila	Baby's breath	*Gypsophila elegans*	Caryophyllaceae
Saponaria	Soapwart	*Saponaria vaccaria*	Caryophyllaceae
Sweet William	-	*Dianthus barbatus*	Caryophyllaceae

Stock		*Matthiola incana*	Cruciferae
Sweet Alyssum	-	*Alyssum maritimum*	Cruciferae
Candytuft	Hyacinth flower	*Iberis spp.*	Cruciferae
Wall flower		*Cherianthus cherii*	Cruciferae
Eustoma/ Lisianthus	Tulip gentian, Blue bells	*Prairie gentian*	Gentianaceae
Phacelia	-	*Phacelia campanulata*	Hydrophyllaceae
Bells of Ireland	-	*Molucella lauvis*	Labiatae
Salvia	Sage flower	*Salvia splendens*	Labiatae
Lupin	-	*Lupinus hartwegii*	Leguminosae
Clianthus	Parrot's bill	*Clianthus dampieri*	Leguminosae
Sweet pea	-	*Lathyrus odoratus*	Leguminosae
Clarkia	-	*Clarkia elegans*	Onagraceae
Statice	Sea lavender	*Limonium sinuatum*	Plumbaginaceae
Phlox	Star flower	*Phlox drummondii*	Polemoneaceae
Larkspur		*Delphinium hybridum*	Ranunculaceae
Nigella	Love in a mist	*Nigella damascena*	Ranunculaceae
Mignonette		*Reseda odorata*	Resedaceae
Antirrhinum	Snapdragon/ Dog flower	*Antirrhinum majus*	Scrophulariaceae
Mimulus	Monkey flower	*Mimulus tigrinus*	Scrophulariaceae
Wish bone	-	*Torenia fournien*	Scrophulariaceae
Petunia		*Petunia hybrida*	Solanaeae
Schizanthus	Butterfly flower/ Poorman's orchid	*Schizanthus wistonensis*	Solanaceae
Nasturtium	Canary bird-flower	*Tropaeolum majus*	Troparolaceae
Lady's lace	-	*Pimpinella monoica*	Umbelliferae
Verbena	-	*Verbena hybrida*	Verbanaceae

15.2 Exotic and Indian bred varieties in different annual flowers:

- Acroclinum: White Hawaii, Blue Hawaii, Royal Hawaii.
- African daisy: Tetra Goliath (tetraploid), Snowball, Monstrosa, Ruby.
- Amaranthus (NBRI, Lucknow): Amar Shola, Amar Kiran, Amar Mosaic, Amar Peet, Amar Jyoti, Amar Parvati, Amar Tetra, Amar Tirang, Amar Prithu, Amar Sri Kiran, Amar Raktabh.
- Cosmos: Alipore Beauty.
- Coreopsis:
  - Exotic: Sunbeam, Sunburst, Early Sunrise.
  - Indian: Pusa Tara. Suitable for cut flower, growing in beds/ mixed borders/ rockeries/ pots/ sunny corners of home garden.
- Candytuft: Iceberg, Empress, White Pinnacle.
- Celosia: Golden Feather, Silver Feather, Lilliput, Jewel Box, Red Fox. Fire Glow.
- Calendula: Gold Star, Golden Gem, Cream Beauty, Orange King, Orange Coronet.
- Gazania: Minister, Carnival hybrids.
- Helichrysum: Fireball, Tall Double, Dwarf Double.
- Larkspur: Blue Bell, Dazzler, Miss California, Elite, Flemingo.
- Nicotiana: Nicki Pink/ Red/ White.

- Portulaca:
  - Exotic: Magic Carpet, Double Red.
  - Indian (NBRI, Lucknow): Zhumka, Karana Pali, Lalita, Mukta, Vibhuti, Ratnam.
- Rudbeckia: Pink Wheel, Red Pillar, Violet Queen, Pygmy.
- Nicotiana: Nicki hybrids are popular.
- Sunflower: 'Amit' is pollen-less variety.
- Sweet pea:
  - Exotic: Grandiflora, Multiflora, Dwarf Cupid and Spencer type have wavy petals. Cv. Spencer is developed by single plant selection.
  - Indian (PAU, Ludhiana): Punjab Sweet Pea-1 (magenta coloured flowers), Punjab Sweet Pea-2 (pink flowers), Punjab Sweet Pea-3 (maroon coloured flowers), Punjab Sweet Pea-4 (purple flowers), Punjab Sweet Pea-5 (cream coloured flowers). All are climbing types and flowers within 42-47 days after sowing.
- Four free-flowering highly floriferous and heat resistant verbena hybrids were developed by hybridizing *V. tenuisecta* and *V. hybrida* at NBRI. Hybrids show GMS and don't set seeds and therefore highly floriferous and free flowering.
- Wall flower: Cloth of Gold, Fire King, Tom Thumb, Purple Queen.

15.3 Seed production of annual flowers:

Crop	Planting time	Planting distance(cm)	Flowering period	Harvesting period
Ageratum houstanianum	Oct-Nov.	45 x 45	Feb-Mar	April
Alyssum maritimum	Oct-Nov.	30 x 20	Feb-Mar	April
Aster amellus	Oct-Nov.	45 x 30	Feb-Mar	April
Calendula officinalis	Oct-Nov.	30 x 30	-	-
Celosia plumosa	June	30 x 20	August	September
Corepsis lanceolata	2nd week Nov.	60 x 45	April	May
Cosmos bipinnatus	Mid-Oct.	45 x 30	Feb-March	April
Dahlia hybrida	Oct-Nov.	45 x 45	-	-
Eschscholzia californica	Nov. end	45 x 30	Feb end	April-May
Gaillardia pulchella	Feb-March	60 x 45	May	June-July
Gazania splendens	1st fortnight Nov.	70 x 45	April	May
Helichrysum spp.	Oct end.	60 x 45	March-April	March-April
Impatiens balsamina	1st week July	30 x 30	August end	Sept-Oct
Mesembryanthemum criniflorum	Oct-Nov.	30 x 25	March	April
Molucella spp.	Oct.	45 x 30	1st week March	Mid May
Papaver rhoeas	Oct.	45 x 30	March	April
Petunia hybrida	Oct-Nov.	45 x 45	March- Mid June	April-June
Phlox drummondii	Feb-May	45 x 30	March-May	June
Tagetes erecta	Oct-Nov.	45 x 30	Feb-March	May
Tagetes patula	Oct-Nov.	45 x 30	Feb-March	May
Verbena hybrida	1st week Nov.	45 x 30	March- April	Mid May
Viola tricolor	Mid Oct.	45 x 30	February-March	March-April
Zinnia elegans	March-April	45 x 30	May	June-July

16. SHRUBS:

- Plants growing upto 1-4 m height with no clear trunk.
- In home garden, shrubbery borders are kept around 15-20%.
- Flowers used for offering worship Lord Shiva: *Thevetia peruviana.*
- Flowers shed like tears or drop down during sunrise: Parijatak.
- May be used as pot plant, specimen pot plant, hanging basket, foliage plants.
- Pruning of parijatak is done in winter.
- Highly suitable for ornamental hedge: *Lantana camera, Murraya panniculata.*
- Indian origin: Barleria, Chandni, Cup and Saucer, *Clerodendron*, Crossandra, Chitra, Parijatak, Rukmini, Weeping merry.
- Yellow bells: Originated in West Indies.
- Optimum pH range for azalea: 4.5-5.5.
- Commercial valuable product of protea flower: Terminal inflorescence.
- Soil pH indicator plant: Hydrangea (acidic soil (pH < 6.0) -Blue flower & alkaline soil-Red flower). Widely used for dehydration purpose.
- Blue colour of hydrangea: Due to presence of more aluminium than pink ones.
- Neelakurinji (*Strobilanthes kunthiana*) blooms once in 12 years.

16.1 Classification:

- Ever flowering: Bougainvillea, Calliandra, Hibiscus, Ixora, Nerium.
- Winter flowering: *Poinsettia pulcherrima, Pyrostegia venusta, Homskioldia* spp., *Doembya* spp.
- Flowering and foliage: *Hamelia patens, Bougainvillea, Buddelia asiatica.*
- Foliage: Acalypha, Aralia, Codium, Eranthemum, Graptophyllum, *Pisonia alba.*
- Fragrance: *Cestrum nocturnum, Cestrum diurnum, Murraya panniculata, Jasminum* spp.,
- Specimen: *Cassia biflora, Hibiscus rosa-sinensis, Hamelia patens, Thevetia peruviana, Murraya panniculata.*
- Salt tolerant: *Bougainvillea, Barleria cristata, Hamelia patens, Russelia juncea.*
- Salt sensitive: *Buddleia asiatica, Lagerstroemia indica, Barleria cristata,*

16.2 Propagation method:

1. Seed: *Calliandra* spp., *Caesalpinia pulcherrima, Putranjiva roxturghii, Stenolobium stans, Thevetia peruviana.*
2. Stem cutting: *Achania malvaviscus, Bougainvillea* spp., *Cestrum diurnum, C. nocturnum, Dieffenbachia amoena, Hibiscus, Hamelia patens, Jasminum sambac, Hydrangea, Pachystachys lutea.*

3. Layering: *Ixora* spp., *J. sambac*, *J. multiflorum*.
4. Ground layering: *J. multiflorum*.
5. Terminal cuttings: *Eunymous japonicus*, *Ficus panda*, *Brunfelsia americana*.
6. Rhizome: *Calathea zebrina*,

Name	Botanical name	Family	Flower colour
Barleria	*Barleria cristata*	Acanthaceae	Violet-blue
Lollipop plant	*Pachystachys lutea*	Acanthaceae	Golden yellow
Joker smile plant/ Water dropwort/ Hairy buttercup	*Oxypolis filiformis*	Apiaceae	White
Tropic snow	*Dieffenbachia amoena*	Araceae	Varigated leaves
Ribbon plant	*Chlorophytum comosum*	Araceae	-
Yellow trumpet bush/ Yellow bells	*Tecoma stans*	Bignoniaceae	Yellow
Japanese spindle tree	*Eunymous japonicus*	Celastraceae	Greenish white
Azalea	*Azalea spp.*	Ericaceae	White, purple, pink
Snow bush/ Leaf flower	*Breynia disticha*	Euphorbiaceae	Variegated leaves
Copper plant	*Acalypha spp.*	Euphorbiaceae	Greenish white
Poinsettia	*Poinsettia pulcherima*	Euphorbiaceae	White
Hydrangea	*Hydron hortensia* (syn. *H. microphylla*)	Hydrangeaceae	Blue & pink
Peacock flower	*Caesalpinia pulcherrima*	Leguminosae	Red, yellow
Butterfly bush	*Buddleia asiatica*	Loganiaceae	White
Pomegranate/ Anar	*Punica granatum*	Lythraceae	Red
Shravani	*Lagerstromia indica*	Lythraceae	White, red, purple
Abutilon	*Abutilon indicum*	Malvaceae	Yellow
China rose/ Shoe flower/ Queen of Tropics	*Hibiscus-rosa sinensis*	Malvaceae	Scarlet
Dancing lady	*Fuchshia hybrida*	Onagraceae	Red, purple
King of Day	*Cestrum diurnum*	Oleaceae	White
Kund	*Jasminum multiflorum*	Oleaceae	White
Mogra	*Jasminum sambac*	Oleaceae	White
Parijatak/ Tree of sadness/ Night flowering jasmine/ Harsingar	*Nyctanthes arbor-tristis*	Oleaceae	White orange
Chitra	*Plumbago auriculata*	Plumbaginaceae	Blue
Protea	*Protea cynaroides*	Proteaceae	-
Ixora	*Ixora perviflora*	Rubiaceae	White, red
Mussaenda/ Dhobi tree	*Mussaenda luteola*, *M. frondosa*	Rubiaceae	Yellow
Kamini	*Murraya exotica*	Rutaceae	White
Weeping merry	*Russelia juncea*	Scrophulariaceae	Red
Queen of night	*Cestrum nocturnum*	Solanaceae	White
Yesterday- Today- Tomorrow	*Brunfelsia calycina*	Solanaceae	Blue
Cup and saucer	*Holmskioldia sanguinea*	Verbanaceae	Red

17. CLIMBERS:

- Generally climbers are suitable for roof gardens.
- Queen of climbers: *Clematis panniculata.*
- Trailers do not form roots at their nodes.

17.1 Classification based on purpose:

- Annual: Sweet pea, *Ipomea lobata, Clitoria ternatea*
- Hedge: *Clerodendron inerme, Bougainvillea.*
- Screening: *Vernonia elegnarfolia, Pyrostegia venusta.*
- Sunny situation: *Quisqualis indica*, *Antigonon leptopus*, *Bougainvillea* spp., *Campsis grandiflora*, *P. venusta.*
- Partial shade: *Clerodendron splendens*, *Petrea volubilis*, *Lonicera japonica*, *Trachelospermum jasminoides*.
- Deciduous nature: *Wisteria sinensis.*
- Indoor decoration: *Pothos*, *Monstera deliciosa*, *Asparagus* spp.
- Pot purpose: *Bougainvillea*, *C. ternatea.*
- Heavy climber: Rangoon creeper, *Bougainvillea*, *Pyrostegia venusta*, *Wisteria sinensis*, *Bignonia magnifolia*, *Beaumontia grandiflora.*
- Light climber: *Lonicera japonica, T. jasminoides, Clitoria ternatea*, *Quamoclit pinnata*.
- Fragrant: *J. grandiflorum*, *T. jasminoides*, *Hiptage benghalensis*, *Clematis panniculata*, *L. japonica*.
- Screening walls: *Ficus repens.*

17.2 Modified organs:

- Avail the support of their special structures like thorns, tendrils, rootlets, modified leaf stalks, prickles, hooks, etc.
- Climbers without any structure climb over support by twining themselves.
- Climbers manage to support themselves over trunks/ stems/ branches of other plants are nicknamed as 'Ramblers/ Stagglers'.
- Climbers are trained on trellies/ pergolas/ arches/ arbours and pillars.
  a) Tendrils: Coral vine, Bignonia, Golden shower, Virgin flower.
  b) Thorns/ Hooks: Bougainvillea, Climbing rose.
  c) Roots and rootlets: Trumpet climber, Indian ivy, Star jasmine.
  d) Sticky substance: Indian ivy.
  e) Twiners/ lianes: *Echitis*, *Hiptage*, *Lonicera.*
  f) Ramblers and stagglers: Rangoon creeper.
  g) Creeper: Morning glory.

Common name	Botanical name	Family	Flower colour	Flowering time
Sky flower/ Black eyed susan	*Thunbergia grandiflora*	Acanthaceae	Blue	February-March
Nepal trumpet creeper	*Beaumontia grandiflora*	Apocynaceae	White	March
Duck flower	*Aristolochia elegans*	Aristolochiceae	White	September
Creeping tuberose	*Stephanotis floribunda*	Asclepidaceae	White	April-August
Vernonia	*Vernonia elaegnifolia*	Asteraceae	-	-
Adenocalymma	*Adenocalymma alliaceum*	Bignoniaceae	Lavender	November
Bignonia	*Bignonia gracilis*	Bignoniaceae	Yellow	March-April
Trumpet climber	*Campsis grandiflora*	Bignoniaceae	Orange	March-November
Golden shower	*Pyrostegia venusta*	Bignoniceae	Orange	February-March
Honey suckle	*Lonicera japonica*	Caprifoliaceae	Cream	May-June
Rangoon creeper	*Quisqualis indica*	Combretaceae	Pink-red	Throughout year
Railway creeper	*Ipomea palmata*	Convolvulaceae	Purple	Round the year
Morning glory	*Ipomea learii*	Convolvulaceae	Purple-red	Throughout year
Cypress vine	*Mina lobata* (*Quamoclit pinnata*)	Convolvulaceae	Red	August-December
Bridal bouquet	*Porana panniculata*	Convolvulaceae	White	October-March
Bauhinia	*Bauhinia vahlii*	Leguminosae	White	April-may
Grape flower vine	*Wisteria sinensis*	Leguminosae	White	March
Butterfly pea creeper/ Shankhapushpi	*Clitoria ternatea*	Leguminosae	Blue, white	June-August
Madhvilata	*Hiptage bengalensis*	Malphigiaceae	White	February-March
Indian ivy	*Ficus repens*	Moraceae	-	-
Eve's Apron	*Ficus roxburghi*	Moraceae	-	-
Chameli	*Jasminum grandiflorum*	Oleaceae	White	June-November
Star jasmine	*Trachelospermum jasmenoides*	Oleaceae	White	May-June
Watch flower	*Passiflora lauriflora*	Passifloraceae	Purple	-
Coral vine	*Antigonon leptopus*	Polygonaceae	Red	September-November
Virgin flower	*Clematis panniculata*	Ranunculaceae	White	July-August
Blue potato creeper	*Solanum seaforthianum*	Solanaceae	-	-
Clerodendron	*Clerodendron splendens*	Verbanaceae	Deep red	December-March
Purple wreath	*Petrea volubilis*	Verbanaceae	Purple	April-May

18. TREES:

- Dendrology: Study of wood plants.
- Among global ladder of forest, India ranks 10th in total forest cover (0.7 million sq.km).
- Planting of trees in avenue i.e. arboriculture was done by Emperor Ashoka (Father of road side avenue planting). He adopted arboriculture 1st time in his state policy.
- Arboretum: Grouping of different trees are planted & maintained for scientific study.

- Silviculture: Growing of trees for forestry purpose.
- Woodland planting: Trees established in large waste lands.
- 1st evidence of an ornamental tree, the peepal (*Ficus religiosa*) comes from Mohenjo-daro.
- *Van Mahotsva* was initiated by Dr. K.M. Munshi in 1950.
- During 2016, tree cover of India is 23.81%.
- Central India and Arunachal Pradesh: Fo efront in total forest area.
- Madhya Pradesh: Maximum area (77,462 sq. km) under forest followed by Arunachal Pradesh (67,248 sq. km), Chhattisgarh, Maharashtra and Odisha.
- Hard wood: Wood obtained from broad leaved tree.
- Tallest living tree of world: Coast redwood (*Sequoia sempervirens*) measuring 115.92 m found in Redwood National Park, California.
- Cricket bats are prepared from *Salix* spp.
- Costliest wood: Agar wood.
- National tree of India: Banyan tree (*Ficus benghalensis*).
- Tree leaves absord 95% of UV radiation.
- King tree of Great Indian Desert: Khejri (*Prosopis cineraria*). Highly drought tolerant because it has phreatophytic root system. It increases fertility status of soil.
- Phreatophyte: Tree species having ability to absorb water from deeper layers through special roots.
- Each 20-30 m width of trees can absorb about 6-8 decibels of sound under city and reduce noise of traffic of national highways.
- Neem, coconut, tamarind reduce noise level up to 6-10 dB (Decibel).
- Amaltas is known as ‘Nature indicator of rain’ or ‘Shower of the forest’.
- Trees with compound leaves are poor dust collectors than simple leaves.
- Neem and Tamarind are highly prized for their ability to filter noise, dust and light.
- Among trees seeds, dormancy is quite serious in Cassia.
- World’s tallest tree Coast redwood (*Sequoria sempervirens*) found in California has height of 115.5 m.
- Leaf type in *Bauhunia purpurea*: Optocordate.
- *Bauhinia racemosa*: *Kalpavriksha* (tree of heaven) of Rajasthan.
- Flowers and leaves of *Callistemon citrinus* have anti-cancerous properties.
- *Taxus baccata*: Known to cure cancer disease.
- Flowers of *Albizia* tree are used for ear decoration.
- Trumpet shaped flowers: *Jacaranda mimosaefolia* (blue colour), *Kigelia pinnata* (crimson colour).

- Bearing fruits in the trunk pattern is specific to *Crescentia cujete.*
- Pongamia (*Pongamia pinnata*): Very cool tree (natural refrigerator).
- Flame of forest can withstand both frost and drought.
- Monkey puzzle: Most attractive plant in Victorian park of Trees in Great Britain. Tree not destroyed even after eruption of volcanoes. Wood used for construction purpose, railway boggies preparations.
- *Cassia lancusteri*: *C. nodosa* x *C. marginata.*
- Two kind of flowering trees blooming at one time-
  - i) *Cassia fistula* (yellow): *Delonix regia* (red).
  - ii) *Grevillea robusta* (yellow): *Jacaranda acutifolia* (blue).
  - iii) *Cassia fistula* (yellow): *Cassia nodosa* (pink).
- Shade tree should have wide oval canopy.
- Trees in garden are planted in 15-20% area.

18.1 Classification based on purpose:

Screening purpose	*Casuarina equisetifolia, Cupressus sempervirens, Grevillea robusta, Eucalyptus* spp., *Populus ciliata, Polyanthia longifolia, Putranjiva roxburghii*
Specimen trees	*Araucaria aculea, Amhersita nobilis, Callistemon lanceolatus, Cassia fistula, Casuarina equisetifolia, Chorisia speciosa, Ficus elastica, Magnolia grandiflora, Plumeria alba, Salix babylonica, Saraca thaipingensis, Platanus orientalis*
Drooping/ cascade type branching	*Salix babylonica, Callistemon lanceolatus*
Ideal avenue trees	*Cassia fistula, Grevillea robusta, Jacaranda acutifolia, Ficus infectoria, Milletia ovalifolia, Kigelia pinnata, Pterospermum acerifolium, Heterophragma adinophyllum, Mellingtonia hortensis, Cassia siamea*
Thorny ornamental trees	*Bombax ceiba, Chorisia speciosa, Erythrina indica, Parkinsonia aculeata, Acacia nilotica*
Sweet smelling flowering trees	*Anthocephalus cadamba, Melingtonia hortensis, Magnolia grandiflora, Aegel marmelos, Michelia champaca, Mesuaferrea, Nyctanthus arbor-tristis, Plumeria alba, Pterospermum acerifolium*
Fowl smelling flowering trees	*Gustavia, Sterculia, Crateva, Careya*
Fast & quick establishing trees	Copper shield tree, *Melia azadirach*, Gulmohar, Neem
Slow growing trees	*Pterocarpus santalinus, Tamarindus indica*
In front of multi-storey house	*Polyalthia longifolia, Cupressus sempervirens*
With round canopy	*Ficus infectoria, Mimusops elengi, Dillenia indica, Plumeria indica, Morus nigra*
With beautiful trunk	*Bombax ceiba, Chorisia speciosa, Adansonia digitata, Platanus orientalis, Eucalyptus hybrida*
Trees for marshy areas	*Eucalyptus hybrida, Plantains, Populus deltoids, Salix babylonica, Tamarix* spp.
Checking air pollution	*Acer negundo, Albizia lebbeck, Anthocephalus cadamba, Azadiracta indica, Betula pendula, Cassia fistula, Cidrus deodara, Ficus infectoria, Ficus religiosa, Ficus*

	benjamina,Morus spp., Michelia champaca, Populus deltoids, Plumeria acutifolia, Robinia pseudocacia, Syzygium cumini, Terminalia arjuna
Dust pollution control	*Bombax ceiba, Betula pendula, Dalbergia sissoo, Ficus benjamina, Grevillea robusta, Juniperus chinensis, Viburnum lantana*
Noise pollution control	Evergreen trees e.g. *Butea monosperma, Mangifera indica, Madhuca indica, Eucalyptus citriodora, Salix planifolia, Azadirachta indica, Cocos nucifera, Tamarindus indica*
Alkaline and saline soil	*Azadirachta indica, Butea frondosa, Bassia latifolia, Casuarina equistifolia, Cassia fistula, Parkinsonia aculeata, Phoenix dactylifera, Thespesia populnea*
Acidic soils	*Pinus wallichiana*
Unique branching habit/ Tiered branching pattern	*Terminalia catappa*
Wide & vigorous root system	*Ficus benghalensis, Sterculia alata*
Queer leaves	*Ficus krishnae*
Twisted flowers	*Couroupita guinensis, Parkia filicodea*
Strange fruits & nuts	*Artocarpus heterophyllus, Bixa orellana, Couroupita guinensis, Kigelia pinnata*
Nectar yielding trees	*Azadiracta indica, Bauhinia purpurea, Bauhinia variegata, Callistemon lanceolatus, Dalbergia sisoo, Eugenia jambolana*
Fruiting trees	*Mangifera indica, Zizyphus mauritiana, Emblica officinalis, Artocarpus heterophyllus, Syzygium cumini, Ficus carica*
Trees with ornamental fruits	*Citrus microcarpa, Hazara orange*
Trees with ornamental foliage	*Averrhoa carambola, Callistemon lanceolatus, Citharexylum subeserratum, Polyalthia longifolia*
Trees for sea shore	*Tamarix indica, Casuarina equisetifolia, Pinus heliopensis, Juniperus vargodensis, Populus simony, Acer rubrum*
Trees as wind break	*Eugenia jambolana,*
Water loving trees	*Bassia latifolia, Terminalia* spp., *Syzygium cumini*

18.2 Important trees:

Common name	Botanical name	Family	Flower colour	Flowering time
Scholar's tree/ Ashok	*Polyalthia longifolia*	Annonaceae	Pale green	April
Pagoda tree	*Plumeria alba*	Apocynaceae	White, yellow, red	Round the year
Temple tree	*Plumeria acutifolia*	Apocynaceae	White with yellow centre	May-September
Devil's tree/ Saptaparni	*Alstonia scholaris*	Apocynaceae	White	July-August
Umbrella tree	*Schefflera actinophylla*	Araliaceae	-	-
Rice paper plant	*Tetrapanex papyriferum*	Araliaceae	Foliage	-
Araucaria	*Araucariacookii*	Araucariaceae	Foliage	-
Birch tree	*Betula alnoides*	Betulaceae	White	-
Nili gulmohar	*Jacaranda acutifolia*	Bignoniaceae	Bluish purple	May-June
Balam khira/ African sausage tree	*Kigelia pinnata*	Bignoniaceae	Blue	April

Monkey tail	*Heterophragma adenophyllum*	Bignoniceae	Blue	April
Akash neem/ Indian cork tree/ Tree jasmine	*Millingtonia hortensis*	Bignoniaceae	White	October-January
Fountain tree/ Indiantree/Tulip tree	*Spathodea campanulata*	Bignoniaceae	Red	February-March
Nili gulmohor	*Jacaranda mimosifolia*	Bignoniaceae	Blue	April
Sausage tree/ Balam kheera	*Kigelia pinnata*	Bignoniaceae	Crimson	May
Lahura	*Tecomella undulate*	Bignoniaceae	Yellow-orange	February-March
Semal/ Red cotton silk	*Bombax malabaricum* (syn. *B. ceiba*)	Bombaceae	Bright-red	March
Indian lavender tree	*Bursera delpechiana*	Burseraceae	Lavender	-
Fern leafed tree	*Filicium decipiens*	Burseraceae	Foliage	-
Bauhinia/ Camel's foot/ Kachnar	*Bauhinia variegata*	Caesalpinaceae	Rose red	March
Amaltas/ Golden shower/ Indian laburnum/ Bahava	*Cassia fistula*	Caesalpinaceae	Deep yellow	March-July
Candle bush/ Popcorn senna	*Cassia alata*	Caesalpinaceae	Yellow	March-April
Pink cassia	*Cassia nodosa*	Caesalpinaceae	Pink	April-May
Java cassia	*Cassia javanica*	Caesalpinaceae	Deep pink	April
Yellow cassia	*Cassia siamea*	Caesalpinaceae	Yellow	July
Jerusalem thorn	*Parkinsonia aculeata*	Caesalpinaceae	Yellow	April-May
Arjun	*Terminalia arjuna*	Combretaceae	Yellow	May-July
False almond	*Terminalia catappa*	Combretaceae	White	May
Monster plant/ Alien plant/Buttonwood/ Button mangrove	*Conocarpus erectus*	Combretaceae	-	-
Himalayn silver fir	*Abies pindrow*	Conifereae	Foliage	Evergreen
Monkey puzzle/ Anti-fire tree	*Araucaria excelsa, A. cookii*	Conifereae	Foliage	Evergreen
Chinese juniper	*Juniperus chinensis*	Conifereae	Foliage	Evergreen
Elephant tree/ Chalta tree	*Dillenia indica*	Dilleniaceae	White	May-August
Child-Life-tree/ Jiva Putra	*Putranjiva roxburghii*	Euphorbiaceae	Light yellow	March-April
Pride of Burma/ Queen of flowering tree	*Amhersita nobilis*	Fabaceaea	Vermillion	Red
Alexandrian Laurel	*Calophyllum inophyllum*	Guttiferae	Dull white	March
White Indian Mountain rose	*Brownea coccinea*	Leguminosae	Scarlet	March-April
Hong Kong orchid tree	*Bauhinia blakenea*	Leguminosae	Dark crimson	December-March
Gulmohar/ May flower	*Delonix regia*	Leguminosae	Orange-red	May-June
Badminton ball tree	*Pakia biglandulosa*	Leguminosae	White	-
Karanj	*Pongamia pinnata*	Leguminosae	Purple	May
Copper pod tree/ Yellow gulmohar	*Peltophorum feruugineum*	Leguminosae	Pale yellow	-

Siris	*Albizzia lebbeck*	Leguminosae	Greenish-yellow	April
Australian wattle	*Acacia auriculiformis*	Leguminosae	Foliage tree	-
Rose of Venezula	*Brownea grandiceps*	Leguminosae	Scarlet red	March-April
Jungal jalebi	*Inga dulcis*	Leguminosae	-	
Sita Ashok	*Saraca indica*	Leguminosae	Scarlet red	April
Queen flower/ Rose of India/ Pride of India	*Lagerstroemia speciosa*	Lythraceae	Deep mauve	April-August
Swarn champa	*Michelia champaka*	Magnoliaceae	White	April-May
Bara champa	*Magnolia grandiflora*	Magnoliaceae	White	April
Pahari papal/ Porda tree	*Thespesia populnea*	Malvaceae	Yellow	Ever blooming
Mexican semal	*Choresia speciosa*	Malvaceae	Pink	October
Neem	*Azadirachta indica*	Meliaceae	White	April
Persian lilac	*Melia azedarach*	Meliaceae	Lilac	April-May
Indian mahagoni	*Cederlla tona*	Meliaceae	White	April
Spanish mahagoni	*Swietenia mahagoni*	Meliaceae	Foliage	
Bodhi tree/ Pipal	*Ficus religiosa*	Moraceae	-	April-May
Makhan katora	*Ficus krishnae*	Moraceae	-	Evergreen
Weeping fig/ Golden fig	*Ficus benjamina*	Moraceae	Yellow	Evergreen
Bargad/ Banyan tree	*Ficus benghalensis*	Moraceae	Red	February-March
Pakan	*Ficus infectoria*	Moraceae	Foliage	Evergreen
Banzo tree	*Ficus lyrata*	Moraceae	-	Evergreen
Chilkan	*Ficus retusa*	Moraceae	Foliage	Evergreen
Flowering gum	*Eucalyptus ficifolia*	Myrtaceae	White to pink	April
Bottle brush	*Callistemon lanceolatus*	Myrtaceae	Red/ scarlet	March-April
Kadam	*Anthocephalus cadamba*	Naucleaceae	Foliage	-
Mother of cocoa	*Gliricidia sepium*	Papilionaceae	Light pink	February-March
Flame of forest/ Palash	*Butea monosperma*	Papilionaceae	Scarlet	March
Indian coral tree/ Parrot flower	*Erythrina variegata* (*E. indica*)	Papilionaceae	Scarlet	April
Silver oak	*Grevillea robusta*	Proteaceae	Golden yellow	April
Weeping willow	*Salix babylonica*	Saliacaceae	Red	March-April
Golden rain tree/ Chienese rain tree	*Koelreutaria panniculata*	Sapindaceae		-
Mahua	*Bassia latifolia* (syn. *Madhuka indica*)	Sapotaceae	Red	April-May
Molsari	*Mimusops elengi*	Sapotaceae	White	May-August
Tree of Heaven	*Ailanthus excelsa*	Simaroubaceae	Foliage tree	April-June
Potato tree	*Solanum grandiflorum*	Solanaceae	Blue-mauve	Throughout year
Kanak champa	*Pterospermum acerifolium*	Sterculiaceae	Yellow	April-June
Himalayan yew	*Taxus wallichiana*	Taxaceae	-	March-May
Tree of life	*Guaicum officinalis*	Zygophyllaceae	Blue	March-April

19. PALMS:

- Eulogized as 'Princes of vegtable kingdom'.

- Monocot and belongs to family Arecaceae.
- Comprises 212 genera and 2,780 species.
- Palms are mostly slow growing plants.
- Arboreal palms in their juvenile stages can be used for decorating large rooms, seminar halls, parlours and *varandas*.
- Palms with dwarf built are mostly used for indoor decoration.
- Calamus: Climbing palm or sprawl on ground. Largest genus comprising 400 species.
- Planted for creating special effects.
- Palm is efficient air purifier. They absorb CO_2 and release O_2.
- Caudex: Marks of scars of fallen leaves.
- Lady palm: Introduction from southern China. Dwarf, multistemmed clump of dense foliage.
- Arrangement of leaves in specific pattern: Traveller's palm.
- Repeated pruning produces a phenomenon known as 'pencil top', a narrowed trunk just below the fronds.
- Best air purifiers for indoor environment: Ornamental palms like Dwarf date palm, Bamboo palm, Broad leaved lady palm, Areca palm.
- **Group/ Types of palms**: They are grouped into feather/ pinnate leaved and fan/ flabelliform leaved.

Solitary palms	*Cocos, Phoenix* spp., *Elaeis* spp.
Clumping palms	*Areca lutescens*, *Rhapis humilis*
Branching palms	*Hyphane indica* (branching above ground), *Nipa fruticans* (branching below ground)
Trunkless palms	*Phoenix acaulis*, *Phoenix pusilla*

Important palms:

Name	Botanical name	Origin	Propagation	Cultural tips & growing conditions
Broad leaved lady palm	*Rhapis excelsa*	China & Japan	Seeds or suckers	Taller upto 3 m; can grow in low light/ partially shaded area; cold hardy
Slender lady palm	*Rhapis humilis*	China	Seeds or suckers	Dwarf upto 1.5 m; can grow in low light/ partially shaded area
Areca palm/ Golden cane palm/ Butterfly palm	*Chrysalido-carpus lutescens* (syn. *Areca lutescens*)	Madagascar	Seeds or suckers	Height 3-4 m; require cool area & adequate light in rooms; suitable for rockeries, background& indoor plant
Parlour palm	*Chamaedbrea elegans*	Mexico	Seeds	Grown in pots; slender stem grows upto 1.2 m height; orange coloured flowers; shaded area with adequate moisture
Panama hat palm	*Carludovica*	Central	Seeds or	Height upto 250 cm; pot plant;

	palmate	America	suckers	grown for mass effect in groups & rockeries
Fish tail palm/ Burmese crested/ Tufted fish tail	*Caryota mitis*	S-E-Asia	Seeds or suckers	Quick growing; fishtail like leaves; suitable for background decoration, pot plant & deep shade
Indian sago palm	*Caryota urens*	Forests of peninsular India	Seeds	Require partial shade; suitable only in juvenile stage (1-3 years) for indoor decoration
Good luck palm	*Chamaedorea elegans*	Mexico	Seeds or suckers	Spineless, grows to height 250 cm; suitable pot culture; cold hardy; produces most popular cut green
Licula	*Licula grandis* (syn. *Pritchardia grandis*)	New Guinea	Seeds or suckers	Dwarf; fan leaved palm growing upto 180-250 cm; very ornamental indoor plant
Chinese fan palm	*Livistona chinensis*	China	Seeds or suckers	Beautiful; grows upto 900 cm; leaves fan like; suitable for ground, avenues & pots
Date palm	*Phoenix roebelenii*	Tropical Asia	Seeds or suckers	Very graceful; dwarf; rough trunk; grown as pot plant
Wild date palm	*Phoenix sylvestris*	Tropical Asia	Seeds	Leaflets are spinescent & difficult to handle; require moderate shade; good indoor plant
Ptychosperma	*Ptychosperma macarthurii*	North-East Australia	Seeds or suckers	Small cluster stem with scattered rings; suitable for ground, avenues
Bamboo palm	*Raphis excelsa*	South China	Seeds or suckers	Bamboo like shrub; leathery leaves; suitable for shade garden & pot
Fan palm	*Thrinax parviflora*	Jamaica	Seeds or suckers	Fan shaped leaves almost circular; grown as pot plant
Washingtonia palm	*Washingtonia filifera*	Arizona	Seeds or suckers	Cylindrical, robust-stemmed; grown as pot plant & in gardens
Cardboard palm	*Zamia furfuracea*	Mexico	Seeds or suckers	Exotic looking cones & instinct for survival; one of 'living fossil' plants; leathery leaf give cardboard like feeling when rubbed; great container plant & specimen plant; used as beachside planting
Bismarck palm	*Bismarkia nobilis*	North America	Seeds or suckers	Beautiful palm; leaves silvery green; best fan leaved palm in world of gardening; cold hardy
Balaka palm	*Balaka seeemannil*	Fiji	Seeds or suckers	Very attractive; suitable for pot culture; grow in plains in cool indoor areas
Sinaloa Hesper palm	*Brahea aculeata*	Mexico	Seeds or suckers	Suitable for hot plains; does not grow well indoors
Sealing wax palm/ Lipstick palm	*Crytostachys renda*	Malaysia	Seeds or suckers	Most beautiful; clustering; slow growing; suitable for tropical area
Royal palm/ Bottle palm	*Oreodoxa regia* (syn. *Roystonea regia*)	North America	Seeds or suckers	Grows upto 200 cm; best suitable as specimen & planted along avenue; tolerant to saline soils

Kentia/ Curly	*Howea for steriana*	Australia	Seeds or suckers	Handsome & graceful; suitable as pot plant
Queen palm	*Arecastrum romanzoffianum*	South America	Seeds or suckers	Handsome; feather like glossy leaves
African red oil palm	*Elaeis guieneesis*	Tropical west Africa	Seeds	Leaves radiate from ground; require plenty of moisture
Sugar palm/ Sago palm	*Arenga pinnata*	Indonesia	Seeds	Good for avenue planting
Rattan palm/ Cane palm	*Calamus lindeni*	Indonesia	Seeds	Thorny & rambling habit; excellent for table decoration when young
Bourbon palm/ Red latan palm	*Latania lontaroides*	Mauritius	Seeds	Most handsome; rare & costly
Cabbage palm	*Livistona australis*	Australia	Seeds	Good for avenue planting
Traveller's palm/ East-West palm	*Ravenula madagas cariensis*	Maadag-ascar	Seeds & division	-
Blue palm/ Dwarf Palmetto	*Sabal adansonii*	South America	Seeds	Almost stemless because stem remains buried in ground
Windmill palm/ Fortunes palm	*Trachycarpus fortune* (*Chamaerops excelsa*)	China & Japan	Seeds	Slow growing; very ornamental

20. HEDGE:

- Shrubs or trees grown below 4 m height at regular intervals to form a continuous screen.

Characteristics of hedge:

- Quick growing.
- Hardy, including drought resistant character.
- Thorny and should be dense in growth habit.
- Respond to frequent pruning and clipping.
- Raised quickly by seeds or cuttings.
- Attractive foliage and/or flowers.

Classification based on purpose:

- Tall protective- *Inga dulcis,* Karonda, Bougainvillea, *Acasia fernesina.*
- Dwarf protective- *Euphorbia bojori*, *Opuntia* spp., *Agave* spp., *Pedilanthus* spp.
- Tall ornamental- Mehendi, Duranta, Casuarina, Hibiscus, *Hamelia patens, Thevetia peruviana, Murraya panniculata.*
- Dwarf ornamental- Acalypha, Clerodendron, Thunbergia, *Lantana* spp.
- Waterlogged areas: Screwpine.
- Saline and alkaline soils: Nerium.

21. EDGE

- Lining of borders of flower beds, paths, lawn and shrubbery with brick, concrete, living plants, etc.
- Mosaiculture: Art of composing a motif, an image, a picture or a sculpture using carefully selected and pruned plants.
- Formal edging: Bricks, tiles, stones, concrete.
- Informal edging: Grass cover.
- Edge and carpet bedding: *Echeveria*, *Clerodendron inerme* (forest jasmine), *Acalypha hispida*, *Alternanthera amoena*, *Coleus salicifolius*, *Impatiens repens*, *Lobelia succulenta* (Nilgiri grass), *Sedum rupestris* (Stone crop), miniature roses, *Pyrethrum aureum*, *Pilea muscosa*, Justicia, Eupatorium, *Iresine lindenii*, Helianthemum.

22. BULBOUS PLANTS:

- Leading bulbous plant producing country: The Netherlands.
- Leading bulbous plant importing country: USA.
- Leading bulbous plant growing country: South Africa.
- Leading bulbous plants growing state in India: Kalimpong (Sikkim).
- Bulbous plant having maximum area under cultivation: Gladiolus.
- Temperature plays an important role in regulation of floral initiation in bulbous species.
- Warm season: Canna, Dahlia, Tuberose, Crinum, *Zephyranthes*.
- Cool season: Gladiolus, Narcissus, Daffodil, Freesia.
- Bulb needs staking: Gladiolus, Dahlia, *Lilium*spp..
- Generally bulbs are planted at 7-10 cm depth & 30 cm x 20 cm planting distance.
- Harvesting at goose neck stage: Narcissus, Daffodil.
- For mass effect: Dahlia, Canna, Zephyranthes.
- Popular climber of Indian origin: *Gloriosa superba*.
- Oxalis had dicot bulb.
- Canna varieties: Bharat (by selection), Agnisikha, Raktima (induced mutation), Butter Cup, Apricot (yellow flowers).

Common name	Botanical name	Family
Tuberose	*Polianthes tuberosa*	Agavaceae
Belladona lily/Night star lily/Trumpet lily	*Amaryllis* spp. (syn. *Hippeastrum* spp.)	Amaryllidaceae
Sudarshan/St. John lily	*Crinum bulbispermum*	Amaryllidaceae
Red cape lily/Blood flower/Foot ball lily	*Haemanthes multiflorus*	Amaryllidaceae
Spider lily	*Hymenocallis litteralis*	Amaryllidaceae
Himalayan giant lily	*Cardiocrinum giganteum*	Amaryllidaceae
Glory lily	*Gloriosa superba*	Amaryllidaceae
Day lily	*Hemerocallis fulva*	Amaryllidaceae
Daffodil/Narcissus	*Narcissus* spp.	Amaryllidaceae

Zephyr lily/Rain lily	*Zephyranthes* spp.	Amaryllidaceae
Torch lily	*Kniphofia aloides*	Amaryllidaceae
Lily of the valley	*Convallaria majalis*	Asparagaceae
Cobra/ Snake lily	*Arisaema* spp.	Araceae
Calla lily/ Lily of the Nile	*Zantedeschia* spp.	Araceae
Indian shot/ American Beauty/ Status of liberty	*Canna indica*	Cannaceae
Magic flower	*Achimene longiflora*	Gesneriaceae
Gloxinia	*Gloxinia speciosa*	Gesneriaceae
Freesia	*Freesia refrecta*	Iridaceae
Flag flower	*Iris* x *germanica*	Iridaceae
Watsonia	*Watsonia* spp.	Iridaceae
Cyclamen	*Cyclamen persicum*	Primulaceae
Wind flower	*Anemone* spp.	Ranunculaceae
Hedychium/ Shell ginger	*Alpinia speciosa*	Zingiberaceae

23. HOUSE PLANTS/ INDOOR PLANTS:

- Greeks and Romans were pioneers of indoor gardening.
- House plants became popular after 2nd World War.
- House plants lend architectural beauty to the house interior.
- For superb performance, these plants require semi-shade.
- Foliage beauty can be enhanced by periodical sponging of the leaves.
- KSG nursery of Bengaluru holds patents on four Aglaonema hybrids namely 'Jewel of India' and 'Emerald Star', 'Silver Ribbon' and 'Silverado'.
- They purify air by removing poisonous gases such as benzene, formaldehyde, trichloroethylene, xylene, toluene and ammonia.
- Modes of propagation: Seed, division, sucker, cutting, and air layering.
- Ideal temperature for indoor plants: 15-21^{0}C and R.H. is 40-60%.
- Optimum bulk density of potting medium: 0.5-0.75 g/cc.
- Light requirement: 15-25 foot candles (16 hr light/day).
- Better growth of indoor plants: Red and blue light.
- Suitable for window garden: Agalonema, Aracaria, Sanseveria, Dieffenbachia, Poinsettia, Zebrina, Begonia, Aspidistra.
- Aspidistra: Pioneer indoor plant. Grows well in dark corner of house.
- Climbing: *Hedera*, *Ficus pumila*, *Cissus*, *Philodendron*, *Epipremum aureum*,
- Bowl/ Terrarium/ Glass bottle gardening: *Begonia*, *Billbergia nutans*, *Fittonia*, *Calathea*.
- Poisonous indoor plant: Dieffenbachia.
- Bryophyllum: Day neutral plant.
- Mode of propagation: Seeds, air layering, stem cuttings, aerial roots, rhizome, suckers, etc.
- Croton varieties: Arkavati, Gnat, Pink Elegance, Valmiki, Vijayanta, Sonar Bangla.

Name	Scientific name	Family	Origin
Shrimp plant	*Beloperone guttata*	Acanthaceae	-
Nerve plant/ Mosaic plant	*Fittonia* spp.	Acanthaceae	Peru
Caricature plant	*Graptophyllum pictum*	Acanthaceae	-
Zebra plant	*Aphelandra squarrosa*	Acanthaceae	Brazil
Chinese evergreen	*Aglaonema commutatum*	Araceae	Tropical Asia
Money plant/ Pothos/ Devil's Ivy/ Marble queen	*Epipremum aureum*	Araceae	South-East Asia
Elephant's ear plant	*Alocasia* x *amazonica*	Araceae	Asia & Australia
White veined anthurium	*Anthurium clarinervium*	Araceae	South America
Dumb cane	*Diffenbachia amoena*	Araceae	Tropical America
Arrowhead plant	*Syngonium podophyllum*	Araceae	Tropical America
Window-leaf/ Bread fruit vine	*Monstera deliciosa*	Araceae	Costa Rica
Caladium	*Caladium hortulanum*	Araceae	South America
Philodendron	*Philodendron* spp.	Araceae	Tropical America
Peace lily	*Spathiphyllum wallisii*	Araceae	Central America
Algerian ivy	*Hedera canariensis*	Araliaceae	-
Ghost tree	*Hedera helix*	Araliaceae	North Africa
Asparagus	*Asparagus tetragonus*	Asparagaceae	Europe
Cast-iron plant	*Aspidistra elatior*	Asparagaceae	China
Ribbon plant	*Chlorophytum comosum* 'Variegatum'	Asparagaceae	Tropical Asia
Rex begonia	*Begonia rex*	Begoniaceae	East Asia & India
Semperflorens begonia	*Begonia semperflorens*	Begoniaceae	East Asia & India
Variegated pineapple	*Ananas comosus* var. *variegatus*	Bromeliaceae	South America
Bromelia	*Bromelia balansae*	Bromeliaceae	Tropical America
Moses in the cradle	*Roheo spathacea*	Commelinaceae	Mexico
Purple Heart	*Setcreasea purpurea*	Commelinaceae	Mexico
Spiderwort	*Tradescantia* spp.	Commelinaceae	Central America
Wondering Jew	*Zebrina pendula*	Commelinaceae	-
Norfolk island pine	*Araucaria heterophylla*	Coniferae	North America
Bryophyllum	*Kalanchoe* spp.	Crassulaceae	Tropical Asia
Croton	*Codiaeum variegatum*	Euphorbiaceae	South India
Black prince/ Indian rubber plant	*Ficus elastic* var. *rubra*	Ficaceae	India
Painted Nettle	*Coleus blumei*	Lamiaceae	South-East Asia
Palm Lilies	*Cordyline terminalis*	Laxmanniaceae	South America
Song of India	*Dracena margineta*	Liliaceae	Madagascar
Butcher's Broom	*Ruscus aculeata*	Liliaceae	Europe
Peacock plant/ Brain plant/ Prayer plant/ Zebra plant	*Calathea zebrina*	Marantaceae	Tropical America
Arrowroot/ Obedience plant	*Maranta arundinacea*	Marantaceae	America
Screw pine	*Pandanus amaryllifolius*	Pandanaceae	America
Pepper face/ Radiator plant	*Peperomia fraseri*	Piperaceae	Tropical America
Bat flower	*Tacca* spp.	Taccaceae	Malaysia
Artillery/ Pistol/Gun Powder plant	*Pilea macrophylla*	Urticaceae	West Indies
Aluminum plant	*Pilea cadierei*	Urticaceae	China

24. TOPIARY:

- Word topiary is derived from Latin word '*Topiarius*' a creator of *topia* or "ornamental gardening".
- Roman art of training plants into different shapes of statues, birds, animals and sculptures.
- Art of clipping and shearing shrubs and small trees and herbaceous perennials into ornamental or abstract shapes.
- Topiary art started in the 1st century A.D.
- Plants used must be of evergreen, small leaves or needles, produce dense foliage or columnar growth habit.
- In India, the hanging gardens of Kamla Nehru park, Mumbai and Ramojirao film city, Hyderabad are famous for topiary work.
- Espalier: Plants that are clipped or pruned into two dimensional forms.
- Most common plants for topiary: *Acacia modesta, Bignonia unguscati, Bougainvillea, Clerodendron inerme, Cupressus macrocarpa, Duranta plumeri, Hibiscus, Inga dulcis, Murraya exotica, Polyalthia longifolia*, *Putranjiva roxburghii*, *Sesbenia egyptica* and *Thuja orientalis*.
- Temperate region; Box (*Buxus sempervirens*) and English yew (*Taxus baccata*)
- Samban-lei-Sekpil (Manipur) is the world's tallest topiary.
- American portable style topiary was introduced to Disneyland around 1962.

25. LAWN:

- Agrostology: Study of grass.
- Eulogized as 'Heart of garden or Natural green carpet'.
- 1st recorded lawns were developed in Europe.
- Axis of lawn is never divergent.
- In home garden, total area under lawn should not be more than 30%.
- Optimum time for planting: February-March or July-August.
- Best site for lawn establishment: Southern side of house, south-east or south-west.
- Most attractive shape of flower bed in midest of lawn: Rectangle.
- Most suitable grass for most parts of India: Hariyali or doob grass.
- Most suitable grass for small area and home garden: Korean grass.
- Grasses for warmer areas: These grasses lose their colour in cold weather and become brown to enter into dormancy.
- Grass for saline water condition: Selection-1.
- Grass for highly drought conditions: Fine fescue grass.
- Perennial rye grass: Fastest grass to establish.

- Kentucky blue grass: Slowest grass to establish. Suitable for salinity places. Very fine texture that gives soft-carpet like feel.
- Kikuyu grass: Grass suitable for acidic soil and higher elevation. It can be laid by dibbling or sod culture.
- Korean grass can be established only from seed, springs or sod.
- Seed colour of *Dechondra repens*: Blue.
- Astro Turf/ Synthetic/ Artificial grass: Synthetic lawn used in roof garden and cricket stadium.
- Chamomile grass: Used in lawn during 11-13th century in UK.
- Warm season grasses ae mostly dought tolerant and can survive temperature up to 45^{0}C and congenial temperature is 25-35^{0}C. Low temperature (-15^{0}C) can kill m[illegible]t of lawns.
- Cool season grasses start growing at 5^{0}C and prevails between 10-25^{0}C. They retain their colour in extreme cold, typically grow very dense, carpet like lawns with little thatch.

Warm season grasses		**Cool season/ Shady area grasses**	
Common name	**Botanical name**	**Common name**	**Botanical name**
Bahia grass	*Paspalum notatum*	Annual blue grass	*Poa an[illegible]a*
Bermuda grass	*Cynodon dactylon*	Annual rye grass	*Lolium multiflorum*
Buffalo grass	*Buchloe dactyloides*	Chewings fescue	*Festuca rubra* ssp. *rubra*
Carpet grass	*Axonopus affinis*	Colonial bent grass	*Agrostis tenuis*
Centipede grass	*Eremochloa ophiuroides*	Creeping bent grass	*Agrostis palustris*
Kikuyu grass	*Pennisetum clandestineum*	Velvet bent grass	*Agrostis canina*
Seashore paspalum	*Paspalum vaginatum*	Red top grass	*Agrostis gigantea*
Japanese lawn / Korean grass	*Zoysia japonica*	Kentucky blue grass	*Poa pratensis*
Mascarene grass	*Zoysia tunifolia*	Perennial rye grass	*Lolium perenne*
Manila grass	*Zoysia matrella*	Rough blue grass	*Poa trivialis*
Elephant grass	*Typha elephantina*	Tall fescue grass	*Fesuca arundinacea*
Alkali grass	*Puccinnellia distans*	Chain grass	*Sporobolus tremulus*
Beach grass	*Ammophila* spp.	Carpet grass	*Axonopus affinis*
Orchard grass	*Dactylis glomerata*	St. Augustine grass	*Stenotaphrum secundatum*
Port Harcourt grass	*Crysopogon aciculatus*		

Major grasses:

- Varieties of bermuda grass: Arizona Common, Jackpot, Princess-77, MS-Choice, Quickstand, Midlawn, GN-1, Celebration, Riviera, Sonesta, Sundevil, Tifsport, Tifgreen, Tifdwarf.
- Varieties of zoysia grass: Meyer, Palisades, Zenith, Cavalier, Diamond, Zorro, Emerald, Z-3.

- Variety of bahia grass: Pensacola.

Name	Suitability to athletic fields
Bermuda/ Doob/ Couch/ /Bahama/ Haryali / Hyderabad grass	All sports & drought resistant
Creeping bent grass, Colonial bent grass	Tennis courts, Bowling & Croquet
Kentucky Blue/ China/ June grass	Baseball, Football, Soccer
Tall Fescue	Baseball, Football, Soccer
Korean/ Velvet/ Mascarene / Japanese grass	Soccer
Ryegrass, Creeping Bent grass, Bahia/ paspalum grass	Golf
St. Augustine/ Charleston grass	Golf & shady areas

- Planting methods:
  a) Seeding: Easiest method to establishment. September-October is best months to seed a new lawn with improved varieties of quality grass and reseeding (over seeding) an established lawn to make it thicker and healthier.
  b) Dibbling of roots: Most common, cheapest, slowest but perfect method. Roots are dibbled at 12-15 cm apart.
  c) Turfing/ Sodding: Quickest but most expensive method
  d) Turf plastering: not suitable for dry areas.
  e) Stolonizing: Stolons are used e.g. St. Augustine grass.
  f) Sprigging: Placing sprigs in narrow furrows spaced 6-8" apart and 2-3" deep.
  g) Hydro seedling (seed + mulch + fertilizer) is one of the latest methods for establishing lawn in large areas.
  h) Planting on polyethylene: Polyethylene thickness of 800 gauge. It is used to create temporary effect.
- Rolling helps in anchorage of grass.
- Lawn mower (cylinder or reel mower): Invented by Edwin Budding in 1830 in England.
- Mowing prevents excessive growth of grass.
- Normal mowing height: 5-6 cm.
- Mowing height is lowest for bermuda grass (0.5-1.5 cm).
- In golfs, turf areas are mowed to lowest height.
- In rotary mower, blades are parallel to surface of ground.
- Slicing, coring, spiking is done for soil aeration.
- Scrapping is done to avoid toughness.
- Raking: Allows the grass blade to breathe and absorb moisture for roots.
- Bricking: To replace unhealthy patches in lawn.
- 'Pop up' sprinklers: Irrigating lawns.
- 1st commercial hydroseeder was invented in USA in 1950 andused in UK in 1960.
- Depth of medium for lawn making: 12-15 cm.

- Seed rate: 12 kg/acre or 25-30 kg/ha or 2.5 g/m^2.
- Seed take about 3-5 weeks for germination from sowing.
- Problematic weed: Motha (*Cyperus rotundus*).
- Diseases: Fairy ring- caused by fungus *Marasmus ordeades, Psalliota campestris, Leipiota morgoni*.
- Other diseases: Brown patch, dollar spot, gray snow.
- Fairy ring: Drench copper fungicide like Copper oxychloride @ 0.3% or bordeux mixture (4:4:50 i.e. 4 Kg $CuSO_4$: 4 Kg lime: 50 litres of water).
- Dried patches in lawn: Termite infestation.
- In north India, grass is injured by frost.
- Best months for top dressing: August-September.
- Apply ammonium sulphate @ 1 kg/ 50 m^2 once in every month.
- Excess N dose of 62 kg/ha/ month reduce Bermuda grass establishment.
- Pale or yellow lawn: Due to N_2 deficiency.
- Pre-emergent herbicide: Pendamethalin, Siduron.
- Post-emergent herbicide: Glyphosate (new generation & widely used), 2, 4-D, MCPP, Dicamb.
- Herbicide for narrow leaf weed: Atrazine 1.0 kg (50% WP)/ ha.
- Management of *Cyprus rotundus*: Glyphosate.

Ground covers:

- Low growing plants used for mass planting or evergreen lawn for covering large area.
- Liriope and Ajuga are ground covers.
- Creeping dogwood vine or Bunchberry dogwood (*Cornus canadensis*): Fastest releasing pollen i.e. pollens are dispersed by stored elastic energy.
  a) Green coloured- *Wadelia trilobata, W. chinensis, Alternanthera ficodea, Cuphea gerlonica, Opheophogon japonicus*.
  b) Red coloured- *Iresine lindenii, Oxalis, Ipomea tricolor, Alternanthera versicolor, Tradescantia flamiensis, Zebrina pendula*.
  c) Golden coloured- *Duranta goldiana, Ipomea charyteuse, Alternanthera variegata*.

26. CACTI AND SUCCULENTS:

- Eulogized as 'Plants of 21st century'.
- Word 'Cactus' is derived from Greek word '*Kaaktos*' meaning 'a kind of prickly plant'.

- Origin: South America
- Dicot
- Regional Plant Resource Centre, Bhubaneshwar has collection of 850 cactus varieties.
- Cactus garden, a unique botanical garden, Kevadia, Gujarat spread over 836 m^2 (25 acre) comprises 450 species.
- Cactus flower petals arise from the top of the ovary.
- Fruit type: Single seeded berry.
- Pigments present in fruits: Betalin.
- Cactus pear is commonly known as ''prickly pear' while its edible fruit is called 'tuna'.
- Prefer neutral water for irrigation.
- Best suitable in sunny location.
- All cacti are succulents but all succulents are not cacti.
- Cacti can be distinguished from succulents by presence of areoles.
- Ideal season for grafting: Spring or Autumn i.e. September.
- Rootstock for cactus: *Acanthocereus tetragonus*.
- Hunt (2006) recognized Cactaceae family has 4 sub-families viz. Pereskioideae (the leaf cactus, 20 spp.), Opuntioideae (300 spp.), Cactoideae (1,000 spp.) and Maihuenioideae (2 spp.).
- Three tribes: Pereskieae, Opuntieae, Cereae.
- Tribe Cereae has 8 sub-tribes: Cereanae, Hylocereanae, Echinocereanae, Echiocactanae, Cactanae, Coryphanthanae, Epiphyelanae, Rhipsolidanae.
- The cacti of sub-tribe 'Echinocereanae' are commonly known as 'Hedgehogs'.
- Epiphytic cacti are known as 'Chain cactus'.
- Melon cactus or Turk's cap is belongs to sub-tribe 'Cactanae' e.g. *Opuntia* and *Discocactus*
- Rapid method of multiplication of rootstock: Cuttings.
- *Espostoaplumosa* 'Cristate' do not perform well on its own roots and have to be grafted.
- *Gymnocalycium mihanovichii* cv. 'Rubrum': Lacks chlorophyll.
- *Trichocereus tephracanthus, Myrtillocactus geometrizans, Cephalocereus palmeri, C. albispinus*: Used as rootstock.
- Leaf cactus/ Barbados gooseberry/ Lemon vine (*Pereskia grandiflora, P. aculeata*) is only genus which has leaves. Used as rootstock. Fruits of *Pereskia aculeata* are used to make sauces.
- Cacti that is almost spineless and most commonly used for fencing: Opuntia.
- Milk of *Euphorbia antiquorum* is taken as purgative.

- A succulent looks like pebbles around it *Lithops hookeri*.
- Succulent having woody stem: Aeonium.
- Day flowering cacti: *Astrophytum*, *Chamaecereus*, *Echinopsis*, *Lobivia*, *Parodia*, *Rebutia*.
- Night flowering cacti: Selenicereus, *Mammillaria*, *Epiphyllum oxypetalum*, *Cereus peruvianus*.
- Photoblastic seed germination: *Mammillaria* and *Pilosocereus gounellei*.
- Most of the succulents originate from Mexico.
- 'Pedilanthus' often used as a hedge border.
- Suitable for hedging, pots and rock garden: *Agave furcarea*.
- Echinopsis: Arise due to sectorial chimera.
- Iron starvation increases succulency in *Tradescantia navicularis*.
- Aloe is easier to cross compared to others.
- Aeonium: Succulent with woody stem.
- Zamia: Cycad.
- R.Q. value during night: Zero.

Name	Botanical name	Family	Purpose
Flowering stone	*Lithops bela*	Aizoaceae	-
Heartleaf ice plant	*Aptenia cordifolia*	Aizoaceae	Stem covered with glistering papillae
Century plant	*Agave americana*	Amaryllidaceae	-
Aloe	*Aloe vera*	Amaryllidaceae	-
Yucca/ Spanish day	*Yucca gloriosa*	Amaryllidaceae	-
Sea onion/ Climbing onion	*Bowea volubilis*	Amaryllidaceae	-
Ponytail palm/ Nolina	*Beaucarnea recurvata*	Amaryllidaceae	Suitable as specimen plant
Howarthia	*Howarthia fasciata*	Amaryllidaceae	Leaves rosette & densely arranged
Mother in Law's tongue	*Sanseveria trifasciata*	Amaryllidaceae	Rhizome propagated
Adenium	*Adenium obesum*	Apocynaceae	Fleshy & twisted stem
Opuntia	*Opuntia cylindrica*	Cactaceae	Planted for fencing purpose
Rat's tail	*Aporocactus flagilleformis*	Cactaceae	-
Chin/ Coloured/ Spider cactus	*Gymnocalycium mihanovichii*	Cactaceae	Globular shape
Bird's nest cactus	*Mammillaria camptotricha*	Cactaceae	Stem covered with silky hair
African milk barrel	*Euphorbia horrida*	Cactaceae	Presence of milky juice
Air plane plant	*Crassula falcata*	Crassulaceae	-
Jade plant	*Crassula argentea*	Crassulaceae	-
Bryophylum	*Kalanchoe calycium*	Crassulaceae	-
Sedum	*Sedum compactum*	Crassulaceae	Creeping habit

Bishop's hood cactus	*Astrophytum myriostigma*	Cactaceae	-
Thanks giving cactus	*Zygocactus*	Cactaceae	-
Golden barrel cactus	*Echinocactus grusonii*	Cactaceae	-
Rainbow cactus	*Echinocereus dasyacanthus*	Cactaceae	-
Curiosity plant/ Night flowering cactus	*Cereus peruvianus*, *C. hexagonus*	Cactaceae	-
Old man cactus	*Cephalocereus senilis*	Cactaceae	Commonly grown cactus
Silver torch cactus/ Cleisto cactus	*Cleistocactus strausii*	Cactaceae	Branching stem; used as rootstock
Barrel cactus	*Coryphantha cornifera*	Cactaceae	Spines looks attractive
Star cactus/ Sea urchin	*Astrophytum asterias*	Cactaceae	Globular shape
-	*Astrophytum capricorne*	Cactaceae	Very difficult to grow
Cob cactus	*Lobivia famatimensis*	Cactaceae	-
Chain plant/ Nargis eye	*Tradescantia navicularis*	Commelinaceae	-
House leek	*Sempervivum* spp.	Crassulaceae	-
Slipper plant. Bird cactus/ Pedilanthus	*Euphorbia tithymaloides*	Euphorbiaceae	Exudes milky latex; popular for foliage beauty
Euphorbia	*Euphorbia bojeri*	Euphorbiaceae	Presence of milky juice
Elephant bush	*Portulacaria afra*	Portuaceae	-
Living stone	*Lithops optica*	Mesembryan-themaceae	-

27. BONSAI/ MINIATURE PLANT/ PLANT SCULPTURE:

- Japanese art of growing miniature trees and shrubs by extreme dwarfing.
- Origin- China 1133 A.D.
- '*Bon*' means a tray or shallow container and '*sai*' means to grow i.e. tray planting.
- Term 'Bonsai' was popularized by Buddhist monks.
- 1st bonsai garden (1990): Kamla Nehru park, Mumbai.
- Daisugi: Means 'table cedar'. This ancient bonsai technique (or Japanese forestry technique) makes the tree looks like we are putting something on a table made from cedar tree. It is usually practiced in Kitayama, Kyoto that can prevent deforestation.
- Tall square type container is good for cascade style bonsai.
- Cascading: Popular art of Japanese for making dwarf bonsai where branches move in semi-circle fashion around main stem.
- Copper wire (10-22 gauge) is most suitable for making bonsai.
- In 1982, Doordarshan telecasted a film on bonsai.
- Most suitable shrub for bonsai making: Bougainvillea.
- Most suitable climber for bonsai making: *Petrea volubilis*.
- Plants suitable for bonsai: Bamboo, Guava, *Ficus* spp., Jacaranda, Citrus, Mango, Neem, Pomegranate, Ber, Semal, Devdar, *Pinus roxburghii*.

- Height of mame bonsai: 15-20 cm (2-6").
- Repotting of old bonsai done in 2-3 year.
- Styles of bonsai:
  a) Formal upright
  b) Informal upright
  c) Wind swept
  d) Slanting
  e) Cascade
  f) Multiple trunks
  g) Raft
  h) Broom
  i) Rock grown

28. FERNS

- Flowerless plant that has feathery or leafy fronds.
- Reproduced by spores.
- Valuable for decoration, indoors or outdoors in houses and gardens.
- Leather-leaf fern is most widely used foliage in round arrangement.
- Can be grown in acidic soil pH 5.0-5.5.
- Optimum potting mixture pH for growth of ferns: 4-6.
- Stag horn fern: *Platycerium*.
- Climbing fern: *Lycopodium*.
- Rumhora fern is most popular as cut green.
- *Pteridium* is poisonous fern containing HCN.
- Diversity in varieties/ species: 1) Brake fern (*Pteris*) 2) Maidenhair fern (*Adiantum*) 3) Button fern (*Tectaria*).

Common name	Botanical name	Family	Propagation	Origin
Asplenium	*Asplenium bulbiferum*	Aspleniaceae	Plantlets	New Zealand
Maidenhair fern	*Adiantum capillus-veneris*	Pteridaceae	Division or spores	N. America
Chinese ladder brake fern	*Pteris vittata*	Pteridaceae	Rhizomes	Asia, Tropical Africa
Squirrel's foot fern	*Davallia trichomanoides*	Davalliaceae	Rhizomes	S-E Asia
Nephrolepis	*Nephrolepis cordifolia*	Davalliaceae	Division	Australia
Microlepia	*Microlepia strigosa*	Dennstaedtiaceae	Spores	Central Asia
Holly fern	*Cyrtomium falcatum*	Dryopteridaceae	Division or spores	East Asia
Leather leaf fern	*Rumhora adiantiformis*	Dryopteridaceae	Division & spores	South Africa
Lemon button fern	*Nephrolepis furcans*	Dryopteridaceae	Division or spores	Thailand
Rabbit foot's fern	*Nephrolepis exaltata*	Nephrolepidaceae	Stolons & rhizomes	N. America
Staghorn fern	*Platycerium bifurcatum*	Polypodiaceae	Offsets	Java, New Guinea
Golden rod fern	*Phymatodes scolopendria*	Polypodiaceae	Rhizomes	Australia

29. BIO-AESTHETIC PLANNING:

- Term 'Bio-aesthetic planning' coined by Prof. Lancelot Hogben.
- It means the proper utilization of the available flora and fauna in the beautification the surroundings or country.
- Bio-aesthetic planning was included as a subject under Ministry of Agriculture and Cooperation.
- 1st evidence of bio-aesthetic planning comes from Mohan-Jo-Daro.
- King Sher Shah Suri (1540-1544 AD) constructed the famous grand trunk road from Kolkata to Lahore.
- Bio-aesthetically planned city: Chandigarh (north India); Bengaluru (south India).
- Idea of systematic planning of Chandigarh city was proposed by Dr. M.S.Randhawa.
- Flag bearer of bio-aesthetic planning in India: Dr. M.S.Randhawa.
- Architects of Chandigarh city: Le Corbusier and his associates, Piere Jeanneret, E. Maxwell Fry and Jane B. Drew.
- Parks: Considered as 'lungs of city'.
- Trees: Source of sink for carbon.
- Government offices: Considered as 'brain'.
- Connecting roads: Considered as 'nervous system'.

30. ESSENTIAL OIL EXTRACTION:

- Perfume city of world or World perfume capital: Grasse, France.
- Largest producer of perfumery products and rose perfume in world: Bulgeria.
- Largest producer of jasmine perfume: Egypt.
- Largest producer of tuberose and carnation perfume: France.
- World production of jasmine essential oil has been estimated to be 10-15 thousand kgs.
- Perfume capital of India or City of *Ittr*: Kannauj, Uttar Pradesh.
- India is 2nd largest producer and exporter of tuberose concrete to world market.
- Global trade: 11.19 billion dollars by 2022.
- India's share in world export of essential oil: 0.4%.
- India produces 25 T oil annually.
- 1st reference of rose perfume: *Charaka Samhita*.
- Rose water and rose perfume were known to Indian civilization before Vedic period.
- Plants suitable for oil extraction: Champaca, Gardenia, Honey-suckle, Hyacinth, Jasmine, Lavender, Plumeria, Magnolia, Marigold, Narcissus, Damask rose, Scented geranium, Sweet violet, etc.

- Archeological excavations in Harappan civilization say that rose-distillation were more than 5000 years old.
- Queen Noorjehan was 1st reported extracted rose oil and named it as *'Attare Jahangiri'*.
- 'Ave Cena' discovered the art of rose distillation in 9th century.
- Quality of essential oil is determined by gas chromatography.
- CIMAP released low cost and multi-utility portable distillation unit 'CIM-ASVIKA'.

Methods of essential oil extraction-

a) Enfleurage or cold fat extraction: e.g. Jasmine.
b) Maceration or hot fat extraction.
c) Steam distillation: e.g. Scented geranium, rose, rosemary, Rhyme, etc.
d) Solvent extraction (petroleum ether or food grade benzene): Most suitable method for extraction of floral perfume e.g. Tuberose.
e) Super-critical fluid extraction: Use of solid CO_2.
f) Primitive copper stills.
g) High performance liquid chromatography (HPLC): Use of helium or nitrogen gas.

- 350-400 kg rose petals yield 1 kg concrete.
- 3-5 tones rose petals are required to extract 1 litre rose oil.
- Damask rose should be harvested between 6-8 AM for maximum oil extraction.
- Rose- (i) *Rosa damascena*- 0.05%; (ii) *R. bourboniana*- 0.04% (iii) *R. centifolia*- 0.01%.
- Jasmine- (i) *J. auriculatum*- 0.29% (maximum oil recovery); (ii) *J. grandiflorum*- 0.25-0.30%; (iii) *J. sambac*- 0.04%.
- Carnation: 0.2-0.3%.
- Tuberose: 0.1%.
- *Michelia champaca*: 0.16-0.2%.
- Rose scented geranium (*Pelargonium graveolens*): 0.16%.
- Reunion or Bourbon type geranium yield more oil.
- Pot marigold, salvia.
- Constituent of essential oil: Rose (citronellol); jasmine (benzyl acetate); tuberose (geraniol); geranium (rhodinol), marigold (piperitone-in leaf; 1-8-cineole-in flower).
- Sesame seeds are used in extraction of jasmine oil.
- Concrete: Non-purified form of essential oil obtained by solvent extraction method containing 45-55% absolute.
- Absolute: Highly concentrated, entirely alcohol soluble and usually liquid perfume material.

- Extrait: Alcoholic solution of odorous part of pomade & intermediate product in preparation of absolute.
- Fixative: Reduces rate of evaporation.
- Sweet pea is commercially grown for oil extraction.
- Storage: In closed containers and kept in dark to avoid oxidation and polymerization.
- Traces of water in essential oil can be removed by using unhydrous sodium sulphate.

I. Jasmine concrete (production of essential oil):

- Oil extraction is done mechanically.
- Process of oil extraction: Flowers are submerged in hexane (which dissolves essential oil, waxes & pigments); liquid mixture is evaporated at low temperature; remaining substance is dried in vacuum; resultant material is dried yellow-brown, waxy & full of jasmine colour; yield varies from 25-30 kg/ha.

II. **Production of absolute:**

- Jasmine concrete is purified by using special grade alcohol.
- Final product is semi-viscous, brown coloured liquid rich in jasmine essential oil known as absolute.
- Its recovery is 49% of the concrete.
- It is used to blend all high grade perfumes through out the world.

31. ACANTHACEAE

31.1 Crossandra

- Eulogized as 'Fire cracker flower'.
- Tranditional flower crop of India.
- Most commonly used in *veni* preparation along with jasmine.
- Flowers: Bisexual, fan shaped with 3-5 asymmetrical petals, non-fragrant, light weight, bright orange and/or yellow coloured.
- Type of inflorescence: Hairy spike.
- Spike takes 15-25 days for complete flowering.
- Flowering season: June-January.
- Flower open in acropetal manner.
- Fruit type: Capsule.
- Pollinating agents: Butterfly, dragonfly.
- Best temperature for seed germination: 25-28^{0}C.
- Number of flowers/ kg: 15,000.
- Alar @ 1000 ppm at 30, 45, 60 days after planting improves growth and yield of triploid crossandra.

Species:

Species	Features
Crossandra infundibuliformis (syn. *C. undulaefolia*)	Most grown commercially. It is highly susceptible to wilt and root knot nematode
C. flava	Unbranched and short stemmed shrub for plains
C. mucronata	Threatened; flowers pale apricot-orange coloured
Neelambari green shrimp (*Ecobolium ligustranium*)	Sister of crossandra having green flowers
C. guineensis	Free flowering; suitable for sunny situation & partial shade; flowers pale lilac coloured
C. subacaulis	Stemless; crowded leaves at base; orange coloured flowered
C. nilotica	Very free flowering; suited for partial shade; red-orange coloured flowers
C. mahatma	Cultivated for saffron coloured flowers

Varieties:

- A mutant named 'Savindi' is released as a novel ornamental variety for international flower trade.
- Selections: Fortuna, Diane, Ghana Red, Orange Marmalade, Tropic Flame, Florida Sunset, Old Orange, Shamrock, Sundance.
- Clonal selections: Mona Wallhead Compti, Mona Wallhead Nile, Mona Wallhead Ane.

Varieties	Breeding method	Features
IIHR, Bengaluru		
Arka Ambara (2009)	Hybridization and selection of 'Local x Lakshmi'	Big orange-red coloured flowers with pleasant odour; yield 6 t/acre/year;
Arka Kanaka (2009)	Hybridization and selection of 'Local Yellow x Delhi Crossandra'	Big orange-red coloured flowers with pleasant odour; yield 5 t/acre/year; tolerant to wilt
Arka Shreeya (2011)	Hybridization and selection of 'Local x Arka Ambara'	Big orange-red coloured flowers; yield 5-6 t/acre/year; do not set seeds; multiplied by terminal cuttings; tolerant to wilt
Arka Shravya (2011)	Hybridization and selection of '*C. nilotica* x Mangalore Local'	Big orange-red coloured flowers; yield 5-6 t/acre/year; do not set seeds; multiplied by terminal cuttings; suitable for landscape & cut flower purpose
Arka Chenna (2019)	Mutant	Flowers 20% bigger than local; orange petals; yield (40 kg/ week/ 1000 plants); shelf life 3.4 days; stalk strength 0.82 kg/cm^2
TNAU, Coimbatore		
Kanakadhara	Mutation using sodium azide to cutting	-

Raj Kankambaram	Mutation using sodium azide to cutting	-
Subasu	Mutation using sodium azide to cutting	-
Lakshmi	Mutation using sodium azide to cutting	-
Maruvur Arasi	Mutation using sodium azide to cutting	-
Dr. A.P.J. Abdul Kalam	Mutation using sodium azide to cutting	-
Neelambari	Mutation using sodium azide to cutting	-
Vijaya Kanakambaram	Polyploid using colchicine to seeds	-
Orange	Polyploidy breeding	Tetraploid (2n=4x=40); orange flowers
Lutea Yellow	Polyploidy breeding	Tetraploid (2n=4x=40); orange yellow flowers
Sebaculis Red	Polyploidy breeding	Tetraploid (2n=4x=40); tolerant to nematode
Delhi (syn. Soundarya)	Polyploidy breeding	Triploid (2n=3x=30); propagated by terminal stem cuttings

Diseases and deficiencies:

- Wilt: Caused by root lesion nematode (*Pratylenchus montrozerii*).
- Chlorosis: Due to iron deficiency: Common problem.
- Purple leaves: Unavailability of 'P'.

32. AGAVACEAE

32.1 Tuberose

- Greek name '*Plios*' mean white or bright and '*anthos*' meaning 'a flower'.
- In tropical and sub-tropical region, it is grown round the year.
- Flowers are used for garland, floral ornament, buttonholes, bouquets and cut flowers for table decoration.
- Night blooming plant.
- Introduced in India by Europeans.
- Single type flowers are highly fragrant than double types.
- Chromosome No. 2n=2x=60 (Single type) and 2n=2x=50 (Double type).
- Petals of single and double cultivars are white and devoid of any colour pigments.
- Variation in petal colour from pink to whitish yellow in tuberose hybrid is due to ratio of anthocyanins and carotenoids.
- Higher temperature (30^0C) and natural light intensity affect petal pigmentation in hybrids.

- Variegated types have golden yellow streaks along leaf margin with longer spike and bear profuse seeds compared to erratic/ no seed set in single/ semi-double/ double types.
- LD_{50} for gamma rays: 2.5 to 3.5 Kr.
- LD_{50} for fast neutrons: 538 rads (single), 375 rads (double).
- Inflorescence: Spike/ terminal raceme of fragrant-waxy florets in one or more rows of corolla segments that bloom in acropetal manner.
- Highly cross pollinated, dichogamy and gametophytic SI is prevalent.
- Bisexual flowers have cylindrical and tubular perianth that bends near base and flare in funnel form.
- Propagation method: Bulbs and bulblets.
- Scape: Presence of single flower at top.
- Flowers borne in pairs in axil of bracts.
- In single type, 6 stamens and all are fertile while in double type, stamen variable in number and mostly sterile.
- Fruit type: Capsule containing tiny black, light and flat seeds.
- Single type takes 55-65 days for appearance of spike from planting.
- Spike appears 26-29 days for opening of florets.
- Spike last on plant for 15-18 days in single and 18-22 days in double type.
- Stigma receptivity: 3-5 days after anthesis.
- Single types are fertile while double types are sterile due to absence of female reproductive organ/ rudimentary pistil.
- On selfing, neither double nor single type produce any seed due to incompatibility.
- Number of spikes varies from 1-3 with 20-35 florets/ spike.
- Size of pollen grains: 45.4 to 75.6 µm.
- Pollen fertility: 86.8% (single), 21.6% (double).
- Seed sterility is due to absence of female reproductive organ.
- Seeds from single exhibit better germination than doubles.
- Days required from seed sowing to flowering: 270.
- Alkaloid present in bulbs: Lycorine.
- Ideal bulb size for planting: 25-30 g (bulb diameter e" 2 cm).
- Bulb dormancy is broken by 4% thiourea for 1 hr.
- About 1150 Kg flowers yield 1 kg of oil (concrete).
- Essential oil extraction method: Solvent extraction.
- Planting distance: 30 cm x 30 cm.
- Ideal planting time in north Indian plains: March.

- October-December is a lean period for tuberose flower yield.
- Oil is extensively used in perfumery.
- Days for flower initiation after planting: 80-100.
- Bulb soaking in GA_3 (10-500 ppm) increased spike length, floret number/spike and bulb production.
- It shows pronounced heterobeltiosis for loose flower yield, recovery of concrete and spike yield.

Species:

- *Polianthes tuberosa*: Cultivated.
- *P. howardii*: Dwarf and coloured tuberose. Display both carotenoid and anthocyanin pigments in petals.
- *P. geminiflora*: Light orange-red coloured flowers.
- *P. graminiflora*: Deep red coloured flowers.
- *P. gracilis*: Mexican species close relative of tuberose.
- *P. tuberosa* is cross compatible with *P. virginica*, *P. muculoda*, *P. geminiflora*, *P. graminiflora*, *P. howardii* and *P. bulliana*.
- *Manfreda* x *Polianthes* are cross compatible. Produce greenish flowers.
- Crossing between single x double types yield more singles (85%) hybrids than doubles (15%).

Varieties:

- Mexican Single, Mexican Double, Hyderabad Single, Hyderabad Double, Calcutta Single, Calcutta Double, Sikkim Selection, Pearl Double.
- Sunset (*P. blisii* x *P. bundrantii*): Orange red coloured single flowers.
- *P. blisii*: F_1 hybrid between (*P. geminiflora* x *P. tuberosa*): Long spike, single type, pink flowers.
- *P. bundrantii* (*P. tuberosa* x *P. howardii*): Long spike, small single type colourful (pink, reddish purple, orange & yellow) flowers.

Name	Breeding method	Features
IIHR, Bengaluru		
Arka Sugandhi (2014)	Clonal selection from seedling lines 'IIHR-5 x IIHR-6'	120 florets/ m^2; tolerant to nematodes
Shringar (2006)	Hybridization & selection of (Mexican Single x Pearl Double)	Single type flowers, off season variety; seed fertile; ideal for garland making & cut flowers; resistant to root knot nematodes
Suvasini (2006)	Hybridization &	Double (multi-whorled) flowers & suited as cut flower;

	selection of (Mexican Single x Pearl Double)	seed sterile; improved essential oil content & recovery
Arka Prajwal (2000)	Hybridization & selection of (Shringar x Mexican Single)	Single type flowers & ideal for garland and spikes suited for cut flowers; yield 20-22 t/ ha/ year
Arka Vaibhav (2001)	Hybridization & selection of (Mexican Single x IIHR-2)	Double type flowers; yield 2.5-3 lakh spikes/ha/year
Arka Nirantara (2010)	Hybridization & selection of (Shringar x IIHR-6)	Single type flowers & used for landscaping; yield 20-25 t/ha
Directorate of Floricultural Research, Pune		
Sahyadri Vaman (2020)	-	Dwarf & suitable for pot purpose
MPKV, Rahuri		
Phule Rajani (GK-T-D-2) 2005)	Hybridization & selection of (Local Single x Shringar)	Single type flowers
Phule Rajat (2019)	Hybridization & selection of (Vaibhav x Phule Rajani)	Double type; 60 florets/spike; 10 days vase life
NBRI, Lucknow		
Rajat Rekha (1974)	Gamma ray mutant (1.5 Kr) of 'Mexican Single'	Single type flowers
Swarna Rekha (1974)	Gamma ray mutant of 'Pearl Double'	Double type flowers
BCKV, Kalyani		
Bidhan Snigdha	-	Single type flowers; 40 florets/spike
Bidhan Ujwal	-	Single type flowers; 63 florets/ spike
Bidhan Jyoti	-	Single type flowers; 33 florets/spike

Pest and disease:

- Serious problem in foliage i.e. Greasy streak: Foliar nematode (*Aphelenchoides besseyi*).
- Stem rot (*Sclerotium rolfsii*). Soil drenching with brassicol 2 g/lit.
- Red spider mite:

33. ALSTROEMERIACEAE

33.1 Alstroemeria

- Eulogized as 'Inca lily or Peruvian lily'.
- Protandrous in nature.
- Optimum day temperature required: 15^{0}C.

- Photoperiod required for flower induction: 11-14 h.
- Propagation method: Rhizome and by tissue culture.
- 10-15 plants from 1 year old plant or 20-25 plantlets from 2 year old plant can be prepared.
- Hot spot for commercial cultivation: Uttarakhand.
- Planting months: October-November.
- Harvesting time: Colour appears on 1st floret.
- Yield: 200-300 shoots/ m^2/ year.
- **Varieties**: Alladdin, Serena, Riana, Amor, Capri, Cindrella, Rosita, Pluto, etc.

Grading system:

- According to length, maturity and weight of flowering stem.
- As per Association of Floral Importers of Florida (AFIF) and Colombian Association of Flower Exporters (Asocolflores).

Grade	Length (cm)	Flowers/stem	Stems/bunch
Super Select (Extra)	75	≥ 4	10
Select	65	≥ 3	10
Fancy	60	≥ 3	10

34. AMARANTHACEAE

34.1 Gomphrena

- Eulogized as 'Globe amaranth or Bachelor's button'.
- Used as dry flower, loose flower, making garlands, crafts and pot pourries.
- It has C_3 and C_4 pathway of photosynthesis.
- Hardy plant tolerant to alkaline soils.
- Flower heads may be terminal/axillary and borne on long thin stem above foliage and long lasting.
- Round, button like/ spherical flower head is cylindrical spike (1-2 cm long & 1 cm diameter).
- Propagation method: Seed.
- Dehusking significantly influence seed germination.
- Pinching at 15 days after transplanting produces large number of bigger sized flowers.
- F_1 hybrid 'Pinball': Developed by Sakata Seed Company is vegetatively propagated.
- Cv. Buddy has intense purple flower heads.
- Cv. Firework is tolerant to heat and drought.
- Used as indicator plant for potato potex virus.
- Symptomless carrier of Bottle Gourd Mosaic virus.

35. AMARYLLIDACEAE

35.1 Amaryllis (syn. Hippeastrum)

- Eulogized as 'Belladonna lily or Trumpet lily or Night star lily or Royal Dutch lily'.
- Amaryllis means 'sparkle'.
- Bulbous ornamental grown around the world for cut flower, potted plant, window garden and floral arrangements.
- Monotypic genus grown in tropical to sub-tropical and warm temperate regions of the world.
- Hippeastrum and amaryllis are synonyms for 'trumpet lily or Night star lily' in Indian gardens.
- Hippeastrum is different from amaryllis: Solid scape and absence of scales between the filaments.
- International Registration Authority located at Royal General Bulb Growers Association, the Netherlands.
- *A. belladonna* (syn. *Callicore rosea*, *H. equstre*): Deciduous, self sterile diploid.
- *H. aulicum*: Origin- South America, *H. blumeracia* (2n=7x=77).
- *H. procera*: frim Brazil has lavender blue or violet blue coloured flowers.
- *H. hybridum*: Known as 'Royal Dutch amaryllis or Dutch amaryllis hybrids'.
- Most significant developments: Development of Reginae and Leopoldii groups of hybrids.
- Bulb produces 30-60 cm tall, 1-2 leafless stems, and bear 2-12 funnel shaped flowers at top.
- Throughout growth period, flower initiation alternates with leaf formation.
- Inflorescence: Terminal cluster (umbel) and bear 2-4 trumpet shaped fragrant flowers.
- Flowers 6-10 cm in dia., with 6 sepals (3 inner petals + 3 outer sepals) with round/ triangular stigma.
- Flowers are protandrous and remain open for 4-6 days.
- At anthesis, style is shorter and as flower matures, style elongates and style and stigma points upwards.
- Anther dehiscence: 8-10 AM and split longitudinally.
- Stigma receptivity: 12-14 h after anther dehiscence.
- Ovary: Tricarpellery.
- Fruit: 3 chambered capsule, globose shaped and contain black/ dark brown, flat and winged seeds.
- Flowering season: March to mid-June (sub-tropical) and late summer (temperate) areas.
- Pollination agents: Moths, honey bees, bumble bees, humming birds and bats.
- Low or lack of seed set: Due to endosperm failure caused by mitotic aberrations.

- Self incompatibility in diploid amaryllis disappears in both tetraploid species and tetraploid hybrids.
- Breeding methods: Line hybrid (superior inbred lines are crossed to exploit heterosis) and group hybrid method (crosses are made among specific hybrids and promising ones are selected for garden use).
- Breeding for double flower (stamen conversion to petal like structure contributes doubleness of floret) was 1st reported by McCann (1937).
- Notching is done in Dutch amaryllis.
- Seeds storage: Orthodox behaviour.
- Propagation method: Bulbs and bulblets.
- Standard method of propagation: Cultivars that produce few or no offsets are multiplied through twin-scaling.
- In twin-scales, thickness and length of outer scale affect the rate of propagation.
- Large bulb produces 2 or more bulblets per season.
- Bulb size for commercial production: 5-10 cm in dia. or 20-22 to >32 cm in circumference.
- There is no absolute dormancy in amaryllis bulbs.
- Under tropical conditions, bulbs do not have dormancy but in sub-tropical and temperate conditions, natural dormancy causes only one flowering period.
- Planting density for cut flower forcing: 50 bulbs/ m^2.
- Light intensity for cut flower forcing: 1000-1500 foot candles.
- Optimum temperature for forcing: 24-27^{0}C.
- CO_2 concentration in greenhouse for forcing: 500-600 ppm.
- Potted hippeastrum are marketed when flower stalk length is 30 cm tall and leaves are 15-30 cm long.
- Fragrance: Due to presence of volatile oil and associated with white coloured spp. (*H. tucumann, H. viridiflora, H. brasiliana, H. fragrantissima*). Absent in Dutch hybrids.
- Fresh pollen grains can be stored in house hold refrigerator for a month at 4-10^{0}C.
- Seed shattering: Major problem in seed production.
- Seed stratification influences germination rate and seed takes 28 days for germination.
- Temperature influences germination rate and constant temperature of 25^{0}C results in higher germination (86%) and germination completed within 4-8 days.
- Within 2 years, bulblets grow into large sized bulb and produce flower.
- Seedlings take 3 years to flower.
- Flower stalk is harvested when buds are fully elongated.
- Seeds stored at 52% R.H. at 15^{0}C remain viable for 12 months.
- Post harvest life of potted amaryllis: 14-21 days.

- Embryo rescue adopted in *H. evansiae*.
- Mosaic virus and red scorch (*Stagonoscora curtisii*): Most destructive in production.

Varieties:

- Today's commercial cultivars of amaryllis are tetraploids.
- 1st reported double amaryllis, a form of *H. puniceum* found wild in Cuba.
- Double flowers: Double Picotte, Lady Jane, Pasadena, Double Record.
- Tetraploid cvs.: Apple Blossom, Lucky Strike, Red Strike, Dasuto.
- *A. belladonna* cvs.: Star of India, White Queen, Pink Indira, Prime Minister, Royal Ruby, Red Majesty, Snow Queen, Silver Lining.
- For pot culture and cut flower: Bhagiraj, Canary Bird, Candidum, Carmine King, Christmas Gift, Double Belle, Honey Moon, Lyric Pink Pearl, Peppermint, Sophia.

Varieties	Breeding method	Features
Maxima, American Express, Bold Leader, Carnival, Cocktail	Introduction	Introduced *Amaryllis* hybrids from USA
Apple Blossom, Fire Dance, Ludwig's Scarlet, Picotee, Pink Favorite	Introduction	Introduced *Hippeastrum* hybrids from USA
IARI, New Delhi		
Surya Kiran	*A. stylossum* Red x *A. stylossum* White	Long flower stem; bears 3-4 bicoloured flowers
NBRI, Lucknow		
Honey Moon, Snow White, Fairy Queen, Five Star, Fire Fly, Cardinal, Candidum, Vermilion Record	Introduction	-
Begum Secunder	Seedling selections	Flowers very soft pink.
Dhruva		Flowers large, flat face, red with no marking, throat greenish yellow with prominent white star.
Shah Najaf		Scarlet flowers, feathered white, greenish white star.
Prof. K.N. Kaul		Flowers pink with faint strips of deeper pink at the edge of petals.
Prakash		Flat face, red coloured markings present on white ground of petals, throat yellowish green; does not produce seeds, but can be used as male parent.
Miss. Deepa Kaul		Inner three petals flushed deep pink, outer pale red, green yellow base.
Mrs. Shiela Kaul		White flowers, green base, greenish white star to end of petal, feathered & lined bright scarlet.
Mrs. Percy Lancaster		Flowers white, deeply feathered scarlet, outer margin scarlet, star greenish white.
Agni	Charm x Pink Pearl	Flowers large, red, throat yellowish green, hybrid does not produce seeds, but can be used as male parent.

Apurb (1991)	Minerva (4x) x Lady Lancaster (4x)	Crimson, greenish white throat at base, eye present in throat, freely seed setting variety.
Chitwan (1991)	Saturn (2x) x Deepali	Diploid bicoloured, female sterile, but crosses as pollen parent freely.
Garima (1992)	Bleeding Heart (4x) x Apollo (4x)	Semi-double flowers with scarlet colour.
Kiran (2008)	Ganymede (4x) x Romeo (2x) (*A. vittata*)	Triploid; evergreen hybrid produces 2 to 3 tall (40-50 cm) scapes in a season; flowers large (18-20 cm across), white with 6-8 scarlet veins running parallel to mid-rib of perianth.
Kiran Rekha	Flame (4x) x Chest (4x)	Flowers current red coloured.
McKean Hybrid Double (2009)	-	Hippeastrum hybrid; multipetalled flower
Niharika (1995)	Minerva (4x) x Candy Cane (4x)	Flowers white with crimson red streaks.
Poonam (1987)	Snow White (2x) x Aphrodets (2x)	White with golden yellow throat at base, hybrid is sexually sterile & does not produce seeds either by self or cross pollination.
Raktamanjari (1990)	Sneezy x Saturn	Red with greenish white throat at base.
Samrat (1987)	Bridegroom (4x) (*A. belladonna*) x Coquette (4x)	Tetraploid; 2-3 tall scapes bear 4 flowers, 16-18 cm across, flat wide, open & reflexed, Dutch vermilion in colour with greenish white throat, 6-8 white parallel veins radiating lengthwise over perianth.
Smriti (1995)	Charm (4x) x Orthelloo (4x)	Bicoloured combination of brilliant current red & white.
Jwala (1992)	Crice (4x) x Minerva (4x)	Dutch vermillion flowers with greenish yellow white throat.
Jyoti (1987)	Snow White (2x) x Fire Fly (2x) (*A. belladonna*)	Semi-double flowers with more than two whorls of perianth lobes, flowers bell shaped, 10 cm across with deep crimson veins radiating towards apex.
Tarang	Spontaenous mutant	Bicoloured red streaks over white appear side by side in the flower
BCKV, Kalyani		
Anjali	Bouquet x White Favorite	Unique pattern of pigment blending in perianth, stamen, and carpel

Inheritance of characters:

Character	Inheritance pattern
High floret number	Dominant & polygenic
Flower doubleness	Dominant
Foliage-white mid-rib leaf stripe	Monogenic dominant to plain green.
Flowering season	Polygenic.
Flower colour	Anthocyanin (red) dominant over carotenoid (yellow); cyanidin (pink to rose) dominant over pelargonidin (salmon to scarlet).
Fragrance	Recessive trait & linked with white or pastel coloured flower
Disease resistance	Species with grayish waxy (glaucous) foliage resistant to red scorch infection.

35.2 Daffodil

- Narcissus flower releases mucilaginous substances in vase water.
- Coronas of narcissi are richest source of carotene.
- Galanthaime alkaloid from narcissi flower is responsible for treating dementias and Alzheimer's disease.
- 600 kg narcissus flowers are required to extract one kg of essential oil.
- In narcissus, fertilizers are not applied while bulb forcing and also at the time of rooting as sprouting is significantly delayed.
- Flower initiation normally starts 2.5 months before optimum lifting time.
- Narcissus flowers have 'tulip type' dormancy.

Disease and pest:

- Basal rot (*Fusarium oxysporum f.sp. narcissi*): Most serious disease.
- Stem and bulb nematode: Most serious.

35.3 Day lily

- Toxic alkaloid: Hamercallin.
- Yellow day lily: *Hemerocallis fulva*.
- Golden or orange lily: *H. aurantica*.
- 1st colchicine induced tetraploid synthetic species: *H. washingtonia*.
- Propagation method: Division of clumps.
- Breeding work was started by A.B. Stout in the New York Botanical Garden, USA and 1st selection 'Mikado' was produced in 1929.

36. APOCYNACEAE

36.1 Periwinkle (syn. Vinca)

- Eulogized as '*Saba bahar* or *sadaphuli*'.
- One of the top 10th best selling plant in USA.
- Seed propagated evergreen bedding plant used for landscape.
- Model plant species for study of plant's secondary metabolites.
- Trap crop for root knot nematode.
- Monocot, pink flowered variety is more tolerant to salinity.
- Plant parts rich in pharmaceutical compounds.
- Indole: Terpenoid alkaloid in leaves and roots possess anti-cancer properties.
- Ajmalicine (Raubasin) and Serpentine- Anti-fibrillic, hypertensive.
- Leaves contain VLB alkaloids i.e. Vincristine, Vinblastine (0.60-0.65%) with anti-neoplastic properties used in curing blood cancer.

- Roots: Rich in ajmalicine, raubacine and reserpine (0.75-1.20%) used in controlling high blood pressure.
- Vincristine sulphate is marketed under trade name 'ONCOVIN' which is used against acute leukemia and Vinblastine sulphate as 'VELBE' to cure Hodgkin's disease.
- Flowers borne in leaf axil, pedicillate, pentamerous, hypogynous, hermaphrodite and white/ rosy purple/ pink coloured.
- Inflorescence: Dichasial cyme.
- Calyx: 5 sepals and velvet.
- Corolla: 5 petals, gamopetalous and twisted.
- Androecium: 5 stamens, epipetalous, inserted atthe mouth of corolla tube.
- Type of placentation: Marginal.
- Seed colour: Brown.
- Pollination agent: Butter fly.
- Propagation method: Seed, terminal stem cuttings.
- Fruit type: Follicle containing many black coloured seeds.
- Seed size: 2.3 mm length x 1.2 mm breadth.
- Anther dehiscence: Simultaneously with anthesis in non-self pollinating strains.
- Intra-flower self pollination in self pollinating strains is due to continuous growth of gynoecium.
- Seed rate: 2-3 kg/ha (direct sowing), 500 g/ha (transplanting).
- Number of seeds/ fruit: 18-24 (intra-flower self pollination); 22-25 (cross pollination).
- Pollen fertility: 71-92%.
- Fruit set in absence of pollinators: 75-85%.
- Shoot is follicle contains many small sized black coloured seeds.
- Harvesting method: Foliage is picked twice at 120-150 days after planting. 3rd leaf picking at uprooting of plants for roots after 200 days after planting.
- Root growth between 150-200 days is high with maximum alkaloid.
- Leaf yield: 14 q/ha (with 4 q/ha of roots and basal stems).
- Crop is dried in shade and foliage, stem and roots lose 80, 70 and 60% moisture during drying, respectively.
- Roots are cut into 15-20 cm pieces before drying.
- Cryptic self incompatibility is observed since self and cross pollinations are equally successful.
- Morphological male sterility i.e. no anther dehiscence due to dominant and recessive genes.
- Major problem in seed production: Natural seed shedding due to fruit shattering.
- Seed viability: Long period under ambient conditions.

- Seed stored in dessicator over calcium chloride for 4 years show 90% germination.
- Flavonol compounds: Useful taxonomic marker.
- Purple hypocotyls and pubescent leaves (30 days old): Morphological markers for easy identification of hybrids in nursery.
- Indehiscent anther: 1st report on linkage in periwinkle by Sreevalli *et al.* (2003).
- Heterosis breeding: Reported only for leaf and root yield in '*C. trichophyllus* x *C. roseus*' but not for alkaloid content.
- Gupta *et al.* (2007) constructed 1st genetic linkage map covering a distance of 1131.9 cM.
- Genome size: 1500 Mbp by Guimaries *et al.* (2012).
- Somatic embryo: Derived from immature zygotic embryo in cv. Madagaskar.
- Hairy root culture: For metabolic engineering of alkaloids in plant.

Species:

- Natural hybrids exist between *C. longifolius* x *C. roseus* and artificial hybrids synthesized between *C. ovalis* x *C. longifolius*.

Species	Characters
C. roseus (Madagascar periwinkle)	Dwarf, much branched; flowers rose or white, solitary; cross compatible
C. longifolius	Found in southern-central Madagascar; contain vindolicine alkaloid.
C. pusillus	Erect; annual herb; commonly occur as weed and restricted to India & Sri Lanka & endemic to Madagascar.
C. coriaceus	Rare species of central Madagascar.
C. lanceus	Endemic to Madagascar.
C. ovalis	Distributed in Madagascar.
C. scitulus	Distributed in Madagascar.
C. trichophyllus	Erect; single stems with high branching; flower colour purple yellow eyed corolla; cross compatible

Varieties:

- No recognized varieties, but 3 types based on flower colour viz. *albus* (white flower); *roseus* (pink rose coloured flower); *ocillatus* (white flower having rose purple spot in the centre).
- Creeping type is good for hanging basket, odd shaped decorative containers and ground covers e.g. Magic Carpet series.
- F_1 hybrids: Patricia White, Peppermint Cooler, Pacifica Apricot, Pacifica Lilac, Blue Pearl, First Kiss series, Garden Leader Splash series, Heat Wave series, Tropicana series, Little Pinki and Titan Burgundy.
- Indehiscent anther mutant: EMS-1-10 is isolated from 'Nirmal'.
- NEU-1-7: Wavy leaf margin mutant with dehiscent anther.
- Non-self pollinating but fertile strains 'Wy and Dw' from cv. Nirmal have been developed by mutation. Contain high alkaloid.

- Suitable for greenhouse production: Pacifica Punch, Pacifica Orchid.
- Resistant to phytophthora aerial blight: Cora series, Nirvana series, Little Pinkie, Little Bright Eye.

Name	Breeding method	Features
CIMAP, Lucknow		
Nirmal (CIMAP-0865)	Selection	White flowers; resistant to wilt & die back
Dhawal	Induced mutant of 'Nirmal' by seed treatment of EMS @ 0.6-0.8% & followed by selection	White flowers; higher leaf yield (2557 kg/ha); leaf alkaloid (0.89-1.40%); root alkaloid (1.60-2.22%); resistant to die back
EC 12083	Introduction	Resistant to wilt & die back
IC 49581	Selection	-
Prabhat	Selection	-

Inheritance of characters:

Character	Number of genes	Inheritance pattern
Wavy leaf margin, pubescent leaves, green hypocotyls, white flowers	Monogenic recessive	-
Purple hypocotyl (stem), normal leaves	Monogenic dominant	-
Intra-flower self pollination	Duplicate recessive	Independently inherited
Indehiscent anther	Monogenic recessive	Linked to gene controlling wavy leaf margin
Functional male sterility (no anther dehiscence)		Recessive & dominant gene
Single flower	Monogenic dominant	Single dominant to doubleness
Flower colour	Digenic and epistatic	-

Genes controlling flower colour:

Genotype	Phenotype
R-W-	Pink corolla and red eye
R-ww	White corolla and red eye
rrww	White
A-R-W-B-	Violet corolla and purple violet eye
A-R-W-bb	Pink corolla and purple violet eye
A-R-ww-B-	White corolla and purple eye
A-R-wwbb	White corolla and reddish purple eye
A-rr—, *aaR—*, and *aarr-*	White corolla
R-W-I-, *R-W-ii-*	Pink corolla and red eye
R-wwI-	Pale pink corolla and red eye
R-wwii	White corolla and red eye
rrW-I-, *rrwwI-*, *rrW-ii*, and *rrwwii*	White corolla
E	Presence o absence of red eye
O	Orange red corolla
ia	Indehiscent anthers
wy	wavy leaf margin

Disease:

- Root rot (*Phytophthora parasitica*): Serious disease. Cora series, Nirvana series, Little Bright Eye, Little Linda and Little Pinkie are resistant.

36.2 Adenium

- Eulogized as 'Desert rose'and considered as 'lucky plant'.
- Other colours in adenium can be achieved by grafting only.
- Once in 2 years, adenium plant is cut back to 2-3 inches.
- Caudex has abundant nutrients.
- Trunk imposes bonsai look.
- Base colour of flower: Pink.

Species:

Botanical name	Features
Adenium obesum	One of parent in many hybrids; summer blooming widely cultivated
A. multiflorum	Slender trunk; bloom in winter without leaf; deciduous; flowers in May-August
A. swazicum	Most popular & parent of many hybrids
A. somalense	Extremely intolerant of cole
A. crispum	Thin stems, quilled petals, sensitive to cold
A. boehmianum	Slow growing & largest leaves in genus
A. oleifolium	Smaller species with underground caudex
A. socotranum	Rare species; giant species of group
A. arabicum	Spherical basal caudex

Varieties: Gujarat Adenium-1, Gujarat Adenium-2.

37. ARACEAE

37.1 Anthurium

- Eulogized as 'Aristocrat of the plant world'.
- Cultivated in countries between 60^0N latitude and 40^0S latitude.
- Cultivated globally for its attractive foliage and flower.
- Ranks 2nd among tropical cut flowers.
- World's largest grower: The Netherlands.
- Mizoram state: Largest producer and exporter in North-East Himalayan region.
- Anthurium festival is held every year in Mizoram state since 2006 to promote tourism and cultivation of this crop.
- International Registration Authority of Ornamental Aroids: Florida, USA.
- Largest and most complex genus in monocotyledonary family.
- Anthra is a world wide knowledge centre for cultivation of anthurium based in Holland & Germany.

- Anthurium derived Greek legendary *Anthos* meaning 'flower' and 'aura' mean 'tail' referring to spadix.
- Major characteristic used to separate different sections: Berry shape.
- Floral fragrance compounds (sabinene, α-pinene, b-pinene, limonene, 1-8-cineole, phenethyl alcohol): Useful as taxonomic markers to clarify phylogenetic relationships.
- Flower is combination of spathe (colourful modified leaf/ bract that encloses flower cluster) and spadix or candle or inflorescence (i.e. cylindrical protrusion arising from base of spathe).
- Major factors in flower trade: Flower colour & spathe shape.
- The standard, upright and heart shaped spathe are mostly preferred in market.
- Double flowering types produce 1 small and 1 large spathe on same stem with single spadix.
- Spathe and spadix are borne on leafless stem/ peduncle.
- Spathe growth: Double sigmoid growth curve.
- Flowers develop acropetally and one flower emerges from each leaf axil.
- 1st imported anthuriums were pastel coloured.
- Most preferred spathe colour: Red followed by pink.
- Pigments in spathe colour: Yellow (carotenoids); green (chlorophyll); white (colourless flavones); red, pink, coral (pelargonidin & anthocyanin), brown (co-pigments of orange & green), white (colourless flavone), liliac (magenta + pink).
- Flower colour: Orange (preferred in Italian market); Red, scarlet and pastel (preferred in European market).
- Less preferred colours: Green, white blush, novelty.
- Dwarf species currently referred as 'andreacola' types.
- Spadix contains approximately 50 to 200 minute flowers arranged in a series of spirals along central axis.
- Prsence of dichogamy: Protogynous.
- Optimum soil pH: 5.2-6.2.
- Irrigation water with E.C. > 0.5 dS/cm should not be used.
- Grows naturally in 75% shade and 80-90% R.H. is ideal for healthy growth.
- Light intensity: 15000-25000 lux (1627 Klux).
- Temperature for initiation of flowering: 20^0C ($18\text{-}24^0$C) and growth and development: $25\text{-}28^0$C.
- Temperature >32^0C may cause foliar burning, faded flower colour and reduced flower life.
- Pfitzer (1957) was 1st time to indicate presence of β-chromosome in anthurium but it does not affect phenotype. It is transmitted through both pollen and eggs.
- Propagation methods: Seeds, division of offshoots, stem cutting, suckers (general) and micropropagation (commercial using leaf segments, spadix segments, vegetative buds, stem sections, etc.).

- For seed production: Spadix need to be pollinated more than once because uneven maturation of female flowers.
- Total duration of tissue culture cycle from leaf explants to complete plantlet: 11 months.
- Days required from spike emergence to full bloom: 21 days.
- Pollination agents: Ants, Bees, Flies, Weevils, humming birds.
- Female phase: Up to 28th day from opening of spathe.
- Receptivity of flowers: 2 weeks.
- Anthesis and dehiscence: 8-10 AM.
- Stigma receptivity: 6-7 days before anther dehiscence.
- Days required from pollination to seed maturity: 180-200 days.
- Days required for seed germination: 6-8.
- Fruit type: Berry (yellow, red, brownish coloured) with 1-2 seeds inside.
- Months required for seedling transplantation: 5-6.
- Hybrid seedlings flower within 30-36 months.
- Ideal angle between spathe and spadix: 30-45^0.
- 3-5 healthy leaves are maintainted per plant.
- Stage of harvest: Spathe completely unfurled and 2/3rd flowers on spadix open.
- Pulsing treatment with BA 50 ppm for 12 hours delays initiation of spathe bluing and spadix necrosis.
- Ideal storage temperature of flower: 14-17^{0}C.
- Flowers are placed in luke warm water (38^{0}C).
- Application of BA @ 750 ppm increases sucker production.
- Planting distance: 45cm x 45 cm.
- Yield: 8-12 flowers/plant/year.
- LD_{50} for *in vitro* mutagenesis: 15 Gy.
- Tetraploid plantlets could be regenerated through aerial roots.
- Skills like tissue culture, ploidy manipulation and molecular markers could be used to speed up flower breeding.
- Anther culture was successfully developed haploids in *A. andreanum* cv. Tropical.
- Somatic embryogenesis: Leaf explants from *in vitro* grown plants of *A. andreanum* formed callus and converted into plantlets.
- Genome breeding in Hawaii is done for enhanced resistance to bacterial blight.
- Isozyme: 1st molecular markers used for genotypic characterization.
- Seed extraction: By squeezing.
- Seed extraction in *A. scherzerianum*: Fruits are soaked in 13% crystalline Sodium carbonate (CSC) at 20^{0}C for 2.5 hours or 6% CSC + 1% pectinase solution at 26-36^{0}C for 1 hr.

- Seeds stored at 10⁰C for 3 weeks give 100% germination in 4 days.
- Seeds remain viable for 20 weeks when stored in low moisture cabinet at 11⁰C with 50-70% germination.
- Seeds per berry: 1 to 6 (2.7 cross pollination) and 1-4 (2.3 self pollination).

Species:

- All anthurium species are aroids i.e. plant that produce spathe and spadix.
- Present day anthuriums are interspecific hybrids between *A. andreanum* x *A.scherzerianum*.
- *A. andreanum* and *A. scherzerianum*: Only species that grow bright red spathe.
- Foliage purpose: *A. amnicola, A. corrugatum, A. crystallinum, A. digitatum* and *A. grande.*
- Fragrance purpose: *A. angustispadix, A. armeniense, A. brownii, A. fatoense, A. fragrantissimum, A. hacumense, A. lindenianum, A. ochranthum, A. salvodorense, A. schlechtendaii, A. standleyl, A. uplaense, A. roseospadix.*

Species	Salient features
A. acutangulum	Spathe green tinged with red-violet; spadix yellow-green coloured
A. amnicola (syn. *A. lilacinum*) (Tulip anthurium or Tulip Flamingo flower)	True miniature (6-8 inch height) from Panama; lilac/ purple coloured spathe & purple spadix; round the year flowering; highly cross compatible with other species & used in numerous interspecific crosses with *A. andreanum*.
A. andreanum (Oil cloth flower or Tail flower or boy flower or Painter's palette)	Secondary polyploid (2n=30 +2B); introduced to Europe in 1876;spathe waxy, 10-15 cm long, heart shaped; spadix yellow & white; cordate leaves; non-coiled spadix; cultivated for cut flower purpose & year round production
A. antioquiense	Resistant to bacterial blight
A. armeniense	Spadix longer than spathe; mint like fragrance.
A. bakeri	Spathe is pale yellow-green and spadix cream white in colour; potted flowering plant
A. brownii.	Spathe is greenish rose tinted & spadix purple; fragrant
A. crystallinum	Leaves variegated (green with contrasting white veins); spathe green, heavily tinged with red-violet
A. x *cultorum*	Complex hybrid involves *A. andreanum, A. lindenianum, A. nymphaeifolum* & *A. ornatum*
A. magnificum	Leaves variegated (green with white veins); spathe and spadix green; peduncle 9 ridged.
A. regale (Regal anthurium)	Coracious leathery leaves, stunningly large (exceed 90 cm).
A. scandens (Pearl lace leaf)	Creeping type with dark green foliage.
A. scherzerianum (Flamingo flower or Flame plant)	1st widely cultivated pot plant; introduced to Europe in 1872;leaves narrow; spathe ovate; spadix spirally twisted, golden-yellow; flowers from February to July; popular house plant
A. veitchii (King anthurium)	Leaves ovate-cordate and bright green; spathe is cup shaped, white turning purplish rose.

Types of anthuriums:

A. Standard: Are common heart shaped spathe lobes ranging from 12 cm x 12 cm to 20 cm x 18 cm.

B. Obake: Have two tone coloration i.e. bicoloured effects of green with a major spathe colour. In some varieties, there is loss of green colour in summer and size of spathe ranges from 8 cm x 7 cm to 28 cm x 23 cm.

C. Tulip: Are upright cupped spathes and straight, erect spadix. Size of spathe is about 10 cm x 6 cm. These are mostly hybrids.

Varieties:

- Whole day fragrant: Tasuta Pink Obake.
- Cvs. Marian Seefurth, Nitta, Lady Jane, Southern Blush, Honeymoon Red are freely used in breeding programme.
- Brazilian cvs: IAC Astral, IAC Eidibel (selection, red spathe and white spadix; 7.5 flowers/ year); IAC Iguape, IAC Isla (better post harvest keeping quality).
- Cvs. Gloria Angara, Pink Obake (largest flower): Popular in Trinidad.
- Taiwan Agricultural Research Institute: Pink Panther, Orange Storm, Green Elf, Pink Girl, Tropical-P (mutant of Tropical).
- Suitable for hydroponics: Red Queen, Kraho, Serenta, Aikara.

Name	Breeding method	Features
University of Hawaii		
Uniwai	Clonal selection	White spathe
Marian Seefurth	Clonal selection	Rose oval spathe
White Green (UH-8)	Clonal selection	Bicoloured
Rose Opal Green (UH-16)	Clonal selection	Bicoloured
Coral Green (UH-39)	Clonal selection	Bicoloured
Princess Aiko (syn. Imperial)	*A. antioquiense* (white) x *A. andreanum* cv. Tatsuta Pink Obake	Sweet scented; pink coloured spathe; high yielding & long lasting flowers
Regina	*A. andreanum* cv. Marian Seefurth x *A. formosum*	Large, purple coloured tulip type spathe
Centennial	Complex cross of White x Lavender hybrid 570-77 [(Uniwai x *A. lindenianum*)] x *A. amnicola*] x A494 (*A. andreanum* x *A. antioquiense*)	Green yellow spadix; tulip type spathe; resistant to bacterial blight
Ruth Morat	*A. antioquiense* x *A.*	Larger red coloured spathe; mean width, length 50 and

(syn. Lady Ruth)	*andreanum* cv. Rotolante	77 mm, respectively.
Southern Blush	*A. andreanum* (large, pink spathe) x *A. amnicola* (dwarf)	Leaves lanceolate; spathe pink with slight lavender tint; suitable for pot culture
Show Biz	*A. andreanum* x *A. amnicola*	Floriferous, compact growth habit, light red spathe & suitable for pot culture
Iga Gold	*A. scherzerianum* x *A. wendlingerii*	Fertile hybrid with grayish orange spathe
Ellsina	*A. scherzerianum* x *A. andreanum*	Fertile hybrid with grayish orange spathe
Red Hot	Southern Blush x Lady Jane	Red spathe; 6-7 cm long & 4-5 cm wide; spadix orange red; suitable for pot culture
Tatsuta Pink Obake (UH-1299)	-	Emit scent at pistillate stage; strong fragrance all the day
Orange Hot	*In vitro* mutagenesis of 'Red Hot'	Orange spathe; spadices like its parent; free branching
IIHR, Bengaluru		
IIHR-26 (1990)	Hybrids of *A. andreanum* (pink) x *A. armeniense* (white)	Spathe orange red with reclining yellow spadix; 8.3 flowers/year
IIHR-139 (1991)		Very floriferous; spathe white with reclining orange spadix; 7.2 flowers/ year
IIHR-243 (1992)		Very floriferous; spathe orange red coloured
IIHR-51 (1992)		Very vigorous; spathe white, spadix pink, highly fragrant & resistant to anthracnose

Grading system:

- CFB box size: 60 x 30 x 23 cm accommodating 70-100 flowers.

European standards			American standards	
Flower size (cm)	**Stem length (cm)**	**No. of stems/ box**	**Grade**	**Inches (avg. length and width)**
> 15	50	8	Extra large	> 6
13-15	45	12	Large	5-6
11-13	40	16	Medium	4-5
9-11	35	11	Small	3-4
8-9	30	15	Miniature	2-3
7-8	25	18	Peewee	Under 2
6-7	20	21	Corsage	Under 2

Diseases, pest and disorders:

- Bacterial leaf blight: Most destructive. 1st reported in Brazil in 1972 and in India during 1992.
- Colour break disorder: Ca deficiency.

- To stabilize spathe colour: Application of lime or $CaNO_3$ @ 5 g/plant.
- Molluscicide used to control snails and slugs: Metaldehyde.

Disease	Causal organism	Resistant/ tolerant cultivars
Stem and spadix rot	*Colletotrichum gloeosporioides*	Marian Seefurth, Manoa Mist, Uniwai (white spathe), Mauna Kea, Avenue
Bacterial leaf blight	*Xanthomonas axonopodis* pv. *dieffenbachiae*	Kalapana, Centennial, Tropic Ice, Tropic Flame, Paradise Pink, Rudolph
Anthracnose	*Colletotrichum gloeosporioides*	Marian Seefurth, Abe Pink, IIHR-51

Inheritance of characters:

- Negative heterosis is recorded for plant height, length and width and leaf blade, days from emergence to maturity of leaves, leaf area, time taken for first flowering and inclination of candle.
- -ve correlation: Sucker production and flower production.
- Genes, *M* and *O*, are responsible for spathe colour in anthurium. Gene *M* controls production of tetraploi-3-rutinoside and gene *O* controls production of pelargonidin-3-rutinoside tetraploids production.

Character	Number of genes	Inheritance pattern
Sucker production	Polygenic	-
Spathe colour	Monogenic	Red dominant over orange
Bacterial leaf blight resistance	Digenic	Additive
Purple spathe	-	Recessive

Spathe colour	Proposed genotypes	Spathe colour	Proposed genotypes
Red	*MMOO, MMOo*, or *MmOO*	Coral	*mmOo* or *mmoo*
Pink	*MmOo*	White	*mmoo* or *Mmoo*
Orange	*mmOo, mmOO* or *mmoo*		

37.2 Calla lily

- Eulogized as 'Arum lily or Aroid lily or Black lily of Nile'.
- Evergreen, perennial herb.
- Grown for cut flower, potted plant/ landscape purpose and variegated foliage for floral arrangements.
- Biggest exporter: New Zealand.
- *Zantedeschia elliottiopica* (*Z. aethiopica* x *Z. elliottiana*): It is cross incompatible with other species.
- *Z. aethiopica* (syn. *Calla aethiopica*, *Rhchardia africana*):
- Multiplied by seeds and rhizome offsets/ disc shaped corm.

- Dormant buds on rhizome produce several shoots on plant and give multibranching growth habit.
- Best temperature for growth: 15-24^{0}C.
- Average light intensity: 40,000 lux.
- Suitable pH: 6.1 to 6.5 and E.C. not less than 1 mS/cm.
- High temperature is harmful after flowering and during tuber growth.
- Ornamental part: Corolla like spathe for cut flower and variegated/ spotted foliage in floral arrangement.
- Floral differentiation occurs when shoot growth begins.
- Pollination agent: Flies.
- Juvenile phase: 1-2 year.
- Petalloid leaves arise from thick rhizome.
- Petioles are hairy below and spongy throughout.
- Flowering season: Late winter to late spring.
- Fruit: Orange coloured beaked berry which becomes yellow and soft (mucilagenous) when ripe.
- Seed: Ovoid, leathery and compressed.
- Seed count: 50-500 seeds/ berry.
- Pulp is removed and seeds are dried off.
- Seeds remain dormant for > 4 months.
- Inflorescence: White yellow or pink spathe, funnel shaped and open with pointed and recurved tip and finger like spadix which is staminate above and pistillate below.
- Flowers: Unisexual with male zone longer than female zone and female flowers with or without stamenoids.
- Flower forcing require 88 days production period.
- Highly cross pollinated due to monoecy and protogyny leads to allogamy.
- Tissue culture and embryo rescue have been widely used to obtain interspecific and intergeneric hybrids.
- Albino hybrid embryos are obtained from successful intersectional crosses. No green hybrids have been reported.
- Bacterial soft rot: Soil borne disease occurs worldwide. Use of streptomycin is recommended.
- Varieties resistant to soft rot (*Erwinia carotovora*): Pink Opal, Dominique, Inspiration and Pacific Pink.

Grading system:

Length (cm)	Inflorescence
80	Appropriate for stem length
70	Appropriate for stem length
60	Appropriate for stem length

Inheritance of characters:

Character	Inheritance pattern
Spathe colour	Four pairs of dominant genes &complementary genes
Leaf shape	Oligogenic
Number of leaf spots	Oligogenic

38. ASTERACEAE (COMPOSITAE)

38.1 Chrysanthemum

- Eulogized as 'Autumn Queen or Queen of Eastor Glory of East or Queen of fall flowers'.
- National flower of Japan.
- Ranks 2nd among commercial flowers in international market.
- It was known to India in the earliest times as mentioned in *Gyaneshwari* (*Marathi* treatise on *Bhagwatgita*) during 13th century and it was in cultivation in north India in 17th century.
- Oldest garden flower and presently highly evolved flower plant.
- Word 'Chrysanthemum' is derived from Greek word '*chrysos*' (golden) and '*anthemon / anthos*'means 'flower'.
- National Chrysanthemum Society of America at New York was founded in 1890.
- National Registration Centre for Chrysanthemum: NBRI, Lucknow.
- National Chrysanthemum Society is located at England.
- International Atomic Energy Agency (IAEA), Vienna maintains database of new varieties developed through induced mutagenesis.
- Wide range of polyploidy level (diploid to decaploid) is found in different species.
- Festival of Happiness (National Chrysanthemum Day): Celebrated in Japan with this flower.
- Resistant to Peroxyacetyl nitrate (PAN).
- Edible and garnish chrysanthemums are grown in Japan.
- All cultivated chrysanthemums are allohexaploids (2n=6x=54).
- Garden chrysanthemum is polyanaeploid complex ranging from 2x to 25x (2n=26,36,45,47,51 to 75).
- Chromosome number: 2n=53-56 (edible cultivars) and 51+â to 55 (garnish cultivars).

- Chromosome number is correlated with flowering period or flower size in edible type.
- No relationship between chromosome number & inflorescence diameter.
- Pot chrysanthemums are called as 'mums' in which one cutting is planted in one pot.
- Indeterminate origin of varieties from *C. morifolium*.
- Optimum pH for cultivation: 6.2-6.7.
- Ideal cutting size for propagation: 4-6 cm.
- Quick dip method for rooting of cuttings: IBA @ 500 ppm.
- Diameter of an ideal bush: 60 cm.
- M.K. Chailakhyan (1937) discovered presence of florigen.

Species	**Common name & features**
C. boreale	Evolution of florist's chrysanthemum
C. carinatum	Tri-colour chrysanthemum & annual; self incompatible
C. chanetii	Salt tolerant
C. cinerarifolium, C. coccineum, C. roseum, C.marshalli, C.tamrutene	Source of pyrethrum insecticide
C. coronarium	Known as garland chrysanthemum & annual
C. frutescens	Grown as pot plant
C. rubellum	Winter hardy species
C. lavandulifolium	Halophyte
C. maximum	Sasta daisy & grown as cut flower
C. multicaule, C. paludosum, C. segetum & *C. spectabilis*	*Annuals*
C. morifolium (syn. *Dendranthema* x *grandiflora, C. indicum* (2n=4x=36), *C. hortorum*)	Florist's chrysanthemum / cultivated garden chrysanthemum/ greenhouse chrysanthemum (2n=6x=54)
C. segetum	Known as Corn marigold; annual; basically an abnoxious weed
C. saga	Analyzed for study of radiosensitivity

- Pollen grains can be used as component of plant introduction.
- Requires long day for vegetative growth and short day for flowering.
- Garden and greenhouse cultivars require 6-8 weeks and 8-14 weeks period of short days for flowering, respectively.
- Short day plant: Photo-sensitive (10 h day light).
- Flowering is dependent on photoperiod, temperature and vernalization.
- Starts flowering at < 13 h day length.
- Day length of 14.5 h is necessary for flower initiation but shorter day length of 13.5 h is required for flower bud development.
- Shading is essential to induce flower bud by using black polyethylene sheet of 150 gauge thickness.

- A 'ten-week' group means blooming after 10 weeks, after the start of short days.
- Reaction time: Time from start of short day period to harvest and is very sensitive to temperature.
- Cathey (1955) classified genotypes based on flowering at different temperature regimes.
  1. Thermozero: Flowering is at any temperature ranging from 10-27^{0}C but consistently at 16^{0}C night temperature e.g. Shasta.
  2. Thermo positive: Require higher temperature (27^{0}C) for bud initiation e.g. 'Cameo'.
  3. Thermo negative: Require higher temperature (27^{0}C) for bud initiation but flowering delayed at higher temperature e.g. Defiance
- Garden chrysanthemum is highly heterozygous.
- Ideal stage of emasculation for hybridization: Fully developed unopened flowers.
- Male sterility: Functional type.
- Male sterility is important for spray type since it induces pollen allergy & reduces flower quality.
- Kinds of florets that compose chrysanthemum bloom are disc flowers (situated in centre) and ray florets (surround the disc florets).
- Disc florets are tubular shaped, contain both reproductive parts and called perfect flower.
- Ray florets are comparatively longer, contain only reproductive part & called imperfect flower.
- Ratio of ray florets to disc florets varies from 1:8-10-12 in different species. Ratio of length of ray florets and its width is 2:1.
- At diploid level, disc floret number is variable & ray floret number is static.
- In short day conditions, maximum number of disc florets are formed in inflorescence.
- In fully double or super double varieties (10 rows of ray florets and 0 rows of disc florets).
- Most preferred colour for cut flower: White & yellow.
- Number of flowers/ plant shows variation:
  - < 100 flowers e.g. Kundan, Flirt (suitable for cut flower & pot culture).
  - > 1000 flowes e.g. Suhag Singar.
  - Most other varieties between 100 and 200 flowers/ plant.
- Duration of flowering: Varies from 30 days (Flirt) to 50 days (Decorative).
- Flower weight (of 100 flowers): 30 g (Suhag Singar) to 200 g (Indira) and average wt. around 150 g in most varieties.
- Tall varieties required more pinching as compared with shorter ones.
- No pinching (without) required in cv. Hemant Singar and Suhag Singar.

- Predominantly self incompatible but cross compatible with other species.
- *C. cinerariifolium* is self incompatible.
- Sporophytic SI occurs at all ploidy levels.
- Pseudo-self compatibility (PSC) exists in garden and greenhouse chrysanthemum which allows seed set following self pollination.It can be transferred from garden to greenhouse types.
- Variability in ovule number in disc florets results in incompatibility.
- Seed dormancy is regulated by hard seed coatin *C. coronarium*.
- Seed set occurs only in disc florets and all varieties do not set seeds.
- Pollination agent: Honey bee (*Apis mellifera*).
- Stigma receptivity: Peak on 11th day and upto 15 daysof anthesis.
- Pollen longevity: > 16 days at ambient temperature and 35-45% R.H.
- Disbudding of standard chrysanthemum is done at 29th short days.
- Pinching or stopping is the most essential for small flowered or spray chrysanthemum. It is done at 14-21 days after planting or 8-10 cm tall plants.
- Soft pinching: Removal of soft tips of shoot along with 2-3 open leaves.
- Hard pinching: Removal of longer portion up to hard shoot. Done in pot plants.
- Roll out pinching: Practiced only in short plants.
- SADH @ 2000-4000 ppm applied after disbudding reduces stem length, produces thicker stem, enhance flower colour and increase vase life.
- Chemicals used for disbudding: Maleic hydrazide and Oxathin.
- *Sen rin tsukuri* (Japanese word): Japanese style of chrysanthemum culture which means growing thousand blooms.
- Cascade form (effect of a water fall in blooming stage): Japanese style of chrysanthemum culture.
- Most critical technique in formation of a cascade: Pinching.
- Standard type chrysanthemum: 3 flowers per plant.
- Anemone and Korean types are suitable for cascade form e.g. Jaya, Mayur, Modella, Perfecta and Flirt.
- 'No Pinch No Stake' (NPNS) type: Suitable for pot culture.
- Small flowered double Korean types: Mostly grown in open field condition.
- Palynotaxonomy i.e. Pollen morphology (number of spores and spines) can be used for species *C. morifolium* and *C. zawadskii* identification.
- Fruit type: Ribbed achene.
- The entire flowering shoot per spray is a compound cyme with a multiple inflorescence.
- Flowering of inflorescences is in subtending manner, the terminal occurs basipetally.
- 'Crown bud' appears in the month of May.

- Best time for taking terminal cuttings: Mid-June to Mid-July.
- Propagation method: Root suckers and terminal cuttings.
- Urea is not applied because it causes phytotoxicity.
- Alar (0.25%) or Phosphon D: Very effective in producing better size blooms on dwarf plants.
- Floral pigmentation is located in ray florets except in anemone flowers with pigmentation in disc and ray florets.
- Pompon type chrysanthemum looks globular.
- Variegated leaved varieties: Niharika, Arun Singar, Dhawal, Subarna.
- Effect of CO_2 injection in greenhouse: Thicker stems and greater plant height.
- Ideal vase solution: 8-HQC @ 200 ppm + 2 % sucrose.
- Most effective biocide: Silver nitrate ($AgNO_3$) @ 25 ppm.
- $AgNO_3$ cause black spot on chrysanthemum.
- Optimum temperature for long holding of chrysanthemum: 2.5^{0}C.
- Phytochemicals viz. flavonoids, carotenoids, chlorophyll and anthocyanins are useful as taxonomic markers a) in large flower cultivars 2) to prepare checklist, 3) identification of varieties and 4) selection of desirable characters for intervarietal breeding programme.
- Ray petal modifications and their relative number per whorl forms the basis of classification of flower types viz. single, double, fully double.
- NCS of America classified cultivars on basis of flower form, corolla shape and arrangements of florets as single, anemone, spoon, decorative, quilled, button, etc.
- Based on number of flowers/ stalk, garden varieties are classified as 1) standard (single bloom per stem and bloom incurved or reflexed type) 2) spray (entire cyme is allowed to bloom).
- LD_{50} for gamma radiation: 1.5-2.5 Krad.
- Optimum dose for X-ray radiation: 2000-4000 rad.
- Mutation rate highest in pink coloured cultivars.
- Pink colouredcultivars produce bronze, yellow or white mutants upon mutation.
- Yellow varieties produce shades of yellow or white or mixture of yellow + white.
- Common medium for rooting of cutting: Perlite + sphagnum peat moss.
- Planting density: 48 plants/ m^2.
- Thermo tolerance in small flowering types for controlled conditions has been developed by creating mutants through irradiation of rooted cuttings over seedlings.

Varieties:

- 1st chrysanthemum known to USA was 'Dark Purple' imported by a scientist John Stevens in 1798.

- 1st record of chrysanthemum hybridization, germination and selection of superior seedlings was published in 1827 by M. Bernet.
- Inbreeding depression results in decreased plant height, seed set, germination and flowering.
- Greenhouse cvs. are double types & contain only gynoecious florets & highly sterile.
- Generation cycle required for sexual breeding: 0.75 to 1.5 years.
- Embryo rescue technique brings down generation cycle to 100 days & allows 3 generations/ year.
- Utility of cultivars as
  1. Large flowered type as exhibit.
  2. Small flowered for pot culture, cut flower and garland purpose.
  3. Bedding and garden decoration purpose.
- 'Queen of Talmuk' is bud sport of 'Casa Grande'.
- 'MODI': Name given by Isreali government to a fast growing chrysanthemum plant.
- Varieties suitable for pot culture: Rakhee, Indira, Kirti, Chandrakant.
- Introduction from USA: Casa Grande, Dream Castle, Mountaineer, Peacock, Potomac, Royal Pomp, Snow Ball, Temptation, Yellow Glow, *C. parthenium*.
- Introduction from UK: Alfred Wilson, Cameo, Pink Cloude, Princess Anne, *C. coronarium*.
- Introduction from Hungary: *C. caucasium*, *C. coccineum*, *C. frutescens*, *C. leucenthemum*, *C. serotimum*, *C. vulgare*.
- Interspecific hybridization between garden chrysanthemum & *C. weyrichii*, *C. grandiflora*, *C. makinoi*, *C. pacificum* are successful.
- Maxi-Mum, My Favorite: Large shrub and extremely winter hardy.
- Low temperature tolerant mutants: Apricot Miros, Bronze Miros, Dark Miros, Golden Horim, White Horim.
- Winter hardy & frost tolerant cvs.: Red Chief, Duluth, Minngopher, Jimba.
- Minn Queen, Minn Ruby, Minn Bronze, Minn White, Minn Yellow: Cushion habit.
- Japanese cv. Chiyo Zakura is resistant to low temperature & winter light conditions.
- Heat delay sensitive greenhouse cvs.: Delano, Yellow Mandalay, Sunny Mandalay.
- Japanese day neutral & heat delay insensitive cvs.: Geongwoon, Mezame.
- Using biotechnology approach, colour of 'Money Maker' cv. has changed from pink to white.
- Varieties registered under PPVFRA: Pusa Anmol and Pusa Centenary.
- Colchi Bahar: Colchicine induced mutant (0.0625%) of *C. maxima* cv. 'Sharad Bahar'.
- NBRI has produced the 1st *in vitro* Chrysanthemum Aspermy Virus (CAV) free plants by shoot meristem culture from *C. morifolium* cv. Pooja.

Name	Breeding method	Features
IARI, New Delhi		
Pusa Aditya (2012)	OP seedling of 'Jaya'	Bushy, 30-35 branches; spray type; yellow colour at periphery with orange red in centre
Pusa Chitraksha (2012)	OP seedling of 'Lal Pari'	Bushy, 24-30 branches; spreading type; single flowers; deep magenta colour; highly floriferous
Pusa Sona (2012)	OP seedling of 'Sadbhavana'	Extremely dwarf (25-30 cm); 20-25 branches; spreading, spray type single yellow flowers, suited for pot mum; can be grown in ice cream cups/ small containers
Pusa Anmol (2005)	Induced mutant of 'Ajay'	Photo-thermo insensitive; highly floriferous, bushy, spray type, yellowish pink; flowers thrice in a year & peak in summer, good suckering ability, response well to *in vitro* propagation
Pusa Centenary (2005)	Induced mutant of 'Thai Chen Queen'	Vigorous, tall, yellow coloured, flowers large, incurving & disc florets are fleshy, good suckering ability, slightly fragrant, suitable for cut flower & exhibition
Pusa Arunodaya (2012)	Induced mutant of 'Thai Chen Queen'	Pink coloured ray florets, semi-double flowers, big in size (7-8 cm dia.); incurving ray florets
Pusa Kesari (2012)	Induced mutant of 'Thai Chen Queen'	Red coloured ray florets, semi-double flowers, bigger size (9-10 cm dia.); incurving ray florets
Pusa Guldasta (2018)	OP seedling of 'Lalpari'	Plant height 58 cm; semi-double flowers of 3.8 cm dia.; orange red ray florets with yellow disc; 48 days life in field condition
Pusa Shwet (2018)	OP seedling of 'Lalpari'	Plant height 41 cm; semi-double flowers of 6 cm dia.; white ray florets with yellow disc; 40 days life in field condition
IIHR, Bengaluru		
Arka Pink Star (2009)	Half sib selection of cv. Punjab Gold	Semi-double, pink coloured flowers, 318 flowers/ plant.
Rakhee (1980)	OP seedling of cv. Lord Doonex	Bushy; primrose yellow, anemone type; 124 flowers/ plant; flower 161 g/ plant & good for potting, veni & religious purpose
IIHR selection-5	Seedling selection	Good for loose flower purpose; high yielding.
IIHR selection-6	Seedling selection	White blooms; good for loose flower purpose; high yielding
Arka Ganga (1999)	Flirt (late flowering) x Red Gold (early flowering)	White with pink tinge, double Korean type & suitable for garland, potted plant & bedding purpose.
Arka Ravi (1999)	Mundial x Arka Swarna	Peach coloured; Korean type (6 cm dia.); early blooming, 65 days flowering duration; 69 flowers/ plant; yield 133 g/ plant; vase life 12 days.

Arka Swarna (1999)	Nanako x CO.1	Yellow coloured, Pompon, 74 flowers/ plant; yield 157 g/ plant cut & loose flower.
Chandrakant (1990)	Angela x G.P.67	White; decorative type; 149 flowers/ plant; yield 272 g flowers/ plant; 124 days to flower; produces more 2.2 times more yield than local white.
Chandrika (1994)	Angela x G.P.1	Plant dwarf, compact, white; decorative type & loose flower; 98 days to flower, 130 flowers/ plant; 4.7 cm across.
Indira (1980)	OP of 'Lord Doonex numbered LD-114 (purple) and a hybrid seedling of [Flirt (deep red) x Valentine (FXV-1, beet root purple]	Early blooming; flower 6 cm dia.; Double Korean type; yellow, decorative type & cut flower; yield (103 flowers/plant); good multiplier.
Kirti (1994)	Angela x G.P.1	Early flowering; dwarf; spreading and compact; flowers double Korean type; white, but fades to pink tinge; 119 flowers/ plant.
Nilima (1992)	Flirt x Valentine	Flowers purple, decorative type, 144 flowers/ plant; flower yield 281 g/ plant & used as cut flower.
Pankaj (1994)	Lord Doonex-14 x (Flirt x Valentine-1)	Pink; decorative type; 140 flowers/ plant; flower yield 363 g flower/plant & cut flower purpose.
Ravikiran (1993)	Flirt x Valentine	Stellate flowers; reddish-brown looks like papery flower; 86 flowers/ plant; used as cut flower.
Red Gold (1980)	Flirt x Valentine	Very floriferous; flower grayish orange, double Korean type (6 cm across), 292 flowers/ plant; flower yield 400 g/plant; good multiplier; suitable for pot culture
Yellow Star (1990)	Flirt x Valentine-22	Yellow; decorative type; 150 flowers/ plant; flowers 272 g/ plant.
Yellow Gold (1992)	Induced mutant of 'Flirt'	Yellow with brick red coloured strips on petals; decorative type; 113 flowers/ plant; flower yield 244 g/plant
Usha Kiran (2001)	Induced mutant of 'Kirti'	Yellow, dwarf, semi-double, 170 flowers/plant; flower yield 367 g/ plant; useful for bedding, pot plant & floral decoration
NBRI, Lucknow		
Appu (1982)	OP seedling selection	Dwarf & early blooming; flowers double & purple, compact, button type; suitable for mini culture.
Apsara (1977)	OP seedling selection	Rosy flue on white flower; pompon type.
Apurva (1987)	OP seedling selection	Flowers pink, very early blooming; No Pinch No Stake type; suitable for pot/ mini culture.
Apurva Singar (1983)	OP seedling selection	Double Korean type; No Pinch No Stake type; suitable for pot culture.
Arun Kumar (1983)	OP seedling selection	Flowers red; plant super dwarf; No Pinch No Stake type; suitable for mini culture.

Arun Singar (1982)	OP seedling selection	Flowers red striped; leaves variegated; No Pinch No Stake type; suitable for pot/ mini culture.
Bindiya (1976)	OP seedling selection	Flowers dark crimson, double Korean type; suitable for pot & mini culture.
Birbal Sahani (1976)	OP seedling selection	Flowers snow white, pompon type with long vase life; suitable for cut flower purpose.
Cameo	OP seedling selection	Suitable for mini culture
Chacko	Selection from 'Jaya'	-
Dhawal	OP seedling selection	Variegated leaves; flowers white
Diana (1999)	OP seedling selection	Small flowered, red, anemone type, mini chrysanthemum; blooms in early December.
Gauri	OP seedling selection	Flowers white, double Korean type; suitable for pot culture.
Gazania Type	Selection from 'Lal Pari'	-
Gulal	OP seedling selection	Flowers bronze, double Korean type; suitable for pot culture.
Guldasta (1986)	OP seedling selection	No Pinch No Stake type, flowers anemone type, bronze, suitable for pot culture.
Haldighati (1988)	OP seedling selection	Off season blooming type; No Pinch No Stake type; double Korean type, dwarf & yellow coloured; suitable for mini culture.
Hemant Singar (1981)	OP seedling selection	No Pinch No Stake type; Korean type, early blooming & dwarf; flowers pink, single, small& very light in weight; yield (700 flowers/ plant); suitable for pot culture.
Himanshu (1982)	OP seedling selection	White, anemone type, double Korean type, off season (summer) blooming; useful for monochromatic landscaping & pot culture.
Jaya (1980)	OP seedling selection	Decorative type; late blooming, crimson flowers; suitable for cut flower & pot culture
Jayanti (1979)	OP seedling selection	Pompon type; yellow flowers, long vase life; suitable for cut flower, pot culture & garland making.
Jubilee (1980)	OP seedling selection	Pompon type; orange-red coloured flowers; suitable for cut flower & pot culture.
Jwala (1981)	OP seedling selection	Off season blooming; double Korean type; red flowers; suitable for cut flower & pot culture.
Jyoti (1980)	OP seedling selection	Off season blooming; flowers Double Korean type, yellow coloured; suitable for cut flower & pot culture.
Jyotsna	OP seedling selection	Flowers double Korean type, white coloured; suitable for cut flower
Kaumudi (1980)	OP seedling selection	Double Korean type; purple flowers; suitable for pot culture.
Kiran (1980)	OP seedling selection	Double Korean type; purple strips on white base; suitable for cut flower & pot culture.
Kirti (1980)	OP seedling selection	Single Korean type; purple strips on white base; suitable for cut flower & pot culture.
Kundan (1980)	OP seedling selectionfrom cv. Jayanti	Dwarf; flowers small, yellow coloured; suitable for cut flower
Lal Kila (1980)	OP seedling selection	Double Korean type; crimson flowers; suitable for cut flower.

Lalima (1990)	OP seedling selection	Double Korean/decorative type; red flowers; suitable for cut flower & pot culture
Lalpari (1989)	OP seedling selection	Single Korean type; red flowers; suitable for ground culture.
Lilith (1989)	OP seedling selection	Double Korean type; white flowers; suitable for cut flower
Maghi (1989)	OP seedling selection	Pompon type; blooms in January, pink flowers.
May-Day (1981)	OP seedling selection	Out of season blooming (May-June/October-November) type; suitable for pot culture.
Mayur (1982)	OP seedling selection	Pin cushion type, yellow flowers; suitable for cut flower & pot culture.
Meghdoot (1982)	OP seedling selection	Blooms during July-August; suitable for pot culture.
Mini Queen (1997)	OP seedling selection	Anemone type, creamy white flowers; suitable for mini pot culture.
Mohini (1997)	OP seedling selection	Decorative type; suitable for pot culture.
Mother Teresa (1997)	OP seedling selection	Anemone type, mini chrysanthemum; No Pinch No Stake type; flowers small white & patented variety
Himanshu (2009)	OP seedling selection	Anemone type, white; blooms in December.
Little Hemant (2009)	OP seedling selection	Yellow, selection from cv. Little Darling, pompon type; suitable for cut flower.
Little Kusum (2009)	OP seedling selection	Bronze colour, selection from cv. Little Darling, pompon type, suitable for cut flower.
Little Orange (2009)	OP seedling selection from cv. Little Darling	Pompon, tubular type, yellow colour; suitable for cut flower.
Little Pink (2009)	OP seedling selection	Purple, selection from cv. Little Darling; decorative type.
Neelima (1980)	OP seedling selection	Double Korean type; bluish purple, late blooming; suitable for pot culture & cut flower.
Nirmal (1981)	OP seedling selection	Anemone type, dwarf, profuse flowers, white ideal for pot culture.
Orange Spoon	OP seedling selection from cv. Jaya	Spoon type flowers
Pancho	OP seedling selection	Single Korean type; flowers with yellow disc & orange petals; suitable for mini culture.
Peet Singar (1980)	OP seedling selection	No Pinch No Stake type; early blooming; yellow coloured; suitable for pot culture
Phuhar (1982)	OP seedling selection	Out of season blooming (rainy season); double Korean type, pink; suitable for pot culture & cut flower
Priya (2000)	OP seedling selection	Single Korean type; purple coloured
Puja (2000)	OP seedling selection	Decorative type, pink coloured
Ragini (2000)	OP seedling selection	Single Korean type; Orange coloured
Rangoli (2000)	Selection from 'Diana'	Dark red colour, double Korean type, No Pinch No Stake type; useful for mini culture
Ratna (1989)	OP seedling selection	Pompon type, red flowers; flowers in December-January.
Sadbhavna (2000)	OP seedling selection	Double Korean type, No Pinch No Stake type; dwarf bushy, floret colour red purple; useful for mini culture

Shanti (2000)	OP seedling selection	Dwarf; small flowered, white colour, decorative type, useful for garland purpose.; 99 flower heads/plant; 199 florets/ flower head
Sharda (1978)	OP seedling selection	Very early blooming, double Korean type, yellow, suitable for pot & garland making.
Sharad Kanti (1976)	OP seedling selection	Decorative type, yellow.
Sharad Kumar (1976)	OP seedling selection	Dwarf, profuse branching, Korean type, No Pinch No Stake type.
Sharad Mala (1976)	OP seedling selection	Earliest among all cvs.; Double Korean type flowers; dull white colour; suitable for cut flower & garland.
Sharad Mukta (1977)	OP seedling selection	Flowers spoon type, purple coloured; blooms in October-November; suitable for pot & cut flower.
Sharad Sandhya (1977)	OP seedling selection	Double Korean type; red flowers; suitable for pot culture.
Sharad Singar (1977)	Chance seedling of 'Original Dwarf'	No Pinch No Stake type variety; flowers yellow with bronze strips; suitable for mini culture
Sharad Shobha (1977)	OP seedling selection	Out of season blooming (September-October); double Korean type; white coloured; suitable for pot culture.
Shizuka (1981)	OP seedling selection	Double Korean type; red, suitable for mini culture.
Shyamal (1981)	OP seedling selection	Fluffy Korean type, deep purple; suitable for pots, cut flowers & loose flowers.
Suhag Singar (1981)	OP seedling selection	Dwarf; No Pinch No Stake type; double Korean type; red coloured; suitable for pot culture.
Sujata (1991)	OP seedling selection	Spray type, compact yellow flowers.
Suneel (1991)	OP seedling selection	Double Korean mauve coloured.
Sunayana (1976)	OP seedling selection	Single Korean type, mauve type; late blooming; ideal for pot culture.
Surya (1982)	OP seedling selection	Single Korean; red tips with yellow base; suitable for pot culture.
Swarna Singar (1982)	OP seedling selection	No Pinch No Stake type; double Korean type; suitable for mini culture.
Sweta Singar (1982)	OP seedling selection	No Pinch No Stake type; white coloured; suitable for mini culture.
Tushar (1982)	OP seedling selection	Off season blooming type; white coloured; suitable for pot culture.
Vandana (1980)	OP seedling selection	Anemone type; mauve with yellow centre.
Vasantika (1980)	OP seedling selection	Very late blooming; Tall; double Korean type flowers; sulphur yellow coloured flowers; suitable for pot culture & cut flower.
Vinaya (2000)	OP seedling selection	Single Korean, white coloured; suitable for pot culture.
White Profile (2000)	OP seedling selection	Double Korean type.
White Charm (2000)	OP seedling selection	Suitable for mini culture.
Yellow Charm (2011)	OP seedling selection	No Pinch No Stake type; single Korean type; suitable for mini culture.

Yellow Prolific (2011)	OP seedling selection	Double Korean, light yellow coloured; ideal for pot & cut flower.
Y2K (2000)	OP seedling selection	White, anemone type &No Pinch No Stake type; dwarf bushy
NBRI-Kaul (2010)	Lalpari x Vijay	Purple, single Korean type, useful for pot & bedding purpose.
NBRI-Khoshoo (2010)	Lalpari x Vijay	Gray-red, single Korean type, useful for pot & cut flower purpose.
NBRI- Little Kusum (2009)	Haldighati x Sharad Kanti suitable for pot culture.	Small flowered, bushy, compact, yellow open disc, single Korean type chrysanthemum;
NBRI-Little Darling	White Charm x Jubilee	Terracotta pompon type mini chrysanthemum; requires No Pinch No Stake type, dwarf, compact round shape
NBRI-Mini Jessie	Cameo x Jessie	Small flowered, cineraria type mini chrysanthemum; requires No Pinch No Stake type; attractive for 'mini culture'.
NBRI-Pushpangadan (2011)	Mutant of 'A-22' (White)	Small, anemone type, tubular shaped; yellow coloured ray florets; floriferous (>150 flowers); ideal for pot culture & bedding.
NBRI-Yellow Bud Sport (2011)	Mutant of 'A-22' (White)	Small, anemone type, tubular shaped, yellow coloured ray florets, floriferous (>150 flowers), ideal for pot culture & bedding.
Ashankit (1974)	γ ray (1.5 Krad) induced mutant of 'Undaunted'	Large flowered, exhibition type, bright mauve coloured flowers; semi-quilled, fringed ray florets with silvery reverse flower.
Cosmonaut (1984)	γ ray (1.5-2 Krad) induced mutant of 'Nimrod' (white)	Small flowered anemone type; white flower colour.
Jhalar (1975)	γ ray (1.5 Krad) induced mutant of 'Undaunted'	Large flowered; exhibition type; mauve coloured flowers; flat & fringed ray florets.
Kargil 99 (2000)	-	Small flowered, spoon shaped, single whorl ray florets with yellow disc, purplish mauve florets; snow white variegation of leaves; 215 flowers/ plant; red floret colour.
Kasturba Gandhi (1961)	Mahatma Gandhi	Spider & tubular type blooms; flowers from October-November; flower dia.12.5 cm, 344 florets/ head; good for cut flower
Kunchita (1974)	γ ray (1.5 Krad) induced mutant of 'Undaunted'	Large flowered, exhibition type, incurved ray florets of mauve colour.
Lalima Head Shape	γ ray (2 Krad) induced mutant of 'Lalima' (red)	Pompon type flower head; yellow-orange coloured; suitable for bedding & pot culture
Lalima Tubular	Mutant of 'Lalima'	Ray florets changed to tubular form; suitable for bedding & pot culture
Niharika (B-7)	-	Chlorophyll variegated leaves; flowers single Korean type; No Pinch No Stake type; snow white petals; suitable for mini-pot culture.
Nirbhaya (1974)	γ ray (1.5 Krad) induced mutant of 'Undaunted'	Exhibition type; semi-quilled fringed flowers of ligher mauve colour.

Nirbhik (1974)	γ ray (1.5 Krad) induced mutant of 'Undaunted'	Exhibition type; lighter mauve flowers.
Shabnam (1987)	Mutant of 'D-5'	Decorative type, magnolia purple coloured flowers
Tulika (1985)	γ ray (1.5 Krad) induced mutant of 'M-24' (purple)	Semi-quilled (brush like appearance of floret); purple coloured flowers
Agnishikha (1987)	γ ray (1.5-2 Krad) induced mutant of 'D-5' (purple)	Decorative type; erythrite red colour.
Anamika (1974)	γ ray (1.5 Krad) induced mutant of 'E-13' (mauve)	Small pompon type; light reddish colour.
Basant (1979)	γ ray (1.5 Krad) induced mutant of 'Paul' (terracotta)	Small flowered pompon type; yellow coloured florets.
Basanti (1974)	γ ray (1.5 Krad) induced mutant of 'E-13'	Early blooming; small flowered pompon type; yellow flower colour; suitable for cut flower
Batik (1994)	γ ray (2 Krad) induced mutant of 'Flirt' (deep red)	Small flowered double Korean type; yellow stripe on red background.
Hemanti (1979)	γ ray (1.5 Krad) induced mutant of 'Megami' (amaranth pink)	Dwarf, decorative type; early blooming yellow flower colour.
Himani (1974)	γ ray (2 Krad) induced mutant of 'E-13'	Pompon type; white flower colour.
Jugnu (1991)	γ ray (1.5-2 Krad) induced mutant of 'Lalima'	Double Korean type; bicoloured flowers.
Kapish (1974)	γ ray (2 Krad) induced mutant of 'E-13'	Pompon type; brownish flowers.
Lohita (1974)	γ ray (2 Krad) induced mutant of 'E-13'	Pompon type, dark reddish flowers.
Manbhawan (1982)	Induced mutant of 'Flirt' (deep red)	Double Korean type, bicoloured (yellow and red) flowers.
Navneet (1987)	γ ray (2 Krad) induced mutant of 'Kalyani Mauve' (pansy violet)	Decorative type, creamish white flowers.
Navneet Yellow (1993)	γ ray (1.5 Krad); induced mutant of 'Kalyani Mauve'	Decorative type, yellow coloured flowers.
Sharad Har (1992)	γ ray (1.5 Krad) induced mutant of 'Sharadmala' (white)	Decorative type, yellow colour.
Sheela (1985)	γ ray (2-2.5 Krad) induced mutant of 'Himani'	Pompon type, canary yellow coloured flowers.

Sonali (1991)	γ ray (2 Krad) induced mutant of 'Ratna' (mauve)	Pompon type, yellow coloured flowers.
Subarna (1991)	γ ray (2 Krad) induced mutant of 'Flirt'	Variegated leaves; double Korean type, yellow coloured flowers.
Surekha Yellow (1992)	γ ray (1.5 Krad) induced mutant of 'Surekha' (deep red)	Yellow coloured flowers.
Alankar (1982)	γ ray (1.5 Krad) induced mutant of 'D-5' (pink)	Large flowered; decorative type; panish orange colour.
Aruna (1982)	Induced mutant of 'Ashankit' (bright mauve)	Exhibition type; dark reddish flowers.
Asha (1974)	γ ray (1.5 Krad) induced mutant of 'Hope' (pink)	Large flowers; reflexed type; creamish coloured florets.
Basant (1979)	Induced mutant of 'Paul'	Pompon type; yellow flower colour.
Gairik (1974)	γ ray (1 Krad); induced mutant of 'Belur Math' (pink)	Incurved flowers; light salmon coloured flowers.
Kanak (1974)	γ ray (1.5 Krad) induced mutant of 'Undaunted' (bright mauve)	Exhibition type; dark brown flowers.
Kansya (1974)	γ ray (1.5 Krad) induced mutant of 'Rose Day' (pink)	Extra large, bronze flower colour & reflexing ray floret shape.
Kum Kum (1987)	γ ray (2-2.5 Krad) induced mutant of 'M-71' (liliac purple)	Brown coloured flowers
Pingal (1974)	Induced mutant of 'Pink Casket' (pink)	Spoon type; terracotta coloured flowers.
Pitika (1974)	γ ray (1.5 Krad) induced mutant of 'Kansya' (brown)	Extra large, reflexing ray florets, lovely yellow flowers.
Pitamber (1977)	Induced mutant of 'Otome Zakura' (pastel lilac)	Pompon type, yellow coloured flowers.
Purnima (1977)	Induced mutant of 'Otome Zakura'	Pompon type, white coloured flowers.
Raktima (1996)	Induced mutant of 'Shyamal' (purple)	Chrysanthemum crimson coloured flowers.
Rohit (1979)	γ ray (1.5 Krad) induced mutant of 'Kingsford Smith' (fuchsia purple)	Reflexed type, rhodonite red coloured flowers.
Shefali (1974)	γ ray (2 Krad) induced mutant of 'Undaunted'	Exhibition type, incurved ray florets of light reddish flower colour.

Sharad Shobha (1980)	γ ray induced mutant of 'Sharada'	Off season blooming; white coloured double Korean type flowers; suiable for pot culture.
Sheveta (1974)	γ ray (1.5 Krad) induced mutant of 'Fish Tail' (pinkish mauve)	Incurving, white coloured flowers.
Shukla	γ ray induced mutant of 'Mrs. H. Gubby'	White coloured flowers.
Swarnim (1974)	γ ray induced mutant of 'Undaunted'	Mauve coloured flowers.
Tamra (1974)	γ ray (2 Krad) induced mutant of 'Goldie' (light apricot)	Intense coppery red (apricot) on yellow background.
Taruni (1979)	γ ray (2.5 Krad) induced mutant of 'Kingsford Smith'	Refluxed type, Azalea pink coloured flowers.
Vijay Kiran (2009)	Induced mutant of 'Vijay'	Early flowering (October blooming), dwarf & small flowered, double Korean type; yellow coloured flowers.
DFR, Pune		
C-1	-	Faint yellow colour; 200 flowers/ plant; suitable for garland & pot purpose
C-2	-	Pink coloured
C-3	-	Dark yellow coloured; 175 flowers/ plant; 5.8 cm dia., suitable for Nov-Dec planting
TNAU, Coimbatore		
CO.1 (1985)	Selection from local	Long lasting flowers; 170 42-50 flowers/ plant; yellow colour; useful for garland & flower decoration
CO.2 (1985)	Clonal selection from introduction from NBRI	Vigorous, rhodamine purple coloured flowers.
MDU 1 (1985)	Selection from local germplas	Early flowering; sulphur yellow coloured flowers
PAU, Ludhiana		
Punjab Garden Beauty (2007)	Selection from local germplasm	Deep maroon coloured flowers; 73 flowers/ plant; suitable for bedding & garden decoration.
Punjab Mohini (2018)	Selection from local germplasm	Single Korean type flowers white with yellow centre; suitable for pot culture; mod. resistant to septoria leaf spot.
Punjab Shingar (2018)	Selection from local germplasm	Flowers white coloured & decorative type; suitable as loose flower; resistant to septoria leaf spot
Punjab Gold	Flirt x Gul-E-Sahir	Red coloured flowers, long flowering duration, resistant to septoria leaf spot.
Punjab Anmol (2007)	Puncho x Rage	Bright yellow flowers; anemone type, late, 4 cm size; 208 flowers/ plant; suitable for pot culture.

Punjab Autumn Joy (2007)	White Bouquet x Flirt	Shiny pink flowers; decorative type; early; 6.6 cm size; 283 flowers/ plant; suitable for bedding & garden decoration.
Punjab Royal Purple (2007)	Bindiya x Rage	Purple pink flowers; anemone type; 5 cm size; late maturing; 200 flowers/plant; suitable for pot culture.
Punjab Yellow Delight (2007)	White Bouquet x Gul-e-Shair	Bright yellow flowers; pompon type; early; 5 cm size; 103 flowers/ plant; suitable for pot culture.
Punjab Winter Queen (2007)	White Bouquet x Flirt	Pink flowers; spoon form; 9 cm size; 125 flowers/ plant; suitable for bedding & garden decoration.
UHS, Bagalkot		
Dundi	Selection	Attractive yellow flower colour
BCKV, Kalyani		
Bidhan Madhuri	Selection	Red purple coloured flowers; decorative type; suitable for loose flower production
Bidhan Jayanti	Selection	50 flowers/ plant; yellow coloured flowers & decorative type
Bidhan Mallika	Selection	110 flowers/plant; double Korean type; suitable for pot culture
Bidhan Tarun	Selection	75 flowers/ plant; red purple coloured flowers; suitable for pot culture
Bidhan Mum	Selection	51 flowers/ plant; yellow-orange coloured flowers; pompon type; suitable for pot culture
Bidhan Purna	Selection	72 flowers/ plant; yellow coloured flowers; single Korean type; suitable for pot culture
Dr PDKV, Akola		
PDKV Ragini	Gamma ray induced mutant (2.0 Krad) of 'Akola Local' (yellow)	Red tinge on yellow petals; flower dia., 6.5 cm; 100 flower weight 645.9 g; flower yield 180 q/ ha; mod. resistant to fusarium wilt
PDKV Shubhra	OP seedling selection	High yielding; white flowers
Bijali Supers	-	Multi-petalled white coloured flowers; dwarf with more spreading habit; high yield

Offseason blooming cultivars developed at NBRI, Lucknow

Blooming season	Varieties
Summer season (April-May/ 2nd flush in October)	Himanshu, Usha, Jwala, Jyoti
May-June/ 2nd flush in October-November	May-Day, Ujawla
June-July/2nd flush in November	Jyoti, Tushar
Rainy season (July-August)	Meghdoot, Phuhar
September-October	Ajay, Sharada
October-November	Makhmal, Megami, Mohini, Sharad Har, Sharad Mala, Sharad Singar, Haldi Ghati
November-December	Makhmal, Mohini
December-January	Jaya, Vasantika
January-February	Suneel, Lilith, Maghi

Grading system: As per Society of American Florists, USA.

Standard chrysanthemum-

Grade	Minimum flower diameter (mm)	Minimum stem length (cm)	Stem strength
Blue	150	76	Strong
Red	125	76	Strong
Green	100	61	Strong
Yellow	-	60	Strong

Spray chrysanthemum-

Grade	Stems per sleeve	Specification
Gold	10	6 flowers or more out and some to come
Silver	15	4 or 5 flowers out and some to come
Bronze	20	3 flowers out and some to come
Make-up	-	All stems not covered above, filling sleeves to same extent as other grades

Pests, diseases and disorders:

- Tomato Aspermy Virus: Less common.
- Aphid: Very serious pest.
- Leaf miner (*Phytomyza syngenesiae*): Cvs. Yellow Night, Nightingale, Promenade, Improved Bonnie Jan.
- Europen corn borer (*Ostrinia nubilalis*): Cvs. Freedom, Classic, Compatriot, Fortune, Pancho are resistant.
- Indian cvs. Baggi (white coloured; sutiable for cut flower purpose) and Ratlam's Selection show multiple disease resistance.
- Ray speck (*Stemphylium lycopersici)*:

- Septoria leaf spot (*Septoria chrysanthemella*): Cvs. Phillips, Flirt, Gumti are resistant.
- Bud borer menace is severe.
- White rust (*Puccinia horiana*):
- Chrysanthemum Stunt viroid (CSVD): Spread worldwide in nurseries & transmitted by mechanical means. Japanese cv. Okayamaheiwa is highly resistant.
- Petal burn: Boron deficiency.
- Quilling of florets.

Inheritance of characters:

- Linkage between increase in disc size & male sterility has been reported.

Character	Number of gene(s)	Inheritance pattern
Flower size	Monogenic	• Anemone type inherits singly
	Digenic	• Incurved type
	4 unnamed genes	• 4 dominant genes-single flower
		• Any 3 set of dominant genes-semi-double flower
		• 1 or no dominant gene-super-double flower.
Branching habit	-	Branching dominant over non-branching
Flower doubleness	Monogenic recessive	• Singleness partially dominant over doubleness; • Tubular ray florets is recessive.
Flower diameter	-	Unclear
Leaf number	Polygenic	-
Petal orientation	-	• Incurved petals by 2 dominant genes *O* & *P*; • Quilled petals unclear inheritance; • Promiscuous ray petal by 2 dominant genes *R* & *S*
Plastid pigmentation	Disomic	Dominant gene inhibited pigmentation
Flower colour	Disomic/ tetrasomic/ hexasomic	Complex & unclear
Carotenoid pigmentation in petal cells	Monogenic	In dominant- white & pink & in recessive-Yellow & bronze
Anthocyanin pigmentation in petal cells	Digenic	• *A* & *I*-pink, carmine, bluish red; • Absence of *A* & *I*-yellow; • *A* without *I*- brownish red; • Absence of '*A*' alone-white
Self incompatibility	Trigenic	Independent gene action with intragenic dominance
Male sterility	Monogenic	Sterility recessive to normal type
Resistance to CSVD	-	Unclear

38.2 Marigold

- Annual and loose flower crop grown all over world.
- Popular due to wider adaptability, good keeping quality, various commercial uses in medicinal and industrial sector and religious and decorative purposes.
- It spread to different parts of the world during early part of 16th century.
- Introduced by Portuguese in India.

- In Kerala, commercial scale extraction of carotenoids is done in homescale/ cottage industries.
- Receptacle-less flower.
- Marigold is not used in making '*gajara*'.
- African marigold: Grown for loose flower, landscaping.
- French marigold: Ideal for rockery, edging, hanging basket and window boxes. It is most effective in lowering root knot nematode population.
- Foliage has musky/ pungent scent.
- Inflorescence: Capitulum/ flower head (1-15 cm dia.).
- Flower head has tubular hermaphrodite disc florets in centre and strap shaped, long and pointed ray florets (colourful and showy part) around periphery.
- Seed type: Achene which is devoid of endosperm and ripens and shed within 2 weeks after bloom.
- Type of dichogamy: Protandrous.
- Seed rate: 1-1.5 kg/ha.
- Seed is non-endospermic.
- Seed cup: Cypsela.
- Apetalous flowerlacks colourful ray florets.
- Ratio of cross and self pollination in *T. erecta* (35: 65) and in *T. patula* (70: 30).
- Many rows of ray florets give pompon like shape to flowers.
- Leaves of all species have oil glands.
- Oil of *T. minuta*: Antiviral, bronchodilatory, tranquilizing and anti-inflamatory properties.
- Essential oil is used in perfumery industry and as flavourant in food and tobacco industry.
- Major constituent of essential oil: Piperitone (50%) in leaf and 1-8-cineole (23%) in flower.
- Kemin yellow oil from Kemin Industries, USA is the product of marigold.
- Highest content of zeaxanthin and xanthophylls (lutein-an anti-oxidant) found in African marigold- dried petal used in poultry industry to increase colour of egg yolk.
- Total carotenoid content in orange petals: 3-5 mg/ g fresh wt.
- Lutein accounts for 80-90% of total xanthophyll content.
- Helenine present in flower colour: Used for eye adaptability to distinct light intensity.
- Male sterility in African marigold is due to female character 'Femina'.
- Use of male sterile lines and tester parents are maintained as inbred lines in F_1 seed production.
- Ratio of 3 MS lines : 1 male fertile is optimum.

- Morphological marker in male sterile plants in *T. erecta*: Pitcher type shape of flower buds.
- Number of back crossings required to transfer male sterility into standard varieties: 5-6.
- For commercial seed production, pollens are collected from male parents through vacuum pump and dusted on male sterile plants.
- Seeds ripen within 45-60 days after pollination.
- Only black seeds within capitulum are viable and produce perfect F_1 hybrid plants.
- For hybrid seed production, hand emasculation and pollination by insects (bees) are used. And in this case, male sterile diploid African marigold and fertile French tetraploids are used.
- Two distinct types of MS as-
  1. Apetalous or femina type i.e. without stamen.
  2. Male sterility of true double form which produce no anthers in disc florets.
- Apetalous MS lines developed in *T. erecta* at IARI are-
  1. MS-5: Tall, late flowering, smaller flower dia., femina form flowers and yellow colour;
  2. MS-7: Semi-tall, late flowering, smaller dia, femina form flowers and light orange colour;
  3. MS-8: Tall, later flowering, smaller dia, femina form flowers and orange colour.
- Fresh seeds exhibit dormancy and require 3 months after ripening period before germination.
- Seeds viability: 21 months (ambient conditions).
- Seed soaking in 0.75% KNO_3 gives rapid and good germination.
- Halo priming with 50 mM $CaCl_2$ for 24 h increases final germination and germination index, shoot and root length and fresh wt. of seedlings.
- Colchiploidy affects significantly on size of capitulum and reduction in plant height.
- *In vivo* polyploidization; Nodal segments in African marigold were used.
- Optimum moisture for long-term storage at low temperature (-20^{0}C): 3-6%.
- Seed moisture injurious during storage: > 9%.
- Seed stored in tin and plastic boxes can be stored upto 10 months.
- Seeds can be dried upto 1.5% moisture content without loosing viability.
- Number of seeds/ gram: 300-350.
- Seed yield: African marigold (170-200 kg/ha); French marigold (370-500 kg/ha).
- In micropropagation, explants collected from September to December gave good proliferation of vegetative shoots.
- Multiplication rate of white marigold (*T. erecta*) is not as fast as yellow marigold due to low seed viability and poor germination (30%).

- Heterosis breeding has been exploited for all flower characters viz. duration of flowering (114.31%), total number of flowers (327.55%), peak of flowering (196.8%), seed wt. (41.85%), plant height (44.13%), flower size (79.59%), flower head dia. (79.59%), number of flower heads andflower yield (310.2%).
- Somatic embryos of African marigold from cotyledon and organogenesis from leaves, florets and hypocotyls have been standardized.
- SRAP marker linked to recessive male sterile '*Tems*' gene in MS line (M525A) and was converted into SCAR marker located within 2.4 cM from *Tems* locus.
- *In vitro* mutagenesis: Tissue culture for genetic improvement and propagation of elite mutants.
- LD_{50} in cv. Pusa Narangi Gainda for *in vivo* and *in vitro* condition: 15 and 20 Gy, respectively.

Species:

- Geatest diversity found in Central Mexico.
- *Tagetes erecta* and *T. patula* show strong reproductive barriers leading to hybrid weakness and sterility but produce very few good seeds in F_1 hybrids.
- Important species from garden point of view in Europe: *T. minuta*, *T. corymbosa*, *T. pusilla*.
- Important species from cultivation point of view & chosen for breeding in India: *T. erecta*, *T. patula*, *T. tenuifolia*.
- Artificial allotetraploid: *T. erectatenuifolia*.
- Mule marigold: Sterile triploid hybrids of tall African and dwarf French marigold.

Common name	Botanical name	2n=	Features & promising varieties
African (syn. American marigold, Rose of Indies)	*Tagetes erecta*	2x=24	self as well as cross compatible; commercially exploited for loose flowers, xanthophyll content and aromatic oil e.g. African Perfection, Cracker Jack, Luxor, Giant Double African Orange, Golden Age, First Lady, Gold Lady, Orange Lady, Crown of Gold
French marigold	*T. patula* (syn. *T. corymbosa*)	4x=48	Dwarf; allotetraploid; self as well as cross compatible; possess bicoloured flowers e.g. Pusa Deep, Rusty Red, Butter Scotch, Valencia, Star of India, Harmony, French Aurora
Single signet (syn. Baby marigold, Stripped Mexican marigold)	*T. tenuifolia* (syn. *T. signata*)	2x=24	Self incompatible;free flowering, small yellow flower having 5 ray florets, edible flower having spicy flavour & foliage has lemon fragrance; suitable for perfume industry e.g. Golden Gem, Lulu, Pumila, Ursula are suitable for edging & rock gardens

Sweet scented marigold	*T. lucida* (syn. *T. florida*)	2x=22	Perennial; 2-3 ray florets; produce in terminal corymbs
Californian marigold	*T. lacera*	-	Discovered in California; grows up to 120-150 cm; flowers profusely; yellow coloured.
Shrubby marigold	*T. lemmonii*	-	Shrubby; grows up to 60-70 cm; flowers showy & 2-3 cm in dia
Mystery marigold	*T. sarmentosa*	-	
-	*T. minuta* (syn. *T. glandulifera*	-	South American spp. produce white flowers in terminal clusters; commercially grown for essential oil (known as tagette) extraction in France, Australia & Brazil; found in North Western Himalaya; widely used in perfumes & cosmetics

Varieties:

- Climax and Toreador: 1st F_1 hybrid in African marigold. Extra large fully double flowers.
- David (1937) developed 'Red and Gold' interspecific hybrids. These belong to French marigold.
- Triploid interspecific hybrids between diploid African (♀) and tetraploid French (♂) marigold e.g. Nugget, Yellow Nugget, Gold, Red Gold, Burpee's Gold, Space Age series (dwarf & early flowering), Gold Coin series, Inca series (fully double flowers), Galore series (long flowering duration), Red Seven Star, Show Boat, Seven Star, Orange Ball.
- In triploids, sterility confers the character of continuous flowering.
- Tetraploid French marigold: Tetra Ruffled Red.
- Moonshot: Ultra-dwarf compact & very free flowering plants.
- French marigold: Royal & Giant Lucifer series.
- Richest source of xanthophylls: Gold Lady, Gold Dollar, Erecter, Diamond Jubilee (9795 µg/g dry weight).
- F_1 hybrids private seed companies in India: French Aurora, African Perfection.
- F_1 hybrids of *T. erecta* from Belgium: First Lady, Gold Lady, Orange Lady.
- White marigold (*T. erecta*): Single plant selection developed in 1999 at IARI. Possess medium size white flower and clonally propagated by shoot tip culture.

Name	Breeding method	Features
IARI, New Delhi		
Pusa Narangi Gainda	Cracker Jack x Golden Jubilee	African marigold; orange colour (carotenoid 2.69 mg/g); suitable for carotenoid extraction & loose flower production purpose.
Pusa Basanti Gainda	Golden Yellow x Sun Giant	African marigold; sulphur yellow coloured (carotenoid 1.37 mg/g); 58 flowers/ plant; ideal for growing both in pots & beds in the gardens.

Pusa Bahar (2015)	-	African marigold; yellow colour; suitable for bedding & floral decorations; 50-60 flowers/plant
Pusa Sankar-1	Apetalous type male sterility	French marigold
Pusa Arpita (2010)	Single plant selection (OP)	Yellow flowers; yield 18-20 t/ha
Pusa Bahar (2018)	OP selection	African marigold, flower dia., 8-9 cm; yellow coloured; 50-60 flowers/ plant; suitable for bedding & floral decoration purpose
Pusa Deep (2018)	OP selection	French marigold; early flowering; flowers dark red coloured; 80-90 flowers/ plant; yield 18-20 t/ha
IIHR, Bengaluru		
Arka Alankara	MGYP-1 x 9-2	African marigold; yellow flowers; suitable as loose flower; carotenoid extraction; 129 flowers/ plant; multiplied by stem cuttings
Arka Agni	Sister line of Arka Alankara	African marigold; orange flowers; suitable as loose flower; carotenoid extraction; 119 flowers/ plant; multiplied by stem-cuttings
Arka Bangara	-	African marigold; suitable as loose flower; carotenoid extraction
Arka Bangara-2 (2019)	-	African marigold; flowers compact, large, yellow-gold coloured; vegetatively propagated, early flowering; suitable for loose flower
Arka Honey (2019)	-	French marigold; dwarf; photo-insensitive; double coloured; 4.8 cm flower dia.; yield 5.8 t/acre
Arka Pari (2019)	-	French marigold; dwarf; photo-insensitive; double coloured; 4.3 cm flower dia.; yield 4.7 t/acre (500-600 flowers/plant)
Arka Abhi (2020)	F_1 hybrid	African marigold; flowers large, bright lemon yellow coloured; yield 10 t/acre; 6-8 days shelf life
Arka Bhanu	F_1 hybrid	African marigold; flowers large, golden yellow coloured; yield 10 t/acre; 7-8 days shelf life
Arka Vibha	F_1 hybrid	African marigold; flowers large, bright orange coloured; yield 10-12 t/acre; 8-9 days shelf life
Arka Shuba (2020)	F_1 hybrid	African marigold; spreading type; flowers large, bright orange coloured; rich in carotenoid (3.25%); yield 12-14 t/acre; 5-6 days shelf life
TNAU, Coimbatore		
MDU-1 (1986)	Selection	African marigold; suitable for loose flower; carotenoid extraction
BCKV, Kalyani		
Bidhan Basanti (syn. Bidhan Marigold-1)	-	French marigold; suitable for garland & long distance transport
Bidhan Gold (Syn. Bidhan Marigold-2)	-	French marigold; suitable for garland & long distance transport
Bidhan Marigold-3	-	French marigold; suitable for garland & long distance transport
CCSHAU, Hisar		
Hisar Beauty		African marigold
Hisar Jafri-2	-	African marigold

Inheritance of characters:

- GMS is controlled by single recessive gene.
- Flower longevity is positively correlated with number of petals/ flower, number of whorls/ flower, shelf life and flower yield.
- Flower yield is positively correlated with number of branches/ plant, number of flowers/plant, flower head diameter, size, weight & xanthophyll content.

Trait	Number of genes	Inheritance pattern
Leaf colour	Partially lethal	Virescent (chlorotic) duplicate recessive over green
Stalk length	-	Non-additive
Flower type	Monogenic	Double flower (*RR*) dominant over single (*rr*)
	Digenic	Carnation type (*RR TuTu CC*) dominant over cupid type (*rr TuTu CuCu*)
	Duplicate epistatic	Carnation type (*RR TuTu CC*) dominant over chrysanthemum type (*rr tutu cc, RR tutu cc*)
Floret shape	Monogenic	Flatness of floret dominant over tubular
	Monogenic	Flat ray florets dominant over tubular ray florets
Flower colour	Polygenic	Corolla anthocyanin (red) dominant (*RR*) over absence
	2 independent genes	Orpiment dominant over yellow. • Orpiment (*TTIIYY, ttIIyy, ttiiyy*), • Tangerine (*TTiiYY, TTiiyy*) and • Yellow (*ttiiYY*) colours
	Polygenic	Carotenoid & lutein content is governed by dominance (non-additive) gene action. Xanthophyll esters both additive & dominance (or non-additive)
Flower number/ plant	-	Additive, non-additive & dominance x dominance
Apetalous sterility	Monogenic recessive	Male fertile (petalous) dominant over male sterile (apetalous)

Diseases, pest and disorder:

- Powdery mildew (*Leveillula taurica*):
- Alternaria leaf spot (*Alternaria*, *Cercospora* and *Septoria* spp.): Golden Guardian, Double Bloom are resistant.
- Blight (*Colletotrichum capsici*): Infects petiole and branches.
- Gray mold (*Botrytis cineraria*): More destructive.
- Aster yellow:
- Alpha terthinyl: Chemical present in roots kills nematodes.
- Heart rot: Boron deficiency.

38.3 China aster

- Genus *Callistephus* is monotypic containing only one species *chinensis*.
- This species is important in Japanese floriculture industry as cut flower.

- Germans developed double forms during 18th century. Hence, also referred as German aster.
- Main centre for development of plant: Branching types which were introduced in USA.
- North (1979) and Watts (1980) grouped China aster under self pollinated crop.
- Pure yellow colour is not found in aster.
- Comet types: (Quilled flowers) released in 1886.
- Best temperature for colour development: 20-30^{0}C (day) and 15-17^{0}C (night) with 50-60% R.H.
- Pigment responsible for flower colour: Flavonoids.
- Propagation method: Seed.
- Seed rate: 2.5-3 kg/ha.
- Optimum soil temperature for seed germination: 21^{0}C.
- Seed count i.e. Number of seeds/ gram: 450-600 (430 approx).
- Blooms in about 3 ½ to 4 months from date of sowing.
- Flower yield: 4-5 t/ acre.
- Seed yield: 40 kg/ acre.
- Flower head contains 1 or 2 rows/ rings of ray florets (red/ pink, purple, violet, white) and yellow disc florets in centre.
- Maximum vase life of flower: 10-12 days.
- Seed viability: 1 year.
- Seed crop is harvested when flower heads are fuzzy.

Varieties:

- Fusarium wilt resistant: Asterix, Matsumoto, Matsumoto Pink, Princess Armida and Jitka

Name	Breeding method	Features
Sarlet Beauty, Blue Beauty, Cascade, Dwarf Queen	Introduction from USA	-
Perfection Rose, Perfection White	From Australia	-
Sky Blue Star, Blood Red	From Canada	-
IIHR, Bengaluru		
Kamini (1992)	Pedigree selection of (AST 6 xAST 36)	Deep pink coloured flowers; 138 days to flower, yields 50 flowers/ plant, 8 days vase life
Poornima (1992)	Pedigree selection of (AST 29 x AST 3)	Pure white flowers; flower dia. 6 cm, yield 25 flowers/ plant, 86 g flowers/ plant; 7 days vase life; root knot nematode resistant
Shashank (1994)	Pedigree selection of [Local x Pure line (Local Pink x AST 2)]	Creamy white, powder puff-type flowers; weighs 2.5 g each, 45 flowers/ plant, vase life of 9 days; root knot nematode resistant

Violet Cushion (1994)	Pedigree selection of [(Local Pink x AST 2)]	Flowers pompon type & violet coloured, flower weigh 2 g each, 70 flowers/ plant; 113 g flowers/ plant; vase life of 8 days
Arka Aadya (2016)	Single plant selection	Spreading type; high flower yield (178.56 g/ plant); pink flowers; tolerance of lodging; suitable for loose flowers & bedding purpose
Arka Archana (2016)	Single plant selection	Spreading type; white flowers; flowers (84.34/ plant), tolerant to lodging; suitable for loose flowers & bedding purpose
Arka Advaika (2020)	Selection	Semi-double; white coloured flowers; flower dia. 3 cm; suitable for cut flower, flower arrangement & bouquet making.
Arka Nirali	Selection	Semi-double; violet coloured flowers; flower dia. 2.8 cm; 43 flowers/ plant; recommended for cut flower, flower arrangement & bouquet making
Arka Shubhi	Selection	Semi-double; light-pink coloured flowers; flower dia. 2.8 cm; 56 flowers/ plant; recommended for cut flower, flower arrangement & bouquet making
MPKV, Rahuri		
Phule Ganesh White	Mass selection	Tall, erect growing, late, snow-white flowers, double chrysanthemum type
Phule Ganesh Pink	Mass selection	Early, semi-erect, double chrysanthemum-type, big size & rosy pink flowers
Phule Ganesh Violet	Mass selection	Early, semi-erect, double chrysanthemum-type, medium size, violet flowers
Phule Ganesh Purple	Mass selection	Semi-erect, bright purple flowers

Inheritance of characters:

Character	Number of genes	Inheriance pattern
Flower colour	Four independent genes	- Violet dominant over all colours - Blue dominant over creamy white - Deep pink dominant over pink, white & incompletely dominant over light pink & white - Pink dominant over light pink and pure white
Flower type	Monogenic	- Doubleness dominant over singleness - Pompon (one row of ray florets & tubular disc florets) dominant over chrysanthemum and fluffy types. - Chrysanthemum type dominant over fluffy type; - Pompon type (four rows of ray florets & tubular disc florets) dominant over pompon (one row of ray florets and tubular disc florets)
Growth habit	One major gene	Drooping incompletely dominant over erect
Apetalous character	-	Recessive to normal flower

Pests, disease and disorders:

- Root knot nematode causes 20-25% loss.
- Phyllody disease: Due to mycoplasma like organisms (MLO).
- Rosetting of leaves: Zn deficiency and day length >14 hours.

38.4 Dahlia

- Diversity of forms and colours make it 'King of flowers'.
- Cultivated dahlia is allotetraploid (2n=4x=32).
- Dahlias are deciduous, dicot, tuberous-rooted hardy perennials.
- Most flamboyant flower of winter season.
- Valued for potted flowering and garden crop world wide.
- International Registration Authority for Dahlia is located at RHS, England.
- National Dahlia Society, England.
- 1st introduced in 1857 by Agri-Horticultural Society of India, Kolkata.
- Optimum temperature for shoot development: 13-25⁰C.
- Optimum temperature for flower initiation and development: 10-15⁰C.
- Facultative short day to day neutral plant.
- Photoperiod determines total number of florets in a capitulum.
- Optimum photoperiod for flowering: 13-14 h and typical limit is 12 h.
- Flower buds remain blind when grown under shorter photoperiod than critical limit.
- Photoperiod of 14 h produces more flowers and 8 h photoperiod drastically reduces it.
- Short day reduces number of ray florets & increases proportion of disc florets & induces abortion.
- Flower opening is centripetal.
- Long stemmed solitary flower head (2-12 inch dia.) may lack ray florets.
- Stigma is protogynous and remains receptive for 77 h.
- Type of fruit: Achene with pappus of scales.
- Pigments present: Apigenin; yellow (chalcones & aurones); orange (anthocyanin); rose & lilac (low chalcones); black (high anthocyanin).
- Giant decorative type: Common popular type in Indiaand world. Take longest time to open fully, and set less seeds than other types.
- Propagation methods: Seed, stem cutting, root tuber, *invitro* method.
- Only dwarf bedding single type are grown from seeds.
- Root tubers have dormancy & sprouts only when attains physiological maturity.
- Breeding is easiest among all flowers.
- Self incompatibility is prevalent in large flowered exhibition type.
- Species with same chromosome number readily hybridize.
- Pollination agent: Bees.
- Hand pollination is resorted when better seeds are desired.
- Ray florets are used in hand pollination than disc florets.

- Rows of petals near to disc florets bear seeds more easily.
- Crossing time: 10 AM to 3 PM.
- Number of seeds/ gram: 98.
- Seed germinate in 10 days at favorable temperature of 18-28^{0}C.
- Seed yield: 10-15 g/plant.
- Seeds are sown in September-October.
- For seed germination, seeds are sown in medium containing equal parts of peat moss & vermiculite.
- In easy seed bearing types, both disc and ray florets form seed.
- In some cvs. ray florets are sterile & only disc florets form seed while in some cvs. both disc & ray florets are sterile & do not produce any seed.
- Common and commercial method of propagation to get large flowers: Terminal stem cutting treated with Seradix B powder.
- Growth regulator to induce flowering: GA_3 @ 100 ppm.
- Reduction in plant height: CCC, MH.
- Ray flowers have all flower colours whereas disc florets are generally yellow.
- Ideal months for inducing irradiation: June-July.
- Mutation theory of dahlia evolution is propounded by Swami Vinayananda.
- Mutation breeding: Only means of crop improvement.
- For induction of somatic mutations 500-1000 rads is recommended.
- LD_{50} for gamma irradiation: 1000-1500 rads.
- LD_{50} for X-ray irradiation to tubers: 2000-3000 rads.
- Garden dahlia cvs. Salmon Rays, Arthur Godfrey, Eldorado give greater number of mutations for flower colour and shape.
- Stopping and thinning is practiced in dahlia.
- Disbudding and deshooting is done to obtain quality bloom.
- Dahlias have 3 buds at end of each branch.
- Disbudding is done at 'pea' stage.
- Major air pollutant to dahlia: Sulphur dioxide (SO_2).
- When seeds are ready, heads are cut off & dried seeds are kept in glass containers to retain viability for longer period.
- Non-viable seeds are produced in hybridization performed between chromosomal races within same species and between different species with female parent having either 2n=32 or 2n=64 genomes.
- Seed shapes in different types: Long & thin (cactus), broad & narrow (decorative), flat (fansy & show), circular (pompon).
- Major disease: Powdery mildew (*Erysiphe polygonii*).

- Ideal temperature for tuber storage: 4-7°C.
- *In vitro* culture through meristem culture is practiced to get rid of mosaic virus and tomato spotted wilt virus.
- Genome size (cDNA value) can be useful to identify chromosome races within species.

Species:

Name	Species	Features
Tree dahlia/ Paenoy flowered dahlia/ Tom Thumb dahlia	*D. imperialis* (syn. *D. arborea, D. excelsa*)	Diploid (2n=32); flowers funnel shaped flowers; white with red tinged flowers
Cactus dahlia	*D. juarezii*	Tetraploid (2n=64); scarlet flowers
Garden dahlia	*D. variabilis*	Ancestor of dahlia; octaploid (2n=8x=128); resulted from *D. imperialis* x *D. coccinea*; self incompatible; promising for mutation breeding
Highly variable spp.	*D. coccinea*	Single yellow flowers; both diploid (2n=32), tetraploid (2n=64); contributed most to present day dahlias
-	*D. merckii*	Lilac and yellow flowers
-	*D. rudis, D. excelsa*	Diploid; purple flowers
-	*D. tenuis*	Flowers small with yellow ray florets & few disc florets
-	*D. pinnata*	Tetraploid; bear large single/ double flowers of bluish red colour
-	*D. rosea, D. purpurea, D. nana, D. crocata*	Tetraploid (2n=64); single rose coloured flowers
-	*D. macdougallii*	Only climbing spp.

Groups of garden dahlias:

- Numerous phenotypes viz. star/ anemone/ paeony/ decorative/ pompon/ cactus/ water lily flowered are available in world market.

Group/type	Originated from	Description	Cultivars
A. Border dahlias: Flower freely for 4-5 months on hills from July onwards until cut down by frost & classified into 12 groups			
I- Single flowered	*D. coccinea*	Flowers up to 4" dia. having 1 row of smooth ray florets surrounding the central disk, suitable for breeding purpose	Bambino, Collarette, Inflammation, Margaret Geerlings, Yellow Hammer
II- Anemone flowered	*D. pinnata, D. crocea, D. coronata* and *D. juarezii*	Flowers double; outer rows of ray florets surround a central group of comparatively long tubular florets	Guinea, Honey, Lucy, Scarlet Comet
III- Collerette	-	Large petals forming an outer ring (the collerette) around a	Can Can, Comet, Lilian Alice, Magic Night, Mrs. H. brown,

		central disc; blooms 5-6" across, usually contrasting in colour.	Nonsense, President Viger, Suntan, Starsister
IV- Water lily (Nymphaea flowered/Double camellia-flowered)		Introduced as a Nymphaea dahlia; flowers fully double; bloom 6" dia, petals edges involute & look like widely open tubes giving saucer shaped appearance; bloom in August.	Helena, Peace Pact, Pearl of Heemstede
V- Decorative	-	Most popular section; fully double flowers showing no central disc, cover wide range of colours & size from globular blooms; flower size 4-6", 6-8", 8-10", >10" dia.	African Queen, Arthur Godfrey, Avalanche, Bhola Baba, Colonel, Croydon Apricot, Kelvin Rose, Kenya,
VI- Ball	-	Fully double ball shaped blooms in 3.5-4" in dia. Globular having central florets like the outer ones. Florets incurved at their margins, short blunt at tips.	Duston Stone, Hot Lips, Nobel, Pipelnoir, Pompon, Sunrise, Swiss Miss, Rotriger, Tam Tam, Yellow Gem
VII- Pompon	-	Similar to ball dahlias, but much smaller & more globular; flower heads up to 2" in dia.	Albino, Barbara, Deepest, Glow, Little Conn, Moon Place
VIII- Cactus	*D. hortensis* x other spp.	Fully double flowers having no central disc & with long pointed ray florets. Straight or incurving petals are partially inturned (revolute) along their length and tend to narrow and pointed and which give the flower a star like appearance	Annapurna, Cardinal, Carnival, Danny, Gens, Garden Glory, Happy Boy, Manali, Margaret, Preference, Pride of Holland, Orgeo, Royal Highness, White Pearl, Center Field, Chatnoir
IX- Semi-cactus	-	Blooms fully double with fully double flowers similar to cactus group.	Autumn Fire, Center Field, Hamari Boy, Latest Flame
X- Miscellaneous	-	Contains small, dissimilar classes.	Akita, Fasciation
XI- Paeony (sunflower type)	*D. coccinea*	They possess 2 or 3 rows of florets which are generally flat with a central disk apparent; flower size up to 7 inch.	Aurantiaca, Magnifica, Roquencourt
XII- Star flowered/ Stellar		Small flowers; recurved at the edges & form a shallow cup shaped flower around a central disk.	Tahoma Hope

B. Bedding dahlias: Grown from seeds. They grow to 30-50 cm height; flowers measure 5-7.5 cm across & appear from June end till frost e.g. Coltness Hybrids, Fascination, Pink Radiance, Redskin

Varieties:

- Many horticultural varieties have arisen by gene mutation (chimera) only.

- 1st pompon was raised in Germany in 1850.
- Breeding work started in Somalia in late 1960.
- Dahlia seeds were introduced in Europe in 1789 & named in honour of Swedish botanist Dr. Andreas Dahl.
- Double flowered varieties are called A) Show type- self coloured & ball like flowers B) Fancy type- Mostly multicoloured.
- Interspecific cross (*D. variabilis* 2n=64) x *D. macdougallii* (2n=32) yield hexaploid hybrid (2n=48).
- Present day cultivars are resulted from crosses between *D. imparialis*, *D. coccinea*, *D. merakii* and *D. pinnata*.
- Species with same chromosome number can readily hybridized.
- India's contribution: Flower pot dahlia forms.
- Swami Vinayananda has done pioneer work in dahlia. He isolated spoon flowered type in 1984 from Giant decorative type. He developed Bhikkus Vivek, Jyotsna, Lord Buddha, Prabodh, Sarada Devi, Swami Gouriswarananda, Swami Lokeswarananda & Swami Madhavananda.
- Rotonde, Ornamental Rays: Gamma ray induced mutants of Salmon Ray.
- Japanese cv. World is mutant developed through ion beam breeding.
- Multiple flower mutant cultivars developed by Broentjes and Bauseso (Holland), 1960 through tuber irradiation (8 Kr gamma rays).
- 1st Indian dahlia selected from planned hybridization in 1973: Bhikkus Mother.
- Black coloured cvs.: Arabian Night, Macop, Magic Night, Black Jack, Kanora, Tisa, Chatnoir.
- Blue coloured cvs.: Blue Light, Blue River, Blue Stone, Twilight, Violet, Blue Lagoon, Nearest Blue.
- Bicoloured cvs. are popular and bicolour characteristic is dominant when white flowered cv. is used as seed parent.

Name	Breeding method	Features
Elegance, Chinese Lantern, Golden Autumn, Light Music, Spectacular	Introduction from Holland & USA	-
Swami Vinayananda	Croydon Monarch x Croydon Masterpiece	Decorative type; bicoloured; long lasting bloom; longer vase life, flowers from November to March; disease resistant.
Trio	Shirly Wright x Croydon Masterpiece	Bicolour dahlia of crimson white tips, produce three types of flowers
Disco	Television x Terry	Small bicolour; informal decorative type which changes to semi-cactus form on ageing; suitable for exhibition, garden display & cut flower

Badlel Stream	Sel. No. 97-1357 x Dapalipi	Double pink coloured ray florets & yellow coloured disc florets
Julita, Krynica, Lucilla, Violetta, Orietta, Melba	-	Early; cross between pompon type anddecorative type; wide range of flower colours; suitable for both garden beds & cut flower purpose.
Pepi, Piko, Noris, Syria	-	Dwarf types; suitable for bedding purpose.
Aida, Kiker, Wrzos, Aga, Etna, Klio, Eros, Dafnis, Aida, Kaprys, Ozyrys, Korona	-	Semi-cactus & cactus types, medium-tall; suitable for cut flower purpose.
Glory of India	Selection	-
NBRI Pinki (2001)	Seedling selection from exotic source	Pompon decorative type
Junita	Spontaneous mutant	-
Manjushri	Spontaneous mutant	-
Manali	Sectorial chimera of White Pearl	-
Padmaja Naidu	Sectorial chimera	-
Kailaspati	Sectorial chimera	-
Dandapani sport	Sectorial chimera	-
Prime Minister Sport	Sectorial chimera	-

Parent cultivar and characteristics	Mutant & salient features
Kenya- tall; stem pinkish green; leaf dark green; flower colour orange red; flower head loose & open; bloom 25 cm dia.	**Pride of Sindri**; stem light green & devoid of pink pigmentation; leaf light green; flower primrose yellow, more compact; bloom 35 cm dia.; flowers more freely. **Bichitra**; tall, stem & leaf light green shade; flower mimosa yellow; bloom 30 cm dia.; petals (ray florets) narrow; compact arrangement. **Jyoti**; plant tall; bloom 37 cm dia.; mallow purple flowers; good form & habit. **Twilight**; tall; bloom 35 cm dia.; purplish red flower. **Jubilee**; tall; bloom 35 cm dia., orange yellow flower colour with pink strips. Kenya Blue, Kenya White, Kenya Yellow
Eagle Stone- plant tall, 16 cm flower dia. & light pink colour	**Netaji**; plant tall; bloom 15 cm dia.; attractive bloom of light primrose yellow colour. **Pearl**; tall; bloom 15 cm dia.& pearl white in colour
Black Out- tall, 20 cm dia. bloom, dark crimson flower colour	**Black Beauty**; plant tall; bloom 28 cm dia.; bloom darkest crimson colour with neyron rose strips; very attractive; size of bloom like parent.
The Master- plant 1.2m tall, bloom 28 cm dia., light apricot colour; good form	**Vivekanand**; plant tall; bloom 28 cm dia.; spirea red colour; ray florets are divided at tip.
Croydon Monarch- plant 40 tall; bloom 30 cm; towny red colour	**Happiness**; plant tall, bloom size 30 cm dia. & as that of parent; deep ruby red coloured. **Yellow Monarch** (yellow petals)

Croydon Apricot- plant 45 cm tall, bloom 22 cm dia,; rich apricot colour; decorative dahlia of good form and habit	**Jayaprakash**; plant tall; bloom 25 cm; phlox pink in colour; compact form & attractive shape.
Alva's Supreme; Rustig (cream)	White Alva's & White Rustig (white)
Bhikkus Mother	Zail Singh, Bhikku & Swamiji
Bronze Symbol	Pink Symbol (dark pink), Lavender Symbol (lavender)
Daleko Jupiter	Pink Jupiter (pink colour)
Frank Hornsey	Pink Frank Hornsey (pink), Yellow Hornsey (yellow), Lemon Hornsey (yellow), Pearl Hornsey (pink and white blend), Rose Hornsey (yellow with rose flush)
Comet (maroon)	Scarlet comet (light red)
Klankstad Kerkrade (cream flowered)	White Kerkrade (white), Majestic Kerkrade (cream and pink blend)
Paul Chester (bronze)	Lemon Chester; Yellow Chester (yellow)
Reginald Keene (Bronze blend)	Candy Keene (pink blend) & Salmon Keene (salmon pink blend)
Shirley Alliance (orange)	Pink Shirley Alliance & Rosemary Clare (pink)
Swamiji	Prabodh

Inheritance of characters:

- Most flower colour genes occur as tetrasomic.
- Yellow and deep anthocyanins are completely dominant.
- White flowered varieties have recessive genes.
- Bicoloured characteristic of seed parent is dominant.
- Crossing of two different monochromatic coloured cultivars (if one parent is white flowered) give bicoured offsprings.

38.5 Gerbera

- Eulogized as 'African daisy or Barberton daisy or Transvaal daisy'.
- Most used cut flower worldwide for domestic as well as export market.
- For flower development studies, gerbera is used as model species.
- It valued as traditional Chinese medicine for curing cold with cough and rheumatism.
- Sensitive to salt.
- Removes variety of chemical vapours (formaldehyde, benzene) from air.
- Potted gerberas are commonly known as 'Samurai'.
- Plant stemless, dwarf and hairy (pappus) throughout and leaves arranged in rosette at the base.
- Bear single solitary flower on long, thin and leafless stalk (scape) arising from ground.
- Inflorescence: Head or Capitulum.
- Flower head consists of 3 whorls of outermost ray florets arranged marginally around central disc floret and several whorls of short, inconspicuous trans and disc florets.

- Trans florets are present in between disc and ray florets, hermaphrodite or bisexual.
- Ray florets are large, have aborted anthers but produce pistils.
- Ray florets have large outer corolla lip (ligule) and 2 rudimentary corolla internal lips.
- Disc florets are very small with 2 corolla internal lips as large as outer corolla lips.
- Number of ray florets/ flower: Few to > 44.
- Colour of disc florets (green/ black/ cream) increases market appeal.
- Flower colour pigments: Flavonoids (red), carotenoids (yellow).
- Flower head is 4-12 cm across, which are single, double or semi-double form with wide range of colours.
- Flower forms:
  1. Single type: 1-2 rows or ray florets on periphery of disc and rest are disc florets.
  2. Semi-double type: Extra row of minipetals around centre eye.
  3. Double type: 5-7 rows of petals that completely cover the flower head.
  4. Spider type: Thinner and more pointed petals.
  5. Standard type: Floral dia. >9 cm.
  6. Mini type: Floral dia. < 9 cm.
- Optimum pH for growth: 5-7.2 produces long flower and stem.
- Best mutagen for inducing single gene mutation to seeds: EMS.
- Tolerant to chlorine which is present in vase water.
- Seed germination is >70% when 1000 seed weight is 5 gram or above.
- Seed production/ inflorescence is greater in 1st year and flower production/ plant in 2nd year.
- Selfing is desirable for production of large number of hybrid seed.
- Harvesting stage: When 2nd circle of disc florets shows pollen development.
- High light intensity cause more compact growth, shorter stems and discoloration of flowers.
- Phytochemical compound 'flavonoid' used as chemotaxonomic marker to acertain inter and intraspecific variability.
- Pre-soaking of seeds in 0.3% $KMNO_4$ for 24 hours at 25-28^{0}C gives good germination.
- Seed viability: 2 years under -18^{0}C in plastic bags.

Species:

- 1st discovered in 1878 in South Africa by botanist R. Jameson.
- 1st scientific description of gerbera: Hooker (1889).
- *G. kunzeana*: Found in Himalaya and cleistogamous.
- *Gerbera jamesonii*: Cultivated and South African species.

- *G. viridiflora*: South African species.
- Present day (*G. hybrida*) cultivars originated from *G. jamesonii* x *G. viridiflora*.

Varieties:

- Breeding was started in 1887 by R. I. Lynch.
- 1st hybrid was evolved in 1912.
- Skipper & Tempo: World's 1st F_1 hybrid mini type (10 cm plant height) pot gerbera series.
- M/S. Terra Nigra of Holland: Leading firm developing excellent cultivars of gerbera.
- OP series 'Happy Pot' is daisy type potted plant in 5 colours other than white by Sakata Seed Company.
- Party Time (Hope x Sumyo): Pink coloured gerbera with semi-double type with brown centre.
- Sunmyo (Red Beauty x Tamara): Semi-double flower with bright golden yellow flower with black centre.
- Suncap: Bicoloured (red/yellow) ray florets with green centre, 13.5 days vase life.

Name	Breeding method	Features
IIHR, Pengaluru		
Arka Nesara (2016)	Half sib-selection (IIHR-1 x mixed pollen of 10 varieties)	Double type; suitable for 50% shade net; 3.23 flowers/ month; suitable for cut flower & flower arrangement
Arka Ashwa (2016)	Half-sib selection (IIHR-3 x mixed pollen of 10 varieties)	Double type; suitable for 50% shade net; 3.23 flowers/ month; suitable for cut flower & flower arrangement
Arka Krishika (2014)	Half-sib selection	3.6 flowers/ month; mod. resis. to thrips; suitable for open condition; used for cut flower & floral decoration
Arka Pink (H-16-8) 2019	Hybridization & selection from Arka Ashwa	Stalk length 62 cm; flower dia., 11 cm; 2.8 flower/plant/ month; vase life 7.2 days
Arka White (H-15-7) 2019	Hybridization & selection from 'IIHR-9'	Semi-double; stalk length 60 cm; flower dia., 10 cm; 2.78 flower/plant/ month; vase life 7 days
Arka Red (H-GO-1) 2019	Hybrid	Double type; yield 40 flowers/ plant/ year; suitable for open condition
TNAU, Coimbatore		
YCD-1 (1992)	Clonal selection	Double flowers with cherry red colour; 9.11 cm dia.; long flowers; free from bent neck, petal necrosis & temporary wilting; suitable for hilly area
YCD-3 (1995)	Selection	Blooms throughout year; 80 flowers/clump; suitable for hilly area
IHBT, Palampur		
Him Glow	IHBT-Gr-2 x IHBT-Gr-3	Double type; yellow orange colour petals; green coloured disc; vase life 18 days
Him Peace	IHBT-Gr-1 x IHBT-Gr-7	Double type; white colour petals; green coloured disc; vase life 15 days

Private sector hybrids: Salvadore, Dana Ellen, Primrose, Savannah, Winter Queen, Himalaya

Inheritance of characters:

- Post harvest longevity, flower productivity, flower diameter controlled by additive gene action.
- Flower colour: Digenic or polygenic.
- Crested and spider flower type: Monogenic and dominant to wild type.
- Disc colour: Monogenic dominant.
- Powdery mildew resistance (*Pmr*-1) and micro hair density (*Mhd*): Unlinked and controlled by 2 major putative genes.
- Vase life positively coorelated with floral diameter and trans floret diameter.

Pests, diseases and disorder:

- Leaf miner (*Liriomyza trifoli*): Serious pest.
- Foot rot (*Phytopthora cryptogea*): Major disease.
- Powdery mildew (*Podosphaerotheca xanthii*): Most common and destructive in production.
- Wilt (*Phytophthora cryptogea*): Most common and destructive in production. Broad petalled genotypes are highly susceptible.
- Stem break disorder: 10 cm below capitulum. Post harvest disorder due to lead deficiency.
- Higher pH leads to chlorosis.

38.6 Gaillardia

- Eulogized as 'Indian blanket flower or Firewheel or Sundance'.
- Summer season annual, frost hardy plant grown for loose flower and garland preparation.
- Plant can withstand to high salinity.
- Sporophytic self incompatibility is prevalent.
- Inflorescence: Racemose.
- Flower head small in diameter with short, narrow and more ray florets.
- Optimum seed moisture: 9%.
- Seed viability: 31 months.
- Seed yield: 500-600 kg/ha.

Species:

Species	Varieties, characters and colour
Gaillardia pulchella (syn. *G. bicolor*, *G. bicolor* var. *drummondii*)	Annual garden hybrid; flowers during summer to late autumn; 30-45 cm height; leaves, Cultivars have single or double flowers with red, orange yellow, yellow-tipped red, red-tipped yellow, bronze-scarlet, coppery-scarlet, orange-brown, golden yellow, orange, crimson-banded yellow coloured flowers; 6-8 cm in dia., var. *Picta*; Bronze red and golden-yellow.

	var. *Picta alba marginata*; reddish-maroon and white.
	var. *Picta aurea*; pure yellow.
	var. *Picta* Chameleon; scarlet, white andyellow.
	var. *Picta* Indian Chief; red.
	var. *Picta* Lorenziana; a curious and decorative hybrid with double flowers and tubular petals, yellow, bronze and red.v
	ar. *Picta* Lorenziana Bicolour; red and yellow.
	var. *Picta* Lorenziana *rubra*;red and white.
	var. *Picta* Lorenziana *sulphurea*; golden yellow,
	var. The Bride; cream-white
G. aestivalis var. *winklerii*	Yellow-flowered var. *winklerii* is white with yellow center
G. amblyodon	Annual; free flowering; reddish maroon flower; 5 cm dia.; flowers during June-October
G. aristata (syn. *G. grandiflora, G. lutea, G. maxima* and *G. perennis*)	Perennial; drought tolerant; blooms from June-October; coppery, yellow, golden yellow, orange, coppery scarlet coloured blooms; suitable for dry land and requires low maintenance
G. fistulosa	Quilled florets e.g. Buffalo Bill (large, pure yellow with a narrow disc), Vivian Grey (yellow-fringed rays & yellow disc).
G. kermesiana splendens	Narrow canary-yellow rays & rich crimson coloured disc.
G. sulphurea oculata	Pale sulphur & bright maroon disc florets.

Classification:

1. **Based on botany**: Cox and Klett (1984):
   a) Annuals derived from *G. pulchella* and *G. amblyodon*.
   b) Perennials derived from *G. aristata*.
2. **Based on flower type**
   a) Picta type- Flowers larger in size and singles e.g. Indian Chief Red, Picta Mixed.
   b) Lorenziana type- Flowers larger in size and doubles e.g. Sunshine, Gaity Double Mixed, Double Tetra, Fiesta.

Varieties:

- Mesa Yellow: 1st F_1 yellow-blooming cv. evolved from seed.
- Introductions: Burgundy, Dazzler, Double Tetra, Fiesta, Gaity Double, Golden Goblin, Lollypop Orange, Lollypop Yellow, Monarch Strain, Red Plume, Sundance, Sunshine Strain.
- Seedling selection: Bellini from cv. Burgundy.

Name	Breeding methods	Salient features
MPUA & T, Udaipur		
MPUAT GOPS 1	OP seedling selection	Yellow double type flowers; yellow hairs with convex disc; more branches (15-28); 4.6-6 cm flower dia.; 100-137 flowers/ plant.
MPUAT GOPS 3	OP seedling selection	Fully dark red double type; more branches (15-22); tooth on ray florets (4-5)
MPUAT GOPS 5	OP seedling selection	Red petals ray florets end yellow; more branches (15-22); flowering duration 90-95 days; flower wt. (1.6-1.7 g); no. of flowers (98-134).
MPUAT GOPS 7	OP seedling selection	Light yellow, semi-double type; flowering duration 90-95 days; flower dia. (5.4-5.8 g); number of flowers (98-130).

38.7 Zinnia

- Eulogized as 'Poor man's rose'.
- Dwarf, compact and double flowered are popular for container gardening.
- Multipurpose ornamental annual cultivated in summer and autumn season throughout world.
- Nematicide flower crop.
- 1st flower grown in space.
- It is water hardy and has long blooming period.
- Flowering season: March-November.
- Large flower head (capitula) 4-7 cm across and has 1-2 several whorls of ray florets on achenes of petals.
- Ray florets have showy legule and disc florets are small, tubular, perfect and less showy.
- Inflorescence: Terminal head/ capitulum on hollow peduncle.
- Achenes from ray florets are larger and shaped differently than disc florets.
- Flower doubleness decreases as day length become shorter.
- In *Z. elegans*, frequency of flower doubleness decreases when seeds are continuously taken by open pollination.
- Quantitative short day plant for flower initiation and development.
- Longer day lengthens time to flowering.
- During summer and fall season, buds initiated are of higher quality.
- Number of pollen grains/ tubular floret: 12000-18000.
- Sporophytic self incompatibility is prevalent.
- Male sterility has been reported and utilized in hybrid seed production.
- Male sterility results in floral abnormality.
- Apetalous male sterile flower is referred as 'feminas' since flower head is entirely pistillate.
- Due to sterility factor, F_1 hybrids have prolonged flowering season.
- Petals of ray and disc florets are degraded as thread like structure and stamens appear as yellow filaments lacking pollens.
- Disc florets are dichogamous.
- Each floret produces single seed (achene) and mostly awned.
- Within a capitulum, florets mature from outermost to innermost whorl.
- Capitula mature in 7-8 weeks from pollination.
- Major cause of low seed set in OP varieties: Poor pollination.
- In *Z. elegans*, gamma irradiation of seeds changes flower shapes i.e. flat ray florets changed to tubular ray florets.
- Capitula with more tubular florets produce more seeds.

- In double flowered capitula, low seed set is noticed.
- Seed viability: 30 months.
- F_1 hybrid seed yieldin *Z. violacea*: 170-335 kg/ha.
- Seed soaking in H_2SO_4 for 1 h or 1000 ppm GA_3 for 48 h improves seed germination.
- Seed treatment with thirum @ 0.3% or captan 0.5% gives freeness from*Alternaria* spp.
- *Z. violacea* seeds can tolerate to dessication like orthodox seeds.
- Air dried seeds can be stored in liquid nitrogen for longer period.

Species:

- Most species are obligate out breeders.
- *Z. peruviana* and *Z. violacea* are cross incompatible & produce non-viable seeds.

Species	Characteristics
Zinnia violacea (syn. *Z. elegans*)	Mexican spp; most widely cultivated, herbaceous annual; self compatible; flowers purple or lilac-pink, e.g. Border Beauty, Canary Bird, Crimson Red, Crimson Monarch, Dreamland, Flore Pleno (1st double flowered developed in 1871), Golden Ball, Red Sun, Short Stuff, Sinnita, Snow Ball, Sunrise, State Fair, Trail Blazer (1st male sterile hybrid), Youth and old age, State Fair (autotetraploid)
Z. pumila (syn. *Z. acerosa*)	Low growing perennial; commonly called as 'desert zinnia', 'wild zinnia', 'white zinnia' & 'spiny leaf zinnia'; requires low water & long blooming period e.g. Cut and Come Again.
Z. grandiflora	Polyploid (2n=4x=44); tall with branching stems. Leaves oppositely arranged, linear in shape, covered in short, rough hairs, flower head has 3-6 bright yellow ray florets; Rocky Mountain zinnia or Plains zinnia are grown as ornamental plants
Z. angustifolia (syn. *Z. linearis*)	Mexican spp; erect or low bushy plant habit; annual; single flowers (1.5-3.5 cm dia.) 2n=2x=22, 24, commonly known as 'narrow leaf zinnia' & multidisease resistant to PM, alternaria blight, bacterial leaf spot e.g. Crystal White, Oklahoma, Classic
Z. haageana (syn. *Z. mexicana*)	Commonly known as 'Persian Carpet' or 'Mexican zinnia'. Erect or decumbent herbaceous annual, flowers from July-November; resistant to disease e.g. Chippendale Daisy, Old Mexico (autotetraploid), Persian Carpet
Z. peruviana (syn. *Z. multiflora*, *Z. pauciflora*)	Erect herbaceous annual;self compatible; flowers from April-October in North America, yield prolific number of seeds
Z. acerosa var. *guanajuatensis*	Prostrate habit, wider inflorescence contains large number of flowers, achenes completely pappose.
Z. zamudiana (syn. *Z. juniperifolia*)	Prostrate habit, inflorescence with short peduncle, shorter & less intensely coloured ligules.
Z. marylandica	2n=4x=46: ornamental artificial hybrid between *Z. angustifolia* var. *angustifolia* (2n=22) x *Z. violacea* (2n=24). Multidisease resistant to PM, alternaria blight & bacterial blight e.g. Rose Pinwheel, Profusion Orange, Profusion White, Profusion Cherry.

Varieties:

- Many private seed companies introduced hybrid cultivars in mid 20th century.
- Liliput type (bright coloured, 1.5 inch dia.): Developed in France in 1880s.
- Double flowered F_1 hybrids: Sunrise, Gold Sun, Red Sun, Tart.
- Orange King: Interspecific hybrid between *Z.angustifolia* and *Z. elegans*.
- Giant Mammoth: Progenitor of large flowered *Z. violacea* available today.
- *Z. marylandica* cvs. Zahara Starlight Rose, Double Zahara Fire, Double Zahara Cherry.
- Cv. Thumbelina released in 1963 breeds true for dwarf habit.
- Popular F_1 hybrids: Peter Pan Pink (PM resistant), Peter Pan Plum, Fruit Bowl Novelty.
- Resistant to bacterial leaf & flower spot and flower blight: Classic, Chippendale Daisy, Old Mexico, Persian Carpet; Cut & Come Again, Tangerine & Ruffles series.
- Resistant to PM: Oklahoma, Profusion, Cristal White, Panorama Red, State Fair and Short Stuff Orange.

Disease and pests:

- Leaf curl virus: Most destructive to garden zinnia.Vector-White fly. 1st reported in India from Dehradoon. *Z. elegans* cv. Single Mixed resistant.
- Powdery mildew: Major problem in greenhouse & garden.
- Alternaria blight: Major problem in greenhouse & garden.
- Bacterial leaf spot: Major problem in greenhouse & garden.

Inheritance of characters:

- Degree of doubleness *I* determined by number & arrangement of ray florets.
- Tight linkage between shape of ray floret and flower doubleness.

Character	Number of genes	Inheritance pattern
Flower colour in *Z. violacea*	Digenic/Polygenic	-
Flower colour in *Z. angustifolia*	Monogenic	-
Pedicel length	-	Maternal & paternal additive
Resistance to PM resistance in leaf	2 independent genes	Resistance in ligule is independent that of
Leaf curl virus resistance	Digenic	-
Dwarf stature	Monogenic recessive	-
Plant height	Polygenic	-
Male sterility & flower doubleness	1 or 3 independent recessive genes	-
Apetalous character	Pleiotropic genes	-
Normal/ ligulate ray florets	Monogenic dominant (*LL*)	-
Shape of ray floret	Monogenic	• Cactus type homozygous recessive *iill*. • Daisy type flower *LLII* & *LiLl*
Crown size	-	Additive & non-additive

38.8 Calendula (Pot marigold)

- Latin word '*Calendae*' meaning 'little calendar' because mostly flowers bloom on first day of month.
- From ancient times Arabs, Egytians, Greeks, Hindus cultivated for beautification.
- Leaves, flowers and seed: Source of acid, oil, pigment and flavonoids.
- Romans cultivated calendula and made a dye as substitute for saffron dye.
- Dried petals used in potpourri and asa poultry feed.
- Flowers have spicy aroma.
- Diploid cvs. are best suited for garden purpose.
- Germplasm is maintained at University Agricultural Sciences and Veterinary Medicine, Romania.
- Uses: Cosmetics, human medicine, veterinary medicine, dietary composition and in salad.
- Seed rate for oil production: 10-20 kg/ha.
- Oil: as base oil in aromatherapy, cosmetic products, curing skin related problems like rashes, acne, eczema and burning.
- Yellow dye is used for colouring fabrics and flavouring food.
- Petals and pollens contain carotenoids.
- Major carotenoid pigments: Flavoxanthin, Auroxanthin.
- β-carotene content: 2.3-8.0 mg/g (fresh wt).
- Seed contain 18-22% oil of which 55-60% calendic acid.
- Long day plant and low photoperiodic cycle (6.5 h) is essential for flowering.
- Capitulum is surrounded by two rows of hairy bracts.
- Disc florets (called petals) are tubular, pseudohermaphrodite and orange coloured.
- Ray florets: Tridentate, sterile, and form fruits.
- Fruit type: Thorny, heterocarp achene, sickle shaped or curved and ringed.
- Seed: Crescent, horse shoe shaped with rough surface.
- Mode of propagation: Seed, cuttings.
- Flowering season: July- September.
- LD_{50} dose for α irradiation: 5 Krad.
- NAA spray @ 10 and 100 ppm 6 hours after pollination results in high seed bearing heads (90-95%) and more number of seeds/ head.
- Seed production: Seed rate 4 kg/ha and high dose of N 40 kg/ha increases seed yield.
- Seed treatment: 200 ppm Iprodione increases seed emergence.
- Seeds on paper soaked in 0.2% KNO_3 after 14 h gives 74.5% germination.

- Seed yield: 400-500 kg/ha.
- Aphid (*Aphis fabae*): Vector for viral disease.

Species:

- *Calendula officinalis*: (2n=32) cultivated for yellow dye extracted from petals.
- C. *agyptiaca*: Only diploid spp. (2n=14) found in Mediterranean region.
- *C. arvensis*: Tetraploid (2n=4x=28): Lead in southern Europe.
- *C. suffrutocisa*: (2n=28) cultivated for yellow dye.
- Germplasm centre: University of Agricultural Science and Veterinary medicine, Romania.

Varieties:

- Sterility barriers exists between inter and intraspecific crosses.
- Major breeding method: Selection and heterosis.
- Basis of selection method: Petal colour; single /double type ligulate flowers for medicinal purpose.
- Hybridization is successful in phylogenetically closed parental genotype.
- Hybridization in genetically diverse parents results in sterility and low seed production.
- Costa: Cultivated for yellow dye and edible petals added to salads.
- Triploid cultivars are best suited for garden purpose.
- *C. officinalis* cvs: Orange King, Campfire, Golden Emperor, Art Shade, Pacific Beauty, Apricot Beauty, Orange Coronet, Flame Beauty, Lemin Beauty, Double Dwarf Fiesta, Bon Bon Mix, Bon Bon Orange.
- Intervarietal hybrids: Tetrana from Romania; Diana and Natali from Maldive.
- Interspecific hybrids: Suggested between *C. officinalis* x *C. arvensis* for medicinal purpose.

Inherirtance of characters:

- Number of leaves on main branches: Additive.
- Heterosis is controlled by partial dominance.
- +ve correlation: Seed weight with plant emergence, number of branches, plant height, number of flowers/ plant.
- -ve correlation: Number of petals with weight and seed germination, plant height, number of flowers/ plant, aphid tolerance.

38.9 Garden cosmos

- Eulogized as 'Mexican aster'.
- Late flowering, rainy season annual.

- Flower extract: Used as natural dye, nematicide, anti-malerial, anti-oxidative, anti-genotoxic agent.
- Plants tolerate dry season and infertile soils.
- Early varieties are insensitive to photoperiod.
- Late varieties are sensitive to short days.
- Species: *C. sulphureus* (sulphur cosmos), *C. bipinnatus* (garden cosmos), *C. atrosanguineus* (chocolate cosmos) and *C. diversifolius* (wild).
- In a flower head, ray florets are sterile and all inconspicuous disc florets are hermaphrodite or bisexual.
- In single type, flower head consist of 8 well developed coloured ray florets and disc florets are short, tubular and bright yellow coloured.
- In double type, disc florets are more tubular in length (quilled) or small ray like development and yield less number of seeds. In ordinary double cosmos, disc florets are changed to ligulate.
- In abnormal or apetalous flower, no tubular ray florets and capitulum comprises of disc florets and produce seeds.
- Flower colour is very variable within different species.
- Pollination agent: Insects.
- Flower with long style is rarely found and is genetic abnormality.
- Syngenesious anthers are imperfect, contain less pollen and do not protrude above disc florets.
- Blooms 40-60 days after transplanting.
- Anthesis period: Centripetal and require 7 days for complete.
- Type of SI: Hetermorphic and homomorphic.
- Embryo rescue: Attempted in *C. bippinatus* x *C. sulphureus* cross.
- Ovary culture: Attempted in *C. atrosanguineus* (2n=48) x *C. sulphureus* (2n=24) cross.
- Hybrid nature of above cross is confirmed by DNA fingerprinting and flow cytometry analysis.
- Seed production: No emaculation of flower is required due to self sterility.
- Seed set occurs within 7-10 days after pollination.
- Seedlings are transplanted in July-August.
- Self fertility increases towards end of growing period and pseudo-self fertility is not observed.
- Seed harvesting: *C. sulphureus* (mid-Sept.-Mid Oct.), *C. bipinnatus* (end of December).
- Single flower types are used as pollen parent to get seeds from double flowered because double flowers are male sterile.

- Compatible pollination produces 20-30 seeds/ head.
- Seed yield: 200-350 kg/ha.
- Polyploidy breeding: Potent method of crop improvement.
- Mutation breeding: Use of X-rays produce more mutants than gamma rays.
- Tubular-petaled and Vestigial-petaled type are different from Non-petaled type-modifier genes.

Different flower types:

1. Single type (S-type): Flower head has 8 well developed ray florets and disc florets are in short tubular form.
2. Malform-petaled type (M-type):
   a) Non-petaled type (Np-type): Flower head of this type develops no ray florets, while disc florets remain short.
   b) Vestigial-petaled type (Vt-type): Short vestigial ray florets more or less developed, a transitionary type between Np-type and Mt-type.
   c) Tubular-petaled type (Mt-type): Ray florets are tubular in form. Top of each tubular ray splits and becomes more or less open, the base remains tubular. The flower heads are hardly distinguishable from Ms-type.
   d) Sub-petaled type (Ms-type): Usually found in F_1 generation of crosses between single type and Np-type.
3. Double flowered type (D-type): Double strain has a higher commercial value. Corolla tube of the disc florets are strongly tubular (quilled). Yield less number of seeds.
   a) Pompon-type (Dp-type): Degree of doubling varies and pompon type is observed.
4. Malform-double mixed type (MD-type): Segregation of 'double' type results into miscellaneous types with combination of disc development and malformation of rays.

Varieties:

- *C. atrosanguineus* cv: New Choco is OP selection. It is tolerant to high temperatures and powdery mildew.
- Alipore Beauty: Indian bred.
- *C. sulphureus*: Fiesta, Mandarin, Orange Flare, Orange Ruffle
- *C. bipinnatus*: Gloria, Dazzler, Gloria, Pink Sensation, Purity Radiance, Rubenza, Single Cimson, Versailles.

Inheritance of characters:

Character	Number of genes	Gene action
Flower pattern, flower form, pollen colour	Digenic	-
Flower size	Monogenic	Large dominant over small
Flower type	Monogenic	Single domiant over non-petalled type;Single incompletely dominant over Sub-petaled type
Flower colour	Digenic	Coloured (*C-c*, *CC*, *Cc*) dominat over white (*cc*);
	Monogenic	Crimson dominant over pink
White streaks on flower	-	Change from dominant to recessive character
Apetalody of flowers	Monogenic	Normal dominant to apetalous condition
Double capitulum	Monogenic	Doubleness dominant to singleness
Long style	Monogenic	Long style recessive to normal

39. BALSAMINACEAE

39.1 Balsam

- Eulogized as 'Bizzy-Lizzy or Patience plant or Zanzibar balsam or or Sultana' in Europe and 'Jewel/ snap weed or touch-me-not and garden or rose balsam' in India.
- Grown as bedding plant, hanging basket.
- Besides marigold, balsam flowers are used in poultry industry.
- Important groups in horticulture industry: *Impatiens wallerana* (Java *Impatiens*), and *I. hawkeri* (New Guinea *Impatiens*).
- Qualitative short day plant.
- Inflorescence: Axillary cyme.
- Flowers type: Hermaphrodie, zygomorphic, cleistogamous, protandrous & chasmogamous.
- Type of fruit: Capsule.
- Type of male sterility: CMS.
- Self pollination occurs in some species including *I. wallerana*.
- Pollination agents: Bees, beetles, birds, moths, and butterflies.
- Flowering months: July-November.
- Anthesis time: 2-3 AM.
- Anther dehiscence occurs one day before anthesis.
- Type of dichogamy: Protandry.
- Outcrossing rate in the strongly protandrous chasmogamous flowers of *I. capensis*: 0.29 to 0.71%.
- Flower pigments: Glycosides of 3 anthocyanidins i.e. pelargonidin, peonidin and malvidin.

- Heterosis was observed for flowers/ plant, branches per plant, plant height, flower size and petals/ flower.
- Treatment for seed germination: H_2SO_4 for 60 sec.
- Seed require red light for good germination.
- Seed matures in 14-21 days.
- Seed yield: 250-300 kg/ha.
- Colchicine dose for induction of polyploidy: 0.2-2 % aqueous solution for 6 hours.
- Embryo rescue is used in crosses of *I. wallerana* x *I. auricoma* and *I. nianniamensis* x *I. wallerana*.
- Hairy root culture was developed for 1st time in *I.hawkerii*.

Species:

- In India, *Impatiens* species occurs in Western Himalayas, N-E hilly regions, and Western Ghats.
- About 230 species were known from Arunachal Pradesh.

Species	Common name	Characteristics
I. wallerana (syn. *I. sultanii, I. holstii*)	Garden balsam or Busy Lizzie or Patience plant or Patient lucy	Perennial tender succulent herb; grows < 3 feet height with foliage as rosette towards the top of stem; leaves alternate, dense towards tip, lanceolate ovate to elliptic; flowers red with 5 petals; suitable for cottage gardens.
I. hawkeri	New Guinea impatiens	One of the sources for the popular New Guinea hybrids.
I. balsamina	Rose balsam or Bush balsam or Gul mehndi	Annual; 20 to 75 cm tall, thick & soft stem, leaves spirally-arranged, with deeply toothed margin. Flowers red, pink, purple, or white & 2.5-5 cm diameter.
I. glandulifera	Himalayan balsam or Indian balsam	1-2 m tall, soft green or red-tinged stem; lanceolate leaves, crushed foliage has a strong musty smell. Flowers pink, with a hooded shape.
I. balfourii	Kashmir balsam	Annual, 15 to 120 cm tall, stem glabrous, reddish, lined, very branched, leaves alternately arranged, oval to lance-shaped.
I. linearifolia hybrida	-	Bushy; leaves lanceolate, variegated green & yellow; flowers carmine red.
I. walongensis	-	Grows upto 1 m; light pink flowers; species from Arunachal Pradesh.
I. arunachalensis	-	Purple flowers and pink throat; critically endangered.
I. zironiana	-	Pale yellow flowers
I. paramjitiana, I. rugosipetala, I. tatoensis, I. pathakiana, I. rugosipetala	-	Found in Arunachal Pradesh.
I. latifolia	Indian angel balsam	Perennial; grows upto 1.5 ft; flowers borne in 2-3 flowered clusters

Varieties:

- Breeding in *Impatiens* began in late 1940s in Costa Rica.
- Claude Hope: Widely regarded as father of modern *Impatiens*.
- 1st hybrid 'Pixie White' was introduced in 1958 by Ball Seed Company followed by 'Jewel' series in 1961.
- F_1 hybrid *Impatiens* of merit is 'Imp' followed by 'Shade Glow' series by Joseph Harris Company.
- In 1968, Claude introduced single flowered seed propagated 'Elfin' series.
- 'Fantasia', 'Futura' and 'Shady Lady' series are popular among growers.
- 'Carpet' and 'Red Ripple' are promising cultivars of *I. wallerana*.
- *I. wallerana* & *I. usambarensis* are known to have naturally hybridized in the wild.
- Popular hybrids: Double Camellia Flowered, Royal Balsam, Rose Flowered, Tall Double, Dwarf Bush Flowered and Tom Thumb.
- New Guinea Impatiens cvs.: Arctic Star, Betsy Ross, Bid Top, Bozo, Charmer, Cotton Candy, Harlequin, Lafayette, Liberty, Lollipop, Morning Star, Orange Crush, Orange Satin, Painted Lady, Paul Revere, Pink Eyes, Preamble, Star Fire, Stop Light, Sweet Sue.
- Circus series: Calliope, Canon Ball, Fortune Teller Chariot, Juggler, Magician, Ring Master, Roustabout, Show Boat, Trapeze, Carnival, Headliner, Majorettee, Roller Coaster, Ring Master Improved and Sky Rocket.
- Seed propagated single flowered F_1 hybrids: Accent, Blitz 2000, Cajun, Candy, Carnival, Dazzler, Expo, Impact, Infinity, Impulse, Minette, Tempo and Super Elfin series.
- Seed propagated double flowered F_1 hybrids: Rosette, Confection series.
- Vegetatively propagated (cutting) double flowered F_1 hybrids: Cameo, Double Diamond, Double-Up, Fiesta series, Fiesta Ole's, Golden, Ice series, Rose Bud and Tioga.

F_1 hybrid	Parents	Characters
Isopo	No. 85/12/2 x Nina	Compact growth; leaves dark green with red underside; flowers red purple with overlapping petals & dia. of 50 mm.
Patula	No. 85-58-03 x Aurore	Compact growth habit; leaves dark green; flowers red purple & mean dia. 52 mm.
Senia	Breeder selections	Plants small, ovate leaves, dark green; flowers simple & red.
Celsia	Caligo and a breeder selection	Plant medium sized; dark green elliptic leaves, serrated margin; flowers simple & red purple with a darker red purple eye zone.
Dunya	Breeder selections	Plant small to medium sized; leaves dark green; flowers simple & red purple.
Anaea	Breeder selections	Plant small with lanceolate to elliptic leaves; dark green above & light green below, simple; flowers red
Lysandra	No. 85-17-8 x Thecla	Plant medium height; leaves dark green with red underside; flowers red purple & dia. 57 mm.

Interspecific hybridization:

Crosses	Result (s)
I. wallerana x *I. auricoma*	Cultured ovules of 6-11 days growth had higher rates of survival than those explanted before 6th day post-pollination. All resulting hybrids were sterile & shared morphological characters of both parents.
I. auricoma x *I. wallerana*	
I. wallerana x *I. epiphytica*	
I. wallerana x *I. nimanimaensis*	
I. wallerana x *I. hawkeri* N463, N47, N514, N568 (all New Guinea cultivars)	
New Guinea spp. x Indonesian spp.	Sterile hybrids

Inheritance of characters:

- Growth habit, seed germination, foliage colour, bicolour flower patterns including star and picottee patterns, thrips resistance, are polygenic.

Character	Inheritance pattern	Remarks
Plant height	Additive in nature and absence of epistasis	Association of excess of recessive genes for all characters
Branches/ plant	Additive and absence of epistasis	
Flowers/ plant	Complementary epistasis	
Petals/ flower	Additive and absence of epistasis	
Flower size	Additive and absence of epistasis	

Genetics of flower colour:

Gene symbol	Character	Inheritance pattern
W,ww	Non-cream vs. cream	(W) Dominant
L,l	Nearly-white lavender vs. white	No dominance
H,h	Hermosa vs. white	(H) partial dominant
P	Pink	-
P^g, $P^{g'}$, $P^{g''}$ *vs P*	Intensity of nearly white pink on petals and of pink on spur	-
p, P^g, $P^{g'}$, $P^{g''}$	Green lower stem	-
P^r, $P^{r'}$, $P^{r''}$	Pink colour on petals and spurs, red on stems with p and P^gseries	-
LH	Hermosa lavender	-
HP^g, $HP^{g'}$ or $HP^{g''}$	Rose	-
LP^g, $LP^{g'}$, $LP^{g''}$	Lavender	-
LHP^g, $LHP^{g'}$	Rose-lavender	-
HP^r, $HP^{r'}$, $HP^{r''}$	Red-stemmed plants	-
LP^r, $LP^{r'}$, $LP^{r''}$	Purple	-
LHP'	Magenta	-
W,L,H and *P*	-	Assort independently
Sc	-	Not linked with L nor with W locus
sc	Affects colour of red and magenta and carried by hermosa	Recessive gene

Pest and diseases:

- Thrips (*Frankliniella occidentalis*):
- Two spotted spider mite (*Tetranychus urticae*):
- Impatiens Necrotic Spot Virus (INSV):
- Tomato Spotted Wilt Virus (TSWV):
- Foliar blight (*Pseudomonas syringae*):
- Damping off (*Pythium* and *Rhizoctonia*):

40. CARYOPHYLLACEAE (PINK FAMILY)

40.1 Carnation

- Eulogized as 'Divine flower or Clove pink or Garden pink'.
- Word 'Carnation' is derived from Greek word '*Coronation*' because of its use as decorating the crowns of Greek athletes during ancient times.
- Bogota region of Columbia is ideal for cultivation of carnation.
- An altitude of 2800 m near Equator is near ideal for cultivation.
- Carnation state in India: Himachal Pradesh.
- Uses: Cut flower, bedding, pots, borders, edging, rock garden purpose.
- 1st introduced in India around 1980 in Nasik (Maharashtra).
- Mr. Firoz Masani of Nashik has made notable contribution in carnation.
- 'FEROZE' is the 1st Indian company to grow carnations to International standards and to be registered at VBA, The Netherlands.
- National Repository for Carnation germplasm: DrYSPUH&F, Solan.
- Pioneer of carnation breeding: Montague Allwood.
- Popular carnation type in India: Clove scented marguerite carnation.
- Volatile oil is used only in sophisticated perfumes(hair oils, talcum powder & soaps).
- Fragrance: Eugenol and benzonic acid derivatives.
- Light coloured flowers are used for perfume production in France & Holland.
- Facultative and qualitative long day (i.e. form flowers during long days) and C_4 plant.
- Photoperiod is important factor than light intensity in flowering.
- Photoperiod influences lateral shoot development and flowering.
- Optimum light intensity: 21.5 Klux (2,000 foot candle) upto 50,000 lux.
- Light for 16 hours. are best for flower size and overall quality.
- Flower quality can be improved by providing long days only for short period of 6-7 weeks at 6-7 pairs of leaves.
- Shoots are sensitive to day length at 6-7 leaf pairs.

- Optimum temperature for growth in standard carnation: 28^{0}C (day) and 16-18^{0}C (night).
- High day and night temperature during flowering results in abnormal flower opening and calyx splitting.
- Ideal soil pH range: 5.5 to 6.5.
- Optimum E.C. during vegetative stage: 1.2 mS/cm and during generative stage 1.5 to 1.7 mS/cm.
- Optimum soil moisture is 300-500 cm tension.
- Optimum R.H. for growth: 80-85% (initial stage); 60-65% (full growth).
- Optimum CO_2 concentration: 800-1000 ppm.
- More CO_2 injection in greenhouse results in increase in yield (38%), weight of flower and stem strength.
- Soil sterilization is indispensable to check fusarium and nematodes (with methyl bromide).
- Methods of soil sterilization:
  - Steam: Not feasible under Indian conditions.
  - Sun: Cover soil with plastic for 6-8 weeks to kill fungi.
  - Chemicals: H_2O_2 @ 8.55 lit in 5700 lit of water; formalin @ 7.5-10 lit/ 100 sq.m; basamid (Dazomet) @ 30-40 g/m^2.
- Methyl bromide should not be used as soil sterilant.
- Rooting hormone for cuttings: NAA @ 500 ppm (quick dip method).
- Night temperature for rooting of cutting: 15-16^{0}C.
- Commercial method of production: Protray/ container system of planting.
- Terminal cuttings can be stored at 1-3^{0}C before root inition.
- Planting distance: 20 cm x 20 cm (Standard) and 30 cm x 30 cm (Spray).
- Support system: Supported with 4-5 layers of support material (metal wire). Botom net (7.5 x7.5 cm); one net of 10 x 10 cm; two nets of 12.5 x 12.5 cm.
- Number of plants/ sq.m.: 20
- Over head sprinkler irrigation during first 3 weeks after planting.
- Drip irrigation (3 tubes/ bed) and at full growth of crop, apply 6-7 lit. of water/ sq.m/ day.
- Type of inflorescence: Spike.
- Number of stamens: 6-10.
- Days for bud formation: 168.
- Days from bud to full development of flower: 16.
- Anthesis time: 10 AM to 2 PM.
- Optimum temperature for pollen production in greenhouse: 23^{0}C.

- Stigma receptivity: 48-72 h after anthesis.
- Fruit set takes place 11 days after anthesis.
- Days require for capsule maturity: 30-60.
- Seeds germinate in dark in 7-10 days at 21^{0}C.
- Number of seeds/ ovary: 6-7.
- Number of seeds/ capsule: 52 (artificial pollination), 42 (selfing).
- Petal removal before pollination give higher seed set and seed number.
- Plant density of 36 plants /sq.m gives highest seed set.
- Pollen viability: 96.26% (fresh), 32% (after 10 days storage at 20-25^{0}C).
- Seed germinate in dark.
- Seed yield increase by application of 10 and 100 ppm GA_3 and 1 ppm NAA.
- Fruit: Tubular capsule.
- Delayed self fertilization is noticed.
- Isolation distance for multiplication of foundation and certified seeds: 600, 300 m, respectively.
- Society of American Florist does not include 'White' grade of carnation.
- Adequate level of potassium in soil: Positive correlation with fusarium wilt resistance.
- Fertigation: From 4th week onwards, start fertigation, since roots are unable to absorb nutrients upto 3 weeks of planting.
- Pinching: Important cultural operation in production of top quality flowers.
- Disbudding: Removal undesirable immature flower buds.
- Harvesting stage: Paint brush (1.25-2.5 cm) or 2-3 petals unfurl.
- Yield: 200 flowers/ sq.m. (from 20 plants).
- Total crop duration: 24 months.
- Preconditioning of cut flower in $AgNO_3$ or Silver Thiosulphate (STS) solution is important to avoid ethylene injury and prolong vase life.
- Cold storage temperature: 5-8^{0}C.
- Tinting: Colouring of white carnation.
- Vase life is short about 5-7 days in normal sim type cultivars.
- Intervarietal grafting is effective when grafted on resistant rootstock viz. Arancio25D, Heidi, May Britt and Excuisite minimizes problems caused by fusarium in problematic soils.

Species:

- *Dianthus caryophyllus*: Greenhouse carnation. Ancestor of border carnation.
- *D. knappi* (2n=30): Source for yellow carnation.

- *D. chinensis* (syn. Indian/Rainbow/ Japanese pink): Tetraploid (2n=4x=60).
- *D. gratianoplitanus*: Hexaploid (2n=90). Require near obligate vernalization (0^0C for >4 weeks).
- *D. barbatus* (syn. Sweet William): Classified as 'Pinks' has cluster of flowers.
- *D. plumarius* (2n=90): Source for white carnation.
- *D. nobilis*: Not cultivated commercially.
- *D. superbus* and *D. arenarius*: Opens at night.
- D. Allwoodii (Hybrid Pink): Hexaploid (2n=6x=90).
- *D. sylvestris* (Woodland Pink): Gynomono/ gynodioecious spp.
- *D. armeria, D. barbatus, D. deltoids, D. sylvestris*: Diurnal spp.
- Species associated with development of modern carnation: *D. barbatus, D. chinensis, D. knappii.*
- Gynodiocy reported in *D. barbatus, D.plumaris, D. superbus, D. acicularis.*
- *D. laucheanus* (*D. barbatus* x *D. deltoides*):

Types:

- Standards or Sim: Have single large flower on stem.
- Sprays (miniature): Bear large number of small flowers.
- Midis (chinensii): Have small flowers, stem shorter, multiple side branches.
- Multiflora: Numerous small flowers.

Perpetual/ Greenhouse/ Perennial/florist carnation	**Annual/ Marguerite/ Chabaud**	**Malmaison/ Tree carnation**	**Border/ Picotee**	**Miniature**
D. caryophyllus x *D. chinensis*	*D. chinensis* x *D. caryophyllus*	Seedling of perpetual carnation	-	*D. chinensis, D. pencicii* and *D. pontederae*
Propagate by terminal cuttings	Seed propagated & sown in winter	-	Seed propagation	-
Grown on large scale	Bush type	-	Massive habit	-
Petaloid stamens	Fused petals	Cut flower type	Symmetrical flower	Pot culture
-	Low shelf life	Fragrant flower	-	-

- **Based on number of petals**:
  - Single type: Upto 5 petals.
  - Semi-double type: 30-60 petals.
  - Double/ superdouble/ bull head type: 100-150 petals.

Pigments:

i) Acyanic group: White, yellow.
ii) Cyanic group: Red, Salmon, Lavender, Pink.
iii) Transition group: Crimson.

Colour	Standards	Sprays
Cherry	Pirandello, Dona Brecas, Laurella, Killer	Cherry Bag, Kortina Chery, Ciska, Ondelia
Orange	Amstel, Orange Pinto Solar, Orange Isac	Niky, Sintonia, Target, Macarena
Pink	Bologna, Petra, Pink Diamante	Happiness, Rossini, Fantasia
Purple	Lavender Lace	Purple Chopin, Roxette
Red	Desio, Master, Impala, Nelson, Dakar	Alister, Darling, Red Arrow, Rony Arony
White	Sansare, White Giant, Bogota, Rivera	Virgo, Close Up, West Crystal
Yellow	Esty, Pinto, Tahiti	Guernsey Yellow, Castillo, Koreno
Variegated: Stripped/fancy		
Red	Minerva, Nicol, Roderic	Challenger
Orange	Orange Prestige, Ivonne Orange	Sintonia, Fuego
White	Forever, Olympus, Tropea, Aledo, Atletico, Giamaica	Saffora, Regis, Manatovani
Yellow	Super Star, Pontiac, Michelle	Naomi, Picaro, Jacobine

Pinching:

- Pinching (6-8 leaf pair stage) and disbudding (removal of visible 5-10 mm undesirable buds) are regular practices.
- Pinching-
  i) Single pinching: below 6th node; to get early and single peak crop.
  ii) Pinch and half: steady production without gap
  iii) Double pinching: to delay flowering period.
- Standard or Sim carnation: Commercial importance and need regular pinching.
- Disbudding is not followed in spray or miniature type carnation.
- Carnation produce cut blooms after 16-20 weeks.

Varieties:

- All the present cultivars with red flowers are regenerated from callus of 'White Sim' cultivar.
- Introduction: Major crop improvement method.
- Variety responsible for major breakthrough in carnation industry: William Sim. It is produced in 1938 in USA
- Thomas Fairchild (1717) bred 1st interspecific hybrid i.e. Mule Pink, crossing 'Sweet William x Florist's carnation. It is sterile with double flowers.
- Most of the present day cultivars are bud sports of 'William Sim' and 'Sydney Little Field'.

- Perpetual flowering carnations developed in France is intervarietal hybrid between cv. Olillesde Mahon x Bisbon.
- F_1 Britannia (scarlet flowers) is cross between Perpetual type x Border carnation.
- 1st introduced 'William Sim' cultivars were of red/ scarlet coloured.
- 1st cultivar : Souvenir de La Malmaison in 1857.
- Arka Tejas (Standard type): Interspecific hybrid (*D. caryophyllus* x *D. chinensis*).
- Arka Flame (spray type): *In vitro* mutant of cv. Tempo. Tolerant to fusarium wilt & root knot nematodes.
- Tetraploid cultivars: Sarafi and Mabdavian.
- 1st spray type: Exquisite.
- F_1 Knight miniature series by Goldsmith Seeds Co. California bears 15-20 flowers/ stem.
- Longest shelf life cv.: Roland.
- Tangerine Sim: Not tolerant to fusarium wilt.
- Miniature cvs.: Tony Red, White Elegance, Salmony, Goldline, Silvery Pink, Ronald, Lima, White Lily, Salmony Exquisite.
- Pot culture: Maldives, Cerratop, Charmtop, White Sunny, Purple Rain.
- Micro-carnation developed by 'Van Staaveren' from Holland, produce compact growth and button-like flowers in large numbers (about 1,000/m^2).
- Pico: Interspecific hybrid (*D.chinensis* x *D. caryophyllus*) released by IHPB, Wageningen is suitable for pot culture.
- Sweet Wivelsfield (*D. Allwoodii* x *D. barbatus*).
- Delight (Sweet Wivelsfield x *D. neglectus* var. roysii).
- Royal carnation is cross of Malmaison x Perpetual type.
- Induced mutants: Enzett Barther Fruhling (EMS), Enzett Folklore, Dione; Pink Sim, White Sim, William Sim (X-rays).
- Moon Dust: 1st GM floriculture crop having violet blue colour. Other cultivars are Moon Shadow, Moon Vista, Moon Shade, Moon Lite and Moon Aqua. They express *F3'5'H* gene from pansy and petunia *DFR*-A gene.All have stable blue colour.

Grading system:

Grade		Minimum flower dia. (mm)	Minimum stem length (cm)
Blue (Fancy)	Tight	50	55
	Fairly tight	62	
	Open	75	
Red (Standard)	Tight	44	43
	Fairly tight	56	
	Open	69	
Green (Short)	Tight	None	30
	Fairly tight	None	

Pests, diseases and disorders:

- Red spider mite is serious during hot months & dry period.
- Flower bud rot is a botrytis disease.
- Vascular wilt is responsible for rapid decline of Nizza carnation.
- Calyx splitting: Genetic factor, more in long days than in short days.

Name	Scientific name	Resistant species & cultivars
Fusarium wilt	*F. oxysporum* f.sp. *dianthii*	*D. knappii, D. cruentus, D. capitatus*, Arbel, Arthur Sim, Novada, Revada, Scarlet, Vanya
Bacterial wilt	*Pseudomonas caryophylii*	*D. capitatus, D. henteri*, Carnation Nou No.1 (Super Gold x *D. capitatus*)
Vascular wilt	*Phialophora cinerescens*	Chabaud, Grenadins, Wener
Rust	*Uromyces caryophyllinus*	Arthur Sim, Minirosa and Rosa
Stem rot	*Rhizoctonia*	Vermillion, William Sim
Gray mold	*Botrytis cinerea*	-
Red spider mite	*Tetranychus urticae*	-

Inheritance of characters:

- Bacterial wilt resistance is linked with undesirable flower quality.
- Presence of red in yellow flowered type is associated with presence of perfect sexual organs.

Character	Number of genes	Inheritance pattern
Dwarfing, excessive branching; premature flowering	Polygenic	Additive
Flower type	Monogenic	Doubleness dominant to singleness
No. of petals	Polygenic	Or due to pleiotropic effect of mutant gene
Flower doubleness	Monogenic	Bull head incompletely dominant to single
Flower colour	-	White is dominant over yellow or red where red is a latent character * Pink, red and crimson dominant over salmon; * Red is recessive to salmon; * Deep pink dominant to light pink Recessive gene control white, variegation and self (clear) colours
Vase life	Polygenic	Additive gene action
Vascular wilt resistance	Digenic	Additive
Fusarium wilt resistance	Digenic	Additive

40.2 Gypsophila

- Eulogized as 'Baby's breath'.
- Generic word is derived from Greek word 'gypsos' meaning gypsum and 'philos' meaning friendship, is due to its ability to grow in calcareous soils.

- Long day plant which requires night temperature > 11^{0}C.
- Excellent for mixed borders, sry-stone wall or rock gardens and prefer alkaline soil.
- Used as filler material in interior decoration, flower arrangement and bouquets.
- Major cut flower in Korea.
- Cut flower of gypsophila is exported from Zimbabwe to the Netherlands.
- Roots of *G. paniculata* and *G. arrostii* (soap root) are known as saponin drugs and used as detergents and expectorants.
- Opening room: Facility having highly controlled conditions of temperature, light and humidity.
- Flowers to be kept in 'opening room' are harvested at 20-30% flower opening stage.
- Propagation method: Seed, stem cutting.
- Weeks taken for seed germination: 11 weeks.
- MH at 1000 ppm inhibited growth and flowering.

Species:

Name	Features
Gypsophila paniculata	Perennial & cut flower; tap rooted; branched; leaves glaucous & hairless; flowers loose and borne on panicles; used for dry flower arrangement
G. elegans	Annual & cut flower; branching; leaves 2-4 cm long; flowers 4 petalled, star-shaped, 1 cm across
G. repens	Alpine gypsophila; perennial and trailing type; plant height 20-50 cm; leaves sickle shaped; flowers star shaped; suitable for rockeries and herbaceous borders
G. acutifolia	Perennial, many branched stems, panicles spreading; flowers 2-5 cm across
G. aretioides	Plants dense, hardy, cushion-forming, evergreen; leaves tiny, oblong; flowers small, usually solitary, star-shaped white
G. cerastioides	Native to Himalayas. Plants mat-forming, perennial; leaves 6-10 mm long, spoon-shaped; flower on loose panicles, 1.5 cm across, trumpet shaped, white coloured, veined and faintly tinged pink
G. tekyra	Source of production of saponin (43.9-52.2%)
G. muralis	Annual; much branched; leaves minute, linear bright green; flowers small but very numerous, flesh pink; useful for dry walls

Varieties:

- *G. elegans*: Bright Rose, Carminea, Covent Garden, Giant White, Red Cloud, Rosea.
- *G. paniculata*: Bristol Fairy, Compacta Plena, Flamingo.
- *G. repens*: Dorothy Teacher, Fratensis, Floriana Mist, Floriana Cascade.

41. CRUCIFERAE

41.1 Stock

- Eulogized as 'Gilly flower'.
- Annual or biennial plant produce flowers in terminal clusters and used as cut flower.
- Potential source of 3-linolenic acid.

- Trisomics carry '*Ss*' genes.
- Trisomic: Production of 100% double flowers suggested by Frost (1928).
- Propagation method: Seed.
- Optimum germination for seed germination: 18-24^{0}C.
- Sowing time: September-October (plains) and February-March (hills).
- Stage of transplanting: 2-3 cm tall or 3-4 leaves.
- Planting distance: 20 cm x 15 cm.
- Potential source of 3-linolenic acid which is used for dietary supplements and industrial uses.
- Under incandescent and sodium lamps, plants are taller.
- Late flowering cvs. initiated flowers only at 12^{0}C, mid-season at 12^0 and 17^{0}C and early cvs. formed flowers at all temperatures.
- Flowering is also influenced by duration of low temperature i.e. early cvs. require less days than late ones.
- Abnormal flowers developed if the plants were transferred to high temperature before first flower primordium was visible microscopically.
- GA_3 at 100 ppm increased overall growth, improved plant appearance, stem thickness and more compactness.
- Harvesting stage: One half or two third of florets opened or with minimum 6 open flowers.
- Seed yield: 750 kg/ ha.
- Paclobutrazol at 0.5 mg/pot produced marketably pot plants.

Species:

- Genus *Matthiola*, is named after P.A. Matthioli, an Italian physician and writer on plants.
- *Matthiola incana*: Annual as well as biennial, up to 80 cm height; flowers 2.5 cm across, mauve, purple, violet, pink and white coloured; large number of cvs. were developed from crosses between *M. incana* x *M. sinuata*.
- *M. sinuata*: Plant erect, branched; leaves oblong, hairy; stigma compressed, velvety.
- *M. fruticulosa*: Dwarf, tufted; woody base up to 60 cm height; leaves simple or pinnatifid; flowers yellow to purplish violet.
- *M. longipetala* ssp. *bicornis*: (syn. *M. bicornis*): Annual; night scented; erect to spreading, single stem or branched; flowers 2 cm across, pink, mauve and purple coloured.
- *M. odoratissima*: Evergreen, sub-shrubby, up to 30-60 cm; leaves hairy; flowers creamy white; sweet scented.
- *M. tricuspidata*: Resistant to bacterial blight.
- *M. tristis*: Perennial, woody base; leaves linear, entire or toothed, hairy; flowers creamy white.

Varieties:

- Identification of flower is based on root system i.e. single (tap root, dark green leaves), double (fibrous root, pale green leaves).
- Single flowers have 4 petals, 4 stamens and a pistil having 30-60 ovules.
- Double flowers have 40-70 petals and male and female sterile.
- An algorithm based on the fuzzy evaluation theory was developed to discriminate double and single flowering stock in seedling stage.
- Cindrella series: Plants 20-25 cm tall, racemes 15 cm long, flowers double, dark, blue-purple, red, rose-pink, silvery blue coloured.
- Mammoth Column series: Plants 75 cm tall, racemes 30 cm long, flowers double, scarlet-red, rose-pink, lavender-blue, white and creamy yellow coloured.
- Midget series: Plants 75 cm tall, racemes 30 cm long, flowers double, white, pink, carmine-red and light to dark blue coloured.
- Ten Week Mixed: Dwarf, 30 cm height, bushy, racemes 15 cm long, flowers double, crimson, pink, lavender-pink, purple and white coloured.
- Trisomic variety: (2n=14+1): Snow Flake. It has slender leaves with an extra segment of chromosome.

Inheritance of characters:

Character	Number of genes	Inheritance pattern
Plant height	Monogenic	Tall dominant to dwarf
Branching	Monogenic	Branching dominant to unbranched
Presence of glands on leaves	Monogenic	Glandless dominant to presence of glands
Embryo colour	Monogenic	Blue dominant to yellow
Seed coat colour	Monogenic	Brown dominant to light yellow
Leaf morphology	Monogenic (*CC*)	* Normal entire leaf dominant to sinuate leaf shape; *c* allele is tightly linked to recessive allele for double flowering *s*. * Sinuate leaf allele reduce frequency & delayed flowering of double-flowered plants.
Flowering time	-	Additive (single flowered plants flowered earlier than double flowered)
Flower colour	Monogenic (*C, R, B, V*)	* *CRBV*-Purple * *CRBv*-Plum * *CRbV*-Red * *CRbv*-Copper * All other genotypes- White * White dominant (*W*) over cream (*w*)
Flower type	Monogenic (*SS*)	Single dominant to double
Leaf hoariness	Polygenic (*Cc, Rr, Kk*) & 3 multiple allelomorphs i.e. H, H_1, h	* CRKH-Hoary * H_1H_1KK-Half hoary * H_1H_1Kk-Mid-hoary; * H_1h_1KK-Quarter hoary; * Others are glabrous

Diseases and pests:

- Bacterial blight (*Xanthomonas campestris* pv. *incanae*):
- Damping off (*Pythium debaryanum* and *Pellicuraria filamentosa*): Excess moisture and high temperature favours occurrence.
- Foot rot (*Phytophthora megasperma*): Drench with Benomyl @ 2 g/ litre.
- Gray mold (*Botrytis cinerea*):
- Wilt (*Fusarium oxysporum* f.sp. *matthioli*):
- Leaf spot (*Alternaria raphani*):
- Downy mildew (*Peronospora parasitica*):
- White rust (*Albugo candida*):
- Aphids (*Aphis mathiolae*):
- Diamond back moth (*Plutella maculipennis*): Spray systemic insecticide.
- Springtails (*Bourletiella hortensis*):

42. GERANIACEAE

42.1 Geranium

- Eulogized as 'Stork bills'.
- Genus name is derived from Greek word '*Pelargos*' meaning 'Stork' referring to long beak like fruits.
- Popular seed and vegetatively propagated bedding and pot plant.
- Essential oil is widely used in perfumery, cosmetics, pharmaceutical, talcum powder, body lotion, and food industries.Oil has anti-microbial and pesticidal activity.
- Scented rose geranium is introduced to south India by Portuguese priests and French planters in 20th century.
- Facultative short-long- day plant i.e. they flower if given perіof of short days with temperature of 10-12^{0}C (*P. gradiflorum* hybrids).
- Inflorescence: Cymose and flowers in umbel like cluster called 'pseudoumbels' of 50-60 buds.
- Type of placentation: Axile.
- Pollination agent: Bees.
- Propagation method: Seed and long terminal cuttings.
- Fruit type: 5 walled pod (3 x 1 mm) containing 5 light brown seeds.
- Pod abortion is frequent phenomenon.
- Planting distance: 4 feet x 1.25 feet (10,000/ acre).
- Harvesting of leaves start after 2.5-3 months.
- Total crop duration: 4 year.

- Harvesting: 1st harvest after 3th month and subsequently after 3 months after.
- Ratooning: Possible at 3-4 times/ year.
- Yield: 4-5 t/acre 1st cutting and 10 ton subsequent cuttings (herbage); 600-800 ml/ 1 ton herb (oil).
- Maximum oil content: Leaf blade.
- Geranium leaf oil content: 0.8-0.15 % (rhodinol) and 60.56% (geranial).
- Commercial value of geranium oil: Total rhodinol content and ratio of citronellol and geranial.
- Flower colour pigments: Pelargonidin and delphinidin.
- Red flower colour of ivy leaved geranium: Mixture of glucosides of pelargonidin, peonidin, cyanidin.
- Pink colour: Malvinidin glucosides.
- Flavonoids: Useful taxonomic marker for phylogenetic relationships among spp.
- HPLC procedure for cultivar identification on the basis of geranium florets.
- Parthenocarpic fruit set occurs in regal pelargonium.
- Number of seeds/ flower in cross pollination: 3.5 (diploid) and 1.25 (tetraploid).
- Diploid seeds germinate faster and plants flower a week earlier than tetraploids.
- Seed propagated geranium cvs. exhibit tall phenotype.
- Seed germination: Slow, erratic and inefficient process.
- Impermeable (waxing) seed coat results in poor (40-50%) germination.
- Seeds require 20 days to complete germination and germinate better at constant 20°C.
- Seed germination: Seeds treatment with 1N H_2SO_4 for 3-5 minute, ethephon @ 50 ppm 12 hours soaking and mechanical scarification.
- pH substrate: 5.6-6.5 gives better plant development.
- Nickling: Quite poor, resulting in low seed set.
- Formation of short filament is associated with male sterility.
- Present oil yielding cvs. suffer from high female and male sterility.
- Cross compatibility:
  1. *P. stenopetalum* is self and cross incompatible as pistillate parent.
  2. Crossability is pelargonium is limited due to unequal basic chromosome numbers and different ploidy levels.
  3. Species having same chromosome number and ploidy level are intercrossable.
  4. Post fertilization barriers in crosses between *P. hortorum*, *P. peltatum* gives low germination of hybrid seeds.

- Hybrid variegation i.e. chlorophyll deficiency, a phenomenon in geranium makes selection work difficult and has biparental inheritance.
- Anther and embryo culture: Production of haploid plants in *P. zonale*.
- Somatic hybridization: Protoplast fusion between *P. hortorum* (susceptible) x *P. domesticum* (resistant) to induce resistance to *Xanthomonas*.
- Somatic embryogenesis: Attempted due to high degree of male and female sterility in conventional breeding. It is reported in *P. capitata* and cv. Frensham.
- Synthetic seed production i.e. desiccated somatic embryos: Reported in zonale and regal geranium. Encapsulation of somatic embryos @ 3% sodium alginate in *P. zonale*.
- Somaclonal variation: Studied in plant height, growth habit, flower shape and size and fertility status, disease and pest resistance.
- Molecular study using TRAP (Target region amplification polymorphism) shows genetic background of tetraploid cultivars.
- Genetically engineered male sterility in pelargonium *P. zonale*, transgenic lines carry no pollen grains in modified anther structure.
- Use of GFP gene as *in vivo* selectable marker has been reported.

Species:

- Number of sections: 16.
- Use of *P. peltatum* as bridging species between *P.* x *hortorum* x *P. domesticum*.

Species	Common name	Characteristics
P. citriodorum	Lemon scented geranium	Lemon scented leaves.
P. citronellum	Citronella mosquito plant	Evergreen, bushy shrub with lemon scented leaves.
P. crispum	Crisped-leaf pelargonium	Erect, much-branched shrub with pink flowers; leaves fan shaped and lemon scented; male sterile
P. x *domesticum*	Regal pelargonium	Perennial; erect; soft and non-succulent stems; require frequent pruning & shapinge.g. Tiny Tot, Lavender Queen, Grand Slam, Azalea, Fire Dancer.
P. x *fragrans*	Nutmeg scented geranium	Perennial, dwarf, rounded leaves having nutmeg scent; pink flowers.
P. graveolens (syn. *P. roseum*)	Rose scented geranium	Octaploid (2n=8x=88); evergreen; rose scented leaves; parent spp. for all commercial varieties; source of essential oil of international importance having anti-microbial & pesticidal activity.
P. capitatum	-	Hexaploid (2n=6x=66); shrubby, low growing plant; rose scented leaves.
P. x *hortorum*	Zonal/ Golden/ Fish type/ Bedding geranium	Most commonly used ornamental plant; grows easily from seed e.g. Red Orbit, White Orbit, Scarlet Orbit, Enchantress
P. inodorum	Scentless geranium	Annual or short-lived perennial herb; summer flowering.
P. odoratissimum	Sweet scented pelargonium	Evergreen perennial; apple scented leaves & whitish flowers.

Classification based on botanical forms:

Class I	Zonal/ Fish type geranium	Include fancy leaved types and botanically classed as *P.* x *hortorum* (*P. zonale* x *P. inquinans*); possess round leaves with a coloured spot (or 'zone') in the centre (hence 'zonal'). Flowers are single, semi-double or double. Seed raised are single flowered; large flowered are propagated by cuttings & ideal for container plants
Class II	Ivy leaved geranium	Classified as *P. peltatum* (*P. inquinans* x *P. peltatum*); trailing stems and hardened leaves & widely used in hanging baskets
Class III	Regal geraniums	Botanically *P.* x *domesticum*. Royal/ French varieties are derived from (*P. grandiflorum* x *P. cucullatum*); woody stems, wrinkled thin leaves, stalky growth habit due to long internodes, mainly grown in greenhouses.
Class IV	Show or Fancy-leaved geranium	Known as pelargoniums. Flowers are very double with neat variations in both leaf form & colour variegation
Class V	Scented leaved geranium	Known as rose geranium *P. graveolens* (*P. radens* x *P. capitatum*); important aromatic plants for geranium oil used in perfume industry.
Class VI	Oak leaf geranium	Botanically *P. quercifolium* & have showy flowers and leaves

Classification based on origin:

- Algerian or Tunisian (slender with dark pink flowers) type: Grown in Nilgiri hills and is unsuitable for wet conditions. Yields 50-60% more oil with a more delicate odour than Reunion type.
- Bourbon or Reunion (sturdy with light pink flowers) type: Oil content higher during summer. Terminal portion with 6-12 leaves contains more oil than basal portion. Suitable for wet conditions and susceptible to wilt.
- Egyptian or African type: High in geranial content. Drought hardy, tolerant to high temperature and wilt.

Varieties:

- Genetic improvement by sexual method is extremely difficult.
- Commercial available seed grown cultivars have single floret and major problem of seed shattering.
- Inbred lines breed true for various flower colours.
- Pre-selection criteria for identification of different characters: General vigour, growth habit, leaf zonation, flower colour, size, number and type, pollen production, earliness and continuity of flowering, seed germination, response to stress, pest resistance.
- Three methods to improve asexually propagated cultivars:
    1. Sports or mutant selection: Diploid and tetraploid cultivars has arisen from sports.
    2. Strain selection: Deleterious mutations are eliminated and beneficial mutations are selected. Plays major role in developing culture index and culture-virus indexed pelargonium.
    3. Hybridization: Recombination of genes from indigenous types as well as between the indigenous and exotic types.

- Somaclonal breeding program proved extremely successful in developing resistant cultivars.
- Backcross breeding is used to induce CMS for hybrid seed production.
- Becker Zens developed 1st efficient embryo culture (14 days age) technique in *P. zonale* hybrids in 1983.
- Sprinter Scarlet: 1st pot plant cv. in pelargonium introduced by Goldsmith Seeds.
- Black Velvet Rose F_1: 1st black leaved cultivar of *P.* x *hortorum* bred at VUKOZ, Czech Republic.
- Gizela: Diploid, green leaved with a standard type leaf zone having bright red flowers.
- New Era: F_1 hybrid introduced by Joseph Haris Seed Company.
- Carefree series: Introduced by PanAmerica Seed Company.
- Snow Storm: Pure white flowered cultivar.
- Percival: Dwarf type having semi-double pure white flowers.
- *P. hybrida* cv. Carpet Red and *P.* x *hortorum* cv. Orange Appeal: Suitable for bedding purpose.
- F_1 hybrid series: Sprinter, Scarlet, Elite, Ringo, Orbit, Pinto, Diamond.
- Gold Smith: Multibloom type.
- Double Dip, Parfait, Marathon: Semi-double flowers.
- Verona: Golden leaf mutant of zonal pelargonium.
- *P.graveolens* cv. Hemanti, Bipuli and Kunti are male sterile.

Name	Breeding method	Features
Iowa State University, Iowa		
Hazel	Intervarietal hybrid of (Will Rogers x Pink Cloud) x Pink Jade	Self branching, increased flowering, resistant to damage from wind & rain; high tolerant to botrytis & two spotted mite
Marian	Intervarietal hybrid of (Galaxy x Summer Time) x (Pink Cloud x Marquise de Castellane)	Self branching, short internodes, 2-3 node flowering cycle, all plant parts pubescent; vivid flower colour; high level of tolerance to botrytis
Pearl Bailey	Intervarietal hybrid of (Orange Crimson Sldg x Crimson Star)	Bushy-compact plant habit, erect, spreading type, inflorescence contain 50-60 buds, short floral cycle; semi-double type; high field tolerance to botrytis
P. quercifolium cv. Mme	Triple hybrid	Continuous flowering
-	Intervarietal hybrid of (Prince Rupert (4x) x Morning Glory)	Dwarf
CIMAP, Lucknow		
BSP-1, 2, 3	Half-sib progeny 'Bipuli x Kunti'	-
BSP-4	Heterotic hybrid of	Large canopy; high essential oil (1.44 times more oil

	'Bipuli x Hemanti'	content) 5 fold more oil yield over Bipuli accession
Narmada	Somaclonal variant of Indian cv. Bourbon (*P. graveolens*)	Contain high rhodinol; total alcohol & high citronellol/ geraniol ratio; received US plant patent
Kelkar (NIC 23414)	OP selection	Egyptian type; much branched; leaves & tender twigs light green; essential oil content 0.05-0.38%; essential oil (79.93 g/plot); rich in citronellol (61.48%)
Bourbon	OP selection from Reunion islands	Highest quality geranium oil; diploid; leaf yield (42.86 kg/ plot); essential oil (72.01 g/plot); rich in citronellol
CIM-Bio-G-171	-	Leaf yield (174.42 q/ha);
CIM-Pawan	-	Leaf yield (160.56 q/ha); essential oil (103.87 g/plot); rich in citronellol (32.60)
CIM-Safal	Heterotic hybrid of 'Bipuli x Hemanti'	High rhodinol (89%) in essential oil; 1: 1 citronellol to geraniol ratio; suitable for commercial scale
CIM-Parimal	Somaclone developed via callus through *in vitro* tissue culture	High herb & oil yield
NIC 23415	-	Plant spreading; stem brownish; essential oil 0.05-0.35%
NIC 23413	-	Essential oil 0.06-0.32%
Ranichauri (IC 212823)	-	Plant spreading to medium erect; essential oil 0.05-0.29%
Velvet Rose	*In vitro* development	1st named cv. derived from tissue culture in *P. graveolens*
IIHR, Bengaluru		
IIHR Sel-8	Clonal selection	Reunion type; highest oil yield
TNAU, Coimbatore		
KKL-1 (1987)	Clonal selection	Algerian type; vigorous, yield of leaves (45.2 T/ha); oil recovery of 0.16%; leaf oil contains 60.56% geraniol; 2.32 ml oil /plant.
Other cvs.		
Black Velvet Scarlet	Polyploid using colchicine @ (0.1% to 2.5%)	Diploid, black leaved cultivar with orange red flowers; failure of blooming; double or full larger flowers
Velvet Pure	Polyploid breeding	(2n=144);
Calliclone	Periclinal chimera	Thick grey green & densely pubescent leaves, stocky, dense plant stature and produces some viable seeds
Kleine Liebling	Polyploid breeding	Haploid

Inheritance of characters:

- Quantitative differences of anthocyanins control flower colour pigments.

Character	Number of genes	Inheritance pattern
Plant height	Monogenic	Dwarf dominant over tall; major gene with incomplete dominance
Presence of spur in semi-double or double flower	-	Pleiotropic effect of single flower gene/ unidentified linked gene
Golden leaf	-	Nuclear gene with incomplete dominance
Blotch	-	White dominant to colour; 5 blotches dominant to 2 blotches

Leaf zonation	Five multiple alleles of one gene *Zo/zo*	Four zone pattern dominant to zoneless pattern/ narrow peripheral/ narrow middle zone
Earliness to flower	Digenic	Earliness dominant to late types
Floret centre colour	Monogenic	Red dominant over white
Vein pattern on petals	Monogenic	Coloured dominant over colourless
Red spotted trichomes	Digenic (*Aur*$^+$/*Aur* golden leaves, *Rst/rst* red spots on petals)	Red spotted trichome dominant over red spotless; two genes segregate independently
Red flower colour	Two dominant & complementary genes (R_1/r_1 and R_2/r_2)	In the absence of dominant allele of either gene flowers are salmon, pink or white coloured. Epistasis & R_2/r_2 provide no evidence for linkage
Pattern in white flowers	Four genes (*Ve/ve, Ba/ba, Pi/pi* or *Ce/ce*)	Dominant alleles control expression of patterns (*Ve* (vein), *Ba* (bar), *Pi, Ce* (picotee). Interaction of two genes (*Ce* with *Ve*= centre pattern; *Ba* with *Ve*= ring pattern)
Mite resistance	Digenic	Dominant genes act in unison
Male sterility	One or two (*ms1, ms2*)	Male sterility is recessive to fertility
Plastid inheritance	Polygenic	Biparental
CGMS	Mitochondrial genes	-
Sensitive to high temperature	-	Dominant in clonal and seed propagated cvs.

Diseases and pests:

- Traditional breeding for disease resistance is not successful.
- Rust (*Puccinia pelargonii*): Most destructive and all cvs. are susceptible. Hybrids between ivy leaved and zonal geraniums are immune to rust.
- Gray mold (*B. cinerea*): Causes damage to stem, leaves and flowers.
- Bacterial blight (*Xanthomonas pelargonii*): Species resistant to this disease lacks desirable horticultural traits.

Disease and pest	Features; species and varieties having resistance
Bacterial leaf spot and stem rot	Lady Washington, Martha Washington (*P. domesticum*), Madame Layal and Marie Vogel (P. x *domesticum*), Torento, Pepper Mint (*P. tomentosum*), Countless of Scarborough (*P. scarboroviae*)
Powdery mildew	Alan Bloom, Buxton's Blue, Biokovo, *G. dalmanicum, G. album*.
Root rot	-
Gray mold (*Botrytis cinerea*)	Waltztime, Hawkeye, Skylark, Pearl Bailey, Berlin, Marian
Pelargonium flower break carom virus (PFBV)	Hampers total production; wild species of *P. zonale* cv. Zink and Elizabeth
Two spotted mites	Hazel

43. HELICONIACEAE

43.1 Heliconia

- Eulogized as 'Parrot plantain or False plantain or Lobster's claws or Parrot flower or False Bird of paradise'.

- Ideal intercrop for coconut garden.
- Two main types: 1) Erect heliconia with standing straight bracts pointing up 2) Pendent heliconia with hanging bracts pointing down.
- Cultivated up to 3,000-4,000 m MSL.
- Optimum temperature for growth: 21-35^{0}C.
- Shoot emergence period: 2 months from planting.
- Inflorescence development: Within 6 months.
- Peak flowering period: September-December.
- 50% production in India: West Godavari district, Andhra Pradesh.
- Ornamental part: Highly modified leaves and bracts.
- Main pollinators: Humming bird and bats.
- Propagation method: Rhizome (40 g), side shoots and suckers.
- Packing: Bunch of 10 in plastic film or weave netting.
- Box size: 150 cm x 50 cm x 25 cm.

Species:

- *Heliconia psittacorum*: Known as Parrot's beak. Excellent for flower arrangement. Bracts pendent and pointing downward.
- *H. bihai*: cv. Lobster Claw One.
- *H. psittacorum* x *H. spathocircinata*: cv. Golden Torch.
- *H. psittacorum*: Excellent for flower arrangement cv. Lady Di, Choconiana.
- *H. rostrata*: Minimum number of suckers. Hardiest species with pendent inflorescence.
- *H. latispatha*: Excellent for flower arrangement.
- *H. stricta*: Inflorescence resembles lobster claws.
- *H. angustifolia*:
- *H. metallica*:
- *H. humilis*:

44. IRIDACEAE

44.1 Gladiolus

- Eulogized as 'Queen of bulbous flowers or Sword lily or Corn flag or King of hill floriculture'.
- Sub-family: Ixioideae.
- 1st person who grew gladiolus in India: Mr. Charles Gray.
- IARI, New Delhi has celebrated the year 2009-10 as 'Year of Gladiolus'.

- Latin word '*gladius'* means 'sword shaped foliage'.
- As per North American Gladiolus Council (NAGC) system of classification 1st digit indicates- floret size and last two digits indicates- florest colour and shade and odd last digit indicates conspicuous mark or blotch.
- Planting season: July-August.
- Pigments in flower colour: Violet red (anthocyanin), ivory, cream, yellow (anthoxanthin), violet (malvidin), blue (delphinidin).
- Double gladiolus: Any gladiolus having > 5 petals.
- It is 7 months crop from planting to lifting of corms.
- Optimum temperature for growth: 10-25^{0}C.
- Full sunshine (80%) is essential for cultivation.
- Favorable temperature for flowering, corm and cormel production: 16^{0}C (lower) and 23-43^{0}C (higher).
- Marked difference in day and night temperature promotes a) contractile roots in shallow planted corms and b) brings early maturity of corms & cormels c) contractile roots also serve as a basis for development of more cormels.
- Both short days and low light intensities increases flower abortion.
- Long day length (> 12 h) improves spike quality.
- Short days at 1st-2nd leaf stage leads to blind shoot.
- 2nd leaf stage: Most sensitive to low night temperature.
- 3rd leaf stage: Flower bud initiation.
- 4-6th leaf stage: Most sensitive to light and most critical stage of irrigation.
- 7th leaf stage (spike emergence): Sensitive to chilling damage.
- Individual flower is called as 'floret', funnel shaped, sessile, protandrous and open in acropetal succession.
- Sepals, petals are alike & are collectively called 'tepals'.
- Inflorescence: Spike.
- Inflorescence initiation follows a definite number of leaves of 8-10.
- Stigma becomes receptive on 3rd day of opening of flowers.
- Fruit type: 3 chamber capsule and contains winged seeds.
- Propagation method: Seeds, corms, cormels (baby corms) and cormlets.
- Corm: Large bulb from inflated lower node of shoot.
- Cormel/ spawn: Smallest propagule developed from stolon.
- Corm is covered by 4-6 dry scales/ husk and the point where scale is attached to corm is called 'node'.
- Planting distance: 30 cm x 15 cm.
- Spacing at 25 x 25 cm increases floret size, corm weight.

- Shallow rooted crop.
- Planting depth: 5-6 cm.
- HDP: 60-90 corms/ m^2.
- Optimum corm size for planting: 5-7 cm diameter.
- Optimum soil pH: 6-7.
- Full sunshine (80%) is essential for cultivation.
- There are 6 categories for classification of corms and cormels.
- Jumbo grade of corm: >5.1 cm diameter.
- Plant population: 1,50,000 corms/ ha.
- Commercial life of any variety: 10-15 years.
- Best season of planting: June, October, November.
- Ammonium sulphate gives better results compared to nitrate nitrogen.
- Higher nitrogen results in taller and soft spikes with dull florets.
- Pollen grains are round (106 μ in dia.), heavy & not carried by wind or bees.
- Pollen viability: 3 months (at low temperature) & 1 week (room temperature).
- Dried pollen grains frozen at -40°C, then thawed, retain viability for >1 year.
- Lower 3-4 flowers are selected for pollination.
- Capsule/pod matures after 4-5 weeks of pollination.
- Maximum 40-60 seeds/ capsule and take four seasons to bloom.
- Seed viability: 1 year (at 14°C, 26% R.H).
- Corms of exotic cultivars can be stored in cold storage at 10 ±2°C & 40-60% R.H.
- Indicator plant for floride pollution. Fluoride toxicity seen on tip of leaves.
- Toxicity is due to heavy application of super phosphate, rock phosphate which contains hydrogen fluoride.
- Earthing up is done upto 10-12 cm deep.It is needed at 4th leaf stage and at spike emergence.
- Some species emit maximum fragrance between 10 AM to 14 PM (*G. orchidiflorus*) and few between 18 PM to 22 PM (*G. tristis*, *G. recurvus*).
- Removal of spikes before flower opening or at 2 flowers open or 8 flowers open resulted in increase of corm weight up to 150 g.
- Number of cormel production was highest at NAA @ 50, 100, 200 ppm concentration.
- Corms are rich source of Vit. C.
- Corm should be treated with 0.2% Bavistin or Captaf.
- Seeds requires 15-20 days to germinate & do not have dormancy like corms.
- Optimum temperature for seed germination: 20°C within 3-5 weeks.
- Dormant corms contain linolinic acid, linoleic acid and palmic acid.
- Soaking of corms in GA_3 (10-50 ppm) accelerates plant height and flowering.

- Dormant corms and cormels contain 5-10 times ABA than non-dormant. It is broken by GA_3@ 100-500 ppm.
- Breaking of corm dormancy: Store corms at 4-5^{0}C for 3-4 months or corm treatment with Thiourea @ 1000 ppm for 12 hours.
- Ethylene chlorohydrine: 1st chemical used to break corm dormancy by Denny (1938).
- Hilling and scoring: Important operations in gladiolus.
- Low temperature induced frost injury is noticed.
- For cut spikes storage temperature: 1-2^{0}C for 2 weeks.
- Preservative solution: 20% sucrose + 200 ppm HQC.
- Hamper: Container used for shipping gladiolus.
- 1st report on *in vitro* propagation: Ziv *et al*. (1970).
- Radio sensitivity is genotype and trait dependent mechanism.
- LD_{50}: 10-15 Krad. 7.2 Kr (for corm germination) and 4.7 Kr (for survival).

Species:

- Species found in Asia Minoı are called 'Corn lilies'.
- South African spp. (tetraploid, 2n=60), European spp. (diploid, 2n=30).
- Orchidiola group is distinct from Pixiola group in both their flower colour pattern and growth duration.
- Lewis *et al.* (1972) divided the genus into 4 groups based on number of well developed leaves viz. Plurifoliati (5-8 or more),Paucifoliati (2-5),Unifoliati (1) and Exfoliati (leaves appar after flowering).
- Fragrant species: *Acidanthera bicolor* var. *murielae* (*G. callianthus*), *G. carinatus*, *G. caryophyllaceus* (syn. *G. hirsutus*), *G.* x *christabel*, *G. liliaceus*, *G. longicollis*, *G. maculatus*, *G. orchidiflorus*, *G. recurvus*, *G. tristis*, *G. virescens*, *G. victorialis* (*G. byzantinus* x *G. cardinalis*), G. *watermeyeri* and *G. watsonius*.
- Frangrant species have smaller florets & spike size.
- Aneuploids are less fragrant than euploids.
- Loss of fragrance is determined by chromosomes at meiosis.

Name	Features
G. cardinalis	Used in breeding scarlet coloured florets
G. dalenii	Used in breeding summer blooming hybrids
G. dracocephalous, G. eckloni	Used in breeding multicoloured florets i.e. green, brown & slate
G. floribundus	Nyctinastic movements
G. natalensis (Parrot gladiolus)	-
G. primulinus (Waterfall gladiolus or Maid of the Mist)	Used for producing miniature type & primrose yellow coloured florets
G. tristis (Sweet scented gladiolus, 2n=30)	White flowers; sweet scented; night blooming & used in breeding winter flowering hybrids
G. recurvus	Sweet scented

Races of gladiolus:

Hybrid/race	Cross	Salient characters
Modern day gladiolus (Gandavensis hybrids)	Belgium race of Parrot gladiolus *G. natalensis* (*psittacinus*) x *G. oppositiflorus*	Funnel-shaped red to reddish yellow flowers; flowers bloom from late spring to summer.
Ghent hybrids (*G.* x *gandavensis*)	*G. cardinalis* x *G. psittacinus*	Bright rich crimson flowers with markings.
G. brencheleyensis	*G. cardinalis* x *G. psittacinus*	Light red colour.
G. citrinus	*G. cardinalis* x *G. psittacinus*	Yellow flowers
Zurich race (*G. turicensis*)	*G. gandavensis* x *G. saundersi superbus*	Purplish crimson flowers white markings on lower segments.
G. x *colvillei*	*G. tristis* var. *concolor* x *G. cardinalis*	Summer flowering and suitable for pot culture.
France race (*G. lemoinei*)	*G. gandavensis* or *G. brenchelyensis* x *G. purpureoauralus*	Pale sulphur-coloured flowers with deep red-brown blotches.
Elegant and fertile race	*G. cardinalis* x *G. blandus*	-
German race (*G.* x *nanceianus*)	*G. lemoinei* x *G. saundersii*	-
G. childsii	*G. gandavensis* x *G. saundersii*	Robust and large flowers.
G. victorialis (1893)	*G. byzantinus* x *G. cardinalis*	

Species	Scent compound
G. liliaceus	Eugenol
G. alatus, *G. maculates*, *G. recurvus* & *G. tristis*	Linalool
G. jonquilliodorus, *G. orchidiflorus*, *G. patersoniae* & *G. scullyi*	Geraniol and Citronellol
G. carinatus & *G. virescens*	B-ionone

Varieties:

- Breeding at polyploid level is widely used in hybridization program.
- Bigeneric homoglad hybrid hybrids were developed in 1967 (*G. tristis* x *Homoglossom watsonius*).
- Shuttle breeding method: Reduce the time span required for release of variety.
- Cv. Grace (Her Majesty x Snow Princess) has been patented in USA.
- Double flowering gladiolus: Multipetal No. 1.
- 1st hybrid: *G.* x *gandavensis* developed in 1841.
- 1st fragrant variety: Lucky Star [2n=4x=80, bigeneric *G. callianthus* (diploid, scented) x Filigree (amphidiploids, non-scented)] developed in New Zealand have pink florets.
- 1st smoky coloured variety: Prince of India.
- Red Majesty: Dutch hybrid.
- Concolor: Whitish yellow florets & emit fragrance at night hours.
- Homoglad: Bigeneric hybrid between *G. tristis* (white flower) x *G. watsonius* (scarlet flower).
- Rose Charm: Virus free & superior in horticultural characters.

- Wood Violet: Mini gladiolus for pot culture purpose.
- Fragrant cvs.: Acacia, Mid Bloom, New Era, Incense, Frilled Fragrance.

Name	Breeding method	Features
IARI, New Delhi		
Agnirekha (1980)	Seedling selection of 'Sylvia' (*G. psittacinus* 2n=75)	Fire red having scarlet strips blended with saffron yellow; 6 florets open at a time
Bindiya (1997)	Seedling selection of 'Ratna's Butterfly'	Florets yellowish cream with fan-shaped red coloration on 2 side falls; spikes 64 cm long; 18 florets/ spike
Jyotsna (2002)	Seedling selection of 'Melodie'	Florets orange coloured with darker streaks on petals; spike length >103 cm; 18 florets/ spike each with 11 cm diameter
Mayur (1980)	Seedling selection of 'Sylvia'	Lilac purple with dark purple throat; 8 florets open at a time; tolerant to all most all diseases.
Pusa Kiran (2009)	Seedling selection of 'Ave'	White coloured florets, 16-19 in number, prolific multiplier; vase life of 10 days.
Pusa Red Valentine (2012)	Seedling selection of 'Regency'	Flowers in 95 days; 17-19 florets on a spike; brick or blood red florets with sunray like small lines on lower tepals
Pusa Sarang (1997)	Seedling selection of 'White Oak'	Florets purple red &mid season variety.
Pusa Sukanya (2000)	Seedling selection of 'Salmon Queen'	Floret colour white with scarlet ring in the lip
Pusa Suhagin (1987)	Seedling selection of '**Sylvia**'	Florets ruby-red with barium yellow streaks
Swapnil (2000)	Seedling selection of 'Viola'	Florets violet with creamy throat; spikes 109 cm long with 17 florets of 11.4 cm dia.
Pusa Sindoori (2018)	Seedling selection of 'Little Fawn'	Florets base colour is bright red with two yellow spots and rainbow type stripe; spike length 99 cm; 19 florets/ spike
Anjali (1997)	Sancerre x Rose Spire	Florets scarlet pink with yellow dusting on falls; spikes 95 cm long; florets 17-19 & 8.5 cm across.
Chandni (1997)	Green Woodpecker x White Butterfly	Florets greenish white; 12 florets/ spike; spikes 80-90 cm long with 14-15 florets
Chirag (1997)	Cygnet x Little Fawn	Florets orange coloured with deeper throat; spikes 85-99 cm long with 16-18 florets
Dhanvantari (1995)	Jr.Prom x Lucky Star	Florets light yellow; 13 florets/ spike; 16-18 florets with 1-2 shoots/mother corm
Gulal (2002)	Snow Princess x Viola	Florets are red purple; spike length 84 cm with >17 florets
Kamini (2000)	Ave x Christian Jane	Orange-red florets
Lohit (2000)	Creamy Green x American Beauty	Floret colour is red with white mid-ribs on 2 side falls; spikes 90-100 cm long with 16 florets.
Mohini (2000)	Ave x Christian Jane	Floret colour red-purple; spike length 75-90 cm with 15 florets/ spike

Neelam (1995)	Sylvia x Patricia	Deep mauve florets; spikes 100 cm long; florets 16-19/ spike.
Pusa Gunjan (2012)	White Oak x Oscar	Soft orange coloured florets; 110 cm plant height; 18 florets/ spike.
Pusa Manmohak (2012)	Mayur x Hunting Song	Florets saffron red with whitish strips on throat of lower tepals; 19-21 florets/ spike.
Pusa Shubham (2009)	Lucky Shamrock x Green Lilac	14-16 florets of cream to yellow colour; flowers in 72 days
Pusa Shweta (1997)	Wind Song x Pink Frost Seedlings	Florets frilled white with green-yellow throat.
Pusa Srijana (2013)	Berlew x Heady Wine	Spikes 86 cm long; 15-17 purple coloured florets
Pusa Unnati (2013)	Berlew x Heady Wine	Florets are purple red/pink in colour with white stripe on inner two tepals. 16-20 florets &produces 2-3 shoots/ corm
Pusa Shanti (2020)	-	Suitable for Delhi condition
Pusa Urvashi (2006)	Snow Princess x Eurovision	Satin-like florets; light purple-orange colour.
Pusa Vandana (1997)	George Mazure x Eurovision	Orange coloured; mid-season variety.
Pusa Vidushi (2012)	Melody x Berlew	15-16 florets/spike; purplish white in colour with grey purple spots on base of throat.
Rangmahal (2000)	Red Bantam x Flaura Belle	Florets ruffled, red-purple spikes 85-95 cm long with 17-18 florets/ spike
Sanjeevani (1959)	Purple Burma x Lucky Star.	16 florets/ spike & white in colour.
Shagun (2001)	White Oak x Oscar	Dazzling red coloured florets; plant height 118 cm; 16 florets/ spike.
Shringarika (2001)	Mayur x Heady Winc	Purple coloured florets; 110 cm plant height; 14 florets/ spike.
Suchitra (1980)	Sylvia x Jo Wagenaar	Camelia rose coloured, stripped vermilion, throat dianthus purple; 22 florets/ spike; tolerant to all most all diseases.
Sunayna (1991)	George Mazure x Eurovision	Early; florets pink with red throat.
Urmil (2000)	Tinker Belle x Break O'Dawn	Florets violet with creamy throat; spikes 91 cm long with 16 florets/ spike; flower dia. 10-11 cm.
Swarnima (2000)	Bud sport of 'Dhanvantari' (light yellow)	Florets coppery yellow; spikes 70-90 cm long; 16 florets.
IIHR, Bengaluru		
Aarti (1980)	Shirley x Melody	11 florets/ spike; florets light orange having red spots with red & yellow blotch; suitable for flower arrangement
Apsara (1980)	Black Jack x Friendship	18 florets/ spike; purple with barium yellow flecks in throat
Arka Aayush (2015)	Gold Medal 412 x Poonam	Red florets, 18 florets/ spike; resistant to fusarium
Arka Amar (2010)	Pedigree selection of Watermelon Pink x Aarti	Florets pink with white blotch; 17 florets/ spike; fusarium wilt resistant.
Arka Gold (2010)	Greenbay x Gold Medal- 412	13 florets/ spike; 10 cm flower dia.; florets yellow with yellow lower lip & red blotch.

Arka Kesar (1999)	Vink's Glory x Sagar	18 florets/spike; 10 cm flowers dia.; saffron coloured florets; moderately resistant to fusarium wilt.
Arka Manorama (2015)	Meera x Picardy	Red purple florets, 13 florets/ spike; 47 cm rachis length; resistant to fusarium
Arka Naveen (2010)	Hybrid 74-39-1 x Tropic Seas	Florets purple violet with pale yellow blotch; 16 florets/ spike; 10.5 cm flower dia.
Arka Suvarna (1999)	Geliber Herald x Vink's Glory	16 florets/ spike; yellow florets arranged in double rows.
Arka Pratham (2019)	Junior Prom x Arka Poonum	Floret colour purple violet (purple margin & green white line on lower lip); suitable for cut flower & bedding purpose
Arka Ranjini (2019)	Arka Poonum x Gold Medal-412	Floret colour purple middle, spike length 104 cm; suitable for cut flower & bedding purpose
Darshan (1993)	Watermelon pink x Shirley	87 cm spike length; 15 florets/ spike; mod.resistant to fusarium wilt.
Dhiraj (1993)	Beauty Spot x *Psittacinus* hybrid	83 cm spike length; 17 florets/ spike; red-purple with yellow & red-purple blotch; resistant to fusarium wilt.
Kum Kum (1993)	Watermelon pink x Lady John	Florets are red with yellow blotch; 83 cm stem length; mod.resistant to fusarium wilt.
Meera (1979)	G.P.I x Friendship	Late flowering; spikes robust, 18 florets per spike; snow white colour; vase life 8 days.
Nazrana (1979)	Black Jack x Friendship	18 florets/ spike; florets cardinal red coloured with barium yellow flash in throat.
Poonam (1979)	Gelliber Herald x R.N. 121	Spikes 100 cm long; 17 florets/ spike; compact; pale yellow with light yellow blotch; tolerant to fusarium wilt.
Sagar (1990)	Melody x Wild Rose	Florets pink with red & yellow blotch, spikes 119 cm long with 20 florets/ spike
Sapna (1979)	Queen Woodpecker x Friendship	Spike length 119 cm; 20 florets/ spike; florets pink with red & yellow blotch
Shakti (1990)	Watermelon Pink x Wild Rose	Florets open faced, red in colour have white lines & blotch; 87 cm spike length; 15 florets/ spike.
Sindur (1993)	Watermelon Pink x Lady John	77 cm spike length; 17 florets/ spike; 8 cm floret dia.; florets red with darker blotches with yellow splashes.
Tilak (1993)	Watermelon Pink x Lady John	94 cm spike length; 15 florets/ spike; floret dark red with red specks, lower lip red with yellow lines; mod.resistant to wilt.
Shobha (1980)	Bud sport of 'Wild Rose'	97 cm spike length; 18 florets/ spike; florets shell pink with empire yellow throat.
NBRI, Lucknow		
Basant Bahar	Seedling selection of 'Tunias Challenge'	Florets are yellow with magenta specks in throat.
Jwala	*G. psittacinus* hybrid	Floret vermillion with blotched yellow; its branching habit makes it suited for bedding purpose.
Kajal	-	Blackish red flowers.

Kalima	Seedling selection of 'Sylvia'	Florets red with 2 side falls blotched yellow.
Menaka	-	Blush pink flowers.
Priyadarshini	Seedling selection of 'Lavanesque'	Florets mauve and throat white.
Sada Bahar	Seedling selection of 'Sylvia'	Florets specked purple with sulphur yellow petal mid-ribs.
Smita	Seedling selection of 'Lavanesque'	Floret rose with dark margins.
Gazal	Seedling selection of 'White Friendship'	Florets are pink with darker lips & linear shading, having yellow throat
Archana (1984)	*G. psittacinus* Sylvia (2n=75) x Friendship (2n=60)	Aneuploid (2n=60); floret colour purple with yellow blotch and white mid-rib, mid-season variety.
Arun (1984)	Sylvia x Fancy (2n=60)	Aneuploid (2n=67); florets Vermillion coloured & it is a late blooming variety.
Hans (1985)	Friendship x *G. tristis* (2n=30)	Triploid (2n=45); florets white with falls having mid-rib.
Indrani (1985)	Friendship x *G. tristis*	Florets crimson with white mid-rib.
Jamuni (syn. Amethyst) (2010)	Lavender Puff x Tropic Sea	Spike length 0.95m; 16-18 florets/ spike; bicoloured florets in combination of purple & yellow-white.
Kohra (1983)	*G. psittacinus* hybrid x King Leaf	Outer four petals slightly frilled, tip pointed & curved outward having 80% purple colour & rest is yellow-white.
Manhar (1983)	Friendship x *G. tristis*	Triploid, florets primrose yellow having splashes of tyrian rose.
Manisha (1983)	Friendship x *G. tristis*	Triploid; florets yellow with purple splashes at tips; late blooming
Manmohan (1981)	Friendship x *G. tristis*	Triploid, florets primrose yellow with orchid purple splashes at tips.
Manohar (1982)	Friendship x *G. tristis*	Triploid; florets purple & throat yellow
Mohini (1982)	Friendship x *G. tristis*	Triploid; florets white, splashed with rose & throat primrose yellow
Mridula (1985)	Friendship x *G. tristis*	Triploid; florets purpled specked at edges with yellow throat & white mid-ribs
Mukta (1981)	Friendship x *G. tristis*	Triploid; florets sulphur-yellow splashes of orchid purple
Neelima (2006)	Snow Princess x Tropic Sea	Bluish-purple coloured florets with purple-white centre
Pitamber (1985)	Friendship x *G. tristis*	Triploid; florets light green with purple steaks in the throat,
Rashmi	Friendship White x My Love	Petals creamish white speckled with purple
Roshni (2010)	Friendship Pink x Red Beauty	Petals having pinkish-red base & central nerve of orange-white
Sanyukta (1984)	Friendship x *G. tristis*	Triploid; florets rose with primrose-yellow throat
Suverna (2008)	Fedelio x Hall Mark	Florets in colour combinations of orange red, red & creamy yellow
Sydney Percy Lancaster (2011)	Friendship Pink x Priscilla	-

Triloki (1984)	Friendship x *G. tristis*	Triploid; florets rose with yellow throat & it is a mid-season blooming
Urvashi (2006)	Snow Princess x Eurovision	Satin like florets in light purple orange colour.
Horticulture Experimentation and Training Centre, Chaubattia (Almora), Uttarakhand		
Chaubattia Ankur	Oscar x Friendship	Spikes 85.8 cm long; florets Dutch Vermilion coloured; 16 florets/ spike.
Chaubattia Arunima	Oscar x Mother Fisher	Spikes 89.1 cm long; florets Mandarin Red with white stripes; 18.6 florets/ spike.
Chaubattia Shobhit	Meria Goretti x Tropic Sea	Spikes 86.2 cm long; florets rose purple coloured; 16.1 florets/ spike.
Chaubattia Tripti	Sunny Boy x Oscar	Spikes 86.9 cm long; florets Charteuse green with Azalea pink stripes, 17.1 florets/ spike.
IHBT, Palampur		
Anurag	Her Majesty x Aldebran	Patented in USA (USPP13, 353)
Brick Beauty	Vink's Glory x Eurovision	Patented in USA (USPP13, 417)
Cute Munni	Bonfire x Eurovision	Patented in USA (USPP13, 591)
Palampur Pride	Her Majesty x Jesters	Patented in USA (USPP13, 980)
Palampur Delight	Her Majesty x Eurovision	Patented in USA (USPP13, 080)
Palampur Princess	Bonfire x Aldebran	Patented in USA (USPP13, 435)
Palampur Queen	Green Woodpecker x Oscar	Patented in USA (USPP13, 418)
Tushar Mauli	Oscar x Friendship	Patented in USA (USPP13, 710)
Grace	Her Majesty x Snow Princess	Patented in USA (USPP14, 979)
The Saint	-	Patented in USA (USPP13, 626)
PAU, Ludhiana		
Punjab Pink Elegance (2010)	-	Mid-season flowering; spike length 85 cm; rachis length 51 cm; floret size > 10 cm; flowering duration 16 days
Punjab Lemon Delight (2010)	-	Late-season flowering; spike length 81 cm; rachis length 30.5 cm; floret size >7 cm; flowering duration 12 days
Punjab Glance (2010)	-	Late-season flowering; spike length 83.5 cm; rachis length 47 cm; floret size > 8 cm; flowering duration 17 days
Punjab Flame (2010)	-	Mid-season flowering; spike length 92 cm; rachis length 49 cm; floret size > 8 cm; flowering duration 16 days
Punjab Morning	-	Spike length 66 cm; rachis length 37 cm; 16 florets/ spike; floret size 8.35 cm
Shan-e-Punjab	-	-
Punjab Glad-1 (2013)	-	Late-season flowering; spike length 85 cm; rachis length 52 cm; floret size > 8 cm; flowering duration 16 days

Punjab Glad-2 (2016)	-	-
Punjab Glad-3 (2019)	-	-
Directorate of Agriculture, Jammu		
Night (2001)	Her Majesty x White Friendship	Number of cormlets 25
Durga (2009)	Seedling selection of 'Congo Song'	Plant height 105 cm; 15florets/ spike; basal floret diameter 10.92 cm; florets pinkish with whitish midribs.
Eighth Wonder (2010)	Melody x Oscar	18-20 florets/ spike; spike length 70 cm; florets bright orange ruffled
Jammu Pride (2006)	Congo Song x Red Beauty	Produce 3 spikes/ corm, vase life 13-15 days.
Red Ginger (2012)	Red Beauty x Summer Sunshine	Early (60-75 days); 15.55 red coloured florets/ spike
Red Majesty (2013)	Red Beauty x Black Beauty	12 florets/ spike; shorter spike length (32 cm)
Sarla (2017)	Summer Sunshine x True Yellow	17 florets/ spike; spike length (50 cm); floret diameter (10-12 cm)
Shobhit Snow (2019)	White Friendship x White Prosparity	White spike; 95 cm spike length; 15 florets/ spike
Dr YSPUH & F, Solan		
Solan Mangla	Interpid x White Dream	17 florets/ spike; red coloured
MPKV, Rahuri		
Phule Ganesh (2001)	Sancerre x Oscar	Yellow white florets; spike 115-120cm; 19 florets/ spike; floret dia., 10-11cm; 2 corms & 70-80 cormels/ corm.
Phule Neelrekha (2004)	Tropic Seas x IIHR-77-59-32	Long spikes (138 cm); 31 florets/ spike; dark purple with fine streaks on the ventral side of the petals; tolerant to wilt.
Phule Prerna (2002)	Tropic Seas x Yellow Stone	Attractive pink coloured florets; spike 120 cm long; 17 florets/ spike; 250 cormels/ corm; yield 1.65 lakh spikes/ ha; less susceptible to wilt
Phule Tejas (2006)	Sancerre x IARI Sel. 3	Spike length 85 cm; leaf narrow short vase life; tolerant to wilt
Dr PDKV, Akola		
PDKV Roshni (AK-GL-04-06-A)	Darshan x White Friendship	Rachis length 48 cm; 16 florets/ spike; 1.73 spikes/ plant
PDKV Gold (AK-GL-04-16)	-	Pinkish yellow flowers, 2.77 lakh flower stalks/ha.
GBPUA & T, Pantnagar		
Shubhangini	-	-
TNAU, Coimbatore (HRS, Kodaikanal)		
KKL-1 (1993)	Selection	Flower red-purple; spike length 89 cm; 16 florets/spike

- **Grading system**: as per the North American Gladiolus Council (NAGC):

Grade	Spike length (cm)	Number of florets (min.)
Fancy (Grade A)	>107	16
Special (Grade B)	96-107	14
Standard (Grade C)	81-96	12
Utility (Grade D)	<81	10

Diseases and disorder:

- Fusarium wilt or Collar rot: Sickle/ curve shaped leaves with leaf tip burn symptoms. Cause 62-100% loss.
- Gladiolic acid is produced by corms affected by *Penicillium gladioli*.
- Dry rot: Leaf turn brown from tips downwards. Hot water treatment with 50-55^{0}C for 30 min.
- Crooked stem: Due to water stress.
- Brown tip/ Tip burn: Exposure to SO_2 gas or injury to roots.

Disease	Causal organism	Resistant species & cultivars
Fusarium wilt/ Soft rot/ Vascular disease	*Fusarium oxysporum* f. sp. *gladioli*	*G. callianthus*, Arka Amar, Arka Aayush, Arka Kesar, Darshan, Dhiraj, Kum Kum, Tilak, Margaret Fulton (USA), Mirgae (USA), Florida Flame, Morning Mist, Snow Princess, Camelia, Melody, Sylvia, May Up, Tiger Flame, Beauty Crest
Core rot/ Spongy rot/ Botrytis rot	*Botrytis gladiolorum*	Soil borne highly destructive fungus
Neck rot/ Dry rot/ corm rot	*Stromatinia gladioli* or *Sclerotinia gladioli*	Soil borne
Storage rot	*Penicillium gladioli*	-
Leaf blight/ Curvularia spot	*Curvularia trifoli* f.sp. *gladioli*	-
Aster yellow	MLO	
Leaf rust	*Uromyces transvesalis*	*G. daleni*, *G. ochroleucus*, *G. papilio*, *G. tristis* var. *concolor* & *G. tristis*

Inheritance of characters:

- Cormel weight: Additive gene action.
- Linkage of characters is observed due to pleiotropy-
  - Heavy substance of petals and sepals and heavy ruffling.
  - Heavy ruffling and short flower heads.
  - Blue violet flower colour or red flower colour and susceptibility to certain diseases.
  - Large floret size and loose floral attachment.
  - Flower colour and corm pigmentation.
  - Production of large cormels and late blooming, etc.

44.2 Iris

- Iris means 'rainbow'.
- Bracts are known as 'spathe valve'.
- Head: Term used to denote the tissue from each spathe or pair of bracts.
- Iris roots are used for oil extraction.
- Propagation method: Corm.
- Falls: Outer parts of iris flowers, which seem to fall downwards or outwards, often bearded.
- **Varieties**: Blue Diamond, Madonna, Blue Magic, Professor Blaauw, Golden Beauty, San Diego.

45. LABIATAE

45.1 Salvia

- 1st common named as 'Lee's scarlet sage' in 1822.
- Herbaceous annual or perennial plant and cultivated as bedding plant.
- Species are strongly aromatic having horticultural, commercial and medicinal values.
- Glandular hairs on leaf surfaces secrete volatile oil that gives distinct aroma to the plant.
- Cool temperature with short days induce flowering.
- Quantitative LD plant.
- Photoperiod > 14 hours delay flowering in 'Bonfire and San John's Fire' cultivars.
- Stem quadrangular and covered with glandular hairs.
- Glandular hairs on leaf surfaces secrete volatile oil that gives distinct aroma to plant.
- Root has medicinal value for cardiovascular diseases.
- Inflorescence type: Cymose, compound raceme or panicle.
- Pollen to ovule ratio indicate facultative xenogamy.
- Flower: Bracteate, hermaphrodite, hypogynous, zygomorphic, and protandrous.
- Lower lip of corolla forms platform for visiting insect.
- Stamens reduced two short structures, the upper part is fertile and lower is imperfect.
- Gynoecium: Bicarpellary, syncarpous with superior ovary.
- Type of fruit: Schizocarp of 1-4 nutlets, each nutlet containing one seed. Seeds with no endosperm.
- 2 ovules in each locule.
- Type of placentation: Axile.
- Anthesis period: June to October.
- Stigma receptivity: 2 days prior to anthesis to 6 hours after opening.

- Flower structure is heteromorphic and homostyly resulting cross pollination.
- Generally large flowered species are outbreeders and species with minute flowers are inbreeders.
- Pollination agents: Ants, black bees, honey bees (*Apis mellifera*), humming birds.
- Seed set in insect pollination: 94-95%.
- Honey bee enhances seed production in *S. splendens*.
- Mature seed develop within 25 days after fertilization.
- No significant difference (23-24 seeds/ floret) in seed set between selfing and outcrossing.
- Heterostyly controls crossing rate and outcrossing rate is controlled by cleistogamy and chasmogamy.
- Propagation method: Seed.
- Explant for micropropagation: Stem segments with axillary buds.
- In hybrid seed production, use of dominant genetic male sterility is recommended.
- 2 different systems of male sterility: 1) Male sterility inherited as single dominant gene, maintained in heterozygous condition in cv. Harbinger. 2) Male sterility inherited as single recessive gene in cv. Bone Fire Early.
- Long flowering period is unfavourable for seed production.
- Seed priming helps in rapid and uniform plant emergence.
- Seed imbibed in distilled water for six days germinate earlier at 6^0C.
- Radiation at 1000 Gy accelerates germination.
- Shade drying for 6-7 days is essential to preserve volatile oil and normal green colour.
- Leaf yield: 1.7-2.3 T/ha (dry leaves for medicinal purpose).
- Space mutagenesis: Induced mutant in space of *S. splendens* cv. Shenzhouhong, derived as a mutant of 'Diwang'.
- Polyploid breeding: Colchicine @ 10 ppm to bud culture.
- Hu *et al*. (2009) suggested that Nested PCR-SSCP is an accurate and rapid tool for detecting gene point mutations.
- All domesticated varieties lack striated stem pigmentation trait which is present in wild relatives. This trait is used as morphological marker while crossing wild types and domesticated varieties.
- Interspecific crosses are successful within close phylogenetic group and species with different chromosome number.
- Malformation frequency is high with heavy ion bombardment at 200 Gy.

Species:

- 3 sub-species viz. *Salvia officinalis* ssp. *major* (Dalmatian); ssp. *lavendulifolia* (Spanish); ssp. *triloba* (Greek).
- Most species have both heterostylic (pin type and thrum type) and homostylic flowers.
- Homostylic flowers are observed in: *S. hispanica, S. reflexa, S. horminum, S. reflexa, S. tilliifolia, S. aegyptica, S. taraxacifolia, S. verbenacea.*
- All types of flowers bearing species: *S. coccinia, S. splendens, S. farinacea, S. pratensis, S. grahamii, S. glutinosa, S. leucantha.*
- Species with homostylic flowers show high degree of seed setting.

Species	Common name	Salient features
S. clevelandii	Blue sage/ Cleveland sage/ Fragrant sage	Evergreen shrub; fragrant; flowers are with numerous whorls.
S. coccinea	Texas sage/ Tropical sage/ blood sage	Herbaceous perennial; small flowers, red, pink or white in colour &cultivated as bedding or pot plant.
S. hispanica	Domesticated Chia	Seeds valued for food, medicine & oil.
S. sclarea	Clary sage	Biennial or perennial; fragrant; 2-6 flowers in each vertical
S. splendens	Cultivated sage	Familiar species in cultivation, commercially important & famous bedding plant.
S. miltiorrhiza	-	Roots have medicinal value for cardiovascular diseases.
S. officinalis	Common sage	Leaves have medicinal value.
S. pratensis	Meadow sage	Herbaceous perennial; flowers are rich violet & violet-blue to bluish white, pink, pure white coloured; high essential oil, used in traditional medicine.
S. verbenacea	-	Protandrous but if receives out crossing pollen, produces heavy seeds
S. verticilata	Lilac sage	Herbaceous perennial; tiny lavender flowers; used in folk medicine & as garden ornamental plant.
S. argentea	Silver sage	Resistant to powdery mildew
S. nemerosa	-	Resistant to powdery mildew

Varieties:

- First F_1 hybrid 'Hot Pants' released in 1972 followed by 'Torch' in 1975 and 'Trail Blazer' and 'Tallyho' in 1976.
- Sakata Seed Company, Japan: Coral Nymph (chimeric tetraploid), Tall Purple, Little Tango (dwarf).
- Day neutral cvs.: St. John's Fire, Fire Ball.
- Photoperid responsive cvs. (flowering is delayed under long day): Red Pillar, Bonfire, Scarlet Sage.
- Resistant to PM (*Erysiphe polygoni*): Blue Hill, Blue Queen, East Friesland, May Night (Mainacht), Rose Queen, Snow Hill.

Cultivar	Species & common name	Salient features
Summer Jewel Pink	(*S. coccinea*)- Pink salvia	Annual; vigorous, dwarf, 3 season bloomer, pink flowers
Victoria	(*S. farinacea*)- Mealy Cup sage	Dwarf, tender perennial; summer bloomer, drought tolerant; self seeding; violet blue flowers
Fairy Queen	(*S. farinacea*)- Mealy Cup sage	Tender perennial; compact, hardy, long blooming; drought tolerant; blue & white flowers
Blue Angel	(*S. patens*)-Gentian Sage	Annual; blossoms 2-2.5 inch wide; blue flowers held horizontally
Light House Purple	*S. splendens*- Common sage	Heat tolerant; deep purple spikes with dark to black corollas
Shenzhouhong (2008)	*S. splendens*- Common sage	Space mutagenesis from 'Diwang'; improved flowering time & high ornamental value

Inheritance of characters:

- Positive correlation: Plant height with flower length, inflorescence, branch number, time to flower.
- Leaf shape, number of nodes: Dominant.
- Plant height, days to flowering, flower number/ stem: Recessive.

Character	Number of genes	Inheritance pattern
Genic male sterility	Monogenic dominant	-
Photoperiodic flowering response & stem splitting	Monogenic dominant	-
Flower colour	Four	Red, rose, salmon & pink governed by two complementary genes (*Int* and *L*) & purple by incompletely dominant gene
		Dominant alleles of both (*Int-L-*) = red colour
		Recessive (*int int L-*) = rose colour
		Salmon colour (*Int-ll*) is a dilution of red
		Double recessive (*int int ll*) = pink colour
	Seven genes (*R, L, P, B, E, Int, V*)	Red (*-R-L-*)
		Rose (*-rrL-*)
		Salmon (*-R-ll*)
		Pink (*-rrll*)
		Int gene when dominant, no effect on the *R* & *L* genes
		Rose- *Int* gene when recessive with dominant *R* & *LL*
		P gene controls coloured P-, versus white pp, flowers
		Purple-*V* gene
		Burgundy-*B* gene
		E gene dilutes the colours produced by the other loci
White seed	Monogenic recessive	
Stem pigmentation	Monogenic dominant	

46. LILIACEAE

46.1 Lilium

- Bulbous ornamental plant produced worldwide.
- Ranks 4th among cut flower trade in international market.
- Shirui lily festival: Annual five day state festival celebrated in Ukhrul district of Manipur.
- It has association with world's cultures, religious feasts & symbolism of purity and innocence.
- Genus *Lilium* is Greek word '*Li*' meaning 'whiteness'.
- Diploid species in Asiatic and Orientals have 2n=24 and less cross fertile.
- Triploid *L. tigrinum* and *L. bulbiferum* have 2n=3x=36 and are sterile.
- Tetraploids are fertile.
- Pollen-less lilium cultivars are preferred by consumers.
- Dutch companies are dominant in lilium breeding.
- Lilies with spike length >50 cm are suitable for cut flower, while potted plants having 20-50 cm height are good.
- In Easter lily, short day reduces plant height while long day induces shoot height double than normal day.
- Gametophytic SI (GSI) prevails in *L. longiflorum*. It retards growth rate of pollen tube in style.
- 2 types of GSI 1) Short growth interspecific incompatibility i.e. growth of pollen tube is inhibited at base of stigma 2) Half growth incompatibility i.e. growth of pollen tube inhibited when it is grown half way down.
- Apomixis is one of the cause of incompatibility in *L. monadelphum*, *L. szovitsianum*, *L. kesslringianum*.
- Modes of propagation: Seeds (*L. formosanum*); scales (from side of bulbs); bulb developing into rhizome/ stolon, offsets, bulbils in leaf axils (*L. wallichianum*, *L. tigrinum*), bulblets (Asiatic lily cv. Sunshine).
- Normal stigmatic pollination technique is performed to overcome pre-fertilization barriers.
- Male gamete takes 5 days to reach ovary & fertilize. In Oriental hybrids, 7 days.
- Seed coat removal as well as high temperature treatment (30^{0}C) hastens seed germination.
- Seed dormancy is broken by chilling the seeds to 5^{0}C for 3-4 weeks.
- Hybrid seed between (*L. speciosum* x *L. auratum*) germinate after washing in running water for 10-14 hours.
- Commercial method of propagation: Multiplication by scales.
- Yearlings: Lily planting stock at the end of first growing season from bulblets.

- Most of lilium hybrids and varieties do not flower in 1st year from seed/ scale due to obligate vernalization requirement and lengthy juvenility.
- Bulbs flower in 3-4 years after scaling.
- Methods to break incompatibility:

1. Heat treatment to style (50⁰C for 6 min.) 2) Use of PGRs 3) Application of genetically inactivated i.e. irradiated, compatible mentor or pioneer pollen on stigma 4) Placement of pollen in base of styler canal 5) Pollination of ovary by cutting styles 6) Pre-fertilization barriers can be overcome through cut style and grafted style method. 7) Post-fertilization barriers can be overcome through ovary slice/ ovule/ embryo/ embryo rescue technique.
2. Interspecific incompatibility experienced in L. longiflorum can be overcome through use of pre-pollination injections to styles with exudates from stigma.
3. Pre-pollination injection of 50 ppm Kinetin in detached styles of Easter lily also removes incompatibility reaction & results in increased fruit set & seed number/ capsule.
4. SI in *L. longiflorum* can be overcome by application of flower organ extract or temperature treatment of pollen at 40⁰C for 10 or 90 min or 50⁰C for 30 or 60 min followed by -20⁰C for 24 hours.

- Flowers borne in raceme/ umbel at the tip of stem.
- Perfect flower contains 6 stamens, 6 tepals and trilobed stigma.
- Pollen grains are dark red/ brown in colour and sticky.
- Fruit type: 3 celled capsule with numerous seeds.
- IAA promotes bulblet formation.
- Longer shelf life: 25% bud colour storage.
- Susceptible to high day temperature (>30⁰C).
- Growth regulator used for controlling height: Ancymidol, CCC and Ethrel.
- Pollen grain storage: Polypropylene bottles at -20⁰C.
- Pollen grains remain viable > 180 days in acetone/ benzene/ ethyl ether.
- Irradiation (0.1 to 0.8 kR) increases viability of stored pollens & produce seeds in different crosses.
- For forcing both the lilies requires 13-17⁰C night and 21⁰C day.
- North American Lily Society is actively involved in lilium improvement program (www.lilis.org).
- Sweetening: Term used to denote odour of lilies after storage under anaerobic conditions.
- Micropropagation: Bulb regeneration from explants (*L. auratum*, *L. speciosum*); excised leaves (*L. leichtinii* var. *maximowiezii*); callus (*L. longiflorum*).
- Anther culture: *L. davidii* var. Willmottiae.
- Embryo culture performed to introduce pink colour and small flower size.

- Somatic hybridization protoplast fusion is used to regenerate new hybrids from sexually incompatible species.
- Molecular biology is used to engineer lilium against LSV, TBV resistance.

Species:

- Temperate species are deciduous and dormant in winter.
- Largest genome size (32 Bbp) in plant kingdom: *L.henryii*.

Name	Features
Easter lily (*Lilium longiflorum*)	Flowers outward facing; trumpet shaped; pure white coloured; distinct fragrance; important holiday potted plant & cut flower; strong GSI found
Turk cap lily (*L. martagon*)	Reflexed petal lily;
L. amximouiczii	Edible
L. elegans (syn. *L. maculatum*)	Dwarf
Madonna lily (*L. candidum*)	Oil yielding
Tiger lily (*L. tigrinum*)	Double flowers; triploid (2n=36); produce bulbils
Torch lily/ Red hot poker (*Kniphofia uvaria*)	Suitable for borders; bloom in June-September; look like stand alone specimen in garden; heat & drought tolerant
Formosa lily (*L. formosanum*)	Flower from seed/scale within first year without vernalization
L. henryii	Resistant to fusarium wilt & tulip breaking virus (TBV)
L. dauricum	Resistant to fusarium wilt
L. candidum	Tolerant to low temperature, low light & year round flowering ability
Torch lily (*Kniphofia loides*)	Suitable for border & as a accent; heat & drought tolerant

Two commercially groups grown in India:

Oriental lily (O-genome) *Archeliron* section	Asiatic lily (A-genome) *Sinomartagon* section
Late flowering (50-55 days from visible bud)	Early flowering (30-35 days from visible bud)
Highly fragrant	Odourless
Leaves parallel to ground	Leaves narrow & upward growing
White & pink coloured flowers	Orange, red, yellow coloured flowers
Bulbs 16-22 cm in dia.	Bulbs 10-16 cm in dia.
Blooms in July-September	Blooms in early June
Bulbs stored at 5^0C for 8-10 weeks	Bulbs stored at 2-4^0C for 8-10 weeks
Flowers up-ward facing (referred as Star gazers); large in size, long lasting, resistant to botrytis but susceptible to fusarium & fetch higher price	Flowers are upright facing (umbrella type), have dark spots, short vase life, fetch low market price, resistant to fusarium but susceptible to botrytis

Varieties:

- Lily breeding was initiated in Europe in mid of 19th century.
- Lilium cvs. of ornamental importance are bred from crosses within *Sinomartagon*, *Archeliron* & *Leucolirion* sections.
- Mid-century hybrids (now called Asiatic hybrids): Released in USA in 1940 and hybrid 'Enchantment' bred by Jan De Graaff in 1944 was breakthrough.

- Oriental hybrids (*L. auratum* x *L. speciosum*) were developed during 1990.
- 'Stargazer': 1st up-facing Oriental hybrid was bred by Leslie Woodriff in 1975.
- 1st crosses within section *Sinomartagon* were produced in Decennia of 20th century in Japan & USA.
- Hybridization between Asiatic, Trumpet & Oriental group is very difficult.
- In early 1990s, a new class of insectional triploid LA hybrids (*L. longiflorum* x Asiatic) were introduced in European market.
- Due to advanced breeding techniques, Asiatic hybrids have been replaced by LA hybrids (75%), OT hybrids (15%), LO hybrids (50%) and form commercial cultivars grown for garden & greenhouse cultivation.
- Insectional triploid hybrids: LO (*L. longiflorum* x Oriental); OT (Oriental x Trumpet); OA (Oriental x Asiatic);
- Hybrids OTO, FA (Pink Pearl, Green Star, Honey Bowl, Cream Star, Glossy Orange), FAA (Pink Pearl), FO (Hanuri), OT (Crimson Glory, Crimson Star, Crimson Lady, Red Bird) & OA are developed by cyt style method and *in vitro* embryo rescue techniques by National Institute of Horticultural & Herbal Science, Korea.
- Through meiotic and mitotic polyploidization, genetic base has been broaden and ALA hybrid 'Fangio' (2n=3x=36) is derived from spontaneous meiotic polyploidization.
- Parkmanni hybrids: Prominently grown in New Zealand.
- KILH-13: Indigenously developed line using *L. formosanum* x *L. longiflorum*.
- *L. longiflorum* cvs. Formobel, Formolongi, Geberia, Snow Hill, Snow Queen, White Europe, White American, White Elegance, White Heaven.
- Asiatic hybrids: Acapulco (pink), Albino, Alpenglow, Aryeo, Asian Flame, Bravo, Butternut, Black Eye, Charisma, Cherub, Chinook, Connecticut King, Enchantment, Endeavour, Elite, Expression (white), Fire Band, Fire Cracker, Golden Pixie, Lovely Girl, Nutmegger, Orange Girl, Sunshine (Loly Pop x Shocking Pink), Sunny Gold, White Superstar, Yellow Blaze.
- Oriental hybrids: Barnini, Bonfire, Casa Blanca (white), Casa Dream, Casendra, Empress of China, Empress of India, Imperial Gold, Imperial Pink, Pink Lady, Star Queen, Swan Beauty.
- Pollenless Asiatic hybrid cultivars have been bred in Europe only.

Cultivars resistant to gray mold

	Parentage	Parental level of infection	Grading of hybrids
Asiatic hybrids			
K-1	Nakts Tango x H-7-92	Moderately susceptible x heavy susceptible	Highly susceptible
K-2 (Otis)	Nakts Tango x Cha-Cha	Moderately susceptible x heavy susceptible	Highly susceptible
K-3	Cha-Cha x My Joe Ann	Healthy x very highly susceptible and vice versa	Intermediate

K-4	Cha-Cha x Silly Girl	Moderately susceptible x heavy susceptible	Highly susceptible
K-5(Balley)	Baltais Lacis x Shirley	Healthy x slightly susceptible & vice versa	Highly susceptible
K-6(Tora)	Tirreno x Honey Pink	Healthy x very highly susceptible & vice versa	Intermediate
K-7 (Saulenini)	Herrold x Solstice	Healthy x healthy	Resistant
K-8 (Kornelija)	Compass x Gran Paradiso	Slightly susceptible x slightly susceptible	Highly susceptible
K-9 (Vigante)	Nepal x Alisa	Healthy x slightly susceptible & vice versa	Susceptibility prevailed
K-10 (Annija)	Patricija x Magic Eye	Healthy x slightly susceptible & vice versa	Susceptibility prevailed
K-11 (Orfo)	Orfejs x Aristo	Healthy x very highly susceptible & vice versa	Resistant
K-12	Olga x Arabeska	Healthy x slightly susceptible & vice versa	Susceptibility prevailed
Trumpet hybrids			
K-13 (Aurelija)	Zemgale x White Henryi	Healthy x Healthy	Resistant
K-14 (Varsma)	Ekzotika x *L. henryii* var. *citrinum*	Healthy x Healthy	Resistant

Inheritance of characters:

- Raised spots & splatters appear on flower tepals is unique in Lilium.
- Tepal spots and splatters are genetically independent.
- Flower longevity has positive & significant correlation with forcing period.

Character	Number of genes	Inheritance pattern
Flower longevity	Polygenic	Additive
Flower colour	-	In Asiatic hybrids orange red dominant to white, yellow and violet; Apricot white incompletely dominant to salmon orange In Oriental hybrids dark pink dominant to white
	Monogenic	Recessive gene give rise to yellow colour
	-	Spotless or brightness is dominant
Flower shape	-	Funnel shape recessive to up-facing & split type perianth
Flowering without vernalization (i.e. Recurrent flowering)	Digenic (*Ver*)	Atleast one dominant allele at one of the loci
Vase life	Polygenic	Additive
Pollen-less nature	-	Cytoplasmic & nuclear genes govern trait

Diseases, pest and disorders:

- Serious pests: Thrips (*T. vancckei*) and mites.
- Gray mold (*Botrytis ellytica* & *B. cinerea*): Most destructive and infect various vegetative organs, leaves, flower buds, flower stem and seed pods.

Name	Cause	Remedy
Fleck	Combination of CMV & lily symptomless virus	-
Leaf tip burn or leaf scorch	Excess Mn and Al salts in soil, high fluoride level, high relative humidity	Spray 70 mM Calcium nitrate
Bud blast or bud abortion	Low light and ethylene	Apply silver thiosulphate (STS) in standing crop
Leaf yellowing	Easter lilies & Oriental hybrids are highly susceptible. Root rot, over watering, moisture stress, etc.	Spray 100 ppm Promalin or Accel
Bulb split	Aphids & high greenhouse temperature	Maintain humidity

Disease	Resistant /tolerant species and cultivars
Tulip Breaking Virus (TBV)	*L. henryii*, Asiatic hybrid lily cv. Connecticut King.
Fusarium oxysporum	*L. dauricum*; *L. henryii*, Asiatic hybrid lily cv. Connecticut King (partial resistance); *L. longiflorum* cv. Gelria; Cvs. Hae-wool, Sinavro, FA 96-16 as highly & Supia & Doran as moderately resistant.
Botrytis	L. *henryii* var. *citrinum*, Oriental hybrids, Herrold, Solstice, Orfejs, Ekzotika, Zemgale, White Henryi.

46.2 Tulip

- Ornamental bulbous geophyte, cultivated for cut flower, potted plant, garden plant and landcape purpose.
- It ranks 2nd among international cut flower trade.
- Garden tulip was introduced into Europe from Turkey in 16th century.
- The Netherlands and France: Major tulip bulb producers.
- In India, tulip thrives well in temperate regions of J & K, H.P, U.P.
- Name 'Tulipa' is derived from the Persian word '*Toliban*' meaning 'Turban'.
- Most prestigious flower among all bulbous ornamentals.
- Richest gene centre: North-West Himalayas.
- Herbacious, perennial geophyte with true bulb.
- Mature bulb has 6 tunicated (circularpapery covering) scales attached to the base of plant and develops roots.
- Axillary buds develop into flowering scape with sessile leaves and daughter bulbs.
- Apical axillary bud form 4leaves and terminal flattened and fleshy flower.
- Lowest leaf is largest called as 'wrapper leaf' which develops on the side of the bulb.
- Bulbs need vernalization i.e. cold period treatment of several weeks for optimal flowering.

- Trap shaped leaves with waxy coating appear in alternate sequence on the stem.
- Flower is large, borne on scape, cup to star shaped.
- Each flower has 3 petals, 3 sepals which are nearly identical and called as 'tepals' (i.e. perianth segments).
- Flower has 6 tepals, 6 anthers and one style with a tri-lobed stigma and superior ovary.
- Flowers are monochromatic or bicoloured or stripped.
- Fruit: 3 valved, loculicidal capsule with leathery covering and ellipsoidal in shape.
- Each capsule contains numerous flat, disc shaped seeds in two rows.
- Number of ovules/ovary: 150 (*T. turkestanica*) and 300-450 (*T. gesneriana*).
- Seeds are light brown to dark brown in colour with thin seed coat and endosperm does not fill the entire seed.
- Tendency of apomixis and production of apomictic seed is observed.
- Pollen grains can be stored for 1-2 years with silica gel and indicator A at 5-7^{0}C.
- Testing of pollen viability: 1% tetrazolium chloride.
- Stamens: Basifixed with filaments shorter than tepals.
- Stamens dominate central portion of flower popularly known as 'eye'.
- Ornamental value of flower: Depend of narrow ratio between stamen length and width of perianth cup i.e. number of perianth.
- Cultivars of Darwin group produce 3-4 bulbs/ year than cvs. of other group (1-2).
- Flower colour and shape are not affected by environmental factors.
- Red flower colour: Anthoxanthin.
- All tulips bloom in spring.
- Planting season: August for early type and November for late flowering types.
- Floral longevity: 8-16 days and can be extended upto 22 days.
- Seeds take 5-6 years to obtain a flowering plant and 10-20 years period for development of a cultivar.
- Capsules are harvested 9-12 weeks after pollination.
- Seeds are kept at 4^{0}C to overcome dormancy.
- Seed treatment with 'Esculetin' alone or in combination with GA, speed up germination.
- Seeds require low temperature to induce germination & to initiate bulb primorpdium.
- Application of *in vitro* pollination offers good prospects in tulip breeding.
- Pre-selection criteria:

1. Screening of juvenile seedlings and clones at nursery stage against fusarium disease;

2. Bulk selection at very young stage to overcome long juvenile period;
3. Breeding line on the basis of bulb diameter or bulb weight for offset production and length of juvenile period;
4. For flowering time: Time of shoot emergence and time of foliage senescence;
5. For forcing ability: Early flowering and length of flowering stem;
6. Selection of tunicated bulbs on skin colour basis when bulbs are harvested in bulk for prediction of earliness in flowering;
7. Breeder select around 0.1 to 1% best plants during forcing as cut flower purpose.

- Flower forcing is attempted with short cold period to fulfill very early or late market demand, to achieve quality cut flower for plant plant under poor light conditions in winter and to increase number of flowers per unit area.
- Eskimo (ice) tulip: Forcing procedure in which tulips are planted in late fall season, rooted at 9^0C & then frozen at -3^0C until defrosted for summer/ fall flowering.
- Techniques to overcome crossing barriers: Ovary slice culture, embryo culture.
- Hybrids from *T. generiana* x *T. agenensis* and *T. gesneriana* x *T. praestans* can be obtained from ovary slice culture.
- Kinds of barriers preventing fertilization in interspecific crosses:
  1. Low pollen germination on stigma
  2. Low pollen tube growth in style
  3. Low pollen tube penetration of ovule
  4. Failure to form zygote
  5. Retarded zygote growth
  6. Embryo abortion.
- Techniques to remove difficulties:
  1. Bud pollination
  2. Use of cut style method or grafted style method
  3. Placental pollination
  4. Pollination of isolated ovules.
- More embryos could be rescued during early developmental stages (4 weeks post pollination) with ovule culture compared to embryo culture.
- Post fertilization barriers cause sterility of F_1 hybrids and fertility can be restored by chromosome doubling.
- Tulip bulbs are renewed annually.
- Thieves: Tulip bulbs that are small, withered and rarely flower.
- 'H' bulb: Small bulblets of tulip located between tunic and fleshy scale.
- During 4th year, small bulbs (planting stock) produce flowers in 5-7 years.

- On an average there are 5-7 daughter bulbs.
- Bulb finger: Irritation caused due to handling of tulip bulbs.
- Bulb units: Annual increment of bulb growth.
- Foot: Lower most internode of floral scape.
- GISH technique has been used to clarify genome composition.
- Micropropagation of cv. Merry Widow is successful.
- Homozygous parental lines can be produced through development of *in vitro* haploids using microspore culture and then their polyploidization.
- Somatic embryogenesis is done in *T. gesneriana* cv. Christmas Marvel.
- Ovule culture is done in *T. gesneriana* cv. Gander.

Species:

- *Tulipa suaveolens*: Wild in southern Europe and plays important role in evolution of garden tulip.
- *T. stellata*: Himalayan origin, diploid (2n=2x=24).
- *T. saxatilis*, *T. lanuta*: Triploid (2n=3x=36)
- *T. bakeri*: Diploid. Identical growth pattern with stolons.
- *T. gesneriana* (Garden tulip).
- *T. kaufmanniana* (Water lily tulip).
- *T. clusiana*: Tetraploid (2n=4x=48).
- *T. systole*: Used as bridging species between species of section Tulipanum & *T. gesneriana*.
- Early flowering tulips are originated from *T. schrenkii* while late flowering types from *T. macedonic*.

Varieties:

- Varieties differ widely in form, size, shape, colour and flowering habit.
- Cvs. from *Hortus Bulborum*: Mendel Triumph, Lily flowered tulips are progenitors of new tulip types for characters like disease resistance, early forcing and keeping quality.
- From inbreeding program, new cultivars viz. Garden Wonder, Red Coral, Red Pearl, Amethyst (Parrot tulip) have been developed for commercial use.
- Tolerant to salinity: Darwin hybrid tulips, Apeldoorn, Elite Diplomate.
- Cytotypes reported in *T. clusiana* cv. Titica (diploid), Stellata (tetraploid), Chrysanrha (pentaploid).
- For cut flower purpose: Lucky Strike, Parade, Purissima, Golden Melody, Cassini.
- For garden decoration purpose: Cantala.
- Suitable for early forcing: Cassini, Mirjoran, Gold Mirjoran.

- Yellow Dover:*T. fosteriana* cv. Queen of Night (2n=24) x *T. gesneriana* cv. Red Emperor (2n=24).

Group	Features & cultivars
Single early tulips	Belladona, Brilliant Star, Charles, Christmas Marvel, Pink Beauty
Double early or paeony tulips	Carlton, Electra (purple colour, bud sport of Murillo), Fringed Beauty (red with fringed golden yellow colour, bud sport of Titan), Monte Carlo, Oranje Nassau (orange brown coloured, bud sport of Murillo), Peach Blossom (deep rose coloured, bud sport of Murillo), Gold Medal, Bonanza
Cottage tulips (Single late type)	Artist, Golden Artist, Princess Margaret Rose, Smiling Queen, White City
Double late tulips	Bonanza, Gold Medal, May Wonder, Orange Triumph
Mendel tulips	Apricot Beauty, Pink Trophy, Athlete (pure white coloured, bud sport of Webber)
Triumph tulips	Orange Wonder, First Lady, Garden Party, Golden Melody, Lucky Strike, Fidelio, Rose Beauty
Darwin hybrid tulips	Interspecific hybrid of (*T. gesneriana* x *T. fosteriana*); sterile triploids (2n=3x=36); more productive, flower earlier, longer, more disease resistant & suitable for cut flower e.g. Big Chief, Beauty of Apeldoorn, Dover, Golden Apeldoorn, Tender Beauty, Orange Sun, Purissima (highly fertile), Yellow Dover
Darwin tulips	Aristocrat, Golden Age, Pink Supreme, Queen of Night, Sweet Harmony, Yellow Flight
Lily-flowered tulips	Aladdin, Aster, China Pink, Maytime, Picotee, West Point
Parrot tulips	Black Parrot, Orange Favorite, Texas Gold, White Parrot, Blue Parrot, Red Parrot
Breeder tulips	May flowering, grow upto 60 cm height; single & enormous oval blooms
Multiflora tulips	May flowering, branched flower stems; 3-6 blooms per bulb & ideal for bedding & cutting
Green tulips	May flowering; depict green colour category; most ideal for flower arrangement, garden display

Pests, diseases & disorder:

Disease	Causal organism	Resistant cultivars, species & remarks
Fusarium bulb rot	*F. oxysporum* f.sp. *tulipae*	*T. tarda*, Water Scheel, Black Parrot, Lucky Strike, Aristocrat, Christmas Fire, Early Sunrise, Pink Mission,
Tulip Breaking Virus	-	Cantata, Juan, Madame Lefeber (tetraploid), Princeps
Gray mold/ Tulip fire	*Botrytis tulipae*	*T. tarda*
Aphid	-	*T. eichleri*, *T. fosteriana*, *T. vvedenskyi*
Tied leaf	-	Flower bending at 45^0.
Bulker	-	Cvs. producing small number of bulbs
Cracking	-	Leaf & scape disorder, Ethylene or B deficiency
Hollow stem	-	Moisture imbalance

Inheritance of characters:

- Positive correlation: Longevity of flower attached to the bulb and vase life; keeping quality and time required for forcing; Width of perianth cup and number of perianth.
- Flower pigmentation: Quantitative trait & red colour is due to anthocyanin.

Character	Inheritance pattern
Floral pigments (delphinidin, quercetin and kaempferol) in tepals	Additive & non additive
Flower colour	Polygenic
Flower shape	Difficult to predict
Keeping quality (senescence) & flower longevity	Additive
Fusarium (sourness) disease resistance	Additive

47. MALVACEAE/ (MALLOW FAMILY)

47.1 Hibiscus

- Eulogized as 'Queen of Tropics or Rose of China or Chinese hibiscus or Blacking plant or Shoe flower'.
- Flowering plant of hot and warm climate.
- Florida: Prominent hibiscus growing centre of the world.
- Hawaii: World's richest collection and centre for evolving new varieties.
- Plant grows back quickly after pruning.
- Propagation method: Semi-hard wood cuttings.
- Propagation of Hawaiian hibiscus: Patch budding and veneer grafting.
- Techniques for mass propagation: Cuttings, Marcottage (96% success), cleft grafting (88% success), patch budding (65% success).
- Self pollinated crop.
- Flowers borne in drooping fashion and are axillary, bisexual, actinomorphic and non-fragrant.
- Style is terminated by 5 lobed stigma whose ends are discoid.
- Pollen fertility: High (53-100%) in species and 27-97% in cultivars.
- Pollen grains are polysiphonous.
- Fruit is 5-10 lobed capsule and takes 40-70 days for seed maturity under Bengaluru condition and 28-38 days under Kerala condition.
- Each capsule contains 10-20 seeds in each lobe.
- Fruit set is higher in August-October compared to January-March.
- Fruit set and seed set is obtained only in crosses involving species belonging to same section and 60 days after pollination.
- Seeds are fuzzy and brown-black coloured.
- Dried calyces of *H. sabdariffa* are used for making an infusion beverage called 'zobo' in Nigeria.
- Flower buds of *H. syriacus* are acidic and used as vegetable.

- Hibiscus cultivars with high ploidy level are more fertile than low ploidy level.
- Use of flow cytometry: Quick identification of ploidy levels & genome sizes.
- Somatic hybridization: Protoplast fusion.
- Hybrids are easy to detect at seedling stage provided parents differ in genotypic & phenotypic characters.
- Witche's broom: Severe and obligate root parasite.

Species:

- *H. coccineus* x *H. moscheutos*: Cold hardy progeny.
- *H. syriacus* is cross compatible with *H. paramutabilis* & *H. sinosyriacus*.
- *H. sabdariffa* var. *sabdariffa* & *altissima:* Tolerant to fusarium wilt.
- *H. syriacus*, *H. sinosyriacus*, *H. paramutabilis*: Belong to temperate regions of world & winter hardy.
- *H. lavateroides*: Lavender coloured flowers.
- *H. diversifolius*, *H. esculentus*, *H. trionus* (syn. *H. africanas*): Annual spp.
- Asian spp. used for making bast fibre (making rops & mats): *H. cannabinus* (also used as minor vegetable), *H. sabdariffa*, *H. surattensis*, *H. planifolius*, *H. flococcus*, *H. macrophyllus*.

Species	Common name	Features
H. rosa chinensis	Shoe flower/ China rose	Day neutral plant
H. mutabilis	Changeable/ Persian rose/ Cotton rose	Only species requires pruning after flowering
H. cameronii	Pink hibiscus	Shrub; cup-shaped flowers (7.5-10 cm dia.); staminal column is red & curved downward
H. sabdariffa	Indian sorrel/ Roselle	Annual or perennial herb; dicot & autogamous; yellow flowers; cultivated for garden hedges used for production of bast fibers & as an infusion/ natural medicine for treating hypertension
H. schizopetalus	African hibiscus/ Chinese lanterns	Short day plant
H. acetosella	Purple leaved hibiscus/ False roselle/ African Rosemallow	Natural polyploid; annual, tall; very vigorous; cold hardy & tolerant to drought; highly resistant to root knot nematode & yellow vein mosaic viruse.g. Blue Bird, Marina, Lucky, Red Heart, Wood Bridge, Pink Giant, Diana, Helene
H. syriacus	Rose of Sharon/ True hollyhock	Long day plant; cold hardy & tolerant to drought
H. moscheutos	Crimson eyed rose mallow/ Wild cotton/ Swamp rosemallow/ Swamp hibiscus	Winter hardy & highly tolerant to drought
Malvaviscus arboreus	Sleeping hibiscus/ Firecracker hibiscus	-
H. arnottianus	-	White flowered
H. brackenridgei	-	Sulphur yellow flowers; cross incompatible & sterile; self seeder
H. youngianus	-	Pink flowered; self seeder
H. kokio	-	Red flowered; self seeder

Varieties:

- 1st hibiscus hybridization was accomplished in 1872 at Hawaii islands.
- Texas A & M Agri Life Foundation Seed, Vernon have developed over 6,000 hybrids during 2009-12.
- Hibiscus improvement and development work has been extensively done at IIHR, Bengaluru.
- Improved variety of 'Chandrika' is 'Punnagai'.
- Cv. Alipore Beauty: Rootstock for Hawaiian hibiscus.
- Archer's Hibiscus (Hibiscus x Archeri): Old hybrid between *H. rosa sinensis* x *H. schizopetalus*. Upright growth, fast growing & red flowers.
- Anjali: Somatic mutation through gamma irradiation in cv. Alipore Beauty.
- Minerva (lavender flowers), Helene (white flowers): Polyploidy breeding.
- 1st blue flowering winter hardy cv.: Blue Angel.
- Cv. Robert Brown: Dual coloured flowers.

Variety	Breeding method	Features
Agnes, Australian Single, Glowing Sunset, Lipstick, My Beauty, Netaji, Viceroy	Introduction	Single flowered
Alipore Beauty, Chitra, Aurora, Daffodil, Dream, Juno, Mahatma	Introduction	Double flowered
Lal Bagh botanical garden, Bengaluru		
Aphrodite	Selection from *H. syriacus*	Erect, multi-stemed, flowers 10-14 cm in dia. Flowering from June to September.
Bharat Sundari (1976)	Selection from 'IIHR-1'	Very floriferous; flowers single, saucer shaped, corolla deep rose with light border.
CO.1 (syn. Punnagai) 1981	Selection from 'Chandrika'	Semi-spreading, flower bigger size (14 cm dia.); crape paper textured petals; 1000 flowers/ plant.
Dr. B. P. Pal (syn. H.S. No.187) 1969	Selection from 'Lahiana'	Flowers polypetalous, base of corolla is whitish pink turns to rose pink; petals are mandarin red (deep gold) in colour.
Gnat	Selection from 'Lahiana'	Shrub with drooping branches, flowers single 17-20 cm across; petals recurved, base of corolla is pink with red margin.
President	Selection from 'Hula Bule'	Flowers single 12 cm across with red base changing to cherry red up to 2/3rd of corolla. Marginal portion rose coloured.
Rashtrapati	Selection from 'Lahiana'	Most prolific bearer; flowers last for 2 days, petals with frilled margin; basal part of corolla is rose opal coloured & terminates to peach colour
Soyang (1997)	Selection from '*H. syriacus*'	Dwarf, flowers funnel shaped, very small in size; reddish pink flower colour with red eye spot.

Aurobindo	Hybrid of 'Leberacea x White Pink Centre'	Leaves cordate-ovate; flowers single (13-16 cm across); corolla aureolin & margin of petals is saffron yellow while back side of petal is lemon yellow.
Mother Teresa (1972)	Hybrid of 'Honi Honi x Comet'	Leaves cordate, ovate, acute & undulate; flowers 15-17 cm across; corolla base is capsicum red & margin of petal is saffron red.
University of Philippines		
Domini M. Torevillas	Marcela x Nelia T. Gonzales	Dark orange flower with dark red eye zone & light red blushes radiating to the petals.
Cynthia A. Villar	Tangerine Orange x Loren B. Legarda	Orange flower with red eye zone surrounded by pinkish halo.
Marilyn D. Maranon	Perla Santos-Ocampo x Loren B. Legarda	Lemon yellow flower with white eye zone surrounded by pinkish halo.
Maria Rosario O. Montejo	Perla Santos-Ocampo x Loren B. Legarda	Red orange flower with pinkish red eye surrounded by yellow edges.
Arlene B. Arcillas	Nazaria x Loren B. Legarda	Carmine rose flower with cardinal red eye.
Connie S. Angeles	Tangerine Orange x Loren B. Legarda	Orpiment orange flower with cardinal red eye surrounded by pinkish halo.
Sylvia P. Lina	Nazaria x Loren B. Legarda	Neyron rose flower with magenta eye.
IIHR, Bengaluru		
Aikta (1976)	Debby Ann x H.S.203	Moderately vigorous, erect lateral branches with post office red coloured corolla.
Anuradha (1978)	Debby Ann x H.S.48	Very floriferous; flowers single, cup shaped, 14-16 cm across, corolla golden buff with reddish border.
Ashirwad (1978)	H.S.121 x Hombe Gowda	Vigorous with prominent lenticels all over the surface of branches, floriferous; flowers single; 18-21 cm across; corolla cadmium orange.
Arunodaya (1972)	IIHR-H-2 x Rachaiah	Vigorous with profuse lateral branches with nasturtium orange corolla colour. Flowers single (16-18 cm across).
Basant (1972)	IIHR-H-1 x Rachaiah	Moderately vigorous with erect lateral branches with sulphur yellow coloured flowers. Flowers single (17-20 cm across).
Benazeer (1972)	H.S. (Red) x H.S.123	Moderately vigorous with drooping lateral branches with capsicum red coloured flowers.
Chitralekha (1976)	Debby Ann x H.S.203	Moderately vigorous, erect lateral branches with china rose coloured corolla. Flower single (15-17 cm dia.). White variegation of different shape & size in the centre of each petal is a unique feature of this variety i.e. novelty in hibiscus.
Dilruba (1976)	Debby Ann x H.S.203	Moderately vigorous, drooping branches with dark golden buff coloured corolla.
Geetanjali (1972)	Debby Ann x Rachiah	Moderately vigorous & Dutch vermilion corolla colour.
Jogan (1972)	IIHR-H-1 x Rachaiah	Moderately vigorous with drooping branches with apricot corolla colour.

Nartaki (1972)	H.S.(red) x H.S.123	Moderately vigorous, drooping branches with marigold orange colour. Flower double (14-16 cm dia.). Outer whorls of petals are recurved & inner whorls are fused with the staminal column.
Nazneen (1972)	H.S.203 x Rashtrapati	Moderately vigorous shrub with slightly pubescent leaves Flowers single, tangerine orange coloured, slightly cup shaped, 18-22 cm dia., petals recurved along the margin & with silky texture.
Neelofer (1979)	Seedling x Aldrin	Moderately vigorous; shinning dark green leaves; flowers single, 18-22 cm across; corolla is Magenta Rose with slightly reddish tinge towards margin.
Pakeezah (1972)	IIHR-H-1 x Rachaiah	Moderately vigorous, erect lateral branches with carmine red coloured corolla.
Phulkari (1976)	H.S.139 x H.S.18	Very vigorous with many erect lateral branches, flower single measuring 17-19 cm across; corolla Delft Rose coloured with prominent light purple rays & yellow border.
Priya (1972)	IIHR-H-2 x Rachaiah	Moderately vigorous, erect lateral branches with Rose Bengal coloured corolla.
Queen of Hessaraghatta (1976)	H.S. x H.S.123	Moderately vigorous, erect lateral branches with orange corolla colour.
Ratna (1979)	H.S. 127 x Ruffle	Vigorous shrub with erect lateral branches; moderately floriferous, flowers single, saucer shaped, 14-15 cm across; petals are slightly frilled towards the margin; corolla yellow with white centre orange red stripes.
Red Gold (1972)	IIHR-H-2 x Cronwell	Early blooming; moderately vigorous, erect lateral branches with Dutch vermillion coloured corolla.
Red Saturn (1978)	H.S. 182 x Red Double	Very vigorous with erect lateral branches & shining dark green foliage, floriferous, flowers double with ruffled petals and 10-12 cm across, corolla signal red coloured without any conspicuous centre.
Shanti (1972)	IIHR-H-1 x Rachaiah	Moderately vigorous, erect lateral branches having Primrose Yellow coloured corolla.
Smt. Indira Gandhi (1974)	H.S.182 x Ruffle	Moderately vigorous, flowers single, saucer shaped, 22-25 cm across; petals recurved along margin, Indian yellow coloured corolla with orange red margin.
Smt. Kamla Nehru (1974)	Debby Inn x Nijalingappa	Moderately vigorous, erect lateral branches with Rose Bengal coloured corolla.
Tribal Queen (1972)	IIHR.H-1 x H.S.481	Moderately vigorous, flowers single, saucer shaped, 16-20 cm across, petals recurved, corolla cardinal red with dark purple base.
TNAU, Coimbatore		
Thilagum (syn. CO.2) 1981	Intergeneric hybrid of '*H. rosa-sinensis* x *Malvaviscus arboreus*	Woody perennial; double flowers (30-36 petals/ flower); highly floriferous (>3,000 flowers/ plant/ year) & suitable for planting as single specimen in lawn
CO.3 (1984)	Bright Yellow x Red Gold	Interclonal hybrid; flowers apricot yellow with signal red throat, highly floriferous(1,300 flowers/plant/ yeaı)

Inheritance of characters:

- Stem pigmentation: Monogenic.
- Leaf shape: Digenic.
- Bushy plant habit and edible calyx: Monogenic dominant.
- Pink flower colour dominant over red.
- Red flower colour dominant over white.
- Pure white is rare colour. In white coloured flowers, no colour pigment is produced.
- Root knot nematode resistance: Monogenic dominant.
- Cold hardiness: Polygenic.

47.2 Hollyhock

- Seed propagated winter flowering annual.
- Cold hardy and long day plant.
- It is facultative xenogamous.
- Fruit type: Schizocarp and contains 35-36 seeds.
- Flowers: Protandrous, herkogamous, allows geitonogamy and produced in axil of leaves.
- Fully opened flower have 5 imbricated petals with adnate base to the stamens.
- 1st report on heterosis: Swaroop *et al.* (1973).
- Heterosis was for number of flowers on main stem (48.33%), side branches (421%) and flower size and flower weight.
- Unusual plant height (2.5-3 m) and delay in flowering are handicaps in its popularity.
- Flowering period lasts for 100-103 days.
- Peak flowering season: June-August.
- Flowers on the main stem form a column.
- Inflorescence: Raceme.
- Flowers at bottom of raceme bloom first.
- Possesses high degree of protandry.
- Anthesis time: 7-9 AM.
- Lower nodes of plant have 3 flowers, each open at a node on same day.
- Fruit: Schizocarp, dry disc divided into 15 locules containing 35-36 seeds.
- Pollination agents: Bees (*A. mellifera*), humming birds, butterflies.
- Vase life of single flower: 3-4 days.
- To produce seeds of F_1 hybrids, hand emasculation and pollination is commonly followed.
- Seed production cost is very high.

Species:

- Black hollyhock (*Althea rosea* var. *nigra*). In Hungery, it is widely used for colouring ingredient in herbal tea, liquors, paintings, as a skin conditioning and dehydrating substance in cosmetic industry.
- Bristly hollyhock (*A. setosa*):
- Fig leafed hollyhock (*A. ficifolia*): Fully double flower type.
- Russian hollyhock (*A. rugosa*):

Varieties:

- Alcea Spotlight' is a true perennial promising variety of hollyhock. 'Charter's Double Mix' series is double flowered hollyhock.
- Dwarf mutants from IARI, New Delhi: Bona Pastel Pink, Bona Red, Bona White and Bona Yellow.

Variety	Breeding method	Features
IARI, New Delhi		
Pusa Gulabi	OP selection	Double flowers; pink coloured flowers.
Pusa Krishna	OP selection	Double flowers; maroon coloured flowers.
Pusa Lalima	OP selection	Double flowers; red coloured flowers.
Pusa Shweta	OP selection	Double flowers; white coloured flowers.
Pusa Apricot Supreme	F_1 hybrid of 'Hungarian Rosea Annua White x Supreme Mixed Yellow'	Apricot coloured flowers
Pusa Pastel Pink	F_1 hybrid of 'Hungarian Rosea Annua White x Supreme Mixed Yellow'	Pink coloured flowers
Pusa Pink Beauty	F_1 hybrid of 'Hungarian Rosea Annua White x Supreme Mixed Yellow'	Deep pink coloured flowers
Pusa Yellow Beauty	F_1 hybrid of 'Hungarian Rosea Annua White x Supreme Mixed Yellow'	Yellow coloured flowers
Deepika (1991)	Selection from 'Hungarian Rosea Annua White x Supreme Mixed Yellow'	Early flowering, tall (120-150 cm); 7-8 large, double flowers with fringed petals; light yellow flowers.
Dulhan (1991)	Selection from 'Hungarian Rosea Annua White x Supreme Mixed Yellow'	Late flowering, tall (120-140 cm); double, deep red coloured flowers.
Gouri (1991)	Selection from 'Hungarian Rosea Annua White x Supreme Mixed Yellow'	Early flowing, short (100-120 cm); flowers pink and white coloured; fringed petals.

- **Disease**: Leaf rust (*Puccinia malvacearum*): Most destructive disease. *A. ficifolia* and *A. rugosa* are resistant.

Inheritance of characters:

- No inbreeding depression is noticed.
- High level of self compatibility results in higher seed set.

Character	Inheritance pattern
Flower weight, Flowers on main stem, Flowers on side branches	Additive
Flower doubleness	Dominant over singleness

48. NELUMBONACEAE

48.1 Lotus

- Eulogized as 'Jewels of water garden or *Makhana*'.
- National flower of India and Vietnam.
- Aquatic perennial herb and commonly known as '*Padma*, *Neeraj*, *Saroj*, *Pushkar*, *Kamal*'.
- Most spectacular flower in the world and occupies special place under water garden.
- Indian lotus (*N. indica*), sacred to Hindus, has very old and close association with Indian culture and religion.
- Flower has agricultural, medicinal, cultural and religious importance.
- 1st fossil recordavailable with Pleistocene epoch of Kashmir.
- Flower: Actinomorphic, hypogynous, solitary/ axillary and pedicillate at the end of long pedicle.
- Flowers yield valuable perfume.
- Flower: Cultivated for ornamental value, environment beautification, water purification, besides for food, Chinese traditional medicine and yield valuable perfume.
- Flowers are thermogenic and physiologically thermoregulatory.
- Flowers recommended as cardiac tonic and used in curing diseases of liver, skin.
- Its dried and powdered rhizomes are used to cure piles.
- Lotus has been found to have 77% anti-oxidant activity.
- Rhizome is known for its hypoglycemic, anti-pyretic, anti-diarrheal, anti-bacterial and anti-inflammatory activity.
- Rhizome possesses anti-fungal activity against *Aspergillus*, *Trichoderma*, and *Penicilium*.
- Bhasinda: Underground stem i.e. rhizomes are edible.
- Swollen rhizome of vegetable lotus is used in culinary preparations.
- The roasted seeds are used as a substitute to coffee.
- Nutrition composition/ 100 g edible portion: Fresh rhizomes contains moisture (83%), crude protein (2.7%), fat (0.11%), reducing sugar (1.56%), sucrose (0.41%), starch

(9.25%), fiber (0.80%), ash (1.10%), calcium (0.06%), thiamine (0.22 mg), riboflavin (0.06 mg), niacin (2.1 mg) and ascorbic acid (15.0 mg).

- Protein content in seed: 10.6-14.8%.
- Seed pods are used in dry flower arrangement.
- Giant red lotus lake (Lake Nong Harn), Thailand: World's strangest lake.
- 1st fossil record is available with Pleistocene epoch of Kashmir.
- Leaf: Waxy and bluish green, attached to long cylindrical leaf stalk and has frilled edge with leaf dia., 45-90 cm.
- Diameter and area of leaf exceed 0.5 and 0.25 m^2, respectively in full growing period.
- Calyx has 4 sepals while petals are numerous (16-24 in single form and 116-160 in double form).
- Temperature for seed germination: 13-20^{0}C.
- Ideal temperature for flowering: 30-35^{0}C.
- Minimum water depth for growth: 30 cm and grows upto 2.5 m depth.
- Common weed: Water hyacinth.
- Propagation method: Seed and vegetative (rhizome).
- Maximum depth of seed sowing: 2.4 cm
- It has long chain of tuberous rhizome creeping underground and recalcitrant to regenerate.
- Pollination agents: Bees and flies contribute 80 and 50% fruit set, respectively.
- Inflorescence: Solitary and axillary.
- Stamens are many (upto 230) with short filaments and spirally arranged and become yellow during anthesis.
- Gynoecium is polycarpellary, very sticky and superior with one ovule in each locule.
- Fruit: Large, funnel shaped, flat topped with perforated recepticle containing many carpels.
- Seed pod: Brown woody in texture upto 10 cm dia., containing 7-15 nut like seedsin sunken cavity.
- Seed size: 1.5 cm length and 1.3 cm breadth.
- Seed has long longevity and easy to preserve.
- Seeds have hard and impermeable seed coatand recalcitrant in nature.
- Time from seedling to flowering: 1-2 years.
- Rhizome harvest during October-November.
- Scarification and stratification of seeds gives better germination.
- Breaking of seed dormancy: Scarification (sand paper rubbing at both ends), H_2SO_4 (24 h), Chromic acid, Potassium hydrate.

- Flower blooming period: June-October.
- In plains of India, lotus blooms between March-October and remains dormant in winter.
- Flower opens each morning for 3 successive days.
- Flowers are self heating during anthesis and produce 1 million pollen grains/ flower.
- Anthesis time: Flower fully open each morning (6-7 h for 3 successive days and closes by 12 h).
- Stigma receptivity: Maximum on 1st day and anther dehiscence occurs on 2nd and 3rd day.
- Pollen viability: Few hours after shedding.
- Crossing program in late July to early August gives good success.
- Hand pollination is effected at 6-8 AM in sunny days.
- Seeds mature 30 days after pollination.
- Optimum pH for seed germination: 7.5-8.5.
- Seed germinate within a week at ambient conditions.
- Within 10-20 days, seedling become ready for transplanting when attains 2 leaf stage.
- Seed rate: 4-5 kg/ acre and 10-12 kg/ha (for nursery).
- Best time for seedling transplanting: April.
- Seed setting takes place in September-October.
- Harvesting of rhizomes is done in the month of October.
- Water percentage in fresh rhizome: 80%.
- No biparental inbreeding is observed.
- Common disease: Leaf spot (*Cercospora* spp.).
- Use of EST-SSR, AFLP markers: *N. nucifera*.
- Low genetic diversity is attributed to asexual reproduction in *N. nucifera*.
- Use of atppb-rbcL chloroplast spacer for genetic relationship between seed vs. rhizome accessions indicate it might have arisen by single domestication event.

Species:

- *Nelumbo* is Ceylonese (Sri Lankan) name.
- China: World's richest germplasm centre of sacred lotus.
- NBRI, Lucknow: Acts as a biodiversity conservation centre.
- *Nelumbo*, genus of aquatic angiosperms belong to monogeneric family Nelumbonaceae is represented by 2 elemental species *N. nucifera* and *N. lutea*.
- Horticultural hybrids have been produced from these 2 geographically different species.

- N. *aureavallis,* known from Eocene fossils from North Dakota, USA is an extinct species from USA.
- *N. nucifera* and *N. lutea* are cross compatible.

Name	Features
Nelumbo lutea (syn. *N. centapetala*, *N. luteum*)	Native to New world; commonly known as American lotus/ Yellow lotus/ Lotus lily; introduced in India from USA during 1993; yellow flower colour; thrive in 60-75 cm deep water; tolerant to cold
N. nucifera (syn. *N. speciosa*, *N. indica*, *N. nelumbo*)	Native to Old world; commonly known as Indian lotus/ Asiatic lotus/ Sacred lotus/ Chinese water lily/ Rose of India/ Sacred water lily of Hinduisum and Buddhisum. Introduced into Egypt in 523 B.C.; flower colour red, white & pink; widely cultivated for food (seeds, rhizome, petiole, leaves & flowers); flowers bowl shaped, fragrant, bisexual, protogynous
N. speciosum	Very beautiful in hot season with white and pink flowers. Require 1-1.5 m deep water

Varieties:

- Krishna: Local selection from West Bengal, pink coloured flowers having 160 petals/ flower.
- Swarna Vaidehi: Variety of Makhana.

Name	Breeding method	Features
Angel Wing (1984)	Interspecific hybrid of '*N. nucifera* Pekimense Rubra x *N*. Shirokunshi- the tulip lotus'	Flowers delicately white & slightly fragrant. Recurrent bloomer & highly suitable for home garden.
Carolina Queen (1984)	Interspecific hybrid of '*N. lutea* x *N. nucifera* Rosea Plancea'	Colour changes from rose with yellow centre to pink & finally creamy yellow at the third day.
Perry's Giant Sunburst (1987)	Interspecific hybrid of '*N. nucifera* Alba Plena x *N. lutea*'	Summer blooming; soft yellow flowers; 25-30 cm dia., suitable for growing in large container.
Mrs. Perry D. Slocum	Interspecific hybrid of '*N. nucifera* x *N. lutea*'	Most beautiful, vigorous; double flowers (30 cm across), rose pink changes to creamy yellow.

49. NYCTAGINACEAE

49.1 Bougainvillea

- Eulogized as 'Glory of the garden'.
- Ornamental bougainvillea is used as pot plant, edge, pergola, standard and bonsai for display.
- Hardy, evergreen, woody, ornamental climbing shrub commonly grown in Indian garden.

- In temperate regions of European countries, it is grown in greenhouses.
- Existing cultivars are diploid i.e. 2n=34, 51, 64, 68 and sterile.
- Air pollution tolerant plant.
- IARI, New Delhi: International Registration Authority for bougainvillea in 2007.
- Concept of 'Walk and Learn Path': For identification of varieties at IARI, New Delhi.
- Bougainvillea Society of India: 1973.
- Best budding season: February-March.
- Bottom heat technique: Used for rooting of semi-hard wood cuttings.
- Two flowering peaks: March-April and November-December.
- Flowers: Nectariferous.
- Colourful flowers are really petalloid papery bracts or modified leaves to which true flowers are attached to midrib.
- True flowers are borne in cluster of 3, small in size, tubular, constricted in middle, white in colour and hermaphrodite.
- Colour of bracts: Presence of betalins pigments i.e. betacyanin and betaxanthin and act as the chemotaxonomic marker for identification of species and hybrid groups.
- Inflorescence: Cyme.
- Anthesis time: 10 AM followed by dehiscence & stigma receptivity.
- Number of anthers: 6-8 and dorsified. Stamens arise from base of flower tube.
- Pollen viability: 22-90% and fails to germination after self pollination.
- Fruit: Narrow, 5 lobed elongated acheneand has dry hard fruit cover.
- Both self and cross pollination occurs.
- Pollination agent: Butterfly.
- Plants fail to set seeds until age of 2-4 years.
- Seed set takes place only after cross pollination.
- Seed setting period in Tamil Nadu: February- April.
- Seed mature within 2-3 months and seedlings flower after a year.
- A cultivar which set seed in one place may prove seed sterile in another place.
- Spontaneous bud sports accounted from *B.* x *buttiana* (50%), *B. peruviana* (26%), *B. spetabilis* (16%), *B.* x *spectoglabra* (6%), *B. glabra* (1%).
- Homomorphic flowers, simultaneous cytokinesis, trinucleate pollen, and absence of pollen grain germination suggest sporophytic SI.
- Sporophytic SI persists in induced tetraploid and bud sport cultivars.
- About 85% of bougainvilleas are both female and male sterile resulting in no seed set. And no new varieties can be expected by genetic recombination.

- Fertility can be restored by colchiploidy.
- Landmark in bougainvillea breeding: Use of polyploids in interspecific hybridization to restore fertility in sterile hybrids through colchicine.
- *In vitro* multiplication of cultivars which do not produce seeds and difficult to root through hard wood cuttings e.g. Mahara, Mahatma Gandhi, Mary Palmer, Scarlet Queen Variegata, Shubhra, Sweet Heart.
- Tissue banks and genetic revolutionary race histories are maintained at NBRI, Lucknow.
- 1st report on shoot tip proliferation in woody ornamental: *B. glabra* cv. Magnifica by Chaturvedi *et al*. (1978).
- Stable character for identification of species and cultivars: Pollen morphology i.e. tips of brochi (differences in size & number of brochi) and exine part.
- RAPD, EST-SSR and AFLP markers: Identification of cultivars, determining diversity and genetic relationship.

Species:

- 1st plant collection was made by French botanist Commerson from Brazil in 1789 under the name *B. spectabilis*.
- 1st species introduced in Indiafrom Europe at Kolkata in 1860: *B. spectabilis*.
- Basic species: *Bougainvillea spectabilis, B. glabra, B. peruviana*.
- *B. glabra*: Commonly called as 'paper flower'.
- *B. spectabilis*: Potential in virus resistance and pollution-tolerance.
- Putative parent: *B. peruviana*.
- Hybrid groups: *B.* x *buttiana, B.* x *spectoperuviana*, *B.* x *spectoglabra*.
- Insulin like compound, pinitol, was 1st isolated from leaves of *B. spectabilis*.
- Reasons for horticultural diversity in cultivars: Variability within species *B. spectabilis*, *B. glabra* and indiscriminate hybridization among them and with *B. peruviana*.

Varieties:

- 1st introductions in India: Mrs. Butt, Princes Margaret Rose (*B. peruviana*), Scarlet Queen (*B.* x *buttiana*) and Splendens (*B. glabra*).
- 1st bougainvillea variety introduced in India by S. Percy Lancaster in 1920: Scarlet Queen.
- Leaves of cv. Mrs. Butt contain anti-viral principle to TMV and Sunhemp Rosette Virus.
- Maximum number of bud sports has been developed from *B.* x*buttiana*.
- Triploid cultivars show more intense pigmentation in bracts.

- Single/normal bracted: Begum Sikandar, Chitra, Dr. H. B. Singh, Dr. R.R.Pal, Dr. B.P. Pal, Golden Glow, Lady Mary Baring, Mahatma Gandhi, Mrs. McClean, Pixie, Shweta.
- Double/multi-bracted: Cherry Blossom (syn. Bridal Bouquet or Double White), Los Banos Beauty (from Pink Beauty), Mahara (from Mrs. Butt), Marietta (from Mahara), Roseville's Delight (from Mrs. McClean).
- Variegated leaves: Archana, Dr. H.J. Bhaba, Gangaswamy, Hawaiian White Variegata, L.N. Birla, Louise Wathen Variegata, Mariegatta, Mataji Agnihotri, Vishakha, Red September.
- Multibract and variegated: Los Banos Variegata, Los Banos Variegata Jayanti, Thimma.
- Thornless: Pink Beauty, Torch Glow.
- Seed setting cultivars: Maharaja of Mysore, Laterita, Formosa, Trinidad, Mrs. Fraser, Thomasii.
- Mutation rate in stem cuttings: 0.74% with 3-3.5 Kr gamma irradiation.
- Cytochimeral varieties: Thimma, Mrs. McClean (induced tetraploid); sporophytic SI persists in them.
- Bud sports in *B. buttiana*: Mrs. Butt, Mrs. Louis Wathen.
- Bud sports selected by private growers: Mrs. H.C. Buck, Mary Palmer, Thimma, Shubhra, Mahara, Roseville's Delight, Los Banos Beauty, Cherry Blossom.
- Sister lines of *B. spectabilis* (Thomasii) x *B. buttiana* (Louise Wathen): Spring festival, Dr. R.R. Pal, Summer Time.
- Sister lines of *B. glabra* x *B. spectabilis*: Pink Beauty, Rose Queen.

Species, hybrid groups & cultivars

a) ***B. glabra***: Cypheri (triploid), Dark Purple, Dream, Dr. R.R. Pal, Formosa, Gopal Glabra, Jennifer, Los Banos, Magnifica, Partha, Sanderiana, Snow White, Typica (has three forms Acuti-bracteata, Obtusi-bracteata & Laeviuscula).

b) ***B. spectabilis***: Barbara Krast (Crimson Lake x Sanderiana), Deep Cherry, Jubilee, L.N. Birla, Mrs. Chico, Mrs. Frazer, Lateritia, Orange King, Pradhan's Profusion, Purple Gem (Mrs. H.C. Buck x Refulgens), Purple Robe, Red Glory, Refulgens (drooping branches), Ruby, Speciosa, Thomasii, Tomato Red (Thomasii x Glabra), Turkey's Special.

c) ***B. peruviana***: Ecuador Pink, Lady Hudson, Mary Palmer (syn. Surprise), Mrs. H.C. Buck, Princes Margaret Rose, Shubhra

d) ***B. x buttiana***: Natural interspecific hybrid group between *B. peruviana* x *B. glabra*. It is grown as hedge, pergola, standard, pot plant & bonsai & utilized for pollution tolerance e.g. Archana, Alick Lancaster, Enid Lancaster, Lady Mary Baring (tetraploid), Louis Wathen, Mahara (tetraploid), Mrs. Butt (bud sport), Mrs. McClean (tetraploid), President Roosevelt (tetraploid), Scarlet Glory, Scarlet Queen Variegata, Surekha, Versicolor, Yellow Queen.

e) ***B.* x *spectoperuviana***: The cultivars of this group combine characters like branched main shoot as in *B. spectabilis* and division of flowering cyme more than twice and recurrent blooming habit as in *B. peruviana* e.g. Elizabeth, Gopal, Mahatma Gandhi, Padmini, Sensation, Sonnet, Spring Festival, Spring Time, Summer Time, Thimma.

f) ***B.* x *spectoglabra***: It is intermediate between parental characters with respect to degree of hairiness & shape of flower tube while being recurrent bloomers like *B. glabra* e.g. Joe, Jubilee, Lilicina, Maharaja of Mysore, Pink Beauty, Pixie, Sanderiana, Rosa Catalina, Rose Queen.

g) **Undetermined group**: Some cultivars because of their anomalous characters can not be grouped under either of the elemental species or the hybrid groups are included in this group e.g. Glady's Hepburn, Isobel Green Smith, Killie Campbell, Lord Willingdon, Magnifica (tetraploid), Partha Variegata, Perfection (triploid), Poultoni, Superba, Tomato Seedling.

Variety	Breeding method	Features
IARI, New Delhi		
Purple Prince, Mauve Queen, Sylvia Delap, Srinivasa, Smoky, Scarlet Queen Variegata & Ceylon Hybrid	Introduced as exotic germplasm	-
Lady Mary Baring	Introduced from Africa; Mrs. Butt sporting to Mrs. McClean, sporting to Golden Glow	Golden yellow bracts produced thick trusses
Poultoni	Introduced from Africa	Triploid; raspberry coloured bracts.
Poultoni Special	Introduced from Africa	Triploid; curled & rhodamine coloured bracts.
Rhodamine	Introduced from Nairobi	Rhodamine purple coloured bracts.
Charles Wilson	Introduced from Nairobi	Brilliant flame coloured bracts.
Mrs. Butt (syn. Crimson Lake)	Introduced from Kenya	Bud sport
Million Dollar (syn. Mahara)	Introduced from Philippines	Tetraploid, 20-40 bracts in cyme; look like clustered roses; bracts rhodamine purple to rosien purple
Scarlet Queen	Introduced from West Indies	Purple red bracts
Vishakha (1976)	Bud sport of 'Mrs. H.C. Buck' (*B. peruviana*)	Variegated leaves along margin; bracts spinel red; flowering in winter & summer
Other seedling selections		
Baby Margaret Rose	Seedling selection of 'Princes Margaret Rose'	Bracts orange coloured, turning to red.
Eisha	Seedling selection of 'Formosa' (*B. glabra*)	Bracts greenish, lilac tipped.
Gopal	Seedling selection of 'Formosa'	Bracts carmine tinged with light magenta

Gagarin (1955)	Seedling selection of 'Trinidad' (*B. glabra*)	Bracts mallow purple & do not touch at base
Jayalakshmi	Seedling selection of 'Meera' (*B.* x *buttiana*)	Bracts brick red turning to purple
Lalbagh (1974)	Seedling selection of 'Lateritia' (*B. spectabilis*)	Bracts dull brick red; flowering profuse
Lilac Queen	Seedling selection of 'Formosa'	Bracts rose mauve coloured.
Mahatma Gandhi	Seedling selection of 'Princes Margaret Rose'	Bracts light shinning pink tinged mauve.
Marigowda (1974)	Seedling selection of 'Glady's Hepburn'	Bracts flesh coloured turn to bluish pink
Meera (1930)	Seedling selection of '*B.* x *buttiana*'	Bracts large, very deep crimson.
Partha (syn. Indian Flame)	Seedling selection of 'Princes Margaret Rose'	Bracts deep orange chang to carmine pink.
Red Glory	Seedling selection of 'Mrs. Fraser'	Bracts deep scarlet.
Sholay	Seedling selection of 'Red Glory'	Bracts deep scarlet
Sonnet (1959)	Seedling selection of '*B. spectoglabra*'	Diploid (2n=34); bracts orchid purple
Srinivasa	Seedling selection of 'Jayalakshmi'	Bracts orange coloured.
Stanza (1964) purple	Seedling selection of '*B. glabra*'	Diploid (2n=34); bracts Rhodamine
Thomasii (1959)	Seedling selection of '*B. spectabilis*'	Bracts purple changing to carmine.
Trinidad (1959)	Seedling selection of 'Snow Queen' (*B. glabra*)	Bracts elliptic, light mauve coloured.
Vernal Nagpal	Seedling selection of 'Gagarin'	Bracts deep lilac coloured.
Dr. R.R. Pal (1959)	Interspecific hybrid of '*B. spectabilis* (Thomasii) x *B.* x *buttiana* (Louise Wathen)'	Aneuploid (2n=3x-2=49); bracts purple red coloured; useful as rootstock for budding.
Spring Festival (1959)	Interspecific hybrid of'*B. spectabilis* (Thomasii) x *B.* x *buttiana* (Louise Wathen)'	*B.* x *buttiana*, diploid (2n=34); bracts orchid purple.
Summer Time (1959)	Interspecific hybrid of'*B. spectabilis* (Thomasii) x *B.* x *buttiana* (Louise Wathen)'	*B.* x *buttiana*, diploid (2n=34); bracts cardinal red coloured; star prominent.
Begum Sikander (1969)	Interspecific hybrid of'*B. peruviana* (Dr. B.P. Pal) x *B. glabra* (Jennifer Fernie)'	Aneuploid i.e. mitotically irregular (2n=3x-2=49); highly pollen sterile; single bracts white centre with light magenta margin; ideal for pot culture.
Chitra (1981)	Interspecific hybrid of'*B. peruviana* (Dr. B.P. Pal) x *B.* x *buttiana* (Tetra Mrs. McClean)'	Tetraploid (2n=4x=68), bracts magenta coloured; ideal as shrub & standard.
Wajid Ali Shah (1974)	Interspecific hybrid of '*B. peruviana* (Dr. B.P. Pal) x *B. spectabilis* (Mrs. Chico)'	Triploid (2n=3x=51), winter bloomer; bracts bicoloured (white and rosien purple) & non-persistent; recommended for pot culture.
Maharaja of Mysore	*B. spectabilis* (Lateritia) x *B. glabra*	Bracts pale rose turning to cinnamon
Pink Beauty	Mauve seedling (*B. glabra*) x *B. spectabilis* (Lady Mountbatten)	Very dwarf; bracts soft pink

Pixie	*B. glabra* x *B. spectabilis*	Single bracts
Rose Queen	Mauve seedling (*B. glabra*) x *B. spectabilis* (Lady Mountbatten)	Bracts cyclamen purple, stars prominent
IIHR, Bengaluru		
Usha (1977)	Half-sib selection of 'Lady Hope (*B. peruviana*)'	Diploid; bracts magenta fade to mandarin red; flowers in winter & summer season
Chitravati (1979)	Intervarietal hybrid of 'Lal Bagh (*B. spectabilis*) x Red Glory (*B. spectabilis*)'	Thorns large; bracts mandarin red.
Dr. H. B. Singh (1977)	Intervarietal hybrid of 'Trinidad (*B. glabra*) x Formosa (*B. glabra*)'	Bracts light violet-purple. It is patented as 'Krishna' in Australia.
Purple Wonder (1979)	Intervarietal hybrid of 'Formosa (*B. glabra*) x Trinidad (*B. glabra*)'	Bracts violet-purple.
Mary Palmer Special (1974)	Intervarietal hybrid of 'Princes Margaret Rose(*B. peruviana*) x Dr. B.P. Pal *(B. peruviana*)'	Triploid (2n=3x=51); vigorous; thorns curved; bract white, magenta or blotched; suitable for pot culture.
Jawaharlal Nehru (1975)	OP seedling of cv. Lal Bagh (*B. spectabilis*)	Variegated leaves along margin; bracts scarlet rose fading to orange red
Sholay (1977)	Bud sport of 'Red Glory (*B. spectabilis*)'	Vigorous; greenish bracts; flowers in winter & summer
Lal bagh botanical garden, Bengaluru		
Laxminarayan (1961)	Bud sport of '*B. spetabilis*'	Vigorous, bracts similar to *B. spectabilis*. Leaves variegated & diffused all over.
Gangaswamy (1974)	Bud sport of 'Lady Mary Baring (*B.* x *buttiana*)'	Vigorous growing; flowering sparse & produce in winter and summer; foliage small, green centre & white margin, glabrous, ovate; thorns straight; bracts golden yellow.
Kuvempu (1960)	Bud sport of 'Rao (*B.* x *buttiana*)'	Foliage creamy white, glabrous & ovate; thorns straight; bracts fuchsia purple; flowering in winter & summer.
Rao (1954)	Bud sport of 'Mrs. Butt (*B. buttiana*)'	Vigorous; foliage small; young pink & later green centre & creamy margin, glabrous, ovate; thorns small, bracts crimson red; flowering in winter & summer.
Sharma (1961)	Bud sport of 'Mrs. Fraser (*B. spectabilis*)'	Leaves variegated, diffused type, cream & green, tendency for lobing; bracts terracotta.
Thimma (1960)	Bud sport of 'Mary Palmer (*B. peruviana*)'	Variegated leaves with green margin & creamy yellow patches in leaf; multibracts with double coloured-magenta & white
Vellayani (1950)	Bud sport of 'Mrs. Butt'	Variegation of leaves has cream & green patches; purple coloured bracts.
Yellow Queen (1960)	Bud sport of 'Mrs. McClean (*B. buttiana*)'	Yellow tinged bracts; malformed flowers.
Zakir Hussain (1963)	Bud sport of 'Maharaja of Mysore (*B. spectoglabra*)'	Foliage light green patches of variegation; bracts cyclamen purple
Dr. H.J. Bhabha	Bud sport of 'Louis Wathen'	Less vigorous; mauve coloured bracts; variegated leaves

NBRI, Lucknow		
Archana (syn. Roseville's Delight Archana) 1973	Bud sport of 'Roseville's Delight (*B.* x *buttiana*)'	Variation in leaf surface; bracts apricot orange; flowering in winter & summer.
Hawaiian Beauty (1990)	Bud sport of 'Hawaiian White'	Leaves variegated; young bract pea green changing to white.
Manohar Chandra Variegated (1985)	Bud sport of 'Manohar Chandra'	Young bract current red changing to magenta.
Nirmal (1982)	Bud sport of 'Mrs. McClean (*B.* x *buttiana*)'	Leaves variegated, young bract orange changing to rose
Parthasarathy (1977)	Bud sport of 'Partha'	Leaves variegated, bracts colour like cv. Partha.
Shubhra (1969)	Bud sport of 'Mary Palmer (*B. peruviana*)'	Vigorous growing; foliage large green, glabrous, ovate; thorns large, curved; bracts white; profuse flowering in winter & summer; hardy & easy to multiply.
Shweta (1979)	Bud sport of 'Trinidad'	Drooping plant habit; thorns curved; leaves green, glabrous, elliptic; flowering profuse at ¼th to ¾th branch; bracts white, elliptic, star prominent.
Spectabilis Variegata (1959)	Bud sport of '*B. spectabilis*'	Leaves variegated; bracts colour fuchsia purple.
Surekha (1981)	Bud sport of 'Scarlet Queen (*B.* x *buttiana*)'	Leaves variegated; bract colour carmine to fuchsia purple; bracts margin is crinkled.
Abhimanyu (2010)	γ ray mutant of 'Arjuna'	Variegated leaves, bracts red coloured.
Arjuna (1974)	γ ray mutant (500 rad) of 'Partha (*B. peruviana*)'	Variegated leaves; bract colour pinkish purple.
Aruna (2008)	γ ray mutant of 'Palekar'	Bracts pink & young bracts orange coloured. Suitable for pot culture, cascade, standard & hanging basket.
Los Banos Variegata (1987)	γ ray mutant (1 Krad) of 'Los Banos Beauty (syn. Mohan) (double bract with green leaf)'	Variegated leaves; double bracted & bract colour mallow purple.
Pallavi (1987)	γ ray mutant (1 Krad) of 'Roseville's Delight (double bract with green leaf)'	Double bracted; variegated leaves, light green in various shades
Mahara Variegata abnormal leaves (2002)	γ ray mutant (1 Krad) of 'Mahara (multi-bract with green leaves)'	Variegation varies from leaf to leaf; old leaves dull yellow green; bracts rhodamine purple coloured.
Los Banos Variegata Silver Margin (2002)	γ ray mutant of 'Los Banos Beauty'	Variegated leaves, bracts colour mallow purple.
Los Banos Variegata Jayanthi (2006)	EMS induced mutant of 'Los Banos Beauty'	Two types of variegated leaves; multibracts mallow purple coloured
Pixie Variegata (2008)	EMS induced mutant of 'Pixie (single bracted)'	Variegated small leaves (periclinal chimera); bracts pinkish purple coloured.
Dr. B.P. Pal (1981)	Induced polyploid of 'Shubhra'	Tetraploid (2n=4x=68); bract white; recurrent bloomer; best among single bracted cultivar.

Tetra Mrs. McClean (1969)	Induced polyploid of 'Mrs. McClean'	Tetraploid (2n=4x=68); bracts empire rose in colour
BARC, Mumbai		
Lady Hudson of Ceylon Variegata (1979)	γ ray mutant of 'Lady Hudson of Ceylon'	Leaves variegated, bracts colour phlox pink.
Jayalakshmi Variegata (1977)	γ ray mutant of 'Jayalakshmi (*B.* x *buttiana*)'	Leaf variegation on margins and lamina bracts brick red while young & turn to fuchsia purple when mature.
Silver Top (1986)	γ ray mutant of 'Versicolour'	Leaves crinkled & boat shaped; bracts narrow.
OUAT, Bhubaneshwar		
Odisse (1977)	Bud sport of 'Mary Palmer'	Leaves dark green, glabrous, bracts large size, white with delicate pink tinge in irregular pattern
AHSI, Kolkata		
Alick Lancaster (1930)	Bud sport of 'Scarlet Queen'	Leaves elliptical with acute tip with cordate base; cyclamen purple coloured bracts
Enid Lancaster (syn. Golden Queen, 1930)	Bud sport of 'Louise Wathen (syn. Orange Glory) (*B.* x *buttiana*)	Bracts yellow shaded spanish orange
Louise Wathen Mediopicta (syn. Louise Wathen Variegata)	Bud sport of 'Louise Wathen'	Variegated leaf with pale yellow patches in centre of lamina; bracts similar to Louise Wathen

50. NYMPHAEACEAE

50.1 Water lily

- Bulbous, rhizomatous, aquatic, perennial herbaceous plant.
- Word '*Nympha*' in Greek and in Roman mythology means 'Nature-goddess'.
- Water lily culture began in 1786 in England with introduction of *N. odorata* from America.
- Nymphacine: Alkaloid present in all parts except seeds and contain 47% starch and fatty oils.
- Flowers: Used as cardiac tonic to relieve pains and cures diseases of liver and skin.
- Rhizomes: Used in tannin industry, seeds for culinary purposes and leaves as dining plates. Dried rhizome powder cure piles.
- Wide range of polyploidy (2x=28 to 16x=224) including aneuploidy, trisomy, polysomaty.
- La-ongsri *et al.* (2009) proposed groups 1) Single flowered (< 25 petals), 2) Intermediate (25-50 petals), 3) Double flowered (> 50 petals (116-160).
- Leaf types: 1) Very thin, fragile and submerged having short petiole, 2) Floating, thick in texture 3) Aerial, leathery leaves.
- Leaves emerge from rhizome in spiral form and float on water surface.
- Leaf have single notch from edge into centre of lily pad.

- Flowers; Solitary, bisexual, perigynous (extra axillary) and day and night blooming habit.
- Each flower has 4 sepals and many petals with inner ones form petalloid stamen and carpels.
- Calyx and corolla are poorly differentiated and form perianth of 6 or more free tepals.
- Ideal temperature for flowering: 30-35^{0}C.
- Flowers open at a particular time of day from 2-7 successive days or nights and go down into water through spiral coiling of peduncle.
- Tropical species adopt autogamy while temperature species allogamy.
- Agamaspory also reported.
- Pollination agents: Beetles and small flies.
- Fruit type: Berry, very tight and contains numerous small seeds.
- Day and night blooming means 8 AM to 2 PM or 9.30 PM to 11 AM.
- Intervarietal crosses are complicated by low stigma receptivity, low seed set and many cases embryo abortion.
- Reproduction: Sexual and viviparous (i.e. bear bulbs at top of petiole in *N. mexicana* syn. *N. flava*) reproduction from spent blossoms.
- Sexual reproduction is dependent on xenogamy, geitonogamy and autogamy.
- Viviparous germination occurs in races: Comanche, Indiana, Mooreana, Solfatore, Sioux, Sunrise.
- Low temperature during fertilization period decreases seed set per flower.
- Placentation: Marginal or parietal.
- Seeds ripen within 6-10 weeks.
- Days for seed germination: 10-15 while scarified seed germinate after 3-4 days.
- Seeds have buoyant aril and float on water surface after fruit burst.
- Seed priming in distilled water for 6 days helps for rapid & uniform plant emergence.
- Mode of seed dispersal: Water.
- LD_{50} dosefor rhizomes of *N. rubra*: 5 Krad.
- LD_{50} dose for *in vitro* mutagenesis: 1-2 Krad γ- or X-ray doses.
- Emasculation deterres crossing success. Flowers are not emasculated to reduce stress on maternal flower.
- Foreign anthers are collected, placed in stigmatic fluid and settled suspension is used for pollination to enhance success.

Species:

- Indian sub-continent is active centre for evolution of diploid forms while polyploid taxa are more diverse in climate of Europe.

- *Nymphea* species is a complex hybrid group.
- Species of single group hybridize readily among themselves and outside of group between apo-carpus (Cabomboideae, Nelumboideae) and syn-carpous (Nymphaeoideae) no genuine hybrids are produced.
- Vegetable *'kamal kakri'* is rhizome of *Nymphae anouchali.*

Species	Ploidy level	2n=
N. pubescence	6x	84
N. stellata	2x	28
N. tetragona	8x	112
N. caerulea	2x, 4x	28, 56
N. gigantea	16x	224
N. lotus	2x, 4x, 6x	28, 56, 84
N. sioux	5x	70
N. alba	4x	56

Species	Common name	Features
N. alba (syn. *N. venusta, N. splendens, Castalia alba*)	Nilofar/Romanian water lily/European water lily/English white water lily	Native perennial herb found in Kashmir, Europe, West Asia & North Africa; flowers white; day blooming (7 AM to 4 PM). Flowering in June-August.
N. caerulea (syn. *N. nouchali* var. *caerulea*)	Egyptian blue water lily	Hardy; day blooming (7.30 AM to 12 noon); flowers star shaped, 8-15 cm across, sky blue coloured with yellow stamen & blue anthers; 14-20 petals/flower. Used extensively in hybridization. Extremely significant in Egyptian mythology e.g. Blue Beauty
N. nouchali (syn. *N. stellata*)	Neelkamal/ Blue water lily/ Blue lotus of India	Perennial; highly similar to *N. caerulea*; largest species found in warmer parts of India in lakes & ponds; native of India & South-East Asia; edible rhizomes; highly fragrant; flower sky blue coloured changing to pale yellow, open for 3 days from 8 am to 2 pm, 11-14 petals; rhizomes used to cure dysentery & diarrhoea
N. candida (syn. *N. nitida, N. biradiata, N. semiapetra*)	Bohemian water lily	Hardy; native of Central & North Europe, Asia & Himalaya. Suitable for shallow water. Flowers large; small red stigmas, white cup shaped, 8 cm across.
N. capensis	Cape blue water lily	Native of South & East Africa & up to Malagasy. Fragrant flowers star like, blue with yellow stamens, opens for 4 days; flowers have 20-30 petals, day bloomer (7 AM to 4 PM).
N. caroliniana	-	Cross between *N. odorata rosea* x *N.tuberosa*. Day blooming, hardy. Flowers star shaped with many petals, white or rosy pink.
N. chromatella	-	Hybrid of *N. mexicana* x *N.alba* or *N. tuberosa*. Flowers bright yellow with golden stamen, 8-15 cm across with numerous incurved petals.
N. daubeniana	Madagascar aquarium lily	German hybrid of *N. micrantha* x *N. caerulea*. Day blooming, tropical water lily; strongly viviparous.

N. dentata	-	Botanical variety of *N. lotus*. Native of Egypt. Night blooming. Leaves glabrous, flowers white, 25-30 cm across.
N. layaekeri	-	Hybrid between *N. alba rubra* x *N. tetragona*; day blooming; suitable for tub culture; flowers small & pink/ rose/ red/ purple coloured.
N. lemonmist	Lemon mist water lily	Perennial introduced herb. Bears quintessential lily pad leaves, mottled with purple splotches. Flowering May-October.
N. marliacea chromatella	Chromatella water lily/ Queen of aquatic lotus	Aquatic perennial; light; canary yellow flowers having sweet strong fragrance. Excellent choice for any size of aquatic water garden.
N. mexicana (syn. *N. flava*)	-	Native of Florida & Mexico; rhizomes erect, tuber like; flowers 10 cm across, slightly fragrant, bright yellow with golden yellow stamens; petals 23-25, day bloomer (11 AM to 4 PM).
N. odorata var. rosea	Cape cod water lily	Hardy, diurnal spp., native to North America; flowers white, fragrant, 7.5-13 cm across, opening for 3 days from 6 to 12 AM
N. panama pacific	Tropical water lily / Panama Pacific	Violet purple to wine red coloured flowers; very sweet fragrance; free flowering; suitable for tub culture, or large water gardens; tolerates partial shade; day blooming
N. pennsylvania	-	Hybrid of *N. caerulea* x *N. zanzibariensis*. Large, deep blue flowers open from 8 AM to 5 PM. Petals 23 & stamens 140.
N. lotus (syn. *N. edulis*, *N. thermalis*)	-	Native of Egypt; day & night bloomer (7.30 PM to 11 AM); flowers star shaped, white; sepals green; petals 19-20
N. pubescence (syn. *N. lotus* var. *pubescens*, *N. purpurea*)	Pink water lily	Perennial, native to India, South-East Asia, America and Australia. Used in hybridization & not in cultivation. Pink flowers with 12-14 shiny petals. Night blooming (8-8.30 PM). Flowering is from August-October.
	White water lily / Kumud	Perennial, native to India & South-East Asia. White flowers are 5-15 cm in dia., with 12-14 shiny petals; referred in ancient Hindu literature.
N. pygmaea 'Rubra' (syn. *N. tetragona* var. *orientalis*, *Castalia pygmaea*)	Chinese pygmy water lily / Red pygmy water lily / Small white water lily	Perennial; beautiful miniature water lily native to Meghalaya (Himalaya & swamps of Khasi hills). Slightly fragrant; bright red flowers, flowering June-September; ideal for aquaria, tub culture, sinks & shallow ponds
N. rubra (syn. *N. rosea*, *N. magnifica*)	Red water lily/ Rakta kamal/ Lal kamal	Beautiful floating plant native to India & widely cultivated in other countries; flowers deep purplish red coloured, opens for 3-4 nights from 8 pm to 11 am; unripe fruits & flowering stalks used as vegetable & salads, respectively.
Victoria amazonica (syn. *V. regia*)	Amazon water lily/ Royal water lily/ Giant water lily	Queen of all water lilies; large leaves (2-3 m dia.), edges turn up to form rim.

Varieties:

- Intervarietal crosses are complicated by low stigma receptivity, embryo abortion & low seed set.

- Les *et al*. (2004) obtained synthetic F_1 hybrid (violet petals) between *N. gigantea* (♀ pink petal, sub-genus *Anecphya* x *N.colorata* ♂ white petal sub-genus *Brachyceras*).
- 1st interspecific hybrid evolved in 1851 between *N. lotus* x *N. rubra*.
- Interspecific hybrids: Frienship Penoy from America; Buddha's Seat, Han Lotus, Sino Japanese Friendship, Yushan Pink from China.
- Sunrise: 2n=28; Panama Pacific 4x=56.

Name	Breeding method	Features
Director G.T. Moore	Interspecific hybrid of '*N. colorata* x unknown'	Trisomic (2n=28+1); free flowering, day blooming, tropical water lily with small fragrant violet flowers; flowers 6-10 cm across
F_1 hybrid	Interspecific hybrid of '*N. gigantea* x *N. colorata*'	Violet petals; >200 stamens; carmine coloured anthers;
George Spencer	Interspecific hybrid of '*N. dentata* x *N. rubra*'	-

Inheritance of characters:

- No correlation among flower size and ploidy level e.g.
  1. Pigmy flower in *N. tetragona* (2n=112) and largest flower in *N. gigantea* (2n=224);
  2. Hexaploid (2n=84) cvs. possess small flowers (4-10 cm); diploids, triploids, tetraploids and higher poly-aneuploids (2n=154 to 206) possess large flowers (12-24 cm).

51. OLEACEAE (OLIVE FAMILY)

51.1 Jasmine

- Eulogized as 'Queen of fragrance'.
- Word 'Jasmine' is derived from Arabic/ Persian word '*Yasmun*' meaning 'fragrance'.
- Ornamental flowering plant cultivated for wide uses ranging from landscape to hair adornments, perfumes and cosmetics.
- Suitable in planting shrubbery, arches and pergolas.
- Leading traditional flower of India.
- Cheap substitute of saffron.
- Maximum area occupied among loose flowers in India.
- Maximum area and production: Tamil nadu.
- Flowers are exported to Sri Lanka, Malaysia, Singapore, West Asian countries.
- Countries growing *J. officinalis*: Egypt, UAE, South Africa, France, Italy, Syria, Algeria, Morocco, China.

- Large genetic variation as deciduous or evergreen, erect/ spreading/ climbing, shrub/ vine.
- World's best quality jasmine perfume: Produced in France.
- Jasmine tea: Popular drink in China.
- Jasmine oil has significant place as an ingredient in cosmetics, ointments, disinfectants, detergents, confectionaries and in pharmaceutical beverages.
- Flowers are white/ yellow/ reddish, typically round, 0.5 cm diameter and very fragrant.
- Calyx: Bell shaped and 4-9 petals.
- Inflorescence: Cymose, in cluster (minimum 3) or solitary at the end of branchlet.
- Fruit type: Berry/ drupe/ capsule, black coloured when ripe with 2 seeds/ fruit.
- Seeds are edible.
- Type of placentation: Axile.
- Flower bud differentiation and formation occur in acropetal succession with sepals develop first followed by petals, stamens and ovary.
- Flowers usually last for a day.
- Planting distance: *J. grandiflorum* (2 m x 2 m= 2,500 plants/ha); *J. sambac* (1.2 m x 1.2 m= 69,444 plants/ ha); *J. auriculatum* and *J. multiflorum* (1.8 m x 1.8 m= 3,086 plants/ ha).
- High degree of heterostyly: *Jasminum auriculatum*.
- Floral dimorphism (morphophytes): Pin (long style & short filament) and thrum (short style & long filament) in *J. grandiflorum* and *J. pubescence*.
- Pin type produce profuse flowering whereas, thrum types are shy bearers.
- Pin type flowers are superior for petal width, style length, and gall mite resistance.
- Thrum type flowers are superior for flower bud length, weight, corolla tube length, and diameter of opened flowers.
- Warm summer and mild winter cause profuse blooms for longer duration.
- Months for peak flower production: June-July (*J. grandiflorum*, *J. auriculatum*), July-October (*J. grandiflorum*), and February-October in other species.
- Time of anthesis is not uniform in all species.
- Anthesis during night hours (6-7 pm).
- Very late (9-10 pm) anthesis: *J. communis*.
- Blooming period: 3-4.5 months in different species.
- Anther dehiscence is 2-4 h earlier than anthesis.
- Commercial method of propagation in *J. sambac*: Hard wood or Semi-hard wood cutting give 60-70% rooting.
- The 15 cm long cuttings having 4 leaves and treated with 4000 ppm IBA results excellent rooting.

- Most successful method of layering: Ground layering.
- Micropropagation: Stems and leaves cultured on modified ½ strength MS medium containing GA_3 @ 1mg/ litre and NAA @ 0.1 mg/ litre.
- In France, *J. grandiflorum* is grafted on *J. officinalis*.
- Only few species set seeds under natural condition: 33-72%.
- Selfing did not result in any seed set in *J. auriculatum* and *J. grandiflorum*.
- Seed viability: Up to 10 months & thereafter rapid decline.
- Seed germination: 75-84% (in *J. auriculatum* and *J. grandiflorum*) and 55% (in *J. flexile*).
- Days for seed germination: 3 weeks to 3 months.
- Harvesting stage: Buds fully developed but not opened.
- Highest concrete yield: *J. grandiflorum*c lone (Lucknow and Thimmapuram); *J. auriculatum* clone (Long Round); *J. flexile*.
- Maximum oil recovery in *J. auriculatum* (between 6-8 AM); *J. grandiflorum* (3-9 AM).
- 1 ton of fresh jasmine flowers gave concrete yield: 2.8-3 kg & absolute yield: 1.3-1.5 kg.
- Gramaxone: Best herbicide in cultivation.
- All species are susceptible to water stagnation.
- Productive life of jasmine plantation: 10-15 years.
- Plants are hardy as compared with other commercial ornamentals.
- Pollen storage at -60°C shows better germination than storage at 4°C and fresh pollens.
- Pollen storage in silica gel under vacuum shows good germination than organic solvents.
- In *J. grandiflorum*, cycocel spray and B-Nine@ 1000 ppm induce early flowering, extends blooming period, improves flower yield and essential oil.
- In *J. sambac*, cycocel spray @ 1000-2000 ppm induces early flowering, and high flower yield.
- Ethylene spray (1500 ppm) increased flower size and concrete yield.
- In *J. auriculatum*, NAA @ 25 ppm enhances number of flowers/plant.
- SADH spray (500 ppm) and GA_3 (25 ppm) during blooming period enhance freshness of flowers and retain fragrance for longer time.
- Treatment of flowers before storage with 1% sucrose, 0.5% boric acid, 0.1% $CuSO_4$, 0.001% silver nitrate or 0.1% aluminium sulphate solutions extend flower freshness to 72 hours.
- Packaging flowers in 200 gauge polythene bags maintains freshness, retains white colour.
- Seed treatment with gamma rays beyond 10 kR is lethal.

- Seed soaking in 0.1% EMS for 72 h is lethal.
- Soft wood cuttings with gamma rays 1-10 kR is lethal.
- In *J. grandiflorum* gamma rays beyond 30 kR is lethal.

Pruning:

- In Morocco, *J. grandiflorum* plants are trained to trellis system.
- Regular pruning from 3rd year onwards is essential.
- Flowering occurs only on new growth.
- Staggered pruning gives flowers over longer period.
- Pinching of new shoots after pruning regulates/ staggers peak flowering productivity in *J. auriculatum* and *J. grandiflorum.*
- Unpruned plants stop to flower between October-January.
- Pruning of unproductive water shoots is essential.
  - *J. sambac*- October end (every after 6 months at 50 cm height from ground level).
  - *J. grandiflorum*- Pruned during mid-December till 1st January leaving 9-11 shoots. Each shoot cut back to 90-100 cm from ground level.
  - *J. auriculatum*- December-January. Shoots cut back 50 cm from ground level.
  - *J. multiflorum*- 3rd week of November at 50 cm height from ground level.
- Chemical defoliants:
  a) Cannot replace manual pruning.
  b) Unable to control plant size.
  c) Used as substitute for pruning to reduce labour cost.
  d) Initial years of planting, following defoliants can be used.
  e) Effective substitute for pruning: Pentachlorophenol (chemical defoliant).
    - *J. grandiflorum* or *J. officinalis*- Pentachlorophenol (3000 ppm) and potassium iodide (4000 ppm).
    - *J. auriculatum*- Pentachlorophenol (0.3%) and NaCl (0.8%).
    - *J. sambac*- Bolls eye (sodium salt of cacodylic acid) @ 3000 ppm.

Species:

- *Jasminum humile*, *J. officinalis*, *J. auriculatum* and *J. grandiflorum* are diploid (2n=2x=26); *J. sambac*, *J. primulinum* is triploid (2n=3x=39) and *J. flexile* is tetraploid (2n=4x=52).
- India: One of the principle Centre of orgin.
- Only 4 species are gorn commercially in India.
- Bailey (1949) gave taxonomic description of jasmine species and key for their identification.

Botanical name	Native of	Common name	Characteristics
J. adenophyllum	India	Bluegrape/ Princess jasmine	Spreading fast growing vine with glossy large 2-3 inch dark green leaves; flowers large (2-3 inch wide) narrow curled petals & extremely fragrant; endemic in India.
J. angular	South Africa	South African jasmine	Evergreen vine; summer blooming; white non-scented flowers in groups of three.
J. angustifolium	India	-	Dwarf; flowers white, star-like & fragrant; flowering from November-February; good seed set.
J. arborescens	India	Mutabela/ Naba mallige/ Tree jasmine	Dwarf; white fragrant flowers; shy bearer; flowering in March-June; extremely low seed/ fruit set; very difficult to root from cuttings % &multiplied through suckers
J. auriculatum	India	Juhi/ Jooee/ Mullai/ Ambur mallige	Day neutral; creeper; sweet scented white flowers; 5-8 petals terminal or axillary; borne in clusters or solitary; high seed set; seed black; flowers during Feb-Dec. with peak during April-August; yield (5655 kg/ ha)
J. beesianum	China	Red jasmine/ Rosy jasmine	Hardy; low climber with slender grooved stem; flowers small, fragrant, pink to deep rose in colour.
J. calophyllum	India	Pendal mallige	Scented white flowers throughout year with peak during July-Nov.; flowers small with less keeping quality; good seed set; grown for garden decoration; resistant to rust, leaf spot & anthracnose
J. dichotomum (syn. *J. ternifolium*)	West Africa	Gold coast jasmine	Vigorous climbing woody vine; small fragrant flowers produced in clusters at intervals throughout year; unopened flower buds are tinted red on outside, but open flowers are pure white inside; endemic in west Africa.
J. dispermum	China, India	-	Deciduous climber; flowers white or slightly pink tinged, fragrant; born in axillary or terminal cymes.
J. faveri	Burma	-	Evergreen; shoots angled, downy & purplish; leaves trifoliate & ovate-lanceolate; flowers borne in terminal clusters; corolla bright yellow in colour.
J. flexile (syn. *J. caudatum*)	China	Climbing jasmine	Profuse scented flowers throughout year with peak from April- November; high fruit set; grown for compound garden
J. floridum	China	Showy jasmine/ Golden-yellow jooee	Evergreen rambler; shoots angled & glabrous; leaf trifoliate; golden yellow coloured flowers with five petals, borne in terminal clusters
J. fluminense	Brazil	Brazilian jasmine	Woody vine; flowers small, very fragrant & borne in loose clusters.
J. fruticans (syn. *J. syricum*)	Mediterranean region	-	Evergreen or semi-evergreen shrub; corolla yellow; calyx with slender lobes.
J. multiflorum (syn. *J. pubescense*, *J. gracillimum*)	India	Indian jasmine/ Star jasmine/ Downy jasmine/ Winter jasmine/ Pink budded jasmine/ Furry jasmine/ Pin wheel jasmine/Kundphool/Kundu/	Hardiest spp. among jasmine; climbing or rambling; flowers large, non- fragrant, very ornamental & white in colour; petals 9 & blooms for 10 month in year, profuse during winter; flowers in bunches (as many as 30); yield (7-8 t/ha/year); least affected by pests & diseases

		Kundam/ Kakda	
J. officinalis (syn. *J.grandiflorum*)	India, Afghanistan and Persia	Royal jasmine/Spanish jasmine/French jasmine/Catalonian jasmine/Chameli/Jai/ Pitchi/Jaji mallige/Jathi mallige	Day neutral; semi-evergreen climber not naturalized in Himalaya; flowers large (1 inch dia.,) white reddish inside, fragrant & born in axillary or terminal with 5 petals; flowers throughout year with peak during July-January; high seed set; highly priced for high grade perfume throughout the world; yield (1595 kg/ ha); sensitive to frost
J. humile (syn. *J. revolutum*, *J. bignoniaceum*, *J. wallichianum*)	Afghanistan, Himalaya and Western China	Italian yellow jasmine or Sem mallige/ Pelli chambell/ Swarna chameli	Hardy; evergreen semi-erect shrub or vine; flowers mildly fragrant, 5 petals, yellow coloured, 2-4 flowers in clusters; flowers from April-June; grown for home gardens
J. maingyi	China	-	Tolerant to white fly and red spider mite
J. nitidum (syn. *J. communis*, *J. laurifolium*)	New Guinea	Angle wing jasmine/ Star jasmine	Triploid; woody vine; flowers very fragrant in clusters; buds tinted pink on outside, but white when open & 4 cm across; non-fruit bearing type; 9 months flowering period.
J. parkeri	Himalaya	-	Potential ornamental species; suitable for rock garden
J. parceflorum	China	-	New species from China
J. polyanthum	China, USA	-	Deciduous or evergreen climber; flowers highly fragrant; corolla white inside & rosy outside; excellent pot plant
J. rex	Thailand	King's jasmine	Shrub; flowers large (5 cm dia.) having nine broad overlapping petals; non-fragrant, pure white, profusely flowers in large terminal cymes.
J. ritchiei	India	-	Grows wild; flowers 3-7 in cyme, milky white coloured; mild fragrant; flowers in Aug-Oct.
J. sambac	India	Arabian jasmine/ Tuscan jasmine/ Mogra	Evergreen shrub;flowers white, single, semi-double or fully double; highly fragrant; flowers from January-June; yield (1014 kg/ha); sensitive to frost; certain varieties set seeds
J. simplicifolium ssp. australiense (syn. *J. volubile*, *J. gracile*)	Australia	Australian stiff/ Wax jasmine	Climbing shrub; simple, opposite & ovate leaf; fragrant white flowers with pink tinge; terminally borne in clusters.
J. x *stephanense*	China	-	Hybrid origin; hardy; simple to pinnate leaf, fragrant pale pink flowers
J. trinerve (syn. *J. acuminatum*)	Vietnam	-	Climbing shrub; glabrous branches, flowers white.
J. undulatum	India	-	Climbing shrub; slender hairy branches; flowers scented; 6-10 in terminal cymes with long tubes.

Varieties:

- Crop improvement methods: OP seedling selection, clonal selection, hybridization, mutation, and polyploidy breeding.
- Supression of polyploids by diploid growth despite pinching is a bottleneck in polyploidy breeding.
- Varieties of *J. sambac* are grouped in 4 classes viz.
  1. Single whorled petals e.g. Sooji mallige.
  2. Globular buds & double whorled petals e.g. Gundu mallige.
  3. Elongated buds & double whorled petals e.g. Madanban, Rambanam.
  4. Rounded buds (2-5 mm dia.) e.g. Idukka mallige, Mungra.

Morphological variants:

Name	Salient features
J. auriculatum	
Long Round, Long Point, Short Point, Medium Point	Variant differing chiefly in flower bud characters; bloom from April-August; susceptible to gall mite pest except Medium Point clone.
Short Round	High percentage of improved floral characters; best for flower yield & concrete recovery.
Aureum	Cultivar with variegated yellow leaves.
Hadagali mallige	-
J. grandiflorum	
Triploid	Large size flowers with pinkish buds; highly sterile.
Mysore mallige	Buds white; highly fragrant & high yielding & endemic.
Thimmapuram, Coimbatore, Lucknow, Pink Thrum, Pink Pin	Buds white to red; highly fragrant & high yielding.
J. sambac	
Iruvatchi	Flowers with shorter corolla tube with 3-4 whorls; high degree of resistance to rust, leaf spot & anthracnose
Gundu mallige/ Madurai mallige	Globular bud with double whorled petals;high yielder; known for its fragrance in world
Sooji mallige	Long buds, single whorled.
Kasturi mallige	Flowers with medium-long flower tube.
Oosi mallige	Long slender buds.
Single mogra	Flowers with three or four whorls.
Double mogra	Flowers with good fragrance resembling white rose; 8-10 whorls.
Rambanam	Elongated bud with double whorled petals; high yielder.
Madanban	Elongated bud with double whorled petals; high yielder.
Virupakshi	Globular bud with double whorled petals.
Motia	Globular bud with double whorled petals.
Bela	Globular bud with double whorled petals.
Mungra	Nearly round buds measuring about 2-2.5 cm dia.; blooms from February-June.
Yelu-suthu mallige	Nearly round buds measuring about 2-2.5 cm dia.; blooms from February-June.
Idukka mallige	Nearly round buds measuring about 2-2.5 cm dia.; blooms from February-June.

Udupi mallige	Mild fragrance & have GI tag.
J. multiflorum	
Kundphool/ Kundu/Kundam	Commercial type; high yielder (7-8 t/ha); hardiest; non-scented, but very attractive; oval unpointed petals, moderate size white flowers; least affected by pests & diseases.
Giant	More floriferous with larger pendulous panicles with elongated petals & large size flowers.
Violet	Resembles 'Kund' except for pointed petals and pink mauve colourations, flowers smaller than 'Kund', petals oval shaped with pink mauve colouration outside. Five sepals, very small with little pubescence.
Natural variant '*Rubescens*'	Mild fragrance; bud slightly pinkish & possess only one row of petals.
Kakda/ *Sullanijooee*	Dark green foliage; very fragrant white flowers with purple on underside of petals and tube & buds are also purple in colour.

Name	Breeding method	Features
Ann Clements	Interspecific hybrid of '*J. rex* x *J. nitidum*'	-
J. stephanense	Interspecific hybrid of '*J. beesianum* and *J. officinale*'	Hardy vigorous climber; simple or pinnate leaves; flowers fragrant, corolla soft & pale pink coloured
IIHR, Benguluru		
Arka Surabhi	Clonal selection from Pink Pin (*J. grandiflorum*)	Highly tolerant to drought; flower yield (10 t/ha) & concrete extraction (0.35%)
Arka Arpan	Clonal selection from *J. multiflorum*	Tolerant to jasmine rust & leaf spot disease; drought hardy; flower yield (6.19 t/ha) & concrete content 0.23%
Arka Aradhana	Clonal selection from *J. sambac* var. Soojimallige	Hardy, double whorled flowers; free from major pests & diseases, flower yield (7.89 t/ha) & concrete extraction (0.18%)
TNAU, Coimbatore		
Parimullai (1971)	Clonal selection from Medium Point variant (*J. auriculatum*)	Long flowering season (9 months); high flower yield (7,800 kg/ha); concrete recovery 0.29 %; gall mite resistant; suffer from undesirable corolla length.
CO.1 Mullai	Seedling selection from Local type Long Round (*J. auriculatum*)	Bold buds; high flower yield with concrete recovery 0.34%; suitable for fresh flower trade
CO.2 Mullai	(Mutant (Sl) x Long Point) of *J. auriculatum*)	Bold pink & long flower buds (4.14 cm); yield (8800 kg), & concrete recovery of 0.34%
Acc. Jn-1	Clonal selection of *J. nitidum*	Year round flowering; mild fragrance & high consumer preference; yield 2.21 kg/ plant/ year
CO.1 Pitchi (1980)	Clonal selection of *J. gradiflorum* Lucknow clone (Jg-3)	Pink flower buds with pleasant fragrance; high yield (10.15 t/ha) & concrete recovery of 0.29%; suitable for fresh flower trade & oil extraction
CO.2 Pitchi	Induced gamma ray mutant of 'CO. 1 Pitchi' using 1.5 kR to stem cuttings	Pink coloured long flower buds (4.14 cm) & high yield (11,680 kg/ha) with concrete recovery of 0.30%

Diseases and pests:

- Leaf blight (*Cercospora jasminicola*): Most serious. Flower production reduced to 50%.
- Rust (*Uromyces hobsoni*): Blister like appearance. Spray Bordeaux mixture (1:1:50) from May to December.
- Leaf spot (*Cercopspora jasminicola* & *Alternaria jasminie*): Serious throughout the world. Fungus destroy foliage during rainy season & lowers yield by 50%. Spray Dithane-M-45 @ 0.2%.
- Wilt (*Fusarium solani* or *Sclerotium rolfsii*): Drench Blitox or Brassicol @ 0.2% or Benlate 0.1%.
- Anthracnose (*Colletotrichum* spp.): Serious throughout the world.
- Bud and shoot worm (*Hendecasis duplifascialis*): Cause serious economic loss.
- Shoot borer (*Sycophylla* spp.): Apply Carbofuron @ 40 g/ buch as basal application & spray Nuvacron 0.2% from May to December.
- Eriophyid mite (*Aceria jasmini*):
- Gall mite (*Eriophid* spp): Spray 3g/lit wettable sulphur or Kelthane 0.01% at monthly interval.
- Yellow ring mosaic virus.

52. ORCHIDACEAE

52.1 Orchids

- Eulogized as 'Botanical jewels'.
- Maximum diversity: North-East Himalaya and Western ghat regions.
- International trade restrictions on orchids through CITES (Convention on International Trade in Endangered Species of Wild Fauna and Flora) to restrict the illegal collections, smuggling and export of important endangered orchids.
- RHS, London: International Authority for Registration of Orchids.
- Japan: World's largest importer of orchids.
- The Netherlands: Largest producer of temperate orchids (*Cymbidium*).
- Thailand: Largest producer of tropical orchids (*Dendrobium*).
- Malaysia: Leading orchid exporting country.
- Taiwan: Largest producer of *Phalaenopsis* in world.
- Hawaii, California, Florida: Major potted *Dendrobium* growing regions in United Nations.
- Orchid form 9% of Indian flora.
- About 20% of recorded Indian taxa are endemic.
- About 60% species of Indian origin are epiphytic while rests are terrestrial.

- N-E hilly region of India is richest in world both in quantity and individual spp. & serves as foundation of orchid industry.
- N-E hilly region of India: Agri-export zone for production of *Cymbidium* orchids.
- Germplasm is protected by using modern tools of bar coding.
- Major importers of fresh orchid flowers: Italy (29%), France (19%), Germany (12%), UK (9%).
- Major growers of orchids: Singapore, Thailand, Malaysia, Indonesia, Japan, Australia.
- Occupy prime position among ornamental plants of the modern world.
- Accounts for 10% share of global floriculture trade both as cut flower and potted plant.
- In India, orchids accounts for 3% share of total cut flower production.
- Dendrobiums are very valuable herbs with wide medicinal and clinical application in China.
- Central America and South America: Orchid paradise.
- Brazilian (*Cattleya*), Mexican (*Laelia*) and Indian (*Cymbidium*, *Dendrobium*, *Vanda*) played important role in development of modern orchid industry.
- Indian *Cymbidiums*, *Dendrobium* and *Vandas* have great potential in floriculture, pharmaceutical, and tourism industry of our country.
- Genome breeding and wider crosses are routinely used to create genetic variability.
- Father of modern orchidology: John Lindley.
- Region famous for orchid cultivation: North-East states of India.
- Kalimpong area of Darjeeling: Called as 'Heaven of orchids'.
- Arunachal Pradesh: 'Orchid Paradise' and 'Orchid State' of India.
- Asia's largest orchidarium is situated at Tipi, Arunachal Pradesh.
- Convenient height of orchid house: 3 m.
- Orchid plants were used as anti-depressants and stimulants in Greece and Asia Minor.
- Indian origin: *Cymbidium, Dendrobium, Paphiopedilum.*
- *Ophioglossum vulgatum* is antidote for snake bite.
- Major factor which played animportant role in orchid breeding: Polyploidy.
- Intergeneric crosses have been commercially exploited in orchids.
- King of orchids: *Cymbidium*.
- Queen of orchids: *Cattleya*.
- Noble orchid: *Cymbidium goeringii*.
- Largest genera *Bulbophyllum* followed by *Dendrobium*.
- Largest Indian orchid: *Galelola falconesi*.

- Smallest Indian orchid: *Eria pusilla*.
- Mirror orchid (*Ophrys speculum*): Produces a flower that looklike female species of large wasp or bee.
- Smallest size of chromosome (<2 μm): *Dendrobium lindleyi*.
- Largest size of chromosome: *Paphiopedilum insigne*.
- Tiny orchid (no leaves and stem): *Taeniophyllum khasianum*.
- Yellow colour is constituted by: *Paphiopedilum insigne*.
- *Eulophia andamanensis* (Pretty Green Bay): Important medicinal indigenous orchid species registered at NBPGR has special characteristics viz. green flowers, long spike and duration of flowering.
- Jewel orchids: Valued for their beautiful leaves.
- Monarchy of orchids in the world: *Paphiopedilum*.
- Most popular cut flower in Asia: *Dendrobium*.
- Most fragrant: *Aerides odoratum* and *Coelgyne ochracea*.
- *Cattleya* orchids are used for hair decoration in Hawaii.
- Alkaloid not present in orchids: Atrazine.
- Pseudobulbs of *Dendrobium tokai* are used as oral contraceptives.
- *Vanda parviflora*: Anti-viral and anti-cancerous properties.
- Drug 'chin shih hu' obtained from dried stem of *Dendrobium nobile* is being used in China as anti-pyretic and tonic.
- Edible parts: Leaves, tubers, pseudobulbs.
- Anoectochilus leaves are used as vegetable in Indonesia and Malaysia.
- Number of alkaloids like Anthocyanins, stilebnoids, tri-terpenoids have been isolated.
- Value added products: Species trade, drying, flower arrangement, herbal medicines, edible products, other aesthetic products.

Common name	**Genera**	**Common name**	**Genera**	**Common name**	**Genera**
Scorpian orchid	*Arachnis*	Sun loving orchid	*Renanthera*	Lady's slipper	*Paphiopedilum*
Dancing lady	*Oncidium*	Spider orchid	*Brassia*	Butterfly orchid	*Oncidium*
Moth orchid	*Phalaenopsis*	Dove orchid	*Peristeria*	Fox tail orchid	*Rhyncostylis retusa*
Vine orchid	*Vanilla*	Bee orchid	*Ophyrys*	Aphid orchid	*Epicactis consimilis*
Necklace orchid	*Coelogyne tomentosa*				

- Pseudobulbs develop in 1st pair of true leaves.
- Most orchids are day neutral.
- Anthocyanin and carotenoid pigments determine colour.
- White or creamy white flowered orchids are strongly fragrant.

- Stamenoids, sepals and petals are richest source of scent.
- *Cymbidium* cvs. with 40-60% florets: Raceme length is recommended for cultivation.
- In *Cymbidium* orchid, fragrance ranges from lemon/ orange/ chocolate/ coconut/ vanilla to menthol.
- Natural compounds for fragrance: Limonene, Pinene, Anisyl acetate, Benzyl acetate, Camphene.
- Most widely cultivated tropical orchid: *Dendrobium*.
- Light requirement: 6000-10000 lux.
- Grows vigorously in 1500-2500 mm rainfall, 70-95% R.H. and 10-25^{0}C.
- Coal and bark: Important constituents of potting media.
- Repotting: Done every year and is done at active vegetative growth stage.
- *Dendrobium peguanum*: Rare spp. located in Satpura hills of Maharashtra. This grows on teak wood and during flowering becomes leafless.
- Breeding behaviour of *Dendrobium*: Self pollination and sibmating results in fruit set.
- Flowers are primitively zygomorphic.
- Inflorescence: Spike (*Oncidium*, *Phalaenopsis*); Raceme (*D.moschatum*); Panicle (*Cleisostoma racemiferum*).
- Inflorescence is terminal in terrestrial orchids and lateral in epiphytic forms.
- Inflorescence is apical in *Cattleya*, axillary in *Vanda*, arise at base of tuber in *Cymbidium*.
- Special feature of orchid flower: Both sepals and petals are coloured.
- Column/ gynandrium/ gynostegium/ gynostemium: Distinguishing feature from other flower and resting place for insects. It is joined structure of anther and style.
- 15 organs in 5 whorls are found in flower.
- Orchid flower contains 7 parts: 3 sepals, 3 petals and 1 gynostegium (triangular ovary).
- Sepals are usually very similar to the petals (called as tepals).
- Flower has 3-sepals and 3 petals, hence called 'tepals'.
- Gynoecium is tricarpellary, syncarpous, inferior and unilocular.
- Modified tepal of orchids: Lip or labellum.
- Pleoric flower: 6-7 petals with 3-4 labellum.
- Pollens are generally waxy masses and aggregate to form 'pollinia (2-8/ stamen)' which avoids self pollination. It is critical determining factor in the genera.
- Out of 6 stamens, only one stamen in 3rd whorl is fertile called 'Monandrae'.

- If 2 or more fertile stamens, the flower is known as 'Pleonandrae'.
- Pollination agents: Insects, snakes, ants, wind, rains, bees, wasps, moths, butterflies, frogs, snails, bats, lizzards, humming birds, human beings.
- Cleistogamy is reported in *Dendrobium antennatum*.
- Anthesis time: Early morning (7-8 h).
- Anther dehiscence: Longitudinal.
- Stigma receptivity: Upto 2-8 days after anthesis.
- Pollen viability: 12 months at 45^0F.
- Days required for seed development from pollination: 80-150.
- Fruit type: Capsule and ripens within 6-12 months depending on species.
- Number of seeds/ capsule: 5,000-6,000.
- Pollen grain storage temperature: 4^0C in refrigerator for several months.
- Dry seed storage temperature: 0-4^0C for storage in organic solvants.
- 1st meristem tip culture in *Cymbidium* spp. by Morel (1960).
- Layer of spongy tissue in orchids: Velamen aroung the root which absorbs water and mineral salts.
- Velamen tissue: Common feature of epiphytic orchids.
- Optimum dose of gamma irradiation: 1.5-2.5 Krad in *Dendrobium*.
- Pollen induced parthenocarpy is reported.
- Polyembryony is reported in *Cymbidium densifolium* and *C. pendulum*.
- Chilling injury is common in tropical orchids.
- *Cymbidium* orchids are winter and spring blooming and suitable for high altitudes.
- Optimum dose of gamma rays: 900 rad/ hr (*cymbidium*); 1.5-2.5 Krad/hr (*dendrobium*).
- Phylogenetic study in orchids uses ribosomal and mitochondrial DNA.
- Genomic markers find application in plant patenting & breeders rights.
- Aromatic spp.: *Aerides multiflorum*, *Cattleya maxima*, *Cymbidium ensifolium*, *Dendrobium nobile*, *Epidendrum floribundum*, *E. nocturnum*, *E. cristatum*, *Oncidium spaceolatum*, *Vanda cristata*, *V. tesselata*.

Classification:

- Commercial orchids grown in temperate zone: Terrestrial orchids.
- Commercial orchids grown in tropical zone: Epiphytic orchids.
- *Dendrobium* belongs to both warm group (night temperature 16^0C) and cool group (night temperature 10^0C).

1. **Based on growth habit**: Small plant (0.5 cm height) to vine (30 m).

a) **Monopodial**: Single stemmed growth (no lateral shoots). They produce single continuous stem without any rhizome or pseudobulb. They produce aerial roots to anchor e.g. *Aerides, Arachnis, Aranda,Phalaenopsis, Renanthera, Vanda, Vanilla*

b) **Sympodial**: Multi stemmed growth. Rank high in export marketor preferred for commercial cultivation. They produce swollen stems (pseudobulbs) to store water and food material. Equally preferred in commercial cultivation e.g. *Bulbophyllum, Cattleya, Cymbidium, Dendrobium, Epidendrum, Oncidium*. Among the sympodial types major share is occupied by *Dendrobium* hybrids.

2. **Based on habitat**:

1. Epiphytes-Grows on tree trunks/ branches, flowering is lateral or axillary e.g. *Aerides, Aranda, Aranthera, Bulbophyllum, Cattleya, Calanthe, Dendrobium, Obernia, Phalaenopsis, Thunia, Vanda.*
2. Terrestrials- Xerophytic/mesophytic and perennial in nature. Flowering is terminal.
3. Lithophytes- Grown on moist and shaded rocks e.g. *Cymbidium munroniamum, Diplomeris hirsuta, Phaius*.
4. Saprophytes- lack green leaves, possess fleshy underground rhizome. Endotrophic mychorrhiza occurs in almost all saprophytic orchids.

3. **Based on leaf characters**:*Vanda* orchids can be divided into two groups-

a) Strap shaped leaves which are fleshy, flat and keeled e.g. *V. coerulea*.

b) Terete leaves which are distichous and leathery texture e.g. *V. teres*.

4. **Based on temperature requirement**:*Dendrobium* can be divided into two groups-

Warm group (night temperature 16^{0}C)	Cool group (night temperature 10^{0}C)
D. phalaenopsis, D. gouldii, D. bigibbum, D. antennatum & D. discolor	*D. lindleyi* (*D. aggregatum, D. parishii, D. pierardii, D. densiflorum, D. chrysotoxum & D. anosmum*)

5. **Carnivorous**: *Schoburgkia tibicinis*.

Modes of propagation:

1. One complete plant of orchids constitutes back bulb, mature bulb and young bulb.
2. Division: *Cattleya, Cymbidium, Dendrobium.*
3. Cutting: *Cattleya, Dendrobium, Cymbidium, Phalaenopsis.*
4. Top cutting: *Vanda.*
5. Air layering: *Vanda.*
6. Rhizome: *Habenaria & Eulophia.*
7. Pseudobulb: Help to survive in drought. Vary from small (1.2 mm in *Bulbophyllum minutissimum*) to 5 m (*Gammotphyllum speciousum*).

- Keikis are more common in *Dendrobium*. They are produced from node region. Takes long time to flower.
- Shoots growing on the plants of orchids: Keikis.
- Pseudobulb is a secondary stem modification.
- Seed dormancy due to immature embryo is common.
- Optimum temperature for seed germination: 20-25^{0}C.
- Time needed for seed germination: 2-10 weeks.
- Mature seeds germinate earlier and develop protocorms.
- At 4th leaf stage, seedlings are transplanted in pots.
- Only 1-2% seeds germinate in nature.
- For natural germination, seeds require symbiotic association with mycorrhiza.
- *Rhizoctonia* spp. For symbiotic seed germination: *R. repens*, *R. mucoroides* and *R. languinosa*.
- Triphenyl tetrazolium chloride and Malachite green dye at 0.1% indicates seed viability in orchids.
- Commercial propagation: Tissue culture.
- 1st floricultural crop successfully mass propagated through tissue culture.
- 1sttissue culture in orchids was done by 'Morel'.
- A.V. Thomas: 1st tissue culture laboratory established in India in 1984.
- Mericloning is very popular in orchids.
- Culture medium for higher and faster seed germination: 'Knudson C' medium.
- Nitsch's medium supplemented with coconut water (15%) is commonly used medium for *Dendrobium* seed germination.
- Pre-treatment of seeds: Sodium hypochlorite (2-6%).
- Polyembrony: *Cymbidium densifolium* and *C. pendulum*.
- Common potting medium for epiphytic orchids: *Osmunda* fibers.
- Virus resistance in *Dendrobium* is transferred by particle gun method.
- Only resistant x resistant parents produce resistant offsprings, indicate genetic control.
- Hybrids are propagated by mericloning.
- Polyembryony is reported in *Cymbidium densiflorum* & *C. pendulum*.
- World orchid conference was held in Miami in 1984 and proposed to start:
  1. Banking of orchid seeds as insurance against loss of species from its habitats in wild
  2. Dry storage of species at -20^{0}C
  3. Extension of life span of orchid seeds in liquid nitrogen.

Selection of parents for orchid breeding-

Orchid species	Breeding utility
Cymbidium aloiifolium	Potential to produce warm growing potted orchids
Cymbidium devonianum, C. lancifolium	Potentialto produce miniature (potted) hybrids
C. sinonsianum	Blooms in July-August & potential parent in creation of late blooming hybrids
C. hookerianum	Potential to produce large sized flowers
C. lowianum	Potential to produce colour variation
C. munronianum	Potential to incorporate fragrance
C. tigrinum	Highly valued in international breeding programme
Dendrobium antennatum	For potted plants
Phalaenopsis mannii	For long lasting flowers & colour breeding
P. equestris & P. stuartiana	Pot culture varieties (small and plentiful flowers)
P. violacea, P. amboinensis & P. venosa	Imparts special fragrance
P. equestris var. *alba*	Pure white flower form
P. equestris var. *aurea*	White flowers with solid yellow lip
P. equestris var. *leucaspis*	Small flowers with white edges on pink petals & sepals
P. equestris var. *leucotante*	Flowers with white lips
P. equestris var. *rosea*	Flowers with even red petals & sepals
Vanda cristata	Compact, floriferous & cold tolerant orchids
V. pumila	Miniature potted orchids with small size & white flowers
V. coerulea	Source for blue orchids

Varieties:

- Maximum number of man made hybrids are in *Cymbidium*, *Dendrobium*, *Phalaenopsis*, *Vanda*.
- Cymbidium cvs. with 40-60% floret; raceme length is recommended for cultivation.
- 1st orchid *Bletia purpurea* (1731) was grown by Peter Collinson who was 1st among the westerns to grown an orchid.
- 1st artificial hybrid *Calanthe dominii* (*Calanthe masuca* x *Calanthe furcata*) by J. Dominy (1852).
- 1st ornamental orchid: *Cypripedium reginae.*
- 1st bigeneric hybrid: *Phaius grandiflorus* x *Calanthe vestia.*
- 1st sexageneric hybrid 'Brilliandeara Gary' was registered in 1982.
- New hybrids of *Cymbidium* from Sikkim: Deen Dayal, Sardar, Namo.
- *Cymbidium* hybrid: Cym 'B.S. Basnett'.
- *Aranda* hybrid: Aranda 'Kunga Gyatso'.
- *Dendrobium* hybrid: Den 'V. Nagaraju'.
- *Vanda* hybrids: Mimi Palmer, Arjuna.
- *Phalaenopsis* hybrids: Blueberry, Brother Purple, Brother Supersonic, Brother Precious Stones, Blueberry, Brother Oconee, Brother Purple Lip, Doris, Golden

Lotus, Golden Buddha, Indigo Bunting, Little Blue Bird, Pink Marble, Sapphire Doll, White Angel, Yellow Marble, Yellow Dream,

- Miniature hybrids: Mini Gem, Doctor Sharif, Mardi.
- CARI Pretty Green Bay: 35-45 flowers/spike; 4-6 spikes/plant; spike length 120-150 cm.

F_1 hybrid & its characters	Parents
Cymbidium	
Alexanderi (large white flowered, diploid, widely used in breeding for pastel coloured hybrids) & Westonbirt (tetraploid)	*C. eburneo-lowianum* x *C. insigne*
Miniature type hybrid (evolved in England in 1944)	*Cymbidium* 'Lois Sander' x *C. pumilum*
C. gammieanum	*C. elegans* x *C. Iridioides*
Dendrobium	
IIHR.38 (Robust; floriferous with 12-15 purple violet sepals with narrow white margin; spike 35-40 cm long; petals red purple; flowers from February-May; flowers lasts for 2-3 months	*D. pompadour* x *D. superbiens*
Autumn Lace Florida Twist (Long arch up to 68 cm, 53 flowers with colour combination of brown, orange, yellow & purple, flowers lasts for 14-20 days; 18 racemes/bulb; vase life 60 days	*D. streblocerasx* x *D. canaliculatum*
Vanda	
IIHR 164 (Robust; spike length 20-35 cm; 10-13 flowers/spike; flowers from September-November	*V. rothschildiana* x *V. coerulea*
Vanda Issel	*V.* Harriet Miyae x *V.* Rothschildiana
Vanda violeta (syn. *V.* x *amoena*)	*V. tessellata* x *V. coerulea*
Vanda Miss Joaquim (2n=38)	*V. teres* x *V. hookeriana*
Albino form of *V.* Miss Joaquim	*V. hookeriana* x *V. teres*
Vanda Paki	*V. cristata* x *V. tricolor*
Vanda Venus	*Vanda* Paki x *Euanthe sanderina*
Vanda David Junka	*V. cristata* x *Vanda* Kultana Gold
Vanda Ben Berliner	*V. cristata* with *V. coerulescence*

Name	Breeding method	Features
KAU, Thrissur		
Deep Blush (2006)	D. Nagoya Pink x D.[Candy Stripe x Tomie Drake]	Long arching inflorescence with 9-10 flowers; flowers large, magenta coloured, double shaded & striped with full appearance
Lemon Glow (2006)	D. Chiangmai Pink x D. [Candy Stripe x Tomie Drake]	Long, arching inflorescence with 10-12 flowers; flowers light pink towards outer side & greenish white towards the centre
Master Delight (2006)	D. Sonia-17 x D.[Candy Stripe x Tomie Drake]	Long, arching inflorescence with10-12 flowers; flower colour dark purple with very faint stripes & sepal tips white
Pink Cascade (2006)	D. Nagoya Pink x D. [Candy Stripe x Tomie Drake]	Long, arching inflorescence with 8-10 flowers; flowers light pink with prominent dark pink stripes throughout.
Velvet Soft (2006)	D. Rungnapa x D. [Candy Stripe x Tomie Drake]	Long, arching inflorescence with 10-12 flowers; flowers purplish magenta coloured & striped with white operculum

- Natural and artificial hybrids
  1. *Phalaenopsis intermedia* (*P.aphrodita* x *P. rosea*).
  2. *Vanda* Miss Joaquim (*V. teres* x *V. hookeriana*): 2n=38.
  3. Darjeeling Nymph (*Cymbidium* Sleeping Nymph x *C. lowianum*).
  4. Darjeeling Delight (*C. lowianum* x *C.* 'Showgirl Coocksbridge').
  5. Tanakara (*Phalaenopsis* x *Aerides* x *Vanda*).

Three classes of *Cymbidiums*:

- Standard: > 1m stem length and 12-15 flowers/spike.
- Intermediate: 8-10 flowers/ spike.
- Miniature: 6-8 flowers/ spike.

Pest, diseases and disorders:

- Snails and slugs: Use Metaldhyde or Methomyl.
- Heart rot (*Phytophthora*).
- Orchid mantis: Insect look like orchid flower.
- Anthracnose spot (*Collitotrichum* spp.)
- Bacterial soft rot (*Erwinia carotovora*)
- Cymbidium mosaic virus: Reported throughout world.Cause floral necrosis. Associated with Cattleya leaf necrosis, Cymbidium black streak & Spathoglottis diamond spot.

Inheritance of characters:

Character	Gene action
Rachis length in *Cymbidium*	Additive
Pseudobulb length and width	Additive
Carbohydrate in back bulbs	Additive
Longevity of flower	Additive
Pansy lip (leaf reverts to petals)	Monogenic recessive
Carbohydrate content in flowering pseudobulb	Non-additive
Leaf length	Non-additive
Chlorophyll in leaf	Non-additive
Flower colour in *Dendrobium*	Purple (two complementary gene pair *C* & *R*)
	Alba (complementary gene action)
Flower colour in *Phalaenopsis*	Red (monogenic dominant)
	Pink (monogenic dominant/ 2 complientory)
	Yellow (two independent dominant duplicate genes)
Floral necrosis in *Dendrobium*	Monogenic dominant

53. PLANTAGINACEAE (SCROPHULARIACEAE)

53.1 Snapdragon

- Eulogized as 'Dragon flower or Dog flower'.
- Decorative ornamental used as model plant for genetic and biochemical study since early 20th century.
- Grown as cut flower, bedding plant and potted plant all over the world.
- Flowers look like 'skulls'.
- Basically temperate plant, but widely cultivated in tropical and sub-tropical regions.
- Inflorescence: Terminal raceme with perfect flower.
- Highly cross pollinated due to gametophytic SI and male sterility.
- Pollination agent: Bumble bee.
- Propagation method: Seeds and soft wood cutting.
- Flowers: Yellow, tubular, bilaterally symmetrical, hermaphrodite, borne on short pedicle along stem.
- Each flower has 5 lobed petals and corolla is fused into a tube.
- 3 lower lips are typically spreading, upper two lips are erect and form a mouth.
- Pollen viability: 8 days.
- 3 kinds of flowers: 1) Normal bunny face or close type (lip like mouth) 2) Intermediate or half open 3) Open throated penstemon type.
- Floral scent: Volatile benzenoids.
- Cross pollination usually done greenhouses without resorting to emaculation.
- Bunny face type is easy to emasculate and pollinate.
- Isolation distance seed production: 600 m (foundation) and 300 m (certified).

Species:

Species	Characters
Antirrhinum blanquetti	Perennial, glabrous, glandular pubescent inflorescence; corolla yellow;capsule oblong, glandular, hairy
A. calycinum	Glabrous annual, height 45 cm, leaves narrow elliptic.
A. coulterianum	Annual, erect; leaves ovate to elliptic, raceme pubescent; corolla white with pale yellow palate coloured petals.
A. filipes	Slender, glabrous, scandent annual, upper leaves linear to lanceolate while lower leaves ovate to oblong; flowers yellow with lower lip golden & palate maroon coloured.
A. glandulosum	Annual, rose coloured flowers with lower portion white yellow
A. glutinosum	Native of Spain, woody & perennial, branches fragile; leaves alternate & oblong to ovate; flowers large, erect & solitary in leaf axil.
A. hispanicum	Dwarf shrub, leaves lanceolate to broadly ovate; corolla white or pink
A. latifolium	Perennial, erect, leaves ovate, obtuse broadly truncate, bracts ovate, calyx lobes broadly ovate; corolla pale yellow in colour.

A. majus	Perennial, cultivated; stem glabrous, erect, corolla purple or pink in colour
A. molle	Dwarf, perennial, corolla pale pink or white in colour
A. multiflorum	Herbaceous perennial, erect, corolla pale pink to carmine in colour
A. nuttallinum	Annual erect, pubescent miniature, corolla lavender to blue-purple, tube & palate white in colour, flower oblique-ovoid
A. orontium	Annual herb, stems erect, sparsely branched, corolla pink, rarely white in colour or shorter than the calyx.
A. ovatum	Annual, height 60 cm, branched, spreading, corolla cream, flushed pink on upper lip & tube, flowers oblique to ovoid.
A. pulverulentum	Species similar to *A. sempervirens* differs only in larger hair, upper leaves alternate, corolla pale yellow in colour.
A. sempervirens	Dwarf woody evergreen shrub, height 40 cm, corolla cream or white in colour, violet on upper lip, palate yellowor white, flower whitish, sub-globose, glandular-pubescent
A. siculum	Perennial herb, erect, free branching, corolla pale yellow

Varieties:

- 1st F_1 hybrid: Christmus Cheer.
- Butterfly type cultivars have open cup-shaped flowers: Due to gene mutation.
- Tetra Giant: Tetraploid cultivar.
- Landscape purpose: Animation, Butterfly, Ribbon, Overture, Freesong, Solastic, La Bella, Kim, Bells, Floral Showers, Magic, Mini Snap.
- Rust resistant: Amber Monarch, Carmine Monarch, Coral Monarch, Lavender Monarch, Scarlet Monarch, White Frredom, Yellow Freedom, Moon Glow, Rainbow Mixture and Victory.
- Tall Giant or Grandiflora group: Butterfly type *viz.*, Bright Butterflies, Madam Butterfly; Rocket Hybrid series (cv. Rocket Bronze, Rocket Lemon, Rocket Pink, Rock Red, Rocket White); Tip Top Canary yellow, Tip Top Apple Blossom, Tip Top White.
- Intermediate or semi-dwarf e.g. Intermediate Bright Pink, Intermediate White, Intermediate Mauve, Bedding Scarlet, Sonnet series, Tetra Ruffled.
- Dwarf: hardly grow 30 cm e.g. Bells Flower, Chimes, Floral Showers, F_1 Floral Carpet, F_1 Kolibre, Little Darling, Orange Scarlet and Tom Thumb, etc.
- Miniature: Cross between *A. majus* and *A. molle* resulted into Magic Carpet series e.g. Magic Carpet, Floral Carpet. Very dwarf, useful for edging and rockeries.
- Super Giants: Plants grow tall and produce standard blossoms e.g. Candle Light, Lollipop, Nanum, Sky Scraper, Sun Set, Tetra Giant, etc.
- Double Azalea series: flowers double like azaleas and bigger e.g. Madame Butterfly.
- Sweet Heart series: a tetraploid type is popular due to double flowers.
- Penstemon type: Florets look like colourful butterfly e.g. Bright Butterflies.
- Pixie series: Orange Pixie, Pink Pixie, White Pixie, Rose Pixie and Red Pixie.

- Scented antirrhinum having soft clove like fragrance e.g. Super Jet, Vanguard and Venus.

Disease and disorder:

- Anthracnose: Serious greenhouse disease.
- Rust (*Puccinia antirrhini*): Most destructive disease affecting greenhouse production.
- Flower shattering: Ethylene injury.

Inheritance of characters:

- Purple colour of stem and leaf are dominant over green.

Character	Inheritance pattern
Floret diameter; number of primary and secondary branches/plant; number of spikes/ plant; rachis length; weight of seeds/ plant	Additive
Weight of spike; Vase life	Non-additive
Flower form/shape	Bunny face is monogenic dominant over penstemon & penstemon over intermediate
Flower colour	* Incomplete dominant * Red maroon flower colour dominant over orange, yellow peach & white
Post harvest longevity (PHL)	Additive & partially dominant
Variegated leaf mutants	Recessive to wild
Spiral phyllotaxy	Epistatic to whorled
Rust resistance	Monogenic & dominant

54. PLUMBAGINACEAE

54.1 Statice

- Eulogized as 'Sea lavender or Ever lasting flower'.
- Generic name is derived from Greek word '*Leimon*' means 'a meadow'.
- Perennial and annual statice is popular in garden decoration and in flower arrangement.
- Plant is hardy, herbaceous, or woody shrub (multistemmed).
- Used as dry flower and cut flower.
- Halophyte (found in salt marshes) and obligate allogamous crop due to reproductive dimorphism.
- Cool temperature is required to induce flowering, flowers are sensitive to frost.
- Propagation method: Seed.
- Reproduction: Seed and apomictic.
- Long days (16 h) are best for advancement of flowering.
- Flowering season: April-September.
- Flowers are produced in cluster and flowers look like fox tail.

- Flowering stems bear only small, brown scaled leaves (bracts).
- Flower is tiny (4-10 mm length), with 5 lobed tubular calyx and corolla and 5 stamens.
- Inflorescence: Branched paniculate corymb.
- Low temperature during growth phase enhances flower formation.
- Fruit type: Capsule containing single seed.
- Seed is produced as a result of apomixis.
- Days taken for seed setting: 35-40.
- Days take for seed germination: 5-9.
- Optimum temperature for seed germination: 13-18^{0}C.
- Seed sowing: September-October (plains); March-April (hills).
- Diplospory: Mechanism for asexual production of seeds and strong correlation exists with tetraploidy.
- Biparental inbreeding: Due to heteromorphic diallelic SI.
- Higher ploidy taxa viz. tetraploids (2n=34), pentaploids (2n=43), hexaploid (2n=52) also occur but in frequency than triploids.
- Harvesting stage: Heads start to open or calyces of individual flowers have opened and showing colour.
- Yield: 7-8 cut flower/ plant.
- Statice is used to investigate the rate of cooling during vacuum cooling.
- Vase life: 1-2 weeks.
- Storage: Flowers are stored for 2-3 weeks at 2^{0}C.
- Moth (*Goniodona limoniella*): An ant (*Messor burbieri*) act as pre and post dispersal seed predator.
- Exhibits self incompatibility linked with pollen (wide/ narrow) reticulum type and stylar (cob (heterozygous *Aa*)/ pop (homozygous *aa*) dimorphism.
- Hindrance for *ex situ* germplasm conservation: Low seed production.
- Explants for cryopreservation: Shoot primordial e.g. Blue Symphonet.
- Facultative apomictic reproduction is correlated with genome combinations.
- Technique used to produce interspecific hybrids: Embryo rescue/ ovule culture.
- Embryo rescue: 12-16 days old embryos from interspecific crosses.

Species:

- Majority of species are triploid (2n=3x=27) and reproduce apomictically.
- Spanish Balearic Island: Hot spot for biodiversity.
- *Limonium sinuatum, L. suworowii*: Grown as annual, cut flower and produce every colour.
- *L. latifolium*, *L. vulgare*: Perennial.
- *L. propsum*: Medicinal purpose.

- *L. cordatum*, *L. braceoli*: Critically endangered species in 2004.
- Apomictic hybrids are *L. palmare* (tetraploid 2n=4x=34), *L. roridum* (pentaploid 2n=5x=43), *L. graecum* (hexaploid 2n=6x=52).

Breeding system in Greek *Limonium* species-

- Dimorphic combinations of A & B are self incompatible i.e. self sterile.
- Four pollen & stigma combinations viz.
  A. Cob like stigma & coarse reticulate pollen grain surface.
  B. Papillate stigma & fine reticulate pollen grain surface.
  C. Papillate stigma & fine reticulate pollen grain surface.
  D. Papillate stigma & coarse reticulate pollen grain surface.
- **Dimorphic combinations of C & D are self compatible i.e. self fertile.**

Taxon	Reproductive mechanism
L. palmare	Dimorphic or monomorphic in respect to their pollen and stigma combination. In each dimorphic population both SI combinations A and B occur, while monomorphic population shows only one combination A or B is present; pollen viability is 0-99% and good seed production. It is facultative apomictic.
L. roridum	Monomorphic (A or B) or dimorphic, high pollen viability, good seed production; facultative apomictic.
L. graecum	Monomorphic with SI combination B, low pollen stainability 0-4% and good seed production, apomictic in behaviour.
L. virgatum	Monomorphic with SI combination B, low pollen stainability 0-35% and good seed production, apomictic in behaviour.
L. narbonense	Dimorphic with both SI combinations A and B, high pollen viability 50-96%, sexually reproduce.

Varieties:

- Mistry: F_1 hybrid of *L. hybrida*.

Name	Breeding method	Features
I.S.F. SOI'50	OP seedling selection from *L. tataricum*	White calyx & corolla
Turbo White	OP seedling selection	Long panicle; cut flower purpose
Montana	Hybrid	25 stems/plant; blue coloured flowers; resistant to low temperature
Chorus Magenta	Interspecific hybrid of (*L. perigrinum x L. purpuratum)*	Stem length 60 cm, but pollen sterile
Ocean Blue	Interspecific hybrid of (*L. latifolium* x *L. caspium*)	Tall (110 cm), compact stems (15 stems/ plant); soft blue coloured flowers
Blue Symphonet	Interspecific hybrid of (*L. altaica* x *L. caspium*)	Blue coloured flowers

Other promising hybrids: Apricot Beauty, Blue Cloud, Bouquet series, California series, Gold Coast, Heavenly Blue, Iceberg, Lavender Queen, Lemon Star, New Art Shade series, Maine Blue, Midnight Blue, Splash Blue, Snow Queen, Sunburst series, Super Lady, Topian Blue, Yellow Star.

Diseases and pests:

- Damping off (*Botrytis cinerea*): Seed soaking in hot water (52^{0}C) for 30 min or 0.5% sodium hypochloride for 2 min.
- Anthracnose (*Colletotrichum gloeosporioides*): Spray with bavistin (0.1%) or dithane Z-78 (0.2%).
- Downy mildew (*Peronospora statices*): Spray Azoxystrobin (0.2%).
- Leaf spot (*Alternaria* spp.): Spray Clorothalonil @ 2 g/litre.
- MLO: Phytoplasma.

55. POLEMONEACEAE

55.1 Phlox

- Used as ground cover in beds, borders, rock gardens and as edging plant.
- Wild and cultivated forms are maintained at Ornamental Plant Germplasm Centre, Florida.
- Planting season: October-November (plains), February-March (hills).
- Planting distance: 45 cm x 45 cm.
- Flowering period: March.
- Number of flowers per inflorescence: 5-10.
- Fragrant flower has 5 petals and 3 ovules/ flower.
- Fruit type: Pod or capsule.
- Seed harvesting: Between 4-12 weeks after pollination.
- Pods are crushed to separate seeds.
- Seed germination: Temperature of 20^{0}C or 0^{0}C in alterations at 5 days interval.
- Seed treatment with B, Zn, Al speed up germination.
- LD_{50} for gamma rays to dry seeds: > 20 Kr (for white cvs.) and (> 30 Kr for yellow cvs).
- Style length determines success of crosses between different species.
  a) Species having style length approximately same to ovary length e.g. *P. divaricata, P. amoenia, P. floridana, P. pilosa, P. drummondii, P. nivalis, P. subulata* and *P. bifida*.
  b) Species having style 2-3 times longer than ovary e.g. *P. ovata, P. pulchra, P. maculata, P. glaberrima* and *P. carolina*.

- Flowers may self pollinate but seed set is very meager.
- Outcrossing rate: 0.88%.
- Selfing leads to inbreeding depression in *P. drummondii* and leads to seed abortion.
- Seed yield: 250-300 kg/ ha.
- In intervarietal hybridization, production of seed is very meager (0.1-1.12 seed/ pollination).
- In intervarietal hybridization, crossing with short style species with long style species is unsuccessful.
- In intervarietal hybridization, rate of seed production, varies greatly from 5.3 to 43% per pollination.
- Anther culture: Androgenic haploid of *P. drummondii*.
- Cross compatibility: Gametophytic under single gene control at *S* locus.

Species:

Common name	Botanical name	Features
Garden or Summer phlox	*Phlox paniculata*	-
Early or meadow phlox	*P. maculata*	-
-	*P. cuspidata*	Predominantly self pollinated i.e. self compatible
-	*P. drummondii*	Predominantly out crossed; most commonly grown ornamental
-	*P. fimbriata*	-
-	*P.* x *arendsii*	Resultant of *P. divaricata* (blue phlox) and *P. paniculata*
-	*P. cuspidata*	Self compatible

Major types of phlox native to eastern North America

- Growth habits: 1) Mat and cushion forming 2) Trailing to tall and erect.

Characters	Upright or mounded type	Mat forming type	Winter annuals
Species	*P. paniculata*, *P. pilosa*, *P. divaricata*, *P. ovata*	*P. subulata*, *P. bifida*, *P. nivalis*	*P. drummondii*, *P. cuspidata*, *P. roemeriana*
Ploidy level	n= 7	n= 7, 14	n= 7
Life cycle	Perennial	Perennial	Annual
Foliage	Deciduous or evergreen	Evergreen	Deciduous
Flowering period	Spring and summer (May-October)	Spring (April-May)	Late winter and spring (February-May)
Special attributes	Wide range in habit; long blooming period	Resistance to foliar diseases	Bold and diverse flower colours.
Limitations	Susceptible to powdery mildew & black leaf spot; some have open, leggy growth habit	Short flowering period (1-3 weeks); some genotypes not widely adaptable	Susceptible to powdery mildew & black leaf spot; not adaptable to hot summer or cold winters.

Varieties:

- For border and rock garden: Beaky Tower, Gold-mine, Rainbow, Cocktail, Beaky Tower, Frosted Elegance, Ruby Mine.
- F_1 hybrids: Patriot, Chanal.
- Twinkle: Star shaped petals developed by spontaneous mutation.
- Resistant to powdery mildew: Goldmine, Flower Power, Peppermint, Twist.

Interspecific hybrid group	Taxa	Putative parentage
a) Natural hybrids	*P.* x *arendsii*	*P. paniculata* x *P. divaricata*
	P. x *glutinosa*	*P. divaricata* x *P. pilosa*
	P. x *rugelii*	*P. amoena* x *P. divaricata*
b) Suspeced natural hybrids	*P.* x *villosissima*	*P. drummondii* x *P. pilosa*
	P. x *pilosa ssp. deamii*	*P. pilosa* x *P. amoena*
	P. x *pilosa ssp. detonsa*	*P. pilosa* x *P. Carolina*
	P. x *pilosa ssp. sangamonesis*	*P. pilosa* x *P. maculata ssp. pyramibalis*
c) Garden origin hybrids	*P.* 'Depressa'	*P. paniculata* x *P. drummondii*
	P. x *decussate*	*P. paniculata* x *P. maculata*
	P. x *procumbens*	*P. sublata* x *P. stolonifera*
	P. 'Sunrise'	*P. adsurgens* x *P. nivalis*

Inheritance of characters:

Character	Number of genes	Type of gene action
Flower shape	Monogenic	Salver shape dominant to funnel shape.
Flower colour	Monogenic (*WW*)	White dominant to cream (ww)
Flower eye colour	Monogenic (*MM*)	Dark dominant to white (mm)
Simple type leaf blade	Three genes (*E*,*A*,*R*)	Simultaneous presence of gene *E* and *A* and chromogene *R* i.e. complementary gene action
Seed viability	Polygenic and/or major recessive genes	Additive
Seed weight	-	Extra-nuclear maternal effect

Disease:

- Powdery mildew (*Erysiphe cichoracearum*): Hampers production but *P. maculata* cv. Pestrushka is immune and cvs. Gold Mine, Rainbow, Ruby Mine, Sherbert Cocktail, Flower Power, Papermint Twist are resistant.

56. ROSACEAE

56.1 Rose

- Eulogized as 'Perfume of god or Queen of flowers orFairest flower or Flower of antiquity'.
- It exists before man (30 million years old).

- Rose cultivation was introduced as an industry in Turkey in 17th century.
- No. 1 cut flower in global market.
- Cut flower having largest area in India.
- 1st consignment of rose was sent by IARI to Paris, Rotterdam, and Frankfurt in 1969.
- In India, damask rose was introduced from Persia at Kannauj, Uttar Pradesh during 17th century.
- Rose day is celebrated on 25th June.
- About 80% of rose flower are utilized for rose water, 10% for attar, 1-2% for *pankhuri* and remaining for manufacture of *gulkand* and *gul-roghan* (a rose hair oil).
- Dried rose petals called as '*pankhuri*', mainly used for preparing cool drinks.
- Rose gulkand: Used as tonic and laxative. It is prepared by mixing petal and sugar in 1: 2 ratio.
- In Czechoslovakia, fruits of wild rose used for preparing hot drinks like tea.
- 'City of Roses' in America: Portland.
- World Federation of Rose Societies (WFRS) was established in 1968 at London. It has now 39 member countries.
- International Cultivar Registration Authority for Roses (IRAR): American Rose Society, Louisiana.
- American Rose Society was established in 1892.
- National Registration Centre of Roses: IARI, New Delhi.
- Rose Society of India was formed in 1961 at New Delhi.
- Rose Society of Pune developed polybag method for nursery purpose.
- French rose: Oldest type of cultivated roses.
- Rose oil is anti-HIV, anti-bacterial against Mycobacterium and anti-oxidant.
- Essential oil content is highest in flowers harvested at 8.30-9.00 AM.
- 1st record of rose perfume is in *Charak Samhita*.
- Extraction of essential oil: Steam distillation method. It was mentioned in Ayurveda by Charaka around 100 A.D.
- Solvent extraction is now more frequently used to extract aroma from blossoms. It yields about 10 times more than steam distillation.
- During distillation, condenser temperature is held at 45⁰C to prevent deposition of waxes in condenser.
- Specific gravity of rose oil (otto): 0.85.
- Product richer in fragrance is obtained by CO_2 extraction only.
- 1 kg oil is produced from 3-5 tones of petals.

- Bulgerian rose oil is recognized as the ultimate best rose oil in the world.
- Bluing of rose petals: Accumulation of NH_3 (ammonia).
- Fragrance of rose is the only fragrance that never tires the human olfactory system.
- Export of rose water started in 8th century from Iran and later in 9th century from India and China mostly to Arabian countries.
- Acetocarmine stain: Used for checking pollen sterility.
- Pollen grains stored at -80^{0}C can be used for pollination.
- Pollen grains stored with dessicants at -18^{0}C remain viable even after 2 years.
- Sprays of GA_3 @ 10, 50 or 250 ppm on 7th or 14th day of pollination increase hip set.
- Fruit of rose: Hip/ hep/ apple; rich source of vit. C (100 mg/100 g).
- *R. beggerana* (Begger rose): Highest vit. C. (7000-20000 mg/100 g).
- Hip is 'etaerio of achenes'. It contains 5-25 seeds.
- Hips of *R. chinensis* applied to wounds, sprains and ulcers in China.
- Hips collection: 4-6 months after pollination.
- Harvested fruits can be kept in refrigerator at 8-10^{0}C for 150 days.
- Seeds require after ripening period for germination.
- Seed extracted from mature fruits (green to red) give high germination.
- Seeds exhibit both exogenous and endogenous dormancy.
- Planting density: 7.5 plants/ sq.m.
- Ideal temperature for growth and development: 28^{0}C (day), 18^{0}C (night) and 65-70% R.H.
- Ideal light intensity: 6000-8000 lux.
- Ideal CO_2 concentration: 1000-1500 ppm.
- 20% greenhouse space should be utilized for ventilation.
- Best time for planting: End of September to middle of October
- Commercial method propagation: 'T' or Shield budding or Top grafting.
- Propagated by root cuttings: *R. nitida, R. blanda, R. virginiana.*
- Climbers are raised by air or ground layering.
- Pruned twice in a year- 1st during November end and 2nd during last week of June.
- Number of prunings at Bengaluru condition: 2 times.
- Maximum pollen receptivity in roses is after 2 days of anthesis.
- Winter grafting is followed in Germany, the Netherlands on *R. canina inermis.*
- Bud union is most susceptible to low temperature than any other part of rose.
- In India, budding is done at 5-7.5 cm above root junction.
- Best time for budding: November to February and temperature is 10-25^{0}C.

- o Budding height in full standards (HT & grandiflora): 1.0-1.15 m.
- o Budding height in half standards (floribunda & polyantha): 45-60 cm.
- o Budding height in weeping standards (climber & rambler): 1.5 m or above.
- Best rooting medium: Sand, Cocopeat.
- Winter chilling is necessary in flower bud formation in *R. damascena*. It is done in western parts of India and is done in September-October.
- Green bending: Special horticultural practice done in 3 months old plants to induce new sprouts in greenhouse.
- Most of varieties take about 60-65 days for blooming after pruning.
- Harvesting stage: Tight bud stage or 1-2 petals unfurl.
- Yield of damask rose flowers: 3.5-5 t/ha.
- More CO_2 injection in greenhouse results in decrease in number of blind shoots, increased stem length and weight, greater number of petals and shorter cropping time in winter.
- Soil-less medium widely used in Western countries in hi-tech production: Rockwool.
- Photographs of cvs. Bhim, Delhi Princess, Jawahar, Mrinalini, Neelam and Sugandha have appeared on postage stamp along with embedded scent by Indian Post's & Telegraph, Govt. of India released during 2007.
- A hand painted rose cultivar developed by M.S. Virraghavan (1966): Priyatama.
- Stenting method (budding on cuttings, which are planted for rooting in mist chamber): Practiced in rose.
- Major problem in rose breeding: Seed setting
- Dry packing: In standard box size 12 cm x 51 cm x 30.5 cm.
- Wet packing: 33 cm x 33 cm x 56 cm.
- In wet storage, roses are stored for 5-7 days at 2-4^{0}C by dipping basal stem in water.
- In dry storage, stems are sealed in polybags at low temperature for about 7 days and longevity is more.
- Cut flowers are shifted to cold room (3-5^{0}C) for precooling.
- In protected cultivation, prolonged exposure to low temperature leads to formation of blind shoots.
- Vase/ preservative solution: 1-3% sugar + 100-200 ppm 8-HQC.
- Silver thiosulphate (STS): Not commonly used.
- Seed dispersal of *R. canina* and *R. rubiginosa* is generally by birds.
- Seeds of *R. rubiginosa* remain viable in soil for 3-4 years.
- Cobalt prevents appearance of bent neck, increases water uptake and extends flower longevity.

- IHBT, Palampur has developed a novel method 'Round Cut method' for emasculation of roses. The method involves making a round cut in the thalamus near the base of the clayx and a longitudinal cut along the buds, anthers, petals and calyx were totally removed exposing only styles and stigmas of the flower bud within a fraction of minute.
- Chimera is common in rose.
- *In vitro* mutagenesis avoids chimera formation.
- Gamma irradiation at 15, 20 or 25 Gy is effective in inducing novel floral variants.
- LD_{50} for white & mauve coloured cvs. is lower than yellow, red or pink flowered.
- Wine prepared from rose petals got patented.

Classification of rose:

- Accepted classification of roses is 'Rehder'.
- Modern rose: Any rose identified after 1867.
- Father of modern roses: Perpetual flowering 'Parson's Pink China Rose'.
- Optimum number of petals in good rose flower: 30-50.
- Old rose group includes roses like China Tea, Moss, Damask, Bourbon, Hybrid perpetual and Noisette roses.
- Modern rose is the results of cross breeding Hybrid tea with polyanthas.
- Popular types in modern roses: Hybrid Tea, Floribunda, Grandiflora.
- Thornless rose: Derived from *R. pendulina*, *R. blanda*, *R. multiflora*.

Class	Features
Hybrid perpetual (HP)	Immediate forerunners of HT and descendents of *R. chinensis, R. gallica* & *R. centifolia*. Resulted due to tetraploid (2n=4x=28) x diploid (2n=2x=14); very hardy & flower almost throughout the year.
Tea roses	Called as 'Tea scented China rose'. Originated from *R. chinensis* x *R. gigantea*; flowers have distinct aroma & free flowering nature
Hybrid Tea (HT)	Cross between 'Hybrid Perpetual x Tea rose'. Most popular rose type of modern days. Perpetual flowering China rose species (*R. chinensis*) when crossed with European species (*R. damascena*) produced Bourbon & hybrid perpetual hybrids which latter crossed with Chinese species (*R. odorata*) gave Tea roses. Possess long stem (125 cm) & single large flower (4 cm); ideal for cut flower & bedding purpose.
Polyantha (Pol)	Polyanthas have ancestry of crosses of *R. multiflora, R. wichuraiana* & Bengal hybrid *R. indica major* (*R. chinensis*). Produce dwarf, bear clusters of small blossoms & cold hardy
Pernetian rose	Cross between Tea rose x *R. lutea* (syn. *R. foetida*) from Central and West Asia produced new flower colours like yellow & orange.
Floribunda	Cross between Hybrid Tea x Polyantha; possess short stem (< 60 cm) & small flowers (2.5 cm); most suitable for hedge
Grandiflora (Gr.)	Cross between Hybrid Tea x Floribundas. Large flowers in small clusters with very vigorous growth

Shrub roses	Perpetual/continuous flowering, taller than bush & shorter than climbers
Miniature (Min.)	Dwarf; small leaves and flowers, hardy; known as 'baby rose or sweet hearts or fairy roses'. Introduced by China as Pigmy rose. Very small buds on a single stem; suited for pot culture, edging, rockeries or window gardening & terrace gardening
Miniflora	e.g. Honeybee™
Climber	Upright, but require support for growth, flowers large in small clusters & at the end of side branches
Rambler	Cross between Hybrid perpetual x *R. multiflora* & *R. wichuraiana*. Small flowers in large clusters, only one flush during a year (late spring) which lasts for several weeks & fades quickly. Suitable for covering fences, pergolas, trellies.
China rose	Present day popular roses belong to this group. Bears red- white flowers in small clusters. The green rose *R. chinensis viridifolia* is member of this class.
Damask rose	Cross between *R. gallica* x *R. phoenicia*. In India, introduced by Mughal king Baber. Bears clusters of fragrant pink to red, double petalled flowers. Mainly belongs to spp. *R. damascena*.
Bourbon roses	Natural cross between China rose x damask rose. In India, introduced by Britishers; flowers large, wide with silky petals and very scented.
Cabbage roses	Belongs to spp. *R. centifolia*; bear large, globular, solitary, very fragrant pink flowers.
Moss roses	Sports of Centifolias and belong to Cabbage rose class; originated as mutation of *R. centifoliamucosa* (thorn type) & *R. centifolia cristata* (crested type); moss like growth of glandular hairs on petals when bruised; flowers are sweet scented, moss like growth of glandular hairs, particularly on the petals; cv. Old Pink Moss
French rose	Oldest type of cultivated roses, developed from *R. gallica*; blooms are large, of varied colours and good fragrance
Albas	Originated from cross between *R. corymbifera* x *R. gallica* and constitute truly old garden roses with Gallicas & Damasks. Bear whitish or pinkish sweet scented flowers & very hardy.
Musk roses	*R. moschata* produce flowers in clusters with pronounced musky fragrance.
Noisette roses	Hybrids of *R. chinensis* & *R. moschata*. Popular climbers like Mme Alfred Carriere, Lamarque, Marechal Niel.
Rugosas	Often called 'Japanese roses (*R. rugosa*), extremely vigorous, hardy, thorny, resistant to cold & grow in poor soils. They bear large red or white flowers
Austrain Briars	This includes Austrain Copper (*R. foetida bicolor*) & Persian yellow (*R. foetida persiana*). These are main sources of yellow roses in modern roses.

Species:

- Damask roses were 1st discovered in Syria by European botanist during 13th century.
- Section *Cinnamomeae* is largest containing 48 species.
- Section *Indicae* and *Synstylae* have exerted styles.
- In India, two strains of damask roses are grown-
  1. 'Chaiti or Fasli gulab or Fossil gulab' which blooms twice in a year.
  2. 'Haldighati gulab' which flower only in March-April.
- Fragrance purpose: *R. damascena, R. centifolia, R. bourboniana, R. gallica, R. moschata* and *R. alba*.
- Short day roses: Caramia, *R. gallica*.

Species	Common name	Salient features and uses
R. acicularis	-	Weak vigour, poor growth rate; poor compatibility; resistant to black spot.
R. alba (*R. corymbifera* x *R. gallica*)	Albas/ White rose of York	Erect bush with glaucous foliage; white, semi-double, fragrant flowers; used for oil extraction in Bulgeria; not commercially cultivated in India.
R. arkansana	-	Tolerant to drought & cold.
R. arvensis	Field rose	Deciduous with creeping habit; white scentless flowers.
R. blanda	Meadow rose or wild rose or smooth rose or prairie rose	Perennial; sturdy, tolerate dry condition; nutrient poor habitats such as roadsides & sandy soil.
R. bourboniana (*R. chinensis* x *R. damascenasemperflorens*)	Edouard rose or Bourbon rose or Baramasi	Hardy, vigorous; hooked prickles; flowers double, deep rosy-red & scented. Poor root system; propagated by cuttings; used as rootstock for budding standards & preparation of gulkand & rose water; widely used in north India; susceptible to PM.
R. bracteata	-	Good growth rate under low temperature; weak vigour; resistant to black spot& heat
R. brunonii (syn. *R. moschata nepalensis*)	Himalayan musk rose	White rose of the lord Vishnu-Brahma; very hardy, vigorous giant musk rose climber; foliage grey green, narrow leaflets; flowers single, white, scented & borne in clusters; capacity to waft fragrance in air; found in Nepal & Garhwal regions.
R. canina	Dog rose	Vigorous; produces normal and apomictic seedlings; propagated by seed; flowers single white or pink, scented; foliage toothed margin; prominent thorns; cuttings difficult to root; used as rootstock; suitable to drought & alkaline soil conditions; widely used in Europe
R. x *centifolia* (complex hybrid of 4 species *viz.*, *R. gallica, R. phoenicia, R. moschata, R. camria*)	Provence rose or Cabbage rose	Loose growing shrub of medium vigour; large solitary, double, pink coloured flowers, overlapping petals; strongly fragrant.
R. chinensis (syn. *R. indica*)	China rose	Large climbing evergreen shrub; small leaflets; flowers single, bluish pink coloured flowers; commercially grown in France for essential oil & rose water.
R. chinensis 'Major'	-	Tolerant to NaCl stress; not commonly used.
R. chinensis semperflorens	Crimson China rose	Climbing shrub with evergreen foliage; flowers crimson or deep pink & solitary.
R. chinensis viridiflora	Green rose or Bengal rose or Monthly rose	Medium vigorous, blue green foliage; fully double flowers with green petals; borne in clusters; originated in 1855.
R. x *damascena* [Summer damask rose (*R. gallica* x	Fossil rose or Damask rose or Fasli gulab or Chaiti gulab	Climber; white/pink/red flowers in clusters; fragrant; soft grey-green foliage; leaflets oval & toothed; branches very prickly with hooked spines. Blooms twice in a year. Contains best quality

R. phoenicia) and Autumn damask rose [*R.* x *bifera* (*R. gallica* x *R. moschata*)]		geraniol (30-35 %) & citronellol (25-30 %) & high percentage of rose oil (0.03 %) in its petals.
R. ecae	Afghan rose	Used as hedge plant in Kargil.
R. eglanteria (syn. *R. rubiginosa*)	Sweet briar or Eglantine rose	Vigorous with dense prickled branches; small leaflets; scented foliage; single flowers in clusters.
R. foetida (syn. *R. lutea*, *R. eglanteria*)	Austrian briar or Persian yellow rose or Golden yellow rose of Iran	Erect stems with prickly stems having delicate foliage; single flowes with unpleasant aroma; given rise to modern yellow roses.
R. fortuniana	-	Nematode resistant.
R. gallica (syn. *R. rubra*)	Gallica rose or French rose	Stiff erect stem; thornless, but small prickles; fragrant flowers; foliage dark green, rounded; prolific seed bearer; not popular in India.
R. hemisphaerica (syn. *R. glaucophylla*, *R. sulphurea*)	Sulphur rose	Loose growing shrub with glaucous foliage; flowers large, double, scented & sulphur yellow coloured.
R. indica var. Major	-	Resistant to nematode; induces early flowering.
R. indica var. Odorata	-	Climbing shrub; used for greenhouse forcing roses; propagates easily through cuttings; adapts to excessive dry/wet soil conditions & suitable for saline soils; tolerant to PM & insect-pest.
R. involucrata (syn. *R. sempervirens*, *R. leschenaultiana*, *R. clinophylla*)	-	Branches downy or hairy; leaves composed of three to nine in pairs; thorns placed in pairs under stipules; petals white & longer than calyx; resistant to heat
R.manetti (syn. *R. noisettiana* Manetti)	-	Used in Europe for propagating dwarf roses & for sandy soils; resistant to verticilium wilt &root knot nematode (*M. hapla*).
R. moschata Hook. (syn. *R.chinensis* x *R.moschata*)	Musk rose or Noisette rose	Vigorous climber with reddish, prickly stems; flowers single/semi-double, white, musk fragrance & borne in terminal clusters. Grows wild in Himalayas.
R. multiflora.	Baby rose or Japanese rose or Seven-sisters rose or Eijitsu rose	Introduction from China; deciduous; flowers, single, scented, borne in clusters; used as shock absorbers or crash barriers; used as rootstock in western & coastal areas; resistant to root knot nematode (*M. hapla*)&tolerant to low winter temperature; very sensitive to crown gall.
Rosa spp. Natal briar	-	Less susceptible for nematode; tolerant to salinity
R. odorata (*R.*	Tea scented China rose	Vigorous climber with purplish stems with prickles; flowers slightly drooping, large, double,

chinensis x *R. gigantea*)		scented & borne singly; used as rootstock.
R. persica (syn. *R. berberifolia*)	Rose of Persia	Dwarf shrub with silvery-grey foliage; possess undivided leaves; flowers single & deep yellow.
R. rugosa	Rugosa rose or Ramanas rose	Vigorous erect bush; shallow root system, fibrous; suckers heavily; budded plants are long lived; colourful bright apple green foliage; flowers in clusters; single; frost resistant & widely used as rootstock in Europe for standard roses
R. sericea (syn. *R. omeiensis*)	Ladakh rose	Vigorous shrub, very thorny stems; leaflets 5-17; petals 4; flowers single, white, occurs at altitude of 3000-4700 m.
R. titri	-	Recommended for Rajasthan.
R. webbiana	Webb's rose	Dense growing bush; deciduous; single, lilac-pink colored flowers; occurs at altitude of 1000-4000 m (dry Kashmir & Western Himalayan belts).
R. x *wichuraiana* (syn. *R. lucillae*)	Memorial rose	Vigorous rambler; single, scented flowers; good compatibility

Species with chromosome number:

Species	Chromosome number
(Asian/Chinese): *R. moschata, R. gigantea, R. multiflora, R. wichuraiana* & *R. chinensis var.* minima	Diploid (2n=2x=14)
R. persica & modern roses	Triploid (2n=3x=21)
(Western/European): *R gallica, R. foetida* & their derivatives viz. *R. damascena, R. centifolia* & *R. hybrida* cv. Akito	Tetraploid (2n=4x=28)
R. fedtschenkoana, R. hybrida cv. Iceberg	Hexaploid (2n=6x=42)

Pigments:

- Anthocyanin pigments producing red colour: Chrysanthemin, Paeonin.
- Delphinidin: Blue to violet;
- Pelargonidin: Orange red to scarlet;
- Cyanidin: Crimson to bluish red;
- Chalcone: Yellow

Varieties:

- Breeding methods: Recurrent selection (for quantitative traits), back crossing (for expressibe of recessive qualitative traits).
- Reason to high pollen sterility: Structural hybridity.
- Number of rose varieties in world: 20,000.
- World's 1st blue rose: Applause developed in 2009 by Australian firm Florigene Ltd. Along with Japanese firm Suntroy Ltd. Other GM blue roses are Blue Moon, Blue Perfume, Blue Nile.
- 1st HT rose-La France by Guillot (1867).
- 1st HT yellow rose-Soleild'or.
- 1st Hybrid perpetual-Princess Helene.
- 1st Floribunda-Rodhatte by Poulsen (1912).
- 1st Grandiflora-Buccaneer (1952).
- 1st Polyantha-La Paquerette (1875).
- Juliet Rose: Most expensive, full cupped shaped, apricot coloured with voluminous petals bred by David Austin.
- Red Cascade: Widely used for landscape design.
- J. Baptiste Guillot discovered 'La France' in a patch of seedlings in Lyon-Monplaisir.
- Some believe that 'La France' was either a seedling of 'Mme Falcot' (Tea) or the cross between 'Mme Victor Verdier' (Hybrid Perpetual) and 'Mme Bravy' (Chinese Tea).
- Peace: 1st rose bred by American Rose Society received gold medal in 1951.
- B.K. Roy Choudhary: 1st Indian rose breeder who raised cv. Dr. S.D. Mookerji (Hadley x Fascination) in 1935.
- B.S.Bhatcharji (father of rose breeding) evolved var. Ramkrishnadev in 1941, Heart Throb, Raja Ram Mohan Roy, Pandit Nehru, Sugandha, Kalima.
- Dr. B.P. Pal: 1st variety Rose Sherbet (1962, crimson, highly fragrant flowers with 0.033% oil content; OP of 'Gruss en Teplitz'), 2nd is Delhi Pink Pearl, Delhi Princess (1st floribunda).

- Although research on rose was started in 1956 at IARI but in 1968, 1st varieties of rose developed were Pusa Soniya and Sarvodaya.
- After every 4 years, World Rose Exhibition is held in different countries.
- Periclinal chimera: Jaguar, Gabriesa derived from Mercedes.
- Fragrant varieties: Oklahoma, Avon, Sweet Afton.
- *R. damascena*: Nurjehan and Ranisaheba (CIMAP, Lucknow) and Jwala and Himroz (IHBT, Palampur), Crimson Red (from USSR).
- Jwala and Noorjehan are suitable for sub-tropical northern plains, mid hills and mild temperate regions up to 1,200 m altitude. Himroz variety is suitable for mild temperate to cold temperate regions 1,200-2,500 m altitude.
- Rooted cuttings are transplanted during monsoon while winter is ideal for establishment in the field.
- Floribunda cv. Sindhoor is also used as cut flower.
- Thornless cultivars belong to category of 'Grand Gala group'.
- Taj Mahal: Indian variety competing with 'First Red'.
- Jacaranda, Cocktail, Konfetti, Ritz: Fragrant greenhouse rose cultivars.
- Varieties for rockery: Fairy Queen, Magic.
- Varieties for pot plants: Baby Darling, Cindrella, Starina.
- Varieties for hangers: Red Cascade, Yellow Doll.
- Variety having spicy fragrance: Golden Afternoon.
- Varieties having longer vase life: Vivaldi, Red Success, Samourai, Ravel, Konfetti.
- New Dawn: Recurrent flowering and received 1st USA patent. It was bred by Henry F. Bosenberg.
- Royalty: Developed through genetic engineering using *Agrobacterium* strain.
- White Lady Banksia: World's largest rose bush about 100 years old located at Tombstone, Arizona, USA.
- Thornless: Basye's Blueberry, Bella Multiflora, Hermosa, Bettyland, Cecile, Brunner, Zephirinc.
- Cv. Front N Center™: Suitable for pot culture miniature rose, show very high level of water stress tolerance.
- EVC: Tetraploid. Arisen from Robinhood (2x) x JG Thornton (4x) by double restitution.
- M.S. Swaminathan: Rich deep purple HT rose growing to 4-5 feet height, sweet scented & resistant to diseases bred by farmer Mr. M. Veer Raghavan from Kodaikanal.

Name	Breeding method	Features
IARI, New Delhi		
Aruna (HT,1968)	Seedling selection of 'Independence'	Vigorous, medium sized; double flowers of velvety orange scarlet coloured.
Ashirwad (1984)	-	Bright current red with golden based petals; slightly fragrant
Aravali Princess (1983)	Seedling selection of 'Sonia'	Porcelain pink blooms; very high number of petals; symmetrically arranged
Dark Boy (HT, 1965)	Seedling selection of 'Nigrette'	Medium sized blooms; velvety, very dark maroon red coloured petals.
Delhi Pastel (HT, 1964)	Seedling selection of 'Una Wallace'	Large pastel pink coloured petals.
Delhi Sunshine (HT, 1963)	Seedling selection of 'Mme Charles Sauvage'	Deep unfading cream blooms; extremely regular arrangement of flowers.
Dr. Homi Bhabha (HT, 1968)*	Seedling selection of 'Virgo'	Very large pure white flowers having 60 petals.
Dil Ki Rani (1985)	-	Very lovely shade of ethereal pink with tinge of lavender; exhibition type;
Dilruba (1984)	-	Glorious blackish-velvety crimson buds; good keeping quality; very hardy
Ganga (HT, 1970)	Seedling selection of 'Sabine '	Pointed buds, colour varies from pale yellow to gold, vigorous.
Gulbadan (1976)	-	Light yellow buds; large blooms; fragrant
Golden Afternoon (1983)	-	Glorious colour; golden apricot on upper side; spicy fragrance; glossy leaves; very floriferous
Golconda (HT, 1968)	Seedling selection of 'Mme Charles Sauvage'	Large, vigorous, yellow to deep apricot coloured flowers; slightly fragrant.
Jawani (1985)	Seedling selection of 'Mme Charles Sauvage'	Buds & flowers of richest shades of gold & apricot; decorative type; delicious fragrance
Kanakangi (HT, 1968)*	Seedling selection of 'Mme Charles Sauvage'	Flexible branches; buds & flowers are of gold & apricot shade; tea type fragrance.
Kulu Belle (HT, 1972)	Seedling selection of 'Sabine'	Deep pink colour; very long tapering buds.
Madhumati (HT, 1973)	Seedling selection of 'General Mac Arthur'	Large, deep rose pink flowers; fragrance of old rose type.
Madhushala (HT, 1973)	Seedling selection of 'African Star'	Large, double flowers of deep mauve colour; bushy growth.
Maharani (HT, 1986)	Seedling selection of 'President Macia'	Large, very long buds of deep pink colour; upright, tall & vigorous growth.
Mechak (HT, 1977)	Seedling selection of 'Samourai'	Dark, long shapely buds of blackest red; free flowering.
Meghdoot (HT, 1972)	Seedling selection of 'Virgo'	Vigorous; long urn shaped buds open to large flowers of shinning white; petals recalling silky texture of poppy flower.
Nazneen (HT, 1969)	Seedling selection of 'Queen Elizabeth'	Large flowers of pale pink colour; flowers profusely.
Pahadi Dhun (HT, 1981)	Seedling selection of 'Lady X'	Medium sized bloms with reflexing petals borne on long stems; dark purple buds open to silvery flowers; pleasant fragrance; very free flowering.
Pale Hands (HT, 1965)	Seedling selection of 'Mc Gredy's Ivory'	Very large flowers with colour ranging from ivory white to pale yellow, buff & peach.

Poornima (HT, 1971)	Seedling selection of 'Fernard Aries'	Long buds with many petals; light yellow coloured flowers.
Pusa Sonia (HT, 1986)	Seedling selection of 'Mc Gredy's Yellow'	Bright golden yellow flowers, borne in singles, freely on long stems, long pointed sharp buds, 55 flowers/season; 14 open at a time; avg. bloom size 7.5 cm & 24 petals.
Raat-Ki-Rani (HT, 1975)	Seedling selection of 'Scaret Knight'	Large pointed buds open to velvety crimson red blooms; free flowering & vigorous.
Rangshala (HT, 1969)	Seedling selection of 'Margaret's Spaull'	Light red buds, open to blooms of peach/apricot/amber yellow colour, medium size, flowers in great profusion, recurrent bloomer.
Scented Bowl (HT, 1965)	Seedling selection of 'General Mc Arthur'	Glowing red with many petals; strong & attractive fragrance.
Sharmili (HT, 1986)	Seedling selection of 'Rose Gaujard'	Vigorous, long pointed buds of milky white flushed with pink edge; moderately fragrant.
Sugandhini (HT, 1969)	Seedling selection of 'Margaret Spaull '	Vigorous, light rhodamine pink coloured blooms; fragrant.
Sujata (HT, 1971)	Seedling selection of 'Sabine'	Deep crimson red; large bloom; 12 cm across; 50 blooms/ season; 40 petals/ bloom; fragrant.
Surekha (HT, 1969)	Seedling selection of 'Queen Elizabeth'	Triploid; coral red, many petalled blooms in abundance; vigorous.
Uttam (HT, 1969)	Seedling selection of 'Elite'	Pointed buds and pastel-pink coloured flowers, vigorous.
White Sun (HT, 1968)	Seedling selection of 'Virgo'	Upright growth; pure white blooms.
Akash Nartaki (F, 1983)	Seedling selection of 'Sterling Silver'	Semi-double flowers; low growing, silvery lilac coloured flowers.
Arunima (F, 1976)	Seedling selection of 'Frolic'	Deep pink flowers, long lasting, produced in small bunches, very compact bush
Chingari (F, 1976)	Seedling selection of 'Charleston'	Blooms have blend of yellow & deep velvety red; handsome foliage.
Chitchor (F, 1972)	Seedling selection of 'Pink Parfait'	Double flowers; white very lightly suffused with pink and deep pink on edges; centre is sometimes illuminated by pale golden glow.
Deepika (F, 1975)	Seedling selection of 'Shepherd's Delight'	Pointed small buds of mandarine red coloured with yellow base.
Delhi Sherbet (F, 1963)	Seedling selection of 'Gruss an Teplitz'	Very vigorous; deep rose pink flowers; highly fragrant; useful as low fragrant hedge.
Delhi White Pearl (Climber, 1963)	Seedling selection of 'Prosperity'	Glossy green leaves, enormous clusters of flowers; faint musky fragrance; pearl white colour.
Fugitive (F, 1965)	Seedling selection of 'Mrs. Oakley Fisher'	Large clusters of single 5-petalled flowers; flowers having shades of buff and pale yellow.
Himangini (F, 1968)	Seedling selection of 'Saratoga'	Vigorous; ivory white flowers in huge trusses; 6 cm across; 50 petals; 310 blooms/ bush; recurrent bloomer; resistant to PM, die back & other diseases.
Kavita (F, 1972)	Seedling selection of 'Margaret Spaull'	Vigorous; 265 blooms, orient pink with light yellow base of petal, 8.5 cm dia. Across; 30 petals per bloom produced in clusters.

Kumkum (F, 1971)	Seedling selection of 'Orangeade'	Single to semi-double flowers; borne in large clusters of dazzling orange scarlet.
Lal Makhmal (1983)	Seedling selection of 'Samourai'	Very dark velvety red with scarlet sheen; rich glowing colour
Loree (F, 1968)	Seedling selection of 'Frolic'	Extremely pale pink, double flowers.
Manasi (F, 1991)	Seedling selection of 'Frolic'	Large flowers with mild fragrance; pointed buds; suitable for bedding.
Orange Cup (F, 1965)	Seedling selection of 'Cocorico'	Very large trusses of orange-scarlet flowers; very vigorous & free flowering; good for hedge.
Paharan (F, 1971)	Seedling selection of 'Anna Wheat Croft'	Large clusters of equisite buds open into small pretty, fully double flowers of pleasing shades of white to pink.
Pusa Virangana (F)	Seedling selection of 'Jantar Mantar'	Large, deep and flowers are produced in bunch. Very good for garden & making standards.
Pusa Barahmasi (F)	Seedling selection of 'Sadabahar'	Deep pink flowers in bunches, very hardy plant, flowers round the year; tolerant to die back, PM& black spot.
Ragini (F, 1972)	Seedling selection of 'Queen Elizabeth'	Delightful clear rose pink coloured flowers.
Rose Sherbet (F, 1962)	Seedling selection of 'Gruss an Tepletz'	Very free flowering, deep pink colour, highly scented with 0.033% oil content; good for mass planting or hedge.
Sadabahar (F, 1969)	Seedling selection of 'Frolic'	Pointed bud, deep pink flowers, medium sized, very vigorous & tolerant to most of diseases.
Shabnam (F, 1975)	Seedling selection of 'Baby Sylvia'	White, compact, small flowers in clusters, upright & vigorous growth.
Sandhya Bela (F, 1971)	Seedling selection of 'Zambra'	Orange coloured double flowers.
Shabnam (F, 1975)	Seedling selection of 'Baby Sylvia'	White, compact small flowers, upright & vigorous growing.
Shola (F, 1969)	Seedling selection of 'Anna Wheatcroft'	Dutch vermilion buds; long lasting, medium sized buds.
Suhasini (F, 1972)	Seedling selection of 'Queen Elizabeth'	Vigorous; abundant blooms of rich translucent coral-pink.
Suryodaya (F, 1968)	Seedling selection of 'Orangeade'	Tall and strong bush; dazzling orange double; 6.3 cm across, 48 petals; well shaped flowers borne in single and clusters of 4-6, abundant flowering; 150 flowers/ bush.
Sungold (F, 1968)	Seedling selection of 'Oklahoma'	Apricot with buff yellow, very fragrant.
Temple Flame (F, 1965)	Seedling selection of 'Orangeade'	Extremely vigorous; blooms of brilliant orange colour; flowers produced singly or in cluster.
Usa (F, 1975)	Seedling selection of 'Orangeade'	Small flowers of deep camellia rose colour.
Martin Luther King (Pol, 1968)	Seedling selection of 'Oklahoma'	Deep red almost black flowered.
Swati (Pol, 1969)	Seedling selection of 'Winifred Coulter'	Deep carmine pink buds with silvery reverse, white flowers; recurrent bloomer; excellent for edging, pot & bedding.
Delhi Starlet (Miniature, 1963)	Seedling selection of 'Goudvlinder'	Dwarf, compact with deep yellow coloured buds.

Anurag (HT, 1980)	Sweet Afton x Gulzar	Upright growth & medium size; sharp bloom; tyrian rose; highly fragrant.
Apsara (HT, 1982)	Sonia Meilland x Sabine	Very long & upright stems; flowers pink with salmon shadings; fragrant.
Arjun (HT, 1980)	Blithe Spirit x Montezuma	Procelin rose colour, 40-155 blooms/ stem; export quality blooms of long lasting quality; hardy
Bhim (HT, 1970)	Charles Mallerin x Delhi princess	Flowers very large, bright red with many petals, slight fragrant, very vigorous & withstand severe cold winters.
Chandragupta (HT, 1974)	Delhi Princess x Eiffel Tower	Vigorous; highly fragrant; very large (12 cm across); high centred; borne singly in abundance (50 blooms).
Chitralekha (HT, 1972)	Montezuma x Baccara	Ruby red flowers, large sized (10 cm across), 25 petals/ bloom; borne freely; long lasting, unfading quality of blooms; floriferous (40 blooms).
Chitwan (HT, 1971)	Western Sun x Golden Splendor	Compact bush; primrose yellow flowers, 75 petals/ bloom; 50 flowers in a season; 10.5 cm across.
Dr. Benjamin Pal (HT, 1993)	Sweet Afton x First Prize	Vigorous and upright stems; long pointed deep pink coloured buds; more than 45 petals; slightly fragrant.
Dr. Bharat Ram (2006)	Sweet Afton x Ganga	High centered; apricot flowers having pink shade; profuse flowering; slightly fragrant
Dr. M.S. Randhawa (HT, 1989)	Sabine x Kiss of Fire	Large, double flowers with >50 flowers; creamy white outside and splashed deep pink inside; fragrant.
Diva Swapna (1981)	Raised from 'Sonia' cross	Exhibition size; lovely buds; good for cutting & exhibition
Dulhan (HT, 1983)	Bonne Nuit x Ena Harkness	Tall, vigorous, flowers freely; rose to red coloured flowers; fragrant.
Eastern Princess (1984)	-	Flowers with novel orange colour with gold base; elegant buds; strongly scented; very free flowering
Gulzar (HT, 1971)	Kiss of Fire x Prelude	Compact & fragrant; deep magenta red coloured flower, 45 petals/ bloom; 11 cm across.
Hans (HT, 1970)	Message x Virgo	Pure white blooms; bloom size 11.5 cm; 18 petals & cold hardy.
Haseena (HT, 1979)	Youki San x Balinese	Soft pink with light lilac coloured petals; flowers long lasting.
Homage (HT, 1986)*	Sonia x Princess Margaret of England	Vigorous and free flowering; high centred flowers; crise red buds, double flowers; exhibition type.
Indian Princess (HT, 1980)*	Super Star x Granada	Large long buds; carmine-vermilion coloured flowers; scented blooms.
Jawahar (HT, 1980)	Sweet Afton x Delhi Princess	Creamy white flower, high centred, 47 petals/ bloom; strong spicy fragrance; excellent for exhibition.
Jawani (HT, 1985)*	Scarlet Queen Elizabeth x Louisiana	Vigorous & orange red coloured flowers.
Kamla Devi Chatto padhyay (HT, 1989)	Sonia x Kathleen O' Rourke	Vigorous; large, double flowers of brilliant orange salmon colour; long lasting & very fragrant.

Lalima (HT, 1978)*	Picture x Jour d'ete	Vigorous; deep rose pink buds; slightly fragrant.
Mother Teresa (HT, 1994)	Sweet Afton x First Prize	Vigorous, upright growing; long pointed soft pink buds.
Mridula (HT, 1975)	Queen Elizabeth x Seedling of Sir. Henry Segrave	Vigorous with upright growth, very long, pinkish white, sharp buds, large, fragrant blooms.
Mrinalini (HT, 1972)	Pink Parfait x Christion Dior	Vigorous; phlox pink, blooms in single; 32 petals/ bloom; long lasting & withstand severe winter; 60 blooms in a season & slightly fragrant.
Mrs. K.B. Sharma (HT, 1989)	White Masterpiece x Michele Meilland	Very long, white buds; petals large & long; lightly scented.
Nehru Centenary (HT, 1989)	Christian Dior x Avon	Dark red, large pointed buds borne on long, strong shoots; slightely fragrant.
Nurjehan (HT, 1980)	Sweet Afton x Crimson Glory	Upright growth; very large blooms; rose Bengal coloured well formed blooms; highly fragrant.
Preyasi (HT, 1991)	Chandra x Queen Elizabeth	Vigorous; highly fragrant fuchsin pink coloured flowers; long sized flowers with 30 petals; exhibition purpose.
Priyadarshini (HT, 1986)	Pink Parfait x First Prize	Flowers large (13.5 cm dia.), rhodomine pink; produce bicolour effect; mild fragrant.
Pusa Ajay (HT, 2005)	Pink Parfait x Queen Elizabeth	Mildly fragrant; foliage pigmented, glossy & dark pink coloured flowers; mod. tolerant to PM & black spot, suitable for cut flower.
Pusa Gaurav (HT, 2001)	Pink Parfait x Arjun	Tolerant to die back & black spot.
Pusa Arum (HT, 2005)	Queen Elizabeth (G) x Jantar mantar	Mild fragrant, petals; tolerant to red scale &PM; suitable for cut flower & exhibition.
Pusa Bahadur (HT, 2009)	Cara Mia x Century Two	Vigorus; red coloured petals; highly floriferous & recurrent blooming.
Pusa Garima (HT, 2002)	Cara Mia x Century Two	Vigorus; highly floriferous & recurrent blooming.
Pusa Mohit (HT, 2002)	Suchitra (pink) x Christion Dior (red)	Completely thornless; long pointed buds, red petals; tolerant to black spot; 9.5 cm dia.,70 petals/ flower.
Pusa Priya (HT, 2009)	Jantar Mantar x Queen Elizabeth	Very long & rose pink coloured petals.
Pusa Ranjana (HT, 2001)	Pink Parfait x Ice Berg	Dwarf compact bush; dark pink flowers; flower dia.5 cm; 10 petals/ flower.
Pusa Sonora (HT, 1983)	Queen Elizabeth x First Prize	Vigorous & upright blooms; soft pink, high centred, stable blooms.
Pusa Shatabdi (HT, 2005)	Jadis x Century Two	Mildly fragrant; petals (35-40) fleshy & pink; tolerant to powdery mildew (PM) & leaf spot; suitable for cut flower & exhibition.
Raja Surendra Singh of Nalagarh (HT, 1977)	Scarlet Knight x Montezuma	Large sized, good, high centred flowers of orange salmon pink colour; buds extremely beautiful & fully double.
Raj Kumari (HT, 1975)	Charles Mallerin x Delhi Princess	Long slender buds, large well formed, deep pink flowers.
Raktima (HT, 1991)	Pink Parfait x Sugandha	Highly scented double flowers of red colour; recurrent bloomer.
Raktagandha (HT, 1975)	Christion Dior x Seedling of Carrousel	Red, large, pointed buds, open to large, high centred flowers with slight

		fragrance.
Rosy Evening (HT, 1985)*	Invitation x Anvil Sparks	Coppery pink to flame orange pink coloured flowers; suitable for exhibition & bedding.
Shanti Pal (HT, 1989)	Sonia x Kathleen O' Rourke	Vigorous, large, high centred double flowers; salmon pink coloured blooms.
Shreyasi (HT, 1994)	Pink Parfait x Christion Dior	Bicoloured flowers of plum red with silver grey on lower side with 40 petals; borne singly.
Sir C.V. Raman (HT, 1989)	Scarlet Knight x First Prize	Vigorous, upright stems; brilliant orange scarlet colour of large double flowers; fragrant, long lasting flowers.
Soma (HT, 1980)	White Bouquet x Virgo	Vigorous, flowers having shades of solferino purple; well formed buds, brone freely.
Surabhi (HT, 1975)	Oklahoma x Delhi Princess	Phlox pink, long, tapering buds, open to large, well shaped flowers with long lasting quality.
Vasant (HT, 1980)	Sweet Afton x Delhi Princess	Flowers Chinese yellow with rose edge of petals.
Belle of Punjab (F, 1965)	Montezuma x Flamenco	Warm pink coloured flowers; upright, vigorous with handsome foliage.
Chandrama (F, 1980)	White Bouquet x Virgo	Dawn pink buds open to moon light white, 11 cm across & double flowers; 23 petals/ bloom; borne in clusters of 4-6 flowers.
Deepshikha (F, 1975)	Sea Pearl x Shola	Dutch vermilion double; flowers in summer & rainy season.
Dr. S.S.Bhatnagar (F, 1994)	Oklahoma x White Christmas	Double, velvety red coloured flowers; vigorous & upright growing bush; slightly fragrant & good for bedding.
Lahar (F, 1991)	Pink Parfait x Ganga	Highly floriferous; tolerant to major diseases & temperature
Madhura (F, 1979)*	Kiss of Fire x Goud Vilinder	H.T. shaped buds of light yellow & pink blend; honey like fragrance.
Manmatha (F, 1989)	Sonia x Princess Margaret of England	Blooms profusely; smoky pink or silvery mauve coloured flowers.
Mohini (F, 1970)	Sea Pearl (4x) x Shola (2x)	Hypertriploid (2n=22 or 21+1) or trisomic; chocholate brown colour with yellow tinge at base of petals; patened in USA in 1974 by M/s. Jackson and Perkins for distribution in the world.
Navneet (F, 1971)	Prelude x Africa Star	Creamy white semi-double flowers; 20 petals/bloom; 20 flowers of large size (10 cm across) in a bunch;
Neelambari (F, 1975)	Blue Moon x Africa Star	Flowers rose form & magenta purple colour, borne in large clusters.
Nutkhut (F, 1969)	Rumba x Cocorico	Large clusters of pompon like flowers of lovely coral red coloured;
Prema (F, 1970)	Sea Pearl (4x) x Shola (2x)	Triploid; sister seedling of 'Mohini'. Petals pink with deep pink edges, tolerant to diseases & pests.
Pusa Manhar (F, 2001)	Jantar Mantar x Lahar	Petals creamy white; magenta shade on outer petals & edges; tolerant to PM & black spot; 60 flowers/plant; 15 flowers/ bunch.
Pusa Muskan (F, 2005)	Pink Parfait x Alinka	Large cluster of flowers, creamy white having pink shade & red coloured

		edges; tolerant to PM; flower dia.6.5 cm & 20 petals/ flower.
Pusa Komal (F, 2005)	Pink Parfait x Suchitra	Completely thornless; 40-45 flowers in winter borne in clusters; mod. tolerant to thrips, PM & black spot.
Rupali (F, 1971)	Sweet Afton x Delhi Princess	Very vigorous, tall; deep rose; large flowers; 10 cm across; 40 petals/bloom; slightly fragrant.
Shringar (F, 1972)	Eiffel Tower x Suryodaya	Deep camellia rose, semi-double flowers (18-24 peatls/bloom); long lasting quality; bloom dia. 7.5 cm across.
Sindoor (F, 1980)	Sea Pearl x Suryodaya	Tall; vigorus; long pointed buds open to geranium lake; double & large blooms
Suchitra (F, 1972)	Lady Frost x Swati	Rhodamine pink with mimosa yellow base & silvery white reverse; large flowers 10 cm across; good for bedding.
Chandrika (Miniature, 1972)	Katharina x Cinderalla	Greenish white flowers in clusters.
Pusa Mansij (2002)	Bud sport of Raja Surendra Singh of Nalagarh (Scarlet Knight x Montezuma)	Long pointed flower buds; orange pink in colour with white strips & spots on both sides of petal; tolerant to PM.
Pusa Abhishek (F, 2001)	Bud sport of 'Jantar Mantar'	Big bunches having 25-30 flowers; long strips of creamy white & yellow appear on red background; tolerant to black spot & PM.
Pusa Urmil (F, 2001)	Bud sport of 'Jantar Mantar'	Brown pink coloured flowers in big clusters (40-50 flowers); tolerant to black spot & PM; 40 petals/ flower.
Madhosh (HT, 1975)	Induced mutant of 'Gulzar'	Deep magenta red with mauve coloured faint & broad streaks on petals
Abhisarika (HT, 1975)	Induced mutant of 'Kiss of Fire'	Apricot colour changes to deep pink with silvery reverse.
Pusa Christina (HT, 1975)	Induced mutant of 'Christian Dior'	Fuchsia pink with yellow base of petals.
Stripped Christian Dior	Induced mutant of 'Queen Elizabeth'	Pink & white strips on red base.
Akash Sundari (1982)	-	Apricot colour changing to deep pink; deep pink to light purplish streaks
Pusa Mahak (HT, 2017)	-	Flowers dark pinkish with outstanding fragrance; flowers semi-double with 22-23 petals; 50-60 flowering shoots/ annum
IIHR, Bengaluru		
Arka Swadesh (HT, 2011)	Half-sib progenies of Corvette	Red coloured flowers, 145 flowers/ sq.m/ year; suitable for polyhouse cultivation.
Arka Parimala (HT, 2009)	Half-sib selection of cv. Red Chief	Fragrant; flower red-purple in colour; 80-100 flowers/ plant/ year; rich in anti-oxidants & used to make rose petal tea &sherbet; mod. resistant to thrips & black spot
Arka Kinnari (HT, 2019)	Seedling selection from half sib population of the variety 'Folklore'	Flower dia. 10-11 cm & 35-40 petals/flower; bicolored flowers consisting vermilion red; suitable for garden display
Arka Sharmeeli (HT, 2019)	Seedling selection from half sib population of IIHRR-11 (IC-0617919)	Ever blooming, suitable for garden display; flower color changes from light pink to different shades of red; 450-500 flowers/ plant/ year; 30- 35 petals

		/flower
Arka Sinchana (F, 2019)	Seedling selection from half sib population of 'Five Star'	Everblooming for garden display; flowers bright red colored; flowers small sized (5.4cm) & with 40-45 petals/flower; 1250-1500 flowers/plant/year
Arka Sukanya (2016)	-	Fragrant; dark purplish red coloured petals; ideal for garden display (landscape garden), cosmetics & perfume industry
Dr. G.S. Randhawa (HT, 1993)	Queen Elizabeth x American Heritage	Floriferous with pointed buds; 60-75 flowers/ plant/ year; peach pink flowers changing to salmon pink along the border.
Kiran (HT, 1993)	Big Red x Blue Moon	Floriferous with pointed buds; 60-75 flowers/ plant/ year; fewer spines; flowers tyrian purple changing to Rose Bengal with white streaks on some petals.
Arka Pride (2016)	IIHR-SG-1 x mixed pollens of six lines	Stem length 70 cm; 120 flowers/ sq.m; orange red flowers; ideal for cut flower production under protected cultivation
Arka Ivory (2016)	IIHR-SG-1 x mixed pollens of six lines	110 flowers/sq. m.; cream white flowers; ideal for cut flower production; mod. resistant to mites
Arka Savi (2017)	-	Purple pink flowers; 30 t/acre/year; suitable for loose flower & gulkand production
Nishant (1993)	-	Belongs to *R. multiflora*; thornless & used as rootstock
IHBT, Palampur		
Himalayan Wonder (HT, 2013)	Selection from 'First Red'	Thornless; stem length 79 cm; 27 flowers/plant; 31 petals/ flower; suitable for cut flower purpose
Himalayan Glory (HT, 2013)	Selection from 'First Red'	Petal colour purple rose; 27 flowers/plant; 31 petals/ flower; 8 days vase life; suitable for cut flower purpose
NBRI, Lucknow		
Sharada	Mutant of Queen Elizabeth	-
Sukumari	Mutant of America'sJunior Miss	-
Yellow Contempo	Mutant of Contempo	-
Tangerine Contempo	Mutant of Contempo	-
TNAU, Coimbatore		
YCD-1	Clonal selection from seedlings	Mod. vigorous; medium branched; flowers has 50-53 petals; flowers in 3-5 clusters; bright yellow flowers with pink tinge; yield 100-200 flowers/ annum; 7 days vase life
YCD-2	Clonal selection from seedlings	Mod. vigorous; medium branched; flowers in 3-5 clusters; bright yellow flowers with scarlet tinge; yield 50-200 flowers/ annum

Pests and diseases:

- Red scale (*Anidella aurantii*): Serious pest.
- Die back or wilt (*Diplodia roseum*): Very serious.
- Black leaf spot (*Diplocarpon rosae*): Resistant cvs. Prairie Princess, Spotless Gold, Spotless Yellow and Spotless Pink.
- Powdery mildew (*Sphaerotheca pannosa* var. *rosea*):
- Rust (*Phragmidium mucronatum*):
- Crown gall (*Agrobacterium rhizogenes*): Bacterial disease.
- Sooty mold (*Alternaria* spp.):
- Downy mildew (*Peronospora sparsa*): Spread by wind.
- Botrytis blight (*Botrytis cinerea*): Fungal disease.
- Topaz: Best chemical for powdery mildew control.
- Bioagent for red spider mite is *Phytoseiulus* and for white fly is *Macrolophus*.
- Rose rosette: -ve sense RNA virus. Transmitted by Eriophyid mite (*Phyllocoptes fructiphilus*).
- Enzyme responsible for loss in post harvest life due to botrytis: Mannitol dehydrogenase (MTD).

Inheritance of characters:

- Strong linkage between damask scent and short vase life of flower.

Character	Number of gene (s)	Inheritance pattern
Growth habit	Monogenic	Climbing dominant to dwarf
Miniature stature in polyantha	Monogenic	Dwarf dominant to erect
Flowering duration	Monogenic	Blooming once a year/season dominant over more than once in a season/ extended period
Glossy foliage	Monogenic	Glossy dominant to dull
Double flowers	Monogenic	Double dominant to single
Flower colour	Additive & Polygenic	• Pink co-dominant to white • Pink dominant to dark red, orange red, orange-yellow, yellow, crimson, white and scarlet • Light yellow dominant to deep yellow • White recessive to cream & light yellow • Greenish white dominant to pure white
Moss character	Monogenic	Dominant
Thornless rose	Monogenic recessive	-
Fragrance	Polygenic	For expressing fragrance in progenies both parents must possess fragrance.
PM resistance	Monogenic	Resistance dominant over susceptibility
Black spot resistance	-	Resistance dominant & additive

57. SOLANACEAE

57.1 Petunia

- Popular bedding plant for landscape/ home garden designs and container garden.
- Model plant for genetics and genetic engineering studies
- Model plant used for growing in space. This is due to strigolactone growth regulator.
- Drought tolerant and energy efficient annual.
- 1st monograph was published by Fries in 1911.
- Phenotypes viz. Grandiflora, Multiflora, Milliflora, Waves & hedgiflora are complex hybrids.
- Sensitive to Peroxyacetyl nitrate (PAN).
- Creeping/ spreading growth habit with trailing branches.
- Flowers: Zygomorphic, solitary, axillary and trumpet (funnel) shaped.
- Five petals join and form trumpet shaped.
- Long days accelerate flowering and induce long terminal growth habit with few lateral branches.
- Short days inhibit flowers and produce rosette growth habit.
- Inflorescence: Cyme.
- Fruit type: Capsule and contains numerous small seeds.
- Seed capsule is conic shaped i.e. wider at base and taper to apex.
- Number of seeds/ capsule: 86-600 of which 70-90% are ripened.
- Maximum somatic hybrids have been released.
- Pollen viability: At -5 or -18^{0}C for 6 months and fertility drops at 30^{0}C.
- Double petunia never set any seeds.
- Strictly cross pollinated crop and vegetative propagation is possible.
- In white coloured flowers, light blue colour can be brought with use of betalins.
- β-ionone compound imparts fragrance in flowers.
- Floral scent compounds: Benzyl aldehyde, benzenoid and phenyl propanoid compounds.
- Gametophytic self incompatibility (GSI) is reported.
- Pseudo-self compatibility (PSC) represents breakdown of SI system giving limited to full seed set after an incomplete pollination.
- PSC in crosses between *P. violacea* and *P. axillaris* is under polygenic control.
- Use of CMS results in reduction of production cost of F_1 hybrid seed.
- Cvs. Snowball, Blue Bedder, Rosymorn are CMS sterile types in *P. hybrida*.
- In CMS, functional pollen is not produced or fails to release at anthesis.

- Heterosis for ornamental traits and vegetative characters is exhibited in double petunia hybrids.
- Double types never set any seeds.
- Grandiflora type is a spontaneous mutant from Multiflora type cv. Defiance strain.
- Induced mutation by seed treatment with EMS are:
  - a) Grandiflora mutant from aneuploid plant;
  - b) Linear leaf mutant from *P. axillaris*;
  - c) Chimeral flowered mutant from *P. hybrida*;
  - d) Height mutant from *P. hybrida*.
- Green florescent protein (GFP) from jelly fish used as vital marker in selection of transgenic petunia hybrid plant.
- Transgenic plants with white anthers exhibit male sterility due to arrest in male gametophyte development.
- Hybrid seed is produced entirely through hand emasculation and pollination only.
- In hybrid seed production, Multiflora is used as seed parent and Grandiflora as pollen parent.
- Seed yield: 150-180 kg/ha.
- Seed germination: Higher in hybrids (92%), Multiflora (77%) and Grandiflora (45%).
- Breaking of seed dormancy: Seed treatment at 35ºC for 4 days in dark followed by chilling at 5ºC for 7 days.
- Seed viability is lost within 4 months in open boxes/ paper packets.
- Seeds stored in paper packets and kept under ambient conditions loose viability within 9 months.
- Seed viability is preserved for 3-4 years in sealed plastic bags with addition of silica gel.
- LD_{50} dose for decrease in plant height: 100 Gy gamma irradiation and 0.1% EMS.
- Botrytis blight (*Botrytis cinerea*): Most serious disease.Cv. Resisto Blue partial resistant.
- 1st anti-sense technology has been used to incorporate anti-sense *CHS* gene to alter flower colour.
- 1st successful application of genetic engineering for flower colour modification-Crimson coloured *AI* gene from maize.
- Transgenic plants with white anthers exhibit male sterility due to arrest in male gametophyte development.

Species:

- Cultivated petunia (*Petunia* x *hybrida*) is hybrid between *P. axillaris* x *P. integrifolia.*

- *P. axillaris* (syn. *P. nyctanginiflora*): Self incompatible. 1st cultivated in 1923. Show hawk moth pollination.
- *P. integrifolia* (syn. *P. violacea*): 1st flowered in 1931. Flower exhibit diurnal opening & closing movements.
- *P. exserta*: Arisen from wild spp. *P. axillaris* x *P. violacea*. Show humming bird pollination.
- *P. parodii*: Most affected by day length & temperature.
- *P. inflata* & *P. integrifolia* are allopatric species & interfertile.

♂	***P. axillaris***	***P. exserta***	***P. integrifolia***	***P. reitzii***	***P. interior***	***P. guarapuavensis***	***P. altiplana***	***P. mantiqueirensis***	***P. scheideana***	***P. saxicola***	***P. bonjardinensis***
P. axillaris (♀)	++	+	-	++	+	-	-	++	+	++	++

(++) = highly cross fertile; (+) = medium fertile; (-) = poorly cross fertile

Varieties:

- 1st F_1 petunia: All Double Victoria Mixed (1934).
- Hybrid vigour was exploited in Japan for 1st time during World War II (1940-50) by producing 'All Double Petunia' hybrids that revolutionized the flower seed industry.
- 1st grandiflora F_1 hybrid: Ballerina introduced by Weddle Seed Company.
- 1st inbred red flowered multiflora cv.: Fire Chief introduced by S. Sinclair of Bodger Seeds of USA in 1950.
- In India, 1st hybrid of petunia was released by Indo-American Hybrid Seed (IAHS) Bengaluru, in 1967.
- Comanche: 1st red flowered F_1 Grandiflora: It is developed from 'Fire Chief' in 1953.
- Cvs. California Giant and Superbissima are allotetraploids (2n=4x=28).
- Cv. Rose: Mutant developed in Japan in 2003 is through ion beam breeding.
- Mutants of *P. axillaris* developed via seed treatment with sodium azide, 2,4-D & alpha rays: Stellata, Campyloflora, Rubriflora Mixed, Grandiflora, Albiflora Mixed.
- Surfinia: White coloured variety developed through anti-sense RNA technology.

Class	**Varietal series/ cultivars**
Multiflora F_1 hybrids (single, small flowers of smooth edged petals). Stress tolerant, vigorous & floriferous	Blue, Blue Star, Comanche, Coral Bells, Coral Satin, Dream Girl, Fairy Land, Fairy Star, Peach Satin, Pinwheel, Pink Joy, Plum Pudding, Tidal Wave, Tiny Tunia, Trail Blazer, Trumpets, Wave, White, White Joy & White Satin.
Multiflora F_1 hybrids (double)	Allegro, Apple Tart, Blue Danube, Bonanza, Peach Tart, Pink Delight, Plum Tart, Raspberry Tart, Scarlet Empress & Snow Berry Tart.

Multiflora F_2 hybrids	Calorona, Canfetti.
Grandiflora F_1 hybrids (single large flowers with ruffled petals)	Apricot Tart, Apple Blossom, Astro, Ballerina, Blue Flash, Blue Lace, Blue Magic, Bravo, Calypso, Cherry Blossom, Red Flash, Red Magic, Super Cascade Red, Super Cascade White, Super Magic Pink, Super Magic Red, White Flair, White Magic & Yellow Magic.
Grandiflora F_1 hybrids (double)	Blue Danube, Blue Luster, Bridal Bouquet, Duet, Nocturne Improved, Rose perfection, Salmon Bouquet, Sky Magic, Snow Cap, Sonata, Tango & Valentine.
Grandiflora F_2 hybrids	Carnival.
Cascade F_1 hybrids	Chiffon, Coral Cascade, Pink Cascade, White Cascade & Fandango.
Trailing type and small flowered	Blue Wonder, Rose Wonder & Rose.
Frilled types	Giants of California, Superbissima, Romona, Snow Storm, Theodosia, Defiance, Super Frills.
Smooth edged Grandiflora types	Bingo, Dazzler, Pop Corn & Purple Prince.
Dwarf and compact bedding types (Nana compacta)	Alderman, Blue Bedder, Blue Bird, Butter Scotch, Cream Star, Erfordia, Fire Chief, Fleming Velvet & Snow Ball.

Inheritance of characters:

- Grandiflora type: Spontaneous mutant from Multiflora type 'Defiance Strain' and is single dominant gene mutant.

Character	Type of gene action
Flower diameter	Large flower dominant over small
Flower colour	Purple dominant over red
	Multiple genes & no complete dominance; 2-6 genes for colour intensity
Colour intensity	Incomplete dominant gene (*Inl*)
Mutant flower form (apetalous condition)	Monogenic recessive
Flower doubleness (increase in number of both petals & stamens)	Monogenic dominant (DD) over single form &linked to female sterility/ abnormality
Flower size; nector volume	Polygenic
Male sterility	Single plasma gene; maternal (cytoplasmic) inheritance
Genic male sterility	Monogenic, recessive gene (*ms*)
Pseudo-self compatibility	Polygenic
Plastid inheritance	Maternal inheritance
PAN (peroxyacetyl nitrate) resistance	Additive & partial dominance
Kanamycin resistance	Monogenic dominant (*NPTII* gene & cDNA of PEPC from green sorghum leaves) co-inherited in transgenics
Narrow leaf form	Pleiotropic

58. STRELITZIACEAE

58.1 Bird of paradise

- Eulogized as 'Crane flower'.
- Evergreen, perennial herbaceous plant.

- Name comes from remarkably shaped and coloured flower clusters, like the crested head of a bird.
- Optimum temperature for growth: 10-24^{0}C.
- Seeds were noticed in *S. reginae* and *S. juncea*.
- Propagation method: Seeds, division of clumps and separation of offsets.
- Temperature required for seed germination: 18-21^{0}C.
- Seed treatment: H_2SO_4 for 5 minutes.
- Offsets take 3-5 years to come into flowering.
- Plant enter in reproductive phase when they attain 14 leaves.
- Number of leaves to be retained on plant for good flowering: 51-55.
- Pollination agent: Bird.
- Flower production is seasonal i.e. low in January-March and December and high in July-September.
- Plant started cropping in 4th to 6th year and enter in reproductive phase when they had 14 leaves.
- Low light intensity results in reduced flowering and promotes flower abortion or blasting.
- Repotting should be done every spring.
- Harvesting stage: First floret opens.

Species:

Name	Features
Strelitzia reginae	Very popular, orange-blue coloured flowers; grows upto 90 cm height;
S. nicopi	Blue coloured petals
S. alba	White bird of paradise
S. nicolai	Giant bird of paradise. Grows up to height of 10 m; clump forming; spathe brownish red, flowers white, 20 cm long, corolla light purplish blue.
S. kewensis	Garden hybrid from *S. augusta* x *S. reginae*; Up to 1.5 m height; leaf blades 60 cm long; flower pale yellow coloured having liliac-pink patches at the base of sepals
S. candida	-
S. augusta	Grows up to 5 m height, leaves 60-90 cm long, inflorescence composed of 2 spathe, shaped like bird's head, from the middle of which white flower emerge

- **Varieties**: Mandela's Gold: Released from Kirstenbosch National Botanical Garden, Cape Town. South Africa.

Grading system:

Stem length (cm)	Bloom size (mm)
100	≥ 16
80	≥ 13
60	≥ 10

Inheritance of characters:

- Number of vegetative shoots was inversely related to length of photoperiod.
- Number of days to flower decreased as photoperiod increased.
- Frequency of leaf emergenc has direct relationship to flower production.

Diseases and pests:

- Root rot (*Fusarium monoliforme*): Seed borne. Pre-soaking seeds at room temperature followed by hot water (57^{0}C) treatment for 30 min. controls disease.
- Leaf spot (*Microsphaerpsis* spp.):
- Soft rot (*Pseudomonas syringae* pv. *delphinii*):
- Gray mold (*Botrytis cinerea*):
- Mealy bug (*Planococcus citri*):
- Scales (*Aspidiotus camolliae*):

59. VERBENACEAE

59.1 Verbena

- Annual, suitable for landscapes, hanging baskets and ground cover as bedding type and rockery.
- Flowers are small with 5 petals and borne in dense spikes.
- Seed hilum contribute to irregular germination.
- Very sensitive to high soil moisture content.
- Verbena of North America diploid and S. America is polyploid.
- Inflorescence: Dense spike.
- Propagation methods: Seed and cutting.
- Seed hilum morphology contributes to irregular germination.
- Chochiploidy can be exploited for improvement in seed set and large flower size in tetraploids over diploids.
- Use of heavy ion beam (HIB) radiation (5 Gy) is effective to create new cvs. within short duration and excellent tool for sterile mutation breeding.
- HIB: Widely used to isolate sterile mutants of cv. Coral Pink and Sakura and to generate self incompatible mutants in *V. hybrida*.
- LD_{50} dose of gamma irradiation: 25 Kr (*V. hybrida*) and 45 Kr (*V. tenuisecta*).
- Low seed set in open conditions is observed in *V. platensis* and *V. peruviana* but hand pollination results in seed set.
- Seed yield: 250-375 kg/ha.
- Seed dormancy period: 2 months.

- Seed dormancy: Broken by soaking for 2 days followed by chilling at 4-5^{0}C for 5-7 days.
- Genic male sterile hybrids are highly floriferous and free flowering having long blooming period.
- Red colour is a basic to genus *Verbena*.
- Genetically stable mutant 'doubleness' in white flowered *V. erinoides*: Recessive gene.
- Tissue bank and Genetic Evolutionary Race History are maintained at NBRI.
- SCAR markers: Useful to assess genetic relationships of *V. officinalis* with all other species.

Species:

- *Verbena hybrida* and *V. bonariensis* show lower chiasmata per bivalent.
- Genus *Verbena* is dibasic i.e.there are two chromosome groups with section *Glandularia* X=5 (polyploid) and section *Verbenacea* X=7 (diploid).
- All *Verbena* species, irrespective of ploidy level are pollen fertile and self compatible.
- Species belonging to two sections do not cross because of strong genetic barrier between them.
- Species of *Verbenacea* section are predominantly self pollinated, while species of *Glandularia* section are cross pollinated. *Verbena hybrida*, *V. incisa*, *V. phlogiflora* are more self pollinated while *V. platensis*, *V. peruviana* are out crossed.
- Species belonging to these sections do not cross and indicate existence of strong genetic barrier between them.

Section	Features & species
Glandularia	*V. hybrida*, *V. tenuisecta*, *V. peruviana*, *V. platensis*, *V. incisa*, *V. phlogiflora* and *V. aubletia*
Verbenacea	Self pollinated; *V. hastata*, *V. urticifolia*

Species	Salient characters
V. rigida	2n=6x=42; flowers in July; PM & drought resistant.
V. hybrida (Garden verbena)	2n=10; annual, tall (100-130 cm), highly showy blue-purple coloured large flowers, less drought tolerant; used for bedding.
V. bonariensis	2n=2x=14; 3x=28; tall (3-4 feet); biennial; summer blooming; bloom colour blue-violet; PM & drought resistant; excellent for cut flower arrangement.
V.canadensis (Rose vervain)	More compact growth, wild species.
V. tenuisecta (Moss verbena)	2n=10; hardy; less colourful, small flowers & used as a ground cover throughout year

Varieties:

- Free flowering hybrids have been developed by NBRI by hybridizing *V. tenuisecta* x *V. hybrida* by repeated back crossing with recurrent parent *V. hybrida*. These hybrids are summer hardy with genes that confer heat resistance and mating habit.

- *V.* x *teasii*: Interspecific hybrid of *V. tenuisecta* x *V. hybrida*. Highly floriferous and long blooming period.
- Popular in USA: Showtime Blaze, Red A, Romance Scarlet.
- Popular in Japan: Temari Sakura, Temari Violet, Tapien Pink, Coral Pink, Sangria.
- Resistant to powdery mildew (*Podosphaera xanthii*): Major depressive factor. E.g. Aztec Dark Red, Aztec Violet, Coral, Candy Cane, Dark Blue Lascar White, Empress Strawberry, Pink Shades, Lanai.
- Temari series: Long blooming period with many flower clusters.
- Temari Coral Pink (*V. hybrida*): Developed by HIB radiation exhibit self compatible.

60. VIOLACEAE

60.1 Pansy

- Eulogized as 'King of annuals or Symbol of thought or Heart's Ease or Sweet violet'.
- Variety of forms, sizes, and shapes of pansies make it 'king of annuals'.
- Cultivated for landscape planting, garden design, container gardening and ground cover.
- Dwarf plants with small sized flowers are called 'Johny Jump-Ups'.
- Facultative autogamous plant.
- Growth habit: Acaulescent (absence of stem).
- Planting distance: 20 cm x 30 cm.
- Flowers are hardy, long lived with complicated morphology.
- Flowers: Zygomorphic, bilateral symmetrical having five petals (2 superior, 2 lateral and 1 inferior).
- Flower oil: Used in perfumes and flavourings.
- Highly self pollinated but protandrous type makes cross pollination.
- Cleistogamy in long days (obligatory self pollinated) and flowers are produced under 14 h of day light.
- Chasmogamy in short days (open cross pollinated) and short petioled leaves are produced under 11 h or less day light.
- Both types of flowers appear on generative plants.
- In different speeies, flowering time overlaps as chasmogamous flowers in spring and cleistogamous flowers in summer.
- Orientation of flower is governed by posture of pedicel.
- Ovary position: Superior.
- Pollination agents: Bumble bees, moths (*Plusia gamma*).
- Flower remain open for 7-15 days in summer.

- Flowering period: January-March ends in May.
- Anthesis time: 8-10 AM.
- Anther dehiscence occurs first in the posterior anther followed by lateral and anterior anthers.
- Pollination did not terminate the life span of flower. Senescence starts after 8 days onward.
- Pollen viability: 6-8 days after start of anthesis.
- Pollen grains germinate only in 5% sucrose solution.
- Pollen grains can be stored up to 90 days at (4^0C).
- Ideal planting time for seed production: Mid October.
- Pollination with the help of camel hair brush is effective.
- Pollination should be continuously done till the last stage of flowering.
- Days taken for capsule maturity: 40.
- Fruit type: Pod (capsule) containing 40-50 light brown seeds.
- Harvest capsule along with small stalk (5 cm long) at yellow green stage.
- Premature dehiscence of capsule results in white seeds.
- Nut like seeds have straight embryos, flat cotyledons and soft, fleshy oily endosperm.
- Seeds dispersal: Ants.
- Seed yield: 70-80 kg/ha (controlled), 200-250 kg/ ha (OP).
- Seed treatment to break dormancy: 100-200 ppm GA_3 solution.
- Digital image analysis permits quantitative evaluation of various horticultural traits.
- Seed priming with 12-20% moisture during storage at 5^0C gives germination between 21-98% after 6 months of storage.
- SSAA (saturated salt accelerated ageing) test credits better seed emergence and longevity.
- Dried seeds can be stored for 2-4 months at 4^0C with KNO_3 treatment.
- Capsule set is very poor (5%) under natural selfing compared to hand selfing (68.7%).
- For seed production, ratio of male and female plants: 1: 2.
- Cleistogamous flowers produce more capsules than chasmogamous flowers.
- Somatic embryos of *V. pedata* from embryonic callus and cell suspension have been established.
- Cercospora leaf spot: Major disease.

Species:

- Genetic diversity is maintained even though presence of high level of cleistogamy and vegetative reproduction.
- Present day large flowered originated from selection from *V. lutea* x *V. tricolor*.

- Nature of ploidy in species: Segmental alloploid.
- Endangered species: *V. elatior*, *V. pumila*, *V. stagnina*.
- Yellow zinc violet (section *Melanium*) *V. lutea* ssp. *calaminaria*.
- Blue violet (section *Melanium*) *V. lutea* ssp. *westfalica*.
- In *V. papilionacea*, chasmogamous flowers are infertile.
- Species in section *Melanium* can be crossed with each other irrespective of chromosome number and produce fertile offsprings.
- Hybrids are easily obtained in section *Melanium*.
- Numerous species hybrids have been known in section *Nominium*.

Species	Salient features
Viola canadensis (Canadian white violet)	Leaves heart shaped.
V. lutea (Mountain pansy)	2n=18; yellow coloured flowers.
V. subdimidiata	-
V. tricolor (Heart'sease or wild pansy)	2n=26; small plant of creeping and ramping; found in partial shade.
V. riviniana (Common violet or Wood violet or Dog violet)	Perennial; flowering from April to June; can be grown as ground cover.
V. x *wittrockiana* (Garden pansy)	-
V. odorata	Dried flowers are used against cough, influenza & lung troubles
V. striata	Chasmogamous;
V. grahamii	Cleistogamous;

Varieties:

- Breeding of modern pansies began in 19th century in UK and in Japan, during 20th century.
- Clausen (1922) 1st time reported hybrids by crossing *V. arvensis* (n=17) x *V. tricolor* (n=13), *V. elegantula* x *V. cornuta* and *V. tricolor* x *V. arvensis*.
- *V.* x *wittrockiana* hybrids: *V. tricolour* x *V. altaica*.
- Hybrids between *V. lutea* x *V. tricolor* and *V. calcarata* x *V. tricolor* are reported.
- Resistant to cercospora leaf spot: Bingo Red, Bingo Yellow, Crown Golden, Crown Blue, Majestic Giant Yellow, Dynamite Red, Dynamite Yellow.
- Tolerant to heat: Pansy Velocity, Pansy Plentiful, Pansy Rain Purple, Beacon.

Name	Features
Alpen Glow, Coronation Gold, Midnight Blue, White Lady, Knight Blue, Hybrid Purple, Majestic Mixed, Blue Carpet, White Perfection, Yellow Charm	Introduced from foreign country
Punjab Purple Wave (2013)	Leaves have purple tinge; flower purple coloured with dark purple blotch; flowering duration 76 days; 71 flowers/ plant

Punjab Choco Gold (2013)	Leaves light green; flower yellow coloured with chocolate blotch; flowering duration 83 days; 83 flowers/ plant; suitable for bedding purpose
Punjab Sunaina (2014)	Dwarf; flower yellow & purple coloured; suitable for pot culture & bedding
Punjab Neelima (2014)	Dwarf; flower purple coloured; suitable for pot culture & bedding
Cool Wave, Wonderful Purple With Face, Pansy Delta, Viola Floral Power Red, Floral Power Sky Blue Blotch	Outstanding F_1 hybrids

Inheritance of characters:

- Hybrids varied in productivity due to incomplete dominance of more productive parents.
- Major target for breeding all over the world: Round flower shape.
- Flower shape is determined by combination of 3 petal shapes.

Character	Number of genes	Inheritance pattern
Hairy & glabrous leaves	Monogenic (*H*)	High hairy dominant to glabrous (hispid type of hairiness of *V. rothomagensis* dominant to glabrous)
Stipule form	Polygenic (basic gene *T*)	Digitate stipule dominant to pinnate
Spathulate middle lobe of stipule	Monogenic (*P*)	Spathulate dominant to non-spathulate
Scarious margin of flower sepal	Monogenic (*C*)	Scarious margin dominant to non-scarious margin
Spur of lowermost petal	Monogenic (*Y*)	Long and slender petaloid spur dominant to short spur
Direction of lateral petals	Polygenic	Inhibiting genes control upward direction in *Melanium* & downward direction in *Nominium* viola
Style spot	3 distinct genes, 1 complementary gene & 2 complementary inhibiting genes	Combined action of these genes complicates segregation of style spot
Flower size	Monogenic	Genes have inhibitory effect & are linked together. Crossing over amounts to 25%. Large incompletely dominant over small
Flower shape	Monogenic	Round dominant stipulate
Geotropic stem	2 polymeric genes	Transversal geotropic dominant to negative geotropic main stem
Flower colour	-	Deep red dominant to deep velvety red border of *V. tricolor*
	Two polymeric genes	Change in colour velvety red to velvety violet or purple
	Three genes	Epistatic & inhibit velvety colouring & turn violet
	Digenic	One gene homozygotically turns violet yellow & other turns full yellow to yellowish white
	Three polymeric genes	When basal genes lack; flower colour becomes either pure white (alba) or alba yellow

Seven genes (*A, M, R, L, W, Pal, V*)	• Polymeric series A_1 to A_6, all are dominant • M_1 to M_3 series dominant & partially epistatic gene • R_1 and R_2 polymeric genes change reddish to violet • *LL* epistatic to violet W • *Ll* indicate blue • *W* epistatic effect • *Pal* bleaching gene on all colours & inherited in Mendelian ratio • *V* epistatic to *A, M, R & L*

61. PROTECTED CULTIVATION OF FLOWER CROPS:

- Production of chrysanthemum stock during 1960s is the main reason for development of greenhouse.
- The bioagent + fertilizer used for rapid decompose of coir pith: Pleurotus + urea.
- Ideal pH range for soil based substrate in greenhouse cultivation: 6.2 to 6.8.
- Ideal pH range for soilless substrates in greenhouse cultivation: 5.4 to 6.0.
- Kerala: Leading state in protected cultivation of orchids.
- Flower crops suitable for protected cultivation: Dutch roses, Cut chrysanthemum, Gerbera, Carnation, Orchids, Anthurium, Calla lily, Gypsophila, Statice, etc.

Special horticultural practices:

- Wintering: An alternative to root pruning. It is done in rose, jasmine in Northern and Eastern India.
- Pinching: Removal of growing point of shoot along with few leaves.
- Pricking: Transfers of young seedlings to another pan or tray.

Practice	Purpose	Crops
Staking	Give support	Sweet pea, Morning glory, Nasturtium
Bending	To maintain source & sink relation & to induce new shoots in greenhouse	Rose
Wintering (Root pruning)	To make dwarf, to induce flowering, fruitfulness & determining flowering time	Rose, Jasmine
Disbudding	To induce showy good quality flowers	Carnation, Chrysanthemum, Dahlia
Pinching/ Stopping	To induce lateral or side shoot production	Carnation, Chrysanthemum, Marigold, Dahlia, Brachycome
Deshooting	To retain single bud at top	Rose, Carnation, Chrysanthemum
Forcing	To produce flowers	Amaryllis, Calla lily, Lilium, Tulip, Daffodil

Orchid (Phalaenopsis):

- Well known white flowered species *P. amabilis*.
- Generic male indicates moth like flower structure (3 sepals + 3 petals + trianugular ovary).

- Plant exhibit monopodial form of growth (no lateral shoots).
- Only one spray of flowers develops from leaf axil on main stem.
- Phalaenopsis has fleshy and distichous leaves.
- Tropical orchid require 15-32^{0}C; growth phase (26-27^{0}C); flowering phase (19-21^{0}C), for spike induction (18^{0}C).
- Ideal R.H. for growth and development: 60-80%.
- CO_2 requirement: CAM plant and require600-800 ppm.
- Light intensity:
  - o Excessive light intensity results in burning of foliage.
  - o Inadequate light intensity results in straggly and poor quality sprays and poor root development in plants.
  - o Growth phase require 5000-8000 lux.
  - o Flowering phase require 8000-15000 lux.
- Cultivation:
  - o On open benches having good air circulation.
  - o White coloured transparent pots of two sizes 5" top dia. with 1.1 lit capacity and 9" pot dia. with 6 lit. capacity.
- Potting media and planting distance:
  - o Initial planting in 5" pot filled with only coco peat.
  - o Transplant after 6 months in 9" pot containing bottom layer with coco fibre and top layer of fcoco peat.
  - o Row to row: 35 cm and plant to plant: 40 cm.
- Sprinkler irrigation: 5 to 12 litres of water per m^2/ hour.
- Hints during flower production:
  - o On an average 12 plants per sq. m.
  - o Complete growing period upto 5 years.
  - o Flowering starts 8 months after planting.
  - o Premature flower are removed during growing phase.
  - o Flower stems are supported with sticks when flower buds begin to swell.
  - o Branches are harvested when last flower is still in bud stage.
  - o Yield: 6-7 stems/ plant/ year.
- PHT:
  - o After harvesting, stems are kept in bucket containing water & stored at 7-10^{0}C.
  - o Vase life: 5 days to 6 weeks.
  - o Box size: 100 x 15 x 11.5 cm.
  - o Depending on number of flowers/ stem, 25-30 stems are packed per box.

- Abnormalities due to climatic factors:
  - Bud loss: Occurs from flower stick during flowering phase due to excess high temperature in relation to light intensity.
  - Dripping spikes and leaves due to moisture drop from stem.
  - Loss of glossiness in flowers due to viral damage/ lack of potassium/ high humidity with dark conditions.
  - Cooling or transport sunken spots on foliage during transplantation (from growing pot to flowering pot)/ or due to stress/ excess of light intensity.

62. PHYSIOLOGICAL DISORDERS OF FLOWER CROPS:

Crop	Disorder	Cause (s)
Alstromeria	Flower abortion	Excessive salt or over watering
Carnation	a) Sleepiness (temporary or permanent wilting of flowers)	- Ethylene injury, Ca deficiency/ High water stress
	b) Calyx splitting	
	c) Slabside	- Night temperature $< 10^{0}$C, low B, N dose
	d) Curly tip (poor flower quality)	- Cool period
	e) Grassiness	- Low light, low temperature & B deficiency
	f) Splitting at node & bushiness/ witches broom	- Genetic factor - Boron deficiency
Chrysanthemum	a) Premature budding	-
	b) Quilling of florets	-
	c) Crooked stem	- Day night temperature variation
	d) Bronze foliage	- Lead deficiency
	e) Bleached petals	- High temperature during flower development
	f) Crown buds	- Insufficient light
	g) Bract buds	- Day-night temperature exceeds 27.2^{0}C
	h) Heat delay	- High temperature ($>28^{0}$C) during production
	i) Tip scorch	- Calcium deficiency, excess humidity
Gladiolus	a) Topple	- Calcium deficiency
	b) Bud rot	- Calcium deficiency
	c) Blindness	- Unfavorable temperature
	d) Negative geotropism	- Uneven distribution of auxin
	e) Flower blasting	- Low light intensity
Lilium	a) Leaf scorch/ Leaf burn/ Tip burn	- Calcium deficiency (high Mn and Al in soil)
	b) Bud blast/ bud abortion	- Storage of water at top of plant & high N level
	c) Puffy foliage	- Frost injury
	d) Bud drop	- Insufficient light condition
	e) Topple or bud rot	- Calcium deficiency
	f) Fleck: Small white and brown spots and streaks appearing on the leaves with deformed flowers.	- Combination of cucumber mosaic virus and lily symptomless virus
Orchids	a) Dry sepal injury	* High humidity & smog
	b) Deformed flowers (flowers with abnormal number of petals/ lip are called 'peloric')	Low temperature & chilling injury (a genetic trait but expression is environmentally influenced & appears random)
Rose	a) Bull head	- Improper pruning, high N dose

	b) Bent neck (limp neck)	- Storage disorder
	c) Blind shoots	- Low light intensity & prolonged exposure to low temperature
Tuberose	Cracking of spikes	Calcium deficiency
Poinsettia	Epinasty	Ethylene injury
Hyacinth	Spitting	-
Daffodil	Bull nose (after reaching goose neck stage of development flower do not open properly)	-
Gerbera	Bending	Calcium deficiency
	Double flowers	Nutrient imbalance
	Uneven stem length	High chlorides, water stress & reduced soil temperature
	Yellowing of old & new leaves	Nitrogen deficiency
	Browning of leaf veins & necrosis	Phosphorous deficiency
	Blackening of leaf stalk	Boron deficiency
	Leaf burning from edge to inside	Potassium deficiency
Tulip	Cracking	Leaf and scape-crack disorder due to ethylene or B deficiency
	Knuckling (shoot grows back into bulb scale instead of upward)	-

63. HORTICULTURE ASSOCIATIONS AND SOCIETIES

1. Agri-Horti Society of India, Kolkata.
2. Hort-Society of India, Bengaluru.
3. The Horticultural Society of Chota Nagpur, Ranchi.
4. All India Kitchen Garden Association, New Delhi.
5. The Indian Association for Ornamental Horticulture, New Delhi.
6. Bonsai Study Group of the Indo-Japanies, Mumbai.
7. Bombay Rose Society, Mumbai.
8. Cactus and Succulents Society, New Delhi.
9. National Cactus and Succulents Society of India, Chandigarh.
10. Chrysanthemum Society of India, New Delhi.
11. Indian Society of Tree Scientists, Solan.
12. South Indian Horticulture Association, Coimbatore.

64. INTERNET AND INFO-TECH SERVICES IN FLORICULTURE INDUSTRY:

1. www.nbpgr.ernet.in
2. www.gardenweb.com
3. www.usplant.com

4. www.thegardenhelper.com
5. www.planthealthcare.com
6. www.rso.cornell.edu
7. www.agriwatch.com
8. www.cals.nesu.edu/hort-sci
9. www.ipm.ucdavis.edu
10. www.postharvest.ucdavis.edu
11. www.hortibizindia.nic.in
12. www.apeda.com
13. www.seeds@iihr.res.in

65. Books on floriculture and landscape gardening:

Book (s)	Name of author
Beautiful Trees and Gardens, Garden Through Ages, Beautiful Cities of India, Flowering Trees	M.S.Randhava
Floriculture in India	G.S. Randhava & A.K. Mukhopadhya
Complete Gardening in India	K. Gopal Swami Iyengar
Ornamental Horticulture, Garden Flowers, Indoor Gardening	Vishnu Swaroop
Introductory Ornamental Horticulture	J.S.Arora
Advances in Horticulture	K.L,Chadha & S.K.Bhattacharjee
Advances in Ornamental Horticulture	L.C. Dey & S.K.Bhattacharjee
Commercial Flowers, Landscape Gardening	T.K. Bose *et al*.
Rose in India, Flowering Shrubs, Survey of Rose Breeding in India, Golap Bari, Search for New Genes, The Beautiful Climbers of India,	B.P.Pal
Beautiful Indian Orchids	B.N. Ghosh
Orchids of India	A.S. Rao
Biology, Conservation and Culture of Orchids	S.P. Vij
Chrysanthemum in India	M.A.Kher
The Bougainvilleas	B.P. Pal & Vishnu Swarup
Ornamental Horticulture	Vishnu Swarup
Design Elements of Landscape Gardening	K.M.P. Nambisan
Garden Design	J. Brooks
Gladiolus	A. Mukhopadhyay
Home Gardening, Beautiful Shrubs	P.P. Trivedi
Ikebana	D. Trivedi
Ikebana in India	S. Thakur
Orchids of India, Garden Plants	T.K. Bose & S.K. Bhattacharjee
Ornamental Bulbous Plants	S.L. Jindal
Ornamental Horticulture in India	K.L. Chadha & B. Choudhary
Prospects of Floriculture in India	G.K. Kaul & N.K. Dadlani
Seasonal Flowers	B.L. Desai
Water Plants	B. Bhadri, B. Singh & B.L. Desai
Wonderland of Tropical Bonsai	J. Parekh & Nilkunj
Poisonous Plants of India	R.L. Bahadur & S. Ghosh
High Altitude Flowering Plants of Western Himalayas	M.A. Rau
Flower Breeding and Genetics	M.S. Patil & A.R. Karale

5

PLANTATION CROPS

1. GENERAL INFORMATION:

- These crops are cultivated in an extensive scale in large contiguous areas, owned and managed by an individual or a company and whose produce is utilized only after processing e.g. Coffee, Tea, Rubber, Coconut, Cocoa, etc.
- Plantation crops occupy 2.3 % of total cultivated area.
- Grown in tropics between 20^0N and 20^0S of equator.
- They maintain ecological balance by their intense forest & vegetative cover.
- They contribute 25% to GDP from an area of 8.5% under these crops.
- Contribute to gross national product: 27% of total from agricultural commodities and 4.8% of total export.
- Small holders' plantation crops: Coconut, Areca nut, Cashew nut, black pepper and cardamom.
- Estate crops or conventional plantation crops: Rubber, Tea, Coffee.
- Leading arecanut producing states: Karnataka (56.2%), Kerala (18.2%), Assam (11.9%).
- Leading coconut producing states: Kerala (32%), Tamil Nadu (28%), Karnataka (21%).
- International Group for the Genetic Improvement of Cocoa (INGENIC) formed in 1993.
- Coconut Research Station (presently CPCRI) was established in 1916. It was taken over by Indian Central Coconut Committee in 1948.
- CPCRI hosts International Coconut Gene Bank for South Asia under the umbrella of Coconut Genetic Resources Network (COGENT) of the Biodiversity International.
- COGENT restricts movement of coconut germplasm through seeds and permits zygotic embryos.
- Member countries of COGENT: Any coconut-producing country can become a member. Currently has 39 member countries that are divided into five sub-networks.
- National Active Germplasm Site (NAGS) for coconut is maintained at CPCRI.
- CPCRI, Regional Station, Vittal was established in 1970.

- Asia Pacific Coconut Community (APCC) or Cocommunity (now International Coconut Community i.e. ICC) was established on 2nd September, 1969.It is an inter-governmental organization of states in Asia-Pacific that produce coconuts. The purpose of the APCC is "to promote, coordinate and harmonize all activities of the coconut industry".
- ICC is the 1st commodity based organization established under the auspices of United Nations-Economic and Social Commission for Asia and the Pacific (UN-ESCAP) in 1969.
- Branch of International Rubber Association was established in 1948 at Kottayam, Kerala. It was renamed as 'Indian Rubber Institute' in 1987.
- Coconut Development Board (CDB) works under Ministry of Agriculture, GOI.
- Rubber Board works under Ministry of Commerce and Industry.
- 1st chief scientific officer of UPASI: Dr. W. S. Shaw.
- 1st Tea research station: Jorhat (1904).
- National Mission on Oil seeds and Oil Palm was introduced in 12th five year plan.
- National Mission on Edible Oils was initiated on 9th August, 2021.
- Report of UNO's committee on climate change indicated that oil palm trees are mainly responsible for vagaries of climate change in the world.
- Restriction on import and export of palm oil have been laid down by UNO.
- ICAR-CPCRI, Kasargod distributing the QR coded coconut seedlings for the past three years.
- Coffee Act: Formed during 1942.
- Dichotomous branching habit is noticed in coconut, palmyra palm, nipa palm.
- Defined rhizosphere is observed in plantation crops.
- Areca-cocoa cropping system has carbon sequestration potential of 2.02 to 3.89 $Mg.ha^{-1}.y^{-1}$.
- Suitable crops for Multi-tier/ multistoried cropping system: Coconut, Elephant yam, Cocoa, Pineapple, Banana.
- 1st industrial park for rubber and rubber wood based industries: Kerala.
- Nitrogen use efficiency of plantation crops is 10-15%, phosphorous use efficiency is 25-30% and potassium is 20-25%.
- Asian tea Alliance launched in China on April 19, 2019 (Members of this association are India, China, Sri Lanka, Indonesia and Japan. Main objective: To enhance tea trade, cultural exchanges and promoting tea.
- To provide Digital mobile extension services for coffee stakeholders, Union Ministry of Commerce & Industry launched 'Coffee Connect & Coffee *Krishitharanga*'.
- Prices of Darjeeling Tea have fell by 20% to 25% due to unchecked flow of Nepal Tea into the country.

2. ARACACEAE/ PALMAE

2.1 Coconut

- Eulogized as 'Tree of Heaven or Nature's supermarket or Tree of life or *Kalpavriksha* or Carbon sequestering crop or Mankind's greatest provider in the Tropics or Wonder palm'.
- Spanish word 'coco' means 'monkey face'.
- Genus *Cocos* is monotypic containing only one species *C. nucifera*.
- Most beautiful and useful tree in the world.
- World's largest coconut germplasm: CPCRI.
- Distribution of coconut: Between 27^{0}N and 27^{0}S latitudes and 600 to 900 m altitudes.
- Grown in 93 countries having 12.20 million ha area under cultivation with production of 70,000 million nuts with productivity of 10,345 nuts/ ha.
- Indonesia has highest productivity in terms of output coconut oil/ ha.
- Major growing countries of the world are found in Asia, West Indies, Central and South America, East and West Africa.
- Philippines leads in world area (36.6%) followed by Indonesia (26.9%), India (15.91%) and Sri Lanka.
- It ranks 6th among the different fruits grown in world.
- 2n=32.
- Origin: South East Asia.
- World Coconut Day: 2nd September and theme of year 2020 is 'Invest in Coconut to Save the World'.
- State tree of Goa.
- India contributes 30.49% of world coconut production.
- World production of coir is estimated to be 0.282 million tonnes of which, India contributes 50%.
- In India, during 2019-20, area under coconut (2.08million ha), production (22,168 million nuts) and productivity (10,611 nuts/ ha).
- Maximum productivity is from Maharashtra (20,621 nuts/ha) followed by Chhattisgarh (16,508 nuts/ha), Andhra Pradesh (13,759 nuts/ha), Tamil Nadu (13,423 nuts/ha).
- Major coconut growing state: Kerala (65%) contributing 43% of country's production.
- Kerala, Tamil Nadu, Karnataka, Andhra Pradesh share 91% coconut production in India.
- Utilization of coconut in India: 50% for consumption and religious purposes; 35% for copra preparation; 11% for tender water; 2% for processing and remaining 2% for other purposes.

- Consumption pattern of coconut oil: 46% used as hair oil, cosmetics and others, 40% for edible purpose and 14% for industrial soap purpose.
- Coconut is mostly traded as mature coconuts, tender coconuts, copra and coconut oil.
- Uses of endocarp or coconut shell: Fuel, household utensils, toys, buttons, making activated carbon/ charcoal and Sri Lanka meets 90% of world demand.
- Coconut contributes about 6% of oil requirement of country.
- Bole: Lowermost (60 cm) swollen region of stem.
- Meat: White albuminous endosperm.
- No cambium tissue in roots and stem is observed.
- Tall palms are known as *Cocos nucifera* var. *typica* while dwarf types are *var. nana*.
- Baby coconut is commercially known as 'coco-nana' or 'coconino' or mini coconut or dwarf coconut or coquito nuts or coker nuts or pigmy coconut or monkey coconuts, measuring upto maximum 1 inch. It is native to Philippines.
- Desiccated coconut and coconut flour is utilized in confectionaries and food industries.
- Composition of nut (by weight): Husk i.e. coir (35%), shell (12%), kernel i.e. meat (28%), water (25%).
- Husk forms 35-45% of weight of whole nut.
- About 30% of husk is fiber and 70% is coir dust and used as soil conditioner.
- Coir/ coconut fibre is obtained from mesocarp (husk).
- Coconut fibre is spun into coir yarn by machine or hand and then made into ropes, mats, mattings, nets, bags and bricks for road construction.
- Major constituents of coconut fiber: Lignin and cellulose.
- 11 months old nuts yield higher coir (50-55%) while 9-10 months yield 70% coir.
- Green husk by bacteriological retting (husk soaked in water for 6-8 months) yield mat fiber/ yarn fiber/ white fiber which is made into ropes, mats, nets, bags and bricks for road construction.
- Hardly 41% of fibre is used for various purposes in India and hardly 16% in Konkan region of Maharashtra.
- Task force has been approved in Maharashtra to develop industries based on coir since it earns substantial amount of foreign exchange.

Classification:

I. Lunger (1920)- 7 varieties as-

   i) Virdis- Green nut.

   ii) Rubescence- Grey brown nut.

iii) Macrocarpa- Very big nut.

iv) Rutila- Very thick husk and little endosperm.

v) Euberna- Albino/ ornamental.

vi) Pumila- Green dwarf early bearing.

vii) Regia- Yellow/ orange/ red dwarf.

II John and Narayana (1949)- 5 varieties as-

i) Spicata- Tall, unbranched inflorescence, male flowers absent, spikelets 1 or 2.

ii) Typica- Tall and monoecious.

iii) Androgens- Male palms.

iv) Javanica- Dwarf/ semi-tall, bearing in 4 years.

v) Nana- Dwarf palms bearing in 3 years.

Among 'Nana' varieties, 'Dwarf Orange' is highest and 'Dwarf Yellow' is lowest in pollen production. 'Dwarf Green' is intermediate in pollen production.

III. Freemond *et al.* (1966) – 2 groups.

i) Allogamic- Cross pollinated and Spicata as separate group includes all tall varieties.

ii) Autogamic- Self pollinated and includes all dwarf varieties.

IV. Based on stature- 2 groups viz. (i) Tall (ii) Dwarf.

- Root spread (i.e. feeding zone): Up to 2m radius from base of palm.
- Heliophile plant (sunlight requirement for profuse growth & productivity).
- Copra yield is reduced with sunlight is < 2000 h / annum or 120 h/ month.
- Highly sensitive to shade.
- Salinity tolerance level of coconut: Up to 8 dS/m.
- Fruit type: One seeded fibrous drupe.
- Seed viability: 16 months.
- Wet meat or kernel or endosperm: Obtained from ripe coconut.
- The moisture content of desiccated coconut should be <3%.
- Four months old nut contains maximum quantity of water and sugar concentration in water increases to maximum (8.8%) in 7th month and minimum (1.4%) in 12th month.
- Calorific value of tender coconut water: 17.4 Kcal/ 100 gram water.
- Coconut sap (*Kalparasa* or *neera*) is 'the life essence' of palm tree.
- Coconut water: Liquid endosperm of tender coconut.
- Nutrient composition: Moisture (10.2%), protein (0.9%), -CHO (83.5%), sucrose (71.8%), glucose and fructose (3.7%).
- Composition of coconut water: -CHO (4%), protein and fat (0.1% each), minerals (0.4%).

- Coconut water is rich source of vit. C, cobalamine, cytokinin having pH 4.8-5.3.
- Composition of kernel/ endosperm/ wet meat of ripe coconut: Milk or cream is obtained by squeezing.
- Composition of fresh kernel: Moisture (45%), protein (4%), fat (37%), -CHO (10%), minerals (4%).
- Kurumba: An immature coconut containing refreshing clear liquid.
- Optimum temperature for growth: 27^{0}C with diurnal range of 6-7^{0}C.
- Severe drought at flowering period seals the growing point and cause inflorescence to abort and delays the production of nuts up to 28-30 months.
- Rainfall during first 3 months of nut development determines size of crop and amount of copra and copra weight/ nut/year.
- Interval between male and female phases is less in dwarf and hybrid varieties (so there are increased chances of self pollination)
- Inflorescence: Spadix is produced in every leaf axil and varies from 12-15 per annum.
- Inflorescence consists of main axis (peduncle) with up to 40 side branches.
- *Selection of mother palm*:
  - Age of mother palm for collection of nuts: Regular bearer with 15-40 years (tall) & 12-30 years (dwarf).
  - Good mother palm should have 35-40 fronds i.e. leaves and frond orientation at almost right angle to main trunk and present umbrella like appearance.
- In each inflorescence, there are 30-35 spikelets, each having 25-40 female flowers and 250-300 male flowers.
- A single anther may produce 1,11,000 to 2,21,000 pollen grains.
- Number of pollen grains in individual inflorescence: 85-196 millions.
- In India, female flower production is high during March-May and low in September-January.
- Sex form in tall coconut: Protandry.
- Flower bud differentiation (i.e. primordia of inflorescence) begins in leaf axil and takes 32 months for spathe opening.
- Male flowers: Small, asymmetric, sweet scented, has 6 perianth leaves surrounding 6 stamens.
- Female flowers: Called as 'buttons', large (2.5 cm long), button shaped having 6 fleshy perianth leaves surrounding white tricarpic pistil with 1 ovule.
- Fruit: Large (20-30 cm long), one seeded fibrous drupe.
- Anthesis time: Begin with male flowers at tip of branch.
- Anthesis continuous for 18-20 days (male phase) and anther splits longitudinally.
- Anther dehiscence: 2 weeks from anthesis.

- Pollen viability: 3-5 days after dehiscence under ambient temperature of 25-30^{0}C.
- Freeze dried pollengrains retain viability for 6 months.
- Pollen grains are collected on 3rd and 8th day after opening of spathe.
- Pollen grains are collected by oven drying of male flowers at 40^{0}C for 20 hours.
- Pollen grain size: 40-46 μm.
- Under refrigeration, pollen grains can be stored for 6 months.
- Receptivity of female flowers: Starts from 21stday onwards and continues for 4-7 days.
- Stigma receptivity: After 1-2 days of anthesis up to 3rd day.
- Percentage of female flowers reach maturity under normal condition: 25-40%.
- Genetically, dwarf palms are autogamous while tall palms are allogamous.
- Pollination agents: Wind, insects, house fly, wasp, beetles, honey bees (*Apis indica*, *A. florae*, *A. dorsata*, *A. mellifera*).
- Propagation method: Only through seeds exhibit considerable genetic variation.
- Selection of seed nuts is made from proven gardens of mother palms.
- New technique for rapid propagation of coconut has been developed by Catholic University, Belgium in collaboration with CIAT.
- Aseptic culturing of single developing embryo with PGR gives more number of embryo sprouts (clones).
- Cryo-preservation of these clonal embryos is possible in liquid nitrogen at -196^{0}C temperature for long duration.
- With this advanced technique, it is possible to achieve both, 1) rapid rate of propagation and conservation of biodiversity of coconut.
- On west coast of India, seed nuts are harvested during February-May and nut should be 11 or 12 months old.
- Seed nuts are arranged in shade vertically over a layer of sand and completely covered with it till planting time.
- Seed beds should be long and width is adjusted to accommodate 4-5 rows of nuts only.
- Soaking seed nuts in water for 2 weeks reduces germination period.
- Horizontal planting of seed nuts is found to be best; but vertical planting (stalk end up position) is widely practiced in India.
- Pre-sowing treatment for higher germination: Soaking the seed nuts in water for 2 weeks.
- Planting of seed nuts during monsoon with variable spacing between nuts from 25-38 cm.
- Roots emerge in about 14 weeks from sowing.

- Nuts of tall variety commence germination in 11-12 weeks after planting.
- Nut which fail to germinate within 6 months are discarded.
- Undesirable plants are removed at different stages.
- In India, 9-12 months old seedlings are transplanted.
- Harvesting of coconut: 12-13 months after inflorescence opening.
- Harvesting for tender nut purpose: 8-10 months from fertilization.
- In Malaysia and Thailand, harvesting is done by trained monkeys.
- Seasoning: Storage of nuts under shade for few days.
- Planting distance for sole cropping: 7.5 m x 7.5 m i.e. 177 plants/ ha.
- Central Agriculture Research Institute (CARI) varieties can be planted at 6 m x 6 m.
- Systems of planting viz. Square, triangular, rectangular, quincunx; of which first two are commonly adapted.
- Triangular system accommodates about 15% more palms in a unit area viz. 10.0 m (115 palms/ ha); 9.2 m (140 palms/ ha); 8.0 m (184 palms/ ha).
- Square system is suitable for tall varieties.
- Hedge system: Suitable for seed garden and dwarf varieties.
- In Sri Lanka, double row system of planting accommodate 600 palms/ ha.
- In hedge system of planting, seedlings more than necessary are transplanted in unit area by adapting wider inter-row spacing and closer intra-row spacing.
- Active root zone of coconut utilize 25% of available land.
- Water requirement/ palm through drip irrigation: 30-35 liters (winter); 40-45 liters (summer) with drippers placed at 1.25 m away from bole.
- Water requirement/ palm through ring method (conventional): 160-180 litres (winter season); 200-240 litres (summer season) at 4 days interval.
- Irrigation once in 10 days is essential.
- Total quantity of water lost through transpiration: 90 liters/day.
- Drought at flowering period kills growing point cause inflorescence to abort.
- Application of fertilizers @ 1 kg N, 500 g P and 1 kg K/ palm/ year through drip irrigation in 8 splits from Oct-May is recommended.
- Suitable mixed crops: Cocoa, pepper, cinnamon, clove, nutmeg.
- Suitable cover crops: *Mimosa invisa, Stylosanthes gracilis, Calapogonium mucunoides.*
- Plant growth regulator for enhancing fruit set: NAA @ 200 ppm or 2,4-D @ 60 ppm.
- Harvesting interval time: 45 days (summer) and 60 days (winter).

- Continuously growing central shoot is called as 'cabbage'.
- Coconut has only one growing point with no cambium tissue.
- Bole region: Swollen basal portion of stem at height of 60 cm from ground.
- Stomata confined to lower surface of leaf. About 200 stomata can be observed per sq.m.
- Saturated fatty acids present in coconut oil: Lauric acid and octanoic acid.
- Virgin oil: Coconut milk is filtered and concentrated and then cream is separated by centrifugation.
- Cream is stirred vigorously to get virgin coconut oil by a process called 'phase inversion'.
- Dried kernel is available in two forms-
  1. Ball copra i.e. whole dry kernel.
  2. Cup copra i.e. splitted into two halves in the form of cup.
- Dried copra on crushing produce 65-70% oil and 33-40% oil cake.
- Coconut cake: Solid matter left after extraction of oil from copra and forms 32-40% of copra crushed.
- Monoluron content of coconut oil has anti-HIV property.
- Annual outturn of copra per palm is much higher (23-25 kg/ palm) from exotic tall types but oil content is generally low (65-69%).
- Average copra outturn per nut (Kg): Tall (0.171), Dwarf (green) (0.038); T x D hybrid (0.187).
- Loss of copra: 6% in 11 months old nut, 16% in 10 month & 33% in 9 months old nut.
- Oil percent: Tall (71.7%); Dwarf (65.6%); T x D hybrid (70.1%).
- Oil content in kernel increases from 31-71% in 8-12 months period.
- Reduction in oil percentage in 11, 10 & 9 months old nuts is 5, 15, 33%, respectively.
- As the fruit matures, nut water is partially replaced by meat.
- Fresh weight of meat is maximum during 10th month while weight of dried kernel (copra) is highest in 12th month.
- Milling copra: Copra with < 6% moisture content used for oil production.
- In south India (Kerala), 60-65% of total coconut product is converted to milling copra (copra used for production of oil).
- Commercially manufacturing copra: Milling copra.
- Globally 50% of total coconut production is converted to copra.
- Edible copra fetches higher price than milling copra.
- Problems in cultivation:
  - Shedding of buttons & immature nuts;

  - Production of barren nuts (without or with imperfectly developed kernels);
  - Production of barren nuts is due to defective fertilization resulting in malformation of embryo.
- Average coconut yield: 44 nuts/ palm/ year. Tall (60-80 nuts/ palm/ year in rainfed & 120 nuts/ palm/ year under irrigated condition).
- Boron deficiency is widely observed in India.
- Germplasm collection and *in vitro* conservation from Indian Ocean islands is via storage embryo culture.
- Toddy: Sugar containing juice obtained by tapping the unopened spadix of palm.
- From this vinegar, jaggery, sugar and arrack (alcohol) are prepared.
- Despite its economic importance, coconut genome (~3 gb) is not available & coconut phytoplasma genomes are still not sequenced.
- Fertilizer recommendation by CPCRI: FYM 50 kg + 10: 5: 20 @ 3.5 kg for rainfed tall variety & 6 kg for hybrids and irrigated talls per palm per year.
- To increase production of any hybrid coconuts, apply double dose of potash fertilizers.
- Cleavage polyembryony is reported.
- Drought tolerance traits: Epicuticular wax on leaf, low stomatal frequency, low stomatal resistance, low leaf water potential.
- Earthworm (*Eudrilus* spp.): Efficient in composting coconut and arecanut leaves.
- Use of radio isotope (p^{32}) shows that uptake efficiency is high if P_2O_5 is applied in entire area around palm up to distance of 2 m from hole.
- Tissue culture technique has been successfully attempted at TNAU, Coimbatore.
- By adopting tissue culture technology, multiplication ratio can be enhanced to 1: 20.

Varieties:

- Area under hybrids:< 2-3%.
- CPCRI maintains largest field gene bank.
- CPCRI released 1st hybrid coconut in world.
- Methods of crop improvement: Introduction, artificial self pollination, mass selection, hybridization, selection from among the selfed lines.
- Mass selection i.e. maternal line selection has formed the standard practice from early times.
- Inbreeding depression is not important.
- New method of tree breeding: Paired cross (i.e. both male & female parents are known in controlled hybridization).
- Large number of deleterious recessive gene appear in selfing and hence not promising method of breeding.

- Genetically dwarf palms are autogamous and tall palms are allogamous. While genetically dwarf-green hybrids are both types.
- 1st report of hybrid vigour from India: J.H. Patel (1937) in cross between WCT and CGD.
- Tall x Dwarf hybrids exhibit hybrid vigour for different characters.
- In D x T hybrids, dwarf palms are used as female parent since they are self pollinated and homogeneous.
- Performance of D x T hybrids is always superior over T x D hybrids.
- Male parents used in T x D hybridization: Dwarf Orange, Dwarf Green, Ganga Bondam, Malayan Dwarf Yellow.
- Undesirable traits in T x D hybrids: Alternate bearing, bunch buckling & less drought tolerance.
- D x T hybrids: Most common types in India. Identified in nursery by colour marker (orange or yellow petiole colour), more vigorous, superior in nut & copra characters and more akin to tall type.
- T x T hybrids are late bearer with high yield potential.
- Inbreeding depression does not appear.
- T x D hybrids exhibit heterosis for nut weight, nut water and kernel content.
- Hartland (1957) gave the concept of pre-potent palm. He suggested role of self pollination since parents are homozygous.
- Pre-potent palms: Genetically superior palms which possess sufficient dominant genes with a capacity to transmit growth characters and high yield to progeny.
- Pre-potent palms can be identified based on seedling characters viz. collar girth, leaf production from 5th month after germination.
- Pre-potency: Ability of palm to transmit high yield to its offsprings in spite of open pollination. It may be due to high additive genetic value. Pre-potent male transmitters can be ascertained by using pollens of high yielding palms.
- Sunramam: Commercially grown in Philippines.
- Drought tolerant: Assam Green, Java Giant Fiji.
- Tall types: Kappadam Tall (Chappadan), Komadan, Philippines Ordinary Tall (PHOT), Spicata.
- Dwarf types: Kenthali Orange Dwarf.
- Private farms: DJ Sampoorna.

Name	Breeding method	Features
Central Agriculture Research Institute, Port Blair		
Surya	Variant of Hari Papua	Ornamental purpose; dwarf; yield 105 nuts/ palm/ year
Omkar	Variant of Niu Oma	Ornamental purpose; dwarf; pear shaped nuts; yield 110 nuts/ palm/ year
Chandan	Variant of Nikkore	Ornamental purpose; dwarf; spherical nuts; yield 98 nuts/ palm/ year
Annapurna	Variant of Niu Lekha	Ornamental purpose; dwarf; drought tolerant; 245g copra/nut; 13.7 kg copra recovery/ palm
CPCRI, Kasargod & Regional stations of AICRP on palms		
Laccadive Micro Tall (LMT)	Selection	Irregular bearer; very small sized nuts; yield 180 nuts/palm/ year; suitablefor making ball copra (whole dry kernel) & oil extraction
Chowghat Green Dwarf (CGD)	Selection	Irregular bearer, leathery copra & low oil content; better pollen parent for root wilt resistance
Chowghat Orange Dwarf (COD) 1991	Selection	Indigenous dwarf; 63 nuts/palm; maximum amount of total sugars (7.0 g/100 ml), rich in sodium (20 ppm) & potassium (2,000 ppm); nut water content (350 ml/ nut); ornamental purpose; used as male parent in hybrid production; sensitive to copper
IND-045S	Selection	Dual purpose variety for copra & tender nut; nut contains 438 ml water having TSS-5.85^{0}Brix, total sugars-4.55 g/100 ml; less eriophyid mite infestation (8.87%); yield 118 nuts/ palm/ year; copra yield 25.54 kg/palm/year
IND-048S	Selection	Dwarf; 400 ml water/ nut; TSS - 6.2^{0}Brix, total sugars - 6.7 g/100 ml; yield 123 nuts/ palm/ year
IND-010S	Selection from 'Federated Malay States Tall'	Yield (148 nuts/palm/year, 26196 nuts/ha); 27.23 kg copra/palm, 4820 kg/ ha; dual purpose; suitable for tender nut & copra; drought tolerant
i) D x T hybrids		
Chandra Kalpa (syn. Laccadive Ordinary Tall i.e. LOT) 1985	Selection from 'Tiptur Tall'	Early & irregular bearer; very small sized nuts; prominent 3 sides of nut; yield 150 nuts/palm/ year; annual out-turn of copra/ palm 19.2 kg; low copra content (60 g/nut); 72% oil; good for ball copra production (whole dry kernel) & oil extraction, tapping sweet toddy &tolerant to drought
Chandra Laksha (1984)	LOT x COD	High nut, oil & copra yield; yield 109 nuts/ palm/year; 21 kg copra/palm; 69% oil; tolerant to drought
Chandra Sankara (1984)	COD x WCT	High nut, oil & copra yield; yield 140 nuts/ palm/year; 22.8 kg copra; 68% oil
Chandra Tara (syn. Double Century) 1995	Selection from 'Philippines Ordinary'	National variety; 12 m height; yield 90-200 nuts/palm/year; copra content 198 g/nut with 66% oil

ii) T x D hybrids		
Kera Bastar (2007)	Selection from 'Fiji Tall'	Starts bearing at 80 months; yield 110 nuts/ palm/ year; annual out-turn of copra/ ha 2.97 t;
Kera Sankara (1991)	WCT x COD	High nut, oil & copra yield; yield 106 nuts/ palm; copra yield 21 kg/ palm/ year; 68% oil in copra
Kera Chandra (1995)	Selection from 'PHOT'	Yield 110 nuts/ palm/ year; 20.8 kg /palm/ year; 66% oil; mean copra/ nut 215 g; annual out-turn of copra/ palm 23.4 kg & 69% oil
Kera Keralam (2007)	Selection from WCT	Tall; adaptive to wide range of cultivation zones; comes to flowering in 58 months; oil content 67.8%
Laksha Ganga (PHC-1) 1989	LOT x GGD	Yield 108 nuts/ palm/ year; copra yield 21 kg & oil content 69%
Kera Ganga (PHC-3) 1989	WCT x GBGD	Yield 100 nuts/ palm/year; 69% oil content
Kera Sree (1992)	WCT x MYD	Yield 112 nuts/ palm/year; 66% oil content
Kera Sowbhagya (1993)	WCT x SSAT	Yield 130 nuts/ palm/year; 65% oil content
Kera Sagara (2006)	Selection from 'Seychelles Tall'	Yield 99 nuts/ palm/ year; 67.8% oil content
Ananda Ganga (1989)	ADOT x GBGD	Yield 95 nuts/palm/year; oil content 68%
Kalpa Samrudhi (2009)	MYD x WCT	Yield (117 nuts/ palm/year), copra out turn (25 kg/ palm/ year) & oil yield (3.04 t/ ha); suitable for tender nut purpose
KalpaRaksha (2007)	Selection from 'Malayan Green Dwarf (MGD)'	Yield 65 nuts/ palm/year; easy to climb; resistant to root wilt; suitable for HDP
Kalpa Sree	Selection from 'CGD'	Tender nut water 240 ml/ nut; TSS 4.8^0 Brix; water contain 150 ppm potassium & 22.4 ppm sodium; tolerant to root wilt
Kalpa Sankara	CGD x WCT	Yield (84 nuts/ palm/ year); copra yield (2.5 t/ha); oil yield (1.69 t/ha); tolerant to root wilt
Kalpa Tharu	Selection from 'Tiptur Tall'	High yield (15,750 nuts/ ha/ year) & drought tolerant
Kalpa Dhenu (2007)	Selection from 'Andaman Giant Tall'	Tall; yield 86 nuts/ palm/ year; 20.8 kg copra/ palm; 65.5% oil in copra; tender water 290 ml; oil is higher in lauric acid content; tolerant to drought
Kalpa Prathiba (2007)	Selection from 'Cochin China Tall'	Regular bearer; Tall; yield 91 nuts/ palm/ year; 67% oil; 450 ml tender water; tolerant to drought; promoted as national variety
Kalpa Mitra (2007)	Selection from 'Java Tall'	Tall; yield 80 nuts/ palm/year; 19.3 kg copra/ palm; 66.5% oil; dual purpose national variety; contain 495 ml tender water; drought tolerant
Kalpa Shatabdi	Selection from IND 034	Yield 105/palm/year; copra yield (28.65 kg/ palm/ year); copra content 272 g; contain 612 ml of

		tender water with TSS of 6.12^0 Brix
Kalpa Jyothi (2012)	Selection from MYD	Dwarf; yellow fruits; yield 114 nuts/ palm/ year; copra yield 16 kg/ palm/ year; oil content 61.5%; suitable for tender nut purpose
Kalpa Surya (2012)	Selection from MOD	Dwarf; orange fruits; yield 123 nuts/ palm/ year; copra yield 23 kg/ palm/ year; oil content 67%
Kalpa Haritha (2012)	Selection	Less incidence of eriophyid mite; yield 118 nuts/ palm/ year; copra yield of 25.5 kg/ palm/ year; suitable for dual purpose
Kalpa Sreshta (2014)	MYD x TPT	Yield 167 nuts/ palm/ year; copra yield 36 kg/ palm/ year; tender water (368 ml); TSS-5.89^{0}Brix; suitable for tender nut purpose
Kalpa Ganga (2013)	GBGD x FJT	Semi-tall; yield (120 nuts/ palm/year. 20880 nuts/ha/year); copra yield 3.38 t/ha; oil content 64.4 %
KalpaRatna (2019)	-	Yield (133 nuts/palm/year); copra out turn (24 kg/palm/year); suitable for tender nut purpose
TNAU, Coimbatore (Coconut Research Station, Veppankulam)		
VHC-1 (1982)	ECT x Dwarf Green	Early bearer; yield 98 nuts/ palm/year
VHC-2 (1988)	ECT x MYD	Yield 107 nuts/ palm/ year; oil content 69%
VHC-3 (2000)	ECT x MOD	Yield (156 nuts/palm/year & 22570 nuts/ ha); copra yield (3.65 T); 70% oil
VHC-4 (2015)	LCT × Cochin China Tall (CCNT)	Yield (161 nuts/palm/year, 28014 nuts/ha/year); copra content 149.8 g/ nut; oil content 70%; tender nut water (368 ml); TSS 4.8^{0}Brix
VHC-5 (2013)	LOT x CCNT	1st of its kind in country involving tall parents in India & South Asia
VPM-3 (syn. Andaman Ordinary Tall i.e. ADOT) 1994	Selection from 'Andaman Ordinary' (AO)	Good toddy yielder; yield 72-92 nuts/palm/year; 15 kg copra/palm/year; high oil content; suitable for drought condition
Aliyarnagar Tall-1 (ALR-1) 2002	Selection from 'Arasampatti Tall'	Tall; circular crown shape; starts flowering at 48 months & yield at 66 months; oil content 66.5%; suitable for drought
ALR-2 (2010)	Selection from Tiptur Tall'	Nut bearing in 5½ years; regular bearer; 12 inflorescences/ year; copra wt. 135 g/nut; copra 2.57 t/ha; oil 64.7%; drought tolerant; mod. resistant to rhinoceros beetle, red palm weevil & leaf blight; yield (140 nuts/palm/year).
Dr BSKKV, Dapoli		
Banawali (2002)	Pure line selection from Ratnagiri local collection	Yield 113-120 fruits/ tree; wider adaptability
Pratap (syn. Banawali Green Round i.e. BGR) 1987	Pure line selection from 'Benaulim Tall'	Tall; better pollen parent for coconut; yield (150 nuts/ palm/year); annual out-turn of copra/ palm 12.9 kg; high oil percent (68%)
D x T (2003)	WCT x COD	Dwarf; early bearer; yield (144 nuts/ palm/year); early bearer
Konkan Bhatye Coconut Hybrid-1 (2007)	GBCD x ECT	Tall; bearing starts at 66 months with green colour; oil content 67%; copra yield (22.08 kg/ palm/year; 3.65 t/ha); copra nut 152 g; yield (122 nuts/palm/year; 20,300 nuts/ha/year)
Konkan Avishkar (2008)	GBGD x ECT	High yield with better copra quality; resistant to stem bleeding, leaf blight & bud rot

AAU, Assam		
Kamrupa (syn. Assam Tall) 2001	Selection from 'Assam Green Tall'	Yield (106 nuts/palm/year); copra yield (16.34 kg/palm/year); oil content 64.50%; tolerant to red palm weevil, rhinoceros beetle, stem bleeding, nut rot, crown choking, grey leaf spot; withstand cold injury
Kahikuchi Coconut Hybrid-1 (2007)	MYD x WCT	Semi-tall hybrid; starts bearing at 64 months; 103 nuts/ palm; copra content (172.8 g/nut); 67.4% oil.
BCKV, Kalyani		
Kalyani Coconut-1 (2007)	Selection from 'Jamaica Tall'	Dual purpose & recommended for West Bengal; mod. tolerant to drought; yield (80 nuts/ palm/ year)
Dr YSRHU, Andhra Pradesh		
Godavari Ganga (1991)	ECT x GBGD	Flowering starts 4-5 years of growth; high yielder (140-150 nuts/ palm/year); oil content 68%; mean copra/ nut 230 g
Gowthami Ganga (2007)	Selection from GBGD	Dwarf; most ideal tender coconut variety (446 ml & potassium content 2035 ppm); ornamental purpose; yield (12813 nuts/ ha/ year);oil content 68%; used as parent in production of D x T hybrids
Vasista Ganga (2013)	GBGD x PHOT	Semi-tall; yield (125 nuts/palm/year & 21750 nuts/ha/year); copra yield (21.9 kg/palm/year, 3.88 t/ha); oil content 69%; water in tender nut 395 ml; TSS 6.2^{0}Brix
Anantha Ganga	GBGD x LOT	-
Vynateya Ganga	PHOT x GBGD	Yield 118 nuts/palm/ year; copra content 190 g/nut; 66% oil content
Abhaya Ganga	GBGD x LCT	Yield 136 nuts/palm/ year; copra content 170 g/nut; 72% oil content
Other varieties		
Arasampatti Tall	Selection	High yielding variety of Tamil Nadu
Benaulium Tall	Selection	Oil is most suitable for industrial uses for manufacture of binder, emollient & cosmetics
East Coast Tall (ECT)	Selection	Parent for production of commercial coconut hybrids
Ganga Bondam Green Dwarf (GBGD)	Selection	Used as male parent in hybrid production; resistant to tatipaka disease
Malayan Green Dwarf (MGD)	Selection	Tolerant to root wilt
Malayan Yellow Dwarf (MYD)	Selection	Alternate bearer; high recovery of hybrids due to homozygosity
Malayan Orange Dwarf (MOD)	Selection	Ornamental purpose; sensitive to copper
West Coast Tall (WCT)	Selection	Parent for production of commercial coconut hybrids
Arsikere Tall	Selection	Polyembryonic
Ramganga	GBGD x WCT	Farmer's selection; flowering within 24-30 months; nut water 500-750 ml

Pests and diseases:

- Rhinoceros beetle and Red palm weevil: Most destructive pests.
- Rhinoceros beetle (*Orycetes rhinoceros*):
  - Characteristic geometric cut (inverted 'V' shape) into unopened fronds and spathes.
  - Remove and destroy affected palms.
  - Fill innermost 2-3 leaf axils with mixture of neem seed kernel powder 100 g + fine sand 150 g/ palm during May, September and December.
  - Release of bio-agent: *Orycetes baculovirus* @ 10-15/ ha and grubs by green muscardine fungus.
  - Exotic predator for rhinoceros beetle: *Platymeris laevicollis.*
  - Entomo-pathogenic fungi for rhinoceros beetle: *Metarhizium anisopliae* @ 5 x 10^{11} spores/ m^3 on manure heaps.
  - Application of Chloranraniliprole 0.4% GR @ 5-10 g in leaf axils.
  - Place Napthalene balls @ 12 g/ palm in leaf axil.
  - Establishment of rhinolure traps @ 1 /ha.
- Red palm weevil (*Rhynchophorus ferrugineus*):
  - Avoid making any cuts causing injury & paste it with CoC @ 3 g/ litre.
  - Tissue borer pest of young palms. Oozing out viscous brown fluid.
  - Destroy affected palms.
  - Prophylactic filling of collar region with Chlorpyrifos dust @ 2-3 g mixed with sand.
  - Spray Imidacloprid @ 1 ml/ litre.
  - Trapping of weevil- 'Ferrugineol' pheromone lure @ 1 trap/ ha
- Eriophyid mite (*Aceria guerreronis*):
  - Serious pest. 1st reported in Mexico in 1965 then in Kerala at Ernakulum and Tamil Nadu in 1988.
  - Apply RDF and micronutrients.
  - Raise green manure crops.
  - Apply neem cake and keraprobio in 2 splits.
  - Spray Azadiractin 1% in Jan-Feb and May-June. Neem oil (30 ml in 1 lit) + Teepol in March-April.
  - Soil moisture conservation by burial of coconut husk.
  - Spraying of palm oil suspension @ 1 lit/ palm.
  - Root feeding Fenpyroxymate 5% EC @ 10 ml + 20 ml water/ palm.
- Black headed caterpillar (*Opisina arenosella*):
  - Most destructive (38-60% in Andhra Pradesh in 2018-19).

   - Release of 10-20 parasites of *Goniozus nephantidis* or *Latoia nephanditis* @ 3100-3500 /ha in March gives 100% control. Release of parasitode *Encarsia guadeloupae* and *Bracon bravicornis*.
- Rugose spirelling white fly (*Aleurodicus rugioperculatus*):
   - Severe in dwarf varieties.
   - Use yellow sticky traps and entomopathogenic fungus *Isaria fumosorosea* and predator *Pseudomallada astur*.
- Slug caterpillar (*Macroplectra nararia*): Sporadic pest. Use *Pediobius imbrues*parasitoid
- Coconut leaf beetle (*Brontispa longissima*): Most serious and devastating to young palms in many countries.
- Root grubs: Light trap for beetles.
- Attack of new exotic pest: Bonder nesting white fly in Maharashtra, Kerala, Karnataka, Tamil Nadu and Andhra Pradesh has been confirmed by Institute of Food and Agril. Sciences, Florida (IFAS) in December, 2021. This pest was introduced in 2017 in Port Blair and Andaman and Nicobar Islands and now spread to other parts of the country.
- Leaf eating caterpillar: Predators- *Braconid* and *Bethylid*.
- Coreid bug: Attacks buttons and tender nuts.
- Stem bleeding (*Chalara paradoxa* syn. *Thielaviopsis paradoxa*):
   - Exudation of reddish brown ooze.
   - Remove infected trees.
   - Apply 10% Bordeaux paste.
   - Apply RDF, neem cake 5 kg with 100 g *Trichoderma virens* / palm/ year.
- Coconut wilt/ Thanjavar wilt/ Trunk and root rot/ Basal stem rot/ Anaberoga (*Ganoderma lucidum*):
   - Phytoplasma bleeding patches at base of trunk.
   - Rotting of root and bole region, size of crown is reduced and tree becomes barren.
   - Drenching of Difolatan @ 100 ppm give good control.
- Bud rot (*Phytophthora palmivora*):
   - Yellowing of two young leaves and emitting foul smell.
   - High humidity limits nutrient uptake and favours rapid spread of disease.
   - Rotten parts should be removed & destroyed.
   - Apply talc formulation of *Pseudomonas fluorescens* or *T. viride* in crown region.
   - Bio-agent for bud rot: *Bacillus amyloliguifaci*.
   - Spray CoC @ 3 g/ litre twice at 15 days interval during monsoon.
- Root wilt (Phytoplasma):

- Coconut root wilt was 1st observed in 1882.
- Vector is Lace bug & Leaf hopper.
- Visual diagnostic symptom: Abnormal bending or ribbing of leaflet termed as 'flaccidity' with yellowing and marginal necrosis of leaflet.

- Tatipaka disease:
  - 1st appeared in Tatipaka village of East Godavari district of Andhra Pradesh in 1949. It is due to phytoplasma.
  - Symptoms:Fasciated appearance of leaves due to improper unfolding of leaflets. Abnormal large crown development, tapering stem, unfolding of leaflets and affected trees produce atrophied barren nuts.
- Leaf blight (grey leaf spot) *Pestalotia palmarum*.
- Weligama/ leaf wilt: Phytoplasma disease.
- Cadang-cadang (syn. Yellow Mottle decline): Virus (vector- *Stephanitis typicus*).
- Sulawesi yellows:
- Coconut foliar decay virus: Transmitted by hopper.

Physiological disorders:

- Button shedding/ Barren nuts / Crown chocking: Due to defective fertilization resulting in malformation of embryo and B deficiency. It is high during August-November & more severe on heavy soils than on lighter soils.
- Rosette/ Little leaf: Zn deficiency.

Inheritance of characters:

- Tall stature is controlled by dominant gene.
- Dwarfness is due to single gene of heterozygous penetrance.
- Earliness to bear: Dominant character transmitted usually by dwarf types.
- Size of nut, husk and shell percentage, copra weight and its oil content: Polygenic.
- Large fruit size dominant to small; spindle fruit shape dominant to oblate type; green and brown petiole colour dominant to yellow, orange or red; green fruit colour dominant to brownish-red or grey-brown and grey copra colour is dominant to black.
- Dwarf Orange/ Yellow as female parent carries general marker to identify pure dwarfs in nursery.

2.2 Arecanut

- Eulogized as 'Betel nut or *Supari*'.
- Raw arecanut is used as *supari* for masticatory/ chewing purposes, while processed nuts are used in *gutkha* industry.
- Important commercial crop in South East Asia.
- Areca word is taken from the Malayan language means the 'cluster of nuts'.

- Country having highest area under arecanut: Indonesia.
- More than half of the world arecanut production comes from Indonesia.
- Other major producers: Myanmar, Bangladesh, Indonesia, Malaysia, Sri Lanka, China, India, and Thailand.
- World productivity: 1.287 t/ha.
- China ranks 1st in productivity with 3.752 t/ha while India ranks 4th in productivity (1.189 t/ha).
- India dominates the world in area (58%) and production (53%) of arecanut.
- Per capita availability in India: 1.58 g/ adult/ day.
- Major arecanut producing state: Karnataka (40%) followed by Kerala (28%), Assam (20%).
- 2n=32.
- It plays prominent role religious, social, cultural functions & economic life of people in India.
- Origin: Malayan Archipelago/ Indonesia.
- Arecanut can be grown up to an elevation of 1000 m MSL but at higher altitudes it is unproductive.
- Cultivation is confined to 28^{0}S and S of equator.
- It is best adapted to coastal regions and grown in areas receiving annual rainfall of 750-4500 mm.
- Optimum temperature for growth: 14-36^{0}C but growth is adversely affected by temperatures below 10^{0}C and above 40^{0}C.
- Nuts harvested from high altitudes have soft kernel and do not possess sufficient weight.
- In sole cropping, 70% land area and 40% solar radiation is wasted.
- Transmits 40% light through its canopy when planted at 2.1 m^2 planting.
- RDF: 100: 40: 40 kg NPK/ palm/ year.
- Root spread: Up to 1m radius.
- Stem is sensitive to sunlight.
- Inflorescence: Spadix.
- Each spadix bears 100-125 flowers.
- Palm produces 6 new leaves per year.
- Economic part: Edible endosperm.
- Fruit type: Single seeded berry.
- Male phase lasts for 25-46 days and female phase for 3-10 days. Overlapping of phase leads to self pollination.

- Pollination agent: Honey bees and wind.
- Fruit set: 12 to 40%.
- About 30% female (button) flowers set fruits (nuts).
- Propagation: Only through seeds.
- Age of mother palm for collection of nuts to raise nursery: >10 years.
- The minimum nut yield specified for mother palm is 300 for Kerala and 700 for Tamil Nadu.
- Only fully ripe nuts with heavier seed nuts (>35 g) and seedlings with 5 or more number of leaves should be selected for planting.
- Time taken for seed germination: 40 days.
- Sprouts are retained in primary nursery till they produce 2-3 leaves which usually take 3-4 months.
- Seedlings with higher selection index value are selected for planting.
- Selection index = Leaf number x 40 – seedling height.
- Generally 12-18 months old seedlings are preferred for transplanting.
- Planting in September-October is recommended.
- Spacing of 2.7 m x 2.7 m is optimum.
- Palms are highly susceptible to sun scorching.
- Quick growing shade plants are planted on southern and western sides of garden.
- Young seedlings are best protected by raising banana crop during early years.
- Inter/ mixed cropping of banana, cocoa, betel vine, black pepper, pineapple, elephant foot yam is more economical.
- Highly profitable intercrop: Black pepper.
- Cover crops: *Mimosa invisa, Stylosanthes gracilis* and *Calapogonium muconoides.*
- Irrigation: About 175 litres of water/ palm is applied in each irrigation.
- Drip irrigation is recommended for efficient water use.
- Watering once in 7 days during November-December, once in 6 days during January-February and once in 3-5 days during March-May is recommended.
- Average pre-bearing age: 5-8 years.
- Colour of fruit during its growth changes from green to different shades of yellow & red during ripening.
- Time taken from flowering to fruit maturity: 240-270 days or 25-37 weeks or 8-9 months.
- Harvesting of nuts: 45-50 days interval in 3 pickings.
- Tender nuts are harvested from July-December.

- Ripe nuts are harvested from December-March or from May to July.
- Three to four pickings are done during the whole season.
- Stage of harvesting depends on type of product to be prepared:

  a) To produce kalipak: about 6-7 months old nuts which are immature, dark green & soft are harvested.

  b) When the end use of chali or kottapak, fully ripe dried nuts are harvested.
- Hardening of arecanut during maturity is due to formation of polysaccharides.
- Size grades (decreasing order): Moti, Srivardhan, Jamnagar, Jini.

Uses of arecanut constituents and byproducts:

- Acid extracted from areca nut used in preparation of black ink: Tannic acid.
- Astringency: Polyphenols and tannins.

1. Tannins:

   a) Polyphenols/ tannins form major constituents of nut.

   b) Tender nut contains 30 to 37% tannins, while ripe nuts have only 16 to 22%.

   c) Areca tannins obtained as byproduct from tender nut processing is utilized for dying clothes & ropes, for making black writing ink, adhesive in plywood manufacturing and even as food colour.

2. Fats:

   a) Nuts contains 8-12% fats, which is rich in myristic acid.

   b) It is substitute for vanaspati in preparations of sweets and biscuits.

3. Alkaloids:

   a) Arecanut has 1.5% of alkaloids viz. arecoline, (accounts for 0.24% & lowers blood sugar) arecaidine, guvacine, iso-guvacine & arecolidine.

   b) Alkaloids possess anti-bacterial & anti-helminthic properties.

4. Areca husk:

   a) Husk constitutes 60-80% of total weight of fresh nut.

   b) Plastic boards, brown wrapping paper, hard boards are prepared from husk.

   c) It is a good source of furfural and xylose for industrial applications.

5. Areca stem and leaf sheath is useful as building material, making plyboards, making cups & plates as substitute to paper plates.

Typically processed products:

- Chali/ Kottapak/ Dry kernel/ White arecanut:

  ° Most processed and popular product in Northern and Western India especially in Kerala, Karnataka, Assam & Maharashtra.

- o Trade type arecanut.
- o Ripe nuts (9 months old) are sun dried for 35-40 days then dehusked and marketed as whole nut.
- o Optimum moisture content is around 12%.
- o To facilitate drying and dehusking, nuts are cut into 2 halves & sundried for 10 days.
- o Kernels are scooped out & given final drying.
- o Mechanical driers can be used to make chali.
- o Drying takes 60-70 h over a period of 7-8 days at 45-75^{0}C.

- Kalipak:
  - o Popular in Kerala and Karnataka.
  - o It is prepared from immature dark green nut (6-7 months old).
  - o Tender nuts are dehusked & cut into pieces-boiled & dried.
  - o 'Kali' is the thick concentrated extract obtained after 3-4 batches of boiling.
  - o Pieces are given coatings with kali till they have glossy appearance and reduces tannin content.
  - o Kalipak is known by different names depending on number, shape & size of cut as:-
    - a) *Api* or *Unde* (without any cuts).
    - b) *Batlu* (transverse cut into halves)
    - c) *Choor* (several longitudinal cuts)
    - d) *Pudi* (both longitudinal & transverse cuts) &
    - e) *Erazel* (transverse thick slices).
- Iylon:
  - o Mainly consumed in Tamil Nadu and Andhra Pradesh.
  - o Made from green & slightly matured nuts, which are cut transversely into 5-6 discs.
  - o It is unboiled type is well known in trade & without 'kali' coating.
- Nuli / Red arecanut:
  - o It is made from very tender nuts.
- Pareha:
  - o It is dried ripe nut product (similar to chali) is popular in Kerala & Karnataka.
- Scented supari:
  - o Popular in north and central India.
  - o It is made both from chali & kalipak.

° Dried nuts are broken into bits.

° Essential oil of spices & synthetic flavours, rose essence or menthol are added.

° These are packed in butter paper/ plastic strips/ tins/ aluminium pouches.

Species:

- Species plantarum, areca has been given status of monospecific genus.

Species	Features
Areca triandra	Originated in Indonesia & mostly used in breeding; ornamental value due to suckering habit & red fruit colour
A. concinna	Suckering palm & scarlet red fruit colour; chewed in Sri Lanka
A. catechu	Only cultivated species used for masticatory.

- Botanical varieties are recognized based on size and shape of fruits and kernel as-

  i) *A. catechu* var. *communis*

  ii) *A. catechu* var. *silvatica*

  iii) *A. catechu* var. *batanensis*

  iv) *A. catechu* var. *longicarpa*

  v) *A. catechu* var. *deliciosa*: Yields sweet kernels from Mysore.

Varieties:

- Seed farm to produce parental lines and quality planting material: Kidu, Karnataka.
- Interspecific hybridization between *A. catechu* and *A. triandra*: F_1 express hybrid vigour for number of female flowers, spadix length and stem girth but show high sterility.
- Area under hybrids < 2-3%.

Name	Breeding method	Features
CPCRI Regional station, Vittal		
Mangala (VTL-3) 1973	Selection from material introduced from China	Semi-tall, round nuts; higher fruit set; yield (8.8 kg ripe nuts/ palm/ year; dry kernel (chali) 3 kg/ palm/ year); good chewing & marketing quality
Su Mangala (VTL-11) 1985	Selection from material introduced from Indonesia	Tall with drooping habit; yield (12.93 ripe nuts/ palm/ year; chali yield (3.28 kg/ palm/ year); high recovery of dry nut (26.50%); tolerant to burrowing nematode
Sree Mangala (VTL-17) 1985	Selection from material introduced from Singapore	Tall with drooping habit; oblong to round nuts; yield (12.82 kg ripe nuts /palm/ year; 3.18 kg dry kernel palm/ year); tolerant to burrowing nematode
Swarna Mangala (2006)	Mohitnagar x HD hybrid (Selection from VTL-12)	Dwarf variety; chali yield (3.88 kg / palm/ year)
Madhura Mangala (VTL-62)	Selection	Chali yield (3.54 kg/ palm/ year; 4500-5000 kg dry kernel/ ha/year); suitable for tender nut & white nut purpose

Shata Mangala (VTL-146)	Selection	Dry kernel yield (3.91 kg/palm/ year) & tender nut yield (3.26 kg/palm/year)
Mohitnagar (1991)	Selection made from indigenous collection from West Bengal (VTL-60)	Indigenous to West Bengal; greater uniformity; bunch well spread; yield (dry kernel 3.67 kg/ palm/ year; & 15 kg ripe nuts/ palm/ year)
VTLAH- 1 (2006)	Hybridization & selection of 'Hirehalli Dwarf x Sumangala'	Dwarf; chali yield 2.54 kg/ palm/year
VTLAH-2	Hybridization & selection of 'Hirehalli Dwarf x Mohitnagar'	Dwarf; chali yield 2.64 kg/ palm/year
Kahikuchi	Selection from VTL-64	Grown in Assam; chali recovery 25.16%
Nalbari (VTL-75)	Selection	Regular bearer; yield (dry kernel (chali) 4.15 kg/ palm/ year); fresh nut recovery 25.18%
CARI, Portblair		
Cal-17/ Samrudhi (1995)	Selection from Andaman Nicobar Islands (VTL-37)	Tall; bold nuts; yield (18.89 kg ripe nuts /palm/ year & dry kernel yield 4.34 kg/ palm/ year); recommended for Andaman and Nicobar Islands
Dr BSKKV, Dapoli		
Sreevardhan (1998)	Selection from Shrivardhan village	Semi-tall; indigenous to Maharashtra; bearing starts from 4th year; marble white kernel, tastier endosperm rated as best quality; higher content of polysaccharides & polyphenols ; dry kernel yield 3.54 kg /palm/ year; 4,500-5,000 kg dry kernels/ ha/ year
UHS, Bagalkot (HRS, Sirsi)		
Sirsi Arecanut Selection-1 (SAS-1) 1995	Selection from 'Sirsi Tall'	Suitable for tender nut & ripe nut processing; yield (18 kg ripe nuts/ palm/ year; 4.6 kg chali/palm/year)
Sirsi Arecanut Selection-2 (SAS-2)	Selection from 'Sirsi Tall'	Yield (4.6 kg chali/palm/year; tender nut yield 4.22 kg/ palm i.e. 55.3 q/ha); tender nut wt. 4.26 g; suitable for tender nut & chali processing; tolerant to koleroga
Sirsi Arecanut Selection-3 (SAS-3)	Selection from 'Sirsi Tall'	Yield (6.2 kg chali/palm/year; tender nut yield 4.08 Kg/ palm i.e.53.4 q/ha); tender nut wt. 3.18 g; suitable for tender nut & chali processing; tolerant to koleroga
Other varieties		
Thirthahalli	Selection	Tall; small & elongated nuts; yield (chali 2.6 kg/palm/ year); grown extensively in Karnataka; preferred for tender nut processing
Hirehalli Dwarf	Natural dwarf mutant	Round to oval nuts; yield (1.2 kg chali kg/palm/ year)
Hirehalli Local	Selection	Grown in Karnataka
Mettupalayam	Selection	Grown in Tamil Nadu
South Kanara Local	Selection	Tall; round, large sized nuts; yield (7 kg ripe nuts/ palm/ year & 1.5 kg chali/ palm/ year); largely grown in Karnataka & Kerala; mainly used for chali purpose
Sagar	Selection	Tall; small & round nuts; yield (7 kg ripe nuts/ palm/year)

Pests, diseases and disorders:

- Spindle bud (*Calvalhoia areceae*): Major pest.
- Mahali/ Koleroga (*Phytophthora arecae*): Nut shedding and water soaked regions.
- Bud rot (*Phytophthora palmivora*): Spindle appearance.
- Anaberoga (*Ganoderma lucidum*): Oozing.
- Yellow leaf disease (MLO): Spindle bug and Water logging condition.
- Inflorescence die back (*Colletotrichum gloeosporioides*):
- Bacterial leaf stripe (*Xanthomonas campestris* pv. *arecae*):
- Band or Hidimundige: Improper drainage.
- Nut splitting.
- Stem breaking/ sun scorching.

2.3 Palmyrah palm/ *Tadgul*

- Eulogized as 'Tree of life or *Kalpaka viruchum*'.
- 2n=36.
- Botanical name: *Borassus flabellifer*.
- Origin: Tropical Africa.
- State tree of Tamil Nadu (1978).
- Most abundant palm found in the world, next to coconut.
- Most primitive among palms.
- Tropical crop can withstand low rainfall, high temperature, drought and heavy winds.
- Source of sweetening agent since time immemorial.
- Palm fibre is exported to > 33 countries.
- Major importing countries of palmyrah fibre: Japan, UK, West Germany, Belgium, Poland.
- Trunk is suitable for poles.
- Leaves are used for thatches, fans, mats, hats and basket work.
- Writing and printing papers are prepared from leaf stalks.
- Sex form: Dioecious.
- Spadix is branching and perianth is double whorled.
- Fruit type: Three seeded drupe.
- Method of propagation: Seed.
- Seeds are monoembryonic and occurrence of polyembryony is also reported.
- Peak flowering month: May.
- Seeds from ripe fruits (80-90%) germinate within 22 days after planting.

- Criteria for selection of mother palm for seed collection:
  a) Between 30-40 years age group.
  b) Dwarf and stout trees with green compact leaves.
  c) Fruit bunches are heaped for 5-6 days to ferment, which facilitates easy removal of mesocarp.
  d) Seeds selected from single nut give female trees & double nuts give one each of female & male tree. Tri-nuts give 2 male and 1 female tree.
  e) Collect 10-15% double nuts to maintain female and male ratio.
  f) Plumule from germinating seed nut goes down into earth as tuber.
  g) When tuber matures, the rooting starts.
- Seed nut raised in nursery give higher (98%) germination than conventional method (56-65%).
- Nursery raised in low cost humid chamber helps in better growth of seedlings.
- Hardening of seedlings in nursery reduces establishment period in main field.
- Best season for *in situ* planting: August-September.
- Planting systems: a) Square (3m x 3m) 450 palms/ ha, b) Triangular spacing at 3 m accommodates 500 palms/ha.
- In dry lands, leaf mulching & pitcher irrigation may be followed to conserve moisture.
- Legumes as cover crops & groundnut, tapioca, ginger, sweet potato, fruit crops as intercrops and jasmine as border crop can be grown.
- Leaf pruning in initial years should be restricted to 1 or 2 and no leaf cutting during summer months.
- Average pre bearing age: 10-12 years.
- Two variants: Black colour and red colour.
- Tending: Act of periodically removing the persisting leaf bases.
- Both male and female palms mature 10-12 years after planting.
- Tapping: Extraction of sap or neera from inflorescence is the most economic product.
- Tapping is done during January and on 7th day onward neera comes out from male inflorescence.
- In female palms, inflorescence bracket is removed before opening and tapped and from cut tip portion, neera starts flowing from 6th day onwards.
- Normally female spathe is tapped for a longer period (April-December).
- Method of extraction of tapping in male palm:
  1. Aripanni (1-1 ½ months old inflorescence) and
  2. Vallupanni (1 month old inflorescence).
- Thattupalai: Young female inflorescence.

- Kaivetty: 2-3 months old female inflorescence.
- From female palms, food products like neera + fruits + edible tubers from seeds are available.
- Yield of neera: Based on soil type, genetic diversity & environmental conditions, yield varies from 10-12 to 18-20 litres/ palm/day.
- Fruit jelly from tender fruits harvested during summer and juice with fibrous yellow pulp from matured fruits harvested after summer.
- Neera, toddy, vinegar, sugar, jaggery and candy are edible products of palm besides wood, leaves, fibre, roots, fruit pulp & fruit fibres are commercial products.
- Nutrient composition of fruit: Moisture (8.9%), protein (1.1%), -CHO (88.3%), sucrose (77.3%), glucose and fructose (2.2%).
- Neera or *padaneer* contains 13-16% sugar, vit. C and vit. Bcomplex i.e. thiamin, riboflavin, niacin and calcium.
- Neera from male trees contain 13% sugar (sucrose) and from female trees contain 16% sugar.
- Sweet juice yields 8-10% jaggery.
- 8 litres of neera is required to produce 1 kg jaggery.
- Use of organic manures 25 kg + SSP 500 g / palm increases yield of neera by 14%.
- Jaggery prepared from palmyrah grown in calcareous soils is more sweet.
- When palms start flowering (10-15 years old) juice is collected.
- Season of collection of juice: November-February.
- Taste of neera is affected by pH.
- Sweet neera becomes slight bitter in taste at pH>10.
- If pH of juice is 8 to 8.1, it does not easily ferment.
- Calorific value of neera: 113.3 Kcal.
- Calorific value of palm sugar: 398 Kcal/ 100g.
- Toddy: Natural uncontrolled fermented product of sugary sap i.e. neera or palm nectar (alcohol content 5-8%).
- Toddy is used to produce 'arrack' by pot still distillation.
- Sweet toddy with pH of 6-7 sterilized and inoculated with wine yeast produce clear straw coloured wine.
- Palm sugar: Boiling of stained and clarified sap to 108-110^{0}C @ 85^0 brix. It contains vit. C and vit. B_{12}.
- Nungu: Tender palmyra fruit-Rich source of carbohydrate, P, Fe, vit. C and riboflavin.
- Fresh sap is boiled to form concentrated crystal sugar candy (*talmishri*) has medicinal value.
- Palm industry is important in terms of productivity, income generation and employment.

- Fruit contains 29.66% pulp and 6.55% fibre.
- Naar (fibre): Fibrous portion extracted from stalk of fronds.
- Palmyrah fibre has high commercial value and 80% of total produce is exported to over 33 countries worldwide.
- Andhra Pradesh accounts for 60% of total export of fibre from country followed by Tamil Nadu.
- Geo-tagging of palmyrah palm has been made mandatory to tap neera and its sale, since yield depends on genetic diversity of palm. On-line permits will be issued only to license holders.

Varieties:

- Indigenous and exotic germplasm is maintained at TNAU.
- SVPR-1: Selection from Srivilliputhur Local. Semi-dwarf variety of TNAU.
- BF-4, BF-6, BF-16, BF-23, BF-34, BF-36: Elite genotypes.

Diseases and pests:

- Bud rot (*Pythium palmivorum*): Damage apical portion.
- Dwarf crown: Mycoplasma disease.
- Rhinoceros beetle (*Orycetes rhinoceros*): Serious pest.
- Red palm weevil (*Rhynchophorus ferrugineus*): Serious pest.

2.4 Oil palm/ *Tel tad* / Red oil palm

- Eulogized as 'Small holders irrigated crop or Crop for future'.
- Humid tropical palm.
- Grown mostly within 10^0N or 10^0S of the equator.
- Grown commercially in latitudes of 17^0 from the equator.
- Crop is grown in 42 countries worldwide and palm oil shares 40% of the world's trade in edible oil.
- Major importers of palm oil: India, China, Pakistan, Middle-East countries & European Union.
- World's largest producer and exporter of palm oil: Malaysia and Indonesia. Account for 90% of both global production and global trade in palm oil.
- The share of Indonesia in global production of palm oil is 30% of which 40% is exported.
- Oil palm is the most productive of all oil crops, with average yield of 3-4 tonnes of mesocarp oil/ ha/ year in major producing countries.
- The productivity is 3-8 times more than most oil seed crops (< 1 t/ha/year).

- Oil yield from oil palm is over 6 times more than oil yields from commercially grown rapeseed.
- Energy balance expressed by ratio of energy output to input is wider for oil palm than other commercially grown oil crops.
- India in world palm oil industry (million tons):
  a) Annual oil production: 0.2% share.
  b) Annual oil imports: 13.2% share.
  c) Annual oil consumption: 11.5% share.
- During 2018-19, India imported 8.85 million ton of crude and refined oil palm oil.
- India depends on palm oil imports of over 25% of its annual edible oil requirement.
- High-value palm palm kernel oil is marketed as lauric oils throughout the world.
- Introduced as an ornamental palm at National Botanic Garden, Kolkata during 1848 out of botanical curiosity.
- Attained status of commercial plantation crop during 1960 at Kerala.
- Highest and cheapest oil yielding crop among perennial oil yielding crops.
- Palm oil is the 2nd most produced oil in the world after soybean.
- Peak production period of palm oil: April to December.
- Maximum area: Andhra Pradesh.
- Godrej Agrowet: Private company in India in palm oil industry.
- Area under cultivation in India: 61,700 ha.
- African oil palm supply 30% world's edible oil.
- C_3 photosynthesis crop.
- Soil suitable: Loamy soils rich in humus. Highly saline, alkaline, water logged & coastal sandy soils are unsuitable.
- Ideal soil pH for growth: 4-7.
- Thrives well in annual temperature range of 19-33^{0}C and rainfall of 2500-4000 mm/ annum, more than 80% humidity and sunshine hours of not less than 5 hours/ day.
- Optimum temperature for growth: 22-24^{0}C (min.) to 29-33^{0}C (max.).
- Optimum humidity for cultivation: 60%.
- Highly cross pollinated.
- Flowering starts 14 to 18 months after planting.
- Inflorescence: Compound spike or spadix.
- Male and female inflorescences are produced separately.
- Palm is monoecious with a tendency towards dioecious habit.
- Period between sex differentiation and anthesis: 2 years.

- Sex ratio: Partly genetic and partly determined by environmental conditions at time of floral differentiation.
- Propagation method: Seed.
- Seeds are extracted by retting using depericarper.
- Old system of raising seedlings in soil bed is replaced by polybags nursery and can be of single or double stage system.
  - i) In single stage system, sprouts are directly placed in bigger polybags (500 gauge) of size 40 x 35 cm and nurtured till planting. Precise stage of planting sprouts is 10-14 days from germination. It is best method.
  - ii) In double stage system, sprouts are first planted in small sized polybags and later planted in bigger bags and maintained till field planting.
- Seeds can be stored in polyethylene bags for 6 months without loosing viability.
- Seed germination is poor and takes several months for germination, results in sporadic germination.
- Seed dormancy is removed as pre-heating seeds in heating chamber at 39-40^{0}C for 80 days.
- Heat treated seeds are again soaked in runner water for 5 days to enhance early germination.
- Days required for seed germination: 10-12 with 90-95% germination.
- F_1 hybrid seed of Tenera types is produced by companies specializing in oil palm breeding.
- Sprouted seeds raised in hi-tech nurseries are also imported from other countries for planting.
- Selection of seedlings: 10-14 months old nursery raised seedlings (1-1.3 m height) having 13 functional leaves & good collar girth are selected for commercial planting.
- System of planting: Triangular planting system at (at 9m x 9m x 9m) accommodate 143 palms/ ha.
- Best period of planting: June to December.
- Juvenile period: 3 years and intercrops like pulses, cereals, vegetables and grasses can be grown.
- Irrigation requirement: 150-200 litres water/ day/palm.
- Any physiological stress shifts sex ratio in favour of male flowers and productivity is reduced.
- In undulating terrains, drip/ micro-sprinkler is advantageous.
- Mulching with organic material is widely practiced.
- Growing of sunhemp & use of weedicide is highly recommended.
- Branching is due to damage in apical cells.

- 'Deli Dura' is used around the world as a female line for production of seeds.
- Continuously growing central shoot (cabbage) is edible.
- Pollinating agent: Weevil (*Elaeidobius kamerunicus*).
- Assisted pollination refers to hand pollination for proper fruit set.
- Basin management: Basins are widened every year & accumulation of soil at collar region is avoided.
- Active root growth zone in basin is kept weed free.
- Sprays of Glyphosate / Monouron/ Diuron/ Paraquat/ Atrazine twice a year controls weeds.
- Inter crops/ cover crops helps in soil and water conservation & checks weed growth.
- Coconut husk/ sugarcane trash/ plastics can be used as mulch.
- Severe pruning of leaves affects growth & yield and is discouraged.
- Ablation/ Disbudding: Removal of male and female flowers produced in early stage of plantation is recommended to gain adequate stem girth, vigour and development of root system.
- It starts about 14 months after field planting and continues until about 26th month, when 70% of the palms are producing inflorescence.
- Usually 4-5 weeks interval is kept between two successive ablation rounds.
- Stripping: Removal of berries from bunches after harvest.
- Each palm produces 24 leaves annually and frond pruning drastically reduces yields.
- Frond pruning helps in easy visual assessment of fruit ripeness, harvest, minimizing loss of loose fruits which are retained in frond bases.
- In juvenile stage, pruning is confined to removal of senescent and useless fronds lying close to soil surface.
- When inflorescence starts developing, two whorls of fronds are left below the lowest developing inflorescence.
- This system continues up to 10th year and from 11th year single frond whorl below the lower most bunch is retained.
- Pruning is organized in such a way that about 32-35 top leaves are left undisturbed on adult palms.
- Flowering starts 14-18 months after planting.
- Period from flowering to harvesting of ripe fruits: 5-6 months.
- First harvest at 36 months after planting.
- Harvesting: Most important activity of whole production process of oil palm because of its high cost (18%) of total cost of farm.
- Highest concentration of oil occurs during final weeks of development of fruit i.e. a week before harvesting.

- Harvesting index: Fruits in a bunch turn yellowish-orange, dropping off 5-10 fruits from each bunch, when pressed hard, orange coloured oil exudes from fruit.
- Correct stage of harvesting (i.e. full ripe stage 80%) is very important.
- Delayed harvesting of bunches cause conversion of fats into free fatty acids and glycerol.
- Permissible limit of free fatty acid (FFA) in food grade palm oil: 5%.
- High FFA causes oil inedible, faster rancidity, colour fixing and increased refining loss.
- Mesocarp or pulp comprises 35-95% fruit with 35-60% oil containing 10-20% fibres.
- Oil recovery in India: 15-17%.
- Oil yield/ palm = Bunch weight ÷ Palm X Fruits/ bunch X Mesocarp/fruit x Oil/ mesocarp.
- Average productivity: 4-6 T oil/ha/year.
- FFB (Fresh fruit bunches); EFB (Empty fruit bunches); RBD (Refined bleached de-odoured); POME (Palm Oil Mill Effluent).
- Expected productivity: 20-25 T FFB/ ha after 6th year.
- Under irrigated conditions, yield level up to 30 T of FFB/ ha/year have been recorded.
- Yield of clonally propagated elite progenies: 20-30% more than seedling origin.
- Number of bunches produced/ palm/year: 10-12 (20-25 t/ha).
- Bunch weight varies from 60-100 kg.
- *Oil palm produces* 2 *distinct types* of edible vegetable *oils* viz. Crude p*alm oil* (extracted from fleshy orange-red mesocarp or fruit pulp) and kernel oil (from kernel & potential source of lauric acid).
- ***Steps involved in palm oil extraction from mesocarp of fruits*:**

a) Sterilization:

   i) Fruits are steam sterilized immediately (within 24 hours. of bunch harvesting since mesocarp is highly perishable) for 30-60 min. at 45 psi to avoid FFA formation, deactivate lipase (fat splitting) enzyme, soften the tissue for better digestion, loose the fruits to facilitate stripping, to coagulate protein, to obtain edible quality raw oil and to kill microorganisms.

   ii) Threshed fruits are cooked/ sterilized using high temperature with steam pressure @ 3 kg/cm^2 for 40-60 min.

b) Digestion process: It is process of releasing oil in the fruit mesocarp through rupture of oil bearing cells. This process also frees nuts from fibres. Oil from digested material is extracted by dry method (mechanical press) or wet method (hot water) to leach out oil.

c) Clarification: It is done to separate oil from its impurities. Purified and vacuum dried oil is stored in tanks around 50^{0}C.

d) Vacuum drying: To reduce moisture level up to 0.1 to 0.15.

e) This oil is called as 'crude palm oil', which in refining becomes palm oil.

- Oil content in mesocarp is strongly related with fruit ripeness.
  - Oil is extracted from mesocarp (70-90%) and kernels (10-30%) through wet rendering process.
  - Oil extracted from mesocarp is known as 'Crude Palm Oil'; which on refining becomes palm oil commercially known as 'Palmolein'.
  - Palmolein extracted from palm oil has thick consistency, flavour, red colour & high smoke point & needs further purification.
  - Crude palm oil is rich in vit. A and E and cholesterol free. It is utilized in diets to overcome vit. A deficiency in children. Rich in palmitic acid.

Dietary value/ 100 gram edible portion

	Oil palm fruit	Palm oil
Water (%)	26	0.5
Calories	540	878
Protein (%)	1.9	0
Fat (%)	58.4	99.1
Carbohydrate (%)	12.5	0.4
Crude fiber (%)	3.2	0
% of US RDA		
Vitamin A	3.5	2.3
Thiamin	13.3	2.0
Riboflavin	5.6	Trace
Niacin	7.0	-
Vitamin C	26.7	-
Calcium	10.3	0.9
Phosphorus	5.9	1.0
Iron	45	55
Sodium	2.4	-
Potassium	5.3	-

- *E. oleifera* produces oil with lower melting point (22^{0}C), higher iodine value and unsaturation (80%) giving large liquid fraction which increases commercial value of oil.
- Kernel oil i.e. oil extracted from palm nut is recovered by pressing of cake. It is utilized for culinary as well as industrial purposes (bio-fuel), in production of margarine and cooking fat like vanaspati. Oil is used in manufacture of biscuits, ice-creams, soaps, detergents and shampoos.

***Steps involved in palm oil recovery from kernels*:**

- Nuts are separated from fibres.
- Kernels are broken into small fragments and to flaking in roller mill,

- o Kernel flakes are conveyed to stack cooker for steam conditioning to separate oil from meal.
- o Meals are cooked to moisture content of 3% at 104-110^{0}C.
- o Cooked meal is fed to screw pressing for oil extraction through barrel.
- o Oil clarification is done through filler press prior to bulk storage.
- o Kernel oil is similar to coconut oil in fatty acid composition and fetches premium price.

- Recovery of kernel oil: 2% on fresh fruit bunch (FFB) basis.
- Increasing the level unsaturation: Diversification in the use of palm oil.
- End product of refining methods: RBDPO (Refined bleached and deodorized palm oil).
- Fruit contain only one seed.
- Mantle fruits (i.e. abnormal fruit type) are rare & occurs due to single dominant mutation.
- Mantled fruits has more mesocarp/ bunch.
- Mantling is advantageous for delayed harvesting.
- Bunch failure can be problem with genetically mantled palms.
- Parthenocarpic fruits are reported in mantle fruited tenera palm & Surinam oleifera palm.
- Economic life of palm: 30-35 years.
- Matured plantation (8-9 years old) yields 20-25 tonnes of FFB's / ha.
- OP seeds are successfully regenerated through de-operculum germination technique.
- *In vitro* clonal propagation suffers a setback due to abnormal flower development when palms are transferred to field.
- Tissue culture technology has potential to develop bi-clonal seeds.
- Cryopreservation: Embryoids can be stored for 15 months.
- Malaysian Palm Oil Board (MPOB) has developed GISH technique.
- MPOB has taken initiative to produce high carotene content planting material PS4.

Species:

- Genetic resources: Oil palms with distinct characters like thornless, mantled fruited tenera and oleiferas are reported.
- *Elaeis* is derived from Greek word '*elaion*' meaning oil while species name '*guineensis*' shows its origin from Guinea coast.
- *E. guineensis*: Grown as wild, semi-wild & cultivated in tropical rain forests of West Africa.

- *E. oleifera*: For incorporating dwarfness, superior oil quantity and resistance to major biotic stresses.
- **Idolatrica/ Thornless oil palm** (*Elaeis guineensis* var. *idolatrica*): Found in Ghana & western Nigeria. Pendent form of fronds makes it useful as ornamental palm. Fruits big sized with mesocarp, endocarp (thick shelled) and large kernel. Fruit setting is low (1.2-2.7%), FFB yield (88 kg/ year with 5 bunches). Palm yield (14.5 % oil/ bunch).
- **Mantled fruited tenera oil palm**: Found in West Godavari district of Andhra Pradesh. The entire frond (100%) with female fruit bunches in spikelets. Average bunch wt. 14 kg and abnormal mantled fruits with average wt. 6.56 kg. More mesocarp/ bunch is desirable character. Delayed harvesting is advantageous but bunch failure (inadequate number of fertilized fruits) is genetic problem. Occurrence of mantled fruits is due to single dominant gene. Seedlings are germinated through de-operculum germination technique.
- **Virescens fruited Pisifera oil palm**: Found in Tanzani & Nigeria. No male inflorescence & female aborted bunches. Unfertilized fruits are albescence & open pollinated ones varies in maturity & weight (1-5 kg). Styler end fruits are green/ yellow and pedicellar ends are creamy white coloured. Orange coloured fruits yield 89% oil & no oil from green/white coloured fruits. Virescens character is controlled by dominant genes. Chevalier (1910) reported this rare character called as 'Gracilinux'.
- **Surinam oleifera oil palm**: Identified in field gene bank by DOPR, Palode in 2006. It has very high fruit setting (43.4%) compared to other oleifera sources. It produces 75 kg FFB/year/palm with 6 bunches. It has marked tendency towards production of parthenocarpic fruits. It has bunch wt. 12.5 kg, mesocarp oil 9.25%, kernel oil 3.1% to bunch. Yields 54% fruits to bunch and 76% mesocarp to fruits. Produces 24 fronds/ year and precocious in bunch ripening (4.5 months).
- **Cithara oleifera I & II palms**: Identified from commercial Tenera plantations by Oil Palm India Limited (OPIL), Thiruvananthapuram. Originated from Nigeria/ Costa Rica/ Malaysia. Oleifera palm-I is vigorous in growth with excellent fronds & regular in bunch production with 12-15 kg wt. Produce big sized fruits with seeds, as well as parthenocarpic fruits weighing 10 kg. Oleifera palm- II is shy bearer and low fruit setting.
- **American oil palm**: has tendency towards production of parthenocarpic fruits and this character is fully dominant in hybrids.

Characters	American oil palm	African oil palm
Botanical name	*E. oleifera, E. odora*	*E. guineensis*
Stature	Dwarf	Tall
Leaflet arrangement on frond	On one plane	Alternative arrangement of leaflets
Quality of oil	Better	Comparatively poor
Yield	Less	More
Distribution	Found only in tropical central & South America	Cultivated in America, Asia and Africa
Carotene content	High (4000 ppm)	Low (500-700 ppm)
Fatty acid content	Low	High

- Three fruit types forms of oil palm viz.:
  1. *Dura* palm: Thick shell (2-8 mm) present & 35-55% mesocarp. Widely used for commercial hybrid seed production program in India.
  2. *Pisifera* palm: It has palms have highest sex ratio followed by Tenera and Dura palms. Usually shell is absent or shell-less and female sterile mostly. Widely used for commercial hybrid seed production program in India.
  3. *Tenera* palm: Hybrid between *Dura* (female) x *Pisifera* (male): Thin shell, prominent fibre rings are present in mesocarp. Widely and commercially cultivated all over the world due to high mesocarp content (60-95%) & high oil content (16-20%). Commercial *Tenera* planting material produced in India has narrow genetic base.

Varieties:

- In India, hybridization work was initiated in 1975 at Research Centre, Palode (Kerala) using Dura parents of Malaysian origin.
- Oil palm improvement work was started in 1976 in Andhra Pradesh.
- Dura and Pisifera are basic breeding populations used in commercial hybrid seed production in India, which has narrow genetic base.
- Breeding program based on reciprocal recurrent selection was initiated in 1984 to select elite *Duras* & *Pisiferas* separately & crossing them to produce D x P seeds.
- Thodupuzha *dura* and Nigerian *pisifera* are basic breeding population used in commercial hybrid seed production in India.
- At IIOPR, Pedavegi, 11 new3rd generation D x P hybrids viz. DOPR 41 to DOPR 51, possessing desirable characters viz., high FFB yield, slow vertical growth and tolerance to drought were developed.
- Indian Dwarf: 1st dwarf tenera from Nigerian germplasm collection.
- DOPR G21-221: Dwarf oil palm.
- IC0597690 (DOPR G23-48): Dwarf Oil Palm (*E. guineensis*x*E. oleifera*): It has 12 cm annual height increment. High fruit set (69.09%).

- AVROS (Algemene Vereniging van Rubberplanters ter Oostkust van Sumatra) pisiferas are from Indonesia. AVROS *pisifera* progenies exhibit a high mesocarp-to-fruit and oil to bunch ratios but are tall.
- *Deli* is the name of a place while *AVROS* is the name of a research station in Indonesia.
- Malaysian hybrids are obtained by crossing 'Deli Dura x AVROS *pisifera*'.
- Interspecific hybrids namely ISH-1 (360Eg x 13Eo) andISH-2 (361 Eg x 11 Eo), 48 (16 Eo x 18 Eg) and 6 (12 Eo x 82 Eg) have been identified from back cross program.
- Palode-I (65 D x 30-103P) and Palode-II (120 D x 30-103P): Indian hybrids with high yield potential released from AICRP on palms at Jorhat in 1998.
- Sources for dwarfness: *E. oleifera*, Dura selections like Dumpy Dura, Pobe-dumpies, Indian Dwarf.
- Nigrescens is a cultivar of oil palm.
- Patron Dolly: Dwarf variety.
- Godavari Swarna:

Inheritance of characters:

- Shell thickness: Controlled by single gene pair. In Dura, gene is dominant (Sh^+Sh^+) and in Pisifera, it is recessive (Sh^-Sh^-). Tenera (Sh^+Sh^-) is monofactorial hybrid between these two.

Diseases and pests:

- Spear rot: Phytoplasma like organism. No control measures. Roguing of diseased palm prevents the spread.
- Bud rot/ Little leaf (*Ermima* spp.). Cause rotting of spindle. Drench the crown with 0.1% Carbendazim.
- Trunk rot: Drought and K deficiency.
- Crown rot: Multiple factors (physiological imbalance, genetic, Mg and K deficiency).
- Fruit rot: Fungal.
- Anthracnose: Severe in nursery.
- Lethal yellowing.
- Spindle bug (*Carvalhoia arecae*): More damage in nursery and during rainy season.
- Red palm weevil:
- Rhinoceros beetle: Severe pest. Use 5-10 g phorate granules/ palm three times in a year.
- Bag worm (*Manatha albipes*/ *Metisa plana*): Cause severe defoliation. Spray 0.1% Carbaryl.

- Vertebrate pests like crows, parrots feed on ripe fruits.
- Rat damage ripe bunches. Cover mature bunches with GI wire mesh.

3. EUPHORBIACEAE (MORACEAE)

3.1 Rubber

- Eulogized as 'Para rubber or Natural rubber': Most commercially used.
- Name 'Para' rubber tree is obtained after the Brazilian port of Para.
- *Hevea brasiliensis* (2n=36).
- Nitrile rubber: Man made rubber.
- Other source of natural rubber: *Manihot glaziovii* (Cera rubber), *Ficus elastica* (India rubber), *Castiolla elastica* (Panama rubber), *Parthenium argentatum* (Guayule rubber) from South America.
- Origin: Brazil (Amazon valley)
- No single plant species has influenced human life as *Hevea* has.
- World cannot think-of without natural rubber.
- Rubber was introduced in Asia in 1876.
- Commercial cultivation in India was commenced in 1902.
- *Hevea* was 1st used as source of rubber by the French.
- *Hevea* is hardy perennial tree and can be cultivated for reclamation of marginal and degraded ecosystems.
- It is grown extensively in Thailand, Indonesia, Malaysia, China, India and Sri Lanka.
- Thailand ranks 1st in area (45%), annual production (48 lakh tonnes) & export of (31.5%) natural rubber & its products in the world.
- Production cost of 1 kg latex in Thailand is around Rs. 125.
- Japan and China are major importers of Thai rubber.
- Asian countries account for 90% of natural rubber exports and India's share is 1.4%.
- India ranks 5th in total area and 4th in production.
- India accounts for 8.9% of total global rubber production.
- Rubber occupies only 0.4% of the gross cropped area in country with highest average productivity of 1796 kg/ha.
- India is 4th largest producer (8.6% of world output) of natural rubber next to Thailand, Indonesia and Malaysia.
- During last 60 years, area, production & productivity has increased by 7.5, 37.8 and 5.5 times, respectively.
- Highest area under cultivation in India: Kerala (83%).

- Kerala accounts for 98% total production.
- India's growth rate in production: 9-10% per year.
- Per capita per year availability: 0.5 kg.
- Formal cultivation of rubber was initiated in India in 19th century.
- In India, rubber is cultivated along the Arabian Sea in East to Western Ghats in west.
- In India, RSS (Ribbed Smoke Sheet) account for 72% of production and 45% of imports.
- In India, block rubber accounts for 10% of production and 40% of imports.
- Non-traditional growing regions having potential areas in India: Andhra Pradesh, Assam, Goa, Karnataka, Madhya Pradesh, Maharashtra, North-East regions, north Konkan, Odisha, Tamil Nadu and West Bengal.
- Two major forms of natural rubber in India: Concentrated latex (11%) & technically specified rubber (10%).
- Kinds of products: From automobile tyres to pencil erasers are manufactured from latex and natural rubber.
- Maximum consumption of rubber in world: Transportation sector (vehicle tyres and tubes).
- Tree is deciduous and leaves are trifoliate with long stalks.
- Crop thrives in tropical belt lying between 15^0N and 10^0S of equator but cultivation is extended up to 29^0N and 23^0S of equator.
- Growth is satisfactory up to 450 m MSL.
- Crop requires bright sunshine amounting to 2000 h/ annum @ 6 h/ day throughout all months.
- It is mainly grown as rainfed crop.
- High rainfall (2000-4000 mm), high R.H. (> 80%), warm and sunny days (> 6 h sunshine/day) throughout year) and 25-28^{0}C temperature are ideal for cultivation.
- Crop performance is better in deep soils (125 cm) with gentle slope & moderate acidic soils.
- Inflorescence: Many branched panicle. Male and female flowers born separately.
- Copious flowers appear in large clusters and flowers are small.
- Fruit type: 3 lobed capsule, each holding 3 seeds.
- Fruit ripens 5-6 months after fertilization.
- Tree has 7 years of immature phase and 25 years of productive phase.
- Seeds ripen during July-September.
- Seeds contain an oily endosperm.

- Seeds acts as morphological marker i.e. clones can be identified by shape and markings on seed coat.
- Seed: Recalcitrant type with viability of 7-10 days.
- Seeds are placed in charcoal powder/ saw dust with 15-20% moisture in container for extending viability to 4-6 weeks.
- Soil pH tolerance of plant: 3.8 to 8.0.
- Pollinating agents: Bees, midges and thrips.
- Systems of planting: Square or rectangular.
- Contour planting is done on slope which exceeds 8%.
- Hedge planting system is adopted.
- Types of planting:
  1. System of planting seeds is called as 'seed at stake' planting and it is followed by field budding. In this method, 2 or 3 germinating seeds are planted in line or triangle and weaker plants are thinned out before budding.
  2. Seedling stumps planting followed by budding.
  3. Polybag planting in field at N-S direction.
- Planting density: 420-445 plants/ha (budded plants) and 445-520 plants/ha (seedling plantation).
  a) For hilly areas: 6.7 m x 3.4 m (455 plants/ ha).
  b) Flat areas with square system: 4.9 m x 4.9 m (420 plants/ ha).
  c) Triangular: 4.9 m x 4.9 m (470 plants/ ha).
  d) Seedlings in hilly areas: 6.1 m x 3 m (539 plants/ ha).
  e) Seedlings in flat areas: 4.6 m x 4.6 m (479 plants/ ha).
- High initial stand is recommended for allowing proper thinning out.
- By selective thinning crop stand is reduced to 310 plants/ ha by 10th year of tapping.
- Common intercrops: Banana, pineapple, ginger, turmeric, vegetables, legume crops and medicinal plants.
- Mulching with dry leaves, paddy straw, grass cutting @ 5 kg / sq.m is effective and November is ideal time for mulching.
- Pre-emergent herbicide: Diuron, Simazine, Alachlor are used.
- Economic product of rubber: Latex (specialized cytoplasm) obtained from bark of tree by tapping.
- Latex vessels are modified sieve tubes, present in all parts of tree except in wood.
- Natural rubber latex is a colloidal dispersion of solid particles of the polymer polyisoprene $(C_5H_8)_n$ in water.

- Latex vessels of tapped trees contain 30-40% rubber in the form of particles.
- Particle size of latex: 0.05 to 3μm.
- pH of fresh rubber latex: 6.5-7.0 (neutral in reaction).
- Specific gravity of fresh rubber latex: 0.97-0.98.
- Natural latex, when present in the latex vessel of the tree, is assumed to be sterile.
- Composition of latex: Latex contain 34% dry rubber, 2% protein.

Rubber	30-40%	Resins	1-2%
Proteins	2-2.5%	Sugars	1-1.5%
Ash	0.7-0.9%	Water	55-65%

  - Coagulants (4%): Acetic acid or Formic acid.
  - Anti-coagulants (10-25%): Formalin, Ammonia, Sodium sulphite.
- Coagulation takes about 12 h.
- Mold growth on sheet rubber is prevented by treatment of para-nitrophenol (PNP) @ 0.05-0.1% for 100 sheets or four days of smoking at low temperature (40-50^{0}C).
- Methods used for drying rubber sheets: Solar-cum-smoke frying/ sun drying / air drying.
- VFA content of un-infected fresh latex is assumed to be zero.
- DRC (Dry Rubber Content) values (minimum 50- 55% of rubber).
- DRC is estimated with metrolac (special type of hydrometer calibrated to directly read the DRC).
- Mastication is process during which the elastic rubber achieves plastic properties.
- Latex is processed into Crepe rubber, Sheet rubber, Block rubber Preserved field latex or Latex concentrate.
- Most common and widely followed processing: Sheet rubber making.
- Sheet rubber is prepared by coagulating latex into suitable containers into thin slabs.
- Crepe rubber is processed from fresh latex coagulum, field coagulum or cutting of RSS through machine. Crinkly, lace like rubber when dried is called 'crepe rubber'.
- Field coagulation can be processed only into Crepe rubber or Block rubber.
- Translucent Specified Rubber (TSR): It is modern marketable form of natural rubber produced from latex and field coagulum.
- TSR is developed to compete with synthetic alternative.
- TSR production is started in 1973 in India and marketed under INSR (Indian Standard Natural Rubber).
- Ammonia is the first and the most popular preservative.
- It is generally added to field latex at about 1% concentration for long-term preservation.

- Combination of ammonia and tetramethyl thiuram disulphide (TMTD) and zinc oxide is found effective in latex preservation.
- Smoking house temperature: 48-50^{0}C + high RH.
- Standard rubber consistency: 12-15%.
- Economic life of plantation: 20-22 years.
- Planting of shade trees (Albizzia & Gliricidia) is advised.
- Cover crops: *Pueraria phaseoloides, Calopogonium mucunoides, centrosema pubescens*.
- Hancock suggested plantation growing of rubber in 1824.
- Rubber processing cooperatives are functioning in Kerala.
- 1st industrial park for rubber and rubber wood based industries: Kerala.
- Goodyear and Hancock discovered vulcanization in 1839.
- Sulphur is used in rubber vulcanization during which, plastic properties of raw rubber are converted to elastic properties.
- Vulcanized rubber has high tensile strength & comparatively low elongation.
- Mulching of dry grass and leguminous cover crops conserve soil and moisture & enhance N levels.
- NPKMg mixture (10:10:4:1) @ 25 kg for every 100 m^2 is recommended during 6-8 week's of planting.
- After 4 years, NPK mixture (12:12:16) @ 500 g/plant during April-May and September-October is recommended.
- In tapping trees, excess Mg cause pre-coagulation of latex on tapping panel.
- Removal of sprouts/ suckers from rootstock and thinning of side shoots is essential during immature phase & early years of tapping.
- Roots have mycorrhizal association.
- Nectar is secreted only on new flush of leaves during flowering.
- Wintering: Tree show annual shedding of mature leaves for short period. Induced by dry weather.
- High grade of rubber colour: Golden brown.
- Rubber latex preservation tank centrifugation should be kept at 1440 rpm.
- Rubber-cacao agroforestry combination is modeled in USA.

Propagation methods:

- Seeds from monoclonal area are preferred.
- Raising of clonal seedlings avoids time loss incurred through budding.
  a) Seeds of clones are termed as clonal seeds.
  b) Kinds of clonal seeds: Monoclonal, polyclonal, legitimate & illegitimate.

c) Three types of budding:
   - Brown budding: Brown coloured buds taken from one year old shoot are budded on to stock plants of 10 months age.
   - Green budding: Both stock (7 months old) & bud wood (6-8 weeks old & green coloured tender buds) are taken from young shoots. Budding success is more during rainy season than in summer.
   - Young budding: Green tender buds are budded on very young plants (< 2 months old stock plants).

d) Depending on part of stock where budding is carried out, budding is classified into-
   - Crown budding: Replacing undesirable crown of a high yielding clone with desirable one.
   - Over budding: Bud wood plants are budded at higher levels (at the basal portion of brown wood before harvesting it) for converting bud wood nursery of a clone to another clone without replanting is termed as 'over budding'.
   - Base budding: It is carried out at the base of stock plant.
   - Stumped budding: Successful green budded plants are cut back above bud patch and allowed to grow.

e) Modified forket budding: Commercial method.

- Clonal seed: Seed collected from clonal stands.
- Monoclonal seeds are produced from single clone while polyclonal seeds from different clones.
- Planting material can be raised by 2 methods viz.
  a) Planting of budded stumps in polybags (60 cm length & 30 cm width & 400 gauge thick).
  b) Planting of germinating seeds in polybags and bud grafted when 5-6 months old.
- Bud wood nursery: Brown bud wood nursery (produce brown buds) and green bud wood nursery (produce green buds).
- Planting material is classified into clones and polyclonal seeds.
- Clones generated through bud grafts are most popular.
- Polyclonal seedlings are recommended in non-traditional and marginal rubber growing areas in India.
- Polyclonal seed gardens: Grouping of high yielding latex clones (3-6) allowed for natural open pollination.
- Polyclonal seedlings have better stress tolerance than bud grafts.
- In India, multiclone planting is recommended by Rubber Board of India.

Tapping:

- It is a process of controlled wounding during which thin shavings of bark are removed.
- Aims of tapping:

  1. To cut open latex vessels in trees tapped first time or

  2. To remove coagulation which is blocks cut ends of latex vessels in trees under regular tapping.
- Vessels are concentrated in soft bark arranged in series of concentric rings of interconnecting vessels.
- Panels are marked on trees selected for tapping.
- Vertical line called front channel line is drawn on panel.
- Another vertical line called black channel line is marked on half spiral point above opening height.
- Tapping technology was invented by Ridley. Latex produced in bark tissue is harvested through this process. It is a controlled wounding process.
- Number of annual tappings: 110-120.
- Number of tapping days in a year: 240-300.
- Generally, vessels run in anti-clockwise direction (2 ½° to vertical). So tapping is done in clockwise direction.
- Two important factors affecting latex yield: Latex flow and regeneration of latex after tapping.
- Latex flow is affected by bursting index, latex total solids, thiols and magnesium content.
- Protein called 'Hevein' causes plugging of vessels and cease of latex flow.
- Tapping stage: 7th year onward (70% trees attain tappable girth).
- Fitness for tapping is gauged by girth of trunk.
- Seedling (55 cm girth & 50 cm height) and budded tree (50 cm girth & 125-150 cm height).50 to 70% trees must reach this size for tapping.
- Tapping depth: < 1 mm close to cambium tissue.
- Tapping task: Number of trees tapped on a day by tapper.
- In rubber, swellings takes place when tapping depth is =1 mm.
- Tapping panel/ cut slope to horizontal: 25^0in seedlings tree (because of thick bark) and 30^0 for budded plants.
- Generally angle of inclination of rubber vessels varies 3-5^0 to right and therefore, cut from high left to low right opens greater number of latex vessels.
- Average latex yield/tapping: 100 ml/tree/ month.
- Average yield: 320-360 kg/ acre from improved planting material.

- Yield of raw latex/ annum: 12-15 q/ha.
- Stimulation of latex yield: 2, 4-D or Ethrel + Coconut oil @ 10 % (thrice a year).
- It is not done in rains.
- During winter and defoliation period, rest of 4 weeks is given.
- Done in morning hours due to high turgor pressure. Since late tapping reduces exudation of latex due to increased transpiration by trees.

Tapping system:

Intensity	Commonly followed tree	Remarks
S_2d_2 (100%)	Budded plants	Tapping alternate days for 6 months
S_2d_3 (67%)	Clonal seedlings	Tapping at every 3 days for 6 months
S_2d_1 (200%)	Followed by small growers	Daily tapping (favours brown blast)
-	Medium yielding clones (RRIM-600, GT-1, PB-28/59)	Alternate daily tapping
d_3, d_4 & d_6	High yielding clones (PRII-105, PB-217)	Low frequency tapping systems with stimulation

- Panel notation: Indicates panel position and renewal success of panel to describe tapping.
- Common panel notations:
  a) BO-1: First basal panel of virgin bark.
  b) BO-2: Second basal panel of virgin bark
  c) BI-3: First renewal bark of BO-1.
  d) BI-4: First renewal bark of BO-2.
  e) BII-1: Second renewal bark of BO-1.
  f) BII-2: Second renewal bark of BO-2.
- First, second, third and fourth high panels of virgin bark above standard height of opening are indicated by HO-1, HO-2, HO-3 and HO-4, respectively.
- Renewed bark is usually not tapped in high panels.
- Slaughter tapping: Intensive tapping prior to felling of old trees.
- Intensive tapping: Done on old trees for few years prior to their removal.
- High level tapping: When tapping of renewed bark on basal panels become uneconomic, new cuts are opened at higher levels i.e. 180 cm from bud union or even higher.
- CUT (Controlled Upward Tapping): Improvement in ladder/ high level tapping. It is practiced for longer exploitation of virgin bark of above the base panel & tapping cut can be ¼ spiral and its angle is 45^0.

- Puncture tapping or micro-tapping: Incision method of tapping which involves making punctures on vertical band of stimulated bark below tapping height. It is followed when tree attain 40-45 cm girth and 1 year before normal opening.
- Slaughter tapping: It means higher intensive (last stage in tapping cycle) prior to replanting.
- Rain guarding: About 35-40 additional tapping days could be obtained every year by rain guarding trees by LDPE to trunk above tapping cut.
- Rain guarding is recommended only in areas where yield is 675 kg/ha/ annum and 25 or more tapping days are annually lost by rain.
- Under low frequency tapping systems, trees are stimulated using ethephon @ 2.5% by panel application method to achieve sustainable yield.

Grades/ marketable forms:

- Preserved latex and latex concentrates: Between 36 to 50% d.r.c.; between 51 to 60% d.r.c.
- Dry ribbed rubber: RMA series.
- Dry crepe rubber: EPC series.
- Dry crumb rubber or Solid Block rubber.
- Tree lace/ Shell scrap/ Earth scrap is processed only into Crepe or Solid Block rubber.
- International grades for sheet rubber: RSS-1X, RSS-1, RSS-2, RSS-3, RSS-4, RSS-5.
- Grades of crepe rubber:
  1. Pale latex crepe (PLC): Used for preparations of pharmaceutical articles, tapes, adhesives, light coloured and transparent goods.
  2. Sole crepe: Used for production of translucent shoe soling materials.

Varieties:

- Methods of breeding: Hybridization and clonal selection.
- Range of heterosis: 2.62 to 74.29%.
- Breeding in *Hevea* involves Generation wise Assortative Mating (GAM) where best clones in one cycle are used as parents for next and so on (Simmonds, 1989).
- Crop improvement program initiated in India in 1954.
- Clones are classified into primary and hybrid clones.
- The planting material approved by Rubber Board:
  1. Clone category-1: Only for 50% of total area.
  2. Clone category-2: 35% area.
  3. Clone category-3: 15% area only.

- Categories of clones:

Category-I	RRII-105, PB-260, RRII-414, RRII-430 (RRIM-600 & GT-1 in non-traditional areas)
Category-II	RRIM-600, GT-1, RRII-5, RRII-203, PB-28/59, PB-217, RRII-417, RRII-422
Category-III	RRII-50, RRII-51, RRII-52, RRII-118, RRII-176, RRII-208, RRII-300, RRII-429, PR-107, PR-225, PR-261, PB-86, PB-5/51, PB-235, PB-255, PB-280, PB-311, PB-312, PB-314, PB-330, RRIM-605, RRIM-701, RRIM-703, RRIM-712, RRIC-100, RRIC-102, RRIC-130, KRS-163, IRCA-111, IRCA-130, SCATC-88-13, SCATC-93-114, Haiken-1, BPM-24, polyclonal seeds

- Clones are named after the estates/ institute/ station from which they originate e.g. (PB- Prang Basar, Malaysia; PR- Profestation Voor Rubber, Indonesia; RRRI- Rubber Research Institute of India, Kerala; RRIM- Rubber Research Institute of Malaysia; GT- Gondang Tapen, Indonesia).
- GM rubber: Gene enzyme MnSDD: Drought tolerance.

Name	Breeding method	Features
RRII 105	Tjir-1 x GL 1	Most popular in country (80% area under cultivation)& highest yield (2400 kg/ha); tolerant to abnormal leaf fall; susceptible to pink & FM, drought; approved for large scale planting
RRII-118	Mil 3/2 x Hil 28	-
RRII-150	-	-
RRII-208	Mil 3/2 x AVROS-255	-
RRII-414	RRII-105 x RRII-100	-
RRII-417	RRII-105 x RRII-100	-
RRII-422	RRII-105 x RRII-100	-
RRII-429	RRII 105 x RRII 100	-
RRII 430	RRII-105 x RRII-100	Extensively planted in Indonesia
RRIM-600	Tjir-1 x PB-86	Extensively grown in world.
RRIM-605	Tjir-1 x PB-49	-
RRIM-203	PB-86 x Mil 3/2	Tapping yield 1818 kg/ha
RRIM-701	44/553 x RRIM-501	-
RRIM-703	RRIM-600 x RRIM-500	-
RRIM-728	GT-1 x RRIM-623	-
GT-1	-	Yield 1420 kg/ha
PB-311	RRIM-600 x PB-235	-
PB-260	PB 5/51 x PB-49	-
PB-217	PB 5/51 x PB 6/9	-
PB-235	PB 5/51 x PB 5/78	-
PB-5/51	PB 56 x PB 24	-
PR-255	Tjir-1 x PR-107	-
PR-261	Tjir-1 x PR-107	-
Dr BSKKV, Dapoli		
Konkan Hevea Rubber-1	Clonal selection	-

Disease and disorder:

- Tapping panel dryness (TPD) or Brown blast: Major physiological disorder due to high intensity of tapping. Excessive meristematic activity and occluded xylem.
- RRII 105, PB 235, PB 260, PB 281: Prone to TPD.
- Powdery mildew is caused by *Oidium haveae*.
- Abnormal leaf fall (*Phytophthora palmivora*): Most destructive disease.
- Pink disease: Mycelia growth in fork region of branches.
- South American late blight (*Microcyclus ulei*):
- Pestalotipips: Serious fungal and air borne disease of rubber causes heavy loss of yield.

Inheritance of characters:

- Most of characters are polygenically controlled.

4. RUBIACEAE (MADDER FAMILY)

4.1 Coffee

- Eulogized as 'King of beverage crop'.
- Stimulating beverage crop.
- Origin: Ethiopia.
- World production of Arabica coffee during 2016-17: 153.9 bags. (1 bag = 160 kg).
- Major producing countries: Brazil (33.16%), Columbia (11.65%), Vietnam (10.61%), Indonesia (5.97%), Mexico (4.59%), India (4.60%) and rest of the countries around 28%.
- World's largest coffee producing region: Latin America and Caribbean.
- World's top 3 producing countries: Brazil, Columbia and Vietnam.
- Brazil: Top producer and contributes 1/5th of global production.
- Vietnam: Highest productivity (1562 kg/ha).
- USA is leading importer (22.68% share) of green coffee at global level, followed by Germany (17.55%), Japan (7.34%) and Italy (3.95%).
- India is 34th rank and constitute 0.38% of the global imports of green coffee.
- Indian coffee is exported to 74 countries and major destination is Europe. Russian federation (14.61%), Germany (8.31%), Belgium (5.55%) and Spain (5.11%) are top 5 destinations for Indian coffee.
- Leading importers of Indian coffee are Italy (33.88%), Germany (12.09%), Belgium (7.42%), Spain (6.60%) and Russia (5.30%).
- India has 11th and 69th position in export of green coffee (3%) and roasted coffee (0.01%) at global levels, respectively.

- India exports 75% of its coffee & contribute about 3.5% of world's production and remaining quantity is consumed in domestic markets.
- India imports from 25 countries. Indonesia and Vietnam alone account for 97% quantity and 96% value.
- India coffee contribute 4% to global production enjoys niche market.
- In India, Kerala is 2nd largest producer (22.3%) next to Karnataka (58.5%).
- India ranks 4th in production (860 kg/ha). Arabica contributes 42% and Robusta has 58%.
- Its use was 1st discovered in Arabica around mid-15th century.
- ORAC (Oxygen Radical Absorbance capacity) value of coffee: 243000.
- Average productivity in India: 947 kg coffee/ha.
- 2nd important commodity in the world trade after petroleum products.
- Coffee beans stand at the 3rd place in the list of legally traded product in the world.
- Till 1989, the ICO (International Coffee Organization) controlled global coffee trade and after that, coffee became a free trade commodity.
- Under NPOP (National Program for Organic Production), Coffee Board is identified as accreditation agency for development and promotion of organic coffee in the country.
- Coffee Board initiated 'project on promotion of organic coffee production' in India during IXth plan period (1997-2002).
- Founder of coffee research in India: Dr. L. C. Coleman.
- Coffee was a food before it was drink. Early East African tribes were 1st to get on the coffee train. They mixed coffee berries with animal fat and turned it into energy packed snack.
- World's most expensive coffee, made from poop of elephant followed by civet cat.
- Civet coffee, also called as 'Luwark coffee' is a drink of elite consumed widely in the Gulf nations and Europe, is sold for Rs 20,000-25,000/kg abroad. It is highly priced because it is claimed to be more nutritious and high cost involved in sourcing the animal dropping, wastage during processing and quality certification.
- Distribution of coffee estates/ holding in India: Karnataka (55%), Kerala (27%), Tamil Nadu (11%), other states (7%).
- Coffees of the highest altitudes are more dense and larger in size than those produced at lower altitudes. Similarly, coffees develop more slowly at higher altitudes and often have the best flavour profiles.
- Coffee contains- Niacin which is used to cure skin diseases.
- It is woody, perennial, evergreen shrub.
- It has main vertical (orthotropic) stem and primary, secondary and tertiary horizontal (plagiotropic) branches.

- India is the only country that grows all of its coffee under shade.
- Short day plant.
- Optimum light requirement: 70%.
- Scuffling/ Soil stirring is done (to control weeds and soil moisture conservation) towards beginning of dry period.
- At flowering and grain filling stage, high temperature and low rains affect production.
- Pollination agents: Wind and bee.
- Fruits parts: Beneath the cherries red, glossy skin (exocarp or outer shell) is fleshy pulp (mesocarp), slimy layer (parenchyma) and parchment like covering of bean (endocarp). Inside these layer, usually 2 beans, which are covered by thin membrane/ coat/ seed skin (spermoderm) is referred to in coffee trade as 'silver skin'.
- Fruit type: Cherry or two seeded drupe (i.e. modified berry).
- Endospermic dicot seeds.
- Days required for cherry development: 8-9 months.
- Coffee seeds contain sucrose synthetase enzyme.
- Planting method: Square system on plains & Contour planting in hills.
- Planting distance: Arabica (6 ft. x 6 ft.; 7 ft. x 7 ft.); Robusta (10 ft. x 10 ft.; 9 ft. x 9ft).
- HDP: (4 ft. x 4 ft. or 5ft. x 4 ft.).
- Optimum soil pH: 6-6.5.
- Lime application is recommended in soil pH < 6.2
- Seed viability: Max. 22 months (Arabica- 47 weeks; Robusta-16 months).
- Propagation methods: Seed (Arabica coffee); Rooted cutting of orthotropic shoots (Robusta coffee to achieve uniformity) and nodal and apical meristem (explant for micropropagation).
- Month of seed sowing: December-January (for Arabica) and February-March (for Robusta).
- Seed bed of 4 x 3 m size is sufficient for 1.5 kg seeds.
- Seedlings at button or toppee stage (before opening of cotyledonary leaves) are transplanted into polybags (23 cm x 15 cm & 150 gauge) or into nursery baskets in February-March when at 'button stage'.
- Single node green wood i.e. semi-hard wood cuttings of 10 cm length & 3-6 months old, taken in June-July from orthotropic shoots are plants in propagation chamber.
- IBA @ 5000 ppm enhances early rooting.
- Cuttings root in 3-4 months after planting. Hardened cuttings are transplanted in main field.
- Cleft grafting: Rejuvenation of unproductive coffee plants.

- Wedge-cleft grafting at seedling stage (2 month old) with Arabica scion and Robusta rootstock is recommended for planting in nematode infested areas.
- Zygotic embryo culture: Rescue incompatible crosses.
- Planting of shade trees:
  1. Two-tier shade canopy for micro-climate development comprising-.
     - Temporary shade tree: Dadap (*Erythrina lithospermum*) & Silver oak.
     - Permanent shade tree: *Albizzia lebbek, A. moluccana, Artocarpus integrifolia, Cedrella tonna, Delbergia latifolia, Ficus glomerata, F. infectoria, F. retusa.*
  2. Optimum shade requirement: 50% for Arabica and 30% for Robusta coffee.
- Six months old seedlings with 5-6 pairs of leaves are transplanted into main field.
- Flower buds appear in leaf axils in clusters of 10-20 during October to March.
- Only one cropping season followed in India.
- Method of irrigation: Sprinkler irrigation during November to April is necessary.
- Summer/ blossom showers are important for flowering.
- For Robusta coffee, blossom showers are essential during February- March.
- Critical growth stages: Flowering, period of berry expansion, period of dry matter accumulation.
- Branches show dimorphic branching and central orthotropic stem.
- Training system:
  1. Single stem: Most common method in India. It is recommended for coffee grown under shade.
  2. Multiple stem system: Practiced in Kenya and Tanzania.
- Topping/ capping is cultural practice to restrict bush to a convenient height. It means decapitation of terminal portion of main stem at prescribed height for spread of lower canopy.
- In tall Arabica, 1st topping at 0.9 m & 2nd topping after harvesting 4-5 crops at 1.5-1.7 m. In dwarf Arabicas and Robustas, single topping at 1.5-1.7 m height is recommended.
- Pruning: It is a thinning process of branches in order to keep balance between the vegetative and reproductive woods as the crop is produced on 2nd year's wood.
- Pruning is done immediately after harvest of crop.
- Arabicas are pruned once in a year while in Robustas, regular pruning is not required.
- Thinning process is done to divert vigour of plant to certain parts by pruning other parts.
- Thinning or handling of young flush arised after main pruning is carried out once during June-July or 2nd round during September.

- Pruning involves:
  a) Centering: Removal of vegetative growth up to 15 cm radius from centre to 1st node of all primary branches.
  b) Desuckering: Removal of orthotropic branches arising from main trunk.
  c) Handling: Removal of small sprouts arising from axis of leaves which otherwise grows towards the inner side and cause shade and become unproductive wood.
  d) Nipping: Growing tip of primary branches is removed to encourage secondary and tertiary branches.
- Harvesting comprises selective picking (harvesting of ripe cherries by hand), stripping (both unripe & over ripe beans are stripped from tree) or mechanical harvesting (collection of all beans using harvesting machine).
- Fly picking: Selective picking of ripe berries.
- Main picking: After fly picking: 4-6 pickings @ 10-15 days interval.
- About 12 to 20 kg export ready coffee is obtained from every 100 kg of coffee cherries harvested.
- Coffee beans = seeds of ripened cherries.
- Arabica cherries ripen after 6-8 months and Robusta beans take 9-11 months to ripen.
- Typically, there is only one harvest in a year.
- Harvesting season:
  i) North of equator- harvesting in September to March.
  ii) South of equator- harvesting in April to August.
  iii) In equatorial countries can harvest fruits all round year.
- Average coffee tree produces 0.45 to 0.70 kg of roasted coffee/ year.
- Approximately 9000 hand picked green coffee beans make 1 kg coffee.
- Blending of coffee: Roots of chicory (*Chicorium intybus*) are used as additive in coffee. It is high in inulin and used as high-fiber dietary supplement.
- Chicory improves colour, odour and taste of coffee.
- Forms of seed berries:
  1. Pea berry (coffee with single seed; due to abortion of embryo after fertilization);
  2. Normal berry (2 ovules);
  3. Triangular berry (3 or more ovules in trilocular ovary);
  4. Elephant bean: Formation of more than one ovule/ locule by pseudo-polyembryony.
- Processing of coffee:
  - Roasting coffee:

- Roasting is heat treatment (of about 287^{0}C) which transforms green beans into aromatic brown nuggets that we buy whole or ground form.
- At temperature of 204^{0}C, beans turn darker brown and oil (called coffee essence/ coffee oil/ caffeol) start to emerge.
- This process, called 'pyrolosis' is heart of roasting and it produces flavour and aroma of coffee.

- Grinding coffee: It is done to get most flavour from beans and done by infusing ground beans in hot water. Faster the infusion, finer the grind.
- Speciality coffee: It denotes high quality coffee and differs from normal coffee in visual quality or cup quality or both. It is a term used to refer to coffee that has scored over 80 points on a 100 point scale by the SCAA (Specialty Coffee Association of America). Specialty is the term 1st used in 1974- in the *Tea & Coffee Trade Journal*- to describe beans of the highest quality.

The Q grade score sheet:

Score	Grade	Specialty (yes/ no)
90-100	Outstanding	Yes
85-89.99	Excellent	Yes
80-84.99	Very good	Yes
Below 80	No grading	No

Speciality coffee is classified into 5 categories based on unique features as:

i) **Decaffeinated coffee**: It means coffee with caffeine removed artificially. Green beans extracted with solvent (ethyl acetate) to reduce caffeine content to less than 0.1%.

ii) **High grown coffee**: means coffee grown at higher elevations (> 1250 m MSL) possess distinct flavour and acidity in cup due to slower development of beans. It is of high quality with dense beans.

iii) **Estate coffee**: It means that originate on single form with distinct identity in terms of flavour and aroma.

iv) **Variety coffee**: It means fruits of different varieties harvested and processed separately to retain their inherent/ intrinsic cup quality e.g. Indian varieties like Kent, CxR, Agaro Cioccie are unique in their cup quality.

v) **Monsooned coffee**:

- It means swelled coffee beans (swelling due to moisture in air) are processed specially, having monsooned flavour, mellow taste and golden look.
- Main grades: (1) Monsooned Malabar AA, (2) Monsooned Basanally (3) Monsooned Robusta AA.

- French coffee: Combination of coffee with chicory.
- Flavoured coffee: Addition of cardamom/ cinnamon/ lemon/ saffron flavor.
- Gahwa coffee: Cardamom flavoured coffee.
- Instant/ Soluble coffee: Concentrates of coffee are extracted in hot water (90-150^{0}C for 3 min) and spray dried/ freeze dried. It is a chicory mixture made from blends of coffee & chicory as 70% + 30%, respectively.
- Parchment/ Washed/ Plantation coffee: Obtained by wet processing method e.g. Arabica coffee. Just ripened berries are ideal for pulping to prepare parchment coffee.
- Cherry coffee: Obtained by dry processing method e.g. Robusta coffee. Cherry coffee due to longer contact with mucilage and fruit skin gives fruity flavour.

- Over/ under ripe berries results in poor cup quality after processing. Over ripe fruits give foxy flavour.
- Cup test results indicate that there is no difference in cup quality coffee processed by different methods.
- Drying is considered complete when sample forlits 40 litres of coffee record the same weight (15.5 kg) for 2 consecutive days.

***Processing steps of coffee beans*:**

1. In wet processing method (preparation of parchment coffee):

- Wet processing of coffee cherries produces 'washed coffee'.
- Pulp is removed from beans by pulping machine within 12-24 hours of harvesting of cherries.
- Enzymatic method by using commercial pectinolytic enzymes or removal of mucilage by fraction (using specific machines).
- Lighter/ immature beans are separated from heavier, mature beans through pre-grader channels.
- Natural fermentation: Allowed to ferment itself for 24-36 hrs in Arabica & 48-72 h in Robusta.
- Treatment with alkali (10% caustic soda i.e. NaOH) solution for 1 hr in Arabica & 1-1/2 h in Robusta.
- Beans are stored in fermentation tanks for 12 h (in regions of low altitude) to 48 h (in higher altitudes).
- Enzymes naturally separates slimy layer (parenchyma) from parchment like covering (endocarp).
- Hulling is also used to remove dried parchment layer surrounding the beans.
- When process is complete, endocarp has peebly feel.
- Endocarp is dried in sun/ dryers to retain 11% moisture.
- After 7-15 days, beans are known as 'parchment coffee'.

2. In dry processing method (preparation of cherry coffee):

- Dry processing of coffee cherries produces 'neutral coffee'.
- Preparation is rather simple.
- Harvested cherries are spread over in sunlight on drying yard (8 cm thickness) & raked at regular intervals to prevent fermentation.
- After 7-10 days, when moisture content of each cherry falls to 11%, it is conditioned that cherries are dry.
- When outer shell turns dark brown & brittle, beans rattle around inside their husk.
- Hulling method is also used to remove husk/ dried outer covering of original cherries or dried cherries are stored in silos where beans continue to lose moisture.
- Test weight for cherry coffee is 16 kg for one forlits (i.e. 40 litres).

- **Polishing of beans**: Is optional process in above two methods of processing. Polishing means any silver skin remained on beans after hulling is removed in polishing machine.
  - Removal of mucilage by fraction (using specific machines)
  - Preparation is rather simple.
- Green coffee: Term is used to describe 'coffee beans before they are roasted'.
- Green coffee traded in market is 'cured coffee'.
- Coffee quality index: Denotes physical appearance in raw & roast as well as liquor qualities like aroma, body & acidity in the cup.
- Treatment of coffee processing effluents (causing pollution) is done by biological methods i.e. anaerobic digestion followed by aerobic lagooning.
- Aroma of coffee is increased due to roasting.
- Green coffee contains 12% moisture.
- Total moisture loss during roasting: 14-20%.
- Caffelite: Type of plastic material made from coffee beans.
- Araku Emerald: Coffee brand signifies organic production in Andhra Pradesh.
- Silver skin: Embryo covered by thin silvery testa.
- Uniform ripening of berries is achieved by ethrel @ 480-720 ppm.
- Cup quality: Attributes of coffee that can be distinguished by senses and can be assessed organoleptically by professional coffee tasters for flavour, acidity and body and cup cleanness.
- Coffee cupping/ tasting: Professional practice of observing the tastes and aromas of brewed coffee by professionals (certified coffee tasters) known as "Q graders".

- Coffee tasters measure aspects of the coffee's taste, specifically the body (the texture or mouth feel such as oiliness), sweetness, acidity (a sharp and tangy feeling, like when biting into an orange), flavor (the characters in the cup), and after taste.

Grading and sorting:

- Beans are first graded by size and then by density.
- Beans are sorted through-
  - Scanner in size grades of 10 to 20 OR
  - By pneumatic (air-jet) method to separate heavy and light beans.
  - Over fermented or unhulled beans are removed.
  - Beans are sorted by hand/ though belts or by electronic colour sorting.
- SCAA have standards for grading coffee beans as number of defects per 300 grams. They are-

Grade 1	Specialty Grade Coffee Beans: no primary defects, 0-3 full defects, sorted with a maximum of 5% above and 5% below specified screen size or range of screen size, and exhibiting a distinct attribute in one or more of the following areas: taste, acidity, body, or aroma. Also must be free of cup faults and taints. Zero quakers allowed. Moisture content between 9-13%
Grade 2	Premium Grade Coffee Beans: Same as Grade 1 except maximum of 3 quakers. 0-8 full defects
Grade 3	Exchange Grade Coffee Beans: 50% above screen 15 and less than 5% below screen 15. Max of 5 quakers. Must be free from faults. 9-23 full defects.
Grade 4	Standard Grade Coffee Beans: 24-86 full defects.
Grade 5	Off Grade Coffee Beans: More than 86 full defects

Coffee grades followed in India:

- Of the 6 export grades, top grade is SHB (also known as liquor) for evaluation of brew & determining characteristics.
- Following 10 criteria are used to describe and categorize coffee:

Type	Robusta, washed, Arabica
Taste	Strictly soft, harsh
Body	Lacking, too heavy
Acidity	Some, too much at the top
Age	Old to fresh
Defects	Sour, grassy, musty
Cup	Roast, watery, burned, old
Overall assessment	Neutral, spicy, hard
Aroma	Weak to strong
Fullness	Slight to considerable

- Size of the bean and are commonly expressed in 1/64 of inch.

- Triage: Defective broken bits of coffee seeds. They are used for preparation of instant coffee.

Garbling Standard and Tolerance:

Grades		Tolerance
Plantation	Clean garbled	2% PB
AA (Arabica Cherry)	Clean garbled	2% PB, 1% Triage
Robusta Cherry	Clean garbled	2% PB, 1% Triage
Arabica Cherry	Clean garbled	2% PB, 2% Triage
A (Robusta Parchment)	Clean garbled	2% PB
Robusta Cherry	Clean garbled	2% PB, 2% Triage
Plantation	-	2% Flats, 2% PB Triage
PB (Arabica Cherry)	Clean garbled	2% Flats, 2% PB Triage
Bold (Robusta Parchment)	Clean garbled	2% Flats, 2% PB Triage
Robusta Cherry	Clean garbled	2% Flats, 2% PB Triage

MNEB (Mysore Nuggets Extra Bold):

- Premium/ best quality coffee from India.
- Beans uniform blush green in colour with clean polished appearance.
- Cup quality exhibits full aroma, fine spicy flavour, good body & good acidity.
- Highest grade of washed Arabica coffee based on very large bean size and virtual absence of visual defects.

Screen No.	Sieve (mm)	Min. Retention %	Garbling status	Tolerance
19	7.50	90	Clean Garbled	No tolerance for any defects
17	6.65	100	-	-

RKR (Robusta Kaapi Royale):

- Prepared from Robusta parchment AB.
- Beans bold, round with pointed ends and gray to bluish-gray in colour.
- Cup quality ensures full body, soft smooth and mellow flavour.
- RKR is Robusta washed coffee that has no defects.
- These coffees do not have the normal rubbery taste that other low grade Robustas have.

Screen No.	Sieve (mm)	Min. retention %	Garbling status	Tolerance
17	6.7	90	Clean Garbled	No tolerance for any defects
15	6.0	100	-	-

***Commercial grades-Sieve specifications*:**

Grades	Arabica						Robusta					
	Plantation			Cherry			Parchment			Cherry		
	Screen No.	Sieve (mm)	Min. retention %	Screen No.	Sieve (mm)	Min. retention %	Screen No.	Sieve (mm)	Min. retention %	Screen No.	Sieve (mm)	Min. retention %
AA	18	7.10	90.0	18	7.10	90.0	-	-	-	18	7.10	90.0
	17	6.65	100.0	17	6.65	100.0	-	-	-	17	6.65	100.0
A	-	-	-	17	6.65	90.0	17	6.65	90.0	17	6.65	90.0
	-	-	-	15	6.0	100.0	15	6.0	100.0	15	6.0	100.0
PB Bold	12 (oblong)	4.75	100.0	12	4.75	100.0	11	4.50	100.0	11	4.50	100.0

***Monsooned Malabar Coffees*:**

- India is single source of monsooned Malabar coffee in the world market.
- Arabica unwashed coffees are exposed to the monsoon rain and winds for a period of about three to four months, causing the beans to swell and lose the original acridity, resulting in a unique flavour profile. Coffee would generally have dense aroma, tint of fruity note, gritty body, and bitter walnut tones.

Species:

- About 70 species are grouped in 4 sections viz.,
  - o *Eucoffea*- all species are diploid (2n=22) except *C. 'arabica*. Most useful species divided into 4 sub-sections viz., *Erythrocoffea*, *Nanocoffea*, *Melanocoffea*, *Mozambicoffea*:
  - o *Mascarocoffea*:
  - o *Agrocoffea*- excluded from coffee since seeds do not resemble coffee.
  - o *Paracoffea*:
- *C. racemosa* and *C. excelsa*: Diploid species. Introduced into genebank at CCRI to develop synthetic varieties.
- *C. eugenoides*: Diploid (2n=22).
- Nearly 70-80% of world's coffee is produced from *C. arabica* and 20% from *C. canephora* and 1% from *C. liberica*.
- *C. arabica*: Introduced in India during 1700 AD by Muslim pilgrim, Baba Budan on the hills near Chikmagalur Dist., Karnataka. Tree is more fragile & produces less fruits.
- Tree coffee/ Liberica coffee (*C. liberica*): Used as filler with other coffee because of bitter taste and poor quality. Act as source of leaf rust, take 1 year to mature. Male sterility genes can be introduced from *C. canephora* and *C. racemosa*. High yielder & beans are more harshly flavoured.
- Robusta coffee: Higher yield, beans are harshly flavoured. It is inferior in taste with high caffeine content. Plants more robust than Arabica.

Character	**Arabica coffee (*C. arabica*)**	**Robusta coffee (*C. canephora*)**
Ploidy	2n= 4x=44 (allotetraploid)	2n=22 (diploid)
Origin	Ethiopia	Central Africa
Adaptability	Higher elevation	Lower elevation
Plant stature	Small tree or bush	Bigger tree than arabica
Leaves	Dark green	Pale green
Blossoming after receipt of blossom showers	Bloom in 9-10 days	Bloom in 7 days
Topping height	9-12 months	18-24 months

Flowers	Scaly, small bracts per axil 4-5 inflorescence of 1-4 flowers/ inflorescence	Leafy and expanded bracts with 5-6 flowers/ inflorescence
Berries	10-20 per node oblong to round	40-60 or more per node
Berry development period	8-9 months	10-11 months
Root system	Small but deep	Large but shallow
Pollination and fertilization	Self pollinated & self fertile	Highly cross pollinated & self sterile
Fermentation time	24-36 hours	48-72 hours
Harvesting season	November-January	December-February
Popularity	Most popular	Least popular
Aroma	Best	Low
Caffeine content	Low	High & preferred for manufacture of instant coffee
Disease reaction	Very susceptible to leaf rust	Rust resistant & relatively tolerant to nematodes
Quality attributes	Superior quality; aroma taste & flavour present; drought tolerant	Inferior quality; deficient in aroma & flavor; susceptible to drought

Varieties:

- CCRI: Only organization in India takes up crop improvement work.
- 'Hibrido-de-Timor/832/2' i.e. HDT: It is spontaneous natural hybrid between *C. canephora* x *C. arabica* spotted in Timor island, shows resistance to leaf rust. It was introduced in India during 1961.
- Tafarikela: An Ethiopian variety. Popular male clone used in coffee breeding.
- Old Chiks:
- Kents: It is a mutant selected by Mr. Vent, an English planter during 1920. Earliest cv. of Arabica, known for its exceptional cup quality and least susceptible to rust.
- Caturra: A natural semi-dwarf mutant of the high quality 'Bourbon' variety from Brazil. Plants short statured with many secondary branches. High production and good quality.
- Devamachy: Spontaneous Robusta x Arabica hybrid.
- Typica: Plants are tall & conical shaped. Very low production but has excellent cup quality. Many Arabica varieties have been developed from it.
- Bourbon: Thrives at higher elevations (1200-2000 MSL). Plants conical shaped with more secondary branches. Fruits small, dense and fall of the branch easily. Cherries mature quickly, Excellent cup quality.
- Catuai: Hybrid developed from a cross between Mundo Novo x Caturra. Plants short statured and high yielding. Fruits does not fall off the branch easily. Suitable for high rainfall areas.

- Catimor: Hybrid between Timor coffee (rust resistant) x Caturra coffee, developed in Portugal in 1959. Early maturing & very high yielding with good cup quality.
- Catimor T-8667 (large coffee fruits & seeds), Catimor T-5269, T-5175 are very productive and robust descendants of Catimor.
- Blue Mountain: Popular variety of Jamaica & Hawaii, known for high quality flavour profile. Suitable for high lands. Resistant to coffee berry disease.
- Maragogype: It is mutant of Typica coffee discovered in Brazil. Plants are larger & taller but low in production. Seeds are very large, bold with superior cup quality.
- Pache colis: Discovered in Guatemala. Tree has profuse secondary and tertiary branches and leaves are roughly textured. Well adapted to 20-21^{0}C. Fruits very large with good cup quality. Resistant to phoma disease.
- Pache comum: Mutant of Typica coffee, discovered in Guatemala. Cup quality is smooth or flat.
- San Ramon: Dwarf mutant variety spotted at Costa Rica. Very compact branching habit, close internodes, deep roots but highly susceptible to rust. Introduced to India to develop dwarf genotypes.

Name	Parentage	Special features
Arabica		
Selection 1 (Sln.-288) 1936	Pure line selection from S.26 (putative natural hybrid between *C. liberica* x *C. arabica*)	Tetraploid; resistant to leaf rust race I & II; very frequent seed abnormality; fruits round with broad discs & orange-yellow to red coloured; popularly known as 'golden drops'. Defective beans (20-30%); yield 8-10 q/ha; liquor quality is rated as fair average quality.
Selection 2 (Sln. 333) 1940	Hybrid of S.31 x S.22	Resistance to leaf rust & high bean abnormalities
Selection 3 (S. 795) 1940	Cross between (S.288 x Kents)	Most widely adaptable & cultivated; bush tall, very vigorous, wide spreading; each node produces 14-16 cherries; beans oblong, bold with 60-65% 'A' grade; yield 15-20 q/ha; resistant to rust races I, II but susceptible to race VIII.
Selection 4	Selection includes three Ethiopian Arabica collections viz. Cioccie, Agaro, and Tafarikela	Beans bluish-green, long & bold with 65% 'A' grade and 25% 'B' grade with excellent liquor quality.
Sln. 5A	Devamachy x S.881 (Wild Arabica Rume Sudan)	Vigorous; erect branching; fruits 8-12/ cluster; yield 12-15 q/ha; produce 40% 'B' grade beans; very popular variety in non-traditional coffee areas.
Sln. 5B	Devamachy x S.333	Semi-drooping; bold beans with 60-65% 'A' grade beans; yield 15 q/ha; resistant to leaf rust
Selection 6 (S. 2828)	Crossing Robusta cv. S:274 x Kents Arabica	60-65% 'A' grade beans; 16-20 fruits/ cluster; bean yield 12-20 q/ha; tolerant to leaf rust
Selection 7	Cross of San Ramon	Dwarf; bean yield 15 q/ha; highly resistant to leaf rust

	(dwarf mutant) with other Arabica's	
Selection 7.1	San Ramon x S. 795	-
Selection 7.3	Dwarf type in Sln.7.1 x HDT	Late ripener; drought tolerant; suitable for marginal areas
Selection 8 (1968)	Pure line selection from HDT	Compact growth with drooping branches; yield 10-12 q/ha; suitable for cultivation in medium altitudes; resistant to leaf rust
Selection 9	Cross between (Tafarikela (Ethiopian Arabica collection) x HDT)	Tall, drooping branches; 12-16 beans/ cluster; 65% 'A' grade beans; excellent liquor quality; distinct flavor; yield 17 q/ha; drought hardy; tolerant to rust
Selection 10	Double cross hybrid of [Caturra x (Cioccie x S.795)]	Compact; semi-dwarf; profuse bearing; 65% 'A' grade beans; resistant to rust; drought hardy; suitable for different coffee zones
Selection 11	Interspecific hybrid of (*C. arabica* x *C. eugenioides*)	Fruits 12-15/ cluster; more 'B' grade beans (40-45%); resistant to rust & drought hardy
Selection 12 (syn. Cauvery) 1985	Descendant of cross between (Caturra x HDT) from F_4 generation	Semi-dwarf; compact; high degree of synchronized flowering; bears in 3 years; berries 14-18/ cluster; yield 20 q/ha; suitable for HDP; 60% 'A' grade beans; cup rating FAQ is too good; resistant to rust
Selection 13 (syn. Chandragiri) 2007	Selfed F_3 progeny of the cross between Villa Sarchi (i.e. a semi-dwarf mutant of Bourbon coffee) x HDT & introduced in India in 1975	Semi-dwarf; bold & long beans; 14-18 beans/cluster; 63-86% 'A' grade beans; highly resistant to rust & drought; best for cultivating in higher elevations (3300 ft. and above); yield 12-19 q/ha
Sln. 16	Interspecific hybrid of (*C. robusta* x *C. arabica*)	-
No. 4631	Cross between (Cauvery x HDT) x Geisha	Highly vigorous; resistant to rust
Sln. 4595	Interspecific hybrid	Improved grain size; cup quality is good
Sln-4600	Interspecific hybrid	Improved grain size; cup quality is good
Robusta		
Balehonur Robustas	Clonal selection from (S. 270 x S.274)	Recommended to Robusta tracts
Sln 1 R (S-274)	Single plant progeny selection	High yield with bold beans
Sln 2 R (S-270)	Single plant progeny selection	-
Sel 3 R	*C. congensis* x *C. Canephora* & back crossed to *C. canephora*	Bushy; poor yield; low-caffeine content
C x R	Interspecific hybrid between *C. congensis* x *C. canephora*	Suitable for HDP; tolerant to drought & rust

Diseases, pests and disorders:

- Die back: Major disorder. Death of young tertiary branches.
- Brown eye-spot (*Cercospora coffeicola*): Spray Dithane M-45 @ 5 g/litre.
- Leaf rust caused by Basidiomycete fungus (*Hamelia vestatrix*) introduced from Sri Lanka on epidemic scale in India in 1869.
- Leaf rust is hyper-parasitised by *Verticillium lecanii* (syn. *Lecanicillium lacanii*).
- White stem borer (*Xylotrechu squadripes*): Wilting and yellowing of leaves. Major problem in coffee cultivation.
- Coffee berry borer (*Hypothenemus hampei*): Most serious pest in world. It is controlled by fungus *Beauveria bassiana*.
- Shot hole borer (*Xylosandrus compactus*): Extensive tunneling.
- Coffee nematode (*Pratylenches coffeae*): Dieback and dislodged.
- Root knot nematode (*Meloidogyne paranaenis*):
- Bean disorders in Arabica coffee: Black bean, Black jolloo, Normal jolloo develop to the extent of 2-10% mainly due to depletion of carbohydrate, defoliation, high shade & low light intensity during berry development.
- Pre-mature fruit drop: Wet feet condition, -CHO and hormonal imbalance. Spray Planofix or Miraculan or Atonik @ 50 ml/ 200 litres of water.
- Star flowers: Due to high temperature, petals remain small, fleshy and stiff. Fail to set fruits.
- Kondli/ Stem wasting: Non-parasitic disorder of young plants due to copper toxicity.

Inheritance of characters:

- Two genes are associated with scent of coffee.
- Self incompatibility in robusta: Controlled by single gene with multiple alleles leading to high heterozygosity in seedling population.
- Male sterility: Single recessive nuclear gene.

5. STERCULIACEAE (MALVACEAE)

5.1 Cocoa

- Eulogized as 'Drink of Gods'.
- Generic name *Theobroma* is derived from Greek words 'Theos' (God) and 'broma' (beverage).
- Origin: Amazon valley/ region in South America.
- Brown revolution: Cocoa production.
- Important beverage crop and occupies 3rd place after tea and coffee.
- Cocoa cultivation is concentrated between the 10 ^{0}N and 10^{0}S latitude.

- Major share of global production: West African countries (70%). Bulk of cocoa is produced in tropical areas of African continent.
- World consumption of cocoa is estimated at 28 lakh tones / year and largest importer are Holland, USA, Germany, Britain and Brazil with average consumption of 6.8 kg/ person/ year.
- Present production of cocoa beans hardly meets 30% of demand of processing industry in India.
- Most popular crop for multiple cropping system in arecanut plantation.
- Grown as companion crop in irrigated coconut/ arecanut gardens in Kerala and Karnataka.
- Kerala accounts for about 76% of area and 78% of total production in country.
- Cocoa production in India is more costly.
- Cocoa is exported in the form of powder.
- Word ‘chocolate’ originated from ‘xocoatl’.
- Cocoa butter obtained from seeds is used in preparation of chocolates, cosmetics, perfumery, lubricants for massaging and as base for ointment.
- Shell is used as conditioner for commercial fertilizers or as fuel.
- Shells are used for extracting theobromine, which possesses diuretic properties and also act as myocardial stimulant and muscle relaxant.
- Cocoa and chocolate contains high level of flavonoids (epicatechin) having beneficial cardiovascular effects on health.
- Xocoatl: Drink made by Spanish people from beans after roasting and grinding.
- Barry Callebaut: World’s largest supplier of high quality chocolate and cocoa products.
- It was introduced into India in 1791, but cultivation began in 1960.
- Cocoa beans, known as ‘nibs’ in the trade, are fermented, dried and ground to make chocolate.
- Maximum area: Kerala.
- Most nutritious among beverage crops.
- Cocoa beans are source of cocoa butter and cocoa mass.
- Seeds are source of non-alcoholic beverage, confectionary and cosmetics.
- The kernel or ‘nib’ is useful part and is bitter without any aroma or flavour.
- Rich source of fat (37%) and protein (7%).
- Wet beans: Beans with pulp.
- Beans are surrounded by pulp & mucilage.
- Optimum soil pH: 6.5-7.0.
- Optimum temperature for cultivation: 25^{0}C (15-32^{0}C).
- Below 10^{0}C causes chilling injury.
- At higher temperature, trees cause excessive vegetative growth.

- Branching habit: Dimorphic.
- Bearing habit: Cauliflorous.
- Cocoa plant flowers from 2nd year of planting.
- Cocoa produces flowers throughout the year.
- Cocoa gives two main crops i.e. September-January (main) and April-June (second).
- Production of leaves on fan branches is by series of 'flushes'.
- 'Crazy' flowering also occurs during any period of a year.
- Flushing in cocoa is referred as 'change of leaf'.
- Anthesis time: 14-16 h and completes next day up to 14-16 hours.
- Anther dehiscence: 4-5 h and completed between 8 to 10 hours.
- Fruiting season: October-March.
- Fruit type: Indehiscent drupe (pod i.e. modified berry).
- Young fruit of 10 cm length is called as 'cherelle' and its wilting prior to maturity is called as 'cherelle wilt'.
- Biomass production is maximum in cocoa than any other crop.
- Cocoa grows naturally in a series of storeys branches i.e. tiers, a layer of fans.
- Jorquette: Vertical continuous stem of cocoa or branching at the tip of branch.
- Preferred height of jorquetting: 1 m.
- Fan/ Jorquette are horizontal (plagiotropic) branches.
- Single main stem/ Chupon: Axillary bud just below the jorquette and grows vertically straight.
- Pollination agents: Midge fly (*Forcipomyia* spp.), small flies & wasp.
- Hand pollination is practiced to enhance fruit set. Total yield increase by 161% through this.
- Limitation in breeding: Narrow genetic base.
- 1st report of gametophytic SI: Harland (1925).
- Site of incompatibility: Embryo sac.
- Fertilization is controlled by single locus having series of 5 '*S*' alleles. $S_a = S_b = S_c > S_d > S_e$.
- Incompatibility operates when parents used in crossing are genetically similar.
- Ratio of pollen parent and female parent in case of polyclonal cocoa orchard: 1:5.
- Cocoa plants found in lower Amazon basin are self incompatible but cross compatible.
- If both parents are self incompatible, all pods can be used for seed purpose.
- For raising the seedlings, seeds of mature pods are taken from high yielding mother plants.

***Selection of mother plant*:**

- High yielder (> 100 pods/ year).

  - They should have medium to large sized green pods.
  - In the pods, average dry bean weight should not be less than 1 g.
  - Seeds are collected from bi-clonal or polyclonal seed gardens having superior self incompatible parents.
- Very narrow genetic base leads to low productivity.
- Type of parthenocarpy: Stimulative.
- Propagation method: Seeds, soft wood grafting, budding.
- Time taken for seed germination: 7 days.
- Seed viability: Max. 4 months (52% germination)
- Seed sowing is done with hilum end down.
- Best time of seed sowing: December-January.
- Budding methods: T, inverted T, patch & modified forkert method are followed and 6-12 months old seedlings are used as rootstock.
- Bud wood from chupons or fan branches is normally preferred for budding to give bushy appearance and spreading habit. Pre-curing of bud wood increases percentage success.
- New method of propagation: Micro-budding.
- For micro-budding, young stock plants less than 15 days old is used.
- Tissue culture through somatic embryogenesis is followed in cocoa.
- Cocoa needs shade for its early establishment and nursery must be located in heavy shaded area allowing only 25-50% sunlight.
- For planting in main field, 4-6 months old seedlings are preferred.
- Planting distance: 2.7 m x 2.7m (sole cropping); 5.4 m x 2.7m (HDP, 689 plants/ha).
- Pod value: Number of pods required to produce 1 kg wet beans. It must be less than 12.
- Best seeds for sowing are from the middle portion of the pod.
- Theobromin is extracted from bark.
- Critical stage of irrigation: Flowering stage.
- Sanitary pruning is practiced in cocoa.
- Drooping fan shoots are pruned once a year when crop load is low (Dec.-Jan.)
- Centering (cultural operation) is a process of removal of all lateral fan branches arising around jorquette.
- Top working: Rejuvenate old and unproductive plants and convert genetically poor yielders to high yielders.
- Leaves required for growth of single pod: 20-30.
- Number of flowers/ cushion/ season: Up to 50.
- Number of beans/ pod: 20-60 embedded in white pulp and higher in Forastero than Criollo.

- Cured beans/ 100 g: 95 (as per International Cocoa standards).
- Maturity indices:
  - o Days taken to maturity from pollination: 150-170.
  - o Change in pod colour: Pods are green when immature, turn yellow on maturity and reddish pods turn yellow to orange.
  - o Change of colour starts from grooves on the pods and spreads to entire surface.
- Harvesting of pods is done at regular intervals of 10-15 days.
- Harvested pods are kept for minimum period of 2 days before manual breaking for fermentation.
- Pods are broken cross wise and placenta is removed with husk and beans are kept for fermentation.
- **Processing:** It involves curing (fermentation) upto 7 days followed by drying.
- Fermentation of beans is essential-
  a) To remove adhering mucilaginous pulp.
  b) To develop flavor/ aroma precursors.
  c) To reduce bitterness.
  d) To kill the germs in seeds.
  e) To loosen the testa.
- Standard methods of fermentation: Heap, box, tray & basket methods are adopted in different countries.

A. Heap method:

i) About 50 kg mass of wet beans is kept over banana leaves to facilitate flow of sweating.

ii) Covered heap is dismantled & beans are mixed on 3rd and 5th days.

iii) It needs about 6 days for complete fermentation & beans are taken out for drying on 7th day.

B. Tray method:

i) Wooden tray of 90 x 60 x 13 cm size contains 45 kg wet beans.

ii) Six trays are stacked one over the other & covered with banana leaves/ gunny sacks.

iii) Empty tray kept at bottom collects drainage of sweating.

iv) No need of mixing beans & fermentation is complete in 4 days.

v) On 5th day, beans are taken out for drying.

C. Box method:

i) Wooden boxes (1.2 x 0.95 x 0.75 m) with holes in bottom & sides are filled with wet beans (approx. 1 ton).

ii) Beans are stirred on alternate days for uniform drying and to prevent clump formation & beans are shifted to other box for next stirring.

iii) Duration of fermentation is for 3-5 days.

- Mixing of beans is effected and transferred to next box (60 cm x 60 cm x 45 cm) wooden box.
- Mixing facilitates uniform fermentation and maintains proper temperature, moisture and aeration during fermentation.
- Temperature of fermentation mass rises to 42-48^{0}C after 48 h of fermentation.
- Again, transferring is done at 72 h of fermentation and final transferring at 24 hours of this fermentation.
- Total 6 days (114 h) are required to complete the fermentation process and then beans are withdrawn for drying. Chocolate flavor is developed during curing process.
- Time taken to ferment Criollo is less than compared to Forastero.
- Beans are skin dried within 24 h of fermentation to avoid mold growth.
- During drying, bio-chemical oxidation of excess acetic acid from beans takes place.
- Drying is attempted in artificial drier for 48 to 96 hours.
- Slow drying gives better quality beans.
- Fermented beans have 55-69% moisture and drying rate depends on temperature and air flow.
- In electric ovens, beans are dried for 8-10 h at 45-55^{0}C for first 2 days followed by continuous drying at 60^{0}C and total drying period is 72-90 hours.
- Moisture content in dry beans should be 6-7% for safe storage.
- Cleaned beans are stored in polybags (150-200 gauge) lined gunny bags.
- Dry cocoa can be stored for longer period.
- At 85% R.H., bean moisture content exceeds by 8%.
- At 95% R.H., storage of cocoa is difficult in rainy months.
- For merchantable quality, cocoa must be cured (fermented, dry) & free from smoky beans.
- Alkalization is done by steeping cocoa beans in 1% Sodium bi-carbonate solution for 3 hours.

Grades:

- Throughout the world, standards of Ghana cocoa are implemented for grading as:
  - Grade I: Max. 3% count each of moldy beans & slaty beans. Insect damaged/ germinated/ flat beans max 3%.
  - Grade II: Max 4% count each of moldy beans & 8% of slaty beans. Max 6% count of insect damaged/ germinated/ flat beans.

Species:

- *Theobroma cocoa*: Only cultivated species among 22 species with 2n=20.
- Pittier (1933) reported 2 sub species viz.:
  1. *T. cocoa* ssp. *cacao* = Criollo;
  2. *T. cocoa* ssp. *sphaerocarpum* (syn. *T. leiocarpum*) = Forastero & Trinitario.
- Cupuassu (*T. grandiflorum*):
- Mountain cocoa (*T. gileri*):
- Macambo (*T. bicolour*): Seeds are used as adulterant.
- Wild cocoa (*T. subincannum*):
- Beans of *T. angustifolium* are mixed with cocoa in Mexico and Costa Rica.

Varieties:

- Crop improvement was started in 1980 at CPCRI, regional station, Vittal, Karnataka and KAU, Vellanikkara, Kerala.
- Three major varietal groups as mentioned below-

Character	Criollo	Forastero	Trinitario
Cotyledons (Beans colour)	Plumpy and white when fresh and turn cinnamon colour on fermentation	Flat and purple when fresh and turn dark chocolate brown on fermentation.	White or nearly black
Plant vigour	Less vigorous	More vigorous	Less vigorous to more vigorous
Number of beans/ pod	20-30	30 or more	30 or more
Immature pod colour	Red	Green	White, green pod or purple
Mature pod colour	Yellow	Yellow	Yellow, orange or red
Pod husk texture	Soft	Hard	Medium
Other pod characters	Pod big, warty, beaked pods with prominent constrictions & deep furrows	Pods small, smooth with inconspicuous ridges, thick walled, melon shaped with rounded end (less prominent beak)	Highly variable, surface ranging from complete smoothness to heavy sculpturing
Flavour and aroma	Bland flavour (mild & delicate)	Strong (harsh flavour, bitter taste)	Medium
Duration of fermentation	3 days	6 days	
Easiness to cultivate	Difficult	Easy	Easy
Adaptability in India	Poor; very sensitive to stresses	Good & bulk share	
Disease susceptibility	Extremely susceptible to bark canker, witches broom & swollen shoot virus	More vigorous	Susceptible/ tolerant
Yield	Low	High	High

- Criollo: Naturally evolved.
- Forastero: Naturally evolved. Commercially grown all over the world. It is high yielding, resistant to pests and diseases and more tolerant to drought compared to Criollo. It is recommended for commercial cultivation by CPCRI.

***Other types include*:**

1. Trinitario from Trinidad (evolved through genetic mixing of Criollo x Forastero): Highly heterozygous. Hardier and more productive than Criollo. Used in making luxury chocolates.
2. Amelonado, a Forastero type bean with melon shaped pod is cultivated in West Africa. Self compatible and do not cross with self incompatible types.
3. Amazon, a relatively new type collected from Amazon forests.
   - Success of hybridization is unidirectional i.e. when cocoa cultivar is used as female parent.
   - CPCRI has recommended selections from Malaya viz. I-21, II-11, II-18, II-67 and II-101 for commercial cultivation (all are high yielders and bean wt. > 1 g).
   - All the superior hybrids have GI-V 5/9 as a parent.
   - Best quality of cocoa with respect to flavour: Criollo type.
   - Criollo types are used for specific chocolate preparations.
   - Indonesian varieties resistant to cocoa moth: DR-1, DR-2, DR-21, DR-35.
   - Tropical Research Station, Trinidad: TSH-999.
   - UF-650, 667, 668: Resistant to swollen shoot disease, released from Costa Rica.
   - Clones resistant to witches broom: ICS-1, ICS-45, ICS-92.
   - Resistant to drought: NC-3, NC-23, NC-29, NC-39, NC-42

Name	Breeding method	Features
CPCRI regional station, Vittal		
Vittal Cocoa Clone-1 (i.e. VTLCC-1) 2006	Selection from 'Nigerian clone 45/53'	Early & heavy bearer; self and cross compatible; 75 pods/ tree/ year; 52.5% fat content; 12% shelling percentage
VTLCH-1 (2006)	Selection from 'II-67 x NC-42/94	Tolerant to water stress; 40 pods/ tree/ year; 12% shelling percentage; suitable for rainfed& irrigated condition; 1.25 kg dry bean yield/ tree
VTLCH-2	Selection from 'ICS-6 xSCA-6'	No. of pods/ tree/ year 70; single dry bean weight 1.15g; dry bean yield 1.15 kg/ tree/ year ; 54% fat with a shelling percentage of 11; tolerant to black pod disease
VTLCH-3	Selection from 'II-67 x NC 29/66'	Yield 45 pods/tree, bean dry weight-1.07 g/bean; fat content in bean 50%, shelling 13%; drought tolerant
VTLCH-4	Selection from 'II-67 x NC-42/94'	yield 40 pods/tree per year; dry weight 1.01 g/bean; fat content in dry beans 50%, shelling 13%; drought tolerant
VTLCH-5 (syn. Nethra Centura)	Hybrid	Precocious, stable & heavy bearer; yield (66 pods/tree/ year), 43 beans/pod, single bean dry wt. of 1.11 g. Highest dry bean yield (3.2 kg/tree/ year & 18 q/ha;

		highly suitable for chocolate industry
VTLC-1	Selection	55 smooth red pods/ tree/ year; pod wt. 360 g; contain 41 beans; fat content in dry beans 52%; shelling 11%; suitable for chocolate industry
VTLC-57	Selection	54 green pods/ tree/ year; pod wt. 400 g containing 41 beans
VTLC-115	Selection	-
VTLC-119	Selection	-
Kalpa Raja (syn. VTLCC-11) 2021	Clonal selection	Tolerant to root wilt
KAU, Vellanikkara		
CCRP-1 (1998)	Selection from local germplasm	Heavy bearer; self incompatible (SI); tolerant to vascular streak dieback; 56 pods/ tree/ year; pod wt. 385 g; 46 beans/ pod; 2.5 kg dry beans/plant
CCRP-2 (2001)	Selection from local germplasm	Heavy bearer; SI; tolerant to vascular streak dieback; 54 pods/ tree/ year
CCRP-3 (2001)	Selection	Heavy bearer; SI; tolerant to vascular streak dieback; 69 pods/ tree/ year
CCRP-4 (1998)	Selection	Heavy bearer; SI; tolerant to vascular streak dieback; 66 pods/ tree/ year; pod wt. 402 g; 45 beans/ pod; 3.9 kg dry beans/plant
CCRP-5 (1998)	Selection	Heavy bearer; SI; tolerant to vascular streak dieback; 38 pods/ tree/ year; pod wt. 425 g; 45 beans/ pod; 1.7 kg dry beans/plant
CCRP-6 (1998)	Selection	Heavy bearer; SI; tolerant to vascular streak dieback; 50 pods/ tree/ year; pod wt. 895 g; 48 beans/ pod; 3.1 kg dry beans/plant
CCRP-7 (1998)	Selection	Heavy bearer; SI; tolerant to vascular streak dieback; 78 pods/ tree/ year; pod wt. 527 g; 47 beans/ pod; 4 kg dry beans/plant
CCRP-8	Hybrid of (CCRP-1 x CCRP-7S.I)	Heavy bearer; pod wt. 389 g; bean No. 48.8; tolerant to vascular streak dieback; 90 pods/ tree/ year
CCRP-9	Hybrid of (CCRP-1 x CCRP-4S.I)	Heavy bearer; pod wt. 370 g; bean No. 36.7; tolerant to vascular streak dieback; 106 pods/ tree/ year
CCRP-10	Hybrid of (CCRP-3 x GVI-68)	Heavy bearer; pod wt. 332 g; bean No. 41.5; tolerant to vascular streak dieback; 80 pods/ tree/ year

Pests, diseases and disorders:

- Stem borer (*Zeuzara aurantii*): Serious pest.
- Black pod (*Phytophthora palmivora*): Rainfall >3000 mm favours disease development & vascular streak die back. Cause damage to diploid pods and Cherelles (young pods). Crop loss is about 30-40%.
- Cocoa mealy bug (*Planoccoccus lilacinus*).
- Cherelle wilt: Multiple factors. It occurs up to 100 days after fertilization with peak wilting at 50-70 days. Several fungi and insects are associated.
- Swollen shoot is transmitted by *Planococcoides njalensis*.

- Witches broom.
- Rodents and squirrel cause damage >10% damage.

Inheritance of characters:

- Foliar resistance to black pod disease: Additive and non-additive gene action.

6. THEACEAE (CAMELLIACEAE)

6.1 Tea

- Eulogized as 'Golden leaf or Queen of beverage crop or Calcifiuge crop'.
- Oldest beverage crop.
- The word 'Tea' originated from Chinese language '*Tey*'.
- Commercialization of tea occurred during 8th century AD through the Arabian travelers.
- Tea grows at 27-43°N up to 2500 m above MSL.
- Origin: China.
- 2n=30.
- Tea cultivation was introduced in India during 1832.
- Da Hong Pao (Big Red Robe Tea): Costliest tea. Wuyi rock *tea* grown in the Wuyimountains. Heavily oxidized, dark oolong *tea.*
- Declared as national drink of Afghanistan and Iran.
- China ranks 1st in tea production followed by India.
- India's account is 20% of world's tea production.
- Sri Lanka: Main rival of India in export.
- Production of tea in India accounts for 27.74% of the global tea production in world.
- Assam share 55% in total tea production in India.
- India is the largest consumer of tea and accounts for 22% of global consumption.
- Per capita consumption in India: 660 g/head/year.
- High fluoride content (50.2 ppm) in leaves prevents tooth decay.
- Bed weeps: Cemented beds provided with rectangular shaped wholes to drain excess water.
- Russia and Egypt: Big market for Indian green tea.
- Green tea is widely used in beverage industry, meat and poultry products to increase flavour, taste and keeping quality.
- Tea clones tolerate 2 to 6 Kr of gamma radiation.
- Central Insecticides Board & Registration Committee recommended use of glyphosate herbicide in tea gardens.
- Special Purpose Tea Fund (SPTF) is approved by GOI under Tea Board for funding re-plantation and rejuvenation activities to improve age profile of tea plantations.

- 1st fortified tea with vit. A, B_2, niacin: 'Brooke Bond A1' by Hindustan Lever Limited.
- 1st introduced by Mr. Robert Kyd (1980).
- 1st consignment of Assam tea was sent to London in 1839.
- World's 1st commercial tea company: The Assam Company.
- 1st auction centre of tea in India: Kolkata in 1861.
- Study of tea is known as 'Tsiology'.
- Four tea research institutes set up in India: Tocklai, UPASI, DTRC & IHBT.
- Tocklai Tea Experiment Station was established in 1911, Jorhat, Assam.
- India is largest producer of organic tea.
- India accounts for 18.5% of total world tea area with 26.2% total world production.
- Among Indian tea, Darjeeling is known for its unique 'muscatel' flavor i.e. distinct sweet flavour; Assam for cup character and Nilgiris have characteristic taste flavor.
- Japan is the third largest buyer of Darjeeling tea.
- Major phenols in green tea: Catechins.
- Health properties in tea: Due to catechins (i.e. epigallocatechin-3-gallate-EGCG).
- Leaves contains caffeine, polyphenols (tannins) & essential oil.
- Caffeine: Bitter principle of tea and coffee.
- Stimulative effect is due to Thein/ caffeine (1.25-4.5%).
- Economic age of tea bush: 40-60 years.
- Tea is exact in its climatic requirements.
- Most tea gardens are located between 1000-1200 m MSL.
- At 1000 m elevation 31.8% area and between 1000-1500 m elevation 34.5% area and above 2000 m elevation 8.2% area.
- In south India, tea areas are located at hilly terrains.
- Optimum temperature for growth: 16-32^{0}C and well distributed rainfall of 150 cm/ annum.
- Temperature affects tea yield by influencing rate of photosynthesis and controlling growth and dormancy.
- Day length influences growth & dormancy in bushes.
- Seasonal dormancy appears around 18^0 N and S latitudes.
- When days are less than 11.15 h duration for 6 weeks, tea bushes become dormant i.e. critical day length for flushing is 11.15.
- In N-E India (25^0-27^0 N latitude) tea bushes remain dormant during winter for 3 months on account of short days and low temperatures.
- Below 12^{0}C and beyond 30^{0}C, tea plants cease flushing.
- Leaves are simple, shiny, alternate and serrated.
- Flower type: Bisexual.

- Ovary position: Superior.
- Fruit: Thick walled capsule and takes 9-12 months to mature.
- Seed viability: Max. 10 months (50% germination).
- For raising 1 lakh plants and hardening, 1500 sq. m land is required.
- Optimum soil pH: 4.5-5.0 especially 4.8.
- Planting season: June-July or September-October.
- East-West orientation of nursery bed is desirable.
- Flowering:
  - Flower bud initiation (75%) takes place during March-June & completed by end of September (97%).
  - Blossoming starts from early October and ends by January with peak period in Nov-Dec.
  - Seeds are produced from peak flowering after 10 months.
  - Seeds ripen by next October.
  - November to May is crucial period for fruit development.
- Tea is virtually self sterile and self incompatibility is reported in Assam jats.
- Highly cross pollinated by small insect (Pserphid).
- Fruit is allowed to dehisce on tree and dropped seeds are collected from ground.
- Seeds vary in size from 10-22 mm in diameter.
- Rotary type shifter is used for grading & elimination of very small seeds.
- One kg of graded & sorted seeds accommodate 300-500 seeds.
- Seeds which sink (sinkers) are used for raising nursery and floating seeds (floaters) are discarded.
- Nursery bed of 30 m x 1.5 c or 37.5 m x 1.2 m size accommodates about 1300 seeds when sown at 20 cm x 20 cm (triangular) spacing.
- Seeds are sown in rows with 'eye' facing downwards or parallel to ground surface.
- Seedlings can be raised in polyethylene sleeves (17 cm wide & 20-30 cm long & 150 gauge thick).
- Vigorous seedlings are planted in the field in April-May when they are 5-6 months old.
- Seed rate: 40-60 kg/ha.
- Chances of getting clone from seedling population: 0.0125 to 0.025%.
- Polyclonal seed: Seeds obtained from crosses involving >2 clones.
- Bi-clonal seed: Seeds resulting from 2 clones.
- Polyclonal or bi-clonal seeds are preferred for seed production.
- Seedlings take 15-18 months for transplanting.

- Commercial propagation: Single node cuttings.
- About 3 cm long cuttings from mid portion of juvenile shoot are preferred.
- Cuttings can be raised in nursery & for raising 1 lakh plants at a time & hardening them, 1500 sq. m land is required.
- Cuttings taken from primaries with dormant apical buds (banji state) gives higher success.
- Cuttings/ clones can be planted directly into sleeves.
- Callusing starts in 4-6 weeks and rooting occurs in 10-12 weeks.
- The 9-12 months old plants become ready for planting in the field.
- Current trend in tea nursery is to grow tube nurseries rather than bed nurseries.
- Cleft grafting on rooted cuttings of UPASI-2 as rootstock gives 90% success.
- Stump or carrot planting: Adopted in drought pone area.
- Single or double hedge style of planting is recommended in tea.
- Planting distance:
  - Up and down style: 1.2 m x 1.2 m (6800 plants/ ha).
  - Contour planting:
    - Single hedge - 1.2 m x 0.75 m (10800 plants/ ha).
    - Double hedge - 1.35 m x 0.75 m x 0.75 m (13200 plants/ ha). Accommodate more number of plants/ unit area.
- In N-E India, at 60 cm x 105 cm distance (7000 bushes/ ha).
- Calcium ammonium nitrate (CAN): Best source of nitrogen in winter in South India.
- Crop tolerates soils with less amount of calcium but high quantities of potassium and silicon.
- Soil amendment for maintaining soil pH: Lime ($CaCO_3$) and Dolomite ($CaMgCO_3$).
- Soil must have more proportion of Fe and N content.
- Ratio of N and P application in plucking tea fields: 1: 1.
- Role of shady tree: Regulate temperature.
- Best permanent shade tree in southern India: Silver oak (*Grevillea robusta*).
- Temporary shade tree: *Indigofera teysmanii* (most commonly used), *Glyricidia sepium*.
- Pollarding: Cutting the main stem to develop lateral branches and it is done when tree attains 50 cm girth at elbow level.
- Annual lopping: Cutting the erect growing branches & retained laterals is lopping and it is done before onset of monsoon.
- Centering: Type of training method: promotes axillary bud or lateral branches. It is removal of growing point of main stem leaving 8-10 matured leaves at height of 20

cm from ground. It is done to induce secondaries. When secondaries reach more than 3-4 leaves and buds then tertiaries are induced.

- In North-East India, tea is pruned every year when bushes enter dormant phase.
- Primary shoots/ periodic shoots: Shoots arising from sticks (frame) of pruned bushes.
- Flush: Growth of apical bud between 2 successive phases of dormancy.
- Formation of frame is achieved by following 3 operations:
  a) Decentering, lung prune, de-budding and
  b) Formative pruning 20-26 months after planting &
  c) Final Frame formation pruning.
- Permanent frame bush architecture consist of 3-tier branching system in proportion of 1: 3: 7 at De-centering/ de-budding, Frame forming prune & Permanent Frame forming prune levels, respectively.
- Height of permanent bush frame: 35-45 cm from ground level.
- Pruning: Bushes are pruned at periodic intervals to vitalize vegetative vigour, regulate plant height, for good yield of crop and to develop good frame.
- Pruning is carried out when tea bush is dormant and there is good reserve of root starch.
- Pruning maintains the bushes permanently in vegetative phase.
- Area of plucking tables, density of plucking points and proportion of banji shoots increases as the age of bush advances from pruning.
- There is direct relationship between pruning and drought-stress.
- Generally, 4 or 5 year pruning cycle is followed.
- Pruning is done between mid-December to mid-January.
- The shoots arising from sticks (frames) of pruned bushes are called 'primaries'.
- Skiffing: Lightest form of pruning above 75 cm from ground level. This is done when bush frame is healthy. Only green stems are removed to obtain uniform level of pruning surface.
- Light pruning: Bushes are pruned at 60-70 cm height.
- Medium pruning: To check the bush growth to a inconvenient height. It stimulates new wood and maintains foliage at lower level. It is done occasionally (once in 12 to 18 years). Medium style of pruning refers to pruning between 45 and 55 cm.
- Hard/ Formative pruning: Done at 5 years after planting (40-50 cm above ground level) to attain proper spread.
- Collar pruning or rehabitation: Severe most pruning (30-40 cm height) for rejuvenation of tea gardens.
- Lung pruning or fringe pruning: Criss-cross branches are removed so that bush maintains a uniform height.

- Rejuvenation pruning: Done to revitalize plant and uprooting is delayed by 10-15 years.
- Cleaning of branches which are less than pencil thick in dia., & removal of knots and snags is undertaken while carrying out this type of pruning.
- The periodic shoots developing on frames of pruned bushes are tipped at appropriate height.
- Height of tipping decreases with increasing height of pruning.
- Tipping: Practice of removal of terminal portion of shoot (4 leaves and a bud) with jats. It is first plucking of recovering bushes. It is first round of harvesting of young shoots.
- Objectives of tipping:
  - o To establish a level plucking surface.
  - o To provide maintenance foliage and
  - o For production of secondary branches.
- Tipping height = Number of leaves that must be left above the pruned cut.
- Tipping material = that portion of terminal shoot which must be tipped off.
- Immediately after rejuvenation or hard pruning, cut ends are smeared with paste of copper oxychloride + linseed oil in 1 : 1 ratio.
- Being a leaf crop, manuring of tea plantations enhances vegetaive growth and suppress the reproductive phase.
- Manuring constitutes 17-24% of total output.
- From total dry matter produced in a pruning cycle, about 10% is diverted to flushing of shoots, 18% to mature foliage, 12% to twigs, 35% to thick wood and 25% to roots.
- For tea sprinkler irrigation in the range of 5-15 mm/ hr is most common.
- For application of 2.5 cm of water in 1 ha, 55,945 gallons of water is required.
- Drip irrigation is confined to seed orchards (baris).
- Cataphylls or Janams: First 1-2 scale leaves.
- Fish leaf: Present above scale leaves.
- Banji is dormant phase/ resting period.
- Banji shoot means 'dormant shoots'.
- Half of the 1st opened leaf or apical bud known as 'Banji bud'.
- Plucking is tea is synonymous with harvesting.
- Plucking involves plucking of tender portions of shoots consisting apical/ terminal bud and 2 or 3 leaves, immediately below it.
- Appropriate harvesting stage: Two leaves and a bud.
- It takes about 18-29 months (1.5 to 2.5 years) from planting to reach regular plucking.

- Plucking: Most labour intensive operation.
- Plucking interval: Every week.
- Plucking standard: Denotes the average size of shoots harvested.
- Plucking system: Denotes the severity of operation and amount of mature foliage left behind on bush while plucking.
  - i) Janam plucking: Most common practice in N-E states of India while in south India, fish leaf plucking is not adopted.
  - ii) Fish leaf plucking: Standard picking.
  - iii) Single leaf plucking.
- Mother leaf plucking is done from January to March.
- Tea shoots are plucked to janam or fish leaf level during December-January and to mother leaf plucking from January-March.
- Light plucking: Plucking of shoots up to mother leaf.
- Hard plucking: Plucking of shoots below mother leaf.
- Coarse plucking: Plucking of terminal bud with more than 2 leaves.
- Single mature plant gives 250-300 pluckings in a year.
- Plucking round: Denotes interval between two successive plucking in one area and vary from 4 to 14 days, although 7 days round is most common.
- Commercial tea plants are subjected to 35-40 rounds of plucking annually.
- In N-E states of India, plucking round varies from 6-8 days.
- Each plant produce 10-15 g green leaves per plucking round.
- Plucking table: Denotes formation of plucking surface.
- Plucking is never done below plucking table and janams are never removed.
- During development of apical bud:
  - i) First two scale leaves (cataphylls) or janams appear.
  - ii) Above the scale leaves (janam), is smooth 'fish leaf'.
  - iii) This is followed by series of 3 or 4 normal leaves, the 1st of which is called the 'mother leaf'.
- Phyllocron/ leaf expansion time: Number of days taken for unfolding of successive leaves (1 leaf + bud in 2 leaves + bud).
- In black plucking, all 1 + buds, all 2 + buds & single banji is removed.
- Dicot weeds cause 12% loss in crop and grasses nearly 21% crop loss.
- Dicot weeds can be controlled by Sodium salt of 2, 4-D @ 1.4 kg/ha or Paraquat dichloride @ 1.12 to 2.25 lit/ ha or glyphosate @ 2-3 lit/ ha is recommended.
- In tea, stimulant is 'Thein' and aroma is due to 'Theol' and bitterness/ astringency is due to 'Tannin' i.e. polyphenols.
- Tolerates 2 to 6 Kr gamma radiation.

Species:

- Free intercrossing among different species made tea population highly heterozygous.
- Three distinct taxa: China type, Assam type, Cambod type.
- *Camellia sinensis* (2n=60) is also known as 'China tea'. Introduced to India in the beginning of 19th century.
- Cambod or Indo-China type (*C. assamica ssp. lasiocalyx*): Natural hybrid. Far superior to China variety. Broad leaved Assam plant. Introduced in India from S.E. Asia in beginning of 20th century.
- *C. irrawadiensis*: Caffeine free species.
- *C. japonica* (2n=30): Diploid. Native of China and Japan. Possesses thick, deep green foliage and large flowers.
- Successful crossing between *C. sinensis* x *C. japonica* is reported.
- Triploid (2n=3x=45) hybrid is derived from interspecific hybridization between tetraploid variety (4x=60) and *C. japonica*.
- Open pollinated progenies often produce natural diploids, triploids, tetraploids and aneuploids.
- In China type, 2 morphological forms viz., Macrophylla (broad & long leaves) and Parviflora (small narrow leaves) are identified.
- In Assam type, 2 types viz., Assam type (light green leaves, flowers appear in cluster of 2-9, high yield) and Manipuri type (dark green leaves, flowers appear singly, poor yield, drought resistant).

Assam jats (*C. assamica*)	China jats (*C. sinensis*)
Tree; far superior to China variety	Shrub; introduced to India in 19th century
Few robust branches	Branches abundant and whippy
Large, glossy leaves	Small leathery leaves
Light to medium green leaves	Dark green colour leaves
High yield and medium quality	Low yield but good quality
Susceptible to drought and frost	Hardy and resistant to cold & drought
Sparse flowering	Profuse flowering

Varieties:

- Two stage selection procedure is applied in tea.
- Release of clones for commercial cultivation takes 10-12 years.
- In tea improvement program, clonal selection is done in bi-clonal progeny because of greater phenotypic uniformity.
- Compatible rootstock series of clones have been released by Tea Research Association (TRA) and UPASI-Tea Research Foundation (UPASI-TRF).
- Tocklai Tea research station, Assam released 1st tea clone (vegetatively propagated) in the world in 1949.

- TES has released 29 TV series clones, 130 TRA/ Garden series clones, 100 industry clones and 9 Tocklai bi-clonal seed stocks.
- Following clones released for commercial cultivation:
  - i) Standard TV series clones: TV-2, TV-3, TV-4, TV-5, TV-6, TV-7, TV-10, TV-11, TV-12, TV-13, TV-14, TV-16, TV-17, TV-20, TV-27 and TV-28 having yield potential of 3000-3500 kg made tea/ ha.
  - ii) High yielding TV series clones: TV-8, TV-9, TV-15, TV-18, TV-19, TV-22, TV-23, TV-25, TV-26 and TV-30 having yield potential of 4000 kg made tea/ ha and above.
  - iii) Quality clones: TV-1 and TV-2 having high quality with yield potential of 2500-2800 kg made tea/ ha.
- Bi-clonal Seed Stocks released by Tocklai till 2002 are: TS-378, TS-379, TS-449, TS-450, TS-462, TS-463, TS-464, TS-491, TS-506, TS-520, TS-557, TS-569 and TS-589.
- Bi-clonal hybrid progeny exhibits hybrid vigour, morphological uniformity and retains genetic diversity. These are released by UPASI.
- Bi-clonal method take long period (23-27 years) to develop a seed cultivar.
- 1st polyclonal seed cv. 'Stock 203' released as 'Gaurishankar' in 1954 in India is developed through hybridization.
- Bi-clonal seed stocks developed through hybridization: TS-397, TS-449, TS-450, TS-462, TS-464.
- Promising clones from Sri Lanka: TRI-2024 (high yielding), TRI-2025 (hardy & average yield).

Name	Features
Tea Research Station,Valparai, Tamil Nadu	
UPASI-1 (Evergreen)	Hardy; bi-clonal variety; yield 11,000 kg/ha; quality- above average
UPASI-2 (Jayram)	Hardy; bi-clonal variety; moderate yielder; tolerant to drought & winds; suitable for all elevations
UPASI-3 (Sundaram)	Natural triploid clone; very high yielding; used as male parent for crossing with diploid clone
UPASI-6 (Brook-Lands)	Clonal selection; moderate yielder; suitable for mid & higher elevations
UPASI-8 (Golconda)	Bi-clonal variety; very high yielding; suitable for all elevations
UPASI-9 (Athrey)	Most suitable for high soil pH, drought tolerant & high yielder
UPASI-10 (Pandian)	Hardy clone; moderate yielder; resistant to drought, winds & suitable for higher elevation only
UPASI-14 (Singara)	Suited to higher elevation; very high yielding
UPASI-15 (Spring Field)	Resistant to drought & tolerant to wind, mild frost, suitable to mild altitude & produce quality tea throughout year; approved by Tea Board of India & released for commercial planting
UPASI-16	High yield

UPASI-17 (Swarna)	Flushes well; high yielding; approved by Tea Board of India & released for commercial planting
UPASI-20	Natural triploid clone; moderate yielder; used as male parent for crossing with diploid clone
UPASI-24	Hardy
UPASI-25	High yielding
UPASI-26	Moderate yielder
UPASI-27	Drought tolerant; very high yielding
UPASI-28 (UPASI 10 x TRI 2025)	Bi-clonal; good strength; high quality; very high yielding
TRF-1	High yielding
BSS-1 (UPASI 10 x TRI 2025)	Bi-clonal;
BSS-2 (UPASI 2 x TRI 2025)	Bi-clonal;
BSS-3 (UPASI 9 x TRI 2025)	Bi-clonal;
BSS-4 (UPASI 15 x TRI 2025)	Bi-clonal;
BSS-5 (CR 6017 x UPASI 8)	Bi-clonal;
Tocklai Tea Experimental Station, Jorhat, Assam	
TV-9	Tolerant to water logging
TV-24 (*C. irrawadiensis* x *C. assamica*)	Interspecific hybrid clone developed by back cross method; high yielding & high quality clone; highly aromatic
TV-29 (1990)	Triploid clone
HPKV, Palampur	
B-26	Resistant to frost
IHBT, Palampur	
Him Sphurti (Selection from Kangra-CEF-02, China hybrid Tea)	Yield 1686 kg/ha; wavy leaf shape; 2.2 internode length; 0.428% the oflavins; 2.14% caffeine
CH-1	Smallest leaf
BGP-156 (Selection)	

Processing:

- Leaves and flushes from *C. sinensis* are transformed into dried leaves for brewing tea.
- Processing steps involves oxidizing of leaves, stopping oxidation, forming tea and drying it.
- Degree of oxidation determines final flavour of tea with curing and leaf breakage contribute to lesser amount flavour.
- Pectinase treatment accelerates tea fermentation and also destroys foam forming property.
- Fermentation denotes enzymatic oxidation.
- Fermentation imparts colour to tea.
- Colour of tea: Theaflavins and Thearubigins.

Biochemical compounds responsible for colour:

Compounds	Colour
Theaflavins	Yellowish brown
Thearubigins	Reddish brown
Flavonol glycosides	Light yellow
Pheophorbide	Brownish
Pheophytin	Blackish
Carotene	Yellow

***Biochemical compounds responsible for taste*:**

Compounds	Taste
Polyphenol	Astringent
Amino acids	Brothy
Caffeine	Bitter
Theaflavins	Astringent
Thearubigin	Ashy and slight astringent

***Biochemical compounds responsible for flavour*:**

Compounds	Flavour
Linalool, Linalool oxide	Sweet
Geraniol, Phenylacetaldehyde	Floral
Nerolidol, Benzaldehyde, Methyl salicylate, Phenyl ethanol	Fruity
Trans-2-Hexanal, n-Hexanal, Cis-3-Hexenol, Grassy, b-Ionone	Fresh flavour

- Moisture content in fermented tea 'dhool': 55-60%.
- Moisture content in finally made tea: 2.5-3%.
- In tea manufacturing, end products of fermentation are theaflavins and thearubigins. Proper balance between them is must for a good of tea and optimum ratio is 1:10 to 1:12.
- CTC (Crush, Tear & Curl): Strong strength tea.
- Orthodox tea: Light strength tea.

***Steps involved in processing*:**

a) Wilting/ withering:

- 1st step in processing of tea is 'withering'.
- Main objective of withering: Remove about 15-20% moisture from green leaves.
- Soon after picking, leaves loose excess water and start wilting with gradual onset of enzymatic oxidation.

b) Bruising: Leaves kneaded or rolled-over by heavy wheels releases leaf juices and aid in oxidation and change the taste profile of tea.

c) Oxidation: Leaves left in closed room turn progressively darker due to oxidation process, which can be stopped at any time. In light Oolong tea, 5-40% oxidation, in darker Oolong tea 60-70% and in Black-tea, 100% oxidation is chosen.

d) Kill-green: It is done to stop tea leaf oxidation at desired level. This process is accomplished by moderate heating/ panning/ baking of leaves in rolling drum. This step deactivates oxidative enzymes, without destroying flavour of tea. In CTC black tea, Kill-green is done simultaneously with drying.

e) Yellowing: Unique to yellow tea, warm and damp tea leaves after Kill-green are allowed to lightly heated in closed container, which causes previously green leaves to yellow.

f) Shaping: Damp leaves are rolled to form into wrinkle strips. Rolling action causes oozing out of sap and juices from leaves, which enhances taste of tea. Strips can be rolled into spirals/ kneaded/ pellets or tied into balls.

g) Drying: It is done to 'finish' the tea for sale. It is done by panning, sunning, air-drying or baking. Total drying time in conventional driers: 20-22 minutes.

h) Curing: Some teas require additional aging, secondary-fermentation or baking to reach drinking potential. Sprays of aroma and flavours are done in manufacturing of special flavoured teas.

***Type specific processing*:**

- Green tea: Without fermentation. Leaves dried in shade. Oxidation process is stopped after minimal amount of oxidation by application of steam heat or dry cooking in hot pans. The tea is processed within 1-2 days of harvesting. This process is time consuming and done with pekoes of higher quality. Contains vit. K.
- Black (red) tea:
  - Leaves dried in sun light.
  - Oxidation process takes 2 weeks to one month period.
  - Black tea us classified as Orthodox or CTC, production method developed in 1932.
  - Orthodox processed black teas are further graded according to post-production of leaf quality by Orange Pekoes system while CTC teas by different grading systems.
  - Rich in B complex, folic acid (anti-ulcer & anti-carcinogenic).
- Oolong/ Blue-green tea: Partially fermented tea or semi-oxidized tea. Oxidation process takes 2-3 days. Oxidation is stopped somewhere between standards for green tea and black tea. Outer edges of leaf's are fermented, while heart of leaf remains unfermented. This tea is consumed in Taiwan and China.

- White tea: No oxidation of young leaves. The new growth of buds is shielded from sunlight to prevent formation of chlorophyll. Very less quantity of tea is produced and very expensive.
- Yellow tea: Special tea processed similarly to green tea but with slower drying phase.
- Kukicha tea: It is made from twigs and old leaves pruned from plants during its dormant season and dry roasted over fire.
- Post-fermented tea: Teas that undergo second oxidation are collectively referred to as secondary/ post-fermented tea.
- Poolee tea in Cantonese is very common in market.

Marketing grades:

- Leaf grades results exclusively from sorting stage (last stage of production).
- Four basic grades in orthodox production are Leaf, Broken, Fanning and Dust.
- These categories specify and indicate different leaf sizes and associated strengths.
- Flowery Pekoe (FP), Pekoe (PK), Broken Orange Pekoe (BOP), Red Dust (RD), Super Red Dust (SRD), Super Fine Dust (SFD).

Pests and diseases:

- Red coffee borer (*Zeuzera coffeae*): Major pest.
- Pink mite (*Acaphylla theae*): Serious.
- Blister blight (*Exobasidium vexans*).
- Black root rot (*Rosellinia arcuata*).
- Red rust (*Cephaleuros* spp.).
- Tea Yellow/ Yellowing of tea leaves- Due to sulphur deficiency.

6

SPICES AND CONDIMENTS

1. GENERAL INFORMATION:

- **Spices**: It is defined as vegetable products (non-leafy parts) or mixture thereof, used for flavouring, seasoning and imparting aroma in food. It may be whole form or in ground form e.g. Pepper, Cardamom, Clove, Cinnamon, etc.
- **Condiments:** Plant products that are used as food adjuncts to add taste only e.g. Turmeric, Ginger, Red chillies, Onion, Garlic, etc.
- Term 'spice' was derived from Latin '*Species aromatacea*' means 'Fruits of the earth'.
- Seed spices: Group of annual spices whose dried fruits or seeds are used as spices.
- Spices and condiments are grouped under food adjuncts.
- Major importers: U.S.A, China, South East Asian countries, U.A.E, U.K, Germany, Saudi Arabia, Thailand, Netherlands, Sri Lanka, Mexico, Bangladesh, Brazil, Pakistan, Japan, France, Egypt, Spain, South Africa and Australia.
- USA is the largest importer of hot spices (black pepper, red chilli & ginger) in the world's demand.
- Countries like Malaysia, Netherlands and Germany are raw spice producers and they act as Spice Trading hubs.
- South Asia (India, Pakistan and Nepal) is leading region, produces 55% of the world's production.
- Of the world's 70 plant species grown as spices, 13 are considered as major spices produced in Asia.
- In last decade, average growth in spice production was 4.3% and trade in spices grew @ 5.8% per year.
- In Asia, particularly India is known as "Land of Spices".
- India is largest producer, consumer and exporter of spices and oleoresin.
- Indian spices fulfill almost 1/3rd of the world demand.
- More than 90% of the spices produced in India are used for domestic consumption and rest exported as raw as value added products.
- Kerala state is known as 'Spice Garden of India or Home of spices or Spice bowl of India'.

- States called as 'bowl of seed spices': Rajasthan and Gujarat.
- Leading spice producing states: Gujarat, Andhra Pradesh, Rajasthan.
- Spice crops are largely grown in tropics between 20^0N and 20^0S latitude.
- Indian monopoly is threatened by China, Brazil, Vietnam, Pakistan, Egypt, Turkey, African & Caribbean countries.
- There are 109 spices listed by International Organization for Standardization (ISO) world over, 63 are grown in India and promoted by Spices Board.
- Contribution of spices to total horticultural exports: 28.5%.
- Contribution of spices to total agricultural exports: 19.37%.
- Export of Indian spices and condiments has been increased by 110-115% from 15-16%.
- Chilli, black pepper and turmeric constitutes >70% of total export among spices.
- Spice share 13% of area and 2% of production of the total horticultural crops in India.
- Total area under spices (2018-19): 3.97 million ha.
- Total production (2018-19): 9.41 million tons.
- Value of export of spices (2018-19): 20013.07 crores (4th place).
- Per capita consumption of spices in India has been estimated at 2.639 kg compared to 1.448 kg in USA.
- India commands 46% in global trade in terms of quantity & 28% in terms of value.
- During last decade, spice exports is moving up with an increase of 210% in quantity and 622% in value.
- During recent years, export has been declined by 12% both in terms of quantity & value due to strict regulations of WTO.
- Contribution to world spice production: India (86%), China (4%), Bangladesh (3%), Pakistan and Turkey (2% each) and Nepal (1%).
- Share of major spices in world trade: Peppers & chilli (57%), seed spices (16.67%), cinnamon & cassia (7.33%), turmeric (6.67%) & ginger (4%).
- India's share of the world trade in spices is 45-50% by volume and 25% by value.
- At present, about 48.1% of Indian soils are deficient in available zinc, 11.2% in iron, 7% in available copper and 5.1% in available manganese.
- Unit value earned by spices is 3.6 times more than that for other horticultural exports.
- Most of the spices are hygroscopic in nature.
- Largest area under seed spices: Rajasthan followed by Gujarat.
- The world demand of seed spices is increasing @ 8-10% annually.
- Total area and production under seed spices: 9.7 lakhs ha and 5-6 lakhs tones annually.
- Seed spices share 38% of area and 18% in production of total spices in India.

- India is exporting only 10.87% of its production of seed spices.
- Export of seed spices accounts for 45-50% in volume and 25-30% in value of total export of spices from India.
- Major seed spices: Coriander, Cumin, Fennel, Fenugreek
- Minor seed spices: Ajowain, Dill, Celery, Anise, Nigella, Caraway.
- Among seed spices, cumin contributes most followed by coriander.
- Among seed spices, Ajowain can be grown in kharif and rabi season.
- Best crops for sodic or calcareous soils: Fennel and Dill.
- IISR, Kozhikode has developed crop specific, soil pH based micronutrient mixtures for foliar application in black pepper, cardamom, ginger, and turmeric crops which guarantees 15 to 25% increase in yield.
- Adoption of GAPs like mulching, planting on broad ridges and furrows helps to increase total production by 30-40%.
- Seed spices are rabi crops and grown in semi-arid and arid regions of India.
- Seed spices are aromatic vegetable products having high value and low volume.
- Seed spices are gold mines since having beneficial bio-active compounds for pharmacology.
- Seed spices: Foreign basket of the country.
- Seed spices have not received attention in national seed production policies.
- Organized research on spices started on pepper at Panniyur in 1948 and on small cardamom at Pampadumpara (Kerala) and Mudigere (Karnataka) in 1953.
- Cardamom Research Station, Pampadumpara, Kerala, established in 1956.
- 1st pepper research scheme initiated by Govt. of Madras, at Panniyur.
- H.Q. of AICRP on spices: CPCRI, Calicut.
- The Spice Board Act, 1986 recognized 52 crops.
- Spice Board of India has prepared a document on organic spices in 1998.
- Indian Central Spice and Cashewnut Committee was established during 1961.
- Directorate of Arecanut and Spices Development was established in 1966.
- All India Spices Development Council was established in 1966.
- All India Coordinated Spices and Cashew improvement Projected started in 1975.
- CPCRI at Calicut was constituted in 1975.In 1986, it acquired the status of NRC for Spices.
- NRC was upgraded to Indian Institute of Spice Research (IISR) at Kozhikode on 1st July 1995.
- Systematic research on seed spices in India was started in 1975.
- USA is major importer and consumer of oleoresins (50%).

- Largest producer and exporter of organic spices: Sri Lanka.
- Non judicial use of pesticide is major hurdle in exporting seed spices from India.
- Perispermic seeds are observed in pepper, cardamom, nutmeg, etc.
- In Apiaceae, presence of coumarins in seed inhibits seed germination.
- Spice oil: Obtained by steam distillation method.
- Paper chromatography was 1st proposed by M.S. Tswett in 1903, after successful separation of plant pigments.
- Modern gas chromatography (GC) was invented by A. J. P. Martin and A.T. James in 1952.
- New method of extraction of volatile oil from pepper, nutmeg and ginger with more quality and yield: Super Critical Fluid Extraction (SCFE).
- The residual solvent in oleoresin should be < 30 ppm.
- Nutmeg Act: 1967.
- Spices Cess Act came into existence during 1986.
- Seed priming and pelleting: Modern concept having potential for seed spices.
- Seed spices slows down process of lipid oxidation.
- Cryogenic grinding/ cryo-mill process/ freeze grinding: Powder spices ensure better quality of produce (retain 30% more volatiles over traditional ground spices). Spices are ground without losing even the sensitive flavour principles.
- Advantages of cryogenic grinding: Improves aroma, minimizes loss of essential oils (3-10% loss compared to 15-43% in conventional processing), thickness of ground spices (50 microns compared to 500-1000 microns in conventional processing), reduced oxidation of spice oils and increased stability due to pasteurizing effect.
- Oleoresin (true essence): Overall flavour profile of spices.
- Technology of chilli oleoresin has been worked out in early 1970s by CFTRI, Mysuru.
- Ground powder: Main processed product of spices.
- Ground spices need to be rehydrated to develop their flavour.
- Whole spice grinding unit were established at Mumbai, Cochin and Virudhunagar.
- All Spices Development Council was established in 1966.
- GIS system application has been used to collect diversity in pepper and *Garcinia*.
- ASTA standards: American Spice Trade Association Standards (cleanliness specifications for spices).
- Agricultural Produce Grading and Marketing (APGM) Act (1937): Indian Spice quality control (cleanliness specifications for spices).
- In IX Plan, the Directorate of Arecanut and Spices Development, Calicut, has sanctioned schemes on seed production, demonstration and minikit distribution.

- Organic seed spices certification agencies: Ecocert (Aurangabad); Skal, IMO, APOF from Bengaluru; SGS and Natureland (Gurgaon); Lacon, Bioinspectra and Indocert (Cochin); IRFT (Mumbai); ISCOP (Coimbatore)
- Out of 26 spices covered under Agmark Grading Scheme, the 13 covered under the 'Compulsory Grading Scheme'.
- Agmark Organization (DMI) called mother of standardization in country, rendered pioneering services in quality control of spices.
- Spices Export Promotion Council- Kochi was set up under Ministry of Commerce. GOI.
- Central Agmark Laboratory, Nagpur (1967).
- 1st AGMARK specification was formulated for Curry powder in 1956; for Cardamom and Chilli in 1962 and for turmeric, Ginger, Coriander, Chilli powder, Onion, Garlic, Ambadi, Cumin, Poppy seed in 1964.
- National Accreditation Body (NAB) under Ministry of Commerce is responsible for Accreditation of organic Certification Bodies in country.
- INDOCERT offers Organic certification as per USDA-NOP standards for products destined for export to the United States. It is accreditation agency for organic certification.
- Parameters for seed production: Physical purity, Germinability, seed health, seed borne diseases and genetic purity.
- Spice logo: Certificate given to export quality spice.
- Use 10 Kg bio-fertilizers for 1 acre field of seed spices.
- Value added products constitute 37% of the total export basket.
- Main value added products of seed spices: Ground spices viz., curry powder, spice extracts, oils and oleoresins, mouth fresheners, confectionery items, medicinal utility products, mixed powders, dried leaves, chutney, jal-jeera, RTS, etc.
- Maximum limit for aflatoxins in spices: 1-2 ppb.
- As per European spice association, maximum limit of extraneous matter is 1% and foreign matter is 2%.
- Moisture content of ground spice: 8-10%.
- Orthodox seeds: Coriander, Cumin, fennel and fenugreek.
- Optimum soil pH for seed spices: 6-7.5.
- Seed spices are grown by broadcasting and line sowing.
- Seed viability of seed spices: 2 years.
- Optimum temperature for seed germination 21-27^{0}C, for growth 15-21^{0}C and for maturity 27-35^{0}C.
- '*Lakhi bagh*' technology has been popularized by Dr.BSKKV, Dapoli.

- Indian Institute of Packaging, Mumbai formulated containers for spices and spice products in international market.
- Bio-pesticides: Use of commercial formulation of *Bt* var. Baculo viruses has been effective in controlling shoot borer of ginger & turmeric and *Matarrhizium* sp. and *Bauveria* sp. in control of root grub of cardamom.
- 'Green technology' for management of cardamom thrips using new generation pesticides derived from actinomycetes was developed by IISR, Kozhikode.
- Virus elimination technique in black pepper through somatic embryogenesis was developed by IISR, Kozhikode.
- Integrated technology for rejuvenating virus affected black pepper plantations was developed by IISR, Kozhikode.
- DIVA-GIS study: 1st report on geographic distribution in spices.
- ORAC (oxygen Radical Absorbance capacity) values of spices: Clove (314446), cinnamon (267537), turmeric (102700), cumin (76800), ginger (28811).
- Higher ORAC, better will be oxygen carrying capacity of blood and lungs oxygen capacity.
- During post QRs free trade period, export of spices is declined by 12%, both in terms of quantity and value.
- Demonstration-cum-Seed Production farm in Abhayapuri, Assam serves as 'Treasure House of Spices' where all the spices grown in North-Eastern States will be maintained and serve as main source of planting material for the region.
- Spices suitable for protected cultivation: Turmeric, Ginger, Mint, etc.

Leading countries in production:

- Black Pepper: Vietnam, Indonesia, India, Brazil.
- Cardamom: Guatemala, India.
- Cinnamon: Sri Lanka, India.
- Ginger: Nigeria, India, China.
- Turmeric: India, Europe, North America.
- Nutmeg and mace: Indonesia (75%), Grenada (20%), India, Malaysia.
- Cumin: Europe, India, Iran.
- Coriander: Turkey, Egypt, Romania, Morocco, Iran, China and India.
- Fennel: Syria, Turkey, India.
- Caraway: Netherlands, India.
- Celery: Pakistan, India.
- Anise: Syria, India.
- Fenugreek: Egypt, India.
- Dill: Europe, India, North America.
- Parsley: USA.

2. Classification of Spices and condiments:

2.1 Based on botany

Family	Name	Botanical name	Fruit type	Origin	2n=
Apiaceae	Coriander	*Coriandrum sativum*	Schizocarp	Mediterranean region	22
	Fennel	*Foeniculum vulgare*	Schizocarp	S. Europe	22
	Anise	*Pimpinella anisum* (syn. *Anisum vulgare*)	Schizocarp	East Mediterranean Region	18, 20
	Cumin	*Cuminum cyminum* (syn. *C. odorum*)	Schizocarp	Egypt	14
	Asafoetida	*Ferula asafoetida*	Schizocarp	Central Asia	22
	Dill	*Anethum graveolens*	Schizocarp	Mediterranean region	20
	Ajowain	*Trachyspermum ammi*	Cremocarp with single seed	Middle East	18
	Nigella	*Nigella sativa*	Schizocarp	South Europe	12
	Caraway	*Carum carvi*	Schizocarp	Asia Minor	14
Iridaceae	Saffron	*Crocus sativus*	-	Mediterranean region	24 (3x)
Myristicaceae	Nutmeg	*Myristica fragrans*	Drupe	Indonesia	42, 44
Myrtaceae	Clove	*Syzygium aromatic*	Mother clove	Indonesia	44
	Cinnamon	*Cinnamomum verum*	Berry	India, China	24
	All spice	*Pimenta dioica*	Two seeded berry	West Indies	22
Orchidaceae	Vanilla	*Vanilla planifolia*	-	Mexico	32
Parmeliaceae	Black stone flower	*Parmotrema perlatum*	Algae	-	-
Piperaceae	Black pepper	*Piper nigrum*	Single seeded berry	India	52
	Betel leaf	*Piper betle*	Berry	India	32
Rutaceae	Curry leaf	*Murraya koenigii*	Drupe	India	18
Zingiberaceae	Small cardamom	*Elettaria car damomum*	Capsule	Western Ghats of South India	48
	Large cardamom	*Amomum subulatum*	Capsule	Eastern Himalayan region	48
	Turmeric	*Curcuma longa*	Drupe	India	32, 62, 64 (3x)
	Ginger	*Zingiber officinale*	Single seeded drupe	Indo-Malayan region	22

2.2 Based on growth habit:

1. Herbs: Chilli, Coriander, Cumin, Fenugreek, Fennel, Parsley.
2. Shrubs: Perennial chilli, Long pepper (creeping shrub)

3. Trees: All spice, Clove, Cinnamon, Curry leaf, Kokum, Nutmeg,Tamarind.
4. Climbers: Black pepper, Vanilla.
5. Rhizome: Asafoetida, Cardamom, Ginger, Turmeric,Greater galanga, Sweet flag.

2.3 Based on plant part used:

1. Aril: Mace.
2. Bark: Cinnamon, Cassia.
3. Root exudates: Asafoetida.
4. Flower buds: Clove.
5. Fruit/ seed: Aniseed, Caraway, Coriander, Dill, Fenugreek, Mustard.
6. Fruit pulp/rind: Kokum, Tamarind.
7. Kernel: Nutmeg.
8. Leaf: Basil, Bay leaf, Curry leaf, Marjoram.
9. Pistil/stigma: Saffron.
10. Root: Angelica, Horse radish, Lovage.
11. Rhizome: Ginger, Turmeric.
12. Whole fruit: All spice, Ajowain, Black pepper, Chilli, Cumin, Fennel.

2.4 Based on important flavor, taste compounds:

- Alkaloids present in spices are responsible for pungency.

Spice	Flavour/ aroma compound	Spice	Flavour/ aroma compounds
All spice	Eugenol, β-caryophyllene	Celery	Limonene
Asafoetida	Ferulic acid	Nutmeg & mace	Sabinine, Myristicin, a-pinene, 1-terpenin-4-ol, Safrimine
Basil	Methyl chavicol	Cumin	Cuminaldehyde
Black pepper	Piperine, β-caryophyllene, S-3-Carene	Fennel, Star anise	(E)-Anethole
Cardamom	a-terpinyl acetate, 1-8-cinole, linalool	Saffron	Safranal
Turmeric	ar-Turmerone, Zingiberene, 1,8-cineole	Vanilla	Vanillin, P-OH-benzyl methyl ether
Ginger	Gingerol, Shogaol, Zingiberene (pungency components); β-sesquiphel-lenbrene & ar-curcumine (ginger flavour); α-terpenol & citral (lemony flavour)	Coriander	Linalool
Chilli	Capsaicin,	Cinnamon	Cinnamaldehyde, eugenol
Fenugreek	Trigonellin	Horse radish	Sinigrin
Clove	Eugenol, Eugenol acetate	Thyme	Thymol
Rosemary	Cineol	Pepper mint	Menthol
Parsley	1, 3, 8-p-menthatreiene	-	-

2.5 Based on colour compounds:

Spice	Colour compound found
Mustard	Reddish orange (β-carotene)
Red chilli, paprika	Red (cryptoxanthin), Dark red (capsanthin 30-60%), Purple red (capsorubin 6-18%); Reddish orange (β-carotene)
Paprika,	Dark red (lutein), Orange (violaxanthin); Red &Yellow components i.e. mixture of carotenoids; Reddish orange (β-carotene)
Saffron	Yellow orange (crocetin), Dark red (crocetin), Reddish orange (β-carotene)
Parsley	Orange yellow (neoxanthin); Dark red (lutein), Orange (violaxanthin)
Turmeric	Orange yellow (Curcumin/ curcuminoid)
Ginger	Yellow (Flavonoid)

2.6 Based on isolation distance for seed spices:

Spices	Distance (m)		Moisture (%)	
	Foundation seed	Certified seed	Foundation seed	Certified seed
Fenugreek (highly self pollinated)	50	25	8	8
Coriander (cross pollinated)	800	400	10	10
Cumin (cross pollinated)	200	100	10	10
Fennel (cross pollinated)	800	400	10	10
Ajowain (cross pollinated)	400	200	8	8
Dill (cross pollinated)	800	400	9	9
Celery (cross pollinated)	800	400	9	9
Anise (cross pollinated)	800	400	10	10
Nigella (cross pollinated)	400	200	9	9

2.7 Based on salinity/ alkalinity tolerance limit in seed spices

Spice	EC dS/m (soil/water)	Tolerance
Coriander	4.0	Sensitive to higher pH in calcareous soil
Cumin	13.5	Sensitive to higher pH in calcareous soil
Fennel	8-10	Tolerance improved with advance crop & sensitive to higher pH in calcareous soil age
Fenugreek	2-4	Seedling stage is more tolerant than later
Dill	5-12	Tolerant to high pH (9.0)
Celery	9-11	Bit sensitive to sodicity
Ajowain	6-8	Medium tolerant to sodicity & mild sensitive to high pH in calcareous soil
Anise	6-8	This tolerance is for germination; least tolerant among seed spices
Nigella	2-7.5	Mild sensitive to high pH in calcareous soil

2.8 Seed standards for seed spices:

- Seed moisture content: 3-7% (base collection), 8-10% (active collection).
- Sampling size: 3000-4000 seeds (fenugreek), 4000-12000 seeds (remaining all seeds).

Spice	Pure seed (min.)		Germination (%)		Moisture (%)	
	Foundation	Certified	Foundation	Certified	Foundation	Certified
Fenugreek	98	98	70	70	8	8
Coriander	97	97	65	65	10	10
Cumin	97	97	65	65	10	10
Fennel	98	98	75	75	10	10
Ajowain	97	97	65	65	8	8
Dill	98	98	75	75	9	9
Anise	98	98	65	65	10	10
Celery	97	97	65	65	9	9
Caraway	97	97	70	70	10	10
Nigella	98	98	70	70	9	9

2.9 Critical stages of irrigating seed spices:

Crop	Crop duration (Days)	Water requirement with surface irrigation (mm)	No. of irrigation	Irrigation schedule
Cumin	110-125	200-250	4-5	At sowing time, at germination (8-10 DAS), at flowering (50 DAS) & seed development stage (70-80 DAS)
Coriander	135-150	250-300	5-6	At germination (8-10 DAS), at vegetative phase (50 DAS), flowering (80 DAS) & seed development stage (110 DAS)
Fenugreek	120-135	300-350	6-7	At germination (8-10 DAS), at vegetative phase (50 DAS), flowering (80 DAS) & pod filling stage (110 DAS)
Fennel	180-210	500-600	10-12	At germination (8-10 DAS), at vegetative phase (70 DAS), emergence of king umbel (120 DAS), secondary and tertiary umbel stage (150 DAS) & seed development stage (180 DAS)
Ajowain	150-180	350-400	7-8	At germination (12-15 DAS), at vegetative phase (80 DAS), flowering stage (110 DAS) & seed development stage (130 DAS)
Dill	180-210	250-300	5-6	At germination (8-10 DAS), at vegetative phase (70 DAS), emergence of king umbel (120 DAS), secondary and tertiary umbel stage (150 DAS) & seed development stage (180 DAS)
Celery	180-210	400-500	8-10	At germination (8-10 DAS), at vegetative phase (70 DAS), emergence of king umbel (120 DAS), secondary and tertiary umbel stage (150 DAS) & seed development stage (180 DAS)
Nigella	115-130	300-350	6-7	At germination (8-10 DAS), at vegetative phase (50 DAS), flowering (80 DAS) & capsule filling stage (100 DAS)
Caraway	135-150	3900-350	6-7	At germination (8-10 DAS), at vegetative phase (70 DAS), flowering (100 DAS) & seed development stage (125 DAS)

SPICE PARKS IN INDIA:

1. Chhindwara (Madhya Pradesh)- 1st spice park. Dehydration plant for chilli and garlic.
2. Puttady (Kerala)- Small cardamom and pepper.
3. Jodhpur (Rajasthan)- Coriander and Fenugreek.
4. Guna (Madhya Pradesh)- Mustard, Coriander, Chilli, Garlic, Ginger.
5. Guntur (Andhra Pradesh)- Chilli.
6. Sivaganga (Tamil Nadu).
7. Kota (Rajasthan).
8. Raebareli (Uttar Pradesh).

3. APIACEAE (UMBELLIFERAE)

3.1 Coriander/ *Dhania*

- *Coriandrum sativum* (only cultivated species).
- Most heavily consumed herb.
- Leaves show stronger anti-oxidant activity than seeds and lower blood sugar.
- Rajasthan: Maximum area and production.
- Germination is adversely affected at >30°C and <10°C.
- Can tolerate salinity upto EC 4.0 dS/m.
- If salinity > 6 dS/m, reduction in 50% growth, flowering and yield is observed.
- Fresh green leaves called 'cilantro' contains 4% volatiles (on wt. leaf basis) primarily 2-decenal and 2-dodecenal.
- Volatile oil determines colour and flavour character.
- Volatile oil content ranges from 0.1 to 1.7% and up to 2.7%.
- Oil content in dry seeds: 0.10 to 1.0% (essential oil) and 19 to 21% fatty oil.
- Seed contain 19-21% fatty oil.
- Seed flavor is due to terpenes i.e. d-linalool (25-80% of volatile oil) also known as Corianderol ($C_{10}H_{17}OH$).
- Andromonoecious plant flowers in July-August.
- Type of dichogamy: Protandrous.
- Inflorescence: Compound umbel with small white or pinkish flowers.
- Highly cross pollinated by honey bee.
- No inbreeding depression observed after 3 generations of selfing.
- Drying is done to maintain moisture level <13% in seeds.
- Seed rate: 10-16 kg/ha (irrigated); 15-20 kg/ha (rainfed).

- Yield: 8-10 q/ha.
- GA_3 spray @ 100 ppm at 5th stage increases male flowers.
- Seed soaking in 50 ppm IAA improves flowering.
- Magnesium chlorate @ 8 kg/ha at waxy stage of ripening makes harvesting easier and improves essential oil content.
- Round, red brown seed capsule is aromatic when ripe.
- Coriander *dal* is obtained from seeds of coriander.
- Seeds shatter after maturity (90 days from planting).

Varieties:

- Karan: Small seeded.
- Pusa Selection-360.
- JD (SI)-l: High oil type coriander (0.67 %).
- CIMPO S-33: Tall, erect, small seeded with high essential oil (1.3%).

Name	Breeding method	Special feature
TNAU, Coimbatore		
CO.1 (1977)	Selection from 'Koilpatti local'	Suitable for green & grains; yield 440 kg/ha (dry)
CO.2 (1982)	Reselection from P_2 cv. of Gujarat	Dual purpose; grown in water logged, drought, saline-alkaline condition; yield 520 kg/ha (dry)
CO.3 (1991)	Reselection from Acc. 695 of IARI type	Dwarf; yield 650 kg/ha (dry); tolerant to wilt, PM & gray mold
CS-287 (1991)	Reselection from Guntur collection	Very early maturing; yield 600 kg/ha (dry); tolerant to wilt & gray mold
CO (CR)-4 (2002)	Reselection from germplasm ATP-77	Early maturing; suitable for rainfed & irrigated areas; essential oil 0.4%; tolerant to wilt & gray mold
NRCSS, Ajmer		
Ajmer Coriander-1 (2006)	Selection from exotic collection	Dual purpose; late maturing; 0.6% essential oil; resistant to stem gall & tolerant to PM
Ajmer Coriander-2 (2018)	Selection	Resistant to stem gall
Ajmer Coriander-3 (2019)	Selection	High volatile oil (0.55 %) with high linalool (75.42 %)
Ajmer Coriander-01-250	Selection	Resistant to stem gall & wilt
IIHR, Bengaluru		
Arka Isha	Mass selection from exotic introduction from Japan	Bushy, multi-cut type; good keeping quality (21 days under refrigeration), rich in vit. C (167 mg/ 100g), yield (12 T/ha) in 3 cuttings in 70 days
CARI, Port Blair		

Broad Dhania	-	Mexican coriander/ Spiny coriander (*Eryngium foetidum*; yield 8-10 T/ha; rich in Phytochemicals & micronutrients
GBPUA & T, Pantnagar		
Pant Haritima (1993)	Selection from local	Tall; dual purpose type; high oil 0.4%; yield 1200 kg/ha (dry); resistant to stem gall
UAS, Dharwad		
DWA-3 (1999)	Pure line selection	Dual purpose variety; 0.27% essential oil; mod. tolerant to PM; black clay soils best suited.
DrYSRHU, Andhra Pradesh (ARS, Lam, Guntur)		
Swathi (Lam CS-6), 1989	Mass selection from local 'Nandyal' collection	Suitable for late sowing; yield 855 kg/ha (dry); tolerant to white fly, gray mold & wilt
Sadhana (CS-4), 1989	Mass selection from local 'Alur' collection	Suitable for rainfed areas; yield 1025 kg/ha (dry); resistant to aphids, white flies & mites; tolerant to salinity
Sindhu (Lam CS-2) 1991	Mass selection from local 'Warangal' local	Matures in 102 days; yield 1050 kg/ha (dry); suitable for intercropping & rainfed area, tolerant to wilt, PM & resistant to aphids
Sonia (Lam CS-7)	Mass selection	Leaf & grain purpose
APAU Dhania-1	Selection	Suitable for rainfed area
Susthira (2018)	Selection	Suitable in rabi
Suguna (2018)	Selection	-
Suruchi	Selection	Off season coriander; suitable for protected cultivation in summer
SDAU, Jagudan		
GCr-1 (1974)	Selection from germplasm	Grain purpose; yield 1100 kg/ha (dry); highly sensitive to salinity; tolerant to wilt & PM
GCr-2 (1985)	Reselection from CO.2	Grain purpose & no lodging; yield 1450 kg/ha (dry); highly sensitive to salinity; mod. tolerant to wilt & PM
GCr-3 (2012)	Selection	-
GC-4	Selection	Resistant to fusarium wilt
RPCAU, Pusa, Samastipur, Bihar (College of Agriculture, Dholi)		
Rajendra Swati (RD-44) 1988	Selection from Muzzaffarpur collection	yield 1300 kg/ha (dry); resistant to stem gall; highly sensitive to salinity
Rajendra Sonia	Selection	Resistant to wilt, aphid, weevil; tolerant to fruit fly
Rajendra Dhania-1 (2018)	Selection	-
Rajendra Dhania-2	Selection	-
Rajendra Dhania-3	Selection	Climatic resilient variety; yield (14.09 q/ha); high oil (0.52 %).
RD 385 (Dr. RPCAU Dhania-1) 2019	Selection	Moderately resistant to stem gall disease & resistant to lodging
RAU, Jobner, Rajasthan		
RCr-41 (1988)	Recurrent half-sib selection from local type	Suitable for irrigated areas; yield 909 kg/ha (dry); small sized grains; highly resistant to stem gall & wilt & tolerant to PM
RCr-20 (1997)	Recurrent half-sib selection from Jaipur local	Suitable as rainfed crop; oval large grains; yield 900 kg/ha (dry); mod. tolerant to PM, wilt & gall fly; highly sensitive to salinity
RCr-435 (1999)	Recurrent selection from local type	Medium sized grains; yield 1000 kg/ha (dry); mod. resistant to root knot nematode, PM

RCr-436 (1999)	Recurrent selection from local type	Matures in 90-110 days; yield 1200 kg/ha (dry); suitable for heavy soils, mod. resistant to root knot nematode
RCr-684 (1999)	Mutation by gamma rays to 'RCr-20'	Bold grains, yield 990 kg/ha (dry); resistant to stem gall & PM
RCr-446 (1997)	Half-sib selection from local type	Higher number of grains; suitable for irrigated cropping system; mod. resistant to stem gall & wilt
UD-446 (2001)	Half-sib selection from local	Yield 1200 kg/ha (dry); resistant to stem gall & wilt
SVBPUA & T, Meerut		
Sarvehari	Mass selection	Sown in kharif & rabi
CSAUA & T, Kanpur		
Azad Dhania-1 (1996)	Mass selection	0.30% essential oil; yield 1800 kg/ha (dry); tolerant to moisture stress, PM & aphids
Azad Dhania-2	Mass selection from Kalyanpur germplasm	Suitable in rabi; 0.29% essential oil; tolerant to moisture stress, PM & aphids
IGKV, Raipur, Chhattisgarh		
Chhattisgarh Dhaniya-1	-	
Chhattisgarh Shri Chandrahasini Dhaniya-2 (2019)	Mass selection	Climatic resilient variety for dual purpose (leaf & seed purpose); mod. resistant to PM & aphids
CCSHAU, Hissar		
Hisar Sugandh (2001)	Mass selection from indigenous germplasm	Suitable in rabi; yield 1500 kg/ha (dry); dual purpose; resistant to stem gall
Hisar Anand (1994)	Mass selection from Haryana collection	Suitable in rabi; 0.35% essential oil; yield 1400 kg/ha (dry); resistant to lodging
Hisar Surabhi (2004)	Mass selection from local germplasm	Bushy; suitable in rabi; 0.425% oil content; tolerant to salinity, frost & less susceptible to aphids
DH-209	Selection	Suitable for Haryana; matures in 130-140 days
DH-5 (1993)	Selection from local	Matures in 120-130 days; yield 1800 kg/ha (dry)
Dr BSKKV, Dapoli		
Konkan Kasturi (2013)	Selection	Leaves have high aroma; suitable for green leaf purpose; suitable for rabi & summer season; 0.02% oil in green leaves & 0.126% in dried leaves; aldehyde mandarin content 8740 ppm; yield 25-40 q/ha
UHS, Bagalkot (HRS, Devihosur)		
Varadevi	Selection	-
SKUAST, Jammu		
Jammu Coriander-07	-	
JNKVV, Jabalpur		
Jawahar Dhaniya-1	Selection	High oil (0.67 %); high yield (14.14 q/ha)
Jawahar Dhaniya-10	Selection	-

Diseases and pest:

- Fusarium wilt. Fungus release toxin (fusaric acid) and block xylem vessels. Use *T. viride*, *T. harzianum*.
- Powdery mildew: *Erysiphe polygoni*.
- Stem gall (*Protomyces macrosporus)* is specific disease. RCr-1: Tolerant to stem gall. Early and late sown corianders are less affected by this disease in comparison to timely sown. Shape of seeds change.
- Aphids (*Hyadaphis coriandri*; > 50% loss), Seed wasp (*Systole albipennis*), Red spider mite.

3.2 Fennel/*Saunf*

- Cultivated species:
  - o *Foeniculum vulgare*: Cultivated in India, Russia, Italy, Hungary, Germany, Rumania.
  - o *F. dulce*: Cultivated in France, Italy, South Europe.
- *F. vulgare* var. *azoricum*: Sweet fennel or Florence fennel. Forms bulb (swollen leaf base) like structure just above the ground.
- Seed used in Italian and French cooking, stems sometimes used raw.
- Sweet fennel is rich in carbohydrates (7.29 g), protein (1.24 g), Vit. A (134 IU).
- Low calorie food: 31 Kcal/100g.
- Common fennel is more drought tolerant than sweet fennel.
- Sweet fennel: Perennial herb, grown as annual is exotic vegetable. Native to southern Europe. It has low calorie food. Ornamental feathery leaves with aromatic leaf stalks are used.
- Volatile oil (i.e. Corianderol $C_{10}H_{17}OH$): Sweet and higher in smaller seed (0.7 to 1.2 %).
- Essential oil in fennel fruits is 3-5% by weight and exhibit anti-bacterial and anti-viral activities.
- Chemical content: Limone.
- Optimum soil pH: 6.5 to 8.
- Seed rate: 10-12 kg/ha.
- Seed replacement rate: 10-14%.
- Spacing: 45 cm x 20 cm.
- Method of sowing: Broadcasting.
- Seed treatment: Seed soaking in water for 5 h and treat with Bavistin @ 2 g/kg.
- Highly susceptible to frost in early fruit setting and flowering stage.
- Crop maturity: 5-6 months.

- Chewing type fennel (Lucknawi) umbel is harvested at 30-40 days after pollination.
- Yield: 10-15 q/ha.

Varieties:

- Sweet fennel: Trieste: Variety of bulbous fennel, Zefafino (from USA), Orion hybrid (resistant to bolting).

Name	Breeding method	Features
SDAU, Jagudan		
S-7-9 (1956)	Selection	Bushy; mod. tolerant to blight, 1.2% essential oil
PF-35 (1973)	Selection from Pilwai local	Tall; 1.9% essential oil; matures within 215-225 days; yield 1280 kg/ha (dry); mod. tolerant to leaf spot; blight & sugary disease
Gujarat Fennel-1 (1984)	Pure line selection	Tall; resistant to seed shattering & lodging; 2.2% essential oil; yield 1695 kg/ha (dry); tolerant to drought, sugary disease
GF-2 (1997)	Pedigree selection from local	Bushy; 2.4% essential oil; yield 1940 kg/ha (dry); suitable for rainfed & irrigated condition
GF-3 (2003)	Selection	Medium maturing; 1.8% essential oil; suitable for rabi season
GF-11	Recurrent selection	Yield 1940 kg/ha (dry); 2.4 % essential oil; suitable for rabi season
GF-12	Selection	Yield 1840 kg/ha (dry); 2.2 % essential oil; suitable for rabi season
RAU, Jobner, Rajasthan		
RF-101 (1999)	Recurrent selection from local germplasm	Erect; long bold grains; suitable for loamy & black cotton soils; yield 1400 kg/ha (dry)
RF-107	Selection	Most sodicity tolerant
RF-125 (1997)	Half-sib selection from exotic collection 'EC-243380'	Dwarf; seed yield (1700 kg/ha dry); matures in 110-130 days; 2.78% essential oil; tolerant to salinity& sugary disease
RF-143	Recurrent selection of individual plant	Seed yield (12 q/ha dry); 1.87% essential oil; recommended for loamy and black soil
RF-157	Selection	Long attractive and bold seeds
RF-178	Selection	Seed yield 18-19 q/ha (dry)
RF-205 (2009)	Selection	Seed yield 29.45 q/ha (dry)
RF-281 (2012)	Selection	Bold, attractive seeds, high volatile oil (2.58%); seed yield 18-19 q/ha (dry)
Rajendra Saurbha (2000)	Selection	Seed yield 18-19 q/ha
CCSHAU, Hisar		
Hisar Swarup (2004)	Mass selection	Bushy; 1.6% essential oil; resistant to lodging; no shattering of grains
HF-107	Selection	Yield 13 q/ha; matures in 160 days
HF-143 (2012)	Selection	Yield 18 q/ha; matures only in 150 days

NRCSS, Ajmer		
Ajmer Fennel-1 (2006)	Selection	Early sowing & rabi season; 1.6% volatile oil; tolerant to *Ramularia* & alternaria blight
Ajmer Fennel-2 (2016)	Selection	Suitable for early & rabi season; high oil content (1.9%); tolerant to ramularia blight
Ajmer Fennel-3	Selection	High yielding (21.43 q/ha) & high oil (1.9%)
NDUA & T, Faizabad		
NDF-7	Selection	-
NDF-9	Selection	-
TNAU, Coimbatore		
CO. 1 (1985)	Reselection from PF-35	Diffuse branching; suitable for intercropping; drought prone, resistant to water logged, saline &alkaline conditions; matures in 210-220 days; yield 570 kg/ha (dry)
CSAUA & T, Kanpur		
Azad Sauf-1 (1996)	Selection from germplasm	Matures in 160-170 days; seed yield 1800 kg/ha (dry); resistant to blight & root rot
GBUA & T, Pantnagar		
Pant Madhurikar	Pure line selection from local germplasm	Tall; big umbels; bold seeds; sweet taste; yield 1500 kg/ha (dry)

Diseases and pest:

- Collar rot: Due to water stagnation.
- Ramularia blight (*Ramularia foeniculi*): Most serious.
- Alternaria blight (*Alternaria tenius*):
- Powdery mildew (*Erysiphe polygoni*):
- Ashy spots: Spray Dithane Z-78 @ 0.2%.
- Gummosis: Wide spread.
- Aphid: Serious pest causing loss up to 50%. Spray neem seed kernel extract @ 5% or neem oil @ 2%.
- Seed wasp: Female wasp lays egg inside seed. Spray neem oil @ 2%.
- Cut worm: Apply phorate 10 kg/ha.

3.3 Anise/*Vilayati saunf*

- Annual and least tolerant to salinity among seed spices.
- Used for different purposes (anti-microbial, anti-fungal, anti-viral, anti-oxidant, insecticidal) in traditional medicine.
- Seed used in medicines, cooking and flavouring liquors.
- Economic part: Fruit.
- Propagation method: Seed.
- Volatile oil: Anithol.

Varieties:

- NRCSS-ANi-1: High volatile oil content (3.2% in seed). Yield 7-8 q/ha.
- NRCSS-ANi-13: Highest salinity tolerant.

3.4 Cumin/*Jeera*

- Highest salinity tolerant crop (13.5 dS/m) from germination to overall growth period but highly susceptible to frost injury in flowering and early fruit setting.
- Black jeera is cultivated in Gurez valley in Kashmir.
- Salinity does not affect essential oil content.
- Seed can germinate up to 20 dS/m.
- Salinity does not markedly affect essential oil content.
- Iran: Main cumin exporter.
- Rich in thymol.
- Dried fruit is called as 'cumin seed'.
- Seeds are good source of iron.
- Seeds yield volatile oil (2.5 to 4.5%)-cuminaldehyde i.e. cuminol (20-40%) exhibit strong larvicidal and anti-bacterial activity, used in perfumery.
- Crop duration: 110-120 days.
- Seed rate: 8-10 kg/ha;
- Seed yield: 8-12 q/ha.
- Tractor mounted cumin planter saves 30% seed.
- Weed competition is major problem at all stages of growth.
- Objectionable weed in seed spice: *Plantago pumila* (jeeri or jeeralu), *Asphadelous tenuifolius*.
- Moisture content in seed before storage: 11%.

Varieties:

Name	Breeding method	Features
NRCSS, Ajmer		
AC-01-3	Selection	Wilt resistant & drought tolerant
SDAU, Jagudan, Gujarat		
5-404 (1952)	Selection from local	Erect, 2.2% essential oil; mod. tolerant to PM
Mc-43 (1970)	Selection from local	Bold grains; withstand lodging; 2.7% essential oil; mod. tolerant to fusarium wilt, alternaria blight & PM; yield 580 kg/ha (dry)
GC-1 (1983)	Single plant selection from local	Bushy, spreading; withstand shattering; 3.6% essential oil; mod. tolerant to Fusarium wilt, alternaria blight & PM; yield 700 kg/ha (dry)
GC-2 (1992)	Pure line selection	Bushy; tolerant to salinity, wilt, blight, PM; 4% essential oil; yield 500 kg/ha (dry)

GC-3 (2000)	Recurrent selection	Bushy; resistant to frost, wilt & suitable for winter season; 4.4% essential oil; yield 663 kg/ha (dry)
GC-4 (2003)	Natural crossing followed by selection	1st wilt resistant variety; no seed shattering
GC-5 (2012)	Selection	High yielding; wilt resistant; 38% high yield than GC-4
RAU, Jobner, Rajasthan		
RZ-19 (1988)	Recurrent selection from 'UC.19'	Erect growth; bold pubescent grains; suitable for late sowing; 2.3-3% oil; tolerant to wilt, blight; yield 500 kg/ha (dry)
RZ-209 (1995)	Recurrent selection	Resistant to wilt & blight; tolerant to blight
RZ-223 (1999)	Mutation breeding in 'UC-216'	Bushy; attractive seeds; 3.5% essential oil; resistant to wilt
RZ-341	Recurrent selection	Highly tolerant to salinity
RZ-345	Recurrent selection	Seeds bold; high volatile oil; mod. resistant to wilt
TNAU, Coimbatore		
CO.1	Selection	Profuse branching; suitable for saline & alkaline soils/ hilly area/ drought prone areas
CCSHAU, Hisar		
Hisar Swarup	Selection	Resistant to lodging & seed shattering

Diseases and pest:

- Leaf blight (*Alternaria burnsii*):
- Fusarium wilt: Soil borne.
- Powdery mildew (*Erysiphe polygoni*): Major disease.
- Thrips: Serious pest.

3.5 Asafoetida/ *Heeng*

- Eulogized as 'Devil's dung'.
- IHBT, has taken up heeng cultivation in the Lahaul valley of Himachal Pradesh.
- Rhizome produce 2 types of plants.
- Male: Produce inflorescence
  Female: Only foliage and no inflorescence.
- Major varieties: Heeng (exudates of *F. asafoetida*), Heengra (exudates of *F. scorodosma*).
- Hadda: Most priced and strongest.
- Heengashakta: An Ayurvedic medicine prepared from *heeng*.
- Odour: Sulphur compound.
- Stage of tapping: Foliage turns green to yellow.
- Tapping is done for extraction of oleogum.
- Asafoetida contains resin (40-64%), gum (2.5%) & volatile oil (10-17%).

- In market, it is available in 3 forms: Tears (purest form of resin), mass, paste.
- Bandhani heeng/ Compounded asafoetida/ Irani or Pathani heeng: Contain one or more varieties.

3.6 Dill/ *Sowa*

- *Anethum graveolens* (European type); *A. sowa* (Indian type).
- It is annual and biannual herb.
- Whole plant is aromatic.
- Young leaves and full grown green fruits used for flavouring purpose.
- Oil is known as 'Dill weed oil'.
- Oil is used in food, flavour and perfume industry.
- Salinity tolerance: 5 to 12 dS/m.
- Tolerates to alkalinity up to pH 9.8.
- Seed sowing: September-October.
- Seed rate: 5 Kg/ha.
- Planting distance: 45 cm x 45 cm.
- Flowering stage is more sensitive for higher pH.
- Essential oil (carvone 1.5-4%) is highest at milky wax stage of seed (fully developed but green fruits).
- Yields and vit. C content increases by herbicidal treatment.
- Seed yield: 8-10 q/ha.

Varieties:

- Ghoda Sowa, Variyali Sowa and Vizag Sowa.
- CSS-1: More adaptive to higher soil pH.

Name	Breeding method	Features
NRCSS, Ajmer		
NRCSS Ajmer Dill-1 (2006)	Selection	European type; matures in 142 days; seed contains 2-5% volatile oil (carvone)
NRCSS Ajmer Dill-2 (2006)	Selection	Indian type; matures in 135 days

Diseases:

- Damping off: Serious disease.
- Powdery mildew.

3.7 Ajowain

- Eulogized as 'Carom seed or Bishop's weed'.
- *Trachyspermum ammi* (Syn. *Carum copticum, C. ajowan*).

- Oil content increases with increase in soil salinity.
- Stripped seeds are used as spice.
- Widely used in bakery industry, wine industry, condiments and Ayurvedic field.
- Economic part: Fruit.
- Propagation method: Seed.
- Essential oil (2.5-5% in dried fruits) is dominated by thymol (35-60%).
- Thymol content (35-60%) makes Ajowain, a potent fungicide.
- Crystal form of thymol: *'Ajowain ka phool* .
- Objectionable weed in seed spice: *Ammi majus*.

Varieties:

- Pratap Ajowain-1

Name	Breeding method	Features
NRCSS, Ajmer		
NRCSS-AA-1 (2006)	Selection	Suitable for both under irrigated & rainfed condition; yield 11-14 q/ha; tolerant to drought & PM; high oil content
NRCSS-AA-2 (2006)	Selection	Suitable for rainfed condition; tolerant to drought & PM; seed contain 3% oil; yield 10-12 q/ha
NRCSS-AA-84	Selection	Suitable for rainfed condition; yield 10-12 q/ha; most tolerant to fusarium
NRCSS-AA-01-19	Selection	Suitable for saline soils
NRCSS Ajmer Ajowain-73 (2019)	Selection	-
GBPUA & T, Pantnagar		
Pant Ruchika	-	-
ANGRAU, Hyderabad (RARS, Guntur)		
Lam Selection-1	-	-
Lam Selection-2	-	-
RAU, Jobner		
Rajendra Mani	-	-
GAU, Jobner		
GA-1	-	Most late maturing
CSAUA & T, Kanpur		
Azad Ajowain-1	-	Sowing in February gives more yield

3.8 Nigella/ *Kala jeera*

- Eulogized as 'Black cumin or *Kalaunji'*
- Tolerates salinity upto 4.0 dS/m.
- Economic part: Seed.
- Seed contain 0.5 to 1.4% essential oil.

- Oil is used in treating skin diseases.
- Crop duration: 140-160 days after sowing.
- Seed rate: 7 kg/ha.
- Spacing: 30 cm x 10 cm.
- Sowing season: October.
- Chemical content: Nigellone.
- Yield: 10-12 q/ha.
- Objectionable weed in seed spice: *Nigella damescena*.
- **Varieties**: NRCSS-AN-1(resistant to root rot), Azad Kalaunji-1, Pant Krishna.

3.9 Caraway

- Eulogized as 'Shiya or *Vilayati jeera*'.
- Plants had fleshy root and slender branched stem.
- Leaves pinnate and small white flowers.
- Dried fruit is brown in colour with pleasant aromatic odour.
- Economic part: Fruit.
- Seeds are used in making bread, cheese, salad, sauce, soups and cakes.
- Propagation method: Seed.
- Seed on steam distillation yield 4-6% aromatic oil which is used in medicine.

4. IRIDACEAE

4.1 Saffron

- Eulogized as 'Golden condiment or Golden spice'.
- Name 'saffron' is derived from Arabic "*za-faran*" which means 'be yellow'.
- World's most expensive spice.
- Saffron revolution is possible in Kashmir under brand name 'Kashmiri saffron'.
- Advanced research centre on saffron at Dusa in was started in collaboration with Sher-e-Kashmir University of Agricultural Sciences and Technology, Jammu.
- Iran occupies 79% area followed by Spain (9%) and India (7%).
- Average productivity in India: 3.13 kg/ha.
- Iran contributes 80% of total world production followed by Spain 10-12%, India 3.3%, Greece 2%, Morocco 0.3%.
- Cultivated only in Jammu and Kashmir as rainfed cropat 1600 m MSL.
- Area to be covered under National Saffron Mission: 3715 ha.
- Saffron production now can be taken up in North-Eastern states.
- Hub of saffron: Pampore of Kashmir.
- IIKSTC: India International Kashmiri Saffron Trading Centre.

- Cultivated saffron (*Crocus sativus*) is considered to be a mutant, derived from *C. cartwrightianus*.
- It is a stem-less perennial grass plant.
- Flower is borne singly on a scape.
- Plant is sterile and does not set viable seeds.
- *C. vernus* flowers when corms are >7 cm in circumference and *C. sativus* at 3-5 cm.
- Perennial herb with globular underground corm 3-5 cm in dia.
- Flower colour: Blue or lavender blue.
- Flowers arise directly from corms.
- Commerce/ Economic part: Dried trilobed (trifid) stigma along with style & deep red in colour.
- Optimum temperature for flower initiation: 23-27^{0}C.
- Cool and wet climate inhibits flowering but enhances mother corms to produce daughter corms.
- Planting season: Mid-July to August.
- Flowering season: Late October-mid. November.
- Flowering starts 40 days after planting and continues for 30-40 days.
- Propagation method: Daughter corms.
- Mother corms reproduce annually 2-12 cormlets.
- Optimum soil pH: 5.5-7.0
- High $CaCO_3$ content in soil is desirable for growth.
- Planting distance: 15 cm x 20 cm.
- About 2.0 lakh dried stigmas from 70,000 flowers make 1 pound of saffron.
- Seed rate: 3.0-4.0 T/ha i.e. (5-6 lakh) seed corms/ ha.
- Yield: 5 kg dried saffron/ha.
- About 14 kg/ha of dry saffron is achieved in 5 years.
- Essential oil content: 0.3-0.8%.
- World's most expensive saffron: Shahi/ Kashmiri (Indian) saffron is finest quality having golden coloured styles and red tips of stigma.
- Mongra and Lacha: Inferior quality saffron consisting parts of stigmas and tops of styles.
- If style portion is longer than 2 mm then it is of inferior quality.
- Quality parameters: Colour (crocin concentration), taste (picrocrocin), odour (safranal).
- Main principle of bitter odour/ flavour: Picrocrocin (water soluble glucoside).
- Aroma and flavour compound of volatile oil: Safranal. It is less bitter than picrocrocin.
- Colour pigment: Cicrocrocin (water soluble carotenoid).

- Water or glycerine oil is used to improve weight & appearance.
- Drying percentage: 20%.
- In dehydration, stigma loses 78-80% its weight.
- Fresh saffron is air dried to 8-10% moisture content.
- Quality depends on colouring power, odour and taste.
- Toasting: Drying process of stigma in Spain.
- Storage of corm: 2.5 months at 23-25^{0}C at 65-75% R.H.
- Corm rot: Soil borne and devastating fungal disease. Drench Carbendazim @ 0.2% and Trichoderma.
- Rabbits, rats and birds: Cause high damage.
- **Grades**: Based on length of threads (stigma + style), colour, aroma and degree of purity.
  - Very select: Stigma length >30 mm, deep brilliant colour and strong aroma.
  - Slack: Broken stigma, stigma length <20 mm, dark in colour.

5. MYRISTICACEAE

5.1 Nutmeg

- Species are distributed from India & S-E Asia to north Australia & Pacific Islands.
- Leading producer countries- Indonesia, Grenada (West Indies).
- Both countries contribute to around 75% and 20%, respectively to world production.
- Remaining 5% production is done by India, Malaysia and Sri Lanka.
- EU, USA & Japan are major nutmeg and mace consuming countries.
- Singapore and Netherlands are main re-exporters of the spice & its derivaties.
- British people introduced nutmeg during 18th century.
- Two distinctly different spices viz. nutmeg and mace are produced.
- Both spices are strong, aromatic, resinous and warm in taste.
- Nutmeg: Dried kernel of seed (brown nut).
- Mace (thin leathery tissue between stone and pulp): Red feathery aril surrounding the seed nut has oil content from 4-17%. More expensive than nutmeg.
- Red arils on drying become orange in colour and are 'mace of commerce'.
- Pericarp is used for making jam, jelly, pickles and is rich source of pectin (12-14%).
- Fatty acid present: Myristic acid.
- Myristicin content ranges from 1.1 to 45.6% in nutmeg oil and 0.21 to 36.6 in mace oil.
- Average wt. of individual nutmeg: 60 g of which seed weight is 6-7 g, mace: 3-4 g and rest is pericarp.
- Nutmeg contains 25-50% fat, 7.5% protein.

- Leaves contain 0.40-0.62% light brown volatile oil.
- Nutmeg essential oil: 5-15% of seed weight which is mostly composed of terpene hydrocarbons (60-90%) terpene derivatives (5-15%) and phenyl propanes (2-10%).
- The unshelled nuts are coarsely crushed in mechanical crackers and steam distilled to obtain yellow to white volatile liquid possessing fresh warm aromatic odour.
- Uses of nutmeg oil:
  1. Aromatherapy: Oil is used for relaxation of muscles and body.
  2. Beverages: To flavour beverages, syrups, food and sweets.
  3. Personal hygiene products: Major ingredients in toothpaste, mouthwash and tooth powders.
  4. Medicinal uses: Oil has therapeutic value and used for diseases related to nervous system and digestive system and preparation of cough syrups.
  5. Oil finds application on cosmetics and pharmaceutical industry.
- Aroma constituent i.e. aromatic ethers trymyristicin & elemicin present in oil & oleoresin.
- Essential oil extracted by steam distillation: 5-15%.
- Oleoresin extracted by solvent extraction: 31-37%.
- Super critical fluid extraction is used to extract oleoresin from nutmeg.
- Yield of oleoresin is 10-12% for seed nut (kernel) and 10-13% for mace.
- Nutmeg butter contains 7-16% nutmeg oil.
  1. It is obtained by pressing the crushed nuts in presence of steam or by extracting wit solvents.
  2. Yield of butter: 25-40%.
  3. It is highly aromatic orange coloured fat with the consistency of butter at ambient temperature.
- Mace yield 27-32% oleoresin and 8.5 to 22% volatile oil.
- Mace oil is more expensive than nutmeg oil. It is colourless to pale yellow liquid possessing organoleptic properties similar to nutmeg oil.
- Nutmeg loses its fragrance quickly when ground.
- Tree thrives well in warm, humid conditions with annual rainfall of 150-300 cm.
- Crop requires 70-95% R.H. throughout the year.
- Crop grows well up to 1300 m above MSL.
- Evergreen, perennial, shade loving and dioecious tree cultivated as an intercrop in coconut and arecanut gardens.
- Permanent shade trees are planted when nutmeg is grown as monocrop.
- Suitable fast growing shade trees like *Albizia* and *Erythrina* are planted in advance.
- Constraints in cultivation: Dioecious nature of tree causes segregation of seedlings into male & female plants and this result in about 50% of unproductive male plants.

- Flowers are structurally hermaphrodite. Male trees flowers throughout year.
- Flowering is confined to 7 months in females.
- Inflorescence: Axillary cyme (male), simple cyme (female).
- Flowers are creamish yellow & fragrant.
- Female flower takes 154 days for complete development.
- Peak anthesis time: 9 PM to 3 AM.
- Anther dehiscence: 24 h prior to anthesis.
- Fruit type: Drupe.
- Fruit is composed of 3 parts: Pericarp or husk; mace and seed (nutmeg of commerce).
- Shoot growth is cyclic. A period of growth followed by quiescence.
- Two growth peaks are observed in May, June and September.
- Fruit follows single sigmoid growth curve.
- Shoot growth is cyclical, a period of growth followed by quiescence.
- Two growth peaks in May-June and September.
- Male inflorescence has more number of flowers (up to 10), while female has less (up to 3).
- Obligatory cross pollinated by wind and insects.
- Planting ratio of female and male trees: 20:1.
- 65% female trees are necessary for optimum yield in plantation.
- Identification of sex of plant at seedling stage is not feasible.
- Sex of tree can be identified only 7-8 years of planting when they begin to flower.
- Seedling progenies segregate into unisexual male, female and bisexual types.
- Propagation method: Seed and vegetative methods.
- Seeds are collected from seed gardens having desirable characters like regular bearing & high yielding (> 10000 fruits/ tree/ year) having 30 g wt./ fruit and 10 g wt. of nut/ fruit.
- Seeds are extracted from pericarp and sown in nursery.
- Seed germinate slowly & seed soaking in GA @ 1000 ppm gives higher (85%) germination.
- Days for seed germination: 40-90 days.
- About 20 days old sprouts are transplanted to polybags.
- About 18-24 months old seedlings are transplanted in main field.
- Epicotyl grafting, approach grafting and patch budding are successful.
- *M. fragrans*: As rootstock gives 80% success in August.
- Epicotyl grafting on Myphal (*M. beddomei*) as rootstock is more promising with 48% survival in August-September.
- For raising rootstock:

i) Naturally split, healthy fruit are harvested during June-July.

ii) Seeds are extracted from pericarp.

iii) Grafting: Germinating seeds of less than 2 weeks old are wedge grafted with mature scion.

iv) Grafting during August-September give 80% success.

- Orthotropic shoots from female trees are used as a scion (with 2 leaves) for grafting.
- Four months old and 8 months old scion sticks gives higher success.
- Graft union takes place after 30-45 days in veneer grafting.
- Grafts having 30 cm height and have put forth minimum of 8-10 leaves are suitable for planting.
- Planting distance: 5m x 5m.
- Top working: Converting unproductive male trees into productive female one with 48% survival in August-September.
- Fruit drop after set: 74%.
- Of the total flowers produced, only 8.74% fruits are harvested.
- Female trees start fruiting from 6th year and peak harvesting period reaches after 20 years.
- Days for fruit maturity: 206-237 or 9 months after flowering.
- Fruits are available throughout the year, but December to May is the peak period.
- Fruits are either plucked from the tree or allowed to drop.
- Harvesting stage: When fruit splits.
- After de-rinding, mace is manually separated from pericarp.
- Nuts and mace are dried separately on drying yard for 3-5 days.
- Nutmeg loose 25% of its weight on drying.
- Ratio of nutmeg to mace : 1: 8.
- Crop does not tolerate water stress.
- Water requirement through drip irrigation: 30 litres/ day/ tree.
- Fruit set is under control of additive gene action.
- Special dryers have been developed for drying of nutmeg and mace, which retains its original colour.

Grades:

- Whole or sound nutmeg.
- Sound shrivels: Used for oil extraction.
- Rejections: Used for oil distillation.
- Broken or wormy: Suitable for oil distillation.

Varieties:

- A-9-71: Source of high sabinene.
- Promising accessions from Dr.BSKKV, Dapoli: N-29, N-49, N-70, N-72, N-74.

Name	Breeding method	Features
IISR, Kozhikode		
Viswashree (2001)	Clonal selection	High quality; bushy; fruit wt. 80-100 g; seed wt. 10-13.5g; mace wt. 2.8-3.7g; 70% nut recovery; 35% mace recovery; 7.14% oil; mace oil 7.13%; oleoresin 2.48%; myristicin 12.48%; yield 1000 fruits/ tree; low incidence of fruit rot
Keralashree (2013)	Seedling selection	1st farmer participatory bred cv. with extra bold fruit mace & nut; 480 kg mace/ha; 9.1% oleoresin; low incidence of fruit rot
Dr BSKKV, Dapoli		
Konkan Sugandha (1998)	Single plant selection	Only hermaphrodite variety; fruiting starts from 6th year; high fruit set; yield 500 fruits/ tree/ year from 10th year onward;
Konkan Swad (2003)	Seedling selection from Ratnagiri district	Female variety; 39.8% essential oil in seed & 10.9% in mace; yield 761 fruits/ tree/ year from 10th year onwards; medium sized seed weighs 5 g & mace 1.2 g; planting of male tree is essential; free from pests & diseases
Konkan Shrimanti (2005)	Seedling selection	Female variety; yield 900 fruits/ tree/ tree from 10th year onward; 39.85% oil; sized seed weighs 10 g & mace 2 g; planting of male tree is essential;
Konkan Sanyukta	-	2nd monoecious variety with bold nuts, high nut oil (27%) and mace oil (17.75%); yield 500 fruits/ tree/ year from 10th year onwards
KAU, Thrissur		
Pullan (2018)	Selection	Oval nut; nut wt. 10.85g; nut yield (22.79 kg/tree); mace yield 2.86 kg/tree
Kochukudy (2018)	Selection	Round nut; nut wt. 11.6g; nut yield (20.88 kg/tree); mace yield 4.48 kg/tree
Mundathanam (2018)	Selection	Oval fruits; dark brown nuts; nut wt. 12.6 g; nut yield (19.7 kg/tree); mace yield 3.89 kg/tree
Poothara (2018)	Selection	Round fruits; nut wt. 10 g; nut yield (22.0 kg/tree); mace yield 4.53 kg/ tree
Punnathanam (2018)	Selection	Round fruits; red coloured mace; nut wt. 13.85g; nut yield 19.39 kg/tree; mace yield 4.23 kg/tree

Diseases and pest:

- Thread blight is caused by *Marasmius equicrenus*.
- Fruit rot: *Diplodia natalensis* and *Phytopthora spp*.
- Scale insect (*Parasaisettia nigra / Pseudaulacaspis cockerelli*): Wilting & drying of seedlings.

6. MYRTACEAE (LAURACEAE)

6.1 Clove

- Ancient valuable spice originated in Indonesia.
- Indonesia accounts for 66% of world production.
- Indonesia produces 3/4th share of total world output and export (1st rank) followed by Grenada on 2nd rank.
- Southern regions of India (Andaman and Nicobar, Karnataka, Kerala and Tamil Nadu) produce large quantities of cloves and most of which is domestically consumed.
- Largest producer: Tanzania followed by Indonesia, Madagascar, Sri Lanka & Malaysia.
- 1st introduced in India by East India Company during 1800 AD in Tamil Nadu.
- Cultivation was extended after 1850 AD to Nilgiri hills & slopes of Western Ghats.
- 2nd most important spice next to black pepper. It is suitable for mixed cropping in coconut and arecanut gardens.
- Clove is traded in international level for derivatives of essential oil and oleoresins.
- In Indonesia, clove is used for making KRETEK cigarette industry.
- Uses of clove oil:
  1. Medicine: It is effective anti-biotic, anti-septic, anti-viral, carminative, expectorant & stimulant.
  2. Aromatherapy: Oil is blended with other oils for its therapeutic value as stimulating, revitalizing, purifying & energizing.
  3. Flavouring industry.
  4. Perfumery
  5. Personel hygiene products like toothpaste, mouthwash & tooth powders.
  6. Nutritional composition of cinnamon/ 100 g:

Composition	USDA (ground)	ASTA
Water (g)	6.86	5.0
Food energy (kcal)	323	430
Protein (g)	5.98	6.0
Fat (g)	20.06	14.5
Carbohydrate (g)	61.22	68.8
Ash (g)	5.88	5.0
Calcium (g)	0.646	0.7
Phosphorous (mg)	105	110
Sodium (mg)	243	250
Potassium (mg)	1102	1200
Iron (mg)	8.68	9.5
Thiamin (mg)	0.115	0.11
Riboflavin (mg)	0.267	Not detected
Niacin (mg)	1.458	1.5
Ascorbic acid (mg)	80.81	81
Vit. A activity (RE)	53	53

- Clove oil is also eulogized as 'caryopil oil' and 'amboynas'.
- Clove oil content in dried bud: 16-21% which contains 70-90% eugenol and 5-12% eugenol acetate.
- Oil content: 1.5-1.8% (leaves), 4-7% (stem), 6.5% (mother clove), 6% (roots).
- Methyl-n-amyl ketone present only in bud oil.
- Thrives well up to an altitude of 1000 m MSL.
- Tropical plant and requires warm humid climate.
- Clove and all spice have practically narrow variability due to autogamy.
- Clove is still used to preserve 'Virginia Ham' food.
- Flowering season: September- October in plains & December - February in high altitudes.
- Inflorescence: Terminal pendulated panicle.
- Number of flowers/ panicle: 3 to 20.
- Flowers are bisexual and inbreeding is common.
- Flower bud: 1-2 cm long having cylindrical thick ovary consisting of 4 fleshy sepals.
- Pollination agents: Ants, thrips, bees.
- Fertilized flower takes 3 months for harvest.
- Collected ripe seed (fruit) is known as 'Mother clove/King clove'.
- Clove tree with very small buds is called 'Lilliput or mini clove'.
- Clove of commerce/ economic part: Fully grown dried unopened reddish brown flower bud having mellow odour.
- Alternate bearing habit.
- Inflorescence: Terminal pedunculated panicle with 3-20 flowers per panicle.
- Flower buds: 1-2 cm long having cylindrical thick ovary consisting of 4 fleshy sepals.
- Best period for pollination: 4th and 6th day after opening.
- Propagation method: Seed and approach grafting on its own rootstock is successful.
- Seed propagation: Most widely adopted method.
- Ripe fruits are collected from mother trees (seed garden) having desirable characters like healthy and high yielding (> 3 kg dry buds/ tree), regular bearer and bushy in nature.
- Ripe fruits collected during July-August are soaked in water overnight & pericarp is removed before sowing for quicker and higher germination.
- Fully developed and uniform-sized seeds showing presence of pink radical are used for sowing.
- Seeds are sown in raised nursery beds at 2-3 cm spacing and 2 cm depth.
- Germination commences with 2 weeks of sowing & lasts for about 6 weeks.
- Sprouts or one year old seedlings are transplanted to polybags (30-35 cm x 15-22 cm).

- About 18-24 months old seedlings having 45 cm height are planted in main field in May-June.
- Spacing of 7m x 7m accommodate 200 plants/ ha.
- Banana can be planted to provide cool & humid atmosphere to tender plants.
- No intercultivation is done for clove.
- Clove trees begins to yield from 7th year of planting.
- Full bearing stage is reached only after 15 years.
- Fertilized flowers take 3 months for harvest.
- Seeds are harvested 80-90 days after fruit set.
- Flower buds are formed on young flush.
- Harvesting stage: Unopended, fully developed bud, colour change of base of calyx from green to pinkish tinge
- At this time, they are less than 2 cm long.
- Such clove buds are picked by hand.
- Opened flowers are not valued as spice.
- Bending of branches or knocking down bud clusters with sticks adversely affect succeeding growth.
- Harvested buds are separated from cluster & spread in drying yard for drying.
- The correct stage of drying when stem of bud become dark brown & rest of the bud ligher brown.
- Dry cloves weigh 1/3rd the weight of green, fleshy cloves.
- Yield: 2 kg/tree; (3-8 q/ha dry flower buds annually).
- About 11,000-15,000 dried cloves make 1 kg.

Species:

- *Syzygium aromatica* (syn. *Eugenia caryophyllata, E. aromatica*).
- Brazilian cherry/ Pitanga (*E. uniflora*):
- **Varieties**: PPI (CL)-1, ICFRI-1, B-95.

Grades:

- Clove Special (good quality),
- Khoker (buds which are fermented during drying),
- Headless (without ball shaped unopened flower bud),
- King clove (extra bold clove buds).

Diseases and pests:

- Sudden death (*Valsa eugeniae*):
- Seedling wilt (*Cylindrocladium* spp., *Fusarium* spp.): Remove affected plants. Soil drench with 0.1% Carbendazim. Spray foliage with 1% Bordeaux mixture.

- Leaf rot (*Cylindrocladium quinqueseptatum*): Spray foliage with 0.1% Carbendazim.
- Leaf spot (*Colletotrichum gloeosporioides*): Spray 1% Bordeaux mixture.
- Stem borer (*Sahyadrassus malabaricus*): Spray 0.1% Quinalphos around bore-hole.
- Scales: Spray 0.05% Monocrotophos.

6.2 a. Cinnamon

- Eulogized as 'Sweet wood or *Dalchini*'.
- Cinnamon is introduced to India from Sri Lanka by the European settlers during 18th century.
- In ancient Egypt, cinnamon was used medicinally and as flavouring for beverages.
- In ancient world, it was more precious than gold.
- Largest producer of cinnamon bark: Sri Lanka.
- In global trade of true cinnamon, Sri Lanka contributes 80% of total production followed by Seychelles, Madagascar and India.
- Major importers: USA, Japan, European Union.
- In global trade of cinnamon oil, Sri Lanka contributes 70% of world's production and has monopolistic control.
- Major importers of oil: France, USA.
- India produces cinnamon leaf oil mostly for domestic consumption.
- Bark has carminative, astringent, stimulative and anti-septic properties.
- Oil is obtained from bark, leaf, root and seeds (unripe fruit).
- Plants with purple leaf flushes record 29% more bark oil than green flushes.
- Nutritional composition of cinnamon/ 100 g:

Composition	USDA (data for *C. verum* & *C. cassia* combined)	ASTA
Water (g)	9.52	10.00
Food energy (kcal)	261	355
Protein (g)	3.89	4.5
Fat (g)	3.18	2.2
Carbohydrate (g)	79.85	79.8
Ash (g)	3.55	3.5
Calcium (g)	1.228	1.6
Phosphorous (mg)	61	50
Sodium (mg)	26	10
Potassium (mg)	500	400
Iron (mg)	38.07	4.1
Thiamin (mg)	0.077	0.14
Riboflavin (mg)	0.14	0.21
Niacin (mg)	1.30	1.9
Ascorbic acid (mg)	28.46	40
Vit. A activity (RE)	26	26

- Come up well up to an elevation of 1000 m.
- Annual rainfall of 200-250 cm is ideal for cultivation with average temperature of 27^{0}C.
- Bark quality is highly influenced by soil and ecological factors.
- Mostly raised as unirrigated crop.
- Dried leaves are used as spice- *Tamalpatra* & unripe dried fruits as *kala nagkesar*.
- Flowering occurs on current season's growth.
- Flesh colour is taken as a criterion for selection of seedlings at nursery stage.
- Fruit: Dark purple one seeded berry surrounded by enlarged perianth. It is small ovoid in shape and dark purple colour.
- Propagation method: Seed (commercial), cutting, layering.
- Seed is recalcitrant and loses viability quickly when stored for 5 weeks.
- Seed viability: 1 week (80% germination) and loses completely after 40 days.
- Fresh seeds give 90-94% germination.
- Germination starts in about 20 days.
- Seed soaking in GA @ 150 ppm or Thiourea @ 1500 ppm results in high germination and days required for commencement of germination is also reduced.
- Seedlings require artificial shading till they become 6 months old.
- Cuttings with one or two leaves can be rooted within 40 days in closed chamber with diffused light.
- Cuttings root within 60 days, if kept in moist coir dust.
- Application of Seradix or Phospho-bacteria hasten rooting percentage.
- Air layering in July on semi-hard wood shoots with application of gallic acid gives 80% rooting and sphagnum moss is the best rooting media.
- Multiple shoots can be induced from seeds on MS media.
- Shoots can be multiplied by sub-culturing hypocotyls & internode segments on MS media + BA or kinetin + NAA & *in vitro* shoots are rooted in Whites medium containing IAA, IBA & IPA.
- About 10-12 months old seedings are planted in the field at a spacing of 2m x 2m.
- Planting is carried out in June-July or October-November when N-E monsoon prevails.
- Two years old trees are cut back periodically (coppiced) during June-July to a height of 12 cm from ground level and stump is covered by earthing up.
- This encourages bunch of canes (peeler shoots) suitable for peeling in about 4 years time and plant assumes shape of low bush.
- Coppicing for bark extraction can be commenced from 4th or 5th year of planting.
- Usually, coppicing is done in alternate years.

- Shoots are harvested from September to November.
- Shoots having finger thickness and uniform brown colour are ideal for bark extraction.
- A 'test cut' (of bark separation) is made on stem with sharp knife for determining time of bark peeling.
- Such shots are bundled after removing leaves & terminal portions & carried out in peeling shed.
- Bark recovery in India: 40%.
- Peeling (by knife) is done to facilitate quick ripping of bark.
- Peels are telescoped one into another, forming a quill & filled with trimmings of same quality bark to maintain cylindrical shape.
- The diameter of 'H-3' grade cinnamon is 38 mm.
- In seedling tree, regular peeling operation is commenced from 4-5th year.
- Yield: 1.6-3.4% (leaf oil); 0.95-3.55% (bark oil).
- Annual yield: 10-12 q/ha (dried leaves); 5-10 q/ha (dry bark).
- In mature plantation, yield is around 180-200 kg quills/ ha.
- Processing and post harvest management:
  i) Moisture content of 12% is recommended for dried quills.
  ii) Pieces of bark less than 107 cm long are categorized as 'quills'.
  iii) Very thin pieces of bark or twisted bark is graded as 'featherings'.
  iv) Small pieces of bark (5-20 cm long) left after preparing quills are graded as 'quillings'.
  v) Chips: Are trimming of quills or bark of coarser canes that are scraped off, instead of peeling.
  vi) Un-scrapped chips mean the bark that is scrapped off without removing outer bark.
  vii) Scrapped chips: denotes that bark of the coarser canes is scrapped after removing the outer bark.

Grading:

- Quills are bleached with SO_2 and sorted according to Sri Lankan system of grading into 4 types.
- Bark quills are graded from '00000' being the finest quality to 0 the coarsest quality.
- Alba grade: less than 6 mm diameter.
- Fine/ Continental grade: 6-19 m dia.,
  i) C-00000 Special thinnest grade-6 mm.
  ii) C-00000- 10 mm.
  iii) C-0000- 13 mm.

iv) C-000- 16 mm.
v) C-00- 17 mm.
vi) C-0- thickest grade- 19 mm dia.

- Mexican grade: 16 mm dia., depending on number of quills/ kg as:
  i) M-00000- Special.
  ii) M-0000- Intermediate.
- Hamburg grade: 23-28 mm dia.,
  i) H-1 grade (23 mm).
  ii) H-2 grade (25 mm).
  iii) H-3 grade (38 mm).
- Packing for marketing:
  1. Dried quills are tightened into small bundles & each bundle contains 30-40 quills.
  2. For whole sum export, quills are packed in compact cylindrical bales of 50 kg.
- Processing:
  1. Bark oil is extracted from broken pieces of bark by hydro or steam distillation. Bark oil contains cinnamaldehyde (65%) as major component.
  2. Leaf oil is extracted by steam or hydro distillation.
     a) Fresh leaves yield 1.8-2.6% oil.
     b) Dried leaves yield 3.75% oil.
     c) Major component of leaf oil- Eugenol (75-80%).
     d) Leaf oil is used as adulterant for bark oil.
  3. Oleoresin:
     a) Extracted with organic solvents. Chips are used for preparation of oleoresins.
     b) Oleoresin recovery from bark of cinnamon: 7-10%.
  4. Cinnamon powder/ ground spice: Different grades of bark are powdered.

Species:

Common name	Botanical name	Features
Ceylon cinnamon	*Cinnamomum veerum* of commerce (syn. *C. zeylanicum*)	Indigenous to Sri Lanka; dried inner bark of 'True cinnamon or cinnamon of commerce'; possess thickest bark
Chinese/ False cinnamon	*C. cassia* (syn. *C. aromaticum*)	Originated in China; sweet bark; used for flavouring food, beverages, pharmaceutical preparations & perfumery
Indonesian cassia	*C. burmannii*	-
Saigon/ Vietnamese cassia	*C. loureirii*	Highest essential oil & cinnamaldehyde content
Indian cassia/ Indian bay leaf or Tejpat	*C. tamala*	Leaves used as spice and inferior to true cinnamon in appearance, flavour and odour

Varieties:

- In Sri Lanka, distinct cultivars are prevalent viz. Sweet Honey cinnamon (commercially cultivated), Camphor cinnamon, Snake cinnamon, Astringent cinnamon, etc.

Name	Breeding method	Features
IISR-Kozhikode		
IISR-Cassia	-	1[st]cassia variety with low coumarin content
TNAU, Coimbatore (HRS, Yercaud and Pechipari)		
Yercaud-1 (1996)	Clonal selection	Good bark recovery; bark oil 2.8%; leaf oil 3.1%; bark recovery 35.3%; bark yield 360 dry kg/ ha;drought tolerant; resistant to major pests & diseases
PPI (Cl)-1 (2003)	OP progeny selection	1st variety with high oil content (6%); high oil recovery; leaf oil 3.3%; bark oil 2.9%; bark recovery 34.22%; bark yield 980 fresh kg/ ha; suitable for higher elevations; released for leaf oil purpose
Dr BSKKV, Dapoli		
Konkan Tej (1993)	Selection from Calicut material	Superior quality; leaf oil 2.28%; eugenol in bark oil 6.93%; bark recovery 29% 3.2% bark oil; bark yield 85 dry g/ tree; cinnamaldyhyde content in bark oil 70.23%; eugenol in bark oil 6.9% & leaf oil 75.5%; yield 250 g cinnamon/tree/ year & 0.5 kg *tamalpatra*; suitable for higher elevations
Konkan Tejpatta (2008)	Seedling selection	Superior quality; leaf oil 2.28%; eugenol in bark oil 6.93%; bark recovery 51.78%; yield more leaves (1.6 kg/tree; 7.8 t/ ha); suitable for higher elevations
KAU, Thrissur (Aromatic & Medicinal Plants Research Station, Odakkali)		
Sugandhini (2001)	Single tree selection	Recommended for leaf oil production; leaf oil 1.6%; bark oil 0.94%; bark recovery 51%; eugenol in leaf oil 93.7%
IISR, Kozhikode		
Nithyashree (1996)	Selection	Higher cinnamaldyhyde & bark oleoresin (10%); bark yield 250 dry kg/ ha; 2.7% bark oil; 2.8% leaf oil; bark recovery (30.7%); cinnamaldyhyde content in bark oil 58% & leaf oil 14%; eugenol in bark oil 5% & leaf oil 62%
Navashree (Sel. 189) 1996	Selection	6-7 shoots/year; yield 56 kg/ha; bark yield 200 dry kg/ ha; high bark recovery (40.6%); excellent quality characters viz. 2.7% bark oil; cinnamaldyhyde content in bark oil 73% & leaf oil 15%; 8% bark oleoresin & 2.8% leaf oil. Eugenol content in bark oil 6% & leaf oil 62%; young flushes are purple which turn green in 7-10 days.
CSIR, Lucknow (RRL, Bhubaneshwar)		
RRL (B)-C-6	Selection	Leaf oil 0.9%; 94% eugenol in leaf oil & 86% cinnamaldehyde in bark oil

Accessions C1, D1 and D3 are superior.

Diseases and pests:

- Leaf spot (*Colletotrichum gloeosporioides*): Pruning of affected branches. Spray 1% Bordeaux mixture.
- Seedling blight (*Diplodia* spp.): Spray 1% Bordeaux mixture.
- Grey blight (*Pestalotia palmarum*): Spray 1% Bordeaux mixture.
- Cinnamon butterfly (*Chilasa clytia*): Most serious pest. Larve defoliate plant. Spray 0.05% Quinalphos.
- Leaf miner (*Conopomorpha civica*): Common during monsoon period. Spray 0.05% Quinalphos.

6.2 b. Cassia

- Eulogized as 'Chinese cinnamon or Lignea or False cinnamon'.
- Oldest spice.
- An evergreen tree, aromatic in all its parts & resembles to true

6.3 All spice

- Eulogized as 'Four Spices-in-One or Jamaican pepper'.
- All spice (*Pimenta dioica* (syn. *P. officinalis*, *Eugenia pimento, Myrtus pimento, M, dioica*).
- Bay rum tree (*P. racemosa*).
- Polygamodioecious, evergreen tree grows up to 15-20 m height with profuse branching.
- Tree spice introduced to India.
- Jamaica (West Indies) contributes 70% of world's production.
- Edible part: Dried immature fruits (berry) and leaves.
- Fully mature but unripe fruits are used as spice & are marketed as 'pimento of commerce'.
- Major producer and exporter: Jamaica.
- Berries contain vitamin A (144 I.U).
- Contain flavour of 4 spices: cinnamon, clove, black pepper and nutmeg.
- Dried berries contain 2-5% volatile oil (yellow to brown coloured).
- Main component of all spice is eugenol (65-90%) followed by methyl eugenol (10%) & myrcene in trace (1%).
- Leaves contain less essential oil (0.7-2.9%) & in composition, it is similar to essential oil from fruits.
- Inflorescence: Axillary cyme.
- Flowering season: March-June.
- Flowers are structurally hermaphrodite but functionally dioecious.

- Male trees flower earlier than female tree.
- Fragrant, white, small flowers does not set fruits in all parts of India.
- Fruit is deep purple coloured two seeded berry.
- Optimum soil pH: 6-8.
- All spice flourishes well in temperature of 18-24^{0}C with low of 15^{0}C & high of 32^{0}C.
- Tree grows well up to an altitude of 1000 m MSL.
- Methods of propagation: Seed must be procured from registered seed gardens during June-July.
- Ripe fruits are light brown in colour.
- Seeds loose viability after 2 months.
- Seed germination begins 9-10 days after sowing & lasts up to 30-45 days.
- On germination, short purplish cotyledon appears above ground, followed by pair of small, opposite leaves.
- Seedlings at 4 leaf stage are lifted from nursery beds & transplanted to polybags (30 x 15 cm size).
- Seedlings of 9-10 months old and 25-30 cm height are planted in main field.
- Vegetative propagation:
  - Air layering in January gives 100% success and requires 18-28 months to separate rooted layers from mother plants.
  - Leafy soft wood cuttings treated with IBA @ 1000-1500 ppm gives 30% rooting.
  - Approach grafting: Two years old seedlings are used as rootstock for grafting.
  - Splice grafting during August-September gives 60% success.
  - Graft union takes place in about 6-8 months.
- Planting: Since it is dioecious, male : female ratio of 1: 10 is kept in plantation.
- Planting distance: 6 m x 6 m.
- All spice is irregular bearer.
- Use of Paclobutrazol @ 1.25-3.75 g induces flowering.
- Since evergreen in nature, avoid water stress.
- From flowering to fruit maturity, 3-4 months are required.
- Economic bearing period: 15-25 years.
- For spice purpose, immature green berries are harvested during July-August.
- Fruits are cured for 3-12 days till they are completely dried.
- After completion of curing, berries become crisp & produce metallic sound.
- Yield: 20-25 kg dried berries/ tree.
- **Varieties**: Jamaican Allspice, Mexican Allspice, Honduran Allspice.

7. ORCHIDACEAE

7.1 Vanilla

- Eulogized as 'Stick's of commerce or Princess of spices'.
- Name came from Spanish word 'vainilla' meaning 'little pod'.
- Only edible fruit of family Orchidaceae.
- 2nd most expensive spice traded in international markets.
- Vanilla flavour was 1st introduced to France and England during the early part of 17th century.
- Cultivation of vanilla started in Mauritius in 1827 and in Madagascar in 1848.
- Major producing countries: Madagascar and Indonesia.
- Vanillin is mainly responsible for fragrance, flavour and aroma of vanilla essence.
- Vanilla production is increasing at global level with average annual growth rate of 4%.
- Vanilla extracts from beans accounts for < 1% of vanillin production and remaining 99% is obtained synthetically.
- Used in preparation of ice creams, chocolates, cakes, pastries, puddings, soft drinks, liquors, pharmaceuticals, perfumery and in nutraceuticals.
- Introduced in India during 1835.
- World's most labour intensive crop.
- Shade loving, perennial climbing vine producing aerial roots (velamen roots) at nodes.
- About 50% of vanilla is used in ice-cream industry.
- 90% of world's vanilla production comes from Madagascar and Indonesia.
- Madagascar vanilla 'bourbon vanilla' fetches highest price in international market.
- World export market for natural vanillin is sourced only from Madagascar (50% share).
- USA, France and Germany's import account for 80% of world's import.
- Major importers of natural vanilla are US (50-60%), France (10%) & Germany (15%).
- These countries are also major re-importers of both vanilla beans and processed vanilla products.
- In India, entire vanilla demand is met by synthetic vanillin.
- Spice Board of India is encouraging vanilla cultivation.
- Thermophilous crop.
- Crop thrives well between 10^0N and 20^0S latitudes.
- It comes well up to 1500 m MSL.
- Vanilla needs warm and moist conditions (80% R.H.) with temperature range of 25-32^0C.

Species:

- o Mexican vanilla (*V. planifolia* syn. *V. fragrans*): Cultivated; produce short thick pods & superior quality vanillin.
- o West Indian vanilla (*V. pompono*): Cultivated; produce largest pods (10-23 cm) & inferior quality vanillin.
- o Tahitian vanilla (*V. tahitensis*): Cultivated. Produce inferior quality vanillin.
- o *V. grandiflora*: Preparing fishing nets.
- o *V. griffithii*: Manufacture of hair conditioners.

- Trees for shade: *Jatropa*, *Plumeria alba*, *Casuarina equisetifolia*, *Erythrina*, *Glyricidia maculata*, *Bauhinia* or silver oak.
- Under Indian conditions, *Glyricidia* is very good standard for support & shade.
- Spacing for erecting standards: 1.2-1.5 m x 2.5-3.0 m (1600-2000 standards/ ha).
- Ideal month of planting vanilla: August-September.
- Thumb rule is that vanilla vines require about 50% shade.
- Flowering and quality of vanilla beans is highly influenced by degree of shade.
- Trailing of vines (growth) should be limited up to 150 cm height to facilitate easy manual pollination.
- Vines are trained horizontally on branches and coiled round the supporting standards.
- If vegetative growth of vine is arrested by pruning, it turns to reproductive phase.
- Usually starts flowering in 3rd year of planting.
- Maximum flower production seen at 7-8 years after planting.
- Flowers during December-February and each flower lasts for only a day.
- Pinching off top 7.5 to 10 cm of vine, 6-8 months before flowering season encourages flower production.
- Flowers borne in axillary racemes and each inflorescence consists 15-20 flowers.
- It takes 45-60 days from flower initiation to opening of flowers and only 1-2 flowers open in a day.
- Flowers are large, pale greenish yellow and bisexual.
- Natural pollination is impossible due to presence of rostellum which prevents contact of anther cap to stigma.
- Pollination agents: Melapona bees and humming birds.
- Discovery of hand pollination: 1841.
- Success of hand pollination: 85-100 %.
- In hand pollination, use of pin or needle or small piece of pointed wood or tooth pick is used.
- Ideal time for pollination on the day of anthesis: 6 AM-1 PM.

- For commercial production, only 10-12 flowers/ bunch are pollinated to get quality beans.
- An efficient pollinator can pollinate 100 to 150 flowers per day.
- Period required to attain pod full size from fertilization: 6 weeks.
- Propagation methods:
  - Stem cuttings of with 2-3 nodes and 60-120 cm long from vines of current year growth.
  - Cuttings can be raised in polybags of 18 x 12 c.n size and 100-150 gauge thickness.
  - Cuttings are ready for field planting in 6-7 months having 50-70 cm vine growth. Stem cutting give faster vine growth compared to tissue cultured plantlets.
  - Coir rope, wooden sticks or agro-shade net strips can be used as support/ trailing material.
  - For micropropagation, 2-3 cm long nodal segments are collected from 2nd to 6th nodes from shoot tip.
  - Explants from field grown vines are collected in November-May or August-September months.
- Immature beans will not develop full aroma and sufficient vanillin content during curing, while over matured beans split open at time of curing and affect quality of processed beans.
- Harvest index: Loose attachment of pod to pedicel. Tender pods harvested.
- Pods ready for harvest 6-9 months after flowering when they change colour from green to pale yellow.
- Right stage of picking pods: Distal end of pods turn yellow and fine yellow streaks appear on pods. Pods are picked by cutting with knife.
- Most desirable size of beans: 18-25 cm long.
- Yield: 300-600 kg cured beans/ ha/ year.
- About 6 kg of green pods produce 1 kg of cured beans.
- Yield of vine declines after 12-14 years.
- Production of beans in a particular area is directly related to conditions of growing of vines during previous year.
- Curing: Vanillin is developed as a result of enzymatic action on the glucosides during process of curing.
- Curing involves killing of vegetative life of the beans to initiate enzymatic action.
- Methods of curing:
  - Mexican process- Killing of beans is done by exposing the beans directly to sun for 5 hours.

- o Bourbon process- Bamboo basket with beans immersed in hot water (63-65^{0}C) for 3 minutes. After rapidly draining the water when beans are still hot, they are kept in wooden boxes lined with blankets. Beans after acquiring chocolate brown colour, are spread in sun on dark colour cotton for 3-4 h and later rolled up to retain heat and stored in wooden boxes. This process is repeated for 6-8 days. Beans are dried by spreading in wooden trays under shade in airy location. Finally, they are graded according to size and kept in iron boxes lined with paraffin paper.
- o Peruvian process-
- o Guyana process-

- To initiate enzyme activity, beans are dipped in hot water (63-65^{0}C) for 3 min.
- Rising of temperature (known as sweating) enhances enzymatic action in beans to achieve rapid drying to prevent harmful fermentation.
- Beans are bundled and stored in air tight container for conditioning.
- Beans take 2 months for drying.
  - o Slow drying for development of fragrant substances.
  - o Conditioning the product by sorting for few months in closed boxes.
- Vanillin crystals appear on surface of bean.
- Oil is called 'Balsam of vanilla' i.e. vanillin.
- Properly cured beans contain about 2-2.5% vanillin.
- Vanillin from green pods is odourless and flavourless.
- Characteristic aroma and flavour is developed due to action of enzymes (ß-glycosidase). It is extracted by hydro-alcoholic extraction.
- Natural vanillin gives brownish to yellow colour to preparations.
- Fine vanilla (French term- *Givre*): Quality vanilla having frosting crystal is produced during induced fermentation.
- Woody vanilla: Shorter, uncrystalized, lighter in colour and slightly bitter is taste.
- Coumarin: Cheap substitute for vanilla.
- Maximum economic life of vanilla: 10 years.
- After curing, seven primary grades of whole beans in descending order of quality are:

1. Extra superior
2. Good superior
3. Superior
4. Good
5. Medium good
6. Medium
7. Ordinary

- Final grading on the basis of length, moisture content, colour, appearance and aroma is as follows:
    1. Top quality/ grade beans are 17 to 25 cm long, fleshy, very dark brown to black in colour with 35-40% moisture content & strongly aromatic. Vanillin content 1.48-2.90%.
    2. Low quality beans are hard, dry, thin, brownish or reddish-brown in colour and possess poor aroma. Poorest grade has as low as 10% moisture.
    3. Splits are also sorted into various categories.
- Vanilla beans of commerce are divided into 5 geographic types as:

Types	Places where grown
Mexican	Mexico
Bourbon	Island of Reunion, Madagascar, Comoros and Seychelles & India
South American	French West Indies
Tahiti	Tahiti
Java	Indonesia

- Indian vanilla grades for international market (Bourbon grading procedure)

1st grade	Whole beans > 14 cm length, moisture content < 25%, no scratches, blemishes, good flavour
2nd grade	Whole beans > 14 cm length, moisture content 25-28%, some scratches are permitted
3rd grade	Whole beans > 14 cm length, moisture > 30%, more scratches or blemishes
4th grade	Whole beans with less flavour, length < 14 cm with more scratches, moisture > 30%
5th grade	Broken, cut, short beans which do not have good flavour. Higher moisture level.

- Each bundle contains 70-100 beans and weighs 150 to 500 g.
- Bundles are wrapped in butter paper and stored air tight boxes.
- Processed products:
    1. Vanilla extract or essence is extracted aroma & flavour characteristics of vanilla beans in an aqueous solution.
    2. Vanilla oleoresin is semi-solid concentrate obtained by complete removal of solvent from vanilla extract with inferior flavour & aroma.
    3. Vanilla flavouring: It is similar to vanilla extract but with ethyl alcohol content always less than 35%.
    4. Vanilla powder: It comprises mixture of vanilla powder or vanilla oleoresin with sugar, food starch or gum acasia.

Pests and diseases:

- Anthracnose (*Calospora vanillae*) is most serious disease.
- Fusarium wilt (*F. oxysporum*): Most serious disease. Remove & destruct affected plants. Drench 0.1% Carbendazim.

- Phytophthora rot (*Phytophthora meadii*): Phytosanitation & spray 1% Bordeaux mixture.
- Root rot (*Sclerotium rolfsii*): Drench 0.1% Carbendazim.
- Dry rot (*Rhizoctonia* spp.):
- Leaf feeding beetles: Spray contact insecticide.
- Sucking bug (*Halyomorpha* spp): Spray contact insecticide.
- Sun scorching: Dry climate along with direct falling of sunlight on the plants.

8. PARMELIACEAE

8.1 Black stone flower

- Eulogized as 'Canary moss or Black edged leaf lichen or *Pathar phool*'.
- Type of dried flower, lichen used as dried spice.
- Grows on acidic bark or oak and hybrid willow tree.
- Rich in secondary metabolites.
- Thallus contains atranorin & chloro-atronorin.
- Highly susceptible to SO_2 pollution.

9. PIPERACEAE

9.1 Black pepper

- Eulogized as 'King of spices or Black gold or Multi-functional spice'.
- Name 'pepper', is derived from Sanskrit word 'pippali' meaning 'berry'.
- It has extensive culinary uses for flavouring and preserving processed food and is important medicinally.
- Of the total spices traded internationally, pepper accounts about 34% by value.
- It is 1st oriental spice introduced into Western world & was well known among the Romans and Greeks.
- Major producing countries: Indonesia, Brazil, India, Malaysia, Cambodia, Sri Lanka, China and Vietnam.
- World's largest producer and exporter: Vietnam.
- India is leading producer, consumer and exporter.
- India with > 40% share of the world area under pepper and contributes about 23% of total production of pepper in the world.
- Black pepper is exported to > 75 countries.
- Major importer of Indian pepper: North America.
- Kerala accounts for 96% of total production.
- Kerala's share in total pepper export from India is around 94% both in terms of volume and value.

- The traditional home of black pepper: Malabar Coast.
- Nutritional composition of black pepper/ 100 g:

Composition	USDA	ASTA
Water (g)	10.51	8.0
Food energy (kcal)	255	400
Protein (g)	10.95	10.0
Fat (g)	3.26	10.2
Carbohydrate (g)	64.81	66.5
Ash (g)	4.33	4.6
Calcium (g)	0.437	0.4
Phosphorous (mg)	173	160
Sodium (mg)	44	10
Potassium (mg)	1259	1200
Iron (mg)	28.86	17.0
Thiamin (mg)	0.109	0.070
Riboflavin (mg)	0.240	0.210
Niacin (mg)	1.142	0.8
Ascorbic acid (mg)	-	Not detected
Vit. A activity (RE)	19	19

- Crop of warm humid tropics.
- Successfully cultivated between 20^0 N & S latitude up to 1500 m MSL.
- Requires 200-250 rainy days (annual rainfall 2000-3000 mm), dry spell of 30-45 days before flowering and high humidity (75-95%).
- Crop tolerates 10-40^{0}C temperature, ideal around 25-35^{0}C.
- Optimum soil pH: 4.5 to 6.6.
- Day neutral plant.
- Vines kept under shade (7% incident light) remained green and healthy.
- About 50% shade boosted growth of cuttings in nursery.
- Illumination above 5000 lux (9.00 μ mol/ s/ m^2) decreased carbon fixation.
- Shade reduction in live standards is an important cultural practice during rainy/ cloudy weather to allow sufficient light for crop growth.
- Use of reflectants is common to reduce stress during summer. Spraying lime over leaf surface enhanced chlorophyll content.
- Sex form: Gynomonoecious.
- Inflorescence- Catkin. .
- Sessile, white, small flowers are borne in pendulous spike of about 50 blossoms each.
- Flowers: Unisexual, with monoecious or dioecious or hermaphrodite.
- Hermaphrodite flowers are protogynous.

- Grown as monocrop (large scale) as well as intercrop in coffee estates.
- Pungency and biting taste is due to alkaloid piperine- $C_{17}H_{19}O_3N$ (1.7-7.4%).
- Other pungent alkaloids: Chavicine, Peperidine & Piperettine.
- Black pepper aroma is due to compound caryophyllene (2-5%).
- Starch accounts for 34% in black pepper and 56.5% in white pepper.
- Being a climber, it is trailed on supports called 'standards'.
- In homestead farming, it is trained on coconut/ arecanut/ jack fruit tree.
- Most popular live standard for pepper: *Erythrina indica*.
- Other standards used: Indian coral tree (*Garuga sepium*), Silver oak (*Grevillea robusta*).
- In mono cropping system, spacing of 2.7 m x 2.7 m accommodates 1,100 vines/ha.
- Optimum spacing for planting: 3m x 3 m in plains.
- Closer spacing of 2m x 2m is adopted when non-living standards are used.
- In multiple cropping system, only 540-560 vines/ha are accommodated.
- Planting distance for bush pepper: 1m x 1m to 1.5m to 1.5 m.
- Bush pepper can be planted in earthen pots.
- Regulation of shade by lopping of branches of standards provides optimum light to vines and also enables straight growth of standards.
- Branching habit: Dimorphic.
- Fruiting/ lateral branches: Plagiotropes (sympodial growth habit).
- Black pepper has 3 types of aerial shoots:

  a) Top / Terminal shoots:

  b) Runner shoots: Arises from base of vine, very vigorous & used for multiplication. Coiled runner shoots are separated from vine during February-March and cuttings of 2-3 nodes each are planted in nursery for rooting and transplanted in May-June.

  c) Fruit bearing lateral shoots with limited growth and on rooting give rise to bush type growth.
- Hanging shoots: Geotropes.
- Pollination agent: Rain water (hydrophily) but naturally self pollinated due to geitonogamy.
- In long pepper, fruiting is apomictic and fruits are produced without pollination.
- When long pepper is grown for roots, only male plants are grown. Male plants are more vigorous growing and produce more quantity of roots.
- Ideal time of propagation: February-March.
- Methods of propagation: Shoot cuttings, seed, tissue culture.

- Commercial/ Pit/ Rapid method of propagation (simple, cheaper & quicker): Single node cutting (runner shoots) from middle 1/3rd portion.
- Rapid multiplication technique is called 'bamboo method'. This technique was developed in Sri Lanka and refined at IISR, Kozhikode.
- Plants are ready within 4 months compared to 6 months in conventional method.
- In conventional method, 4 node cuttings are used.
- Continuous regeneration and about 4 harvestings of rooted cuttings can be taken in a year, giving multiple rate of 1: 40 in a year.
- Serpentine method for production of quality planting material.
- Column method of propagation is practiced.
- Micropropagation: Direct regeneration from explants of leaf, stem, terminal/ side buds/ nodal segments gives 4000 explants.
- *In vitro* mass multiplication technique was developed by KAU, Thrissur, and shoot tips and eye bud explants are best and results in speedier establishment of cultures.
- By planting one year old lateral branches with 3-4 nodes (i.e. plagiotropic (top) fruiting branches), pepper can be grown as bush.
- Bush pepper is ideal under-storey crop in coconut garden, agro-forestry systems and suitable for terrace gardens and can be grown in pots.
- Under planting (i.e. new re-planting of vines) is attempted when regular decline trend in yield appears.
- Old and senile vines are removed 3-5 years after under planting.
- Irrigation from November-December till March and withholding thereafter till onset of rains increases yield by 50%.
- Depth of irrigation: 10 mm (100 lit. water/ irrigation at 8-10 days interval).
- Water requirement through drip irrigation: 7-10 liters/ day/ vine.
- Mulching of basins with green or dry leaves/ saw dust/ arecanut husk @ 5 kg/ vine is highly advantageous during summer months.
- Sprays of 2% lime solution in summer months reduces leaf scorching.
- Chemical weed control is not recommended.
- Fertilization: 100: 40 : 100 g NPK/ vine/ year for Penniyur region.
- Black pepper starts yielding after 3rd year onward.
- Duration from flowering to full maturity: 6-7 months or 180-230 days.
- At higher altitudes, berries take 210-245 days for full maturity.
- Harvesting at immature stage reduces bulk density.
- Bulk density of pepper ranges between 425-850 g/ litre.
- Early harvesting of spikes results in 15-20% reduction in weight or processed material.

- Harvesting period: December-January (in plains) and January-April (in hills).
- During ripening stage, weight of pepper decreases.
- Moisture content is reduced from 82.5% at pin head stage to 60% and 40% at ripening stage.
- Harvesting before maturity leads to loss in berry wt., while delayed harvesting leads to berry shedding.
- Harvesting stage: One or two berries on spike turn bright yellow/ orange or red.
- Berries are harvested at different maturity levels depending on product preparations as mentioned below:

Products	Maturity at harvest
Pepper in vine/ canned pepper	Green & tender (4-5 months)
White pepper	Fully matured (ripened)
Black pepper	Fully mature & near ripe
Dehydrated green pepper	10-15 days before full maturity
Oil & oleoresin	15-20 days before maturity
Pepper powder	Fully matured with maximum starch

- De-spiking: If the harvested spikes are kept in bag for 12-24 h or heaped and covered over night, de-spiking is easy.
- Trampling with legs is traditionally followed technique for de-spiking.
- Yield: 1.09-2.67 t/ha.
- Average pepper yield in India: 273 kg/ha compared to 425 kg/ha (Indonesia); 431 kg/ha (Sri Lanka); 2000 kg/ha (Malaysia).
- Yield of bush pepper: 100-150 g dried black pepper berries/ bush/year.
- Blanching:
  a) It is done to give waxy coating to dried pepper grains & uniform black colour.
  b) It helps in disinfection of berries.
  c) Pepper can be dried in 3-4 days as against 5-6 days required in traditional practice.
  d) Blanched pepper fetches better price in the market.
  e) Blanching is done by immersing threshed berries in boiling water.
- Drying:
  a) Green pepper contains 80-85% moisture.
  b) Sun dried berries contain only 10-12% moisture.
  c) Generally, black pepper recovery is 28-38%, which is about 1/3rd of green berries.
  d) Drying process enhances activity of enzymes.
  e) Fenugreek coated bamboo mat is ideal to dry black pepper.
- For bush type peppers, frequent weeding in basins is essential.

- Starch content in black pepper is 34% and in white pepper is 56.5%.
- Sterilization is done by steam and High Temperature Short Time (HTST) treatment.
- Slightly immature pepper contains highest level of piperine (6-8%).
- Oleoresin (8.1-13.8%) is extracted by solvent extraction (acetone/ ethylene dichloride) of pepper powder.
- SO_2 treatment reduces darkening of dehydrated green pepper.
- Cover crops used: *Calapogonium mucanoides, Mimosa invisa.*
- Fruit setting percentage: 50%.
- Spike shedding occurs during almost all the months from spike emergence to harvest.
- Spike shedding percentage: 14-65%.
- Spray IAA @ 50 ppm at berry setting stage to reduce spike shedding.
- Spray Bordeaux mixture @ 1% and apply 10% Bordeaux paste on stems up to 1 m height.

Processing and grading:

- Primary processing consists of sun drying of matured berries for 3-5 days after separation from spikes.
- Heat treatment: Collect separated berries in perforated basket and dipped in boiling water for 1 min and drain and spread for sun drying.
- Recovery: 100 kg matured berries yield 33 kg black pepper i.e. 30-33%.
- White pepper i.e. 'white inner corn' is produced by retting of matured berries in clean water for 5-7 days after removing pericarp (outer skin) by different methods viz. water steeping, steaming or boiling & decortication.
- Recovery: 100 kg matured green berries yield 25 kg white berries i.e. 22-27%.
- Green pepper is converted to white pepper by using microbial consortium.
- A chemical process for white pepper have been patented by Josi (1962) and Omanakutty *et al.* (2006).
- For decortications purpose, pectinase enzyme is very effective for both dried and fresh pepper.
- Specific gravity for white pepper preparation: >1.12.
- Retting: Traditional method to prepare white pepper.
- Green and tender pepper is harvested for preparation of canned pepper.
- Green colour of pepper is maintained in 12% brine solution (i.e. salinity of steeping liquid).

***Grading*:**

- Grading of green berries is done by using wire mesh to remove light berries and pin heads.

- AGMARK grade specifications: 19.
- Quality factors for pepper grading: 1) Extraneous matter 2) Light berries 3) Moisture content 4) Sieve size 5) General characteristics.
- Garbling: Removal of dust, chaff and grade pepper according to densities.
- Grades: Malabar Garbled (MG), Garbled Light Pepper and Pin heads.
- Foreign matter other than black pepper in solid state is considered as 'extraneous matter'.
- Pin heads: Under developed berries can be separated by passing through sieve of mesh size 3 mm.
- Light berries: Berries of pepper with light weight of 0.01 to 0.02 mg and which float freely in methylated spirit of specific gravity ranging from 0.8 to 0.82.
- Bold pepper is classified into 3 types 1) Berries with 4 mm sieve mesh size 2) 4.25 mm 3) 4.75 (TGSEB).
- Major cause for black listing of black pepper by United States Food and Drug Administration (USFDA): Presence of excreta viz, mammalian excreta originated from animals/ rodents. This is because of our age old practice of using cow dung for smearing over bamboo mats and other surfaces for drying pepper. The value was 180 mg/ pound.
- The ASTA tolerance limit for presence of mammalian excreta is 1 mg/ pound; insect infected berries 1% by weight; light berries 2-20%; storage pest 2 numbers by count; moisture 11% and molds 2%.
- The harmonized Commodity coding and description System (HS) is the classification system followed internationally for trading of goods.
- The Indian Trade classification is the eight digit ITC (HS) code which is the extension of six digit HS code.

ITC(HS) code	Description
070990.04	Green pepper
071190.01	Green pepper in brine
090411.01	Pepper long
090411.02	Light black pepper
090411.03	Black pepper, garbled
090411.04	Black pepper, ungarbled
090411.05	Dehydrated green pepper
090411.06	Pepper pinheads
090411.07	Freeze dried green pepper
090411.08	Frozen pepper
090411.11	White pepper
090411.19	Other pepper
090412.00	Pepper, crushed or ground

Species:

- Cultivar diversity is one of principal components of diversity.
- IISR, Kozhikode: Largest germplasm collection in the world.
- Order: Piperales.

Species	Features
Piper wightii (hexaploid), *P. galeatum*	Wild; dioecious but cultivated are gynomonoecious
P. nigrum (black pepper)	2n=4x=52; dioecious in wild condition & cultivated form are monoecious; thick leaves, bold berries.
P. betle (betel vine)	2n=6x=78; used for *pan* industry
P. colubrinum (Brazilian pepper)	Used as rootstock as it is resistance to quick wilt/ foot rot (*Phytophthora capsici*); propagated by cuttings
P. ornatum	Resistant to quick wilt & root knot nematode
P. barberi, P. chaba, P. hymenophyllum, P. longum (long pepper)	Pubescent leaves, creeping habit; erect cylindrical spikes & fused laterally; tolerant to pollu beetle
P. crocatum, P. magnificum	Ornamental value
P. cubeba (Tailed pepper), *P. retrofractum*	Indigenous medicinal plant
P. sarmentosum	Culinary and medicinal spp.
P. barberi	Endangered& listed in red data book
P. ribesioides	Wild culinary spice of Andaman Islands; substitute for black pepper; imparts pungent flavour & is considered digestive & carminative
Schinus molle	Pepper tree

Varieties:

- For white pepper purpose: Valiakaniakadan.
- Thekkan.
- Vishwam: Released variety of long pepper (*P. longum*).

Varieties	Breeding method	Special features
KAU, Thrissur (Pepper Research Station, Panniyur)		
Panniyur-1(1966)	Intervarietal hybrid of 'Uthirankotta x Cheriyakaniakadan'	1st released F_1 hybrid; bold berries; yield (2.5 kg green berries/ vine; 11.8 kg dry pepper/vine; 1242 kg/ha dry pepper); do not tolerate shade; performs better in half shade sunlight; 5.3% piperine; 11.8% oleoresin; essential oil 3.5%
Panniyur-2 (Krishna, 1991)	Clonal selection from OP progeny of 'Balankotta'	Shade tolerant; suitable for intercropping; 10.9% oleoresin; 6.6% piperine; 35.7% dry recovery; essential oil 3.4%; yield (2570 kg/ha dry pepper)
Panniyur-3 (Shima, 1989)	Intervarietal hybrid of 'Uthirankotta x Cheriyakaniakadan'	F_1 hybrid, late maturing; suitable for all pepper growing regions; 5.2% piperine; 12.7% oleoresin; essential oil 3.1%; yield (1953 kg/ha dry pepper)
Panniyur-4(1991)	Clonal selection from 'Kuthiravally type II'	Stable yielder; yield (1277 kg/ha dry pepper); 9.2% oleoresin; 34.7% dry recovery; 4.4% piperine; essential oil 2.1%

Panniyur-5 (1996)	OP progeny of 'Perumkodi'	35.7% dry recovery; 5.3% piperine; 12.33% oleoresin; 3.8% essential oil; yield (1098 kg/ha dry pepper); suitable for mixed cropping, tolerant to drought, nursery diseases & shade
Panniyur- 6 (2000)	Clonal selection from 'Karimunda type III'	Regular bearer; 4.9% piperine; 8.3% oleoresin; 1.3% essential oil; yield (2127 kg/ha dry pepper); tolerant to drought & shade
Panniyur-7 (2000)	OP progeny of 'Kalluvally'	5.6% piperine; 10.6% oleoresin; 1.5% essential oil; yield (1410 kg/ha dry pepper); tolerant to drought & shade
Panniyur-8	Intervarietal hybrid of 'Panniyur 6 x Panniyur 5'	Regular bearer; yield (2,130 kg/ha dry pepper; 12.17% oleoresin, 5.68 % piperine; 1.17% volatile oil content; drought tolerant; withstand water stress; tolerant to Phytophthora foot rot
Panniyur-9 (2018)	-	Spike length 10.2 cm; 90 berries/ spike; 1000 berry wt. 150 g; piperine 6.11%; volatile oil 5%; oleoresin 12.71%; suitable for open condition; tolerant to phytophthora foot rot; quick wilt & drought; yield (fresh 7.2 kg /tree) & dry 2.86 kg/ tree)
IISR, Kozhikode		
Sreekara (1990)	Selection from 'Karimunda' (K.S. 14)	High essential oil (7%) & oleoresin (13%); yield (2677 kg/ha dry pepper); 5% piperine; tolerant to drought
Subhakara (1990)	Selection from 'Karimunda' (K.S. 27)	High yield; high piperine (12.4%) & essential oil (6%); 3.4% oleoresin; yield (2352 kg/ha dry pepper)
Panchami (1991)	Selection from 'Aimpirian'	Late maturing; oleoresin 12.5%, piperine 4.7%; essential oil 3.4%; high yield (2828 kg/ ha dry pepper) with excellent fruit set; spike twisted in appearance due to high fruit set
Pournami (1991)	Selection from 'Ottaplackal-1' type	Tolerant to root knot nematode; high yield; yield (2333 kg/ ha dry pepper)
IISR-Thevam (2006)	Clonal selection from 'Thevanmundi'	Tolerant to fruit rot; suitable for high altitude areas; yield 5.17 kg/vine
IISR-Malabar Excel	Hybrid of 'Cholamundi x Panniyur-1'	F_1 hybrid; suitable for higher elevations& plains; recommended for rainfed condition; yield 2.78 kg/vine; 2.4% piperine; oleoresin 11.7%; 2.8% essential oil; 32% dry recovery
IISR-Girimunda (2004)	Hybrid of 'Cholamundi x Panniyur-1'	F_1 hybrid; medium maturing; yield 6.14 kg/vine; 2.2% piperine; oleoresin 19.65%; 47 fruits/ spike; essential oil 3.4%; 32% dry recovery
IISR-Shakti (2004)	OP seedling of 'Perambramundi'	3.3% piperine; essential oil 3.7%; 49 berries/ spike; yield (5.22 kg/vine dry pepper); resistant to foot rot
Vijay (2013)	Hybrid of 'Panniyur-2 x Kottanadan'	Medium long spikes; bold berries, oil, oleoresin, piperine more; field tolerant to phytophthora foot rot
Arka Coorg Excel (2012)	Seedling selection	Medium mature; 99 fruits/ spike; yield (7.15 kg/vine dry pepper)
NRC Oil palm, Palode		
PLD-2 (1996)	Clonal selection	Late maturity; 3% piperine; oleoresin 15.45%; essential oil

	from 'Kottanadan'	4.8%; suitable for plains & higher elevations; yield (2475 kg/ha dry pepper)
Other popular varieties		
Balankotta	Local cv.	Self fertile; 9% oleoresin; 4.2% piperine; 5% essential oil; fresh berry yield (1-3 kg/vine); drought tolerant; tolerant to foot rot; suitable for white pepper purpose
Kalluvally	Local cv.	Self fertile; 8.5-12% oleoresin; 2.5-5.4% piperine; 3% essential oil; fresh berry yield (1-2 kg/vine); drought tolerant; tolerant to foot rot; suitable for white pepper purpose
Aimpirian	Local cv.	12-13% oleoresin; 4-5% piperine; 3% essential oil; fresh berry yield (4-5 kg/vine)
Arakkulammunda	Local cv.	9.8% oleoresin; 4.4% piperine; 4.7% essential oil; fresh berry yield (1-2 kg/vine)
Karimunda	Local cv.	7-13% oleoresin; 4.5-6.2% piperine; 3.5% essential oil; fresh berry yield (3-5 kg/vine); high spiking intensity
Kottanadan	Local cv.	17.8% oleoresin; 6.6% piperine; 2.5% essential oil; fresh berry yield (5 kg/vine)
Kuthiravally	Local cv.	15% oleoresin; 6% piperine; 4.5% essential oil; fresh berry yield (3 kg/vine)
Narayakodi	Local cv.	11 % oleoresin; 5.4% piperine; 4% essential oil; fresh berry yield (1.5-2 kg/vine); tolerant to phytophthora foot rot; berries got persistent stigma
Neelamundi	Local cv.	14% oleoresin; 4.6% piperine; 3.3 % essential oil; fresh berry yield (2 kg/vine); tolerant to phytophthora foot rot
Vadakkan	Local cv.	Triploid; 10.8% oleoresin; 4.2% piperine; 3.2 % essential oil; fresh berry yield (3 kg/vine)

Pests, diseases and disorders:

- Pepper yellow/ Slow decline: Caused by burrowing nematodes and foot rot.
- Basal wilt (*Sclerotium rolfsii*):
- Scale insect (*Lepidosaphes piperis*): Serious pest at higher altitude. Spray systemic insecticide.
- Pollu (*Colletotrichum gloeosporioides*): Serious disease. Spray 1% Bordeaux mixture.
- Pollu beetle or Lanka ramkrishnae (*Longitarsus nigripennis*) is major destructive pest.
- Leaf gall thrips (*Liothrips karnyi*): More serious at higher altitudes. Spray systemic insecticide.
- Top shoot borer (*Cydia hemidoxa*): Serious in young vines.
- Quick wilt/ Phytophthora foot rot in pepper was 1[st]noticed in Waynad district of Kerala.
- Biological control against foot rot (*Phytophthora capsici*) is *Trichoderma harzianum* and *Pseudomonas fluorescens*.

- Anthracnose disease causes spike shedding in pepper.
- Nematodes: Drenching 0.1% Carbosulfan 25 EC (0.125 a. i.) @ 5 litres/ plant at the base of plant twice a year (pre-monsoon -May and post-monsoon - October).
- Rosetting: Zn deficiency.
- Little leaf: Caused due to Cucumber Mosaic Virus. Eradicate affected plant.
- Phyllody (Phytoplasma+Anthracnose): Eradicate affected plant.

9.2 Betel vine/ *Tambuli*/ *Pan*

- Eulogized as 'Neglected green gold' of India.
- India is major exporter of betel vine and its products to UK, Africa, Canada, USA & many Islamic countries.
- Cultivated in hot and damp regions of the world.
- Cultivation in India was confined to members of particular community known as Chaurasia's who were raising the crop from time immemorial.
- Cash crop of India and referred in ancient Indian literature dating back to 340 BC.
- Leaves are of great religious importance particularly in traditional Indian Hindu way of life.
- In auspicious occasion such as celebrations, marriages, rituals, religious gatherings, etc. *Pan* is used in worship of god.
- Geographically it belongs to regions bounded by 68^0E to 118^0W longitudes and 30^0N to 12^0S latitudes.
- Optimum rainfall: 225-475 cm and grown from sea level to altitude of 900 m in Western Ghats.
- Leaves are aromatic, carminative, anti-septic, astringent, mildly stimulant, expectorant and exhalent in nature. Rich in vit. A, B, C, 21 essential oils, alkaloids and arecolins.
- Leaves composition: Moisture (85.4%), proteins (3.1%), fats (0.08%), fibres (2.3%), -CHO (6.1%), mineral matter (2.3%) and carotene (9600 IU), high content of KNO_3 (0.26-0.42%), sugar as glucose (1.4-3.2%), reducing sugar as sucrose (0.6-2.5%), starch (1-1.2%), essential oils (0.81-1.8%), tannins (1-1.3%), vit. A (9.365 mg/ 100 g), vit. C (4.8 mg/ 100 g fresh wt.).
- Leaves for chewing should contain little starch but high proportion of sucrose.
- Sugars present: Glucose, fructose, maltose, sucrose.
- Leaf juice is acidic in nature and Malic and Oxalic acids are reported.
- Aromatic value of leaf is based on essential oil content and varies from 0.7-2.6%.
- During bleaching, oil content increases from 1.2% in unbleached to 4.2% in bleached leaves.
- Oil is bright yellow to dark brownish coloured.
- Bleaching process improves concentration of phenols in oil.

- Eugenol is predominant phenolic constituent.
- Higher the proportion of phenols in oil, better is the quality.
- Leaves clear mouth and throat.
- Acts as tonic for brain, liver and heart.
- Essential oils of betel vine are important for medicines and *pan masala* industry.
- Chemo-preventive effects against cancer, anti-oxidant, anti-mutagenic, anti-inflammatory.
- 1st betel vine research centre was established in 1962 at Ramtek & now functions under Dr. PDKV, Akola.
- 2nd research centre was established in Akot tehsil of district Akola, Maharashtra.
- Perennial dioecious evergreen creeper and produces orthotropic (vegetative) and plagiotropic (reproductive) shoots.
- Moisture loving and shade tolerant plant.
- Alternate leaves on vine which grips the support firmly with adventitious roots.
- Leaves gathered from branches are called as *'Hatvan'* (best quality).
- Leaves gathered from nodes on main stem are called *'Angwan'* (medium quality).
- Leaves at nodes on main stem are called *'Madwan'* (inferior quality).
- On the basis of colour and maturity on the vines, the new leaves are called as 'Nevati'; second flush as 'Parati', third flush as 'Terti' and those kept on vines for long time till good market conditions are called as *'Junwan'*.
- Sexual dimorphism is expressed in leaf length: breadth ratio.
- Being dioecious, cross poilination must occur.
- Inflorescence: Dense catkin, the naked compactly arranged flowers are sunk in fleshy axis of spike.
- Flowers: naked, very minute, in dense spike, flattened (peltate), bracteate, bisexual/unisexual.
- Number of stamens: 2-6 and dehisce by longitudinal slits.
- Spp. *P. nigrum*, posses only 2 stamens and the posterior one of inner whorl is abortive.
- Number of carpels, 2-5 and coalescent.
- Ovary is superior, unilocular with single basal orthotropus ovule.
- Number of stigma 1-5 and corresponds to number of carpels.
- Fruit: Small drupe, often described as berry.
- Seeds: Small, endospermic with minute embryo.
- Male spikes long, cylindrical, dense, patuous or defieted.

- Female spikes deflexed, shorter than male, pendulous and 2.5-5 cm long.
- In betel vine, artificially created shed for shade i.e. conservatories & training which is locally known as 'Boroj/ Bareja/ Bheet/ Baras'.
- Suitable supportive plants: *Sesbania grandiflora, Erythrina indica, Moringa oleifera.*
- Aroma is due to phenols and terpenes.
- Propagation method: Stem cutting (with 3-5 nodes and 30-45 cm long) taken from 2 year old from top portion.
- Sets are prepared from single node with one leaf (mother leaf).
- Planting season varies in different tracts in the country.
- When the vines reach a height of 3 m, they are rejuvenated by lowering.
- Trailing: Vines require tightening with support to facilitate climbing and is done every 10-15 days depending upon growth rate of vines.
- Ratooning: It is done year after year in same orchard.
- Vines become full grown in 10 months.
- Vine lasts for 3-12 years.
- Picking of leaves starts from 4-6 months after plantation and leaves are picked from branches and not from main stem.
- Harvesting method:
    - Matured/ tender leaves along with portion of petiole.
    - Leaves are plucked by hand without any aid & or iron nail is used to facilitate plucking.
    - Leaves are arranged vertically in layers forming 3-4 circles of leaves in each layer.
    - Leaves are packed in baskets (60-75 cm dia. and 30-45 cm high).
    - A vertical empty space is left out in centre for aeration.
- Three grades are practiced: Babla (large sized), Adke (medium), Modwan (small sized).
- In Uttar Pradesh, commercial grades are recognized on the basis of place of origin as: Desi (local), Maghai (Bihar), Bangla (Bengal), Jaggnnathi (Odisha), Kapoori (Chennai).
- Good demand in market: Bleached betel leaves.
- Bleaching:
    - Fresh leaves used for chewing are subjected to bleaching/ blanching / curing.
    - Bleaching process consist of moistening the leaves & allowing them to stand warm in ventilated place in absence of light.
    - Lots of 25-35 kg leaves (comprising 16,000-20,000 in number) are bleached at a time.

  - Leaves are sprinkled with water.
  - During bleaching, leaves turn gradually yellowish white.
  - After 5-6 days, leaves are taken out of container for inspection & whole process normally takes 10-15 days in summer & 15-20 days in winter.
  - Bleached leaves are dried to remove surface moisture & packed for marketing.
- Market grades: Kali, Fafada, Hakkal.
- Unit of sale:
  1. In Maharashtra and Andhra Pradesh, basket (*daag*) containing 3000-6000 leaves (based on leaf size).
  2. In Coimbatore, unit of packaging as one *Palagai* of 2000 leaves while one *Kavali* consisting of 200 leaves.
- N @ 200 kg/ha in organic and inorganic forms is essential for better growth and leaf production.
- Cultivation is labour intensive job.
- Yield: 100-150 q/ha (green leaves).
- Cold storage: Temperature of 5.5-7.0^{0}C and 85-90% R.H. for 5-6 days and not more than 10-15 days.
- Polybags without respiration vents is advocated.
- Sprays of Althroann @ 50 ppm and Neystatin @ 100 ppm increases shelf life > 30 days.
- Utility of leaves: *Pan masala*, oil industry (as preservative) and in medicinal industry.
- Hydroxy-chavicol (4-allyl pyrocatechol) isolated from leaves exhibits strong anti-oxidant effect and checks the development of rancidity in ghee.
- Terminologies used:
  - Propping: Fastening of growing betle vine to sesbania plants with the help of Typha grass from time to time in regular intervals of 20-25 days.
  - Kalli: Means leaves that are born on branches are plucked for market.
  - Papada: Means leaves born on main stems, are of lower quality and not much relished on markets.

Varieties:

- Two different types: Pungent (wild type) and non-pungent.
- Cultivated types in different states clustered into 6 different varieties: Assam Patti, Banaras, Calcutta, Karpura Kodi, Karapaku, Kalli Patti, Magai pan, Poona, Vellai Kodi (kodi means 'vine').

Bangla	Vigorous, very pungent; leaves with 7-9 prominent secondary veins; petioles 8-10 cm long; lamina 8.5 to 15.5 x 11-19 cm; light green with yellowish ting, cordate- roundish shaped leaves; widest part of lamina is below middle point; petiole glabrous, base auriculate & short, fibrous with nearly 82% essential oil comprises eugenol
Desawari	Large cordate leaves, short, pointed acuminate with curved apex; lamina glabrous, less conspicuous basal lobes; 4-6 prominent secondary veins; mild sweet taste due to low anethole content
Kappori	Vines moderately vigorous, aromatic; leaves narrow & ovate; lamina thin, margins entire; light yellowish to green in colour; glabrous & soft in texture; apex acuminate; leaf base lobed; lamina with prominent mid-ribs & 4-6 secondary veins; trichomes rare; aroma due to high level (20%) of terpenyl acetate
Khasi	Wild in characters; mainly grown in N-E hilly areas; leaves large, cordate to elliptical shaped, thicker & leathery; leaf apex short, pointed & curved; secondary veins thick & originate from different points; 4-6 in number, leaf colour dark green
Meetha	Leaves thin & waxy, cordate to broadly ovate shaped, dark green in colour with characteristic pale yellowish spots; apex short but pointed; high preponderance of trichomes; aroma is of anethole that gives it alternative name Saunfia.
Sanchi	Pungent; leaves medium to large (9 to 21 x 5.5 to 13.2 cm), narrow & ovate with long base; lobes less prominent, leaf margin entire, venation reticulate, multicostate with 6-8 prominent secondary veins; leaves dark green & fibrous

- Multiple resistant cultivar: Halisahar Sanchi.
- DPB-6, 7, Kapoori Local, Kapoori Uttukar, Kapoori Chittikavati.
- Kumbachola: Tolerant to foot rot.

Name	Breeding method	Features
TNAU, Coimbatore (ARS, Sirugamani)		
SGM-1 (1994)	Clonal selection	Bushy female vine; tolerant to pests & diseases; ideal homestead variety; leaf yield 110 lakh/ha
SGM-2 (2004)	Clonal selection	Multilateral vine; leaf yield 100 lakh/ha; slightly pungent; tolerant to pests & bacterial leaf spot; suited for open conditions
SGM-BV-2	Pure line selection from Dindigul Local	Resistant to linear scale insect; mod. resistant to phytophthora, stem rot, blight, mite & nematodes
OUAT, Bhubaneshwar		
Utkal Sudam (1999)	Clonal selection	Short internodes; tolerant to major diseases; suitable for Bareja type cultivation
BCKV, Kalyani		
Bidhan pan (2002)	Clonal selection	Bangla type; cordate leaves; high leaf yield; tolerant to pest & diseases
MPKV, Rahuri		
Krishna pan (2001)	Clonal selection	Less pungent; 320 leaves/ vine; 10 days shelf life; yield (47.13 lakh leaves/ ha); oblong leaves; thick & light green colour; 16 days storage life; mod. resistant to foot rot; susceptible to betelvine bug & nematode

Pests and diseases:

- Betel vine mired bug (*Disphincuts politus*): Major pest.
- Reniform and Root knot nematodes: Serious nematodes.
- Powdery mildew: (*Oidium piperis*): Most serious disease.
- Foot rot (*Phytophthora parasitica*): Severe during water logging. It is a terrestrial fungus known as plant destroyer and 1st noticed in 1925.

10. RUTACEAE

10.1 Curry leaf

- Perennial aromatic tree cum spice leaf vegetable.
- *Murraya koenigii* (syn. *Bergera koenigii* or *Chaleas koenigii*): Cultivated and true diploid.
- *M. exotica* (syn. *Chaleas paniculata*): Ornamental &scented hedge.
- Introduced to south India from Persia (Middle-East).
- Nutrition composition 100 g leaf: -CHO (8.7g), protein (6g), fat (1g), Ca (83 mg), Fe (0.93 mg), vit. A (12600 I.U).
- Self pollinated crop.
- It is high temperature tolerant (26-37^{0}C) crop.
- Below 16^{0}C, vegetative buds become dormant and growth is affected.
- Peculiar aroma is due to sulphur containing essential oil.
- Oil content in fresh leaves: 2.6%.
- Leaves contain oxalates in higher concentration.
- Leaves yield volatile oil and a crystalline glucoside from leaves 'koenigiin' and from flowers 'murrayin or muragin' are industrial products.
- Oil has strong spicy odour and pungent clove like taste.
- Carotenoids are present in leaves.
- Major anti-oxidant present in leaves: Carbazole compounds
- Flowers: Terminal corymbose panicle (cymes).
- Fruit type: Indehiscent berry (thin pericarp and mucilaginous pulp) & contains 2-3 seeds.
- Propagation method: Seeds & root suckers.
- Clones obtained from root suckers.
- Polyembryony in nature.
- Dehydrated at 50^{0}C and made into powder.
- Harvesting of leaves starts 10-12 months after planting.
- Leaves are picked at 15 months after planting at 2 ½ to 3 months interval.

- Yield: 20-25 T/ ha.
- Two distinct types observed in cultivation—small leaf type and large leaf type.
- Small leaf type has more fragrant, greater flavour than large leaf type. Used in extraction of essential oil.
- Extraction of essential oil: Steam distillation under high pressure.

Varieties:

- Highly aromatic varieties are developed through clonal selection and OP seedling progeny.
- Senkaampu: Red petioled local type developed by farmer, popular in Tamil Nadu. Leaves highly aromatic.

Name	Breeding method	Features
UAS, Dharwad		
DWD-1 (syn. Suvasini)	Clonal selection	Oil- 5.22%, sensitive to low winter temperatures results in poor growth; dehydrated at 50^{0}C without loss in quality; chlorophyll content 0.1629 mg/g fresh leaf
DWD-2	OP seedling progeny of unknown source	8 times higher yield than DWD-1; winter insensitive; oil-4.09%; less aromatic

Diseases:

- Sap rot (*Fomes pectinatius*):
- Collar rot of seedlings (*Rhizoctonia solani*):
- Leaf spot (*Phyllosticdina murrayae*):

11. ZINGIBERACEAE

11.1 Small cardamom

- Eulogized as 'Queen of spices or Grains of paradise'.
- India is known as the home of cardamom.
- Major producers: Guatemala, India, Sri Lanka, Papua New Guinea and Nepal.
- Guatemala produces 2/3rd of global production.
- Guatemala exports 68.08% of volume and 64.81% by value.
- In Arab countries, it is traditionally used for flavouring coffee.
- Major oriental spice.
- 2nd national spice; third most expensive spice after saffron and vanilla.
- Cardamom occurs in its natural state only in tropical evergreen forests of Western Ghats in south India.
- Cardamom Hill Reserve: Travancore area Dist. Idukki. World heritage site by UNESCO.

- Indian cardamom is low in fat, high in protein, iron, vit. B and C.
- India is 2nd largest consumer in world after Saudi Arabia.
- Major importers of Indian cardamom: Saudi Arabia (42%) and Japan (39%).
- Major import markets of value added products of Indian cardamom: Germany, Netherlands, and UK.
- West Asia is the major consumer of cardamom contributing 59% of total world consumption.
- Kerala occupies 1st position in both area (56%) and production (78%).
- Karnataka has 37% share in area and 14% share in production.
- India's productivity: 149 kg/ha; Guatemala's productivity: 250 kg/ha.
- Idukki district in Kerala is having highest productivity (200 kg/ha).
- India exports 5-8% of its total production and 90% of produce is consumed within nation.
- Order: Scitaminae.
- 1st descriptor for cardamom: Prepared by IPGRI, Rome in 1994.
- Classification based on fruit size viz. *E. cardamomum* var. Major and var. Minor is not accepted due to lack of demarcation on size and shape of fruits.
- Nature of panicle is accepted for classification.
- Grows within an altitude between 600-1200 m MSL.
- Annual rainfall between 1500-4000 mm and temperature range of 10-35^{0}C is congenial for good growth.
- Ideal soil pH: 4.2 to 6.8.
- Pseophyte (shade loving) and grown as rainfed crop.
- Light intensity for growth: Medium to high (45-65%).
- Cardamom grows well at an altitude between 600 to 1200 m above MSL.
- *Erythrina* is planted for temporary shade.
- Trees suitable for permanent shade: Palangi (*Artocarpus fraxinifolius*), Jackfruit, Red cedar (*Cedrella toona*), Karimaram (*Diospyros ebenum*), *Vernonia arborea*, *Cassia fistula*, *Terminalia tomentosa*, and Elangi (*Mimusops elangi*) are suitable.
- Alleppey cardamom (designated as Alleppey Green): Best and reserved for export.
- Commercial propagation method: Seed and suckers.
- Seed viability is very low.
- Seed storage for 15 days decreases germination by 20% and 3-5 months storage decreases it up to 94%.
- Best time of seed sowing: September.
- Cardamom has hard seed coat which prevents germination.

- For higher seed germination, seeds are treated with concentrated Sulphuric acid for 2 min or 2.5% nitric acid for 10 min.
- Seed germination commences 20-25 days after sowing and continues for further 30-40 days.
- Seed rate: 30-50 g per 6 x 1 m size raised bed.
- One kg seed capsules produce 5000 seedlings.
- Seedlings can be raised in secondary nursery or in polybags.
- Seedlings at 3-4 leaf stage are transplanted into black polybags (20 cm x 20 cm size & 100 gauge thickness) for better establishment.
- By this method, nursery period can be reduced to 5-6 months as against 10-12 months in secondary nursery.
- Propagation method for true to type planting material: Sucker and micropropagation.
- Suckers grow continuous for 18 months from time of emergence.
- Rate of linear growth is maximum in June-July.
- Explants used in micropropagation: Shoot buds from young sprouting tillers.
- Rate of multiplication is quite high through this technique (3 shoots/ explant with 86-93% rooting).
- Virus free plants are produced through meristem culture.
- Rhizome multiplication can be taken from March-October.
- New shoots arise from the rhizome and constitute a clump.
- On an average, 20-30 suckers/ initial planting unit can be produced within 1 year of planting.
- About 10-18 months old seedlings are used for planting in main field.
- Close planting (2 x 1 m) is advisable along the contour.
- Planting distance: Malabar type (2m x 2 m); Mysore & Vazhukka type (2.4m x 2.4 m or 3m x 3m).
- Number of plants/ ha: 1000-1250 (in India) and 1500-2200 (in Guatemala).
- Plant seedlings up to collar region.
- Shade regulation (50-60%) and mulching are important practices.
- Tuberous underground rhizome is its real stem.
- Aerial shoot is pseudo-stem formed by enriching leaf sheaths.
- Throughout year flowering on current as well as previous season panicle takes place.
- Summer showers during February- April are essential for panicle initiation.
- Development of inflorescence (panicles) takes place in about 10-12 months.
- Type of fruit: Tri-locular oblong capsule containing 15-20 seeds, covered with mucilaginous membraneous aril & attached to axile placenta.

- Flowers: Hermaphrodite & zygomorphic.
- Pollination agents: Honey bee (*Apis cerana, A. indica* and *A. dorsata*).
- For assured pollination, 2-3 bee hives are maintained.
- Days required from flower bud initiation to reach full bloom stage: 26-34.
- Days required from full bloom to capsule development: 110-120.
- Cool humid weather is necessary during flowering for fruit set.
- Plants take about 2 years to bear capsules.
- Fruit setting percentage: Morning time (72%) and evening time (24%).
- During June-July, fruit set is 50-58% while in December-January no fruit set.
- Mixed cropping of coffee, arecanut and coconut is more beneficial than sole cropping.
- Foliar sprays of $ZnSO_4$ @ 250 g/100 liters of water during April-May and September-October is recommended.
- Soil application of Borax @ 7.5 kg/ ha is recommended.
- Regular irrigation (25-37 mm) helps in initiation of panicles, flowering and fruit set.
- Water requirement through drip irrigation: 10-15 liters/ plant/ day.
- Soil moisture level should be maintained above 45-50%.
- Trashing: Removal of old and dry leaves, tillers & leaf sheaths is done 1 or 2 times in a year.
- Recommended herbicide: Paraquat (625 ml/ 500 lit of water/ ha).
- Maturity indices:
  - Distinctly developed shoulders of capsule.
  - Clear cut line between two segments of the shell.
  - Triangular deep cut at point of attachment.
  - Loosed attachment of capsules to panicle.
  - Change of seed colour to brownish black or black.
- Two types of pickings:

  a) Light picking:

    i) Only green & mature capsules are harvested & naturally gives lower green crop/ pick.

    ii) Gap between picking rounds: 20-30 days.

  b) Hard picking:

    i) Semi-mature capsules are also removed and this process reduces curing percentage.

    ii) Increases picking average.

    iii) Gives green coloured capsules upon curing.

    iv) Gap between picking rounds: 30-45 days.

- Harvesting in rainy days results in lower out turn.
- Out turn increases with progress of harvest into December-January and there after declines.
- Peak harvesting time: October-November.
- Capsules from younger plants will have higher percentage of recovery.
- Capsules are picked up only at physiologically mature to fully ripened stage to obtain higher recovery.
- Cardamom recovery is highest in fully ripen capsules (29%) followed by harvest at physiological maturity (24%) and immature stage (14%).
- Picking of over ripened capsules causes splitting at time of curing.
- Storing of harvested capsules should be avoided.
- Yield: 500 kg/ha (150 kg dry/ha).
- Curing: It is a process in which, moisture of freshly harvested capsules is reduced from 80% to 10-12% at 50^0C to retain green colour to maximum extent.

Two types of drying:

a) Natural sun drying has very high use of thermal efficiency.

b) Artificial drying using fire wood (artificial flue pipe system) imparts better green colour.

c) ICRI (Spices Board) suggested use of LPG/ kerosene as source of fuel.

- After drying, capsules are polished when they are hot by rubbing against hard surface or using polishing machine.
- Dried capsules are stored in black polythene lines gunny bags to retain green colour.
- MELCARD (Modern Economical Low Cost Cardamom Drier).
- Economic life of cardamom: 8-10 years.
- Cardamom products:
  1. Essential oil: contains esters & treatment of steam distillation to crushed fruits for 4 h is needed.
  2. Oleoresin: comprises volatile oil & resins, solvent extraction method is used to obtain it. One kg oleoresin = 20 kg of ground spice.
- Most cardamom varieties contain 5-9% oil.
- Volatile oil in cardamom seeds: 6.6-10.6%.
- Cardamom grading and marketing rules were formed in 1962.
- Best oil is obtained from Alleppey Green.
- Important constituent of oil: Cineol.
- Taste of cardamom is due to oil: 1, 8-cineole & α-terpinyl acetate.
- White cardamom: SO_2 treatment given to green cardamom.

- Bleached (creamy-white or golden yellow coloured) cardamom is prepared by using SO_2, KMS (25% containing 1% HCl for 30 min.) and H_2O_2 (4-6% at pH 4.0).
- Freshly harvested green (wet) capsules are soaked in 2 % washing soda (sodium carbonate) alkali solution for 10 min. prior to drying stabilizes chlorophyll and to retains original green colour.
- Dry capsule recovery: 20% in fully ripe capsules, followed by 24% in matured (physiologically ripe) & 14% in immature stage of capsules.

Grades:

Bold/ Export grade	Capsules have > 6.5 mm dia., & greenish colour; Lt. wt 415 g
Super bold/ Special grade	Matured green capsules have > 8 mm dia., Lt. wt. > 450 g
Extra bold	Matured green capsules have > 7 mm dia., Lt. wt. 435 g
Bulk grade	Contains all sizes, mature & immature capsules, black, yellow & splited cardamom
Small	Size between 5.5 to 6 mm, cleaned & black capsules, Lt. wt. 385 g
Open/ Splits	Matured capsule colour may be partly green/ partly yellow & size > 6.5 mm
Seeds	Husks are fully removed with brown coloured seeds. Lt. wt. around 550 g to 600 g
Fruit	Over matured capsules with slight yellow colour & Lt. wt. > 425 g

AGMARK Grade Specifications for spices, Spices Board:

Grade designation	Trade name	Colour	Unclipped capsules (% by count) max.	Empty & malformed capsules (% by count) max.	Immature & shriveled capsules (% w/w) max.	Blacks & splits (% by count) max.	Size, dia., of the sieve hole on which retained (mm)	Wt. of G/L by wt. (max.)
Alleppey Green Cardamom								
AGEB	Cardamom extra bold	Deep green, green or light green	-	2.0	2.0	0.0	7.0	435
AGB	Cardamom bold	-do-	-	2.0	2.0	0.0	6.0	415
AGS	Cardamom superior	-do-	-	3.0	5.0	0.0	5.0	385
AGS-1	Shipment-1	-do-	-	5.0	7.0	10.0	4.0	350
AGS-2	Shipment-3	-do-	-	7.0	9.0	12.0	4.0	320
AGL	Light	-	-	-	-	15.0	3.5	260
Coorg Green Cardamom								
CGEB	Extra bold	-	0.0	0.0	0.0	0.0	8.0	450
CGB	Bold	-	0.0	2.0	3.0	0.0	7.5	435
CG-1	Superior	-	0.0	3.0	5.0	0.0	6.5	415
CG-2	Coorg green or Motta green	-	3.0	5.0	10.0	0.0	6.0	385
CG-3	Shipment	-	5.0	10.0	15.0	10.0	5.0	350
CG-4	Light	-	-	-	-	15.0	3.5	280
Bleached or half bleached cardamom								
BL-1	-	-	-	0.0	0.0	-	8.5	340
BL-2	-	-	-	0.0	0.0	-	7.0	340
BL-3	-	-	-	0.0	0.0	-	5.0	300

Species:

- Indian cardamom (*Elettaria cardamomum*): True cardamom.
- Sri Lankan wild cardamom (*E. ensal*): For flavouring and medicinal purpose.
- Malaysian wild cardamom (*E. longituba*):
- Indonesian type: *E. rubida*, *E. stolonifera*, *E. kapitensis*, *E. surculosa*, etc.
- The species comprises freely inter breeding population.
- Polycross method of breeding is ideal to get better varieties.

Distinguishing characters of cultivars:

- Vazhukka type: Natural hybrid between Malabar and Mysore type.
- Malabar type: Most pleasant and mellow aroma and flavour. It has short span of flowering & highly suitable for high density planting (HDP) accommodating 5,000 plants/ha.

Character	Malabar	Vazhukka	Mysore
Adaptability	Lower elevation	Higher	Higher
Area	Karnataka	Kerala	Kerala, Tamil Nadu
Tolerance to drought	Withstand long dry spells	Prefer well distributed rain	Prefer well distributed rain
Plant stature	Dwarf (2-3 m)	Tall (3-5 m)	Tall
Leaf petiole	Short	Long	Long
Panicle	Prostrate (spreading on ground)	Semi-erect (pendent)	Erect
Bearing nature of capsule	Early, short span of flowering	Late, long	Late, long
Colour at maturity	Pale/ golden green	Green	Green

Varieties:

- In small cardamom, two varieties based on size of fruits are recognized as:
  a) *E. cardamomum* var. major is primitive variety from which cultivated var. minor is derived. It comprises wild indigenous cardamom of Ceylon or Greater oblong cardamom or Long cardamom.
  b) *E. cardamomum* var. minor: comprises all cultivated races included under the names Malabar and Mysore types.
- All the varieties and races are inter-fertile and observed variations are due to natural crossing.
- Intervarietal hybridization produces high heterotic recombinations.
- Intergeneric hybridization between *Cardamom* and allied genera viz. *Alpinia*, *Aframomum* and *Amomum* indicate compatibility barriers (no fruit setting).
- Planting of single cardamom clone is not recommended because of self incompatibility.

- Njallani Green Gold: Farmer's selection in Kerala. Dry capsule yield 2475 kg/ha.
- Local landraces: Vali Green Gold, Vander Cardamom, Palakkudi, Panikulangara, PNS Vaigai, PR-1.
- MHC-10 and MHC-18: Heterotic hybrids.

Name	Breeding method	Features
UAS, Bangalore (RRS, Mudigere)		
Mudigere-1 (1984)	Clonal selection	Malabar type; prostrate type panicles; oval bold capsules; 8% oil; 1,8 cineole content 36%; á-terpenyl acetate 42%; dry capsule yield 275 kg /ha; mod. tolerant to thrips, hairy caterpillar; suitable for HDP; best suited for Karnataka
Mudigere-2 (1996)	Clonal selection	Malabar type; early maturing; 8% oil; 1,8 cineole content 45%; á-terpenyl acetate 38%; dry capsule yield 475 kg/ha; suitable for HDP
KAU, Thrissur (CRS, Pampadumpara)		
PV-1 (1987)	Selection from 'Walayar collection'	Prostrate type panicles; long and bold capsules; early maturing; 6.8% essential oil; dry capsule yield 260 kg/ha; 1,8 cineole content 33%; á-terpenyl acetate 46%; best suited for Karnataka
PV-2 (2018)	OP selection of PV-1	Malabar type; unbranched panicle; essential oil 10.45%; dry capsule yield 982 kg /ha; tolerant to stem borer; thrips, clump rot, capsule rot; suitable for elevation range of 1000-2000 m MSL
PV-3 (2018)	OP selection	Vazhukka type; ovoid capsule, 153 number of capsules/ panicle; dry recovery 18%; tolerant to drought, thrips & capsule borer; dry capsule yield 594 kg/ha
ICRI, (Spice board), Myladumpara		
ICRI-1 (1992)	Clonal selection	Malabar type; early maturing; essential oil 8.7%; 1,8 cineole content 29%; α-terpenyl acetate 38%; dry capsule yield 375 kg /ha; best suited for Kerala & TN
ICRI-2 (1992)	Clonal selection	Perform well at high altitude; tolerant to azukkal disease; 1,8 cineole content 29%; α-terpenyl acetate 36%; dry capsule yield 375 kg/ ha; best suited for Kerala & TN
ICRI-3 (1993)	Selection	Malabar type; non-pubescent leaves; essential oil 6.6%; 1,8 cineole content 54%; α-terpenyl acetate 24%; dry capsule yield 440 kg/ ha; tolerant to rhizome rot; suitable for hill zone of Karnataka
ICRI-4 (1997)	Clonal selection	Malabar type, early mature; essential oil 6.4%; suitable for low rainfall areas; tolerant to rhizome rot & capsule borer; dry capsule yield 455 kg /ha
ICRI-5 (2006)	Hybrid of 'MCC-260 x MCC-49'	Malabar type; 1st hybrid; early mature; mod. tolerant to drought; high yield under intensive management; oil 7.13%; dry recovery 23.15%
ICRI-6 (2006)	Clonal selection (MCC-73) from germplasm	Malabar type; high yield; tolerant to drought; oil content 7.33%; dry recovery 19%

ICRI-7	MCC-12 x MCC-35	Yield (1,400 kg dry capsule/ha; recovery 22.24% (dry capsules), angular bold (69.87%) capsules, high volatile oil (8.84%) & high oleoresin content (7.99%); mod. tolerant to drought
IISR (CRC, Appangala)		
IISR- Suvasini (1997)	Clonal selection	Malabar type; high yield, early maturing; essential oil 8.7%; 1,8 cineole content 42%; α-terpenyl acetate 37%; dry capsule yield 745 kg /ha; suitable for HDP
IISR- Vijetha (Natural Katte Escape, line-12) 2001	Clonal selection	Malabar type; essential oil 7.9%; 1,8 cineole content 45%; α-terpenyl acetate 23.4%; dry capsule yield 979 kg /ha; tolerant to Katte disease
IISR, Avinash (1999)	Clonal selection from hot spot areas	Malabar type; essential oil 6.7%; 1,8 cineole content 30.4%; α-terpenyl acetate 34.6%; dry capsule yield 847 kg /ha; tolerant to rhizome rot, shoot & capsule borer
Appangala-1	Clonal selection	Malabar type; 5% oil; dry capsule yield 678 kg/ha
Appangala-2	Appangala-1 x NKE-19	Malabar type; 1st Katte disease resistant hybrid; essential oil 6.3%; dry capsule yield 927 kg/ ha; tolerant to capsule borer
Coorg Cardamom Selection-1	OP selection of clone 37	Maiabar type; prostrate type panicles; suited for HDP; dry capsule yield 408 kg/ ha; 8.7% essential oil; best suited for Karnataka
SKP-14	-	Prostrate type panicles; best suited for Karnataka

Pests and diseases:

- Major constraint in vegetative propagation: Katte disease.
- Katte: Viral disease transmitted by suckers and aphids (*Pentalonia nigronervosa*). Use disease free planting material.
- Azhukkal or capsule rot (*Phytophthora meadii*). Malabar and Vazhukka types are more susceptible than Mysore type. Apply *Trichoderma harzianum* @ 2.5 kg/ clump.
- Rhizome rot/ Clump rot/ *Pythium* and *Rhizoctonia* spp. are most serious diseases.
- Kokke Kandu (cardamom vein clearing virus): Causes quick decline & death of clumps.
- Nilgiri necrosis: Another viral disease like 'katte'. Gradual reduction in vigour and productivity of clumps but not death of clumps.
- Clump rot and damping off (*R. solani*, *P. vexans*): Nursery management with *Trichoderma harzianum* @ 50 g/ sq. m before seed sowing.
- Leaf spot (*Phyllosticta elettariae*): Reduces vigour of seedlings in nursery. Apply Bordeaux mixture 1% during March-April.
- Cardamom shoot and capsule borer (*Conogethes* (*Dichocrocis*) *punctiferalis*): Serious pest.
- Shoot fly, hairy caterpillar, root grubs, root knot nematodes: Serious pests.

- *Lecanicillium psalliotae*: Entomopathogenic fungus, for thrips management @ 3-4 times soil application (108 cfu/g) during May-September with 3 sprays of Spinosad 0.0135% (derived from *Saccharopolyspora spinosa*) during March, May and August.

11.2 Large cardamom

- Eulogized as 'Black cardamom or Fragrant cardamom or Greater Indian cardamom or Winged Bengal cardamom or Life line of Sikkim or *Badi elaichi*'.
- India roughly exports 19-20% of its production to various countries and Pakistan, UK and UAE are major importers.
- Sikkim is largest producer and constitute lion's share.
- It contains 2-3% of essential oil and possesses medicinal properties like carminative, stomachic, diuretic, cardiac stimulant and anti-emetic.
- Nutritional composition of cardamom seed/ 100 g:

Composition	USDA (ground)	ASTA
Water (g)	8.28	8.0
Food energy (kcal)	311	360
Protein (g)	10.76	10.0
Fat (g)	6.70	2.9
Carbohydrate (g)	68.47	74.2
Ash (g)	5.78	4.7
Calcium (g)	0.383	0.3
Phosphorous (mg)	178	210
Sodium (mg)	18	10
Potassium (mg)	1119	1200
Iron (mg)	13.97	11.6
Thiamin (mg)	0.198	0.18
Riboflavin (mg)	0.182	0.23
Niacin (mg)	1.102	2.3
Ascorbic acid (mg)	-	Not detected
Vit. A activity (RE)	Trace	Not detected

- Pseophyte i.e. plant grows under shade of Utis (*Alnus nepalensis*) trees which fixes atmospheric nitrogen.
- It is widely cultivated in eastern Himalaya i.e. Sikkim, West Bengal and Assam.
- Cultivation confined to 600-2350 m MSL.
- During severe winter, plants remain dormant & can withstand up to 2°C.
- Rainfall range: 2000-3000 mm per annum.
- Optimum soil pH: 4.5-6.0.
- Anthesis time: Early morning around 5.30 AM.
- Inflorescence: Condensed spike on short peduncle, bearing 40-50 flower buds in acropetal sequence.

- Type of fruit: Capsule.
- Fruit: Dark red brown, globose capsule.
- Flower bud differentiation occurs from August (in lower altitude) to October (in higher altitude).
- Late flowering at higher altitudes by 2-3 months compared to lower elevations.
- Continuous rains during flowering results in poor capsule set and barren spikes.
- Pollination agents: Bumble bees, honey bees.
- Nectar secretion begins at 9 h on day of anthesis and reaches peak at 14 hours.
- Stigma is protogynous and receptive 12 h before anthesis and remain receptive after 15 h of floral senescence.
- Best time of pollination: 6-9 h on day of anthesis.
- Propagation method: Seed and suckers.
- Seed germination is very poor (20-30%).
- Seed treatment with 25% nitric acid for 10 min. gives early, uniform & better germination.
- Seed soaking in 10 ppm GA_3 give 60% germination.
- Seeds are sown in primary nursery in September-October.
- Germination commence after 25-30 days of sowing.
- About 10 g seed is enough for 1 m area of nursery bed.
- When seedlings attain 3-4 leaf stage, they are transplanted to secondary beds 3-4 months after germination.
- Over-head pendal is erected for providing shade.
- Seedlings of 8-10 months age having 45-60 cm height with 2-3 tillers are planted in main field during June-July of subsequent year.
- Sucker multiplication nursery can be established under shade of forest trees or black shade net.
- Month of planting: May-June.
- Multiplication ratio in this method is about 1: 8 in one year's time.
- Micropropagation technique is used.
- Through meristem culture, virus free clones of cardamom can be developed.
- Planting distance: Less vigorous varieties (1.5 m x 1.5 m); robust varieties (1.8 m x 1.8 m).
- 1st crop is ready for harvest after 2 ½ years of planting in both cases of sucker and seedlings plantation.
- Ideal time of harvesting: August-September (low altitude), November-December (high altitude).
- Bearing spikes are removed at collar region using sharp edged knife.
- Harvest index: Seeds of top most capsule turn brown.

- Raw capsules are fleshy and contain up to 85% moisture.
- Capsules are immediately cured to retain only about 10-13% moisture in dry weight basis.
- Traditionally, capsules are dried by direct heating at 50-55^{0}C. This causes direct contact with smoke and capsules turns black or dark brown coloured with smoky smell and hance not recommended.
- Natural colour and flavour constituents are highly volatile and easily lost due to direct heat and higher temperature (> 55^{0}C) during curing.
- Curing: ICRI Spice Board has approved *Bhatti* system in which cardamom is dried by use of indirect heating at 50-55^{0}C.
- Curing causes fall in moisture content (up to 10% level) and gives metallic sound.
- Cured capsules are rubbed on wire mesh for cleaning and removal of calyx.
- Dry recovery of capsules after curing: 24%.
- Annual yield: 10-15 q/ha (dry fruits).
- Seeds on steam distillation yield 1 to 3.5% essential oil rich in 1,8-cineole.
- Colour of cured cardamom is important factor in consumers market.

Species:

- There is controversy over grouping of cardamom.
- International Standards Organization (ISO) has recognized 9 species of cardamom under 3 main groups:
  I. Group I: *Elettaria cardamomum*.
  II. Group II: Four species of *Aframomum* as:
    1. Madagascar cardamom (*A. angustifolium*):
    2. Cameroon cardamom (*A. hanburyi*):
    3. Korarima cardamom (*A. korarima*):
    4. Grains of paradise or Guinea grains (*A. melegueta*):
  III. Group III: Four species of *Amomum*:
    1. Bengal/ Nepal/ Sikkim cardamom (*A. aromaticum*):
    2. Round cardamom of Java (*A. kepulaga*):
    3. Thailand/ Cambodian cardamom (*A. krervanh*):
    4. Greater Indian/ Large/ Nepal/ Sikkim cardamom (*A. subulatum*): Used as ingrediant in several traditional medicine.
- False cardamoms belong to *Aframomum* of large cardamom. Used as spice.
- West African cardamom (*Aframomum sanguineum*):
- Black amomum (*Aframomum granum-paradisi*):
- Khasi and Eastern Himalaya cardamom (*Amomum dealbatum*):
- Chester or Siam cardamom (*Amomum cardamom*):

- Java cardamom (*Amomum maximum*):
- Chinese round cardamom (*Amomum globosum*):
- *Amomum* species are known in north-east India and South-East Asian countries.
- Fruits of *Amomum* (Indian region) and *Aframomum* (African region) are much larger in size compared to *E. cardamomum* and very easy to distinguish them but seed size and anatomy are very similar in all the three genera.

Varieties:

- ICRI Sikkim-1, ICRI Sikkim-2: Belong to Sawney cultivar.
- Cultivars found in Arunachal Pradesh: Bebo, Boklok, Tali, Jaker, Belal.
- Other selections: SBLC-5, SBLC-47, SBLC-42, SBLC-44, SBLC-50, SBLC-51.

Ramsay	Suitable for high altitude 1515 m MSL	Plants robust; require high shade; tiller maroon coloured with narrow leaves; flowers in May & harvest in Oct-Nov.; capsule contain16-30 seeds; grown in north Sikkim; essential oil content 1-1.8%; susceptible to chirkey & foorkey disease at lower altitudes
Bebo		Grown in Basar area of Arunachal Pradesh; unique feature of rhizome & suckering habit; rhizomes are raised above ground; & young suckers are covered under thick leaf sheath; long peduncle; seed contain 2% essential oil; tolerant to drought, foorkey viral infection
Golsey	Suitable for low altitude < 975 m MSL	Require less shade; suitable to area below 1500 m MSL; suited for close planting; capsule contain 40-50seeds; essential oil content 2.3-5%; tolerant to chirkey & susceptible to foorkey disease
Green Golsey	Suitable for low altitude 975-1515 m MSL	Leaves narrow & erect; big capsule with 50-70 seeds
Ramla	Suitable for high altitude 1515 MSL	Natural hybrid of (Golsey x Ramsey); leaves broad & long; capsule dark pink & contain 25-38 seeds; seeds contain 2.2-3% volatile oil; susceptible to foorkey but tolerant to chirkey
Sawney	Suitable for high altitude < 975 m MSL	Plants robust; leaves slender, papery textured & dark green coloured; flowering starts in March-May & harvest in Sept-Nov.; big capsule with 30-40 seeds; essential oil content 1.8-2.5%; susceptible to viral diseases
Barlangey	Suitable for high altitude 1515 m MSL	Plants tall up to 2.8 m with stout pseudostem & large leaves; Narrow leaves with wavy margin; grown in east Sikkim & higher altitudes of Darjeeling; 20 capsules/ spike with 50-65 seeds; yield 500 kg of cured capsules/ ha; susceptible to foorkey & chirkey.
(Dzongu) Seremna (syn. Sharmney or Lephrakey)	Suitable for low altitude < 975 m MSL	Grown in west Sikkim; leaves drooping type; 2-3 spikes/ tiller; 10 capsules/ spike with 65-70 seeds/ capsule;
Varlangey	Suited for mid-high altitudes	Plants robust; spike & productive tiller ratio is high; 50-70 bold seeds/ capsule; flowering in May at medium altitude & during June-July at higher altitude

Pests and diseases:

- Leaf eating caterpillar (*Artona chorista*): Major pest and outbreak in 1978 in Sikkim.
- Hairy caterpillar (*Eupterote* spp., *Clelea plumbiola*): Severe defoliator. Feed on chlorophyll & leave behind skeleton of mid-ribs and veins.
- Cardamom moth and psocids: Incidence is more in flue cured cardamom.
- Grass hopper (*Mecopoda elongata*): Damage > 5%.
- Shoot fly (*Merochlorops dimorphus*):
- Stem borer (*Glypheterix* spp.): Cause substantial loss and active during July-September.
- Capsule borer (*Synoxy* spp.): Serious pest making capsules hollow.
- Leaf hoppers, thrips, mealy bugs: Suck sap from developing capsules and vectors of Foorkey viral disease.
- Root knot nematode: Cause reduction in yields up to 47%. Treat nursery beds with Phorate @ 5 kg/ ha.
- Chirkey: Viral disease transmitted by mechanical sap and spread by aphid (*Micromyzus kalimpongensis*).
- Foorkey: Viral disease cause stunted shoots.
- Leaf streak disease (*Pestalotiopsis royenae*): Most serious foliar disease.

11.3 Turmeric

- Eulogized as 'Ancient sacred spice of Asian countries or Indian saffron or Golden crop'.
- Used as spice, dye and in cosmetic industry and religious ceremonies.
- Monocot and triploid (2n=3x=63).
- World production: 11 lakh tones.
- Major exporting countries: India, Vietnam, Indonesia, Burma, Netherlands.
- Major importing countries: America, Iran, Germany, England.
- India won patent right under leadership of Dr. Raghunath Mashelkar.
- India ranks 1st in total production of turmeric in the world.
- India accounts for 80% of total world production.
- It has a share of 19% in the total production of spices.
- India exports only raw turmeric in international market.
- Export of turmeric powder has decreased by 11% in August 2021.
- Turmeric powder is exported to UAE, Bangladesh, USA, Germany, Iraq, Saudi Arabia, Malaysia, Iran, and Tunisia.
- Major growing states: Telangana, Maharashtra, Kerala, Andhra Pradesh, Tamil Nadu.
- These states contribute 40% to countries production.
- Annually 4.5 lakh ton production in India.
- Maharashtra ranks 1st in area (84066 ha) followed by Telangana (56000 ha).

- Bihar has highest productivity (26.1 t/ha) and ranks 1st followed by Maharashtra (20.3 t/ha) and ranks 2nd.
- Andhra Pradesh leads 1st position in area and production & 3rd in productivity.
- Erect, perennial herb grown as an annual crop.
- Used as spice, dye & in cosmetic industry and religious ceremonies.
- Marketing unit in India: 1 bag= 70 kg.
- Molecular formula of curcumin: $C_{21}H_{20}O_6$.
- Curcumin (2-6%): Principle colouring pigment, used as therapeutic and anti-cancer property.
- Solvent used to separate curcumin from dried powder: Ethyl alcohol.
- Curcumin is safe even at high doses (12 g/ day) in humans.
- Institute contested the US patent on use of turmeric in wound healing: CSIR.
- CFTRI, Mysuru has developed steam distillation procedure to separate oleoresins (5-7%) & volatile oil (18-20%) from powder.
- Rhizomes contain 2.5-7.2% essential oil and leaves contain 1-1.5% oil.
- Major aroma principle in oil: Ar-tur-merone.
- Oleoresin: Orange red colour & yields 7.9 to 10.4%.
- Volatile oil has yellowish orange colour & highly scented.
- Oleoresin is obtained by solvent extraction and is highly concentrated (25-55% curcumin).
- Fragrant oil (1-1.5%) is extracted from leaves at 6-7 months old.
- For medicinal purpose, pills of curcumin are available in market.
- Turmeric is anti-oxidant due to phenolic compound curcumin.
- Alleppey turmeric: Famous for its colour in trade.
- Alleppey finger turmeric and Madras turmeric: High curcumin (5.44%) content.
- Curcumin content in cv. Salem: 4.5%.
- Shade crops: Castor, Agathi (*Sesbania grandiflora*).
- Seed rate: 1.5 to 2.5 q/ acre and 20,000 plants/ acre.
- Propagation method: Whole or split mother rhizomes.
- Each planting unit consist bits of 20-25 g each.
- Planting methods:
  - Raised beds- 30 cm x 15 or 20 cm (in beds).
  - Ridges and furrow- 40-60 cm x 25 cm.
  - Flat bed system- 50 cm x 15 cm.
- Crop is mulched immediately after planting.
- Earthing up: 1st on 50-60 days after planting and next after 40 days.
- Crop cannot withstand prolonged water logging and heavy shade.

- Favorable temperature for rhizome germination: 35-40^{0}C.
- Planting in May and harvesting in November, yield 30% more curcumin than harvesting at full maturity.
- Days require from planting to germination: 3-4 weeks.
- Crop requires 45 days for attaining two leaf stage.
- Yield: 25-30 t/ha.
- Number of irrigations: 13-15.
- Grown as intercrop in coconut garden or as mixed crop with vegetables.
- Maize is not recommended as intercrop because it affects yield up to 15-20%.
- Value added products: Ground turmeric, turmeric oil, oleoresin, curcumin.
- Yellow turmeric paper can be used as a test for alkalinity which turns it brown.
- Polyploidy breeding may be useful.
- Protray method for raising seedlings for transplanting.
- *Peva*: Underground special storage structure for turmeric constructed in Maharashtra.
- Cured turmeric is sorted as Fingers, Round & Splits.
- Processing 3 types: Curing!Polishing!Colouring.
- Mother and finger rhizomes are cured (boiled & dried) separately.
- It takes 40-60 minutes to complete the cooking process to reach soft stage.
- Slight alkaline condition (100 g of $NaHCO_3$ in 100 liters of water) is maintained during cooking.
- Drying process takes about 10-15 days.
- Dried turmeric is subjected to polishing in power operated drums.
- Drying recovery: 15-30% depending on variety.
- Yield of polished turmeric from raw material varies from 15-25%.
- Processing techniques for raw turmeric have been developed in Taiwan and Denmark.

Classification based on maturity group:

1. Short duration: Thick, long rhizome, low curcumin and early maturity (180-200 days) e.g. Dindigram, Udayagiri, Kasturi, Amalapuram.
2. Medium duration: Mature in 230-240 days e.g. Rajapuri.
3. Long duration: Mature in 8-9 months. Possess long, stout, smooth and hard rhizome e.g. Duggirala, Tekurpet, Sugandham.

Species:

- Highest diversity is observed in the Indo-Burma regions.
- Genetic differentiation is due to mutation followed by selection.
- *C. longa*: Taxonomically no distinct varieties are established.
- *C. domestica*: Arise by process of triploidy from *C. aromatica* or a form similar to it with 42 chromosomes.

Species	Features
Curcuma longa (syn. *C. domestica, C. rotunda*)	Cultivated (2n=32, 62, 64); highest area under cultivation; mature in 9 months
C. aromatica (Cochin/Kasturi turmeric)	Native of India; used in cosmetics as dye but not as a spice; grown in Andhra Pradesh & Tamil Nadu; mature in 7 months; rich in starch
C. amada (Mango turmeric)	Rhizome has mango flavour & taste; possess aphrodisiac properties; used as spice, medicine, salad &pickles in India; rich in starch
C. caesia (Black turmeric)	Used in cosmetics & local medicine; rhizome contain camphor
C. angustifolia (East Indian arrow root)	High starch content (35-40%) in rhizome; used as cattle feed
C. zedoaria (*C. xanthorrhiza*)	Largest species; rich in starch (35-40%); used in perfume industry, arrow root industry, medicine & starch extraction
Berberis aristata (Tree turmeric)	Possess thorns
C. aeruginosa	Cultivated in Malaysia as medicinally
C. mangga	Wild; used a seasoning for food
C. purpurascens	Cultivated in Java; used as seasoning for food
C. caulina, C. montana	Rich in starch (35-40%)

Varieties:

- More than 53 varieties are cultivated in India.
- Progressive farmer Mr. P. Chandrashekar Azad has been nominated by A.P. govt.-brand Ambassador of 'Pratibha' variety.
- Armoor: Long duration (9 months) and resistant to leaf blotch.
- Nano-curcumin has 2.5 fold increased solubility in both water as well as in virgin coconut oil.
- Resistant to rhizome rot: Shillong, PCT-13 and PCT-14.
- Resistant to leaf blotch: Alleppey, Amalapuram.

Name	Breeding method	Specific features
TNAU, Coimbatore		
CO.1 (1983)	X-ray mutant of 'Erode Local'	Bold & bright orange yellow rhizome; crop duration 285 days; fresh rhizome yield 30.5 t/ha; dry recovery 19.5%; curcumin 3.2%; oleoresin 6.7%; essential oil 3.7%; suitable for drought prone, hilly areas, saline areas
BSR-1 (1986)	X-ray mutant of 'Erode Local'	Yellow rhizome; crop duration 285 days; fresh rhizome yield 30.7 t/ha; curcumin 4.2%; oleoresin 4%; essential oil 3.7%; dry recovery 20%; suitable for drought prone areas
BSR-2 (1994)	Induced mutant of 'Erode Local'	crop duration 285 days; fresh rhizome yield 30.7 t/ha; curcumin 4.2%; oleoresin 4%; essential oil 3.7%; dry recovery 20%; short duration; resistant to scale insects
IHBT, Palampur		
Him Haldi	Clonal selection	*C. aromatica*; antidote to snake bite
CSK HPKV, Palampur		
Palam Pitamber	Selection	Curcumin (5%); essential oil (7%); yield 33 t/ha
Palam Lalima	Selection	Curcumin (7%); yield 35.7 t/ha
CIMAP, Lucknow		
CIM- Pitamber	Selection	Mature in 190 days, 12.5 % curcumin, tolerant to common leaf botch; 50% more yield (60-65 t/ha)
PAU, Ludhiana		
Punjab Haldi-1	Selection	Mature in 215 days; curcumin (3.33%); oleoresin (6.76 %); yield 27.2 t/ha
Punjab Haldi-2	Selection	Mature in 238 days; curcumin 2.91%; oleoresin (7.61%); yield 30 t/ha
MPKV, Rahuri (ARS, Kasbe Digraj)		
Krishna (1983)	Clonal selection from Tekur	Plumpy rhizome; curcumin 2.8%; oleoresin 3.8%; essential oil 2%; crop duration 240 days; fresh rhizome yield 9.2 t/ha; dry recovery 16.4%;
Phule Swarupa	Clonal selection	High curcumin (5.19%); tolerant to pests & diseases, high seed multiplication ratio (1:5); curing recovery 22%
Dr PDKV, Akola		
PDKV Waigao	Local	GI tag; mature in 220 days; 6.7% curcumin; more fragrant; yield 26 t/ha; resistant to leaf spot
GAU, Jagudan (Spice Research Station, Jagudan)		
Sugandham (1984)	Germplasm selection	Thick round rhizome with short internodes; crop duration 210 days; curcumin 3.1%; oleoresin 11%; essential oil 2.7%; fresh rhizome yield 15-20 t/ha; dry recovery 23%
NAU, Navsari		
Gujarat Navsari Turmeric-1	Clonal selection	Mature in 252-260 days; compact rhizomes; curcumin (2.84 %); oleoresin (8.68 %); fibreless rhizome & non-lodging; yield 33.6 t/ha; resistant to rhizome rot; scented
High altitude research station, (OUAT, Pottangi)		
Roma (1988)	Clonal selection	Crop duration 250 days; fresh ginger yield 20.7 t/ha; dry recovery 31%; curcumin 9.3%; oleoresin 13.2%; essential oil 4.2% suitable for hilly areas, rainfed & irrigated condition
Suroma (1989)	X-ray mutant of	Crop duration 253 days; fresh ginger yield 20 t/ha; dry

	cv. 'Sunder'	recovery 26%; curcumin 9.3%; oleoresin 13.1%; essential oil 4.4%; suitable to drought areas
Ranga (1992)	Clonal selection from 'Rajapuri Local'	Spindle shaped rhizome; crop duration of 250 days; fresh ginger yield 29 t/ha; dry recovery 24.8%; curcumin 6.3%; oleoresin 13.5%; essential oil 4.4%; resistant to leaf blotch, scales
Rashmi (1992)	Clonal selection from 'Rajapuri Local'	Spindle shaped rhizome; crop duration 240 days; fresh ginger yield 31.3 t/ha; dry recovery 23%; curcumin 6.4%; oleoresin 13.4%; essential oil 6.4%; suitable for rainfed & irrigated condition
RAU, Dholi		
Rajendra Sonia (1989)	Selection from local	Plumpy rhizome; crop duration of 225 days; fresh ginger yield 4.8 t/ha; dry recovery 18%; curcumin 8.4%; essential oil 5%; grows widely under north Indian conditions
Godavari	Selection from local	Plumpy rhizome; grows widely under north Indian conditions; curcumin 8.34%; essential oil 5.5%
ICAR Research Complex for NEH Region, Meghalaya		
Megha Turmeric-1 (1996)	Selection from 'Lakadong' type	Suitable for NEH region; crop duration of 315 days; fresh ginger yield 20 t/ha; dry recovery 16.37%; curcumin 6.8%;
Lakadong	Selection	Suitable for NEH region; curcumin 6.35%; dry recovery 16.37%
UBKVV, Pundibari		
Uttar Suranjana (2000)	Clonal selection	Suitable for open & shaded condition; suitable for rainfed & high rainfall areas; curcumin 5.7%; essential oil 4.1%; oleoresin 10.9%; tolerant to rhizome rot & leaf blotch; resistant to rhizome scale & shoot borer
Uttar Rupanjana (TCP-64) 2018	Selection	-
Uttar Rangini (TCP-129) 2019	Selection from 'Uttar Rupanjana'	Dry recovery (26.5%); curcumin 5.1%; tolerant to leaf spot and leaf blotch
IISR, Kozhikode		
IISR-Suguna (1991)	Selection from 'PCT-13'	Short duration crop of 190 days; fresh rhizome yield 29.3%; dry recovery 12%; curcumin 7.3% oleoresin 13.5%; essential oil 6%; resistant to rhizome rot
IISR: Suvarna (1991)	Selection from 'PCT-8'	Crop duration 200 days; curcumin 4.3%; oleoresin 13.5%; essential oil 7%; fresh ginger yield 17.4 t/ha; dry recovery 20%; tolerant to rhizome rot, leaf blotch, leaf spot, rhizome scale & shoot borer
IISR: Sudarsana (1991)	Selection from 'PCT-14'	Short duration crop of 190 days; fresh ginger yield 28.8 t/ha; dry recovery 12%; curcumin 5.3%; oleoresin 15%; essential oil 7%; tolerant to rhizome rot & leaf blotch
IISR: Prabha (1996)	OP seedling selection	crop duration of 205 days; fresh ginger yield 37.5 t/ha; dry recovery 19.5%; curcumin 6.5%; oleoresin 15%; essential oil 6.5%
IISR: Prathiba (1996)	OP seedling selection	High quality line; crop duration of 225 days; fresh ginger yield 39.1 t/ha; dry recovery 18.5%; curcumin 6.2%; oleoresin 16.2%; essential oil 6.2%
IISR: Alleppey Supreme (2004)	Clonal selection from Alleppey turmeric	Crop duration of 220 days; fresh ginger yield 5.6 t/ha; dry recovery 18.9%; high colour variety; curcumin 5.55%; oleoresin 16%

IISR: Kedarum (2004)	Clonal selection from 'Thodupuzha collection'	Crop duration of 220 days; fresh ginger yield 5.3 t/ha; dry recovery 19.3%; curcumin 5.5%; oleoresin 13.6%; tolerant to leaf blotch
IISR: Rajapuri	Clonal selection	Yield 17.46 t/ha; resistant to leaf spot
IISR-Pragati	Clonal selection	Short duration (180 days), mod. tolerant to nematode; yield (35 t/ha)
KAU, Thrissur		
Kanthi (1996)	Selection	Erect leaf; crop duration of 250 days; fresh ginger yield 7.9 t/ha; dry recovery 20.2%; curcumin 7.18%; oleoresin 8.25%; essential oil 5.15%
Sobha (1996)	Clonal selection	Close internodes; crop duration of 250 days; fresh ginger yield 5.74 t/ha; dry recovery 19.4%; curcumin 7.39%; oleoresin 9.65%; essential oil 4.24%
Sona (2002)	Clonal selection	Crop duration of 250 days; fresh ginger yield 4 t/ha; dry recovery 18.9%; curcumin 7.12%; oleoresin 10.25%; essential oil 4.4%; tolerant to leaf blotch
Varna (2002)	Clonal selection	Crop duration of 250 days; fresh ginger yield 4 t/ha; dry recovery 18.9%; curcumin 7.87%; oleoresin 10.8%; essential oil 4.56%; tolerant to leaf blotch
NDUA & T, Faizabad		
Narendra Haldi-1	Clonal selection	Source of natural â-turmerone & á-turmerone
NDH-98	Clonal selection	Tolerant to salinity
NDH-8 (syn. Narendra Saryu)	Clonal selection	High curcumin content (5-6%), more number of primaries; suitable for powder industry
CSAUA & T, Kanpur		
Azad Haldi	Selection	Yield 260 q/ha
Other varieties		
Duggirala	Selection	25 t/ha yield; curcumin 4.1%; long duration (9 months) and resistant to leaf blotch
Tekurpettah, Erode Local, Cudlapah, Nizamabad	Selection	Long duration,

Diseases and pest:

- Rhizome rot (*Pythium graminicolum*):
- Leaf blotch (*Taphrina maculans*): Oily looking spots on leaves cause blighting & loss of photosynthetic area.
- Leaf spot (*Colletotrichum capsici*): Most serious diseases. Spray mancozeb @ 0.1% during June to September.
- Rhizome fly (*Mimegralla coeruleifrons*): Serious pest.
- Rhizome scale (*Aspidiella hartii*): Soak seed rhizome in Quinolphos @ 0.1% prior to storage and sowing.
- Shoot borer (*Conogethes punctiferalis*): Spray Malathion @ 0.1% or Monocrotophos @ 0.05%.

- Root knot nematode (*Meloidgyne* spp.) and burrowing nematode (*Radopholus similis*): Severe problem leading to reduced vigour & tillering. Cvs. Kodur and Chayapasupu are resistant.

11.4 Ginger

- Monocot, herbaceous perennial with unbranched aerial stems, distichous leaves, open sheaths and hypogeal germination.
- Largest producers: Nigeria and China followed by India.
- Major exporter in world: China (70%) followed by Thailand, Peru.
- Largest importers: USA followed by Japan, Netherlands, United Arab Nations, Pakistan, Malaysia.
- Bangladesh: Major importer of Indian ginger.
- Jamaican ginger: Best in world followed by Cochin ginger (i.e. Indian ginger).
- Major states growing ginger: Kerala, Meghalaya, Arunachal Pradesh, Odisha.
- Kerala leading producer (60% area).
- More demand in world market is for fresh green ginger followed by dry ginger & juice.
- India: Largest producer of dry ginger (70%) in the world and 50% in world export.
- Only about 3.5% of our produce is exported in fresh/ dry form, oil and oleoresin form.
- Crop exhibits annual growth rate of 4.6% in area, 7.4% in production and 2.7% in productivity.
- Indian dry ginger is known in world market as Cochin ginger (NUGC) and Calicut ginger (NUGK).
- Optimum elevation for successful cultivation: 300-900m.
- Nutrient exhaustive crop.
- Nutrition score: 49.
- Calorific value: 80 Kcal/ 100g.
- Inflorescence is spike and fruit is capsule.
- Pungency: Gingerol (22%).
- Estimation of pungency: By gravimetric method devised by Garnett and Grier.
- Fiber content: 5.19%.
- Ginger oleoresin is commercially known as 'Gingerin'.
- Oleoresin content: 3.5-9.5%.
- Starch content: 40.4 to 59%.
- Presence of volatile oil: 1.5 to 2.7%. The oil possesses only aroma and not flavour of spice.

- Amount of essential oil in oleoresin in different growing areas varies from 7 to 28%.
- Essential oil in trade is known as 'oil of ginger' have greenish to yellow in colour, is extracted from unscraped dried ginger or from ginger scrapings by steam distillation.
- Oil cells are present just below the outer skin.
- Aroma of oil: Zingiberene.
- Volatile oil is higher during 150-180 days after planting than at final harvest stage.
- Solvents used for extraction of oleoresin: Alcochol, acetone, ethylene dichloride.
- Propagation method: Portion of rhizome called 'seed rhizome'.
- Seed rhizome or sets or rhizome bits of 15-20g and 2.5-5.0 cm length each having one or two good buds.
- Tissue culture: Direct regeneration from pseudostem.
- Micro-tuber: Disease free planting material.
- Water requirement: 1320-1520 mm.
- Critical stages of irrigation: Germination stage, rhizome initiation and rhizome development.
- Mulching is done at 40 and 90 days after planting.
- Spiny stigmatic surface is cause for no seed set.
- Lack of viable seed is major barrier in breeding.
- Planting distance: 30 cm x 30 cm.
- Seed rate: 1.5-1.8 T/ha (Kerala); 2.0-2.5 T/ha (higher altitude).
- Yield: 15-30 T/ha (fresh).
- Harvesting period: 6-8 months, when leaves turn yellow and start drying.
- For green (fresh) ginger, harvested after 6 months after planting.
- For dry ginger, harvested after 7-8 months after planting.
- Delayed harvesting decreases volatile oil, develop fibres and pungency.
- Ginger should be dried to safe moisture level of 8-10%, above which it causes development of aflatoxins.
- For dry ginger, produce is soaked in water for 6-7 hours. and outer skin is removed with bamboo splinters having pointed ends.
- Recovery of dry ginger: 19-25% of green ginger.
- Two types of dried gingers produced in India are: Bleached and unbleached.
- Bleached/ limed ginger: Peeled rhizomes are soaked in 1.5-2% slaked lime for 6 h and sun dried for 10 days.
- Dehydrated ginger: Green ginger is placed in wire-gauge cage & dipped in boiling solution of 20, 25 or 50% NaOH for 5, 1 or 0.5 minutes. Cage is removed and rhizomes are placed in 4% citric acid for 2 h, then washed and dried.

- Loss in weight due to lye-peeling is 12.5%.
- Finger ginger (relatively low fibre) harvested at 170-180 days after planting can be used for preparing salted ginger.
- Fibre in ginger and curcumin in turmeric varies with location, season and variety.
- Value added products: Ginger powder, salted ginger, crude fibre, oleoresin, ginger oil, ginger beer, ginger *murabba*, ginger candy, ginger pickle, etc.
- Technology for preparing salted ginger from immature fresh ginger has been developed at CFTRI.
- Bio-priming for protecting seed rhizomes has been patented.
- For good germination, seed rhizomes are to be stored properly in pits under shade.
- Farmers use leaves of *Glycosmis pentaphylla* to preserve seed rhizome.

Species:

- Cultivated ginger (*Z. officinale*):
- Black/ Midnight ginger (*Z. malaysianum*): Ornamental purpose. Bracts sulphur yellow and turn to pink as ages.
- *Z. zerumbet* and *Z. caumunnar* (syn. *Z. purpureum*): Used in indigenous medicine.
- Ornamental ginger (*Z. spectabile*): Look like honeycomb.
- Gold brush ginger (*Burbidgea schizocheila*):
- Malay rose (*Etlingera vensuta*): World's rare and most beautiful ginger.

Varieties:

- Varieties are named after the localities where they are grown.
- Nadia and Eyezol: Largely grown in Assam have difference in rhizome structure. These cultivars contain 5-7% alcohol and 5.4% crude fibre.
- Cv. Corbi Anglong have medicinal value.
- Ornamental ginger: Singapore Gold, Pink Maraca, Dancing Jewels, Dancing Ladies, White Dragon, Red Leaf, Malay Rose.
- Sanshu and Buderim Gold: Tetraploid grown in Japan.

Name	Breeding method	Special features
Rio-de-Janeiro	Introduction	Most popular & highest oleoresin
High altitude research station, OUAT, Pottangi, Bhubaneswar		
Suprabha (PGS-35), 1988	Clonal selection from 'Kunduli Local'	Plumpy rhizome; high field resistance to soft rot; high dry ginger recovery (20.5%); fresh ginger yield 16.6 t/ha; crude fibre 4.4%; oleoresin 8.9%; essential oil 1.9%
Suruchi (PGS-19), 1990	Clonal selection from 'Kunduli Local'	Profuse tillering; high field resistance to soft rot; high dry ginger recovery (23.5%); fresh ginger yield 11.6 t/ha; crude fibre 3.8%; oleoresin 10%; essential oil 2%

Surabhi (1991)	Induced mutant of 'Rudrapur Local'	Plumpy rhizome; suitable for dry & irrigated areas; 10.2% oleoresin; 2.1% essential oil; duration 225 days
Suravi (1991)	Gamma ray (1 kR) mutant of 'Rudrapur Local'	Fresh ginger yield 17.5 t/ha; dry recovery 23%; crude fibre 4%; oleoresin 10.2%; essential oil 2.1%; suitable for rainfed & irrigated condition
Kuruppampadi	Local selection	-
Wynad	Local selection	Raw ginger varieties
Ernad	Local selection	-
DrYSPUH & F		
Himgiri	Clonal selection from 'Himachal collection'	Best for green ginger & tolerant to rhizome rot; crop duration 230 days; oleoresin 4.29%; fresh ginger yield 13.13 t/ha; dry recovery 20.2%; crude fibre 6.05%; essential oil 1.63%
Solan Giriganga (2018)	Clonal selection	Plumpy & bold rhizomes suitable for western Himalayas; dry matter recovery 21%; essential oil 1.45%, oleoresin 4.69%, crude fibre 4.47%; < 10%incidence of rhizome rot
IISR, Kozhikode		
IISR: Mahima (2002)	Germplasm selection	Fresh ginger yield 23.2 t/ha; dry recovery 21.1%; high essential oil (1.72%); 4.48% oleoresin; crude fibre 3.26%; root knot nematode resistant
IISR: Rejatha (2002)	Germplasm selection	Fresh ginger yield 22.4 t/ha; dry recovery 20.8%; high essential oil (2.36%) ; 6.34% oleoresin; crude fibre 4%; root knot nematode resistant
IISR: Varada (1996)	Germplasm selection	20.7% dry recovery; fresh ginger yield 22.6 t/ha; crude fibre 3.29%; oleoresin 6.73%; essential oil 1.75%; tolerant to rhizome rot
GCP-49	Selection	Bold rhizomes with dry recovery of 21.7%
KAU, Kerala		
Athira (2010)	Clonal selection from somaclones of cv. Maran	Yield 25-30 t/ha; Zingiberene (35.76%); essential oil (3.1%); crude fibre (3.4%); tolerant to soft rot & bacterial wilt
Karthika (2010)	Selection	Tolerant to soft rot & bacterial wilt
Aswathy (2013)	Selection	Recommended for green ginger; tolerant to Phyllosticta leaf spot disease
Chandra (2018)	Selection	Volatile oil 1.6%; oleoresin 5.17%; good for fresh and dry ginger; suitable for moist humus rich soils of tropics. Fresh yield 23.51 t/ha; dry yield 5.23 t/ha
Chitra (2018)	Selection	Volatile oil 1.6%; oleoresin 4.71%; ideal for dry ginger; fresh yield 22.06 t/ha; dry yield 5.16 t/ha
Karakkal	Local selection	Highest essential oil
MPKV, Rahuri		
Mahim	Selection	Very bold rhizomes; resistant to root knot nematode
Other varieties		
Manantody, Himachal, Maran	Local selections	Dry ginger varieties
Jamaica, Bangkok, China	Introduction	Less fibre varieties

Diseases and pests:

- Soft rot/ Rhizome rot (*Pythium aphanidermatum*): Most serious, seed borne. Spreads very fast during rainy season. Treat rhizomes with *Trichoderma viride* @ 8 g/ litre.
- Bacterial wilt (*Ralstonia solanacearum*): Do rhizome solarization.
- Leaf spot (*Phyllosticta zingiberi*) and leaf blight: Drastic reduction in yield. Spray 1% Bordeaux mixture.
- Shoot borer (*Conogethes punctiferalis*): Most serious pest. Spray Dipel @ 0.3% at 21 days interval during July-October.
- Rhizome scale (*Aspidiella hartii*). Serious pest infests in storage. Seed dipping in Fenthion (0.05%) before storage + foliar spray of Deltamethrin 1.5 ml/ litre.
- Rhizome fly: Spray systemic insecticide followed by soil application of Furadan 10 kg/ha.
- Root knot nematode (*Meloidogyne* spp.); Burrowing nematode (*Radopholus similis*): Treat rhizomes with hot water (50^{0}C) for 10 min.
- Leaf roller (*Udaspes folus*): Spray Carbaryl @ 0.1%.

12. Other minor spice

Common Name	Family	Economic part	Propagation method
Terragon (*Artemisia dracunculus*)	Asteraceae	Young leaves & shoots	Stem cuttings

7

MEDICINAL AND AROMATIC PLANTS

1. GENERAL INFORMATION:

- Medicinal plants are non-food non-plantation crops.
- These are rich in secondary metabolites viz. alkaloids, glycosides, coumarins, flavonoides and steroids, etc.
- Union government of India has started a project on 'Traditional Knowledge Digital Library' under which it is documenting all Ayurvedic formulations in a digital form to avert patent threats from companies in the developed world.
- Total area under medicinal and aromatic crops (2018-19): 6.55 lakh ha.
- Total production (2018-19): 8.18 lakh tons.
- The international market of medicinal plants is growing @ 7% per annum.
- India's herbal export trade is 150 million annually.
- India is 2nd largest exporter of raw medicinal plant material next to China.
- India exported raw herbs worth USD 330.18 million during 2017-18 with growth rate of 14.22%.
- India's share in world herbal medicinal trade: 0.5% as against China (55%).
- India exports crude drugs to 6 developed countries viz., USA, Germany, France, Switzerland, UK and Japan.
- 400% cropping intensity is possible because of short/ medium duration.
- More than 80% of these plants are collected from 17 million ha of Indian forest land.
- About 8,000 herbal remedies have been codified in AYUSH systems in India.
- Ayurveda and Unani Medicine are most developed and widely practiced in India.
- Earliest treatises on Indian medicine the *Charak Samhita* 1000 BC records the use of >340 drugs of vegetable origin.
- *Rig veda* records the use of plants in medicine.
- More details are available in *Atharvaveda*.
- Number of medicinal herbs account to 1500.
- This knowledge came through oral folklore.
- These studies are now classified in 'Ethnobotany'.
- Major constraint of medicinal plants: Lack of genuine planting material.

- Maximum number of medicinal plants belongs to Asteraceae family.
- Maximum demand in world market: 1. Senna leaves 2. Isabgol seeds 3. *Cassia tora* seeds.
- India is largest producer of 1. Kewada oil 2. Senna 3. Davana oil 4. Isabgol.
- India is 2nd largest producer of 1. Opium latex 2. Jasmine concrete 3. Tuberose concrete
- India is 3rd largest exporter of periwinkle.
- Mint and products export: 22.7 t; oils and oleoresins export 14 t.
- China is largest producer of 1. Geranium oil 2. Citronella oil.
- *Dioscorea* producing countries: Mexico, Guatamala, Costa Rica.
- Essential oils: Odoriferous steam volatile constituents evaporating at ambient temperature.
- Hippocrates: Father of modern medicine.
- Theophrastus: Father of pharmacognosy.
- The world production of essential oil is estimated at about 1,00,000-1,10,000 tones and India is 3rd with share of 16-17%.
- USA: Largest producer and consumer of essential oil.
- Good Agricultural Practices (GAPs) were developed for safed musli, lemon grass, palmarosa grass, senna, etc.
- RRL- Jammu: Oldest research station credited with introduction of Japanese mint and hops.
- A 'Programme on G-15 gene' of National Immunity Science Institute is being carried out for medicinal and aromatic plants.
- CIM-Jeevan is a variety of Bhumyamlaki.
- Asalio or Garden cress: *Lepidium sativum*.
- Annato (*Bixa orellana*): Natural carotenoid present in outer seed coat.
- Annato dye is non toxic and used for colouring edible materials like butter, ghee, chocolate & cosmetics.
- Annato seed meal is used in poultry feed, floor polishes, shoe polishes, hair oils.
- Glory lily (*Gloriosa superba*): Yield colchicine ($C_{22}H_{25}O_6N$) alkaloid.
- Government of Himachal Pradesh has launched '*Vanaspati Van Yojana*' in Chamba and Kullu districts.
- CIMAP works on industrial utilization of medicinal and aromatic plants.
- Black wattle (*Acacia meaensii*) is harvested after 10 years of growth.
- 'Trikatu' an Ayurvedic medicine contains *Piper nigrum*, *P. longum* and ginger.
- Prishnparni (*Uraria picta*) a critically endangered dashmool drug.
- ORAC (oxygen Radical Absorbance capacity) values of tulsi (67553), thyme (27426).

2. CLASSIFICATION OF MEDICINAL AND AROMATIC PLANTS

Family	Common name	Botanical name	Origin	2n=
Medicinal plants				
Acanthaceae	Adathoda	*Adathoda vasica*	India	34
	Kalmegh	*Andrographis paniculata*	Taiwan	50
Apiaceae	Dill	*Anethum graveolens*	Europe	20
	Indian pennywort	*Centella asiatica*	India	18,36, 54
Apocynaceae	Sarpagandha	*Rauvolfia serpentina*	India	22
Araceae	Sweet flag	*Achorus calamus*	Europe	36, 54,72
Asclepidaceae	Madhunashini	*Gymnema sylvestre*	India	22
Asteraceae	Bhrangraj	*Eclipta alba*	India	22
	Stevia	*Stevia rebaudiana*	Paraguay	22
	Sweet worm wood	*Artemisia annua*	China	18
	Chrysanthemum	*Chrysanthemum cinerarifolium*	China	54
Burseraceae	Guggul	*Commiphora wightii*	Africa	26
Combretaceae	Behada	*Terminalia bellirica*	India	48
Convolvulaceae	Shankhpushpi	*Convolvulus microphyllus*	India	16, 24
Costaceae	Costus	*Costus igneus, C. pictus*	S. America	18
Dioscoreaceae	Medicinal yam	*Dioscorea floribunda*	Mexico	36, 72
Euphorbiaceae	Aonla	*Phyllanthus niruri*	India	36
Fabaceae	Babchi	*Psoralea corylifolia*	India	20, 22
	Cow hedge/ Velvet bean	*Mucuna pruriens*	Tropical Asia	22
	Indian liquorice	*Glycyrhiza glabra*	India	14
Ginkgoaceae	Siberian ginseng	*Ginkgo biloba*	Siberia	24
Lamiaceae	Medicinal coleus/ Pasan bhendi	*Coleus forskohlii*	India	16
Leguminosae	Senna	*Cassia angustifolia*	Europe	22, 24, 26,28
Liliaceae	Safed musli	*Chlorophytum borivilianum*	Africa	42
	Aloe	*Aloe vera*	India	14
	Shatavari	*Asparagus racemosus*	India	22,30,40
Menispermaceae	Giloe/ Gulvel	*Tinospora cordifolia*	India	22
Papaveraceae	Opium poppy	*Papaver somniferum*	Europe	22
Plantaginaceae	Isabgol	*Plantago ovata*	Persia	8
	Brahmi	*Bacopa monnieri*	India	64
Piperaceae	Long pepper/ Pipali	*Piper longum*	India	24, 96(4x)
Plumbaginaceae	Chitrak	*Plumbago zeylanica*	India	16
Rubiaceae	Cinchona	*Cinchona officinalis*	South America	34
	Ipecac	*Cephaelis ipecacuanha*	Brazil	22
Scrophulariaceae	Foxglove	*Digitalis purpurea, D. lanata*	Europe	56
Solanaceae	Ashwagandha	*Withania somnifera*	Africa	48
	Belladonna	*Atropa belladonna*	Europe	72
	Datura	*Datura innoxia, D. metel*	Mexico	24, 48(4x)
	Henbane	*Hyoscyamus niger* (Indian)	Europe	34
	Medicinal solanum	*Solanum khasianum*	New Zealand	72
Zingiberaceae	Insulin plant	*Costus speciosus*	South East Asia	18

Aromatic plants				
Asteraceae	Davana	*Artimisia pallens*	India	
	Chamomile	*Matricaria chamomilla*	Europe	18
Apiaceae	Celery	*Apium graveolens*	Mediterranean region	22
Cannabinaceae	Hops	*Humulus lupulus*	East Europe	20
Euphorbiaceae	Jamalgota	*Croton tiglium*	South-East Asia	20
Lamiaceae	Patchouli	*Pogostemon patchouli*, (syn. *P. cablin*)	South-East Asia, China	30
	Indian basil	*Ocimum* spp.	Africa	32, 48(3x)
	Rosemary	*Rosemarinus officinalis*	Europe	20
	Melissa	*Melissa officinalis*	Europe	64
	Thyme	*Thymus vulgaris*	South Europe	30
	Lavender	*Lavandula officinalis*	Mediterranean region	42
	Mint	*Mentha* spp.	Mediterranean region	36, 72, 96
Malvaceae	Ambrette	*Abelmoschus moschatus*	India	72
Myrtaceae	Eucalyptus	*Eucalyptus citriodora*	Australia	22, 24
Pandanaceae	Screw pine	*Pandanus fascicularis*	Tropical Africa	60
Poaceae	Lemon grass	*Cymbopogon flexuosus*	India	20
	Java citronelia	*Cymbopogon winterianus* (syn. *C. nardus*)	Sri Lanka	20, 40
	Palmarosa grass	*Cymbopogon martinii* var. Motia	Sri Lanka	20, 60
Rosaceae	Rose	*Rosa spp.*	India	14(2x), 21(3x), 28(4x)
Santalaceae	Sandalwood	*Santalum album*	India & Australia	20
Viteveraceae	Vetiver	*Vetivaria zizanioides*; (syn. *Chrysopogon zizanioides*)	India	20, 40

3. MEDICINAL PLANTS

3.1. ACANTHACEAE

3.1.1 Adathoda

- Commonly known as 'Adulsa or Malabar nut or Basaka'.
- Economic parts: Leaves and roots.
- Chemical content/ Alkaloid: Vasicine.
- Uses: Asthma, Chronic bronchitis, Cough.
- Crop duration: 5-6 years.

3.1.2 Kalmegh

- Eulogized as 'King of bitters or Rice bitters'.

- Economic parts: Whole herb excluding root.
- Chemical content/ Alkaloid: Andrographolide (leaves), Andrographidin A, B, C, D, and E (roots).
- Uses: Treat snake bite & acute jaundice; curing fever, worms, dysentery, curing general weakness.
- **Varieties**: Megha, AK-1, KI-5.

3.2. APIACEAE

3.2.1 Dill

- Eulogized as 'Sowa'.
- Biennial and long day plant.
- Oil content in seed: 2.5-3.0%.
- Seed rate: 5-10 kg/ha.
- Seed yield: 1-1.4 t/ha.
- Indian dill oil is not preferred in pharmacy due to presence of Dillapiole.
- Economic parts: Seeds and leaves.
- Stems and blossom heads used for making pickles and seasoning soups.
- Chemical content/ Alkaloid: Carvone.
- Uses: Improve digestion, preparing of gripe water.
- **Varieties**: Soona, ALFT-2.

3.2.2. Indian pennywort

- Eulogized as 'Mandukaparni'.
- Economic part: Leaf.
- Uses: Blood purifier, memory enhancer, treating leprosy; tuberculosis.
- **Varieties**: Majjaposhak & Kayakirti (CIMAP), RK-1, Vallabh Medha, Arka Prabhavi, Arka Divya.

3.3. APOCYNACEAE

3.3.1 Sarpagandha

- Thailand: Largest exporter of sarpagandha leaves.
- Propagation method: Seeds and cuttings.
- Harvesting: 2-3 years after planting.
- Economic part: Root.
- Alkaloids: Serpentine, Reserpine, Saponins.
- Uses: Treatment for hypertension as sedative; tranquillizer; asthma; gastric ulcers.
- **Variety**: RI-1

3.4. ARACEAE

3.4.1 Sweet flag

- Eulogized as '*Vekhand*'.
- Aquatic perennial herb.
- Economic part: Rhizome.
- Chemical content/ Alkaloid: Acorin.
- Uses: Improving memory power, treating insomnia, dysentery, stomachache, kidney disease; flavouring drinks, perfumery & insecticides; powdered roots used as vermifuge; rhizome has anti-bacterial activity; rhizome oil has sedative & analgesic property.
- **Variety**: CIM- Balya.

3.5. ASCLEPIDACEAE

3.5.1 Madhunashini

- Eulogized as 'Australian cow plant'.
- Economic part: Leaf.
- Chemical content/ alkaloid: Gymnemic acid.
- Use: Anti-diabetic.

3.6. ASTERACEAE

3.6.1 Bhrangraj

- Economic part: Whole plant.
- Use: Hair cosmetics, night blindness, headache, anti-viral agent against Ranikhet viral disease.

3.6.2 Stevia

- IHBT, Palampur: Developed green technology for production of steviol glycosides from stevia.
- Economic part: Leaf.
- Chemical content/ alkaloid: Stevioside (15-20%).
- Concentration of stevioside increases under long day conditions just before flowering.
- Use: Calorie free bio-sweetner.
- **Variety**: Him-Stevia.

3.6.3 Sweet worm wood

- Eulogized as 'Aromatic herb of 21st century'.
- Economic part: Leaf.

- Chemical content/ alkaloid: Artimisinin (0.05-0.17%).
- Use: Anti-malarial drug.

Varieties:

Name	Breeding method	Features
CIMAP, Lucknow		
CIM-Arogya	-	High artemisinin content
Jeevanraksha	-	
Suraksha	-	
Surekha	-	
Asha	-	

3.6.4 Chrysanthemum

- Highest pyrethrin found in achenes (93%).
- Maturity index: 3-4 rows of disc florets opened.
- **Varieties**: C-793, KKL-1, Hansa, Jhelum, Sel-2.

3.7. BURSERACEAE

3.7.1 Guggul

- Eulogized as 'Indian bdellium tree'.
- Economic part: Oleogum resin having yellow colour.
- Chemical content/ alkaloid: Guggul lipids (phenyl butazone).
- Contain Z- and E-guggul sterones chemical.
- Tapping: Annual pruning is practiced in guggul.
- Uses: Obesity, arthritis, anti-inflammatory, hypoglycemic, reduce cholesterol in blood.
- **Variety**: Marusudha.

3.8. COMBRETACEAE

3.8.1 Behada

- Economic part: Fruit.
- Uses: Stomach disorders; brain tonic; constituent of *triphala churna*; tannin industry, ink & dyeing cloth.

3.9. CONVOLVULACEAE

3.9.1 Shankhapushpi

- Economic part: Leaves.
- Uses: Brain tonic.

3.10. COSTACEAE

3.10.1 Costus

- Eulogized as 'Insulin plant or Spiral flag or Step ladder'.
- Economic part: Leaf.
- Active principle: Diosgenin.
- Use: Anti-diabetic.

3.11. DIOSCOREACEAE

3.11.1 Medicinal yam

- Medicinal spp.: *Dioscorea floribunda* (introduced from Mexico), *D.composita*.
- *D. lanata* and *D. purpurea* contains lanatoside A,B,C which on hydrolysis yield digitoxin, gitoxin and digoxin of which last one is very important.
- Edible spp.: *D. alata* and *D. esculenta*.
- Economic part: Tuber.
- Planting distance: 2 feet x 1 feet (55,000 plants/ ha).
- Nutrition: 300 kg N + 150 kg P + 150 kg K.
- Recommended as 2 year crop.
- Tuber wt. for planting material: 50-70 g but should not less than 40 g.
- To improve diosgenin recovery, freshly harvested & homogenized tubers are incubated at 37^{0}C for 24 hours.
- Diosgenin content in tubers: 2-7%.
- Uses: Production of sex hormones and oral contraceptive pills.
- Propagation method: seed, crown portion of tuber or leaf node cutting.

Varieties: Arka Upkar, FB (C)-1(tuber yield 1 kg/plant/year; 30-35 t/ha; free from diseases).

Disease:

- Tuber rot: Major depressive factor. Dip planting material in 3000 ppm Benlate for 5 min. Dusting of cut ends with 0.3% Benlate in storage.

3.12. EUPHORBIACEAE

- Economic part: Fruits.
- Active principle: Phyllanthin.
- Uses: Hepatitis B and Jaundice.

3.12.1 Jamal gota

- Eulogized as 'Physic nut'.
- Economic part: Fruits.
- Use: Oil used as biodiesel, violent purgative; mouth wash (leaves); oil used for curing skin diseases like eczema, herpes, itch, sores and bleeding wounds, fresh latex applied to piles, scabies, ringworms and decayed teeth.

3.13. FABACEAE

3.13.1 Babchi

- Type of fruit- Single seeded pod.
- Uses: Leucoderma, leprosy & psoriasis; anthelmintic & antibacterial.

3.13.2 Cow hedge

- Eulogized as 'Velvet bean'.
- Economic part: Seed.
- Chemical content: Mucunine & active principle: L-DOPA.
- Uses : Parkinson disease, sexual disorders, elephantiasis, nerve tonic.

Varieties: CIM- Azar

Name	Breeding method	Features
IIHR, Bengaluru		
Arka Shubra	Pedigree selection	White seeds; seed yield (4.5-5.5 t/ha with support & 2.25-2.75 t/ha under surface cultivation); high L-dopa content & yield (5.43%; 269.67 kg/ha) with non-irritant trichomes on pods; matures in 180-190 days
Arka Charaka	Pedigree selection	Black shiny seeds; seed yield (4.0-4.25 t/ha with support & 2.0-2.25 t/ha under surface cultivation); high L-dopa content & yield (4.80%; 200 kg/ha); non-irritant trichomes on pods; matures in 155-165 days
Arka Shukla	Pure line selection	White medium bold seeds; seed yield (3.0-3.5 t/ha under support & 2.0 t/ha under surface cultivation); L-dopa content 3.86%; matures in 155-165 days
Arka Daksha	Pure line selection	Bold black seeds with brown mottling; seed yield (3.5 to 4 t/ha with support & 1.8-2.2 t/ha without support); L-dopa content (3.72%); yield 150.39 kg/ha; matures in 150-160 days
Arka Dhanvantari	Selection	Seed yield of 4.2 t/ha; L-DOPA yield of 190 kg/ha; crop duration (185-190 days); purple flowers on long rachis; shiny black seed coat/ medium sized seeds
Arka Aswini	Selection	Seed yield of 2.31 t/ha; L-DOPA content 3.5-4.0%; L-DOPA yield 80.62 kg/ha; non-irritant trichomes; short duration (120-130 days); purple flowers on short rachis; fruits black

3.13.3 Indian liquorice

- Eulogized as '*Mulethi* or *Jeshthamadh*'.
- Sweet herb used as medicine for gastric ulcer, confectionary (root extraction).
- Long day plant.
- Propagation method: Semi-hardwood cutting (300 kg/ha).
- Economic part: Whole plant including roots.
- Yellow colour of roots: Isoliqril.
- Active principle: Glycyrrhizin (50 times sweeter than sugar). Highest in older roots.
- Uses: Anti-inflammatory, taste modulator, cure intestinal & peptic ulcers, purgative, aphrodisiac; sour throat, bronchitis, abdominal pains & epilepsy; diuretic and confectionary (root extraction).
- **Variety**: Haryana Mulethi-1

3.14. GINKGOACEAE

3.14.1 Siberian ginseng

- Eulogized as 'Living fossil'.
- Uses: anti-depressant, asthma, bronchitis, memory enhancer.

3.15. LAMIACEAE

3.15.1 Medicinal coleus

- Common name: *Pasan Bhendi* in Sanskrit and *Patharchur* in Hindi.
- Commercially cultivated in Himalayan regions (Kumaon), Gujarat, Rajasthan, Maharashtra, Karnataka and Tamil Nadu.
- Crop prefers sub-tropical to warm temperate climate, 600-1800 m MSL.
- Optimum soil pH for cultivation: 6.4-7.9.
- Herbaceous crop growing up to 50-60 cm.
- Flowers borne on long terminal raceme.
- Economic part: Root.
- Roots are fleshy and succulent, highly aromatic, orange to pink fleshed with yellowish brown tuber skin.
- Uses:Treatment to hypertension, eczema (atopic dermatitis), asthma, psoriasis, cardiovascular disorders, glaucoma; coleus oil has useful application in flavour and fragrance in aromatherapy.
- Propagation methods: Seeds and terminal stem cuttings of 10-12 cm long.
- Planting season: June-July and September-October.
- Planting distance: 60 cm x 45 cm (37,037 plants/ ha).

- Crop duration: 180 days after planting.
- Period required for harvesting: 135-150 days after planting.
- Harvest index: a) 50% leaves dry and shed off a) tubers are uprooted manually, cleaned and cut off into small bits and sun dried for 10 days.
- Yield/plant: 250-300 g (fresh tuber) and 60-90 g (dry tuber).
- Yield/ ha: 15-20 ton (fresh tubers) and 2 t (dry tubers).
- Fresh tubers yield 12% dry matter & 0.45% forskolin.
- Chemical content: Forskolin (syn. Coleonol; a diterpenoid activates cyclic adenosine monophosphate or cyclic AMP in cells).
- Forskolin content: 0.40%.
- Forskolin enhances fat loss without loss of muscle mass.
- Planting of marigold as intercrop is recommended.
- Extreme drought and waterlogged conditions affect tuberization.
- Drip-fertigation gives higher economic returns.

Varieties:

- Two types of varieties:
  1. Flowering type available in nature have less forskolin content.
  2. Non-flowering types are cultivated due to high forskolin.
- K-8, Hy 08-53, Garmai, Clone CF-36.

Disease and pest:

- Bacterial wilt: Major disease.
- Root knot nematode: Major pest.
- Leaf eating caterpillar:

3.16. LEGUMINOSAE

3.16.1 Senna

- Eulogized as 'Sonamukhi'.
- Oldest medicinal plant.
- Leaves are used in herbal tea in Western Europe. Powder is mixed in bread dough to make product more digestible.
- Uses: Laxative.
- Day neutral plant.
- Crop thrives at soil pH 7-8.5.
- Number of seeds/ pod: 5-8.
- Predominantly self pollinated but outcrossing very high (20%) through beetles.

- Indian senna (*Cassia angustifolia*):
- Alexandrian senna(*C. acutifolia*):
- Though legume crop lacks nodule formation.
- Foliage is picked periodically 3 times in growing period of 130 days.
- Sennoside A, B, C, D content: 1.5-3.0% (Indian), 4-4.5% (Alexandrian).
- Sennoside content is maximum at flowering stage and minimum at pod maturity stage.
- Foliage and dry pods possess 2.5 and 3% total sennoside, respectively.
- Seed rate: 5 kg/ha.
- 3 pickings of leaves and pods at 50, 90 and 130 days after sowing.
- Mature leaves and 15-25 days old pods are harvested.
- Yield: 1.2-1.5 T/ha (leaves) and 3-4 q/ha (pods).
- HPLC technique is used for extraction of alkaloids.

Varieties:

Name	Breeding method	Features
AAU, Anand		
ALFT-2	Selection	Late flowering; 75% high dry matter
Anand Late Selection (1989)	Selection	-
CIMAP, Lucknow		
Sona	Selection	Yield (11 q/ha dry leaf & 4 q/ha pods); 3.5% sennoside; 100-115 days to flower
TNAU, Coimbatore		
KKM Sel.-1 (2001)	Selection	Yield (712 kg/ha dry leaves & 266 kg/ha pods); crop duration 135-140 days; 2.54% sennoside; good export potential
Tirunelveli Local	Selection	Semi-spreading; suitable for rainfed areas

Grades:

In the market, 3-4 grades based upon size and colour-

1. Grade A / first grade: The extra large and bold leaves and pods having yellowish green colour.
2. Grade B /second grade: Produce having brownish leaves and pods.
3. Grade C /lower grade: Smaller and broken leaves and pods.

3.17. LILIACEAE

3.17.1 Safed musli

- Eulogized as '2nd shilajeet or White gold'.
- Crop maturity: 90 days.

- Root/ tuber contains steroid sapogenine (1-2%), protein (10-12%) and calcium.
- Tubers are fat free.
- Basic ingredient in *chavanprash*.
- Uses: Effective against diabetes, leucorrhoea, renal calculus, blood purification, as vital tonic, cure general diabetes.
- Roots are harvested after 5 months.
- Yield: 1 T/ha.
- **Variety**: Jawahar Safed Musli-405.

3.17.2 Aloe

- Eulogized as 'First aid plant or Two in one plant or Mini pharmacy or Miracle plant or Treasure of medicine'.
- *Aloe* word derived from Arabic word *'Alloeh'* meaning 'bitter substance' while '*vera*' is a Latin word meaning 'true'.
- *Aloe vera* (syn. *A. barbadensis*): Indian aloe.
- *A. ferox*: Renowned for medicinal qualities.
- *A. africana*, *A. spicata*: Yield aloe of lesser importance.
- Dichotomous branching habit is observed in *A. dichotoma*.
- Purify air by removing benzene and formaldehyde.
- Economic part: Leaves.
- Spacing: 60 cm x 30 cm or 60 cm x 45 cm.
- Parenchyma cells contain transparent mucilaginous jelly referred as 'Aloe gel'.
- Aloe gel contains 'biogenic stimulators', 'wound healing hormones'.
- Constituent of yellow sap in aloe: Aloin (syn. Barbaloin).
- Aloin oil (Amine): Mixture of glycosides, used as purgative.
- Barbaloin: Main glycoside present in aloin that varies from 3.8 to 22.1%.
- Uses of gel (aloin): Skin tonic, herbal cosmetics, laxative, peptic ulcers, hepatitis, treatment of burns and pain killer, moisturizing agent, anti-wrinkle, stabilizer in preparation of gold and silver nanoparticles.
- Propagation method: Root sucker/ seeds/ rhizome cuttings.
- Root suckers of 3-4 months old having 4-5 leaves.
- Crop is cut 9-10 months after planting and 3-4 pickings/ year.
- Yield: 15-20 T/ha.

Varieties: IIHR AV-4 (High juice 1.16 ml/leaf), Sheetal, INGR 06023 (aloin 20-23%), INGR 06024 (aloin 20-23%), INGR 13043 (aloin 20-23%).

3.17.3 Asparagus

- Eulogized as '*Shatavari*'.
- Major cultivators: India, Nepal, South Australia & Sri Lanka.
- Economic part: Roots.
- Active principle: Saponin.
- White *shatavari* is found in forest areas of Maharashtra, M.P. and U.P.
- Yellow or Nepali *shatavari* is found in hilly terrains of Himalayas.
- Powdered form has export potential in America, European and Arabian countries.
- *Khadashatavari*: Dried form obtained in pieces from peeled roots.
- Uses: Weight gain, hormonal imbalance, tuberculosis, leprosy, tumor, night blindness.
- **Variety**: Shakti.

3.18. LYTHRACEAE

3.18.1 Henna/ Mehendi

- *Lawsonia inermis*
- Used as medicine as antidote for boils and industrial use for staining skin.

3.19. MENISPERMACEAE

3.19.1 *Giloe/ Gulvel*

- Economic part: Stem and bark.
- Uses: Anti-periodic and aphrodisiac.
- Widely used as remedy to control Corona virus disease.

3.20. PAPAVERACEAE

3.20.1 Opium poppy

- Eulogized as 'Sleep inducing poppy'.
- 1st exotic plant brought under cultivation in later part of 10th century.
- Takes 3 years for maturity.
- Seeds contain 52% edible oil.
- Drugs isolated from milky latex: Morphine, Heroin, Codeine and Papaverine.
- Seed colour of opium poppy is dark, black and white.
- Terminal capsule yields more latex.
- Papaverine: As anti-spasmodic.
- Heroine: Semi-synthetic derivative of morphine.
- Economic part: Latex and fruit (Capsule).

- Seeds are small, kidney shaped and dark blue in colour.
- Seed contain 44-50% fixed oil.
- Principal component of oil: Linoleic and Oleic acid.
- Lancing: Done at 20-25 days after petal fall.
- Seed rate: 7-8 kg/ha (broadcasting) & 4-5 kg/ha (line sowing).
- Alkaloids: Morphine, Codeine, Narcotine.
- Uses: Pain killer, Analgesic, used to cure leukemia.

Varieties:

- BROP-1, Ranghatak, Shyama, Swetha, Talia, Dholia, Vivek, Sanchita & Shubhra (high morphine content in straw).

Name	Breeding method	Features
JNKVV, Mandsaur, Jabalpur		
Jawahar Aphim-16 (1984)	Selection	White flowered; 2-3 capsules/plant; 60-65 kg/ha latex; 12.5% morphine
Jawahar Opium-539 (1997)	Selection	2 capsules/plant; 65 kg/ha latex; 14.85% morphine
Jawahar Opium-540 (1998)	Selection	75 kg/ha latex; 13% morphine
NDUA & T, Faizabad		
Kirtiman (1990)	Selection	Height 1 m; white flowered; 45-50 kg/ha latex yield
RAU, Udaipur		
Chetak (1994)	-	-
NBPGR, New Delhi		
Trishna (1989)	Selection	Pink flowers; 5-7 capsules/plant; 49-53 kg/ha latex; 14.78% morphine
CIMAP, Lucknow		
Sujata	Selection	Opiumless

3.21. PLANTAGINACEAE

3.21.1 Isabgol/ *Psyllium*

- Small, stem-less, soft hairy annual herb and gives large number of tillers from base.
- Rabi crop grown in India particularly in Gujarat and Rajasthan.
- Economic parts: Seed and husk absorb water up to 40-90%.
- Albuminous boat shaped seed.
- Mucilaginous covering swells 11-20 times on wetting.
- Seed embryo is rich in unsaturated fatty oil (50% Linoleic acid).
- Seed husk is rosy white membranous covering (epidermis) which constitute drug in commerce.
- Husk contains mucilage consist of xylose, arabinose and galacturonic acid.

- Uses: Anti-diarrhoea, soothing & cooling agent, used against irritation in gastrointestinal tract; infections of kidney and bladder; embryo oil prevents arteriosclerosis.
- Coating of seed provides husk on mechanical milling.
- Mucilage contain glucoside-Acubin.
- Roots contain Saussurine alkaloid.
- Seed have 17.4% protein, 6.7% fat, 24.6% dietary fibres and combustion heat of 4.75 Kcal per gram.
- Inflorescence: Spike.
- Flowers: Bisexual and protogynous.
- Fruit: Capsule, each contains oval shaped two seeds which are dull white in colour.
- Seed rate: 4-6 kg/ha
- Maturity: Spike turns brownish purple.
- Yield: 1 t/ha
- Husk: seed ratio is 25:75 by weight.
- Yield of husk: 28-30% of unhusked seed.
- Downy mildew is serious at spike initiation.
- Swelling factor is worked out by 1 g of seed in 20 cc cylinder- volume 20 ml- read final volume after 6 hours. It is expressed as 'cc/gram'.

Varieties:

Name	Breeding method	Features
AAU, Anand		
Gujarat Isabgol-1	Selection	Dark green leaf; spike length 4-4.5 cm; plant height 50 cm; yield 10 q/ha
Gujarat Isabgol-2	selection	Pale green leaf; spike length 3.8-4.6 cm; plant height 58-64 cm; resistant to downy mildew; yield 10 q/ha
Gujarat Isabgol-3	Selection	Pale green leaf; spike length 4-4.2 cm; plant height 52 cm
Gujarat Isabgol-4	Selection	Dark green leaf; spike length 3-4 cm; plant height 45 cm;
DMAP, Anand		
Vallabh Isabgol-1	Mutant of Gujarat Isabgol-2	Dark green leaves; yield 1400 kg/ha
Vallabh Isabgol-2	Mutant of GI-2	Erect growth; dwarf; seed yield 1104 kg/ha;
Vallabh Isabgol-3	Mutant of GI-2	Early maturing 100-105 days; seed yield 1048.85 Kg/ha;
CCSHAU, Hisar		
Haryana Isabgol-4	Selection	Matures in 140-145 days; yield 1000-1200 kg/ha; husk 25%
Haryana Isabgol-5	selection	Long spike; resistant to DM; seed possess 30% husk
RVSKVV, Mandsaur, Madhya Pradesh		
Jawahar Isabgol-4	Selection	Matures in 140-145 days; yield 1300-1500 kg/ha; husk 25%
CIMAP, Lucknow		
Mayuri	Gamma ray irradiation to seed	Early maturing; high yielding; distinct pigment marker of the panicles related to the maturity thereby indicating the right harvesting stage;
Niharika	-	

Grades of husk powder after grinding and sieving:

- Khakho: Contain small husk powder and sand.
- Lali: Contains embryo and seed pieces.
- Gola: Husked grain.

3.21.2 *Brahmi*

- Economic part: Whole herb.
- Active principles: Brahmine,Herpestine.
- Uses: Enhance memory & vitality.
- **Varieties**: Pragyashakti & Subodhak

3.22. PIPERACEAE

3.22.1 Long pepper/ *Pipali*

- Economic part: Catkins.
- Active principles: Piperine (0.2-0.25%).
- Uses: Stimulant, appetizer, laxative; rheumatic pains & paralysis; decoction from dried fruits used in chronic bronchitis.
- **Variety**: Vishwam.

3.23. PLUMBAGINACEAE

3.23.1_Chitrak

- Economic part: Leaves & roots.

3.24. RUBIACEAE

3.24.1 Cinchona

- Introduced in India mainly to fight menace of malaria.
- *Cinchona caulisaya.*
- Prefer acidic (pH 6-6.5) soil.
- Crop duration: 12-15 years.
- Economic part: Bark.
- Alkaloid: Quinine sulphate forms one of most important groups of cmpounds.
- Use: Anti-malarial drug.
- Propagation methods: Seed, cuttings, stooling, layering, patch budding.
- Harvesting of cinchona is called as coppicing. It is followed at 8-10 years interval.
- Yield: 5-10 q/ha (dry bark).

Variety: Clone No. 701.

3.24.2 Ipecac

- Introduced in India mainly to fight menace of diarrhoea.
- Prefer acidic (pH 6-6.5) soil.
- Economic part: Root.
- Alkaloid: Cephaline, Emetin.
- Use: Induce vomiting, used against amoebeiosis.

Variety: Metograsso.

3.25. SCROPHULARIACEAE

3.25.1 Foxglove/ *Tilpushpi*

- Annual herb used as medicine for weak heart, ointment for burns and wounds.
- *Digitalis lanata* (1-1.4% glycosides). No side effects.
- *D. purpurea* (0.2-0.4% glycosides).
- Require cool climate.
- Seed rate: 8 kg/ha.
- Crop duration: 140-160 days.
- Economic part: Dried leaves and entire plant.
- Alkaloids: Digoxin, Digitoxin, Getanin.
- Uses: Carminative, Cardiotonic; to cure heart diseases; diuretic for dropsy & renal obstruction, ointment for wounds and burns, medicine for weak heart.

Varieties: EC-115996, D-76, D-21.

3.26. SOLANACEAE

3.26.1 Ashwagandha

- Eulogized as 'Winter cherry or Indian ginseng'.
- Oldest medicinal plant grown in India. Grown in drier regions of India.
- Other spp. *Withania coagulans*. Occurs in N-W India.
- Of 8 different types of alkaloids, Ethenin, Withaferin & Somniferin are important.
- With aferine- anti-biotic, anti-carcinogenic and anti-tumor activity found in leaves.
- Propagation method: Seeds.
- Seed germinate in 5-8 days after treating with GA 500 ppm overnight.
- 35 days old seedlings are transplanted.
- Planting distance: 30 cm x 10 cm.
- Seed rate: 10-12 kg/ha and transplanting 5 kg/ha.
- Pencil thick roots are valued in trade.

- Economic part: Roots, leaves, green fruits, seeds.
- Roots contain 0.2-0.5% alkaloids (Withanine, Somniferine)
- Uses: Immune-modulator, anti-stress; improve male potency, cure skin disease; rheumatism, diuretic; root powder applied locally on ulcers, inflammation health improvement, physical fitness; fruit powder useful against skin problems, high blood pressure, piles.

Varieties:

- Rakshita, Poshita. IIHRWS 3, Nimiti, Nagori

Name	Breeding method	Features
RVSKVV, Mandsaur, Madhya Pradesh		
Jawahar Asgand-20	Selection	Plant height 5.5 cm; dry root yield 5-6 q/ha; number of roots 16
Jawahar Asgand-134	Selection	Dry root yield 6-8 q/ha
Rai Vijay Asagandh-100	Selection	Dry root yield 6-7 q/ha
IIHR, Bengaluru		
Arka Ashwagandha	Selection	Plant height 6.3 cm; high dry root yield (12 q/ha); number of roots 17;

3.26.2 Belladonna

- Eulogized as 'Deadly night shade'.
- Propagation method: Seeds (1 kg/ha)
- Indian belladonna (*Atropa acuminata*) and European belladona (*A. belladonna*).
- Total alkaloid content depend upon stage of development i.e. very low during flowering and very high at green berry stage.
- Drug decreases secretion of sweat, salivary and gastric glands.
- Economic parts: Leaves, other aerial parts & roots.
- Active principle- Tropane alkaloids (0.13-0.7%).
- Uses: Atropine drug in neurologic pains, Ampholinergic property; strong anti-spasmodic in intestinal colic; sedative, useful in asthma & whooping cough; useful in eye drop preparation; used as antidote in certain poisoning cases.
- Drug Hyoscine, Hyoscyamine as truth confessor in criminal investigations.

A. belladonna	*A. acuminata*
purple flower	yellow flower
More active principle	Less active principle
Distributed in southern parts of Europe, UK, USSR	Distributed in temperate region of Himalayas

3.26.3 Datura

- Eulogized as 'Thorn apple'.
- Economic part: Whole herb.
- Active principles: Hyoscyamine, Scopolamine & Atropine
- Uses: Pre-anesthetic in surgery & child birth, ophthalmology.
- **Varieties**: RRL-Neel Lohit, RRL- Green.

3.26.4 Henbane

- Egyptian *henbane (Hyoscyamus muticus)*: Cultivated in Kashmir. Leaves are smoked for intoxication.
- Indian henbane (*H. niger*).
- Long day plant.
- Annual, flowers during summer and set seeds.
- Biennial produces tuft of leaves in one season and flowering in spring.
- Economic parts: Leaves and flowers.
- Dried leaves are smoked as cigarette against asthma.
- Cataplasm of fresh leaves is used as pain killer.
- Chemical content/ alkaloid: Hyoscyamine to cure asthma & whooping cough. Anti-spasmodic & anti-cholinergic property; relieves painful spasmodic conditions of muscles; dilates pupil of eye; intense narcotic property.
- Seed rate- 2-3 kg/ha.
- **Varieties**: Aela (pink anthers); IC-66, HMI-80-1.

3.26.5 Medicinal solanum

- Eulogized as 'Tropical soda apple' (*Solanum viarum*).
- Kangroo apple (*S. laciniatum*).
- Highest solasodine content species: *S. incanum* (1.8-2.0%)
- Glucoalkaloid: Solasodine content in berries (1.0-1.75%).
- 60% in seeds and 40% in pericarp.
- Seed rate: 1.25 kg/ha.
- Economic part: Fruit.
- Yield- 6-8 T berries/ha.
- Uses: As corticosteroids, contraceptive, sex hormones.
- **Varieties**: RRL- 20-2, RRL-SL-6 (spineless mutant), Arka Mahima (4x), GLAXO, BARC, Arka Sanjeevani (2x, Spineless), RRL-SL-6 (spineless mutant).

4. AROMATIC PLANTS

4.1. ASTERACEAE

4.1.1 Davana

- Propagation method: Seed (1.5 kg/ha).
- 1 g contains 1600 seeds.
- Related spp.: *A. annua* (0.3-0.4% oil).
- Economic part: Leaves & flower tops.
- Chemical content: Davonone.
- Uses: Delicate fragrance for floral decoration, cosmetics, anthelmintic drug 'santonin' calming down anxiety.

4.1.2 Chamomile

- Economic part: Flowers.
- Active principle: Chamzulene.
- Uses: Pain relieving balms, anti-bacterial & anti-fungal.
- **Variety**: Vallary.

4.2. APIACEAE

4.2.1 Celery

- Flower: Protandrous
- Seed oil contain Selinene, d-limonene
- Seed rate: 1 kg/ha
- Seed shattering is major problem.
- Crop matures in 3 months after transplanting.
- Uses: Seasoning and flavouring sauces.
- **Variety**: RRL-85-1.

4.3. CANNABINACEAE

4.3.1 Hops

- World's costliest vegetable.
- Economic part: Flowers, fruit, stem.
- Use: Beverage industry, beer industry, making anti-biotics, treating tuberculosis.
- Flowers are called as 'hop-cones or strobile' which are used as stability agent in beer making.
- Rich source of anti-oxidants.

- Shoots are used as flavouring agent in beer.
- Acid present in shoot: Humulones.
- Lupulones in humulones is effective in killing cancer cells.

4.4. LAMIACEAE

4.4.1 Patchouli

- Short day plant and used as catch crop.
- Good intercrop in coconut and rubber plantation.
- Oil has fixative property & used to preserve currency notes, agarbatti making, perfumery, etc.
- In natural condition never flower.
- Propagation method: Terminal cuttings.
- Highest oil content: Top 3 leaves.
- Oil content in leaves: Patchouliol (2-6%) & oil recovery (3-3.5%).
- Most odour intensive constituent of oil: Alcohol (32-37%).
- Uses: Fixative property, perfumes, insect repellent
- Steam distillation duration: 6-8 hours.
- Sodium sulphate @ 20-30 g/l is used to remove moisture in oil.
- Major pest: Nematodes.
- **Varieties**: Johore (best quality oil), Malaysian, CIM-Sheshta, CIM-Samarth, IIHR-1.

4.4.2 Basil/ *Tulsi*

- Eulogized as 'Indian basil or Holy basil or Queen of herbs or Elixir of life'.
- French/ Roman basil: *Ocimum basilicum*. Highly susceptible to cercospora leaf spot.
- Holy basil: *O. tenuifolium*.
- *O. basilicum* var. *hispidium*: Dried plants used for fumigation to repel mosquitoes and flies.
- Local variety 'Kamakasturi' shows field resistance to cercospora leaf spot.

Four varieties identified in India-

- Var. *album* (lettuce leaf basil).
- Var. *differme* (curry leafed basil).
- Var. *purfurascens* (violet red basil).
- Var. *thyrsiflorum* (Thai basil/ common white basil). Commercially cultivated in North India.

- Dark Opal: *O. basilicum* x *O. forskolei*.
- Rich natural source of camphor: *O. kilimandscharicum* and *O. canum*.
- Egyptian basil contains higher amount of methyl chavicol.
- European type sweet basil i.e. Sabja, contains highest quality aroma with linalool and methyl chavicol as major oil content.
- Methyl cinnamate rich basil has been commercially produced in Bulgaria, India and Pakistan.
- Clove flavoured foliage used on seasoning, meats, soups and salads.
- Protandrous flower.
- Pollination: Honey bee.
- Difficulty in nomenclature: Polymorphism and cross pollination.
- Oil recovery: 0.5%.
- Time required for extracting essential oil: 4-6 hours.
- Sweet basil contains eugenol, linalool, Methyl chavicol (70-80%).
- Clocimum: Substitute of clove oil.
- Seed rate: 250 g/ha.
- Oil yield: 66-70 kg/ha.
- Herbage yield: 20-30 T/ha
- Herbage yield: 20-30 T/ha
- Seeds when steeped in water, liberate mucilage (9.3%) which is semi-transparent and tasteless.
- Economic part: Leaves and inflorescence.
- Use: Flavoring foods.

Varieties: RRL-011, Kusumohak, Vikarsudha (methyl chavicol rich), Chandni, Sharada, CIM- Ayu, CIM- Saumya, CIM-Angana, CIM- Surabhi, GAB-1, HYBL-1: Perennial, evergreen, cold tolerant, with high herb, essential oil yield (200 kg/ ha), linalool rich strain(75-80%).

4.4.3 Rosemary

- Evergreen, hardy, perennial and widely used in aromatherapy.
- Ancient Latin name means 'sea-dew'.
- Essential oil has anti-fungal and anti-bacterial properties.
- Oil is used as an insect repellent, remedy for headache.
- Rosemary tea makes mouthwash for halitosis and anti-septic gargle.
- Used in herbal shampoo as hair tonic.
- Inflorescence: Spike.
- Economic part: Leaves & flowers.
- Needle shaped, dark green & highly aromatic leaves are used for seasoning.
- Pale blue flowers appear in early spring to early summer or in early autumn.

- Fruit: Oval shaped, four sectioned cremocarp.
- Propagation method: Seeds, layering and rooted soft wood cuttings, semi-hard wood cuttings & layerings of 10-15 cm length.
- Seed germination need bottom heat technique of 27-32^{0}C.
- After 6-8 weeks, cuttings are planted.
- Planting distance: 60 cm x 60 cm or 60 cm x 75 cm.
- Variety: Ooty (Rm)-1.
- Number of plants/ acre: 12,000.
- 1st cutting starts at 8 months age.
- Crop duration: 25-30 years.
- Fresh leaves and tender tops are distilled to yield 0.5-1.5% essential oil.
- Main chemical content: Cineol, borneol, mentoterpene (linalool &verbenol).
- Alkaloids present: Rosemarinic acid, camphor, caffeic acid, ursolic acid, betulinic acid, etc.
- Uses: Anti-cancer & anti-oxidant property.
- Pruning / trimming once or twice in each season to maintain thickness.
- Dried leaves retain green colour and has bitter sweet flavour.
- Yield of dry leaf: 6-12 T/ha.

Species:

- Other promising varieties of *R. officinalis* are- Beneden Blue rosemary, Severn Sea, Primley Blue, Sudbury Blue, Majorca Pink, Fota Blue, Sissinghurst Blue.

Common name	Botanical name
White rosemary	*R. officinalis var. albiflorus*
Corsican blue rosemary	*R. officinalis var. angustssmus*
Golden rosemary	*R. officinalis var. aureus*
Pink rosemary	*R. officinalis var. roseus*
Prostrate rosemary	*R. officinalis var. prostratus*
Beneden Blue rosemary	*R. officinalis var. angustissimus*

4.4.4 Melissa

- Economic part: Whole herb.
- Chemical content: Citrol, nerol.
- Uses: Perfumery, cosmetics.

4.4.5 Thyme

- Perennial, ancient herb used by Egyptians in oil form for embalming.
- The Greeks used it in baths and as incense in temples.
- The Romans used it to purify rooms.

- Thyme oil from leaves used in treatment of bronchitis.
- Leading producer of thyme oil: France.
- It has anti-septic, anti-spasmodic, anti-oxidant, anti-microbial and carminative properties.
- The tea makes a gargle or mouthwash and is an excellent remedy for sore throats and infected gums and also good for hangovers.
- Essential oil is anti-bacterial, anti-fungal and used in manufacture of toothpaste, mouthwash, gargles and other toilet articles.
- Oil is also used to ease rheumatic pains and often used in liniments, massage oils and also used to kill mosquito larvae.
- Economic part: Leaves and flowers.
- Used both as fresh, dried whole and grounded form.
- Leaves used for seasoning soups, gravies, stews, sauces and meats.
- Propagation methods: Seed, leaf cuttings, root divisions.
- Seeds are very fine & need bottom heat technique (15-22^{0}C) for germination.
- Hardened seedlings are planted in late spring or early summer in main field at 25-40 cm apart.
- Seedlings thinned at 15 cm between plants in nursery.
- Soft wood cuttings (5-8 cm length) from new growth is used for planting.
- Division of aerial roots of creeping thymes can be used for planting.
- Mound layers from matured, woody thymes can also be prepared for planting.
- It can be grown in containers.
- Poor and low fertile soils with good drainage impart better flavour to thymes.
- Planting in rich fertile soils impairs flavour and plants become soft.
- Trimming back after flowering maintains shape of plants, promotes new growth, stops the plants becoming woody & sprawling in wrong direction.
- Sunlight is essential for good growth and also to impart better flavour to leaves.
- Dried leaves are curled and usually not longer than 6-7 mm.
- Planting distance: 90 cm x 30 cm.
- Fruit: Smooth, dark coloured, 4 sectioned nutlet.
- Replanted at every 3 years.
- Since it is, evergreen plant, it can be harvested in fresh form all the year round.
- For preservation, crop is harvested before flowering.
- 2-3 harvest every year.
- Herbage is gathered when plants are in full bloom.
- Flowering tops are clipped together with part of leafy stem.
- Shade dried to preserve grayish green colour.
- Leaves can be dried or can be kept in vinegar or oil.

- Yield: 1-1.5 t/ha.
- Volatile oil: Thymol (0.8-2.0%).
- Phenol is major constituent of this essential oil.
- Chemical content: Thymal 23.63%
- Uses: Perfume & flavour.
- Tolerant to root rot, nematodes and white fly.

Species:

- Genus contains numerous species that are very diverse in appearance & come from many different parts of the world, although majority grows in Mediterranean region.

Common name	Botanical name	Features
Silver Posie thyme	*Thymus vulgaris*	Evergreen, hardy, perennial, 30 cm height; leaves grey/ silver variegation with pink tinge on underside; pale pink/ lilac flowers; good culinary thyme used in salads
Common (garden) thyme	*T. vulgaris*	Evergreen, hardy, perennial, 30 cm height; thin green aromatic leaves; mauve flowers; used in stews, sauces, salads; medicinal properties are anti-fungal & anti-bacterial
Lucy thyme	*T. vulgaris*	Evergreen, hardy, perennial, 30 cm height; large green leaves with mild flavour & scent; pink flowers; excellent culinary thyme; medicinal properties are anti-bacterial & anti-fungal
Orange scented thyme	*T. fragrantissimus*	Evergreen, hardy, perennial, 30 cm height; leaves small, narrow, grayish green & smell of spicy orange; pale pink/ white flowers; good for puddings
Caraway thyme	*T. herbabarona*	Evergreen, hardy, perennial, 2 cm height; dark green small leaves with unique caraway scent; rose coloured flowers; good for culinary purpose
Broad-leaved thyme	*T. pulegioides*	Evergreen, hardy, perennial, 8 cm height; large round, green leaves with strong thyme flavour; pink/ mauve flowers; good for culinary purpose; excellent for ground cover & in hanging basket
Russeting thyme	*T. serpyllum*	Evergreen, hardy, perennial, prostrate form, a creeper; small green leaves; purple/ mauve flowers; decorative, aromatic & good ground cover
Snow-drift thyme	*T. serpyllum*	Evergreen, hardy, perennial, prostrate form, a creeper; small green round leaves & masses of white flowers; decorative, aromatic & good ground cover
Wild creeping thyme/ Mother of thyme/ Creeping thyme	*T. polytrichus ssp. britannicus*	Evergreen, hardy, perennial, 2 cm height & 20 cm spread; small, dark green leaves with mild scent; very valuable herb
Lemon thyme	*T. x citriodorus*	Evergreen, hardy, perennial, 30 cm height; large green leaves with strong lemon scent; pink flowers; good for culinary purpose
Golden King thyme	*T. x citriodorus*	Evergreen, hardy, perennial, 2 cm height; large green leaves variegated with gold, strongly lemon scented; pink coloured flowers; excellent culinary purpose & for salad dressing

Variety: Ooty-1.

4.4.6 Lavender

- France: Largest supplier of lavender oil in the world.
- *Lavendula angustifolia*: True lavender.
- *L. latifolia*: Spike lavender.
- Species having highest quality of essential oil: *L. officinalis*.
- Prefers temperate climate.
- Flowers, leaves and stalks used for their pleasant fragrance, also used on medicines.
- Oil: Linalool and Linalyl acetate.
- Propagation method: Seeds or cuttings.
- Harvesting: 3 years after planting.
- Specific gravity of oil: 0.88-0.89%.
- **Variety**: Karlovo, Akash, Sher-e-Kashmir.

4.4.7 Japanese mint

- Eulogized as 'Menthol mint or Corn mint or Field mint'.
- Aromatic crop having maximum area.
- *Mentha arvensis* var. *piperascens*.
- Grown in hilly region part in Jammu and Kashmir.
- Shallow rooted and long day plant but never set seeds.
- High menthol content spp.
- Inflorescence: Spike.
- Crop duration: 2-3 years.
- Propagation method: Suckers 500-600 kg/ha.
- Qualitative long day plant.
- Show facultative apomixes.
- Crop maturity determined by Clevenger's apparatus.
- Oil yield: 150 kg/ year.
- Oil percent: 0.1 to 0.5%.
- Oil recovery: 75-80 kg/ha.
- Time required for extracting essential oil: 4-5 hours.
- All mints are harvested on sunny days because in rainy/cloudy season convert menthol to menthone, lowering value of produce.
- Used as carminative, stimulant.
- Oil is used needed for cigarettes.
- Pest: Leaf webber (*Syngamia obruptallis*).

Varieties:

Name	Breeding method	Features
CIMAP, Lucknow		
CIM-Kushal	-	Tolerant to leaf spot, rust & powdery mildew
CIM-Saksham	Screening of somaclones	High essential oil;
CIM-Damroo		High essential oil;
Gomti	-	Better regeneration after 1st harvest
Himalaya	-	resistant to pests & diseases
Kosi	-	High menthol; high biomass & high oil yield with symmetrical branching
Kalka	-	-
Sambhav	Somaclonal variant of cv. Himalaya	Extra wide canopy; insect tolerant, high essential oil and methanol
Neerkalka	Intervarietal hybrid of *Mentha arvensis* (cv. Kalka) x & *Mentha spicata* (cv. Neera)	Propagated by suckers or stem cuttings & stable for commercial cultivation.
Saryu	-	-
Kranti	Half-sib selection from 'Gomti'	-
Krant	-	Tolerant to cold
Shivalik	-	Most popular variety

4.4.8 Common mint

- Eulogized as 'Spear mint or Garden mintor Multi-utility mint'.
- *Mentha spicata*.
- Perennial.
- Leaves are used as medicine for cough and industrial use for flavouring food products.
- Green or dried leaves used for seasoning soups, sauces & meats; also used for flavouring puddings and gelatin desserts.
- Contain 70-80 % menthone.
- Contain 0.57% oil.
- Oil is rich in carvone (65%).
- Oil is useful in dentifrice, confectionary and pharmaceutical products.
- Plants bear lanceolate, stalkless, light green narrow leaves.
- Flowering spikes are long with lilac flowers.
- Oil yield: 120 litres/ ha.

Varieties:

Name	Breeding method	Features
CIMAP, Lucknow		
CIM- Ganga		Oil has anti-insect & anti-microbial activity; highly useful for agrochemical & pharmaceutical purposes.
Neera	-	
Supriya	-	
MSS-1	-	
MSS-2	-	
MSS-5	-	-
PAU, Ludhiana		
Punjab Spearmint-1	-	

4.4.9 Bergamot mint

- Eulogized as 'Lemon mint or Orange mint'.
- *Mentha cardiaca, M.citrata* (syn. *M. viridis*).
- Tolerant to frost.
- Rich in linalool & linalyl acetate.
- Oil yield: 75-150 kg/ha.

Variety: Kiran (mutant of bergamot mint from CIMAP).

4.4.10 Pepper mint

- Eulogized as '*Vilayati pudina*' (*Mentha piperita*).
- Contains menthol (25-40%) and menthone (30-40%).
- Perennial and prefers temperate climate.
- Qualitative long day plant
- Use: Anti-tussive.
- Oil yield: 0.3 to 1%.
- On chilling oil, menthol separates out as crystals.
- Used as medicine for controlling vomiting, head ache and flavouring purpose.

Varieties:

Name	Breeding method	Features
CIMAP, Lucknow		
CIM- Indus	-	High menthofuran (22 to 30%) & high pulegone (9.0 to 18%).
CIM-Patra	-	
CIM-Pranjal	Mutation	High menthol rich essential oil; deep purplish green foliage; purplish white flowers; tolerant Bihar hairy caterpillar (*Spilarctia obliqua*)
Kukrail	-	-
CIM-Madhuras	-	-
Black Mitcham	-	-
EC- 41911	-	-

4.5. MALVACEAE

4.5.1 Ambrette

- Eulogized as *'Muskdana'*.
- Economic part: Seed.
- Chemical content: Farnesol & Ambrettolide.
- Uses: Musk odour used in incense sticks.

4.6. MYRTACEAE

4.6.1 Eucalyptus

- Used as shade/ wind break and in industry for oil/ perfumery.
- Economic part: Leaves.
- Oil denotes 3 distinct group of essential oils: Medicinal type, perfumery type and Phellandrene rich type.
- Lemon scented/ Tasmanian/ Blue gum (*E. globulus*)- high cineol content. Deodorant is manufactured besides utilization of oil for asthama, bronchitis, perfumery, etc.
- Phellandrene rich type: *E. citriodora* (most widely grown in hill stations of south India). The source of citronellal and menthol from leaves and terminal buds is famous for perfumery industries.
- Economic parts: Leaves and terminal buds- along with trunk.
- Coppicing is practiced in every 4th year.
- Pollarding is method of harvesting.
- Leaf harvesting time: March-May.
- Essential oil content; 1.3-3.5%.

4.7. PANDANACEAE

4.7.1 Screwpine

- Eulogized as *'Kewada'*.
- Three morphotypes: wild spinous, spineless and ketaki types.
- Tolerant to drought and floods.
- Aerial root is characteristic feature.
- Propagation method: Crown suckers.
- Economic part: Flowers.
- Flower period: May-June.
- Chemical content: Lupulin
- Uses: Kewada water.

4.8. POACEAE (GRAMINAE)

4.8.1 Lemon grass

- Eulogized as 'Sugandh rohisha grass'.
- *Cymbopogon flexuosus*: East Indian lemon grass.
- *C. citrates*: West Indian lemon grass.
- *C. pendulus*: North Indian/ Jammu lemon grass.
- Good soil binding nature so used in soil conservation purpose.
- Hardy drought tolerant and short day plant.
- Commercially grown in Kerala and Assam.
- Stemless perennial hedge.
- Economic part: Leaves.
- Citral is starting material for preparation of Ionone.
- Propagation method: Seeds (4-5 kg/ha).
- Economic life for commercial cultivation: 5 years.
- Cut at 20 cm above ground and left for withering for 4-6 hours in field.
- Distilled in steam distillation unit.
- Time required for extracting essential oil: 4-6 hours.
- Oil content: 0.5-0.8%.
- Oil yield/ ha: 80-100 kg (rainfed) and 150-180 kg (irrigated).
- Chemical content: Citral (75-80%), Farnesol, Citronellol, Geraniol.
- Flavour compound: Citral.
- Produce flowers and set seeds luxuriantly during autumn (short day condition only).
- Inflorescence: Long terminal branched panicle.
- Spike consists of 5-11 spikelets in pairs, of which one is sessile and others stalked.
- Sessile spike is awned and holds bisexual florets with 4 blooms.
- Stalked spikes are awnless with 3 blooms and a staminate floret.
- Crop harvest after 90 days during 1st year and 60-65 days thereafter.
- Uses: 'β-Ione' from citral in manufacture of vit. A tablets, insect repellent, pesticide, preservative, anti-fungal & 'α-Ione' used in flavours, cosmetics, perfumes, soaps & disinfectant.
- Uses of byproducts: Printing paper/ writing paper, cattle feed, fuel.

Varieties:

Name	Breeding method	Features
CIMAP, Lucknow		
CIM- Nima		Suitable for high pH & sodic soil. Rich in citral
CIM-Chirharit	Selection from OP progeny 'Cauvery'	Tetraploid variant; frost resistant; does not show reduction in yield over the years
CIM-Shikhar	-	-
Sugandhi	Selection from OD-440	Old cv. grown in Kerala & drought tolerant
Praman	-	Tetraploid mutant of *C. pendulus*
Pragati	Clonal selection	Popular in Himalayan regions
Krishna	-	Wider adaptability
Cauvery	-	-
GRL-1	-	Geraniol rich
CKP-25	Intergeneric hybrid of (*C. khasianus* x *C. pendulus*)	-
CIM-Suwarna	-	Suitable for drought prone area
OD-19	-	-
OD-23	-	-
OD-440	-	-
SD-68	-	-
RRL-16	-	-
NLG-84	-	-

4.8.2 Java citronella

- Economic part: Leaves.
- Chemical content: Citronellal, Geraniol, Citronellal.
- Time required for extracting essential oil: 4-6 hours.
- Crop duration: 5 years.
- Planting distance: 3 feet x 3 feet.
- 1st cutting after 6 months and subsequent at 2-3 months interval.
- Yield: 2-3 t/ha (herbage); 5-10 q/ha (oil).
- More oil yield in summer months than rainy season.
- Uses: Mosquito repellent, deodorants, scented soaps.

Varieties:

Name	Breeding method	Features
CIMAP, Lucknow		
Mandakini	-	-
Manjusha	-	-
Manjari	-	-

Jal Pallavi	Selection of somatic variant of 'Jorlab-2'	Tolerant to water logging
CIM-Jiva	-	-
Jorlab-2	-	-
Java Sel. 2	-	-
Medni	-	-
Bio-13	-	-

4.8.3 Palmarosha grass

- Eulogized as 'Sweet scented grass or Rosha grass'.
- Drought hardy and produce profuse illering.
- Crop has maximum oil content at flower opening stage.
- 1st coppicing in October-November.
- Yield: 150-200 kg oil/ha.
- Time required for extracting essential oil: 4-6 hrs.
- Chemical content of oil: Geraniol.
- Uses: Soaps, perfumery, cosmetics, mosquito repellent, anthelmintic against nematodes, skin diseases, and confectionary.

Varieties:

Name	Breeding method	Features
CIMAP, Lucknow		
Trishna	-	-
Jamrosa	-	Flowers twice in a year & does not form seed; hence raised by rooted slips
PRC-1	-	-
Motia	-	-
Rosha Grass-49	-	-
CI-80-68	-	-
CIM- Harsh	-	Leaf yield 399 q/ha
CIM-Vaishnavi	-	-
CIM-Tripta	-	-

4.9. SANTALACEAE

4.9.1 Sandalwood

- Obligatory root parasite.
- Economic part: Heart wood and takes about 30-60 years to form good heart wood.
- Propagation method: Seed.
- Yield of heart wood: 19-50 kg/tree.
- Oil contains α and β-santalols (90-93% oil).

- Use: Astringent, arrest discharge of blood, mucus, etc.
- Seed germination is major problem.
- Sandal wood is affected by spike disease (MLOs).

4.10. VITEVERACEAE

4.10.1 Vetiver grass

- Eulogized as 'Khus grass'.
- World production of vetiver oil: 300-350 t /year.
- India's production of vetiver oil: 100-150 t /year
- Soil binding property and hence grown in flood, undulated, soil eroded lands, carbon sequestration, water conservation.
- Average root strength is 75 mpa and roots will improve shear strength of soil by 30-40%.
- Xerophytic grass.
- Known to live for a long time. Longest recorded period: 60 years (at Msamfu Research Station in Zambia).
- Ratooning is not possible.
- Propagation method: Root division.
- Tolerant to alkalinity and flooding.
- Maturity period: 18 months.
- Economic part: Root slips.
- Chemical content: Viteverol/ Hydrosol.
- Uses: Carminative, cosmetics & aromatherapy.
- Herbage yield: 15-30 t/ha.
- Time required for extracting essential oil: 60-70 hrs.
- Oil content: 0.2-0.8% (north Indian type); 0.6-1.2% (south Indian type).
- North Indian oil quality is best in the world.
- Genetics of essential oil yield: Non-additive gene action.

Varieties:

Name	Breeding method	Specific features
IARI, New Delhi		
Pusa Hybrid-1	-	-
Pusa Hybrid-2	-	-
Pusa Hybrid-7	-	-
Pusa Hybrid-8	-	-

NBPGR, New Delhi		
HYB-08	-	-
CIMAP, Lucknow		
CIM-Vriddhi	-	-
CIM-Samriddhi	-	20% higher essential oil; oil yield (30 kg/ha);
CIM- Khus-15	-	-
CIM- Khus-22	-	-
CIM-Khusinolika	Recurrent selection through polycross	Spreading type; 45-50% Khusinol (v/v);
ODV-3	-	-
KS-1	-	-
KS-2	-	-
KS-3	-	-
CIMAP-KS-40	Polyploidy	Autopolyploid (4x=40) clone; useful for carbon sequestration and soil conservation
Nilambore	-	-
Sugandha	-	-
MS-1	-	-
Gulabi	-	-
Kesari	-	-
Dharini	-	-

8 POST HARVEST TECHNOLOGY

GENERAL INFORMATION

- About 25% of world's total food production is lost due to insects, bacteria and rodents after harvesting.
- India's exports of Processed Food was Rs. 31,503.43 Crores in 2014-15, which includes products like Mango pulp (Rs. 841.59 Crores), Dried and Preserved vegetable (Rs. 842.14 Crores), Other Processed [illegible]

8

POST HARVEST TECHNOLOGY

1. GENERAL INFORMATION:

- About 25% of world's total food production is lost due to insects, bacteria and rodents after harvesting.
- India's exports of Processed Food was Rs. 31563.43 Crores in 2014-15, which includes products like Mango pulp (Rs. 841.39 Crores), Dried and Preserved vegetable (Rs. 847.11 Crores), Other Processed Fruit and Vegetable (Rs. 2,569.93 Crores), Pulses (Rs. 1,209.51 Crores), Groundnuts (Rs. 4,675.35 Crores), Guargum (Rs. 9,480.00 Crores), Jaggery and Confectionary (Rs. 1,161.81 Crores), Cocoa Products (Rs. 848.62 Crores), Cereal preparations (Rs. 3,038.79 Crores), Alcoholic and Non-alcoholic beverages (Rs. 2,231.58 Crores) and Miscellaneous preparations (Rs. 2,437.77 Crores).
- Export of fruit and vegetable products is also growing @ 15%.
- In India, less than 5% fruits are being sold by organized supply chain management and E-commerce companies and only about 3% of the total produce gets processed.
- Organized supply chain management companies in India like Reliance Fresh, Big Bazaar, Aditya Birla Retail Ltd., Safal or E-commerce companies like Big Basket or Grofers, etc. account for procurement of less than 5% of the total fruits produced in the country.
- Fruit and vegetable processing: USA (65%), Brazil (70%), Philippines (78%), South Africa (80%), Malaysia (83%), Thailand (30%)
- Most of Indian varieties have been bred for table consumption, hence less suitable for processing.
- In India, processing industry is a high risk-low margin proposition.
- 30-35% fruits and vegetables perish due to want of post-harvest facilities.
- Of the total horticulture production, only 67% is used for local consumption, 30% is subjected to post harvest losses, 2% for export and 0.8% for processing.
- As per Ministry of Food Processing Industries (MOFPI), only 2-2.2% fruits and 1% vegetables are processed in India.
- Huge post harvest losses (25-40%) in horticultural produce is >Rs. 30,000 crore per year.
- Losses in fruits and vegetables both qualitative and quantitative occur between harvesting and consumption.

- Post harvest losses in fruits and vegetables: Mango (15-35%), papaya (20-35%), citrus (10-30%), pineapple (20-40%), grape (10-25%), banana (25-40%), guava (10-32%), Sapota (10-20%), jamun (30-60%), phalsa (20-35%), potato (30-40%), onion (25-40%), tomato (10-35%), cabbage and cauliflower (8-25%), chilli (5-35%), carrot (5-10%), radish (3-5%), garlic (1-3%), tapioca (5-10%), green pea (7-10%).
- Nature of losses at farmer's field (15-20%), in packaging (15-20%), in transportation (30-40%) and in marketing (30-40%).
- Fruits and vegetables processing industry is growing @ 10% per annum.
- Contribution of the food processing industry to agricultural sector: 9%.
- Contribution of the food processing industry to manufacturing sector: 11%.
- APEDA belongs to Ministry of Commerce and Industry.
- Regulatory bodies for food irradiation in India: Atomic Energy Regulatory Board (AERB) and Department of Atomic Energy (DAE).
- Ministry of Food Processing Industries has taken interest in radiation processing technology as a means of preservation of perishable fruits and vegetables, pest control and enhancement of quality.
- Union Ministry of Agriculture and Farmers Welfare launched online software for processing applications, AGMARK quality certification mark for agricultural products is- AGMARK Online system.
- Total number of 'Mega Food Parks' in India approved by Ministry of Food Processing Industries: 57.
- Cold storage capacity of Mega Food Parks till 2019: 32 Metric tones.
- India's 1st Aqua Mega Food Park established at Bhima Varammandal of West Godavari, Andhra Pradesh. (14th February, 2019).
- Minimum land required for setting up a Mega Food Park: 50 acres.
- Total cold storage capacity of India: 34 MT (Million tones).
- In India, cold storage facility is available for only 10% of fruits.
- More number of cold storage units: Uttar Pradesh (2285), Gujarat (753), Punjab (655), Maharashtra (581), West Bengal (511).
- 100% FDI is allowed in cold storage, ware houses and Food Processing sector.
- Physiological maturity: It is the stage when a fruit is capable of further development or ripening when it is harvested. It refers to maximum growth and maturation has occurred.
- Horticultural maturity: It refers to the stage of development when plant and plant part possesses the pre-requisites for use by consumers for a particular purpose i.e. ready for harvest.
- AICRP on Post Harvest Technology was started in 1978.
- Preservation of fruit and vegetables began in 18th century.

- Work on preservation in India started at Layalpur in 1934.
- Ministry of Food Processing was established in 1999.
- Central AGMARK Laboratory is located at Nagpur (Maharashtra).
- AGMARK is related with food quality.
- Bureau of Indian Standards (BIS) earlier Indian Standards Institution (ISI), was National Standard Body of *India* established under the BIS Act 2016. It was established during 23rd December, 1986 under Ministry of Consumer Affairs.
- Operation Green: Project approved by the Ministry of Food Processing Industries launched in 2018 with the target to stabilize the supply of tomato, onion and potato crops in India, as well as to ensure their availability around the country, year-round without price volatility. It is implemented to promote farmer producers' organization, agri-logistics, processing facilities and professional management.
- 1st fruit product research laboratory in India: Kodour.
- 1st fruit and vegetable processing industry in India: Mumbai (1935).
- 1st Fruit Preservation and Canning Institute: Lucknow (1949).
- 1st example of use of bio-agent for controlling post harvest diseases: *Bacillus subtillis*.
- 1st commercial flexible film: Cellophane.
- Retortable pouches can replace canning and hermitically sealed glass jars.
- Machine harvesters are used for grape, raspberry, cranberry, blackberry and strawberry.
- 1st fruit harvested by machine: Cranberry.
- Machine harvested potatoes show slow decrease in defects due to bruising.
- 1st 'British Patent' on canning of foods in tin container was received by Peter Durand in 1810.
- Only pathogen penetrating fruit skin: *Colletotrichum* spp.
- Hydrochloric acid is used for removing the residues of Arsenic (As) and Lead (Pb) from the fruits.
- King of acids: Sulphuric acid.
- Country having minimum quarantine restrictions for Indian fresh produce: Iran.
- Refractometer: Sugar content of ripe fruits is measured using hydrometer/ refractometer. It is calibrated in balling or brix scale and read directly in percent sugar/ weight (gram sugar per 100 gram of solution).
- Hydrometer test: It measures specific gravity (weight per unit volume as compared with pure water).
- Term 'brix hydrometer' is used to designate the instrument and degree brix is used for values.
- The percent soluble solids and refractometer reading is the same values as degree brix.

- Principle of hand refractometer: Refraction of light.
- Refractometer sugar test: Refractometer measures the refractive index of a solution (light bending property as compared with pure water).
- Refractive index of a sucrose solution is an accurate measure of concentration of dissolved substances. This instrument also measures TSS as percent sugar from fruits and extracted juices.
- Most brix hydrometers are standardized at 20^{0}C.
- Hydrolase enzymes: Amylase, cellulose, protease and pectinase.
- Sweetness of fruit: Due to increase á-amylase activity.
- Immobilized enzymes: Enzymes that are localized in some part of space with retention of their activity and used repeatedly and continuously.
- Shaffer micro method: Estimation of sugar.
- Salometer: Measurement of salt concentration (^{0}SAL).
- Penetrometer: Measurement of fruit firmness (psi).
- Succulometer: Measures maturity/ moisture / juice content (12-22%) of sweet corn.
- Nature's acidulant: Citric acid.
- Ultrafiltration is also called as cold process.
- B.V.O.: Brominated Vegetable Oil.
- PEM: Protein Energy Malnutrition.
- NAFPP: National Associations of Fresh Produce Processors.
- TASTE: Thermally Accelerated Short Time Evaporation.
- ERH: Relative humidity at which product neither gains nor loses the moisture.
- D value: At which 90% microorganisms are killed.
- F value: Combination of time and temperature.
- Danger point: Point which is 5% lower R.H. than critical point.
- Extinction point: Oxygen concentration at which anaerobic respiration commence.
- Thermal Death Time (TDT): Time required at a given temperature to kill a stated number of organisms under specific conditions.
- Respiratory Quotient (R.Q.)= Ratio of CO_2 evolved to O_2 consumed.
- Harvest Watch Technology: Based on principle of respiratory quotient.
- Respiration rate: Major indicator of potential storage life of fruits and vegetables.
- Maillard reaction in fruit products is non-enzymatic.
- Sensory evaluation is done by texture, taste, size, colour, etc.
- Aroma, taste and feel leads to flavour.
- Hedonic scale: Used to determine sensory quality.
- 9-point Hedonic scale: Most widely used sensory scale in the world.

- Complete inhibition of microorganism: CO_2 @ 46 g/ litre.
- Brine flotation technique is used for 'garden pea and beans'.
- Ionomer: New family of thermoplastics & introduced as 'surlyn'.
- Polyethylene: Largest thermoplastic single film used in packaging industry.
- Amylase film (Ediflex film): Sold by American Maize products. It is edible and made from corn starch.
- Extrusion: Size enlargement process in food processing.
- Sulphuring (sulphur burning for 60-70 min.): Done to prevent discolouration.
- Ethylene concentration suitable for climacteric fruits: 0.1 to 1.0 ml/ lit.
- Anthocyanins (flavins) change its colour with soil pH.
- Deaeration in orange juice: Done to prevent destruction of vitamin C.
- Word 'Umami' is derived from Japanese language meaning 'pleasant savory taste'.
- Umami refers to the taste of 'monosodium glutamate' i.e. glutamic acid.
- Foods that have strong umami flavour include meats, shellfish, fish, tomatoes, mushrooms, hydrolyzed vegetable protein, cheeses, meat extract and soy sauce.
- Major organic acid used in respiration: Malic acid.
- Coeliac disease: Consumption of gluten enriched foods.
- Characteristic of palmitic acid: Waxy flavour.
- Oxidation of fats in potato chips is prevented by N_2 gas packaging.
- Barium chloride: Salt having sweet taste while NaCl have salty taste.
- To get rid of minute particles and colloidal particles, fruit juices are clarified by boiling e.g. pomegranate.
- Most reliable maturity index for several fruits: Soluble solid concentration.
- Appearance of visible shrinkage of freshly harvested fruits and vegetables: Moisture loss around 10-15%.
- Term 'pH' was coined by Sorensen.
- pH stands for Potential of hydrogen ion.
- Dividing line of pH between acidic and non-acidic food= 3.5 pH.
- Specific gravity indicates physiological maturity.
- Specific gravity is useful in judging maturity of guava, cherry, mango, ber, and in potato it is used in measurement of quality.
- Specific gravity = Weight/ volume x 100.
- As fruit matures, specific gravity increases (> 1.0).
- Fruits that float in water (floaters) have lower TSS, low specific gravity and hence immature while fruits that sink in water (sinkers) have high TSS.
- Main microbiological hazard in unpasteurized citrus juice: *E. coli* & Salmonella.

- Compounds responsible for bitterness of citrus juice: Flavonoids and Limonoids.
- Four limonoids namely, limonin, nomilin, ichangin and nomolinic acid are bitter in taste.
- Commercially accepted technology for debittering of citrus juices: Use of immobilized enzymes.
- Instrument used to measure consistency of mango juice: Brookfield viscometer.
- Oxidation product of ascorbic acid: á-ketoglutonic acid.
- Fixation of green colour in vegetables through 'veri-green' process involves use of copper salts.
- Polyphenol oxidase (PPO) is inactivated by heat at 83-98^0 C.
- The most appropriate PPO substrate: Quercetin.
- Quality of tomato puree is dependent on tomato solids, lycopene content and inactivation of PPO.
- Economic threshold level of ethylene in fruits and vegetables: 0.01 µl or 0.1 ppm.
- Ethylene in cold storage can be removed by UV light, ventilation and low pressure.
- Citric acid is commercially produced by *Aspergillus niger*.
- Indicator used for estimation of acidity: Phenolphthalein ($C_{20}H_{14}O_4$).
- Indicator used for estimation of total sugar: Methylene Blue ($C_{16}H_{18}CIN_3S$).
- Mycobacterium is used to absorb ethylene from storage chamber.
- Softening of fruits occurs due to breakdown of pectic substances.
- Case-hardening of dried fruits and vegetables is prevented by increasing the R.H.
- The density that distinguishes HDPE from LDPE is 0.94.
- $CaCl_2$ is used in water to raise temperature up to 121.1^{0}C.
- Equilibrium R.H. of saturated salt solution of potassium sulphate is 97%.
- Permissible limit of tin content in processed food: 2 ppm.
- Senescence: Last stage of fruit development.
- Red colour of grapefruit juice is due to lycopene.
- Chemical used for NaOH standardization during acidity estimation: Potassium thalate.
- The term 'Carry Over' applies to priming and foaming.
- Soy protein: Foaming agent.
- 'Brimstone' i.e. burning stone; stands for Sulphur.
- Kidd (1934) attributed sudden rise in respiration of few fruits during ripening due to presence of activated fructose in cytoplasm.
- Hardness of water can be removed by caustic soda and sodium carbonate.
- Boiler feed water should have hardness below 0.2 ppm.
- More oxygen will be absorbed by water when it is impure.

- Mohr titration method is used for estimation of salt.
- Texture measurement equipment for vegetables are 'General Food Texturometers and Universal Testing Machines'.
- Response Surface Methodology (RSM) is a kind of effective method to optimize process conditions, and it can determine the influence of various factors and their interactions on the indexes under investigation during technological operation.
- Fruit powders are prepared from apples, plums, chocoberries, cranberries, mango, banana, etc.
- In laser printing, no ink or glue is used and printed part is edible. There is no adverse effect on fruit taste or storage capacity.
- Use of plastic stickers (food label stickers) can be avoided with use of laser technique.
- Laser print labeling is possible on fruits and vegetables (avocado, watermelon, cucumber, potato).
- Pathogenic growth of most fungi is completely stopped at 0^0C.
- Dicloran: Fungicide effective to control *Rhizopus stolonifer* in stone fruits.
- Sulphur dioxide: Used to fumigate grape to check *Botrytis cinerea*.
- Benomyl and Carbendazim is used to control molds in citrus, stem-end rot and brown rot in stone fruits, lenticel rot in apples, anthracnose in banana, papaya and mango and black rot in pineapple.
- Essential oils from *Melaleuca leucadendron*, *Ocimum* spp., *Citrus medica* protect from *Aspergillus flavus*.
- Plant extracts of eucalyptus, pomegranate, *Lawsonia inermis*, datura are effective in controlling fruit rots.
- Banana puree in aseptic drums is demanded by dairy and baby food industry.
- Guava (yellowish white, pink) is demanded by dairy industry and multifruit drinks.
- Papaya pulp (25^0 Brix) is in demand in yoghurt and baby food.
- Beginning of food irradiation program in many countries including India was started in 1950.
- Commercial application of irradiation in fruits in India was started in the year 2000.
- Irradiation cost may range from Rs. 0.25 to 0.50 /kg for low dose application such as sprout inhibition of potato, onion and insect disinfection in cereals and pulses to Rs. 1-3 /kg for high dose application such as treatment of spices for microbial decontamination.
- The cost of phytosanitary treatments like hot water, vapour treatment and cold treatment is 2-10 times higher than irradiation.
- 'Aspire', a bio-product used for control of post harvest diseases contains *Candida oleophila*.
- Punnet packing is practiced for cherry, apple, pear, grapes, kiwi fruit, strawberry.

- Frozen dessert contains edible vegetable oil.
- Arka herbiwash: Formulation developed by IIHR, Bengaluru to remove residue of insecticides from fruits and vegetables. It removes residue up to 80-100%.
- Price look-up (PLU) code: Denote method of production viz. organic way/ genetically modified/ conventional method. Non-organic produce is randomly assigned four-digit PLU codes in the 3000 and 4000 series. Organic produce may be designated by prefixing the four-digit, non-organic PLU with a "9". E.g. non-organic bananas are 4011, while organic bananas are 94011.
- Non GMO certification from exporting countries will be compulsory from August, 2020 while importing items in India viz. Soybean seeds & oil, maize products like flakes, French bean & saffron.
- West Bengal celebrated the 'Rosogolla Dibas' or Rasgulla Day on 14 November 2019 to mark the granting of Geographical Indication (GI) tag of 'Banglar Rosogolla' or Bengal's Rasgulla.
- Kisan Mitra OP-01 instrument has been innovated by Dr. O.P. Kulkarni which detects storage rots and losses in different fruits (mango) & vegetable crops (onion, potato).

2. INVENTIONS AND DISCOVERIES:

- Needham (1749) 1st time explained cause of spoilage of stored food.
- Clearance Birdseye (1937): Father of frozen food industry (vegetable freezing). He developed refrigerator in 1930.
- Saddington: 1st to describe canning method (1807).
- Nicolas Appert: He was a French inventor of airtight food preservation. He was known as 'father of canning' was a confectioner. He wrote a book entitled 'The Art of Preserving All Kinds of Animal and Vegetable Substances for Several Years'
- Canning of fruits introduced in USA on commercial scale by William Underwood (1817).
- Fruit and vegetable processing was 1st started in organized manner in 1857.
- Canning of fruits and vegetables started in 1927. It is also known as appertizing.
- Papain (1861): Cooling of food by means of pressure.
- A.L. Shriver: Discovered pressure cooker.
- Louis Pasteur (1864): Pasteurization.
- Dr. W.B. McGlasson: Mechanism of ethylene action in fruits through system I and II.
- K. Ikeda (1909): Flavour enhancing property of Monosodium glutamate.
- Peter Durand: Metal container (1800).
- Augustus de Heine: Iron container (1800).

- Cameron and Esty: Classified fruits and vegetables according to their pH.
- Esty and Meyor: 12 D concept (1922).
- Farrow and Green: 5 groups of lacquering (1941)
- Gore: Concentrates from fruit juices by freezing (1914).
- James Harrison: Father of modern refrigeration (1857).
- Martin: Aseptic canning (1950).

3. FOOD LAWS:

- Agricultural Produce Act is also known as AGMARK act.
- AGMARK (Grading and Marketing) Act: 1937
- Central Food Advisory Board: 1937.
- Central Committee for Food Standards: 1941.
- Food and Agriculture Organization (FAO): 1945.
- International Standards Organization (ISO): 1945.It is related with food safety management.
- Head quarter of ISO is situated at Geneva.
- Vegetable Oil Products Order: 1947.
- Indian Standard Institute (ISI): 1951.
- Essential Commodity Act: 1954.
- Integrated Food Safety & Standard Bill: 2005.
- Prevention of Food Adulteration (PFA) Act: 1954.
- FPO (Fruit Products Order) was passed by Government of India in 1955.
- Licensing authority of FPO: Govt. of India (Ministry of Food Processing Engineering).
- Food Safety and Standards Act: 2006.
- Export (Quality control and Inspection) Act: 1963.
- Export (Quality control and inspection) Rules: 1964.
- Cold Storage Order: 1964.
- The Consumer Protection Act: 1986.
- Food Safety and Quality Control Act: 2001. It is issued by MOFPI.
- Food Safety and Standards Authority of India (FSSAI) Act: 2005.
- The modern concept of quality management flows through GMP to HACCP to ISO to TQM.
- HACCP: Hazard Analysis Critical Control Point. This system is 1st introduced in USA (1971) by Pilsburry Company to supply food to NASA.
- Basic principle of HACCP: Doing only what is needed.

- HACCP concept is developed in 1960 to ensure safety of food products. It is a part of CAC/FDA quality control standard.
- 3rd principle of HACCP: Establishment of Critical Control Point.
- National Centre for HACCP certification: Thiruvananthapuram.
- There are 7 principles for HACCP.
- CODEX is the common name for the Codex Alimentarius Commission (CAC).
- CAC was cleared by FAO and WHO in 1963.
- Currently, 183 countries are members of codex and one member organization, the European union.
- CODEX alimentarius is food code which speaks about 12 steps for achieve hygiene.
- Food Safety and Standard Authority of India (FSSAI) is the National Codex Contact Point of India. It belongs to Ministry of Health and Family Welfare. It does not provide license to alcoholic beverages.
- FSSAI: Statutory body related to food safety and regulation, protecting and promoting public health through the regulation and supervision of food safety in India.
- FSSAI notifies standards for honey and its products to curb adulteration. It will help farmers to fetch better prices for their products.
- Mandate: To develop food standards, guidelines, recommendations and codes of practices with objective of protecting health of consumers and ensuring fair practices in food trade.
- EUREPGAP: Euro Retailer Produce Working Group (1977). Certification required for fresh fruits and vegetables to sell in European market. Emphasize on following of practices during production of horticultural produce.

4. CONTAINERS AND PACKING:

- Alcoholic containers are packed only in PVC.
- Black steel plate: Non-acid foods.
- Edible packaging: Acetylated monoglyceride and amylopectin product.
- EVA is used as additive for waxes.
- Frozen foods are packed in polycarbonate.
- GPPS: General Purpose Poly Styrene.
- HIPS: High Impact Poly Styrene.
- Nylons are known as polyamides.
- Opaque materials are barrier to light.
- Open mesh bags are mostly used for vegetables.
- Polysterene: Tubes of ice cream, jam bottles.
- PVC: Soft drinks, vinegar bottles.

- Self heating can contain Calcium silicate and Fe_2O_3 or Fe_3O_4 produce 50^0C for 4-5 minutes used by defence forces.
- Shellac laminated plastics are used for dried products.
- String opening composite container: Baby food, confectionary powder.
- Tin thickness: Steel plate of low carbon content, highly coated inner side of tin metal have thickness of 0.00025 cm or 2.5 μm; tin weight: 0.681 kg.
- Type L container: Low metalloid for corrosive foods.
- Type M container: Similar to MC but not rolled.
- Type MC container: Rephosphorised steel to give high temper.
- Type MR container: Similar to L. Less restricted in residual.
- A typical 'Tetrapak' has 4 layers comprising of polyethylene and aluminium layers.
- Packaging provides 3 basic functions: Preservation, protection, presentation.

Packaging containers	Products packed
A. **Glass bottles**	Beverages (RTS, squash, syrup, cordial, wine, cider, vinegar), jam, jelly, chutney, etc.
B. **Glass jar**	Preserve pickles
C. **Cans**	
i) Plain can	Canned products of mango, guava, litchi, apricot, banana, papaya
ii) AR lacqured can (R-enamel)	Canned products of strawberry, plum, coloured acidic products grapes
iii) SR lacqured can (C- enamel) non-acidic product	Canned products of pea, asparagus, beans, mushrooms
iv) Midget can (picnic pack)	Mango juice, coconut water
D. **Plastic packing**	
i) Pouches (made of laminates & multi-layer film)	Fruit juice concentrates, fruit juice based beverages, wine & country liquor
ii) Metalized laminates	Dry fruits (pecan nuts, cashew nuts)
iii) Polyethylene bag	Frozen fruits & vegetables
iv) Thermo formed cups & tubes	Jelly, portion packs of pickles, chutney, ketchups, jams
v) Tetra packs	Non carbonated beverages
vi) Stretched blow moulded bottle of PET & PVC	Beverages, alcoholic beverages (wine, cider, vinegar) & ketchup
vii) Printed wrappers of laminates	Fruit bar & cheese

5. POST HARVEST MANAGEMENT OF HORTICULTURAL CROPS:

- Ascorbic acid (100 g) for retention of colour, flavour and carotene.
- TSS of mango puree: 30^0Brix.
- Preservative used in squash preparation: Sirka (potassium meta-bi-sulphite i.e. KMS).
- Concentration of chlorine in washing solution of vegetables: 100-150 ppm.
- pH of washing solution: 6.5-7.5.

- Temperature of all enzymes losing their activity: e" 80^{0}C.
- Heat application checks both microbial and enzyme spoilage.
- Sealing temperature: Not less than74^{0}C.
- Caramelization: Decomposition of sugar at high temperature (melting point) forming a brown mass.
- Enzymatic browning is due to polyphenol oxidase, phenolase, pectic methyl esterase.
- 30 % fruits decay due to *Penicillium* spp.

5.1. Post-harvest losses:

- Total post harvest losses in fruits and vegetables: 20-40 %.
  a) Mechanical losses- bruising, cracking and cuts.
  b) Microbial losses- fungi and bacteria.
  c) Physiological losses- changes in respiration, transpiration, pigments, organic acid & flavour.

Nature of losses:

1. Loss in weight due to transpiration of water.
2. Shrinking and wilting.
3. Change in colour due to high temperature and drying e.g. litchi become brown, spinach and lettuce become pale yellow, white head of cauliflower become yellow.
4. Change in texture e.g. softness in tomato
5. Change in taste e.g. flat sour and unpleasant odour in fruits e.g. potato at low temperature become sweet.
6. Bruising
7. Sprouting
8. Toughening
9. Greening e.g. Potato and Sweet potato exposed to light- Solanin development is toxin.
10) Rotting- Mostly by fungi.

Biochemical changes during ripening:

- Rate of respiration and metabolic activities increase 2-3 folds for every 10^{0}C rise in temperature.
- Respiration causes loss of sugars, flavour compounds and produces heat known as 'vital heat'.
- Usually organic acids are converted into sugars.
- During senescence, level of free amino acids increases and decrease metabolic activity (except banana and pineapple where acidity increases during ripening).

- Phenols in fruits give astringent taste.
- Phenolics such as tannins are polymerized to insoluble compounds resulting in reduction of astringency in ripe banana fruit.
- Sensitive to ethylene: Apples, pears, tomato, muskmelons.
- Critical temperature for sugar accumulation: 10^0C for potato and 15^0C for sweet potato.
- Activity of enzymes in fruit, vegetables and ornamentals decline at 30^0C.

5.1.1.Pre-harvest factors to reduce losses:

1. Cultural operations-
    - Pruning or thinning increases fruit size while decreases TSS and acidity.
2. Pre-harvest treatment-
    - Pre-harvest treatment of maleic hydrazide (MH) @ 1500-2000 ppm, after 75-90 days of transplanting reduces sprouting of onion, carrot, garlic and potato during storage in ventilated structures.
    - Pre-harvest spray of MH @ 500 ppm, 15 days before harvest of bulbs will prevent sprouting of onion bulb in storage and keep the bulbs healthy for about 6-7 months.
    - Pre-harvest spray of 0.2% Difolatan control post harvest diseases of tomato and onion.
    - Pre-harvest spray of N-Benzyladenine (BA) @ 10-20 ppm prolongs shelf life of vegetables.

5.1.2. Post-harvest factors:

5.1.2.1. Degreening:

- It is applicable to Banana, Mango, Citrus, Tomato.
- Most widely used growth regulator: Ethrel.
- Done to increase aesthetic value of fruits.
- Low concentration of ethylene (20-50ppm) is applied.
- Best degreening temperature: 27^0C and R.H. is 85-90%.
- CO_2 level below 1% does not allow higher colouring.

5.1.2.2. Pre-cooling:

- Rate of cooling is often expressed as either the cooling coefficient (C) or half of the cooling time, which is time required to reduce the temperature difference between produce and cooling medium by one-half.
- Rapid removal of field heat before shipment or storage from freshly harvested produce and is done within 2-4 hours.

- Conduction and convection are the two main heat-transfer mechanisms used for cooling produce.
- In precooling mostly water are removed by conduction.
- For tropical and sub-tropical fruits precooling at 10-13^{0}C is adequate.
- Berries, peaches, plums, grapes, early apples, mature peas are precooled to 5^{0}C.
- Peas and okra which deteriorate fast, needs prompt cooling.
- Most common precooling technique: Room cooling for produce in boxes, cartons, bulk containers and other packages.
- In hydrocooling, ice-cold water is the heat transfer medium.
- Hydrocooling: Rapid cooling method. It is used for root, stem and flower type vegetables, melons and some tree fruits.
- Hydrocooling at 12-15^{0}C with 500 ppm Carbendazim increase shelf life of mango.
- Forced air cooling: Commonly used for fruits (grapes, berries, tomatoes), many leafy vegetables, watermelons and cut flowers.
- Package icing used for root and stem vegetables, Broccoli and Brussels sprouts.
- Vacuum cooling: Best modern method of precooling for leafy vegetables, celery, cauliflower.
- Hydro-vacuum cooling process is called as 'hydrovac' cooling.
- Vacuum and water spray vacuum cooling are usually reserved for leafy vegetables.

5.1.2.3. Curing:

- It is an essential part of tuber and bulb crops to strengthen the skin.
- Tuber and bulb crops exposed to high temperature and high R.H. at farm level, cause suberization of outer tissue followed by development of wound periderm.
- Done in onion, garlic, potato, sweet potato, cassava, colocasia, yam, turmeric, ginger, spices, etc.

5.1.2.4. Disinfection:

- Papaya, Mango. Melons are susceptible to fruit fly attacks.
- Disinfection is done either by vapour heat treatment (VHT) at 48^{0}C or by ethylene di-bromide fumigation (18-22 g/m^3).
- Chlorine (free chlorine) concentration of 200 ppm is generally used in hydrocoolers.
- Chlorine compounds are most popular sanitizers and have many advantages except stability in presence of hard water salts.

5.1.2.5. Waxing:

- Term 'wax' is derived from Anglo-Saxon word '*weax*' which was used to describe the material present in honeycomb of bees.
- Wax is lipid i.e. polysaccharides.

- Cuticular waxes are isolated by immersion or washing tissues with hexane or chloroform.
- Wax was 1st coating used on citrus fruits especially on oranges and lemons during 12th or 13th century in China.
- During 1930, hot-melt paraffin was commercially available.
- Waxing reduces transpiration.
- Waxing can be done by foaming, brushing and dipping.
- Natural wax on the fruit surface is called as 'bloom'.
- Application of fungicides/ growth substance along with edible wax e.g. apple, pomegranate.
- Waxing reduce moisture loss (transpiration), improve appearance, minimize physiological weight loss and incidence of storage diseases.
- Storage wax: When horticultural produce not to be marketed immediately.
- Pack-out wax: When horticultural produce are to be marketed immediately.
- High-shine wax: For giving a very high grace on market demand.
- Thickness of edible coating applied to fruit: < 0.3 mm.
- Particle film technology (PFT):
- Commercially available PFs: Surround, Raynoux, Eclipse, Cocoon, Parasol, Antistress-500, Purshade, Screen, processed particle film technology.
- Bio-degradable fruit covers are used litchi, pomegranate.
- Using wax emulsion, it is possible to store mangoes for 2 ½ months at 5-8^{0}C.
- Bio-coating of cassava starch is suitable for extending shelf life of mango and guava.

***Trade names of extensively used waxes*:**

- Frutox: Emulsion of different waxes with 12% solids.
- Waxol (3%) is more efficient in retaining freshness of fruit than Tal Prolong (1-1.5%).
- Waxol-O-12: Oil emulsion wax containing 12% solids. Impart gloss to fruits.
- Waxol-W-12: Water emulsion was containing 12% solids. Does not impart gloss to fruits.
- Tal-Prolong.
- Semper-fresh.
- Fruit and vegetable kleen.
- Decco Luter.
- Chitosan: Bee wax and nitrogen containing edible film recommended for strawberry.

5.1.2.6. Ripening:

- Calcium carbide (CaC_2): Synthetic ripening & releases acetylene gas. It is carcinogenic.
- Cheap source of ripening: CaC_2.
- Cycocel (500 ml/ litre), Alar, GA, Menadione sulphur retard ripening.
- Purafil (Alkaline $KMnO_4$): Ethylene absorber or scavenger or scrubber (banana held in sealed polyethylene bags).
- Concentration of CO_2>1% delay ripening,
- Fruitox (Fungicide with waxo (0.3%) and Tat prolong (1-1.5%) retard ripening in mango.
- Ethylene inhibitor: Silver thiosulphate (STS), Silver nitrate ($AgNO_3$), 1-MCP (1-Methylcyclo propane).
- 1-MCP is a non-toxic gaseous compound having antagonistic impact on ethylene production.
- Use of 1-MCP is standardized in apple, kiwi fruit and plum.
- Foliar sprays of IPC (Isopropyl-N-phenyl carbamate) reduces respiration rate, ripening and spoilage of sapota during storage.
- Chemicals like 2,4-D, 2,4,5-T enhances storage life of Coorg mandarin oranges.

5.1.2.7. Packaging:

- Preston (1967), Heiss (1971) and Taylor (1966) gave information on packaging of foods in containers.
- Individual seal shrink wrapping technique is Modified Atmospheric packaging (MAP) for individual fruit.
- MAP is effective to prevent the built up of CO_2 and acetylene.
- Wrapping: Covering fruits after harvest with any material to improve its post harvest life e.g. Tissue paper, waxed paper, plio film, cellophane paper, aluminium foils and alkathene paper.
- Packaging film used for better MAP: Polypropylene.
- Opaque package should be used for potatoes for delaying greening.
- Vacuum packaging: Removal of air within the package without deliberate replacement with another gas e.g. Guava.
- Vacuum packaging is a simple method than other method.
- Seal/ shrink packing: Apple, pear, kiwifruit, citrus and pomegranate.
- Shrink wrapping technology developed by IARI to enhance shelf life of pomegranate by 20 days.
- Thickness of heat shrinkable plastic film: 9 µ.

- Citrus fruits can be preserved for few weeks as room temperature by wrapping individual fruit in HDP envelops.
- Packing of mushrooms: Polyethylene (PE) and polypropylene (PP) bags of 100 gauge.
- PE and PP bags: Used for minimally processed products.
- Polyvinylchloride (PVC): Used for overwrapping.
- Environment friendly packaging material containers: Sal leaves (*Shorea robusta*) and arecanut leaf sheath.
- Palletization: Term used to refer packaging fruits/ vegetables boxes in huge containers at airport/ sea port before shipment.
- Loading and unloading are done manually in India. Due to low unit load, there is tendency to throw, drop or mishandle the package, damaging the commodity. This loss can be considerably reduced by using pallet system.
- Commonly used cushioning material: Paddy straw, Banana leaves, dry grass, wheat straw.
- Use of CFB boxes in mango and other fruit crops is becoming popular.

5.1.2.8. Ethylene absorbents:

- Brominated activated carbon, Celite with $KMnO_4$ proved effective as ethylene absorbents and prolongs shelf life of tomato and grapes.

5.1.2.9. Anti-transpirants:

- Stomata closing anti-transpirants: Phenyl mercuric acetate (PMA), ABA, Atrazine.
- Reflective type anti-transpirants: Kaoline, $ZnSO_4$.
- Kaoline, Mobileaf is beneficial to leafy vegetables to check transpiration loss.

5.1.2.10. Transportation:

- For highly perishable commodity, there should be minimum temperature rise during transit.

5.1.2.11. Storage:

- For perishable commodities, the relative humidity (R.H.) inside the cold room should be maintained at 90-95%.
- To store fruits and vegetables, low temperature and high humidity (90-95%) are required except in onion and garlic which require low R.H. (70-75%)
- 90% capacity of cold store is being utilized for storage of potato including seed potato.
- Among fruits, mainly apples are kept in cold storage.
- Normally storage temperature should be 0 to 1.1^0C for most of the temperature fruits.

- Maximum temperature inside cool chamber is 2-8^{0}C.
- Methyl bromide: Fumigant used to control pests of post harvest storage.

Physical and biochemical changes during storage:

Parameters	Different changes in storage
A) Physical	
Weight loss	Increased loss of moisture due to transpiration
Shriveling	Increases even 5% of loss of wt. results in shriveling.
Firmness	Firmness of fruit is due to calcium pectate. Breakdown of substance reduces firmness and causes softness in fruits and vegetables.
Colour	Colour development takes place in mango, banana, papaya, limes & lemons take place. While discolouration in litchi, grape, strawberry occurs
Flavour	In the beginning of storage, flavour development in peach, pineapple, pear & guava and long storage results acidic flavour in many fruits
B) Biochemical	
Hormone	Level of ethylene increases in climacteric fruits. Excess of ethylene stimulates softening and pathological disorders in many fruits and vegetables. ABA increase in pear fruits and stimulates ripening in storage
Respiration	Increased level of ethylene during storage increases rate of respiration which leads to breakdown of glucose and other organic compounds
Sugar	In beginning of storage it increases then decreases. In table variety of potato it increases
Pigment	Chlorophyll and anthocyanin decreases and carotenoid increases
Pectic substances	Increase in pectic acid & decrease in protopectin e.g. guava
Amino acids	Argenine, proline increase in grape but total amino acid decreases
Enzymes	An increased level of amylase, pectin esterase, malic enzyme, catalase, peroxidase & polyphenol oxidase
Lipids	Palmitic acid & palmitoleic increase and linoleic acid decrease in avocado fruits
Volatile compounds	Ethylene, esters, aldehyde, ketone increase & cause harmful effects
Phenolic compounds	Tannins, flavons & total phenols decrease
Vitamins	Ascorbic acid decrease and beta carotene increase

5.1.2.11.1 Low cost cold storage technology:

- Evaporative cooling is nature's very own method (i.e. require no energy).
- Zero Energy Cool Chamber (ZECC): Based on principle of evaporative cooling system. It was developed by Dr. S.K. Roy and Dr. S.R. Khurdiya at IARI.
- Cool chamber can reduce temperature by 17-18^{0}C & maintains R.H. 95% during peak summer months when atmospheric humidity falls below 20%.
- In winter months, average maximum temperature of cool chamber remains 5^{0}C less than ambient temperature.
- ZECC is ideal for short term storage of fresh fruits and vegetables.
- Night ventilation (air cool storage): Widely used storage structure in high hill region.
- ZECC can be constructed in remote villages.

- Recently, 5 metric tons capacity with ducts for recirculation of cool air has been successful for bulk storage of potato and Kinnow fruits.
- Ventilated storage structure for onion and garlic.
- Based on principles of evaporative cooling, low cost solar energy input cool chamber called 'Pusa Farm Sunfreezer' has been developed by IARI, New Delhi (Chopra and Singh, 2021).
- **Features of sunfreezer:**
  - This is ideal for short term storage (15 days) of all sorts of fruits and vegetables up to 2 tonnes capacity.
  - It is possible to shift this sunfreezer from one place to another place.
  - It can be erected on farm lands.
  - This structure (3x3x3 m size) can maintain internal temperature of 8-10^{0}C during day time and 12-15^{0}C during night hours and high humidity 95% throughout day.
  - This structure has been made from RCC base, nylon fabrics walls, Styrofoam panels, 5 solar panels (produce 5 KW energy), modified minisplit inverter air conditioner unit and heat exchanger drum (120 lit capacity).
  - Once these low cost sunfreezers are set up by small farmers, they can build up few day's stock before dispatching to wholesale market.

5.1.2.11.2 High cost cold storage technology:

- Widely used refrigerants in cold/ refrigerated storage: Freon, ammonia and methyl chloride.
- Commonly used refrigerant in India: Ammonia.
- Freon is most popular, odourless and non-toxic.
- Controlled atmosphere storage.
- Modified atmosphere storage.
- Low pressure storage / hypobaric storage.

Recommended temperature and R.H. conditions under cold storage:

Name of commodity	Temperature (^{0}C)	Relative humidity (%)	Approximate storage life
Fruits			
Apple	-1 to -4	90-95	4-8 months
Apricot	-0.5 to 0.0	85-90	1-2 weeks
Banana	13-15	85-90	2-3 weeks
Black currant	0.5 to 0	90-95	21-28 days
Black sapote	10	85	29 days
Blueberry	0.0	90-95	21-28 days
Fig	0	90	1 week

Grape	-0.5-0	90-95	3-6 weeks
Guava	6-8	90-95	2-3 weeks
Kiwi fruit	-0.5 to 0.0	90-95	3-5 weeks
Litchi	1-2	90-95	3-5 weeks
Lemon	8.9 to 10.0	85-90	1-6 months
Limes	9 to 10	90	1-2 months
Mandarin (Kinnow)	4 to 5	90-95	2 months
Mango	13	85-90	2-4 weeks
Olive	7.2 to 10.0	85-90	4-6 weeks
Papaya	7.2	85-90	1-2 weeks
Peach	0.0 to 3.0	85-90	2-4 weeks
Pineapple	10 to 13	90	3-4 weeks
Pomegranate	5	90-95	2-3 months
Sapota	12.2	85-90	2-3 weeks
Strawberry	0	90-95	7-10 weeks
Vegetables			
Asparagus	0-2	95	2-4 weeks
Beans	4-7	90-95	7-10 days
Bitter gourd	10-12	85-90	2-3 weeks
Broccoli	0	95-100	10-14 days
Cabbage (head)	0	95-98	1-6 months
Cabbage (Chinese)	0	98-100	2-3 months
Lettuce	0	98-100	2-3 weeks
Summer squash	7-10	95	1-2 weeks
Winter squash	10-12	60	1-3 months
Sweet corn	0	95-98	5-8 days
Carrot	0	90-95	6-8 months
Celery	0	98-100	1-2 months
Cauliflower	0	90-95	3-4 weeks
Brinjal	10-12	90-95	1-2 weeks
Peas	0	90-95	1-2 weeks
Tomato (mature green)	10-13	90-95	1-3 weeks
Tomato (fully ripe)	8-10	90	2-3 weeks
Ginger	8.3-10	85-90	15 weeks
Knol khol	5-6	85-90	13 weeks
Potato	3 to 4.4 (seed) & 4 to 6 (vegetable)	85	34 weeks
Cucumber	10 to 13	90	1-2 weeks
Okra	8.9	90	2 weeks
Onion bulbs	0	70-75	20-24 weeks
Garlic	0	70-75	28-36 weeks
Sprouting broccoli	4	65	1-2 weeks

5.1.2.11.3 Controlled atmosphere (CA) storage:

- Systems where atmospheric control (concentration of CO_2 and O_2) is accurately controlled.
- Low O_2 and high CO_2 around fruit or by lowering the temperature.
- Best method of storage in which rate of respiration is reduced and ageing is delayed.
- Invented by Kidd and West.
- 1st suggested by W.R. Phillips.
- Started in England before World War II.
- Most fruits and vegetables tolerate O_2 levels down to 1-5% and CO_2 levels up to 5-10%.
- O_2 required for apple storage: 3%.
- Pre-wrapping of produce establishes CA package.
- Under CA storage, the acidity of the stored materials increases.
- No CA recommended for citrus fruits.

***Benefits of CA storage*:**

- Slow down respiration and ethylene production rates, softening and retard senescence of horticultural produce.
- Reduce fruit sensitivity to ethylene action.
- Alleviate certain physiological disorders such as chilling injury of various commodities, russet spotting in lettuce, and some storage disorders including, scald of apples.

***Harmful effects of CA storage*:**

- Initiation or aggravation of certain physiological disorders can occur, such as black heart in potatoes, brown stain on lettuce, and brown heart in apples and pears.
- Irregular ripening of fruits, such as banana, mango, pear and tomato, can result from exposure to O2 levels below 2% or CO2 levels above 5% for more than 2 to 4 weeks.
- Off- flavors and off-odours at very low O2 or very high CO2 concentration may develop as a result of anaerobic respiration and fermentative metabolism.

Recommended CA storage conditions for selected fruits and vegetables:

Commodity	Temperature (°C)	% O_2	% CO_2	Inference
Apple	0-5	1-2	0-3	-
Banana	14	2-5	2-5	Sensitive to reduced O_2 (<1%) & high CO_2 (>10%), MAP commercially for transportation
Grape fruit	10-15	3-10	5-10	Short term tolerant to reduced O_2 (1%) post harvest disinfestation

Lemon & lime	10-15	5-10	5-10	Minimize water loss & MAP commercial
Orange	0-5	5-10	5-10	Potential for MAP & reduce water loss
Guava	8-10	5-8	5	Sensitive to reduced CO_2 (<5%), retard chilling injury & fruit softening
Litchi	5-12	3-5	3-5	Reduced pericarp browning
Mango	10-15	3-5	5-8	Commercially used for transportation & potential for postharvest disinfestation
Pineapple	7.5-12	2-5	5-10	Reduced internal browning
Papaya	7-13	2-5	5-8	Not used commercially, reduce chilling injury
Pomegranate	5-10	3-5	5-10	Inhibit husk scald & chilling injury
Beans (green)	5-10	2-3	4-7	-
Broccoli	0-5	1-2	5-10	-
Cabbage	0-5	2-3	3-6	-
Onion	0-5	1-2	0-10	-
Tomato	10-15	3-5	3-5	-

5.1.2.11.4 Modified atmosphere (MA) storage:

- Modifying the composition of air in storage environment with less accuracy i.e. control of gas concentration is less precise.
- This technique utilizes polymeric films with selective permeability for CO_2, O_2 and water vapour.
- Recommended R.H. for storage of green, root and tuber vegetables to prolong storage life: 90-95%.
- Most commonly used O_2 absorber in MAS: Ferrous oxide (FeO): Iron powder.
- Most commonly used CO_2 absorbers: Hydrated lime, activated charcoal, magnesium oxide.
- Most commonly used C_2H_4 absorbers: Purafil (Alkaline $KMnO_4$), vermiculite, silica gel or alumina pellets, brominated activated carbon, activated earth, tetrazine film (pink colour turns brown when saturated with ethylene).
- Bio-degradable plastic: Laminate of polyhydroxy butyrate, chitoson-cellulose and polycaprolactone as a film for fresh produce e.g. lettuce, cabbage, cut broccoli, whole broccoli, tomatoes, sweet corn, blueberries.
- Edible films (LLDPE) and coatings: Polysaccharides, proteins, lipids e.g. Netfilm.
- Polymeric film: Semi-permeable film used as packing material.
- Uptake of O_2 by produce & evolution of CO_2, C_2H_4, H_2O & other volatiles and at same time, specific restricted permeation of these gases through packaging film.

5.1.2.11.5 Hypobaric (HB) storage:

- Also known as 'Reduced atmospheric storage or low pressure storage or vacuum storage or sub-atmospheric storage'.
- Very expensive method and used in case of high value commodities.
- Principle used-

- º Ethylene gas is removed from storage atmosphere and partial pressure of O_2 is lowered which leads to slow ripening to keep fruits for longer time.
- º Low O_2 reduces the respiration rate and low ethylene delays ripening e.g. cut flowers, mango, banana, pineapple, papaya, guava, apple, pear, avocado, lemon have better storage and transportation life.
- º Low pressure of O_2 (102 mm Hg) reduces growth of pathogens such as *Aspergillus niger*, *Rhizophus nigricans*, *Alternaria* and *Botrytis* spp.

- 1st described by Burg and Burg (1966).
- Fruits are held at 0.2 to 0.5 atmospheric pressure at 59 to 75ºF (15-24ºC) and humified air is passed through chamber to maintain humidity, to remove ethylene and other volatile compounds given off by fruits and vegetables.
- Storage of produce at low atmospheric pressure (200 mm Hg) under vacuum tight, refrigerated condition, continuous ventilation and high R.H.
- Modified CA storage: Use of sub-atmospheric pressure to store the horticultural produce.
- Hypobaric storage involves the cold storage of horticultural produce under partial vacuum.

Mobile cool chambers

- Thermal Management System i.e. an insulated box with TMS could be used.
- This box can hold 8 plastic creates in two layers each. About 100 kg vegetables or fruits can be transported.
- Pusa Mobile Vendor Cart: Developed by IARI to minimize post-harvest losses in horticultural crops.

Refrigerated van

- Precise control on temperature and relative humidity keep produce fresh for long time.

5.1.2.11.6 Use of ultra-high pressure:

- At pressure of 4000-9000 atmosphere enzymes and bacteria are inactivated but taste and flavor remain unaffected.
- It improves rheological and functional properties of food.
- It is environmental friendly causing less affluent problems.
- High pressure with 4000-9000 bars extends refrigerated produce shelf-life from 2-6 months at 4ºC.

5.1.2.11.7 Super critical extraction technology:

- It is an alternative method for new or improved applications in food processing.
- It is environmentally friendly green processing technique.

- Can replace traditional organic solvent based extraction technique like supercritical CO_2, ethanol and water.

5.2 Post harvest management of flower crops:

Important terms:

1. Pulsing/ loading:
   - Short term pre-shipment or pre-storage treatment.
   - Sucrose is main component.
   - It is given to cut flowers before packing and transportation.
   - Time for pulsing: 12-24 h under a light intensity of 1000 lux @ 20-27ºC.
   - Pulsing promote opening and increase in shelf life of flowers.
2. Bud opening solution:
   - It is procedure for harvesting flowers at storage earlier than normally coincided by cutting stage.
   - Low concentration of sucrose (2-5%).
   - 8-HQC, STS, KCl, Al_2SO_4, 4% sucrose are used for bud opening.
3. Holding/ vase solution:
   - Holding solution used in vases to keep flowers for extending their vase life.
   - Prepared by mixture of chemicals (sugar + germicide + growth regulator + organic acid + ethylene inhibitor).
   - Commonly used chemicals: Sucrose + citric acid + 8-HQC.
   - Use of preservative in form of tablets.
4. Conditioning/ hardening:
   - Flowers are kept standing loosely in big container, so that air can circulate around the stems.
   - Purpose: Restore turgidity of cut flower from water stress during storage and transportation.
   - Water + germicide + citric acid @ 500 ppm and pH: 4.5-5.0.
5. Impregnation:
   - Ends of cut flower stems are impregnated for short time with chemicals.
   - Prevent blockage of xylem vessels by microbial growth and stem decay.
   - Commonly used chemicals: $AgNO_3$, $NiCl_2$, $CoCl_2$ for 10-15 min.

5.2.1. Harvesting stages of flowers:

- Common symptom of chilling injury: Pitting and discoloration.

Flower	Stage of harvest
Alstroemeria	2 florets open
Anthurium	Spathe fully open & spadix 2/3rd mature
Antirrhinum	1/3rd florets open
Bird of paradise	First floret opens
Calendula	Fully open flowers
Carnation	Paint brush (1.25-2.5 cm) or 2-3 petals unfurl
China aster	Fully open flowers
Cattleya orchid	4-5 days after opening
Chrysanthemum	
* Standard	When outer florets expanded
* Spray	Flower open but before shedding of pollens
* Pompons & decorative	Centre of oldest flower fully open
* Anemones	Open but before central disc florets begin to elongate
Cymbidium orchid	3-4 days after opening of all flowers
Daffodil	Goose neck stage
Dahlia	Fully open flowers
Dendrobium orchid	Fully open flowers
Carnation	
* Standard	Paint brush stage
* Spray	At least 2 flowers fully open
Freesia	Coloured buds
Gerbera	Flowers open and when 2nd circle of disc florets shows pollen development
Gladiolus	Basal 1-3 florets show colour
Gypsophila	Flowers just open
Iris	Coloured buds
Jasmine	Buds fully developed but not opened
Lilium	Coloured buds
Narcissus	Goose neck stage
Rose	Tight bud stage or 1-2 petals unfurl
Statice	Heads start to open or calyces of individual flowers have opened and showing colour
Stock	One half or two third of florets opened or with minimum 6 open flowers
Tuberose	Lower buds fully open
Tulip	Half coloured buds
Zinnia	Fully open flowers

Particulars	Flowers
Highly sensitive to ethylene	Alstroemeria, Antirrhinum, Bird of paradise, Camellia, Carnation, Daffodil, Euphorbia, Freesia, Gardenia, Hibiscus, Lilium, Nerium, Petunia
Insensitive to ethylene	Anthurium, Asparagus, Aster, Chrysanthemum, Day lily, Delphinium, Gladiolus, Gerbera, Gypsophila, Iris, Orchids, Rose
Highly sensitive to chilling injury	Anthurium, Bird of paradise, *Vanda* and *Cattleya* orchids, Tulip
Less sensitive to chilling injury	Chrysanthemum, Gerbera, China aster
Highly susceptible to gray mold	Gladiolus, Bird of paradise
Highly sensitive to fluorides	Gladiolus, Freesia, Gerbera, Chrysanthemum, Rose
Sensitive to geotropic bending	Freesia, Snapdragon, Gladiolus

5.2.2. Grading, packing and transport:

- Flowers are generally packed in telescope type boxes made of corrugated fiberboard (CFB) boxes i.e. cardboard boxes.
- The quality board usually 4-5 ply boxes are used.
- New packaging system 'Procona' (Producer to Consumer in Aqua) uses plastic container and cardboard sleeves & allows transport of flowers in upright position.

Campanula:

Length (cm)	Blooms	Flowers/stem	Stems/bunch
60	≥ 3 open	≥ 8 total	10
50	≥ 2 open	≥ 8 total	10

Bells of Ireland:

Length (cm)	Inflorescence (%)	Stems/bunch
90	60	10
80	60	10
70	60	10
60	60	10

5.2.3. Storage techniques of flowers:

- Storage is not recommended: Dahlia, Pot marigold, Zinnia.
- Storage temperature for tropical flowers viz. Anthurium, *Cattleya*, Poinsettia: 10-15^{0}C.
- Storage temperature for sub-tropical flowers: Gladiolus, bird of paradise, anemone: 2-8^{0}C.
- Low oxygen is responsible for reducing rate of respiration & ethylene production.
- High CO_2 reduces or inhibits rate of enzymatic reactions & also reduces transpiration.
- CO_2 level higher than 4% cause injury to many flowers.
- O_2 level lower than 0.4% produce anaerobic conditions.
- 8-HQC: Phytotoxic to daffodil.
- Refrigerated storage is most widely used method for storage of cut flowers. It is of 2 types-
- Dry storage:
  - Flowers are sealed in plastic bags to prevent loss of moisture.
  - Used to hold flowers for longer duration.
  - Most flowers prone to freezing injury below -2^{0}C.

- Wet storage:
  - Flowers with their base kept in water or preservative solution.
  - Used to hold the flowers for short duration and for their day to day handling.
  - Temperature kept is 2-4^{0}C i.e. slightly higher than dry storage.

Storage	Crop	Storage temperature (^{0}C)	Maximum storage period
Dry	Carnation	0 to 1	16-24 weeks
	Chrysanthemum	1	3 weeks
	Gerbera	2	2 days
	Gladiolus	4	2-3 weeks
	Rose	0.5 to 2	2 weeks
Wet	Anthurium	13	2-4 weeks
	Antirrhinum	1	8 days
	Carnation	4	4 weeks
	Dendrobium	5 to 7	10-14 days
	Gerbera	4	3-4 weeks
	Gladiolus	0.5 to 1.6	10 days
	Tuberose	7 to 10	3-5 days
	Lilium	1	4 week
	Tulip	-0.5 to 0	2-3 days

- Sodium hypochlorite (Clorex): Common household bleach. Used for sterilization of greenhouse benches & tools.
- Floral preservative have two basic constituents: Sugar and biocide.
- Relative humidity of air during pre-cooling and shipment of cut flower: 95-98%.
- pH of vase water for cut flowers during shipment: 3.5-4.5.
- Optimum TSS in vase water for cut flowers: < 200 ppm.
- Sugar provides an additional food to cut flower.
- Most commonly used sugar in vase solution: Sucrose @ 0.5-2.0%.
- Most commonly used acidifying agent in vase solution: Citric acid.
- Bio-cide: Inhibit microbial growth in vase solution.
- Most commonly used bio-cide: Quinoline salts e.g. 8-Hydroxy quinoline citrate (8-HQC), 8-Hydroxy quinoline sulphate (8-HQS).
- Other biocides: $AgNO_3$ (50-100 ppm), Aluminium sulphate, Citric acid.
- 8-HQC: Broad spectrum biocide & partial closure of stomata.
- Anti-ethylene compounds: Salts of cobalt and nickel e.g. $CoCl_2$, $NiCl_2$.
- Presence of sodium ion in vase solution is detrimental for flowers.
- Flowers sensitive to geotropic bending must be transported in upright position e.g. Gladiolus.
- New promising fresh flower preservative: Amino-oxyacetic acid (AOA).

- Best preservative for cut flowers: Silver thiosulphate (STS).
- STS is not used to enhance flower longevity in rose.
- Boiling water treatment given to base of cut flowers for 30 sec.: Dahlia, Zinnia and Rose.
- Burning the base of cut flowers for 15 min.: Poinsettia and Nerium.
- IAA promotes petal senescence in carnation by enhancing ethylene production.
- Gibberellin (GA_3) helps in promoting bud opening in carnation.
- In cut rose, cv. Raktagandha, 25-100 Krad of gamma irradiation prolonged vase life.
- Important postharvest disease is due to humidity and temperature: Gray mold (*Botrytis cinerea*).
- Cut foliage is stored at 2-5^{0}C.
- Florissant 500 is a germicide i.e. bactericide.
- Major disadvantage of vacuum container transport of cut flower is reduced vase life i.e. yellowing of leaves.
- Slow release chlorine compounds: DICA, DDMH.
- Enzyme inhibitors: Sodium azide (NaN_2), 2,4-dinitrophenol (2,4-DNP), Cycloheximide.
- Cyclopropanes like 1-MCP & 1-OCP are highly effective for ethylene insensitive flowers.
- 1-MCP is marketed under brand name Smart Fresh™ and Ethyle Bock®.
- Polyamines like spermine, spermindine and puttresine enhance flower longevity in gladiolus influencing free radical metabolism i.e. by alleviation of anti-oxidant activities.
- Besides anti-oxidants like α-Lipoic acid, sodium benzoate, citriç acid also influences vase life of cut flowers.
- Ethylene exerts its effect by altering gene expression.
- Ethylene forming enzyme (EFE): ACC oxidase.
- Ethylene inhibitors: Nitric oxide, Aminoethoxy vinyl glycine (AVG), Methoxy vinyl glycine (MVG) @ 0.7-0.13 mM.
- Ethylene induces senescence of many flowers.
- Effects of ethylene:
  - Epinasty in poinsettia.
  - Abscission of petals or whole flowers.
  - Inhibition or promotion of bud opening in roses.

Modified atmosphere (MA) storage of flowers:

Flower	CO_2 (%)	O_2 (%)	Storage temperature (°C)	Storage period (days)
Carnation	5	1-3	0-1	30
Freesia	10	21	1-2	20-22
Gladiolus	5	1-3	1-5	21
Rose	5-10	1-3	0	20-30
Tulip	5	21	1	10
Lilium	10-20	21	1.0	10

6. HORTICULTURAL CROP RESIDUE AND PROCESSING WASTE FOR VALUE ADDED PRODUCTS

- During processing of fruits/vegetables large quantity of waste material is left over e.g. peels, corings, pomace, seeds, stones, rind, etc.
- These wastes varies from 10-25% in leafy vegetables, 28% cabbage, 48-58% cauliflower and 25-35% in mango, 40-50% citrus and pineapple, 30-40% guava, 25-30% grape and apple, 15-20% banana, 20-25% peach, pear, apricot.
- Ripe banana peel waste constitutes 20% while 35-40% of peel waste is generated in banana chip industry.
- Utilization of solid waste (10-50%) will reduce cost of major products and minimizes the pollution.
- Value added products can be made from waste.

Crop	Waste	Utilization of by-product
Water melon	Rind	Pickles & candy
Coconut	Husk	Coir industry
Peach, apricot, cherry tomato	Seeds	Edible oil
Jack fruit	Seeds	Flour
Mango	Kernels	Powdered starch, flour, fat
Banana	Peel	Cheese
Banana	Pseudostem	Paper pulp, other articles, clothes
Tomato/ apple/ citrus	Pomace/ rags	Cattle feed
Citrus	Peel	Oil & pectins
Pineapple	Pomace/ rags	Cake/ cattle feed
Beet root/ tomato/ blue grapes	Pomace	Natural colours

I. Phytochemicals and functional foods from horticultural wastes-

- Dietary fibres can be obtained from orange peel, mango peel and fruit pomace, carrot pomace, grape and apple pomace. These can be used in bread and bakery products and beverages.
- Grape seed oil has cholesterol thinning property with abundance of vit. E.
- Citrus wastes are rich source of essential oils and pectins.

- Citrus skin and residue contains 2.5-5.5% pectin.
- Tomato processing waste is rich in carotenoids, can be used as natural food colour items.
- Orange peel yields 0.54% citrus oil and has use in cosmetic and confectionary industry.

II. Particle boards and fibres from horticulture waste-

- Particle boards and agrofibres from kiwi pruning, date palm leaves, banana leaf sheath.
- Banana leaves, coffee husk, coconut husk, pineapple leaves for high quality fibres for textile industry.
- Banana leaves are used for dinner plates.
- Banana fibre used to print currency notes (Yen) in Japan.
- Mushroom spent logs are better substitute for bio-ethanol production.
- 50-60% waste originating from vegetables is used for bio-methanation in European countries.

III. Bio-conversion of horticulture waste-

- Grape skin and pulp- good substitute for production of 'Pullulan', an industrially important polysaccharide.
- Pineapple residue- free phenolics through *Rhizopus oligosporus*.
- Grape pomace for animal feed.

IV. Pectin production-

- Majority of pectins produced in the world are extracted from citrus Galgal and lime peels, mangosteen rind and mango ripe fruit peels and utilized for jam, jelly making and pharmaceutical industries.

V. Starch production-

- Banana pseudostems give about 5% edible starch.
- Mango seed kernels.
- Vegetable waste from roots of cassava and tuber crops are rich sources of starch.

VI. Fats production-

- Industrial processing of fruits and vegetables generate wastes e.g.
  1. Mango seed kernels contain 8.85 g/100 g fats;
  2. Sweet orange seeds contain higher fats (36.9 g/100 g);

3. Jackfruit (inner and outer portion) yield higher amount of fats (11.82 g/ 100g);
4. Tomato peels, seeds, cores and culls contains 10% fats.

VII. Essential oil production-

- Citrus fruits generate large wastes in processing units.
  1. Orange peel yield oil (2.05 ml/ 100 g peel)
  2. Malta peel (1.21% oil) followed by lemon peel (1.12% oil).
  3. Mango seed kernels contain essential oil and used in manufacture of soap, shaving cream & other cosmetic products.
  4. Tomato seeds as solid waste is non-traditional source of oil up to 38%.

VIII. Production of natural colours/ plant pigments-

- Natural colours of blue grapes, kokum, phalsa, jamun, beet roots, carrot and tomato fruits can be used for food colours.
- Rind of kokum yields fat soluble yellow pigments known as garcinol.
- Safflower pigments have wide use in food industry.

IX. Bio-gas production-

- Biomass (agricultural/ forest/ crop residues/ solid & liquid waste) can be diverted for bio-gas generation (0.68 m^3/ kg volatile solids, with methane content of 52%).
- Total bio-gas yield from wastes of fruits and vegetables is 158 kg dry matter which is 3 times more than mixture of cow dung.

X. Animal feed production-

- Livestock feed (carbohydrate concentrates & molasses) is prepared in California and Florida from organic waste (in form of peels, rages and seeds).
- Poultry feed is prepared in Vietnam from ripe banana peels.
- Pineapple bran as cattle feed in Hawaii islands.
- Drying of mango peels and kernels can replace 20% corn for feeding dairy and beef cattle.
- DTP (Dried Tomato Pomace) is used as an alternative feed stuff in lying hen's diet improves egg quality.

XI. Waste for composting-

- Organic fertilizers can be prepared from bio-degradable fruit wastes of mango, banana, sapota and vegetables.
- Vermicompost can be prepared from banana waste (suckers + leaves) + dung in ratio of 70:30.

XII. Other uses of waste-

- Fermentation of fruit waste can yield number of beverages (cider, beer, wine, brandy, vinegar).
- From pineapple processing waste- RTS beverages, vinegar & wine.
- Apple and guava pomace- production of cider.
- Fermented papaya yield ethanol (3.83 to 5.19% v/v).
- Mango peels can yield good quality vinegar with 4.5-5.05% acetic acid.

7. PROCESSING TECHNOLOGY OF HORTICULTURAL CROPS

Sl. No.	Processing methods	Principles involved	Products
1.	**Drying**		
	i) Sun drying ii) Dehydration	Removal of water prevents growth & multiplication of micro-organisms	Raisin, dried fig, date, apricot, litchi, potato chips
	Preservatives		
	a) Natural		
	i) Sugar	Acts as osmosis	Jam, jelly, marmalade, preserve, candy, glazed fruits etc.
	ii) Salt	Acts as osmosis	Pickle, sauce, chutney etc.
	iii) Oils	Create anaerobic condition where aerobic microorganisms cannot be grown causes plasmolysis of microbial cell	Fruit & vegetable pickles
	b) Chemicals		
	i) Sodium/potassium meta-bi-sulphite	Kill or inhibit the growth of micro-organisms	Beverages- juices, pulps, squashes, concentrates
	ii) Sodium benzoate	Kill or inhibit the growth of micro-organisms	Tomato products, coloured juices, pulps, squashes, syrups etc.
	iii) Acetic acid	Germicidal & anti-septic properties	Pickle, sauce, chutney etc.
2.	**Thermal processing/ heat treatment**		
	i) Sterilization	Complete destruction of all forms of micro-organisms & inactivation of enzymes	Canned fruits & vegetables
	ii) Pasteurization	Killing of microorganisms & inactivate enzymes	Juice, nectar, RTS
3.	**Freezing/ low temperature**	Microbial growth retarded or prevented by low temperature	Frozen fruits & vegetables
4.	**Fermentation**		
	i) Alcoholic ii) Acetic acid iii) Lactic acid	Inhibit mold growth or product is preserved by organic acid formed by microbial fermentation	Wine, bear, cider, vinegar, fermented pickles, such sour crates, green olives, string beans
5.	Filtration	Removal of microorganism through sterilized bacterial proof filter	Juices, wines, soft drinks
6.	Asepsis	Microbial contamination prevented by providing protective covering or aseptic packaging	A wide variety of fruit pulps & concentrates

7.	Anti-biotics (Subtelin)	Inhibit growth of microorganisms	Canned asparagus, peas, tomato, corn etc.
8.	Irradiation	High potency radiation kills the microorganism	Irradiated potatoes & onion
9.	Minimal processing	Inhibit growth of microorganism by mild treatment, packing in flexible polymeric films & storing at low temperature	Salad vegetables, leafy vegetables, tubers, diced fruit chunks etc.
10.	Hurdle technology	Application of combination of treatments or hurdles (heating, drying, reducing water activity & addition of preservatives) disturb the homeostasis of the microorganisms there by retarding the growth resulting in microbial stability	Fruit & vegetable products

Aseptic processing:

- It is a high temperature short time heat processing (HTST).
- Process is based on enzyme inactivation rather than microbial destruction.
- Technique for processing liquid food products by exposure to intense heating.
- Product and packaging material both are sterilized separately and filled in aseptic atmosphere.
- Temperature ranges from 90-110^{0}C for acidic product (pH 4.6 or less) and 121^{0}C for low acidic food (pH> 4.6).
- Process involves sterilization, holding, cooling, sterilization of packaging material, chilling and sealing.
- This rapid heating and cooling process reduces energy use and nutrient lossess associated with conventional sterilization.
- Fruit juices, pulp, concentrate, wines are packed by using this method.

Minimal processing:

- Minimally processed: Term used to refer 'lightly processed' or 'partially processed' or 'fresh processed' or 'pre-prepared'.
- Unique operation involves washing, peeling, cutting to required size and shape-pretreatment-packaging in polymeric films and storing at low temperature.
- Flavour, colour and texture are not changed significantly.
- Products are ready-to-use in great demand in urban areas.
- Minimally processed form (ready to cook) of fruits and vegetables have great significance for generation of employment and income in production catchment areas.
- Minimally processed fruits and vegetables: Peeled and cored pineapple, peeled citrus fruits, peeled and sliced potatoes, leafy vegetables such as shredded lettuce and

cabbage, cleaned and sliced onion, washed and trimmed spinach, micro-waveable fresh vegetable trays, chilled peach, mango, other fruit slices, melon and vegetable snacks such as carrot, celery sticks, cauliflower and broccoli florets.

- Most widely used preservation technology for fresh cut vegetables.
- For safe storage, high level of CO_2 (5-10%) and low O_2 (1-3%) concentration is used.
- The modified atmospheres that best maintain the quality and storage life of minimally processed products have an O_2range of 2-8 % and CO_2 concentrations of 5-15%.

Hurdle technology:

- Concept was introduced by Leistner is another paradigm shift in preserving fruits and vegetables.
- It is a combination of processing techniques/ treatments such as heating, drying, addition of preservatives, water activity controls, irradiation, high pressure processing, freezing, pH, water activity controls, ultrasonication, etc. used in synergistic fashion to bring about microbiological safety and sensory acceptability.
- This offers viable alternative to canning and dehydration.
- Microbial stability and safety of food is based on combination of several preservative factors (called *hurdles*). Thus hurdles in stable product control spoilage.
- Hurdle technology was developed as a new concept of food preservation employing a combination of preservation procedures or *hurdles* to inhibit the growth of spoilage causing microorganisms for the realization of safe, nutritious, tasty and economical food. It is called as combined method technology.
- Qualities of HT products: Convenience + safety + microbiological stability + fresh-like appearance.

Important hurdles for food preservation-

Symbol	Parameter	Application
F	High temperature	Heating
T	Low temperature	Chilling and freezing
aw	Reduced water activity	Drying, curing & conserving
pH	Increased acidity	Acid addition or formation
Eh	Reduced redox potential	Removal of oxygen or addition of ascorbate
Pres.	Preservatives	Sorbate, sulphite and nitrite
c.f.	Competitive flora	Microbial fermentations

Examples of hurdles used to preserve foods

Type of hurdle	Examples
Physical hurdles	Aseptic packaging, microwave, high temperature (blanching, pasteurization, sterilization, evaporation, extrusion, baking, frying), ionic radiation, low temperature (chilling freezing), modified atmospheres, packaging films, UV radiations, ultrasonication
Physico-chemical hurdles	Carbon dioxide, ethanol, lactic acid, low pH, low redox potential, Maillard reaction, organic acids, oxygen, ozone, phenols, smoking, sodium nitrite/ nitrate, sodium sulphite, surface treatment agents
Microbially derived hurdles	Anti-biotics, bacteriocins, competitive flora, protective cultures

7.1 Preservation by high temperature

- Asepsis (Absence of infection through general cleanliness during handling and processing): Keeping out of microorganisms using high temperature. It protects the processed contents from contamination by microorganisms e.g. Food packaging.
- Filtration: Removal of micro-organisms through sterilized bacterial proof filter.

i) **Pasteurization**:

- Thermal/ heat treatment < 100ºC.
- Partial destruction of microbes.
- Most common method of preservation for fruit juices, RTS and nector.
- Pasteurization: Heating of fruit juices @ 85-90ºC for 30 min.
- Vitamin that increase in fruits & vegetables during heat pasteurization: Niacin.
- Flash pasteurization: Fruit juice is heated rapidly about 5.5ºC higher than pasteurization temperature. Commonly used for apple, canning of natural orange juice and grape juices.
- Bottle or holding pasteurization: Most commonly used for preservation of fruit juices at home.
- RTS and Nectar are pasteurized at about 85ºC for 25-30 min.
- Overflow method: Juice is heated rapidly about 2.5ºC higher than the pasteurization temperature. Most suitable for grape juice.
- Pasteurization temperature for vinegar: 77ºC.
- Mold spores are destroyed by heating at 79ºC for 5-10 min.
- Yeast and acid tolerant bacteria are killed at 66ºC.
- Pectic enzymes in juice can be destroyed by heating the juice at about 85ºC for 4 min or 88ºC for 1 min.

Hot water treatment for controlling diseases in fruits after harvesting

Fruit	Hot water dip		Disease controlled
	Temperature (^{0}C)	Time (min)	
Apple	45	10	Botrytis rot &penicillium rot
Avocado	40-42	20-30	Colletotrichum rot
Ber	50	5	Anthracnose rot
Cherry	52	2	Codling moth & botrytis rot
Guava	46	35	Botrytis rot
Kinnow	50	2	Penicillium rot
Lemon	52-53	5-10	Alternaria, penicillium, brown rot
Litchi	52	2	Brown rot
Mango	52	5	Anthracnose rot
Orange	53	5	Blue and gray mold
Papaya	43-47	20	Fungal disease
Peach	50	2.5-3	Brown rot, rhizopus rot
Plum	45-50	30-35	Rhizopus rot
Pear	47	30	Botrytis rot

ii) **Sterilization**:

- Thermal/ heat treatment at 100^{0}C and above.
- Complete destruction of all forms of microbes and inactivate enzymes.
- Commonly used for canned fruits and vegetables.
- Hot pack or hot fill is generally used in home for jam preparation.
- Heat sterilization: Most effective process of food preservation.
- Aseptic canning/ martin aseptic canning/ ultra high temperature (UHT) sterilization: 149^{0}C for 1-2 sec.
- Fruits and tomato products should be heated at 100^{0}C for 30 min. to kill the spore forming bacteria.
- Sterilization temperature for spore forming bacteria: 110^{0}C, 30-90 min.
- Spore forming bacteria: *Bacillus subtilis* and *B. mesentericus*.

iii) **Ohmic heating:**

- Developed by Lima in 2008.
- Used in aseptic processing system.
- Low frequency alternating current (50 or 60 Hz) is passed through the food product to heat as a result of its inherent electrical resistance.
- Principle: Electrical energy is transformed into thermal energy.

iv) **Microwave processing:**

- Preferred to pasteurization and sterilization through conventional heating.
- Require less time
- Cause reduced nutrient losses particularly of thermolabile components.

7.2 Preservation by low temperature i.e. freezing

- Most harmless, cheaper than canning and latest method of preservation.
- Standard unit of expressing refrigeration capacity or load: Ton.
- It is low temperature preservation process where product is frozen at -40^{0}C and stored at -20^{0}C.
- Vegetables are washed, peeled (potato, carrot), cut (pepper, brinjal, zucchini), shelled (legume seeds) and immediately frozen.
- Frozen products are of better quality than canned products and close to fresh products.
- Based on principle of crystallization (converting water molecules into ice crystals i.e. removal of heat) without major changes in its physiochemical property.
- This causes cell wall rupture & texture of produce becomes much softer than when raw. Tomato, celery & lettuce are not frozen for above reasons.
- Freezing retards metabolic activities and spoilage due to post harvest chemical changes.
- It is done for inactivation of microbial growth.
- Cellar storage (15^{0}C) e.g. Root crops, potatoes, onions and apples are most suitable.
- Freezing temperature: -18^{0}C to -40^{0}C.
- Best way preserving pure fruit juice: Freezing
- Frozen foods should always be kept at below -1 to -5^{0}C.
- Household refrigerators run at 4.4 to 7.2^{0}C.
- Fruit juices are frozen at -12 to -17^{0}C (quick freezing: 0-4^{0}C for 30 min).
- Frozen fruits are good for making preserves.
- Freezing with cryogenic liquids like liquid N_2 (-196^{0}C) & liquid CO_2 (-43^{0}C).
- Freeze drying has < 4 mm Hg pressure.
- Process involved in freeze drying: Lyophilization.
- Fruits for freezing: Mango slices and pulp, guava slices, pineapple slices and orange segments.
- Vegetables for freezing: Peas, spinach, cauliflower, beans and carrot.
- Quick freezing is preferred over slow freezing for the formation of large crystal e.g. Peas.
- Freezing storage temperature: -18^{0}C (microbial growth is completely stopped but chemical reaction continues).
- Sublimation is associated with freeze drying.
- Thawing: Change form solid ice to liquid water followed by melting of the central portions.
- Colour retention in stored foods is more in freezing method than canning technique.

- Staphylococcus bacterium survives during freeze drying.
- Methyl cellulose is foaming agent for apple, peach, cherry drying.
- Indicator bacteria for freezing: *Enterococci*.
- Retention of ascorbic acid and Vit. C are reliable index for estimating quality deterioration.
- Frozen spinach is most susceptible to Vit. C degradation.
- Vitamin C is generally destroyed during freezing due to oxidation.
- Loss of ascorbic acid is enhanced by activity of ascorbate oxidase and depends on pH of vegetable.
- Vegetables susceptible to chilling injury: Tomato, brinjal, pepper, cucumber, snap bean, summer squash, pumpkin, lettuce, celery and water melon.
- Non-chilling sensitive commodities: Broccoli and peas.
- Blanching process (in broccoli and Spinach) is used before freezing to inactivate enzymes and to destroy microbes.
- Fruits are not blanched.
- Rancid oxidative flavour (a chemical change occurs in frozen product) develops due to contact of air & controlled by using vital wrapping material.
- Chilling injury is also known as 'low temperature breakdown'.
- It occurs in tissues exposed to temperature above freezing point or even at temperature as high as 14^0C.
- This type of spoilage is more acute in tropical fruits.
- High or low temperature conditioning, intermittent warming, controlled atmosphere, application of growth regulators or other chemicals (NO, methyl jasmonate, salicylic acid, polyamines), waxing and packaging are reported to reduce chilling injury in fruits.
- Cause more economic losses during storage or in refrigerated shipments.
- Chilling injury symptoms: Internal discoloration & electrolyte leakage.

Tropical fruits	Symptoms of chilling injury
Mango	Uneven ripening, dull & blemished skin, loss of sweetness
Banana	Fails to ripen properly, increase in tannin content, hardening of central placenta, inhibition of starch / sugar conversion, reduced ascorbic acid content
Lime & lemon	Skin pilling, slow degreening, membrane discolouration, oil glands darker than surrounding areas
Papaya	Fails to ripen properly, skin pitting, conversion of sucrose to reducing sugar inhibited
Pineapple	Uneven ripening, discolourtion of flesh, crown wilting, fails to develop ideal flavour
Litchi	Skin colour becomes dull

- Methods of freezing-
  a) Plate freezing: Food products are placed in contact with cold surface & surface suitable for packed food products.
  b) Blast freezing: Vigorous circulation of cold air for freezing the products. Air temperature is -18^{0}C to -30^{0}C or even lower. Variety of sizes and shapes are accommodated.
  c) Individual Quick Freezing (IQF): Fluidization of the product in the freezing conveyer and circulating cold air at -40^{0}C. Advantage of IQF is reconstitution property due to quick freezing.
  d) Ice bank cooling: Recent development in refrigeration with positive ventilation. Quicker cooling & removal of large amount of heat in short period of time.
- Problems during storage:
  1. Sublimation occur when water vapour pressure of ice is higher than vapour pressure of surrounding air. As a result tissues of frozen product become dry, tough and brownish. Wrapping of products as moisture proof barrier is used as preventive.
  2. Recrystallization: Many small ice crystals combine and form large crystals. Fluctuation is storage temperature and prolonged storage enhances crystallization which decreases product quality.
  3. Denaturation: Protein alteration during storage can cause toughness in frozen products.
  4. Changes in chemical quality: Accumulation of volatile compounds and oxidation of lipids cause off odours/ flavours. Enzymatic browning, los of vitamins particularly ascorbic acid, pigments and recontamination of microorganisms decrease the quality and product become unsafe. These changes are faster at higher storage temperature.

7.2.1 Isocoric freezing technology:

- New technique of food freezing developed by American Agricultural scientists.
- Energy saving and low release of CO_2 is possible with this new technique.
- Isoccoric freezing technique can be used in home scale refrigerators for long term preservation/ storage of tomatoes, cherries, potatoes.
- Principle of crystallization is totally eliminated in this new technique.
- Microbial growth is completely stopped.
- This new freezing technique can be used when food products are in sealed (either in plastic or metal or any other container) conditions.

7.3 Preservation by chemical preservatives

- Any substance that is capable of inhibiting, retarding or arresting the process of fermentation, acidification or other decomposition of food.

- Class I preservatives: Common salt i.e. NaCl, sugar, spices, vinegar, honey, wood smoke and vegetable oil. Salts and sugar acts on the principle of osmosis. Oil prevents anaerobic condition reaction.
- In fruit canning and pickling, salt act as anti-oxidant.
- Class II preservatives: KMS, Calcium sorbate and benzoic acid.

a) **Sulphur dioxide:**

- Kills or inhibit growth of microorganisms.
- Common stable source of SO_2: Potassium meta-bi-sulphite (KMS) i.e. $K_2S_2O_5$.
- SO_2 content in pure KMS: 57.7 %.
- Most effective preservative action by releasing SO_2 gas in presence of acidic medium and retards growth of bacteria, fungi and molds.
- Used to preserve most of juices/ mango pulp.
- As per FPO, maximum limit in fruit juice: 700 ppm.
- Concentration of SO_2 in concentrated juice: 1500 ppm.
- The toxicity of SO_2 increases at high temperature.
- Germicidal effect of KMS is due to H_2SO_3.
- Beverages, juices, pulps, squashes and concentrates are preserved by this chemical process.

b) **Benzoic acid:**

- Kills or inhibit growth of microorganisms.
- Salt of sodium benzoate.
- Recommended level of sodium benzoate in fruit juice: 0.06 to 1.0%.
- Most effective against yeast.
- Used for coloured juices with citric acid (only in non-acid fruits).
- As per FPO, maximum limit in RTS and nectar is 100 ppm.
- Effectiveness of benzoic acid increases in presence of CO_2.
- Tomato products, coloured juices, pulps, squashes and syrups are preserved by this chemical process because it does not bleach the anthocyanin pigment.

- Any substance added to food by the process of curing is known as 'smoking'.
- Common salt exerts its preservative action by causing high osmotic pressure resulting in plasmolysis of microbial cells.
- Salt @ 15-25% act as preservative and acts on osmotic principle.
- Sugar @ 62-65 % act as preservative in fruit syrup, jam, jelly, marmalade, candy, preserve, crystallized fruit and glazed fruit.
- Alcohol @ 14% acts as preservative in wine.
- Acetic acid (vinegar), citric acid (lime juice) and lactic acid are commonly used for preservation.

- About 2% acetic acid is enough to prevent spoilage of products.
- Acetic acid has germicidal and anti-septic properties.
- Acetic acid checks aerobic and anaerobic fermentation and pickles, sauces and chutney are preserved by this process.
- Citric acid is added to many fruit squashes, jams and jellies to increase the acidity and prevent mold growth.
- Oils create anaerobic condition where aerobic microorganisms cannot be grown and causes plasmolysis of microbial cells.
- Turmeric, pepper, salt and asafoetida have bacterio-static effect.
- Mostly fruit and vegetable pickles are preserved by this method.
- Permitted preservatives in all countries: Sulphur dioxide and Benzoic acid.

Permissible limits of preservatives in food products

Food product	Sulphur dioxide (SO_2)	Benzoic acid
Pickle & chutney	100 ppm	250 ppm
Jam, jelly & marmalade	40 ppm	200 ppm
Cherry juice	5000 ppm	-
Strawberry juice	2000 ppm	-
Fruit juice	700 ppm	-
Dried fruit	2000 ppm	-
Raisins	750 ppm	-
Crystallized candy & glazed fruit	150 ppm	-
Dehydrated vegetables	2000 ppm	-
Cider	200 ppm	-
Tomato puree, paste	-	250 ppm
Tomato sauce	-	750 ppm
Preserve	-	200 ppm
More effective against	Bacteria, mold	Yeast inhibits enzymes
Usage	Not used in coloured products	Mostly used in coloured juices
-	Act as anti-oxidant	Anti-bacterial action is increased in presence of CO_2 and acid

7.4 Preservation by carbonation/carbonated beverages

- Beverages are preserved by carbonation.
- In carbonated drinks, oxygen of air is displaced with CO_2.
- It is a process of mixing of CO_2 gas under pressure with water or beverages and mixed with certain additives at low temperature.
- These are based on synthetic, colouring & flavouring agents which are potentially allergenic.
- Fruit juice can be directly carbonated or fruit juice concentrate can be used for carbonation.

- Fruit based syrups such as pineapple, orange, lime, grape, guava can be used.
- It is a mixture of fruit juice + sugar + water + acid + CO_2.
- Molds and yeast which require oxygen for their growth become inactive in presence of CO_2.
- CO_2 @ 1-8g/litre is added to carbonated beverages.
- CO_2 @ 14.6 g/litre completely inhibit microbial activity.
- Keeping quality is enhanced by adding 0.005% sodium benzoate and light heat processing.
- It provides anaerobic condition and reduces the oxidation of ascorbic acid.
- E.g. Pepsi Cola, Thums Up, Seven Up, Gold Spot, Limca, Sprite, etc.

7.5 Preservation by irradiation

- Also known as cold sterilization i.e. food is free of microorganisms, insect parasites that cause disease and spoilage of food products without high temperature treatment.
- Food is exposed to radio isotopes (gamma rays or X-rays).
- Irradiation destroys microorganisms, enzymes and also alters physiology of fruits.
- Irradiation is done for quarantine purpose and extension of shelf life.
- Ionizing radiation has potential to extend shelf life of perishables.
- Approved under preservation of Food Adulteration (Act) Rule, 1955, Ministry of Health and Family Welfare.
- Govt. of India has permitted use of irradiation technology in preservation of food items like potato, onion, rice, semolina (*sooji* or *rawas*), wheat *atta* or *maida*, mango, raisins, figs, dried dates, ginger, garlic, shallots (small onion) and meat products including chicken.
- Gamma radiation helps in destruction of microorganisms & alters physiology of fruits.
- Increase shelf life of bulbs and tubers and delay ripening of fruits.
- Ultra-filtration or cold process: To remove microbes from fruit juices, wines and beers.
- Food preserved by ionizing radiation (gamma rays) at 4-5^{0}C.
- WHO and IAEA have recommended that radiation dose up to 1 mili rad is not hazardous.
- Radiation technology in horticultural produce is safe for consumption and economical also.
- Technology is suitable for heat sensitive material, absence of harmful residues and adaptable for prepackaged material.

- Irradiation plants are established as Vashi (Mumbai), Lasalgaon (Nashik) for onion, potato and spices.
- A thick concrete shield (1.5-1.8 m thick) is essential surrounding the irradiation room.
- Isotope when not in use for food treatment is stored in 5-6 m deep well.
- Cobalt-60 is produced by neutron bombardment in a nuclear reactor of metal cobalt-59. It has half-life of 5.3 years.
- Gamma rays are highly penetrating and used to treat full boxes of fresh or frozen food.
- Over 80% of the global Cobalt-60 is produced in Canada.
- India also produces few some quantity of Cobalt-60.
- Radiation dose: Quantity of radiation energy absorbed by food as it passes through radiation field during processing.
- Radiation dose is now measured in Grays (Gy) or kilo Grays (kGy).
- Earlier unit of radiation was 'rad'.
- 1 Gray is equivalent to 1 Joule of energy absorbed by 1 Kg of irradiated food.
- Maximum dose recommended by the Codex General Standard for food irradiation: 10 kGy.
- Minimum gamma irradiation dose approved by USDA-APHIS for importing mango in USA: 400 Gy.
- Ionizing radiation has numerous applications (Khader, 1985) as
  a) Inhibits sprouting in tubers, bulbs, and root crops.
  b) Delaying stem elongation and cap opening in button mushrooms.
  c) Disinfection f insects causing spoilage in fresh fruits/ fry fruits/ nuts in international trade.
  d) Controls growth of fungal pathogens in stored fruits.
  e) Delaying process of ripening and senescence of certain climacteric fruits and strawberries (irradiation dose 1.5 to 3 kGy).
- Radiation sensitivity of different organisms-
  - Insect disinfection and destruction of parasites: <1 kGy i.e. 10^2 to 10^3 rad. Used in stored grains, pulses and food products and destruction of parasites in meat and meat products;
  - Humans: 10^3 to 10^6 rad.
  - Microorganisms: 1-10 kGy i.e. 10^3 to 10^7 rad.
  - Food and production of stable food: >10 kGy.
- Sprouting of tubers (potato), bulbs (onions), carrots and rhizomes are inhibited at 10^3 to 10^4 rad (0.03-0.15 k Gy).

- ° Onion: (0.03-0.09 kGy), garlic: (0.075 kGy).
- ° Potato, yam, ginger, chestnut: 0.06-0.15 kGy.
- ° Delay in fruit ripening: 0.25-0.75 kGy.
- Sterilizing dose: Bacterial endospores (3 x 10^6); yeasts and fungi (5 x 10^4).
- Sterilizing dose for canned foods: > 25 kGy.
- Source of ionizing radiation:
  1. Radioisotopes: Cobalt-60 (CO^{60}) and Caesium-137 (CS^{137}).
  2. Machine: X-rays and Gamma rays.
- Technology fails to kill viruses.
- Adverse changes in loss of sugars, vitamins in treated fruits and vegetables are observed.
- Irradiation with 25-35 Kr delay initiation of natural ripening of banana without interfering ethylene induced ripening or affecting fruit quality.

Fruits	Recommended dose for control of diseases (Gy)	Fruits	Recommended dose for control of diseases (Gy)
Apple	150	Apricot, peaches, nectarine	200
Avocado, Banana,	1000 (max.)	Lemon	150-200
Orange	200	Tomato	300
Strawberry	200 to 5000	Grape	150
Mango	750	Spices	6000-14000

Doses of radiations required for killing organism

Organism	Approximate lethal dose (kGy)
Insects	0.22 to 0.93
Viruses	10 to 40
Yeasts (fermentative)	4 to 9
Yeasts (film)	3.7 to 18
Molds (with spores)	1.3 to 11
Bacteria (cells of pathogens)	1.4 to 4.8
Gram-negative	1.8 to 2.3
Gram-positive	0.23 to 8.8
Bacterial spores	3.1 to 50

7.6 Preservation by anti-biotics

- An anti-biotic is a chemical substance produced by microorganisms which have capacity of inhibiting growth.
- The target organism for commercial sterility is *Clostridium botulinum*.
- Nisin:An anti-biotic produced by *Streptococcus lactis* commonly found in milk, curd, cheese and other fermented milk products. It is commonly used for canning of

mushrooms, tomatoes and milk products. It suppresses growth of gas, spore forming and toxin producing *Clostridium botulinum*.

- Pimaricin: An anti-fungal anti-biotic is commonly used for treating fruits and fruit juices.
- Subtelin: An anti-biotic produced by *Bacillus subtilis*. It is used in preservation of asparagus, corn and peas. It is most effective against gram positive bacteria and spore forming organisms.
- Recommended dose for canned peas and tomatoes: 10 and 20 ppm, respectively.

7.7 CANNING

- Most ancient method of preservation of fruits and vegetables.
- It is process of heating i.e. thermal processing and sealing food stuffs hermetically in containers and sterilizing them by heat for long storage.
- Air is driven during heating and forms vacuum seal.
- Fruit softening of canned chilli/ paprika is minimized with $CaCl_2$ (0.02%) treatment.
- The cans used are known as open top sanitary cans or 3 piece cans.
- Generally electrolyte coated tin cans are used for food processing.
- Rossogolla: 1st and only canned food product manufactured in country.
- In canning, fruits and vegetables mostly get damaged by 'Flat sour'.
- Toughening effect in canned bean is due to calcium.
- Clinching is related to canning.
- Peach is canned after halving.
- High temperature kills microorganisms and block enzymes.
- Canned chilli fruits have maximum shelf life of 2 years and citric acid is commonly used to preserve chilli.
- Methods of canning:
  I. Water bath (boiling water) e.g. Fruits, tomato, pickled vegetables, jam, jellies are high acid foods (pH < 4.6).
  II. Pressure canning: Low acid foods (pH > 4.6) e.g. all vegetables are processed by this method.

FPO specifications for canned fruits/ vegetables:

- Head space in the can should not be more than 1.6 cm.
- Drain weight not less than 50% for fruits and 55% for vegetables except tomato 50%.
- No addition of preservative and artificial colour except for peas.
- Can should not show any sign of bacterial growth when incubated at 37^{0}C for a week.

Difference in canning of fruits and vegetables:

Process	Fruit	Vegetable
Blanching	Non required	Required
Syruping	Used	Not used
Brining	Not used	Used
Processing	In boiling water & temperature is lower	In steam/ cooker pressure & temperature is higher

- Fruits for canning: Mango slices, Pineapple slices, Litchi, Cherry, Apricot, Strawberry, Peach, Grapes, Loquat, Plum, Papaya pieces, Banana slices, Guava cuttings into halves/ quarters.

Thermal processing of vegetables:

- Safe method of food preservation.
- Consist of placing vegetables (after washing-cutting-trimming-slicing-shelling) in a container (glass/ jar/ tin/ can/ tetrapack) at temperatures from 100-135^{0}C.
- High temperature kills microorganisms and block the enzymes responsible for undesirable changes in organoleptic properties (flavor, colour & texture).
- Air is driven during heating & forms vacuum seal.
- Before heating a brine with chemical additives viz. ascorbic acid, citric acid, acetic acid is added to flavor heat conductivity during thermal processing & to avoid oxidation reactions to compromise product quality.

Methods of canning:

I. Water bath (boiling water): e.g. Fruits, tomato, pickled vegetables, jam, jellies are high acid foods (pH< 4.6) are canned by using water bath.

II. Pressure canning: Low acid foods (pH value > 4.6) e.g. all vegetables (except tomato) are processed by this method.

  - Within 30-40 minutes, lethal temperature close to 121^{0}C is reached.
  - Being sterilized, canned vegetables can be stored up to 3 years at room temperature.
  - Canned carrots & green peas has higher carotenoid content than fresh samples.
  - In legumes, thermal treatment cause turgor loss & leads to decrease in firmness/ crisp succulence & affect textural variability.
  - Canning process does not affect fibre content, but make it more soluble & are comparable to fresh and frozen products.
  - In soybean, brine composition & blanching duration affect quality. To retain desirable colour and texture, add 150 g NaCl + 2.9 g $CaCl_2$ per litre at pH 6.5 & thermal treatment for 9 min.

Vegetable cultivars for canning

Vegetable	Cultivars
Tomato	Pearl Harbour, Marglobe, Kullu Valley, Sioux, Italian Red Pear, Mountain Delight, Mountain Fresh, Mountain Gold, Red Top, Red Rose, Roma, Rupali
Potato	Kufri Jyoti, K. Chandramukhi, K. Surya, K. Frysona, K. Himsona, etc.
Okra	EMS-8, Punjab-7, Punjab Padmini, Pusa Sawani, Vaishali Vadhu
Cabbage	Lucknow Local, PusaDrum Head, Infusion of Glory, Pride of India, Golden Acre
Bitter gourd	BG-14, C-96
French bean	Selection No. 572, Contender, Blue Lake
Beet root	Wisconsin, New York, Washington, Detroit Dark Red
Cauliflower	-
Mushroom	-
Carrot	Chantaney
Peas	American Wonder, Alaska, Canners, Delwiche Commando, Early Perfection, Early Crop, Early Giant, Frosty, Gregory's Surprise, Marrow Fat, Model, NP-291, Telephone, William Wonder, Yates
Beans	Tender Crop, Cascade

7.7.1 Peeling

- Removal of outer covering of fruits.
- Hand peeling: Mango & papaya.
- Steam peeling: Potato, tomato, free stone and clingstone peaches.
- Mechanical peeling: Apple, peach, pineapple, cherries and root crops (carrot, turnip & potato).
- Lye peeling is done by 1-2% NaOH (Boiling caustic soda 93^{0}C) for 30 sec. to 2 minutes.
- Lye peeling: Fruits (apricot, aonla, mandarin, peach, sweet orange); vegetables (carrot, sweet potato) and medicinal plant (safed musli).
- Flame peeling: Garlic and onion.
- Specific term used for peeling in vegetables: Peas (shelled), Carrot (scraped), Beans (snipped).
- Infra-red heating: Apple and tomato.

7.7.2 Blanching

- Also known as scalding, paraboiling or pre-cooking.
- Blanching loosens skin, inactivates natural enzymes, do sterilization i.e. inactivates microbes in fruits and vegetables.
- It acts as pre-treatment (boiling water exposure for vegetables) e.g. Okra, cabbage, beans.
- Hot water blanching: Most commercially used blanching technique in canning industry.

- Blanching temperature: 82.2- 93.3^{0}C (180-200^{0}F) @ 2-5 min.
- Average blanching time: 6 min (2-5 min).
- Most commonly used vegetables: Green beans, yellow carrots, okra, turnip, cabbage.
- During blanching Vitamin C loss is 10-50%.
- Chemical added for prevention of chlorophyll conversion into pheophytin during blanching: Sodium bicarbonate.
- Browning: Many cut fruits and vegetables have tendency to turn brown when exposed to air due to polyphenol oxidase activity.

7.7.3 Sulphuring

- Commonly used for fruits.
- Exposure of whole fruits, slices or pieces into burning sulphur fumes is done in sulphur box.
- Used to prevent the oxidation and darkening of fruits.
- Timing for exposure in sulphur box: 30-60 min.
- SO_2 fumes used to check mold growth.
- Sweating: Keeping dried products in boxes or bins to equalize moisture content.

7.7.4 Syruping

- Solution of sugar in water.
- It is done only for fruits.
- Sucrose syrup is used for canning.
- Syruping concentration: 20-55^{0}brix.
- Syrup should be filled at 79-82^{0}C, leaving head space of 0.32-0.47 cm.
- Fruit syrup (sharbat) contains more than 66% sugar that generally doesn't ferment.

7.7.5 Brining

- Solution of salt in water.
- Brining is done only for vegetables.
- Brine floatation technique: Commonly used in peas and beans.
- Maximum solubility of common salt in water is above 26.5%.
- Salt concentration in pickle is measured by Salometer.
- When Salometer reading is 60S, then salt is 15%.
- Brine concentration: 1-3% or 2-2.5%.
- Brining filled at 79-82^{0}C, leaving head space of 0.32-0.47 cm.
- Exhausting: Removal of air from cans.

- Time of exhausting: 6-10 min.
- Exhausting is done at 79°C temperature.
- During sealing of cans, the temperature should not fall below 74°C.
- Almost all fruits and acidic vegetables can be processed at 100°C.
- Fruits and acid vegetables (Tomato and Rhubarb) are generally processed in open type cookers, continuous non-agitating cookers and continuous agitating cookers.
- Vegetable processing temperature: 115-121°C under a pressure of 0.70-1.05 kg/ cm^2.
- Non-acid vegetables are processed under steam pressure in closed resorts known as automatic pressure cookers.
- After processing, the cans are cooled rapidly to 39°C for stopping cooking process and to prevent stack burn.

7.7.6 Classification of fruits and vegetables based on pH content

Class	pH	Fruits/ vegetables/ products
Low acid/ non-acid	>5.0	Peas, Asparagus, Cauliflower, Spinach, Beet, Corn, French bean, Lima bean
Medium acid	4.5-5.0	Okra, Carrot, Cabbage, Pumpkin, Beet, Green bean
Acid	3.7-4.5	Tomato, Mango, Banana, Pineapple, Jack fruit, Apple, Pear, Peach, Sweet cherry
High acid	< 3.7	Rhubarb, Citrus juice

- Lacquering is the process of coating the inside of can with lacquer (golden coloured enamel) which prevents discoloration without affecting flavour.
- Lacquering may be acid resistant or sulphur resistant.
- Thickness of tin coating is usually <0.0001 inches (0.025 mm).
- Acid resistant lacquer or R-enamel or AR cans: Acidic fruits and vegetables.
- Sulphur resistant lacquer or C-enamel or SR cans: Vegetables and non-acid foods.
- AR cans are suitable for packing fruits having water soluble pigments viz. red plum, strawberry, coloured grapes.
- SR cans used for non-acid foods only like peas, cauliflower, sweet potato, corn, lima bean, and red kidney beans.
- The fruits which have pigments insoluble such as pineapple, peach, apricot are suitable for packing in plain cans.
- Tin containers/ glass (bottle) containers/ plastic containers and heat sealable pouches are popular in recent years.
- Corn enamel are SR lacquers.
- Springer can: A can in which the vacuum is low that mechanical shock will produce distortion of one or both ends.
- In can size, the 1st number of the symbol devotes diameter.

7.7.7 Spoilage of canned foods

- Thermophilic bacteria is common at 100°C.
- *Flat sour*: *Bacillus sterothermophilus*: Common in non-acid foods and vegetables.
- 'Panelling' in large sized cans is due to hydrogen swells.
- Sulphur stinker spoilage: *Clostridium nigrificans*: Common in low acid fruits.
- Mesophilic micro-organism spoilage below 38°C.
- Pink discolouration is a problem in canned cabbage and peach is due to low cooling.
- TA (Thermophilic acid) spoilage i.e. swelling is due to CO_2 and hydrogen, developed in low and medium acid foods when stored in hot conditions.
- TA spoilage is due to *Clostridium thermosaccharolyticum*.
- *Clostridium botulinum* exotoxin can be destroyed at the temperature of 80°C.
- *Clostridium botulinum*: Cause lethal poisoning in canned foods.
- Pathogenic microorganisms/ parasites: *Escherichia coli*, *Salmonella*, *Campylobacter jejuni*, *Listeria monocytogenes*, *Vibrio* and *Trichinella spiralis*.

Problem	Indication and prevention
Hydrogen swell	Due to reaction between tin plate and acids in food and formation of hydrogen gas. Product become cloudiness and off flavoured. Common in low and medium acid foods. Using good quality tin, addition of citric acid (0.5%) to syrup, proper exhausting, firm placing of lid, proper head space (0.6-0.9 cm) and storing the canned product under cool and dry condition will minimize problem.
Leaker	Leaking is due to defective or faulty seaming, corrosion both inside and outside the can and physical damage during handling. Precaution must be taken.
Discoloration of products (black, brown and pink)	Due to biological reasons such as enzymatic and non-enzymatic browning or metallic contamination. Enzymatic browning can be prevented by regulation of exhausting process and placing the fruit and vegetable cut pieces in 2% salt solution. Metallic contamination caused by iron (iron sulphide) and copper (copper sulphide). This can be avoided by eliminating the use of iron and copper vessels and using lacquered can, glass containers, stainless steel equipment, etc.
Flat souring	Caused by microorganism i.e. thermophilic bacteria. Two organisms causes flat sour taste i) *Bacillus sterothermophilus* and *B. coagulans*. Problem can be minimized by cleaning and washing the material thoroughly prior to canning and by using proper exhausting, processing time and temperature. These are heat resistant bacteria and require higher temp for killing.
Formation of acid and gases	Caused by microorganism i.e. thermophilic anaerobic bacteria i.e. *Clostridium thermosaccharolyticum*. This attacks carbohydrates and forms acid and gases (CO_2, H_2) which develop pressure to cause bulging. Problem occurs in acid and low acid fruit/ vegetables. Problems can be prevented by appropriate processing and cooling of cans at about 39°C before stacking.
Sulphide spoilage	Organism responsible for this is *Clostridium nigrificans* or *Desulphomaculum nigrificans*. This also causes swelling of cans. SO_2 is produced by bacteria which reacts with cans and cause darkening or browning of the product. It is present in low acid fruit and vegetable products. Problem can be minimized by proper processing or avoid under processing.

Fermentation & bulging	Mesophilic spore forming organism such as *Clostridium butyricum* and *C. pasteurianum* which are anaerobic bacteria spoil the product of acid and low acid fruits by forming fermentation. Some species of *Bacillus* such as *B. subtilis* (aerobic bacteria) causes bulging and spoil the product of low acids fruits. Problems can be minimized by adequate processing.
Leakage	It is due to air which may contain many types of spoilage agent such as yeast, mold and non-spore forming bacteria. It is mixed type of spoilage which gives various types of odours. Precautions should be taken.

7.8 Preservation by dehydration

- Process of removal of moisture (water) by application of artificial heat under controlled conditions of temperature, R.H. and air flow. It prevents microbial growth responsible for quality decay.
- Share of dried and preserved vegetables is 30.9% over horticultural produce.
- Drying or dehydration is the most widely used, cheapest method of preservation and require less storage space e.g. raisins, dried figs, dates, potato chips, etc.
- Technique consists of reduction in weight and volume of fruits and vegetables.
- It reduces many moisture mediated degenerative reactions.
- Many structural and physico-chemical changes occur in dry conservation viz.
  1. Physical and structural changes as shrinkage, cell damage & volatile retention.
  2. Chemical and organoleptic changes as browning reactions, pigments degradation, enzyme inactivation, lipid oxidation.
  3. Nutritional changes- Protein denaturation, vitamin degradation.
  4. Colour and dehydration ratios are important quality attributes.
- Drying methods:
  I. Adiabatic: Consist of heat vaporization and heat transfer from product by convection and conduction i.e. hot air drying.
  II. Non-adiabatic: Using radiation from electromagnetic waves in which heat flows directly into solid from the sources.
- Dehydrated/concentrated products are called as high sugar acid foods or high value low volume foods.
- Drying/dehydration reduces the bulk (1/4 or more) of fresh fruits.
- Initial temperature of the dehydrator: 43°C.
- Optimum dehydration temperature for vegetables: 60-66°C.
- Residual moisture in vegetables should not be more than 6-8% and in fruits10-20%.
- Dehydration temperature for fruits:
  - 67-71°C (grape drying at 66-80°C for 20-30 h up to moisture content of 15-20%,
  - Dates dried at 45-50°C up to moisture content of 10-20%,

- Fig dried at 55-60^{0}C for 10-20 h up to moisture 10-20%,
- Mango pulp dried at 45-50^{0}C up to moisture 10-15% and
- Banana pulp pieces dried at 55-90^{0}C for 18-20 h).

- Psychometric relation: Relationship between moisture content and temperature of air during drying.
- Most useful fumigant used in spices and condiments: Ethylene oxide.
- Fluidized bed and foam mat drying are mainly used for vegetables.
- Most used package desiccants for partial dehydration of vegetables: Calcium oxide or fumed silicas.
- Rehydration of dried fruits is done at 54-65^{0}C.
- Suitable fruits- Apple, Apricot, Banana, Ber, Grape, Fig, Mandarin orange, Peach, Pear, Pineapple, Pomegranate, Sapota, Strawberry, Sweet orange, etc.
- Suitable vegetables: Brinjal, Beet root, Cabbage, Carrot, Cauliflower, Celery, Chilli, Cluster bean, Coriander, Corn, Cucumber, Curry leaf, Drumstick, Fenugreek, Garlic, Mint, Mushroom, Okra, Onion, Peppers, Potato, Tomato, Zucchini, etc.

Vegetable	Cultivars for drying
Okra	Pusa Sawani, Selection-2-2.
Tomato	Pusa Ruby
Pea	Little Marvel, Varanasi Sweet, Duke of Albany, Morris, Bonneville
Onion	Pusa White Round, Pusa White Flat, Udaipur 101, Udaipur-102

- Types of drying techniques:
  1. Sun/ Solar drying: Sun drying is slow as evaporation takes place continuously, but nutrient loss is minimal e.g. leafy vegetables, onion flakes, kokum, raw mango, potato, chilli, spices, condiments, etc.
  2. Hot air drying: Widely used method for production of dehydrated vegetables e.g. Onion.
  3. Microwave drying: Takes least time for drying e.g. Peach.
  4. Infrared drying e.g. Onion.
  5. Vacuum drying: Most suitable for low moisture/ low sugar fruits like peaches and apricotsand Asian White radish slices.
  6. Microwave-vacuum drying e.g. Onion slices.
  7. Osmotic drying e.g. Onion slices and tomato fruits.
  8. Freeze drying e.g. Strawberry and corn.
- Manuka/ Manakka: Raisins prepared from seeded white/green grapes.
- Kishmish: Raisins prepared from seedless black grapes.
- Bedana: Raisins prepared from seedless white/ green grapes.

- Pind (soft & fully ripened)khajoor is processed to dried form as chhuhara (kharik) in Middle-East countries.
- Dried ripe kokum rind is known as '*amsol*' and drying ratio in cabinet drier (60^{0}C) is 6.24:1 and in sun drying 7.77: 1.
- Drying ratio of vegetables: Beans and potato (7:1), Onion (10:1), Okra (12:1), Bitter gourd (16:1), Cabbage, carrot (18:1), Tomato (27:1), Cauliflower (35:1), Drumstick pieces(6.4: 1).
- Tunnel and continuous belt driers are most commonly used for dehydrating fruits and vegetables.
- Solar tunnel dryer: Aonla candy, Potato chips, Leafy vegetables, Turmeric, Chilli, Safed musli, long pepper. Use of 200 micro film is used.
- Dryer used for fruit juices: Cabinet dryer.
- Spray drying at 200^{0}C is suitable for juice concentrates.
- Vacuum puff drying should not be allowed for tomato.
- Packing is fundamental to preserve quality of dehydrated vegetables.
- Freeze drying technique preserves structural properties of whole vegetable with 90% of water without shrinkage and cell collapse.

FPO specifications:

a) Moisture content shall not exceed 20% in fruits and 24% in vegetables by w/w.

b) Fruits and vegetables used for drying should be clean, wholesome & free from insect/ fungal attack.

c) Dehydrated may contain permitted preservatives.

d) Dehydration process is distinct from sun drying.

7.9 Jam

- Jam is prepared by cooking fruit pulp.
- Boiling fruit pulp with sufficient sugar which make thick consistency e.g. Mango, Strawberry.
- Jam contains invert sugar should not be more than 40%.
- Judging end point of jam by sheet or flake test and temperature test at 105^{0}C.
- In jam: < 30% sugar crystallization will form and > 50% sugar-Honey like mass will form.
- To avoid crystallization of jam, corn syrup or glucose must be added.
- Sticky or gummy jam can be solved by addition of pectin or citric acid or both.
- Premature setting of jam is due to low TSS and high pectin.
- Surface graining and shrinkage is due to high evaporation of moisture of jam during storage.

- Storage R.H. is 80%.
- Microbial spoilage (mold) when jam is exposed to more than 90% R.H.
- Citrus fruits are not suitable for jam making.
- Raspberry and strawberry jam contain: 25% fruit pulp.
- Jam is well preserved by action of sugar called exosmosis.

FPO specifications for jam:

- TSS (68.5%);
- Acidity (0.5-0.6%);
- Minimum percentage of fruit juice in final product should be 45.

7.10 Jelly

- 'Fibril' theory of jelly formation is given by W.V Cruess.
- According to 'Spencer' theory, pectin particles are negatively charged.
- According to Hinton's theory, pectins are complex mixtures of variable composition.
- Most important constituent of jelly: Pectin (0.5-1.0%).
- Methoxyl content of pectin: 7-10%.
- Pectin is also known as 'Galacturonic acid'.
- Enzyme used for clarification of fruit pectin: Pectin lyase.
- An ideal fruit for making jelly should be rich in pectin and acids.
- For preparation of fruit jelly addition of sugar depends on pectin.
- Suitable temperature required for extracting pectin from fruits: 80^{0}C.
- Jelly is prepared from strained juice/ clear water extract of fruit, free from pulp.
- Fortification is done in jelly.
- Pectin solution is most stable at neutral pH range and increase in acidity or alkalinity decreases its stability.
- The optimum pH of jelly is 3.2 & that of good jelly is 3.46.
  - 60^0 B of jelly pH: 3.0.
  - 65^0 B of jelly pH: 3.2.
  - 70^0 B of jelly pH: 3.4
- Alcohol test and jelmeter test is used to determine pectin content.
- Jelmeter test is performed at 21-38^{0}C.
- When jel meter shows its reading ¾th then 750 g sugar is to be added.
- Recommended acid for jelly: Citric acid (2g/kg of fruit).
- Judging end point: Sheet or flake test, drop test and temperature test.
- End point of jelly: 65% TSS @ 105^{0}C.

- Pectin and sugar is present in the ratio of 1: 65.
- Enzyme responsible for converting protopectin into pectin: Proto-pectinase.
- Enzyme responsible for converting pectin to pectic acid: Pectic Methyl Esterase (PME).
- Ripe fruits: Protopectin (water insoluble); pectin (water soluble, pectinic acid).
- Overripe fruits: Pectin-Pectic methyl esterase (PME) and pectic acid (water insoluble).
- Firm ripe fruits: Most suitable for jelly making.
- Firmness is due to calcium pectate.
- Premature gelation is due to excess of pectin.
- Suitable fruits for jelly: Guava, Wood apple, Jamun, Gooseberry, Loquat, Karonda and Plum.
- Quality of jelly: It should be clear, transparent, sparkling, attractive colour, keep its shape when cut and not breaking or flowing.
- **FPO specifications** for jelly: TSS (65%), acidity (0.5-0.75%) and minimum 25% fruit juice.
- **Problems in jelly**:
  1. Failure to set: Cooking below end point, lack of acid/ pectin, cooking beyond end point, slow cooking for a long time.
  2. Crystal formation: Use of excess sugar and less cooking.
  3. Syneresis/ weeping jelly: Phenomenon of oozing of fluid from a gel. It is due to excess of acid, too low concentration of sugar, insufficient pectin, premature gelation and pectin degradation.
  4. Cloudy or foggy jelly: Due to use of immature fruits or non-clarified juice, over cooking, overcooling and non-removal of scum.
- Jelly with high sugar and low acid: Soft jelly.
- Tough jelly: High pectin content.
- Removal of scum or foam by addition of edible oil.
- Tartaric acid is best for jelly preparation.

7.11 Marmalade

- Fruit jelly with addition of its peel e.g. Sweet orange.
- Pectin content is slightly higher.
- Browning and fermentation is common problem in storage. It is prevented by addition of KMS/ NaMS @ 0.09 g/ kg of finished product.
- Cooking temperature for marmalade: 103-105^{0}C.
- Cooling temperature for marmalade: 82-88^{0}C.

- End point of marmalade: 65% TSS @ 105°C.
- Jelly marmalade: Clarified extract of pectin is used.
- Jam marmalade: Whole pulp is used.
- Avoid tin containers for packaging.
- FPO specifications are same as for jelly.

7.12 Other products

- Preserve, jelly and candy are Intermediate Moisture Foods (IMF).
- Moisture content in IMF: 20-40%.
- Water activity (a_w) in most IMF: 0.75-0.85.
- **Preserve**: Mature fruit/ vegetable impregnated with heavy sugar syrup till it become tender and transparent. Preserve- sugar syrup should have 68-70% concentration.
  - It is made by quick, slow and vacuum processes.
  - Shrinkage of preserve is due to fruit boiled in heavy syrup.
  - Stickiness in preserve is due to inconsistency of syrup.
  - Strawberry, Aonla, bael, karonda, apple, mango, papaya, raspberry and vegetables such as gourds and carrots are used for making preserve.
  - **FPO specifications** for food preserve: Minimum percentage of TSS in final product (w/w) should be 68 and minimum percentage of prepared fruit in final product (w/w) should be 55.
- **Candy**: Mature fruit/ vegetable impregnated with cane sugar syrup and subsequently drained free of syrup and dried. Dehydrating by osmotic pressure of sugar solution (osmotic dehydration) e.g. Ginger, Ber, Aonla, Pointed gourd, Bottle gourd, Ash gourd, Citrus peel, Karonda, Cherry, Cashew apple and Carambola.
  - **FPO specifications** of candied fruit: TSS (should not be less than 75%), reducing sugar (as of total sugar should not be less than 25%).
- Problems and precautions in preserve/ candy:

Problem	Cause	Precaution
Shrinkage	Fruit boiled in heavy syrup	Blanching first and use low sugar syrup to increase sugar absorption
Toughening	Inadequate blanching	Adequate blanching till it becomes tender/ soft
Floating	Packing the preserve without cooling	Cooling the preserve prior to packing or filling
Stickiness	Insufficient consistency of syrup	Maintain proper consistency of syrup
Fermentation	Low concentration of syrup	Use proper concentration of sugar syrup i.e. 68-70%

- **Glazed fruit**: Covering of candied fruit/ vegetable with a thin transparent coating of sugar for glossy appearance.

- o Temperature for glazed fruits: 113-115⁰C.
- **Crystallized fruit**: Candied fruit when covered or coated with crystals of sugar.

  Diversified products can be prepared from pulpy fruits and have scope for cottage and small scale industry.

- **Toffee**: Ingredients are fruit pulp, glucose sugar, steamed milk powder, butter, essence and colour can also be added. Pulp is cooked or concentrated to 1/3rd of original volume, spreading into thin (0.5-0.75 cm) sheet and drying at 50-60⁰C to a final moisture of 5-10⁰C are important steps. Suitable fruits: Mango, Banana, Guava, Papaya, Bael, Aonla.
- **Fruit bar**: Prepared by drying fruit pulp after mixing suitable ingredients (sugar, citric acid, KMS). Fruit bars are sou ce of carbohydrates, minerals and vitamins. Banana, Mango, Jamun, Pineapple, Guava, Papaya fruit bars are popular.
- **Fruit butter**: Prepared from pulp of apple and pear fruits. Mango butter is made from kernels & used in cosmetics as lip care, body lotions and decorative element. Fruit butter can be easily spread on breads due to soft consistency. Fruit pulp is mixed with sugar, spice powder (cinnamon, clove, ginger) and essence of vanilla/ lemon if required.
- **Cheese**: Preparation is more or less jam type.
- **FPO specifications** for cheese:
  1. Minimum percentage of fruit in final product on fresh weight basis (w/w) 45.
  2. Minimum percentage of TSS in final product should be 68.
  3. The finished product should have heavy consistency e.g. Guava.

7.13 Vinegar

- Word vinegar is derived from French '*vin* (wine) *aigre* (sour)' means 'sour wine'.
- Vinegar means a liquid obtained from alcoholic and acetous fermentation of any sugary material.
- Vinegar made from fruits is called 'fruit vinegar'.
- Vinegar contains 1-5% acetic acid. It is oldest known product of fermentation.
- About 2% acetic acid prevents spoilage of many products.
- Acetic acid vinegar has germicidal and anti-septic properties and inhibit bacterial growth.
- It is obtained through alcoholic and acetic acid fermentation.
- Production of vinegar: Acetic acid fermentation (acetobacter, acetibacteria is used for oxidation of ethyl alcohol into acetic acid).
- Fresh vinegar is turbid liquid and has raw biting taste. Hence, aging for 3-6 months to develop good flavor and aroma is essential.

- Amount of acid in vinegar is expressed as 'grain strength'.
- 1% acetic acid is termed as 10 grain strength.
- Fermentation temperature for vinegar production: 21-27°C.
- Aging or maturation time for vinegar: 4-8 months.
- Ideal vinegar should contain only 0.3% sugar.
- Pasteurization of vinegar is done at 77°C for 15-20 min.
- Bacteria are involved in production of vinegar.
- Optimum temperature for the activity of vinegar bacteria: 27-30°C.
- A lactic acid bacterium is more common in fermented juice of vinegar.
- Wine flower, lactic acid bacteria, vinegar flies (*Drosophila cellaris*), vinegar cels are problem in vinegar production. It is prevented by addition of 20-25% unpasteurized mother vinegar.
- Vinegar eels (*Anguillula*) is killed by heating the vinegar at 60°C.
- Anti-microbial activity of acetic acid increases as pH decreases.
- Jamun vinegar is most popular.
- Problems in vinegar:
    1. Disagreeable mousy flavour due to presence of lactic acid and bacteria in fermented juice which produce lactic acid and other acids responsible for disagreeable flavor
    2. Formation of wine flower (a film of yeast forms on surface of liquid when unfermented juices are exposed to air). Both these problems can be prevented by using 20% unpasteurized mother vinegar.
- **FPO specifications** for fruit vinegar: Minimum percentage of acidity (acetic acid) 3.75; it should contain at least 15% w/w of total solids and should not contain any foreign substance or coloring matter except caramel.

7.14 Pickles/ Chutney

- 29th May: Pickle day.
- Preservation of food in common salt or in vinegar or oil or in combination along with spices is called pickling.
- Most ancient method of preservation of fruits & vegetables.
- Pickling is the result of fermentation by lactic acid bacteria.
- Salt concentration of e" 15% prevents microbial growth in pickles.
- Seedling varieties of mango are preferred because of rich in acidity and high fibre content.
- Suitable fruits: Mango, Lime, Lemon, Aonla, Karonda.

- Mango pickle: Ranks 1st followed by cauliflower, onion in India.
- Lime pickle (National pickle of India).
- Cucumber (gherkin) pickle ranks 1st in world.
- Vegetables rank 1st in pickle making: Cucumber, Cauliflower, Onion, Turnip.
- In pickle, salt concentration should be 10%.
- Salt concentration in dilute pickle is 5.3%.
- 1% acetic acid is used in pickle to prevent scum.
- Temperature for pickle making should be 30°C.
- Mango pieces are dipped before pickling in solution of 2% salt.
- Salt concentration in kokum agal (brined kokum juice from rind or pulp) is 15-16%.
- Boiled product: Chutney.
- Major export chutney in India: Mango chutney.
- Apple and apricot chutney are favoured in India.
- Lactic acid bacteria are most active at 30°C.
- Lactic acid bacteria grow in 8-10% of salt solution.
- Growth of majority of spoilage organisms is inhibited by 15% of salt.
- Advisable to place vegetables in 10% salt solution for vigorous lactic acid bacteria.
- Preservation by salt (15% or above) method of preservation is mostly used in vegetables.
- Pickles preserved by oil: Mango, Cauliflower.
- Finished pickle should not be less than 2% acetic acid.
- Recommended vinegar strength for vegetables or fruit pickle: 10%.
- Softness and slipperiness is due to use of weak brine or inadequate covering with oil and brine.
- Cloudiness of pickle is due to use of inferior quality of vinegar e.g. onion.
- Sodium bisulphate (0.5-1% by wt.) is the most common preservative in pickled chilli.
- Blackening is due to iron in the brine solution.
- Scum formation is due to growth of wild yeast.
- Shriveling of pickles is due to vegetables placed in very strong solution of salt or sugar or vinegar e.g. Cucumber, Gherkin.
- Gassy spoilage of olive pickle due to *Enterobacter*, *Bacillus*, and *Clostridium* spp. are called as 'fish eye'.
- Zapatera: Spoilage in green olive pickle.

Problems of pickles & their prevention

Problems	Cause	Measures
Blackening	Reaction of iron in brine or processing equipment with ingredients of pickle	Avoid contamination
Shriveling	Use of very strong solution of salt or sugar or vinegar	Proper concentration of these should be used
Bitter taste	Use of strong vinegar, excess spice & prolonged cooking of spice	Use proper concentration of vinegar, spice & avoid long cooking
Dull & faded appearance	Use of poor quality materials & insufficient curing	Use better quality ingredients & proper curing
Softness & slipperiness	Inadequate covering with oil or brine	Keep the pickles below the surface of oil or brine

- **FPO specifications for oil pickles:**
  1. Any edible vegetable oil (rape seed, mustard, olive can be used).
  2. Fruits used in preparation should be wholesome.
  3. Add only spices, salt, oil, sugar, jaggery, condiments and preservatives.
  4. Permissible limits of preservative: SO_2 (100 ppm) and Benzoic acid (250 ppm).
  5. In case of salt pickle, minimum percentage of salt should be 12.
  6. All ingredients used shall be thoroughly clean & free from extraneous matter.
- Chutney may be hot and sweet.
- Chutney improves digestion and are good appetizer.
- Fruits based chutney is prepared from Mango, Aonla, Gooseberry, Karonda, Apple, Pear, Plum, Apricot.
- Vegetable based chutney is prepared from Tomato, Ginger.
- **FPO specifications for fruit chutney:**
  1. Minimum percentage of prepared fruit in final product should be 40.
  2. Permissible limits of preservative are same as in pickles.
- Problems in chutneys: Rancidity and black compound formed in product due to contamination of iron with tannin of fruits and spices and adversely affects colour, taste and flavour.

7.15 Fruit based beverages

- For beverage preparation, excellent quality of fruits with high pulp content, low fiber, excellent flavour, taste, pulp colour, high TSS with low acidity are required.
- Fruits based beverages are easily digestible, very refreshing, invigorating, thirst quenchers & appetizers.
- Dietic value is far greater than synthetic/ aerated drinks due to their taste, flavour, & nutritional qualities.

- CO_2 content in carbonated fruit juice beverages: 1-8 g/lit.
- Dietic value of fruit based beverages is far greater than of synthetic/ aerated drinks due to its taste, flavour and nutritional quality.
- Fruits suitable for nectar making: Papaya, Mango, Guava, Peach, Apricot.
- Fruits suitable fruits for juice making: Pineapple, Apple, Mango, Guava, Mandarin orange, Grape, Litchi, Pomegranate, Jamun, Guava, etc.
- Fruits suitable fruits for cordial making: Grape, phalsa, guava, citrus.
- pH level of majority of fruit juices: 3.5-4.0.
- General pH in citrus squashes and cordials: 2.5-3.5.
- pH range for growth:
  - Molds: 1.5 to 8.5
  - Yeasts: 2.5 to 8.0
  - Bacteria: 4.0 to 7.5

Products	Fruit juice (%)	TSS (%)	Acidity (%)	Preservative
Undiluted before serving				
Unsweetened juices	100	Natural	Natural	350 ppm SO_2
Sweetened juices	85	10	-	350 ppm SO_2
RTS	10	10	0.3	70 ppm SO_2/ 120 ppm benzoic acid
Nectar	20	15	0.3	Dilution is not required before serving; 70 ppm SO_2/ 120 ppm benzoic acid
Nectar of orange & pineapple	40	15	-	
Cordial (lime & lemon)	25	30	1.5	350 ppm SO_2
Barley water (is a type of fruit beverage made from limes & lemons)	25	30	1.0	0.25% barley starch
Fruit juice concentrate	100	32	-	1500 ppm SO_2
Cashew squash	25	40	3.5	350 ppm SO_2
Cashew syrup	25	65	3.5	350 ppm SO_2
Cashew RTS	10	10	-	70 ppm SO_2
Diluted before serving				
Squash	25	40-50	1.0	350 ppm SO_2 or 600 ppm sodium benzoate
Crush	25	55	1.0	350 ppm SO_2 or 600 ppm sodium benzoate
Syrup & sherbet	25	65	1.3-1.5	350 ppm SO_2 or 600 ppm sodium benzoate

- **FPO specifications for unsweetened juice:**
  1. Minimum TSS: 10%.
  2. Minimum fruit juice: 85%.
  3. Permissible limit of preservative as SO_2: 350 ppm.

I. **Ready-to-serve**:
- Most popular bottled or tetrapack products which contains at least 10% fruit juice and 10% TSS.
- Suitable fruits: Mango, Apple, Citrus Fruits, Pineapple, Papaya, Plum, Litchi, Guava, Bael, Jamun.
- Excellent quality of soft drink can also be prepared from Phalsa & blend of Aonla & Ginger.

- **FPO specifications**:
  1. Minimum TSS: 10%.
  2. Minimum fruit juice: 10%.
  3. Permissible limit of preservative: 70 ppm SO_2 & 120 ppm benzoic acid.

II. **Fruit juice powder:**
- Fruit juice which is dried into powder.
- Powder has great scope where there are no refrigerator facilities.
- Offers convinces, versatility & storage ability.
- Stored at room temperature and instantly soluble even in cold water.
- Prepared from Mango, Guava, Banana, Bael, Oranges.
- Techniques to prepare powders:
  1. Vacuum drying (Freeze drying & vacuum puff drying).
  2. Air drying (Drum drying, spray drying & foam mat drying).

Classification of beverages:

Unfermented/ Non-alcoholic beverages	Fermented/ Alcoholic beverages
Natural sweetened juices	Wine
Ready to serve (RTS)	Champaigne (sparkling white wine from grape)
Nectar	Port (sweet fortified red wine)
Cordial	Sherry (Spanish wine)
Squash	Tokay (Fortified wine)
Crush	Muscat (Muscat grapes)
Syrup	Perry (Pear)
Fruit juice concentrate	Orange wine (Orange juice)
Fruit juice powder	Berry wine (Strawberry, Black berry, Elder berry)
Barley water	Nira (Palmyarah palm)
Carbonated beverages	Cider (Apple, bael), Feni (Cashew apple juice)

7.15.1 Unfermented/ Non-alcoholic fruit beverages

- Synthetic drinks contain only water (88%) and total carbohydrates (12%).
- Synthetic drinks provide 48 Kcal.
- Tannin-gelatin method is most widely used for clarifying fruit juices.
- Filter acid @ 0.1-0.2% is used for filteration of unfermented beverages.
- Most important filter acids are supercel, kieselguhr and Spanish clay.
- Suspended matter passes through ultrafiltration.
- Commonly used pectic enzymes for destroying the pectin in fruit juices: Pectinol and Filtragol.
- Pectinol is obtained from *Penicillium glauccum*.
- Fining agent: Gelatin, albumen and casein.
- Maltotylsin enzyme is used for fining apple juices.
- Gelatin is mostly used for apple and cashew apple juices.
- Fruit juices, RTS and nectars are preserved by pasteurization.
- Acid content in nector- 0.3%.
- Cordial: Sparkling clear, sweetened fruit juice from which pulp & other suspended material are completely eliminated pulp. It is most suitable for blending with wines.
- Squashes, crushes and cordials are preserved only by chemicals.
- Fruit juices containing 66% or more sugar do not ordinarily ferment.
- General head space for bottled fruit juice beverages 1.5-2.5 cm.
- To stop the enzymatic action in fruit juices is heated by 77^{0}C for 30 min.
- All juices are sweetened by adding sugar except grape and apple.
- Recommended fortification of ascorbic acid and â-carotene (water soluble form) in juices: 250-500 mg/ litre and 7-10 mg/ litre, respectively.
- Recommended acid for cola type beverages: Phosphoric acid.
- In all types of beverages, citric acid is used.
- Sinigrin: Bitter principle of mustard and horse radish.
- Fruits for making squash: Mango, Mandarin Orange, Pineapple, Jamun, Phalsa, Pomegranate, Litchi, Bael, Papaya, Limes/ Lemons, Plums, etc.
- Fruits used for making syrup: Phalsa, Aonla, Jamun, Pomegranate, Grape, Lemon, Orange, and Ginger.
- Synthetic syrup contains 70-75% sugar.
- Fruit juice concentrate: Fruit juice which are concentrated by removing water either by heat/ freezing). It is easy to handle due to reduced weight and bulk.
- Juice concentrates can be used for preparation of various types of beverages including carbonated beverages.
- Barley water is prepared from citrus fruits such as lime, lemon, grapefruit and oranges.

7.15.2 Fermented fruit beverages

- Definition: Bacterial decomposition of simple hexose's sugar into alcohol and CO_2.
- Decomposition of carbohydrates (-CHO_8) by microorganisms or enzyme ($C_6H_{12}O_6$+ yeast $\rightarrow$ $2C_2H_5OH + 2CO_2$).
- Fermentation is only process where both donor and accepter are organic.
- Master Sommelier Diploma Exam: World's toughest exam for blind testing of wines conducted in UK.
- Wine, beers, cider, vinegar, fermented drinks and fermented pickles are preserved by fermentation process.
- Greek word 'cider' means strong drink and defined as beverage made wholly or partly from fermented juice of apple. It is also prepared from guava, pear, peach and raspberry fruits.
- Word 'wine' strictly signifies fermented alcoholic beverage produced by grape juice without distillation (wine = fermented grape juice by yeasts).
- Wines can be broadly classified into two major groups-
  1. Natural wine having 9-14% alcohol. Such wines are still wines (dry table wine) and sparkling wine. Nature and keeping quality depends on complete yeast fermentation.
  2. Dessert and appetizer wine having 15-21% alcohol. Nature and keeping quality depends on addition of wine spirits. Such wines are sweet wines (white, pink, red colour), sherries (white, sweet or dry wines) and flavoured speciality wines (vermouth).
- Alcohol content of wine: 7-21%.

Types of wine	% alcohol
Light wine	7-9 %
Medium wine	9-16 %
Strong wine	16-21 %
Cider	4-6 %
Sherry wine	18-21 %
Sparkling wine	Retains considerable amount of CO_2
Still wine	Do not retain CO_2 produced during fermentation
Fortified wine	Addition of alcohol in the form of brandy
Red wine	From coloured grapes (skin intact)
White wine	From white/ green grapes (skin removed); lower in tannin & extract
Dry wine	Very little/ no unfermented sugar is detected & aged for 2-5 years at 60-70^{0}F
Sweet wine	High sugar content can be detected

- Wines prepared are named after the grape varieties e.g. Muscati (prepared from Muscat variety), Tokay (prepared from Takay variety).

- Fruits utilized for wine preparation: Guava, pomegranate, bael, mahua flower, pear, mulberry, pineapple, jack fruit.
- Addition of wine yeast inoculum @ 4 ml thick yeast suspension per kg or grape.
- Degree proof: Measurement of strength of alcohol in alcoholic beverages.
- Word 'must' in grape industry refers to crushed grapes.
- 'Must' of grape wine is an indicator of starch.
- Terms related to wine preparation:
  - Racking means siphoning of fermented wine to separate the yeast cells and other solid deposits from wine.
  - Fining means new wine may not be clear and require fining agent (bentonite) to be added to settle down colloidal matter.
  - Filtration means clear wine is siphoned off or filtered.
  - Maturation (aging): Wine is allowed to mature for 6-8 months at room temperature (in cool place) the process is known aging.
- Development of biochemical principles of fermentation was originated by Lavoisier (1789) in France.
- Barrels of oak wood are preferred for wine maturing as they impart fine bouquet to wine.
- Principle changes during wine aging: Oxidation and formation of esters e.g. Ethyl acetate, ethyl isobutyrate, ethyl succinate.
- Honey wine is known as 'mead' e.g. Pomegranate, jamun.
- Jamun wine is commercially known as 'Resvera' is prepared in Nashik, Maharashtra.
- Types of jamun wine: Jamun Pure and Jamun Light Rose.
- Acid content in grapes for wine: 0.6-0.8%.
- pH of grape wine: 3.5-4.0
- Optimum temperature for fermentation of grape wine: 23-28^{0}C.
- Wine yeast: *Torulopsis sphaerica*.
- Common yeast used in wine: *Saccharomyces cerevisiae* var. *ellipsoideus* (20 ml/kg of grapes).
- Common yeast used in cider: *S. carlbergensis*.
- Organisms for spoilage of wine: *Acetobactor*, *Lactobacillus* and *Leuconostoc*.
- Generally wines are pasteurized at 82-88^{0}C for 1-2 min.
- Cider is a product of normal alcoholic fermentation of fruit juice (particularly apple juice) contains >8% alcohol.
- Fruits with higher tannin are preferred for cider making.
- Fruit cider with 5-8% alcohol and TSS: acid of 25-30 is most ideal.
- In USA, apple cider means non-clarified apple juices while in India, apple cider means fermented apple juice.

- Cider is referred as 'ladies wine' due to their mild sweetness and very low pungency.
- Cider apple contain higher percentage of sugar i.e. fructose 12.5%.
- Fruits suitable for cider making: Guava, Bael, Jamun, Phalsa, Aonla.
- Common preservative used in cider: SO_2 @ 100 ppm or KMS @ 0.22 g/kg.
- Cider is mostly prepared from fermentation of special grades of apples.
- For cider preparation apple should have 10% sugar & 0.1-0.3% acidity or tannin.
- Champagne(sparkling wine) is made chiefly in Champagne district of France from grape cvs. Chardonay and Pinot Noir.
- Grape varieties used for making white wine: Muscat, Palomino, Malaga and Thompson Seedless.
- Fortified wine 'Tokay' is made in Hungary.
- Sweet fortified red wine 'Port' is made in Portugal.
- Canded krusei: Cocoa fermentation.
- Acetic acid content in white wine is 0.12g/ 100 ml and in red wine is 0.14g/ 100 ml.
- Bottom yeast is used in beer preparation.

a) Lactic acid fermented products:

- Food is preserved chemically.
- NaCl is useful in lactic acid fermentation of food.
- Fresh vegetables can be preserved by lactic acid fermentation.
- Quality of fermented products is better at low temperature (20-25^{0}C) than at higher temperature.
- Kanji prepared from black carrot- takes 7-10 days for lactic acid fermentation.
- Production of pickles and sauerkraut (lactic acid forming bacteria such as *Bacillus subtilis, B.licheniformis, B. coagulans, Dendrocalamus hamiltonii, Enterococcus durans, Pediococcus pentasaceous*, *Lactobacillus cellubiosus*, *L. mesenteroides, L. fermentum, L. brevis, L. plantarum*, *Phyllostachys assamica, Streptococcus lactis*).
- 'Soibum' prepared from succulent bamboo shoots of *Dendrocalamus hamiltonii, D. giganteus, Melocanna bambusoides, Bambusa tulda*, *B. balcowa*, *Melocanna humilis*.

Raw material	Product
Cabbage	Sauerkraut (sour cabbage)
Leaves of mustard/ radish/ cauliflower	Gundruk
Lettuce	Lettucekraut
Cucumber, tomato, mango, lemon	Pickle
Cucumber	Khalpi
Mustard	Rai, Ziangsang
Black carrot	Kanji
Turnip	Saurruben
Radish root	Sinki
Cowpea	Phalaphal (popular in Egypt)
Vegetables + milk	Tarhana
Vegetables + rice	Sajurasin
Mixed vegetables + cabbage + turnip + radish	Paw Tsay
Mixed vegetables + Chinese cabbage	Kimchi
Taro corms	Poi (acidic product)
Bamboo shoots	Tenga, Soibum, Soidon, Kardi, Hikhu, Hiring, Ekung, Eup, Lungsiej
Magane-saag (*Cardamine macrophylla*)	Goyang
Tannia tubers	Fufu
Cassava tubers	Gari/ farinha de manioca (popular in African contries)

b) Alcoholic fermented products:

- Wine → Alcohol (7-21%), sparkling wine retains considerable amount of CO_2.
- Nira → Product from palm tree.
- Toddy → Product from coconut.
- Feni → Product from cashew apple juice.
- Cider → Product from apple and guava.
- Poi → Product from corm of taro.
- Vodka → Product from potato.
- Khalpi → Product from cucumber.
- Whisky → Product from malt.
- Pulque → Product from agave & contain 6% alcohol.

7.16 Stepping preservation of vegetables

1. Potassium meta-bi-sulphite as preservative helps in retaining ascorbic acid in vegetables.
2. Preserved vegetables can be stored for 6-8 months at ambient temperature.
3. Blanched cauliflower with 2% NaCl, 1% acetic acid with 350 ppm SO_2 and 400 ppm benzoic acid is preferred most and acceptable for 3 months at room temperature.
4. Unblanched carrots stepped with 25% sugar, 0.4% citric acid, 400 ppm benzoic acid and 700 ppm SO_2 and acceptable to 5-6 months of storage at room temperature.

5. Blanched bitter gourd slices with stepping 2% NaCl, 0.5 to 1% citric acid, 200 ppm SO_2 and 400 ppm benzoic acid and acceptable for 2 months during storage at room temperature.

7.17 Bio-preservation of vegetables

1. Bacteriocin has activity against undesirable food borne pathogenic bacteria. It is used as preservative in heat processed and low pH foods.
2. Nisin, a natural preservative effectively controls gram positive bacteria. It is useful against gram negative bacteria when used in conjunction with other preservatives.

7.18 Sauces/ ketchups

- Sauces/ ketchup are more or less same except little difference in total solids content.
- Generally TSS content of ketchup (28%) and sauces (30%).
- Sauces are mixture of spices and other ingredients infused in vinegar and later strained off.
- Sauces/ ketchups are prepared more or less from same ingredients as chutneys except that fruit from which it is prepared is sieved after cooking to give the finished product a smooth consistency.
- Fruits and vegetables suitable for sauce preparation: Aonla, Apple, Plum, Papaya, Chilli, mixed vegetables (red pumpkin + carrot + potato + onion + ginger + garlic), mushroom, tomato.
- Apple pulp is mostly used as thickening agent in sauce preparation.
- Hot chilli varieties of *C. annuum*, *C. frutescens* and *C. chinense* are used to produce bottled hot chilli sauce.
- Hot chilli 'Tabasco sauce' produced from fruits of *C. frutescens* is aged for 3 years in oak barrels.
- Problems in sauces: Black ring formation at the neck of bottle (due to formation of ferric tannate, which is black in colour). Iron gets into product from the cap or crown cork through the action of acid. This iron contact with tannins in spices and forms ferrous tannate, it is oxidized to black ferric tannate and hence 'black ring' is formed. This can be prevented by:
  1. Filling the hot product at a temperature of 85^{0}C or above.
  2. Head space in the bottle should not be more.
  3. Iron contamination should be minimized.
  4. Addition of 100 mg per litre of ascorbic acid or 100 ppm sulphur dioxide.
  5. Use of corn or glucose syrup which contains sulphur for partial replacement of sugar.
  6. Storing of bottles in horizontal position or upside down position.

- **FPO specifications** for fruit sauce (other than tomato):
  - Minimum TSS 15%, minimum acidity as acetic acid 1.2% and mold count not an excess of 125 per 1/60 c.mm and bacteria not an excess of 100 million per cc, permissible limit of preservative as benzoic acid is 750 ppm.

7.19 Tomato processing

- Many products are influenced by consistency (viscosity).
- Fruit pH affects heating time required to achieve sterilization of processed commodity.
- Longer the time required, the product pH increases.
- Tomato sauce and apple sauce are popular in India.
- Super Hot Break Tomato Concentrate: Commercial method for obtaining of tomato paste. This type of paste is rich in fibres and very high consistency. It is produced by heating tomato pulp up to 105^{0}C.
- Solan Gola, Yashwant, Rupali and MTH-6: Most preferred cultivars for juice making.
- Winter tomatoes are superior quality because of more total solids.
- Lycopene is the self oxidizing isomer of carotene.
- Lycopene turns brown when it comes in contact with iron.
- Iron also forms black compounds with tannin when tomato and spices used.

FPO specification for tomato products

Tomato product	TSS (^{0} Brix)	Other specifications
Juice	5	Sugar 1%, salt 0.5%, citric acid 0.4%
Soup	7	-
Crush	-	Tomato pulp with skin & seeds
Puree	-	Tomato pulp without skin & seeds
Medium tomato puree	9	Benzoic acid @ 250 ppm
Heavy tomato puree	12	Benzoic acid @ 250 ppm
Tomato paste	25	Made from strained tomato juice or pulp, benzoic acid @ 250 ppm
Concentrated tomato paste	33	
Sauce/ ketchup	25	Tomato solids 12%, 1% acetic acid, benzoic acid @ 750 ppm

- Sugar content of tomato ketchup/ sauces: 10-26%.
- Salt content of tomato ketchup/ sauces: 1.3-3.4%.
- Sauces are generally thinner and contain more TSS (min. 30%) than ketchup (min. 25%).
- Acidity percent in good quality juice: 0.4%.
- Acetic acid content in ketchup/ sauces: 1.25-1.5%.
- Jalapino pepper used in sauce is considered to be most pungent.

- Pasteurization temperature is 85-90^{0}C for 30 min.
- Ketchup should be filled at 88^{0}C.
- Heating of tomato juice @ 82-88^{0}C for 1 min.
- Sterilization tomato soup @ 115^{0}C for 40-45 min.
- Tomato juice/ pulp is extracted by hot pulping (superior quality) and cold pulping.
- Colour of sauce should be light.
- End point of cooking puree and paste determined by refractometer.
- Water activity for tomato paste is 0.93- 0.98.

7.20 Major products

- To have normal kraut fermentation the salt should be 2.5%.
- Sauerkraut means acid/sour cabbage.
  - 2-3 organisms are involved.
  - Aroma is due to diacetyl.
  - Fermented product (2.25-2.5% salt), lactic acid (1.5%).
  - Suitable cabbage type: white cabbage.
  - Stimulate laxative property due to acetylcholine and lactylcholine (ester).
  - Common bacteria: *Leuconostoc mesenteroides*.
  - *L. brevis*: continues to grow when there is no mannitol.
  - Ideal temperature for fermentation: 18-22^{0}C (rapid fermentation).
  - Pasteurization temperature: 73.9^{0}C.
  - *Enterobactor glocae* is 1st organism to notice on fermentation.
- Mango slices (amchur): Suitable stage for amchur product: Green, mature.
- Mango leather synonym to mango slab, amawat, ampaper.
- Suitable stage for mango leather: Ripe and juicy fruits.
- Fruit cheese: Guava, apple, pear and plum: Suitable stage for fruit cheese: Firm and ripe fruits.
- Fruit butter: Apple, peach, plum (suitable stage: Firm and ripe).
- Fruit toffee: Mango, guava, papaya (suitable stage: Firm and ripe).
- Syrup from kokam rind (Amrit kokum): By adding cane sugar @ 1:2 and preservative sodium benzoate (610 mg/ kg of syrup).

7.21 Papain

- According to CFTRI, papain extraction is highest during rainy season.
- Prepared from dried latex of 'unripe papaya'.
- Suitable drying temperature: 50-55^{0}C.
- Dried papain moisture content: 5%.

7.22 Jaggery preparation

- Jaggery made from palmyra palm (*Borassus flabellifer*), coconut (*Cocos nucifera*), fishtail palm (*Caryota urens*) and wild date palm (*Phoenix sylvestris*).
- Jaggery recovery from sweet juice: 8-10%.
- Extraction begins 10-15 years of planting when flowering starts.
- 2-2.5 kg juice per single palm per day.
- 30 kg jaggery per palm per year.
- 97% jaggery is prepared from palmyra palm and wild date palm.

Jaggery preparation palm juice

Ingredient	Palmyra palm	Coconut	Fishtail palm	Date palm
Water (%)	8.9	10.2	9.1	9.1
Protein (%)	1.1	0.9	2.2	1.4
-CHO (%)	88.3	83.5	84.8	86.2
Sucrose (%)	77.3	71.8	84.8	72.2
Glucose + Fructose (%)	2.2	3.7	0.5	1.4

- Neera is sweet in taste, special flavour, transparent with more sucrose content and ferment easily.
- pH of juice: 8-8.1.
- Neera extraction time: November to February.
- Fermentation can be extended by adding calcium oxide.

7.23 Food colour

- As per FPO recommendations, use of metallic colours are completely banned.
- 1st carotenoid pigment was extracted from carrot.
- 1st synthetic colour: Coaltar.
- Eco-friendly natural colours:
  - Beet root: Red/ pink.
  - Turmeric: Yellow.
  - Eucalyptus rind: Chocolate.
  - Heena: Black.
  - Aonla fruit powder: Black.
  - Blue coloured flowers of hibiscus-Blue.
  - Flowers of 'Flame of forest' tree: Orange.
  - Arrow root (maranta) powder: Used as base for preparation of all colours.
  - To prepare light colours, use more quantity of arrow root powder and for dark colours use less quantity.

- Coaltar dye or mixture of dye which added to any food product should not exceed 0.2 g/ kg of final product.
- Maximum permissible colour in food preservation: 200 ppm.
- Most stable colour in fruits: Yellow.
- Colour is measured by Tintometer.
- Chlorophyll a: b (3:1) in plants.
- Carotenoids: Fat soluble, orange yellow pigment e.g. Tomato (Lycopene); Black pepper (Capsanthin); Annatto (Bixin).
- Extract of carrot, avocado, palm oil contain â-carotene.
- Kokum rind (2-3% anthocyanin) is promising source of natural colorant for food.
- Anthocyanin: Water soluble- Red, Blue, Purple pigment e.g. Cherry, Apple, Jamun, Mulberry.
- Flavonoides: Cream white colour e.g. Potato, Cauliflower.
- Tanninis responsible for astringency in brinjal, apple, bottle gourd, mango (mangiferin), beet (betalins).
- Carmoisine: Synthetic red colour.
- Erythrosine: Synthetic colour used to obtain red shades.
- Curcumin gives bright yellow colour even at 5-200 ppm dose.
- Curcuminoids as a food colour has been allotted low ADI (acceptable daily intake) of 0 to 1.0 mg/ kg body wt./ day.

7.24 Food additives

- Anti-oxidants: BHA (Butylated hydroxyl anisole), BHT, propyl gallate, $SnCl_2$
- Preservatives: SO_2, Benzoic acid, Sorbic acid.
- Surface active agent: Monosodium phosphate.
- Stabilizers/thickners: CMC (Carboxy methyl cellulose), Pectin, Gelatin, Starch.
- Sweetners: Aspartane, Glycyrrhizic acid.
- Zero calorie sweetner: Sucralose.
- Flavouring agent: Monosodiumglutamate i.e. MSG (most widely used & somewhat controversial flavour enhancer).
- Colouring agent: Titanium dioxide. Carbon black
- Bleaching agent: Benzoyl peroxide, H_2O_2.

7.25 Food spoilage

7.25.1 Useful bacteria:

1. **Vinegar bacteria**: *Acetobacter* spp.
   - Aerobic bacteria.
   - Important spp. *A. aceti, A. orleansis, A. schzenbachi*.

2. **Lactic acid bacteria**: *Lactobacillus* spp.
   - Facultative thermophiles.
   - Most active at 30^0C.
   - Used in lactic acid production (cheese and dairy products).
   - *L. plantarum*: Pickles preparation.
   - An example of hetero-fermentor is *Lactobacillus brevis*.
3. **Yeast**:
   - Unicellular fungi.
   - Prefer low concentration of sugar for growth.
   - Commonly used for wine and beer production.
   - Yeast candida is the problem in high acid food and salty food.
   - Ammonium hydrogen sulphate is added as nutrient for yeast.
4. **Molds**:
   - Multicellular, filamentous fungi.
   - Sensitive to heat.
   - Blue mold: *Penicillium*.
   - Black mold: *Asparagus*.
   - Gray mold: *Mucor* spp.
   - Spoilage of canned fruits: *Byssochlamys* spp.
   - Microbes require atleast 13% free water in foods for their growth.
5. **Browning reaction**:
   - Browning reactions due to enzymatic and non-enzymatic.

5.1 **Enzymatic browning:** Apple, banana, brinjal.
   - Browning is due to polyphenol oxidase, tyrosinase and catecholase.

5.2 **Non-enzymatic browning:**
   - Sugar and sugar related compounds.
   - Maillard browning: Roasted coffee beans.
   - Caramelization: Due to high temperature.

- At >7 water activity (a_w) non-enzymatic browning start in dried foods.

6. **Natural toxins**:
   - Potato: Protease inhibitors.
   - Saponins: Spinach and asparagus.
   - Goitrogens: Cabbage.
   - Oxalic acid: Rhubarb, spinach, beet.
7. **Other processed products**:
   - Churno: Freezed potato.

- Tunta: Sun dried potato.
- Calcium acetate is used to improve texture of French fries.
- French fries are frozen potato chips.
- Canned potatoes should have low dry matter of 18-20%.
- High specific gravity (1.085) potatoes preferable for chips.

7.25.2 Type of spoilage:

Food	Type of spoilage	Causal organism
Fresh fruits and vegetables	1. Gray mold rot 2. Rhizopus soft rot 3. Blue mold rot 4. Black mold rot 5. Sliminess or souring	*Botrytis cinerea* *R. nigricans* (white cottony growth) *Penicillium italicum* (blue mold of citrus), *P. digitatum* (green mold of citrus), *P. expansum* (blue mold of apple).*Aspergillus niger*, *Alternaria* spp., *Saprophytic bacteria*
Pickles	1. Black pickle 2. Soft pickle	*Bacillus nigricans* *Bacillus*
Mango	Mechanical damage	Stem end rot
Banana		Crown rot
Citrus		Green mold
Pineapple		Pedicel rot

7.25.3 Post-harvest diseases of fruit crops:

Fruit	Disease	Causal Organism
Banana	Crown rot	*Colletotrichum musae*, *Fusarium semitectum*
Ber	Fruit rot	*Alternaria* spp., *Phomopsis* spp., *Colletotrichum* spp.
Citrus	Black rot	*Alternaria citri*
	Gray mold	*Botrytis cinerea*
	Green mold	*Penicillium digitatum*
	Stem end rot	*Diaporthe citri*, *D. medusa*, *D. natalensis*
Guava	Anthracnose	*Colletotrichum gloeosporioides*
Kiwi fruit	Stem rot	*Botrytis cinerea*
	Ripe rot	*Botryosphaeria dithodea*
Litchi	Skin injury	*Aspergillus* spp., *Penicillium* spp.
Mango	Stem end rot	*Botryodiplodia theobromae*
	Black mold	*Aspergillus niger*
	Dry rot	*Mycosphaerella* spp.
	Wet rot	*Phomopsis* spp.
	Alternaria spot	*Alternaria alternata*
	Fusarium rot	*Fusarium solani*
	Internal yellowing	*Enterobacter clocae*
Pear	Blossom end rot	*Alternaria* spp., *Botrytis* spp.
Pineapple	Black rot	*Chalara paradoxa*
	Fruitlet core rot	*Penicillium funicalosum*, *Fusarium moniliformi*
Pomegranate	Heart rot	*Aspergillus niger*, *Alternaria* spp.
	Penicillium rot	*Penicillium* spp.
Papaya	Anthracnose	*Colletotrichum gloeosporioides*

7.25.4 Chemicals used to extend shelf life of fruits

Fruit	Chemical & its concentration	Time of application	Response
Apple	Boric acid (0.1 to 0.2%)	45 & 60 days before harvest	Improve calcium status of fruit
	Alar (1000 ppm)	60 days before harvest	Improve storability
	$AgNO_3$ (75 ppm) or DNP (30 ppm)	6 weeks before harvest	Improve storability
	Diphenylamine (0.1-0.25%)	Post harvest dip for 30 sec.	Control superficial scald
Mango	Maleic hydrazide (1000-2000 ppm)	Post harvest dip	Delayed ripening
	$CaNO_3$ (1%) or $CaCl_2$ (0.6%)	Post harvest spray	Enhanced keeping quality
Banana	Tal Prolong (1-2%)	Post harvest dip	Extended storability
	GA_3 (50 ppm) & kinetin (20 ppm)	Post harvest dip	Retarded ripening
Ber	Calcium compounds (1.7g/l)	Post harvest spray	Delayed fruit ripening
Kinnow	Wax emulsion (6%) with benomyl (0.1%)	-	Reduced weight loss during 2 months storage
Nagpur santra	Waxing with benlate (0.1%)	-	Reduced rotting at ambient storage
Grape	$CaNO_3$ (0.75%), Cycocel (2000-4000 ppm)	10 days before harvest	Reduced weight loss & delay ripening, reduced berry rot
Guava	$CaNO_3$ (1%)	Post harvest dip	Retained quality for 6 days
	Morphactin (2.5 and 5 ppm) & chloroflurenol methyl ester	Pre & post harvest application	Extended shelf life
Passion fruit	4% $CaCl_2$ for 3 min	5 days after harvest	Controls storage rot, reduced storage losses, higher sugars & vit C content
Olive	BA (150 & 300 ppm), TIBA (50 & 100 ppm), GA_3 (50 & 100 ppm), CEPA (150 & 300 ppm)	At full bloom	Reduction of fruit drop, increased fruit set in self incompatible cultivars
	NAA	At full bloom	Helps in fruit thinning
	Cycocel @ 200 or 500 ppm, ethephon 200 ppm, SADH 2000 ppm	-	Bud burst & flower bud formation, increase in perfect flowers
Longan	Fumigation with 6 g SO_2/ 0.07 m^2 & packed in plastic film bags	Stored at 3^0C	Storage, colour & overall quality good